Comparative Corporate Law

Comparative Corporate Law

United States, European Union, China and Japan

Cases and Materials

Larry Catá Backer

Carolina Academic Press
Durham, North Carolina

ISBN: 0-89089-526-0
LCCN: 2001088034

Carolina Academic Press
700 Kent Street
Durham, North Carolina 27701
Telephone (919) 489-7486
Fax (919) 493-5668
www.cap-press.com

Printed in the United States of America

Summary of Contents

Contents

Table of Cases

Table of Authorities

Gensler, Howard, *Company Formation and Securities Listing in the People's Republic of China*, 17 Hous. J. Int'l L. 399 (1995), 250, 727

Gevurtz, Franklin A., *The Business Judgment Rule: Meaningless Verbiage or Misguided Notion?*, 67 S. Cal. L. Rev. 287 (1994), 1199, 1209

Gillespie, John, *Private Commercial Rights in Vietnam: A Comparative Analysis*, 30 Stan. J. Int'l L. 325 (1994), 790

Goldman, Berthold, *The Convention Between the Member States of the European Economic Community on the Mutual Recognition of Companies and Legal Persons*, 6 C.M.L.Rev. 104 (1968), 656

Grace, Michael J., *Proposed "Check-the-Box" Regulations Would Streamline But Not Eliminate Entity Classification Process*, 37 Tax Mgmt. Memorandum 295 (1996), 300

Hahn, Elliott J., Japanese Business Law and the Legal System (1984), 56

Haley, John Owen, Authority Without Power: Law and the Japanese Paradox (1991), 136, 1282

Halsbury's Laws of England, Law of the European Communities, 93, 110

Hamson, Executive Discretion and Judicial Control (1954), 92

Han, Anna M., *China's Company Law: Practicing Capitalism in a Transitional Economy*, 5 Pac. Rim L. & Pol'y J. 457 (1996), 164

Hanna, Christopher H., *Initial Thoughts on Classifying the Major Japanese Business Entities Under the Check-the-box Regulations*, 51 SMU L. Rev. 75 (1997), 233, 302

Harris, Brian, *"Social Charter": The Legal Basis*, New Law Journal; vol. 139, No. 6410, 1099

Hartley, T., *Constitutional and Institutional Aspects of the Maastricht Agreement*, 42 Int'l & Comp. L. Q. 213 (1993), 91

Hawke, Neil, Coporate Liability (2000), 1076

Hawke, Neil and Marston, John, *Facades and Corporate Veils*, Law Society's Gazette (3 May 1989), 1060

Heftel, Christopher Lee, *Survey, Corporate Governance in Japan: The Position of Shareholders in Publicly Held Corporations*, 5 U. Haw. L. Rev. 135 (1983), 237, 1152

Henderson, Dan Fenno, *Security Markets in the United States and Japan: Distinctive Aspects Molded by Cultural, Social, Economic, and Political Differences*, 14 Hastings Int'l & Comp. L. Rev. 263 (1991), 726, 967, 1153, 1301, 1357

Hessen, Robert, *A New Concept of Corporations: A Contractual and Private Property Model*, 30 Hastings L.J. 1327 (1979), 324

Hofstetter, Karl, *Parent Responsibility for Subsidiary Corporations: Evaluating European Trends*, 39 Int'l & Comp. L. Q. 577 (1990), 1087

Hoshi, Takeo, *Japanese Corporate Governance as a System, in* Comparative Corporate Governance: The State of the Art and Emerging Research 847 (Klaus J. Hopt, Hideki Kanda, Mark J. Roe, Eddy Wymeersch and Stephan Prigge, eds., 1998), 305, 315

Howson, Nicholas C., *China's Company Law: One Step Forward, Two Steps Back? A Modest Complaint*, 11 Colum. J. Asian L. 127 (1997), 789, 973, 1126, 1285

Huckaby, S. Todd, Note: *Defensive Action to Hostile Takeover Efforts in Japan: The Shuwa Decisions*, 29 Colum. J. Transnat'l L. 439 (1991), 1272, 1358

Hudson, Alex Maitland, France: Practical Commercial Law (1991), 66

Iwai, Katsuhito, *Persons, Things and Corporations: The Corporate Personality Controversy and Comparative Corporate Governance*, 47 Am. J. Comp. L. 583 (1999), 403

Jackson, David and Frumkin, Joseph B., *The Global Role of Corporate Law*, 25 Del. J. Corp. L. 106 (2000), 438

Jianhua, Zhong and Guanghua, Yu, *China's Uniform Contract Law: Progress and Problems*, 17 U.C.L.A. Pac. Basin L.J. 1 (1999), 789

Keller, Perry, *Sources of Order in Chinese Law*, 42 Am. J. Comp. L. 711 (1994), 156

Kitchin, Alan W.N. and McClenahan, John, *Doing Business in Asia: Focus on Japan, India, and Vietnam*, 1 Pac. Rim L. & Pol'y J. 127 (1992), 668, 722

Klein, William A., *The Modern Business Organization: Bargaining Under Constraints*, 91 Yale L.J. 1521 (1982), 307

Klein, William A. and Coffee, John C. Jr., Business Organization and Finance: Legal and Economic Principles (7th ed., 2000), 177

Kline, Carol L., *Protecting Minority Shareholders in Close Corporations: Modeling Czech Investor Protections on German and United States Law*, 23 B.C. Int'l & Comp. L. Rev. 229 (2000), 1351

Kommers, Donald P., *The Constitutional Jurisprudence of the Federal Republic of Germany*, 364

Kondō, Mitsuo, *The Management Liability of Directors*, 20 Law in Japan 150 (Donald C. Clarke, trans., 1987), 1228

Kostel, Mary E., Note: *A Public Choice Perspective on the Debate over Federal Versus State Corporate Law*, 79 Va. L. Rev. 2129 (1993), 571

Langbein, John H., *Cultural Chavinism in Comparative Law*, 5 Cardozo J. Int'l & Comp. L. 41 (1997), 61

Lasok, D. & Bridge, J.W., Law and Institutions of the European Communities (5th ed., 1991), 75, 91, 92, 93, 582

Lastres, José Manuel Otero, *Company Law, in*, Spanish Business Law 153 (Bernardo M. Cremades, Gen Ed. 1985), 715, 882

Licht, Amir N., *The Mother of All Path Dependencies Toward a Cross-cultural Theory of Corporate Governance Systems*, 26 Del. J. Corp. L. 147 (2001), 1149

Lin, Yabo, *New Forms and Organizational Structures of Foreign Investment in China Under the Company Law of the PRC*, 7 Transnat'l Law. 327 (1994), 164

MacLennan, Bruce W., *Establishing a Stock Corporation in Japan after the 1990 Revision of the Commercial Code*, 1 Pac. Rim L. & Pol'y J. 127 (1992), 670, 722

Macey, Jonathon, *Institutional Investors and Corporate Monitoring: A Demand-Side Perspective in a Comparative View, in* Comparative Corporate Governance: The State of the Art and Emerging Research 903 (Klaus J. Hopt, Hideki Kanda, Mark J. Roe, Eddy Wymeersch and Stephan Prigge, eds., 1998), 309

McKinney's Consolidated Laws of New York, Annotated Business Corporation Law, 431

Mengozzi, Paolo, European Community Law: From the Treaty of Rome to the Treaty of Amsterdam (2nd ed., 1999), 80

Winter, *State Law, Shareholder Protection and the Theory of the Corporation*, 6 J. LEGAL STUD. 251 (1977), 558

WINTER, AUDREY, ET AL., EUROPE WITHOUT FRONTIERS: A LAWYER'S GUIDE (1989), 77, 110

WOOLDRIDGE, FRANK, COMPANY LAW IN THE UNITED KINGDOM AND THE EUROPEAN COMMUNITY: ITS HARMONIZATION AND UNIFICATION (1991), 123, 630, 724, 745, 920

WYATT, DERRICK AND DASHWOOD, ALAN, THE SUBSTANTIVE LAW OF THE EEC (1987), 123

Preface

It is true enough that the world is becoming a smaller place. Business enterprises today contemplate venturing into places they would not have considered even thirty years ago. This venturing has been made infinitely easier since the mid 1990s with the advent of the Internet as a tool of commerce. Electronic commerce is revolutionizing the nature of retail as well as wholesale commerce. The legal and economic ramifications of this change in commercial practice will be worked out in this century. The pace of the harmonization of commercial practice has accelerated in response to these rapid changes. The recent work of the United Nations Commission on International Trade Law in creating a Model Law on Electronic Commerce is a case in point. *See, e.g.*, <http://www.un.or.at/unicitral/english/texts/electcom/>.

At the same time, the world is becoming a more consolidating place. Changes in commercial practice are inducing change in the organization and strategies of commercial enterprises. The most significant of these changes have resulted from the challenges faced by enterprises increasingly pulled from within the borders of their places of formation. Political transformation has mirrored changes in commercial practice. Groups of countries are increasingly uniting for diverse purposes. These political and trade groupings are meant to take advantage of the greater flexibility and power that unity brings. That has been the case In the area of trade in the United States has taekn advantage of this flexibility through its participation in the North American Free Trade Association composed of the United States, Mexico and Canada, as well as in the World Trade Organization.

The tendency to consolidate has not been reserved to the arena of mutually advantageous foreign relations. Increasingly, nation-states have begun to surrender a portion of their sovereignty to effect more intimate unions with other nations. Sometimes the process has been extraordinarily successful—consider the union of the states which has become known as the United States of America. Sometimes they have been unsuccessful—consider the fates of the former Union of Soviet Socialist Republics, Yugoslavia and Czechoslovakia. Latin America has seen the emergence of a number of economic unions patterned, to some extent on the European Community. The largest of the South American regional trade associations, MERCOSUR, for example, unites Brazil, Argentina, Uruguay and Paraguay. It is still too early to gauge the success of these new economic combinations. However, the pattern emerging at the end of the twentieth century is clear enough: the nation-state has increasingly become a hindrance, rather than a help for expanding trade and economic development. Law and political organization is slowly shifting to recognize the economic realities of patterns of world wide commerce.

Europe is of particular interest in this regard. Since the end of the Second World War, the nations of Western Europe have been attempting to create of a new form of a union of sorts—a community of nations producing a "Europe without borders" while retaining the separate national characters of the member states. This process started in the early 1950s when six nations, France, West Germany, Italy, Belgium, Luxembourg, and the Netherlands, created three distinct, but related, functional "communities"—the European Economic Community ("EEC" now the "EC"), the European Coal and Steel Community ("ECSC") and the European Atomic Energy Community (EurAtom"). This union of six nations had grown to twelve by 1991: Portugal, Spain, The United Kingdom, France, Germany, Belgium, the Netherlands, Luxembourg, Denmark, Ireland, Greece, and Italy. In 1994 three additional Member States were admitted: Sweden, Austria and Finland (Norway chose not to join but to remain associated with the Communities). Today, the three Communities have expanded their scope and become the nucleus of a European Union ("EU"). The impetus within the EU is for even greater union among the Member States.

The aim of the EU is to create, as between its members, a unified geographic and political area characterized by free trade and free circulation of goods, services, capital and persons. To aid in this effort, the members of the Communities created a number of central governing institutions with supra-national authority to effect the necessary integration. The goal of creating a unified market has resulted in a significant effort to harmonize the laws of the EU's Member States. The result, it is hoped, will be a union with the economic advantages of the US, but without the loss of the political authority which the states of the US have suffered since 1789.

In contrast to the coming together of the nations of the European continent stands Japan. Since the Second World War, Japan, like Europe, has risen to become among the most powerful of the industrialized nations of the world. However, Japan has not chosen to seek economic or political union with its neighbors. Yet Japan has managed to extend its markets worldwide to a remarkable degree. It has, perhaps deliberately, avoided creation of a political system mimicking that of the United States. Japan is an important source for the comparative study of systems of corporate governance because, unlike most other nations in the world, Japan has had to successfully absorb not one but two distinct systems of law into its own governance traditions, and all within the space of a century. The first was the absorption of European governance principles during the second half of the nineteenth century. The second was the absorption of American principles during the forced democratization of social, political and economic organizations during the military occupation of Japan after 1945. To that extent alone Japan provides fertile ground for studying the ability of a socially and culturally distinct community to absorb the norms of another, and the conditions under which such absorption is possible. The lessons are important for the emerging economies of Asia as well as the nations which emerged from under the influence of the Soviet Union after 1991.

Increasingly important to the United States, the European Union, and Japan is the People's Republic of China ("PRC" or China). A political union with significant restive ethnic and political communities, the PRC has successfully reconstituted itself in the eyes of the outside world as a unified nation. The PRC is expected to dominate trade, if only because of its population and size. Yet the PRC remains unwilling to freely participate in the rush toward convergence. China has begun to transform itself from a backwater militaristic totalitarian dictatorship state organized as a blend of traditional Chinese norms and Eastern European Marxist-Socialist totalitarian practices into a control economy participating in the emerging worldwide market economy. It is accomplishing this transformation by aping, for benefit of the market, the forms of market organization, while retaining, at the same time, its core normative organization as an anti-capitalist state. As such, China provides evidence of the power of the emerging world market to induce convergence in even the most hostile state. On the other hand, to the extent that China is able to devise a viable non-capitalist alternative to enterprise organization, it will provide an important point of divergence for a host of states which have yet to participate in this world-wide market. It will also exert a strong pull for convergence to proceed along the lines pioneered by China. The ability of the Chinese leadership to overcome the contradictions of the position it has staked out will make China among the most interesting places to observe in this new century. The PRC is thus an important subject of study for any person interested in issues in comparative enterprise governance.

But comparisons with the United States raise very real questions about the extent to which harmonization and uniformity is necessary to achieve the free circulation of people, goods, services and capital between nation-states. This is especially so in the area of the regulation of business enterprises, particularly enterprises operating in corporate form. For example, the EU has been working toward internal harmonization of its Company (Corporate) Law and its securities' markets, while the United States has achieved a fairly uniform internal market with a substantially decentralized regulation of corporations, but with a highly centralized regulation of its securities markets. Japan, on the other hand, has remained aloof from regimes for regional or supra-national integration. Japan, however, has made serious efforts to conform its practices to at least outward conformity with emerging global norms. The PRC, even more than Japan, offers an example of resistence to wholesale absorption of global norms which do not have a "Chinese face." Each, in its own very different way, avoids succumbing wholesale to the norms of cross border harmonization, except to the extent necessary to preserve their respective overseas markets and to participate in international markets for capital.

Moreover, consolidation and harmonization remain partial accomplishments. Political borders remain real and significant barriers for enterprises seeking to trade across borders. Enterprises organized as companies, like merchants in an earlier age, can still be stopped at a political border. And like those merchants, modern enterprise organizations can still be required to conform to the trading and organizational rules of the political community in which they seek to profit. Consequently, and especially with respect to larger market areas, it becomes important to understand the rules by which "insiders" can organize and "outsiders" can penetrate these borders.[1]

The European and Japanese approaches to the organization and regulation of economic enterprises has become of increasing importance to the American business lawyer. As the harmonization of European Company Law becomes more of a reality, as the governing institutions of the EU become more important in the regulation of corporations, and as Americans become more involved in business activities in the EU, an understanding of the approaches of the European Communities to the regulation of its most significant form of business enterprise becomes important. The same, of course, applies to Japan. In both cases divergence and convergence of business practices as well as regulation will have a singular impact on American enterprises venturing abroad. Moreover, in the emerging world order, Japan becomes singularly important because of

1. A more concentrated study of these rules is usually reserved for the standard course in international business transactions, and will not be the focus of the materials in this book.

its proximity to China. As China emerges from its self-imposed economic isolation to join the world economic community, it is likely that the PRC will look to Japan for acceptable models of corporate governance. Moreover, the experience of the EU and Japan may provide valuable lessons for American businesses and legislatures as they grapple with the periodic calls for formal change in the regulatory structure of American business. For example, Japan may provide lessons for isolationists, but especially for those in the US who mean to resist the regularizing regimes of international, commercial and enterprise organizational norms. Europe provides a model of the benefits and travails of the sort of federalization of corporate law that has been advocated in the United States from time to time. *See, e.g.*, Cary, *Federalism and Corporate Law, Reflections Upon Delaware*, 83 YALE L.J. 663 (1974).

The purpose of these materials is to introduce readers to the comparative analysis of American, European, Chinese and Japanese approaches to the regulation of business enterprises operating in corporate form. The goal is to provide the student with a basic understanding of the fundamental, and perhaps fundamentally different, approaches taken by governments in the US, the EU, China, and Japan to the regulation of the corporation. The focus will be on giving a basic flavor of difference to the beginning student in a number of significant areas of corporate governance. As such, the materials concentrate on the formal sources of law and thereafter highlight some ways in which the difference in approach is manifested in actual regulation. While an understanding of the approaches of the systems for the regulation of corporations of other nations might also be useful, the sole emphasis of these materials is on the laws and approaches of the nations comprising the US, the EU, Japan, and China.[2] The ultimate aim of this focus is to understand the ways in which systems adjust to the existence of other, and sometimes competitive systems of corporate governance, in an era of global trade. The power of harmonization, emulation, penetration, convergence, and separation is inseparably linked to the comparative study of governance systems. The perhaps problematic notion of technological determinism, that different systems reach similar results when confronted by the same problem, provides a sub-text of this study.

These materials are intended for a basic course in comparative corporate law. It also may be appropriate for use in courses taught overseas in short or semester long programs of study. These materials may be used either for a "lecture" course or as the basic readings of a seminar. Depending on the time available and the interest of the students and faculty, the course instructor can utilize all of the materials, or she may limit the scope of the course to a review of the materials which cover the United States and some, but not all of the other systems included in the materials. In past years, when teaching from these materials in Europe, I have concentrated on the US and the EU and limited the discussion of issues of Chinese and Japanese law. Conversely, the course can emphasize the comparative study of US and Asian systems, minimizing the considerations of issues of European law.

---

2. Other systems of corporate governance are also worthy of study. The governance systems of Latin America, the Indian subcontinent and Africa merit discussion in their own right. India and the States of Latin America evidence the effects of the colonial experience on systems of law, but in two different contexts. India, like Japan, grafted western, and in India's case English, systems of corporate governance onto a strong and vibrant indigenous culture. Latin America's experience was different. There, as in the United States, the indigenous population was marginalized, and Spanish, and then French systems of law, introduced wholesale. Considerations of space, the similar experiences of some of the nations covered, and the focus on primary systems of corporate governance in the emerging world economy militated against an in depth treatment of the systems of these states.

The course is best utilized by students who have taken a basic course in enterprise organization or are taking concurrently with it. However, there are enough materials provided so that even students who have not taken the basic course may profit from a study of these materials. The course materials are meant to provide a sound grounding for courses in international business transactions and international or cross border dispute resolution courses as well as provide a close study of materials usually treated lightly in Conflicts of Laws courses. The materials assume no familiarity with Japanese, Chinese, European national or EU law, but do assume some familiarity with basic US law. For classes in which students have already taken a basic enterprise organization law course, the materials can be explored at a deeper level.

The materials are divided into eleven chapters. Chapters One and Two introduce the basic concepts which will be useful throughout the rest of the study. Chapter One introduces the student to the basic parameters of comparative law, and particularly, comparative law focused on issues of corporate governance. The materials provided introduce students to the basic themes and tensions in comparative study, with a focus on issues of enterprise governance. Chapter Two provides a very basic introduction to the political regimes of the governments that constitute the objects of study. In particular, there is a substantial amount of introductory material on the organization of the European Union, and the political and social organization of Japan and the People's Republic of China. Because the assumption is that students know very little about the political or social organization of at least some for the countries or supra-national organizations studied, the materials cover much basic ground. To the extent that students are better grounded in this introductory material, teachers may choose to skip this material, referring back to it from time to time as needed, rather than teaching through it.

Chapter Three introduces the student to the regulatory context of enterprise organization. The first part of the chapter introduces the student to the patterns of formal organization of corporations in the U.S., some of the Member States of the EU, Japan and China. The second considers the way a state determines which pattern of enterprise regulation is best for them. Particular emphasis is placed on a consideration of legal, economic and sociological characterizations of the corporation as a form of enterprise organization, and raises issues about the efficient regulation of these enterprises based on these characterizations. Introduced here also are issues of legal personality and their effects on regulatory regimes. Thus, these Chapters cover both the formal characteristics of corporate form, what makes a corporation different from other forms of business organization, and the problems of corporate reification. The concentration on reification is used as the introduction to the comparative analysis of American, European and Japanese approaches to the regulation of the corporation.

Chapter Four draws on the discussions in prior chapters, particularly in the last parts of Chapter Three, to consider the way in which conceptions of legal personality affect the form and substance of corporate regulation. The first part of the Chapter considers external regulation, and in particular the availability of constitutional or fundamental rights for corporations. The second part of the Chapter turns to the effect of different conceptions of legal personality on internal regulation of corporations. Chapter Four provides the basis for much of the discussion in the rest of the materials. Moreover, this chapter provides materials which illuminate the sharp differences possible among the various systems reviewed. Most importantly, it shows the way in which different views of corporate personality *within* a system can have a significant effect on the way in which corporations are regulated.

Chapters Five and Six introduce students to issues peculiar to corporate governance within multi-level federal or supra-national systems. As such, these chapters concentrate on the regulatory systems of the U.S. and EU. Japan and the PRC, as integrated unitary systems, do not encounter the formal problems of regulation considered in these chapters. Both chapters, however, point to patterns of regulation which might form a basis for worldwide harmonization in the future. Chapter Five concentrates on an area of fundamental difference between the corporate law of the U.S. and EU—how most efficiently to harmonize the corporate law of an integrated political union. In the United States such harmonization has occurred from the bottom up, by way of the so-called incorporation or "internal affairs" doctrine. Under this doctrine, the laws of the state of incorporation of a corporation determine its validity and the extent of the rights and obligations of the participants in the corporate enterprise. Once determined to be valid in the state of incorporation, such an enterprise must be recognized as valid and permitted to operate as such in all other states in the U.S. In contrast, most European states have embraced the "siège social" doctrine, under which a corporation, to be validly established, must be registered in compliance with all of the company laws of the state in which its primary operations are located. The Chapters also introduce students to the means certain states, notably, California and New York, have sought, with limited success to import the concept of "siège social" into the American corporate jurisprudence, as well as the ways in which the European Court of Justice may be incorporating the English model of corporate organization into the constitutional law of the European Union.

Chapter Six continues the study of the problems of corporate governance in integrated federal unions by considering the potential for and effects of the federalization of corporate law in the U.S. and EU. The first part of the chapter considers arguments for the federalization of American corporate law. The latter part of the chapter is taken up with a consideration of the sources of Community Law affecting company law. Particular focus is directed to the characteristics and effects of EC directives and regulations to harmonize corporate law within the Member States.

Chapters Seven through Eleven provide four distinct and separable areas of comparative study of corporate governance. Chapter Seven introduces the student to issues of liability for the pre-incorporation obligations of the enterprise, and the liability of the corporation for ultra vires actions. The chapter considers the imposition of this liability under two circumstances—when the incorporators or promoters enter into agreement prior to the filing of the requisite documents which establish the existence, in law, of the corporation, and when people enter into contract or incur other obligations on behalf of an invalidly formed corporation. On the American side, the emphasis will be on general common law, with some consideration of the approach suggested under the Revised Model Business Corporation Act. On the European side, the chapter considers how the First and Second Council directives on company law harmonization treat these issues in the European Community. The nuance of Chinese and Japanese law round out the study.

Chapter Eight considers issues touching on state regulation of capital and capital requirements for companies. In the US, the emphasis will be on the approach taken by Delaware, a representative of the traditional approach to the maintenance of capital requirements. Consideration will also be given to the "modern" approach of the Revised Model Business Corporation Act, and the approach taken by California. Capital requirements form a far more important part of European and Japanese company law than they do in the US, and for reasons largely rejected as irrelevant in the US—the protection of creditors and other strangers to the corporate enterprise. The chapter examines the attempts to harmonize capital maintenance requirements set forth in the Second Company Law Directive and the Japanese system of minimum capital requirements. China's distinctive approach is also considered.

Chapter Nine takes up a study of a core value of enterprise organization in corporate form–limited liability for investors. Much of the law in this area in the United States remains a matter of state law. The same can, to some extent, be said of the law in the Member States of the EU. Japanese law provides a nice example of the way in which reception of foreign law that is not culturally compatible can be reworked to achieve a harmonious result. The Chinese approach to limited liability, based on the appointment of a natural person to stand in the place of the corporate legal person, is unique and ties the study of this area more closely to earlier considerations of the effect of conceptions of legal personality on corporate governance. The Chapter highlights the different approaches to the application of the doctrines of disregard of corporate personality in cases of multi-corporate enterprises, that is, of enterprises operating through a series of related corporations.

Chapters Ten and Eleven take up another core area of corporate governance–the supervision and disciplining of a corporation's managers and dominant shareholders. Chapter Ten explores judicial and legislative approaches to the regulation of managers. It starts with a review of the American common law and statutory rules defining the nature of a manager's duties to the enterprise. It then contrasts these rules of fiduciary duty with the more formal, but also more narrowly tailored approaches in Europe. The European approach is contrasted with the Japanese hybrid of American and European approaches. Chinese construction of a system of monitoring managers will then be considered. The principal focus will be on what are known in the United States as the duties of care and loyalty.

Chapter Eleven considers the special case of shareholder duty to the enterprise. It considers the circumstances under which shareholder discretion with respect to her holdings are properly the subject of regulation or control by the state. The American fiduciary duty approach, adopted by some, but by no means all, of the states, is contrasted with the approaches of continental Europe and Japan. Particular attention is paid to the problems of shareholder regulation in states where the state has or had a dominant position in the economy. In this connection, the focus is on Russia as a transitional economy and the People's Republic of China as a nation still wed to the concept of state ownership of the means of production.

My hope is that the study of some or all of the issues raised in these materials will provide students with a broader perspective for understanding the benefits and limitations of American systems of governance, and an appreciation for differences in governance in other economically important parts of the world. I also hope that the study of these materials provide the basis for understanding the limited number of patterns existing or used for the regulation of enterprise organizations, and the ways in which these patterns manifest themselves in the context of different political systems.

I am grateful to all those who have helped this project along. In particular I want to thank the students enrolled in programs of study abroad sponsored by St. Thomas University Law School in El Escorial, Spain, and those sponsored by the University of Tulsa College of Law in Bratislava, Slovakia, Buenos Aires Argentina and London, England, whose feedback on earlier versions of this material proved invaluable.

I am especially grateful to my students and colleagues at the Pennsylvania State Univeresity–Dickinson School of Law, whose comments, suggestions, questions and insights were instrumental in moving from draft to finished product. My thanks to all of you. In addition, I extend special thanks to Kim Kraviec (North Carolina), Barbara Buckholtz (Tulsa), and Ediberto Roman (St. Thomas) for bravely using earlier versions of these materials in their own courses. Nicholas Cicero (Tulsa), Ryan Barnett (Penn. State), and Seema Lal (Penn. State) provided very able research assistance. My thanks also to my colleague from the Ukraine, Alexander Merezhko, for his insights into the realities of Socialist law, and very special thanks to Paul Finkelman (Tulsa) and Carolina Academic Press for helping me realize this project. This book is dedicated to the late Bernard Schwartz (NYU and Tulsa), who first encouraged me in this endeavor.

Larry Catá Backer

October 2001

Acknowledgments

I gratefully acknowledge the authors and publishers that permitted me to reprint excerpts of copyrighted works. They are

Andre, Thomas J. Jr., Cultural Hegemony: The Exportation of Anglo-Saxon Corporate Governance Ideologies to Germany, originally published in 73 Tul. L. Rev. 69-171 (1998). Reprinted with the permission of Tulane Law Review Association, which holds the copyright.

Andre, Thomas J. Jr., Some Reflections on German Corporate Governance: A Glimpse at German Supervisory Boards, originally published in 70 Tul. L. Rev. 1819–1879 (1996). Reprinted with the permission of Tulane Law Review Association, which holds the copyright.

Antunes, Jose Engracia, The Liability of Polycorporate Enterprises, 13 Conn. J. Int'l L. 197 (1999). Copyright © 1999 by the Connecticut Journal of International Law. Reprinted by permission.

Art, Roberts C., Gu, Minkang, China Incorporated: The First Corporation Law of the People's Republic of China, 20 Yale J. Int'l L. 273 (1995). Copyright © Yale Journal of International Law. Reprinted by permission.

Backer, Larry Catá, Forging Federal Systems Within a Matrix of Contained Conflict: The Example of the European Union, 12 Emory Int'l L. Rev. 1331 (1998). Copyright © 1998 by Emory International Law Review. Reprinted by permission.

Backer, Larry Catá, Harmonization, Subsidiarity and Cultural Difference: An Essay on the Dynamics of Opposition Within Federative and International Legal Systems, 4 Tulsa J. Comp. & Int'l L. 185 (1997). Copyright © 1997 Tulsa Journal of Comparative and International Law. Reprinted by permission.

Baev, Andrei A., The Transformation of the Role of the State in Monitoring Large Firms in Russia: From the State's Supervision to the State's Fiduciary Duties, 8 Transnat'l Law. 247 (1995). Copyright © 1995 by The Transnational Lawyer. Reprinted by permission.

Balotti, R. Franklin, Elson, Charles, M. & Laster, J. Travis, Equity Ownership and the Duty of Care: Convergence, Revolution, or Evolution?, 55 Bus. Law. 661 (2000). Copyright © 2000 by ABA Publishing. Reprinted by permission.

Bebchuk, Lucian Arye and Roe, Mark J., A Theory of Path Dependence in Corporate Ownership and Governance, 52 Stan. L. Rev. 127 (1999). Reprinted with the permission of the Stanford Law Review. Copyright © 2000 by the Board of Trustees of the Leland Stanford Junior University.

Bell, John, Boyron, Sophie, & Whittaker, Simon, Principles of French Law (1998). Copyright © 1998 by Oxford University Press. Reprinted by permission of Oxford

University Press. Reprinted from Colin J. Bennett, Regulating Privacy: Data Protection and Public Policy in Europe and the United States. Copyright © 1992 by Cornell University. Used by permission of the publisher, Cornell University Press.

Bennett, Colin J., Regulating Privacy & Data Protection and Public Policy in Europe and the United States. Copyright © 1992 by Cornell University. Used by permission of the publisher, Cornell University Press.

Berger, David J., Exporting the Twin Towers: The Development of a Transnational Business Judgment Rule, 9 St. Louis U. Pub. L. Rev. 169 (1990). Reprinted with permission of the Saint Louis University *Public Law Review* © 1990 St. Louis University School of Law, St. Louis, Missouri.

Blackburn, Terence L., The Societas Europeana: The Evolving European Corporation Statute, 61 Fordham L. Rev. 695 (1993). Copyright © 1993 by Fordham Law Review. Reprinted with permission.

Blackburn, Terence L., The Unification of Corporate Laws: The United States, the European Community and the Race to Laxity, 3 Geo. Mason Independent L. Rev. 1 (1994). Copyright © 1994 by George Mason Independent Law Review. Reprinted with permission.

Blackmore, Thomas J. and Yazawa, Makoto, Japanese Commercial Code Revisions Concerning Corporations, 2 Am. J. Comp. L. 711 (1953). Copyright © 1953 by American Journal of Comparative Law. Reprinted by permission.

Blumberg, Phillip I., The Law of Corporate Groups: Tort, Contract and Other Common Law Problems in the Substantive Law of Parent and Subsidiary Corporations (1987). Reprinted by permission of the author.

Bradley, Michael & Schipani, Cindy A., The Relevance of the Duty of Care Standard in Corporate Governance, 75 Iowa L. Rev. 1, 3–9 (1989) (Reprinted with permission).

Bradley, Michael, Schipani, Cindy A., Sundaram, Anant K. & Walsh, James P., The Purposes and Accountability of the Corporation in Contemporary Society: Corporate Governance at a Crossroads, 62 Law and Contemporary Problems 9 (1999). Copyright © 1999 by authors. Reprinted by permission.

Breskovski, Vassil, Director's Duty of Care in Eastern Europe, 29 Int'l Law. 77 (1995). Copyright © 1995 by American Bar Association. Reprinted by permission.

Buxbaum, Richard M. & Hopt, Klaus J., Legal Harmonization and the Business Enterprise: Corporate and Capital Market Law Harmonization Policy in Europe and the U.S.A. (1988). Copyright © 1988 by Walter de Gruyter GmbH & Co. Reprinted by permission.

Cao, Lan, Chinese Privatization: Between Plan and Market, 63 Law and Contemporary Problems 13 (2000). Copyright © 2000 by Law and Contemporary Problems. Reprinted by permission.

Cary, William L., Federalism and Corporate Law: Reflections Upon Delaware, 83 Yale L.J. 663 (1974). Reprinted by permission of The Yale Law Journal Company and William S. Hein Company from The Yale Law Journal, Vol. 83, pages 663–705.

Cohn, E.J. and Simitis, C., "Lifting the Veil" in the Company Law of the European Continent, 12 Int'l & Comp. L.Q. 189 (1963). Copyright © 1963 by Oxford University Press. Reprinted by permission.

Company Law: Lifting the Veil, Estates Gazette 25 July 1992, Issue No. 9229, p. 115. Copyright © 1992 by The Estates Gazette Ltd. Reprinted by permission.

Cowles, Maria Green, The Changing Architecture of Big Business, in Collective Acton in the European Union: Interests and the New Politics of Associability (1998). Copyright © 1998 by Routledge. Reprinted by permission.

Craig, Paul and de Búrca, EU Law: Text, Cases and Materials, (2nd ed. 1998). Copyright © 1998 by Oxford University Press. Reprinted by permission of Oxford University Press.

Cunningham, Lawrence A., Commonalities and Prescriptions in the Vertical Dimensions of Global Corporate Governance, 84 Cornell L. Rev. 1133 (1999). Copyright © 1999 by the Cornell Law Review. Reprinted by permission.

Cunningham, Lawrence A., Comparative Corporate Governance and Pedagogy, 34 Ga. L. Rev. 721 (2000). Copyright © 2000 by Georgia Law Review. Reprinted by permission.

Deering's California Codes, Corporations Code, § 500. Reprinted by permission Lexis Nexis.

DeVries, Henry P. & Juenger, Friedrick K., Limited Liability Contract: The GmbH. This article originally appeared at 64 Colum. L. Rev. 866 (1964). Reprinted by permission.

Dobson, Juan M., Lifting the Veil in Four Countries: The Law of Argentina, England, France and the United States, 35 Int'l & Comp. L.Q. 839 (1986). Copyright © 1986 by Oxford University Press. Reprinted by permission.

Doing Business in France, Price Waterhouse World Firm Services BV, Inc. (1995). Reprinted by permission.

Drexl, Josef, Was Sir Francis Drake a Dutchman?—British Supremacy of Parliament After Factortame, 41 Am. J. Comp. L. 551 (1993). Copyright © 1993 by American Journal of Comparative Law. Reprinted by permission.

Edwards, Vanessa, EC Company Law (1999). Copyright © 1999. Reprinted from EC Company Law by Vanessa Edwards (1999) by permission of Oxford University Press.

Eisenberg, Melvin A., Corporate Law and Social Norms. This article originally appeared at 99 Colum. L. Rev. 1253 (1999). Reprinted by permission.

Ellard, George, Constitutional Rights of the Corporate Person, 91 Yale L.J. 1641 (1982). Reprinted by permission of The Yale Law Journal Company and William S. Hein Company from The Yale Law Journal, Vol. 91, pages 1645–1751.

English, Richard D., Company Law in the European Single Market, 1990 B.Y.U. L. Rev. 1413 (1990). Copyright © 1990 Brigham Young University Law Review. Reprinted by permission.

Ercklentz, Enno W. Jr., Modern German Corporation Law (1979). Copyright © Oceana Publications Inc. Reprinted by permission.

Farrar, John H. & Hannigan, Brenda M., Farrar's Company Law 4th Edition (1998). Copyright © 1991 by Butterworths Division of Reed Elsevier (UK) Limited. Reproduced by permission of The Butterworths Division of Reed Elsevier (UK) Limited.

Ferran, Eilís, Company Law and Corporate Finance (1999). Copyright © Eilís Ferran 1999. Reprinted from Company Law and Corporate Finance by Eilís Ferran (1999) by permission of Oxford University Press.

Fischel, Daniel R., The "Race to the Bottom" Revisited: Reflections on Developments in Delaware's Corporation Law, 76 Nw. U. L. Rev. 913 (1982). Reprinted by special permission of Northwestern University School of Law, Law Review.

Fisher, Howard D., The German Legal System and Language, 2nd ed., 1999, London: Cavendish Publishing. Reprinted by permission.

Folk on Delaware General Corporation Law: A Commentary and Analysis (3rd ed. 1992). Copyright © 1992. Reprinted with permission of Aspen Law & Business.

Foster, Nigel, German Legal System and Laws 1–4 (2nd ed 1996). Copyright © 1996 by Blackstone Press Limited. Reprinted by permission.

Frommel, S.N. & Thompson, J.H., Company Law in Europe (1975). Copyright © 1975. Reprinted with the kind permission of Kluwer Law International.

Fu, Tingmei, Legal Person in China, 41 Am. J. Comp. L. 261 (1993). Copyright © 1993 by American Journal of Comparative Law. Reprinted by permission.

Fukushima, Masao, The Significance of the Enforcement of the Company Law Chapters of the Old Commercial Code in 1893, 24 Law in Japan 171, William Horton trans. (1991). Copyright © 1991Japanese American Society for Legal Studies. Reprinted by permission.

Gensler, Howard, Company Formation and Securities Listing in the People's Republic of China, 17 Hous. J. Int'l L. 399 (1995). Copyright © 1995 by Houston Journal of International Law. Reprinted by permission.

Gevurtz, Franklin A., The Business Judgment Rule: Meaningless Verbiage or Misguided Notion?, 67 S. Cal. L. Rev. 287–337 (1994). Reprinted by permission of Southern California Law Review.

Gillespie, John, Private Commercial Rights in Vietnam: A Comparative Analysis, 30 Stan. J. Int'l L. 325 (1994). Reprinted with the permission of the Stanford Journal of International Law. Copyright © 1994 by the Board of Trustees of the Leland Stanford Junior University.

Goldman, Berthold, The Convention Between the Member States of the European Economic Community on the Mutual Recognition of Companies, 6 C.M. L. Rev. 104 (1968). Copyright © 1968 by the Common Market Law Review. Reprinted with the kind permission of Kluwer Law International.

Hahn, Elliott J., Japanese Business Law and the Legal System. Copyright © 1984 by Quorum Books. Reproduced with permission of Greenwood Publishing Group, Inc., Westport, CT.

From Authority Without Power: Law and the Japanese Paradox by John Owen Haley, copyright © 1994 by Oxford University Press, Inc. Used by permission of Oxford University Press, Inc.

Han, Anna M., China's Company Law: Practicing Capitalism in a Transitional Economy, 5 Pac. Rim. L. & Pol'y J. 457 (1996). Copyright © 1996 by Pacific Rim Law and Policy Journal. Reprinted by permission.

Hanna, Christopher H., Initial Thoughts on Classifying the Major Japanese Business Entities Under the Check-the-box Regulations, 51 SMU L. Rev. 75 (1997). Originally appearing in Vol. 51, No. 1 of SMU Law Review. Reprinted with permission from the SMU Law Review and the Southern Methodist University School of Law.

Harris, Brian, "Social Charter": The Legal Basis, The New Law Journal, V. 139, no. 6410, p. 764 (1989). Copyright © 1989. Reprinted by permission of author.

Hawke, Neil & Marston, John, Facades and Corporate Veils, Law Society's Gazette (1989), 3 May 1989, V. 86, No. 17, p. 32. Copyright © 1989. Reprinted by permission of the authors.

Heftel, Christopher Lee, Survey, Corporate Governance in Japan: The Position of Shareholders in Publicly Held Corporations, 5 U. Haw. L. Rev. 135 (1983). Copyright © 1983 by University of Hawaii Law Review. Reprinted by permission.

Henderson, Dan Fenno, Security Markets in the United States and Japan: Distinctive Aspects Molded by Cultural, Social, Economic, and Political Differences, 14 Hastings Int'l & Comp. L. Rev. 263 (1991). Copyright © 1991 by University of California, Hastings College of the Law. Reprinted from Hastings International and Comparative Law Review.

Hessen, Robert, A New Concept of Corporations: A Contractual and Private Property Model, 14 Hastings L.J. 1327 (1979). Copyright © 1979 by University of California, Hastings College of the Law. Reprinted with permission from Hastings Law Journal, Vol 30, Number 5, May 1979, 1327–1350.

Hofstetter, Karl, Parent Responsibility for Subsidiary Corporations: Evaluating European Trends, 39 Int'l & Comp. L.Q. 577 (1990). Copyright © 1990 by Oxford University Press. Reprinted by permission.

Hoshi, Takeo, Japanese Corporate Governance as a System (1998). Copyright © 1998 K. Hopt, H. Kanda, M. Roe, E. Wymeersch, and S. Prigge. Reprinted from Comparative Corporate Governance—The State of the Art and Emerging Research edited by Klaus J. Hopt, Hideki Kanda, Mark J. Roe, Eddy Wymeersch, & Stefan Prigge (1998) by permission of Oxford University Press.

Howson, Nicholas C., China's Company Law: One Step Forward, Two Steps Back? A Modest Complaint, 11 Colum. J. Asian L. 127 (1997). Copyright © 1997, originally published in the Columbia Journal of Asian Law. Reprinted by permission.

Huckaby, S. Todd, Note: Defensive Action to Hostile Takeover Efforts in Japan: The Shuwa Decisions, 29 Colum. J. Transnat'l L. 439 (1991). Copyright © 1991 by Columbia Journal of Transnational Law. Reprinted by permission.

Hudson, Alexis Maitland, France: Practical Commercial Law (1991) Copyright © 1991 by Sweet & Maxwell Limited. Reprinted by permission.

Iwai, Katsuhito, Persons, Things and Corporations: The Corporate Personality Controversy and Comparative Corporate Governance, 47 Am. J. Comp. L. 583 (1999). Copyright © 1999 by American Journal of Comparative Law. Reprinted by permission.

Jackson, David & Frumkin, Joseph B., The Global Role of Corporate Law, 25 Del. J. Corp. L. 106 (2000). Copyright © 2000 by Delaware Journal of Corporate Law. Reprinted by permission.

Jianhua, Zhong & Guanghua, Yu, China's Uniform Contract Law: Progress and Problems, 17 U.C.L.A. Pac. Basin L.J. 1 (1999). Copyright © 1999. Reprinted by permission of authors.

Keller, Perry, Sources of Order in Chinese Law, 42 Am. J. Comp. L. 711 (1994). Copyright © 1994 by American Journal of Comparative Law. Reprinted by permission.

Kitchin, Alan W.N. and McClenahan, John, Doing Business in Asia: Focus on Japan, India, and Vietnam, in Going International: International Trade for the Nonspecialist, pp. 184–185. Copyright © 1994 by The American Law Institute. Reprinted with the permission of the American Law Institute-American Bar Association Committee on Continuing Professional Education.

Klein, William A. & Coffee, John C., Business Organization and Corporate Finance (7th ed. 2000). Copyright © 2000 by Foundation Press. Reprinted by permission.

Kline, Carol L., Protecting Minority Shareholders in Close Corporations: Modeling Czech Investor Protections on German and United States Law, 23 B.C. Int'l & Comp. L. Rev. 229 (2000). Copyright © by B.C. International & Comparative Law Review. Reprinted by permission.

Kommers, Donald J., The Constitutional Jurisprudence of the Federal Republic of Germany (2nd ed. 1997). Copyright © 1997 by Duke University Press. Reprinted by permission.

Kondō, The Management Liability of Directors, 20 Law in Japan 150 (1987). Copyright © 1987 Japanese American Society for Legal Studies. Reprinted by permission.

Kostel, Mary E., Note: A Public Choice Perspective on the Debate over Federal Versus State Corporate Law, 79 Va. L. Rev. 2129 (1993). Copyright © 1993 by Virginia Law Review. Reprinted by permission.

Langbein, John H., Cultural Chauvinism in Comparative Law. This article originally appeared in 5 Cardoza J. Int'l & Comp. L. 41 (1997). Reprinted by permission.

Lasok, D. & Bridge, J.W., Law and Institutions of the European Communities (5th ed. 1991). Copyright © 1991 by Butterworths Division of Reed Elsevier (UK) Limited. Reproduced by permission of The Butterworths Division of Reed Elsevier (UK) Limited.

Lastres, Jose Manuel Otero, Company Law in Spanish Business Law, p. 153, Bernardo M. Cremades, ed (1985). Copyright © 1985. Reprinted with the kind permission of Kluwer Law International.

Licht, Amir N., The Mother of All Path Dependencies Toward a Cross-cultural Theory of Corporate Governance Systems, 26 Del. J. Corp. L. 147 (2001). Copyright © 2001 by Delaware Journal of Corporate Law. Reprinted by permission.

Lin, Yabo, New Forms and Organizational Structures of Foreign Investment in China Under the Company Law of the PRC, 7 Transnat'l Law. 327 (1994). Copyright © 1994 by The Transnational Lawyer. Reprinted by permission.

MacLennan, Bruce W., Establishing a Stock Corporation in Japan after the 1990 Revision of the Commercial Code, 1 Pac. Rim L. & Pol'y J. 127 (1992). Copyright © 1992 by Pacific Rim Law and Policy Journal. Reprinted by permission.

Macey, Jonathon R., Institutional Investors and Corporate Monitoring: A Demand-Side Perspective in a Comparative View (1998). Copyright © 1998 K. Hopt, H. Kanda, M. Roe, E. Wymeersch, and S. Prigge. Reprinted from Comparative Corporate Governance—The State of the Art and Emerging Research edited by Klaus J. Hopt, Hideki Kanda, Mark J. Roe, Eddy Wymeersch, & Stefan Prigge (1998) by permission of Oxford University Press.

McKinney's Consolidated Laws of New York Annotated, Chapter 4 of the Consolidated Laws, Article 13, § 1319. Reprinted by permission of West Group.

Mengozzi, Paolo, European Community Law: From the Treaty of Rome to the Treaty of Amsterdam, (2nd ed. 1999). Reprinted with the kind permission of Kluwer Law International. Reprinted by permission of author.

Merezhko, Alexander, Problems of Stylistics in Ukrainian Legislation on the Example of the Draft of the Law "On Securing Performance of Obligations with Moveable Property," Legal Practices Newspaper, No. 16 (122), April 20, 2000. Reprinted by permission.

Mesnooh, Christopher Joseph, Law and Business in France: A Guide to French Commercial and Corporate Law (1994). Reprinted with the kind permission of Kluwer Law International.

Michalowski, Sabine & Woods, Lorna, German Constitutional Law: The Protection of Civil Liberties (1999). Copyright © 1999 by Ashgate Publishing Ltd. Reprinted by permission.

Miller, Sandra K., Minority Shareholder Oppression in the Private Company in the European Community: A Comparative Analysis of the German, United Kingdom, and French "Close Corporation Problem," 30 Cornell Int'l L.J. 381 (1997). Copyright © 1997 by the Cornell International Law Journal. Reprinted by permission.

Miller, Sandra K., Piercing the Corporate Veil among Affiliated Companies in the European Community and in the U.S.: A Comparative Analysis of U.S., German, and U.K. Veil Piercing Approaches, 36 Am. Bus. L.J. 73 (1998). Reprinted by permission of author.

Miwa, Yoshiro, Symposium, Corporate Social Responsibility: Dangerous and Harmful, Though Maybe Not Irrelevant, 84 Cornell L. Rev. 1227 (1999). Copyright © 1999 by Cornell Law Review. Reprinted by permission.

Mussa, Michael, Factors Driving Global Economic Integration, presented in Jackson Hole, Wyoming at a symposium sponsored by the Federal Reserve Bank of Kansas City on Global Opportunities and Challenges, August 25, 2000. Available at <www.imf.org/external/np/speeches/2000/082500.htm>. Reprinted by permission of International Monetary Fund.

Nader, Ralph & Green, Mark, The Case for Federal Charters, The Nation, Febrary 5, 1973 at 173. Reprinted by permission. From the February 5, 1973 issue of The Nation.

Nikkel, Michael Irl, Note: "Chinese Characteristics" in Corporate Clothing: Questions of Fiduciary Duty in China's Company Law, 80 Minn. L. Rev. 503 (1995). Copyright © 1995 by Minnesota Law Review. Reprinted by permission.

Noda, Yosiyuki, Introduction to Japanese Law. Copyright © 1976 by University of Tokyo Press. Reprinted by permission.

Oda, Hiroshi, Japanese Law (2nd ed. 1999). Copyright © 1999 by Oxford University Press. Reprinted by permission of Oxford University Press.

Ogus, Anthony, Competition Between National Legal Systems: A Contribution of Economic Analysis, 48 Int'l & Comp. L.Q, 405 (1999). Copyright © 1999 by Oxford University Press. Reprinted by permission.

Ong, Kingsley T.W. & Baxter, Colin R., A Comparative Study of the Fundamental Elements of Chinese and English Company Law, 48 Int'l & Comp. L.Q. 88 (1999). Copyright © 1999 by Oxford University Press. Reprinted by permission.

Peng, Chuan Roger, Limited Liability in China: A Partial Reading of China's Company Law of 1994, 10 Colum. J. Asian L. 263 (1996). Copyright © 1996 by Columbia Journal of Asian Law. Reprinted by permission.

Raiser, Thomas, The Theory of Enterprise Law in the Federal Republic of Germany, 36 Am. J. Comp. L. 111 (1988). Copyright © 1988 by American Journal of Comparative Law. Reprinted by permission.

Ramseyer, Mark & Nakazato, Japanese Law: An Economic Approach (1999). Copyright © 1999 by University of Chicago Press. Reprinted by permission.

Restatement (Second) Conflict of Laws, §§ 298, 302, 309, 311. Reprinted by permission of American Law Institute.

Revised Model Business Corporation Act, Sections 2.04; 6.21; 6.40, and portions of the official comments and illustrations of those sections, Copyright © 2000 by ABA Publishing. Reprinted by permission.

Roe, Mark J., German Codetermination and German Securities Markets, 5 Colum. J. Eur. L. 199 (1999). Copyright © 1999 by Columbia Journal of European Law. Reprinted by permission.

Rojo, Angel, The Typology of Companies, in European Company Laws: A Comparative Approach (1991). Copyright © 1991 by Ashgate Publishing Limited. Reprinted by permission.

Romano, Roberta, The State Competition Debate in Corporate Law. This article originally appeared in 8 Cardozo L. Rev. 709 (1987). Reprinted by permission.

Ruskola, Teemu, Conceptualizing Corporations and Kinship: Comparative Law and Development Theory in a Chinese Perspective, 52 Stan. L. Rev. 1599 (2000). Reprinted with the permission of the Stanford Law Review. Copyright © 2000 by the Board of Trustees of the Leland Stanford Junior University.

Samara-Krispis, Anastasia and Steindorff, Ernst, Joined Cases C-19/90 and 20/90, M. Karella and N. Karellas v. Ypourgos viomichanias, energias kai technologias, Organismos Anasygkrotiseos Epicheiriseon AE, Preliminary ruling of 30 January 1991, requested by the Greek Council of State on the interpretation of Articles 25, 41 and 42 of the Second Directive on company law, not yet reported, 1992 C.M.L. Rev. 615 (1992). Copyright © 1992 by Common Market Law Review. Reprinted with the kind permission of Kluwer Law International.

Schmitthoff, Clive M., Social Responsibility in European Company Law, 30 Hast. L.J. 1419 (1979). Copyright © 1979 by the University of California, Hastings College of the Law. Reprinted from Hastings Law Journal with permission.

Seita, Alex Y., Globalization and the Convergence of Values, 30 Cornell Int'l L.J. 429 (1997). Copyright © 1997 by the Cornell International Law Journal. Reprinted by permission.

Simon, William H., The Legal Structure of the Chinese "Socialist Market" Enterprise, 21 J. Corp. L. 267 (1996). Copyright © 1996 by Journal of Corporation Law. Reprinted with permission.

Takayangi, K., A Century of Innovation: The Development of Japanese Law 1868–1961. Reprinted by Permission from Law In Japan the Legal Order in a Changing Society, edited by Arthur von Mehren, Cambridge, Mass. Harvard University Press, Copyright © 1963 by the President and Fellows of Harvard College, Copyright © renewed 1991.

Takeuchi, Akio, How Should We Abolish the Ultra Vires Doctrine in Corporate Law?, 2 Law in Japan 140, Dan Fenno Henderson, trans. (1968). Copyright © 1968 Japanese American Society for Legal Studies. Reprinted by permission.

Teubner, Gunther, Enterprise Corporatism: New Industrial Policy and the "Essence" of the Legal Person, 36 Am. J. Corp. L. 130 (1988). Copyright © 1988 by American Journal of Comparative Law. Reprinted by permission.

Thompson, Robert B., Preemption and Federalism in Corporate Governance: Protecting Shareholder Rights to Vote, Sell and Sue, 62 Law and Contemporary Problems 215 (1999). Copyright © 1999 by author. Reprinted by permission.

Varallo, Gregory V. and Dreisbach, Daniel A., Fundamentals of Corporate Governance: A Guide for Directors and Corporate Counsel (1996). Copyright © 1996 by ABA Publishing. Reprinted by permission.

Wang, Joseph En-Pao, Selected Legal Documents of the People's Republic of China. Copyright © 1979 by UPA, Greenwood Publishing Group. Reproduced with permission of Greenwood Publishing Group, Inc., Westport, CT.

West, Mark D., The Pricing of Shareholder Derivative Actions in Japan and the United States, 88 Nw. U. L. Rev. 1436 (1994). Reprinted by special permission of Northwestern University School of Law, Law Review.

West's Annotated California Codes, Title 1, Division 1, Chapter 21, §2115. Reprinted by permission of West Group.

Winter, Audrey, The Origins and Constitutional Framework of the Single Market. Reproduced with permission from Europe Without Frontiers: A Lawyer's Guide (Corporate Practice Series), pp 5–8. Copyright © 1989 by the Bureau of National Affairs, Inc. (800-372-1033) <http://www.bna.com>

Wooldridge, Frank, Company Law in the United Kingdom and the European Community: Its Harmonization and Unification (1991). Copyright © 1991 The Continuum International Publishing Group Ltd. Reprinted by permission.

Wyatt, Derrick & Dashwood, Alan, The Substantive Law of the EEC (1987). Copyright © 1987 by Sweet & Maxwell Limited. Reprinted by permission.

Comparative Corporate Law

Chapter 1

An Introduction to Comparative Corporate Law

In this course you will be engaged in the task of making comparisons. More specifically, you will be making comparisons in connection with issues relating to the regulation of business enterprises operating in corporate form. Before commencing, it might be worth your while to pause to reflect on the nature of the task. What is there to compare? Why compare at all?

Corporations have become a dominant form of enterprise organization in virtually every part of the industrialized world. The modern corporation emerged in the 19th century as people sought an efficient means of aggregating their resources and organizing large scale organs for the production of wealth. Corporations, an ancient device of intangible organization, provided a convenient foundation for this aggregation. A variety of nations sought to provide a legal basis for this organization while preserving, to some extent, authority to control abuses of the form. However, while the 19th century provided the socio-economic foundation for the creation of organizations for the aggregation of wealth and the deployment of resources in industry and commerce, it also marked the high water mark for the socio-political disaggregation of political communities. The 19th century saw the triumph of the nation-state in the legal sphere. The century opened with the promulgation of the Napoleonic Code—a fully developed self-contained codex of legislation arising from and reflecting the peculiar and unique genius of the people of France—and closed with the promulgation of the German and Japanese Empire's legislative codes—fully developed and self contained codices reflecting the particular genius of the German and Japanese *Volk*. The opening of the twentieth century also saw the triumph of territorial jurisprudence in common law states—the development of state corporate law codes in the United States and within the realms of the British Empire.

As a result, a universal need for a mechanism for the deployment of resources was met by a profusion of different techniques for their organization. The 20th century has seen a tremendous expansion of the operations of enterprises organized as corporations, many with worldwide, or at least multi-national operations. It has also seen the breakdown of strict separation between the legal orders of states. Especially since the mid 20th century, states have begun to organize themselves within a variety of multistate organizations, from quasi-federal states such as the European Union, to loosely based regional trade associations such as MERCOSUR in Latin America. Interaction at both economic and political levels have resulted in a push for regularization—unification or harmonization—of the legal regimes within which economic enterprises are organized, recognized and regulated. Conversely, the 20th Century saw the rise of resistance to integration. Socialist systems of law, based on assumptions of ownership and political organization ostensibly incompatible with those that gave rise to the law of enterprise organization at one point covered a large part of the world. Reduced now, in its purest form to China and some smaller states, these states remain self-conscious points of resistance to systems of organization based on non-state aggregations of resources. Also, systems of theocratic political organization, increasingly popular in certain parts of the world, suggests that the 19th century European manifestations of community "genius" have not yet seen their last expression as political acts of communities seeking to impose or export their own notions of appropriate organization.

Thus, it is necessary to understand regimes of enterprise organization because global trade results in the operation of enterprises in communities with regulatory regimes different from that of the enterprise's countries of origin. Borders of regulatory regimes remain effective barriers to foreign enterprises, which along with tariffs, produce effective barriers to trade. These barriers tend to advantage those within, and disadvantage those without, the barriers. Conversely, to the extent that political communities more closely integrate, it may be necessary to understand the range of enterprise organization and regulation for the purpose of unification or harmonization. Lastly, the limits of integration must be understood—either as a function of culture, religion, or politics.

This chapter provides the student with an introduction to the major themes of the comparative method. This introduction focuses on problems of the regulation of enterprises operating in corporate form. The chapter starts with the familiar—at least for students of American law—exploring the ways in which comparison has become basic to the common law system in the United States. The chapter concludes with an introductory exploration of the major issues involved in the comparative study of corporate organization—the reasons people compare systems, and the limits of the value of comparison. The themes of unification, harmonization, and resistance form the outer boundary of the study. As you read the materials that follow, consider the effects of trade, technology, culture, politics and economics on convergence and divergence of enterprise organization in today's world.

A. Why Make Comparisons?

1. *Indigenous Comparative Law in the United States*

American lawyers are natural comparativists. American lawyers, judges and legislators look to other jurisdictions for solutions to similar problems. Legislators, in particular, have done much to harmonize the laws as between the states. This harmonization has been accomplished through the adoption of uniform laws, developed, in part through the efforts of non-governmental organizations, like the American Law Institute.[1] The essence of legal training for American lawyers is built on a foundation of

1. The American Law Institute (ALI) is a non-governmental organization, whose members are primarily practicing lawyers, judges and law professors from the United States. The ALI is devoted to the reformulation and modernization of law. The ALI develops uniform codes representing their view of the best accepted approach to a particular body of law. Its work has been highly influential. For more information see the ALI website, <http://www.ali.org>.

multi-jurisdictional analysis. It is not unusual for American lawyers and judges, to seek answers to legal questions within the law of their own jurisdiction first, and then look to the law of sister jurisdictions for persuasive approaches where the answer is not locally available. American legislators look to the legislative approaches of sister states in fashioning legislation. Sometimes other states have innovated in particularly successful ways, sometimes other states have found a solution to a problem which had yet to be addressed in the home state. American non-governmental organizations have also been at the forefront of harmonization of law. The Model Business Corporations Act, now adopted by close to a majority of the states in some form, attests to the naturalization in the United States of the comparative law process. Thus, the American legal system is accustomed to the use of the comparative method: (i) as a model, (ii) to gain perspective; (iii) as a means to harmonize the laws between jurisdictions; or (iv) as part of a plan of unification of the law.

The cases that follow give the student a taste of the way in which Americans habitually approach comparative law. How is the comparative method used in each of the cases? Is there any reason the courts could not also have consulted the law of jurisdictions outside the United States? Under what circumstances?

Thomas Berreman, Appellant, v. West Publishing Company, et al., Respondents

Court of Appeals of Minnesota, No. CX-00-110
615 N.W.2d 362, Aug. 1, 2000

LANSING, Judge.

Thomas Berreman appeals from summary judgment dismissing his action against West Publishing Company and three West directors (collectively "West"). Berreman alleged three causes of action: breach of fiduciary duty, unfairly prejudicial conduct in violation of Minn.Stat. § 320A.751, subd. 1(b)(3) (1994), and fraud. Berreman's claims were based on his assertion that West had a duty to disclose to him, before Berreman retired from West and sold his stock back to the company in June 1995, that three of West's directors had begun to consider the sale of West and had engaged an investment-banking firm to explore West's options. On cross-motions for summary judgment, the district court granted summary judgment to West on all of Berreman's claims. Because West did not breach a fiduciary duty, unfairly prejudice Berreman within the meaning of Minn.Stat. § 302A.751, subd. 1(b)(3), or commit fraud, we affirm.

FACTS

The facts are undisputed. In April 1995, Thomas Berreman, a 25-year employee of West Publishing Company, told West's Chief Executive Officer, Dwight Opperman, that he intended to retire effective June 1, 1995. Berreman had worked for West's lawschool division since 1970. West promoted him to assistant manager of the division in 1977 and to division head in 1992.

Beginning in 1974, Berreman bought West stock through a stock-option program for high-level managers and sales representatives that granted options at Dwight Opperman's discretion. In June 1995, Berreman owned 1,600 shares of stock. Berreman bought his stock subject to a written agreement for purchase, sale, and resale, which provided that if he decided to sell his stock or in the event of his death, incompetency, or termination of employment, West could exercise an option to repurchase the stock at book value. The agreement placed no ultimate limitation on Berreman's ability to sell his stock outside the company, but historically West had always exercised its option to redeem its stock. When Berreman told Dwight Opperman of his plans to retire, Opperman looked at Berreman's records and told him that he should "do all right."

Berreman's last day at West was May 31, 1995. On June 1, 1995, with Berreman's authorization, West redeemed Berreman's stock at the current book value of $2,088.90 per share and paid off a bank loan secured by the stock. On June 15, 1995, Chief Financial Officer Grant Nelson gave Berreman a check for approximately $2.8 million.

As of May 31, 1995, West had about 200 employee shareholders, 25 non-employee shareholders, and 328,908 shares outstanding. Dwight Opperman, Nelson, and board president Vance Opperman, in addition to being directors, were each shareholders. Together they held 23 percent of West's outstanding shares. Until its sale to Thomson Corporation in 1996, West was a privately held corporation. And until West announced the possibility of a sale in August 1995, West directors had publicly expressed their commitment to remaining privately held.

During 1994 and 1995, West was facing an increasingly competitive legal publications market. Two of West's competitors, Mead Data, owner of Lexis-Nexis, and Prentice Hall Law & Business, merged into international publishing companies in 1994. That same year West received unsolicited materials on possible mergers from investment-banking firms Goldman-Sachs and A.G. Edwards, which included information about Thomson Corporation. In response to the increasingly competitive conditions, West's board increased its acquisition fund from $70 million to $300 million in October 1994.

During the second week of May 1995, while on vacation, Nelson reflected on the future of West in light of the changing legal-publications market. Nelson was concerned about West's future given increasing competition, changing technology, and pending antitrust investigations. Nelson concluded that rather than making an acquisition, West should consider being acquired or entering into a joint venture.

On May 15, 1995, Nelson met with Dwight Opperman, who listened to Nelson's concerns and told him, "I think you may be right." Nelson and Dwight Opperman met with Vance Opperman the next day, and the three decided to engage A.G. Edwards to explore West's options. Nelson called Ray Kalinowski at A.G. Edwards the same day and told him that West wanted advice on the company's future financial options, including a possible sale of the company. On May 17, 1995, A.G. Edwards representatives met with the West directors. The directors authorized A.G. Edwards to retain another investment-banking firm if necessary.

The West board met on May 23, 1995. During that meeting, the board again addressed its potential acquisitions and authorized A.G. Edwards to explore financing options beyond West's local bank. The board did not discuss the possibility of selling the company. This meeting was the last board meeting before Berreman's June 1 retirement.

On August 28, 1995, A.G. Edwards made a presentation to the West board outlining four options: recapitalization, public offering, status quo, and sale. The board engaged A.G. Edwards and Goldman-Sachs to advise and assist West in evaluating its options and authorized West management to take necessary steps, including contacting potential buyers and developing acquisition proposals.

On August 29, 1995, West announced to its employees and to the public that it had engaged investment bankers and was considering alternative financial options including public offering, entering into a joint venture, joining a strategic partner, recapitalization, sale, or any other available option. In September 1995, West sent invitations for bids to 45 potential purchasers. The bids were due by February 1996, and West eventually received four bids, including one from Thomson Corporation. West accepted Thomson Corporation's bid, and the companies entered into a merger agreement on February 25, 1996. After a shareholder vote and review by the Department of Justice, West concluded the sale to Thomson in June 1996. Thomson paid $10,445 per share to acquire West, about five times the amount Berreman received when he sold his stock back to the company in June 1995. Berreman's action against West followed.

ISSUES

I. Did the district court err by granting summary judgment to West on Berreman's fiduciary duty claim?

II. Did the district court err by granting summary judgment to West on Berreman's claim of unfairly prejudicial conduct under Minn.Stat. § 302A.751, subd. 1(b)(3) (1994)?

III. Did the district court err by granting summary judgment to West on Berreman's fraud claim?

ANALYSIS

I

This court reviews appeals from summary judgment to determine if there are any genuine issues of material fact and if the district court erred in its application of the law. Reads Landing Campers Ass'n, Inc. v. Township of Pepin, 546 N.W.2d 10, 13 (Minn.1996)....

Common Law Fiduciary Duty

At common law, the shareholders in a close corporation owe one another a fiduciary duty. See Fewell v. Tappan, 223 Minn. 483, 494, 27 N.W.2d 648, 654 (1947); Pedro v. Pedro, 489 N.W.2d 798, 801 (Minn.App.1992) (Pedro II), review denied (Minn. Oct. 20, 1992); Evans v. Blesi, 345 N.W.2d 775, 779 (Minn.App.1984). Courts impose the fiduciary duty because they find that close corporations are really more like "partnership[s] in corporate guise." Westland Capital Corp. v. Lucht Eng'g Inc., 308 N.W.2d 709, 712 (Minn.1981); see also Fewell, 223 Minn. at 494, 27 N.W.2d at 654 (concluding that two men who co-owned corporation and agreed not to sell stock without other man's consent, "stood in the relationship of copartners"); Pedro II, 489 N.W.2d at 801 ("relationship among shareholders in closely held corporations is analogous to that of partners"); Donahue v. Rodd Electrotype Co., 367 Mass. 578, 328 N.E.2d 505, 512 (1975) ("Commentators and courts have noted that the close corporation is often little more than an 'incorporated' or 'chartered' partnership.").

Attributes of Close Corporation

Courts generally identify common law close corporations by three characteristics: (1) a small number of shareholders; (2) no ready market for corporate stock; and (3) active shareholder participation in the business. Donahue, 328 N.E.2d at 511; see also Westland, 308 N.W.2d at 712 (describing close corporations). In addition, dividends are rarely distributed in a close corporation. Westland, 308 N.W.2d at 712. Rather, "shareholders derive their income mainly from salaries and perquisites." Id.

In May 1995, West exhibited characteristics of a close corporation. First, West was not publicly traded; thus, there was no ready public market for its stock. See Sundberg v. Lampert Lumber Co., 390 N.W.2d 352, 354, 357 (Minn.App.1986) (no ready public market for stock that was never registered for sale and was not traded on any securities market), review denied (Minn. Sept. 22, 1986), superseded by statute on other grounds, Minn.Stat. § 302A.751, subd. 2 (1994)....

Second, the rationale for distinguishing close corporations from other corporations supports the characterization of West as a close corporation. Courts have recognized that because majority shareholders of a close corporation can deny minority shareholders income from their investment, minority shareholders are in a vulnerable position. See, e.g., Westland, 308 N.W.2d at 712. Majority shareholders can "freeze out" minority shareholders by refusing to employ them, refusing to declare any dividends, siphoning off profits through excessive salaries to officers or directors or self-dealing leases and contracts, selling business assets to majority shareholders or their affiliates, forcing redemption of shares, or "cashing out" minority shareholders at an unfairly low price through a merger. Daniel S. Kleinberger, Why Not Good Faith? The Foibles of Fairness in the Law of Close Corporations, 16 Wm. Mitchell L.Rev. 1143, 1152 (1990). In combination with the lack of a public market for the shares, these actions effectively hold the minority shareholders' investments hostage. That West's corporate structure would have allowed this type of "freeze out" supports its characterization as a close corporation.

On the other hand, West's 200 shareholders far exceed the number of shareholders in any corporation that Minnesota courts have recognized as a close corporation. To categorize West as a close corporation under Minnesota common law would substantially extend the definition's numerical boundaries. Berreman argues that because 94% of the stock was held by employees and subject to repurchase agreements, West's decision-making was concentrated in only a few individuals, and West's numerical structure should be analyzed from that viewpoint. These arguments have persuasive force and a fact-finder could draw inferences that would credit Berreman's arguments. Because we are reviewing a summary judgment against Berreman's claims, he is entitled to review in a light most favorable to the evidence supporting his claims, and thus we assume for purposes of our analysis that West may be categorized as a close corporation. See Martin v. Spirit Mountain Recreation, 566 N.W.2d 719, 721 (Minn.1997) (reviewing court must view evidence in light most favorable to party opposing motion).

Effect of Minnesota Business Corporation Act on Common Law Fiduciary Duty

West argues that even if it could have been characterized as a common law close corporation, the legislature abrogated the common law definition by enacting the Minnesota Business Corporations Act (MBCA), Minn.Stat. §§ 302A.01-.917 (1994 & Supp.1995). First, the MBCA did not completely abrogate the common law fiduciary duty in the context of a close corporation. See Pedro II, 489 N.W.2d at 802 (affirming judgment based on breach of fiduciary duty). In fact, the MBCA specifically recognizes "the duty which all shareholders in a closely held corporation owe one another to act in an honest, fair, and reasonable manner." Minn.Stat. § 302A.751, subd. 3a (1994). But, significantly, the MBCA defines closely held corporations as those with 35 or fewer shareholders. Minn.Stat. § 302A.011, subd. 6a (1994). West asserts that adoption of this definition abrogates common law fiduciary duty claims involving companies with more than 35 shareholders. Berreman, in turn, argues that a statutory closely held corporation is distinguishable from the common law close corporation and that the common law close corporation survives for purposes of determining fiduciary duties.

Although West's abrogation argument has merit, we conclude for several reasons that it does not prevail....

Scope of Common Law Fiduciary Duty

We turn next to the scope of the common law fiduciary duty. While it is well established that shareholders in a close corporation owe a fiduciary duty to one another, the scope of the duty has never been well defined. In Donahue v. Rodd Electrotype Co.—often cited as a leading case on fiduciary duty in the close corporation context—the Massachusetts Supreme Court held that "stockholders in a close corporation owe[d] one another substantially the same fiduciary duty in the operation of the enterprise that partners owe one another." 328 N.E.2d at 515 (footnote omitted). The court described the duty as one of "utmost good faith and loyalty" and went on to hold that a corporation that buys shares from one shareholder must offer to buy shares from all other shareholders at the same rate. Id. at 515, 518. This has since been called the equal-opportunity rule. Donahue is probably the broadest statement of the fiduciary duty in the close-corporation context. Even the Massachusetts Supreme Court later qualified its holding by recognizing that there may be legitimate business reasons for treating shareholders differently. Wilkes v. Springside Nursing Home, Inc., 370 Mass. 842, 353 N.E.2d 657, 663 (1976) (establishing that when corporation demonstrates legitimate business interest, plaintiff, to succeed on fiduciary claim, must show less harmful alternative to achieve that interest).

"Freeze-out" situations are the classic situations in which courts have found and enforced fiduciary duties. Thus, courts have found breaches of fiduciary duty based on majority shareholders' preferential use of corporate assets. See Crosby v. Beam, 47 Ohio St.3d 105, 548 N.E.2d 217, 221 (1989) (stating that majority shareholders breach fiduciary duty when they use their control to give themselves benefits not enjoyed by the minority); Tillis v. United Parts, Inc., 395 So.2d 618, 619 (Fla.Dist.Ct.App.1981) (recognizing that allowing only majority shareholder to sell shares to corporation constitutes preferential distribution of corporate assets and is inconsistent with fiduciary duty); Comolli v. Comolli, 241 Ga. 471, 246 S.E.2d 278, 281 (1978) (same); Donahue, 328 N.E.2d at 518 (same). The courts also have found breaches of fiduciary duties based on majority shareholders' withholding of dividends or exclusion of minority shareholders from employment. Wilkes, 353 N.E.2d at 663 (holding that majority shareholders breached fiduciary duty when they terminated 25-percent shareholder from his position as officer, director, and employee).

Minnesota appellate cases addressing fiduciary duty in the close-corporation context, while sparse, are consistent with the fiduciary duty cases in other jurisdictions. In Fewell v. Tappan, the Supreme Court held that the co-owners of a close corporation owed each other "the highest standard of integrity and good faith in their dealings with each other." 223 Minn. at 494, 27 N.W.2d at 654. In Fewell and Evans v. Blesi, the courts found breaches of the fiduciary duty when shareholders threatened or deceived other shareholders into selling their shares. Fewell, 223 Minn. at 494, 27 N.W.2d at 654 (co-owner of close corporation breached duty by misleading other owner to believe business was in danger of receivership and thus inducing the other owner to sell his shares for a fraction of their value); Evans, 345 N.W.2d at 779–80 (partner in closely held corporation breached fiduciary duty by using intimidating tactics to gain majority share of stock and forcing plaintiff's resignation). In essence, the Minnesota courts have held that shareholders in a close corporation have a duty to deal " 'openly, honestly, and fairly with other shareholders.' " Pedro II, 489 N.W.2d at 801 (quoting Evans, 345 N.W.2d at 779).

The Minnesota cases have not addressed whether the fiduciary duty in a close corporation context includes a duty to disclose. The Supreme Court has, however, ruled that "[o]ne who stands in a confidential or fiduciary relation to the other party to a transaction must disclose material facts." Klein v. First Edina Nat'l Bank, 293 Minn. 418, 420, 196 N.W.2d 619, 622 (1972). And this court has applied the duty to disclose material facts in the analogous partnership context. See Appletree Square I Ltd. Partnership v. Investmark, Inc., 494 N.W.2d 889, 892 (Minn.App.1993) (holding partners had duty to disclose to their other partners existence of asbestos in office building), review denied (Minn. Mar. 16, 1993).

Relying on the principles expressed in the Minnesota cases addressing disclosure, we conclude that the fiduciary duties of shareholders in a close corporation include the duty to disclose material information about the corporation. Our holding is consistent with federal cases recognizing the duty to disclose material facts as within the fiduciary duties of shareholders in a close corporation. Jordan v. Duff & Phelps, Inc., 815 F.2d 429, 435 (7th Cir.1987) (stating that "[c]lose corporations buying their own stock, like knowledgeable insiders of closely held firms buying from outsiders, have a fiduciary duty to disclose material facts"); Helms v. Duckworth, 249 F.2d 482, 487 (D.C.Cir.1957) (stating that "holders of closely held stock in a corporation...bear a fiduciary duty to deal fairly, honestly, and openly with their fellow stockholders and to make disclosure of all essential information").

Materiality of Undisclosed Facts

The recognition that shareholders in a close corporation have a duty to disclose material facts leads us to the second part of the question: What facts are material and thus fall within the scope of that duty? In the context of the federal securities laws, the U.S. Supreme Court has held that an omitted fact is material "if there is a substantial likelihood that a reasonable shareholder would consider it important in deciding how to vote." Basic Inc. v. Levinson, 485 U.S. 224, 231, 108 S.Ct. 978, 983, 99 L.Ed.2d 194 (1988) (citation omitted). Or, put another way, "there must be a substantial likelihood that the disclosure of the omitted fact would have been viewed by the reasonable investor as having significantly altered the 'total mix' of information made available." Id. at 231–32, 108 S.Ct. at 983 (citation omitted). See also Black's Law Dictionary 991 (7th ed.1999) (defining material as "[o]f such a nature that knowledge of the item would affect a person's decision-making process"). Materiality, then, depends on the specific facts of each case. Basic, 485 U.S. at 239, 108 S.Ct. at 987.

In Basic v. Levinson, the Supreme Court adopted the probability-magnitude approach for determining whether preliminary merger discussions are material. Under that test, materiality "will depend at any time upon a balancing of both the indicated probability that the event will occur and the anticipated magnitude of the event in light of the totality of the company activity." Id. at 238, 108 S.Ct. at 987 (citation omitted). Probability should be assessed by evaluating the "indicia of interest in the transaction at the highest corporate levels." Id. at 239, 108 S.Ct. at 987. Magnitude should be assessed by considering "such facts as the size of the two corporate entities and of the potential premiums over market value." Id.

Addressing circumstances similar to Berreman's, the federal courts have held that tentative or preliminary merger discussions were not material. See Taylor v. First Union Corp., 857 F.2d 240, 243 (4th Cir.1988) (holding discussions between two companies on "the possibility of a future merger" were not material); Panfil v. ACC Corp., 768 F.Supp. 54, 58 (W.D.N.Y.1991). In Panfil, the plaintiff alleged that ACC breached a duty to him by failing to inform him, before he sold his stock, that it intended to approach another company "to facilitate a combination" of the two businesses. 768 F.Supp. at 58. The court found that the facts were not material, reasoning that "there were not 'tentative' discussions" about merger, "there were no discussions." Id. The court concluded that "[t]he mere intention to pursue a possible merger at some time in the future, without more, is simply not a material fact.... The probability of merger prior to contact with potential suitors—prior to any evidence that a suitor is in any way interested in merger—is too remote." Id.

The Supreme Court has recognized, however, that facts that would not be material in the context of a publicly held corporation may be material, and thus subject to the duty to disclose, when they relate to a close corporation:

> Since a merger in which it is bought out is the most important event that can occur in a small corporation's life, to wit, its death, we think that inside information, as regards a merger of this sort, can become material at an earlier stage than would be the case as regards lesser transactions—and this even though the mortality rate of mergers in such formative stages is doubtless high.

Basic, 485 U.S. at 238, 108 S.Ct. at 987 (citation omitted). Consistent with this analysis, the Seventh Circuit Court of Appeals has held that a close corporation's initial decision to seek buyers may be material. Jordan, 815 F.2d at 434 (reasoning that a jury could conclude "that the board's decision...to seek a buyer...—coupled with the fact that at least one putative buyer thought Duff & Phelps worth $50 million...—was material"); Michaels v. Michaels, 767 F.2d 1185, 1197 (7th Cir.1985) (concluding that "a jury could reasonably find that Littlejohn's agreement to contact prospective buyers on behalf of Hyman-Michaels was material").

Application of Probability-Magnitude Test to Undisclosed Facts

Applying the probability-magnitude test to this case, we hold that the facts known to West at the time Berreman resigned were immaterial as a matter of law. By the end of May 1995, Nelson, Dwight Opperman, and Vance Opperman had decided to explore options for the future of West including a possible sale, and they had hired an investment-banking firm to investigate West's options. West, however, had made no decision to solicit bids for the sale of West, much less initiated discussions with any potential buyers. The federal courts have been reluctant to find materiality in the absence of evidence that the corporation engaged in discussions with potential buyers. Even in the close-corporation context, the Seventh Circuit has gone no further than to say that a corporation's decision to seek a buyer may be material. We agree that tentative, speculative discussions about merger are not material.

Berreman urges that the early discussions among the West directors about the possibility of merger should be found material because the magnitude of any potential merger was substantial. West had always been a privately held corporation, and until August 1995, its directors were vocally committed to being privately held. That any merger would have been such a sharp departure from West's long history of being privately held supports the magnitude of the merger discussions. But the magnitude of the discussions does not overcome the low probability that the merger would ever occur. The initial discussions were among West's top directors, which supports probability. But even these three directors had decided only to explore West's financial options. Thus, the discussions were not material.

II

Berreman next claims that West's conduct was unfairly prejudicial to him and that he is thus entitled to equitable relief under the MBCA. See Minn.Stat. §302A.751, subd. 1(b)(3) (1994). The district court did not directly address Berreman's theory that West's failure to disclose the initial merger discussions was unfairly prejudicial under section 302A.751. West argues that the district court implicitly rejected this theory-based on its conclusion that there were no material facts that would trigger a duty to disclose. But Berreman contends that materiality is not dispositive of the analysis under section 302A.751 and that the district court should have separately considered his statutory claim.

We agree that materiality is not an element of unfairly prejudicial conduct under section 302A.751, subd. 1(b)(3), and thus Berreman's statutory claim warrants separate consideration. We believe, however, that the circumstances would be rare when a director's failure to disclose immaterial facts would constitute unfairly prejudicial conduct under the statute. We also conclude that because the issue has been fully briefed, we need not remand to the district court for a specific determination on this issue. Holen v. Minneapolis-St. Paul Metro. Airports Comm'n, 250 Minn. 130, 135, 84 N.W.2d 282, 286 (1957) (stating that appellate court may address issues when fully briefed and no possible advantage or disadvantage to either party in not having prior ruling).

The MBCA allows the courts to grant equitable relief to a shareholder in a corporation that is not publicly held when the directors of that corporation have "acted in a manner unfairly prejudicial" toward that shareholder in his capacity as shareholder or director. Minn.Stat. §302A.751, subd. 1(b)(3). The term "unfairly prejudicial" should be liberally construed. Minn.Stat. Ann. §302A.751 (West 1985) (Reporter's Notes 1982–84); McCallum v. Rosen's Diversified, Inc., 153 F.3d 701, 703 (8th Cir.1998). The statute does not define the term, however, and its plain meaning is not apparent.

Breaches of fiduciary duty are probably unfairly prejudicial within the meaning of section 302A.751, subd. 1(b)(3). Section 302A.751, subd. 3a, specifically directs that courts, in deciding whether to grant equitable relief, should consider the "duty which all shareholders in a closely held corporation owe one another to act in an honest, fair, and reasonable manner." Minnesota courts' application of this section is consistent with that understanding. See Pedro II, 489 N.W.2d at 802–03 (affirming judgment on fiduciary duty claim along with award of equitable relief under Minn.Stat. §302A.751). Unfairly prejudicial conduct also is distinct from fraudulent or illegal conduct, which is addressed elsewhere in the statute. See Minn.Stat. §302A.751, subd. 1(b)(2) (1994) (court may grant equitable relief based on directors' fraudulent or illegal conduct); Minn.Stat. §645.17 (1994) (statute must be considered as a whole to harmonize and give effect to all provisions).

Seven other states refer to "unfair prejudice" or "unfairly prejudicial" in their business corporation statutes. See Kiriakides v. Atlas Food Sys. & Servs., Inc., 338 S.C. 572, 527 S.E.2d 371, 386 (S.C.Ct.App.2000) (listing Alaska, California, Minnesota, Missouri, Montana, Wisconsin, and Wyoming in addition to South Carolina). Other states follow the Model Business Corporations Act by referencing "oppressive conduct." O'Neal, supra, § 9.29, at 131–32. Only South Carolina, which has a statute that references both oppressive and unfairly prejudicial conduct, has explicitly defined unfairly prejudicial. According to the South Carolina Court of Appeals, oppressive or unfairly prejudicial conduct is:

1) A visible departure from the standards of fair dealing and a violation of fair play on which every shareholder who entrusts his money to a company is entitled to rely; or

2) A breach of fiduciary duty of good faith and fair dealing; or

3) Whether the reasonable expectations of the minority shareholders have been frustrated by the actions of the majority; or

4) A lack of probity and fair dealing in the affairs of a company to the prejudice of some of its members; or

5) A deprivation by majority shareholders of participation in management by minority shareholders.

Kiriakides, 527 S.E.2d at 387–88 371.

Kiriakides's definition of oppressive or unfairly prejudicial conduct is consistent with other jurisdictions' application of oppressive conduct. The courts have primarily defined "oppressive" as one of the first three prongs of the Kiriakides definition. See O'Neal, supra, § 9.29, at 132 (collecting cases). The most often applied definition of oppressive asks whether the actions of majority shareholders have frustrated a minority shareholder's reasonable expectations. See id.

We conclude that the reasonable-expectations approach is most consistent with the Minnesota legislature's intent in adopting the unfairly prejudicial language. The advisory task force indicated that one of its goals was to draft a law that would "provide, as rules, all of the provisions that would normally be expected to result from associative bargaining if all parties were represented by counsel, coupled with the expressed flexibility to vary those rules whenever necessary to reflect the actual associative bargain." Advisory Task Force Report, supra. Further, the statute explicitly directs the courts to consider the expectations of shareholders in a closely held corporation. Minn.Stat. § 302A.751, subd. 3a. Although this section of the statute does not directly apply in this case, it demonstrates the importance that the legislature has placed on shareholder expectations.

We conclude that unfairly prejudicial conduct under Minn.Stat. § 302A.751, subd. 1(b)(3), is conduct that frustrates the reasonable expectations of shareholders in their capacity as shareholders or directors of a corporation that is not publicly held or as officers or employees of a closely held corporation.

West argues that the buy-back agreement compels a conclusion that West's conduct did not frustrate Berreman's reasonable expectations. See Minn.Stat. § 302A.751, subd. 3a (written agreements between the parties are presumed to represent their reasonable expectations). We disagree that the repurchase terms are dispositive of reasonable expectations in all circumstances. Berreman's reasonable expectations would not have been frustrated if the buy-back agreement had been triggered by events outside Berreman's control, i.e., if West terminated his employment. In this case, however, Berreman chose the course of action that triggered the buy-back agreement, i.e., retirement, and contends that he would not have retired if West had disclosed the merger discussions to him. Under these circumstances the presumed reasonableness of the buy-back agreement is not dispositive.

Nonetheless, we conclude that West's conduct did not frustrate Berreman's reasonable expectations as a shareholder. In a typical close corporation, a shareholder may have an expectation of a job, a share of corporate earnings, and a place in management. Pedro II, 489 N.W.2d at 802; see also Balvik v. Sylvester, 411 N.W.2d 383, 387 (N.D.1987). At-will employees who are allowed to buy stock subject to a buy-back-on-termination agreement may have lower expectations. See Coleman v. Taub, 638 F.2d 628, 636 (3d Cir.1981) (holding that shareholder who signed buy-back agreement bargained for right to be shareholder only while employed). Berreman did not have a reasonable expectation that he would be informed of any speculative discussions West's directors had about the financial future of West. See Balvik, 411 N.W.2d at 387 (N.D.1987) (reasoning that "[d]isappointment alone should not necessarily be equated with oppression") (citation omitted). Therefore, West's conduct was not unfairly prejudicial to Berreman, and he is not entitled to equitable relief under the MBCA.

III

[Court considers and rejects the claim of fraud for failing to disclose the initial merger discussions]

DECISION

As a matter of law West did not breach a fiduciary duty, unfairly prejudice Berreman within the meaning of Minn.Stat. 302A 751, subd. 1(b)(3), or commit fraud. Accordingly, we affirm summary judgment for West on each of Berreman's claims.

Marsha L. Hunt and PMH, Inc., Appellees, v. Data Management Resources, Inc., William C. Estes, and Aubrey Richardson, Appellants

Court of Appeals of Kansas, 26 Kan.App.2d 405, 985 P.2d 730
No. 80,686. Aug. 27, 1999.

ELLIOTT, P.J.:

Marsha L. Hunt sold her stock in Data Management Resources, Inc. (DMR) to PMH, Inc. (PMH). DMR and its officers, William C. Estes and Aubrey Richardson, appeal the trial court's order in mandamus requiring DMR to transfer the stock to PMH on its corporate books.

We affirm.

The facts are essentially undisputed. DMR is a closely held Kansas corporation formed in 1992. Estes and Richardson are the directors and officers of DMR and are shareholders as well. Hunt was a minority shareholder.

Hunt offered to sell her shares to Estes and Richardson for $50,000, informing them that if they rejected her offer, she would transfer her shares to an entity which would disqualify DMR from subchapter S corporation tax status. Hunt explained she wanted to reduce her personal tax liability on undistributed income. Hunt received no reply; her husband formed PMH and capitalized it with $25,000 from his personal account. PMH then offered to buy Hunt's shares for $25,000.

As required by DMR's articles, Hunt gave Estes and Richardson a 30-day option to buy her shares for $25,000, explaining she would accept PMH's offer if they did not exercise their option. Estes and Richardson rejected the option to buy.

PMH then purchased Hunt's shares for $25,000; Hunt deposited the PMH check in an account she held jointly with her husband, who then wrote a check on the joint account for $25,000 and deposited it in his personal account.

When DMR refused to transfer the shares on the corporate books and issue a certificate to PMH, Hunt and PMH filed a mandamus action against DMR and against Estes and Richardson in their official capacities. Appellants DMR, Estes, and Richardson accused Hunt of violating her fiduciary duty as a shareholder in a close corporation, and also argued the PMH offer was not bona fide. The trial court disagreed and issued its mandamus order requiring that the transfer be recorded and a certificate be issued to PMH.

Appellants argue Hunt owed a fiduciary duty to Estes and Richardson as shareholders. The mandamus action, however, was not against them as shareholders but as officers of DMR. Mandamus is a proceeding to compel, inter alia, a corporation or a person to perform an official duty. See K.S.A. 60-801. Mandamus is appropriate to compel a corporation or its officers to transfer stock on its corporate books. See Steele v. Telephone Association, 95 Kan. 580, 148 P. 661 (1915).

Here, the trial court ordered Estes and Richardson to perform an official duty, and they brought no counterclaims for personal damages. As a result, Hunt's behavior would be a defense only if she owed a fiduciary duty to the corporation itself.

The law does not impose a strict fiduciary duty on a shareholder to act in the best interests of the corporation; a shareholder is free to act in his or her own self-interest. Resolution Trust Corp. v. Fleischer, 890 F.Supp. 972, 978 (D.Kan.1995). As a general proposition, then, Hunt owed no fiduciary duty to DMR.

Appellants rely on Rexford Rand Corp. v. Ancel, 58 F.3d 1215, 1219 (7th Cir.1995). There, in an equitable action, the court held minority shareholders owe a duty of loyalty to a close corporation under certain circumstances. The reliance is misplaced.

Our examination of Kansas law shows DMR was not a close corporation. While the parties stipulated DMR was a close corporation, we are not bound by stipulations as to questions of law. See City of Lenexa v. Board of Johnson County Comm'rs, 237 Kan. 782, Syl. ¶ 1, 703 P.2d 800 (1985). The legislature has statutorily defined close corporations. See K.S.A. 17-7201 et seq.; Hecker, Close Corporations and the Kansas General Corporation Code of 1972, 22 Kan. L.Rev. 489, 546 (1974).

A close corporation is one whose articles provide for a specified number of shareholders, not exceeding 30; one or more restrictions on transfers of stock, as found at K.S.A. 17-6426; and no public offering of stock. K.S.A. 17-7202(a)(1)-(3). A close corporation must also include a heading to that effect in its articles of incorporation. K.S.A. 17-7203(a). In the present case, DMR's articles did not restrict the number of shareholders, did not prohibit a public offering of stock, and did not include the required heading.

While the Rexford Rand court held a corporation not organized under the Illinois close corporation statute was still a close corporation under common law, 58 F.3d at 1217 n. 1, the Delaware Supreme Court has refused to create protective rules where a corporation is a "closely-held, but not statutory 'close corporation.' " Nixon v. Blackwell, 626 A.2d 1366, 1380 (Del.1993). The Delaware court held the legislature had preempted the field by statute and any effort to construct a special rule outside the statutory framework would amount to inappropriate judicial legislation. 626 A.2d at 1380-81.

Since the Kansas statute is based on the Delaware statute, decisions of the Delaware court are persuasive. See Achey v. Linn County Bank, 261 Kan. 669, 676, 931 P.2d 16 (1997). We, therefore, adopt the Delaware holding and reject the holding of Rexford Rand.

Simply put, appellants cannot claim any special treatment accorded close corporations because DMR did not fit within the statutory framework. Further, appellants were not powerless to protect their interests. They could have required prior approval of any transfer or transferee. K.S.A. 17-6426(c)(3). They could have prohibited transfers to reasonably designated classes of persons. K.S.A. 17-6426(c)(4). And a restriction for the purpose of maintaining subchapter S tax status would be conclusively reasonable. See K.S.A. 17-6426(d). Here, DMR, Estes, and Richardson simply failed to take these steps.

* * *

Since Hunt was under no fiduciary duty, she was free to negotiate for the sale, Hunt's offer and eventual sale to PMH did not violate the articles of incorporation, and the trial court properly issued its mandamus order requiring the transfer of the stock to PMH.

Affirmed.

Comments and Questions

1. The Court in *Berreman* and *Hunt* each utilized the comparative method to solve different problems with which each was confronted. The *Berreman* court looked to the law of other states and other levels of government (federal securities laws) to help find answers to issues of Minnesota law. The court in *Hunt* was faced with an issue of interpretation of transplanted law—the Kansas statute was adopted from Delaware law. To help resolve the question, the *Hunt* court considered the way the courts of Delaware had dealt with the issue. In either case was it necessary for the courts to look beyond their borders for the answers to the issues in dispute in the cases? On what forms of law did the courts rely in the cases?

2. Are the purposes of comparison the same for courts as they may be for legislators? What may be the differences?

3. What is harmonization of laws? Does harmonization of laws require that all states adopt the same law? Does it suggest that all laws be interpreted identically?

B. Framing the Study of Comparative Corporate Law

Before embarking on the comparative study of issues in the legal governance of corporations between major national corporate governance regimes, it may be worthwhile to pause long enough to contemplate the question: why undertake this study at all? The general answer is usually given in the following form:

> Three main tasks can be identified for comparative law. The first is to investigate differences between legal systems and, in particular, to distinguish between "real" differences, where the outcomes of the application of principles diverge between legal systems, and "superficial" differences, where similar outcomes are masked by the conceptual structures of the relevant systems. The second is to trace developments in the relationships between legal systems and thus to explore tendencies of convergence or divergence (in terms of "real" differences), noting that in some areas convergence may be required under international legal instruments. The third task is to explain and to evaluate such developments: why do systems converge or diverge? Is convergence or divergence desirable or undesirable?

Anthony Ogus, *Competition Between National Legal Systems: A Contribution of Economic Analysis to Comparative Law*, 48 INT'L & COMP. L. Q. 405 (1999).

The materials that follow build on this general comparative framework. Each of the readings that follow also suggests reasons why the study of comparative corporate law is necessary and worthwhile. The first, by Lawrence Cunningham, suggests the parameters of the comparative study of corporate governance. He also suggests one of the reasons for comparative study—the possibility that different systems will converge. In reading that excerpt consider to what extent Professor Cunningham's approach to comparative corporate governance is driven by an essentially American focus on finance. Professor Cunningham suggests that as world markets grow, and as multi-national enterprises become more important, worldwide variations in corporate governance may converge. Are you as optimistic as the author is about the inevitability of the convergence? Do you believe that this version of the American model of corporate governance characterized by local (state-centered) regimes of internal corporate governance subject to a unified scheme of capital market regulation is the most sensible approach to convergence or harmonization of corporate regulation? The excerpt from Colin Bennett's *Regulating Privacy*, explores the convergence imperative more deeply from a political science perspective. It does so by studying the way in which four countries, the United States, Sweden, Germany and Britain responded to the problem of data protection. In reading that excerpt, consider to what extent the comparative corporate law project ought inevitably lead to convergence. The excerpt from the work of Professors Bebchuk and Roe provides a different perspective on the nature of incentives (and disincentives) toward convergence, and suggest an explanation for the fact that convergence has not resulted in a more complete harmonization or unification of law to date. The work introduces notions of culture and habit, including the habit of law, as important factors in comparative law.

Lawrence A. Cunningham, *Comparative Corporate Governance and Pedagogy*

34 GA. L. REV. 721 (2000)
(excerpts from pages 722–724)

I. WHAT IS COMPARATIVE CORPORATE GOVERNANCE

I take the phrase "governance" to mean the collection of law and practice that regulates the conduct of those in control of a business organization. The collection is grounded in fiduciary duties and their application. It also includes the other provisions commonly contained in charters and similar documents or custom, such as the manner of calling and holding meetings, qualifications for office, and so on. When we refer to "corporate governance," I take the talk to be mainly about business organizations formed as corporations, as distinct from partnerships, LLCs, joint ventures and others, although there will undoubtedly be analogues among the various forms when it comes to the mechanisms regulating those in control of the organizations.[2]

"Comparative corporate governance," then, is the collection of mechanisms in use in selected parts of the world to regulate those in control of business organizations, with attention to the origins and durability of the differences between countries or regions. The United States is commonly compared to countries such as the United Kingdom and those in continental Europe,[3] and Asia (chiefly Japan), and to a lesser extent Australia, Canada, Israel and South Africa.

Comparisons of these models typically emphasize their finance characteristics. In the United States and the United Kingdom, capital traditionally has been supplied by debt financing offered by banks and other financial institutions while equity financing is offered by public investors in organized stock markets and private placements (characteristics that may be changing).[4] In Germany and other European nations capital historically has tended to be supplied by banking institutions that offer both debt and equity financing for their industrial clients. Ownership of industrial companies therefore tended to be fragmented in Anglo-Saxon countries and concentrated on the Continent.

Corporate governance regimes in these countries differed substantially as a result of this relative fragmentation or concentration—at least in the abstract. United States and United Kingdom managers were to focus on the shareholder interest according to a complex system of checks and balances intended to compel them to put shareholders first. German and other European corporations were to operate not by putting shareholders first but by commanding corporate boards and managers to operate the firm in the best interests of all its constituencies.

The traditional Japanese model is different yet again, with the system of lifetime employment and interlocking corporate ownership (*keiretsu*). [Contrasted to the Anglo-Saxon tradition of employment-at-will and the United States aversion to concentrations of power (which may be waning).] The list of potential comparative countries is increasing as privatization breaks out the world over, and could go on to include countries in economic and political transition such as former republics of the Soviet Union,[5]

---

2. *See* ROBERT HAMILTON & RICHARD BOOTH, BUSINESS BASICS FOR LAW STUDENTS 284 (2nd ed. 1998) (noting that limited number of courts that have considered issues raised in context of limited liability companies have turned to corporate law for guidance).

3. The chief focus tends to be on the most economically productive of these countries: Germany, The Netherlands, France, Italy, and Austria; the focus may also include Belgium, Switzerland, Spain, Portugal, Norway, Sweden, Finland and Denmark. *See, e.g.*, Ronald J. Gilson, & Reinier Kraakman, *Investment Companies as Guardian Shareholders: The Place of the MSIC in the Corporate Governance Debate*, 45 STAN. L. REV. 985 (1993) (discussing Sweden).

4. Repeal of the Glass-Steagall Act could change the features of American finance.

5. Armenia, Azerbaijan, Belorussia, Estonia, Georgia, Kazakhstan, Kyrgyzstan, Latvia, Lithuania, Moldovia, Russia, Tajikstan, Turkmenistan, Ukraine, and Uzbekistan. J. Robert Brown, Jr., *Of Brokers, Banks and the Case for Regulatory Intervention in the Russian Securities Markets*, 32 STAN. J. INT'L L. 185 (1996); Philip M. Nichols, *The Viability of Transplanted Law: Kazakhstani Reception of a Transplanted Foreign Investment Code*, 18 U. PA. J. INT'L ECON. L. 1235 (1997).

former members of the Soviet Union's Council for Mutual Economic Assistance (COMECON),[6] and former Republics of Yugoslavia.[7]

As these transitions go forward, new variations on governance approaches are emerging, often blending aspects of the models usually treated as polar. These polar models may also be seen to be converging with one another as transnational corporations increasingly dominate global capital, labor and products markets. Indeed, one of the most important recent corners of corporate-law scholarship has been the question of such convergence and the challenge it seems to pose to the abstract conception of modular polarity.[8]

Colin J. Bennett, *Regulating Privacy: Data Protection and Public Policy in Europe and the United States*

(1992)

(excerpts from pages 4–8)

So how have Sweden, the United States, West Germany, and Britain responded to this problem, and why have they responded in the way they have? The point of departure is the argument that there will be strong pressures for these states to respond in similar ways—there will be a policy *convergence* in other words. This result flows from a familiar thesis that technological and economic development has a leveling impact on diverse social structures, cultural traditions, and public policies. The "convergence thesis" says that modernization brings processes and implications in its wake: an emphasis on planning and rationalization; a replacement of an ideological with a pragmatic imperative; a centrality for a technocratic elite; and a pervasive role for high technology.[4]

General theories of convergence often result, however, in formulations that are imprecise about what is supposed to be converging and that obscure the different processes through which convergence might occur. The logic of the convergence thesis is overly deterministic; policy responses will supposedly converge because states at the same level of development face similar problems. The common "policy prob-

---

6. Bulgaria, Cuba, Czechoslovakia, German Democratic Republic, Hungary, Mongolia, Poland, Romania, and the Soviet Union itself. John C. Coffee, Jr., *Inventing a Corporate Monitor for Transnational Economies: The Uncertain Lessons From the Czech and Polish Experiences, in* COMPARATIVE CORPORATE GOVERNANCE: THE STATE OF THE ART AND EMERGING RESEARCH 68–138 (Klaus Hopt et al. eds. 1998).

7. Bosnia-Herzegovina, Croatia, and Slovenia.

8. *See, e.g.*, John C. Coffee, Jr., *The Future as History: The Prospects for Global Convergence in Corporate Governance and its Implications*, 93 NW. L. REV. 641 (1999) (concluding that corporate law is converging toward U.S. style regime of securities regulation even as overall corporate law convergence has been frustrated); Lawrence A. Cunningham, *Commonalities and Prescriptions in the Vertical Dimensions of Global Corporate Governance*, 84 CORNELL L. REV. 1133 (1999) (examining how market, structural and regulatory forces have promoted convergence of global corporate mechanisms, particularly vertical mechanisms that address director duties and responsibilities to the organization); Jeffrey N. Gordon, *Pathways to Corporate Convergence? Two Steps on the Road to Shareholder Capitalism in Germany*, 5 COLUM. J. EUR. L. 219 (1999) (using recent privatization of Deutsche Telekom and merger of Chrysler and Daimler-Benz to explore German tolerance for shareholder capitalism).

4. The convergence literature is reviewed and evaluated in CLARK KERR, THE FUTURE OF INDUSTRIAL SOCIETIES: CONVERGENCE OR CONTINUING DIVERSITY? (Cambridge: Harvard University Press, 1983).

lem" plays the role of independent variable. Policy analysis that relies too heavily on this logic may easily collapse into an apology for economic or technological determinism, may lead to a premature rejection of no less important explanations for convergence, and may obscure critical divergences.[5] It is an empirical question whether the same problems predetermine the same solution. The *technological determinism* hypothesis is the first, but only one, possible explanation for policy convergence in this area.

The second is *emulation*, because policy makers imitate or adapt the efforts of other countries. Data protection is an example of policy innovation, and as several studies have demonstrated, the incentives to copy or at least draw lessons form the pioneers in such circumstances can be strong. When innovation is required, there may be no readily available solution within the existing repertoire of policy and procedural techniques. Without the opportunity to learn from one's own experience, there is a natural tendency to look abroad, to see how other states have responded, to share ideas, and to bring foreign evidence to bear on the domestic decision–making process. Convergence is then the result of a pressure to conform in an insecure and tentative policy–making climate.

A third, and related, explanation may be termed *elite networking*. Here, convergence results form the shared beliefs of a relatively coherent and enduring network of elites bound by expertise on an issue and a common concern for its resolution. Convergence is the result not of constraints imposed by the problem or of collective insecurity but of a consensus among members of a trans-national "policy community" or "issue network." This interaction occurs at first among above the fray of domestic politics, the point at which a consensus of motivation and concern crystallizes. The participants then go forth to spread the word to their respective societies and governments. Similar responses then emanate as the result of the presentation and debate of similar evidence.

The fourth explanation is *harmonization*. Explicit attempts to harmonize policy require not only a coherent group of transnational actors, a broad consonance of motivation and concern, and regular opportunities for interaction, they also require authoritative action by opportunities for interaction, they also require authoritative action by an international organization or regime. The harmonization of policy by intergovernmental organizations is driven by recognition of interdependence and of the need to avoid unnecessary discrepancies and incompatibilities. Convergence occurs because international regimes recognize this interdependence, realize that the problem cannot be properly resolved at the national level, and decide that the benefits of convergence outweigh these alternatives.

One final possibility, which contrasts with the seemingly cooperative relations under harmonization, is that states may be forced to conform to the actions of others. This process is termed *penetration*. It is based on the assumption that policy action within one jurisdiction (either a nation-state or an international organization) may carry certain costs that are then exported to those which have not yet responded. In a penetrative process foreign officials participate in the domestic policy processes of another state, consulting, advising, and giving the strong message that the country concerned has no alternative but to follow the lead taken elsewhere.

* * *

5. For a more complete discussion of these problems, *see* Colin J. Bennett, *Review Article: What is Policy Convergence and What Causes It?* BRITISH JOURNAL OF POLITICAL SCIENCE 21 (1991): 215–33.

The central theoretical argument is that these forces for convergence confront and interact with distinctively Swedish, German, American, and British beliefs and institutions. The extent to which states did not converge depends on obstacles or constraints peculiar to these particular states. The familiar metaphor of the prism is helpful here. A common problem with common properties flows around advanced democratic countries and is then confronted with a set of obstacles to be overcome in each state, some of which might block the dispersal, some of which might refract it in peculiar and interesting ways. The familiar conditions of postindustrialism (bureaucracy and information technology) have created a frequently recognized problem that enters four different prisms at roughly the same time. Whether, and in what ways, the resulting outcomes converge because of some or all of these trans-national forces, or diverge because of distinctive culture, constitutional, economic, or bureaucratic factors, is another way of stating the central question of this book.

* * *

The concepts of convergence and divergence have also been associated with questions about the relative autonomy of the democratic state. Some have assumed that evidence of convergence is also evidence that states have been forced to conform to an inexorable set of trans-national forces. What does the evidence of convergence and divergence in data protection policy tell us about the relative autonomy of these four states? Which has been able to fashion a policy independently and in response to its own agenda? Which have been more influenced by forces beyond their control? The central conclusion here is that evidence of convergence per se should not be interpreted as evidence of lack of autonomy. The key evidence is the *reason* for that convergence, hence the need in any study of this nature to explore various propositions that rest on different assumptions about the behavior and autonomy of state actors. Closely associated with this question is that of "policy style." Which were more anticipatory, which more reactive? In which was the process more conflictual, in which more consensual? How do generalizations about policy style drawn from other cases stand up to examination here?

Lucian Arye Bebchuk and Mark J. Roe
A Theory of Path Dependence in Corporate Ownership and Governance

52 Stan. L. Rev. 127 (1999)
(excerpts from pages 134–138; some footnotes omitted)

1. Globalization and the drive toward efficient structures.

It might be thought that the advanced economies should by now display similar patterns of corporate structure. Companies in these countries face similar governance problems. All large-scale firms share some key common functions: Capital must be gathered, management must be selected and disciplined, and information must be transmitted to core decision-makers. Organizational imperatives could demand organizational imperatives. And other powerful forces, it might be argued, drive countries and firms to adopt the most efficient corporate rules and structures. Not to do so in our competitive global village runs the risk that firms and the economy will fall behind. A firm that did not adopt the best structure would be hurt either in its profits and value or in its ability to raise new capital. Countries that fail to adopt efficient rules would inflict costs on their corporations, which would then be worth less and would then be less able to raise capital; as a result, firms, factories, and businesses might suffer, or they might migrate away from the country.[6]

Another way of stating the above view is that, as efficient new technologies can spread rapidly, one might expect (by analogy) that new corporate technologies, if better, should spread rapidly. Corporate governance could be seen as a technology—similar to a manufacturing technique, an inventory management system, or an engineering economy of scale—and firms face powerful incentives to adopt the best corporate technologies possible:

> The corporation and its securities are products in financial markets to as great an extent as the sewing machines or other things the firm makes. Just as the founders of a firm have incentives to make the kinds of sewing machines people want to buy, they have incentives to create the kind of firm, governance structure, and securities the customers in capital markets want.[7]

The adoption of the same efficient corporate governance technologies across the advanced economies might be facilitated, on the view under consideration, by the easy flow of information about corporate technologies. Cross-border investors and multinationals bring with them familiarity with foreign practices.[8] National reports regularly consider practices seen elsewhere and identify them as beneficial.[9]

---

6. *See* Frank H. Easterbrook & Daniel R. Fischel, The Economic Structure of Corporate Law 212–18 (1991) (arguing that competition induces convergence in state rules); Roberta S. Karmel, *Is It Time for a Federal Corporation Law?*, 57 Brook. L. Rev. 55, 90 (1991) ("Despite these historical differences in corporate governance practice in the United Kingdom and continental countries, the laws will soon become more congruent...."); cf. Harold Demsetz, *The Structure of Ownership and the Theory of the Firm*, 26 J.L. & Econ. 375, 375–77 (1983) (arguing that there is an ineluctable pressure on corporate structures toward efficiency).

7. Easterbrook & Fischel, *supra* note 6, at 4–5 (emphasis added).

8. In the late 1990s, this cross-border investment force tends to make corporate governance converge more towards American patterns than otherwise, because the international investors most active so far in pushing corporate governance initiatives have been Americans. *See* Martine Orange & Enguerand Renault, *Les patrons francais se sont convertis aux exigences des actionnaires* [*The French Owners Have Converted to Stockholders' Demands*], Le Monde, Apr. 23, 1998, at 21 (noting that foreign, typically Anglo-Saxon, stockholders in large French firms are pressing managers to be more concerned about shareholder value); John Tagliabue, *Compliments of U.S. Investors: New Activism Shakes Europe's Markets*, N.Y. Times, Apr. 15, 1998, at D1 (noting spread of American shareholder activism); Sara Webb, *Calpers Sees New Targets Overseas*, Wall St. J., Oct. 20, 1997, at C1, available in 1997 WL-WSJ 14170443 (noting Calpers' attempts to improve the corporate governance of overseas companies). Daimler's takeover of Chrysler might bring German governance practices in line with American ones (or further spread American governance practices in Germany).

9. *See generally* Corporate Governance Forum of Japan, Corporate Governance Principles—A Japanese View (Interim Report) (1997) (discussing in general corporate governance); Competitiveness Policy Council, Reports of the Subcouncils (1993) (discussing value of large institutional blockholding); Peter Mulbert, Empfehlen sich gesetzliche Regelungen zur Einschran-ung des Einflusses der Kreditinstitute auf Aktiengesellschaften? [Are Rules Limiting Bank Influence Desirable?] (1996) (discussing usefulness of alternative governance systems); Organization for Economic Cooperation and Development, Business Sector Advisory Group on Corporate Governance, Institutional Modernisation for Effective and Adaptive Corporate Governance: Challenges and Responses (1997) (seeking basic worldwide principles of corporate governance); Michael E. Porter, *Capital Disadvantage: America's Failing Capital Investment System*, Harv. Bus. Rev., Sept.–Oct. 1992, at 65–82 (advocating adoption of foreign-based corporate governance innovations).

2. Persistence.

Given these pressures to whittle down corporate differences, the question arises as to why corporate ownership and governance structures have continued to differ.

To be sure, it is possible to point out movements that are reducing certain differences—e.g., the efforts to encourage wider stock ownership in Europe,[10] German banks' statements that they will sell off their stockholdings,[11] the takeover headlines in Europe,[12] and the rising influence of American institutional investors in the United States (with the possibility that they will acquire the influence sometimes had by financial institutions in continental Europe and Japan).[13] But these stories are balanced by considerable persistence.

For example, German banks, despite their rhetoric of withdrawal from stock ownership, have thus far held on to their stock. In fact, over the past decade, Germany's banks have increased the number of influential blocks they own in the one hundred largest German firms from forty to over fifty. Thus, while German banks seem to have failed at their monitoring job in publicized cases, and while they have regularly been the target of populist sentiment, their considerable stock ownership has thus far persisted. Similarly, concentrated family ownership of Germany's largest firms persists.

With respect to Japan, given the breakdown of the Japanese banking system, and the widespread recognition of the problems of Japanese corporate governance, one might have expected to observe a decline in banks' ownership of large corporate blocks in Japan. Yet, the ownership data for the largest Japanese firms hardly indicate any movement in bank and insurer ownership in the largest firms over the past three decades.[16]

In any event, it does not matter for our purposes whether the overall variance among countries in ownership structures has been recently narrowing somewhat, remaining the same, or increasing—a question which the data is insufficient to resolve. What is clear is that, notwithstanding the forces of globalization and efficiency, some key differences in corporate structures among countries have persisted. This observation raises important questions for researchers: Why have such differences persisted? And will they persist in the future?

---

10. *See* Jeffrey N. Gordon, *Pathways to Corporate Convergence? Two Steps on the Road to Shareholder Capitalism in Germany*, 5 COLUM. J. EUR. L. 219, 220 (1999).

11. *See, e.g.*, Brian Coleman & Dagmar Aalund, *Deutsche Bank to Cash Out of Industrial Stakes*, WALL ST. J., Dec. 16, 1998, at A17 (noting that Deutsche Bank announced plans to sell stock holdings); Role of the Financial Services Sector: Hearings Before the Task Force on the International Competitiveness of U.S. Financial Institutions of the Subcommittee on Financial Institutions Supervision, Regulation and Insurance of the House Committee on Banking, Finance and Urban Affairs, 101st Cong. 164–65 (1990) (noting that Deutsche Bank executive revealed intention to sell stock holdings).

12. *See, e.g.*, Sophie Fay & Pascale Santi, *L'offensive de la BNP plonge le monde bancaire dans la confusion [BNP's offensive plunges the banking world into confusion]*, LE MONDE, Mar. 12, 1999, at 23 (noting that French bank made simultaneous hostile bids for two other large banks).

13. *See* MARK J. ROE, STRONG MANAGERS, WEAK OWNERS: THE POLITICAL ROOTS OF AMERICAN CORPORATE FINANCE 223–24 (1994)....

16. *See generally* Michael S. Gibson, "Big Bang" Deregulation and Japanese Corporate Governance: A Survey of the Issues (Federal Reserve Int'l Fin. Discussion Paper No. 624, 1998) (concluding that reforms of financial institutions in Japan have thus far had a limited effect on corporate governance).

C. Sources of Path Dependence

Our focus will be on the role that is played by path dependence in creating and maintaining differences in corporate structures. There are two sources of path dependence. One type of path dependence... is structure driven. By structure-driven path dependence, we mean the ways in which initial ownership structures in an economy directly influence subsequent ownership structures. As we shall see, there are two ways through which an economy's ownership structures might depend on its initial pattern of corporate ownership structures.

The other type of path dependence arises from corporate rules. Such rules can influence corporate ownership and governance structures. In particular, such rules can shape choices between ownership structures that have and do not have a controlling shareholder. Corporate rules affect ownership and governance structures in at least three ways.

First, concentrated ownership might be discouraged by the presence of legal rules that make it more difficult or costly for financial institutions to accumulate and hold large blocks.[17] Such rules are strongly present in the United States, but not as strong in other countries.[18]

Second, in corporate systems that enable controllers to extract large private benefits of control, "rent-protection" considerations might lead to concentrated ownership.[19] When private control benefits are large, those who set up the corporate structure in an IPO would be reluctant to leave control up for grabs, because doing so would attract attempts to grab control and render the chosen structure unstable. Furthermore, when private benefits of control are large, controlling shareholders of publicly traded companies will be reluctant to relinquish their lock on control when raising extra capital, because they will not be compensated by existing shareholders for forgoing the larger benefits that come with a lock on control.

Third, some countries have mandatory corporate rules that constrain, or push in a certain direction, the choice of governance structure. For example, some rules affect the constitution of the board of directors and the degree of labor influence in the firm. American stock exchange rules and state corporate law doctrines militate in favor of a high proportion of independent directors. Japanese employee-oriented norms lead to insiders dominating corporate boards.[21] And German rules mandate that labor has half of the board seats of large firms.[22]

Thus, given how important corporate rules are, substantial differences in such rules among countries might be sufficient to produce substantial differences in ownership patterns.... By rule-driven path dependence we mean the additional, indirect (but important) channel through which initial corporate structures might affect sub-

---

17. *See* Roe, *Strong Managers, supra* note 13, at 26–49.

18. *See id.* at 167–97.

19. *See generally* Lucian Arye Bebchuk, A Rent-Protection Theory of Corporate Ownership and Control (National Bureau of Econ. Research Working Paper No. 7203, 1999)...(analyzing how rent-protection considerations affect the choice of ownership structure at the IPO stage)....

21. *See* Yasu Izumikawa, *Amidst Calls for Corporate Governance Reform, Nissan Questions Role of Non-Executive Directors*, IRRC Corp. Governance Bull., July–Sept. 1997, at 21 (noting the Japanese view that nonexecutives contribute little to corporate governance).

22. *See* Katharina Pistor, *Co-determination in Germany: A Sociopolitical Model with Governance Externalities*, in Employees' Role in Corporate Governance (Margaret Blair & Mark J. Roe eds., 1999).

sequent structures—by affecting future business rules. As we shall show, the corporate rules of an economy, which will have an effect on choices of ownership structures, are themselves influenced by the economy's initial pattern of corporate structures

---

Comments and Questions

1. Professors Bebchuk and Roe suggest a limit to the convergence of systems of corporate governance. The authors also suggest an important basis of resistance to the harmonization or unification of regulatory systems. Yet, how effective, in practical terms, is this a source of resistance to harmonization? If corporations are free to migrate from less to more congenial regulatory regimes, does convergence become irrelevant? Or does migration promote greater convergence among those states uneasy about losing corporate domiciliaries?

2. Do your answers to the questions in paragraph 1 change when you consider the following excerpt?

> The forces of regulatory competition also are driving forum-shopping by corporations that look to locate in host countries with attractive laws, thereby further promoting sovereign-state competition.[72] To give a simple example, most European countries do not permit tax deductions for amortization expense of goodwill or other intangible assets. However, Italy, the Netherlands, and Spain do allow these deductions. This difference creates an incentive for corporations that acquire assets elsewhere (France, for instance) to sell the assets to a related entity in one of those countries and then to lease the assets back to the French entity.[73] The sale-leaseback device neutralizes the cross-border difference, thereby subverting French tax policy. Thus, a little creative contracting quickly can minimize legal differences among nations.[74]

Lawrence A. Cunningham, *Commonalities and Prescriptions in the Vertical Dimension of Global Corporate Governance*, 84 CORNELL L. REV. 1133, 1151 (1999).

3. Resistance, at least since the nineteenth century, has acquired a strong cultural and nationalist dimension. Are our notions about comparative law and convergence more an arrogant expression of the current dominant position of Western European and American models of economic and political organization, or do they reflect something that transcends this momentary preeminence? In that connection, consider the following:

---

72. For a few excellent articles on international regulatory competition in securities regulation, *see* James D. Cox, *Regulatory Competition in Securities Markets: An Approach for Reconciling Japanese and United States Disclosure Philosophies*, 16 HASTINGS INT'L & COMP. L. REV. 149 (1993); James D. Cox, *Rethinking U.S. Securities Laws in the Shadow of International Regulatory Competition*, LAW & CONTEMP. PROBS. (Autumn 1992), at 157; Bevis Longstreth, *A Look at the SEC's Adaptation to Global Market Pressures*, 33 COLUM. J. TRANSNAT'L L. 319 (1995). For an excellent article on regulatory competition in general, *see* William W. Bratton & Joseph A. McCahery, *Regulatory Competition, Regulatory Capture, and Corporate Self-Regulation*, 73 N.C. L. REV. 1861 (1995).

73. [CLIFFORD CHANCE, BUYING A EUROPEAN BUSINESS: A GUIDE TO NEGOTIATED ACQUISITIONS IN WESTERN EUROPE (2d ed. 1997)] at 24.

74. *See generally* Bernard S. Black, *Is Corporate Law Trivial?: A Political and Economic Analysis*, 84 NW. U. L. REV. 542 (1990) (arguing that state corporate law in the United States is trivial because it can be contracted around to enable corporations to use whatever governance structure they desire).

> One of the most important benefits of comparative law is that it can provide a knowledge of the different patterns of legal thinking current in the world and show that the personal way of thinking that everyone considers without reflection to be that of everyone else is in fact only one of the many ways.... Although the study of any foreign legal system teaches something about this relativity, the Japanese system provides material which brings out the relativity in an accentuated way. Japan is situated both geographically and historically in a special position. On the one hand it is isolated in the Pacific and, being at some distance from the continent, was free from foreign invasion until 1945. On the other hand the distance from the continent was not so great as to prevent all communication. For these reasons Japan freely adopted ideas and habits from foreign civilizations. The ideas took root in Japanese soil, and cut off from their native cultural surroundings, they have developed and been transformed into something quite different from the original. This pattern is in direct contrast with that of Europe, where nations have been fighting violently for thousands of years and where differing ideas have mixed with and complemented each other to form the basis of a single European type of thought. Though it is possible to speak of Oriental ideas, there is nothing in this conception or in those ideas which can compare with the cohesion found in European thought.
>
> Japanese thought has a further characteristic which results from the policy of isolationism during the two hundred and fifty years which preceded the Meiji era (1868–1912). While European nations were engaged in fierce political and economic competition, Japan was enjoying the idleness of peace. The effects of this isolation are difficult to gauge, but one thing is sure—isolation assured Japanese thought of an excessive accentuation of its natural characteristics and had a great influence on the Japanese conception of law.

YOSIYUKI NODA, INTRODUCTION TO JAPANESE LAW 5–6 (Anthony H. Angelo, trans. 1976).

4. ***Social norms and convergence.*** The idea that practice follows law may not be invariably true, even in the United States. Is it possible that law, and business practice, to some extent are captives of, and merely memorialize, the practices of localized economic communities? Yet if this is true, then the possibly of harmonization exists as the business practice community expands beyond national or ethnic borders. Is it possible that worldwide harmonization is attainable without the primary intervention and guidance of governments, but rather by the formalization of patterns of behavior among worldwide communities? Melvin Eisenberg explains that:

> Corporate law serves both to facilitate and to regulate the conduct of the corporate enterprise. Insofar as corporate law is regulatory, it provides incentives and disincentives to the major actors in the corporate enterprise—directors, officers, and significant shareholders—through the threat of liability. In significant part, however, these actors are motivated not by the desire to avoid liability, but by the prospect of financial gain, on the one hand, and by social norms, on the other. Much work has been done on the way in which these actors are motivated by the threat of liability and the prospect of financial gain, but relatively little work has been done on the operation of social norms.
>
> The neglect of the operation of social norms in the field of corporate law parallels the neglect of the operation of social norms in the law generally.[1] In recent

1. *See* Eric A. Posner, *Efficient Norms, in* 2 NEW PALGRAVE ENCYCLOPEDIA OF LAW AND ECONOMICS 19, 20 (1998).

years, a small but important group of scholars has begun to remedy this neglect.[2] By and large, however, the work has not concerned the interrelation of law and social norms in specific fields of law. Instead, most of the new work has either concerned the operation of social norms in general, using illustrations from various fields, or has concerned occupational communities whose members choose to be governed by their own social norms rather than law in their dealings with each other.[3] Furthermore, much of this work has concerned only those social norms that impose obligations, and little of the work has concerned the role of belief-systems in the origin and adoption of social norms.

* * *

B. Three Categories of Social Norms

Social norms can be divided into three categories according to the degree of self-consciousness and obligation that they involve.

The first category consists of behavioral patterns that neither entail a sense of obligation nor are self-consciously adhered to or engaged in. One type of behavioral pattern consists of functional responses to the facts of the natural world, like putting on warm clothes when it's cold. Another consists of statistical regularities, like the fact that automobile accidents peak during holidays. Still another consists of habits, like drinking coffee at breakfast.

The second category of social norms consists of rules and regularities that are self-consciously adhered to or engaged in, but do not entail a sense of obligation. For example, it is a practice in some law schools to begin "one-hour" classes on the hour and finish at ten minutes of, and in others to begin at ten minutes after the hour and finish on the hour. These practices are self-consciously adhered to and engaged in, and indeed have the look and feel of rules, but they do not involve a sense of obligation. A law school would normally not be criticized for changing from one practice to the other, or to a third practice entirely. A faculty member could normally depart from the practice—make an exception to the rule—without criticism, as long as she

---

2. *See, e.g.*, ROBERT C. ELLICKSON, ORDER WITHOUT LAW: HOW NEIGHBORS SETTLE DISPUTES (1991); Lisa Bernstein, *Merchant Law in a Merchant Court: Rethinking the Code's Search for Immanent Business Norms*, 144 U. PA. L. REV. 1765 (1996); Lisa Bernstein, *Opting Out of the Legal System: Extralegal Contractual Relations in the Diamond Industry*, 21 J. LEGAL STUD. 115 (1992) [hereinafter Bernstein, Opting Out]; David Charny, *Illusions of Spontaneous Order: Norms in Contractual Relationships*, 144 U. PA. L. REV. 1841 (1996); Robert D. Cooter, *Decentralized Law For a Complex Economy: The Structural Approach to Adjudicating the New Law Merchant*, 144 U. PA. L. REV. 1643 (1996) [hereinafter Cooter, Decentralized Law]; Robert D. Cooter, *Expressive Law and Economics*, 27 J. LEGAL STUD. 585 (1998) [hereinafter Cooter, Expressive Law and Economics]; Robert Cooter, *Normative Failure Theory of Law*, 82 CORNELL L. REV. 947 (1997); Jody S. Kraus, *Legal Design and the Evolution of Commercial Norms*, 26 J. LEGAL STUD. 377 (1997); Lawrence Lessig, *The Regulation of Social Meaning*, 62 U. CHI. L. REV. 943 (1995); Richard H. McAdams, *The Origin, Development, and Regulation of Norms*, 96 MICH. L. REV. 338, 341 (1997); Richard H. Pildes, *The Destruction of Social Capital Through Law*, 144 U. PA. L. REV. 2055 (1996); Eric A. Posner, *Law, Economics, and Inefficient Norms*, 144 U. PA. L. REV. 1697 (1996) [hereinafter Posner, Law, Economics, and Inefficient Norms]; Eric A. Posner, *Symbols, Signals, and Social Norms in Politics and the Law*, 27 J. LEGAL STUD. 765 (1998) [hereinafter Posner, Symbols, Signal, and Social Norms]; Eric A. Posner, *The Regulation of Groups: The Influence of Legal and Nonlegal Sanctions on Collective Action*, 63 U. CHI. L. REV. 133 (1996) [hereinafter Posner, Regulation of Groups]; Cass R. Sunstein, *On the Expressive Function of Law*, 144 U. PA. L. REV. 2021 (1996); Cass R. Sunstein, *Social Norms and Social Roles*, 96 COLUM. L. REV. 903 (1996)....

3. *See, e.g.*, Bernstein, Opting Out, *supra* note 2.

could comfortably fit the schedule of her class into the schedules of other classes, and adhered to the related norm that a one-hour law school class lasts 50 minutes.

Another type of norm in this category consists of usages that attach meanings to words, symbols, or stylized conduct. Here is an example from the Restatement Second of Contracts.

> A contracts to sell B 1,000 feet of San Domingo mahogany. By usage of dealers in mahogany, known to A and B, good figured mahogany of a certain density is known as San Domingo mahogany, though it does not come from San Domingo. Unless otherwise agreed, the usage is part of the contract.[5] Another example is the posture and hand signal used to hitchhike: As a matter of usage, standing in a certain posture by the side of a road and holding up your hand in a certain way means that you want a lift.

I will call norms in this second category practices, and I will call behavioral patterns and practices, taken together, nonobligational norms.

The third category of social norms consists of rules or practices that actors not only self-consciously adhere to or engage in, but feel obliged in some sense to adhere to or engage in, although (by hypothesis) the rule or practice is neither a legal nor an organizational rule. I will call such norms obligational norms. An operational test of whether a social norm is obligational is whether a departure from the norm is likely to involve either self-criticism or criticism by others.

Moral norms are one extremely important type of obligational norm. Much human conduct can only be convincingly explained on the basis of moral norms. Even conduct that could be explained on instrumental grounds often has a moral dimension whose explanatory power cannot be safely ignored.[6] But a social norm may be obligational without being moral. For example, if it is a practice to wear formal dress to Metropolitan Opera premieres, then [those who attend] regular Metropolitan Opera opening nights will probably believe there is an obligation, although not a moral obligation, to follow along. Correspondingly, those who attend a premiere in informal dress will be criticized. Similarly, the social norms concerning what kinds of foods should be eaten with utensils, rather than with one's hands, are not moral norms, but they are obligational norms.

Melvin A. Eisenberg, *Corporate Law and Social Norms*, 99 COLUM. L. REV. 1253, 1253–54, 1256–57 (1999).

5. As we study the materials in this course, think about the extent to which social norms hinder or facilitate the process of harmonization. Social norms are not necessarily national norms. Social norms can be religious (the need to apply rules derived from Shar'ia in business dealings between Muslims in the United States, for example), ethnic, or class based. The law, itself, may recognize economic classes and treat them differently in some contexts. Western law, for example, distinguishes between "merchants" and others in connection with the law of sales.[1] As such, harmonization that is extra-national may be, to some extent, a means of rearranging political organization with the

5. Restatement (Second) of Contracts § 222 cmt. b, illus. 2 (1996).

6. See ROBERT AXELROD, THE COMPLEXITY OF COOPERATION 40 (1997).

1. *See*, for example, the UNIFORM COMMERCIAL CODE in the United States. European Civil Law countries also distinguish between merchants (*commerçants*) and others in their commercial codes. We study this further in Chapter 2.

consequence that the power to legislate formally moves from the nation-state to other social, economic or political communities.

6. The two excerpts that follow suggest two different perspectives on the inevitability of harmonization, and the realities of resistance. As you read them consider whether the views expressed in each are irreconcilable. Is it possible to argue that the authors of each excerpt are concerned about harmonization at different, and perhaps critically different levels of generality?

Alexander Merezhko, *Problems of Stylistics in Ukrainian Legislation on the Example of the Draft of the Law "On Securing Performance of Obligations with Moveable Property"*

Newspaper "Yuridicheskaya Praktika" ("Legal Practices")
No. 16 (122) April 20, 2000 (Kiev)
("Problemy stilistiki ukrainskogo zakonodatel'stva na primere proekta zakona "Ob obespechenii ispolneniia obiazatel'stv dvizhimym imuschestvom")
(translated by the author)

Development of the Ukraine's legal system is impossible without taking into consideration the experience of other states in the field of legislative drafting, as well as without borrowing some of the most advanced foreign legal institutes and legal solutions. At the same time, it is always important to keep in mind that moving even the most advanced institutes and the most successful legal solutions from the realm of foreign law to Ukrainian legal soil requires extreme carefulness and attention, since peculiarities of the Ukraine's legal system must be taken into consideration. From the perspective of legal technique, it is rather important that the foreign legal institute, which is being borrowed by the Ukrainian legislators, nicely fits into the current legal infrastructure of Ukraine's legal system, without damaging this system.

As regards foreign lawyers, who sincerely try to help our country in creation of authentic rule-of-law state by way of assisting in adoption and development of new draft laws based on the legal norms of foreign countries, they should be especially attentive in taking into account Ukraine's legal context as well as its legal traditions.

Since American lawyers in particular appear to be especially active in influencing our legislative process (which is very useful and commendable in itself), they must be well aware of the differences in approaches to the process of legislative drafting between the Anglo-Saxon common law system and the continental system of law.

Black and White

Let's consider some differences of stylistic nature between the legislative drafting process in the framework of common law on the one hand, and the system of continental law, to which Ukraine belongs, on the other hand.

First of all, while in both systems of law, laws have a priority position in the hierarchy of sources of law, at the same time they perform different functions. In Ukraine, just like in other continental law countries, the basis of the legislation is made up of codes, containing legal principles and norms of general character, and the codes are supplemented by legislative acts on certain specific issues.

On the other hand, laws in the common law system supplement the existing precedent law, and are supplemented by subsequent precedents. To put it differently, provisions of the laws exist here in the atmosphere of precedent law.

Peculiarities of legislative style are conditional upon the functions performed by laws in the two legal systems under consideration.

If codes and laws of the continental law system are characterized by conciseness and laconicism (so called French style), laws within framework of common law are characterized by preciseness and distinctness (so called English style).

Laws in the continental law system, as a rule, contain the minimum of legal definitions, and their provisions are formulated in very general phrases, since the purpose is to govern a wide circle of possible situations.

In their turn, laws in the common law systems are distinguished by a significant number of rather detailed definitions used in the text of the law, by the carefully written and distinct sphere of its application, as well as by huge number of exclusions therefrom.

All these stylistic peculiarities result from the fact that norms of the laws in continental legislation are formulated broadly enough, have an exhaustive character, and, as a rule, are not subject for restrictive interpretation.

Laws in the common law system, on the contrary, must not be concessive and laconic, but rather distinct and precise, since courts in the common law system interpret laws not broadly, but narrowly, restrictively, i.e. limit the sphere of their application exclusively with regard to those facts and situations for the regulation of which such laws have been designed. In common law, laws are interpreted against the background of the precedent law. In contrast, laws in continental legal system have independent meaning and constitute the major source of law.

When in Rome...

In the light of the above said, let's analyze the draft law of Ukraine "On Securing Performance of Obligations with Moveable Property" (registered number 4245, and has already passed through the first reading in the Ukrainian Parliament (Verkhovna Rada), drafters of which were obviously inspired by the respective provisions of the Uniform Commercial Code of the USA (Section 9) to the detriment of the prevalent system of Ukrainian legislation.

Let's emphasize from the very beginning that we are not trying to question economic content of the draft law and practical expediency of implementation of its main idea. Quite the contrary, this idea is quite urgent, and its correct implementation will only facilitate the creation of a legal basis for a civilized market in Ukraine. We are talking exclusively of such details as legal form and style of the given draft law. However, as Americans say "the devil is in the details".

The problem is, first of all, related to the fact that the draft law has been created in Anglo-American legislative style and, if passed, may cause significant harm to the system of Ukrainian legislation.

First, totally in the manner of Anglo-American law, a disproportionately large part of its provisions is composed of legal definitions. In total, there are more than 25 of them, which constitutes almost one third of the draft law. Such an excessive, from the point of view of continental law, number of definitions, significantly complicates perception of the draft law. Some of these definitions are written in such a way that their meaning may only be understood by addressing a number of other definitions. The following "masterpiece of tautology" is of especially high interest: "A secured obligation is one or several obligations secured by security interest" (Article 4(1)). In order to comprehend the depth of this esoteric phrase, it is necessary to consider three more definitions contained in the draft law ("security interest", "moveable property", "account").

Among the definitions used in the draft law there are also definitions of the civil law terms, which must be contained not in the separate law, but in the apparatus of definitions of the Civil Code to avoid situation when one and the same civil law term is used in different meanings. In particular, the terms "debtor", "account", "proceeds", "moveable property", "goods", "value", etc. are among such terms.

It is also not quite clear why the authors of the draft law needed to complicate the text of this draft by dividing the notion of "goods" into four separate categories ("consumer goods", "farm products", "inventory" and "equipment").

The authors of the draft law are also trying without proper consideration some specific notions of Anglo-American law, which are not familiar to Ukrainian legislation, Ukrainian soil. In particular, such a specific notion as "fixtures to immovable property" is a case in point.

The scope of the law is formulated in a typical Anglo-American style, i.e. it contains excessively detailed indication of four cases when the law should be applied, as well as indicates nine exclusions.

In general, the question arises whether it is at all worthwhile to adopt separate law on collateral, or it may be more expedient to adopt respective amendments to the current Ukrainian law "On the Pledge"?

The Law without Citizenship

Overall impression about this draft law is that it is not an integral part of the Ukraine's legal system, but rather a separate autonomous legal system with its own apparatus of terms and definitions.

Yet worse, the authors of the draft law claim to amend five existing laws, which will automatically lead to replication of the shortcomings of this draft law.

Hence, this draft law at the moment is an alien body to Ukrainian legislation, which will inevitably cause the reaction of rejection by this legislation in the event that the said draft law is nevertheless adopted by the Verkhovna Rada.

In our opinion, this draft law should be composed of the legal definitions and institutes already existing in the modern Ukrainian legislation, with consideration of current laws (the law "On the Pledge" in particular), as well as based on the draft Civil Code of Ukraine, adopted by the Verkhovna Rada in the second reading.

Besides, adoption of this law before the draft Civil Code is passed will mean putting the cart in front of the horse, since the draft law must logically flow from the new Civil Code and supplement it. In our opinion, the situation with the draft law "On Securing Performance of Obligations with Moveable Property" testifies one more time to the necessity of urgent adoption of the draft Civil Code, which must become the nucleus around which and on the basis of which all further legislative drafting in the sphere of commercial legislation must be done.

The elementary logic of legislative drafting in Ukraine requires that not the whole legal system of Ukraine adjust itself to the new draft law, but on the contrary, that the new draft law is formulated in such a manner that it organically fits into the existing legal context.

Finally, I would like to turn to foreign lawyers providing expertise to Ukrainian legislative drafters and ask them to treat legal traditions and peculiarities of the Ukrainian legal system more carefully, since imposing their opinion on what this system must be like, may only decrease the efficiency and quality of Ukrainian laws aimed at creation of civilized market relations in Ukraine. After all, Ukraine is not a defeated Japan of the 1945-model, where it was possible to impose rules and laws ignoring peculiarities of its legal system and culture.

Michael Mussa,[1] *Factors Driving Global Economic Integration*

presented in Jackson Hole, Wyoming at a symposium sponsored by the Federal Reserve Bank of Kansas City on "Global Opportunities and Challenges," August 25, 2000 <http://www.imf.org/external/np/speeches/2000/082500.htm> (footnotes, charts and references omitted)

Introduction

Global economic integration is not a new phenomenon. Some communication and trade took place between distant civilizations even in ancient times. Since the travels of Marco Polo seven centuries ago, global economic integration—through trade, factor movements, and communication of economically useful knowledge and technology—has been on a generally rising trend. This process of globalization in the economic domain has not always proceeded smoothly. Nor has it always benefitted all whom it has affected. But, despite occasional interruptions, such as following the collapse of the Roman Empire or during the interwar period in this century, the degree of economic integration among different societies around the world has been rising. Indeed, during the past half century, the pace of economic globalization (including the reversal of the interwar decline) has been particularly rapid. And, with the exception of human migration, global economic integration today is greater than it ever has been and is likely to deepen going forward.

Three fundamental factors have affected the process of economic globalization and are likely to continue driving it in the future. First, improvements in the technology of transportation and communication have reduced the costs of transporting goods, services, and factors of production and of communicating economically useful knowledge and technology. Second, the tastes of individuals and societies have generally, but not universally, favored taking advantage of the opportunities provided by declining costs of transportation and communication through increasing economic integration. Third, public policies have significantly influenced the character and pace of economic integration, although not always in the direction of increasing economic integration.

1. Economic Counselor and Director of Research IMF [International Monetary Fund]. The views expressed in this paper are those of the author and do not reflect those of the IMF.

These three fundamental factors have influenced the pattern and pace of economic integration in all of its important dimensions. In particular, this paper discusses three important dimensions of economic integration: (1) through human migration; (2) through trade in goods and services; and (3) through movements of capital and integration of financial markets. After examining how fundamental forces have influenced economic integration in these dimensions, the paper concludes with reflections on three issues of general importance to the future course of global economic integration: the importance of communication as an influence on integration; the possibility that we may see a sharp reversal in the general trend of increasing integration, as occurred in the interwar period; and the apparent end of imperialism as a mechanism of integration. Before turning to this agenda, however, it is important emphasize a key theme that will recur in subsequent discussion: the main factors that drive the process of economic integration exert not only independent influences but also interact in important and complex ways.

Interactions Among the Fundamental Factors Driving Economic Integration

Although technology, tastes, and public policy each have important independent influences on the pattern and pace of economic integration in its various dimensions, they clearly interact in important ways. Improvements in the technology of transportation and communication do not spontaneously in an economic vacuum. The desire of people to take advantage of what they see as the benefits of closer integration—that is, the taste for the benefits of integration—is a key why it is profitable to make the innovations and investments that bring improvements in the technology of transportation and communication. And, public policy has often played a significant role in fostering innovation and investment in transportation and communication both to pursue the benefits of closer economic integration (within as well as across political boundaries) and for other reasons, such as national defense.

The tastes that people have and develop for the potential benefits of economic integration are themselves partly dependent on experience that made possible by cheaper means of transportation and communication. For example, centuries ago, wealthy people in Europe first learned about the tea and spices of the East as the consequence of limited and very expensive trade The broadening desire for these products resulting from limited experience hastened the search for easier and cheaper means of securing them. As a by-product of these efforts, America was discovered, and new frontiers of integration were opened up in the economic and other domains. More recently, if less dramatically, it is clear that tastes for products and services produced in far away locations (including tastes exercised through travel and tourism), as well as for investment in foreign assets, depend to an important degree on experience. As this experience grows, partly because it becomes cheaper, the tastes for the benefits of economic integration typically tend to rise. For example, it appears that as global investors have gained more experience with equities issued by firms in emerging market countries, they have become more interested in diversifying their portfolios to include some of these assets.

Public policy toward economic integration is also, to an important extent, responsive to the tastes that people have regarding various aspects of such integration, as well as to the technologies that make integration possible. On the latter score, it is relevant to note the current issues concerning public policy with respect to commerce conducted over the internet. Before advances in computing and communications technology, there was no internet over which commerce could be conducted; and, accordingly, these issues of public policy simply did not arise. Regarding the influence of tastes on public policy, the situation is complicated. Reflecting the general desire to secure the perceived benefits of integration, public policies usually, if not invariably, tend to support closer economic integration within political jurisdictions. The disposition of public policy toward economic integration between different jurisdictions is typically more ambivalent. Better harbors built with public support (and better internal means of transportation as well) tend to facilitate international trade—both imports and exports. Import tariffs and quotas, however, are clearly intended to discourage people from exercising their individual tastes for imported products and encourage production of domestic substitutes. Sadly, the mercantilist fallacy that seems to provide common-sense support for these policies often finds political resonance. Even very smart politicians, such as Abraham Lincoln (who favored a protective tariff, as well as public support for investments to enhance domestic economic integration) often fail to understand the fundamental truth of Lerner's (1936) symmetry theorem—a tax on imports is fundamentally the same thing as a tax on exports.

It should be emphasized that the interactions between public policy and both tastes and technology in their effects on economic integration can be quite complex and sometimes surprising. Two examples help to illustrate this point. First, for several centuries, there has been active trade between Britain and the Bordeaux region of France, with Britain importing large quantities of Bordeaux wine. This trade, however, was seriously interrupted (if not completely suppressed) during various periods of hostility between the two countries when one side or the other wished to suppress trade with the enemy. Partly as a result of being cut off from Bordeaux wines, and partly as a means of strengthening its alliance with Portugal, Britain sought to develop imports of Portuguese wines. The existing Portuguese wines, however, did not meet British requirements. A solution was found in creating a new product—Portuguese red wine from the Duoro region, fortified with grape brandy that gave the wine an extra alcoholic kick, retained some of the fruit sugar that would otherwise have been absorbed in fermentation, and helped protect the wine during shipment in hot weather. The result of this technological innovation was a new product—modern Port—that developed and retained a considerable market, especially in Britain, even after barriers to the acquisition of French wines were reduced.

The second example concerns U.S. public policy toward international trade in sugar which, in a bizarre way, is partly the consequence of policies pursued by Napoleon Bonaparte and Admiral Lord Nelson. For many years, the United States has maintained tight import quotas on sugar to keep the domestic price typically at roughly three times the world market level. The domestic political interests that support this policy include some sugar refiners, some producers of cane sugar in the deep south and Hawaii, and a few thousand sugar beet farmers primarily in the upper midwest. Production of sugar from beets is a "new" technology, dating back to the Napoleonic period. Before that time, sugar was produced from cane grown primarily in the West Indies. Admiral Lord Nelson's establishment of naval supremacy over the French enabled Britain to cut off Napoleon's empire from imports of West Indian sugar. In response, Napoleon established a prize for finding a substitute for cane-based sugar which could be produced within his empire. The sugar beet was discovered, and has been with us ever since.

This story becomes even more complicated when we consider reactions to the U.S. governments' sugar policy. Responding to the high domestic price of sugar, users have searched for alternatives. High fructose corn syrup is a cheaper and attractive alternative, especially for producers of soft drinks who are major users of sweeteners. A key by-product of high fructose corn syrup is corn gluten meal which can be used as animal feed and which the U.S. both uses domestically and exports, notably to the European Union. Thus, through this round-about channel of public policies and product innovations, what was started by Napoleon and Nelson has come back to European shores.

Human Migration

Evidence from DNA has established that all modern humans are descended from common pre-human ancestors living in Africa roughly one million years ago. From that time until a few centuries ago, the most important mechanism for interaction among and integration of the activities of different human societies was undoubtedly people moving from one place to another, predominantly by foot. In the great span of pre-history up to roughly fifty thousand years ago, humans walked out of Africa and settled across the Eurasian land mass. Settlement of the Americas came later; my mother's native American ancestors probably walked across the land bridge between Asia and North America now submerged under the Bering Strait roughly ten thousand years ago.

Throughout most of historical time, extending back roughly five thousand years, human migration has remained the predominant mechanism of interaction and integration of different societies. Use of the horse and other beasts of burden changed somewhat the technology of human movement (and had a larger effect on methods of warfare), and boats were used to cross water barriers. However, most people most of the time continued to travel by foot. Although migration was slow (by the standards of present speeds of human transport) and often posed considerable risks, it proceeded on a vast scale. Indeed, even for many societies that pursued agriculture (as well as hunting and gathering) migration was a very common phenomenon up until quite recent times—as is testified to by the waves of migration out of Asia and across Europe extending up to roughly 1000 AD. What fundamental factors were driving these waves of human migration? Relevant technologies (e.g., use of horses) presumably had some effect, and changing tastes may also have mattered somewhat. But, the key factor was surely public policy. In some cases a society would see that it was exhausting the productive opportunities in a particular location and decide to move on. Also, if one society thought it had the military might to improve its welfare by taking over the territory and other property of one of its neighbors and perhaps also enslave its citizens, it would launch an attack. Seeing discretion as the better part of valor, the society under attack might decide to move on—and perhaps attack somebody else.

For the victor who succeeded in subjugating or driving out a rival society, the result would probably be an improvement in economic welfare. The loser, of course, would lose. The overall result presumably was negative sum. Indeed, in the first work in the entire field now known as social science, Thucydides opens his History on the Peloponnesian War with the following observation:

> "...it is evident that the country now called Hellas had in ancient times [i.e., well before 400 BC] no settled population; on the contrary, migrations were of frequent occurrence, the several tribes readily abandoning their homes under pressure of superior numbers. Without commerce, without freedom of communication either by land or sea, cultivating no more of their territory than the necessities of life required, destitute of capital, never planting their land (for they could not tell when an invader might not come and take it all away, and when he did come they had no walls to stop him), thinking that the necessities of daily sustenance could be sup-

> plied at one place as well as another, they cared little about shifting their habitation, and consequently neither built large cities nor attained to any other form of greatness. Their richest soils were always subject to this change of masters...The goodness of the land favored the enrichment of particular individuals, and thus created faction which proved a fertile source of ruin. It also invited invasion."

This ancient observation remains highly relevant today. It reminds us that good governance at the national and international level—especially maintenance of reasonable security for peoples' lives and property—is essential for economic progress. It also reminds us that not all forms of economic interaction among different societies are necessarily beneficial. Globalization by means of the sword, the gun boat, or the slave ship is very different from globalization through voluntary movements of people, goods, services, and physical and financial assets.

Turning to human migration in more recent times, it is useful to distinguish between mass migrations which have continued to occur in response to wars and political and social turmoil, and migrations of individuals and families undertaken primarily for economic reasons. Of course, the two categories are not completely distinct; individual and family decisions about migration are often affected by both economic and non-economic factors. Nevertheless, events such as the mass migrations in Europe that occurred during and immediately after World War II clearly reflect different fundamental factors than those that were primarily at work in influencing migration to the United States during the past two centuries.

As the noted historian Oscar Handlin observed, America is a nation of immigrants. The greatest surge of immigrants came during the period from the end of the Civil War up to the start of World War I, especially during the first decade of this century.... Economic considerations, including the cost of transportation mainly explain why immigration was particularly high during this period, with fluctuations in annual immigration flows reflecting (with a short lag) business cycle conditions in the United States.

Even in the early part of the 19th century, the United States was, relatively, a rich country. Average per capita income was roughly comparable to that in England, but the average American worker and his family probably lived better than the average English working family. The gap between America and much of the rest of Europe was substantial. However, travel from Europe to America was neither cheap nor fast nor without risks. A sailing ship could easily take a month to make the voyage. During colonial times, if a poor man wanted to immigrate, he could secure passage by agreeing to become an indentured servant, usually for five to seven years.

By the middle of the 19th century, the cost, speed, and safety of human transport across the Atlantic had all progressively improved, especially with the replacement of wooden sailing vessels by iron-made steam ships. These improvements in passenger transportation continued through the 19th and into the 20th century. By 1907 when my father's family migrated from Paris to New York, the cost of passage was down to a couple of months' wages. Indeed, my grandmother Marie Noel earned sufficiently good wages as a skilled seamstress for high fashion houses in New York (where speaking French was an important advantage), and was sufficiently suspicious of American doctors, that she sailed back to France in 1908 to give birth to her fourth son, before returning to live out the rest of her life—generally quite happily—in America. Some of my father's Italian relatives and friends also made trips back and forth between Europe and both the United States and Argentina. A couple of them, after experience in the new world, returned permanently to Italy. Beyond these anecdotes, there is evidence of significant back and forth movement of people between Europe and the Americas in the period shortly before World War I.

This phenomenon of back-and-forth movement is significant. It suggests that by no later than the early part of this century, the costs and risks of transportation had fallen to the point that (in contrast to earlier times) they were no longer a substantial factor in economic decisions about migration. Also, this reduction in transportation costs probably interacted with tastes in a way that enhanced the likelihood of migration. Even if, as is often the case, one knows family or friends who have migrated to a new country and culture, there must be uncertainty and concern about adapting to a new environment. If the decision to migrate is seen as practically irreversible, deterrence to migration is relatively high. If the costs of reversal are comparatively low, it is possible to experiment and see whether one's tastes are compatible with or adaptable to the new environment.

Undoubtedly, the transportation costs of migration have continued to decline since World War I. Why has the pace of immigration into the United States slowed? For migration from Europe, the answer is partly that income differentials have narrowed and so too have the economic and non-economic incentives for migration. However, economic incentives for migration to the United States (and most other industrial countries) from developing countries remain very large. Here, it is clear that public policies restricting migration—even though not fully effective—are the key reason why migration has declined from the high rates prevailing before World War I. Indeed, for the United States, there was no restriction on inward migration until the Chinese Exclusion Act of 1882 (adopted because of domestic political opposition, especially in California and other western states, to further immigration of Chinese laborers for railroad construction and other work). General restrictions on immigration from other countries did not come until the National Origins Act of 1924. Interestingly, as will be discussed further below, enactment of this highly restrictive measure was part of the general retreat of the United States into isolationism during the interwar period. This retreat, which was not limited only to the United States, reflected a general shift in tastes toward opposition to many forms of involvement and interaction with foreign countries.

Trade in Goods and Services

Traditionally, economists tend to focus on trade in goods and, to a lesser extent, services as the key mechanism for integrating economic activities across countries and as a critical channel (but not the only important one) for transmitting disturbances between national economies. Indeed, in the economic theory of international trade (specifically the Hecksher-Ohlin-Samuelson theory described in most textbooks), trade in goods is seen as a substitute for mobility of factors of production. Under certain restricted conditions, which do not apply completely in practice, the theory says trade in the outputs of production processes may be an essentially perfect substitute for mobility of factors, with the result that factor returns are equalized internationally—i.e., factor price equalization is achieved—without the necessity for factors to move internationally to achieve this equalization.

If the conditions for factor price equalization did apply, there would be no economic benefit from international mobility of factors of production. Full economic efficiency could be achieved exclusively through trading outputs. A key reason why the conditions for factor price equalization do not fully apply is because of barriers to trade in outputs that effectively prevent the equalization of relative output prices at different locations.

These barriers take two forms: natural barriers to trade in the form of transportation costs and also costs of information about product prices and availabilities at different locations; and artificial barriers to trade arising from tariffs, quotas, and other public policy interventions. Indeed, even if the broader conditions for factor price equalization (e.g., identical technologies with constant returns to scale) and, consequently trade in goods alone (without factor mobility) is not sufficient to achieve full international economic integration, a focus on natural and artificial barriers to trade is still important in assessing the extent to which international economic integration through trade achieves as much as is possible through this channel. Specifically, if there were literally no natural or artificial barriers to trade in goods or services, then the relative prices of all goods and services would be equalized everywhere, and integration through the channel of trade would be perfect and complete. In practice, of course, there are important natural and artificial barriers to trade which preclude such perfection. In general, the higher are the barriers to trade, the lower will be the degree of international integration through trade, and conversely. Thus, it is relevant to consider what has been happening to barriers to trade as a means of assessing what has been happening to international economic integration through this important channel.

The development of ocean-going sailing vessels beginning in the late 15th century expanded the horizons for trade to a truly global scale. However, despite gradual and cumulatively substantial improvements in transportation technology, during the era of sail high sea transportation costs (including risks from piracy or misadventure) generally remained an important barrier to trade over substantial distances. For most goods, shipping by land for more than a few score miles was prohibitively expensive. Shipping by water across the Atlantic or, even more so, between Europe and Asia was mainly restricted to goods with high ratios of value to weight and substantial disparities in relative prices between distant trading locations. Unlike recent times when there is a good deal of two-way intra-industry trade in very similar products, trade over long distances consisted primarily of products which were not produced domestically or of payment flows of gold and silver. Gradually, as sailing vessels became larger and piracy and other hazards to ocean-borne commerce were reduced, ocean-borne shipping costs did decline significantly and longer-distance trade expanded as a result. Nevertheless, well into the 1800s, transportation costs remained an important natural barrier to global trade.

The invention and development of steam-powered iron ships during the second half of the 19th century further reduced the costs of ocean shipping. By the end of the century, the cost of shipping a ton of cargo across the Atlantic was probably less than one-fifth of what it had been at the start of the century. This reduction in shipping costs contributed importantly to the expansion of world trade and to the range of products participating in that trade.

Artificial barriers to trade in the form of import tariffs and other public policy interventions have a very long history. No doubt, there has always been some interest in such measures as means of providing protection to domestic producers (often including monopolists and cartels) from foreign competition. Owners of warehouses in ancient Rome, for example, supposedly objected to the construction of the new harbor at Ostia which would improve the city's ability to deal with food shortages by increasing imports from around the Mediterranean. However, raising revenue for the state probably remained the most important reason for the imposition of tariffs until the 19th century. In the United States, in particular, tariffs were generally the most important source of revenue for the federal government up to World War I.

Despite the continuing importance of revenue as a reason for imposing tariffs, it appears that interest in these measures as a means of providing protection to domestic producers increased as natural barriers to trade from transportation costs declined and as the revolution in manufacturing technology created important new competitive threats to more traditional and higher cost producers. Interestingly, the tariff proposed by Treasury Secretary Alexander Hamilton in President Washington's first administration was intended both to raise much needed revenue for the new federal government and to provide protection to domestic manufactures. Manufactured products typically had quite high ratios of value to weight, and even the quite high transatlantic shipping costs of the 1790s offered comparatively little natural protection for American producers of such products.

By the end of the 19th century, ocean shipping costs for high valued products like most manufactures had generally declined to the point that they were no longer a substantial natural barrier to trade among the industrialized countries bordering the Atlantic. Import tariffs imposed by most of these countries—except for Great Britain which retained a policy of free trade—were, by this stage, generally far more important barriers than transportation costs.

The interwar period witnessed a collapse in the volume of world trade. This collapse reflected both the worldwide depression of economic activity in the 1930s and the widespread and massive increase in tariffs and other trade restrictions during this period. The retreat into protectionism included, and to an important degree was probably stimulated by, two massive increases in tariffs imposed by the United States. The first was imposed just after the end of World War I and was intended as both a revenue measure (to absorb the elimination of the wartime income tax and to help pay-off debts accumulated during the war). The second was the infamous Smoot-Hawley tariff of 1930 which must be seen largely as an effort of protectionism.

Since World War II, the world economy has enjoyed a remarkable era of prosperity that has spread quite broadly, but not universally, across the globe. Over the past five decades, real world GDP has risen at somewhat more than a 4 percent annual rate, with real GDP in developing countries (as a group) growing in per capita terms at about the same pace as the industrial countries. The result has been that real living standards, as measured by real per capita GDP, have improved on average about three-fold in just half a century;... During this era of remarkable economic growth, world trade in goods and services has expanded at nearly double the pace of world real GDP. As a result the volume of world trade in goods and services (the sum of both exports and imports) rose from barely one-tenth of world GDP in 1950 to about one-third of world GDP in 2000. By this measure—and by others as well—there has indeed been an increase in the degree of global economic integration through trade in goods and services during the past half century.

The two fundamental factors that appear to have driven this increasing global economic integration are continuing improvements in the technology of transportation and communication and a very substantial, progressive reduction in artificial barriers to international commerce resulting from public policy interventions.

* * *

Looking forward, how might the fundamental factors of technological developments affecting natural barriers to trade and of public policies affecting artificial barriers to trade be expected to evolve and thereby to influence the extent of global economic integration through international trade in goods and services. Almost surely, technological improvements will continue to reduce the costs of transportation and communication, both domestically and internationally. For transportation, because costs cannot go negative, further absolute cost reductions cannot generally be as large as what has been achieved in the past century. Even in proportional terms, it seems likely that the pace of advance will slow from the pace of the past century. In fact, during the past quarter century, while there have been continuing efficiency gains in transportation, the main technologies of land, sea, and air transport have not changed. Nevertheless, as the natural barriers to international trade for most goods arising from transportation costs are already quite low, technological limits on the likely pace of future cost reductions will probably not be very important, at least for the industrial countries. For developing countries, where the infrastructure of modern transportation is generally less well developed, opportunities for reductions in transportation costs that would enhance economic integration (both within the domestic economy and internationally) are clearly greater.

For communications (as discussed further below), the situation is very different. A technological revolution is underway and appears likely to continue for some time. Costs of communication, domestic and international, have fallen rapidly; and these declines also seem likely to continue. International trade surely benefits from improvements in communications. As previously discussed, the areas likely to benefit the most are those that rely particularly heavily on communications, with financial services being an important example.

Concerning the future of public policies toward trade, the successful postwar effort to reduce trade barriers has virtually eliminated most significant restrictions on trade in most goods among industrial countries, with notable exceptions for a number of agricultural products and a few manufactured products. To make further meaningful progress, the industrial countries need to address the few remaining hard cases (especially agriculture) in goods trade and deal with a complex of restrictions that artificially suppress opportunities for trade in services—trade that is increasingly being made feasible by advances in communications and other technologies. For developing countries, the agenda includes both reducing import restrictions that remain relatively high for products where industrial country barriers are already quite low and securing from the industrial countries reductions in barriers against exports of products for which developing countries have an important comparative advantage.

* * *

There is no doubt that advances in information and communications technology are the most important technological advances of the past quarter century. In the United States, technological advances in these areas account for much of the rise in total factor productivity in recent years. As a result of these technological advances, the costs of processing and communicating forms of information have been all declining very rapidly; i.e., by a factor of two or more within a two year period. By nature, much of the activity in the financial services industry has to do with the processing and communication of information. It stands to reason, therefore, that the financial services industry would be particularly strongly affected by rapid advances in information and communications technology—and, it has been. This is readily apparent in a number of phenomena. For example, the costs of making stock exchange transactions for both retail and wholesale traders has dropped enormously (and the gap between them has narrowed significantly) during the past twenty years, with the predictable result that there has been an explosion of the volume of transactions and (perhaps somewhat more surprisingly) a large increase in the number of retail investors. The cost of bank transactions at the wholesale and interbank level has also dropped precipitously; and this, among other things, is reflected in the continuing rise in the volume of bank transactions relative to nominal GDP. Some indication of how advances in technology are affecting (and likely to continue to affect) retail banking transactions is suggested by Chart 7.

As information and communications technology has advanced and the costs of doing virtually all forms of financial business have declined, the meaningfulness of the differences associated with different locations or with different sectors of the financial services industry appear to have eroded. This reflects the fact it is much cheaper now than a few years ago to do financial business over a wider geographic range and over a wider scope of activities. As a consequence, there has been a tendency toward restructuring of institutions in the financial sector in the direction of broader geographic and functional scope. This tendency is apparent in recent efforts to integrate and/or consolidate trading activities on different stock and commodity exchanges. It is also apparent the restructuring of banking systems and the integration of banks with other types of financial institutions.

Public policy in most countries has been accommodating or facilitating these developments. In the United States, the last restrictions on nation wide banking have been removed; and, with the passage of the Gramm-Leach-Bliley Act last year, most remaining restrictions on bank holding company participation in the full range of financial services have been removed. In the European Union, under the auspices of directives from the European Commission, the banking sector is becoming more competitive; and the advent of the EMU at the start of 1999 is providing important additional impetus to restructuring in the financial sector. In Japan, partly as a consequence of difficulties of recent years, public policy is also pushing, reform and restructuring in the financial sector....

Not surprisingly, the same types of changes that have been taking place within the financial service sectors of individual countries have also been occurring internationally—and in response to the same principal driving force. The advances in information and communication technology which make it efficient to do financial business across a wider geographic and functional scope domestically, also operate across national boundaries. And, the effects are seen, for example, in the efforts to integrate the activities of stock and commodity markets internationally and in the international diversification of a number of leading firms providing financial services. As in the domestic arena, public policies are, by and large, facilitating these developments or at least accommodating them. In particular, seeing the advantages of allowing (sophisticated) foreign financial institutions to provide services in domestic markets, a number of emerging market countries have liberalized or are liberalizing to permit such participation....

Going forward, it is clear that advances in information and communications technology that have already been achieved and those that are in the pipeline will continue to drive the evolution of the financial services industry. People will want to take advantage of the opportunities rapid advances in technology allow—in financial services, as well as elsewhere. Public policy can influence, to some degree, the pace and pattern of developments. It can spur or retard them; but it is unlikely to stop them.

At the international level, this implies that we have strong reason to expect an increasing degree of capital market integration in the future. Information and communications costs are a natural barrier to integration of capital markets and financial services—just as transportation costs are for trade in physical goods. As these costs come down, integration should increase.

There is, however, one important worry. Many empirical studies have confirmed the common-sense appraisal of the postwar experience with trade liberalization: open policies toward international trade are an important factor contributing to stronger economic growth. Similarly persuasive evidence is not available for liberal policies toward international capital flows, particularly for portfolio flows rather than direct investment flows. Indeed, the experience in recent financial crises could cause reasonable people to question whether liberal policies toward international capital flows are wise for all countries in all circumstances. The answer, I believe, is probably not. High openness to international capital flows, especially short-term credit flows, can be dangerous for countries that have weak or inconsistent macro-economic policies or inadequately capitalized and regulated financial systems. For such countries, public policy has important challenges to meet in preparing for a world economy that is being driven toward higher degrees of capital market integration.

The Particular Importance of Communications

In many discussions of international economic integration, the focus is on integration through trade and factor movements, both labor and capital. There is, however, clearly another important mechanism through which economic activities in different parts of the world affect each other; namely, through the communication of economically relevant information and technology. It may, or may not, be true that Marco Polo carried back from China to Italy the concept of noodles—and thus multiple forms of Italian pasta were born. The lesson nevertheless is clear. It is not necessary to transport large quantities of noodles (by expensive and slow camel caravans) from China to Italy to produce a culinary revolution. It is necessary only to transport the concept of a noodle and an understanding of how noodles are made to have this effect. And clearly, noodles are but one example. International trade and movements of people and capital are undoubtedly important for the spread around the world of the fundamental technological innovations that underlie the broad advance of human productivity—from the use of the wheel through the modern personal computer. Societies that cut themselves off from commerce with the rest of humanity do tend to stagnate. However, the volume of international commerce is probably not the critical determinant of the spread of useful innovations—provided that channels of communication remain reasonably well open.

* * *

[T]he recent and continuing advances in communications promise to have a profound effect on innovation across a very broad spectrum and on a global scale. We are seeing the beginnings of this now, in the financial services. It promises to be a profound force driving global economic integration in the future

A Reversal in the Trend of Increasing Global Economic Integration?

During the interwar period between World Wars I and II, there was a sharp reversal in the generally rising trend of global economic integration. The volume of world trade contracted sharply.... [T]his contraction of world trade was particularly pronounced during the early 1930s, and was partly attributable to, the general decline of economic activity in the great depression. The decline in world trade, however, was much greater than the decline in economic activity (or in goods production). The rise of protectionism, particularly the Smoot-Hawley tariff imposed by the United States in 1930 and the retaliatory responses to it, clearly contributed importantly to the collapse of world trade. At around the same time, capital market linkages among countries weakened substantially, as the international gold standard collapsed and as several countries, led by Nazi Germany, began to impose highly restrictive controls on capital movements.

A complex of factors undoubtedly contributed to the general sharp reversal of global economic integration in the interwar period, including especially the economic effects of the great depression. Several studies have suggested economic and political economy explanations for this reversal, especially as relates to developments in the United States.... However, I believe that it is not possible to explain an important part of this worldwide phenomenon without recognizing that there was an important change of tastes in the body politic of several key countries away from sympathy to involvement in an economically integrated global economy and toward nationalism and isolationism. In Europe, the tragedy of the Great War and its aftermath explains much of the change. Russia after the devastation of the war and Bolshevik revolution was invaded by some of its former allies. Mutual suspicion and hostility between communist Russia and most of the rest of the world was reflected in Russia's economic isolation. In Germany, a bitter defeat and a bitter peace fed a new spirit of nationalism. In the United States, the symptoms of the shift toward isolationism took many forms. The Senate refused to ratify the League of Nations Treaty in 1920. The government took repressive action toward imported political ideologies in the red scare. The Ku Klux Klan was reborn and gained prominence outside of the south, expressing antipathy not only to blacks but also to most things foreign. Prohibition was passed, partly based on campaigns that attributed alcoholism to foreign influences. The National Origins Act sharply restricted foreign immigration. All of this transpired during the roaring twenties, before the great depression; the Smoot-Hawley tariff was also passed before the depression took hold. From all of these developments, it seems clear that after World War I and partly in reaction to it, many Americans decided that they wanted substantially less involvement with most things foreign.

What are the chances that something similar might happen again? The protesters in Seattle demonstrated that globalization has its detractors; and we have hardly seen or heard the last of them. However, while we need to remain cognizant of the risk that such protests may gain political momentum, I do not believe that the conditions are ripe for a return to isolationism. The plain fact is that the U.S. economy, and the world economy more generally, have prospered enormously under, and partly because of, favorable policies toward international economic integration—policies that have been championed by the United States in the post World War II era. Despite occasional difficulties such as the recent emerging market financial crises, nations around the world are not seeking to withdraw from the increasingly integrated global economic system. Rather, those that are not yet full participants are generally seeking to become so.

The End of Empire

In the public park above the great Rheingau vineyard near Rudesheim, there stands a large, rather ugly statue commemorating Prussia's victory in the Franco-Prussian War of 1870–71. Notably, this was the last important European war in which the victor ended up better off because of the conflict. The defeat of the French, after earlier victories over the Danes and the Austrians, solidified the basis for a unified Germany under Prussia's leadership. Subsequently, in both World War I and World

War II, none of the combatants, victor or vanquished, gained as a result of the conflict. The United States and the Soviet Union did emerge as the two global super powers after World War II. But, the Soviet Union suffered horribly during the war, and the postwar prosperity enjoyed by the United States was not the consequence of its military victory. Indeed, the defeated Axis powers recovered relatively rapidly from wartime devastation and prospered impressively thereafter. Exploiting its wartime victory, for forty-five years, the Soviet Union maintained effective control over most of central and eastern Europe and may have gained economically as a result. But, under the stress of economic stagnation and political dissatisfaction, this empire collapsed in 1990; and by 1992, the Soviet state itself split apart into politically independent republics. Earlier than this, efforts by each of the super powers to impose their military wills on much smaller countries—the United States in Vietnam and the Soviet Union in Afghanistan—ended in failure.

Before the 20th century, these things often turned out quite differently. For those who were good at it, military aggression and imperialism often paid off economically. The Vikings, for example, pillaged with enthusiasm and success along the coasts and rivers of Europe in the 9th and 10th centuries. Spain grew rich on the new world plunder gathered up by a few hundred conquistadors early in the 16th century. Britain prospered during the 17th, 18th, and 19th centuries from its far flung empire. The other European imperialists who came relatively early to the game—the Portuguese, the Dutch, the French, and (to some extent) the Belgians—also profited, although the late comers—the Germans and the Italians—did not. Austria's central European empire generally prospered and expanded from the 16th through the 19th century. Over six centuries, the Czars built the huge Russian Empire. For 1600 years Constantinople (now Istanbul) retained its importance as an imperial capital, under the Romans, Byzantines, and Ottoman Turks. Indeed, by the end of the 19th century, the political map of the world was, to an impressive extent, a patch quilt of different empires. And, this political reality clearly influenced patterns of global economic integration, which tended to be stronger within rather than across imperial domains.

By the end of the 20th century, all of this had changed. Except for a few bits and pieces, the empires that had existed a century before (and many for long before that) were gone. Efforts to create new empires during the 20th century—by the Germans, Italians, Japanese, and Soviets—all failed. As a consequence of this substantial change in the political organization of the world, there were important changes in its economic organization as well. Flows of trade, capital, and people that a century ago were channeled within empires now generally take place on a more diversified basis. This is true, for example, of Great Britain where trade with colonies and commonwealth partners has declined substantially relative to trade with former rival imperial powers in Europe. It is also dramatically true for the transition countries of Central and Eastern Europe and the former Soviet Union where, since 1990 trade among them has declined enormously, while trade with the rest of the world has picked up substantially.

Not that we should regret it, but it is relevant to ask why the 20th century was so unkind to imperialism? Obviously, imperialism is a matter of public policy; so the short answer is that public policy changed. But, why this policy change on a global scale? Tastes are probably part of the answer. Just as moral revulsion against slavery was critical to its suppression in the 19th century, revulsion at the great carnage of war and the brutality of oppression have helped turn the tide against imperialism. Mass communications that graphically portray carnage and brutality have contributed to the change in public attitudes. Perhaps more important, however, is the shift in technology that has made imperialism an inefficient, if not counter productive, means of improving economic welfare.

Although he apparently did not fully appreciate his own wisdom, Napoleon once observed, "A bayonet is good for just about anything, except to sit on." The 20th century has been a very uncomfortable time for imperialists to seek to impose their will on other peoples, either for economic gain or for other reasons. Unwelcome efforts to exert control over an alien people, especially in the face of armed opposition, tends to be very expensive in blood and treasure. In contrast, devoting resources to domestic economic development through efficient investments in physical and human capital and development and exploitation of new technologies is an attractive and reliable path to improved national economic well-being. This is the experience and the lesson of the past century.

As this lesson becomes broadly understood and appreciated, the prospect is that the process of global economic integration—which is being driven by essentially irresistible forces of technological advance—will take place through voluntary means. People around the world will decide to participate—through trade, through movements of people and capital, and through accessing information and taking advantage of new technologies—because they see the benefit to them of such participation. Unlike too many unfortunate episodes in the past, participation in the global economy will not occur at the point of a sword or facing the muzzle of a gun. This, perhaps more than anything else, provides the reasonable assurance that the fundamental forces that are driving global economic integration are, in fact, driving the world toward a better economic future.

Comments and Questions

1. The preceding excerpts raise important questions about the role of cultural difference in the context of globalization. It is possible to think of cultural difference, and history as merely aesthetics—that is, as nothing more than the outward expression of taste. As such, cultural difference is reducible to a question of marketing. It is also possible, then, to suggest that uniformity can be achieved, at least at the level of fundamental or basic ideas, and that cultural difference can be contained as merely a matter of flexibility with respect to detail, that is, at the level of the particular, bounded only by the limits of the fundamental agreement on principles at a more general level. What implications might this insight hold for the convergence of enterprise law?

2. Is the propensity toward convergence more a question of technology than of culture? Consider the arguments made in Colin J. Bennett, *Regulating Privacy: Data Protection and Public Policy in Europe and the United States* with the arguments made by Dr. Mussa in the excerpt above.

3. Is resistance reducible to questions of detail—that is of the ability to understand the local language in order to better translate the workable form of harmonizing rules? Do details make the difference? The answers to these question may depend on the relationship of corporations, of enterprise organization, to the socio-cultural foundations of the communities from which they spring. It is possible to suggest that

corporations—any sort of enterprise organization—merely reflect the foundational assumptions on which the greater community is organized. The democratic principle is important in American corporate law because it is a foundational principle for the organization of the American Republic. That model may work less well in communities organized on the basis of the principle of family allegiance. Societies built on webs of kin or clan relationships may resist notions of social organization based on the treatment of all relationships as occurring between strangers "at arm's length."

4. How important is law, as an independent basis of norm making, within the context of unification, harmonization and resistance, when different normative systems meet? It is possible to consider the arguments made in the readings as covering merely one small, and perhaps, except for its formal and official character, insignificant part of the basis on which community mores are constructed and maintained. It is possible that because of the formal memorialized character of legal norms that scholars tend to concentrate on them to the exclusion of equally important bases of a community's normative foundations. Legal norms, as opposed to other normative bases of social organization, are constructed in an imperative-attributive tense—laws impose obligations, but command rights. Non-legal norms are purely imperative in character—these norms impose obligations, the reward for which is in their performance. Social norms, political norms, religious norms and moral norms may constitute significant impediments or lubricants to the enterprise of unification, harmonization or resistance.

5. As the excerpt from Alexander Merezhko suggests, law in different cultures has different meanings. The process of observation of difference and comparison may therefore lead not to harmonization or unification, but to confirmation of the value of difference to a particular culture. What are some reasons that exercise of comparison might lead to a rejection of the object of comparison as a model for reform? How would Dr. Mussa approach the issues raised by Merezhko?

C. Does Comparative Corporate Law Have a Mission?

The excerpts from the articles that follow present a different, perhaps far more active, conception of globalization. They illustrate some of the issues raised when scholars, politicians, economists, and business people compare emerging regimes of corporate goverance in the context of globalization: now that globalization has been identified, what will/does/can it do? Some argue that globalization will occur in one form or another and that state power can be harassed to guide that globalization. Moreover, it is to the economically dominant states that the task of guidance must fall. Others argue that theories of path dependence, and cultural uniqueness make globalization a fact without a mission. Still others suggest that economic and legal globalization are not inseparably linked. With which do you agree?

Alex Y. Seita, *Globalization and the Convergence of Values*

30 Cornell Int'l L.J. 429 (1997)
(excerpts pages 469–491; some footnotes and tables omitted)

IV. Shaping the Content of Globalization

Despite its ubiquity, globalization is not a given, the inevitable consequence of the confluence of current human events. It is a highly probable long-term outcome, that should be supported in the face of opposing forces, in order to ensure its survival.[129] Although there is no inevitability that the process of globalization will continue, it seems very likely for economic and technological reasons. Autarky and isolationism are disfavored national policies. Absent major international calamities, globalization will grow as market integration, economic interdependence, and technological advances continue.

Nor is the precise shape of globalization a settled outcome. There is not just one distinct type of globalization. The activities, the principles, and the value-converging features of globalization are variables influenced by the leadership of nations such as the United States and international organizations such as the United Nations and the World Trade Organization. How globalization proceeds, especially in its preeminent economic form, is crucial because globalization can be a double-edged sword. It can create international problems as well as elevate human beings into a better world.[130]

For example, the basic values that globalization spreads can sometimes be at odds with each other and with other important values. Free market practices can weaken democracy through a race to the bottom in permitting unethical business practices, and democracy can suppress human rights through a tyranny of the majority. All three convergent values can conflict with the desire to protect the environment, a desire that is predominantly a concern of industrialized countries. Also, economic and technological interdependency can facilitate the activities of rogue nations and terrorist groups, and make members of the global community vulnerable to transnational crime.[132] Finally,

---

129. Opposition to economic globalization, and the integration of markets, is a strong, though not dominant, movement in the United States as well as in other industrialized countries. Politicians often blame the global integration of markets for declining wages and increasing unemployment or underemployment. Cf. David E. Sanger, *A Flare-Up of Passions on Trade and Jobs*, N.Y. Times, Feb. 20, 1996, at A1 (Pat Buchanan, candidate for the Republican presidential nomination, denouncing the World Trade Organization and the North American Free Trade Agreement, and pledging to pull the United States out of both organizations); David LaGesse, *Silence on NAFTA Could Prove Fleeting: Candidates May Have to Face Issue if Perot Runs, Mexico Finances Sink*, Dallas Morn. News, Apr. 6, 1996, at 1A, available in LEXIS, News Library, Curnws File (documenting 1992 presidential candidate Ross Perot's opposition to U.S. participation in the World Trade Organization and the North American Free Trade Agreement).

130. It is well recognized that the effects of globalization are not always economic or beneficial. *See, e.g., It's the Global Economy, Stupid: The Corporatization of the World*, The Nation, July 15–22, 1996 (series of articles on the harmful consequences of the global economy); David C. Korten, When Corporations Rule the World (1995); Richard J. Barnet & John Cavanagh, Global Dreams: Imperial Corporations and the New World Order (1994)....

132. At one time the Bank for Credit and Commerce International (BCCI) was the seventh-largest private bank in the world, with assets of over $20 billion. BCCI's involvement with widespread international banking fraud eventually led to its collapse in 1991. *See, e.g.*, Raj K. Bhala, Foreign Bank Regulation After BCCI 3–13 (1994); John Kerry & Hank Brown, 102d Cong., The BCCI Affair: A Report to the Committee on Foreign Relations, United States Senate (Comm. Print 102–140 1992). According to the report produced by Senators Kerry and Brown, BCCI was involved in more than just bank fraud. It was also engaged in laundering drug money, supporting terrorism and arms trafficking, training drug cartel death squads, and supplying prostitutes. *See id.* at 61–72.

how globalization copes with the paradoxical trend of diversification (e.g., ethnic, political, or religious differentiation) is important.

Managing globalization will require policies and programs that carefully nurture, accommodate tensions among, and emphasize the universality of convergent values. These values need to be supported because the presence of free markets, democracy, and human rights in some countries may represent currently ascendant economic and political systems—existing superficial conditions—rather than fundamental values. Citizens of more countries may now describe their economic system as "market" based, their structure of government as "democratic," and their panoply of civil liberties as the protection of "human rights." Yet, for newly formed capitalist democracies, their citizens may not completely accept these conditions as fundamental values—deeply felt beliefs of what is right.[134]

Balancing these values, when they conflict with each other or with the protection of the environment, it is necessary to avoid, primarily, a race to the bottom in economic practices and the unreasonable dominance of economic activities over political and environmental concerns. The universality of convergent values essentially means that human beings will work to ensure that the same general rights—including the satisfaction of basic needs—are available in all countries. The idea that particular rights should be universally present, without geographic limitation, is important not just to the convergence of fundamental values but also to the belief that all human beings belong to the same society and are entitled to the same rights.

A. Fulfilling Western Responsibilities

The industrialized democracies have an essential, indispensable role in determining the policies and programs for globalization that will promote common values, balance competing values, solidify respect for the rule of law, and increase empathy among nations. This role is given not by the grace of God but by a simple fact of economics and by the deep roots of liberal democratic values in the industrialized democracies. They have the lion's share of world wealth, and by it, the ability to finance and influence heavily the course of globalization. In addition, free markets, democracy, and the pro-

---

"BCCI cannot be taken as an isolated example of a rogue bank, but a case study of the vulnerability of the world to international crime on a global scale that is beyond the current ability of governments to control." *Id.* at 17. International crime, of course, involves more than just bank fraud. From bases in one country and supported financially by another country, terrorists can launch attacks into a third country. *See, e.g.*, WESTERN RESPONSES TO TERRORISM (Alex P. Schmid & Ronald D. Crelinsten eds., 1993). Illegal drugs, especially those consumed in the United States, often have transnational origins. *See, e.g.*, Office of National Drug Control Policy, Executive Office of the President, The National Drug Control Strategy, 1996: Program, Resources, and Evaluation 17–20. Finally, from anywhere in the world, one can access pornography or recipes for homemade bombs through the internet.

134. The belief of many people in these nations in the values of liberal democracy may be quite fragile. Further, the shift in economic or political systems for nations previously under command economies or authoritarian political regimes has created substantial numbers of losers as well as winners. It would be in the self-interest of the industrialized democracies to support those countries in transition from command and authoritarian systems to market and democratic systems. Russia, in particular, should receive generous financial and political help. Without the bold actions of the former Soviet leadership, the end of the Cold War—and the subsequently reduced threat of nuclear war, freedom for the east European countries from Soviet domination, and reunification of Germany—would not have occurred. *See* PHILIP ZELIKOW & CONDOLEEZZA RICE, GERMANY UNIFIED AND EUROPE TRANSFORMED: A STUDY IN STATECRAFT 4–19, 369–70 (1995).

tection of human rights are fundamental values, permanent and enduring, in the industrialized democracies.

It is undeniable that the industrialized nations dominate the world economically. These nations are bound together by the common values of liberal democracy, and are either allied or on friendly terms with the United States. Table 1, below [omitted], provides figures for the population, economy, contributions to the United Nations, foreign aid (official development assistance, or ODA), and numbers of the world's largest corporations from the twenty-three industrialized nations collectively referred to as the "West": the United States, Japan, the fifteen-nation European Union, and six other rich industrialized nations.

[Table 1 omitted]

As Table 1 shows, the West, with less than 15% of the world's population, generates over 75% of the world's GNP, and has the financial resources to pay most of the U.N.'s regular budget, provide substantial amounts of foreign aid, and produce nearly all of the world's largest corporations. Just America and Japan together account for over 40% of world GNP.

The hand of the West is also dominant in the major international economic institutions which provide substantial flows of financial capital to developing countries and to countries in economic transition from socialism to capitalism.[139] Table 2, below [omitted], shows that the big five and the other industrialized democracies of the West together have a commanding share of the voting power in such major international economic institutions as the International Bank for Reconstruction and Development (IBRD), International Finance Corporation (IFC), and International Development Association (IDA) of the World Bank Group, the International Monetary Fund (IMF), the Asian Development Bank (ADB), and the European Bank for Reconstruction and Development (EBRD).

---

139. As of June 30, 1996, the International Bank for Reconstruction and Development (IBRD) had approved loans totaling $164,766,000,000, of which $110,246,000,000 was outstanding. *See* [World Bank, Annual Report 1996] at 173. Also providing substantial funding to developing countries are the IBRD's two affiliates, the International Development Association (IDA), which provides low-interest rate credits (loans) to the poorer developing countries, and the International Finance Corporation (IFC), which finances private sector ventures and projects primarily in less developed countries. As of June 30, 1996, the IDA approved $97,450,000,000 in development credits, of which $72,821,000,000 was outstanding. *See id.* at 203. As of June 30, 1996, the IFC provided cumulative gross commitments of $30,380,906,000 for 1707 enterprises. See International Finance Corporation, Annual Report 1996, at 143 (1996) [hereinafter IFC]. As of April 30, 1996, the IMF had total loans outstanding of SDR 42,040,000,000 (approximately $60.961 billion)....

Other important multilateral economic institutions include regional development banks such as the Asian Development Bank (ADB) and the European Bank for Reconstruction and Development (EBRD), which provide funding and technical assistance for development in their respective regions. As of December 31, 1995, the ADB had approved loans totaling $31,426,926,000, of which $17,530,101,000 were outstanding, to member countries in the Asian and Pacific region. *See* Asian Development Bank, Annual Report 1995, at 154 (1995) [hereinafter ADB]. As of December 31, 1995, the European Bank for Reconstruction and Development provided ECU 7,853,000,000 (approximately $10.072 billion) in financing through loans, equity participation, and guarantees to countries and projects in central and eastern Europe. *See* European Bank for Reconstruction and Development, Annual Report 1995, at 15–17, 53 n.2 (1995) (using ECU 1.2826 = $1 exchange rate) [hereinafter EBRD]....The ECU will be replaced by the Euro on January 1, 1999. *See* The Road to Economic and Monetary Union (visited Oct. 15, 1996) <http://europa.eu.int/en/agenda/emu/en-scsc.html> (from website of the European Union).

[Table 2 omitted]

While there are different ways of calculating the collective economic power of the West, there is no question of the West's economic importance to the world. As much as possible, the West—principally the economic giants of the United States, Japan, and the European Union—should act collectively to create a humane globalization. These three entities should undertake to cooperate even more extensively than they already do. This will require American acceptance of a greater role for the European Union and Japan in western decision-making, a process that historically has been carried out mostly by American leadership. It will also require a more vigorous and creative Japanese presence in international affairs.

The United States, Japan, and the European Union are singled out, not because their citizenry are inherently wiser and more capable than those of other nations, but because their economic power tempered by the humanitarian constraints of their political systems make them best suited to shape a better world if they so choose. There is also the reality that although it is the world's richest country and only superpower, the United States cannot manage or finance globalization on its own. Because the three are so important economically, it would be a mistake, as some have gratuitously suggested, for the United States and the European Union to unite to isolate Japan politically and economically.

When necessary, the West should also use its economic power to flesh out the details of market economies, democratic governments, and human rights in the globalization context. While the devil may lie in details, some refinement of principles may be required to create a "level playing field" for business competition and to balance competing values. That may open up the charge that the views of the West are being imposed upon, and not necessarily to the benefit of, the rest of the world.

While such an allegation would have substantial historical validity, it could be deflected by the promulgation of rules based on those internal practices of the industrialized democracies. These rules would be a modification of the "Golden Rule." Nations should do unto others what the nations of the West do unto themselves. That undeniably involves the value judgment that the industrialized democracies are better models for economic and political development. It is a value judgement, however, that seems to be shared by most human beings: the flow of immigration between the West and the rest of the world is decidedly one-sided in the former's favor.

B. Adhering to the Rule of Law

The process of converging values through the activities of globalization is facilitated by procedural mechanisms and substantive principles. Without them, globalization might eventually consist solely of the intermingling of peoples and the economic interdependence of countries without the sharing of values. Convergence is reinforced by procedural mechanisms that implement substantive principles which are derived from and flesh out the meaning of convergent values. One mechanism might consist of unilateral action in which one nation, particularly the United States, imposes its views of appropriate economic behavior on another country. While an economically dominant nation may get its way, the subordinate country may not accept the substantive principle used to justify the unilateral action. The latter country may simply see the "principle" of "might makes right."

Another mechanism exists in multilateral agreements in which nations collectively determine the international legal rights of individual nations. Multilateral agreements often contain dispute settlement procedures that attempt, in theory, to administer impartially the rule of law in judging national, firm, or individual conduct.[146] The "law" would be made up of substantive principles that reflect or accommodate clashes among convergent values. The use of the rule of law is today one of the most effective means to reinforce common values, especially in the areas connected with international trade. The rule of law also avoids the antagonism generated when one nation imposes its views on other nations.

In a broad sense, the rule of law requires respect for substantive principle, not merely power or chance, to settle disputes.[147] Implicit, too, in the rule of law is that disputes are peacefully settled whenever possible, and that negotiations and economic sanctions are utilized before military operations are commenced. In the globalization context, acceptance of the rule of law means that most nations will not only acknowledge the applicability of substantive principles to a transnational problem but also accept a solution recommended by an impartial international body. The absence of either condition precludes the existence of a rule of law, and also militates against the development of convergent values.

First, without the recognition that there are substantive principles which are relevant to analyzing a conflict, there is no rule of law because there are no laws to apply. Without substantive principles, convergent values are less likely to emerge. Second, a nation should respect the decisions of a mediating or adjudicatory international organization. If a nation chooses to settle a dispute unilaterally, there is no rule of law since any principle, even if meritorious, would be enforced unequally. The unilateral actor would be a law enforcer against other nations only, and presumably never the object of enforcement.[149] Such discriminatory enforcement diminishes the validity of substantive principles because they do not apply to all nations, and impedes the acceptance of their values as convergent values.

At the same time, the international tribunal or body that implements the rule of law must be impartial and competent, for nations are more likely to abide by the rule of law when they believe that it can be administered fairly and wisely. Further, before abiding

---

146. The dispute settlement procedure of the World Trade Organization applies to the agreement establishing the WTO as well as the numerous WTO agreements. *See* Understanding on Rules and Procedures Governing the Settlement of Disputes, Apr. 15, 1994, Marrakesh Agreement Establishing the World Trade Organization, Annex 2, 33 I.L.M. 112 (1994) [hereinafter Dispute Settlement Understanding]. Many bilateral agreements do not have dispute resolution procedures....

147. Cf. GRANT GILMORE, THE AGES OF AMERICAN LAW 105 (1977) (the rule of law "emphasizes principally the importance of procedural due process, the nice observance of established rules, the right of the accused to confront his accuser in open court before he is sent to jail"). For purposes of this Article, the rule of law is briefly discussed only to show its role in facilitating the convergence of values....

149. Unilateral measures by one country, even if ostensibly taken to protect desirable principles, may engender ill will among other countries affected by those measures. These countries may react by questioning the justifications of the unilateral actor. Eventually, the validity of the principles may come into question if they are applied only to protect one country's interests. For example, the United States frequently takes a unilateral approach to solving economic problems with its trading partners. *See, e.g.*, Trade Act of 1974, Pub. L. No. 93-618, §301, 88 Stat. 1978 (1974) (codified as amended at 19 U.S.C. §2411 (1988)) (authorizing the United States to take unilateral action against unfair, even though not internationally unlawful, economic practices of foreign countries). This has not generated feelings of goodwill among U.S. allies. *See, e.g.*, European Commission, Report on United States Barriers to Trade and Investment 1996, at 9–10 (criticizing section 301); Hiroshi Nakamae, *U.S. Worst Violator of Trade Rules, MITI Says*, NIKKEI WKLY., June 6, 1994, at 2 (in its 1994 Report on Unfair Trade Policies by Major Trading Partners, the Japanese Ministry of International Trade and Industry accuses the United States of pursuing unfair trade practices such as section 301).

by the rule of law in a particular area, nations usually must conclude that the substantive principles of law are generally acceptable to them. Of course, some principles may be imprecise in order to accommodate different national views about how detailed these principles should be. Because nations may have varying opinions on the desired details of substantive principles and may make political compromises to arrive at their language, these principles may be vague or incomplete. The tribunal or other body that interprets these principles may have considerable leeway to refine, embellish, or expand the meaning of the substantive law.

While an immediate benefit of the rule of law is that current disputes are resolved, a long-term benefit is that the utilization of reason and rules are substituted for power or force. If powerful and weak nations alike will follow the rule of law, then the law, not military or economic power, will determine rights and resolve conflicts. Recognition of the rule of law also means that the substantive principles used to resolve disputes are automatically enhanced since their selection legitimizes them (they are the "law") and reinforces the values that they represent. While these principles are likely to be popular and respected in order to have been chosen as the substantive bases for conflict resolution, their selection is likely to strengthen and broaden their appeal, enhancing the durability of their values. Thus, the choice of interpreters and the selection of substantive principles are important decisions.

At times, the viability of the rule of law may require enforcement to ensure adherence to the rule of law. In economic disputes, there could be collectively authorized sanctions. When there are acts of aggression over territorial disputes and economic sanctions have failed to prevent a breach of the peace, the use of military force could be authorized. For example, in 1990, Iraq invaded Kuwait over alleged disputed property rights and territory; in response, the United Nations authorized the use of force by the United States and its allies against the Iraq in the 1991 Gulf War.

For countries like North Korea and Iraq that are not democracies and do not protect human rights, the industrialized democracies should present a unified front in encouraging change and discouraging political oppression and the use of force. While the ad hoc international criminal tribunals for Bosnia and Rwanda are important, the establishment of a permanent international criminal court will better solidify the idea that war crimes must be condemned and adjudicated by the international community. Although it is late, there ought to be a tribunal for Cambodia. There is still no justice for the atrocities against the Cambodian people that occurred in the mid to late 1970s, in what many have called the equivalent of genocide. The establishment of a standing emergency peacekeeping force might prevent the future reoccurrence of atrocities that took place in Cambodia, Rwanda, Burundi, Bosnia, and elsewhere.

Also, although there has been a general convergence of economic and political values, the application of these values to specific situations is, in most cases, yet to be determined. When it becomes important to specify how these values will apply to particular cases, the use of a multilateral forum will help to win international acceptance of the principles selected to implement these values. The process of filling out the details of these values, that is, determining their principles, is facilitated because there is agreement over basic values. Once a broad framework has been agreed upon, nations can resolve particular difficulties as necessary.

The most fruitful area of further refinement of values is in the economic realm. There is already a process of greater harmonization of rules and practices that affect trade, investment, and intellectual property.[159] Establishing ground rules for international competition will eliminate the perceived unfair advantages of some nations. At the same time, there should be agreement on the proper conduct of governments, businesses, and individuals in transnational activities. Determining proper behavior will create a level playing field for international competition and will avoid actual or perceived disadvantages for some nations.

C. Setting Global Standards and Balancing Values

A major issue raised by globalization is the harmonization of business practices and the accommodation of competing values. Without common rules to govern business behavior, companies from one country might compete at a disadvantage against those of another because each country could have dissimilar rules for acceptable corporate behavior in international business. Setting up the "rules of the game" in international business is important not just to promote economic competition under fair conditions but also to determine the proper balancing of competing values.

As with other policies, the single-minded pursuit of free markets, democracy, or human rights can be destructive when carried to an extreme. Any single principle, right, or value has its limits and becomes constrained before taken too far because it will invariably clash with other principles, rights, or values.[161] Like the conflict between liberty and order, or freedom of the press and a defendant's right to a fair trial, there can be conflicts among the activities of the free market, a democratic government, and protection of human rights. While frictions may always be present, they need to be managed by a balancing of values, to determine how far a particular value should be pursued, to prevent one value from unduly dominating the others.

In particular, the dynamism of economic globalization has produced a number of serious, and often novel problems that involve the clashing of economic objectives with democratic values, human rights, and environmental goals. To be solved effectively, these problems require internationally agreed upon rules of behavior which accommodate competing values. For example, an unfettered capitalism can produce a "race to the bottom" in economic behavior, producing deplorable political and environmental effects. Also, nations might engage in economic activities that have harmful transnational environmental effects—"externalities" or "spillover effects."

The industrialized democracies should therefore have two main, interconnected, priorities. First, they should "harmonize" their economic practices that have a significant international effect. Second, they must harmonize practices in a way that optimally accommodates other competing values when conflicts arise. Some judgment about the desirable balance of competing values is unavoidable. Presumably, it would be undesirable to have a harmonized rule that all western corporations may engage in bribery when doing business overseas because that rule would weaken the integrity of political institutions in foreign, primarily developing nations.

---

159. The European Union is the outstanding example at an international regional level. *See generally* KLAUS-DIETER BORCHARDT, EUROPEAN INTEGRATION: THE ORIGINS AND GROWTH OF THE EUROPEAN UNION 31–58 (1995). On a global scale, the WTO is potentially of enormous importance in establishing and refining global trade rules. *See generally* Transmission of Legislation and Related Documents to Implement Agreements Resulting from GATT—Uruguay Round—Message from The President of the United States, H.R. Doc. No. 103-316 (1994).

161. Cf. Hudson County Water Co. v. McCarter, 209 U.S. 349, 355 (1908) (Holmes, J.) ("All rights tend to declare themselves absolute to their logical extreme. Yet all in fact are limited by the neighborhood of principles of policy which are other than those on which the particular right is founded, and which becomes strong enough to hold their own when a certain point is reached.").

Harmonization has already occurred to a degree. Some important examples of ground rules are found in various GATT and WTO agreements, such as those which prohibit dumped and subsidized goods in international trade. Another is the agreement reached by the industrialized democracies on capital adequacy requirements for international banks. There could be global standards on industrial espionage, a problem that directly afflicts western countries rather than developing countries, and the wisdom of harmful exports such as tobacco products.

The area of foreign corrupt practices is another that could be harmonized. There is now no rule that prevents western multinational corporations from committing corrupt practices overseas. Companies from an industrialized country with lax laws on foreign corrupt practices can steal business away from companies headquartered in a country with stringent laws by offering bribes or engaging in other corrupt practices. Without an agreement, western firms from different countries would not compete on equal terms for business contracts in the developing world.

The industrialized democracies are now in the process of reaching an agreement to prohibit bribes and other corrupt business practices in doing business abroad. All the industrialized countries currently make it illegal for companies to engage in corrupt practices at home. The proposed agreement will simply extend that prohibition to activities abroad, and possibly lead to higher ethical standards in developing countries where corruption is endemic. This agreement would be enforceable against the companies most likely to violate the agreement because the great majority of banks and corporations engaged in international business transactions come from the industrialized democracies.

Setting up the "rules of the game" is important not just to promote competition under fair conditions. Common ground rules also balance competing values. In particular, they avoid an injurious race to the bottom in business practices that elevate economic objectives over all others. There are business activities that need global standards because the practices or the secondary effects of economic globalization can directly conflict with the protection of human rights. For example, there could be restrictions on investments in countries that violate human rights, standards on employment conditions by foreign investors in developing nations, and curbs on the involvement of western tourists in the sex industries of developing nations. Global standards can balance economic globalization with the protection of human rights.

Only an international agreement can effectively address the issue of fair labor conditions in facilities operated or utilized by western corporations in developing countries. Otherwise, there might be a race to obtain the lowest possible costs by western corporations, and developing nations might, for economic gain, condone exploitative activities by foreigners. These companies could profit from cheap labor in developing countries, contributing to or preventing improvement in deplorable labor practices, such as thirteen and fourteen-year-old children working fifteen to twenty-hour workdays under armed guard.

Obviously, however, foreign investment can provide sorely needed jobs, for children as well as adults, in developing nations.[173] The condition of child labor is a complex

---

173. At the same time, the desperation of developing countries and their workers should not allow western companies to use their superior bargaining position to extract unconscionable concessions. A basic human right should be the right to work for an "appropriate" wage under "decent" work conditions. Without global standards, there might be a race to the bottom in providing the lowest wages and the worst working conditions. *See* David Holmstrom, *One Man's Fight Against Sweatshops*, CHRIST. SCI. MONITOR, July 3, 1996, at 12. Western investors might give their domestic employees barely minimal advantages over prevailing miserable foreign wages and employment

problem involving the shortages of alternatives for children in developing countries. These nations may lack the educational infrastructure to keep all young teenagers in primary or middle schools, and national governments may not fully realize that educating children, rather than making them work, makes more sense for economic growth in the long run.

There is also the growing problem of child prostitution, mostly in economically poorer countries but also in industrialized countries, with increasing transnational traffic. Teenage children have become trapped in prostitution, exploited by pimps who extract most of the children's "earnings" and use the children as virtual slaves. While the growth of child prostitution in developing countries has been fueled to a certain extent by sex tourists from the industrialized world, most exploiters of children are domestic ones. "Employment" for children and local community standards of morality should never justify the use of child prostitutes to satisfy local and western lust. The trade in child sex is just part of the general problem of prostitution present in every country but especially widespread in the developing world.

The sex "market" in the poorer countries attracts male "buyers" from the industrialized countries—Europeans, Americans, Japanese, Australians, Canadians, New Zealanders, and others—who are able to pay higher prices than local customers and thereby increase the supply of prostitutes. Yet, like child prostitution, adult prostitution in developing nations is not a problem caused by the industrialized countries; domestic patrons outnumber foreign ones. Poverty, the lack of economic and educational opportunities for children and women, cultures that tolerate prostitution, and affluent western sex tourists combine to create thriving sex industries in many developing countries.

Another important conflict is with the principle of environmental protection, a value that is generally more strongly held among the industrialized than the developing countries. There is often a clash between the policies of protecting the environment and encouraging economic development. Domestic activities would not be an international problem if their effects were substantially confined within national boundaries. But local activities can have detrimental spillover effects—harmful externalities that have transnational or global effects: radioactive fallout (from nuclear power plant accidents),

---

conditions. The problem of child labor in developing countries, however, is not purely one of western creation. The use of child labor is rampant throughout the developing world. *See, e.g.*, Timothy P. McElduff, Jr. & Jon Veiga, *The Child Labor Deterrence Act of 1995: A Choice Between Hegemony and Hypocrisy*, 11 St. John's J. Legal Comment., 581, 584–88 (1996); Timothy A. Glut, *Changing the Approach to Ending Child Labor: An International Solution to an International Problem*, 28 Vand. J. Transnat'l L. 1203, 1205–10 (1995). *See generally* Press Releases Index (visited Apr. 24, 1997) <http:// www.ilo.org/public/english/235press/pr/index.htm> (containing press releases on the problem of child labor, from the website of the International Labor Organization, a specialized agency of the United Nations). If the industrialized nations used their economic power to force developing nations to prohibit the use of child labor, tens of millions of poor children would be out of work and possibly forced into even more dangerous occupations. *See* Gordon Fairclough, *Child Labour: It Isn't Black and White*, Far East. Econ. Rev., Mar. 7, 1996, at 54. Also, western corporations may show more social responsibility than they are commonly given credit for. Some, perhaps most, western multinationals apparently carry out policies in developing countries that would meet with approval in the industrialized countries. *See, e.g.*, Matt Moffett, *A Racial "Democracy" Begins Painful Debate on Affirmative Action: Blacks Make up 45% of Brazil But Stay Marginalized*, Wall St. J., Aug. 6, 1996, at A1 (quoting a Brazilian Justice Ministry official as saying that "The companies that discriminate the most in Brazil [against blacks] are Brazilian companies. The best are multinationals, and when multinationals do discriminate it's usually because the directors are Brazilian.").

acid rain, ozone depletion, global warming, and depletion of tropical rain forests. Other local economic activities, while not directly affecting the welfare of foreigners, can cause environmental concern: the decimation of wild fish stocks in the world's oceans by modern industrial fishing,] the destruction of coastal areas by economic activities, [and the trade in endangered species.

Thus, there should be a balance between the right of nations to utilize their resources and engage in economic activity, and the right of other nations to be free from harmful externalities. Whether this conflict is characterized as one between protection of the environment and free market principles (or democracy or human rights), there is a clash between the value of protecting the environment and a convergent value. Views regarding environmental protection may eventually converge if global standards are agreed upon. Major steps towards possible future convergence have emerged from the Rio Conference, with its aspirational but nonbinding Agenda 21 and Rio Declaration on Environment and Development, which address, among other issues, the problem of "sustainable development." In time, the protection of the environment may become another converging value.

Elliott J. Hahn, *Japanese Business Law and the Legal System*

(1984)

(excerpts 124–125; some footnotes omitted)

Those who contend that the United States should adopt an industrial policy of its own similar to that in Japan are ignoring, I believe, some of the cultural features of the system idiosyncratic to the Japanese that make the system so successful there. Such factors as the high respect accorded to the bureaucracy, the key role of the elite bureaucrats, the virtual unity of values and attitudes in Japan between government and business, and the unwillingness of business to contest government "suggestions" in court as to what course of action it should adopt all contribute in strong measure to the enormous success of Japan's industrial policy. The absence of these factors in the U.S. system, though, makes the transplanting to the United States of Japan's national industry policy system extremely difficult. In addition, a variety of other factors have contributed to Japan's economic success. Some of them are the influence of Confucianism[48] in the Japanese culture which encourages, *inter alia*, hard work and thrift; low taxes;[49] high savings rate;[50] low unemployment; less restrictive antitrust laws; the commitment to quality control; and the ease, by and large, with which the Japanese have been so far able to borrow technology from abroad rather than spending huge sums on its development themselves.

48. In *The Eastasian Edge*, Roy Hofheinze and Kent Calder argue that the values of Confucianism shared by the Eastasian nations have contributed to the enormous economic success enjoyed by most of them recently. R. Hofheinze and K. Calder, *The Eastasian Edge* 41–52 (1982).

49. From 1951 to 1970, Japan's gross national product grew at an average rate of 9 percent per year. During the same period, total national and local taxes (not including social security) dropped from 22.4 percent of national income to 18.9 percent. In the United States, on the other hand, the percentage rose to 31.3 percent from 28.5 percent. D. Henderson, "A Difference of Opinion," *Fortune International*, August 8, 1983, at 113, 114.

50. In 1980, savings in Japan were 19.4 percent of personal income, more than three times the American rate. This high savings percentage leads to capital formation, thus spurring economic growth. *Id.* at 114.

For the United States to adopt Japan's national industrial policy system and its concomitant features would violate some of our most basic principles. Administrative guidance as it is practiced in Japan most likely would be unconstitutional here. For the government to favor some industries while urging others to scale down their operations due to their lack of competitiveness would violate our strict constitutional requirements of separation of powers and due process. Even more fundamentally, the underpinnings of our constitutional system would not tolerate a concept of government largesse that is available to some companies but not to others.

Anthony Ogus, *Competition Between National Legal Systems: A Contribution of Economic Analysis to Comparative Law*

48 Int'l & Comp. L. Q. 405 (1999)
(excerpts pages 405–406; 415–418; some footnotes omitted)

The convergence issue has been the subject of an intense debate among comparative lawyers.[2] As regards the positive dimension, the majority view appears to be that, except in relation to the domain of moral or religious norms (e.g., family law), and at least as between jurisdictions at an equivalent stage of social and economic development, there has been a tendency for legal principles from different jurisdictions to converge.[3] Others believe that such convergence is superficial: apparent consensus on principles has been unable to overcome real differences emanating from divergent legal cultures.[4] So also on the normative dimension. The orthodox line is that to facilitate dealings with the law, particularly in the context of international trade, harmonisation is—with the exception of the moral and religious domain—desirable.[5] Conversely, the dissidents hold that the genuine transplantation of concepts from one legal tradition to another is impossible[6] or at least produces unintended and unwanted consequences. [7]

The article aims to contribute to the debate with the aid of economic analysis....

The normative issue is of immense importance to the current debate on harmonisation or subsidiarity in European law, but the contribution of comparativists to the debate has tended to be superficial because the costs and benefits of harmonisation are not investigated with any rigour and little or no notice has been taken of the rich economics literature on the question.

---

2. Cf. B. De Witte, "The Convergence Debate" (1996) 3 Maastricht J. European and Comparative Law 105.

3. W. Van Gervan, "Bridging the Unbridgeable: Community and National Tort Laws After *Frankovich* and *Brasserie*" (1996) 45 I.C.L.Q. 507; and more generally, K. Zweigert and H. Kötz, *An Introduction to Comparative Law* (2nd ed., 1987), pp. 23–27.

4. Notably P. Legrand, "European Legal Systems are not Converging" (1996) 45 I.C.L.Q. 52.

5. R.g. O. Lando, "Why Harmonize the Contracts Law of Europe," in P. Sarcevic (Ed.) *International Contracts and Conflicts of Law* (1990), chap. 1; B.S. Markensis, "Learning from Europe and Learning in Europe", in B.S. Markensis (Ed.), *The Gradual Convergence: Foreign Ideas, Foreign Influences and English Law on the Eve of the 21st Century* (1994), chap. 1.

6. P. Legrand, "The Impossibility of 'Legal Transplants'" (1997) 4 Maestricht J. European and Comparative Law 111; "Against a European Civil Code" (1997) 60 M.L.R. 44.

7. G. Teubner, "Legal Irritants: Good Faith in British Law or How Unifying Law Ends Up in New Divergences" (1998) 61 M.L.R. 11.

* * *

E. The Normative Dimension

[T]he normal process of trade and the existence of competition between jurisdictions should lead to the convergence of principles in some areas of law. The main question to be addressed in this section is the desirability of more proactive harmonisation, whether this is by a mandatory unification measure, as imposed by European directive and international treaties, or by voluntary codes, and exemplified by the output of UNIDROIT and the Lando Commission,[71] which serve as model laws that States are free to adopt or which may influence courts in the development of judicial doctrine.

Comparative lawyers have been committed advocates for, and active participants in, both harmonisation processes, particularly the second. Indeed it seems obvious that substantial benefits may be acquired thereby: those engaged in international transactions will incur reduced costs in acquiring information as to the governing legal principles and, if necessary, in enforcing rights and obligations. But the ready appreciation of these advantages often blinds commentators to the costs which unifying laws may generate.[74]

Let us first take homogeneous legal products. As we have seen, competition between jurisdictions should spontaneously induce some convergence towards least-cost legal principles. The very process of evolution from a pattern of diverse laws enables jurisdictions to experiment with different legal arrangements.[75] Spontaneous convergence has the additional, and perhaps even more significant, over imposed or more formal harmonisation that the evolution towards common solutions should occur only where it is economically appropriate; that is, where the benefits of convergence exceed it costs. Now, while the reduction in information and other costs of harmonising legal principles may be substantial, such benefits may be outweighed by the costs of formulating uniform principles, reaching agreement on, and subsequently adapting national legal systems to, them. And, as regards to the latter, we should note that private law is more problematic than regulatory law. Since it is generally deeply entrenched in national legal culture.[77]

Of course, as we have seen, private interest groups, particularly practising lawyers, may be able to obstruct the processes of competition between jurisdictions, thus impeding evolution towards economically justifiable common principles. Should that occur, the case for mandatory harmonisation is strengthened. At the same time, we should recognise that comparative lawyers have themselves an interest in the harmonisation process: it generates a demand for their services and confers on them significant non-financial utility, such as that derived from increased prestige and agreeable meet-

---

71. O. Lando and H. Beale (Eds.), *Principles of European Contract Law* (1995).

74. [R. Van den Bergh, "The Subsidiarity Principle in European Community Law: Some Insights from Law and Economics" (1995) 2 Maastricht J. European and Comp. L. 337]. See also [L.E. Ribstein and B.H. Kobayashi, "An Economic Analysis of Uniform State Laws" (1996) J. Legal Studies 131].

75. [S. Woolcock, "Competition Among Rules in the Sigle European Market", in W. Brattan, J. McCahery, S. Picciotto and C. Scott (Des.), *International Regulatory Competition: Perspectives on European Regulation in Europe and the United States* (1996)] at 299; [L.E. Ribstein and B.H. Kobayashi, "An Economic Analysis of Uniform State Laws" (1996) J. Legal Studies 131] at pp. 140–141. Both this, and the last, proposition are derivable from the Hayekian theory of law: F.A. Hayek, *Law, Legislation and Liberty* (1979); and see A. Ogus, "Law and Spontaneous Order: Hayek's Contribution to Legal Theory" (1989) 16 J. Law and Society 393.

77. Van den Bergh, op. cit. Supra n. [74], at pp. 146–147.

ings in attractive locations! We may therefore expect comparative lawyers to promote harmonisation even when it is not objectively justifiable.

The arguments against harmonisation and a heterogeneous legal product are, in general, even stronger. Here, as we have seen, citizens in different jurisdictions may have different preferences regarding the level of protection to be imposed and the price to be paid for it. Obviously, such preferences may be overreached, with attendant welfare losses, if the uniform legal principles are imposed on purely domestic arrangements. Even when harmonisation is confined to activities with an international dimension, selection of the uniform principle may involve the supplanting of one jurisdiction's preferences by those of another, an outcome which may be avoided through a principle of mutual recognition or by appropriate choice of law rules.[78] Arguments for the harmonisation of *minimum* standards of protection[79] stand on a different footing since this may proceed on the assumption of homogeneity of preferences: it is reasonable to infer that the citizens of all affected jurisdictions would agree on the relevant threshold.

There remain two oft-cited justifications for uniformity of legal principles: trans-boundary externalities and fair competition. We have seen that the ability of firms to export to other countries the harmful effects of their activities, while capturing the benefits of those activities for themselves and others in their jurisdictions, *may* lead to the promulgation of lax standards. This would appear to be the paradigm case for mandatory harmonisation,[80] and yet we should not rush to that conclusion without recognising that it is a costly exercise and that alternative, cheaper solutions may be available.[81]

The ideal alternative solution would be to offer to those affected in the receiving jurisdiction the level of protection which would meet their preferences if they had to pay the increased costs of complying with that standard. In the case of product liability this may be feasible. A tort claim made by victims in their own jurisdiction would be governed by the law of that jurisdiction and the costs of meeting such potential claims would be reflected in the prices charged by importers and retailers. The same would apply if the import and sale of the product were governed by regulatory standards imposed by receiving jurisdictions. With trans-boundary pollution this solution would not be viable, since there is no direct way of internalising to the pollution victims the costs of higher environmental protection. It would be necessary for the application of the receiving jurisdiction's environmental law to the polluter—itself a problematic task—to be combined with the system of subsidies to offset the necessary abatement costs incurred by pollution exporters and financed, at least in part, by a tax on those residents in the affected State.[83]

---

78. [D.W. Leebron, "Lying Down with Procrustes: An Analysis of Harmonization Claims", in J.N. Bhagwati and R.E. Hudec (Eds.), Fair Trade and Harmonization, Vol. 1: Economic Analysis (1996)].

79. This is now the policy favoured by the European Commission towards harmonisation of regulatory standards: see J. Pelkmans, "The New Approach to Technical Harmonization and Standardization" (1987) 25 J. Common Market Studies 249.

80. Leebron, *op. cit. supra* n. 78, at pp. 55–57.

81. R.L. Revesz, "Rehabilitating Interstate Competition: Rethinking the 'Race-to-the-Bottom' Rationale for Federal Environmental Regulation" (1992) 67 N.Y.U.L.R. 1210; R. Van den Bergh, M. Faure and J. Lefevere, "The Subsidiarity Principle in European Environmental Law: An Economic Analysis", in E. Eide and R. Van den Bergh (Eds.), *Law and Economics of the Environment (1996)*, pp. 121–166.

83. [J. Bhagwati and T.N. Srinivasan, "Trade and the Environment: Does Environmental Diversity Detract from the Case for Free Trade?", in Bhagwati and Hudec, *Fair Trade and Harmonization*, Vol. 1 *Economic Analysis* (1996)].

Finally, there is the familiar assertion that diversity of interventionist legal principles can create non-tariff barriers to international trade and thus impede fair competition. I cannot in this article adequately address the broad and complex range of economic and non-economic issues which this justification raises. I will limit myself to some general observations, suggesting that caution should be exercised in invoking this set of arguments.

In the first place, there is the traditional economic reasoning, dating from Adam Smith:[85] while laxer interventionist laws in one jurisdiction confer a competitive advantage in firms subject to those laws, the consequence should be lower prices of the products and services available in the international market with welfare gains to those in the States of the industries whose prices have been undercut. The resources hitherto used for the latter can then largely be shifted to other, more productive uses. Subject to short-term frictional losses, the aggregate welfare consequences for both jurisdictions are likely to be beneficial. In other words, the problem—if any—is distributional rather than economic:[86] for the more general good, some losses will be incurred by the industries previously complying with the stricter laws.[87]

Second, if the argument is for harmonisation at a higher level of protection than that provided in some jurisdictions, why should the preferences of their citizens for lower standards at a lower cost be overreached?[88] One answer is that there may be legitimate doubts as to whether the law in fact reflects those preferences, but it is far from clear that foreign observers are in a good position to decide whether or not there is political failure of this sort. Another possible answer is that the standards may be so low as to infringe widely held perceptions of human rights. Rights may, in this instance, justifiably "trump" efficiency;[89] or the matter may, rather, be characterised as a negative externality, foreigners deriving this utility from observing the plight of victims in the offending State. In either case there is still the difficulty of determining the legitimate boundaries of human rights or the disutility function of foreigners.[90]

Comments and Problem

1. Can the views of Professor Seita be reconciled with those of Professors Hahn and Ogus? It is possible to argue that the differences between the universalists and those who stress the unique culture and cultural differences between participants in worldwide commerce really reflect not so much a divergence of views as a tendency to focus on different parts of a problem. The universalists focus on the macro aspects of enterprise culture. At this level of generality, many differences due to culture, history or taste become reduced in size to insignificance. Looking down from the 40th floor of an office building, it is hard to distinguish the differences between the cars driving down the street. At this level, generalizations about street traffic, and its reg-

85. *The Wealth of Nations* (Ed. W.R. Scott, 1921), Book IV.

86. Judged by the Kaldor-Hicks measure of economic efficiency: cf. [A. Ogus, *Regulation: Legal Form and Economic Theory* (1994) 11 J. Law and Economics] at pp. 24–25.

87. Leebron, *op. cit. supra* n. [78].

88. A.K. Klevorick, "Reflections on the Race to the Bottom", in Bhagwati and Hudec, *op. cit. supra* n. 83] chap. 12.

89. R. Dworkin, *Taking Rights Seriously* (1977), chap. 4.

90. [M. Trebilcock and R. Howse, "Trade Liberalization and Regulatory Diversity: Reconciling Competitive Policies" (1998) 6 European J. Law and Economics 5] at pp. 14–15.

ulation and harmonization, appear possible. On the other hand, culturalists stress the micro aspects of enterprise culture. Culturalists are the people watching the same cars at street level. For them, the great differences between cars—size, color, equipment, styling, tires, etc.—suggest the difficulty of harmonization. As such, the argument between culturalists and universalists is more an argument about the parties to the argument than about the object of the argument. Both culturalists and universalists may be right but their focus misdirected and as such ultimately unhelpful. Do you agree?

2. Critics have argued that globalization in reality masks the creation of a modern fascist style super-state in which the organs of the highest level of government are corporate and that traditional nation-states assume a secondary role as provinces within the domain of the international corporate state. Do the arguments made by Professor Seita provide a convincing counter to those arguments? If not, can you think of arguments that might?

In considering the faults of American systems of civil procedure, at least one German proceduralist has rejected the arguments based on cultural difference and the value of resistance on nationalist grounds.

> Some Americans do not want to admit the dimensions of our failure in civil justice. Powerful vested interests, especially at the trial bar, thrive from this dysfunctional system. They do not want it subjected to the searching critique that results from comparative study. Cultural chauvinism—the claim that cultural differences prevent us from adopting and adapting the superior procedural devices of other legal systems—is an effort to switch off the searchlight of comparative law. In truth, the cultural differences that touch on the basic choices in civil procedure are trivial. The real explanation for the tenacity of our deeply deficient system of civil justice is not culture, but a combination of inertia and the vested interests of those who profit from the status quo.

John H. Langbein, *Cultural Chauvinism in Comparative Law*, 5 CARDOZO J. INT'L & COMP. L. 41, 48–49 (1997). As applied to the context of the study of systems of corporate governance, do you think Professor Langbein has a point?

3. Professor Ogus refocuses the analysis, drawing from the perspective of economic theory. He suggests that diversity might be efficient in the aggregate but may not be across individual communities. Is it possible, however, to argue that the problem with Professor Ogus' analysis is not the need to harmonize, but the choice of units within which to conduct the analysis? For example, applying the economic principles specified by Professor Ogus, might a different result follow if the communities of measure were the communities of "merchants" rather than the "people" of "nations?" To base economic analysis on the territorial principle may not be realistic in this century.

4. **Problem:** The newly freed nation of East Freemore is in the early stages of reconstruction. A predominantly Roman Catholic South Asian country, it was administered by the Portuguese for a number of centuries under a combination of Portuguese law, derived from French civil law, and the indigenous law of the Freemorese people. For a number of years before liberation, it had been under occupation by the military of Spindonia, a predominantly Muslim country, which in the years prior to liberation of East Freemore, had imposed Islamic religious law on East Freemore. The government has just received a report that a famous American television actress and an American manufacturer of athletic shoes are contemplating establishing enterprises in Freemore. Representatives of these enterprises would like to meet with government officials to discuss the "improvement" of the commercial, corporate and labor laws of Freemore. They have suggested that a showing of

willingness to reform Freemorese law would be beneficial to the country, bring it "into the twentieth" century, allow Freemore to participate fully in the global economy, and make it more likely that these enterprises would indeed establish a presence in Freemore. You are an advisor to the new President of East Freemore. He asks your opinion: how should he respond to the suggestions of these enterprises? Please be prepared to discuss the different alternatives and the anticipated arguments in defense of and in opposition to each.

Chapter 2

Basic Regulatory Regimes: An Introduction

Not all systems of enterprise organization are the same. The sources of these differences are complex and varied. Many differences, however, might reflect the social, cultural, political, economic and legal regimes in which these systems of enterprise organization operate. Thus, it is difficult to study different systems of enterprise governance without at least some basic knowledge of the formal and informal organizational structures the political and legal systems from which these governance systems are created.

Formally, the United States is a federation of member states in which power is shared between state and national governments. Basic governance systems, and basic socio-political mores, derive in large part from English Common Law and are substantially homogenous across the federation. The trend in the United States, especially since the American Civil War, has been for power to flow upwards to the federal (now national) government, and for a favoring of legislative over judge made law.

The European continent is divided into an unstable number of formally independent states stretching from the Atlantic Ocean to the Ural Mountains. Religion, language and ethnicity still divide Europe. These independent states share long histories of warfare, based on a complex and constantly changing set of social, political, ideological, religious, ethnic and imperialist factors. Yet European, and especially Continental European countries, share a common ancestral source of lawmaking—the Roman law in the West, and the Roman-Byzantine law in the East. These systems are based on notions of legislative supremacy, in which authoritative lawmaking is vested in a legislative body and memorialized in a (usually) written code of law. The English speaking countries share a much younger legal tradition—the common law. These systems acknowledge legislative supremacy but do not treat formal institutional statutory lawmaking as the exclusive source of law; the judge has a more significant role to articulate law. Since the late 1950s, an increasing number of Western European States have joined together in a supra-national organization, the functions of which have begun to mimic those of a traditional federation. The European Union has become a great producer of law in its own right.

Japan and China were constituted as empires for many centuries. Both have experienced long periods of political fragmentation, as well as long periods of stability under centralizing regimes. Japanese society is roughly homogenous, reflecting both its geography (a group of islands at a significant distance from the Asian mainland) and its history. Japan has remained virtually invasion free for most of its history. That part of Asia today commonly included within what we know as the People's Republic of China, on the other hand, is less homogenous. Moreover, unlike Japan, it has been shaped to a greater degree by periodic invasions and mass migrations, the populations of which the indigenous population largely has managed to assimilate and absorb. China has experienced periods of aggressive imperialist expansion (into Tibet, Turkish Asia and the Mongol lands) and periods of contraction and internal fracture. Japan remains an Empire, though now organized as a constitutional monarchy. China today is a centralized Marxist-Socialist state. Japanese and Chinese legal systems are a fusion, more or less successful, of traditional indigenous law systems with European systems of lawmaking and governance. In Japan, the principal sources of borrowing came from Germany, France and England before the Second World War, and the United States after 1945. The Chinese state borrowed from French and German systems at the end of the Imperial period. After the victory of the Communist Party, the principal sources of borrowing have been from Marxist/Socialist States, primarily the Soviet Union, a traditional Roman/Byzantine state. The normative basis of such systems were bureaucratic, hierarchical, and centralizing. This Marxist/Socialist-Roman/Byzantine European normative structure was overlaid on traditional Chinese governance systems which were themselves ancient bureaucratic, hierarchical and centralizing systems. As such, at least in China, new norms are in harmony with traditional approaches to governance.

The purpose of this chapter is to acquaint (or re-acquaint) students with the rudiments of different national systems in Europe and Asia within which issues of corporate or enterprise governance are determined.[1] The materials in this chapter can be covered with an attention appropriate to the focus of the course. In some instances, it may make sense to cover the materials that follow extensively, to prepare the student for more sophisticated analysis of the material in the subsequent chapters. In other cases, it may be appropriate to use these materials as a supplement or resource when studying the materials that follow starting with Chapter 3, referring to the materials as necessary

A. The United States

By now, you should be familiar with the basic formal organization of American government. This section will not attempt even a short summary of that system. There are, however, some aspects of American political organization a student should keep in mind as she studies the materials in the rest of this chapter. These can be summarized as follows:

1. The basic postulate of American political organization is that the power of governance—sovereignty—proceeds from and is retained by the people. The people retain the power to form and reform their system of political organization, consistent with the principles of democratic representative government. Individuals acting in their capacity as government officials owe a duty of utmost loyalty to the people they serve and on whose behalf they act.
2. The American system of government is based on written constitutions. These constitutions alone provide the sources and limitations of governmental authority. The federal constitution operates as the supreme law of the land; state constitutions operate as the supreme law of the state, subject to the superior authority of the federal government.

1. For a basic refresher, see among the many valuable works in the field, DANIEL FARBER AND SUZANNA SHERRY, A HISTORY OF THE AMERICAN CONSTITUTION (1990).

3. Although governmental authority is divided between the states and the federal government, all governments in the United States share a common approach to law and lawmaking. This approach is based on shared common norms. The legal tradition of the United States derives in large part from the common law tradition of England. Portions of the United States, including those territories purchased from France and Spain, as well as the territories conquered from Mexico, retain a residue of the civil law tradition of France (especially in the case of Louisiana) or Spain and Mexico.
4. Governmental authority in the United States is divided between the federal government, in which the people of all of the states of the Union are represented, and the states themselves. Federal authority is limited to that power granted by the federal constitution to the national government. The authority of the states consists of all power not reserved to or exercised by the federal government, and not otherwise prohibited by state constitutions. Since the founding of the Republic, and with some exceptions, the federal courts have tended to broadly interpret the powers of the federal government, and to restrict the assertion of authority of the states, especially with respect to issues of commerce and foreign relations. Increasingly since the adoption of the Fourteenth, 16th (income tax) and 17th (direct election of senators) Amendments, the federal government has become a significant source of legislation and funding for the operation of government in the United States.
5. The power of the federal government is regulated by principles of separation of powers and concurrent authority. Governmental power is divided among an executive, a legislative and a judicial branch, each with its own core group of powers. Yet, most government action requires the concurrence of at least two branches of government.
6. The judicial branch of the federal government has been recognized to be vested with the power to render authoritative interpretations of the federal constitution. In this capacity, the federal courts may review the constitutionality of legislative and executive acts. State legislation and case law can be reviewed for conformity to federal constitutional limits on state power.
7. The regulation of commercial law and the organization of business enterprises traditionally have been left to the states. In modern times, federal and state governments have shared authority over the regulation of the sale of corporate shares and of securities markets. Federal securities regulation is based on the offer of securities to the public and is grounded on the imposition of reporting obligations on enterprises subject to federal regulation. State securities regulation is generally limited to shares offered for sale within the state.

You should ask yourself, from time to time as you explore the materials that follow, whether, or to what extent, American forms of enterprise organization can be understood as a necessary function of the structure of the American political system and the political culture that underlies it. Are corporations, and corporate constitutions, a private law version of the American political model? Are notions of shareholder democracy and institutional transparency the equivalent of federal constitutional notions of a right to vote and a right to be informed? Consider also whether the corporate organization of other political cultures also tends to reflect the political organization of those societies, and whether that reflection is necessary? Alternatively, you might want to test the theory that enterprise organization is not a prisoner of the political cultures of the places where those organizations are formed. Instead, it might be possible to think of the norms of enterprise organization as transnational—based on universal principles of economic efficiency. Thus, corporate organization is merely the applied expression of an optimizing form of economic organization. Yet, might such universal principles have an effect on political organization as well?

B. National Organization in Europe

Unlike the United States, which though divided politically constitutes a country in which all political units share the same approach to law and lawmaking, Europe is made up of a large number of states few of which share the same legal tradition. European legal traditions, and approaches to law, can be divided into four large "families" of law: (i) common law approach; (ii) Latin civil law approach, (iii) Germanic civil law approach; and (iv) Scandinavian law approach. This section is meant to provide you with a very basic introduction to the different legal approaches of France and Germany, the most influential members of the European legal families. As you read through these materials consider how the way a legal culture is structured may affect the form and substance of regulation. Also consider the similarities as well as the differences between the systems described.

1. *France: Latin Civil Law Approach*

French law is the most influential source of law making within the Latin Civil Law approach. The materials that follow provide you with a very short introduction to the French approach to law and legal issues.

Alexis Maitland Hudson, *France: Practical Commercial Law*

(1991)

(excerpts from pages 1–10)

For anyone with common law legal knowledge or training, approaching French legal problems for the first time there is the obvious hurdle of coming to terms with a codified system of law in which legal precedent has a much lesser significance. In truth, the divide is not so complete, since large sections of English law are now substantially codified in the form of statutes (e.g., The Sale of Goods Act 1979) whilst French practitioners do indeed look to the cases to clarify and expand codified legal precepts which are often startlingly lapidary in their formulation.

For the purposes of this work the principal sources of the law are:

(i)	*Code Civil*	Civil Code	CC
(ii)	*Code de Commerce*	Commercial Code	CoC
(iii)	*Code du Travail*	Employment Code	EC
(iv)	*Code Général des impôts*	Tax Code	TC

These texts are published in separate volumes annually by two legal publishers *Dalloz* and *Litec* and incorporate any new laws which have been passed since the last edition with consequential amendments to the old texts. They are the invaluable source material to be consulted whenever the practitioner wishes to find a statement of the law. These primary sources contain numerous footnotes and references to case law which serve to illustrate the effect of any particular disposition.

For the common law lawyer the most worrying feature of dealing with a legal problem by reference to the relevant Code is the discovery that the law typically appears at first glance to be stated simplistically. As an illustration of this point 1382 of the Civil Code reads:

> 'A person who commits any wrongful act whatsoever which causes damage to another is obligated to make good that damage.'

However, there then follows many pages of footnotes and case references which seek to clarify and expand this brief statement contained in the Code. Thus at the end of the day the common law approach and the French approach are seen to produce similar results for the student or the practitioner wishing to inform himself.

Nevertheless, the French courts do not invent new remedies or restate the law and have no right to do so. It may be said that the French system in this way offers more certainty.

Amongst the most significant differences in practice between English and French law, in a commercial context, is a positive duty under the latter to execute contractual obligations in good faith. Article 1134 of the Civil Code provides:

> 'A legally binding contract must be respected by the parties to it. It may only be brought to an end by mutual consent or in a way which the law allows. It must be performed in good faith.'

It is therefore possible to reproach a party to a contract for doing or omitting to do something which is manifestly in bad faith even if it is within the scope of the contract. This example goes some way to explaining the relative brevity of French contractual documentation, since the Court has a discretion, in cases of dispute, to consider the good faith of the parties. As a result they are more prepared to accept general provisions rather than feeling obliged to be totally exhaustive and compendious.

Another significant practical difference which is crucial to doing business in France concerns the value accorded to evidence in commercial litigation. Article 109 of the Commercial Code provides that any means of evidence is admissible in the Commercial Court but as a matter of practice only written evidence of any fact or correspondence will have much effect. The Court fully expects the parties themselves to be less than objective in what they say and there is very seldom any oral evidence. Equally, any expert appointed unilaterally by a party will have his impartiality questioned. The Courts, in general, and Commercial Courts in particular, maintain lists of court experts (*experts judiciares*) to whom complex issues of fact, mostly technical in nature, are delegated and whose findings are generally determinative of the issues upon which their views are sought.

The involvement of court experts in disputes, frequently even before proceedings are issued, coupled with the absence of any duty to produce documents in a contentious matter analogous to the common law Discovery Procedure, should lead a non-French party to exercise considerable care in what he writes and what he expects to see confirmed in writing. French law also has a very limited notion of privilege in relation to settlement negotiations in commercial disputes. Only exchanges in writing between *av-*

ocats marked *'confidentiel'* are privileged. Any other document may be produced in court and thus any 'without prejudice' correspondence which exists may be shown to the court by either side, often with highly prejudicial results.

As any student of comparative law knows there are more similarities than differences between most systems of substantive law. The means by which a legal result is achieved are, however, frequently diverse....

The Courts

There are three levels of jurisdiction in the French legal system. The choice of the first level will depend both on the subject matter of the dispute, the nature of the parties and the amount in issue. Commercial disputes between commercial people (*commerçants*) as defined are always heard before the relevant Commercial Court (*tribunal de commerce*) by a lay judge. The lay judge has been elected to office from the local commercial community, either sitting alone or with two assessors in an appropriate case.

The quality of *'commerçant'* is conferred by the nature of the activity he performs and in certain cases by the holding of a specific document (*carte de commerçant*). All commercial companies, both French and foreign have the necessary status to appear in the Commercial Court.

Non-commercial cases at first instance are heard by either the local inferior court (*tribunal d'instance*) or superior court (*tribunal de grande instance*) depending on the monetary value and subject matter. The judge is a professional magistrate, but may sit with two lay assessors in an appropriate case.

Appeal from these first instance courts lies without leave to the appropriate chamber of the local Court of Appeal (*cour d'appel*). The appeal judges are professional magistrates, three of which hear any case—one presides (*président*) and the two others assist (*assesseurs*). All appeals from first instance courts are reheard *de novo* on the facts and the law.

An appeal lies from the court of appeal without leave to the appropriate section of the Supreme Court (*Cour de Cassation*) in Paris. Such an appeal may not re-open issues of fact and is on matters of law only. At least five judges hear such appeals, although in practice the hearing is often very short and there is seldom oral argument. The judges are all senior professional magistrates.

Tax causes and claims by and against the State have a separate hierarchy of tribunals (*tribunaux administratifs*) leading to ultimate appeal on legal issues to the *Conseil d'Etat*.

French courts are inquisitorial in nature. Rather than allowing the parties alone to develop their respective cases, the judge will have to read the pleadings, any court expert's report (*rapport d'expertise*) and other relevant documents before the case opens and will frequently ask the parties' lawyers about them. In certain circumstances he may himself raise matters of law pertinent to the case and is bound to raise matters of public order. Oral argument is brief and frequently somewhat histrionic by English standards. Costs generally follow the event, but very seldom include a significant element in respect of lawyer's fees, although there are now signs of change in this respect.

All originating process and judgments are required to be served by a court bailiff (*huisser*) and certain other procedural matters will also be dealt with in this way.

Common law observers are inclined to think, and not without some justification, that the French legal system is based upon the premise that all litigants do not tell the truth and will seek to falsify all evidence. This is a grotesque over-simplification but it does help one appreciate why many significant differences between (say) English and French practice and procedure exist and explains why the court mistrusts the parties' own experts, oral evidence and any proof which is not written.

* * *

In order to negotiate contracts successfully in France or to resolve commercial disputes which may have arisen it is plainly desirable to have a feel for the legal culture which affects the thinking of your French counterpart.....The cost of legal proceedings in France is still generally lower than in England, not least because of the different standards of proof and absence of witnesses and oral argument in court. There is, therefore, a greater readiness to resolve matters in court if no other way can be found.

By and large the French will perform their contractual obligations in accordance with the spirit of the agreement they have made. They will not be slavishly literal minded nor Machiavellian in their interpretation. They are, however, strongly influenced by notions the English may not have, such as the overriding duty of good faith, or the importance of the written word as a matter of proof. They are haunted by tax considerations which do not exist in the UK...and they have concerns about company law requirements which are less developed in the UK.

2. *Germany: Germanic Civil Law Approach*

The German legal system, like that of the French, is based on a civil law approach. Legal regulation is comprehensively set forth in codes of law, and courts have only a limited role in the construction of legal principles. Unlike France and like the United States, Germany is a federal Republic in which power is shared between the federal government with its capital in Berlin, and the states (*Länder*).

Howard D. Fisher, *German Legal System and Legal Language: A General Survey Together With Notes and a German Vocabulary*

(1996)

(excerpts pages vii; 5–6; 29–30)

Germany has one of the most scientific legal systems anywhere in the world. For a person with English as his or her mother tongue to seek to understand that system is not easy, even with a legal education. Why is this so? The principle reason lies in the fact that, for historical reasons, the methods and sources of German and English law have developed differently. Another reason is the German language and its seemingly endless supply of formal terminology. Certainly, legal and everyday language are not the same anywhere, but where can it be more so than in Germany?

If the linguistic complexities were not enough, the enormous codification of practically every area of law in Germany will remain a formidable obstacle to comprehension of the German system for a foreigner, even after the dawn of the new Europe after 1993.

* * *

Readers with a love for plenty of case-law should always remember that it is a fact that the German legal system is almost entirely based on codifications.....

* * *

The Federal State
The Division of Power

In Germany, state power (*staatsgewalt*) is not centralised. Germany is divided into the Federal Republic (*Budesrepublik* or *Bund*) as the main state (*Zentralstaat*) and its constituent states (*Länder*).[1]

Each state (*Land*) is a member of the whole, but at the same time maintains its own state power; it is not fully independent, as otherwise the Federal Republic would be a confederation of states (*Staatenbund*). The *Bund* is a federal state (*Bundesstaat*), a new state created together by the joining together of its members.

The Passing of Laws

The *Bund* and the *Länder* are each entitled to pass laws (*Gesetz*) and their respective competence to do so (*Gesetzbungskompetenz*) is laid down in the (federal) constitution (*Grundgesetz*/GG/Basic Law).[2]

Article 70 GG lays down a presumption in favour of the competence of the *Länder*, but the constitution allocates to the *Bund* the right to pass laws in the most important fields; this right is either exclusive (*ausschließlich*: Article 71 GG) or concurrent (*konkurrierend*: Article 72 GG) or permits the *Bund* to lay down a general framework (*Rahmen*) for legislation by the *Länder* (Article 75 GG). The law of the Bund takes precedence over that of the *Länder* (Article 31 GG; *Bundesrecht bricht Landesrecht)*.[3]

* * *

Public and Private Law
Introduction

German law divides itself strictly into public law (*öffentliches Recht*)—dealing with the relationship of the individual to the state and other carriers of public power—and private law (*Privatrecht*)—dealing with the relationship of citizens amongst each other.

---

1. The *Bund* and its member states (*Gliedstaaten*) together form the *Gesamtstaat* (whole state)....Only the *Bund* enjoys full sovereign authority in external relations....

2. The immediate precursors of the *Grundgesetz* were the constitution of the (unified) German Empire of 16 April 1871 and the constitution of the Weimar Republic (the *Weimare (Reichs) Verfassung*) of 11 August 1919. The latter lasted until the *Ermächtigungsgesetz* (Enablement Law) of 24 March 1933 empowered Hitler to override it.

The constitution of the Weimar Republic had, for the first time, enacted (in its second part) a catalogue of *Grundrechte* (Basic Rights), which were later suspended by Hitler....

3. For a review of the relationship between the *Bund* and the *Länder* see [Wesel, Fast alles, was Recht ist (Eichborn, 1994, Study edn)] chapter 2 (*Der Bund und die Länder*). Wesel points out that in the field of legislation, the *Länder* are merely left with residual areas (*Restbestände*; for example police and building law) and that the decisions of the (federal) courts of the *Bund* have a significant influence on the judicature in the courts of the *Länder*.
Only in the area of administrative law do the *Länder* remain predominant....

German private law has two main branches:

• Civil law (*bürgerliches Recht*), the main source of which is the *Bürgerliches Gesetzbuch* (Civil Code (BGB)); and

• commercial and company law (*Handelsrecht* and *Gesellschaftsrecht*).

It is important to note here, however, that the subject-matter of private law in Germany is dealt with in numerous secondary and special statutes (*Nebenund Sondergesetze*), apart from the BGB and the statutes relating to commercial and company law eg in the fields of property and landlord and tenant law, employment law, traffic and public liability law, insurance and intellectual property law.

The main branches of German public law are:

• state and constitutional law (*Staats- und Verfassungsrecht*);

• administrative law (*Verwaltunssrecht*);

• tax law (*Steuerrecht*);

• criminal law (*Strafrecht*);

• procedural law (*Prozeßrecht*);

• public international law (*Völkerrecht*)....

Distinguishability of Norms

There are various theories as to how to establish whether a particular norm falls within the area of private or public law, for example:

• the interest theory, which asks if the norm serves the interests of the state or those of the individual;

• the subordination theory, which asks if the legal relationship between the parties is on equal terms (*auf der Grundlage der Gleichordnung*) or one of dominance and subordination (*Über und unterordnung*); and

• the modified subject or special rights theory (Sonderrechtstheorie), which asks if the norm necessarily only benefits or is directed as a carrier of public power (*ob eine Norm nur ein Träger öffentlicher Gewalt berechtige oder verpflichtet*).

Norms can also be distinguished according to whether they:

• are norms of material or formal law. Formal law (*formelles Recht*) deals with the application (*Anwendung*) and carrying out (*Durchsetzung*) of material law (*materielles Recht*), which contains the substantive provisions. Examples of formal law are procedural law (*Prozeßrecht/Verfahrensrecht*) and the law governing the various court jurisdictions (*Gerichtsbarkeiten*);

• are norms of federal or state law or norms with only more limited application....

• are compulsory norms (*zwingende Normen: ius cogens*) or dispositive norms (*nachgiebige Normen/dispositives Recht: ius dispositivum*). Dispositive norms are largely to be found in private law, where the important principles of freedom of contract (*Vertragsfreiheit*) and private autonomy (*Privatautonomie*) prevail. Thus, the contract law of the BGB usually only applies in the absence of an agreement between free contracting parties;

• emanate from statute/statutory instrument (*Gesetz*) or custom (*Gewohnheit*).

Nigel Foster, *German Legal System and Laws*

(2nd ed. 1996)
(excerpts from pages 1–4; some footnotes omitted)

The distinctive features of the German legal system arise in large part from the relatively comprehensive and rapid assimilation of Roman principles of law in the middle ages, the codification of the nineteenth century, in part influenced by the codification in France, and more recently the changes introduced as a result of the restructuring of Germany following the Second World War. At the turn of the last [nineteenth] century it was true to say that a vast difference existed between the German and English legal systems. For a number of reasons these systems are now coming closer together. This is in part due to the increasing importance of case law in Germany, the consolidation of statute in the UK and the membership of both countries of the European Communities.

3. THE CLASSIFICATION AS A CIVIL LAW COUNTRY

The German legal system belongs to the central European family of legal systems, broadly classified as civil law countries. German law contrasts, at least in theory and basic principles, quite strongly with the UK legal system.

The term 'civil law country' is not a very useful term but unfortunately is in widespread usage. One of its basic features is that a country which has adopted the civil law tradition will usually have as the core of its legal system five codes, normally including civil law in the roman law definition, criminal law, civil procedure law, criminal procedure law, and commercial law. This is in fact just what the German legal system has, although it is adding to these. The Germanic type of legal system, which includes German, Austrian, and Swiss legal systems, has influenced, to a large extent, Turkish, Greek, Japanese and Brazilian law amongst others, and more recently the former eastern bloc countries such as the Czech Republic.

4. THE DIVISION OF PUBLIC AND CIVIL(PRIVATE) LAW

The term 'civil law' is also used to describe a particular division of law. Despite the fact that all German laws, at least in theory, have an equitable status within a unified system of law, the German legal system has been influenced by the Roman legal system division between civil and public law.

Public law is concerned with the legal relationships between the citizen and the state, or the manifestations of the state in the form of public authorities. Most of the public law actions take place in the administrative courts.

Civil law (*Privatrecht*) contains the concentration of legal principles concerned with the regulation of civil life, i.e., the affairs between individuals as private individuals. Transactions undertaken between a public body and an individual which concern civil law are governed by civil law and not public law rules. The classic roman formulation of civil law includes the laws of obligations (contract and tort), succession, family law and property law, but has been extended in the modern setting to further include commercial law, company law and labour law. Labour law has, however, been subject to such considerable state influence, and now contains extensive public law elements, that it is difficult strictly to regard it as civil law any longer.

The division would have been more distinct in the past. The greater power of the state inherent in public law is a major reason for the distinction between public and private law. Public law was as a result more rigid and insisted on a stricter relationship of rights between the state and the citizen. Civil law, concerned with equals, could afford to be based on much more flexible foundations and was left very much to the parties to determine exactly how their relations should be governed. This greater emphasis on the classification or division into private and public law subject areas had and still has an influence on the organization of the courts, the form and style of legal education and, to some extent, on the legal professions of Germany but no great effect on the law itself and how it is applied in individual circumstances.

Areas of law within public law are primarily constitutional law and administrative law and, amongst others, criminal law, procedural law (applicable in both public and civil jurisdictions), international law, law governing the public professions, social law, and revenue law. As the concern and the influence are manifested in ever more regulation, the boundaries and intervention of the state in areas of law becomes ever more great. This is resulting (and will continue to result) in the erosion of the reasonably clear boundaries between civil and public law as seen in the past. The clearest example of this can be observed in the birth and development of the law of economic administration (*Wirtschaftsverwaltungsrecht*) which is entirely concerned with the state's intervention in the economy and thus the civil and commercial affairs of individuals. This hybrid area of law will without doubt grow as exampled by environmental law.

5. CODE AND STATUTE-BASED LAW

The high degree to which German laws are contained in codification and in statutory form originally distinguished them from the UK system with its predominant base in common law. This has allowed the description of a 'written law country' to be applied. A number of major codes exist, most notably the civil and criminal codes amongst the original five, but the process of codification continues. Codification is more than simple assimilation or compilation or, as in the UK, the consolidation of a number of statutes in particular areas of law. It is the presentation of these laws in a complete and systematic form, free from contradiction and complete with general and specific principles. The very many statutes and case decisions that exist in a particular area of law are completely reviewed, the general principles that exist are filtered out and presented at the beginning of the code with the specific rules in following books of the code. The style of codified law differs greatly from UK law. It is an attempt to present an area of law as a unified whole, to contain not only the specific rules but also the general and abstract rules and principles which apply to all of the specific circumstances. Thus in the German legal system the codes contain what at first seem to be vague legal concepts but which can be applied to new legal problems to achieve a result. The codes can be used to interpret everyday problems and agreements without the need for going into great detail in the agreements themselves. Codification continues with environmental law, further additions to the social law code and the proposed labour law code.

6. SOURCES OF LAW

Only two sources of law are formally recognized in the German legal system—statute and customary law—although other influences so without doubt have an impact.

6.1 Statute (*Gesetz*)

Statute, translated above as *Gesetz*, as a source of law includes the German Constitution of the present Republic; the *Grundgesetz*,[2] the comprehensive codes and amending or

2. The term *Grundgesetz* will be used throughout the text to mean 'Constitution,' which words are intended to be synonymous and interchangeable. The term 'basic law' will not be used but will be found in many texts on German law....

additional individual statutes of both the Federation (*Bund*) and individual states (*Länder*). *Gesetz* in a wider sense may further encompass legal acts, which could be equated to the term 'secondary legislation', of the Federation, Ministries of the Federation, *Länder* and other law-making bodies under public law. Predominantly these include regulations and byelaws (*Verordnungen* and *Stazungen*). The internal rules promulgated by the local authorities do not have the force of law or the same status as *Gesetz.*

6.2 Custom (*Gewohnheitsretch*)

This includes all regular and general public practice recognized as binding. There is no strict time requirement for customary law in Germany and it is now a very limited source of new law.

More recent legal developments, although not formally acknowledged as sources of law, must undoubtedly include the case law of the courts. Another recent influence is the membership of the European Communities.

6.3 The role of the courts, judiciary and precedence

The courts and case law in the modern German legal system play no formal part as a source of law. In Germany, judges are supposed only to apply law and not create it. However, this view is increasingly regarded as unrealistic, and the role judges do play is clearly far greater than legal theory permits and is quite extensive as interpreters and developers of law. The German courts need to interpret law, hence there is plenty of scope for judicial creativity and legal development. The judiciary in Germany do, however, clearly play a far more active role in the administration of court proceedings than in the UK.

In theory, precedence in the common-law countries is a strictly applied principle, but in practice the ability to distinguish a case means that precedence can be circumvented when it suits the purposes of the court. In Germany, the theory is that with no system of binding precedence the judges are completely free to decide every case on its merits and not be hindered by previous decisions. In practice previous decisions are observed and considered. There are also exceptions to the basic rule that there is no system of *stare decisis* in Germany.... The clearest example is in the case of the decisions of the Federal Constitutional Court (*Bundesvefassungsgericht:* BverfG) which are binding rules of law. Generally, decisions of higher courts are studied carefully and consistency is maintained wherever possible. Indeed, major or radical changes proposed by the courts to principles of law must be sanctioned by special senates of the Federal Court of Justice. However, courts increasingly pay a great deal of attention to previous decisions, especially those of higher courts. German courts, in contrast to those in the UK, have adopted the practice of giving greater respect to more recent decisions. Additionally, the writings of academics and jurists command considerable persuasive authority, especially if a dominating opinion (*herrschende Meinung*) appears to exist. There is thus a much greater influence of legal theory and private legal research.

C. The European Union

In this section, you will be introduced to the supra-national, perhaps even federal, structure, created among the Member States of the European Communities ("EC") now known, in its broadest manifestation, as the European Union ("EU").[1] It is from this supra-national grouping that much of the impetus for the trend towards harmonizing EC law arises. The EU system has provided a significant impetus for the harmonization of European Company law. In order to understand the notion of European company law harmonization, it is necessary to understand the emerging structures of the EU. In this section, we will cover first the sources of EC law, how it operates, what areas of law it covers, and what areas are left to the member states to regulate. In going through the materials which follow, consider the similarities and differences between the system created for European economic union, and that effected in the United States.

1. *Brief History of Formation of the European Union*

The Treaty of Paris established the first of the European Communities, the European Coal and Steel Community ("ECSC"), in 1951. (Treaty Establishing the European Coal and Steel Community (ECSC Treaty)). The original members of the ECSC were France, West Germany, Belgium, the Netherlands, Luxembourg and Italy. The organization of the ECSC—split into a High Authority (executive body), a Common Assembly (made up of representative parliamentarians from Member States), a Special Council (ministers of state), and a Court of Justice, laid the institutional framework for the modern EU (ECSC Treaty, Tit. II, Art. 7-45).

The primary purpose of the ECSC was to place the production of coal and steel under a common authority. The goal was to make it harder to wage war by this transfer of authority over the basic materials used for war-making to a supra-national organization.

D. Lasok and J.W. Bridge, *Law and Institutions of the European Communities*

(5th ed. 1991).

(excerpts pages 12–13)

Several lessons could be drawn from this experiment [the creation of the ECSC]. It proved that supra-national institutions could function in spite of diverse national interests; that far from being an economic disaster, this first European Common Market greatly contributed to the economic progress of the Member States. The enlarged market activated industries far beyond those directly connected with coal and steel. The greatest benefit accrued to Italy, the economically weakest member. However, all was not well all the time. In 1959 there was a crisis in the coal industry caused mainly by over-production and an increase in the use of oil which rendered coal mines, especially in Belgium and Germany, redundant. The [ECSC] High Authority endeavored to finance stock-piling, to reduce production and even to lower wages, but the Council of Ministers refused to sanction these measures clearly because national interests were at

---

1. The terms EC and EC are used interchangeably in the text. As you will see from the materials that follow, as a technical matter, the EC and the EU refer to different aspects of the various agreements of community between the Member States.

stake. The High Authority was, therefore, forced to provide a special aid to Belgium which was hit very badly, for the rehabilitation and retraining of minors and to restrict imports from outside the Community. The very existence of the Community enabled it to relieve at least one country but it also became clear that there must be a common European policy in the field of energy. Whilst the Community was successful in its field it was not able to cope with other economic problems and its limited success certainly did not satisfy those who worked for a United Europe in their lifetime.

Two Treaties of Rome of 1957 created two additional European Communities—the European Atomic Energy Community ("EURATOM"), (Treaty Establishing the European Atomic Energy Community [Euratom Treaty]), and the European Economic Community ("EEC") now the EC, (Treaty Establishing the European Economic Community [EEC Treaty]). The ECSC, EC and EURATOM, together, constitute the European Communities ("EC"). The original members of the EC were France, West Germany, Belgium, the Netherlands, Luxembourg and Italy (together, and along with later additions to the Community, the "Member States"). The organization of the EC and EURATOM were modeled on that of the ESCS. Initially, the institutions of all three communities remained separate.

Like the ESCS, the other Communities were initially created to serve specific purposes. The primary purpose of EURATOM was to create a specialist supra-national structure for the management of atomic power. It provides the focus for the development of a common European energy policy. EURATOM will not be considered directly in these materials. The primary purposes of the Economic Community was to provide a supra-national framework for the creation and regulation of a common market for its members, without sacrificing the political independence of any of its members. This common market was to be effected by the implementation of rules to further the harmonizing policies underlying the basic rights accorded under the EC Treaty. At the heart of these rights were the "Four Freedoms"—the free movement of people, goods, services and capital between Member States. The free movement of goods was to establish by creation of a customs union between Member States and a common external tariff for goods from nonmember States (completed around 1968). Additional measures were implemented to promote the free movement of persons, services and capital. Other goals included the creation of common policies for agriculture, transportation, and external trade.

Thus, by 1957, three legally separate "communities" of European states were constituted—each focused on distinct and different purposes. After 1957, the Member States of the European Communities began a process of consolidating the governing bodies of the three Communities. A Convention entered into simultaneously with the Rome Treaties in 1957 established a single Parliamentary Assembly and a single Court of Justice for all three Communities. The Commissions, High Authorities, and Councils of the three Communities were not merged until 1967 by Treaty Establishing a Single Council and a Single Commission of the European Communities the "Merger Treaty"), entered into in 1965 but effective in 1967. The Merger Treaty also merged the auditing departments created by the three Communities. While the organs of governance of the communities have merged, each of the three Communities remains a distinct legal entity, subject to and limited by the provisions of its own treaty of creation.

Audrey Winter, et al., *Europe Without Frontiers: A Lawyer's Guide*

(1989)

(excerpts pages 5–8; footnotes omitted)

* * * * [T]he 1960's and 1970s were difficult times politically and financially for the Community. On the political front in the '60s, the first applications for membership by the United Kingdom, Ireland, and Denmark in 1961 were not successful. On the financial front, the establishment of the Common Agricultural Policy beginning in 1962—pursuant to which common market organizations were set up to guarantee the price of many agricultural commodities through the European Agricultural Guidance and Guarantee Fund—brought with it the need for additional financing. Simultaneously, the European Commission was boldly proposing to give the Community its own resources—thereby making it in large part financially autonomous—by allocating to it the import duties collected on goods coming in from third countries. In response, the French government in 1965 declared the Community to be in a state of crisis, recalled its permanent representative to Paris, and did not participate in Community meetings for the next seven months. [The crisis was resolved in 1966 with the Luxembourg Compromise which required unanimous consent for EC Council decisions. This accord was replaced with weighted voting on the adoption of the Single European Act in 1986.]

The 1970s were characterized by wild exchange rate fluctuations, two oil shocks, and widespread economic recession. These events led the Member States to give priority to national interests over Community interests.... [A degree of monetary stability was achieved after 1972 by controlling the ranges of fluctuations of Member States' currencies.] This system was further strengthened in 1979, when the European Monetary System was brought into effect. [This system introduced the European Currency Unit and other means of maintaining monetary stability.]

* * *

Moreover, [in the 1980s] competition from the United States, Japan and other Asian nations prompted the Commission to begin to take steps to combat the "eurosclerosis" for which the Community had come to be known.

The interest in a single European market began again in earnest in the early 1980's. In 1982 the European Council instructed the Council to prioritize measures which were in need of adoption for the completion of the European internal market. The pressure to work towards greater unification intensified in the early 1980's as a result of the passage by the European Parliament of the draft European Union Treaty. That Treaty, though ultimately rejected, would have conferred on the E.E.C. substantial powers over economic, monetary and foreign policy. The recommendations of a White Paper, (Completing the Internal Market: White Paper From the Commission to the European Council, COM(85)310 final (June, 1985) [the "White Paper"]), were presented as an alternative (along with what became the Single European Act of 1986 ("SEA")) to the rejected European Union Treaty.

The White Paper contained a plan for achieving a more effective economic union among the Member States. It identified three different types of barriers to a European internal market: (i) physical barriers (checks on goods and people as they cross borders between Member States); (ii) technical barriers (differing national standards for goods and services which affect the free movement of those items between Member States); and (iii) fiscal barriers (differing types and rates of indirect taxes). Physical barriers were to be overcome by reducing the inconvenience of border checks. Technical barriers were to be minimized by replacing national with pan-European standards for health and safety requirement, professional qualifications (lawyers, doctors, accountants, etc.), and by creating suitable conditions for industrial cooperation (by harmonizing company law, etc.). Fiscal barriers were to be overcome by harmonizing VAT (value added tax, which forms an integral part of the tax systems of many European countries) and excise tax rates between the Member States. The heart of the White Paper consisted of nearly three hundred legislative proposals for overcoming the identified barriers and a timetable for adoption of each. Among these were proposals for greater "harmonization" of company law. A portion of the White Paper follows.

The White Paper

Completing the Internal Market: White Paper From the Commission to the European Council, COM(85)310 final
June, 1985
(excerpts ¶¶4–5, 7–8, 136–137)

4. The Treaty [E.E.C. Treaty] clearly envisaged from the outset the creation of a single integrated internal market free of restrictions on the movement of goods; the abolition of obstacles to the free movement of persons, services and capital; the institution of a system ensuring that competition in the common market is not distorted; the approximation of laws as required for the proper functioning of the common market; and the approximation of indirect taxation in the interest of the common market.

5. In the early days attention concentrated on the common customs tariff, which was established eighteen months ahead of the 12-year programme set out in the Treaty.... But thereafter momentum was lost partly through the onset of the recession, partly through a lack of confidence and vision.

* * *

7. But the mood began to change, and the commitment to be rediscovered: gradually at first, but now with increasing tempo. The Heads of State and Government at the European Council meeting in Copenhagen in 1982 pledged themselves to the completion of the internal market as a high priority. The pledge was repeated at Fountainbleau in June 1984; at Dublin in December of that year; and, most recently, in Brussels, in March, 1985. The time for talk has now passed. The time for action has come. That is what this White Paper is about.

8. The case for the completion of the internal market has been argued elsewhere: and as the communiques at successive European Councils have indicated, it has been accepted by the Heads of State and Governments of the Member States. But it is worth recalling that the objective of completing the internal market has three aspects:

   – First, the wielding together of the ten, soon to be twelve, individual markets of the Member States into one single market of 320 million people;

- Second, ensuring that this single market is also an expanding market—not static but growing;
- Third, to this end, ensuring that the market is flexible so that resources, both of people and materials, and of capital and investment, flow into the areas of greatest economic advantage.

* * *

136. The absence of a Community legal framework for cross-border activities by enterprises and for cooperation between enterprises of different Member States has led—if only for psychological reasons—to numerous potential joint projects failing to get off the ground. The Community is now, for the first time, setting the stage for a new type of association to be known as the "European Economic Interest Grouping" that will be governed by uniform Community legislation and will make it easier for enterprises from the different Member States jointly to undertake specific activities.

137. Also, it is worth noting that a Council decision is still awaited on the proposed statute for a European Company. The Commission is conscious that the creation of an optional legal form at the Community level holds considerable attraction as an instrument for the industrial cooperation needed in a unified Internal Market. A decision on the proposed statute will clearly be needed in 1992. In the interim period, the Commission intends to concentrate on measures to approximate national laws and does not preclude the possibility of amending its European Company proposal in order to build on results achieved in discussion of approximation measures.

The White Paper reflects both frustration with the pace of European integration and optimism that such integration would proceed—at least on an economic level. The 1980s saw not only the movement toward economic integration envisioned by the White Paper, but increasingly, political integration as well. This movement for integration was reflected in the changes brought about by a number of significant revisions to the original EEC Treaty commencing with the Single European Act.

The Single European Act was meant to serve as a substitute for the rejected European Union Treaty. While it included some of the concepts of the European Union Treaty, it shied away from the formal merger of the traditional three Communities—ECSC, EURATOM and EEC, instead offering a further formalized merging of the workings of the three. Thus, the Single European Act amounts to a constitutional amendment of the Communities treaties. At the same time it sought to provide a lukewarm expansion of European Community integration by providing a formalized means of coordinating Member State foreign policy. The SEA also formalized the European Council; SEA, Arts. 1–3.

The primary economic purpose of the Treaty was expressed in SEA Arts. 13–15, adding Arts. 8A–8C to the EEC Treaty (now articles 18–20)—to adopt measures with the aim of establishing an internal market by the end of 1992. "The internal market shall comprise an area without internal frontiers in which the free movement of goods, persons, services and capital is ensured in accordance with the provisions of the" SEA. EC Art. 19.

The SEA also made it easier for the EC Council to adopt measures for the implementation of the integration of European Communities by permitting the EC Council to adopt the measures on the internal market by a "qualified majority" made up of weighted votes, with some escape clauses. SEA, Art. 18, adding Art. 100a (now Art. 95) to the EC Treaty. For the definition of "qualified majority, see EEC Treaty, Art. 148 (now Art. 205). Measures includes directives, regulations, decisions and recommendations (but with the preference given to the use of directives.

The reading that follows provides a summary of the movement toward integration after adoption of the Single European Act. As you read this consider whether European integration remains merely economic or whether integration is a precursor to political union.

Paolo Mengozzi, *European Community Law: From the Treaty of Rome to the Treaty of Amsterdam*

(2nd ed., 1999) (Patrick Del Duca, trans.)
(excerpts pages 3–9; some footnotes omitted)

Since 1957, the European integration process has both broadened and deepened. The entry into force of the Single European Act on July 1, 1987 is the first of three fundamental developments which overcame the Member State resistence to the Union Treaty proposal adopted on February 1, 1984 by the European Parliament. The second fundamental development is the Maastricht Treaty on European Union (TEU) which became effective November 1, 1993, and the third is the October 2, 1997 signing of the Treaty of Amsterdam.

The Single European Act introduced more democratic decision making mechanisms, provided for the passage from a common market to a single internal market through the abolition of customs controls between the Member States (known as "Objective 92"), extended Community competence to new fields of activity including the environment, research and economic and social cohesion and formalized, outside the European Economic Community framework, a European political cooperation between the Member States. Meanwhile, as the scope of the European Community widened, its membership also increased.

The broadening of the collective goals pursued under the EEC Treaty and particularly the success in achieving them, necessarily affected the United Kingdom's initial negative response to the several invitations extended to it to join the common market. Once the opposition of France was overcome following the conference of the Hague on December 1 and 2, 1969, serious negotiations began with regard to the admission to the Communities, not only of the United Kingdom, but also of Ireland, Denmark and Norway. In the meantime Denmark and Norway had joined with the United Kingdom in the European Free Trade Association ("EFTA"). By the adoption of two treaties and of related acts effective January 1, 1973, Denmark, Ireland, and the United Kingdom joined the three Communities. Norway, although it signed the two treaties, did not ratify them, and accordingly did not join.

Additional admissions to the Community followed. The first was that of Greece, perfected by the January 1, 1981 effectiveness of two treaties, signed at Athens on May 28, 1979, and of related acts.[8] Spain and Portugal joined with the coming into effect on January 1, 1986 of a treaty signed on June 12, 1985 at Lisbon and Madrid, along with its

8. OJ L 291/1 (November 19, 1979).

annex containing the terms for adhesion and adaptation of the Treaty regarding the three Communities.[9] Three others—Austria, Finland and Sweden—joined with the entry into force of a treaty[10] negotiated among all Member States and with Norway, which once again declined membership due to failure to ratify following an unsuccessful referendum.

* * *

2. Factors leading to the Maastricht Treaty

The implementation of the Single European Act caused much of the preconceived visions which preceded its adoption to be reexamined. Factors, both internal to the Communities and outside them, highlighted the insufficiency of the European integration which it had achieved.

Within the Communities, the following needs became apparent:

(1) to move more quickly towards a single currency so as to eliminate trade distortions due to fluctuating exchange rates and the cost of exchanging money;[13]

(2) to augment Community social policy so as to neutralize the risks of social dumping potentially associated with development of a purely "free market";

(3) to confront the democracy deficit resulting form increased powers of the Community institutions unaccompanied by popular control by the persons subjected to them; and

(4) to institute new and improved mechanisms to address at a Community level the risks of increased international crime, drug trafficking, terrorism and illegal immigration resulting from the elimination of internal; customs controls.

At the external level, a need was perceived to strengthen the Community in the face of profound changes in the geopolitical structure of the continent following:

(1) the collapse of the Central and Eastern European Bloc, beginning in 1989, and then of the Soviet Union;

(2) German reunification, which led the other Member States to seek reinforcement of the European Community so as to have a European Germany rather than a German Europe; and

(3) the end of the Cold War, which created urgency to modify the foreign policy structures and arrangements for the defense of Western Europe in order to avoid repeating events such as the insufficient Community response to the 1990–1991 Gulf War.

These needs led to two intergovernmental conferences, one on economic and monetary union and another on political union. These conferences, preceded by various summits (Hanover, Madrid, Strasbourg, Dublin I and II, and Rome) were held between 1988 and 1990 and concluded in 1991. The Treaty on European Union (TEU), signed at Maastricht on February 7, 1992 was the result. After the necessary Member State's ratifications, it took effect on November 1, 1993.

During the two intergovernmental conferences, two distinct views arose. Some Member States, with the aim of maintaining their own sovereignty in matters of foreign

9. OJ L 302/1 (November 15, 1985).

10. OJ 241 (August 29, 1994).

13. The original Article 102A, introduced into the EEC Treaty by the Single European Act, for the first time attributed the Community a "monetary competence."

policy, security, justice and internal affairs, wanted to preserve a clear distinction between matters falling within the Community sphere of action and those of political cooperation. Other states, with a more federal view, pushed to overcome such distinctions so as to avoid deviations from the model of the European Communities and to more decisively in the direction of a federal type of integration.

The Maastricht Treaty reflects both views. It contains important modifications to the Treaties instituting the European Communities. It develops and integrates intergovernmental cooperation between the Member States, initiated in the Single European Act, with the creation of the Common Foreign and Security Policy (CFSP) and the Cooperation in Justice and Home Affairs (CJHA). It places the workings of the modified Community and the implementation of the CFSP and the CJHA under a single treaty structure, described as corresponding to a Greek temple, where its pediment is constituted of common provisions, resting on three pillars or columns, corresponding to the European Communities, the CFSP and the CJHA.

Regarding the first point... the Member States, in adopting and ratifying the TEU, amplified the EEC's objectives by European Community ("EC"). They also outlined an economic and monetary union designed, with some features astonishing in their boldness, to function within the framework of the EC.[15] Community powers already established in certain sectors were expanded. In addition, they introduced two important structural elements: union citizenship and the principle of subsidiarity. The Member States addressed the risk of increasing democratic deficit determined by the new Community powers by increasing the role of the European Parliament in the Community decision-making process, in the nomination of the President and other members of the Commission, and in monitoring respect for the rights of Union citizens. They also addressed the United Kingdom's objection to any increase in Community competence to avoid the risks of social dumping, by inserting into the text of the EC Treaty a protocol authorizing all Member States other than the United Kingdom to call upon the Community institutions to adopt legislation in social matters outside the scope of what the EC Treaty contemplated, and having effect in the Member States other than the United Kingdom....

With respect to the single institutional framework for the functioning of each of the Community, the CFSP and police and judicial cooperation, TEU Article C (now Article 3) provides:

> The Union shall be served by a single institutional framework which shall ensure the consistency and the continuity of the activities carried out in order to attain its objectives while respecting and building upon the *acquis communautaire*.[16]

TEU Article B (now Article 2) provides that the Union is: "...to maintain in full the *acquis communautaire* and to build on it..."

The Maastricht Treaty drafters thus overcame the initial resistance to the evolution of the Community and created new means of action in the fields covered by the CFSP and

---

15. The third phase of Monetary Union began January 1, 1999, when the Euro became the common currency of 11 Member States. The various national currencies, however, remain in circulation until June 30, 2002....

16. Article M of the TEU (now Article 47) confirms the principle of respect for the *acquis communautaire* by providing that no provisions of the TEU "shall affect the Treaties establishing the European Communities or the subsequent Treaties and Acts modifying or supplementing them." [Ed: the *acquis communautaire* includes all derivative law of the Communities as supplemented by judgments of the European Court of Justice].

CJHA. The creation of the CFSP and the CJHA as forms of collaboration to be realized according to loosely defined mechanisms outside the established framework of Community law, is recognized as subject to an evolution, whose development is planned but whose content remains to be seen.

3. 1996 Intergovernmental Conference and the Treaty of Amsterdam

The drafters of the Maastricht Treaty, conscious of the dynamic nature of the European integration process, had provided in Article N.2 for a 1996 conference of Member State government representatives to examine and revise the Treaty in light of the objectives established in Articles A and B. This conference opened on March 29, 1996 and concluded on October 2, 1997 with the signing of the Treaty of Amsterdam. This Treaty amended the Treaty on European Union and, once again, the EC Treaty. It simplified them, eliminated obsolete text, and renumbered their articles.

Article N.2 contemplated examination only of certain provisions expressly contemplated to be revised; however, in light of the Union's potential enlargement to include countries from central and eastern Europe, as well as certain Mediterranean states, the European Council attempted more ambitious institutional and financial reform. This attempt was not entirely successful. No specific innovations were adopted to address the most pressing questions of expansion, such as the composition of the Commission or voting in the Council. Other questions also went unresolved, such as the establishment of a clear hierarchy of categories of Community action, creation of a common defense system and integration of the WEU into the EU. The ultimate goal of European integration remains undefined, as do aspects of economic and monetary union.

Nevertheless, those reforms which the Treaty of Amsterdam did achieve are not to be underrated. The structure of the European Union as resting on three pillars was maintained, but reorganized, particularly with respect to the third pillar. This reorganization "communitarized" much of the material covered and improved the internal organization so as to preserve and develop the Union in areas of freedom, security and justice.

Additional innovations... include:

(1) express statement that: the Union is founded on principles of freedom, democracy, respect for human rights and fundamental freedoms, and the rule of law; these principles are common to the Members States; and their serious and persistent breach is punishable by sanctions.

(2) empowering the Council to take appropriate measures to combat discrimination based on gender, race or ethnic origin, religion or personal creed, disability age or sexual orientation.

(3) emphasis on social elements by the introduction of a new Title into the EC Treaty, dedicated to employment and incorporating into the Community pillars the Agreement on social policy—including the participation of Great Britain—referenced in Maastricht Treaty Protocol 14. To a large extent, these elements may be considered a response to the social sacrifces acceted by Member States so as to satisfy the requirements for participation in monetary union.

(4) greater attention to environmental preservation, consumer protection and public health.

(5) further specification of the principles of subsidiarity and proportionality, thus "constitutionalizing" previous instruments.

(6) greater transparency in decision making.

(7) strengthening the European Parliament's role, thereby increasing democracy in the operations of the institutions.

(8) reinforcement of the figure of the President of the Commission, whose nomination the European Parliament must now approve.

(9) broader Court of Justice Jurisdiction.

(10) greater participation of the Economic Committee and the Committee of the Regions through increased consultation.

(11) recognition, under certain circumstances, of the possibility of forming closer cooperation between a majority of the Member States, which may lead to the definition of the ultimate goal of European integration.

Comments and Questions

1. Since the adoption of the SEA and the presentation of the White Paper, the EC has been working on the programs for European economic integration. While the goal of full integration was not completely met by the end of 1992, the EC continued down the path laid out by the White Paper. There have been some bumps on the road to integration. For example, the Maastricht Treaty had a rocky road to ratification by the member states. In Denmark the electorate initially rejected the Treaty. France and Britain narrowly approved. In Germany it resulted in significant constitutional litigation which resulted in an opinion of the German Federal Constitutional Court suggesting structural limits to the integrative powers of the institutions of the EU and the supremacy of EU legislation. The adoption of the Treaty of Amsterdam, in contrasty, was more easily ratified by the Member States.

2. The political integration that has followed economic integration has given rise among some Member States to a fear of over-centralization. In an attempt to assuade those fears, the EC treaty was modified to include the principle of "subsidiarity." Subsidiarity is meant to provide a legislative rule of choice of locus for enacting legislation. As written into the Treaty, subsidiarity is set forth as follows:

> In areas which do not fall within its exclusive competence, the Community shall take action, in accordance with the principle of subsidiarity, only if and in so far as the objectives of the proposed action cannot be sufficiently achieved by the Member States and can therefore, by reason of the scale or effects of the proposed action, be better achieved by the Community.

The principle of subsidiarity should act as a "choice of lawmaking" rule with respect to the determination of the appropriate level at which lawmaking on particular issues ought to be assigned. Its purpose is to break the tendency of lawmaking power to flow upward in a federal system to the jurisdiction of greatest generality. For an extensive discussion of the subsidiary principle from a comparative perspective, see, George A. Berman, *Taking Subsidiarity Seriously: Federalism in the European Community and the United States*, 94 Colum. L. Rev. 331 (1994).

> The recently incorporated principle of subsidiarity, imposes on the European federative system a constitutional choice of the political level at which legislative action must be taken within the European Union. Critics of the principle have ar-

gued that subsidiarity will give the Member States, as independent political entities, significant leverage in negotiating the extent of E.U. actions within the E.U. Council. They note that an argument can always be made that while an action falls within the competence of the E.U., the matter has not been shown to be better achieved by the Community.[18]

The United States has no equivalent principle of deference to its constituent states. We rely on politics. And yet politics can be very effective. Consider the subsidiarity issues within the Contract with America[20] on which the Republican party rode to political domination in the legislative branch of the federal government in the 1994 elections.

Larry Catá Backer, *Harmonization, Subsidiarity and Cultural Difference: An Essay on the Dynamics of Opposition Within Federative and International Legal Systems*, 4 TULSA J. COMP. & INT'L L. 185, 191–92 (1997) (some footnotes omitted). Do you think that subsidiarity can be used as a precise basis for the partitioning of power between levels of government in a federal or supra-national system?

3. Subsidiarity has also resulted in greater attention to regional differences within the E.U. The Treaty now provides in Art. 151 that the "*Community shall contribute to the flowering of the culture of the Member States, while respecting their national and regional diversity and at the same time bringing the common cultural heritage to the fore.*" However, no body of the E.U. has been given any affirmative power to act on this provision directly. It's collateral effect on the shaping of European Union enactments, however, could be significant. The provision remains hortatory, as a statement of principle, but we shall see what the future brings.

4. The themes of the Maastricht Treaty were further developed in the latest of the revisions of the Treaties. The Maastricht Treaty tied together, within the institutional framework of a supra-national organization the previously existing Communities, which became the first of three "pillars" of the union. The first pillar strengthened the institutional and legal structure of the Communities. The two additional pillars of union, the Common Foreign and Security Policy (Art. J, Maastricht Treaty) and Co-operation in Justice and Home Affairs (Art. K, Maastricht Treaty), were excluded from the institutional structure of the Communities pillar, and functioned largely at the level of the Member States. With the ratification of the Treaty of Amsterdam, October 2, 1997, 1997 O.J. C 340/1 (November 10, 1997), the Justice and Home Affairs Pillar was restructured to link it more closely to the institutional structure of the Communities Pillar. Thus, what is popularly conceived of as the government of the European "Union," over which the institutions of the Euro-

---

18. *See* STEPHEN WEATHERILL, LAW AND INTEGRATION IN THE EUROPEAN UNION 170 (1995). Note, though, that subsidiarity, as a formal matter, is only relevant in the areas of shared competence between Member States and the Community. In areas of exclusive Community competence, it has no role to play. Of course, the Treaty is singularly unhelpful in defining areas of exclusive and joint competence. One can argue (broadly) that any area covered by the EC Treaty would be exclusively within Community competence. The only exceptions would be in those areas where the EC Treaty expressly give the Member States a role to play (for example, Article 129 (now Art. 152 and vocational training; Article 128 (now Art. 151) and cultural solicitude). Conversely, areas of exclusive Community competence might be defined as limited to those areas in which the Member States are expressly forbidden to legislate. For a discussion of these issues, see, for example, [George A. Berman, *Taking Subsidiarity Seriously: Federalism in the European Community and the United States*, 94 COLUM. L. REV. 331 (1994)], at 344–47.

20. REPUBLICAN NATIONAL COMMITTEE, CONTRACT WITH AMERICA: THE BOLD PLAN BY REP. NEWT GINGRICH, REP. DICK ARMEY, AND THE HOUSE REPUBLICANS TO CHANGE THE NATION (1994).

pean Communities have authority—the European Council, the European Commission and the European Court of Justice—is actually limited to those matters within the competence of the old Communities treaties, mostly economic (common market) regulation. The CFSP and, to some lesser extent, the CJHAP, function on a more traditionally intergovernmental basis. As such, it is deceiving, to some extent, to speak of the governance of Europe in the singular. Something far more complicated is being devised. However, "the Amsterdam Treaty, though formally confirming the three pillar structure, blurred the institutional and constitutional divide between the EC and the intergovernmental strains of the non-EC EU....At the very least, the label 'European Union law', previously misleading in its intimation of a unified constitutional pattern, has begun to attain credibility, albeit that the evolving creature represents an unsettling combination of mutating legal strains."[21]

Paul Craig and Gráinne de Búrca, *EU Law: Text, Cases and Materials*

(2nd ed. 1998)
(excerpt page 35; footnotes omitted)

The semi-communautarisation of the third pillar and the simultaneous infiltration of the Community Treaty by third-pillar features emphasise the increasing complexity and mixity of the European Union constitutional order, and an inevitable move away from the clarity and simplicity of the Community legal order of the past.

In some ways, this is a paradoxical feature of the Amsterdam Treaty. One of the key concerns articulated by the European institutions themselves and by the Reflection Group of Member State representatives which was established to prepare the agenda for the 1996 IGC [intergovernmental conference] was that of *simplification*: bringing the EU closer to the ordinary person and making it more comprehensible. And indeed, Part Two to the ToA [Treaty of Amsterdam] consists of a tidying up section, which sets out to delete lapsed and obsolete provisions from the EC Treaty and to adapt others accordingly. Further, the final provisions of the ToA set out to renumber all of the Articles, titles and sections of the [Maastricht Treaty] and the EC Treaty. While this latter change is bound to confuse a generation of lawyers and students working with the old and the new numbers simultaneously, it might eventually make the Treaty layout somewhat less clumsy and awkward. However, it becomes quickly obvious that any simplification brought about by the ToA will be superficial only, and that the overall constitutional structure of the European Union is increasingly complex and tangles. To expect substantive simplification would, however, be entirely unrealistic. That the EU legal and constitutional order should be so complex and labyrinthine may not be very satisfactory, but it is hardly surprising, given that it is largely a reflection of the political compromises and differences of approach across a vast range of policy areas among fifteen different Member States.

---

21. Stephen Weatherhill & Paul Beaumont, EU Law: The Essential Guide to the Legal Workings of the European Union 23 (1999).

2. *The Legal Structure of the EU*

The legal basis of the institutions of the Communities is set forth in the EC TREATY, as supplemented and modified by subsequent treaties. The materials which follow present a condensed description of these institutions. For a fuller discussion of the institutional organs of the EU, *See* STEPHEN WEATHERHILL & PAUL BEAUMONT, EU LAW (3rd ed. 1999); PAUL CRAIG AND GRÁINNE DE BÚRCA, EU LAW: TEXT, CASES AND MATERIALS (2nd ed. 1998). For a basic reader on issues within the European Union, see THE EVOLUTION OF EU LAW (Paul Craig and Gráinne de Búrca, eds. 1999); The basic Treaties of the EC may be found on the web site maintained by the institutions of the European Union: <http://www.europa.eu.int>. The institutional organization of the modern EU is complex. This section provides a brief introduction to the institutions which together comprise the government of the EU.

a. European Council

The European Council is comprised of the heads of government of the Member States and the President of the Commission of the European Community, assisted by the ministers of foreign affairs and by a member of the EC Commission (formalized in the Single European Act, tit. I, Art. 2). The European Council meets twice a year. Its purpose is primarily advisory; it represents a direct means by which the heads of the governments of the Member States may influence the direction of EC integration. Thus, while it hasn't supplanted the EU Council (recall that the EU Council also consists of persons holding ministerial positions in the governments of the Member States), it has begun to acquire substantially more Community authority. It provides progress reports on the State of the EU to Parliament (influence). It sets broad guidelines on economic policy. It is heavily involved in monetary integration and foreign policy.

b. EC Council, or Council of Ministers

The EC Council is generally charged with enactment of "legislation" within the EU system. The EC Council is also the body which directly represents the interests of the Member States, as governmental units, within the formal structure of the EU. In some respects this harkens back to the time when a similar arrangement prevailed within the American federal system—the appointment of senators to the federal Congress before the enactment of a constitutional amendment mandating the direct popular election of senators.

The composition of the EC Council is determined in accordance with Art. 2 of the Merger Treaty. Unlike the members of the EC Commission, EC Council members are specifically intended to represent the interests of the Member State which each represents (and usually acts on instruction of the Member States they represent). Because membership is by "representatives," the actual representative at EC Council meeting will depend on the subject being discussed. As such, several EC Council meetings can be held simultaneously, although, as a legal matter, there is only one EC Council. The Office of President of the EC Council is held on a rotating basis by a representative of all Member States for a six month period.

Meetings of the EC Council are closed to the public and the records are confidential. Meetings can be called by the President or any member of the EC Council. Merger

Treaty Art. 3; Maastricht Art. 147. The EC Council operates pursuant to its own rules of procedure. Merger Treaty, Art. 5 (Rules of Procedure of the Council 79/868, 22 O.J. Eur. Comm. (No.L268) 1 (October 25, 1979), *modified by* 30 O.J. Eur. Comm. (No. L 291) 27 (Oct. 15, 1987).

The EC Council is served by a secretariat and by the Committee of Permanent Representatives ("COREPER"). Maastricht Art. 151. The secretariat services the President and the various committees set up by the EC Council (on which the EC Commission is usually entitled a representative). COREPER was officially created by the Merger Treaty. Merger Treaty, Art. 4. COREPER is responsible for preparing the work of the EC Council and carrying out such other tasks as may be presented by the EC Council. COREPER acts as a gatekeeper for the EC Council. It is divided into two groups (i) a technical group COREPER I, which does specialized work, and (ii) COREPER II which is made up of the representatives themselves and which handles the more politically delicate work. COREPER determines the agenda of the EC Council and advises the EC Council of issues which have and have not been agreed upon by COREPER II members.

The general powers of the EC Council are set forth at Art. 145 of the EC Treaty. The EC Council is the formal decision making body of the EC. It is the organ with the power to make decisions, but generally acts only on proposals presented to it by the EC Commission. *See, e.g.*, EC Treaty, Arts. 43(2), 100A.

Voting by the EC Council is accomplished in one of three ways, depending on the matter to be voted on: simple majority, unanimous consent, or qualified majority.

Simple majority voting is reserved for the following measures: (i) EC Council's rules of procedure (Merger Treaty, Art. 5); (ii) vocational training (EC Treaty, Art. 128); (iii) procedural rules of committees (EC Treaty, Art. 145); (iv) calling for a meeting to amend the Treaty (EC Treaty, Art. 236). A good basic explanation can be found in Stephen Weatherhill and Paul Beaumont, EU Law 79–92 (1999).

Unanimous consent is required for measures taken in the following areas: (i) constitutional measures changing the core powers and membership of the Communities (EC Treaty, arts. 235, 237); (ii) derogations from the EC Treaties (EEC Treaty, Art. 93(2), 76, 145); (iii) adoption of provisions relating to the free movement of people, the rights and interests of employed people and fiscal matters (EC Treaty, Art. 100a(2)); (iv) measures relating to the environment (SEA, Art. 25, EC Treaty, Art. 130s); joint projects with non-Member states, and scientific and technological programs (EC Treaty Art. 130Q(1)); where the EC Council seeks to amend a proposal submitted by the EC Commission (EC Treaty, Art. 149(1)).

Voting by qualified majority (as described at Art. 148, EC Treaty) is permitted for measures taken in the following areas: (i) measures to complete the internal market (EC Treaty, Art. 100a); (ii) certain research and technological development programs (EC Treaty, Art. 130Q(2)); (iii) certain economic and social cohesion programs, after unanimous adoption of a comprehensive proposal in this regard by the EC Council (EC Treaty, Art. 130E). Every Member State is assigned a "value" for its votes. In order to pass a measure, the number of "value votes" must exceed a certain number—now 62 votes cast by at least 10 Member States. The new formula has the effect of requiring more than two large states and two small states, or more than one large state and five small states, to block action by qualified majority. Qualified majority voting is designed to prevent dominance by a small coterie of states as well as to provide some power to large states to prevent measures from being passed. But this was passed more for the large states than for the small ones. Thus at least three large states can now block any measure.

c. *The European Commission (EC Commission)*

The EC Commission is generally charged with the proper execution of the Treaty and the administration of the Treaty obligations of the Member States. It is also the EU institution with the primary authority to originate EU legislation.

The Commission consists of 20 members who are to be independent of their national governments. Maastricht, amending EC Art. 157. Currently, France, the United Kingdom, Spain, Germany and Italy nominate two commissioners, the other Member States nominate one each. No Member State can have more than two members on the Commission. Maastricht Art. 157. Commissioners serve five (5) year terms. Maastricht Treaty, Art. 158(1). Through custom, the president of the EC Commission is chosen from among the members of the EC Commission after consultation with the Members States. The Maastricht Treaty now also requires consultation with the EU Parliament before the appointment of the President (Art. 158(2)). All Commission Members, together, must then be approved by the EU Parliament. This started January 7, 1995 (Art. 158(3)). Prior to Maastricht, Vice Presidents (six (6) in number) usually include at least one each from the larger Member States. All serve for two year terms. Merger Treaty, Art. 14. EC Commission action is approved by absolute majority vote. Merger Treaty, Art. 17. Maastricht reduces the number of Vice Presidents to a maximum of two (2). (Maastricht Art. 161)). The Commission acts by a majority of the total members (currently 9 votes). (Maastricht Art. 163).

Dismissal can occur in one of two ways: (i) The European Parliament has the power to dismiss the entire EC Commission on affirmative vote of 2/3 of the majority of its members. EC TREATY, Art. 144; ECSC TREATY, Art. 24, EURATOM TREATY, Art. 114; (ii) On petition of the EC Council or the EC Commission to the European Court of Justice, individual commissioners may be "retired" for failure to fulfill conditions required for the performance of his duties, or for serious misconduct. Merger Treaty, Art. 13, Maastricht Art. 160.

Organization of the EC Commission. Each EC Commissioner has his own personal staff, headed by a *chef de cabinet*, and each EC Commissioner oversees one or more of the EC Commission's subdivisions ("*directorates general*"). Five auxiliary services also serve the EC Commission: (i) Secretariat General; (ii) the Legal Service; (iii) Joint Interpreting and Conference Service; (iv) Statistical Office; and (v) Customs Union Service. Rules of Procedure of the Commission 63/41, Art. 16, 6 J.O. COMM. EUR. (No. 17) 181 (January 31, 1963) (These procedural rules have been enacted under authority of Merger Treaty, Art. 16).

The general powers of the EC Commission are set forth in Art. 155 of the EC TREATY. In connection therewith, you should note the following:

The EC Commission's more important function is to initiate substantially all Community legislation for adoption by the EC Council. EEC TREATY, Art. 43(2)3.

The EC Commission has very limited authority to adopt legislation. However, it is charged with the implantation of the rules the EC Council adopts (Art. 145, EEC TREATY, as amended by the SEA) In addition, the EC Commission has some authority to impose fines in addition to implementation authority in certain areas: usually in connection with the implementation of anti-trust policy, agricultural policy, anti-dumping and anti-subsidy policy.

The EC Commission can exercise power delegated to it by the EC Council. This power is overseen by the EC Council. *See* Einfuhr-und Vorratsstelle fur Getreide un Futtermittel v. Köster, Berodt & Co., Case 25/70, [1970] ECR 1161 (confirming power of the EC Council to oversee the delegation of rulemaking authority to the EC Commission).

The EC Commission also enforces compliance with the Community Treaties in two ways: (i) by addressing opinions to the Member States, and (ii) on failure to comply with the opinion, by an enforcement action brought before the European Court of Justice. EEC TREATY, Art. 169.

d. European Parliament ("EP")

The European Parliament consists of representatives of the people of the Member States. EC TREATY, Art. 137. With the entry of Sweden, Finland and Austria, the total number of Parliament members is 626, elected by direct universal suffrage (since 1979). ACT CONCERNING THE ELECTION OF THE REPRESENTATIVES OF THE ASSEMBLY BY DIRECT UNIVERSAL SUFFRAGE (the "Universal Suffrage Act"), Art. 2. The distribution of seats among the Member States corresponds roughly to relative population. Act Concerning the Election of the Representatives of the Assembly by Direct Universal Suffrage, Art. 2. Representatives serve five (5) year terms. Universal Suffrage Act, Art. 3. The President of the Parliament is elected by secret ballot from among the members. EEC TREATY, Art. 140. The Maastricht Treaty created the office of Ombudsman. This person (office) is entitled to receive complaints from an EU citizen or resident (Maastricht Art. 138e) and report on his findings to Parliament.

The members of the Parliament are affiliated with political groups, but cannot be members of the government of the Member State which they represent. Maastricht encourages the formation of political parties at the European level. Maastricht Art. 138a. They are supposed to represent the European people rather than the governments of the member States and so are elected on the basis of Euro-party affiliation, and sit with other members of their party in the Parliament.

The European Parliament acts by absolute majority. EEC TREATY, art. 141. It operates through committees on the basis of procedures that it adopts. EEC TREATY, art. 142. The Parliament generally has no independent legislative power. However, the Parliament has been given an increasingly important voice in influencing legislation through its powers under the consultation, co-operation and co-determination procedures required for the enactment of certain provisions. Parliament may also ask questions of the EC Commission and the EC Council. EEC TREATY, Art. 140. The questions are published in the Official Journal of the European Union (OJ).

Under a number of provisions of the EEC TREATY, the Parliament must be consulted by the EC Commission and the EC Council—but both bodies are free to disregard Parliament's opinion. On consulting, *see* EC Treaty, Arts. 43 (agricultural policy), 54 (right of establishment), 56 (same), 87 (rules about competition), 130Q (scientific and technical programs), 130S (environmental programs); EURATOM TREATY Arts. 31, 76, 85, 90). Failure to consult can void the adoption of any measure. *See* S. A. Roquette Freres v. EC Council, Case 138/79, [1980] ECR 3333.

Since the adoption of the Single European Act, the EC Parliament acquired additional indirect power to influence legislation. EC Treaty, Art. 149. this new authority applies wherever the EC Treaty requires the EC Commission or EC Council to co-operate with the Parliament on any measure. This would include all legislation with respect to the elimination of discrimination on the grounds of nationality, free movement of workers and establish, free movement of services, and harmonization measures relating to the establishment and functioning of the Communities' internal market. SEA, Art. 6(1). This procedure amounts to a mandatory second reading of proposals. For a description of the new procedures, *see* D. LASOK & J.W. BRIDGE, LAW AND INSTITUTIONS OF THE EUROPEAN COMMUNITIES 230–31 (5th ed. 1991).

Since the adoption of the Maastricht Treaty, the EP has also enjoyed a power of co-decision with respect to certain measures. Maastricht Art. 189 now states that "the European Parliament acting jointly with the Council, the Council and the Commission shall make regulations and issue directives, take decisions, make recommendations or deliver opinions." Co-decision requires submission of proposals by the Commission to both the Parliament and Council, the requirement for adoption of a common position, in the absence of which the Commission and Council may still pass the provision, but only by unanimous vote of the Council. If Parliament seeks to reject the proposal (rather than work out a common position or seek amendment), then a conciliation process is initiated. If conciliation fails, the Council may still adopt the measure by unanimous vote, but, for the first time, the Parliament may veto the passage of the proposal by vote of an absolute majority of its members. For a detailed analysis of the cooperation and co-determination processes, see, T. Hartley, *Constitutional and Institutional Aspects of the Maastricht Agreement*, 42 INT'L & COMP. L. Q. 213 (1993).

e. The Court of Auditors

This body was established by Maastricht Treaty (new EC Art. 188b), the purpose of which is primarily to examine the revenue and expenditure of the Community.

f. EC Committee of the Regions

In order to provide the poorer or less populous regions of the EU some measure of protection, a Committee of Regions is established under the Maastricht Treaty Art. 198. It is meant to provide consultation whenever such is deemed necessary. Its effectiveness is as yet unproven. It has, however, proven to be a place in which regional differences have been sharpened, and regional positions clarified during the course of law making within the EU.

Consider by comparison the Constitutional formulation of a House of Representatives; does it accomplish the same things?

g. The EC Economic and Social Committee

The Economic and Social committee was established by the EC Treaty, Art. 193, and given advisory status. It must consist of representatives of various economic and social activities, "in particular, representatives of producers, farmers, carriers, workers, dealers, craftsmen, professional occupations, and representatives of the general public." EC Treaty, Art. 193. The representatives are selected by the EC Council by unanimous vote for four year terms, each Member State entitled to a number of representatives roughly corresponding to its relative population within the Community. EC Treaty, Art. 194. They are normally selected from lists submitted by the Member States containing twice as many candidates as there are slots allotted. EC Treaty, Art. 195. While the Economic and Social Committee may be consulted by the EC Council or the EC Commission whenever either body deems it appropriate, both must consult with the Committee when required to do so by the terms of the EC Treaty. EC Treaty, Art. 198. Failure to do so when required could well void any action taken by the EC Council or EC Commission. (See discussion below).

h. Court of Justice of the European Communities ("ECJ")

The composition and organization of the ECJ is treated in the following sources: EEC Treaty, Arts. 165–168 (as amended by the adjusted First Act of Accession 1972, Arts. 17–19, Second Act of Accession 1979, Arts. 16 and 135, Third Act of Accession 1985, Arts. 17–19, 384, and SEA, Arts. 11–12) and the Protocol on the Statute of the Court of Justice, tits. I–II. The ECJ consists of 15 Judges. EC Treaty, Art. 165. Each serves six (6) year renewable terms, the terms of six and seven of which expire in three year intervals. EC Treaty, Art. 167. While the judges are supposed to be appointed by "common accord of the governments of the Member States" *Id.* in practice, each Member State has a judge of its nationality on the ECJ. Much of the procedure of the ECJ is largely derived from French law. The ECJ sits in Luxembourg.

The ECJ is assisted by eight (8) *advocates general.* They are charged with the task of preparing non-binding "reasoned submissions" on cases before the ECJ in advance of the ECJ's ruling. EEC TREATY, Art. 166. These submissions are to be made in open court with complete impartiality and independence. These submissions are usually published along with the decisions in the case. The function of the advocates general are roughly similar to those of the *Commissaire du Gouvernement* at the French *Conseil d'Etat,* to act as the embodied "conscience of the ECJ." HAMSON, EXECUTIVE DISCRETION AND JUDICIAL CONTROL 80 (1954). *See* D. LASOK & J.W. BRIDGE, LAW AND INSTITUTIONS OF THE EUROPEAN COMMUNITIES 283 (5th ed. 1991). In practice, each of the four (4) larger Member States selects an advocate general of its nationality. Since 1993, Spain has joined the group of states entitled to select an advocate general. The remaining three advocates general positions are chosen from among the nationals of the other Member States by rotation.

The ECJ is subdivided into six (6) panels—four (4) of which consist of three (3) judges, and the remaining two (2) consist of six (6) judges. *See* EC TREATY, Art. 165. Decisions of the full court are valid if seven members are sitting. Protocol on the Statute of the Court of Justice, Art. 15. The ECJ remains permanently in session. *Id.*, Art. 14.

The general procedure of the ECJ is set forth in Title III of the Protocol on the Statute of the Court of Justice (Arts. 17–45). These may be amended by unanimous vote of the EC Council. EC Treaty, Art. 188. The ECJ may supplement its procedures by adopting rules of procedure—all of which require the unanimous approval of the EC Council. *Id.* Such rules of procedure have been adopted. *See* Rules of Procedure of the Court of Justice. The current rules were adopted in 1974. *See Rules of Procedure,* O.J. EUR. COMM. (No. L 238) (1979), as amended by O.J. EUR. COMM. (No. L 199) (1981), O.J. EUR. COMM. (No. L 165) (1987), O.J. EUR. COMM. (No. L 241) (1989). Very generally, the procedures (following French legal tradition) are divided into three stages: (i) a written stage (the most important), (ii) a preparatory stage, and (iii) an oral stage. For a description of court procedure, *see* D. LASOK & J.W. BRIDGE, LAW AND INSTITUTIONS OF THE EUROPEAN COMMUNITIES 285–290 (5th ed. 1991).

The SEA permitted the ECJ, subject to consultation with the EC Commission and the unanimous approval of the EC Council, to create Courts of First Instance. These courts are empowered to hear cases on points of law, subject to appeal to the ECJ. EC TREATY, Art. 168A. For a thorough discussion of the Courts of First Instance, see, T. WILLET, THE COURT OF FIRST INSTANCE OF THE EUROPEAN COMMUNITIES (1990). The Courts of First Instance have become a vital source of relief for the ECJ. Their jurisdiction has been expanded in the years since the adoption of the SEA. It is even possible that the Courts of First Instance will someday form the core of a system of lower courts with general appeal up to the ECJ.

The overall purpose of the ECJ is to "ensure that in the interpretation and application of this Treaty the law is observed." EC Treaty, Art. 164. The ECJ, like our own federal courts, has used its overall review authority in an integrationist manner. It has powerfully insisted on the adherence by Member States of the doctrines of direct effect (whereby Community law is said to confer direct rights on individuals which must be enforced by the courts of the Member States), supremacy and preemption in favor of the Community Treaties. *See* 1 CAPPELLETTI, SECCOMBE & WEILER, INTEGRATION THROUGH LAW: EUROPE AND THE AMERICAN FEDERAL EXPERIENCE bk 2 at 30 (1986); LAW OF THE EUROPEAN COMMUNITIES 1301 (Vaughan, ed.), *in* 51 HALSBURY'S LAWS OF ENGLAND (4th ed. 1986).

The jurisdiction of the ECJ is broad, and generally covers four (4) principal categories: (i) adversarial proceedings based on the Community Treaties or rights/obligations created by Community law; (ii) interlocutory rulings on legal points raised by national courts; (iii) advice to other EC institutions on specified points; and (iv) certain EURATOM TREATY appeals. Both individuals (persons and companies) and Member States have standing to bring actions before the ECJ. EC Treaty, Art. 173. The ECJ has such power to assess penalties as may be accorded it by the EC Council. EEC TREATY, Art. 172. The ECJ has broad jurisdiction over four types of actions: (i) Direct Actions Against a Member State for Failure to Fulfill a Treaty Obligation; (ii) Direct Actions to Annul Acts of the EC Commission or EC Council; (iii) Direct Actions for Failure of EC Institutions to Act; (iv) Preliminary Rulings on matters affecting Treaty rights and obligations presented by the national courts of Member States.

I. *Direct Actions Against a Member State for Failure to Fulfill a Treaty Obligation.* EEC TREATY, Arts. 169 & 170. Before the EC Commission can bring an action under Article 169, the EC Commission must give the Member State a chance to submit its "observations." Generally, in the context of Company Law harmonization, such actions are brought where a Member State fails to enact legislation required under a Community Directive. Upon a finding of failure to comply with Community obligations, the Member State is obligated to take the necessary measures to comply with the judgment of the ECJ. EC Treaty, Art. 171. The EC Commission has been aggressive in its attempts to compel Member States to apply the directives in the area of company law harmonization, and the ECJ has been receptive to its arguments, adopting an expansive reading of the applicability of Council directives. In that connection, consider the following.

II. *Direct Actions to Annul Acts of the EC Commission or EC Council.* EC Treaty, art. 173. Such actions can be brought by the EC Council, EC Commission, a Member State, or under very limited circumstances, an individual (*see, e.g.* Transocean Marine Paint Ass'n v. EC Commission [1974] E.C.R. 1063; Calpak SpA v. EC Commission, [1980] E.C.R. 1949 at 1961, set forth below). On a finding that the action is well founded, the

ECJ will annul the act. However, if a regulation is voided, the ECJ may determine that some of the effects of the regulation voided will remain "definitive." EC Treaty, Art. 174. The following cases illustrate both the power the ECJ has respecting the nullification of EC Council action and the difficulty of the bringing of a direct action by an individual citizen of a Member State.

The two cases that follow are intended to provide students with an introduction to the form of opinions of the ECJ, and the relationship between the opinion of the Advocate General and the Court itself. The cases also introduce the student to issues of the regulation of the lawmaking power of the institutions of the EU. In particular, the cases illustrate the basic procedural rights accorded in the EU system and the nature and limitations of EU regulatory power over individuals and enterprises. In reviewing the following cases, consider the extent to which the doctrines set forth therein on the power of the ECJ to nullify actions of Community institutions and to limit the right of individuals to bring such actions to the ECJ parallel or depart from the model of US federal constitutional law. Can the developing European doctrines be said to follow US federal rules of the powers of the Supreme Court to declare the Constitutionality of statutes and of the federal doctrine of standing?

Transocean Marine Paint Association v. EC Commission

(Case 17/74) European Court of Justice
[1974] ECR 1063, [1974] 2 CMLR 459
23 October 1974

* * *

J. P. Warner, the Advocate-General delivered his opinion on 19 September 1974.

'Marine paint' is a technical generic term used to describe those kinds of paint that are applied to ships. It is common ground between the parties in this case that the technically more advanced marine paints, about 80% of the total, cannot be used for other purposes.

An important characteristic of the marine paint market is that the customers, i.e. shipowners, demand a world-wide service, in the sense that the paint chosen for a particular ship must be available, not only at the yard where she is built, but subsequently, for maintenance purposes, at any port, or at all events any major port, where she may call. Moreover, the supplier of marine paint must in general be prepared to provide on the spot technical advice and assistance.

Those characteristics make it difficult for a small or medium-sized manufacturer of marine paint in any country to compete with the multinational groups. So it was that, in 1959, a number of medium-sized manufacturers in different countries joined together to form the Transocean Marine Paint Association, their essential idea being that together they would be able to provide that world-wide service that none of them could afford alone.

A basic feature of the Association is that each member manufacturers paint of the same composition and quality and sells it under the same 'Transocean' trade-mark. In order to achieve this object, the members exchange technical know-how, afford each other preferential treatment in the matter of patent-licensing and submit to quality control. One consequence is that, in effect, they pool the results of their research. This, in itself, strengthens their competitive position vis-a-vis the multinationals.

It is of crucial importance to the Association that it should, so far as possible, have a member in each major maritime country, so that 'Transocean' paints may be readily available wherever ships may call, backed up by the necessary technical service. The evidence in the case evinces the anxiety that has been caused to the Association by the loss of its Norwegian and Swedish members, the former through a take-over bid and the latter because it ceased production for economic reasons. Similar anxiety was engendered recently by a threat, in circumstances that I shall detail, that the Association might be compelled to shed its French and Spanish members.

The membership of the Association has not remained fixed. It appears that at its foundation it had 18 members. With some losses and some gains over the years it now numbers 20. Of the 20, seven are established in the EEC, namely in Belgium, Denmark, the Federal Republic, France, Italy, the Netherlands and the United Kingdom respectively. One is established in an associated territory, namely Curacao and the remaining twelve are established in third countries, namely in Spain, Turkey, south Africa, Mauritius, Thailand, Malaysia, Singapore, Hong-Kong, the Philippines, Japan, Australia and the U.S.A., respectively.

The marine paint turnover of the members is unequal, the Japanese member by itself accounting for some 60% of the total of it.

Thus the Association, though its Central Office is in Rotterdam, is not preponderantly European.

Under the Charter of the Association, each member undertakes to promote sales of Transocean marine paints, and to supply such paints, in its own country and 'allocated territories.' It also undertakes not to participate, directly or indirectly, in any other similar organization relating to marine paints. But no member has an exclusive right to supply marine paints in its territory. There have always been, in the Charter of the Association, provisions envisaging the 'export' of marine paints by any member into the territory of another as well as provisions envisaging the securing of orders by members for each other. Those provisions have been accompanied by a system of 'commissions' payable by members to each other in various circumstances, though it is expressly stated in the Charter that the scale of 'commissions' there set out is 'for guidance only' and that 'Members are expected to negotiate in good faith a suitable commission rate contingent with the particular requirements of the case'.

The Association is not in any way a price-ring: each member is free to fix its own prices.

I should add, in order to make what follows clear, that the affairs of the Association are managed by a Board of Directors representative of the members, and that the Charter contains an arbitration clause.

On 29 October 1962, following the coming into force of the EEC Treaty and of Regulation No 17 of the Council, the Association applied to the Commission for negative clearance of its Charter under Article 2 of that Regulation and, failing that, for exemption under Article 85 (3) of the Treaty.

On 27 June 1967 the Commission issued its Decision. It is plain from this that, in the meantime, the Association had amended its Charter in a number of ways, at the behest of the Commission. having regard to those amendments the Commission felt able, not indeed to grant negative clearance, but to grant exemption under Article 85 (3) until 31

December 1972, subject to certain conditions, contained in Article 4 of the Decision (OJ 163 of 20. 7. 1967).

Those were that:

'1. The following should be notified without delay to the Commission:

(a) all alterations which may take place in the composition of the Association;

(b) all amendments and additions to the Charter;

(c) all the decisions of the Board of Directors and all arbitral awards relating to the application or interpretation of the provisions of the Charter taken into consideration in the present Decision.

2. The Commission should be supplied once annually, and on the first occasion for the year 1967, with a report on the activity of the Association, on the volume of production and on the volume and amount of the sales of each of the members in the marine paint sector, making a distinction between the 'Transocean' paints and the other marine paints which they manufacture, on the volume of deliveries of marine paints for which the members of the Association established in the Common Market are reciprocally required to pay commissions and on the amount and rates of the relevant commissions.'

By letter dated 27 October 1972 the Association applied to the Commission for an extension of its exemption for a further ten years. This brought forth from the Commission a notice of objections dated 27 July 1973, in which two main points were taken.

First the Commission observed that the most important competitors of the members of the Association were the large chemical concerns and that by far the most important change in the situation since it had issued its Decision of 27 June 1967 was that the French and Spanish members had each been taken over by one of these: the French member, 'Astral', by the Dutch group AKZO and the Spanish member, 'Urruzola', by the German BASF. The Commission pointed out that, in reaching its Decision, it had had particular regard to the fact that by combining and coordinating their sales networks as medium-sized undertakings the members would be in a position to compete more effectively with the large marine paint manufacturers already represented in all the important countries. It would be inconsistent with that approach to permit the members of the Association to include subsidiaries of such large manufacturers. The Commission would therefore make it a condition of granting an extension that either Astral and Urruzola withdraw from the Association or AKZO and BASF dispose of their holdings in those undertakings.

The second point taken by the Commission was that the Charter contained two restrictions which, having regard to the growing strength of the Association, could no longer be justified. The first was a provision under which a member was precluded from exporting marine paint other than 'Transocean' into the territory of another without the latter's consent. The second was a provision under which a member exporting 'Transocean' paint into the territory of another, or supplying it to a ship from another's territory, was to pay a commission to that other. The Commission intimated that it would make any extension of the exemption conditional on the removal of these restrictions.

Without any explanation at all, the Commission added that it would make the extension conditional on a further requirement and it is in this that lies the germ of the dispute in this case.

My Lords, the original of the notice of objections was in Dutch. The commission has supplied to the Court (Annex 1 to the Defense) an unrevised translation of it into English. In this translation the material paragraph, paragraph 3 (c), reads as follows:

> 'In addition to complying with the conditions laid down in Article 4 of the Decision of 27 June 1967, the Transocean associates must notify the commission without delay regarding any change in the participatory position of the associates.'

In a letter dated 6 February 1974 (Annex 2 to the Reply) written by the Commission, in English, to the Association's Counsel, in circumstances to which I shall come, the crucial phrase ('iedere wijziging in de deelnemingsverhoudingen van de leden') is translated as 'every change in the financial interests of the members'.

There are also before the Court two versions of that phrase in French. The first is in a translation of the relevant parts of the notice of objections made by the Court's own translation service. In this, paragraph 3 (c) reads as follows:

> 'outre les conditions figurant a l'article 4 de la decision du 27 juin 1967, les membres de Transocean doivent notifier sans delai a la Commission toute modification intervenant dans l'importance respective de la participation des membres a l'association.'

The other was put forward by Counsel for the Commission at the hearing, by way of correction of an earlier French translation submitted by the Commission. It was: 'toute modification qui interviendrait dans la situation des liens et participations des membres'.

Such, my Lords, is the material on which those of us who do not have the advantage of knowing Dutch must prima facie form a view to the meaning and content of paragraph 3 (c). I say 'prima facie' because I think that in fact the way in which the Association, which was represented throughout by Dutch Counsel, reacted to that paragraph is very significant.

On the basis of the translations alone I would have formed the view that, in paragraph 3 (c), the Commission was foreshadowing only a requirement that it should be kept informed as to the relations between the members of the Association—a requirement that would have been readily understandable.

That seems to have been the understanding of the Association. It treated paragraph 3 (c) as innocuous. It made its observations on the notice of objections first by letter dated 6 September 1973 and then at a hearing held by the commission on 27 September 1973. On neither occasion was paragraph 3 (c) even referred to. (See annexes 4 and 5 to the Application and II and III to the Defense). On both occasions—apart from seeking to show that the Charter did not come within Article 85 (1) of the Treaty at all—the Association addressed itself only to the two main points raised in the notice of objections. As the subsequent Decision of the Commission shows, it did so with marked success.

That Decision (Annex 7 to the Application) was issued on 21 December 1973. It extended the exemption under Article 85 (3) until 31 December 1978 without any condition whatever relating to Astral or Urruzola. Moreover it did not require the complete removal of the provision in the Charter about the payment of commission on export orders, but merely its modification so that it should not apply irrespective of the services rendered by the recipient member in obtaining or executing the order in question. But Article 3 of the Decision declared that is was subject to the following obligations (I read from the authentic text, which is in English, and in which the Charter of the Association is referred to as 'the Agreement'):

'1. That the Commission shall be informed without delay of the following matters:

(a) Any amendment or addition to the agreement.

(b) Any decision taken by the Board of Directors or the result of any arbitration held, pursuant to the restrictive provisions of the Agreement...

(c) Any change in the composition of membership,

(d) Any links by way of common Directors or managers between a member of the Association and any other company or firm in the paints sector or any financial participation by a member of the Association in such outside companies or firms or vice versa including all changes in such links or participations already in existence.

2. A report is to be submitted by the Association annually to the Commission on the activities of the Association and in particular on improvements in the production and marketing of marine paint products achieved.'

The Association at once protested to the Commission about paragraph (1) (d). In a letter written to the Commission on its behalf by its Counsel on 21 January 1974 (Annex 1 to the Reply) he pointed out that the obligation contained in that paragraph had not been mentioned in the notice of objections or in any other statement, formal or informal, made by the Commission to the Association. He contended that the Commission was accordingly in breach of Article 4 of Regulation No 99/63/EEC of the Commission (OJ 127 of 20. 8. 1963), which provides:

> 'The Commission shall in its decisions deal only with those objections raised against undertakings and associations of undertakings in respect of which they have been afforded the opportunity of making known their views.'

He explained that, in inserting this obligation it its Decision, the Commission placed the Association in a difficulty. The information available at the Central Office of the Association pertained only to members' activities in the marine paint field. With regard to their activities in other fields the members, particularly those in Asia and in the USA, tended 'to cover themselves in clouds of secrecy of varying density'. He expressed the fear that the non-EEC members might regard the provision of the information required by the Commission too high a price to pay for the retention of the EEC members in the Association. (In his pleadings he expresses an alternative fear, that the members who are remote from Europe might in fact fail to supply the information and so place the other members in jeopardy of fines). He suggested an alternative formulation of the obligation, which would confine it to any link 'between a member of the association situated within the EEC and any other company or firm in the Marine Paint sector, or between a member of the association and any other company or firm situated within the EEC in the Marine Paint sector'.

By the letter of 6 February 1974 to which I have already referred, the Commission replied that it was unable to agree that reference to the obligation in question was not made in the notice of objections. 'It was made very clear', the letter said, 'that the commission was most concerned with the links between the members of Transocean, including the members outside the Community and other paint producers, and the objections expressly referred to the obligation of informing the Commission of every change in the financial interests of the members ("iedere wijziging in de deelnemingsverhoudingen van de leden")'. The letter concluded by stating that the Association's complaint could not therefore be entertained and by observing that it was of course open to the Association to challenge the Decision of the Commission before the Court.

It is in those circumstances that the Application in this case was lodged on 1 March 1974 by 16 of the members of the Association. The Application is made under Article 173 of the Treaty and the Applicants thereby claim, in effect, that paragraph (1) (d) of Article 3 of the Decision be declared void. In support of this claim they advance two contentions.

First they say that the Decision is vitiated by, to use the words of Article 173, an 'infringement of an essential procedural requirement', because the Commission was in breach of Articles 2 (1) and 4 of Regulation No 99/66/EEC. Article 4 of that Regulation I have already read. Article 2 (1) is merely the one that provides that the Commission shall inform undertakings and associations of undertakings in writing of the objections raised against them.

Secondly the Applicants contend that the Commission acted ultra vires because, in formulating the obligation in paragraph 1 (d), it failed to distinguish—

(a) between the marine paint market and the markets for paint in general, and

(b) between links relevant to the common Market and those not.

With regard to the first contention the Commission argues in the first place that it is not bound to inform applicants for exemption under Article 85 (3) of conditions or obligations that it is considering attaching, pursuant to Article 8 (1) of Regulation No 17, to a decision in their favour. It says that Articles 2 and 4 of Regulation No 99/63/EEC—and, I would suppose, Article 3 too, for Articles 2, 3 and 4 of that Regulation form a coherent scheme—apply only to 'objections' that may lead to a decision unfavorable to the undertaking or to the association concerned. In the second place the commission submits that, in any event, the Applicants in the present case were apprised of what it had in mind.

My Lords, I hope that I shall be acquitted of discourtesy towards the Commission if I deal with the latter submission shortly. It seems to me plainly inconsistent with the facts, which I have recited. The Commission relies of course on paragraph 3 (c) of the notice of objections. But this was, at best, ambiguous and, as subsequent events showed, it certainly failed to convey to the Applicants that the Commission was envisaging anything on the lines of Article 3 (1) (d) of its Decision. Your Lordships will remember that, at the hearing, Counsel for the Applicants expressed himself as having been 'amazed' by the Commission's interpretation of it. For the rest, the arguments of the Commission in support of this submission amount to no more than saying that the applicants ought to have divined what it had in mind from the anxieties it had expressed about the links between some members of the Association and multinational groups. This, in my opinion, just will not do. I would agree, of course, that, if the commission was under a duty to inform the Applicants of what it had in mind, it would fulfill that duty by giving them an indication of it in general terms and need not formulate it in every precise detail. But some unambiguous communication there must be.

So the question is whether, as a matter of law, the Commission was under such a duty. I agree with the Commission that Articles 2, 3 and 4 of Regulation No 99/63/EEC are not here in point. A reading of Regulation no 17, together with Regulation No 99/63/EEC, evinces clearly that the authors of those Regulations distinguished between 'objections' of the kind with which those Articles are concerned and 'conditions and obligations' of the kind that may be imposed by the Commission under Article 8 of Regulation No 17. I do not overlook that Regulation No 99/63/EEC was adopted in implementation of Article 19 of Regulation No 17 and that the latter Article expressly refers to Article 8 of the same Regulations. But it does so in terms that indicate that it is concerned only with 'objections' that may lead to a refusal of exemption under Article 85 (3) of the Treaty. It could indeed hardly do otherwise. One can readily figure a case where, at the outset, the Commission has only objections to granting exemption, and is subsequently persuaded, by representations made by the undertakings concerned, to grant it subject to conditions or obligations. One could hardly expect the Commission, in such a case, to anticipate those conditions or obligations in its notice of objections.

That, however, is, in my opinion, far from being the end of the question.

There is a rule embedded in the law of some of our countries that an administrative authority, before wielding a statutory power to the detriment of a particular person, must in general hear what that person has to say about the matter, even if the statute does not expressly require it. 'Audi alteram partem' or, as it is sometimes expressed, 'audiatur et altera pars'. I say that the rule applies 'in general' because it is subject to exceptions, as are most legal principles.

In the law of England the rule is centuries old, firmly established and of daily application. It is considered to be a 'rule of natural justice', a somewhat flamboyant and sometimes criticized phrase embodying a concept akin to what is, in French-speaking countries, more soberly and, I think, more accurately, referred to as 'les principes generaux du droit'. The late Professor de Smith, in his book 'Judicial Review of Administrative Action' (3rd Ed. at p. 134 et seq.), traced its origins and development. I will not take up your Lordships' time with an account of them. The most often cited expression of the rule is in the judgment of Byles J. in Cooper v Wandsworth Board of Works (1863) 14 C.B.N.S. 180, where he said that 'although there are no positive words in a statute requiring that the party shall be heard, yet the justice of the common law will supply the omission of the legislature'. In England today there is no scope for controversy about the existence of the rule, but only about the circumstances in which it may be held inapplicable and about the manner in which it is to be applied in particular instances—consider the judgments in the House of Lords in Ridge v Baldwin [1964] A.C. 40. I know, my Lords, of no exception to the rule, acknowledged in English law, which could have deprived the Applicants in the circumstances of the present case of the right to be heard before being subjected to an obligation such as that contained in Article 3 (1) (d) of the commission's Decision.

There can be no doubt that the rule forms part also of the law of Scotland (consider Malloch v Aberdeen Corporation 1971 S.L.T. 245; [1971] 1 W.L.R. 1578) and of the laws of Denmark (see Andersen, 'Dansk Forvaltningsret', at p. 337 et seq.), of Germany (See Forsthoff, 'Lehrbuch des Verwaltungsrechts', 10th Ed., at p. 235 et seq.) and of Ireland (see Kelly, 'Fundamental Rights in the Irish Law and Constitutions', at p. 313–314).

It has been said by Professor Vedel that the rule 'audi alteram partem' does not exist in French administrative law (see, for instance, his 'Cours de Droit Administratif', p. 536). Professor Waline, on the other hand, in an article on the rule ('Livre Jubilaire' du Conseil d'Etat du Grand-Duche de Luxembourg, 1957, pp. 495–506) suggests on the contrary that it does. In my opinion, it matters little whether the applicable rule is subsumed under the title 'audi alteram partem' or, as Professor Vedel would prefer, under the concept of the 'droits de la defense'. What is undoubted is that French administrative law does acknowledge the existence of those 'principes generaux du droit' which I {1088} have mentioned and which are applicable even in the absence of any specific legislative provision. The relevant decisions of the Conseil d'Etat are collected by Professor Waline in his article, and I need not rehearse them. It appears that the principle here in question is of fairly recent origin in French law, and that its scope is not yet settled. The decisions of the Conseil d'Etat evince three different approaches: the narrowest being to apply it only when the decision of the administrative authority concerned is in the nature of a sanction; a slightly wider approach which would apply it in any case where the decision of that authority is based on the character or on the behaviour of the person to be affected; and a third approach which is virtually as wide as that of the English common law. I should perhaps add that Professor Vedel refers to French law as being in this respect 'plutot retardataire' and 'en voie d'evolution (see 'Cours de Droit Administratif', p. 534, and 'Droit Administratif' 5th Ed., p. 279); and this is echoed by Professor Waline who refers to the principle 'audi alteram partem' as 'un principe en voie de developpement' (p. 496).

The position in Belgium and in Luxembourg is similar, though the conseils d'Etat of those countries seem to have been less hesitant in developing the principle than that of France (see as to Belgium an article by Professor L. P. Suetens in Tijdschrift voor Bestuurswetensschappen en Publiek Recht, 1970, et p. 388, and as to Luxembourg the decisions of the Conseil d'Etat of 13 April 1961 in Lorse v Ministre des Transports (Aff. No 5811), of 5th August 1966 in Roth v Ministres de l'Interieur, de la Sante Publique et des Travaux Publics (Aff. No 5968) and of 9th July 1971 in Colot v Ministre du Tresor (Aff. No 6136).

In Italy the consiglio di Stato has held that there is no general principle of law requiring an administrative authority to inform those concerned of its proposals so as to enable them to comment (Sez. IV, 15 May 1970, n. 345, Rass. Cons. di Stato 1970, I, p. 828, at p. 834). And it seems that the law of the Netherlands is similar, in this respect, to that of Italy.

My Lords, that review, which I have sought to keep short, of the laws of the Member States, must, I think, on balance, lead to the conclusion that the right to be heard forms part of those rights which 'the law' referred to in Article 164 of the Treaty upholds, and of which, accordingly, it is the duty of this Court to ensure the observance.

I would therefore reject the contention of the Commission that it was under no duty to inform the Applicants of what it had in mind before imposing on them the obligation contained in Article 3 (1) (d) of its Decision.

In support of that contention, the Commission pointed to Article 11 of Regulation No 17, which enables the commission, in carrying out the duties assigned to it by Article 89 of the Treaty and by provisions adopted under Article 87 thereof, to 'obtain all necessary information from the Governments and competent authorities of the Member States and from undertakings and associations of undertakings'. The commission's argument was that that Article contains no express provision entitling the undertakings and associations of undertakings there referred to to make observations on the question whether they should be required to supply the information called for by the Commission. So it does not. But it is, to my mind, significant that Article 11 envisages a two-stage procedure. First the Commission is to send out its 'request for information' to an undertaking or association of undertakings, with copy to the competent authority of the Member State in whose territory the seat of the undertaking or association of undertakings is situated. In its request the Commission is, by paragraph 3 of Article 11, to state the legal basis and the purpose of the request and also the penalties for {1089} supplying incorrect information. Then, by paragraph 5 (OJ 13 of 21. 2. 1962):

> 'When an undertaking or association of undertakings does not supply the information requested within the time limit fixed by the Commission, or supplies incomplete information, the Commission shall by decision require the information to be supplied. The decision shall specify what information is required, fix an appropriate time limit within which it is to be supplied and indicate the penalties

provided for...and the right to have the decision reviewed by the Court of Justice.'

What possible purpose can this two-stage procedure serve, unless it be to afford an opportunity for any observations of the 'undertaking or associations of undertakings' concerned, as well as of the competent authorities of the relevant Member State or Member States, to be made and considered before the Commission reaches a final decision?

Thus, to my mind, far from bolstering the contention of the Commission, reference to Article 11 serves only to underline that that contention is misconceived.

I conclude that, in the present case, the members of the Association were entitled to be heard on the merits of the order proposed to be made by the Commission. Indeed, there is, to my mind, in this respect, no sensible dividing line between the withdrawal of the exemption and its extension subject to conditions to be imposed by the Commission. As the Commission was bound to hear the members of the Association before the exemption could be withdrawn, so it was bound to hear them before imposing the requirement which the Applicants have challenged.

* * *

I am therefore of the opinion

1. that Article 3 (1) (d) of the Decision of the Commission should be declared void;

2. that the case should be remitted to the Commission to determine, after having heard the members of the Association, what obligation should be imposed on them to supply to the Commission information about their links with undertakings outside the Association; and

3. that the Commission should be ordered to pay the costs of this action. {1092}

DECISION:

1. By Decision of 21 December 1973 the Commission, pursuant to Article 85 (3) of the EEC Treaty, renewed, subject to new conditions, the exemption from the prohibition contained in Article 85 (1), which had been granted, by Decision of 27 June 1967, to an agreement restricting competition on the market in marine paints, concluded between the undertakings constituting the Transocean Marine Paint Association (hereinafter referred to as the Association).

2. Inter alia, Article 3 (1) (d) of the Decision requires members of the Association to inform the Commission without delay of 'any links by way of common directors or managers between a member of the Association and any other company or firm in the paints sector or any financial participation by a member of the Association in such outside companies or vice-versa including all changes in such links or participations already in existence'.

3. This action has been brought for the purpose of annulling that single provision.

4. The applicants firstly state that the obligation in issue was mentioned neither in the 'notice of objections' of 27 July 1973, nor at the time of the hearing on 27 September 1973, and that furthermore it was not mentioned in any letter or memorandum from the Commission, prior to the Decision, so that they were never given the opportunity to make their views known on this subject. Accordingly, as regards the clause in issue, the Commission is said to have infringed rules of procedure laid down by Regu-

lation No 99/63 of the Commission of 25 July 1963 (OJ 127 of 20. 8. 1963), on the hearings provided for in Article 19 of Regulation No 17 of the Council of 6 February 1962 (OJ 13 of 21. 2. 1962) and in particular Articles 2 and 4 of the said Regulation no 99/63.

5. Secondly, the applicants allege an infringement of Article 85 of the Treaty and of Article 8 (1) of Regulation No 17, in that the obligation imposed upon the undertakings is wider in scope than anything which may be imposed upon them under Article 85.

6. In communication of 27 July 1973 entitled 'notice of objections', drawn up in Dutch, the Commission stated that a simple renewal of the exemption could not be envisaged, since the position of the members of the Association on the marine paints market had changed as a result of the increase in the number of undertakings composing the Association, the increased size of certain of them and the links which two of the members, Astral and Urruzola, had forged with large industrial chemical concerns.

7. The Commission added that it was nevertheless willing to renew the exemption for a period of five years, but at the same time making it subject to fresh conditions and obligations, one of which was formulated so as to involve, for the members of the Association, apart from the obligations contained in Article 4 of the Decision of 27 June 1967, the further obligation to notify to the Commission without delay 'iedere wijziging in de deelnemingsverhoudingen van de leden' (literally: any change in the participatory relationships of the members).

8. The applicants claim that at no time could they infer from this statement that the Commission intended to impose on them a condition such as that contained in the provision in issue, and one to which they would not be able, by reasons of its breadth, to adhere and which, without good reason, would harm their interests. If they had been in a position to realize the Commission's intentions they would not have failed to make known their objections on this matter so as to draw the Commission's attention to the inconvenience which would result from the obligation in issue and to the illegality by which it is vitiated. Since they were not given this opportunity, they allege that the Decision, insofar as the obligation in issue is concerned, must be annulled since it is vitiated by a procedural defect.

9. The defendant replies, firstly, that the requirement laid down in Article 2 of Regulation No 99/63, according to which 'the Commission shall inform undertakings and associations of undertakings in writing of the objections raised against them', in the same way as the obligation imposed upon it by Article 4 of the same Regulation, to deal only with 'those objections raised against undertakings and associations of undertakings in respect of which they have been afforded the opportunity of making known their views', do not relate to the conditions which the Commission intends to attach to a decision granting exemption.

10. The Commission adds that the concern which is given expression in the clause in issue was known to the applicants, in particular because of the importance attached to the case of the companies Astral and Urruzola, and this both in the communication of 27 July 1973 and during the course of the hearing.

11. According to Article 19 of Regulation No 17 of the Council, the Commission, before taking decisions as provided for in Articles 2, 3, 6, 7, 8, 15 and 16 of that Regulation, shall give the undertakings or associations of undertakings concerned the opportunity of being heard on the matters to which the Commission has taken objection. In referring to Article 6, this provision relates to decisions taken pursuant to a request for the application of Article 85 (3).

12. According to Article 24 of the same Regulation the Commission shall have power to adopt implementing provisions in this context, which it did in Regulation No 99/63.

13. It is clear both from the title and from the first recital of this Regulation that it is concerned with all the hearings provided for in Article 19 of Regulation No 17 of the Council and, accordingly, also applies to procedures with regard to Article 85 (3). However, the obligation imposed upon the Commission by Articles 2 and 4 of Regulation No 99/63 to inform an undertaking, in writing or by giving notice in the Official Journal, of the objections raised against it and to deal, in its decisions, only with these objections, is essentially concerned with the statement of the reasons which would lead it to apply paragraph (1) of Article 85, either by ordering that an infringement be terminated or imposing a fine upon the undertakings, or by refusing to give the latter negative clearance or the benefit of paragraph (3) of the same provision.

14. On the other hand, the Commission cannot be expected to anticipate the conditions and obligations to which it is entitled to subject the exemption laid down in Article 85 (3). In fact, the investigation of a request for exemption may bring to light various ways in which the operation of an agreement or the control of that operation may be undertaken, this prompting the Commission to withdraw the objections which it had raised against the request and justifying the grant, possibly subject to certain conditions, of the benefit of Article 85 (3).

15. It is clear, however, both from the nature and objective of the procedure for hearings, and from Articles 5, 6 and 7 of Regulation No 99/63, that this Regulation, notwithstanding the cases specifically dealt with in Articles 2 and 4, applies the general rule that a person whose interests are perceptibly affected by a decision taken by a public authority must be given opportunity to make his point of view known. This rule requires that an undertaking be clearly informed, in good time, of the essence of conditions to which the Commission intends to subject an exemption and it must have the opportunity to submit its observations to the Commission. This is especially so in the case of conditions which, as in this case, impose considerable obligations having far-reaching effects.

16. Since Article 85 (3) constitutes, for the benefit of undertakings, an exception to the general prohibition contained in Article 85 (1) the Commission must be in a position at any moment to check whether the conditions justifying the exemption are still present. Accordingly, in relation to the detailed rules to which it may subject the exemption, the Commission enjoys a large measure of discretion, while at the same time having to act within the limits imposed upon its competence by Article 85. On the other hand, the exercise of this discretionary power is linked to a preliminary canvassing of objections which may be raised by the undertakings.

17. It is clear from the file that this requirement was not fulfilled in respect of the obligation in issue.

18. The statement contained in the communication of 27 July 1973 could be interpreted in widely differing ways, inter alia, as requiring merely that the information which had already to be supplied under Article 4 of the Decision of 27 June 1967 be supplemented by the notification of any links which might exist between the undertakings which are members of the Association. The ambiguity of this statement is highlighted by the fact that during the proceedings before the Court the Commission suggested different versions of it both in English, which is the language chosen by the applicants as the language of the case, and in French, in the translation in the statement of defense and in the correction proposed during the oral procedure.

19. Although it is clear from the minutes of the hearing that the links between two members of the Association, the companies Astral and Urruzola, and two important industrial chemical concerns were examined in dept—which moreover prompted the Commission to dispense with its requirement that these two members should leave the Association—the said minutes show that at no time was the general condition later contained in the Decision the subject of an exchange of points of view. This fact confirms the applicants' assertion that they were convinced that the obligation as stated in the 'notice of objections' concerned only the mutual relations between members of the Association and not such links as might exist with outside undertakings, including those operating outside the Common Market and concerned with the manufacture of paints other than marine paints.

20. Accordingly, the condition stated in Article 3 (1) (d) of the Decision was imposed in breach of procedural requirements and the Commission must be given the opportunity to reach a fresh decision on this point after hearing the observations or suggestions of the members of the Association.

21. Notwithstanding the importance of the subject matter of this part of the decision, it is nevertheless capable of being severed, for the time being, from the other provisions, and a partial annulment is therefore possible and is justified by the fact that, taken as a whole, the Decision is favourable to the interests of the undertakings concerned.

22. The provision in issue should therefore be annulled and the case remitted to the Commission.

Costs

23. Under Article 69 (2) of the Rules of Procedure, the unsuccessful party shall be ordered to pay the costs, if a submission has been made to that effect.

24. The defendant party has failed in its pleas.

25. The defendant party should therefore be ordered to pay the costs. {1081}

THE COURT hereby:

1. Annuls Article 3 (1) (d) of the Decision of 21 December 1973;

2. Refers the case back to the Commission.

3. Orders the Commission to pay the costs.

Mannesmannrohren-werke AG and Another v. EC Council

(Case 333/85) Court of Justice of the European Communities (6th Chamber) [1987] ECR 1381, [1988] 2 CMLR 627, 17 March 1987

DECISION:

By application lodged at the Court Registry on 11 November 1985, Mannesmannrohren-Werke AG and Paderwerk Gebr Benteler GmbH & Co, having their registered offices in Dusseldorf and Paderborn-Schloss Neuhaus respectively, brought an action under Article 173(2) EEC for a declaration that Council Regulation (EEC) 2355/85 of 6

August 1985 supplementing Regulation (EEC) 60/85 on the restriction of exports of steel pipes and tubes to the United States of America is void.

The Council, the defendant, has contested the admissibility of the application in the light of certain considerations which it is appropriate to consider first.

With regard to the legal background to the dispute reference is made to the Report for the hearing and the submissions and arguments of the parties, which are mentioned or discussed hereinafter only in so far as is necessary for the reasoning of the Court.

The Council states in the first place that the contested regulation supplements Council Regulation 60/85 on the restriction of exports of steel pipes and tubes to the United States of America and that the two regulations constitute an indivisible whole. Regulation 60/85 produces legal effects with regard to categories of persons described in a generalised and abstract manner, namely present and future producers and exporters of pipes and tubes. Regulation 2355/85, which merely inserts a table concerning tubes of a certain type in Annex III to Regulation 60/85, should therefore be regarded as a true regulation against which individuals have no right of action.

Moreover, the Council points out that if the amendment of Annex III is treated as an autonomous provision, the allocation of the Community quota among the member-States under that provision should be regarded as a decision addressed to the member-States. That decision is not of direct concern to the applicants since the apportionment among undertakings of the sub-quota allocated by the Council to a member-State is to be carried out by the authorities of that State. The contested measure is not of individual concern to the applicants because the allocation of the Community quota among the member-States under that measure affects the interest of Community exporters as a whole, including any new undertakings specialising in trade in pipes and tubes which may be set up.

The applicants consider that the contested measure is of direct and individual concern to them. The member-States may not freely share out among undertakings the sub-quotas allocated to them but should apply the objective criteria laid down by Regulation 60/85. Accordingly, if the share of the quota allocated to the Federal Republic of Germany is objectively too small, as the applicants maintain, the six German undertakings engaged in manufacturing the products referred to in Regulation 2355/85 will be obliged to make a further reduction in their deliveries over and above that resulting from the Arrangement with the United States of America.

Next, the applicants emphasize that in the Federal Republic of Germany there are only six undertakings which produce steel pipes and tubes and that no other undertaking could join that group and penetrate the export market until it had made extremely lengthy preparations. Those six undertakings are individually distinguished by the fact that, at the time of the adoption of Regulation 2355/85, they held provisional export (licenses covering the period between 1 January 1985 and the entry into force of that regulation. Since that regulation has retroactive effect from 1 January 1985, the circle of undertakings concerned is definitively circumscribed.

In considering those arguments, it must in the first place be borne in mind that, according to the terms of the Arrangement with the United States of America concerning trade in steel pipes and tubes, approved by Council Regulation 59/85, the level of Community exports of steel pipes and tubes originating in the Community is fixed at 7.6 per cent of United States apparent consumption for the calendar years 1985 and 1986. However, in the case of pipes and tubes described as 'oil country tubular goods', or

OCTG tubes, that level is fixed at 10 per cent of United States apparent consumption, within the overall limit of 7.6 per cent.

The purpose of Regulation 60/85 is to introduce in the Community, in order to ensure the application of that Arrangement, certain restrictions on the amount of the products in question exported to the United States. According to the preamble to that regulation, for practical and management reasons, the quantitative export limits agreed by the Community must be allocated among the member-States and, in order to do so, an allocation method must be established which takes account of traditional patterns of trade. Thereafter, the member-States must 'share out the amounts allocated to them among undertakings in accordance with objective criteria'.

According to Article 2 of Regulation 60/85, the Community export limit for steel tubes and pipes and for OCTG tubes is to be calculated by the Commission on the basis of the level of apparent consumption of those products in the United States, as laid down in the Arrangement. The limits thus calculated are to be adjusted by the Commission so as to take account of revisions of United States apparent consumption. Article 3 provides that the Commission is to allocate among the member-States the quantitative export limits established and calculated pursuant to the method set out in Article 2 in accordance with Annex III. That allocation may be adjusted by the Commission, subject to the conditions laid down in Article 4, so as to ensure the best use of the quantitative export limits.

Annex III to Regulation 60/85 shows the quantity of pipes and tubes allocated to the member-States, each State being allotted a figure indicating its share of United States consumption (in the case of Germany: 2.82 per cent). As regards OCTG tubes, the annex contained, in the regulation as originally enacted, a separate entry to the effect that the allocation among the member-States would be decided on by the Council before 31 January 1985. The Council did not adopt Regulation 2355/85 supplementing Annex III with regard to OCTG tubes until 6 August 1985. That regulation replaces the OCTG entry in Annex III with a table showing the proportion of United States consumption for each member-State (in the case of Germany: 4.38 per cent).

Article 5 of Regulation 60/85 provides that export licenses are to be issued by the competent authorities of each member-State within the limits of the amounts allocated to it pursuant to Article 3. The licenses are to be issued in accordance with the following criteria set out in Article 5(2): compliance with the rules prescribed by the regulation, in particular those concerning the quota allocated by the Commission pursuant to Article 3; compliance with the traditional export patterns of undertakings taking account of the reduction principles established by the regulation and possibly the situation of new producers of pipes and tubes; compliance with the rates of exports to the United States as traditionally spread out over the year; optimum use and administration of the export possibilities afforded by the regulation; best use being made of any new possibilities provided for, where appropriate, by the regulation.

That survey of the applicable rules shows that the opportunities for undertakings to export OCTG tubes originating in the Community to the United States are determined not by a single act on the part of a Community or national institution but by a series of measures and decisions concerning the restriction of exports by the Community, the member-States and the undertakings, successively. The quantity of OCTG tubes which may be sold on the United States market is limited by the Arrangement, for the Community as a whole, to a percentage of United States apparent consumption. The Community fixes the Community export limit on the basis of that percentage and adjusts it if necessary. Thereafter, exports of OCTG tubes originating in a given member-State may not exceed the percentage of United States consumption fixed for that member-State in Annex III. The Commission allocates the Community export limit among the member-States on the basis of that percentage and adjusts it where appropriate. Finally, the authorities of those States issue export licenses within the limits thus laid down. In so doing, they must take due account of certain criteria which may be objective but whose implementation involves the exercise of a discretion and whose significance must be determined having regard to the combination of different criteria.

It follows that the fixing of the percentage of the sub-quota for the Federal Republic of Germany by Regulation 2355/85 does not directly affect the legal position of the undertakings producing OCTG tubes in that country, since the issue of export licenses to those undertakings is not based directly on that percentage but depends in the first place on the manner in which the Commission has calculated and adjusted the Community export limit and fixed Germany's sub-quota on the basis of that percentage, and secondly on the apportionment of that sub-quota by the national authorities among the undertakings concerned, which is no way an automatic process but is based on a number of criteria.

Accordingly, Annex III to Regulation 60/85, as supplemented by Regulation 2355/85, is not of direct concern to the applicants.

The applicants claim in the alternative that Regulation 2355/85 should be declared void only for the period from 1 January 1985 to 20 August 1985, the date on which it entered into force, on the ground that, in any event, the fact that the regulation had retroactive effect was of individual concern to them. Since the court has established that the regulation was not of direct concern to the applicants, the alternative submission cannot lead to a different outcome.

It follows from the foregoing considerations that the application is inadmissible.

Costs

Under Article 69(2) of the Rules of Procedure, the unsuccessful party is to be ordered to pay the costs. Since the applicants have failed in their submissions, they must be ordered to pay the costs.

On those grounds, THE COURT (Sixth Chamber) hereby:

1. dismisses the application as inadmissible.
2. Declares that the applicants are jointly and severally liable for the costs.

Comments and Questions

1. In *Transocean Marine*, did the Court adopt the position of the advocate general? In what ways was the decision different from that of those advocate general?

2. Following the practice of many civil law countries, ECJ opinions are not authored by particular named judges. In addition to following the civil law practice of per curiam

decisions, the ECJ does not permit dissenting or concurring opinions. Do you think this increases or decreases the utility of opinions for lawyers and others seeking guidance?

3. In the absence of concurring and dissenting opinions, the opinions of the advocate generals take on more significance. They are the only source of information about the Court's decision written by someone close to the Court that is available other than the decision itself. Usually, advocate general opinions delve into significantly more detail than do the opinions themselves. As a lawyer advising clients on EU law, would you pay attention to advocate general opinions? Note that even the opinions of advocate generals that are rejected in the decisions are valuable. In the absence of dissenting or concurring opinions, the advocate general's opinion may provide clues to ideas rejected by the majority, but which might be advanced in other cases. Are there other ways in which an advocate general's opinion can be useful?

4. For American lawyers, even American lawyers used to the prolixity of Supreme Court opinions, the opinions of advocate generals and the ECJ may come as a bit of a shock. Much of the material in the opinions may, from an American lawyer's perspective be tangential or beside the point. For lawyers and business people seeking clues about the direction and thinking of the Court, however, such verbiage proves valuable from time to time. Also valuable, especially for American law students, is the ability to be able to read through the opinions to pick out what may be important in a given context. These opinions provide students with some practice.

5. The advocate general in *Transocean Marine* extracts and applies a principle of due process, applicable on a Community wide basis. What is the nature of the due process right extracted and from what sources did the advocate general extract this right? How does the due process right described in *Transocean Marine* compare to due process in the American system? See *Matthews v. Eldrige*, 424 U.S. 319 (1976).

> In recent years this Court increasingly has had occasion to consider the extent to which due process requires an evidentiary hearing prior to the deprivation of some type of property interest even if such a hearing is provided thereafter. In only one case, *Goldberg v. Kelly*, 397 U.S. at 266–271, has the Court held that a hearing closely approximating a judicial trial is necessary. In other cases requiring some type of pre-termination hearing as a matter of constitutional right the Court has spoken sparingly about the requisite procedures. *Sniadach v. Family Finance Corp.*, 395 U.S. 337 (1969), involving garnishment of wages, was entirely silent on the matter. In *Fuentes v. Shevin*, 407 U.S. 67, 96–97 (1972), the Court said only that in a replevin suit between two private parties the initial determination required more than an *ex parte* proceeding before a court clerk. Similarly, *Bell v. Burson*, 402 U.S. 535, 540 (1971), held, in the context of the revocation of a state-granted driver's license, that due process required only that the pre-revocaton hearing involve a probable-cause determination as to the fault of the licensee, noting that the hearing "need not take the form of a full adjudication of the question of liability."... More recently, in *Arnett v. Kennedy*... we sustained the validity of procedures by which a federal employee could be dismissed for cause. They included notice of the action sought, a copy of the charge, reasonable time for filing a written response, and an opportunity for an oral appearance. Following dismissal, an evidentiary hearing was provided.
>
> These decisions underscore the truism that "'[d]ue process', unlike some legal rules, is not a technical conception with a fixed content unrelated to time, place

> and circumstances." *Cafeteria Workers v. McElroy*, 367 U.S. 886, 895 (1961). "[D]ue process is flexible and calls for such procedural protections as the particular situation demands." *Morrissey v. Brewer*, 408 U.S. 471, 481 (1972). Accordingly, resolution of the issue whether the administrative procedures provided here are constitutionally sufficient requires analysis of the governmental and private interests that are affected. More precisely, our prior decisions indicate that identification of the specific dictates of due process generally requires consideration of three distinct factors: First, the private interest that will be affected by the official action; second, the risk of an erroneous deprivation of such interest through the procedures used, and the probable value, if any, of additional or substitute procedural safeguards; and finally, the Government's interest, including the function involved and the fiscal and administrative burdens that the additional or substitute procedural requirement would entail....

Matthews v. Eldridge, 424 U.S. at 330–31.

III. *Direct Actions for Failure of EC Institutions to Act.* EC TREATY, Art. 232 (ex 175). This action can be maintained only if the complaining party has sought action from the defendant prior to institution of the suit and the EC institution has failed to act. The complainant is given two (2) months to initiate suit after the failure to act. The ECJ can require the EC Institution to take the actions necessary to comply with the judgment of the ECJ.

IV. *Preliminary Rulings.* EC TREATY, Art. 234c (ex 177). In order to ensure uniformity of interpretation and application of Community law, national courts are given the authority to refer matters of Community Law to the ECJ. The ECJ's interpretation in these cases is authoritative and binding on the national courts. Referral to the ECJ is permissive, and made in the discretion of the referring court. Referral is mandatory only from a court against whose judgment there is no appeal (that is the highest national court of the Member State). The process for referral is set forth in the statute, and requires notice to all parties, as well as most EC institutions. *See* Protocol on the Statute of the Court of Justice art. 20. Article 177 has provided the most effective means for individual to litigate EC law before the ECJ. Article 177 permits the individual to avoid the standing problems of litigation under Articles 173 and 175, and to begin the dispute resolution in the national courts (with which he is more familiar). It is an especially useful vehicle for challenging a Member State's compliance with EC Directives. As such, this procedure is particularly important in dealing with the Company Law harmonization efforts of the Communities, since those are usually effected through Directives. *See* STEPHEN WEATHERHILL & PAUL BEAUMONT, EU LAW 314–356 (1999); AUDREY WINTER ET AL., EUROPE WITHOUT FRONTIERS: A LAWYER'S GUIDE 38–39 (1989); LAW OF THE EUROPEAN COMMUNITIES 290 (Vaughan, ed.), *in* 51 HALSBURY'S LAWS OF ENGLAND (4th ed. 1986).

3. *Lawmaking Within the European Union*

The process of enactment of Community legislation is complex, and since the adoption of the Single European Act, even more so. What follows is a brief outline of the process for the enactment of legislation. Legislation may be enacted in one of three ways: (i) via the consultation process (the traditional method), (ii) via the cooperation procedure (adopted after the adoption of the Single European Act), and (iii) via the co-determination process. The EU Treaties specify the method of enactment necessary for passage of legislation with respect to individual provisions. As a result, and in contrast to law making under the US Constitution, a determination of the appropriate legal basis for enactment of legislation is a critical part of EU law making. The legal basis of regulation provides the method of enactment as well.

a. The Consultation Process. The EC Commission is normally the source of all legislative efforts within the EEC. The EC Council is substantially the only body that may enact such legislation. Normally, the EC Commission formulates and sends proposals for regulations, directives, and other measures to the EC Council. The Council can also request the submission of particular proposals. Generally, such measures are developed through a process of informal consultation between the staffs of the various directorates general of the Commission and interested functionaries of the Member States as well as private parties before a proposal is drafted. Once drafted, the proposal is circulated to all of the chefs de cabinets of the EC Commission, and if approved, sent on the EC Council. If not approved, the proposal is debated in the EC Commission, and passed on if it receives a majority of votes. At this point it is first published in the official reporter of the Community—the Official Journal of the European Communities ("OJ") as a Commission Document.

Once at the EC Council, the proposal is usually sent to the EC Parliament and the Economic and Social Committee for comments (this is required where specific EEC Treaty provisions require consultation). After study (which can take as much time as the Parliament wishes), the EC Parliament will generally vote on the passage of a "resolution" which either approves the proposal or contains amendments to the proposal. Normally, such amendments are discussed informally between the EC Parliament, the EC Council and the EC Commission well before a formal vote of the Parliament. Because the consultation process has no time limit, the Parliament can assert some power by holding up consideration of a particular proposal. The Economic and Social Committee follows a similar process. With the formal opinions of the EC Parliament and the Economic and Social Committee, the EC Council sends the proposal to a working committee for further review and submission to the Committee of Permanent Representatives of the EC Council. If the working group approves the Proposal, it is sent to the full Council for fast track approval. If there is no agreement, the proposal comes up for debate before the full Council. The EC Commission may amend the proposal until the EC Council adopts it. Once adopted, the proposal becomes law. If the proposal is adopted, the Member States are also notified, so that they can begin the process of amending their national laws in conformity with the directive.

b. The Cooperation Procedure. The cooperation procedure is set forth at Article 252 (ex 189c) of the EC TREATY. Under this process, both the EC Parliament and EC Council review the proposal twice before it can be enacted. The cooperation process is substantially the same as the consultation procedure through the consideration of the proposal by the EC Parliament and the Economic and Social Committee. However, under the cooperation procedure, this is deemed to constitute a first reading of the proposal. After the first reading, the Council, along with the Commission, adopts a "common position" by qualified majority vote, unless the EC Council amends the proposal, in which event, the vote must be unanimous. The Common position is then transmitted back to the EC Parliament along with an explanation of the EC Council's reasons for adopting the position transmitted. There is no time limit for the formulation by the EC Council of its common position.

At this point, the proposal is transmitted between the EC Council, the EC Commission and the EC Parliament, depending on the actions taken by them. All of these actions are subject to strict time limits. The EC TREATY, Art. 252 (ex 189c), provides a reasonable explanation of the procedure:

> (b) The Council's common position shall be communicated to the European Parliament. The Council and the Commission shall inform the European Parliament fully of the reasons which led the Council to adopt its common position.
>
> If within three months of such communication, the European Parliament approves this common position or has not taken a decision within that period, the Council shall definitively adopt the act in question in accordance with the common position.
>
> (c) The European Parliament may within the period of three months referred to in point (b), by an absolute majority of its component members, propose amendments to the Council's common position. The European Parliament may also, by the same majority, reject the Council's common position. The result of the proceedings shall be transmitted to the Council and the Commission.
>
> If the European Parliament has rejected the Council's common position, unanimity shall be required for the Council to act on a second reading.
>
> (d) The Commission shall, within a period of one month, re-examine the proposal on the basis of which the Council adopted its common position, by taking into account the amendments proposed by the European Parliament.
>
> The Commission shall forward to the Council, at the same time as its re-examined proposal, the amendments of the European Parliament which it has not accepted, and shall express its opinion on them. The Council may adopt these amendments unanimously.
>
> (e) The Council, acting by a qualified majority, shall adopt the proposal as re-examined by the Commission.
>
> Unanimity shall be required for the Council to amend the proposal as re-examined by the Commission.
>
> (f) In the cases referred to in points (c), (d) and (e), the Council shall be required to act within a period of three months. If no decision is taken within this period, the Commission proposal shall be deemed not to have been adopted.

Some of these periods may be extended for no more than one month by agreement between the Council and the EC Parliament. Consequently, if the Parliament amends or rejects the common position, the EC Commission is given one month to review the Parliaments's amendments and revise its proposals, all of which it then submits to the EC Council as a "re-examined proposal" along with the EC Parliament amendments it rejected (along with reasons for the rejection). The EC Council then has three months to : (i) adopt the "re-examined proposal" by qualified majority; (ii) adopt an amended "re-examined proposal" by unanimous vote; (iii) adopt the EC Parliament's amendments not approved by the Commission by unanimous vote; (iv) otherwise amend the re-examined proposal, by unanimous vote; (v) fail to act, in which event the proposal lapses. Since adoption of the Treaty of Amsterdam, the cooperation procedure has been supplanted by the co-decision process. The purpose is to make the process of legislation more democratic by increasing the participation of the EU Parliament. *See* STEPHEN WEATHERHILL & PAUL BEAUMONT, EU LAW 129 (1999).

c. The Co-decision Procedure. The co-decision process was introduced by the Maastricht Treaty (Art. 189b (after the Treaty of Amsterdam Art. 251. This procedure for enactment substantially increased the power of Parliament with respect to the passage of legislation. Under certain circumstances, the new procedure gave the European Parliament a veto over Council and Commission action on a measure. Legislation based on many of the more important sources of Community power were made subject to this enactment process. These include legislation based on the freedom of movement for workers, the freedom of establishment, and measures for the approximation of laws for the purpose of implementing the internal market.

The co-decision procedure is substantially the same as the cooperation procedure through the first reading stage of enactment and the development of a common position. Article 251(2) specifies that where the EC Council adopts all the amendments proposed by the European Parliament or where the European Parliament makes no proposals, the provision may be adopted.

Otherwise, with respect to the communication of the common position, if the European Parliament, within three months of the communication:

> (a) approves the common position or has not taken a decision, the act in question shall be deemed to have been adopted in accordance with the common position;
>
> (b) rejects, by an absolute majority of its component members, the common position, the proposed act shall be deemed not to have been adopted;
>
> (c) proposes amendments to the common position by an absolute majority of its component members, the amended text shall be forwarded to the Council and to the Commission, which shall deliver an opinion on such amendments.

EC Treaty, Art. 251(2). If the European Parliament sends amendments back in this manner, they will be deemed adopted if approved by the Commission and adopted by qualified majority vote of the EC Council, but if the Commission rejects the amendments the EC Council may stll adopt, but only by unanimous vote. EC Treaty, Art. 251(3). A Conciliation Committee is convened in the event the Council does not approve all the amendments. The Conciliation Committee is made up of equal numbers of representatives of the Council and the EU Parliament, with the Commission's representatives taking an important but less formal role in the proceedings. EC Treaty, Art. 251(4). Where a joint text is approved by the Conciliation Committee, such text can be enacted on a vote of a qualified majority of the EC Council and an absolute majority of the members of the EU Parliament. Failure to approve a joint text or failure to attain the necessary votes in the EC Council and the EU Parliament effectively kills the measure. EC Treaty, Art. 251(5) and (6).

4. *Forms of Law*

The basic documents establishing the EU, the Treaties, set forth the forms and hierarchy of law making within the EU. These forms and hierarchy differ in some substantial respects from those of traditional federations such as the US or Germany. Within the EU, four sources of law are recognized: (i) the Treaty provisions themselves, which correspond to the provisions of the US Constitution; (ii) regulations, which correspond to US federal statutes; (iii) directives, commands to the Member States to enact the legislation described; and (iv) decisions affecting individuals.

a. Treaty Provisions

The Treaties comprising the basic laws of the European Union constitute the basis of a constitutional order as between the Member States of the European Union. Community law preempts the laws of the Member States. While the ECJ has held on numerous occasions that the EC Treaty is superior to even the Constitutional law of the Member States, several Member States, through their constitutional courts, have taken the position, at least in theory, that the EC Treaty is either subordinate or co-equal to Member State Constitutional law. Among these Member States are Germany, Italy and Spain. This issue is unresolved. Also, while the obligations under the Treaty are ostensibly directed to the Member States and not directly to the citizens of the European Union, the ECJ under the doctrine of "direct effect" discussed below, has ruled that certain treaty provisions, along with other measures taken by the institutions of the EU are directly applicable in the law of the Member States without any legislative action on their part.

Costa v. Ente Nazionale per L'energia Elettrica (ENEL)

Giudice Conciliatore Di Milano (1a Sezione)
[1968] CMLR 267, 14 May 1966

FACTS: The plaintiff, a lawyer, resides at 3 Via Afredo Oriani, Milan and was the consumer of electricity supplied to him at those premises by Messrs Edisonvolta SPA, in which he is also a shareholder.

He received a request for the payment of 1,925 lire in respect of electricity submitted by EMEL and on 8 December 1963 he applied to the Court for a declaration that this sum was not due by him to the defendant with whom he had never entered into contractual relations; in addition to a declaration to this effect, he also claimed costs.

At the preliminary hearing before the Conciliatore on 16 October 1963 ENEL argued by way of defence that on 22 May 1963 Messrs Edisonvolta SPA had handed over to ENEL all its assets and therefore the whole of its undertaking which from that date was run by ENEL in its own name. In pursuance thereof, ENEL had maintained the supply of electricity which formed the object of contracts concluded by Edisonvolta including that with the plaintiff. In the defendant's submissions it followed from this that since ENEL had performed its part of the contract, it had a right to claim from electricity consumers what was due in respect of electricity supplied and that anyhow the plaintiff, had he thought fit to do so, could have availed himself of the provisions contained in Article 1406 of the Italian Civil Code. (Article 1406 of the Italian Civil Code, which appears under the heading 'Assignment of contractual rights and obligations' reads as follows: Each party can substitute a third party to itself in all relations deriving from a contract with mutuality of performance, provided that performance has not yet taken place and the other party thereto agrees to the substitution.) For all these reasons it was submitted that the plaintiff's application was misconceived.

At the hearing the defendant produced a copy of the minute recording the handing over on 22 May 1963 of Edisonvolta assets to ENEL which took place before the local 'Intendent di Finanza' of Milan Province. This resulted in an adjournment by mutual consent of the parties and a further hearing on 11 December 1963 whereat ENEL produced a copy of an Order made by the Milan Conciliatore on 10 September 1963 whereby the matter was referred to the Constitutional Court. On his part the plaintiff asked that the proceedings be suspended by referring the matter both to the Constitutional Court and to the European Court of Justice in Luexmbourg. The request for a suspension of the proceedings was opposed by the defendant and at that stage the Conciliatore reserved judgment. By a subsequent Order issued in Chambers on 16 January 1964 and deposited in Chancery on 21 January 1964 the same Conciliatore held that the question of constitutional legality of Law No 1643 of 5 December 1962 and of the subsequent relative Presidential decrees (No 1670 of 15 December 1962, No 36 of 4 February 1963, No 138 of 25 February 1963 and No 219 of 14 March 1963) was not manifestly unfounded in view of Articles 81, 47, 5, 102, 113, 25 and 76 of the Constitution of the Italian Republic and accordingly ordered a suspension of the proceedings by virtue of Article 23 of Law No 87 of 11 March 1953 and the reference of the proceedings to the Constitutional Court against the background of the provisions of the Constitution previously referred to.

The Conciliatore further ordered that, in view of Article 177 of the Treaty that created the EEC on 25 March 1957 and of its reception in the Italian legal system (by Law No 1203 of 14 October 1957) and in consideration of the violation of Articles 102, 93, 53 and 37 of that same Treaty by the aforesaid Law No 1643 of 6 December 1962 and subsequent Presidential decrees, the proceedings should be suspended and an authenticated copy of the file remitted to the Court of Justice of the European Committee in Luxembourg for their interpretation of the Articles aforesaid.

On 15 July 1964 (Costa v. ENEL (6/64), 15 July 1964: [1964] CMLR 425; (1964) 1-0 Recueil 1141) the Court of Justice of the European Community rejected the argument that it lacked jurisdiction under Article 177 of the EEC Treaty and held that the questions referred for decision to the Milan Conciliatore are, in accordance with Article 177 aforesaid, capable of being entertained, since they relate to the interpretation of certain provisions of that same Treaty, it being understood that no subsequent unilateral Act can prevail over Community provisions.

On 15 July 1965 the Italian Constitutional Court declared unfounded the allegations of constitutional illegality.

Pursuant upon an order made on 6 August 1965 a decision on the merits of the case was once more referred to the Milan Conciliatore before which, at the hearing that took place on 24 November 1965, the parties reiterated and amplified their previous contentions [the contentions of the parties are omitted]

DECISION: The present controversy originates primarily in the allegation put forward in ENEL's defence dated 16 October 1963. It was there argued that the defendant was not subject to the provisions of Article 1406 et seq of the Civil Code. These provisions entail that the plaintiff should be notified of the assignment of the whole of the undertaking of Edisonvolta SPA to ENEL. The basis for discussion (that is to say, whether, on the facts, the provisions of Article 1406 could be said to have been complied with) was therefore extended to two further questions:

1. The question whether the law that created ENEL and the subsequent Presidential decrees, exonerated ENEL from complying with those provisions.

2. The question whether the law that created ENEL was in the first instance applicable on the facts.

The applicability of such law to the facts was immediately disputed by the plaintiff who argued that the provisions thereof were constitutionally unlawful and in violation of the EEC Treaty. This gave rise to two preliminary issues.

On the first one, the Constitutional Court has declared unfounded the allegations of constitutional illegality made against the law creating ENEL (and certain presidential decrees) by reference to Articles 81, 25, 102(2), 113 and 76 of the Constitution, although in part of the reasoning adduced in its judgment of 12 July 1965 it could not entirely accept certain objections raised by ENEL as regards the admissibility or otherwise of the allegations, whilst at the same time putting on one side 'the numerous amplifications put forward before that court' which were deemed to go beyond the order of the judge of first instance.

On the other hand, the first step of the European Court of Justice was to adjudge upon the preliminary objections by the Italian government and by ENEL.

Dealing with the objection as to jurisdiction based upon Article 177 that Court decided as follows:

'The questions referred by the Milan Conciliatore in accordance with Article 177, are admissible since, in the particular case, they relate to the interpretation of provisions of the EEC Treaty, it being understood that no subsequent unilateral statute can prevail over community provisions'.

Resulting from this, the European Court of Justice also declared that:

(1) Article 102 contained no provisions which ascribe to individuals rights that national judges are bound to protect;

(2) Nor do the provisions of Article 93 relating to the subject-matter ascribe any such rights.

(3) Article 53 is a Community rule which is capable of ascribing to individuals the rights which national judges are in fact bound to protect. This Article prohibits any new provision having as its aim the submission of citizens of Member-States to a more rigorous discipline than is normally reserved to nationals of such States, regardless of the type of undertaking adopted.

(4) All the provisions of Article 37(2) are Community rules capable as such of ascribing to individuals rights which national judges are bound to protect.

When related to the question raised in these proceedings their aim is to prohibit any new measure which might conflict with the principles of Article 37(1), that is to say, to prohibit any new measure having as its object or from which might follow a discrimination between citizens of member-States in matters of supply and marketing through monopolies and bodies having as their object dealings in commercial products which lend themselves to competition, and to exchanges between Member-States, and which also carry some weight in such exchanges.

Upon an examination of the judgment of the European Court it must be remarked that the Community provision contained in Article 37(2) of the EEC Treaty grants to individuals—and therefore also to the present plaintiff—certain rights which this court is bound to protect.

Such Article 37(2), in its second paragraph, aims at prohibiting any new measure that might conflict with the principles laid down in its first part.

In the European Court's judgment it is pointed out that any measure having as its object, or from which might follow, a discrimination between citizens of member-

States in matters relating to supply and marketing, by means of monopolies or bodies having as their objects dealings in commercial products which lend themselves to competition and to exchanges between such member-States and also carry a real weight in such exchanges, is in open contradiction to the principles contained in the first half of Article 37 aforesaid of the Treaty.

There can be no doubt that, both before and after the coming into operation of Law No 1643 of 6 December 1962, electricity was and is a commercial product which lent itself, and still does, to competition and to exchanges between EEC member-States.

Prior to the coming into force of Law No 1643 the competition in matters of supply of electricity appeared quite free amongst Italian firms when compared to firms in other EEC member-States. As a result of Article 1 of Law No 1643 there is reserved to ENEL the exclusive function of carrying out, within the territory of the Italian state, the activities of production, importation, exportation and sale of electricity regardless of its source: this is where the monopoly lies.

It is the opinion of this Court that, by creating ENEL, there has been created a new monopolistic measure from which flows a discrimination between the citizens of the Italian state and those of other member-States of the EEC in matters appertaining to the supply of electricity. As a body exercising a monopoly, ENEL carries a real weight in all exchanges of electricity with foreign countries and therefore also with the holders of rights that belong also to other EEC member-States. On the basis, therefore, of Article 37(2) of the EEC Treaty there is a prohibition upon the creation of ENEL as constituted, since ENEL represents a new measure which is in patent conflict with the principles contained in the provisions of Article 37(1), as enumerated and discussed above. It also follows that Law No 1643 of 6 December 1962 (and the relative presidential decrees) are the legalistic regulation of ENEL and as such contain this new measure prohibited by the EEC Treaty.

Having thus established that, according to the authentic interpretation given by the European Court, Law No 1643—viewed as a whole and more particularly in its Articles 1 and 3(11)—was promulgated in contravention of provisions laid down in the EEC Treaty (such as those contained in Article 37 thereof, first and second parts) and having also established that, according to such interpretation, by that same judgment the Community provisions contained in Article 37 are capable of ascribing to individuals, and therefore also to the present plaintiff, rights which this court not only can, but indeed must, protect: in consideration of all this it must be acknowledged, and consequent protection afforded to him, that the plaintiff has a right to a declaration that Law No 1643 (and the relative Presidential decrees) are inoperative and inapplicable even to the present situation.

Despite the foregoing, however, this Court feels it must investigate whether there are any general provisions of national law which might preclude such a declaration.

In its judgment No 14 of 7 March 1964 (dealing with an alleged violation of Article 11 of the Constitution), the Constitutional Court (COSTA V ENEL (Corte Costituzionale, 24 February/7 March 1964—14/1964): [1964] CMLR 425; [1964] I Foro It 465) has excluded that such a violation took place but, outside the Constitutional problem that was put to it, has also voiced considerations and arguments which (as is apparent in the European Court judgment of 15 July 1964) have provoked the EEC Commission to complain that the Italian Constitutional Court 'may have laid down a principle destined to have repercussions in the Community legal system as a whole'.

This observation by the EEC Commission formed the basis for the following remarks contained in the judgment of the European Court:

> 'This Court points out that, thus differing from ordinary international treaties, the EEC Treaty has created its own legal system which has been integrated with that of Member-States at the time the Treaty itself came into force and which, as such, national judges are duty bound to observe. In fact, by creating a Community without limits of duration, having its own organs, as well as its own personality, legal capacity and ability to be represented on the international plane, but more particularly having real powers derived either from limitations on jurisdiction or transfers of functions from the Member-States of the Community, the same member-States have, albeit in circumscribed fields, limited their own sovereign powers and created accordingly a whole system of law binding upon themselves and their citizens.'

The integration of rules which emanate from Community sources within the law of each member-State and, more generally, the spirit and the terms of the treaty, have as their corollary the inability, on the part of member-States, to cause to prevail, against a legal order which they themselves have accepted on conditions of reciprocity, a subsequent unilateral provision, which cannot therefore affect the common order. If the efficacy of the laws of the Community were to vary from one State to the next depending upon subsequent local laws, this would endanger the realisations of the aims of the EEC Treaty envisaged in Article 5(2) and would provoke a discrimination which as such is prohibited by Article 7 of the Treaty. The obligations undertaken with the signing of the EEC Treaty would not be performed, but merely conditionally adhered to, if the contracting parties could exempt themselves from the observance thereof by means of subsequent legislation.

Cases where member-States have a right to act unilaterally are expressly provided for (see, for example, Articles 15, 93(3), 223–225) and in any event applications for exemptions by member-States are subject to authorisation procedures (see, for instance, Articles 8(4), 17(4), 25, 26, 73, 93(2) (3) and 226) which would be entirely meaningless if the member-States could exonerate themselves from compliance by means of a simple local statute.

The pre-eminence of Community law finds its endorsement in Article 189 according to which regulations are obligatory and directly operative in each member-State. This provision, which is unaccompanied by any reservation, would be devoid of meaning if a member-State could unilaterally nullify the effects thereof by means of legislative action which prevailed over Community texts. It follows from all this that because of its very nature, and as derived from an autonomous source, the laws which originate from the Treaty could find limitations in any internal provision only at the cost of losing their own Community character and of shaking the legal foundations of the Community.

There is no doubt that the transfer, by Member-States in favour of the Community legal system, of rights and obligations corresponding to Treaty provisions implies a final limitation upon their sovereign right against which a subsequent unilateral act (which is not compatible with the Community system) is entirely devoid of effect. Article 177 of the Treaty is therefore to be applied regardless of any national law every time a question of interpretation of the Treaty should arise.'

Should this not suffice, the judgment of the European Court goes further in establishing the principle according to which: '... national judges whose judgments, as in this particular case cannot be appealed against, must ask the Court to decide, as preliminary points, questions of interpretation of the Treaty whenever these are raised before them.'

It is in application of this reasoning that the European Court goes on to decide: 'the questions referred to us by the Milan Concilatore in accordance with Article 177 are admissible since, on the facts, they deal with the interpretation of provisions of the EEC Treaty it being understood that no subsequent later Act can prevail over Community provisions'.

It is therefore this very judgment of the European Court which precludes, in our case, the efficacy of the theory according to which law No 1643 can prevail over Law No 1203 of 14 October 57 which gave execution in Italy to the EEC Treaty, since it comes second in time: such a theory does not concern constitutional law directly, although it has been argued before the Constitutional Court. On the other hand, it is still possible that a law which is formally perfect may lose its validity, quite apart from any problem of a constitutional nature, because of its anti-legality. In this context there is undoubted relevance in the plaintiff's argument when dealing with the case of Law No 4 of 7 January 1929 which is still in force, and which in practice (in its Articles 1 and 23) lays down the principle according to which the mere unlawfulness of a law can be determined by a later law.

It is therefore the opinion of this Court that by virtue of Article 37 of the EEC Treaty, Law No 1643 (and the relative presidential decree) can have no effect in this case because they are unlawful vis-a-vis the Community system to which the Italian system is bound to adapt itself, in accordance with the authentic interpretation contained in the judgment given on 15 July 1964 by the European Court of Justice.

From this it follows that the minute recording the hand-over to ENEL of the assets of Messrs Edisonvolta, recorded in the Milan Registry of Public Deeds at No 51382, Form 1, Vol 1483 on 24 May 1963, is to be considered as a separate legal transaction which stands on its own two feet in fact, and which in law is independent of the statutory provisions mentioned in it (Presidential decree of 4 February 1963 No 36 and Law No 1643 of 6 December 1962), which are unlawful.

Once this stage is reached, we must consider also those questions which derive from the interpretation of the other Articles of the Treaty rendered by the European Court in its judgment.

In its reasoning, such judgment acknowledges that 'by virtue of Article 102, whenever there is reason to fear that the adoption of a legislative provision might cause a distortion, the member-State intending so to proceed shall consult the Commission which may recommend to the other member-States measures apt to avoid the feared distortion'. The Court goes on to add that 'this Article, which is contained in the heading entitled "harmonization of laws", aims at avoiding increases in differences between the various national legal systems as regards the scope of the Treaty. With these provisions, member-States have limited their freedom of initiative and have accepted a submission to appropriate consultation procedures. By expressly undertaking a prior consultation of the commission in all the cases where their legislative programme might create a risk, albeit slight, of distortion, the member-States have thus accepted, vis-a-vis the Community, an obligation which binds them as states'.

In view of this interpretation and in view of the fact that the risk of distortion vis-a-vis the Community existed in the Bill which was then transformed into Law No 1643 as well as in those which preceded the relative presidential decrees—(at any rate in the acknowledged violation of Article 37 of the Treaty) , it is obvious that Article 102 of the Treaty has been violated by the Italian Government since the compulsory procedure of consultation with the EEC Commission was not followed.

This violation constitutes a further consideration and a further cause of illegality in law No 1643 (and the relative presidential decrees) inasmuch as that Law came into force within the framework of the Italian legal system without there having been followed the legislative route which was prescribed for it, since prior communication was not made to the EEC Commission. From this stems the illegality of the relative presidential decrees.

It is of course true that the Court of Justice went on to say that Article 102 does not contain provisions which grant to individuals rights that national judges are bound to protect but, in the opinion of the present Court, this statement concerns solely the right of individuals, within the framework of Community law, to apply to Community bodies. It is hardly possible that the Court of Justice meant to go further than its sphere of influence by excluding that within the framework of national systems any citizen can act in accordance with the requirements of national procedural law whenever a national law has been passed without the prescribed legislative procedure having been followed. The consequences that flow as far as internal national law is concerned from a provision of the Treaty once such provision has been authoritatively interpreted fall within the exclusive jurisdiction of the national judge and, in this case, of this Tribunal.

Put differently, it is the opinion of this Tribunal that by accepting into the national system Article 102 of the Treaty, the Italian State has introduced, into such system, a provision which is additional to the existing ones relating to the formation of laws. This provision (Article 102 of the EEC Treaty) was subsequently ignored in the legislative procedure which gave rise to Law No 1643 of 6 December 1962: and such an omission has legal significance.

Whereas the individual cannot avail himself of it as far as the Community system is concerned, he can certainly raise it as a ground of objection within the national framework where all laws, even those relating to the formation of the laws themselves, must be observed, and where any violation of the same offends against the perfect subjective right which every citizen has in ensuring that the prescribed rules are followed whenever laws are created, amended, or repealed.

There follows from this that whenever a law comes into being without due observance of an ordinary law which prescribes certain requirements for its formation, even if (in accordance with the above-mentioned judgment of the Constitutional Court) such law should not be constitutionally unlawful, it is nevertheless affected by illegality, because no state organ can, in carrying out its functions, fail to apply the laws of the state unless the same are repealed through other acts having the same force and features of those to be repealed.

Therefore, the violation of the EEC Treaty has resulted in a further illegality of the law which brought such violation into being, and even if we assume that the parties cannot raise this as a ground of objection, the court can certainly point to it of its own motion. Because in so doing, rather than protecting the right of an individual, the judge protects the rights of all individuals.

The same reasoning also applies to the Community provision contained in Article 93 which, according to the reasoning contained in the judgment of the Court of Justice of 15 July 1964, has been violated by the Italian Government inasmuch as the Commission was not given sufficient notice of the plans for aids contained in the Bill that later became law No 1643, thus failing to comply with the relative prescribed procedure, as indeed is apparent from the reasoning aforesaid.

As regards the interpretation of Article 53, this Court inclines to the view that it cannot be extended to the situation where the Italian citizen can freely establish electrical undertakings in the other member-States of the Community whereas the citizens of those States cannot do likewise in Italy.

Dealing with the other grounds adduced by the plaintiff, it is to be noted that the defendant, in its defence, has suggested to the plaintiff that for the future he avail himself of the provisions contained in Article 1406 of the Italian Civil Code. In this connection, the Court would wish to point out that it is up to the assignee (ENEL) to notify to the party being assigned (the plaintiff herein) the fact of the assignment of contractual rights so that the party assigned can give his consent which represents a constituent in the assignment of a contract with reciprocal obligations. There is no doubt that the benefit of the contract, containing mutual obligations, for the supply of electricity to the plaintiff in this action was included in the minute made at the time Messrs Edisonvolta handed over to ENEL its own assets. As a result of Article 1406 et seq in the Civil Code, it was up to ENEL to notify to the plaintiff the fact that his contract had been assigned to them as a result of the transfer of assets previously referred to.

It was only once such notification had been made and accepted by the party assigned (that is to say, our plaintiff) that ENEL could have become a contracting party. It was only at such time that the request for payment of the sum of 1,925 lire could have been treated as lawful; but this stage, according to the documents before us, has not yet come about.

For this reason it goes without saying that the defendant must fail, as regards the consequences that follow from Article 91 of the Code of Civil Procedure, in these proceedings which are of extraordinary importance for the subject-matter.

Whereas expenditure incurred in connection with the proceedings before the Constitutional Court cannot be recovered as a result of the principle laid down in Article 19 of the Rules of Interpretation relating to the procedure of that court dated 16 March 1956, as endorsed in judgment No 75 of the Constitutional Court of 6 December 1965 (in the case of Costantini v the State Revenue Administration), the expenses relating to the judgment before the Court of Justice of the European Community can indeed be recovered. In fact, according to the judgment dated 15 July 1964 of that court, it is expressly declared that:

'It is up to the Milan Conciliatore to decide upon the expenses in these proceedings.'

In the opinion of this Court, the defendant must be deemed to have failed also in the proceedings before such Court of Justice, both because the arguments adduced by the plaintiff are amply acknowledged when dealing with the interpretation of Article 37 of the EEC Treaty as well as because the defendants' contentions as regards the interpretation of Articles 102, 93, 53 and 37 of the Treaty aforesaid are not accepted.

For all these reasons, the Milan Deputy Conciliatore, having read the pleadings and the documents relating to this matter, as well as the judgments of 15 July 1964 of the Court of Justice of the European Community and 12 July 1965 of the Constitutional Court of the Italian Republic, having heard the Attorneys for the parties,

DECIDES, rejecting any diverse and contrary argument and contention:

1. In the present case, Law No 1643 of 6 December 1962 and the relative Presidential decrees have no legal effect as a result of Article 37 of the EEC Treaty as expressly interpreted by the judgment of the Court of Justice of the European Communities dated 15 July 1964.

2. Accordingly, as matters stand at present the plaintiff does not owe the defendant the sum of 1,925 lire which were requested by the defendant with the invoice that gave rise to these proceedings.

3. The defendant is bound to pay the costs of the present proceedings which are taxed in the sum of 220,000 lire (of which 20,000 for disbursements, 50,000 for solicitors' fees and 150,000 for barristers' fees) as well as the costs of the judgment and any resulting therefrom. The defendant is also bound to repay to the plaintiff the costs of the proceedings before the Court of Justice of the European Community in Luxembourg which are taxed in a total of 400,000 lire.

4. Each party shall bear its own costs of the proceedings before the Constitutional Court.

Comments and Questions

1. Since the 1960s, the European Court of Justice has articulated three fundamental general principles of law which give legitimacy to the organization created. These are the autonomy of the European Community, the supremacy of the Community within the ambit of its authority, the direct relationship between the Community and the citizens of the Member States, and the sole competence of the European Court of Justice to determine the nature and scope of the powers ceded to the Community by the Member States. The Community, in its own eyes, has been transformed from a self-styled regional organization of sovereign states to—something else. The Italian court in *Costa* provides an interesting reaction of a national court to one of the early cases in this project of creating an independent government for the EU. The *Costa* case reproduced above provides an example of the way in which national courts have begun to confront the European Court of Justice's theory of EC independence, supremacy, and direct relationship. Not all courts have accepted the pronouncements of the ECJ without question. Is the European Community (Union) a supra-national organization or is it a federation-confederation? Does the fact that the EU is based on a Treaty rather than on a constitution supply an important consideration in this respect? For a discussion, see Larry Catá Backer, *The Extra-National State: American Confederate Federalism and the European Union*, 7 Colum. J. Eur. L. 173 (2001).

2. The question of the nature of the EU has become very sensitive. On its resolution depend questions of preemption, the hierarchy of laws and the status and authority of the Member States vis-avis each other and the other nations of the world. That resolution, though, is likely to be a long time coming, at least *de jure*. After *Costa*, do you think the EU is more a federation or a supra-national organization? Does it make a difference for the study of enterprise regulation? Why?

---

b. Regulations (EC Treaty, Arts. 249, 253–256) (ex Arts. 189–192)

The quasi-federal nature of the Community by the EC Treaty is most clearly evidenced by the legislative power with which the EC Council has been vested, which is binding on the Member States to the same extent as if such had been enacted by national legislatures. The Member States have agreed, that "[i]n order to carry out their task, the Council and the Commission shall, in accordance with the provisions of this Treaty, make regulations, issue directives, take decisions, make recommendations, or deliver opinions." EC TREATY, Art. 249 (ex Art. 189). Regulations and directives have binding effect. They will be considered in more detail below.

Regulations are given direct general application by the EC Treaty by Art. 249 (ex. Art. 189) ("A regulation shall have general application. It shall be binding in its entirety and directly applicable in all Member States.).

> ....national courts must take cognizance of regulations as legal instruments whose validity and recognition by national courts must not be conditioned on national procedures of incorporation into the national legal order. Whether or not *particular provisions* of such an instrument in fact give rise to rights in individuals which national courts must safeguard is a matter of interpretation of the provisions concerned, in light of the criteria established by the Court of Justice with respect to the direct application of provisions of the Treaty. This is the better view and is quite consistent with the decided cases, though the Court has gone out of its way to clarify the matter.
>
> * * *
>
> Regulations, in short, are to be treated as "law" in every sense of the word. National courts must take judicial notice of them in their entirety; specific provisions contained therein may bestow on individuals rights as against other individuals or Member States; and their effect in a particular area may be to preempt national legislative competence. DERRICK WYATT & ALAN DASHWOOD, THE SUBSTANTIVE LAW OF THE EEC 39, 41 (1987).

Regulations have been used infrequently in the process of company law harmonization. In particular, these regulations represent an attempt to further the policies and aims of the EC as expressed in Art. 44(3)(f) (ex Art. 54(3)(f)) of the EC Treaty ("by effecting the progressive abolition of restrictions on freedom of establishment...."), and have been effected pursuant to the authority of Arts. 189, and 235 of the EC Treaty. With respect to company law, the EU has created the European Economic Interest Grouping ("EEIG") by Council Regulation (EEC) No. 213/85 (July 25, 1985). The EEIG is discussed at Chapter 6.

Another sort of supra-national entity is being considered—the *Societas Europeae* ("SE"). The SE would operate outside the national laws of the Member States and be subject to the new European company law. The proposal for the creation of such an entity has had a very long, complex and controversial history. The idea of such an entity has been considered seriously since at least 1970, when the EC Commission proposed a European Company Statute (see 13 J.O. Comm. Eur. (No. C 124) 1 (October 10, 1970). The major points of controversy currently appear to be the insistence that the SE follow German practice and permit worker participation in management, and the inability of the Member States to satisfactorily harmonize their business accounting practices. For a short discussion of the SE, see FRANK WOOLDRIDGE, COMPANY LAW IN THE UNITED KINGDOM AND THE EUROPEAN COMMUNITY: ITS HARMONIZATION AND UNIFICATION 117–134 (1991); and Terence L. Blackburn, *The Societas Europeana: The Evolving European Corporation Statute*, 61 FORDHAM L. REV. 695 (1993).

c. Directives (EC Treaty, Arts. 249, 253–256) (ex Arts. 189–192)

Unlike regulations, which are directly binding on the Member States, Directives are only "binding, as to the result to be achieved, upon each Member State to which it is addressed, but...leave[s] to the national authorities the choice of form and methods." EC Treaty, Art. 249. As such, they are not meant to serve as a means of uniformity—they serve primarily to effect the approximation of the laws of the Member States, leaving enough flexibility to accommodate the political realities of each of the Member States. Thus, the EC Treaty directs the "Council [to] issue directives for the approximation of such provisions laid down by law, regulation or administrative action in Member States as directly affect the establishment or functioning of the common market." EC Treaty, Art. 94 (ex Art. 100).

Directives are addressed to the Member States, and are in the nature of commands, imposing specific obligations on the Member States. Member States are obligated to implement such directives by binding acts. Advisory or other non-binding practices will not suffice. The EC Treaty gives the EC Commission the authority to enforce directives against recalcitrant Member States. EC Treaty, Art. 226 (ex Art. 169). Generally, neither the EC Commission, nor the ECJ has been particularly receptive to excuses respecting the failure of a Member State to implement directives. Consider, in that connection, the following cases. Each suggests the ways in which the ECJ has substantially curtailed the ability of Member States to raise objections to compliance with their Treaty obligations otherwise available under principles of international law.

EC Commission v. Ireland

(Case C-236/91) Court of Justice of the European Communities
[1993] 1 CMLR 320, 17 November 1992

Herr Claus Gulmann, Advocate General delivered the following opinion:

1. The Commission has brought this action seeking a declaration that Ireland has not implemented Council Directive 87/328 on the acceptance for breeding purposes of pure-bred breeding animals of the bovine species [1987] OJ L167/54). According to Article 6 of the directive, it should have been implemented by 1 January 1989.

2. In its defence the Irish Government concedes that it has still not adopted the legislation needed to implement the directive. It submits, however, that the directive is observed in practice. The Court has consistently held that 'mere administrative practices, which by their nature are alterable at will by the authorities and are not given the appropriate publicity, cannot be regarded as constituting the proper fulfillment of obligations under the Treaty (Case 168/58, EC Commission v. Italy: [1986] ECR 2945, [1988] 1 CMLR 580, para [13].'

3. I therefore propose that the Court should uphold the Commission's claim and order Ireland to pay the costs.

Decision:

By application lodged at the Court Registry on 17 September 1991, the EC Commission brought an action before the Court under Article 169 EEC for a declaration that by failing to bring into force the laws, regulations and administrative provisions necessary to comply with Council Directive 87/328 on the acceptance for breeding purposes of pure-bred breeding animals of the bovine species hereinafter referred to as 'the directive' ([1987] OJ L167/54)), Ireland had failed to fulfill its obligations under directive and in particular Article 6 thereof and under the EEC Treaty.

Article 6 of the directive provides that: 'member-States shall bring into force the laws, regulations and administrative provisions necessary to comply with this directive by 1 January 1989. They shall forthwith inform the Commission thereof.'

The Commission contends that the mandatory character of directives required Ireland to adopt the legislative provisions necessary to transpose the directive into national law.

Ireland concedes that the legislative provisions necessary to give effect to the directive have still not been enacted. It maintains, however, that pending the adoption of the necessary legislation, the rules laid down by the directive are observed in practice.

Ireland's argument cannot be accepted.

As the Court has consistently held in judgments concerning the implementation of directives, mere administrative practices, which by their nature are alterable at will by the authorities and are not given the appropriate publicity, cannot be regarded as constituting the proper fulfillment of a member-State's obligations under the Treaty: Case 168/85, EC Commission v. Italy ([1988] ECR 2945, [1988] 1 CMLR 580, para [13]).

Consequently, Ireland, which does not dispute its obligation to adopt the legislative provisions necessary to transpose the directive into national law cannot, even temporarily, evade that obligation by relying on the application of an administrative practice alleged to be in accordance with the rules laid down by the directive.

It follows that the Commission is entitled to a declaration of infringement in the terms sought.

Costs

Under Article 69(2) of the Rules of Procedure, the unsuccessful party is to be ordered to pay the costs. Since Ireland has failed in its submissions, it must be ordered to pay the costs.

On those grounds, THE COURT hereby:

1. Declares that by failing to bring into force the laws, regulations and administrative provisions necessary to comply with Council Directive 87/328 on the acceptance for breeding purposes of pure-bred breeding animals of the bovine species, Ireland has failed to fulfil its obligations under that directive and in particular Article 6 thereof and under the EEC Treaty.

2. Orders Ireland to pay the costs.

EC Commission v. Kingdom of Belgium

(Case 301/81) European Court of Justice
[1983] ECR 467, 1 March 1983

PANEL: J. Mertens de Wilmars, President, P. Pescatore, A. O'Keeffe and U. Everling (Presidents of Chambers), Lord Mackenzie Stuart, G. Bosco and Y. Galmot, Judges

DECISION:

By application lodged at the Court Registry on 30 November 1981 the Commission of the European Communities brought an action under Article 169 of the EEC Treaty for a declaration that, by failing to adopt within the prescribed period the provisions necessary to comply with Council Directive No. 77/780/EEC of 12 December 1977 on the co-ordination of the laws, regulations and administrative provisions relating to the taking up and pursuit of the business of credit institutions (Official Journal 1977 No. L 322, p. 30), the Kingdom of Belgium failed to fulfil its obligations under the third paragraph of Article 189 of the Treaty.

The case must be considered in the light of the background to the directive and the events which preceded the commencement of these proceedings.

Council Directive No. 77/780 constitutes the first stage in the harmonization of banking structures and the supervision thereof. The purpose of such harmonization is to permit the gradual attainment of freedom of establishment for credit institutions and the liberalization of banking services. In that respect the directive introduces certain minimum conditions for the authorization of credit institutions which all Member States must observe. In order to facilitate the taking up and pursuit of business as a credit institution the directive aims in particular to reduce the discretion enjoyed by certain supervisory authorities in authorizing credit institutions.

Article 14 (1) of the directive provides that Member States must bring into force the measures necessary to comply therewith within 24 months of its notification. That period expired in the present case on 15 December 1979. As a result of the directive a bill was prepared in Belgium but had not yet been introduced into the Belgian Parliament when the action for a declaration was brought by the Commission.

In its defence the Belgian Government emphasized first of all the extent of the technical, institutional and political difficulties which explain why, in spite of the efforts it has made, it has not yet been possible to place the bill incorporating the directive into national law before Parliament. Moreover, special problems are said to have arisen from the fact that it was decided to use the directive as an occasion for recasting the Belgian banking legislation in relation to all credit institutions.

Although those circumstances may explain the difficulties in applying the directive, they cannot expunge the Kingdom of Belgium's failure to fulfil its obligations. The Court has consistently held that a Member State may not plead provisions, practices or circumstances in its internal legal order to justify a failure to comply with obligations under Community directives.

The Belgian Government also consider that insufficient grounds are given both in the reasoned opinion and in the Commission's application, in so far as there is no reference to the difficulties entailed by the application of the directive or to any degree of inertia or opposition on the part of the Belgian State in that regard. Further, it is argued that the period allowed in the reasoned opinion is inadequate.

In that respect if must be observed that the admissibility of an action based on Article 169 of the Treaty depends only on an objective finding of a failure to fulfil obligations and not on proof of any inertia or opposition on the part of the Member State concerned. As the Court has already stated, the opinion referred to in Article 169 must be considered to contain a sufficient statement of reasons to satisfy the law when it contains a coherent exposition of the reasons which led the Commission to the conviction that the State concerned had failed to fulfil an obligation under the Treaty. To that extent the Commission was not required to refer to any difficulties entailed by the application of the directive in the Member State concerned.

Finally, the directive allowed the Member States a period of 24 months for the adoption of implementing measures. The period of two months laid down in the reasoned opinion merely constitutes an additional period in which the Member State is invited to put an end to the failure with which it is charged. Further, the Commission waited almost two years after sending the reasoned opinion before bringing the matter before the Court. It is therefore futile for the Kingdom of Belgium in those circumstances to challenge the period of two months laid down in the reasoned opinion.

The Belgian Government further submits that the action is unfounded because the period of 24 months for implementing the directive is patently inadequate. It also argues that Council Directive No. 77/780 raises problems of interpretation with regard to the very nature of the obligations which it imposes upon Member States and the directly applicable nature of certain provisions.

In that respect attention should be drawn to the fact that the governments of the Member States participate in the preparatory work for directives and must therefore be in a position to prepare within the period prescribed the legislative provisions necessary for their implementation. If, nevertheless, the period allowed for the implementation of a directive proves to be too short, the only means of action compatible with Community law available to the Member State concerned consists in taking the appropriate initiatives within the Community in order to obtain the necessary extension of the period by the competent Community institution.

As for the difficulties in interpreting the directive, they cannot have been such as to sanction the Belgian Government in exceeding the periods it had accepted, especially as it had other means to enable it to determine the scope of its obligations.

Moreover, even if certain provisions of the directive were directly applicable, that does not exempt the Belgian State from its obligation of implementing the directive by adopting national provisions. As the Court has already observed in the judgment of 6 May 1980 in Case 102/79 (Commission v Belgium [1980] ECR 1487), the right of persons affected to rely in law on a directive as against the defaulting Member State constitutes a minimum guarantee arising from the binding nature of the obligation imposed on Member States by the effect of directives under the third paragraph of Article 189 and cannot justify a Member State's absolving itself from taking in due time implementing measures sufficient to meet the purpose of each directive.

Finally, in its statement of defence the Belgian Government observes that the requirements of the directive are already satisfied in national legislative provisions properly so called or in administrative rules of a general nature which have received sufficient publicity. In its rejoinder the Belgian Government states that those provisions cannot be regarded simply as administrative practices but are in fact administrative rules. It was only after a request addressed to it by the Court that the Belgian Government lodged, on 11 October 1982, at the Court Registry a document to which were annexed the various national provisions which, in its view, ensure implementation of the directive in Belgian law.

However, the Belgian Government invoked that argument only during the course of the action before the Court and confined itself during the procedure prior to action to stating that for the purpose of implementing the directive in question legislation was in preparation.

That manner of proceeding does not comply with the obligation imposed by Article 14 (1) of Directive No. 77/780, which requires Member States immediately to supply the Commission with all necessary information concerning the measures which have been taken to comply with the directive.

However, the action brought by the Commission seeks solely a finding that the Kingdom of Belgium failed to fulfil its obligations under the EEC Treaty "by failing to bring into force within the prescribed period the provisions necessary to comply with Council Directive No. 77/780/EEC" and thus does not concern the obligation under Article 14 of the directive to supply information. It is thus within those limits that the Belgian Government's submission must be answered.

The submission must nevertheless be rejected. Various clear breaches of the directive may be cited here by way of example. In the first place, there appears to be no law at present in force embodying various obligations, imposed inter alia by Articles 3 (7), 8 (5) and 9 (2) of the directive, to notify decisions taken by the Belgian supervisory authorities.

As regards the performance of the obligation upon the competent authorities of the Member States to supply one another with all information likely to facilitate supervision of credit institutions (Article 7 of the directive), the Kingdom of Belgium submits that such an obligation is laid down by Article 40 of Royal Decree No. 185 of 9 July 1935. It is true that that article releases members of the Banking Commission and auditors from the duty of professional secrecy which binds them when they communicate information to a foreign supervisory authority, but it imposes no obligation on the Belgian authorities to collaborate with the authorities of the other Member States.

Furthermore, the document supplied by the Belgian Government does not mention any provision implementing Article 5 of the directive relating to the right of branches of credit institutions to use the same name as they use in the Member State in which their head office is situated. Finally, certain provisions relating to the withdrawal of authorization (Article 8) do not have any equivalent in Belgian law. That is true of the provision which empowers the authorities to withdraw authorization if the institution does not carry on business within 12 months.

It is therefore proper to declare that, by failing to adopt within the prescribed period the provisions necessary to comply with Council Directive No. 77/780 of 12 December 1977, the Kingdom of Belgium failed to fulfil its obligations under the Treaty.

Costs

Under Article 69 (2) of the Rules of Procedure the unsuccessful party is to be ordered to pay the costs. Since the defendant has failed in its submissions it must be ordered to pay the costs.

On those grounds, THE COURT hereby:

1. Declares that, by not adopting within the prescribed period the provisions necessary to comply with Council Directive No. 77/780 of 12 December 1977 on the co-ordination of laws, regulations and administrative provisions relating to the taking up and pursuit of the business of credit institutions (Official Journal 1977 No. L 322, p. 30), the Kingdom of Belgium failed to fulfil its obligations under the EEC Treaty;

2. Orders the defendant to pay the costs.

---

d. A Note on Direct Effect of Directives

While Directives are usually addressed to the Member States, the ECJ has developed a doctrine of direct effect, permitting private individuals to have directives enforced directly by Member States even when the Member State has failed to implement the directive. While the ECJ has applied this principle of direct effect only in special cases, the ECJ has consistently reaffirmed its authority to order the direct enforcement of unimplemented directives under the proper circumstances. Generally, the ECJ has directly applied an unimplemented directive only where the provisions of the directive are sufficiently detailed and explicit to make transformation into national legislation a mere formality. In such a case, the ECJ will oblige the Member State by treating the directive as so transformed into national legislation. The case that follows illustrates the judicial approach to the doctrine of direct effect.

Ursula Becker v. Finanzamt Munster-Innenstadt

(reference for a preliminary ruling from the Finanzgericht Munster)
(Case 8/81) European Court of Justice
[1982] ECR 53, [1982] CMLR 499, 19 January 1982

DECISION: ....

The background to the dispute

It should be recalled that the Sixth Directive, which was adopted on 17 May 1977, provided in Article 1 that the Member States were to adopt by 1 January 1978 at the latest the necessary laws, regulations and administrative provisions in order to modify their value added tax systems in accordance with the requirements of the directive. A number of Member States, including the Federal Republic of Germany, were unable to make the necessary modifications within the prescribed period and therefore the Council, by the Ninth Directive, No. 78/583/EEC of 26 June 1978 on the harmonization of the laws of the Member States relating to turnover taxes (Official Journal 1978 No. L 194, p.16), extended, in the case of those Member States, to 1 January 1979 the period laid down in Article 1 of the Sixth Directive.

It was not until the adoption of the Law of 26 November 1979 (Bundesgesetzblatt I, p.1953), which took effect on 1 January 1980, that the Federal Republic of Germany implemented the Sixth Directive.

It is apparent from the order making the reference to the Court that in her monthly returns in respect of turnover tax for the period from March to June 1979 the plaintiff in the main action, who carries on the business of a self-employed credit negotiator, applied for exemption from tax in respect of her transactions, claiming that Article 13 B (d) 1. compelled the Member States to exempt from value added tax inter alia "the granting and the negotiation of credit" and that that directive had been part of national law since 1 January 1979.

It appears from the file on the case that the plaintiff in the main action informed the Finanzamt [Tax Office] of the amount of her turnover and of the input tax which she had paid and at the same time claimed that she was entitled to the exemption provided for by Article 13 B (d) 1. of the directive. Consequently, in each case she declared the amount of tax payable and the deduction in respect of input tax to be "nil".

The Finanzamt did not accept those returns and, in its provisional notices of assessment for the months in question, charged turnover tax on the transactions of the plaintiff in the main action, in accordance with the national legislation which had not yet been amended, subject to a deduction in respect of input tax.

Following the dismissal of her objection, the plaintiff in the main action appealed against those assessments to the Finanzgericht, relying upon the above-mentioned provision of the directive....

Substance of the case

The Finanzamt, the Government of the Federal Republic of Germany and the Government of the French Republic do not dispute the fact that the provisions of directives may in certain circumstances be relied upon by individuals, as is clear from the case-law of the Court, but maintain that such an effect is not to be attributed to the provision in question in the main action....

The effect of directives in general

According to the third paragraph of Article 189 of the Treaty, "a directive shall be binding, as to the result to be achieved, upon each Member State to which it is addressed, but shall leave to the national authorities the choice of form and methods".

It is clear from that provision that States to which a directive is addressed are under an obligation to achieve a result, which must be fulfilled before the expiry of the period laid down by the directive itself.

It follows that wherever a directive is correctly implemented, its effects extend to individuals through the medium of the implementing measures adopted by the Member State concerned (judgment of 6 May 1980 in Case 102/79 Commission v Belgium [1980] ECR 1473).

However, special problems arise where a Member State has failed to implement a directive correctly and, more particularly, where the provisions of the directive have not been implemented by the end of the period prescribed for that purpose.

It follows from well-established case-law of the Court and, most recently, from the judgment of 5 April 1979 in Case 148/78 Pubblico Ministero v Ratti [1979] ECR 1629, that whilst under Article 189 regulations are directly applicable and, consequently, by their nature capable of producing direct effects, that does not mean that other categories of measures covered by that article can never produce similar effects.

It would be incompatible with the binding effect which Article 189 ascribes to directives to exclude in principle the possibility of the obligations imposed by them being relied on by persons concerned.

Particularly in cases in which the Community authorities have, by means of a directive, placed Member States under a duty to adopt a certain course of action, the effectiveness of such a measure would be diminished if persons were prevented from relying upon it in proceedings before a court and national courts were prevented from taking it into consideration as an element of Community law.

Consequently, a Member State which has not adopted the implementing measures required by the directive within the prescribed period may not plead, as against individuals, its own failure to perform the obligations which the directive entails.

Thus, wherever the provisions of a directive appear, as far as their subject-matter is concerned, to be unconditional and sufficiently precise, those provisions may, in the absence of implementing measures adopted within the prescribed period, be relied upon as against any national provision which is incompatible with the directive or in so far as the provisions define rights which individuals are able to assert against the State.

The question put to the Court by the Finanzgericht seeks to determine whether Article 13 B (d) 1. of the directive may be considered to be of such a nature....

Consequently, the reply to be given to the question put to the Court is that as from 1 January 1979 it was possible for the provision concerning the exemption from turnover tax of transactions consisting of the negotiation of credit contained in Article 13 B (d) 1. of the Sixth Council Directive of 17 May 1977 on the harmonization of the laws of the Member States relating to turnover taxes—Common system of value added tax: uniform basis of assessment to be relied upon, in the absence of the implementation of that directive, by a credit negotiator where he had refrained from passing that tax on to persons following him in the chain of supply, and the State could not claim, as against him, that it had failed to implement the directive.

Costs

The costs incurred by the Government of the Federal Republic of Germany, the Government of the French Republic, the Council and the Commission of the European Communities, which have submitted observations to the Court, are not recoverable. As these proceedings are, in so far as the parties to the main action are concerned, in the nature of a step in the action pending before the national court, the decision on costs is a matter for that court.

On those grounds, THE COURT, in answer to the questions submitted to it by the Finanzgericht Munster by order of 27 November 1980, hereby rules:

As from 1 January 1979 it was possible for the provision concerning the exemption from turnover tax of transactions consisting of the negotiation of credit contained in Article 13 B (d) 1. of the Sixth Council Directive No. 77/388/EEC of 17 May 1977 on the harmonization of the laws of the Member States relating to turnover taxes—Common system of value added tax: uniform basis of assessment to be relied upon, in the absence of the implementation of that directive, by a credit negotiator where he had refrained from passing that tax on to persons following him in the chain of supply, and the State could not claim, as against him, that it had failed to implement the directive.

D. Japan and China

Japan and China can be viewed as variations on a theme. Each was confronted with a technologically superior and aggressive amalgam of European and North American states and each confronted these invasions, especially from the 19th Century on, by resisting the invaders in a way that would preserve what independence each could retain. For both, this meant, in part, "modernization" or "westernization." The object of these efforts was to match the technological superiority of the invaders with indigenous versions of the modern European state. Both Japan and China attempted to incorporate those institutions, theories and habits of the invaders which might be turned to their respective advantages. By the end of the 19th Century, Japan had begun to absorb the capitalist and legal traditions of Western Europe, principally Germany and France.

Japan then turned outward to duplicate the successful aggression of the Western powers, first against Korea, and then against the Russian Empire and China. China remained fractured and more heavily dominated by foreign powers through this period. Despite this, China also sought to modernize by attempting the same sort of systems assimilation. By the middle of the twentieth century, however, Japan, defeated in a war and occupied by the United States, was required to reorient its social and legal systems on an American model. China chose a different path. Upon the victory of the Chinese Communist Party in the great Chinese civil war of the late 1940s, China also was required to absorb a European system of governance. Unlike Japan, which adopted an American overlay, the Chinese Communist Party imported and imposed a different European system in China—a form of Soviet centralizing totalitarian Marxism-Socialism. By the end of the century, however, China began another process of transformation. This time the change constituted an attempt to reform its internal system to be able to effectively deal with an increasingly unified worldwide system of capitalist trade and finance based on the organization of economic enterprises. As you read the materials that follow, consider whether or to what extent, the process of assimilation, complex, contradictory and incomplete in the case of both China and Japan, has contributed to the uniqueness of the development of their respective approaches to the formation and regulation of enterprises.

1. *Japan*

Japan today is classified as a democratic free market constitutional monarchy. The monarchy stretches back to before the beginning of Japanese recorded history. The modern origins of Japanese government and socio-political structure occurred in two waves. The first wave of modernization occurred in the context of political revolution within Japan in the last half of the nineteenth century, when the Emperor recaptured power from the Shogun and attempted the modernization of the nation's legal and economic structure. The model for this modernization was France, and to a greater extent, Germany, with which the Japanese elite thought there was a greater social and cultural connection. This modernization attempt had internal and external components. It's internal component was meant, in some respects, to solidify and institutionalize the power of government under the Emperor. It's external component was focused on industrialization and the acquisition of wealth for the purpose of retaining the independence of Japan in the face of the aggressive military and economic imperialism of the European and American West. Japan's success in this regard was phenomenal. In its rise as a modern industrial power, however, Japan began mimicking the behavior of the West, acquiring a colonial Empire around its periphery and eventually seeking the domination of its greatest historic partner and adversary—China. The eventual result, after a disastrous alliance with Germany and Italy, was military defeat and occupation by the Allied powers in 1945. This occupation brought the second great wave of social, political and economic reform, this time based on an American model of a democratic, free market state. As you read through the introductory materials that follow, think about the ways in which the transplants from the West were integrated within the socio-political culture of Japan and to what extent such transplants were themselves transformed in the process of naturalization in Japan.

Yosiyuki Noda, *Introduction to Japanese Law*

(Anthony H. Angelo, trans. 1976)
(excerpts from pages 39; 58–62; 187–189; some footnotes omitted)

What is the real importance of the old Japanese law to the modern law of Japan? As will be seen, the modern state has no connection with the former Japanese law. The modern law considers itself rather as an heir of Western law. It is only rarely that studies of the former Japanese law are used to interpret the law currently in force.... An eminent Japanese student of Romano-Germanic law, Haranda, in his work *Genealogical Studies of the Japanese Civil Code*, makes clear that all of the articles of the Japanese Civil Code had their origin in modern Western law or in Roman law and not in early Japanese law. It could therefore be said that the history of early Japanese law is, for the present at least, a luxury.

All this does not mean, however, that early Japanese law has no place in an extensive or profound study of contemporary law. There may be a marked difference between the modern and the old law at the level of state law, but at the level of living law there was no break in continuity. The latter evolved spontaneously and unconsciously. Historical continuity interrupted in the conscious continues into the subconscious, and this subconscious plays an important role in the social life of the Japanese people today. It surprises non-Japanese to see that in the studies of jurisprudence in Japan no mention is made of Japanese legal thought, although there is a detailed analysis of Western ideas from Socrates to Geny. The relationship between the old and the new law is one that has not yet been fully studied, and the historical study of Japanese legal thought itself is still a virgin field.

* * *

Although Japan succeeded in faithfully and skillfully imitating the French and German legal systems, its own culture could not help but give an original character to the system that was received. The rapid Europeanization was limited to the field of state law, which dealt only with a small section of Japanese society. Further, it must not be forgotten that the modernized law was put into operation by men whose outlook was determined by a peculiar set of geographical and historical factors. As Koschaker said, "No legislator could avoid leaving some area for the application of indigenous law, and even if he envisaged an en bloc reception it is doubtful that he could even then completely exclude indigenous law. For though the law can be changed from one day to the next, the men to whom it is applied and those who have to apply it in the future cannot be changed this way."[26] Japan was destined to remain a long time subject to social rules that were quite foreign to the received law.

The modern codes predicated a bourgeois society in which every individual is presumed free and equal with everyone else, in which all legal relations constitutive of rights and obligations are formed by the individuals themselves, and where legal relationships are created by the exercise of the individual's free will. This is of course an ideal which no real society fully attains, though it is true that any modern society worthy of the name does attain the ideal to a greater or lesser degree. There was no important difference between the archetypal society on which the French Civil Code was based and the society to which it applied.... Japanese society, on the other hand, retained an essentially archaic morality from the preceding period after the reception of

26. Koschaker, Europa und das römische Recht, p. 145.

Western law. There was a great gap between the society presumed by the modern-style codes and that which existed almost independently of them. Japanese society had no knowledge of ideas of right and duty before the reception, and so the school of *Begriffsjurisprudenz* prospered in Japan after the promulgation of the codes. Japanese jurists did not concern themselves with the actual life of the people because this life followed rules of quite a different kind from those of state law. Even the people did not want state law to be interpreted for their benefit, so that judges contented themselves with giving logical coherence to their decisions without trying to convince the parties. A former professor commenting on the judicial practice of the prewar judges said, "A good judge was considered to be the one who disposed of contrary arguments by saying that they were ill founded in as few words and possible. The judge's merit was in his being able to formulate his decisions in an extremely laconic manner and in his having some knowledge of the German language."

Why was Japanese society able to continue in this way for such a long time in spite of the rapid progress of modern capitalism? The development of capitalism in Japan was dominated from the beginning by political rather than economic considerations. The Meiji Restoration of 1868 was not brought about by the bourgeoisie. The lower ranking samurai, who were the main engineers of the political reform, had absolutely no intention of abandoning the feudal principles which they considered constituted a morality far superior to the European. They understood that they could not preserve Japan's independence without recourse to the material means that the Western powers controlled, but they believed that it was possible to adopt the material civilization of Europe and to harmonize it with Oriental morality. Even the most progressive intellectuals toward the end of the Edo period expressed this idea, and their motto was "Western techniques, Oriental morality." As a consequence the Meiji government intended to modernize Japan only to the extent necessary to make it an equal of the great powers of the world. It was necessary to be wealthy and strong; thus the basic principle of government was embodied in the motto *fokoku kyohei* (rich country and strong military).

* * *

After World War I jurists had begun a critical and sociological study of law, and also a very lively movement toward democracy was growing among a large section of the populace. This tendency coincided with the movement for social rights in Europe, but in Japan it was nothing more than the beginning of true liberalism and democracy. The dominant class feared his development, and in 1925 it had a law, which is well known in Japan for its severity, voted by the Diet. This was the *chian-iji-ho*, the law on the maintenance of public security.... This law was used, with the assistance of the police and the special secret police, *tokubetsu koto keisatu*, to repress progressive ideas. Originally it was used to repress communist activities, but in the end it was used to stifle any idea that could, in the eyes of the ruling class, constitute the slightest danger to the existing political regime....

* * *

In Japan, the starting point for a study of the sources of law is article 3 of the decree of *Dajokan* no. 103 of 8 June 1875.... The decree is entitled "Directives for the Administration of Justice," and article 3 provides that in civil matters a judge must, in the absence of written laws, decide according to custom; in the absence of custom he must decide taking into account *jori*.[4] This text, which has not been abrogated, shows

4. *Jo* (straight line) and *ri* (reason); *jori* corresponds therefore to *recta ratio* in the Ciceronian sense. The term *jori* is much used by jurists at present in those cases where French lawyers would in-

that Japanese law admits a hierarchy of sources of law. Legislation constitutes the primary source, then comes custom, and *jori* is a subsidiary source. The article does not mention case law, though in Japan as in Europe case law is very important, nor is the text of 1875 exclusive. Even between law and custom the hierarchical order is not always clearly indicated. Article 1 of the Commercial Code provides that, "In commercial matters commercial custom shall apply in the absence of provisions in this code, and in the absence of custom the provisions of the Civil Code shall apply." Commercial custom therefore takes precedence over the civil law enactments in commercial affairs.

The Japanese word corresponding to "legislation" is *horitsu.* It may be interpreted widely or restrictively. In the broad sense *horitsu* means law in its entirety, whether written or not. Used in this esense there are the expressions *horitsugaku* (science of law), and *horitsu ka* (jurists). In the narrower and more technical sense *horitsu* means the rules of law established by Parliament. Article 59 of the Constitution uses the term in this narrow sense when it speaks of a bill becoming *horitsu* after it was voted by the two Houses. Not all rules of law voted by Parliament are, however, in the form of *horitsu.* The budget, for example, which is considered by most Japanese public lawyers to have the characteristics of a rule of law, is called *yosan.*

Legislation in Japan, as in Romano-Germanic systems, is the most important of the formal sources of law, and a judge is required to apply it to the cases that come before him in preference to all other sources of law. Legislation is not, of course, as the school of exegesis would have it, the sole source of law, and a judge can refer to other sources of law in the case of the absence, obscurity, or inadequacy of the legislation, for his function is not so much to apply the preexisting law faithfully as to give a reasonable solution to the social conflicts that arise, without the parties having to ask whether laws exist to regulate their dispute or not. In the usual run of cases the judge finds the legislation to apply, since all the important matters likely to cause legal disputes are now regulated by legislation. In this sense, and in this sense only, legislation is the primary source of law.

* * *

The rules promulgated by Parliament have a value superior to that of all other state rules.

The Constitution established by Parliament has a peculiar character and is considered a supreme norm and distinct from other legislation.

* * *

Subordinate to the Constitution a great number of laws regulate all the legal life of the Japanese people. An attempt is being made to codify them to facilitate access to the law by the people, but the end is not yet in sight, and the bulk of the law remains uncodified. There are so far six codes: the Constitution, the Civil Code, the Commercial Code, the Code of Civil Procedure, the Criminal Code, and the Code of Criminal Procedure.

---

voke general principles of law. The term, however, was not invented at the time of the reception of Western law, but was known in the Edo period too. An original Japanese philosopher, Miura Baien, understands this term to mean reason or the universal law which dominates all the physical and moral world. It is not known, however, whether the legislator in 1875 took the word from this source.

John Owen Haley, *Authority Without Power: Law and the Japanese Paradox*

(1991)

(excerpts 139–144; 153–155; 160–163; 166–168; some footnotes omitted)

Bureaucrats and Business: Administrative Powers Constrained

The paradigm of the administrative state has long been the dominant vision of governance in the modern Japanese state. Governmental intrusion into all areas of life has been widely viewed as characteristic of Japan since the Meiji era. The power, prestige, and ubiquitous presence of Japanese officialdom has been a constant theme. Views may vary from Robert Ward's restrained understatement that "since the Meiji restoration... the bureaucracy has been very important in the Japanese political system"[1] to Dan Henderson's hyperbole that in Japan, "[r]ather than a rule of law, a rule of bureaucrats prevails."[2] Some even see in Japan new and menacing models of bureaucratic domination to achieve mercantilist economic goals as "Japan Incorporated,"[3] "Japan's New Capitalism,"[4] or the "Developmental State."[5] Whatever the name, and however varied the harmony, the melody remains the same. Whether a "triumvirate"[6] or "a system,"[7] political, economic, and bureaucratic leaders in Japan form a powerful elite that directs the political economy to achieve self-centered, nationalist aims. Japanese society is thus directed by a state controlled by a small clique of power holders.

Each of these views presupposes the capacity of the state or "system" to exercise power with authority in conscious, willed aims and directions. Japan's economic success is thus the product of intentional, planned policies executed effectively by the state. To the extent that market forces have played any role, this would primarily also be a consequence of intentional choice by prescient officials and their political and business partners in governance. Such analyses leave little room for accident, luck, or circumstance. The operating premise is that what Japanese bureaucrats wanted, they got.

By all appearances such observations are quite accurate. The administrative state has been a preeminent pattern of governance in Japan since the sixth century. It is also the dominant model in all industrial democracies. Many features of Japanese bureaucratic presence are merely reflections of the expanded role of the administrative organs of the state in all societies, industrial and developing. They sometimes appear to Americans as well as Japanese who tend to use the United States as the measure for self-defining comparisons to be peculiar to Japan because the organization and diffusion of political and administrative authority (with power) of the American presidential system are mistakenly taken as the norm against which Japan is compared.

Many of the features considered from an America viewpoint to be distinctively Japanese are in fact, however, reflections of distinctively American institutional

---

1. [Robert E. Ward, Japan's Political System (2nd ed. 1978)], at p. 163.
2. [Dan Fenno Henderson, Foreign Enterprise in Japan (1973)], at p. 195.
3. The person who coined the expression "Japan Incorporated" may now be lost to history, but one of the earliest published uses of the label appears in Eugene J. Kaplan, Japan: The Government-Business Relationship (Washington, D.C.: U.S. Department of Commerce, 1972).
4. William W. Lockwood, *Japan's 'New Capitalism,'* in [The State and Economic Enterprise in Japan (W.W. Lockwood, ed., 1965], at pp. 447–522.
5. Chalmers Johnson, MITI and the Japanese Miracle [(1982)].
6. *See, e.g.*, Joji Watanuki, Politicis in Postwar Japan [(1969)], at p. 11.
7. Karel van Wolferen, The Enigma of Japanese Power [(1969)], at pp. 43–44.

arrangements. Take, for example, the policy-making or legislative code of the bureaucracy. Bureaucratic involvement in setting the legislative agenda and determining the content of legislation is prevalent in all industrial societies, the United States included. However, many Japan specialists in the United States use data on the dearth of private or member bills introduced in the Diet and the overwhelming percentage of government-sponsored and bureaucracy-drafted legislation as an indication of an unusually influential bureaucratic establishment. Chalmers Johnson, for example, sees in such data evidence that "the influence of former bureaucrats in the Diet has tended to perpetuate and actually strengthen the prewar pattern of bureaucratic dominance."[9] However accurate this conclusion may be on other grounds, the bureaucracy's influence on legislation does not provide its proof.

Bureaucratic Influence in Japan: A Comparative Perspective

With respect to legislation, Japan's experience does not differ significantly from that of the United Kingdom, Germany, France, or other parliamentary systems. In the United Kingdom, for example, legislation is prepared and drafted as a matter of course within the administrative department with jurisdiction over its subject matter after consultation with affected interests.[10] Private member bills in the United Kingdom constitute a "very small proportion of the work of Parliament, and then only those which embody policies acceptable to the government are passed."[11] In the Federal Republic of Germany, three-quarters of all legislation is estimated to originate in the ministries.[12] The same is true for France.[13] "The political system of the Fifth Republic," writes Ezra Sulieman, "has conspired to place the deputy in an impotent position, at the mercy of the government and the administration."[14]

Another often-stated source of bureaucratic influence in the legislative process in Japan is the participation by former bureaucrats within the ruling Liberal Democratic Party. The presence of a significant proportion of former bureaucrats in leadership positions in the Party is commonly cited as an explanation for the Japanese bureaucracy's pronounced influence.[15] After all, it is noted, during the thirty-four-year period between 1946 and 1980, for all but five years (1947–48, 1954–57, 1972–76) Japan has been governed by cabinets led by prime ministers who began their careers in one of five national ministries. It is argued that former bureaucrats within the political parties and the Diet tend to retain ties and allegiances to their former ministries analogous to the relationships maintained by former union officials to labor union bureaucracies under Labor Party governments in the United Kingdom, Australia, and New Zealand.

Direct participation by former bureaucrats in the Liberal Democratic Party is explained in large part by the near monopoly of power that elite civilian bureaucrats enjoyed under and immediately after the Allied Occupation. As Chalmers Johnson points out:

---

9. Johnson, *MITI*, op. cit., at p. 47.

10. Brian Smith, Policy-making in the British Government: An Analysis of Power and Rationality [(1976)], at p. 86.

11. Ibid.

12. Gerhard Loewenberg, Parliament in the German Political System [(1967)], at p. 267.

13. Henry W. Ehrmann, Politics in France [(1983)], at p. 307.

14. Ezra N. Suleiman, Politics, Powers, and Bureaucracy in France: The Administrative Elite [(1974)], at pp. 302–305.

15. *See, e.g.*, Daniel I. Okimoto, *Ex-Bureaucrats in the Liberal Democratic Party*, in [Inside the Japanese system, (D.I. Okimoto and T.R. Rohlen eds., 1988)], at pp. 187–190.

> Ironically, it was during the Occupation that one of the fondest dreams of the wartime "control bureaucrats" (*tosei kanryu*) were finally realized. With the militarist gone, the *zaibatsu* facing dissolution and SCAP's [Supreme Commander for the Allied Powers] decision to try to set the economy on its feet, the bureaucracy found itself working for the *tennō* [MacArthur] who really possessed the attributes of "absolutism" (*zettai-shugi*).[17]

The decision by SCAP to rule occupied Japan indirectly, unlike occupied Germany, through the existing civilian bureaucracy precluded any massive purges of civilian officials who had supported and participated in Japan's war effort and secured the political influence of Japan's bureaucratic elite for at least a generation. The members of this elite created the ruling political parties of postwar Japan. The contrast between the postwar and wartime careers of Shigeru Yoshida and Konrad Adenauer or between Nobusuke Kishi and Ludwig Erhard is instructive. The political leadership of postwar Japan was drawn form the prewar or wartime bureaucracy. In postwar Germany, they were either prewar political figures opposed to Hitler's National Socialist regime or political newcomers. Bureaucratic influence in the postwar political process in Japan was thus more a consequence of Occupation policies than some less mutable institutional or cultural feature of Japanese politics.

Gradually, almost imperceptibly, however, the postwar constitutional order has functioned to reduce rather than increase this influence. Except for the 1949 Diet election, in which 37 former government officials, including 25 of Prime Minister Yoshiga's recruits, entered the Diet, and 1952, in which 48 former officials, including several depurgees such as Nobosuki Kishi, were elected; ex-bureaucrats have not made significant political gains in any postwar election. Rarely has the number of newly elected former bureaucrats exceeded a dozen. As the careers of former Prime Minister Kakuei Tanaka and Yasuhiro Nakasone illustrate, the political influence of career politicians and members of their staffs with strong bases of local support has slowly increased from election to election during the postwar period at the expense of bureaucratic elites at the center.

Even granting that former officials exercise significant influence in the ruling party and the Diet, here too Japan's experience merely approximates other parliamentary systems. Aberbach, Putman, and Rockman, for example, show that in 1973 about 38 percent of the members of the West German Bundesrat were government officials on leave.[20] Of those elected a decade later, over ten percent were high civil service officials in federal, state, or local government, at the time of their election. With about 20 percent of the LDP members of the Japanese House of Representatives identified as former government officials, Japan is thus comparable to the Netherlands.

From an American perspective, the coercive powers of the Japanese bureaucracy seem impressive also for their reach. The scope of corrosive bureaucratic intrusion into the economic and social life of Japan is often described as if it were several degrees greater than in the United States or other industrial democracies. Japanese officialdom appears to be "so confident, prestigious, and effective, as well as officious."[23] Such ob-

---

17. Chalmers Johnson, *Japan, 'Who Governs?' An Essay on Official Bureaucracy,* [2 JOURNAL OF JAPANESE STUDIES 16 (1975).

20. JOEL D. ABERBACH, ROBERT D. PUTNAM, AND BERT A. ROCKMAN, BUREAUCRATS AND POLITICIANS IN WESTERN DEMOCRACIES [(1987)], at p. 277, fn. 16.

23. Henderson, *Foreign Enterprise,* op. cit., at p. 208.

servations are equally flawed. Government in the United States is far more intrusive in its coercive impact than in Japan. Except perhaps for family registration and the neighborhood police, there is little if any evidence that the average Japanese citizen has any more contact with the government than his or her American counterpart. The volume and coercive intrusiveness of governmental controls in the United States—from taxation through consumer and environmental regulation—is in fact greater than in Japan. The volume of new regulatory enactments in the United States each week exceeds the annual quota of all new legislation and administrative regulation combined promulgated by Japanese authorities. There is in fact no evidence to support the widespread belief that bureaucratic influence is any greater in Japan than in other developed parliamentary democracies. Once again, we confront a persistent and unyielding myth.

Even in comparison with the United States the extent of administrative intervention in Japan is hardly remarkable. Despite differences in priorities and emphasis, governmental measures designed to foster economic growth were at least as extensive in 19th century America as Meiji Japan. The Meiji government's efforts to encourage industrial development through model factories, new government-managed enterprises, and subsidies pale in comparison with the massive transfer of public land and timber and mineral resources for promotion of the railroad, timber, and mining industries. By the 1880s, however, as the Meiji government completed its liquidation of government enterprises and the remaining mining and other resources owned by its Tokugawa predecessors, the United States had already begun the regulatory era. Whereas the Japanese continued to pursue their goal of economic growth through the promotion of private industry, by the late nineteenth century the United States was regulating major sectors of the economy purportedly in the public or consumer interest. The result in the United States was the burgeoning state and federal administrative apparatus of regulatory commissions departments, and agencies. As Kenenth Culp Davis reminds us, "almost one-third of all federal peace-time administrative agencies were created before 1900 and another third before 1930."[24] The array of regulatory controls quite familiar in the United States by the eve of World War I were unknown in Japan until after World War II. Those who describe the power and presence of the postwar Japanese bureaucracies generally ignore the fact that nearly all of Japan's basic regulatory legislation in effect today was drafted and imposed by its American occupiers between 1945 and 1952. No Japanese Diet has extended the powers granted to the Japanese bureaucracies by the Occupation authorities.

Nor at any time in modern Japanese history has Japan maintained as large a bureaucratic establishment as the United States. In 1910, for example, Japan had estimated 185,045 advisory national government civilian employees, including imperial appointees, minor officials, and other salaried government employees—that is, one government employee per 265.8 persons. In the United States in 1910 there were an estimated 388,708 federal government employees, including postal workers, or 1 federal employee per 237.7 persons. By 1970 both the absolute numbers and ratios had increased significantly in both countries, with as might be expected, the United States leading Japan by a wide margin. By 1970 the number of Japanese civilian government employees had increased to 832, 174, almost doubling the number of government employees per capita to 1 per 146.9 persons. During the same period the number of United

24. Kenneth Culp Davis, I Administrative Law Treatise [(2nd ed., 1982)], at p. 17.

States federal government employees rose to 2,981,574 or 1 government employee to every 68.4 persons.

What makes the role of the bureaucracy distinctive in Japan is neither its influence nor its size. It is instead the conjunction of broad, seemingly limitless authority without, however, even a relatively normal degree of coercive legal powers. That most assessments of the Japanese bureaucracy fail to convey its role accurately can best be explained by fundamental differences in language and conceptual premises.

Seldom articulated with much precision, governmental regulation and bureaucratic influence in most industrial democracies is assumed by economists, political scientists, and lawyers alike to relate to politics articulated in legislation or legally binding administrative pronouncements and then implemented by governmental authorities exercising a variety of coercive legal powers. The prevailing paradigm of the administrative state in the West depicts legislatures, administrative agencies, and, occasionally, the courts as the fora with legislators, administrative officials, and judges, the primary actors. Despite formal procedural controls, particularly in the United States, most administrative activities tends to be informal. Moreover, by necessity or design those whose economic, ideological, and political interests are affected usually participate both in the process formulating policy and in its implementation. Notwithstanding procedural requirements structuring how decisions are to be made, informal negotiation and compromise are dominant aspects of the process. There is thus always some element of consent by those most affected. Government officials remain, however, the primary actors. They are the ones who make the decisions, they decide whether to accept or reject a compromise and issue the final rule or order.

Administrative regulation in the Western democracies also has limits. Governmental controls are restricted to specific areas of activity. As exemplified by economic regulation, governmental directives and control do not cover a broad expanse of economic matters but instead reflect in conception particularized intervention as a substitute for otherwise private or marketplace decisions. Whether a regulated or command economy, however, the nature of state coercion through statutory or administrative fiat is essentially the same. The difference between the two lies more in the pervasive scope of state direction not in the nature or the efficacy of the state's coercion or control in areas subject to state intervention. In both law is the primary instrument of the coercive powers of the state.

The Japanese pattern must be distinguished. In terms of *authority* governmental activity in Japan tends to be as unlimited in scope as in a command economy. In terms of *coercive power,* however, government officials have only the legal powers granted to them by statute plus whatever extra-legal levers of influence or persuasion may be available. The result is that pervasive, ostensibly unrestrained capacity to intervene without, however, the means of coercive legal control that may be necessary to achieve official aims unilaterally lacking the consent of those affected.

The Japanese administrative process is more aptly described therefore as a form of *consensual administrative management.* Yet even this phrase may mislead insofar as it implies as exercise of power by state officials in determining or implementing policy. In the context of contemporary Japan, consensual management encompasses a process of governance in which the state may have the authority to intervene but not necessarily the power to insist on unilateral decisions. Ministries and other administrative bodies become in consequence the situs for decisions, but officials are not the primary actors. Their influence and control depend upon their ability to achieve consent among those most directly affected by the policies being implemented and whose cooperation is necessary for their effective implementation. Behind the appearance of official direction and control is a process of governance by negotiation in which the state must by necessity bargain in both the making of policy and its enforcement. In such circumstances, distinctions between "public" and "private" blur and "regulation" takes on new meaning, as those apparently subject to governmental direction gain a significant and often determinative voice in the process of formulating and implementing policy. Unlike expressions of consent expressed through formal electoral and similar institutionalized channels in other industrial democracies, the consent of those governed in Japan is less the product of intentional political choice than necessity born of Japan's unique institutional history.

* * *

A Mission to Manage

A sense of mission is widely recognized as one of the chief attributes of the Japanese bureaucracy. John Maki, writing in 1947 as a critic of bureaucratic influence, viewed the select economic ministries as a small elite sharing "a common training, a common tradition, a common ideology, and a common desire to monopolize what the group regarded as the skills of government."[70] Writing three decades later Ezra Vogel elaborated:

> The esprit that unites a ministry's five hundred or so elite bureaucrats rests on a sense of group mission. Although not immune form political pressures, bureaucrats do not hestitate to unite against politicians who obstruct their perceived mission. Responsibility for success in any important matter rests with the work unit, and all in the unit are judged by the unit's contribution to the ministry. Superiors do not promote someone who cannot win the liking and cooperation of his peers. For an individual's value to his unit is determined by his capacity to work effectively with his peers, his superiors and his subordinates. Each bureaucrat is personally identified with the mission of his work unit and the ministry as a whole.[71]

Generally absent, however, from such descriptions of the esprit and sense of mission of the MITI and other economic bureaucracies is any clear definition of what that mission is. Chalmers Johnson comes close. In his study of the Ministry of International Trade and Industry, he demonstrates how MITI officials by choice and chance emerge as one of the dominant actors in setting Japan's economic agenda. Theirs was no narrow, technocratic mission to manage or control carefully defined sectors of Japan's economy. Their objective was instead a broad, undefined mission to manage the economy overall.[72] In effect, Japan's bureaucratic establishment divided the totality of Japanese economic life and allocated to each ministry responsibility for the management in their respective spheres with MITI at the center. As a result, governmental intervention in the economy appears to be totalitarian in scope with unbounded administrative discretion. Ministry establishment laws [*setchi ho*] became blueprints for territorial divisions, allocating managerial jurisdiction over specific segments of the total terrain. This claim to authority above all other factors sets the Japanese governmental agencies apart from the regulatory, policing agencies of the United States as well as the more "managerial" approach of bureaucracies in other industrial democracies. The managerial mission of Japan's economic officialdom establishes an underlying premise that it had as

---

70. John M. Maki, *The Role of the Bureaucracy in Japan*, PACIFIC AFFAIRS (1947), at p. 396.
71. EZRA F. VOGEL, JAPAN AS NUMBER ONE: LESSONS FOR AMERICA [(1979)], at pp. 56–57.
72. Johnson, *MITI*, op. cit., at p. 40.

much to do with their organization and behavior as history or even shared values and expectations of the Japanese society at large.

The mission of Japan's bureaucracies is not, however, unrelated to either history or culture. Both are central aspects of bureaucratic authority that cannot be separated form the more general societal acceptance of the bureaucracy's role. While denying the utility of cultural explanations for Japanese economic success, Johnson nevertheless subscribes—perhaps inadvertently—to what is essentially a cultural analysis of the bureaucracy's role. As he explains:

> The "aura" formerly attached to samurai can still be found in some of the terminology now associated with bureaucrats. For example, the common term for governmental authorities is "those above" (*okami*). It is also said that Japanese do not normally question the authority of the government because they respect its "samurai sword" (*denka no hoto*), which refers directly to a samurai family's heirloom sword. Such a jeweled sword symbolized the status of a samurai household rather than being a weapon designed for killing people. Yamanouchi says that use of the term reflects the popular consciousness of the law as being a symbol of authority, not something the possessor of authority need actually use. The change from the old constitution to the new, Yamanouchi argues, did little to change this attitude.[75]

In other words, Japanese bureaucrats enjoy widespread public acceptance of their authority to govern, an authority that, like the heirloom samurai sword, is symbolic and does not necessarily denote the powers of actual rule. The postwar constitution did not radically alyter the prewar system. Continuity exists. Popular sovereignty may have replaced imperial rule but the bureaucracy has managed to perpetuate its claim to authority absent imperial delegation nonetheless. The ultimate justification for the postwar bureaucracy's mission to manage has thus been a shared societal expectation, a general public consensus, based on a perceived tradition and historical perspective. Bureaucratic authority in Japan does not necessarily include the prerogatives of power.

* * *

Administrative Guidance: A Reflection of Authority Without Power

As a result of the lack of formal legal powers and the weakness of the few legal penal fines that do exist for noncompliance with administrative orders, Japanese government officials have been forced by necessity to rely on informal, extra-legal sanctions when coercion is required. Denied express legal powers to make and implement desired economic policies, Japan's economic ministries have had resort to indirect means of persuasion. Barely able to pressure much less expand any express legitimizing statutory powers, MITI, in the late 1950s and 1960s increasingly relied on controls bequeathed by the Occupation. Foremost among these were foreign exchange and foreign trade controls. The threat of denial of foreign exchange or import licenses for essential; raw materials in many instances was sufficient to achieve desired ends.

The promotional thrust of Japanese economic policy coupled with extensive bureaucratic involvement in the economic life of an industry or firm generally made overt threats unnecessary. The mechanisms of postwar economic policy ensured continual, cooperative relationships between Japan's leading corporations and government officials. Few adversarial issues arose, and those that did could be resolved cooperatively. For this reason, the inadequacy of formal legal sanctions seldom posed a problem. Most

---

75. Johnson, *MITI*, op. cit., at p. 40.

governmental actions were designed as benefits and therefore the question of how to compel compliance rarely surfaced. Even where an official request for action may have had some adverse consequences, in most instances the recipient could expect protection from major losses and thus could accommodate official policy. The prevalence of administrative guidance [*gyōsei shidō*] as an informal means of governmental persuasion by Japan's economic ministries is thus partially explained by the policies being implemented to foster economic growth and industrial development. Not all uses of administrative guidance fall into this category, however.

The economists and the lawyers tend to define the term administrative guidance differently. In the literature on Japan's postwar economy, administrative guidance is often equated with the content or substance of Japan's postwar industrial policy. For the lawyer, however, the term is descriptive of a process used to implement public policies as distinguished from the policies themselves. Administrative guidance is defined quite simply as advice or direction by government officials carried out violently—that is, without formal legal coercion—by the recipient. By definition it does not involve either formal legal action on the part of the government or direct legal coercion. Compliance is voluntary therefore only in a narrow legal sense.

As noted in a recent Japanese study,[87] administrative guidance is an academic concept not a technical legal term. As such, it has been the topic of considerable scholarly analysis in Japan, the United States, and Western Europe. Japanese legal scholars usually treat the subject in relation to more fundamental issues of administrative law, ranging from direct judicial review or other forms of redress by objecting recipients to the ultimate if more abstract question of the legality of particular instances of administrative guidance.[88]

These are, of course, critical questions for those concerned with the legal issues administrative guidance poses within the Japanese legal system. For instance, the restrictive approach adopted by Japanese courts in defining administrative measures subject to judicial review has insured that neither the recipients nor third parties adversely affected by administrative guidance have had the access to the courts except in a few instances through damage actions.[89] Moreover, as a closed process of continuous interaction between government officials and a limited number of private parties, official resort to administrative guidance is also excoriated for exclusion of public participation and political review.[90]

At least in part because Japanese perceive the administrative process in the West to be a formal and more clearly defined procedural process, Japanese observers think of administrative guidance as a uniquely Japanese phenomenon. It is commonly regarded as

87. *Gyōsei shidō ni kansuru chōsa kenkyū hōkokusho* (Report on investigative study of administrative guidance) (Tokyo... 1981) (hereafter *Administrative Guidance Research Report).* The Report was prepared for the Administrative Management Agency [Gyōsei Kanri Chō] by a committee of Japan's leading legal scholars in administrative law and select businessmen and government officials.

88. *See, e.g.*, Narita Yoriaki, *Gyōsei shidō, in* Gendaihō (Contemporary Law) Vol. 4 [(1966)], at pp. 131–168, translated ("Administrative Guidance") in [2 Law in Japan: An Annual](1968), at pp. 45–79.

89. *See*, for example, the summary of Japanese requirements for standing in Ichiro Ogawa, *Judicial Review of Administrative Actions in Japan,* [43 Wash. L. Rev. 1075–1094 (1968)]. For a study of judicial review by means of damage actions, *see* Michael K. Young, *Judicial Review of Administrative Guidance: Governmentally Encouraged Consensual Dispute Resolution in Japan*, [84 Colum. L. Rev. 923–83 (1984)]...

90. *See, e.g.*, Yamanouchi Kazuo, *Administrative Guidance and the Rule of Law,* [7 Law in Japan, 22, 31–33 (1974)]. See also Watanabe Yoshifusa, *Gyōsei shidō o meguru shomondai* (Problems with administrative guidance), Jurisuto, No. 342 (1966), at. pp. 46, 48–49.

the product of Japan's particular historical and social context and thus endemic as an aspect of the "Japanese climate."[91] Many Western observers similarly emphasize the uniqueness of administrative guidance to Japan. Although all major studies in English and German recognize that practices analogous to administrative guidance can be found in the West, most emphasize the cultural factors that seem to explain administrative guidance as a peculiar Japanese institution. They find the underpinnings for administrative guidance in a neo-Confucian deference to authority and related desire to maintain harmony and cooperation and to avoid adversarial posturing, in other words, in the special social psychology of the Japanese. Paul Davis, for example, lists the persistence of patron-client relations, the continuity of traditional attitudes towards officials, a strongly held desire to avoid confrontation, and a weak "legal consciousness" as its main cultural props.[92] Elaborating upon these points, Wolfgang Pape is more sweeping:

> [T]he vertical structure of Japanese society allows open intercourse between those "above and below" and demarcates only in perpendicular fashion the interests of each group. This prevents formation of class consciousness and leads to a high degree of permeability in the traditional hierarchy from the Emperor to the common people (*shimojimo*). The structure of the smallest community of interest is transmitted to all other social units. Consequently, corresponding patterns of conduct are manifested between teacher and pupil, employer and employee, large firm and sub-contractor and in like manner between public administrators and private enterprises, without regard to any identity of interest on a horizontal level.[93]

Pape adds the "average man's longing for *amae*" and "the reciprocal obligatory effect [*giri*] of all kinds of favors or acts of benevolence [*on*]"[94] to his list.

Such analyses cannot be dismissed out of hand. Some explanation is necessary to explain what appears to be an extraordinary feature of the Japanese system of governance—that informal requests to produce compliance—for Japanese and Western commentators alike assert or seem to presume that administrative guidance is an effective means of implementing policy. "Compliance," Jeffrey Lepon claims, "is the typical Japanese corporate response to administrative guidance."[95] Chalmers Johnson makes a similar claim, coining the term "developmental" as the new rubric under which administrative guidance as a cooperative process for implementing economic policy is viewed as a cornerstone of Japan's postwar recovery.[96] Although many duly note the role of private business in formulating economic policy and a Japanese stress on consensus, they appear uniformly to believe that what officials want, officials get by voluntary compliance. Were this true, Japan would indeed be a unique case.

The mist clears and an array of fundamental misconceptions disappear, however, when administrative guidance is viewed simply as a Japanese species of informal enforcement. As such, administrative guidance is not peculiarly Japanese, except perhaps for its ubiquity. Informal enforcement by official suggestion, advice, recommendations,

---

91. *Administrative Guidance Research Report*, op. cit., at pp. i–iii.

92. Paul A. Davis, *Administrative Guidance, Sophia University Socio-Economic Institute Bulletin*, No. 41 (1972), at pp. 7–11.

93. Wolgang Pape, *Gyōsei shidō and the Antimonopoly Law*, [15 Law in Japan: An Annual 15 (1982)]. *See also* Wolfgang Pape, Gyoseishido un das Anti-Monopol-Gesetz in Japan (Administrative Guidance and the anti-monopoly law in Japan) (1980)], at pp. 41–50.

94. Ibid. at 16.

95. Jeffrey M. Lepon, *Administrative Guidance in Japan*, [2 Fletcher Forum] (1978), at p. 143.

96. Johnson, *MITI*, op. cit.

or pointed direction is not only common to all legal systems, it is indeed the most common form of law enforcement. All legal systems depend upon voluntary compliance with the law from the payment of taxes to regulatory control. No regime except perhaps one of absolute terror relies principally upon direct coercion, and even then compliance is usually not involuntary in the narrow sense of a response to legally binding orders backed by immediate and direct threats of coercion.

Informal enforcement by United States antitrust authorities may contrast starkly with MITI practice in policy but not as process.... Whether labeled administrative guidance or informal enforcement, and whether carried out by the Japanese FTC and MTI or United States Federal Trade Commission and Justice Department officials, the process is the same.

What distinguishes Japan is the persuasive resort to informal enforcement in contexts that seem to require formal regulation in other industrial states. In Japan informal enforcement is not *a* process of governing, but has become the process of governing. It is used to implement nearly all bureaucratic policy, whether or not expressed in statute or regulation, at all levels of government and all administrative offices. Japanese officials use informal enforcement to implement policy in every conceivable situation from antitrust violations and price controls to regulation of financial institutions. Even bowling alley business hours have been informally curtailed by the police as a means of reducing juvenile crime.[100]....

* * *

Consensual Governance

The avoidance of legal regulation and coercive state control must be viewed as among the most prominent characteristics of governance in postwar Japan. As Richard Samuels insightfully observes: "Although the Japanese state pervades the market, it does not lead, guide or supervise private interests. There is little evidence that state actors have ever been able to resist political pressures in the absence of alliances with part of the private sector."[103].... Samuels concludes, "The Japanese bureaucracy does not dominate, it negotiates."[105]

Governmental decisions are not and cannot be unilateral. Legal ordering and state controls are accepted more often than not as a last resort. Individuals ad private corporate interests alike seek governmental assistance and protection only out of necessity and the failure of extralegal, non-governmental mechanisms for preserving a desired status quo or effecting a desired change. The jurisdictional authority of those with political and legal authority may seem pervasive and boundless in scope. However, a myriad of social and political arrangements—not the least of which is the postwar constitutional system of executive and political accountability to the electorate—hem in those with any pretensions to authority by reducing and restraining their coercive powers. Authority to command thus may seem limitless in practice but not so the power to coerce.

This separation of power from authority in postwar Japan does not, however, render officials impotent. They remain managers whose capacity to perform their appointed

100. The *Administrative Guidance Research Report*, op. cit., includes detailed studies of administrative guidance by each of the economic ministries in transportation, petroleum, agriculture, forestry, fisheries, pharmaceuticals, labor and construction.

103. Richard Samuels, The Business of the Japanese State: Energy Markets in Comparative and Historical Perspective [(1987)], at p. 260.

105. Ibid.

tasks effectively depends upon their skills in achieving consensus and assent. Japan's postwar officialdom thus does not govern in any Western sense of the word. Instead, they participate in the processes of governance as mediators, brokers, cajolers, and above all, presiding officials responsible for bargained-for, negotiated policymaking and implementation by reciprocal consent. To quote Samuels once more:

> Reciprocal consent is not uniquely Japanese. In Western Europe similar negotiations over the nature and extent of state intervention have resulted in a market presence for the state—often with considerable support from industry and a labor. In Japan the state has been diverted away from market competition entirely. What makes Japan different is the routinization of economic policy which the durability of elites and their constituencies makes possible. Japan is not merely a vat of competing interests; neither is Japan a European government in an American business environment. Rather, the institutionalized routine of negotiation, reciprocal consent, is the tie that binds.[106]

The political, social, and economic consequences of this institutionalized routine are particularly significant for those outside the select enclosures of the system. Reciprocal consent does not work very well when there are too many players. Hence Japan's bureaucratic managers expend considerable efforts in reducing the number of participants. This means keeping outsiders out. Even within the system, hierarchical order prevails with those who have the greatest bargaining power taking leading roles. Above all, the process to work by necessity precludes transparency. By opening it to public participation or scrutiny, it becomes unmanageable and out of control. Frank Upham is surely correct therefore in his assessment that:

> [T]he bureaucracy does retain a surprising degree of control over the pace and course, if not the substance, of social change in Japan, and one of the major instruments for such control is the manipulation of the legal framework within which social change and its harbinger, social conflict, occur.... Just as the government uses institutionalized mediation, compensation systems, and affirmative action grants to avoid or influence the course of conflict in the pollution and discrimination areas, MITI mediates interfirm ad interindustry conflict with the goal of facilitating eventual agreement on policy that is satisfactory to the participants and also within government guidelines. The relative power of the bureaucracy vis-a-vis the private sector may be significantly less in industrial policy than in the other cases, but the underlying role of the government as mediator and facilitator within an informal process of conflict management remains unchanged.[107]

In the end, however, the pressures of the marketplace—be it political or economic—become determinative in the formation of policy and its implementation. Law, as most Japanese take for granted, does not control. But it does provide the framework within which consensual ordering occurs or a means of legitimating norms around which a consensus can be formed, and thereby channels behavior. Law is therefore only one of several factors that drive the mechanisms of societal ordering in Japan: social controls.

---

106. Ibid.

107. [Frank K. Upham, Law and Social Change in Postwar Japan (1987)], at pp. 17, 24–25.

Comments and Questions

1. The concept of *consensual administrative management* described in the excerpt of Professor Haley provides a useful basis for understanding the relationship of Japanese law to Japanese practice not only with respect to law in general, but perhaps also with the "rules" for the regulation of enterprises. Does the reading suggest that an appreciation of Japanese corporate governance requires an understanding of more than the black letter law? But would this also apply to an understanding of corporate practice in the United States?

2. Professor Haley makes the point that the Americans used the indigenous bureaucracy in Japan as the instrument of the implementation of its program of democratization during the Occupation. In Germany, the Americans purged the Occupied Zones of the indigenous bureaucracy but left the civil law structure substantially intact (other than to remove the now offensive accretions to law made during the dictatorship of Hitler and his party). Do you think that this difference in treatment affected the ways in which law was received in each country?

3. How important do you think is the concept of separation of power from authority? Can you think of an examples of situations in the United States in which power is separated from authority? The readings also highlight the relationship between law and social controls. Americans are sometimes taught to believe in the primacy of law, and its importance in molding social norms. Is it possible that social norms also exert a strong influence on formal lawmaking, especially in the area of enterprise regulation?

4. Do the excerpts above make a case for convergence theory—that is that ostensibly different cultures will tend to solve the same problem in similar ways? Think about that question as you look at the way in which the People's Republic of China has attempted to create what it considers a unique and superior system of governance.

---

2. China

Like Japan, China has seen two great waves of social, cultural and economic transformation, reflected in its law, and grafted onto a vibrant ancient, imperialist and hegemonic indigenous system of social organization. Both waves occurred at roughly the same time as the great transforming waves in Japan—with a substantially different focus and effect. The first wave occurred at the end of the nineteenth century, leading to the demise of the old Chinese Empire and the attempt to establish a Western style democracy, with Chinese characteristics under the leadership of Sun Yat-Sen. But China, unlike Japan, had been partially occupied by the Western powers for a long time before this revolution, and the Chinese elites were significantly fractured in terms of the direction they sought for China. The ultimate result was political fracture and the continued interference of the Western powers, and, after the 1920s, by Japan. The 1930s brought invasion by Japan, and civil war between the factions of the Chinese elites. These factions were roughly divided into two great camps; one led by Chiang Kai-Chek, the long-time leader of the Chinese Nationalist Party and ally of the Western powers, sought a modernization of an independent and strong China, free of foreign interference, on the model of Western European states and Japan. The other, led by Mao-Tse-

Tung, the leader of the Chinese Communist Party, sought the same modernizing transformation, but on the model of Eastern European states, particularly those of the Marxist-Socialist totalitarian republics of the Soviet Union. The civil war continued after the end of the Japanese occupation in 1945, and culminated in the victory of the Chinese Communist Party under the leadership of Mao Tse-Tung.

The Constitution of the People's Republic of China

Adopted March 5, 1978 by the Fifth National People's Congress of the People's Republic of China at its First Session, reprinted and translated, in II Selected Legal Documents if the People's Republic of China (Joseph En-Pao Wang, ed. 1979) (excerpt pages 127–158)

Preamble

After more than a century of heroic struggle the Chinese people, led by the Communist Party of China headed by our great leader and teacher Chairman Mao Tsetung, finally overthrew the reactionary rule of imperialism, feudalism and bureaucrat-capitalism by means of people's revolutionary war, winning complete victory in the new-democratic revolution, and in 1949 founded the People's Republic of China.

The founding of the People's Republic of China marked the beginning of the historical period of socialism in our country. Since then, under the leadership of Chairman Mao and the Chinese Communist Party, the People of all our nationalities have carried out Chairman Mao's proletarian revolutionary line in the political, economic, cultural and military fields and in foreign affairs and have won great victories in socialist revolution and socialist construction through repeated struggles against enemies both at home and abroad through the Great Proletarian Cultural Revolution. The dictatorship of the proletariat in our country has been consolidated and strengthened, and China has become a socialist country with the beginnings of prosperity.

Chairman Mao Tsetung was the founder of the People's Republic of China. All our victories in revolution and construction havwe been won under the guidance of Marxism-Leninism-Mao Tsetung Thought. The fundamental guarantee that the people of all nationalities will struggle in unity and carry the proletarian revolution through to the end is always to hold high and staunchly to defend the great banner of Chairman Mao.

The triumphant conclusion of the Great Proletarian Cultural Revolution has ushered in a new period of development in China's socialist revolution and socialist construction. In accordance with the basic line of the Chinese Communist Party for the entire historical period for socialism, the general task for the people of the whole country in this new period is: To persevere in continuing the revolution under the dictatorship of the proletariat, carry forward the three great revolutionary movements of class struggle, the struggle for production and scientific experimentation, and make China a great and powerful socialist country with modern agriculture, industry, national defense and science and technology by the end of the century.

We must persevere in the struggle of the proletariat against the bourgeoisie and in the struggle for the socialist road against the capitalist road. We must oppose revision-ism and prevent the restoration of capitalism. We must be prepared to deal with subversion and aggression against our country by social-imperialism and imperialism.

We should consolidate and expand the revolutionary united front which is led by the working class and based on the worker-peasant alliance, and which unites the large numbers of intellectuals and other working people. Patriotic democratic parties, patriotic personages, our compatriots in Taiwan, Hongkong and Macao, and our countrymen residing abroad. We should enhance the great unity of all the nationalities in our country. We should correctly distinguish and handle the contradictions among the people and those between ourselves and the enemy. We should endeavor to create a among the people of the whole country a political situation in which there are both centralism and democracy, both discipline and freedom, both unity of will and personal ease of mind and liveliness, so as to help bring all positive factors into play, overcome all difficulties, better consolidate the proletarian dictatorship and build up our country more rapidly.

Taiwan is China's sacred territory. We are determined to liberate Taiwan and accomplish the great cause of unifying our motherland.

In international affairs, we should establish and develop relations with other countries on the basis of the Five Principles of mutual respect for sovereignty and territorial integrity, mutual non-aggression, non-interference in each other's internal affairs, equality and mutual benefits, and peaceful coexistence. Our country will never seek hegemony, or strive to be a superpower. We should uphold proletarian internationalism. In accordance with the theory of the three worlds, we should strengthen our unity with the proletariat and the opposed people and nations throughout the world, the socialist countries, and the third world countries, and we should unite with all countries subjected to aggression, subversion, interference, control and bullying by the social imperialists and the imperialist superpowers to form the broadest possible international united front against the hegemonists of the super powers and against a new world war, and strive for the progress and emancipation of humanity.

Chapter One
General Principles

Article I

The People's Republic of China is a socialist state of the dictatorship of the proletariat led by the working class and based on the alliance of workers and peasants.

Article 2

The Communist Party of China is the core of leadership of the whole Chinese people. The working class exercises leadership over the state through its vanguard, the Communist Party of China.

The guiding ideology of the People's Republic of China is Marxism-Leninism-Mao Tsetung Thought.

Article 3

All power in the People's Republic of China belongs to the people. The organs through which the people exercise state powers are the National People's Congress and the local people's congresses at various levels.

The National People's Congress, the local people's congresses at various levels and all other organs of state practise democratic centralism.

Article 4

The People's Republic of China is a unitary multi-national state.

All the nationalities are equal. There should be unity and fraternal love among then nationalities and they should help and learn from each other. Discrimination against, or oppression of, any nationality, and acts which undermine the unity of the nationalities are prohibited. Big-nationality chauvinism and local-nationality chauvinism must be opposed.

All the nationalities have the freedom to use and develop their own spoken and written languages, and to preserve or reform their own customs and ways.

Regional autonomy applies in an area where a minority nationality lives in a compact community. All the national autonomous areas are inalienable parts of the People's Republic of China.

Article 5

There are mainly two kinds of ownership of the means of production in the People's Republic of China at the present stage: socialist ownership by the whole people and socialist collective ownership by the working people.

The state allows non-agricultural individual labourers to engage in individual labour involving no exploitation of others, within the limits permitted by law and under unified arrangement and management by organizations at the basic level in cities and towns or in rural areas. At the same time, it guides these individual labourers step by step onto the road of socialist collectivization.

Article 6

The state sector of the economy, that is, the socialist sector owned by the whole people, is the leading force in the national economy.

Mineral resources, waters and those forests, undeveloped lands and other marine and land resources owned by the state are the property of the whole people.

The state may requisition by purchase, take over for use, or nationalize land under conditions prescribed by law.

Article 7

The rural people's commune sector of the economy is a socialist sector collectively owned by the masses of working people. At present, it generally takes the form of three-level ownership, that is, ownership by the commune, the production brigade and the production team, with the production team as the basic accounting unit. A production brigade may become the basic accounting unit when its conditions are ripe.

Provided that the absolute predominance of the collective economy of the people's commune is ensured, commune members may farm small plots of land for personal needs, engage in limited household side-line production, and in pastoral areas they may also keep a limited number of livestock for personal needs.

Article 8

Socialist public property shall be inviolable. The state ensures the consolidation and development of the socialist sector of the economy owned by the whole people and of the socialist sector collectively owned by the masses of working people.

The state prohibits any person from using any means whatsoever to disrupt the economic order of the society, undermine the economic plans of the state, encroach upon or squander state and collective property, or injure the public interest.

Article 9

The state protects the right of citizens to own lawfully earned income, savings, houses and other means of livelihood.

Article 10

The state applies the socialist principles: "He who does not work, neither shall he eat" and "from each according to his ability, to each according to his work."

Work is an honourable duty for every citizen able to work. The state promotes socialist labour emulation, and, putting proletarian politics in command, it applies the policy of combining moral encouragement with material reward, with the stress on the former, in order to heighten the citizens' socialist enthusiasm and creativeness in work.

Article 11

The state adheres to the general line of going all out, aiming high and achieving greater, faster, better and more economical results in building socialism, it undertakes the planned, proportionate and high speed development of the national economy, and it continuously develops the productive forces, so as to consolidate the country's independence and security and improve the people's material and cultural life step by step.

In developing the national economy, the state adheres to the principle of building our country independently, with the initiative of our hands and through self-reliance, hard struggle, diligence and thrifts, it adheres to the principle of taking agriculture as the foundation and industry as the leading factor, and it adheres to the principle of bringing the initiative of both the central and local authorities into full play under the unified leadership of the central authorities.

The state protects the environment and natural resources and prevents and eliminates pollution and other hazards to the public.

Article 12

The state devotes major efforts to developing science, expands scientific research, promotes technical innovation and technical revolution and adopts advanced techniques wherever possible in all departments of the national economy. In scientific and technological work we must follow the practice of combining professional contingents with the masses, and combining learning from others with our own creative efforts.

Article 13

The state devotes major efforts to developing education in order to raise the cultural and scientific level for the whole nation. Education must serve proletarian politics and be combined with productive labour and must enable everyone who receives an education to develop morally, intellectually and physically and become a worker with both socialist consciousness and culture.

Article 14

The state upholds the leading position of Marxism-Leninism-Mao Tsetung Thought in all spheres of ideology and culture. All cultural undertakings must serve the workers, peasants and soldiers and serve socialism.

The state applies the policy of "letting a hundred flowers blossom and a hundred schools of thought contend" so as to promote the development of the arts and science and bring about a flourishing socialist culture.

Article 15

All organs of state must constantly maintain close contact with the masses of the people, rely on them, heed their opinions, be concerned for their weal and woe, streamline administration, practise economy, raise efficiency and combat bureaucracy.

The leading personnel of state organs at all levels must conform to the requirements for successors in the proletarian revolutionary cause and their composition must conform to the principle of the three-in-one combination of the old, the middle-aged and the young.

Article 16

The personnel or organs of state must earnestly study Marxism-Leninism-Mao Tsetung Thought, wholeheartedly serve the people, endeavour to perfect their professional competence, take an active part in collective productive labour, accept supervision by the masses, be models in observing the Constitution and the law, correctly implement the policies of the state, seek truth from facts, and must not have recourse to deception or exploit their position and power to seek personal gain.

Article 17

The state adheres to the principle of socialist democracy, and ensures to the people the right to participate in the management of state affairs and of all economic and cultural undertakings, and the right to supervise the organs of state and their personnel.

Article 18

The state safeguards the socialist system, suppresses all treasonable and counter-revolutionary activities, punishes all traitors and counter-revolutionaries, and punishes new born bourgeois elements and other bad elements.

The state deprives of political rights, as prescribed by law, those landlords, rich peasants and reactionary capitalists who have not yet been reformed, and at the same time it provides them with the opportunity to earn a living so that they may be reformed through labour and become law-abiding citizens supporting themselves by their own labour.

Article 19

The Chairman of the Central Committee of the Communist Party of China commands the armed forces of the People's Republic of China.

The Chinese People's Liberation Army is the workers' and peasants' own armed force led by the Communist Party of China; it is the pillar of the dictatorship of the proletariat. The state devotes major efforts to the revolutionization and modernization of the Chinese People's Liberation Army, strengthens the building of the militia and adopts a system under which our armed forces are a combination of the field armies, the regional forces and the militia.

The fundamental task of the armed forces of the People's Republic of China is: To safeguard the socialist revolution and socialist construction, to defend the sovereignty, territorial integrity and security of the state, and to guard against subversion and aggression by social-imperialism, imperialism and their lackeys.

Chapter 2
The Structure of the State

Section 1
The National People's Congress

Article 20

The National People's Congress is the highest organ of state power.

Article 21

The National People's Congress is composed of deputies elected by the people's congresses of the provinces, autonomous regions, and municipalities directly under the Central Government, and by the People's Liberation Army....

Article 22

The National People's Congress exercises the following functions and powers:

(1) to amend the constitution;

(2) to make laws;

(3) to supervise the enforcement of the Constitution and the law;

(4) to decide on the choice of the Premier of the State Council upon the recommendation of the Central Committee of the Communist Party of China;

(5) to decide on the choice of other members of the State Council upon the recommendation of the Premier of the State Council;

(6) to elect the President of the Supreme People's Court and the Chief Prosecutor of the Supreme People's Procuratorate;

(7) to examine and approve the national economic plan, the state budget and the final state accounts;

(8) to confirm the following administrative divisions: provinces, autonomous regions, and municipalities directly under the Central Government;

(9) to decide on questions of war and peace; and

(10) to exercise such other functions and powers as the National People's Congress deems necessary.

* * *

Article 24

The Standing Committee of the National People's Congress is the permanent organ of the National People's Congress. It is responsible and accountable to the National People's Congress....

* * *

Article 25

The Standing Committee of the National People's Congress exercises the following functions and powers:

(1) to conduct the election of deputies to the National People's Congress;

(2) to convene the sessions of the National People's Congress;

(3) to interpret the Constitution and laws and to enact decrees;

(4) to supervise the work of the State Council, the Supreme People's Court and the Supreme People's Procuratorate;

(5) to change and annul inappropriate decisions adopted by the organs of state power of provinces, autonomous regions, and municipalities directly under the Central Government;

(6) to decide on the appointment and removal of individual members of the State Council upon the recommendation of the Premier of the State Council when the National people's Council is not in session;

(7) to appoint and remove Vice-Presidents of the Supreme People's Court and Deputy Chief Prosecutors of the Supreme People's Procuratorate;

(8) to decide on the appointment and removal of plenipotentiary representatives abroad;

(9) to decide on the ratification and abrogation of treaties concluded with foreign states;

(10) to institute state titles of honor and decide on their conferment;

(11) to decide on the granting of pardons;

(12) to decide on the proclamation of a state of war in the event of armed attack of the country when the National People's Congress is not in session; and

(13) to exercise such other functions and powers as are vested in it by the National People's Congress.

* * *

Section II
The State Council

Article 30

The State Council is the Central People's Government and the executive organ of the highest organ of state power, it is the highest organ of state administration.

The State Council is responsible and accountable to the National People's Congress, or, when the National People's Congress is not in session, to its Standing Committee.

Article 31

The State Council is composed of the following members: the Premier; the Vice Premiers; the ministers; and the ministers heading the commissions.

The Premier presides over the work of the State Council and the Vice Premiers assist the Premier in his work.

Article 32

The State Council exercises the following functions and powers:

(1) to formulate administrative measures, issue decisions and orders and verify their execution, in accordance with the Constitution, laws and decrees;

(2) to submit proposals on laws and other matters to the National People's Congress or its Standing Committee;

(3) to exercise unified leadership over the work of the ministries and commissions and other organizations under it;

(4) to exercise unified leadership over the work of local organs of state administration at various levels throughout the country;

(5) to draw up and put into effect the national economic plan and the state budget;

(6) to protect the interests of the state, maintain public order and safeguard the rights of citizens;

(7) to confirm the following administrative divisions: autonomous prefectures, counties, autonomous counties, and cities;

(8) to appoint and remove administrative personnel according to the provisions of the law; and

(9) to exercise such other functions and powers as are vested in it by the National People's Congress or its Standing Committee.

* * *

Article 36

Local people's congresses at various levels, in their respective administrative areas, ensure the observance and enforcement of the Constitution, laws and decrees; ensure the implementation of the state plan; make plans for local economic and cultural development and for public utilities; examine and approve local economic plans, budgets and final accounts; protect public property; maintain public order; safeguard the rights of citizens and the equal rights of minority nationalities; and promote the development of socialist revolution and socialist construction.

Local people's congresses may adopt and issue decisions within the limits of their authority as prescribed by law....

Article 37

Local revolutionary committees at various levels, that is, local people's governments, are the executive organs of local people's congresses at the corresponding levels and they are also local organs of state administration....

Local revolutionary committees carry out the decisions of people's congresses at the corresponding levels as well as the decisions and orders of the organs of state administration at higher levels, direct administrative work of their respective areas, and issue decisions and orders within the limits of their authority as prescribed by law. Revolutionary committees at the county level and above appoint or remove the personnel of organs of state according to the provisions of law....

Perry Keller, *Sources of Order in Chinese Law*

42 Am. J. Comp. L. 711 (1994)
(excerpts pages 717–729; some footnotes omitted)

The late Qing law reformers enjoyed reasonably good access to European civil and common law materials, principally through diplomatic collections gathered abroad and contacts with European legal scholars. But it was Japan, a country which also possessed a related Confucian heritage, that furnished a convenient model for the reception of western legal concepts.[31] At the turn of the century, Japan's Meiji government had already acquired decades of experience in the translation and adaptation of European law. In 1898 the Japanese had felt sufficiently confident in their mastery of European law to adopt the German civil code, the Burgerliches Gesetzbuch (BGB), only two years after its German promulgation. The apparent success of Japan's programme of political and economic modernization provoked strong Chinese interest. Many Chinese officials and scholars gained their first thorough appreciation of European civil law concepts of legislative organization through these Sino-Japanese exchanges.[32]

The exposure of the Chinese to the German civil code is particularly significant. The BGB represents a remarkably sustained attempt to realise a formalist idealization of law's coherence and rationality within the form and structure of positive law.[33] In this attempt to elaborate a consistent statement of the principles of civil law through careful organization and precise phrasing, Chinese jurists discovered a novel conception of formal law which profoundly affected legislative development during the republican period and continues to echo dimly in contemporary legal reform. It was not however until Chiang Kai-shek's Nationalist Party consolidated its control over the central regions of China in the late 1920's that another comprehensive reform of Chinese law was attempted. The Nationalist programme of legal reform centred on the adoption of codifications of constitutional law, criminal law, criminal procedure and administrative law. These codifications, known as the Six Codes, were heavily indebted in both organization and substance to German legislative precedents. They remain the basis of the Nationalist legal order in Taiwan and more recently have become a source of inspiration for law makers and academics within the People's Republic of China (PRC).

The promulgation of the Six Codes in the 1930's appeared to herald China's complete reception of the Romano-German civil law tradition. However, the implementation of Nationalist law was largely restricted to major urban areas under the central government's control.[35] Undermined by corrupt and authoritarian central administration, semi-autonomous regional warlords, civil war with the Communists and finally war with Japan, the Nationalist legal regime had little impact on Chinese society.

Soviet Theory and Chinese Bureaucracy

When the Communist Party came to power in 1949 it possessed an experience of law and administration which was rather different from that of the Nationalists. In their re-

---

31. Henderson, "Japanese influences on Communist Chinese Legal Language," in Jerome Cohen (ed.) Contemporary Chinese Law 158 (1973).

32. Id. at 169.

33. See Konrad Zweigert & Hein Kotz, An Introduction to Comparative Law 149–62 (2nd ed. 1992).

35. John King Fairbank, China: A New History 301 (1992). For a specific example, see Zelin, "Merchant Dispute Mediation in Twentieth-Century Zigong, Sichuan," in Kathryn Bernhardt & Philip Huang (eds.) Civil Law in Qing and Republican China 249–86 (1994).

mote rural base areas, the Communists had created a style of administration adapted to the Party's proclaimed tasks of political and social revolution. The simple legal system developed by the Party in these wartime conditions consisted of major principles and rules of conduct concerning the suppression of political opposition and common crimes as well as reforms concerning land holding and the structure of the family.[36] The structure of these laws tended to be simple and transitory. Processes of enactment and distinctions of form were largely unnecessary in a system where the commands of Party leaders carried overriding authority.[37]

As the Communist Party secured its victory over the Nationalists, it began to build on its administrative experience in the base areas to create a new legal order. Well before the official founding of the PRC, the Central Committee decreed the complete abolition of the Six Codes and all other Nationalist legislation.[38] But in view of the rudimentary state of the Communist legal system, the Central Committee also ordered that where the "new laws of the people" did not exist, judicial work should be carried out in accordance with the policies of the Party.[39] In effect, this decree formalized the legal authority of Party policy directives, which in the early years of the PRC served as the mainstay of Communist administration. The awkward balance created between law and Party policy set out in this decree exemplifies what was to become the enduring conundrum of the Communist legal order; how is it possible to assert the authority of law within a state founded on Leninist principles of Communist party supremacy?

Whilst content to avoid the use of formal laws or legal procedures in most areas, the Communist leadership moved quickly to create a constitutional foundation for the new state. The Common Programme, a temporary constitutional instrument issued in 1949, set out a general structure for national, regional and local administration.[40] And although the Common Programme had little practical significance in the militarized administration of the early People's Republic, it did create an important precedent for subsequent Chinese legislative practice. Its drafters sought to balance ideological and practical demands for a strong, unitary state with the equally important need to allow for regional diversity. Their solution was to include a grant of subordinate law making power to regional and local governments.[41] This in effect created a multi-tiered hierarchy of legislation in which law making authority at each level was, in principle, circumscribed by the content of all higher level laws and regulations.

During the early 1950's, Soviet legal theory, in particular the work of the Stalinist jurist and chief prosecutor A.Y. Vyshinsky, had a decisive impact on the construction of Chinese socialist law. Chinese theorists embraced Vyshinsky's rigid positivist view that law is a formal, normative expression of the will of the ruling class, as formulated and

36. Wu Daying and Liu Han, supra at n. 6, 20. O'Brien, supra at n. 8, 20–25.

37. Wu Daying and Liu Han, id. at 18.

38. Guanyu Feichu Guomindang Liufa Quanshu Yu Queding Jiefangqu de Sifa Yuanze de Shishi, (Directive Concerning the Abolition of the Nationalist Six Codes and the Establishment of Principles of Law in the Liberated Areas), issued by the Central Committee of the CCP, February 1949, Zhonghua Renmin Gongheguo Falu Quanshu, supra at n. 1, 1426.

39. Id.

40. Zhongguo Renmin Zhengzhi Xieshanghuiyi Gongtong Gangling (The Common Programme of the Chinese People's Political Consultative Conference), Zhonghua Renmin Gongheguo Zuzhi Fagui Xuanbian 3 (Selected Organizational Laws of the P.R.C.) (1985) (hereinafter Zuzhi Fagui).

41. Liu Han, "Zhongguo Xianxing Zhengzhi Tizhi he Fazhi de Lishi yu Xianzhuang" (The History and Circumstances of China's Current Political Structure and Legal System), in Wu Daying & Liu Han (eds.), Zhengzhi Tizhi Gaige Yu Fazhi Jianshe (Political Structural Reform and Legal Construction) 1-77, 54 (1991).

enforced by the state in the interests of that class.[42] In a socialist state, according to Vyshinsky, the Communist Party, as the representative of the ruling proletariat, should enjoy absolute control over the creation of positive law by the organs of the state. The Party should also determine the form and content of these laws according to the requirements of its evolving programme of economic and social development.

The consolidation of Chinese Communist legal doctrine brought about an increasingly decisive break with the legislative concerns of the republican era. Vyshinsky's Leninist rejection of any autonomy of law from politics carried with it an abandonment of rationality as an essential characteristic of law. There was no longer a theoretical imperative to achieve internally constructed order and consistency of meaning in the law, either through the positive language of legislation or through its doctrinal elaboration. This is not to say that consistency in legal doctrine or practice was no longer of any importance. However its appeal to Chinese administrators was clearly only functional. Having rejected capitalist rule of law theories, coherence in law only appealed to the extent that it improved the effectiveness or convenience of state administration.[43]

The Communist Party's instrumental conception of law marked an official return to a much more contextualist approach to the issue of legislative meaning. According to Chinese adaptations of Vyshinsky's work, the function of law is to express, in a positive, normative form, current Party policy.[44] The Party therefore holds incontrovertible authority over the determination of the content of the law. But by giving absolute primacy to Party policy and denying the validity of any dissenting interpretation of the needs of socialist development, Party leaders ensured that statutory language could not provide a basis from which to challenge Party authority. Official doctrine has therefore ensured that the authority of any law is in practice contingent on its accurate reflection of the current state of Party policy. Laws which are in this sense inaccurate require re-interpretation, amendment or, as is frequently the case in China, may simply be ignored.[45]

In fashioning its new legislative order, Party leaders adopted the Soviet principle that all state power should rest exclusively in the hands of a supreme legislature.[46] This principle was expressed in the PRC's first fully fledged constitution which was promulgated in 1954 by China's new national legislature, the National People's Congress (NPC). In

---

42. Yu Xingzhong, "Legal Pragmatism in the People's Republic of China," 3 Journal of Chinese Law 28–51, 36 (1980). See also, Xu Yongkang, "Qianping Weixinsiji Falu Lilun," (A Short Review of Vyshinsky's Theory of law) 6 Faxue 1–3 (1988). For an account of Vyshinsky's life and work, see Sharlet & Beirne, "In Search of Vyshinsky: The Paradox of Law and Terror," in Piers Beirne (ed.) Revolution in Law 136–56 (1991).

43. Liberal theories of the rule of law make greater demands on legal coherence. The essential liberal requirement that there should be a distinct separation of law and politics necessarily implies that law should possess a high degree of internal rationality and coherence capable of supporting the consistent application of legal principles and rules without direct resort to external political considerations. A useful account and defense of liberal legal theory can be found in Andrew Altman, Critical Legal Studies: A Liberal Critique (1990).

44. Chen Hanfeng, "Zhengdang, Zhengce, Quanli, Falu Zhi Guanxi," (The Relationship of Political Parties, Policy, Power and Law) Fazhi Ribao 3 (30 October 1987).

45. One of the more significant examples of this practice occurred in 1987, when the Party approved experimental land leases in selected areas despite constitutional and legal prohibitions on land leasing. Keller, "Legislation in the People's Republic of China," 23 U. Bri. Colum. L. Rev. 653–88, 658 (1989).

46. For a discussion of Soviet legislative principles, see Rene David & John Brierly, Major Legal Systems in the World Today 226–30 (3rd ed. 1985). Also see, Huskey, "A Framework for the Analysis of Soviet Law," 50 The Russian Review 53–70 (1991).

this Soviet inspired Constitution the NPC rescinded the legislative structure established by the Common Programme in 1949 and radically centralized the exercise of law making powers. Only the NPC and its executive body, the Standing Committee, retained authority to enact national laws (falu) or decrees (faling).[48] Regional and local governments, with the exception of autonomous minority areas, were stripped of all formal legislative power.[49] The 1954 legislative structure accommodated Soviet doctrinal requirements and also responded to the leadership's desire to curb the growth of regional powerbases.[50] It did not however produce a framework which could sustain a workable system of law. The country clearly could not be governed on the scanty output of a national legislature which met in two week annual sessions, or even its somewhat more productive Standing Committee, which met in poorly attended, monthly sessions. But it is also obvious that the Party never intended that it should be, because the development of normative administration was already occurring elsewhere.

The use of positive norms in Communist administration emerged out of early Party and state systems of bureaucratic communication. In the first years of the People's Republic, the Communist Party found that its documentary communication systems, developed in the base areas, could not meet the demands of national government. After initially relying on inherited Nationalist government documents and procedures, the Party developed its own complex methods of written and verbal bureaucratic communication. As these methods evolved, officials and academics began to use the Soviet derived term normative documents (guifanxing wenjian) to refer to all administrative directives purporting to establish or modify norms of public or official behaviour.[53] Documents of this type were issued at all levels of the administrative hierarchy, from the State Council down to village and neighbourhood authorities. They appeared in innumerable forms and were used to set general principles as well as precise rules of conduct. Throughout most of the Communist era, normative documents have constituted the basis of normative administration. Indeed, as this article describes, China's current legal order was in many respects developed out of the pre-existing normative document system.

For some Chinese officials, the 1954 constitutional changes created an obvious conflict between the express restriction of most formal law making powers to the NPC and the widespread use of normative documents by other state bodies. As the courts had no power to challenge the authority of normative documents or legislation, there appeared to be little more than a procedural distinction between these two categories. In some instances, normative documents were even issued using common legislative designations, such as the much favoured term "tiaoli" (regulations).[54] In 1956 Mao Tse-Tung addressed this issue when he stated that, "under the Constitution, legislative power is concentrated at the centre. But where central policies are not violated and it is in accordance with the needs of the situation and the work at hand, localities may issue regulations ("zhangcheng, tiaoli,

---

48. Articles 27 and 31, Zhonghua Renmin Gongheguo Xianfa 1954 (Constitution of the PRC), Zuzhi Fagui, supra at n. 40, 7 and 9.

49. Liu Han, supra at n. 41, 56.

50. Maurice J. Meisner, Mao's China 130–33 (1977).

53. ....The term 'normative document' (guifanxing wenjian) is most frequently used to refer to any document issued by state or quasi state bodies which has a normative content. In this broad sense, 'normative documents' include both formal laws and administrative directives. In this article 'normative document' is used in a narrower sense to mean, for the sake of clarity, a document having normative content but which is not included in the recognized categories of formal law.

54. See, Zhonghua Renmin Gongheguo Fagui Huibian (1955) (Collected Laws and Regulations of the PRC) (1956) which contains several State Council normative documents that are styled as 'regulations' tiaoli.

banfa"). The Constitution certainly does not prevent this."[55] In this statement Mao accomplished two important things. First he decisively affirmed the authority of normative documents. Second, by endorsing the role of normative documents he forestalled any argument that formal law should move beyond the general principles expressed in the NPC legislation and become more specific and technical in character. The Chinese legal order therefore effectively remained split between the formal legal powers of the NPC, which symbolized the unitary nature of the state, and the administrative powers of the central and regional bureaucracies to issue and enforce normative documents.

The enactment of the 1954 Constitution marked the beginning of a period of legal reform which some officials expected would produce a comprehensive body of substantive law patterned after the Soviet model. In a short period of time legislative drafters made considerable progress in creating important draft legislation, including a criminal and a civil code. However the onset of the Anti-Rightist Campaign in 1957 brought an abrupt end to any hopes of replacing institutional reliance on Party and state administrative directives with even a basic core of substantive legislation. During this devastating political campaign to identify and silence the Party's critics, advocates of greater legal control over the Party's activities were purged from legal and academic institutions. The 1950's legislative programme did not recover from this onslaught. Draft legislation was shelved and the NPC did not enact any further legislation for another two decades. Despite the apparent return to political stability during the early 1960's, many of China's leaders, in particular Mao Tse-tung, had come to believe that law in any form represented an unnecessary fetter on the Party's ability to govern and develop a socialist society. Legal bureaucracies, such as the Ministry of Justice, were gradually abolished as the role of law in state administration continued to be downgraded. What remained of the formal legal order and its institutions finally disappeared in the chaos of the Cultural Revolution era (1966–1976).

The Return to Legal Modernization

Chinese legal literature usually portrays the Cultural Revolution as a time in which there was literally no law at all; an era of legal nihilism "bereft of the laws of man or heaven" (wufa wutian). But whilst anarchy and civil war threatened in its initial phase, military forces soon restored a semblance of central authority. And even though government administration during these years was characterized by mass mobilization campaigns, there is abundant evidence that administrative authorities continued to rely on normative documents to implement policy through much of this period. Even Chinese public records show only a three year hiatus in the issue of national level directives in important areas such as the regulation of industry and commerce.[63] The re-establishment of Party and State bureaucratic systems in the early 1970's coincided with a recorded increase in the use of normative documents, some of which have been retrospectively accorded the status of law.[64] However, as Guo Daohui points out, these instruments were not produced by designated law making bodies or through fixed procedures and were otherwise indistinguishable from the administrative process itself. Not

55. Liu Han, supra at n. 41, 55.

63. Zhou Zhenxiang & Zhao Jingchun (eds.), Xin Zhongguo Fazhi Jianshe Sishi Nian Yaolan (A Survey of Forty Years of New China's Legal Construction) 361 (1990).

64. See, for example, Guanyu Tushu Banben Jilu de Guiding, (Regulations Concerning Records of Book Editions), issued by the Publications Office of the State Council, 7 December 1972, contained in Zhonghua Renmin Gongheguo Xianxing Xinwen Chuban Fagui Huibian (1949–1990) (Collected Press and Publication Regulations of the PRC Currently in Effect) (1990).

only were they produced in a non-systematic, piecemeal fashion, they were not governed by what H.L.A. Hart would describe as authoritative secondary rules capable of determining their validity. The use of normative documents during the Cultural Revolution therefore only amounted to an informal system of law in the broadest possible sense. But the experience of normative governance acquired through the issue and implementation of these regulatory instruments subsequently provided the wellspring for China's current programme of legal modernization.

The Communist Party officially renewed its interest in law reform in 1978 with the Central Committee's ratification of Deng Xiaoping's ambitious plans for economic revival. Legislative officials were instructed to dust off the draft legislation of the 1950's and prepare these and other new laws for promulgation. However, as legal reform gathered pace, it became apparent that the constitutional allocation of law making powers was at odds with the needs of the new legislative programme as well as the realities of bureaucratic power. Under the cautiously reformist Constitution of 1978, the NPC and its Standing Committee retained exclusive authority over the enactment of law.[66] Legislative planners were consequently faced with the same problem that Mao Tse-tung had papered over in his declaration of 1956. China's cumbersome supreme legislature was simply not equipped to deliver the torrent of legislation required if China was to move to a legally based system of administration.

In theory the Communist Party could have reconstituted the NPC and its Standing Committee to work throughout most of the year considering and enacting legislation. The NPC could also have delegated the authority to issue subordinate regulations for specific national laws to central or regional administrative bodies. But this model, in which all law issues directly or indirectly from a single legislative authority, would have flown in the face of the practical divisions of state power within China. The State Council, along with the commissions, ministries and other departments under its authority, was and still is the central administrative organ of the national government. At provincial and local levels, People's Governments and their departments have served a similar function. At the outset of the legal modernization programme, these bureaucracies were not only the experienced centres of government administration in China, they also formed important institutional power bases within the structure of the Communist Party. During this transitional period, I suggest, powerful interests within these bureaucracies demanded formal recognition of their quasi-legislative functions.

The extension of law making authority to these bodies was not long in coming. By 1979 the Central Committee had already acknowledged the need to decentralise administrative power and had caused the NPC to enact legislation extending subordinate law making powers to the provincial level People's Congresses.[67] Three years later, the NPC completely overhauled the country's formal legislative structure with the adoption of China's current constitution.[68] The last extension of legislative power came in 1986 when the NPC granted law making powers to regional People's Governments and to selected local People's Congresses and People's Governments.[69] However, as this article de-

66. Article 20, Zhonghua Renmin Gongheguo Xianfa 1978, (Constitution of the PRC), Zuzhi Fagui, supra at n. 40, 21. For a general description of this Constitution, see Cohen, "China's Changing Constitution," (1978) China Quarterly, No. 76, 794–841.

67. Article 7, para one, Zhonghua Renmin Gongheguo Difang Geji Renmin Daibiao Dahui he Difang Geji Renmin Zhengfu Fa, supra at n. 9, 122.

68. Zhonghua Renmin Gongheguo Xianfa 1982 (Constitution of the PRC), Changyong 1.

69. Article 7, para. two Article 51, Zhonghua Renmin Gongheguo Difang Geji Renmin Daibiao Dahui he Difang Geji Renmin Zhengfu Fa, supra at n. 9, 122 and 130.

scribes, the acquisition of law making powers has been a mixed blessing. It has brought expectations of order, coherence of meaning and even openness which pose a threat to the secrecy and flexibility of administrative practice. The failure to meet these expectations has no doubt fueled theoretical arguments within China that these administrative rule making powers cannot properly be described as 'legislative powers'.

China's legislative structure combines two different forms of legislative hierarchy. The first is a unified hierarchy of institutional bodies possessing law making authority. This hierarchy is crowned by the full NPC and descends directly through its Standing Committee to the State Council. Below these central government institutions, law making powers are divided between the territorial bureaucracies of regional and local government and the functional bureaucracies of central government administration. The special powers granted to the autonomous minority area legislatures provide the third leg to this division of law making authority.

The second is a hierarchy of legislative categories, which can be simplified into three levels. Primary legislation stands at the top of this pyramid, just below the Constitution in legal authority. This type of legislation is often narrowly categorized as " falu," a term which is usually translated as "law" and hence gives rise to considerable confusion in foreign accounts of Chinese law. At the second legislative level, there are " fagui" which are issued in different forms by the State Council and the regional People's Congresses. Although the term " fagui" is usually translated as "regulations," there are in fact many other Chinese legislative terms which, out of a lack of English language alternatives, must also be translated as 'regulations'. This provides yet another source of confusion in the use of English language translations of Chinese law. Finally, at the tertiary level, there are " guizhang" which are issued in different forms by central government ministries and regional and local governments. This term is also commonly translated as "regulation." This article adopts the terms "secondary regulations" and "tertiary regulations" to maintain a clear distinction between these two categories. The special legislative category of " autonomous and special regulations" (zizhi & danxing tiaoli) created for autonomous minority areas rests uneasily in a poorly defined space between the primary and secondary legislative levels.[70]

Although the development of formal sources of law in China has been driven by the practical interests of state administrative bureaucracies, theoretical arguments have also had their influence. In resurrecting the theme of legal modernization, Party officials returned to the theoretical doctrines as well as the draft legislation of the 1950's. Vyshinsky's instrumentalism reappeared in force. Even official pronouncements on the need to institute the "rule of law" in place of the "rule of men," made plain that law should still be subordinated to Party policy.[72] Yet since the early 1980's the intellectual climate in China has changed beyond recognition. In the legal sphere, the growth of a community

70. Autonomous and special regulations are a problematic category of subordinate law. In principle they are the legal instruments which designated minority area administrations use to pursue special policies related to ethnic needs. However legislative commentators have yet to show convincingly how they are to be distinguished from other subordinate legislation. (See, for example, Liu Jinghai, Minzu Quyu Zizhifa Shishi Zhong de Jige Wenti' (Several Issues Concerning the Implementation of the Minorities Autonomy Law) (1991) 5 Zhongguo Faxue 41–45.) Therefore, for the purposes of this article, any observations made regarding regional regulations (difangxing fagui) should be regarded as applying, mutatis mutandis, to autonomous and special regulations.

72. A useful summary of the officially approved theory of socialist legal construction in China is contained in the Shehuizhuyi Fazhi (Socialist Legal System) entry of the Faxue (Legal Science) volume of the Zhongguo Dabaike Quanshu (The Chinese Encyclopedia) (1984).

of academics, officials and professionals involved in legal affairs has engendered a more sophisticated understanding of China's own legal history as well as the function of law in contemporary Chinese society. In periods of relative tolerance, legal writers have even been able to express new views on the relationship between the Communist Party and the laws of the state.[73] Without challenging the ultimate authority of the Party, writers have also argued for the creation of a rationally ordered and internally consistent legislative order. For some officials and academics, the reorganization of positive law on a more coherent basis is essential if law is to become the pre-eminent framework for public and private life.

The Legislative Structure of the People's Republic of China [omitted]

Nonetheless, the importance of these ideas should not be overstated. As described below, China's legislative structure has yet to approach the formal rationality and coherence promoted by these officials and academics. Chinese legislative practice is more often characterized by narrow instrumentalism than by the bending of administrative practice to the demands of legal consistency. Moreover, many officials involved in the development of Chinese law appear content that the legal system should derive consistency and coherence primarily from the dictates of Party and state policy and perhaps even the commonly held values of Chinese society.

Comments and Questions

1. The Constitution of the PRC was amended in significant respect in 1993.

"The momentum of nurturing a rational market economy culminated in a landmark, and perhaps irreversible amendment to the Constitution of the People's Republic of China by the National People's Congress (NPC) in March 1993. This amendment drastically changes 'the State shall implement a planned economy on the basis of socialist public ownership system,'[8] a sacred motto in China for more than four decades, to 'the State shall implement a socialist market economy. The State shall strengthen economic legislation to improve macro regulation and control.'[9] This amendment paved an indispensable path for the legislation of the

73. See, for example, Ding Bangkai, "Dang Zheng Fenkai de Faxue Sikao," (Thoughts on the Legal Aspect of the Separation of the Party and the State) 3 Faxue Yanjiu 15 (1988).

8. Zhonghua Renmin Gongheguo Xianfa [Constitution of the PRC], Art. 15, Reprinted in the LAWS OF THE PEOPLE'S REPUBLIC OF CHINA (1979–1982) 1 (Foreign Language Press 1987).

9. Zhonghua Renmin Gongheguo Xianfa Xiuzheng An [Amendment to the Constitution of the PRC], Art. 7, reprinted in 1993 Ni emphasis added). A much more pragmatic and less ideological policy underpins this Amendment an Quanguo Lushi Zhige Kaoshi Fuxi Fagui Huibian [COMPILATION OF LAWS AND REGULATIONS FOR NATIONAL BAR EXAMINATION OF 1993] n. 20 (Ministry of Justice of China ed., Economic Administration Publishing House, 1993). Its significance is at least two-pronged. First, it provides a constitutional recognition of Chinese reform and opening-up during the past fourteen years. In addition, by writing the notion of socialist market economy into the Constitution to replace that of a planned economy as the cornerstone of socialism, it lays down a constitutional justification for future growth in private sectors including foreign investment, and for the fledgling legislation protecting the private economy. Since this is contrary to the traditional socialist principles in China, a question may be raised as to the reliability of this Amendment. Retrospectively viewed in the context of Chinese legislation and policies aimed at an efficient market economy since 1979, this Amendment is nothing but a natural summary of developments. In addition, Article 3 of this Amendment adds new language, "[t]he State shall stick to reforms and opening to the outside world," to the Preamble of the Constitution, thus further assuring the irreversible

Company Law. The Company Law will fill some of the legislative vacancies in the area of commerce, and gear the process of privatization of Chinese stateowned enterprises towards a legal track.

Yabo Lin, *New Forms and Organizational Structures of Foreign Investment in China Under the Company Law of the PRC*, 7 TRANSNAT'L LAW. 327, 331–332 (1994).

2. Article 11 Chapter 1 of the PRC Constitution speaks of the principles underlying Chinese economic development. How are these principles reconciled with the opening of foreign investment into China and the incorporation of Western capitalist forms of economic organization? Does Article 17 of Chapter 1 affect the power of the state to permit enterprises which completely mimic the forms of enterprise organization and conduct consistent with Western notions of free enterprise?

3. Does Chapter 2 of the Constitution of the People's Republic of China suggest the institution of a system of government based on the notion of separation of powers? How do the powers of the National People's Congress compare to those of the Congress of the United States of America? Does the Standing Committee of the National People's Congress assert authority in addition to that assigned to the National People's Congress itself? Why?

4. How many levels of government may be involved in the development, implementation and administration of company law rules within the People's Republic of China? Does the current system promote the operation of enterprises free of the interference of the state or its organs? Does the current system comprehend the ownership of property as understood in the West?

5. The excerpt of the article that follows integrates the basic understanding of the formal set up of the government of the People's Republic with the actual context in which business is regulated. In reading the excerpt, think about whether the formal expression of law in China is reflected in its practice. If it is not, should that disjunction concern those who might wish to participate in commercial or enterprise activity in China?

Anna M. Han, *China's Company Law: Practicing Capitalism in a Transitional Economy*

5 PAC. RIM L. & POL'Y J. 457 (1996)
(excerpts pages 461–477; some footnotes omitted)

To gain a better understanding of how a company will operate in China's transitional economy and to better appreciate the obstacles facing the Chinese company, an overview of some of the key economic levers which affect the Chinese economy is essential.

A. A Brief History

When it came to power in 1949, the Chinese Communist Party adopted an economic system and management style patterned after the Soviet model. Property was owned either by the State or by collectives.[14] Until 1978, China's economic system did not allow

---

direction of market reform in China. For an official comment on this Amendment, *see China's Constitution to Be Amended*, 36 BEIJING REV. 4 (1993).

14. Private ownership officially existed for a short period until the early 1950s. It consisted primarily of providers of skilled trades, which had not been subsumed by the collective work groups. During the "Great Leap Forward," such private ownership was virtually eliminated. Today, a very small segment of the economy, primarily the service industry, is privately owned. For a discussion

any of the normal market mechanisms found in other countries to function. The economic system was almost fully centralized and decisions that were made through administrative organs were duly executed by the enterprises.[15] Every aspect of the economy was planned.[16] The government engaged in both macro and micro planning. The macro planning included a master list of priority industries which would receive material and funds first. Then, the various levels of government administrators micro-managed the enterprises on every aspect of their operation, including purchasing, production, quality control, and labor practices. Those industries on the priority list were supplied with raw materials at state-plan prices which were unrelated to market conditions.[20] The system of controlling everything from the purchasing of raw materials to the sale of goods was implemented in both the state-owned enterprises and in the collectively-owned enterprises.[21] This centralized management approach governed nearly every aspect of all enterprises from 1958 to 1978, covering nearly eighty-five percent of the total economy of China.

China engaged in what is known as "directive planning" (Ziling Jihua), where production units were given specific production targets to meet.[23] Under directive planning, management of China's enterprises were nominally controlled by the state, and the actual power resided in the hands of the various administrative organs and the bureaucrats who staffed these organs.[24] Numerous problems resulted from this arrangement. Enterprises lacked the most basic decision making powers. Managers lacked the authority to make production and sales decisions, such as determining what to produce, what to purchase, whom to hire, when to borrow money and repay loans, and how to distribute products. All of these decisions were determined by the State's plan as interpreted by several layers of bureaucracy.[25]

---

of these changes *see* Du Mengkun, *Government Budgets*, in CHINA'S ECONOMIC REFORM [(George Totten & Zhou Shulian eds., 1992)], at 39–40.

15. *See generally* Chen Jiyan, *The Planning System*, in CHINA'S ECONOMIC REFORM (Gene Tidrick & Chen Jiyuan eds., 1987).

16. Although the attempt was made, China never claimed that its planning was perfect. Many gaps existed, and the planning often led to terrible economic consequences such as the widespread famines after the so-called "Great Leap Forward." [PETER M. LICHTENSTEIN, CHINA AT THE BRINK 80 (1991)] at 80; [A. JAMES GREGOR, MARXISM, CHINA, & DEVELOPMENT (1995)] at 80 (1995).

20. Indergit Singh, China: Industrial Policies for an Economy in Transition, World Bank Discussion Papers No. 143, 1992, at 15.

21. Such planning had the advantage of predictability, to the extent that the targeted goals were met. However, its disadvantages were significant. Enterprises which produced goods lacked decision-making power, management lacked incentive to be innovative and workers failed to share in the profitability (or failure) of the enterprise. *See* Gene Tidrick, *Planning and Supply, in China's Industrial Reform, supra* note 15, at 196–97. For a discussion of centrally planned economies in Eastern Europe and their similarities to China, *see* Richard Portes, *From Central Planning to a Market Economy, in* MAKING MARKETS: ECONOMIC TRANSFORMATION IN EASTERN EUROPE AND THE POST SOVIET STATES 20–36 (Shafiqul Islam & Michael Mandelbaum eds., 1993).

23. ROBERT C. HSU, ECONOMIC THEORIES IN CHINA, 1979–1988 35 (1991)....

24. Every Chinese enterprise is run by two heads, the manager or factory director and the party secretary. For most of the past four decades since the Communists took power, any ultimate decision rested with the party secretary. Theoretically, the manager was in charge of production and the party leader was to ensure conformity to party policy. However, if the two objectives clashed, which they often did, the party policy always prevailed. As with any creature with two heads, reaching any particular objective efficiently became difficult if not impossible. LICHTENSTEIN, *supra* note [16], at 37.

25. [Zhou Shulian, *Reform of the Economic Structure, in* CHINA'S ECONOMIC REFORM, (George Totten & Zhou Shulian eds., 1992)] at 2–5. *See also* Zheng Guangliang, *The Leadership System, in* CHINA'S INDUSTRIAL REFORM, *supra* note 15, at 304. In China, the decision to expand operations

The centralized system took away any incentive for Chinese enterprise to be innovative and profitable. To the enterprises, profits were irrelevant since excess earnings were not retained but simply turned over to the government. Losses did not decrease jobs, output, or salaries since the government subsidized these losses. The net effect of this system was to encourage, across the economy as a whole, complacency and resignation to the point of stagnation.

B. Role of Law

China's legal system prior to 1978 was devoid of economic legislation. It did not have any of the most fundamental legislation such as contract law, tax codes, and corporation codes. Such laws were unnecessary since all economic agreements entered into were between government units. If one party were to breach a contract, any damages ordered would be paid from one government fund to another, a rather meaningless exercise which the Chinese avoided. If a party breached an agreement and the government felt that the breach affected central planning, private enforcement under a judicial proceeding was unnecessary because the government simply ordered specific performance. This method sufficed in a planned economy where production units were under direct government control.

With the decision to marketize in 1978, the rules changed. After experiencing governmental control for over thirty years, Chinese enterprises were suddenly called upon to produce market efficiency. The first effort to implement elements of a market system was directed at attracting foreign investment. But given China's lack of laws, foreigners were unwilling to invest in China, and expressed a reluctance to invest without legal protection and procedures to address breaches. The Chinese government recognizes that its ability to attract such investors depended on the foreign confidence in China's legal processes. Legal regulations served to engender greater foreign confidence. Therefore, a crucial part of marketization was the adoption of a system of economic regulation. While China recognized the need for economic legislation to replace the command economy with market values, it was also conscious of the loss of power which accompanied the transition. To address this issue, China took its first step toward marketization in a controlled environment by carefully monitoring the type and quantities of foreign investment projects. Each project required approval by the government.

China's efforts to change its political and economic systems by legislation which would encourage more reliance on market factors began long before the promulgation of the Company Law. As early as 1979, soon after China's decision to "open its doors" to the rest of the world, China enacted a set of joint venture laws, which enabled foreign investors to invest in China by joint venturing with Chinese entities.[31] The joint venture laws were the first introduction of private ownership in China. Although the Chinese partner of a joint venture was almost always a government entity, at least the portion of the joint venture's assets owned by the foreign party was in private hands.

---

due to growing demand was not made within the operating enterprise, but was instead made by an administrative bureaucrat. Usually, this bureaucrat has little or no understanding of the enterprise's product or concern about its market position. The administrator may also have a political agenda which is inconsistent with the welfare of the enterprise. An example of inconsistent goals may be when a factory's resources, machinery, labor, and raw materials are ordered to produce military uniforms which are then "sold" to the government at set low prices to meet a political need when those same resources would be economically more profitable producing consumer clothing in greater demand and selling for higher prices. *See supra* LICHTENSTEIN, note [16], at 36.

31. *The Law of the People's Republic of China on Sino-foreign Joint Equity Ventures*, reprinted in CHINA L. FOREIGN BUS. (CCH Austl.) P 6-500, Art. 1 (1979).

Pressure from foreign companies desiring more flexible forms of investment in China led to enactment of further legislation allowing for other forms of business, such as cooperative joint ventures and, very importantly, wholly-owned foreign enterprises.[32] The creation of these wholly-owned foreign enterprises meant that at least small parts of China's economy became privately owned and managed by foreigners. The percentage of such foreign enterprises was so small that it had negligible impact on China's economy, but it was, nevertheless, an important policy change. China also established various special economic zones along the coastal regions to encourage foreign investment and trade.[33] These zones provided flexible forms of investment to foreign investors and lower tax rates. Most of these zones have been very successful economically. Investment by Hong Kong, Macao, and Taiwan Chinese is especially concentrated in these zones.

Reflected in these past economic laws, and in the Company Law, is the delicate balance of allowing some independent decision making on the enterprise level to achieve maximum operating efficiency while giving up the minimum amount of political control. The laws are typically designed to facilitate activities the government wishes to encourage without relinquishing the rights that would limit state power. Chinese laws tend to contain, paradoxically, provisions which are vague and broadly drafted, accompanied by detailed restrictions. The former gives maximum room for interpretation by bureaucrats, which can vary as government policies change. The latter allows the government to prohibit activities which it deems to be harmful.[34]

Some of this economic legislation has achieved significant success by attracting foreign investment, although foreign investors still often complain of the difficulties in dealing with Chinese partners who are not motivated by profits and bureaucrats who are obstructionists.[36] The question is whether the same success can be achieved when the scope of the marketization is expanded to individual domestic enterprises.

C. Creating a Socialist Market System

While China has taken steps to transform its economy from one that is planned to one that is driven by market forces, that process is far from complete. Vestiges of the planned economy and its instruments remain and continue to control significant portions of the Chinese economy today.

Much has been written in the western press about this "fundamental change" in China's policies and many commentators have advanced the idea that this change sig-

---

32. *Law of People's Republic of China Concerning Enterprises With Sole Foreign Investment,* reprinted in CHINA L. FOREIGN BUS. (CCH Austl.) P 13-506 (1986).

33. For background information pertaining to the formation and development of the Special Economic Zones, *see generally* CHINA'S REGIONAL DEVELOPMENT (David S.G. Goodman ed., 2d ed. 1990); GEORGE T. CRANE, THE POLITICAL ECONOMY OF CHINA'S SPECIAL ECONOMIC ZONES (1990); CAROL LEE HAMRIM, CHINA AND THE CHALLENGE OF THE FUTURE (1990); HARRY HARDING, CHINA'S SECOND REVOLUTION (1987); ROBERT KLEINBERG, CHINA'S "OPENING" TO THE OUTSIDE WORLD (1990); COLIN MACKERRAS ET AL., CHINA SINCE 1978: REFORM, MODERNIZATION & 'SOCIALISM WITH CHINESE CHARACTERISTICS' (1994).

34. For example, specific laws encouraging foreign investment would detail the sectors of economy which foreign investment is encouraged but be vague as to the benefits foreign investors would receive when investing in those sectors. Law on Encouragement of Foreign Investment, Arts. 2 & 15. Often, laws are broad policy statements which promise unspecified "relevant regulations" to clarify the ambiguities. Until such regulations are issued, interpretation of any ambiguity is left to the bureaucrats who are in charge of enforcement. *See supra* note 32.

36. Julia S. Sensenbrenner, *The Evolving Enterprise,* CHINA BUS. REV., Mar.–Apr. 1987, at 35.

nals the end of Communism and represents concrete proof of the superiority and basic correctness of western capitalism. However, China's decision to change its system is markedly different from the changes occurring in the former Soviet Union and various eastern European countries. For example, China's decision was self-made, not forced upon her by the collapse of the previous system. China was able, at a relatively early date, to perceive the need for this transformation and to take measured steps to implement changes. Other differences in population, size, culture, stage of economic development, natural resources, and political structure render comparisons between China's transformation and those occurring in Eastern Europe inappropriate.[39]

Another major distinction between China's transformation and that occurring in Eastern Europe and Russia is that China's change, at least nominally, is only in the economic sphere. Politically, China continues to adhere to Marxist/Maoist doctrines.

China is one of a few countries in the world which still professes adherence to communism. Of these countries, China is the only one with any significant economic power. Recognizing that continued adherence to the rigid, centrally planned economic system of traditional Communism would not induce the desired type of progress and growth, China has embarked on a path to create a "socialist system with Chinese characteristics" or "socialist market economy," which essentially consists of injecting certain market aspects into a planned economy. To China, it matters little that "socialism" and "market system" are contradictory terms. The Chinese leadership would like to keep the facade of socialism, as it is the basis which the Chinese Communist came to power, while adopting as much of capitalism in substance as it can in the economic sector. To avoid the appearance of abandoning socialism, China initially called the new system a "commodity production economy" and later changed the label to a "socialist market economy."[43]

---

39. None of the Eastern European countries or the Soviet Union have a population anywhere near China's. China's economic development has been considered to be further along than most, with the possible exception of Hungary. Politically, China's leadership is attempting to marketize without dismantling its own power base, in marked contrast to the toppling of the Communist Party in most of the Eastern European countries. Peter Harold, China's Reform Experience to Date, World Bank Discussion Papers No. 180, 1992, at 1–4. For those interested in the experience and analysis of Eastern European countries and the former Soviet Union, *see generally* CAPITALIST GOALS, SOCIALIST PAST: THE RISE OF THE PRIVATE SECTOR IN COMMAND ECONOMIES (Perry L. Patterson ed., 1993); ECONOMIC ADJUSTMENT & REFORM IN EASTERN EUROPE & THE SOVIET UNION (Joseph C. Brada et al. eds., 1987); ECONOMIC TRANSFORMATION IN CENTRAL EUROPE: A PROGRESS REPORT (Richard Portes ed., 1994); THE ECONOMIC TRANSFORMATION OF EASTERN EUROPE (Bernard S. Katz & Libby Rittenberg eds., 1992); PRIVATIZATION & ECONOMIC REFORM IN CENTRAL EUROPE (Dennis A. Rondinelli ed., 1994); ROMAN FRYDMAN & ANDRZEJ RAPACZYNSKI, THE PRIVATIZATION PROCESS IN CENTRAL EUROPE (1993); ROMAN FRYDMAN & ANDRZEJ RAPACZYNSKI, PRIVATIZATION IN EASTERN EUROPE: IS THE STATE WITHERING AWAY? (1994); MARKET SOCIALISM OR THE RESTORATION OF CAPITALISM? (Anders Aslund ed., 1992); REFORMING THE ECONOMIES OF CENTRAL & EASTERN EUROPE, ORGANIZATION FOR ECONOMIC CO-OPERATION & DEVELOPMENT (1992); 1 THE TRANSITION IN EASTERN EUROPE (Oliver Jean Blanchard et al. eds., 1994); 2 THE TRANSITION IN EASTERN EUROPE, *id.*; TRIALS OF TRANSITION: ECONOMIC REFORM IN THE FORMER COMMUNIST BLOC (Michael Keren & Gur Ofer eds., 1992).

43. The label "commodity production economy" or "commodity economy" was used early in the reform process in 1983 and 1984 to avoid antagonizing the more conservative factions of the communist party. *See* JOSEPH FEWSMITH, DILEMMAS OF REFORM IN CHINA: POLITICAL CONFLICT AND ECONOMIC DEBATE 133 (1994). In 1992, after the Fourteenth Party Congress, when the reform movement was more secure, the use of the term "socialist market economy" was adopted. *Id.* at 146. *See* LICHTENSTEIN, *supra* note 12, at 41. Apparently, the purpose of introducing market mecha-

Some scholars may be interested in debating whether China is "maintaining a socialist economy with unique Chinese characteristics" as its leaders declare, or whether it has become capitalist and is simply continuing outdated political rhetoric for the convenience of those in power. Others may well adopt Deng Xiao Ping's pragmatic (and much touted) slogan: "It doesn't matter what color the cat so long as it catches mice."[44] This attitude allows the Chinese government to maintain a pretense that it has not abandoned the principles upon which the Communist Party was founded while implementing reform measures which look more and more like capitalism.

D. The Key Economic Levers

The following is a more detailed discussion of the major economic levers which propel the Chinese economy. Particular emphasis is placed upon the factors which closely relate to the operation of a company in China's transitional economy. The specific factors also relate clearly to certain fundamental preconditions of a market economy: the ability to decide what to produce, how much to produce, the number and specifics of employees, prices of goods and services provided and allocation of profits.

1. Production

In planned economies, factories produce goods to meet government specifications and not market demands. Since purchase decisions are also made by the State, no real incentive exists for the enterprises to produce innovative goods with better quality. In contrast, enterprises in market economies manufacture to meet market demands. As China's economic growth is highly dependent upon export, Chinese enterprises are now beginning to plan their production and design their products according to the demands of the international market. Without price de-control, access to investment and raw material, and the ability to hire and fire workers as needed, the ability of individual factories to respond to market signals remains limited.

Furthermore, making efficient production decisions depends on access to market information which in turn allows decisions to be made according to the information received. While it clearly is true that market economies do not always have perfect access to information, in China, the type of information available to a production unit is particularly skewed and inadequate. The government is the primary, if not the sole source, of such information and often, the statistics reflect political agenda and not actual facts. The problem is further complicated when portions of the economy remain under central planning and portions attempt to operate under market rules. Information and statistics cannot reflect true market conditions, only partial or mixed messages.[47]

---

nisms into a socialist system is to make the planning more efficient and flexible, not change the system to a capitalist economy.

44. Zhou, *supra* note[25], at xi.

47. Under a planned economy, information is gathered by the government and the decisions are made accordingly. Although this information was not perfect, at least it was as close to complete as the government could make it. With part of the enterprises in state hands and part private, the collection and dissemination of information will be much more difficult. One of the greatest challenges facing a transition economy is the task of facilitating information flow and exchange to allow for informed decisions. China is no exception. Raimund Dietz, *Ten Propositions Towards a Theory of Transformation, in From Command to Exchange Communication,* in The Transition from Command to Market Economies in East-Central Europe 77 (Sandor Richter ed., 1992).

There is also the question whether market information, to the extent it is available, will lead to appropriate production responses by the enterprise. A possible example of a perverse response in a transitional economy is that a factory would raise prices to counterbalance the decreased demand for its products. This decision could well be the result of a need for full employment or the vestiges of an older system which dictated production units. Chinese enterprises are so accustomed to their monopolistic practices that their response to competition may not be the same of an enterprise familiar with operating under market rules.[49]

2. Prices

In China, the government is the arbiter of prices of goods rather than the supply and demand of market forces. Often, these prices are arbitrary and bear no relationship to the cost of manufacturing or market prices.

The danger of massive price reform—relinquishing governmental control and allowing price to be determined by market demand and supply—is the possibility of runaway inflation once price control is lifted. Due to long term price control and shortage of goods, the sudden lifting of controls may cause certain prices, especially of goods in short supply, to increase unchecked. These increases may far outpace the real income earnings of the people. To prevent this problem, the Chinese government has kept the prices of basic commodities such as rice and oil stable while allowing more fluctuations with non-essential goods such as television and fans.

3. Labor Policies

A central factor in planning production and setting prices is the cost of labor. In China, where there is an abundance of labor, efficient allocation and pricing of labor have previously been unimportant. Instead, the goal of labor allocation was to achieve full employment. This goal is hardly surprising, for the Chinese communists came into power during an era of great labor unrest. In that era, the need to keep workers occupied, however inefficiently, far exceeded the need for efficient allocation.[55]

As a direct result of the need to solidify control and gain worker support, the government guaranteed the state sector life long employment. The term "iron rice bowl" is

---

49. For example, one author has noted how readily Chinese distributors accept pricing policies and leads set by others in the distribution chain. This acquiescence is attributed to vestiges of old state pricing policies. Jane Greaver, *The Right Price.* CHINESE BUS. REV., Sept.–Oct. 1995, at 31.

55. Chinese workers do not choose the fields which they wish to enter. Rather, upon graduation from high school or other educational institutions, workers are assigned to various enterprises. William Byrd & Gene Tidrick, *Factor Allocation and Enterprise Incentives, in* CHINA'S INDUSTRIAL REFORM, *supra* note 15, at 67–69. Therefore, it is often possible to find a worker in a toy factory whose interest lies in garment design, or a worker in a botanical garden whose major in college was English. With this type of labor allocation, China's labor system is, at best, inefficient.

In the 1960s and early 1970s, the problem of too many urban laborers was solved by simply sending high school and college graduates to the countryside to learn from the peasant class. [Bill Brugger, *Democracy and Organization in Chinese Industry-New Directions?*, in CHINA: DILEMMAS OF MODERNIZATION 62–63 (Graham Young ed., 1985)] at 87; *see also* Zhao Lukuan & Lu Guotai, *Employment and Wages in Cities and Towns,* in CHINA'S ECONOMIC REFORM, *supra* note [16] at 188. Workers could be recalled if they were needed. If they were not needed, they would simply be left on semi-permanent agricultural duty. Brugger, *supra* note 42, at 86–88. While this system of allocation did not take into account the talents or desires of the worker, it is accepted by most as a better alternative to unemployment. For an interesting discussion of the history of the assignment system, *see* Zou Ji, *The Assignment of Jobs to College Graduates,* in CASE STUDIES OF CHINESE ECONOMIC REFORM 51–79 (Timothy King & Zhang Jiping eds., 1992).

used to describe the notion that one could not be fired regardless of one's performance on the job. While this practice has been somewhat curtailed in China, the concept of lifelong, or at least long-term, guaranteed employment prevails. Because vestiges of the "iron rice bowl" remain, enterprises find it is still difficult to fire an inefficient worker in China today. The government is equally afraid to change the status quo.

In China's labor market, a new form of state sanctioned nepotism has emerged. It is not uncommon for a person who is retiring to be replaced by his or her child, regardless of the child's background or training. In fact, this practice of handing a job to one's offspring has been used by many industries to induce early retirement of older workers. The replacement worker, however, may neither be experienced nor have any interest in the job. While inefficient, the system of replacement by a child insures that retiring workers receive their share of a pension for a set amount of time, and the children are guaranteed a job.

Traditionally, wages in Communist China were set by the government and responded to neither productivity nor efficiency. The Marxist ideal of "from each according to his ability, to each according to his need" undermined any incentive to work,[62] because the State theoretically provided for each citizen's needs regardless of an individual's employment status. In the last few years, officials have been touting a new slogan: "compensation according to work done."[64] Various enterprises have introduced bonus systems, which theoretically award bonuses according to the workers' performance. In reality, many of the bonuses are still awarded on a massive company-wide basis, without singling out individual workers based on merit. Years of indoctrination with egalitarian theory make it hard for workers and managers to adopt to radically different ideas such as paychecks which are not all identical and to accept merit based compensation.

Labor issues played an important role in the events which led to the 1949 revolution in China. Chinese officials are certainly sensitive to this issue and will go to great lengths to avoid actions which would result in widespread unemployment. China also refuses to officially recognize unemployment as problem and has made no provision for unemployment compensation. This refusal to confront the existence of unemployment has also created an anomaly in China's labor statistics: an entire class of youth who are "waiting for assignment" do not appear in China's official unemployment numbers. The State would like to see some of these young people enter the newly emerging private sector, but many of these prospective workers are afraid to risk their chance to grasp the "iron rice bowl" by forsaking public-sector employment.

4. Sources of Capital: Loans and Investors

In the past, the government was the sole source of funding and allocation of capital by the government did not necessarily correspond to the efficiency of the enterprise, and inefficient enterprises which operated continually at a loss could still obtain capital from the government. Unlike capitalist societies where only enterprises with good or excellent performance would be able to obtain additional capital, the Chinese government continually subsidized enterprises without regard to efficiency or profitability, often

62. ALVIN W. GOULDNER, AGAINST FRAGMENTATION: THE ORIGINS OF MARXISM AND THE SOCIOLOGY OF INTELLECTUALS 47 (1985).

64. Du Peirong, *Motivating Workers in a Large State-Owned Enterprise, in* CHINA'S ECONOMIC REFORM, *supra* note [15], at 89; *Shekou Industrial Zone Marks 15th Anniversary*, Xinhua News Agency, Oct. 2, 1994, available in LEXIS, ASIAPC library, XINHUA file.

only to further governmental policy objectives. Much of the government subsidies were designed to keep enterprises in operation in order to avoid unemployment of the workers, a political rather than economic decision. As a result, well-connected but inefficient enterprises often were able to obtain large capital infusions to continue operating.

Even as China moves towards a system where capital is acquired from sources other than direct government grants, such as bank loans, problems still exist with the system. Often banks are pressured by officials seeking loans for specific pet projects of the local officials. Banks operating locally must respond to pressure from local officials who have a special interest in seeing a particular project funded. The notion that "official notes could become bank notes" (*Tiaozi Bian Piaozi*) has become an accepted phrase.[74] With this type of inefficient allocation of capital where banks lend based on the amount of pressure received rather than the feasibility of the project, well-connected but inefficient enterprises will often receive funding instead of the efficient ones.

Some portions of China's economy, especially those funded by foreign investment, operated under some pressure to be efficient. For example, joint ventures often borrowed funds from foreign banks based on economic projections in the joint ventures' feasibility reports. These loans were usually guaranteed by the investors or the Bank of China. The success and failure of these joint ventures taught lessons of fiscal responsibility to Chinese enterprises unaccustomed to such notions.

Another traditional source of capital in market economies is accumulated profits. However, in Chinese enterprises, the notion of accumulating profits for future expansion is not always attractive to the managers and owners of the enterprise. Although theoretically an enterprise may now keep some of its profits, the managers and owners often fear the ever present possibility that the government will take its "share," either by direct collection or by changing the tax laws. Also, because managers do not necessarily benefit from capital expansion, the incentive is to spend profits on the type of expenditure which would immediately benefit the workers (e.g., a cafeteria, more cars for management, bonuses to management and workers, etc.) and not on expanding production.

Even if an enterprise wanted to expand and could set aside funds for that purpose, the inability to acquire property or competitors without government approval hinders efficient expansion. In China, since each enterprise is under the supervision of a ministry, the target company or adjacent facility which one enterprise may wish to acquire are often under the administration of different ministries, each of whose approval would be required for merger or acquisition. Therefore, the normal economies of scale that might be achieved by combining certain enterprises do not occur naturally in China. Unfortunately, the Company Law does nothing to eliminate this bureaucratic roadblock as it explicitly states that the administrative organs in charge of the enterprises owned by the State would remain in charge of the company after incorporation. The Law also specifies that mergers of companies limited by shares are subject to approval of the state authorized departments after the shareholders have adopted a merger resolution.

Comments and Questions

1. Does the Japanese concept of administrative guidance carry over into an understanding of the political culture of China? What sorts of formal and informal relation-

74. [Robert C. Hsu, Economic Theories in China, 1979–1988 (1991)] at 100.

ships do you expect to encounter in China? Does the role of the Communist party as an ex-officio partner of government and business change your analysis?

2. The governing principles of the Constitution of the People's Republic of China express ideas which are not commonly accepted in industrialized democratic states. How large a role do these constitutional principles play in the organization of the state? There is a temptation, perhaps, to downplay the full import of these principles in a West eager to participate in the potential markets of China and used to re-characterizing systems to fit their own fundamental understanding of the ordering of the world. How much of an impediment is the Constitution of the PRC to the establishment of Western style enterprises within China? Does it matter? Would other nations content themselves by the creation of exceptions to the internal organization of Chinese society as long as the integrity and operation of foreign enterprises are respected within China? But if this is the system to be created, does it not, in some ways, replicate the old pre-communist imperial system of trade, positing an essentially closed China in which the state is the sole actor, but in which foreigners are granted special trading privileges in special places?

3. What is the relationship between formal law and more generalized socio-moral rules of good conduct in China? Does that relationship help shape the way in which constitutionalism, and the notion of the "rule of law" is approached in China, irrespective of the economic and political system currently accorded pride of place within the nation?

> The Confucian concept of "li," or standards of social conduct, was traditionally considered far superior to narrow legalistic rules, known as "fa." Codified law was seen as unnecessary and abhorrent. Since 1979, however, this view has bowed to the demands of foreign investors, and modifications of traditional ideology and a "frenzy of codification" have resulted. Barbara Campbell Potter, *China's Equity Joint Venture Law: A Standing Invitation to the West for Foreign Investment?*, 14 U. PA. J. INT'L BUS. L. 1, 4–6 (1993).

Robert C. Art and Minkang Gu, *China Incorporated: The First Corporation Law of the People's Republic of China*, 20 YALE J. INT'L L. 273, 274 (1995). The authors of that article noted that:

> "The Corporation Law represents a key element in the program of economic reform that China began in 1978. Through this program, the Chinese government aims to standardize and modernize enterprise organization and practice. The Corporation Law of 1993 thus supersedes provisional corporate regulations of the central government and two municipalities. It also constitutes one part of a general process of "legalization," the replacement of the traditional emphasis on policy and propriety with codified law and legal institutions.

Id., at 274.

Chapter 3

The Regulation of Corporations

What is a corporation? What makes a business enterprise operating in corporate form different from other forms of business organization? In this Chapter we will look at a corporation from several perspectives. We will look behind the unity of the corporate form to its constituent elements. We then examine the motivations of and constraints on these actors in creating an enterprise in corporate form.[1] From that examination we proceed to a review of the legal basis for the treatment of the corporation as something different from other forms of organization. We do this by examining the legal attributes which are said to distinguish corporations. Lastly we touch on the different theoretical conceptions of the corporate entity—is a corporation an independent and autonomous entity, a series of contractual arrangements or is it the sum of its components (equity investors, creditors, managers, employees, suppliers, etc.) or the creature of the political entity from which it receives its charter?

The materials also concentrate on governmental regulation as a constraint and definer of the nature of corporate form and function in the United States, among the Member States of the European Communities, and non-Western systems. In that context, we also begin to explore an increasingly important regulatory issue—should corporate regulation be viewed as constituting an invariably separate and unique category requiring its own systems of regulation or are corporations merely a subset of enterprises generally, and regulated as such? Do corporations share a set of unique organizational constraints requiring particularized regulation? The emerging theories of enterprise law worldwide point to an acceptance of the idea that corporations are merely one variety of enterprise, like an individual is merely one form of "person", unique in themselves, but sharing a large number of common characteristics. It follows from this view that corporations can, with other forms of enterprise organization, in whatever form organized, be regulated as a group.

A primary object of this Chapter is to introduce the student to the sources of American, European, Chinese and Japanese corporate law. Another object of these materials is to describe and contrast these corporate regulatory regimes: centralization of company regulation versus local regulation of corporations; multi-state harmonization versus insular regimes of rules relating to governance. In reviewing the materials that follow, you should concentrate on the examination of the fundamental differences between the approaches taken by the United States, Japan, China and the European Union and its Member States. In the United States, the regulation of corporations is substantially decentralized. Federal regulation (harmonization) is limited to specific areas of corporate

1. This subject is treated more fully in WILLLIAM A. KLEIN AND JOHN C. COFFEE, JR., BUSINESS ORGANIZATION AND FINANCE (7th ed. 2000); *see also* William A. Klein, *The Modern Business Organization: Bargaining Under Constraints*, 91 YALE L. J. 1521 (1982).

activity: for example the sale of corporate securities to the public (securities law) and the attempt to dominate an industry through monopolistic practices (antitrust law). Other areas, such as accounting practices, are left substantially in the hands of private organizations (the Accounting Standards Review Board). Conversely, the European Union is moving deliberately (if not with much speed!) towards a centralized approach by way of the harmonizing directives of the European Union.

A. The American Regulatory Context: A Regime of State Law

In the absence of federal regulation of corporations, states have retained the power to regulate and charter corporations. In examining the materials that follow, keep in mind the following elementary legal rules which have characterized American corporate jurisprudence for at least the past century.

First, corporation laws are general, rather than special (they are available to all who meet the statutorily prescribed requirements and do not require the approval of bureaucrats or the legislatures like ancient charters).

Second, the determination of the state in which to incorporate is made by the incorporators, and is not dictated by law or the condition of the enterprise (for example by doctrines such as that of the *siege social*, which compels incorporation in the state where the primary economic activity of the enterprise takes place).

Third, corporation laws are limited to the internal governance of the corporation—the relationship between officers, directors and shareholders, and the manner in which ownership of the corporation can be evidenced and affected.

Fourth, corporate laws are "enabling" (permitting incorporation on the terms agreeable to the shareholders, such to the minimum requirements of the statute) and not "regulatory" (imposing extensive restrictions on the discretion of managers and shareholders to determine the nature of their relationship).

1. *The Participants in the Corporate Business Enterprise*

The structure of the legal form of the corporation recognizes, as a formal matter, three different groups: shareholders, directors and officers. The corporate law gives each of these groups certain rights and imposes certain obligations with respect to the operation of the enterprise. It also regulates the distribution of rights and duties between the three groups. The excerpt from the book authored by William A. Klein and John C. Coffee, Jr., *Business Organization and Finance: Legal and Economic Principles*, which follows, briefly outlines these relationships and obligations.

William A. Klein and John C. Coffee, Jr., *Business Organization and Finance: Legal and Economic Principles*

(7th ed. 2000)
(excerpts pages 118–133)

II. The Basic Structure

A. INTRODUCTION

The formal structure for control and operation of a corporation can best be described by reference to three basic groups—shareholders, directors, and officers. The shareholders, who may also be called stockholders, collectively own the residual or equity interest in the corporation; this interest entitles them to a learning and appreciation in the value of the corporation's assets after the fixed claims of the corporation's senior security holders (i.e. creditors and referred shareholders) are satisfied. Absent extraordinary circumstances and a few special statutes, shareholders have no liability for the debts of the corporation.... The interests of individual shareholders are reflected in "shares of common stock" issued by the corporation and held by them.... Shareholders can control the operation of the corporation only by electing directors who form the board of directors and collectively exercise general supervisory control over the business. The directors are responsible for hiring and monitoring the officers, who perform or supervise the day-to-day managerial functions and who are likely, as well, to prepare and submit to the board for approval plans for long-term investment and operations strategy. The three roles—shareholder, director, and officer—may be filled by the same people, but they need not be.

In overview, the most basic structural fact about corporate law is that it delegates broad authority from shareholders through directors to managers. Given the complexity of most business decisions, day-to-day shareholder control, at least in the public corporation, is not feasible. Broad delegation of authority is protected by a legal doctrine, known as the "business judgement rule," that largely immunizes managerial decisions from judicial review or shareholder challenge.... Nonetheless, because managerial and shareholder interests can conflict in some areas, corporate law balances its broad delegation of authority with a system of checks that seeks to maintain the accountability of corporate managers to their shareholders. The tension between the need to delegate wide discretionary authority to managers and the need to maintain accountability generates most of the important issues in corporate law.

B. SHAREHOLDERS

1. Shareholder Voting. By statute, common shareholders have the right to vote (at annual or specially called meetings) for the election of directors and on certain "fundamental matters." Under most state statutes, the "fundamental matters" that require a common shareholder vote include: (1) mergers involving the corporation (except, under some statutes, when the corporation acquires a much smaller firm), (2) any amendment to the certificate of incorporation, (3) the sale of substantially all the corporation's assets and (4) liquidation. Legally, the shareholders are neither agents nor principals of the corporation, and they can neither act on behalf of the corporation nor give orders to officers or other employees of the firm. Their right to vote is much like that of citizens in a representative democracy; that is, they vote to elect directors, who are expected to use their own best judgment. In addition, shareholders can generally

only vote on a merger or charter amendment if it has been first approved by the board of directors.[9] Some commentators have criticized this statutory pattern on the ground that shareholders, as owners, should not need the approval of the board to sell or restructure the firm. Still, the impact of this requirement for prior board approval is probably not very significant, except in special circumstances, such as a takeover battle, where a hostile bidder can acquire a majority of the shares and still may not be able to control the board of directors until the next annual election.[10]

Generally shareholders vote in proportion to the number of shares they hold. Since the mid-19th Century, shareholder democracy has traditionally meant "one share, one vote." This principle may be modified by specific provisions in the certificate of incorporation, giving different classes of stock either greater or lessor voting rights.... It is important to distinguish between, however, between those situations in which a corporation (a) sells newly issued nonvoting or low-vote shares to the public and those in which it (b) engages in a "recapitalization"—that is, beginning with a single class of shares held by the public, it creates a new, lower vote class and provides the public shareholders with an incentive to exchange existing shares for the new, lower-vote shares. In the former situation, the use of differential voting rights may have benign purposes and effects and, with a willing buyer and seller, it may be difficult to find any sound basis for objection to the difference in voting power. In the latter situation, on the other hand, the purposes and effects are more suspicious... and there may be an element of coercion of public shareholders....

....In 1994, however, the three principle exchanges—the New York Stock Exchange, the American Stock Exchange, and NASDAQ—all adopted a rule that substantially restricts the freedom of corporations to reduce the voting power of outstanding shares, but protects dual-class structures that had been accomplished before the rule was adopted.

Exchange rules (and the SEC) do not require that preferred stock have equivalent voting power on a share for share basis. Typically, preferred stock does not vote, except in certain limited contingencies (such as when dividends have not been paid for a specified period). The rationale for disenfranchising the preferred shareholders is that they can rely on their contractual rights and do not need as much to participate in corporate governance. That is, preferred shareholders are promised a fixed, but limited, return (such as 10% of the face value of their stock certificates), which must be paid before the common shareholders receive anything. Their rights to a prior, but limited, dividend more closely resemble the rights of creditors, who also rely on their contractual rights and do not vote in the election of directors. In contrast, because the common shareholders are entitled to the forms residual earnings, after all prior claims are paid, they

---

9. A few states, including New York, permit shareholders to amend the certificate of incorporation at a shareholders' meeting without prior board approval of the resolution.

10. In most states (but not Delaware), shareholders may not remove a director between annual meetings except "for cause," meaning for some specific act of disloyalty or incompetence. Determining that such an act occurred requires a formal hearing before the assembled shareholders of a public corporation. A minority of the states permits removal without cause, but even then the ability of the shareholders to call a special meeting to do so may be limited by by-law or charter provisions that chill this right as a practical matter. Under a few statutes (such as § 228 of the Delaware General Corporation Law), shareholders may act by majority consent in lieu of a shareholders' meeting, unless the certificate of incorporation provides otherwise. Such a statute would effectively allow a hostile bidder to assume control immediately, unless its effect were cancelled by a provision in the target's certificate of incorporation.

have a greater need to monitor management in order to ensure that the firm's returns are maximized, so they elect directors as their agents.

2. Voting by Proxy. Shareholders may vote only at a meeting called for that purpose. Because the shareholders of a publicly held corporation will generally not find it worthwhile to attend a meeting, especially at a distant site, a system known as "proxy voting" has been devised to permit them to vote through designated agents. Under this system, shareholders are permitted to give to another person a *proxy*, which is a document transferring to that person the right to vote the shareholder's shares in the manner indicated on the proxy. Generally, this proxy is revocable at the discretion of the shareholder, who can change his or her mind up to the moment of the election. In the case of corporations with many thousand of shareholders, most of the voting is done by proxy, as it must be for practical reasons.

In most public corporations, the managers (officers or directors or both) use the corporate shareholder list and corporate funds to solicit proxies. Thus, management is said to control the *proxy machinery*, but other shareholders who wish to seek election to the board are generally entitled to access to the corporation's shareholder list. The proxies sent out by management to shareholders for signature will seek authority to vote in favor of a list (or "slate") of people to serve on the board of directors. Generally, these will be people selected by management or of whom management approves.... Management, in its proxy solicitations, may also seek authority to vote on other issues requiring shareholder approval (such as amendments to the certificate of incorporation, approval of stock options for management, appointment of the independent auditors, etc.). Historically, both on the election of directors and on specific issues, shareholders have tended to vote overwhelmingly in support of the management's recommendations.....

* * *

C. DIRECTORS

The directors, collectively called the "board of directors" or "board," have the legal power and duty to manage the affairs of the firm. Traditionally, state corporation laws have provided that the business and affairs of a corporation "shall be managed" by its board of directors. More recently, these statutes have been updated to state that the business "shall be managed by or under the direction of the board." This reflects the growing recognition that the principal responsibility of the board is to monitor rather than to manage. Directors are not full-time employees of the corporation, although some officers of the corporation will invariably be elected to the board. Directors meet as a board periodically (typically monthly or quarterly, but various committees of the board may meet more frequently or as needed) to review and approve significant investment and operational decisions, such as building a new plant or adding a new product line, to approve or review a budget, to decide financial matters, such as issuance of new securities or payment of dividends, and, of most importance in many situations, to appoint, monitor, and determine the compensation of the person chiefly responsible for the front-line operation of the business—the person who has in recent years come to be known as the chief executive officer or "C.E.O." As with shareholders, individual directors have no inherent authority to bind the corporation; their authority is only collective—as the board, as a delegated committee, or as an agent thereof.

Although the directors are not agents of the shareholders in the legal sense, they are considered to be quasi-trustees who are subject to "fiduciary duties" owed to the corporation; in essence, these duties amount to the same kind of duty of loyalty and duty of care than an agent owes to his or her principal....

Directors are accorded wide discretion in their conduct of the corporation's business. Courts almost never interfere with a decision reached by the board, or impose liability on board members, unless it appears that there was a background of self-dealing, conflict of interest, or illegality. The principle relied upon by courts in deferring to the board's decision is known as the "business judgment rule." ... However, there are limits to the breadth of the directors' discretion. In a classic statement, those limits were defined in *Dodge v. Ford Motor*, where the court said:

> A business corporation is organized and carried on primarily for the profit of the stockholders. The powers of the directors are to be employed for that end. The discretion of directors is to be exercised in the choice of means to attain that end, and does not extend to a change in the end itself, to the reduction of profits, or to the nondistribution of profits among stockholders in order to devote them to other purposes.

In short, directors have great discretion over how to maximize the return to shareholders, but not whether to. Certain deviations from the goal of shareholder wealth maximization, such as in the case of charitable contributions, are tolerated but are subject to a "rule of reason" standard.

Shareholders can choose not to re-elect directors upon the expiration of their terms of office and can vote to remove them from office (for any reason in some jurisdictions, but only "for cause" in other jurisdictions). If state law or the certificate of incorporation permits directors to be removed without cause, a new majority shareholder may be able to remove an old board quickly by calling a special meeting of shareholders; otherwise this shareholder must wait until the next annual meeting of shareholders to take action. This point has considerable significance in takeover battles. Still, the shareholders of a publicly held corporation generally lack the legal power to interfere directly in the directors' managerial functions. In practice, of course, directors generally pay heed to shareholders with meaningful voting power.

1. The Closely Held Corporation. In closely held corporations, directors are usually controlling shareholders, or people selected by, and responsive the wishes of, these shareholders. Put simply, it is the shareholders, not the directors, who will be calling the shots. There are exceptions to this generalization, usually arising when the shareholders are at odds with one another; then voting rules and procedures may become important. But, for the most part, in a closely held corporation the board of directors acts as a rubber stamp. Indeed, under some modern statutes no directors are required in a closely held corporation, and shareholders may directly manage the corporation if the certificate of incorporation so provides.

Shareholders of closely held corporations often enter into various forms of agreement relating to control. For example, three shareholders holding 60 percent of the voting shares might enter into an agreement to vote all their shares according to the wishes of a majority of them or in some specified manner. Of considerable significance are agreements designed to assure that particular individuals will have jobs in the firm, with designated duties or salaries or both. These agreements help protect the expectations of the parties and prevent abuse by controlling shareholders, who might otherwise divert dividend income into overly generous salaries for themselves and their associates. Shareholder agreements permit the minority shareholders to be assured of some participation in control of the corporation plus a current return (the salary). In other words, the minority shareholder is protected, to some degree, against being left out in the cold, holding shares worth less than their pro rata share of the total value of the firm.

Another common kind of protective agreement relating to control is one that assures a shareholder a seat on the board of directors. Standing alone, this may assure a minority shareholder somewhat better access to information about the operations of the firm than would otherwise be available. Beyond that, board membership, if combined with a requirement in the articles of incorporation or by-laws that certain proposals be unanimously approved by the board, can give a shareholder (as director) veto power over these proposals—for better or worse....

The law today will uphold shareholders' agreements, subject to an important exception where these agreements bind a director's discretion in his or her capacity to vote as a director. That is, while shareholders may agree to vote their shares to elect each other to the board, an agreement to vote as a director to elect themselves or a third party to be a corporate officer has traditionally been held to be unenforceable....

2. The Public Corporation. In the case of public corporations, the directors may be divided into three categories: (a) insiders (Officers and other employees of the corporation); (b) persons having some other significant relationship with the corporation's management (such as the corporation's ouside lawyers or investment bankers); and (c) true outsiders or "independent" directors (those who do not fit into either of the other two categories). Most of the independent directors of large corporations will be people (mostly men) who are top executives of other corporations, although there may also be a sprinkling of university presidents, Nobel Prize winners, ex-generals, ambassadors, and other public figures.

Available data shows a marked trend over the last decade toward boards with a majority of independent directors, at least in the case of corporations listed on major stock exchanges. Today, the majority of the board of most New York Stock Exchange listed corporations is composed of non-management directors. Less clear is the degree to which these non-management directors have other less visible affiliations with the managements they are supervising. Surveys by management consulting firms and the SEC suggest, however, that the number of non-management directors falling into this intermediate category because of other affiliations with management has also dropped sharply; in particular, it has become increasingly uncommon for a corporation's outside lawyer or its commercial banker to serve on the board.

The question remains, however, whether a lack of economic affiliation with management makes these directors tough minded evaluators of management's performance. Some indications do exist that boards have fired the chief executive officer with more frequency over the last decade, but such internal coup d'etat still remain the exception rather than the rule and are vastly dwarfed by the number of externally induced changes in corporate control. Those who are skeptical of the ability of independent directors to monitor management point to the limited information and incentives that outside directors possess to question management closely. Because most boards lack any staff to develop information for them, directors are largely dependent on the data that management provides them. Although an outside director may question the chief executive closely for a half-hour or more at a board meeting, it is the rare (and probably inept) chief executive who cannot easily withstand this polite assault. Typically, their dialogue involves a mismatch between a full time professional (the c.e.o.) And a part time observer (the director) who, while intelligent, neither wants to be so skeptical as to seem offensive nor has the same depth of knowledge about the specific matter under consideration. Thus, some critics worry that the trend toward independent directors may lead courts to defer excessively to decisions actually reached by corporate managers who may be self-interested.[20]

On the other side of this debate, a persuasive argument can be made that the independent directors have significantly improved corporate governance, even if they are not informed or motivated enough to resist management on all, or even most, occasions. When independent directors are in the majority, the possibility that ineffective senior managers can be removed presumably increases. Not only is removal itself more likely, but the fear of removal for poor performance may have a salutary effect, because it probably deters shirking and managerial consumption of excessive perquisites. Persistent questioning by informed directors may also have an impact by requiring management to articulate its policies and to seek consistency among them, even if the board seldom actually rebuffs the chief executive officer.

The proponents of the independent director would also point to considerably revised structure of the modern board of directors to support their thesis that the board makes a significant difference. Today, the work of the board is chiefly done in committees, where independent directors may specialize and focus their attention. Within such a structure, independent directors may be more effective. Over the last decade, there has been a significant movement toward the institution of two more important committees of outside directors—the audit committee and nominating committee.

The use of an audit committee of independent directors is now required by the New York Stock Exchange, and has been widely adopted by probably a majority of corporations trading on other stock exchanges. Typically, this committee meets regularly with the corporation's independent auditors to conduct a general review of the corporation's financial statements and the audit process. Because these outside auditors are hired (and fired) by the corporation's senior managers, there is always the possibility that the auditors will not be candid with the board as a whole, particularly if they are asked in effect to criticize the corporation's management in the latter's presence. The importance of the audit committee then is that it affords a forum at which the independent directors can learn from the firm's auditors outside the presence of these senior managers about any deficiencies in the firm's auditing controls or accounting policies. For example, if these accountants believe that the corporation is pursuing overly aggressive policies in reporting earnings or if there are legal problems or other contingent liabilities of which the directors were not adequately apprized, the audit committee is the place where these problems can be candidly discussed. Because the firm's independent auditors are in effect the "inspector general" of the corporation, this channel of communication through the audit committee to the independent directors can do much to restore the information imbalance between management and the board.

The nominating committee is probably even more important and more controversial. Today, in most public corporations, the chief executive still plays a dominant role in selecting the outside directors whom the board, in its proxy statement, will propose to the shareholders for election. Almost invariably, the c.e.o. also handpicks his or her successor as c.e.o. When the chief executive officer selects the outside directors, it is at least possible (some would say certain) that these directors will feel a personal loyalty to the c.e.o. An

20. For expression of this concern, see Victor Brudney, *The Independent Director—Heavenly City or Potemkin Village?*, 95 Harv. L. Rev. 597 (1982); Note, *The Propriety of Judicial Deference to Corporate Boards of Directors*, 96 Harv. L. Rev. 1894 (1983).

independent auditing committee may thus increase the objectivity and change the orientation of the outside directors, even if it produces individuals who are no more qualified or energetic. Although only a minority of publicly held corporations have to date adopted an independent nominating committee, its use appears to be significantly growing.

In contrast, there no longer seems to be much political or legislative interest in requiring that the board of directors represent particular non-shareholder constituencies (such as consumers, labor, minority groups, etc.). Proposals for such a constituency based board were floated by Ralph Nadar and others during the 1970's but have subsequently received little discernable support. Shareholders seem generally to be indifferent to the composition of the board of directors, and tend to be concerned with its performance chiefly in dramatic circumstances, such as a hostile takeover or a leveraged buyout, where the board's decisions will have an immediate effect on the corporation's stock price.

D. OFFICERS

Legally, the officers (and other employees) of the corporation are agents of the corporation whose authority comes from a delegation by the board. Authority may be delegated either pursuant to a by-law (such as one authorizing the president to act as the general manager of the corporation and manage its day-to-day affairs) or by a resolution of the board (such as one instructing a manager to buy or sell a specific asset) or by implication (for example, the foregoing resolution might also grant authority by implication to hire lawyers and brokers to negotiate the purchase). The president will also likely be found by most courts to have some implied or "inherent" authority by virtue of his or her office to conduct day-to-day affairs and enter transactions in the ordinary course of business. Still, no officer has the right to bind the corporation in a major transaction, such as borrowing a significant sum of money in the corporation's name, without board approval.

Litigation over authority to bind the corporation is recurrent and often involves a fact pattern where the corporation, after a deal has turned sour, seems to be "welshing" on a commitment made by its officer. In these situations, courts often find that the officer had "apparent authority" (or, in some cases, "inherent agency power"). Under the doctrine of apparent authority, when a prior course of conduct on the corporation's part (involving conduct by person's in addition to the unauthorized agent) gives the appearance to reasonable persons that the agent was authorized to act as he or she did, the corporation is held responsible for creating the impression that the agent had actual, delegated authority to so act and may not avoid or invalidate the transaction. Generally, the party seeking to use this doctrine must have been aware of some prior instances in which the corporation permitted its agent to act in such a fashion. In effect, courts decide in these cases who should bear the risk of the unauthorized agent's acts—the corporation of the "innocent" third party. When it would have been possible for the third party to ascertain the agent's authority at low cost to itself, courts have sometimes declined to find that the agent had apparent authority.[22] The case law in this area is far from consistent, and a variety of factors have been given weight by different courts.

22. For example, in South Sacramento Drayage Co. v. Campbell Soup Co., 220 Cal. App. 2d 851, 34 Cal.Rptr. 137 (3rd Dist. 1963), the court declined to find that a California traffic manager for Campbell Soup, a New Jersey company, had authority to enter into a fifteen year exclusive dealing contract for the intrastate hauling of tomatoes in California. In so doing, the court emphasized that the other party to the contract had not contacted Campbell Soup to ascertain the scope of its agent's authority. In terms of relative costs, it seems clear here that it would have been much cheaper for the other party to inquire of Campbell Soup as to its agent's authority than for Campbell Soup to attempt to broadcast to unknown future contracting parties the same information.

Still, from an economic perspective, the efficient rule of law would seemingly place the risk of loss on the superior "cost avoider"—that is the party which at a lower cost could have prevented the loss from occurring. If the corporation is held liable because the agent is found to have had apparent authority, the corporation could in theory hold its agent liable for acting beyond the scope of his or her delegated authority. In practice, however, the agent's pocket will seldom be deep enough to cover the corporation's loss.

State corporation codes typically provide that a corporation shall have four officers; a president, a secretary, a treasurer, and one or more vice-presidents. Generally, the by-laws will spell out the authority of each of these officers. One person can occupy more than one of these positions, subject to a standard limitation that the same person cannot be both president and secretary. This last limitation arises because the corporate secretary's primary function is to certify that the person signing as the c.e.o. is in fact that person and has been duly authorized. It would make little sense for the c.e.o. to certify as to his or her own status and authority, because an imposter would happily certify these facts as well.

Comments and Questions

1. The foregoing discussion of the formal corporate structuring of group relations is both incomplete and misleading, primarily because it places too much emphasis on the corporation as an entity and ignores the complex web of economic relations that exist between the real participants in the business enterprise. Lenders, employees, trade creditors also have a strong and continuing relationship with the enterprise. In American law, these actors define their relationship to the either through private law (loan agreements and contracts), or through other sets of legal rules (for example labor law). Others may have a more generalized interest in the enterprise—customers, the public in general and the government that serves them, for example. In what ways does law provide these actors with a mechanism for regularizing their relationships with corporate enterprises?

2. European corporate law does not always make the same distinctions as American law between shareholders, officers, directors, creditors, employees and the public. In the section that follows, you will consider the ways in which European corporate law attempts to reconcile the differing interests of shareholders, officers, directors, creditors, employees and the public.

3. American corporate law involves not only choices among the principal participants in the corporate enterprise. A fundamental question of corporate law in the United States involves a choice of corporate home. The section that follows examines this peculiarity of American corporate law.

2. A Note on the Primacy of Delaware Corporate Law

As creatures of state law, one might expect that corporations would "naturally" tend to incorporate in the state in which their principal place of business is located. Three reasons can be advanced for this assumption: (1) convenience; (2) familiarity with local legal setting and (3) greater potential for influencing corporate legislation (a large local corporation may have the ear of the local legislators more than those of legislators in a foreign jurisdiction with whom the only connection is the incorporation).

Yet, it turns out that this is not the case in the US; instead, many corporations, and a large proportion of large publicly traded corporations, tend to incorporate in a handful of states, and primarily Delaware. The materials that follow examine the reasons for this behavior. The corporate law of the state of Delaware has been among the most important since the end of the nineteenth century. The following excerpt provides an interesting perspective on the reasons for the dominance of Delaware state corporate law.

Roberta Romano, *The State Competition Debate in Corporate Law*

8 Cardozo L. Rev. 709 (1987)
(excerpt pages 720–725)

2. Why is Delaware the Destination State of Choice?

The transaction cost explanation of the corporate charter market provides a different perspective on state competition. Delaware's persistent large market share is maintained by a first-mover advantage created by the reciprocal relation that develops between the chartering state and firms due to their substantial investment in assets that are specific to the chartering transaction. The concept of a transaction specific asset, developed by Oliver Williamson, arises in an intertemporal context and refers to an asset that cannot be redeployed in an alternative use at a price anywhere comparable to its value in the original contract should that contract be disrupted.[23] Contracts involving such assets transform the parties' exchange relationship from a competitive market transaction into a bilateral monopoly. A simple example of a transaction specific asset is the specialized racks that are used to transport finished automobiles to market. Such racks are customized for specific car models and cannot be used to transport models of different manufacturers. As a consequence, they are valuable only in certain transactions, and both transporter and car manufacturer are vulnerable and have holdup power. At the outset, there a number of transporters and automobile manufacturers with which to negotiate, but once parties enter into an agreement, the manufacturer needs that particular hauler to get its cars to market and the hauler needs that manufacturer to earn a return on the racks.

The key feature for analysis is that the nonredeployable character of the asset makes the parties to a contract vulnerable and necessitates additional institutional arrangements—which Williamson terms "governance structures"—that reduce the possibility of exploitation and safeguard investments in the transaction specific asset. One such mechanism is the bilateral use of hostages—the contracting party may place him or herself in an analogously vulnerable position to the asset owner by giving up something of value, by posting a bond so to speak. This action credibly guarantees his or her performance and thereby maintains the other party's incentive to invest in the transaction

---

23. For a complete exposition of the theory, *see* O. Williamson, The Economic Institutions of Capitalism 163–206 (1985).

specific asset.[24] In cases of asset specificity, the exchange of hostages may be prerequisite for the transaction itself to occur.

How does this analysis apply to the corporate charter market?[25] Because the transactions between a firm and its incorporation state extend over a long period of time and reincorporation is not costless, relocation makes a firm vulnerable to exploitation by the state. In particular, the state may charge a premium for incorporation and then alter its code or simply not implement the latest innovations, to the firm's detriment, knowing that the firm cannot quickly migrate again without incurring additional expenses. Hence, due to this nonsimultaneity in performance, a state with a favorable corporation code must guarantee its code's continued responsiveness to be successful in the corporate charter market.

Of all the states, Delaware is best positioned credibly to commit itself to responsiveness because it has so much to lose. For unlike states less dependent on franchise revenues, Delaware has no readily available alternative source to which it can turn in order to maintain expenditures. It cannot afford to lose firms to other states by failing to keep its code up-to-date. In this way, Delaware offers itself as a hostage by its reliance on franchise taxes to finance its expenditures.

Second, an additional institutional mechanism warranting responsiveness is Delaware's constitutional provision mandating that all changes in the corporation code be adopted by a two-thirds vote of both houses of the state legislature.[26] This makes it difficult to renege on provisions already in the code and, correspondingly, on the overall policy of being responsive to firms. While the provision would appear to make future changes equally difficult, if firms are risk averse when it comes to corporation codes, they might favor a maximum strategy in which the constitutional provision would be desirable, since it helps to ensure that the legal regime will never be worse than it is at the time of incorporation. This provision thus complements Delaware's high proportionate franchise tax, for while the constitution is backward-looking, as the state reacts to the high proportion of franchise tax revenues in the past by maintaining its responsiveness in incremental change in the future.

Third, Delaware has invested in assets that have no use outside of the chartering business. These assets, which can best be characterized as legal capital, consist of a store of legal precedents forming comprehensive body of case law, judicial expertise in corporate law, and administrative expertise in the rapid processing of corporate filings. These

---

24. *See id.* The typical solution to the automobile racks example discussed in the test involves informal contracting in conjunction with ownership of the racks by the carrier, rather than a bilateral exchange of hostages; the typical solution for the shipment of automobile parts, which also require specialized racks, is ownership by the shipper. Palay, *Avoiding Regulatory Constraints: Contracting Safeguards and the Role of Informal Agreements*, 1 J.L. ECON. & ORG. 155 (1985). Good examples of pure hostages are far too complex to be useful for the text's pedagogic point of an illustration of a transaction specific asset. For specific examples, *see* O. Williamson, *supra* note 32, at 180–189, 197–203.

25. The discussion in the text sets out the thesis put forth in Romano, *supra* note 1, at 235–36, 240–42, 257–60, 273–79. I state the thesis in detail for those who have not read or do not wish to read the longer article, and for those who did not understand it. In a recent paper, Jonathan Macey and Geoffrey Miller, after citing my article for the data, state that they are offering a new explanation of state competition in which Delaware "offers a reliable promise—one that cannot be matched by its competitors—that its corporation law will remain highly attractive to managers for many years into the future." Macey & Miller, INTEREST GROUPS AND DELAWARE CORPORATE LAW 26 (preliminary draft 1986) (available at Cardozo Law Library). The central insight that they are advancing as their theory of the corporate charter market is precisely that of my earlier article.

26. Del. Const. Art. IX § 1. Only one other state, Iowa, has such a constitutional provision. Iowa Const. Art. 8, § 12.

features are not as easily duplicated by other states as the provisions of a corporation code because of the start-up costs in developing expertise and the dynamic precedent-based nature of adjudication by courts.[27]

The combination of these factors—the high proportion of franchise tax revenue, the constitutional supermajority requirement, and the investments in legal capital—create an intangible asset with hostage-like qualities, a reputation for responsiveness,[28] that firms weigh in their incorporation decision. The large number of firms already incorporated in Delaware further solidifies its commanding position in the market by giving it a first-mover advantage. There is safety in numbers—the more firms there are the higher the level of franchise tax paid and the more the state relies on its incorporation business for revenue, which provides the incentive to behave responsively. In addition, the large number of firms makes it more likely that any particular issue will be litigated and decided in Delaware, providing a sound basis for corporate planning. This attracts even more firms for the more responsive a state and the more settles its law, the cheaper it is for a firm to operate under that legal regime. The first-mover advantage is self-sustaining because the more firms there are paying a franchise tax, the greater the return Delaware earns on its reputation for responsiveness, and the stronger its incentive to not engage in an end game strategy of exploiting firms that would damage, if not destroy, its investment in a reputation.

This brings us to the demand side of the market, which also aids Delaware in maintaining an edge. There is a third party affected by the incorporation system, legal counsel, and the features of Delaware's legal regime that are attractive to firms—a well-developed case law with a pool of handy precedents and means for rapidly obtaining a legal opinion on any issue—are also advantageous to corporate lawyers. For these features of Delaware law lower the cost of furnishing advice to clients. This is especially important for outside counsel, who service firms that are headquartered in different states, and who are instrumental in choosing the incorporation state.[29] They realize cost savings by having clients operate under one legal regime. In addition to encouraging the choice of Delaware as the incorporation site for clients, specialization also provides an incentive for advising firms to remain in Delaware, because moving will diminish the attorney's human capital.

27. While a state could explicitly legislate the principle of statutory construction that when it enacted a Delaware law it intended to include all of the existing judicial interpretations, *see, e.g.*, Wilmington City, Ry., v. People's Ry., 47 A. 245, 251 (Del. Ch. 1900), this would not protect firms concerning future adjudicative issues. The state would have to bind its courts to follow future Delaware precedents, and hope that no case of first impression decided by its own courts would conflict with a subsequent Delaware decision. Such a system would involve overwhelming problems of constitutional delegation and parties' right of appeal, in addition to problems concerning the coherency of local decisional law and the granting of retroactive relief should the hypothesized conflict arise.

28. The connection between reputations and hostages is straightforward: in the corporate charter market where both firms and states have potentially infinite lives, the party with the reputation, Delaware, has an incentive to maintain it because the costs of building up its reputation will not be recouped if it behaves irresponsively in the short run. For then, domestic firms will relocate, new firms will not migrate to it, and tax revenues in later periods will be lost. In other words, a cooperative equilibrium can emerge from a "tit-for-tat" strategy. *See generally* R. AXELROD, THE EVOLUTION OF COOPERATION (1984) (reciprocity strategies are self-reinforcing and powerful tools to create cooperation).

29. .... Macey and Miller question these results, stating that "the questionnaire...used did not list investment banks as potential parties to suggest reincorporation." Macey and Miller, *supra* note 34, at 25. The questionnaire included investment bankers as an explicit choice; the respondents did not choose that answer.

Counsel's desire to recoup the investment in mastery of the institutional detail of Delaware law ties firms reciprocally to Delaware, just as Delaware is tied to firms.

Human capital is important in another way. Delaware's stake in the chartering business exceeds the revenues it receives from the franchise tax. A number of its citizens specialize in providing services to nonresident Delaware corporation. Accordingly, it is in the interest of those individuals that Delaware be responsive to corporations so that the demand for their services does not decline.[30] Delaware's supermajority constitutional provision therefore serves an important function aside from credibly precommitting it to be responsive to firms: It protects the value of these individuals' personal investments by making it more difficult for a political realignment in the state to alter the longstanding course of corporate responsiveness.

This transaction specific human capital, which creates a "mutual reliance relation"[31] between firms and Delaware, joins the parties in long-term cooperation because of their reciprocal vulnerability, and cements Delaware's market position, as it makes it difficult for rival state to compete successfully. Another state cannot simply offer corporations the same code at a lower price and attract the marginal firm, because a switch would increase operating and legal costs, and more importantly, the state cannot provide a credible commitment of superior service. In particular, a rival state cannot place itself in the same vulnerable position as Delaware because it starts from a low franchise tax ratio and has not yet invested in legal capital. In order for a state to begin to complete, a significant number of firms would have to agree to move in to it in concert. But there is no incentive for corporations to move in another state so long as Delaware continues to cooperate, and there are powerful incentives for Delaware to continue to do so.

Professor Romano has described a peculiarity of American corporate law that tends to be treated as a defect in the American approach to corporate regulation by people outside the United States. As you read the materials that follow, consider the ways in which European corporate statutes create the sort of stable corporate law environment produced in Delaware. In chapter 5 we will consider directly the issue of the way in

---

30. .... A number of years ago, Joe Bishop made the point concerning the importance of lawyers in Delaware's lack of a security-for-expenses requirement for shareholder derivative suits. He wrote: "It might... occur to a cynical mind that this curious anomaly of the Delaware's law may not be wholly unconnected with the fact that the prosecution or defense of a derivative suit in a Delaware court requires the retention of Delaware counsel." Bishop, *New Cure for an Old Ailment: Insurance Against Directors' and Officers' Liability*, 22 Bus. Law. 92, 94–95 (1966). Macey and Miller, *supra* note 34, also stress the importance of lawyers in Delaware. They appear to suggest that the input of lawyers in Delaware's legislative process has a negative implication for a theory of state competition. Such a conclusion could be wrong—the role of lawyers is peripheral to the debate, particularly from the transaction cost view of state competition that they appear to be advancing. If Delaware passes corporate laws that systematically favor lawyers to the detriment of firms on a large scale, it would lose its chartering business to another state whose lawyers were not as avaricious. Delaware maintains its position by mutual cooperation with, and not by exploitation of, firms. This is not to say that lawyers do not profit in Delaware. While lawyers are actively and intimately involved in Delaware's profitable chartering business, their participation provides no clear-cut insight concerning whether it benefits managers at the shareholders' expense. The important question, which Macey and Miller do not address, is how any rents are divided between Delaware, the bar, and firms.

31. The term is from *Williamson, Credible Commitments: Using Hostages to Support Exchange*, 73 Am. Econ. Rev. 519, 528 (1983).

which states regulate the ability of an enterprise to choose the laws under which it will be regulated.

B. Establishing the European Regulatory Context: Laws of the Member States

In this section, we will take a brief look at European company law—company law is usually regulated by each Member State. General enabling statutes are the basis for the national company laws of all Member States of the European Communities. Despite structural uniformity, there are considerable differences in the manner in which individual states implement their respective statutes.

1. *Development and National Sources of Company Law*

There are four basic approaches to basic corporate law in the Member States of the European Community: (i) common law approach; (ii) Latin civil law approach, (iii) Germanic civil law approach; and (iv) Scandinavian law approach. The major differences between them include (1) formation and financing, (2) internal organization, (3) disclosure requirements, (4) choice of the company's legal form, and (5) limitations on groups of companies and business combinations. The following excerpts give a flavor of the differences and similarities of Western European Company Law as well a short history of its development.

S.N. Frommel and J.H. Thompson, *Introduction*

in Company Law in Europe
(S.N. Frommel & J.H. Thompson eds., 1975)
(excerpts pages 15–16; 55–56)

IV. FORMS OF BUSINESS ORGANIZATION

Terminology: companies and partnerships

48. All the countries under discussion have two basic forms of business organization: the partnership, where either all of the members are responsible for the liabilities of the firm, and the limited company, where none of the members is liable for the company's debts.

49. On the Continent, in contrast with England, there is a single word which comprises both partnerships and companies: this word, in French *société*, in German *Gesellschaft*, depending on the context in which it is used, may refer to a partnership, or a company, or to both. Thus, the *société en nom collectif* (SNC) and the *offene Handelsgesellschaft* (OHG) are general commercial partnerships; the partnership governed by the Civil Code is the *société civile* pr *BGB-Gesellschaft*; and the limited partnership is the *société en commandite simple* (SCS) or *Kommanditgesellschaft* (KG).

'Public' and 'private' companies

50. The Latin and Germanic countries have two basic types of limited companies: the 'share' company (French: *société anonyme* (SA); German: *Aktiengesellschaft* (AG), and the 'limited liability' company (French: *société á responsabilité limitée* (SARL); German: *Gesellschaft mit beshränkter Haftung* (GmbH).[1]

51. Until 1973 all Scandinavian countries had only one type of company, the share company (Sweden: *Aktiebolag* (A/B); Denmark: *Aktieselskab* (A/S), but in that year Denmark introduced the second type, the limited liability company (*Anpartsselskab*).

52. The strict English equivalent of the Continental 'share' company is the registered company limited by shares which may in turn be public or private. The expression 'public' can be misleading because it does not mean, technically, at least, that its shares are publicly held or that they are listed on a Stock Exchange; they may, but need not, be held by the public. Some experts maintain that English public and private companies are respectively the equivalent of the Continental share company with or without a public issue of shares. Others contend, however, that the English private company, though not the subject of separate legislation as on the Continent, is nevertheless the equivalent of the Continental limited liability company.[2]

53. It is easier to distinguish between share companies and limited liability companies on the Continent than between public and private companies in England. For instance, on the Continent the name of each type of company includes a different designation, whereas in England the names of both types of company have the same designation 'limited' (or 'Ltd'). In addition, while in England the private company is merely a form of the company limited by shares, on the Continent the limited liability company is a second type of company quite distinct from the share company. These terms have been left in the original language in each chapter, but are referred to in English as the 'public' company (i.e., the Continental share company) and the 'private company (i.e. the limited liability company) respectively.

54. There are two expressions which are roughly equivalent to the English words 'partnership' and 'company', but they are rather cumbersome: *sociétés de personnes, Personengesellschaften*, indicating the former, and *sociétés de capitaux, Kapitalgesellschaften*, the latter. This distinction is mainly used in tax law. It is not entirely accurate because individuals (*personnes* are needed by the company as well as by the partnership, and capital (*captaux* is required not only by the company, but also by the partnership.

55. In those countries where the limited liability company more closely resembles the partnership (e.g., Belgium and Luxemburg), it is considered to be a *société de personnes*, whereas in others (e.g. Italy and Germany), as it has more characteristics of the share company, it is a *société de capitaux*.

* * *

1. The terminology is summarized in the chart which follows the reading excerpted from Clive Smithhoff, *Social Responsibility in European Company Law*, below.

2. Zweigert and Goldman, 'Report on the possibility of harmonizing member states' legislation on private limited companies (or similar bodies) (*societé à responsabilité limitée*)', Council of Europe (1969), 21.

Contiinental Equivalents to the English Private and Public Company		
Country	"Private" Company (Limited liability company)	Public Company (Share company)
Austria	*Gesellschaft mit beschränker Hafttung* (GmbH)	*Aktiengesellsc haft* (AG)
Belgium	*Société de Personnes à Responsabilité Limité* (SPRL)	*Société Anonyme* (SA)
Denmark	*Anpartsselskab* (ApS)	*Aktiese lskab* (A/S)
France	*Société à responsabilité limitée* (SARL)	*Société Anonyme* (SA)
Germany	*Gesellschaft mit beschrånkter Haftung* (GmbH)	*Aktiengesellsc haft* (AG)
Italy	*Società a responsabilità limitata* (Srl)	*Società per Azioni* (SpA)
Liechtenstein	*Gesellschaft mit beschrånkter Haftung* (GmbH)	*Aktiengesellsc haft* (AG)
Luxemburg	*Société à responsabilité limitée* (SRL)	*Società Anonyme* (SA)
Netherlands	*Besloten Vennotschap met beperkte aansprakelijkheid (BV)*	*Namm loze Vernootschap (NV)*
Spain	*Sociedad de responsabilidad limitada* (SRL or SL)	*Socied ad anónima* (SA)
Sweden	*Aktiebolag* (A/B)	
Switzerland	In French: *Société à responsabilité limitée* (SRL) In German: *Gesellschaft mit beschrånkter Haftung* (GmbH)	in French: *Societé Anonyme* (SA) in German: *Aktiengesellschaft* (AG)

While the various European states chose to go their own way in setting up regulations for companies, the different approaches adopted share many commonalities. And to some extent, European nations tend to borrow from each other when faced with similar problems. The excerpt below provides some historical background on the development of modern company law in Europe from the nineteenth century.

Richard M. Buxbaum and Klaus J. Hopt, *Legal Harmonization and the Business Enterprise: Corporate and Capital Market Law Harmonization Policy in Europe and the U.S.A.*

(1988) (excerpts pages 176–189; footnotes omitted or renumbered)

B. The Development of Different National Company and Capital Market Laws

The European attempt to harmonize national company and capital market laws is confronted with considerable, sometimes fundamental, diversity of such laws, not only between Civil and Common Law states, but among the Civil Law states themselves.

Some of the more important characteristics of this diversity will be considered below. It should be emphasized that despite all differences this diversity is only relative. Unlike such areas as constitutional law administrative law, public economic law, or family and inheritance law, the basic assumptions of commercial and company law are generally similar among the Western industrialized countries. The goal of company law everywhere is to find an organizational form suitable to the economic activity of the types of firms operating within an economy. All such law attempts to reconcile the differing interests of the shareholders, the creditors, and possibly the employees and the public. In general, the diversity of organizational laws is not the result of ideological conflict, apart from the questions of worker participation and representation of the public interest in the firms.

Similarly, capital market law, which has grown out of company law and in various countries become quite independent of it, is generally the subject of ideological agreement among the various states. This is particularly true to the extent that most countries agree that recourse to the capital market by firms should be linked with obligations of disclosure and conduct. Not until one considers the detailed structures of national capital markets do considerable differences appear, in such areas as access to the capital market, the constitution of the individual markets and government intervention in their function. Most of these differences may be attributed to national tradition.

1. Development of National Company Laws

The development of national company laws began in the nineteenth century. Industrialization, which had begun in the first half of the century, had transformed the economy of the Western world by the second half, leading to the development of new company structures. The trend was toward the formation of large corporations, particularly in the German *Reich* and the United States, and to a smaller extent in Great Britain and France as well. Company law played a key part in this growth, by allowing the external expansion of firms and promoting capital concentration.

Developments in company law principles also spread to the banking sector, increasing capital concentration. The state played its part in promoting this process by freeing the corporate structure from historical restrictions. Originally, permits from the individual states were required to constitute a corporation as a legal person, but this concession system was gradually replaced by general enabling and normative provisions.[1] Under this new system, every firm meeting the organizational conditions of the enabling statutes had a right to be constituted as a corporation. The states no longer exercised investment supervision over companies, either as protection for investors, as a restriction on company objectives, or as general control over economic power.

Today, general enabling statutes are the basis for the national company laws of all Member States of the European Community. Even the Netherlands, where a certificate of government approval from the Justice Minister is still necessary to form a corporation, is an exception only in form, since issuance of the certificate has become a mere formality. Despite this structural uniformity, however, there are consid-

1. England (1844), Joint Stock Companies Act 1844, ...; France (1867), Loi No. 15.328 sur *les* Societes, du 24 juillet 1867, Arts. 21 & 47, *Bull. des Lois,* No. 1513, Tome 30, p. 95 (1866–1870); Germany (1870), Gesetz betr. die Kommanditgesellschaft auf Aktien u. die Aktiengesellschaften vom 11.6.1870, BGBI. Norddeutscher Bund 1870, 375.

erable differences in how the various nations' company laws implement their respective enabling statutes. These differences will be discussed in the following sections, particularly in the context of national company laws governing (a) formation and financing, (b) internal organization, (c) disclosure requirements, (d) choice of the company's legal form, and (e) limitations on groups of companies and business combination.

a. Formation and Financing of the Corporation

The concession system of company law was abolished in England in 1844, in France in 1867, and in Germany in 1870. In each case, the respective legislature felt that market forces and disclosure requirements applicable to the formation of corporations would suffice for the protection of shareholders and creditors. This optimism, evidenced by Gladstone's pathbreaking legislation of 1844, very soon proved unjustified. After the special legislative charter controls were abandoned, corporations were frequently used fraudulently in Britain (after 1866) and in Germany after 1870, during the "*Grunderzeit.*"

As a consequence of these abuses, formation and financing provisions of company law were tightened in all countries. In Germany, for example, this came about through the Companies Act of 1884.[2] However, as each country reformed its statutes, the diversity of issues requiring regulation and the variety of protection mechanisms chosen led inevitably to a divergence of national company laws. This differentiation can be seen today in such areas as: statutes on the adequacy of stated capital versus a fixed company capital requirement; provisions for raising and maintaining these amounts; provisions for contribution of property as well as, or instead of, money as capital; issuance of nonvoting shares; limitations on the validity of shares with more than one vote; limitations on authorization of corporate reacquisition of shares; requirements for capital increases and reductions; requirements for minimum contents of company charters; and provisions for control and definition of the duty to observe these regulations.

b. Organs and Internal Organization of the Corporation

For the first half of the nineteenth century, creation of company organs and regulation of their tasks was largely left up to the individual articles of association. The company laws of the time contained few if any of the organizational norms familiar today. This situation changed with the abandonment of the concession system, and by about 1870 the basic features of this area were regulated, or at least sketched out in the case law.

In Common Law countries the development of organization law was traditionally in the hands of the courts. Similarly, in France, the important initiatives also came from the courts, since the organization law enacted in 1867 was left unamended by the legislature for a long time. In Germany, by contrast, the legislature made a considerable contribution to the development of internal controls through the reform statute of 1884.

Even at this early date, German organization law was intended primarily to serve the capital interests of shareholders. Apart from the corporations with majority shareholders, who were usually entrepreneurs, shareholder interests and managerial functions were already largely separate.

2. ....L.C.B. Gowir, J.B. Cronin, A.J. Easson & Lord Wedderburn, Gower's Principles of Modern Company Law 39–52 (4th ed., London 1979) [hereinafter cited as Gower].

* * *

i. Control of Management

The problem of management control was seen as more or less fundamental everywhere it was considered, but only a few legal regimes developed a true independent supervisory body in the sense of a division of the board of directors between management and supervision. This board of directors, frequently conceived of as a committee of shareholders, concerned itself with decisions of principle, while the day-to-day business was generally controlled by inside directors or special managers. The personal overlap between board and management rendered impartial control difficult from the outset. The board was in a strong legal position vis-a-vis management, but because the outside directors were not actively involved in the day-to-day business of the corporation, they could not effectively control management's activity as a practical matter.

A similar situation prevailed in France, where overall management was handled by an administrative board *(conseil d'administration)* whose competence was confined to decisions of principle. The daily business of the corporation was run by "managers:' some of whom were members of the administrative board and some of whom were not. Legally, the administrative board could supervise management, but it was not obliged to do so because it was ultimately responsible only for business policy. The administrative board itself was supervised by "*commissaires*" who were appointed by the [shareholders'] general assembly, but these *commissaires* were primarily responsible for supervising the accounting aspect of the corporation, without any entrepreneurial initiative.

The first compulsory provision for a functional separation between management and the supervisory organ was enacted in France, but only in the case of limited-share partnerships. The company structure known as the share partnership had, in contrast to the corporation, been available without government permission for decades and had become an instrument of serious abuses. As a result, the legal regulation of the share partnership, enacted in 1856, provided for an obligatory "*conseil de surveillance.*"

This legal structure also reached Germany, via the Nuremberg Conference on the preparation of the All-German Commercial Code. Accordingly, the Company Reform Act of 1870 brought about the abandonment of the concession system, but at the same time as a safe-guard introduced the obligatory supervisory board for corporations. This structure was tightened even further in 1884 through additional limitations providing that the supervisory board members could not also be members or permanent representatives of the board of directors, or part of the management staff of the corporation.

* * *

The supervisory board proved one of the most important factors in modern economic concentration. Made up of the most important business partners of the corporation and representatives of the large corporate banks, these supervisory boards became instruments for the expansion of large corporations. Supervisory boards were also a key to the growth of the universal banking system. There has been little significant change in this function to date.

All the important arguments for and against the one-tier and two-tier systems had been developed by the turn of the century. Little has been learned since from experience. The extent to which practice can accommodate itself to any system was shown by the result of the French legislative experiment of 1966, which allowed corporations to choose between either a single board of directors or a two-tier system incorporating a supervisory board. This opportunity was taken advantage of by only a small number of French corporations (some of them economically quite important it is true), although French scholars have been unable to fully explain this development on objective grounds.

A more fundamental divergence of company law has developed with the emergence in some Member States[3] of laws requiring worker participation (codetermination). The German Federal Republic became the primary example of this trend in 1976 when it adopted a model for worker participation on the supervisory board. The model is based on equal representation of capital and labor, and places a final tie-breaking vote with capital through the chairman of the supervisory board. A weaker form of worker participation was introduced in the Netherlands in 1973. Under the Dutch model, the managerial board of directors, the central works council and the shareholders' general assembly each makes proposals for appointments to vacant supervisory posts. The supervisory board then chooses from among those proposed. More limited attempts at codetermination have been made in other countries, with participation restricted to particular industries, or introduced on a voluntary basis. Unlike other issues of company law, these decisions have not been based on technical issues of corporate organization, but involve fundamental questions about economic systems, which are more often decided on the basis of emotion and ideology.

ii. Shareholders' General Assembly

The shareholders' general assembly, found in the company laws of all Member States, does not act as the supreme organ of the firm, although it is frequently assigned this position by the legislature. In Germany, the reform act of 1884 was intended to strengthen the shareholders' control by increasing the powers of the general assembly. In reality, however, management generally ran matters independent of this assembly.... Shareholder democracy was ultimately regarded as both unworkable and undesirable, and the company law reform of 1937 made the board of directors the most important organ of the company.

The German Companies Act of 1965, in force today, was intended to improve the position of the small shareholder. The general assembly's influence on the use of profits was strengthened, and legal protections for the individual shareholder were improved. In practice, however, this reform did not change the limited influence of the general assembly, particularly in public companies without major shareholders. The general assembly continues to play a decisive role only as to basic structural decisions, which can only be made by a qualified majority of three-quarters of the share capital participating in the decision (unless the articles of association, within specific limits, provide otherwise).

---

3. For a survey on the state of codetermination in different Member States *see* EC Commission, "Employee Participation and Company Structure" *Bull EC,* SUPP. 8/1975, at 51 ("Green Paper"); F. Gamillscheg et al., *Mitbestimmung der Arbeitnehmer in Frankreieh, Grossbritannien, Schweden, Italien, den USA under der Bundesrepublik Deutschland* (Frankfurt 1978); Symposium, "Worker Participation in Management" 4 *Comp. L. Yearbook* 3-163 (1981) (USA, Austria, Belgium, Germany, Holland, Italy, Japan, Switzerland, Yugoslavia); Hopt, "Grundprobleme der Mitbestimmung in Europa: Eine rechtsvergleichende Bestandsaufnahme und Einschatzung der Vorschlige zur Rechtsangleichung der Arbeitnehmermitbestimmung in den Europiischen Gemeinschaften" 13 *ZfA* 207 (1982) (also available in French version: "Problemes fondamentaux de la participation en Europe," 34 *Rev. droit comm. et droit econ.* 401 (1981)),....

Attempts to give greater power to the general assembly have failed in other jurisdictions as well. In France, for example, the legislature sought to strengthen the position of the general assembly by giving to it the right to amend the articles of association, elect the supervisory board, and approve the balance sheet. This failed to change the passivity and absenteeism of the shareholders. In Britain, the ultimate decisions were intended to be reserved to the shareholders through the use of their powers of election and removal, and the case law there tended toward recognition of the separation of powers between the board and shareholders. But this model also failed to increase the shareholders' control.

Today, in order to fill the vacuum created by this impotence of the general assembly in the internal organization of corporations, the Member States have adopted various reforms in national company law, particularly on the issue of proxy voting (also called nominee voting). In this area, there is a fundamental difference between the US, British and French laws and the statutes of, for example, Germany. Under the former laws, shareholders are generally free to transfer their voting rights to board members. But even though such proxy voting implies the possibility of instructing the board to make particular decisions, it became apparent long ago that it actually does little to change the dominance of the board, even where it is buttressed by comprehensive disclosure requirements. As Cower comments: "Although proxy voting gave an appearance of democratic freedom, this appearance was often deceptive and in reality the practice helped to enhance the Dictatorship of the board."[4] Despite recent procedural improvements in proxy voting, little has changed in practice.

German law took an opposite position on proxy voting, but only in theory. While German law made proxy voting impermissible, it allowed the transfer of voting rights to parties other than managers. After the turn of the century this practice led to the development of so-called depository voting rights whereby shareholders who deposited their shares at a bank transferred their voting rights to the bank as part of the deposit transaction. This depository voting right, which was generally adopted, has meant that banks have frequently set the tone in the general assemblies of public companies.

* * *

iii. Board of Directors

Today, despite important differences in legal regulations, the board of directors is the dominant body in public companies without major shareholders. This dominance can be demonstrated in a variety of areas, but we shall examine only a few here. These are (1) the legal position of the board of directors vis-a-vis the other organs of the company; (2) the legal power of the board to represent the corporation; and (3) the obligations of the board with respect to the proper execution of its role.

An example of the evolution of the dominant legal position of the board of directors is provided by the German company law reform of 1937. Said to be the transfer of the "Fuhrer principle" to corporate law, this statute greatly strengthened the board's position in the company. The statute required the board of directors to pursue not only the interests of the shareholders but also the interests of the company, the interests of its workers, and the public interest in general. Although this provision has since been abolished, the board remains the preeminent organ in the company. The debate continues on the board's responsibility to set the interests of the workers and the public above profitability.

---

4. Gower, *supra* note [1], at 538....

The extent to which the board of directors is permitted to bind the company to third parties also provides an excellent example of an area where, despite differing regulations, the power of the board remains preeminent. Here, the older *ultra vires* doctrine of Common Law countries, even though moderated today by appropriate wording of the articles of association and by exculpatory legislation, can be compared to the widespread Continental view that business activity would be excessively restricted by such a limitation on the power of representation. In the European view, the *ultra vires* doctrine would ultimately compel fidelity to the articles of association over the obligations of any individual transaction, and would be an unacceptable restriction on the power of the board. It should be noted, however, that although theoretically the Continental view is clearly more liberal than the Common Law view, there has been little practical difference between the two systems.

The differences under various national laws in the fiduciary duty of the board have rarely been dealt with before. National statutes have had little to say on these issues, so that differences have arisen chiefly through developments in case law. In the Common Law countries, the theoretical basis for regulation of the board's duties is the idea that the board of directors occupies the position of a trustee, and is subject to the wide-ranging duties of a trustee. This definition of the board's obligation results in the imposition of extensive behavioral obligations in such areas as conflict of interests, use of inside information, making of takeover offers, etc. Continental European legal systems, in which the concept of the trust is alien, are only gradually beginning to appreciate the extent of these problems, and to regulate these aspects of the board's role. This is still generally true even though some countries do have some quite highly developed rules in specific fields; for example, France has developed rules on personal self-dealing of board members with their corporation and Germany has gone far in regulating competition with one's own corporation. Even less homogeneous are the views on what legal duties the board members have concerning corporate social responsibility.

c. Corporate Disclosure Requirements

The area of disclosure reveals yet another aspect of the divergence of European company and capital law evolution. In most European company law systems, the translation from the concession system to the enabling system of incorporation went hand in hand with the development of compulsory minimum disclosure requirements. State control through concessions was replaced by shareholder control through disclosure. By the second half of the last century, legislatures began to recognize the special relation between disclosure and such diverse issues as the growth of free competition, the protection of shareholders and the protection of the proper function of the stock market. Despite their common goals, however, the various countries originally took quite different approaches to the use of disclosure as a means of control over the corporation.

This difference is highlighted by the contrasting approaches developed by the Common Law countries, such as Great Britain, and the Continental systems, such as Germany. While British company law has pursued far-reaching disclosure since the time of Gladstone, disclosure developed only gradually and hesitantly in German company law. Disclosure was introduced to German company law in 1870 by the All-German Commercial Code, which originally required disclosure only of the corporate balance sheet and profit-and-loss statements in public documents. It was not until 1931, in the wake of the world economic crisis, that the law was amended to require a compulsory audit of final accounts by special auditors. Broader company disclosure was not imposed until 1969, when a new law was passed requiring disclosure of the annual account based on the size of the firm, not the company's legal form (i.e., whether or not a corporation). Under this statute, the disclosure obligation arises when two out of three characteristics are present: gross assets of more than DM 125 million, an annual turnover of more than DM 250 million, and more than 5,000 employees. This approach emphasizes the economic importance of the individual firm and covers even sole proprietorships.

d. Choice of the Company's Legal Form

In contrast to such countries as Britain, France and Switzerland, the corporate company structure has steadily lost importance in Germany over the last two decades. The number of corporations, as well as the number quoted on the stock exchange, has fallen considerably. Implementation of economic and social policies through company law has led to greater burdens placed on corporations, as compared with other company structures. These differences arise particularly in such areas as disclosure requirements, tax burdens, and labor and codetermination laws....

On the other hand, the limited-liability company has steadily gained ground in Germany. Historically, this type of company structure was developed for medium and small firms that were more simply regulated than the corporation. The external stimulus to the growth of these companies was provided by the German company law reform act of 1884, which tightened the normative enabling provisions applicable to corporations. The 1892 Limited-Liability Companies Act was a pioneering statute,[5] which soon found imitators in neighboring European countries. While the legal concept of the Act relied heavily on a small or close corporation model, which had traditionally restricted the influence of the capital provider to setting guidelines and supervising business policy, what made the 1892 Act so revolutionary was the recognition that participants in the company were free to use a more individual organization structure. The Act allowed far-reaching contractual freedom in choosing and adapting company structures, and this freedom led to extensive development of the limited-liability company. The only important limitation of the Act, which prevented large capital-intensive firms from abandoning the corporate form, was the difficulty surrounding the transfer of company shares. An unintended consequence was that a limited-liability company can obtain practically no equity capital from the general public on the capital market.

The freedom of choice among company forms and the broad contractual freedom within most of these forms (other than the corporation) led German lawyers to experiment with company constructions, mixing corporate and individual structural elements. In 1922, when the court of last instance recognized the GmbH & Co. KG (limited-liability joint stock partnership) there was no stopping the trend toward mixed structures. This mixed structure of the limited-liability company partnership expanded rapidly in Germany, even though in most other Member States it plays no significant role, and is explicitly forbidden in Switzerland. Originally, this expansion was attributable to the tax advantages of the mixed structure, but since the corporate tax reform act of 1977, the company law advantages have been the key attraction of this structure. Today, a company so structured may enjoy the benefits of a limited liability company, while also having flexibility in the appointment of outsiders to the management organs (thereby facilitating the choice of management and succession) and freedom of form.

---

5. Clive Schmitthoff, *The Future of the European Company Law Scene*, in THE HARMONIZATION OF EUROPEAN COMPANY LAW 3, 11 et seq. (C.M. Schmitthoff ed., London 1973).

Moreover, since the 1970's, practice has developed yet another type of GmbH & Co., the so-called personal public company or mass company. While the circulation of shares of limited-liability companies (GmbHs) is not allowed, there is nothing in German law that prevents trading in shares of commercial partnerships, since in their case unlimited liability supposedly functions as a regulator. Thus, the GmbH & Co. made direct access to the capital market possible and removed the threat of personal liability, without requiring use of the corporate legal form. The success of the GmbH & Co. has been pervasive. In recent years more new capital has flowed into such public companies than into corporations. Moreover, despite widespread abuses, the legislature has been unable to decide on a capital market act to regulate this trend (a point dealt with below). It therefore has been up to the case law to deal with this phenomenon and to treat it as what it really is, a corporation in the disguise of a partnership....

* * *

The European system of a functional division of corporate organization, based on the character of share ownership went substantially unchanged until the 1960s. By that time, a sense had arisen that corporate organization was no longer used for the purposes for which each had been envisioned. Private companies controlled wealth which rivaled that of the more heavily regulated public companies. Moreover, public companies were using private companies as subsidiaries in an effort to avoid some of the burdens of public company regulation with respect to certain of their operations. As a result, a series of reforms of company law were begun, principally in England and Germany, which resulted in the overlaying of the traditional regulation of companies by form of internal organization with new regulation based on criteria other than formal organization—principally size and character. The excerpt below provides a taste of the concern and the result.

Clive M. Schmitthoff, *Social Responsibility in European Company Law*

30 Hast. L.J. 1419 (1979)
(excerpt pages 1422–25)

A New Classification of Companies

The traditional classification of companies in Europe is into public and private companies. The private company originated in Germany as the *Gesellschaft mit beschränkter Haftung* (GmbH), where it is still regulated by the Law of April 20, 1892. This Law is at present under revision. Professor H. Wurdinger writes in his *German Company Law:* "The private company...is an invention of the legislature, and was created by the Law of 20th April, 1892 (GmbHG) without any historical precedent in German or European law."[6] The idea of the private company was to make the form of the limited-liability company available to small business. This idea spread from Germany to France and the other European countries. The private company was introduced into French law by the Law of March 7, 1925 which admitted the creation of the *société à responsibilité limitée* (SARL). In Belgium this form is known as the *société des personnes à responsibilité lim-*

---

6. H. Würdinger, German Company Law 183 (1975).

itée (SPRL). In the United Kingdom the private company was introduced by the Company Law Reform of 1907 and 1908.[7]

The traditional distinction between public and private companies is no longer in accordance with economic reality. The private company is used for two different purposes, as the small family company and as a subsidiary of large enterprises, particularly of the public-company type. The United Kingdom Companies Act 1948 sought to distinguish between these two types of the private company. The Act attempted to grant the privilege of balance-sheet secrecy from subsidiary private companies, the shares of which were owned by other companies. This arrangement proved to be too complicated, and, since the Companies Act 1967, all private companies in the United Kingdom, large or small have had to publish their balance sheets. However, it is now widely recognized in the United Kingdom that that measure went too far and that small family companies require special regulation. In the leading case of *In re Westbourne Galleries Limited*[8] the House of Lords recognized that the so-called partnership company[9] enjoyed a special status and that the shareholders in such a company were under an equitable obligation not to exercise their legal rights in a manner contravening the expectations of the other members.

The modern classification of companies that is closer to economic reality is that between large public companies listed at the Stock Exchange and family companies which use the corporate form only for purposes of convenience, such as to avail themselves of the benefit of limited liability or for tax reasons. Between these two poles of large listed public companies and small family companies is a spectrum of large private companies and unlisted public companies. The concept of the large company[10] is recognized in many European countries, although no unanimity exists on what constitutes a large company. Thus, in Germany, where the GmbH in principle enjoys balance-sheet secrecy, following the United Kingdom Companies Act 1967, the so-called *Publizitätsgesetz* of 1969 was introduced which lays down three criteria for the GmbH:

(a) the total balance of the annual balance sheet exceeds DM 125,000,000;

(b) the turnover in the last twelve months exceeds DM 250,000,000;

(c) the enterprise has employed more than 5,000 employees during the last twelve months.

If two of these criteria are satisfied, the GmbH must publish its balance sheet, like the public company (*Aktiengesellschaft*, A.G.). Sometimes different criteria are employed for the large company with respect to balance-sheet secrecy and the requirement of employee participation. Thus in Germany a GmbH must have a supervisory board and employee participation if it has more than 500 employees. In the Netherlands every company, whether public or private, must publish its balance sheet if it satisfied the following three cumulative criteria:

(a) according to its balance sheet the issued capital and the reserves amount to at least D.Fl. 10,000,000;

(b) the company or any other company in which it holds at least half of the issued shares for its own benefit is compelled by law to establish a works council; and

---

7. I Palmer, Company Law, ¶ 2-09 (2d ed. 1976).

8. [1973] A.C. 360; *see* Bushell v. Faith, [1970] A.C. 1099; Schmitthoff, *How the English Discovered the Private Company*, in QUO VADIS IUS SOCIETATUM? 183 (1972).

9. *See generally* Morse & Tedd, *Partnership Companies*, 1971 J. BUS L. 261.

10. *See generally* Schmitthoff, *New Concepts in Company Law*, 1973 J. BUS. L. 312.

(c) the company or any such other company usually employs at least 100 employees in the Netherlands.

In Denmark, according to an Act of June 13, 1973, a company must have a supervisory board with employee participation if it has more than fifty employees and the employees so desire. According to the Fifth Draft Directive of the EEC, which deals with company structure and applies only to public companies, all these companies must have a supervisory board but employee participation is on principle only provided for companies having 500 or more employees.

It would be desirable if in the course of time a uniform concept of the large company could be established in the EEC for the purposes of publicity and employee participation, but at present there is no indication for a development in that direction.

In the United Kingdom an interesting change in attitude is noticeable which is necessary in order to comply with the Second Council Directive of the EEC of December 13, 1976. So far the public company was the residual form in the United Kingdom and every company that was not a private company was treated as a public company. In compliance with the Second Council Directive, however, a change will be carried out that is already indicated in the Government White Paper on Changes in Company Law.[11] Every company will henceforth be a private company unless it satisfied the requirements for a public company which include, inter alia, a minimum capital of £50,000. If that suggestion is accepted by Parliament, the private company will be the residual form of company.

---

2. *France*

Christopher Joseph Mesnooh, *Law and Business in France: A Guide to French Commercial and Corporate Law*

(1994)

(excerpt pages 32–39)

1. GENERAL PRINCIPLES APPLICABLE TO ALL COMMERCIAL COMPANIES

The majority of foreign investors wishing to carry out business in France through the creation of a subsidiary will choose one of the five forms of commercial companies (*sociétés commerciales*). These five forms of companies are treated by the fundamental law on commercial companies, Law No. 66-537 of July 24, 1966 (the "1966 Law"). The 1966 Law is complemented by Decree No. 67-236 of March 23, 1967 (the "1967 Decree"); numerous subsequent modifications have been brought to this legislation. Commercial companies are in addition governed by a variety of other laws and decrees in areas such as bankruptcy, taxation, antitrust and listing of shares on stock exchanges.

In addition to applicable French law, a number of European Community directives have been issued in the context of commercial companies, inspired by Article 58 of the Treaty of Rome on the freedom of establishment for commercial companies, and these have been in many cases incorporated into French law (while others are still under review). Mention may be made of the Second Directive on corporations, the Sixth Direc-

---

11. CMND. No. 7291 (1978).

tive on Spinoffs, and the Eighth directive on single shareholder SARLs. Additionally, European Community Legislation in areas such as mergers...., while not having a direct impact on the methods of creating commercial companies, can have important consequences on the ways in which their operations and expansions are carried out.

The five forms of commercial companies treated by the 1996 Law are:

- the *société anonyme* (the "SA"), which is the French law equivalent of a corporation;
- the *société à responsabilité limitée* (the "SARL"), which possesses many of the characteristics of an SA but is more suited for small- and medium-sized undertakings;
- the *société en nom collectif* (the "SNC"), which is the equivalent of a general partnership;
- the *société en commandite par actions* (the "SCA"), which is the equivalent of a limited share partnership; and
- the *société en commandite simple* (the "SCS") which is the equivalent of a limited partnership.

In addition, other entities which may carry out commercial activities or related activities include the Economic Interest Group, branches and liason offices.

The 1966 Law and 1967 Decree set forth a number of provisions which govern all five forms of commercial companies (unless a specific exception is made relating to a particular form of company). Before discussing the particularities of each of the forms of commercial company which exist under French law, it is worthwhile to briefly review those elements which are common to all commercial companies.

– Forms of companies: Any of the five forms of companies treated by the 1966 Law is a "commercial" company, as opposed to a "civil" company. (A civil company (*société civile*) may also take a variety of forms but may not carry out commercial activities and may not assume any of the five legal forms set out above. The shareholders of a civil company may be held personally liable for acts carried out by a civil company which are deemed to be commercial. Civil companies are defined as those to which another form has not been attributed.)

The consequences for an entity to be classified as commercial include the fact that it is subject to the competence of the Commercial Court and to the publicity requirements for commercial companies, it must conform to certain accounting standards..., it can part in elections to the Commercial Courts and it can be placed in judicial reorganization.... Virtually all of the activities normally assumed to be of a commercial nature are deemed commercial law.

A preliminary distinction is made, within the context of commercial companies, between companies formed by persons (*sociétés des personnes*) and capital companies (*sociétés de capitaux*).

Companies formed by persons are created by associates (*associés*) for whom the identity of each associate is an essential consideration (*intuitu personae*); consequently, the entry or departure of any associate is subject to significant restrictions. Additionally, companies of persons are in most cases transparent for tax purposes (unless election to be taxed as a capital company is specifically made...), with profits earned passed on to the associates themselves and subsequently taxed under either personal or corporate income taxation (depending upon whether the associate is an individual or a legal entity, respectively). The two forms of commercial companies which are deemed companies formed by persons are the SNC and the SCS.

A capital company is a company in which the personality of each associate is generally of much less significance; their interests in the entity are thus usually freely transferable, unless the bylaws provide otherwise. The SA is the preeminent form of capital company. In addition, the SRL, while technically a hybrid form, is considered to be a capital company by virtue of the many similarities which it bears to an SA in its operations; it is nonetheless akin to a company of persons with respect to the restrictive rules for the transfer of associates' interests. The SCA is governed by the rules applicable to capital companies with respect to its limioted partners and the rules for companys formed by persons with respect to its general partners.

– Legal capacity: Capacity of the associates of a commercial company is an essential consideration. Of particular interest to the foreign investors are two issues relating to capacity. A foreign associate with capacity under laws of its own country will in most cases be deemed to have such capacity in France. The foreigner who wishes to carry out a commercial or industrial activity, occupy certain management-level positions (such as chief executive officer or manager) or be associates in certain types of commercial companies may be required to obtain a trader's card (*carte de commerçant étranger*).... Citizens of any of the Member States of the EC as well as persons holding the ten year resident's card... are not required, however, to obtain the trader's card to carry out such activities.

Secondly, a commercial company can under most conditions be an associate in another commercial company in France and can even serve, through the appointment of a permanent representative, on the Board of Directors of an SA....

– Purpose: The purpose of a company (*objects social*) contained in the company's bylaws, must be legal. The purpose clause also defines the limits of the powers which can be exercised by the company's officers and directors and thus obligates the company, in the majority of cases, vis a vis third parties in cases where such third party was unaware of the scope of the purpose clause. The associates have great freedom in determining the purposes of the company; and clauses are often drafted to indicate a number of specified activities followed by a general "catch-all" clause authorizing any related activities.

– Contributions to a Commercial Company: There are three kinds of contributions which can be made to commercial companies: cash or its equivalent (*apports en numéraire*), in-kind (*apports en nature*) and services (*apports en industrie*) (this latter being extremely infrequent). These contributions serve as the basis of the company's existence. Each contribution must have a genuine value; fictitious contributions, such as assets encumbered by debts far in excess of their real value, can lead to the nullification of the creation of the company.

The person who has made a contribution to the company is remunerated by an interest in the company (shares or other interests) and may also receive exceptional advantages (such as a preferential right to dividends). The contributor is required to make the contribution to the company which it has undertaken to make, and the other associates or the creditors of the company can seek a court order requiring the party in question to make its contribution.

Contributions in cash are the most common form of contribution made to a company. The bylaws of the company set forth the provisions for paying in these contributions; there are particular rules applicable for SAs and SARLs concerning the method of making such contributions and the time period by the end of which such contributions made be completely paid in.

In-kind contributions may be tangible or intangible property including intellectual property, real property, going businesses and many other forms. Two principal kinds of in-kind contributions depending upon the nature of the rights being transferred are to be distinguished.

When the contribution is of actual ownership of the assets (*apport en propriété*), the company in fact becomes the owner of that asset. Ownership is transferred to the company on the date on which the company is registered on the Commercial Register. When the contribution is merely for the right to use the property (*apport en jouissance*), such right is transferred for a defined period of time, but no ownership rights are actually transferred to the company. The owner of the goods rather than the company itself, remains responsible for all harm or loss which occurs to them.

It should finally be noted that, in light of the type of assets being contributed, particular formalities may need to be complied with (for example, the transfer of real or intellectual property contributions must be noted on particular registers and the documentation prepared by a notary in the case of contributions of real property).

– Life of the company: The maximum time frame permitted for the existence of a commercial company is ninety-nine years from the date of the registration of such company on the Commercial Register. The term of the company is set forth in the by-laws. The term of a company can be extended by a decision of the associates at least one year prior to the end of the company, by unanimous decision of the associates (unless the by-laws require a different majority).

– Name: Each commercial company must be given a corporate name (*dénomination social*) which must be accompanied by the abbreviation referring to the juridical form of company (e.g. SA, SARL, etc.). The name of one or more of the associates can in most cases form a part of the company name.

The choice of the company name is free, provided that the rights which others may have over the name are respected; this can be avoided by requesting the National Institute of Industrial Property to carry out a name and trademark search and by consulting local commercial registries and directories. A company cannot use as its corporate name a trademark registered by another party; even if such name is already in use, however the courts will generally restrain the second party from adopting the name for areas in which they compete or in which a risk of confusion exists in the mind of the public. Any change in the company name necessitates a corresponding change in the by-laws and in each form of commercial company thus requires a meeting...under the same conditions as one for the modification of the by-laws....

The rights to a commercial name (*nom commercial*), which is distinct from the company name, are acquired by first use, and such commercial name is only protected if other businesses selling similar products, or otherwise competitive attempt to use it (unless such commercial name is widely known).

– Head Office: Every company must have a head office (*siège social*) where its management and administrative services are located. This location must be specified in the by-laws. These offices can be situated in real property owned, leased or sub-leased by the company. No request for registration on the Commercial Register can be made unless the associates can show that they have the right to use defined premises for their commercial activity.

Several options are available to a newly formed company, the first being the purchase or leasing of space to serve as the site of the head office. Alternatively, a new company can be located in the offices of another company, either related or unrelated. Another possibility, often used by French subsidiaries of foreign parent companies not yet ready to expend the funds to acquire office space, is a "domiciliation contract" with a company, which offers leases for office space to a large number of companies (as well as associated services, such as mail forwarding and acceptance of legal documents). Finally, a company can be located in the residence of its legal representative for a period not exceeding two years.

– Profits and losses: The sharing of profits and losses is an essential element of all forms of commercial companies. Clauses exonerating an associate from all losses or imposing all losses on a single associate are prohibited. Profits and losses are generally shared in proportion to the amount of the contributions made by each of the associates; by-laws may contain provisions which modify this general rule, providing for example that associates whose contributions were equal will nonetheless share unequally in the profits (or losses), or that an associate may bear profits in a proportion which is different from that to be borne with respect to losses.

– Liability: A company can be held liable on civil grounds, in accordance with the provisions of Articles 1382 and 1383 of the Civil Code, for harm caused to third parties by the legal representatives of the company. It is also held responsible for harm suffered by property under its responsibility and for acts of its employees. This liability is not contingent upon any finding of responsibility on the part of the body within the corporation having made the decision.

Criminal liability traditionally could not be imposed upon companies, for the necessary element of intent could not be established. However, recent legislation was enacted imposing penal liability upon companies in a wide variety of circumstances. The penal code, reformed in 1992 and effective as of March 1, 1994, now provides that legal entities can be held criminally responsible for "violations committed, for their benefit, by their governing bodies or representatives", without this provision precluding a similar finding toward the individuals who actually carried out or were accomplices to the criminal act. Among the sanctions which can be levied against companies include dissolution, prohibition from carrying out any of its activities for a period not exceeding five years, closure of any of its establishments definitively or for a period not exceeding five years, or confiscation of the property which served to commit the offense. Fines can also be levied in an amount equal to five times those levied against individuals.

– Transformation: During the life of the company, the associates may wish to transform the juridical form of the company, for example, from an SARL to an SA. Such a decision will have to be taken in accordance with the terms of the by-laws with respect to their modification as well as particular legal provisions concerning transformation. In addition, all of the requirements of the new legal form (such as number of associates and minimum capital) need to be complied with at the time the company is transformed.

The legal personality of the entity is maintained and a new entity is not deemed to have come into existence. More particularly, upon decision of the associates, the accounts of the former legal entity are closed and approved and the profits or losses carried over to the new company (whose tax regime, it should be noted, may or may not be the same as the previous form of the company). The officers and directors are removed from their duties to make way for the new management structure provided for by law. The creditors of the prior company form retain their rights vis a vis the new company. Salaried employees continue to be employed in the transformed entity under the provisions of Article L 122-12 of the Labor Code....

– Dissolution and liquidation: There are numerous causes for the dissolution of a commercial company, including the end of the term, of the company (unless extended by the associates); the satisfaction of the corporate purpose or the impossibility of carrying it out due to a change of law or circumstances; the decision of the associates; a judicial order upon the request of one of the partners in the case of a failure of another partner to satisfy his obligations or upon paralysis blocking the functioning of the company; and for any reason which has been provided for in the by-laws. There are also reasons particular to each form of commercial company....

Any of the above grounds for dissolution leads to the liquidation of the company. The legal personality continues for purposes of liquidation until the publication of the closing of the process. During the procedure, the company name must be followed by an indication of its status: *société en liquidation*. The management bodies must report on their mandate through the date of the dissolution. The interests of the associates continue through liquidation, and the shares of an SA remain negotiable until the date of the closing of the liquidation proceeding. Creditors also maintain their rights during this period. The dissolution is only enforceable against third parties beginning on the date on which notice has been published in the Commercial Register....

John Bell, Sophie Boyron, and Simon Whittaker, *Principles of French Law*

(1998)

(excerpts from pages 445–449; some footnotes omitted)

(a) *Société anonymes*

The designation '*société anonyme*' is a reflection of the impersonal character of the members' involvement: whereas the SNC traditionally had to include the names of its members in its name, the name of an SA indicated its purpose, not its members (who would be a potentially fluctuating body). The SA is the form favoured by large companies, and one of its main attractions is the fact that, in common with the SCA, an SA can 'go public', raising money by inviting the public to invest in shares or debentures. However, to be able to do this, an SA must satisfy certain criteria, and not every SA does so; and, in any event, the members may prefer to remain private. This distinction between private and public SAs is increasingly important in practice, because the latter are subject to special rules; and it may be added, the existence of such a distinction clearly means that the standard equation of the SA with the English public limited company is not entirely accurate.

For the creation of an SA, there must be at least seven shareholders, who may be natural or moral persons.[58] During the lifetime of the *société*, the number of members may drop temporarily below this figure, but if the deficiency is not rectified within a year, any interested party can apply for the *société* to be wound up.[59] There are also restric-

---

58. Art. 73, of the '966 *loi*.

59. Art. 241.

tions with respect to the share capital of a *société*: if it is to raise money from the public, the share capital must be at least 1,500,000 F otherwise it must be 250,000 F.[60]

The traditional management structure of an SA is based on the *conseil d'administration*, the equivalent of the English board of directors. Article 95 of the 1966 *loi* provides that its members (*administrateurs*) must all be shareholders and article 90 provides that, apart from any worker directors elected by the employees, they are elected by the shareholders' meeting. There must be at least three *administrateurs*, and the statutes of the *société* may provide for as many as twenty-four (article 89). Article 98 provides that the *conseil* is 'invested with the widest powers to act in any circumstance in the name of the *société*'. Nevertheless, the effective day-to-day management of the *société* is in the hands of the chairman (*président*) of the *conseil*, assited by up to five executive officers (*directeurs généraux*), who may or may not be members of the *conseil*.

While preserving the traditional management structure, the *loi* of 24 July 1966 introduced as an alternative a new structure which follows the model of German law.[61] This involves a two-tier arrangement which draws a sharp line between those controlling and those carrying out the management of the *société*. In place of the single *conseil d'administration* article 129 provides for a supervisory board (*conseil de surveillance*), similar in size to the *conseil d'administration*, and a smaller executive board (*directoire*).[62] Like the members of the *conseil d'administration*, the members of the supervisory *conseil de surveillance* must be shareholders (article 130), but since they are not involved directly in the management of the *société*, article 250 provides that they can only be held personally liable for negligence in supervision. The members of the executive *directoire*, for their part, do not have to be shareholders: they are, in effect, specialist managers. The memberships of the two bodies are mutually exclusive (article 133).

The majority of SAs continue to use the traditional structure. Those that adopt the new form must indicate the fact in their corporate name.[63]

The members of an SA hold transferable shares. These may take a number of forms, including preference shares *(actions priviégiées)*[64] and, for loyal members who have remained with the *société* for at least 2 years, shares with double voting rights (*actions avec droit de vote double*).[65] Given that the personality of the individual members is not critical to the success of the *société*, shares are, in principle, freely transferrable. Nevertheless, in practice the elements of personality may be reintroduced by the statutes of the SA, which may contain a *clause d'agrément* subjecting transfers to third parties to the approval of the *société*.[66] This acts as a filter for new shareholders; however, it cannot be used to lock in a member who wishes to leave: if a transfer is disapproved, the *société* must buy the shares itself or provide a third party who is willing to do so.[67] In the case

60. Art. 71.
61. The German *Aktiengesellschaft* has a *Vorstand* (managing board of directors) and an *Aufsichtstrat* (supervisory board)....
62. The rules for the size of the *directoire* vary according to the share capital of the *société* and according to whether the shares are quoted on the stock exchange (*Bourse*): Art. 120.
63. An SA using the new structure must be designated as a '*société* anonyme à directoire et conseil de surveillance': art. 56 of *decrét* no. 67-236 of 23 March 1967 (as amended by *decréet* no. 88-418 of 22 April 1988, which did away with the more cumbersome designation....
64. Art. 269 of the *loi* of 24 July 1966, which also provides for non-voting preference shares (*actions à dividende prioritaire sans droit de vote*).
65. *Ibid.*, Art. 175.
66. *Ibid.*, Art. 274.
67. *Ibid.*, Art. 275.

of SAs quoted on the official market of the stock exchange, *clauses d'agrément* cannot be relied on.

* * *

3. *Sociétés à responsabilité limitée*

The *sociétés à responsabilité limitée* (SARL) is the most popular form of *société*, and it is something of a hybrid, having some of the qualities of a *sociétés de personnes* and a *société par actions.* On the one hand, the members' shares are not freely transferrable, but on the other hand, they enjoy limited liability and they do not have the status of *commerçants.* Traditionally, a SARL (like any other *société*) had to have at least two members. Since the *loi* no. 85-697 of 11 July 1985 (the '1985 *loi*'), however, sole traders have been able to incorporate themselves as an SARL and benefit from limited liability, in which case the *société* is known as an *enterprise unipersonnelle à responsabilité limité* (EURL).

(a) The traditional *Sociétés à responsabilité limitée* (SARL)

The *sociétés à responsabilité limitée* must have a capital of at least 50,000 F[70] and it may have no more than 50 members (if it grows too large it must convert to an SA).[71] There are certain limits to the permissible activities of an SARL: for example, insurance companies and savings institutions cannot take this form.[72]

The management of an SARL is in the hands of one or more managers (*gérants*), who have extensive powers as set out in article 49 of the 1966 *loi.* The managers, who need not be members, are appointed by the membership. Unlike the case of the SA, there is no special body monitoring the managers: they are simply under the control of the members.

Unlike the members of an SA, the members of an SARL do not have freely negotiable *actions.* A member may assign his share in the *société*, but only subject to limitations. Transfers to someone who is not already a member generally require the consent of a majority of the membership who must hold between them at least three-quarters of the capital of the *société* (article 45). But, as where a *clause d'agrément* figures in the statutes of an SA, this requirement of consent cannot be used to lock an unwilling member in. If consent is refused, the other members must find a buyer or buy the shares themselves, or else reduce the capital of the *société.* By contrast, transfers can generally be made freely by one member to another (article 47) or by one member to his or her spouse, ascendants or descendants (article 44). However, restrictions can be imposed by the statutes of the *société*, provided that they are no more onerous than those imposed by law on transfers to outsiders.

* * *

In practice the [*enterprise unipersonnelle a resonsabilité limité*] EURL has found only limited popularity. In part, this is because the limited liability achieved by incorporation is compromised by the fact that institutions making loans to an EURL will usually require the single member to provide a personal guarantee. In addition, there are no tax advantages gained by incorporation.

---

70. Art. 35 of the 1966 *loi.*
71. *Ibid.*, Art. 36.
72. *Ibid.*, Art. 490.

Comments and Questions

1. The SARL has proven to be a very versatile vehicle for enterprise organization in countries following the French model. In revising the Spanish law applicable to the similar sociedad de responsabilidad limitada ("SRL") (Ley 2/1995, de 23 de marzo, BOE num. 71 de 24 de marzo), the introduction to the legislation set forth three basic postulates that guided the legislature in its conceptualization of the SRL laws. First, the law had to harmonize the elements of organization that push SRLs in different directions—while the SRL is not a miniature SA, neither is it purely a partnership. Second, the law had to protect the closed character of SRL organization, by providing strong limitations on investment and transfer of interests in the enterprise. Third, the law had to permit maximum flexibility in organizational form consistent with the other limits of SRL organization.

2. In revising their corporate statutes in 1995, the Spanish government suggested that while there does not exist a complete correspondence between the SA and the large publicly owned business enterprise, it would be inadvisable for the small or non-public enterprise to elect to register as an SA. The reasons for this include the inflexibility of the organizational form of the SA, the expense of creating and maintaining the SA, and the significant public disclosure requirements imposed on SAs. Are there reasons why a small or non-public enterprise might still consider registration as an SA? Should the attitudes of lenders with respect to the risk of lending to SAs versus SRLs make a difference? Should cultural norms about the character of nature of these forms of enterprise organization also make a difference?

3. A number of changes in French law were effected after 2000 by the New Economic Regulations. The new regulations applicable to SAs move the French public company more towards the German model. For example, under the NEA, the board fo directors now is explicitly given a strategic role in corporate management—to establish the general goals and objectives of the company, to monitor the company's progress toward those goals, and to investigate the company's activities as the board may deem appropriate. It is also now possible to split the offices of chairman of the board of directors and general manager of the company, though the same person can serve in both offices. Management of the company is to be effected either through the chairman of the board or through the general manager (and up to 5 deputy managers) as specified in the bylaws. The choice of form of management remains with the board rather than with the shareholders. Since the general manager need not be a member fo the board of directors, foreign companies establishing subsidiaries in France may be able, if they elect this model, to appoint a local as the general manager while reserving the chairmanship to an employee of the parent company.

A number of other reforms have been made. First, boards of directors now have the option of meeting by means of videoconferencing. Under certain circumstances the rules extend to meetings of the shareholders as well. This effects a significant liberalization of the prior law that required presence at meetings for all practical purposes. In addition, the rights of workers, through works councils (required of companies with more than 50 salaried employees) has been strengthened by requiring the company to provide the works councils with more company information. Works councils now also have greater rights in connection with certain sales of the company, and permits works councils to call a shareholder meetings in certain exceptional circumstances (*urgence*—the term is not defined in the statute) and may participate in general shareholder meetings.

In an attempt to limit the possibilities of self dealing, the law has been modified to limit the number of offices that a single individual can hold. Individuals now may not hold offices in more than five SAs. In addition, the management's report to shareholders will now have to disclose substantially more information on officer compensation .

3. *Germany*

The German system of corporate regulation is similar to that of France. There are some differences. You were introduced to some of the basics of German business organization in the materials excerpted above from RICHARD M. BUXBAUM & KLAUS J. HOPT, LEGAL HARMONIZATION AND THE BUSINESS ENTERPRISE. Review those materials. The materials that follow provide more of a basic introduction to the German approach to corporate regulation. As you read the materials that follow, see if you can identify the differences between the German and the French systems.

Thomas J. Andre, Jr., *Some Reflections on German Corporate Governance: A Glimpse at German Supervisory Boards*

70 TUL. L. REV. 1819 (1996)

(excerpts pages 1823–1826; some footnotes omitted)

II. A Brief Overview of the Governance of the German Aktiengesellschaft

All German publicly traded companies are formed under the Aktiengesetz.[9] The Aktiengesetz requires that each company (Aktiengesellschaft or AG)[10] have two separate boards, a supervisory board (Aufsichtsrat) and a management board (Vorstand[11]). Each board has distinctly different legal duties. Briefly, the supervisory board appoints the members of the Vorstand[12] which in turn is charged generally with actually operating the business. The supervisory board is in turn charged generally with supervision of the management board.[13] Individuals on both boards are expected to "employ the care of a diligent and conscientious manager."[14] Additionally, the Aktiengesetz imposes certain

---

9. Stock Company Act, Aktiengesetz [AktG], 1965 BGB1. I 1089.

10. Of the DAX 30 companies surveyed below, see infra text accompanying notes 77–81, all but Henkel KGaA are AGs. Henkel is a Kommanditgesellschaft auf Aktien, the basic equivalent of a publicly traded limited partnership. AktG s 278. For purposes of this Essay, the differences between the two forms are negligible, and the concentration will be on the AG.

11. The term " Vorstand" will be used throughout to avoid any confusion between the two boards.

12. AktG § 84, P 1. This does not mean that the Vorstand has no role in the selection of its own members. Indeed, the Vorstand often has a decisive role. *See, e.g.*, Padraic Fallon, *The Battle Plans of Hilmar Kopper*, EUROMONEY, Jan. 1994, at 39 (containing an interview with the CEO of Deutsche Bank, who notes that the Vorstand actually initiates the appointment of a new Vorstand member, requests that the supervisory board approve the recommendation, and that, "[s]o far the Deutsche Bank Aufsichtsrat has always been kind enough to do so").

13. AktG § 111, P 1.

14. *Id.* §§ 93, P 1, 116.

other duties on the supervisory board, and gives the supervisory board the right to receive certain information regarding the operation of the company.[15]

Viewed in terms more familiar to American readers, the supervisory board theoretically plays a monitoring role somewhat similar to that played by outside directors on a unitary board.[16] But the analogy is clearly a limited one. In a narrow legal sense, the directors of a U.S. board acting in their capacity as directors generally have identical responsibilities whether they are outsiders or insiders. By contrast, the supervisory board concept originated as a kind of substitute for regulation that had previously been undertaken by the state,[17] and indeed, the Aktiengesetz itself clearly envisions a much stricter separation of board functions than exists on a unitary board.

The Aktiengesetz stresses this strict separation in a number of ways. Except in rare instances, the statute explicitly forbids an individual from serving simultaneously on both the Vorstand and the supervisory board.[18] Moreover, management or executive functions cannot lawfully be delegated to the supervisory board or any individual member of the board.[19] The supervisory board may remove members of the Vorstand, but only for "important cause" (wichtiger Grund).[20] By contrast, in the United States senior executives typically serve at the will of the board, subject only to whatever contract rights they have. Finally, the fact that the Aktiengesetz only requires supervisory board meetings twice annually further underscores the independence of the Vorstand.[21] Members of the Vorstand would appear to have far more independence, therefore, than typical inside employee directors would have in a unitary system.[22] Specifically, members of the Vorstand have far more independence than would the typical CEO-director[23] or other inside directors of a U.S. public com-

---

15. *Id.* §90, P 1. For a more thorough discussion of directors' duties, *see* Willi Joachim, *The Liability of Supervisory Board Directors in Germany*, 25 INT'L LAW. 41 (1991).

16. Christian J. Meier-Schatz, *Corporate Governance and Legal Rules: A Transnational Look at Concepts and Problems of Internal Corporate Management Control*, 13 J. CORP. L. 431, 443 n.67 (1988).

17. Detlev F. Vagts, *Reforming the "Modern" Corporation: Perspectives from the German*, 80 HARV. L. REV. 23, 50–51 (1966).

18. AktG s 105, P1.

19. Under the articles of incorporation (Satzung), supervisory board approval of specified management action may be required. Even in this case, however, the statute underscores the independence of the Vorstand by allowing it to sidestep the supervisory board and obtain shareholder approval where the supervisory board has denied its approval to the Vorstand's action. *Id.* §111, P4. Finally, the Act provides a specific process by which the supervisory board may seek judicial assistance if the Vorstand refuses to provide certain specific information to the supervisory board. *Id.* §§90, 407, P1.

20. *Id.* §84, P3.

21. *Id.* §110, P3. In practice some boards follow the statutory "preference" for four yearly meetings. Gerhard Liener, *The Future of German Governance*, CORP. BOARD, May 1995, at 1 (noting that most supervisory boards meet three or four times annually). One slightly older study found that 86% of the AGs surveyed met only twice a year. JEREMY EDWARDS & KLAUS FISCHER, BANKS, FINANCE AND INVESTMENT IN GERMANY 213 (1994).

22. For a brief comparison of the UK and Germany models, *see* C.H. Putt, *A Comparison of the General Powers and Duties of the Directors of UK and German Companies*, 15 COMPANY L. INT'L 253 (1994).

23. In Germany, the chairman of the Vorstand is usually referred to as the Vorsitzender (or Sprecher, usually for banks). The chairman of the Vorstand is more or less equivalent to the chief executive officer of the company. To avoid any confusion in the use of the term "chairman," which in the United States refers to the chairman of the board, in this Essay, the term "CEO" will be used to denote the Vorsitzender, or Sprecher.

pany, a point that Germany supervisory board members have frequently stressed when questioned about some of the asserted breakdowns of the two-board governance system.[24]

Notwithstanding the relative independence of the Vorstand, it is the case in Germany, as in the United States, that the supervisory board normally receives the great bulk of the criticism whenever internal corporate controls fail to prevent catastrophic or near-catastrophic behavior by individual members of the Vorstand or other senior managers, or whenever a company merely performs poorly. In turn, that criticism inevitably turns into criticism, not so much of individual members of the supervisory board (although such criticism certainly does occur[26]), but rather into criticism of the composition of the supervisory board itself.

Henry P. deVries and Friedrich K. Juenger, *Limited Liability Contract: The GmbH*

64 Colum. L. Rev. 866 (1964)

(Excerpts pages 867–881; some footnotes omitted)

German law provides for two principal categories of business organization: the *Aktiengesellschaft* (AG), or corporation, and the *Gesellschaft mit beschränkter Haftung* (GmbH), or limited liability company. Since the AG is the counterpart of the American public issue corporation, the GmbH might be described as the "German close corporation." Yet its actual significance is much broader. Section 1 of the GmbH Statute provides: "Limited liability companies may be formed, in accordance with the provisions of this law, for any legally permissible purpose."[7] As this language suggests, the GmbH is really a device to carry out any legitimate objective with the protection of limited liability. It can be utilized to serve small companies as well as enterprises with multi-million

---

24. A common theme has been that the supervisory board was misled by the Vorstand or its individual members, that the Vorstand failed to keep the supervisory board properly informed, and that no supervisory system is capable of detecting what amounted to criminal activity. E.g., In the Line of Fire—Metallgesellschaft, *supra* note 2, at 40 (quoting the chairman of the Metallgesellschaft supervisory board: "The supervisory board of MG never had any clue that there had been—let me put it drastically—any criminal energy at the level of the managing board.").

26. E.g., John Eisenhammer, *Metallgesellschaft Meeting in Uproar*, The Independent (London), Feb. 25, 1994, at 33 (stating that shareholders referred to the chairman of the supervisory board as a "hypocrite" and "gangster"); John Templeman, *The Shocks for Daimler's New Driver*, Bus. Wk., Aug. 21, 1995, at 38 (suggesting that Daimler-Benz's supervisory board, chaired by a member of Deutsche Bank's Vorstand, was to blame for Daimler's unsuccessful diversification).

7. Gesetz betreffend die Gesellschaften mit beschränkter Haftung (Statute Concerning the Limited Liability Companies), Law of April 20, 1892, [1892] R.G.Bl. 480, as amended, Bundesgesetzblatt III. 4123 (1961) [hereinafter cited as GmbH Statute]. GmbH Statute § 13, paras. 2–3 state:

> The limited liability company has, as such, independent rights and duties; it can acquire title and other rights in real property, sue in court and be sued.
>
> For liabilities of the company only the assets of the company are answerable to its creditors.

Despite this language, the juridical personality of the GmbH had initially been doubted by some, but today it is clear that the GmbH is a legal entity. *See* [Baumbach & Hueck, GmbH-Gesetz (10th ed. 1962)], annot. 1 before § 13, at 54; 1 [Hachenburg, Kommentar zum Gesetz Betreffend die Gesellschaftern mit Beschränkter Haftung (16th ed. 1956)] § 13, annots. 1–3, at 327–28; [Scholz, Kommentar zum GmbH-Gesetz (4th ed. 1960)] §13, annot. 2, at 158.

dollar capital, one man proprietorships and partnerships, as well as companies open to broad membership. It is well suited to provide a means of formalizing subsidiaries, holding companies, and joint ventures, and has been used to form pools, combines, and cartels. Its objective need not be an activity for gain. Trade associations, pension funds, professional associations of auditors, accountants or business advisors may choose this form, and it is open likewise to political, social, scientific, and religious organizations. Even a judicial settlement may conveniently be organized as a GmbH. The usefulness of the GmbH to serve as a vehicle for a particular purpose is broadened further by the possibility of combining one GmbH with another, or with an AG, in the form of a partnership. Nor need the interests which use this form be private in nature. GmbHs have been used as instrumentalities of government, both for publicly owned industrial enterprises and as bodies exercising sovereign functions.

Private parties using the GmbH find in it an exceedingly pliable device because of the freedom of contract they enjoy with respect to the charter. The legislative technique for giving the members of the GmbH this autonomy is the use of "dispositive norms," i.e., statutory rules that apply only in the absence of specific stipulations. Thus, while the GmbH Statute regulates in some detail various aspects of internal organization and operation, most of these rules are merely designed to obviate the necessaity for specific charter provisions.[15] They do not hinder the parties from adopting solutions differing from those suggested in the statute.

II. History

Unlike the AG, the GmbH came into being without historical antecedent and exclusively by virtue of legislative fiat. The German GmbH legislation was largely caused by a reform in 1884 of the law governing Ags, which had attempted to curb abuses of the corporate form by imposing a more stringent examination of contributions in kind, strengthening the role of shareholders and minority rights, increasing the power of the supervisory board, and establishing more thorough accounting procedures. The tightening of formal and substantive requirements rendered the AG impractical for other than large business organizations. This led to a movement within the German business community for a less cumbersome and expensive entity to serve the need of smaller enterprises. Various proposals were submitted by the proponents of this movement, which were considered and became the basis of a draft by the German Ministry of Justice. This bill was passed, in slightly modified form, by the German Parliament effective as of April 20, 1892.

From its very beginning this novel form was readily accepted by the German business world and the idea copied in a number of other civil-law countries.[19] The statutory changes that have occurred since then have not materially affected the substance of the law.

III. Comparison With the AG

* * *

15. The *Gesellschaftsvertrag* or *Stazung* combines the function of both certificate of incorporation and by-laws. This instrument will be called "charter" since it is the organizational document.

19. Portugal (1901); Austria (106); Poland (1919); Brazil (1919); Chile (1923); Bulgaria (1923); France (1925); Liechtenstein (1926); Turkey (1926); Hungary (1929); Cuba (1929); Argentina (1932); Luxembourg (1933); Uruguay (1933); Mexico (1934); Belgium (1935); Switzerland (1936); Spain (1953).

B. The GmbH

The principal distinguishing feature of the GmbH in relation to the AG is the fact that the capital of the GmbH is divided into quotas rather than shares. This difference in name signifies an important difference in substance, for while shares are generally readily negotiable (and, in Germany, customarily issued in bearer form), quotas require a notarial record of both the transfer and the executory contract to transfer. This last requirement, which is designed to prevent public speculation in GmbH interests, is bolstered by a number of other provisions in the GmbH Statute having the same aim. For example, the statute permits quotas of unequal amounts, inhibits the splitting of quotas, encourages restraints on alienation, and bars embodying quotas in negotiable certificates.

The minimum stated capital of the GmbH is DM 20,000, one-fifth that required for the AG, and of this only one-fourth need be paid upon formation. Only two incorporators are required [Ed: this has subsequently been amended to permit formation with a single incorporator]. Contributions in kind are permissible if they are specified in the charter, and, unlike the case of the AG, there is no examination into the value of such contributions. Liability of the quota holders to the company need not be limited to their capital contribution. The charter may impose continuing obligations on quota holders, such as the rendering of services, and furnishing of additional funds, as well as rendering other contributions.

Management of the GmbH can be in the hands of one person. A supervisory board is required only if a GmbH has more than 500 employees. The formality of quota holders' meetings may be dispensed with. No recordation of such meetings is required. No annual reports need be filed or published, except in the case of banks.

C. Comparison

The amount of the minimum stated capital, the cumbersome and expensive formalities of a supervisory council and board and shareholders' meetings, the publicity requirements, and the lessor flexibility with respect to permissible charter provisions render the AG unsuitable to serve as a corporate vehicle except in the case of vary large corporations contemplating public marketing of shares or when psychological reasons suggest using the more prestigious form of the AG. This conclusion is reflected in the statistics: While the combined capital of AGs in the Federal Republic of Germany and West Berlin more than doubles that of the GmbHs, the latter outnumber the former by roughly fifteen to one.

IV. Internal Organization of the GmbH

A. Membership in the GmbH

The GmbH Statute contains no restrictions with respect to the parties that can become quota holders in a GmbH. Natural persons, entities recognized by the civil or commercial laws, and even commercial partnerships (which are not considered to have legal personality under German law) may become quota holders.

.... [T]he acquisition of all quotas by one party is not a ground for the nullity or dissolution of the company. Thus, incorporated single proprietorships and wholly owned subsidiaries are permissible.

The German authorities would give effect to charter provisions restricting membership in a particular GmbH to certain persons or groups of persons, such as nationals of a specified country or members of a particular family, organization or trade. Provisions of this type would permit utilizing the GmbH device to perpetuate control similar to testamentary, trust, or foundation provisions.

B. Restraints on Alienation

Apart from specifying initially the parties that can become quota holders of a GmbH, other methods that preclude intrusion by unwanted outsiders can be adopted in the charter. Section 15, paragraph 5 of the GmbH Statute, specifically permits making the transfer of a quota interest dependent "on other conditions, in particular the consent of the company." It is doubtful whether this provision is broad enough to cover an express prohibition against any form of alienation of quotas. Essentially the same effect can, however, be achieved by requiring the unanimous consent of all quota holders for any transfer of quotas, and it has been held that the reasons for withholding consent will not be reviewed by the courts. Provisions for the consent of a majority of the quota holders or of management, or for a right of first refusal in favor of the company or quota holders, are frequent in German practice.

While it is questionable whether inheritability of quotas can be excluded, the charter may effectively provide that specified persons shall become quota holders upon the death of a member, or that upon the death of a quota holder his quopta shall be cancelled or the company dissolved.

Thus, the extent to which outsiders should be allowed to join the GmbH can be maintained in a fashion similar to the rules prevailing with respect to partnerships.

C. Functions of Quota Holders

Section 45 of the GmbH Statute provides:

> The rights of the quota holders and their exercise with respect to the affairs of the company, in particular its management, shall be determined by the charter in the absence of statutory provisions to the contrary.
>
> Absent specific provisions in the articles of incorporation, the provisions of §§46 to 51 shall apply.

This provision gives the parties a large measure of freedom in shaping the organization of the company in the charter. Action by the quota holders as a body is indispensable only to effectuate organic changes such as charter amendments,[39] capital increases,[40] and decreases,[41] and changes of corporate form.[42] Such action requires a majority of three-fourths of the votes cast, a notarial protocol and filing with the Commercial Register, as well as the consent of all those quota holders whose rights are affected by such a change.[44] To safeguard the status quo, the statute provides that the charter may make such changes dependent upon "additional requirements," which would include unanimity.

In all other instances, quota-holder action may be dispensed with. Thus the charter may delegate functions normally within the competence of quota holders to management or special committees. Rights and powers may also be reserved, partially or exclu-

39. GmbH Statute §§53–54.
40. GmbH Statute §§55–57.
41. GmbH Statute §58.
42. Aktiengesetz §§249–83.
44. GmbH Statute §53, para. 3. This requirement of consent of adversely affected quota holders is applicable even when the newly created duty concerns all quota holders alike....

sively, to certain specifies quota holders, and the charter may create privileges of which quota holders cannot be deprived, for example, to be a member of management, to use the facilities of the company, or to purchase its output.

The same flexibility prevails with respect to corporate meetings. Apart from such mandatory provisions as those designed to guarantee fair notice,[50] the parties are free to provide in the charter the manner of passing resolutions in any fashion they choose. There is no requirement of regular annual meetings. Meetings may be held at any place in or outside of Germany. The consent of all quota holders in writing to a specific resolution, or the prior agreement to be bound by a written votes makes a formal meeting unnecessary.[51] The charter may even authorize voting by telephone. While, as a practical matter, minutes are important for evidentiary purposes, there is no recordation requirement.

The charter may establish quorum and majority requirements, including unanimity, for all or certain categories of resolutions. Absent such provision in the charter no quorum is required and a bare majority of the vote cast suffices to pass a resolution.

D. Quota-Holders' Duties

An additional measure of flexibility is provided by the possibility of imposing duties of various kinds in the charter that are binding on the members. Except for certain specific instances of continuing duties, such as the liability for additional contributions to capital (up to a specified amount or unlimitedly),[55] the statute contains no general enabling provisions to that effect. However, section 3, second paragraph, which refers to "other obligations vis-a-vis the company," seems to take it for granted that duties can be imposed and so do the German authorities on this point.

This possibility has a wider range of application. For example, the charter may require a quota holder to act as a manager, to transfer new inventions to the company, to sell exclusively to it, to transfer his quota upon ceasing to be a member of another association, to make loans to the company, or to guarantee its debts. As in a partnership, the charter of a GmbH can therefore give expression to the fact that the motivating force in contracting with a particular party is his peculiar facilities, financial resources, or special abilities as a manager or inventor.

The possibility that the charter may impose duties of exclusivity and abstention from doing certain acts had made the GmbH a popular device for cartels and combines.

The remedies in case of breach of such corporate duties are damages and injunctive relief, and, if stipulated, contractual penalties. In addition, a quota holder who violates his obligations to the company may be expelled.

E. Minority Protection

A quota holder may not be deprived by the majority of privileges granted to him in the charter. And he also has the right to litigate the question whether a quota holders' resolution is void or voidable. But beyond that, he enjoys very little protection if he happens to be in the minority.

Apart from the power of a twenty-five percent interest to block organic changes, only three statutory minority rights exist: Quota holders representing a minimum of one-

---

50. *See* GmbH Statute § 51.
51. GmbH Statute § 48, para. 2. Implied consent suffices....
55. See GmbH Statute §§ 26–28.

tenth of the stated capital may (a) request convocation for a quota-holders' meeting...; (b) sue for dissolution of the company in cases in which it becomes impossible to achieve the corporate purpose or where other "important reasons" for dissolution exist; and (c) request the court to appoint liquidators in case of dissolution of the company. In addition, a rather limited right to inspection of books and records has been developed by the courts. A greater degree of minority protection can be achieved in numerous ways. In truly close GmbHs, the requirement of unanimity for all or specified important transactions is quite customary. Other devices for the protection of minority rights depend on the imagination of the draftsman and success at the bargaining table. Given both, a minority can achieve ample protection and even be put in a [position of control.

F. Capital Structure

Since rights and duties inherent in each quota need not be equal, a GmbH may have non-voting quotas and quotas with multiple voting rights, or preferences with respect to distributions or upon liquidation.

This possibility of having classes of quotas, together with that of issuing bonds and hybrid securities, would permit the formation of a GmbH with a capital structure similar to that of a public issue corporation....

A GmbH may acquire its own quotas by purchase or gift. These treasury quotas remain independent and can be transferred to third parties, but rights and duties connected with their ownership remain dormant as long as they are held by the company. Although the statute in general prohibits distribution that would impair the "trust fund" of stated capital, the acquisition by the GmbH of its own paid up quotas is effective even if such acquisition can not be made out of surplus. This exception may have been motivated by the consideration that the interest of a GmbH to keep out third parties should be of overriding importance.

G. Management

In dealing with third parties, the GmbH is represented by one or more managers who must be natural persons. A board of supervisors is optional,[88] except for GmbHs having 500 or more employees.[89]...

Normally, any transaction entered into by the managers acting for the GmbH in proper form is binding on the company. This is true even when the managerial action is in disregard of express directives issued by the quota holders or restrictions contained in the charter. Although such restrictions require the managers to act accordingly, they do not affect their power to bind the company. However, under certain circumstances a third party may be estopped from relying on the validity of a transaction entered into by the manager in disregard of his duties.

While the rules relating to the power of managers to bind the company are mandatory, other aspects concerning management such as the manner of representation, the election of the managers, and their role in the conduct of the company's business, are subject to the provisions of the charter. Thus, while the statute envisages joint representation in the case of a plurality of managers, the charter may provide for the power to

88. GmbH Statute § 52.

89. Betriebsverfassungsgetsetz, Law of Oct. 11, 1952, §§ 76–77, [1952] B.G.Bl.I. 681. Where a board is required, one third of the members must be labor representatives.

represent the company to be exercised by a single representative, a majority of managers, or a manager acting jointly with another party.

The managers need not be elected. The quota holders may effectively delegate their powers to appoint managers to other quota holders, the supervisory board or even to outsiders. If managers are elected by a quota-holders' meeting, the manner of their election—cumulative or simple voting, quorum and majority requirements, or the right to majority and minority directorships—can be specified in the charter.

Apart from laying down rules for their powers as legal representatives, the GmbH Statute makes no provision as regards the functions of the managers to conduct the business of the company. It merely enumerates a number of specific duties (such as the duty to notify the Commercial Register of transactions requiring such notification, to keep proper books of account, to prepare balance sheet and profit and loss statements, and to file a petition in bankruptcy in case of insolvency), establishes a standard of care and provides for liability if they breach their duties. The actual scope of managerial functions depends, therefore, entirely on provisions in the charter, quota holders' directives, the managers' employment contracts, and the pattern of conduct of the company's business. Thus, while managers are indispensable as legal representatives of the company, their powers internally vary greatly and it is left to the quota holders whether to take an active interest in running the business or to defer to management's expertise.

Comments and Questions

1. One of the most important features of the GmbH contributing to its popularity is its "dispositive norms." In effect, the statute provides default provisions which may be invoked when the parties choose not to deviate from the defaults in constructing the GmbH's organizational documents, the *Satzung*. To what extent can you argue that American corporate statutes exhibit "dispositive norms"?

2. Do you think that the structure or philosophy of the GmbH is culturally unique to Germany?

3. The GmbH law does not create a uniquely self-contained form of organizational enterprise. The law recognizes that, at least with respect to size, at some point a GmbH may assume practice characteristics that make the core portions of the GmbH law problematically applicable to it. Thus, for example, larger GmbHs, those with more than 500 employees, are subject to stricter requirements, that is, the range of flexibility in organizational form is restricted. One of the more interesting restrictions on flexibility is the requirement that large GmbHs install a board with a mandatory minimum number of labor representatives. Would these provisions of the GmbH law be difficult to export to other systems?

---

4. *England*

One would expect the English system of corporate regulation to most resemble our own in the United States. In many respects, English corporate regulation is closer in spirit to that of the United States than any other. However, like differences between the

German and French systems of corporate governance, the English systems exhibits characteristics unique to it.

The sources of English company law are similar to those of corporate law in the US. They consist of a national company statute which provides an incomplete and flexible template of company regulation. The current corporate code in England is the Companies Act of 1985, as amended. It and related statutes incorporate European law to the extent required. These incorporations can be found in the Companies Act of 1985 or related statutes. The statute is supplemented in significant respect by case law, including in important areas such as fiduciary duties of directors. Public companies, like publicly traded companies in the US, are also subject to exchange rules and a national securities act, the Public Offers of Securities Act of 1995 (SI 1995/1537). Lastly, individual arrangements of companies are set forth in the critical basic corporate documents—the corporate constitution (corresponding to the American corporate charter or articles of incorporation) and articles of association (in some respects fulfilling the role of the American corporate bylaws).

As you look at the materials that follow, see if you can focus on those aspects of English corporate regulation which distinguish it from its American counterparts.

John H. Farrar and Brenda M. Hannigan, *Farrar's Company Law*

(1998)
(excerpts pages 42–44)

Legal Classification of Companies Under the Companies Acts

There are two basic systems of legal classification of companies under the Companies Acts, neither of which is now directly concerned with size, but both of which have some bearing on the raising of capital. These are (1) by reference to the liability of members and (2) the public/private dichotomy.

Dealing with (1), registered companies may be :

(a) companies limited by shares (this was introduced in 1855);

(b) companies limited by guarantee (this was introduced in 1862);

(c) unlimited companies (this is the oldest type of company and ultimately dates back to 1844).

In the case of (a), which is the most common type in practice, each member must contribute to the company's assets the amount unpaid on his or her shares. Under §74(1) of the Insolvency Act of 1986, past members are also liable if they were members within one year before the commencement of the winding up and it appears to the court that the existing members are unable to satisfy the contributions required of them; but past members are only liable to the extent unpaid on their former shares before they ceased to be members and for debts contracted before they ceased to be members. The limited liability of members effectively transfers the risk of business failure from them to the creditors. In practice this means trade creditors and involuntary creditors, since finance creditors usually take security and personal guarantees in the case of small firms. In the case of larger firms, the limited liability greatly facilitates capital raising from the public.

In the case of (b), the member is contingently liable for the amount which he or she has undertaken to contribute in the event of insolvent winding up. In the case of (c) the member's liability is unlimited if the company is insolvent, although the company has legal personality.

In practice, (b) and (c) are rare. (b) is mainly used for educational or other charitable bodies as an alternative to the trust mechanism.

Until 1907, there was just one basic type of company under the Companies Acts. In that year the public/private dichotomy was introduced. The introduction of the private company was almost by accident. Originally the Loreburn Committee had simply intended it as the basis of exemption from the statement in lieu of prospectus but in the House of Lords it was successfully proposed that it should be exempt from filing a balance sheet. English law did not, as German law, recognise the private company as an instituton, sui generis but simply as a species of the genus, limited company.[90]

The basis of the dichotomy was restrictions on offers to the public of its shares, share transfers and the number of shareholders. Thus to some extent size entered into the classification. The private company was intended for small businesses, the public company for large businesses. However, the method of capital raising was fundamental to the classification.

Because public companies are able to incorporate private companies as subsidiaries, the 1948 Act limited the privilege of not filing accounts to the exempt private company, which corresponded roughly to the small incorporated firm. This continued until the Companies Act of 1967 abolished the concept. Apart from the accounting advantages conferred on small and medium sized companies by CA 1985, private companies have had basically the same disclosure obligations as a public company. However, the Companies Act of 1989 has relaxed a number of the legal requirements as part of a policy of 'de-regulation'....

The rational basis of classification of the 1900s was abandoned in 1980 in order to implement the Second Directive of the EU. Now CA 1985 defines a public company explicitly and a private company by exclusion. A public company is defined in § 1(3) as a company limited by shares or limited by guarantee and having a share capital (a) whose memorandum states that it is to be a public company and (b) which has complied with the provisions for registration of such a company. This means that its memorandum must be in the form specified by regulation under the Act by virtue of § 3 and it must have a minimum capital of at least £ 50,000. With effect from 22 December 1980, a company cannot be formed as or become a company limited by guarantee with a share capital. A private company is a company which is not a public company. The only provision still expressly concerned with size and capital raising is § 81 which makes it a criminal offense for a private company (other than a company limited by guarantee and not having a share capital) to offer its securities to the public directly or indirectly. This is now the only real disadvantage of incorporation as a private company which otherwise has substantial advantages over public companies.

The following is a list of the other legal differences between public and private companies:

90. *See* C.M. Schmitthoff 'How the English Discovered the Private Company' in *Quo Vadis, Jus Societatum?* Ed. P. Zonderland (1972), p 183.

(i) public companies must have a least two directors whereas private companies need only have one (CA 1985, § 282(1));

(ii) in the case of public companies, two or more directors cannot be appointed by a single resolution unless a resolution that it shall be so has first been agreed to without any vote being given against it (§ 292);

(iii) proxies appointed to attend and vote instead of a member of a private company has the same right to speak as the member;

(iv) accounting records need only be kept for three years in the case of a private company whereas they must be kept for six years in the case of a public company (§ 244(1));

(v) the period for laying and delivering accounts by a private company is 10 months after the end of the account period whereas it is seven months for public companies (§ 244(1));

(vi) the company secretary of a public company must be suitably qualified (§ 286);

(vii) certain pre-emptive rights conferred by §§ 89 and 90 may be excluded by a provision in the memorandum or articles of a private company (§ 91);

(viii) the stringent rules for payment for shares which regulate non-cash consideration only apply to public companies (§ 99 et seq);

(ix) the obligation to convene an extraordinary general meeting in the event of a serious loss of capital only applies to a public company (§ 142);

(x) the rules relating to treatment of shares held by or on behalf of a company in itself only apply to public companies;

(xi) the rules restricting liens and charges by a company on its shares applies only to public companies (§ 150);

(xii) the rules restricting payment of dividends to an amount which does not diminish a company's net assets below its called up share capital and undistributable reserves only apply to public companies (§ 264);

(xiii) the directors of a private company are under fewer restrictions in their financial relationship to their company and need make less disclosure in the accounts (§ 330 et seq);

(xiv) the public company registered as such on its original incorporation must obtain a certificate before it carries on business or borrows. The principal significance of this is that the private company does not have to have a minimum capital;

(xv) a private company may purchase or redeem its own shares out of capital (§ 171 et seq);

(xvi) a private company may provide financial assistance for the purchase of its own shares (§ 155 et seq);

(xvii) private companies are not subject to the disclosure of interests in shares provisions of Pt VI of the Act;

(xviii) private companies have been 'deregulated' by CA 1989, §§ 113, 116 by allowing written resolutions and elective resolutions to relax formalities in respect of authority to allot shares, laying accounts before general meetings, holding annual general meetings, short notice of meetings and dispensing with the annual appointment of auditors.

Comments and Questions

1. The scope of company law differs under French, German, English and US law. Among these, US and English law take the most restrictive view of the scope of company law—limited essentially to enterprises we know as corporations. German and French systems take a much broader view of the sorts of enterprises subject to regulation as companies.

> The German definition of company law is considerable wider than the one employed in the UK, which applies quite narrowly to the regulation of particular forms of business enterprise; the public and private limited liability companies. Thus partnership law is excluded from the considerations of company law, although it may be the focus of comparison for some aspects.
>
> In Germany, the definition of company law (*Gesellschaftsrecht*) includes any association by agreement to conduct joint pursuits, hence all forms of commercial and non-commercial enterprise come under this heading, as can be seen from the German texts on company law cited below. 'Company' is used, therefore, more in its literal sense in Germany.
>
> Company law in Germany is governed by a number of principal enactments in the absence of a company code. Thus elements of the civil and commercial codes apply, as well as statutes on distinct business forms such as the Joint Stock Corporation Act (*Aktiengesetz: AktG*) and the Limited Liability Companies Act (*Gesetz betreffend die Gesellschaften mit beschränkter Haftung:* GmHG). Additionally in this noncodified area, case law has adopted a more important role.
>
> The principle distinction in German company law is the division into partnerships which do not have legal personality, and corporations which are legal persons. The partnerships do, however, enjoy such legal rights concerning the name and ability to sue and be sued in the partnership name as to render the absence of full legal personality almost inconsequential.

Nigel Foster, German Legal System and Laws 327–328 (2nd ed. 1996).

2. Are there functional equivalents of the SARL or the GmbH in English corporate law? In what ways are English private limited companies similar or different from closely held corporations in the US?

3. To what extent are corporate regulations in English (or Germany or France) focused on attributes other than form—for example, how do factors such as size of enterprise, participation in particular markets (telecommunications, transportation, banking, insurance or the like) affect the nature of the regulation of the particular form of the corporation? Can it be argued that the classification of companies by type within the context of European corporate law suggests that corporate regulation is merely a reflection of larger policy concerns affecting the regulation of particular types of enterprises (irrespective of form of organization) rather than a struggle over the peculiarities of the corporate form itself?

C. The Asian Approach: Japan and China

The experience of both Japan and China show the influence of Western corporate models under very different circumstances. The Japanese imported and adapted Western forms of law in the late 19th century, a time during which the country was undergoing internal unification under the Emperor and attempting to eliminate foreign concessions within its borders. A century later the Chinese began an attempt to accomplish a similar absorption of Western company law models, but under very different circumstances. China in the late 20th century had already undergone a half century of absorption and adaptation of Western models of Marxist/Socialist/Totalitarian forms of governance. The importation of Western models of company law thus required an assimilation through a double filter: first company law had to adapt to indigenous customary forms of enterprise organization, and second, company law had to conform to the formal requirements of a Maoist Marxist state.

1. *Japan*

As you read the materials that follow, consider how the effects of history have influenced the way company law has been absorbed in Japan. If the absorption of foreign forms of legal organization of enterprises is "skin deep," does the lack of internalization of company law principles matter? Does the discipline of international capital markets or that of the needs of worldwide business transactions provide effective policing of corporate norms in places where it has only recently naturalized? Would indigenous forms of enterprise organization have developed the same way in the absensce of the absorption of foreign laws?

Yoshiro Miwa, *Symposium: Corporate Social Responsibility: Dangerous and Harmful, Though Maybe Not Irrelevant*

84 CORNELL L. REV. 1227 (1999)

(excerpts pages 1231–1232; some footnotes omitted)

A Brief Overview of Japanese CorporateLaw

The Japanese Diet enacted the Sho-ho, or Commercial Code, shortly before the turn of the century.[7] The Diet revised the Commercial Code, which the drafters modeled on Prussian law,[8] after World War II to reflect more closely U.S. commercial law. [9] Despite these postwar modifications, the Code remains more detailed and less flexible than its statutory counterpart in the United States.

The kabushiki kaisha, or public corporation, is the most popular business form for both large and small Japanese businesses.[10] It shares many fundamental features with

7. *See* KENZO TAKAYANAGI, HISTORICAL INTRODUCTION TO THE 1 COMMERCIAL CODE OF JAPAN ANNOTATED ix, xxxiv (Codes Translation Comm., League of Nations Ass'n of Japan 1931).

8. *See id.* at xxxi.

9. *See* Elliott J. Hahn, *An Overview of the Japanese Legal System*, 5 NW. J. INT'L L. & BUS. 517, 522 (1983).

10. *See* YUKIO YANAGIDA ET AL., LAW AND INVESTMENT IN JAPAN 271 (1994).

the prevailing U.S. corporate form.[11] Shareholders of Japanese public corporations are subject to liability only to the extent of their capital contributions.[12] They generally have one vote per share[13] and usually can recover their investment only by selling their shares. They exercise influence over corporate management by holding shareholder meetings, which the Code requires them to hold at least once a year.[14] Shareholders also may hold meetings at the request of the board of directors,[15] with court permission,[16] and at the request of a group of shareholders that collectively owns at least three percent of the firm's outstanding shares.[17] The Code requires a majority vote to pass shareholder resolutions unless the resolution falls within a statutory exception or the firm's articles of incorporation provide otherwise.[18]

The shareholders elect directors at their annual meeting[19] to manage the corporation.[20] Each director serves on the board for a term that lasts no longer than two years,[21] and shareholders can remove directors before their terms expire.[22] The Code vests broad statutory authority in the board to manage the corporation.[23] Enumerated responsibilities of Japanese boards include convocation of general shareholder meetings,[24] approval of transactions between directors and the company,[25] and financial reporting to auditors.[26]

Japanese corporate law does not require boards of directors to delegate management authority to corporate officers. In Japan, individuals whom U.S. companies would consider "senior management" are directors. The Code requires that Japanese boards of directors appoint at least one "representative director" who has actual authority to bind the corporation on certain enumerated issues.[27] A duty of care and a duty of loyalty govern the relationship between directors and the firm, and a breach of either is grounds for a shareholder law suit.[28] The board must monitor the activities of each individual director, and the Code prohibits the board from delegating decision-making authority on certain key issues to specific directors.[29] Shareholders also can petition a court to enjoin action by directors when irreparable damage to the firm otherwise will result.

---

11. *See id.*
12. *See* Shoho Art. 200, para. 1, reprinted in 2 Law Bulletin Series: Japan (EHS) at JA 49 (1997) [hereinafter Shoho] (English translation).
13. *See id.* Art. 241, para. 1.
14. *See id.* Art. 234, para. 1.
15. *See id.* Art. 231.
16. *See id.* Art. 237, para. 2.
17. *See id.* Art. 237, para. 1.
18. *See id.* Art. 239, para. 1.
19. *See id.* Art. 254, para. 1.
20. *See id.* Art. 260, para. 1.
21. *See id.* Art. 256, para. 1.
22. *See id.* Art. 257, para. 1. Directors, however, can seek damages when removed without cause. *See id.*
23. *See id.* Art. 260.
24. *See id.* Art. 231.
25. *See id.* Art. 265, para. 1.
26. *See id.* Art. 274, para. 2.
27. *See id.* Art. 261.
28. In 1950, the Commercial Code incorporated the kabunushi daihyo sosho, or shareholders' derivative suit. Oddly, the provision does not include a requirement that the representative "fairly and appropriately" represent the shareholders' interests. For comprehensive treatment of this provision, *see* Yoshiro Miwa, *kabunushi daihyo sosho*, in Yoshiro Miwa et al., Kaisha-Ho No Keizaigaku 151 (1998).
29. *See* Shoho, *supra* note 12, Art. 260, para. 2.

Masao Fukushima, *The Significance of the Enforcement of the Company Law Chapters of the Old Commercial Code in 1893*

24 Law in Japan 171 (1991)
(William Horton, trans.)
(excerpts from pages 171–183; some footnotes omitted)

It has been thought that private law did not develop in old Japan, the laws of the period having been primarily criminal laws, exemplified by feudal dominant law. However, it is clear that commercial law based on customary law became highly developed in the Edo Period, the exchange bills and notes laws being the best example of this....

However, prior to the Meiji Restoration, commercial customary law was defective in that it lacked a company system in the current sense. All businesses, from small to large, raised capital within the house (*ie*) (family associations), and there was no custom of raising capital on a large scale from a large number of investors through shares with limited liability.[3] This is understandable when compared to the history of company formation in Western countries, which began with colonization companies and trading companies that had been granted royal patents. By comparison, Japan was under seclusion orders and thus lacked the conditions for establishment of such companies and incentive to establish and develop a company system. The company laws of the European nations gradually developed as they ventured to the various continents in search of profit during the age of exploration (*daihankai jidai*), and this development continued as the industrial revolution spread throughout domestic commerce.

Following the Meiji Restoration, the popularization of a company system patterned on such conditions abroad and the channeling of investable capital (*yoshi*) to the establishment of enterprises became a powerful method of implementing the fundamental governmental policy of "fostering commerce and strengthening industry." The government expended significant efforts in promoting this new concept throughout Japan....

Meiji absolutist political authority was thus used to enhance national strength through an improved understanding of finance and the formation of industrial capital by drawing on a variety of sources of funding, and it was argued that these policies were necessary to stimulate the development of economic activity, and this would naturally include the establishment of a legal system.... However, the first comprehensive plan to establish various laws was not made until September 28, 1876.... However, it is not clear from the historical materials whether or not a draft of the commercial law was actually made by the Justice Department at this time.

3. In the late Tokugawa Period, kinship and geographically based joint enterprises existed, but these are said to have been in the nature of partnerships, limited liability partnerships companies and limited associations (*toumei kumiai*). However, there was no custom of a company system having transferable shares with limited liability. Toshimitsu Imuta, *kindai shin'yo seido no keisei to kabushiki kaisha no fukyo [The Spread of the Joint Stock Corporation and the Establishment of a Modern Credit System]*, I KOZA NIHON SHIHONSHUGI HATTATSU SH RON [COLLECTED ESSAYS ON THE HISTORY OF THE DEVELOPMENT OF CAPITALISM IN JAPAN] 177. Also, the appearance at the end of the Tougawa Period and early Meiji Period in the newly opened port towns of "companies" modeled after European and American practice is as described below in connection with an examination of the commercial code.

Thereafter, a Committee for the Investigation of Company and Association Regulations was set up by the Senate (*Genru-in*) on September 22, 1880.... This committee was dissolved in March 1882, and a Commercial Code Investigation Committee was established in its place.... In other words, the work expanded to a general code.

However, this organ was changed from time to time. In May 1884, the Commercial Code Compilation Committee was dissolved, and another Company Regulations Compilation Committee was established under the newly established Institutional Reform Bureau [to work on draft company regulations based on a draft of a commercial code prepared by Karl Friedrich Hermann Rössler]....

This is the first mention of the Rössler draft.... Rössler was charged with the drafting of the Commercial Code, and he completed it in January of 1884.

In the meantime, this period saw the Matsukata fiscal reform begin in 1882 and the fiscal austerity resulting therefrom threw the Japanese economy into a depression, which ended in 1885....

* * *

Companies at the time were referred to as "*gappon gaisha*" or "*shimei gaisha*", meaning "joint stock corporation," and the liability of the shareholders was not at all clear under the law in either case. This posed no problem in periods when the economy was going well, but it was a major problem in the deflationary conditions arising from the Matsukata currency reform....

Certainly this was the state of affairs, and we learn that there was a legal debate over limited liability and at the very least suits were filed in courts of the first instance.

That the defects in the legal regulation of the company were deleterious was clearly shown in the deflationary period, and although the Matsukata currency reform that took effect from 1887 resulted in the improvement of commercial and industrial sectors and the tendency for enterprises to proliferate, the significant defects in the law continued unchanged. This circumstance shows how a rational company system was used to change the nature and purpose of Japanese society, in which a number of pre-modern elements remained, and the later experience of the overseas Chinese is representative of this....[10]

* * *

---

10. Koji Iizuka, Sekai Shi Ni Okeru Toyo Shakai [Oriental Society in World History] 172 (1948); Iizuka Koji Chosaku Sho [Collected Writings of Koji Iizuka] 291 (1975). The following is quoted from *A Case in Which the Legal System of Modern Society was Used for Opposite Purposes by the Pre-Modern Overseas Chinese*, published by the overseas Chinese economic scholar, W.J. Ketter (1936):

> Although European law does not fully satisfy the needs of the overseas Chinese, the overseas Chinese, without being limited by this, took as much advantage of European law as they could. When it came to be known that a method was available by which individual liability could be easily avoided, and an opportunity existed to participate in commercial transactions as investors while protecting the safety of personal assets, there were no examples where share companies were established in great numbers by the overseas Chinese in the Dutch East Indies.... Moreover, the cases in which the corporations which were established by the overseas Chinese were family companies were numerous... and... there were cases in which the president of the company engaged in his individual capacity in the same business as that of the company, leaving the unprofitable transactions to the company.... It is necessary to make the penal regulations relating to share companies more severe.

See You Chung Hsun, Kakyo Keizai No Kenkyo [Studies on the Economies of Overseas Chinese], Chapter 6 "Characteristics of the Businesses of Overseas Chinese" (1969).

Through such stages, the government came to recognize that it was necessary to regulate companies as soon as possible, and it ultimately produced a draft, titled the "Commercial Company Law," and submitted it to the Senate. This was in 1886....

The entire draft was approved by all the Deliberating Officers, who expressed the view that the current conditions could not be permitted to continue and that legal regulation was urgently necessary....

* * *

Notwithstanding this, after the Senate passed the bill for adoption, it was not promulgated....

The reason is not at all clear. On essential condition was the urgency of the compilation of a Commercial Code and other laws, which had become part of the preparation for renegotiation with the various advanced countries of the unequal treaties (loss of right to impose customs, extra-territorial jurisdiction, etc.), which was the Tokugawa legacy....An Anglo-German proposal was presented...on June 15 [1886]. With respect to its contents, as a condition to the revocations of the judicial power of the consulates, Japan was required to compile and promulgate a commercial law, a personal liability limit [bankruptcy] law and other important laws, and to approve the appointment of foreign judges to Japanese courts in civil and criminal cases relating to foreigners....

The promulgation of the Company Law draft which had proceeded through the Senate was stopped by the Foreign Ministry and the government, which was concentrating all its attention on these negotiations....

In the meantime, a great deal of opposition both within and without the government had arisen to the negotiations being conducted by [the] Foreign Minister...on the grounds that he was ceding too much sovereign authority.

....Governmental and public opposition to [the] Foreign Minister...eventually became so strong that [he] had to announce to the foreign powers in July 1987 that the Treaty Revision Conference was indefinitely postponed....Then, in the last half of October 1887, the Legislation Investigation Committee [charged with finalizing the Commercial Code and Company Law] was transferred to the Ministry of Justice....At the end of November 1888, [the Justice Minister] submitted a report to the various ministries, and by year end, the Civil Code, the Commercial Code, the Procedure Law (Civil) and the Court Organization Law were completed and submitted to the Senate....

....The government requested that proceedings be undertaken rapidly with respect to this legislation in particular, and both Houses, after some minor revisions, postponed the enforcement date to June 1893 and approved the bills. This was the first legal regulation of the company to be recognized in Japan.

K. Takayangi, *A Century of Innovation: The Development of Japanese Law 1868–1961*

page 1, in Law in Japan: The Legal Order in a Changing Society
(Arthur Taylor von Mehren, ed., 1963)
(excerpt pages 31–32)

As in the case of the Civil Code, there also were an Old Commercial Code and a New Commercial Code. The old Code was based on a draft written by Hermann Roessler, a

German advisor to the government and professor at the Imperial University. Roesler's draft was eclectic and not exclusively French, since German and English law were also taken into account. The Old Commercial Code was promulgated on 27 April 1890, but shared the fate of the Old Civil Code in the heat of the postponement controversy. However, unlike the Old Civil Code, which never came into force but only served as convenient material for the court in exercising 'reason,' some sections of the Old Commercial Code, especially those parts relating to companies, came into operation on 1 July 1893, and remained in force until the coming into effect of the New Commercial Code. Book III of the Old Commercial Code, which provided for bankruptcy of companies, also came into effect on 1 July 1893, and was in force until replaced by the Bankruptcy Law of 1922. These temporary measures were necessitated by a business panic. The New Commercial Code, drafted by a committee consisting of Ume, Okano, and Tabe, was promulgated on 9 March 1899, and took effect on 16 June of the same year.

The Commercial Code of 1899 consisted of five books: General Provisions, Companies, Commercial Acts, Bills, and Maritime Commerce. Book IV, dealing with bills of exchange, promissory notes and checks was stricken from the code simultaneously with the enactment of two statues, one on bills of exchange and promissory notes (1932) and the other on checks (1933). These enactments followed the ratifications of two international treaties entered into at Geneva providing for uniform laws on those topics.

In view of the marked development of industry and commerce after World War I, the Commercial Code, especially Book II, was radically amended, and the amended code came into force on 1 January 1940. A separate statute providing for limited liability companies (*yugen kaisha*) came into force on the same date, thus amplifying the forms available for business enterprise. The law on companies was again radically revised during the Allied military occupation as one phase of the democratization of Japan, and in this process American corporation law was taken as a model.

Thomas J. Blackmore and Makoto Yazawa, *Japanese Commercial Code Revisions Concerning Corporations*

2 Am. J. Comp. L. 12 (1953)
(excerpts from pages 12–19; some footnotes omitted).

The story of the conception, enactment, content, and acceptance of the recent revisions of the Japanese Commercial Code is not inspiring nor entirely a credit to American legal leadership. Nevertheless it should interest the legal scholars of other countries for, like the medical data obtained from German concentration camp experimentation during World War II, the present revision probably will remain unique. This account also possibly might prove instructive to military governors, if in the future there again are those who regard a reformation of all areas of law as their duty.

I. Background

The Commercial Code which the Allied Occupation authorities found when they took over Japan in September 1945 was an easily identified member for the continental family. It has been transplanted to Japan from Germany approximately fifty years before, as one part of the unprecedented reception of Western law in the Meiji period, and had replaced almost all elements of feudal Japan's indigenous law merchant. The principal author was Herman Rössler, a German legal advisor to the Department of Justice, whose draft of 1884, after being roundly criticized as a foreign innovation, was partially accepted but was soon replaced by a new Code in 1899. The revised Code was politically acceptable in having been drafted by Japanese scholars, but nevertheless, in form and substance closely resembled the (then) draft German Commercial Code which took effect later at the onset of the twentieth century. Subsequent amendments to the Code in 1911, 1933 and 1938 in the field of corporate law also tended to reflect German developments. Almost alone among the major Japanese codes, the Commercial Code was not regarded by Japanese scholars as one ripe for reform when the Allied Occupation commenced in 1945.

II. Occupation Policies

During the first years of occupation, the General Headquarters for the Supreme Commander for Allied Powers (...SCAP) paid slight attention to conventional commercial law. Its attention was on bigger game. Following the program officially described as the "Promotion of Democratic Force Manifested in the Basic Post Surrender Policy for Japan,"[3] SCAP revamped the economic framework of Japan, first by the dissolution of the huge combines peculiar to Japan called the Zaibatsu,[4] then by the imposition of legislation designed to further decentralize economic power, and power, and finally by the enactment of a most advanced variety of antitrust legislation. Only in connection with the implementation of the last program and late in the course of the occupation did the Commercial Code finally come under the scrutiny of the Anti-Trust and Cartels Decision of the Economic and Scientific Section of SCAP which then was exorcizing monopoly in every field of law to which it had access.

The initial step in SCAP's reform of corporate law was the abolition in 1948 of those provisions of the Commercial Code which permitted the issuance of shares in return for only a part of the face value and left the time of collection of the remainder subject to the decision of directors. Later that year, the Japanese Attorney General's Office was instructed by the Economic and Scientific Section of SCAP to assemble a group of Japanese officials and scholars to join representatives of the Occupation as a committee for the preparation of revisions of the Commercial Code for the stated purpose of "strengthening the status of shareholders." This committee commenced operations in 1949 and, after more than fifty sessions which lasted until the middle of the following year, formulated the revisions of the Commercial Code which, but with slight modifications, came into effect in 1951.

---

3. A statement of policy by the Far Eastern Commission of July 11, 1947, at page 27, Nippon Kanri Horei Kenkyu, vol. 27, provided:

> "Policies shall be laid down with the object of insuring a wide and just distribution of income and the ownership of the means of production and trade. Encouragement shall be given to those forms of economic activity, organization and leadership deemed likely to strengthen the democratic forces in Japan and to prevent economic activity from being used in support of military ends. To this end it shall be the policy of the Supreme Commander...to require a program for the dissolution of the large industrial and banking combinations accompanied by their progressive replacement by organizations which would widen the basis of control and ownership."

This policy was enunciated first in the United States Initial Post Surrender Policy for Japan in 1945 in similar language.

4. Some European scholars see parallels to the Zaibatsu in European cartels, especially the German. The Zaibatsu were dissolved in compliance with the SCAP "Memorandum Concerning Dissolution of Holding Companies," of 6 November, 1945. The acts of dissolution were Imperial Ordinances No. 65 of 1945 and No. 23 of 1946.

Since the necessity for strengthening the status of shareholders was not apparent to or acknowledged by the Japanese government or the Japanese members of the committee, and since the Occupation officials in charge were vehemently determined that changes should be made, the committee procedures were of a character unknown to Roberts Rules of Order. Normally, the committee chairman offered drafts of revised articles of the code which the committee was invited to consider and, after a proper interval and opportunity for debate as to phraseology and techniques of adoption, was required to adopt without substantial revision. The ultimate decision whether or not such provision should be adopted was not before the committee. These proposals followed closely the provisions of the Uniform Stock Transfer Act of 1909 and the Illinois Business Corporation Act of 1933, whose use apparently was not the result of the excellence of the legislation of that state but simply of the fact that the particular SCAP officials in charge of revision hailed form Chicago.

* * *

Upon completion of a draft incorporating all the changes both required of and desired by the Japanese members of the committee, that draft was presented to a reviewing body of scholars, businessmen, lawyers, and officials, nominated by the Office of the Attorney General. This body, called the Legislative Counsel, registered strong objections to certain portions of the proposed draft but also did not succeed in obtaining a relaxation of the Occupation's policies. Reluctantly, the revisions were presented to the Japanese Diet, without change, as a government-proposed bill whose enactment was an occupational necessity. The revised Code was enacted in 1950, but, in the period intervening before its application in July 1951, a last opposition effort within the Diet, using the argument that there was insufficient time for preparation, did succeed in bargaining with SCAP officials for the deletion of several objectionable provisions regarding shareholders' rights and deferred enforcement of certain other provisions until the end of 1951.

III. Content of Reform

Classified by substance rather than origin, the amendments to the Japanese Commercial Code made in 1950 fall into three major categories, namely (a) the rearrangement of corporate powers as between the shareholders' meeting, the board of directors, and the corporate auditors, (b) the provision of new methods of attracting and inducing capital investment, and (c) the strengthening of the rights of individual shareholders.

(a) Rearrangement of Corporate Powers.... Before the recent amendments, the Japanese Commercial Code afforded unlimited power to the shareholders meeting. Every resolution of shareholders, on whatever subject, bound the corporation. As now amended, the powers of shareholders are limited to matters enumerated by law or stated in the articles of incorporation. These powers now afforded by law to shareholders are: to amend the articles of incorporation,[15] to decrease the stated capital,[16] to consolidate or dissolve,[17] to approve financial statements and to declare dividends,[18] and to elect direc-

15. Art. 342.
16. Art. 375.
17. Art. 408, 404.
18. Art. 283. Note that Japanese law differs from American in that the power to give formal approval to financial statements and to declare dividends is afforded to shareholders rather than the board of directors.

tors and auditors.[19] The authority to issue bonds and shares which previously had been held by shareholders was assigned to the board of directors unless otherwise provided by the articles of incorporation.

The concept of a board of directors as an institution holding and exercising corporate managerial functions did not exist previously in Japanese law. Under former law, every director had a general authority to act on behalf of the corporation and to represent it in transactions, except as otherwise limited by the articles of incorporation or the resolution of shareholders. As amended, the directors have no such powers individually, but their authority is now exercised collectively as a board. Representation of the corporation is afforded only to representative directors elected by the board, who resemble the officers of an American company. Directors are elected at two year intervals by the corporate shareholders in general meeting and by a special quorum of one third of the shareholders.[25]

Another innovation which was much debated and opposed by Japanese scholars was the element of cumulative voting. Unless otherwise restricted or prohibited by the articles of incorporation, directors must be elected by cumulative voting upon the request of any shareholder.... This procedure appears to have been stillborn, for, up to the present, no instances have been reported in which this voting method has been used. Without exception known to the authors, an exclusion of cumulative voting is specified in the articles of incorporation of every Japanese corporation.

The only substantial point of difference which now remains between the Japanese and American corporate organizational patterns is that of the existence of the auditor. Formerly, Japanese auditors had power to inspect corporate assets, examine the business affairs of the corporation, and to audit and examine financial statements. The recent amendment removes all authority other than that of auditing financial statements and the power of reporting to the shareholders meeting. This provision of law resembles the English Companies Act of 1948....

*(b) New Methods of Corporate Financing.....*In the 1950 amendment, the institutions of authorized capital stock, as well as nonpar stock, were introduced from American corporate law in an effort to provide financing flexibility.... The board of directors also is free to determine the consideration which a corporation will receive for the issuance of shares without par value and to provide that one fourth of the consideration paid for such shares may be set aside as paid-in-surplus. The previous requirement for court approval in the event of issuance of shares for consideration other than cash continues.[35]...

Other inducements to corporate investors which are afforded by the 1950 amendment are redeemable stock, stock dividends, stock split-ups, and transfers from reserves to stated capital.

Since previous revisions of the Japanese Corporations Act of 1938 had provided for convertible bonds and stock, and nonvoting stock, it now appears that Japanese corporations have a variety of means with which to seek their new capital requirements....

(c) Strengthening Shareholders' Rights. [discussed at Chapter 7, infra. LCB].

---

19. Arts. 254, 280.

25. Arts. 256, 256-2. Previously, the maximum term of office was three years. According to the original proposal of the American component for the drafting committee, the term was to be one year as in American law. The two-year term represents a compromise between the two.

35. Art. 280–8.

Comments and Questions

1. The excerpts of the Blackmore and Yazawa article provide hints of the nature of the reception of American corporate law in occupied Japan. Incorporation was not an enthusiastic event, yet the result was likely, once naturalized by the Japanese themselves, to become permanent fixtures of Japanese law. That was the pattern of the first reception of Western law in Japan. Compare the process of reception in the late 19th century as described in the excerpt by Fukushima, above, with that of the reception of American corporate law after 1945. Recall that the initial form of the Commercial Code, drafted by a German on the Japanese payroll, was quickly replaced by a new Commercial Code, written by Japanese, but based substantially on the new German Commercial Code. Is this a case of nationalism as form over function or is something more profound at work here in the methodology of incorporation?

2. The article identified Thomas L. Blackmore, one of the authors of the article, as an American associated with the Institute of Current World Affairs in the study of Japanese law before the Second World War. Blackmore worked as a lawyer for the Americans in Japan from 1946 to 1949 and then stayed on to practice law. His co-author, Makoto Yazawa, was an academic, Assistant Professor at Tokyo University serving as a member of the committee that prepared the revisions to the Commercial Code and secretary to the Legislative Counsel of the Japanese Attorney General's Office that had been assembled for the purpose of Code revision. To what extent might the backgrounds of these men informed their perspective on corporate law reform in Japan after 1945?

3. The American revisions reflected a view, still popular in the United States, that changing formal written law is an effective means of effecting radical social change. Social and political democratization was to be reflected in all economic and as well political organizations. As such, shareholder democracy and dispersed ownership of corporations was to reflect the democratization and diffusion of political power in the Post-War Japan.

> Japanese corporate law is so lax that independent stockholders are deprived of opportunity to know what management is doing or to exercise any voice in corporate affairs. The regulations concerning partially-paid stock assist insiders in erecting large structures of control upon a narrow base of ownership and squeezing out independent stockholders when they see fit. If enterprises with diffused ownership are to be prevalent in Japan, protection of the small stockholders' interest and limitation upon arbitrary power of management will be indispensable.

Dr. Corwin D. Edwards, quoted in Pacific Affairs, September 1946 and *reprinted in* Thomas J. Blackmore and Makoto Yazawa, *Japanese Commercial Code Revisions*, 2 Am. J. Comp. L. 12, n.7 (1953). In reading the materials that follow in this chapter, consider to what extent this belief in the power of institutional law has been justified. Consider also, whether there are lessons here for Americans and Western Europeans eager to reform the commercial law of the nations of the former Soviet Empire, or of Shar'ia based nations in the image of the West by the expedient of formal legal reform alone.

Christopher H. Hanna, *Initial Thoughts on Classifying the Major Japanese Business Entities Under the Check-the-box Regulations*

51 S.M.U. L. Rev. 75 (1997)
(excerpts pages 76–81; some footnotes omitted)

II. OVERVIEW OF MAJOR JAPANESE BUSINESS ENTITIES

Under the Japanese income tax laws,[1] corporation ("HEojin") refers to an organization that has juridical (or legal) personality under the Commercial Code, Civil Code, or any other laws. In addition to the stock companies, it includes various partnerships, cooperatives, non-profit organizations, and other types of organizations. It does not include a simple partnership under the Japanese Civil Code ("nin-i kumiai"), which is generally a joint venture without legal personality carried on by taxpayers. The term corporation also does not include a secret partnership or anonymous association under the Japanese Commercial Code ("tokumei kumiai"). As a result, the nin-i kumiai and the tokumei kumiai are not subject to the Japanese corporate income tax.

Corporations are classified into one of two categories: domestic and foreign. A domestic corporation ("naikoku HEojin") is one maintaining its head office ("honten") or principal office ("shutaru jimusho") in Japan.[6] A foreign corporation ("gaikoku HEojin") is simply defined as a corporation that is not a domestic corporation.

There are four primary Japanese organizations that are classified for tax purposes as corporations under the category of ordinary corporations and that are the focus of this article. These are: the joint stock company ("kabushiki kaisha"); the limited company ("yugen kaisha"); the unlimited partnership company ("gomei kaisha"); and the limited partnership company ("goshi kaisha"). All four of these ordinary corporations are subject to the Japanese corporate income tax on their taxable income. Three of the business entities, the kabushiki kaisha, the gomei kaisha, and the goshi kaisha, are companies ("kaisha") under the Commercial Code.[9] The yugen kaisha is a company under the

---

1. [A]ny reference to Japanese income tax laws includes both the individual and the corporate income tax laws of Japan. Generally, the Income Tax Law ("Shotokuzei HEo") applies to individuals, and the Corporate Tax Law ("HEojinzei HEo") applies to corporations, but certain withholding provisions of the Income Tax Law also apply to corporations....

6. *See* Corporation Tax Law, Art. 2(1)(iii) (translated in Yuji Gomi, Japan Corporation Tax Law (1996)). Under the Commercial Code, the permanent establishment of a company is at the seat of its principal office. *See* Commercial Code, Art. 54(2). Under the Civil Code, the permanent establishment of a company is at the seat of its principal office. *See* Civil Code, Art. 50. The two provisions are translated identically by one translation service. But some commentators have noted that the Commercial Code is actually referring to the head office while the Civil Code is referring to the main office. *See* Uematsu, *supra* note 2, at 584 n.105; *see also* Darcy, *supra* note 3, P 105.10. Nevertheless, it should be noted that principal office should mean the head office (under the Commercial Code) or main office (under the Civil Code) and not the principal place of business.... Under the United States-Japan Income Tax Treaty, the term "Japanese corporation" means a juridical person that has its head or main office in Japan or any organization without juridical personality treated for purposes of Japanese tax as a Japanese juridical person. *See* Convention for the Avoidance of Double Taxation and the Prevention of Fiscal Evasion with Respect to Taxes on Income, March 8, 1971, U.S.-Japan, Art. 2(1)(e)(ii).

9. *See* Commercial Code, Arts. 52, 53, 54.

Limited Company Law, which incorporates by reference many provisions of the Commercial Code applicable to the kabushiki kaisha.[10]

The joint stock company, or kabushiki kaisha, is organized under the Commercial Code.[11] It has been described in detail many times, and no attempt will be made to do so here.[12] It is used by large Japanese businesses and by an overwhelming number of foreign organizations conducting business in Japan, either as a wholly owned subsidiary or as a joint venture with Japanese partners. All of the shareholders of the kabushiki kaisha have limited liability.[14] It is very similar to the United States corporation.

The limited company, or yugen kaisha, is organized under the Limited Company Law which, as noted earlier, incorporates by reference many provisions of the Commercial Code applicable to the kabushiki kaisha. It is commonly used by small Japanese businesses, such as family owned businesses. It can be owned by a single member, but can have a maximum of only fifty members with limited exceptions.[16] All of the members of the yugen kaisha have limited liability.[17] It is similar in many ways to the kabushiki kaisha, except that it is generally smaller and its procedures and requirements are simpler.[18]

The kabushiki kaisha has been used much more frequently by foreign investors than the yugen kaisha. Several commentators have noted, however, that the yugen kaisha seems to be the perfect Japanese business entity for foreign investors because of its simpler procedures and requirements. But others have noted that the yugen kaisha is not a suitable entity for structuring foreign investment. Commentators have given a number of reasons for the lack of interest in the yugen kaisha by foreign investors, including: (1) the lack of prestige associated with it; (2) difficulty in obtaining bank credit and developing business relationships (because of the lack of prestige); (3) delays in dealing with Japanese authorities because of their unfamiliarity with the yugen kaisha; (4) the lack of flexibility in certain corporate matters; and (5) in actual practice, the simpler procedural requirements may only be minimally simpler than the procedures for a kabushiki kaisha.

The unlimited partnership company, or gomei kaisha, is organized under the Commercial Code.[23] It is similar in many respects to the United States general partnership. Its members have unlimited liability for the debts of the partnership.[24] More specifically, the partners are jointly and severally liable for the debts of the partnership if the assets

---

10. *See* Limited Company Law, Art. 1.

11. *See* Commercial Code, ch. IV, Arts. 165-456.

12. For a detailed description of the kabushiki kaisha in English, *see, e.g.*, Griffith Way et al., Business Operations in Japan, in Tax Management A-5 to A-19 (BNA Portfolio 51-7th 1990); Michio Matsueda & Kazuo Ihara, *Business Organization*, in 4 Doing Business in Japan pt. 7 (Zentaro Kitagawa ed., 1996); Yasuyuki Kawabata, *Japan*, in 2 Taxes and Investment in Asia and the Pacific 9–24 (Supp. No. 138, 1996).

14. *See* Commercial Code, Art. 200(1) ("The liability of a shareholder shall be limited to the value at which he has taken his own shares.")

16. ....Prior to the 1990 change, Limited Company Law art. 69(1)(v) stated that the yugen kaisha would dissolve whenever only one member remained.

17. *See* Limited Company Law, Art. 17 ("The liability of a member, except as otherwise provided for in this Law, shall be limited to the amount of his contribution.")....

18. [John W. Darcy, Japan-U.S. International Tax Transactions (1994)] at ¶ 105.20....

23. *See* Commercial Code, ch. II, Arts. 62–145.

24. *See id.* Art. 80.

of the partnership are insufficient to fully satisfy creditors.[25] In addition, a company cannot be a partner in the gomei kaisha.[26]

The limited partnership company, or goshi kaisha, is also organized under the Commercial Code.[27] Many of the provisions applicable to the gomei kaisha are also applicable to the goshi kaisha.[28] It is similar in many respects to the United States limited partnership. The articles of incorporation must specify which partners have limited liability and which partners have unlimited liability.[29] There must be at least one partner with unlimited liability and one partner with limited liability.[30] Partners with limited liability may make contributions only in the form of cash or property.[31] A company can be a limited partner but not an unlimited partner.[32] A limited partner may not participate in the management of the goshi kaisha.[33] If it does, it may be treated as a partner with unlimited liability.[34]

The gomei kaisha and the goshi kaisha are not popular with foreign investors because they have many disadvantages with very few advantages. Many of the previously discussed disadvantages of the yugen kaisha relative to the kabushiki kaisha are equally applicable to the gomei kaisha and the goshi kaisha, such as the lack of prestige and the lack of familiarity with the gomei kaisha and goshi kaisha. In addition, all of the partners of the gomei kaisha have unlimited liability while at least one partner of the goshi kaisha has unlimited liability. Also, all of the partners of the gomei kaisha and the unlimited partners of the goshi kaisha cannot be companies, thereby limiting their use in the business world. In the case of the gomei kaisha, a partner cannot engage in transactions of the same type of business as the gomei kaisha without the consent of all the partners, further limiting its use in the business world. Finally, the gomei kaisha and the goshi kaisha are subject to the Japanese corporate income tax and, therefore, are not flow-through entities for tax purposes.

In addition to the category of ordinary corporations, there are three more categories of organizations subject to the Japanese corporate income tax: public interest corporations ("koeki HEojin"),[39] cooperatives ("kyEodEo kumiai"),[40] and non-juridical organizations ("jinkaku no nai shadan").[41] Public interest corporations are generally religious, educational, or charitable corporations. Some examples of public interest corporations are the National Space Development Agency of Japan, National Health Insurance Organization, Securities Dealers Association, and the Japan Chamber of Commerce and Industry. Cooperatives are generally mutual aid organizations "established by persons engaged in specific occupations or by consumers." Some examples of cooperatives are Federation of Fisheries Cooperative Associations, Consumer's Cooperative Union, and Forest Owners' Cooperative Associations.

---

25. *Id.*
26. *See id.* Art. 55; Limited Company Law, Art. 4.
27. *See* Commercial Code, ch. III, Arts. 146–64.
28. *See id.* Art. 147.
29. *See id.* Art. 148.
30. *See id.* Art. 146; *see*, e.g., [Takashi Kuboi & Yoichi Asakawa, *Partnering in Japan: Form of Entry and Recent Tax Issues*, 13 TAX NOTES INT'L 446 (1996)] at 447. . . .
31. *See* Commercial Code, Art. 150.
32. *See id.* Art. 55; Limited Company Law, Art. 4. . . .
33. *See* Commercial Code, Art. 156. . . .
34. *See* Commercial Code, Art. 159. . . .
39. *See* Corporation Tax Law, Art. 2(1)(vi).
40. *See id.* Art. 2(1)(vii).
41. *See id.* Art. 2(1)(viii).

The last category is probably the most interesting. Non-juridical organizations are unincorporated organizations that have designated managers or representatives.[45] This category was formed in 1957 under the Juridical Persons' Tax Law (the predecessor of the Corporation Tax Law) because of a perceived abuse that was taking place. A group of individuals would enter into a profit-making activity and act not as a mere collection of individuals but rather pursuant "to a single will and whose continued existence transcend[ed] the individuality of the various component members."[47] Because the organization of individuals did not have juridical personality, the organization was not subject to the Juridical Persons' Tax Law. It was also argued that the Income Tax Law did not apply to the organization because it was thought that the Income Tax Law applied only to natural persons. Furthermore, it did not seem appropriate to tax the legal representatives of the organization under the Income Tax Law. As a result, legislation was enacted in 1957 to remedy this loophole in the law. From that point on, non-juridical organizations were treated as corporations for corporate income tax purposes.[51]

Even if an organization is classified as a corporation for Japanese income tax purposes, it may be subject to corporate income tax on only a portion of its income or, in some cases, may be entirely exempt from the corporate income tax. Generally, all domestic corporations are subject to the corporate income tax.[52] Foreign corporations are subject to corporate income tax only on income from sources within Japan.[53]

Ordinary corporations and cooperatives are taxed on their entire income.[54] Public corporations are not subject to the corporate income tax.[55] Public corporations include the Government of Japan, Japanese agencies and local public entities (such as prefectures and municipalities), and corporations established by government entities (such as the Government Housing Loan Corporation). Public interest corporations, however, are taxed, but only on income from profit-making activities. A non-juridical organization is taxed like a public interest corporation, that is, only on its income from profit-making activities.

Japan also has special rules for a family corporation ("dozoku kaisha"), which is defined as a corporation with three or fewer shareholders owning fifty percent or more of its stock.[59] An example of a family corporation is a wholly owned subsidiary. The general consequence of family corporation status is that the Japanese tax authorities can deny certain transactions of a family corporation that they determine unreasonably decrease the corporation's tax liability.

---

45. *See* Corporation Tax Law, Art. 2(1)(viii).
47. [Morio Uematsu, *Computation of Income in Japanese Income Taxation: A Study in the Adjustment of Theory to Reality in Law*, in JAPAN: THE LEGAL ORDER IN A CHANGING SOCIETY 566 (Arthur Taylor von Mehren ed., 1963).] at 583–84.
51. *See* Corporation Tax Law, Art. 3.
52. *See id.* Arts. 4(1), 5, 6.
53. *See id.* Arts. 4(2), 9.
54. *See id.* Arts. 4(1), 5, 6.
55. *See id.* Arts. 2(1)(v), 4(3)
59. [Corporation Tax Law] Art. 2(1)(x).

Christopher Lee Heftel, Survey, *Corporate Governance in Japan: The Position of Shareholders in Publicly Held Corporations*

5 U. Haw. L. Rev. 135 (1983)
(excerpts from pages 152–164; some footnotes omitted).

Part 2 of the Commercial Code is the primary source of Japanese law affecting the internal corporate governance of stock companies.[87] The stock company is the most widely used corporate form in Japan....

Although the Commercial Code is based on an American model, it is more detailed and less flexible than its statutory counterparts in the United States "where procedures and formalities have been eliminated to the extent possible."[91] The Code originally applied uniformly to all stock companies, but various amendments passed over the years interjected distinctions among companies based on size and whether or not their stock was listed. The major amendments to the Commercial Code and related laws passed in 1981 expanded these distinctions. Thus, while most of the description below applies to all stock companies, distinctions are noted that in particular affect Japan's...publicly listed stock companies.

1. Directors

Every stock company must have at least three directors. Directors are elected at shareholder meetings and serve terms of office of two years or less. The board of directors is granted broad statutory powers to "manage" the corporation. Japanese boards do not delegate their management powers to corporate "officers" who do not exist in Japan. Everyone who would be considered "senior management" by American standards occupies a place on the board of directors. Consequently, Japanese boards tend to be large, often numbering over thirty.

The directors are split into a hierarchy of several ranks. Seniority usually determines ranking. The lower ranking directors tend to be salaried employees, such as department chiefs. Higher up are "managing directors" who have in essence retired from employee status. Above the one or more ranks[102] of managing directors are a variety of vice presidents[103] and a president.[104] The most senior members of the typical board take on such titles as vice-chairman,[105] chairman,[106] advisor[107] and senior advisor.

The size of the typical Japanese board of directors necessitates division into more compact decision making units. Directors often form working and executive commit-

87. "*Kabushiki gaisha.*"

91. [Birmingham, *The Japanese Corporation as a Business Vehicle for Foreign Business, in* Current Legal Aspects of Doing Business in Japan and East Asia (J.O. Haley ed. 1978)] at 61.

102. For example, in addition to "managing directors," some companies have "senior managing directors" ("*senmu torishimariyaku*").

103. "*Fuku shacho.*"

104. "*Shacho.*"

105. "*Fuku kaicho.*"

106. "*Kaicho.*"

107. "*Sodan yaku.*"

tees that meet more frequently than the full board. These committees are not recognized by statute. However, the Code does recognize the position of "representative director."[109] Representative directors are appointed by the board from its ranks to act on behalf of the corporation.[110] The boards of most large stock companies appoint several directors, including the president, to function as representative directors to deal with third parties on behalf of the company. Representative directors implement decisions made at shareholders' or board meetings and are empowered to make decisions on matters delegated by the board.

Beginning with incidents such as the Lockheed scandal, concern grew that the individual directors needed to be more accountable to the board as a whole and that the board's supervising authority needed to be strengthened. Disagreement existed over what kind of matters could be delegated by the board to a representative director. Thus, the 1981 Commercial Code amendments specifically enumerated four subjects[115] which the board may *not* have a director decide and further prohibits the board from delegating the "execution of any other important business affairs."[116]

The new Code has other provisions designed to exact greater responsibility on the part of individual directors. For example, the amended Code provides that "[a] director shall report to the board of directors the status of execution of business affairs not less than once every three months."[117] These reports must include concrete descriptions of how corporate affairs are being handled, thus providing the entire board with all the information necessary to enable proper supervision. The new Code also imposes heavier duties and liabilities on directors, increases an individual director's ability to carry out his duties, and specifies criteria for the disqualification of directors.

The board has other enumerated obligations including: convocation of general meetings of shareholders, approval of transactions between a director and the company, submission of certain financial reports to the auditors prior to each ordinary general meeting, transfer from statutory reserve to stated capital, and declaration of stock-splits, and interim dividends. Unless stricter requirements are provided in the articles of incorporation, a majority of the board constitutes a quorum, and all board resolutions must be passed by a majority of those present at a board meeting.

In practice many boards have been ineffective in overseeing the affairs of the company, often being considered just "hollow shells" controlled by powerful presidents. Regardless of how actively these directors in fact supervise the company, their loyalties are

109. "*Daihyo torishimariyaku.*"

110. Commercial Code, Art. 261, para. 1. Representative directors are those with authority to represent the company. They usually have a title such as president, executive vice president, senior managing director or managing director. To protect bona fide third parties, the Commercial Code provides that a company shall be liable to a bona fide third person for any act done by an apparent representative director. *Id.*, Art. 262. An apparent representative director is a director with a title from which it may be assumed he has authority to represent the company, although he actually has no such power....

115. Commercial Code, Art. 260, para. 2. The four subjects which the board as a whole must decide upon are: (1) disposal or acquisition of substantial assets; (2) borrowing in substantial amount; (3) appointment or removal of a manager or other senior employee; and (4) substantial organizational changes.

116. *Id.*

117. *Id.*, para 260, para. 3. While normally only representative directors would be in a position of responsibility requiring such reports back to the board, this provision places the duty to report on all directors, thus anticipating occasions where other directors might be in a position of such responsibility....

not generally to the shareholders but to the corporate insiders and the employees. While the trend for publicly held firms in the U.S. has been toward greater numbers of "outside directors," Japanese boards continue to be comprised almost entirely of "inside directors." Most of these directors are the survivors of the seniority system in which they worked their way up to the position of director after many years with the same firm. Outsiders are few in number and are usually not independent from the company in the American sense of outside directors. Instead, they are transplanted or retired from major bank creditors, sister companies and government agencies that regulate the company.[137]

2. Auditors

The shareholders must appoint auditors,[138] who are in charge of supervising the management track record set by the directors. They are appointed for two year terms and may not concurrently serve as directors or employees of the company. Most companies fill these positions with retiring employees who did not quite excel enough to become directors; in some cases middle level directors who are not going to be promoted to a more powerful position on the board are appointed as auditors. Auditors may be employed on a full time or part time basis.

Amendments in 1974 strengthened auditor's powers and duties. Auditors are empowered to: investigate corporate affairs and documents,[147] make reports to the directors and at the shareholders' meetings[148], enjoin directors' illegal acts[149] and bring certain suits on behalf of the corporation.[150] Auditors are jointly and severally liable to the company for damages due to nonperformance of their duties. In spite of the 1974 amendments, auditors often function as mere "rubber stamps" for the board of directors and often lack the professional expertise to carry out their duties.[152]

In an effort to strengthen the self-regulating functions of the company, the auditors' powers and duties were greatly enlarged by the 1981 Code revisions. Large companies must now have at least two auditors, of which at least one must be full-time. Auditors have the option of obtaining employee reports from the directors or can circumvent the directors and obtain the report directly from the employee.[155] Auditors may also de-

---

137. ....The practice of placing on a company's board retired government officials who used to regulate the company is referred to in Japan as "*amakudari*" which translates as "descent from heaven."....

138. Commercial Code, Arts. 254, 280; Special Audit Law, Art. 18, "*Kansayaku*," also translated as "Statutory auditor." Because auditors are individuals who usually work solely for the company in question and who were previously employed by that company in other capacities, they are also known as "inside auditors."

147. Commercial Code, Arts. 274, 275.

148. *Id.*, Arts. 260–3, 275.

149. *Id.*, Art. 275-2.

150. *Id.*, Arts. 247, para. 1, 275-4, 280-15, para. 2, 380, para. 2, 415. 428, para. 2.

152. ....The auditor's role in the company is sometimes so insignificant that some Japanese, instead of saying "*kansayaku*" ("auditor"), jokingly make a play on words and say "*kansanyaku* which translates as "official of leisure." [*Ato Ikkagetsu! Kaisei ho Norikiri Sodo—Gurei-zon Jissen Nanatsu no Pointo* (Only One Month Left! The Cahos Following the Amended Law: Seven Pointers Concerning the "Grey Zone" in Practice), in Shukan Daiyamondo (Weekly Diamond), September 4, 1982 at 16] at 19.

155. Commercial Code, Art. 274, para. 2. A director has the duty to immediately report to an auditor facts which give rise to an apprehension that significant damage may be incurred by the stock company. *Id.*, Art. 274-2.

mand the convocation of a meeting of the board of directors whenever necessary. Auditors' right to remuneration and compensation for expenses have been increased. This further shields auditors from undue influence by directors and makes it easier for them to hire specialists to assist in their auditing and other technical duties. The duties which expose auditors to liability to the company have been expanded and clarified. The new Code imposes liability against third persons as well where false statements have been made in any audit report.

* * *

3. Accounting Auditors

In large companies financial statements must not only be audited by company auditors but also by outside "accounting auditors."[164] An accounting auditor must be a certified public accountant or an audit corporation. Accounting auditors were previously appointed and removed by the board of directors but the new Code shifts these powers to the general meeting of shareholders.[166] Other new provisions further insulate accounting auditors from undue influence by directors or inside auditors.[167] Accounting auditors are liable to the company and to third parties for damages caused by their negligence.

4. Shareholders

a. Stock System

Although different classes of stock are allowed, almost all stock issued in Japan is voting common stock. Until October, 1982, most stock had a par value of fifty yen, which is considered excessively low given the current value of the yen. Consequently, the 1981 amendments provide for raising the unit par value to a minimum of 50,000 yen, which for most companies will require consolidating 1000 shares of stock (at par of fifty yen each) into new stock "units." The burden imposed on large investors is minimal since the nominal lot size for trading on the exchanges has been 50,000 yen. However, those investors holding less than one "unit" of stock in a company will lose their right to vote this stock....

b. Voting

While the unit stock system eliminates almost one quarter of Japan's shareholders from participating in general meetings, the procedures for share voting have essentially remained the same. The Commercial Code enumerates a limited number of matters upon which shareholders have the power to vote at a general meeting. These can be extended by the articles of incorporation. Cumulative voting is possible for the election of directors, but the practice is rarely, if ever, used.

---

164. "*Kaikei kansanin.*"

166. [Special Audit Law] Arts. 3, 6. The accounting auditors may also be removed by the inside auditors. *Id.*, Arts. 6-2.

167. For example, where the dismissal of an accounting auditor is considered at a shareholders' meeting, the accounting auditor may speak directly to the shareholders so that the shareholders do not have to rely solely on the opinions of the directors and inside auditors. Special Audit Law, Arts. 6-2, 6-3. Accounting auditors may have no other associations with the company. *Id.*, Art. 4, para. 2, item 2.....

Most matters may be passed upon by a simple resolution of the shareholders. Some of the matters which may be passed by ordinary resolution include: declaration of cash dividends,[183] declaration of stock dividends,[184] approval of financial statements, and election of auditors,[186] and accounting auditors.[187] This requires a quorum of a majority of the outstanding voting shares and affirmative votes of a majority of the shares represented at the meeting.[188] These quorum and voting requirements for simple resolutions can be changed by the articles of incorporation,[189] but elections for directors and auditors must in any event have a quorum of not less than one-third of the outstanding voting stock.[190]

Certain matters can only be passed by special resolution requiring a quorum of a majority of the outstanding stock and the favorable vote of two-thirds of the shares represented at the meeting. These requirements cannot be relaxed by the articles of incorporation. Some of the matters requiring a special resolution include: amending the articles of incorporation,[192] removing directors and auditors prior to the expiration of their terms,[193] approving mergers and consolidations,[194] reducing paid in capital[195] and issuance of new shares at favorable prices to persons other than shareholders.[196] There are certain matters which require even more stringent voting or quorum requirements; for example, releasing directors and auditors from liability for various acts usually requires unanimous consent.[197]

c. Dissenting Shareholders

When a shareholders' meeting has passed a special resolution with regard to matters such as disposition of all or an important part of a company's business, merger, consolidation or a restriction on stock transfer, any shareholder who has notified the company in writing prior to the meeting that he opposes the resolution and then does in fact oppose the resolution at the meeting, may demand that the company purchase his shares at the fair market value of the shares prior to the resolution.[198] Where the price cannot be agreed upon the shareholder may apply to the appropriate court for an appraisal remedy.[199]

Comments and Questions

1. What does the experience of Japan since the nineteenth century suggest are the limits of translation of legal doctrine or practice? Is one of the implications of Japan's experience with Western law that unification of law is impossible?

183. Commercial Code, Art. 293.
184. *Id.*, Art. 293-2....
186. Commercial Code, Art. 280; Art. 254, para. 1.
187. Special Audit Law, Art. 3, para. 1.
188. Commercial Code, Art. 239.
189. *Id.*, Art. 239, para. 1.
190. *Id.*, Art. 256-2, 280.
192. *Id.*, Art. 342, para. 1, 343.
193. *Id.*, Art. 257, paras. 1 and 2, 280, 343.
194. *Id.*, Art. 408, paras. 1 and 3, 343.
195. *Id.*, Art. 375, para. 1, 376, para. 1, 343.
196. *Id.*, Art. 280-2, para. 2, 343.
197. *Id.*, Art. 266....
198. Commercial Code, Art. 245-2....
199. Commercial Code, Art. 245-3.

2. The experience of Japan suggests a certain serendipity in the way laws or legal systems are transposed from one system to another. Transposition requires not merely reception, but, as between systems from among which translation is possible, a choice between them. Sometimes those choices are made for reasons of convenience or familiarity. It might be possible, for example, to argue that the Americanization of the Japanese corporate law system might have been more successful had the drafters used as a model the Delaware Code, and thus provided a means for the great Japanese corporations to harmonize their practices with those of their American counterparts. Consider in this respect the efforts to "democratize" and "Westernize" the laws of the nations which emerged out of the breakup of the Soviet Empire in the early 1990s.

3. **Problem:** Assume that the Marxist-Socialist government of Cuba has been overthrown and a democratically and capitalist minded government has been installed in its place. You represent a number of law firms which have banded together for the purpose of proposing changes to the corporate law of Cuba. Prior to the Marxist-Socialist revolution, Cuban company law had been modeled on the French system. But fifty years of state Socialism has effectively obliterated that system, and little memory of the old ways of enterprise organization exist on the island. On the other hand, many European companies, principally German, have been operating in Cuba since the 1960s, some of which have employed loyal members of the Cuban Communist Party. Some of these people have now assumed positions within the new government. Be prepared to discuss (1) how you would go about determining what system of corporate governance to recommend, and (2) the actual outlines of the system. In preparing your answer, consider the Chinese approach to company law at the end of the 20th century in the excerpt below.

---

2. *China*

The Chinese experience is a distorted mirror of the Japanese experience. China, expelling Western European colonialism after the Second World War, found itself absorbing Eastern European Marxist-Socialism after 1949. By the end of the 20th century, however, China also found itself confronting change again, this time in the form of the organization of worldwide commerce in goods and funds. The excerpt by William Simon, *The Legal Structure of the Chinese "Socialist Market" Enterprise* suggests the different dimensions of resistance and absorption represented by the Chinese experience. As you read the excerpt consider again your answer to the questions raised in connection with the Japanese experience, in light of the very different experiences of a different ancient Eastern "system" which chose to absorb the political and economic traditions of Europe's East rather than its West.

William H. Simon, *The Legal Structure of the Chinese "Socialist Market" Enterprise*

21 J. Corp. L. 267 (1996)

(excerpts pages 286–294; some footnotes omitted)

The focus of debate over legal reform has now shifted to corporatization. A large body of literature has emerged; though some of it is skeptical, most writers have argued that some form of corporatization would improve the SOEs [State Owned Enterprises]. The appeal of the corporate form seems to rest for some on little more than the glamour of its perceived association with economic modernity. Others favor it as a means of facilitating foreign investment or the development of a domestic capital market.

But the strongest emphasis has been on the potential contribution of the corporate form to balancing official and managerial power and limiting state economic responsibility. The Central Committee's program document argues that "corporations can effectively accomplish the separation between the ownership of investors and the rights of enterprise" and are "conducive to...enabling enterprises to get rid of reliance on administrative organizations and enabling the state to get rid of its unlimited responsibility for enterprises."[78] In fact, however, the literature is not very specific as to how corporatization is to contribute to these goals.

The rhetoric of the "separation of ownership and control" in the modern corporation, popularized in the 1930s in the West by Adolph Berle and Gardner Means, has played a distinctive role in recent discussions in China. For Berle and Means, the separation of ownership and control represented a problem—managerial unaccountability—that called for imposing responsibility on management. Some recent Chinese reformers have seized on Berle and Means's rhetoric as if "separation" were a solution to an entirely different problem— the interference of government officials in the operation of enterprises. Thus, ironically, Berle and Means's rhetoric is identified in some recent Chinese debates with proposals that tend to enlarge managerial discretion to degrees they would have considered implausible.

The closest thing to a comprehensive picture of what a corporatized SOE would look like is the Company Law enacted in late 1993.[79] The Company Law represents the convergence of the corporatization project, focusing primarily on corporate governance, with a partially distinct "securitization" project, focusing primarily on finance.

During the 1980s, central and provincial governments permitted a few enterprises to experiment with issuing securities. Local markets for the exchange of these securities were permitted in several areas. In 1990 Shanghai opened a stock exchange listing secu-

78. Decision of the CPC Central Committee, *supra* note 2, at 24. A sampling of the literature on corporatization in English translation includes State Commission for Restructuring Economic System, Production System Department, Properly Run Joint-Stock System Pilot Projects According to Standardized Requirements, JPRS Rep. China (JPRS), at 34–39 (Aug. 3, 1992); Liu Guoliang, Market Economy: State Enterprises Facing Serious Tests, JPRS Rep. China (JPRS), at 9–10 (Jan. 22, 1993); Liu Hongru, Probe for a Correct Path—Questions on the Experiments in Joint Stock Companies and the Stock Market, JPRS Rep. China (JPRS), at 20–27 (Oct. 21, 1993); Chao Qian & Xin Yi, Some Thoughts on Overhauling Enterprise Operating Mechanisms, JPRS Rep. China (JPRS) (Sept. 23, 1992); Sun Xiaoliang, A Contradiction in Continuing Enterprise Reform, JPRS Rep. China (JPRS), at 21–23 (Sept. 15, 1992); Zhan Zhongde & Ma Ping, Use Shareholding System to Revitalize State Enterprises, JPRS Rep. China (JPRS), at 30–33 (Jan. 8, 1993). An influential early work by the leading academic proponent of corporatization is Li Yinning, A Conception of Reform of the Ownership System of Our Country, Daily Rep. China (FBIS), at K5–11 (Oct. 22, 1986). For a well known article by a lawyer expressing skepticism about corporatization, *see* Wang Liming, Lun Gufen Z: *Qiye Shuoyouqian De Erchong Jiegou (On the Dual Structure of Stock Enterprise Ownership)*, 1 Zhongguo Faxue (Juris. China) 47, 47–56 (1989). Some of the literature is cited and summarized in Jianfu Chen, *Securitisation of State-Owned Enterprises and the Ownership Controversy in the PRC*, 15 Sydney L. Rev. 59 (1993).

79. *Company Law*, Daily Rep. China (FBIS), at 27–48 (Jan. 26, 1994).

rities in a few state enterprises; in 1992 Shenzhen opened its exchange, listing a few more SOE securities.

Though these securities were sometimes called "shares," most looked more like bonds, with fixed payment guarantees and no control rights. In 1992, however, the State Council endorsed limited experimentation with corporatization, contemplating the issuance of shares with control rights. It also published proposed company legislation, and Shanghai and Guangdung province (where Shenzhen is located) enacted provincial company laws.[80] These were pre-empted the following year by the national Company Law, which applies to SOE stock companies, as well as private ones.

The 1993 Central Committee policy statement authorized reformers to "experiment with the corporate system." It cautioned, however, that only a "small number" of SOEs should have publicly traded shares.[81] Several thousand SOEs have since been converted to stock companies, though only a few hundred have had their shares traded on exchanges. In most of the new corporations, shares not held by the state directly are held by other enterprises and organizations ("legal persons"), most of which are themselves state-owned, or by managers and workers of the enterprise itself. Typically, "legal person" shares can be traded only among organizations; two organized national markets for trading "legal person" shares now operate. Manager and worker shares typically cannot be traded outside the enterprise (though some transfer restrictions lapse after a period of time).[82]

The Company Law is a more or less wholesale importation of a European, notably German, model. This cross-cultural borrowing reflects the prestige of the economic institutions of the pioneer capitalist countries. It also represents a desire to encourage foreign investors by providing a legal regime familiar to them.

The choice of the German model over competing capitalist ones probably reflects historically embedded intellectual affinities. China's legal system was strongly influenced by civil, especially German, law in the late Qing and Republican periods, and the influence survived in the system the Guomindang developed on Taiwan. Moreover, the Soviet Union, which remained the dominant foreign intellectual influence on China until well into the reform period, had incorporated extensively civil law principles and rhetoric in its legal system. In adopting the Principles of Civil Law in 1986, PRC law makers had signalled an attraction to civil law models.[83]

It comes as no surprise to Western lawyers that a corporation code adopted wholecloth from the West leaves many key questions about Chinese enterprise structures

80. *See* Chen, *supra* note 78, at 60–64; *see also*, Pitman B. Potter, *The Legal Framework for Securities Markets in China: The Challenge of Maintaining State Control and Inducing Investor Confidence*, 7 China L. Rep. 61 (1992).

81. [Decision of the CPC Central Committee on Some Issues Concerning the Establishment of a Socialist Market Economic Structure, Daily Rep. China (FBIS) (Nov. 17, 1993)] at 24.

82. Transfer of legal person shares was previously restricted by general regulation. The Company Law now provides in Article 143 that all "shares may be transferred in accordance with law." Transfer restrictions now take the form of charter provisions or contracts specific to the particular enterprise.

83. The Qing Company Law of 1904 was influenced by Germany by way of the German-influenced Japanese Code. The Republican Company Law of 1929 was directly influenced by the German model, and this influence survived in the 1949 revision. William C. Kirby, *China Unincorporated: Company Law and Business Enterprise in Twentieth Century China*, 54 J. Asian Stud. 43, 47, 49, 54–55 (1995). On Russia's reliance on civil law principles, *see* Andrei Baev, *Legal Mechanisms of Monitoring State Property in Russia* 27–58 (1995) (unpublished Ph.D. dissertation, Stanford University). Taiwan's Company Law is also said to have specifically influenced the PRC's. *See* Republic of China Ministry of Economic Affairs, Company Law (1995); Norbert Horn et al., German Private and Commercial Law: An Introduction 251–79 (Tony Weir trans., 1982).

unanswered. Few European or American lawyers would argue that their corporation statutes are functionally well-adapted to their own practical circumstances, much less to China's. In both Europe and America, much of the most important corporate law is nonstatutory—for example, fiduciary duties—and many preoccupations of the statutes seem anachronistic—for example, the legal (registered) capital regimes.

Moreover, recent Western scholarship has suggested that the key issues of corporate governance are largely outside corporate law, as conventionally defined. Corporate codes are largely devoted to regulating the interaction of shareholders, managers, and creditors. But the most important practical distinctions now seem to depend on how shares are allocated among different types of investors, which in turn depends on a variety of rules outside the corporate code. In Germany and Japan, financial intermediaries holding substantial blocks of shares deal directly with management. In the United States, where shares are more dispersed and intermediaries more constrained, the stock market (and the takeover) play more important roles.[84] Like its Western counterparts, the PRC Company Law is silent about to whom shares in large corporations will be allocated. The leadership's commitment to state ownership as the "mainstay" of the economy would seem to imply that the state own at least a controlling block of the shares in most enterprises, which most proposals seem to contemplate.[85]

How will the state's shareholder rights be exercised? Surprisingly, the corporatization experiment was launched before any definite answer to this question was reached, and apparently even before much thought had been given to it. For the moment, a large fraction of state shares are held by the industrial ministries or, in some instances, the holding company structures that have taken their places. Most of the rest are held by the National Administrative Bureau of State-Owned Property, created in 1988 as an arm of the State Council to superintend the state's interest in the reformed enterprises.

Few regard the current arrangements as satisfactory, however. The industrial minis tries often try to continue their old ways of commanding enterprise management. The National Administrative Bureau of State-Owned Property is primarily an auditing agency; it has neither adequate staffing nor expertise to participate actively in corporate governance.

Recent discussions of institutionalizing the state's shareholder role appear to be converging on a structure that, if implemented successfully, would constitute a new form of market socialism. The structure has three tiers. The corporatized operating companies are the bottom tier. The middle tier would consist of intermediaries of various types holding the operating company shares. The intermediaries would include holding companies, investment companies, charitable foundations, and pension funds. Most of these intermediaries would in turn be owned wholly or in part by state agencies forming the top tier, perhaps by an expanded National Administrative Bureau of State-

84. See generally MARK J. ROE, STRONG MANAGERS, WEAK OWNERS: THE POLITICAL ROOTS OF AMERICAN CORPORATE FINANCE (1994).

85. Li Yinning's influential proposal suggested that the state should retain a controlling interest but that "one-third, two-fifths, or even less" of outstanding shares would be sufficient for control. Yinning, supra note 78, at K7. According to Shanghai officials I spoke to in 1995, in the 92 listed companies formed from former SOEs controlled by the Shanghai government, the government holds on average 53% of the shares. The Central Committee program document says, "Companies that turn out special-category products and those producing armaments should be held by the state alone. In key enterprises in 'backbone' and basic industries, the state should have controlling shares and at the same time bring in non-state capital...." Decision of the CPC Central Committee, supra note [81], at 24. The implication that the state might take a minority position in other industries is unelaborated.

Owned Property, or perhaps as some would prefer, a new agency accountable directly to the National People's Congress and its Standing Committee.

One promising feature of the model is that it would make possible competition among intermediaries in monitoring. As long as intermediary managers are given incentives to maximize returns and many intermediaries are free to invest or disinvest in any given enterprise, competition might induce effective monitoring of the operating companies.

Competition at the top level would not be possible, but it should be possible to specify a set of fairly simple rules for officials at the top that would make it easy for a separate government agency to audit performance. In essence, top level officials would be instructed to move capital into and out of the intermediaries in accordance with their relative performances.[86] This approach presupposes that the government will pursue social goals distinct from profit maximization through the regulation and the tax-transfer system, rather than through ownership. Many reformers are quite clear about this, fearing that social goals are too vague to permit monitoring and accountability through corporate institutions. A compromise would be to set up a separate set of investment and monitoring institutions for "social" investing.

At the moment, the banking system plays no role in corporate monitoring. The law forbids banks to hold shares. But many proposals contemplate an important role for banks. Banks have a substantial fraction of China's economic expertise. Moreover, banks hold massive debt claims on the SOEs that are uncollectible in their current forms and need restructuring. One alternative popular with reformers is a swap of debt for equity, which would give enterprises more flexibility and turn banks into major shareholders.[87]

The few publicly traded SOE corporations typically have dispersed individual shareholders. However, there is little expectation that they will play any direct role in corporate monitoring. (The Company Law does not provide for cumulative voting or derivative suits, nor does it give majority shareholders duties to minority ones.) On the other hand, some reformers have expressed the hope that the share prices in the public market of these companies will provide an important signal to controlling shareholders of how well management is doing. Others doubt that the market in the near term will become sufficiently informationally efficient to perform such a role.

The Company Law represents a dilution of the three distinctive themes of the 1980s rhetoric, but the themes are still notably present.

Authority. For the reformers, the greatest appeal of the corporate form is as a model for the "separation of administration and management." Corporatization converts the

86. Many experiments with intermediary structures for managing state enterprises have been tried in recent decades, though they have generally not contemplated competition among the intermediaries. *See generally* ANJALI KUMAR, STATE HOLDING COMPANIES AND PUBLIC ENTERPRISES IN TRANSITION (1993). China's size and the fragmentation of its government structure offer a distinctively auspicious setting for trying to achieve a competitive structure.

87. .... *Financial System Reform in China: Lessons from Japan's Main Bank System*, in THE JAPANESE MAIN BANK SYSTEM: ITS RELEVANCE FOR DEVELOPING AND TRANSFORMING ECONOMIES 552, 575–78 (Masahiko Aoki & Hugh Patrick eds., 1994). A 1985 World Bank report on China focused attention on the idea of exercising corporate control through multiple independent public intermediaries. WORLD BANK, CHINA: LONG TERM DEVELOPMENT ISSUES AND OPTIONS 165–66 (1985). *See also* the interesting interpretation of "socialism with Chinese characteristics" by Bo Yibo, an elder of the revolutionary generation, which does not mention clarifying property rights and suggests that the "initial conditions for developing joint stock enterprises on the basis of public ownership" have been created by the diffusion of SOE control among different public institutions. Bo Yibo, *Correctly Handle the Relationship Between Planning and the Market*, DAILY REP. CHINA (FBIS), at 28, 39 (Feb. 3, 1993).

state from a sovereign with plenary powers to a corporate shareholder. In this way, corporatization purports to limit the state's power of unprincipled or ad hoc intervention in the affairs of the business.

Managers of a corporation are not agents subject to the general authority of the shareholders. Under the new Company Law, as under its Western counterparts, share holders have the power to elect and remove the senior managers (directors) and to veto certain fundamental alterations of the business, such as mergers, revisions of the share structure, or liquidations. Aside from this limited class of decisions, however, while they are in office, managers have general authority to run the business. Moreover, though shareholders can remove directors with whom they are displeased, the Company Law permits removal during their terms only for "proper justification."[88]

On the other hand, though corporatization is vaunted as a way of constraining state power, some aspects of the Company Law in theory represent steps back from the extreme managerialism of the Enterprise Law. The meeting of shareholders is declared the "highest power organ" in the enterprise.[89] Furthermore, managerial power is fragmented among, first, a "manager" with responsibility to "take charge of the company's operation (and) management"; second, a chairman of the board of directors, who is the "company's legal representative"; third, a board of directors charged with formulating the company's operating and strategic plans and hiring, firing, and supervising senior management; and, fourth, a board of supervisors charged with "monitoring" managers and directors to insure they "perform their duties to the company."[90]

Whether the statute gives management more or less power than its Western counterparts is debatable. On the one hand, the statute gives the shareholders several powers that American (and to a lesser extent, German) shareholders normally do not have. In addition to the power to elect directors and veto major "strategic" transactions, the statute prescribes shareholder power over the fixing of director's compensation, issuance of bonds, and dividend payments.[91] It also gives shareholders the right of "approval" of the board of directors' business plan, which if construed as a right to veto it, is a power not normally enjoyed by Western shareholders. From this perspective, the Company Law is less managerial than Western ones.

On the other hand, if we understand "management" to include not all members of both boards, but primarily the Board of Directors, which typically consists of senior full-time management, then arguably the PRC Law is more managerial. In the German system, the shareholder-elected members of the supervisory board, who are part-timers meeting only a few times a year, are usually thought of as "outside" directors acting (though not necessarily effectively) as watchdogs on management. German law gives to the supervisory board the power to appoint the managing board.[92] But the PRC Law gives this power to the shareholders. Thus the PRC supervisory board is weaker. If, as is

88. Company Law, *supra* note 79, Art. 115. The Company Law authorizes three separate types of corporations: (1) limited liability companies, which have relatively smaller capital requirements, simpler governance structures, and less readily tradable shares; (2) limited liability stock companies, which are generally large companies with broadly traded stock; and (3) wholly state-owned companies, which have a simpler governance structure—since there is only a single shareholder, they dispense with shareholders' meetings. The focus above is on limited liability stock companies, which seem to be the most important variation for SOE reform.

89. *Id.* Art. 110.

90. *Id.* Arts. 126, 119, 112.

91. *Id.* Art. 103.

92. 84 Aktiengesetz I (1965) (F.R.G.); Horn et al., *supra* note 83, at 260.

often assumed, shareholders have more difficulty monitoring than supervisory directors, full-time management is stronger under the PRC Company Law.

Inevitably, the statute (even if we assume it will be enforced in good faith) is not a guarantee against either official or managerial abuse. Although shareholders have no right to instruct managers directly on a broad range of matters, their power to remove them (even if, in the absence of cause for midterm removal, they must wait until the end of their terms) may give them sufficient leverage to enforce their will on managers continuously. On the other hand, while they are in office, managers have great power to dispose of the corporation and its assets. In particular, given the concern about manage rial asset stripping, it is surprising that the Company Law constraints on managerial self-dealing are as brief and vague as they are.[93]

Despite all the ambiguity and the retreat from some of the managerial rhetoric of the Enterprise Law, Yingyi Qian reports that managers are wildly enthusiastic about corporatization. The dominant popular connotation of corporate status is managerial independence. At least in the absence of a developed system for the exercise of the state's rights as majority shareholder, the monitoring provisions of the Company Law do not seem threatening. Another benefit of corporatization is to avoid constraints on wage levels and dispersion; the constraints do not apply to dividend payments.

The worker theme remains salient in the Company Law. Two sections of the Law require the company to "invite" or "heed" worker opinions, and to allow worker attendance at management meetings on issues of "immediate concern" to workers and "important issues relating to production and operation."[95] The Board of Supervisors must include an "appropriate" number of "democratically elected" worker representatives.[96] (The number is to be decided by promoters or shareholders.) This is a substantial step back from the German model which prescribes that half the supervisory positions must go to workers,[97] but most other Western countries prescribe no worker board representation at all.[98]

Membership. The membership theme survives explicitly in the Company Law principally in the requirement—foreign to American and German law—that a company set

93. The Law forbids directors and managers to "use their positions and powers in the company to seek personal gains" and to "sign contracts or conduct transactions with the company." Company Law, *supra* note 79, Arts. 123, 61. These provisions could be interpreted to forbid all conflict-of-interest transactions, but it seems more likely that they will be construed to permit transactions that are fair and provide benefits to the corporation, even if managers benefit too, so long as managers do not contract in purely personal capacities with the corporation (as opposed to through affiliated entities or relatives). If the latter interpretation is likely, then a plausible procedural safeguard would have been a provision requiring conflict-of-interest transactions to be ratified by independent directors or shareholders.

95. Company Law, *supra* note 79, Arts. 121–22.

96. *Id.* Art. 124. Somewhat different norms apply to companies that are wholly state-owned and to limited liability companies (the presumptively smaller type of corporation with less readily transferable shares) formed wholly or "primarily" by state-owned investors. First, these companies must practice "democratic management." *Id.* Art. 16. Though the meaning of the term is far from clear, it could be construed to require a more ambitious measure of worker participation than the consultation procedures mandated for limited liability stock companies. Second, these companies must include elected worker representatives on their boards of directors. (These companies need not have supervisory boards.)

97. The German requirement of one-half worker members applies to companies with more than 2,000 employees; in companies with more than 500 but fewer than 2,000, a third of the supervisory seats go to employees. Horn et al., *supra* note 83, at 277.

98. *See, e.g.*, Terence L. Blackburn, *The Societas Europea: The Evolving European Corporation Statute*, 61 FORDHAM L. REV. 695, 749 (1993) (noting that of EC states, only Germany and Netherlands require employee board representation).

aside five to ten percent of its profits in a "common welfare fund" to be used for "collective welfare programs of the company's workers."[99] As mentioned above, the 1994 Labor Law provides for tenure, but only after ten years of employment.

In fact, SOEs continue to be encompassing communities with a reduced but substantial range of collective cultural and consumption responsibilities. Nevertheless, there is a trend, particularly in SOEs converting to stock companies, to try to spin off housing and other consumption activities into separate organizations. These separate organizations operate on a fee-for-service basis.

One aspect of corporatization that bears on the membership theme is worker shareholding. Together with managers, workers hold substantial blocks in most corporatized enterprises. In some respects, the shareholder relation is the opposite of the membership relation. Corporate shares are typically individual financial interests that can be traded like commodities. However, worker shares in corporatized SOEs function a little differently. They typically cannot be sold outside the enterprise and have to be relinquished on departure. The reformers see their purpose as to counter worker pressures for short-term income distribution by giving them a capital stake designed to reflect long-term enterprise performance.[100] On the other hand, shareholding weakens norms of internal egalitarianism reflected in the constraints on wage dispersion since shares and dividends are typically distributed much more unequally than wages.

Reinvestment. The reinvestment constraints of the Company Law are much weaker than under the Enterprise Law, but they remain stronger than the Western counterparts. As under the Western models, amounts paid for the company's stock become the measure of its "registered capital," and distributions to shareholders that would reduce its assets below this sum are prohibited. In addition, the company is obliged to contribute ten percent of its profits annually to a reserve fund until the fund equals fifty percent of its registered capital, and distributions that would impair the reserve fund are also prohibited.[101] The company can invest in other companies, but such outside investments are not supposed to exceed fifty percent of its net assets.[102] In the West, the reserve fund is understood as a safeguard for creditors rather than a commitment by owners to develop the enterprise. Nevertheless, the unusually demanding requirement of the Company Law may partly reflect a commitment to internal reinvestment as desirable in itself.

---

99. Company Law, *supra* note 79, Arts. 177, 180.

100. A significant step away from the membership theme is the Company Law's rejection of "enterprise shares." Some commentators had urged that major blocks of stock in corporatized shares should be held by the enterprise itself in its corporate capacity. Some pre-Company Law corporatization experiments had involved this, and two commentators suggested that the "enterprise shares" were "the essential difference between the system of shares in China and stock corporations in the West." Gu Peidong & Liu Xirong, *Study on Turning State-Owned Enterprises into Stock Companies*, 9 Soc. Sci. China 25, 36–40 (1988). To Western lawyers the notion of "enterprise shares" begs the question of who within the enterprise is to have the financial and control rights of the shares and invites confusion and sharp practice. Thus, Western codes typically forbid voting or distributions on shares held by the issuing enterprise. However, the appeal of enterprise shares to some of the commentators might be interpreted as a desire to preserve a larger role for more informal and collective modes of decision-making and distribution. The Company Law rejects such ideas by providing that the corporation cannot issue stock to itself and must cancel repurchased shares. Company Law, *supra* note 79, Art. 149.

101. Id. Art. 177. In Germany, the reserve fund need be only 10% of basic capital. 57 Aktiengesetz I (1965) (F.R.G.); Horn et al., *supra* note 83, at 268.

102. Company Law, *supra* note 79, Art. 12.

Howard Gensler, *Company Formation and Securities Listing in the People's Republic of China*

17 Hous. J. Int'l L. 399 (1995)

(excerpts pages 401–427; some footnotes omitted)

II. IN GENERAL

There are three types of companies: companies with limited liability (limited companies), limited stock-companies (stock companies), and companies wholly owned by the state (state companies).[6] A limited company is the smaller of the three.[7] The new law is also applicable to enterprises with foreign investment.[8] Companies and enterprises have a limited amount of time to comply with the law.[9]

III. LIMITED COMPANIES

A. Formation

To form a limited company in China, several steps must be taken. First, two to fifty stockholders must contribute capital.[10] Second, the stockholders must draft the company constitution.[11] Finally, the company must establish permanent residence.[12]

The company constitution must provide: (i) the name of the company; (ii) the residence of the company; (iii) the business scope; (iv) the amount of registered capital; (v) the names of the stockholders; (vi) the rights and responsibilities of the stockholders; (vii) the amount and form of stockholders' capital contributions; (viii) the company procedures for formation and operation; (ix) the company's powers and rights; (x) the identity of the legal representative; (xi) the dissolution and liquidation procedures;[13] (xii) the procedural rules for conducting stockholders' meetings and voting;[14] (xiii) the regular (periodic) stockholders' meetings;[15] (xiv) the procedures for selecting the chair and vice-chair(s) of the board of directors;[16] (xv) the term for members of the board of directors (not to exceed three years);[17] (xvi) the proportion of members of the board of supervisors representing stockholders and employees;[18] and (xvii) the procedural rules

---

6. [Company Law (P.R.C.) (Howard Gensler, trans.) (manuscript on file with the author) (hereinafter Co. L.).], Arts. 19–128 (discussing the establishment and organization of limited companies, stock companies, and state companies).

7. One may think of limited companies as closely held corporations, and stock companies as general corporations, though the analogy is only illustrative for comparison purposes in a gross sense.

8. Co. L., *supra* note [6], Art. 18.

9. *Id.* Arts. 21 & 229. The amount of time is not specified. Detailed regulations will be issued subsequently. *Id.* Art. 229.

10. *Id.* Art. 20.

11. *Id.* Art. 19(3).

12. *Id.* Art. 19(5).

13. *Id.* Art. 22.

14. *Id.* Art. 39.

15. *Id.* Art. 43.

16. *Id.* Art. 45.

17. *Id.* Art. 47.

18. *Id.* Art. 52.

for conducting meetings of the board of directors and voting.[19] The company constitution must also be signed and sealed by the stockholders.[20]

The registered capital of the company is the amount of capital actually contributed by the stockholders. The registered capital must be reported to the Registrar of Companies.[21] The minimum amount of capital required to form a company depends upon the industry: (i) the manufacturing industry requires 500,000 yuan Renminbi (RMB); (ii) the wholesale industry requires 500,000 RMB; (iii) the retail industry requires 300,000 RMB; and (iv) the technological development, consultation, and services industries require 100,000 RMB.[22]

If an industry requires higher minimum amounts, such amounts shall be established in separate regulations.[23] Capital contributions may be in cash or in kind.[24] The value of assets must be verified.[25] In the case of land, an appraisal must be obtained pursuant to regulations.[26] The value of industrial property rights and nonpatented technology contributed cannot exceed twenty percent of the registered capital unless an exception for high technology has been made by the state.[27] Cash contributions should be paid in full in accordance with the company constitution.[28] Contributions made prior to the formation of the company should be deposited in the temporary bank account for the company under formation.[29] Contributions in kind should be transferred pursuant to the law.[30] Stockholders who fail to make declared contributions are liable for the full amount.[31] After the shareholders' capital contributions are made in full, a legal appraisal institution should appraise the assets and issue a certificate.[32]

Once the appraisal has been obtained, a representative of the stockholders may apply to the Registrar of Companies for a company registration and business license.[33] The following documents must be submitted: (i) the application for registration of a company; (ii) the company constitution; (iii) the certificate of appraisal; and (iv) any necessary governmental approvals.[34]

After the company has been established, share certificates should be issued to the stockholders.[35] Share certificates should set forth the following: (i) the name of the company; (ii) the registration date of the company; (iii) the registered capital of the company; and (iv) individual stockholder information.[36]

Share certificates must bear the company seal.[37] A stockholder's register must be maintained by the company, recording the name and address of each stockholder, the

19. *Id.* Art. 49.
20. *Id.* Art. 22.
21. *Id.* Art. 23.
22. *Id.* Art. 23(1)-(4).
23. *Id.* Art. 23.
24. *Id.* Art. 24.
25. *Id.*
26. *Id.* Art. 26.
27. *Id.*
28. *Id.* Art. 25.
29. *Id.*
30. *Id.*
31. *Id.*
32. *Id.* Art. 27.
33. *Id.*
34. *Id.*
35. *Id.* Art. 30.
36. *Id.*
37. *Id.*

amount of each stockholder's capital contribution, and the number of share certificates issued to each stockholder.[38]

If the actual value of the capital contributed by any shareholder has been found to be overstated after the company has been established, the shareholder who made the deficient contribution must make up the difference.[39] Other stockholders who similarly subscribed in the establishment process are jointly liable.[40] Once the company is registered, stockholders may not withdraw their capital contribution.[41]

B. Branch Businesses

A company may apply for the establishment of branch businesses at the same time it is applying for its own establishment.[42] Application must be made to the Registrar of Companies for establishment, and a business license must be obtained for each branch business.[43] If the company has already been established, the application may be made by the company's legal representative.[44]

C. Shareholder's Rights

Stockholders have the following rights: (i) the right to inspect the minutes of the stockholders' meetings;[45] (ii) the right to inspect the company accounting reports;[46] (iii) the right to share in profits in proportion to their capital contribution;[47] (iv) the right to transfer shares to another stockholder;[48] (v) the right to purchase any shares offered by a shareholder to an outsider on the same terms as the offer to the outsider;[49] (vi) the right to attend the stockholders' meeting;[50] (vii) the right to vote in proportion to shareholdings;[51] and (viii) the right to receive fifteen days advance notice of stockholders' meetings.[52] In addition, the company may grant stockholders a preemptive right to new issuances of stock.[53]

D. Stockholders' Meeting

The following fundamental company decisions are made by the stockholders at the stockholders' meeting: (i) the structure of investment plans and management strategies; (ii) the election of members to the board of directors; (iii) the removal of members from the board of directors; (iv) the determination of compensation for directors; (v) the election of members to the board of supervisors; (vi) the removal of members from the board of supervisors; (vii) the determination of compensation for supervisors; (viii)

---

38. *Id.* Art. 31.
39. *Id.* Art. 28.
40. *Id.*
41. *Id.* Art. 34.
42. *Id.* Art. 29.
43. *Id.*
44. *Id.*
45. *Id.* Art. 32.
46. *Id.*
47. *Id.* Art. 33.
48. *Id.* Art. 35.
49. *Id.*
50. *Id.* Art. 37.
51. *Id.* Art. 41.
52. *Id.* Art. 44.
53. *Id.* Art. 33.

the examination and approval reports from the board of directors; (ix) the examination and approval of reports from the board of supervisors; (x) the examination and approval of the budget; (xi) the examination and approval of the accounts; (xii) the examination and approval of the dividend distribution plan; (xiii) the examination and approval of the plan to make up any deficit; (xiv) the approval of any resolution to change the amount of registered capital; (xv) the approval of any resolution to issue bonds;[54] (xvi) the approval of the transfer of stock to outsiders;[55] (xvii) the approval of a change of form in the company, including mergers, separations (spin off or split-up), dissolution, or clearance of debt or liquidation; and (xviii) the amendment of the company constitution.[56]

The first stockholders' meeting shall be presided over by the stockholder with the most shares. Subsequent stockholders' meetings will be convened by the board of directors, and presided over by the chairman of the board, or the vice-chair, or other designated director in the absence of the chairman.[57] Minutes of the stockholders' meeting must be kept and must record the adoption of any resolution.[58] Resolutions to change the amount of registered capital, change the form of the company, or amend the company constitution must be passed by a two-thirds majority vote.[59] All stockholders who attended the meeting should sign the minutes.[60]

A special stockholders' meeting may be called by stockholders holding one-fourth of the voting stock, one-third of the directors, or one-third of the supervisors.[61]

E. Board of Directors

A limited company in the PRC must have a board of directors with three to thirteen members.[62] Where a company is small or has only a few stockholders, the company may have one executive director who may serve concurrently as manager.[63] If the company has been formed by two or more state-owned enterprises,[64] at least one member must be elected by and from the employees.[65] The board of directors must have a chair who will be the legal representative of the company and may have up to two vice-chairs.[66] The board of directors has the following rights and duties: (i) calling stockholders' meetings; (ii) reporting on the performance of the company; (iii) determining the budget; (iv) determining the investment plan; (v) drafting the dividend distribution plan; (vi) drafting the plan to satisfy any budget deficit; (vii) drafting the plan to change the registered capital; (viii) drafting the plan for a change in the company form; (ix) determining the company's management structure; (x) appointing and removing the manager; (xi) appointing and removing the vice-manager and chief financial officer; (xii)

---

54. *Id.* Art. 38.
55. However, stockholders who vote against such transfer must be willing to purchase the stock or else they will be deemed to have voted in favor. *Id.* Art. 35.
56. *Id.* Art. 38.
57. *Id.* Art. 43.
58. *Id.* Art. 44.
59. *Id.* Art. 39.
60. *Id.* Art. 44.
61. *Id.* Arts. 43, 54.
62. *Id.* Art. 45.
63. *Id.* Art. 51.
64. This includes investment companies. *Id.* Art. 45.
65. *Id.*
66. *Id.*

the right to receive ten days advance notice of board meetings;[67] and (xiii) setting the compensation of the manager, the vice-manager, and the chief financial officer.[68]

Directors may be re-elected to subsequent terms.[69] Directors may not be dismissed by the stockholders without cause.[70] The meetings of the board of directors are called and presided over by the chair of the board of directors, or the vice-chair or another designated director in the absence of the chairman.[71] A meeting of the board of directors may be called by a proposal supported by at least one-third of the members of the board of directors.[72] Minutes of board meetings should record all resolutions passed by the board, and should be signed by those board members in attendance.[73] Whenever a matter of employee welfare is examined, opinions of the employees should be solicited, and representatives of the employees (or the union) should attend the meeting as nonvoting delegates.[74] Whenever a matter of operation is examined, or important rules are being formulated, opinions of the employees should be solicited.[75]

F. General Manager

The general manager (manager) reports to the board of directors.[76] The manager: (i) leads and controls the administration; (ii) implements resolutions of the board of directors; (iii) implements the budget; (iv) implements the investment plan; (v) organizes the management structure; (vi) formulates company regulations; (vii) nominates the vice-manager and chief financial officer; (viii) recommends the removal of the vice-manager and chief financial officer; (ix) hires and fires other management personnel; and (x) has any other power granted by the company constitution or the board of directors.[77]

G. Board of Supervisors

Large companies shall establish a board of supervisors consisting of at least three members.[78] Small companies (few stockholders) may establish a board of supervisors with less than three members.[79] The members shall elect one of them to be the convenor.[80] The members shall represent the stockholders and the employees in a proportion established by the company constitution.[81] The employee representative(s) must be elected by and from the employees.[82] Current directors, the manager, and the chief financial officer are ineligible to serve on the board of supervisors.[83] Supervisors serve

67. *Id.* Art. 49.
68. *Id.* Art. 46.
69. *Id.* Art. 46.
70. *Id.* Art. 47.
71. *Id.*
72. *Id.* Art. 48.
73. *Id.*
74. *Id.* Art. 49.
75. *Id.* Art. 55.
76. *Id.* Art. 56.
77. *Id.* Art. 50.
78. *Id.*
79. *Id.* Art. 52.
80. *Id.*
81. *Id.*
82. *Id.*
83. *Id.*

three-year terms and may be re-elected.[84] The board of supervisors: (i) examines financial records; (ii) oversees the propriety of the manager's activities; (iii) oversees the propriety of the board of directors' activities; (iv) directs that action taken by the board of directors or the manager which harms the company be corrected; (v) convenes a stockholders' meeting; and (vi) has other rights and duties as provided in the company constitution.[85]

H. Disqualification from Office

The following conditions disqualify a person from holding the position of manager, director, or supervisor: (i) mental impairment; (ii) a conviction within five years of graft, bribery, theft, embezzlement, crimes against the social economic order, and crimes resulting in the deprivation of political rights; (iii) the bankruptcy of a company within three years due to such individual's poor management;[86] (iv) the loss of a business license within three years; or (v) the failure to make timely payment of substantial debts.[87]

If any of these conditions has occurred, the appointment of any such person is void.[88] No current government official may serve as director, supervisor, or manager.[89]

I. General Fiduciary Duties

The directors, supervisors, and manager must: (i) observe the company constitution; (ii) perform all duties faithfully; and (iii) protect the interests of the company.[90]

The directors, supervisors, and manager shall not: (i) personally profit from exploitation of the position held with the company; (ii) accept any bribe; (iii) steal or embezzle;[91] or (iv) deal with the company.[92]

The directors and manager shall not: (i) lend company funds;[93] (ii) deposit any assets of the company into a personal account of their own or another's; (iii) use the company assets to guarantee any individual's debt;[94] (iv) operate a competitive business for themselves or others;[95] (v) engage in any activity harmful to the interests of the company;[96] or (vi) reveal any confidence of the company.[97] Any manager, director, or supervisor who violates any law, regulation, or provision of the company constitution in the execution of a duty to the company is liable for all resulting damage to the company.[98]

---

84. *Id.* Art. 53.
85. *Id.* Art. 54.
86. The three-year period is counted from the date of revocation of the company's business license. *Id.* Art. 57(3).
87. *Id.* Art. 57.
88. *Id.*
89. *Id.* Art. 58.
90. *Id.* Art. 59.
91. *Id.*
92. The managers may not do so unless allowed by the company constitution or agreed on by the stockholders at a meeting. *Id.* Art. 61.
93. *Id.* Art. 60.
94. *Id.*
95. In such case, the income shall be forfeited to the company. *Id.* Art. 61.
96. *Id.*
97. *Id.* Art. 62.
98. *Id.* Art. 63.

IV. STATE COMPANIES

A state company is a limited liability company established under the CL by a governmental department or organization authorized to make investments.[99] Such a public body is known as the founder of the state company. The companies in certain special industries using this form of organization must be solely owned by the state.[100]

A. Formation

A state company is formed as follows: (i) the founder provides the capital;[101] (ii) the founder or the board of director drafts the company constitution and submits it to the founder for approval;[102] and (iii) the company establishes a permanent residence.[103]

The company constitution must provide: (i) the name of the company; (ii) the residence of the company; (iii) the business scope; (iv) the registered capital; (v) the names of the founders; (vi) the rights and responsibilities of the founder; (vii) the amount and form of the founder's capital contributions; (viii) company procedures for formation and operation; (ix) company powers and rights; (x) the identity of the legal representative; (xi) dissolution and liquidation procedures;[104] (xii) procedures for selecting the chair and vice-chair(s) of the board of directors;[105] (xiii) the term for members of the board of directors (not to exceed three years);[106] (xiv) the number of members of the board of supervisors representing employees;[107] and (xv) procedural rules for conducting meetings of the board of directors and voting.[108] The company constitution must also be signed and sealed by the founder.[109]

B. Board of Directors

A state company must have a board of directors with three to nine members.[110] Where the company has been formed by two or more state-owned enterprises,[111] at least one member must be elected by and from the employees.[112] The board of directors may appoint a chair, who shall be the legal representative of the company, and one or more vice-chairs.[113] The board of directors of the state company has the following rights and duties:[114] (i) reporting on the performance of the company; (ii) determining the budget; (iii) determining the investment plan; (iv) drafting the dividend distribution plan; (v) drafting the plan to satisfy any budget deficit; (vi) drafting the plan to change the registered capital; (vii) drafting the plan for a change in the company form; (viii) determining the company's management structure; (ix) appointing and removing the manager;

---

99. *Id.* Art. 64.
100. *Id.* Arts. 20, 21, 64 (referring to companies that produce special products or belonging to industries regulated by the State Council).
101. *See Id.* Arts. 64, 71.
102. *Id.* Art. 65.
103. *Id.* Art. 19.
104. *Id.* Art. 22.
105. *Id.* Art. 45.
106. *Id.* Art. 47.
107. *Id.* Art. 52.
108. *Id.* Art. 49.
109. *See Id.* Arts. 22, 65, 66.
110. *Id.* Art. 68.
111. This includes investment companies. *Id.* Art. 45.
112. *Id.* Art. 45.
113. *Id.* Art. 68.
114. *See Id.* Arts. 45, 46, 66, 68.

(x) appointing and removing the vice-manager and chief financial officer; (xi) the right to receive ten days advance notice of board meetings,[115] subject to the the manager's recommendation; and (xii) setting the compensation of the manager, the vice-manager, and the chief financial officer.[116]

Directors may be re-elected to subsequent terms.[117] The meetings of the board of directors are called and presided over by the chair of the board of directors, the vice chair or other designated director in the absence of the chairman.[118] A meeting of the board of directors may be called by a proposal supported by at least one-third of the members of the board of directors.[119] Minutes of board meetings should record all resolutions passed by the board, and should be signed by those board members in attendance.[120] Whenever a matter of employee welfare is examined, opinions of the employees should be solicited, and representatives of the employees (or the union) should attend the meeting as nonvoting delegates.[121] Opinions of the employees should also be solicited whenever a matter of operation is examined, or important rules are being formulated.[122]

A state company does not hold stockholder meetings.[123] The following fundamental company decisions may be delegated to the board of directors by the founder: (i) determination of investment plans; (ii) determination of management strategies; (iii) examination and approval of the budget; (iv) examination and approval of the accounts; and (v) proposal of amendments to the company constitution.[124]

The following fundamental company decisions are made by the founder: (i) administration of the state-owned assets;[125] (ii) selection of members to the board of directors; (iii) removal of members from the board of directors; (iv) determination of compensation for directors; (v) examination and approval of reports from the board of directors; (vi) examination and approval of the budget; (vii) examination and approval of the accounts; (viii) examination and approval of the dividend distribution plan; (ix) examination and approval of the plan to make up any deficit; (x) approval of any resolution to change the amount of registered capital; (xi) approval of any resolution to issue bonds;[126] (xii) approval of the transfer of state assets;[127] (xii) determination of the procedures for the transfer of state assets;[128] (xiii) approval of a change of form in the company;[129] and (xiv) amendment of the company constitution.[130] Large state companies with appropriate management systems and operating conditions may exercise full ownership powers over assets upon State Council authorization.[131]

115. *Id.* Art. 49.
116. *Id.* Art. 46.
117. *Id.* Art. 47.
118. *Id.* Art. 48.
119. *Id.*
120. *Id.* Art. 49.
121. *Id.* Art. 55.
122. *Id.* Art. 56.
123. *Id.* Art. 66.
124. *See id.* Arts. 38, 66.
125. *Id.* Art. 67.
126. *Id.* Arts. 38, 66.
127. *Id.* Art. 71.
128. *Id.*
129. *Id.* Arts. 38, 66.
130. *Id.*
131. *Id.* Art. 72.

C. General Manager

State companies employ managers, who may serve concurrently as directors.[132] The manager reports to the board of directors.[133] The manager: (i) leads and controls the administration; (ii) implements resolutions of the board of directors; (iii) implements the budget; (iv) implements the investment plan; (v) organizes the management structure; (vi) formulates company regulations; (vii) nominates the vice-manager and chief financial officer; (viii) recommends the removal of the vice-manager and chief financial officer; (ix) hires and fires other management personnel; and (x) has any other power granted by the company constitution or the board of directors.[134]

D. Disqualification from Office

The following conditions disqualify a person from holding the position of manager or director: (i) mental impairment; (ii) a conviction within five years of graft, bribery, theft, embezzlement, crimes against the social economic order, and crimes resulting in the deprivation of political rights; (iii) the bankruptcy of a company within three years due to such individual's poor management;[135] (iv) the loss of a business license within three years; or (v) the failure to make timely payment of substantial debts.[136] If any of these conditions has occurred the appointment of any such person is void.[137] No current government official may serve as director, supervisor, or manager.[138]

E.General Fiduciary Duties

The directors and managers shall: (i) observe the company constitution; (ii) perform all duties faithfully; and (iii) protect the interests of the company.[139]

The directors and managers shall not: (i) personally profit from exploitation of the position held with the company; (ii) accept any bribe; (iii) steal or embezzle;[140] (iv) deal with the company;[141] (v) lend company funds;[142] (vi) deposit any assets of the company into a personal account of their own or another's; (v) use the company assets to guarantee any individual's debt;[143] (vi) operate a competitive business for themselves or others;[144] (vii) engage in any activity harmful to the interests of the company;[145] or (viii) reveal any confidence of the company.[146]

Any manager or director who violates any law, regulation, or provision of the company constitution in the execution of a duty to the company is liable for all resulting

---

132. *Id.* Art. 69.
133. *Id.* Arts. 50, 69.
134. *Id.*
135. The three-year period is counted from the date of revocation of the company's business license. *Id.* Art. 57(3).
136. *Id.* Art. 57(5).
137. *Id.* Art. 57.
138. *Id.* Art. 58.
139. *Id.* Art. 59.
140. *Id.*
141. Unless allowed by the founder. *See Id.* Arts. 61, 69, 70.
142. *Id.* Art. 60.
143. *Id.*
144. In such case, the income shall be forfeited to the company. *Id.* Art. 61.
145. *Id.* Art. 61.
146. *Id.* Art. 62.

damage to the company.[147] No manager, director, chair, or vice-chair may hold a management or fiduciary position in another company without permission from the founder.[148]

V. LIMITED STOCK-COMPANIES

A. Formation

A stock company is formed as follows: (i) the minimum amount of capital is fully subscribed; (ii) the company is organized at a stockholders' meeting; (iii) the issuance of stock conforms to the regulations; (iv) the company formation conforms to the regulations; (v) the initiators draft the company constitution; (vi) the company has an appropriate name; (vii) the company has an appropriate organization; (viii) the company has established a permanent residence; (ix) the company has adequate resources to begin operation;[149] (x) the board of directors applies to the Registrar of Companies for registration of the company by submitting the appropriate documents;[150] and (xi) appropriate governmental approval is given.[151]

The application for registration must be made within thirty days of the stockholders' meeting.[152] The approval of the application must be issued within thirty days of receipt of the application.[153] The date of the issuance of the business license is the date of the establishment of the company.[154] An announcement of the establishment of the company should then be published.[155] If stock was sold to the public, a report must be filed with the securities administration department.[156]

Initiators are the initial investors who organize the limited stock company.[157] There must be at least five initiators, more than half of which reside in China.[158] Where a state-owned enterprise is being converted to a stock company, there may be less than five initiators.[159]

A subscription is the initial agreement to purchase stock in the company.[160] A public sale is the actual purchase of stock.[161] The registered capital is the total amount of capital actually contributed to the company and registered at the Registrar of Companies.[162] The minimum amount of registered capital for a stock company is 10,000,000 RMB. This minimum amount may be increased by the states for special cases.[163] Initiators may make capital contributions in cash or in kind.[164] The value of assets must be verified, and must

147. *Id.* Art. 63.
148. *Id.* Art. 70.
149. *Id.* Art. 73.
150. *Id.* Arts. 82, 94.
151. *Id.* Art. 77.
152. *Id.* Art. 94.
153. *Id.* Art. 95.
154. *Id.* Art. 95.
155. *Id.*
156. *Id.*
157. *Id.* Arts. 74, 76.
158. *Id.* Art. 75.
159. *Id.*
160. *Id.* Art. 74.
161. *Id.*
162. *Id.* Art. 78.
163. *Id.*
164. *Id.* Art. 80.

be neither overvalued nor undervalued. In the case of land, an appraisal must be obtained pursuant to regulations.[165] The contributed value of industrial property rights and nonpatented technology cannot exceed twenty percent of the registered capital.[166] It is strictly forbidden to undervalue the assets of a state-owned enterprise, or to sell such assets at below their fair market value.[167] An underwriter must be retained to manage the offering.[168] A bank must be retained to receive subscription payments. The bank should issue receipts to subscribers and account statements to appropriate parties.[169]

Subscriptions must be paid up in full once the minimum capitalization requirements of the company established in the company constitution have been met by sales and subscriptions.[170] In kind assets are to be transferred pursuant to law.[171] Once all amounts owed under the subscription agreements have been paid, assets must be appraised by an authorized appraiser who issues a certificate. A stockholders' meeting must then be convened within thirty days or subscribers may obtain a refund with interest.[172] Subscribers must be given fifteen days advance notice of the meeting. Over half of the value of the stock must be represented at the meeting.[173]

The stockholders' meeting is conducted in the following order: (i) a quorum of stockholders is present and votes;[174] (ii) the initiators' company preparation report is examined;[175] (iii) the company constitution is adopted;[176] (iv) the board of directors is elected;[177] (v) the board of supervisors is elected;[178] and (vi) the expenditure accounts are prepared and examined.[179] Alternatively, the stockholders may resolve not to establish the company because of significant unanticipated changes adversely affecting the company have occurred.[180]

The company constitution must provide: (i) the name of the company; (ii) the residence of the company; (iii) the business scope; (iv) the registered capital; (v) the total number of shares of stock and the par value; (vi) the names of the initiators and the number of shares subscribed to by each; (vii) the rights and responsibilities of the stockholders; (viii) the authority, tenure, and procedures of the board of directors and board of supervisors; (ix) the legal representative of the company; (x) the profit distribution provisions; (xi) the dissolution and liquidation procedures; (xii) the procedural rules for sending notices; and (xiii) for any other matters decided by the stockholders.[181]

Initiators must purchase at least thirty-five percent of the stock if stock is sold to the public.[182] Approval to sell stock publicly must be obtained from the securities adminis-

165. *Id.*
166. *Id.*
167. *Id.* Art. 81.
168. *Id.* Art. 89.
169. *Id.* Art. 90.
170. *Id.* Art. 82.
171. *Id.*
172. *Id.* Arts. 91, 93.
173. *Id.* Art. 92.
174. *Id.* Art. 73.
175. *Id.* Art. 92.
176. *Id.* Arts. 73, 92.
177. *Id.* Arts. 82, 92.
178. *Id.*
179. *Id.* Art. 92.
180. *Id.*
181. *Id.* Art. 79
182. *Id.* Art. 83.

tration department of the State Council.[183] The application to sell stock to the public must include the following documents: (i) the company registration; (ii) the company constitution; (iii) a projected budget; (iv) initiator information;[184] (v) a certificate of appraisal; (vi) a prospectus; (vii) the name and address of the bank where stock purchase payments are to be made; (viii) the name of the underwriter; and (ix) the underwriter agreements.[185]

If any material condition is misrepresented in the application documents, approval to issue stock will be denied or revoked[186] and stock purchasers may obtain a refund with interest from the initiators.[187] Stock may be sold outside of China pursuant to detailed regulations to be issued.[188]

The company constitution and the prospectus must be given to prospective stock purchasers. The prospectus must state:[189] (i) the subscription amount of the initiators; (ii) par value; (iii) the issue price; (iv) the total issuance of nonregistered stock; (v) subscriber rights and duties; and (vi) the fundraising term.[190]

The initiators must prepare the letter of subscription for subscribers to use in purchasing stock.[191] The letter must restate the main points of the prospectus, as well as advise the purchaser of the prospectus. The subscriber shall enter the number of shares desired, the purchase price, and the subscriber's address. The subscriber shall then sign and seal the letter. Shares so subscribed must be paid for.[192]

If the issuance is not sold out by the ending date of the fundraising period, the subscribers may rescind their subscriptions.[193] In the event that the establishment process is not completed, the debts and expenses incurred are to be borne by the initiators.[194] The initiators are liable for return of stock purchase money paid with interest. If the establishment process damages the company's interests in any way, the initiators are liable.[195]

A limited company may reorganize itself as a stock company by completing the relevant procedures.[196] The amount of stock converted should equal the net assets of the company. New stock sales to the public to raise new capital should follow the procedures for public stock sales.[197] The debts and obligations of the limited company that reorganizes as a stock company are assumed by the new company.[198]

183. *Id.* Art. 84.
184. *Id.* Art. 84(4) (including names, amount of stock, form of capital payment, and certificate of appraisal).
185. *Id.* Art. 84.
186. *Id.* Art. 86.
187. *Id.*
188. *Id.* Art. 85.
189. *Id.* Art. 87.
190. *Id.*
191. *Id.* Art. 88.
192. *Id.*
193. *Id.* Arts. 87, 93.
194. *Id.* Art. 97(1).
195. *Id.* Art. 97(2).
196. *Id.* Art. 98.
197. *Id.* Art. 99.
198. *Id.* Art. 100.

A stock company must maintain the following company documents:[199] (i) a company constitution; (ii) minutes of stockholders' meetings; (iii) stockholders' register; and (iv) accounting reports.[200]

B.Branch Businesses

A stock company may apply for the establishment of branch businesses[201] at the same time it is applying for its own establishment.[202] Application must be made to the Registrar of Companies for establishment, and a business license for each branch business must be obtained.[203] If the company has already been established, the application may be made by the company's legal representative.[204]

C.The General Meeting of the Stockholders

The following fundamental company decisions are made by the stockholders at the stockholders' meeting: (i) the structure of investment plans and management strategies; (ii) the election of members to the board of directors; (iii) the removal of members from the board of directors; (iv) the determination of compensation for directors; (v) the election of members to the board of supervisors; (vi) the removal of members from the board of supervisors; (vii) the determination of compensation for supervisors; (viii) the examination and approval of reports from the board of directors; (ix) the examination and approval of reports from the board of supervisors; (x) the examination and approval of the budget; (xi) the examination and approval of the accounts; (xii) the examination and approval of the dividend distribution plan; (xiii) the examination and approval of the plan to make up any deficit; (xiv) the approval of any resolution to change the amount of registered capital; (xv) the approval of any resolution to issue bonds;[205] (xvi) the approval of the transfer of stock to outsiders;[206] (xvii) the approval of a change of form in the company, including mergers, separations (spin off or split-up), dissolution, or clearance of debt or liquidation; and (xviii) the amendment of the company constitution.

The general meeting of the stockholders is held annually.[207] A provisional general meeting of the stockholders shall be held within two months of the following: (i) the number of members of the board of directors falls below the number set forth in the CL, or less than two-thirds the number in the company constitution; (ii) the deficit reaches one-third of the amount of the capital stock; (iii) stockholders holding ten percent of the stock request; (iv) the board of directors considers it necessary; and (v) the board of supervisors proposes a meeting.[209]

General stockholders' meetings will be convened by the board of directors, and presided over by the chair of the board, the vice chair, or another designated director in the absence of the chair.[210] Stockholders are to be notified of the agenda of the meeting

---

199. *Id.* Art. 101.
200. *Id.*
201. *Id.* Art. 96.
202. *Id.*
203. *Id.*
204. *Id.*
205. *Id.* Art. 38(9).
206. However, stockholders who vote against such transfer must be willing to purchase the stock or else they will be deemed to have voted in favor. *Id.* Art. 35.
207. *Id.*
209. *Id.* Art. 104(5).
210. *Id.* Art. 43.

thirty days in advance. Holders of nonregistered stock who will attend the meeting must deposit their stock with the company five days before the meeting until the conclusion of the meeting.[211] Stockholders who attend the meeting have one vote per share.[212] Stockholders may vote by proxy by giving a letter of authorization to the company.[213] Resolutions may be passed with a simple majority vote, except for resolutions on a change of company form, liquidation, or amendments to the company constitution[214] which require a two-thirds majority vote.[215]

Minutes of the stockholders' meeting must be kept recording discussions on all matters.[216] All directors who attended the meeting should sign the minutes.[217] The stockholders who attend should sign an attendance register. Proxies and minutes of the meeting should be maintained with the register.[218]

Stockholders have the right to inspect the books, company constitution, minutes, financial reports and accounts, make suggestions, and pose questions.[219] Stockholders may bring legal action to terminate any action by the stockholders or board of directors which is illegal or violates the rights of stockholders.[220]

D. Board of Directors

A limited stock company must have a board of directors with five to nineteen members.[221] The director's term shall be set in the company constitution, but shall not exceed three years. Directors may be re-elected.[222] The stockholders may not dismiss a director without cause.[223]

The board of directors must meet at least twice per year. Directors should be given at least ten days advance notice of a meeting. The procedures for convening a provisional meeting of the board of directors may be set separately.[224] A quorum for a board meeting is half the number of directors.[225] Resolutions may be adopted by a simple majority vote of the directors in attendance.[226] Directors should attend meetings personally or authorize another director in writing to vote with explicit instructions. The minutes of the meeting should record all resolutions, and be signed by each director who attended. Directors are liable for action taken that violates law or company policy unless such director dissented.[227]

The board of directors has the following rights and duties:[228] (i) convening the general meeting of the stockholders; (ii) reporting on the performance of the company;

211. *Id.* Art. 105.
212. *Id.* Art. 106.
213. *Id.* Art. 108.
214. *Id.* Arts. 106, 107.
215. *Id.*
216. *Id.* Art. 109.
217. *Id.*
218. *Id.*
219. *Id.* Art. 110.
220. *Id.* Art. 111.
221. *Id.* Art. 112.
222. *Id.* Art. 115.
223. *Id.*
224. *Id.* Art. 116.
225. *Id.* Art. 117.
226. *Id.*
227. *Id.* Art. 118.
228. *Id.* Art. 112.

(iii) determining the budget; (iv) determining financial plans; (v) determining investment plan; (vi) drafting the dividend distribution plan; (vii) drafting the plan to satisfy any budget deficit; (viii) drafting the plan to change the registered capital; (ix) drafting the plan for a change in the company form including a mergers, split up spin off, or liquidation; (x) determining the company's management structure; (xi) appoint and remove the manager; (xii) appointing and removing the vice-manager and chief financial officer on the manager's recommendation; and (xiii) setting the compensation of the manager, the vice-manager, and the chief financial officer.

E. The Chair of the Board of Directors

The board of directors may appoint a chair, who shall be the legal representative of the company, along with one or two vice-chairs.[230] The chair and vice-chair(s) must be elected by a majority of all directors. The chair is the legal representative of the company. The chair: (i) presides over the general stockholders' meeting; (ii) presides over the board of directors' meeting; (iii) examines the implementation of directors' resolutions; and (iv) signs company stocks and bonds.[233] The vice-chair(s) assist the chair. If the chair is unable to carry out any duty, a vice-chair or designated director will substitute. The board of directors may delegate part of their authority to the chair in appropriate situations.[234]

F. General Manager

A stock company employs a manager, who is appointed by the board of directors and may also be removed by the board of directors. The manager reports to the board.[236] The manager may serve concurrently as a member of the board of directors.[237] The manager: (i) leads and controls the administration; (ii) implements resolutions of the board of directors; (iii) implements the budget; (iv) implements the investment plan; (v) organizes the management structure; (vi) formulates company regulations; (vii) nominates the vice-manager and chief financial officer; (viii) recommends the removal of the vice-manager and chief financial officer; (xi) hires and fires other management personnel; and (xii) has any other power granted by the company constitution or the board of directors.[238] The manager attends the meetings of the board of directors as a nonvoting member.[239]

G. Board of Supervisors

A stock company shall establish a board of supervisors consisting of at least three members.[240] The members shall elect one of them to be the convenor. The members shall represent the stockholders and the employees in a proportion established by the company constitution. The employee representative(s) must be elected by and from the employees. Current directors, the manager, and the chief financial officer are ineligible to serve on the board of supervisors. Supervisors serve three year terms and may be reelected.[243] The procedures of the board shall be set in the company constitution.[244] The board of supervisors has the following rights and duties: (i) examining financial

230. *Id.* Art. 113.
233. *Id.* Art. 114.
234. *Id.* Art. 120.
236. *Id.* Art. 119.
237. *Id.* Art. 120.
238. *Id.* Art. 119.
239. *Id.*
240. *Id.* Art. 124.
243. *Id.* Art. 125.
244. *Id.* Art. 127.

records; (ii) overseeing the propriety of the manager's activities; (iii) overseeing the propriety of the board of director's activities; (v) directing that a harmful action taken by the board of directors or the manager be corrected; (vi) convening stockholders' meetings; (vii) attending the meetings of the board of directors as nonvoting members; and (viii) other rights and duties as provided in the company constitution.[245]

H. Disqualification from Office

The following conditions disqualify a person from holding the position of manager, director, or supervisor: (i) mental impairment; (ii) a conviction within five years of graft, bribery, theft, embezzlement, crimes against the social economic order, and crimes resulting in the deprivation of political rights; (iii) the bankruptcy of a company within three years due to such individual's poor management;[246] (iv) the loss of a business license within three years; or (v) the failure to make timely payment of substantial debts.[247] If any of these conditions has occurred the appointment of any such person is void.[248] No current government official may serve as director, supervisor, or manager.[249]

I. General Fiduciary Duties

The directors, supervisors, and manager shall observe the company constitution, perform all duties faithfully, and protect the interests of the company.[250]

The directors, supervisors, and manager shall not personally profit from exploitation of the position held with the company, accept any bribe, steal or embezzle, or deal with the company.[251]

The directors and manager shall not: (i) lend company funds; (ii) deposit any assets of the company into a personal account of their own or another's; (iii) use the company assets to guarantee any individual's debt; (iv) operate a competitive business for themselves or others;[252] (v) engage in any activity harmful to the interests of the company; or (vi) reveal any confidence of the company.[253]

Any manager, director, or supervisor who violates any law, regulation, or provision of the company constitution in the execution of a duty to the company is liable for all resulting damage to the company.[254]

J. Issuance of Stock

Openness, impartiality, and fairness are the guiding principles in the issuance of stock.[255] Each share of stock should be of equal value, and if sold at the same time, should be sold at the same price.[256] Stock may not be issued at below par value.[257] Stock

245. *Id.* Art. 126.
246. The three-year period is counted from the date of revocation of the company's business license. *Id.* Art. 57(3).
247. *Id.* Art. 57(5).
248. *Id.* Art. 57.
249. *Id.* Art. 58.
250. *Id.* Art. 123.
251. They may not do this unless the company constitution allows it, or it is agreed on by the stockholders at a meeting. *Id.*
252. In such case, the income shall be forfeited to the company. *Id.* Art. 61.
253. *Id.* Art. 123.
254. *Id.* Art. 123.
255. *Id.* Art. 130.
256. *Id.* Arts. 129, 130.
257. *Id.* Art. 131.

may be issued above par value with authorization from the securities administration department. Above par premiums must be included in the company capital accumulation fund.

Each stock certificate must state: (i) the company name; (ii) the company registration date; (iii) the category of stock; (iv) the par value; and (v) the number of shares and sequence number.[260] Each certificate of stock must be signed by the chair of the board of directors and sealed with the company seal.

Stock issued to initiators, the underwriter, or a legal entity should be registered stock. The holders of registered stock should be recorded on the stock. Stock issued to the public may be registered or nonregistered stock.[261] A stock register should be maintained for registered stock recording the following: (i) the stockholders' names and residences; (ii) the number of shares held by each stockholder; (iii) the sequence numbers of stock held by each shareholder; and (iv) the dates stocks were obtained.[262] For nonregistered stock, the company should record the amount of stock, issuance date, and sequence numbers.[263] Stock may not be issued until the company is registered. Once the company receives its registration, stock certificates should be delivered directly.

For a new issuance of stock, the following rules apply: (i) the previous issue must be fully subscribed; (ii) it must have been at least one year since the last issuance; (iii) the company must have earned profits in each of the last three years; (iv) the company must have been able to pay dividends for the last three years;[265] (v) there has been no false statement in any financial report of the company in the last three years; (vi) expected profits must at least meet the interest rate on bank deposits; [266] (vii) the stockholders must adopt a resolution providing the category of stock, the amount of stock assuming price, the start and end dates of the issuance period, the category and amount of new stock issued to former stockholders;[267] and (viii) the board of directors must apply to the government for approval. If public sales are to be made, the securities administration department must approve.[268] Upon approval of a public sale, the company prepares a prospectus, financial statements, supplementary statements, and a certificate of subscription.[269]

The company must then engage an underwriter.[270] Pricing of the issue should be determined by the profit history and capital accumulation record.[271] When the subscription is sold out, the records at the Registrar of Companies should be amended, and an announcement should be made.[272]

K. Transfer of Stock

Stock must be traded in an established securities exchange market.[273] Registered stock is transferred by endorsement. The company must record the purchaser's name in the

260. *Id.* Art. 132.
261. *Id.* Art. 133.
262. *Id.* Art. 134.
263. *Id.* Art. 134.
265. This does not apply to newly formed companies. *Id.*
266. *Id.* Art. 137.
267. *Id.* Art. 138.
268. *Id.* Art. 139.
269. *Id.* Art. 140.
270. *Id.*
271. *Id.* Art. 141.
272. *Id.* Art. 142.
273. *Id.* Art. 144.

stock register. No changes in the stock register are allowed within thirty days of a stockholders' meeting or within five days of the record date of a dividend distribution.[274]

Nonregistered stock is transferred on delivery through a securities exchange market.[275] Initiators may not transfer stock for three years from the registration date of the company.[276] Directors, supervisors, and managers may not transfer stock during their tenure in office.[277] The founder (of a state company) may transfer stock pursuant to regulations.[278]

If a company purchases its own stock, it must cancel such stock within ten days, reduce its capital accordingly, amend its registration, and make an announcement.[279] A company may not accept its own stock as security for a pledge. A company may not hold its own stock as treasury stock.

If registered stock is lost or stolen, the stockholder may petition the court to void the stock. The stockholder may then apply to the company for a reissuance.[281]

VI. THE LISTED COMPANY

A listed company is a company whose stocks are listed on an approved securities exchange.[282] To become a listed company, the following conditions must be met: (i) the securities administration department has approved the stock issuance; (ii) the total capital stock is at least 50,000,000 RMB; (iii) the company has been in business for three years;[283] (iv) the company has not committed any major unlawful act for three years; and (v) the company has not made a false statement in any financial report for three years.[284]

For small companies, the procedures are: (i) the company has earned profits in the last three years; (ii) there are more than 1000 stockholders; (iii) the par value of the stock exceeds 1000 RMB; and (iv) at least twenty-five percent of the stock is held publicly.[285]

For large companies, the procedures are: (i) the capital stock exceeds 400,000,000 RMB; and (ii) at least fifteen percent of the stock is held publicly.

Conforming companies may submit an application for listing. The application must be accompanied by all relevant documents.[287] Once the application is approved, the report for listing must be published by the company and the application documents must be made available for inspection by the public. Financial statements must be published semi-annually, and financial reports and operational statements must be provided periodically.[288]

A company's stock may be suspended from trading for the following reasons: (i) the capital stock falls below minimum listing requirements; (ii) the distribution requirements for stock holdings falls below minimum listing requirements; (iii) reports are not filed timely; (iv) false reports are filed; (v) a major unlawful practice is committed; or (vi) the company sustains three consecutive years of losses.

---

274. *Id.* Art. 145.
275. *Id.* Art. 146.
276. *Id.* Art. 147.
277. *Id.*
278. *Id.* Art. 148.
279. *Id.* Art. 149.
281. *Id.* Art. 150.
282. *Id.* Arts. 151, 154.
283. Former state-owned enterprises may include the period of operation as a state-owned enterprise. *Id.* Art. 152(2)-(3).
284. *Id.* Art. 152(5).
285. *Id.* Art. 152(4).
287. *Id.* Art. 153.
288. *Id.* Art. 156.

Voluntary or involuntary bankruptcy proceedings will result in a termination of a listing.[290] Serious violations or chronic violations may result in a termination of listing.

Comments and Questions

1. Given the power of the State to intervene in the affairs of companies, and the position of the State in many companies as a majority or controlling shareholder, are Chinese companies corporations, in basic respect, as understood under general principles common to American, European and Japanese corporations? Are PRC companies better described as quasi-independent administrative units of the State? Are Chinese companies potentially sui generis? Is that uniqueness a valuable commodity in the context of global patterns of trade and commerce?

D. Convergence of Corporate Governance Systems?

The emphasis in this chapter has been both on convergence and differences between the corporate governance regimes of the United States, Europe, Japan, and China. The article that follows, *The Purposes and Accountability of the Corporation in Contemporary Society: Corporate Governance at a Crossroads*, makes the case for convergence of these systems of corporate governance. In reading the excerpt consider whether you think convergence is either necessary or appropriate today. In considering this question, think about the situation of countries other than Japan, the member states of the European Union and the United States. The article that follows, Teemu Ruskola's *Conceptualizing Corporations and Kinship* takes a different approach, one that suggests that neither lock-step convergence, nor convergence on the American model are inevitable. That excerpt will serve as a bridge to a broader consideration of the regulation of corporations as enterprises on a comparative basis.

Michael Bradley, Cindy A. Schipani, Anant K. Sundaram, and James P. Walsh, *The Purposes and Accountability of the Corporation in Contemporary Society: Corporate Governance at a Crossroads*

62 Law and Contemporary Problems 9 (1999)
(excerpts pages 67–77; some footnotes omitted)

b. Changes in the Governance Systems. The three governance systems are, of course, not static. The past decade has witnessed evolutionary shifts in all three systems, but ar-

290. *Id.* Art. 158.

guably, the nature of changes in Germany and Japan, relative to their underlying focus historically, has been more dramatic than that in the United States.

There are a number of changes underway in the U.S. system of corporate governance including the increasing influence of the sentiments reflected in the ALI Project on Corporate Governance;[358] the shifting roles of institutional shareholders and independent directors on boards;[359] the attempts to delink the jobs of chairpersons and CEO;[360] the recent changes in proxy-voting rules instituted by the SEC;[361] the Delaware court rulings on the importance of incumbent-firm strategy in takeover contests;[362] the regulatory moves away from director liability;[363] and the increasingly contractarian imperatives of the global financial markets. However, as discussed earlier, these changes do not appear to challenge in any fundamental way the United States's outsider orientation or its focus on shareholder value and financial returns. Indeed, many of the changes in the U.S. governance system may be in the direction of actually strengthening its underlying contractarian focus. Further, there do not appear to be any systematic or widespread moves either in boardrooms or in the realm of public policy to make U.S. firms more communitarian in their approach to governance. On the other hand, the changes in Germany and Japan appear to be moving firms in a direction away from their traditional insider/communitarian focus.

Consider the German case first. Although the German governance system continues to meet stiff resistance from unions and employees and although some of the changes may

---

358. *See* Carol B. Swanson, *Corporate Governance: Sliding Seamlessly into the Twenty-First Century*, 21 J. Corp. L. 417, 430–32 (1996). *See generally* [American Law Institute, Principles of Corporate Governance: Analysis and Recommendations (1994)].

359. The increased role of institutional investors is apparent in the various corporate governance principles that have been proposed and promulgated by large pension funds such as the California Public Employees Retirement System ("CalPERS") and in the annual rankings of "governance grades" given to various companies. A recent study uses the governance grades given by CalPERS as a control variable in assessing corporate performance and finds that there are significant improvements in corporate performance, as measured by Economic Value Added, for those companies graded higher by CalPERS. *See* Ira Millstein & Paul MacAvoy, *The Active Board of Directors and Improved Performance of the Large Publicly Traded Corporation*, 98 Colum. L. Rev. 1283 (1998). Millstein and MacAvoy document substantial evidence on the governance pressures faced by U.S. corporations from large public pension funds. With respect to the heightened roles of independent directors, the article cites an impressive array of evidence from a number of surveys of board composition during the 1990s which have found increased roles for outside and independent directors....

360. *See* Harold M. Williams & Irving S. Shapiro, The 1979 Benjamin F. Fairless Memorial Lectures, Power and Accountability: The Changing Role of the Corporate Board 18 (1979); see also Jay W. Lorsch & Elizabeth MacIver, Pawns of Potentates: The Reality of America's Corporate Boards 184–87 (1989); Martin Lipton & Jay W. Lorsch, *A Modest Proposal for Improved Corporate Governance*, 48 Bus. Law. 58 (1992).

361. *See generally* Joseph Evan Calio & Rafael Xavier Zahralddin, *The Securities and Exchange Commission's 1992 Proxy Amendments: Questions of Accountability*, 14 Pace L. Rev. 459 (1994). *See also* Norma M. Sharara & Anne E. Hoke-Witherspoon, *The Evolution of the 1992 Shareholder Communication Proxy Rules and their Impact on Corporate Governance*, 49 Bus. Law. 327 (1993).

362. *See* Randall S. Thomas, *Judicial Review of Defensive Tactics in Proxy Contests: When is Using a Rights Plan Right?*, 46 Vand. L. Rev. 503, 514–24 (1993). *See generally* Richard C. Brown, *The Role of the Courts in Hostile Takeovers*, 93 Dick. L. Rev. 195 (1989); Lawrence A. Cunningham & Charles M. Yablon, *Delaware Fiduciary Duty Law After QVC and Technicolor: A Unified Standard (and the End of Revlon Duties?)*, 49 Bus. Law. 1593 (1994); Alex Devience, Jr., *A Hindsight Review of the Business Judgment Rule in a Takeover Environment: The State of the Business Judgment Rule after the Fall*, 5 DePaul Bus. L.J. 113 (1992–93).

363. [*See, e.g.*, Del. Code Ann. tit. 8, § 102(b)(7) (Supp. 1998)].

be halting, many basic features of the system appear to be under severe stress. The sources of such stress include regulatory changes both at home and from the European Union directives, the imperatives of corporate decisionmaking in the context of eroding competitiveness in globalized financial and product markets, and grassroots shareholder activism.

During the past decade, many of the regulations prohibiting or constraining the issuance of equity and market debt have been dismantled in Germany.[365] Insider trading laws have been passed;[366] consideration is being given to changes in corporate law to allow firms to repurchase shares;[367] firms are now allowed to pay their sick workers only eighty percent of full pay;[368] banks are being encouraged to divest their corporate shareholdings and to reduce their lending exposures to individual companies;[369] major revisions of bankruptcy laws are under discussion;[370] efforts are underway to develop a new set of standards for financial disclosure;[371] German investors are now required to reveal the details of share ownership of more than five percent in a company;[372] a new supervisory authority for securities trading is in the process of being created;[373] special tax incentives are being offered for start-up firms in high-risk industries;[374] foreign share ownership rules have been relaxed;[375] and, as a result, foreigners now own nearly twenty percent of the shares in Germany, up from negligible amounts in the 1950s.

Substantial changes are underway at the German corporate level as well. An increasing number of firms are listing their shares abroad, especially in the Anglo-American markets; some degree of corporate restructuring through sale of unprofitable units, spin-offs to increase shareholder value, downsizing, and deconglomeration appear to be underway; and a few major companies have introduced stock-option schemes as part of top-management compensation.

* * *

The significant increase in merger and acquisition activity for German firms is another sign that the governance structure of these corporations is changing toward a more Anglo-American system. In the United States, M&A activity was 232% greater (60,407/26,000) in the 1990s than in the 1980s. In comparison, the number of successful acquisitions of German firms grew by 1,959% (8,246/421) over the same period. For

365. *See* [Stephen Prowse, Corporate Governance in an International Perspective: A Survey of Corporate Control Mechanisms Among Large Firms in the United States, the United Kingdom, Japan, and Germany, Bank for International Settlements Economic Papers No. 41, (July 1994)] at 27.

366. *See* [Organization for Econ. Cooperation and Dev., Organization for Economic Cooperation and Development Economic Surveys: Germany 87 (1995)] at 120.

367. *See* Stefan Wagstyl et al., *Crumbs from the Table*, Fin. Times, Sept. 25, 1996, at Comment & Analysis 27.

368. Until recently, firms were required to pay 100%; this change resulted in major strikes and work stoppages in Germany in the last quarter of 1996. *See* Edmund Andrews, *New Hard Line by Big Companies Threatens German Work Benefits*, N.Y. Times, Oct. 1, 1996, at A1 (noting that "the Parliament approved a broad new bill that reduces the minimum required sick pay from 100% of pay for six weeks to 80%")....

369. OECD Germany, *supra* note [366], at 120.

370. *See* [Mitsuhiro Fukao, Financial Integration, Corporate Governance, and the Performance of Multinational Corporations 123 (1995)].

371. *See* OECD Germany, *supra* note [366], at 120.

372. *See Stakeholder Capitalism: Unhappy Families*, Economist, Feb. 10, 1996, at 23.

373. *See* OECD Germany, *supra* note [366], at 120.

374. *Id.*, at 121.

375. See *Business in Europe: Investor Power*, Economist, Nov. 23, 1996, at 11–12.

continental Europe as a whole, M&A activity was 1,275% greater (33,687/2,643). Interestingly, while the number of successful hostile acquisitions of U.S. targets has fallen dramatically in the most recent decade—163 between 1981 and 1989 compared to fifty-six between 1990 and 1998—the number of hostile takeovers of firms in continental Europe has actually increased from eight to seventeen.

Finally, the number of German firms that recently have listed their shares on the New York Stock Exchange indicates a trend toward a more Anglo-American governance structure. None of the eight German firms with American Depositary Receipts ("ADRs") currently trading on the NYSE was listed before 1996.[390]

* * *

Similar changes are occurring elsewhere in Europe. The OECD reports that the governance systems of France, Switzerland, the Netherlands, and Sweden are moving closer to the Anglo-American model, whereas they previously had more closely followed the German model.[392] There are significant corporate governance debates underway in France. Many of the changes in both the regulations and the conduct of French corporations parallel those chronicled above for the German case.[393] France is currently debating the introduction of private-pension-funding schemes along the lines of those in the United States. In both France and Italy, there is an increasing number of high-profile cases in which minority shareholders are demanding and obtaining adequate rights, especially in matters concerning takeover premia.[394] Norms are also being developed to limit multiple-board memberships among a small group of financial and corporate elites.[395] Perhaps most telling, since 1998, there have been five hostile acquisitions of French companies, each with a market value in excess of one billion dollars.[396]

....Competition laws and antitrust regulations are being strengthened and more forcefully applied in the European Union.[399] Moreover, there are significant moves to-

---

390. The eight firms are Celanese (1999), Deutsche Telekom (1996), Epcos (1999), Fresenius Medical Care (1996), Pfeifer Vacuum (1996), SAP Aktiengesellschaft (1998), SGL Carbon (1996), VEBA (1997). *See* New York Stock Exchange (visited Jan. 24, 2000) <www.nyse.com/international.htm>.

392. *See* OECD Germany, supra note [366], at 19.

393. The French phrase for corporate governance is "le corporate governance." *See* Allanna Sullivan & Thomas Kama, *Continental Shift: Elf Aquitane's Chief Illustrates the Changes in Europe's Executives*, WALL ST. J., Apr. 9, 1996, at A1.

394. For a chronicle of such cases, *see* [*Business in Europe: Investor Power*, ECONOMIST, Nov. 23, 1996, at 11–12]; *see also* John Tagliabue, *A Specter in Europe: Shareholders Demand Rights*, INT'L HERALD TRIB., Apr. 28, 1998, at 11; *France's Boardroom Revolution*, WALL ST. J., Oct. 17, 1995, at A20. For a comprehensive description of the corporate governance reform efforts underway, including a "Marini Report" of the French Senate to reform the rights of minority shareholders in France, see Organization for Econ. Cooperation and Dev., Organization for Economic Cooperation and Development Economic Surveys: France 128–29 (1997)...(noting that "[o]verall, the transition appears to have gone on the direction of shareholder (outsider) model and...the French system is now closer to the Anglo-American model").

395. This recommendation is contained in the Vienot Report, the report produced by a corporate governance committee formed in France and headed by Marc Vienot, the CEO of Societe Generale. *See* OECD France, *supra* note 394, at 130 (summarizing the Vienot Report and comparing it to the so-called Cadbury Report in the United Kingdom)....

396. Data are derived and calculated by the authors from the online mergers and acquisitions database of the Securities Data Corporation....

399. *See The Irritating Commissioner*, ECONOMIST, Jan. 31, 1998, at 72 (describing the increase in the aggressiveness and "free market zealotry" of antitrust enforcement in the European Union under the new Competition Commissioner).

ward the adoption of a common set of accounting and disclosure rules under the International Accounting Standards.[400]

In Japan, financial markets were liberalized to a significant degree during the 1980s.[401] The Japanese government also recently announced new plans for further deregulation of the banking, securities, foreign exchange, and insurance sectors to take effect by 2001, along the lines of the "Big Bang" in London.[402] Other changes are similarly underway that challenge the status quo in Japanese corporate governance: Some keiretsu firms are reportedly beginning to sell their stockholdings;[403] the notion of lifetime employment is under serious debate;[404] after a few years of slowdown, 1996 saw a resurgence in the market for mergers and acquisitions, with more than 600 deals valued at more than one trillion yen being completed;[405] a significant number of large corporations have moved toward arms-length relations with their main banks as Japanese banks are losing their capacity to act as enforcers of financial discipline;[406] Japanese firms have become far more dependent on international capital markets for their global funding needs for both debt and equity, and the proportion of bank financing to total capitalization has steadily declined during the past decade; and the number of firms listing their shares in the Anglo-American stock markets has risen substantially during the past decade, to the point where thirty-four percent of the largest, by market capitalization, 100 Japanese firms listed on the Tokyo stock exchange are also now listed on either the U.S. or the U.K. stock markets.

The Asian economic crises that began in the latter half of 1997—with the attendant economic contraction, currency depreciation, plummeting stock markets, soaring unemployment, and banking crises—affecting Japan, Thailand, Indonesia, Malaysia, the Philippines, and Korea have brought into sharper focus the nature of corporate governance practices in those economies. Numerous writers, policymakers, and commentators have alluded to the opacity and crony capitalism in the governance systems in these economies, arguing that these attributes have exacerbated the crises, if not actually en-

---

400. *See* International Accounting Standards Committee, International Accounting Standards Committee Insight 15 (Oct. 1997). The International Accounting Standards Committee ("IASC") is an international group of financial institutions, corporations, and policymakers, such as stock exchange authorities and central bankers, that has undertaken the task of formulating a common set of accounting standards worldwide. The Insight reports that as of the end of 1996, 56 of 67 countries that they surveyed either used the International Accounting Standards ("IAS") as their national standards or based their national standards primarily on IAS. The United States, however, has decided to continue with its own standards. *See id.*

401. [Stephen Prowse, Corporate Governance in an International Perspective: A Survey of Corporate Control Mechanisms Among Large Firms in the United States, the United Kingdom, Japan, and Germany, Bank for International Settlements Economic Papers No. 41, (July 1994)] at 26.

402. *See Laying the Charge for the Big Bang,* Banker, July 1, 1997, at 108, 108–09; *see also Changing Japan: Whispering Reform,* Economist, Jan. 11, 1997, at 19, 19; *see also Survey Japanese Finance,* Economist, June 28, 1997, at 2, 2–3.

403. *See Stakeholder Capitalism: Unhappy Families,* Economist, Feb. 10, 1996, at 25 (noting that "some keiretsu may have begun to unravel; under financial pressure, some partners have recently started to sell their cross-shareholdings"); *see also Japan Inc. Frays at the Edges,* Economist, June 3, 1995, at 67, 67 (noting that "[a] sluggish economy is putting unprecedented pressure on the system of cross-shareholdings that binds Japanese companies and banks together").

404. *See Stakeholder Capitalism, supra* note 403, at 25 (noting that "the lifetime employment of core workers is increasingly under threat" and that "Japanese firms are redefining 'lifetime employment,' ...")

405. *See* Velisarios Kattoulas, *Japan Catches Merger Fever Again,* Int'l Herald Trib., Jan. 2, 1997, at 9.

406. *See* OECD Germany, *supra* note [366], at 20.

gendered them.[408] Of course, it is too early to forecast just how these events will transform these economies, their politics, laws, institutions, and corporate governance practices. However, it is clear that these economies, like the post-communist economies of Eastern Europe and the former Soviet Union, are in transition into a new and uncharted governance territory. At a minimum, these events legitimately have raised questions about the efficacy of communitarian styles of governance and their ability, or lack thereof, to cope with a world in which international capital flows, globalization, and human-capital-intensive technologies have become the norm. Arguably, they also have resulted in the increasing acceptance of the notion that the adoption of some form of contractarian governance mechanisms in the Anglo-American tradition—with their transparent, market-driven, shareholder-oriented styles—may be the long-term solution.

A particularly compelling example of such acceptance comes from Japan. A 1998 statement of corporate governance principles for Japan, issued by a Corporate Governance Committee of the Corporate Governance Forum of Japan,[409] derives its principles based on the primacy of creation and management of shareholder value as the basic managerial goal and role of board independence in achieving that goal.[410] The report notes that Japanese boards of directors as currently constituted have not been "equipped with sufficient governance authority or capability, while the board of auditors has been little more than a cosmetic shell,"[411] that "the board of directors tends not to have real decision making power,"[412] and that currently "a sufficient supply of independent external directors does not exist in Japan."[413] It points out that "in the medium term, the uniquely Japanese system of cross-shareholding might begin to unravel, which will necessitate a system of governance more reliant on independent and external directors, in turn leading to the creation of a market for such individuals."[414] The report argues for the creation of a U.S.-style concept of fiduciary duty to shareholders and implies that the current Japanese concepts of such duty may be somewhat vague, covered as they are by legal concepts such as bona fide loyalty duty and the duty of honest manager's care.[415]

In both Continental Europe and Asia, many other such examples abound. But the evidence presented here reveals that the evolutionary shifts underway in both these geographic areas appear to be posing significant challenges to their traditionally insider-oriented, stakeholder-based, relatively communitarian systems of corporate governance. Moreover, the governance systems of the three major industrial economies of the world—the United States, Germany, and Japan—seem to be inexorably moving toward some practical form of convergence. The nature of this movement is inarguably in the Anglo-American direction rather than the other way around.

---

408. Although there have been voluminous viewpoints on the Asian economic crisis, all of it is in the realm of the public media at the time of this writing, and, unfortunately, little has yet to appear in the academic realm....

409. *See generally* Corporate Governance Committee, Corporate Governance Forum of Japan Corporate, Governance Principles: A Japanese View (Final Report) (May 26, 1998). The Committee, constituted in 1994, consists of 17 leading Japanese corporate executives, institutional investors, media representatives, and lawyers. Details on the Committee, its meetings, and its deliberations, can be found in the Report. *See id.* at 33, 35.

410. *See id.* at 45–54.

411. *Id.* at 37.

412. *Id.* at 41.

413. *Id.* at 42.

414. *Id.*

415. *See id.* at 43.

This conclusion is quite different from the prevailing sentiment in the literature on comparative corporate governance. W. Carl Kester, for example, captures the prevailing sentiment quite clearly:

> Since the early 1980s a kind of competition among systems of corporate governance has emerged. Despite the twentieth century international hegemony of first the United Kingdom, followed by the United States, it is by no means certain that the Anglo-American system of governance as currently configured will win this competition.[416] Additionally, Kester mentions that Mark J. Roe has tied these shifts to the political roots in their respective settings but Roe notes that it may be a mistake to pronounce one system as more advantageous than another.[417] Andrei Shleifer and Robert W. Vishny, in a similar vein, argue that "all these economies have the essential elements of a good governance system, [and] the available evidence does not tell us which one of their governance systems is the best."[418]

Our conclusion that the economies of the world, and the corporate forms residing therein, are evolving toward a more contractarian structure follows from our analysis above and is rooted in the following assessment of the purposes and accountability of the public corporation in an ever-changing, global economy.

Teemu Ruskola, *Conceptualizing Corporations and Kinship: Comparative Law and Development Theory in a Chinese Perspective*

STAN. L. REV. 1599 (2000)

(excerpts pages 1713–1728; some footnotes omitted)

But even if every law needs a story, and even if some functionally similar arrangements can be justified by very different stories, there remains the question of how the stories of one system will interact with those of another. What happens when the indigenous Chinese corporate tradition comes into contact with the new Company Law?

At one end of the spectrum are comparativists whose answer is, "Nothing much." For example, Pierre Legrand maintains that, as a general matter, the much-advertised convergence of legal systems within the European Community is only apparent. Superficial similarities on the level of legal rules cannot overcome "differences arising between the common law and civil law mentalites at the epistemological level": Such differences are, in the end, "irreducible." Among scholars of Chinese law, Thomas Stephens has offered an extreme formulation of this view. According to Stephens, the essence of Chinese "law" is the maintenance of discipline within a status hierarchy, rather than adjudication with the aid of universally applicable neutral principles. In ef-

416. [W. Carl Kester, *Industrial Groups as Systems of Contractual Governance*, 8 OXFORD REV. ECON. POL'Y 24 (1992).]

417. *See* W. Carl Kester, *American and Japanese Corporate Governance, Convenience to Best Practice?*, *in* NATIONAL DIVERSITY & GLOBAL CAPITALISM 107–37 (Suzanne Berger & Ronald Dore eds., 1996). *See generally* Mark J. Roe, *The Political Roots of American Corporate Finance*, J. APPLIED CORP. FIN., Winter 1997, at 19.

418. [Andrei Shleifer & Robert W. Vishny, *A Survey of Corporate Governance*, 52 J. FIN. 737 (1997)] at 739.

fect, Stephens expels China from his definition of law: Study of traditional Chinese law is not fit to be denominated as comparative law—comparative philosophy, perhaps. Ultimately, no real encounter is possible with this tradition and Western systems of law: It is like trying to mix "oil and water." Or, as Samuel Huntington would put it, law is but one dimension in the clash of civilizations in a "West versus the Rest" world.

At the opposite end of the spectrum are those who emphasize the universal rather than culturally particular aspects of law: They believe in an ongoing process of apparently natural global "harmonization." The new subfield of comparative law and economics shares some of this optimism regarding at least the functional, if not doctrinal, convergence of legal systems. In contrast to Alan Watson, the pioneering student of legal transplants who believes that express borrowing of rules is the main engine of legal change, Ugo Mattei has put forth the thesis that much legal evolution is in fact driven by the pressure for law to find "efficient" solutions: The comparativist's task is to identify "this common core of efficient principles hidden in the different technicalities of the legal systems."[584] This effort is, in the end, not unlike Hohfeld's classic attempt to arrive at "fundamental legal conceptions" which will reveal to us the underlying "unity and harmony in the law." In just this manner, some enterprising students of Chinese law indeed claim to have found equivalents in the Chinese tradition for various purported fundaments of our system.

Between the prophets of divergence and convergence, which group speaks (more) in the voice of God? The divergence theorists are in a constant danger of lapsing into cultural essentialism. Yearning for a simple explanation of the successes of Chinese economic organization among overseas Chinese, they frequently underscore the "cash value of Confucian values" and attribute the peculiar features of Chinese economic organization to differences of culture and tradition. But to observe that the Chinese family business is "peculiarly well adapted to its socio-cultural milieu" is to state a truism, approximately as useful as the observation in Moliere's Le Malade imaginaire that opium makes its users sleepy because of the dormitive principle of poppies. Just as anthropologists warn comparative lawyers against the sort of cross-cultural study that, inevitably, finds "Frenchmen Cartesian and Englishmen Lockean," to label certain aspects of Chinese legal and economic culture "Confucian" or "traditional" verges on tautology. Indeed, it echoes back to Marx's curiously timeless notion of an "Asiatic mode of production" as the defining feature of Asian economies, and it brings to mind the similarly static notions of East Asian cultures held by nineteenth-century comparative legal scholars. In the words of Henry Maine, for example, in "those great and unexplored regions which we vaguely term the East...the distinction between the Present and the Past disappears."[593] The Sinologist Edward Parker put it even less delicately, announcing that to study Chinese law is to enter into "a living past, and to converse with fossil men."[594]

In contrast, the prophets of convergence at least allow for a certain dynamism in relations among legal systems. Alas, that dynamism tends to work in one direction only: "Non-Western" law will converge toward "Western" law—or "colonial" to "metropolitan," "primitive" to "advanced," depending on the particular narrative of redemption. Not only are the choices binary—either "our" way or "their" way—but the telos of legal development is a foregone conclusion, too obvious to be stated. It has

584. Ugo Mattei, *Efficiency in Legal Transplants: An Essay in Comparative Law and Economics*, 14 INT'L REV. L. & ECON. 3, 18 (1994).

593. [HENRY SUMNER MAINE, VILLAGE COMMUNITIES IN THE EAST AND WEST (London, John Murray, 2d ed. 1872)], at 7.

594. [Edward Harper Parker, *Comparative Chinese Family Law*, 8 CHINA REV. 67 (1879)], at 69.

become fashionable to refer to the Chinese economy and legal system as being "in transition," just as the post-Socialist states of Eastern Europe are said to be. The unstated implication of this seemingly innocuous phrase is that, whatever hybrid form China may have adopted for now, this form is ultimately not authentic: Until China has fully "modernized," it will remain in transit. Of course, to the extent that "we," "the West," are not in transition, then by implication "we have arrived" at the ultimate destination: a (highly idealized) Western-style market economy. While the colonial mission civilisatrice as well as the naive evangelism of the Law and Development movement may have receded into history, they have been replaced with the ostensibly more generous assumption that China and the rest of the world will, one day, simply "catch up" with the West. Benign as this may sound, it is still one more example of neo-Hegelian evolutionary schemes "in which China always furnishes a beginning to be improved upon."

In other words, this view of Chinese legal development still leaves the West in the center and everybody else in the periphery, little more than "victims and silent witnesses" of their own primitivity. It also suggests that the "progress" of Chinese law is ultimately a response to the influence of the West. Just as this "impact-response" paradigm has come under fire among Sinologists in the social sciences, legal scholars too ought to keep in mind that the relation between the Chinese legal tradition and transplanted contemporary corporation law is likely never an entirely one-sided affair with the West providing all the important features of a "modern" legal order.

In the end, "modernity" and "tradition" need not be mutually exclusive historical trajectories: A legal culture can surely "modernize" in one aspect while remaining—or becoming even more—"traditional" in others. For instance, anthropologists remind us that urbanization need not spell the end of customary notions of kinship; quite the contrary, "the urban milieu presents new possibilities for extended kinship organizations."[605] Likewise, in the Taiwanese countryside technological advances have reinvigorated, not dampened, customary practices: "Improved methods of communication have widened the range of kinsmen with whom significant interaction is possible."[606] In fact, in his study of contract law in late-Qing Taiwan Rosser Brockman discovered a "highly developed, sophisticated system of contract" that permitted "commerce to flourish through the use of long-range, impersonal bargains."[607] As Brockman puts it, "Studies of the impact of Western legal systems on Taiwan and China in general in the twentieth century and the resulting 'legal modernization' will have to take full account of the vitality of the traditional legal forms."[608] Indeed, "it may be that the 'legal modernization' which has taken place in China and Taiwan owes its success as much or more to the strength of the traditional institutions as to any contribution made by Western law."[609]

---

605. Morton H. Fried, *Some Political Aspects of Clanship in a Modern Chinese City*, in POLITICAL ANTHROPOLOGY 285, 300 (Marc J. Swartz, Victor W. Turner & Arthur Tuden eds., 1966) (emphasis added).

606. [Myron L. Cohen, *Family Partition as Contractual Procedure in Taiwan: A Case Study from South Taiwan*, in CHINESE FAMILY LAW AND SOCIAL CHANGE IN HISTORICAL AND COMPARATIVE PERSPECTIVE 109, 119 (David C. Buxbaum ed., 1978)], at 195.

607. [Rosser H. Brockman, *Commercial Contract Law in Late Nineteenth-Century Taiwan*, in ESSAYS ON CHINA'S LEGAL TRADITION 76 (Jerome Alan Cohen, R. Randle Edwards, & Fu-mei Chang Chen eds., 1980)], at 129.

608. *Id.* at 129.

609. *Id.* at 130. The once absolute condemnation of traditional Chinese law has softened somewhat, from acknowledging its preference for mediation as a "fine tradition" of the Chinese people to

The possibility that several opposing tendencies may be simultaneously entrenching in a legal system also throws into doubt the fundamental distinction between domestic and foreign law as the objects of comparative study. A view of the world in which the two categories live independent lives has certainly made it easy for legal scholars to focus on one to the exclusion of the other and has contributed to the marginalization of the entire field of comparative legal studies. Yet with growing political, social, commercial, financial, and cultural interaction on a global scale, it is difficult for legal systems to maintain their (real or imagined) purity. To borrow Clifford Geertz's terminology, living in the contemporary "confusion of legal tongues" calls for "an hermeneutics of legal pluralism,"[612] an understanding of intersystemic and cross-cultural legal influences that have little respect for the Romantic dream of national legal systems, each reflecting its unique Volksgeist.

In fact, one might argue that today both Chinese and American law are in a dynamic process of convergence from opposite directions, not only on the level of legal rules but even on the deeper level of conceptualization: Increasingly, American corporate law scholars alienated by contractarian models are turning to communitarian solutions, and calls for strengthening the fiduciary aspects of the corporation are proliferating. Of late some states have expressly authorized corporate directors to take into account in their decisionmaking processes constituencies other than shareholders, resulting, in effect, in a broader notion of the community which corporations are expected to serve and of which they partake. Poignantly, at the very same time, China's legal elites are reacting to the Communist state's (and, ultimately, even the imperial state's) inability to make good on the promise to create a true fiduciary community on a national scale. Strikingly, as the appeal of orthodox notions of community fades, legal theorists are turning to contract, which for many stands for nothing less than the freedom and autonomy of the human subject. The current pro-reform legal literature teems with approving references to Maine's thumbnail sketch of progress as a move from Status to Contract, which is reportedly cited more often by legal thinkers than even the views of Marx himself. For an Anglo-American observer, to peruse recent mainstream writings is to enter into a strange hall of mirrors where the key rights are "life, liberty, and property," and, in a disorienting echo of laissez-faire, the market is hailed as the key to humanity's salvation.

Is corporation law thus simply the latest chapter in the evolution of another jus commune, a new global common law freed of the "excesses of nation-worship"? Perhaps we will get a completely new kind of corporation law, freely combining various elements of all or most legal traditions. Or perhaps the global marketplace will function as a great "melting pot" of particularistic legal systems and tribal jurisdictions, and the end result will be a more democratically constituted "multicultural" corporation law, in the construction of which each legal system gets to participate.

---

praising faintly even the imperial preference for flexible standards over rigid rules in legislation, *see* Perry Keller, *Sources of Order in Chinese Law*, 42 AM. J. COMP. L. 711, 749 n. 191 (1994). But even today, it is the mainstream view that, "[o]bviously, China's traditional legal concepts are incapable of accommodating the rich essence of modern legal concepts.... We must expose and criticize past history and consciously recognize the traditions that we inherited unintentionally." Liang Zhiping, *Explicating "Law": A Comparative Perspective of Chinese and Western Legal Culture*, 3 J. CHINESE L. 55, 91 (1989) (emphasis added). This rejection of China's legal heritage is largely an artifact of the Marxist need to discredit all vestiges of an irredeemably "feudal" past.

612. [Clifford Geertz, *Local Knowledge: Fact and Law in Comparative Perspective*, in LOCAL KNOWLEDGE: FURTHER ESSAYS IN INTERPRETIVE ANTHROPOLOGY 185 (1983)], at 225.

For better or worse, this is highly improbable—or at least not very meaningful. It might hold true on the level of some fairly technical legal rules, but, as John Merryman has long admonished comparative lawyers, "a focus on rules is superficial and misleading: superficial because rules literally lie on the surface of legal systems whose true dimensions are found elsewhere; misleading because we are led to assume that if rules are made to resemble each other something significant by way of rapprochement has been accomplished."[621] In the end, the stories we—and the Chinese—tell about corporation law are not simply incidental ornaments on the surface of legal rules: We have no choice but to tell stories about law. In order to make sense and carry meaning, every legal rule must be informed by a justification, and, as Robert Cover puts it, "Narrative is the literary genre for the objectification of value."[622] It is relatively easy to see that grand constitutional concepts such as "due process" grow out of deeply held cultural notions and legends of Founding Fathers, yet the rules of corporation law are no less submerged in socio-cultural assumptions: "Even the seemingly most insignificant or neutral doctrines and rules, taken as a whole, have a story to tell, if we are willing to listen to them."[625] The problem with an "international law of corporations" is that, to be meaningful, it would require a truly globally shared metanarrative that would inform it. It seems unlikely that such a monolithic narrative will arise anytime soon out of the "emerging world disorder."

Indeed, even national legal systems remain always more or less diverse, or, as Francis Bacon put it, "we see in any one kingdom, which is most at unity in itself, there is diversity of customs for the guiding of property and private rights."[627] The likelihood of China's evolving any one shared narrative, indigenous or transplanted, is perhaps especially bleak because of its heterogeneous heritage. Although China does not have a federal system, its regional differences are remarkable, and the central state's inability to maintain uniform administration of the laws is notorious. Indeed, a student of Chinese corporation law "should start with the assumption that there are wide local variations in the governance of individual enterprises."[629] For one thing, even the "central" Chinese state, constituted as it is of multiple bureaucracies and centers of power, is likely to use law for many, often contradictory purposes. In the battle between the ideologies of the market and communism, the state's interpretations of its laws are guided by at least two invisible hands: the right one belonging to Adam Smith, and the left one identified with the Party.

Besides, even if the Party is still the red eminence behind the Chinese state, it has contenders. That Confucius is alive and still roams the landscape was evident in the

---

621. John Merryman, *On the Convergence (and Divergence) of the Civil Law and the Common Law*, in New Perspectives for a Common Law of Europe 195, 223 (Mauro Cappelletti ed., 1978). *See also* Pierre Legrand, *Strange Power of Words: Codification Situated*, 9 Tul. Eur. & Civ. L. For. 1, 18 (1994) (criticizing the rule-bound conception of law as an "epistemological barrier to legal knowledge").

622. Or, in the parlance of legal realism, every law must have a "purpose." *See, e.g.*, Karl N. Llewellyn, *Remarks on the Theory of Appellate Decision and the Rules or Canons About How Statutes Are To Be Construed*, 3 Vand. L. Rev. 395, 400 ("A statute merely declaring a rule, with no purpose or objective, is nonsense.").

625. J.M. Balkin, *Deconstructive Practice and Legal Theory*, 96 Yale L.J. 743, 762 (1987).

627. Francis Bacon, *A Preparation Toward the Union of the Laws of England and Scotland*, in 5 Lord Bacon's Works, Lord Chancellor of England 83–84 (Basil Montagu ed., London, William Pickering 1826).

629. Andrew G. Walder, *The County Government as an Industrial Corporation*, in Zouping in Transition: The Process of Reform in Rural North China 62, 64 (Andrew G. Walder ed., 1998).

fervor with which he was campaigned against in the Cultural Revolution—surely the Great Helmsman would not have bothered attacking somebody already dead. When talk of Confucian capitalism was de rigueur in the roaring economies of the East Asian Tigers, the Master experienced a minor rehabilitation even in the PRC. In any event, continuation of the patrilineage still matters in China; an underground market in heirs persists, and trafficking in women is on the rise as well. Although customary law has no official place in the PRC legal system, the Supreme Court has judicially recognized customary landholding arrangements dating to the imperial era. Even today, rural households continue to execute traditional household division (fen-jia) contracts which theoretically enjoy no legal recognition. Other aspects of custom, as I have suggested, persist without express recognition. There are even signs that the clan and other family institutions are growing increasingly prominent in South China—which is, perhaps not coincidentally, also in the forefront of economic growth. To the extent clans have received attention in recent legal literature, it has been largely colored by the need to make them agree with the Marxist demonization of China's past, but some authors have nevertheless called for a selective rehabilitation of the institution.

Furthermore, even the official legal system has a complex genealogy. In retooling their initially Soviet-inspired legal system, Communists have studied the reforms of their predecessors, who in turn were influenced primarily by the German model—mostly as it was interpreted in Japan—but who also studied legal systems worldwide. Especially in commercial law, PRC lawyers make wide (if unacknowledged) use of the Taiwanese experience in Sinicizing civil law institutions. But even though China may be formally following mostly the civil law model, actual legal practices are being shaped more and more by encounters with common lawyers. Some locales, of course, have their own international heritages whose continuing influence is difficult to gauge, but which surely matters—as in the case of Shanghai, for example.

Further complicating the PRC legal system is the continued coexistence of two separate regimes. At least in the area of commercial legislation, there are, effectively, two parallel legal universes—one for the Chinese, another for foreign investors. This arrangement uneasily echoes the history of foreign rights of extraterritoriality. Although on paper China is moving toward integrated legislation, the so-called "Special Economic Zones" have their own mini-regimes that are in many respects exempted from national legislation. Moreover, although one of the purported goals of the new Company Law is to harmonize the enterprise law governing foreign and domestic businesses, the Company Law expressly states that any conflicting provisions of laws governing foreign joint ventures trump the Company Law. In an even more striking echo of the era of Unequal Treaties, the Securities Committee of the State Council has formulated a set of mandatory provisions to be included in the bylaws of companies planning to list on foreign stock exchanges; by administrative fiat, these provisions essentially rewrite the Company Law governing partly foreign-owned corporations.

The reincorporation of Hong Kong into the motherland presents perhaps the ultimate test case of intrasystemic pluralism: What are the constitutional implications of having "one country, two Grundnormen"? Just how many different—and how different—stories can one system tolerate? To start with, the task of translating Hong Kong's English common law into Chinese has proven complex and controversial, as one might well expect when a law embodying one vision of the world is being molded into the idiom of another vision. Furthermore, the PRC's pledge to respect Hong Kong's pre-handover legal system has the rather stunning implication that Qing custom remains the law of the land on sovereign PRC territory. It was part of the British colonial policy to permit the application of local custom to the native populations of the outlying areas of Hong Kong, where ancestral trusts enjoyed customary recognition up until the handover, and presumably continue to do so even today. Indeed, over the years some Hong Kong trusts have even incorporated as companies. Quite simply, Chinese legal "history" may not be history quite yet: As recently as 1987, a Hong Kong court faced with a land dispute among the beneficiaries of an ancestral trust expressly asked an expert witness to consider "how... a Chinese magistrate might have reacted if the same problem had been submitted to him."[653]

Nor is traditional Chinese "corporation law" limited to a particular geographic space. Clan organizations and ancestral trusts have traveled wherever Chinese emigrants have—most prominently, to Southeast Asia, Europe, and the United States. In far-flung places, they have performed multiple functions as community service providers, business associations, and tribunals for the enforcement of customary legal institutions. In the Chicago of the 1930s, Chinatown was seen as "'extra-territoriality' by way of the Chinese method,"[658] and its associations functioned according to their own laws: "[W]e open a hall or temple for our meetings and family worship. We elect our officers, who are usually the oldest in our group, and our organization functions according to our ways of life, in old China."[659] Even today, Chinatowns remain in some ways beyond the reach of formal American law (which, of course, does not in itself make Chinatowns any different from many other American communities that are governed by their "indigenous" law).

Given China's pluralistic legal history, the harmonization of corporation law remains unlikely, despite insistent demands for the global unification of private law. Even though the ever-faster pace of globalization has helped us perceive that nations are, in the end, "imagined communities" with no necessary, fixed boundaries, we ought to keep in mind that the very phenomenon of globalization is itself as much a discursive condition as a set of material processes: It has become a new metanarrative in its own right—and, to those weary of modernist disenchantment with the world, an enchantingly postmodern one at that. Yet a truly global community, too, consists of more than planes and electronic communications crossing borders: No less than nations, a global community also has to be summoned into existence through creative acts of imagination.

As far as corporation law is concerned, the capacity of human beings to imagine various ways of organizing factors of production is vast, if not limitless, and our facility in telling different stories that justify those arrangements is even greater. It surely is noteworthy that even the relatively homogeneous European Community's attempt to create a European company law— societas europaea —faces bleak prospects. While corporate finance has grown global with a vengeance, corporate governance arrangements have maintained a far more local character, and it is entirely possible that growing pressure from international competition will entrench, rather than disturb, existing corporate governance systems. Despite our technical facility in communicating globally, the process whereby human beings reach shared understandings regardingthe economic,

653. Kan Fat-tat v. Kan Yin-tat, [1987] H.K.L.R. 516, 543.

658. Remigio B. Ronquillo, *The Administration of Law Among the Chinese in Chicago*, 25 J. Am. Inst. Crim. L. 205, 205 (1934–35).

659. *Id.* at 221.

social, political, and moral ordering of their lives still remains far slower than the speed at which money traverses the globe.

Of course, this does not mean that Americans and Chinese cannot interact commercially and legally; as Pound observed, "unity of law is by no means necessary to close economic and commercial relations" between China and the rest of the world. Yet it does mean that the Chinese and their commercial partners may have different subjective views and interpretations of the nature and purpose of their interactions: There may be several cosmologies that can support (what we would call) "capitalist" institutions. One might regard these divergent interpretations as misunderstandings, but undoubtedly many of them are "working misunderstandings." Perhaps what we will see is a kind of "pidgin corporation law," analogous to the pidgin English that evolved out of the interactions of early European traders and their Chinese counterparts in the nineteenth century (the word "pidgin" being simply the pidgin pronunciation of the English word "business"). To be sure, as linguists tell us, even a pidgin, which by definition has no native speakers, can evolve over time into an authentic linguistic community and thereby become a creole, a "real" language in its own right. Rather than homogenization, globalization may signal the creolization of law and the emergence of entirely novel legal subcultures.

Or it may not.

Comments and Questions

1. The points raised in the excerpts above provide a good place to take stock of the issues of comparative corporate law you have thus far considered. To what extent do the materials you read in Chapter 1 suggest that convergence, on the US model, is proceeding or do you agree with Carl Kester, quoted at the end of the excerpted materials above?

2. To what extent are the issues in the convergence debate issues of corporate governance, narrowly understood, or of the regulation of enterprise organization, more generally, in the context of cross-border economic activity? This question points us in the direction the materials will take you next—a consideration of the meaning of corporate "regulation." More importantly, the materials that follow provide a means of understanding corporate regulation as perhaps a small part of the much larger and more important field of the regulation of enterprises. The focus shifts from the status of an enterprise, to the characteristics of enterprises generally that may form common bases of regulation, irrespective of the differences of formal organization.

E. The Attributes of Corporate Organization

What is it that makes the corporate form of enterprise different from other forms of business organization? Do these characteristics carry over from the curiosities of internal organization to issues affecting the general regulation of business enterprises? Should they carry over? Corporations, partnerships, trust and sole proprietorships are all means for carrying on a business, that is, for engaging in work, either alone or with others, for the purpose of generating income from the activity and dividing the profits between the participants. All of these forms of organizations are forms of business enterprises. While these enterprises may be different in forms of organization, in other respects they may exhibit similar characteristics. For example, all business enterprises may be very large or very small. Just as there are very small corporations, there are very large partnerships. Corporations, partnerships and business trusts may each consist of a large number of investors, lenders and employees, each of whom seeks to derive benefits from their respective investment in the enterprise. As such, business enterprises might more logically be understood as a variation of a common legal form—the single or multi-participant combinations created for the purpose of conducting business independent of the participants in the enterprise. It might then follow that the legal regulation of the organization of enterprises might be better organized by dividing enterprises on the basis of characteristics other than form of legal organization—perhaps on the basis of size or common characteristics.

The materials which follow suggest the uncertainties which characterize any possible answer to these questions, or the viability of alternative approaches to enterprise regulation. The first excerpt establishes the context. It is meant to provide a basis for considering the possibility of regulation of enterprises on the bases of characteristics other than the peculiarities of formation.

Ironically, some of the answers to these questions have been the object of consideration by the courts and the U.S. Internal Revenue Service in the course of interpreting the tax laws, rather than state judicial or legislative organs, interpreting the corporate law. The Internal Revenue Service is particularly interested because the tax obligations of business enterprises depend, to a substantial extent, on the legal characterization of the enterprise. This is particularly the case with corporations, because they are taxed independently of their shareholders. A corporation must pay taxes on its income. Corporate shareholders also pay taxes on all dividends paid by the corporation. In contrast, a partnership is not taxed on its income. Rather, partnership income (and loss) is generally distributed directly to the partners who are then taxed on the amounts passed through to them.

The *Morrissey* case, and the Internal Revenue Service Regulations which follow provide an important discussion of the issue of the nature of a corporation. When reading the case, consider whether it should make a difference that the discussion takes place in the context of the federal tax laws rather than in the context of state corporate law. Consider also whether the Supreme Court in *Morrissey* is describing universal principles of corporate organization.

Thomas Raiser, *The Theory of Enterprise Law in the Federal Republic of Germany*

36 American Journal of Comparative Law 111 (1988)
(excerpts from pages 111–115)

In the Federal Republic of Germany, as in other countries of the Continental and Anglo-American legal families, the organizational law of economic enterprises lies in the commercial and company law as developed during the 19th century. The basic provisions are found in the Commercial Code which, with the Civil Code, came into force in the year 1900. The former's fundamental organizing concepts are those of the "merchant," the "commercial company," and the "commercial transaction."[1].... The concept of the enterprise occurs only incidentally and is used without either explanation or in any autonomous definitional sense.

Since World War I, and in increased measure after the end of World War II, the concept of "enterprise" has gained in significance both in general and in the legal terminology. It is the basic concept and object of numerous laws which use it in place of the concepts "merchant" and "company."[4] In jurisprudence, too, it is used broadly.[5] As a result, legal science has developed a theory of enterprise law which claims to demonstrate the newer economic, social, and legal evolution in its area of legal application, and which therefore, in a sense, understands itself as in counterposition to the traditional doctrines of commercial and company law....

* * *

1. Enterprise law reflects the new macro-economic and legal environment, which is particularly characterized by anti-trust law, favoring competition while at the same time depriving it of its absolute status, and by the increased power of the state to control and guide the economic process to the point of allowing certain elements of central planning as well as the participation of the state in the economic process in the form of state-owned production and service enterprises (including banks). Enterprise law also is an expression of a reawakened attentiveness toward the social and political influence of large enterprises as producers of economic well-being, guarantors of jobs and income, and centers of social domination which can achieve political weight. To speak of enterprise law in this sense is to indicate that social transactions no longer are a purely private matter but entail a social and public responsibility....

2. In contrast to traditional commercial and company law, the style of enterprise law is further shaped by the predominance of production and service enterprises, which have overtaken traditional trade and commerce as important factors of economic life. From this perspective enterprise law is to be understood as a comprehensive theory which embraces all autonomous enterprises without concern for their legal form or for the nature of their activity.

3. Enterprise law emphasizes the size of an enterprise instead of the legal form for the company. Its paradigm is the large firm, especially the corporation.... Enterprise law is based upon the separation of ownership from control, on the existence of a professional management which derives its legitimation not from ownership of the means of production but from personal skill, on the growing importance of experts and staff functionaries, and on the development of a bureaucratic organization....

5. Last, not least, the concept of enterprise law includes the participation and codetermination rights of employees and trade unions. It links company law and labor law in order to clarify in detail the legal rights and duties of the representatives of employees and the negotiation processes of owners, employees, and managers....

---

1. Commercial Code (Handelsgesetzbuch) §§ 1 ff., 105 ff., 230 ff.

4. E.g., in Gesetz gegan Wettbewerbsbeschränkingen (Law Against Restraints on Competition) §§ 15 ff., 291 ff., Corporations Code (Aktiengesetz) (1965) §§ 291 ff.; Codetermination Law (Mitbestimmungsgesetz) (1976) et al.

5. E.g., the "Codetermination" decision of the Federal Constitutional Court, in 50 BverfGE 290 (1976).

Morrissey v. Commissioner of Internal Revenue

296 U.S. 344; 56 S. Ct. 289
October 18, 1935, argued; December 16, 1935, decided
(some footnotes omitted)

MR. CHIEF JUSTICE HUGHES delivered the opinion of the Court.

Petitioners, the trustees of an express trust, contest income taxes for the years 1924 to 1926, inclusive, upon the ground that the trust has been illegally treated as an "association." The Circuit Court of Appeals affirmed the decision of the Board of Tax Appeals, which sustained the ruling of the Commissioner of Internal Revenue. 74 F.2d 803. We granted certiorari because of a conflict of decisions as to the distinction between an "association" and a "pure trust," the decisions being described in one of the cases as "seemingly in a hopeless state of confusion." Coleman-Gilbert Associates v. Commissioner, 76 F.2d 191, 193.[6]

The facts were stipulated. In the year 1921 petitioners made a declaration of trust of real estate in Los Angeles. They were to be designated in "their collective capacity" as "Western Avenue Golf Club." The trustees were authorized to add to their number and to choose their successors; to purchase, encumber, sell, lease and operate the "described or other lands"; to construct and operate golf courses, club houses, etc.; to receive the rents, profits and income; to make loans and investments; to make regulations; and generally to manage the trust estate as if the trustees were its absolute owners. The trustees were declared to be without power to bind the beneficiaries personally by "any act, neglect or default," and the beneficiaries and all persons dealing with the trustees were required to look for payment or indemnity to the trust property. The beneficial interests were to be evidenced solely by transferable certificates for shares which were divided into 2,000 preferred shares of the par value of $ 100 each, and 2,000 common shares of no par value, and the rights of the respective shareholders in the surplus, profits, and capital assets were defined. "Share ledgers" showing the names and addresses of shareholders were to be kept.

The trustees might convene the shareholders in meeting for the purpose of making reports or considering recommendations, but the votes of the shareholders were to be advisory only. The death of a trustee or of a beneficiary was not to end the trust, which was to continue for twenty-five years unless sooner terminated by the trustees.

During the years 1921 and 1922, the trustees sold beneficial interests and paid commissions on the sales. About 42 acres (of the 155 acres described by the declaration of trust) were plotted into lots which were sold during the years 1921 to 1923, most of the sales being on the installment basis. On the remaining property a golf course and club house were constructed, and in 1923 this property with the improvements was conveyed to

6. Post, p. 369, Nos. 78–79. *See also*, post, pp. 362, 365, No. 108, Swanson v. Commissioner, and No. 238, Helvering v. Combs.

Western Avenue Golf Club, Inc., a California corporation, in exchange for its stock. Under a lease from the corporation petitioners continued the operation of the golf course until January 12, 1924. After that date petitioners' activities were confined to collections of installments of principal and interest on contracts of purchase, the receipt of interest on bank balances and of fees on assignments by holders of purchase contracts, the execution of conveyances to purchasers, the receipt of dividends from the incorporated club, and the distribution of moneys to the holders of beneficial interests. On December 31, 1923, the total number of outstanding beneficial interests was 3016, held by 920 persons; by December 31, 1926, the number of interests had been gradually decreased to 2172, held by 275 persons. The holdings by the trustees ranged approximately from 16 to 29 per cent.

Petitioners contend that they are trustees "of property held in trust," within §219 of the Revenue Acts of 1924 and 1926, and are taxable accordingly and not as an "association." They urge that, to constitute an association, the applicable test requires "a quasi-corporate organization in which the beneficiaries, whether or not certificate holders, have some voice in the management and some control over the trustees and have an opportunity to exercise such control through the right to vote at meetings"; and that, in any event, the activities in which petitioners were engaged, during the tax years under consideration, did not constitute "a carrying on of business" within the rule applied by this Court. [n2 43 Stat. 275; 44 Stat. 32.]

The Government insists that the distinction between associations and the trusts taxed under §219 is between "business trusts on the one side" and other trusts "which are engaged merely in collecting the income and conserving the property against the day when it is to be distributed to the beneficiaries"; that Congress intended that all "business trusts" should be taxed as associations.

1. The Revenue Acts of 1924 and 1926 provided:

"The term 'corporation' includes associations, joint-stock companies, and insurance companies." 1924, §2 (a) (2); 1926, §2 (a) (2). [43 Stat. 253; 44 Stat. 9]

A similar definition is found in the earlier Revenue Acts of 1917, §200, 1918, §1, and 1921, §2 (2), [40 Stat. 302; 40 Stat. 1058; 42 Stat. 227.] and also in the later Acts of 1928, §701 (a) (2), 1932, §1111 (a) (2), and 1934, §801 (a) (2). [45 Stat. 878; 47 Stat. 289; 48 Stat. 771.]

The Corporation Tax Act of 1909, which imposed an excise tax upon the privilege of doing business in a corporate capacity, embraced associations having a capital stock represented by shares and "organized under the laws of the United States or of any State or Territory." Flint v. Stone Tracy Co., 220 U.S. 107, 144; Eliot v. Freeman, 220 U.S. 178, 186. The Income Tax Act of 1913, taxed the net income of "every corporation, joint-stock company or association, and every insurance company, organized in the United States, no matter how created or organized, not including partnerships." The case of Crocker v. Malley, 249 U.S. 223, arose under the latter Act. The Court found that the declaration of trust in that case, relating to mill property was on its face "an ordinary real estate trust of the kind familiar in Massachusetts," and that the function of the trustees was "not to manage the mills but simply to collect the rents and income of such property as may be in their hands, with a large discretion in the application of it, but with a recognition that the receipt holders are entitled to it subject to the exercise of the powers confided to the trustees." The Court thought that, if it were assumed that the words "no matter how created or organized" applied to "association," still it would be "a wide departure from normal usage" to call the beneficiaries a joint-stock association when they were not partners and had "no joint action or interest and no control over the fund." Nor could the trustees "by themselves" be treated as a joint-stock association within the meaning of the Act "unless all trustees with discretionary powers are such." Id., pp. 232–234.

The decision in Crocker v. Malley was rendered in March, 1919, and the Treasury Department thereupon assumed that the degree of control exercised by the beneficiaries over the management of the trust was determinative of the question whether the trust constituted an "association." See statement of the rulings of the Bureau by the Board of Tax Appeals in Woodrow Lee Trust v. Commissioner, 17 B. T. A., pp. 111, 112. It was in that view, that the Regulations under the Revenue Acts of 1918 and 1921, in distinguishing an "association" from a "trust," provided as follows:

> "If, however, the cestuis que trust have a voice in the conduct of the business of the trust, whether through the right periodically to elect trustees or otherwise, the trust is an association within the meaning of the statute." Regulations Nos. 45, 62, Art. 1504.

This ruling continued until our decision in May, 1924, in Hecht v. Malley, 265 U.S. 144, and furnished the test which the Board of Tax Appeals applied in its determinations for earlier years. Accordingly, the Board in the case now before us, holding that under the trust instrument the shareholders "had no control over the trustees or the management of the business," determined that the trust was taxable as such and not as an association, for the years 1921, 1922 and 1923.

The case of Hecht v. Malley related to the excise taxes imposed upon "associations" by the Revenue Acts of 1916, §407, and 1918, §1000 (a). [39 Stat. 789; 40 Stat. 1126] The provision of the Act of 1916 retained the qualifying words of the Corporation Tax Act of 1909—"organized under the laws of the United States, or any State or Territory"—and the Court followed the construction placed upon those words in Eliot v. Freeman, supra. But the Act of 1918 omitted this qualification, and the excise tax as laid upon corporations applied to "associations" under the general definition. The Court thus found the terms of the Act of 1918 to be in significant contrast to the provisions of the Acts of 1909 and 1916. The omission of the qualification showed the intention of Congress "to extend the tax from one imposed solely upon organizations exercising statutory privileges, as theretofore, to include also organizations exercising the privilege of doing business as associations at the common law." 265 U.S. p. 155. Shorn of the restriction, the word "association" appeared to be used in its ordinary meaning, and we referred to several definitions found in standard dictionaries, as, e. g., "a body of persons united without a charter, but upon the methods and forms used by incorporated bodies for the prosecution of some common enterprise"; "a body of persons organized for the prosecution of some purpose, without a charter, but having the general form and mode of procedure of a corporation"; "an organized but unchartered body analogous to but distinguished from a corporation." Id., p. 157. We expressed the view that the word "association," as used in the excise tax provision of the Revenue Act of 1918, clearly included "Massachusetts trusts," of the sort there involved, "having quasi-corporate organizations under which they are engaged in carrying on business enterprises." We were careful to say that it was then unnecessary to determine "what other form of 'associations,' if any," the Act embraced. Id.

In the Hecht case, the trustees of the Hecht and Haymarket trusts relied strongly upon the decision in Crocker v. Malley as conclusively determining that those trusts could not be held to be associations, unless the trust agreements vested "the shareholders with such control over the trustees as to constitute them more than strict trusts within the Massachusetts rule." Reviewing the reasoning of that decision, we pointed out that it was not authority for the broad proposition advanced. We concluded that, when the nature of the trusts was considered, as the petitioners were "not merely trustees for collecting funds and paying them over," but were "associated together in much the same manner as the directors in a corporation for the purpose of carrying on business enterprises," the trusts were to be deemed associations within the meaning of the Act of 1918. This was true "independently of the large measure of control exercised by the beneficiaries." And we rejected the view that Congress intended that organizations of that character "should be exempt from the excise tax on the privilege of carrying on their business merely because such a slight measure of control may be vested in the beneficiaries that they might be deemed strict trusts within the rule established by the Massachusetts courts."

Following this decision, the Treasury Department amended its regulation so as to provide that the distinction between an association and a trust should no longer depend upon beneficiary control. The new provision read:

"Operating trusts, whether or not of the Massachusetts type, in which the trustees are not restricted to the mere collection of funds and their payment to the beneficiaries, but are associated together in much the same manner as directors in a corporation for the purpose of carrying on some business enterprise, are to be deemed associations within the meaning of the Act, regardless of the control exercised by the beneficiaries." Regulations No. 65, Art. 1504, issued in October, 1924, under the Revenue Act of that year.

This provision was amended in August, 1925, so as to read as follows:

> "If, however, the beneficiaries have positive control over the trust, whether through the right periodically to elect trustees or otherwise, an association exists within the meaning of section 2. Even in the absence of any control by the beneficiaries, where the trustees are not restricted to the mere collection of funds and their payment to the beneficiaries, but are associated together with similar or greater powers than the directors in a corporation for the purpose of carrying on some business enterprise, the trust is an association within the meaning of the statute." T. D. 3748, IV-2 Cumulative Bulletin 7.

The text of the regulations relating to associations, so far as pertinent here, promulgated under the Act of 1924, is set forth in the margin. Regulations No. 65, Arts. 1502, 1504, as amended.[7] These regulations were continued substantially unchanged under the Revenue Acts of 1926 and 1928. No. 69, Arts. 1502, 1504; No. 74, Arts. 1312, 1314.

---

7. "Art. 1502. Association.—Associations and joint-stock companies include associations, common law trusts, and organizations by whatever name known, which act or do business in an organized capacity, whether created under and pursuant to state laws, agreements, declarations of trust, or otherwise, the net income of which, if any, is distributed or distributable among the shareholders on the basis of the capital stock which each holds, or, where there is no capital stock, on the basis of the proportionate share or capital which each has or has invested in the business or property of the organization...."

"Art. 1504. Association distinguished from trust.—Where trustees merely hold property for the collection of the income and its distribution among the beneficiaries of the trust, and are not engaged, either by themselves or in connection with the beneficiaries, in the carrying on of any business, and the beneficiaries have no control over the trust although their consent may be required for the filling of a vacancy among the trustees or for a modification of the terms of the trust, no association exists, and the trust and the beneficiaries thereof will be subject to tax as provided by section 219 and by Articles 341–347. If, however, the beneficiaries have positive control over the trust, whether through the right periodically to elect trustees or otherwise, an association exists within the meaning of section 2. Even in the absence of any control by the beneficiaries, where the trustees are not restricted to the mere collection of funds and their payment to the beneficiaries, but are associ-

The corresponding regulations under the Act of 1932 were somewhat modified, No. 77, Art. 1314; and these were considerably expanded by the regulations issued under the Act of 1934, No. 86, Art. 801-2, 801-3.

2. As the statute merely provided that the term "corporation" should include "associations," without further definition, the Treasury Department was authorized to supply rules for the enforcement of the Act within the permissible bounds of administrative construction. Nor can this authority be deemed to be so restricted that the regulations, once issued, could not later be clarified or enlarged so as to meet administrative exigencies or conform to judicial decision. Compare Murphy Oil Co. v. Burnet, 287 U.S. 299, 303–307. We find no ground for the contention that by the enactment of the Revenue Act of 1924 the Department was limited to its previous regulations as to associations. And, while the case of Hecht v. Malley was concerned with the special excise tax provision of the Revenue Act of 1918, the ruling of the Court that the degree of the control by beneficiaries was not a decisive test in that relation could by similar reasoning be applied to the general income taxes laid by the revenue acts upon corporations and thus upon associations. These general income taxes covered both those taxes which in their nature were excise taxes on business, and as such could have been laid prior to the Sixteenth Amendment, and those taxes on other income which were permitted by that Amendment. Stanton v. Baltic Mining Co., 240 U.S. 103, 107, 114. We think that the Department did not exceed its powers in rewriting its regulation, in the light of the decision in Hecht v. Malley, so as to provide with respect to the income taxes, in general, to be paid by associations, that the extent or lack of control by the beneficiaries of a trust should not in itself determine whether there was an association within the meaning of the statute. That the revised regulation had congressional approval is persuasively evidenced by the fact that the regulation, as amended in 1925, was continued without substantial alteration until 1933, and meanwhile Congress reenacted without change the general provision as to associations in the Revenue Acts of 1926, 1928, and 1932. See Brewster v. Gage, 280 U.S. 327, 337; McCaughn v. Hershey Chocolate Co., 283 U.S. 488, 492; Murphy Oil Co. v. Burnet, supra; Helvering v. Bliss, 293 U.S. 144, 151.

The question is not one of the power of Congress to impose this tax upon petitioners but is simply one of statutory construction,—whether Congress has imposed it. See Burk-Waggoner Oil Assn. v. Hopkins, 269 U.S. 110, 114. The difficulty with the regulations as an exposition was that they themselves required explication; that they left many questions open with respect both to their application to particular enterprises and to their validity as applied. The so-called "control test" had led to much litigation, and the change in the regulations after the decision in Hecht v. Malley caused increased uncertainty. That situation is put in a strong light by the action of Congress, in order to afford relief to taxpayers, in enacting § 704 of the Revenue Act of 1928 as a "retroactive" provision applicable, as stated, to trust returns which had been filed for a taxable year prior to 1925 under previous regulations and rulings, and also by giving an option to a trustee, in specified circumstances, in relation to the Revenue Act of 1926 and prior Acts. While it is impossible in the nature of things to translate the statutory concept of "association" into a particularity of detail that would fix the sta-

---

ated together with similar or greater powers than the directors in a corporation for the purpose of carrying on some business enterprise, the trust is an association within the meaning of the statute."

tus of every sort of enterprise or organization which ingenuity may create, the recurring disputes emphasize the need of a further examination of the congressional intent.

3. "Association" implies associates. It implies the entering into a joint enterprise, and, as the applicable regulation imports, an enterprise for the transaction of business. This is not the characteristic of an ordinary trust—whether created by will, deed, or declaration—by which particular property is conveyed to a trustee or is to be held by the settlor, on specified trusts, for the benefit of named or described persons. Such beneficiaries do not ordinarily, and as mere cestuis que trustent, plan a common effort or enter into a combination for the conduct of a business enterprise. Undoubtedly the terms of an association may make the taking or acquiring of shares or interests sufficient to constitute participation, and may leave the management, or even control of the enterprise, to designated persons. But the nature and purpose of the cooperative undertaking will differentiate it from an ordinary trust. In what are called "business trusts" the object is not to hold and conserve particular property, with incidental powers, as in the traditional type of trusts, but to provide a medium for the conduct of a business and sharing its gains. Thus a trust may be created as a convenient method by which persons become associated for dealings in real estate, the development of tracts of land, the construction of improvements, and the purchase, management and sale of properties; or for dealings in securities or other personal property; or for the production, or manufacture, and sale of commodities; or for commerce, or other sorts of business; where those who become beneficially interested, either by joining in the plan at the outset, or by later participation according to the terms of the arrangement, seek to share the advantages of a union of their interests in the common enterprise.

The Government contends that such an organized community of effort for the doing of business presents the essential features of an association. Petitioners stress the significance of, and the limitations said to be implied in, the provision classifying associations with corporations.

4. The inclusion of associations with corporations implies resemblance; but it is resemblance and not identity. The resemblance points to features distinguishing associations from partnerships as well as from ordinary trusts. As we have seen, the classification cannot be said to require organization under a statute, or with statutory privileges. The term embraces associations as they may exist at common law. Hecht v. Malley, supra. We have already referred to the definitions, quoted in that case, showing the ordinary meaning of the term as applicable to a body of persons united without a charter "but upon the methods and forms used by incorporated bodies for the prosecution of some common enterprise." These definitions, while helpful, are not to be pressed so far as to make mere formal procedure a controlling test. The provision itself negatives such a construction. Thus unincorporated joint-stock companies have generally been regarded as bearing the closest resemblance to corporations. But, in the revenue acts, associations are mentioned separately and are not to be treated as limited to "joint-stock companies," although belonging to the same group. While the use of corporate forms may furnish persuasive evidence of the existence of an association, the absence of particular forms, or of the usual terminology of corporations, cannot be regarded as decisive. Thus an association may not have "directors" or "officers," but the "trustees" may function "in much the same manner as the directors in a corporation" for the purpose of carrying on the enterprise. The regulatory provisions of the trust instrument may take the place of "by-laws." And as there may be, under the reasoning in the Hecht case, an absence of control by beneficiaries such as is commonly exercised by stockholders in a business corporation, it cannot be considered to be essential to the existence of an association that those beneficially interested should hold meetings or elect their representatives. Again, while the faculty of

transferring the interests of members without affecting the continuity of the enterprise may be deemed to be characteristic, the test of an association is not to be found in the mere formal evidence of interests or in a particular method of transfer.

What, then, are the salient features of a trust—when created and maintained as a medium for the carrying on of a business enterprise and sharing its gains—which may be regarded as making it analogous to a corporate organization? A corporation, as an entity, holds the title to the property embarked in the corporate undertaking. Trustees, as a continuing body with provision for succession, may afford a corresponding advantage during the existence of the trust. Corporate organization furnishes the opportunity for a centralized management through representatives of the members of the corporation. The designation of trustees, who are charged with the conduct of an enterprise,—who act "in much the same manner as directors"—may provide a similar scheme, with corresponding effectiveness. Whether the trustees are named in the trust instrument with power to select successors, so as to constitute a self-perpetuating body, or are selected by, or with the advice of, those beneficially interested in the undertaking, centralization of management analogous to that of corporate activities may be achieved. An enterprise carried on by means of a trust may be secure from termination or interruption by the death of owners of beneficial interests and in this respect their interests are distinguished from those of partners and are akin to the interests of members of a corporation. And the trust type of organization facilitates, as does corporate organization, the transfer of beneficial interests without affecting the continuity of the enterprise, and also the introduction of large numbers of participants. The trust method also permits the limitation of the personal liability of participants to the property embarked in the undertaking.

It is no answer to say that these advantages flow from the very nature of trusts. For the question has arisen because of the use and adaptation of the trust mechanism. The suggestion ignores the postulate that we are considering those trusts which have the distinctive feature of being created to enable the participants to carry on a business and divide the gains which accrue from their common undertaking,—trusts that thus satisfy the primary conception of association and have the attributes to which we have referred, distinguishing them from partnerships. In such a case, we think that these attributes make the trust sufficiently analogous to corporate organization to justify the conclusion that Congress intended that the income of the enterprise should be taxed in the same manner as that of corporations.

5. Applying these principles to the instant case, we are of the opinion that the trust constituted an association. The trust was created for the development of a tract of land through the construction and operation of golf courses, club houses, etc. and the conduct of incidental businesses, with broad powers for the purchase, operation and sale of properties. Provision was made for the issue of shares of beneficial interests, with described rights and priorities. There were to be preferred shares of the value of $ 100 each and common shares of no par value. Thus those who took beneficial interests became shareholders in the common undertaking to be conducted for their profit according to the terms of the arrangement. They were not the less associated in that undertaking because the arrangement vested the management and control in the trustees. And the contemplated development of the tract of land held at the outset, even if other properties were not acquired, involved what was essentially a business enterprise. The arrangement provided for centralized control, continuity, and limited liability, and the analogy to corporate organization was carried still further by the provision for the issue of transferable certificates.

Under the trust, a considerable portion of the property was surveyed and subdivided into lots, which were sold and, to facilitate the sales, the subdivided property was improved by the construction of streets, sidewalks and curbs. The fact that these sales were made before the beginning of the tax years here in question, and that the remaining property was conveyed to a corporation in exchange for its stock, did not alter the character of the organization. Its character was determined by the terms of the trust instrument. It was not a liquidating trust; it was still an organization for profit, and the profits were still coming in. The powers conferred on the trustees continued and could be exercised for such activities as the instrument authorized.

6. Petitioners contend that the trust was not taxable as an association, by reason of the retroactive provisions of § 704 (a) of the Revenue Act of 1928. The contention is plainly unavailing and does not require an extended discussion. Section 704 (a) of the Act of 1928 provides, in substance, that where a taxpayer filed a return as a trust for a taxable year prior to 1925, the taxpayer shall be taxable as a trust, and not as a corporation, if the taxpayer was considered to be so taxable either (1) under the regulations in force at the time the return was made, or (2) under a departmental ruling then applicable and in force. Prior to the time for filing petitioners' return for the year 1924 the regulations had been amended, following the decision in Hecht v. Malley, supra, so as to provide that operating trusts in which the trustees were not restricted to the mere collection of funds and their payment to beneficiaries, but were associated together in much the same manner as directors in a corporation for the purpose of carrying on a business enterprise, should be deemed to be associations, regardless of the control exercised by the beneficiaries. Treasury Regulations No. 65, Art. 1504, October, 1924. It does not appear that there were regulations or rulings in force, at the time of the return for the taxable year 1924, under which the trust in this instance would be taxable as a trust and not as an association.

The judgment is

Affirmed.

Comments and Questions

1. Does the opinion provide a basis for being able to define a corporation? From what sources does the Supreme Court draw to describe the defining characteristics of corporations? Do corporations, trusts and partnerships share the same legal basis for organizations? How do they differ from one another?

2. *Morrissey* seems to make clear that the enterprise characteristics which define a corporation as a unique form of organization are shared with other forms of enterprise organization in the United States, partnerships and trusts. How is it that these different forms of enterprise organization, created and governed by the different internal regulatory systems (Partnership law, corporate codes, and the like) of the states, can all exhibit the same characteristics?

3. If enterprises organized on different legal bases can exhibit the same core characteristics, then why does the law bother to recognize these different forms of enterprise organization as distinct? For what purposes are these organizations treated as distinct?

4. Are the characteristics of a corporation identified in *Morrissey* universal? In answering this question consider this description of the fundamental characteristics of Spanish companies:

> "The company is born out of a contract, but once created, it becomes a new entity with a juridical personality. The inherent effects in the creation of the company as a legal entity, distinct from its members, are the following:... It has the condition of being subject to the law, that is, it has separate legal personality and has full legal capacity to make acquisitions to bind itself. It is granted proprietary independence. The liability of the company is separate from that of its members. The company has its own name. The company has a domicile and a nationality. The company acts by means of organs and representatives." DOING BUSINESS IN SPAIN §12.02 (2000).

4. The general approach adopted by the *Morrissey* Court was eventually adopted as legislative rule by the Internal Revenue Service. Do the regulations which follow faithfully incorporate the Supreme Court's views? Do the regulations clarify differences between corporations, trusts and partnerships, in the way they may be created, or the form in which they may function? On what sorts of enterprises do the regulations tend to concentrate?

Code of Federal Regulations

Title 26—Internal Revenue
Chapter I—Internal Revenue Service, Department of the Treasury
Subchapter F—Procedure and Administration
Part 301—Procedure and Administration
Definitions
Treas. Reg. § 301.7701-1 Through 301.7701-4
Current through August 18, 2000;
65 FR 50593

§ 301.7701-1 Classification of organizations for federal tax purposes.

(a) Organizations for federal tax purposes—(1) In general. The Internal Revenue Code prescribes the classification of various organizations for federal tax purposes. Whether an organization is an entity separate from its owners for federal tax purposes is a matter of federal tax law and does not depend on whether the organization is recognized as an entity under local law.

(2) Certain joint undertakings give rise to entities for federal tax purposes. A joint venture or other contractual arrangement may create a separate entity for federal tax purposes if the participants carry on a trade, business, financial operation, or venture and divide the profits therefrom. For example, a separate entity exists for federal tax purposes if co-owners of an apartment building lease space and in addition provide services to the occupants either directly or through an agent. Nevertheless, a joint undertaking merely to share expenses does not create a separate entity for federal tax purposes. For example, if two or more persons jointly construct a ditch merely to drain surface water from their properties, they have not created a separate entity for federal tax purposes. Similarly, mere co-ownership of property that is maintained, kept in repair, and rented or leased does not constitute a separate entity for federal tax purposes. For example, if an individual owner, or tenants in common, of farm property lease it to a farmer for a cash rental or a share of the crops, they do not necessarily create a separate entity for federal tax purposes.

(3) Certain local law entities not recognized. An entity formed under local law is not always recognized as a separate entity for federal tax purposes. For example, an organi-

zation wholly owned by a State is not recognized as a separate entity for federal tax purposes if it is an integral part of the State. Similarly, tribes incorporated under section 17 of the Indian Reorganization Act of 1934, as amended, 25 U.S.C. 477, or under section 3 of the Oklahoma Indian Welfare Act, as amended, 25 U.S.C. 503, are not recognized as separate entities for federal tax purposes.

(4) Single owner organizations. Under §§301.7701-2 and 301.7701-3, certain organizations that have a single owner can choose to be recognized or disregarded as entities separate from their owners.

(b) Classification of organizations. The classification of organizations that are recognized as separate entities is determined under §§301.7701-2, 301.7701-3, and 301.7701-4 unless a provision of the Internal Revenue Code (such as section 860A addressing Real Estate Mortgage Investment Conduits (REMICs)) provides for special treatment of that organization. For the classification of organizations as trusts, see §301.7701-4. That section provides that trusts generally do not have associates or an objective to carry on business for profit. Sections 301.7701-2 and 301.7701-3 provide rules for classifying organizations that are not classified as trusts.

(c) Qualified cost sharing arrangements. A qualified cost sharing arrangement that is described in §1.482-7 of this chapter and any arrangement that is treated by the Commissioner as a qualified cost sharing arrangement under §1.482-7 of this chapter is not recognized as a separate entity for purposes of the Internal Revenue Code. See §1.482-7 of this chapter for the proper treatment of qualified cost sharing arrangements.

(d) Domestic and foreign entities. For purposes of this section and §§301.7701-2 and 301.7701-3, an entity is a domestic entity if it is created or organized in the United States or under the law of the United States or of any State; an entity is foreign if it is not domestic. See sections 7701(a)(4) and (a)(5).

(e) State. For purposes of this section and §301.7701-2, the term State includes the District of Columbia.

(f) Effective date. The rules of this section are effective as of January 1, 1997.

§301.7701-2 Business entities; definitions.

(a) Business entities. For purposes of this section and §301.7701-3, a business entity is any entity recognized for federal tax purposes (including an entity with a single owner that may be disregarded as an entity separate from its owner under §301.7701-3) that is not properly classified as a trust under §301.7701-4 or otherwise subject to special treatment under the Internal Revenue Code. A business entity with two or more members is classified for federal tax purposes as either a corporation or a partnership. A business entity with only one owner is classified as a corporation or is disregarded; if the entity is disregarded, its activities are treated in the same manner as a sole proprietorship, branch, or division of the owner.

(b) Corporations. For federal tax purposes, the term corporation means—

(1) A business entity organized under a Federal or State statute, or under a statute of a federally recognized Indian tribe, if the statute describes or refers to the entity as incorporated or as a corporation, body corporate, or body politic;

(2) An association (as determined under §301.7701-3);

(3) A business entity organized under a State statute, if the statute describes or refers to the entity as a joint-stock company or joint-stock association;

(4) An insurance company;

(5) A State-chartered business entity conducting banking activities, if any of its deposits are insured under the Federal Deposit Insurance Act, as amended, 12 U.S.C. 1811 et seq., or a similar federal statute;

(6) A business entity wholly owned by a State or any political subdivision thereof;

(7) A business entity that is taxable as a corporation under a provision of the Internal Revenue Code other than section 7701(a)(3); and

(8) Certain foreign entities—(i) In general. Except as provided in paragraphs (b)(8)(ii) and (d) of this section, the following business entities formed in the following jurisdictions:

[Ed: there follows a listing of the names of the form of companies permitted to sell shares to the public and have those shares on the public markets in a majority of the globe's countries]

(c) Other business entities. For federal tax purposes—

(1) The term partnership means a business entity that is not a corporation under paragraph (b) of this section and that has at least two members.

(2) Wholly owned entities—(i) In general. A business entity that has a single owner and is not a corporation under paragraph (b) of this section is disregarded as an entity separate from its owner.

(ii) Special rule for certain business entities. [omitted]

(e) Effective date. [omitted]

§ 301.7701-3 Classification of certain business entities.

(a) In general. A business entity that is not classified as a corporation under § 301.7701-2(b)(1), (3), (4), (5), (6), (7), or (8) (an eligible entity) can elect its classification for federal tax purposes as provided in this section. An eligible entity with at least two members can elect to be classified as either an association (and thus a corporation under § 301.7701-2(b)(2)) or a partnership, and an eligible entity with a single owner can elect to be classified as an association or to be disregarded as an entity separate from its owner. Paragraph (b) of this section provides a default classification for an eligible entity that does not make an election. Thus, elections are necessary only when an eligible entity chooses to be classified initially as other than the default classification or when an eligible entity chooses to change its classification. An entity whose classification is determined under the default classification retains that classification (regardless of any changes in the members' liability that occurs at any time during the time that the entity's classification is relevant as defined in paragraph (d) of this section) until the entity makes an election to change that classification under paragraph (c)(1) of this section. Paragraph (c) of this section provides rules for making express elections. Paragraph (d) of this section provides special rules for foreign eligible entities. Paragraph (e) of this section provides special rules for classifying entities resulting from partnership terminations and divisions under section 708(b). Paragraph (f) of this section sets forth the effective date of this section and a special rule relating to prior periods.

(b) Classification of eligible entities that do not file an election—(1) Domestic eligible entities. Except as provided in paragraph (b)(3) of this section, unless the entity elects otherwise, a domestic eligible entity is—

(i) A partnership if it has two or more members; or

(ii) Disregarded as an entity separate from its owner if it has a single owner.

(2) Foreign eligible entities—(i) In general. Except as provided in paragraph (b)(3) of this section, unless the entity elects otherwise, a foreign eligible entity is—

(A) A partnership if it has two or more members and at least one member does not have limited liability;

(B) An association if all members have limited liability; or

(C) Disregarded as an entity separate from its owner if it has a single owner that does not have limited liability.

(ii) Definition of limited liability. For purposes of paragraph (b)(2)(i) of this section, a member of a foreign eligible entity has limited liability if the member has no personal liability for the debts of or claims against the entity by reason of being a member. This determination is based solely on the statute or law pursuant to which the entity is organized, except that if the underlying statute or law allows the entity to specify in its organizational documents whether the members will have limited liability, the organizational documents may also be relevant. For purposes of this section, a member has personal liability if the creditors of the entity may seek satisfaction of all or any portion of the debts or claims against the entity from the member as such. A member has personal liability for purposes of this paragraph even if the member makes an agreement under which another person (whether or not a member of the entity) assumes such liability or agrees to indemnify that member for any such liability.

(3) Existing eligible entities—(i) In general. Unless the entity elects otherwise, an eligible entity in existence prior to the effective date of this section will have the same classification that the entity claimed under §§301.7701-1 through 301.7701-3 as in effect on the date prior to the effective date of this section; except that if an eligible entity with a single owner claimed to be a partnership under those regulations, the entity will be disregarded as an entity separate from its owner under this paragraph (b)(3)(i). For special rules regarding the classification of such entities for periods prior to the effective date of this section, see paragraph (f)(2) of this section.

* * *

(c) Elections—(1) Time and place for filing—(i) In general. Except as provided in paragraphs (c)(1)(iv) and (v) of this section, an eligible entity may elect to be classified other than as provided under paragraph (b) of this section, or to change its classification, by filing Form 8832, Entity Classification Election, with the service center designated on Form 8832. An election will not be accepted unless all of the information required by the form and instructions, including the taxpayer identifying number of the entity, is provided on Form 8832. See §301.6109-1 for rules on applying for and displaying Employer Identification Numbers.

* * *

(d) Special rules for foreign eligible entities—(1) Definition of relevance. For purposes of this section, a foreign eligible entity's classification is relevant when its classification affects the liability of any person for federal tax or information purposes. For example, a foreign entity's classification would be relevant if U.S. income was paid to the entity and the determination by the withholding agent of the amount to be withheld under chapter 3 of the Internal Revenue Code (if any) would vary depending upon whether the entity is classified as a partnership or as an association. Thus, the classification might affect the documentation that the withholding agent must receive from the entity, the type of tax or information return to file, or how the return must be prepared. The date that the classification of a foreign eligible entity is relevant is the date an event occurs that creates an obligation to file a federal tax return, information return, or statement for which the classification of the entity must be determined. Thus, the classification of a foreign entity is relevant, for example, on the date that an interest in the entity is acquired which will require a U.S. person to file an information return on Form 5471.

(2) Special rule when classification is no longer relevant—If the classification of a foreign eligible entity which was previously relevant for federal tax purposes ceases to be relevant for sixty consecutive months, the entity's classification will initially be determined under the default classification when the classification of the foreign eligible entity again becomes relevant. The date that the classification of a foreign entity ceases to be relevant is the date an event occurs that causes the classification to no longer be relevant, or, if no event occurs in a taxable year that causes the classification to be relevant, then the date is the first day of that taxable year.

(e) Coordination with section 708(b). [omitted]

(f) Changes in number of members of an entity—(1) Associations. The classification of an eligible entity as an association is not affected by any change in the number of members of the entity.

(2) Partnerships and single member entities. An eligible entity classified as a partnership becomes disregarded as an entity separate from its owner when the entity's membership is reduced to one member. A single member entity disregarded as an entity separate from its owner is classified as a partnership when the entity has more than one member. If an elective classification change under paragraph (c) of this section is effective at the same time as a membership change described in this paragraph (f)(2), the deemed transactions in paragraph (g) of this section resulting from the elective change preempt the transactions that would result from the change in membership.

(3) Effect on sixty month limitation. A change in the number of members of an entity does not result in the creation of a new entity for purposes of the sixty month limitation on elections under paragraph (c)(1)(iv) of this section.

(4) Examples. The following examples illustrate the application of this paragraph (f):

Example 1. A, a U.S. person, owns a domestic eligible entity that is disregarded as an entity separate from its owner.

On January 1, 1998, B, a U.S. person, buys a 50 percent interest in the entity from A. Under this paragraph (f), the entity is classified as a partnership when B acquires an interest in the entity. However, A and B elect to have the entity classified as an association effective on January 1, 1998. Thus, B is treated as buying shares of stock on January 1, 1998. (Under paragraph (c)(1)(iv) of this section, this election is treated as a change in classification so that the entity generally cannot change its classification by election again during the sixty months succeeding the effective date of the election.) Under paragraph (g)(1) of this section, A is treated as contributing the assets and liabilities of the entity to the newly formed association immediately before the close of December 31, 1997. Because A does not retain control of the association as required by section 351, A's contribution will be a taxable event. Therefore, under section 1012, the association will take a fair market value basis in the assets contributed by A, and A will have a fair market value basis in the stock received. A will have no additional gain upon the sale of stock to B, and B will have a cost basis in the stock purchased from A.

Example 2. (i) On April 1, 1998, A and B, U.S. persons, form X, a foreign eligible entity. X is treated as an association under the default provisions of paragraph (b)(2)(i) of this section, and X does not make an election to be classified as a partnership. A subsequently purchases all of B's interest in X.

(ii) Under paragraph (f)(1) of this section, X continues to be classified as an association. X, however, can subsequently elect to be disregarded as an entity separate from A. The sixty month limitation of paragraph (c)(1)(iv) of this section does not prevent X from making an election because X has not made a prior election under paragraph (c)(1)(i) of this section.

Example 3. (i) On April 1, 1998, A and B, U.S. persons, form X, a foreign eligible entity. X is treated as an association under the default provisions of paragraph (b)(2)(i) of this section, and X does not make an election to be classified as a partnership. On January 1, 1999, X elects to be classified as a partnership effective on that date. Under the sixty month limitation of paragraph (c)(1)(iv) of this section, X cannot elect to be classified as an association until January 1, 2004 (i.e., sixty months after the effective date of the election to be classified as a partnership).

(ii) On June 1, 2000, A purchases all of B's interest in X. After A's purchase of B's interest, X can no longer be classified as a partnership because X has only one member. Under paragraph (f)(2) of this section, X is disregarded as an entity separate from A when A becomes the only member of X. X, however, is not treated as a new entity for purposes of paragraph (c)(1)(iv) of this section. As a result, the sixty month limitation of paragraph (c)(1)(iv) of this section continues to apply to X, and X cannot elect to be classified as an association until January 1, 2004 (i.e., sixty months after January 1, 1999, the effective date of the election by X to be classified as a partnership).

(5) Effective date. This paragraph (f) applies as of November 29, 1999.

(g) Elective changes in classification. [omitted]

§ 301.7701-4 Trusts.

(a) Ordinary trusts. In general, the term "trust" as used in the Internal Revenue Code refers to an arrangement created either by a will or by an inter vivos declaration whereby trustees take title to property for the purpose of protecting or conserving it for the beneficiaries under the ordinary rules applied in chancery or probate courts. Usually the beneficiaries of such a trust do no more than accept the benefits thereof and are not the voluntary planners or creators of the trust arrangement. However, the beneficiaries of such a trust may be the persons who create it and it will be recognized as a trust under the Internal Revenue Code if it was created for the purpose of protecting or conserving the trust property for beneficiaries who stand in the same relation to the trust as they would if the trust had been created by others for them. Generally speaking, an arrangement will be treated as a trust under the Internal Revenue Code if it can be shown that the purpose of the arrangement is to vest in trustees responsibility for the protection and conservation of property for beneficiaries who cannot share in the discharge of this responsibility and, therefore, are not associates in a joint enterprise for the conduct of business for profit.

(b) Business trusts. There are other arrangements which are known as trusts because the legal title to property is conveyed to trustees for the benefit of beneficiaries, but which are not classified as trusts for purposes of the Internal Revenue Code because they are not simply arrangements to protect or conserve the property for the beneficiaries. These trusts, which are often known as business or commercial trusts, generally are created by the beneficiaries simply as a device to carry on a profit-making business which normally would have been carried on through business organizations that are classified as corporations or partnerships under the Internal Revenue Code. However, the fact that the corpus of the trust is not supplied by the beneficiaries is not sufficient reason in itself for classifying the arrangement as an ordinary trust rather than as an association or partnership. The fact that any organization is technically cast in the trust form, by conveying title to property to trustees for the benefit of persons designated as beneficiaries, will not change the real character of the organization if the organization is more properly classified as a business entity under §301.7701-2.

(c) Certain investment trusts—(1) An "investment" trust will not be classified as a trust if there is a power under the trust agreement to vary the investment of the certificate holders. See Commissioner v. North American Bond Trust, 122 F. 2d 545 (2d Cir. 1941), cert. denied, 314 U.S. 701 (1942). An investment trust with a single class of ownership interests, representing undivided beneficial interests in the assets of the trust, will be classified as a trust if there is no power under the trust agreement to vary the investment of the certificate holders. An investment trust with multiple classes of ownership interests ordinarily will be classified as a business entity under §301.7701-2; however, an investment trust with multiple classes of ownership interests, in which there is no power under the trust agreement to vary the investment of the certificate holders, will be classified as a trust if the trust isformed to facilitate direct investment in the assets of the trust and the existence of multiple classes of ownership interests is incidental to that purpose.

(2) The provisions of paragraph (c)(1) of this section may be illustrated by the following examples:

Example 1: A corporation purchases a portfolio of residential mortgages and transfers the mortgages to a bank under a trust agreement. At the same time, the bank as trustee delivers to the corporation certificates evidencing rights to payments from the pooled mortgages; the corporation sells the certificates to the public. The trustee holds legal title to the mortgages in the pool for the benefit of the certificate holders but has no power to reinvest proceeds attributable to the mortgages in the pool or to vary investments in the pool in any other manner. There are two classes of certificates. Holders of class A certificates are entitled to all payments of mortgage principal, both scheduled and prepaid, until their certificates are retired; holders of class B certificates receive payments of principal only after all class A certificates have been retired. The different rights of the class A and class B certificates serve to shift to the holders of the class A certificates, in addition to the earlier scheduled payments of principal, the risk that mortgages in the pool will be prepaid so that the holders of the class B certificates will have "call protection" (freedom from premature termination of their interests on account of prepayments). The trust thus serves to create investment interests with respect to the mortgages held by the trust that differ significantly from direct investment in the mortgages. As a consequence, the existence of multiple classes of trust ownership is not incidental to any purpose of the trust to facilitate direct investment, and, accordingly, the trust is classified as a business entity under §301.7701-2.

Example 2: Corporation M is the originator of a portfolio of residential mortgages and transfers the mortgages to a bank under a trust agreement. At the same time, the bank as trustee delivers to M certificates evidencing rights to payments from the pooled mortgages. The trustee holds legal title to the mortgages in the pool for the benefit of the certificate holders, but has no power to reinvest proceeds attributable to the mortgages in the pool or to vary investments in the pool in any other manner. There are two classes of certificates. Holders of class C certificates are entitled to receive 90 percent of the payments of principal and interest on the mortgages; class D certificate holders are entitled to receive the other ten percent. The two classes of certificates are identical except that, in the event of a default on the underlying mortgages, the payment rights of class D certificate holders are subordinated to the rights of class C certificate holders. M sells the class C certificates to investors and retains the class D certificates. The trust has multiple classes of ownership interests, given the greater security provided to holders of class C certificates. The interests of certificate holders, however, are substantially equivalent to undivided interests in the pool of mortgages, coupled with a limited recourse guarantee running from M to the holders of class C certificates. In such circumstances, the existence of multiple classes of ownership interests is incidental to the trust's purpose of facilitating direct investment in the assets of the trust. Accordingly, the trust is classified as a trust.

Example 3: A promoter forms a trust in which shareholders of a publicly traded corporation can deposit their stock. For each share of stock deposited with the trust, the participant receives two certificates that are initially attached, but may be separated and traded independently of each other. One certificate represents the right to dividends and the value of the underlying stock up to a specified amount; the other certificate represents the right to appreciation in the stock's value above the specified amount. The separate certificates represent two different classes of ownership interest in the trust, which effectively separate dividend rights on the stock held by the trust from a portion of the right to appreciation in the value of such stock. The multiple classes of ownership interests are designed to permit investors, by transferring one of the certificates and retaining the other, to fulfill their varying investment objectives of seeking primarily either dividend income or capital appreciation from the stock held by the trust. Given that the trust serves to create investment interests with respect to the stock held by the trust that differ significantly from direct investment in such stock, the trust is not formed to facilitate direct investment in the assets of the trust. Accordingly, the trust is classified as a business entity under §301.7701-2.

Example 4: Corporation N purchases a portfolio of bonds and transfers the bonds to a bank under a trust agreement. At the same time, the trustee delivers to N certificates evidencing interests in the bonds. These certificates are sold to public investors. Each certificate represents the right to receive a particular payment with respect to a specific bond. Under section 1286, stripped coupons and stripped bonds are treated as separate bonds for federal income tax purposes. Although the interest of each certificate holder is different from that of each other certificate holder, and the trust thus has multiple classes of ownership, the multiple classes simply provide each certificate holder with a direct interest in what is treated under section 1286 as a separate bond. Given the similarity of the interests acquired by the certificate holders to the interests that could be acquired by direct investment, the multiple classes of trust interests merely facilitate direct investment in the assets held by the trust. Accordingly, the trust is classified as a trust.

(d) Liquidating trusts. Certain organizations which are commonly known as liquidating trusts are treated as trusts for purposes of the Internal Revenue Code. An organization will be considered a liquidating trust if it is organized for the primary purpose of liquidating and distributing the assets transferred to it, and if its activities are all reasonably necessary to, and consistent with, the accomplishment of that purpose. A liquidating trust is treated as a trust for purposes of the Internal Revenue Code because it is formed with the objective of liquidating particular assets and not as an organization having as its purpose the carrying on of a profit-making business which normally would be conducted through business organizations classified as corporations or partnerships. However, if the liquidation is unreasonably prolonged or if the liquidation purpose becomes so obscured by business activities that the declared purpose of liquidation can be said to be lost or abandoned, the status of the organization will no longer be that of a liquidating trust. Bondholders' protective committees, voting trusts, and other agencies formed to protect the interests of security holders during insolvency, bankruptcy, or corporate reorganization proceedings are analogous to liquidating trusts but if subsequently utilized to further the control or profitable operation of a going business on a permanent continuing basis, they will lose their classification as trusts for purposes of the Internal Revenue Code.

(e) Environmental remediation trusts. (1) An environmental remediation trust is considered a trust for purposes of the Internal Revenue Code. For purposes of this paragraph (e), an organization is an environmental remediation trust if the organization is organized under state law as a trust; the primary purpose of the trust is collecting and disbursing amounts for environmental remediation of an existing waste site to resolve, satisfy, mitigate, address, or prevent the liability or potential liability of persons imposed by federal, state, or local environmental laws; all contributors to the trust have (at the time of contribution and thereafter) actual or potential liability or a reasonable expectation of liability under federal, state, or local environmental laws for environmental remediation of the waste site; and the trust is not a qualified settlement fund within the meaning of § 1.468B-1(a) of this chapter.

* * *

(f) Effective date. The rules of this section generally apply to taxable years beginning after December 31, 1960. Paragraph (e)(5) of this section contains rules of applicability for paragraph (e) of this section. In addition, the last sentences of paragraphs (b), (c)(1), and (c)(2), Example 1 and Example 3 of this section, are effective as of January 1, 1997.

Comments and Questions

1. The Internal Revenue Regulations reproduced above created a system permitting the election of tax status based on entity characteristics effective January 1, 1997. For a discussion of the new system see, e.g., Hugh M. Dourgan et al., *Check the Box—Looking Under the Lid*, 75 Tax Notes 1141 (1997); Michael J. Grace, *Proposed "Check-the-Box" Regulations Would Streamline But Not Eliminate Entity Classification Process*, 37 Tax Mgmt. Memorandum 295 (1996). For a discussion of the new regulations in the context of international tax planning, see, e.g., Bruce Davis, *International Tax Planning Under the Final Check-the-Box Regulations*, 26 Tax Mgmt. Int'l J. 3 (1997).

2. The system of income taxation of business ventures exemplified by the U.S. system can be said to be an example of the regulation of enterprises, rather than of corporate entities. It represents regulation of enterprises based on factors or characteristics other than the formal organization of the enterprises regulated. What was the

basis of regulation under the Internal Revenue Service Regulations? Are there bases of enterprise regulation other than those adopted in the Internal Revenue Service Regulations?

2. Enterprise regulation depends, in part at least, on the ability of enterprises formally organized in different ways, to exhibit the same organizational or business characteristics. What is the relation between the internal law of corporate (or partnership or trust) organization, and the external law of enterprise organization? Can they said to be two aspects of the same general category of lawmaking? Does it make a difference?

3. Do the answer to these questions depend on the basis of enterprise organization possible under the laws of a state? Consider in this light the approach of the Restatement (Second) Conflict of Laws.

> "An organization in one state will be considered a corporation within the meaning of a statute or rule of another state if the attributes the organization possesses under the local law of the state of its formation are sufficient to make it a corporation for the purpose of the statute or rule."[1]

The materials which follow suggest that corporate organization, and its relation to the regulation of business enterprises generally, may depend on the underlying social or economic public policy of the states under which such organizations are given legal effect.

4. On the universalism of Western style corporate organization for business enterprises, consider in reading the excerpts below on the Japanese and Chinese systems, whether the worldwide adoption of a standardized form of corporate organization is a function of its universally applicable efficiency. Can you argue that the adoption of the Western form of enterprise organization is more likely a function of something else, perhaps the predominance of worldwide financial markets in which a standardized corporate form provides the basic form of investment?

5. The excerpts that follow suggest a broader contextualization of corporate law as a subset, perhaps merely a subset of technical rules, of the broader category of enterprise regulation that applies to enterprises organized as corporations, partnerships or trusts. Even with respect to the technical regulations which might be deemed to form the core of the corporate law as a separate body of regulation, we have seen that, even in the US context, the technical details of organizational regulation can produce enterprise organization the character of which is shared among a variety of enterprise organizational forms. The excerpts describing the basis of the commercial law of Spain and France that follow suggest the more traditional basis of enterprise regulation—the merchant or trader, the *kaufmann* of German commercial law. The excerpts focusing on Japanese and Chinese law suggest a different, though no less broad context of enterprise (as opposed to mere corporate) regulation. As you read these materials, consider the many bases on which the regulation of economic enterprises can be based, and see if you can find any basis of regulation unique to the regulation of corporations.

---

1. Restatement (Second) Conflict of Laws § 298. The determination of corporate status is to be made on the basis of a comparison of the attributes of the organization in question with the "attributes an organization must possess to be a corporation for purposes of the statute or rule. Restatement (Second) Conflict of Laws § 298 comment a.

John Bell, Sophie Boyron, and Simon Whittaker, *Principles of French Law*

(1998)

(excerpt from pages 441–442)

As in English law, those involved in commerce come in many different guises. An individual wishing to engage in business may act on his own as a sole trader or he may combine with others in setting up some kind of business organization. A wide variety of business organizations are possible under French law, most being legal or 'moral' persons, i.e. having a legal personality in their own right, distinct from that of the natural persons involved.... [S]ome organizations are automatically considered to be *commerçants*, and their acts are deemed to be commercial acts subject to commercial law. For others, however, their character as *commerçants* derives from the nature of their activities....

The general term used in French law for a profit making organization is *société*. It is generally established by contract between two or more persons (the *associés*), although it is possible, in certain exceptional cases laid down by legislation, for it to be established by a single person,[2] and the *société* becomes a legal person through being registered. It is tempting to translate *société* as 'company', but this would in fact be misleading, for it encompasses what English lawyers would recognize as partnerships as well as companies. This is not to say that French law does not distinguish between these different types of organization: it is only natural to draw a distinction according to the nature of the participation involved, and partnerships find their equivalent in the category of société de personnel. Nevertheless, this is simply a sub-species of the single genus, société, and the fact that French lawyers do not draw a sharp distinction here in the way that English lawyers do is significant for it reflects the differing approaches of the two systems to the question of legal personality. In English law, the distinction between partnerships and companies is vital because the former do not have personality whereas the latter do. In French law, on the other hand, société de personnel are capable of having legal personality (although this is not mandatory).

Not every *société* is involved in commerce. French law draws a distinction between civil and commercial *société*, the former governed by *droit civil* and the latter by *droit commercial*. Whether a *société* is commercial, a *commerçant*, depends in part on the nature of the *société* and in part on what it does....

Christopher H. Hanna, *Initial Thoughts on Classifying the Major Japanese Business Entities Under the Check-the-box Regulations*

51 SMU L. Rev. 75 (1997)

(excerpts from pages 76–81; some footnotes omitted)

Reread the excerpts that appeared earlier in this Chapter.

---

2. Art. 1832 Code Civil, as amended by *loi* no. 85-697 of 11 July 1985, which made provision for a *société à resonsibilité limitée* with only one associé....

Kingsley T.W. Ong and Colin R. Baxter, *A Comparative Study of the Fundamental Elements of Chinese and English Company Law*

48 International & Comparative Law Quarterly 88 (1999)
(excerpts from pages 92–93)

The most common type of business entity in today's world is perhaps the company. With the advent of China's domestic economic growth, it is a natural development for the company again to play an important role in the economy. The concept of "company" was re-introduced into Chinese jurisprudence in the late 1970s.

* * *

The rapid establishment of economic entities, particularly companies, highlighted the need for a comprehensive and systematic set of laws which would govern the organization and activities of business enterprises. The Chinese government had adopted such laws and regulations. But these were encapsulated in separate pieces of legislation, each of which applied to a specific type of entity/company.[27] All these laws had their individual worth. However, the fact that they were enacted separately constituted a major problem. Each different law and set of regulations provided different standards for the organization and operation of different types of company. This was not conducive to the healthy development of a market economy. Furthermore, it made supervision by government regulatory authorities difficult. As more companies became interested in being listed on stock exchanges within and outside China, the Chinese Government felt compelled to adopt company legislation that would provide standard requirements on a nationwide basis.

F. On Actors in the Corporate Enterprise

When we speak of corporate enterprises in a colloquial sense, we tend to think of a singular entity, much like the ancient Greeks conceived of wisdom as a woman with an overripe fondness for owls, whom they called Athena. But, is General Motors Corp. or Xerox Corp., or even Steve's Corner Drug Store, Inc., someone that you can invite to

27. For example, the National People's Congress adopted the Law of the PRC on Industrial Enterprises Owned by the Whole People on 13 April 1988. To implement this law, the State Council further promulgated the Regulations for Converting the Status of the Enterprises Owned by the Whole People on 23 July 1992. These laws ensured a legal framework governing State-owned enterprises. China also adopted laws and regulations governing enterprises with foreign investment like the Chinese-foreign equity joint ventures, Chinese-foreign contractual joint ventures and wholly foreign-owned enterprises. For privately owned enterprises, the State Council promulgated the Provisional Regulations of the PRC on Private Enterprises on 25 June 1988. In 1992, Deng Xiaoping visited Southern China to promote further economic reforms and to advocate the establishment of a market economy in China. Following this, the State Economic Structure Reform Commission of the State Council took a major step by promulgating the Opinion on the Standardisation of Joint Stock Companies of 15 May 1992. This Opinion provides for the establishment of limited liability companies and joint stock companies in China and made it possible for Chinese companies to be listed on stock exchanges outside of China. Local Governments like Shenzhen Municipality and Guangdong Provincial People's Government have also adopted provisions in respect of business enterprises: [Wang Guiguo, China's Company Law: The New Legislation 12 (1994)].

your mother's house for supper? Our legal codes tend to conspire to induce us to think in this way. After all, corporations, our codes and statutes tell us, are juridical persons for a large variety of purposes. Indeed, for some purposes a corporation, like Athena, can be capable of committing a crime or of bearing the burden of a tax in the eyes of the law.

As such, the corporation can be characterized as nothing more than a legal construct having an existence separate from that of the participants in the enterprise it represents. But that characterization tends to oversimplify the reality of the corporate enterprise. In a very real sense, individuals enjoy the benefits, take the risks and assume the responsibilities we lump together under the legal concept of corporation. Though standing apart from its participants, the corporate enterprise is, in a fundamental sense, the sum of a complex aggregation of contractual arrangements between people with conflicting interests in the enterprise subject to legally specified (constraining) powers and duties. And it is the varying and conflicting nature of that interest that gives individuality to a particular corporate enterprise. Indeed, only by considering the characteristics and constraints of the participants in the corporate business enterprise might the student better comprehend the ultimate nature of the relationship between the state, acting either as regulator or as grantor of legal status, and the complex series of relationships we call the corporate enterprise.

Let us consider briefly the principal participants in the corporate enterprise in pure and idealized form. The primary participants are the owners and managers (employees). Lenders play a secondary role, and suppliers, customers, franchisees and other people who may affect the business play subsidiary roles. Owners have a residual or equity interest in the revenues generated by the enterprise. All of the funds that the business generates, and the value of the business itself (in the event it is sold) are the property of the owner. The more successful the enterprise, the greater the residual (revenues and aggregate value of the enterprise) which is available to the owner, and to the owner alone. However, the converse is also true. To the extent the business does not generate revenue or loses value, the owner must bear this loss. An owner also has control of the manner in which the business is run. This makes intuitive sense, especially where the owner has a full residual claim on revenues and value. Where there is more than one owner, the owners, as between themselves must determine the manner in which the claim to revenues, value and control are divided.

The owner's claim to the revenues and value of the enterprise, and the owner's right of control can be limited. Owners lose control to the extent they must delegate decision making authority to employees. The larger (and more successful) the enterprise, the less likely the owner(s) will be able to run the enterprise without help. Managerial employees do not perform tasks for free (much to the chagrin of owners). Managers sell labor, and the price of labor is usually a fixed claim to the revenues of the enterprise—salary. A managerial employee's claim to wages is fixed—the amount of salary is fixed at the time of hire and generally does not depend on the success of the business. Fixed claims are normally paid before an owner can claim his residual interest.

An owner's claim to revenues and control can also be ceded to lenders. While managerial employees sell their labor, lenders sell capital to the enterprise. Why? Because many times, owners do not have sufficient capital to fund the organization or expansion of the enterprise with their own funds. Like labor, the claim of lenders to the revenues of the enterprise are fixed. Lenders charge interest for the use of their money. Interest is paid periodically and is set as a percentage of the amount borrowed. It does not vary with the performance of the enterprise. An enterprise that is wildly successful will make the residual claimant to revenues (the owner) much money—the other claimants to enterprise revenues, lenders and employees, continue to receive the amount of their fixed claim. The same is true if the revenues are insufficient to cover the expenses of the firm. In that case, the owner must make up the difference, the amount of the claims of lenders and employees remains unchanged.

The ideal types—owners, lenders, and managers—are useful for understanding the ends of the spectrum of the characteristics of enterprise participants. In reality, the ideal types merge. For instance, many managers receive compensation in the form of a bonus based on the performance of the enterprise. To that extent, the manager has a residual claim which moves the manager closer to the status of owner. The manager can also bargain for the right to hire and fire subordinate employees, gaining some control reserved for the ideal owner type. Likewise, lenders can acquire attributes of owners by bargaining for the right to control some basic decisions of the enterprise (in the form of positive and negative covenants in loan agreements) and for the right to receive payments based on the gain from the sale of enterprise property. Moreover, to the extent that the lender has more capital invested in the enterprise than the owner, the lender's risk begins to resemble that of the owner.

Takeo Hoshi, *Japanese Corporate Governance as a System*

Chapter 11, in COMPARATIVE CORPORATE GOVERNANCE: THE STATE OF THE ART AND EMERGING RESEARCH 847
(Klaus J. Hopt, Hideki Kanda, Mark J. Roe, Eddy Wymeersch and Stephan Prigge, eds., 1998)
(excerpts from pages 851–852, some footnotes omitted)

The agency problems between shareholders and managers is the most important aspect of corporate governance.[5] The problem arises because managers have an informational advantage that can be misused against the shareholders' interest. There are several possible mechanisms that can alleviate the problem, but we can classify those into two types. First, the shareholders can closely monitor the manager so that the manager does not harm the shareholders' interest. Alternatively, the shareholders can try to align the manager's incentive with theirs.... I will refer to "control-oriented" shareholding and "arms-length" shareholding.

Control-oriented shareholders monitor the behavior of management and, if necessary, intervene in the management. The monitoring is often delegated to the board of directors elected by the shareholders.... Since it is costly to monitor the board's performance and start proxy fights if necessary, control-oriented shareholders are more likely to be large shareholders whose benefits from such active intervention are sufficiently large....

Arm's-length shareholders, on the contrary, do not actively intervene in the management of a corporation. When they are not satisfied with the corporation's performance,

5. Some large firms in Japan, such as many insurance companies, are mutual companies and do not have shareholders. This paper does not address the issue of corporate governance of mutual companies or co-ops, which do not have shareholders.

however, they can take some actions that hurt the management. For example, they can sell their shares, which lowers the share price and makes a firm a target for hostile takeover....

.....Arm's-length shareholding and control-oriented shareholding co-exist in the same economy. They coexist even at the firm level: some shareholders can provide control-oriented shareholding while others provide arm's-length shareholding.

* * *

What one find's however, is that arm's-length shareholding is more prominent in some economies compared with other economies, and that control-oriented shareholding is more prominent in other economies. For example, the U.S. economy has more liquid stock markets and more frequent hostile takeovers compared with other economies, and takeover threats help discipline the managers. In this sense, the U.S. economy is characterized more by arm's-length shareholding. In contrast, hostile takeovers rarely happen in the Japanese economy, and the main bank, which is also one of the largest shareholders of the firm, takes the responsibility of monitoring and disciplining the management.

* * *

Constraints on Bargaining Between Enterprise Participants.

The ideal types—owners, lenders, and managers—bargain with respect to four interrelated fundamental underlying elements. These serve to define (limit) the outer bounds as well as the language of bargaining about the character of the enterprise. Bargaining with respect to each, in turn, is driven by the fundamental economic notion that people will tend to act to maximize their welfare (monetary, economic, or however else welfare is defined). The four elements are *risk of loss, return, control and duration.* These, in turn, are constrained by notions of *conflict of interest, governmental regulation,* and *the inability to fully specify all terms of the relationships between the participants.*

All actors in a business enterprise bargain about the allocation of *risk of loss.* This refers to who will bear the risk that the enterprise will fail or not perform as well as expected. Traditionally, the extent of the risk of a claim is dependant on the residual nature of the claim. High risk claims include equity claims (stocks), contingent claims (performance bonuses), and other residual claims (options and warrants). Low risk claims include debt claims (bank loans), and other fixed claims (salary). The risk of hybrid claims, the most likely to exist after bargaining among the participants, will depend on the resemblance of the claim to the ideal high or low risk claim. All actors bear some risk—lenders for the amount loaned, managers for salary unpaid, owners for capital invested. Questions respecting the priority of risk, who realizes risk first, and to what extent do each of the actors bear this risk is a fundamental part of the discourse of corporate organization. For example, who is entitled to any remaining assets in the event a corporation fails, and in what order. The lender will want priority to take assets up to the amount owed it before anyone else, but the manager will want to receive all sums due him for his labor before the lender is paid, and the owner might wish to bargain for the priority of payment for at least part of her investment, or for pro rata payout of remaining assets along with certain classes (especially unsecured) of lenders.

Return focuses on the opposite side of risk of loss. Return describes what the participants expect to receive if the enterprise is successful. Residual returns bear both the highest risk and the greatest possibility of positive return. They include profits, royalties, and perhaps even the interest of managers in continued employment. Participants of residual returns are interested in the profit maximization of the enterprise. They tend, therefore, to have an incentive to take risks if the rewards (in terms of profit maximization) are great enough. Fixed returns, on the other hand, are limited to a finite amount—the principal amount of a bank loan for instance. Lenders and others receiving a fixed return are less interested in profit maximization and more interested in maximizing the probability that they will be paid. As such, lenders tend to be far more risk averse than residual return holders, they have far more to lose and nothing to gain by a risky strategy that may return in an enormous residual return (they are entitled to none of this "excess" return after all). Lenders therefore have an incentive to attempt to limit the borrower's freedom to make business decisions.

The allocation of *control* determines who has the right to make certain business decisions affecting the conduct of the enterprise. Generally control attaches to the residual claimant. However, since there is rarely one well defined or sole holder of residual claims, control can be diffused among the various participants. Managers have an interest in control, since the success of the business may affect their income as well as their reputation in the business community. Owners are interested in control because they bear a substantial amount of the financial risk should the enterprise fail. Lenders seek control to the extent they deem necessary to minimize the risk of non-payment of their loan.

Duration determines the intensity and complexity of the bargain between the participants in the enterprise. At the greatest level of generality, durational issues touch on the conditions with respect to which the business can be terminated, or a participant's interest in the enterprise transferred to another. Restrictions on transfer can lock a participant into an enterprise and affect the manner in which he calculates risk of loss and the requisite need to control the enterprise. As duration increases, the contingencies with which a participant must deal increases as well. Not all participants experience the same durational time lines. Lenders, managers and owners approach their involvement with a business enterprise differently. The participation of lenders is generally fixed both as to amount and time. A loan comes due at the maturity date and must be paid then or be renegotiated to avoid a default. The term of the loan may be quite long (a mortgage secured by real property may extend to forty years or more) or quite short (terminating in a matter of months). Likewise managers may expect a three to five year tenure with an enterprise, the bargaining as between managers and owners usually revolves around the establishment of a definitive term of employment. "The relationship between lender and borrower may be at will (loan callable on demand) but often is for a specified term. The relationship among shareholders of a corporation (including the relationship between common and preferred shareholders) is ordinarily of indefinite duration; the corporation continues until terminated by a majority of the shareholders or, in unusual circumstances, by judicial decree." William A. Klein, *The Modern Business Organization: Bargaining Under Constraints*, 91 Yale L. J. 1521, 1549 (1982).

The basis on which the participants in an enterprise bargain about the allocation of risk of loss, return, control, and the duration of their relationship with the enterprise is limited by and subject to three overarching constraints—*conflict of interest, governmental regulation, and the inability to fully specify all terms of the relationships between the participants.*

Conflict of interest follows from the fact that our economic system postulates that people tend to act in their own best interests, and that such personal utility maximization behavior may be hard to detect or control. Conflicts of interest arise because the different participants tend to have different fundamental objectives and perceptions on the kinds of strategies that will maximize their personal returns. In the most fundamental sense, these differences may result in conflicting reactions to the taking of risks in the running of the enterprise. Thus, for instance, lenders would tend to urge an enterprise to pursue more conservative strategies than owners might prefer, because the additional value added to the enterprise from the successful pursuit of the more risky strategy would inure almost entirely to the owner and not to the lender (whose claim on the enterprise, as you will recall, is usually fixed). More sharply drawn conflicts arise when the interests of one participant can be advanced only at the expense of that of another participant. Thus, for instance managers whose claim on an enterprise is limited to a fixed claim for salary might be more inclined to divert an opportunity of value to the enterprise to his own personal use if he has the ability to make use of the opportunity personally (and thereby appropriate the entire value). Conflict may be control by protective rules, limiting the discretion or power of participants to act in certain ways. Where an owner fears that a manager will have less of an interest in overseeing the affairs of the enterprise than the owner (because the owner and not the manager has a residual claim on the revenues of the enterprise), an owner can control conflict by tying at least some portion of the manager's compensation to the performance of the enterprise.

Governmental regulation, which provides the primary focus of the materials in this book, provides a significant and fairly well defined set of constraints. Indeed, lawyers tend to think about constraints on corporations almost purely in terms of these formal, legal constraints. As I have indicated, that is likely an excessively narrow way of conceiving of the forces shaping the form of corporate enterprises. At the most general level of understanding, governmental regulation may restrict participants' freedom to define the relationships between them in the manner they might otherwise prefer. For instance, managers who have effective control of the management of the enterprise owned by a large number of individuals with small interest in the enterprise might have been able to bargain for the elimination of any right of the shareholders to inspect the corporate books and records. Corporate statutes generally prohibit this kind of bargain. Governmental regulation can impose costs on particular transactions that may make alternatives more economically palatable than they might otherwise be. Thus, the reporting and informational requirements of the Federal securities laws impose costs and delays on an enterprise's ability to raise capital through the public offering of securities which may make the raising of capital through debt more attractive. On the other hand, governmental regulation also provides a "pre-bargained" package of fundamental agreements respecting the nature of the relationships between the participants that may reduce substantially the transaction costs of creating an enterprise in corporate form.

Lastly, the practical inability of the parties to set out their agreements with *complete specificity* limits the ability of the participants to anticipate and provide for solutions to all contingencies that may arise in the course of the existence of the enterprise. To the extent that specificity is impossible, participants must rely on more or less acceptable substitutes, primarily vague general rules and reliance on the honesty and good faith of the participants. Honesty and good faith is a powerful proxy for information. As a result, personal reputation in the business world has some significant positive economic value. The problem of specificity is particularly suited to the lawyer's craft. Legal rules can serve as an efficient proxy for specificity. Indeed, much state corporate legislation over the course of the twentieth century has been targeted towards crafting general rules which can serve as the base for dealing with issues common to corporate enterprises. The limits of specificity and governmental regulation are complementary and provide a reasonable basis on which the participants in the corporate enterprise can order their relationships on a general level.

Jonathon R. Macey, *Institutional Investors and Corporate Monitoring: A Demand-Side Perspective in a Comparative View*

Chapter 12, in COMPARATIVE CORPORATE GOVERNANCE: THE STATE OF THE ART AND EMERGING RESEARCH (Klaus J. Hopt, Hideki Kanda, Mark J. Roe, Eddy Wymeersch and Stephan Prigge, eds., 1998) (excerpts pages 903, 907–908; some footnotes omitted)

I believe that a consensus exists on at least two important issues. There seems to be agreement among scholars and commentators about: (1) the incomplete nature of the corporate contract, and the need for corporate governance principles that fill in the gaps in these incomplete, contingent contracts; and (2) the need to control managerial shirking, i.e. to control agency costs.

It is well known that corporate law provides, *inter alia*, a set of standard, off-the-rack terms that permit participants in a corporation to economize on contracting costs. The formal contracts among entrepreneurs, managers, investors, etc., are necessarily incomplete, and corporate law provides an important mechanism for supplementing the actual bargains that people make by supplying background terms and filling in the gaps in contracts.

* * *

A second goal of a properly functioning system of corporate governance is controlling managerial shirking. While this goal can also be characterized as a subset of the first goal of enforcing contracts, it is important enough to deserve special mention. Any corporation of any size will have outside investors. The presence of these outside investors requires the separation of management and finance, commonly described as the separation of ownership and control. Takeovers, proxy fights and public contest for control are among the ways that capital-markets-oriented corporate governance systems (such as the U.S. and the U.K.) deal with the problem of agency costs. In corporate governance regimes with a weak or non-existent market for corporate control, but relatively strong banks, a company's relationships with its main bank, its corporate shareholders, its corporate group, and other institutional investors may substitute, to some extent, for the role played by the market for corporate control in its various incarnations.[6]

---

6. Misahiko Aoki, *Towards an Economic Model of the Japanese Firm*, 28 J. ECON. LIT. 1 (1990); Misahiko Aolki, Hugh Patrick and Paul Sheard, *The Japanese Main Bank System: An Introductory Overview*, in THE JAPANESE MAIN BANK SYSTEM: ITS RELEVANCY FOR DEVELOPING AND TRANSFORMING ECONOMIES 1 (Misahiko Aoli and Hugh Patrick, eds. 1994).

Mark J. Roe, *German Codetermination and German Securities Markets*

5 COLUM. J. EUR. L. 199 (1999)
(excerpt pages 200–206; some footnotes omitted)

II. The German Boardroom

One might begin to analyze the German boardroom with a handful of observations from the U.S. about what makes for a good board:

1. Small size, with specialized sub committees;
2. Frequent meetings;
3. Intense information flow; and
4. Low conflicts of interest.

To an American, the German boardroom seems poor on all four characteristics. That observation might be taken as advice for German boardroom players—a start on a conversation about how to improve the German boardroom. Or, second, that observation might initiate an analysis of German boardroom origins: Did shareholder voice in the firm through banks' indirect ownership and their control of the proxy system combine to induce codetermination legislation to give labor a louder voice in the firm? Once both shareholder voice and labor voice are firmly in place, is it easy for one to be lowered without lowering the other as well? Or, third, that observation might reflect back on the United States. Because German companies have until now been internationally competitive, maybe these features are not crucial to good operations, and other features, not yet well identified in the corporate governance literature, are.

I shall focus here on the second inquiry: I assume that these four boardroom features are desirable, that German boards lack every one, and that one might want to speculate on the origins and persistence of that deficit. For the U.S., I have argued elsewhere that some prevalent forms plausibly have political origins,[5] and one might speculate similarly for the German boardroom. Mundane features might be linked to German social politics. In reaction to German codetermination, players inside the firm, namely managers and shareholders, seem to have sought to weaken the large firm's supervisory board or, more properly, to keep it weak, despite global business changes that led to its strengthening elsewhere.[6]

Moreover, German businesspeople, the German business press and business academics at times point to Germany's lack of a vibrant securities markets that would take innovative firms public and help charge-up the German economy. Standard accounts identify the lack of an equity-holding culture (a demand-side perspective), the lack of an entrepreneurial culture of business people who create new firms (a supply-side perspective), inappropriate securities laws, opaque accounting, and the influence of the banks (in business and politics) to explain the lack of a vibrant German stock market. While I do not deny these explanations, even if these problems (which are common in

5. *See* [MARK J. ROE, STRONG MANAGERS, WEAK OWNERS: THE POLITICAL ROOTS OF AMERICAN CORPORATE FINANCE (1997)].

6. *See, e.g.*, Richard H. Schmidt, Korreferat zum Referat W. von Schimmelmann, Sonderdruck aus Finanzmärkte 1 5 (1997) (employee's presence on the supervisory board moves critical discussions, especially those critical of management, out from the supervisory board meetings, so that the important decisions are taken before the meetings, in informal meetings and telephone conferences).

several continental European countries) were overcome, Germany would face an additional, and perhaps even more intractable, difficulty in developing vibrant securities markets with many initial public offerings (IPOs), namely, that the codetermined structure fits poorly with diffuse ownership. Codetermination and concentrated blockholding fit together as complements and continued blockholding will mean diffuse securities markets will not develop deeply and well. The poor fit between codetermination and diffuse ownership makes firm founders less willing to sell their blocks of stock into IPOs and makes distant potential buyers much more wary of owning stock in the German firm than they would be otherwise.

III. Codetermination and Boardroom Reaction

We begin by examining what seem to be the details of a board's structure and function: information flow, the size of the board, and the frequency of board meetings. Could these features strongly link up to German codetermination? Take the size of the board. American studies find that smaller boards are more effective than big ones; here linkage is quite explicit because the codetermination statute mandates the board's size by requiring that the board's size vary between twelve and twenty members depending on the company size.[7]

The other features of German boards, like the infrequency of board meetings, the formalized but weak information flow, and the frequently conflicted composition of the shareholder side, are not mandated by statutes but can also be seen as buttressed by codetermination. Begin with the frequency of meetings: American boards tend to meet more frequently, about eight times per year. Many German boards typically meet two to four times per year. Although the German statute sets the minimum frequency of two meetings annually, the board is free to meet more frequently—but many do not, and those that do typically only meet four times a year. (True, some boards meet even more often and perhaps recent governance problems have induced a trend to hold more frequent meetings.) Obviously, a board that seldom meets will, all else being equal, be less informed and less able to monitor management than one that meets frequently.

Moreover, information flow to the German board that meets infrequently is further constricted, as oftentimes key documents are placed in front of the board members only at the meeting. This practice renders directors unable to intensely prepare to examine the firm's current operations (if they were so inclined), and to closely question managers. But even motivated and capable directors will have a hard time being strong monitors if the company's basic information is placed in front of them only moments before a formalized meeting begins and then is whisked away shortly thereafter.

As said, the linkage between board size, which is mandated, and codetermination is clear. The deeper question is whether variable matters, like meeting frequency and information flow, also link up to codetermination. Let us assume that intense information flow and more frequent meetings are functional. If so, German boards could have evolved consciously to get better information and to meet more frequently. After errors and missteps, boards could have decided that they needed to meet more often to be effective. (To be sure, a few have.) Or German managers and board members, aware that meeting frequency and information flow could improve the board's functions, could have led boards to meet more often even before the firm made any errors. Or boards

---

7. ....Companies with more than 20,000 employees must have a twenty-one person board; those with less than 10,000 must have a twelve person board; and those between 10,000 and 20,000 get a sixteen person board.

might have stumbled onto more frequent meetings as effective and then continued the practice.[11]

If in fact these processes could have occurred but for the most part did not, what could explain the roadblock? Once again, dysfunctionality or irrelevance cannot be rejected, but the American experience suggests the contrary. A simple economic analysis suggests a hypothesis. If there are gains to be made by strengthening governance, but it is not strengthened, then perhaps increasing its strength also would brought on costs, either to the firm or to players inside the firm. Here codetermination might play a role in the internal calculus of the firm's players, and perhaps in the firm's performance as well.

That the German supervisory board was never formally intended to have a hands on role is not critical to this discussion. We ask here why the German boardroom did not evolve to be more hands on. True, one cannot dismiss the possibility that, for the German supervisory boards to evolve, the players needed a formal legal mandate and that, absent that mandate, the board could not evolve even if business pressures pushed to increase activity.[13] But this too begs our question. Even if the lack of formal authority to go beyond nomination of management board personnel blocked evolution (presumably because formalities are more important in determining the authority of the German than of the American boardroom), we would still not know why the German corporate players did not turn to the parliamentary granters of formal authority to request that parliament upgrade the players' authority. The hypothesis I offer in this paper could help explain why there was no demand for formal change, if formal change was a necessary precursor to substantive change.

The German firm can be analyzed by abstracting it into three parts: management, labor and capital. Managers who face the possibility that an independent board may scrutinize them might perform better than those who do not worry about facing that kind of scrutiny. But for boards to be able to scrutinize the managers, they need to meet frequently and to get good information about the firm. Capital might insist on this scrutiny, or managers might form time to time ask for it, or firms with this scrutiny might tend to grow and those without it to contract. Normally the board would be the vehicle for this scrutiny.

Now let us look at capital vis-a-vis labor and assume that capital does not want labor to be well informed. Capital's desire could be functional, dysfunctional or neutral, but is easy to understand. Their desire could be functional in the sense that labor could sometimes damage the firm, especially when labor's representatives pursue the goals of employees with only a few years left to work at the firm; greater employee voice and information in corporate affairs could increase that damage. Conflict, even if not arising from capital-labor disputes, is a critical cause of failure in closely held firms when owners fight to divide value and thereby harm the firm. Increased information could increase conflict, and increased conflict could fritter away firm value.

Capital's desire could here also be neutral to the total size of the pie. Internal rent-seeking between capital and labor could be in play; capital might want to keep labor in

---

11. Thus one would hypothesize that recent boardroom failures in Germany would have increased the pressure on supervisory boards to meet more often. *See* [GERHARD LIENER, THE FUTURE OF GERMAN GOVERNANCE, CORP. BOARD, 1 (May 1995), cited in Thomas J. André, Jr., *Some Reflections on German Corporate Governance: A Glimpse at German Supervisory Boards*, 70 TUL. L. REV. 1819, 1825 n. 21 (1996)].

13. The supervisory board cannot take on management functions. *See* André, *supra* note [11], at 1824 n. 19 (citing §4 AktG).

the dark so that labor is less effective in internal rent seeking and capital more effective. Or capital's desire could be dysfunctional because some labor-management decisions require trust, and well informed labor that gets good information through the board could enhance that trust in shop-floor activities. But if this enhanced firm performance is offset by capital's perception that it would lose value because labor would eb able to rent-seek more effectively (or capital's rent-seeking would be less effective), or by management's fear that consulting labor would constrict their own autonomy, then capital's (and management's) desire to keep labor in the dark becomes dysfunctional.

It is easy to see that capital (and sometimes management) might prefer that labor be ill-informed. But if the supervisory board is theoretically the best (or a good) conduit for information to capital as well, then capital, cutting down on (or by failing to increase) the information flow to the board, would be constricting the information flow to itself. This self imposed constriction could be rational if the costs to capital from labor being better informed were greater than the gains to capital by better form performance: capital might prefer to take its chance with unmonitored managers than with well informed labor.

Or capital might decide it can get enough information elsewhere—through informal discussions, through control of the speaker's seat of the supervisory board (the chair of the supervisory board is from the shareholder side), through separate meetings between management and the shareholder bench of the board, or through bank loan channels. Capital may know that these channels could be enhanced with better boardroom information, but if the better boardroom channel would come with the price of better informed labor, they may prefer the codetermined board to be less well informed than it could be. In any case, bankers believe they get no more information from their seats on the supervisory board than they could get as a creditor of the firm.[16]

Shareholders and managers may look at meeting frequency similarly to how they look at information flow to the board. They may know that more monitoring should somewhat improve operations, at least at critical junctures, and they may believe that more meetings should improve monitoring. But more meetings would enhance labor's voice in the codetermined boardroom, making management and capital shy away from asking to have more meetings.

The board's size might also naturally lead to reduced information flow and fewer meetings by making it harder for its members to coordinate meeting times than if the board were smaller. This is the reason often given by German board members on why meetings are infrequent, but I wonder whether those who use it do so to avoid confronting the deeper structural questions that codetermination raises.

The large size of the firm's board also increases the inside-the-boardroom free-rider problem. ("Why prepare, if I am a small player inside the boardroom?"). If free-riding board members will not prepare well, then there is little reason to get the reports out to the supervisory board for early study (because they will not be studied by the free rid-

16. Peter O. Mulbert, *Empfehlen sich gesetzliche Regelungen zur Einschränkung des Einflusses der Kreditinstitute auf Aktiengesellschaften?*, Gutachten E, zum 61. Deutschen Juristentag 49 (1996). Labor could similarly seek alternative information channels, through the works councils or straightforward union negotiation. Board seats may also become a patronage item, one that compensates employee-side players who enter the boardroom and become less likely to confront the firm and its managers in other arenas. As such, capital and managers may have other reasons to maintain the current system of few meetings and limited work, as a means of coopting some players who could disrupt the firm elsewhere.

ers); small benefits (like maintaining general confidentiality) from last minute distribution could thereby keep the flow of information low.

The evidence available, although indirect, is consistent with this view of a deliberately weakened supervisory board in the face of the 1976 expansion of German codetermination. Early studies suggest that managers and shareholders sought to weaken the labor side of the codetermined board via, say, equity-dominated sub-committees. More than half of the German boards adopted one or more of these "equity-enhancing" characteristics:

1. Additional stockholder Vice Chairs of the board (the German corporate law's default rule is that the Vice-Chair come from the labor side, the Chair from the equity side);
2. Equity-controlled subcommittees;
3. Enhanced power of the Chair (who is from the shareholder side) to control the agenda;
4. Quorum rules that favored equity;
5. Additional authority of the Chair to postpone a substantive action if he or she could not be present;
6. Requirement that the Chair cast the tie-breaking vote if a board vote was tied; or
7. Restraint on board members from making statements outside of the boardroom.[18]

But it is puzzling to this observer that when corporate governance becomes a hot topic in Germany, as it has, the number of seats that the bankers take becomes an issue, as it should be, and custodial voting becomes an issue, as it should likewise be. But the reports we see in the U.S. do not indicate codetermination's effects as an issue also, which may be just as powerful.[19] This is partly because the topic of codetermination is academically passé in Germany, partly because it is a sacred cow that is above direct criticism, and partly because this kind of functional analysis (as opposed to formalist and doctrinal analysis) is not central to German legal scholarship.

Tests are plausible here. The most obvious one is to conduct a sociological survey wherein supervisory board members would be asked whether or not the frequency of meetings and information flow are issues to them or not and if codetermination affected decisions on whether to change or not.[20] A more sophisticated test would take a sample of firms and divide them into two: one, where internal rent-seeking should be low, and the other, where it could be high. If the hypotheses I advanced earlier are cor-

---

18. Elmar Gerum, Horst Steinman & Werner Fees, Der Mitbestimmte Aufsichtsrat—Eine Empirische Untersuchung 98–115 (1988). The study, however, dealt with data from 1979 and so is now stale.

19. The Ministry of Finance thought to reduce board size from 20, limiting the number of chairmanships that a single person can hold, and moving the authority to appoint auditors from the management board to the supervisory board. The leading shareholder associations focused on these matters, and also proposed to limit to 10 the boards a single person can sit on, to upgrade board committees, and to increase required board meetings to four per year. *See* Corinna Arnold, *Recent Scandals Place German Boards Under Attack* (IRRC Corporate Governance Bulletin), July–Sept. 1996, at 16, 17. As Professor Kübler reports, German unions persuaded Chancellor Kohl to kill off the proposal to reduce boards to a less unwieldy size. Friedrich Kübler, *Comment* 5 Colum. J. Eur. L. 213 (1999).

20. "[C]ritical questions are not asked because you have to take account of the employees." This quotation, said to be radical, is attributed to the head of the Federation of German Industry [BDI]....

rect, then the low rent seeking firms should have more frequent meetings, better information, and more diffuse ownership.

Takeo Hoshi, *Japanese Corporate Governance as a System*

Chapter 11, in COMPARATIVE CORPORATE GOVERNANCE
THE STATE OF THE ART AND EMERGING RESEARCH 847
(Klaus J. Hopt, Hideki Kanda, Mark J. Roe,
Eddy Wymeersch and Stephan Prigge, eds., 1998)
(excerpts from pages 857–863; some footnotes omitted)

The aspects of corporate governance are not only related with each other, but also with some other economic institutions. Here I list four important institutions that influence the nature of corporate governance. Those are (a) system of human resource management, (b) managerial labor market, (c) product market competition, and (d) corporate law....

The first one is the system of human resource management.....There are many types of arrangements that can mitigate this type of agency problem, but we can again identify two broad classes of approaches: the arm's length approach that relies on a well-organized labor market, and the control oriented approach that relies more on long term relation in internal labor markets.

In the arm's-length approach, the manager finds workers in a well organized labor market, where each worker is priced according to the market assessment of his productivity....

A control-oriented approach creates an internal labor market that enhances the learning of workers' abilities and gives the right incentive for workers to exert their efforts....

Note that the control-oriented human resource management requires a long term commitment of both the employers and the employees. An employer needs a long time to find out the quality of her employees and the employees need a long time to climb up the ranking hierarchy to achieve high earnings (that come with high ranks). Thus, a corporate governance mechanism that relies on corporate takeovers to reduce the agency problem between shareholders and management may be too disruptive to control oriented human resource management. Control oriented shareholding, in which management changes are carried out by stable shareholders, may be more conducive to such a labor management.

The second institution that influences the nature of corporate governance is the labor market for managers. If there is a well-organized market for managers, any misconduct by a manager toward stakeholders may hurt the reputation of the manager in the labor market and reduce the probability of getting a lucrative management position in the future. This pressure from the managerial labor marker can prevent managers from abusing their informational advantage against the stakeholders. In this sense, a well functioning labor market for managers can be a substitute for corporate governance.

Third, the product market competition also disciplines managers and may substitute for corporate governance....

In the sense that a competitive product market provides valuable information about how a company is performing, it may well be complementary to the system of corporate governance that uses such information. Without a reasonably competitive product market, even control oriented stakeholders may have trouble assessing the performance of the firm.

Finally, corporate laws influence corporate governance. Roe[Mark J. Roe, *Political and Legal Restraints on Ownership and Control of Public Companies*, 27 J. Financial Economics 7-41 (1990)] points out many impediments in the corporate law in the U.S. that discourage or prohibit control-oriented shareholding. Fukao [Mitsuhiro Fukao, *Financial Integration, Corporate Governance, and the Performance of Multinaitonal Companies*, The Brookings Institution, Washington, D.C. 1995] also finds obstacles for shareholders who want to intervene in the management actively in the U.S. and the U.K. while shareholders in Japan, Germany, and France do not encounter many of the restrictions. He also finds that there are many legal constraints on cash distributions in Japan, Germany, France, and the U.K., while few restrictions exist in the U.S. Thus, the stakeholders in Japan, Germany, France and the U.K do not have to worry much about the possibility of the manager (colluding with shareholders) making too much distribution to shareholders. This influences the nature for corporate governance developed in these countries.....

* * *

Shareholding in Japan is closer to control-oriented than arm's length. The majority of shares of major corporations in Japan are held by stable shareholders, which include other corporations in the same business group, major creditors, and major customers/suppliers....As a consequence of stable shareholding, a hostile takeover is very difficult and in fact rarely happens. Thus, arm's length shareholding, which relies on takeover threats to discipline managers, would not work.

Instead, shareholders in Japan are more control oriented. Stable shareholders, especially banks, often place their retired employees as board members. The cases of financially distressed firms accepting the executives dispatched by their main banks to senior directors' positions are well documented....The cases of financial distress are the clearest evidence for the control-oriented nature of Japanese corporate governance, but directors dispatched by stable shareholders are also observed during normal times....

A relatively more concentrated shareholding structure in Japan compared with the U.S. makes it easier to have control-oriented shareholding because a collective action problem among small shareholders is mitigated....

It is important to note that the dominant majority of stable shareholders in Japan are corporations that have business relations with the company. They are shareholders but also other stakeholders at the same time. They are creditors, suppliers, and customers. Thus, even though we observe control-oriented shareholding, it is exercised by the corporations, which also have other types of stake in the company, and the role played by individual shareholders is minimal.

In addition to being major shareholders, creditors (especially banks) in Japan influence the management through another mechanism. Again, their approach is control-oriented rather than arm's length. Rather than relying on the threat of bankruptcy, banks monitor the management of a corporation and intervene when the company gets into financial trouble.

....The other creditors delegate monitoring to the main bank, which is expected to represent the interests of all creditors....

Japanese workers do not have formal representation in a supervisory board....Nevertheless, they are considered important stakeholders, and consideration of workers' welfare influences major decisions relating to corporate governance, such as mergers and rescue operations of financially troubled firms led by their main banks....

Thus, even though Japanese workers do not have a mechanism to formally represent themselves in the board, they can influence corporate decisions in critical times.... [T]he ability of labor to influence corporate decisions seems to be related to the Japanese labor practice characterized by lifetime employment and seniority wages.

Suppliers and customers are often members of stable shareholders. This is especially the case when a series of suppliers are organized under a prime manufacturer to form production *keiretsu*, or when a series of distributors are organized under a manufacturer to form distribution *keiretsu*.[15]....

The Japanese government did not intervene in the economy by owning companies. The government ownership was limited to some industries, such as communications and railroads, and has been declining since the 1980s. Nonetheless, the Japanese government has been very actively influencing private business. A device used by the Japanese government to direct private business without owning shares is the industrial policy, which is often implemented through administrative guidance without specifically relying on formal laws.

Another tool is *amakudari*, which is a practice for retired government officials to be invited to be board members of private companies. As other stakeholders, such as banks and firms in the same business group, send their employees to sit on the board, the government, though not a shareholder, sends in the retired officials to be board members. This in itself shows the influence of the government over private firms, and it gives the government a communication channel to intervene in the management, if necessary....

* * *

To summarize the arguments in this section, Japanese corporate governance is characterized by (1) control-oriented shareholding, (2) shareholding by creditors and control-oriented lending, (3) involvement of labor without formal representation, (4) shareholding by suppliers/customers and long term relationship, and (5) interventionist government without shareholding.

Yoshiro Miwa, *The Economics of Corporate Governance in Japan*

in COMPARATIVE CORPORATE GOVERNANCE
THE STATE OF THE ART AND EMERGING RESEARCYH 877
(Klaus J. Hopt, Hideki Kanda, Mark J. Roe,
Eddy Wymeersch and Stephan Prigge, eds., 1998)
(excerpts from pages 881, 885)

In most large Japanese firms, the controlling group is the body of employees. In such firms, the directors and managers are selected from among the firm's employees, and are almost always able to expect strong support from the majority of employees, as long as their actions are generally consistent with the interests of these employees. Large

15. Toyota *keiretsu* organized by Toyota Auto is an example of production *keiretsu*. Many Japanese consumer electronics manufacturers, such as Matsushita and Hitachi, form their own distribution *keiretsu*. *See* [MICHAEL GERLACH, ALLIANCE CAPITALISM: THE SOCIAL ORGANIZATION OF JAPANESE BUSINESS (1992)] for more on *keiretsu*.

shareholders remain as such and faithfully support existing management. They maintain the right as large shareholders under the present corporate law and legal system to deprive the existing management of their leadership in the firm. However, we are in a world of exchange by agreement rather than by coercion, therefore, these shareholders have no incentive to unite for this purpose. Otherwise, nothing prevents them from uniting in order to realize the benefits. If such a situation were to occur, the positions of directors and managers would not be stable....

* * *

When the body of employees establishes its controlling group position within a firm and is supported by friendly shareholders, it is costly for large shareholders to unite in order to deprive the existing management of their leadership in the firm. Management is strongly supported by the body of employees. New management, whether invited from the outside or selected from the inside among employees, intent on changing the nature of the organization or corporate policy will face strong resistence from the body of employees since its accumulated human capital is organization-specific. Moreover, as a result of the prevalence of such firms, the external market for managers is not well developed. It is difficult to find a new body of management capable of improving the firm's performance for shareholders. When a bank with a large share of a firm's equity appoints its manager as the president of the firm, there is unlikely to be any significant change in the firm. Unless accepted by the body of employees as its representative, the director cannot change corporate policy. Hence, appointing a leading director from the outside is rarely effective in improving the firm's performance.

* * *

Since the time of Adam Smith, the separation of ownership and management, or the separation of management from control, within a large modern corporation has gathered wide attention....In postwar Japan the same argument has prevailed, and many have insisted that the separation was even more clearly realized in Japan than in the U.S.

My argument presents a different view of this ownership-management separation. The classical view states that each shareholder is so small that the cost of uniting is prohibitive, limiting the effective control of management. In Japan, however, a small number of shareholders own the dominant portion of equity, and for them the cost of uniting is not high. They support the existing management as friendly shareholders, since it is more profitable for them to do so than to manage the firm by themselves or replace the management. Here the separation of ownership and management, and that of management from control, is not a serious social problem.

Comments and Questions

1. The German and Japanese systems have approached the problem of managerial shirking in different ways. Are each of the systems constructed to optimize managerial performance given the constraints of each system, or is there a unified culture-neutral way to account for the differences, each producing optimal results?

2. In the U.S. system of governance, employees, like lenders, are treated as outsiders to the economics of "internal" enterprise organization. Each regulates their relationship to an enterprise on a contract theory approach—the relationship between employees

and the enterprise are governed by the private law of the employment contract or collective bargaining agreement. The relationship between lenders and enterprises is also substantially a matter of private law—this relationship is governed by the loan agreements between lenders and the enterprise. In each case, however, law reduces the absolute flexibility of contract. State and federal labor regulation constrains the "freedom of contract" in the labor area; the regulation of lending at state and federal levels, including regulation of interest rates, consumer lending and the limitations within the corporate law on the ability of actors to deviate from the statutory model, constrain the freedom of lenders and borrowers to shape a law of relationship between them.

The German and Japanese systems have taken a substantially different approach. Employees join shareholders and managers as integral parts of enterprise organization. Moreover, in Germany and Japan, Banks play an important role in corporate governance.

> German universal banks,[301] and traditionally the three GroSSbanken, Deutsche Bank, Dresdner Bank, and Commerzbank,[302] occupy a unique position in German corporate governance that has no analogue in the United States. With resources and capital that are substantial in relation to the size of the capital markets, and without significant numbers of competing institutional investors,[303] collectively these three banks, and perhaps not more than two or three others that are not officially classified as GroSSbanken, are able to exert an influence on nonbanking firms beyond anything that would be comparable in the United States.[304] International institutional investors will of necessity have to confront this influence, or what the Germans themselves often refer to simply as Bankenmacht (bank power).
>
> The collective role of the GroSSbanken in the governance of German industrial concerns has been extensively documented[305] and the subject of extensive debate

301. In addition to their "pure" banking functions, German universal banks are also able to engage in traditional securities businesses such as underwriting, brokerage and investment banking, and they are able to offer various insurance products as well. For general descriptions of German universal banking, *see* Theodor Baums, *Universal Banks and Investment Companies in Germany*, in UNIVERSAL BANKING 124 (Anthony Saunders & Ingo Walter eds., 1996) [hereinafter Baums, Universal Banks]; George J. Benston, *Universal Banking*, 8 J. ECON. PERSPECTIVES 121 (1994).

302. This is the classification used by many, including, for example, the Association of German Banks. *See* Bundesverband deutscher Banken, Private Banken: GroSSbanken (visited Oct. 30, 1998) <http:// www.bdb.de/privat/gross.htm>.

303. Germany does have a relatively small but growing mutual fund industry. *See, e.g.*, Rick Smith, *New Generation, Casting Aside Traditional Mistrust, Plunges Into Equities*, INT'L HERALD TRIB., Dec, 7, 1997, available in LEXIS, World Library, Allwld File. However, effectively most of it is controlled by the German banks. *See id.*

304. *See* Mark. J. Roe, *German Populism and the Large Public Corporation*, 14 INT'L REV. L. & ECON. 187, 193 (1994).

305. *See, e.g.*, JEREMY EDWARDS & KLAUS FISCHER, BANKS, FINANCE AND INVESTMENT IN GERMANY 202–05 (1994); Johannes Kondgen, *Duties of Banks in Voting Their Clients' Stock*, in INSTITUTIONAL INVESTORS AND CORPORATE GOVERNANCE, 531, 539 (Theodor Baums et al. eds., 1994); Baums, Corporate Governance, *supra* note 169, at 511; cf. Josef Esser, *Bank Power in West Germany Revised*, 13 W. EUR. POL. 17, 26 (1990) ("Juggling with numbers—shareholdings in industry, supervisory board seats, involvement of banking personnel, etc—has become almost a national pastime among critics of the banks...."). *See generally* Jeremy Edwards & Sheilagh Ogilvie, *Universal Banks and German Industrialization: A Reappraisal*, 49 ECON. HIST. REV. 427 (1996) (describing the historical relationships among banks and industry).

for years.[306] While criticism of the banks is somewhat episodic,[307] becoming most strident whenever a German industrial company fails or finds itself in financial difficulty, in fact the large German banks, and Deutsche Bank in particular,[308] have long been favorite "whipping boys" of many German politicians,[309] the press,[310] and more generally the public.[311]

The three most direct components of bank influence in the governance process are their equity holdings in German industrial companies, their representation on the supervisory boards of individual companies (or in some cases, major affiliates) and their near monopoly over the actual voting of shares held by public stockholders.[312]

Thomas J. Andre, Jr., *Cultural Hegemony: The Exportation of Anglo-saxon Corporate Governance Ideologies to Germany*, 73 TUL. L. REV. 69, 127–128 (1998). In what ways have the Japanese and German systems of governance "internalized" the participation of employees and lenders? In what way is this internalization different from the American approach?

---

306. For views that would probably reflect the general position of the German banks in the debate, *see generally* Ulrich Schroder, *Corporate Governance in Germany: The Changing Role of the Banks*, 5 GERMAN POL. 356 (1996) (arguing that although the banks have influence in companies, they do not dominate companies); Ulrich Schroder & Alexander Schrader, The Changing Role of Banks and Corporate Governance in Germany: Evolution Towards the Marketplace (American Inst. Contemp. German Studies, Johns Hopkins Univ. Working Paper No. 13, 1997).

307. The chief executive of Deutsche Bank has suggested that the issue of bank power emerges once a year like the Loch Ness monster. *See Mit dem Euro eine Fusionswelle*, FOCUS MAGAZIN, May 26, 1997, at 242, available in LEXIS, World Library, Allwld File.

308. *See* David Crossland, *Deutsche No Stranger to Debacles in Recent Years*, REUTER EUR. BUS. REP., Apr. 16, 1997, available in LEXIS, World Library, Allwld File ("Deutsche is so big... that it frequently bears the brunt of criticism of perceived excessive bank power and of German banks in general."). Deutsche Bank is not infrequently referred to as the spider in the German web of industrial companies. *See, e.g., Deutsche Bank*, FIN. TIMES, July 1, 1996, at 18; Hermannus Pfeiffer, *Nichts geht gegen den Willen der Deutschen Bank*, TAZ-DIE TAGESZEITUNG, Sept. 26, 1997, at 3 (stating "Deutsche Bank is the spider at the heart of the web of shareholdings that dominate corporate scene").

309. *See Cherchez la Banque*, EUR. BANKER, Apr. 23, 1997, at 8 ("The relationship between German banks and politicians has never been good."); Don't Bank on Change, Economist, July 26, 1980, at 68 ("Wicked bankers have been the bogymen of red-blooded German socialists since the nineteenth century.").

310. See, e.g., Kurt Breme, Angriff auf die Macht der Banken [Attack on the Power of the Banks], Die Woche, Sept. 19, 1997, at 1, available in LEXIS, World Library, Allwld File. This includes the foreign press. *See, e.g., Daimler and Deutsche Bank*, WALL ST. J. EUR., Aug. 14, 1995, at 6 ("[A] key structural problem of Germany's cozy corporate culture... [is the] excessive influence of banks on industry.").

311. *See* Josef Esser, *Bank Power in West Germany Revised*, 13 W. EUR. POL. 17, 17 (1990) (tracing briefly the "century-old debate on the power of banks in Germany"); *Panic Over; The Gessler Commission Has Given West Germany's Banking System a Pretty Clean Bill of Health*, ECONOMIST, May 26, 1979, at 82 (discussing some of the traditional criticisms). According to one survey, three out of four Germans believe that Bankenmacht should be restricted. *See Bankenmacht soll starker beschrankt werden*, DIE WELT, Apr. 4, 1997 (visited Oct. 30, 1998) <http://www.welt.de/archiv/1997/04/04/0404wi01.htm.>; *see also Arbeitslose demonstrieren gegen Bankenmacht* [Unemployed Demonstrate Against Bank Power], REUTERS NEWS SERV., Oct. 30, 1997, available in Reuters Bus. Briefing (visited Oct. 30, 1998) <http://www.bbriefing.reuters.com>.

312. There are other indirect but significant sources of bank influence. For example, banks in the aggregate control over 80% of Deutsche Borse AG, which in turn operates the Frankfurt Stock Exchange. *See* Deutsche Borse AG, Corporate Structure (visited Sept. 18, 1998) <http:// www.exchange.de/structure.html>. The Deutsche Bank chairman is also the chairman of the Deutsche Borse supervisory board. *See* David Crossland, *"Mr. Financial Markets" Takes Helm at Deutsche*, REUTER EUR. BUS. REP., May 20, 1997, available in LEXIS, World Library, Allwld File.

3. The excerpts suggest the ways in which different countries approach the issue of managerial shirking. How is managerial shirking minimized in the Japanese and German systems? In what ways do these methods differ from those common in American corporations?

4. In the U.S., managers have a duty to act solely in the best interests of the corporation. That duty is translated in the American context as requiring managers to maximize share value. It is possible, however, to interpret this duty in a different way. It is possible that acting in the best interests of the corporation can require optimizing the interests of other participants in the enterprise—including employees and managers. The excerpts above indicate that German and Japanese corporations have internalized employee and lender participation. Do German and Japanese managers translate their duty to the corporation in the same way as their American counterparts, that is, as limited to maximizing share value?

5. Professor Roe cites studies that indicate that smaller boards are more effective than larger boards. Yet the Japanese corporate governance model is based on larger boards. In what way does the Japanese example corroborate or disprove the American studies, or otherwise limit its utility to political cultures like those of the U.S.?

Chapter 4

Legal Personality and Corporate Regulation

We have been exploring the problem of locating the appropriate level of corporate regulation. Is it "better" to regulate corporations externally, that is, by regulation based on some basis other than its legal character? Some alternative bases of enterprise regulation were suggested—based on actual attributes of particular enterprise, or based on the size of the enterprise, or the commercial character of the enterprise. A theory of enterprise organization and regulation was described. In contrast to this mode of regulation, we examined the traditional mode of corporate regulation—internal regulation based on the legal form of the enterprise, and characterized by the internal regulation of that form.

In this context we began to examine the characteristics of the corporate form of enterprise organization. We discovered that there is no simple answer to the question: what is a corporation? Instead, the answer may vary by perspective. We then began exploring the nature of the corporation as a separate legal entity from these different perspectives. First we considered the corporate entity as the sum of certain attributes, and then the extent to which those attributes were shared by other forms of business organization. This brought us to an exploration of the nature of the uniqueness of the corporate form. We then explored these attributes in the context of entity formation—we explored the interchangeability of corporate, partnership and trust forms of enterprise organization.

These now traditional modes of analysis pose significant problems for determining an optimal or at least unitary characterization of corporations for purposes of regulation. The different bases of corporate organization described suggest different approaches to regulation. The entity theory focuses on the legal entity created. The contract theory focuses on the nexus of relationships through which participants in the corporate enterprise pursue their individual interests. A license theory focuses on the power of the state to order the relationships between the participants in the enterprise and the relationship between the state and the enterprise. The license theory tends to treat the corporation as a passive devise wholly at the mercy of the state for its characteristics. A corporation can be understood strictly as an individual entity, existing separate and apart from those with an interest in it. In such a case, the entity created would be understood as one of limited powers, its characteristics, powers, and those of the individuals with an interest in it wholly defined and limited by the state (or the unit of government with the power to create it). Alternatively, a corporation might be better understood as a series of bargains between actors with conflicting interests and legally specified powers and duties. Such a bundle of bargains might be regulated in some manner by the state, the chartering agency, but is not defined by the charter. The charter, and corporate law rules, in general, represent no more than a set of rules which must be followed as the participants in the corporate enterprise order their relationships. Alternatively, a corporation can constitute a separable legal and economic system in which contracts between individuals and licensing by the state merely provide the formal recognition of an organization that exists independent of such recognition. Lawyers have been taught to understand that the bundle of legal obligations created by the state, in the aggregate, define the corporation. Economists consider the inter-participants contracts as the prime focus of corporate personality. Sociologists might focus on the independence of the bundle of human systems represented by the word "enterprise" or "corporation."

Agreement about the exact nature of that distinct legal personality remains elusive. Consider the following statements: "In order to exist [a corporation] must obtain a charter. A corporate charter is in effect an agreement whereby a government gives the corporate entity existence and that entity, in return, agrees to serve the public interest." Nader & Green, *The Case for Federal Charters*, THE NATION, February 5, 1973, at 173. "[A] corporation is simply and literally a voluntary association of individuals, united by a network of contracts, who are entitled to the same rights and legal protections as all other individuals and organizations. [The contract model] holds that corporations are not the recipients of special privileges, that they do not require governmental permission to exist, and that their 'charters' do not contain any promise (express or implied) to place public service ahead of private profit." Robert Hessen, *A New Concept of Corporations: A Contractual and Private Property Model*, 30 HASTINGS L. J. 1327, 1330 (1979).

The materials which follow present these issues in more concrete form. Section A explores the consequences of divergent views of legal personality in the United States and the European Union from the perspective of external regulation. Section B considers the same issues in the United States, the European Union, Japan and China from the perspective of internal regulation.

A. External Regulation: The Constitutional or Fundamental Rights of Corporations

Because the law tends to regulate this "singularity" it has "created," and because the nature of that regulation may vary significantly depending on the underlying understanding of that singularity, the way in which European, American and Japanese institutions approach corporate regulation is substantially affected by the underlying understanding of the nature of the "corporate personality." Differences over the nature of corporate personality can have a spectacular effect on corporate regulation. This is most dramatically illustrated when a state wrestles with the question of the applicability of fundamental human or constitutional rights to the legal person it has created.

In reading the materials which follow, begin to consider to what extent the presumption of the nature of corporate personality affected the approaches followed and rejected as courts wrestle with the issue of fundamental rights and the corporation. Which basis of corporate personality makes most sense? Is there really much difference between them? Is your approach based on fear (of aggregations of wealth and power) or something else?

1. *Fundamental Rights in the United States*

First National Bank of Boston et al., Appellants, v. Francis X. Bellotti, etc.

No. 76-1172.
Argued Nov. 9, 1977. Decided April 26, 1978.
Rehearing Denied June 26, 1978.
435 U.S. 765, 98 S.Ct. 1407
(some footnotes omitted)

Mr. Justice POWELL delivered the opinion of the Court.

In sustaining a state criminal statute that forbids certain expenditures by banks and business corporations for the purpose of influencing the vote on referendum proposals, the Massachusetts Supreme Judicial Court held that the First Amendment rights of a corporation are limited to issues that materially affect its business, property, or assets. The court rejected appellants' claim that the statute abridges freedom of speech in violation of the First and Fourteenth Amendments. The issue presented in this context is one of first impression in this Court. We postponed the question of jurisdiction to our consideration of the merits. 430 U.S. 964, 97 S.Ct. 1642, 52 L.Ed.2d 354 (1977). We now reverse.

I

The statute at issue, Mass. Gen. Laws Ann., ch. 55, §8 (West Supp. 1977), prohibits appellants, two national banking associations and three business corporations,[1] from making contributions or expenditures "for the purpose of... influencing or affecting the vote on any question submitted to the voters, other than one materially affecting any of the property, business or assets of the corporation." The statute further specifies that "[n]o question submitted to the voters solely concerning the taxation of the income, property or transactions of individuals shall be deemed materially to affect the property, business or assets of the corporation." A corporation that violates §8 may receive a maximum fine of $50,000; a corporate officer, director, or agent who violates the section may receive a maximum fine of $10,000 or imprisonment for up to one year, or both.[2]

---

1. Appellants are the First National Bank of Boston, New England Merchants National Bank, the Gillette Co., Digital Equipment Corp., and Wyman-Gordon Co.

2. Massachusetts Gen. Laws Ann., ch. 55, §8 (West Supp. 1977), provides (with emphasis supplied): "No corporation carrying on the business of a bank, trust, surety, indemnity, safe deposit, insurance, railroad, street railway, telegraph, telephone, gas, electric light, heat, power, canal, aqueduct, or water company, no company having the right to take land by eminent domain or to exercise franchises in public ways, granted by the commonwealth or by any county, city or town, no trustee or trustees owning or holding the majority of the stock of such a corporation, no business corporation incorporated under the laws of or doing business in the commonwealth and no officer or agent acting in behalf of any corporation mentioned in this section, shall directly or indirectly give, pay, expend or contribute, or promise to give, pay, expend or contribute, any money or other valuable thing for the purpose of aiding, promoting or preventing the nomination or election of any person to public office, or aiding, promoting or antagonizing the interests of any political party, or influencing or affecting the vote on any question submitted to the voters, other than one materially af-

Appellants wanted to spend money to publicize their views on a proposed constitutional amendment that was to be submitted to the voters as a ballot question at a general election on November 2, 1976. The amendment would have permitted the legislature to impose a graduated tax on the income of individuals. After appellee, the Attorney General of Massachusetts, informed appellants that he intended to enforce § 8 against them, they brought this action seeking to have the statute declared unconstitutional. On April 26, 1976, the case was submitted to a single justice of the Supreme Judicial Court on an expedited basis and upon agreed facts, in order to settle the question before the upcoming election.[3] Judgment was reserved and the case referred to the full court that same day.

Appellants argued that § 8 violates the First Amendment, the Due Process and Equal Protection Clauses of the Fourteenth Amendment, and similar provisions of the Massachusetts Constitution. They prayed that the statute be declared unconstitutional on its face and as it would be applied to their proposed expenditures. The parties' statement of agreed facts reflected their disagreement as to the effect that the adoption of a personal income tax would have on appellants' business; it noted that "[t]here is a division of opinion among economists as to whether and to what extent a graduated income tax imposed solely on individuals would affect the business and assets of corporations." App. 17. Appellee did not dispute that appellants' management believed that the tax would have a significant effect on their businesses.[4]

---

fecting any of the property, business or assets of the corporation. No question submitted to the voters solely concerning the taxation of the income, property or transactions of individuals shall be deemed materially to affect the property, business or assets of the corporation. No person or persons, no political committee, and no person acting under the authority of a political committee, or in its behalf, shall solicit or receive from such corporation or such holders of stock any gift, payment, expenditure, contribution or promise to give, pay, expend or contribute for any such purpose. "Any corporation violating any provision of this section shall be punished by a fine of not more than fifty thousand dollars and any officer, director or agent of the corporation violating any provision thereof or authorizing such violation, . . . shall be punished by a fine of not more than ten thousand dollars or by imprisonment for not more than one year, or both."

3. This was not the first challenge to § 8. The statute's legislative and judicial history has been a troubled one. Its successive re-enactments have been linked to the legislature's repeated submissions to the voters of a constitutional amendment that would allow the enactment of a graduated tax. The predecessor of § 8, Mass. Gen. Laws, ch. 55, § 7 (as amended by 1946 Mass.Acts, ch. 537, § 10), was first challenged in Lustwerk v. Lytron, Inc., 344 Mass. 647, 183 N.E.2d 871 (1962). Unlike § 8, § 7 did not dictate that questions concerning the taxation of individuals could not satisfy the "materially affecting" requirement. The Supreme Judicial Court construed § 7 not to prohibit a corporate expenditure urging the voters to reject a proposed constitutional amendment authorizing the legislature to impose a graduated tax on corporate as well as individual income. After Lustwerk the legislature amended § 7 by adding the sentence: "No question submitted to the voters concerning the taxation of the income, property or transactions of individuals shall be deemed materially to affect the property, business or assets of the corporation." 1972 Mass.Acts, ch. 458. The statute was challenged in 1972 by four of the present appellants; they wanted to oppose a referendum proposal similar to the one submitted to and rejected by the voters in 1962. Again the expenditure was held to be lawful. First Nat. Bank of Boston v. Attorney General, 362 Mass. 570, 290 N.E.2d 526 (1972). The most recent amendment was enacted on April 28, 1975, when the legislature further refined the second sentence of § 8 to apply only to ballot questions "solely" concerning the taxation of individuals. 1975 Mass.Acts, ch. 151, § 1. Following this amendment, the legislature on May 7, 1975, voted to submit to the voters on November 2, 1976, the proposed constitutional amendment authorizing the imposition of a graduated personal income tax. It was this proposal that led to the case now before us.

4. Appellants believe that the adoption of a graduated personal income tax would materially affect their business in a variety of ways, including, in the words of the court below, "discouraging highly qualified executives and highly skilled professional personnel from settling, working or remaining in Massachusetts; promoting a tax climate which would be considered unfavorable by business corporations, thereby discouraging them from settling in Massachusetts with 'resultant adverse

On September 22, 1976, the full bench directed the single justice to enter judgment upholding the constitutionality of § 8. An opinion followed on February 1, 1977. In addressing appellants' constitutional contentions, [...] the court acknowledged that § 8 "operate[s] in an area of the most fundamental First Amendment activities," Buckley v. Valeo, 424 U.S. 1, 14, 96 S.Ct. 612, 632, 46 L.Ed.2d 659 (1976), and viewed the principal question as "whether business corporations, such as [appellants], have First Amendment rights coextensive with those of natural persons or associations of natural persons." 371 Mass. 773, 783, 359 N.E.2d 1262, 1269. The court found its answer in the contours of a corporation's constitutional right, as a "person" under the Fourteenth Amendment, not to be deprived of property without due process of law. Distinguishing the First Amendment rights of a natural person from the more limited rights of a corporation, the court concluded that "whether its rights are designated 'liberty' rights or 'property' rights, a corporation's property and business interests are entitled to Fourteenth Amendment protection.... [A]s an incident of such protection, corporations [also] possess certain rights of speech and expression under the First Amendment." Id., at 784, 359 N.E.2d, at 1270 (citations and footnote omitted). Accordingly, the court held that "only when a general political issue materially affects a corporation's business property or assets may that corporation claim First Amendment protection for its speech or other activities entitling it to communicate its position on that issue to the general public." Since this limitation is "identical to the legislative command in the first sentence of [§ 8]," the court concluded that the legislature "has clearly identified in the challenged statute the parameters of corporate free speech." Id., at 785, 359 N.E.2d, at 1270.

The court also declined to say that there was "no rational basis for [the] legislative determination," embodied in the second sentence of § 8, that a ballot question concerning the taxation of individuals could not materially affect the interests of a corporation. Id., at 786, 359 N.E.2d, at 1271. In rejecting appellants' argument that this second sentence established a conclusive presumption in violation of the Due Process Clause, the court construed § 8 to embody two distinct crimes: The first prohibits a corporation from spending money to influence the vote on a ballot question not materially affecting its business interests; the second, and more specific, prohibition makes it criminal per se for a corporation to spend money to influence the vote on a ballot question solely concerning individual taxation. While acknowledging that the second crime is "related to the general crime" stated in the first sentence of § 8, the court intimated that the second sentence was intended to make criminal an expenditure of the type proposed by appellants without regard to specific proof of the materiality of the question to the corporation's business interests.[5] Id., at 795 n. 19, 790–791, 359 N.E.2d, at 1276 n. 19,

---

effects' on the plaintiff banks' loans, deposits, and other services; and tending to shrink the disposable income of individuals available for the purchase of the consumer products manufactured by at least one of the plaintiff corporations." 371 Mass., at 777, 359 N.E.2d, at 1266.

5. For purposes of this decision we need not distinguish between the "two crimes" identified by the Supreme Judicial Court. Mr. Justice White, dissenting, conveys an incorrect impression of our decision when he states, post, at 1430, that we have not disapproved the legislative judgment that the personal income tax issue could not have a material effect on any corporation, including appellants. We simply have no occasion either to approve or to disapprove that judgment. If we were to invalidate the second sentence of § 8, thereby putting a ballot question concerning taxation of individuals on the same plane as any other ballot question, we still would have to decide whether the "materially affecting" limitation in the general prohibition of § 8 could be squared with the First Amendment. The court below already has held that appellants' proposed expenditures would not meet that test and therefore would be proscribed. This is a finding of fact which we have no occasion to review.... Conversely, we would have to reach the question of the constitutionality of the

1273–1274. The court nevertheless seems to have reintroduced the "materially affecting" concept into its interpretation of the second sentence of §8, as a limitation on the scope of the so-called "second crime" imposed by the Federal Constitution rather than the Massachusetts Legislature. Id., at 786, 359 N.E.2d, at 1271. But because the court thought appellants had not made a sufficient showing of material effect, their challenge to the statutory prohibition as applied to them also failed.

Appellants' other arguments fared no better. Adopting a narrowing construction of the statute,[6] the Supreme Judicial Court rejected the contention that §8 is overbroad. It also found no merit in appellants' vagueness argument because the specific prohibition against corporate expenditures on a referendum solely concerning individual taxation is "both precise and definite." Id., at 791, 359 N.E.2d, at 1273–1274. Finally, the court held that appellants were not denied the equal protection of the laws....

II

Because the 1976 referendum has been held, and the proposed constitutional amendment defeated, we face at the outset a question of mootness....

Nor can there be any serious doubt that there is a "reasonable expectation," Weinstein v. Bradford, supra, that appellants again will be subject to the threat of prosecution under §8. The 1976 election marked the fourth time in recent years that a proposed graduated income tax amendment has been submitted to the Massachusetts voters. Appellee's suggestion that the legislature may abandon its quest for a constitutional amendment is purely speculative....Appellants insist that they will continue to oppose the constitutional amendment, and there is no reason to believe that the Attorney General will refrain from prosecuting violations of §8....

[W]e conclude that this case is not moot and proceed to address the merits.

III

The court below framed the principal question in this case as whether and to what extent corporations have First Amendment rights. We believe that the court posed the wrong question. The Constitution often protects interests broader than those of the party seeking their vindication. The First Amendment, in particular, serves significant societal interests. The proper question therefore is not whether corporations "have" First Amendment rights and, if so, whether they are coextensive with those of natural persons. Instead, the question must be whether §8 abridges expression that the First Amendment was meant to protect. We hold that it does.

"second" and more restrictive crime only if we first concluded that it is permissible under the First Amendment to limit corporate speech to matters materially affecting the corporation's business, property, or assets. Because the "materially affecting" limitation bars appellants from making their proposed expenditures under either the first or second sentence of §8, we must decide whether that limitation is constitutional.

6. The court stated that §8 would not prohibit the publication of "in-house" newspapers or communications to stockholders containing the corporation's view on a graduated personal income tax; the participation by corporate employees, at corporate expense, in discussions or legislative hearings on the issue; the participation of corporate officers, directors, stockholders, or employees in public discussion of the issue on radio or television, at news conferences, or through statements to the press or "similar means not involving contributions or expenditure of corporate funds"; or speeches or comments by employees or officers, on working hours, to the press or a chamber of commerce. 371 Mass., at 789, 359 N.E.2d, at 1272.

A

The speech proposed by appellants is at the heart of the First Amendment's protection. "The freedom of speech and of the press guaranteed by the Constitution embraces at the least the liberty to discuss publicly and truthfully all matters of public concern without previous restraint or fear of subsequent punishment.... Freedom of discussion, if it would fulfill its historic function in this nation, must embrace all issues about which information is needed or appropriate to enable the members of society to cope with the exigencies of their period." Thornhill v. Alabama, 310 U.S. 88, 101–102, 60 S.Ct. 736, 744, 84 L.Ed. 1093 (1940). The referendum issue that appellants wish to address falls squarely within this description. In appellants' view, the enactment of a graduated personal income tax, as proposed to be authorized by constitutional amendment, would have a seriously adverse effect on the economy of the State. See n. 4, supra. The importance of the referendum issue to the people and government of Massachusetts is not disputed. Its merits, however, are the subject of sharp disagreement.

As the Court said in Mills v. Alabama, 384 U.S. 214, 218, 86 S.Ct. 1434, 1437, 16 L.Ed.2d 484 (1966), "there is practically universal agreement that a major purpose of [the First] Amendment was to protect the free discussion of governmental affairs." If the speakers here were not corporations, no one would suggest that the State could silence their proposed speech. It is the type of speech indispensable to decisionmaking in a democracy,[7] and this is no less true because the speech comes from a corporation rather than an individual.... The inherent worth of the speech in terms of its capacity for informing the public does not depend upon the identity of its source, whether corporation, association, union, or individual.

The court below nevertheless held that corporate speech is protected by the First Amendment only when it pertains directly to the corporation's business interests. In deciding whether this novel and restrictive gloss on the First Amendment comports with the Constitution and the precedents of this Court, we need not survey the outer boundaries of the Amendment's protection of corporate speech, or address the abstract question whether corporations have the full measure of rights that individuals enjoy under the First Amendment.[8] The question in this case, simply put, is whether the corporate identity of the speaker deprives this proposed speech of what otherwise would be its clear entitlement to protection. We turn now to that question.

B

The court below found confirmation of the legislature's definition of the scope of a corporation's First Amendment rights in the language of the Fourteenth Amendment. Noting that the First Amendment is applicable to the States through the Fourteenth, and seizing upon the observation that corporations "cannot claim for themselves the liberty which the Fourteenth Amendment guarantees." Pierce v. Society of Sisters, 268 U.S. 510, 535, 45 S.Ct. 571, 573, 69 L.Ed. 1070 (1925), the court concluded that a cor-

7. Freedom of expression has particular significance with respect to government because "[i]t is here that the state has a special incentive to repress opposition and often wields a more effective power of suppression." T. EMERSON, TOWARD A GENERAL THEORY OF THE FIRST AMENDMENT 9 (1966). *See also* A. MEIKLEJOHN, FREE SPEECH AND ITS RELATION TO SELF-GOVERNMENT 24–26 (1948).

8. Nor is there any occasion to consider in this case whether, under different circumstances, a justification for a restriction on speech that would be inadequate as applied to individuals might suffice to sustain the same restriction as applied to corporations, unions, or like entities.

poration's First Amendment rights must derive from its property rights under the Fourteenth.[9]

This is an artificial mode of analysis, untenable under decisions of this Court. "In a series of decisions beginning with Gitlow v. New York, 268 U.S. 652, 45 S.Ct. 625, 69 L.Ed. 1138 (1925), this Court held that the liberty of speech and of the press which the First Amendment guarantees against abridgment by the federal government is within the liberty safeguarded by the Due Process Clause of the Fourteenth Amendment from invasion by state action. That principle has been followed and reaffirmed to the present day." Joseph Burstyn, Inc. v. Wilson, 343 U.S. 495, 500–501, 72 S.Ct. 777, 780, 96 L.Ed. 1098 (1952) (footnote omitted) (emphasis supplied). Freedom of speech and the other freedoms encompassed by the First Amendment always have been viewed as fundamental components of the liberty safeguarded by the Due Process Clause, see Gitlow v. New York, 268 U.S. 652, 666, 45 S.Ct. 625, 629, 69 L.Ed. 1138 (1925); id., at 672, 45 S.Ct., at 632 (Holmes, J., dissenting);...., and the Court has not identified a separate source for the right when it has been asserted by corporations.[10]..., the Court rejected the very reasoning adopted by the Supreme Judicial Court and did not rely on the corporation's property rights under the Fourteenth Amendment in sustaining its freedom of speech.[11]

---

9. The Massachusetts court did not go so far as to accept appellee's argument that corporations, as creatures of the State, have only those rights granted them by the State. *See* Brief for Appellee 4, 23–25. Cf. Mr. Justice White's dissent, post, at 1433; Mr. Justice Rehnquist's dissent, post, at 1439. The court below recognized that such an extreme position could not be reconciled either with the many decisions holding state laws invalid under the Fourteenth Amendment when they infringe protected speech by corporate bodies, e.g., Linmark Associates, Inc. v. Township of Willingboro, 431 U.S. 85, 97 S.Ct. 1614, 52 L.Ed.2d 155 (1977);...., or with decisions affording corporations the protection of constitutional guarantees other than the First Amendment. e.g., United States v. Martin Linen Supply Co., 430 U.S. 564, 97 S.Ct. 1349, 51 L.Ed.2d 642 (1977) (Fifth Amendment double jeopardy); G.M. Leasing Corp. v. United States, 429 U.S. 338, 353, 97 S.Ct. 619, 628, 50 L.Ed.2d 530 (1977) (Fourth Amendment). In any event, appellee's argument is inapplicable to two of the appellants. National banks are creatures of federal law and instrumentalities of the Federal Government,... and their existence is in no way dependent on state law. *See* 7A Michie, Banks and Banking, ch. 15, §§1, 5 (1973 ed.). In cases where corporate speech has been denied the shelter of the First Amendment, there is no suggestion that the reason was because a corporation rather than an individual or association was involved.... Corporate identity has been determinative in several decisions denying corporations certain constitutional rights, such as the privilege against compulsory self-incrimination, Wilson v. United States, 221 U.S. 361, 382–386, 31 S.Ct. 538, 545–546, 55 L.Ed. 771 (1911), or equality with individuals in the enjoyment of a right to privacy,... but this is not because the States are free to define the rights of their creatures without constitutional limit. Otherwise, corporations could be denied the protection of all constitutional guarantees, including due process and the equal protection of the laws. Certain "purely personal" guarantees, such as the privilege against compulsory self-incrimination, are unavailable to corporations and other organizations because the "historic function" of the particular guarantee has been limited to the protection of individuals. United States v. White, 322 U.S. 694, 698–701, 64 S.Ct. 1248, 1251–1252, 88 L.Ed. 1542 (1944). Whether or not a particular guarantee is "purely personal" or is unavailable to corporations for some other reason depends on the nature, history, and purpose of the particular constitutional provision.

10. It has been settled for almost a century that corporations are persons within the meaning of the Fourteenth Amendment. Santa Clara County v. Southern Pacific R. Co., 118 U.S. 394, 6 S.Ct. 1132, 30 L.Ed. 118 (1886); *see* Covington & Lexington Turnpike R. Co. v. Sanford, 164 U.S. 578, 17 S.Ct. 198, 41 L.Ed. 560 (1896).

11. The appellant in Grosjean argued that "[t]he liberty guaranteed by the fourteenth amendment against deprivation without due process of law is the liberty of NATURAL not of artificial persons." Brief for Appellant in Grosjean v. American Press Co., O.T. 1935, No. 303, p. 42; *see* 297 U.S., at 235, 56 S.Ct., at 445. *See also* Hague v. CIO, 307 U.S. 496, 518, 59 S.Ct. 954, 965, 83 L.Ed. 1423 (1939) (opinion of Stone, J.). *But see* NAACP v. Alabama ex rel. Patterson, 357 U.S. 449, 78 S.Ct.

Yet appellee suggests that First Amendment rights generally have been afforded only to corporations engaged in the communications business or through which individuals express themselves, and the court below apparently accepted the "materially affecting" theory as the conceptual common denominator between appellee's position and the precedents of this Court. It is true that the "materially affecting" requirement would have been satisfied in the Court's decisions affording protection to the speech of media corporations and corporations otherwise in the business of communication or entertainment, and to the commercial speech of business corporations. See cases cited in n. 14, supra. In such cases, the speech would be connected to the corporation's business almost by definition. But the effect on the business of the corporation was not the governing rationale in any of these decisions. None of them mentions, let alone attributes significance to, the fact that the subject of the challenged communication materially affected the corporation's business.

The press cases emphasize the special and constitutionally recognized role of that institution in informing and educating the public, offering criticism, and providing a forum for discussion and debate.[12] ... But the press does not have a monopoly on either the First Amendment or the ability to enlighten.[13].....Similarly, the Court's decisions in-

---

1163, 2 L.Ed.2d 1488 (1958); NAACP v. Button, 371 U.S. 415, 83 S.Ct. 328, 9 L.Ed.2d 405 (1963). The semantic reasoning of the court below would lead logically to the conclusion that the protection afforded speech by corporations, or, for that matter, other artificial entities and associations, would differ depending on whether the source of the alleged abridgment was a State or the Federal Government. But the States do not have greater latitude than Congress to abridge freedom of speech. The dissenting opinion of Mr. Justice Rehnquist, post, at 1440, is predicated on the view that the First Amendment has only a "limited application... to the States." *See also* Buckley v. Valeo, 424 U.S. 1, 291–292, 96 S.Ct. 612, 760–761, 46 L.Ed.2d 659 (1976) (opinion of Rehnquist, J.). Although advanced forcefully by Mr. Justice Jackson in 1952, Beauharnais v. Illinois, 343 U.S. 250, 287–295, 72 S.Ct. 725, 746–750, 96 L.Ed. 919 (1952) (dissenting opinion), and repeated by Mr. Justice Harlan in 1957, Roth v. United States, 354 U.S. 476, 500–503, 77 S.Ct. 1304, 1317–1319, 1 L.Ed.2d 1498 (1957) (dissenting opinion), this view has never been accepted by any majority of this Court.

12. By its terms, § 8 would seem to apply to corporate members of the press. The court below noted, however, that no one "has... asserted that [§ 8] bars the press, corporate, institutional or otherwise, from engaging in discussion or debate on the referendum question." 371 Mass., at 785 n. 13, 359 N.E.2d, at 1270 n. 13. Because none of the appellants claimed to be part of the institutional press, the court did not "venture an opinion on such matters." *Ibid.* The observation of Mr. Justice White, post, at 1432 n. 8, that media corporations cannot be "immunize[d]" from restrictions on electoral expenditures, ignores the fact that those corporations need not make separately identifiable expenditures to communicate their views. They accomplish the same objective each day within the framework of their usual protected communications.

13. If we were to adopt appellee's suggestion that communication by corporate members of the institutional press is entitled to greater constitutional protection than the same communication by appellants, the result would not be responsive to the informational purpose of the First Amendment. Certainly there are voters in Massachusetts, concerned with such economic issues as the tax rate, employment opportunities, and the ability to attract new business into the State and to prevent established businesses from leaving, who would be as interested in hearing appellants' views on a graduated tax as the views of media corporations that might be less knowledgeable on the subject. "[P]ublic debate must not only be unfettered; it must also be informed." Saxbe v. Washington Post Co., 417 U.S. 843, 862–863, 94 S.Ct. 2811, 2821, 41 L.Ed.2d 514 (1974) (Powell, J., dissenting). Mr. Justice White's dissenting view would empower a State to restrict corporate speech far more narrowly than would the opinion of the Massachusetts court or the statute under consideration. This case involves speech in connection with a referendum. Mr. Justice White's rationale would allow a State to proscribe the expenditure of corporate funds at any time for the purpose of expressing views on "political [or] social questions" or in connection with undefined "ideological crusades," unless the expenditures were shown to be "integrally related to corporate business operations." Post, at 1430, 1431, 1436, 1438, 1439. Thus corporate activities that are widely viewed as educational and socially constructive could be prohibited. Corporations no longer would be able safely to support—

volving corporations in the business of communication or entertainment are based not only on the role of the First Amendment in fostering individual self-expression but also on its role in affording the public access to discussion, debate, and the dissemination of information and ideas.[14]... Even decisions seemingly based exclusively on the individual's right to express himself acknowledge that the expression may contribute to society's edification. Winters v. New York, 333 U.S. 507, 510, 68 S.Ct. 665, 667, 92 L.Ed. 840 (1948).

Nor do our recent commercial speech cases lend support to appellee's business interest theory. They illustrate that the First Amendment goes beyond protection of the press and the self-expression of individuals to prohibit government from limiting the stock of information from which members of the public may draw. A commercial advertisement is constitutionally protected not so much because it pertains to the seller's business as because it furthers the societal interest in the "free flow of commercial information." Virginia State Bd. of Pharmacy v. Virginia Citizens Consumer Council, Inc., 425 U.S. 748, 764, 96 S.Ct. 1817, 1827, 48 L.Ed.2d 346 (1976); ....[15]

C

We thus find no support in the First or Fourteenth Amendment, or in the decisions of this Court, for the proposition that speech that otherwise would be within the protection of the First Amendment loses that protection simply because its source is a corporation that cannot prove, to the satisfaction of a court, a material effect on its business or property. The "materially affecting" requirement is not an identification of the boundaries of corporate speech etched by the Constitution itself. Rather, it amounts to an impermissible legislative prohibition of speech based on the identity of the interests that spokesmen may represent in public debate over controversial issues and a requirement that the speaker have a sufficiently great interest in the subject to justify communication.

---

by contributions or public service advertising—educational, charitable, cultural, or even human rights causes. Similarly, informational advertising on such subjects of national interest as inflation and the worldwide energy problem could be prohibited. Many of these "causes" and subjects could be viewed as "social," "political," or "ideological." No prudent corporate management would incur the risk of criminal penalties, such as those in the Massachusetts Act, that would follow from a failure to prove the materiality to the corporation's "business, property or assets" of such contributions or advertisements. *See* n. 21, *infra*.

14. The suggestion in Mr. Justice White's dissent, post, at 1432, that the First Amendment affords less protection to ideas that are not the product of "individual choice" would seem to apply to newspaper editorials and every other form of speech created under the auspices of a corporate body. No decision of this Court lends support to such a restrictive notion.

15. It is somewhat ironic that appellee seeks to reconcile these decisions with the "materially affecting" concept by noting that the commercial speaker would "have a direct financial interest in the speech," Brief for Appellee 19, and n. 12. Until recently, the "purely commercial" nature of an advertisement was thought to undermine and even negate its entitlement to the sanctuary of the First Amendment. Valentine v. Chrestensen, 316 U.S. 52, 62 S.Ct. 920, 86 L.Ed. 1262 (1942); *see* Bigelow v. Virginia, 421 U.S. 809, 822, 95 S.Ct. 2222, 2232, 44 L.Ed.2d 600 (1975); Virginia State Bd. of Pharmacy v. Virginia Citizens Consumer Council, Inc., 425 U.S. 748, 96 S.Ct. 1817, 48 L.Ed.2d 346 (1976). Appellee would invert the debate by giving constitutional significance to a corporation's "hawking of wares" while approving criminal sanctions for a bank's expression of opinion on a tax law of general public interest. In emphasizing the societal interest and the fact that this Court's decisions have not turned on the effect upon the speaker's business interests, we do not say that such interests may not be relevant or important in a different context.

Section 8 permits a corporation to communicate to the public its views on certain referendum subjects—those materially affecting its business—but not others. It also singles out one kind of ballot question—individual taxation—as a subject about which corporations may never make their ideas public. The legislature has drawn the line between permissible and impermissible speech according to whether there is a sufficient nexus, as defined by the legislature, between the issue presented to the voters and the business interests of the speaker.

In the realm of protected speech, the legislature is constitutionally disqualified from dictating the subjects about which persons may speak and the speakers who may address a public issue. Police Dept. of Chicago v. Mosley, 408 U.S. 92, 96, 92 S.Ct. 2286, 2290, 33 L.Ed.2d 212 (1972). If a legislature may direct business corporations to "stick to business," it also may limit other corporations—religious, charitable, or civic—to their respective "business" when addressing the public. Such power in government to channel the expression of views is unacceptable under the First Amendment.[16] Especially where, as here, the legislature's suppression of speech suggests an attempt to give one side of a debatable public question an advantage in expressing its views to the people,[17] the First Amendment is plainly offended. Yet the State contends that its action is necessitated by governmental interests of the highest order. We next consider these asserted interests.

IV

The constitutionality of § 8's prohibition of the "exposition of ideas" by corporations turns on whether it can survive the exacting scrutiny necessitated by a state-imposed restriction of freedom of speech. Especially where, as here, a prohibition is directed at speech itself,[18] and the speech is intimately related to the process of governing, "the

16. Even assuming that the rationale behind the "materially affecting" requirement itself were unobjectionable, the limitation in § 8 would have an impermissibly restraining effect on protected speech. Much valuable information which a corporation might be able to provide would remain unpublished because corporate management would not be willing to risk the substantial criminal penalties—personal as well as corporate—provided for in § 8.... As the facts in this case illustrate, management never could be sure whether a court would disagree with its judgment as to the effect upon the corporation's business of a particular referendum issue. In addition, the burden and expense of litigating the issue—especially when what must be established is a complex and amorphous economic relationship—would unduly impinge on the exercise of the constitutional right. "[T]he free dissemination of ideas [might] be the loser." Smith v. California, *supra*, 361 U.S., at 151, 80 S.Ct., at 218; *see* Freedman v. Maryland, 380 U.S. 51, 59–60, 85 S.Ct. 734, 739–740, 13 L.Ed.2d 649 (1965).

17. Cf. City of Madison, Joint School Dist. No. 8 v. Wisconsin Employment Relations Comm'n, 429 U.S. 167, 175–176, 97 S.Ct. 421, 426–427, 50 L.Ed.2d 376 (1976). Our observation about the apparent purpose of the Massachusetts Legislature is not an endorsement of the legislature's factual assumptions about the views of corporations. We know of no documentation of the notion that corporations are likely to share a monolithic view on an issue such as the adoption of a graduated personal income tax. Corporations, like individuals or groups, are not homogeneous. They range from great multi-national enterprises whose stock is publicly held and traded to medium-size public companies and to those that are closely held and controlled by an individual or family. It is arguable that small or medium-size corporations might welcome imposition of a graduated personal income tax that might shift a greater share of the tax burden onto wealthy individuals. *See* Brief for New England Council as Amicus Curiae 23–24.

18. It is too late to suggest "that the dependence of a communication on the expenditure of money itself operates to introduce a nonspeech element or to reduce the exacting scrutiny required by the First Amendment." Buckley v. Valeo, 424 U.S., at 16, 96 S.Ct., at 633; *see* New York Times Co. v. Sullivan, 376 U.S., at 266, 84 S.Ct., at 718. Furthermore, § 8 is an "attempt directly to control speech... rather [than] to protect, from an evil shown to be grave, some interest clearly within the

State may prevail only upon showing a subordinating interest which is compelling," Bates v. City of Little Rock, 361 U.S. 516, 524, 80 S.Ct. 412, 417, 4 L.Ed.2d 480 (1960);...., "and the burden is on the Government to show the existence of such an interest." Elrod v. Burns, 427 U.S. 347, 362, 96 S.Ct. 2673, 49 L.Ed.2d 547 (1976). Even then, the State must employ means "closely drawn to avoid unnecessary abridgment...." Buckley v. Valeo, 424 U.S., at 25, 96 S.Ct., at 638; ....

The Supreme Judicial Court did not subject § 8 to "the critical scrutiny demanded under accepted First Amendment and equal protection principles," Buckley, supra, 424 U.S., at 11, 96 S.Ct., at 631, because of its view that the First Amendment does not apply to appellants' proposed speech.... For this reason the court did not even discuss the State's interests in considering appellants' First Amendment argument. The court adverted to the conceivable interests served by § 8 only in rejecting appellants' equal protection claim.[19] Appellee nevertheless advances two principal justifications for the prohibition of corporate speech. The first is the State's interest in sustaining the active role of the individual citizen in the electoral process and thereby preventing diminution of the citizen's confidence in government. The second is the interest in protecting the rights of shareholders whose views differ from those expressed by management on behalf of the corporation. However weighty these interests may be in the context of partisan candidate elections,[20] they either are not implicated in this case or are not served at all, or in other than a random manner, by the prohibition in § 8.

---

sphere of governmental concern." Speiser v. Randall, 357 U.S., at 527, 78 S.Ct., at 1343. Cf. United States v. O'Brien, 391 U.S. 367, 88 S.Ct. 1673, 20 L.Ed.2d 672 (1968).

19. The court reasoned that the inclusion of business corporations in § 8, but not entities such as unincorporated associations, partnerships, labor unions, or nonprofit corporations, might be attributable to the fact that the latter entities do not have shareholders: "Section 8 could represent a legislative desire to protect such shareholders against ultra vires activities...." *Id.* at 794, 359 N.E.2d, at 1275. The court found justification for the noninclusion of other entities that have shareholders, such as business trusts and real estate investment trusts, in the supposition that "the Legislature may justifiably have concluded that such trusts did not present the type of problem in this area presented by general business corporations." *Ibid.* The court did not specify which "type of problem" it meant.

20. In addition to prohibiting corporate contributions and expenditures for the purpose of influencing the vote on a ballot question submitted to the voters, § 8 also proscribes corporate contributions or expenditures "for the purpose of aiding, promoting or preventing the nomination or election of any person to public office, or aiding, promoting, or antagonizing the interests of any political party." *See* n. 2, *supra.* In this respect, the statute is not unlike many other state and federal laws regulating corporate participation in partisan candidate elections. Appellants do not challenge the constitutionality of laws prohibiting or limiting corporate contributions to political candidates or committees, or other means of influencing candidate elections.... About half of these laws, including the federal law, 2 U.S.C. § 441b (1976 ed.) (originally enacted as the Federal Corrupt Practices Act, 34 Stat. 864), by their terms do not apply to referendum votes. Several of the others proscribe or limit spending for "political" purposes, which may or may not cover referenda. *See* Schwartz v. Romnes, 495 F.2d 844 (CA2 1974). The overriding concern behind the enactment of statutes such as the Federal Corrupt Practices Act was the problem of corruption of elected representatives through the creation of political debts. *See* United States v. United Automobile Workers, *supra*, 352 U.S., at 570–575, 77 S.Ct., at 530–533; Schwartz v. Romnes, *supra*, at 849–851. The importance of the governmental interest in preventing this occurrence has never been doubted. The case before us presents no comparable problem, and our consideration of a corporation's right to speak on issues of general public interest implies no comparable right in the quite different context of participation in a political campaign for election to public office. Congress might well be able to demonstrate the existence of a danger of real or apparent corruption in independent expenditures by corporations to influence candidate elections. Cf. Buckley v. Valeo, *supra*, 424 U.S., at 46, 96 S.Ct., at 647; Comment, *The Regulation of Union Political Activity: Majority and Minority Rights and Remedies*, 126 U. Pa. L. Rev. 386, 408–410 (1977).

A

Preserving the integrity of the electoral process, preventing corruption, and "sustain[ing] the active, alert responsibility of the individual citizen in a democracy for the wise conduct of government"[21] are interests of the highest importance.... Preservation of the individual citizen's confidence in government is equally important....

Appellee advances a number of arguments in support of his view that these interests are endangered by corporate participation in discussion of a referendum issue. They hinge upon the assumption that such participation would exert an undue influence on the outcome of a referendum vote, and—in the end—destroy the confidence of the people in the democratic process and the integrity of government. According to appellee, corporations are wealthy and powerful and their views may drown out other points of view. If appellee's arguments were supported by record or legislative findings that corporate advocacy threatened imminently to undermine democratic processes, thereby denigrating rather than serving First Amendment interests, these arguments would merit our consideration. Cf. Red Lion Broadcasting Co. v. FCC, 395 U.S. 367, 89 S.Ct. 1794, 23 L.Ed.2d 371 (1969). But there has been no showing that the relative voice of corporations has been overwhelming or even significant in influencing referenda in Massachusetts,[22] or that there has been any threat to the confidence of the citizenry in government. Cf. Wood v. Georgia, 370 U.S. 375, 388, 82 S.Ct. 1364, 1371, 8 L.Ed.2d 569 (1962).

Nor are appellee's arguments inherently persuasive or supported by the precedents of this Court. Referenda are held on issues, not candidates for public office. The risk of corruption perceived in cases involving candidate elections, e. g., United States v. United Automobile Workers, supra; United States v. CIO, supra, simply is not present in a popular vote on a public issue.[23] To be sure, corporate advertising may influence the outcome of the vote; this would be its purpose. But the fact that advocacy may persuade the electorate is hardly a reason to suppress it: The Constitution "protects expression which is eloquent no less than that which is unconvincing." Kingsley Int'l Pictures Corp. v. Regents, 360 U.S., at 689, 79 S.Ct., at 1365. We noted only recently that "the concept that government may restrict the speech of some elements of our society in order to enhance the relative voice of others is wholly foreign to the First Amendment...." Buckley, 424 U.S. at 48–49, 96 S.Ct. at 649.[24] Moreover, the people in our democracy are en-

21. United States v. United Automobile Workers, *supra*, 352 U.S., at 575, 77 S.Ct., at 533.

22. In his dissenting opinion, Mr. Justice White relies on incomplete facts with respect to expenditures in the 1972 referendum election, in support of his perception as to the "domination of the electoral process by corporate wealth." Post, at 1434; *see id.*, at 1433–1434. The record shows only the extent of corporate and individual contributions to the two committees that were organized to support and oppose, respectively, the constitutional amendment. It does show that three of the appellants each contributed $3,000 to the "opposition" committee. The dissenting opinion makes no reference to the fact that amounts of money expended independently of organized committees need not be reported under Massachusetts law, and therefore remain unknown. Even if viewed as material, any inference that corporate contributions "dominated" the electoral process on this issue is refuted by the 1976 election. There the voters again rejected the proposed constitutional amendment even in the absence of any corporate spending, which had been forbidden by the decision below.

23. ....

24. Mr. Justice White argues, without support in the record, that because corporations are given certain privileges by law they are able to "amass wealth" and then to "dominate" debate on an issue. Post, at 1433, 1439. He concludes from this generalization that the State has a subordinating interest in denying corporations access to debate and, correspondingly, in denying the public access to corporate views. The potential impact of this argument, especially on the news media, is unsettling. One might argue with comparable logic that the State may control the volume of expression by the wealthier, more powerful corporate members of the press in order to "enhance the relative voices"

trusted with the responsibility for judging and evaluating the relative merits of conflicting arguments.[25] They may consider, in making their judgment, the source and credibility of the advocate.[26] But if there be any danger that the people cannot evaluate the information and arguments advanced by appellants, it is a danger contemplated by the Framers of the First Amendment. Wood v. Georgia, supra. In sum, "[a] restriction so destructive of the right of public discussion [as § 8], without greater or more imminent danger to the public interest than existed in this case, is incompatible with the freedoms secured by the First Amendment."[27]

B

Finally, appellee argues that § 8 protects corporate shareholders, an interest that is both legitimate and traditionally within the province of state law. Cort v. Ash, 422 U.S. 66, 82–84, 95 S.Ct. 2080, 2089–2091, 45 L.Ed.2d 26 (1975). The statute is said to serve this interest by preventing the use of corporate resources in furtherance of views with which some shareholders may disagree. This purpose is belied, however, by the provisions of the statute, which are both underinclusive and overinclusive.

The underinclusiveness of the statute is self-evident. Corporate expenditures with respect to a referendum are prohibited, while corporate activity with respect to the passage or defeat of legislation is permitted,... even though corporations may engage in lobbying more often than they take positions on ballot questions submitted to the voters. Nor does § 8 prohibit a corporation from expressing its views, by the expenditure of corporate funds, on any public issue until it becomes the subject of a referendum, though the displeasure of disapproving shareholders is unlikely to be any less.

---

of smaller and less influential members. Except in the special context of limited access to the channels of communication, *see* Red Lion Broadcasting Co. v. FCC, 395 U.S. 367, 89 S.Ct. 1794, 23 L.Ed.2d 371 (1969), this concept contradicts basic tenets of First Amendment jurisprudence. We rejected a similar notion in Miami Herald Publishing Co. v. Tornillo, 418 U.S. 241, 94 S.Ct. 2831, 41 L.Ed.2d 730 (1974). There we held that the First Amendment prohibits a State from requiring a newspaper to make space available at no cost for a reply from a candidate whom the newspaper has criticized. The state court had held that "free speech was enhanced and not abridged by the Florida right-of-reply statute, which in that court's view, furthered the 'broad societal interest in the free flow of information to the public.'" *Id.*, at 245, 94 S.Ct., at 2833. Far more than in the instant case, allegations were there made and substantiated of a concentration in the hands of a few of "the power to inform the American people and shape public opinion," and that "the public has lost any ability to respond or to contribute in a meaningful way to the debate on issues." *Id.*, at 250, 94 S.Ct., at 2836.

25. Government is forbidden to assume the task of ultimate judgment, lest the people lose their ability to govern themselves. *See* Thornhill v. Alabama, 310 U.S. 88, 95, 60 S.Ct. 736, 740, 84 L.Ed. 1093 (1940); Meiklejohn, The First Amendment is an Absolute, 1961 S.Ct.Rev. 245, 263. The First Amendment rejects the "highly paternalistic" approach of statutes like § 8 which restrict what the people may hear.... The State's paternalism evidenced by this statute is illustrated by the fact that Massachusetts does not prohibit lobbying by corporations, which are free to exert as much influence on the people's representatives as their resources and inclinations permit. Presumably the legislature thought its members competent to resist the pressures and blandishments of lobbying, but had markedly less confidence in the electorate. If the First Amendment protects the right of corporations to petition legislative and administrative bodies, ... there hardly can be less reason for allowing corporate views to be presented openly to the people when they are to take action in their sovereign capacity.

26. Corporate advertising, unlike some methods of participation in political campaigns, is likely to be highly visible. Identification of the source of advertising may be required as a means of disclosure, so that the people will be able to evaluate the arguments to which they are being subjected....

27. Thomas v. Collins, 323 U.S. 516, 537, 65 S.Ct. 315, 325, 89 L.Ed. 430 (1945).

The fact that a particular kind of ballot question has been singled out for special treatment undermines the likelihood of a genuine state interest in protecting shareholders. It suggests instead that the legislature may have been concerned with silencing corporations on a particular subject. Indeed, appellee has conceded that "the legislative and judicial history of the statute indicates... that the second crime was 'tailor-made' to prohibit corporate campaign contributions to oppose a graduated income tax amendment." Brief for Appellee at 6.

Nor is the fact that § 8 is limited to banks and business corporations without relevance. Excluded from its provisions and criminal sanctions are entities or organized groups in which numbers of persons may hold an interest or membership, and which often have resources comparable to those of large corporations. Minorities in such groups or entities may have interests with respect to institutional speech quite comparable to those of minority shareholders in a corporation. Thus the exclusion of Massachusetts business trusts, real estate investment trusts, labor unions, and other associations undermines the plausibility of the State's purported concern for the persons who happen to be shareholders in the banks and corporations covered by § 8.

The overinclusiveness of the statute is demonstrated by the fact that § 8 would prohibit a corporation from supporting or opposing a referendum proposal even if its shareholders unanimously authorized the contribution or expenditure. Ultimately shareholders may decide, through the procedures of corporate democracy, whether their corporation should engage in debate on public issues.[28] Acting through their power to elect the board of directors or to insist upon protective provisions in the cor-

28. Appellee does not explain why the dissenting shareholder's wishes are entitled to such greater solicitude in this context than in many others where equally important and controversial corporate decisions are made by management or by a predetermined percentage of the shareholders. Mr. Justice White's repeatedly expressed concern for corporate shareholders who may be "coerced" into supporting "causes with which they disagree" apparently is not shared by appellants' shareholders. Not a single shareholder has joined appellee in defending the Massachusetts statute or, so far as the record shows, has interposed any objection to the right asserted by the corporations to make the proscribed expenditures. The dissent of Mr. Justice White relies heavily on Abood v. Detroit Board of Education, 431 U.S. 209, 97 S.Ct. 1782, 52 L.Ed.2d 261 (1977), and International Assn. of Machinists v. Street, 367 U.S. 740, 81 S.Ct. 1784, 6 L.Ed.2d 1141 (1961). These decisions involved the First Amendment rights of employees in closed or agency shops not to be compelled, as a condition of employment, to support with financial contributions the political activities of other union members with which the dissenters disagreed. Street and Abood are irrelevant to the question presented in this case. In those cases employees were required, either by state law or by agreement between the employer and the union, to pay dues or a "service fee" to the exclusive bargaining representative. To the extent that these funds were used by the union in furtherance of political goals, unrelated to collective bargaining, they were held to be unconstitutional because they compelled the dissenting union member "to furnish contributions of money for the propagation of opinions which he disbelieves...." Abood, *supra*, 431 U.S., at 235 n. 31, 97 S.Ct., at 1799 (Thomas Jefferson as quoted in I. Brant, James Madison: The Nationalist 354 (1948)). The critical distinction here is that no shareholder has been "compelled" to contribute anything. Apart from the fact, noted by the dissent, that compulsion by the State is wholly absent, the [shareholder] invests in a corporation of his own volition and is [free to withdraw his investment at any time and for any reason.] A more relevant analogy, therefore, is to the situation where an employee voluntarily joins a union, or an individual voluntarily joins an association, and later finds himself in disagreement with its stance on a political issue. The Street and Abood Courts did not address the question whether, in such a situation, the union or association must refund a portion of the dissenter's dues or, more drastically, refrain from expressing the majority's views. In addition, even apart from the substantive differences between compelled membership in a union and voluntary investment in a corporation or voluntary participation in any collective organization, it is by no means an automatic step from the remedy in Abood, which honored the interests of the minority without infringing the majority's rights to the

poration's charter, shareholders normally are presumed competent to protect their own interests. In addition to intracorporate remedies, minority shareholders generally have access to the judicial remedy of a derivative suit to challenge corporate disbursements alleged to have been made for improper corporate purposes or merely to further the personal interests of management.

Assuming, arguendo, that protection of shareholders is a "compelling" interest under the circumstances of this case, we find "no substantially relevant correlation between the governmental interest asserted and the State's effort" to prohibit appellants from speaking. Shelton v. Tucker, 364 U.S., at 485, 81 S.Ct., at 250.

V

Because that portion of § 8 challenged by appellants prohibits protected speech in a manner unjustified by a compelling state interest, it must be invalidated. The judgment of the Supreme Judicial Court is Reversed.

Mr. Chief Justice BURGER, concurring.

I join the opinion and judgment of the Court but write separately to raise some questions likely to arise in this area in the future.

A disquieting aspect of Massachusetts' position is that it may carry the risk of impinging on the First Amendment rights of those who employ the corporate form—as most do—to carry on the business of mass communications, particularly the large media conglomerates. This is so because of the difficulty, and perhaps impossibility, of distinguishing, either as a matter of fact or constitutional law, media corporations from corporations such as the appellants in this case.

Making traditional use of the corporate form, some media enterprises have amassed vast wealth and power and conduct many activities, some directly related—and some not—to their publishing and broadcasting activities. See Miami Herald Publishing Co. v. Tornillo, 418 U.S. 241, 248–254, 94 S.Ct. 2831, 2835–2838, 41 L.Ed.2d 730 (1974). Today, a corporation might own the dominant newspaper in one or more large metropolitan centers, television and radio stations in those same centers and others, a newspaper chain, news magazines with nationwide circulation, national or worldwide wire news services, and substantial interests in book publishing and distribution enterprises. Corporate ownership may extend, vertically, to pulp mills and pulp timberlands to insure an adequate, continuing supply of newsprint and to trucking and steamship lines for the purpose of transporting the newsprint to the presses. Such activities would be logical economic auxiliaries to a publishing conglomerate. Ownership also may extend beyond to business activities unrelated to the task of publishing newspapers and magazines or broadcasting radio and television programs. Obviously, such far-reaching ownership would not be possible without the state-provided corporate form and its "special rules relating to such matters as limited liability, perpetual life, and the accumulation, distribution, and taxation of assets...." Post, at 1433 (White, J., dissenting).

In terms of "unfair advantage in the political process" and "corporate domination of the electoral process," post, at 1433, it could be argued that such media conglomerates as I describe pose a much more realistic threat to valid interests than do appellants and

---

position adopted by the dissent which would completely silence the majority because a hypothetical minority might object.

similar entities not regularly concerned with shaping popular opinion on public issues. See Miami Herald Publishing Co. v. Tornillo, supra; ante, at 1423 n. 29. In Tornillo, for example, we noted the serious contentions advanced that a result of the growth of modern media empires "has been to place in a few hands the power to inform the American people and shape public opinion." 418 U.S., at 250, 94 S.Ct., at 2836.

In terms of Massachusetts' other concern, the interests of minority shareholders, I perceive no basis for saying that the managers and directors of the media conglomerates are more or less sensitive to the views and desires of minority shareholders than are corporate officers generally.[1] Nor can it be said, even if relevant to First Amendment analysis—which it is not—that the former are more virtuous, wise, or restrained in the exercise of corporate power than are the latter. Cf. Columbia Broadcasting System v. Democratic National Committee, 412 U.S. 94, 124–125, 93 S.Ct. 2080, 2097–2098, 36 L.Ed.2d 772 (1973); 14 The Writings of Thomas Jefferson 46 (A. Libscomb ed. 1904) (letter to Dr. Walter Jones, Jan. 2, 1814). Thus, no factual distinction has been identified as yet that would justify government restraints on the right of appellants to express their views without, at the same time, opening the door to similar restraints on media conglomerates with their vastly greater influence.

Despite these factual similarities between media and nonmedia corporations, those who view the Press Clause as somehow conferring special and extraordinary privileges or status on the "institutional press"—which are not extended to those who wish to express ideas other than by publishing a newspaper—might perceive no danger to institutional media corporations flowing from the position asserted by Massachusetts. Under this narrow reading of the Press Clause, government could perhaps impose on nonmedia corporations restrictions not permissible with respect to "media" enterprises. Cf. Bezanson, The New Free Press Guarantee, 63 Va.L.Rev. 731, 767–770 (1977).[2] The Court has not yet squarely resolved whether the Press Clause confers upon the "institutional press" any freedom from government restraint not enjoyed by all others.

I perceive two fundamental difficulties with a narrow reading of the Press Clause. First, although certainty on this point is not possible, the history of the Clause does not suggest that the authors contemplated a "special" or "institutional" privilege. See Lange, The Speech and Press Clauses, 23 UCLA L.Rev. 77, 88–99 (1975). The common 18th century understanding of freedom of the press is suggested by Andrew Bradford, a colonial American newspaperman. In defining the nature of the liberty, he did not limit it to a particular group: "But, by the Freedom of the Press, I mean a Liberty, within the Bounds of Law, for any Man to communicate to the Public, his Sentiments on the Important Points of religion and Government ; of proposing any Laws, which he apprehends may be for the Good of his Country, and of applying for the Repeal of such, as he Judges pernicious...."This is the Liberty of the Press, the great Palladium of all our

1. It may be that a nonmedia corporation, because of its nature, is subject to more limitations on political expression than a media corporation whose very existence is aimed at political expression. For example, the charter of a nonmedia corporation may be so framed as to render such activity or expression ultra vires; or its shareholders may be much less inclined to permit expenditure for corporate speech. Moreover, a nonmedia corporation may find it more difficult to characterize its expenditures as ordinary and necessary business expenses for tax purposes.

2. It is open to question whether limitations can be placed on the free expression rights of some without undermining the guarantees of all. Experience with statutory limitations on campaign expenditures on behalf of candidates or parties may shed some light on this issue. Cf. Buckley v. Valeo, 424 U.S. 1, 96 S.Ct. 612, 46 L.Ed.2d 659 (1976).

other Liberties, which I hope the good People of this Province, will forever enjoy...." A. Bradford, Sentiments on the Liberty of the Press, in L. Levy, Freedom of the Press from Zenger to Jefferson 41–42 (1966) (emphasis deleted) (first published in Bradford's The American Weekly Mercury, a Philadelphia newspaper, Apr. 25, 1734). Indeed most pre-First Amendment commentators "who employed the term 'freedom of speech' with great frequency, used it synonymously with freedom of the press." L. Levy, Legacy of Suppression: Freedom of Speech and Press in Early American History 174 (1960).

Those interpreting the Press Clause as extending protection only to, or creating a special role for, the "institutional press" must either (a) assert such an intention on the part of the Framers for which no supporting evidence is available, cf. Lange, supra, at 89–91; (b) argue that events after 1791 somehow operated to "constitutionalize" this interpretation, see Bezanson, supra n. 3, at 788; or (c) candidly acknowledging the absence of historical support, suggest that the intent of the Framers is not important today. See Nimmer, supra n. 3, at 640–641.

To conclude that the Framers did not intend to limit the freedom of the press to one select group is not necessarily to suggest that the Press Clause is redundant. The Speech Clause standing alone may be viewed as a protection of the liberty to express ideas and beliefs,[4] while the Press Clause focuses specifically on the liberty to disseminate expression broadly and "comprehends every sort of publication which affords a vehicle of information and opinion." Lovell v. Griffin, 303 U.S. 444, 452, 58 S.Ct. 666, 669, 82 L.Ed. 949 (1938).[5] Yet there is no fundamental distinction between expression and dissemination. The liberty encompassed by the Press Clause, although complementary to and a natural extension of Speech Clause liberty, merited special mention simply because it had been more often the object of official restraints. Soon after the invention of the printing press, English and continental monarchs, fearful of the power implicit in its use and the threat to Establishment thought and order—political and religious—devised restraints, such as licensing, censors, indices of prohibited books, and prosecutions for seditious libel, which generally were unknown in the pre-printing press era. Official restrictions were the official response to the new, disquieting idea that this invention would provide a means for mass communication.

---

4. The simplest explanation of the Speech and Press Clauses might be that the former protects oral communications; the latter, written. But the historical evidence does not strongly support this explanation. The first draft of what became the free expression provisions of the First Amendment, one proposed by Madison on June 8, 1789, as an addition to Art. 1, §9, read: "The people shall not be deprived or abridged of their right to speak, to write, or to publish their sentiments; and the freedom of the press, as one of the great bulwarks of liberty, shall be inviolable." 1 Annals of Cong. 434 (1789). The language was changed to its current form, "freedom of speech, or of the press," by the Committee of Eleven to which Madison's amendments were referred. (There is no explanation for the change and the language was not altered thereafter.) It seems likely that the Committee shortened Madison's language preceding the semicolon in his draft to "freedom of speech" without intending to diminish the scope of protection contemplated by Madison's phrase; in short, it was a stylistic change. Cf. Kilbourn v. Thompson, 103 U.S. 168, 26 L.Ed. 377 (1881); Doe v. McMillan, 412 U.S. 306, 93 S.Ct. 2018, 36 L.Ed.2d 912 (1973) (Speech or Debate Clause extends to both spoken and written expressions within the legislative function).

5. It is not strange that "press," the word for what was then the sole means of broad dissemination of ideas and news, would be used to describe the freedom to communicate with a large, unseen audience. Changes wrought by 20th century technology, of course, have rendered the printing press as it existed in 1791 as obsolete as Watt's copying or letter press. It is the core meaning of "press" as used in the constitutional text which must govern.

The second fundamental difficulty with interpreting the Press Clause as conferring special status on a limited group is one of definition.... The very task of including some entities within the "institutional press" while excluding others, whether undertaken by legislature, court, or administrative agency, is reminiscent of the abhorred licensing system of Tudor and Stuart England—a system the First Amendment was intended to ban from this country. Lovell v. Griffin, supra, 303 U.S., at 451–452, 58 S.Ct., at 668–669. Further, the officials undertaking that task would be required to distinguish the protected from the unprotected on the basis of such variables as content of expression, frequency or fervor of expression, or ownership of the technological means of dissemination. Yet nothing in this Court's opinions supports such a confining approach to the scope of Press Clause protection.... Indeed, the Court has plainly intimated the contrary view:

"Freedom of the press is a 'fundamental personal right' which 'is not confined to newspapers and periodicals. It necessarily embraces pamphlets and leaflets.... The press in its historic connotation comprehends every sort of publication which affords a vehicle of information and opinion.'... The informative function asserted by representatives of the organized press... is also performed by lecturers, political pollsters, novelists, academic researchers, and dramatists. Almost any author may quite accurately assert that he is contributing to the flow of information to the public...." Branzburg v. Hayes, 408 U.S. 665, 704–705, 92 S.Ct. 2646, 2668, 33 L.Ed.2d 626 (1972), quoting Lovell v. Griffin, supra, 303 U.S., at 450, 452, 58 S.Ct., at 668, 669.

The meaning of the Press Clause, as a provision separate and apart from the Speech Clause, is implicated only indirectly by this case. Yet Massachusetts' position poses serious questions. The evolution of traditional newspapers into modern corporate conglomerates in which the daily dissemination of news by print is no longer the major part of the whole enterprise suggests the need for caution in limiting the First Amendment rights of corporations as such. Thus, the tentative probings of this brief inquiry are wholly consistent, I think, with the Court's refusal to sustain § 8's serious and potentially dangerous restriction on the freedom of political speech.

Because the First Amendment was meant to guarantee freedom to express and communicate ideas, I can see no difference between the right of those who seek to disseminate ideas by way of a newspaper and those who give lectures or speeches and seek to enlarge the audience by publication and wide dissemination. "[T]he purpose of the Constitution was not to erect the press into a privileged institution but to protect all persons in their right to print what they will as well as to utter it. '... the liberty of the press is no greater and no less...' than the liberty of every citizen of the Republic." Pennekamp v. Florida, 328 U.S. 331, 364, 66 S.Ct. 1029, 1046, 90 L.Ed. 1295 (1946) (Frankfurter, J., concurring).

In short, the First Amendment does not "belong" to any definable category of persons or entities: It belongs to all who exercise its freedoms.

Mr. Justice WHITE, with whom Mr. Justice BRENNAN and Mr. Justice MARSHALL join, dissenting.

The Massachusetts statute challenged here forbids the use of corporate funds to publish views about referenda issues having no material effect on the business, property, or assets of the corporation. The legislative judgment that the personal income tax issue, which is the subject of the referendum out of which this case arose, has no such effect was sustained by the Supreme Judicial Court of Massachusetts and is not disapproved by this Court today. Hence, as this case comes to us, the issue is whether a State may prevent corporate management from using the corporate treasury to propagate views having no connection with the corporate business. The Court commendably enough squarely faces the issue but unfortunately errs in deciding it. The Court invalidates the Massachusetts statute and holds that the First Amendment guarantees corporate managers the right to use not only their personal funds, but also those of the corporation, to circulate fact and opinion irrelevant to the business placed in their charge and necessarily representing their own personal or collective views about political and social questions. I do not suggest for a moment that the First Amendment requires a State to forbid such use of corporate funds, but I do strongly disagree that the First Amendment forbids state interference with managerial decisions of this kind.

By holding that Massachusetts may not prohibit corporate expenditures or contributions made in connection with referenda involving issues having no material connection with the corporate business, the Court not only invalidates a statute which has been on the books in one form or another for many years, but also casts considerable doubt upon the constitutionality of legislation passed by some 31 States restricting corporate political activity,....as well as upon the Federal Corrupt Practices Act, 2 U.S.C. §441b (1976 ed.). The Court's fundamental error is its failure to realize that the state regulatory interests in terms of which the alleged curtailment of First Amendment rights accomplished by the statute must be evaluated are themselves derived from the First Amendment. The question posed by this case, as approached by the Court, is whether the State has struck the best possible balance, i. e., the one which it would have chosen, between competing First Amendment interests. Although in my view the choice made by the State would survive even the most exacting scrutiny, perhaps a rational argument might be made to the contrary. What is inexplicable, is for the Court to substitute its judgment as to the proper balance for that of Massachusetts where the State has passed legislation reasonably designed to further First Amendment interests in the context of the political arena where the expertise of legislators is at its peak and that of judges is at its very lowest....Moreover, the result reached today in critical respects marks a drastic departure from the Court's prior decisions which have protected against governmental infringement the very First Amendment interests which the Court now deems inadequate to justify the Massachusetts statute.

I

There is now little doubt that corporate communications come within the scope of the First Amendment. This, however, is merely the starting point of analysis, because an examination of the First Amendment values that corporate expression furthers and the threat to the functioning of a free society it is capable of posing reveals that it is not fungible with communications emanating from individuals and is subject to restrictions which individual expression is not. Indeed, what some have considered to be the principal function of the First Amendment, the use of communication as a means of self-expression, self-realization, and self-fulfillment, is not at all furthered by corporate speech.[1] It is clear that the communications of profitmaking corporations are not "an integral part of the development of ideas, of mental exploration and of the affirmation of self."[2] They do not represent a manifestation of individual freedom or choice. Undoubtedly, as this Court has recognized, see NAACP v. Button, 371 U.S. 415, 83 S.Ct. 328, 9 L.Ed.2d 405 (1963), there are some corporations formed for the express purpose

---

1. *See* T. Emerson, Toward a General Theory of the First Amendment 4–7 (1966); West Virginia Board of Education v. Barnette, 319 U.S. 624, 63 S.Ct. 1178, 87 L.Ed. 1628 (1943).

2. Emerson, *supra*, at 5.

of advancing certain ideological causes shared by all their members, or, as in the case of the press, of disseminating information and ideas. Under such circumstances, association in a corporate form may be viewed as merely a means of achieving effective self-expression. But this is hardly the case generally with corporations operated for the purpose of making profits. Shareholders in such entities do not share a common set of political or social views, and they certainly have not invested their money for the purpose of advancing political or social causes or in an enterprise engaged in the business of disseminating news and opinion. In fact, as discussed infra, the government has a strong interest in assuring that investment decisions are not predicated upon agreement or disagreement with the activities of corporations in the political arena.

Of course, it may be assumed that corporate investors are united by a desire to make money, for the value of their investment to increase. Since even communications which have no purpose other than that of enriching the communicator have some First Amendment protection, activities such as advertising and other communications integrally related to the operation of the corporation's business may be viewed as a means of furthering the desires of individual shareholders.[3] This unanimity of purpose breaks down, however, when corporations make expenditures or undertake activities designed to influence the opinion or votes of the general public on political and social issues that have no material connection with or effect upon their business, property, or assets. Although it is arguable that corporations make such expenditures because their managers believe that it is in the corporations' economic interest to do so, there is no basis whatsoever for concluding that these views are expressive of the heterogeneous beliefs of their shareholders whose convictions on many political issues are undoubtedly shaped by considerations other than a desire to endorse any electoral or ideological cause which would tend to increase the value of a particular corporate investment. This is particularly true where, as in this case, whatever the belief of the corporate managers may be, they have not been able to demonstrate that the issue involved has any material connection with the corporate business. Thus when a profitmaking corporation contributes to a political candidate this does not further the self-expression or self-fulfillment of its shareholders in the way that expenditures from them as individuals would.[4]

The self-expression of the communicator is not the only value encompassed by the First Amendment. One of its functions, often referred to as the right to hear or receive information, is to protect the interchange of ideas. Any communication of ideas, and consequently any expenditure of funds which makes the communication of ideas possible, it can be argued, furthers the purposes of the First Amendment. This proposition does not establish, however, that the right of the general public to receive communications financed by means of corporate expenditures is of the same

3. *See* United States v. CIO, 335 U.S. 106, 122–123, 68 S.Ct. 1349, 1357–1358, 92 L.Ed. 1849 (1948).

4. This distinguishes the regulation of corporate speech from the limitations upon individual political campaign expenditures invalidated in Buckley v. Valeo, 424 U.S. 1, 96 S.Ct. 612, 46 L.Ed.2d 659 (1976). The Court there struck down the limitations upon individual expenditures because they impermissibly restricted the right of individuals to speak their minds and make their views known. *Id.*, at 48, 52, 96 S.Ct. at 648, 651. At the same time, however, the Court sustained limitations upon political contributions on the ground that such provisions entail a much lesser restriction upon the individual's ability to engage in free communication than expenditure restrictions. *Id.*, at 20–23, 96 S.Ct. at 635–637. In the case of corporate political activities, we are not at all concerned with the self-expression of the communicator.

dimension as that to hear other forms of expression. In the first place, as discussed supra, corporate expenditures designed to further political causes lack the connection with individual self-expression which is one of the principal justifications for the constitutional protection of speech provided by the First Amendment. Ideas which are not a product of individual choice are entitled to less First Amendment protection. Secondly, the restriction of corporate speech concerned with political matters impinges much less severely upon the availability of ideas to the general public than do restrictions upon individual speech. Even the complete curtailment of corporate communications concerning political or ideological questions not integral to day-to-day business functions would leave individuals, including corporate shareholders, employees, and customers, free to communicate their thoughts. Moreover, it is unlikely that any significant communication would be lost by such a prohibition. These individuals would remain perfectly free to communicate any ideas which could be conveyed by means of the corporate form. Indeed, such individuals could even form associations for the very purpose of promoting political or ideological causes.[5]

I recognize that there may be certain communications undertaken by corporations which could not be restricted without impinging seriously upon the right to receive information. In the absence of advertising and similar promotional activities, for example, the ability of consumers to obtain information relating to products manufactured by corporations would be significantly impeded. There is also a need for employees, customers, and shareholders of corporations to be able to receive communications about matters relating to the functioning of corporations. Such communications are clearly desired by all investors and may well be viewed as an associational form of self-expression. See United States v. CIO, 335 U.S. 106, 121–123, 68 S.Ct. 1349, 1356–1358, 92 L.Ed. 1849 (1948). Moreover, it is unlikely that such information would be disseminated by sources other than corporations. It is for such reasons that the Court has extended a certain degree of First Amendment protection to activities of this kind.[6] None of these considerations, however, are implicated by a prohibition upon corporate expenditures relating to referenda concerning questions of general public concern having no connection with corporate business affairs.

It bears emphasis here that the Massachusetts statute forbids the expenditure of corporate funds in connection with referenda but in no way forbids the board of directors of a corporation from formulating and making public what it represents as the views of

5. This is in contrast to the limitations upon individual campaign expenditures in Buckley v. Valeo, *supra*, which the Court viewed as heavily burdening the exchange of ideas between individuals and the forming of associations for that purpose. 424 U.S., at 19–20, 47–48, 96 S.Ct., at 634–635, 648–649.

6. In addition, newspapers and other forms of literature obviously do not lose their First Amendment protection simply because they are produced or distributed by corporations. It is, of course, impermissible to restrict any communication, corporate or otherwise, because of displeasure with its content. I need not decide whether newspapers have a First Amendment right to operate in a corporate form. It may be that for a State which generally permits businesses to operate as corporations to prohibit those engaged in the dissemination of information and opinion from taking advantage of the corporate form would constitute a departure from neutrality prohibited by the free press guarantee of the First Amendment. *See* Stewart, *Or of the Press*, 26 Hastings L.J. 631 (1975); Bezanson, *The New Free Press Guarantee*, 63 Va.L.Rev. 731 (1977). There can be no doubt, however, that the First Amendment does not immunize media corporations any more than other types of corporations from restrictions upon electoral contributions and expenditures.

the corporation even though the subject addressed has no material effect whatsoever on the business of the corporation. These views could be publicized at the individual expense of the officers, directors, stockholders, or anyone else interested in circulating the corporate view on matters irrelevant to its business.

The governmental interest in regulating corporate political communications, especially those relating to electoral matters, also raises considerations which differ significantly from those governing the regulation of individual speech. Corporations are artificial entities created by law for the purpose of furthering certain economic goals. In order to facilitate the achievement of such ends, special rules relating to such matters as limited liability, perpetual life, and the accumulation, distribution, and taxation of assets are normally applied to them. States have provided corporations with such attributes in order to increase their economic viability and thus strengthen the economy generally. It has long been recognized however, that the special status of corporations has placed them in a position to control vast amounts of economic power which may, if not regulated, dominate not only the economy but also the very heart of our democracy, the electoral process. Although Buckley v. Valeo, 424 U.S. 1, 96 S.Ct. 612, 46 L.Ed.2d 659 (1976), provides support for the position that the desire to equalize the financial resources available to candidates does not justify the limitation upon the expression of support which a restriction upon individual contributions entails,[7] the interest of Massachusetts and the many other States which have restricted corporate political activity is quite different. It is not one of equalizing the resources of opposing candidates or opposing positions, but rather of preventing institutions which have been permitted to amass wealth as a result of special advantages extended by the State for certain economic purposes from using that wealth to acquire an unfair advantage in the political process, especially where, as here, the issue involved has no material connection with the business of the corporation. The State need not permit its own creation to consume it. Massachusetts could permissibly conclude that not to impose limits upon the political activities of corporations would have placed it in a position of departing from neutrality and indirectly assisting the propagation of corporate views because of the advantages its laws give to the corporate acquisition of funds to finance such activities. Such expenditures may be viewed as seriously threatening the role of the First Amendment as a guarantor of a free marketplace of ideas. Ordinarily, the expenditure of funds to promote political causes may be assumed to bear some relation to the fervency with which they are held. Corporate political expression, however, is not only divorced from the convictions of individual corporate shareholders, but also, because of the ease with which corporations are permitted to accumulate capital, bears no relation to the conviction with which the ideas expressed are held by the communicator.[8]

The Court's opinion appears to recognize at least the possibility that fear of corporate domination of the electoral process would justify restrictions upon corporate expenditures and contributions in connection with referenda but brushes this interest aside by asserting that "there has been no showing that the relative voice of corporations has been overwhelming or even significant in influencing referenda in Massachusetts," ante, at 1423, and by suggesting that the statute in issue represents an attempt to give an unfair advantage to those who hold views in opposition to positions which would otherwise be financed by corporations. Ante, at 1420-1421. It fails even to allude to the fact, however, that Massachusetts' most recent experience with unrestrained corporate expenditures in connection with ballot questions establishes precisely the con-

7. Buckley v. Valeo, 424 U.S., at 48–49, 54, 56–57, 96 S.Ct., at 648–649, 651, 652–653.

trary. In 1972, a proposed amendment to the Massachusetts Constitution which would have authorized the imposition of a graduated income tax on both individuals and corporations was put to the voters. The Committee for Jobs and Government Economy, an organized political committee, raised and expended approximately $120,000 to oppose the proposed amendment, the bulk of it raised through large corporate contributions. Three of the present appellant corporations each contributed $3,000 to this committee. In contrast, the Coalition for Tax Reform, Inc., the only political committee organized to support the 1972 amendment, was able to raise and expend only approximately $7,000. App. to Jurisdictional Statement 41; App. to Record 48–84. Perhaps these figures reflect the Court's view of the appropriate role which corporations should play in the Massachusetts electoral process, but it nowhere explains why it is entitled to substitute its judgment for that of Massachusetts and other States,... as well as the United States, which have acted to correct or prevent similar domination of the electoral process by corporate wealth.

This Nation has for many years recognized the need for measures designed to prevent corporate domination of the political process. The Corrupt Practices Act, first enacted in 1907, has consistently barred corporate contributions in connection with federal elections. This Court has repeatedly recognized that one of the principal purposes of this prohibition is "to avoid the deleterious influences on federal elections resulting from the use of money by those who exercise control over large aggregations of capital." United States v. International Union United Automobile Workers, 352 U.S. 567, 585, 77 S.Ct. 529, 538, 1 L.Ed.2d 563 (1957).... Although this Court has never adjudicated the constitutionality of the Act, there is no suggestion in its cases construing it, cited supra, that this purpose is in any sense illegitimate or deserving of other than the utmost respect; indeed, the thrust of its opinions, until today, has been to the contrary....

II

There is an additional overriding interest related to the prevention of corporate domination which is substantially advanced by Massachusetts' restrictions upon corporate contributions: assuring that shareholders are not compelled to support and financially further beliefs with which they disagree where, as is the case here, the issue involved does not materially affect the business, property, or other affairs of the corporation. The State has not interfered with the prerogatives of corporate management to communicate about matters that have material impact on the business affairs entrusted to them, however much individual stockholders may disagree on economic or ideological grounds. Nor has the State forbidden management from formulating and circulating its views at its own expense or at the expense of others, even where the subject at issue is irrelevant to corporate business affairs. But Massachusetts has chosen to forbid corporate management from spending corporate funds in referenda elections absent some demonstrable effect of the issue on the economic life of the company. In short, corporate management may not use corporate monies to promote what does not further corporate affairs but what in the last analysis are the purely personal views of the management, individually or as a group.

This is not only a policy which a State may adopt consistent with the First Amendment but one which protects the very freedoms that this Court has held to be guaranteed by the First Amendment. In West Virginia Board of Education v. Barnette, 319 U.S. 624, 63 S.Ct. 1178, 87 L.Ed. 1628 (1943), the Court struck down a West Virginia statute which compelled children enrolled in public school to salute the flag and pledge allegiance to it on the ground that the First Amendment prohibits public authorities from requiring an individual to express support for or agreement with a cause with which he disagrees or concerning which he prefers to remain silent. Subsequent cases have applied this principle to prohibit organizations to which individuals are compelled to belong as a condition of employment from using compulsory dues to support candidates, political parties, or other forms of political expression which members disagree or do not wish to support. In International Assn. of Machinists v. Street, 367 U.S. 740, 81 S.Ct. 1784, 6 L.Ed.2d 1141 (1961), the Court was presented with allegations that a union shop authorized by the Railway Labor Act, 45 U.S.C. § 152 Eleventh, had used the union treasury to which all employees were compelled to contribute "to finance the campaigns of candidates for federal and state offices whom [the petitioners] opposed, and to promote the propagation of political and economic doctrines, concepts and ideologies with which [they] disagreed." 367 U.S., at 744, 81 S.Ct., at 1787. The Court recognized that compelling contributions for such purposes presented constitutional "questions of the utmost gravity" and consequently construed the Act to prohibit the use of compulsory union dues for political purposes. Id., at 749–750, 81 S.Ct., at 1789–1790. Last Term, in Abood v. Detroit Board of Education, 431 U.S. 209, 97 S.Ct. 1782, 52 L.Ed.2d 261 (1977), we confronted these constitutional questions and held that a State may not, even indirectly, require an individual to contribute to the support of an ideological cause he may oppose as a condition of employment....

Presumably, unlike the situations presented by Street and Abood, the use of funds invested by shareholders with opposing views by Massachusetts corporations in connection with referenda or elections would not constitute state action and, consequently, would not violate the First Amendment. Until now, however, the States have always been free to adopt measures designed to further rights protected by the Constitution even when not compelled to do so. It could hardly be plausibly contended that just because Massachusetts' regulation of corporations is less extensive than Michigan's regulation of labor-management relations, Massachusetts may not constitutionally prohibit the very evil which Michigan may not constitutionally permit. Yet this is precisely what the Court today holds. Although the Court places great stress upon the alleged infringement of the right to receive information produced by Massachusetts' ban on corporate expenditures which, for the reasons stated supra, I believe to be misconceived, it fails to explain why such an interest was not sufficient to compel a different weighing of First Amendment interests and, consequently, a different result in Abood. After all, even contributions for political causes coerced by labor unions would, under the Court's analysis, increase unions' ability to disseminate their views and, consequently, increase the amount of information available to the general public.

The Court assumes that the interest in preventing the use of corporate resources in furtherance of views which are irrelevant to the corporate business and with which some shareholders may disagree is a compelling one, but concludes that the Massachusetts statute is nevertheless invalid because the State has failed to adopt the means best suited, in its opinion, for achieving this end. Ante, at 1424–1426. It proposes that the aggrieved shareholder assert his interest in preventing the expenditure of funds for nonbusiness causes he finds unconscionable through the channels provided by "corporate democracy" and purports to be mystified as to "why the dissenting shareholder's wishes are entitled to such greater solicitude in this context than in many others where equally important and controversial corporate decisions are made by management or by a predetermined percentage of the shareholders." Ante, at 1425, and n. 34. It should be obvious that the alternative means upon the adequacy of which the majority is willing to predicate a constitutional adjudication is no more able to satisfy the State's interest than a ruling in Street and Abood leaving aggrieved employees to the remedies provided by union democracy would have satisfied the demands of the First Amendment. The interest which the State wishes to protect here is identical to that which the Court has previously held to be protected by the First Amendment: the right to adhere to one's own beliefs and to refuse to support the dissemination of the personal and political views of others, regardless of how large a majority they may compose. In most contexts, of course, the views of the dissenting shareholder have little, if any, First Amendment significance. By purchasing interests in corporations shareholders accept the fact that corporations are going to make decisions concerning matters such as advertising integrally related to their business operations according to the procedures set forth in their charters and bylaws. Otherwise, corporations could not function. First Amendment concerns of stockholders are directly implicated, however, when a corporation chooses to use its privileged status to finance ideological crusades which are unconnected with the corporate business or property and which some shareholders might not wish to support. Once again, we are provided no explanation whatsoever by the Court as to why the State's interest is of less constitutional weight than that of corporations to participate financially in the electoral process and as to why the balance between two First Amendment interests should be struck by this Court. Moreover, the Court offers no reason whatsoever for constitutionally imposing its choice of means to achieve a legitimate goal and invalidating those chosen by the State.[10]

Abood cannot be distinguished, as the present Court attempts to do,... on the ground that the Court there did not constitutionally prohibit expenditures by unions for the election of political candidates or for ideological causes so long as they are fi-

10. The Court's additional suggestion that the aggrieved shareholder pursue judicial remedies to challenge corporate referenda disbursements, *ante*, at 1426, is untenable in light of its holding precluding Massachusetts from defining the powers of corporations active within its borders so as to prohibit the expenditure of funds in connection with referenda campaigns not material to their business functions. The Court also asserts that Massachusetts' interest in protecting dissenting shareholders is "belied" by its failure to prohibit corporate activity with respect to the passage or defeat of legislation or to include business trusts, real estate investment trusts, and labor unions in its prohibition upon electoral expenditures. *Ante*, at 1424–1425. It strongly implies that what it views as "underinclusiveness" weakens the consideration to which the interest asserted by Massachusetts is entitled by this Court. Such a conclusion, however, is without justification. No basis whatsoever is offered by the Court for rejecting the conclusion reached by the court below in dismissing appellants' equal protection challenge that the state legislature could permissibly find on the basis of experience, which this Court lacks, that other activities and forms of association do not present problems of the same type or the same dimension. 371 Mass. 773, 794, 359 N.E.2d 1262, 1275 (1977). Indeed, the Court declines to consider appellants' equal protection challenge. *Ante*, at 1414 n. 8. The Court's further claim that "[t]he fact that a particular kind of ballot question has been singled out for special treatment undermines the likelihood of a genuine state interest in protecting shareholders [and] suggests instead that the legislature may have been concerned with silencing corporations on a particular subject," *ante*, at 1425, ignores the fact that, as earlier acknowledged by the majority, *ante*, at 1412 n. 3, the statutory provision stating that the personal income tax does not materially affect the business of corporations was enacted in response to prior judicial decisions construing the "materially affecting" requirement as not prohibiting corporate expenditures in connection with income tax referenda. To find evidence of hostility toward corporations on the basis of a decision of a legislature to clarify its intent following judicial rulings interpreting the scope of a statute is to elevate corporations to a level of deference which has not been seen at least since the days when substantive due process was regularly used to invalidate regulatory legislation thought to unfairly impinge upon established economic interests.

nanced from assessments paid by employees who are not coerced into doing so against their will. In the first place, the Court did not purport to hold that all political or ideological expenditures not constitutionally prohibited were constitutionally protected. A State might well conclude that the most and perhaps, in its view, the only effective way of preventing unions or corporations from using funds contributed by differing members or shareholders to support political causes having no connection with the business of the organization is to absolutely ban such expenditures. Secondly, unlike the remedies available to the Court in Street and Abood which required unions to refund the exacted funds in the proportion that union political expenditures with which a member disagreed bore to total union expenditures, no such alternative is readily available which would enable a corporate shareholder to maintain his investment in a corporation without supporting its electoral or political ventures other than prohibiting corporations from participating in such activities. There is no apparent way of segregating one shareholder's ownership interest in a corporation from another's. It is no answer to respond, as the Court does, that the dissenting "shareholder... is free to withdraw his investment at any time and for any reason." Ante, at 1425 n. 34. The employees in Street and Abood were also free to seek other jobs where they would not be compelled to finance causes with which they disagreed, but we held in Abood that First Amendment rights could not be so burdened. Clearly the State has a strong interest in assuring that its citizens are not forced to choose between supporting the propagation of views with which they disagree and passing up investment opportunities.

Finally, even if corporations developed an effective mechanism for rebating to shareholders that portion of their investment used to finance political activities with which they disagreed, a State may still choose to restrict corporate political activity irrelevant to business functions on the grounds that many investors would be deterred from investing in corporations because of a wish not to associate with corporations propagating certain views. The State has an interest not only in enabling individuals to exercise freedom of conscience without penalty but also in eliminating the danger that investment decisions will be significantly influenced by the ideological views of corporations. While the latter concern may not be of the same constitutional magnitude as the former, it is far from trivial. Corporations, as previously noted, are created by the State as a means of furthering the public welfare. One of their functions is to determine, by their success in obtaining funds, the uses to which society's resources are to be put. A State may legitimately conclude that corporations would not serve as economically efficient vehicles for such decisions if the investment preferences of the public were significantly affected by their ideological or political activities. It has long been recognized that such pursuits are not the proper business of corporations. The common law was generally interpreted as prohibiting corporate political participation.... Indeed, the Securities and Exchange Commission's rules permit corporations to refuse to submit for shareholder vote any proposal which concerns a general economic, political, racial, religious, or social cause that is not significantly related to the business of the corporation or is not within its control....

The necessity of prohibiting corporate political expenditures in order to prevent the use of corporate funds for purposes with which shareholders may disagree is not a unique perception of Massachusetts. This Court has repeatedly recognized that one of the purposes of the Corrupt Practices Act was to prevent the use of corporate or union funds for political purposes without the consent of the shareholders or union members and to protect minority interests from domination by corporate or union leadership.... Although the Court has never, as noted supra, adjudicated the constitutionality of the Act, it has consistently treated this objective with deference. Indeed, in United States v.

CIO, 335 U.S. 106, 68 S.Ct. 1349, 92 L.Ed. 1849 (1948), the Court construed a previous version of the Corrupt Practices Act so as to conform its prohibitions to those activities to which the Court believed union members or shareholders might object. After noting that if the statute "were construed to prohibit the publication, by corporations and unions in the regular course of conducting their affairs, of periodicals advising their members, stockholders or customers of danger or advantage to their interests from the adoption of measures or the election to office of men, espousing such measures, the gravest doubt would arise in our minds as to its constitutionality," id., at 121, 68 S.Ct., at 1357, the Court held that the statute did not prohibit such in-house publications. It was persuaded that the purposes of the Act would not be impeded by such an interpretation, because it "is unduly stretching language to say that the members or stockholders are unwilling participants in such normal organizational activities, including the advocacy thereby of governmental policies affecting their interests, and the support thereby of candidates thought to be favorable to their interests." Id., at 123, 68 S.Ct. at 1357.

The Court today purports not to foreclose the possibility that the Corrupt Practices Act and state statutes which prohibit corporate expenditures only in the context of elections to public office may survive constitutional scrutiny because of the interest in preventing the corruption of elected representatives through the creation of political debts.... It does not choose to explain or even suggest, however, why the state interests which it so cursorily dismisses are less worthy than the interest in preventing corruption or the appearance of it. More importantly, the analytical framework employed by the Court clearly raises great doubt about the Corrupt Practices Act. The question in the present case, as viewed by the Court, "is whether the corporate identity of the speaker deprives this proposed speech of what otherwise would be its clear entitlement to protection," ante, at 1416, which it answers in the negative. But the Court has previously held in Buckley v. Valeo, that the interest in preventing corruption is insufficient to justify restrictions upon individual expenditures relative to candidates for political office. If the corporate identity of the speaker makes no difference, all the Court has done is to reserve the formal interment of the Corrupt Practices Act and similar state statutes for another day. As I understand the view that has now become part of First Amendment jurisprudence, the use of corporate funds, even for causes irrelevant to the corporation's business, may be no more limited than that of individual funds. Hence, corporate contributions to and expenditures on behalf of political candidates may be no more limited than those of individuals. Individual contributions under federal law are limited but not entirely forbidden, and under Buckley v. Valeo expenditures may not constitutionally be limited at all. Most state corrupt practices Acts, like the federal Act, forbid any contributions or expenditures by corporations to or for a political candidate.

In my view, the interests in protecting a system of freedom of expression, set forth supra, are sufficient to justify any incremental curtailment in the volume of expression which the Massachusetts statute might produce. I would hold that apart from corporate activities,... which are integrally related to corporate business operations, a State may prohibit corporate expenditures for political or ideological purposes. There can be no doubt that corporate expenditures in connection with referenda immaterial to corporate business affairs fall clearly into the category of corporate activities which may be barred. The electoral process, of course, is the essence of our democracy. It is an arena in which the public interest in preventing corporate domination and the coerced support by shareholders of causes with which they disagree is at its strongest and any claim that corporate expenditures are integral to the economic functioning of the corporation is at its weakest.[11]

I would affirm the judgment of the Supreme Judicial Court for the Commonwealth of Massachusetts.

Mr. Justice REHNQUIST, dissenting.

This Court decided at an early date, with neither argument nor discussion, that a business corporation is a "person" entitled to the protection of the Equal Protection Clause of the Fourteenth Amendment. Santa Clara County v. Southern Pacific R. Co., 118 U.S. 394, 396, 6 S.Ct. 1132, 30 L.Ed. 118 (1886). Likewise, it soon became accepted that the property of a corporation was protected under the Due Process Clause of that same Amendment. See, e. g., Smyth v. Ames, 169 U.S. 466, 522, 18 S.Ct. 418, 424, 42 L.Ed. 819 (1898). Nevertheless, we concluded soon thereafter that the liberty protected by that Amendment "is the liberty of natural, not artificial persons." Northwestern Nat. Life Ins. Co. v. Riggs, 203 U.S. 243, 255, 27 S.Ct. 126, 129, 51 L.Ed. 168 (1906). Before today, our only considered and explicit departures from that holding have been that a corporation engaged in the business of publishing or broadcasting enjoys the same liberty of the press as is enjoyed by natural persons, Grosjean v. American Press Co., 297 U.S. 233, 244, 56 S.Ct. 444, 446, 80 L.Ed. 660 (1936), and that a nonprofit membership corporation organized for the purpose of "achieving... equality of treatment by all government, federal, state and local, for the members of the Negro community" enjoys certain liberties of political expression. NAACP v. Button, 371 U.S. 415, 429, 83 S.Ct. 328, 336, 9 L.Ed.2d 405 (1963).

The question presented today, whether business corporations have a constitutionally protected liberty to engage in political activities, has never been squarely addressed by any previous decision of this Court.[1] However, the General Court of the Commonwealth of Massachusetts, the Congress of the United States, and the legislatures of 30 other States of this Republic have considered the matter, and have concluded that restrictions upon the political activity of business corporations are both politically desirable and constitutionally permissible. The judgment of such a broad consensus of governmental bodies expressed over a period of many decades is entitled to considerable deference from this Court. I think it quite probable that their judgment may properly be reconciled with our controlling precedents, but I am certain that under my views of the limited application of the First Amendment to the States, which I share with the two immediately preceding occupants of my seat on the Court, but not with my present colleagues, the judgment of the Supreme Judicial Court of Massachusetts should be affirmed.

Early in our history, Mr. Chief Justice Marshall described the status of a corporation in the eyes of federal law: "A corporation is an artificial being, invisible, intangible, and

11. The exemption provided by the Massachusetts statute for contributions and expenditures in connection with any referendum question "materially affecting any of the property, business or assets of the corporation" affords any First Amendment protection to which corporate electoral communications may be entitled. *See* Mass. Gen. Laws Ann., ch. 55, § 8 (West Supp. 1977).

1. Our prior cases, mostly of recent vintage, have discussed the boundaries of protected speech without distinguishing between artificial and natural persons. *See, e.g.*, Linmark Associates, Inc. v. Township of Willingboro, 431 U.S. 85, 97 S.Ct. 1614, 52 L.Ed.2d 155 (1977); Buckley v. Valeo, 424 U.S. 1, 96 S.Ct. 612, 46 L.Ed.2d 659 (1976). Nevertheless, the Court today affirms that the failure of those cases to draw distinctions between artificial and natural persons does not mean that no such distinctions may be drawn. The Court explicitly states that corporations may not enjoy all the political liberties of natural persons, although it fails to articulate the basis of its suggested distinction. *Ante*, at 1416 n. 13.

existing only in contemplation of law. Being the mere creature of law, it possesses only those properties which the charter of creation confers upon it, either expressly, or as incidental to its very existence. These are such as are supposed best calculated to effect the object for which it was created." Dartmouth College v. Woodward, 4 Wheat. 518, 636, 4 L.Ed. 629 (1819). The appellants herein either were created by the Commonwealth or were admitted into the Commonwealth only for the limited purposes described in their charters and regulated by state law.[2] Since it cannot be disputed that the mere creation of a corporation does not invest it with all the liberties enjoyed by natural persons, United States v. White, 322 U.S. 694, 698–701, 64 S.Ct. 1248, 1251–1252, 88 L.Ed. 1542 (1944) (corporations do not enjoy the privilege against self-incrimination), our inquiry must seek to determine which constitutional protections are "incidental to its very existence." Dartmouth College, supra, 4 Wheat. at 636.

There can be little doubt that when a State creates a corporation with the power to acquire and utilize property, it necessarily and implicitly guarantees that the corporation will not be deprived of that property absent due process of law. Likewise, when a State charters a corporation for the purpose of publishing a newspaper, it necessarily assumes that the corporation is entitled to the liberty of the press essential to the conduct of its business. Grosjean so held, and our subsequent cases have so assumed. E. g., Time, Inc. v. Firestone, 424 U.S. 448, 96 S.Ct. 958, 47 L.Ed.2d 154 (1976); New York Times Co. v. Sullivan, 376 U.S. 254, 84 S.Ct. 710, 11 L.Ed.2d 686 (1964).[3] Until recently, it was not thought that any persons, natural or artificial, had any protected right to engage in commercial speech. See Virginia State Board of Pharmacy v. Virginia Citizens Consumer Council, 425 U.S. 748, 761–770, 96 S.Ct. 1817, 1825–1829, 48 L.Ed.2d 346 (1976). Although the Court has never explicitly recognized a corporation's right of commercial speech, such a right might be considered necessarily incidental to the business of a commercial corporation.

It cannot be so readily concluded that the right of political expression is equally necessary to carry out the functions of a corporation organized for commercial purposes.[4] A

2. Appellants Wyman-Gordon Co. and Digital Equipment Corp. are incorporated in Massachusetts. The Gillette Co. is incorporated in Delaware, but does business in Massachusetts. It is absolutely clear that a State may impose the same restrictions upon foreign corporations doing business within its borders as it imposes upon its own corporations. Northwestern Nat. Life Ins. Co., 203 U.S. 243, 254–255, 27 S.Ct. 126, 129, 51 L.Ed. 168 (1906). Appellants First National Bank of Boston and New England Merchants National Bank are organized under the laws of the United States. In providing for the chartering of national banks, Congress has not purported to empower them to take part in the political activities of the States in which they do business. Indeed, it has explicitly forbidden them to make any "contribution or expenditure in connection with any election to any political office." 2 U.S.C. §441b(a) (1976 ed.). Thus, there is no occasion to consider whether Congress would have the power to require the States to permit national banks to participate in political affairs. Cf. McCulloch v. Maryland, 4 Wheat. 316, 4 L.Ed. 579 at 14–15 (1819).

3. It does not necessarily follow that such a corporation would be entitled to all the rights of free expression enjoyed by natural persons. Although a newspaper corporation must necessarily have the liberty to endorse a political candidate in its editorial columns, it need have no greater right than any other corporation to contribute money to that candidate's campaign. Such a right is no more "incidental to its very existence" than it is to any other business corporation.

4. However, where a State permits the organization of a corporation for explicitly political purposes, this Court has held that its rights of political expression, which are necessarily incidental to its purposes, are entitled to constitutional protection. NAACP v. Button, 371 U.S. 415, 428–429, 83 S.Ct. 328, 335–336, 9 L.Ed.2d 405 (1963). The fact that the author of that opinion, my Brother Brennan, has joined my Brother White's dissent in this case strengthens my conclusion that nothing in Button requires that similar protection be extended to ordinary business corporations. It should not escape notice that the rule established in Button was only an alternative holding, since the Court also ruled that the National Association for the Advancement of Colored People had standing to as-

State grants to a business corporation the blessings of potentially perpetual life and limited liability to enhance its efficiency as an economic entity. It might reasonably be concluded that those properties, so beneficial in the economic sphere, pose special dangers in the political sphere. Furthermore, it might be argued that liberties of political expression are not at all necessary to effectuate the purposes for which States permit commercial corporations to exist. So long as the Judicial Branches of the State and Federal Governments remain open to protect the corporation's interest in its property, it has no need, though it may have the desire, to petition the political branches for similar protection. Indeed, the States might reasonably fear that the corporation would use its economic power to obtain further benefits beyond those already bestowed.[5] I would think that any particular form of organization upon which the State confers special privileges or immunities different from those of natural persons would be subject to like regulation, whether the organization is a labor union, a partnership, a trade association, or a corporation.

---

sert the personal rights of its members. *Ibid.*, citing NAACP v. Alabama ex rel. Patterson, 357 U.S. 449, 458–460, 78 S.Ct. 1163, 1169–1171, 2 L.Ed.2d 1488 (1958). The holding, which has never been repeated, was directly contrary to an earlier decision of this Court holding that another political corporation, the American Civil Liberties Union, did not enjoy freedom of speech and assembly. Hague v. CIO, 307 U.S. 496, 514, 59 S.Ct. 954, 963, 83 L.Ed. 1423 (1939) (opinion of Roberts, J.); *id.*, at 527, 59 S.Ct., at 969 (opinion of Stone, J.).

5. My Brother White raises substantially these same arguments in his dissent, *ante*, at 1433. However, his heavy emphasis on the need to protect minority shareholders at least suggests that "[t]he governmental interest in regulating corporate political communications," *ante*, at 1433, might not prove sufficiently weighty in the absence of such concerns. Because of my conclusion that the Fourteenth Amendment does not require a State to endow a business corporation with the power of political speech, I do not find it necessary to join his assessment of the interests of the Commonwealth supporting this legislation. The question of whether such restrictions are politically desirable is exclusively for decision by the political branches of the Federal Government and by the States, and may not be reviewed here. My Brother White, in his dissenting opinion, puts the legislative determination in its most appealing light when he says, *ibid.*: "[T]he interest of Massachusetts and the many other States which have restricted corporate political activity... is not one of equalizing the resources of opposing candidates or opposing positions, but rather of preventing institutions which have been permitted to amass wealth as a result of special advantages extended by the State for certain economic purposes from using that wealth to acquire an unfair advantage in the political process...." As I indicate in the text, supra I agree that this is a rational basis for sustaining the legislation here in question. But I cannot agree with my Brother White's intimation that this is in fact the reason that the Massachusetts General Court enacted this legislation. If inquiry into legislative motives were to determine the outcome of cases such as this, I think a very persuasive argument could be made that the General Court, desiring to impose a personal income tax but more than once defeated in that desire by the combination of the Commonwealth's referendum provision and corporate expenditures in opposition to such a tax, simply decided to muzzle corporations on this sort of issue so that it could succeed in its desire. If one believes, as my Brother White apparently does, *see ante*, at 1432, that a function of the First Amendment is to protect the interchange of ideas, he cannot readily subscribe to the idea that, if the desire to muzzle corporations played a part in the enactment of this legislation, the General Court was simply engaged in deciding which First Amendment values to promote. Thomas Jefferson in his First Inaugural Address made the now familiar observation: "If there be any among us who would wish to dissolve this Union or change its republican form, let them stand undisturbed as monuments of the safety with which error of opinion may be tolerated where reason is left free to combat it." J. Richardson, A Compilation of the Messages and Papers of the Presidents 310 (1897). One may entertain a healthy skepticism as to whether the General Court left reason free to combat error by their legislation; and it most assuredly did not leave undisturbed corporations which opposed its proposed personal income tax as "monuments of the safety with which error of opinion may be tolerated." But I think the Supreme Judicial Court was correct in concluding that, whatever may have been the motive of the General Court, the law thus challenged did not violate the United States Constitution.

One need not adopt such a restrictive view of the political liberties of business corporations to affirm the judgment of the Supreme Judicial Court in this case. That court reasoned that this Court's decisions entitling the property of a corporation to constitutional protection should be construed as recognizing the liberty of a corporation to express itself on political matters concerning that property. Thus, the Court construed the statute in question not to forbid political expression by a corporation "when a general political issue materially affects a corporation's business, property or assets." 371 Mass. 773, 785, 359 N.E.2d 1262, 1270 (1977).

I can see no basis for concluding that the liberty of a corporation to engage in political activity with regard to matters having no material effect on its business is necessarily incidental to the purposes for which the Commonwealth permitted these corporations to be organized or admitted within its boundaries. Nor can I disagree with the Supreme Judicial Court's factual finding that no such effect has been shown by these appellants. Because the statute as construed provides at least as much protection as the Fourteenth Amendment requires, I believe it is constitutionally valid.

It is true, as the Court points out, ante, at 1418–1420, that recent decisions of this Court have emphasized the interest of the public in receiving the information offered by the speaker seeking protection. The free flow of information is in no way diminished by the Commonwealth's decision to permit the operation of business corporations with limited rights of political expression. All natural persons, who owe their existence to a higher sovereign than the Commonwealth, remain as free as before to engage in political activity. Cf. Maher v. Roe, 432 U.S. 464, 474, 97 S.Ct. 2376, 2382, 53 L.Ed.2d 484 (1977).

I would affirm the judgment of the Supreme Judicial Court.

Comments and Questions

1. The *Bellotti* opinion provides an important example of the effect of different conceptions of the nature of a corporate enterprise on the extent to which that entity may be accorded legal (and constitutional) rights. Notions of what a corporation *is*, then, can have significant political effect, both in terms of the rights which a state may feel compelled to provide to the entity (as an economic unit) and the obligations it may impose on corporations to minimize its threat to the political order.

2. The Courts have recognized a distinction between legal persons and natural persons for purposes of applying the fundamental rights protections of the federal Constitution. This difference in treatment permits States greater regulatory powers with respect to legal than natural persons.

> "A corporation is not a citizen within the meaning of the privileges and immunities clause of Article IV, §2 of the United States Constitution, although it is a person within the meaning of the equal protection clause of the Fourteenth Amendment. A State has greater power to regulate the circumstances under which the corporation of a sister State may conduct activities within its territory than it has in the case of an individual domiciled in a sister State or of a partnership organized in a sister State." Restatement (Second) Conflict of Laws §311 comment a.

3. The Court's incompatible notions of the nature of the corporation again resulted in different approaches to the question of the extent to which corporations, as entities independent of their owners, managers and employees, may be prohibited from in-

volvement in the political process, *Austin v. Michigan Chamber of Commerce*, 494 U.S. 652 (1990). Can you reconcile *Austin* with *Bellotti*?

In *Austin* the four dissenters in *Bellotti*, together with two others, held that the State of Michigan could prohibit corporations from using corporate funds for contributions or independent expenditures in support or opposition of any candidates in elections for state office. In so holding, Justice Marshall, for the Court, explained that

> ...the mere fact that corporations may accumulate large amounts of wealth is not the justification for [this statute]; rather, the unique state conferred corporate structure that facilitates the amassing of large treasuries warrants the limit on independent expenditures. Corporate wealth can unfairly influence elections when it is deployed in the form of independent expenditures, just as it can when it assumes the guise of political contributions. We therefore hold that the State has articulated a sufficiently compelling rationale to support its restriction on independent expenditures by corporations.

Justice Scalia, in a scathing dissent argued that

> The Court's opinion says that political speech of corporations can be regulated because "[s]tate law grants [them] special advantages," and because this "unique state conferred corporate structure...facilitates the amassing of large treasuries." This analysis seeks to create one good argument by combining two bad ones. Those individuals who form that type of voluntary association known as a corporation are, to be sure, given special advantages—notably, the immunization of their personal fortunes from liability for the actions of the association—that the State is under no obligation to confer. But so are other associations and private individuals given all sorts of special tax advantages that the State need not confer, ranging from tax breaks to contract awards to public employment to outright cash subsidies. It is rudimentary that the State cannot exact as the price of these special advantages the forfeiture of First Amendment rights....Which is why the Court puts forward its second bad argument, the fact that corporations "amas[s] large treasuries." But that alone is also not sufficient justification for the suppression of political speech, unless one thinks it would be lawful to prohibit men and women whose net worth is above a certain figure from endorsing political candidates. Neither of these two flawed arguments is improved by combining them and saying, as the Court, in effect does, that "since the State gives special advantages to these voluntary associations, and since they amass vast wealth, they may be required to abandon their right of political speech."
>
> * * *
>
> But even if the object of the prohibition could plausibly be portrayed as the protection of shareholders [argued by Justice Brennan in his concurring opinion], that would not suffice as a "compelling need" to support this blatant restriction upon core political speech. A person becomes a member of that form of association known as a for-profit corporation in order to pursue economic objectives., i.e. to make money. Some corporate charters may specify the line of commerce to which the company is limited, but even that can be amended by shareholder vote. Thus, in joining such an association, the shareholder knows that management may take any action that is ultimately in accord with what the majority (or a specified supermajority) of the shareholder wishes, so long as that action is designed to make a profit. That is the deal. The corporate actions to which the shareholder

exposes himself, therefore, include many things that he may find politically or ideologically uncongenial: investment in South Africa, operation of an abortion clinic, publication of a pornographic magazine, or even publication of a newspaper that adopts absurd political views and makes catastrophic political endorsements. His only protection against such assaults upon his ideological commitments are (1) his ability to persuade a majority (or the requisite minority) of his fellow shareholders that the action should not be taken, and ultimately (2) his ability to sell his stock.... It seems to me entirely fanciful, in other words, to suggest that the Michigan statute makes any significant contribution towards insulating the exclusively profit-motivated shareholder from the rude world of politics and ideology.

4. The result in *Austin* is even more interesting when compared to another recent case involving the power of the state to regulate the political participation of groups—*Romer v. Evans*, 116 S.Ct. 1620 (1996). In that case the Supreme Court held, again over a vigorous dissent by Justice Scalia, that an amendment to the Colorado state constitution, effected through a statewide voter referendum, which precluded all legislative, executive or judicial action at any level of state or local government designed to protect the status of persons based on their "homosexual, lesbian or bisexual orientation, conduct, practices or relationships" violated the Equal Protection Clause of the federal Constitution. Justice Kennedy declared the Constitutional Amendment invalid as a violation generally of our cultural "commitment to the law's neutrality where the rights of persons are at stake,"[1] and specifically of the Equal Protection Clause of the Federal Constitution. The amendment impermissibly created a solitary class of people for the purpose of withdrawing from them specific legal protections against discrimination as well as forbidding the reinstatement of those legal protections. Why aren't these sentiments applicable to corporations as well? Consider this question in light of the discussion of the different theoretical bases of corporate personality summarized in the following excerpt.

5. **Problem:** Harry Berlusconi is president, chairman of the board of directors, and the owner of a controlling (though not majority) interest in Newsco, a corporation that operates a nationwide chain of newspapers, several cable television stations, and two news magazines with national circulation. Mr. Berlusconi is running for President of the United States. Three years ago, Congress passed and the President signed into law the 'Corporate Influence Act' that provides in part that: 'no corporation doing business in the United States shall directly or indirectly give, pay, expend or contribute, or promise to give, pay, expend or contribute any thing of value to any political party any of whose members seek or hold elective office of any kind, if such member or members seeking or holding elective office is also an officer, director or shareholder of said corporation.' During the election campaign, the newspapers, cable television stations, and magazines owned by Newsco devoted a tremendous amount of coverage to Mr. Berlusconi, who subsequently won the election. The coverage for Mr. Berlusconi far exceeded that given any other candidate. A federal prosecutor is now investigating Newsco for violation of the Corporate Influence Act in connection with their coverage of Mr. Berlusconi during the election campaign. Newsco has indicated that it believes the Act is unconstitutional in whole or as applied to Newsco in this case. Can you think of arguments that can be made to support or oppose these positions? To what extent do your assumptions about the nature of the corporation and its 'personality' affect those

1. Romer v. Evans, 116 S.Ct. 1620 (1996).

arguments? Revisit your answers after you read the excerpt that follows; have your answers changed?

George Ellard, Note: *Constitutional Rights of the Corporate Person*

91 YALE L.J. 1641 (July 1982)

(excerpt pages 1645–1651; footnotes renumbered, some footnotes omitted)

II. Traditional Explanations of Corporate Personality

To understand the action taken by First National Bank in Bellotti, a suit brought by a corporation in its own name for a declaration of rights, one would have to examine the nature of the person petitioning the court. There has been no dearth of speculation as to the kind of person attorneys for the body corporate represent, though the many theories advanced to explain the corporate person can be reduced to three paradigms that have successively dominated judicial opinion. The rise of a new theory usually does not signify the complete disappearance of the view that has been superseded. Earlier views continue to exist as part of the judicial common sense, ready to be resurrected if the dominant view fails to guide decision-making in peculiar circumstances or leads to unpalatable consequences.

A. Fiction Theory

The earliest complete view of corporate personality, the fiction theory, explains the presence of corporate parties before a court by referring to a political event: the decision of the sovereign to create a social unit by grant of legal status.[1] The corporation thus exists as a person only because it is recognized by the law, and it is granted standing in the court only because it has been brought into being by the state.[2]

Under this view, the corporate entity can do only that which the sovereign allows. Of its own power, the corporation "does no act, speaks no word, thinks no thoughts."[3]

---

1. "Ten men do not become in fact one person because they associate themselves together for one end any more than two horses become one animal when they draw the same cart." J. SALMOND, JURISPRUDENCE 350 (1902),.... An act of the legislature is necessary to become one in the eyes of the law. Those who, "without the sanction of the legislature, presume to act as a corporation, are guilty of a contempt of the King, by usurping on his prerogative." Duvergier v. Fellows, 5 Bing. 248, 268, 130 Eng.Rep. 1056, 1064 (C.P.1828), aff'd, 34 Rev.Rep. 578 (K.B.1830).

2. Thus, Coke distinguishes "persons incorporate or politique created by the policy of man" and "persons natural created by God." The former—also known as corporations aggregate—are "invisible, immortal, and rest only in the intendment and consideration of the law." Quoted in 2 J. DAVIS, CORPORATIONS 214 (1905). The doctrine that corporations are fictions was first applied to ecclesiastical bodies....

3. Maitland, Introduction to O. VON GIERKE, *supra*, note 3, at xxi. The several meanings given to the term fiction theory in the literature can be distinguished along ontological and political lines. All advocates of this view agree that the law calls forth the corporation out of nothing, that is, no extra-legal entity exists prior to the sovereign's act. Dispute arises, however, as to whether the sovereign creates some thing which then acquires a life of its own. Compare Coke, quoted in J. DAVIS, supra note [2] at 214 (corporation exists only in the "intendment and consideration of the law") with Machen, *Corporate Personality*, 24 HARV.L.REV. 253, 257 (1910) ("If a corporation is 'created,' it is real, and therefore cannot be a purely fictitious body having no existence except in the legal imag-

This limiting vision of the powers of the corporate person filtered through the common law tradition to govern the legal status of corporations in the English colonies and the early United States.[4]

Though the fiction theory has long since fallen from dominance, judicial decisions regarding the powers and responsibilities of corporations often appear, even today, to rest on political assumptions that are reasonable only in the context of a fiction-like view. In Bellotti, for instance, when Justice White refers to the First National Bank as a creature of the state, he implies that the very existence of the corporation is the result of an extraordinary political act that should be tailored to the needs of the commonweal.[5] If the grant bestowing life to the corporation does not serve those needs, it can be rewritten or even withdrawn. Thus, although the view historically known as the fiction theory has lost much of its persuasive power, the political implications of that view die hard: the corporation is a creature of the state and can be made to answer its maker.

---

ination."). This Note adopts the more traditional view: to say that corporate personality is a fiction is to claim that no extra-legal ens underlies these non-natural, juristic persons; they exist only according to the "intendment" of the state. Quasi-fictional views, which assert that the act of the sovereign creates a being with a life of its own, are treated as instances of realism....

Fiction theories can also be distinguished along political lines. A strong version of the theory (sometimes referred to as the "concession" view) maintains that the centrality of the sovereign's act to the corporation's existence makes all corporate acts in effect acts of the government, corporate officers being ultimately accountable to the state. *See* R. Winter, Government and the Corporation 1 (1978). This version of the fiction view makes most sense if restricted to that era when incorporation occurred only through special charter, that is, only through a royal grant of exclusive monopoly. As the term is used in this Note, the fiction theory does hold the state ultimately responsible for overseeing the exercise of corporate power, but only in setting the bounds of that power in the corporate charter. Any activity beyond those bounds is ultra vires.

4. Thus, well into the nineteenth century, legislatures granted charters of incorporation tailored to specific social needs. Because the powers conferred by charter were deemed special privileges granted by the sovereign, charters were strictly construed by the courts. *See* J. Hurst, the Legitimacy of the Business Corporation in the Law of the United States 13–57 (1970). The state frequently challenged unauthorized acts of corporations through a quo warranto proceeding, the same action by which allegedly wrongful assertions of public powers were tested. D. Vagts, Basic Corporation Law 101 (1979). An act not covered by the warrant or charter was ultra vires and as such was "void, illegal, and a nullity." H. Henn, Handbook of the Law of Corporations and Other Business Enterprises § 184 (2d ed. 1970). For a rare example of the ultra vires remedy used to keep corporate funds out of the political arena, *see* McConnell v. Combination Mining & Milling Co., 31 Mont. 563, 79 P. 248 (1905). *See generally* L. Friedman, A History of American Law 453–54 (1973) (detailing the rise and fall of ultra vires doctrines). The state supreme court in Bellotti saw the Massachusetts statute as an attempt to guard against ultra vires acts of corporate managers....

5. *See* First Nat'l Bank v. Bellotti, 435 U.S. 765, 778 (1978) (White, J., dissenting). Justice Rehnquist also declined to grant First Amendment protection to the political expression of business corporations. Like Justice White, he argued that corporations, created by the state and granted special privileges, are entitled to only those constitutional protections "incidental to [their] very existence" and implied by their charter. Liberty of political expression, Justice Rehnquist concluded, is not "necessary to effectuate the purposes for which States permit commercial corporations to exist." *Id.* at 825–26 (Rehnquist, J., dissenting).

Justice Powell rejected a fiction-like analysis of the corporate person. He congratulated the Massachusetts court for rejecting appellant's argument that corporations, as creatures of the state, possess only those rights granted by the state. This "extreme position," the Justice explained, "cannot be reconciled with the many judicial decisions holding invalid under the Fourteenth Amendment, state laws that infringe on protected corporate speech." *Id.* at 778 n. 14.

B. Contract Theory

The view that incorporation is a privilege accorded by the sovereign came into growing disfavor in the nineteenth century amid charges of monopoly and corruption.[6] As access to corporate status became a right of the many,[7] the corporation came to be regarded progressively less as a creation of the sovereign and increasingly more as a product of contractual agreement.[8] The resulting contract view of corporate personality interprets the corporate form as but a convenient summarizing device for the limited rights and duties of the private parties who contractually create the corporation.[9] The authority of the sovereign toward the corporation, the contract theorist concludes, is no greater and no less than its authority toward any other private agreement among contracting parties.[10] This trend toward greater freedom of contract, however, could not as-

---

6. Exclusive franchises, it was generally believed, were never granted but for political or monetary consideration. J. HURST, *supra* note [4]. Furthermore, an economy geared to expansion in space and productive capacity could not long tolerate the anti-competitive character of the monopolistic grants of privilege the fiction theory historically sanctioned. M. HORWITZ, THE TRANSFORMATION OF AMERICAN LAW, 1780–1860, at 108–39 (1977).

7. General legislative acts gradually replaced specific charters as the mode of incorporation, thus making the corporate form a more common mode of business enterprise. *See* L. FRIEDMAN, *supra* note [d] at 447 ("It was cheap and easy to incorporate under general laws—a few papers filed, a few forms and signatures; the privilege of incorporation lay open to whoever wanted it...."). In 1811, New York State enacted the first general incorporation law for certain kinds of manufacturing companies. By 1835, general incorporation statutes had been passed in several states. Dodd, *American Business Association Law a Hundred Years Ago and Today*, in 3 LAW: A CENTURY OF PROGRESS 254, 289 n. 85 (A. Repply ed. 1937). General laws of incorporation at first contained severe restrictions on corporate size, lifespan, and scope of activities; permission to incorporate "for any lawful purpose" was not common before 1875. *See* Clark, *The Four Stages of Capitalism: Reflections on Investment Management Treatises*, 94 HARV.L.REV. 561, 562 n. 4 (1981).

8. *See* Trustees of Dartmouth College v. Woodward, 17 U.S. (4 Wheat.) 518 (1819). The case involved an act of the New Hampshire legislature altering, without the consent of the corporation, the charter granted by the British Crown to the original trustees of Dartmouth College. In effect, the legislature converted the college into a state instrument by giving the governor of New Hampshire the right to expand the board of trustees and to fill all vacancies. Chief Justice Marshall declared that while the power of the state may be necessary to create and sustain a corporation, the corporation does not thereby become a public institution: "It is no more a state instrument than a natural person exercising the same powers would be." *Id.* at 636. Since the certificate of incorporation is a contract first between the state and the incorporators and secondly among the incorporators themselves, Dartmouth College is shielded from unreasonable state interference by the constitutional provisions securing contractual arrangements.

The language of Chief Justice Marshall's opinion in Dartmouth College often suggests a fiction theory of corporate personality: "[A] corporation is an artificial being, invisible, intangible, and existing only in contemplation of law. Being the mere creature of law, it possesses only those properties which the charter of its creation confers upon it, either expressly or as incidental to its very existence." *Id.* at 636. Chief Justice Marshall in fact subsequently came to regret this and other such descriptions of the corporate person. Louisville, C. & C.R.R. Co. v. Letson, 43 U.S. (2 How.) 497, 555 (1844) (Wayne, J.); 1 W. FLETCHER, CYCLOPEDIA OF THE LAW OF PRIVATE CORPORATIONS § 24, at 99 n. 37 (rev. perm. ed. 1975). Although strong protest greeted the Dartmouth decision, *see* L. FRIEDMAN, *supra* note [4], at 174–75, state courts had already started to draw the new distinction between public and private corporations....

9. *See* V. MORAWETZ, A TREATISE ON THE LAW OF PRIVATE CORPORATIONS § 1, at 2 (1882) ("[T]he existence of a corporation independently of its shareholders is a fiction;...the rights and duties of an incorporated association are in reality the rights and duties of the persons who compose it, and not of an imaginary being.").

10. As with the fiction view, there seem to be several conflicting versions of the contract theory in the literature. The formulation most widely held reduces the corporate person (or, as it is some-

suage lingering doubts about the legitimacy of private centers of economic power, doubts given judicial expression in opinions based on peculiar amalgamations of contract and fiction theories.[11]

The state court's opinion in Bellotti reflected no such doubt, at least insofar as it came to legitimizing the state's power to regulate corporate expenditures in the political arena. Such regulation is "reasonably related to a legitimate public purpose": the protection of shareholders against ultra vires acts of management.[12] This notion that managerial authority is carefully circumscribed by a fiduciary duty to shareholders developed as the contract view came to dominate Anglo-American jurisprudence and declined in importance as that view lost its centrality....

---

times said, the corporate name) to a simple "contrivance" for referring summarily to the contractual rights and duties of the incorporators.... Another formulation of the contract view asserts that these contractual bargains create an entity which is not reducible to the collective prerogatives and obligations of shareholders. *See* Pollock & Maitland, *Corporation and Person*, in ANTHROPOLOGY AND EARLY LAW 303 (L. Krader ed. 1966) (corporation created through contract becomes indivisible unit comparable to human being).

As the term is used in this Note, the contract view accepts the ontological conclusion of the fiction theory that there is no extra-legal, corporate entity other than the collective powers and responsibilities of the incorporators, but rejects the political premise that the incorporator is really the sovereign or the state. Private parties, by adopting the corporate form, simply draw the attention of the judiciary to the fact that they have reached one kind of contractual agreement and not another.... Those theories that reject a minimalist ontology will be treated as instances of realism.

The difference between the fiction and contract views is illustrated in Continental Tyre & Rubber Co. v. Daimler Co., 84 L.J.K.B. (n.s.) 926 (1915). The plaintiff-corporation was chartered under English law; its directors were German nationals, residing in Germany; and all its shares but one were held by German citizens. The controversy turned on the question of whether the company was an English subject who could bring suit independently of its German directors and stockholders, thus avoiding the terms of the Enemy Trading Act. The court held that the corporation was "a different person altogether from the subscribers to the memorandum, or the shareholders on the register," *id.* at 937, and, therefore, could sue in an English court as a British subject. Lord Buckley, however, insisted on reducing the corporate form to the contracting parties who had created it. "The artificial legal entity has no independent power of motion," he declared. "It is moved by the corporators... [who are] German in fact, but British in form." *Id.* at 945 (Buckley, L.J., dissenting). *See* F. HALLIS, *supra* note 3, at vi; Smith, Legal Personality, 37 YALE L.J. 283, 297 n. 53 (1928).

11. Thus, in Bank of Augusta v. Earle, 38 U.S. (13 Pet.) 519 (1839), the Taney Court declared that a corporation was not a "citizen" within the meaning of the privileges and immunities clause of the United States Constitution. A corporation, therefore, could not as a matter of constitutional right do business in a state other than the one in which it has been incorporated. The Court also held, however, that states would be presumed, as a matter of comity, to have recognized the acts of other states, their fellow sovereigns. This dual holding is said to mirror "the tensions of mid-nineteenth century public policy toward the legitimacy of the corporation." J. HURST, *supra* note [4], at 64–65. On the one hand, the denial of the protection afforded by the privileges and immunities clause signifies that the rights of the corporation are not those of the incorporators and reflects the same distrust of private power inherent in the notion that the act of the sovereign fully circumscribes the powers of his creatures. On the other hand, the presumption of comity reflects legislative practices which accorded corporate status as a matter of statutory right to almost any businessman applying for it.

Subsequent decisions removed much of the substance of the Augusta decision insofar as it limited the rights of corporations to do business outside the state of incorporation.....

12. First Nat'l Bank v. Attorney Gen., 371 Mass. 773, 794, 359 N.E.2d 1262, 1275 (1977), rev'd sub nom. First Nat'l Bank v. Bellotti, 435 U.S. 765 (1978). For a discussion of the ultra vires doctrine, *see* Brudney, *supra* note 4, at 243–52 (examining corporate political speech as ultra vires violation of management's duty not to act wastefully)....

C. Realism

The final explanation of the corporate person is ontologically the most daring of the three views. The law does not create its own subjects, realism asserts; rather, it is forced to recognize the extra-legal existence of certain "persons"—some natural, others not.[13]

To the realist, a corporation is more than a legal fiction[14] and more than the sum of shareholder rights and duties.[15] The business corporation is a complex mode of produc-

---

13. The classical expression of this view is found in O. VON GIERKE, DIE GENOSSENSCHAFTSTHEORIE (1887). "Natural persons" should not be identified with physical persons. A natural person is as much a legal construct with implied rights and responsibilities as is an artificial person (like the corporation). Often large classes of physical persons—Jews, monks, serfs in medieval England, minors and mental incompetents in the United States—are not deemed natural persons by the law. 1 F. POLLOCK & F. MAITLAND, THE HISTORY OF ENGLISH LAW 461–75 (1898).

The realist understanding of the corporate person first came to prominence in American jurisprudence in the latter part of the nineteenth century as the Supreme Court rapidly expanded the number of constitutional protections afforded artificial persons against state regulation. In 1886, for example, even before arguments had been heard in the case, Justice Waite announced from the bench that:

The court does not wish to hear argument on the question whether the provision in the Fourteenth Amendment to the Constitution, which forbids a State to deny any person within its jurisdiction the equal protection of its laws, applies to these corporations. We are all of the opinion that it does. Santa Clara County v. Southern Pac. R.R., 118 U.S. 394, 396 (1886). In subsequent decisions, the Court decided that corporations might seek protection of "liberty" (to transact business) and of "property" (against unreasonable state laws). Chicago, M. & St. P.R. Co. v. Minnesota, 134 U.S. 418 (1890); Smith v. Ames, 169 U.S. 466 (1898). In so extending constitutional rights to corporate persons, the Court vitiated much of the force of the Augusta decision. *See supra* note 32. States could still supervise the affairs of artificial persons, but only to the extent that they could constitutionally limit the activities of natural persons under the Fourteenth Amendment.

Charles and Mary Beard have made popular a "Conspiracy Theory of the Fourteenth Amendment," which alleges that the constitutional provision had been drafted so as surreptitiously to include corporations among its intended beneficiaries. THE RISE OF AMERICAN CIVILIZATION 113 (1927). *But see* J. HURST, *supra* note [4], at 66–69 (attacking the Beards' argument); Graham, *The Conspiracy Theory of the Fourteenth Amendment*, 47 YALE L.J. 371 (1937) (same). If Santa Clara and the cases following it are explained as a change in the framework by which the judiciary understood the corporate person, there is no longer any need to explain this radical transformation in terms of a conspiracy theory.

Whether the product of conspiracy or not, this line of cases has made every act of state and local government that touches adversely the rights of corporate persons subject to review by the Supreme Court. For a general review of the Court's handling of such cases, *see* Wheeling Steel Corp. v. Glander, 337 U.S. 562, 576 (1949) (Douglas, J., dissenting); Connecticut Gen. Life Ins. Co. v. Johnson, 303 U.S. 77, 83 (1938) (Black, J., dissenting). Both Justices conclude that Santa Clara should be overruled.

14. To get a taste of this "more," consider Berle's account of what would happen if a large corporation were suddenly shorn of its legal existence by an act of the state:

> Clearly it is not the law, with its fiction of juristic personality, that supplies the life blood and beating heart of those vast mechanisms. If the law, acting through some instrumentality, declared that they did not exist, the entities would be found to be not fictitious, but factual.... In vain would some lawyer complain that the directors could no longer fix policy, or the president give orders.... The huge machine would keep right on rolling. This is the essence of an institution, and not of a legalistic creation.

A. BERLE, THE TWENTIETH CENTURY CAPITALIST REVOLUTION 18–19 (1954).

In general, realism asserts that the corporation—at least the modern, business corporation—is not a creature of the state, even though the laws that govern it are. The corporation is "the first new autonomous institution that has emerged in Western society since the collapse of the medieval order.... It is the local self-government of modern society, the logical successor to manor, village and town." Drucker, *The Meaning of Mass Production*, 57 COMMONWEAL 547 (1953). *See generally* C. LINDBLOM, POLITICS AND MARKETS (1977) (describing the effect of corporate economies on democratic processes).

15. J.J. McCaskill Co. v. United States, 216 U.S. 504, 514 (1910) ("Undoubtedly a corporation is, in law, a person or entity distinct from its stockholders and officers."). Cf. V. MORAWETZ, *supra* note 30, § 1, at 2 ("[T]he existence of a corporation independently of its shareholders is a fiction."). The

tive organization with a logic of its own. Corporate managers are often left with few options as they try to satisfy the conflicting pressures of investors and the state, while protecting the organization's capacity to respond to market opportunities.[16] Sound business judgment is all the law can reasonably demand of those who must respond to the needs of complex economic institutions within a hostile environment.[17]

In reinforcing the power of management over the corporate fisc, the Supreme Court's majority opinion in Bellotti reflects a realist understanding of the modern, business corporation as something other than the natural persons who constitute it. In arguing that the Massachusetts statute would limit the stock of information available to

---

corporation, moreover, does not act or hold property as an agent of the stockholders. 1 W. FLETCHER, *supra* note 29, § 30, at 130.

The attack on the nineteenth century assumption that equity interests are the defining concern of the corporate person has taken many forms. The first assault was made against the notion that shareholders effectively control the modern corporation. *See* A. BERLE & G. MEANS, THE MODERN CORPORATION AND PRIVATE PROPERTY 346–47 (1932) (distinguishing "passive property" or the rights of ownership retained by equity and "active property" or the power entrusted to management to use economic resources).

Equity's loss of power over business operations has been accompanied by a move in the law from a rule of unanimous shareholder consent for significant alterations of the corporate structure to a simple majority rule, further strengthening management's control over the corporation. *See* Carney, *Fundamental Corporate Changes, Minority Shareholders and Business Purposes*, 1980 AM.B.FOUND. RESEARCH J. 69. For additional changes in corporate charters diminishing equity power over corporate affairs, see J. COLEMAN, POWER AND THE STRUCTURE OF SOCIETY 44–50 (1974). For an analysis of the "de facto autonomy" these developments have brought to management, *see* Rostow, *To Whom and for What Ends Is Corporate Management Responsible?*, in THE CORPORATION IN MODERN SOCIETY 46 (E. Mason ed. 1959).

16. These managers, according to the realist, have fiduciary duties to the corporate person, which are distinct from and often in conflict with their duties to shareholders. *See* J. COLEMAN, *supra* note 37, at 49. Increased return on equity is not an exclusive goal, but merely one of several constraints (like wages and federal guidelines) which must be taken into account by those who control the corporation. See Mason, *The Apologetics of Mangerialism*, 31 J.BUS. 1, 3 (1958) (noting views of chairman of Standard Oil that managers of corporations must conduct its affairs "in such a way as to maintain an equitable and working balance among the claims of the various directly interested groups—stockholders, employees, customers, and the public at large"); A.P. Smith Mfg. Co. v. Barlow, 13 N.J. 145, 147, 98 A.2d 581, 583 (1953) (citing views of Standard Oil chairman).

The classic debate as to whom the duties of corporate management ultimately run was conducted by Professors Berle and Dodd some fifty years ago. Berle began with a thesis compatible with the older contract view: corporate powers are held in trust, "necessarily and at all times exercisable only for the ratable benefit of all the stockholders as their interest appears." Berle, *Corporate Powers as Powers in Trust*, 44 HARV.L.REV. 1049, 1049 (1931). Professor Dodd replied in a realist vein: directors should be legally understood as trustees for the enterprise and not merely as attorneys for stockholders. Dodd, *For Whom Are Corporate Managers Trustees?*, 45 HARV.L.REV. 1145 (1932). Berle finally accepted Dodd's initial position in A. BERLE, THE TWENTIETH CENTURY CAPITALIST REVOLUTION (1954). The View That the Duties of Corporate Managers Go Beyond Maximizing Shareholder Profit Has Been Attacked as "A Fundamentally Subversive Doctrine." M. FRIEDMAN, CAPITALISM AND FREEDOM 133–36 (1962).

17. Under the business judgment rule, directors are not liable for honest errors of judgment, "even though the errors may be so gross that they may demonstrate the unfitness of the directors to manage the corporate affairs." 3A W. FLETCHER, *supra* note [8], § 1039. In effect the business judgment rule allows corporate directors uninhibited discretion, absent self-dealing, bad faith, or lack of due care. The rule has come to replace the moribund notion of ultra vires, which limited corporate activity to those privileges specifically granted by the sovereign in the charter of incorporation. See *supra* notes 25–26. Under the realist approach, an ultra vires act is not illegal unless it is a public wrong. H. HENN, *supra* note [4], § 184. For a brief account of the replacement of ultra vires by the business judgment rule, *see* L. FRIEDMAN, *supra* note [4], at 453–54.

the public,[18] Justice Powell cannot be referring to the purely personal views of corporate management, for corporate officers would still be free under the law to express themselves in their private capacities.[19] The Justice must be alarmed, then, by the threat the Massachusetts law poses to the views of the corporation itself, views which management is under a fiduciary obligation to express when it speaks in its corporate capacity or when it allocates corporate funds to influence a political question.

The notion that soulless, inarticulate corporations could even hold a political view, let alone insist on the right to express it, would be incomprehensible to the scholastic philosophers and the classical economists who provided the conceptual ground for earlier explanations of corporate personality. The organizations they knew as corporations, however, would be deficient in many respects when compared with this modern form of production.[20]

---

2. *The Fundamental Rights of Legal Persons in Europe*

Europeans, like their American counterparts, have constructed complex systems of human rights, based in large part on written instruments. The Europeans also have wrestled with the question of the applicability of the basic guarantees of human rights to business enterprises. The German constitutional court has extended the protections of the Basic Law (*Grundgesetz*), the Constitution of the Federal Republic of Germany, to legal as well as natural persons. Thus, the "right to personality...has not been confined to natural persons. Freedom of action has been extended by interpretation to corporations and legal persons."[1] However, as in the United States, legal and natural persons are not necessarily treated identically for all purposes of the Basic Law. Consider, for example, the extension of privacy rights in Germany:

> Article 13(1) declares: "The home shall be inviolable." Paragraph 2 authorizes judges to order searches as prescribed by law, and paragraph 3 permits "encroachments" (Eingriffe) and "restrictions" (Beschränkungen) of the home's inviolability only "to avert a common danger or a mortal danger to individuals or, pursuant to law, to prevent imminent danger to public safety and order." In the *Dry Cleaning* case (1971) the court rules that the term "home" within the meaning of Article 13 is to be interpreted broadly as a "private living sphere"

---

18. First Nat'l Bank v. Bellotti, 435 U.S. 765, 783 (1978).

19. As one brief in Bellotti stated,

> If there is speech involved here, it must be the speech of management. But corporate managers are free to speak as they wish, and to spend money to promote their beliefs and ideas. What they claim is that their speech is abridged by their inability to use their employer's treasury to promote political viewpoints.

Brief for Appellee at 18, First Nat'l Bank v. Bellotti, 435 U.S. 765 (1978). Justice Powell's concern for those voters "interested in hearing appellants' views" on referendum issues, Bellotti, 435 U.S. at 782 n. 18 (emphasis added), must be understood in terms of the frequent references to "the corporate identity of the speaker."...

20. *See* Rostow, *supra* note [15], at 50 (comparing modern corporations to "puny institutions" of eighteenth and nineteenth century).

1. Donald P. Kommers, The Constitutional Jurisprudence of the Federal Republic of Germany 575 & n.30 (2nd ed. 1997).

that would include rooms for study, work and business. But it drew a sharp distinction between this private sphere and a commercial business office. The state could thus permissibly inspect records that would disclose the exact nature of a business for tax purposes. In the *Bauer Company* case (1976), however, the court laid down carefully circumscribed standards for the judicial authorization of such a search. [Excerpted from DONALD P. KOMMERS, THE CONSTITUTIONAL JURISPRUDENCE OF THE FEDERAL REPUBLIC OF GERMANY 335 (2nd ed. 1997)].

Moreover, the German Federal Constitutional Court has expressed its doubts that the German Basic Law's protection of association rights extends to all corporate entities.[2] In the Codetermination Case ((1979) 50 BverfGE 290) the Federal Constitutional Court was presented with a challenge to the Codetermination Act of 1976 which called for the representation of employees on the supervisory boards of large public corporations. In rejecting the challenge, the Federal Constitutional Court stated that the Codetermination Act does not:

> impair the fundamental right to form associations. It may even be doubtful that the protected right set out in Article 9(1) of the Basic Law and the substance of this provision permit an application of the guarantee to larger joint-stock companies. Unlike the type of association and society which the Basic Law primarily safeguards, the personal element in such larger companies dwindles to the point of insignificance. However, this issue can remain unresolved since the contested provisions do not infringe Article 9(1) of the Basic Law even if we assume in principle that it is inapplicable in this case....[3]

The issues of fundamental rights for corporations and other associations with legal personality has become more complicated in Europe since the second half of the Twentieth Century. The fundamental rights encompassed in the treaties established in the European Union and the human rights guarantees in the European Convention for the Protection of Human Rights and Fundamental Freedoms have added two additional layers of lawmaking with respect to the protection of the "personhood" of enterprises, particularly corporations. The complexities, ambiguities and conflicts resulting from the institutionalization of a system where two orders of human rights exist side by side has resulted in an approach to the "human rights" of corporations somewhat distinct from that developed in the U.S.

In the materials which follow, consider whether the approach of the European Courts is similar to that adopted by the Supreme Court. To the extent the approaches are different, are the differences significant? Are the differences based on a different view of the nature of corporate legal personality?

---

2. Article 9(1) of the German Basic Law provides that "All Germans have the right to form associations and societies." Translated in DONALD P. KOMMERS, THE CONSTITUTIONAL JURISPRUDENCE OF THE FEDERAL REPUBLIC OF GERMANY App. A at 509 (2nd ed. 1997). Sabine Michalowski and Lorna Woods translate that provision differently: "All Germans have the right to form associations and companies." SABINE MICHALOWSKI AND LORNA WOODS, GERMAN CONSTITUTIONAL LAW: THE PROTECTION OF CIVIL LIBERTIES 277 (1999).

3. Codetermination Case, (1979) 50 BverfGE 290, excerpted from DONALD P. KOMMERS, THE CONSTITUTIONAL JURISPRUDENCE OF THE FEDERAL REPUBLIC OF GERMANY 270 (2nd ed. 1997) (official Summary). Professor Kommers notes: "The *Codetermination* case consumes ninety-one pages of the official German reports. In addition, the Federal Constitutional Court's public relations office issued a short summary of the case....A full English translation of the case appears in *European Commercial Cases* 2 (1979): 324–86." *Id.*, at 268.

Hoechst AG v. EC Commission

Joined Cases 46/87 and 227/188
European Court of Justice
[1989] ECR 2859, [1991] 4 CMLR 410
21 September 1989

DECISION:

By applications lodged at the Court Registry on 16 February 1987 and 5 August 1988 respectively, Hoechst AG brought two actions under the second paragraph of Article 173 of the EEC Treaty for declarations that three Commission decisions adopted in Cases IV/31.865—PVC—and IV/31.866—Polyethylene—under Regulation No 17 of the Council of 6 February 1962 (First Regulation implementing Articles 85 and 86 of the Treaty (Official Journal, English Special Edition 1959–1962, p 87)) were void. The first action is directed against Decision K(87) 19/5 of 15 January 1987 concerning an investigation under Article 14(3) of Regulation No 17 and Decision K(87) 248 of 3 February 1987 imposing a periodic penalty payment under Article 16 of Regulation No 17. The second action is directed against Decision K(88) 928 of 26 May 1988 fixing the definitive amount of a periodic penalty payment under Article 16 of Regulation No 17.

Having grounds for suspecting the existence, as between certain producers and suppliers of PVC and polyethylene in the Community, of agreements or concerted practices concerning the fixing of prices and delivery quotas for those products, the Commission decided to carry out an investigation into several undertakings, including the applicant in respect of which it adopted the above-mentioned contested decision of 15 January 1987 (hereinafter referred to "the decision ordering the investigation").

On 20, 22 and 23 January 1987, the Commission sought to carry out the investigation in question, but the applicant refused to submit to the investigation on the ground that it constituted an unlawful search. The applicant expressed the same point of view in its reply to a telex in which the Commission called upon it to undertake to submit to the investigation and set a periodic penalty payment in the event of non-compliance of 1 000 ECU for each day of delay. The Commission then adopted the above-mentioned contested decision of 3 February 1987, in which it imposed the periodic penalty payment mentioned above on the applicant (hereinafter referred to as "the decision imposing the periodic penalty payment").

By decision of 12 February 1987, the Amtsgericht [Local Court] Frankfurt am Main dismissed an application by the Bundeskartellamt [Federal Cartel Office] whose assistance had been sought in accordance with Regulation No 17, for a search warrant on the ground that no facts had been put before it to justify the suspicion of the existence of agreements or concerted practices.

By order of 26 March 1987, the President of the Court of Justice dismissed the applicant's application for suspension of the operation of the decision ordering the investigation and the decision imposing the periodic penalty payment.

On 31 March 1987 the Bundeskartellamt obtained from the Amtsgericht Frankfurt am Main a search warrant issued directly in the name of the Commission. The latter carried out the investigation on 2 and 3 April 1987.

After giving the applicant an opportunity to express its views and after hearing the Advisory Committee on Restrictive Practices and Dominant Positions, the Commission, in the above-mentioned contested decision of 26 May 1988 (hereinafter referred to as "the decision fixing the definitive amount"), fixed the definitive amount of the periodic penalty payment at 55 000 ECU, that is to say, 1 000 ECU per day from 6 February to 1 April 1987 inclusive.

Reference is made to the Report for the Hearing for a fuller account of the background to the dispute, the course of the procedure and the submissions and arguments of the parties which are mentioned or discussed hereinafter only in so far as is necessary for the reasoning of the Court.

The decision ordering the investigation:

The applicant relies on three submissions against the decision ordering the investigation, alleging that the Commission exceeded its powers of investigation, that the statement of reasons for the decision was inadequate and that the procedure followed was irregular.

(a) The Commission's powers of investigation

The applicant considers that the contested decision is unlawful inasmuch as it permitted the Commission's officials to take steps which the applicant describes as a search, which are not provided for under Article 14 of Regulation No. 17 and which infringe fundamental rights recognized by Community law. It adds that if that provision is to be interpreted as empowering the Commission to carry out searches, it is unlawful on the ground that it is incompatible with fundamental rights, for the protection of which it is necessary that searches should be carried out only on the basis of a judicial warrant issued in advance.

The Commission contends that its powers under Article 14 of Regulation No. 17 extend to the adoption of measures which, under the law of some Member States, would be regarded as searches. It nonetheless considers that the requirements of judicial protection deriving from fundamental rights, which it does not contest in principle, are fulfilled in so far as the addressees of decisions ordering investigations have an opportunity, on the one hand, to contest those decisions before the Court and, on the other, to apply for suspension of their operation by way of interim order, which permits the Court to check rapidly that the investigations ordered are not arbitrary in nature. Such review is equivalent to a judicial warrant issued in advance.

It should be noted, before the nature and scope of the Commission's powers of investigation under Article 14 of Regulation No. 17 are examined, that that article cannot be interpreted in such a way as to give rise to results which are incompatible with the general principles of Community law and in particular with fundamental rights.

The Court has consistently held that fundamental rights are an integral part of the general principles of law the observance of which the Court ensures, in accordance with constitutional traditions common to the Member States, and the international treaties on which the Member States have collaborated or of which they are signatories (see, in particular, the judgment of 14 May 1974 in Case 4/73, Nold v. Commission [1974] ECR 491). The European Convention for the Protection of Human Rights and Fundamental Freedoms of 4 November 1950 (hereinafter referred to as "the European Convention on Human Rights") is of particular significance in that regard (see, in particular, the judgment of 15 May 1986 in Case 222/84, Johnston v. Chief Constable of the Royal Ulster Constabulary [1986] ECR 1651).

In interpreting Article 14 of Regulation No. 17, regard must be had in particular to the rights of the defence, a principle whose fundamental nature has been stressed on numerous occasions in the Court's decisions (see, in particular, the judgment of 9 November 1983 in Case 322/81, Michelin v. Commission [1983] ECR 3461, paragraph 7).

In that judgment, the Court pointed out that the rights of the defence must be observed in administrative procedures which may lead to the imposition of penalties. But it is also necessary to prevent those rights from being irremediably impaired during preliminary inquiry procedures including, in particular, investigations which may be decisive in providing evidence of the unlawful nature of conduct engaged in by undertakings for which they may be liable.

Consequently, although certain rights of the defence relate only to the contentious proceedings which follow the delivery of the statement of objections, other rights, such as the right to legal representation and the privileged nature of correspondence between lawyer and client (recognized by the Court in the judgment of 18 May 1982 in Case 155/79, AM & S v. Commission [1982] ECR 1575) must be respected as from the preliminary-inquiry stage.

Since the applicant has also relied on the requirements stemming from the fundamental right to the inviolability of the home, it should be observed that, although the existence of such a right must be recognized in the Community legal order as a principle common to the laws of the Member States in regard to the private dwellings of natural persons, the same is not true in regard to undertakings, because there are not inconsiderable divergences between the legal systems of the Member States in regard to the nature and degree of protection afforded to business premises against intervention by the public authorities.

No other inference is to be drawn from Article 8(1) of the European Convention on Human Rights which provides that: "Everyone has the right to respect for his private and family life, his home and his correspondence". The protective scope of that article is concerned with the development of man's personal freedom and may not therefore be extended to business premises. Furthermore, it should be noted that there is no case-law of the European Court of Human Rights on that subject.

Nonetheless, in all the legal systems of the Member States, any intervention by the public authorities in the sphere of private activities of any person, whether natural or legal, must have a legal basis and be justified on the grounds laid down by law, and, consequently, those systems provide, albeit in different forms, protection against arbitrary or disproportionate intervention. The need for such protection must be recognized as a general principle of Community law. In that regard, it should be pointed out that the Court has held that it has the power to determine whether measures of investigation taken by the Commission under the ECSC Treaty are excessive (judgment of 14 December 1962 in Joined Cases 5 to 11 and 13 to 15/62, San Michele and Others v. Commission [1962] ECR 449).

The nature and scope of the Commission's powers of investigation under Article 14 of Regulation No. 17 should therefore be considered in the light of the general principles set out above.

* * *

Although Article 14 of Regulation No 17 thus confers wide powers of investigation on the Commission, the exercise of those powers is subject to conditions serving to ensure that the rights of the undertakings concerned are respected.

In that regard, it should be noted first that the Commission is required to specify the subject-matter and purposes of the investigation. That obligation is a fundamental requirement not merely in order to show that the investigation to be carried out on the premise of the undertakings concerned is justified but also to enable those undertakings to assess the scope of their duty to co-operate while at the same time safeguarding the rights of the defence.

It should also be pointed out that the conditions for the exercise of the Commission's investigative powers vary according to the procedure which the Commission has chosen, the attitude of the undertakings concerned and the intervention of the national authorities.

* * *

It follows from Article 14(6) that it is for each Member State to determine the conditions under which the national authorities will afford assistance to the Commission's officials. In that regard, the Member States are required to ensure that the Commission's action is effective, while respecting the general principles set out above. It follows that, within those limits, the appropriate procedural rules designed to ensure respect for undertakings' rights are those laid down by national law.

Consequently, if the Commission intends, with the assistance of the national authorities, to carry out an investigation other than with the co-operation of the undertakings concerned, it is required to respect the relevant procedural guarantees laid down by national law.

The Commission must make sure that the competent body under national law has all that it needs to exercise its own supervisory powers. It should be pointed out that that body, whether judicial or otherwise, cannot in this respect substitute its own assessment of the need for the investigations ordered for that of the Commission, the lawfulness of whose assessments of fact and law is subject only to review by the Court of Justice. On the other hand, it is within the powers of the national body, after satisfying itself that the decision ordering the investigation is authentic, to consider whether the measures of constraint envisaged are arbitrary or excessive having regard to the subject-matter of the investigation and to ensure that the rules of national law are complied with in the application of those measures.

In the light of the foregoing, it must be held that the measures which the contested decision ordering the investigation permitted the Commission's officials to take did not exceed their powers under Article 14 of Regulation No. 17. Article 1 of that decision merely requires the applicant "to permit officials authorized by the Commission to enter its premises during normal office hours, to produce for inspection and to permit copies to be made of business documents related to the subject-matter of the enquiry which are requested by the said officials and to provide immediately any explanations which those officials may seek".

* * *

The submission alleging that the Commission exceeded its powers of investigation must therefore be rejected.

(b) The statement of reasons

According to the applicant, the decision ordering the investigation infringes Article 190 of the Treaty and Article 14(3) of Regulation No. 17 on the ground that it is imprecise, in particular in regard to the subject-matter and purpose of the investigation.

[The Court, considered and rejected this claim].

(c) The procedure under which the decision was adopted

[The Court, considered and rejected this claim].

Since none of the submissions raised against the decision ordering the investigation can be accepted, the application for a declaration that that decision is void must be dismissed.

The decision imposing the periodic penalty payment

* * *

It should be pointed out that the undertakings concerned must be given the opportunity "of being heard on the matters to which the Commission has taken objection", pursuant to Article 19(1) of Regulation No. 17, before the adoption of various decisions, including those provided for in Article 16 concerning periodic penalty payments.

That hearing is an essential part of the rights of the defense. It is necessary in order for undertakings and associations of undertakings to be able "to submit their comments on the whole of the objections raised against them which the Commission proposes to deal with in its decisions" (third recital in the preamble to Regulation No 99/63 of the Commission of 25 July 1963 on the hearings provided for in Article 19(1) and (2) of Council Regulation No. 17 (Official Journal, English Special Edition 1963–1964, p 47)).

With regard to the Advisory Committee on Restrictive Practices and Dominant Positions, Articles 16(3) provides that "Article 10(3) to (6) shall apply". Those provisions govern the powers, composition, and procedure for consulting the Advisory Committee.

According to Article 1 of Regulation No 99/63, "before consulting the Advisory Committee on Restrictive Practices and Dominant Positions, the Commission shall hold a hearing pursuant to Article 19(1) of Regulation No. 17". That provision confirms that the hearing of the undertakings concerned and the consultation of the Advisory Committee are necessary in the same situations.

In determining whether the Commission was required to hear the applicant and consult the Advisory Committee before adopting the decision imposing the periodic penalty payment, it should be borne in mind that the fixing of periodic penalty payments under Article 16 of Regulation No. 17 necessarily involves two stages. In its first decision, referred to in Article 16(1), the Commission imposes a periodic penalty payment expressed in terms of a number of units of account per day of delay, calculated from a date fixed by it. Since that decision does not determine the total amount of the periodic penalty payment, it cannot be enforced. That amount can be definitively fixed only in another decision.

Therefore, the obligation to hear the undertaking concerned and to consult the Advisory Committee on Restrictive Practices and Dominant Positions is fulfilled if the hearing and consultation take place before the fixing of the definitive amount of the periodic penalty payment, so that both the undertaking concerned and the Advisory Committee are then in a proper position to express their views on all the matters on the basis of which the Commission has imposed the periodic penalty payment and fixed the definitive amount thereof.

Furthermore, the requirement to hear the undertaking and consult the Advisory Committee before the adoption of a decision imposing a periodic penalty payment on an undertaking which has refused to submit to an investigation would entail delaying the date of adoption of that decision and, therefore, jeopardizing the effectiveness of the decision ordering the investigation.

It follows from the foregoing that the adoption of the decision imposing the periodic penalty payment was not vitiated by a breach of essential procedural requirements. The application for a declaration that that decision is void must therefore be dismissed.

The decision fixing the definitive amount of the periodic penalty payment.

[The Court, considered and rejected this claim].

It follows from the foregoing that the applications must be dismissed.

Costs

Under Article 69(2) of the Rules of Procedure, the unsuccessful party is to be ordered to pay the costs if they have been asked for in the successful party's pleading. Since the applicant has failed in its submissions, it must be ordered to pay the costs.

On those grounds,

THE COURT

hereby:

(1) Dismisses the applications;

(2) Orders the applicant to pay the costs.

Niemietz v. Germany (search of law offices)

European Court of Human Rights
Series A, No, 251-B
Application No. 13710/88
16 E.H.R.R. 97
16 December 1992
(some footnotes omitted)

The Facts

I. *The Particular Circumstances of the Case*

6. Mr. Niemietz lives in Freiburg im Breisgau, Germany, where he practises as a lawyer (*Rechtsanwalt*).

7. On 9 December 1985 a letter was sent by telefax from the Freiburg post office to Judge Moisga of the Freising District Court (*Amtsgericht*). It related to criminal proceedings for insulting behavior (*Beleidigung*) pending before the court against Mr. J, an employer who refused to deduct from his employees' salaries and pay over to the tax office the church tax to which they were liable. The letter bore the signature of one Klaus Wegner—possibly a fictitious person—followed by the words 'on behalf of the Anticlerical Working Group (*Antiklerikaler Arbbeitskries*) of the Freiburg *Bunte Liste* (multicloured group)' and a post-office box number....

8. The applicant had, as a city councillor, been chairman for some years of the Freiburg *Bunte Liste*, which is a local political party. He had also played a particularly committed role in, although he had never been a member of, its Anti-clerical Working Group, which sought to curtail the influence of the church.

Until the end of 1985 certain of the mail for the *Bunte Liste*, which had as its address for the correspondence only the post-office box number that had been given in the letter to Judge Miosga, had been delivered to the office (*Bürogemeinschft*) of the applicant and a colleague of his; the latter had also been active on behalf of the party and had acted for it professionally.

9. On 13 January 1986, the Director of the Munich I Regional Court (*Landgericht*) requested the Muhich Police Prosecutor's Office (*Statsanwaltschaft*) to institute criminal proceedings against Klaus Wegner for the offense of insulting behaviour, contrary to Article 185 of the Criminal Code. Attempts to serve a summons on him were unsuccessful. The applicant's colleague refused to give any information about Klaus Wegner or his whereabouts and other attempts to find him failed.

10. In the context of the above-mentioned proceedings the Munich District Court issued, on 8 August 1986, a warrant to search the law office of the applicant and his colleague and the homes of Ms. D and Ms. G. [The contents of the search warrant is omitted]....

11. The search of the law office, the need for which the investigating authorities had first tried to obviate by questioning a witness, was effected by representatives of the Freiburg Public Prosecutor's Office and the police on 13 November 1986. According to a police officer's report drawn up on the following day, the premises were entered at about 9:00 a.m. and inspected in the presence of two office assistants. The actual search began about 9:15 a.m., when the applicant's colleague arrived, and lasted until about 10:30 a.m. The applicant himself arrived at 9:30 a.m. He declined to give any information as to the identity of Klaus Wegner, on the ground that he might thereby expose himself to the risk of criminal prosecution.

Those conducting the search examined four filing cabinets with data concerning clients, [and various files contained in those cabinets along with a client index and other materials]. Those searching neither found the documents they were seeking nor seized any materials. In the proceedings before the [Human Rights] Commission, the applicant stated that he had been able to put aside in time documents pointing to the identity of Klaus Wegner and had subsequently destroyed them.

12. The homes of Ms. D and Ms. G were also searched; documents were found that gave rise to a suspicion that the letter to Judge Miosga had been sent by Ms. D under an assumed name.

13. On 10 December 1986 the Chairman of the Freiburg Bar Association, who had been informed about the search by the applicant's colleague, addressed a formal protest to the President of the Munich District Court. The Chairman sent copies to the Bavarian Minister of Justice and the Munich Bar Association and invited the latter to associate itself with the protest.

In a reply of 27 January 1987, the President of the Munich District Court stated that the search was proportionate because the letter in question had constituted a serious interference with a pending case; hence no legal action on the protest was necessary.

14. The criminal proceedings against 'Klause Wegner' were later discontinued for lack of evidence.

15. On 27 March 1987, the Munich I Regional Court declared an appeal (*Beschwerde*) lodged by the applicant, pursuant to Article 304 of the Code of Criminal Procedure, against the search warrant to be inadmissible, on the ground that it had already been executed (*wegen prozessualer Überholung*). It considered that in the circumstances there was no legal interest in having the warrant declared unlawful. It had not been arbitrary, since there had been concrete indications that specified material would be found. There was no ground for holding that Article 97 of the Code of Criminal Procedure[1] had been circum-

1. *See* para. 21 below.

vented: The warrant had been based on the fact that mail for the Freiburg *Bunte Liste* had for some time been delivered to the applicant's office and it could not be assumed that that mail could concern a lawyer-client relationship. In addition, personal honour was not so minor a legal interest as to render the search disproportionate. There could be no question in the present case of preventing a lawyer from freely exercising his profession.

16.On 28 April 1987 the applicant lodged a constitutional complaint (*Verfassungsbeschwerde*) against the search warrant of 8 August 1986 and the Munich I Regional Court's decision of 27 March 1987. On 18 August a panel of three judges of the Federal Constitutional Court (*Bundesverfassungsgericht*) declined to accept the complaint for adjudication, on the ground that it did not offer sufficient prospects of success.

The Federal Constitutional Court also found that the Munich I Regional Court's decision of 27 March 1987 that the applicant's appeal was inadmissible was not objectionable in terms of constitutional law. Furthermore, as regards the actual execution of the warrant, Mr. Niemietz had not exhausted the remedy available to him under section 23(10) of the Introductory Act to the Courts Organization Act (*Einführungsgesetz zum Gerichtsverfassungsgesetz*).

II. *Relevant domestic law*

17. The search complained of was ordered in the context of criminal proceedings for insulting behavior, an offense punishable by imprisonment for a maximum, where no physical violence is involved, of one year or a fine.[2]

18. Article 13(1) of the Basic Law (*Grundgezetz*) guarantees the inviolability of the home (*Wohnung*); this provision has been consistently interpreted by the German courts in a wide sense, to include business premises.[3]

19. Article 103 of the Code of Criminal Procedure that the home and other premises (*Wohnung und andere Räume*) of a person who is not suspected of a criminal offence may be searched only in order to arrest a person charged with an offence, to investigate indications of an offence or to seize specific objects and provided always that there are facts to suggest that such a person, indications or objects is or are to be found on the premises to be searched.

20. Search warrants may be challenged, as regards their lawfulness, in proceedings instituted under Article 304 of the Code of Criminal Procedure and, as regards their manner of execution, in proceedings instituted under section 23(1) of the Introductory Act to the Courts Organisation Act.

21. In Germany, a lawyer is an independent organ in the administration of justice and an independent counsel and representative in all legal matters.

An unauthorised breach of secrecy by a lawyer is punishable by imprisonment for a maximum of one year or a fine.[4] A lawyer is entitled to refuse to give testimony concerning any matter confided to him in his professional capacity.[5] The last-mentioned provisions in conjunction with Article 97, prohibit, with certain exceptions, the seizure of correspondence between lawyer and client.

---

2. Art. 185 of the Criminal Code.
3. *See*, in particular, the Federal Constitutonal Court's judgment of 13 October 1971—*Entscheidungssammlung des Bubdesverfassungsgerichts*, vo. 32, p.54.
4. Art. 203(1)(3) of the Criminal Code.
5. Art. 53(1)(2) and (3) of the Code of Criminal Procedure.

III. *Case law of the Court of Justice of the European Communities*

22. In its judgment of 21 September 1989 in Joined Cases 46/87 and 22/88 HOECHST V. COMMISSION [1989],[6] the Court of Justice of the European Communities stated as follows

> [the opinion quoted the language from the *Hoechst* opinion analyzing the applicability of Article 8(1) of the European Convention on Human Rights which is set forth in the excerpt of the *Hoechst* case set forth above in section 1 of this Chapter].

This statement was affirmed in the same court's judgments of 17 October 1989 in Case 85/87 Dow Benelux v. Commission [1989][7] and Joined cases 97 to 99/87 Dow Chemical Ibérica and Others v. Commission [1989].[8]

PROCEEDINGS BEFORE THE COMMISSION

23. In his application lodged with the Commission on 15 February 1988, Mr. Niemietz alleges that the search had violated his right to respect for his home and correspondence, guaranteed by Article 8 of the Convention, and had also, by impairing the goodwill of his law office and reputation as a lawyer, constituted a breach of his rights under Article 1 of the Protocol No. 1. In addition, he submitted that, contrary to Article 13 of the Convention, he had no effective remedies before German authorities in respect of those complaints.

24. By decision of 5 April 1990, the Commission declared the complaints under Article 8 of the Convention and Article 1 of the Protocol No. 1 admissible and the remainder of the application inadmissible.

In its report of 29 May 1991 (Art. 31), the Commission expressed the unanimous opinion that there had been a violation of Article 8 of the Convention and that no separate issue arose under Article 1 of Protocol No. 1. The text of the Commission's opinion is published below.

[The Commission's opinion is omitted]

Judgment

I. *Alleged violation of Article 8 of the Convention*

26. Mr. Niemietz alleged that the search of his law office had given rise to a breach of Article 8 of the Convention, which reads as follows:

> 1. Everyone has the right to respect for his private and family life, his home and his correspondence.
>
> 2. There shall be no interference by a public authority with the exercise of this right except as is in accordance with the law and is necessary in a democratic society in the interests of national security, public safety or the economic wellbeing of the country, for the prevention of disorder or crime, for the protection of health or morals, or for the protection of the rights and freedoms of others.

This submission was accepted by the Commission, on the basis that the search constituted an unjustified interference with the applicant's private life and home.

---

6. HOECHST V. COMMISSION, [1989] E.C.R. 2859 at 2924.
7. Dow Benelux v. Commission [1989] E.C.R. 3137 at 3157.
8. Dow Chemical Ibérica and Others v. Commission [1989] E.C.R. 3165 at 3185–6.

A. *Was there an 'interference'?*

27. In contesting the Commission's conclusion, the Government maintained that Article 8 did not afford protection against the search of a lawyer's office. In their view, the Convention drew a clear distinction between private life and home, on the one hand, and professional and business life and premises, on the other hand.

28. In arriving at its opinion there had been an interference with Mr. Niemietz's 'private life' and 'home,' the Commission attached particular significance to the confidential relationship that exists between lawyer and client. The Court shares the Government's doubts as to whether this factor can serve as a workable criterion for the purposes of delimiting the scope of the protection afforded by Article 8. Virtually all professional and business activities may involve, to a greater or lesser degree, matters that are confidential with the result that, if that criterion were adopted, disputes would frequently arise as to where the line should be drawn.

29. The Court does not consider it possible or necessary to attempt an exhaustive definition of the notion of 'private life.' However, it would be too restrictive to limit the notion to an 'inner circle' in which the individual may live his own personal life as he chooses and to exclude therefrom entirely the outside world not encompassed within that circle. Respect for private life must also comprise to a certain degree the right to establish and develop relationships with other human beings.

There appears, furthermore, to be no reason of principle why this understanding of the notion of 'private life' should be taken to exclude activities of a [professional or business nature since it is, after all, in the course of their working lives, that the majority of people have a significant, if not the greatest, appertained of developing relationships with the outside world. This view is supported by the fact, as was rightly pointed out by the Commission, it is not always possible to distinguish clearly which of an individuals activities form part of his professional or business life and which do not. Thus, especially in the case of a person exercising a liberal profession, his work in that context may form part and parcel of his life to such a degree that it becomes impossible to know in what capacity he is acting at a given moment of time.

To deny the protection of Article 8 on the ground that the measure complained of related only to professional activities—as the Government suggested should be done in the present case—could moreover lead to an inequality of treatment, in that such protection would remain available to a person whose professional and non professional activities were so intermingled that there was no means of distinguishing between them. In fact, the Court has not heretofore drawn such distinctions: it concluded that there had been an interference with private life even where telephone tapping covered both business and private calls[21]; and, where a search was directed solely against business activities, it did not rely on the fact as a ground for excluding the applicability of Article 8 under the head of 'private life.'

30. As regards the word 'home,' appearing in the English text of Article 8, the Court observes that in certain Contracting States, notably Germany,[22] it has been accepted as extending to business premises. Such an interpretation is, moreover, fully consonant

21. *See* Huvig v. France (1990) 12 E.H.R.R. 528, paras. 8 and 25.
22. *See* para. 18 above.

with the French text, since the word '*domicile*' has a broader connotation 'home' and may extend, for example, to a professional person's office.

In this context also, it may always be possible, to draw precise distinctions, since activities which are related to a profession or business may well be conducted form a person's private residence and activities which are not so related may well be carried on in an office or commercial premises. A narrow interpretation of the words 'home' and '*domicile*' could therefore give rise to the same risk of inequality of treatment as a narrow interpretation of the notion of 'private life.'

31. More generally, to interpret the words 'private life' and 'home' as including certain professional or business activities or premises would be consonant with the essential object and purpose of Article 8, namely to protect the individual against arbitrary interference by the public authorities.[25] Such an interpretation would not unduly hamper the Contracting States, for they would retain their entitlement to 'interfere' to the extent permitted by Article 8(2); that entitlement might well be more far reaching where professional or business activities or premises were involved than would otherwise be the case.

32. To the abovementioned general considerations, which militate against the view that Article 8 is not applicable, must be added a further factor pertaining to the particular circumstances of the case. The warrant issued by the Munich District Court ordered a search for, and seizure of, 'documents'—without qualification or limitation—revealing the identity of Klaus Wegner. Furthermore, those conducting the search examined four cabinets with data concerning clients as well as six individual files; their operations must perforce have covered 'correspondence' and materials that can properly be regarded as such for the purposes of Article 8. In this connection, it is sufficient to note that that provision does not use, as it does for the word 'life' any adjective to qualify the word 'correspondence.' And, indeed, the Court has already held that, in the context of correspondence in the form of telephone calls, no such qualification is to be made.[26] Again, in a number of cases relating to correspondence with a lawyer, the Court did not event advert to the possibility that Article 8 might be inapplicable on the ground that the correspondence was of a professional nature.

33. Taken together, the foregoing reasons lead the Court to find that the search of the applicant's office constituted an interference with his rights under Article 8.

B. *Was the interference 'in accordance with the law'?*

34. The applicant submitted that the interference in question was not 'in accordance with the law,' since it was based on suspicions rather than facts and so did not meet the conditions laid down by Article 103 of the Code of Criminal Procedure[27] and since it was intended to circumvent the legal provisions safeguarding professional secrecy.

35. The Court agrees with the Commission and the Government that that submission must be rejected. It notes that both the Munich I Regional Court and the Federal Constitutional Court considered that the search was lawful in terms of Article 103 of the aforesaid Code and sees no reason to differ from the views from the views which those courts expressed.

---

25. *See*, for example, Marck X v. Belgium (1979) 2 E.H.R.R. 330, para. 31.
26. *See* Huvig v. France (1990) 12 E.H.R.R. 528, paras. 8 and 25.
27. *See* para. 19 above.

C. *Did the interference have a legitimate aim or aims?*

36. Like the Commission, the Court finds that, as was not contested by the applicant, the interference pursued aims that were legitimate under Article 8(2), namely the prevention of crime and the protection of the rights of others, that is the honor of Judge Miosga.

D. *Was the interference 'necessary in a democratic society'?*

37. As to whether the interference was 'necessary in a democratic society,' the Court inclines to the view that the reasons given therefore by the Munich District Court can be regarded as relevant in terms of legitimate aims pursued. It does not, however, consider it essential to pursue this point since it has formed the opinion that, as was contended by the applicant and was found by the Commission, the measure complained of was not proportionate to those aims.

It is true that the offense in connection with which the search was effected, involving as it did not only an insult to but also an attempt to bring pressure on a judge, cannot be classified as no more than minor. On the other had, the warrant was drawn in broad terms, in that it ordered a search for and seizure of 'documents,' without any limitation, revealing the identity of the author of the offensive letter; this point is of special significance where, as in Germany, the search of a lawyer's office is not accompanied by any special procedural safeguards, such as the presence of an independent observer. More importantly, having regard to the materials that were in fact inspected, the search impinged on professional secrecy to an extent that appears disproportionate in the circumstances; it has, in this connection, to be recalled that, where a lawyer is involved, an encroachment on professional secrecy may have repercussions on the proper administration of justice and hence on the rights guaranteed by Article 6 of the Convention. In addition, the attendant publicity must have been capable of affecting adversely the applicant's professional reputation, in the eyes both of his existing clients and of the public at large.

E. *Conclusion*

38. The Court thus concludes that there was a breach of Article 8.

* * *

For these reasons, the court unanimously

1. *Holds* that there has been a violation of Article 8 of the Convention.....

Comments and Questions

1. The *Hoechst* and *Niemietz* decisions point to the conditionality of a legal person's fundamental rights within Europe. As in the United States, legal persons are not treated like natural persons in the context of the availability of fundamental rights. As in the United States, the bases on which rights are accorded, or even conceived as possibly available to a legal person, depend to some extent on the way in which legal persons are conceived. Yet the cases do not enunciate a unitary view on that conceptualization. Nor do the cases even appear to agree on the proper allocation of rights to legal persons. Which of the two decisions do you believe make more sense? What theory of legal personality underlay each of the decisions?

2. The discussion thus far has proceeded on the basis of the standard theories of corporate personality—licensee, entity and contractarian. Other theories of legal personality have emerged in recent years. Among the more interesting, perhaps, are those of Gunther Teubner. Professor Teubner conceives of corporate personality in the way one can conceive of the personality of any integrated social system. In effect, perhaps theories of the state are best suited for understanding the nature of corporate personality. Do you agree?

Gunther Teubner, *Enterprise Corporatism: New Industrial Policy and the "Essence" of the Legal Person*

36 Am. J. Corp. L. 130 (1988)

(excerpts from pages 138–148; some footnotes omitted)

....The corporate actor is "fictional" because it is not identical with the real organization but only with the semantics of its self-description. It is "real" because this fiction takes on structural effect and orients social actions by binding them collectively. Max Weber came closes to capturing this ambivalence by treating collectivities only as "ideas" in the heads of judges, officials and the public, while at the same time assigning them "a powerful, often decisive, causal influence on the course of action of real individuals."[43]....

* * *

The first interim result might then be as follows: the social substratum of the legal person is neither an assemblage of people nor a pool of resources nor a mere organizational structure. Nor is it adequately characterized as an action system or as a formal organization. The substratum is conceived properly as a "collectivity" or "corporate actor", i.e. the self-description of a (usually formally) organized social action system that brings about a cyclical linkage of self-referentially constituted system identity and system elements.

* * *

From the standpoint of theory of self-referential systems, too, the autonomy of the law in the construction of its own environment and in the choice of its distinctions must be stressed. This is external observation of a self-observation: the legal system observes, using its own conceptualizations, how the organized social system observes itself as a "collectivity," or else how it is observed as such by its environment. The legal system is in no way "bound" by the self-observation, nor by other (e.g. psychological, sociological or "life world") external observations of this self-observation.[49] There is therefore no contradiction between on the one hand stressing the social reality of the substratum and on the other defending a positivist or constructivist concept of the legal person. The most decisive advocate of this position was perhaps Kelson: the legal person is a partial legal suborder, a complex of norms relating to a particular legally defined entity (contrast, corporation, association, federation, mu-

---

43. [Max Weber, Economy and Society 13 ff (1978)].

49. From this point of view one may sympathize with Hart, *Definition and Theory of Jurisprudence*, 70 L. Q. Rev. 37 (1954), when he calls for abandonment of the "ever baffling question" of "what is any association or organized group?" and its replacement by the question "Under what conditions do we refer to numbers and sequences of men as aggregates of individuals and under what conditions do we adopt instead unifying phrases extended by analogy form individuals?"

nicipality, state). In the personification, the norm complex is nothing but a point of attribution.[50]....

Accordingly, nothing prevents the legal system from taking any object whatever—divinities, saints, temples, plots of land, art objects—as points of attribution and giving them legal capacity. Trees particularly are prominent candidates. In legal theory and legal policy discussion they are continuously raised as potential legal subjects—quite rightly today. ("Should trees have standing?")[51]

It is amazing that, despite an extremely high degree of freedom and choice, there are nevertheless such great structural similarities between "collectivity" and "legal person." It is not only that the social and legal mechanisms of action attribution to constructs produced within the system (individual/collectivity in the social world, natural person/legal person in the legal world) are in principle structured in a parallel fashion. It is more striking that the law today makes practically no use of its positivist freedom and exclusively promotes "collectivities" to the status of legal persons.... Flume has argued forcefully that it makes no sense to subsume the complex reality of the legal person under a "unitary concept"; "What meaning is it supposed to have if one covers the reality of the state, of municipalities, of churches, of a corporation, of a foundation, of a sporting association, etc., in a unitary concept?"[54] But the concept of a "collectivity" or "corporate actor" developed above (i.e. self-description of an organized social system as the link between identity and capacity for action) shows instead that it certainly does it make sense to subsume social phenomena under a unitary concept.

* * *

The thesis is that, without being normatively compelled to do so, the law regularly binds up legal capacity with a large set of prerequisites of a particular social reality, which can be described by a "unitary concept." These prerequisites are: (1) (formally) organized action system; (2) a self-description of a collective identity; and (3) a cyclical linkage of identity and action via mechanisms of attribution. And thus we return to the social system's unitary concept of the collectivity. The reasons for the close correspondence between law and society, astonishing from the viewpoint of positivist freedoms, are neither of natural law nor of legal logic, but merely of legal policy. Giving legal capacity to social formations makes policy sense only when they have a highly developed internal order. Social capacity for action, i.e. the capacity for attributing external effects to the social systems as such, implies that actions of certain individuals are attributed to all participants, socially entitling and obligating them....

* * *

The second reason supporting a correspondence between the social and legal structure lies deeper. It concerns the social function of legal personification. This is understood quite inadequately if only the advantages of limited liability are taken into consideration and if the disadvantages are partially compensated for by "piercing the

50. Kelson, Allgemeine Staatslehre 66 ff. (1925) (English translation, General Theory of Law and State 96 ff. (1954)....

51. Kohler, Lehrbuch des buergerlichen Rechts I 230 (1906); Wolff, I Organbschaft und juristische Person 62 (1933); Stone, Should Trees Have Standing? Toward Legal Rights for Natural Objects (1974).

54. Flume, Die Juristische Person 25 (1983).

corporate veil."[58] Much more important aspects are, for example, the saving in transaction costs and the coordination advantages of "resource pooling"; efficiency gains deriving from the legal support of the capacity for action of the system as such; the positional advantages for the organization in contacts with the environment; or, last but not least, the well known "legal immortality." The really interesting "emergent property" lies, however, in the building up of a (second order) autopoietic system.[63] By the cyclical linkage of identity and action perfected in the legal person, the organization acquires a hitherto unachieved autonomy vis-a-vis its environment, both the external environment of market and politics and the internal environment of members and others involved in the organization. The legally supported personification is a decisive step toward complete operational closure, which at the same time means a new type of environmental openness, i.e., a step towards that linkage between closure and openness which is typical of autopoietic systems and is the basis of their evolutionary success.

This clears the way for transferring the profit motive motive from shareholders to the *Unternehmen an sich* (enterprise in and of itself), and would make the criteria of social responsibility apply not only to the personal actors, but also to the organization in terms of "corporate social responsibility." The development of autopoietic autonomy thereby also opens up far-reaching perspectives of economic and social control....

* * *

Of what concern is all this to the practicing lawyer? A great deal, for apart from consequences in legal theory, this view of the "essence" of the corporate personality also has implications for legal doctrine. If its "essence" lies not in resources nor in people, but in the legal reconstruction of a collectivized action system, this has immediately foreseeable consequences for such exotic legal phenomena as the one-man company, and the "personless corporation."... But consequences also have to be drawn for the legal conceptualization of corporate membership and of corporate bodies (Organe), since in the glaring light of systems theory corporate members and corporate bodies evaporate into mere bundles of roles. When the issue of the disregard of the corporate entity is raised, the legal person is to be "taken seriously" in a different sense than that recently proposed. And the relationship between "unity and multiplicity in the group enterprise" should be rethought in relation to the legal capacity for action of the group enterprise as a whole....

* * *

It is striking how many arguments for and against Meunchhausen accumulate around the topic of the legal person. There is the time honored argument that the fiction theory is false because the State itself, as a legal person, would then have to be a fiction, whereas the State could not, like Muenchhausen, have erected itself by mere motion into a legal fiction.[78] Then, by contrast with Flume, who angrily rejects this argument as speculation, Hofstadler of Goedel-Escher-Bach would joyfully welcome

---

58. This seems to be the prevailing trend, and not only in Germany: see the collective volume by Bastid, David & Luchaire, *La personnalite morale et ses limites* (1960), with country by country reports;...

63. On this, using the construction of the hypercycle, *see* [Teubner, *Hypercycle in Law and Organization*, in EUROPEAN YEARBOOK IN THE SOCIOLOGY OF LAW (1988)]. On second order autopoiesuis, cf. MATURANA AND VARELA, AUTOPOIESIS AND COGNITION 107 ff (1980), Mossakowski and Nettman, *Is there a Linear Hierarchy of Biological Systems?*, in [SELF ORGAINIZING SYSTEMS 39ff (Roth and Schwegler, eds., 1981)]; Jessop, *Relative Autonomy and Autopoiesis in Economy, Law and State*, in TEUBNER, STATE LAW, ECONOMY AS AUTOPOIETIC SYSTEMS (1988).

78. 1 BESELER, SYSTEM DES GEMEINEN DEUTSCHEN PRIVATRECHTS 236 (1847). SALEILLES, DE LA PERSONNALITÉ JURIDIQUE 354 (1922)....

it: "Reflexivity of law!"[79] We also find that Kelson's concept of legal person of legal person as legal suborder and point of attribution has been objected to on the grounds that the statement that the legal suborder is itself a bearer of norms is a tautology: the construction would have to support itself "like the late Baron Muenchhausen."[80] And in this same context we are confronted with the attempt of German corporation law to circumvent Muenchhausen by making the enterprise have a "subject" (*Traeger*) different from itself, namely, the legal person, which is turn is supposed to have a substratum different from itself, namely, the association of persons or the resource pool. Obviously, this is an attempt to avoid such tautologies and circular arguments as that the firm "represents" itself or that the legal person is "based" on itself.

But perhaps the mendacious Baron was not so wrong after all? Perhaps there really are, in the area of the legal person, circular relationships. May not the legal person's function indeed consist in making self-reference possible and in increasing self-reference still further in the interest of organizational autonomy? This, at any rate, is what the theory of self-referential systems, which has been successfully applied in such varied fields as logic, computer science, neurophysiology, sociology, business organization and legal theory would suggest.

This prompts the following two theses: (1) the traditional demarcations between the enterprise, the legal person, and its substratum are to be interpreted as attempts to avoid self-referentiality in corporation law. Under this smokescreen, however, self-referentiality was actually able to make its way into the reality of the enterprise: (2) If the taboo of self-referential circularity is broken, the view opens up on to a self-supporting construction: the "subject" (*Träger)* of the enterprise is the collectivity, constituted as legal person; the "substratum" of the legal person is the enterprise personified as collectivity.

B. Internal Regulation: Legal Personality and Corporate Law

1. *Corporate Personality and the U.S. Courts*

In areas of traditional corporate law, the Delaware courts have developed a theory of corporate personality which is well articulated in the two cases that follow. In reading the cases, see if you can determine what theory of corporate personality underlies the Delaware courts' interpretive approach. Is it a singular approach?

79. Hofstadter, Goedel, Escher, Bach: An Eternal Golden Braid, esp. 692 ff. (1979). About the connections between self-reference and paradox law, *see* Suber, The Paradox of Self-Amendment, Law, Omnipotence and Change (1982); Fletcher, *Paradoxes in Legal Thought*, 85 Colum. L. Rev. 1263 ff. (1985).

80. Wilff, [I Organschaft un Juristiche Person 69 (1933)] with other references.

Lawson v. Household Finance Corp.

Supreme Court of Delaware
Feb. 27, 1930
17 Del.Ch. 343, 152 A. 723

RICHARDS, J., delivering the opinion of the Court:

The general proposition that no power or authority can be conferred upon a corporation by its charter, which was not provided by the statute under which it was created is not disputed.

All corporations created in this state and powers thereby granted must be sanctioned by an Act of the Legislature. Constitution, article 9.

Corporate existence and powers were well defined by Chief Justice Marshall in the celebrated Dartmouth College Case, when he said, 'A corporation is an artificial being, invisible, intangible, and existing only in contemplation of law. Being the mere creature of law, it possesses only those properties which the charter of its creation confers upon it, either expressly, or as incidental to its very existence. These are such as are supposed best calculated to effect the object which it was created.' Dartmouth College v. Woodward, 4 Wheat. 518, 636, 4 L. Ed. 629.

The same rules which govern the construction of statutes, contracts and other written instruments, are made use of in construing the provisions and determining the meaning of charters and grants of corporate powers and privileges. Hartford Bridge Co. v. Union Ferry Co., 29 Conn. 210; Dempster Mfg. Co. v. Downs, 126 Iowa, 80, 101 N. W. 735, 106 Am. St. Rep. 340, 3 Ann. Cas. 187; State v. Noyes, 47 Me. 189; Casper v. Kalt-Zimmers Mfg. Co., 159 Wis. 517, 149 N. W. 754, 150 N. W. 1101.

An examination of the General Corporation Law of this state, being chapter 65 of the Revised Code of 1915, as amended, discloses that the following powers are expressly granted to every corporation organized under its provisions.

Section 2, par. 6: 'To make by-laws not inconsistent with the Constitution or laws of the United States or of this State, fixing and altering the number of its directors, for the management of its property, the regulation and government of its affairs and for the certificate and transfer of its stock....

Section 3: 'In addition to the powers enumerated in the second section of this Chapter, every corporation, its officers, directors and stockholders, shall possess and exercise all the powers and privileges contained in this Chapter, and the powers expressly given in its charter or in its certificate under which it was incorporated, so far as the same are necessary or convenient to the attainment of the objects set forth in such charter or certificate of incorporation.'

Section 16: 'The shares of stock in every corporation shall be deemed personal property and transferable on the books of the corporation in such manner and under such regulations as the By-laws provide.'

Did the Household Finance Corporation, under the above mentioned provisions of the General Corporation Law, have the authority to place such restrictions and regulations upon the alienation of its Class B. Common Stock, as are found in its charter and by-laws? Was it justified in refusing to transfer the stock in question?

Section 2 gives it the right to make by-laws for the management and government of its affairs, provided such by-laws do not conflict with the constitution or laws of the

United States or of this state; Section 3 confers upon it the additional right to possess and exercise all the powers and privileges contained and expressly given in its certificate of incorporation which are necessary or convenient to the attainment of the objects therein set forth; and section 16 provides that its shares shall be personal property and grants it the privilege of regulating their transfer.

Article 9 of its charter sets forth fully the restrictions and limitations placed upon the selling or transferring of its Class B. Common Stock and they are also contained in the by-laws which were adopted thereafter. But does it appear that these restrictions and limitations are necessary or convenient to the attainment of the objects set forth in the charter? The object of the business as outlined by the charter, is to loan its own money, to act as agent in procuring money for loans, to endorse, guarantee the payment of, buy, sell, and otherwise deal in notes, open accounts and obligations of like character. In enlarging upon the nature of the business, the answer sets out that it consists of making small loans not exceeding Three Hundred Dollars, averaging from One Hundred Dollars to One Hundred and Fifty Dollars, such loans being made largely upon the reputation of the borrower without security, with branch offices in various cities throughout the country. A business of this kind is certainly a very precarious one and one which requires the employment of trained, competent and honest persons who can always be depended upon to protect the company's interests. Such persons can best be secured by providing them with an interest in the business and in order to be able to do this the company must have the privilege of purchasing its own stock in preference to others. Certainly the provision that the company should be notified of the stockholder's desire to sell his stock and have a prior right to purchase the same is necessary to the attainment of the objects set forth in the charter and the success of the company would be in danger without this right to purchase the stock. It should not be forgotten that the restrictions contained in the charter and by-laws under consideration do not restrict the sale of the stock of Household Finance Corporation to its board of directors, but simply provide that notice of the desire to sell should be given the directors and they should have the refusal thereof. It cannot be denied that as a general proposition, and independent of valid charter or statutory provisions, a corporate by-law which unreasonably restrains the power of a stockholder to transfer his stock, has been held invalid as against public policy....

There seems to be a conflict of decisions as to the validity of a by-law of that character, requiring a stockholder before selling his stock, to give the corporation or other stockholders an opportunity to purchase it. The cases of Victor G. Bloede Co. v. Bloede, and Ireland v. Globe Milling & Reduction Co., above cited, hold that such a by-law is an unreasonable restraint upon the power to alienate the stock.

But [other] cases sustain by-laws containing such provisions though statutes were involved in some of them. In Nicholson v. Franklin Brewing Company, supra, the company was incorporated under the laws of this state. One of its by-laws required a stockholder who desired to sell his stock to notify the secretary of the company in writing, stating the amount he desired to sell and the market value thereof, after which the company should have an option on it for thirty days. In holding this by-law valid, the Ohio Court referred to section 3 of the General Corporation Law, and used the following language: 'The by-law here called in question contains no suggestion of a purpose to prevent the alienation of stock nor to restrict it beyond reasons suggested by a consideration of the welfare of the corporation and the express provisions of the statute. It interposes no permanent impediment to the transfer, providing only for an option in the directors for 30 days as a reasonable opportunity to them to dispose of stock to persons deemed desirable as holders.' In the cases of Casper v. Kalt-Zimmers Mfg. Co. 159 Wis. 517, 149 N. W. 754, 756, 150 N. W. 1101; Sweetland v. Quidnick Co., 11 R. I. 328; and Farmers', etc., Co. v. Laun, 146 Wis. 252, 131 N. W. 366, there were charter provisions requiring a shareholder desiring to sell his stock first to offer the same to the Board of Directors or remaining shareholders and giving them an option thereon for a certain time.

The following language was used by the Court in the case of Casper v. Kalt-Zimmers Mfg. Co.... 'The personal element is as important in the make-up and management of a corporation as it is in almost every other undertaking. Restrictions, therefore, reasonably protecting incorporations or stockholders in their interests by permitting them first to purchase stock offered for sale, should be held lawful as promotive of good management and sound business enterprise.'

The restrictions placed upon the transfer of stock in the last three cases cited are very similar to the restrictions in the case now before the Court, and the reasons there expressed for holding them valid apply with equal force to this case. We think that reasonable restrictions upon the transfer of stock of a corporation, such as are necessary and convenient to the attainment of the objects for which the company was incorporated, as the restrictions in this case appear to be, are valid and are within the powers delegated to corporations by our General Corporation Law.

In fact, practically the same general principle was involved in McDowell v. Bank of Wilmington & Brandywine, 1 Har. 27. In that case though the corporate charter was granted by legislative act it authorized the bank to 'establish such other laws, regulations and ordinances as to them shall seem necessary and convenient for the government of said corporation.' Under this provision a by-law prohibiting the transfer of any stock owned by a person who was indebted to the bank was held valid.

We are not compelled, however, to rest the decision of this case on that point alone as there is another reason why the restrictions placed upon the transfer of the stock of this corporation should be upheld, and one which is supported by the weight of authority. We refer to the contractual relation existing between the corporation and its stockholders. Ever since the decision in the Dartmouth College Case above referred to, it has been generally recognized in this country that the charter of a corporation is a contract both between the corporation and the state and the corporation and its stockholders. It is not necessary to cite authorities to support this proposition.

As was pointed out by the Chancellor, section 19 of our General Corporation Law confers upon all corporations created under it the right to purchase, hold, sell and transfer shares of their own capital stock. The ninth article of the charter sets forth the provisions of a contract by which every person who becomes a stockholder binds himself to give the corporation an opportunity to purchase his stock in pursuance of its statutory power. The provisions with respect to notice of his desire to sell, naming appraisers, disregarding good will and giving the Board of Directors an option to purchase are all terms of the contract equally binding upon the corporation and the stockholder....

It has been strongly urged on behalf of the Appellant, that the conditions of the charter and by-laws on question constitute a restraint upon the alienation of property and in consequence thereof are void as against public policy. Our attention is called to the fact that section 16 of the General Corporation Law, makes stock in every corporation personal property.

In this connection it is contended that one of the primary characteristics of personal property is the right to dispose of it, and that this right still exists regardless of the limitations which may be placed upon it. We agree with the contention that one of the essential incidents to the ownership of property is the right to dispose of it in the manner provided by law. This right has always been zealously guarded by the Courts, and there has been a tendency for years to remove many of the old restraints upon alienation. This tendency has not been so strong in the development of the law of corporations, the voting trust being an example. In this case, however, the restrictions are not absolute and do not prevent the ultimate alienation of the stock. They simply regulate the transfer by giving the Board of Directors an option on the stock for a specified time. The cases of Wynehamer v. People, 13 N. Y. 378, and Dixon v. People, 168 Ill. 179, 48 N. E. 108, 39 L. R. A. 116, relied upon by appellant in support of his position, involve the construction of criminal statutes and are not the best authority in a case of this nature.

In the cases of Straus v. Victor Talking Machine Co., 243 U. S. 490, 37 S. Ct. 412, 61 L. Ed. 866, L. R. A. 1917A, 1196, Ann. Cas. 1918A, 955, and Dr. Miles Medicine Co. v. Park & Sons Co., 220 U.S. 373, 31 S. Ct. 376, 55 L. Ed. 502, which were also relied upon, the conditions practically amounted to an absolute restriction of the right to sell the property. In the other cases cited in support of this point the regulations were more stringent than those now being considered. Another reason which has been presented and argued with much force, why the conditions placed on the sale of the stock should be held void, is that good will cannot be considered in appraising the value thereof.

It is argued that this term embraces the great number of elements which are so necessary to the success of any undertaking, and of which no record is kept. The fact that good will is essential in almost every business enterprise cannot be denied. But what is it, and how can its value be accurately estimated? Counsel has referred to the financial statements of some of the strongest corporations of the country in order to show the great value which they place upon good will. It is not surprising that they do for without it they might soon find themselves in financial difficulty. A man may start an enterprise and by his pleasing personality, close application, dependability and honesty build up an enormous business in which the value of the good will would be very large; while one to whom he might sell the same business, by his disagreeable manner, carelessness, unreliability, and questionable honesty might get it in such a condition that the good will would have no value whatever. Consequently good will is a fleeting, intangible something which depends largely upon the individual or the personality and ability of the officers and employees of the corporation. The cases of Trego v. Hunt, [1896] App. Cas. 7; Didlake v. Roden Grocery Co., 160 Ala. 484, 49 So. 384, 22 L. R. A. (N. S.) 907, 18 Ann. Cas. 430; Washburn v. National Wall-Paper Company (C. C. A.) 81 F. 17; and Borden's Estate, 95 Misc. Rep. 443, 159 N. Y. S. 346, which were cited to show the value of good will are not in conflict with the view above expressed.

* * *

The judgment of the Court below is, therefore, affirmed.

STAAR Surgical Co. v. Thomas R. Waggoner and Patricia L. Waggoner

Supreme Court of Delaware
588 A.2d 1130

[Shareholders brought action to determine validity of common shares of stock. The Chancery Court, New Castle County, granted shareholders equitable relief. Corporation appealed. The Supreme Court, reversed, holding that: (1) common shares of stock which were derived from invalid preferred stock were void, and (2) trial court erred in granting shareholders equitable relief.]

MOORE, Justice.

In this latest dispute between the parties we determine the validity of two million shares of STAAR Surgical Company ("STAAR") common stock issued to STAAR's former President and CEO, Thomas R. Waggoner and his wife, Patricia Waggoner ("Waggoner" or "Waggoners"). This is a continuation of the controversy between Waggoner and STAAR. We have already ruled that a provision of the preferred stock STAAR issued to Waggoner, purportedly giving him super-majority voting control of the company, was invalid. See Waggoner v. Laster, Del.Supr., 581 A.2d 1127 (1990) ("Waggoner I "). In Waggoner I, we did not otherwise decide the validity of the Waggoners' preferred and common shares.

* * *

II.

The Court of Chancery specifically assumed that the preferred shares "were invalidly issued" because the board failed to formally adopt both the December 17 resolution and the certificate of designation as required by 8 Del.C. § 151. See Waggoner II, slip op. at 14 n. 7. Nonetheless, the trial court found that the Waggoners were entitled to an order "akin to specific performance" authorizing the issuance of the common shares and declaring them eligible to vote. Id. at 9. The court reasoned that Waggoner was equitably entitled to receive the two million shares of common stock as consideration for his personal guarantee of STAAR's debts. Id. at 9–10.

* * *

D.

We must reject the Waggoners' attempt to separate the common shares from the preferred stock. We also reject their very limited interpretation of Triplex. Stock issued without authority of law is void and a nullity.

It is undisputed that Waggoner could not receive his common stock without exercising the conversion option of at least one preferred share. The December 17, 1987 resolution and the certificate of designation purportedly authorized the issuance of the preferred shares. Without validly issued preferred stock, there was simply no other legal mechanism by which the common shares could be issued. Simply stated, if the preferred shares were void, as the Court of Chancery assumed, then the common stock could not be created out of whole cloth.

Based on the trial court's findings, it is clear that the preferred convertible shares originally issued to the Waggoners were invalid and void under Delaware law. There was no compliance with the terms of 8 Del.C. § 151. The directors never formally adopted either the December 17, 1987 resolution or the certificate of designation.

The Waggoners' attempt to trivialize the unassailable facts of this case as mere "technicalities" is wholly unpersuasive. The issuance of corporate stock is an act of fundamental legal significance having a direct bearing upon questions of corporate governance, control and the capital structure of the enterprise. The law properly requires certainty in such matters.

There are many interacting principles of established law at play here. First, it is a basic concept that the General Corporation Law is a part of the certificate of incorporation of every Delaware company. See 8 Del.C. § 394. Second, a corporate charter is both a contract between the State and the corporation, and the corporation and its shareholders. See Lawson v. Household Finance Corp., Del.Supr., 152 A. 723, 727 (1930). The charter is also a contract among the shareholders themselves. See Morris v. American Public Utilities Co., Del.Ch., 122 A. 696, 700 (1923). When a corporation files a certificate of designation under § 151(g), it amends the certificate of incorporation and fundamentally alters the contract between all of the parties. See 8 Del.C. §§ 104, 151(g). A party affecting these interrelated, fundamental interests, through an amendment to the corporate charter, must scrupulously observe the law....

Finally, it is a basic concept of our corporation law that in the absence of a clear agreement to the contrary, preferred stock rights are in derogation of the common law and must be strictly construed....

This principle of "strict construction" applies with equal force to the creation of preferred stock and its attendant rights, powers, designations and preferences. Accordingly, a board's failure to adopt a resolution and certificate of designation, amending the fundamental document which imbues a corporation with its life and powers, and defines the contract with its shareholders, cannot be deemed a mere "technical" error.

Thus, we must reject the trial court's authorization of the two million shares of common stock on equitable grounds. Stock issued in violation of 8 Del.C. § 151 is void and not merely voidable. See Triplex, 152 A. at 347; D. Drexler, L. Black & A. Sparks, Delaware Corporate Law and Practice, § 17.02 at 17–23 n. 89 (1990). A court cannot imbue void stock with the attributes of valid shares.

E.

The Waggoners argue that the board's failure to ratify its resolution to issue the convertible preferred shares merely rendered the common stock voidable, not void. The Waggoners claim that, unlike Triplex, where this Court found that the corporation did not have the power or authority to issue no par stock, STAAR's charter specifically authorized the issuance of their two million shares of common stock. Therefore, the Waggoners conclude that the issuance of the two million shares of common stock was merely a voidable act.

The Court of Chancery has correctly recognized that the available form of equitable relief depends on the facts of each case. If the stock is indeed void, then "cancellation is the proper remedy." However, if the stock is voidable then a court may grant " 'that form of relief [that] is to be most in accord with all of the equities of the case.' " See Diamond State Brewery, Inc. v. De La Rigaudiere, Del.Ch., 17 A.2d 313, 318 (1941) (quoting Blair v. F.H. Smith Co., Del.Ch., 156 A. 207, 213 (1931)).

We have already rejected the Waggoners' narrow reading of Triplex in Waggoner I, 581 A.2d at 1137–38. We cited to Triplex in Waggoner I for the proposition that the equitable doctrine of estoppel is inapplicable to agreements or instruments that violate either express law or public policy. Id. We also rejected the Waggoners' argument that Triplex was limited only to instances where a corporation illegally issued stock. Id. Accordingly, we ruled that the Waggoners could not invoke the equitable doctrine of estoppel to validate the super-majority voting rights associated with their preferred shares after the court had already declared those rights void under the corporation law. Id.

Parity of reason compels us to reach a similar result here. Under the present circumstances, the Court of Chancery had no basis to grant equitable relief "akin" to specific performance after it concluded that the Waggoners' preferred shares were invalid. Neither logic nor equity compel the validation of a legally void act.[1]

The judgment of the Court of Chancery is

REVERSED.

Comments and Questions

1. How many different conceptions of corporate legal personality does Delaware apply in each of these cases?

It is possible to argue that Delaware applies two different conceptions of corporate personality in the cases. First it applies a fiction concession theory with respect to the contract between the state and the corporation. The state, through its corporate law, is free to create the terms of its relationship with any entity it chooses to license into existence. The terms of that relationship are set forth in the state's corporate law. This is a conception of the corporation in line with Justice Rehnquist's views as expressed in *Bellotti.* Once set forth, that concession of personality, that license, assumes the attributes of a contract as between the state and the corporation so chartered. As a contract it cannot be modified without the consent of both parties without effecting a breach. That, effectively was the thrust of the *Dartmouth College* case discussed above. The State preserves its right to modify the terms of its license by reading into its contract with the corporation the condition that the license is granted subject to this governmental right of modification. The only recourse for the licensee, the corporation, is to re-incorporate elsewhere (exit) dissolve, or invoke the political process to avoid or repeal the modification.

As between the corporation and its participants—shareholders, officers and directors—a different basis of corporate personality applies. With respect to this relationship the Delaware courts apply a realist/contractualist basis of corporate personality to interpret the respective duties and obligations of the parties. The participants are free to arrange their relationships as they like, subject only to the ground rules, the limits, set forth in the agreement between the state and the corporation itself. This contract between the participants in the corporation is set forth in the corporation's charter and by-laws. As such, as between the state and the enterprise, the corporation exists as a unified entity. However, as between the participants in the corporate enterprise, the corporation dissolves into the contractual relations between the participants as described in the charter and by-laws of the entity.

---

2. *Corporate Personality and the Courts of the Member States of the EU*

In England, the traditional view has been that the corporation is, indeed, a fiction, wholly dependent on an act of state for its existence. As a result, such a dependent en-

1. Again, we emphasize that our courts must act with caution and restraint when granting equitable relief in derogation of established principles of corporate law. *See* Alabama By-Products Corp. v. Neal, Del.Supr., 588 A.2d 255, 258 (1991).

tity can have only such powers and characteristics as the state permits. Other common law countries have adopted this rule as well. In reviewing the cases below, ask yourselves whether the English conceptualization of the corporation as articulated in the cases differs from that in the United States.

Sutton's Hospital Case

10 Co. Rep. 23 a (1613)

* * *

[29b] * * * * Now it is to be seen what things are of the essence of a corporation. 1. Lawful authority of incorporation: and that may be by four means, by the common law, as the King himself, &c by authority of Parliament: by the King's charter...; and by prescription. The 2d, which is of the essence of the incorporation, are persons to be incorporated....3. A name by which they are incorporated....4. Of a place, for without a place no incorporation can be made;....5. By words sufficient in law, but not restrained to any certain, legal, and prescript form of words....

* * *

[32b] * * * * And it is great reason that an hospital, &c. in expectancy or intendment or nomination, should be sufficient to support the name of an incorporation when the corporation itself is only *in abstracto*, and rests only in intendment and consideration of the law; for a corporation aggregate of many is invisible, immortal, and rests only on intendment and consideration of the law....They cannot commit treason, nor be outlawed nor excommunicate, for they have no souls, neither can they appear in person, but by attorney....A corporation aggregate of many cannot do fealty, for an invisible body can neither be in person nor swear,...and it is not subject to imbecilities, death of the natural body, and diverse other cases.

The Irish Permanent Building Society et al. v. Seamus Cauldwell (sued as Registrar of Building Societies), et al.

High Court Irish Republic
[1981] ILRM 242
5 December 1980

BARRINGTON J.:

The first named plaintiff is a building society which has its registered office at Lower O'Connell Street in the City of Dublin. It is the largest building society in the State with assets of more than £400,000,000 and it transacts about 40% of the building society business carried on in the State.

The second named plaintiff is an agent of the first named plaintiff, he is a citizen of Ireland, and became a member of the second named defendant (the Irish Life Building Society) in the circumstances hereinafter described. He was added as a plaintiff during the course of the hearing at the request of counsel for the plaintiffs to facilitate the plaintiffs in making out the case already pleaded by them in their statement of claim as amended, but not so as to authorise them to make a new case arising out of his membership of the Irish Life Building Society.

The first named defendant was the registrar of building societies at the date of the institution of these proceedings.

The second named defendant is a body registered as a building society by the registrar of building societies on 4 January, 1979.

The third named defendant is the Irish Life Assurance Company Ltd. and is a corporation carrying on the business of insurance. Its registered office is at the Irish Life Centre, Lower Abbey Street in the City of Dublin. It has assets of approximately £700,000,000 and, like the first named plaintiff, it ranks as one of the major financial institutions in our society. Approximately 90% of its shares are owned by the State.

The last ten defendants are the founder members of the Irish Life Building Society and are also executives of the Irish Life Assurance Company Limited.

In these proceedings the plaintiffs claim a declaration that the second named defendant (the Irish Life Building Society) is not a 'Building Society' within the meaning of the Building Societies Act, 1976; a declaration that the purported registration of the rules of the Irish Life Building Society by the registrar of building societies and the issue of a certificate of incorporation by the registrar of building societies to the Irish Life Building Society are null and void; a declaration that the registration of the second named defendant under the name of the 'Irish Life Building Society' is undesirable and not in the interests of the orderly and proper regulation of Building Society business; a declaration that the rules of the Irish Life Building Society do not comply with the requirements of the Building Societies Act 1976; an injunction restraining the defendants (other than the first named defendant) from carrying on building society business within the State and further and other relief....

The facts surrounding the incorporation of the second named defendant are scarcely in dispute.

The major shareholder in the third named defendant (Irish Life Assurance Company Limited) is the Minister for Finance. The Minister for Finance, for reasons arising from his view of what the national interest required, brought pressure to bear on the Irish Life Assurance Company Limited to provide funds, by way of mortgage, for house purchase. The Irish Life Assurance Company Limited was not anxious to get involved with mortgage finance for house purchase as its Board considered that it could invest its policy holders money in ways which would be more rewarding to it and to them. However the Board considered it to be in the interests of the company to retain the goodwill of the Minister and for that reason set aside a sum of three quarters of a million a year to provide finance for house purchase.

It was this predicament of the Board of the Irish Life Assurance Company Limited which led to the formation of the Irish Life Building Society. The Board thought that if it formed a building society and provided funds in the order of three quarters of a million pounds to it annually for a period of five years, that at the end of that period, the building society would be self financing and the Assurance Company would, accordingly, be free of its obligation to provide funds annually for house purchase finance and at the same time retain the good-will of the Minister.

The Assurance Company had other reasons for establishing the building society. These included access to the short term savings market; providing career opportunities for the staff of the Assurance Company; and enhancement of the investment returns of the Assurance Company.

Ten executives of the Insurance Company were invited to be the founding members of the building society. I have no doubt that these men were willing to act and considered it an honour to be invited. The money to pay for their share subscription was provided by the Assurance Company. Each man acknowledged that he held his shares in trust for the Assurance Company; undertook to pay any interest earned on his shares to the Assurance Company; and undertook to use his shares to vote as the Assurance Company would direct.

The deposit of £20,000 which a building society must maintain with the Central Bank pursuant to §20 of the Building Societies Act, 1976 was provided by the Assurance Company.

The share capital of the building society was divided into savings shares and investment shares. A shareholder was to have two votes, on a poll, for each £10 of savings shares held by him and a hundred votes for each £100 in investment shares held by him. The investment shares therefore carried five votes for each one vote carried by the savings shares.

I am satisfied, on the basis of the evidence of the second named plaintiff Mr. Bolger, that it was not the intention, at least in the early days of the building society, that investment shares would be easily available to members of the public. Mr. Bolger, who was at all times unknown to the defendant society, acting in the interests of the plaintiff society, attempted to obtain investment shares in the defendant society but could only obtain savings shares.

The Assurance Company provided for each of the ten founder members £10,000 worth of savings shares and £10,000 worth of investment shares.

The Assurance Company also acquired investment shares in its own name and by May 1980 had acquired three million three hundred thousand pounds worth of investment shares in its own name and controlled a further hundred thousand pounds worth of investment shares through the founder members.

Moreover the Assurance Company lent to the building society a sum of 1.6 million pounds and the loan agreement contained a clause entitling the lender to convert the loan into investment shares.

Under these circumstances I am satisfied that the building society was at all material times, and still is, totally under the control of the Assurance Company. In the circumstances it is not surprising that in an advertisement advertising a managerial post in the Building Society, placed in the newspapers by a firm of management consultants, the building society should have been described as a 'subsidiary' of the Assurance Company.

I consider it entirely reasonable that the Assurance Company having made such a substantial investment in the building society should seek to protect its interest n that society in any manner which the law allows.I also accept the evidence of Mr Willis that he and the other directors of the building society, despite their close connection with the Assurance company, will in their capacity as directors of the building society, put the interests of the building society first. It is also quite clear that the founders of the building society disclosed fully to the registrar of building societies, prior to registration, the close connection which would exist between the building society and the Assurance company.

The issue is whether a building society bearing such a close connection with an Assurance Company is registerable under the Building Societies Act 1976.

BUILDING SOCIETIES ACT, 1976

The Statute law relating to building societies is now contained in the Building Societies Act, 1976. The Act defines the kind of 'society' to which it relates as: 'a Building Society established under this Act for the purposes of raising, in accordance with this Act, funds (by the subscription of the members, the acceptance of deposits and loans) for making loans to members on security by the mortgage of freehold or leasehold estate or interest'. § 8 of the Act provides that any ten or more persons, not disqualified under the Act, may establish a society, by agreeing on rules for the government of the society which comply with § 10 and by complying with the requirements of § 11 sub-§ 1.

Section 9 provides that the words 'Building Society' or their Irish equivalent 'Cumann Foirgniochta' are to be included in the name of the society. These words may not now be used to describe any new society unless it is a building society incorporated under the Act.

Section 10 sets out the matters to be covered by the rules. Among these (at sub-§ 1(R)) are: 'the voting rights of members, the right of a member to appoint a proxy and demand a poll and the manner in which a poll is to be taken'.

Section 11 of the Act reads as follows:

> 1. Where ten or more persons not disqualified under this Act agree on rules for the purpose of establishing a society they shall deliver two copies of the rules, signed by not less than ten of the persons, to the registrar.
>
> 2. Where copies of rules are delivered to the registrar in accordance with sub-section 1, the register may at his discretion, but subject to this section, register or refuse to register the rules.
>
> 3. The registrar, if he is satisfied that the rules comply with the relevant requirements of this Act, shall not refuse to register rules delivered to him under sub-section 1 unless he is of the opinion that the rules are not substantially in accordance with any rules prescribed under § 10 sub-§ 3 or that the name of the proposed society is undesirable or so resembles the name of another society or the name of a person carrying on in the State banking business within the meaning of the Act of 1971 as to be calculated to deceive, or that registration would not be in the interest of the orderly and proper regulation of building society business.
>
> 4. Whenever the registrar decides to refuse to register rules delivered to him under sub-§ 1, he shall, within six months of such delivery, notify the signatories of the rules of his decision and of his reasons for it, and an appeal may be made to the court against the decision by not less than ten such persons.
>
> 5. Where copies of rules are delivered to the registrar under sub-§ 1 and he does not decide to refuse to register the rules, he shall retain and register one copy, return the other copy to the society, together with a certificate of incorporation of the society in a prescribed form, and notify the registration to the Minister, the Minister for Finance and the Central Bank.
>
> 6. From the date of its incorporation a society shall be a body corporate (with the name contained in its rules) having perpetual succession and a common seal.
>
> 7. A certificate of incorporation given under this section by the registrar shall be sufficient evidence until the contrary is shown that all the requirements of this Act relating to registration of rules and matters precedent and incidental to registration of rules have been complied with and that the society is a society authorized to be incorporated and was duly incorporated under this Act.

[Section] 17 provides that every person holding one or more shares in a society shall be a member of the society. Subject to its rules however a society may allow a person to whom a loan is being or has been made to become a member without holding a share in the society. § 77 provides that the Minister may make regulations providing the maximum amount that a society may lend to a body corporate. It is clear therefore that a body corporate can be a member of a society but cannot be a director of it.(See § 40 sub-§ 2).

The society may admit to membership persons under the age of 21 but a person under the age of 18 years is not entitled to vote at a meeting of the society. Likewise only members who, at the end of the previous financial year before the date of the meeting, held shares to which voting rights attach and which were issued by the society under § 22 sub-§ 1 to a value of not less than £ 10, and at the date of the meeting continued to hold such shares, are entitled to vote.

In general a society may not issue shares under § 22 of the Act to which voting rights do not attach. The only exception is in favour of societies which, on or before the 5 December 1975, had issued such shares.

A society may from time to time raise funds for the purposes of the society by the issue of shares, either with or without accumulating interest, and may repay such funds when they are no longer required. A society may also borrow money by accepting deposits or loans at interest. Societies usually prefer however to issue shares. The shareholder is usually issued with a book showing the amount of his share capital at any one time. The shareholder is allowed to redeem his shares with the minimum of formality and, so far as ease of withdrawal is concerned, his position is very similar to that of a depositor with a savings bank or with the post office. As a result the membership of a large building society and its share capital, are in a constant state of flux.

Part 3 of the Act confers extensive powers of control of societies on the registrar. Section 85 of the Act provides that the registrar of Friendly Societies is to be the registrar of building societies for the purposes of the Act.

Five sections of the Act make certain provisions in the rules of the building society void. Under § 71, and subject to the exceptions, therein contained, any provision in the rules for exempting an officer of a society from, or for indemnifying him against, any liability which by virtue of any rule of law would otherwise attach to him in respect of any negligence, default, breach of duty or breach of trust is to be void. The other sections avoiding rules of a building society all appear to relate to the summoning or conduct of meetings or to the voting rights of members. Under § 12 sub-§ 5 any provision in the rules of a society that the rules may be altered without passing a special resolution is to be void. Under § 51 sub-§ 1 any provision in a society's rules providing for the calling of a meeting of the society, other than an adjourned meeting, by a shorter notice than 21 days is to be void. Under § 54 any provision in the rules of a society which would require an instrument appointing a proxy to be received by the society more than 48 hours before a meeting is to be void. Under § 55 any provision in the rules of a society which would either exclude the right to demand a poll or make ineffective a demand for a poll is to be void.

Section 56 deals with special resolutions. It is as follows:

> 56.1 A resolution of a society shall be a special resolution when it has been passed by a majority of such members of the society as, being entitled to do so, vote in person or by proxy on a poll on the resolution at a meeting of the society in rela-

tion to which notice specifying the intention to propose the resolution as a special resolution has been duly given.

Sub-§ 2. Notwithstanding anything in the rules of a society, the business which may be dealt with at any meeting of the society may include any resolution to be passed as a special resolution.

Sub-§ 3. The terms of any special resolution before a general meeting of a society may be amended by ordinary resolution moved at the meeting if the terms of the resolution as amended will still be such that adequate notice of the intention to pass the resolutions can be deemed to have been given.

THE PLAINTIFFS SUBMISSIONS

The plaintiffs submitted that the name of the defendant society was so undesirable that the registrar could not, in the proper exercise of his discretion, have permitted the defendant society to be registered with the name 'Irish Life Building Society'. More fundamentally the plaintiffs submitted that the defendant society was not a building society at all and therefore not registerable. They based this submission on a number of far-reaching propositions. They said the defendant society was not established for the purposes contemplated by the Act. They submitted that being in effect a subsidiary of a large financial institution it was not the kind of society which building society law contemplated. All the founding members were nominees of the Irish Life Assurance Company Limited. So far as the forming of a building society was concerned they were not free agents and it could not therefore be held that they had agreed together to form a building society or that they had, in any real sense, agreed on rules or delivered agreed rules to the registrar. Finally they submitted that the society was not registerable because the draft rules violated the Act and, in particular § 56.

FIRST SUBMISSION—THE NAME IS UNDESIRABLE

[omittted]

SECOND SUBMISSION:

[omitted]

THIRD SUBMISSION

The society is not registerable because it is not an autonomous co-operative society but is the subsidiary of another body.

I accept that the society is, in all respects, the creature of the Irish Assurance Company Limited. That company decided to set up; provided its deposit at the Central Bank; assigned employees to be the founding members and the Board of Directors of the society; provided the founding members with their share capital on their undertaking to hold these shares in trust for the company and to use them to vote as directed by it; arranged the share capital so that its nominees could control the constitution of the society and outvote any opposition for the foreseeable future and generally provided the finance to set the society up in business.

I hasten to add that there is nothing reprehensible about any of this. The Assurance Company has a huge investment in the society and it is totally understandable that the Assurance Company should seek to protect its investment at any rate in the early days of the society. The plaintiffs however submit that such control of a society by an outside body is not permissible under the Building Societies Act.

That Act, they say, was designed to consolidate the preexisting law in relation to building societies. Such societies they say, had, traditionally, been autonomous co-operative societies whereby people of modest means could help one another to build houses.

The spirit of the building society movement they submit is illustrated by the preamble to the Building Societies Act, 1836 which begins:

> Whereas certain societies commonly called building societies have been established in different parts of the Kingdom principally among the industrial classes, for the purposes of raising by small periodical subscriptions a fund to assist the members thereof in obtaining a small freehold or leasehold property, and it is expedient to afford encouragement and protection to such societies and the property obtained therewith... it was never intended, the plaintiffs submit, that building societies should be the 'creatures' or 'subsidiaries' of large financial institutions like banks or insurance companies. The law concerning building societies in the United Kingdom, they submit, is broadly similar to the law here but no society bearing a relationship as close to a bank or insurance company as the Irish Life Building Society bears to the Irish Life Assurance Company has been formed there. If, they say, it is permissible for a large financial institution to form its own building society in the way which the Irish Assurance Company has done in this case then building societies will merely become front organizations for large financial institutions and the building society, as traditionally conceived, will become a thing of the past.

This the plaintiffs say will open the way for many abuses some of which they suggest, are illustrated by the circumstances of the present case.

They point to three specific actual or potential abuses which they say have resulted, or might result, from the kind of control which the Irish Life Assurance Company exercises over the Irish Life Building Society. The first relates to the surplus funds of the building society. The Building Society Act contemplates that these funds be kept for the purposes of the society and § 38 of the 1976 Act contains provisions as to how the surplus funds of a building society may be invested.

Prior to deciding to form the building society the Assurance Company received a report from four of its executives discussing the advantages and disadvantages of forming a building society. Section 4 of the report deals with the return to the Assurance Company on its investment in the building society and touches on the problem of the surplus generated by the society. It points out that as the Assurance Company will only be an investor in the society, it would rank pari passu with other investors. It continues '...our rights as regards the surplus generated are questionable. We certainly could not overtly remove the surplus but methods such as inflated management charges are always-available'. Subsequently to receiving this report which recommended the establishment of the building society the board of the Assurance Company decided to form the society. But it would be quite wrong to conclude from this that the board approved of every detailed recommendation in this long and complex report. In particular I am sure it would not and did not approve the proposal to remove the surplus from the building society by charging 'inflated management charges'. One would feel happier, however, if one had seen evidence that this suggestion had been specifically repudiated by the board.

Secondly the plaintiffs pointed to the fact that the account of the defendant building society for the period ended 31 December 1979 disclosed the society as having made a surplus of £26,223. In fact however the first instalment of interest under the societies loan of £1,600,000 from the Assurance Company fell due during the relevant period. Had this been paid the society instead of making a surplus of £26,000 would have made a loss in excess of £100,000. The society was saved from making a loss only because the assurance company waived the first installment of interest due to it on foot of its loan. This waiver is not revealed in the accounts themselves or in any note appended to them. I would have thought that a potential investor in the building society should be interested to know whether the surplus had accrued in the normal course of business or whether it existed merely by the grace and favour of the promoters and principal creditor of the building society. Mr. Francis Barrett, the distinguished accountant, who was called to give evidence by the plaintiffs said that the facts set out above would cause him serious doubts as to whether the accounts of the building society had been properly prepared. Mr. Willis however stated in evidence that full disclosure of all relevant facts was made to the building society's own accountants who are a distinguished and reputable firm, and who certified the accounts and advised that no note was necessary. I fully accept this, though, as the accountants in question were not called to give evidence to explain their advice I cannot say that the question raised by Mr. Barrett's evidence has been totally answered.

Thirdly the plaintiffs point to §75 of the 1976 Act which prohibits a building society from paying commission for the introduction of mortgage business and which, subject to exceptions, makes it illegal for a building society to require a borrower to take out, in consideration of or in connection with the making of the loan, a life assurance policy other than a mortgage protection policy. Presumably this provision exists because the Oireachtas recognises that a person looking for a mortgage to buy a house is in a vulnerable position and wishes to ensure that he will not be pressed to take out endowment insurance which he does not require or cannot afford. There is no doubt that the founders of the defendant building society appreciated that commercial advantage could be derived from a close link between an insurance company and a building society and this the plaintiffs say is undesirable. It is not clear however that §75 has any direct bearing on the matter.

The real issue in the present case is whether the law permits the kind of relationship which exists between the Irish Assurance Company and the Irish Life Building society. If such a relationship is permissible in law it is permissible and this abstract issue cannot be determined by whether a particular relationship does or does not give rise to possibilities of abuse. If abuses exist they are to be dealt with by the agencies set up to control the activities of building societies and insurance companies.

The defendants submit that the plaintiffs have failed to grasp the significance of the fact that a building society, under the 1976 Act, is an incorporated body and that certain incidents attach to the fact of incorporation. They submit that it is quite unreal for a great financial institution like the Irish Permanent Building Society to compare itself with the small unincorporated building societies contemplated by the 1836 Act. when, they say, §9 of the Building Societies Act, 1874 provided for the incorporation of building societies it opened the way to the formation of a society such as the Irish Life Building Society.

The defendants submit that the plaintiffs have missed the significance of the concept of incorporation, and to illustrate their point, they refer to the judgment of the Court of Appeal in Salomons Case (1895) 2 CD 323.

In that case Salomon caused a limited liability company to be incorporated and the seven subscribers of the memorandum of association consisted of Mr Salomon, his wife, his daughter and his four sons. Twenty thousand shares were issued to Mr Saloman and one share only to each of the other six subscribers to the memorandum of association. Mr Salomon transferred his business to the company, took a floating charge over the company, became managing director, and carried on his business as before. The other members of the company were merely his nominees.

Lopes L.J. (at page 340 of the report) commented on this situation and his comments are interesting as they almost exactly reproduce the submissions made on behalf of the plaintiffs in the present case. He said:

> The incorporation of the company was perfect—the machinery by which it was formed was in every respect perfect, every detail had been observed; but notwithstanding, the business was, in truth and in fact the business of Aron Salomon; he had the beneficial interest in it; the company was a mere nominis umbra, under cover of which he carried on his business as before, securing himself against loss by a limited liability of £1 per share, all of which shares he practically possessed, and obtaining a priority over unsecured creditors of the company by the debentures of which he had constituted himself the holder. It would be lamentable if a scheme like this could not be defeated. If we were to permit it to succeed, we would be authorizing a perversion of the Joint Stock Companies Acts. We would be giving vitality to that which is a myth and a fiction. The transaction is a device to apply the machinery of the Joint Stock Companies Act to a state of things never contemplated by that Act—an ingenious device to obtain the protection of that Act in a way inconsistent with and opposed to its policy and provisions. It never was intended that the company to be constituted should consist of one substantial person and six mere dummies, the nominees of that person, without any real interest in the company. The act contemplated the incorporation of seven independent bona fide members, who had a mind and a will of their own, and were not the mere puppets of an individual who, adopting the machinery of the Act, carried on his old business in the same way as before, when he was a sole trader. To legalize such a transaction would be a scandal.

The significance of these comments for the purposes of the present case is that they were totally rejected by the House of Lords (see 1897 Appeal Cases page 22) as revealing a failure to understand what was involved in the incorporation of a limited liability company under the Companies Act.

In his speech in the House of Lords Lord Herschell said (at page 45):

> It was said that in the present case the six shareholders other than the appellant were mere dummies, his nominees, and held their shares in trust for him. I will assume that this was so. In my opinion it makes no difference. The statute forbids the entry of the seven persons subscribing the memorandum must be beneficially entitled to the share or shares for which he subscribes. The persons who subscribe the memorandum, or who have agreed to become members of the company and whose names are on the register are alone regarded as, and in fact are the shareholders. They are subject to all the liability which attaches to the holding of the share. They can be compelled to make any payment which the ownership of the share involves. Whether they are beneficial owners or trustees is a matter with which neither the company nor creditors have anything to do: it concerns only them and their cestuis que trust if they have any. If, then, in the present case all the requirements of the Statute were complied with, and the company was effectually constituted and this is the hypothesis of the judgment appealed from, what warrant is there for saying that what was done was contrary to the true intent and meaning of the companies Act?

The defendants submit that the Oireachtas, in the 1976 Act, by providing that a building society must have at least ten founding members and that it must make a deposit of not less than £20,000 with the Central Bank, has accepted that building societies have changed greatly from the small associations of working men contemplated by the 1836 Act. Likewise, they say the Minister by providing, in effect, by SI No. 119 of 1977 that the share qualification of directors must be £10,000 each has recognized the financial importance of building societies and has sought to protect the public by having them run by men of substance. Moreover the defendants say that shortly before the enactment of the 1976 Act the Norwich Union Insurance Group caused to be formed the Norwich Irish Building Society and the legislature could have been expected to intervene had it considered such a close relationship between an insurance company and a building society to be undesirable.

It therefore appears to me that I should approach this case on the basis that the incidents of incorporation attach to building societies as they do to limited liability companies except in so far as they are affected by the differing provisions of the Companies Act and the Building Societies Act.

The plaintiff submit that there are relevant distinctions between the Companies Act 1963 and the Building Societies Act 1976 concerning the formation of a company or building society. Section 5 of the 1963 Act provides that any seven or more persons, or in the case of a private company, any two or more person 'associated for any lawful purpose' may be 'subscribing their names' to a memorandum of association form an incorporated company. Section 8 of the 1976 Act on the other hand provides that any ten or more persons not disqualified by law may form a building society by 'agreeing on rules'.

The plaintiffs submit that an 'agreement' of ten persons contemplates ten individuals will converging on a particular course but, they submit, there can be no agreement if all of the ten persons are nominees of the same person and each is expressing not his own will but the will of the person who nominated him. For the same reason they submit that there can be no delivery of 'agreed' rules under § 11 of the Building Societies Act as there has a in fact been no agreement.

This submission appears to me to be answered in part by the extract from the speech of Lord Herschell in Salomon's case. As a matter of fact I am satisfied that each of the ten founder members of the building society was pleased to act in the formation of the building society and that each of them accepted the rules. In these circumstances I reject the plaintiffs submission on this score as being based on too fine and metaphysical a distinction to be useful in dealing with practical affairs.

* * *

RELIEF

In these circumstances the question arises as to what relief if any, the plaintiffs are entitled to in the present case. In my view they are not entitled to any relief. In so far as the second named plaintiff, as a member of the society, may be entitled to any relief the Act provides the machinery whereby he may obtain it. He is not entitled to it in these proceedings. In the course of my judgment I have had necessarily to advert to the fact that there is a serious defect in the defendant society's rules. If as a result of developments in the law it is possible for large financial institutions to promote, and in some measure, control Building Societies then it is all the more necessary that the interests of those persons of modest means for whose benefit Building Societies were originally created and granted certain privileges in law, should be protected. But that does not give the plaintiffs any rights against the defendants. I will merely draw the matter to the attention of the registrar.

Judgment accordingly.

Comments and Questions

1. Do the English courts take the same dual contract approach as the American courts?

2. Recall the readings of earlier in the chapter—Note, *Constitutional Rights of the Corporate Person*, and Gunther Teubner, *Enterprise Corporatism: New Industrial Policy and the "Essence" of the Legal Person*. On the basis of what understanding of the nature of corporate personality are the cases excerpted above based?

3. The reading that follows suggests both that, (a) like the United States, European states tend to approach a polyglot approach to corporate regulation, shifting their basis of understanding of the nature of the corporation to suit their legislative or judicial aims, and (b) statutory rules recently adopted particularly reflects this schizophrenia. As you read the excerpt that follows, consider whether or to what extent you are inclined to agree with this assessment.

Eilís Ferran, *Company Law and Corporate Finance*

(1999)
(excerpts pages 9–13)

Fiction Theory

The fiction theory of the company is that corporate personality is a fiction to which the law gives effect: companies are able to incur rights and obligations because the law endows them with capacity to act. The fiction theory provides a ready justification for state regulation of the activities of companies because the state can intervene to impose whatever restrictions it deems appropriate on those creatures whose very existence depends on the operation of law. The concession theory of incorporation can be seen to be an aspect of the fictional approach and, just as the establishment of incorporation by administrative act rapidly made it unrealistic to view incorporation as a privilege granted as a concession by the state, so too have legal developments undermined other aspects of a fiction-based analysis.[40] Consistent with fiction theory, it used to be the case that companies were regarded as having limited capacity; they were required by the companies legislation to state their objects in their constitution and the constitutional statement operated as a limit on capacity, with any purported act which was not authorised by the constitution being regarded as void. The rule of limited capacity was undermined by companies taking matters into their own hands by drafting ever wider statements of their objects. The result is that, nowadays, companies incorporated under the Companies Act of 1985 typically have such long objects that their capacity is practically unlimited. This illustrates how the consequences of corporate personality can stem more from the actions of the human beings who are involved in the company—in the specific example,

40. Stokes, M, 'Company Law and Legal Theory' in Wheeler, S (ed), *The Law of the Business Enterprise* (1994) 80 (reprinted from Twining W. (ed), *Legal Theory and Common Law* (1986) 155); Bratton, WW, 'The Nexus of Contract Corporation: A Critical Appraisal' (1989) 74 Cornell Law Review 407; Eisenberg, MA, 'The Structure of Corporation Law' (1989) 89 Cornell Law Review 1461.

the action of the company's shareholders in adopting the constitution—than from the intervention of the state. It is generally accepted that it is now implausible to rest any justification for state intervention in a company's affairs on the fact that its existence is derived from a state concession or privilege.[41] Fiction theory is a model that does not fit with the realities of modern corporate practice.

Contractual Theory

An important economic model of the company views it as a nexus of contracts between the various constituencies, shareholders, managers, creditors and employees, who have an interest in the firm. 'Contract' is used in a loose sense to include voluntary associations of whatever nature. Corporate legislation and judge made rules on such matters as fiduciary duties are seen as a form of standard form contract which the constituencies can adopt or depart from as they think fit. An example of the contractual approach to company law is to say that one of its distinctive features—limited liability for shareholders in limited companies—is a standard form provision which removes the need for costly negotiations in order to contract out liability on a case by case basis. In this model, corporate personality is no more than a convenient shorthand for the complex arrangements worked out between the various constituencies who have an interest in the company. As so stated, the contractual theory seems to rule out the existence of mandatory corporate law, but this is to oversimplify a complex and highly developed analytical model. Proponents of the contractual approach accept that some mandatory legislation may be justifiable but suggest that this should be kept to a minimum: wherever possible, the state should allow the parties to have an involvement in a company to make their own bargain in accordance with prevailing market forces.

Although there is a large element of contract in company law, contractual theory does not explain fully the present day structure and operation of company law.[46] As well as the existence of a considerable amount of mandatory legislation, the theory struggles to explain convincingly the basic fact of separate legal personality.[48] As a mater of legal analysis, the company is a legal entity which is itself capable of incurring rights and obligations. If a company were not something more than a convenient shorthand for a network of voluntary arrangements, and in the absence of some other legislative mechanisms such as are now being considered in relation to limited liability partnerships, its shareholders would automatically be fully liable for the debts of the business except to the extent of contractual exclusions worked out on an individual basis. Another reason why it may be potentially misleading to overemphasise the existing role of contract in company law is that even in the paradigm case of a contractual relationship within a company, namely that between its shareholders which, according to the Companies Act of 1985, is a contract on the terms of the company's constitution,[50] the contract is of a special type and lacks certain of the features that are normal to arrangements in contractual form.[51]

---

41. Bratton, WW, 'The New Economic Theory of the Firm: Critical Perspectives from History' (1989) 1 Stanford Law Review 1471.

46. 'Nothing, however, beats a theory like a practice and reference to practice makes the pure contractual corporation untenable.' Bratton, WW, 'The Economic Structure of the Post-Contractual Corporation' (1992) 87 Northwestern Law Review 180, 185.

48. *Gas Lighting Improvement Co. Ltd. v. IRC* [1923] AC 723, HL, 740–1 per Lord Sumner.

50. Companies Act 1985, § 14.

51. *Bratton Seymour Service Co Ltd. v Oxborough* [1992] BCC 471, CA per Steven LJ. The statutory contract is unlike an ordinary contract in the following ways: (a) it derives its binding force not from a bargain struck between the parties but from the terms of the statute; (b) it is binding only in

The normative role played by this analytical perspective is important. One of the most valuable aspects of the contractual theory is that it puts the spotlight firmly on the need to justify mandatory company law rules so as to ensure that businesses in corporate form are not subjected to regulation that does not produce beneficial outcomes measured in terms of economic efficiency or on the basis of other criteria. Yet contractual theory, as a normative tool, is also open to criticism. It is based on the classical idea of contract in which the parties have personal autonomy and can fix their bargain as they please. That the general process of contracting really operates in this way is a notion that is widely discounted by specialists in that field. More specifically, the idea of negotiation and bargain does not seem an entirely apt description of the dynamics of many typical relationships within a company: for example, a person who buys shares in a public company through an organised securities market does not engage in the process of negotiation with the company prior to making the investment; the investor's personal discretion is limited to deciding whether to pay the price at which the shares are trading and, in making that decision, the investor may lack the knowledge and understanding of the implications of the investment that classical contract theory would ascribe to the maker of a bargain. These considerations indicate that although removal of excessive regulation should be the driving factor in any reform process, it is also important not to overestimate the ability of persons who have an interest in a company to protect that interest by contract and by the operation of market forces.

Realist Theory

The realist view of the company is that a company is a real person brought into existence by the actions of a group of individuals acting together for a common purpose. As a real rather than a fictitious person, its existence does not depend on state intervention. As a real person, the company is deemed to have organs to think and act on its behalf. This view of the company was originally popularized by German theorists in the nineteenth century.[55] At a theoretical level, however, new life has been breathed into this theory with a suggestion that the recognition of the company as a distinct social entity, rather than as a product of private contract, could provide the basis for a shift towards a shareholder model of company law. This would involve recognising that the that the duty of management to act in the interests of the company extends beyond looking after the collective interests of only one constituency, namely, the shareholders, and also embraces the interests of other groups, especially creditors and employees.[56]

Political Theory

This analytical perspective is linked to the previous one and also views the company as a social institution. Here the argument is that political theory about the legitimacy of private

---

so far as it affects the rights and obligations between the company and its members acting in their capacity as members; (c) it can be altered by special resolution, ie without the consent of all of the contracting parties; (d) it is not defeasible on the grounds of misrepresentation, common-law mistake, mistake in equity, undue influence or duress; (e) it cannot be rectified on the grounds of mistake. Also terms cannot be implied on the basis of business efficiency: *Stanham v National Trust of Australia* (1989) 15 ACLR 87, NSW SC-EqD, 90-1.

55. Gierke O, *Political Theories of the Middle Ages* (translated with introduction by FW Maitland).

56. Kay, J and Silberston, A, 'Corporate Governance' (August 1995) *National Institute Economic Review* 84.

power has an application in relation to companies: although companies are private institutions, they are in a position to yield considerable power which could lead to damaging results if left unregulated. The state can intervene in company affairs in the public interest with a view to curbing misuse of power and achieving socially desirable outcomes. The political theory, either on its own or in combination with the reification of the company, is the main theoretical alternative to the contractual approach. It rejects the notion that a company is simply the creature of a private bargain between participants and, in particular, the suggestion that the role of management is simply to maximize profits for the benefit of shareholders. This theory suggests that, in the public interest, the management of a company should be legally required to act in a way that recognizes the impact that the exercise of their powers can also have on employees, creditors and even the wider community.

Whilst some elements of existing company law are consistent with the stakeholder model of the company, this is more an aspirational vision of what companies and company law might be than an explanation of how they operate at present. Reservations that have been expressed about political theory as a normative tool include: that the legitimate public interests that company law should be designed to serve have not been precisely articulated,[59] and that it is not clear that the interests of, say, employees would be better served by the full scale reorganization of company law than by the enactment of specific obligations and requirements in their favour.....[A] general shift towards adoption of the stakeholder model would require fundamental aspects of company law to be redrawn.

Henry P. deVries and Friedrich K. Juenger, *Limited Liability Contract: The GmbH*

64 Colum. L. Rev. 866 (1964)

Review the excerpted materials from Chapter 3.

Comments and Questions

1. One can agree that "fiction theory is a model that does not fit within the realities of modern corporate practice," as Eilís Ferran suggests, but still understand that many courts have not yet been able to free themselves of its hold in a variety of contexts. The same, of course, applies to legislatures. Thus, though it is true enough that the idea of corporate limited legal capacity has been overcome, for practical purposes, by the breadth of the imagination of clever lawyers, it does not suggest that the state cannot, on a fiction concession theory basis, regulate the capacity of corporations. To some extent, legislatures regulate in this manner all the time. A common illustration in the United States, is the prohibition imposed on general corporations to engage in banking or insurance activities, areas reserved for special regulation.

2. Professor Ferran suggests that contract theory does not provide a basis for fully explaining the state of corporate regulation. Can you make a stronger case for the contract

---

59. McGuinness, K, Rees, B and Copp, S, 'Recent Perspectives on Company Law: A Review Article' (1998) 19 Co Law 290.

theory in the construction of private limited companies, GmbH and SARLs than for public limited companies, AGs and SAs?

3. How does the English version of the realist theory differ from the realist theory described in Note, *Constitutional Rights of the Corporate Person*, excerpted earlier in this Chapter? Is this realist theory more closely linked to the systems theory of Gunther Teubner, *Enterprise Corporatism: New Industrial Policy and the "Essence" of the Legal Person*, also considered earlier in this Chapter?

4. The German GmbH provided the model for a truly flexible, contractually based organization of enterprises in corporate form. What theories or approaches to understanding corporate personality appear to inform that approach? Can you argue that the GmbH is a model of a nearly pure contractarian approach to corporate organization?

---

3. *Approach of the European Court of Justice*

The European Court of Justice, the chief judicial body of the European Communities, has also applied a variant of the fiction-concession theory interpreting the nature of the relationship between the corporate legal "entity" and the state. The formal rule-making bodies of the European Communities were discussed in Chapter 3, above. How does the general European approach differ from that employed in the United States?

Regina v. HM Treasury and Commissioners of Inland Revenue ex parte Daily Mail and General Trust plc

(Case 81/87)
Court of Justice of the European Communities
[1988] ECR 5483, [1988] 3 CMLR 713
27 September 1988

* * *

In that regard it should be borne in mind that, unlike natural persons, companies are creatures of the law and, in the present state of Community law, creatures of national law. They exist only by virtue of the varying national legislation which determines their incorporation and functioning.

As the Commission has emphasized, the legislation of member-States varies widely in regard to both the factor providing a connection to the national territory required for the incorporation of a company and the question whether a company incorporated under the legislation of a member-State may subsequently modify that connecting factor. Certain States require that not merely the registered office but also the real head office, that is to say the central administration of the company, should be situated on their territory, and the removal of the central administration from that territory thus presupposes the winding-up of the company with all the consequences that winding-up entails in company law and tax law. The legislation of other States permits companies to transfer their central administration to a foreign country but certain of them, such as the United Kingdom, make that right subject to certain restrictions, and the legal consequences of a transfer, particularly in regard to taxation, vary from one member-State to another.

* * *

Comments and Questions

1. The ECJ defers to the laws of the Member States for determination of the nature of corporate personality of Member State resident corporations. Does this determination to defer to the Member States suggest a particular, EU-specific understanding of the nature of corporate personality?

2. Is it possible to equate, by analogy, the attributes of corporate personality to the attributes of citizenship for natural persons? If that is the case, is it possible to better appreciate the approach of the ECJ as citizenship based?

---

4. *Japanese and Chinese Approaches to Corporate Personality and Corporate Governance*

The materials that follow consider Japanese and Chinese law approaches to corporate personality.

a. Japan

Japanese corporate law was originally modeled, for the most part, on German law. The Japanese corporate law was significantly modified during the American occupation of Japan to add some features of American corporate law.[1]

Katsuhito Iwai, *Persons, Things and Corporations: The Corporate Personality Controversy and Comparative Corporate Governance*

47 Am. J. Comp. L. 583 (1999)
(excerpts pages 592–612; some footnotes omitted)

2. The Corporation as a Person/Thing Duality

A starting point for our analysis of the internal structure of the corporation is one of the most elementary facts in corporate law. If I take away a gadget from the factory of the corporation I am a shareholder of, I will be immediately subject to arrest as a thief. Why? Because a corporate shareholder is not the legal owner of the corporate assets. Who, then,

1. *See* Hideki Kanda, *Comparative Corporate Governance Country Report: Japan, in* Comparative Corporate Governance: The State of the Art and Emerging Research 921, 924 (Klaus J. Hopt, Hideki Kanda, Mark J. Roe, Eddy Wymeersch and Stephan Prigge, eds., 1998).

owns those corporate assets? The corporation does, of course. It is the corporation itself as a "person" that legally owns the corporate assets. Then, what does a corporate shareholder own? The corporation, of course. It is the corporation itself as a "thing" that a corporate shareholder legally owns. A corporate shareholder is literally a holder of a corporate share, a bundle of participatory and pecuniary rights in the corporation. And to hold a share of the corporation is, unlike a partnership share, to own a fraction of the corporation as a "thing" independent of the remaining fraction and separate and distinct from the underlying assets. This is so commonplace a fact that no corporate law textbook has ever failed to make note of it. But its implications, I believe, have not been fully worked out. What it is telling us is that, in contrast to a sole proprietorship firm or a partnership firm, an incorporated firm is composed of not one but two ownership relations: the shareholders own the corporation, and the corporation in turn owns the corporate assets.

We have already seen that the corporation is a legal device which simplifies the external relations a business firm has to have with employers, suppliers, creditors and customers. We now see that the same legal device has the effect of complicating the internal structure of a business firm by, so to speak, doubling the ownership relations within it. In fact, in this two-tier ownership structure the corporation is playing the dual role of a "person" and a "thing." It owns assets and it is owned by shareholders. In other words, in regard to things, a corporation acts legally as a person, as a subject of property right; and in regard to persons, a corporation is acted on legally as a thing, as an object of property right. Naturally, of course, a corporation is neither a person nor a thing. Legally, however, it is endowed with both personality and thingness. The corporation has thus trespassed across that great divide between persons and things at least in the province of law.

The past controversy on the nature of the corporation has focused exclusively on its legal personality. Yet, its being a "legal thing," separate and distinct from underlying corporate assets, is no less important. Even the die-hard corporate nominalists would concede that the corporation has a "thingness" independently of the underlying assets. Because of the limited liability, any person can own a fraction of the corporation in the form of a certain number of shares, just like any other "things" in the economy. In capitalistic society every "thing" can become a commodity, and the corporation as a thing is no exception. Indeed, the stock market is there for people to buy and sell a share of the corporation as a valuable thing; that is, as a commodity, separate and distinct from the underlying corporate assets. Note that the stock market is not directly trading the corporate assets, though its day-to-day valuation certainly influences the way they are managed and accumulated. And here lies perhaps the most important advantage of the corporation, especially of the publicly held corporation, over the partnership or sole proprietorship. No matter how rapidly the corporate shares are changing hands in the stock market, the productive assets for business activities forever remain in the hands of the same corporation as a legal person. The dual ownership structure thus accomplishes a dual task: it simultaneously "liquidifies" the shareholders' ownership of the corporation and 'solidifies' the corporation's ownership of productive assets. The former serves to attract a large amount of investments, while the latter works to maintain the stability of business operations. This, however, is only half of the story because we have not yet brought in the role of managers. We will discuss the problems of corporate governance in Sections 8 and 9.

It is my belief that it is not the personality per se but the person/thing duality of the corporation that is responsible for most of the confusion in the past debate on its "essence." In fact, if we for some reason ignore or suppress or forget its personality, the corporation appears merely as a thing owned and controlled by shareholders, and we draw near to the position of corporate nominalists. If for some other reason we ignore or suppress or forget its thingness, the corporation appears fully as a person owning and managing corporate assets, and we draw near to the position of corporate realists. The recent important theorization by Professor Meir Dan-Cohen, who pictured the corporation as "a machine endowed with artificial intelligence," might be interpreted as an attempt, indeed an ingenious attempt, to reconcile the inherently irreconcilable person/thing duality of the corporation by invoking an image which amalgamates persons and things.[20]

One must note, however, that even within the province of law a corporation appears to be neither fully a person nor merely a thing. The fact that it can be owned by other persons makes it less than a person even legally, and the fact that it can own other things makes it more than a thing even legally. The task of the following two sections is to demonstrate that there are ways to eliminate either personality or thingness from the person-cum-thing corporation, thereby turning it into a mere "legal thing" or a full "legal person," respectively.

3. How to Make a "Nominalistic" Corporation

The way to eliminate the personality from a corporation is simple: it is to have someone own more than fifty percent of its shares. That someone then commands a majority block of votes in shareholders meetings and acquires an absolute control over the corporation.[21] The corporation is then deprived of its subjectivity and turned into a mere object of property right. Legally speaking, the corporation is still the sole owner of the corporate assets, but in practice it is the dominant shareholder who can exercise the ultimate control over them. She can direct the managerial policies at her will. She can even dissolve the corporation and sell off all the accumulated assets to second-hand markets. The business corporation is reduced de facto to a single ownership relation between the dominant shareholder and the productive assets. We are certainly in the world of the corporate nominalists here.

This is too familiar a fact to warrant any further elaboration. What I should like to do in this section is to suggest that the so-called corporate raiders are daily putting this legal mechanism into practice in the real economy.

That there are two kinds of "things"—the corporate assets and the corporation itself—in an incorporated business firm means that there are also two kinds of values residing in it. They are, respectively, the value of corporate assets and the value of the corporation as a thing. The latter is simply given by its total share price in the stock market. The former is slightly more complex; but for our immediate purposes let us simply define it as the present discounted value of the future profit stream that would accrue from the most efficient use of these assets, with a due consideration of the risk premium. It is often called the "fundamental" value of the corporation. Can these two values be different from each other? Can the stock market value of the corporation be, for instance, smaller than the fundamental value of its assets? The answer is yes. On the one hand, the stock market is notoriously myopic, and its day-to-day valuation may fail to reflect the long-run profitability of the underlying corporate assets. On the other hand, some managers are incompetent or opportunistic, and their management may fail to realize fully the potential value of corporate assets.

---

20. [Meir Dan-Cohen, Rights, Persons, and Organizations: A Legal Theory for Bureaucratic Society (1986)], at 49 and thereafter.

21. With a proviso that many countries (as well as many states in the case of the United States) have various rules which protect the interests of minority shareholders

In any case, it is the business of a corporate raider to search for a corporation whose stock market value is substantially lower than the value of the underlying assets. As soon as she has identified such corporation, she starts negotiating a leveraged buyout (LBO) plan with her banks. By an LBO I mean a form of financing which allows the corporate raider to borrow the funds for acquiring a corporation by pledging the very assets of the target corporation as collateral. Such an acrobatic arrangement is possible only if the borrower can convince the lenders that the stock market value of the target corporation is substantially lower than the value of its assets to be used as the collateral. No sooner is the LBO plan approved, than our corporate raider begins a takeover bid (TOB), offering publicly to buy the shares of the target corporation at a price higher than the current market price. Most of the shareholders are only interested in higher prices and are willing to sell their holdings as long as the offered price premium is large enough.[22] A takeover bid, however, especially a hostile one, seldom goes without challenge. The current management team, fearful of losing their jobs, often deploy various defensive tactics to block it.[23] They may even launch a counterattack by announcing their own buyout plan. And other corporate raiders may suddenly enter into contention.

Suppose, however, that it is our corporate raider who has finally managed to survive the bidding war and to emerge as its ultimate winner. She would immediately call a shareholders meeting with a majority of shares in hand. She now has an absolute power over the fate of the corporation and an absolute control over the use of the corporate assets. She then closes off the corporation from the stock market. If she wants quick money, then she as the de facto owner sells off part or all of the corporate assets in second-hand asset markets. If she is patient, she replaces the incumbent managers by new and (she hopes) better ones, and closely monitors their management. If the corporate restructuring goes well, she can enjoy the improved stream of profits in the long-run. And if the stock market eventually comes round to appreciate the fundamental value of the corporate assets, she can even make the corporation public again and resell all her shares at the improved price. In any of these cases, the profit for her undertaking is the difference between the values of corporate assets and corporate shares, minus the price premium for TOB and the interest payment for LBO. It could be a huge prize if her original estimate of the "fundamental" value of the corporate assets was not wide of the

---

22. As was pointed out by Grossman and Hart, there is, however, a free-rider problem in making a successful tender offer for a corporation. The fact that the raider makes a tender offer means that she has a private information about the way to improve the share price much above the tender price. Current shareholders thus find it to their advantage not to tender now but to hold on to their shares until after the raider takes over the corporation and boosts its share price sufficiently high, as long as their shares are small. Hence, the raider never succeeds in raiding the target corporation. Grossman & Hart, *Takeover Bids, the Free-Rider Problem, and the Theory of the Corporation*, 11 Bell Journal of Economics 42 (1980). It is to avoid this free rider problem that several devices have been designed. One of them is to write a corporate charter that allows the raider to exploit minority shareholders if she succeeds in a takeover. Such right of dilution would certainly induce the shareholders to tender. But it is by no means a costless device as least for current shareholders, because it tends to lower the tender price as well as the returns when the takeover succeeds. On this point, see Bebchuk, *The Pressure to Tender: An Analysis and a Proposed Remedy*, in J. Coffee, L. Lowenstein, & S. Rose Ackerman (eds.), Knights, Raiders, and Targets: The Impact of Hostile Takeovers 371 (1988).

23. Such as super-majority amendments, fair price amendments, reduction in cumulative voting rights, greenmail, and poison pills. For a useful discussion on various anti-takeover strategies, *see* Jarrell, Brickley & Netter, *The Market for Corporate Control: The Empirical Evidence since 1980*, 2 Journal of Economic Perspectives 49 (1988).

mark. And the important thing to note is that this whole operation can be, if successful, self-financing. At least in theory, our corporate raider did not have to prepare any of her own capital to carry it out. Something has come out of nothing, indeed.

We all know that money and hubris are what motivate our corporate raiders. Whatever their subjective motives, their day-to-day business in effect consists of an attempt to eliminate the personality from person-cum-thing corporations and restore the simple person-owning-things relation of the classical firm. Whether they like it or not, corporate raiders appear to be helping to realize the idea of corporate nominalism in this world. In fact, it is often claimed that even if they are not daily raiding corporations, the mere perception that they may at any time enter the scene works as an effective threat to the incumbent managers, steering them away from management policies that may fail to realize the fundamental value of corporate assets. If this is indeed the case, the stock market is said to function efficiently as the "market for corporate control."

Does this mean that by the mere existence of corporate raiders the corporate personality controversy has finally been settled in favor of corporate nominalism? The answer is, "No." Corporate realism can be achieved in fact as well as in theory.

4. How to Make a "Realistic" Corporation

"All human beings are born free and equal in dignity and rights": so declared the United Nations in 1948.[25] The fundamental premise of modern civil society is that every human being is free from any coercion or constraint imposed by another human being and is free to pursue the ends he or she sets for himself or herself. A human being is treated as a self-determining subject.

In the system of law a corporation is treated equally to a human being as a legal person, that is, as a subject of property right. It, however, is also an object of property right, a thing owned and controlled by other beings, human or otherwise. So long as it retains this thingness, a corporation can never be a self-determining subject even within the province of law. Yet, as I shall now demonstrate, there exists a legal mechanism able to eliminate this thingness from the person-cum-thing corporation.

We know that as a legal person a corporation can own things, and that as a legal thing a corporation can be owned by persons. This implies that a corporation as a person can in principle own another corporation as a thing. In fact, since the state legislature of New Jersey in the United States legalized holding companies in 1889, corporations all over the world have been buying and holding the shares of other corporations in order to combine horizontally or in order to integrate vertically. A holding company is a corporation which is created solely for the purpose of owning other corporations. It thus acts as a person in regard to these corporations it owns. Indeed, the holding company has opened a way to an important organizational innovation: the pyramidal system of ownership and control. At the top is a natural person (or a group of natural persons) who owns a corporation as a thing, which as a legal person owns other corporations as things, each of which again as a legal person owns other corporations as things, and so on. Such ownership hierarchy can extend ad infinitum.[27] Nonetheless,

25. Cf. Article One of the Universal Declaration of Human Rights, the United Nations (1948).

27. *See* section 2 of Barca, Iwai, Pagano & Trento, T*he Divergence of the Italian and Japanese Corporate Governance Models: The Role of Institutional Shocks*, 23 ECONOMIC SYSTEMS 35 (1999). It is this pyramidal system of ownership and control that allowed Japanese economy to develop Zaibatsu groups before the WWII and Italian economy family empires both before and after the WWII.

the holding company still falls short of shedding its thingness entirely, because it has its own dominant shareholders watching over it.

One can go a step further at least in theory. A corporation as a person can own itself as a thing. Indeed, nothing prevents us from imagining a corporation which becomes its own controlling shareholder by holding a majority block of its own shares under its own name. If this were indeed possible, that corporation would be free from any control by real human beings and become a kind of self-determining subject. It would remove the thingness from itself and acquire a full personality in the province of law. (In order not to complicate the discussion here, we have for the time being set aside the fact that the incorporeal corporation can act only through flesh and blood human beings. We will take up this problem later in Sections 7–9).

One might dismiss all this as idle speculation with no practical content. Many countries prohibit a corporation from repurchasing its own outstanding shares.[28] And even though share repurchase is allowed in several countries (as long as it does not impair capital), the repurchased shares generally lose their voting rights in shareholders meetings. In the real economy, therefore, it appears impossible for the corporation to become its own owner.

There is, however, an important leeway to this. Imagine a situation where two corporations, A and B, hold a majority of each other's shares. The corporation A as a person owns the corporation B as a thing, and the corporation B as a person in turn owns the corporation A as a thing. Even though each corporation does not own itself directly, it does indirectly through the intermediacy of the other corporation. It is true that this involves a bewildering infinite regression of A owning B owning A owning B..., but it should be noted that even the seemingly simpler single self-ownership (including that of a modern human being) implicitly involves an infinite regression of A owning A owning A owning A.... In any case, we can at least say that the cross-shareholding between two corporations allows each of them to eliminate real human beings as their dominant owners. Though in a much more attenuated manner than in the case of single self-ownership, we have here a pair of corporations owning themselves and becoming free from the control of any human beings.

One might still object to the practical possibility of this leeway by pointing out that some countries impose legal limits on the extent of cross-shareholdings between corporations. For instance, French law prohibits a corporation from owning the shares of another corporation that holds more than 10 percent of its shares.[30] Equally important, many countries place ownership limits on the percentage of shares that banks and other financial institutions may own in an individual corporation. For instance, Japanese law forbids a bank from owning more than 5 percent of the shares of any domestic corporation. American law is even more restrictive, and prohibits a bank from owning any shares directly. It does, however, allow a bank to control up to 5 percent of the voting shares of another corporation indirectly through its parent corporation (bank holding company).

Yet, it is possible to circumvent even these limits. Suppose that twelve corporations (which may include a bank holding company) get together and that each holds 5 percent of each of the other's shares but none of its own. Then, simple arithmetic ((12-1) 5% = 55%) tells us that a majority block of each corporation's shares could be effectively sealed

28. German law and French law in principle prohibit the repurchase of the outstanding shares. Great Britain had made it illegal to acquire its own shares until 1980, but since then the repurchase was allowed under certain conditions. (*See* the Company Act of 1985, Section 143 for these conditions.) Japan also used to prohibit share buybacks, but the ban was partially lifted in June 1995.

30. In many countries including U.S., Great Britain, Germany, Sweden, Japan and France, a subsidiary is generally prohibited from holding the shares of its parent corporation.

off from real human beings, without violating any of the above-mentioned legal restrictions on cross-shareholding. These twelve corporations would indeed become their own owners at least as a group. And if fifty-two corporations can get together, they only have to hold 1 percent of each other's shares to secure the majority block for each. It is therefore practically impossible to prevent corporations from becoming their own owners, if they so wish.

We are not the first to note the possibility of a corporation owning itself, either directly or indirectly through cross-shareholding. That possibility has been discussed from various angles by Martin Wolff, by Alfred Conard, and more recently by Professor Meir Dan-Cohen, among others. It should be noted, however, that these authors have characterized the self-owning corporation as "personless" or "ownerless" (Dan-Cohen) or "holderless" (Conard) or "something resembling a foundation" (Wolff). True, the self-owning corporation eliminates human beings as its owners, but this by no means implies that it has eliminated all its owners. The corporation is a legal thing, and being a legal thing makes it impossible for it to be "personless" or "ownerless" or "holderless," at least legally. And indeed, as the name implies, the self-owning corporation as a thing is owned by itself as a legal person. It thus takes the place of human beings, natural subjects of property right, and becomes a self-determining subject itself. What Professor Dan-Cohen called a "personless" corporation is in fact the most "personified" corporation in the province of law.

We have now come very close to the paradigm of corporate realism. We have indeed seen that a self-owning corporation is a self-determining subject, just as a real human being is, in the eyes of the law. However, this is as close as we can come to the corporate realist paradigm, so long as we remain in the province of law. This is because the claim of corporate realism is not merely that the corporation has a full-fledged legal personality but also that this legal personality is only an outer expression of the underlying social reality. And we have so far refrained from saying anything about the social nature of the corporation. In order to go further into the corporate personality controversy, we now have to face that perennial problem of legal science—the relationship between law and society. But to gain perspective we must first make a detour via Savigny and his fiction theory.

5. The Fiction Theory and the New Indeterminacy Thesis

Nothing appears more diametrically opposed than corporate realism and corporate nominalism. Yet, these two competing legal theories, I believe, share at the most fundamental level the same stance with respect to the relationship between law and society. Corporate realism asserts that the corporate personality is a full-fledged legal entity simply because this theory views the corporation as an organizational being capable of having its own will and pursuing its own goals in society. Corporate nominalism dismisses corporate personality as a mere legal symbol simply because it views the corporation as no more than an association of individual human beings forming a contractual agreement among themselves in the society. The former asserts and the latter dismisses the corporate personality as a legal entity simply because the former asserts and the latter dismisses the corporate personality as a social entity. In either theory the legal concept is subservient to the sociological or economic or political theory, and their opposition in regard to the corporation's legal status is nothing but the reflection of their opposition in regard to the corporation's social being.

In contradistinction to these two theories, the now defunct fiction theory separated the system of law from the actual world of society and tried to locate the concept of corporate personality strictly within the system of law. Or so we can interpret the work of F.C. von Savigny, the best-known German Romanist in the first half of the nineteenth century and the principal proponent of the fiction theory of corporate personality. "Persons as the Subjects of Legal Relations" is the title of the second volume of his famous System of Roman Law, [34] and he made it clear at the outset that his object of inquiry was first and foremost the system of legal relations. "Every legal relation consists in the relation of one person to another person," he wrote. "The first essential element of that relation," he continued, "is the nature of the persons whose reciprocal relation is capable of producing it."[35] Here, by "person" Savigny meant not an empirical human being but a legal entity that is capable of assuming the role of a subject by serving as one of the two elements that constitute a legal relation. It is this separation of the legal from the empirical that prompted Savigny to pose the following seemingly paradoxical question: "who can be the bearer or subject of a legal relation?" or more concisely, "who can be a person?" Of course, every human being is naturally a person, though that legal capacity may wholly or partially be denied to minors and lunatics.[36] And, besides these natural persons, Savigny also found a wide variety of non-natural or artificial beings equally capable of functioning as persons in the system of law. He called them "legal persons" in order to differentiate them from natural persons.[37] One species of this class of legal subjects is the corporation.

As regards the corporation, Savigny said that its essential quality consists in "that the subject of the right does not exist in the individual members thereof, not even in all the members taken collectively, but in the ideal whole."[38] Savigny was well aware that such characterization was in direct opposition to the nominalistic view that identifies "the joint act of all the individual members of a corporation" with the "act of the corporation itself," but he was firm in his assertion that "the totality of the members is rather wholly distinct from the corporation itself, and even when all the individual members without exception act together, this is not to be regarded as if the ideal being, whom we call a legal person, had acted."[39] This by no means implies that Savigny is any closer to the corporate realists. On the contrary, Savigny repeatedly referred to the legal person as an "artificial subject admitted by means of a pure fiction" and went on to insist on "the necessity of State sanction for the creation of every legal person."[40] Because of this insistence, Savigny has sometimes been ridiculed for having littered the legal world with State-created Frankensteins, or worse, he has often been criticized for having reduced the legal person to "a wheel in the State's machinery."[41] He might indeed deserve ridicule or criticism if he actually depicted legal persons as fictitious creatures of the State. Savigny was, however, far more subtle in his handling of the concept of legal personality.

34. Jurial Relations: or, the Roman Law of Persons as Subjects of Jurial Relations: being a Translation of the Second Book of Savigny's System of Modern Roman Law, translated by W. H. Rattigan, (1884), at 181 and 204.

35. *Id.* at 1. Here, I have substituted the word "legal person" for "juristical person" as an English translation of "juristischen Personen."

36. *Id.* at 2.

37. *Id.* at 176 and thereafter.

38. *Id.* at 181.

39. *Id.* at 210.

40. *Id.* at 206.

41. "The Savignian corporation is no "subject" for "liberties and franchises" or "rights of self-government." Really and "publicistically" it can hardly be other than a wheel in the State's machinery." (Maitland, *supra* n. 2, at xxi.)

* * *

To recapitulate, Savigny defined the person, both natural and legal, as the subject of a legal relation. But, as every relation requires at least two elements, every legal relation requires at least two subjects. This means that the legal notion of the person is inherently an inter-subjective one. In order for a human being or a corporation or some other entity to serve as a subject of a legal relation, she or he or it has to be recognized as such by the other subject of the same legal relation. In fact, it is because of this inter-subjective nature of personality that Savigny had to make a distinction between natural persons and legal persons even within the province of law. A natural person can become a person not because she or he is a creature of Nature but because she or he can be recognized as a person naturally. A legal person can become a person only with the sanction of the State not because it is a fictitious creature of the State but because it can be recognized as a person only with the assistance of the State.

There is therefore a good deal of parallelism between the theory of corporate personality Savigny developed in his System of Roman Law and the one we have developed in this article. Both have treated the corporate personality as a mere legal construct, thereby contradicting corporate realism, and both have treated the corporate personality as a full-fledged legal entity, thereby contradicting corporate nominalism. Equally important, both have separated the formal system of law from the real system of actions and studied the concept of corporate personality strictly within the province of law. In this sense both appear to share the methodological orientation of legal positivism, in particular, of the pure theory of law a la Hans Kelsen, which contends that the positive analysis of legal concepts must be distinguished from sociological inquiries into the actual world (as well as from the normative analysis of transcendental justice).[47] In fact, if we were to stay in the province of law, our analysis would surely be taken as an exercise of the Kelsenian pure theory of law.

But our having remained so far in the province of law is merely strategic. Indeed, one purpose of the present article is to demonstrate that it is logically impossible to separate the formal system of law from the actual world of society. And our starting point was the observation, shared with Savigny, that the corporate personality is an inter-subjective concept which has been introduced into the legal system as a legal device to simplify the web of contractual relations between a group of individuals and a multitude of outside parties. We, however, then went beyond this Savignian observation and found that such a simplification of external relations at the same time works to complicate the internal structure of the corporation. Indeed, we saw that the "essence" of the concept of the corporation is its person/thing duality, and we then elucidated two legal mechanisms, one capable of turning the corporation into a mere thing and the other into a full person. What does all this mean? It amounts to saying that the concept of the corporation is essentially indeterminate even within the system of law. The corporation can signify whatever law makes it signify.

This sounds very much like what John Dewey said of the corporate personality in his 1926 article. It should be emphasized, however, that Dewey's indeterminacy thesis was a

---

47. HANS KELSEN, PURE THEORY OF LAW, translated by Max Knight (also Kelsen's *The Pure Theory of Law and Analytical Jurisprudence*, in WHAT IS JUSTICE? JUSTICE, LAW AND POLITICS IN THE MIRROR OF SCIENCE; COLLECTED ESSAYS 266 (1957). It should be mentioned here that Kelsen's theory of the notion of legal personality as presented in PURE THEORY OF LAW was wholly nominalistic.

direct application of his pragmatic philosophy that asserts that a thing is defined not by its essence, but by its consequences or by what it does.[49] The definition of a legal subject, he said, is only "a matter of analysis of facts, not of search for an inhering essence,"[50] and the factual analysis of "the history of western culture," he claimed, "shows a chameleon-like change" in the use of the concept of corporate personality. He thus criticized corporate nominalism and corporate realism alike not for their theoretical content but for their very attempt to "introduce unity into a conception where the facts show utmost divergence."[51]

In contrast to this, our new indeterminacy thesis is a purely theoretical proposition, the validity of which is totally independent of whether the facts show utmost divergence or not. The "essence" of the legal concept of corporation is its person/thing duality, and it is this very "essence" that is responsible for the persistence of divergent views on the nature of corporate personality.

This by no means implies that the "facts" do not matter. Far from it. Our new indeterminacy thesis has opened up a new way of linking the formal system of law with the actual world of society. Law is incomplete and is unable to determine the nature of the corporation within its own system. But at least it is able to provide a "menu" of corporate structures from which a society can choose. Indeed, each society can choose any position along a long spectrum that runs from a purely "nominalistic" to a purely "realistic" structure, on the basis of or at least under the influence of economic efficiency, political interests, ideological forces, cultural traditions, historical evolution and other extra-legal factors. That the law has really served as an effective 'menu' is evidenced by the well-known fact that even among advanced industrial societies the dominant corporate form varies widely from country to country, with America (and Britain) standing the nearest to the "nominalistic" pole, Japan the nearest to the "realistic" pole, and most of continental European countries somewhere in between.

It is time to look at the real world.

6. Two Capitalisms

What goes under the name of capitalism differs widely from country to country and even among advanced industrial societies. Nowhere is this difference more marked than in views about the "purpose" of the public corporation in society.

The traditional assumption in America is that the whole purpose of the business corporation is to maximize the returns to its shareholders and that the task of its managers is to exercise their powers solely for that purpose. [52] However, the following tables suggest that this assumption has no place in Japan and in some of the European countries.

---

49. [Dewey, *The Historical Background of Corporate Legal Personality*, 35 YALE L. J. 655 (1926)], at 660–661.

50. Dewey, *supra* n. [49], at 661.

51. Dewey, *supra* n. [49], at 671.

52. In the famous case of Dodge v. Ford Motor Co., the Michigan Supreme Court ruled as follows: "A business corporation is organized and carried on primarily for the profit of the stockholders. The powers of the directors are to be employed for that end. The discretion of directors is to be exercised in the choice of means to attain that end, and does not extend to a change in the end itself, to the reduction of profits, or to the nondistribution of profits among stockholders in order to devote them to other purposes...." 204 Mich. 459, 170 N.W. 668 (Mich. 1919).

TABLE 1: IMPORTANT MANAGEMENT GOALS

	America	Japan	Europe (%)
Sustenance & Improvement of ROI	78.1	35.6	64.2
Capital Gains of Shareholders	63.0	2.7	10.6
Maintenance & Expansion of Market Share	53.4	50.6	61.8
Improvement of Product Portfolio	28.8	11.5	26.0
Maximization of Sales Volume	15.1	27.9	17.9
Increase in Own Capital Ratio	13.7	21.8	18.7
Rationalization of Production & Distribution Systems	13.7	27.0	27.6
Reinforcement of Global Strategy	12.3	32.8	30.9
Expansion of New Products & New Operations Ratio	11.0	60.8	14.6
Improvement of Corporate Social Image	6.8	18.6	18.7
Retention of Employees	1.4	3.8	6.5
Improvement of Employees' Benefits	0.0	7.7	0.8

Source: Keizai Doyu Kai, Showa 63 nendo Kigyou Hakusho (1988 White Paper on Corporations) (1988).
Note: Number of corporations responding to questionnaire: 73 in America, 724 in Japan and 123 in Europe (58 in Italy, 33 in Germany, 18 in France and 14 in Great Britain).

The first table reports the results of a 1988 survey that asked corporate managers in America, Japan and Europe to pick out the three most important goals of their management policies. Answers given by American corporate managers were entirely consistent with the traditional assumption of the primacy of shareholders' interests—they ranked ROI (the rate of return on investments) at the top and capital gains of shareholders second. In stark contrast, the Japanese corporate managers placed capital gains of shareholders at the very bottom of their ranking. They also did not rank ROI as high. Instead, they put the ratio of new products and new operations at the top and ranked market share second. These goals are more or less related to the survival and growth of the corporation as a business organization in the ever-changing market environment. The answers given by European corporate managers, however, were somewhat murky. This is probably due to the diversity of the countries in this category.

TABLE 2: CRITERIA CONSIDERED VERY IMPORTANT FOR ENTRY DECISION INTO A NEW LINE OF BUSINESS

	America	Japan	Europe (%)
ROI	57.7	42.1	45.9
Competitive Advantage	56.3	25.7	38.3
Growth Potential of Market	56.3	69.4	48.8
Synergy Effects	49.3	20.0	38.8
Size of Market	45.1	32.2	38.5
Magnitude of Risk	40.8	28.0	25.8
Effective Use of Existing Managerial Resources	34.3	32.6	39.3

Source: Keizai Doyu Kai, Showa 63 nendo Kigyou Hakusho (1988 White Paper on Corporations) (Keizai Doyu Kai, 1988).

The same study also asked the corporation managers the importance of the listed criteria in their decision to enter into a new line of business. Table 2 reports the percentage of the managers in America, Japan and Europe who termed each listed criterion "very important." While the American managers emphasize the ROI calculation even in their decision to open up a new business operation, the first and foremost concern of the Japanese managers is the growth potential of the market their corporation is about to enter. (The answers of European managers again give us no clear-cut picture.)

Care is needed in interpreting the above two tables, which are taken from an unevenly sampled questionnaire study. But they appear to be more than sufficient to bring home the striking difference in attitudes towards the purpose of the public corporation among advanced industrial societies, especially between America and Japan.[53] While in America it is generally believed that the whole task of the corporate managers is to maximize the returns to the shareholders, in Japan it is generally believed that the job of the managers is to seek the survival and growth of the corporation itself as a going concern. The attitudes of the corporate managers in Europe seem to be an admixture of those of their American and Japanese counterparts with a tone somewhat closer to the latter.

The above dichotomy, popularly dubbed "shareholder capitalism" versus "corporate capitalism," is certainly a simplification. There is a wide disparity as well as a wide fluctuation both in theory and in practice within each type of capitalism. For example, since the Michigan Supreme Court affirmed the traditional assumption of the supremacy of the shareholders' interests in Dodge v. Ford Motor Co. in 1912, America has experienced a swing away from it at least twice. The first swing took place after the famous debate between E. Merrick Dodd and Adolf Berle, Jr. in 1932.[54] In this debate Berle took exception to Dodd who argued that the corporation is an "economic institution which has a social service as well as a profit-making function,"[55] but he soon converted himself to a view similar to Dodd's.[56] The second swing came in the 1990s. In the aftermath of the frenzied wave of hostile takeovers in the 1980s, more than forty states rushed to enact statutes instructing corporate directors to take account of the interests of constituencies other than shareholders in employing their powers.[57] In Japan (and in some of the continental European countries as well), on the other hand, we are currently witnessing a strong swing in the opposite direction. Disgusted with a series of corporate scandals, alarmed by the deep and prolonged recession, and fearful of the prospect of losing global competitiveness in the post-industrial era, a growing number of academics, public officials, business leaders, and journalists have begun to pressure their "inflexible" and "outmoded" corporate system to become more like the Americans'.

The dichotomy between shareholder capitalism and corporate capitalism is thus a simplification. And yet, this is merely a simplification, not an oversimplification. Notwithstanding large variations within each type of capitalism, we still find it a use-

---

53. There have been a number of studies which report very similar results. *See*, for instance, Kagono, Nonaka, Okumura, Sakakibara, Komatsu & Sakashita, Strategic vs. Evolutionary Management: A US-Japan Comparison of Strategy and Organization (1985), Table 2-5.

54. Dodd, *For Whom Are Corporate Managers Trustees?*, 45 Harv. L. Rev. 1145 (1932); and Berle, *For Whom Corporate Managers Are Trustees: A Note*, 45 Harv. L. Rev. 1365 (1932).

55. Dodd, op. cit., at 1148.

56. Already in Chapter 4, Part 4 of Modern Corporation and Private Property (1932), he co-authored with G.C. Means, Berle expressed a view which is similar to Dodd's. *See also* Adolph Berle, Jr., The 20th Century Capitalist Revolution (1954).

57. *See* Mark Roe, Strong Managers, Weak Owners: The Political Roots of American Corporate Finance (1994), at 151–68, for an informative account of this movement.

ful working hypothesis to assume that American managers are generally expected to maximize the returns to shareholders and that Japanese managers are generally expected to emphasize the survival and growth of the corporation as an organizational entity.

It is not the intention of the present article to pass judgment on which type of capitalism is ethically more just or politically more democratic or economically more efficient. We shall merely take the coexistence of two capitalisms as a given "fact" and proceed with our investigation on that factual foundation. My thesis here is that these two seemingly contradictory capitalisms are but two variants of the genus Capitalism and by no means contradictory. I have already established that the legal concept of the corporation is not determinate itself and that what law is able to do is to offer to each society a menu of possible corporate structures ranging from the purely "nominalistic" to the purely "realistic." I would now argue that from this long legal menu the American economy and the Japanese economy have chosen as their dominant corporate structure one close to the "nominalistic" end and one close to the "realistic" end, respectively.

TABLE 3: AVERAGE ANNUAL VOLUME OF COMPLETED DOMESTIC MERGERS AND CORPORATE TRANSACTIONS WITH DISCLOSED VALUES 1985–89

	America	Japan	Britain	Germany
Total Volume (in billions of US$)	1,070.0	61.3	107.6	4.2
As a Percentage of Total Market Capitalization	41.1	3.1	18.7	2.3

Source: Stephen Prowse, "Corporate Governance in an International Perspective: A Survey of Corporate Control Mechanisms among Large Firms in the United States, the United Kingdom, Japan and Germany," BIS Economic Papers, No. 41 (July 1994); Table 12. Original sources cited in the paper are Securities Data Corporation, Merger and Corporate Transactions database for the U. S., the UK. and Germany, and Yamauchi Securities Corporation for Japan.
Note: The total value of market capitalization is for 1987.

In Section 3 we saw how the day-to-day activities of corporate raiders in the stock market work to turn a person/thing corporation into a "nominalistic" corporation with little or no personality of its own. I would now suggest that the American corporate system very much fits in with this picture. The first row of Table 3 compares the average annual value of completed mergers and acquisitions between America and Japan for the second half of the 1980s. It includes the figures for Great Britain and Germany as well. The second row normalizes this value by dividing it by the total value of market capitalization in 1987. Although both America and Japan are comparable in regard to the value of total market capitalization—about 2,600 billion dollars in America and 2,000 billion dollars in Japan in 1987—their difference in the volume of completed mergers and acquisitions is simply enormous in both absolute and relative magnitude.[58] (In Great Britain corporate mergers and acquisitions were much more active than in Japan but not so much as in America, whereas in Germany they were even less active than in Japan.) When we examine the frequency of hostile takeovers, the difference becomes even more conspicuous. Takeover bids

58. These figures are taken from Prowse, "Corporate Governance in an International Perspective: A Survey of Corporate Control Mechanisms among Large Firms in the United States, the United Kingdom, Japan and Germany," BIS Economic Papers (No. 41, July 1994).

(TOBs) are the most commonly used means for hostile takeovers in America, and they were legally instituted in Japan in 1971 when its Securities and Exchange Acts were revised along the lines of their American counterparts. Hence, the legal apparatus has since been at least formally neutral in terms of comparing the two countries. And yet, from 1971 to 1990, only three (!) TOBs were ever reported in Japan, whereas the Securities and Exchange Commission (SEC) in America received 1,032 reports of TOBs for the much shorter period of 1985 to 1990.[59] In fact, it is said that almost 10% of American corporations included in the Fortune 500 in 1980 have since been acquired in a transaction that was hostile or started off as hostile.[60] The stock market in America serves as the 'market for corporate control' far more effectively than that in Japan.

Why then have hostile takeovers been so rarely observed in Japan? To this question we can readily provide an answer: it is because there are extensive cross-shareholdings among large Japanese corporations.

TABLE 4: CROSS-SHAREHOLDINGS AMONG CORE 20 CORPORATIONS OF SUMITOMO GROUP, 1993
[omitted]

That Japan has six major corporate groups—Mitsubishi, Mitsui, Sumitomo, Fuyo (Fuji), Sanwa, and Daiichi-Kangin (DK) is well-known.[61] Each group is clustered around a main bank, extended over the whole industry, and connected through intricate cross-shareholdings. To get a sense of this, Table 4 exhibits the matrix of shareholdings among 20 corporations which constitute the core members (that is, the member corporations of the prestigious Presidents' Club) of the Sumitomo group. What is remarkable is that their network of cross-shareholdings is so tight-knit that this matrix has few vacant cells except the row for Sumitomo Life Insurance, which is a mutual company issuing no shares, and the column for Sumitomo Light Metals which is essentially a subsidiary of Sumitomo Metals.[62] For instance, Sumitomo Bank holds shares of Sumitomo Marine Insurance, Sumitomo Corporation, NEC, Sumitomo Metals, etc.; Sumitomo Marine Insurance in turn holds shares of Sumitomo Bank, Sumitomo Corporation, NEC, Sumitomo Metals, etc.; and so on. (Sumitomo Life Insurance holds shares of almost all the other corporations in the group.) The average ratio of the mutually held shares within the Sumitomo group was 27.5% in 1989. The average of the averages of the six groups

59. Since the revision of the Securities and Exchange Act in 1990, there have been a few more cases. American data are taken from various issues of the SEC Annual Report.

60. According to W. Carl Kester, Japanese Takeovers: The Global Quest for Corporate Control (1991).

61. It is Hiroshi Okumura who first noted the importance of the system of cross-shareholdings among corporations in understanding the structure and performance of post-war Japanese economy. *See* Hojin Sihonshugi no Kozo [The Structure of Corporate Capitalism], (Nihon Hyoron Sha, 1975; rev. ed., Gendai Kyoyo Bunko, 1991); Nihon no Rokudai Kigyou Shudan [Six Giant Corporate Groups in Japan], (Daiamondo sha, 1976; (rev. ed., Asahi Bunko, 1993); Hojin Sihonshugi [Corporate Capitalism], (Ochanomizu Shobo, 1984; rev. ed., Asahi Bunko, 1991). The term "corporate capitalism" was due to him.

62. Among 20 Japanese life insurance companies established before 1975, 16 are mutual companies while only four of them are incorporated. (In the case of the United States 27 out of 41 life insurance companies were mutual companies in 1985. The ratio has, however, been steadily declining since then.)

was 21.6%.[63] Since these ratios are calculated only among the core corporations, they would go up much higher if we include lesser group members and subsidiaries.

If we combine the core members of the six major corporate groups, they as a whole account for about 15% of total assets, total sales and total profits of the entire economy (excluding the financial sector).[64] If we include lesser members and subsidiaries, their total share would certainly become much larger (perhaps as large as a quarter of the entire economy). Apart from them, there are several other corporate groups with much looser networks of cross-shareholdings; and there are many large independent corporations with little or no cross-shareholdings. Table 5 reproduces the results of a questionnaire sent to all the public corporations in Japan. Its first column shows that, while a third of the respondents have mutual shareholdings ratios of less than 10%, almost a half of them have more than 20% of their shares held mutually. The average ratio is 23%, which is, even taking account of the difference of data sets, a figure comparable to that of the six major corporate groups.[65] Note that the mutual shareholdings ratio may not fully capture the extent to which each corporation is protected from hostile takeovers. Some of the shares may be owned by friendly corporations which maintain long-term mutual relations by buying up a large block of each other's products, by sending directors to each other's board, by sharing important information in the meetings of group corporations, and so on. Those shareholders that are expected to resist the temptation of tender offers by outside raiders are called "stable shareholders" in Japan. The second column of Table 5 indicates that as much as 84% (!) of Japanese public corporations have succeeded in securing more than half of their shares for what they believe to be their stable shareholders.[66] They of course consider themselves largely immune to the threat of corporate raiders.[67]

---

63. Kosei Torihiki Iinkai (Fair Trade Commission), Kigyo Shudan no Jittai ni tsuite [On the Reality of Corporate Groups] (1992).

64. *Id.* The average ratios of the Mitsubishi, Mitsui, Fuyo, Sanwa and DK groups are, respectively, 35.5%, 19.5%, 16.4%, 16.5% and 14.6%.

65. By contrast, in the case of 397 closed corporations responding to the same questionnaire, the average ratio of mutual shareholdings is 16.3%. *See* Fuji Sogo Kenkyujo (Fuji Research Institute Corporation), Mein Banku Sisutemu oyobi Kabushiki Motchiai' ni tsuite no Chosa Hokoku [Reports on the Study of Main Bank System and Cross-Shareholdings], (April 30, 1993).

66. According to Fuji Research Institute Corporation, *supra* n. 62, of those stable shareholders 20% are banks, 8% life insurance companies, 4% liability insurance corporations, 35% other corporations (of those about 10% are parent corporations), 15% individuals, and 2% employees' holding cooperatives.

67. In August, 1999, Daiichi-Kangyo Bank and Fuji Bank, together with Japan Industrial Bank, announced plans to merge their operations through a bank-holding corporation by 2002, and in October of the same year Sumitomo Bank and Sakura Bank (the main bank of Mitsui group) also announced a plan to unite, forming a single bank, by 2002. These announcements heralded a major transformation in the Japanese financial sector, but it is still early to see whether this will lead to the complete transformation of the entire Japanese corporate system or to a mere consolidation of its corporate group structure.

TABLE 5: RATIOS OF MUTUAL SHAREHOLDINGS AND STABLE SHAREHOLDINGS AMONG PUBLIC CORPORATIONS IN JAPAN[1]

	Mutual shareholdings[2]	Stable shareholdings[3] (%)
Less than 10%	31.3	2.2
10-20%	19.1	0.3
20-30%	17.5	1.0
30-40%	12.8	3.8
40-50%	10.9	8.7
50-60%	5.4	25.9
60-70%	3.0	34.3
70-80%	0.5	17.1
More than 80%	0.2	6.7
Average	23.4	61.0

Source: Fuji Sogo Kenkyujo (Fuji Research Institute Corporation), 'Mein Banku Sisutemu oyobi Kabushiki Mochiai' ni tsuite no Chosa Hokokusho (Reports on the Study of 'Main Bank System and Cross-Shareholdings') April 30, 1993.
Notes: 1. The figures are based on the answers given by 586 publicly-held corporations. 2. Percentage of the shares held by the corporations whose shares are also held by the corporation in question. 3. Percentage of the shares held by the corporations which are regarded as stable shareholders by the corporation in question.

In Section 4 we saw how extensive cross-shareholding among a group of corporations works to turn each of the person-cum-thing corporations into a "realistic" corporation with little or no trace of thingness in itself. The Japanese corporate system is now seen to fit in with this picture quite well. Thus, in spite of their seemingly irreconcilable differences, shareholder capitalism in America and corporate capitalism in Japan are but two extreme forms of the genus Capitalism. They assume their particular forms by selecting, respectively, the most "nominalistic" position and the most "realistic" position along a long continuum of possible corporate structures that the law has supplied each society as a menu to choose from.

---

b. China

The official organs of the Chinese state have claimed that their form of corporate organization has combined the core structures and goals of the Marxist state with the efficiency characteristics of corporate organization. Putting aside the question of whether Chinese-style state involvement, direct or indirect, with Chinese corporations is not perhaps better characterized as fascism with a Marxist face, consider whether corporations in China under current law enjoy a distinct legal personality, or whether legal personality is a formal rather than substantive distinction.

Kingsley T.W. Ong and Colin R. Baxter, *A Comparative Study of the Fundamental Elements of Chinese and English Company Law*

48 INTERNATIONAL & COMPARATIVE LAW QUARTERLY 88 (1999)
(excerpts from pages 94–97, 118–120; some footnotes omitted)

China has been ruled under the Marxist ideology since the Communist Party took control in 1949. However, ever since the open door policy adopted in 1978, China has gradually moved away from traditional Marxism. A significant problem posed by Marxism to the open door policy is that it is ambiguous about the value of legal construction.[33] However, it is undeniable too that law and order are important in every society.[34] This is especially true in a highly competitive business environment—which the open door policy seeks to create—where law is essential in setting up the framework within which business must compete. In implementing laws suitable for a business environment, China adopts some concepts capitalistic in origin. The "company" presents an immediate example of a capitalist legal fiction. Some Chinese Marxists have justified this development by arguing that it is essential for China to utilise some capitalist tools to allow the country to develop and eventually reach a communist utopia.[35] While the company concept is *prima facie* in conflict with the dominant Marxist ideology, China retains its socialist character through the State. China is unique in this sense, and therefore provides a testing ground for legal theorists who believe in the Marxist approach.

In employing the company concept, China has adopted a hybrid of two capitalist concepts. On the formation of companies, China adopts the early English concessionary approach. Therefore, the State is justified in its strict regulation of incorporation. On internal governance, China adopts the managerial approach. According to managerialism, the objective of company law is to ensure that managers run the company in the interests of shareholders, given the inevitability and desirability of centralised management. These approaches allow the Chinese State to maintain ultimate control of companies and regulate them.

B. Legal Personality and Property Rights

Owing to traditional Marxist ideologies, one of the major obstacles for the Chinese in adopting capitalist concepts such as the company was the inevitable recognition of the Western concept of property ownership. Property ownership is particularly sensitive in China.[36] Chinese law has shown a strong reluctance to make a unified and clear declaration as to the property ownership rights of various legal persons.[37] Prior to the [first national corporation law of China "CL")] there were differing views on property rights of Chinese legal persons. Some believed that legal persons have the right to ownership

---

33. Marx believed that there would be no need for law in the ideal classless communist society.....

34. Chiam Boon Keng, Registrar of the Supreme Court of Singapore, *cited in* SIA SAU HURA, BUSINESS FIRMS AND COMPANIES 5 (4th ed., 1996).

35. HU YEBI, CHINA'S CAPITAL MARKETS (1993), pp. 67–68. This view was endorsed by Premier Li Peng in 1991....

36. Sobel, M.A. and Zhang, D. "The Evolution of Foreign Secured Lending in China: Socialism and Property" (1989) Vol. 52, No. 3, LAW & COMTEMP. PROBS. 185.

37. For further references and discussion on this issue *see* [Fu Tingmei, *Legal Persons in China: Essence and Limits*, 41 AM. J. COMP. L. 261 (1993)].....

of their property.[38] Others argued that shareholders should also be able to enjoy ownership rights.[39] There were also those who felt that the property of a limited company was owned by its shareholders, and merely managed by its managers.[40]

The CL confers property rights on legal persons for the first time. The company, as a legal entity, has rights over all its assets purchased by the investment of shareholders and enjoys the rights and assumes responsibilities under civil law.[41]....

However, property rights of Chinese companies are complicated by the last sentence of Article 4 of the CL. This provides that ownership of State assets of the company belongs to the State. The ambiguity over "State assets" results in uncertainty over property ownership.[43] Chinese companies bear civil liability for the property they manage. However, under Chinese law, the property of State-owned enterprises is owned by the State but managed by the enterprises. This could have severe implications for creditors, especially where companies go into liquidation.... {I]f the assets of Chinese companies are owned by the State and not the companies *per se*, then in the event of insolvency or liquidation there may be no legal recourse for the creditors, since the assets belonging to State cannot be realised. While the CL makes provision for thorough examination of the assets of the company during liquidation,[44] it is not clear how "State-owned assets" in the company are to be dealt with.

When China was working on drafting its Company Law, there was opposition from the more conservative members in the Communist Party. They could not accept the Western concept that companies, being legal persons, could be capable of owning assets. (Even the ownership rights of natural persons in China are limited.) While they could agree that State enterprises could take the new form of existence under the then proposed Company Law, they insisted that the Law should state expressly that State assets still belonged to the State. Not being legally trained, they did not realise the implications of such a provision. This Chinese misconception of company law, and reluctance to accept capitalistic ownership wholesale, blurs the whole idea of a legal person. Article 14 of the CL further provides that when engaging in business activities a company shall abide by the law, observe professional ethics, enhance building of socialist spiritual civilization and accept supervision by the government and the general public. The socialist tradition has thus been very much preserved.[48]

* * *

A distinctive feature to be specified in the articles of a Chinese legal person is the "legal representative."[215] The importance of the legal representative can be seen in its being classified as a basic element of the CL.

---

38. Guo Feng, *Gufenzhi Qiye Suoyouquan Wenti de Tantao* (Discussion of the Issue of Ownership Right of Joint Stock Companies) (1988) 3 ZHONGGUO FAXUE 3.

39. Wang Liming, *Lun Gufenzhi Qiye Suotouquan de Erchong Jieguo* (On the Two Tier Structure of Ownership Rights of Limited Companies) (1989) 1 ZHONGGUO FAXUE 47.

40. Tong Rou and Shi Jichun, *Woguo Quanmin Suoyouzhi 'Lianquan Fenli' de Caich anquan Jieguo* (The Property Rights Represented by the Separation of Ownership and Management in Our State Ownership System) (1990) 3 ZHONGGUO SHEHUI KEXUE 159.

41. CL, Art. 4.

43. *See* C.A. Png, *Some Concerns About Chinese Company Law* (1996) 17 CO. LAWYER 199, 200–201, for a further discussion of the uncertain nature of property rights in the PRC.

44. *See* CL, Arts. 189–198.

48. *See* [C.A.] *Png*, ["Some Concerns About Chinese Company Law" (1996) 17 CO. LAWYER 199,] at p. 200.

215. CL, Art. 22(9).

While the Chinese adoption of the Western concept of limited liability for shareholders remains significant, the CL does not adopt the concept wholesale. It provides for the distinctly Chinese idea of a human "legal representative", who is subject to sanctions for improper corporate activities.

Limited liability entails entitling a business to enjoy the profits if it succeeds but insulating it from liability from losses if it fails. This concept denies recovery to creditors where the company is bankrupt. This concept is accepted in Western countries like the United Kingdom because it is thought that the benefits to society in encouraging commerce in this manner outweigh the detriments to creditors. England's long history of such policy decisions, motivated by the predominant capitalistic ideology, led to the principle of limited liability appearing basic or commonplace to English society.

However, acceptance of the limited liability principle cannot be assumed in China. China lacks a comparable history of orientation toward private enterprise. Even earlier versions of Chinese company regulations provided for limited liability in only some forms of companies. This explains the importance played on the "legal representative" concept to the Chinese. The "legal representative"[218] concept is integrated into the CL as an encroachment on the limited liability principle.

A legal representative is the natural person authorised to act on behalf of and to bind the company. [219] This is similar to directors acting as company "agents" in the United Kingdom, or acting *as* the company in most of the rest of Europe. He is either the chairman, president[220] or executive director[221] of the company. However, the Chinese legal representative bears greater risks than an ordinary Chinese director[222] or an agent under UK law.

The legal representative is subject to sanctions for the legal person's misconduct.[223] For example, the legal representative is personally at risk if the corporation engages in business beyond its authorised scope, conceals facts from registration and tax authorities, or hides property to evade repayment of debts.[224] The legal representative may also be fined or subjected to administrative sanctions,[225] with attendant loss of prestige, status and face. If the offense constitutes a crime, the legal representative may also be prosecuted. This is in contrast with the English approach, where a company's *criminal* liability is limited owing to the difficulty of identifying the company's *mens rea*.[226] The Chinese "legal representative" approach ensures that no company committing a crime would be exonerated. Although the representative is not personally liable for company debts, the extent of responsibility is nevertheless serious.

218. Known in Chinese as the *fading daibiaoren.*

219. General Principles of Civil Laws of the PRC, Art. 43, 12 Apr. 1986.

220. CL, Arts. 45, 68, 113.

221. CL, Arts. 51.

222. *See* CL, Art. 214, for reference to directors, supervisors and managers. These provisions are similar to the UK provisions for fraudulent and wrongful trading (Companies Act 1985, §§. 213–214). *See also* CL, Arts. 208, 209, 211, 212, 217 and 218 for a comparison.

223. CL, Art. 49.

224. *Ibid.*

225. *Ibid.*

226. *See* J.C. SMITH AND B. HOGAN, CRIMINAL LAW (7th edn. 1992), p. 182. However, where the person committing the crime can be identified as the "directing mind and will" of the guilty company, the company can be held guilty of intent to deceive (*DPP v. Kent & Sussex Contractors* [1944] K.B. 146), and even guilty of manslaughter (*R. V. P&O Ferries* (1990) 93 Cr.App. Rep. 72). Nevertheless, while normal criminal sanctions may be applied to the Chinese "legal representative" (natural person), they cannot be applied to the company *per se* (artifiial legal person).

Consistent with the managerial approach of ensuring the accountability of managers to shareholders of the company, China adopts a cautious approach towards extending the wholesale implementation of the limited liability concept. The "legal representative" concept represents a means of ensuring the accountability of the Chinese company to the shareholders and creditors, notwithstanding the grant of limited liability to the rest of the company.

Despite this encroachment on limited liability, China's adoption of capitalist principles of liability for corporate obligations parallel to the West is significant because of China's long socialist traditions. For example, the CL provides that a company is a legal person, and enjoys civil rights and owes civil responsibilities to the full extent of its assets.[228] The CL also explicitly protects shareholders from liability beyond their capital contributions.[229] This is necessary in order for the CL to be consistent towards the development of a "socialist market economy.

Comments and Questions

1. Reread the provisions of the Constitution of the People's Republic of China in Chapter 2. In light of the basic organizational structure of the Chinese political system, can there ever be a substantive division between the state and enterprise organizations with legal personality? Are enterprises organized as corporations merely another organ of the state, rather than an independently operating entity? Is the nature of the relationship between the organs of state administration and corporation in China more like that between the American federal government and quasi-independent state administrative agencies such as the National Labor Relations Board?

2. Whatever the reality of legal personality in Chinese law, it is clear that the Chinese State has attempted to create a new class of citizen, or a new form of administrative organ through the device of legal personality.

> The Civil Law of 1986 expanded upon the statutory revisions and re-established a legal basis for private business in its corporate form. The Civil Law provides for the regulation of business and personal relationships among Chinese citizens, between "legal persons," and between citizens and "legal persons." Entities such as joint ventures, SOEs and new companies are examples of the "legal persons" contemplated by the law. In other words, the "legal persons" the law creates can be fictional corporate persons. They obtain this status when the enterprises are established in accordance with the appropriate law. Accordingly, the Civil Law guarantees that once establishment and registration are complete, an enterprise is a "legal person" that has the capacity for civil rights in conducting lawful activities—it may lawfully conduct business under the protection of law. As a "legal person," the entity gains a judicial remedy in the event of a contractual or other breach of law by another company, a joint venture, an SOE or a Chinese citizen.

Michael Irl Nikkel, Note: *"Chinese Characteristics" in Corporate Clothing: Questions of Fiduciary Duty in China's Company Law*, 80 MINN. L. REV. 503, 509–510 (1995) (footnotes omitted).

---

228. CL, Arts. 3, 4.
229. CL, Art. 3.

3. How would you describe the nature of the legal personality of Chinese enterprises in terms of the conceptions of legal personality discussed in this chapter? Do you think that the "Political Theory" approach—the stakeholder model, with its implications for the role of the state, as described in the excerpt from EILÍS FERRAN, COMPANY LAW AND CORPORATE FINANCE reproduced above in this Chapter—is a better normative basis for understanding the Chinese approach to corporate law?

Chapter 5

Systems for Division of Regulatory Authority in Multi-State Systems: The Incorporation and Siège Social Doctrines

The fact that states have the authority to create legal persons—corporations for example,—and endow them with certain legal effects, merely opens the door to a host of difficult questions of governance. The most important of these relate to the distribution of power among the states to regulate the corporate entities created by any of them. Three possible regimes of power distribution come to mind. Under one regime, the state of the domicile of the legal person has sole authority to regulate its internal affairs. The second is based on an acceptance of the rule that the state in which the legal entity is formed has sole authority to regulate matters of internal corporate governance. The third regime is based on a failure to agree among possible regulating states. It suggests that any state may regulate those affairs of a legal person over which it has accorded itself authority to the extent of the state's power to assert jurisdiction.

The first regime forms the basis of continental European and Japanese regulation of corporations. This is commonly known as the *siège social* or seat theory of governance and will be discussed later in this chapter. The second, known as the foundation or incorporation theory, forms the basis of regulation in the United States the United Kingdom, Ireland and the Netherlands. American courts sometimes refer to this as the "internal affairs" doctrine.[1] The third remains largely untried today.

Conceptual problems are not eliminated merely by the choice of a common basis of dividing regulatory power among governmental institutions. For example, choosing the seat theory merely opens the door to a host of ambiguities and disjunctions relating to the definition of a seat and the activities that might entitle one state among many claim an entity as a domiciliary. All theories have to wrestle with the question of the characterization of "internal affairs" subject to the governing theory. Special problems arise where corporations operate in states adhering to different theories.

Ultimately, the problem arises because of a critical and fundamental disjunction in the regulation of enterprises. The governmental units which are charged with the cre-

1. In this chapter the terms incorporation, foundation and internal affairs doctrines are used interchangeably.

ation and regulation of legal persons are no longer co-extensive with the geography over which the legal personality conducts its business. Corporate regulation has remained local while the political units within which these enterprises operate are now generally federal and supra-national. As such, local regulation has become more problematic, whether the basis of that regulation is the foundation theory or the seat theory. As you read the materials in this chapter consider to what extent the arguments make or miss this point. Consider also whether, indeed, there is still space for local governance of entities subject to the predominant economic policies of supra-local political entities—the state, the federation, the supra-national organization, and the regional or world trade organization.

This chapter explores the problems of choosing, maintaining and arranging for the regulation of legal persons. States must not only determine the scope of issues regulated under the seat or foundation theories, but also the limits of the theories themselves. More problematic, especially in the European Union, but increasingly a cause for friction in the United States, is the situation where different states seek to enforce forms of the seat and the foundation theories within the same system.

A. The Foundation or Incorporation Doctrine in the United States

In the absence of federal preemption of corporate governance, a corporation validly created in any state will be recognized by other states (Restatement (Second) Conflict of Laws § 297).[2] Any corporation generally can operate in every other state,[3] it can reincorporate in any other state with little tax or other consequences, and the internal affairs of the corporation will be governed by the law of the state of incorporation.[4] The federal Constitution has added some protection in this regard.

Thus, for example, the Commerce Clause has been interpreted to limit the power of states to discriminate in favor of their citizens or their activities or to burden interstate commerce (*see, e.g,* Baldwin v. Selig, 294 U.S. 511 (1935) (invalidating discriminatory treatment of out of state milk sellers) Raymond Motor Trans. v. Rice, 434 U.S. 429 (1978)), and the Due Process Clause has been interpreted to limit the power of states to deprive corporations of liberty or property without due process of law (*see, e.g., Bellotti,* 435 U.S. 765 (1978)).

The materials below introduce you to the foundation or incorporation doctrine, currently accepted as the basis of the division of regulatory power between states over a corporation operating outside the state of its incorporation. Under the incorporation doctrine, the state of incorporation is given regulatory authority of the internal affairs

2. "A distinction must here be drawn between recognition of a foreign corporation and permitting a foreign corporation to do various kinds of acts." Restatement (Second) Conflict of Laws §297 Comment a.

3. "The States have rarely sought to prohibit foreign corporations from doing business, or conducting other activities, within their territories. Generally, they have attempted only to impose conditions upon the privilege by demanding compliance with their qualification requirements." Restatement (Second) Conflict of Laws § 311 Comment b.

4. Restatement (Second) Conflict of Laws §§ 301–310.

of a corporation, any state may exercise such other regulatory power over a corporation as it may assert. While it is accepted that "a corporation's internal affairs are involved whenever the issue concerns the relations *inter se* of the corporation, its shareholders, directors, officers or agents,"[5] this section also introduces the student to the problems that can be involved in determining whether a particular issue of governance forms part of a corporation's internal affairs. The materials also point to the difficulties of determining the limits of a state's power to regulate entities given legal personalities in other states. As you read the materials consider whether the incorporation doctrine is constitutionally mandated, or if it is merely a choice of law principle.

Restatement (Second) of Conflict of Laws

§ 302

(1) Issues involving the rights and liabilities of a corporation, other than those dealt with in § 301, are determined by the local law of the state which, with respect to the particular issue, has the most significant relationship to the occurrence and the parties under the principles stated in § 6.

(2) The local law of the state of incorporation will be applied to determine such issues, except in the unusual case where, with respect to the particular issue, some other state has a more significant relationship to the occurrence and the parties, in which event the local law of the other state will be applied.

* * *

Comment:

a. Scope of section. The rule of this section is to be contrasted with that of § 301. The rule of this Section is concerned with issues involving matters that are peculiar to corporations and other associations, whereas the rule of § 301 is concerned with issues arising from corporate acts of a sort that can also be done by individuals. Many of the matters that fall within the scope of the rule of this Section involve the "internal affairs" of a corporation—that is the relations inter se of the corporation, its shareholders, directors, officers or agents—and hence likewise fall within the scope of the rules of §§ 303–310. Other such matters affect the interests of the corporation's creditors.

Matters falling within the scope of the rule of this Section and which involve primarily a corporation's relationship to its shareholders include steps taken in the course of the original incorporation, the election or appointment of directors and officers, the adoption of bylaws, the issuance of corporate shares, preemptive rights, the holding of directors' and shareholders' meetings, methods of voting including any requirement for cumulative voting, shareholders' rights to examine corporate records, charter and bylaw amendments, mergers, consolidations and reorganizations and the reclassification of shares. Matters which may also affect the interests of the corporation's creditors include the issuance of bonds, the declaration and payment of dividends, loans by the corporation to directors, officers and shareholders, and the purchase and redemption by the corporation of outstanding shares of its own stock.

The rule of this Section will be applied in the absence of a local statute that is explicitly applicable to the situation at hand. All States of the United States have statutes

---

5. Restatement (Second) Conflicts of Law § 313 comment a.

which regulate in various ways the affairs of foreign corporations within their territory. Blue Sky laws and statutes regulating the activities of public utilities are typical examples....

Comment to Subsection (1):

*b. Rationale.....*The factors listed in...of the rule of §6 vary somewhat in importance from field to field. Those which come to the fore in the field of corporations are the needs of the interstate and international systems, certainty, predictability and uniformity of result, protection of the of the justified expectations of the parties, implementation of the relevant policies of the state with the dominant interest in the decision of the particular issue, and ease in the application of the law to be applied. These factors, for reasons stated in Comments *e–h*, will usually lead to the application of the local law of the state of incorporation, which in the situation dealt with here is a contact of great significance.

* * *

Comment on Subsection (2):

e. Rationale. Application of the local law of the state of incorporation will usually be supported by those choice-of-law factors favoring the needs of the interstate and international systems, certainty, predictability and uniformity of result, protection of the justified expectations of the parties and ease in the application of the law to be applied. Usually, application of the law will also be supported by the factor looking toward implementation of the relevant policies of the state with the dominant interest in the decision of the particular issue.

Uniform treatment of directors, officers and shareholders is an important objective which can only be attained by having the rights and liabilities of those persons with respect to the corporation governed by a single law. To the extent that they think about the matter, these persons would usually expect that their rights and duties with respect to the corporation would be determined by the local law of the state of incorporation. This state is also easy to identify, and thus the value of ease of application is attained when the local law of this state is applied.

In addition, many matters involving a corporation cannot practicably be determined differently in different states. Examples of such matters, most of which have already been mentioned in Comment *a*, include steps taken in the course of the original incorporation, the election or appointment of directors and officers, the adoption of by-laws, the issuance of corporate shares (see Comment *f*), the holding of directors' and shareholders' meetings, methods of voting including any requirement for cumulative voting, the declaration and payment of dividends and other distributions, charter amendments, mergers, consolidations, and reorganizations, the reclassification of shares and the purchase and redemption by the corporation of outstanding shares of its own stock.

Matters such as these must be contrasted with the acts dealt with in §301, which include, for example, the making of contracts, the commission of torts and the transfer of property. There is no reason why corporate acts of the latter sort should not be governed by the local law of different states. There is no reason, for example, why an issue involving one corporate contract should not be governed by the local law of state X while an issue involving another corporate contract is governed by the local law of state Y. On the other hand, it would be impractical to have matters of the sort mentioned in the previous paragraph, which involve a corporation's organic structure or internal administration, governed by different laws. It would be impractical, for example, if an election of directors, an issuance of shares, a payment of dividends, a charter amendment, or a consolidation or reorganization were to be held valid in one state and invalid in another. Possible alternatives would be either to have matters of this sort governed by the local law of a particular state or else to hold applicable the local law of any state having a reasonable relationship to the corporation which imposed the strictest requirement. Under this latter view, for example, a corporation could not amend its charter or declare a dividend without satisfying the requirements of all states with which the corporation has a substantial relationship. In the absence of an explicitly applicable local statute to the contrary, the first alternative has almost invariably been adopted and the local law of the state of incorporation has been applied to determine issues involving corporate acts of the sort under consideration.

It should be added that certain issues which are peculiar to corporations or to other organizations do not affect matters of organic structure or internal administration and need not, as a practical matter, be governed by a single law. An example is the transfer of individual shares of a share issue. There is no practical reason, for example, why a corporation incorporated in state X should not comply with the requirements of state Y when it seeks to sell its shares in the latter state. Even as to such matters, however, the local law of the state of incorporation has usually been applied in the absence of an explicitly applicable local statute. Section 8-106 of the Uniform Commercial Code provides that the "validity of a security and the rights and duties of the issuer with respect to registration of transfer are governed by the law (including the conflict of laws rules) of the jurisdiction of organization of the issuer.

* * *

g. When local law of state of incorporation will not be applied. In the absence of an explicitly applicable local statute, the local law of the state of incorporation has been applied almost invariably to determine issues involving matters that are peculiar to corporations.... [T]he local law of the state of incorporation should be applied except in the rare situation where a contrary result is required by the overriding interest of another state in having its rule applied.

Among the factors that bear upon the question are (1) the nature and extent of a corporation's relationship to the state of incorporation, (2) the nature and extent of the corporation's relationship to the state whose local law is sought to be applied, and (3) whether the act is...one which cannot practicably be governed by the local law of more than one state.

The reasons for applying the local law of the state of incorporation carry less weight when the corporation has little or no contact with this state other than the fact that it was incorporated there. In such situations. Some other state will almost surely have a greater interest than the state of incorporation in the determination of the particular issue. Nevertheless, in the absence of an explicitly applicable local statute, the local law of the state of incorporation has almost invariably been applied.... Nevertheless, it is in situations where the corporation has little contact with the state of its incorporation that the local law of some other state is most likely to be applied when (1) the relevant local law rules of the other state embody an important policy of that state, and (2) the matter involved does not affect the corporation's organic structure or internal administration and therefore does not fall within the category of issues which, for reasons stated in Comment *e*, cannot practicably be determined differently in different states.

The local law of a state other than the state of incorporation will not be applied to govern matters covered by the rule of this Section unless that state has the dominant interest in having its local rule applied to determine the particular issue.... Application of the local law of such a state is a particularly drastic step when the matter involved can only be governed by the local law of a single state. For example, only one law can be applied to determine whether a corporation either must, or need not provide for cumulative voting. If the local law of one state is applied to require a corporation to provide for cumulative voting, the corporation must so provide even though perhaps the local law rule of the state of incorporation and of all other states in which it does business or has shareholders is to the contrary. By so applying its law, a state is therefore forcing its policy upon other states. A state which is not the state of incorporation should not apply its local law in such circumstances unless it clearly has an interest superior to that of all other states in the issue to be decided or unless its local law rule is the same as that prevailing in many of the other states in which the corporation does business or has shareholders.... Application of the local law of a state other than the state of incorporation can most easily be justified in situations where the corporation does all, or nearly all, of its business in that state and most of the corporation's shareholders are domiciled there....

* * *

Illustrations:

1. The A corporation is incorporated in state X and does business in states X, Y, and Z. In Y, A issues certain share to B without satisfying the requirements of Y's Blue Sky Law. As a result, the transfer is voidable under Y local law; it is, however, valid and effective under the local law of X. B, who is domiciled in Y, brings suit in a Y court for a rescission. According to the majority rule, the Y court will apply X local law and uphold the transfer unless the Y statute is explicitly applicable to foreign corporations (see Comment *f*). There is good reason, however, why Y local law should be applied. Y is almost surely the state of dominant interest since the purpose of the Y role was undoubtedly to protect persons dealing with corporations in Y. Also application of the Y rule to avoid the particular transfer would not affect the organic structure and internal administration of A.

2. The A corporation is incorporated in state X and does 20 percent of its business in X, 40 percent of its business in state Y, 20 percent of its business in state Z and the remaining 20 percent of its business in a number of other states. A's shareholders are scattered numerically in approximately the same proportions among the above-mentioned states. Y local law requires corporations to provide for cumulative voting. The local law rule of S, Z and the other states is to the contrary. A proceeding is brought in a Y court to prevent A from eliminating cumulative voting on its stock. This relief should be denied unless the Y statute was clearly intended to apply to the facts of the instant case. Application of the Y rule would require the corporation to provide for cumulative voting contrary to the policy of X, Z and the other states. Under the circumstances, Y does not have a sufficiently dominant interest to justify application of its rule in disregard of the policies of the other states.

---

1. Legislative Inroads on the Foundation of Incorporation Doctrine

The notion of corporate personality implicit in the incorporation or foundation doctrine has come under increasing attack from the legislatures of several of the larger commercial states. In particular and in recent years, New York and California have attempted to apply portions of their own corporate law to corporations the majority of whose activities occur within the state. As we will see, however, the foundation or incorporation theory has never been accepted by most of the nations of Europe (with the notable exception of the United Kingdom).

McKinney's Consolidated Laws of New York; Annotated Business Corporation Law

Chapter 4 of the Consolidated Laws
Article 13—Foreign Corporations

§ 1319. Applicability of other provisions

(a) In addition to articles 1 (Short title; definitions; application; certificates; miscellaneous) and 3 (Corporate name and service of process) and the other sections of article 13, the following provisions, to the extent provided therein, shall apply to a foreign corporation doing business in this state, its directors, officers and shareholders:

(1) Section 623 (Procedure to enforce shareholder's right to receive payment for shares).

(2) Section 626 (Shareholders' derivative action brought in the right of the corporation to procure a judgment in its favor).

(3) Section 627 (Security for expenses in shareholders' derivative action brought in the right of the corporation to procure a judgment in its favor).

(4) Sections 721 (Exclusivity of statutory provisions for indemnification of directors and officers) through 727 (Insurance for indemnification of directors and officers), inclusive.

(5) Section 808 (Reorganization under act of Congress).

(6) Section 907 (Merger or consolidation of domestic and foreign corporations).

West's Annotated California Codes

Corporations Code
Title 1. Corporations
Division 1. General Corporation Law
Chapter 21. Foreign Corporations

§ 2115. Foreign corporations subject to corporate laws of state; tests to determine subject corporations; laws applicable; time of application

(a) A foreign corporation (other than a foreign association or foreign nonprofit corporation but including a foreign parent corporation even though it does not itself transact intrastate business) is subject to this section if the average of the property factor, the payroll factor and the sales factor (as defined in Sections 25129, 25132 and 25134 of the Revenue and Taxation Code) with respect to it is more than 50 percent during its latest full income year and if more than one-half of its outstanding voting securities are held of record by persons having addresses in this state. The property factor, payroll factor and sales factor shall be those used in computing the portion of its income allocable to this state in its franchise tax return or, with respect to corporations the allocation of whose income is governed by special formulas or which are not required to file separate or any tax returns, which would have been so used if they were governed by such three-factor formula. The determination of these factors with respect to any parent corporation shall be made on a consolidated basis, including in a unitary computation (after elimination of intercompany transactions) the property, payroll and sales of the parent and all of its subsidiaries in which it owns directly or indirectly more than 50 percent of the outstanding shares entitled to vote for the election of directors, but deducting a percentage of the property, payroll, and sales of any subsidiary equal to the percentage minority ownership, if any, in the subsidiary. For the purpose of this subdivision, any securities held to the knowledge of the issuer in the names of broker-dealers, nominees for broker-dealers, (including clearing corporations) or banks, associations, or other entities holding securities in a nominee name or otherwise on behalf of a beneficial owner (collectively "Nominee Holders"), shall not be considered outstanding. However, if the foreign corporation requests all Nominee Holders to certify, with respect to all beneficial owners for whom securities are held, the number of shares held for those beneficial owners having addresses (as shown on the records of the Nominee Holder) in this state and outside of this state, then all shares so certified shall be considered outstanding and held of record by persons having addresses either in this state or outside of this state as so certified, provided that the certification so provided shall be retained with the record of shareholders and made available for inspection and copying in the same manner as is provided in Section 1600 with respect to that record. A current list of beneficial owners of a foreign corporation's securities provided to the corporation by one or more Nominee Holders or their agent pursuant to the requirements of Rule 14b-1(c) or 14b-2(e) as adopted on December 9, 1986, promulgated under the Securities Exchange Act of 1934 shall constitute an acceptable certification with respect to beneficial owners for the purposes of this subdivision.

(b) The following chapters and sections of this division shall apply to a foreign corporation subject to this section (to the exclusion of the law of the jurisdiction in which it is incorporated):

Chapter 1 (general provisions and definitions), to the extent applicable to the following provisions;

Section 301 (annual election of directors);

Section 303 (removal of directors without cause);

Section 304 (removal of directors by court proceedings);

Section 305, subdivision (c) (filing of director vacancies where less than a majority in office elected by shareholders);

Section 309 (directors' standard of care);

Section 316 (excluding paragraph (3) of subdivision (a) and paragraph (3) of subdivision (f)) (liability of directors for unlawful distributions);

Section 317 (indemnification of directors, officers and others);

Sections 500 to 505, inclusive (limitations on corporate distributions in cash or property);

Section 506 (liability of shareholder who receives unlawful distribution);

Section 600, subdivisions (b) and (c) (requirement for annual shareholders' meeting and remedy if same not timely held);

Section 708, subdivisions (a), (b) and (c) (shareholder's right to cumulate votes at any election of directors);

Section 710 (supermajority vote requirement);

Section 1001, subdivision (d) (limitations on sale of assets);

Section 1101 (provisions following subdivision (e)) (limitations on mergers);

Chapter 12 (commencing with Section 1200) (reorganizations);

Chapter 13 (commencing with Section 1300) (dissenters' rights);

Sections 1500 and 1501 (records and reports);

Section 1508 (action by Attorney General);

Chapter 16 (commencing with Section 1600) (rights of inspection).

(c) Subdivision (a) shall become applicable to any foreign corporation only upon the first day of the first income year of the corporation commencing on or after the 30th day after the filing by it of the report pursuant to Section 2108 showing that the tests referred to in subdivision (a) have been met or on or after the entry of a final order by a court of competent jurisdiction declaring that such tests have been met.

(d) Subdivision (a) shall cease to be applicable at the end of any income year during which a report pursuant to Section 2108 shall have been filed showing that at least one of the tests referred to in subdivision (a) is not met or a final order shall have been entered by a court of competent jurisdiction declaring that one of such tests is not met, provided that such filing or order shall be ineffective if a contrary report or order shall be made or entered before the end of such income year.

(e) This section does not apply to any corporation (1) with outstanding securities listed on the New York Stock Exchange or the American Stock Exchange, or (2) with outstanding securities designated as qualified for trading as a national market security on the National Association of Securities Dealers Automatic Quotation System (or any successor national market system) if such corporation has at least 800 holders of its equity securities as of the record date of its most recent annual meeting of shareholders, or (3) if all of its voting shares (other than directors' qualifying shares) are owned directly or indirectly by a corporation or corporations not subject to this section. For purposes of determining the number of holders of a corporation's equity securities under clause (2) of this subdivision, there shall be included, in addition to the number of recordholders reflected on the corporation's stock records, the number of holders of the equity securities held in the name of any Nominee Holder which furnishes the corporation with a certification pursuant to subdivision (a) provided that the corporation retains the certification with the record of shareholders and makes it available for inspection and copying in the same manner as is provided in Section 1600 with respect to that record.

Comments

Consider whether the approach adopted by New York and California is incompatible with the approach of the foundation doctrine of the Restatement (Second) Conflict of Laws and traditional corporate law. Does the approach make sense in the American regulatory context? The importance of this new approach (from the American perspective) is that it may resemble the traditionally applied approach of many European countries with respect to the determination of the law applicable to the internal governance of a corporation. Consider the extent to which the approach of California and New York actually mimics the "*siege social*" approach of the majority of the member states of the European Communities. The European approach is discussed below. The reaction of traditional American jurisdictions to the "siege social" approach has not been positive.

The cases below set out the major arguments in support of and in opposition to the approach, as well as the judicial complexities which arise from these issues. *Arden-Mayfair* shows the difficulty for corporations faced with collateral attacks on the structure of their governance on the basis of the pseudo-foreign corporations laws of non-state of incorporation jurisdictions. Wilson v. Louisiana-Pacific Resources, Ltd., 187 Cal. Rptr. 852 (Cal. App. 1982)) and Havlicek v. Coast-to-Coast Analytical Services, 46 Cal. Rptr. 2d 696 (Cal. App. 1995) are examples of the ways in which the courts of California have essentially justified the imposition by California of a form of the siege social rule in the United States. McDermott, Inc. v. Lewis, 531 A.2d 206 (Del. 1987) provides a spirited legal and constitutional defense of the incorporation or foundation regime.

Arden-Mayfair, Inc., et al. v. Louart Corp., et al.

434 F.Supp. 580
United States District Court, D. Delaware.
July 19, 1977

CALEB M. WRIGHT, Senior District Judge.

I. INTRODUCTION

This declaratory judgment action was originally filed in state court and removed to this Court pursuant to 28 U.S.C. §§ 1441 and 1446 by petition filed on March 15, 1977. Presently before the Court is plaintiff's Motion to Remand.[1] Remand is sought on the grounds that this Court lacks jurisdiction because the action does not present a federal question and that the removal was defective because of the failure of some defendants to join in the removal petition. The Court concludes that it does not have federal question jurisdiction of this case, and in light of this conclusion, it is unnecessary to discuss the failure of some defendants to join in the removal petition.

---

1. Shortly after removal, certain defendants filed a Motion to Dismiss on the ground that under Barber-Greene Co. v. Walco National Corp., 428 F.Supp. 567 (D.Del.1977), the Court lacked jurisdiction due to the impropriety of substituted service under 10 Del.C. § 365. Shortly thereafter, plaintiffs filed the instant Motion to Remand. The Court conducted independent research and gave full consideration to letter memoranda filed by the parties on the issue of which motion should be disposed of first. Finding authority in support of both sequences, see Walker v. Savell, 335 F.2d 536 (5th Cir. 1964), and Moltke v. Intercontinental Shipping Corp., 86 F.Supp. 662 (S.D.N.Y.1949), the Court agreed with Judge Tuttle that "it may be that the district court should be free to dispose of the case upon whichever of the two grounds may appear to it to be the more convenient." Walker v. Savell, supra at 539, quoting from Garden Homes v. Mason, 238 F.2d 651, 654 (1st Cir. 1956). The Court informed counsel by letter dated May 13, 1977 that in this case it was more appropriate to dispose of the Motion to Remand first in that the Court felt "an obligation to address issues relevant to and only relevant to its own jurisdiction before addressing issues relevant to the jurisdiction of both the state court and this Court."

II. BACKGROUND

Plaintiff, Arden-Mayfair, a Delaware corporation, brought this action in state court naming as defendants (1) Louart Corporation, a California corporation, and a substantial shareholder of Arden-Mayfair, Marshall I. Kass, and Henry L. Melczer, Louart's President and Vice-President (collectively "the Louart defendants"); (2) each of Arden-Mayfair's incumbent directors; (3) nine named Delaware resident Arden-Mayfair shareholders; and (4) John Doe 1 to John Doe 12,000 intended to represent individually and as class action representatives Arden-Mayfair shareholders.

The underlying controversy in this case is a direct result of recent California legislation which became effective January 1, 1977, expanding applicability of the California General Corporation Law ("G.C.L."). Section 2115 of the G.C.L. makes corporations not incorporated in California, which have no "outstanding securities listed on any national securities exchange", subject to certain provisions of the G.C.L. governing internal corporate affairs if: "... the average of the property factor, the payroll factor and the sales factor (as defined in Sections 25129, 25132 and 25134 of the Revenue and Taxation Code) with respect to it is more than 50 percent during its latest full income year and if more than one-half of its outstanding voting securities are held of record by persons having addresses in this state (California)." §2115(a). Any corporation which satisfies the above tests is required by §301(a) of the G.C.L. to conduct annual election of the entire board of directors, and under §708(a) thereof to permit cumulative voting with respect to the election of directors.[2]

Arden-Mayfair is a Delaware corporation. Under its Certificate of Incorporation and by-laws, it prohibits cumulative voting. It maintains a staggered board of directors whereby three directors are elected annually for terms of three years. These provisions are conceded by the Louart defendants to be valid under the General Corporation Law of Delaware. Thus, should Arden-Mayfair satisfy the tests set forth in §2115 of the G.C.L., the requirements of the California law would be in direct conflict with certain aspects of Arden-Mayfair's current internal corporate structure as sanctioned by Delaware law.

By letter dated December 30, 1976, Louart Corporation notified Arden-Mayfair of the impending effectiveness of the above described changes in the G.C.L. and stated its position that Arden-Mayfair satisfied the tests set forth in §2115 and that it was therefore required to comply with the requirements of the California law in the conduct of its 1977 annual meeting. Apparently in response, Arden-Mayfair filed this declaratory judgment action in the Court of Chancery of the State of Delaware in and for New Castle County "to set at rest the conflicting claims and contentions of the parties." (Complaint P 20). The Louart defendants removed the case to this Court by petition filed March 15, 1977, claiming jurisdiction under 28 U.S.C. §1331(a). Arden-Mayfair has moved to remand on the ground that federal jurisdiction is lacking under that provision, in that the case is not one which "arises under the Constitution, laws, or treaties of the United States."

III. FEDERAL QUESTION

The removal statute provides, inter alia : "Except as otherwise expressly provided by Act of Congress, any civil action brought in a State court of which the district courts of

2. G.C.L. §708(a) allows a shareholder to "cumulate such shareholder's votes and give one candidate a number of votes equal to the number of directors to be elected multiplied by the number of votes to which the shareholder's shares are entitled, or distribute the shareholder's votes on the same principle among as many candidates as the shareholder thinks fit."

the United States have original jurisdiction, may be removed by the defendant or the defendants, to the district court of the United States...." 28 U.S.C. § 1441(a). "Any civil action of which the district courts have original jurisdiction founded on a claim or right arising under the Constitution, treaties or laws of the United States shall be removable without regard to the citizenship or residence of the parties." 28 U.S.C. § 1441(b). "Thus, in order to remove a civil action from the state court pursuant to this statute, the District Court of the United States must have original jurisdiction of the action." Coulston v. Int'l Brotherhood of Teamsters, etc., 423 F.Supp. 882, 883 (E.D.Pa.1976). The Louart defendants in their removal petition, Docket Item No. 1, at P 5, and in their briefs and oral argument rely exclusively on 28 U.S.C.§ 1331(a) as providing this Court with original jurisdiction. That section provides: "The district courts shall have original jurisdiction of all civil actions wherein the matter in controversy exceeds the sum or value of $10,000, exclusive of interest and costs, and arises under the Constitution, laws, or treaties of the United States." The value of the amount in controversy appears to exceed the jurisdictional minimum and the focus of the Court's inquiry is whether or not this case "arises under the Constitution... of the United States."

There are several well established tests which must be considered in determining whether a given case arises under federal law. (A) right or immunity created by the Constitution or laws of the United States must be an element, and an essential one, of the plaintiff's cause of action. The right or immunity must be such that it will be supported if the Constitution or laws of the United States are given one construction or effect, and defeated if they receive another. A genuine and present controversy not merely a possible or conjectural one, must exist with reference thereto, and the controversy must be disclosed upon the face of the complaint, unaided by the answer or the petition for removal. Indeed, the complaint itself will not avail as a basis of jurisdiction insofar as it goes beyond a statement of the plaintiff's cause of action and anticipates or replies to a probable defense. Gully v. First Nat'l Bank, 299 U.S. 109, 112–113, 57 S.Ct. 96, 97, 81 L.Ed. 70 (1936) (citations omitted).[3]

This last test, limiting inquiry to the "well-pleaded" portions of the complaint, i. e., those portions which are necessary to plaintiffs' claim and do not anticipate or reply to a defense,[4] is "deceptively simple", since its application "necessarily introduces into the process of determining jurisdiction the question of what is well-pleaded and with it, a host of procedural rules and distinctions." Mishkin, The Federal "Question" in the District Courts, 53 Colum.L.Rev. 157, 176 (1953). "(T)he rule has been heavily criticized for making the existence of federal jurisdiction depend on technicalities that are irrelevant to the interests underlying federal jurisdiction and for requiring adherence to pleading niceties rejected for civil practice." Goldberg, The Influence of Procedural Rules of Federal Jurisdiction, 28 Stan.L.Rev. 397, 410–411 (1976) (citations omitted).

As difficult and complex as the application of this test is to a traditional lawsuit, it is far more so in a declaratory judgment action. Skelly Oil Co. v. Phillips Petroleum Co., 339 U.S. 667, 70 S.Ct. 876, 94 L.Ed. 1194 (1950) was a declaratory judgment action in which the plaintiff sought a declaration that certain contracts it had with defendant

3. The continuing importance of these rules was reaffirmed recently by the Supreme Court in Phillips Petroleum Co. v. Texaco, Inc., 415 U.S. 125, 94 S.Ct. 1002, 39 L.Ed.2d 209 (1974); and Oneida Indian Nation of New York v. County of Oneida, New York, 414 U.S. 661, 94 S.Ct. 772, 39 L.Ed.2d 73 (1974).

4. A classic application of this rule may be found in Louisville & Nashville R.R. v. Mottley, 211 U.S. 149, 29 S.Ct. 42, 53 L.Ed. 126 (1908).

were still in effect and binding. The continued validity of the contracts turned on whether or not plaintiff had received a certificate of public convenience and necessity from the Federal Power Commission under The Natural Gas Act, 15 U.S.C. §717f(c). Justice Frankfurter, observing that the Declaratory Judgment Act is procedural only, in that it enlarges the range of remedies but does not extend jurisdiction, ruled that the jurisdictional issue "must be determined without regard to the procedural possibilities made available by the Declaratory Judgment Act." Bills v. Shaw, Hooker & Co., 398 F.Supp. 161, 163 n. 4 (N.D.Cal.1975). See, Potomac Passengers Ass'n v. Chesapeake & Ohio Railway Co., 171 U.S.App.D.C. 359, 520 F.2d 91, 96–97 (1975). Since the federal issue would have arisen only by way of defense had the suit been a coercive action for damages or enforcement of the contracts, the Court held that the case did not "arise under" federal law, saying: "To sanction suits for declaratory relief as within the jurisdiction of the District Courts merely because, as in this case, artful pleading anticipates a defense based on federal law would contravene the whole trend of jurisdictional legislation by Congress, disregard the effective functioning of the federal judicial system and distort the limited procedural purpose of the Declaratory Judgment Act." 339 U.S. at 673–74, 70 S.Ct. at 880.

The refusal to allow federal question jurisdiction to be enlarged by declaratory judgment actions was reiterated in Public Service Commission v. Wycoff Co., Inc., 344 U.S. 237, 73 S.Ct. 236, 97 L.Ed. 291 (1952)....

Notwithstanding these pronouncements, a number of courts have apparently disregarded this approach and entertained declaratory judgment actions in which the plaintiffs were attempting to establish defenses based on federal law to threatened actions based on state law.[5] Nonetheless, it is well established that a declaratory judgment action seeking to establish the invalidity of a threatened claim based on federal law "arises under" federal law,[6] while a declaratory judgment action seeking to establish a federal defense to a threatened proceeding based on state law does not.[7]

Applying these principles to the instant case mandates the conclusion that if this action had been brought initially in federal court, it would not have been within federal question jurisdiction. The complaint seeks a declaration that "the claims and contentions asserted by Arden-Mayfair as hereinabove alleged are valid and the claims and contentions of any defendants to the contrary are invalid." Complaint at 9–10. The defendants assert that the G.C.L. applies to the plaintiff corporation and requires it, inter alia, to have annual elections of the entire board, and to allow cumulative voting. The

5. *See* General Foods Corp. v. Henderson, 334 F.Supp. 19 (D.N.M.1971); Zaconick v. City of Hollywood, 85 F.Supp. 52 (S.D.Fla.1949); Regents of N.M. College of Agriculture and Mechanic Arts v. Albuquerque Broadcasting Co., 158 F.2d 900 (10th Cir. 1947); Rambusch Decorating Co. v. Brotherhood of Painters, Decorators and Paperhangers of Amer., 105 F.2d 134 (2nd Cir. 1939); and Teeval, Inc. v. City of New York, 92 F.Supp. 827 (S.D.N.Y.1949). *See also*, Serio v. Liss, 300 F.2d 386, 391–92 (3rd Cir. 1961) (Hastie, J. dissenting).

6. *See, e.g.*, Tokyo Shibaura Elec. Co., Ltd. v. Zenith Radio Corp., 548 F.2d 88 (3rd Cir. 1977); Thiokol Chemical Corp. v. Burlington Ind., Inc., 448 F.2d 1328 (3rd Cir. 1971), cert. denied, 404 U.S. 1019, 92 S.Ct. 684, 30 L.Ed.2d 668 (1972); First Nat'l Bk. of Shawnee Mission v. Roeland Park State Bk. and Tr. Co., 357 F.Supp. 708 (D.Kan.1973).

7. *See, e.g.*, Allegheny Airlines, Inc. v. Pennsylvania Pub. Util. Com'n, 465 F.2d 237 (3rd Cir. 1972); McCorkle v. First Pennsylvania Banking and Trust Co., 459 F.2d 243 (4th Cir. 1972); Chandler v. O'Bryan, 445 F.2d 1045 (10th Cir. 1971); Daniel Hale Williams Memorial Health Foundation v. City of Chicago, 407 F.Supp. 342 (N.D.Ill.1976); Bills v. Shaw, Hooker & Co., 398 F.Supp. 161 (N.D.Cal.1975); Safeguard Mutual Ins. Co. v. Commonwealth of Pennsylvania, 372 F.Supp. 939 (E.D.Pa.1974).

plaintiff contends that its internal affairs are subject to regulation by the corporate laws of Delaware, the state in which it is incorporated, and that a wide variety of constitutional provisions would be abridged if it were required to comply with the G.C.L. as well. Plaintiff is relying on Delaware state law and the United States Constitution, in support of its position while defendant has asserted rights only under California state law. Had defendant initiated the threatened coercive action and sought an order requiring the plaintiff to comply with the provisions of the G.C.L., its claim would have been based entirely on state law, with the federal issue being introduced only by way of defense when plaintiff asserted its constitutional claim. As discussed above, in that situation, there would be no federal question jurisdiction.

* * *

Accordingly, plaintiff's Motion to Remand is granted.

Comments and Questions

1. *Arden-Mayfair* suggests that a corporation may not file pre-emptively in a federal court any action which seeks to vindicate its right to be governed strictly by the laws of the state of its incorporation. The well pleaded complaint rule and its application to declaratory judgement actions foreclose that option.

2. But why not file in state court? The problem in this case is that the court may not be able to assert personal jurisdiction over all of the parties. Indeed that seemed to be the problem in this case. The result was some fairly interesting procedural hurdles for the Delaware courts as recounted by A. Gilchrist Sparks, III, in David Jackson, Joseph B. Frumkin, *The Global Role of Corporate Law*, 25 Del. J. Corp. L. 106, 130 (2000):[1]

> There was a case called Arden-Mayfair v. Louart Corp.[16] Arden-Mayfair was a Delaware corporation that did not provide for cumulative voting in its charter and had an insurgent, Louart, that wanted to have cumulative voting. The company qualified for requirements of the California pseudo-corporation law, which mandated cumulative voting.[17] There was an action in California in which the insurgent sought a declaratory judgment that cumulative voting was required.[18] An action was brought by Arden-Mayfair in Delaware to ask then Chancellor Brown to declare that Delaware law governed such that there was no cumulative voting.[19]
>
> The party that was causing the trouble, the plaintiff in the California action, refused to appear in Delaware.[20] Louart was not a Delaware corporation. So Chancellor Brown was faced with the question of how to proceed to adjudicate this very real controversy which directly challenged the internal affairs doctrine, which is the core of why our law governs how Delaware corporations are run, notwithstanding the absence of an adverse party before the court.

---

1. Mr. Sparks was a commentator on a panel on The Global Role of Corporate Law as part of a Symposium on the Next Century of Corporate Law, May 20, 1999.

16. 385 A.2d 3 (Del. Ch. 1978).

17. *Id.* at 3–4.

18. Palmer v. Arden-Mayfair, Inc., No. 5549, 1978 Del. Ch. LEXIS 699, at *7 (Del. Ch. June 20, 1978).

19. Louart Corp., 385 A.2d at 4.

20. *Id.*

Chancellor Brown appointed an amicus to argue the side of the absent raider, who had refused to come into Delaware.[21] And that case was fully litigated. It was resolved. It was resolved in favor of Delaware law in Delaware.[22] The lower court in California resolved it in favor of California law. But an intermediate court in California respected Delaware law and, therefore, the case never made it to the U.S. Supreme Court where I figured it was headed if we had kept down the original track.

3. Why not wait for an action to enforce the pseudo-foreign corporation statute? The answer to that question, perhaps, lies in the *Wilson* case which follows. As you read the case, ask yourself whether the decision of that case was foregone once the California courts were asked to consider the question. Are state court reluctant to void local statutory law? In connection, consider how the Delaware courts might have decided *Wilson.* The Delaware approach is illustrated in *McDermott v. Lewis*, reproduced below.

Ross A. Wilson, Plaintiff and Respondent, v. Louisiana-Pacific Resources, Inc., Defendant and Appellant

Civ. 48939.
Court of Appeal, First District, Division 2.
Dec. 17, 1982; As Modified Jan. 11, 1983.
Hearing Denied Feb. 16, 1983.
138 Cal.App.3d 216, 187 Cal.Rptr. 852

GRODIN, Presiding Justice.

The question presented by this appeal, one of first impression and considerable significance, is whether the State of California may constitutionally impose its law requiring cumulative voting by shareholders upon a corporation which is domiciled elsewhere, but whose contacts with California, as measured by various criteria, are greater than those with any other jurisdiction.

Section 2115 of the California Corporations Code[1] provides for the application of various provisions of that code to a foreign corporation which (on the basis of a three-factor formula including property, payroll and sales) does a majority of its business in this state, where in addition a majority of its outstanding voting securities are held of record by persons having addresses in this state. Among the provisions are subdivisions (a), (b) and (c) of section 708,[2] which provide for cumulative voting.

---

21. Palmer, 1978 Del. Ch. LEXIS 699, at *10.

22. *Id.* at *25.

1. Unless otherwise noted, all references are to the Corporations Code. Section 2115 [is set forth in the materials reproduced above].

2. Section 708, as relevant, provides: "(a) Every shareholder complying with subdivision (b) and entitled to vote at any election of directors may cumulate such shareholder's votes and give one candidate a number of votes equal to the number of directors to be elected multiplied by the number of votes to which the shareholder's shares are normally entitled, or distribute the shareholder's votes on the same principle among as many candidates as the shareholder thinks fit. "(b) No shareholder shall be entitled to cumulate votes (i.e., cast for any candidate a number of votes greater than the number of votes which such shareholder normally is entitled to cast) unless such candidate or candidates' names have been placed in nomination prior to the voting and the shareholder has given notice at the meeting prior to the voting of the shareholder's intention to cumulate the shareholder's votes. If any one shareholder has given such notice, all shareholders may cumulate their votes for

Plaintiff Ross A. Wilson brought this action against Louisiana-Pacific Resources, Inc., a Utah corporation, seeking a declaratory judgment that the defendant met the tests of section 2115, and that he was therefore entitled to cumulative voting in accordance with section 708. The trial court found that in the years preceding the action, the average of the defendant's property, payroll, and sales in California as defined by the California corporations statute exceeded 50 percent, and that more than 50 percent of its shareholders entitled to vote resided in California, so that the statutory conditions had been met. It also found that except for being domiciled in Utah and having a transfer agent there, defendant had virtually no business connection with Utah, that its principal place of business has been in California since at least 1971, that its meetings of shareholders and directors are held in California, and that all of its employees and all of its bank accounts are in California. Finally, the court concluded, contrary to defendant's contentions, that there existed no constitutional obstacle to the application of the cumulative voting requirement to defendant, and that its "[c]umulative voting will be in effect a judicial addendum to defendant's articles of incorporation, and all of its shareholders are entitled to cumulative voting whether they are California residents or not."

Defendant appealed from this judgment, challenging the trial court's finding that the statutory criterion with respect to shareholder residency had been met and renewing its constitutional challenges as well. During the pendency of the appeal, the California Corporations Commissioner certified the Pacific Stock Exchange, upon which appellant's securities are listed, under subdivision (o) of section 25100. This action made section 2115 inapplicable to defendant. (s 2115, subd. (e).) Both parties strenuously urge us, however, to decide the constitutional issues presented, since there appear to be no published decisions on the constitutionality of section 2115. Appellant, moreover, urges that these issues are not moot as to it, since delisting from the Pacific Stock Exchange is a possibility, and since it is contemplating acquisition of new businesses in California which might be subject to section 2115. Because the constitutional issues presented are of general public interest and are likely to recur, we have decided to confront them as the parties request. (DeRonde v. Regents of University of California (1981) 28 Cal.3d 875, 880, 172 Cal.Rptr. 677, 625 P.2d 220; North San Diego County Transit Development Bd. v. Vial (1981) 117 Cal.App.3d 27, 31, 172 Cal.Rptr. 440; Grasko v. Los Angeles City Board of Education (1973) 31 Cal.App.3d 290, 299, 107 Cal.Rptr. 334.)

Discussion

The law of the State of Utah provides for straight voting in an election of directors, but permits cumulative voting if the articles of incorporation so provide. (Utah Bus.Corp.Act (1953) § 16-10-31.) Neither the articles of incorporation nor the bylaws of appellant provide for cumulative voting. Appellant contends that for California to require cumulative voting under these circumstances would violate (1) the full faith and credit clause of the United States Constitution; (2) the commerce clause of the United States Constitution; (3) the "property and vested right protections" of the United States and California Constitutions; (4) the contract clauses of the United States and California Constitutions; and (5) the equal protection clause of the United States Constitution.

---

candidates in nomination. "(c) In any election of directors, the candidates receiving the highest number of votes of the shares entitled to be voted for them up to the number of directors to be elected by such shares are elected."

Finally, appellant challenges the trial court's declaration concerning the impact of section 2115 on its articles. We consider these contentions in turn.

I. Full Faith and Credit

The full faith and credit clause of the federal Constitution (art. IV, § 1) requires that "Full Faith and Credit...be given in each State to the public Acts, Records, and Judicial Proceedings of every other State...." Although the phrase "public Acts, Records and Judicial Proceedings" has been construed to include statutes as well as judicial decisions (e.g., Bradford Elec. Co. v. Clapper (1932) 286 U.S. 145, 52 S.Ct. 571, 76 L.Ed. 1026), the Supreme Court has recognized that "[a] rigid and literal enforcement of the full faith and credit clause, without regard to the statute of the forum, would lead to the absurd result that, wherever the conflict arises, the statute of each state must be enforced in the courts of the other, but cannot be in its own. Unless by force of that clause a greater effect is thus to be given to a state statute abroad than the clause permits it to have at home, it is unavoidable that this Court determine for itself the extent to which the statute of one state may qualify or deny rights asserted under the statute of another." (Alaska Packers Assn. v. Comm'n (1935) 294 U.S. 532, 547, 55 S.Ct. 518, 523, 79 L.Ed. 1044.)

Under the doctrine of Alaska Packers, supra, determination as to application of conflicting statutes was to be made "by appraising the governmental interests of each jurisdiction, and turning the scale of decision according to their weight." (294 U.S. at p. 547, 55 S.Ct. at p. 523.) In this balancing process it was presumed that "every state is entitled to enforce in its own courts its own statutes, lawfully enacted. One who challenges that right, because of the force given to a conflicting statute of another state by the full faith and credit clause, assumes the burden of showing, upon some rational basis, that of the conflicting interests involved those of the foreign state are superior to those of the forum." (Id., at pp. 547–548, 55 S.Ct. at p. 523.)

Since Alaska Packers, the Supreme Court has abandoned the weighing-of-interests requirement in favor of a less exacting standard corresponding to the requirements of the due process clause. (Allstate Ins. Co. v. Hague (1981) 449 U.S. 302, 308, fn. 10, 101 S.Ct. 633, 637, fn. 10, 66 L.Ed.2d 521.) In determining whether a state's choice-of-law decision exceeds federal constitutional requirements, the current rule is that "for a State's substantive law to be selected in a constitutionally permissible manner, that State must have a significant contact or significant aggregation of contacts, creating state interests, such that choice of its law is neither arbitrary nor fundamentally unfair." (Id., at pp. 312–313, 101 S.Ct. at p. 640.)

We consider that test is met here; the criteria which a foreign corporation must meet in order to be subject to section 2115 assure the existence of significant aggregation of contacts. And the state interests created by those contacts are indeed substantial. California's present law requiring cumulative voting by shareholders continues in effect a policy which has existed in this state since the Constitution of 1879.[3] In Western Air

---

3. Article XII, section 12 of the 1879 Constitution provided: "In all elections for directors or managers of corporations, every stockholder shall have the right to vote, in person or by proxy, the number of shares of stock owned by him, for as many persons as there are directors or managers to be elected, or to cumulate said shares and give one candidate as many votes as the number of directors multiplied by the number of his shares of stock shall equal, or to distribute them, on the same principle, among as many candidates as he shall think fit; and such directors or managers shall not be elected in any other manner, except that members of cooperative societies formed for agricultural, mercantile, and manufacturing purposes, may vote on all questions affecting such societies in manner prescribed by law." Although this constitutional provision was repealed in 1930 (Stats.1931,

Lines, Inc. v. Sobieski (1961) 191 Cal.App.2d 399, 12 Cal.Rptr. 719, the court, observing that "[i]t would seem too evident to require protracted dissertation that the right of cumulative voting is a substantial right" (id., at p. 414, 12 Cal.Rptr. 719), held that even in the absence of express statutory mandate, the Corporations Commissioner was justified in refusing to permit the elimination of cumulative voting by a "pseudo foreign" corporation, i.e., "one with its technical domicile outside of this state but one which exercises most of its corporate vitality within this state." (Id., at p. 412, 12 Cal.Rptr. 719.) A contrary holding, the court reasoned, "would enable a foreign corporation to destroy the rights which the State of California has deemed worthy of protection by the enactment of the Corporate Securities Act." (Id., at pp. 413–414, 12 Cal.Rptr. 719.) Section 2115 incorporates the policy reflected in Sobieski and applies it more generally, to all pseudo-foreign corporations meeting the statutory criteria.

Utah, on the other hand, has no interests which are offended by cumulative voting; and, whatever interest it might have in maintaining a laissez faire policy on that score would seem to be clearly outweighed by the interests of California, in which a majority of shareholders and the corporation's business activity is located. Thus, even on the earlier analysis of Alaska Packers, the full faith and credit clause provides no bar to the application of California's statute.[4]

Appellant relies upon Broderick v. Rosner (1935) 294 U.S. 629, 55 S.Ct. 589, 79 L.Ed. 1100, which held that the full faith and credit clause required a New Jersey court to entertain a suit by a New York corporation seeking assessment from shareholders pursuant to a New York statute, despite a New Jersey law which barred suits based on foreign assessment statutes. That case, however, is explainable on the basis that while New York had a clear interest in the application of its policy, New Jersey "had declared no conflicting policy of protecting its residents, as stockholders, against such liability. Neither had it suggested any reason relating to the administration of its courts why actions to enforce such liability should not be brought in New Jersey. It had only a pretended concern for the procedural aspects of such actions...." (B. Currie, Selected Essays on the Conflict of Laws (1963) 347; see also Ross, "Full Faith and Credit" in a Federal System (1936) 20 Minn.L.Rev. 140, 178 ["It is submitted the case of Broderick v. Rosner goes no further than to hold that a state may not deny recovery on foreign facts when its own domestic law would award recovery on parallel facts occurring within its own borders"].) Even if there were vitality left in Broderick after Allstate (and it is perhaps significant that it is not cited in the latter case), Broderick is clearly distinguishable from a situation such as this, involving the application of an explicit state policy of substance to a pseudo-foreign corporation with its "center of gravity" (cf. Hanson v. Denckla (1958) 357 U.S. 235, 254, 78 S.Ct. 1228, 1240, 2 L.Ed.2d 1283) in this state.

---

p. lvi), the General Corporation Law in 1931 continued the right of cumulative voting formerly guaranteed by the Constitution (Stats.1931, ch. 862, § 320, pp. 1780–1781). In the new California General Corporations Law, which became effective January 1, 1977, the Legislature rejected a State Bar committee's recommendation that cumulative voting be permissive (*see* Mattes, *The Burden of the Corporate Director Elected Noncumulatively* (1975) 63 CAL.L.REV. 463, 464), and retained the state's mandatory policy (*see* Corp.Code, § 708, added by Stats.1975, ch. 682, § 7, p. 1569).

4. Justice Stevens, in his concurring opinion in Allstate Ins. Co. v. Hague, *supra*, 449 U.S. at pp. 320–332, 101 S.Ct. at pp. 644–650, would have the court distinguish between whether the state of the forum is required by the full faith and credit clause to apply the law of a different state, and whether it is prevented by the due process clause, from applying its own law. While we need not decide the question here, it would appear that California's interests are sufficient to require the application of its statute by any state which considers the issue.

The "internal affairs doctrine," according to which courts traditionally looked to the law of the state of incorporation in resolving questions regarding a corporation's internal affairs (see Oldham, California Regulates Pseudo-Foreign Corporations—Trampling Upon the Tramp? (1977) 17 Santa Clara L.Rev. 85, 85–90), has no application here. That doctrine has never been followed blindly in California (see Wait v. Kern River Mining etc. Co. (1909) 157 Cal. 16, 21, 106 P. 98; see also Western Air Lines, Inc. v. Sobieski, supra, 191 Cal.App.2d 399, 12 Cal.Rptr. 719); it is inconsistent with the "comparative impairment" approach used by this state in resolving conflict of law problems (Offshore Rental Co. v. Continental Oil Co. (1978) 22 Cal.3d 157, 164–165, 148 Cal.Rptr. 867, 583 P.2d 721); and it is in any event not determinative of the constitutional issue. This is not a common choice-of-law question; the Legislature has resolved the conflicts issue by mandating application of this state's law under certain conditions. The question is whether that mandate is constitutional. (See Allstate Ins. Co. v. Hague, supra, 449 U.S. at pp. 307–308, 101 S.Ct. at p. 637.) For the reasons we have discussed, we conclude that it is, so far as the full faith and credit clause is concerned.

II. Commerce Clause

Although Article I, section 8, clause 3 of the federal Constitution grants Congress power "[t]o regulate commerce... among the several States," Congress has not chosen to regulate the subject in litigation here nor has it undertaken to establish guidelines for regulation by the states. Appellant's commerce clause argument is based, therefore, upon the negative implications of dormant congressional authority.

The United States Supreme Court has established the standard for determining the validity of state statutes in such situations: "Where the statute regulates even-handedly to effectuate a legitimate local public interest, and its effects on interstate commerce are only incidental, it will be upheld unless the burden imposed on such commerce is clearly excessive in relation to the putative local benefits. [Citation.] If a legitimate local purpose is found, then the question becomes one of degree. And the extent of the burden that will be tolerated will of course depend on the nature of the local interest involved, and on whether it could be promoted as well with a lesser impact on interstate activities." (Pike v. Bruce Church, Inc. (1970) 397 U.S. 137, 142, 90 S.Ct. 844, 847, 25 L.Ed.2d 174; see also, Raymond Motor Transportation, Inc. v. Rice (1978) 434 U.S. 429, 441–442, 98 S.Ct. 787, 794, 54 L.Ed.2d 664.)

We observe, initially, that the challenged statute "regulates even-handedly" within the meaning of the Pike guidelines; it applies to covered foreign corporations the same rules which are applied to corporations domiciled within the state. The statute thus imposes no special or distinct burden upon out-of-state interests. (See Tribe, American Constitutional Law (1978) pp. 326–327.)

The nature, strength, and duration of California's interest in the cumulative voting principle, and in the application of that principle to pseudo-foreign corporations have previously been considered in this opinion. There remain to be considered the effects of that application upon interstate activities.

One effect of section 2115 may well be to deter corporations from making their legal homes elsewhere for the purpose of avoiding California's protective corporate legislation, and thus to diminish the practice of "charter-mongering" among states (see Jennings, The Role of the States in Corporate Regulation and Investor Protection (1958) 23 Law & Contemp.Prob. 193, 194–196); but that, presumably, is not an effect which would offend the policies of the commerce clause; and appellant does not so contend. Rather, appellant contends that the application of cumulative voting requirements to pseudo-foreign corporations as provided by section 2115 will have the effect of causing it and other foreign corporations already operating in California to reduce their property, payroll, and sales in this state below the 50 percent level, and will deter foreign corporations contemplating the transaction of business in this state from increasing their business activities above that level.

There is no suggestion, or evidence, that section 2115 was adopted for the purpose of deterring foreign corporations from doing business in this state; nor is there any direct evidence that it has had or will have such an effect. On the contrary, what evidence there is in the record on this point consists of testimony by appellant's president that he knew of no adverse effect on appellant's business which would be caused by cumulative voting.

Appellant argues that adverse consequences are predictable from "potentially conflicting claims of shareholders as to which state [law] governs" the method of voting by shareholders,[5] and from the "transient nature of the applicability of the California statute." It is perhaps true that "[i]n corporation law, uncertainty about what the law is or what law is applicable to a given transaction constitutes a far more serious problem than in areas of the law which do not require comprehensive and continuous planning." (Halloran & Hammer, Section 2115 of the New California General Corporation Law—The Application of California Corporation Law to Foreign Corporations (1976) 23 UCLA L.Rev. 1282, 1283.) Professor Kaplan advises, however, that while the specter of "unbearable chaos and uncertainty" resulting from dual or variable sets of rules constitutes the "primary argument against the application of local law to a foreign corporation," the "precise details of such confusion are seldom stated," and the argument is "seldom challenged, though it is probably neither so cogent nor so compelling as it might at first seem." (Kaplan, Foreign Corporations and Local Corporate Policy (1968) 21 Vand.L.Rev. 433, 476.) Professor Kaplan observes that no such unbearable confusion has appeared from the operations of the New York statutes imposing certain duties upon foreign corporations, and opines that the "contention of the Restatement and of other commentators that avoidance of confusion and difficulty makes it imperative to look to the law of the state of incorporation seems belied by the experience of New York." He notes also that while extensive overlaps in state and federal regulation of many corporate matters, particularly in the area of corporate internal affairs, "has created a situation of theoretical conflict, the practical results have been accepted and viable, and the duplication of controls has resulted not so much in conflict as in cumulative standards." (Id., at pp. 476–477, fn. omitted.)

The potential for conflict and resulting uncertainty from California's statute is substantially minimized by the nature of the criteria specified in section 2115. A corporation can do a majority of its business in only one state at a time; and it can have a majority of its shareholders resident in only one state at a time. If a corporation meets those requirements in this state, no other state is in a position to regulate the method of voting by shareholders on the basis of the same or similar criteria. It might also be said that no other state could claim as great an interest in doing so.[6] In any event, it does not

5. Appellant's argument is actually broader than we have stated it, encompassing other provisions of the Corporations Code made applicable to pseudo-foreign corporations by section 2115. For purposes of this case, however, it is necessary to consider only the cumulative voting requirement.

6. The high threshold requirements of section 2115 distinguish this case from Edgar v. MITE Corp. (1982) — U.S. —, 102 S.Ct. 2629, 72 L.Ed.2d 269, where the United States Supreme Court struck down an Illinois statute regulating tender offers as violative of the commerce clause. The Illi-

appear that any other state has attempted to do so.[7] If California's statute were replicated in all states, no conflict would result. We conclude that the potential for conflict is, on this record, speculative and without substance.

What appellant refers to as the "transient nature" of the statute's applicability, i.e., its application from year to year based upon the prior year's activity, could conceivably be a problem for a corporation whose business activity within the state fluctuated widely, but the "worst-case" scenario—that such a corporation might find it necessary to adopt cumulative voting as a means of assuring compliance on a continuing basis—does not appear to be so burdensome as to result in a significant restraint upon commerce among the states. We are not told, for example, of any diminution of activity in this state by foreign corporations as a result of Western Air Lines, Inc. v. Sobieski, supra, 191 Cal.App.2d 399, 12 Cal.Rptr. 719.

Commentators have generally applauded the California Legislature for "providing an apparently simple and thorough determination of state interest in foreign corporations," thus resolving the uncertainties which resulted from Western Air Lines, Inc. v. Sobieski, supra (Comment, California's New General Corporation Law: Quasi-Foreign Corporations (1976) 7 Pacific L.J. 673, 693), and establishing a "rational means to allocate the regulation of a corporation to the state to which it is primarily related" (Note, The Pseudo-Foreign Corporation in California, supra, 28 Hastings L.J. 119, 147), through a "narrow exception to the internal affairs doctrine in situations where California's interests are clearly paramount." (Oldham, California Regulates Pseudo-Foreign Corporations—Trampling Upon the Tramp?, supra, 17 Santa Clara L.Rev. 85, 98; but cf. Halloran & Hammer, Section 2115 of the New California Corporation Law—The Application of California Corporation Law to Foreign Corporations, supra, 23 U.C.L.A. L.Rev. 1282, 1283.) We conclude that to the extent that the cumulative voting require-

---

nois statute applied to target companies of which shareholders located in Illinois owned 10 percent of the stock subject to the offer, or for which any two of the following three conditions are met: the corporation has its principal executive office in Illinois, is organized under the laws of Illinois, or has at least 10 percent of its stated capital and paid-in surplus represented within the state. (102 S.Ct. at p. 2633.) Obviously, several states could apply such statutes to a company; such is not the case with section 2115. The court noted that the Illinois law on its face would apply even if not a single one of a company's shareholders were a resident of Illinois. (*Id.*, at p. 2641.) "Thus the Act could be applied to regulate a tender offer which would not affect a single Illinois shareholder." (*Ibid.*) The court found it apparent that the statute "is a direct restraint on interstate commerce and that it has a sweeping extraterritorial effect." Such regulation by other states would stifle securities transactions. (*Ibid.*) We find the higher degree of contact with the state which the California statute requires, the significantly decreased if not eliminated possibility of conflicting regulation, and the minimal burden on commerce present here provide a principled distinction between this case and MITE. (*See also* Great Western United Corp. v. Kidwell (5th Cir. 1978) 577 F.2d 1256, revd. for lack of venue sub nom. Leroy v. Great Western United Corp. (1979) 443 U.S. 173, 99 S.Ct. 2710, 61 L.Ed.2d 464, invalidating on both preemption and commerce clause grounds an Idaho statute regulating tender offers where only two percent of the Idaho corporation's stockholders were residents there.)

7. Of the statutes pointed out by respondent as being similar to Corporations Code section 2115, only the New York statute is currently in effect. (*See* N.Y.Bus.Corp.Law, §§ 1317–1320 (McKinney 1963 & Supp.1981.) It should be noted, however, that while the specific aim of the California statute "is to extend to pseudo-foreign corporations its traditional protection of the rights of shareholders and creditors[,] New York... was as interested in liberalizing its entire statute to keep pace with the more permissive states as it was in foreclosing use of foreign incorporations as a means of escaping local regulation." (Note, *The Pseudo-Foreign Corporation in California* (1976) 28 HASTINGS L.J. 119, 126, fn. omitted.) The resulting doubt as to whether the New York statute has had an impact on foreign corporations is heightened by the dearth of reported cases under them. (*Ibid.*)

ment imposed by section 2115 upon pseudo-foreign corporations is shown to have any effect upon interstate commerce, the effect is incidental, and minimal in relation to the purpose which that requirement is designed to achieve.

III. Due Process

Appellant contends that section 2115 is a retrospective law which impairs property rights and destroys vested rights in violation of due process. Before 1977 the California Corporations Code did not purport to apply directly to foreign corporations, and appellant made substantial investments in California before section 2115 was enacted in 1977. Its 5,000 shareholders had a vested voting right, it argues, to insist that their directors be elected by the straight voting procedure authorized by Utah law. This right, it asserts, was violated by section 2115.

The standard of review of economic legislation such as section 2115 is clear. Such legislative acts are clothed with a presumption of constitutionality and "...'the burden is on one complaining of a due process violation to establish that the legislature has acted in an arbitrary and irrational way.' [Citation.]" (Duke Power Co. v. Carolina Env. Study Group (1978) 438 U.S. 59, 83, 98 S.Ct. 2620, 2635, 57 L.Ed.2d 595.)

We discern neither arbitrariness nor irrationality in section 2115. As one comprehensive comment on the statute has pointed out, the section "attempts to insure that the social policies of California, as manifested in its corporations code, will no longer be circumvented by such [pseudo-foreign] corporations pursuant to the internal affairs doctrine." (Oldham, California Regulates Pseudo-Foreign Corporations—Trampling Upon the Tramp?, supra, 17 Santa Clara L.Rev. 85, 90.) Such a desire to assert control over the affairs of foreign corporations has been upheld by no less an authority than Justice Cardozo: "[W]hen countless corporations, organized on paper in neighboring states, live and move and have their being in New York, a sound public policy demands that our legislature be invested with [a] measure of control." (German-American Coffee Co. v. Diehl (1915), 216 N.Y. 57, 109 N.E. 875, 877.) In sum, "Section 2115 reflects a legislative judgment that California has the most significant relationship to a pseudo-foreign corporation which satisfies the section 2115 tests, and that California has the greatest interest in regulating such a corporation, since its principal place of business [is] in California and the majority of its shareholders reside in California." (Oldham, California Regulates Pseudo-Foreign Corporations—Trampling Upon the Tramp?, supra, 17 Santa Clara L.Rev. 85, 98, fn. omitted.) Such a judgment—in view of the significant social costs which might result if pseudo-foreign corporations could ignore the public policies of this state—is not irrational.

Nor can appellant claim that California is applying its law to a matter with which the state has no significant contacts. (Cf. Home Ins. Co. v. Dick (1930) 281 U.S. 397, 408, 50 S.Ct. 338, 341, 74 L.Ed. 926.) Section 2115 only applies when a corporation has significant—and predominant—contacts with California. Under those circumstances, there is no due process violation in the application of a statute such as section 2115....

IV. Contract Clause

Appellant next argues that section 2115 impermissibly infringes on its corporate charter from the State of Utah in violation of the contract clause of the federal and state Constitutions. (U.S. Const., Art. I, § 10, cl. 1; Cal. Const., Art. I, § 9.)

The Supreme Court set forth the definitive standard for contract clause analysis in Allied Structural Steel Co. v. Spannaus (1978) 438 U.S. 234, 244–245, 98 S.Ct. 2716, 2722, 57 L.Ed.2d 727: "[T]he first inquiry must be whether the state law has, in fact, operated as a substantial impairment of a contractual relationship. The severity of the impairment measures the height of the hurdle the state legislation must clear. Minimal alteration of contractual obligations may end the inquiry at its first stage. Severe impairment, on the other hand, will push the inquiry to a careful examination of the nature and purpose of the state legislation."

In Spannaus, the court struck down a Minnesota law which provided that a private employer of 100 employees or more which provided pension benefits under a qualified plan was subject to a "pension funding charge" if it either terminated the plan or closed a Minnesota office. The charge was assessed if the pension funds were not sufficient to cover full pensions for all employees who had worked at least 10 years. (438 U.S. at p. 238, 98 S.Ct. at p. 2719.) The company "relied heavily, and reasonably" on legitimate contractual expectations in calculating its annual contributions to its pension funds (id., at p. 246, 98 S.Ct. at p. 2733); the effect of the state law on its contractual obligation was "severe" (ibid.) since the company was assessed an immediate pension funding charge of approximately $185,000 when it proceeded to close its Minnesota office. (Id., at p. 247, 98 S.Ct. at p. 2723.)

Here, on the other hand, defendant shows only that its charter agreement has been changed to provide for cumulative voting; no showing whatever of hardship is made. This is a paradigm case of "minimal alteration" of contract (id., at p. 245, 98 S.Ct. at p. 2722). Section 2115's requirement of cumulative voting is "a mild one indeed, hardly burdensome...but nonetheless an important one to the State's interest. The Contract Clause does not forbid such a measure." (El Paso v. Simmons (1965) 379 U.S. 497, 516–517, 85 S.Ct. 577, 588, 13 L.Ed.2d 446.)

V. Equal Protection

Appellant contends that section 2115 violates the equal protection clause of the Fourteenth Amendment to the federal Constitution because foreign corporations whose securities are listed on a national securities exchange certified by the California Commissioner of Corporations are exempt from its application.

Classifications made by economic regulations are upheld if a rational basis supports them. "It is no requirement of equal protection that all evils of the same genus be eradicated or none at all." (Railway Express v. New York (1949) 336 U.S. 106, 110, 69 S.Ct. 463, 465, 93 L.Ed. 533.) "States are accorded wide latitude in the regulation of their local economies under their police powers, and rational distinctions may be made with substantially less than mathematical exactitude." (New Orleans v. Dukes (1976) 427 U.S. 297, 303, 96 S.Ct. 2513, 2516, 49 L.Ed.2d 511.)

We have no difficulty discerning a rational basis behind the exemption for corporations listed on certified stock exchanges. While some of the internal affairs covered by section 2115 are not covered by federal securities regulations (see Comment, California's Statutory Attempt to Regulate Foreign Corporations: Will it Survive the Commerce Clause? (1979) 16 San Diego L.Rev. 943, 951), the Legislature may well have reasoned that the disclosure requirements and other forms of regulation imposed upon listed securities, combined with the presumably greater liquidity of such investments, and the higher degree of scrutiny to which they are subjected in the marketplace, provide an adequate substitute, in the case of foreign corporations,[8] for the regulations imposed by

8. Appellant, as a foreign corporation, is not in a position to claim denial of equal protection arising from the state's more restrictive treatment of domestic corporations, which cannot claim ex-

section 2115. There is no reason to suspect that the Legislature, in providing for the challenged exemption, was motivated by favoritism toward corporations whose securities are listed on certified exchanges, or by animosity toward corporations whose securities are not. The criterion is neutral, and appears to serve a legitimate legislative objective. We find with it no constitutional fault.

VI. "Judicial Addendum"

Appellant's final contention is that the trial court improperly "amended" its articles when it declared that cumulative voting should be allowed all shareholders, Californians and non-Californians alike.

This contention is without merit. Section 2115 applies to a covered foreign corporation "to the exclusion of the law of the jurisdiction in which it is incorporated." (§2115, subd. (b).) As we have already concluded that California's public policy favoring cumulative voting outweighs Utah's neutral policy relating to shareholder voting—especially where, as here, the corporation's business is centered in California and it does no business in Utah—the trial judge properly held that section 2115 allows cumulative voting for all shareholders. Any other result would be unworkable. Nor does such a result work any hardship on appellant, since Utah law allows a corporation to provide for cumulative voting in its articles.

The judgment is affirmed.

MILLER and SMITH, JJ., concur.

Hearing denied; GRODIN, J., did not participate.

Comments and Questions

1. Does the Restatement (Second) Conflict of Laws §311, reproduced below, help in determining whether the *Wilson* case was rightly decided?

RESTATEMENT (SECOND) CONFLICT OF LAWS
§311 NEED TO QUALIFY TO DO BUSINESS

Whether a foreign corporation must comply with the qualification requirements of a state before doing business or conducting other activities there is determined, subject to constitutional limitations, by the local law of that state.

Comment:

a. Rationale:....Subject to constitutional limitations, a State may prohibit a foreign corporation from doing business, or conducting other activities, within its territory or may impose conditions as the price of permitting the corporation to do such business or such other acts.

* * *

c. Effect of Constitution of United States. The Constitution of the United States prevents a State from unconditionally refusing to allow a corporation to do busi-

---

emption based upon listing with certified exchanges. The distinction between domestic and foreign corporations in that respect would, however, likewise appear reasonable.

ness in interstate or foreign commerce within the State.... A State may likewise be under a constitutional obligation to permit a foreign corporation to enter its territory for the purpose of doing certain acts which do not amount to the actual doing of business.

d. Imposition of terms.....A State may not compel a foreign corporation, as a condition of doing or continuing to do business in the State, to relinquish rights secured by the Constitution of the United States.... Nor can a State impede a foreign corporation from doing business in interstate or foreign commerce within its territory be seeking to impose conditions which place an undue burden upon such commerce.... It is not within the scope of the Restatement of this Subject to determine what constitutes an "undue burden."

e. Corporations engaged solely in interstate or foreign commerce.....A State's power to satisfy local qualification requirements depends both upon the character of those requirements and upon the quantum of the corporation's activity within the state. Such requirements cannot be discriminatory or unduly burdensome. Nor can they be imposed as the price of permitting the corporation to engage in one or more isolated acts of interstate or foreign commerce within the State. When, however, the corporation does all, or a substantial portion, of its business within the State, it can be subjected to appropriate penalties, such as inability to sue in the local courts, for its failure to comply with reasonable qualification requirements.

2. The problem of establishing the boundaries of state regulation, and the limitations of the internal affairs doctrine to police that boundary, might provide the basis for rethinking the American adherence to a state based regulation of corporations, with a division between "internal" affairs and other matters affecting corporate organization. The section which follows makes the case for a uniform regulation of corporations at the federal level.

2. California courts continue to enforce, and perhaps expand the reach of its corporate law to corporations with their primary residence in California. As you read the case which follows, consider to what extent the arguments made in the case suggest the validity of a rule of corporate governance which accords the state of a corporation's primary residence the authority to regulate its domiciliary corporation's internal affairs. Consider also whether there is any difference between California's pseudo-foreign corporation doctrines and policy and those of the European siège social.

Havlicek v. Coast-to-Coast Analytical Services, Inc.

Court of Appeal, Second District, Division 6, California.
39 Cal.App.4th 1844, 46 Cal.Rptr.2d 696 (1995)

YEGAN, Associate Justice.

Appellants Mary Havlicek and Stephen C. Havlicek, directors of respondent Coast-to-Coast Analytical Services, Inc. (CCAS), sought an order from the superior court allowing them to inspect the books and records of CCAS. In addition, appellants unsuccessfully sought to enjoin a pending merger by CCAS until they had completed their inspection. Appellants contend they have an "absolute right" to review all CCAS documents and are not required to explain or justify their inspection demands. (Corp.Code, § 1602.)[1]

CCAS objected to the inspection on the theory that Delaware law applied because CCAS is a Delaware corporation. Pursuant to the Delaware statute, a director may review corporate documents only for "a purpose reasonably related to his position as a director[,]" and the Delaware Court of Chancery has exclusive jurisdiction to enforce inspection rights. (Del.Code Ann. tit. 8, § 220, subd. (d) (1995).) The trial court agreed with CCAS and denied appellants' request, stating that it lacked "jurisdiction" to order an inspection.

We conclude that the trial court erred in applying Delaware law and in refusing to grant appellants, at the very least, an "inspection with just and proper conditions." (§ 1603, subd. (a).)[2]

Facts

CCAS is a Delaware corporation. When appellants filed their request in the superior court, CCAS maintained its principal executive office in Camarillo, California. Appellants are two of the five directors of CCAS and control 40 percent of its stock. They reside in California. The three remaining directors of CCAS are employees of respondent ISS International Service System, Inc. (ISS), which owns 60 percent of CCAS stock.

Appellants allege that, on April 24, 1994, they were constructively terminated from their positions as officers and employees of CCAS. In early May, CCAS announced plans to merge its assets with those of two other corporations to form Pace Incorporated. Appellants opposed the merger and demanded broad access to CCAS documents. Although CCAS allowed appellants to review certain documents, other documents were withheld because CCAS became suspicious that appellants would use them to establish a competing business.

A majority of the CCAS directors approved the merger on June 6, 1994. Appellants voted against it and continued, unsuccessfully, to demand access to company documents. They filed this action on July 27, 1994, five days before the merger was scheduled to close. At the hearing on July 28, the trial court denied relief. On August 1, 1994, we also denied appellants' petition for writ of mandate.

---

1. All statutory references are to the Corporations Code unless otherwise stated.

Section 1602 provides: "Every director shall have the absolute right at any reasonable time to inspect and copy all books, records and documents of every kind and to inspect the physical properties of the corporation of which such person is a director and also of its subsidiary corporations, domestic or foreign. Such inspection by a director may be made in person or by agent or attorney and the right of inspection includes the right to copy and make extracts. This section applies to a director of any foreign corporation having its principal executive office in this state or customarily holding meetings of its board in this state."

2. Section 1603 subdivision (a) provides: "Upon refusal of a lawful demand for inspection, the superior court of the proper county, may enforce the right of inspection with just and proper conditions or may, for good case shown, appoint one or more competent inspectors or accountants to audit the books and records kept in this state and investigate the property, funds and affairs of any domestic corporation or any foreign corporation keeping records in this state and of any subsidiary corporation thereof, domestic or foreign, keeping records in this state and to report thereon in such manner as the court may direct."

On August 3, 1994, CCAS merged with Pace. CCAS no longer maintains an office in California. Although it continues to exist as a corporation, its only assets are shares of stock in Pace. Pace, located in New York, now owns the documents appellants wish to inspect but CCAS has represented that they continue to exist and can be made available for inspection. The controversy is not over. Litigation between the parties is extant.

The Relocation of CCAS's Principal Office and Removal of the Documents from California Does Not Render This Action Moot.

CCAS argues this appeal is moot because CCAS has transferred its documents and assets to Pace and no longer maintains an executive office in California....

The fact that CCAS has relocated and removed the documents from California is insufficient to render the action moot. Changed circumstances render a matter moot only when they occur "'without any fault of the defendant....'" (Id., at p. 10, 244 Cal.Rptr. 581.)

CCAS is, of course, responsible for closing the California office and its moving of the documents out of state. We need not decide whether section 1603 subdivision (a) limits the right of a director to inspect "...books and records kept in this state..." or whether the "in the state" aspect of the statute applies only to court-appointed inspectors or accountants. Where, as here, the books and records are moved, section 1603 cannot be used as a shield to defeat inspection. This rule is but a variation of the equitable maxim, "[n]o one can take advantage of his own wrong." (Civ.Code, § 3517.) Moreover, an "... appeal reviews the correctness of the judgment or order as of the time of its rendition...." (Karrin v. Ocean-Aire Mobile Home Estates (1991) 1 Cal.App.4th 1066, 1070, 2 Cal.Rptr.2d 581; see also In re Elise K. (1982) 33 Cal.3d 138, 149, 187 Cal.Rptr. 483, 654 P.2d 253.)

Choice of Law

Appellants insist that California law governs the inspection issue. CCAS argues that Delaware law applies because CCAS is a Delaware corporation. To determine the correct choice of law, we apply a three-step analysis. First, we determine whether the two concerned states have different laws. Second, we consider whether each state has an interest in having its law applied to this case. Finally, if the laws are different and each state has an interest in having its own law applied, we apply the law of the state whose "interests would be more impaired if its policy were subordinated to the policy of the other state." (North American Asbestos Corp. v. Superior Court (1986) 180 Cal.App.3d 902, 905, 225 Cal.Rptr. 877. See also Bernhard v. Harrah's Club (1976) 16 Cal.3d 313, 320, 128 Cal.Rptr. 215, 546 P.2d 719.)

The California statute provides: "Every director [has] the absolute right at any reasonable time to inspect and copy all books, records and documents of every kind...." (§ 1602.) Under the analogous Delaware statute, a director has "the right to examine the corporation's...books and records for a purpose reasonably related to his position as a director." (Del.Code Ann. tit. 8, § 220, subd. (d) (1995)). In addition, the Delaware statute grants its Court of Chancery exclusive jurisdiction to resolve disputes concerning inspections by corporate directors. (Id.)

If Delaware law applies, the Delaware Court of Chancery has exclusive jurisdiction and appellants must prove that they have a proper purpose for their request. The California statutory scheme does not impose a "proper purpose" requirement (Valtz v. Penta Investment Corp. (1983) 139 Cal.App.3d 803, 810, 188 Cal.Rptr. 922), and appellants have never articulated the purpose for their inspection demand. Thus, while the California statutory scheme would grant appellants an inspection, the same would not necessarily be true under the more restrictive Delaware statute.[3]

The directors of a corporation owe a fiduciary duty to the corporation and its shareholders. (Hartman v. Hollingsworth (1967) 255 Cal.App.2d 579, 581–582, 63 Cal.Rptr. 563.) Section 1602 represents a legislative judgment that directors are better able to discharge those duties if they have free access to information concerning the corporation. Thus, California has a public policy favoring broad inspection rights for the directors. The Legislature has also declared that it is the public policy of California to apply the same standards to foreign corporations whose principal executive offices are located in California. We may not ignore that declaration of public policy. (California Casualty Indemnity Exchange v. Pettis (1987) 193 Cal.App.3d 1597, 1605, 239 Cal.Rptr. 205.)

Delaware also has important interests at stake. Because CCAS is a creation of Delaware law, Delaware has an interest in prescribing the powers of CCAS, imposing uniform regulations on its internal affairs, and controlling its rights and liabilities. (Riley v. Fitzgerald (1986) 178 Cal.App.3d 871, 877, 223 Cal.Rptr. 889.) The Delaware statute expresses a public policy which attempts to protect corporations against unreasonable or burdensome inspections by directors.

We must decide which state's interests would be more impaired if its policy were subordinated to the policy of the other state. (Offshore Rental Co. v. Continental Oil Co. (1978) 22 Cal.3d 157, 166, 148 Cal.Rptr. 867, 583 P.2d 721.) Delaware's interest in regulating the activities of its domestic corporations is less substantial where, as here, its only contact with the corporation is in issuing a certificate of incorporation. CCAS has no Delaware shareholders or directors. It does not have an office or store its documents in Delaware. The record does not reflect whether CCAS ever conducted business in Delaware. By contrast, California has strong contacts with CCAS. CCAS maintained its principal office and most of the documents at issue in this state until the merger occurred. CCAS also conducted business in California and employed California residents. Forty percent of its stock and two of the five seats on its board of directors are controlled by California residents.

California's interests would be impaired by the application of Delaware law because Delaware cannot at the same time honor a director's "absolute" inspection right and limit inspections to a "purpose reasonably related to his position as a director." However, as we shall explain, the trial court can protect Delaware's interest in avoiding a burdensome inspection by imposing reasonable conditions. We conclude, therefore, that California's interest would be more impaired by the application of Delaware law than Delaware's interest would be impaired by the opposite result. California law applies to the inspection issue.[4]

---

3. Appellants place great reliance on Valtz v. Penta Investment Corp., *supra*, 139 Cal.App.3d 803, 188 Cal.Rptr. 922. There, owners of over 5 percent of the shares sought to enforce their "absolute right" to inspect and copy the shareholders list. The corporation refused, alleging that the information would be used in a competing business. (*Id.*, at p. 806, 188 Cal.Rptr. 922.) The opinion does observe that the "unclean hands" defense was tantamount to the "proper purpose" rule and therefore inapplicable. (*Id.*, at p. 810, 188 Cal.Rptr. 922.) The opinion, however, is silent with respect to section 1603 subdivision (a) and its provision for a protective order.

4. Our construction of section 1603 subdivision (a) (*see* post, at pp. 12–14 does not render the conflict of laws issue moot. The California and Delaware rules for director inspection remain different. Were we to rule that Delaware law applied to this inspection controversy, a director's right to inspect would not only be chilled, it might be frozen. Whether appellants would suffer the burden of litigating the inspection issue in the Delaware chancery court is unknown.

Section 2115 Does Not Render Section 1602 Inapplicable.

CCAS argues that it need not comply with section 1602 because it does not meet the test provided in section 2115 for the application of California law to a foreign corporation. Section 2115 provides that portions of the Corporations Code, including section 1602, apply to a foreign corporation if, among other things, "more than one-half of its outstanding voting securities are held of record by persons having an address in this state." (§2115, subd. (a).) ISS owns 60 percent of the CCAS voting securities and does not have an address in California.

CCAS fails the test under section 2115, but that does not settle the question because section 1602 contains a separate and distinct test; i.e., a "long arm" provision. The statute provides that it "applies to a director of any foreign corporation having its principal executive office in this state...." (§1602.) CCAS meets this test but argues that section 1602 applies only where the corporation also meets the test established in section 2115.

Section 1602 was amended to apply to foreign corporations after section 2115 was enacted. We assume that the Legislature was aware of section 2115 when it amended section 1602 and that it intended to maintain a consistent body of statutes. (Schmidt v. Southern Cal. Rapid Transit Dist. (1993) 14 Cal.App.4th 23, 27, 17 Cal.Rptr.2d 340.) We must also avoid an interpretation of section 2115 which requires that section 1602 be ignored unless " 'the two acts are so inconsistent that there is no possibility of concurrent operation....' " (Hays v. Wood (1979) 25 Cal.3d 772, 784, 160 Cal.Rptr. 102, 603 P.2d 19.)

Here, although the two sections contain different tests, they are capable of concurrent operation. Each section may be given effect because each establishes a separate and distinct test for determining whether a foreign corporation must comply with section 1602. CCAS met one such test and is therefore required to comply with section 1602, regardless of whether it also meets the other available test.

The Internal Affairs Doctrine Does Not Require Application of Delaware Law.

CCAS argues that Delaware law must be applied because the appellants' claim involves the internal affairs of a Delaware corporation, a matter traditionally controlled by the state of incorporation. (Valtz v. Penta Investment Corp, supra, 139 Cal.App.3d at p. 807, 188 Cal.Rptr. 922.) "The internal affairs doctrine is a conflict of laws principle which recognizes that only one State should have the authority to regulate a corporation's internal affairs...because otherwise a corporation could be faced with conflicting demands." (Edgar v. MITE Corp. (1988) 457 U.S. 624, 645, 102 S.Ct. 2629, 2642, 73 L.Ed.2d 269.) Here, complying with California law will not require CCAS to violate Delaware law. The Delaware statute allows, but does not require that a corporation restrict the inspection rights of its directors. CCAS will not violate Delaware law by granting appellants greater access to its documents. The internal affairs doctrine does not apply.

Section 1602 Does Not Violate the Commerce Clause.

CCAS also argues that application of California law in this case would violate the commerce clause of the United States Constitution. (U.S. Const., art. I, §8, cl. 3.) We disagree. The commerce clause prohibits states from discriminating against interstate commerce. (Fort Gratiot Sanitary Landfill v. Mich. Dept. of Natural Resources, (1992) 504 U.S. 353, 359–360, 112 S.Ct. 2019, 2023–2024, 119 L.Ed.2d 139, 147.) It also "precludes the application of a state statute to commerce that takes place wholly outside of the State's borders...," (Edgar v. MITE Corp., supra, 457 U.S. at pp. 642–643, 102 S.Ct. at p. 2641) and invalidates regulations that "adversely...affect interstate commerce by subjecting activities to inconsistent regulations." (CTS Corp. v. Dynamics Corp. of America (1987) 481 U.S. 69, 88, 107 S.Ct. 1637, 1649, 95 L.Ed.2d 67, 84.)

Section 1602 does not suffer from these defects. It does not discriminate against foreign corporations because it imposes on those corporations the same burdens imposed upon domestic corporations. It does not apply to activities occurring wholly outside the borders of California because, until the merger, most CCAS documents were located in California. The same would probably be true for any foreign corporation maintaining its principal office in this state. Finally, section 1602 does not subject CCAS to conflicting regulatory demands. Application of section 1602 to CCAS does not, therefore, violate the commerce clause.

Section 1602 Does Not Violate the Full Faith and Credit Clause.

Similarly, section 1602 does not violate the full faith and credit clause. (U.S. Const., Art. IV, § 1 ["Full Faith and Credit...be given in each State to the public Acts, Records and Judicial Proceedings of every other State...."]) A state's choice of law decision does not violate the full faith and credit clause if the state has significant contacts with the dispute " 'such that choice of its law is neither arbitrary nor fundamentally unfair.' " (Wilson v. Louisiana-Pacific Resources, Inc. (1982) 138 Cal.App.3d 216, 222–223, 187 Cal.Rptr. 852.) For purposes of the full faith and credit clause, the location of a corporation's principal executive office within a state is a "significant contact." (Valtz v. Penta Investment Corp., supra, 139 Cal.App.3d at p. 807, 188 Cal.Rptr. 922.)

CCAS located its principal executive office in this state and has more substantial contacts with California than it does with Delaware. Accordingly, the choice of California law as opposed to Delaware law is neither arbitrary nor fundamentally unfair. Application of section 1602 does not violate the full faith and credit clause.

The Trial Court May Impose Limitations on Appellants' Inspection Rights Under Sections 1602 and 1603.

The trial court must apply California law but is not obligated to grant appellants unfettered access to every document ever created by CCAS. Instead, the trial court may impose "just and proper conditions" upon appellant's otherwise "absolute" inspection rights. We admit that the Legislature's choice of the word, "absolute," in section 1602 does give us pause. But one hypothetical illustrates that "absolute" cannot mean "absolute." A disgruntled director unambiguously announces his or her intention to violate his or her fiduciary duties to the corporation and the shareholders by using inspection rights to learn trade secrets, gain access to confidential customer lists, and compete with the corporation. In this situation, does the Legislature want the judiciary to come to the aid of the disgruntled director, enforce the "absolute right" to inspect and help the director commit a tort against the corporation? No.[5] " 'The literal meaning of the words of

5. We also note the recent case of Chantiles v. Lake Forest II Master Homeowners Assn. (1995) 37 Cal.App.4th 914, 45 Cal.Rptr.2d 1. There, an analogous provision in section 8334, provided for an "absolute right" of inspection for a homeowner's association director. Notwithstanding the use of the word "absolute," a majority of the court were of the opinion that the right to privacy could, and there did, outweigh the "absolute" right of inspection. (Id., at pp. 925–926, 45 Cal.Rptr.2d 1.)

a statute may be disregarded to avoid absurd results....' [Citation.]" (Unzueta v. Ocean View School Dist. (1992) 6 Cal.App.4th 1689, 1698, 8 Cal.Rptr.2d 614.)

The "absolute right" to inspect documents is the general rule in California. However, section 1602 must be read in pari materia with section 1603. (Unzueta v. Ocean View School Dist., supra, 6 Cal.App.4th at p. 1695, 8 Cal.Rptr.2d 614.) The language of section 1603 subdivision (a) is expansive. It is not expressly limited to an inspection request by a shareholder. Being a remedial statute, it must be liberally construed. (Ford Dealers Assn. v. Department of Motor Vehicles (1982) 32 Cal.3d 347, 356, 185 Cal.Rptr. 453, 650 P.2d 328.) Where the corporation determines that an unfettered inspection will result in a tort against the corporation, it may decline the request for inspection. In this situation, "...directors can enforce their inspection rights by court action.... [§ 1603]." (Friedman, Cal.Prac.Guide, Corporations (The Rutter Group (1995)) ¶ 6.502, pp. 6–98; see also 15 Cal.Jur.3d ed., Corporations, § 263, p. 367.)

Upon a director's request for inspection pursuant to section 1603 in the superior court, the corporation must demonstrate, by evidentiary showing, that a protective order is necessary to prevent a tort against the corporation. Whether there are other situations where a director's inspection rights may be curtailed is not before us and we offer no opinion thereon. The superior court may then exercise its broad discretion under section 1603, subdivision (a) to fashion a protective order imposing just and proper conditions on the inspection. Precisely what "just and proper conditions" are necessary in this case, if any, is a question we leave to the superior court.

Conclusion

The trial court erred in applying Delaware law and denying appellants any inspection rights. We reverse and remand the matter to allow the trial court to enter an order granting appellants an appropriate inspection. Each party shall bear its own costs.

STONE, P.J., and GILBERT, J., concur.

Note on the California Approach

1. Is it clear, after *Havlicek*, whether California has adopted either the internal affairs rule or the domiciliary state rule for determining which state has the authority to legislate the internal affairs of a corporation? Could one argue that California has adopted a third approach—that based on the notion that any state may regulate such portions of the internal (and external) affairs of a corporation as it deems itself vested with personal and subject matter jurisdiction over the parties?

2. California is not the only state to seek regulation of the internal affairs of corporations resident within the state. Other states, too, have sought to test the limits of the foundation (internal affairs) doctrine when dealing with corporations whose only connection with the state of incorporation is the corporate charter itself. An example is *Yates v. Bridge Trading Co.*, 844 S.W.2d 56 (Mo.App. 1992), involving the validity of a contract for the issuance of stock for a promissory note. One of the issues raised was whether the law of Missouri, the state of the principal office of the corporation, or the law of Delaware, the state of incorporation, applied with respect to the contract, as the contract involved the issuance of stock. The issue in that case was complicated by the insertion, in the stock purchase agreement, of a choice of law provision which selected

the law of Missouri as governing the agreement. Relying on Restatement (Second) Conflicts of Laws § 302 the Missouri court determined that Missouri law was applicable.

> One of the principal policy reasons for the internal affairs doctrine is to avoid the application of inconsistent or conflicting sets of laws to corporate affairs. Because the stock purchase agreement at issue applied to all Old Trading stock, the uniform application of Missouri law would not run afoul of this policy. The cases discussed above indicate that courts and legislatures have increasingly regulated what was once rigidly designated as the internal affairs of a foreign corporation, especially if the foreign corporation has significant contacts with the forum. In light of the flexibility of the internal affairs doctrine as applied to pseudo-foreign corporations, and the low risk that stockholders would be subjected to inconsistent laws in this case, we find that the internal affairs doctrine does not, in and of itself, bar the application of Missouri corporate law to the issue of stock by a Delaware corporation. The parties were free to choose the law governing their stock issuance so long as there was a uniform law applied to all shareholders, and the parties and the corporation had substantial contacts with the state whose law was selected. 844 S.W. 2d at 62 (footnote omitted).

But the Yates court also determined, in the alternative, that the result would have been the same had the court applied Delaware law. *Id.,* 844 S.W.2d at 63–64.

3. New York and Ohio have also applied its law to a foreign corporation where the corporation has most of its contacts in New York. *See* Application of Dohring, 142 Misc.2d 429, 537 N.Y.S.2d 767 (N.Y.S. 1989) and Gries Sports Enterprises, Inc. v. Modell, 15 Ohio St. 3d 284, 473 N.E.2d 807 (1984) (referencing the Restatement (Second) Conflict of Laws).

4. But these statutory and choice of law attempts to overcome the presumptions of the incorporation doctrine have not gone unchallenged. The Delaware Supreme Court has delivered a strong defense of the policy behind the internal affairs rules. It has also advanced the argument that the incorporation doctrine is nor merely a choice of law rule, but is constitutionally grounded. As you read the case which follows, consider whether the Delaware court in *McDermott* or the California court in *Wilson* makes the stronger argument.

McDermott, Inc. v. Lewis

Supreme Court of Delaware
Submitted: Dec. 9, 1986
Decided: Sept. 16, 1987
531 A.2d 206

(Some footnotes omitted)

Before CHRISTIE, C.J., HORSEY and MOORE, JJ.

MOORE, Justice:

We confront an important issue of first impression—whether a Delaware subsidiary of a Panamanian corporation may vote the shares it holds in its parent company under circumstances which are prohibited by Delaware law, but not the law of Panama. Necessarily, this involves questions of foreign law, and applicability of the internal affairs doctrine under Delaware law.

Plaintiffs, Harry Lewis and Nina Altman, filed these consolidated suits in the Court of Chancery in December, 1982 seeking to enjoin or rescind the 1982 Reorganization under which McDermott Incorporated, a Delaware corporation ("McDermott Delaware"), became a 92%-owned subsidiary of McDermott International, Inc., a Panamanian corporation ("International"). Lewis and Altman are stockholders of McDermott Delaware, which emerged from the Reorganization owning approximately 10% of International's common stock. Plaintiffs challenged this aspect of the Reorganization, and the Court of Chancery granted partial summary judgment in their favor, holding that McDermott Delaware could not vote its stock in International.

We conclude that the trial court erred in refusing to apply the law of Panama to the internal affairs of International. There was no nexus between International and the State of Delaware. Moreover, plaintiffs concede that the issues here do not involve the internal affairs of McDermott Delaware. Thus, we decline to follow Norlin Corp. v. Rooney, Pace Inc., 744 F.2d 255 (2d Cir.1984), which prohibited a similar device involving a Panamanian subsidiary seeking to vote the shares it held in its Panamanian parent. Accordingly, we reverse. In so doing, we reaffirm the principle that the internal affairs doctrine is a major tenet of Delaware corporation law having important federal constitutional underpinnings.

I.

International was incorporated in Panama on August 11, 1959, and is principally engaged in providing worldwide marine construction services to the oil and gas industry. Its executive offices are in New Orleans, Louisiana, and there are no operations in Delaware. International does not maintain offices in Delaware, hold meetings or conduct business here, have agents or employees in Delaware, or have any assets here.

McDermott Delaware and its subsidiaries operate throughout the United States in three principal industry segments: marine construction services, power generation systems and equipment, and engineered materials. McDermott Delaware's principal offices are in New Orleans.

Following the 1982 Reorganization, McDermott Delaware became a 92%-owned subsidiary of International. The public stockholders of International hold approximately 90% of the voting power of International, while McDermott Delaware holds about 10%.

The stated "principal purpose" of the reorganization, according to International's prospectus, was to enable the McDermott Group to retain, reinvest and redeploy earnings from operations outside the United States without subjecting such earnings to United States income tax. The prospectus also admitted that the 10% voting interest given to McDermott Delaware would be voted by International, "and such voting power could be used to oppose an attempt by a third party to acquire control of International if the management of International believes such use of the voting power would be in the best interests of the stockholders of International." An exchange offer, and thus the Reorganization, was supported by 89.59% of McDermott Delaware stockholders.[1]

The applicable Panamanian law is set forth in the record by affidavits and opinion letters of Ricardo A. Durling, Esquire, and the deans of two Panamanian law schools, to support the claim that McDermott Delaware's retention of a 10% interest in Interna-

1. After expiration of the exchange offer, McDermott announced that a preliminary count of the McDermott Delaware common shares tendered totalled approximately 33,740,000, or approximately 89.59% of the total number of outstanding shares. Of these, 30,000,000 shares were ultimately accepted for exchange pursuant to the terms of the Exchange Offer.

tional, and its right to vote those shares, is permitted by the laws of Panama. Significantly, the plaintiffs have not offered any contrary evidence.

[The court describes the evidence offered by the Panamanian law experts]

* * *

This evidence of Panamanian law is uncontroverted. Plaintiffs have offered no proof whatever on the subject. Instead, they rely on Norlin. By letter dated March 9, 1987, McDermott informed the Court of a postargument change in the facts relevant to this appeal. McDermott International has recently registered with the National Securities Commission of Panama, thereby making Article 35 of Panamanian Cabinet Decree No. 247 applicable to the company. Thus, McDermott Delaware cannot now vote its International shares. This change in circumstances technically renders the appeal moot. Normally, we decline to decide moot issues. Sannini v. Casscells, Del.Supr., 401 A.2d 927, 930 (1979). However, where the question is of public importance, and its impact on the law is real, this Court has recognized an exception to the above rule.... Given the importance of this matter to Delaware corporation law, and the state in which it otherwise would be left, we are compelled to decide this case based on the facts presented to the trial court.

II.

We note at the outset that if International were incorporated either in Delaware or Louisiana, its stock could not be voted by a majority-owned subsidiary. 8 Del.C. § 160(c);[3] La.Rev.Stat.Ann. § 12:75(G).[4] No United States jurisdiction of which we are aware permits that practice.

Relying on Norlin Corp. v. Rooney, Pace Inc., 744 F.2d 255 (2d Cir.1984), the Court of Chancery concluded that Panama in effect would refrain from applying its laws under the facts of this case. On that basis, the trial court then concluded that since both Delaware and Louisiana law prohibit a majority-owned subsidiary from voting its parent's stock, the device was improper. We consider this an erroneous application of both Delaware and Panamanian law.

Our analysis requires a two-step inquiry. First, we must determine if Panamanian law, in the factual context addressed by the Court of Chancery, permits International to vote its own shares through the device of McDermott Delaware's ownership. If it does not, then the inquiry ends. However, if Panamanian law permits the practice, we must consider the multifaceted issues inherent in the application of the internal affairs doctrine.

---

3. 8 Del.C. § 160(c) provides:

Shares of its own capital stock belonging to the corporation or to another corporation, if a majority of the shares entitled to vote in the election of directors of such other corporation is held, directly or indirectly, by the corporation, shall neither be entitled to vote nor be counted for quorum purposes. Nothing in this section shall be construed as limiting the right of any corporation to vote stock, including but not limited to its own stock, held by it in a fiduciary capacity.

4. La.Rev.Stat.Ann. § 12:75(G) provides:

Neither (1) treasury shares, nor (2) unissued shares, nor (3) shares of a parent corporation held by a subsidiary corporation in which the parent holds a majority of the shares entitled to vote for the election of directors, shall be voted, or counted in calculating the voting power of shareholders of a corporation.

A.

It is apparent that under limited circumstances the laws of Panama permit a subsidiary to vote the shares of its parent. Article 35 of Panamanian Cabinet Decree No. 247 of July 16, 1970, which is part of the General Corporation Law of Panama, restricts the exercise of voting rights on shares of certain Panamanian corporations, but Article 37 limits the scope of Article 35 to "corporations registered in the National Securities Commission [of Panama] and those whose shares are sold on the market..." Opinion of Ricardo A. Durling, supra p. 5. Based on the facts before the Court of Chancery, it is undisputed that International was not required to register, nor had it registered, with the National Securities Commission. Further, International's shares were not "sold on the market," as that term is defined by the Attorney General of Panama.[5] Reading Articles 35 and 37 together, it is apparent that Article 35's prohibition did not apply to International.

B.

Plaintiffs argue that McDermott Delaware may not vote shares held in International, since Panama law does not expressly permit such corporate action. Further, they contend, and the Vice Chancellor ruled, that Article 37 simply provides "that where a Panama corporation's shares are not registered in Panama and not publicly traded in Panama (i.e., such as the shares of International at bar) the laws of Panama will not be imposed on that corporation." According to plaintiffs, this means that Panama has "declined to assert its own jurisdiction and laws on Panamanian corporations that choose to limit their contact with Panama."

We cannot accept either of those propositions. The uncontroverted evidence clearly and unambiguously rejects the contention that Panamanian law prohibits all conduct not otherwise expressly permitted. All three legal experts agreed that McDermott Delaware could vote the shares it held in International. Further, Dean Fernandez specifically stated that it "is a principle of law that in matters of public law one can only do what is expressly allowed by the law; while in private law all acts not prohibited by law can be performed." This fully accords with basic principles of Delaware corporate law. Unocal Corp. v. Mesa Petroleum Co., Del.Supr., 493 A.2d 946, 957 (1985); See Providence and Worcester Co. v. Baker, Del.Supr., 378 A.2d 121, 123–24 (1977).

C.

We also reject plaintiffs' contention that Article 37 articulates Panama's intent to decline jurisdiction over corporations which are neither registered with the National Securities Commission nor sell shares on the Panamanian "market." Were this the intent of the Panamanian Cabinet Decree, the language of Article 37 would not expressly limit its applicability to Articles 34, 35 and 36.

While offering no proof on this point, plaintiffs cite Norlin Corp. v. Rooney, Pace Inc., 744 F.2d 255 (2d Cir.1984)....

We decline to follow Norlin for several reasons. First, we reject the notion that Panamanian law is inapplicable on the basis of some factually unsupported theory of absten-

5. An opinion of the Executive Director of the National Commission of Securities of Panama, dated May 2, 1984, states that the phrase "sold on the market" requires that shares of a Panamanian corporation be made in Panama to more than ten persons annually. None of International's shares had been so traded. Appendix to Appellant's Opening Brief at A-185 to A-188 (original) and A-189 to A-192 (English translation).

tion. Cf. Hart v. General Motors Corp., N.Y.App.Div., 129 A.D.2d 179, 517 N.Y.S.2d 490 (1987). Second, Norlin applies the law of New York because of the defendants' substantial contacts with that State.[6] Third, Norlin neither cited nor distinguished the earlier contrary decision of Hausman v. Buckley, 299 F.2d 696 (2d Cir.), cert. denied, 369 U.S. 885, 82 S.Ct. 1157, 8 L.Ed.2d 286 (1962), although both opinions were authored by the same member of the Court. Hausman holds that the right of shareholders to bring a derivative action on behalf of a corporation is determined by the laws of the state of its incorporation. The Second Circuit rejected an argument that New York courts would refuse to apply the internal affairs doctrine for reasons of public policy. Id. at 705. Significantly, Hausman recognized that the doctrine was "well established" and had been applied "repeatedly" to determine matters governing the relations of stockholders and corporations inter se. Id. at 702. The failure to even mention Hausman can only further undermine Norlin's persuasiveness.

Finally, Norlin arose in the context of a hostile takeover threat. The Norlin board issued over 800,000 shares of voting stock to a subsidiary, as the final step in a series of transactions designed to place 49% of the voting power in the friendly hands of the board of directors, and with the clear intention of thwarting any hostile bids for control of the company.[7] In contrast, McDermott Delaware emerged from the Reorganization holding only 10% of International's voting power, and there is no serious suggestion that this circumstance, alone, would thwart a determined bidder.

Given the uncontroverted evidence of Panamanian law, establishing that a Panamanian corporation may place voting shares in a majority-owned subsidiary under the limited circumstances provided by Article 37, we turn to the fundamental issues presented by application of the internal affairs doctrine.

III.

Internal corporate affairs involve those matters which are peculiar to the relationships among or between the corporation and its current officers, directors, and shareholders. Edgar v. MITE Corp., 457 U.S. 624, 645, 102 S.Ct. 2629, 2642, 73 L.Ed.2d 269 (1982). Restatement (Second) of Conflict of Laws § 313, Comment a (1971). It is essential to distinguish between acts which can be performed by both corporations and individuals, and those activities which are peculiar to the corporate entity.

Corporations and individuals alike enter into contracts, commit torts, and deal in personal and real property. Choice of law decisions relating to such corporate activities are usually determined after consideration of the facts of each transaction. See Reese and Kaufman, The Law Governing Corporate Affairs: Choice of Law and the Impact of Full Faith and Credit, 58 Colum.L.Rev. 1118, 1121 (1958) (hereinafter "Reese and Kaufman"). In such cases, the choice of law determination often turns on whether the corporation had sufficient contacts with the forum state, in relation to the act or transaction in question, to satisfy the constitutional requirements of due process. The internal

6. Putting aside the question whether Delaware would apply a grouping of contacts or most significant relationship test in other areas of the law, International has no contacts whatever with Delaware. Given that circumstance, and Delaware's long adherence to the internal affairs doctrine, there is no basis for us to impose our own law upon a foreign corporation.

7. While International cites some rather insubstantial federal tax savings as the motivating factor for issuing voting shares to McDermott Delaware, we recognize the potential of McDermott Delaware's voting interest to aid International in a hostile fight for control. However, we do not rest our decision solely on the justifications urged by International, i.e., the possible tax savings provided by the reorganization.

affairs doctrine has no applicability in these situations. Rather, this doctrine governs the choice of law determinations involving matters peculiar to corporations, that is, those activities concerning the relationships inter se of the corporation, its directors, officers and shareholders.

The internal affairs doctrine requires that the law of the state of incorporation should determine issues relating to internal corporate affairs. First Nat'l City Bank v. Banco Para el Comercio Exterior de Cuba, 462 U.S. 611, 621, 103 S.Ct. 2591, 2597, 77 L.Ed.2d 46 (1983). Under Delaware conflict of laws principles and the United States Constitution, there are appropriate circumstances which mandate application of this doctrine.

A.

Delaware's well established conflict of laws principles require that the laws of the jurisdiction of incorporation—here the Republic of Panama—govern this dispute involving McDermott International's voting rights. Beard v. Elster, Del.Supr., 160 A.2d 731, 735 (1960); Elster v. American Airlines, Inc., Del.Ch., 100 A.2d 219, 224–25 (1953); Ringling v. Ringling Bros.-Barnum & Bailey Combined Shows, Inc., Del. Ch., 49 A.2d 603, 607 (1946), modified, Del.Supr., 53 A.2d 441 (1947); Mau v. Montana Pacific Oil Co., Del.Ch., 141 A. 828, 831 (1928); Bruch v. National Guarantee Credit Corp., Del.Ch., 116 A. 738, 744 (1922).[9]

The traditional conflicts rule developed by courts has been that internal corporate relationships are governed by the laws of the forum of incorporation. See Macey & Miller, Toward an Interest-Group Theory of Delaware Corporate Law, 65 Tex.L.Rev. 469, 495 (1987). As early as 1933, the Supreme Court of the United States noted:

> It has long been settled doctrine that a court—state or federal—sitting in one state will, as a general rule, decline to interfere with, or control by injunction or otherwise, the management of the internal affairs of a corporation organized under the laws of another state but will leave controversies as to such matters to the courts of the state of the domicile....

Rogers v. Guaranty Trust Co. of New York, 288 U.S. 123, 130, 53 S.Ct. 295, 297, 77 L.Ed. 652 (1933) (citations omitted).

However, in Western Air Lines, Inc. v. Sobieski, Cal.App., 191 Cal.App.2d 399, 12 Cal.Rptr. 719 (1961), a California court upheld an order of the California Commissioner of Corporations directing a Delaware corporation having major contacts with California to follow the cumulative voting requirements imposed by California law. After the Western Air decision, commentators noted that the case signaled the alleged start of a "conflicts revolution." See Kozyris, Corporate Wars and Choice of Law, 1985 Duke L.J. 1 (hereinafter "Kozyris"); Kaplan, Foreign Corporations and Local Corporate Policy, 21 Vand.L.Rev. 433 (1968) (hereinafter "Kaplan"). The "new" conflicts theory weighs the interests and policies of the forum state in determining whether the law of the forum—lex fori—should be applied. See Restatement (Second) of Conflict of

9. As the Supreme Court of the United States just recently observed:

> It thus is an accepted part of the business landscape in this country for States to create corporations, to prescribe their powers, and to define the rights that are acquired by purchasing their shares. A State has an interest in promoting stable relationships among parties involved in the corporations it charters....

CTS Corp. v. Dynamics Corp. of America, 481 U.S. 69, 107 S.Ct. 1637, 1650–51, 95 L.Ed.2d 67 (1987) (reversing 794 F.2d 250).

Laws, §§ 302–06, 309 (1971). Thus, the Western Air Lines case "was to be the harbinger of a new conflicts approach in corporate law that would limit or perhaps discard the lex incorporationis." Kozyris, supra at 17.

A review of cases over the last twenty-six years, however, finds that in all but a few, the law of the state of incorporation was applied without any discussion. Id. at 17–18. In fact, twenty-six years after Western Air the following statement remains apt:

> The umbilical tie of the foreign corporation to the state of its charter is usually still religiously regarded as conclusive in determining the law to be applied in intracorporate disputes. The fundamental reexamination of the nature of conflict of laws over the past few years has virtually left foreign corporation matters remaining as a pocket of the past in a subject area which has otherwise been characterized by free inquiry, change and flux.

Kaplan, supra at 464.[10]

The policy underlying the internal affairs doctrine is an important one, and we decline to erode the principle:

> Under the prevailing conflicts practice, neither courts nor legislatures have maximized the imposition of local corporate policy on foreign corporations but have consistently applied the law of the state of incorporation to the entire gamut of internal corporate affairs. In many cases, this is a wise, practical, and equitable choice. It serves the vital need for a single, constant and equal law to avoid the fragmentation of continuing, interdependent internal relationships. The lex incorporationis, unlike the lex loci delicti, is not a rule based merely on the priori concept of territoriality and on the desirability of avoiding forum-shopping. It validates the autonomy of the parties in a subject where the underlying policy of the law is enabling. It facilitates planning and enhances predictability. In fields like torts, where the typical dispute involves two persons and a single or simple one-shot issue and where the common substantive policy is to spread the loss through compensation and insurance, the preference for forum law and the emphasis on the state interest in forum residents which are the common denominators of the new conflicts methodologies do not necessarily lead to unacceptable choices. By contrast, applying local internal affairs law to a foreign corporation just because it is amenable to process in the forum or because it has some local shareholders or some other local contact is apt to produce inequalities, intolerable confusion, and uncertainty, and intrude into the domain of other states that have a superior claim to regulate the same subject matter....

Kozyris, supra at 98.

---

10. For an excellent discussion of the post-Western Airlines application of the internal affairs doctrine in the context of takeover litigation, *see* Kozyris, *supra* at 18–19. Since Professor Kozyris' article was published prior to the release of the Norlin opinion, the author did not have the opportunity to note that Norlin is the only known case which ignored the internal affairs doctrine in the context of corporate takeover litigation. Suffice it to say that in many leading cases the internal affairs doctrine was treated as axiomatic. *See* Martin-Marietta Corp. v. Bendix Corp., 690 F.2d 558, 565–68 (6th Cir.1982); Dan River, Inc. v. Icahn, 701 F.2d 278, 280–83, 291–92 (4th Cir.1983); Lewis v. Knutson, 699 F.2d 230, 235 (5th Cir.1983); Panter v. Marshall Field & Co., 646 F.2d 271, 277–78, 293 (7th Cir.), cert. denied, 454 U.S. 1092, 102 S.Ct. 658, 70 L.Ed.2d 631 (1981); Wylain, Inc. v. TRE Corp., Del.Ch., 412 A.2d 338, 344 (1980).

B.

Given the significance of these considerations, application of the internal affairs doctrine is not merely a principle of conflicts law. It is also one of serious constitutional proportions—under due process, the commerce clause and the full faith and credit clause—so that the law of one state governs the relationships of a corporation to its stockholders, directors and officers in matters of internal corporate governance. The alternatives present almost intolerable consequences to the corporate enterprise and its managers. With the existence of multistate and multinational organizations, directors and officers have a significant right, under the fourteenth amendment's due process clause, to know what law will be applied to their actions. Stockholders also have a right to know by what standards of accountability they may hold those managing the corporation's business and affairs. That is particularly so here, given the significant fact that in the McDermott Group reorganization, and after full disclosure, 89.59% of the total outstanding common shares of McDermott Delaware were tendered in the exchange offer. Compare Norlin. Thus, by an overwhelming choice those stockholders received shares in International, and thereby selected the laws of Panama to govern inter se the corporate relations between themselves, International, its directors, officers and agents. (See note 1, supra.) Such issues have been the subject of litigation and scholarly discussions for decades. However, an attitude has developed in some quarters which exalts local interests over more fundamental doctrines. We approach such teachings with reservations.

Under the commerce clause Pike v. Bruce Church, Inc., 397 U.S. 137, 142, 90 S.Ct. 844, 847, 25 L.Ed.2d 174 (1970), determined that a state may regulate interstate commerce indirectly, but emphasized that the burden placed upon interstate commerce may not be excessive in relation to the local interests served by the regulation. In Edgar v. MITE Corp., 457 U.S. 624, 102 S.Ct. 2629, 73 L.Ed.2d 269 (1982), the Supreme Court ruled that under the commerce clause a state "has no interest in regulating the internal affairs of foreign corporations." Id. at 645–46, 102 S.Ct. at 2642. If that is so, then a court or state which attempts to displace the internal affairs doctrine carries a heavy burden to justify its actions.

The recent decision in CTS Corp. v. Dynamics Corp. of America, 481 U.S. 69, 107 S.Ct. 1637, 95 L.Ed.2d 67 (1987), (reversing 794 F.2d 250), seems to support this interpretation of MITE:

> This Court's recent Commerce Clause cases also have invalidated statutes that adversely may affect interstate commerce by subjecting activities to inconsistent regulations... The Indiana Act poses no such problem. So long as each State regulates voting rights only in the corporations it has created, each corporation will be subject to the law of only one state. No principal of corporation law and practice is more firmly established than a State's authority to regulate domestic corporations, including the authority to define the voting rights of shareholders... This beneficial free market system depends at its core upon the fact that a corporation—except in the rarest situations—is organized under, and governed by, the law of a single jurisdiction, traditionally the corporate law of the state of its incorporation.

CTS Corp., 481 U.S. at ——, 107 S.Ct. at 1649 (citations omitted) (emphases added).[11]

---

11. *See* United Air Lines, Inc. v. Illinois Commerce Commission, Ill.Supr., 32 Ill.2d 516, 207 N.E.2d 433, 437–38 (1965) (commerce clause prohibits Illinois from requiring that a Delaware corporation comply with various requirements concerning a stock issuance); United Air Lines, Inc. v. Nebraska State Ry. Comm'n, Neb.Supr., 172 Neb. 784, 112 N.W.2d 414, 422 (1961); State ex rel

Thus, we conclude that application of the internal affairs doctrine is mandated by constitutional principles, except in "the rarest situations."[12]

In the early part of the twentieth century, the internal affairs doctrine was deemed to have constitutional support under the full faith and credit clause.[13] See Broderick v. Rosner, 294 U.S. 629, 643, 55 S.Ct. 589, 593, 79 L.Ed. 1100 (1935); Converse v. Hamilton, 224 U.S. 243, 256–57, 32 S.Ct. 415, 418–19, 56 L.Ed. 749 (1912). However, in 1935 the Supreme Court developed a balancing test to be used when evaluating whether full faith and credit was applicable. Alaska Packers Ass'n v. Industrial Accident Comm'n, 294 U.S. 532, 55 S.Ct. 518 (1935). A party bringing a full faith and credit claim thereafter bore the burden of establishing that conflicting interests of a foreign state were superior to those of the forum state. Id. at 547, 55 S.Ct. at 523–24.

Order of United Commercial Travelers of America v. Wolfe, 331 U.S. 586, 67 S.Ct. 1355, 91 L.Ed. 1687 (1947) is the last Supreme Court decision which mandates application of the law of the state of organization to an entity's internal dealings under the full faith and credit clause. In Wolfe, the Supreme Court held that full faith and credit required that a dispute involving the internal affairs of a fraternal benefit society be governed by the laws of the state where the society was formed. Id. at 623–25, 67 S.Ct. at 1373–74. Although we recognize that there are lingering uncertainties concerning the vitality of Wolfe,[14] we believe that full faith and credit commands application of the internal affairs doctrine except in the rare circumstance where national policy[15] is out-

---

Utilities Comm'n v. Southern Bell Tel. and Tele. Co. N.C.Supr., 288 N.C. 201, 217 S.E.2d 543, 549 (1975); Panhandle Eastern Pipe Line Co. v. Public Util. Comm'n, Ohio Supr., 56 Ohio St.2d 334, 383 N.E.2d 1163, 1169–70 (1978).

12. CTS Corp. v. Dynamics Corp. of America, provides strong support for a conclusion that the commerce clause mandates that a state apply the internal affairs doctrine to disputes involving corporations organized under the laws of a sister state. CTS Corp. involved a challenge to Indiana's second generation corporate takeover statute. The Indiana statute applies only to Indiana corporations, and is thus distinguishable from the first generation of statutes struck down in Edgar v. MITE Corp., which purported to govern the internal affairs of foreign corporations. In MITE, the Supreme Court held that Illinois violated the commerce clause by burdening interstate commerce when regulating the internal affairs of a foreign corporation. In CTS Corp., the Court ruled that a state does not violate the commerce clause, notwithstanding heavy burdens imposed upon interstate commerce, if a state is merely regulating the internal affairs of its own corporations.

13. This clause directs that "Full Faith and Credit shall be given in each State to the Public Acts, Records, and judicial Proceedings of every other State..." U.S. Const. Art. IV, § 1.

14. *See* Allstate Insurance Co. v. Hague, 449 U.S. 302, 101 S.Ct. 633, 66 L.Ed.2d 521 (1981); Wilson v. Louisiana-Pacific Resources, Inc., Cal.App., 138 Cal.App.3d 216, 187 Cal.Rptr. 852, 856–58 (1982) (contra). *See also* Kaplan, *Foreign Corporations and Local Corporate Policy*, 21 VAND.L.REV. 433, 446–47 (1968). However, Professor Kaplan relies on Clay v. Sun Insurance Office, Ltd., 377 U.S. 179, 84 S.Ct. 1197, 12 L.Ed.2d 229 (1964) to support his assertion that Wolfe will not be extended to general business corporations. In Clay, plaintiff purchased an insurance policy which contained a one year statute of limitations clause enforceable under existing Illinois law. The Supreme Court held that a Florida statute requiring a minimum five year statute of limitations period was applicable, in an action brought in Florida, thus striking the one year limitation period provided by the Illinois contract. Petitioner was not a "shareholder" of respondent insurance company, and this case in no way involves the internal affairs of an organization—i.e., those matters peculiar to the officers, directors and shareholders of an organization acting in such capacities. In stark contrast, Wolfe involved the rights of a member of a fraternal benefit society, in his capacity as a member (shareholder) as against the benefit society (corporation). The Supreme Court held that the full faith and credit clause required that the law of the state wherein the benefit society was established be applied in litigation between the member and the society.

15. *See, e.g.*, Kozyris, *supra* at 34: "Elementary considerations of predictability, practicality, and equality call for both corporate governance and the common rights and obligations of shareholders

weighed by a significant interest of the forum state in the corporation and its shareholders. Reese and Kaufman, supra at 1141.

Addressing the facts originally presented to the trial court and to us, we must conclude that due process and the commerce clause, in addition to principles of Delaware conflicts law, mandate reversal. Due process requires that directors, officers and shareholders be given adequate notice of the jurisdiction whose laws will ultimately govern the corporation's internal affairs. Under such circumstances, application of 8 Del.C. § 160(c) to International would unfairly and, in our opinion, unconstitutionally, subject those intimately involved with the management of the corporation to the laws of Delaware.

Moreover, application of Section 160(c) to International would violate the commerce clause. Delaware and Panama law clearly differ in their treatment of a subsidiary's voting rights under the facts originally presented here. For Delaware now to interfere in the internal affairs of a foreign corporation having no relationship whatever to this State clearly implies that International can be subjected to the differing laws of all fifty states on various matters respecting its internal affairs. Such a prohibitive burden has obvious commerce clause implications, and could not pass constitutional muster. The substantial effect that would impose on interstate commerce triggers the Pike v. Bruce Church, Inc. balancing test. Since a state has no interest in regulating the internal affairs of a foreign corporation under MITE, Delaware has nothing left with which to counterbalance the burden that application of Section 160(c) on International would impose on interstate commerce. Given all the circumstances, the trial court's ruling cannot stand.[16]

IV.

Plaintiffs protest the issuance of voting stock to McDermott Delaware on public policy grounds, relying on the following statement from Norlin:

> [The] statutes seek to safeguard minority shareholders from management attempts at self-perpetuation. If cross-ownership and cross-voting of stock between parents and subsidiaries were unregulated, officers and directors could easily entrench themselves by exchanging a sufficient number of shares to block any challenge to their autonomy....

744 F.2d at 262 (citation omitted).

In that regard, Delaware law prohibits cross-voting of stock by majority-owned subsidiaries of Delaware corporations. 8 Del.C. § 160(c). But here, we are called upon to apply the laws of Panama to a Panamanian corporation having no contacts with Delaware. We are not altering existing law governing Delaware corporations.

On the record before the Court of Chancery, we are not faced with some "Draconian" measure for the effectuation of a scheme designed solely to entrench existing management to the detriment of the corporation's shareholders. See Unocal Corp. v. Mesa Petroleum Co., Del.Supr., 493 A.2d 946, 955 (1985). The facts here do not support an entrenchment claim. The size of the voting interest placed in McDermott Delaware, its stated principal purpose being for tax advantages, and the timing of the transaction, all sustain this conclusion. In short, there was no threat of any kind

---

to be subject to a single law. Full faith and credit gives primacy to the statute chosen by the parties with the consent of the state of incorporation.

16. However, we recognize that as a Panamanian corporation, McDermott International's rights here do not derive from the full faith and credit clause, which applies only to the laws of American states.

which implicated the policies discussed by us in Unocal. Id. at 954–59. If such issues should arise in a takeover context, they can be addressed in a proper way and at the proper time. See Moran v. Household International, Inc., Del.Supr., 500 A.2d 1346, 1357 (1985).

In conclusion, the trial court erred as a matter of law in ignoring the uncontroverted Panamanian law, and in applying Delaware and/or Louisiana law to the internal affairs of International contrary to established Delaware law and important constitutional principles. Accordingly the judgment of the Court of Chancery is REVERSED.

Comments and Questions

1. Assume that Wyoming passes a pseudo-foreign corporation law substantially the same as California Corporations Code Section 2115. Pottery World, a California corporation, has its principal place of business in Wyoming. All of Pottery World's employees, managers, plant and equipment are located in Wyoming. Five of Pottery World's ten shareholders (each holding five shares of stock) reside in Wyoming, Four reside in California and the other resides in Delaware. Wyoming's corporation's statutes forbids cumulative voting as inimical to modern notions of democratic corporate governance. The Wyoming shareholders of Pottery World have informed the Board of Directors that under the new Wyoming pseudo-foreign corporation statute, cumulative voting cannot be permitted at the upcoming shareholder's meeting.

   A. Can the California resident shareholder bring a declaratory judgement action in California state court seeking to prohibit the imposition of the Wyoming pseudo-foreign corporation act? Assume that no shareholder, other than the California resident shareholders have any contacts with California.

   B. Assume an action to enforce the Wyoming pseudo-foreign corporations law is brought by Pottery World in Wyoming. How should the Wyoming court decide the case?

2. Assume that in the period after the decisions in *Wilson* and *McDermott*, the states of New York, Texas, Illinois, Florida, New Jersey, Pennsylvania, and Michigan all pass laws substantially the same as California's Corporations Code Section 2115. You are an aid to the Governor of Delaware. The Governor read a report suggesting that, as a result of these enactments, most corporations have begun to conform their incorporation practices to the laws of these states. As a result, the report suggests, many corporations will consider reincorporating in the state of their principal residence and begin lobbying those states for modifications of their corporations codes to conform more to the laws of Delaware. The report concludes that corporations tend to prefer predictability and are not loyal to the principles of the internal affairs doctrine. The Governor has asked you to be prepared to discuss the report and the likelihood that states could, in this manner, impose without federal intervention, a siège social rule in the United States.

3. Assume that a majority of states adopt a rule which provides that the law of the state of the domicile of a corporation applies to the internal affairs of that corporation. Would such a rule eliminate all problems of determining the state with the power to regulate a corporation's internal affairs? Consider in that light a situation where the law of California defined domicile as the place where more than fifty percent of the opera-

tions of a corporation are based, and that Utah defined domicile as the state where a corporation establishes its executive offices.

B. Systems for the Regulation of Corporate Internal Affairs Within the EU

Unlike the United States where there is a general adherence to the foundation or seat rule, and pseudo-foreign corporation rules are the exception, Europe has two dynamic systems of determining which state may regulate corporations. Ireland, England and the Netherlands follow the American rule that the internal affairs of the corporation are governed by the law of the state of incorporation. Under this regime, the general corporate laws of the state of incorporation are deemed to be applicable to corporations, irrespective of the place of operations of the corporation. In contrast, in all other E.C. countries the prevailing rule is that the internal affairs of corporations are subject to the law of the state where the company has its headquarters (*the siège social or seat rule*). In effect, under this regime, a corporation must be domiciled (and incorporated) in the state in which it establishes its principal place of business. Should such principal place of business change, the corporation may have to wind up in the state of its former domicile and reincorporate in the state of its new primary residence. As you read the materials that follow, consider to what extent the European internal affairs doctrine is similar to that described by the Delaware Supreme Court in *McDermott*, and to what extent the rule of California Corporations Code § 2115 is similar to the European siège social.

Richard D. English, *Company Law in the European Single Market*

1990 B.Y.U. L. Rev. 1413 (1990)
(excerpts pages 1433–35)

Among the primary concerns of corporate law in the United States and in Western Europe is the "internal affairs of the corporation"—the relations of the company with its shareholders, its boards, it officers, and among the shareholders themselves. In American corporate law, it is familiar rule that corporations' internal affairs are subject to the law of the state of incorporation. In continental Europe, the prevailing rule is that the internal affairs are subject to the law of the state where the company has its headquarters. In the EC, only in Ireland, the United Kingdom, and the Netherlands does the "state of incorporation" rule prevail.

The problem of determining the legal system that should govern corporations' internal affairs must be distinguished from related problems. First, recognition of foreign companies is concerned with the acceptance of the foreign company's legal personality and of its capacity to contract and sue in its own name. In the original six members of the EC, only a company validly incorporated in the country where it had its central office or principal place of management (its *siège social*) was considered validly incorporated. The *siège social* is required to be the real central office (*siège reel*) and not just a formal registered office (*siège statutaire*). This rule remains valid among most of the Member States including those that became members of the EC after its initial formation. However, in Italy, companies incorporated abroad that have their principal place of business or activity in Italy are regarded as Italian companies, and they must comply with the provisions of Italian law. Secondly, the right of establishment, a basic provision of the Treaty of Rome, assures a wide range of business associations that they will be able to open branches in the other EC nations. Finally, companies formed outside the EC may form subsidiaries organized under the laws of the Member States to take advantage of the provisions of the Treaty of Rome guaranteeing such companies the right of establishment. In addition, these companies may be concerned about the problems associated with the transfer of the headquarters of a company from outside the Community to a location within a Member State. These interrelated issues have had great importance for the shaping of company law in Europe and permeate provisions of the EC's legislation on company law.

The acceptance of the *siège social* rule among most of the Member States has arguably removed a force that would naturally and informally tend to harmonize European company law. The adoption of the opposite rule, the common law's internal affairs doctrine, would have precipitated a European "race of laxity," a downward spiral of competitive deregulation as a governments competed to serve as the incorporator of companies. The obvious response to this contention is that such harmonization would have been achieved only at the cost of lower levels of protection for the interests of shareholders, creditors, and other parties—in other words, protection determined by the lowest common denominator of company law.

---

1. The Seat Theory

Some theorists have argued that the *siège social* or seat rule tends to remove the possibilities that the laws of corporate governance would progressively evolve into a state of greater convergence, on the model of corporate codes in the United States. It has served to preserve the highly protective nature of the company laws of certain Member States, and is one of the causes for the push for harmonization through the rule-making power of the European Communities. Do you agree?

Richard English, *Company Law in the European Single Market*

1990 B.Y.U. L. Rev. 1413
(excerpts pages 1435–36)

The prevalence of the *siège social* rule, a distinctive feature of the laws in most Member States, has tended to remove the possibility that the laws of corporate governance would progressively evolve into a state of greater convergence. While it has preserved the more highly protective nature of Western European company law, it must be seen as one of the conditions necessitating the single market program's company law proposals.

In contrast, the convergence in the corporation laws of the American states was achieved without the conscious design of a single mind or even a single governmental institution, legislative body or political process. In the United States, the celebrated race of laxity had the effect of producing more uniformity and liberality at the same time. The differing conditions in Europe, where the *siège social* rule has served to shield protective rules from erosion, are the basis for the struggle for a more uniform company law for the twelve Member States.

Re Expatriation of a German Company

(Case 3Z BR 14/92)
Bayerisches Oberstes Landesgericht
(Bavarian Provincial Court of Appeal) (3rd Civil Chamber)
[1993] 2 CMLR 801
7 May 1992

The firm—GmbH is registered in the Commercial Register with its seat in Munich. At the notarially authenticated meeting of the company on 13 August 1991 the sole member resolved inter alia to amend the relevant clause of its Articles so as to remove the company's seat to London, England. On 2 September 1991 the company applied for that change in its articles to be entered in the Register. By decision of 23 September 1991 the Registrar refused the application on the ground that the change of the company's seat to a foreign country would remove its legal capacity under German law, so that an application would have to be made for it to be wound up. The objection to that decision, which was not accepted by the Registrar or the sole judge, was dismissed by the Landgericht (Commercial Chamber) as unfounded by its decision of 5 December 1991. The company now appeals further against that decision.

DECISION:

The appeal is unfounded.

The Landgericht reasoned that a German private limited company (Gesellschaft mit beschrankter Haftung) must have its seat in the Federal Republic of Germany; it was impossible to pass a valid resolution to transfer the seat abroad while maintaining the company's identity. A resolution to that effect therefore could not be entered on the Register. Although it was doubtful whether that conclusion was compatible with the EEC Treaty requirement of freedom of movement, the relevant Articles of the Treaty-Articles 52 and 58 were only programmatic.

In the result that decision withstands a review on matters of law.

1. Under the German legal system there are no conflicts of law rules on legal persons. For that reason there is also no set of statutory rules on the treatment of cross-border transfers of the seat of a legal person. The legal system that governs the relationships of such persons, that is to say the personal law applicable to them, must therefore be determined by reference to case law and academic writing. For these purposes the starting point has generally been the 'seat theory', although the 'foundation theory,' which is predominant especially in Anglo-American and Dutch academic thinking, also has its supporters. The difference between these two theories, put simply, lies in the fact that under the foundation theory the personal law applicable to the company is governed by the legal system under which it was founded,

while under the seat theory the legal system of the actual seat of administration is decisive.

(a) The resolution of the sole member to remove the company's seat to London, that is, to a foreign country, evidently entailed the transfer of the registered seat as well as the administrative seat. For that reason it is not necessary for present purposes to decide the question whether the transfer of the registered seat alone to a foreign country would entail other legal consequences than would the transfer of the administrative seat.

(b) If a limited company subject to German law transfers its actual seat of administration to another country then, according to the seat theory, which is adopted almost universally by the courts and predominantly by learned writers, it changes its personal law, whereas according to the foundation theory it retains it. The Court is aware that the foundation theory has recently found supporters in the literature who say that it should also be applied in the European Community sphere in particular, referring to the freedom of establishment guaranteed under Articles 52 and 58 EEC. Among variations of this theory, which are intended to circumvent its weaknesses in certain areas, reference should be made to the differentiation theory, which attempts to combine freedom of formation with protection of third parties' interests, and the overlay theory, under which the application of the rules of the place of incorporation will be ousted by the rules of the place of its seat in certain circumstances.

(c) On further consideration the Court still sees no reason to abandon the seat theory which it has adopted hitherto. This theory, which is a protective one, is still supported by the better arguments. It ensures that in general the law of the state that is most affected will be implemented; it has the advantage of being appropriate to the issues arising, it makes effective state supervision possible, and offers the greatest possible protection for creditors. A state which, out of concern for its own national economy, is wary of the encroachment of the interests of the founders of the company and the state of incorporation will in principle choose a connecting factor independent of the statutory seat and place of registration and concentrate on the law of the place from which the company is actually controlled.

As already mentioned, on the seat theory the transfer of the actual seat of administration to another country leads to a change in the personal law applicable to the company. Its continued existence is only guaranteed if there is co-operation between the old and the new applicable laws. If the state from which it departs requires the company to be dissolved, for that reason alone it is impossible for it to change its applicable law while retaining its identity, regardless of whether the adopted state also requires it to be reconstituted.

2. (a) On the prevailing view the resolution to move the actual seat of administration and the registered seat abroad entails the dissolution of the company. That cannot be prevented either by a contrary intention on the members' part or by a provision in the articles. On another view such a resolution to transfer the seat is void. The Court has no doubts about treating such a resolution to move as a resolution to dissolve, because where a resolution to that effect is unanimous (in this case it was made by the sole member) in transferring the seat account is also taken of the dissolution of the company. But further exposition of this point is unnecessary because regardless of which view one adopts the application to transfer the seat must be dismissed in any event.

(b) Nor is this result affected by the fact that this is a transfer of the seat of a German private company from one EC State to another.

It is true that this Court in its judgment of 18 September 1986, after holding that the European Court evidently proceeded on the basis that Article 58 EEC is immediately applicable, expressed doubts whether Article 58 might not require the application of the foundation theory within the area covered by the Article. But since this issue was not relevant to the decision in that case there was no question of a reference to the European Court. In the meantime it has been made unnecessary because that Court has already decided the question.

(1) The preliminary ruling procedure under Article 177 EEC also applies to cases that are not inter partes. Under Article 177(3) in conjunction with 177(1)(a) a court against whose decisions there is no judicial remedy under national law must make a reference if the interpretation of the Treaty is at issue. For these purposes the prevailing view is that the relevant factor is whether an appeal can still be brought against the decision in the specific case. On that basis, in the present proceedings, a last instance decision is being given for the purposes of Article 177. It is relevant to the decision in the present case whether Article 58 is to be interpreted as meaning that the application of the seat theory is prohibited as regards the removal of the seat of a German private limited company to another EC State.

However, the duty to make a reference under Article 177 EEC does not apply without restriction. It does not arise if, in pending proceedings, a question of Community law is posed but it is not relevant to the decision of the case, and also if the correct application of Community law is so obvious as to leave no scope for reasonable doubt and, finally, if the European Court has already decided an equivalent question raised in other proceedings. The last case applies here.

(2) In its judgment of 27 September 1988 the European Court explained, inter alia, that in some member-States not only the registered office but also the real seat or head office—that is to say the central administration—must be situated in the state's territory; the removal of the corporate leadership from that territory therefore presupposes the dissolution of the company with all the consequences entailed by such winding-up in company and tax law. The differences in the rules of the various national laws were known when the EEC Treaty came into being, and it took account of differences in national laws.

The Treaty did not intend, for example, to solve the problems thrown up by such differences through rules on the right of establishment; rather, in Articles 54(3)(g) (directives) and 220(3) (treaties) it only created the legal basis for legislative measures or conventions, which had not yet come into existence.

Nor have the relevant conventions or legislative measures been forthcoming in the meanwhile.

In the view of the European Court Articles 52 and 58 EEC in the present state of Community law do not accord a company founded under the law of a member-State and having its registered seat there the right to transfer the seat of its corporate leadership to another member-State.

(3) The appeal is certainly correct in pointing out that the subject-matter of the present case is not immediately comparable with that of the case on which the European Court's judgment was based. There, two member-States were involved under whose rules of private international law the foundation theory is relevant (namely the United Kingdom and Holland). Behrens in his critical note on the European Court judgment explains, inter alia, that the Court 'strictly speaking was answering a different question from that referred to it' because it had no cause to express its views on

the consequences of the seat theory under private international law. But that does not alter the fact that the European Court clearly answered the present question in the sense that the seat theory is compatible with Article 58 EEC, and that this provision accords the right of establishment to legal persons only in so far as there are no provisions of national law to the contrary. The scope for the formulation of rules under national company and tax laws therefore has precedence over the freedom of companies to emigrate.

(4) Accordingly this Court's duty to refer the question to the European Court under Article 177(3) EEC is removed. Although there is still a right to make a reference under Article 177(2) and also a duty to do so if the Court did not wish to follow the case law of the European Court since Community law does not recognize an obligation of the European Court to follow its precedents, this Court must refrain from making a reference in the present case because it regards the European Court's exposition of the law as correct, and its doubts expressed in earlier decisions as to whether Article 58 EEC may possibly require the application of the foundation theory are therefore removed.

Appeal dismissed with costs.

Comments and Questions

1. The Bavarian Court expressed the generally given rationales for the use of the seat theory within Europe. How similar are these reasons to the state policies furthered by California Gen. Corp. Code Section 2115?

2. The Bavarian court speaks expressively about the need for nations to regulate legal persons whose relationships with that nation is strongest. The Bavarian court's rationale for the utility of the seat theory appears to apply to any nation. Does the rationale offered by that court imply that national governments, not subordinate governments, ought to be the locus of corporate regulation? What if the nation with respect to which protection against the abuse of legal persons is an important matter of state policy were the European Union and not the federal Republic of Germany? If this is true, might this suggest that, in federal republics and supra-national economic organizations at least, the seat theory is most appropriate where corporate regulation is made at the same level of government as economic policy?

3. Does the use of both the seat and foundation theories in Europe militate against the convergence of corporate law doctrine? If so, why?

---

2. Attacks on the Supremacy of the Seat Theory in the EU

The problems posed by the difference in effect and implementation between the foundation doctrine and that of the siège social, has complicated the movement towards approximation and harmonization of the company laws of the Community. Consider, in this context, the following materials.

Treaty Establishing the European Economic Community

Arts. 43–48 (ex 52–58)

Consolidated Version of the Treaty Establishing the European Community
http://www.europa.eu.int/eur-lex/en/treaties/indext.html
pages 57–59

Chapter 2
Right of establishment

Article 43 (ex Article 52)

Within the framework of the provisions set out below, restrictions on the freedom of establishment of nationals of a Member State in the territory of another Member State shall be prohibited. Such prohibition shall also apply to restrictions on the setting-up of agencies, branches or subsidiaries by nationals of any Member State established in the territory of any Member State.

Freedom of establishment shall include the right to take up and pursue activities as self employed persons and to set up and manage undertakings, in particular companies or firms within the meaning of the second paragraph of Article 48, under the conditions laid down for its own nationals by the law of the country where such establishment is effected, subject to the provisions of the Chapter relating to capital.

* * *

Article 48 (ex Article 58)

Companies or firms formed in accordance with the law of a Member State and having their registered office, central administration or principal place of business within the Community shall, for the purposes of this Chapter, be treated in the same way as natural persons who are nationals of Member States. "Companies or firms' means companies or firms constituted under civil or commercial law, including cooperative societies, and other legal persons governed by public or private law, save for those which are non-profit-making.

Regina v. HM Treasury and Commissioners of Inland Revenue ex parte Daily Mail and General Trust plc

(Case 81/87)
Court of Justice of the European Communities
[1988] ECR 5483, [1988] 3 CMLR 713
27 September 1988

M Marco Darmon (Advocate General):

The issue in the main proceedings lies at the point where company law meets tax law. In the United Kingdom, the connecting factors governing the application to a legal person of those branches of law are not necessarily the same. The concept of incorporation, as it is understood in English law, makes it possible to dissociate a company's domicile, expressed through its registered office, and its nationality, on the one hand, from its residence, which largely determines the tax rules applicable to it, on the other. The proceedings pending before the national court arise from the possibility of such a separation.

In that regard, the legislation of the member-States is very diverse, and that situation is aggravated by differences in the content of the relevant concepts. In order to overcome the resulting difficulties recourse must be had to harmonisation at Community level or agreements concluded by the member-States. In any event, the function of the Court of Justice is to interpret Community law as it now stands. Thus the context of the case in which the Queen's Bench Division of the High Court has referred questions to the Court for a preliminary ruling, as it appears from the file, calls for certain general observations in order to attempt to reply to the questions. Those questions raise delicate problems concerning the interpretation of the Community provisions in regard to the right of establishment which have not until now been considered by the Court. What is involved in this case is the claim by a company to exercise the right of establishment and, in particular, the conditions to which the member-State of origin in which its registered office is situated may make subject the transfer of its central management and control to another member-State.

Does such a transfer come within the scope of the right of establishment guaranteed by the Treaty? Establishment 'means integration into a national economy' (J Schapira, G Le Tallec and JB Blaise, Droit Europeen des Affaires (Paris: PUF, Themis, 1984) p 534). Thus, it is not contested that establishment within the meaning of the Treaty involves two factors: physical location and the exercise of an economic activity, both, if not on a permanent basis, at least on a durable one. (See, for example, J Renauld, Droit Europeen des Societes (Brussels: Bruyland et Vander, 1969) p 2.08; M Colomes, Le Droit de l'Etablissement et des Investissements dans la CEE (Paris: J Delmas, 1971) p 78; F Burrows, Free Movement in European Community Law (Oxford: Clarendon Press, 1987) p 187).

Let me point out that the right of establishment, as laid down in Articles 52 to 58 of the Treaty, applies to 'companies or firms formed in accordance with the law of a member-State and having their registered office, central administration or principal place of business within the Community' (Article 58(1)). The right of establishment can manifest itself in two different ways. (See, for example, J Temple Lang, 'The right of establishment of companies and free movement of capital in the European Economic Community', in WR Lafave and P Hey (ed), International Trade, Investment and Organization, (University of Illinois Press, 1967) p 302, in particular pp 302 and 303). On the one hand, subsidiaries, branches oragencies may be set up. That is known as secondary establishment. The Court, in its judgment of 4 December 1986 EC Commission v Germany (Case 205/84 [1987] 2 CMLR 69), stated that an undertaking is established in a member-State as soon as it has a permanent presence there even if that presence consists merely of

> an office managed by the undertaking's own staff or by a person who is independent but authorised to act on a permanent basis for the undertaking, as would be the case with an agency'.

Establishment may also take the form of the setting up of a new company or the transfer of the central management and control of the company, often regarded as its real head office. That is called 'primary establishment'. It has been said in that regard that 'central management and control is not a legal concept but an economic one' (M Schwartz, Le Droit d'Etablissement des Societes Commerciales dans le Traite instituant la Communaute Economique Europeenne (Geneva: Editions medecine et hygiene, 1963) p 61) and that it 'is located where the company organs take the decisions that are essential for the company's operations' (U Everling, The Right of Establishment in the Common Market (Commerce Clearing House, 1964) p 75).

The concept of establishment itself is essentially an economic one (J Renauld, op cit, pp 2.19 and 2.35). It always implies a genuine economic link (RW Harding, 'Freedom of establishment and the rights of companies', [1963] Current Legal Problems, 162 and 163). The transfer of the central management and control of a company, understood by reference to 'criteria which are more economic than legal' (J Renauld, op cit, p 2.43), is covered by the right of establishment in so far as it is necessary to determine in concrete terms 'the economic centre of gravity of the undertaking'. Thus 'the concept of central management and control... corresponds... not merely to the physical location of the principal administrative services but also, and perhaps principally, to the place from which the company is actually run.' The real head office is normally the place where the company's central management and administration is located, since that is 'the place in which the decisions concerning the company's independent activity are made and from which that activity is set in motion; in other words, it is the centre from which that activity is exercised...' B Goldman and A Lyon-Caen, Droit commercial europeen, 4th ed (Paris: Dalloz, 1983), p 357).

The parties to the main proceedings take entirely opposite views on the question whether the transfer of the management of a company constitutes 'establishment' within the meaning of the Treaty. According to Daily Mail and General Trust, such a transfer comes within the scope of the right of establishment. Arguing on the basis of Articles 52 to 58 of the Treaty and the General Programme for the abolition of restrictions on freedom of establishment (OJ Spec Ed, 2nd series, IX p 7), the applicant considers that the location in a member-State of the central management and control of a company is sufficient to permit the existence of a 'real and continuous link' (Expression borrowed from the general programme, Title I) with the economy of that State to be presumed, and thus constitutes 'establishment' within the meaning of the Treaty. Conversely, the United Kingdom takes the view that a change of residence by a company does not constitute establishment. It does not necessarily imply a change in the company's economic activities, especially since a company wishing to conduct economic activity in another member-State can do so through secondary establishments. Finally, the Commission is of the opinion that it is for national law to determine whether a company may transfer its residence without being wound up. It considers that Article 52 applies where national legislation permits a company to transfer its residence without losing its nationality.

In my view, the problem should be expressed in different terms. The concept of central management is difficult to pin down. Even where it designates the place at which the board of directors meets, it is not sufficient to provide a satisfactory connecting factor. As has been noted, 'owing to the progress made by means of communication, it is no longer necessary to arrange formal board meetings. The telephone, telex and telecopier enable each director to state his point of view and to take part in the decision-making without being physically present in a given place. The board meetings each director will attend via television will soon form part of company's everyday life. The board of directors can meet in a place chosen arbitrarily, which bears no real relation with the decision centre of the company' (J-M Rivier, 'General Report: The Fiscal Residence of Companies', Studies on International Fiscal Law, Volume LXXIIa, p 75). The place in which the board of directors meets cannot, therefore, constitute the sole criterion making it possible to designate with certainty in each case the place in which the central management is located. That designation cannot be arrived at by means of a formal legal assessment which does not take account of a number of factual elements the respective scope of which may vary according to the type of company involved.

In order to determine whether the transfer of the central management and control of a company constitutes establishment within the meaning of the Treaty it is therefore necessary to take into consideration a range of factors. The place at which the management of the company meets is undoubtedly one of the foremost of those factors, as is the place, normally the same, at which general policy decisions are made. However, in certain circumstances those factors may be neither exclusive nor even decisive. It might be necessary to take account of the residence of the principal managers, the place at which administrative and accounting documents are kept and the place at which the company's principal financial activities are carried on, in particular, the place at which it operates a bank account. That list cannot be regarded as exhaustive. Moreover, those factors may have to be given different weight according to whether, for example, the company is engaged in production or investment. In the latter case, it may be perfectly legitimate to take account of the market on which the company's commercial or stock exchange transactions are mainly carried out and the scale of those transactions.

In the light of the judgment in Leclerc (Case 229/83, Association Des Centres Distributeurs Edouard Leclerc V sarl 'AU BLE VERT'; [1985] ECR 1, [1985] 2 CMLR 286) it is clear that Community law offers no assistance where 'objective factors' show that a particular activity was carried out 'in order to circumvent' national legislation. The fact that the essential activities of a company take place on the territory of a member-State other than that to which it intends to transfer its central management may not be ignored. Such circumstances may, in certain cases, constitute an indication that what is involved is not genuine establishment, in particular when the effect of the transfer of the central management is to cause the company to cease to be subject to legislation which would otherwise apply to it. I believe that that conclusion can be drawn from the judgments of the Court in Van Binsbergen (Case 33/74 [1974] ECR 1299, [1975] 1 CMLR 298) and Knoors (Case 115/78 [1979] ECR 399, [1979] 2 CMLR 357). As a general rule it appears that the national court may assess whether, in a specific case and having regard to the circumstances, there is a suggestion of abuse of a right or circumvention of the law and whether it should decide not to apply Community law.

However, when the proper conclusion to be drawn from the circumstances is that the transfer of the central management genuinely constitutes establishment within the meaning of the Treaty, the question then arises whether the right to make such a transfer may be made subject to the authorisation of the national authorities and whether those authorities may object to the transfer for fiscal reasons.

Generally, in most of the member-States, the transfer of the central management of a company, in the sense of its real head office, may take place only through the winding up of the company and its reconstitution in the host member-State. That solution, the 'legal death' of the company, involves the settlement of its tax position, determined on the day of the winding up, both in regard to the existing debt and in regard to matters in respect of which the event normally giving rise to tax liability has not yet occurred. Capital gains are thus taxed even though no disposition of assets has taken place. In regard to the member-States referred to above, the transfer of the central management of a company without loss of legal personality or nationality may take place under agreements between member-States of the kind provided for in Article 220 of the Treaty.

No prior authorisation may be required for the exercise of a fundamental freedom laid down in the Treaty. Similarly, a member-State cannot prevent a company from exercising its right of establishment on the ground that such exercise entails a loss of revenue in respect of taxes which would have been due on the basis of the company's future activities if it had remained subject to the tax laws of that State.

However, I consider that as Community law now stands, member-States are not prevented from requiring a company to settle its fiscal position upon any transfer of its central management, even where winding up is not required. It is generally accepted that the winding up required by national legislation as a condition for the emigration of a company is not contrary to Community law (J Renauld, op cit, p 2.47). It would be paradoxical if a member-State not requiring winding up were to find itself placed by Community law in a less favourable fiscal position precisely because its legislation on companies is more consistent with Community objectives in regard to establishment. A company set up under the legislation of a member-State in which 'fiscal allegiance' (This expression comes from J-M Rivier, op cit, p 15) is determined in the light of the location of the central administration will maintain its registered office in that country and continue to have that country's nationality even after transferring its residence or, more precisely, the seat of its management, to another member-State. However, for the reasons indicated above, that does not seem to me, in the present state of Community law, to preclude national authorities from attaching to such a transfer fiscal consequences similar to those of winding up.

The guidelines which I propose should enable the Court to reply to the first and third questions referred to it by the Queen's Bench Division of the High Court. They make a reply to the fourth question unnecessary. The remaining question does not require any long discussion. Although the first paragraph of Article 58 provides that companies or firms are, for the purposes of the provisions of the Treaty on freedom of establishment, to be treated in the same way as natural persons who are nationals of member-States, they clearly cannot be placed entirely on the same footing; along with the United Kingdom and the Commission, therefore, I consider that Council Directive 72/148 does not apply to legal persons.

Consequently, I propose that the Court should rule that:

> The transfer to another member-State of the central management of a company may constitute a form of exercise of the right of establishment, subject to the assessment by the national court of any elements of fact showing whether or not such a transfer reflects a genuine integration of the said company into the economic life of the host member-State;
>
> Under Community law a member-State may not require a company wishing to establish itself in another member-State, by transferring its central management there, to obtain prior authorisation for such transfer;
>
> However, Community law does not prohibit a member-State from requiring a company established on its territory, upon establishing itself in another member-State by transferring its central management there, to settle its tax position in regard to the part of its assets affected by the transfer, the value of which is to be determined at the date of transfer;

Council Directive 72/148 is applicable only to natural persons.

DECISION (by the Court):

By an order of 6 February 1987, which was received at the Court on 19 March 1987, the High Court of Justice, Queen's Bench Division, referred to the Court for a preliminary ruling under Article 177 EEC four questions on the interpretation of Articles 52 and 58 of the Treaty and Council Directive 73/148 of 21 May 1973 on the abolition of restrictions on movement and residence within the Community for nationals of member-States with regard to establishment and the provision of services ([1973] OJ L172/14).

Those questions arose in proceedings between Daily Mail and General Trust plc, the applicant in the main proceedings (hereinafter referred to as 'the applicant'), and HM Treasury for a declaration, inter alia, that the applicant is not required to obtain consent under United Kingdom tax legislation in order to cease to be resident in the United Kingdom for the purpose of establishing its residence in the Netherlands.

It is apparent from the documents before the Court that under United Kingdom company legislation a company such as the defendant, incorporated under that legislation and having its registered office in the United Kingdom, may establish its central management and control outside the United Kingdom without losing legal personality or ceasing to be a company incorporated in the United Kingdom.

According to the relevant United Kingdom tax legislation, only companies which are resident for tax purposes in the United Kingdom are as a rule liable to United Kingdom corporation tax. A company is resident for tax purposes in the place in which its central management and control is located.

Section 482(1)(a) of the Income and Corporation Taxes Act 1970 prohibits companies resident for tax purposes in the United Kingdom from ceasing to be so resident without the consent of the Treasury.

In 1984 the applicant, which is an investment holding company, applied for consent under the abovementioned national provision in order to transfer its central management and control to the Netherlands, whose legislation does not prevent foreign companies from establishing their central management there; the company proposed, in particular, to hold board meetings and to rent offices for its management in the Netherlands. Without waiting for that consent, it subsequently decided to open an investment management office in the Netherlands with a view to providing services to third parties.

It is common ground that the principal reason for the proposed transfer of central management and control was to enable the applicant, after establishing its residence for tax purposes in the Netherlands, to sell a significant part of its non-permanent assets and to use the proceeds of that sale to buy its own shares, without having to pay the tax to which such transactions would make it liable under United Kingdom tax law, in regard in particular to the substantial capital gains on the assets which the applicant proposed to sell. After establishing its central management and control in the Netherlands the applicant would be subject to Dutch corporation tax, but the transactions envisaged would be taxed only on the basis of any capital gains which accrued after the transfer of its residence for tax purposes.

After a long period of negotiations with the Treasury, which proposed that it should sell at least part of the assets before transferring its residence for tax purposes out of the United Kingdom, the applicant initiated proceedings before the High Court of Justice, Queen's Bench Division, in 1986. Before that court, it claimed that Articles 52 and 58 EEC gave it the right to transfer its central management and control to another member-State without prior consent or the right to obtain such consent unconditionally.

In order to resolve that dispute, the national court stayed the proceedings and referred the following questions to the Court of Justice:

1. Do Articles 42 and 48 of the EEC Treaty preclude a member-State from prohibiting a body corporate with its central management and control in that member-

State from transferring without prior consent or approval that central management and control to another member-State in one or both of the following circumstances, namely where:

(i) payment of tax upon profits or gains which have already arisen may be avoided;

(ii) were the company to transfer its central management and control, tax that might have become chargeable had the company retained its central management and control in that member-State would be avoided?

2. Does Council Directive 73/148/EEC give a right to a corporate body with its central management and control in a member-State to transfer without prior consent or approval its central management and control to another member-State in the conditions set out in Question 1? If so, are the relevant provisions directly applicable in this case?

3. If such prior consent or approval may be required, is a member-State entitled to refuse consent on the grounds set out in Question 1?

4. What difference does it make, if any, that under the relevant law of the member-State no consent is required in the case of a change of residence to another member-State of an individual or firm?

Reference is made to the Report for the Hearing for a fuller account of the facts and the background to the main proceedings, the provisions of national legislation at issue and the observations submitted to the Court, which are mentioned or discussed hereinafter only in so far as is necessary for the reasoning of the Court.

First question

The first question seeks in essence to determine whether Articles 52 and 48 of the Treaty give a company incorporated under the legislation of a member-State and having its registered office there the right to transfer its central management and control to another member-State. If that is so, the national court goes on to ask whether the member-State of origin can make that right subject to the consent of national authorities, the grant of which is linked to the company's tax position.

With regard to the first part of the question, the applicant claims essentially that Article 58 expressly confers on the companies to which it applies the same right of primary establishment in another member-State as is conferred on natural persons by Article 52. The transfer of the central management and control of a company to another member-State amounts to the establishment of the company in that member-State because the company is locating its centre of decision-making there, which constitutes genuine and effective economic activity.

The United Kingdom argues essentially that the provisions of the Treaty do not give companies a general right to move their central management and control from one member-State to another. The fact that the central management and control of a company is located in a member-State does not itself necessarily imply any genuine and effective economic activity on the territory of that member-State and cannot therefore be regarded as establishment within the meaning of Article 52 of the Treaty.

The Commission emphasizes first of all that in the present state of Community law, the conditions under which a company may transfer its central management and control from one member-State to another are still governed by the national law of the State in which it is incorporated and of the State to which it wishes to move. In that regard, the Commission refers to the differences between the national systems of company law. Some of them permit the transfer of the central management and control of a company and, among those, certain attach no legal consequences to such a transfer, even in regard to taxation. Under other systems, the transfer of the management or the centre of decision-making of a company out of the member-State in which it is incorporated results in the loss of legal personality. However, all the systems permit the winding-up of a company in one member-State and its re-incorporation in another. The Commission considers that where the transfer of central management and control is possible under national legislation, the right to transfer it to another member-State is a right protected by Article 52 of the Treaty.

Faced with those diverging opinions, the Court must first point out, as it has done on numerous occasions, that freedom of establishment constitutes one of the fundamental principles of the Community and that the provisions of the Treaty guaranteeing that freedom have been directly applicable since the end of the transitional period. Those provisions secure the right of establishment in another member-State not merely for Community nationals but also for the companies referred to in Article 58.

Even though those provisions are directed mainly to ensuring that foreign nationals and companies are treated in the host member-State in the same way as nationals of that State, they also prohibit the member-State of origin from hindering the establishment in another member-State of one of its nationals or of a company incorporated under its legislation which comes within the definition contained in Article 58. As the Commission rightly observed, the rights guaranteed by Articles 52 et seq would be rendered meaningless if the member-State of origin could prohibit undertakings from leaving in order to establish themselves in another member-State. In regard to natural persons, the right to leave their territory for that purpose is expressly provided for in Directive 73/148, which is the subject of the second question referred to the Court.

In the case of a company, the right of establishment is generally exercised by the setting up of agencies, branches or subsidiaries, as is expressly provided for in the second sentence of the first paragraph of Article 52. Indeed, that is the form of establishment in which the applicant engaged in this case by opening an investment management office in the Netherlands. A company may also exercise its right of establishment by taking part in the incorporation of a company in another member-State, and in that regard Article 221 of the Treaty ensures that it will receive the same treatment as nationals of that member-State as regards participation in the capital of the new company.

The provision of United Kingdom law at issue in the main proceedings imposes no restriction on transactions such as those described above. Nor does it stand in the way of a partial or total transfer of the activities of a company incorporated in the United Kingdom to a company newly incorporated in another member-State, if necessary after winding-up and, consequently, the settlement of the tax position of the United Kingdom company. It requires Treasury consent only where such a company seeks to transfer its central management and control out of the United Kingdom while maintaining its legal personality and its status as a United Kingdom company.

In that regard it should be borne in mind that, unlike natural persons, companies are creatures of the law and, in the present state of Community law, creatures of national law. They exist only by virtue of the varying national legislation which determines their incorporation and functioning.

As the Commission has emphasized, the legislation of member-States varies widely in regard to both the factor providing a connection to the national territory required for the incorporation of a company and the question whether a company incorporated under the legislation of a member-State may subsequently modify that connecting factor. Certain States require that not merely the registered office but also the real head office, that is to say the central administration of the company, should be situated on their territory, and the removal of the central administration from that territory thus presupposes the winding-up of the company with all the consequences that winding-up entails in company law and tax law. The legislation of other States permits companies to transfer their central administration to a foreign country but certain of them, such as the United Kingdom, make that right subject to certain restrictions, and the legal consequences of a transfer, particularly in regard to taxation, vary from one member-State to another.

The Treaty has taken account of that variety in national legislation. In defining, in Article 58, the companies which enjoy the right of establishment, the Treaty places on the same footing, as connecting factors, the registered office, central administration and principal place of business of a company. Moreover, Article 220 of the Treaty provides for the conclusion, so far as is necessary, of agreements between the member-States with a view to securing inter alia the retention of legal personality in the event of transfer of the registered office of companies from one country to another. No convention in this area has yet come into force.

It should be added that none of the directives on the co-ordination of company law adopted under Article 54(3)(g) of the Treaty deal with the differences at issue here.

It must therefore be held that the Treaty regards the differences in national legislation concerning the required connecting factor and the question whether—and if so how—the registered office or real head office of a company incorporated under national law may be transferred from one member-State to another as problems which are not resolved by the rules concerning the right of establishment but must be dealt with by future legislation or conventions.

Under those circumstances, Articles 52 and 58 of the Treaty cannot be interpreted as conferring on companies incorporated under the law of a member-State a right to transfer their central management and control and their central administration to another member-State while retaining their status as companies incorporated under the legislation of the first member-State.

The answer to the first part of the first question must therefore be that in the present state of Community law Articles 52 and 58 of the Treaty, properly construed, confer no right on a company incorporated under the legislation of a member-State and having its registered office there to transfer its central management and control to another member-State.

Having regard to that answer, there is no need to reply to the second part of the first question.

Second question

In its second question, the national court asks whether the provisions of Council Directive 73/148 on the abolition of restrictions on movement and residence within the Community for nationals of member-States with regard to establishment and the provision of services give a company a right to transfer its central management and control to another member-State.

It need merely be pointed out in that regard that the title and provisions of that directive refer solely to the movement and residence of natural persons and that the provisions of the directive cannot, by their nature, be applied by analogy to legal persons.

The answer to the second question must therefore be that Directive 73/148, properly construed, confers no right on a company to transfer its central management and control to another member-State.

Third and fourth questions

Having regard to the answers given to the first two questions referred by the national court, there is no need to reply to the third and fourth questions.

Costs

The costs incurred by the United Kingdom and the Commission of the European Communities, which have submitted observations to the Court, are not recoverable. Since these proceedings are, in so far as the parties to the main proceedings are concerned, in the nature of a step in the action pending before the national court, the decision on costs is a matter for that court.

On those grounds, the Court, in answer to the questions referred to it by the High Court of Justice, Queen's Bench Division, by order of 6 February 1987,

HEREBY RULES:

1. In the present state of Community law, Articles 52 and 58 of the Treaty, properly construed, confer no right on a company incorporated under the legislation of a member-State and having its registered office there to transfer its central management and control to another member-State.

2. Council Directive 73/148 of 21 May 1973 on the abolition of restrictions on movement and residence within the Community for nationals of member-States with regard to establishment and the provision of services, properly construed, confers no right on a company to transfer its central management and control to another member-State.

Comments and Questions

1. Both the Advocate General and the Court distinguish between primary and secondary establishment. What are the differences between them? Is the right of secondary establishment unconditional?

2. Did the Court adopt the position of the Advocate General? If not, what were the differences in their approaches? Does the difference depend on the construction of the meaning of primary establishment for purposes of the "constitutional" right of establishment in the Treaty of Rome? If so, how? Is the primary right of establishment protecting the right of a company to move its principal place of business or administrative offices without loss of the company's incorporation citizenship or is the right protected merely the right to migrate, that is, to dissolve in the place of current incorporation and reincorporate in another place? Would the answer have been different if many of the Member States of the E.U. did not adhere to the seat doctrine?

3. **Problem.** Helga and her spouse are the sole shareholders in a pottery business, Herr Pots GmbH. The company is registered in Trier, where Helga and her spouse reside. All pots are made in Trier from clay imported from Ireland. After several years Helga determines that most of Herr Pots' sales are made in Ireland, now the richest country in the E.U. Helga also knows that she might be able to significantly reduce Her Pots' costs of production and transportation if Helga relocates it to the Dingle Peninsula in Ireland, near the source of her clay. Helga and her spouse establish a division of Herr Pots in Ireland, duly registered with the Irish authorities as "Mr. Pots." This division does not operate in corporate form. Once established, Herr Pots transfers all of its operations to its Irish division. At the end of the year, Helga receives a notification from

the authorities in Trier declaring that Herr Pots GmbH is no longer established in Trier and announcing that dissolution proceedings would begin shortly. Helga comes to see you in your offices in Cork, Ireland. She wants to know if this action on the part of the German authorities violates Herr Pots' establishment rights under the Treaty of Rome. Is she right?

Centros Ltd. v. Erhvervs-og Selskabsstyrelsen

(Case C-212/97)
Court of Justice of the European Communities
[2000] All ER (EC) 481
19 May, 16 July 1998, 9 March 1999

16 July 1998. The Advocate General (La Pergola) delivered the following opinion (translated from the Italian):

I—OBJECT OF THE QUESTION REFERRED BY THE NATIONAL COURT, FACTS AND RELEVANT NATIONAL PROVISIONS

1. The Hojesterets Anke-og Kaeremalsudvalg (Appeals and Objections Committee of the Danish Supreme Court) (the Hojesterets or Supreme Court), has asked the Court of Justice of the European Communities, within the meaning and for the purposes of art 177 of the EC Treaty (now art 234 EC), to interpret the Community provisions on the right of establishment with regard to a case of alleged circumvention of the domestic provisions of a Member State requiring a minimum capital for certain types of company. The question referred by the national court is:

'Is it compatible with Article 52 of the EC Treaty, in conjunction with Articles 58 and 56 thereof, to refuse registration of a branch of a company which has its registered office in another Member State and has been lawfully founded with company capital of £ 100 (approximately D Kr 1000) and established under the legislation of that Member State, where the company does not itself carry on any business but it is desired to set up the branch in order to carry on the entire business in the country in which the branch is established, and where, instead of incorporating a company in the latter Member State, that procedure must be regarded as having been employed in order to avoid paying in company capital of not less than D Kr 200,000 (at present D Kr 125,000)?'

2. I propose to begin with a brief account of the facts that gave rise to the main proceedings. In the summer of 1992, Mrs Bryde, a member and the sole director of Centros Ltd., which had been registered as a private limited company in England and Wales in May of that year, approached the Erhvervs-og Selskabsstyrelsen (the trade and companies board) seeking recognition of the company's memorandum of association with a view to registering a branch. It is apparent from the order for reference that, according to its memorandum of association, the company's object is to carry on business within an extensive range of commercial areas, including the provision of loans. However, the partners intended it only to be a wine import and export business. Since its formation the company has never done any business. The only other member is Mrs Bryde's husband. Mr and Mrs Bryde, both Danish citizens resident in Denmark, acquired the company shortly after it was formed and hold the only two shares that have been issued. The company's share capital, amounting to the legal minimum of £ 100, has not actually been paid in and is kept in a cash box at Mr Bryde's home. The company address is that of a friend of the Brydes in the United Kingdom.

3. The registration of branches of foreign limited companies in Denmark is governed by the rules on limited companies, which, at the time of the events at issue in this case, were embodied in arts 117 to 122 of the Lovbekendtgxrelse (Consolidating Regulation) No 660 of 25 September 1991. It follows from the provisions of that regulation that a limited company established in a member state may do business in Denmark through a branch established in Danish territory, managed by one or more directors authorised to act on its behalf. The branch must be registered by the companies board in order to do business and it may not do business if registration is refused. The branch is subject to Danish law and decisions of the Danish courts in respect of its business dealings in Denmark. It should also be noted for the purposes of this opinion that-as expressly mentioned in the question referred by the national court at the time of the events at issue in this case-companies established in Denmark were required to have paid-up capital of not less than D Kr 200,000 (This was subsequently reduced to D Kr 125,000 by Law No 378 of 22 May 1996. At the same time, however, other rules designed to secure company capital were tightened, in particular (i) the prohibition on acquiring own shares or shares in the parent company; (ii) the conditions governing the acquisition of the company by shareholders within two years of registration if the consideration paid amounts to at least D Kr 50,000 and corresponds to at least 10% of the capital; and (iii) the obligations incumbent on the directors, in the event of losses equal to at least 40% of the share capital.). The commentary on the draft law, subsequently adopted as Law No 886 on 21 December 1991, states that the reason for the increase in the minimum capital required to establish companies of the type in question (and also establish public limited companies (Law No 886 of 21 December 1991 set the requirement as to paid-up capital for public limited liability companies at D Kr 500,000, that is to say, much more than the minimum amount of ECU 25,000 laid down in Second Council Directive (EEC) 77/91 (on co-ordination of safeguards which, for the protection of the interests of members and others, are required by member states of companies within the meaning of the second paragraph of art 58 of the Treaty in respect of the formation of public limited liability companies and the maintenance and alteration of their capital, with a view to making such safeguards equivalent) (OJ 1977 L26 p 1), as subsequently amended.)), compared with the amount previously stipulated, was to strengthen the financial soundness of the companies, to protect the state and other public creditors which, unlike private creditors, cannot demand security or sureties to cover outstanding debts. The new provisions were also intended to prevent the risk of abusive bankruptcy proceedings arising from the insolvency of companies with insufficient paid-up capital. Danish law does not impose any requirement as to minimum capital for companies from other Community countries seeking to establish a branch in Danish territory. However, the practice followed by the companies board in such cases seems to be to ascertain whether the establishment of the existing company abroad is designed to circumvent the Danish rules on minimum capital. In the present case, having failed to obtain from Mrs Bryde the information it had requested about Centros' activities in England and Wales, the board rejected the application for registration. That decision was upheld by the Ostre Landsret (Eastern Regional Court) in a judgment delivered on 8 September 1995, in which it found that the Treaty provisions on freedom of establishment did not allow companies of any member state, whose activity is directed entirely towards the territory of any other member state, to circumvent binding rules of that other state. Appearing as a witness in the proceedings before that court, Mr Bryde said he did not know if the purchase of Centros and the subsequent establishment of a branch in Denmark could be called a circumvention of Danish law but admitted that 'it

is certainly easier to find £ 100 than D Kr 200,000' (free translation). An appeal against the decision of the Court of First Instance of the European Communities is now pending before the Hojesterets, which, in view of the circumstances, has approached the Court of Justice with a request for interpretation in the terms cited above.

II—SUBMISSIONS OF THE PARTIES, THE INTERVENING GOVERNMENTS AND THE COMMISSION

[omitted]

III—LEGAL ANALYSIS OF THE QUESTION REFERRED TO THE COURT

11. The order for reference has defined the reason for referring the question clearly in the following terms. It is not disputed in the main proceedings that properly incorporated private companies limited by shares with registered offices in England or Wales have a right to establishment in Danish territory through branches, despite the fact that the minimum paid-up capital required under United Kingdom law for that type of company is considerably less than is required under Danish law for companies of the same type established in Denmark. Moreover, according to the Danish government representative's statements at the hearing, limited companies of Community member states, particularly the United Kingdom, in fact make wide use of the right of establishment in Denmark without the companies board taking measures of the kind at issue in this case to prevent them from doing so. The point at issue is a different one, namely, is a company lawfully exercising the right to set up a secondary establishment when it intends to carry on its own business exclusively in the country in which the branch is registered and when it is clear that the original decision to incorporate the company in a member state other than the state in which it is intended to do business was motivated solely by a desire to avoid the stricter legal requirements in respect of minimum company capital imposed by the law of the member state in which the secondary establishment was to be set up? According to the Danish government, in view of the circumstances in the case at issue, the answer should be that it is not (and the measure mentioned in the question referred to the court should consequently be declared to be compatible with the rules of the Treaty). To be more precise, the facts in the case at issue are being used by the Danish authorities to advance a two-pronged line of argument, namely that the refusal to register the branch of Centros does not represent a restriction on freedom of establishment contrary to art 52 of the Treaty and, in the alternative, if there is any restriction it is in any event covered by the provisions for special treatment for foreign companies which member states are allowed to adopt under art 56 of the Treaty on grounds of public policy, inter alia. I propose to examine both these arguments in due course. Before doing so, however, I should like if I may to give a brief survey of the court's case law on the subject and to consider what function a secondary establishment in another country performs in the organisational structure of a company.

12. The rule contained in art 52 of the Treaty, which has been directly applicable since the end of the transitional period, is intended to ensure that all nationals of member states who establish themselves in another member state, even if that establishment is only secondary, for the purpose of pursuing activities there as self-employed persons receive the same treatment as nationals of that state. The right of establishment includes the right to set up and manage undertakings under the conditions laid down for its own nationals by the law of the host country and the setting up of agencies, branches or subsidiaries by Community nationals having their principal establishment in the territory of another member state. And under art 58 of the Treaty, the right of establishment also includes the right of companies or firms formed in accordance with the law of a member state and having their registered office, central administration or principal place of

business within the Community to do business in another member state through a secondary establishment. Three further rights are a logical corollary of this fundamental freedom: first, company business may be conducted in a member state through a company incorporated in that state or in another member state; second, companies have the right to decide whether a secondary establishment is to be a subsidiary or a branch; and lastly, foreign companies have the same rights in the state in which the secondary establishment is set up as the companies of that state (see E Werlauff EC Company Law (Copenhagen, 1993) pp 17–22). As the liberal provision of art 58 could be interpreted as meaning that the freedom to set up a secondary establishment is also extended to legal persons having their registered office but not their 'real' head office, that is to say their central administration or principal place of business, within the Community, it very soon became clear that the conditions governing that freedom in the case of companies whose principal establishment was outside the Community would have to be defined (See S Poillot-Peruzetto and M Luby Le Droit Communautaire Applique a l'Entreprise (Paris, 1998) p 141. Yvon Loussouarn observed, with regard to the origin of the criterion of connection examined later in this opinion, that the Community authorities and the delegates of the member states had proceeded on the assumption that art 52 governed the right with respect to a secondary establishment of natural persons having their (primary) establishment in the territory of a member state, hence the requirement of Community residence as well as Community nationality. However, simply to transpose that requirement to companies by insisting on a real head office as well as a registered office would be in open and irremediable breach of art 58 (see 'Le rattachement des societes et la Communaute economique europeenne' in Etudes de Droit des Communautes Europeennes: Melanges Offerts a Pierre Teitgen (Paris, 1984) p 239 (in particular pp 245 and 246) and 'Le droit d'itablissement des societes' [1990] Revue Trimestrielle de Droit Europien 229 (in particular p 236)).). For that purpose, as explained in the general programme for the removal of restrictions on freedom of establishment adopted by the Council on 18 December 1961 ((JO 1962 No 2 p 36) OJ English Sp Ed IX, Resolutions of the Council and of the Representatives of the Member States, p 7), it is necessary to satisfy the further criterion of an economic connection, an 'effective and continuous' link with the economy of a member state (Such a link may consist precisely of a non-Community company having a branch in the territory of a member state, provided that the activities of the territorial extension are permanent, effective and relevant (not just, eg, branch offices or showrooms that are not active in the market or employ only a very small number of people). On the other hand, the nationality of the partners or members of the company's managerial and governing bodies is immaterial in this connection.). However, I need scarcely add, that criterion applies only to non-Community companies.

13. As to the scope of the right to set up a secondary establishment, it is apparent from the case law of the court that it is the seat of the company in question in the sense of the three possibilities mentioned above (see para 12) which-

> 'serves as the connecting factor with the legal system of a particular State, like nationality in the case of natural persons. Acceptance of the proposition that the Member State in which a company seeks to establish itself may freely apply to it a different treatment solely by reason of the fact that its seat (Reporter's note: The text reads 'registered office' at this point as well as earlier in para 18, but it is generally accepted that in this instance 'registered office' is a mistranslation of the French 'sihge' and is incorrect (see eg Judge Edward 'Corporations and the Court' in Corporate Law: The European Dimension (1991) p 149 (at p 152) and Vanessa

> Edwards EC Company Law (1999) p 345.) is situated in another Member State would thus deprive that provision [art 52 of the Treaty] of all meaning.' (See ex multis EC Commission v France Case 270/83 [1986] ECR 273 (para 18 and also paras 13 and 14.) (See also Sodemare SA v Regione Lombardia Case C-70/95 [1997] ECR I-3395 (paras 25 and 26) and Imperial Chemical Industries plc v Colmer (Inspector of Taxes) Case C-264/96 [1998] All ER (EC) 585, [1998] ECR I-4695 (para 20)).

When the two requirements for Community nationality laid down in art 58 are satisfied, ie when a company is lawfully constituted and belongs to a member state, it is entitled to receive the same treatment as companies of a member state other than the state in which its principal establishment is situated, even if it carries on its business solely in that other state through an agency, branch or subsidiary (Segers v Bestuur van de Bedrijfsvereniging voor Bank-en Verzekeringswezen, Groothandel en Vrije Beroepen Case 79/85 [1986] ECR 2375 (paras 14 and 16) (In that judgment, the court held that it was incompatible with arts 52 and 58 of the Treaty for a director of a company to be refused sickness benefit under the national sickness insurance scheme by the competent authorities of the member state in which a secondary establishment (subsidiary) of the company is situated solely by reason of the fact that the parent company was formed in accordance with the laws of another member state and has its registered office in the territory of that state, although it does not conduct any business in that state but operates exclusively in the member state in which the secondary establishment is situated.)). Thus, it follows from the case law of the court that-

> 'the rules regarding equality of treatment forbid not only overt discrimination by reason of nationality or, in the case of a company, its seat, but all covert forms of discrimination which, by the application of other criteria of differentiation, lead in fact to the same result.' (See R v Inland Revenue Comrs, ex p Commerzbank AG Case C-330/91 [1993] 4 All ER 37, [1993] ECR I-4017 (para 14) and Halliburton Services SA v Staatssecretaris van Financien Case C-1/93 [1994] STC 655, [1994] ECR I-1137 (para 15).)

Similarly, the court has ruled that national measures are incompatible with the Treaty where those measures, even though they are applicable without discrimination, are liable to hamper or to render less attractive the exercise by Community nationals (or companies) of fundamental freedoms guaranteed by Community law (see ex multis Kraus v Land Baden-Wurttemberg Case C-19/92 [1993] ECR I-1663 (para 32)).

14. Under art 56 of the Treaty, member states may, moreover, derogate from the prohibition on measures restricting establishment in their territory and apply provisions providing for special treatment for foreign nationals (natural and legal persons) with recognised rights under Community law on grounds of public policy, public security or public health. Inasmuch as it represents a derogation from a fundamental principle of the Treaty, art 56 must be interpreted strictly. For it to apply, there must therefore be a genuine and sufficiently serious threat affecting one of the fundamental interests of society, including the need to combat possible abuse and to ensure the proper implementation of the national social security legislation (see ex multis R v Bouchereau Case 30/77 [1981] 2 All ER 924, [1977] ECR 1999 (para 35) and Segers' case (para 17)). It follows that it cannot be invoked in support of economic aims (see ex multis Stichting Collectieve Antennevoorziening Gouda v Commissariaat voor de Media Case C-288/89 [1991] ECR I-4007 (para 11)); furthermore, the measures taken to protect the interests which it seeks to safeguard must be limited to what is strictly necessary and must obey the principle of proportionality....

Thus, when the restrictive measure at issue is not discriminatory-that is, for present purposes, when it is applicable without distinction to national companies and to companies of other Community countries-it may be justified by overriding reasons relating to the general interest (These include professional rules intended to protect recipients of a service, protection of intellectual property, protection of workers, consumer protection, conservation of the national historical and artistic heritage, turning to account the archaeological, historical and artistic heritage of a country and the widest possible dissemination of knowledge of the artistic and cultural heritage of a country, and reasons of cultural policy (see ex multis the Stichting Collectieve case (paras 14 and 27)); protection of the recipients of services for monitoring and renewing patents (Sager v Dennemeyer & Co Ltd. Case C-76/90 [1991] ECR I-4221 (para 17)); the need to preserve the cohesion of the tax system (Bachmann v Belgium Case C-204/90 [1992] ECR I-249); the prevention of crime and the maintenance of order in society in view of the damaging consequences of excessive demand in the gambling sector (Customs and Excise Comrs v Schindler Case C-275/92 [1994] 2 All ER 193, [1994] ECR I-1039 (paras 58 and 59)); maintaining the good reputation of the national financial sector (Alpine Investments BV v Minister van Financien Case C-384/93 [1995] All ER (EC) 543, [1995] ECR I-1141 (para 44)); the effectiveness of fiscal supervision (Futura Participations SA v Administration des Contributions Case C-250/95 [1997] ECR I-2471 (para 31)); and fair trading (Konsumentombudsmannen (KO) v De Agostini (Svenska) Forlag AB, Konsumentombudsmannen (KO) v TV-Shop I Sverige AB Joined cases C-34-36/95 [1997] All ER (EC) 687, [1997] ECR I-3843 (para 53)).), provided that (i) those reasons are not already satisfied by the rules imposed on the foreign company in the state in which it is established and (ii) the measure is necessary and proportionate (see ex multis the Stichting Collectieve case (paras 13 and 15)).

15. That being said, I come now to the concepts of 'branch' and 'subsidiary' ([in Italian] 'filiale' or to be more precise 'affiliata' ('"Societe affiliate" rather than "filiali" used in Article 52 of the Treaty is the term which, in Italian legal usage, corresponds to the Dutch "dochterondernemingen," English "subsidiaries," French "filiales" and German "Tochtergesellschaften."' (See the opinion of Advocate General Mancini in EC Commission v France.) See also GM Ruggiero and M De Dominicis 'Article 52' in R Quadri, R Monaco and A Trabucchi (ed) Trattato Istitutivo della Comunita Economica Europea. Commentario (Milan, 1965) vol 1 p 399 (in particular pp 412 and 413). But see footnote 15, post.)), referred to in art 52 which in turn refers to art 58 of the Treaty (I leave aside the term 'agency', which has no bearing here). What is the criterion for distinguishing between these two forms of permanent territorial division that a company may set up, possibly in the territory of member states other than the state of origin, generally with the intention that they should deal with third parties? The essential difference is that a branch has no independent legal personality but is defined as part of a de facto whole or simply as a limb of the company, allowing a measure of decentralisation (see M Cabrillac 'Unite ou pluralite de la notion de succursale en droit prive' in Melanges en l'Honneur du Doyen Joseph Harnel (Paris, 1981) p 119 and Yvon Loussouarn 'La succursale, technique juridique du commerce international' [1985] Droit et Pratique du Commerce International 359 (in particular p 362)). A subsidiary, on the other hand, is legally independent of the parent company by which it is controlled (However, see A Pietrobon L'Interpretazione della Nozione Comunitaria di Filiale (Padua, 1990) pp 101–115 (in particular pp 103, 114 and 115). According to the author, the use of legal form as a method for interpreting the concepts of agency, branch and subsidiary-ie the use of concepts and methods pertaining to national laws as though those laws considered individually or in comparison with one another must necessarily provide the

model for interpreting the Treaty-seems inappropriate in that it does not admit certain types of branch which there is no reason to exclude. Moreover, a functional interpretation of the concept of 'secondary establishment' shows its essential characteristics (the fact that the branch is subject to the administrative choices of the parent company, which is responsible for all decisions concerning the existence, functions and basic modus operandi of the territorial division) to be such as to lead inevitably to the conclusion that an independent undertaking, with its own organisation and business, cannot be the secondary establishment of another undertaking. The author adds that it consequently appears doubtful whether this is applicable to the concept of the societe affiliata which, as she has pointed out, is not mentioned in the Italian version of art 52. In her view, the establishment by an undertaking incorporated in one member state, of a subsidiary (societe affiliata) in another member state is an operation that should more properly be regarded as a primary establishment (of the subsidiary). However, she considers that the question is of no practical importance, since both interpretations recognise the possibility of establishing subsidiaries (societe affiliate).). As learned writers have observed (see Yvon Loussouarn (pp 363–368)), the distinction between these two legal devices employed by companies to set up establishments in other countries is important in various respects. Above all, since nationality is an attribute of personality, a branch whose activity is the same as that of its parent company cannot have a different nationality from that company; and its legal status is governed by the legal order to which the parent company, of which it is merely a limb, is subject. The opposite applies to subsidiaries. Moreover, although a branch may enjoy a degree of managerial independence, the parent company alone is responsible for the business activity conducted on its behalf by the person appointed to run the branch. A subsidiary, on the other hand, can legitimately conclude contracts, though in some cases the parent company may intervene in the transaction as a contracting party. And lastly, on the principle of unity of assets and liabilities, any debts contracted (or, conversely, credits accumulated) by a branch in the course of its activities are chargeable to the company (so that it is incorrect to speak of a branch's debts) inasmuch as, for reasons of practical convenience, creditors are normally allowed in such cases to bring an action against the company before the court of the place where the branch is established (see para 18, post). A subsidiary, on the other hand, has its own funds to settle any debts it has contracted; the subsidiary with its own separate legal personality thus acts as a protective screen between parent company and creditors.

IV—THE ANSWER TO THE QUESTION REFERRED BY THE NATIONAL COURT

Compatibility of the refusal to register the Danish branch of Centros with the fundamental freedom of establishment

16. In my view, the measure taken by the Danish authorities is contrary to the Treaty provisions on freedom of establishment. As I shall explain more clearly, that measure does not merely limit the exercise of the right of companies of other Community countries to set up secondary establishments, it absolutely precludes it. In the present case, Mr and Mrs Bryde are effectively prevented from carrying on a business activity in Denmark through a company that is lawfully established and has its registered office in another member state of the Community. The companies board appears to consider, in effect, that because the persons concerned intend to do business only in the Danish market they must therefore comply with the rules imposed under Danish law with respect to the type of company they have chosen. This, in my opinion, is contrary to art 52 of the Treaty. The case must also be considered in the light of art 58. In that regard, it is clear that Centros has been treated differently from companies established in accor-

dance with Danish legislation, which have no such obstacles to overcome when they set up branches in Denmark. The measure at issue in this case also indirectly affects the appellant company's right to decide whether to open a branch or establish a subsidiary in Denmark. It seems to me obvious that the Danish authorities would not have taken exception to Centros if the company established in the United Kingdom had preferred to set up its overseas establishment in the form of a subsidiary rather than a branch since a subsidiary, being separate from the parent company, must by definition satisfy the requirements imposed by the relevant national law, including the requirements as to minimum capital. But the second sentence of the first paragraph of art 52 of the Treaty expressly leaves traders free to choose the most appropriate legal form in which to pursue their activities in another member state and that freedom of choice must not be limited, as it is in the present case, by discriminatory provisions (EC Commission v France (para 22)).

17. I shall now take a closer look at the arguments advanced by the Danish authorities against the points I have found it necessary to raise. They contend that Centros cannot legitimately claim the right to freedom of establishment within the meaning of the Treaty. As the company established by the Brydes in the United Kingdom does not conduct any business there, they maintain that it has no real and continuous link with the economic life of that country and that the situation is consequently of purely domestic concern and as such has nothing to do with Community law; in other words, according to the Danish authorities, this is patently a case of abusive and devious exercise of the right of establishment enshrined in the Treaty.... These arguments do not convince me for reasons I shall explain below and also because they take no account of the fact that the requirement that the parent company effectively carry on business is not only debatable as to substance but difficult to apply owing to its indeterminate nature. What kind of business must the parent company conduct, for how long and on what scale, for it to be at liberty to exercise the right to set up a secondary establishment?

18. Further to the views expressed above, I should point out that the rules on freedom of establishment are inapplicable-as the Danish government maintains they are in the present case-only where there is no connecting factor between the situation of those concerned, be they nationals or companies of a member state, and the provisions of Community law, which consequently has no bearing on the case (see ex multis Batista Morais v Ministere Public of Portugal Case C-60/91 [1992] ECR I-2085). For my own part, I do not think that this is true of the situation at issue in the main proceedings. Centros was formed in accordance with the law of England and Wales and has its registered office in the United Kingdom. Those circumstances alone are sufficient to bring the company's situation within the scope of arts 52 and 58 of the Treaty. In my view, no further information is needed about the nationality of the members or directors or about the territorial scope of the company's activities (see Segers' case (para 14); also footnote 12, above, and footnote 27, post, together with the relevant points in the text; see also the judgment in TV10 SA v Commissariaat voor de Media Case C-23/93 [1994] ECR I-4795 (para 15) (According to which the circumstance that a broadcasting body has established itself in another member state in order to avoid the legislation applicable in the receiving state to domestic broadcasters does not preclude its broadcasts being regarded as services within the meaning and for the purposes of art 59 of the Treaty. The situation of Centros is consequently different, for example, from the situation examined by the court in Esso Espanola v Administracion de la Comunidad Autonoma de Canarias Case C-134/94 [1995] ECR I-4223 (paras 12–17), which had to do purely with the extension, within the territory of a member state, of the activities of a company

having its head office in that state and pursuing its activities there.)). Moreover, the court has held that the reference in art 52 to 'nationals of a Member State' who wish to establish themselves 'in the territory of another Member State' cannot be interpreted in such a way as to exclude from the benefit of Community law a given member state's own nationals when the latter, owing to the fact that they have taken advantage of the facilities existing in the matter of freedom of movement and establishment, are, with regard to their state of origin, in a situation which may be assimilated to that of any other persons enjoying the rights and liberties guaranteed by the Treaty (Knoors v Secretary of State for Economic Affairs Case 115/78 [1979] ECR 399 (paras 20 and 24)). The Danish authorities insist that the principal establishment must really pursue the activities stated to be the object of the company. However, that line of reasoning leads them to see in art 58 of the Treaty an additional condition to which the right to set up a secondary establishment is subject. However, in my view, the formal requirements set out in art 58, for the purpose of identifying companies that have that right, are definitive. The legal form of the company is decisive and there is no need to inquire into the nature and content of the activities the company is pursuing or intends to pursue.... See also mutatis mutandis Pafitis v Trapeza Kentrikis Ellados AE Case C-441/93 [1996] ECR I-1347 (paras 18 and 19), in which the court held: 'It is clear from the title and Article 1 of the Second Directive that it applies to the companies referred to in the second paragraph of Article 58 of the EC Treaty constituted in the form of public limited liability companies. The criterion adopted by the Community legislature to define the scope of the Second Directive is therefore that of the legal form of the company, irrespective of its business.'). Moreover, on the subject of freedom of establishment for natural persons, the court has already had occasion to rule, in Micheletti v Delegacion del Gobierno en Cantabria Case C-369/90 [1992] ECR I-4239, on a member state's claim that the exercise of that right should be subject to an additional condition (in that case, actual residence in the territory of the state in question) over and above the requirement that the person be a national of a member state, which is the only condition art 52 imposes in respect of persons. The court held that claim to be contrary to Community law. According to the court in Micheletti's case (paras 10 and 11):

> '(10)...it is not permissible for the legislation of a Member State to restrict the effects of the grant of the nationality of another Member State by imposing an additional condition for recognition of that nationality with a view to the exercise of the fundamental freedoms provided for in the Treaty. (11) Consequently, it is not permissible to interpret Article 52 of the Treaty to the effect that, where a national of a Member State is also a national of a non-member country, the other Member States may make recognition of the status of Community national subject to a condition such as the habitual residence of the person concerned in the territory of the first Member State.'

See also Ministere Public v Auer Case 136/78 [1979] ECR 437 (para 28), in which the court held:

> 'There is no provision of the Treaty which, within the field of application of the Treaty, makes it possible to treat nationals of a Member State differently according to the time at which or the manner in which they acquired the nationality of that State, as long as, at the time at which they rely on the benefit of the provisions of Community law, they possess the nationality of one of the Member States and that, in addition, the other conditions for the application of the rule on which they rely are fulfilled.'

The comparison-suggested by the companies board-between the present case and the case that was the subject of the ruling in Levin's case is therefore, in my opinion, impracticable in view of the difference in wording between art 52, which guarantees in abstract terms the simple opportunity to engage in business activities (see para 19, post), and art 48(3) of the Treaty, which sets out in detail the content of the activities covered by the right of movement guaranteed to employed persons (The court observed in Levin's case (paras 20 and 21): '(20) Under Article 48(3) of the Treaty the right to move freely within the territory of the Member States is conferred upon workers for the "purpose" of accepting offers of employment actually made. By virtue of the same provision workers enjoy the right to stay in one of the Member States "for the purpose" of employment there. Moreover, it is stated in the preamble to Regulation (EEC) No 1612/68 that freedom of movement for workers entails the right of workers to move freely within the Community "in order to" pursue activities as employed persons, whilst Article 2 of Directive 68/360/EEC requires the Member States to grant workers the right to leave their territory "in order to" take up activities as employed persons or to pursue them in the territory of another Member State. (21) However, these formulations merely give expression to the requirement, which is inherent in the very principle of freedom of movement for workers, that the advantages which Community law confers in the name of that freedom may be relied upon only by persons who actually pursue or seriously wish to pursue activities as employed persons...').

19. In support of the position they have taken in the present case, the Danish authorities also cite other decisions handed down by the court in the context of the Brussels Convention (see para 6, above). Those decisions are, however, irrelevant for the purposes of this case. They are, as we have seen, interpretative decisions concerning the applicability in those particular cases of the provision on special jurisdiction contained in art 5(5) of the Brussels Convention (In derogation from the general rule laid down in art 2 of the Brussels Convention, art 5(5) provides that a person domiciled in a contracting state may, in another contracting state, be sued, as regards a dispute arising out of the operations of a branch, agency or other establishment, in the courts for the place in which the branch, agency or other establishment is situated. 'This concept of operations comprises on the one hand actions relating to rights and contractual or non-contractual obligations concerning the management properly so-called of the agency, branch or other establishment itself such as those concerning the situation of the building where such entity is established or the local engagement of staff to work there. Further it also comprises those relating to undertakings which have been entered into at the above-mentioned place of business in the name of the parent body and which must be performed in the Contracting State where the place of business is established and also actions concerning non-contractual obligations arising from the activities in which the branch, agency or other establishment within the above defined meaning, has engaged at the place in which it is established on behalf of the parent body.' (See Somafer v Saar-Ferngas AG Case 33/78 [1978] ECR 2183 (para 13).) It should also be noted that, in derogation from the provisions of art 4 of the Brussels Convention, art 8 provides that an insurer who is not domiciled in a contracting state but has a branch, agency or other establishment in one of the contracting states shall, in disputes arising out of the operations of the branch, agency or establishment, be deemed to be domiciled in that state; the same rule applies, under art 13 of the Brussels Convention, to a party who has entered into a contract with a consumer and who is not domiciled in a contracting state.). In those cases, the court confined itself to considering the characteristics of the concept of secondary establishment that may from time to time be relevant for the purpose of answering questions referred to it by the national courts. It is required to ensure that the

Brussels Convention is given full effect and it has thus had to rely on an independent interpretation of the concepts of subsidiary and branch. Those conventional concepts are restrictive inasmuch as they are primarily concerned with the need to avoid multiple jurisdiction, with its corollary of forum shopping, and with any 'protectionist' motives underlying the original provisions on special jurisdiction in the legal orders of the contracting states that may be detrimental to foreign defendants (See Pietrobon, cited in footnote 15, above, pp 162–164.). Thus, in those cases the court's statement in Ets A de Bloos SPRL v Bouyer Case 14/76 [1976] ECR 1497 (para 20) that: 'One of the essential characteristics of the concepts of branch or agency is the fact of being subject to the direction and control of the parent body' led inevitably to the conclusion that when the grantee of an exclusive sales concession is subject neither to the control nor to the direction of the grantor, he cannot be regarded as being at the head of a branch, agency or other establishment of the grantor within the meaning of art 5(5) of the Brussels Convention and that-

> 'an independent commercial agent, who merely negotiates business... and... transmits orders to the parent undertaking without being involved in either their terms or their execution, does not have the character of a branch, agency or other establishment within the meaning of art 5(5) of the Brussels Convention...' (Blanckaert & Willems PVBA v Trost Case 139/80 [1981] ECR 819 (para 13) (my emphasis).

And again, it was solely in order to enable the German court to decide whether it had jurisdiction to try an action brought by a German undertaking against a French undertaking, the registered office of which was in French territory but which had an office or place of contact in the Federal Republic of Germany described on its notepaper as 'Representation for Germany', that the court established in Somafer's case the condition that a branch, agency or other establishment must be easily recognisable by third parties as an extension of the parent body, implying-

> 'a place of business which has the appearance of permanency, such as the extension of a parent body, has a management and is materially equipped to negotiate business with third parties so that the latter, although knowing that there will if necessary be a legal link with the parent body, the head office of which is abroad, do not have to deal directly with such parent body but may transact business at the place of business constituting the extension' (see para 12).

The clearest evidence that the normative content of the concept of 'agency, branch or other establishment' in the context of the Brussels Convention is different from that of the concept of 'agency, branch or subsidiary' in the context of the Treaty, with contradictory implications in some cases (see Pietrobon, p 94), is provided by the guidance given by the court on the situation in which a company acts, essentially, as though it were a branch or subsidiary of a different 'parent' company, although it is in fact legally independent and may even hold all the company capital, as was the case in SAR Schotte GmbH v Parfums Rothschild SARL Case 218/86 [1987] ECR 4905. In that case too, in order to protect the confidence of third parties, the special jurisdiction provided under art 5(5) of the Brussels Convention must apply because the situation apparently created by 'the way in which these two undertakings behave in their business relations and present themselves vis-a-vis third parties in their commercial dealings' is such as to determine a close connection between the dispute and the court called upon to hear it. It should be noted that, according to the judgment in Rothschild's case (para 17), that provision applies-

> 'to a case in which a legal entity established in a Contracting State maintains no dependent branch, agency or other establishment in another Contracting State

> but nevertheless pursues its activities there through an independent company with the same name and identical management which negotiates and conducts business in its name and which it uses as an extension of itself.'

That case law was developed for purposes that are entirely different from those at issue here and it certainly cannot be held to imply that an establishment is secondary, rather than primary, only if it concerns commercial activities undertaken as an extension of a principal establishment which is actively engaged in business and to whose direction and control the secondary establishment must be subject.

20. I must also consider another argument advanced by the companies board and by the Danish government, namely that Mr and Mrs Bryde's wish to carry on business through a limited company in Denmark is not eligible for protection under arts 52 ff of the Treaty inasmuch as they deliberately chose to establish the company in the United Kingdom with abusive intent. Their aim was allegedly to avoid the rules on minimum capital in force in the state in which it was proposed to set up the secondary establishment, rules which on this view should have been applicable to what was in effect a 'primary establishment'. It is true that the court has consistently upheld in its case law the principle that 'rights conferred under Community law may not be relied on for fraudulent or abusive ends' (Kefalas v Greece Case C-367/96 [1998] ECR I-2843 (para 20) and the other cases cited earlier in this opinion (The court has consequently held that 'Community law does not preclude a Member State from adopting, in the absence of harmonization, measures designed to prevent the opportunities created under the Treaty from being abused in a manner contrary to the legitimate interests of the State.' (See Kraus v Land Baden-Wurttemberg Case C-19/92 [1993] ECR I-1663 (para 34).))), which is among the general principles of Community law. It is, however, by no means easy to define the precise scope of that principle. According to the recent judgment in Kefalas' case, a person abuses the right conferred on him if he exercises it unreasonably to derive, to the detriment of others, 'an improper advantage, manifestly contrary to the objective' pursued by the legislator in conferring that particular right on the individual (see para 28, with reference to an action brought by certain shareholders for a declaration that the increase in capital of a public limited liability company in financial trouble was invalid (I should point out that the formulation of the principle of abuse of rights adopted by the court is based essentially on the common law of member states with a civil law system (see L N Brown 'Is there a General Principle of Abuse of Rights in European Community Law?' in Institutional Dynamics of European Integration: Essays in Honour of Henry G Schermers (Dordrecht, 1994) vol II (D Curtin and T Heukels (eds)) p 511 (in particular p 515)).)). On this aspect of the abuse of rights, there appears to be a certain affinity between the general principle regarding such abuse and the principle of proportionality as a criterion for limiting the exercise of power (See Brown, in footnote 23, above, pp 521 and 522, and W van Gerven 'Principe de proportionaliti, abus de droit et droits fondamentaux' [1992] Journal des Tribuneux 305 (in particular pp 307 and 308).). Furthermore, as learned authors have pointed out, the famous statement of the French authority on civil law, Planiol, that 'law ceases where abuse begins' (le droit cesse la ou l'abus commence) still holds good and shows very clearly that the problem of abuse is resolved in the last analysis by defining the material content of the particular situation and thus the scope of the right conferred on the individual concerned. In other words, it is claimed that to determine whether or not a right is actually being exercised in an abusive manner is simply to define the material scope of the right in question (See C Nizzo 'L'abuso dei "diritti comunitari": un quesito non risolto' [1997] Diritto del Commercio Internazionale 766 (in particular p 770).). If that is the

case, I should like if I may to revisit the ideas on freedom of establishment developed earlier (see paras 13 and 16, above). That freedom certainly includes, for the purposes of the present case, the right to establish companies in accordance with the legislation of a member state to carry on business in that state or, equally, in any other member state. In other words, the newly formed company may set up its principal—and indeed its secondary—establishment wherever it wishes within the Community.

The right of establishment is essential to the achievement of the objectives set in the Treaty, the purpose of which is to guarantee to all Community citizens alike the freedom to engage in business activities through the instruments provided by national law, thus giving them the chance to enter the market, irrespective of the motives that may actually have prompted the person concerned. In other words, it is the opportunity to exercise business activities that is protected, and with it the contractual freedom to make use of the instruments provided for that purpose in the legal systems of the member states. In the present case, the right of establishment was exercised by setting up the company in accordance with the requirements of the law of the host country. So long as that right is exercised in accordance with the Treaty, the motives, calculations and particular personal interests underlying the choice do not come into consideration and are consequently not open to judgment (see mutatis mutandis Levin v Staatssecretaris van Justitie Case 53/81 [1982] ECR 1035 (paras 20–22) (In which the court held that, provided that a worker actually pursues or wishes to pursue an activity as an employed person in another member state and as such is among those enjoying the rights conferred under art 48(3) of the Treaty and the relevant secondary legislation (see para 18, above), the motives which may have prompted the worker to seek employment in another member state are of no account as regards his right to enter and reside in the territory of the latter state and must not be taken into consideration.)). What is relevant, however, is whether the activities pursued (if there be such) are compatible with the domestic rules of public law in the state in which the establishment (primary or secondary) is situated, which may justify measures restricting the exercise of the right in question. The right of establishment is recognised in those terms precisely with a view to the completion of the single market. This is clear from the fact that different treatment is accorded under the Treaty to legal persons outside the Community who, to enter the circle of the Community, must satisfy the criterion of an effective and continuous link with the economy of a member state (see para 12, above).

In support of what I have just said, I should like if I may to draw attention to the frequently cited case of Segers, in which a Netherlands national had incorporated his one-man business, which had its registered office in the Netherlands, into a private limited liability company formed in accordance with English law, which he had acquired at the same time and which did not conduct any business itself but operated solely through the secondary establishment. In fact, it appeared from the documents in the case that the reason for this arrangement was simply that he wanted to use the designation 'Ltd' which he considered more attractive than its Netherlands equivalent, 'BV', and to avoid the statutory time limit presented by Netherlands law for such a change (see Advocate General Darmon's opinion (para 1)). This did not prevent the court from ruling that the situation of the company and of its director, Mr Segers, was covered by the provisions on freedom of establishment and that the applicant was therefore entitled to receive the treatment accorded to Netherlands nationals (See footnote 12, above, and the relevant part of the text. Similarly, the court appears to have recognised (albeit implicitly) that the registration in the register of British fishing vessels of vessels originally registered in Spain and flying the Spanish flag and the acquisition of British vessels flying the British flag by companies, incorporated under the laws of the United Kingdom, owning or operating such vessels, most of whose directors and shareholders were Spanish nationals, did not constitute an 'abuse of the right of establishment', despite the fact that the wholesale recourse to such registrations in the British shipping register had resulted in the practice known as 'quota hopping', that is to say 'plundering' the fishing quotas allocated to the United Kingdom under the Common Fisheries Policy, and had led in effect to 'circumvention' of the system of national fishing quotas designed to conserve fish stocks and guarantee a reasonable standard of living for the communities dependent on fishing. See R v Secretary of State for Transport, ex p Factortame Ltd. Case C-221/89 [1991] 3 All ER 769, [1991] ECR I-3905 (para 4), in which the court held that legislation on the registration of a fishing vessel in the register of a member state containing restrictive conditions relating to the nationality, residence and domicile of the owners, charterers and operators (and of the shareholders and directors in the case of a company), such as the legislation enacted in 1988 by the United Kingdom to put a stop to quota hopping by vessels flying the British flag but lacking any genuine link with that country, was contrary to art 52 of the Treaty. The court added (at para 34) that freedom of establishment in another member state may legitimately be made subject to a requirement for the registration of a vessel to the effect that it must be managed and its operations directed and controlled from within the member state in which it is to be registered, a requirement which, in the court's view, essentially coincides with the actual concept of establishment within the meaning of art 52 ff of the Treaty. See also Brown, in footnote 23, above (pp 523–525). It is consequently not easy to see why the opposite conclusion should be reached in a situation where—as in the present case—a company is incorporated in the United Kingdom because the founders wish to avail themselves of the opportunity to operate with paid-up capital commensurate with the resources at their disposal and less than is required under Danish law. That situation, whether one likes it or not, is the logical consequence of the rights guaranteed under the Treaty. Moreover, it is consistent with the objective behind the inclusion of the freedom of establishment in the Treaty, namely the need to promote the free movement of persons (and capital) and, by the same token, the achievement of a common market. 'In that respect, the fact that a national of a Member State may take advantage of the flexibility of United Kingdom company law... must be viewed in that context.' (That is, in the context of the Community system.) (See Advocate General Darmon's opinion in Segers' case (para 6).)

In short, in the absence of harmonisation, competition among rules must be allowed free play in corporate matters (See C D Ehlermann 'Compitition entre systhmes riglementaires' [1995] Revue du Marchi Commun et de l'Union Europiene 220 (at 223), according to which there is no possibility of 'free competition' between the company laws of the member states degenerating into a kind of 'Delaware effect'—that is a process whereby newly-formed companies are attracted to the systems which afford a lower level of protection to investors and creditors, as happened in the United States in the case of company laws in New Jersey and, more recently, in Delaware—since member states can have recourse to the mechanism for the harmonisation of company laws within the meaning of art 54(3)(g) of the Treaty. According to D Charny in 'Competition among Jurisdictions in Formulating Corporate Law Rules: An American Perspective on the "Race to the Bottom" in the European Communities' [1991] Harv Int LJ 423 (in particular pp 424 and 425), harmonising the provisions of company law of the member states seems, from the perspective of American corporate theory, to be 'a process in search of a justification', since such harmonisation of national systems may result indirectly from competition between them.). In the present case, as in Segers' case, the above-mentioned freedoms are part of the material content of the right in question and it cannot be held that Mr and Mrs Bryde took 'an improper advantage, manifestly contrary to the objective' pursued by arts 52 ff of the Treaty in abusively avoiding the application of binding rules of the state where the secondary establishment was to be set up. Far from contradicting the conclusion I have reached, the case law cited by the Danish government seems to me ultimately to support it. In fact, it follows from the judgments in those cases that the question of abusing the law can arise only if the rule that is apparently being avoided undoubtedly applies to the legal situation at issue (This is true both in the case of national legislation governing a person's access to or exercise of a profession in the territory of the country concerned (in particular rules relating to organisation, qualifications, professional ethics, supervision and liability), as in van Binsbergen v Bestuur van Bedrijfsvereniging voor de Metaalnijverheid Case 33/74 [1974] ECR 1299, or his trade qualifications, as in Knoors v Secretary of State for Economic Affairs Case 115/78 [1979] ECR 399; and also in the case of national legislation imposing obligations with respect to conduct in relation to the organisation of a specific commercial sector, such as the fixing of retail book prices by publishes or importers (Association des Centres distributeurs Edouard Leclerc v Sarl 'Au ble vert' Case 229/83 [1985] ECR 1 (para 27)), or obligations with respect to the pluralist and non-commercial content of programmes broadcast in national territory (TV10 SA v Commissariaat voor de Media Case C-23/93 [1994] ECR I-4795 (para 21)).). If the apparent avoidance concerns a provision of national law, it is therefore essential to ascertain, first, that the national provision it is hoped to apply in the case at issue can be relied on by the court as being consistent with Community law. And it is on precisely this point that the companies board's arguments appear, if I may say so, to beg the question: by insisting that the national provisions must apply with respect to the minimum capital limited companies are required to have when they are formed, the Danish authorities exclude the possibility that the opposite result may be brought about-as it has been in the present case-through the exercise of the freedom of choice, guaranteed to individuals under the Treaty, as to the company instrument best suited to their purposes of all the instruments available under the various national systems of the member states. The contested measure of the companies board is contrary to Community law precisely because it was adopted on the implicit but clear assumption that business activities conducted by Danish nationals and directed essentially at the Danish market must inevitably be carried on through their principal establishment in Danish territory. This view cannot, however, be sustained at the present stage of European integration, which is characterised by the almost full completion of a single market thanks to the abolition of national obstacles to freedom of movement for persons and capital (see art 3(c) of the Treaty). The interpreter must draw the necessary conclusions from the developments that have already taken place in the Community system; it is for the court to ensure that the spirit of the Treaty prevails by applying the doctrine in Rewe-Zentral AG v Bundesmonopolverwaltung fur Branntwein Case 120/78 [1979] ECR 649 (the 'Cassis de Dijon' doctrine) on mutual recognition in a consistent manner, to, inter alia, corporate mobility (See T Mortimer 'The Removal of Barriers to Corporate Mobility: An Analysis of Cases Pertinent to Articles 52 and 58' in A Caiger and D A Floudas (ed) 1996 Onwards: Lowering the Barriers Further (Chichester, 1996) p 135 (in particular pp 150 and 154). According to the judgment in the 'Cassis de Dijon' case (paras 14 and 15), in the absence of a purpose which is in the general interest and such as to take precedence over the requirements of the free movement of goods, any member state is required to permit goods to be introduced into its territory provided that have they been lawfully produced and marketed in another member state, even if they were produced in accordance with technical or quality requirements other than those in force in the importing state.). This does not, in my view, mean that a foreign company which does no business in the country in which it was formed is not subject, in respect of the exercise of activities by a branch opened in another member state, to binding rules of that state applicable to national companies of the same type. The secondary establishment is, in fact, such as to create an appropriate link between the foreign company and the economic system of the country in which it is set up. But the fact that binding local rules may apply must never mean that the Community company is prevented from exercising its right of establishment. It follows, in my view, that in the present case the companies board's claim that the secondary establishment should be accorded the treatment provided under national law for primary establishments, particularly in respect of minimum capital, can be upheld only if there are suitable reasons to justify it.

Possible justifications for the contested measure:

21. This is the last aspect of the question that remains to be considered. Could the restrictive measure at issue in this case be justified, within the meaning of Community law, as being genuinely based on grounds of public policy and proportionate with respect to the aims it seeks to achieve? The companies board cites the need to combat fraud and, more precisely, the need to protect future creditors of Centros in relation to the activities of the Danish branch: in view of the 'undercapitalisation' of the company, at least by Danish standards, and the limited liability of the partners, the board considers that registration of the branch in Denmark would expose Danish traders and public creditors to the risk of incurring financial losses, should Centros subsequently fail. That is undeniably a risk inherent in all limited liability companies but it seems to me to be very far from constituting 'a genuine and sufficiently serious threat affecting one of the fundamental interests of society', as required by art 56 of the Treaty, a derogating provision that in my view is better suited to cases where the actual object or activities of the foreign company threaten public policy.

Apart from that, while fair trading is an overriding reason relating to the general interest that could, in theory, justify national measures (applicable without distinction) restricting the right of establishment, I do not think that that has any bearing on the present case. Various considerations support this view. First of all, it is doubtful whether, in the case of limited liability companies, the criterion of presumed adequacy of minimum capital alone may be relied upon to protect or (in the words of the fourth recital in the preamble to the second directive, in relation to public limited liability companies) 'ensure' the protection of creditors. It is worth noting that that criterion is not employed in United Kingdom legislation, as the United Kingdom authorities have pointed out (The United Kingdom government considers that minimum capital requirements imposed on private limited companies can act as a disincentive to enterprise and innovation and that they are contrary to the policy of encouraging small and medium-sized undertakings.). As the required minimum capital can easily be dissipated, creditors would in practice be wiser to rely on the more recent information disclosed by the company's annual accounts and, if necessary, seek appropriate security from the directors. But without wishing to overturn the sacred idol of nominal capital (See ex multis G La Villa Introduzione al Diritto Europeo delle Societe (Turin, 1996) p 55, according to which the approach based on regulations designed to protect the integrity of companies' nominal capital has long been criticised and is apparently in the process of being superseded in more advanced economic systems, which tend to revise regulations based on the concepts of nominal capital and nominal value in favour of criteria that are closer to the market and to the real state of a company's assets and liabilities at a given time, and G B

Portale and C Costa 'Capitale sociale e societe per azioni sottocapitalizzate: le nuove tendenze nei paesi europei' in P Abadessa and A Rojo (ed) Il Diritto delle Societe per Azioni: Problemi, Esperienze, Progetti (Milan, 1993) p 133 (in particular pp 144 and 145), according to which fixing 'minimum' company capital actually performs a function entirely different from the function of fixing capital that is 'not manifestly inappropriate' to the company's object: it creates an instrument for choosing between various types of company, and it guarantees a 'reliability threshold' for certain collective business undertakings.), in a case such as this the contested measure is certainly not essential to protect the private creditors of Centros with regard to the operations of a hypothetical Danish branch. In fact, that requirement can be met without any need to adopt measures such as the one at issue in this case, thanks to the results achieved by the Community process of co-ordinating the company law of the member states. As the United Kingdom government has rightly observed, Mr and Mrs Bryde hold themselves out as they are, not a Danish company but the Danish branch of a company incorporated under English law. The limitations on the liability of such a company, that anyone in Denmark having dealings with the company's branch is fully entitled to know, are the limitations resulting from the Danish minimum capital requirement. The protection of persons who have dealings with a company of another member state through a branch of that company is secured under the system of the Treaty through the co-ordinated disclosure requirements of the member state in which the branch is situated (Under arts 1–6 of the eleventh directive, a branch is required to disclose, pursuant to the law of the member state in which it is situated, the information necessary to protect the public, including: (i) the name, address and activities of the branch, (ii) the name of the company of which it forms part, (iii) the names and addresses of the persons who are authorised as permanent representatives of the company for the activities of the branch, or who may represent the company in dealings with third parties and in legal proceedings, (iv) the annual accounts and annual reports relating to the company or group of companies to which it belongs, drawn up in accordance with the fourth and seventh company directives (if necessary translated into the language of the state in which the branch is registered), (v) the closure of the branch, (vi) the winding-up of the company or insolvency proceedings to which it is subject, (vii) particulars of the register in which the company file is kept, together with the registration number in that register, and (viii) the existence of any other branches in the same member state. Also, the member state in which the branch has been opened may require it to disclose further information about the company of which it is a branch, in particular concerning: (i) the instruments of constitution and the memorandum and articles of association (if necessary translated into the language of the state in question), (ii) an attestation from the register in which the company file is kept relating to the existence of the company, and (iii) an indication of the validity of the securities on the company's property situated in the member state in question. Lastly, the registers in which the branch and the company are entered, together with their registration numbers in those registers, the registered office and legal form of the branch (and if necessary the relevant subscribed and paid-up capital) must also be stated in letters and order forms used by the branch.); in this way, third parties are afforded the opportunity to obtain adequate protection for their interests by demanding appropriate guarantees (usually in the form of demanding security from the members) or through pre-emptive proceedings.

22. Then there is the imperative need to protect non-contractual public creditors, such as the social security and tax authorities. In this case, the creditor is not free to choose whether or not to enter into a contract with the branch of a foreign company, nor-as

the Hojesterets' order for reference explains-can it demand guarantees or security from the company's directors. Nevertheless, I consider that the refusal to register the branch, essentially on the ground that there was not an effective principal establishment, is unrelated to the imperative need to protect public creditors: that is to say, the supposed causal connection between that need and the contested measure appears to be too tenuous and indirect to be regarded as relevant for the purposes of Community law. This conclusion is based on the fact that, as the Danish authorities admitted in the course of the oral procedure, Centros would have encountered no obstacle to opening branches in Denmark if it had actually been engaged in business activities in the United Kingdom, though in that event its initial paid-up capital would still have been £ 100. It therefore remains to be seen how the effective possibilities of protecting the Danish social security and tax authorities' rights as creditors might have been affected, had Centros actually been engaged in business activities in its country of origin. Quite apart from any other considerations, it should be possible for the requirement mentioned by the Danish authorities to be satisfied by measures that are less restrictive than the one at issue in this case, which effectively denies the right to set up a secondary establishment. This seems to me to be sufficiently clear not to require lengthy explanations but some clarification is nevertheless called for. In my opinion, the measure suggested by the Commission (see para 10, above) of making registration of the branch in Denmark subject to the condition that the foreign parent company have capital amounting to no less than the capital required under the relevant national provisions for the establishment of companies of the same type in Denmark is not among the measures that could be regarded as acceptable—in the sense of being justified by the imperative need mentioned above, and consistent with the criteria of necessity and proportionality. Like the measure at issue in this case, that condition would essentially be tantamount to indirectly applying the treatment prescribed under national law for a primary establishment to an act exercising the right to set up a secondary establishment. It would therefore still have the result of precluding Mr and Mrs Bryde from availing themselves of 'the flexibility of United Kingdom company law' to operate freely in any part of Community territory with an initial capital that is consistent with the requirements of the provisions on the constitution of companies even if it is less than that required under the laws of other member states (notably the member state in which it is intended to open a secondary establishment). In my view, therefore, not even the objective of protecting public creditors is sufficient a reason not to number the absolute refusal to register the branch among the measures that are incompatible with the Community rules on freedom of establishment. I therefore conclude that—on the assumption that, once the administrative obstacle to its registration is removed, the Danish branch of Centros will be governed by the national provisions on the exercise of business activities to which companies of the same type established in Denmark are subject—the answer to the question referred by the national court should be in the negative, in the absence of any valid justification for the measure at issue.

CONCLUSION

In the light of the foregoing considerations, I propose that the Court of Justice give the following answer to the question submitted by the Hojesterets Anke-og Kaeremalsudvalg:

Articles 52 ff of the EC Treaty prohibit the competent authorities of a member state from refusing to register a branch of a limited liability company formed in accordance with the law of another member state and having its registered office in the territory of that state, if the reasons for refusing are that: (i) the company itself is not engaged in any business activities, (ii) the intention in establishing the branch is to carry on all the company's activities in the state in which the branch is to be set up, and (iii) that way of organising the operation allows the members to avoid the requirement to have a higher minimum capital than would have been the case had the company been established in the member state in which it is intended to open the branch.

DECISION:

9 March 1999. The Court of Justice delivered the following judgment.

1. By order of 3 June 1997, received at the Court of Justice of the European Communities on 5 June 1997, the Hojesterets Anke-og Kaeremalsudvalg (Appeals and Objections Committee of the Danish Supreme Court) (the Hojesterets) referred to the Court of Justice for a preliminary ruling under art 177 of the EC Treaty (now art 234 EC) a question on the interpretation of arts 52, 56 and 58 of the Treaty (now arts 43, 45 and 48 EC).

2. That question was raised in proceedings between Centros Ltd., a private limited company registered on 18 May 1992 in England and Wales, and Erhvervs-og Selskabsstyrelsen (the trade and companies board) (the board) which comes under the Danish Department of Trade, concerning that authority's refusal to register a branch of Centros in Denmark.

3. It is clear from the documents in the main proceedings that Centros has never traded since its formation. Since United Kingdom law imposes no requirement on limited liability companies as to the provision for and the paying-up of a minimum share capital, Centros' share capital, which amounts to £ 100, has been neither paid up nor made available to the company. It is divided into two shares held by Mr and Mrs Bryde, Danish nationals residing in Denmark. Mrs Bryde is the director of Centros, whose registered office is situated in the United Kingdom, at the home of a friend of Mr Bryde.

4. Under Danish law, Centros, as a 'private limited company', is regarded as a foreign limited liability company. The rules governing the registration of branches ('filialer') of such companies are laid down by the Anpartsselskabslov (law on private limited companies).

5. In particular, art 117(1) of the law provides:

> 'Private limited companies and foreign companies having a similar legal form which are established in one Member State of the European Communities may do business in Denmark through a branch.'

6. During the summer of 1992, Mrs Bryde requested the board to register a branch of Centros in Denmark.

7. The board refused that registration on the grounds, inter alia, that Centros, which does not trade in the United Kingdom, was in fact seeking to establish in Denmark, not a branch, but a principal establishment, by circumventing the national rules concerning, in particular, the paying-up of minimum capital fixed at D Kr 200,000 by Law No 886 of 21 December 1991.

8. Centros brought an action before the Ostre Landsret (Eastern Regional Court) against the refusal of the board to effect that registration.

9. The Ostre Landsret upheld the arguments of the board in a judgment of 8 September 1995, whereupon Centros appealed to the Hojesterets.

10. In those proceedings, Centros maintains that it satisfies the conditions imposed by the law on private limited companies relating to the registration of a branch of a foreign company. Since it was lawfully formed in the United Kingdom, it is entitled to set up a branch in Denmark pursuant to art 52, read in conjunction with art 58, of the Treaty.

11. According to Centros the fact that it has never traded, since its formation, in the United Kingdom has no bearing on its right to freedom of establishment. In its judgment in Segers v Bestuur van de Bedrijfsvereniging voor Bank-en Verzekeringswezen, Groothandel en Vrije Beroepen Case 79/85 [1986] ECR 2375, the court ruled that arts 52 and 58 of the Treaty prohibited the competent authorities of a member state from excluding the director of a company from a national sickness insurance scheme solely on the ground that the company had its registered office in another member state, even though it did not conduct any business there.

12. The board submits that its refusal to grant registration is not contrary to arts 52 and 58 of the Treaty since the establishment of a branch in Denmark would seem to be a way of avoiding the national rules on the provision for and the paying-up of minimum share capital. Furthermore, its refusal to register is justified by the need to protect private or public creditors and other contracting parties and also by the need to endeavour to prevent fraudulent insolvencies.

13. In those circumstances, the Hojesterets has decided to stay the proceedings and to refer the following question to the Court of Justice for a preliminary ruling:

> 'Is it compatible with Article 52 of the EC Treaty, in conjunction with Articles 58 and 56 thereof, to refuse registration of a branch of a company which has its registered office in another Member State and has been lawfully founded with company capital of £ 100 (approximately D Kr 1000) and established under the legislation of that Member State, where the company does not itself carry on any business but it is desired to set up the branch in order to carry on the entire business in the country in which the branch is established, and where, instead of incorporating a company in the latter Member State, that procedure must be regarded as having been employed in order to avoid paying in company capital of not less than D Kr 200,000 (at present D Kr 125,000)?'

14. By its question, the national court is in substance asking whether it is contrary to arts 52 and 58 of the Treaty for a member state to refuse to register a branch of a company formed in accordance with the legislation of another member state in which it has its registered office but where it does not carry on any business when the purpose of the branch is to enable the company concerned to carry on its entire business in the state in which that branch is to be set up, while avoiding the formation of a company in that state, thus evading the application of the rules governing the formation of companies which are, in that state, more restrictive so far as minimum paid-up share capital is concerned.

15. As a preliminary point, it should be made clear that the board does not in any way deny that a joint stock or private limited company with its registered office in another member state may carry on business in Denmark through a branch. It therefore agrees, as a general rule, to register in Denmark a branch of a company formed in accordance with the law of another member state. In particular, it has added that, if Centros had conducted any business in England and Wales, the board would have agreed to register its branch in Denmark.

16. According to the Danish government, art 52 of the Treaty is not applicable in the case in the main proceedings, since the situation is purely internal to Denmark. Mr and Mrs Bryde, Danish nationals, have formed a company in the United Kingdom which does not carry on any actual business there with the sole purpose of carrying on business in Denmark through a branch and thus of avoiding application of Danish legislation on the formation of private limited companies. It considers that in such circumstances the formation by nationals of one member state of a company in another

member state does not amount to a relevant external element in the light of Community law and, in particular, freedom of establishment.

17. In this respect, it should be noted that a situation in which a company formed in accordance with the law of a member state in which it has its registered office desires to set up a branch in another member state falls within the scope of Community law. In that regard, it is immaterial that the company was formed in the first member state only for the purpose of establishing itself in the second, where its main, or indeed entire, business is to be conducted (see, to this effect, Segers' case (para 16)).

18. That Mrs and Mrs Bryde formed the company, Centros, in the United Kingdom for the purpose of avoiding Danish legislation requiring that a minimum amount of share capital be paid up has not been denied either in the written observations or at the hearing. That does not, however, mean that the formation by that United Kingdom company of a branch in Denmark is not covered by freedom of establishment for the purposes of arts 52 and 58 of the Treaty. The question of the application of those articles of the Treaty is different from the question whether or not a member state may adopt measures in order to prevent attempts by certain of its nationals to evade domestic legislation by having recourse to the possibilities offered by the Treaty.

19. As to the question whether, as Mr and Mrs Bryde claim, the refusal to register in Denmark a branch of their company formed in accordance with the law of another member state in which it has its registered office constitutes an obstacle to freedom of establishment, it must be borne in mind that that freedom, conferred by art 52 of the Treaty on Community nationals, includes the right for them to take up and pursue activities as self-employed persons and to set up and manage undertakings under the same conditions as are laid down by the law of the member state of establishment for its own nationals. Furthermore, under art 58 of the Treaty, companies or firms formed in accordance with the law of a member state and having their registered office, central administration or principal place of business within the Community are to be treated in the same way as natural persons who are nationals of member states.

20. The immediate consequence of this is that those companies are entitled to carry on their business in another member state through an agency, branch or subsidiary. The location of their registered office, central administration or principal place of business serves as the connecting factor with the legal system of a particular state in the same way as does nationality in the case of a natural person....

21. Where it is the practice of a member state, in certain circumstances, to refuse to register a branch of a company having its registered office in another member state, the result is that companies formed in accordance with the law of that other member state are prevented from exercising the freedom of establishment conferred on them by arts 52 and 58 of the Treaty.

22. Consequently, that practice constitutes an obstacle to the exercise of the freedoms guaranteed by those provisions.

23. According to the Danish authorities, however, Mr and Mrs Bryde cannot rely on those provisions, since the sole purpose of the company formation which they have in mind is to circumvent the application of the national law governing formation of private limited companies and therefore constitutes abuse of the freedom of establishment.

In their submission, the Kingdom of Denmark is therefore entitled to take steps to prevent such abuse by refusing to register the branch.

24. It is true that, according to the case law of the court, a member state is entitled to take measures designed to prevent certain of its nationals from attempting, under cover of the rights created by the Treaty, improperly to circumvent their national legislation or to prevent individuals from improperly or fraudulently taking advantage of provisions of Community law....

25. However, although, in such circumstances, the national courts may, case by case, take account—on the basis of objective evidence—of abuse or fraudulent conduct on the part of the persons concerned in order, where appropriate, to deny them the benefit of the provisions of Community law on which they seek to rely, they must nevertheless assess such conduct in the light of the objectives pursued by those provisions (the Paletta case (para 25)).

26. In the present case, the provisions of national law, the application of which the parties concerned have sought to avoid, are rules governing the formation of companies and not rules concerning the carrying on of certain trades, professions or businesses. The provisions of the Treaty on freedom of establishment are intended specifically to enable companies formed in accordance with the law of a member state and having their registered office, central administration or principal place of business within the Community to pursue activities in other member states through an agency, branch or subsidiary.

27. That being so, the fact that a national of a member state who wishes to set up a company chooses to form it in the member state whose rules of company law seem to him the least restrictive and to set up branches in other member states cannot, in itself, constitute an abuse of the right of establishment. The right to form a company in accordance with the law of a member state and to set up branches in other member states is inherent in the exercise, in a single market, of the freedom of establishment guaranteed by the Treaty.

28. In this connection, the fact that company law is not completely harmonised in the Community is of little consequence. Moreover, it is always open to the Council, on the basis of the powers conferred upon it by art 54(3)(g) of the EC Treaty, to achieve complete harmonisation.

29. In addition, it is clear from Segers' case (para 16) that the fact that a company does not conduct any business in the member state in which it has its registered office and pursues its activities only in the member state where its branch is established is not sufficient to prove the existence of abuse or fraudulent conduct which would entitle the latter member state to deny that company the benefit of the provisions of Community law relating to the right of establishment.

30. Accordingly, the refusal of a member state to register a branch of a company formed in accordance with the law of another member state in which it has its registered office on the grounds that the branch is intended to enable the company to carry on all its economic activity in the host state, with the result that the secondary establishment escapes national rules on the provision for and the paying-up of a minimum capital, is incompatible with arts 52 and 58 of the Treaty, in so far as it prevents any exercise of the right freely to set up a secondary establishment which arts 52 and 58 are specifically intended to guarantee.

31. The final question to be considered is whether the national practice in question might not be justified for the reasons put forward by the Danish authorities.

32. Referring both to art 56 of the Treaty and to the case law of the court on the imperative requirements in the general interest, the board argues that the requirement that private limited companies provide for and pay up a minimum share capital pursues a dual objective: first, to reinforce the financial soundness of those companies in order to protect public creditors against the risk of seeing the public debts owing to them become irrecoverable since, unlike private creditors, they cannot secure those debts by means of guarantees and, second, and more generally, to protect all creditors, whether public or private, by anticipating the risk of fraudulent bankruptcy due to the insolvency of companies whose initial capitalisation was inadequate.

33. The board adds that there is no less restrictive means of attaining this dual objective. The other way of protecting creditors, namely by introducing rules making it possible for shareholders to incur personal liability, under certain conditions, would be more restrictive than the requirement to provide for and pay up a minimum share capital.

34. It should be observed, first, that the reasons put forward do not fall within the ambit of art 56 of the Treaty. Next, it should be borne in mind that, according to the court's case law, national measures liable to hinder or make less attractive the exercise of fundamental freedoms guaranteed by the Treaty must fulfil four conditions: they must be applied in a non-discriminatory manner; they must be justified by imperative requirements in the general interest; they must be suitable for securing the attainment of the objective which they pursue; and they must not go beyond what is necessary in order to attain it....

35. Those conditions are not fulfilled in the case in the main proceedings. First, the practice in question is not such as to attain the objective of protecting creditors which it purports to pursue since, if the company concerned had conducted business in the United Kingdom, its branch would have been registered in Denmark, even though Danish creditors might have been equally exposed to risk.

36. Since the company concerned in the main proceedings holds itself out as a company governed by the law of England and Wales and not as a company governed by Danish law, its creditors are on notice that it is covered by laws different from those which govern the formation of private limited companies in Denmark and they can refer to certain rules of Community law which protect them, such as the Fourth Council Directive (EEC) 78/660 (based on art 54(3)(g) of the Treaty on the annual accounts of certain types of companies) (OJ 1978 L222 p 11), and the Eleventh Council Directive (EEC) 89/666 (concerning disclosure requirements in respect of branches opened in a member state by certain types of company governed by the law of another state) (OJ 1989 L395 p 36).

37. Second, contrary to the arguments of the Danish authorities, it is possible to adopt measures which are less restrictive, or which interfere less with fundamental freedoms, by, for example, making it possible in law for public creditors to obtain the necessary guarantees.

38. Lastly, the fact that a member state may not refuse to register a branch of a company formed in accordance with the law of another member state in which it has its registered office does not preclude that first state from adopting any appropriate measure for preventing or penalising fraud, either in relation to the company itself, if need be in co-operation with the member state in which it was formed, or in relation to its members, where it has been established that they are in fact attempting, by means of the formation of the company, to evade their obligations towards private or public creditors established on the territory of a member state concerned. In any event, combating fraud

cannot justify a practice of refusing to register a branch of a company which has its registered office in another member state.

39. The answer to the question referred must therefore be that it is contrary to arts 52 and 58 of the Treaty for a member state to refuse to register a branch of a company formed in accordance with the law of another member state in which it has its registered office but in which it conducts no business where the branch is intended to enable the company in question to carry on its entire business in the state in which that branch is to be created, while avoiding the need to form a company there, thus evading application of the rules governing the formation of companies which, in that state, are more restrictive as regards the paying-up of a minimum share capital. That interpretation does not, however, prevent the authorities of the member state concerned from adopting any appropriate measure for preventing or penalising fraud, either in relation to the company itself, if need be in co-operation with the member state in which it was formed, or in relation to its members, where it has been established that they are in fact attempting, by means of the formation of a company, to evade their obligations towards private or public creditors established in the territory of the member state concerned.

Costs

40. The costs incurred by the Danish, French, Netherlands, Swedish and United Kingdom governments and by the Commission, which have submitted observations to the court, are not recoverable. Since these proceedings are, for the parties to the main proceedings, a step in the action pending before the national court, the decision on costs is a matter for that court.

On those grounds, the Court of Justice in answer to the question referred to it by the Hojesterets Anke-og Kaeremalsudvalg by order of 3 June 1997, hereby rules: It is contrary to arts 52 and 58 of the EC Treaty for a member state to refuse to register a branch of a company formed in accordance with the law of another member state in which it has its registered office but in which it conducts no business where the branch is intended to enable the company in question to carry on its entire business in the state in which that branch is to be created, while avoiding the need to form a company there, thus evading the application of the rules governing the formation of companies which, in that state, are more restrictive as regards the paying-up of a minimum share capital. That interpretation does not, however, prevent the authorities of the member state concerned from adopting any appropriate measure for preventing or penalising fraud, either in relation to the company itself, if need be in co-operation with the member state in which it was formed, or in relation to its members, where it has been established that they are in fact attempting, by means of the formation of a company, to evade their obligations towards private or public creditors established in the territory of the member state concerned.

Comments and Questions

1. The *Centros* case may have left more questions unanswered than answered. Among the most important is whether after *Centros* a Member State is now prohibited from applying its own law to the internal affairs of the branch operating in its territory. The decision in the case does not speak directly of this. It is possible to suggest that the European Court of Justice opinion necessarily implied that a branch operating in Member State "A" of a

company lawfully registered in Member State "B" must, as to its internal affairs, be regulated solely by the law of the company law of Member State "B." It might, however, be argued that Member State "A" is now merely required to register the branch. It may continue to apply that portion of its company law to the branch necessary to prevent fraud and to ensure that within its territory all companies, however formed, with principal operations in its territory, must submit to uniform regulation. The first argument parallels the views of the Delaware courts. The second argument parallels the views of California courts.

2. The ways in which some of the governments of the Member States may react to *Centros* may be gauged by their position with respect to the merits of the case. Do the positions of the governments, expressed below as summarized by Advocate General La Pergola help?

> "5. [T]he United Kingdom government,... considers that the refusal to register the branch is tantamount to denying Centros a right which is at the very core of the freedom of establishment and that it is contrary to the principle of mutual recognition of companies. The legitimate interest of protecting the creditors of limited companies can be adequately protected by means that are less restrictive than the measure at issue in this case and that are moreover already provided by Community law. The United Kingdom authorities cite, for example the co-ordinated disclosure requirements covering numerous documents and particulars relating to branches opened in a member state by companies governed by the law of another member state introduced by Eleventh Council Directive (EEC) 89/666 (concerning disclosure requirements in respect of branches opened in a member state by certain types of company governed by the law of another state) (OJ 1989 L395 p 36)....
>
> 6. The companies board contends that the Brydes may not, on the basis of a 'pro forma' company incorporated in the United Kingdom, rely on arts 52 and 58 of the Treaty to avoid payment of the minimum capital laid down by law. In the circumstances described, the branch which Centros, in the person of Mrs Bryde, sought to register in Denmark was in reality the parent company.... It must then, according to the companies board, consistently meet the requirements for constituting the principal, not the secondary, establishment. The fact that it is essential to the exercise of the right to set up a secondary establishment that the parent body actually pursue a business activity may, in its view, also be deduced, mutatis mutandis, from the case law on the free movement of workers.... The defendant argues that it is perfectly legitimate for a member state to impose this obligation, since, at the present stage of development of Community law, the establishment and running of companies are still governed by the national rules on the subject. Furthermore, as the court has stated, the host state has the right to require that nationals of other member states abide by the rules applicable to its own nationals or companies in exercising their activities, provided this does not prevent the nationals of other member states from exercising properly their right of establishment.... In short, the companies board contends that, even if Centros was entitled to exercise the right to freedom of establishment within Community territory, the fact remains that the requirement in respect of the minimum capital for limited companies, imposed by Danish law to protect the interests of companies and their employees and creditors, is a perfectly legitimate measure despite the absence of harmonisation on the subject at Community level.... Above all, the protection of the financial interests of creditors is not, in its opinion, an economic objective and consequently not within the scope of art 56 but is intended to preserve a legal system based on fair dealing in contractual relations.

> 7. The views of the companies board are shared by the Danish government and by the French and Swedish authorities.... In any event, the Danish government considers that the court's judgment in Segers' case cannot apply to the main proceedings in the present case, in which there is no element of discrimination on the grounds of nationality.
>
> 8. The French government, for its part, maintains that the principle that for the purposes of the right of establishment it is immaterial that the foreign company does not conduct business in the country in which it is incorporated—a principle established by the court in Segers' case and relied upon in the present case by Centros (see para 4, above)—applies only if there appear to be legitimate reasons for setting up a secondary establishment and there is no abusive or devious intent. This is not so where, as in the present case, the sole purpose of the operation is to circumvent rules of company law in the state where the secondary establishment is being set up. That state may then refuse to register the branch on the assumption that the conduct in question is abusive or devious. For this reason, the competent authorities in France may be obliged to investigate whether there has been an abusive exercise of the right of establishment on the part of the foreign company if the activities of its branch are 'regulated', that is to say if they are subject to supervision, authorisation or certification.
>
> 9. The Netherlands government, for its part, concedes that the companies board's decision is contrary to art 52 of the Treaty but maintains that that provision is of limited application in the present case. In particular, while admitting the need for a consistent interpretation of all the Community rules on the fundamental freedoms, it draws attention to the principle—established by the court in its judgment in Rutili v Minister for the Interior Case 36/75 [1975] ECR 1219 (para 28 (On the interpretation of arts 7 (now art 6 EC) and 48 of the EC Treaty.)) on the free movement of workers—that restrictive national measures based on the personal conduct of the individual concerned may be justified by a genuine and sufficiently serious threat to public policy. The Netherlands government considers that the court's statement in Segers' case, to the effect that the need to combat fraud may justify a difference of treatment for companies formed in accordance with the law of another member state, should be interpreted in the light of these considerations, a contention that is in fact also based on the concept of public order referred to in art 56 of the Treaty."

Centros, opinion of Advocate General La Pergola, ¶¶ 5–9.

3. **Problem:** Assume that, in response to *Centros*, the government of France enacts the following ordinance: every company seeking to do business within the territory of France must establish a branch for that purpose. Said branch must conform to all of the rules applicable to French *sociètès à responsibilitié limité*. You are the assistant to a member of the EU Commission. She has asked you to prepare a position paper, describing the validity of the French law in light of Community Law and the position that the Commission ought to take. In preparing your response, you review the following:

> "10. Finally, the Commission proposes a different and more complex view of the case at issue. On the one hand, it maintains that Centros was simply exercising the right of establishment in the member state that offered it the most favourable conditions in respect of the paid-up capital requirement, a procedure which—it follows from the judgment in Segers' case—is exactly one of the objectives freedom of establishment is designed to achieve. The ability to take advantage of the opportunities offered by different types of company in other countries and differ-

ences in the regulations of member states does not in itself constitute unlawful circumvention of national rules. The Commission therefore maintains that, in the circumstances at issue in the main proceedings, the administrative procedure followed by the companies board in its investigations as described (see para 3, above) and the subsequent refusal to register a branch of a company that meets the requirements laid down in art 58 of the Treaty amount to discrimination on grounds of nationality, which is prohibited under art 52. A state in which it is sought to set up a secondary establishment may not make registration of the branch subject to the condition that the parent company must satisfy all the requirements for the establishment of companies imposed by its national law. On the other hand, when—as in the case which concerns us here—there is no co-ordination at Community level, the Commission considers that the member state in which it is sought to set up a secondary establishment may impose conditions for the registration of the branch based on its domestic rules and designed to secure, for persons in its own territory who enter into relations with the foreign company, a greater measure of protection than is afforded by that company's memorandum of association. In the present case it appears at least probable, if not certain, that the Danish rules on paying up capital achieve the declared objective of protecting public creditors. With respect to that objective, the Commission considers, however, that it is disproportionate to refuse permission for the secondary establishment purely and simply on a presumption of intent to circumvent laws currently in force. Such refusal cannot be justified on any of the grounds mentioned in art 56 of the Treaty, which do not apply to economic objectives and would in any event presuppose actual proof that the foreign company intended to defraud creditors in Denmark. According to the Commission, in view of the facts and the legal background in the main proceedings, an appropriate and less restrictive means of protecting creditors in this case would be to make registration of the branch subject to the condition that the foreign parent company has paid-up capital corresponding to that required under the relevant national provisions for the establishment of companies of that type in Denmark."

Centros, opinion of Advocate General La Pergola, ¶ 10. What position do you suggest the Commission take and why?

4. How far do you think a state may go in regulating branches under the "fraud" exception discussed in *Centros*? Does your answer depend on whether you adopt a broad or narrow construction of the meaning of the European Court of Justice's opinion?

5. The *Centros* case has sent ripples throughout the Member States adhering to the *siege social* (seat) rule. A broad reading of the case might suggest that any corporation may now establish itself in a non-siege social jurisdiction and then freely establish its principle office within the territory of another member state, irrespective of the incorporation rules in effect there.

It is easy, on this basis to decry the result—a U.S. style "race to the bottom" to the detriment of those groups most vulnerable within a corporation. But is this the necessary result? An enterprise theory of business regulation, considered in Chapter 1, suggests that even if the "constitution" of the E.U. now permits U.K. corporations to establish their primary offices in Berlin, Germany might still be able to effectively legislate with respect to matters of direct concern to Germans.

6. **Problem:** Assume that you are an assistant to the Danish Prime Minister. She has asked you to be prepared to discuss with her the ways in which the government of Den-

mark ought to react to the *Centros* holding, and to propose alternative means of protecting shareholders, workers and lenders in Denmark. Be prepared to discuss your proposals, as well as the limits of lawmaking.

7. The advocate general went to some lengths to distinguish branches form subsidiaries. There is still some confusion within the EU with respect to definitions of branches, and the legal effects of that form of presence within the Member States. This was expressed by the Danish companies board in *Centros*:

> "6. The companies board contends that the Brydes may not, on the basis of a 'pro forma' company incorporated in the United Kingdom, rely on arts 52 and 58 of the Treaty to avoid payment of the minimum capital laid down by law. In the circumstances described, the branch which Centros, in the person of Mrs Bryde, sought to register in Denmark was in reality the parent company. As to the Community concept of 'branch', the defendant proposes, in the absence of any acceptable definition in the relevant legislation, to employ the concept used by the court in its rulings interpreting the Convention on Jurisdiction and the Enforcement of Judgments in Civil and Commercial Matters 1968 (the Brussels Convention) (OJ 1972 L299 p 32) (The consolidated version of the Brussels Convention, as amended by previous Accession Conventions (the most recent being the Convention on the Accession of the Republic of Austria, the Republic of Finland and the Kingdom of Sweden to the Rome Convention), was published in OJ 1998 C27 p 1.) [set out in Sch 1 to the Civil Jurisdiction and Judgments Act 1982]. It claims that it follows from that case law (Ets A de Bloos SPRL v Bouyer Case 14/76 [1976] ECR 1497 (para 20), Somafer v Saar-Ferngas AG Case 33/78 [1978] ECR 2183 (para 12), Blanckaert & Willems PVBA v Trost Case 139/80 [1981] ECR 819 (para 12)), in particular, that if there is no parent body with effective powers of direction and control over the activities of the branch, the branch will constitute the company's principal place of business."

Centros, opinion of Advocate General La Pergola; ¶6. We discuss the differences between branches, agencies and subsidiaries in the section that follows.

C. Branches and Agencies

The European Union has attempted to facilitate cross border business enterprise by encouraging the use of agencies, branches and subsidiaries by enterprises resident in the Member States. The aim of fostering that sort of secondary establishment was made clear by the decision in both *Daily Mail* and *Centros*. Moreover, in furtherance of the aim of fostering secondary establishment, the Eleventh Company Law Directive[1] has been promulgated.

As you will see from the *Somafer* case, below, the use of branches and agencies, unlike the use of subsidiaries, has generated additional problems. Among the most impor-

1. 11th Council Directive (EEC) 89/666 of 21 December 1989 concerning disclosure requirements in respect of branches opened in a Member State by certain types of company governed by the law of another State [1989] OJ L395/36.

tant of these problems have been the definition of branches and agencies, the power of states to regulate branches and agencies, and the effect of registration of branches and agencies in a Member State.

Somafer SA v. Saar-Ferngas AG

(preliminary ruling requested by the Oberlandesgericht Saarbrucken)
(Case 33/78)
European Court of Justice
[1978] ECR 2183, [1979] 1 CMLR 490
22 November 1978

Facts: The order making the reference to the Court and the written observations submitted under Article 20 of the Protocol on the Statute of the Court of Justice of the EEC may be summarized as follows:

I—Facts and procedure

The company Etablissements Somafer, the defendant in the main action and appellant on the appeal (hereinafter referred to as "Somafer"), whose principal place of business is at Uckange (France) engages in demolition and blasting and in 1974, on behalf of the Ministry of the Interior of the Saarland, blew up a bunker. since there were in the immediate vicinity of the bunker gas mains belonging to Saar-Ferngas AG (hereinafter referred to as "Ferngas"), the plaintiff in the main action and respondent to the appeal, the latter took safety measures, by agreement or without it—the parties are at variance on the issue—to protect the gas mains and sought reimbursement of the expenses from Somafer. In the Federal Republic of Germany Somafer uses in its dealings with its customers note-paper headed:

"SOMAFER

Vertretung fur Deutschland [Representationfor Germany] 6639 Beckingen (Saar)

Tel. 0 68 35/28 24

Bankverbindung [Bankers]: Credit Lyonnais Saarbrucken Nr. [No] 10146"

At the bottom of this note-paper there appears "Hauptverwaltung Uckange (Frankreich)" ["Central Administration Uckange (France)]. A representative or employee of Somafer stays at Beckingen occasionally and Ferngas alleges that it was with him that it agreed the security measures to be taken. Since it did not receive satisfaction Ferngas summoned Somafer for payment before the Landgericht Saarbrucken. When Somafer demurred that the court had no jurisdiction, Ferngas countered by claiming first that the action related to enforcement of a contractual obligation which had to be performed in Germany so that under Article 5(1) of the Convention of 27 September 1968 the German courts had jurisdiction and alternatively that it related to the operations of a branch, agency or other establishment within the meaning of Article 5(5) of the said Convention and that this also gave the court jurisdiction.

In the view of Ferngas, the facts which it cites, namely the existence of an address with a telephone number and the presence of a representative show that Somafer has an establishment or agency at Beckingen or that at least by the establishment of this connexion it has created the appearance of such an establishment or agency. In both cases it must be inferred in the circumstances that the German courts have jurisdiction. Somafer maintains on the other hand that its representation is completely dependent on its principal place of business in Uckange and that its representative for Germany conducted the negotiations with the Saarland authorities in close co-ordination with Uckange. Furthermore it does not even have its own office accommodation and furniture in Beckingen, there is no separate accounting and it is not entered in the commercial register as a branch (Zweigniederlassung) so that the German courts have no jurisdiction.

When the matter came before the Oberlandesgericht Saarbrucken by way of appeal the latter took the view that the case involved questions of the interpretation of the Convention of 27 September 1968 and by order of 21 February 1978 referred the following questions to the Court of Justice for a preliminary ruling:

'1. Are the conditions regarding jurisdiction in the case of "the operations of a branch, agency or other establishment" mentioned in Article 5(5) of the said Convention to be determined:

(a) under the law of the State before the courts of which the proceedings have been brought; or

(b) under the law of the States concerned (qualification according to the law to be applied in the main action); or

(c) independently, i.e. in accordance with the objectives and system of the said Convention and also with the general principles of law which stem from the corpus of the national legal systems (Judgment of 14 October 1976 in Case 29/76 LTU Lufttransportunternebmen GmbH & Co. KG v Eurocontrol [1976] ECR 1541)?

2. What criteria apply in the case of the last question (1(c)) for interpreting the expressions "branch" and "agency" with reference to capacity to take independent decisions (inter alia to enter into contracts) and also to the extent of the outward manifestation?

3. In this connexion are the principles governing liability for holding oneself out in law to others, i.e. to third parties, to be applied to the question whether there is in fact a branch or agency, with the legal consequences that anyone who creates the appearance of such a situation is to be treated as having operated a branch or agency—as is for example the case under German law (cf. Article 21 of the Zivilprozessordnung [Code of Civil Procedure]) Baumbach, 36th Edition, Note 2 A, Stein-Jonas, 19th Edition, Note II 2; Oberlandesgericht Koln, neue Juristische Wochenschrift 1953, 1834, Oberlandesgericht Breslau hochstrichterliche Rechtspreschung 1939 (Case No 111)?

The order making the reference to the Court of Justice was lodged at the Court Registry on 13 March 1978.

The United Kingdom and the Commission of the European Communities submitted written observations under Article 5 of the Protocol of 3 June 1971 in accordance with Article 20 of the Protocol on the Statute of the Court of Justice of the EEC.

After hearing the report of the Judge-Rapporteur and the views of the Advocate General, the Court decided to open the oral procedure without any preparatory inquiry.

II—Observations under Article 20 of the Protocol on the Statute of the Court of Justice of the EEC

A—Observations of the United Kingdom

The first question.

After stating that in the present case in addition to dOmicile (Article 2(2)) and operations of a branch, agency or other establishment (Article 5(5)) other bases of jurisdiction may be in point such as the place of performance of a contract (Article 5(1)), or the place of occurrence of the harmful event (Article 5(3)), the United Kingdom observes that the basic principle of the Convention on territorial jurisdiction is contained in Article 2 and the bases of jurisdiction listed in Section 2 of the Convention should therefore be construed restrictively as the Court has already recognized in Case 21/76 Bier v Mines de Potasse d'Alsace [1976] ECR 1735. Where such an exception is provided for there are considerable advantages in applying the law of the State before the courts of which the proceedings have been brought for the determination of grounds of jurisdiction. In interpreting the Convention according to its national law the court will avoid inconsistencies which would otherwise inevitably result from the fact that the same term has a different meaning in the Convention, that is to say for determining jurisdiction, from that in the law of the national court charged with deciding the substance of the action. The Convention itself recognizes this advantage by referring in Articles 52 and 53 to the national law of the court for the interpretation of the concept of domicile. However this method should not be applied to the interpretation of the provision in Article 5(5). The forum which this provision establishes is mainly intended to be invoked in cases of a commercial nature arising from economic relations which are the objective of Article 2 of the EEC Treaty. Such relations could be hampered if the actions to which they give rise could be brought before different courts applying different laws. This is particularly so where the jurisdictional rules in some countries make it particularly easy to bring proceedings against foreign traders. Having regard to the fact on the one hand that the general rule of jurisdiction of the defendant's court offers sufficient protection within the scheme of the Convention to the plaintiff and on the other hand that the exceptions provided for in Article 5(1) (contractual) and Article 5(3) (tort) suffice in the majority of cases, the exceptional jurisdiction provided for in Article 5(5)—which will need to be invoked only where the transaction itself has no close links with the foreign country in question—should be available only if the defendant had established in the foreign country a basis for conducting business of a firm and lasting character. National laws do not offer satisfactory criteria in this respect because they have been adopted in a different context, namely: to bring a defendant before a national court on the basis that the plaintiff has no guarantee of obtaining judgment elsewhere. The United Kingdom illustrates these considerations with an example from its national law from which it appears that the national provisions relating to an "agency" would provide an inappropriate test for the meaning to be given to the word "agency" in Article 5(5) of the Convention and concludes therefore that test should be applied uniformly by all courts.

The United Kingdom therefore considers that Question 1(a) and 1(b) asked by the Oberlandesgericht Saarbrucken should be answered in the negative and that question 1(c) should be answered in the affirmative.

The second question

As regards the concepts of branch and agency, the United Kingdom considers that although the law of certain Member States and in particular the law of Scotland (Section 6 of the Sheriff Courts (Scotland) Act 1907) may provide valuable guidance, it is unlikely that the rules of national law command a wide consensus in the context of the Community. Fresh guiding lines therefore need to be formulated which should be directed to establishing (1) that the foreign firm should be conducting business of a continuing nature through one or more representatives operating from a base in the country of the court and (2) that that base should consist of premises firmly set up on a lasting basis.

As regards the independent decision of the agent, the question whether he has authority to bind his principals is not material so long as persons dealing with the representative, operating from an appropriate base, have reason to believe that in so doing they are dealing with the foreign firm.

The third question

In the United Kingdom's view the application of any rules regarding estoppel by conduct are a matter for the procedure of the court concerned and not a question arising on the interpretation of Article 5(5).

B—Observations of the Commission

The first question

The question as to which law should govern interpretation of the concepts used in the Convention has been dealt with in various judgments of the Court of Justice. After declaring in paragraph 11 of the judgment of 6 October 1976 in Case 12/76 Tessili [1976] ECR 1473 that "neither of these two options (namely an independent interpretation or reference to the substantive rules of the law applicable under the rules of conflict of laws of the court before which the matter is first brought) rules out the other since the appropriate choice can only be made in respect of each of the provisions of the Convention" the Court took the view in its judgments of 14 October 1976 in Case 29/76 LTU v Eurocontrol [1976] ECR 1541 and 14 July 1977 in Joined Cases 9 and 10/77 Bavaria v Eurocontrol [1977] ECR 1517 at p. 1525, paragraph 4, that "the principle of legal certainty in the Community legal system and the objectives of the Brussels Convention... require in all Member States a uniform application of the legal concepts and legal classifications developed by the Court in the context of the Brussels Convention". Finally the judgment of 12 November 1977 in Case 43/77 Industrial Diamond Supplies [1977] ECR 2175 gave a uniform and independent interpretation of the concept "ordinary appeal" within the meaning of Articles 30 and 38 of the Convention.

In view of the guiding lines of this case-law the Commission takes the view that the interpretation of the concept of "branch, agency or other establishment" must be uniform and based on the Convention. The Court of Justice rightly began in the judgment of 6 October 1976 in Case 14/76 De Bloos [1976] ECR 1497 to interpret the concepts in question in this way.

The second question

On the basis of the above-mentioned judgment in Case 14/76 De Bloos in which the Court declared (at paragraphs 20 and 21) "One of the essential characteristics of the concepts of branch or agency is the fact of being subject to the direction and control of the parent body. It is clear... that... the Convention requires that the concept of 'establishment' appearing in the said article shall be based on the same essential characteristics as a branch or agency," the Commission considers that the concept of "direction and control of the parent body" should be defined. In its view this concept implies in respect of the organization: that there should be an outward manifestation of a certain significance such as premises, a bank account, a telephone number. As regards independent management: the manager of the branch, agency or other establishment should be authorized to transact business independently subject to the direction and control of the parent body in such a way as to bind the parent body in important transactions without having to consult it each time. As regards the permanent nature: the commercial activities of the branch should not be temporary.

The third question

In view of the fact that by no means all the Member States apply the principle of German law based on appearance, the Commission hesitates to recommend its extension to the Convention. Such interpretation does not facilitate the independent application of the Convention and risks resulting in the neglect, where arising, of the question of the existence of criteria of a branch, agency or other establishment.

The Commission therefore concludes that the simple appearance of a right is not sufficient to give jurisdiction....

H. Mayras, the Advocate General delivered his opinion at the hearing on 11 October 1978:

I—Etablissements Somafer, Uckange, Lorraine, submitted a tender pursuant to an invitation to tender by the Ministry of the Interior of the Saarland to carry out certain demolition work on the perimeter of the Rochling-Burbach factories.

Since the security measures proposed by the French undertaking appeared inadequate the German company SaarFerngas, whose gas mains were in the immediate vicinity of the intended demolition work, considered it necessary itself to take additional protective measures of which it notified Etablissements Somafer on 16 January 1974.

After duly informing the Gewerbeaufsichtsamt of the Saarland, whose functions correspond to those of the Ponts et Chaussees and of the Service des Mines in France, Etablissements Somafer on 29 January 1974 obtained a licence to carry out the work from the Mayor of Volklingen.

On 29 October 1974 the German company with a view to obtaining compensation sent its bill to Etablissements Somafer in respect of the costs incurred.

The representative (Vertretung) for the Federal Republic at Beckingen in the Saar of the main establishment (Hauptverwaltung) Uckange contended that the claim was barred. Saar-Ferngas therefore brought an action against Etablissements Somafer before the local court of the "representative" in the Federal Republic, the Landgericht Saarbrucken. Let me observe incidentally that in France actions relating to administrative contracts and damages for public works come within the jurisdiction of the administrative courts.

The part played by the representative at Beckingen in the discussions conducted between the Ministry of the Interior on the one hand and Etablissements Somafer on the other is disputed by the parties and it is to settle this question that the Oberlandesgericht Saarbrucken has referred the matter to you.

Before starting to consider the questions which have been referred to you it is appropriate to remember that Saar-Ferngas brought the case before the Landgericht Saarbrucken at first instance on the basis that Etablissements Somafer had a branch at Beckingen within the meaning of German law (Article 21 of the German Code of Civil Procedure) and further on the basis that that court was that of the "place of performance of the obligation in question" within the meaning of Article 5(1) of the Brussels Convention of 1968.

The court of first instance accepted neither of these arguments but regarded itself as having jurisdiction under Article 5(5) of the Convention because in its view this goes further than German national law: it recognizes that a connexion with the operation of a branch or agency can give jurisdiction to the courts for the place in which the branch or agency is situated. The court considered that Somafer had at Beckingen at least an agency within the meaning of Article 5(5) of the Convention; it used its office in that area to deal with third parties or in any event it gave Saar-Ferngas the impression that that office was such an agency. In doing this the court relied on criteria of German law but it considers that they could equally be relevant in the application of Article 5(5) of the Convention.

The Saarland undertaking adopted this argument on the appeal. It therefore dropped the claim that it put forward in the alternative at first instance based on Article 23 of the German Code of Civil Procedure. That article which constitutes an excessive rule of national law on jurisdiction provides that in the absence of any other court having jurisdiction in German territory actions relating to property brought against a person not resident within national territory come within the jurisdiction of the court of the place where the goods or objects in question are situate; this however can no longer be relied upon in view of Article 3 of the Convention of 1968.

II—The first question basically asks whether the concepts of "branch, agency or other establishment" must be interpreted by reference to national law or on the contrary independently.

1. In favour of reference to national law for determining place of the court having jurisdiction it may be said that in general there is every advantage in applying the law of the State before whose courts the matter comes or the law applicable to the main action: it is important for questions of jurisdiction to be resolved speedily. It is always easier for a court to apply its own law; further almost all the criteria for jurisdiction referred to in the Convention are connected with concepts which are found used in the national law of the Member States for purposes other than the determination of jurisdiction.

As regards the concepts of domicile of natural persons or the seat of companies or legal persons, in respect of which after all the concepts of Article 5(5) represent only a breakdown or subclass, the Convention refers expressly to the application of the internal law of the court seized of the matter (first paragraph of Article 52) or its rules of private international law (Article 53).

An independent interpretation of the concepts referred to in Article 5(5) would not, strictly, be in accord with "the simplification of formalities governing the reciprocal recognition and enforcement of judgments of courts or tribunals" which is the objective assigned to the Convention by Article 220 of the EEC Treaty; on the contrary it would have been more expeditious for Saar-Ferngas to bring the action against Somafer before the court of the place where the head office of that undertaking is situate to obtain a judgment against it which would have been directly enforceable in France.

Moreover it may be doubted whether the authors of the Convention intended to give a common and independent definition of the branch, agency or establishment. Such a definition would risk being overtaken by the development of the national laws and case-law. The very fact that they used the word "other," which is a type of "residuary" class to cover all other cases, would confirm that they have not sought to give a precise definition at least to the concept of establishment. Such an objective which would come within the sphere of uniform legislation would be alien to the Convention.

Finally the Court decided in the judgment of 6 October 1976, Tessili ([1976] ECR 1473) in connexion with the interpretation of the Convention in general that in certain circumstances the words and concepts used by the Convention (that case was concerned with the concept used in Article 5 of "place of performance of the obligation in question") must be regarded as referring to the substantive rules of the law applicable under the rules of conflict of laws of the court before which the matter is first brought.

2. In favour of the independent nature of the words in Article 5(5) the following considerations on the other hand may be put:

Even if the national law of the court before which the matter is brought or if the private international law applicable to the main action make jurisdiction dependent on criteria more or less identical to those referred to in Article 5(5) of the Convention, it is not likely that the current interpretation of those criteria by the national court is appropriate to cases falling under the Convention.

In the judgment in De Bloos of 6 October 1976 ([1976] ECR 1497) the Court itself began to interpret the concepts referred to in Article 5(5) uniformly and independently in seeking to define the concept of "branch". This precedent does not appear to me completely decisive in itself for the definition—not a full one—given in that judgment is purely negative and was arrived at in relation to the internal relationship between the grantee and grantor of an exclusive sales concession

A little later on 14 October 1976 the Court in the case of the Lufttransportunternehmen ([1976] ECR 1541) ruled that the concept "civil and commercial matters" used in Article 1 of the Convention cannot be interpreted solely in the light of the division of jurisdiction between the various types of courts existing in certain Member States and that the concept in question must therefore be regarded as independent and must be interpreted by reference, first, to the objectives and scheme of the Convention and, secondly, to the general principles which stem from the corpus of the national legal systems.

On 14 July 1977 in Joined Cases Bavaria Fluggesellschaft Schwabe and Germania Bedarfsluftfahrt ([1977] ECR 1517) the Court ruled that this interpretation was based on the desire to ensure in relation to Community law that the Contracting States and parties concerned have equal and uniform rights and duties under the Brussels Convention and that the principle of legal certainty in the Community legal system and the objectives of the Convention in accordance with Article 220 of the EEC Treaty, which is at its origin, require in all Member States a uniform application of the legal concepts and legal classifications developed by the Court in the context of the Convention.

In the case of Industrial Diamond Supplies the Court ruled on 22 November 1977 ([1977] ECR 2175) that if the concept of "ordinary appeal" were interpreted by reference to a national system, whether the legal system of the State in which the judgment was given or that of the State in which recognition or enforcement is sought, it would in certain cases be impossible to classify a specific appeal with the required degree of certainty for the purposes of Articles 30 and 38 of the Convention and that the interpretation of the concept of "ordinary appeal" may usefully be sought only within the framework of the convention itself.

The Court adopted the same attitude in the judgment of 21 June 1978 in Case 150/77 Bertrand v Ott [1978] ECR 1431 in relation to the "sale of goods on instalment credit terms".

On the basis of these precedents I think that the jurisdiction for disputes "arising out of the operation of a branch, agency or other establishment" must be determined independently, that is to say having regard to the objectives and the scheme of the Convention of 1968 and the general principles of the national legal systems.

This "independent" interpretation must be based on the laws and case-law of the Member States which are parties to the Convention as regards the consequences, from the point of view of the forum, of the concepts of branch, agency or other establishment and on the national case-law on the forum for subsidiary establishments of legal persons provided for in certain bilateral Conventions entered into between Member States before the Brussels Convention.

These bilateral Conventions recognize the criterion of attachment either on the basis of direct jurisdiction or on the basis of indirect jurisdiction by means of choice of domicile. It might be said that the Brussels Convention has "codified" and multinationalized the bilateral provisions without in so doing unifying the case-law of the various States relating to their application.

The immediate predecessor of Article 5(5) of the Brussels Convention thus appears to be Article 4(1)(d) of the German-Netherlands Convention of 30 August 1962 which reads:

"The courts of the State where the decision has been given are recognized as having jurisdiction for the purposes of the present Convention:

...if in the State where the decision has been given the defendant has been served at his place of business or at a branch in relation to disputes arising out of the operation of the said establishment or branch."

It must be observed that Article 5(5) of the Brussels Convention provides a criterion of connexion on the basis of direct jurisdiction for the purposes of recognition and enforcement and a presumption of choice of domicile.

Still following this line of reasoning I shall invite you to answer Question 1(b) also in the negative for recourse in a case before a national court to the law applicable in the main action would finally lead to reference to national laws which are probably different.

III—In the event of jurisdiction relating to the operations of a branch, agency or other establishment having to be determined independently, the national court wishes to know by its second question what criteria of interpretation should be applied to the expressions "branch" and "agency" with reference to capacity to take independent decisions (inter alia to enter into contracts) and also to the extent of the outward manifestation. It must be observed that the question does not mention "establishment," but it appears to me necessary to consider it.

Two observations will guide me in this endeavour. First of all whatever the connexion chosen, the concepts referred to in Section 2 of the Convention ("special jurisdiction") and in particular Article 5(5) must be interpreted strictly because the fact must not be lost sight of that there is another general criterion for jurisdiction, namely the defendant's domicile (Article 2). This rule is contained in the judgment in Bier of 30 November 1976 ([1976] ECR 1735).

In the second place it is generally difficult to determine the characteristics of an establishment or agency to which the rule of jurisdiction in Article 5(5) applies. Although the definition of a branch may be relatively precise, the concepts of agency or establishment are very often tinged with questions of fact which in national case-law are generally left to the exclusive decision of the court trying the main action. Even if it is decided that the concepts of Article 5(5) are independent, it inevitably follows that in order to define them it is necessary to clarify questions of fact and this is a task for the national court.

1. The question concerns the concept of "operations" as much, if not more than, that of a branch, agency or other establishment. It must therefore be a question of a dispute involving the operations of one of these entities and not of a dispute in relation to what comes simply under the activity of the parent company or is tied up with it. In other words it is necessary for the foreign trading company to operate in the Federal Republic and it is necessary for the entity in question to be able to develop its own activity there distinct from that of the parent company without nevertheless being a legal person.

The Convention reveals a remarkable absence of precision: it refers not only to branch or agency, which never have legal personality, although they are governed by fairly precise legal regulations, at least the branch is, but also to "other establishment". The common aspect of the concepts to which Article 5(5) refers is therefore of entities not having legal personality; it should be observed in particular that the subsidiary of an undertaking is not referred to for the good reason that such a subsidiary has legal personality and may therefore be brought before the courts where it is established.

Consequently it is necessary for the company to have a sufficient industrial or commercial outward manifestation abroad for there to be operations. Certain criteria contained in the convention on the Mutual Recognition of Companies and Bodies Corporate of 29 February 1968 could be applied by way of analogy, with the necessary adjustments, although this Convention has a different objective and has not yet entered into force: in order to obtain recognition it is necessary (Article 3) for the company or body corporate to have a genuine connexion with the economy of one of the territories to which the Convention applies; the company or body corporate in question must show that it has in fact exercised its activity for a reasonable period in the Contracting State under whose law it was incorporated (Article 4).

2. Although the entity referred to in Article 5(5) must have a certain independence in taking decisions and although in particular it must have power to carry out operations on behalf of and binding the parent company, it must nevertheless be subject to the latter's control and direction.

The Court propounded this principle in the judgment in De Bloos which has already been cited:

"One of the essential characteristics of the concepts of branch or agency is the fact of being subject to the direction and control of the parent body" (paragraph 20).

This criterion was extended to the establishment:

"it is clear from both the object and the wording of this provision that the spirit of the Convention requires that the concept of 'establishment' appearing in the same article shall be based on the same essential characteristics as a branch or agency" (paragraph 21).

However it cannot automatically be inferred a contrario that in its relations with third parties every "representation" which is bound by instructions emanating from the parent company can be described only as a branch or agency.

The delicate question of burden of proof arises here: on whom is the burden to show the existence of such control and direction by the parent company? Is it necessary to require that such control and direction should be based on the internal articles of the parent company and of the subordinate entity so that the latter is legally able to bind the former or does it suffice that in the eyes of third parties the branch, agency or other establishment acts as though it had power even if in law it has exceeded its powers? The answer to this question thus merges with consideration of the third question raised by the national court.

IV—I think that having regard to the special nature of the jurisdiction under Article 5(5) appearances should be disregarded and the realities considered and it is for third parties who wish to rely on this exception to adduce evidence that the entity which they wish to bring before the court was in fact subject to the control and direction of the parent company and that in particular the operation giving rise to the dispute was within the competence of the branch or agency and that there was sufficient connexion with that operation.

In the present case it is for the Saarland company to show that the Saarland manager of the office of the Lorraine company was not a simple executive or technical agent but had the power and status to conclude the operation and that discussions were conducted by this representative and not by the head office.

In this respect it may be useful to refer to a provision of the Franco-German Treaty on the Saar of 26 October 1956, although that provision gave only indirect jurisdiction and is no longer in force. It is Article 46 of the Treaty which provided:

"Where a French national has in the Saar or a citizen of the Saar has in France an establishment or branch of an industrial, commercial or other nature they may, in respect of contracts concluded directly by such establishment or branch, be brought before the courts of the country where the establishment or branch is situate."

In these circumstances I think the argument based on appearances to which the Court refers in its last question should be rejected. I do not know how far such a doctrine is recognized in German law in respect of simple establishments and even if it is accepted that the question of the "practical effects" of appearances is not something peculiar to such law, it appears to me doubtful whether it is part of the legal system of all the Member States which are parties to the Convention. Above all, if such a criterion was resorted to it would open the door to all interpretations and would renationalize, in a manner of speaking, a term which the premises require should be independent. I think there is support for this view too in the case-law of the Court according to which acts giving rise to inferences by one party to a contract cannot take the place of the express extension of jurisdiction required by Article 17 of the Convention (Case 24/76 Estasis [1976] ECR 1831 and Case 25/76 Segoura [1976] ECR 1851).

My opinion is that the Court should hold that in civil and commercial matters for the purposes of Article 5 (5) of the Brussels Convention of 1968 it is sufficient that the entity which is referred to therein has entered directly into the contract out of which the claim arises.

DECISION: 1. By order dated 21 February 1978, received at the Court on 13 March 1978, the Oberlandesgericht Saarbrucken referred to the Court under the Protocol of 3 June 1971 concerning the interpretation of the Convention of 27 September 1968 on Jurisdiction and the Enforcement of Judgments in Civil and Commercial Matters (Official Journal 1978, No L 304, p. 77) (hereinafter referred to as "the Convention") three questions on the interpretation of Article 5(5) of the Convention. According to the provision, interpretation of which is sought, a person domiciled in a Contracting State may, in another Contracting State, be sued:..."(5) as regards a dispute arising out of the operations of a branch, agency or other establishment, in the courts for the place in which the branch, agency or other establishment is situated."

2. The questions put must enable the national court to decide whether it has jurisdiction under the said provision—without prejudice to its jurisdiction on the basis of other provisions of the Convention—to try an action brought by a German undertaking against a French undertaking, the registered office of which is in French territory but which has an office or place of contact in the Federal Republic of Germany described on its notepaper as "Vertretung fur Deutschland" ["Representation for Germany"], for the recovery of the expenses incurred by the German undertaking to protect gas mains belonging to it from any damage which might be caused by demolition work which the French undertaking was carrying out in the vicinity on behalf of the Saarland.

The first question

3. The first question asks

"Are the conditions regarding jurisdiction in the case of 'the operations of a branch, agency or other establishment' mentioned in Article 5(5) of the said Convention to be determined.

(a) under the law of the State before the courts of which the proceedings have been brought; or

(b) under the law of the States concerned (qualification according to the law to be applied in the main action); or

(c) independently, i.e. in accordance with the objectives and system of the said Convention and also with the general principles of law which stem from the corpus of the national legal system (Judgment of 14 October 1976 in Case 29/76 LTU Lufttransportunternehmen GmbH & Co. KG v Eurocontrol [1976] ECR 1541)?"

4. The Convention, concluded pursuant to Article 220 of the EEC Treaty, is intended according to the express terms of its preamble to implement the provisions of that article on the simplification of formalities governing the reciprocal recognition and enforcement of judgments of courts or tribunals and to strengthen in the Community the legal protection of persons therein established. In order to eliminate obstacles to legal relations and to settle disputes within the sphere of intra-Community relations in civil and commercial matters the Convention contains, inter alia, rules enabling the jurisdiction in these matters of the courts of Contracting States to be determined and facilitating the recognition and execution of courts' judgments. Accordingly the Convention must be interpreted having regard both to its principles and objectives and to its relationship within the Treaty.

5. The Convention frequently uses words and legal concepts drawn from civil, commercial and procedural law and capable of a different meaning from one Contracting State to another. The question therefore arises whether these words and concepts must be regarded as having their own independent meaning and as being thus common to all the Contracting States or as referring to substantive rules of the law applicable in each case under the rules of conflict of laws of the court before which the matter is first brought. The answer to this question must ensure that the Convention is fully effective in achieving the objectives which it pursues.

6. The meaning of the words "dispute arising out of the operations of a branch, agency or other establishment," which are the basis of the jurisdiction give by Article 5(5), are different from one Contracting State to another, not only in the respective laws but also in the application given to bilateral conventions on the recognition and enforcement of foreign judgments.

7. Their function in the context of the Convention must be decided in relation to the general rule conferring jurisdiction contained in Article 2(1) of the Convention which states "Subject to the provisions of this Convention, persons domiciled in a Contracting State shall, whatever their nationality, be sued in the courts of that State." Although Article 5 makes provision in a number of cases for a special jurisdiction, which the plaintiff may choose, this is because of the existence, in certain clearly-defined situations, of a particularly close connecting factor between a dispute and the court which may be called upon to hear it, with a view to the efficacious conduct of the proceedings. Multiplication of the bases of jurisdiction in one and the same case is not likely to encourage legal certainty and the effectiveness of legal protection throughout the territory of the Community and therefore it is in accord with the objective of the Convention to avoid a wide and multifarious interpretation of the exceptions to the general rule of jurisdiction contained in Article 2. This is all the more so since in national laws or in bilateral conventions the similar exception is frequently due, as the United Kingdom rightly points

out in its written observations, to the notion that a national State serves the interests of its nationals by offering them an opportunity to escape the jurisdiction of a foreign court and this consideration is out of place in the Community context, since the justification for the exceptions contained in Article 5 to the general rule of jurisdiction in Article 2 is solely in the interests of due administration of justice.

8. The scope and limits of the right given to the plaintiff by Article 5(5) must be determined by the particular facts which either in the relations between the parent body and its branches, agencies or other establishments or in the relations between one of the latter entities and third parties show the special link justifying, in derogation from Article 2, the option granted to the plaintiff. It is by definition a question of factors concerning two entities established in different Contracting States but which in spite of this must be considered in the same way, whether from the point of view of the parent body or of an extension or extensions which the parent body has established in the other Member States or from that of the third parties with whom legal relations are created through such extensions. In these circumstances the need to ensure legal certainty and equality of rights and obligations for the parties as regards the power to derogate from the general jurisdiction of Article 2 requires an independent interpretation, common to all the Contracting States, of the concepts in Article 5(5) of the Convention which are the subject of the reference for a preliminary ruling.

The second and third questions

9. In the event of the words referred to being interpreted independently, the second question asks what criteria apply with reference to the capacity to take independent decisions (inter alia to enter into contracts) and also to the extent of the outward manifestation. The third question asks

"Are the principles liability for holding oneself out in law to others, i.e. to third parties, to be applied to the questions whether there is in fact a branch or agency, with legal consequences that anyone who creates the appearance of such a situation is to be treated as having operated a branch or agency—as is for example the case under German law (cf. Article 21 of the Zivilprozessordnung [Code of Civil Procedure] Baumbach, 36th Edition note 2 A, Stein-Jonas, 19th Edition, Note II 2; Oberlandesgericht Koln Neue Juristische Wochenschrift 1953, 1834, Oberlandesgericht Breslau Hochstrichterliche Rechtsprechung 1939 (Case No 111))?"

10. These two questions must be taken together.

11. Having regard to the fact that the concepts referred to give the right to derogate from the principle of jurisdiction of Article 2 of the Convention their interpretation must show without difficulty the special link justifying such derogation. Such special link comprises in the first place the material signs enabling the existence of the branch, agency or other establishment to be easily recognized and in the second place the connexion that there is between the local entity and the claim directed against the parent body established in another Contracting State.

12. As regards the first issue, the concept of branch, agency or other establishment implies a place of business which has the appearance of permanency, such as the extension of a parent body, has a management and is materially equipped to negotiate business with third parties so that the latter, although knowing that there will if necessary be a legal link with the parent body, the head office of which is abroad, do not have to deal directly with such parent body but may transact business at the place of business constituting the extension.

13. As regards the second issue the claim in the action must concern the operations of the branch, agency or other establishment. This concept of operations comprises on the one hand actions relating to rights and contractual or non-contractual obligations concerning the management properly so-called of the agency, branch or other establishment itself such as those concerning the situation of the building where such entity is established or the local engagement of staff to work there. Further it also comprises those relating to undertakings which have been entered into at the above-mentioned place of business in the name of the parent body and which must be performed in the Contracting State where the place of business is established and also actions concerning non-contractual obligations arising from the activities in which the branch, agency or other establishment within the above defined meaning, has engaged at the place in which it is established on behalf of the parent body. It is in each case for the court before which the matter comes to find the facts whereon it may be established that an effective place of business exists and to determine the legal position by reference to the concept of "operations" as above defined.

14. The above considerations make it unnecessary to answer the third question.

Costs

15. The costs incurred by the Government of the United Kingdom and by the Commission of the European Communities, which have submitted written observations to the Court, are not recoverable and as the proceedings are, so far as the parties to the main action are concerned, a step in the action pending before the national court, the decision on costs is a matter for that court.

On those grounds, the Court in answer to the questions referred to it by the Oberlandesgericht Saarbrucken by order of 21 February 1978, hereby rules:

1. The need to ensure legal certainty and equality of rights and obligations for the parties as regards the power to derogate from the general jurisdiction of Article 2 requires an independent interpretation, common to all the Contracting States, of the concepts in Article 5 (5) of the Convention.

2. The concept of branch, agency or other establishment implies a place of business which has the appearance of permanency, such as the extension of a parent body, has a management and is materially equipped to negotiate business with third parties so that the latter, although knowing that there will if necessary be a legal link with the parent body, the head office of which is abroad, do not have to deal directly with such parent body but may transact business at the place of business constituting the extension.

3. The concept of "operations" comprises:

– actions relating to rights and contractual or non-contractual obligations concerning the management properly so-called of the agency, branch or other establishment itself such as those concerning the situation of the building where such entity is established or the local engagement of staff to work there;

– actions relating to undertakings which have been entered into at the above-mentioned place of business in the name of the parent body and which must be performed in the Contracting State where the place of business is established and also actions concerning non-contractual obligations arising from the activities in which the branch, agency or other establishments within the above defined meaning, has engaged at the place in which it is established on behalf of the parent body.

4. It is in each case for the court before which the matter comes to find the facts whereon it may be established that an effective place of business exists and to determine the legal position by reference to the concept of "operations" as above defined.

Comments and Questions

1. While the Convention on Mutual Recognition has gone unratified, and unenforced,[1] the European Court of Justice has applied from its principles from time to time in connection with the determination of issues under related conventions. In what way does the Convention on the Mutual Recognition of Companies and Legal Persons influence, if at all, the interpretation of the related Convention on the Jurisdiction and the Enforcement of Judgments in Civil and Commercial Matters and the understanding of the judiciary of the nature of branches as forms of enterprise organization?

2. To what extent is the Court's definition of branches binding on the Member States? Should it matter that branches are subject to multiple and potentially inconsistent definitions with different effect?

3. In the United States, issues of personal jurisdiction are a matter of an evaluation of the nexus of contacts between a defendant and the jurisdiction in which contacts are asserted. It is an analysis based on substance over form. (International Shoe Co. v. State of Washington, Office of Unemployment Compensation and Placement, 326 U.S. 310 (1945)). For jurisdiction to be asserted with respect to a claim (specific jurisdiction) there must be sufficient contacts between the forum and the defendant related to the claim. (Burger King Corp. v. Rudzewicz, 471 U.S. 462 (1985) (purposeful availment of privilege of conducting activities in forum state and existence of no factors which render jurisdiction unreasonable)). At its extreme, even a single act directly aimed at a particular person in a form may be sufficient to support personal jurisdiction. (McGee v. International Life Ins. Co., 355 U.S. 220 (1957)). For jurisdiction over a defendant to be asserted with respect to all matters or claims (general jurisdiction) the contacts between the defendant and the forum must be continuous and systematic. (Perkins v. Benguet Consolidated Mining Co., 342 U.S. 437 (1952) (Philippine corporation subject to general jurisdiction in Ohio where administrative center in Ohio)). Personal jurisdiction is available by consent of the defendant as well. (Carnival Cruise Lines, Inc. v. Shute, 499 U.S. 585 (1991)). Thus, for example, in the United States, registering in a state as a foreign corporation may constitute a consent to general jurisdiction within the state.

The *Somafer* court appears to take a different direction. It bases jurisdiction on a formalist analysis: do the activities of the defendant constitute a branch within the meaning of the Convention; if yes, then Germany has jurisdiction; if the activities do not fall within the definition of a branch, then Germany may not assert jurisdiction over the case in its courts. However, is it possible to argue that the court in *Somafer* essentially applied a minimum contacts analysis to determine whether jurisdiction was appropriate in German courts? Look beneath the formalist analysis the court used to determine whether the activity was significant enough to constitute a branch. There appears to be significant amount of contacts analysis supporting the judicial analysis. If the court had applied a different theory of legal personality, could it have reached a different result? Consider in this respect the definition of a branch adopted by the court. It is possible to

---

1. The Convention on the Mutual Recognition of Companies and Legal Persons is discussed in more detail at Chapter 6.C.1, below.

argue that the definition itself encapsulates the sort of contacts analysis with which American lawyers are familiar. Do you agree?

4. Do you agree that the court should not be bound by national definitions of branches for purposes of determining the applicability of jurisdictional provisions? Should convenience and predictability trump the substantive policy of Member States reflected in state definitions of branches?

5. The definition of a branch for purposes of jurisdiction suggests some problems. To what extent is this definition useful in the business context? Does it supply the necessary certainty that makes application easy and sure? Would a more formalist definition be better by providing certainty of formation?

6. *Somafer* teaches us that, at least for purposes of applying jurisdictional rules, the branches are defined independent of the definitions of the Member States, though with reference to such definitions and common understandings. That definition, however, may not be effective for purposes of registration or regulation of a branch within a Member State. These issues may have become more complicated in the aftermath of *Centros*. For example, if a branch does not have independent legal personality, may a Member State regulate the internal affairs of the branch after *Centros* if by doing so the regulating Member State effectively regulates the internal affairs of the parent company? The materials that follow provide information about the treatment of branches within Europe. As you review them, think about how *Centros* may affect their reach.

Doing Business in France

Price Waterhouse World Firm Services BV, Inc. (1995)
(excerpts pages 90–91)

Branch of a foreign corporation
(*Succursale*)

For legal and tax purposes a branch (*succursale*) is not a legal entity separate from its foreign head office.

The formation of a branch is relatively simple. It is registered with the Clerk of the Commercial Court (*Tribunal de Commerce*) by filing a French-language version of the corporate bylaws of the foreign head office as well as an application for a commercial card (*carte de commerçant*) or a resident visa (*carte de résident*) for the manager of a branch if the manager (*gérant*) is not a national of an EU country. The registered name of the branch is the corporate name of the foreign head office.

The cost and time required to forma branch are about the same as for incorporating a SARL. There is no public disclosure of financial statements.

There is no minimum legal capital requirement for branches of foreign companies. For direct investment purposes, however, the Treasury may require assigned capital (*dotation*) sufficient to cover the branch's capital expenditure and operating expenses for at least three to six months.

Branches of foreign corporations are managed by one or more managers (*directeurs*), whose powers are set and may be limited by the foreign head office. The requirements for books and records are those applicable to SARLs, except that there are no board and shareholders' minutes or reports. Except for branches conducting banking activities, there are no statutory audit requirements.

Liason Office

Under French law, a liaison office can be used for certain limited activities without attracting French tax and without the prerequisite of prior authorization because such activities are not considered an investment in France. The role of the liaison office must be limited to activities of a preliminary or limited nature, such as market research, arranging for advertising, and collecting or disseminating information, as long as the nature and extent of operations do not rise to the level of "commercial" activity.

The liaison office should not be separately incorporated in France but rather exists as a French office of a foreign legal entity. Generally, liaison offices are not required to be inscribed in the local Commercial Registry, since their activities are not considered to be of a commercial nature. Because of its noncommercial nature a liaison office can be established and then discontinued with a minimum of requirements and cost.

Comments and Questions

1. Member States require registration of operations of foreign companies, which is done other than through a domestic subsidiary, for a variety of reasons. The two principal reasons are taxation and amenability to suit. As *Somafer* illustrates, amenability to suit may be dependent on the proper characterization of a foreign corporation's operations in a host state as a "branch." Registration may ensure this outcome. On the benefit side for registrants, registration opens access to the host state's courts. Moreover, Member States will tax the income generated by the host state operations of foreign corporations. Registration provides a means of administering the tax consequences of host state operations. In addition, as the excerpt above suggests, registration provides a means of regulating the operations of the registrants, at least to some extent. Are there any aspects of registration as a subsidiary in France, as excerpted above, that may now be subject to attack on the basis of *Centros*? If you were representing France, are there any arguments you could make in support of the validity of the registration requirements attacked? Are there means of redrafting the regulations to accomplish the same purpose without violating the right of establishment as specified in *Centros?*

2. Spain requires branches of foreign corporations to comply with the registration requirements of the Commercial Code. This includes registration in the 'Registro Mercantil' (Commercial Code, tit. II, cap. 1, § 81; and cap XI, § 259–273). Registration includes the deposit of information about the company and its branch for publication in local and national commercial registries. Changes in the legal status of the company must be communicated to the local registrar in which the branch operates.

3. It is worth comparing the rules for the establishment of branches in Europe with those in Japan. "Under Japanese law a foreign company doing more than sporadic business in Japan must appoint a representative in Japan, establish a place of business, and register information with the Japanese government regarding the representative and the place of business.[11] No license or other special permission is

11. Commercial Code Art. 479.

needed to set up a branch office in Japan (except for regulated businesses such as banks)." ELLIOTT HAHN, JAPANESE BUSINESS LAW AND THE LEGAL SYSTEM 52 (1984).

4. There is a law of branch offices in the United States as well. Registration as a foreign corporation with the authorities in a host state provides an opportunity for regulation of the corporations of sister states within the United States.

DHM Segers v. Bestuur Van De Bedrijfsvereniging Voor Bank-En Verzekeringswezen, Groothandel En Vrije Beroepen

(Case 79/85)
Court of Justice of the European Communities
(2nd Chamber)
[1986] ECR 2375, [1987] 2 CMLR 247
10 July 1986

M Marco Darmon, Advocate General, delivered the following opinion:

1

From 1980 Mr Segers, a Dutch national, ran a commercial undertaking known as 'Free Promotion International' which had its registered office in the Netherlands. Being anxious to extend his activities, inter alia, to brokerage on the financial market, he decided to transform his business into a limited liability company. Since he considered that the time required under Dutch law for completing such an operation was too long and that designation 'Ltd' was more attractive than its Dutch equivalent, 'BV,' he took the following steps:

He set up in the United Kingdom a private company limited by shares, known as 'Slenderose Ltd;' and

He converted the Dutch undertaking into a subsidiary of the British company under the name of 'Free Promotion International Company Ltd,' which in fact conducts all of Slenderose's business.

Following that operation and in order to obtain sickness benefits provided for by the Ziektewet (the Dutch Act establishing a general sickness insurance scheme) Mr Segers applied to the competent institution, the Bestuur van de Bedrijfsvereniging voor Bank-en Verzekeringswezen, Groothandel en Vrije Beroepen (Banking, Insurance, Wholesale Trade and Professions' Association, hereinafter referred to as 'the Association').

The Association rejected his application on the ground that Mr Segers could not be regarded as an employed person in his business since his employment did not entail a subordinate relationship with an employer. He was equally unsuccessful before the court of first instance. He then appealed to the Centrale Raad van Berope (Court of last instance in social security matters), which made an order requesting a preliminary ruling from the Court of Justice on the problem of interpretation.

2

The Ziektewet applies to persons with the status of employees and that status is defined in terms of the existence of a subordinate relationship with an employer. As the Dutch court points out, in principle such status cannot be attributed to the director of a company who holds 50 per cent of the shares of his undertaking whilst his wife owns the other 50 per cent. Nevertheless, in view of the legislature's desire to co-ordinate social security law and tax law in that matter, the Centrale Raad van Beroep departed from its previous case law. By two judgments of 10 December 1968, it held that the director of a company holding 50 per cent or more of the shares of a company was to be regarded as an employee.

It is the Association's contention that the effect of that ruling should be limited solely to directors who are majority shareholders of companies whose registered office is the Netherlands. That is why it considers that although Mr Segers is a Dutch national he cannot rely on that decision because he is the director of a company whose registered office is in London.

The Centrale Raad van Beroep therefore decided to refer to the Court for a preliminary ruling the following two questions:

1. Do the principles of freedom of establishment within the EEC and freedom to provide services within the EEC—in particular the last sentence of Article 52 read with Article 58 of the EEC Treaty and the last sentence of Article 60 read with Article 66 of that Treaty—mean that, when deciding whether there is an insurance obligation under Dutch social security legislation, Dutch Courts may not make any distinction between the director/major shareholder of a private company incorporated under Dutch law and a director/major shareholder of a private company incorporated under the laws of another member-State, even if the foreign company clearly does not carry on any actual business in the other member-State concerned but carries on business only in the Netherlands?

2. If that question is answered in the negative, does Community social security law (in particular Article 3(1) of Regulation 1408/71) or any other provision of Community law prohibit such a distinction?

3

In order to define the scope of the problem of interpretation before the Court and to provide the Dutch court with a useful reply, it is necessary to make the following two preliminary observations.

In the first place, it must be stressed that the difference in treatment in question is not based on the nationality of the person concerned. The factor which determines entitlement to benefits under the social security scheme is the location—in the Netherlands and not in another member-State—of the registered office of the patent company.

Secondly it must be noted that Mr Segers, the director of Slenderose Ltd., is established in the Netherlands where he also runs that company's subsidiary, through which, it may be recalled, all the parent company's business is conducted. He does not therefore come within the scope of the provisions of Article 59 EEC, which guarantee the freedom to provide services. Indeed, as the Court has consistently held, those provisions

> 'entail the abolition of all discrimination against a person providing a service on the grounds of his nationality or the fact that he is established in a member-State other than that in which the service must be provided' (Cases 62–63/81, Seco v Evi ([1982] ECR 223).

Ultimately the different treatment which, in the Association's view, should be accorded to Mr Segers is not based either on the nationality or place of residence of the person concerned but on the establishment in another member-State of the registered office of the parent company of which he is the director. It follows that it is necessary to consider Articles 52 to 58 of the Treaty concerning freedom of establishment in order to determine whether a national of a member-State may be deprived, solely for that reason, of his entitlement under national social security legislation.

Beyond that question, in the order requesting the preliminary ruling and the observations which have been submitted to the Court it is suggested that, in view of the finding that the Dutch subsidiary of Slenderose Ltd. in fact conducts all of the company's business, it may also be necessary to consider whether such a difference of treatment may be justified in order to prevent any attempt at fraud.

I propose to consider those two aspects of the problem of interpretation in turn.

4

Article 52(2) EEC provides that:

> Freedom of establishment shall include the right to...set up and manage undertakings, in particular companies or firms within the meaning of Article 58(2), under the conditions laid down for its own nationals by the law of the country where such establishment is effected...

Article 52(1) extends the removal of restrictions on the freedom of establishment of nationals of one member-State in the territory of any member-State.

> to restrictions on the setting up of agencies, branches or subsidiaries by nationals of any member-State established in the territory of any member-State.

That provision must be read in conjunction with Article 58 of the Treaty, according to which:

> companies or firms formed in accordance with the law of a member-State and having their registered office, central administration or principal place of business within the Community shall, for the purposes of this Chapter, be treated in the same way as natural persons who are nationals of member-States.

The fundamental principle of equal treatment of nationals of the member-States, which is thus guaranteed by Article 52 after the expiry of the transitional period and independently of the directives provided for in Articles 54 and 57 for its implementation (see Case 2/74 Reyners ([1974] ECR 631, [1974] 2 CMLR 305)), therefore applies not only to natural persons but also to companies, provided that they fulfil the two cumulative conditions laid down in Article 58(1), namely that they must be formed in accordance with the law and that they must have the requisite connection with one of the member-States.

Freedom of establishment therefore consists of the right for any national of a member-State to establish, even on an ancillary basis, a company in another member-State under the conditions which its law imposes on its nationals Article 52(2) and the right for a company to conduct its business in another member-State through an agency, branch or a subsidiary (Article 52(1).)

On that last point the Court, in its judgment in Case 270/83 (EC Commission v France ([1987] 1 CMLR 401 (Re Tax Credits)) concerning the refusal of France to grant tax exemption to French branches and agencies of insurance companies whose registered office is in another member-State, stated in the following terms the extent of which companies are treated as natural persons for the purposes of Article 58 of the Treaty:

> With regard to companies, it should be noted in this context that it is their registered office in the... sense [of Article 58] that serves as the connecting factor with the legal system of a particular State, like nationality in the case of natural persons.

The Court concluded that:

> Acceptance of the proposition that the Member-State in which a company seeks to establish itself may freely apply to it a different treatment solely by reason of the fact that its registered office is situated in another member-State would... deprive that provision of all meaning.

As I have just stated, the fact that the registered office of Mr Seger's company is in London is the sole basis for the rejection of his application. From that point of view the rejection must therefore be regarded as discriminatory.

But that is not all. In addition to that first finding of principle, another conclusion is to be drawn from the facts of the case. There is no danger that such a difference of treatment in the application of social security provisions may have the effect of dissuading a national already established in the Netherlands, irrespective of his nationality, from setting up a company abroad or from becoming a majority shareholder in such a company. Seen in that light, it is the right of natural persons guaranteed by Article 52(2) EEC to set up and manage companies in another member-State which would ultimately be deprived of any meaning.

From that point of view again, the difference in the application of social security provisions which the Association seeks to establish appears to constitute an obstacle to the exercise of the right of establishment of Community nationals residing in the Netherlands inasmuch as it withdraws from the companies run by such persons the entitlement to equal treatment with national companies accorded to companies whose directors have maintained their registered office in the territory of that State.

5

I consider that none of the arguments put forward by the Association in order to establish that Articles 52 and 58 do not apply is tenable.

In the first place, although it is true that Article 58 EEC does not expressly provide that companies of foreign origin are to be treated as national companies, that does not mean that the provision does not apply in this instance. By bringing companies within the scope of Article 52 EEC, Article 58 accords them the same freedoms as individuals, and requires member-States to accord companies whose registered office is in another member-State of the Community equality of treatment with national companies.

Secondly, I cannot accept the Association's view that the fact that this case concerns a Dutch national residing in the Netherlands where he in practice conducts all his business means that it is a purely internal matter. As I have repeatedly stressed, the different treatment which the Association seeks to apply to Mr Segers is based exclusively on the fact that the parent company's registered office is established in the United Kingdom. The circumstances of this case therefore come within the scope of the Community rules laid down in Articles 52 and 58 of the EEC Treaty. Moreover, it makes no difference that the subsidiary in fact conducts all the business of the United Kingdom company provided that company was formed in accordance with United Kingdom law and is linked to that State by one of the three alternative connecting factors listed in Article 58, in this case the establishment in London of the registered office.

Finally, in reply to the complaint relating to discrimination, the Association contends that nationals of the member-States may, in full knowledge of the circumstances, choose to set up a company either in the Netherlands or in another member-State. In reality that argument amounts to depriving the freedom of establishment of companies of any meaning: although it implies, misleadingly, that the parties concerned are given freedom of choice, foreign companies are dissuaded from establishing themselves in the Netherlands by the refusal to accord them protection under social security provisions. Such an effect is to be regarded as a restriction contrary to Article 52 in conjunction with Article 58. As the Commission stated, the rule of equal treatment for foreign nationals applied to companies whose registered office is in another member-State entails for the members of their staff, whether they are directors or not, the application of the social security provisions which apply to their opposite numbers in companies whose registered office is in the member-State in which they are established. In that connection, as the Court has stated (see, for example, its judgment in Case 197/84, Steinhauser ([1986] 1 CMLR 53), 'useful guidance' may be found in the General Programme for the abolition of restrictions on freedom of establishment of 18 December 1961 ([1961] OJ Spec Ed 2nd Series IX, p87) according to which restrictions on the freedom of establishment include those which

> 'deny or restrict the right to participate in social security schemes...' (Title III Section A point (i)).

It follows that the refusal to accord the directors of a company the advantages provided for by the national legislation on sickness insurance, which advantages are however accorded to the directors of companies whose registered office is in the Netherlands, solely because the registered office of the company in question is in another member-State, must be regarded as a restriction on the freedom of establishment prohibited since the end of the transitional period by Article 52 of the EEC Treaty in conjunction with Article 58, not only because it has the effect of restricting the right of companies established in another member-State to carry out their business in the Netherlands through the intermediary of a branch, agency or a subsidiary set up for that purpose, but also because it may dissuade nationals established in the Netherlands from setting up such a company or from becoming majority shareholders therein.

6

It remains to consider the possibility of fraud.

In the Association's view, the conversion of an undertaking of one member-State into a subsidiary of a company established in another member-State could make it possible for the nationals of the first State to circumvent their national rules. It is therefore in the public interest to limit the right of establishment in order to prevent abuses of that nature.

That argument calls for the following observations.

The operation described above is made possible by the combination of the right which is accorded to natural persons of setting up a company in another member-State and that, for legal persons, including companies created in that way, of conducting their business through the intermediary of a subsidiary in the country of origin of the natural person.

However paradoxical that situation may appear, it is the logical consequence of the rights guaranteed under the Treaty. Moreover, it is consistent with the objective behind the inclusion of the freedom of establishment in the EEC Treaty, namely the need to promote the free movement of persons and, by the same token, the achievement of a common market. In that respect, the fact that a national of a member-State may take advantage of the flexibility of United Kingdom company law and may exploit the effect of the attraction, which in his view, an Anglo-Saxon designation has for his customers must be viewed in that context.

Consequently, and although the Association acknowledged at the sitting that its refusal was not based on any attempt at fraud on the part of the plaintiff in the main proceedings, the possibility cannot be excluded that an operation of the same type as that carried out by him could have a fraudulent purpose. Nevertheless, the mere possibility of that happening cannot justify a general restriction on the right of establishment of natural and legal persons. On the other hand, the national authorities must be permitted to verify in individual cases that the companies thus formed have been, as is expressly provided in Article 58 of the EEC Treaty, formed in accordance with the legal provisions laid down to that effect. Similarly, they may control the activities of such companies with regard to the requirements of public policy. In that respect Article 56 EEC provides that the rules of the Treaty

> shall not prejudice the applicability of provisions laid down by law, regulation or administrative action providing for special treatment for foreign nationals on grounds of public policy, public security or public health.

Subject to those reservations and notwithstanding the legality of its supervisory power a member-State must ensure that companies form other member-States may be set up and may conduct their business under the same conditions as those laid down for 'national' companies.

It is therefore not necessary to consider the second question submitted by the Centrale Raad van Beroep and I propose that the Court shouldrule as follows:

The refusal to accord the advantages of a social security scheme to the director of a company solely because the registered office of that company is in another member-State constitutes a restriction on the freedom of establishment contrary to Articles 52 and 58 of the EEC Treaty.

By an order of 29 January 1985 which was received at the Court on 1 April 1985, the Centrale Raad van Beroep referred to the Court for a preliminary ruling under Article 177 EEC two questions, the first concerning the interpretation of Articles 52, 58, 60 and 66 EEC, and the second that of Article 3 of Council Regulation 1408/71, with a view to determining whether it is compatible with those provisions to apply the Ziektewet (Dutch Act establishing a general sickness insurance scheme) in a way which results in a difference of treatment, as far as admission to the scheme is concerned, for a director of a company according to whether or not the company is incorporated under Dutch law.

The questions were raised in connection with an action brought by Mr Segers, a Dutch national and the director of a company incorporated under English law, against the refusal of the Dutch authorities specifically the Bedrijfsvereniging voor Bank—en Verzekeringswezen, Groothandel en Vrije Beroepen (Banking, Insurance, Wholesale Trade and Professions' Association, hereinafter referred to as 'the Association') to accord him sickness insurance benefits under the Ziektewet.

In April 1981 the private limited liability company Slenderose Ltd., whose registered office is in London, was formed in accordance with English law. In June 1981 Mr Segers and his wife took over that company, each holding an equal number of shares. In July

1981 Mr Segers incorporated into Slenderose Ltd. as a subsidiary of that company his one-man business, Free Promotion International, whose registered office is in the Netherlands. At the same time, he became a director of Slenderose. In practice all of Slenderose's business is conducted by its subsidiary and solely in the Netherlands.

In July 1981, in order to obtain sickness insurance benefits, Mr Segers registered as sick with the Association. That body refused to grant him such benefits on the grounds that he had no employment contract with Slenderose and that consequently he was not subordinate to an employer. The Ziektewet provides, inter alia, that any person who is in a subordinate position in relation to another person, an employer, is insured.

Following the rejection by the court of first instance of his action against that decision, Mr Segers appealed to the Centrale Raad van Beroep. That court referred to its own decisions according to which the director of a company who himself holds 50 per cent or more of the shares of that company must be deemed to work for that company in a position subordinate to it. The Association, however, contended before the national court that that case law should apply only to directors of companies whose registered office was in the Netherlands and not to a company incorporated under foreign law.

The Centrale Raad van Beroep took the view that the Association's argument had some force and that an interpretation of Community law was required. It therefore stayed the proceedings and referred the following questions to the Court of Justice for a preliminary ruling:

1. Do the principles of freedom of establishment within the EEC and freedom to provide services within the EEC—in particular the last sentence of Article 52 read with Article 58 of the EEC Treaty and the last sentence of Article 60 read with Article 66 of that Treaty—mean that, when deciding whether there is an insurance obligation under social security legislation, Dutch courts may not make any distinction between the director/major shareholder of a private company incorporated under Dutch law and a director/major shareholder of a private company incorporated under the laws of another member-State, even if the foreign company clearly does not carry out any actual business in the othermember-State concerned but carries on business only in the Netherlands?

2. If that question must be answered in the negative, does Community social security law (in particular, Article 3(1) of Regulation 1408/71) or any other provision of Community law prohibit such a distinction?

The first question

The first question seeks essentially to establish whether Articles 52 and 58 EEC and Articles 60 and 66 must be interpreted as meaning that the competent authorities of a member-State may not exclude the director of a foreign company from a national sickness insurance benefit scheme solely on the ground that the company in question was formed in accordance with the law of another member-State, where it also has its registered office, even though it does not conduct any business there.

Mr Segers considers that in view of the direct effect of the provisions of the EEC Treaty concerning freedom of establishment and in the light of the General Programmes of the Council for the abolition of retrictions on freedom of establishment and the freedom to provide services the competent national authorities must abolish national provisions restricting the right of directors of companies incorporated under foreign law to be admitted to sickness insurance schemes. He notes in addition that in this case the provisions of the Treaty concerning the freedom to provide services do not apply.

The Association considers that the provisions of the EEC Treaty concerning freedom of establishment and the freedom to provide services do not apply in this instance. In its views, those provisions do not require that companies formed in accordance with the laws of other member-States be treated in the same way as those formed in accordance with Dutch law. As far as admission to sickness insurance benefits is concerned, a difference of treatment as between the directors of a company incorporated under Dutch law and those of a company incorporated under the law of another member-State cannot be regarded as unlawful discrimination since the two types of companies are not comparable. Any person who forms a company under Dutch law is subject to the same conditions regarding insurance, irrespective of his nationality or his place of establishment. Similarly, persons who form a company under foreign law do so under identical conditions. Any person may form a company under Dutch law or under foreign law, irrespective of his nationality or place of establishment. It is always open to the persons concerned to consider the advantages and disadvantages from the point of view of social security and tax, or any other advantages or disadvantages, of those two forms of company.

It also maintains that the difference in treatment in question is justified by the need to combat abuse and to ensure that the Dutch social security legislation is properly implemented. It is necessary to ensure that directors do not elect to form a company under foreign law solely in order to circumvent the restrictions provided for in the Dutch legislation concerning the formation of private limited companies. In addition, the Association draws attention to the difficulty of collecting social security contributions in other member-States.

The Commission takes the view that, by virtue of Article 52, EEC a company formed in accordance with the law of another member-State is entitled to conduct its business in the Netherlands under the same conditions as those applying to companies formed under Dutch law. Those conditions include inter alia the right to be affiliated to a specific social security scheme. The legal conditions for affiliation to such a scheme must be the same for employees of a foreign company as for employees of companies formed under the law of the Member-State concerned. To refuse to apply to the director of a company formed in accordance with the law of another member-State social security legislation applying to the directors of companies formed in accordance with the law of the member-State concerned must therefore be regarded as contrary to the principle of freedom of establishment.

In order to reply to the question submitted it is necessary to consider in the first place Article 52 et seq of the Treaty. In that respect it should be noted that Article 52 is one of the fundamental provisions of the Community and has been directly applicable in the member-States since the expiry of the transitional period. By virtue of that provision, freedom of establishment for nationals of a member-State in the territory of another member-State includes inter alia the right to set up and manage undertakings, in particular companies within the meaning of Article 58(2), under the same conditions as those laid down for its own nationals by the law of the country where such establishment is effected.

The question submitted to the Court concerns a case in which the refusal to grant benefits is based not on the nationality of the director but on the location of the registered office of the company which he directs. However, as far as companies are concerned, it should be recalled that according to the judgment of the Court in Case 270/83, EC

Commission v France ([1987] 1 CMLR 401 (Re Tax Credits)), the right of establishment includes pursuant to Article 58 EEC, the right of companies or firms formed in accordance with the law of a member-State and having their registered office, central administration or principal place of business within the Community to pursue their activities in another member-State through an agency, branch or subsidiary. With regard to companies, it should be noted that it is their registered office in the abovementioned sense that serves as the connecting factor with the legal system of a particular State, as does nationality in the case of natural persons.

In that respect the Court would observe that a company which has been formed in accordance with the law of another member-State and which conducts its business through an agency, branch or subsidiary in the member-State in which it seeks to establish itself cannot be deprived of the benefit of the rule set out above. As the Court has already stated, in EC Commission v France, acceptance of the proposition that the member-State in which a company seeks to establish itself may freely apply to it a different treatment solely by reason of the fact that its registered office is situated in another member-State would deprive Article 58 of all meaning.

It is established that entitlements of sickness costs pertains to a person and not to a company. However, the requirement that a company formed in accordance with the law of another member-State must be accorded the same treatment as national companies means that the employees of that company must have the right to be affiliated to a specific social security scheme. Discrimination against employees in connection with social security protection indirectly restricts the freedom of companies to another member-State to establish themselves through an agency, branch or subsidiary in the member-State concerned. That proposition is supported by the fact that according to the Council's General Programme for the abolition of restrictions on freedom of establishment of 18 December 1961 (OJ Spec Ed Second Series IX, p7), which provides useful guidance for the implementation of the relevant provisions of the Treaty (see Case 71/76, Thieffry ([1977] ECR 765, [1977] 2 CMLR 373) and Case 197/84, Steinhauser ([1986] 1 CMLR 53)), all provisions and administrative practices which 'deny or restrict the right to participate in social security schemes, in particular sickness... insurance schemes' are to be regarded as restrictions on the freedom of establishment.

As regards the doubt expressed by the national court concerning the significance of the fact that the English company clearly does not conduct business in the United Kingdom, it should be noted that for the application of the provisions on the right of establishment, Article 58 requires only that the companies be formed in accordance with the law of a member-State and have their registered office, central administration or principle place of business within the Community. Provided that those requirements are satisfied, the fact that the company conducts its business through an agency, branch or subsidiary solely in another member-State is immaterial.

As regards the grounds put forward by the Association to justify its refusal, namely the need to combat possible abuse and to ensure the proper implementation of the national social security legislation, it should be noted that Article 56 EEC allows within certain limits special treatment for companies formed in accordance with the law of another member-State provided that that treatment is justified on grounds of public policy, public security or public health. Although the need to combat fraud may therefore justify a difference of treatment in certain circumstances, the refusal to accord a sickness benefit to a director of a company formed in accordance with the law of another member-State cannot constitute an appropriate measure in that respect.

The reply given to the first question is based on the provisions of the Treaty concerning the freedom of establishment. It is therefore not necessary to consider the provisions concerning the freedom to provide services.

In the light of all the foregoing considerations, the reply to the first question referred to the Court by the Centrale Raad van Beroep should be that the provisions of Articles 52 and 58 of the EEC Treaty must be interpreted as prohibiting the competent authorities of a member-State from excluding the director of a company from a national sickness insurance scheme solely on the ground that the company in question was formed in accordance with the law of another member-State, where it also has its registered office, even though it does not conduct any business there.

The second question

Since a reply to the second question was required only in the event of a negative reply to the first question, the second question has become devoid of purpose.

Costs

The costs incurred by the Commission of the European Communities, which has submitted observations to the Court, are not recoverable. Since these proceedings are, in so far as the parties in the main proceedings are, concerned, in the nature of a step in the proceedings pending before the national court, the decision on costs is a matter for that court.

On those grounds the Court (Second Chamber), in reply to the questions referred to it by the Centrale Raad van Beroep by order of 29 January 1985,

HEREBY RULES

The provisions of Articles 52 and 58 of the EEC Treaty must be interpreted as prohibiting the competent authorities of a member-State from excluding a director of a company from a national sickness insurance benefit scheme solely on the ground that the company in question was formed in accordance with the law of another member-State, where it also has its registered office, even though it does not conduct any business there.

Eleventh Council Directive

89/666/EEC of 21 December 1989 concerning disclosure requirements in respect of branches opened in a Member State by certain types of company governed by the law of another State Official Journal L 395, 30/12/1989 p. 0036–0039
Finnish special edition....: Chapter 17 Volume 1 p. 99
Swedish special edition...: Chapter 17 Volume 1 p. 99
CONSLEG—78L0660—01/01/1995—54 p.
CONSLEG—83L0349—01/01/1995—41 p.
389L0666
Amendments:
Incorporated by 294A0103(72) (OJ L 001 03.01.1994 p.517)

Text:

ELEVENTH COUNCIL DIRECTIVE of 21 December 1989 concerning disclosure requirements in respect of branches opened in a Member State by certain types of company governed by the law of another State (89/666/EEC)

THE COUNCIL OF THE EUROPEAN COMMUNITIES,

Having regard to the Treaty establishing the European Economic Community, and in particular Article 54 thereof,

Having regard to the proposal from the Commission (1),

In cooperation with the European Parliament (2),

Having regard to the opinion of the Economic and Social Committee (3),

Whereas in order to facilitate the exercise of the freedom of establishment in respect of companies covered by Article 58 of the Treaty, Article 54 (3)(g) and the general programme on the elimination of restrictions on the freedom of establishment require coordination of the safeguards required of companies and firms in the Member States for the protection of the interests of members and others;

Whereas hitherto this coordination has been effected in respect of disclosure by the adoption of the First Directive 68/151/EEC (4) covering companies with share capital, as last amended by the 1985 Act of Accession; whereas it was continued in the field of accounting by the Fourth Directive 78/660/EEC (5) on the annual accounts of certain types of companies, as last amended by the 1985 Act of Accession, the Seventh Directive 83/349/EEC (6) on consolidated accounts, as amended by the 1985 Act of Accession, and the Eighth Directive 84/253/EEC (7) on the persons responsible for carrying out the statutory audits of accounting documents;

Whereas these Directives apply to companies as such but do not cover their branches; whereas the opening of a branch, like the creation of a subsidiary, is one of the possibilities currently open to companies in the exercise of their right of establishment in another Member State;

Whereas in respect of branches the lack of coordination, in particular concerning disclosure, gives rise to some disparities, in the protection of shareholders and third parties, between companies which operate in other Member States by opening branches and those which operate there by creating subsidiaries;

Whereas in this field the differences in the laws of the Member States may interfere with the exercise of the right of establishment; whereas it is therefore necessary to eliminate such differences in order to safeguard, inter alia, the exercise of that right;

Whereas to ensure the protection of persons who deal with companies through the intermediary of branches, measures in respect of disclosure are required in the Member State in which a branch is situated; whereas, in certain respects, the economic and social influence of a branch may be comparable to that of a subsidiary company, so that there is public interest in disclosure of the company at the branch; whereas to effect such disclosure it is necessary to make use of the procedure already instituted for companies with share capital within the Community;

Whereas such disclosure relates to a range of important documents and particulars and amendments thereto;

Whereas such disclosure, with the exception of the powers of representation, the name and legal form and the winding-up of the company and the insolvency proceedings to which it is subject, may be confined to information concerning a branch itself together with a reference to the register of the company of which that branch is part, since under existing Community rules all information covering the company as such is available in that register;

Whereas national provisions in respect of the disclosure of accounting documents relating to a branch can no longer be justified following the coordination of national law in respect of the drawing up, audit and disclosure of companies' accounting documents; whereas it is accordingly sufficient to disclose, in the register of the branch, the accounting documents as audited and disclosed by the company;

Whereas letters and order forms used by a branch must give at least the same information as letters and order forms used by the company, and state the register in which the branch is entered;

Whereas to ensure that the purposes of this Directive are fully realized and to avoid any discrimination on the basis of a company's country of origin, this Directive must also cover branches opened by companies governed by the law of non-member countries and set up in legal forms comparable to companies to which Directive 68/151/EEC applies; whereas for these branches it is necessary to apply certain provisions different from those that apply to the branches of companies governed by the law of other Member States since the Directives referred to above do not apply to companies from non-member countries;

Whereas this Directive in no way affects the disclosure requirements for branches under other provisions of, for example, employment law on workers' rights to information and tax law, or for statistical purposes;

HAS ADOPTED THIS DIRECTIVE:

SECTION I

Branches of companies from other Member States

Article 1

1. Documents and particulars relating to a branch opened in a Member State by a company which is governed by the law of another Member State and to which Directive 68/151/EEC applies shall be disclosed pursuant to the law of the Member State of the branch, in accordance with Article 3 of that Directive.

2. Where disclosure requirements in respect of the branch differ from those in respect of the company, the branch's disclosure requirements shall take precedence with regard to transactions carried out with the branch.

Article 2

1. The compulsory disclosure provided for in Article 1 shall cover the following documents and particulars only:

(a) the address of the branch;

(b) the activities of the branch;

(c) the register in which the company file mentioned in Article 3 of Council Directive 68/151/EEC is kept, together with the registration number in that register;

(d) the name and legal form of the company and the name of the branch if that is different from the name of the company;

(e) the appointment, termination of office and particulars of the persons who are authorized to represent the company in dealings with third parties and in legal proceedings;

– as a company organ constituted pursuant to law or as members of any such organ, in accordance with the disclosure by the company as provided for in Article 2 (1) (d) of Directive 68/151/EEC,

– as permanent representatives of the company for the activities of the branch, with an indication of the extent of their powers;

(f) the winding-up of the company, the appointment of liquidators, particulars concerning them and their powers and the termination of the liquidation in accordance with disclosure by the company as provided for in Article 2 (1) (h), (j) and (k) of Directive 68/151/EEC,

– insolvency proceedings, arrangements, compositions, or any analogous proceedings to which the company is subject;

(g) the accounting documents in accordance with Article 3;

(h) the closure of the branch.

2. The Member State in which the branch has been opened may provide for the disclosure, as referred to in Article 1, of

(a) the signature of the persons referred to in paragraph 1 (e) and (f) of this Article;

(b) the instruments of constitution and the memorandum and articles of association if they are contained in a separate instrument in accordance with Article 2 (1) (a), (b) and (c) of Directive 68/151/EEC, together with amendments to those documents;

(c) an attestation from the register referred to in paragraph 1 (c) of this Article relating to the existence of the company;

(d) an indication of the securities on the company's property situated in that Member State, provided such disclosure relates to the validity of those securities.

Article 3

The compulsory disclosure provided for by Article 2 (1) (g) shall be limited to the accounting documents of the company as drawn up, audited and disclosed pursuant to the law of the Member State by which the company is governed in accordance with Directives 78/660/EEC, 83/349/EEC and 84/253/EEC.

Article 4

The Member State in which the branch has been opened may stipulate that the documents referred to in Article 2 (2) (b) and Article 3 must be published in another official language of the Community and that the translation of such documents must be certified.

Article 5

Where a company has opened more than one branch in a Member State, the disclosure referred to in Article 2 (2) (b) and Article 3 may be made in the register of the branch of the company's choice.

In this case, compulsory disclosure by the other branches shall cover the particulars of the branch register of which disclosure was made, together with the number of that branch in that register.

Article 6

The Member States shall prescribe that letters and order forms used by a branch shall state, in addition to the information prescribed by Article 4 of Directive 68/151/EEC, the register in which the file in respect of the branch is kept together with the number of the branch in that register.

SECTION II

Branches of companies from third countries

Article 7

1. Documents and particulars concerning a branch opened in a Member State by a company which is not governed by the law of a Member State but which is of a legal form comparable with the types of company to which Directive 68/151/EEC applies shall be disclosed in accordance with the law of the Member State of the branch as laid down in Article 3 of that Directive.

2. Article 1 (2) shall apply.

Article 8

The compulsory disclosure provided for in Article 7 shall cover at least the following documents and particulars:

(a) the address of the branch;

(b) the activities of the branch;

(c) the law of the State by which the company is governed;

(d) where that law so provides, the register in which the company is entered and the registration number of the company in that register;

(e) the instruments of constitution, and memorandum and articles of association if they are contained in a separate instrument, with all amendments to these documents;

(f) the legal form of the company, its principal place of business and its object and, at least annually, the amount of subscribed capital if these particulars are not given in the documents referred to in subparagraph (e);

(g) the name of the company and the name of the branch if that is different from the name of the company;

(h) the appointment, termination of office and particulars of the persons who are authorized to represent the company in dealings with third parties and in legal proceedings:

– as a company organ constituted pursuant to law or as members of any such organ,

– as permanent representatives of the company for the activities of the branch.

The extent of the powers of the persons authorized to represent the company must be stated, together with whether they may do so alone or must act jointly;

(i) – the winding-up of the company and the appointment of liquidators, particulars concerning them and their powers and the termination of the liquidation;

– insolvency proceedings, arrangements, compositions or any analogous proceedings to which the company is subject;

(j) the accounting documents in accordance with Article 7;

(k) the closure of the branch.

Article 9

1. The compulsory disclosure provided for by Article 8 (1) (j) shall apply to the accounting documents of the company as drawn up, audited and disclosed pursuant to the law of the State which governs the company. Where they are not drawn up in accordance with or in a manner equivalent to Directives 78/660/EEC and 83/349/EEC, Member States may require that accounting documents relating to the activities of the branch be drawn up and disclosed.

2. Articles 4 and 5 shall apply.

Article 10

The Member States shall prescribe that letters and order forms used by a branch state the register in which the file in respect of the branch is kept together with the number of the branch in that register. Where the law of the State by which the company is governed requires entry in a register, the register in which the company is entered, and the registration number of the company in that register must also be stated.

SECTION III

Indication of branches in the company's annual report

Article 11

The following subparagraph is added to Article 46 (2) of Directive 78/660/EEC:

'(e) the existence of branches of the company'.

SECTION IV

Transitional and final provisions

Article 12

The Member States shall provide for appropriate penalties in the event of failure to disclose the matters set out in Articles 1, 2, 3, 7, 8 and 9 and of omission from letters and order forms of the compulsory particulars provided for in Articles 6 and 10.

Article 13

Each Member State shall determine who shall carry out the disclosure formalities provided for in this Directive.

Article 14

1. Articles 3 and 9 shall not apply to branches opened by credit institutions and financial institutions covered by Directive 89/117/EEC (8).

2. Pending subsequent coordination, the Member States need not apply Articles 3 and 9 to branches opened by insurance companies.

Article 15

Article 54 of Directive 78/660/EEC and Article 48 of Directive 83/349/EEC shall be deleted.

Article 16

1. Member States shall adopt the laws, regulations and administrative provisions necessary to comply with this Directive not later than 1 January 1992. They shall forthwith inform the Commission thereof.

2. Member States shall stipulate that the provisions referred to in paragraph 1 shall apply from 1 January 1993 and, with regard to accounting documents, shall apply for the first time to annual accounts for the financial year beginning on 1 January 1993 or during 1993.

3. Member States shall communicate to the Commission the texts of the provisions of national law which they adopt in the field covered by this Directive.

Article 17

The Contact Committee set up pursuant to Article 52 of Directive 78/660/EEC shall also:

(a) facilitate, without prejudice to Articles 169 and 170 of the Treaty, the harmonized application of this Directive, through regular meetings dealing, in particular, with practical problems arising in connection with its application;

(b) advise the Commission, if necessary, on any additions or amendments to this Directive.

Article 18

This Directive is addressed to the Member States.

Done at Brussels, 21 December 1989.

For the Council

The President

E. CRESSON

(1) OJ No C 105, 21. 4. 1988, p. 6.

(2) OJ No C 345, 21. 12. 1987, p. 76 and OJ No C 256, 9. 10. 1989, p. 27.

(3) OJ No C 319, 30. 11. 1987, p. 61.

(4) OJ No L 65, 14. 3. 1968, p. 8.

(5) OJ No L 222, 14. 8. 1978, p. 11.

(6) OJ No L 193, 18. 7. 1983, p. 1.

(7) OJ No L 126, 12. 5. 1984, p. 20.(8) OJ No L 44, 16. 2. 1989, p. 40.

Comments and Questions

1. How would *Segers* have been decided had it arisen in the United States? Does the 11th Council Directive obviate the need for independent national legislation with respect to branches of companies with a registered or administrative seat in another Member State?

2. What is the difference between a subsidiary and a branch? Should a Member State's authority to regulate a subsidiary be different from its authority to regulate a branch? On what theory do you justify the difference in treatment?

Chapter 6

The Federalization and Harmonization of Corporate Law

Enterprise regulation, and especially corporate law, is no longer solely the province of those jurisdictions which traditionally have claimed the right to create and regulate legal personalities. Within the United States, chartering states no longer have sole or exclusive rights regulate corporations. Moreover, states share the right to charter corporations with the Federal Government. Within the European Union, the Member States now share power to regulate corporate activity with the institutions of the EU. The last century also saw, in federal states, like the United States, and in supra-national organizations, like the European Union, serious consideration given to the replacement of the current system of corporate regulation with national or supra-national corporate laws. Neither Europe nor the U.S. has resolved the question of which units of government ought to have the authority to regulate corporations in federations or other unions with multiple levels of government sharing political authority. The materials that follow provide a discussion of the issues in that debate.

Terence L. Blackburn, *The Unification of Corporate Laws: The United States, the European Community and the Race to Laxity*

3 Geo. Mason Independent L. Rev. 1 (1994)
(excerpts pages 22–28; some footnotes omitted)

B. The Methods of Unification of Corporate Laws

Corporate laws in federal political systems may be harmonized by a number of different methods: (1) national and mandatory methods which are quicker to implement and achieve greater degrees of unification; and (2) local and voluntary methods which allow room for experimentation and permit greater degrees of diversity.

The selection of a method of unification is generally not a matter of free choice. It is affected by a number of different factors that are specific to each separate federal system. The political history of a particular federal system and the attendant legal requirements and customary traditions, such as deference to local law or reliance on national law, significantly affect the choice of the method of unification. Another factor affecting the choice of method is the strength of perceptions that federal level issues exist, requiring federal level solutions.

The following portion of Part I briefly describes and evaluates five methods of unification of corporate laws available in federal political systems: (1) national preemptive rules; (2) national harmonizing rules; (3) national supplementary rules; (4) local voluntary agreements; and (5) local voluntary coordination. Although this discussion deals primarily with the experiences of the United States and the European Community, it can also be applied to other multi-jurisdictional legal and political systems.

1. National Preemptive Rules

National preemptive rules are the quickest and most controlled method of unifying company laws in a federal political system. This method creates a single rule applicable throughout the system and overrules or replaces contrary local rules. It has the benefit of establishing a single standard of behavior for all actors within the political system while providing a high degree of predictability. It is equally effective whether it is used to unify rules to accomplish enabling goals or to unify protective goals. In federal political systems with complex, regulated economies, national preemptive rulemaking may well be the preferred method of unification.[46]

Interestingly, in both the United States and the European Community, national preemptive rules have not frequently been used to unify laws to enable companies to conduct cross-border operations. However, such rules occasionally have been used to unify laws to achieve protective goals. In the United States, national preemptive rules have been used to establish unified laws concerning the rights of debtors and creditors in bankruptcy situations[47] and certain rights of customers[48] and employees.[49] National preemptive rules have not been used to unify laws to enable companies to conduct business across state borders, even though the Interstate Commerce Clause probably would support such an exercise of power by the federal government,[50] because of the tradition of deference to state law in such matters. In the European Community, although the Council of Ministers and the Commission have the power to enact regulations which are directly applicable in the member states,[51] legislation establishing the common mar-

---

46. In examining the Supreme Court's comment concerning state rulemaking and the Commerce Clause, that "the states may interfere with interstate commerce, but not very much," Buxbaum and Hopt have stated:

> Is even that much of a conclusion possible today, or do we not have a more important shift: that in an era of governmental regulation of production, labor and credit factors, centralization is a bureaucratic imperative? If productive activity is too important to be left to the marketplace, it may be too important to be left to the weaker member of a dual sovereignty.

[Richard M. Buxbaum & Klaus J. Hopt, Legal Harmonization and the Business Enterprise: Corporate And Capital Market Law Harmonization Policy In Europe And The USA (1988)] at 51–52.

47. 11 U.S.C. § 101 (1993)....

48. *See, e.g.*, 15 U.S.C. § 1 (1993) (Sherman Act); 15 U.S.C. § 12 (1993) (Clayton Anti-Trust Act); 15 U.S.C. §§ 13, 13a, 13b, 21a (1993) (Robinson-Patman Price Discrimination Act).

49. *See, e.g.*, 29 U.S.C. § 151 (1992) (National Labor Relations Act)....

50. The Supreme Court used the Dormant Commerce Clause to strike down numerous attempts by states to restrict the right of foreign companies to conduct business there. See infra part II.A.1.b. Congress instead could choose to use the Commerce Clause as a basis for establishing either preemptive or supplementary federal incorporation law....

51. A Regulation of the European Community has general application, is binding on the member states, and is directly applicable in those states without the necessity of additional member state legislation....

ket and concerning the right of free establishment of companies must take the form of harmonizing directives.[52] The European Community does, however, have the power to pass mandatory regulations to protect employees.[53]

2. National Harmonizing Rules

A second method of unification of company laws is the use of national harmonizing rules. These harmonizing rules establish standards that local jurisdictions must comply with. Although harmonizing rules may be used to invalidate non-complying local rules, they do not directly impose specific substantive requirements on the local jurisdictions. The degree of freedom that harmonizing rules allow to local jurisdictions varies with the nature of the particular federal political system.

Both the United States and the European Community have used national harmonizing rules to unify company laws. The Dormant Commerce Clause, for example, has been used in the United States to set limits on state restrictions on the entry of foreign corporations and on state taxation of those corporations. Similarly, the European Community has made substantial use of harmonizing directives to unify company laws of the member states concerning taxation and the public sale of securities.

Because they require action by local rulemakers, or simply set limits on local rulemaking, national harmonizing rules are less certain of result[56] (depending on their degree of specificity) and generally take longer to implement than national preemptive rules.[57] They are particularly useful, however, in unifying laws in federal systems that accord a high degree of autonomy to local rulemaking processes.

3. National Supplementary Rules

A third national method of unifying company laws is the use of national supplementary rules. These rules do not preempt or require changes to local rules. Instead, they set up federal rules that either may or must be complied with in addition to the local rules.*

The United States has occasionally used national supplementary rules to unify company laws. For example, the Securities Act of 1933, and certain portions of the Securities Exchange Act of 1934, set federal requirements for the issuance and the purchase and sale of securities, but do not preempt state laws dealing with the same subject.

The European Community has used supplementary rules to unify company laws by creating European Economic Interest Groupings, which are joint ventures among companies organized in different jurisdictions. Another notable attempt by the European Community to utilize national supplementary rules to unify company law is the proposed European Corporation statute. This proposed statute would permit, but not require, certain compa-

---

52. *See* [Treaty Establishing the European Economic Community (Treaty of Rome)] Art. 100 (establishment of the common market); *id.* Arts. 49, 54.2, 56.2 (free establishment of nationals).

53. *See* Treaty of Rome, *supra* note[52], Art. 49.

56. For example, the Supreme Court noted in Northwestern Cement v. Minnesota, 358 U.S. 450 (1959), that analyses of commerce clause limitations on state power to tax interstate commerce had occupied the court in approximately "three hundred full-dress opinions spread through slightly more than that number of our reports." *Id.* at 457–58.

57. For example, member states of the European Community have occasionally been slow to adopt legislation required by Community Directives. In 1982 the Commission brought actions against Italy, Belgium, Luxembourg and Ireland for failing to implement the Second Company Law Directive (establishing minimum disclosure and capital requirements for all public companies organized in the European Community). Commission v. Italy, 1982 E.C.R. 3547; Commission v. Belgium, 1982 E.C.R. 3555; Commission v. Luxembourg, 1982 E.C.R. 3565; Commission v. Ireland, 1982 E.C.R. 3573....

nies to organize themselves as European corporations, rather than, for instance, French or German corporations. However, this proposed statute has not yet been adopted.

National supplementary rules are an ineffective technique for unifying company laws to enable companies to conduct interstate business. Because they permit local laws to remain in place, companies still must meet state requirements to conduct their operations. National supplementary rules are a somewhat more effective technique to unify laws for the purpose of achieving protective goals. If these rules are mandatory, they may provide a minimum standard of protection to non-management participants.[61] If the rules are merely permissive, they may assist companies in doing business in foreign jurisdictions, but will not necessarily achieve protective goals of unification because companies choosing not to subject themselves to such rules will avoid them by not doing business in the jurisdictions that adopt them.[62] In some situations, national supplementary rules may provide a basis for voluntary local coordination of company laws, as the United States federal securities laws have provided a basis for state regulation. Even though national supplementary rules are less effective in unifying laws, they may be more desirable to rule makers, because they are easier to adopt than preemptive or harmonizing rules, and they do not displace local laws.

4. Voluntary Local Agreement (Treaty)

Occasionally, where national unifying rules have not been used to unify company laws, local jurisdictions attempt to unify those laws instead. Because no local jurisdiction has control over the rulemaking process in any other jurisdiction, such unification may take place through concerted action in the form of a treaty or other agreement among the local jurisdictions.

Voluntary local agreements have been used in the United States and the European Community only to achieve enabling goals of unification. In the United States, for example, twenty states are parties to an agreement concerning uniform apportionment of income for state tax purposes.[65] In the European Community, member states have attempted to unify local rules concerning the recognition of foreign corporations by means of a treaty.[66]

The use of voluntary local agreements is a very weak method of unifying company law in a federal political system. One reason for its weakness is that it is only binding on those jurisdictions that agree to be bound by it.[67] In addition, depending upon the nature of the treaty, it may be abandoned by local jurisdictions whenever such action is

---

61. The United States' federal securities laws are a good example of mandatory national supplementary rules that fail to achieve enabling goals, but do achieve protective goals of unification.... If the requirements of the federal supplementary laws are strict enough, they may make the further regulation of the matter by state law unnecessary, and prevent a race to laxity with respect to the subject matter of the rule.

62. The proposed European Corporation statute is an example of a permissive national supplementary rule that achieves the enabling goals of unification but does not achieve protective goals.... The proposed statute would only achieve protective goals if the form of organization were so desirable that companies would choose to use it even though it imposed additional protective rules on those companies.

65. Multistate Tax Compact, All States Tax Guide (RIA) 551, 1962 (hereinafter All States Tax Guide (RIA)).

66. Convention on the Mutual Recognition of Companies and Bodies Politic, 1968 O.J. (L35) 6 (hereinafter Convention on Mutual Recognition).

67. The European Community's Convention on Mutual Recognition never came into force because of The Netherlands' refusal to ratify it....

seen to be to their benefit.[68] These difficulties make the use of voluntary local agreements a relatively ineffective method to unify company laws for the purpose of achieving either enabling or protective goals.

5. Voluntary Coordination of Local Laws

Even if local jurisdictions do not enter into agreements to unify their corporate laws, local unification may still occur. Local rulemakers may voluntarily decide to adopt laws that are similar to laws of other jurisdictions within the federal system. In some situations, the common perceptions of rulemakers from different jurisdictions concerning societal or business needs may result in voluntary local coordination. In other situations, jurisdictions may adopt similar laws as a result of competition among the jurisdictions to attract or retain companies. This type of competition took place in the early part of the Twentieth Century in the United States. Unification at the local level may also be assisted by the development of model acts that are then adopted by the various jurisdictions.

The process of voluntary local coordination and competitive convergence has been much more common in the United States than it has in the European Community. In part, this difference may result simply from the fact that the states of the United States have had fairly integrated economies and similar social and political structures and customs for much longer than have the member states of the European Community.[72] The difference has also been attributed to the absence in the European Community of national professional organizations to perform harmonization work.[73] Finally, this difference may also result from a concern that voluntary coordination and competition will not result in the degree of unification of laws desired in the European Community.[74]

The use of voluntary local coordination and competition is the least efficient method to unify company laws because it is unreliable and time consuming. Voluntary coordination of laws may be used for the purpose of achieving both enabling goals or protective goals of unification. For example, the Uniform Limited Partnership Act has been adopted in forty-nine states and successfully enables partnerships to conduct business across state borders. Similarly, numerous states have adopted shareholder protective statutes concerning the duty of loyalty of directors and officers, thus accomplishing unification of protective laws.

On the other hand, local competition among jurisdictions is effective only to achieve enabling goals of unification. Rulemakers will compete to unify laws which enable companies to conduct cross-border business because such rules will attract man-

68. Seven states, or 25% of the total number of states that have adopted the Multistate Tax Compact, have repealed their adoption of it. All States Tax Guide (RIA), *supra* note 65, 564.

72. The Member States are not, however, so diverse that no voluntary unification of laws is possible. The European Community has made significant use of national harmonizing rules to unify company law. Since the adoption of harmonizing directives requires either unanimous approval or approval of a qualified majority of the member states, it is possible that the use of this method of unification has made the United States' method of voluntary coordination of laws less necessary in the European Community.

73. Buxbaum & Hopt, *supra* note [46], at 230–31.

74. The Treaty of Rome requires that, in protecting the freedom of establishment of companies, the Commission and the Council shall coordinate "the safeguards which, for the protection of the interests of members (shareholders) and others, are required by member states...with a view to making such safeguards equivalent throughout the Community...." Treaty of Rome, *supra* note [52], Art. 54.3(g) (emphasis added).

agers who seek increased business opportunities. Rulemakers have no incentive to compete in unifying laws for the purpose of achieving protective goals because even if the laws are attractive to shareholders or other non-management participants in corporations, these persons rarely have the power to move their corporations to take advantage of such laws.

Comments and Questions

1. Professor Blackburn suggests that national supplementary rules are a means of indirect harmonization, and that the federal securities laws have been an effective means of achieving this sort of harmonization in the United States. Do you agree with the characterization of the federal securities laws as national supplementary legislation? Does your answer depend on the way you define the scope of corporate law? If, indeed, the definition of corporate law is as fungible as Professor Blackburn suggests, then would it not be possible for a federal entity seeking to "federalize" corporate law merely to redefine that field of law in a way that leaves only those portions of corporate law with which it is not interested in harmonizing in the hands of the state?

2. **Problem:** Defend or challenge the following proposed federal statute. Be prepared to discuss the practical effects of the statute as well as the public policy issues affected by the proposal. Defend any possible changes you might make to the proposal:

> The statute provides that all corporations engaged in interstate commerce, defined to include all corporations other than those that have no shareholders, employees, managers, directors, property, plant, equipment or sales outside the state of its incorporation, will be subject to federal law respecting the (1) fiduciary duties of shareholders, directors and employees; (2) corporate restructuring, including mergers, sales of assets and other reorganizations or recapitalization; (3) shareholder and board meetings; (4) dissolution; (5) issuance of shares; and (6) voting rights of shareholders and directors. States retain full power to charter corporations and also power over the fees and other charges in connection with the chartering of corporations. The authors of the statute emphasize that states will retain all rights with respect to the corporate law; the federal statute is meant merely to regulate certain specific enterprises engaged in the national economy for which federal oversight is necessary.

A. The Context of Federalization in the United States

There has never been a general federal corporation law. However, the argument has been made that the federal government is not precluded from enacting such a nationally applicable set of provisions. In considering the materials which follow, compare the arguments made in favor of a deregulated system of corporate law in the United States (states being free to create their own bodies of corporate law), with those made by European commentators in favor of the establishment of a harmonized corporate law among the Member States of the EU. In particular, compare the similarities between the call for the setting of minimum federal standards for corporate governance in the United States, and the discussion of the value of harmonization among the Member States of the EU.

William L. Cary, *Federalism and Corporate Law, Reflections Upon Delaware*

83 YALE L.J. 663 (1974)
(excerpt page 703; footnotes omitted)

* * * * [G]oing all the way—federal incorporation—would be constitutional. The legislative history of various securities acts using the commerce clause as a basis for regulating firms that are "in or affect interstate commerce" are often devoid of discussion or consideration of the act's constitutionality. No one has questioned the constitutionality of amended § 12(g) of the Securities Exchange Act of 1934 enacted in 1964. Referring to the securities acts, one writer in 1936 said, "[I]f the courts are convinced that there is a paramount public necessity for centralized and uniform control of all industrial or commercial corporations, Congress will be found to have the power of regulation to the fullest extent." [citing Berlack, *Federal Incorporation and Securities Regulation*, 49 HARV. L. REV. 396, 411 (1936)].

* * *

---

1. *Federal Sources*

The Federal Constitution does not give Congress the direct power to regulate corporations—that power is nowhere explicitly mentioned in the Constitution. But the federal government may have the power to impose a federal corporations law under the Commerce Clause (William L. Cary, *Federalism and Corporate Law, Reflections Upon Delaware*, 83 YALE L.J. 663, 703 (1974)). Federal chartering would have one of two consequences for the traditional authority of states to charter and regulate corporations. A federal corporate law could preempt all state laws under the Supremacy Clause. It is also possible to create a federal corporate law that functions as a supplement to state law, so that entities that qualify for chartering under either regulatory regime could choose. For example, a federal corporate law limited to companies whose stock is publicly traded would lease intact a state's power to charter other corporations.

Currently, the absence of direct federal chartering of corporations, that power is left to the states under the Reserved Powers Clause, subject to the limitations contained in the Commerce Clause (respecting discrimination against non-citizens of a state) and the Equal Protection and Due Process Clauses (no deprivation of liberty or property of a corporation without due process of law, no disparate treatment of corporations; (*see* cites in the *Bellotti* case, discussed in Chapter 4).

Constitution of the United States

* * *

Art. I., § 8, cl.3: "The Congress shall have Power * * * * To regulate Commerce with foreign Nations, and among the several States, and with the Indian Tribes; * * * * "

Art. 6, cl.2: "This Constitution, and the Laws of the United States which shall be made in Pursuance thereof; and all Treaties made, or which shall be made, under Authority of the United States, shall be the Supreme Law of the Land; and the Judges in every State shall be bound thereby, any Thing in the Constitution or Laws of any State to the Contrary notwithstanding. * * * *"

Amend. X: "The powers not delegated to the United States by the Constitution, nor prohibited to it by the States, are reserved to the States respectively, or to the people."

Amend. XIV: "* * * * nor shall any State deprive any person of Life, liberty, or property without due process of law; nor deny to any person within its jurisdiction the equal protection of the laws."

Robert B. Thompson, *Preemption and Federalism in Corporate Governance: Protecting Shareholder Rights to Vote, Sell and Sue*

62 L. & Contemp. Probs. 215 (1999)
(excerpts pages 216–225; some footnotes omitted)

II

The Traditional Federal and State Realms in Corporate Governance

A. The State Law Pattern

Under corporate law in all states, directors manage the business and affairs of the corporation. Shareholders have only a limited role: They can vote, sell, or sue.

1. Vote. The shareholder franchise is a key part of corporate law, but that does not mean that shareholders vote on very many things. Most business decisions are left entirely to the board of directors or those to whom they delegate such authority. Shareholders participate only infrequently in a limited set of decisions, including the election of directors, fundamental corporate changes, and ratification.

a. Election of directors. Directors are usually elected annually, but this pattern can be varied by the corporation's articles of incorporation or other private ordering. Shareholders also have the power to remove directors in some circumstances.

b. Fundamental corporate changes. Mergers and similar transactions require the approval of shareholders as well as directors and, thus, are an exception to the usual rule that leaves corporate decisions entirely in the hands of the directors. Of course, even here the directors act as gatekeepers: The shareholders can vote only on those transactions that are recommended to them by the directors.

c. Ratification. Shareholders occasionally vote on the ratification of self-dealing transactions by interested directors. The vote can cleanse the transaction of any taint or shift the burden of proof in a legal challenge.

2. Sell. The ability to sell one's shares is a core right for shareholders and one that corporate law has, for the most part, left to the market. Appraisal—or dissenter's rights—is a rare exception where corporate law guarantees shareholders the right to sell their shares. Ordinarily, under corporate norms, a shareholder must obtain liquidity not from the corporation but from the market, if there is one. That is not to say that corporate law does not assume an important role for the ability to exit. Free transferability of shares and limited liability—both core characteristics of the corporate form—facilitate liquidity through the market.[14] Many corporate rules take their specific shape because they exist in the shadow of a market for shares.

3. Sue. In addition to voting and selling, a shareholder's ability to sue serves as a constraint on the actions of managers and is a regular part of the governance matrix. Litigation rights of shareholders include derivative suits, direct suits and class actions, and inspection and other ancillary rights.

a. Derivative suits. In particular circumstances, such as breaches of fiduciary duty by those in control of the corporation, all states permit a shareholder to bring a suit in the name of, and on behalf of, the corporate entity. This type of suit is an exception to the usual rule that directors act for the corporation. It occurs when directors are disabled by conflict or are otherwise unable to meet their fiduciary duty. In response to the fear that a self-appointed shareholder would bring a "strike suit" to harass the corporation or its directors, various procedural rules developed to balance the potential for abuse against the monitoring value of such lawsuits.

b. Direct suits and class actions. Shareholders can also bring direct suits, which may be class actions if numerous shareholders are affected by common questions. In contrast to derivative suits, in which the loss to the shareholder is derivative of the harm to the collective enterprise, direct suits may be brought for an injury that the shareholder feels individually, such as deprivation of a right to vote or a contract right. Such suits under state corporate law have increased in recent years. They may be based on fraud under state common law or on statutory remedies.

c. Inspection and other ancillary rights. Shareholders also have ancillary rights at state law, such as the right to inspect the books and records of the corporation, including the list of shareholders. Such inspection may be the first salvo in a litigation battle, an effort to sell shares, or a voting campaign.

B. The Federal Role

1. As to Corporate Governance. Federal legislation passed in the midst of the Great Depression reflected dissatisfaction with the state law corporate governance system.[23] In

---

14. *See* Henry G. Manne, *Our Two Corporation Systems: Law and Economics*, 53 VA. L. REV. 259, 262 (1967) (noting that publicly held corporations with many small shareholders could not exist without limited liability).

23. Federal incorporation, which had been discussed as far back as the late 19th century, was proposed again during the debate over the 1934 Act. *See* 1 LOUIS LOSS, SECURITIES REGULATION 109 (2d ed. 1961).

> The Roper-Dickinson Report of early 1934, which is part of the legislative history of the Securities Exchange Act of 1934, recommended federal incorporation as the most effective way to deal with certain evils connected with market manipulation by directors and officers, the issuance of stock to insiders for inadequate consideration, incomplete publicity of corporate accounts and similar problems... [,] and others insisted that what are now §§ 12, 13, 14 and 16 of the 1934 Act—the securities registration, reporting, proxy and insider trading provisions—had no place in a stock exchange bill and that the proper solution was federal incorporation.

that same period, Adolf Berle and Gardiner Means wrote their well-known book, The Modern Corporation and Private Property,[24] which detailed the separation of ownership from control in modern corporations and called for additional legislation to constrain the discretion of managers. The congressional response, the Securities Exchange Act of 1934 ("the 1934 Act"), did not provide a federal law of corporations to replace the state system described above, but it did seek to enhance shareholder rights, primarily through disclosure. The 1934 Act reflects what I have termed the "BASF model" of corporate governance, a term taken from the frequent television commercials for the international chemical firm that say, in effect, "We don't make the cars you drive; we make them stronger. We don't make the clothes you wear; we make them brighter." The approach of the federal securities laws has not been to define or create the internal corporate relationship between directors and shareholders, but to make that relationship better for shareholders. For federal securities laws, "better" usually has been defined through greater disclosure requirements. Louis Loss, the most noted securities commentator of the twentieth century, described the function of the federal law as "disclosure, again disclosure, and still more disclosure."[27]

Section 14 of the 1934 Act authorized the Securities and Exchange Commission ("SEC") to regulate proxies, which managers used primarily to solicit shareholder votes in advance of a meeting.[28] The House report noted that the section stemmed from a congressional belief that fair "corporate suffrage is an important right that should attach to every equity security bought on a public exchange."[29] As the Senate report noted, "[t]oo often proxies are solicited without explanation to the stockholder of the real nature of the questions for which authority to cast his vote is sought."[30] Thus, federal legislation was intended to "control the conditions under which the proxies may be solicited with a view to preventing the recurrence of abuses which [had frustrated] the free exercise of the voting rights of shareholders."[31]

The voting decision that disclosure supports is often the election of directors. Many of the proxy regulations address the format and substance of proxy solicitations relating to the annual election of directors.[32] Much of the litigation, as well as the first Supreme Court cases addressing Section 14, concerned proxies to solicit approval of a merger.[33]

Id. See also Edward Ross Aranow & Herbert A. Einhorn, *Proxy Regulation: Suggested Improvements*, 28 Geo. Wash. L. Rev. 306, 306 (1959) ("Notwithstanding the basic importance of the solicitation of proxies in determining the destiny of corporate management and affairs, and the temptations and abuses which almost inevitably accompany unrestricted power, the states did virtually nothing to cope with the problem.").

24. Adolf A. Berle, Jr. & Gardiner C. Means, The Modern Corporation and Private Property (1933).

27. Loss, *supra* note 23, at 21; *see also* Louis Loss & Joel Seligman, Securities Regulation 29 (3d ed. 1989).

28. *See* 15 U.S.C. § 78n (1994).

29. H.R. Rep. No. 73-1383, at 13 (1934).

30. S. Rep. No. 73-792, at 12 (1934).

31. H.R. Rep. No. 73-1383, at 14 (1934).

32. *See, e.g.*, 17 C.F.R. § 240.14a-4(b)(2) (1998) (SEC Rule 14a-4(b)(2)) (form of proxy for election of directors); *id.* § 240.14a-11 (SEC Rule 14a-11) (provisions applicable to election contests); id. §240.14a-101 (SEC Schedule 14A, Item 7) (required disclosure for election of directors).

33. *See* TSC Indus. v. Northway, Inc., 426 U.S. 438 (1976) (defining the standard for "materiality" in lawsuits under Section 14a); Mills v. Electric Auto-Lite Co., 396 U.S. 375 (1970) (finding that material misrepresentation in a merger requires only that proxy solicitation, and not a particular misleading statement, be an "essential link" in the accomplishment of the transaction); J.I. Case Co. v. Borak, 377 U.S. 426 (1964) (recognizing for the first time a private right of action under the fed-

These cases developed the core of federal law and enhanced shareholder voting rights otherwise available at state law.[34]

When hostile tender offers provided a realistic alternative to proxy battles as a means to acquire control of a corporation, Congress extended the shareholder protection just discussed.[35] Again, shareholders were being asked to make a decision without sufficient information. Here, it was not a decision about voting, but rather whether to sell their shares in response to a bidder's tender offer.

Federal law has developed more slowly to protect another shareholder decision arising out of a corporate change: a dissenting shareholder's pursuit of appraisal rights after a merger or similar transaction. The Supreme Court left open that question in Virginia Bankshares, Inc. v. Sandberg,[36] but the four dissenting justices suggested that federal law protected that decision as well.[37] Subsequent federal appellate court decisions have held that "a minority shareholder, who has lost his right to a state appraisal because of a materially deceptive proxy" may seek relief under federal law.[38]

2. As to Securities Transactions. Apart from enhancing shareholder governance decisions, the first Congress of the New Deal also enacted federal legislation to regulate the purchase and sale of securities. The Securities Act of 1933 ("the 1933 Act") sought to protect those who purchased securities, principally by requiring disclosure to those who bought stock in an initial public offering.[39] A year later, the 1934 Act, which regulated the proxy solicitations already discussed, expanded federal disclosure protection to include sellers and purchasers who traded in secondary markets.[40] Although originally overshadowed by the disclosure obligations of the 1933 Act, the provisions of the 1934 Act have grown considerably, and this regulation is now the centerpiece of federal securities regulation. In 1964, Congress expanded the disclosure coverage beyond companies traded on a national stock exchange to include all companies that met minimum thresholds of assets and number of shareholders.[41] The mandatory disclosure required

---

eral securities laws; suit involved shareholders complaining of a merger between their corporation and another).

34. For example, the shareholder proposal rule, 17 C.F.R. § 240.14a-8 (1998) (SEC Rule 14a-8), permits shareholder access to the company's proxy solicitation statement. Ostensibly, state law could permit such access, but state law precedent often does not exist.

35. *See* Williams Act of 1968, Pub. L. No. 90-439, 82 Stat. 454. Analogy was also made to transfer of control through the offer of securities in the acquiring company, which would require disclosure under the provisions of the Securities Act of 1933 as an issuance of security.

36. 501 U.S. 1083, 1108 & n.14 (1991) (leaving open the appraisal issue because bank mergers, such as the one at issue in the case, were expressly excluded from Virginia's appraisal statute).

37. *See id.* at 1121 (Kennedy, J., dissenting) ("The majority avoids the question of whether a plaintiff may prove causation by demonstrating that the misrepresentation or omission deprived her of a state law remedy. I do not think the question difficult, as the whole point of federal proxy rules is to support state law principles of corporate governance.").

38. Wilson v. Great Am. Indus., 979 F.2d 924, 931 (2d Cir. 1992); *see also* Howing Co. v. Nationwide Corp., 972 F.2d 700, 707 (6th Cir. 1992); cf. Scattergood v. Perelman, 945 F.2d 618, 626 & n.4 (3d Cir. 1991).

39. *See* 15 U.S.C. §§ 77a–77l (1994).

40. *See id.* §§ 78m–n (requiring periodic disclosure by companies with securities registered under the 1934 Act and additional disclosure if proxies were solicited).

41. *See* Securities Acts Amendments of 1964, Pub. L. No. 88-467, 78 Stat. 565 (codified as amended in scattered sections of 15 U.S.C.). The 1964 amendments applied to companies with one million dollars in assets and 500 holders in a class of equity securities. *See id.* Under Rule 12g-1, the minimum threshold is now $10 million. *See* 17 C.F.R. § 240.12g-1.

of those companies, now found in Regulation S-K, has expanded to include more than forty items and one hundred pages in the Code of Federal Regulations.[42] Rule 10b-5,[43] an antifraud provision promulgated under the 1934 Act, has been interpreted to expand the disclosure obligations of companies so that it approaches an obligation to disclose any material fact.[44]

This disclosure regime at first glance seems market-based (that is, triggered by the purchase or sale of securities) like the 1933 Act, rather than governance-based, as are the corporate rules discussed in the previous section. Such a market/governance distinction has been attractive to some who advocated federal preemption of the regulation of market transactions discussed later in this article. Yet, any clear division between corporate governance and regulation of market transactions has blurred to such an extent that the line seems difficult to preserve. The transactions regulated by the 1934 Act are different from those regulated by the 1933 Act because members of the protected class usually do not transact with the issuer—the alleged wrongdoer—but rather with another member of the public. Disclosure obligations are imposed on the issuer, a non-party to the transaction, to protect the parties' investment decisions. The duties owed in that setting are not unlike traditional corporate law duties—albeit usually imposed on the directors rather than the corporation—to protect other shareholder decisions. Damages, if any, usually are paid from the corporate treasury, in effect from the pockets of the larger body of shareholders for the benefit of a subgroup of shareholders.

Modern financial theory recognizes the direct link between market rules and governance rules, in which the existence of market constraints can reduce the need for legal rules of governance.[45] Political scientist Albert Hirschman noted the relationship between exit and voice: If investors are denied market remedies, voice via voting or other political access will become more important.[46]

3. Traditional Limits on the Federal Role Reflecting Respect for State Law. For most of this century, there has been tension between the reach of state and federal regulation of shareholder-manager relations. Yet, at the federal level, there has been continuous recognition of the limited role of the federal government. Congress has repeatedly refused to enact a federal incorporations act, and federal courts often have restricted the reach of federal securities laws, citing a desire to preserve federalism and traditional state regulation of corporate matters.

---

42. *See* 17 C.F.R. §§229.10-.911 (1998).

43. *See id.* §240.10b-5 (1999).

44. Judicial interpretation has not gone as far as saying that there is a duty to disclose all material facts. *See, e.g.*, In re Time Warner, Inc., 9 F.3d 259, 267 (2d Cir. 1993) (noting that "a corporation is not required to disclose a fact merely because a reasonable investor would very much like to know that fact"). Rather, the disclosure obligation has a series of triggers—periodic disclosures, proxy solicitations, tender offers, initial distributions, insider trading, misrepresentations, and half-truths in voluntary disclosures—which, together with sometimes judicially imposed duties to update or correct, approach an obligation to disclose any material fact. *See id.* at 270.

45. *See generally* Lucian Ayre Bebchuck, *Limiting Contractual Freedom in Corporate Law: The Desirable Constraints on Charter Amendments*, 102 HARV. L. REV. 1820 (1989); John C. Coffee, Jr., *The Mandatory/Enabling Balance in Corporate Law: An Essay on the Judicial Role*, 89 COLUM. L. REV. 1618 (1989)....

46. *See* ALBERT O. HIRSCHMAN, EXIT, VOICE AND LOYALTY: RESPONSES TO DECLINE IN FIRMS, ORGANIZATIONS AND STATES (1970); *see also* Richard M. Buxbaum, *The Internal Division of Powers in Corporate Governance*, 73 CAL. L. REV. 1671 (1985) (discussing the framework of exit, voice, and loyalty in corporations and suggesting that the reduction of shareholder participation reflects judicial and administrative decisions on governance).

a. Rejecting a federal law of corporations. The supportive, supplemental approach of the federal system to the rights created at state law is evidenced both in the laws passed by Congress and in other proposed legislation Congress chose not to enact. Both the 1933 and 1934 Acts contained savings clauses that preserved existing state law systems and remedies.[47] These clauses most often are discussed in the context of state securities laws but also are relevant to state corporate laws. Before World War I, there had been recurring proposals to enact a federal incorporations law, made first by President Theodore Roosevelt and then by Presidents Taft and Wilson. Mention has already been made of the debate over federal incorporation at the time of the enactment of the 1934 Act. In the early 1940s, there was another effort to enact a federal incorporation law, which evolved later in the decade into the Model Business Corporation Act, a basis for subsequent state statutes. In the 1960s and 1970s, concern about the laxity of state regulation—highlighted by Professor William Cary's 1974 article on the race to the bottom among the states—led to increased calls for federal regulation.[51] Even the American Law Institute's Principles of Corporate Governance—later to be vigorously criticized as making overregulatory suggestions for state corporate law—began as an effort to minimize the need for federal corporate law.[52] None of these federal incorporation efforts succeeded.

b. Limiting broad judicial interpretation of federal disclosure laws. Federalism concerns have also been prominent in judicial decisions. In Santa Fe Industries, Inc. v. Green,[53] the Supreme Court refused to include alleged director misconduct within the fraud prohibited by the 1934 Act and Rule 10b-5 when there had been full disclosure. The majority opinion emphasized judicial reluctance to interfere with state corporate law principles.[54] The Court, however, did not address how to resolve federalism concerns in the much more common situation where corporate directors do not fully disclose possible wrongdoing in the misuse of their position.[55] A series of federal appellate cases after Santa Fe held Rule 10b-5's prohibition of fraud to include nondisclosure or omissions that shielded alleged misuse of corporate position as defined by state law.[56]

---

47. *See* 15 U.S.C. §77p (1994) ("The right and remedies provided by this subchapter shall be in addition to any and all other rights and remedies that may exist at law or in equity."); *id.* §78bb(a) ("The rights and remedies provided by this chapter shall be in addition to any and all other rights and remedies that may exist at law or in equity.").

51. William L. Cary, *Federalism and Corporate Law: Reflections Upon Delaware*, 83 YALE L.J. 663 (1974).

52. *See generally* Roswell B. Perkins, *The Genesis and Goals of the ALI Corporate Governance Project*, 8 CARDOZO L. REV. 661 (1987).

53. 430 U.S. 462 (1977).

54. *See id.* at 478–79 ("The result would be to bring within the Rule a wide variety of corporate conduct traditionally left to state regulation.... Absent a clear indication of congressional intent, we are reluctant to federalize the substantial portion of the law of corporations that deals with transactions in securities, particularly where established state policies of corporate regulation would be overridden.").

55. *See id.* at 475 (distinguishing a prior appellate case that "included some element of deception" and noting that the Santa Fe facts contained full disclosure).

56. *See* Goldberg v. Meridor, 567 F.2d 209, 217 (2d Cir. 1977) ("Schoenbaum, then, can rest solidly on the now widely recognized ground that there is deception of the corporation (in effect, of its minority shareholders) when the corporation is influenced by its controlling shareholder to engage in a transaction adverse to the corporation's interests (in effect, the minority shareholder's interests) and there is nondisclosure or misleading disclosures as to the material facts of the transaction."); *see also* Kas v. Financial Gen. Bankshares, Inc., 796 F.2d 508, 512 (D.C. Cir. 1986); Healey v. Catalyst Recovery, 616 F.2d 641, 645–47 (3d Cir. 1980); Alabama Farm Bureau Mut. Cas. Co. v. American Fidelity Life Ins. Co., 606 F.2d 602, 613–14 (5th Cir. 1979); Kidwell ex rel. Penfold v.

Placed within the structure suggested by this article, these decisions interpreted federal law to protect not just voting decisions but also shareholders' decisions to sell their shares or to sue to enforce their rights. The Supreme Court denied certiorari in several of these cases and has yet to resolve this issue. Commentators have discussed the coverage of such "shame facts" or "sue facts,"[57] but cases based on this theory seem to be brought less frequently today than in earlier decades.[58] To the extent federal action intruded into state law, it was consistent with other examples of federal intrusion that enhanced the shareholder position.

Federal deference to state corporate governance law can also be seen in cases such as Business Roundtable v. SEC[59] where the D.C. Circuit invalidated SEC Rule 19c-4, which sought to deter companies listed on stock exchanges from changing their corporate structure to include dual-class voting. By giving extra voting rights to one class of stock—likely held by management—the changes had the potential to disenfranchise majority shareholders permanently.[60] Although such changes usually required a shareholder vote, the SEC was concerned about possible collective action problems. The SEC was also concerned that existing safeguards would be insufficient if companies influenced shareholders' votes to change to a dual-class voting structure by offering "sweeteners," such as higher dividends on the limited voting rights shares.[61] The federal appellate court struck down the SEC's effort to protect fair corporate suffrage because it exceeded what had been authorized in the 1934 Act and impinged on the tradition of state regulation of corporate law.[62] The court focused on congressional regulation of disclosure and limited its disclosure discussion to one context: shareholders making decisions at a shareholders' meeting.[63]

Another area of restrictive judicial interpretation occurred in the 1980s and related to the reach of the Williams Act, a 1968 amendment to the 1934 Act, that regulated hostile tender offers.[64] The Williams Act imposed disclosure requirements designed to protect shareholders when they were deciding how to respond to a tender offer for their shares. When state legislatures imposed additional, often onerous, requirements on bidders, the Supreme Court struck down such state laws as violative of the Commerce Clause.[65] The Court's decision did not reduce the states' desire to protect target compa-

---

Meikle, 597 F.2d 1273, 1291–92 (9th Cir. 1979); Wright v. Heizer Corp., 560 F.2d 236, 249–51 (7th Cir. 1977).

57. *See* Harvey Gelb, *Rule 10b-5 and Santa Fe—Herein of Sue Facts, Shame Facts and Other Matters,* 87 W. Va. L. Rev. 189 (1985) (defining a "sue fact" as one material to a litigation decision and a "shame fact" as one that would have shamed management into abandoning a proposed transaction).

58. *See, e.g.,* Virginia Bankshares, Inc. v. Sandberg, 501 U.S. 1083, 1100 n.9 (1991) (declining to use sue facts or shame facts as a basis for meeting the "essential link" of Mills v. Electric Auto-Lite Co., 396 U.S. 375 (1970)); LHLC Corp. v. Cluett, Peabody & Co., Inc., 842 F.2d 928, 932 (7th Cir. 1988) (noting that "[w]e have held repeatedly in recent years that the securities laws do not ensure that people will receive information sufficient to make correct decisions about filing or pursuing lawsuits").

59. 905 F.2d 406 (D.C. Cir. 1990).

60. *See* Jeffrey N. Gordon, *Shareholder Initiative: A Social Choice and Game Theoretic Approach to Corporate Law,* 60 U. Cin. L. Rev. 347 (1991).

61. *See* Exchange Act Release No. 24,623, [1987 Transfer Binder] Fed. Sec. L. Rep (CCH) P84,143, at P 88,773–74 (June 22, 1987).

62. *See* Business Roundtable v. SEC, 905 F.2d. 406 (D.C. Cir. 1990).

63. *See id.* at 410 ("The goal of federal proxy regulation was to improve those communications [with potential absentee voters] and thereby to enable proxy voters to control the corporation as effectively as they might have by attending a shareholder meeting.").

64. *See* 15 U.S.C. §§ 78m(d)–(f), 78n(d)–(f) (1994).

65. *See* Edgar v. MITE Corp., 457 U.S. 624, 631–34 (1982).

nies from hostile takeovers, and the legislatures returned to the drawing board and crafted second-generation statutes that equaled or exceeded their first-generation counterparts in their dampening effect on hostile takeovers. The newer statutes were framed as permissive authorizations of what corporate managers could do in contrast to the earlier statutes' restrictive limitations on what bidders could do.

Several federal courts interpreted the Williams Act to protect a shareholder's ability to sell shares by defining the space within which takeovers would be permitted to function unimpeded by state law. A Seventh Circuit decision emphasized that Congress, through the Williams Act, sought to preserve a shareholder's ability to receive tender offers through the market so that any state law that blocked the use of the market should be preempted.[66] The Supreme Court reversed that decision and interpreted the Williams Act as having a limited purpose that focused on the conduct of the bidder vis-a-vis the shareholders who were to receive the offer and not on the shareholder's ability to receive an offer unimpeded by management defensive tactics.[67] The effect was to leave to state law the determination of what rights shareholders would have to use the market as a means to constrain management prerogatives.

Comments and Questions

1. It is possible to argue that many of Professor Cary's concerns have been met, at the federal level, without the need for formal federalization of the corporate law. Could the excerpt from Professor Thompson's work provide arguments in that regard?

2. The gradual federalization of significant aspects of law "touching" on the organization and functioning of corporate enterprises since the Great Depression has effectively federalized a great deal of law affecting the management and governance of the largest and most economically significant national corporations. This is a clever federalization—it depends for its success on the ability to narrow the definition of "corporate" law, and then federalize aspects of enterprise regulation that do not touch on this now more narrow definition of 'corporate' law. Is it really possible to argue that securities laws are not 'corporate' law at all, but part of something 'independent' of corporate law—in this case securities law? Do you think that Professor Thompson's article makes a case for this 'death' of corporate law at the state level by taxonomy' argument?

---

2. *The Federalization of U.S. Corporate Law*

There have been periodic attempts to federalize corporate law, but with no significant result. The "problem" with state regulation of corporate law was set out in cases: *see Louis K. Liggett Co. v. Lee*, 288 U.S. 517, 53 S. Ct. 481 (1933) (excerpted below); and by academics, *see* Cary, *Federalism and Corporate Law, Reflections Upon Delaware*, 83 YALE L.J. 663 (1974). Justice Brandeis, in his dissenting opinion in *Louis K. Liggett Co.*, argues that the large aggregations of wealth in corporations, which is directed by people

66. Convention on the Mutual Recognition of Companies and Bodies Politic, 1968 O.J. (L35) 6 (hereinafter Convention on Mutual Recognition).

67. *See* CTS Corp. v. Dynamics Corp., 481 U.S. 69 (1987).

who are not tied to that wealth by rights of ownership, creates institutions which may dwarf in power the very states which must regulate them. Professor Cary concentrates on arguments that state competition for the chartering business and the revenues it brings has the effect of substantially eroding the ability of the state to protect shareholders from management. For a very powerful counter to this argument, *see* Winter, *State Law, Shareholder Protection and the Theory of the Corporation*, 6 J. LEGAL STUD. 251 (1977), who asserted that the rapaciousness of managers should affect share value negatively, and yet the evidence suggests the opposite occurring. The positions of the proponents of this debate are described in the materials that follow. Are you convinced?

As we will see, the European approach, since the creation of the European Communities has been nearly the opposite of that in the United States. As you read the materials in this chapter, ask yourself, whether there is value in harmonization, and whether national (or in the case of Europe, supra-national) uniformity serves to create a common market.

Louis K. Liggett Co. et al. v. Lee, Comptroller of State of Florida, et al.

288 U.S. 517, 53 S.Ct. 481
Decided March 13, 1933
(some footnotes omitted)

Mr. Justice ROBERTS delivered the opinion of the Court.

Chapter 15624 of the Laws of Florida, 1931 (Ex. Sess.), declares it unlawful for any person, firm, corporation, association, or copartnership, foreign or domestic, to operate any store within the state without first having obtained a license, designates the officer to whom application shall be made, regulates the procedure for issuance of licenses, and provides for annual renewal. The act requires the payment of a filing fee, and by section 5... fixes the amount of the license fee. A tax greater than that exacted for a single store is fixed for each store in excess of one, but not exceeding fifteen, owned or operated by the same person or corporation. The fee for each store is stepped up in amount as the number constituting the chain reaches certain specified limits. This graduated scale applies to stores all of which are within a single county; but, if the same number of stores is located in more than one county, the license fee for each is materially increased.)....

Three chain store owners filed in the circuit court of Leon county, Fla., a class bill, in which twelve others intervened and became coplaintiffs, praying that the tax officials be enjoined from enforcing the act. The complainants are corporations of Florida and other states. They challenge the statute as violative of various provisions of the Constitution of Florida, of the due process and equal protection clauses of the Fourteenth Amendment, and of the commerce clause of the Federal Constitution....

The defendants moved to dismiss. The cause was heard upon this motion and a decree entered dismissing the bill at complainants' costs. The Supreme Court of Florida affirmed the decree. The present appeal presents only the questions arising under the Federal Constitution.

1. In support of the allegation of arbitrary and unreasonable discrimination, the bill recites facts from which appellants claim the conclusion is inevitable that there is no dif-

ference between the method of conducting chain stores and those employed in department stores, so-called voluntary chains, and singly operated units. This is but a reiteration of the contention made and overruled in State Board of Tax Commissioners v. Jackson, 283 U.S. 527, 51 S.Ct. 540, 75 L.Ed. 1248, 73 A.L.R. 1464....

* * *

2. The statute lays a tax of a stated sum per store on any given number of stores in the same ownership located within the same county; but, if one happens to be in a county other than that in which the remainder are situate, imposes an increased tax, not only on the single one lying in the second county, but on all. Thus, if an owner has fourteen stores, he may add a fifteenth in the same county, and the only additional tax will be in the amount of $10 attributable to the privilege of conducting the new store. But, if the new store happens to be in another county, the license fee for it will be increased to $15, and that for each of the other fourteen, which have long since been opened and operated in the original county, will be increased from $10 to $15.

We are unable to discover any reasonable basis for this classification. As we have held, gradation of the tax according to the number of units operated cannot be said to be so unreasonable as to transcend the constitutional powers of the Legislature.....

* * *

The suggestion is made that the statute is in reality aimed solely at large corporate chains; and that, as none other are parties to this suit, we may ignore any discriminatory features as respects individual owners of multiple units. But this is to construe the act by pure speculation and not by what it says, nor by any declared purpose, nor by anything contained in the record. Conceding for the purpose of the argument that in levying the tax the Legislature might have drawn a distinction between corporate owners and individuals, and again between small owners, whether corporate or individual, and large owners, we are not permitted to guess at any such undisclosed purpose in the minds of those who adopted the statute. Assuming power to suppress by taxation a form of organization deemed inimical to the public interest, we can attribute no such motive to the present statute in the absence of legislative declaration or record proof. The act taxes ownership and operation of stores, not corporate nor large corporate operation. The exaction is based on the doing of a business, not on the personality of the merchant.

The title declares it 'An Act Requiring Licenses for the Operation, Maintenance, Opening or Establishment of Stores in this State. * * *' Section 1 enacts 'That from and after the first day of October A.D. 1931, it shall be unlawful for any person, firm, corporation, association or co-partnership, whether foreign or domestic, to operate, maintain, open or establish any store in this State without first having obtained a license. * * *'

It would violate every principle of statutory construction to hold that this plain language really means that individuals and small local corporations are not within the intendment of the act, but that it in fact applies only to so-called giant corporations. To attribute such a covert, hidden, and indirect purpose to those who passed the statute is, in effect, to charge the lawmakers with saying one thing and meaning another. Nothing said in O'Gorman & Young v. Hartford Fire Insurance Co., 282 U.S. 251, 51 S.Ct. 130, 75 L.Ed. 324, or any other decision of this court, justifies such a pronouncement. The Legislature of Florida has declared the purpose and object of the statute to be to tax every store owner and operator, and we should not go behind that declaration and attribute to the lawmakers some other ulterior design. Corporations are as much entitled to the equal protection of the laws guaranteed by the Fourteenth Amendment as are natural persons.... Unequal treatment and arbitrary discrimination as between corporations and natural persons, or between different corporations, inconsistent with the declared object of the legislation, cannot be justified by the assumption, that a different classification for a wholly different purpose might be valid.

Those provisions of section 5 which increase the tax if the owner's stores are located in more than one county are unreasonable and arbitrary, and violate the guaranties of the Fourteenth Amendment....

* * *

The judgment is reversed and the cause remanded for further proceedings not inconsistent with this opinion.

So ordered.

Mr. Justice BRANDEIS (dissenting in part).

In my opinion, the judgment of the Supreme Court of Florida should be affirmed. Florida Laws 1931 (Ex. Sess.), chapter 15624, is legislation of the type popularly called Anti-Chain Store Laws. The statute provides for the licensing of retail stores by the state, the counties, and the municipalities—a system under which large revenues may be raised. But the raising of revenue is obviously not the main purpose of the legislation. Its chief aim is to protect the individual, independently-owned, retail stores from the competition of chain stores. The statute seeks to do this by subjecting the latter to financial handicaps which may conceivably compel their withdrawal from the state. An injunction against its enforcement is sought on the ground that the law violates rights guaranteed by the Federal Constitution.

The Florida law is general in its terms. It prohibits the operation, after September 30, 1931, of any retail store without securing annually a license; and provides, among other things, for annual fees which are in part graduated. If the owner operates only one store, the state fee is $5; if more than one, the fee for the additional stores rises by step increases, dependent upon both the number operated and whether all operated are located in a single county. The highest fee is for a store in excess of 75. If all of the stores are located in a single county, the fee for each store in excess of 75 is $40; if all are not located in the same county, the fee is $50. Under this law, the owner of 100 stores not located in a single county pays for each store operated, on the average, $33.65; and, if they were located in a single county, the owner would pay for each store, on the average, $25.20. If the 100 stores were independently owned (although operated co-operatively as a so-called 'voluntary chain'), the annual fee for each would be only $5. The statute provides that the licenses shall issue to expire on September 30th of each calendar year. This suit was begun September 30, 1931. The first license year had expired before the case was heard in this Court.

In its main features, this statute resembles the Indiana law discussed in State Board of Tax Commissioners v. Jackson, 283 U.S. 527, 51 S.Ct. 540, 75 L.Ed. 1248, 73 A.L.R. 1464. For the reasons there stated, the Court sustains like provisions in the Florida statute. But it declares arbitrary, and hence invalid, the novel provision imposing heavier license fees where the multiple stores of a single owner are located in more than one county, because it is 'unable to discover any reasonable basis for this classification.'...

There is, however, another ground on which this provision should be, and the whole statute could be, sustained—a ground not considered in the Jackson Case and not pertinent there. Jackson was an individual. The plaintiffs here are all corporations. Though the provisions of the statutes in the two states are similar, certain rules of law applicable to the parties to the litigation are different.

The plaintiffs are thirteen corporations which engage in Florida exclusively in intrastate commerce. Each (except one) owns and operates a chain of retail stores within the state and some operate stores in more than one county. Several of the plaintiffs are organized under the laws of Florida; the rest under the laws of other states. No claim of discrimination as between the foreign and domestic corporations is made, compare Southern R. Co. v. Greene, 216 U.S. 400, 30 S.Ct. 287, 54 L.Ed. 536, 17 Ann.Cas. 1247; Hanover Fire Insurance Co. v. Harding, 272 U.S. 494, 47 S.Ct. 179, 71 L.Ed. 372, 49 A.L.R. 713; nor could it be, since the statute affects both classes of corporations alike. The suit is brought as a class suit, for the benefit of all merchants similarly situated who may desire to avail themselves thereof. From certain allegations in the bill it may be inferred that there are at least two natural persons within the state who own and operate more than one store. But, as no such person has intervened in the cause, we have no occasion to inquire whether the discrimination complained of would be fatal as applied to natural persons. The plaintiffs can succeed only if the discrimination is unconstitutional as applied to them; that is, as applied to corporations. One who would strike down a statute must show not only that he is affected by it, but that as applied to him it exceeds the power of the state. This rule, acted upon as early as Austin v. Boston, 7 Wall. 694, 19 L.Ed. 224, and definitely stated in Albany County v. Stanley, 105 U.S. 305, 314, 26 L.Ed. 1044, has been consistently followed since that time.... For the reasons to be stated, the discrimination complained of, and held arbitrary by the court, is, in my opinion, valid as applied to corporations.

First. The Federal Constitution does not confer upon either domestic or foreign corporations the right to engage in intrastate commerce in Florida. The privilege of engaging in such commerce in corporate form is one which the state may confer or may withhold as it sees fit.... Florida might grant the privilege to one set of persons and deny it to others; might grant it for some kinds of business and deny it for others; might grant the privilege to corporations with a small capital while denying it for those whose capital or resources are large. Or it might grant the privilege to private corporations whose shares are owned mainly by those who manage them and to corporations engaged in co-operative undertakings, while denying the privilege to other concerns called private, but whose shares are listed on a stock exchange—corporations financed by the public, largely through the aid of investment bankers. It may grant the privilege broadly, or restrict its exercise to a single county, city, or town, and to a single place of business within any such subdivision of the state.

Whether the corporate privilege shall be granted or withheld is always a matter of state policy. If granted, the privilege is conferred in order to achieve an end which the state deems desirable. It may be granted as a means of raising revenue; or in order to procure for the community a public utility, a bank, or a desired industry not otherwise obtainable; or the reason for granting it may be to promote more generally the public welfare by providing an instrumentality of business which will facilitate the establishment and conduct of new and large enterprises deemed of public benefit. Similarly, if the privilege is denied, it is denied because incidents of like corporate enterprise are deemed inimical to the public welfare and it is desired to protect the community from apprehended harm.

Whether the citizens of Florida are wise in seeking to discourage the operation of chain stores is, obviously, a matter with which this Court has no concern. Nor need it, in my opinion, consider whether the differences in license fees employed to effect such discouragement are inherently reasonable, since the plaintiffs are at liberty to refuse to pay the compensation demanded for the corporate privilege and withdraw from the state, if they consider the price more than the privilege is worth. But a review of the legislation of the several states by which all restraints on corporate size and activity were removed, and a consideration of the economic and social effects of such removal, will help to an understanding of Anti-Chain Store Laws; and will show that the discriminatory license fees prescribed by Florida, even if treated merely as a form of taxation, were laid for a purpose which may be appropriately served by taxation, and that the specific means employed to favor the individual retailer are not constitutionally objectionable.

Second. The prevalence of the corporation in America has led men of this generation to act, at times, as if the privilege of doing business in corporate form were inherent in the citizen; and has led them to accept the evils attendant upon the free and unrestricted use of the corporate mechanism as if these evils were the inescapable price of civilized life, and, hence, to be borne with resignation. Throughout the greater part of our history a different view prevailed. Although the value of this instrumentality in commerce and industry was fully recognized, incorporation for business was commonly denied long after it had been freely granted for religious, educational, and charitable purposes by corporations. So at first the corporate of encroachment upon the liberties and opportunities of the individual. Fear of the subjection of labor to capital. Fear of monopoly. Fear that the absorption of capital by corporations, and their perpetual life, might bring evils similar to those which attended mortmain.[1] There was a sense of some insidious menace inherent in large aggregations of capital, particularly when held by corporations. So at first the corporate privilege was granted sparingly; and only when the grant seemed necessary in order to procure for the community some specific benefit otherwise unattainable. The later enactment of general incorporation laws does not signify that the apprehension of corporate domination had been overcome. The desire for business expansion created an irresistible demand for more charters; and it was believed that under general laws embodying safeguards of universal application the scandals and favoritism incident to special incorporation could be avoided. The general laws, which long embodied severe restrictions upon size and upon the scope of corporate activity, were, in part, an expression of the desire for equality of opportunity.[2]

(a) Limitation upon the amount of the authorized capital of business corporations was long universal. The maximum limit frequently varied with the kinds of business to be carried on, being dependent apparently upon the supposed requirements of the effi-

---

1. It was doubtless because of this that the earlier statutes limited the life of corporations to fixed terms of 20, 30, or 50 years. See the statutes cited in subsequent notes. The power of Legislatures to grant special charters was sometimes strictly limited, even before the adoption of constitutional amendments withdrawing that power entirely. Thus the New York Constitution, adopted in convention in November, 1821, and by popular vote in January, 1822, required the assent of two-thirds of each house for any act 'creating, continuing, altering, or renewing any body politic or corporate'—Article 7, § 9; L. 1822–24, p. x. Similar provisions were included in the Delaware Constitution of 1831, Art. 2, § 17; in the Florida Constitution of 1838, Art. 13, § 2 (with an additional requirement of three months' public notice); and in the Michigan Constitution of 1835, Art. 12, § 2. The Rhode Island Constitution of 1842, Art. 4, § 17, required a bill for a corporate charter to be continued to the next Legislature. The Constitution of Illinois, adopted in 1848, provided that no act authorizing the formation of a corporation with banking powers should be effective unless ratified by popular vote—Article 10, § 5; and a similar provision was included in the Constitution of Wisconsin 1848, Art. 11, §§ 4, 5.

2. That the desire for equality and the dread of special privilege were largely responsible for the general incorporation laws is indicated by the fact that many states included in their constitutions a prohibition of the grant of special charters. The first constitutional provision requiring incorporation under general laws seems to be that in the New York Constitution of 1846, Article 8, § 1 (except where objects of incorporation were not thus attainable). Other states followed in later years.....

cient unit. Although the statutory limits were changed from time to time, this principle of limitation was long retained. Thus in New York the limit was at first $100,000 for some businesses and as little as $50,000 for others. Until 1881 the maximum for business corporations in New York was $2,000,000; and until 1890, $5,000,000. In Massachusetts the limit was at first $200,000 for some businesses and as little as $5,000 for others. Until 1871 the maximum for mechanical and manufacturing corporations was $500,000; and until 1899 $1,000,000. The limit of $1,000,000 was retained for some businesses until 1903.

In many other states, including the leading ones in some industries, the removal of the limitations upon size was more recent. Pennsylvania did not remove the limits until 1905. Its first general act not having contained a maximum limit, that of $500,000 was soon imposed. Later, it was raised to $1,000,000; and, for iron and steel companies, to $5,000,000. Vermont limited the maximum to $1,000,000 until 1911, when up to amount over $10,000,000 was authorized if, in the opinion of a judge of the Supreme Court, such a capitalization would tend 'to create a monopoly or result in restraining competition in trade.[3] Maryland limited until 1918 the capital of mining companies to $3,000,000; and prohibited them from holding more than 500 acres of land (except in Allegany county, where 1,000 acres was allowed). New Hampshire did not remove the maximum limit until 1919. It had been $1,000,000 until 1907, when it was increased to $5,000,000. Michigan did not remove the maximum limit until 1921. The maximum, at first $100,000, had been gradually increased until in 1903 it became $10,000,000 for some corporations and $25,000,000 for others; and in 1917 became $50,000,000. Indiana did not remove until 1921 the maximum limit of $2,000,000 for petroleum and natural gas corporations. Missouri did not remove its maximum limit until 1927. Texas still has such a limit for certain corporations.

(b) Limitations upon the scope of a business corporation's powers and activity were also long universal. At first, corporations could be formed under the general laws only for a limited number of purposes—usually those which required a relatively large fixed capital, like transportation, banking, and insurance, and mechanical, mining, and manufacturing enterprises. Permission to incorporate for 'any lawful purpose'[4] was not common until 1875; and until that time the duration of corporate franchises was generally limited to a period of 20, 30, or 50 years. All, or a majority, of the incorporators or directors, or both, were required to be residents of the incorporating state. The powers which the corporation might exercise in carrying out its purposes were sparingly conferred and strictly construed. Severe limitations were imposed on the amount of indebtedness, bonded or otherwise. The power to hold stock in other corporations was not conferred or implied. The holding company was impossible.

(c) The removal by the leading industrial states of the limitations upon the size and powers of business corporations appears to have been due, not to their conviction that maintenance of the restrictions was undesirable in itself, but to the conviction that it was futile to insist upon them; because local restriction would be circumvented by foreign incorporation. Indeed, local restriction seemed worse than futile. Lesser states, eager for the revenue derived from the traffic in charters, had removed safeguards from

---

3. Act of January 28, 1911, No. 143, L. 1910, pp. 140, 141, 142. This provision was repealed by General Corporation Act, April 1, 1915, No. 141, L. 1915, p. 222.

4. New York—Laws 1866, c. 838, p. 1896; Laws 1875, c. 611, p. 755. Illinois—July 1, 1872, Laws 1871–72, p. 296. Massachusetts—Act of April 14, 1874, c. 165, §1. Maine—February 3, 1876, c. 65, Laws 1876, p. 51. Other states followed shortly.

their own incorporation laws. Companies were early formed to provide charters for corporations in states where the cost was lowest and the laws least restrictive. The states joined in advertising their wares. The race was one not of diligence but of laxity. Incorporation under such laws was possible; and the great industrial States yielded in order not to lose wholly the prospect of the revenue and the control incident to domestic incorporation.

The history of the changes made by New York is illustrative. The New York revision of 1890, which eliminated the maximum limitation on authorized capital, and permitted intercorporate stockholding in a limited class of cases, was passed after a migration of incorporation from New York, attracted by the more liberal incorporation laws of New Jersey. But the changes made by New York in 1890 were not sufficient to stem the tide. In 1892, the Governor of New York approved a special charter for the General Electric Company, modeled upon the New Jersey act, on the ground that otherwise the enterprise would secure a New Jersey charter.[5] Later in the same year the New York corporation law was again revised, allowing the holding of stock in other corporations. But the New Jersey law still continued to be more attractive to incorporators. By specifically providing that corporations might be formed in New Jersey to do all their business elsewhere, the state made its policy unmistakably clear. Of the seven largest trusts existing in 1904, with an aggregate capitalization of over two and a half billion dollars, all were organized under New Jersey law; and three of these were formed in 1899. During the first seven months of that year, 1336 corporations were organized under the laws of New Jersey, with an aggregate authorized capital of over two billion dollars. The Comptroller of New York, in his annual report for 1899, complained that 'our tax list reflects little of the great wave of organization that has swept over the country during the past year and to which this state contributed more capital than any other state in the Union.' 'It is time,' he declared, 'that great corporations having their actual headquarters in this State and a nominal office elsewhere, doing nearly all of their business within our borders, should be brought within the jurisdiction of this State not only as to matters of taxation but in respect to other and equally important affairs.'[6] In 1901 the New York corporation law was again revised.

The history in other states was similar. Thus the Massachusetts revision of 1903 was precipitated by the fact that 'the possibilities of incorporation in other states have become well known, and have been availed of to the detriment of this Commonwealth.'[7]

---

5. N.Y. Laws 1892, c. 323. 'The measure is approved because it is claimed that its objects cannot well be secured under general laws, and because its approval will keep within the State a corporation which professes to be ready to invest a large amount of capital, and which, without the concessions allowed by its proposed charter, would be incorporated under the laws of New Jersey.' Public Papers of Governor Flower, 1892, p. 104. Quoted in James B. Dill, 'Some aspects of New Jersey's Corporate Policy,' Address before the Pennsylvania Bar Association, June 29, 1903, Rep. Pa. Bar Ass'n, 1903, pp. 265, 267.

6. Report of Comptroller of New York, 1890, p. xxvii.

7. Report of Committee on Corporation Laws, Massachusetts (1903) p. 19. The Governor of Michigan, in his Message to the Legislature in 1921, said of the corporation laws of that state: 'Because of their inadequacy to meet modern needs and requirements, and the failure to accord domestic corporations the same rights granted to those organized outside of the state, most of our business corporations are being organized in other states, only to return here as foreign corporations.' Journal of House of Representatives of Michigan, 1921, pp. 31, 37; reprinted in Messages of the Governors of Michigan (Michigan Historical Commission, 1927) vol. 4, pp. 775, 784. In 1921 the corporation laws of Michigan were revised, eliminating, among other things, the maximum limitation on capital stock. *See* note 20, *supra*. The effect of the policy of West Virginia was described by President Henry M. Russell in an address before the West Virginia Bar Association in

Third. Able, discerning scholars have pictured for us the economic and social results of thus removing all limitations upon the size and activities of business corporations and of vesting in their managers vast powers once exercised by stockholders—results not designed by the states and long unsuspected. They show that size alone gives to giant corporations a social significance not attached ordinarily to smaller units of private enterprise. Through size, corporations, once merely an efficient tool employed by individuals in the conduct of private business have become an institution—an institution which has brought such concentration of economic power that so-called private corporations are sometimes able to dominate the state. The typical business corporation of the last century, owned by a small group of individuals, managed by their owners, and limited in size by their personal wealth, is being supplanted by huge concerns in which the lives of tens or hundreds of thousands of employees and the property of tens or hundreds of thousands of investors are subjected, through the corporate mechanism, to the control of a few men. Ownership has been separated from control; and this separation has removed many of the checks which formerly operated to curb the misuse of wealth and power. And, as ownership of the shares is becoming continually more dispersed, the power which formerly accompanied ownership is becoming increasingly concentrated in the hands of a few. The changes thereby wrought in the lives of the workers, of the owners and of the general public, are so fundamental and far-reaching as to lead these scholars to compare the evolving 'corporate system' with the feudal system; and to lead other men of insight and experience to assert that this 'master institution of civilized life' is committing it to the rule of a plutocracy.

The data submitted in support of these conclusions indicate that in the United States the process of absorption has already advanced so far that perhaps two-thirds of our industrial wealth has passed from individual possession to the ownership of large corporations whose shares are dealt in on the stock exchange; that 200 nonbanking corporations, each with assets in excess of $90,000,000, control directly about one-fourth of all our national wealth, and that their influence extends far beyond the assets under their direct control; that these 200 corporations, while nominally controlled by about 2,000 directors, are actually dominated by a few hundred persons—the negation of industrial democracy. Other writers have shown that, coincident with the growth of these giant corporations, there has occurred a marked concentration of individual wealth; and that the resulting disparity in incomes is a major cause of the existing depression. Such is the Frankenstein monster which states have created by their corporation laws.

Fourth. Among these 200 corporations, each with assets in excess of $90,000,000, are five of the plaintiffs. These five have, in the aggregate, $820,000,000 of assets; and they operate, in the several states, an aggregate of 19,718 stores. A single one of these giants operates nearly 16,000. Against these plaintiffs, and other owners of multiple stores, the individual retailers of Florida are engaged in a struggle to preserve their in-

1891. In the six years ending January 1, 1889, he stated, 330 charters were issued by the state to corporations having their principal places of business elsewhere. Of these, 101 were to be in the District of Columbia, and 65 in New York. 'The neighboring State of Pennsylvania has adopted very stringent laws for the government of its corporations. * * * So our Pennsylvania friends who have patent rights or gold mines, come to West Virginia. * * * Of our 330 corporations, 80 were to have their principal offices in Pennsylvania. Our other neighbor, the State of Ohio, carries upon its statute book a law imposing a double liability on the stockholders for the debts of the corporation * * * and 30 out of the 330 have their principal offices in Ohio. Thus 284 of the 330 are found in the cities of Washington and New York and the States of Pennsylvania and Ohio. * * * It is unjust to our sister States.' 27 American Law Review, p. 105.

dependence—perhaps a struggle for existence. The citizens of the state, considering themselves vitally interested in this seemingly unequal struggle, have undertaken to aid the individual retailers by subjecting the owners of multiple stores to the handicap of higher license fees. They may have done so merely in order to preserve competition. But their purpose may have been a broader and deeper one. They may have believed that the chain store, by furthering the concentration of wealth and of power and by promoting absentee ownership, is thwarting American ideals; that it is making impossible equality of opportunity; that it is converting independent tradesmen into clerks; and that it is sapping the resources, the vigor and the hope of the smaller cities and towns.

The plaintiffs insist that no taxable difference exists between the owner of multiple stores and the owner of an individual store. A short answer to the contention has already been given, so far as required for the decision of this case. It is that the license fee is not merely taxation. The fee is the compensation exacted for the privilege of carrying on intrastate business in corporate form. As this privilege is one which a state may withhold or grant, it may charge such compensation as it pleases. Nothing in the Federal Constitution requires that the compensation demanded for the privilege should be reasonable. Moreover, since the authority to operate many stores, or to operate in two or more counties, is certainly a broader privilege than to operate only one store, or in only one county, there is in this record no basis for a finding that it is unreasonable to make the charge higher for the greater privilege.

A more comprehensive answer should, however, be given. The purpose of the Florida statute is not, like ordinary taxation, merely to raise revenue. Its main purpose is social and economic. The chain store is treated as a thing menacing the public welfare. The aim of the statute, at the lowest, is to preserve the competition of the independent stores with the chain stores; at the highest, its aim is to eliminate altogether the corporate chain stores from retail distribution. The legislation reminds of that by which Florida and other states, in order to eliminate the 'premium system' in merchandising, exacted high license fees of merchants who offered trading stamps with their goods....

Whether chain stores owned by individuals may be subjected to the discrimination here challenged need not, however, be decided. This case requires decision only of the narrower question—whether the state may freely apply discrimination in license fees against corporate chain stores. The essential difference between corporations and natural persons has been recognized by the federal government in taxing the income of businesses when conducted by corporations, while exempting a similar business when carried on by an individual or partnership. Flint v. Stone-Tracy Co., 220 U.S. 108, 158, 31 S.Ct. 342, 55 L.Ed. 389, Ann. Cas. 1912B, 1312. It has, at other times, imposed upon businesses conducted by corporations heavier taxes than upon those conducted by individuals. The equality clause of the Fourteenth Amendment presents no obstacle to a state, likewise, taxing businesses engaged in intrastate commerce differently according to the instruments by which they are carried on; provided the purpose of the discrimination is a permissible one, the discrimination employed a means appropriate to achieving the end sought, and the difference in the instruments so employed vital. Compare Fort Smith Lumber Co. v. Arkansas, 251 U.S. 532, 40 S.Ct. 304, 64 L.Ed. 396; Quong Wing v. Kirkendall, 223 U.S. 59, 32 S.Ct. 192, 56 L.Ed. 350; Amoskeag Savings Bank v. Purdy, 231 U.S. 373, 34 S.Ct. 114, 58 L.Ed. 274; Singer Sewing Machine Co. v. Brickell, 233 U.S. 304, 34 S.Ct. 493, 58 L.Ed. 974. The corporate mechanism is obviously a vital element in the conduct of business. The encouragement or discouragement of competition is an end for which the power of taxation may be exerted. And discrimination in the rate of taxation is an effective means to that end.

The requirement of the equality clause that classification 'must rest upon some ground of difference having a fair and substantial relation to the object of the legislation,' Louisville Gas & Electric Co. v. Coleman, 277 U.S. 32, 37, 48 S.Ct. 423, 425, 72 L.Ed. 770, is here satisfied. Mere difference in degree has been widely applied as a difference justifying different taxation or regulation. The difference in power between corporations and natural persons is ample basis for placing them in different, classes. Even as between natural persons, where the equality clause applies rigidly, differences in size furnish an adequate basis for discrimination in a tax rate. The size of estates, or of bequests, is the difference on which rest all the progressive inheritance taxes of the states and of the nation.... Differences in the size of businesses present, likewise, an adequate basis for different rates of taxation....

The state might justify progressively higher license fees for corporations of larger size, or a more extended field of operation, on the oft-asserted ground that such concerns are more efficient than smaller units, and hence that they can, and should, contribute more to the public revenues. But the state need not rest the difference in tax rates on a ground so debatable as the assertion that efficiency increases with size. The Federal Constitution does not require that taxes (as distinguished from assessments for betterments) be proportionate to the differences in benefits received by the taxpayers, compare Illinois Central R. Co. v. Decatur, 147 U.S. 190, 197, 13 S.Ct. 293, 37 L.Ed. 132....; or that taxes be proportionate to the taxpayer's ability to bear the burden.

Since business must yield to the paramount interests of the community in times of peace as well as in times of war, a state may prohibit a business found to be noxious and, likewise, may prohibit incidents or excrescences of a business otherwise beneficent.... Businesses may become as harmful to the community by excessive size, as by monopoly or the commonly recognized restraints of trade. If the state should conclude that bigness in retail merchandising as manifested in corporate chain stores menaces the public welfare, it might prohibit the excessive size or extent of that business as it prohibits excessive size or weight in motor trucks or excessive height in the buildings of a city. Compare Morris v. Duby, 274 U.S. 135, 47 S.Ct. 548, 71 L.Ed. 966;...., that the Sherman Anti-Trust Act (15 USCA §§ 1–7, 15 note) did not forbid large aggregations; but the power of Congress to prohibit corporations of a size deemed excessive from engaging in interstate commerce was not questioned.

The elimination of chain stores, deemed harmful or menacing because of their bigness, may be achieved by leveling the prohibition against the corporate mechanism—the instrument by means of which excessive size is commonly made possible. Or, instead of absolutely prohibiting the corporate chain store, the state might conclude that it should first try the more temperate remedy of curbing the chain by imposing the handicap of discriminatory license fees....'Taxation is regulation just as prohibition is.' Compania General De Tahacos v. Collector, 275 U.S. 87, 96, 48 S.Ct. 100, 103, 72 L.Ed. 177. And the state's power to make social and economic experiments is a broad one.

Fifth. The mere fact that the taxpayer is a corporation does not, of course, exclude it from the protection afforded by the equality clause. Corporations and individuals, aliens and citizens, are for most purposes in the same class. Ordinarily, they have the same civil rights; are entitled to the same remedies; are subject to the same police regulations; and are also subject to the same tax laws. Where such is the case, the corporation taxpayer is entitled, like the individual, to the protection of the equality clause against discrimination, however effected. Compare Iowa-Des Moines National Bank v. Bennett, 284 U.S. 239, 52 S.Ct. 133, 76 L.Ed. 265....

It is true that the Florida Anti-Chain Store Law, like others, is not drawn so as to apply only to giant corporate chains. In terms, it applies to the small corporations as well as to the large; and also to natural persons. But the history of such legislation indicates that these laws were aimed at the huge, publicly-financed corporations; and that the statutes were couched in comprehensive terms in the hope of thereby avoiding constitutional doubts raised by judicial statements that the equality clause applies alike to natural persons and corporations. It was said in Quaker City Cab Co. v. Com. of Pennsylvania, 277 U.S. 389, 402, 48 S.Ct. 553, 72 L.Ed. 927, that the equality clause precludes making the character of the owner the sole fact on which a discrimination in taxation shall depend. And in Frost v. Corporation Commission, 278 U.S. 515, 522, 49 S.Ct. 235, 238, 73 L.Ed. 483, it was said.... 'that a corporation is as much entitled to the equal protection of the laws as an individual.' These statements require, in my opinion, this qualification. Whenever the discrimination is for a permitted purpose—as when a state, having concluded that activity by corporations should be curbed, seeks to favor businesses conducted by individuals—the corporate character of the owner presents a difference in ownership which may be made the sole basis of classification in taxation, as in regulation.[8] The discrimination cannot, in such a case be held arbitrary, since it is made in order to effect the permitted hostile purpose and is appropriate to that end....

Sixth. The plaintiffs contend, for a further reason, that there is no taxable difference justifying the discrimination in license fees. They assert that the struggle between them and the independently owned stores is, in fact, not an unequal one; and, in support of this assertion, they call attention to those paragraphs in the bill which describe the co-operative chains of individual stores and their rapid growth. These paragraphs allege that by 'affiliations and cooperative organizations single grocery (and other) store owners have adopted the best features of chain store merchandising and have secured substantially all the benefits derived therefrom, while at the same time they have avoided burdens of capital investment, insurance, etc., incident to the carrying of a large stock in a central warehouse.' The bill sets forth how this has been achieved, describing in detail the recent advances in efficiency of such co-operative merchandising. It alleges, moreover, that the members of a co-operative chain have the superior advantage of the good will and personal interest of the individual owners, as compared with the hired managers of the regular chains; and that all these facts were known to the Legislature when it enacted the statute here challenged.

---

8. Compare Ernst Freund, Standards of American Legislation (1917) pp. 40, 41: 'So far as the businesses of banking and insurance have been carried on under corporate charters they have been the subject of thorough and detailed regulation, while private banking and the unincorporated forms of fraternal insurance remain to this day in the main unregulated and uncontrolled. Railroads have been built and operated from the beginning by corporate enterprise; thus legislation was called for and was made the instrument of exercising public power over operation, service and in some cases over rates; the express business, on the other hand, which happened to be carried on chiefly by unincorporated concerns, or at least did not seek special charters, practically escaped regulation and was not placed under administrative jurisdiction until the Rate Act of 1906; this tends to show that it was not merely the fact of being a common carrier subject to special power, but more particularly the fact of being a corporation asking for powers, which subjected the railroad company to the extensive and intensive legislative regime which it has experienced.'

These allegations are admitted by the motion to dismiss; and they are supported by recent experience of which we may take notice. But it does not follow that, because the independently owned stores are overcoming through co-operation the advantages once possessed by chain stores, there is no taxable difference between the corporate chain and the single store. The state's power to apply discriminatory taxation as a means of preventing domination of intrastate commerce by capitalistic corporations is not conditioned upon the existence of economic need. It flows from the broader right of Americans to preserve, and to establish from time to time. such institutions, social and economic, as seem to them desirable; and, likewise, to end those which they deem undesirable. The state might, if conditions warranted, subject giant corporations to a control similar to that now exerted over public utility companies. Or the citizens of Florida might conceivably escape from the domination of giant corporations by having the state engage in business. Compare Jones v. City of Portland, 245 U.S. 217, 38 S.Ct. 112, 62 L.Ed. 252.... But Americans seeking escape from corporate domination have open to them under the Constitution another form of social and economic control—one more in keeping with our traditions and aspirations. They may prefer the way of co-operation, which leads directly to the freedom and the equality of opportunity which the Fourteenth Amendment aims to secure. That way is clearly open. For the fundamental difference between capitalistic enterprise and the co-operative—between economic absolutism and industrial democracy—is one which has been commonly accepted by Legislatures and the courts as justifying discrimination in both regulation and taxation....

There is a widespread belief that the existing unemployment is the result, in large part, of the gross inequality in the distribution of wealth and income which giant corporations have fostered; that by the control which the few have exerted through giant corporations individual initiative and effort are being paralyzed, creative power impaired and human happiness lessened; that the true prosperity of our past came not from big business, but through the courage, the energy, and the resourcefulness of small men; that only by releasing from corporate control the faculties of the unknown many, only by reopening to them the opportunities for leadership, can confidence in our future be restored and the existing misery be overcome; and that only through participation by the many in the responsibilities and determinations of business can Americans secure the moral and intellectual development which is essential to the maintenance of liberty. If the citizens of Florida share that belief, I know of nothing in the Federal Constitution which precludes the state from endeavoring to give it effect and prevent domination in intrastate commerce by subjecting corporate chains to discriminatory license fees. To that extent, the citizens of each state are still masters of their destiny.

Mr. Justice CARDOZO, dissenting in part.

[omitted]

Justice Brandeis's dissent has survived in more elaborated form within U.S. law in the context of the participation of American corporations in the political process. Reread Chief Justice Berger's concurrence in *Bellotti*, and the discussion in Chapter 4. The fear of corruption, a subordinate but important theme in *Bellotti*, finds an analogue in *Liggett*. But in *Liggett*, the corruption is not political but economic. The question is one of authority to regulate the economy—is that an authority ultimately vested in the enterprise or in the member state of a federation, or in the nation-state itself?

If that authority flows from a control of economic power, that is from the control of labor, capital and markets, it might now be possible to suggest that some economic enterprises now essentially rival the nation-state. Indeed, from the perspective of the large multi-national corporation, a small nation-state may appear to be little more than the holder of labor or capital, a consumer, or even an economic rival. States within the United States have modified their legal and tax structures to induce large enterprises to use a state's goods and services (its labor and infrastructure). Small nation-states are in a similar position. Small nations, like the Bahamas or Liberia, it has been suggested, have been amenable to adopting maritime registration laws suitable to the needs of global shipping and passenger line enterprises in return for ship registry revenues. It is not clear, in the relations between state and enterprise, where power lies.

Another echo of the dissent finds expression in the enterprise corporatism theory of Gunther Teubner excerpted in Chapter 2. It is possible to argue that state theory is no longer an adequate basis for the conceptualization of the relationship of the largest corporate entities with traditional post-Westphalian nation-states, or their subordinate units. A large multi-national corporation may not be the domiciliary of any state, neither may a large national enterprise in a federal republic like the United States. Moreover, such entities may, in terms of employees (citizens) and property, plant and equipment, dwarf the power of all but the largest nation-states. In that context, it may be difficult to correctly discern which entity regulates and which entity is regulated. Where, as a matter of nation-state policy, it is important to maximize the interests of natural persons irrespective of their citizenship (whether by means of share ownership or employment, creditor, or other relationship) in economic enterprises whose operations cross nation-state borders, it may be necessary to locate the power to regulate at a level of governance larger, or superior, in scope to that of the entities to be regulated. For Brandeis, speaking in the first half of the 20th century, the appropriate level might be the federal government, or the states, backed by the authority of the federal government. Consider whether, in the 21st century, even the largest nation-state can effectively regulate the largest multi-state corporate enterprise.

The worry expressed by Justice Brandeis has been echoed in the work of a number of influential American commentators, among the most important of which was William Cary, a former member of the Securities Exchange Commission. Professor Cary proposed the creation of federal minimum standards for corporate governance, and the abandonment of the notion of the "internal affairs" doctrine as currently conceived. Professor Cary's proposal has generated significant opposition among academics. The strongest criticisms have come from those who argue that Professor Cary's proposal ignores modern American economic theory and reality. Consider the similarities between Professor Cary's proposal and the notions underlying the efforts at the harmonization of European corporate law. The materials which follow outline the American federalization debate.

William L. Cary, *Federalism and Corporate Law, Reflections Upon Delaware*

83 Yale L.J. 663 (1974)

(excerpt pages 700–702; footnotes omitted)

In my opinion, however, [federal incorporation] is politically unrealistic. It has been raised many times in Congress and in the literature but has no public appeal. American business would unanimously reject such a convenient vehicle for government control of the major industries of this country.

* * *

However, in order to remedy the Delaware syndrome it does appear that federal standards of corporate responsibility are called for. This can best be achieved by prescribing minimum corporate law provisions which shall be applicable to companies doing business in interstate commerce and construed by federal judicial standards. Uniformity is of the essence. Efforts must be made to insure that provisions are not interpreted differently owing to varying state interpretations of public policy....

* * *

The proposal is to continue allowing companies to incorporate in the jurisdiction of their choosing but to remove much of the incentive to organize in Delaware or its rival states. Such companies, nevertheless must be subject to the jurisdiction of the federal courts under certain general standards. To illustrate, some of the major provisions of such a federal statute must include: (1) federal fiduciary standards with respect to directors and officers and controlling shareholders; (2) an "interested directors" provision prescribing fairness as a prerequisite to any transaction; (3) a requirement of certain uniform provisions to be incorporated into the certificate of incorporation: for example, authority to amend by-laws, initiate corporate action, or draw up the agenda of shareholders' meetings shall not be vested exclusively in management; (4) a more frequent requirement of shareholder approval of corporate transactions,...; (5) abolition of non-voting shares; (6) the scope of indemnification of directors specifically prescribed and made exclusive; (7) adoption of the long-arm provision of comparable to § 27 of the Securities Exchange Act....

* * *

Mary E. Kostel, *Note: A Public Choice Perspective on the Debate over Federal Versus State Corporate Law*

79 VA. L. REV. 2129 (1993)
(excerpt pages 2129–2135; some footnotes omitted)

INTRODUCTION

Scholars have been debating the wisdom of adopting a federal body of corporate law for the last twenty years, and there are few signs that the dispute between state and federal law will be resolved soon. Some commentators argue that a federal body of regulation would be more efficient than state regulation simply because it would be created federally, others argue that the same fact would make federal regulation necessarily worse, and a third group argues that federal regulation is best suited for some areas of corporate law and state regulation for others.

Many of the scholars who recommend federal regulation have made specific proposals regarding the content of that legislation. However, the recommendation of sophisticated scholars is not enough to get a bill passed by the United States Congress. These scholars have failed to examine the political forces that will come into play in the actual drafting and passing of such regulation.

The Williams Act[1] provides a recent example of federal regulation of corporations. Examining its legislative history, as well as its effects on corporate efficiency and shareholder welfare, may offer some basis for predicting the general contours of a federalized corporate law. The history and effects of the Williams Act suggest that federal regulation is unlikely to monitor better the behavior of corporate management in the gaps where the market for corporate control fails.[2]

Part I of this Note describes the development of the debate over creation of a federal corporation law, coming to rest at a recent and influential contribution to the debate, Professor Lucian Arye Bebchuk's Federalism and the Corporation: The Desirable Limits on State Competition in Corporate Law.[3] Bebchuk aptly points out some of the problems that exist in state regulation but he fails to examine potential federal regulation with the same rigor. Part II briefly describes the public choice theory of the legislative process, which provides the theoretical framework for the Note. Part III examines the legislative history of the Williams Act, concluding that the Act was in all respects pro-management legislation. Part IV explores some of the existing empirical research on the effects of tender offers on shareholder welfare, and the more specific effects of the Williams Act on tender offers and shareholder welfare. This evidence suggests that the disclosure required by the Williams Act is harmful to shareholder welfare in general because it encourages inefficient behavior on the part of management.

Based on the evidence reviewed in Parts III and IV, Part V utilizes the public choice framework and reasons that interest groups are as likely to skew legislation toward management interests—and away from shareholders' interests—at the federal level as at the state level. At best, federal legislation will be equally efficient to that produced by the states. Further, drawing on Bebchuk's own argument, this Part points out that management interest groups will expend more resources lobbying federal legislators than they would spend lobbying state legislators—all to achieve, at best, the same results. This Part concludes that the additional resources expended lobbying federal legislators is pure social waste and should be avoided by leaving corporate regulation to the states.

I. THE CURRENT DEBATE

There are three different theoretical camps concerning the effect of state competition on corporate regulation and the likely consequences of replacing state regulation with a federal monopoly. The first embraces the theory that competition among states results in a "race for the bottom"; the second takes the opposite view, that competition produces a "race for the top"; and the third strikes a middle ground that mixes the conclusions of the first two. All three camps agree on two fundamental points. First, they agree that states have an interest in attracting corporations to incorporate within their boundaries.[7] Incorporation generates state revenues from franchise taxes and fees and in-

1. 15 U.S.C. §§m-78n (1988). Enacted in 1968, Pub. L. No. 90-439, 82 Stat. 454, the Williams Act amended the Securities Exchange Act of 1934, ch. 404, 48 Stat. 881 (codified as amended in scattered sections of 15 U.S.C. (1988)), by requiring disclosure of certain information by tender offerors.

2. *See infra* notes 28–33 and accompanying text for a description of the market for corporate control.

3. 105 Harv. L. Rev. 1435 (1992).

7. *See, e.g.*, William L. Cary, *Federalism and Corporate Law: Reflections Upon Delaware*, 83 Yale L.J. 663, 668–69 (1974); Roberta Romano, *The State Competition Debate in Corporate Law*, 8 Cardozo L. Rev. 709, 710 (1987); Ralph K. Winter, Jr., *State Law, Shareholder Protection, and the Theory of the Corporation*, 6 J. Legal Stud. 251, 254–55 (1977).

creases patronage for "in-state law firms, corporation service companies, and other businesses."[8] Second, they agree that this interest creates an incentive for states to design their laws to attract corporations to incorporate initially, and, more importantly, to reincorporate within their boundaries,[9] thus making the corporations subject to that state's laws.[10] The three camps diverge, however, in their description and evaluation of the effects of such competition among the states, and the efficiency of the corporate regulation it ultimately produces.[11]

A. "Race for the Bottom"

Professor William L. Cary initiated the debate over state versus federal regulation in 1974 with his seminal article, *Federalism and Corporate Law: Reflections Upon Delaware.*[12] He proposed that competition between states to attract corporations produced incentives for the states to design laws that failed adequately to protect shareholders' interests.[13] Cary assumed that states competing for corporate charters have an incentive to design laws that are favorable to management because managers actually decide where to reincorporate.[14] He further reasoned that, because management's interests often do not coincide with those of shareholders,[15] competition would lead to a body of corporation law that would grow less and less favorable to the shareholder.[16] Once a competitive process has begun, states will compete to offer the least shareholder protection, resulting in the so-called "race for the bottom."[17] Cary attributed Delaware's success in state charter competition[18] to its lead in loosening corporate restrictions on management,[19] a development he found alarming.[20]

---

8. Bebchuk, *supra* note [c], at 1451. Theorists within the three camps place differing emphasis on the various rewards to states for attracting corporate charters. For example, compare Cary, *supra* note 7, at 668–69 (emphasizing the generation of tax revenue for the state) with John C. Coffee, Jr., *The Future of Corporate Federalism: State Competition and the New Trend Toward De Facto Federal Minimum Standards*, 8 CARDOZO L. REV. 759, 762–64 (1987) (emphasizing benefits to the corporate bar and "satellite industries" in the state).

9. Bebchuk argues persuasively that reincorporation decisions are more important, for the purposes of this debate, than initial decisions to incorporate. *See* Bebchuk, *supra* note 3, at 1458–61.

10. *See, e.g.*, Cary, *supra* note 7, at 664–66; Romano, *supra* note 7, at 710; Winter, *supra* note 7, at 254–55.

11. The ultimate goal of corporate law is the protection of shareholder wealth. By protecting and increasing such wealth, corporate regulation can encourage investment in ventures that probably would not otherwise take place. *See, e.g.*, Roberta Romano, *The Political Economy of Takeover Statutes*, 73 VA. L. REV. 111, 113 (1987) (describing "the core goal of corporation law" as "the maximization of equity share prices"). The theorists in all three camps accept this fundamental goal of corporate law, but they disagree about the effect of state competition on achieving the goal.

12. 83 YALE L.J. 663 (1974). Cary's argument actually originated with Justice Louis Brandeis' dissent in Louis K. Liggett Co. v. Lee, 288 U.S. 517, 557–64 (1933).

13. *See* Cary, *supra* note 7, at 663–68.

14. *See id.* at 668. This argument was clarified by Jonathan R. Macey and Geoffrey P. Miller in *Toward an Interest-Group Theory of Delaware Corporate Law*, 65 TEX. L. REV. 469, 487 (1987).

15. This premise derives from Professors Berle and Means' idea of the separation of ownership and control, which suggests that managers have interests separate from and often adverse to shareholder's interests. *See* ADOLF A. BERLE, JR. & GARDINER C. MEANS, THE MODERN CORPORATION AND PRIVATE PROPERTY 119–25 (1933).

16. *See* Cary, *supra* note 7, at 696–700.

17. *Id.* at 664–66.

18. At the time of Cary's article, Delaware was "setting the pace" in the race for corporate charters. See id. at 668. That is still the case today. *See, e.g.*, Roberta Romano, *Competition for Corporate Charters and the Lesson of Takeover Statutes*, 61 FORDHAM L. REV. 843, 845–46 (1993).

19. *See* Cary, *supra* note 7, at 668–70.

20. *See id.* at 705.

Concluding that state competition for corporate charters harmed shareholders' interests, Cary urged federal displacement of state regulation.[21] In Cary's view, federal regulation would eliminate the negative effects to shareholders of a competition for corporate charters by eliminating competition altogether.[22] Corporations can flee more readily to another state for incorporation purposes than they can flee from the United States altogether.[23] Because they would be free from the incentive to attract management to their jurisdiction, federal legislators could be more attentive to the protection and advancement of shareholders' interests.[24]

B. "Race for the Top"

Judge Ralph K. Winter, Jr., along with a substantial following, agrees with Cary that states have an incentive to design laws that will attract corporate charters, but sharply disagrees with his conclusion.[25] Winter and his supporters argue instead that competition between states is likely to produce the optimal amount of shareholder protection.[26]

These theorists attack Cary for ignoring an important force constraining corporate management: the market for corporate control.[27] Henry G. Manne first developed the theory of the market for corporate control in 1965.[28] Manne argued that proxy contests and, especially, the tender offer create market-based incentives for efficient corporate management and thus make legal regulation largely irrelevant.[29] According to Manne, the threat of a takeover induces current management to run the corporation efficiently: inefficient management signals corporate raiders that there are profits to be made by takeover, whereas less "fat" means fewer returns to be gained from a takeover.[30] The more efficiently a corporation is run, the less likely it is that a potential competitor for control would want to acquire the corporation.[31] This market-produced check on man-

---

21. *See id.* at 696–701.

22. *See id.*

23. Cf. Charles M. Tiebout, *A Pure Theory of Local Expenditures*, 64 J. Pol. Econ. 416, 418 (1956) (describing how "consumer-voters" will choose to live in the community whose local government most closely satisfies their revenue and expenditure preferences and noting that the provision of public goods at the federal level does not produce similar opportunities for selection).

24. Cary, *supra* note 7, at 701–02. Cary notes, though, that federal legislators would also be subject to political pressure from big business. *See id.* at 702–03.

25. *See* Winter, *supra* note 7; *see also* Peter Dodd & Richard Leftwich, *The Market for Corporate Charters: "Unhealthy Competition" versus Federal Regulation*, 53 L. Bus. 259 (1980) (concluding that competition among states allows management to select the state with rules most favorable to the firm's planned investment and activities, thus benefitting shareholders); Frank H. Easterbrook, *Managers' Discretion and Investors' Welfare: Theories and Evidence*, 9 Del. J. Corp. L. 540 (1984) (asserting that competition among states, by creating a market for corporate control, leads managers to act in the best interests of investors); Frank H. Easterbrook & Daniel R. Fischel, *Voting in Corporate Law*, 26 J.L. & Econ. 395 (1983) (rejecting proposals for federal regulation as more detrimental to shareholders' interests); Daniel R. Fischel, *The "Race to the Bottom" Revisited: Reflections on Recent Developments in Delaware's Corporation Law*, 76 Nw. U. L. Rev. 913 (1982) (criticizing the "race for the bottom" thesis and arguing that managers, in choosing among competing states, will act in the shareholders' best interests).

26. *See generally* sources cited supra note 25.

27. *See* Easterbrook, *supra* note 25, at 549–50, 564–71; Fischel, *supra* note 25, at 916–20; Winter, *supra* note 7, at 256.

28. *See* Henry G. Manne, *Mergers and the Market for Corporate Control*, 73 J. Pol. Econ. 110 (1965).

29. *See id.* at 113.

30. *See id.* at 112–13.

31. *Id.*

agement, Manne argued, aligns the interests of management with those of shareholders, obviating the need for a body of law[32] that constrains the behavior of management.[33]

Proponents of state regulation embraced Manne's hypothesis, arguing that because the market for corporate control aligns management and shareholder interests, states will have incentives to offer shareholder-favorable law. Indeed, state competition for corporate charters will produce a body of law that approaches optimal protection of shareholders' interests.[34] Far from creating a "race for the bottom," competition instead will produce a "race for the top." Thus, this group of scholars concludes that corporate regulation is best left in the hands of the individual states.[35]

C. Third Camp: A Mix of the Two Theories

More recent scholarship has drawn from both theories to better reflect the empirical evidence about the effects of competition among the states. Essentially, the third camp distinguishes among the market effects on management behavior, positing that the market for corporate control efficiently checks the behavior of corporate management in some areas but fails in others.[36]

One of the proponents of this approach, Roberta Romano, counters Cary's interpretation of the evidence of Delaware's outstanding success in the competition for charters.[37] Romano argues that Delaware's success is due to the state's ability to "race for the top" with regard to some issues and "race for the bottom" with regard to others, and the stable and predictable body of law that it offers corporations and managers.[38] Romano suggests a number of factors, specific to Delaware, that help ensure such stability and predictability. First, because the revenues generated by corporate regulation make up a larger percentage of total state revenues in a small state such as Delaware than they would in larger states, Delaware has more to lose than larger states by alienating resident corporations.[39] Second, Delaware's initial success in the competition for corporate charters has resulted in the development of a judiciary that is very sophisticated in corporate matters and thus more likely to render individual decisions with an eye toward developing a cohesive body of corporate law.[40] Third, the state's success in attracting corporations also has produced a substantial industry—including the corporate bar—with a special interest in retaining a body of law with which it is familiar.[41] Romano suggests that, although she does not think it perfect, "[a] middle ground between Cary's

---

32. Manne specifically addressed the body of antitrust law in the merger context. *See id.* at 119.

33. *See id.* at 112–13, 119–20.

34. Easterbrook, *supra* note 25, at 570–71; Fischel, *supra* note 25, at 919–20; Winter, *supra* note 7, at 273–76, 289–92.

35. *See* Dodd & Leftwich, *supra* note 25, at 281–82; Easterbrook, *supra* note 25, at 571; Fischel, *supra* note 25, at 921–23; Winter, *supra* note 7, at 290–92.

36. *See, e.g.*, Bebchuk, *supra* note 3, at 1440; Romano, *supra* note 7, at 752–53.

37. *See* Romano, *supra* note 7, at 720–25.

38. *Id.* Bebchuk calls this the "race for predictability and stability." Bebchuk, *supra* note 3, at 1446.

39. Romano, *supra* note 7, at 721–23.

40. *Id.* at 722.

41. *Id.* at 723–24. Public choice theory similarly posits that laws reflect preferences of interest groups. *See infra* Part II. Cary makes this point as well, but as support for an argument that on some issues the state will make management-unfavorable law (i.e., law that encourages more litigation) to curry the favor of the powerful corporate bar. *See* Cary, *supra* note 7, at 686–88. John C. Coffee, Jr., describes the corporate bar as an interest group and asserts that it is the primary force driving corporate law in Delaware. *See* Coffee, *supra* note 8, at 761–64.

and Winter's positions...[is] the most reasonable position...given current knowledge."[42]

Building on Romano's work, Bebchuk argues in a recent article that although competition between states generally produces law that protects shareholders' interests, there are three specific areas of corporate governance where competition has the opposite effect—that of producing management-favorable law at shareholders' expense—that therefore require federal regulation.[43] Bebchuk identifies those areas as follows:

> First,...issues that involve a potential transfer of significant value from shareholders to managers [relative to the size of the potential efficiency consequences of the arrangement governing the issue]...includ [ing] self-dealing transactions, taking of corporate opportunities, and insider trading. Second,...issues that directly affect the strength of market discipline [of management], such as the regulation of takeover bids and proxy contests. Third,...issues that involve potential transfers between public shareholders and controlling shareholders, such as the regulation of going-private and parent-subsidiary freezeouts.[44]

Daniel R. Fischel, *The "Race to the Bottom" Revisited: Reflections on Recent Developments in Delaware's Corporation Law*

76 Nw. U. L. Rev. 913 (1982)
(excerpts pages 913–917, 919–920; some footnotes omitted)

The extent to which state corporation law provides adequate protection for shareholders' interests has been a subject of considerable controversy in recent years.[1] The debate has been particularly heated with respect to the Delaware corporation law, due to the high percentage of firms that have chosen to incorporate, or reincorporate, in Delaware.[2] In a highly publicized article, Professor William Cary, former Chairman of the Securities and Exchange Commission, has argued that Delaware has achieved this

---

42. Romano, *supra* note 7, at 752–53.

43. Bebchuk, *supra* note 3, at 1441, 1458–84.

44. *Id.* at 1441. Bebchuk also argues that state competition for corporate charters leads to socially undesirable results regarding the interests of externalities, including creditors, potential buyers, and other third parties. *Id.* at 1456, 1485–95....

1. Most commentators have argued that state statutes provide inadequate protection for shareholders' interests. *See, e.g.*, Cary, *Federalism and Corporate Law: Reflections Upon Delaware*, 83 Yale L.J. 663 (1974); Folk, *Corporation Statutes: 1959–1966*, 1966 Duke L.J. 875; Kaplan, *Fiduciary Responsibility in the Management of the Corporation*, 31 Bus. Law. 883 (1976); Jennings, *Federalization of Corporation Law: Part Way or All the Way*, 31 Bus. Law. 991 (1976); Schwartz, *Symposium—Federal Chartering of Corporations: An Introduction*, 61 Geo. L.J. 71 (1972); Young, *Federal Corporate Law, Federalism, and the Federal Courts*, 41 Law & Contemp. Probs. 146 (1977). *But see* R. Wintyer, Government and the Corporation (1978); Arsht, *Reply to Professor Cary*, 31 Bus. Law. 1113 (1976) (arguing that Delaware corporation law adequately protects shareholders); Manning, *Thinking Straight About Corporation Law Reform*, 41 Law & Contemp. Probs. 3, 15–19 (1977).

2. For a statistical demonstration of Delaware's dominance in the market for incorporations, and particularly, in the market for reincorporations, *see* Dodd & Leftwich, *The Market for Corporate Charters: "Unhealthy Competition" versus Federal Regulation*, 53 J. Bus. 259 (1980).

dominance by virtue of its liberal or "enabling" corporation statute (as interpreted by judicial decisions) which allows management to further its own interests at the expense of those of the shareholders.[3] In Cary's view, Delaware's prominent role in corporation law has been achieved as a result of its success in the "race for the bottom."[4]

Cary's attack on the laxity of state corporation laws, and of Delaware law in particular, has been echoed by numerous leading law professors and social reformers, who have advocated various forms of federal regulation of corporations.[5] Federal regulation is necessary, proponents argue, to ensure that shareholders receive the necessary protection which has not been provided under state corporation law....[6]

* * *

Professor Cary and the other proponents of the "race to the bottom" thesis have focused on the revenue that is produced for a state which attracts corporate incorporations. The search for revenue, the argument runs, has led states, particularly Delaware, to attempt to create a favorable climate for management in order to attract new business. The result has been the enactment of enabling statutes which allow management to run the corporation's affairs with little interference from shareholders or the courts.[11] These enabling statutes "have watered the rights of shareholders vis-a-vis management down to a thin gruel."[12] This effect has been exacerbated by the Delaware courts which,

---

3. Cary, note 1, *supra*.

4. *Id.* The phrase, "race for the bottom," is Cary's. *See id.* at 666.

5. *See, e.g.*, R. Nader, M. Green & J. Seligman, Constitutionalizing the Corporation: The Case for the Federal Chatering of Giant Corporations (1976); Cary, note 1 *supra*; Schwartz, *Towards New Corporate Goals: Co-existence with Society*, 60 Geo. L.J. 57(1971). *See generally* Hearings on Corporate Rights and Responsibilities Before the Senate Comm. on Commerce, 94th Cong., 2d Sess. (1976) [hereinafter cited as Senate Hearings on Corporate Rights]; *Symposium on Federal and State Roles in Establishing Standards of Conduct for Corporate Management*, 31 Bus. Law. 859–1213 (1976).

6. *See generally* Senate Hearings on Corporate Rights, note 5 *supra*. Entered into the record as a part of these hearings was the following statement, signed by 80 law professors at 62 different law schools:

> As law teachers who have had a special opportunity to study the law of corporations from an independent perspective and to reflect on the proper function of corporation law and the extent to which the law in its current state fulfills that function, we have a particular interest in the current hearings on the possibility of an expanded federal role in corporation law.
>
> While we believe that it would be difficult if not impossible at this time to achieve a consensus among us as to the precise role the federal government should play in shaping the organic law of corporations, we are in general agreement that state corporation statutes and case law have suffered over the years from what Professor William Cary of Columbia University has called a "race to the bottom," and that as a consequence they no longer adequately serve to guide and regulate the activity of large corporations and their managers, as is the proper role of organic law. We also believe that, with the Supreme Court apparently in the process of drawing limits against the further expansion of federal regulation of corporations through the medium of the securities laws, and with public concern about various kinds of corporate impropriety running at a high level, there is a particular urgency at this time for the Congress to consider some form of federal intervention in this area, whether through the means of a federal chartering statute, through federal "minimum standards" for state corporation laws, or some other mechanism.

Id. at 344.

11. Cary, *supra* note 1, at 666.

12. *Id.*

as a result of an incestuous relationship with legislators and the practicing bar,[13] have adopted a "laissez-faire attitude"[14] and thus have "contributed to shrinking the concept of fiduciary responsibility and fairness."[15]

Widespread reform is thought necessary to remedy this "race to the bottom." There is no reason, Professor Cary argues, why "the policy of a single state occupying a critical position should be permitted to grant management unilateral control untrammeled by other interests."[16] Rather, "[t]here is a need for uniformity in standards to prevent the application of Gresham's law."[17] To provide this uniformity, Cary advocates increased federal regulation of corporations. He proposes a "Federal Corporate Uniformity Act" that would "remove much of the incentive to organize in Delaware or in rival states."[18] This proposed statute would include, inter alia, federal minimum fiduciary standards, a requirement that certain uniform provisions be included in the certificate of incorporation to ensure more shareholder control, and a requirement of more frequent shareholder approval of corporate transactions.[19]

Other proposals for federal regulation to fill the gap left by the absence of meaningful state regulation go even further. The recently proposed Corporate Democracy Act of 1980[20] and Protection of Shareholders' Right Act of 1980,[21] would, for example, require that a majority of a corporation's board be composed of independent directors; that some committees be composed entirely of such directors; that extensive disclosure be made in regard to such matters as planned plant closings and compliance with environmental controls; that a shareholder vote be conducted on major corporate transactions; and that cumulative voting be used in all Directors' elections. Thus far, none of the proposals for federal regulation have been adopted.

* * *

The difficulty with... the "race to the bottom" thesis itself is that these theories are based on a model of shareholder irrationality.[23] Why, given the infinite number of alternative investment opportunities, do shareholders voluntarily entrust their money to managers who have no incentive to maximize their welfare? And why would shareholders ever voluntarily invest in firms located in Delaware, given its alleged promanagement bias which supposedly exacerbates the detriment to shareholders caused by the separation of ownership and control?[24] The extreme unlikelihood that investors would behave in this irrational manner suggests that the Berle-Means-Cary thesis is based on an erroneous premise regarding the structure of the modern publicly held corporation. Recent contributions to the literature on the theory of the firm suggest that the premise is indeed flawed.

---

13. *Id.* at 690–92.
14. *Id.* at 690.
15. *Id.* at 696.
16. *Id.* at 698.
17. *Id.*
18. *Id.* at 701–02.
19. *Id.*
20. H.R. 7010, 96th Cong., 2d Sess. (1980).
21. S. 2567, 96th Cong., 2d Sess. (1980).
23. For a persuasive refutation of the "race to the bottom" thesis, *see* R. Winter, note 1 *supra*.
24. Shareholders would not be acting irrationally if shares of corporations incorporated in Delaware traded at a lower price....

* * *

.... The decision of where to incorporate is one of countless decisions that managers must make as agents for the firm. For the reasons discussed above, managers have compelling incentives to make this decision in the shareholders' best interests. If incorporation in Delaware were really harmful to shareholders, shares of firms located there would trade for less, managers would reduce the value of their services, and the firm might be an attractive takeover candidate with the probable result that existing managers would be displaced. Since managers have no incentive to injure themselves in this fashion, a far more likely explanation is that Delaware has achieved its prominent position because its permissive corporation law maximizes, rather than minimizes, shareholders' welfare. Delaware's preeminence, in short, is in all probability attributable to success in a "climb to the top" rather than to victory in a "race to the bottom."

Comments and Questions: Is Federalizing Corporate Law the Answer?

1. There is power in the federal government to federalize corporate law. There appears to be little political will at the moment to actually legislate a federal corporate statute. Were the political climate to change, there would be at least two means of federalizing corporate law. The first would impose a uniform federal corporate law that preempts state power over incorporation. This would be the "cleanest" and the most politically difficult approach. Moreover it is not clear that constitutional principles of federalism, among others, might not make this approach legally impossible, do you agree? The other approach would involve the enactment of a federal corporate statute, but one preserving the rights of states to continue to make incorporation available under state law. What purpose would this approach serve? Would the result be a migration of corporations from state to federal incorporation? What would be the effect on statutes such as California Corporations Code Section 2115 discussed in the prior chapter?

2. Even if the federal government chose to enact a federal corporate statute, it can limit the availability of federal incorporation, for example to enterprises meeting certain criteria, perhaps only those companies subject to the federal securities acts. What would be the benefit of this approach?

3. Even in the absence of federal legislation, is it possible to suggest that corporate law has, to some extent, already been federalized? It is possible to argue that corporate law has been federalized since the Great Depression, when the United States enacted the first of a number of provisions regulating the markets for transactions in shares. The regulation was indirect—interests in corporations, not corporations themselves, were the object of regulation. However, these regulations had a practical effect on the order of the fundamental relationships between shareholders, officers and managers. This practical effect was accomplished through the application of the extreme principle of transparency at the foundation of the securities acts of the 1930s and thereafter. Corporations were required to modify their behavior, at least to the extent that disclosure raised expectations of conduct. These intrusions into corporate conduct were limited not only by their character as indirect legislation, but also because their application was limited to companies whose securities were offered to the public. Yet even this limitation might be seen as more theoretical than real. To the extent that lenders, other creditors, and other partici-

pants in the corporate enterprise expect uniformity and predictability in business formation and conduct, the model will likely be the large, public corporation. To the extent that this is true, the expectations among those who may be asked to participate in even the smallest corporate enterprise might therefore require modeling the enterprise on those subject to federal securities legislation, at least to some degree. Failure to do so may raise the cost of borrowing, because lenders may interpret the failure as raising the risk of their security, or may make employees, lenders or others unavailable to the corporate enterprise, because of the perception that deviation increases risk. To what extent do you agree with this analysis? Are there credible counterarguments? Can you make them?

4. **Problem:** A new President has been elected in the United States. He has secured the election, in part, on a promise to federalize corporate law—"for the benefit of all the little people, grandma shareholders and others who need protection of their share of the American dream..." The president, through the Secretary of Commerce, has announced the creation of a blue ribbon panel to be chaired by the Secretary of Commerce, for the purpose of drafting a new federal corporate law. You are the Senior Vice President of Strategic Planning at the corporate offices of Conglomo, Inc., a Delaware corporation. The President of Conglomo, Mr. Hugehead, is the director of a large trade association that has been asked to provide a member of the President's blue ribbon committee. Mr. Hugehead has asked you to take that position, provided you are able to convince him that you understand the issues involved, including the nature of all possible options the committee might consider and their ramifications for American corporations. Prepare a presentation for delivery to the Board of Directors of the trade association discussing this topic in detail.

B. The Context of Federalization Within Europe

EU company law harmonization efforts are based on the authority given the EC Commission and EU Council to legislate. While treaties, regulation, and conventions are of some importance in EU legislation generally, in the area of company law harmonization, the EC harmonization efforts are contained in a number of directives (the effect of which are discussed below). This focus is "suggested" by the EC Treaty which provides that, in connection with its work on the abolition of restrictions of free establishment, "the Council shall, acting on a proposal from the Commission, in co-operation with the European Parliament and after consulting with the Economic and Social Committee, issue directives...." EC Treaty, Art. 44(2) [ex Art. 54(2)]. However, the Council is not strictly limited to legislating by directive in the area of company law. "If action by the Community should prove necessary to attain, in the course of the operation of the common market, one of the objectives of the Community and this Treaty has not provided the necessary powers, the Council shall, acting unanimously on a proposal from the Commission and after consulting the Assembly, take the appropriate measure." EC Treaty, Art. 308 [ex Art. 235]. The legislative bodies of the Communities have taken a fairly broad view of the scope of powers granted through this provision, and the Council has, from time to time contemplated legislation by regulation in the area of company law harmonization.

Company harmonization directives and harmonization efforts in general have concentrated in the following areas: (i) disclosure of corporate information; (ii) the formation, capitalization, and management requirements for public companies, (iii) mergers and divisions of companies, (iv) accounting principles and audits, (v) employee participation in the management of public companies, (vi) uniform requirements for small and medium sized enterprises, and (vii) management of company groups. Regulation has generally been limited to proposals for the creation of supra-national corporate entities, the European Economic Interest Grouping and the Societas Europae.

In this section, you will be introduced to the sources of Community law. In the next section, the process of legislation in the European Community is discussed.

1. At the Constitutional Level: Treaties

Member States are bound by international law to carry out the terms of the Treaties which they have adopted. In the case of the ECSC Treaty, the EURATOM Treaty, and the EEC Treaty (including amendment) Member State treaty obligations have assumed quasi-constitutional status.

The actual status of those treaties within the constitutional orders of the Member States is not uniform. The treaties can be deemed either to be self-executing or merely creating obligations on the part of the signatory's government to enact implementing legislation. In that connection consider the following:

Foster v. Neilson

2 U.S (Pet.) 253 (1829)

[Dispute as to title to certain land in territory ceded from Spain to the United States. The issue resolved around the interpretation of the Treaty of St. Ildefonso, pursuant to which Spain ceded the territory in question. The treaty provided that all land grants made by the King of Spain before January 24, 1818 were to be ratified and confirmed to the persons in possession. The Supreme Court held that the provision was not self-executing—the ratification called for by the treaty required an act of the legislature to implement. Until Congress passed legislation confirming such grants, the courts were constrained to follow existing legislation with respect to land claims in the territory. The opinion continues at 2 U.S. (Pet.) 314–315:]

A treaty is in its nature a contract between two nations, not a Legislative Act. It does not generally effect, of itself, the object to be accomplished, especially so far as its operation is intraterritorial; but is carried into execution by the sovereign power of the respective parties to the instrument.

In the United States a different principle is established. Our Constitution declares a Treaty to be the law of the land. It is, consequently, to be regarded in the courts of justice as equivalent to an Act of the Legislature, whenever it operates of itself without the aid of any legislative provision. But when the terms of the stipulation import a contract—when either of the parties engages to perform a particular act—the treaty addresses itself to the political, not the judicial department; and the Legislature must execute the contract before it can become the rule for the court.

The article under consideration does not declare that all grants made by His Catholic Majesty before the 24th of January, 1818, shall be valid to the same extent as if the ceded territories had remained under his dominion. It does not say that those grants are hereby confirmed. Had such been the language, it would have acted directly on the subject, and it would have repealed those Acts of Congress which were repugnant to it; but its language is that the those grants shall be ratified and confirmed to those persons in possession, etc. By whom shall they be ratified and confirmed? This seems to be the language of contract; and if it is, the ratification and confirmation which are promised must be the Act of the Legislature. Until such Act shall be passed, the court is not at liberty to disregard the existing laws on the subject.....

* * *

Many commentators, and the ECJ, have taken the position that the founding treaties are all self-executing. At the time they were ratified, they became the law of the ratifying nation without the need to adopt legislation enacting the actions contemplated by the treaty. Thus, the EC Treaty, ECSC Treaty, and the EURATOM Treaties are the law of the land in each of the Member States. As the law of the land, the applicable provisions of the Treaties must be applied and enforced by the national courts of the Member States. "Member States shall take all appropriate measures, whether general or particular, to ensure fulfillment of the obligations arising out of this Treaty or resulting from action taken by the Institutions of the Community." EEC Treaty, Art. 5. Indeed, as discussed above, the signatories of these treaties have invested a supra-national court, the ECJ, with the power to enforce and interpret such obligations, and has given this court the power to bind individual subjects of the Member States, not just the Member States themselves. The ECJ has explained that the "EEC Treaty has created its own legal system which, on the entry into force of the Treaty, became an integral part of the legal; systems of the Member States and which their courts are bound to apply." *Costa v. ENEL* [1964] E.C.R. 585, 593. Note, however, that opinion in this regard is not unanimous. Some believe that the founding treaties are no more than a collection of contractual obligations which must be implemented by Member States. This seems to be the minority view at the moment. For the argument of the majority view, see, D. Lasok & J.W. Bridge, Law and Institutions of the European Communities 113–118 (5th ed. 1991).

Treaty Establishing the European Economic Community

Arts. 44 (ex 54); 95 (ex 100a)

Consolidated Version of the Treaty Establishing the European Community available at
http://www.europa.eu.int/eur-lex/en/treaties/indext.html
pages 57–59

Chapter 2
Right of establishment

Article 44 (ex Article 54)

1. In order to attain freedom of establishment as regards a particular activity, the Council, acting in accordance with the procedure referred to in Article 251 and after consulting the Economic and Social Committee, shall act by means of directives.

2. The Council and the Commission shall carry out the duties devolving upon them under the preceding provisions, in particular:

a) by according, as a general rule, priority treatment to activities where freedom of establishment makes a particularly valuable contribution to the development of production and trade;

(b) by ensuring close cooperation between the competent authorities in the Member States in order to ascertain the particular situation within the Community of the various activities concerned;

(c) by abolishing those administrative procedures and practices, whether resulting from national legislation or from agreements previously concluded between Member States, the maintenance of which would form an obstacle to freedom of establishment;

(d) by ensuring that workers of one Member State employed in the territory of another Member State may remain in that territory for the purpose of taking up activities therein as self-employed persons, where they satisfy the conditions which they would be required to satisfy if they were entering that State at the time when they intended to take up such activities;

(e) by enabling a national of one Member State to acquire and use land and buildings situated in the territory of another Member State, insofar as this does not conflict with the principles laid down in Article 33(2);

(f) by effecting the progressive abolition of restrictions on freedom of establishment in every branch of activity under consideration, both as regards the conditions for setting up Treaty establishing the European Community agencies, branches or subsidiaries in the territory of a Member State and as regards the subsidiaries in the territory of a Member State and as regards the conditions governing the entry of personnel belonging to the main establishment into managerial or supervisory posts in such agencies, branches or subsidiaries;

(g) by coordinating to the necessary extent the safeguards which, for the protection of the interests of members and other, are required by Member States of companies or firms within the meaning of the second paragraph of Article 48 with a view to making such safeguards equivalent throughout the Community;

(h) by satisfying themselves that the conditions of establishment are not distorted by aids granted by Member States.

Article 45 (ex Article 55)

The provisions of this Chapter shall not apply, so far as any given Member State is concerned, to activities which in that State are connected, even occasionally, with the exercise of official authority. The Council may, acting by a qualified majority on a proposal from the Commission, rule that the provisions of this Chapter shall not apply to certain activities.

Article 46 (ex Article 56)

1. The provisions of this Chapter and measures taken in pursuance thereof shall not prejudice the applicability of provisions laid down by law, regulation or administrative action providing for special treatment for foreign nationals on grounds of public policy, public security or public health.

2. The Council shall, acting in accordance with the procedure referred to in Article 251, issue directives for the coordination of the abovementioned provisions.

* * *

Chapter 3

Approximation of laws

Article 94 (ex Article 100)

The Council shall, acting unanimously on a proposal from the Commission and after consulting the European Parliament and the Economic and Social Committee, issue directives for the approximation of such laws, regulations or administrative provisions of the Member States as directly affect the establishment or functioning of the common market.

Article 95 (ex Article 100a)

1. By way of derogation from Article 94 and save where otherwise provided in this Treaty, the following provisions shall apply for the achievement of the objectives set out in Article 14. The Council shall, acting in accordance with the procedure referred to in Article 251 and after consulting the Economic and Social Committee, adopt the measures for the approximation of the provisions laid down by law, regulation or administrative action in Member States which have as their object the establishment and functioning of the internal market.

* * *

Josef Drexl, *Was Sir Francis Drake a Dutchman?—British Supremacy of Parliament After Factortame*

41 Am. J. Comp. L. 551 (1993)

(excerpts pages 553–554; some footnotes omitted)

Although none of the three European Treaties provided for such a principle explicitly, the European Court of Justice made clear that Community law overrides inconsistent national law (supremacy of Community law).

In *Van Gend en Loos*, the European Court of Justice acknowledged that—under certain circumstances—provisions of the Treaties, on the basis of a new legal order, distinct from international law, are possible sources of individual rights with direct effect in the Member States and those rights will supersede national law.[9] In *Costa v. ENEL*, the European Court of Justice extended the doctrine of direct effect and primacy of Treaty provisions to conflicts with subsequent national law.[10] The Court held:

> The transfer, by member States, from their national orders in favour of the Community order of the rights and obligations arising from the Treaty, carries with it a clear limitation of their sovereign right upon which a subsequent unilateral law, incompatible with the aims of the Community, cannot prevail.

In the *Simmenthal* case, the European Court of Justice decided how national courts have to deal with conflicts between national and superseding Community law. The Court held:[11]

---

9. Case 26/62, Van Gend en Loos v. Nederlandse Asministratie der Belastingen [1963] E.C.R. 1.

10. Case 6/64, Costa v. ENEL, [1964] E.C.R. 585.

11. Case 106/77, Amministrazione delle Finanze dello Stato v. Simmenthal spa, [1978] E.C.R. 629, 643 et seq.

> [I]n accordance with the principle of the precedence of Community law, the relationship between provisions of the Treaty and directly applicable measures of the institutions on the one hand and the national law of the member states on the other is such that those provisions and measures not only by their entry into force render automatically inapplicable any conflicting provisions of current national law but—in so far as they are an integral part of, and take the precedence in, the legal order applicable in the territory of each of the member States—also preclude the valid adoption of new national legislative measures to the extent to which they would be incompatible with Community provisions.

And furthermore:

> [E]very national court must, in a case within its jurisdiction, apply Community law in its entirety and protect rights which the latter confers on individuals and must accordingly set aside any provision of national law which may conflict with it, whether prior or subsequent to te Community rule.

The principle of supremacy of Community law can be summed up as follows:

(1) Community law creates a new legal order that supersedes the legal systems of the Member States.

(2) Community regulations (Art. 189, EC Treaty) are directly applicable and provisions of the Treaties and directives (Art. 189, EC Treaty) may—under certain conditions—have direct effect in the national legal system.

(3) Whenever a conflict of Community law and national law arises, Community law prevails.

(4) Individuals can invoke rights granted by community law in national courts.

(5) National courts have to disregard domestic law whereever community law prevails. there is no automatic invalidation.[12]

Richard M. Buxbaum and Klaus J. Hopt, *Legal Harmonization and the Business Enterprise: Corporate and Capital Market Law Harmonization Policy in Europe and the U.S.A.*

(1988)

(excerpt pages 194–195; some footnotes omitted)

* * *

Article 2 of the EEC Treaty states the objectives that should be legally binding on the European Economic Community. It identifies two intermediate objectives and five ultimate goals. Initially, a Common Market was to be established and the economic policies of the Member States were to be progressively approximated. This was expected to bring

12. National law is applicable where a conflict does not arise. The Treaties, with some exceptions, only deal with transborder cases and, only to this extent, vest rights in individuals. Hence, Germany may not restrict imports of beers from other Member States that do not comply with the strict German brewing laws, but Germany may apply such rules under community law, to domestic production. Harmonizing community legislation, on the other hand, applies both to transborder and exclusively national situations.

about the ultimate objectives of the Treaty: harmonious development of economic activities throughout the Community, the continuous and balanced economic expansion of the Community, an increase in economic stability within the Community, an accelerated raising of the standard of living, and closer relations between all Member States.

Article 3 of the Treaty then summarizes eleven specific activities for the Community which were designed to achieve the goals discussed above. One of these, stated as Article 3(c), is "the abolition, as between Member States, of obstacles to freedom of movement for persons, services and capital." Similarly, Article 3(h) provides for "the approximation of the laws of Member States to the extent required for the proper functioning of the Common Market." Both of these methods are described in more liberal detail later in the Treaty. In 1987 Article 8A of the Treaty added a new policy objective as to the establishment of the internal market by 1992.

The company law harmonization process is described in Article 54(3)(g), and the approximation of the laws is discussed in Article 100 and, as far as the realization of the internal market is concerned, in Article 100A (since 1987). The purpose of these means follow only in general terms. The Treaty states that company law harmonization is to be carried on "to the necessary extent" (Article 54), and that general approximation of laws is to be pursued only in respect of such legal and administrative provisions "as directly affect the establishment or functioning of the common market" (Article 100; without this restriction, now Article 100A). These provisions are further supported by the basic principle of the Community embodied in the general ban on discrimination contained in Article 12 [old Art.6] of the Treaty. This states that within the scope of the application of the Treaty any discrimination on the grounds of nationality is prohibited. The ban applies to legal persons and companies as well as sovereign governments.

* * *

---

2. *Regulations (EC Treaty, Arts. 249–256, ex Arts. 189–192)*

The quasi-federal nature of the Community by the EC Treaty is most clearly evidenced by the legislative power with which the EC Council has been vested, which is binding on the Member States to the same extent as if such had been enacted by national legislatures. The Member States have agreed, that "In order to carry out their task, the Council and the Commission shall, in accordance with the provisions of this Treaty, make regulations, issues directives, take decisions, make recommendations, or deliver opinions." EC Treaty, Art. 249. Regulations and directives have binding effect. They will be considered in more detail below.

Regulations are given direct general application by the EC Treaty by Art. 249.

> "....national courts must take cognizance of regulations as legal instruments whose validity and recognition by national courts must not be conditioned on national procedures of incorporation into the national legal order. Whether or not *particular provisions* of such an instrument in fact give rise to rights in individuals which national courts must safeguard is a matter of interpretation of the provisions concerned, in light of the criteria established by the Court of Justice with respect to the direct application of provisions of the Treaty. This is the better view

and is quite consistent with the decided cases, though the Court has gone out of its way to clarify the matter."

* * *

Regulations, in short, are to be treated as "law" in every sense of the word. National courts must take judicial notice of them in their entirety; specific provisions contained therein may bestow on individuals rights as against other individuals or Member States; and their effect in a particular area may be to preempt national legislative competence. DERRICK WYATT & ALAN DASHWOOD, THE SUBSTANTIVE LAW OF THE EEC 39, 41 (1987).

The EEIG

Regulations have been used infrequently in the process of company law harmonization. In particular, these regulations represent an attempt to further the policies and aims of the EC as expressed in Art. 44(3)(f) of the EC TREATY ("by effecting the progressive abolition of restrictions on freedom of establishment...."), and have been effected pursuant to the authority of Arts. 249, and 308 of the EC TREATY. The... regulation of principal interest in the area of company law harmonization [is] Council Regulation (EEC) No. 213/85 (July 25, 1985), creating European Economic Interest Grouping ("EEIG").

The EEIG is aimed at facilitating cooperation among companies registered in the Member States which are engaged in joint activities. It is modeled on the French *Groupement a l'Interet Economique.* The EEIG permits companies to jointly conduct a portion of their economic activity—research and development, a particular project, etc.—while retaining their economic and legal independence within a structure which is treated as a separate legal entity. It is meant primarily to provide a vehicle enabling the members to undertake activities they could not otherwise undertake, for instance, joint production or joint bidding on large projects. The entity itself is not supposed to be a profit making operation. It is created by contract and acquires its status as a separate legal entity upon its registration in accordance with the requirements of the Regulation. That legal personality will be dependant on the law of the Member State in which it is registered. The EEIG is managed by its members and a group of managers, as provided in the contract of formation. Except to the extent covered in the regulation, the EEIG is subject to the laws of the Member States in which it operated and in which it is registered. Last, EEIG's have certain other limitations—they may not employ more than 500 people, be involved in the management or ownership of its members or participate in another EEIG. While a step in the creation of a real supra-national entity, the EEIG is still substantially bound by the (differing) laws of the Member States.

The Saga of the European Company

While theorists and advocates in the United States have been urging consideration of federal corporate law legislation, the institutions of the European Union have gone much farther. Over the course of the last third of the 20th century, and continuing today, the institutions of the European Community have proposed the creation of an EU wide form of "federally chartered" corporation, the *Societas Europeae* ("SE"). The

SE would operate outside the national laws of the Member States and be subject to the new European company law. The proposal for the creation of such an entity has had a very long, complex and controversial history. The idea of such an entity has been considered seriously since at least 1970, when the EC Commission proposed a European Company Statute (see 13 J.O. Comm. Eur. (No. C 124) 1 (October 10, 1970). The major points of controversy currently appear to be the insistence that the SE follow German practice and permit worker participation in management, and the inability of the Member States to satisfactorily harmonize their business accounting practices.[1] The excerpts that follow discuss the SE in various contexts. Terence L. Blackburn, *The Societas Europeana: The Evolving European Corporation Statute*, 61 FORDHAM L. REV. 695 (1993), explores the SE itself. Vanessa Edwards, in *EC Company Law*, provides an analysis of the politics of missed opportunities and the reluctant federalism of the Member States of the European Union. The idea of a 'federal' statute for an EU Corporation law remains very much alive today. The impediments to enactment however, have not changed much either.

European Communities Commission, Statute for a European Company

Proposal for a Regulation on a Statute for a European Company
presented by the Commission to the Council, 25 August 1989
Document drawn up on the basis of COM(89) 268 final
Bull. Supp. 5/89
(Preface; pages 7–9)

Background

Nearly 20 years ago the Commission proposed a statute for a company to be created under European law, since it considered that the existence of such a statute was necessary for the establishment of the common market.

Since then the importance of such a company has become quite obvious in the context of completing the single market of 1992. At its meeting in Brussels in June 1987 the European Council requested the institutions concerned 'to make swift progress with regard to the company law adjustments required for the creation of a European company.' For this reason, at the suggestion of its President Mr. Delors, the Commission decided to relaunch this initiative by means of a memorandum addressed to the Council, the European Parliament and the two sides of industry.

The conclusions reached by the Internal Market Council of 18 November 1988 made it clear that the majority of the Member States were in favour of the guidelines proposed by the Commission, both as regards the optional character of a European company and its independence of national laws and as regards the principle of rules dealing with the involvement of employees in the future European company.

In November 1988 the Economic and Social Committee, by a large majority adopted an opinion which was also favourable to the suggestions made in the Commission's memorandum, including those of the involvement of employees.

---

1. *See* FRANK WOOLDRIDGE, COMPANY LAW IN THE UNITED KINGDOM AND THE EUROPEAN COMMUNITY: ITS HARMONIZATION AND UNIFICATION 117–134 (1991).

Finally, on 16 March 1989 the European Parliament also approved the Commission's proposal, emphasizing particularly the fact that the European company would be a useful instrument for restructuring European businesses and especially for making them more competitive on the world market.

On the basis of these preliminary discussions the Commission on 12 July 1989, on the proposal of its Vice-President Mr. Bangemann, adopted a proposal for a statute for a European company. The objective was to free the companies of Member States from the legal and practical constraints arising from the existence of 12 distinct legal systems by creating a single European instrument.

Why a Statute for a European Company?

The European Company:

(i) is the first instrument that will enable businesses to carry out cross frontier restructuring by means of an international assets merger rather than merely by means of a takeover bid. This is because in the present state of our law assets mergers are not legally possible until the proposal for a 10th Directive, which at present is held up, can be adopted by the Council;

(ii) will also be a very useful instrument for creating joint subsidiaries or holding companies of international groups. This Statute based on European law will be a means of overcoming major psychological obstacles, since it will avoid placing the firms concerned in the position of having to choose the structure of a particular Member State in order to develop their activities in several Member States;

(iii) will make it easier to manage transnational groups, since it will be possible for all the companies in a group to be managed in accordance with a common strategy;

(iv) will be useful not only to large businesses but also small ones.[1] At present the latter find it very difficult to cooperate on a cross frontier basis since they have to submit themselves to as many different legal systems as there are Member States involved.

The Commission has received requests from a number of firms for such a statute for all the reasons just mentioned but those interested will find on examining the text that there are a number of additional advantages:

(i) as regards the tax aspect, the Statute takes into account the specific nature of the European company, which will carry on its taxable activities through the medium of permanent establishments situated abroad. In this context the losses incurred by those establishments may be set against the company's profits;

(ii) as regards the disclosure of information and the audit of annual and consolidated accounts European companies will enjoy all the options open to the Member States under the fourth Directive (78/660/EEC) and the seventh Directive (83/349/EEC);

(iii) in order not to delay its adoption, the Statute does not contain any rules on groups or companies, which are not legally recognized in the majority of the Member States. However, in the States where a law on groups exists (the Federal Republic of Germany and Portugal) the European company will ensure for minority shareholders and third parties the protection they enjoy under that law when their company is controlled by another.

1. For this purpose the minimum capital has been reduced from ECU 250000 to ECU 100000.

The essential characteristics of the Statute

The European company will be based on an independent law distinct from national laws, where reference will be made to the law harmonized at European level. The Statute will coexist with other forms of companies created under national law and will provide businesses with an additional option. The proposed Statute is thus an instrument that is:

(i) optional for public limited companies from at least two Member States which desire to merge or to create a holding company. For creating a joint subsidiary the Statute is much more widely available, to all companies or firms or other legal bodies from at least two Member States;

(ii) transnational, since it will make it possible to overcome the legal difficulties involved in associations or mergers between companies established in two different Member States;

(iii) attractive from a tax point of view since the basis of assessment for the European company will be calculated after setting off the losses incurred by permanent establishments abroad.

The involvement of employees in the European company

The Statute proposed by the Commission also deals with the involvement of employees in the company. The substance of this may be summarized in a brief formula: no European company without a certain form of involvement, namely regular information for the employees, and consultation of them before implementation of decisions in certain defined cases.

In practice the employees will be consulted on the company's main strategic decisions:

(i) the closure or transfer of establishments or a substantial part thereof;

(ii) substantial reduction, extension or alteration of the activities of the company;

(iii) the setting-up of a subsidiary or of a holding company;

(iv) the establishment of long term cooperation with other businesses, or its termination;

(v) substantial organizational changes within the company;

On the other hand, the day-to-day management of the European company will be solely the responsibility of the management.

The Commission is submitting to the Twelve an optional system based on three models defining the involvement of employees in the company:

(i) representation of the employees on the supervisory board or the administrative board;

(ii) creation of a separate body representing the employees;

(iii) other models drawn up by agreement between employers and employees.

A Member State will be permitted to limit the choice of models for European companies having their registered office on its territory. Where several models are available the management of each of the founder companies must choose one of the basis of an agreement with the representatives of the employees. Since equivalence between the different models is ensured by the Statute it is for the management of the company to choose the model of representation of the employees which it regards as the most appropriate.

* * *

The Commission considers that the European company will facilitate cross-frontier cooperation between limited companies from different countries and hence will avoid the partitioning of the internal market into national markets. It will thus contribute to attainment of the 1992 objective.

Comments and Questions

1. Do you think, like the EC Commission above, that a European Company Statute is necessary for the common market? If, indeed, the answer is yes, then why was the creation of a common market possible in the United States without benefit of a federal corporate statute?

2. Do you think that the ECJ's decision in *Centros*, discussed in the previous chapter, makes the case for a supra-national company law stronger or weaker? Why? It is possible that one of the repercussions of *Centros* will be that companies will no longer find it "very difficult to cooperate on a cross frontier basis since they have to submit themselves to as many different legal systems as there are Member States involved." Do you agree?

3. The materials that follow may help focus and answer these questions. After reading the materials that follow, consider whether you agree with the Commission that "the European company would be a useful instrument for restructuring European businesses and especially for making them more competitive on the world market." If so, why? Do you believe, as the Commission does, that multi-national enterprise organization would be facilitated by a European company act? Could the same result be achieved by the regulation of the securities markets at the European level on a model similar to that used in the United States?

Terence L. Blackburn, *The Societas Europeana: The Evolving European Corporation Statute*

61 Fordham L. Rev. 695 (1993)
(excerpts pages 702–711; 763–770; some footnotes omitted)

II. THE NEED FOR A EUROPEAN CORPORATION STATUTE

Despite the enormous growth in inter-European commerce among the member states of the EC that has occurred since the creation of the European Economic Community in 1958, companies that conduct business across borders through branches or subsidiaries, rather than through purchases and sales or licensing agreements with unrelated companies, continue to face substantial barriers. The varying and conflicting laws that exist within the member states that comprise the EC make both the creation and the operation of such international enterprises difficult, and occasionally legally or practically impossible.[39]

The legal systems of the member states of the EC are based on three different traditions-the common law system, the civil law system, and the Scandinavian law system. Each of the twelve member states has developed its own body of law within these traditions. Great Britain actually has three different legal systems. Some of the member states' laws differ substantially from each other with respect to such matters as employee partic-

39. *See* Dominique Carreau & William L. Lee, *Towards a European Company Law*, 9 NW. J. Int'l L. & Bus. 501, 505–07 (1989).

ipation in management and the recognition of single shareholder limited liability corporations. Therefore, a company seeking to conduct business in more than one member state of the EC must consider the laws of up to fourteen different legal systems.[46]

Although these fourteen different legal systems have significantly similar approaches to many basic business law issues, differences still remain. For example, all of the member states of the EC recognize the concept that a publicly owned enterprise provides limited liability to its owners for enterprise debts. However, not all of the member states recognized single shareholder limited liability enterprises until after 1989, when the Council adopted a directive that required them to do so.[49] Corporate laws on a variety of other subjects, such as whether subscribers' capita must be fully paid in to the corporation, or whether workers have rights to be informed of or involved in major decisions concerning the corporation, also differ significantly from country to country.

The EC Commission[52] has recognized that the varying laws of the member states create significant barriers both to the efficient conduct of business and to the creation of an economically unified market within the EC. The Commission, therefore, has identified various needs of European companies that should be satisfied in order for them to perform more efficiently on an inter-European basis. At the same time, the Commission has recognized that the growth of European (as distinct from national) companies makes it necessary to provide additional protections to persons and groups that do business with those corporations.[54]

A. Enabling Goals of the Proposed Statute

The Commission's general goal of enabling corporations to operate on a fully integrated European basis can be broken down into two related sub-categories: the improvement of companies' ability to make decisions and conduct business operations without regard to national boundaries; and the improvement of companies' ability to organize or reorganize without regard to such boundaries.

1. Operational Goals

In its 1970 proposal for a European corporation statute, the Commission expressed concern about the barriers to Community-based company planning and operations. In the preamble to this proposal, the Commission stated that the creation of an economic union within the EC presupposed "a reorganization of the factors of production and distribution on a Community scale in order to ensure that the enlarged market will op-

---

46. *See* Richard D. English, *Company Law in the European Single Market*, 1990 B.Y.U. L. Rev. 1413, 1418–19 (1990).

49. The directive requires the member states to adopt laws and regulations that allow a company to have "a sole member when it is formed also when all of its shares come to be held by a single person." Twelfth Council Company Law Directive 89/667 of 21 December 1989 on Single Member Private Limited-Liability Companies, Art. 2(1), at 41, 1989 O.J. (L 395) 40 [hereinafter Twelfth Directive]. The member states were required to comply by January 1, 1992, with respect to the formation of new companies, and by January 1, 1993, with respect to existing companies. *See id.* Art 8(1), 8(2), at 42.

52. The 1991 Proposed Regulation was drafted by the Commission and will not become effective until it is adopted by the Council. Accordingly, this Article regards the proposal as being the work of the Commission.

54. [Amended proposal for a Council Regulation on the Statute for a European Company, 1991 O.J. (C 176) 1 [hereinafter 1991 Proposed Regulation]], pmbl.

erate similarly to a domestic market."[55] The Commission sought to improve companies' activities and competitiveness at the Community level, noting that the development of businesses at the national level could "fragment markets and so constitute an impediment to economic integration" of the Community.[56]

Similarly, in 1991, upon concluding that the completion of the internal market of the EC required that "the structures of production...be adapted to the Community dimension,"[57] the Commission called for the "management of companies with a European dimension, free from the obstacles arising from the disparity and the limited territorial application of national company laws."[58] The Commission, moreover, called for the creation of Community-based company law, that would be applicable in all member states, so that companies could operate legally, as well as economically, on a Community-wide basis.[59]

In addition to the need for a general company law that encourages the operation of SEs on a community-wide basis, the Commission has continually recognized the need to allow European companies to coordinate their tax and fiscal policies. In its 1970 proposal, the Commission stated that SEs should be allowed to deduct from their profits any losses incurred by branches or subsidiaries in the other member states.[60] This goal of treating the SE as one entity for tax, as well as operational purposes, has been incorporated into the 1991 proposal.[61]

These statements by the Commission demonstrate that the encouragement of effective operations on a European basis, rather than on a national basis, constitutes one of the major goals of the European corporation statute. Under the fully integrated market sought by the Commission, companies would be able to make operational decisions, such as choosing sources of supply and locations of production and sale, based solely on market considerations.[62] Decisions would not be affected by managers' unfamiliarity with the laws of other member states, or their perceptions of the favorable or unfavorable nature of "competing" national laws. Consequently, inconsistent national laws dealing with corporate governance and control and with tax issues would be harmonized or unified to a Community-wide standard.[63] It is against this standard that the 1991 proposals will be evaluated.

---

55. [Proposal for a Council Regulation embodying a Statute for European Companies, 3 Bull. Eur. Comm. Supp. 8/70 (1970) [hereinafter 1970 Proposed Regulation]] at 5.

56. *Id.* Based on the Commission's stated goals, it is apparent that the Commission believed that the use of companies organized under national laws would render it difficult to operate efficiently on a European basis, partly because of conflicting national laws, and partly because of lingering nationalistic prejudices against "foreign" European businesses. The only other European form of business organization, the European Economic Interest Grouping, does not provide an effective alternative to European businesses because of significant limitations that are placed on its size, and because it must be operated as a partnership, rather than an integrated business entity....

57. 1991 Proposed Regulation, *supra* note [54], at 1.

58. *Id.* at 2.

59. *See id.*

60. *See* 1970 Proposed Regulation, *supra* note [55], at 7–8.

61. *See* 1991 Proposed Regulation, *supra* note [54], at 4.

62. *See id.* at 1–5.

63. It has been suggested that current levels of harmonization of Member State corporate law are insufficient to minimize the "race to the bottom" tendencies that may result from the growing unification of the EC market as governments compete for companies to incorporate and establish their headquarters in their countries. *See* Clark D. Smith, Note, *Federalism and Company Law: A "Race to the Bottom" in the European Community*, 79 GEO. L.J. 1581, 1593–99 (1991).

2. Organizational Goals

Since the time of its first proposal for a European corporation statute, the Commission has recognized that the goal of operational integration of European companies could not be achieved solely by harmonizing the laws of the member states. The Commission noted in 1970 that the harmonization of laws could not eliminate the barriers to either the movement of company headquarters from one member state to another, or the combination of companies across national borders. It also noted that the harmonization of laws would not eliminate the necessity of choosing a single country of "citizenship" and identity for European companies. For this reason, the Commission believed that it was necessary to free European companies from legal ties to any particular country. To accomplish this, the Commission concluded that a "full set of standard provisions" would have to be created to govern "the founding, structure, operation and winding up of the European company." [66]

In 1988, more than six years after the Council had last considered the idea of a European corporation law, and more than eighteen years after it first proposed the adoption of a European corporation statute, the Commission issued yet another call to action. The Commission warned that cross-frontier cooperation had become "imperative" not only for achieving economic integration of the EC market, but also for maintaining the EC's competitive position in relation to the United States and Japan, especially in the high-technology and financial services industries.

In its Memorandum, the Commission pointed out that the absence of a European company statute impeded the development of EC-based companies. The Commission also criticized the resulting failure in the development of legal methods for accomplishing the "obvious economic need to restructure companies." According to the Commission, the reorganization of such companies was made frustrated by: (1) the impossibility of accomplishing cross-frontier mergers and other business combinations under existing laws; (2) inconsistent and conflicting national tax laws resulting in double taxation and tax-oriented rather than market-oriented decisions by managers; and (3) inconsistent national laws regarding the establishment and recognition of groups of companies. The Commission solicited comments from the Council, Parliament, workers, and corporate managers for their use in the formulation of a new European company law proposal.

The resulting proposal, made in 1989 and amended in 1991, reasserts the need to permit the organization of corporations on a European basis. The preamble to this proposal states that European companies should be able to "carry out the reorganization of their business on a Community scale" without reference to the laws of individual member states, and expresses concern over the obstacles to the creation of groups of companies that was produced by the divergent national laws. The Commission concludes that it is essential to create a European corporate form of organization "as a means of enabling companies from different Member States to merge or to create a holding company and...to form a joint subsidiary." A significant addition to the 1989 Proposed Regulation would enable certain companies to become European companies without the need for mergers or other corporate reorganizations. Although the Commission briefly addresses the tax implications of subjecting the corporations to tax in the individual member states, the 1989 and 1991 proposals give much less emphasis to these problems than the 1988 Memorandum had provided. Moreover, because of the

66. *See* 1970 Proposed Regulation, *supra* note [55], at 6–7.

progress made in harmonizing member state company law, the Commission, in the 1991 proposal, places much less emphasis on the need for adopting a full set of European company laws covering all aspects of the annual financial reporting requirements and the winding up of European companies.[76]

B. Protective Goals of the Proposed Statute

The Commission has consistently acknowledged that if companies were allowed to operate and organize on an EC basis, rather than on a national basis, various protective mechanisms commonly found in member state company laws would need to be adopted. The Commission's main concern has been the protection of the rights of workers in such enterprises. In addition, the Commission has been concerned to a somewhat lesser extent about protecting the rights of minority shareholders and creditors.

1. Protection of Employees

The preamble to the 1970 Proposed Regulation, in an effort aimed at achieving "uniformity in the system of management of the European company," warned against the use of national laws in providing a model of employee representation in European company decision-making. [77] The 1970 proposal, however, went far beyond this goal of uniformity, and asserted that it was "necessary... to provide for the formation of a European Works Council"[78] in all European companies, and "equally necessary to allow representation of workers on the Supervisory Boards."[79] The proposal would therefore allow workers to become involved in matters of company management and the appointment of executive officers of the companies.[80] The preamble offered no justification for these worker participation goals other than citing the need for uniformity.[81] In the explanatory notes to the proposal, the Commission stated that European companies

---

76. ....The Fourth, Seventh, and Eighth Company Law Directives eliminate nearly all variations in member state laws on these topics. *See* Fourth Council Directive of 25 July 1978, based on Article 54(3)(g) of the Treaty on the annual accounts of certain types of companies, 1978 O.J. (L 222) 11, 11 [hereinafter Fourth Company Law Directive]; Seventh Council Directive of 13 June 1983, based on the Article 54(3)(g) of the Treaty on consolidated accounts, 1983 O.J. (L 193) 1, 1–2 [hereinafter Seventh Company Law Directive]; Eighth Council Directive of 10 April 1984, based on Article 54(3)(g) of the Treaty on the approval of persons responsible for carrying out the statutory audits of accounting documents, 1984 O.J. (L 126) 20, 20 [hereinafter Eighth Company Law Directive].

77. 1970 Proposed Regulation, supra note [55], pmbl., at 7.

78. *Id.* The European Works Council, which is based on French and Italian systems of employee participation, is a committee of employees in EC scale businesses, that is charged with the responsibility of safeguarding the rights of employees. The committee must be informed and consulted on issues concerning (1) major changes in the business, and (2) conditions of employment. The creation of European Works Councils was finally formally proposed by the Commission in 1990. *See* Proposal for a Council Directive on the Establishment of a European Works Council in Community-scale Undertakings or Groups of Undertakings for the Purposes of Informing and Consulting Employees, 1991 O.J. (C 39) 10.

79. 1970 Proposed Regulation, *supra* note [55], pmbl., at 7.

80. *See id.*

81. *See id.* At the time, the 1970 proposal was made, only Belgium, France, Germany, Italy, Luxembourg, and The Netherlands were members of the EC. In addition, only the laws of Germany provided for worker participation in larger public companies. *See generally* Law on Works Organizations of 1952 & 1972, translated in Heinrich Beinhauer, German Works Council Act 1972 (1972); 1970 Regulation, *supra* note 6, pmbl., at 173. Strong opposition to worker participation in the management of the European company has come from Great Britain and Ireland, which did not join the EC until 1973. *See* CCH, *supra* note 40, ¶¶ 40-424, 40-663, 40-664.

should encourage worker participation in management as a means of improving efficiency through the increased level of cooperation both between employees and management and between employees of the same business entity who worked in different member states.[82]

In 1988, the Commission expressly acknowledged that its proposals on the European company statute were designed to do more than simply establish uniform laws. In its 1988 Memorandum, the Commission commented that the necessary restructuring of European companies on an international level would be more readily accepted by European workers if they participated in that restructuring, and their interests were safeguarded. In the Commission's view, worker participation in the management of the European company was essential both as a means of ensuring the smooth operation of such enterprises and as a matter of "social rights." Therefore, the Commission stated that in addition to encouraging efficient European-wide operations, the European company statute should "at the same time pioneer worker involvement in the decision-making structures of European industry."

The 1989 and amended 1991 draft directives on worker participation in the European company moderated the Commission's language on the social rights aspect of the proposals. Although the Commission stated that the participation of workers in the supervision of the European company was necessary for achieving the economic and social goals of the EC, the Commission placed greater emphasis on the need for coordinating the diverse laws of member states on this issue. In addition, the 1991 draft expressed concern over preventing the competitive inequalities that would arise if equal levels of worker participation were not "guaranteed" to all workers.[87]

2. Protection of Creditors and Shareholders

In articulating the goals of the 1970 proposal, the Commission took the position that protection was required for creditors and certain shareholders of parent-subsidiary groups of companies that were SEs.[88] The Commission believed that the growth of such groups of companies had already caused problems for the creditors and minority shareholders of the controlled companies. As European companies were created, and more and larger groups of companies were formed, the Commission foresaw increasing problems and the need for additional regulation. The Commission also thought that its regulation would serve as a model for the member states' revision of their national laws on the subject.[90]

82. *See* 1970 Proposed Regulation, *supra* note [55], pmbl., at 87.

87. *See* 1991 Proposed Directive, *supra* note [54], pmbl., at 9. The Commission's position on this point lacks a certain amount of internal logic. If it is true that European companies operate more smoothly and effectively when workers participate in management, then a competitive inequality would result from the statute's failure to require worker participation. Under such circumstances, it would hardly seem necessary to guarantee worker participation, because companies would be led by market pressures to allow worker participation (except that such guarantees of worker participation might avoid a damaging period of non-competitiveness until the companies restructured their operations). If, on the other hand, worker participation would have no effect, then no competitive inequality would result from the adoption of this model of management. If, conversely, worker participation would make European companies less efficient, then it would again be necessary to guarantee worker participation, in order to prevent companies without such participation from gaining a competitive advantage.

88. *See* 1970 Proposed regulation, *supra* note [55]bl., at 173–74. The term "creditor" was not defined in the proposal. Because the proposal simply makes parent companies liable for the "obligations" of their subsidiaries, it apparently protects bondholders as well as trade creditors. *See id.*

90. Of the six member states of the EC in 1970, only Germany had passed laws dealing with the protection of creditors and minority shareholders in groups of companies. *See* 1970 Proposed Regulation, *supra* note [55] pmbl., at 173.

The Commission also recognized, in the 1970 Proposed Regulation, that controlling companies and minority shareholders did not have common interests. A controlling company might not act in the best interests of minority shareholders of the controlled company because the controlling company was not necessarily interested in improving the profitability of the controlled company. It might instead use the controlled company for the purpose of improving the controlling company's profitability. The Commission therefore provided special protection for minority shareholders by enabling them to redeem their shares in the controlled company in exchange for either cash or shares in the controlling company.[91]

With respect to creditors, the Commission was more vague about the need for special protection in groups of companies. The Commission only referred to the "threat... for creditors who rely on the protection provided for by law" when one company controlled and directed another.[92] Nevertheless, the Commission's proposal made controlling companies liable for the debts of their controlled companies.[93]

The Commission's views on the special protections needed in groups of companies remained unchanged for several years. In its 1975 amended proposal, the Commission noted Parliament's strong support for such provisions, and retained the provisions of the 1970 proposal.

In 1988, the Commission acknowledged that it had changed its views on the protection of minority shareholders and creditors in groups of companies. Although the Commission still believed that the legal principle of independence conflicted with the economic demands of groups of companies, the Commission noted that it was "open to question... whether the European Company Statute is the proper place to create a body of rules governing groups."

By 1989, the Commission had fully reversed its position on the need for creating special rules for European companies that operated in groups. The Commission acknowledged that under existing law, the rights of shareholders and creditors in a group were governed by the law of the controlled company. Consequently, specific rules were not required for a European company that acted as part of a group of companies. This approach was continued in the 1991 amended proposal.[97]

3. Protection of Others

Aside from its goal of protecting minority shareholders and creditors in groups of companies, the Commission apparently did not see any significant need for providing special protection to creditors and shareholders of European companies that were not members of such groups. The Commission did express a mild concern for proper capitalization of such companies. The Commission wanted to "ensure that such undertakings [would] operate on an acceptable scale," and consequently specified that a minimum paid-in capital would be required.[98] The 1970 proposal also gave creditors the opportunity to oppose a merger in the European Court of Justice if their rights would be affected by the merger.[99]

The provisions of the 1970 proposal that dealt with shareholders' rights were more the product of normal corporate housekeeping concerns (e.g., liability of the board of

---

91. *See id.* Arts. 228–238, at 179–87.
92. *Id.* at 173.
93. *See id.* Art. 239, at 187–88.
97. *See* 1991 Proposed Regulation, *supra* note [54], pmbl., at 4.
98. 1970 Proposed Regulation, *supra* note [55], pmbl., at 6.
99. *See id.* Art. 27, at 29.

management for wrongful acts, and rights of the shareholders to convene shareholder meetings, place items on the agenda, and bring derivative suits) than concerns for the special problems of European companies, and were not separately discussed by the Commission in the preamble or the notes to the proposal.[100]

The Commission has not changed its view that such additional protective measures are not required. The 1989 and 1991 proposals generally followed the pattern of the 1970 proposal on these issues, with the exception that the right of creditors to contest merger in the European Court of Justice has been eliminated.[101]

* * *

IV. EVALUATION OF THE 1991 PROPOSED STATUTE

Although the 1991 Proposed Regulation and the 1991 Proposed Directive take significant steps toward accomplishing the goals and filling the needs identified by the EC, they fall short in several respects. These proposals should not be viewed as an expression of concepts that have already been accepted by all of the participants in the EC. Many provisions of the statute and a number of gaps in it are the result of hard won compromises; others reflect the political realities of what can be accomplished at this stage of the development of the EC itself. Nevertheless, it is important to evaluate the proposed statute against the EC's own statements concerning what the statute is designed to accomplish, in order to determine the extent to which the proposals meet these goals and the extent to which they fail.

A. Goals of the Proposed Statute

The basic purpose of the proposed statute, as identified by the Commission, is to promote the fully integrated internal market of the EC.[399] The Commission has identified four principal means of accomplishing this integration: (1) enabling companies to conduct their daily operations on a true European basis, based solely on market considerations, without regard to national laws pertaining to their operation, governance or tax matters; (2) enabling companies to operate free of any particular national identity; (3) enabling companies to transfer their headquarters within the EC without regard to national borders; and (4) enabling companies to restructure and form new business combinations across national borders.[401] The Commission has also sought to include the employees in the process by giving them a voice in the operation of these new companies and giving them a sense of loyalty to the European nature of the companies. Although the Commission initially attempted to protect the interests of other participants in the European corporation, it has essentially abandoned this goal (except for traditional shareholder protection provisions) in the most recent draft of the proposal.

With these goals in mind, one can now proceed to a final evaluation of whether the 1991 Proposed Regulation and the 1991 Proposed Directive succeed or fail.

B. Formation of the SE

The proposed European corporation statute is only fairly successful in enabling companies to take advantage of the SE form of organization. The proposal does, at least, succeed in making available many of the common methods of structuring or restructur-

---

100. *See, e.g., id.* Arts. 71, 81, 85(1), 85(3), at 62–63, 69, 73.
101. *See* 1991 Proposed Regulation, *supra* note [54], Arts. 4, 17–31, at 7, 12–20.
399. *See* 1991 Proposed Regulation, *supra* note [54], pmbl., at 2.
401. *See* 1991 Proposed Regulation, *supra* note [54], pmbl., at 1–4.

ing companies, including the merger, and the use of holding companies and joint subsidiaries. The only major method of business combination that had been omitted from the 1989 and earlier drafts was the straight acquisition of shares or assets of another company. The addition in the 1991 draft of the conversion method of forming an SE enables companies to become SEs when they either already have operations in other states or simply wish to acquire the shares or assets of companies in other states. Without this provision, companies would have to either forgo a portion of their independence or control over their operations (as a result of their use of a merger, joint holding company or joint subsidiary) or combine with various shell companies in order to fit within the proposed statute.

Unfortunately, the Commission has allowed only public limited liability companies to use the conversion and merger methods of forming SEs. This decision has substantially limited the usefulness of the proposed statute.

For example, under the proposal, a company that wished to form an SE through a merger would first have to become a public limited liability company in the state in which it was organized; in order to do this, the company might have to make a number of changes in its structure, capitalization, and organization. After the company merged with another public company to form an SE, it would no longer be subject to the national laws that had required it to make those changes, even if it were the surviving company. The European corporation statute might not have required some or all of the changes that were made. Consequently, the company would have undertaken a series of changes, in order to be able to form an SE through a merger, that were not required once it became an SE.

The proposed statute raises similar problems for companies that wish to convert to SEs. A company might have to undertake a change in its structure so that it could become eligible to convert into an SE.

The joint holding company and joint subsidiary methods of forming SEs are the only forms that are directly available to private limited liability companies without the intervening step of first becoming a public limited liability company. These two methods of forming SEs are designed to preserve the essential nature and independence of the founding company, while leaving the SE separate and apart from the founding company. This result is often not desirable for companies that wish to create fully integrated, truly European companies.

Finally, the proposed statute is surprisingly inflexible in its requirements of diversity in the operations of the founders of SEs, especially in view of the Commission's announced goal of encouraging the creation of truly European companies. The most flexible rule for the formation of SEs (short of not requiring any diversity of operations at all) would have been to require that the SE, immediately following its formation, have operations in at least one member state besides the state of its central administration, regardless of the method of formation that had been used. This rule, which the 1991 Proposed Regulation included with regard to the formation of SEs by conversion, would have ensured that companies wishing to take advantage of the benefits of the SE form of organization possessed a truly European character.

Instead, the proposed statute sets up more restrictive rules. Companies that wish to form an SE through a merger must have their central administrations in different states, regardless of the diversity of their other operations. Companies that wish to create SEs by holding companies or subsidiaries must either have their places of central administrations located in different member states, or must each have foreign operations before the time that the SE is formed. There is no valid reason for requiring such extended levels of diversity for companies that wish to form SEs through a merger, or the use of a holding company or joint subsidiary.

In summary, the restrictive nature of the proposed statute frustrates the Commission's goal of enabling the greatest number of companies to take advantage of the SE form of organization. The merger and conversion methods of formation are limited by the requirement that each of the founding companies must be publicly held, and the merger, holding company and joint subsidiary methods of formation are limited by excessive diversity requirements. The proposed statute could be simplified, and the Commission's goals could be achieved if all public and private companies were eligible to use each of the methods of forming SEs, and if the diversity test that presently applies to the conversion method of formation were applied to the other three methods of forming SEs.

C. Cross-Border Combinations

The proposed statute is successful in providing companies with a method of combining businesses that are organized under the laws of different member states. Under existing member state laws, there is no procedure that allows companies to fully combine ongoing operations. They can make share acquisitions, create parent-subsidiary relationships, or arrange the purchase and sale of assets, but they cannot actually merge. Such mergers could be accomplished under the proposal if the surviving company were to become an SE. Consequently, this portion of the proposed statute will be very helpful in achieving the Commission's goal of enabling companies to restructure on a European basis.

D. Capital Structure

The inflexibility of the SE's capital structure, as prescribed by the 1991 Proposed Regulation, has the effect of discouraging companies from using the SE form of organization. The proposed statute institutionalizes some of this inflexibility; other problems arise from the Commission's decision to allow the laws of the member states to govern these issues even though no effective harmonization of such laws has taken place.

The minimum capitalization that is required for SEs, although greater than the level that is required for national companies, is not so high as to discourage the formation of SEs. The mandatory use of nominal value shares, and the maintenance of stated capital before dividends can be declared, although anachronisms to many Americans, remain familiar concepts to most Europeans. Therefore, these provisions should not prevent the formation of SEs.

Other provisions of the proposal present greater difficulty. The statute unnecessarily limits the capital formation process by allowing each member state to place limitations on the initial issuance and new issuance of shares and other equity and debt instruments by SEs that are registered in that member state. Consequently, an SE may be at a competitive disadvantage to an SE that is registered in another member state if a disparity exists between the two member states' restrictions on the issuance of financial instruments.

Under the proposed statute, the member state laws may also regulate or prevent the general meeting's prior authorization of the issuance of new shares and the repurchase of shares already issued. These rules make the process of capital formation even more cumbersome for SEs. Furthermore, the Regulation requires that all new issuances of shares must be offered on a preemptive basis to the existing shareholders (first to the shareholders of the same class of shares, followed by offerings to the shareholders of other classes of shares) before a public offering can be made. Regardless of the member states' laws governing national companies, a waiver of these preemptive rights may only be obtained with respect to the particular shares then being issued, rather than pursuant to prior authorization. Because this rule is more restrictive than some of the member states' laws that are applicable to national companies, SEs in such states will be at a disadvantage compared to national companies registered in the same states.

Managers or controlling shareholders may be unwilling to use the SE form of organization if they can obtain greater flexibility by using national forms of organization. Moreover, they may be hesitant to locate their central administrations in those member states that do not allow the issuance of a sufficiently wide range of financial instruments. Furthermore, because the proposed statute allows for a disparity in the laws that regulate an SE's capital structure insofar as some member states are more restrictive in their regulation of national companies than others, it may be impossible for SEs to transfer freely their places of central administration. These results are not desirable in view of the Commission's goal of creating European companies that can organize and operate without reference to the laws of individual member states.

E. Management and Worker Representation

The proposed statute, on its face, appears to grant SEs a great deal of freedom in creating management structures that fit their needs and interests by presenting a choice between a two-tier and one-tier board, and among various models of worker participation in management. Unfortunately, in an attempt at preserving the various traditions that have evolved in the different member states, the proposed statute allows each member state to restrict the choices available to SEs, and further allows member states to require SEs to adopt specific management structures and models of employee representation. The resulting ability of member states to require that SEs adopt a particular management structure and model of worker participation that may differ from the particular forms mandated by another member state, deprives the SE form of organization of much of its usefulness.

This reliance on mandatory member state law in establishing basic matters relating to management destroys the hope of attaining uniformity among SEs that are registered in different member states. Instead of creating border-blind companies, that are truly Community enterprises, the Commission has institutionalized the creation of enterprises that purport to be European, but which retain many of the essential characteristics of the countries in which they are organized. In view of the member states' determination to impose their own national characters on SEs within their borders, it is possible that there will be German SEs, French SEs, and even Northern Ireland SEs.[427]

Moreover, the Commission's attempt to accommodate the interests of a number of member states affects the protection that is provided to an SE's workers. Despite the Commission's assertions to the contrary, the various models of worker participation fail to provide employees with uniform levels of participation and influence. The current proposal thus institutionalizes national variations in worker participation models, and accentuates the disparity in employee rights among the various member states. The proposal also fails to accomplish the Commission's goal of promoting em-

---

427. The proposed statute accepts the laws of territorial units within member states as binding on SEs. *See* 1991 Proposed Regulation, *supra* note [54], Art. 7(2)(b), at 9.

ployee loyalty to a truly European business entity, instead of to a national business entity. Rather than minimizing the importance to employees of the place of central administration of the SE in which they work, the 1991 proposed statute emphasizes that issue.

Because of the variations that will exist in the required management structures and models of worker participation, the selection of an SE's place of central administration will be of vital importance to both the SE and its employees. An SE might not be able to transfer its place of central administration without effecting wrenching changes in its management structure, the composition of its supervisory or administrative board, and the nature of the body that is designated for accomplishing worker participation in accordance with the prescribed model. An SE's transfer of its state of central administration may also become a political issue; member states may vie to retain local SEs or to persuade foreign SEs to transfer their central administrations there. Sadly, it appears that the Commission's economic and philosophic goal of creating a new form of business organization that truly reflects the unified character of the EC, has been subordinated to the strong desires of the member states to preserve their own local traditions with respect to the management of business and employee rights.

F. Operations and Accounts

The proposed European corporation statute also relies heavily on member state law in providing rules that govern the general operation of SEs. Among the events governed by member state law are the procedures to be followed by the general meeting of shareholders, the determination of the actions that require prior board approval, the election of employee representatives and their corresponding duties and status within the SE, and the winding up of SEs. Generally, the most significant of these issues have already been harmonized by other Council directives. Therefore, in contrast to the proposed statute's reliance on member state laws governing capital structure, management structure and employee rights, the reliance on member state law with respect to an SE's operations and financial reporting requirements is unlikely to affect an SE's choice of its place of central administration.

G. Insolvency and Liquidation

The application of member state law to SEs also presents a significant potential for disparity in the laws that apply to an SE's insolvency and liquidation. Here, the Commission has allowed the application of "national law" without limiting the definition of the this term to the law of the member state in which the SE has its central administration. This approach could subject an SE to the varying or conflicting laws of different member states, thereby raising the level of uncertainty faced by managers and requiring managerial familiarity with the laws of other member states besides the one in which the SE has its place of central administration. The Commission had expressed a desire to avoid such a result, and this particular portion of the proposed statute should be reexamined.

H. Taxation

The provisions of the 1991 Proposed Regulation that deal with losses from foreign establishments are helpful, but not vitally important. The member states, under tax treaties, already allow for either the integration of profits and losses or the taking of credits for taxes paid on profits of foreign branches. Under the 1991 Proposed Regulation, the choice between the two methods available to an SE is left to the member state in which the SE has its central administration. The proposed statute ensures that one of these methods will be applied to an SE's foreign operations, but generally does not change the law that would have been applicable if the SE had remained a national company. Furthermore, because the Commission has proposed a harmonization of the rules that apply to national companies, variations among the laws applicable to SEs in different member states will be substantially reduced.

Vanessa Edwards, *EC Company Law*

(1999)

(excerpts pages 399–404; some footnotes omitted)

The European Company

Of all the outstanding Proposals for company law instruments, the European Company goes back the furthest: the idea was first mooted forty years ago in 1959 by Professor Sanders in an inaugural lecture at the Rotterdam School of Economics.[108] Six years later, the Commission, prompted by the French Government, set up a working group of experts chaired by Professor Sanders to prepare a draft Statute for a uniform type of limited company which could be used throughout the Community without being subject to national law. Straddling frontiers, the European Company would enable a business to operate across borders without the administrative burdens involved in setting up and running subsidiaries, all of which typically remain subject to domestic law. The draft was completed by the end of the following year and served as the basis for the Commission's first Proposal, issued in 1970.[109]

The Proposal was for a Statute to be enacted by way of a regulation based on Article 235 of the Treaty, in contrast to Sanders draft which had proposed an international convention. The draft regulation would permit a European Company (or Societas Europea, abbreviated to SE, the linguistically neutral term preferred by Professor Sanders) to be formed by public companies from different Member States by way of either a merger between such companies or forming a holding company or joint subsidiaries. The draft Statute was a daunting and ambitious instrument comprising 284 Articles; it sought to regulate all aspects of the European Company, dealing with constitution, capital, organs, employee representation, accounts and audit, groups of companies, amendment of statutes, dissolution and liquidation, transformation into a national company, fusion, and tax. The draft sowed the seeds of its ultimate destruction in the requirement that the company have a two tiered board, executive and supervisory. The supervisory board was to 'exercise permanent control over the management of the company by the executive board';[113] it also had power to advise the executive board on any mater of im-

---

108. Sanders, P., 'Towards a European Company?' Published also in French [1960] Le droit européen 9, German [1960] Aussenwirtschaftsdienst des Betriebsberaters 1, and Italian [1959] Rivista delle Società 1163. The Dutch, English, French, German and Italian texts are collected in Sanders, P., *European Stock Corporation* (1969).... Suggestions for a similar proposal had also been put forward earlier in 1959 at the 57th Congress of French Notaries in Tours.

109. COM (70) 600 final, 24 June 1970; [1970] JO C124; EC Bull Supp 8/70. For further discussion of the early history leading up to the 1970 proposal *see* Stein, E., *Harmonization of European Company Laws* (1971) and the sources listed at 424–6, n. 267....

113. Art. 73(1).

portance to the company, either on request or of its own initiative,[114] although it was not to intervene directly in the management of the company.[115] Between one-third and one-half of the members of the supervisory board were to be employees' representatives, with the balance appointed by the general meeting.[116]

In 1972 the Economic and Social Committee delivered a broadly favourable Opinion on the 1970 Proposal.[117] The Parliament was also generally supportive, subject to numerous suggested amendments. In 1975 the Commission submitted to the Council an amended Proposal, incorporating many of the Parliament's suggestion including an amendment to the composition of the supervisory board which would consist of one-third shareholders' representatives, one-third employees' representatives and one-third members co-opted by both groups and representing general interests.[118] The amended Proposal was even more complex than the original Proposal. The Council appointed an ad hoc working party which between 1976 and 1982 worked its way through the first reading of the Proposal. It proved impossible to reach a consensus on such issues as the rules governing groups of companies and the tax provisions, as well as the two tier board structure and workers' representation. Discussions were eventually suspended in 1982 when completion was made conditional on 'seeing Commission proposals for harmonization of Member States' legislation of groups of companies.'[119]

In the late 1980s the Commission relaunched the Proposal, issuing first a memorandum on the Societas Europea and shortly thereafter a fresh Proposal for a Council Regulation on the Statute for a European Company.[121] The 1989 Proposal abandoned the earlier models of the mandatory two-tier board and employee representation discussed above. Instead, it provided for either a two-tier (management and supervisory) or a one-tier (administrative) board system;[122] employee representation was to be dealt with in a separate directive complementing the Statute for a European company with regard to the involvement of employees in the European company, a Proposal for which was submitted by the Commission to the Council on the same day as the fresh Proposal for the European Company Statute.[123] The proposed directive describes itself as 'an indissociable complement'[124] and 'an essential supplement'[125] to the regulation, the preamble to which states that the directive forms an 'indissociable complement to this Regulation and must be applied concomitantly.'[126]

114. Art. 73(2).

115. Art. 73(3).

116. Art. 137.

117. [1972] JO C131.

118. COM (75) 150 final, 19 March 1975; EC Bull Supp 4/75. For commentaries see Sanders, P., 'The European Company' (1976) 6 Georgia Journal of International and Comparative Law 367 and Zec, CE, 'The "Societas Europea"—a European Company—and United States Corporation Laws: a Comparison' [1977] Comparative Law Yearbook 285.

119. *See* Memorandum from the Commission to Parliament, the Council and the two sides of industry, "Internal Market and Industrial Cooperation—Statute for the European Company—Internal Market White Paper, point 137 COM (88) 320 final, 15 July 1977; EC Bull Supp 3/88.

121. [1989] OJ C263/41; COM (89) 268 final, 25 August 1989; EC Bull Supp 3/88. For an interesting discussion of the background to the 1989 Proposal, *see* Gordon, M W, 'European Community Company Law' in Folsom, RH, Lake, R and Nanda, VP (eds) *European Community Law After 1992* (1993), 547–52…

122. Art. 61.

123. COM (89) 268 final, 25 August 1989; [1989] OJ C263/69.

124. 6th recital in the preamble.

125. Art. 1.

126. 19th recital in the preamble.

The proposed directive provided that employee participation was to be determined in accordance with one of the following models:[127] (a) appointment of between one-third and half of the members of the supervisory or administrative board by the company's employees or their representatives or, subject to veto by the employees' representatives or the shareholders in general meeting, co-opted by the board;[128] (b) representation of employees by a separate body, whose composition was to be laid down in the statutes in consultation with the representatives of the employees of the founder compnaies;[129] or (c) establishment of another model by agreement between the management and administrative boards of the founder companies and representatives of the employees of those companies.[130] The choice of model was to be determined by agreement between the founder companies' boards and the representatives of their employees provided for by the laws and practices of the Member States; in default of agreement, the choice was to be for the boards.[131]

Further changes since the earlier Proposals included the dropping of provisions seeking to regulate groups (1989 Proposal simply referred to certain provisions of the law of the State where the SE had its registered office and the legal system governing the controlling undertaking[132]) and the abandonment of the ambitious attempt to provide a tax framework for the SE's operations (the 1989 Proposal contained only one fiscal provision, relating to the taxation of permanent establishments of an SE[133]). These changes, together with the slimming down of the provisions on accounts and audit made possible by reference to the Fourth, Seventh, and Eighth Directives which had been adopted since the earlier Proposals, and the increasing use of references to national law to govern certain issues, resulted in a shorter document: 137 Articles, together with a further thirteen in the complementary worker participation firective.

More fundamentally, the legal basis for the proposed regulation changed from Article 235, which requires unanimity in the Council, to Article 100a, which provides for the adoption by qualified majority in accordance with the cooperation procedure of 'measures for the approximation of the provisions laid down by law, regulation or administrative action in Member States which have as their object the establishment and functioning of the internal market'. It has been argued that, since the European Company is a new entity, a regulation for its statute cannot be a measure for the approximation of national law. Since Article 100a cannot be used for measures relating to the rights and interests of employed persons, the complementary directive is based on Article 54 of the Treaty, which concerns measures for the attainment of freedom of establishment: the choice of Article 54 for a directive concerning the participation of employees in in a supra-national entity also seems anomalous.

After delivery of the Opinions to Parliament,[136] and the Economic and Social Committee,[137] the Commission issued an amended Proposal in May 1991.[138] This extended the circumstances in which an SE could be formed to include the conversion of a public limited

127. Art. 3(1).
128. Art. 4.
129. Art. 5.
130. Art. 6.
131. Art. 3(1).
132. Art. 114.
133. Art. 133.
136. [1991] OJ C48/72.
137. [1990] OJ C124/40.
138. COM (91) 174 final, 6 May 1991; [1991] OJ C176/1. Commentaries include Wehlau, A, 'The Societas Europea: A Critique of the Commission's 1991 Amended Proposal' (1992) 29 CMLR

company with a subsidiary or branch in a Member State other than that of its central administration.[139] For some years thereafter the Proposal stalled as a result of disagreement at a political level, mainly centering on the complementary worker provisions: Germany in particular considered that the legislation should contain mandatory provisions so as to prevent German companies from choosing to form an SE solely in order to avoid national provisions, while other Member States, including the United Kingdom, considered the Proposals excessive.[140] In November 1995 the Commission sent a communication to the Council presenting several options for forms of worker participation in inter alia the management of the SE.[141] A year later, the Commission established a high level group, chaired by Viscount Davignon, to seek a solution to the deadlock. While the Davignon group was deliberating, the Commission was no doubt encouraged by the fact that a majority of the respondents to its consultation paper on company law (Member States, academics and organizations representative of economic interest groups) expressed hope that the European Company Statute would be adopted rapidly, in order to enable companies to take full advantage of the potential of the single market.[143]

The Davignon group reported in May 1997,[144] proposing that, in respect of each European company, the management and the employees should seek to reach an agreement on a system of worker participation, failing which, default 'reference rules' would come into play. In addition, the group proposed that one-fifth of the members of the administrative or supervisory board should be employees' representatives, with a minimum of two members. The reaction of the Commission and Member States, including Germany and the United Kingdom, was initially favourable and negotiations within the Council were resumed in June 1997. However, the United Kingdom soon resumed its former stance, finding the proposed default rules for worker participation unacceptable.

Negotiations in the Council continued for another year, enmired in particular in the context of the default provisions, the correct legal basis for the regulation, whether an existing company should be permitted to convert into an SE, and a requirement in the Proposal that the SE's head office be in the same State as its registered office. There was however, broad agreement that, in addition to the Davignon principles of free negotiation and default rules, in each case there should be a Special Negotiating Body made up of employee representatives and management in accordance with specified geographical and proportional criteria and that employee' rights to information and consultation should broadly reflect those laid down in the Works Council Directive.[145]

In April 1998 the United Kingdom, in a last-ditch bid to secure agreement on the regulation during its Presidency on the Council, put forward a further compromise on

473; Israel, S, 'The European Company Statute—"SE" in Wymeersch, E (ed), *Further Perspectives on Financial Integration in Europe* (1994)....

139. Arts. 2(3) and 37a.

140. The UK also has concerns about the protection of creditors in the event of an SE transferring its head office from one Member State to another.

141. Communication on worker information and consultation, COM (95) 547 final, 14 November 1995.

143. *Analysis of Replies to Commission Consultation Paper on Company Law* (XV/6013/97), point 1(a).

144. The text of the report may be found in Dine, J and Hughes, P, *EC Company Law* (1991) (which, since the work is loose-leaf, is up to date to 1998), A3.77–A3.126.

145. Council Directive (EC) 94/45 on the establishment of a European Works Council or a procedure in Community-scale undertakings and Community-scale groups of undertakings for the purposes of informing and consulting employees [1994] OJ L254/64.

worker participation. It proposed that inter alia, where an SE was formed by merger of existing companies, the employee participation rights applying to employees of the merging companies should continue to apply to the SE, except where two-thirds of the employees decide otherwise, and that in other situations there should be no obligation to introduce worker participation to the SE subject to agreement to the contrary within the Special Negotiating Body. This compromise was substantially accepted,[146] although other areas remained contentious. Finally, however, the Proposal stalled once again. In view of its forthcoming Parliamentary elections in September 1998 and the politically explosive nature of any concession on employees' participation, Germany requested that consideration of the Proposal be postponed for a few months. Moreover two stumbling blocks remained, namely the voting rules within the Special Negotiating Body (France, Spain and Italy objected to the proposal whereby one-third of the employees could in effect insist on importing participation provisions from another Member State) and the question whether an SE may be constituted by transformation of an existing company (Ireland, supported by Italy, Spain, the United Kingdom and Greece, objecting to the proposed dropping of that possibility).

Whether the European Company Statute will be adopted remains to be seen. For a brief window, the requisite but elusive political will seemed to be there. If it is adopted, the compromise as to worker participation which that would necessarily represent may well pave the way for a resumption of negotiations on the draft Tenth Directive, also deadlocked as a result of German fears that its employee participation legislation will be undermined by the structures put in place by the directive.

Comments and Questions

1. In 2001, and to the surprise of many, the EU adopted a Statute for a European Company, Council Regulation (EC) No 2157/2001 of 8 October 2001 on the Statute for a European company (SE), OJ L 294 , 10/11/2001 P. 0001–0021, substantially in the form of the previously abandoned version (absent provisions on the participation of workers in the enterprise). The Statute provides for EU chartering of companies whose shares are intended to be publicly held. The announcement of this event by the European Union is set forth below.

> More than 31 years after negotiations had begun on the creation of the European company, the Council definitively adopted the two legislative instruments necessary for its creation and, following examination of the European Parliament amendments, confirmed the texts as reviewed favourably at the meeting of the Employment and Social Policy Council on 20 December 2000.
>
> The Statute for the European company will provide enterprises with an optional new instrument, which will make cross-border enterprise management more flexible and less bureaucratic and should help improve the competitiveness of Community enterprises. It will make it possible for a company to be set up within the territory of the Community in the form of a public limited-liability company, with the Latin name Societas Europaea (SE). The SE will make it possible to operate Community-wide while being subject to Community legislation directly ap-

146. The Economic and Social Committee, which issued an opinion on the proposed compromise, also broadly endorsed it subject to certain suggestions: [1998] OJ C129/3.

plicable in all Member States. Several options will be available to enterprises from at least two Member States wishing to form an SE: a merger, a holding company, the creation of a subsidiary, or transformation into an SE. The statute will allow a public limited-liability company which has its registered office and head office within the Community to transform itself into an SE without going into liquidation. The SE will be entered in a register in the Member State where its registered office is situated. Every registered SE will be publicised in the Official Journal of the European Communities. An SE must take the form of a company with share capital. To ensure that such companies are of a reasonable size, a minimum amount of capital of at least EUR 120 000 has been set.

The rules relating to employee involvement in the SE are the subject of the directive whose provisions seek to ensure that the creation of an SE does not entail the disappearance or reduction of practices of employee involvement existing within the companies participating in the establishment of an SE. Given the diversity of rules and practices in the Member States as regards the manner in which employees' representatives are involved in decision-making within companies, a single European model is not intended. Nevertheless, procedures for the information and consultation of workers at transnational level will be ensured. When rights to participate exist within one or more of the companies establishing

an SE, those rights will be preserved through their transfer to the SE, once established, unless the parties involved decide otherwise within the special negotiating body, which brings together the employees' representatives of all companies concerned. Procedures for the information and consultation of workers at transnational level will also be ensured.

The regulation on the statute for a European company and the Council directive supplementing the statute for a European company with regard to the involvement of employees will enter into force together, three years after adoption.

Bulletin EU 10-2001 available at <http://europa.eu.int/abc/doc/off/bull/en/200110/p103046.htm> [OJ L 294, 10.11.2001].

2. The text of the Statute for a European Company, Council Regulation (EC) No 2157/2001 of 8 October 2001, may be found at http://europa.eu.int/eur-lex/pri/en/oj/dat/2001/l_294/l_29420011110en00010021.pdf. The regulation will enter into force on 8 October 2004. In the meantime, Member States will have to adjust their statutes, and prepare their corporate registers, for this new corporate form.

3. The law to be applied to the governance of SEs is derived from three primary sources. *See* Art. 9 of the Statute. The first is the Statute for a European Company, the second is from national law transposing the directive on worker participation in the management of an SE, and the third is national law applicable to the public limited companies of the Member State in which the SE is registered. The recitals of the Statute for a European Company state in this regard that:

(9) Since the Commission's submission in 1970 of a proposal for a Regulation on the Statute for a European public limited-liability company, amended in 1975, work on the approximation of national company law has made substantial progress, so that on those points where the functioning of an SE does not need uniform Community rules reference may be made to the law governing public limited-liability companies in the Member State where it has its registered office.

OJ L 294, 10/11/2001 P.002.

An example of the interweaving of community and national law in connection with the law applicable to an SE is found in Art. 4, which provides for a minimum subscribed capital of no be less than EUR 120000, but requires that where the laws of a Member State require a greater subscribed capital for companies carrying on certain types of activity, local law is to apply to SEs with registered offices in that Member State. Moreover, the capital of an SE, its maintenance and changes thereto, together with its shares, bonds and other similar securities shall be governed by the provisions which would apply to a public limited-liability company with a registered office in the Member State in which the SE is registered. In addition, the formation of an SE is to be governed by the law of the Member State in which the SE is to be registered. To what extent does this combination of applicable laws contribute to uniformity among SEs? If the Member States still retain substantial responsibility for the governance of SEs, to what extent does the Statute advance the integration of company law? Does the answer depend on the willingness of the EU to continue to harmonize the laws of the Member States through directives?

4. If the laws of the Member States apply to SEs to some large extent, then what is the incentive for corporations to become SEs? One answer may be the ease with which an SE can change the site of its registered office (and in so doing the laws applicable to it). Art. 8 provides that the registered office of an SE may be transferred to another Member State without requiring the winding up of the SE or in the creation of a new legal person. Do you think that the ability of the largest companies in the EU to change their state of residence will lead to a race to the bottom with respect to corporate regulation in the way it has in the United States? Does it make a difference that a change of legal residence requires the movement of the principal offices of the company as well as its registered office?

5. Employee involvement in the enterprise has always been a sticking point for approval of an EU company law. The issue seems to have been resolved by creating a statute without mandatory employee participation rules, and adopting a directive setting out the general rules and objects of employee participation but allowing Member States some leeway in the manner in which the rules are transposed into national law. The Statute for a European Company recites in this connection that "(21) Directive 2001/86/EC is designed to ensure that employees have a right of involvement in issues and decisions affecting the life of their SE. Other social and labour legislation questions, in particular the right of employees to information and consultation as regulated in the Member States, are governed by the national provisions applicable, under the same conditions, to public limited-liability companies." OJ L 294 , 10/11/2001 P. 0002. It is clear that the directive intends that Member States develop a default rule by which the SE must inherit the employee participation rules which are the most expansive. This generally will tend to favor the German model of employee participation where one or more of the companies merging to form an SE include a German company. Even where that is not the case, the directive will provide for extensive worker information and consultation rights. This would seem to require the greatest change for English and Irish companies, whose governance systems have been grounded on the exclusion of employees from the governance process as employees (though employees have always been free to participate in governance as shareholders to the extent they are willing to buy interests in the company).

6. The SE is not intended to supplant companies chartered by the Member States—at least not yet. It is meant for the large company whose business is not limited to one Member State. The preamble of the Statute for a European Company notes that "For

that purpose it is essential that companies the business of which is not limited to satisfying purely local needs should be able to plan and carry out the reorganisation of their business on a Community scale." OJ L 294, 10/11/2001 P. 0001. Consider whether, in the long term, the availability of the SE will eventually limit the utility of chartering under the laws of a Member State to those enterprises of a purely local character? It is possible to argue that as the internal market becomes more of a reality, and as borders between Member States become less of a barrier, that the incentive will increase to register as an SE and thus avoid regulation.

7. Art. 7 of the Statute requires that the registered office of an SE be located within the Community, in the same Member State as its head office. A Member State may in addition impose on SEs registered in its territory the obligation of locating their head office and their registered office in the same place. It seems clear that through the Statute, the EU has rejected the Anglo-American rule and adopted the siege social rule we studied in Chapter 5. Does this provision effectively attempt a legislative overturning of the rule in *Centros*?

8. It appears that, since the Statute places such a heavy emphasis on the company law of the Member States for the governance of SEs, integration of company law through the SE may depend for its long term success on the ability of the EU to effectively harmonize Member State company law.

Indeed, as the readings below suggest, federalization of company law through the SE may be as unnecessary in the EU as it has become in the United States. In the the federalization of the markets for shares may have effectively federalized the regulation of enterprises corresponding to European public limited companies. Thus regulated in important respects, the need to harmonize directly regulation of the internal affairs of corporations might be unnecessary. Moreover, the regulation of public limited companies through the securities laws might also effectively serve to indirectly regulate private limited companies (closely held corporations in the United States). The model of governance of the public limited companies may provide a form-of-governance base which will serve as the standard for lenders and investors. Each may then require compliance with these forms of regulation of all companies in which they invest. In the case of the European Union, piecemeal federalization, through harmonization of the most important, and politically innocuous aspects of internal governance may eventually provide the framework for the unification of European corporate law. As you read the section that follows, consider whether or not a case can be made for this view, and whether, there is a lesson here that the Europeans have learned from the Americans, or a lesson that Americans might learn from the European experience.

---

3. *Directives (EC Treaty, Arts. 249–256, formerly Arts. 189–192)*

Unlike regulations, which are directly binding on the Member States, directives are only "binding, as to the result to be achieved, upon each Member State to which it is addressed, but...leave[s] to the national authorities the choice of form and methods." EC TREATY, Art. 249. As such, they are not meant to serve as a means of uniformity—they serve primarily to effect the approximation of the laws of the Member States, leaving enough flexibility to accommodate the political realities of each of the Member States. Thus, the EC

Treaty directs the "Council [to] issue directives for the approximation of such provisions laid down by law, regulation or administrative action in Member States as directly affect the establishment or functioning of the common market." EC TREATY, Art. 94, formerly Art. 100.

Directives are addressed to the Member States, and are in the nature of commands, imposing specific obligations on the Member States. Member States are obligated to implement such directives by binding acts. Advisory or other non-binding practices will not suffice. The EC Treaty gives the EC Commission the authority to enforce directives against recalcitrant Member States. EC TREATY, Art. 226. Generally, neither the EC Commission, nor the ECJ has been particularly receptive to excuses respecting the failure of a Member State to implement directives.

Phonogram Ltd. v. Brian Lane

English Court of Appeal (Civil Division)
[1982] 3 CMLR 615
10 March 1981

THE MASTER OF THE ROLLS [Lord Denning]: In 1973 there was a group of 'pop' artists. They included two gentlemen called Brian Chatton and John McBurnie. The suggestion was that they should perform under the name 'Cheap Mean and Nasty'. A company was going to be formed to run the group. It was to be called 'Fragile Management Ltd.'

Before the company was formed, negotiations took place for the financing of the group. It was to be financed by one of the subsidiaries of a big organization called the Hemdale Group. It was eventually arranged that money should be provided by Phonogram Ltd. The agreed amount was £12,000, and the first installment was to be £6,000. The first instalment of £6,000 was paid.

But the new company was never formed. The group never performed under it. And the £6,000 was due to be repaid. But it was never repaid. Phonogram Ltd. then tried to discover who was liable to repay the money. Mr Roland Rennie was the man who had negotiated on behalf of the new company which was to be formed. I will read the letter from Mr Rennie to Mr Lane of 4 July 1973. It is the subject-matter of this action:

'Brian Lane, Esq,

Fragile Ltd.,

39, South Street, London, W1.

Dear Brian,

In regard to the contract now being completed between Phonogram Ltd. and Fragile Management Ltd. concerning recordings of a group consisting of Brian Chatton, John McBurnie and one other with a provisional title of "Cheap Mean and Nasty" and further to our conversation this morning, I send you herewith our cheque for £6,000 in anticipation of the contract signing, this being the initial payment for the initial LP called for in the contract.

In the unlikely event that we fail to complete within, say, one month you will undertake to repay us the £6,000.

As per our telephone conversation the cheque has been made payable to Jelly Music Ltd.

For good orders sake, Brian, I should be appreciative if you could sign the attached copy of this letter and return it to me so that I can keep our accounts people informed of what is happening.

Yours sincerely,

Roland G Rennie

SIGNED BY...

For and on behalf of FRAGILE MANAGEMENT LTD.'

That was signed by Mr Lane. So there is the written contract embodying the agreement between those concerned. An invoice was sent forward by Phonogram Ltd:

'Invoice

To contract between Fragile Management and Phonogram Ltd.

Re "Cheap Mean & Nasty		6,000.00
	VAT	600.00
		£6,600.00

Initial Payment for first album as in contract.'

The money was paid over. According to the accounts, it went into the account of Jelly Music Ltd., which was one of the subsidiaries of the Hemdale Group of which Mr Lane, with others, was a director.

The first question is whether, on the true construction of the contract, Mr Lane made himself personally liable. As I read the words of the contract—'I send you herewith our cheque for £6,000' and 'In the unlikely event that we fail to complete within, say, one month you will undertake to repay us the £6,000'—the word 'you' referred to Mr Lane personally. The cheque was made out in favour of Jelly Music Ltd. only as a matter of administrative convenience (as the judge found). It did not effect the fact that the agreement to repay was made by Brian Lane: especially when it is realized that it was known to all concerned that Fragile Management Ltd. had not been formed. So I would have construed the contract, without recourse to any other aids, as making Mr Lane personally liable.

But Phillips J construed the contract differently. He had heard a lot of evidence. He said in his judgment at page 5B:

'But I am quite satisfied that the events of the 4th July did not of themselves involve a contract with Mr Lane personally.'

I will accept for the moment that the judge was correct in so holding. Even so Phonogram Ltd. say that the law of England has been much altered by section 9(2) of the European Communities Act 1972. It says:

> 'Where a contract purports to be made by a company, or by a person as agent for a company, at a time when the company has not been formed, then subject to any agreement to the contrary the contract shall have effect as a contract entered into by the person purporting to act for the company or as agent for it, and he shall be personally liable on the contract accordingly.'

That seems to me to cover this very case. The contract purports to be made on behalf of Fragile Management Ltd., at a time when the company had not been formed. So he is to be personally liable for it.

Mr Thompson, on behalf of Mr Lane, argued very skillfully that section 9(2) did not apply. First, he said: 'Look at the directive under the European Community law which led to this section being introduced.' It is the directive of 9 March 1968. (1st Company Law Directive [1968] OJ Spec Ed 41, [1978] 1 Commercial Laws of Europe 325.) It was written in French. (In 1968 English was not one of the official languages of the European Community). So Mr Thompson referred us to the French text of Article 7 of the directive:

> 'Si des actes ont ete accomplis au nom d'une societe en formation, avant l'acquisition par celle-ci de la personnalite morale, et si la societe ne reprend pas les engagements resultant de ces actes, les personnes qui les ont accomplis en sont solidairement et indefiniment responsables, sauf convention contraire.'
>
> (The authentic English text of Article 7 provides:
>
> 'If, before a company being formed has acquired legal personality, action has been carried out in its name and the company does not assume the obligations arising from such action, the persons who acted shall, without limit, be jointly severally liable therefor, unless otherwise agreed.')

Mr Thompson says that, according to the French text, that directive is limited to companies which are 'en formation,' that is companies which have already started to be formed.

Mr Thompson's submission is reinforced by a passage from a French textbook—Ripert et Roblot Traite Elementaire de Droit Commercial (1970). As I read the passages at pages 601 and 604 of that treatise—interpreting the French as best I can—in the case of a French company or societe there may be, recognised by law, a period of time while a company is in the course of formation when people have put their signatures to what I may call 'the articles of association.' That period is called the period when the societe is 'en formation.' At page 604 a parallel is drawn with a baby at the time of gestation—between the time of conception and the time of birth—and a company when it is 'en formation.'

I reject Mr Thompson's submission. I do not think we should go by the French text of the directive. It was drafted with regard to a different system of company law from that in this country. We should go by section 9(2) of our own statute, the European Communities Act 1972. Under Article 189 of the Treaty, these directives are to be binding only in so far as the spirit and the intent are concerned. Article 189 says:

> 'A directive shall be binding, as to the result to be achieved, upon each member-State to which it is addressed. But shall leave to the national authorities the choice of form and methods.'

Section 9(2) is in accordance with the spirit and intent of the directive. We should go by our own statute, and not by the directive.

That brings me to the second point. What does 'purports' mean in this context? Mr Thompson suggests that there must be a representation that the company is already in existence. I do not agree. A contract can purport to be made on behalf of a company, or by a company, even though that company is known by both parties not to be formed and that it is only about to be formed.

The third point made by Mr Thompson was that a company can be 'a person' within the second line of section 9(2). Mr Thompson say that Jelly Music Ltd. was 'a person' which was purporting to contract on behalf of Fragile Management Ltd. I do not agree. Jelly Music Ltd. were not entering into a contract. Mr Lane was purporting to do so.

So all three of Mr Thompson's points fail.

But I would not leave the matter there. This is the first time the section has come before us. It will have much impact on the common law. I am afraid that before 1972 the common law had adopted some fine distinctions. As I understand Kelner v. Baxter ((1866) LR 2 CP 174) it decided that, if a person contracted on behalf of a company which was non-existent, he himself would be liable on the contract. Just as, if a man signs a contract for on behalf 'of his horses,' he is personally liable. But, since that case was decided, a number of distinctions have been introduced by Hollman v. Pullin ((1884) Cab & E 254); Newborne v. Sensolid (Great Britain) Ltd. ([1954] 1 QB 45) and Black v. Smallwood in the High Court of Australia (117 CLR 51 (1965)). Those three cases seem to suggest that there is a distinction to be drawn according to the way in which an agent signs a contract. If he signs it as 'agent for "X" company'—or 'for and on behalf of "X" company'—and there is no such body as 'X' company, then he himself can be sued upon it. On the other hand, if he signs it as 'X' company per pro himself the managing director, then the position may be different: because he is not contracting personally as an agent. It is the company which is contracting.

That distinction was disliked by Windeyer J in Black v. Smallwood. It has been criticised by Mr Treitel in The Law of Contract (5th ed at p 559). In my opinion the distinction has been obliterated by section 9(2) of the European Communities Act 1972. We now have the clear words. 'Where a contract purports to be made by a company, or by a person as agent for a company, at a time when the company has not been formed.' That applies whatever formula is adopted. The person who purports to contract for the company is personally liable.

There is one further point on section 9(2) which I must mention. In the latest edition of Cheshire and Fifoot's Law of Contract at page 462, after reciting section 9(2), it says:

> 'How far it in fact does so will depend on the meaning given to the words "subject to any agreement to the contrary" since it could be argued that words showing that A signs as agent express an agreement that he is not to be personally liable. If this were correct Newborne v. Sensolid (Great Britain) Ltd. would still be decided the same way. But it may be suspected that the courts will try to give more content to the subsection.'

We certainly will. The words 'subject to any agreement to the contrary' mean—as Shaw LJ suggested in the course of the argument—'unless otherwise agreed.' If there was an express agreement that the man who was signing was not to be liable, the section would not apply. But, unless there is a clear exclusion of personal liability, section 9(2) should be given its full effect. It means that in all cases such as the present, where a person purports to contract on behalf of a company not yet formed, then however he expresses his signature he himself is personally liable on the contract.

I think that Phillips J was right on the section 9(2) point. I would dismiss the appeal.

SHAW LJ: I agree. Like my Lord I would have read into the letter of 4 July 1973 an undertaking on the part of Mr Lane to be personally liable for the repayment of the £6,000 if the contemplated contract with Fragile Management Ltd. was not in the event entered into. But the learned judge found otherwise on the facts, and it is not open to this court—as there is no cross-notice in regard to this—to depart from that finding. So one has to look to the basis upon which the learned judge himself came to the conclusion in favour of the plaintiffs.

The general principle is, of course, that a person who makes a contract ostensibly as an agent cannot afterwards sue or be sued upon it, subject to the qualifications where there is a foreign principal or a del credere agent. The real problem in any given situation is to determine the status of the persons who enter into the engagement. Are they entering into it—whatever form of description they may use—as agents or as principals? It may be that a similar formula in different cases will lead to a different conclusion because the surrounding facts have a different impact upon the interpretation of phrases such as 'for and on behalf of,' as in Kelner v. Baxter. There, notwithstanding the use of that phrase, the judgment proceeded upon the basis that the reality of the matter was that the parties so subscribing themselves were acting as principals, and this was so notwithstanding that reference was made to a company which was in contemplation though not incorporated when the contract was signed.

It could of course happen—and did happen—that in some cases where an agent enters into a contract for a company whose incorporation is contemplated but which had not yet been effected, the third party would be left without redress. He could not sue the agent on the contract itself because the agent had acted as such; nor could the third party sue the agent for breach of warranty of authority if it was known to the third party that the ostensible principal was not in existence. Section 9(2) of the European Communities Act

1972 gives a remedy in such a situation.

Mr Thompson, in his careful analysis of it, put forward a number of propositions, but I agree with the result described by my Lord in dealing with the effect of subsection (2) in the light of the directive. I also think that the note in Cheshire and Fifoot requires to be reconsidered.

I would dismiss this appeal.

OLIVER LJ: I also agree. Speaking for myself I am not convinced that the common law position apart from the Act depends upon the narrow distinction between a signature 'for and on behalf of' and a signature in the name of a company or an association. The question I think in each case is what is the real intent as revealed by the contract? Does the contract purport to be one which is directly between the supposed principal and the other party, or does not purport to be one between the agent himself—albeit acting for a supposed principal—and the other party? In other words, what you have to look at is whether the agent intended himself to be a party to the contract. So in Kelner v. Baxter where the correspondence was directed to the agents and referred to 'the proposed company which everybody knew was not yet in existence, there really was no room for the suggestion that the purchasers were acting in any other capacity than personally. On the other hand, in Newborne v. Sensolid, where the contract was on the company's notepaper, it was clearly intended to be a company's contract (nobody realising that it had not yet been registered) and it could not be said that the individual plaintiff's signature in the company's name could possibly have been intended to make him a party to the contract.

The case, in my judgment, does not rest on any narrow point as to the way in which the contract was actually signed. The result would have been exactly the same, in my judgment, as if the signature there had been accompanied by some such formula as 'for and on behalf of' or 'per prop.' The judgment of Parker J and the judgments in the Court of Appeal of Lord Goddard and Morris LJ (as he then was) show that the case turned on what the contract purported to do; and precisely the same applies I think in the case of Hollman v. Pullin ((1884) Cab & E 254), were a contract, albeit signed by the plaintiff as chairman of the association, was clearly intended to be, and intended only to be, a contract directly with the association by which the defendant's services were intended to be retained. The same again I think applies to the Australian case of Black v. Smallwood. The contract there on its face purported to be a contract between the vendor and the company as purchaser and nothing else, nobody then realising that the company had not been incorporated.

Whether that is right or not, any such subtle distinctions which might have been raised are rendered now irrelevant by section 9(2) of the European Communities Act 1972 in a case where a contract is either with a company or with the agent of a company. It has been suggested that an agreement to the contrary may still be inferred by the fact that the contract was signed by a person acting as agent so as to exclude the section. That I am bound to say seems to me to be wholly unarguable when the section itself in terms provides 'Where a contact purports to be made... by a person as agent for a company,' and to interpret it in the way suggested would defeat the whole purpose of the section.

For the reasons which my Lords had given in the instant case, I agree that the appeal should be dismissed.

Appeal dismissed with costs. Application for leave to appeal to the House of Lords refused.

4. EU Company Law Harmonization

The EU has been able to federalize company law between its Member States, to some extent, through the extensive use of directives. As a result, direct harmonization of company law, with a tolerance of some national deviation, rather than unification, has been the norm. American federal legislation, on the other hand, has been indirect and unifying, with little tolerance for state based deviation, but indirect. This section explores the policy and legal basis for company law harmonization within the EU. Materials that follow introduce you to some of the main issues and arguments in the debate about harmonization of company laws.

Company law harmonization is said to be linked to the core objectives of the EC Treaty. The EC Commission has, over the course of the last decade, taken this position in the strongest of terms.

The White Paper, Completing the Internal Market: White Paper From the Commission to the European Council

COM(85)310 final
June, 1985
¶¶ 219–222

219. Europe stands at the crossroads. We either go ahead—With resolution and determination—or we drop back into mediocrity. We can not either resolve to complete the integration of the economies of Europe; or, through a lack of political will to face the immense problems involved, we can simply allow Europe to develop into no more than a free trade area.

220. The difference is crucial. A well developed free trade area offers significant advantages: it is something much better than that which existed before the Treaty of Rome; better even than that which exists today. But it would fail and fail dismally to release the energies of the people of Europe; it would fail to deploy Europe's immense economic resources to the maximum advantage; and it would fail to satisfy the aspirations of the people of Europe.

221. The free movement of goods is an important, valuable and possibly indispensable step which has to be taken before economic integration can be achieved. But it is not the ultimate goal; at best it is the indispensable precursor. This philosophy is clearly reflected in the Treaties themselves. The Customs Union was the first objective of the Treaty of Rome. But that it was by no means intended as the last is clearly demonstrated by the fact that what the Treaty established was the European Economic Community. The preamble to the Treaty starts with the declaration :

> "Determined to lay the foundations of an ever closer union among the peoples of Europe, resolved to ensure the economic and progress of their countries by common action to eliminate the barriers which divide Europe".

222. Just as the Customs Union had to precede Economic Integration, so Economic Integration has to precede European Unity. What this White Paper proposes therefore is that the Community should now take a further step along the road so clearly delineated in the Treaties. To do less would be to fall short of the ambitions of the founders of the Community, incorporated in the Treaties; it would be to betray the trust invested in us; and it would be to offer the peoples of Europe a narrower, less rewarding, less secure, less prosperous future than they could otherwise enjoy. That is the measure of the challenge which faces us. Let it never be said that we were incapable of rising to it.

In particular, harmonization is said to foster the freedom of establishment under Article 43 et seq. [old Art. 52 et seq. of the EEC Treaty. The source of the power to harmonize Member State legislation is found specifically in Art. 44(3)(g) [Art. 54(3)(g)]: "The Council and the Commission shall carry out the duties devolving upon them [to abolish existing restrictions on the freedom of establishment], in particular:...(g) by coordinating to the necessary extent the safeguards which, for the protection of the interests of members and others, are required by Member States of companies or firms within the meaning of the second paragraph of article 58 with a view to making such safeguards equivalent throughout the Community."

Article 44, formerly Article 54, nicely illustrates the tensions underlying unification within Europe. On the one hand, the creation of a single economic unit within Europe is premised on the basic necessity of freedom for business enterprises to operate throughout the EU without impediment on account of the form of its organization. Without the freedom of enterprises to operate unfettered within the whole of the EU, the creation of an integrated market would not be possible. Without this freedom to establish throughout the EU, the cost of business rises and impediments to the creation of a single economic unit within the EU rise as well. An indirect consequence, of course, is increased cost of goods and services to the consumer. The cost of regulatory compliance with the different requirements of each of the Member States raises basic operating costs to the enterprise as a whole. These costs are sometimes reflected in the price consumers pay for the goods or services. Sometimes, however, where the competitive environment makes it difficult to pass these costs along, the enterprise might choose to forego entry into a market. Alternatively, the enterprise might entirely forgo the production of a good or service, especially if economies of scale require a multi-Member State market. In either case, EU businesses, and the economies of the Member States, would suffer. Smaller business might mean less employment, less consumption, and less production of retained wealth within the EU.

On the other hand, the drive for efficiency underlying the freedom of establishment may have significant costs as well, especially with respect to strongly held regulatory preferences among the Member States. To the extent that such regulatory preferences are both strongly held and differ significantly between Member States, the result of an unfettered and broadly interpreted right of corporate 'freedom of establishment' throughout the EU could effectively undercut the ability of any Member State to regulate the corporate enterprises operating from within its borders. This undercutting has become a particularly sensitive political issue with respect to regulations regarded as important for the protection of shareholders from management. Broadly read then, the right of establishment could enable a corporation, validly existing under the laws of one Member State, to operate directly or indirectly in all other Member States through branches or subsidiaries, or to establish principal or significant offices in other Member States, without being subject to the peculiar rules of these other Member States. If this is the case, corporations would tend to operate from out of those Member States with the least onerous demands on managers, and likely with the lowest level of protection for shareholders. Member States wishing to retain control over enterprises operating within its borders would have to match the regulatory regimes of the most 'popular' Member States, all to the detriment of the Member States. The political will of Member States would thus be bent to the will of the business elite, rather than reflect that of the electorate. Member State corporate law meant to protect investors and lenders would be dead letter, since corporations operating within the jurisdiction would be subject to the presumably more 'lax' law of another Member State. This, of course, is the 'Delaware effect' with a European face.

Thus, the very problems the EU is meant to cure, fractionalization and the economic inefficiencies associated with it, in turn creates the possibility of a troublesome 'Delaware effect' in Europe. The antidote to this Delaware effect enacted through the EU Treaty comes in the form of harmonization and coordination, rather than unification. Harmonization offers the possibility of requiring all Member States to impose certain minimum requirements on corporations. These minimum requirements would be the product of political discourse at the 'federal' level—the institutions of the EU. But, at the same time, harmonization would permit each Member State to implement these minimum requirements in their own way, in order to incorporate these requirements within the peculiar political or institutional set up of each Member State. In this way, it is thought, freedom of establishment becomes politically feasible, and the 'Delaware effect' is muzzled in a manner that minimizes any interference with a Member State's regulation of its economic enterprises.[1] In effect, some have argued, it makes no sense to provide for a Europe-wide integrated market managed by the institutions of the EU, while at the same time permitting the regulation of an important component of that market—enterprises—to be managed by a sub-part of that integrated market—the Member States. To permit Member States exclusive authority over enterprise regulation

1. For a discussion of these issues, *see generally* the essays in HARMONIZATION OF COMPANY AND SECURITIES LAW (B. Wachter et al., eds., 1989).

would effectively privilege some segments of the unified market (those Member States willing to forego shareholder or other important protections to attract enterprise creation within its borders) while damaging other segments (those Member States holding such protections important), without control or direction from the regulators of the market itself. This form of organization is inefficient, because it ultimately reduces the optimal performance of the unified market as a whole. It is also undemocratic, because it effectively imposes the will of the people of one segment of the integrated unit on the people of all other segments.

Not everyone examining the call for harmonization in European company law has come to believe that harmonization, as currently proposed, is useful or has any prospect of real success. Consider the following criticism in light of any arguments in favor of harmonization.

Richard M. Buxbaum and Klaus J. Hopt, *Legal Harmonization and the Business Enterprise: Corporate and Capital Market Law Harmonization Policy in Europe and the U.S.A.*

(1988)

(excerpt pages 15–20; footnotes omitted)

* * *

For some, integration as such is a value. We doubt, however, whether economic or cultural integration, not to mention the range of political and social integration possibilities lying between these two, is *eo ipso* better than diversification without a definition of and consensus about values underlying that conclusion. Certainly at the level of cultural integration there would be no intuitive choice to abandon richness and diversity of experience, let alone to assume that these losses in fact would be balanced by gains of harmony, peace, justice or other social virtues.

To the extent law is an element of a nation's culture, legal integration, too, should be valued for its functional purposes, not as an end in itself. The proper questions are whether, for example, an accepted value—such as a given level of consumer protection, environmental preservation or labor co-determination—is better served by a more centripetal or more centrifugal policy....

It is still unclear whether any existing economic or political theory of integration is already able to offer a fully developed, operational model of how to draw rational dividing lines between federal and state regulation of company and capital market law. It is clear that in the European Community of today the institutions responsible for the harmonization of law have not yet even taken up those bits and pieces of any theory which might be helpful to that effort. Instead, they explicitly understand themselves to be political actors, rather than social engineers, and seem inclined to reach politically feasible compromises at the outset rather than to construct a theoretically optimal dual legislative system in this field.

* * *

* * * * [G]iven in addition the possible theoretical flaws of any model, the financial drain of embarking on a search for empirical data, and not least the uncertainty of

whether the outcome of a theoretical or empirical effort in fact would strengthen the institutional quest for harmonization, the situation is rather such as to discourage European law-making agencies from engaging in these efforts. What these institutions then provide is an explicitly politicized lawmaking process under certain institutional and organizational framework limitations.

In this process the Commission of course has traditionally seen itself as the advocate of more centripetal forces, albeit a politically sensitized advocate; and as such it naturally comes under attack from those forces which are centrifugal in not only political but also technical law-making orientation. Most articulate in this context in recent years have been the English courts, which have contested much of what the Commission is doing in the area of harmonization of laws. Even here, however, the battle is waged on explicitly political or legal "turf" grounds. Even if it would make sense for Member States to rely on economic theses..., which basically favors the political stance of reserving maximum jurisdiction to state lawmaking bodies, their positions tend to be articulated rather in explicit political terms. Specifically, these groups tend to argue in favor of restricting harmonization to the least and absolutely necessary extent, of respecting national legal traditions and positions because they predate the new traditions and positions being proposed as alternatives, and finally and simply of encroaching as little as possible upon national sovereignty. In short, the reality of present European harmonization activity, whether seen from the perspective of the federal or of the state actor, is that of explicit political thrust and counter thrust.

* * *

* * * * [P]rospects for efficient implementation of appropriate harmonization policies in the company law and capital market fields are relatively dim. Of course, in time the law of the Member States will adapt to a reasonable degree to comply with the harmonization compromises presently or soon to be reached at the European level. It is quite another question whether this degree of harmonization will have significant effects in the near future on overall corporate structure and business behavior as these bear on the developing integration of the national markets and legal institutions serving the Common Market.

* * *

Comments and Questions

1. The excerpts from the White Paper suggest the impetus for greater harmonization—the idea that unity in a mere free trade zone would do little to release the synergistic possibilities of a closer union within the boundaries of the EU. Can you describe the nature of the synergies which could be released by harmonization and closer integration among the Member States that would not be realized in the context of a free trade zone?

2. While the differences between the corporate regulatory regimes of states in the United States has not been significant enough to warrant sustained politically significant debate about the 'Delaware effect' in the United States, the opposite has been the case within Europe. Yet, the American debate on the 'Delaware effect' has been held in the context of increasingly pervasive regulation of the offer of securities to investors at the federal level. Federal securities laws, the American people have been told, offer a rel-

atively efficient market in information about corporations whose shares are offered for investment, and also provide a mechanism for easy exit through the maintenance of significant markets for shares and other investment instruments. These capital markets, to a great extent, have not been available within Europe. Nor has the system of enterprise organization been dependant on the existence of large capital markets within most of the states of the EU, at least until very recently. To what extent might these differences account for the different reaction to the 'perils' of the 'Delaware effect' within the EU and the US? Would you expect the European view to change as the EU develops its capital markets? Would your answer depend on the way these capital markets are organized?

3. Professors Bauxbaum and Hopt present an interesting twist on the arguments against harmonization. First, they suggest that harmonization may not be permitted at all. Like the freedom of establishment, the EU has raised as a basic right, the freedom of culture within the EU law, Bauxbaum and Hopt, argue, is an expression of the culture of a nation. As such, harmonization violates the cultural rights of a Member State—rights which ought to be accorded equal dignity with an enterprises's right of freedom of establishment. They also argue that, cultural freedom aside, harmonization will not be achieved in fact, whatever its benefits, in the absence of agreement as between the Member States on the underlying values on which harmonization is to be based. However, the Member States have reached no such consensus—even as harmonization progresses. As such, harmonization is either Member State cultural imperialism (the imposition of one Member State's approach applied to the whole of the EU) or has become an unprincipled end in itself. They suggest, indeed, that harmonization in the company law area has devolved into a game of political compromise, with the goal being harmonization at any price, and no underlying unifying vision supporting it. Do you agree?

4. Professors Buxbaum's and Hopt's concerns have recently been echoed in the writings of other commentators, and some courts of the Member States, especially those of the United Kingdom. The commentators have expressed concern about the way in which harmonization may be distorting traditional patterns of corporate formation in ways that may make no sense in light of the traditional means of organizing corporations in the Member States forced to accept the new forms. The harmonization becomes more pernicious as traditional forms are given substantial new characteristics by means of incorporating the characteristics of similarly named forms from other jurisdictions. The courts have tended to "fight" harmonization by adopting a very narrow interpretation of the scope and effect of Council directives. In this regard, the arguments of Angel Rojo, and of the English court in *Phonogram Ltd. v. Brian Lane* provide further insight. Those excerpts provide an insight into the difficulty of harmonization even as between similarly structured systems. Thus, even in a civil law regime distinguishing between public and private limited companies, the cross border regulation of these forms may have uneven effect where national patterns in one state favor one form of organization in a manner unmatched in the other state. In this case national practice distorts an otherwise similar theoretical basis of organization. Can you identify the source of the difference at the heart of the court's analysis in *Phonogram*?

5. Vanessa Edwards' evaluation of the harmonization process offers a more hopeful perspective. As you read the materials that follow recall that, as a conceptual matter, it would be easy enough to harmonize or unify the company law of the European Union formal law making. The same also could be said for the company law of the United States. But as we have seen, formal lawmaking power is only the beginning of the analy-

sis, and usually not its most interesting or important part. Larry Catá Backer provides a larger systems structure perspective on the dynamics of harmonization. The suggestion is both one of tension between the existing levels of government in a federal system, something well understood by Americans under the name "federalism," and the instability of any division of authority between levels of governance. Harmonization, as such, is inherently a temporary affair.

6. As you read these materials, consider whether unification of the company law of the European Union will be possible as a political matter. Can you suggest other or additional approaches to harmonization?

Angel Rojo, *The Typology of Companies*

in EUROPEAN COMPANY LAWS: A COMPARATIVE APPROACH
(Robert R. Drury & Peter G. Xuereb eds. 1991)
(excerpts pages 43, 44–47)

Under current law, the *societe anonyme* form serves two different and antithetic models by reason of type: the classic *societe anonyme* (SA) model and the *Aktiengesellschaft* (AG) one. The former comes from traditional French law, through the existing law of 24 July 1966 is influenced by the opposed model and generally by the Latin models, and also, in some peculiar aspects..., by English law.

The second has its principal legislative manifestation in the German laws on companies limited by shares of 1937 and 1965 and in the Austrian law of 1966.

In order to appreciate the radical variety of conceptions.... [consider that] while in the Federal Republic of Germany the proportion of [AG's to SARL's] is 1:150,...in Spain, just to mention an extreme example within the Latin family, the proportion is 1:0.25....

These statistical data show that the *societe anonyme* form fulfills different functions in different legal orders, and that the relationship between form and type has different characteristics depending on the legislative system.

* * *

The *Societe anonyme* form in the German laws of 1937 and 1965 is intended for large enterprises. It is for the open company of big dimensions which seeks finance in the capital market—a *Publikumgesellschaft*. For this reason, it is characterized by a clear separation between ownership and management ('hetero-organicism' or 'third parties organicism' principal). That is why, interposed between the shareholders' general meeting and the organ entrusted with the management (*Vorstand*) there is an intermediate organ, the Supervisory Board, which in the majority of the German AGs is composed of an equal number of shareholders' and employees' representatives....

Now adopting a historical perspective, it is possible to appreciate that the AG is a form in regression. Since the end of the Second World War, there has been a move towards the SARL in Germany. There are fewer AGs being formed as such, while many of the existing AGs are being transformed into private companies....The AG is not a wide and adaptable cloth which facilitates movement; it is a veritable suit of armor within which only the movements previously envisaged by its constructor are possible—freedom of choice and of contract have a very restricted scope.

* * *

Societe anonyme compared to the model of the AG, the *societe anonyme* of French and Belgian law, the *societa per azioni* of Italian law, and the *sociedad anonima* of Spanish law [corresponding roughly to the English public company and the American general corporation, ed.] are facultative [that is, flexible and adaptable in use, ed.] and not exclusive forms, and they therefore have poly-valency. Although the legal form is designed with the model of the large company in mind, the legal design incorporates sufficient flexibility to allow the use of the *societe anonyme* form by small- and medium-sized undertakings. That is why, in the Latin and Anglo-Saxon countries, the use of the *societe anonyme* is not restricted to large enterprises....

* * *

Some legal systems developed this neutrality to its ultimate conclusion. An example is the Spanish law of 17 July 1951. Under this law, companies in which the shareholders' liability was limited and which had a share capital of more than 50 million pesetas were obliged to adopt the form of *societe anonyme*. This is the so-called technique of the 'reserve of the form;' however, it was provided that the *societe anonyme* form could be used even where the company's capital was below that amount, without the existence of a fixed minimum capital. The consequence of this legally committed freedom of choice was clear: the smallest companies could be *societes anonyme*. Even companies with a nominal capital which could barely afford to pay the cost of the deed and registration were able to adopt this corporate form....

* * *

Viewed from a comparative law perspective, the coexistence of two typological models in relation to one and the same corporate form would not matter if there did not exist a tendency to minimize or even to disregard the differences between them.

Due to a certain lack of awareness or lack of sufficient analysis, there has been a tendency to treat as equivalent the various legal regimes for the SA or, which is even more dangerous, there has been an endeavour to extend completely or partially the legislative regime of the *Aktiengesellschaft* (which is considered to be technically superior) to the other legal regimes which allow the SA form to be functionally poly-valent, thereby restricting this polyvalency without addressing on precise criteria the underlying typological questions.

The process of selection between one form or another is a matter of legislative policy, but the increasing penetration of the Latin SA with ingredients coming from the AG is not acceptable if the difficult task of the typological organization of the different corporate forms is not addressed first.

Although the negative effects of treating as equivalent corporate forms which are topologically non-equivalent started long ago, it is basically during the advance in legislative harmonization due to the incorporation of the EEC directives into national laws that these negative effects have manifested themselves clearly. For example, the incorporation of EEC Directive 77/91 of 13 December 1976 [OJL 26–31 Jan. 1977, P.1, the Second Council Directive on co-ordination of safeguards which, for the protection of the interests of Members and others, are required in respect of the formation of the formation of public limited liability companies and the maintenance and alteration of their capital, with a view to making such safeguards equivalent] has a completely different meaning and a completely different material scope in German law to that which it has in Spanish or Italian law. The Germanization of the EEC Member States' laws or the Europeanization of German law, as it is sometimes put, involves the extension of the rules contained in the *Aktiengesetz* of 1965 to corporate forms of business organizations of identical or similar name but which do not ascribe to the precise and limited typological model of the AG.

The fundamental initial mistake of the Community's harmonization process—although to be partially remedied later—was to consider as identical different forms of business organization, and to fail to take into account the typological reality of the forms of business organization in the laws of the different Member States. The export of the German rules meant that, whilst that legislation was applicable in Germany only to large enterprises constituted as *Aktiengesellschaften*, in other countries it had to be applied to medium- or even to small-sized enterprises, precisely those which in German company law are normally constituted as limited liability companies or under some other different form. Although formally the scope of application of the Second Directive was unitary—and the same could also be said about EEC Directive 77/855 [9 October 1978, the Third Council Directive based on Article 54(3)(g) concerning mergers of public limited liability companies] and to a lesser extent (due to its relative imperativity) about EEC Directive 82/891 of 17 December 1982 [Sixth Council Directive concerning the division of public limited liability companies]—*materially* that unity did not exist.

In order to counteract the effects of the imperialism of the AG over the Latin type of SA, a criterion of size is applied in EEC Directive 78/660 on Capital Accounts. The introduction of this criterion implies the disregard of the "form criterion." The rules are not applied to all SAs, limited liability companies or *societe en commandite par aciones*, but only to some of them, and this irrespective of their form, that is only to those which meet certain determinate requirements of size. Obviously, this is a defense technique against the German model's supremacy. But at the same time, this technique is a guarantee for the subsistence of the neutral types. A law based on the 'dimensional criterion' is superimposed on the law based on the corporate form criterion. The application of the rules is dictated more by the dimension criterion than by the business organization form criterion.

Vanessa Edwards, *EC Company Law*

(1999)

(excerpts pages 11–14; some footnotes omitted)

Evaluation of the Harmonization Process

Certain criticisms of the company law harmonization programme have been touched upon above, in the context of the suitability of directives as the instrument of harmonization. Assessing the success or failure of harmonization also raises more general issues.

Problems where legal notions are not coterminous

A particular problem in seeking to harmonize the laws of the numerous member States with disparate legal traditions is the difficulty of dovetailing legal concepts. A directive may purport to regulate an area in which specific concepts are essential to one State's application and understanding of the law but alien and difficult to comprehend in another legal culture. An example is the introduction into Community company law of the concept of the company organ in the law relating to ultra vires transactions: a notion borrowed from German law which is familiar to the States whose legislation is derived from the Napoleonic Code but which lies uneasily with the United Kingdom's analysis of company transactions within the framework of agency. Similar problems arise—at least pending definitive interpretation by the Court of Justice—from the use of the terms which may not be sufficiently proximate in the different language versions of a directive and in the Member States' implementing legislation. An analogous difficulty, albeit an extreme example, is provided by the Community legislature's abandonment of any attempt to impose a uniform meaning in the despairing admission of the Public Offers Prospectus Directive that it proved impossible to 'furnish a common definition of the term "public offer" and its constituent arts', a notion fundamental to the whole structure of the directive.

The fields harmonized

More generally, criticisms of the harmonization process are directed at the Commission's priorities as illustrated by the topics which are the subject of adopted directives or the undertakings which are subject to them. Thus, for example, the wisdom of restricting the Second Directive to public companies is frequently questioned (although equal vigour has been deployed against the Commission's recent suggestion of extending the Second Directive to private companies). There is a significant disparity between the pattern of incorporation as public and private companies in the different Member States, which distorts the harmonizing effect of measures applying only to one category of companies. The United Kingdom and Germany, for example, have relatively small numbers of public as compared to private companies, whereas in France and Italy, in contrast, many small undertakings use the form of public company.[62] A similar point arises concerning the use of the corporate form generally: because incorporating a company in the United Kingdom is simple and swift, many small businesses operate as companies which on the continent would be more likely to choose to conduct business as a sole trader or small partnership. Legislation directed at companies therefore affects a higher proportion of commercial businesses in the United Kingdom than in many other Member States.

Particular criticism has been levelled at the failure to promote any harmonization of the law relating to groups of companies.... An associated problem is that a directive will have to leave to domestic law areas linked with the topic which it seeks to harmonize, thus further undermining its harmonizing effect: the Third Directive, for example, leaves much to national law. All these problems however are perhaps inevitable consequences of the practical constraints fettering an ambitious programme: in the context of an ever growing number of Member States whose company law diverges widely in certain areas, the alternatives to 'salami tactic' harmonization would almost certainly have been less rather than more effective legislation.

Moreover, and particularly in the early days of the harmonization programme. the Commissions steps toward company law harmonization had significant indirect effect on the national company law of several Member States: in a process graphically described by Professor Schmitthof as the 'radiation effect of Community thinking', various domestic company law reforms were considerably influenced by the Community's harmonization endeavours which 'operated as a leaven on the otherwise rigid company laws of the Member States' and 'fertilised the national companies legislations'.[64] More recently, a similar effect arises from the implementation throughout the Community of directives which marry principles and techniques derived from the legal traditions of

62. The accounting directives resolve this problem by using size criteria rather than corporate form for certain exemptions and concessions.

64. 'The Success of the Harmonization of European Company Law' (1976) 1 ELR 100, 100–1, 107.

different Member States: for example, the United Kingdom concept of the true and fair view in company accounts, and of legal control as a criterion for the preparation of consolidated accounts have now, thanks to national implementation of the Fourth and Seventh Directives, found their way into continental law and practice.

Timescale

The Council's General Programme for the abolition of restrictions on the freedom of establishment,[67] drawn up at the end of 1961, expressly envisaged completion of the co-ordination of company laws in accordance with Article 54(3)(g) by the end of 1963.[68] In 1965, the Commission, replying to a questionnaire sent by the *Commission du marché intérieur*, indicated that its company law harmonization programme undertaken on the basis of Article 54(3)(g) of the Treaty would enable it to draw up, before the end of 1966, draft legislation regulating public and private limited companies.[69] Over thirty years later, although considerable progress has been made, agreement has still not been reached on several important items of legislation the origin of which may be traced back almost as far: the seeds of the European Company Statute were first sown in 1959, the preliminary draft of the Convention on international mergers, now the draft Tenth Directive, was prepared in 1967 and the original proposal of the Fifth Directive dates back to 1972. Why has it taken so long?

Reasons for delays in the early days of the harmonization programme have already been discussed. Progress in finalizing certain directives, such as the Fourth Directive on annual accounts and the Seventh Directive on consolidated accounts, was substantially hindered by difficulties experienced in bridging major differences between national attitudes and practices. There are moreover understandable practical reasons which have so delayed the adoption of, specifically, the Fifth and Tenth Directives, the Thirteenth Directive on Takeovers and the Regulation for a European Company Statute, closely linked to the Fifth Directive, and the complementary directive on worker participation in European Companies....

More generally, perhaps it is misconceived to deduce from the Commission's original aims, which, however laudable, appear with the benefit of hindsight to be ambiguous to the point of naivety, that the harmonization programme has proved unjustifiably long-winded. The issue in the 1960s was the harmonization of the company laws of the six Member States which, even allowing for differences of approach between, for example, the Netherlands and the other five, or between Germany and France, had many common points of origin and many similarities (although even in that context it must not be overlooked that differences in national laws often reflect divergences of policy which may be harder to bridge). A more measured response to the timescale of company law harmonization which has seen the Community grown from six to fifteen Member States, embracing more divergent legal orders, was expressed by the late Professor Gower:

> although progress has indeed been slow, what is surprising to me is that it has not been slower. Any form of law reform is painfully slow and that which involves

67. 18 December 1961, OJ Spec Ed IX, Resolution of the Council and of the Representatives of the Member States, 7.

68. Title VI of the General Programme.

69. Berkhouwer, MMC, 'Rapport fait au nom de la Commission du marché intérieur' [1966] Revue trimestrielle de droit européen 434.

harmonization of the laws of States with different legal roots is slowest of all. Considering the inevitable dislocations caused where new Member States have been admitted, I find it remarkable that so much progress has been made.[73]

Larry Catá Backer, *Forging Federal Systems Within a Matrix of Contained Conflict: The Example of the European Union*

12 Emory Int'l L. Rev. 1331 (1998)
(excerpts pages 1337–1339)

Harmonization, subsidiarity and cultural solicitude describe the variables of the matrix within which the union of Europe develops. The particular way in which a federal system is manifested, as well as the relationships between supra-national, national and local power, will be a function of the intersection of these three parameters. Within these parameters, federal systems can assume an almost unlimited number of forms, and the form of any federal system can shift depending on the relative importance of each of the parameters in every federal system. The European Union today presents an example of one point of intersection of the values of the three parameters; the United States represents another; GATT and the United Nations represent still others.

Three consequences, significant for the development of the EU, flow directly from this construction. First, there is an inverse relationship between the power to set norms, inherent in harmonization, and the efficacy of subsidiarity. The power to declare fundamental rules at one level of government is the power to limit the possibility of the assertion of power by all subsidiary governments. Historically, the Community has been one in which the European Court of Justice ("ECJ") has itself acquired the power to articulate fundamental norms governing all assertions of power by any government within the EU. The necessary consequence of this assertion has been to limit the discretion of subsidiary units of government, the Member States of the Community, to order their "internal affairs."[7]

Second, cultural solicitude is grounded in exceptionalism, and, as such, is subversive. The gravamen of cultural solicitude is the cry "this cannot apply to me!" But what "cannot apply"? If the inapplicable is merely incidental, *and* the alternative is re-

---

73. Buxbaum, Hertig, Hirsch, Hopt (eds.), *European Business Law* (1991) 311. Although Professor Gower was speaking of harmonization generally, he referred in a footnote to the text cited to company law as an example of an area where much progress had been made. For a more humorous slant, see Lempereur, C, 'Myth and Reality in the European Harmonization Process' in Wymeersch, E (ed), *Further Perspectives in Financial Integration in Europe* (1994) 241, 247: 'the [company law, accounting and securities regulation] harmonization process, as it now is, could also be compared to a bottle of wine looked at, at the same time, by a pessimist and by an optimist. The pessimist would say: my bottle of wine is already half empty. The optimist would say: my bottle of wine is still half full.'

7. This should not be confused with the jurisprudential notion of internal affairs, that is, the rule that "the provisions of the Treaty... cannot be applied to situations which are purely internal to a Member State." Case 115/78, Knoors v. Secretary of State for Economic Affairs, [1979] 2 C.M.L.R. 357, 367 (1979).

lated to the imposition rejected, then the subversion exists only as irritant. If the inapplicable involves a rejection of norms set either at the national or supra-national level, then it implies metaphysical secession. Europe has had a tragic history with secession of this type. Since the Second World War, Europe has attempted a delicate balance between permitting subnational peoples the power to express their "identity" and enforcing a uniform application of "really important" socio-political norms at the nation-state and federal levels. For the moment, the Member States have reduced cultural solicitude to touristic artifacts, such as colorful costumes and exotic languages. Yet within this construct lies the possibility of real redirection in the flow of power.

Third, European constitutionalism is inherently unstable. No one place within the matrix provides the perfect mix of harmonization, subsidiarity and cultural solicitude. The optimal combination, and thus the expression of European constitutionalism, will always be a function of the values placed on the three variables by peoples with the power to implement such valuation. The particular mix of harmonization, subsidiarity and cultural solicitude represented by any one place within the matrix will endure only for as long as the valuations producing that mix of the three variables have currency or the people implementing such a mix have the power to maintain it.

Comments and Questions

1. Do the materials you have read make a case for federalization of company law within the EU that is stronger than that made for federalization of the corporate law in the United States? How important to your argument is the ability to harmonize rather than integrate law?

2. What do the arguments for and against "federalization" in the EU and the US have in common? To what factors can differences of perspective of policy be traced? The EU, unlike the US, has a choice as to methods of federalization. The EU can choose to harmonize laws or to unify them. The flexibility of approach is made possible by the existence of the directive as a legislative device. Does the absence of legislation by directive in the US make a difference in the federalization debate? Can you think of devices or practices in the United with the functional effect of directives?

---

5. The Process of Convergence in the European Union

The process of harmonization of the corporate law within the European Union has been slow. Harmonization remains far from complete. As you read the materials that follow think about whether the difficulties are insurmountable. On the other hand, consider whether informed harmonization within Europe is much farther along than the official institutional process.

Maria Green Cowles, *The Changing Architecture of Big Business*

in COLLECTIVE ACTION IN THE EUROPEAN UNION: INTERESTS AND THE NEW POLITICS OF ASSOCIABILITY 108–125 (Justine Greenwood and Mark Aspinwall, eds. 1998) (excerpts pages 108–109)

One of the most important developments in the European Union (EU) has been the mobilisation of large multinational firms.[1] The collective action of European big business signalled the arrival of new politically powerful actors in the Brussels policy making process. Today, the European Roundtable of Industrialists (ERT)—an organization of chief executive officers from forty-five leading European companies—is arguably the most influential interest group in Brussels. Unlike most Brussels based organizations, the ERT directs its agenda setting strategies at the European Council as well as the European Commission. The EU Committee of AmCham—the group of American multinational corporations—is recognised as one of the most efficient interests groups. Every month, the EU Committee sends out more than 10,000 documents—position papers, reports, letters, and so on—to specifically targeted Commission, Council, European Parliament and media officials. European big business has even emerged as an important international actor in the EU. In the transatlantic Business Dialogue (TABD), large companies, with support from national industry associations, have organised themselves to shape the US-EU trade and investments agenda.

Perhaps due to the important role of firms today, some scholars of European integration have mistakenly assumed that European big business organised early on in the Community's development and actively participated in the policy making process. In fact, the collective action of European big business has been a slow process, characterised by a number of different phases throughout EU history. In each phase, European companies have mobilsed for different selective and collective incentives.... They have created different forms of organisation, and have focused on different industrial concerns. For example, members of the earliest big business group were company leaders who organised for selective social incentives and gathered over sumptuous dinners and cocktails. Learning about the Community's institutional arrangements and industrial programmes that might impact their firms were of secondary concern. By contrast, today's large firm organisations generally mobilise for collective political incentives (see [D. Plotke, *The Political Mobilization of Business, in* THE POLITICS OF INTERESTS: INTEREST GROUPS TRANSFORMED (M.P. Petracca, ed. 1992)] and [D. Coen, *The Evolution of the Large Firm as a Political Actor in the European Union*, 4 J. OF EUROPEAN PUB. POL'Y 1, 91–108 (1997)]). Many of these groups are small, direct-firm organisations dedicated to shaping the agenda on specific Community issues through the use of organised, well financed lobbying schemes.

This changing architecture of European big business is significant in that it challenges traditional forms of industrial collective action in Europe. The creation of European-level big business organisations has allowed large companies to bypass long established European as well as national industry associations in influencing EU legislation and programmes. Thus European and national industry associations—long recognised as the

1. This chapter is largely drawn from Maria Green Cowles, *The Politics of Big Business in the European Union*, forthcoming.

voice of industry—must now coordinate or compete with large companies not only for influence in EU industrial and regulatory policy, but also for membership and dues.

Comments and Questions

1. The last excerpt highlights an interesting relationship between government and enterprises. It could be argued that the trend highlighted in the last excerpt is significant evidence of the growing power of the EU in matters of enterprise regulation. Business tends to be represented, and lobbying tends to congregate, in the vicinity of power. And the congregating habits of big business suggest that power over their businesses seems to be gravitating away from the capitals of the Members States and to the supra-national capital of the EU in Brussels. This migration of power is nothing new for Americans. American big business has been migrating from the states to Washington, D.C. since the early 1900s. Businesses not operating near the national capital have retained representatives there or seek a voice through their trade association offices. At the same time, business has not abandoned state. But as the locus of power has shifted to Washington, D.C., so have the efforts of business. One reason might be that it is easier to deal with one national legislature than with fifty state legislatures. As such, once purely local business issues, like tort reform and product regulation, have become issues of national concern. Does the migration of power to Brussels (like the migration of power to Washington, D.C.) mean that business will abandon efforts to influence Member State (or state) legislation? Why or why not?

2. In the area of company law, do you think that large corporations with multi-state operations would tend to favor or oppose harmonization within the EU? What criteria do you think such businesses would use to judge the value of such efforts?

A Note on the EU's Company Law Directives

The institutions of the EU have been substantially unsuccessful in the attempt to unify Community company law through regulation. The EU has been far more successful in its attempt to harmonize the company laws of the Member States through focused interventions in company law starting in the 1960s. The principal vehicle for company law harmonization has been the directive. The section which follows considers some of the most important directives.

Currently, the EC Council has enacted nine directives applicable to the company law of the Member States. In addition, the EC Commission has proposed a number of additional directives, some of which are highly controversial. These are summarized below. For a fuller treatment of the company law directives, especially as they affect company law in the United Kingdom, see Frank Wooldridge, Company Law in the United Kingdom and the European Community: Its Harmonization and Unification 4–7, 16–100 (1991) and Vanessa Edwards, EC Company Law (1999). The full text of the Company Law Directives may be accessed at the official web site of the European Union, <http://www.europa.eu.int/eur-lex/en/consleg/reg/en_register_1710.html>. The full text of directives may also be accessed using the data retrieval services of Lexis/Nexis, and Westlaw, Inc. For access on Lexis, proceed to the LEGIS file (EC Legislation). For access on Westlaw, proceed to the EU-LEG file (European Union Legislation) in the "International/Worldwide Materials" library.

The enacted directives include the following:

1. First Council Directive of 9 March 1968 on co-ordination of safeguards which, for the protection of the interests of members and others, are required by member states of companies within the meaning of the second paragraph of Article 58, now Art. 48, of the EC Treaty, with a view to making such safeguards equivalent throughout the community (OJ L65, 14.3.1968, p. 41).

This directive represented the EC Council's first venture into the harmonization of European company law, and was first produced in draft form in 1964. The directive, in final form, was enacted in 1964 [JO 1964, 3295]. It deals with three topics—disclosure, the validity of obligations entered into by a company, and the nullity of a company. It is applicable to public and private limited companies. Disclosed materials must be made available to the public by publication in public registers or national gazettes. The material to be published includes the articles of incorporation (Articles of Association), the address of the registered office, the names of the members of the company's board of directors and corporate agents and the subscribed capital. Public companies are also required to disclose annual financial results. The Directive also provides for joint and several liability for the pre-incorporation contracts of a company, and for the protection of creditors and others in the event of a defective incorporation (very generally, the concept of corporate "nullity"). Lastly, the Directive significantly limits the defence of ultra vires by a company as against third party creditors. Transactions or acts of a company which are beyond the stated powers or purposes of the corporation remain binding in favor of a third party unless the third party has knowledge of the corporation's formal lack of power to act in connection with the disputed transaction.

2. Second Council Directive of 13 December 1976 on coordination of safeguards which, for the protection of the interests of members and others, are required by member states of companies within the meaning of the second paragraph of Article 58, now Art. 48, of the EC Treaty, in respect of the formation of public limited liability companies and the maintenance and alteration of their capital, with a view to making such safeguards equivalent.

The second directive was adopted in 1976, six years after it was proposed. It overlaps, in many significant respects, with the First Directive. Unlike the first directive, however, the second directive is focused on European public companies. The Second directive requires that Member States provide a mechanism for distinguishing between public and private companies. (Art. 1). In the United Kingdom, this is accomplished by requiring the name of public limited companies to end with the words "public limited company" or the initials "p.l.c." (U.K. Companies Act of 1985, §§25(1) & 27(4)). The directive requires a substantial amount of disclosure by public companies, and imposes additional requirements for the liabilities incurred for on behalf of a public company prior to the time it is actually authorized to commence business. (Art. 4). The most extensive provisions in the second directive concern the imposition of rules governing the raising of capital when the public company us formed, increases and reductions in, and maintenance of capital. The directive provides for a minimum issued capital amount for public companies, and restricts the distribution of dividends to shareholders which erode this minimum capital. Public companies are also restricted in their ability to repurchase their own shares or reduce their capital, and shareholders are given substantial preemptive rights with respect to new share issuances.

3. Third Council Directive of 9 October 1978 based on Article 54(3)(g), now Art. 44(3)(g), of the EC Treaty concerning mergers of public limited liability companies.

Like the second directive the third directive was first proposed in 1970. It was not enacted until 1978, after the EC Council eliminated from its scope provisions respecting the division of companies (which is now covered in the Sixth directive). It is concerned with mergers between public companies in the same Member State and was much influenced by continental legislation. It does not cover cross-border mergers (the subject of the proposed tenth directive), and is silent on the tax consequences of the mergers contemplated. It's purpose is to provide a certain measure of protection to creditors and shareholders in connection with the merger of public companies within a single Member State. The mergers contemplated include mergers by acquisition and mergers by formation of a new company. The directive provides for the publication of the terms of the merger, and written reports to the shareholders from management and certain independent experts. Approval of mergers require an affirmative vote of 2/3 of the subscribed capital of each of the merging entities. Special provisions are provided where the acquiring company holds at least 90% of the shares of the acquired company.

4. Fourth Council Directive of 25 July 1978 based on Article 54(3)(g), now Art. 44(3)(g), of the EC Treaty on the annual accounts of certain types of companies.

The fourth amendment, contemplated on the enactment of the first directive, was first proposed in 1971, amended in 1974, and finally enacted in 1978. The directive as amended in 1990 to extend its coverage to certain types of limited partnerships. Its purpose is to attempt the establishment of maximum equivalent legal requirements for the disclosure of financial information by companies which are competitive with each other. The directive contains fairly extensive rules for the presentation and content of balance sheets, profit and loss accounts and annual financial reports. The directive provides limited exemptions from the reporting requirements for certain small and medium sized companies. As such large private limited liability companies may still be required to comply with all of the requirements of the directive.

5. Sixth Council Directive of 17 December 1982 based on Article 54(3)(g), now Art. 44(3)(g), of the EC Treaty, concerning the division of public limited liability companies.

This directive is the counterpart of the third directive and was enacted in 1982. It is meant to apply to split ups of public companies, whether or not in connection with an acquisition of additional operation: for example, where a public company (which has acquired an additional business or is merely contemplating the division of its operations, i.e. hotel and airline operations) transfers all of its assets to several newly established companies, the shares of which are held by the shares of the original company roughly in proportion to their ownership interests in the original company (and a payment not exceeding 10% of the nominal value if the shares allotted). Upon the split up, the original company is wound up and dissolved without going through a formal liquidation proceeding. In addition to protection for shareholders and employees, the directive provides for creditor protection in the form of joint liability to creditors (as between the newly created companies) for pre-split up liabilities.

6. Seventh Council Directive of 13 June 1983 based on the Article 54 (3) (g) of the treaty on consolidated accounts.

The purpose of this provision is to provide financial information of all of the members of a consolidated group of companies to persons and institutions with an interest in any member of that consolidated group. The directive, much influenced by German legal principles, was first proposed in 1976, revised in 1978 and enacted in 1983. It was amended in 1990 in conformity with the amendments to the fourth directive. Consolidated financial statements are required where a holding company has the majority of voting rights in its subsidiary or has the right to appoint or remove a majority of the members of the governing boards of directors (administrators or supervisors, depending on the company law applied), or has a contractual right to exercise a dominant influence over the subsidiary. The directive requires the preparation of consolidated accounts by a parent if that company, or any of its subsidiaries, is established as a private or public company in any one of the Member States. Thus, even where a holding company is established outside the European Community, but a subsidiary is so established, the directive applies. The directive, however, gives Member States the option of exempting compliance with the seventh directive in such a case, if the outside holding company prepares worldwide consolidated financial statements in accordance with the provisions of the directive. Exemptions are also provided for small groups (unless one of the companies is listed on a stock exchange). In the U.K. this was implemented by § 13(1) of the Companies Act of 1989.

7. Eighth Council Directive of 10 April 1984 based on Article 54(3)(g), now Art. 44(3)(g), of the EC Treaty on the approval of persons responsible for carrying out the statutory audits of accounting documents (84/253/EEC) (OJ L126, 12.5.1984, p. 20).

This directive applied to the auditing of annual accounts of companies which are covered by the fourth and seventh directives. It sets educational and professional qualification standards for auditors. This directive also had a long study period before enactment. It was first proposed in 1978, amended in 1979 and adopted in 1984. In addition to setting the qualifications of the auditors, the directive requires the public disclosure of the identity of the company's auditors.

8. Eleventh Council Directive of 21 December 1989 concerning disclosure requirements in respect of branches opened in a member state by certain types of company governed by the law of another state (89/666/EEC).

The Eleventh directive, adopted in 1989, deals with the disclosure requirements applicable to branch offices opened in a Member State by companies governed by the laws of another state. Branches of companies of other Member states are required to disclose certain information, similar, in many respects, to the disclosure required under the first directive. Accounting information must be disclosed for the branch, but only with respect to documents which must be disclosed pursuant to the law of the state of the home company. The directive does not require disclosure of the accounts of the branch itself. For branches of companies from non-Member States, the disclosure requirements are roughly the same, except that more detailed information is required, and the accounts must be produced in conformity with EEC legislation.

9. Twelfth Council company law directive of 21 December 1989 on single-member private limited-liability companies (89/667/EEC).

Adopted in 1989, the twelfth directive attempts the harmonization of the company laws with respect to single owner corporations. Prior to the enactment of this directive some Member States had not recognized such entities. The types of companies to which the directive applies are identified—for the most part, these include the private companies limited by shares or the continental SARLs. A single member company may be created as such or may result from the purchase by a single member of the share interests of other shareholders. The directive requires that decisions of the single member with respect to the company, and transactions between the company and the sole shareholder be drawn up in writing. Member States which already recognize single member corporations are not obligated to implement the directive.

In addition to the directives already enacted, several directives have been proposed (some have remained "proposed" for well over a decade). A number of these proposed directives have generated a substantial amount of debate. Three of the more significant of the proposed directives include:

1. Amended proposal for a Fifth Directive on the structure of public limited companies, and the powers and obligations of their organs.

This directive was first proposed in 1972, and amended in 1983. It remains highly controversial. The proposal deals with the structure and administration of public companies. It is controversial because it borrows much of its substance from German (and to some extent French) law, especially with respect to the requirement of employee representation on corporate governing boards. Pursuant to the proposed directive, the member states would have the choice of requiring public companies to adopt a one or two-tiered board system—consisting of a supervisory board and a management board, the former retaining overall and general supervisory and executive control of the company and of the decisions of the management board, and the later charged with the overall management of the corporation. The maintenance of a one-tiered system, however, would be subject to a number of restrictions aimed at harmonizing the functioning of the one-tiered system to that of the two-tiered system. Employee participation in the management of the enterprise would be required for public companies with more than 1000 employees, unless a majority of the company's employees objected to representation. Employee participation could be achieved in one of four ways: by representation on the supervisory board (with employees electing between 1/3 and 1/2 of the members of the board); by participation in an employee representative council at the company level; by participation in a manner similar to that employed under Dutch law; or by representation through a collectively bargained system corresponding roughly to one of the other three models. The provisions relating to shareholders meetings cover the convening and notice of shareholder meetings, the request for new items on the meeting agenda, the right to attend and be represented at the meeting, the amount and extent of information to be presented to shareholders, the right to vote and the regulation of shareholder agreements, provisions relating to majority vote requirements, and proceedings to void unlawful resolutions.

2. Proposal for a Tenth Directive on cross-border mergers of public limited companies.

The proposal deals with cross-border mergers, an activity not covered in the third directive. It was first submitted by the EC Commission in 1985. The proposal is said to facilitate mergers between companies from different Member States. Present law makes such mergers extremely difficult, as a result of tax consequences of such transactions and legal hurdles (such as the requirement of unanimous shareholder consent, or the attachment of complex conditions precedent to the consummation of such transactions). As a result, cross-border "mergers" are currently effected by creating a holding company holding controlling interest in the companies to be merged, followed by the transfer of assets within the newly created group of companies. The proposed directive seeks to synchronize the steps in the process of merger in each of the Member States of origin of the participants in the merger. The proposal contains a provision which would give a Member State the power, for practical purposes, to veto a merger which would result in the termination of employee participation in the enterprise. (Art. 1(3)). In other respects, the detailed provisions for the effectuation of a merger follow the provisions of the third directive.

3. Proposed Directive on Takeover Bids (Thirteenth Company Law Directive).

The proposed thirteenth directive was originally submitted by the EC Commission in 1988, and amended once in 1990. A substantial amount of opposition has come from business groups likely subject to the measures of this Directive. The British business community, for example, fears the effect of the directive on Britain's Takeover Board. The Commission does not appear to have discerned a satisfactory answer. Rather, in answer to the question posed in the EU Parliament, the Commission's representative noted only that:

> The proposed directive requires Member States to designate one or more supervisory authorities which must supervise the bid. Because of differences in legal tradition, the question to what extent recourse against the decisions of a supervisory authority is possible before the courts is left to Member States. The proposed directive does however contain guidance on how to police cross-border take over bids which involve supervisory authorities in more than one Member State.[1]

The proposal reflects some of the influence of U.S. securities laws, particularly the Williams Act. It applies to companies whose shares are listed on one or more stock exchanges in the Community. It requires the offerer to issue an offer prospectus aimed at the shareholders of the target company, which must contain a substantial amount of information. The offer circular must be published in a newspaper of mass circulation or otherwise made available. Offerors owning more than 1/3 of the shares of the target are obligated to make a bid for all of the outstanding shares of the target. Once made, an offer may not be withdrawn until the passage of the deadline for acceptance unless a competing bid is made, the conditions announced in the offer are not met or securities required to be authorized are not. The proposal also treats modifications to offers and the extent to which a target can take defensive measures to ward off a hostile offer.

a. First Directive

The First Company Law Directive sought to harmonize the corporate law of Member States with respect to mandatory disclosure rules, liability for pre-incorporation transactions, and rules for dealing with defective incorporation. The policy underlying the Directive's disclosure rules is straightforward. This policy reflects a determination that shareholders can be protected by an adequate and uniform system of corporate disclosure. A similar policy forms the foundation of the disclosure and reporting requirements of the federal securities laws.

Review the First Company Law Directive before reading the cases that follow. The Directive can be accessed at the official web site of the European Union: <http://www.europa.eu.int/eur-lex/en/consleg/reg/en_register_1710.html>. The first case that follows illustrates the way in which the European Court of Justice has approached the implementation of the First Company Law Directive. More importantly, perhaps, the case also highlights the difficulties some Member States have encountered when attempting to transpose the directive into national law. This difficulty is exacerbated in Member States with federal systems, such as that of the Federal Republic of

1. Answer given by Mr. Bolkestein on behalf of the Commission (17 February 2000) to a question posed in the European Parliament by Theresa Villiers, Official Journal C 225E, 08/08/2000 p. 190; (OJ 2000 C225E/190).

Germany. The cases also serve to remind the student that though the company law directives are each self-contained, they remain significantly related to each other. The relationship between the First Company Law Directive's disclosure rules and the Fourth Company Law Directive's accounting standards rules are a case in point.

EC Commission v. Federal Republic of Germany

Case C-191/95

29 September 1998 (1)

1. By application lodged at the Registry of the Court on 16 June 1995, the Commission of the European Communities commenced proceedings under Article 169 of the EC Treaty for a declaration that, by failing to provide for appropriate penalties in cases where companies limited by shares fail to disclose their annual accounts, as prescribed in particular by the First Council Directive 68/151/EEC of 9 March 1968 on coordination of safeguards which, for the protection of the interests of members and others, are required by Member States of companies within the meaning of the second paragraph of Article 58 of the Treaty, with a view to making such safeguards equivalent throughout the Community (OJ, English Special Edition 1968 (I), p. 41, hereinafter 'the First Directive'), and the Fourth Council Directive 78/660/EEC of 25 July 1978 based on Article 54(3)(g) of the Treaty on the annual accounts of certain types of companies (OJ 1978 L 222, p. 11, hereinafter 'the Fourth Directive'), the Federal Republic of Germany has failed to fulfil its obligations under the EC Treaty and those directives.

The rules in question

The First Directive

2. In terms of Article 1, the First Directive is to apply, in Germany, to the Aktiengesellschaft (public limited company), the Kommanditgesellschaft auf Aktien (partnership limited by shares), and the Gesellschaft mit beschränkter Haftung (limited liability company).

3. Article 2 of the First Directive provides that the Member States are to take the measures required to ensure compulsory disclosure by companies of at least the documents and particulars that it lists. Under Article 2(1)(f) the disclosure requirement is to apply in particular to 'the balance sheet and the profit and loss account for each financial year'.

4. However, the third sentence of Article 2(1)(f) provides, inter alia in respect of the Gesellschaft mit beschränkter Haftung, that the above-mentioned obligation to make disclosure is to 'be postponed until the date of implementation of a Directive concerning coordination of the contents of balance sheets and of profit and loss accounts and concerning exemption of such of those companies whose balance sheet total is less than specified in the Directive'. According to the last sentence of Article 2(1)(f), the Council is to adopt such a directive within two years following the adoption of the First Directive.

5. Under Article 3(2) and (4) of the First Directive, all documents and particulars which must be disclosed are to be entered in the register opened in each Member State and their disclosure is to be effected by publication in the national gazette appointed for that purpose by the Member State, either of the full or partial text, or by means of a reference to the document which has been deposited in the file or entered in the register.

6. Article 6 of the First Directive provides inter alia:

'Member States shall provide for appropriate penalties in case of:

– failure to disclose the balance sheet and profit and loss account as required by Article 2(1)(f);

– ...'

7. Under the first paragraph of Article 13 of the First Directive, the Member States were to transpose the directive into national law within 18 months following its notification, which took place on 11 March 1968.

The Fourth Directive

8. The Fourth Directive lays down, for the forms of company which it lists, provisions concerning annual accounts. Article 2 provides: 'The annual accounts shall comprise the balance sheet, the profit and loss account and the notes on the accounts. These documents shall constitute a composite whole.'

9. With regard to disclosure of annual accounts, Article 47(1) of the Fourth Directive provides:

'The annual accounts, duly approved, and the annual report, together with the opinion submitted by the person responsible for auditing the accounts, shall be published as laid down by the laws of each Member State in accordance with Article 3 of Directive 68/151/EEC.

The laws of a Member State may, however, permit the annual report not to be published as stipulated above. In that case, it shall be made available to the public at the company's registered office in the Member State concerned. It must be possible to obtain a copy of all or part of any such report free of charge upon request.'

10. According to Article 55(1), the Fourth Directive was to be transposed into national law within two years of its notification, which took place on 31 July 1978.

The national legislation

11. In Germany the Gesetz über die Rechnungslegung von bestimmten Unternehmen und Konzernen of 15 August 1969 (Law on the Accounts to be disclosed by certain Undertakings and Groups, BGBl. I, 1969, p. 1189, hereinafter 'the Publizitätsgesetz' (Disclosure Law)) entered into force on 21 August 1969.

12. Paragraphs 9 and 10 of the Publizitätsgesetz contained specific provisions on the requirement to file annual accounts and the annual report in the commercial register and to publish annual accounts in the Bundesanzeiger (Official Gazette of the Federal Republic).

13. The Publizitätsgesetz was recast in particular by the Bilanzrichtlinien-Gesetz of 19 December 1985 (Accounting and Reporting Law, BGBl. I, 1985, p. 2355), which transposed the Fourth Directive together with the Seventh Council Directive 83/349/EEC of 13 June 1983 based on Article 54(3)(g) of the Treaty on consolidated accounts (OJ 1983 L 193, p. 1) and the Eighth Council Directive 84/253/EEC of 10 April 1984 based on Article 54(3)(g) of the Treaty on the approval of persons responsible for carrying out the statutory audits of accounting documents (OJ 1984 L 126, p. 20). The version currently in force provides, in Paragraph 9, that undertakings covered by the Law are to ensure that their annual accounts and annual report are disclosed, in particular by filing them in the commercial register. Compliance with that obligation may be enforced, under Paragraph 21, first sentence, point 8, of the Bilanzrichtlinien-Gesetz, by means of a periodic penalty payment.

4. The Bilanzrichtlinien-Gesetz also introduced into the Handelsgesetzbuch (German Commercial Code, hereinafter 'the HGB') Book III (Paragraphs 238 to 339) concerning accounting records.

15. Paragraph 325 of the HGB contains provisions relating to disclosure, in particular those concerning the requirement that the legal representatives of companies limited by shares present their annual accounts to the commercial register and inform the public thereof by an announcement in the Bundesanzeiger.

16. Paragraph 335 of the HGB provides for periodic penalty payments to be set where the members of the body authorised to represent a company limited by shares do not comply with the requirement to disclose its accounts laid down in Paragraph 325 of the HGB. However, under Paragraph 335, first sentence, point 6, of the HGB, in conjunction with the second sentence of that paragraph, the periodic penalty payment procedure may not be initiated except at the request of a member, a creditor, the central works council or the company's works council.

17. The Bilanzrichtlinien-Gesetz was notified to the Commission early in January 1986. That notification was made subsequent to an application by the Commission, in Case 18/85, for a declaration that the Federal Republic of Germany had delayed in transposing the Fourth Directive. The Commission withdrew its application and the proceedings were terminated by an order of 11 February 1987 (OJ 1987 C 80, p. 6) removing the case from the register.

Pre-litigation procedure and forms of order sought by the parties

8. By letter of formal notice of 26 June 1990 the Commission informed the German Government that, according to the publications available to it, 93% of German companies limited by shares had not complied with the obligation to disclose their annual accounts, which constituted a breach of the combined provisions of Article 3 of the First Directive and Article 47 of the Fourth Directive. The Commission pointed out that under Article 6 of the First Directive Member States are required to provide for appropriate penalties in case of breach of the disclosure requirement laid down in the directive. It called upon the Federal Government, pursuant to Article 169 of the Treaty, to submit its observations within a period of two months.

19. In a communication of 30 July 1990, the German Government denied that there had been a breach of the combined provisions of Article 3 of the First Directive and Article 47 of the Fourth Directive. Relying on its own statistics and referring to the provisions of German law in force, the Federal Government disputed the figures put forward by the Commission and concluded that there was no need to introduce additional penalties for cases where companies limited by shares had not complied with their obligations of disclosure.

20. In those circumstances, on 2 June 1992 the Commission sent a reasoned opinion to the Federal Republic of Germany, complaining that it had failed to fulfil its obligations under the First and Fourth Directives by not making provision for appropriate penalties in cases where companies limited by shares failed to disclose their annual accounts as prescribed in particular by those directives. The Commission called upon the Federal Republic of Germany to adopt the necessary measures within a period of two months in order to comply with the reasoned opinion. At the request of the German Government that period was extended until 30 September 1992.

21. On 25 August 1993 the German Government declared itself ready to reinforce the penalties in cases where documents concerning annual accounts had not been disclosed, provided that the Commission indicated that it agreed to the legislative amendments

envisaged and refrained from commencing proceedings before the Court. It therefore submitted to the Commission a draft concerning the introduction of reinforced penalties to enter into force, for all companies limited by shares, with progressive effect from 1 January 1995 to 1 January 1999.

In that connection, the German Government pointed out that if such provisions were introduced with immediate effect, the Länder, which had competence in such matters, would be unable to ensure immediate compliance, in view of the large number of proceedings that would have to be brought and the sizeable number of civil servants in the former Länder who had been assigned to the reconstruction of the new Länder following German reunification.

22. On 3 March 1994, the Commissioner responsible replied that the penalties envisaged must be applicable immediately and without distinction to all companies of the types concerned which were not complying with their obligation of disclosure. He nevertheless stated that he was prepared to propose that the Commission suspend the procedure if the Federal Government presented, during the current legislative session, a draft Law amended to that effect.

23. By letter of 19 May 1994 the German Government informed the Commission that it was not able, under those conditions, to withdraw from its position of principle, to the effect that Article 54(3)(c) of the EC Treaty did not require any reinforcement of the existing penalties under German law.

24. Subsequent discussions failed to produce a solution and the Commission decided to bring the present action, in which it asks the Court to declare that the Federal Republic of Germany has failed to fulfil its obligations and to order it to pay the costs.

25. The German Government asks the Court to dismiss the action, principally, as inadmissible, or, in the alternative, as unfounded, and to order the Commission to pay the costs.

Admissibility

26. The German Government has put forward three pleas of inadmissibility alleging, first, breach of the principle of collegiality as regards the issuance of the reasoned opinion and the commencement of proceedings, second, a change in the subject-matter of the dispute and, lastly, erroneous assessment as regards the alleged failure to fulfil obligations.

Breach of the principle of collegiality as regards the issuance of the reasoned opinion and the commencement of proceedings

27. The German Government maintains that the reasoned opinion was issued and proceedings before the Court commenced under the delegation procedure. In its view, although recourse to that procedure is compatible with the principle of collegiality for the purpose of adopting measures of management or administration, it is excluded for decisions of principle such as the adoption of a reasoned opinion and the commencement of proceedings before the Court.

Article 169 of the Treaty requires the reasoned opinion and the bringing of proceedings before the Court to be the subject of a decision by the Commission acting as a college.

28. The Commission replies that the decisions to send the letter of formal notice, to notify the reasoned opinion and to commence proceedings before the Court were taken at meetings of the Commission acting as a college.

29. By order of 23 October 1996, the Court (Sixth Chamber) ordered the Commission to produce the decisions, authenticated in accordance with its Rules of Procedure,

which it had adopted, as a college, to issue the reasoned opinion sent on 2 June 1992 to the Federal Republic of Germany and to bring the present action for failure to fulfil obligations.

30. The Commission responded by producing to the Court minutes of a number of meetings and a number of documents to which those minutes refer.

31. At the hearing on 9 December 1997, the German Government claimed that, in the light of the documents produced, the Commission had not established that the members of the college, when they decided to issue the reasoned opinion and commence proceedings before the Court, had sufficient information available to them as regards the content of those measures. The college of Commissioners ought to have had available all the relevant information of fact and law to enable it to ensure that its decisions were devoid of ambiguity and to guarantee that the measures notified had actually been adopted by the college and corresponded to its intention, since it is the college which takes political responsibility for them.

32. The Commission states that for reasons of efficiency, given the number of proceedings for failure to fulfil obligations, Commissioners do not have available draft reasoned opinions when they adopt the decision to issue such measures; this is not necessary in view of the fact that reasoned opinions do not have immediate binding legal effect. However, the crucial information is available to the members of the college, in particular the facts complained of and the provisions of Community law which, in the view of the Commission's services, have been breached. Thus the college reached its decision on the proposals of its services to issue the reasoned opinion and to commence proceedings before the Court in full knowledge of the facts. Drafting of reasoned opinions takes place at administrative level, under the responsibility of the member of the Commission with competence in the matter, following the adoption of the decision by the college to take such a step.

33. It is important to remember, at the outset, that the functioning of the Commission is governed by the principle of collegiate responsibility (Case C-137/92 P Commission v. BASF and Others [1994] ECR I-2555, paragraph 62).

34. It is common ground that the decisions to issue the reasoned opinion and to commence proceedings are subject to that principle of collegiate responsibility.

35. Recourse to Article 169 provides one of the means by which the Commission ensures that the Member States give effect to the provisions of the Treaty and those adopted under the Treaty by the institutions (Case C-422/92 Commission v. Germany [1995] ECR I-1097, paragraph 16). The decisions to issue a reasoned opinion and to commence proceedings before the Court thus come within the general scope of the supervisory task entrusted to the Commission under the first indent of Article 155 of the EC Treaty.

36. In issuing a reasoned opinion, the Commission formally sets out its position with regard to the legal position of the Member State concerned. Moreover, by formally stating the infringement of the Treaty with which the Member State concerned is charged, the reasoned opinion concludes the pre-litigation procedure provided for in Article 169 (Case 74/82 Commission v. Ireland [1984] ECR 317, paragraph 13). The decision to issue a reasoned opinion cannot therefore be described as a measure of administration or management and may not be delegated.

37. The same is true of the decision to apply to the Court for a declaration of failure to fulfil obligations. In its role as guardian of the Treaty, the Commission is competent to

decide whether it is appropriate to bring proceedings against a Member State for failure to fulfil its obligations (see, to that effect, Case C-431/92 Commission v. Germany [1995] ECR I-2189, paragraph 22). Such a decision falls within the discretionary power of the institution (see, in particular, Case C-200/88 Commission v. Greece [1990] ECR I-4299, paragraph 9) and cannot be described as a measure of administration or management.

38. Thus the first plea of inadmissibility, as refined during the current proceedings, concerns the consequences of compliance with the principle of collegiality as regards the conditions in which the college could, first, consider that the Federal Republic of Germany had failed to fulfil one of its obligations under the Treaty and issue a reasoned opinion on that matter and, second, when it considered that that State had not complied with that opinion within the period prescribed, decide to bring the present action.

39. According to settled case-law, the principle of collegiality is based on the equal participation of the Commissioners in the adoption of decisions, from which it follows in particular that decisions should be the subject of collective deliberation and that all the members of the college of Commissioners should bear collective responsibility at political level for all decisions adopted (Case 5/85 AKZO Chemie v. Commission [1986] ECR 2585, paragraph 30; Joined Cases 46/87 and 227/88 Hoechst v. Commission [1986] ECR 2859, and Case 137/92 P Commission v. BASF and Others, cited above, paragraph 63).

40. The Court has also held that compliance with that principle is of concern to individuals affected by the legal consequences of a Commission decision (see, to that effect, Commission v. BASF and Others, cited above, paragraph 64).

41. Nevertheless, the formal requirements for effective compliance with the principle of collegiality vary according to the nature and legal effects of the acts adopted by that institution.

42. Thus the Court has held that, with regard to decisions adopted for the purpose of ensuring observance of the competition rules, in which the Commission finds that there has been an infringement of those rules, issues directions to undertakings and imposes pecuniary penalties upon them, that the undertakings or associations of undertakings addressed by such decisions must be assured that the operative part and the statement of reasons were actually adopted by the college of Commissioners (see, to that effect, Commission v. BASF and Others, cited above, paragraphs 65 to 67).

43. In this case the detailed procedure governing the collective deliberation by the college of Commissioners concerning the issue of the reasoned opinion and the bringing of an action for failure to fulfil obligations must therefore be determined in the light of the legal effects of those decisions with regard to the State concerned.

44. The issue of a reasoned opinion constitutes a preliminary procedure (Joined Cases 142/80 and 143/80 Essevi and Salengo [1981] ECR 1413, paragraph 15), which does not have any binding legal effect for the addressee of the reasoned opinion. It is merely a pre-litigation stage of a procedure which may lead to an action before the Court (Joined Cases 6/69 and 11/69 Commission v. France [1969] ECR 523, paragraph 36). The purpose of that pre-litigation procedure provided for by Article 169 of the Treaty is to enable the Member State to comply of its own accord with the requirements of the Treaty or, if appropriate, to justify its position (Case C-157/94 Commission v. Netherlands [1997] ECR I-5699, paragraph 60; Case C-158/94 Commission v. Italy [1997] ECR I-5789, paragraph 56; and Case C-159/94 Commission v. France [1997] ECR I-5815, paragraph 103).

45. If that attempt at settlement is unsuccessful, the function of the reasoned opinion is to define the subject-matter of the dispute. The Commission is not, however, empowered to determine conclusively, by reasoned opinions formulated pursuant to Article 169, the rights and duties of a Member State or to afford that State guarantees concerning the compatibility of a given line of conduct with the Treaty. According to the system embodied in Articles 169 to 171 of the Treaty, the rights and duties of Member States may be determined and their conduct appraised only by a judgment of the Court (see, to that effect, Essevi and Salengo, cited above, paragraphs 15 and 16).

46. The reasoned opinion therefore has legal effect only in relation to the commencement of proceedings before the Court (see Essevi and Salengo, cited above, paragraph 18) so that where a Member State does not comply with that opinion within the period allowed, the Commission has the right, but not the duty, to commence proceedings before the Court (see, to that effect, Case 247/87 Star Fruit v. Commission [1989] ECR 291, paragraph 12).

47. The decision to commence proceedings before the Court, whilst it constitutes an indispensable step for the purpose of enabling the Court to give judgment on the alleged failure to fulfil obligations by way of a binding decision, nevertheless does not per se alter the legal position in question.

48. It follows from all the foregoing considerations that both the Commission's decision to issue a reasoned opinion and its decision to bring an action for a declaration of failure to fulfil obligations must be the subject of collective deliberation by the college of Commissioners. The information on which those decisions are based must therefore be available to the members of the college. It is not, however, necessary for the college itself formally to decide on the wording of the acts which give effect to those decisions and put them in final form.

49. In this case it is not disputed that the members of the college had available to them all the information they considered would assist them for the purposes of adopting the decision when the college decided, on 31 July 1991, to issue the reasoned opinion, and approved, on 13 December 1994, the proposal to bring the present action.

50. In those circumstances, it must be held that the Commission complied with the rules relating to the principle of collegiality when it issued the reasoned opinion with regard to the Federal Republic of Germany and brought the present action.

51. Consequently the plea of inadmissibility alleging breach of the principle of collegiate responsibility must be dismissed as unfounded.

Change in the subject-matter of the dispute

52. The German Government maintains that the action is inadmissible because the contents of the application differ from those of the letter of formal notice. The Commission stated in its letter of formal notice that the Federal Republic of Germany had failed to fulfil its obligations under the combined provisions of Article 47 of the Fourth Directive and Article 3 of the First Directive, whereas in the reasoned opinion and the application it alleged that there was a breach of Articles 2(1)(f), 3 and 6 of the First Directive. Consequently the subject-matter of the dispute was modified in the course of the pre-litigation procedure.

53. The Commission replies that the wording of both the letter of formal notice and the communication from the German Government of 30 July 1990 shows that the Commission's concerns were clearly expressed and properly understood.

54. The preliminary point must be made that, although the reasoned opinion provided for in Article 169 of the Treaty must contain a coherent and detailed statement of the reasons which led the Commission to conclude that the State in question has failed to fulfil one of its obligations under the Treaty, the letter of formal notice cannot be subject to such strict requirements of precision, since it cannot, of necessity, contain anything more than an initial brief summary of the complaints. There is therefore nothing to prevent the Commission from setting out in detail in the reasoned opinion the complaints which it has already made more generally in the letter of formal notice (Case C-279/94 Commission v. Italy [1997] ECR I-4743, paragraph 15).

55. It is true that the letter of formal notice from the Commission to the Member State and then the reasoned opinion issued by the Commission delimit the subject-matter of the dispute, so that it cannot thereafter be extended. The opportunity for the State concerned to be able to submit its observations, even if it chooses not to avail itself thereof, constitutes an essential guarantee intended by the Treaty, adherence to which is an essential formal requirement of the procedure under Article 169 (Case 124/81 Commission v. United Kingdom [1983] ECR 203, paragraph 6). Consequently, the reasoned opinion and the proceedings brought by the Commission must be based on the same complaints as those set out in the letter of formal notice initiating the pre-litigation procedure.

56. However, that requirement cannot be carried so far as to mean that in every case the statement of complaints in the letter of formal notice, the operative part of the reasoned opinion and the form of order sought in the application must be exactly the same, provided that the subject-matter of the proceedings has not been extended or altered but simply limited (see, to that effect, Case C-279/94 Commission v. Italy, cited above, paragraph 25).

57. In this case, it is clear from the file that in its letter of formal notice the Commission sufficiently identified the alleged failure of the Federal Republic of Germany to fulfil its obligations, in stating that the combined provisions of Article 3 of the First Directive and Article 47 of the Fourth Directive had been infringed since a large proportion of companies limited by shares were failing to comply with the disclosure requirements, and in reminding it of the obligation incumbent on the Member States, pursuant to Article 6 of the First Directive, to provide for appropriate penalties where the disclosure requirement was breached. That letter therefore informed the German Government of the nature of the complaints against it and gave it the opportunity to put forward a defence.

58. Accordingly, the fact that the Commission did not persist in the complaints based on the fact that a large proportion of companies limited by shares were failing to comply with the disclosure requirements, whilst it detailed the complaints based on the need to provide appropriate sanctions, which it had already set out more generally in the letter of formal notice, merely limited the subject-matter of the action.

59. It follows that the second plea of inadmissibility must also be dismissed as unfounded.

Erroneous statement of reasons as regards the alleged failure

60. In the submission of the German Government, the Commission was not entitled to question the conformity with Community law of the German provisions concerning the requirement to disclose annual accounts by basing itself on unverified figures relating to the level of compliance with that requirement on the part of undertakings. It should have conducted its own investigation to ensure that the figures which it was using to support its allegation of such a failure were accurate. The Commission cannot therefore

be considered to have given a coherent and detailed statement of the reasons which led it to conclude that the Federal Republic of Germany should be charged with having failed to fulfil its obligations under Community law.

61. The Commission replies that it remains convinced that there was such a failure and points out that the Federal Republic of Germany admitted as much itself in its communication of 25 August 1993.

62. In that connection it need merely be pointed out that, at the stage of the proceedings before the Court, the Commission did not persist in its complaint to the effect that a large proportion of companies limited by shares were failing to comply with the disclosure requirements. The third plea of inadmissibility therefore refers to an alleged failure at the pre-litigation stage which does not form part of the subject-matter of this action, and must thus be dismissed.

63. It follows that the action must be held admissible in its entirety.

Substance

64. The Commission claims that an examination of the provisions existing in German law shows clearly that although disclosure of the annual accounts of companies limited by shares is governed by Paragraph 325 et seq. of the HGB, the German legislature has not created any effective legal means of imposing the disclosure requirement. Paragraph 335, first sentence, point 6, of the HGB provides for the imposition of periodic penalty payments where the members of the body authorised to represent a company limited by shares do not comply with the disclosure requirement, but the court responsible for the register cannot impose such penalties of its own motion.

65. The German Government maintains that the obligation to introduce appropriate penalties for failure to disclose the balance sheet and profit and loss account as required by Article 6 of the First Directive is not yet applicable to German limited liability companies. In the alternative, it submits that Article 6 of the First Directive was correctly transposed. Pursuant to Article 54(3)(g) of the Treaty, the coordination of national company legislation is aimed at protecting the interests of members and others. The latter do not comprise all natural and legal persons but only those who have a legal connection with the company. Lastly, because of the very large number of small and medium-sized limited liability companies, it would be disproportionate to the purpose of the system defined in Article 54(3)(g) of the Treaty to take legal action against them.

66. In that connection, it is sufficient to note that the Court held in Case C-97/96 Daihatsu Deutschland [1997] ECR I-6843, at paragraphs 14 and 15, that the legislative lacuna left by the First Directive was filled by the Fourth Directive. The Fourth Directive coordinated the national provisions concerning the presentation and content of annual accounts and reports, the valuation methods used therein and their publication in respect of companies limited by shares, including inter alia German limited liability companies.

67. In Daihatsu Deutschland, cited above, the Court ruled that Article 6 of the First Directive was to be interpreted as precluding the legislation of a Member State from restricting to members or creditors of the company, the central works council or the company's works council the right to apply for imposition of the penalty provided for by the law of that Member State in the event of failure by a company to fulfil the obligations regarding disclosure of annual accounts laid down by the First Directive.

68. Lastly, it must be pointed out that the lack of appropriate penalties cannot be justified by the fact that, because of the large numbers involved, application of such penalties to all companies that do not publish their accounts would create considerable diffi-

culties for the German administrative authorities which would be disproportionate to the aim pursued by the Community legislature. The Court has consistently held that a Member State may not plead internal circumstances in order to justify a failure to comply with obligations and time-limits resulting from rules of Community law (see, in particular, Case C-374/89 Commission v. Belgium [1991] ECR I-367, paragraph 10; Case C-45/91 Commission v. Greece [1992] ECR I-2509, paragraph 21; and Joined Cases C-109/94, C-207/94 and C-225/94 Commission v. Greece [1995] ECR I-1791, paragraph 11).

69. Consequently, it must be held that, by failing to provide for appropriate penalties in cases where companies limited by shares fail to effect compulsory disclosure of their annual accounts as prescribed, in particular, by Articles 2(1)(f), 3 and 6 of the First Directive, in conjunction with Article 47(1) of the Fourth Directive, the Federal Republic of Germany has failed to fulfil its obligations under those directives.

Costs

70. Under Article 69(2) of the Rules of Procedure, the unsuccessful party is to be ordered to pay the costs if they have been applied for in the successful party's pleadings. Since the Commission applied for an order that the Federal Republic of Germany pay the costs and the latter has been unsuccessful in its defence, it must be ordered to pay the costs.

On those grounds,

THE COURT hereby:

1. Dismisses the pleas of inadmissibility;

2. Declares that, by failing to provide for appropriate penalties in cases where companies limited by shares fail to effect compulsory disclosure of their annual accounts as prescribed, in particular, by Articles 2(1)(f), 3 and 6 of the First Council Directive 68/151/EEC of 9 March 1968 on coordination of safeguards which, for the protection of the interests of members and others are required by Member States of companies within the meaning of the second paragraph of Article 58 of the Treaty, with a view to making such safeguards equivalent throughout the Community, in conjunction with Article 47(1) of the Fourth Council Directive 78/660/EEC of 25 July 1978 based on Article 54(3)(g) of the Treaty on the annual accounts of certain types of companies, the Federal Republic of Germany has failed to fulfil its obligations under those directives;

3. Orders the Federal Republic of Germany to pay the costs.

The case that follows illustrates the difficulty of transposing the harmonization objectives of EC directives in cases where those objectives expand rights against corporations available under pre-existing national law. Again, the case involves the Federal Republic of Germany, but the same problem occurs in many Member States.

Verband deutscher Daihatsu-Händler eV and Daihatsu Deutschland GmbH

Case C-97/96

4 December 1997 (1)

1. By order of 22 November 1995, received at the Court on 26 March 1996, the Oberlandesgericht Düsseldorf (Düsseldorf Higher Regional Court) referred to the Court for a

preliminary ruling under Article 177 of the EC Treaty a question on the interpretation of Article 6 of the First Council Directive 68/151/EEC of 9 March 1968 on co-ordination of safeguards which, for the protection of the interests of members and others, are required by Member States of companies within the meaning of the second paragraph of Article 58 of the Treaty, with a view to making such safeguards equivalent throughout the Community (OJ, English Special Edition 1968 (I), p. 41, hereinafter 'the First Directive').

2. That question was raised in proceedings brought by the Verband Deutscher Daihatsu-Händler eV ('the Verband'), an association of German dealers in Daihatsu motor vehicles, before the Amtsgericht (Local Court). In Germany, each Amtsgericht is responsible for maintaining the Commercial Register within its area of jurisdiction. The Verband applied to the Amtsgericht Kempen (Kempen Local Court) for an order requiring Daihatsu Deutschland GmbH, the general agent responsible for the importation of Daihatsu vehicles into Germany, to publish its annual accounts, which it had not done since 1989, or, in default, to pay a fine in the form of a periodic penalty payment.

3. That application was dismissed by the Amtsgericht Kempen by decision of 24 October 1994, which was confirmed by decision of the Landgericht Krefeld (Krefeld Regional Court) of 13 December 1994.

4. Like the Amtsgericht, the Landgericht based its decision on point 6 in the first sentence of Paragraph 335 of the German Commercial Code in conjunction with the second sentence of that paragraph, pursuant to which proceedings for the imposition of a fine in the form of a periodic penalty payment may be brought only by a member or creditor of the company, the general works council or the company's works council. The Verband does not fall within any of those categories.

5. On appeal by the Verband, the Oberlandesgericht Düsseldorf confirmed the decision of the lower courts.

6. It considered, nevertheless, that Paragraph 335 of the German Commercial Code incorrectly transposed Article 6 of the First Directive, which requires Member States to provide for appropriate penalties 'in case of failure to disclose the balance sheet and profit and loss account as required by Article 2(1)(f)'.

7. Article 2(1)(f) provides:

> '1.Member States shall take the measures required to ensure compulsory disclosure by companies of at least the following documents and particulars:
>
> ...
>
> (f) the balance sheet and the profit and loss account for each financial year. The document containing the balance sheet shall give particulars of the persons who are required by law to certify it.
>
> However, in respect of the Gesellschaft mit beschränkter Haftung, société de personnes à responsabilité limitée, personenvennootschap met beperkte aansprakelijkheid, société à responsabilité limitée and società a responsabilità limitata under German, Belgian, French, Italian or Luxembourg law, referred to in Article 1, and the besloten naamloze vennootschap under Netherlands law, the compulsory application of this provision shall be postponed until the date of implementation of a Directive concerning co-ordination of the contents of balance sheets and of profit and loss accounts and concerning exemption of such of those companies whose balance sheet total is less than specified in the Directive from the obligation to make disclosure, in full or in part, of the said documents. The Council will adopt such a directive within two years following the adoption of the present Directive;

...'

8. In those circumstances, the Oberlandesgericht Düsseldorf referred the following question to the Court for a preliminary ruling:

> 'Does Article 6 of the First Council Directive on company law of 9 March 1968 have direct effect if under German law the (sole) penalty to ensure enforcement of the duty to disclose the annual accounts of a private limited company is the imposition by the Registration Court of an administrative fine of up to DM 10,000, but the Registration Court may intervene only on application from a member or creditor of the company, the central works council or the company's works council and does any such possible direct effect of that provision mean that, in addition to the persons entitled under German law to make an application, any person may apply for an administrative fine to be imposed or that such a right is available at least to an association of traders which under its articles of association must protect the interests of its members who have a contractual relationship with the private limited company which has failed to comply with its duty to disclose those accounts?'

9. That question raises three distinct issues.

10. First, the national court is essentially asking whether Article 6 of the First Directive must be construed as precluding the legislation of a Member State from restricting to members or creditors of the company, the central works council or the company's works council the right to apply for imposition of the penalty provided for by national law in the event of failure by a company to fulfil the obligations regarding disclosure of annual accounts laid down by the First Directive.

11. If the answer to that question is in the negative, the national court wishes to know whether Article 6 of the First Directive is sufficiently clear, precise and unconditional to have direct effect in the domestic legal order of a Member State.

12. If the answer to the latter question is in the affirmative, the national court wishes to know whether an individual may rely on the First Directive in order to apply to the competent national authority for the imposition of a penalty on a company which has failed to disclose its annual accounts where that individual is excluded under the national rules from the class of persons entitled to make such an application.

The transposition of the Directive

13. The German Government maintains, as a preliminary point, that the obligation to provide for appropriate penalties for failure to disclose the balance sheet and profit and loss account, as required by Article 6 of the First Directive, is not yet applicable to German private limited companies. It submits that, as far as those companies are concerned, Article 2(1)(f) of the First Directive postponed the entry into force of the disclosure obligation 'until the date of implementation of a Directive concerning coordination of the contents of balance sheets and of profit and loss accounts'. According to the German Government, no directive has yet been adopted in that regard.

14. In that connection, it is sufficient to note that the legislative lacuna left by the First Directive was filled by the Fourth Council Directive 78/660/EEC of 25 July 1978 based on Article 54(3)(g) of the Treaty on the annual accounts of certain types of companies (OJ 1978 L 222, p. 11, hereinafter 'the Fourth Directive').

15. The Fourth Directive, the second recital in the preamble to which expressly refers to Article 2(1)(f) of the First Directive, coordinated the national provisions concerning the presentation and content of annual accounts and annual reports, the valuation

methods used therein and their publication in respect of joint-stock companies, including inter alia German limited liability companies (see the first recital in the preamble to the Fourth Directive).

16. As regards the publication of annual accounts, Article 47(1) of the Fourth Directive provides:

> '1.The annual accounts, duly approved, and the annual report, together with the opinion submitted by the person responsible for auditing the accounts, shall be published as laid down by the laws of each Member State in accordance with Article 3 of Directive 68/151/EEC.
>
> The laws of a Member State may, however, permit the annual report not to be published as stipulated above. In that case, it shall be made available to the public at the company's registered office in the Member State concerned. It must be possible to obtain a copy of all or part of any such report free of charge upon request.'

17. Next, the German Government maintains that the Federal Republic of Germany has correctly transposed Article 6 of the First Directive. In accordance with Article 54(3)(g) of the EC Treaty, the coordination of national systems of company law is designed to safeguard the interests of members 'and others'. The latter do not comprise all natural and legal persons but only those who have a legal relationship with the company. In that regard, it is generally recognized in German academic legal writing that the term 'others', within the meaning of Article 54(3)(g) of the Treaty, covers only creditors of the company.

18. It must be pointed out that Article 54(3)(g) must be read in the light not only of Articles 52 and 54 of the EC Treaty, which clearly show that the coordination of systems of company law forms part of the general programme for the abolition of restrictions on freedom of establishment, but also of Article 3(h) of that Treaty, which provides that the activities of the Community are to include the approximation of national laws to the extent required for the functioning of the common market.

19. Furthermore, the very wording of Article 54(3)(g) of the Treaty refers to the need to protect the interests of 'others' generally, without distinguishing or excluding any categories falling within the ambit of that term.

20. Consequently, the term 'others', as contemplated in Article 54(3)(g) of the Treaty, cannot be limited merely to creditors of the company.

21. Moreover, the objective of abolishing restrictions on freedom of establishment, which is assigned in very broad terms to the Council and the Commission by Article 54(1) and (2) of the Treaty, cannot be circumscribed by the provisions of Article 54(3). Article 54(3) merely sets out a non-exhaustive list of measures to be taken in order to attain that objective, as is borne out by the use in that provision of the words 'in particular'.

22. As regards Article 6 of the First Directive, the fourth recital in the preamble shows that disclosure of annual accounts is primarily designed to provide information for third parties who do not know or cannot obtain sufficient knowledge of the company's accounting and financial situation. Article 3 of the First Directive, which provides for the maintenance of a public register in which all documents and particulars to be disclosed must be entered, and pursuant to which copies of the annual accounts must be obtainable by any person upon application, confirms the concern to enable any interested persons to inform themselves of these matters. That concern also finds expression in the recitals in the preamble to the Fourth Directive, which refer to the need to establish in the Community minimum equivalent legal requirements as regards the extent of

the financial information that should be made available to the public by companies that are in competition with one another (see, in particular, the third recital).

23. In view of the foregoing considerations, the answer to this part of the question must be that Article 6 of the First Directive is to be interpreted as precluding the legislation of a Member State from restricting to members or creditors of the company, the central works council or the company's works council the right to apply for imposition of the penalty provided for by the law of that Member State in the event of failure by a company to fulfil the obligations regarding disclosure of annual accounts laid down by the First Directive.

The question whether Article 6 of the First Directive is unconditional and sufficiently clear, and whether it may be relied upon by an individual for the purposes of applying to the competent public authority for the imposition of penalties on a private company:

24. As the Court has consistently held, a directive may not of itself impose obligations on an individual and may therefore not be relied upon as such against such a person (see, in particular, Case 152/84 Marshall I [1986] ECR 723, paragraph 48, Case C-91/92 Faccini Dori v. Recreb [1994] ECR I-3325, paragraph 20, and Case C-192/94 El Corte Inglés v. Blázquez Rivero [1996] ECR I-1281, paragraph 15). Consequently, there is no need to examine whether Article 6 of the First Directive is capable of having direct effect in the domestic legal order of a Member State.

25. This finding is without prejudice to the possible applicability of the principle that Community law requires Member States to make good loss and damage caused to individuals by reason of their failure to transpose a directive or their failure to do so correctly (Joined Cases C-46/93 and C-48/93 Brasserie du Pêcheur and Factortame [1996] ECR I-1029, paragraph 51, and Case C-392/93 The Queen v. H.M. Treasury, ex parte British Telecommunications [1996] ECR I-1631, paragraph 39).

26. In view of the foregoing considerations, the answer to the national court's question must be that, since a directive cannot of itself impose obligations on an individual, and cannot therefore be relied upon as such against such a person, there is no need to examine whether Article 6 of the First Directive has direct effect.

Costs

27. The costs incurred by the French, German and Spanish Governments and by the Commission of the European Communities, which have submitted observations to the Court, are not recoverable. Since these proceedings are, for the parties to the main proceedings, a step in the proceedings pending before the national court, the decision on costs is a matter for that court.

On those grounds,

THE COURT (Fifth Chamber), in answer to the question referred to it by the Oberlandesgericht Düsseldorf by order of 22 November 1995, hereby rules:

1. Article 6 of the First Council Directive 68/151/EEC of 9 March 1968 on co-ordination of safeguards which, for the protection of the interests of members and others, are required by Member States of companies within the meaning of the second paragraph of Article 58 of the Treaty, with a view to making such safeguards equivalent throughout the Community, must be interpreted as precluding the legislation of a Member State from restricting to members or creditors of a company, the central works council or the company's works council the right to apply for imposition of the penalty provided for by the law of that Member State in the event of failure by a company to fulfil the obligations regarding disclosure of annual accounts laid down by the First Directive 68/151.

2. Since a directive cannot of itself impose obligations on an individual, and cannot therefore be relied upon as such against such a person, there is no need to examine whether Article 6 of the First Directive 68/151 has direct effect.

---

b. Fourth Directive

The First Company Law Directive was meant to provide shareholders with a minimum amount of information relative to their investment. However, because the means by which that information was conveyed varied widely between the Member States of the EU, the information provided was not as useful for investors with holdings within more than one of the Member States.

The Fourth Company Law Directive represents an attempt to harmonize the way in which companies prepare their annual accounts. The purpose is to harmonize communication within the EU with respect to the presentation of financial information. Where the rules for the preparation of accounting reports vary from jurisdiction to jurisdiction, it is difficult to assess companies (especially companies in the same industry) operating in different jurisdictions. The Member-States reluctantly have come to conform their practices to those of the Fourth Company Law Directive. Review generally the Fourth Company Law Directive, <http://www.europa.eu.int/eur-lex/en/consleg/reg/en_register_1710.html>, before considering the following case.

EC Commission v. Italian Republic

(Case 17/85)
European Court of Justice
[1986] ECR 1199
20 March 1986

Opinion of M. Darmon, Advocate General:

1. This case concerning the failure of a Member State to fulfil its obligations under the EEC Treaty relates to the failure of the Italian Republic to implement within the prescribed period, which expired on 31 July 1980, the Fourth Council Directive of 25 July 1978 (No 78/660/EEC) based on Article 54(3)(g) of the Treaty on the annual accounts of certain types of companies. The directive was aimed principally at "the co-ordination of national provisions concerning the presentation and content of annual accounts and annual reports, the valuation methods used therein and their publication in respect of certain companies with limited liability..." (first recital in the preamble) whether private or public (Article 1).

The period allowed for transposing into national law the provisions of the regulation, laid down in Article 55(1), was two years from the date of its notification; the same provision required the Member States to inform the Commission as soon as the laws, regulations and administrative provisions necessary to comply with the directive had been adopted.

2. The Commission received no response from the Italian Government either to its letter (No SG (82) D/13781) of 19 October 1982 inviting the Government, in the ab-

sence of any communication from it concerning the adoption of the directive into national law, to submit its observations on the matter to the Commission, or to the reasoned opinion it issued on 14 June 1984 requesting the Italian Government to adopt the measures necessary to comply with the opinion within a period of two months. Having thus complied with the preliminary procedure laid down in Article 169 of the Treaty, the Commission brought this action on 21 January 1985.

The sole argument put forward in its defense by the Italian Government was that consideration of a draft law on the adoption of the directive was now "at an advanced stage" and it hoped that it would be adopted shortly.

3. The Court then asked the Commission to inform it of the measures which had been adopted by the Member States to implement the directive, indicating the dates on which the measures were adopted, and it asked the Italian Government to inform it of the stage actually reached in the procedure for implementing the directive referred to in its defense.

According to the reply received from the Commission six Member States have adopted implementing measures:

Denmark (two laws adopted on 10 June 1981)

United Kingdom (the Companies Act of 30 October 1981)

France (a law adopted on 30 April 1983; Ministerial Decree of 27 April 1982 publishing the new form for companies' accounts; Decree of 22 November 1983)

Belgium (two laws adopted on 1 July 1983 and 5 December 1984; Royal Decrees adopted on 12 September 1983)

Netherlands (a law adopted on 7 December 1983; Decrees of 22 and 23 December 1983)

Luxembourg (a law adopted on 4 May 1984).

Two actions for failure to fulfil obligations are pending before the Court against the Federal Republic of Germany (Case 18/85) and against Ireland (Case 16/85). Note that in the case of Germany a law dated 19 December 1985 concerning the adoption of the Fourth, Seventh and Eighth Directives of the Council harmonizing company law is scheduled to enter into force on 1 January 1987. As regards Ireland, a draft law is at present before the Irish parliament (the Dail), and its provisions may be adopted in the course of the first quarter of 1986.

Finally, proceedings against Greece for breach of its obligations have been initiated under Article 169 of the EEC Treaty.

The reply of the Italian Government was that the draft law, although at an advanced stage, was still in the course of preparation. At the hearing the representative of the Italian Government declared that the situation had not changed.

4. The number of actions which have been brought by the Commission regarding the adoption into national law of the directive in question, and the fact that no Member State was able to comply with the time-limit laid down therefor, are evidence of the difficulty which has been experienced in implementing provisions relating to highly technical subject-matter, affecting a particularly vital area of economic life in which commercial companies play a leading role.

Nevertheless, we are compelled to the conclusion in this case that the Italian Republic—as it has admitted—has not been able to show that the least effort has been made to introduce the measures necessary to implement its obligations under Article 189 of the EEC Treaty. The Court has consistently held, as was recalled by the Commission and re-stated in one of your most recent judgments (that of 6 November 1985 in Case 131/84, Commission v. Italian Republic):

"A Member State may not plead provisions, practices or circumstances existing in its internal legal system in order to justify failure to comply with obligations and time-limits laid down in Community directives" (paragraph 6 of the decision).

5. In conclusion I suggest that the Court Declare that by failing to adopt within the prescribed period the measures necessary to comply with Council Directive No 78/660/EEC of 25 July 1978 the Italian Republic has failed to fulfil its obligations under the EEC Treaty; Order the Italian Government to pay the costs.

DECISION [of the Court]:

By an application lodged at the Court Registry on 22 January 1985 the Commission of the European Communities brought proceedings under Article 169 of the EEC Treaty to obtain a declaration that the Italian republic has failed to fulfil its obligations under that Treaty by not adopting within the prescribed period the measures necessary to comply with Council Directive No 78/660 of 25 July 1978 on the annual accounts of certain types of companies (the Fourth Council Directive).

The Fourth Council Directive, which was based on Article 54(3)(g) of the Treaty, contains measures to co-ordinate national provisions concerning the presentation and content of annual accounts and annual reports, the valuation method used therein and their publication in respect of certain companies with limited liability. There was an urgent need for such co-ordinating measures, as is stated in the second recital in the preamble to the directive, because the activities of such companies frequently extend beyond the frontiers of their national territories and they offer no safeguards to third parties beyond the amounts of their net assets.

Article 55 of the directive provides that the Member States shall bring into force the laws, regulations and administrative provisions necessary for them to comply with the directive within two years of its notification and that they are to inform the Commission thereof. The directive was notified on 31 July 1978, so that that period expired two years thereafter.

The Commission received no communication on the subject from the Italian Government and therefore initiated the procedure under Article 169. Neither its letter of 19 October 1982 calling upon the Italian Government to act nor the reasoned opinion issued on 14 June 1984 elicited a response from the Italian authorities. Accordingly, the Commission brought this application on 22 January 1985.

The Italian Government concedes that it has failed to fulfil its obligations but submits that the subject-matter is a complex one which will entail an amendment to its Civil Code. It claims that draft legislation to implement the directive in question is at an advanced stage of consideration and it hopes that the draft will be adopted within a reasonable period of time. At the hearing it stated that could be done fairly soon, but it could not be sure precisely when the problem would finally be resolved.

The Court would point out that it has consistently held that Member States may not plead provisions, practices or circumstances existing in their internal legal systems in order to justify failure to comply with obligations and time-limits laid down in directives.

Accordingly, the Court finds that by failing to adopt, or inform the Commission of, the measures referred to in Council Directive No 78/660/EEC of 25 July 1978 within the prescribed period the Italian Republic has failed to fulfil its obligations under the EEC Treaty.

Costs

Article 69(2) of the Rules of Procedure provides that the unsuccessful party shall be ordered to pay the costs. Since the defendant has been unsuccessful in its arguments it must be ordered to pay the costs.

On those grounds, THE COURT hereby declares:

By failing to adopt, or to inform the Commission of the adoption of, the measures referred to in Council Directive No 78/660/EEC of 25 July 1978 on the annual accounts of certain types of companies within the prescribed period the Italian republic has failed to fulfil its obligations under the EEC Treaty.

The Italian Republic is ordered to pay the costs.

Comments and Questions

1. The Italian government argued that it had failed to transpose the Fourth Company Law Directive into national law because of the complexity of the directive. Advocate General Darmon noted that neither Germany nor Ireland had been able to transpose the Directive within the time limits set forth in that Directive. Though the European Court of Justice rejected this argument, would you agree, after reviewing the Fourth Company Law Directive (http://www.europa.eu.int/eur-lex/en/consleg/reg/en_register_1710.html), that it was too complex to easily transpose into national law? Would your answer depend on the similarity of the requirements of the Fourth Company Law Directive to current practice under national law? Might Member States have avoided the complexity argument by enacting the Fourth Company Law Directive substantially verbatim? Are there reasons such a verbatim transposition would have been politically unrealistic?

2. Even were all Member States of the EU to eventually harmonize their accounting rules with respect to the preparation of reports of the financial condition of corporations, it would still be difficult for European and American investors to communicate effectively. The Fourth Company Law Directive, like the financial accounting rules of the individual Member States that preceded it, continues to differ from American generally accepted accounting practices in a number of important respects. Among the most important of these are in rules for revenue recognition, accounting for goodwill, pension accounting, and accounting for stock options. Do you think that the reasons for adopting uniform systems of accounting conventions throughout the EU (and the US) also support the creation of a single universal system of accounting conventions applicable to all business enterprises? If so, how would you propose such a global standard be implemented? Are there any exceptions you might create based on the size of the enterprise, or if its securities were publicly traded?

3. Do your answers to the questions posed in Note 2, above, change in light of the materials that follow in Note 4? For an interesting discussion of some of the issues involving foreign companies participating in American securities markets, see Eric M. Sherbet, *Bridging the GAAP: Accounting Standards for Foreign SEC Registrants*, 29 Intl Law. 875 (1995). There has been preliminary work attempted on the creation of a set of

international accounting principles. This work has been done by the International Accounting Standards Committee, an organ of the International Organization of Security Commissions. For a discussion of the development of worldwide accounting standards through the work of the IASC, see Charles Canfield, *FASB v. IASC: Are the Structure and Standard Setting Process at the IASC Adequate for the Securities and Exchange Commission to Accept International Accounting Standards for Cross-border Offerings?*, 20 Nw. J. Int'l L. & Bus. 125 (1999).

4. The United States has largely avoided the problem of legislatively imposing a standard accounting language throughout the United States. Rather than impose a uniform system of accounting through legislation, the United States has traditionally relied on a system of voluntary regulation by the accounting profession. Self-regulation has come through the work of professional bodies affiliated with the American Institute of Certified Public Accountants. These include principally the Financial Accounting Standards Board (FASB), and the Accounting Principles Board (APB). These bodies have developed the principle elements constituting a system of generally accepted accounting principles (GAAP), which has become the body of standards used in the preparation of corporate financial statements.[1] Deviations from GAAP, or a determination not to use GAAP at all, are now customarily noted on financial reports, and might expose the reporting entity to litigation in the event the alternative system can be characterized as misrepresenting the financial condition of the reporting company. Because the American business community for the most part has come to rely on the uniformity and predictability of GAAP for transactions in the financial markets, a failure to abide by GAAP can have serious consequences for the reporting corporation.[2] One of the great strengths of this system of voluntary regulation has been its flexibility—old rules can be modified or abandoned, and new approaches adopted fairly quickly as business practice changes. The strong acceptance of this voluntary system has also resulted in little pressure for governmental regulation of accounting practice in the United States.

5. **Problem**: You work for the Director of a large trade association with significant lobbying expertise in Washington, D.C. The Director of the trade association has heard through his contacts in Congress that the President is considering replacing the current system of voluntary accounting rule regulation with a statutory system based on the Fourth Company Law Directive. He has been heard to argue that such a system would be great for American companies because it would permit investors to apply a uniform system of evaluation to the financial statements of companies throughout the United States and the EU. The president also believes that voluntary regulation of financial statements is anti-democratic, because only a small, unelected elite segment of the American body politic has usurped authority to impose definitive rules in an area of significant national concern. Uniform accounting rules are of significant national concern because they form a fundamental component of the reporting requirements under

1. The federal government has incorporated principles of GAAP into reporting requirements for publicly traded companies subject to the federal securities laws, supplementing GAAP from time to time through the SEC's Accounting Series Releases and Regulation S-X. *See* Martin A. Miller & Larry Bailey, GAAP Guide 1993, § 4.13 (1991).

2. Only companies whose shares are traded on securities markets are required to comply with GAAP in their accounting practices. The large majority of corporations, private and usually small, are not required to comply with GAAP in the preparation of their financial statements. One reason many don't is that GAAP accounting can be expensive. GAAP accounting also tends to be conservative, erring in favor of minimizing revenue recognition and maximizing liabilities.

the federal securities laws, and in this way are pivotal to ensuring the integrity of the financial markets on which American capitalism is based. The Director is particularly concerned because these ideas are coming from a Republican President. He wants you to prepare a memo to him, presenting, in detail, the arguments that can be made in favor of the present system and against a system of legislative standards for accounting rules.

6. Harmonization as an alternative in the United States: The United States has always taken an all or nothing approach to legislation. That is, legislation serves as a command to those to whom the statutes are directed. The alternative to legislation by statute is no legislation. This approach is venerable, the mirror to another age. It is also inflexible. Legislation by directive offers a more flexible alternative—federal direction of the goals and objectives of governmental regulation, with flexibility attained by leaving it to subordinate governmental units, the states, to transpose these goals and objectives in statutes that accord to local practice and tradition. Do you think that harmonization in the EU manner provides the basis for a better approach to solving the 'Delaware effect' in the United States? Do you think it offers a better alternative to federal regulation of accounting practice? Would this sort of harmonization work better in the United States if, rather than the states, private regulatory groups recognized by the federal government, would be charged with transposing federal directives?

C. An Alternative to European Federalization: The Convention on the Mutual Recognition of Legal Persons

The EC Treaty did not contemplate that all "legislation" as between the Member States would derive from the actions of the EC organs—EC Council, EC Commission, and EC Parliament. The EC Treaty directed that "Member States shall, so far as necessary, enter into negotiations with each other with a view to securing for the benefit of their nationals....the mutual recognition of companies or firms within the meaning of the second paragraph of Art. 58[now Art. 48], the retention of legal personality in the event of transfer of their seat from one country to another, and the possibility of mergers between companies or firms governed by the laws of different countries...." EC Treaty, Art. 293. By this provision, the EC Treaty imposed an obligation on Member States to enter into binding Conventions, with the force of treaties, with respect to the subject matter described in Art. 293, which, as noted above, included matters related to company law harmonization. Member States have been somewhat cautious about entering into Conventions within the ambit of Art. 293: the courts have tended to hold that conventions entered into by Member States cannot alter existing Community law, and as such, read the ambit of Conventions narrowly. *Betriebskrankenkasse der Heseper Torfwerk GmbH v. Koster (nee van Dijk)* (Case 33/64) [1965] ECR 97, 104, [1966] CMLR 191 at 208. But this position has been subject to attack even at the level of the ECJ, especially by the advocates-general. *Federal Republic of Germany v. Commission*, (Case 24/62) [1963] ECR 63, [1963] CMLR 347 at 361–362. As a consequence, the Member States have rarely used the Convention as a means of effecting the Common Market. Indeed, since the creation of the EC only four conventions have been signed.

The tendency has been for the EC Council to adopt the subject of conventions as regulations or directives.

---

1. A Failed Convention: Convention on the Mutual Recognition of Companies

The single convention affecting company law—the Convention for the Mutual Recognition of Companies and Legal Persons—signed by the original six Member States of the EC in 1968 never came into force because the Netherlands failed to ratify it. The Convention has been supplemented by a 1971 protocol giving the ECJ competence to make preliminary rulings on the interpretation of the Convention in the same way that Art. 234, formerly Art. 177, of the EC Treaty gives the ECJ competence to interpret the EC Treaty itself. However, neither has had significant effect in European law, and efforts to revive the Convention in one form or another have met with some resistance from the academic community (a significant force in EC legal matters!).

Berthold Goldman, *The Convention Between the Member States of the European Economic Community on the Mutual Recognition of Companies and Legal Persons*

6 C.M.L.Rev. 104 (1968)
pp. 118–119
(footnotes omitted)

We have kept until now the most difficult question, that of the *criterion of attachment* of the companies and legal persons to one of the contracting States. In what circumstances would they be regarded as companies or legal persons "of that State" and therefore as able to benefit from the Convention?

The difference which informs this question is too well known to require a lengthy description: on the one side is the Anglo-American concept of *incorporation*, which attaches the company to the State under the laws of which it was formed (and the provisions of which, relating to registration and publicity, it has consequently followed, where necessary, in order to "take shape"); on the other side, is the "continental" concept—especially German, French and Belgian—which attaches it contrariwise to the country in which it places its *actual* head office (*i.e.* according to the definition currently accepted, the country in which its central administration is established; see Article 5 of the Convention). Far from being a matter of theory, this difference reflects the legal (and also economic) expansionism of those holding the first concept and the territorialism, which some regard as supercilious, of the supporters of the second. The draftsmen of the Hague Convention came up against this, and were only able to surmount it by including in its principle the criterion of incorporation (Art. 1), but leaving it open to those States which are hostile to it to refrain from recognizing the foreign companies whose real head office is in their territory or in the territory of a third State whose law takes it likewise into account (Art. 2).

This is not a very satisfactory solution, for in the end it does not guarantee generality of application of the recognition principle, which is after all the aim of every international convention on this subject; in any case, it could not be wholly adopted in the Convention between the States of the Community [because it was contrary to the principles of mutual recognition set forth in the EEC TREATY Art. 48(1)].

* * *

But once this major concession was made, and ineluctably so, it remained to take account of the concept and of the legitimate interests of the States which are hostile to the incorporation system. * * * *

The divergence is not purely doctrinal; rightly or wrongly, those States [hostile to the incorporation doctrine] fear that companies whose decision-making centre is outside the Common Market might take advantage of the possibility of creating a fragile link with one of the Member States so as to benefit from *ipso jure* recognition in the others; or that companies might be formed in Holland with the intention of remaining in reality in their own territory, because their founders wanted to escape the latter's company law.

Richard D. English, *Company Law in the European Single Market*

1990 B.Y.U. L. REV. 1413 (1990)
(excerpts pages 1435–1436)

It has also been suggested that Articles 52 and 58 of the Treaty of Rome, concerning the free movement of persons and the right of establishment, should be applied to prevent the Member States' application of the *siege social* rule, since it could result in non-recognition of a company's legal capacity. The *siege social* rule severely restricts the movement of enterprises within the Community, since the movement of the headquarters would *ipso facto* change the law applicable to the entirety of the company's internal relations. The rule may, therefore, violate the articles on the right of establishment. This issue was addressed by the Convention on the Mutual Recognition of Legal Persons, which provided as a general principle that a company incorporated in one Member State but having its registered office anywhere in the Community would be recognized in all other Member States and have the validity and capacities provided by the state of incorporation. Unfortunately, the Convention has never come into force because of the Netherlands' failure to ratify it.

The prevalence of the *siege social* rule, as the distinctive feature of the laws in most Member States, has tended to remove the possibility that the laws of corporate governance would progressively evolve into a state of greater convergence. While it has preserved the more highly protective nature of Western European company law, it must be seen as one of the conditions necessitating the single market program's company law proposals. In contrast, the convergence in the corporation laws of the American states was achieved without the conscious design of a single mind or even a single governmental institution, legislative body or political process. In the United States, the celebrated race of laxity had the effect of producing more uniformity and liberality at the same time. The differing conditions in Europe, where the *siege social* rule has served to shield protective rules form erosion, are the basis for the struggle for a more uniform company law for the... Member States.

---

2. *Other Conventions*

Of somewhat more importance has been the Convention on the Jurisdiction and the Enforcement of Judgments in Civil and Commercial Matters, signed in 1969 and in force since 1973.

The Judgments Convention was meant to make it easier to enforce judgments rendered in the courts of the signatories. It applies to civil and commercial matters, with some exceptions. The most important provisions of the Judgments Convention harmonizes the jurisdiction of the courts of the participating nations and provides a basis for determining the proper court for the resolution of disputes. With respect to corporations, Article 53 provides that: "For purposes of this Convention, the seat of a company or other legal person or association of natural or legal persons shall be treated as its domicile. However, in order to determine that seat, the court shall apply its rules of private international law."

The Judgments Convention has its detractors; although the arguments made seem to run counter to the direction EC harmonization efforts have taken since the 1980's. Indeed, the most significant criticism seems to be that the Judgments Convention makes it easier for Member States to prevent corporations from jurisdictions with more liberal company law from operating with ease outside their own jurisdictions. As such, the Judgements Convention can be seen as another means of preventing the "Delaware effect," and imposing uniformity through action of the EC Council.

Tropical Shipping Company v. Dammers & Van Der Heide's

Scheepvaart En Handelsbedrijf BV
Gerechtshof (Court of Appeal), the Hague
[1982] ECC 353
29 February 1980

FACTS:

After the respondent, Dammers, had on 19 January 1979 with leave of the President of the Arrondissementsrechtbank (RB) of Rotterdam had the motor vessel 'Dabema', lying at Rotterdam in the Merwehaven by Uniport and belonging to the appellant, Tropical, taken into conservatory (alien-property) sequestration, Dammers, by summons dated 23 January 1979, summoned Tropical with the permission of the above-mentioned President on shortened notice before the RB of Rotterdam.

On the basis of the facts asserted in the statement of claim, which coincides with the writ, Dammers claimed that Tropical should be ordered to pay to it, Dammers, a sum of 1,452,574.09 guilders plus statutory interest from the date of summons to date of payment, that the sequestration of the motor vessel 'Dabema' notified to Tropical in the above-mentioned summons should be declared valid, and that Tropical should be ordered to pay the costs of the proceedings, including those of the sequestration.

Following this, Tropical raised by way of reasoned submission (with exhibits) in advance of any defence the objection that the Rotterdam RB should declare itself to have no jurisdiction in respect of Dammers' claim for the payment of 1,452,174.09 guilders.

On this interlocutory issue, Dammers in a submission in reply (with exhibits) opposed this objection and submitted that the Rotterdam RB had jurisdiction to admit the claim.

After the parties had by their counsel argued the case on this interlocutory point and Dammers had by formal declaration introduced a number of further documents into the proceedings, the RB, by a judgment of 25 May 1979 on the interlocutory issue, declared that it had jurisdiction to admit the claim in question and fixed a fresh date on which the main action was to be brought on for trial. The RB based its decision on the following views of law.

DECISION:

In raising the objection as to jurisdiction, Tropical adopted the standpoint that its real base is Bouliac in France, so that, under Article 53 in conjunction with Article 2 of the EEC Judgments Convention, the French court (the Tribunal de commerce at Bordeaux) and not the Rotterdam RB has jurisdiction to admit Dammers' claim for payment of the sum of 1,452,174.09 guilders.

The RB did not agree with Tropical on this point and, reproduced in summary and objectively, took the view that, in accordance with Dutch private international law (which, by virtue of Article 53 of the above-mentioned convention is also decisive for the determination of jurisdiction in Community cases), the seat under the memorandum of incorporation is treated as the place where Tropical is based, that this is Monrovia (Liberia) and therefore, since Liberia has not acceded to the EEC Judgments Convention, this Convention does not apply and the Rotterdam RB has jurisdiction on the basis of the (normal) jurisdiction rules in accordance with Dutch law, to admit Dammers' above-mentioned claim against Tropical.

In the first ground of appeal and in its elucidation, Tropical disputes the view taken by the RB. It insists in particular that Dutch private international law does not force one to the conclusion that Tropical's base under the memorandum of incorporation is decisive for the determination of the judge's jurisdiction, but that this must lead to the result that the real base (seat) is the decisive factor and that this is in Bouliac.

This ground of appeal fails. Under current Dutch private international law, the place of a company's base is that determined in the memorandum of incorporation, that is, the 'base by memorandum'. This follows from the development of that law, in which, at present, with regard also to formal law (which is in issue in the present case) this standpoint has been chosen. Tropical's assertion that, under French law, it has a 'seige reel' at Bouliac—which moreover Dammers disputes in reasoned argument—does not therefore fail to be considered nor does the assertion that Tropical's seat under its memorandum is no more than fiction.

In the second ground of appeal, Tropical asserts that the RB wrongly disregarded its arguments with reference to its true seat ('siege reel'). Since the first ground of appeal has been rejected, Tropical's assertions about a real seat are no longer relevant; nor, therefore, is it relevant that Dammers, as Tropical argues in the elucidation of this ground of appeal, always wrote on matters concerning Tropical to Mme Rechenmann's address in Bouliac, which Dammers disputes.

In so far as it would have to be inferred from the elucidation to the second ground of appeal that Tropical likewise feels aggrieved by what the RB considered in the second paragraph under the heading 'In relation to II', this ground of appeal must also fail. For, as the RB correctly considered, it by no means follows from the exhibited documents from the proceedings brought before the President of the Bordeaux Tribunal de Commerce that the latter must adjudicate on the present monetary claim by Dammers on the merits.

From what has been hereinbefore considered, it follows that the RB correctly rejected the objection raised as to jurisdiction and that the judgment must be reaffirmed, with the proviso that the main action can be brought on again in the list of the Rotterdam RB by the party which is ready first.

Appeal dismissed.

Tropical Shipping Company v. Dammers & Van Der Heide's

Scheepvaart En Handelsbedrijf Bv
The Arrondissementsrechtbank (District Court), Rotterdam
[1982] ECC 353
25 May 1979

DECISION:

Dammers bases its claims in the main action on the following assertions (reproduced in abbreviated form):

—as from 26 May 1977, it has carried out on behalf and for the account of Tropical the commercial and technical management of the motor vessels 'Bilinga' and 'Dabema' belonging to Tropical;

—in this connection, it has made payments and advances and has also received freight monies;

—Dammers has every month sent Tropical accounts of costs incurred and payments received;

—since about August 1977, Tropical has failed to pay the negative balances of these accounts;

—up to and including 12 December 1978, Tropical owed a sum of 1,452,174.09 guilders to Dammers, which sum had still not been paid despite formal reminder.

Tropical has appeared solely in order to dispute the RB's jurisdiction. It bases its arguments on the Convention of 27 September 1968 on Jurisdiction and the Enforcement of Judgments in Civil and Commercial Cases, (hereinafter to be referred to as the EEC Judgments Convention), and in particular on:

I. Article 53 in conjunction with Article 2, and

II. Articles 21 to 23 inclusive of the Convention.

and it argues, in summary and in so far as now relevant:

I. (a). Under Article 53 of the Convention, the seat of a company is equated with domicile. In order to determine this place of domicile, the judge applies the rules of private international law which apply to him.

(b). Although Tropical has been incorporated in and is by its memorandum of incorporation based in Monrovia, Liberia, its real seat is in Bouliac, France, the domicile of Madame Rechenmann, who manages Tropical.

(c). The question of where Tropical has its forum-determining seat must not be decided in accordance with Dutch national law, since Tropical has not been incorporated in nor does it have its real seat in Holland, but in accordance with French law as the law of the country where Tropical in fact has its principal office and is managed.

(d). In accordance with French law, a company has its seat where it has its 'siege reel.'

(e). Under Liberian law too, should that law be applicable as the law of the country of incorporation, the place where a company is managed and actually maintains an office is regarded as its seat.

Therefore, in accordance with Article 2 of the Convention, Dammers should have summoned Tropical before the Tribunal de Commerce at Bordeaux as the court of Tropical's domicile.

II. The present claim has already been brought by Dammers in September 1978 before the President of the Tribunal de Commerce at Bordeaux, so that, by virtue of Articles 21 to 23 inclusive of the Convention, the Rotterdam RB will have to declare itself to have no jurisdiction in favour of this Tribunal de Commerce.

Dammers, on the other hand, takes the view that the Rotterdam RB has jurisdiction to admit the present claims. It argues:

In relation to I. Under Dutch private international law, the question of where Tropical has its seat must be answered by the law under which the legal person has been incorporated, that is, in casu, Liberian law.

Contrary to what Tropical asserts, Liberian law regards the seat under the memorandum of incorporation as the place where a company is based.

Even if, however, the question of where Tropical has its seat had to be answered in accordance with French law, then French law in this case nonetheless carries out a renvoi to Liberian law, in view of the fact that, under French law, Tropical does not have any 'siege reel' recognised as such in France. For Tropical—says the defendant to this issue—has not complied with the formalities required in France, while, in addition, its office at Bouliac is ordinarily no more than an 'empty shell' with no one there for months on end.

Therefor the Convention does not apply, and the Rotterdam RB has jurisdiction on the basis of the provisions of the Code of Civil Procedure (Wetboek van Burgerlijke Rechtsvordering (Rv).)

In relation to II. Since the Convention does not apply, nor do its Articles 21 to 23 inclusive.

Moreover, Dammers denies that the present claim is pending before the Bordeaux Tribunal de Commerce, in view of the fact that an order has been made by the President of the latter court that the sequestration imposed on the motor vessel 'Bilinga' could be raised on the giving of security, which has in fact happened.

The RB considers with regard to this:

In relation to I. The question of whether this RB has jurisdiction to admit the present claim must be answered by reference to the rules laid down in the EEC Judgments Convention. This Convention (save for a single exception not relevant here) applies if the defendant is domiciled in the territory of a Convention State; if the defendant has no domicile here, then, under Article 4 of the Convention, jurisdiction is regulated in each Convention State (including Holland) by the legislation of the latter State. It must therefore be examined whether Tropical is domiciled in a Convention State.

As Tropical has rightly argued, the place where a company is based is under Article 53 of the Convention equated with domicile, while the judge applies the rules of private international law applicable to him in order to determine where the company is based. In this case, the base must thus be determined in accordance with Dutch private international law. In accordance with this law, the seat under the memorandum of incorporation is regarded as the seat of a legal person or company. It is established as common ground that Tropical was incorporated in and is under its memorandum based in Monrovia, Liberia, so that its seat—which is to be equated with domicile—under Dutch private international law lies in Liberia. Since Liberia has not acceded to this Convention, Tropical has no domicile on the territory of a Convention State, so that the jurisdiction of the Dutch judge is in the present case determined by Dutch law.

Because the seat of a legal person or company must under Dutch private international law be qualified as the seat under the memorandum, and not as the 'siege reel,' the Court can disregard the parties' arguments with reference to Tropical's true seat.

Nor is the argument relating to—possibly—applicable French or Liberian law helpful. Although, in private international law, domicile is one of the linking concepts in the determination of an applicable system of law, the mere fact of whether the defendant is domiciled inside or outside the territory over which the Convention extends determines, under the Convention, whether the relevant rules of the Convention or the national laws of the judge invoked apply to his jurisdiction. There can be no question on this point of rules for reference to other possible applicable systems of law, let alone of renvoi.

In relation to II. Since the rules of the Convention, as considered above, do not apply in this case, nor do Articles 21 to 23 inclusive of the Convention apply, which dictate transfer to the court where the claim was first brought.

This does not, however, take away the fact that, under Dutch principles of law too, the judge can declare himself to have no jurisdiction or, in order to avoid mutually incompatible judgments, postpone his judgment, if a dispute has been brought before him which is already pending between the same parties before a judge in another State. It must, of course, be a condition that the foreign judge has at his disposal the same, or similar, powers to decide and to enforce his decision as the Dutch judge invoked. This does not appear to be the position in casu either. Having regard to sections 853 et seq, and in particular to sections 872 and 877 of the French New Code of Civil Procedure, and in view of the introductory remarks in the judgment of the President of the Bordeaux Tribunal de Commerce, exhibited by Tropical, which reads: 'Tous droits, moyens, exceptions des parties demeurant au fond reserves et sans y prejudicier...', ('All rights, arguments and objections of the parties remaining reserved for the trial of the principal action and without prejudice thereunto...') the proceedings, as brought before him cannot be equated with a full hearing on the merits (be it said with all respect to the President at Bordeaux). Rather, these French proceedings, in so far as they are still in fact pending, must be put on a par with Dutch summary proceedings which, by virtue of section 292 Code of Civil Procedure, do not prejudice the main issue in the case either.

Therefore, Tropical's arguments under II cannot avail it either.

Thus this RB has jurisdiction by virtue of Dutch law, namely section 767 Code of Civil Procedure, to admit the present claim, since Dammers has imposed conservatory (alien-property) sequestration on the motor vessel 'Dabema' belonging to Tropical and lying in the Merwehaven at Rotterdam.

Tropical appealed against this judgment by summons dated 23 August 1979. In its notice of appeal, it adduced two grounds of appeal against the judgment and submitted, in accordance with the appeal summons, that the Hof, annulling that judgment, should also declare that the Rotterdam RB or the Dutch judge has no jurisdiction to admit the claim for payment of 1,452,174.09 guilders brought against Tropical by Dammers by summons of 23 January 1979, and should remit the case to the Rotterdam RB solely in order for it to proceed further in respect of the claim, brought at the same time by Dammers for a declaration of validity of the conservatory (alien-property) sequestration on the motor vessel 'Dabema' imposed on 19 January 1979 on Dammers' application or with such further decision as the Court shall deem just, with costs according to law. Dammers, in a submission in reply, took issue with Tropical's grounds of appeal, after which the parties, after lodging the documents, applied for judgment to be given.

Comments and Questions

1. It is possible to argue that the effect of the Judgments Convention attains the result sought in the failed Convention on the Mutual Recognition of Companies. Do you agree?

2. To what extent does the Judgments Convention appear to be motivated by a desire to avoid the 'Delaware effect' within Europe? To what extent has the Judgments Convention appeared to be successful in that regard? For a comparative analysis, see John Fitzpatrick, *The Lugano Convention and Western European Integration: A Comparative Analysis of Jurisdiction and Judgments in Europe and the United States*, 8 CONN. J. INT'L L. 695 (1993).

Chapter 7

Pre-Incorporation Transactions: Defective Incorporation and Ultra Vires Transactions

This chapter introduces the student to the differences in conceptual approaches to a series of related problems in corporate law: the liability of people for the pre-incorporation obligations of the enterprise, the effects of corporate contractual actions when the corporate formation is defective, and the liability of the corporation (or its participants) for engaging in ultra vires activities. On the American side, the emphasis will be on general common law, with some consideration of the approach suggested under the Revised Model Business Corporation Act. On the EU side, the chapter considers the approach of the First and Second Council directives and its effect on the resolution of the same problems within the EU. In the case of China and Japan, the chapter highlights the differences and similarities of these systems with those of the West. In both systems, and in contrast to the American approach, there is an emphasis on the law regulating ultra vires activities, and a relative indifference to developing a complicated approach to issues of pre-incorporation or defective corporation liability.

In reviewing the materials on liability for pre-incorporation transactions and for actions taken by defectively formed corporations, think about the factors that may account for the different approaches followed by the United States Japan, China, and the EU. Consider whether ease of corporate formation might also affect the seriousness of the problems within each jurisdiction.

A. Introduction: A Note on Corporate Formation

1. *Corporate Formation in the United States*

Corporate formation in the United States is a simple and fast process, except where the shareholders contemplate a complex capital structure from the moment of incorporation (but even in that case, the shareholders might be able to incorporate using a simple model and then amending the core corporate documents). Incorporation is accomplished by an "incorporator." In some jurisdictions one incorporator suffices, in others more than one (but usually no more than three) are required. In several jurisdictions the incorporator need not even be a natural person—a corporation might be an incorporator.

The incorporator is responsible for signing and filing the critical document in the legal process of corporate formation—the articles of incorporation, or the certificate of incorporation. This document is filed with the Secretary of State or a comparable official of the state in which incorporation is desired. Formal corporate existence commences in some jurisdictions upon the filing of the articles of incorporation (assuming that they have been properly drafted and executed and accompanied by all documents and fees required under the law of the incorporating jurisdiction). In other jurisdictions, corporate existence commences when the appropriate state official actually issues a certificate of incorporation.

The drafting of the articles of incorporation is intended under most corporate statutes to be a simple document, and in the simplest cases it need be no longer than about one page. It generally is required to contain no more than the name of the corporation, the number of shares the corporation's board of directors will be authorized to issue, the name and address of the agent for service of process, the name of the incorporator(s), and the purposes of the corporation (i.e. "for any lawful business purpose"). Of course, the articles of incorporation can be significantly more complex, including within its provisions a statement of the rights, preferences and privileges of the various classes of securities (common and preferred stock) which the corporation, through its board of directors, may be authorized to issue, provisions exculpating members of the Board of Directors from personal liability from breaches of certain duties (of care) otherwise owed to the corporation, and such other provisions as the participants may wish to include in the articles of incorporation.

After the corporation has come into formal existence, most state statutes require an organizational meeting at which an initial board of directors is named, shares are issued (for such consideration as may lawfully be accepted), the bylaws of the corporation are adopted, officers are appointed, a depository bank is designated, and other such matters are resolved. Thus organizational meeting need not be held by the incorporators in person. In most jurisdictions, the incorporators may adopt the necessary resolutions by unanimous consent in lieu of a meeting. The matter of incorporation is so routine in most jurisdictions that the work is often times performed (for a fee) by an incorporation service under the instruction of an attorney. The service provides stock forms, in which the "blanks" are filled in under the direction of the attorney for those seeking the creation of the corporation. These companies will also usually comply with the minimal annual reporting requirements of the state of incorporation. The Revised Model Business Corporation Act ("RMBCA") and the Delaware General Corporation Law ("DGCL") provide typical models of the process of corporate formation. *See* RMBCA §§ 2.01–2.06, 10.20-10.22, and DGCL §§ 101-109.

2. *Corporate Formation Within the European Communities*

Like European companies created under civil law corporate codes (for example those of France and Germany), English (and Irish) corporate law recognizes two general sorts of corporate forms, the public and the private limited company. Yet, like the process of incorporation in the American system, the process of incorporation in the United Kingdom and Ireland contemplates only the most minimal ministerial role for the state. An entity incorporates under the Companies Act of 1985[1] by completing the statutorily required forms and sending them, along with the properly calculated fees, to the English registrar of companies, an entity serving a function similar to that of the corporations departments, or the office of the secretary of a state government in the United States. The requirements with respect to these forms, and fees, are not the same for a private limited company and a public limited company. For example, private limited companies may be incorporated with as few as a single incorporator; public limited companies require at least two, and each must be a shareholder of the resulting company. Like American state officials entrusted with registering corporations, the English registrar of companies preforms merely ministerial tasks, checking only that the formal minimum statutory requirements have been met. If all the requirements are met, then the registrar must issue a certificate of incorporation. A corporation begins its existence with the issuance of that certificate.[2] That certificate of incorporation serves as evidence of corporate status as well as a presumption that all formalities necessary for incorporation have been met.[3]

In contrast to the ease of formation which generally characterizes incorporation in the United States and England, incorporation in any of the Member States of the EU can be a complex process in which error, fatal to the incorporation, can occur more easily than in the United States. A brief review of the laws of the most influential civil law jurisdictions, France (with Spain) and Germany, illustrates the basic differences between American and European methods of corporate formations.

In Germany, public companies (*Aktiengesellschaft*, "AG") require at least five founder shareholders to sign the statutes (articles of incorporation) before a notary public. The founders appoint a supervisory committee (*Aufsichtsrat*) and the management board (*Vorstand*), which then file the formation documents with the trade register at the local court responsible for the district where the company is to have its primary seat (*siege social* or *siege reel*). Registration documents include confirmation from the directors that the minimum share capital has been paid, and an opening balance sheet. The appropriate registration tax on shares must be paid prior to the completion of registration. Public company formation takes roughly six to eight weeks and the company acquires legal status once registration is effected and published. The German private company (*Gesellschaft mit beschrankter Haftung*—GmbH) is easier to form. Notarized articles are still required, as is the payment of the share registration tax. The GmbH, however, may be formed by one or more natural or legal persons, and its minimum share capital is substantially less than that required for the AG.

---

1. Companies Act 1985, §§ 1, 10–11.

2. *Id.*, § 13. Compare the Revised Model Business Corporation Act: "Unless a delayed effective date is specified, the corporate existence begins when the articles of incorporation are filed." REV. MODEL BUS. CORP. ACT §2.03(a).

3. *Id.*, at § 13(7). Compare the Revised Model Business Corporation Act: "The secretary of state's filing of the articles of incorporation is conclusive proof that the incorporators satisfied all conditions precedent to incorporation except in a proceeding by the state to cancel or revoke the incorporation or involuntarily dissolve the corporation." REV. MODEL BUS. CORP. ACT §2.03(b). Under English law, the Attorney-General has similar authority to have the incorporation of a public or private limited company quashed. *See* R. v. Registrar of Companies ex p. Attorney-General, (Court of Appeals, 1980), [1991] BCLC 476.

The Spanish *sociedad anónima* (SA) and French *société anonyme* (SA) are formed by public deed (articles of incorporation) executed before a civil law notary. The articles must include, in addition to the information required in U.S. articles, the bylaws of the company. The share capital that has been paid in, as well as the address of the company (to determine the place of its "seat"), must be included in the articles. The articles must be entered in the Mercantile or Commercial Registry within a short period of time after its execution (two months in Spain), and the transfer tax on shares paid. Corporate existence commences at the time of this registration, if properly effected. Corporate formation generally takes about eight weeks in Spain. Like their German counterpart, formation of an SA requires a minimum number of shareholders, seven shareholders are required for formation of a French SA. Private companies (*sociedad de responsibilidad limitada*, or *société à responsibilité limité*) are formed in substantially the same manner. Private companies can have as few as a single shareholder.

3. *Corporate Formation in Japan*

The formation of corporations in Japan, especially of *kabushiki kaisha*, Japanese corporations similar to the German AG or the French SA, can be a highly complicated affair. The process involves many steps and review by governmental authorities at various stages of incorporation. Consider the similarities and differences between Japanese incorporation of the large public corporation and the European and American corporation.

Alan W.N. Kitchin and John McClenahan, *Doing Business in Asia: Focus on Japan, India, and Vietnam*

in Going International: International Trade for the Nonspecialist, American Law Institute—American Bar Association Continuing Legal Education, ALI-ABA Course of Study, September 29, 1994, C942 ALI-ABA 177, page 177
(excerpts pages 184–185)

Establishing a Company

The Articles of Incorporation of the subsidiary must be signed by the promoters and notarised. At least one promoter is necessary and the parent company can be a promoter.

The Articles of Incorporation must contain inter-alia the company's objects, trade name and the number of shares. It must be signed by its promoter (the parent company can be a promoter), stamped and notarised.

A report which includes the corporate objectives, the amount of capital to be paid in and the date for commencement of business must be filed by the company to the Ministry of Finance and the Minister in charge of the relevant industry through the Bank of Japan.

The constituent meeting of subscribers is then held and three or more directors, and one or more statutory auditors, are elected. Following the constituent general meeting, the first meeting of the board of directors is held to elect a representative director and decide upon the location of the head office.

Registration

The new company must be registered with the local Legal Affairs Bureau in the administrative district where its head office is to be located. The application must be accompanied by documents evidencing the existence of the company, its business and the qualifications of its Japanese representative, each of which must be certified by government agencies. Registration must be completed within two weeks of the organisational meeting and within three months of the filing of the stock acquisition report. The Japanese corporation comes into existence only upon this registration.

On-going Requirements

A subsidiary must file an annual report with the Fair Trade Commission, a report on securities at the Ministry of Finance, hold an annual general meeting, prepare a quarterly report by the representative directors for the board, file various accounts and tax reports and pay various taxes....

Establishment of a Branch Office

Notification

In accordance with the Foreign Exchange and Foreign Trade Control Law, when a branch office is established in Japan by a foreign company a "Report Concerning Establishment of Branch Office" must be filed in advance with the Ministry of Finance through the Bank of Japan.

Registration

When establishing a branch office a foreign company must appoint a representative person in Japan, set up a place of business and then apply for registration at the Local Legal Affairs Bureau. A public announcement must also be made within three weeks of the setting up of the place of business. It is illegal for a foreign company to carry on business in Japan until after the registration. There is a flat registration fee payable. The application must be accompanied by documents evidencing the existence of the company and its business, and a document evidencing the qualifications of the representative person in Japan.

Each of the documents must be verified or certified by appropriate government agencies in the place of incorporation of the company, or by an agency of such foreign government such as its embassy or consulate in Japan.

Ongoing Requirements

- To file an annual report with the Fair Trade Commission.
- To file a report on securities at the Ministry of Finance.
- To hold a general meeting once a year.
- The representative directors to give a quarterly report to the board of directors.
- To file a balance sheet, a profit and loss account, business report and proposals relating to the distribution of profit and loss.
- To appoint at least one statutory auditor.

- To file a tax report and pay tax to the prefectural and municipal tax offices.
- To withhold employees' social security, pension contributions, and tax, and to pay it to the relevant local office on a monthly basis.

Comments and Questions

1. The details of the incorporation process of the *kabushiki kaisha* are quite complex and detailed. The excerpt above provides only a flavor of the mechanics of the process that can take several months to complete. For a more detailed description of the process, see, Bruce W. MacLennan, *Establishing a Stock Corporation in Japan after the 1990 Revision of the Commercial Code*, 1 PAC. RIM L. & POL'Y J. 127 (1992).

2. The Japanese promoter serves the same purpose as the American incorporator. Only one promoter is needed to form a *kabushiki kaisha*. Yet the responsibilities and liabilities of the promoter is significant in Japan. For a discussion see the materials that follow in this Chapter 7 at Section C.1, *Liability for Pre-Incorporation Transactions in the EU and Japan*.

3. The *kabushiki kaisha*, like the French SA and the German AG are subject to significant minimum capital requirements. But in addition, the *kabushiki kaisha* is subject to the American system of par value for its issued shares. Here is an instance of hybridization resulting in the merging of the requirements of two distinct systems caused, in part, by the history of Japanese legal development first in the 19th century and then during the American Occupation after 1945. For a discussion, see the materials in Chapter 8.

4. Establishing a branch for a foreign corporation appears to be a less onerous alternative to establishing a subsidiary. Are there any reasons a corporation wishing to operate in Japan would consider establishing a *kabushiki kaisha* rather than a branch?

5. Is the process of incorporation in Japan more like that in the United States or in Europe? Which system is more efficient? Which system provides greater governmental control? Which system is better? Does your answer to the last question depend on the values and policies you value more than others?

4. Corporate Formation in China

The process of incorporation in China presents issues which are no longer relevant in the West. As you read the materials that follow, consider whether the Chinese process of incorporation reflects the ambivalence of the Chinese Marxist-Socialist state to the substance of enterprise organization even as it exalts the form. Is it possible that the PRC can tolerate the organs of the state and the Chinese Communist Party as the only substantive legal persons within the Chinese state? In other words, does the Chinese process of corporate formation suggest the desire to create corporations in name only, as hollow institutions serving as indirectly managed vehicles of state enterprise funded by non-state actors?

Robert C. Art and Minkang Gu, *China Incorporated: The First Corporation Law of the People's Republic of China*

20 Yale J. Int'l L. 273 (1995)
(excerpt pages 288–291)

A. Incorporation by Approval, Not by Right

The law tightly regulates incorporation, maintaining state control over this form and its attendant privilege of limited liability. Government departments wielding authority granted by the State Council or the provinces[95] must approve the establishment of a company, and may do so only after the enterprise meets certain conditions.[96] Each company must apply for registration and obtain a "certificate of operation."[97] The scope of a corporation's permissible operations is limited to those specified in the registration unless the government department approves an amendment to the registration.[98] Public stock offerings require State Council permission[99] and are subject to detailed rules.[100]

The processes of incorporation, operation, and capitalization of a business are thus plainly matters of governmental control and permission, not of right. The Law condones and even endorses private business activity but handles it warily nevertheless. The operative attitude appears to be that corporations are a necessary evil to be closely regulated rather than an economic engine to be encouraged and released.

The current Chinese approach is comparable to the "special" incorporation processes followed in England and the United States until the early 1800's. At that time, each instance of incorporation required special legislation. Current American policy, in contrast, grants corporate status to any enterprise fulfilling nominal filing requirements.[102]

95. Corporation Law, Art. 77.

96. The prerequisites for establishing a corporation are set out in Articles 19 (for LLCs) and 73 (for Joint Stock Companies). Administrative regulations provide more details. A corporation must: (1) have its own name, organizational structure, and articles of association; (2) have a fixed place of business and the necessary facilities; (3) have funds and personnel of an amount and number which conform with State regulations and which are in proportion with the scale of its production and services; (4) have the ability to bear civil liability independently; and (5) have a scope of business that conforms with the provisions of State laws, statutory regulations, and policies. Administrative Regulations of the People's Republic of China Governing the Registration of Legal Corporations, Art. 7, promulgated June 3, 1988 by the State Council. The Administrative Regulations of the People's Republic of China Concerning the Registration of Corporations (promulgated July 1, 1994 by the State Council) also state detailed items of registration concerning the establishment of a corporation.

97. Corporation Law, Arts. 94–95.

98. *Id.* Art. 11. Companies might circumvent this regulation of operations by investing in another company.The statute limits that possibility by prohibiting any company from investing more than fifty percent of its assets in another company. *Id.* Art. 12.

99. *Id.* Arts. 84–85.

100. *Id.* Art. 86–91.

102. In the early years of the United States, and in England during that period, corporate status and limited liability were regarded as extraordinary privileges, or "concessions" of governmental power. The sovereign (the Crown, Congress, or state legislature) granted corporate charters only in specific instances, and only for companies with an evident connection to public welfare, such as railroads, banks, and traders with foreign lands. Norman Lattin, The Law of Corporations §54, at

Chinese legislators consciously considered whether to require prior approval to incorporate, and deemed such approval necessary. They concluded that this prior screening would ensure the healthy development of corporations and would "protect against corporations being established wantonly."[103] In addition, registration protects the public fisc because the enterprise must arrange to pay taxes on business income[104] and obtain all licenses necessary to conduct its particular line of business before being incorporated.

Most importantly, the prior registration requirement is designed to minimize fraud and abuses. In particular, registration may forestall the organization of "briefcase" companies—private corporations that have no greater substance than the contents of a briefcase and that enter into business deals and then disappear after receiving the first payments. Registration is also intended to prevent foreigners from persuading Chinese investors to contribute equipment and other resources to enterprises in which foreigners contribute only a small down payment and empty promises to contribute more later. The funds that these fly-by-night operators appear to have may be borrowed or subsequently diverted to other purposes. Similarly, promoters may promise to contribute capital in stages: a portion at the outset and the rest in the future. The future amounts may never materialize, or if they do, they may be the original contributions that the promoter has surreptitiously withdrawn. Creditors then suffer the consequences when the company cannot pay its obligations.[105]

In a mature private economy, experienced businesses and individuals contemplating substantial transactions are accustomed to protecting themselves. They investigate the credit and reputation of the other party and often demand collateral, letters of credit, or other forms of protection. The principle of caveat emptor is familiar. Parties are suitably cautious.

China presents different circumstances. The vast majority of enterprises in China continue to be government-owned, accustomed to dealing only with other government-owned entities. These enterprises are oriented toward meeting production goals and administrative requirements, not generating profit. Sharp or dishonest entrepreneurs may

---

174–175 (2d ed. 1971). Corporate powers and purposes were defined narrowly, which generated litigation over "ultra vires" actions—conduct by a corporation outside the lines of business permitted to it. Subsequently, Jacksonian populists viewed the requirement of special legislation for each grant of corporate status as unfairly benefitting the rich and powerful. The solution was "general incorporation" legislation, under which corporate status became inexpensive and freely available to anyone fulfilling fairly minimal filing requirements. *Id.* at 181. In the United States, general incorporation acts appeared first in New York in 1811 and became standard between 1875 and 1925. *Id.* at 175–76. These modern statutes authorize corporations to engage in "any lawful purpose"—which means virtually any conduct permitted to a natural person. *Id.* at 177.

103. Quanguo Renda Falu Weiyuanhui Guanyu 'Zhonghua Renmin Gongheguo Gongsifa (Chaoan)' Shenyijieguo de Baogao [The Law Committee of the National People's Congress, Report Concerning the Examination of Chinese Corporation Law (draft)] (Dec. 17, 1993).

104. Business income taxes are new to China, and the system of assessment and collection remains uncertain. In the case of Sino-foreign mining joint ventures, for example, a government official said that the 33% profit tax and 17% value-added tax applicable to other businesses would apply. However, those ventures would also be subject to a "resources-compensation tax" at a rate that has not yet been decided. Julia Leung, *As China Opens Up Mining, Foreigners are Confused about Ownership, Taxes*, Wall St. J., Mar. 21, 1994, at A7.

105. Zhongguo "Gongsifa" Jijiang Shishi [The Chinese "Corporate Law" Will Be Put into Effect], Asia Today, July 14–20, 1994, at 7....

easily mislead or cheat them. Registration serves to deter or minimize such abuse by assuring, for example, that a corporation meets minimum capitalization requirements.

Despite the burden of registration prior to incorporation, the Corporation Law relaxes regulation to some extent. Establishment of a new enterprise previously required approval to engage in the intended activity from the administrative agency in charge of the particular industry. The administrative agencies followed rigid, highly centralized planning processes. A new enterprise could seek registration as a legal entity only after receiving this preliminary approval. The new legislation, consistent with the policy to establish a socialist market economy, removes this first prerequisite in almost all cases.[106]

B. Liability for Pre-Incorporation and Defective Incorporation Transactions in the United States

Liability for pre-incorporation transactions, as well as for transactions undertaken on behalf of what turns out to be a defectively incorporated entity, remains largely a creature of the common law of the state of incorporation. However, the authors of the Revised Model Business Corporation Act [RMBCA] have adopted a "statutory" approach in the hopes of bringing some form of "harmonization" and regularity to the common law formulas as applied in the various states. Consider, as you review the materials which follow, whether such statutory harmonization is needed, and which approach, that of the common law or that proposed in the RMBCA, makes more sense.

1. *Liability for Pre-Incorporation Transactions in the United States*

Since the late nineteenth century, U.S. courts have developed a fairly coherent set of common law rules respecting the imposition of liability to incorporators or others who enter into transaction for or on behalf of a corporation not then legally existing.

---

106. The Corporation Law preserves the possibility of requiring approval, if laws and regulations outside the Corporate Law so provide. Corporation Law, Art. 8. This provision could apply, for example, to aircraft production. The provision follows the pattern of prior Chinese regulation of companies, which prohibited private enterprises from engaging in military or financial industries or dealing in cultural objects, antiques, jewelry, stamps, firearms, ammunition, cars, and explosives. Conner, *supra* note 4, at 24. Some literature uses the term "socialist market economic macro-control system" to describe the policy of regulating only at the macroeconomic level, not at the level of the individual enterprise. *See, e.g.*, Geng Yuxin, Greeting the Year for Enterprise Reform, Beijing Rev., Jan. 2–8, 1995, at 4.

Goodman v. Darden, Doman & Stafford Associates

Supreme Court of Washington,
En Banc.
100 Wash.2d 476, 670 P.2d 648
Oct. 20, 1983.

DIMMICK, Justice.

John Goodman signed a contract as president of a corporation "in formation." The narrow issue in the instant appeal is whether Goodman, as an individual, is a party to arbitration proceedings brought under the contract. The trial court held he was not. The Court of Appeals reversed, holding the evidence was insufficient to support the trial court's conclusion. We affirm the Court of Appeals.

Goodman, a real estate salesman, sold an apartment building to Darden, Doman & Stafford Associates (hereafter DDS), a general partnership. The apartments needed extensive renovation and Goodman represented that he personally had experience in renovation work. During the course of negotiations on a renovation contract, Goodman informed Don Doman, managing partner of DDS, that he would be forming a corporation in order to limit his personal liability.

A contract was executed in August 1979 between DDS and "BUILDING DESIGN AND DEVELOPMENT INC. (In Formation) John A. Goodman, President." The partners of DDS knew that the corporation was not yet in existence and they testified at trial that they never agreed to look solely to the corporation for performance of the contract. The contract required that work be completed by October 15 and contained an arbitration clause. Goodman immediately subcontracted the work. The work was not completed by October 15 and the work which was done was allegedly of poor quality. On November 1, after this apparent default, Goodman filed articles of incorporation. A corporate license was issued the next day.[1] The first meeting of the board of directors was not held until February 1980.

Between August and December 1979 DDS made five progress payments on the contract. The first check was made out to "Building Design and Development [Sic] Inc.—John Goodman." Goodman struck out his name and endorsed the check "Bldg. Design & Dev. Inc., John A. Goodman, Pres." He instructed DDS to make further payments to the corporation only.

In May 1980, after attempts to remedy the alleged breaches, DDS served Goodman with a demand for arbitration. The demand named both the corporation and Goodman. The record is not clear as to the present status of the corporation although it shows some effort on Goodman's part to sell the corporation. Goodman moved for a stay of arbitration and an order dismissing him from the arbitration proceedings. The trial court entered an order dismissing Goodman, as an individual, from the arbitration. The Court of Appeals reversed. Goodman v. Darden, Doman & Stafford Assocs., 33 Wash.App. 278, 653 P.2d 1371 (1982).

The issue in this appeal is whether Goodman, as a promoter,[2] is a party to the preincorporation contract and as such whether he is required to take part in the arbitration.

---

1. 1. The corporation's name when formed was "Building Renovation and Design Consultants, Inc."

2. A promoter is one who alone or with others forms a corporation and procures for it the rights, instrumentalities and capital to enable it to conduct its business. 1 W. Fletcher, Private Corporations § 189 (1974).

As a general rule where a corporation is contemplated but has not yet been organized at the time when a promoter makes a contract for the benefit of the contemplated corporation, the promoter is personally liable on it, even though the contract will also benefit the future corporation. *Harding v. Will*, 81 Wash.2d 132, 139, 500 P.2d 91 (1972); *Heintze Corp., Inc. v. Northwest Tech-Manuals, Inc.*, 7 Wash.App. 759, 760, 502 P.2d 486 (1972);[3] *Refrigeration Eng'g Co. v. McKay*, 4 Wash.App. 963, 972, 486 P.2d 304 (1971); 18 Am.Jur.2d Corporations § 127 (1965); Annot., *Personal Liability of Promoter to Third Person on or With Respect to Contract Made for Corporation or in Aid of Promotion*, 41 A.L.R.2d 477 (1955). There is a "strong inference that a person intends to make a present contract with an existing person." *White & Bollard, Inc. v. Goodenow*, 58 Wash.2d 180, 184, 361 P.2d 571 (1961).

An exception to the general rule is that if the contracting party knew that the corporation was not in existence at the time of contracting but nevertheless agreed to look solely to the corporation for performance, the promoter is not a party to the contract....

As the proponent of the alleged agreement to look solely to the corporation, Goodman has the burden of proving the agreement. *Johnson v. Nasi*, 50 Wash.2d 87, 309 P.2d 380 (1957). As with any agreement, release of the promoter depends on the intent of the parties. The parties did not manifest their intentions in the contract. Goodman argues that the language indicating that the corporation was "in formation" was an expression by the parties of their intent to make the corporation alone a party to the contract. Some courts do look to such language in the contract and contemporaneous documents to determine intent to release the promoter.... Those cases and others cited by Goodman do not analyze the agreements in light of a "strong inference" that one intends to contract with an existing party—an inference we must keep in mind. The mere signing of a contract with a corporation "in formation" does not suffice to show an agreement to look solely to the corporation. It simply begs the question to say that such language in a contract with a promoter in and of itself constitutes an agreement to release the promoter from the contract. Rather, the language raises the question of the parties' intent. Given the "strong inference" that DDS intended to contract with an existing party, the "in formation" language drafted by Goodman is at best ambiguous as to the parties' intentions.

Courts of other jurisdictions differ in their approach as to how specific the agreement must be to release a promoter from a contract and what evidence they will consider in determining the parties' intent. See generally Annot., 41 A.L.R.2d 447. As noted by the Court of Appeals: Some jurisdictions require that the contract show clearly on its face that there is no intent to hold the promoter liable before he is released. *Vodopich v. Collier Cy. Developers, Inc.*, 319 So.2d 43, 45 (Fla.App.1975). The agreement must be "specific" or "express." *Malisewski v. Singer*, 123 Ariz. 195, 598 P.2d 1014 (Ct.App.1979); *Spence v. Huffman*, 15 Ariz.App. 99, 486 P.2d 211 (1971). In *RKO-Stanley Warner Theatres, Inc. v.*

---

3. The *Heintze* court held that RCW 23A.44.100 codified this rule. That statute states: "All persons who assume to act as a corporation without authority so to do shall be jointly and severally liable for all debts and liabilities incurred or arising as a result thereof." The Supreme Court of Oregon has criticized this reasoning, stating that RCW 23A.44.100 was only intended to abolish the doctrine of de facto corporations and not to alter the liability of promoters. *Sherwood & Roberts-Oregon, Inc. v. Alexander*, 269 Or. 389, 525 P.2d 135 (1974). *Roberts* nonetheless held that the common law rule is the same as that applied in *Heintze*. Because the common law in this state is well settled as to promoter liability and the parties rely on that common law, we expressly decline at this time to decide whether the purpose of RCW 23A.44.100 is to codify these common law principles on promoter liability or to abolish de facto corporations.

Graziano, 467 Pa. 220, 223, 355 A.2d 830, 832 (1976), the contract stated: "It is understood by the parties hereto that it is the intention of the Purchaser to incorporate. Upon condition that such incorporation be completed by closing, all agreements, covenants, and warranties contained herein shall be construed to have been made between Seller and the resultant corporation and all documents shall reflect same." The court held that "while [this paragraph] does make provision for recognition of the resultant corporation as to the closing documents, it makes no mention of any release of personal liability." 467 Pa. at 226. Since the paragraph did not expressly provide for release on closing, the court found it ambiguous and construed it to hold the promoter liable until the corporation actually ratified the contract. 33 Wash.App., at 281–82, 653 P.2d 1371.

We do not believe the agreement to release a promoter from liability must say in so many words, "I agree to release." Where the promoter cannot show an express agreement, existence of the agreement to release him from liability may be shown by circumstances. Of course, where circumstantial evidence is relied on, the circumstances must be such as to make it reasonably certain that the parties intended to and did enter into the agreement. *Kellogg v. Gleeson*, 27 Wash.2d 501, 178 P.2d 969 (1947).

Goodman cites *Quaker Hill, Inc. v. Parr*, 148 Colo. 45, 364 P.2d 1056 (1961) and *Sherwood & Roberts-Oregon, Inc. v. Alexander, supra*, as cases similar to this one. The courts in those cases found that the promoter had been released from liability. Among the circumstances considered by those courts was the fact that the parties seeking personal liability on the part of the promoter actually urged that the contract be made in the name of the proposed corporation. DDS did not so urge Goodman or even suggest incorporation to him.

The trial court did not make a written finding that the parties intended to look solely to the corporation for performance. Thus we may look to the oral decision to clarify the theory on which the trial court decided the case. *Heikkinen v. Hansen*, 57 Wash.2d 840, 360 P.2d 147 (1961). From its oral opinion it is clear that the trial court relied on three considerations in holding that the parties agreed to release Goodman from the contract: (1) DDS knew of the corporation's nonexistence; (2) Goodman told Doman that he was forming a corporation to limit his personal liability; and (3) the progress payments were made to the corporation.

The fact that DDS knew of the corporation's nonexistence is not dispositive in any way of its intent. The rule is that the contracting party may know of the nonexistence of the corporation but nevertheless may agree to look solely to the corporation. The fact that a contracting party knows that the corporation is nonexistent does not indicate any agreement to release the promoter. To the contrary, such knowledge alone would seem to indicate that the members of DDS intended to make Goodman a party to the contract. They could not hold the corporation, a nonexistent entity, responsible and of course they would expect to have recourse against someone (Goodman) if default occurred. This consideration also relates to another factor the trial court apparently had in mind—that the members of DDS were all educated people. Goodman argues that as such they should have expressly requested that he be personally liable. This was unnecessary because under the law as set out above, Goodman was liable until the partners of DDS agreed otherwise. Thus, they were not required to specify personal liability.

The fact that Goodman expressed a desire to form the corporation to limit his liability also is not dispositive of the intentions of the members of DDS. No one from DDS objected to his incorporating but this failure to object does not indicate an affirmative assent to limit Goodman's personal liability. Apparently Goodman believed that incorporation would automatically limit his liability thus misunderstanding the rules regarding promoter liability. The Court of Appeals correctly held in this regard: Even if the expression of desire constituted an offer to make release a term of the contract, silence is acceptance only when there is a duty to speak. *American Aviation, Inc. v. Hinds*, 1 Wash.App. 959, 465 P.2d 676 (1970). DDS had no duty to correct, or even perceive, Goodman's mistaken interpretation of the promoter liability rules. 33 Wash.App. at 282, 653 P.2d 1371.

The only other evidence of the parties' intent to make the corporation the sole party to the contract is that the progress payments were made payable to the corporation. However, they were so written only at the instruction of Goodman and in fact the first check written by DDS after the signing of the contract was written to the corporation and Goodman as an individual. This evidence does not show by reasonable certainty that DDS intended to contract only with the corporation....

Goodman argues that we should not examine the evidence in this manner because in doing so we improperly reweigh it. We acknowledge appellate review is limited to determining whether a trial court's findings are supported by substantial evidence and, if so, whether the findings in turn support the conclusions of law. *Holland v. Boeing Co.*, 90 Wash.2d 384, 390, 583 P.2d 621 (1978). From the oral decision it is clear that the court made a finding that DDS intended to look solely to the corporation as a party to the contract based on the items of evidence discussed above. We can uphold this finding of intent only if the evidence supporting it is substantial; we find that it is not.

The trial court erred in dismissing Goodman from the arbitration proceedings. We therefore remand.

WILLIAM H. WILLIAMS, C.J., ROSELLINI, BRACHTENBACH and PEARSON, JJ., and HAMILTON, J. Pro Tem., concur.

DORE, Justice (dissenting).

The trial court found that Darden, Doman and Stafford Associates (DDS) intended to look solely to the corporation as the party of the contract. There is substantial evidence in the record to substantiate this finding. I would affirm the trial court and dismiss Goodman from the arbitration proceedings.

As the majority states at page 3, as a general rule where a corporation is contemplated but has not yet been organized at the time when a promoter makes a contract for the benefit of the contemplated corporation, the promoter is personally liable on it, even though the contract will also benefit the future corporation....

Promoters are not personally liable, however, on contracts made in the name of a corporation not in existence at the time of contracting, where the intention to make the contract in the future corporation's name is known to the other contracting party. *Heintze Corp., Inc. v. Northwest Tech-Manuals, Inc.*, 7 Wash.App. 759, 760, 502 P.2d 486 (1972).

The issue on appeal is thus whether there is substantial evidence in the record that DDS accepted the obligation of a yet-to-be-formed corporation and did not hold John Goodman as an individual responsible. I believe there is.

The record indicates that Goodman was a licensed real estate salesman for West & Wheeler Associates, Inc. from 1973–1978, and the department manager of its property management division. In May 1979, he sold an apartment house, Suncrest Apartments, to his friend Dick Gimperle, an architect. As sales agent, he received a small amount of cash, the remainder of his commission to be paid by a $4,000 promissory note. Gimperle assigned his interests in the property to DDS. The partnership was a highly educated and qualified group which included an architect, a PhD, and a lawyer. The managing partner was an architect who had extensive experience in constructing condominiums, office buildings and single-family homes. The Suncrest Apartments needed considerable renovation and had about 10-12 vacancies at the time of the sale. Gimperle introduced Goodman to DDS' managing partner, Doman, as a possible contractor to do the renovation work. Originally, Goodman wanted only to be a consultant and not the actual contractor, but Gimperle and Doman persuaded him to do the contracting work. Toward the end of the negotiations, Goodman told Doman that he would be forming a corporation to insulate against liability. The record indicates Doman had no objection to Goodman forming a corporation to insulate against liability.

Doman insisted the parties sign an American Institute of Architects' Standard Form of Agreement Between Owner and Contractor. Doman prepared the contract, including the schedule of the repairs, indexed exterior renovation, interior renovation and specifications for the floor plans, etc. Goodman was the first to sign on August 9. On August 18, the other parties signed the contract and it became operative. The first page of the contract contains a typewritten provision stating, "This is a two party agreement. Where ever [sic] third party responsibilities are assigned in this agreement to a third party (Architect) as agent of the Owner, those third party responsibilities are to be assumed by the Owner unless the context clearly indicates to the contrary....

I

Immediately after signing the contract, Goodman went to his attorney and directed him to prepare articles of incorporation to insulate against his personal liability. His attorney prepared incorporation documents, which were signed on October 2, 1979. The name they had selected for incorporation was not available, however, and they had to select a new name, "Building Renovation and Design Consultants, Inc." This caused further delay and incorporation was not completed until November 1, 1979. Doman scheduled the project completion date of October 15. The work went slowly, however, and the work was not completed at that time.

Doman made all checks out to the corporate name, Building Design and Development, Inc., at Goodman's request. The original check had been made out to both the corporation and Goodman individually, but Goodman had his name deleted and a new check issued in the name of the corporation only. Doman had no objection to this and impliedly acknowledged that he would look to the corporation and not to Goodman as an individual. All of such checks were deposited in the corporation's bank account at Rainier National Bank, Westlake branch. Neither Goodman nor the corporation profited from the Suncrest Apartments contract, and there was no commingling of the personal assets and liabilities of Goodman with the corporation.

On November 1, 1979, a certificate of incorporation was issued to Goodman. The court found that at that time the corporate entity was fully capitalized and operating. DDS was aware of the incorporation and continued to make the checks payable to the corporation. Subsequently, Goodman had the corporation ratify the contract as an action of the corporation.

II

It is clear from the actions of DDS, and its failure to insist upon a personal guaranty from Goodman, that DDS impliedly agreed to look solely to the corporation for performance.

I cannot agree with the majority's conclusion that Goodman's expressed desire to form a corporation to limit his liability does not reflect on the intentions of the members of DDS. If they did not agree with Goodman to look solely to the corporation as the legally responsible entity, the DDS members should have made this clear at the time Goodman brought it up, before the contract was signed. I also cannot agree with the majority that the progress payments made payable to the corporation do not show with reasonable certainty and probability that DDS intended to contract only with the corporation.

Conclusion

The trial court found, in written findings, that DDS knew that the corporation which was a party to the renovation contract was not yet in existence at the time the contract was signed; that the members of DDS, by their actions, impliedly agreed to look solely to the corporation for performance under the contract. The trial court further found that at no time did any member of DDS request of Goodman that he be personally liable on the contract; that all monies received by the corporation went into the corporate bank account and were used to pay corporate obligations; neither Goodman nor the corporation profited from the contract, and there was no commingling of the personal assets and liabilities of Goodman and the corporation; and that Goodman exercised good faith in moving to have the corporation formed.

There was substantial evidence to support such findings and we must recognize their verity....

I would affirm the order of the trial court staying arbitration proceedings as to John Goodman individually.

DOLLIVER and UTTER, JJ., concur.

Nathan Jacobson, Appellant, v. Martin Stern, Jr., Respondent

Supreme Court of Nevada.
96 Nev. 56, 605 P.2d 198
Jan. 16, 1980.

PER CURIAM OPINION

This action was brought by Martin Stern for architectural services rendered to Nathan Jacobson in Jacobson's development of a hotel and casino, known as the Kings Castle, on the north shore of Lake Tahoe, Nevada. Jacobson prevailed on a summary judgment motion, and we subsequently reversed and remanded the case for trial. Stern v. Jacobson, 90 Nev. 113, 520 P.2d 614 (1974).

These parties were involved in two projects during the time involved in this action: the Bonanza in Las Vegas and the Kings Castle in Incline Village. The case at bar concerns only the Kings Castle project.[1]

In January, 1969, Jacobson contacted Stern and asked him to draw plans for Jacobson's new hotel/casino at Lake Tahoe. Stern immediately began preliminary work on the

---

1. *See also* Bonanza Hotel v. Bonanza No. 2, 95 Nev. 463, 596 P.2d 227 (1979).

project and contacted soil engineers and surveyors in this regard. At this time Stern dealt directly with Jacobson, who referred to the project as "my hotel," and with Taylor of Nevada which was to be the general contractor.

On February 18, 1969, Stern wrote to Jacobson detailing, among other things, the architect's services and the fee. Stern's plans were subsequently discussed by the two men and Stern's fee was agreed to be $250,000. Stern was told by Jacobson to proceed, and he completed the preliminary plans by March, 1969. The highrise foundation plans were finished on May 1, 1969 and the scope of the work plans were initiated on May 6, 1969. Stern testified at trial that by May 6, 1969, at least 60% of the architectural services were complete, and the architectural plans and drawings were completed by July 31, 1969. At trial, Jacobson disagreed with these figures, since the theatre and dining room had to be redrawn, but he did not give his own estimate. A letter from Jacobson to Stern, written March 10, 1970, acknowledges that the parties entered into a contract in April, 1969, but no written contract was ever admitted into evidence despite Jacobson's testimony that such a document was executed.

At the same time as the plans for the building were being developed by Stern, Jacobson was negotiating financing and setting up business structures to own and manage the property. On May 1, 1969, Jacobson acquired all of the stock of A.L.W., Inc., a corporation which had previously operated a casino on this site, and which was to operate the Kings Castle. Levin-Townsend Computer Corporation subsequently purchased 20% of the A.L.W., Inc. stock for $300,000. On May 9, 1969, a business structure for ownership of Kings Castle was set up and a number of documents were executed. The business structure included the formation of Lake Enterprises, a corporation of which Jacobson was the sole stockholder and president. Kings Castle, Limited Partnership was formed with Lake Enterprises, Inc. as the general partner and Jacobson and others as limited partners. Jacobson was the most substantial investor in Kings Castle, Limited Partnership, with investments in excess of $3 million.

After May 9, 1969, A.L.W., Inc. operated the hotel and casino and Kings Castle, Limited Partnership, leased the land. All monies were subsequently paid and received through these two entities. Stern billed Jacobson beginning in June of 1969. Some of the billings were disputed, but Stern was in fact paid $30,000 on June 13, 1969; $30,000 on August 11, 1969; $58,000 on September 12, 1969, and $32,000 on October 17, 1969. All of the checks were drawn on the account of A.L.W., Inc.; only one of the checks was signed by Jacobson.

The Kings Castle opened in July 1970. On February 3, 1972, A.L.W., Inc., as owner of Kings Castle and Casino, filed its petition for arrangements under Chapter XI of the Bankruptcy Act. Stern did not file a claim in that proceeding.

This case was set for trial November 17, 1975. On the first day of trial Jacobson's attorney was unable to be in court and co-counsel requested a continuance. The judge granted the continuance but, as a condition, allowed a fee of $2,000 to be given to Stern for his costs of delay. Later, after a three week trial, judgment was rendered for Stern in the amount of $132,590.37, plus interest.

In this appeal Jacobson contends: (1) that there was insufficient evidence presented at trial to support the judgment of his personal liability; (2) that the obligations of Jacobson were adopted by A.L.W., Inc., and that such adoption constituted a novation; and, (3) that it was improper for the court to assess costs against Jacobson for a continuance of the trial.

1. Appellant contends there is no evidence to support the district court's findings that Stern was not dealing with any of the existing corporate entitles; Levin-Townsend Computer Corporation; Bonanza No. 2; J.J. Enterprises;[2] Jacobson as agent for any of these; or with Jacobson as agent for Kings Castle or any other principal.

The evidence shows that Jacobson was, in the early months of 1969, President of J.J. Enterprises, which wholly owned Bonanza No. 2, and Chairman of the Board of Caesar's Palace. There is no evidence, however, that at that time Jacobson was acting on behalf of any of these entities in contracting for the building of Kings Castle Casino, and this is born out by the fact that none of these entities subsequently became involved with the Kings Castle Casino. Although Stern may have known of Jacobson's affiliations, and known that many of the same people who owned and managed the Bonanza were involved in the Kings Castle project, there is little evidence, if any, that he contracted with Jacobson in any capacity connected with those existing corporations. There is no evidence the Levin-Townsend Computer Corporation had anything more than a 20% Ownership interest in A.L.W., Inc. The record is also devoid of evidence that they were involved with Stern directly, or that Jacobson ever represented them in negotiations with Stern.

Kings Castle, Limited Partnership, and Lake Enterprises, Inc., did not exist until May 9, 1969. A.L.W., Inc. existed from 1965, but Jacobson had no connection with it at all until he purchased the stock on May 1, 1969. The contract for architectural services, which was certainly for the benefit of A.L.W., Inc. and Kings Castle, Limited Partnership, was made before May 1, 1969. Stern maintains that he had a contract with Jacobson from February 18, 1969, and Jacobson admits a contract as of April 1969, but in any event the contract was in existence before Kings Castle, Limited Partnership, and Lake Enterprises, Inc., and before Jacobson's involvement with A.L.W., Inc. Thus, none of these corporations could contract, or have Jacobson contract for them because they were not yet organized. Peters Grazing Association v. Legerski, 544 P.2d 449 (Wyo.1975).

Appellant, citing Gillig & Co. v. Lake Bigler Road Co., 2 Nev. 214 (1866), further argues that a course of conduct between the parties created a presumption that Jacobson was acting as agent of J.J. Enterprises, as owner of the Bonanza. The record supports the determination that there was no course of dealing or custom and practice between these parties which would tend to establish Jacobson's agency for J.J. Enterprises in his relationship with Stern in the Kings Castle.

In the absence of any evidence to the contrary, and in the presence of testimony by Stern that he thought he was dealing with Jacobson as an individual, the district court concluded that the contract was made between Jacobson, as promoter of the Kings Castle project, and Stern. A contract with the promoter is not one with the corporation absent some subsequent corporate act or agreement. Paxton v. Bacon Mill & Mining Co., 2 Nev. 257 (1866); Peters Grazing Association v. Legerski, supra. Thus, the district court properly found Jacobson, as promoter, liable on the contract.

2. Under Nevada law, if a pre-incorporation contract made by a promoter is within the corporate powers, the corporation may, when organized, expressly or impliedly ratify the contract and, thus, make it a valid obligation of the corporation. Chartrand v. Barney's Club, Inc., 380 F.2d 97 (9th Cir. 1967). If the corporation accepts the benefits of the contract, it will be required to perform the contractual obligations. Id. The

2. These corporations were involved in the Bonanza project in Las Vegas.

evidence supports a finding that the A.L.W. corporation accepted the benefits of the contract for architectural services, and in fact adopted the contractual obligations and made partial payments on the obligation. However, liability of the corporation by adoption does not, absent a novation, end the liability of the promoter to the third party. Allen Steel Supply Co. v. Bradley, 89 Idaho 29, 402 P.2d 394 (1965).

Appellant argues that there was, in fact, a novation by A.L.W., Inc. in its adoption of all agreements as its corporate liabilities. Where there is a valid express or implied novation, the corporation is substituted for the promoter as a party to the contract in all respects, and the promoter is divested of his rights and released of his liabilities.... In order to constitute a valid novation, however, the creditor must assent to the substitution of a new obligor, but this assent may be inferred from his acceptance of part performance by the new obligor, if the performance is made with the understanding that a complete novation is proposed. Nev. Bank Comm. v. Esquire R. E., Inc., 86 Nev. 238, 468 P.2d 22 (1970).

Appellant contends that, because the evidence shows that after May 1, 1969, Stern probably knew, or should have known, that he was performing for the benefit of A.L.W., Inc., and was paid by A.L.W., Inc., he impliedly consented to a novation. There is no evidence, however, showing that Stern agreed to the substitution of A.L.W., Inc. for Jacobson in the contract, or that he performed with the knowledge or understanding that a novation was proposed. See Nev. Bank Comm. v. Esquire R. E., Inc. supra. In fact he maintained throughout that he had contracted with Jacobson and felt that Jacobson was personally liable on the contract. The intent of the parties to cause a novation must be clear.... The trial court found there was no novation and that Stern never agreed to release Jacobson from his obligations. We agree with this finding.

* * *

Accordingly, the judgment of the district court is affirmed.

---

2. *The Common Law Effects of Defective Incorporation in the United States*

Over the course of the last century, U.S. courts were confronted with the issue of the consequences of defective incorporation. This situation could arise in a variety of contexts. A common and fairly innocuous example would involve the failure to properly execute the articles of incorporation or to fail to send the amount required for the filing fee. In either case, the submission of the articles of incorporation would be rejected by the state official, and the corporation would not be given legal effect. What consequences ought to arise if, in reliance on the proper incorporation of the enterprise, the "board of directors" or "shareholders" of the defective corporation enter in transactions with third parties in the name of the corporation? Should these transactions be treated in the same way as pre-incorporation transactions for purposes of imposing liability? Ought other rules apply? To resolve these issues, the courts at common law developed a fairly complex set of doctrines, the effect of some of which were to limit the ability of creditors to reach the "shareholders" of defectively incorporated corporations under certain circumstances. These doctrines include the concepts of *de facto corporation*, and *corporation by estoppel*. The Revised Model Business Corporation Act has tended to group such transactions together with other pre-incorporation transactions. As you go through the materials which follow, determine which approach is more appealing, and why.

Albion C. Cranson, Jr. v. International Business Machines

Court of Appeals of Maryland.
234 Md. 477, 200 A.2d 33
April 30, 1964

HORNEY, Judge.

On the theory that the Real Estate Service Bureau was neither a de jure nor a de facto corporation and that Albion C. Cranson, Jr., was a partner in the business conducted by the Bureau and as such was personally liable for its debts, the International Business Machines Corporation brought this action against Cranson for the balance due on electric typewriters purchased by the Bureau. At the same time it moved for summary judgment and supported the motion by affidavit. In due course, Cranson filed a general issue plea and an affidavit in opposition to summary judgment in which he asserted in effect that the Bureau was a de facto corporation and that he was not personally liable for its debts.

The agreed statement of facts shows that in April 1961, Cranson was asked to invest in a new business corporation which was about to be created. Towards this purpose he met with other interested individuals and an attorney and agreed to purchase stock and become an officer and director. Thereafter, upon being advised by the attorney that the corporation had been formed under the laws of Maryland, he paid for and received a stock certificate evidencing ownership of shares in the corporation, and was shown the corporate seal and minute book. The business of the new venture was conducted as if it were a corporation, through corporate bank accounts, with auditors maintaining corporate books and records, and under a lease entered into by the corporation for the office from which it operated its business. Cranson was elected president and all transactions conducted by him for the corporation, including the dealings with I.B.M., were made as an officer of the corporation. At no time did he assume any personal obligation or pledge his individual credit to I.B.M. Due to an oversight on the part of the attorney, of which Cranson was not aware, the certificate of incorporation, which had been signed and acknowledged prior to May 1, 1961, was not filed until November 24, 1961. Between May 17 and November 8, the Bureau purchased eight typewriters from I.B.M., on account of which partial payments were made, leaving a balance due of $4,333.40, for which this suit was brought.

Although a question is raised as to the propriety of making use of a motion for summary judgment as the means of determining the issues presented by the pleadings, we think the motion was appropriate. Since there was no genuine dispute as to the material facts, the only question was whether I.B.M. was entitled to judgment as a matter of law. The trial court found that it was, but we disagree.

The fundamental question presented by the appeal is whether an officer[1] of a defectively incorporated association may be subjected to personal liability under the circumstances of this case. We think not.

---

1. Although we are concerned with the liability of an 'officer' in this case, the principles of law stated herein might under other circumstances be applicable to a determination of the liability of a member or shareholder of a defectively organized corporation.

Traditionally, two doctrines have been used by the courts to clothe an officer of a defectively incorporated association with the corporate attribute of limited liability. The first, often referred to as the doctrine of de facto corporations, has been applied in those cases where there are elements showing: (1) the existence of law authorizing incorporation; (2) an effort in good faith to incorporate under the existing law; and (3) actual user or exercise of corporate powers. Ballantine, Private Corporations, § 23; 8 Fletcher, Cyclopedia of the Law of Private Corporations, § 3777; 13 Am.Jur., Corporations, §§ 49–56; 18 C.J.S. Corporations § 99. The second, the doctrine of estoppel to deny the corporate existence, is generally employed where the person seeking to hold the officer personally liable has contracted or otherwise dealt with the association in such a manner as to recognize and in effect admit its existence as a corporate body. Ballantine, op. cit., § 29; Machen, Modern Law of Corporations, §§ 278–282; 18 C.J.S. op. cit. § 109.

* * *

In the Boyce case, an action in assumpsit against a defectively incorporated religious society, the Court... in holding that the society was not estopped to deny its corporate existence, said: 'We think it would be extending the doctrine of estoppel to an extent, not justified by the principles of public policy, to allow it to operate through the conduct of the parties concerned, to create substantially a de facto corporation, with just such powers as the parties may by their acts give to it.'

* * *

When summarized, the law in Maryland pertaining to the de facto and estoppel doctrines reveals that the cases seem to fall into one or the other of two categories. In one line of cases, the Court, choosing to disregard the nature of the dealings between the parties, refused to recognize both doctrines where there had been a failure to comply with a condition precedent to corporate existence, but, whenever such noncompliance concerned a condition subsequent to incorporation, the Court often applied the estoppel doctrine. In the other line of cases, the Court, choosing to make no distinction between defects which were conditions precedent and those which were conditions subsequent, emphasized the course of conduct between the parties and applied the estoppel doctrine when there had been substantial dealings between them on a corporate basis.

Whether or not the decisions in the Boyce and Maryland Tube cases had the effect of repudiating the de facto doctrine in this state, as some of the text writers seem to think, is a question we do not reach in this case and therefore need not consider at this time. On the other hand, since it is clear that the Maryland Tube and National Shutter Bar cases are inconsistent with other Maryland cases insofar as they held (in relying on the statements in Jones v. Aspen Hardware Co., supra) that the doctrine of estoppel cannot be invoked unless a corporation has at least a de facto existence, both cases—Maryland Tube and National Shutter Bar—should be, and are hereby, overruled to the extent of the inconsistency. There is, as we see it, a wide difference between creating a corporation by means of the de facto doctrine and estopping a party, due to his conduct in a particular case, from setting up the claim of no incorporation. Although some cases tend to assimilate the doctrines of incorporation de facto and by estoppel, each is a distinct theory and they are not dependant on one another in their application. See 8 Fletcher, op. cit., § 3763; France on Corporations (2nd ed.), § 29; 18 C.J.S. op. cit. § 111h. Where there is a concurrence of the three elements necessary for the application of the de facto corporation doctrine, there exists an entity which is a corporation de jure against all persons but the state. On the other hand, the estoppel theory is applied only to the facts of each particular case and may be invoked even where there is no corporation de facto. Accordingly, even though one or more of the requisites of a de facto corporation are absent, we think that this factor does not preclude the application of the estoppel doctrine[5] in a proper case, such as the one at bar.

I.B.M. contends that the failure of the Bureau to file its certificate of incorporation debarred all corporate existence. But, in spite of the fact that the omission might have prevented the Bureau from being either a corporation de jure or de facto,[6] Jones v. Linden Building Ass'n, supra, we think that I.B.M. having dealt with the Bureau as if it were a corporation and relied on its credit rather than that of Cranson, is estopped to assert that the Bureau was not incorporated at the time the typewriters were purchased. Laflin & Rand Powder Co. v. Sinsheimer, supra. See also Tulane Improvement Co. v. S. A. Chapman & Co., 129 La. 562, 56 So. 509 (1911). In 1 Clark and Marshall, Private Corporations, § 89, it is stated:

> 'The doctrine in relation to estoppel is based upon the ground that it would generally be inequitable to permit the corporate existence of an association to be denied by persons who have represented it to be a corporation, or held it out as a corporation, or by any persons who have recognized it as a corporation by dealing with it as such; and by the overwhelming weight of authority, therefore, a person may be estopped to deny the legal incorporation of an association which is not even a corporation de facto.'

In cases similar to the one at bar, involving a failure to file articles of incorporation, the courts of other jurisdictions have held that where one has recognized the corporate existence of an association, he is estopped to assert the contrary with respect to a claim arising out of such dealings....

Since I.B.M. is estopped to deny the corporate existence of the Bureau, we hold that Cranson was not liable for the balance due on account of the typewriters.

---

5. A third doctrine, called the modern 'enterprise-entity theory,' which in many respects is not unlike the estoppel theory applied in Maryland, is described in 1 Oleck, Modern Corporation Law, § 592. For an excellent analysis of the law concerning defective incorporation in general, *see* Chapter 25 of Vol. 1, §§ 584–595. *See also* the last sentence in § 591 (p. 839) where the author says that 'in time the doctrine of 'de facto' corporation may become merely an historic example of legal conceptualism at its worst.'

6. Those states which recognize the de facto doctrine are not in accord as to whether a corporation de facto may be created in spite of the failure to file the necessary papers. Some courts, without making clear in every instance whether a de facto corporation was meant or not, have stated that failure to file the required papers prevented the organizations from becoming a corporation and have held in effect that the persons acting as a corporation are a mere association or partnership. *See*, among others, Slocum v. Head, 105 Wis. 431, 81 N.W. 673, 50 L.R.A. 324; Perrine v. Levin, 63 Misc. 327, 123 N.Y.S. 1007; H. J. Hughes Co. v. Farmers' Union Produce Co., 110 Neb. 736, 194 N.W. 872, 37 A.L.R. 1314; Elroad Slug Casting Mach. Co. v. O'Malley, 57 F.Supp. 915 (D.Neb.). Other courts, without expressly deciding whether a de facto corporation was created, hold that the statutes of the state imply corporate existence prior to the filing of articles of incorporation. *See*, for example, Merrick v. Reynolds Eng. & Gov. Co., 101 Mass. 381; Granby Min. & Smelt. Co. v. Richards, 95 Mo. 106, 8 S.W. 246. Still other courts hold that a de facto existence is not precluded by failure to file the articles of incorporation. *See* Mason v. Stevens, 16 S.D. 320, 92 N.W. 424; Frawley v. Tenafly Transportation Co., 95 N.J.L. 405, 113 A. 242, 22 A.L.R. 369; Tisch Auto Supply Co. v. Nelson, 222 Mich. 196, 192 N.W. 600; Berlin State Bank v. Nelson, 231 Mich. 463, 204 N.W. 92; A. W. Mendenhall Co. v. Booher, 226 Mo.App. 945, 48 S.W.2d 120; Culkin v. Hillside Restaurant, 126 N.J.Eq. 97, 8 A.2d 173. Numerous other cases on the problem are collected in 22 A.L.R. 376, 37 A.L.R. 1319. *See also* 1 Oleck, Modern Corporation Law, § 585, and the cases cited in the footnotes.

Judgment reversed; the appellee to pay the costs.

3. *Approach under the Revised Model Business Corporation Act*

The Revised Model Business Corporation Act has gained much acceptance among state legislatures since the 1970s. Among the many 'modernizing' changes attempted by the Revised Model Business Corporation Act is § 204. This provision seeks to streamline the various strains of the common law rules regarding the liability of promoters and others who purport to act for a corporation not yet formed. Consider whether the RMBCA approach is closer to the U.S. common law or to the approach of the European Community directives.

Revised Model Business Corp. Act §2.04 & Commentary

§2.04 Liability for Preincorporation Transactions

All persons purporting to act as or on behalf of a corporation knowing there was no incorporation under this Act, are jointly and severally liable for all liabilities created while so acting.

OFFICIAL COMMENT

Earlier versions of the Model Act, and the statutes of many states, have long provided that corporate existence begins only with the acceptance of articles of incorporation by the secretary of state. Many states also have statutes that provide expressly that those who prematurely act for or on behalf of a corporation are personally liable on all transactions entered into or liabilities incurred before incorporation. A review of recent case law indicates, however, that even in states with such statutes courts have continued to rely on common law concepts of de facto corporations, de jure corporations, and corporations by estoppel that provide uncertain protection against liability for preincorporation transactions. These cases caused a review of the underlying policies represented in earlier versions of the Model Act and the adoption of a slightly more flexible or relaxed standard.

Incorporation under modern statutes is so simple and inexpensive that a strong argument may be made that nothing short of filing articles of incorporation should create the privilege of limited liability. A number of situations have arisen, however, in which the protection of limited liability arguably should be recognized even though the simple incorporation process established by modern statutes has not been completed.

(1) The strongest factual pattern for immunizing participants from personal liability occurs in cases in which the participant honestly and reasonably but erroneously believed the articles had been filed. In Cranson v. International Business Machines Corp., 234 Md. 477, 200 A.2d 33 (1964), for example, the defendant had been shown executed articles of incorporation some months earlier before he invested in the corporation and became an officer and director. He was also told by the corporation's attorney that the articles had been filed, but in fact they had not been filed because of a

mix-up in the attorney's office. The defendant was held not liable on the "corporate" obligation.

(2) Another class of cases, which is less compelling but in which the participants sometimes have escaped personal liability, involves the defendant who mails in articles of incorporation and then enters into a transaction in the corporate name, the letter is either delayed or the secretary of state's office refuses to file the articles after receiving them or returns them for correction. E.g., Cantor v. Sunshine Greenery, Inc., 165 N.J.Super. 411, 398 A.2d 571 (1979). Many state filing agencies adopt the practice of treating the date of receipt as the date of issuance of the certificate even though delayed and the review process may result in the certificate being backdated. The finding of nonliability in cases of this second type can be considered an extension of this principle by treating the date of original mailing or original filing as the date of incorporation.

(3) A third class of cases in which the participants sometimes have escaped personal liability involves situations where the third person has urged immediate execution of the contract in the corporate name even though he knows that the other party has not taken any steps toward incorporating. E.g., Quaker Hill v. Parr, 148 Colo. 45, 364 P.2d 1056 (1961).

(4) In another class of cases the defendant has represented that a corporation exists and entered into a contract in the corporate name when he knows that no corporation has been formed, either because no attempt has been made to file articles of incorporation or because he has already received rejected articles of incorporation from the filing agency. In these cases, the third person has dealt solely with the "corporation" and has not relied on the personal assets of the defendant. The imposition of personal liability in this class of cases, it has sometimes been argued, gives the plaintiff more than he originally bargained for. On the other hand, to recognize limited liability in this situation threatens to undermine the incorporation process, since one then may obtain limited liability by consistently conducting business in the corporate name. Most courts have imposed personal liability in this situation. E.g., Robertson v. Levy, 197 A.2d 443 (D.C.App.1964).

(5) A final class of cases involves inactive investors who provide funds to a promoter with the instruction, "Don't start doing business until you incorporate." After the promoter does start business without incorporating, attempts have been made, sometimes unsuccessfully, to hold the investors liable as partners. E.g., Frontier Refining Co. v. Kunkels, Inc., 407 P.2d 880 (Wyo.1965). One case held that the language of section 146 of the 1969 Model Act ["*persons who assume to act* as a corporation are liable for preincorporation transactions"] creates a distinction between active and inactive participants, makes only the former liable as partners, and therefore relieves the latter of personal liability. Nevertheless, "active" participation was defined to include all investors who actively participate in the policy and operational decisions of the organization and is, therefore, a larger group than merely the persons who incurred the obligation in question on behalf of the "corporation." Timberline Equipment Co. v. Davenport, 267 Or. 64, 72–76, 514 P.2d 1009, 1113–14 (1973).

After a review of these situations, it seemed appropriate to impose liability only on persons who act as or on behalf of corporations "knowing" that no corporation exists. Analogous protection has long been accorded under the uniform limited partnership acts to limited partners who contribute capital to a partnership in the erroneous belief that a limited partnership certificate has been filed. Uniform Limited Partnership Act § 12 (1916); Revised Uniform Limited Partnership Act § 3.04 (1976). Persons protected under § 3.04 of the latter are persons who "erroneously but in good faith" believe that a limited partnership certificate has been filed. The language of section 2.04 has essentially the same meaning.

While no special provision is made in section 2.04, the section does not foreclose the possibility that persons who urge defendants to execute contracts in the corporate name knowing that no steps to incorporate have been taken may be estopped personal liability on individual defendants. This estoppel may be based on the inequity perceived when persons, unwilling or reluctant to enter into a commitment under their own name, are persuaded to use the name of a nonexistent corporation, and then are sought to be held personally liable under section 2.04 by the party advocating that form of execution. By contrast, persons who knowingly participate in a business under a corporate name are jointly and severally liable on "corporate" obligations under section 2.04 and may not argue that plaintiffs are "estopped" from holding them personally liable because all transactions were conducted on a corporate basis.

Timberline Equipment Company, Inc., Respondent, v. Kenneth L. Davenport, Jr., and John R. Gorman, Defendants, Forrest G. Bennett, Dba Aero-Fabb Co., Appellant

Supreme Court of Oregon. In Banc.
Decided Oct. 11, 1973.
267 Or. 64, 514 P.2d 1109

DENECKE, Justice.

Plaintiff brought this action for equipment rentals against the defendant Dr. Bennett and two others. In addition to making a general denial, Dr. Bennett alleged as a defense that the rentals were to a de facto corporation, Aero-Fabb Corp., of which Dr. Bennett was an incorporator, director and shareholder. He also alleged plaintiff was estopped from denying the corporate character of the organization to whom plaintiff rented the equipment. The trial court held for plaintiff. Dr. Bennett, only, appeals.

On January 22, 1970, Dr. Bennett signed articles of incorporation for Aero-Fabb Co. The original articles were not in accord with the statutes and, therefore, no certificate of incorporation was issued for the corporation until June 12, 1970, after new articles were filed. The leases were entered into and rentals earned during the period between January 22nd and June 12th.

Prior to 1953 Oregon had adopted the common-law doctrine that prohibited a collateral attack on the legality of a defectively organized corporation which had achieved the status of a de facto corporation. See, for example, Marsters v. Umpqua Oil Co., 49 Or. 374, 377, 90 P. 151, 12 LRA(ns) 825 (1907).

In 1953 the legislature adopted the Oregon Business Corporation Act. Oregon Laws 1953, ch. 549. The Model Business Corporation Act was used as a working model for the Oregon Act. 1952 Oregon State Bar Committee Reports, p. 5.

ORS 57.321 of the Oregon Business Corporation Act provides:

> 'Upon the issuance of the certificate of incorporation, the corporate existence shall begin, and such certificate of incorporation shall be conclusive evidence that all conditions precedent required to be performed by the incorporators have been com-

plied with and that the corporation has been incorporated under the Oregon Business Corporation Act, except as against this state in a proceeding to cancel or revoke the certificate of incorporation or for involuntary dissolution of the corporation.'

This section is virtually identical to § 56 of the Model Act. The Comment to the Model, prepared as a research project by the American Bar Foundation and edited by the American Bar Association Committee on Corporate Laws, states:

'Under the Model Act, de jure incorporation is complete upon the issuance of the certificate of incorporation, except as against the state in certain proceedings challenging the corporate existence. In this respect, the Model Act provisions are the same as those in many states, although in a number of them some further action is required before the corporation has legal existence, such as local filing or recording or publication.

'Under the unequivocal provisions of the Model Act, any steps short of securing a certificate of incorporation would not constitute apparent compliance. Therefore a de facto corporation cannot exist under the Model Act.

'Like provisions are made throughout the Model Act in respect of the conclusiveness of the issuance by the secretary of state of the appropriate certificate in connection with filings made in his office. * * *

'In some states, however, issuance of the certificate of incorporation and compliance with any additional requirements for filing, recording or publication is not conclusive evidence of incorporation. In those states, such action is stated to be only prima facie evidence of incorporation, and in others the effect is merely one of estoppel preventing any question of due incorporation being raised in legal actions by or against the corporation.' Model Business Corporation Act Annotated § 56, p. 205 (2d ed. 1971).

ORS 57.793 provides:

'All persons who assume to act as a corporation without the authority of a certificate of incorporation issued by the Corporation Commissioner, shall be jointly and severally liable for all debts and liabilities incurred or arising as a result thereof.'

This is merely an elaboration of § 146 of the Model Act. The Comment states:

'This section is designed to prohibit the application of any theory of de facto incorporation. The only authority to act as a corporation under the Model Act arises from completion of the procedures prescribed in sections 53 to 55 inclusive. The consequences of those procedures are specified in section 56 as being the creation of a corporation. No other means being authorized, the effect of section 146 is to negate the possibility of a de facto corporation.

'Abolition of the concept of de facto incorporation, which at best was fuzzy, is a sound result. No reason exists for its continuance under general corporate laws, where the process of acquiring de jure incorporation is both simple and clear. The vestigial appendage should be removed.' 2 Model Business Corporation Act Annotated § 146, pp. 908–909 (2d ed. 1971).

In Robertson v. Levy, 197 A.2d 443 (D.C.Ct. of App.1964), the court held the president of a defectively organized corporation personally liable to a creditor of the 'corporation.' The applicable legislation was similar to Oregon's. The court held the legislation ended the common-law doctrine of de facto corporation.

The Alaska court upheld the cancellation ground that the applicant had not yet been issued its certificate of incorporation at the issued its certificate of incorporation at the time the permit was issued. Swindel v. Kelly, 499 P.2d 291 (Alaska 1972). Alaska has a statute similar to Oregon's. The court commented: 'The concept of de facto corporations has been increasingly disfavored, and Alaska is among the states whose corporation statutes are designed to eliminate the concept.' 499 P.2d at 299, n. 28.

Vincent Drug Co. v. Utah State Tax Com'n, 17 Utah 2d 202, 407 P.2d 683 (1965), cited by defendant, involved a statute similar to that of Oregon; however, the court held the de facto corporation doctrine continued to exist. No reasoning is stated and we find the case unpersuasive.

We hold the principle of de facto corporation no longer exists in Oregon.

The defendant also contends that the plaintiff is estopped to deny that it contracted with a corporation.[1]

The doctrine of 'corporation by estoppel' has been recognized by this court but never fully dissected. Rutherford v. Hill, 22 Or. 218, 29 P. 546, 17 L.R.A. 549 (1892); Nickum v. Burckhardt, 30 Or. 464, 468, 47 P. 888, 60 Am.St.Rep. 822 (1897); Thompson Optical Institute v. Thompson, 119 Or. 252, 260, 237 P. 965 (1925); Doehler v. Lansdon, 135 Or. 687, 696, 291 P. 392, 298 P. 200 (1931); Brandtjen & Kluge v. Biggs, 205 Or. 473, 482–483, 288 P.2d 1025 (1955). Corporation by estoppel is a difficult concept to grasp and courts and writers have 'gone all over the lot' in attempting to define and apply the doctrine. One of the better explanations of the problem and the varied solutions is contained in Ballantine, Manual of Corporation Law and Practice §§ 28–30 (1930):

> 'The so-called estoppel that arises to deny corporate capacity does not depend on the presence of the technical elements of equitable estoppel, viz., misrepresentations and change of position in reliance thereon, but on the nature of the relations contemplated, that one who has recognized the organization as a corporation in business dealings should not be allowed to quibble or raise immaterial issues on matters which do not concern him in the slightest degree or affect his substantial rights.' Ballantine, supra, at 92.

As several writers have pointed out, in order to apply the doctrine correctly, the cases must be classified according to who is being charged with estoppel. Ballantine, supra, at 91; 1 Hornstein, Corporation Law and Practice § 30, p. 31, n. 6 (1959).

When a defendant seeks to escape liability to a corporation plaintiff by contending that the plaintiff is not a lawful corporate entity, courts readily apply the doctrine of corporation by estoppel. Thompson Optical Institute v. Thompson, supra (119 Or. 252, 237 P. 965), well illustrates the equity of the doctrine in this class of cases R. A. Thompson carried on an optical business for years. He then organized a corporation to buy his optical business and subscribed to most of the stock in this corporation. He chaired the

1. Robertson v. Levy, *supra* (197 A.2d 443), held the adoption of the provisions of the Model Business Corporation Act eliminated the concept of corporations by estoppel as well as de facto corporations. Fletcher follows this view. Fletcher, *supra*, § 3890. However, the same court that decided Robertson v. Levy, with the same panel, held a party was estopped to deny the existence of the corporation. Namerdy v. Generalcar, 217 A.2d 109 (D.C.Ct. of App. 1966). Robertson v. Levy was not mentioned. In view of our decision that the defense of estoppel was not established, we do not need to decide the effect of the new Business Corporation Act on the doctrine of estoppel. We observe, however, that '(a)lthough some cases tend to assimilate the doctrines of incorporation De facto and by estoppel, each is a distinct theory and they are not dependent on one another in their application.' Cranson v. International Business Machine Corp., 234 Md. 477, 200 A.2d 33, 38 (1964).

first meeting at which the Board resolved to purchase the business from him. The corporation and Thompson entered into a contract for the sale of the business which included a covenant by Thompson not to compete. Thereafter, Thompson sold all of his stock to another individual. Some years later Thompson re-entered the optical business in violation of the covenant not to compete. The corporation brought suit to restrain Thompson from competing. Thompson defended upon the ground that the corporation had not been legally organized. We held, 'The defendant cannot be heard to challenge the validity of the contract or the proper organization of the corporation.'[2] 119 Or. at 260, 237 P. at 968.

The fairness of estopping a defendant such as Thompson from denying the corporate existence of his creation is apparent.

On the other hand, when individuals such as the defendants in this case seek to escape liability by contending that the debtor is a corporation, Aero-Fabb Co., rather than the individual who purported to act as a corporation, the courts are more reluctant to estop the plaintiff from attacking the legality of the alleged debtor corporation. Ballantine, supra, at 96; 8 Fletcher, Cyclopedia of the Law of Private Corporations (perm.ed.) §3914, p. 228.

The most appealing explanation of why the plaintiff may be estopped is based upon the intention of the parties. The creditor-plaintiff contracted believing it could look for payment only to the corporate entity. The associates, whatever their relationship to the supposed corporate entity, believed their only potential liability was the loss of their investment in the supposed corporate entity and that they were not personally liable. Cranson v. International Business Machine Corp., 234 Md. 477, 200 A.2d 33, 38–39 (1964); Namerdy v. Generalcar, 217 A.2d 109 (D.C. Ct. of App. 1966); E. Merrick Dodd, Jr., Partnership Liability of Stockholders in Defective Corporations, 40 Harv.L.Rev. 521, 552 (1927).

From the plaintiff-creditor's viewpoint, such reasoning is somewhat tenuous. The creditor did nothing to create the appearance that the debtor was a legal corporate entity. The creditor formed its intention to contract with a debtor corporate entity because someone associated with the debtor represented, expressly or impliedly, that the debtor was a legal corporate entity.

We need not decide whether the doctrine of corporation by estoppel would apply in such a case as this. The trial court found that if this doctrine was still available under the Business Corporation Act defendants did not prove all the elements necessary for its application, and, moreover, it would be inequitable to apply the doctrine.[3]

Under the explanation stated above for the application of the doctrine of estoppel in this kind of case, it is necessary that the plaintiff believe that it was contracting with a corporate entity. The evidence on this point is contradictory and the trial court apparently found against defendants.

The trial court found, and its findings are supported by the evidence, that all the defendants were partners prior to January 1970 and did business under the name 'Aero-Fabb Co.' Not until June 1970 were the interests in this partnership assigned to the corporation 'Aero-Fabb Co.' and about the same time the assumed business name 'Aero-Fabb Co.' was cancelled.

---

2. The court also based its decision upon a finding that the plaintiff was a de facto corporation.

3. The trial court made these as conclusions of law, but these statements are in effect general findings of fact.

The trial court found, and the evidence supported the finding, that two of the leases entered into by plaintiff were with 'Kenneth L. Davenport, dba Aero-Fabb Co.' The other was with 'Kenneth L. Davenport, dba Aero-Fabb Corp.' 'Aero-Fabb Corp.' was never the corporate name; the name of the corporation for which a certificate was finally issued was 'Aero-Fabb Co.' The correspondence and records of plaintiff sometimes referred to the debtor as 'Aero-Fabb Co.' and others as 'Aero-Fabb Corp.'

Plaintiff's bookkeeper testified that she thought it was a corporation because, 'This was the way the information was given to me.' It is uncertain whether the information was given to her by someone employed by plaintiff or by a company with whom she made a credit check. In any event, plaintiff's salesman said Mr. Davenport, speaking for the organization, stated several times that he was in a partnership with Drs. Gorman and Bennett. The salesman was dubious and checked the title to the land on which the debtors' operation was being conducted and found it was in the name of the three defendants as individuals.

A final question remains: Can the plaintiff recover against Dr. Bennett individually?

In the first third of this century the liability of persons associated with defectively organized corporations was a controversial and well-documented legal issue. The orthodox view was that if an organization had not achieved de facto status and the plaintiff was not estopped to attack the validity of the corporate status of the corporation, all shareholders were liable as partners. This court, however, rejected the orthodox rule. In Rutherford v. Hill, 22 Or. 218, 29 P. 546, 29 Am.St.R. 596, 17 L.R.A. 549 (1892), we held that a person could not be held liable as a partner merely because he signed the articles of incorporation though the corporation was so defectively formed as to fall short of de facto status. The court stated that under this rule a mere passive stockholder would not be held liable as a partner. We went on to observe, however, that if the party actively participated in the business he might be held liable as a partner.

This controversy subsided 30 or 40 years ago probably because the procedure to achieve de jure corporate status was made simplier; so the problem did not arise.

The Model Act and the Oregon Business Corporation Act, ORS 57.793, solve the problem as follows:

> 'All persons who assume to act as a corporation without the authority of a certificate of incorporation issued by the Corporation Commissioner, shall be jointly and severally liable for all debts and liabilities incurred or arising as a result thereof.'

We have found no decisions, comments to the Model Act, or literature attempting to explain the intent of this section.

We find the language ambiguous. Liability is imposed on '(a)ll persons who assume to act as a corporation.' Such persons shall be liable 'for all debts and liabilities incurred or arising as a result thereof.'

We conclude that the category of 'persons who assume to act as a corporation' does not include those whose only connection with the organization is as an investor. On the other hand, the restriction of liability to those who personally incurred the obligation sued upon cannot be based upon logic or the realities of business practice. When several people carry on the activities of a defectively organized corporation, chance frequently will dictate which of the several active principals directly incurs a certain obligation or whether an employee, rather than an active principal, personally incurs the obligation.

We are of the opinion that the phrase, 'persons who assume to act as a corporation' should be interpreted to include those persons who have an investment in the organization and who actively participate in the policy and operational decisions of the organization. Liability should not necessarily be restricted to the person who personally incurred the obligation.

The trial court found that Dr. Bennett 'acted in the business venture which was subsequently incorporated on June 12, 1970.'

The proposed business of the corporation which was to be formed was to sell airplanes, recondition airplanes and give flying lessons. Land was leased for this purpose. Equipment was rented from plaintiff to level and clear for access and for other construction.

There is evidence from which the trial court could have found that while Drs. Bennett and Gorman, another defendant, entrusted the details of management to Davenport, they endeavored to and did retain some control over his management. All checks required one of their signatures. Dr. Bennett frequently visited the site and observed the activity and the presence of the equipment rented by plaintiff. He met with the organization's employees to discuss the operation of the business. Shortly after the equipment was rented and before most of the rent had accrued, Dr. Bennett was informed of the rentals and given an opinion that they were unnecessary and ill-advised. Drs. Bennett and Gorman thought they had Davenport and his management 'under control.'

This evidence all supports the finding that Dr. Bennett was a person who assumed to act for the organization and the conclusion of the trial court that Dr. Bennett is personally liable.

Affirmed.

Joe Micciche, Petitioner, v. David Billings and the Industrial Commission of the State of Colorado, Respondents

Supreme Court of Colorado,
En Banc.
727 P.2d 367
Nov. 3, 1986.

QUINN, Chief Justice.

We granted certiorari to review the decision of the court of appeals in Billings v. Micciche, 691 P.2d 1155 (Colo.App.1984), concerning the effect of section 7-3-104, 3 C.R.S. (1973), of the Colorado Corporation Code[1] on the personal liability of a corporate officer for corporate debts and liabilities incurred during a period when the corporation had been suspended from transacting business in Colorado as a result of its failure to file the corporate report required by section 7-10-102(1), 3 C.R.S. (1979 Supp.). The court of appeals construed section 7-3-104 to impose joint and several liability

---

1. All citations to the Colorado Corporation Code will be to volume 3 of the 1973 Colorado Revised Statutes and, where appropriate, to the 1979 Supplement, since the statutory law applicable to this case is contained in those sources. The present version of the Colorado Corporation Code is found in volume 3A of the Colorado Revised Statutes (1986).

upon the petitioner, Joe Micciche, a vice president and one of three shareholders of Mountain States Welding and Sheetmetal, Inc. (Mountain States), a Colorado corporation, for work-related injuries sustained by the respondent, David Billings, in the course of his employment with Mountain States. We reverse the judgment of the court of appeals and remand the case for further proceedings.

I.

David Billings was employed by Mountain States as a welder and sheet metal worker. On August 21, 1980, Billings sustained a fracture of both knees when a stack of sheet metal fell on him in the course of his employment. He filed a claim for workmen's compensation on October 31, 1980.

Prior to Billings' accident, the secretary of state in 1979 had suspended Mountain States from transacting business as a Colorado corporation due to its failure to file the corporate report required by section 7-10-102. For a time, however, Mountain States continued to transact business in the state without seeking reinstatement of its corporate status under section 7-10-109(4), 3 C.R.S. (1979 Supp.).[2]

On December 4, 1980, a hearing officer of the Department of Labor entered a workmen's compensation award in favor of Billings for his medical expenses and disability benefits and also assessed statutory penalties against Mountain States for its failure to timely admit or deny liability and for its failure to carry workmen's compensation insurance. On February 10, 1981, Billings moved to reopen his claim and sought to impose liability on Joe Micciche and two other officer-shareholders of Mountain States, alleging that Mountain States did not exist as a corporation. Billings' claim against the other two officers was subsequently settled.

After several hearings, the hearing officer ruled that the suspended status of Mountain States rendered Micciche, as vice president of the corporation, personally liable for workmen's compensation benefits to Billings. The Industrial Commission reversed the ruling of the hearing officer, concluding that a suspension for failing to file a corporate report did not extinguish the corporate entity and that corporate officers, including Micciche, were not liable for corporate debts. The commission, however, remanded the case to the hearing officer for the purpose of determining whether the corporate entity should be disregarded and liability imposed on Micciche under the equitable doctrine of "piercing the corporate veil."

Both Micciche and Billings appealed the decision of the commission to the court of appeals. The court of appeals held that under section 7-3-104, 3 C.R.S. (1973), Mountain States' transaction of business while under suspension rendered Micciche, as an officer of the suspended corporation, personally liable for the corporation's obligation to Billings. We thereafter granted Micciche's petition for certiorari to consider whether the court of appeals erred in holding that section 7-3-104 authorized the imposition of personal liability for corporate obligations on a corporate officer solely because he was an officer when the obligation was incurred. We conclude that the court of ap-

2. In a memorandum brief submitted in support of Micciche's petition for review by the Industrial Commission, the statement is made that Mountain States was dissolved on January 1, 1983, pursuant to section 7-8-113(6), 3 C.R.S. (1979 Supp.). That statute states in relevant part: Commencing on January 1, 1979, and continuing thereafter on January 1 of each successive year, corporations which were suspended for the preceding three-year period under the provisions of [section] 7-10-109 shall be dissolved by operation of law without the necessity of any other action under the provisions of this section and sections 7-8-114 and 7-8-115.

peals erred in its construction of section 7-3-104, and we accordingly reverse the judgment and remand the case for further proceedings on the unresolved issue of whether personal liability might be appropriately imposed on Micciche by "piercing the corporate veil."

II.

Pertinent provisions of the Colorado Corporation Code and applicable case law provide the legal context for our resolution of the issue before us. Under the Colorado Corporation Code, which was originally enacted as the Colorado Corporation Act of 1958, ch. 32, sec. 1-149, 1958 Colo.Sess.Laws 119–203, corporate existence begins when the certificate of incorporation is issued. §7-2-104, 3 C.R.S. (1973). Incorporation results in the creation of a new legal entity with an identity separate and apart from the shareholders. H. Henn & J. Alexander, Laws of Corporations 144–46 (3d ed. 1983). Since a validly formed corporation has an independent legal identity, the corporation itself is legally responsible for its own activities, and adverse economic consequences to the shareholders based on obligations are generally "limited to what the shareholder has invested in the corporation." Id. at 130.

Section 7-3-104, 3 C.R.S. (1973), which is central to this case, was originally enacted as part of the Colorado Corporation Act of 1958 and provides as follows: All persons who assume to act as a corporation without authority to do so shall be jointly and severally liable for all debts and liabilities occurring or arising as a result thereof. Ch. 32, sec. 140, 1958 Colo.Sess.Laws 119, 202. This statute is identical to section 139 of the 1950 Model Business Corporation Act, which was designed to impose personal liability in those situations in which persons hold themselves out and improperly act as a corporation without having made any good faith effort to achieve corporate status under state law. A 1969 revision of the Model Act renumbered section 139 as section 146. Although the statutory text was not changed in the 1969 revision, the comments were rewritten to indicate that the intention underlying section 139 was to make the issuance of a certificate of incorporation the sole determinant of corporate existence, thereby eliminating the doctrine of de facto incorporation. See 1 Model Business Corp. Act Annot. §2.04 comment at 135–36 (3d ed. 1985). Because courts, however, continued to permit limited liability in situations where individuals reasonably but erroneously believed that they had authority to act as a corporation, see, e.g., Cranson v. International Business Machines Corp., 234 Md. 477, 200 A.2d 33 (1964); Cantor v. Sunshine Greenery, Inc., 165 N.J.Super. 411, 398 A.2d 571 (1979), the drafters of the Model Act amended section 146 in 1985 in order to reflect the more flexible standard expressed in case law. 1 Model Business Corp. Act Annot. §2.04 comment at 130–33. The current provision, renumbered section 2.04 and entitled Liability for Preincorporation Transactions, reads: "All persons purporting to act as or on behalf of a corporation, knowing there was no incorporation under this Act, are jointly and severally liable for all liabilities created while so acting." The effect of the 1985 version of section 2.04 is to impose liability only on persons who act as or on behalf of a corporation "knowing" that no corporation exists. Id.[3]

The Colorado Corporation Code requires a corporation to file a biennial report with the secretary of state setting forth various matters, including the character of the busi-

3. The current version of section 7-3-104 was amended in 1985 (Ch. 66, sec. 14, §7-3-104, 1985 Colo.Sess.Laws 318) to require that liability can be imposed only on those "without good faith belief" in their authority to act. §7-3-104, 3A C.R.S. (1986). Although the revision does not apply to this case, it does clarify the implicit meaning of the original version.

ness in which the corporation is engaged, the names and addresses of corporate directors and officers, and a statement regarding the nature and extent of authorized and issued corporate stock. §7-10-101, 3 C.R.S. (1973 & 1979 Supp.). If a corporation fails to file the report, the secretary of state, pursuant to section 7-10-109(1), 3 C.R.S. (1979 Supp.), must give written notice to the corporation of its failure to file, and unless the report is filed within thirty days after such notice, the corporation shall be suspended. Section 7-10-109(2), 3 C.R.S. (1979 Supp.), states:

> Any domestic corporation which is suspended...shall be inoperative and no longer competent to transact business in this state; but the shareholders of such corporation may hold their annual or special meetings of shareholders for the election of directors, and such corporation may hold or continue to hold, encumber, sell, or convey real estate and make such reports as are required by the laws of the United States and this state and elect corporate officers. The suspension of such corporation shall not take away any remedy given against such corporation, its shareholders, or its officers for any liability incurred prior thereto.

A suspended corporation may be reinstated by paying a reinstatement fee of fifty dollars, filing a corporate report and paying the fee due upon such filing for the year in which the corporation is to be reinstated, paying a late penalty of twenty-five dollars for a current year's report filed after May 1, and paying a fee of seventy dollars for each year that a corporate report was not filed. §7-10-109(4), 3 C.R.S. (1979 Supp.). The effect of section 7-10-109 is not to dissolve a corporation. Rather, the obvious effect of the statute is to render a corporation incompetent to transact business while it is in default of its statutory obligations. People v. Zimbelman, 194 Colo. 384, 387–88, 572 P.2d 830, 833 (1977). Although several sections of the Colorado Corporation Code deal specifically with penalties imposed upon corporations, officers, and directors for various forms of conduct, §§7-10-111 and -112, 3 C.R.S. (1979 Supp.),[4] the statutory fees in section 7-10-109(4) are the only provisions that expressly address the matter of penalty in the case of a corporation suspended for failure to file a biennial report.

Prior to 1958, Colorado statutory law provided that officers and directors of a corporation that failed to file a corporate report were jointly and severally liable for corporate debts incurred during the delinquent period. Ch. 102, sec. 11, 1911 Colo.Sess.Laws, 257, 259. This statute was termed "penal in nature" as to the liability of a corporate officer and director but "remedial in character" as to creditors of the corporation. Credit Men's Adjustment Co. v. Vickery, 62 Colo. 214, 161 P. 297 (1916). A later version of the statute limited joint and several liability of corporate officers and directors to a total of one thousand dollars. Ch. 41, §80, 1935 C.S.A. This latter section was ultimately repealed when the Colorado Corporation Act was enacted in 1958. Ch. 32, sec. 148, 1958 Colo.Sess.Laws 119, 203.

Under case law, a corporation reinstated after suspension is deemed to have had continuous existence throughout the period of suspension, with the result that the corporation's loss of authority to transact business does not affect its continued existence as a

4. Section 7-10-111, 3 C.R.S. (1979 Supp.), for example, imposes a civil penalty of twenty-five dollars upon each domestic corporation "not declared suspended that fails or refuses to file its corporate report and pay the fee prescribed therefor by May 1." Section 7-10-112, 3 C.R.S. (1979 Supp.), subjects each officer and director of a domestic corporation to a misdemeanor conviction and fine of not more than one thousand dollars for failure or refusal to answer truthfully interrogatories propounded by the secretary of state or who signs a statement or report or other document filed with the secretary of state which is known to be false in any material respect.

legal entity. Zimbelman, 194 Colo. 384, 572 P.2d 830; Dominion Oil Co. v. Lamb, 119 Colo. 62, 201 P.2d 372 (1948); Smith v. Highland Mary Mining, Milling & Power Co., 82 Colo. 288, 259 P. 1025 (1927). Colorado case law also holds that when a suspended corporation is reinstated, corporate officers are not personally liable for debts incurred during a period of suspension. Rocky Mountain Sales & Service, Inc. v. Havana RV, Inc., 635 P.2d 935 (Colo.App.1981).

III.

We conclude that section 7-3-104, 3 C.R.S. (1973), does not impose liability upon corporate officers for corporate obligations incurred while the corporation was operating under a suspended status but was still a valid legal entity. Several factors lead us to this conclusion.

Since legislative intent is the guiding principle of statutory construction, e.g., Dawson v. Public Employees' Retirement Association, 664 P.2d 702, 707 (Colo.1983), we look initially to the legislative object sought to be attained by section 7-3-104. That object is quite obvious from the statute's source, namely, section 139 of the 1950 Model Business Corporation Act. The purpose of that section was to impose personal liability upon those persons who take it upon themselves to act as a corporation without having undertaken any bona fide effort to achieve corporate status by complying with the statutory requirements for incorporation. 1 Model Business Corp. Act Annot. § 2.04 comment at 130–33. The construction of section 7-3-104 which we adopt herein is consistent with that purpose. Furthermore, such construction finds support in case law from other jurisdictions holding that no personal liability should be imposed on corporate officers for corporate obligations solely on the basis of the corporation's failure to comply with statutory requirements relating to franchise taxes, annual reports, and filing fees. E.g., United States v. Standard Beauty Supply Stores, Inc, 561 F.2d 774 (9th Cir.1977) (failure to pay franchise tax); Creditors Protective Association, Inc. v. Baksay, 32 Or.App. 223, 573 P.2d 766 (1978) (failure to file annual report and to pay annual fee); Tagliani v. Colwell, 10 Wash.App. 227, 517 P.2d 207 (1973) (failure to pay annual license fee).

Our construction of section 7-3-104 finds further support in the circumstances under which the statute was enacted. As already noted, prior to the enactment of section 7-3-104 in 1958, Colorado statutory law imposed personal liability on the officers and directors of any corporation for corporate debts if the corporation failed to file a corporate report, ch. 102, sec. 11, 1911 Colo.Sess.Laws, 257, 259, and a later version of this statute limited liability to one thousand dollars, § 31-7-15, 1953 2 C.R.S. However, the Colorado Corporation Act of 1958, of which section 7-3-104 was an integral part, expressly repealed that statutory penalty. If the legislature intended section 7-3-104 to apply to officers of a validly formed but suspended corporation, it is reasonable to assume that it would have made its intent as clear as it had done in its prior enactments. Moreover, the legislative decision to expressly provide for reinstatement of a suspended corporation upon filing of a corporate report and the payment of statutory penalty fees, § 7-10-109(4), 3 C.R.S. (1979 Supp.), reinforces the conclusion that section 7-3-104 was simply not intended to apply to an officer of a corporation which was validly formed in the first instance but which had been subsequently suspended due to its failure to file a corporate report.[5]

---

5. This conclusion is further supported by the statutory penalty scheme. Section 7-10-112, 3 C.R.S. (1979 Supp.), expressly provides for a one thousand dollar penalty for an officer or director

Finally, we believe it appropriate to consider the consequences of a contrary construction. Given the fact that the Colorado Corporation Code permits a suspended corporation to be reinstated, with the result that corporate powers of a reinstated corporation are regarded as having continuous existence throughout the period of suspension, e.g., Zimbelman, 194 Colo. at 388, 572 P.2d at 833, and in light of the further fact that under Colorado case law corporate officers conducting business are not liable for debts incurred during the period of suspension, Rocky Mountain Sales & Service Co., 635 P.2d at 935, it would be anomalous in the extreme to construe section 7-3-104 in a manner that exposes corporate officers to substantial legal obligations solely on the basis of the corporation's failure to seek reinstatement. We thus limit the scope of section 7-3-104 to those instances when persons act as a corporation without making any bona fide effort to achieve corporate status by complying with the statutory requirements for incorporation.

IV.

[omitted]

The judgment is reversed and the case remanded to the court of appeals with directions to return the case to the hearing officer for further proceedings consistent with the views herein expressed.

Comments and Questions

1. The Revised Model Business Corporation Act §2.04 is said to provide a slightly more relaxed and flexible standard for the determination of pre-incorporation liability of corporate actors than the standard under the old Model Act. Applying the standard of §2.04 to the facts of *Timberline Equipment Company, Inc.*, do you think that the court could have reached a different result? While many jurisdictions adopting the Model Business Corporation approach have adopted provisions similar to §2.04, some jurisdictions continue to operate under the earlier Model Business Corporation Act provisions.

2. The Revised Model Business Corporation Act approach to personal liability for pre-incorporation transactions limits those situations in which, under the common law, some states had limited personal liability. Can you describe factual situations in which liability would be imposed under the Revised Model Business Corporation Act but might not be imposed under common law approaches?

3. The problem posed by the suspended corporation is highlighted in the *Micciche* case. The court in that case concludes that corporate officers do not incur personal liability for corporate obligations incurred while the corporation was operating under a suspended status, but was still a valid legal entity. The Colorado Supreme Court rejected the trial court's determination that corporate suspension caused the corporation to revert to partnership status pending reinstatement. Can you make a policy argument justifying the older approach that imposed joint and several liability on corporate officers and directors for debts incurred during the delinquency period? Would your argument depend on the reasons for or the nature of the suspension?

---

who signs a false report, but makes no mention of a penalty for an officer or director of a corporation which fails to file an annual report. *See* note 4, *supra*.

4. Even if you generally agree with the policy underlying *Micciche* can you think of situations in which a corporate suspension ought to result in reversion of the suspended corporation to partnership status for the duration of the suspension?

5. Where a corporation ceases to exist for any time, courts appear to be more willing to impose personal liability on corporate officers and shareholders. This is the case even when corporate actors move quickly to reincorporate. Thus, in *Adams v. Mt. Pleasant Bank & Trust Co.*, 355 N.W.2d 868 (Iowa 1984), the court, construing a statute similar to section 105 of the 1969 Model Business Corporation Act, determined that the doctrine of de factor corporations no longer applied in Iowa, and on that basis imposed personal liability on shareholders for corporate obligations. In that case, shareholders sought to avoid liability for the time after the old corporation expired and prior to the time that the entity was properly reincorporated, during which the corporation had not been a valid legal entity. Could you develop an argument under common law principles to support the contention that shareholders ought not to incur personal liability when the corporation continues to operate but ceases to be a valid legal entity during a short period of time?

A Note on Hybrid Approaches

Some jurisdictions, adopting the approach suggested by the Revised Model Business Corporation Act, have not treated that approach as the exclusive means of determining liability in the context or pre-incorporation or defective incorporation activities. The materials which follow illustrate the approach taken in a hybrid jurisdiction.

Harry Rich Corp., Appellant, v. Ira Feinberg, et al., Appellees

No. 86-3028.
Third District Court of Appeal of Florida
Dec. 29, 1987.
518 So.2d 377

PEARSON, J:

This appeal arises out of a creditor's attempt to hold an individual liable on a contract he signed on behalf of a corporation which did not at that time exist. After a non-jury trial, the trial court entered judgment for the individual, Ira Feinberg, predicated on two factual findings: that Feinberg did not actually or constructively know that the business on whose behalf he had contracted was not incorporated and that the plaintiff, Harry Rich Corporation (Harry Rich), did not rely on Feinberg's individual assets or credit in making the contract. The trial court therefore concluded that Section 607.397, Florida Statutes (1983),[1] under which the plaintiff sought to recover from Feinberg, was

1. Section 607.397 provides: "All persons who assume to act as a corporation without authority to do so shall be jointly and severally liable for all debts and liabilities incurred or arising as a result thereof."

inapplicable. The trial court's findings are supported by substantial competent evidence and we agree with its legal conclusion.

I.

Sometime between August and November 1984, Feinberg became president of a business called Young Sophisticates Warehouse (Warehouse) upon the resignation of Jack Lavin. Feinberg, who had been an officer of Warehouse, was told in August that Warehouse had been formed by Lavin's son, an attorney. On November 15, 1984, Feinberg, as president of Warehouse, signed a contract with Harry Rich to purchase carpeting for Warehouse. Later that same month, when Feinberg went to his attorney to amend the corporate documents to reflect the change in officers and resident agent, he learned that Warehouse had never been incorporated. By December 5, 1984, Warehouse was incorporated at Feinberg's instructions.

After a dispute over the carpeting contract arose, Harry Rich sued Warehouse and some related corporations which allegedly had been unjustly enriched by the contract. When Harry Rich learned through pre-trial discovery that Warehouse had not been incorporated on the date that the contract was signed, Harry Rich amended its complaint to add Feinberg as a defendant.

After a non-jury trial, the court found the corporations liable and exonerated Feinberg. It explained:

"The Plaintiff never had reason to believe that Mr. Feinberg was acting in the personal capacity and [it] certainly didn't rely upon Mr. Feinberg individually in extending the credit and in entering into the contract.

"[Feinberg] was acting in good faith in the sense that he believed he was [representing] a corporation at the time he signed the contract and in fact the moment he found out it wasn't [incorporated], he directed his attorney to incorporate, which was done two weeks later...."

Harry Rich appeals.

II.

Harry Rich does not contest the trial court's finding that it did not rely upon Feinberg individually in extending the credit and in entering into the contract. Instead Harry Rich contends, first, that Feinberg's asserted lack of knowledge of the unincorporated status of Warehouse—or his good faith belief that Warehouse was incorporated—is entirely irrelevant, that is, an individual who signs a contract on behalf of a corporation not then in existence is ipso facto liable on the contract; second, that if, arguendo, Feinberg's lack of knowledge is relevant, the trial court's factual finding on this issue is not supported by competent evidence; and, third, that Harry Rich was entitled to an award of attorney's fees against the related corporations which, although not parties to the contract, were found to have benefited from it. Finding the second and third points to be without merit, we now turn our attention to the first.

III.

A.

The long-standing rule that an association, until it comes into existence as a corporation, cannot be bound by acts done or promises made in its behalf and cannot therefore be subject to the entry of a judgment against it, 8 W. Fletcher, Cyclopedia of the Law of

Private Corporations ¶ 4059 (rev. perm. ed. 1982), would produce harsh results if applied without resort to equitable doctrines. One such doctrine is "corporation by estoppel,"[2] under which private litigants are estopped to assert the nonexistence of the corporation if they have by their conduct or words affirmed or relied on its existence. Id. at ¶ 3889. See Cranson v. I.B.M., 234 Md. 477, 200 A.2d 33 (1964) (officer signing contract for business, erroneously believing it to be incorporated, held not individually liable; creditor estopped from asserting that debtor not a corporation where creditor dealt with debtor as if it were a corporation and relied on corporation's credit rather than the individual's). This doctrine has been codified in Section 607.401, Florida Statutes, which provides:

> "Estoppel.—No body of persons acting as a corporation shall be permitted to set up the lack of legal organization as a defense to an action against them as a corporation, nor shall any person sued on a contract made with the corporation or sued for an injury to its property or a wrong done to its interests be permitted to set up the lack of such legal organization in his defense."

In other words, the corporation may sue and be sued as if it existed if the parties to the contract behaved as if it existed. This allowed Harry Rich to successfully sue the defendant corporation, since Harry Rich believed it dealt with a corporation. The question remains, however, under what circumstances should the law provide a creditor with the additional remedy of a suit against the individual who acted for the corporation? Stated otherwise, should Section 607.397, Florida Statutes (1983)—which provides that "all persons who assume to act as a corporation without authority to do so shall be jointly and severally liable for all debts and liabilities incurred or arising as a result thereof"—be read to impose unconditional liability upon the individual where the corporation for which the individual acted is estopped to deny its existence.

B.

In Futch v. Southern Stores, Inc., 380 So.2d 444 (Fla. 1st DCA 1979), the First District held that Futch, a non-active director, officer, and fifty-per-cent shareholder of Fuco Oil and Chemical Co., Inc., was not liable for contracts entered into by another officer on behalf of the corporation when, unknown to Futch, the corporation was temporarily dissolved by the state for failure to file required annual reports and filing fees.[3]

---

2. Another is the doctrine of "de facto corporation," which is applicable where an attempt to incorporate is defective and the abortive entity is nonetheless considered a corporation for most purposes. *See generally* Robertson v. Levy, 197 A.2d 443, 445 (D.C. 1964). It has been suggested that the Model Business Corporation Act (adopted substantially by Florida in Chapter 607), having established a bright line for the beginning of corporate existence, *see* § 607.167, Florida Statutes, eliminated the concept of de facto corporation. Clear support for this view can be found in the comments to section 146 of the 1969 version of the Model Business Corporation Act ("This section is designed to prohibit the application of any theory of de facto incorporation."). See also 8 W. Fletcher, *supra,* ¶ 4069. Indeed, some courts have agreed. E.g., Bowers Building Co. v. Altura Glass, Co., 694 P.2d 876 (Colo. Ct. App. 1984); Robertson v. Levy, 197 A.2d 443 (D.C. 1964); Cahoon v. Ward, 231 Ga. 872, 204 S.E.2d 622 (1974); Timberline Equipment Co. v. Davenport, 267 Or. 64, 514 P.2d 1109 (1973). However, the 1984 version of the Model Act (not adopted in Florida) contains no clear statement on de facto corporations, and the comment states that the newer rule provides a "slightly more flexible or relaxed standard." Model Business Corporation Act Annotated § 2.04, at 131 (3d ed. 1987). This court, in Ratner v. Central National Bank, 414 So.2d 210 (Fla. 3d DCA 1982), left open the question of whether Chapter 607, Florida Statutes, abolished de facto corporations. The question remains open, as the present case does not involve a de facto corporation.

3. Although the case before us involves a contract signed before incorporation, we find no distinction between such a contract and one signed where a corporation which once existed has been

Rejecting the plaintiff's argument that Futch was liable under Section 607.397 as a matter of law because the contracts were transacted while she "assumed to act" as a corporation, the court announced:

> "[W]e believe the correct rule is that in the absence of any action inducing reliance on the individual assets of a person acting on behalf of a corporation, the plaintiff's action should be limited to one against the corporation. There is nothing in the record showing that appellant induced any reliance on appellee's part, or indeed that she participated in the transaction in any manner."
>
> Id. at 446.

This court, "without disagreeing with Futch," found it to be distinguishable where the complaint against the active corporate officer was based on fraud. Nessim v. DeLoache, 384 So.2d 1341, 1343 (Fla. 3d DCA 1980).

In Mobil Oil Corp. v. Thoss, 385 So.2d 726, 727 (Fla. 5th DCA 1980), the court, correctly observing that in Futch the contract in question was entered into not by Futch, but by another officer, nonetheless described the holding of Futch as being "that directors, officers, and agents of a dissolved corporation are not personally liable in the absence of a showing that the creditor relied upon the individual assets of the person acting as a corporation." The court proceeded then to expressly disagree with Futch and to hold that the liability of an individual under Section 607.397 is not restricted, as it believed Futch proclaimed, to situations where the creditor relied on the individual assets of the person acting on behalf of a corporation.

We do not read Futch, as we believe the court in Mobil Oil did, to stand for the proposition that a creditor to recover from an individual must prove that it relied on the individual's assets. Instead, because Futch, unlike Feinberg, never acted at all, much less assumed to act as a corporation, see Anderson v. Hillsborough Sheet Metal Inc., 513 So.2d 1359 (Fla. 2d DCA 1987), we read Futch to stand for the proposition that a creditor to recover from an individual who has not acted on behalf of the Corporation must prove that it relied on the individual's assets. Since Feinberg clearly acted on behalf of the corporation, he can take no comfort in Futch.

He can, however, take comfort in the holding of Mobil Oil. There, interpreting Section 607.397, the court held that a creditor to recover from an individual who has acted on behalf of the corporation must prove that the individual knew or should have known of the nonexistence of the corporation when he acted on the corporation's behalf. This construction, said the court, gives content to the word "assume" in the phrase "assume to act":

> "[W]e do not think the Legislature intended to impose liability on every director or agent of a dissolved corporation who does not act or who has no knowledge of the dissolution. We find it significant that Section 607.397 is worded, 'all persons who assume to act....' (Emphasis added). It does not impose liability on all persons who act, only those who assume to act. We conclude that the use of this language reflects an intent to limit the statute's application to those persons who knew or, because of their position, should have known."
>
> Id. at 727.[4]

---

dissolved. *See* Richmond Wholesale Meat Co. v. Hughes, 625 F. Supp. 584, 588 (N.D. Ill. 1985); Barker-Chadsey Co. v. W. C. Fuller Co., 16 Mass.App. 1, 448 N.E.2d 1283, 1285 (1983).

4. The Second District agrees with this reading of the statute and follows Mobil Oil. Anderson v. Hillsborough Sheet Metal, Inc., 513 So.2d 1359 (Fla. 2d DCA 1987); Wayne-Dalton Corp. v. Klinge, 506 So.2d 52 (Fla. 2d DCA 1987). See Steve's Equipment Service, Inc. v. Riebrandt, 121 Ill.App.3d

We agree with the Fifth District's reading of Section 607.397. Its reading is supported not only by the language of the statute, but by equitable considerations as well. Fairness dictates that a creditor dealing with what it believes to be a corporation should be able to recover from that entity. The doctrine of corporation by estoppel, found in Section 607.401, Florida Statutes, provides the creditor with that opportunity. To provide this same creditor with the unconditional right to recover from the individual—when the creditor at no time believed it was dealing with or could look to the individual—is to give to the creditor the unjustified right to recover from two defendants. We observe that in those jurisdictions which, like Florida, have enacted statutes modeled on the Model Business Corporation Act, but which, unlike Florida, have not provided for corporation by estoppel, the determination that the individual will be unconditionally liable provides no windfall to the creditor, since he is concomitantly deprived of the right to sue any but a fully qualified and certified corporation. See Robertson v. Levy, 197 A.2d 443 (D.C. 1964) (construing Business Corporation Act of District of Columbia to have eliminated estoppel and de facto corporation, thus rendering individual acting on behalf of putative corporation unconditionally liable).[5] In contrast, in states such as Florida, where corporation by estoppel (which allows recovery from the corporation) is retained alongside a statute imposing liability on an individual who assumes to act as a corporation, recovery from the individual should be permitted only where the individual acts with actual or constructive knowledge that no corporation exists.[6] This slight windfall to the creditor can be justified on the ground that the individual has not been completely forthcoming to the creditor and should suffer the consequences.

C.

The appellant suggests that regardless of Mobil Oil's construction of Section 607.397, this court in Ratner v. Central National Bank, 414 So.2d 210 (Fla. 3d DCA 1982), adopted a rule that an individual who acts on behalf of a nonexistent corporation is unconditionally liable. We disagree that Ratner adopted such a rule.

Ratner must be understood as being a case about a promoter. As is well known, a promoter is "one who undertakes to bring about the incorporation and organization of a corporation, procure for the corporation the rights and capital by which it is to carry

---

66, 459 N.E.2d 21, 76 Ill. Dec. 612 (1984) (construing similar statute; liability when individual acted with actual or constructive knowledge of corporate nonexistence); *see also* Richmond Wholesale Meat Co. v. Hughes, 625 F. Supp. 584 (N.D. Ill. 1985).

5. The result in Robertson has been criticized as unnecessarily abolishing the concept of estoppel when the statute called only for the abolition of de facto corporations. Note, 43 N.C.L.Rev. 206 (1964).

6. Section 607.397, Florida Statutes, is derived from the 1969 version of the Model Business Corporation Act. The promulgators of the Act—the Committee on Corporate Laws, Section of Corporation, Banking, and Business Law, American Bar Association—noted that despite the Act, courts have "continued to rely on common law concepts of de facto corporations, de jure corporations, and corporations by estoppel that provide uncertain protection against liability for pre-incorporation transactions." 1 Model Business Corporation Act Annotated § 2.04 official comment, at 131 (3d ed. 1987). They concluded that it was "appropriate to impose liability only on those persons who act as or on behalf of corporations 'knowing' that no corporation exists," *Id.* at 133, and the section of the Act (renumbered as 2.04) was accordingly amended in 1984 to read "All persons purporting to act as or on behalf of a corporation, knowing that there was no incorporation under this Act, are jointly and severally liable for all liabilities created while so acting" (emphasis supplied). Cf. Micciche v. Billings, 727 P.2d 367 (Colo. 1986) (comparing old and new provisions). These amendments to the Act simply reflect the existing law in states, such as Florida, which recognize corporate liability by estoppel and thus the need to condition individual liability with the requirement of knowledge.

out the purposes set forth in its charter, and establishes it as able to do business." 8 Fla.Jur.2d Business Relationships ¶23, at 146 (1978); 18 C.J.S. Corporations ¶119 (1939). By definition, a promoter is a person who knows that the business on whose behalf he acts is not incorporated since its incorporation is the very thing he seeks to bring about. If the person dealing with the promoter also knows that the business represented by the promoter is not yet incorporated, as appears to be the case in Ratner, then the contract is a pre-incorporation contract governed by the long-standing common law rule, set forth in Ratner, "that the promoter of a corporation is liable on his contract although the contract was made on behalf of the corporation to be formed, unless the other party agrees to look to another fund for payment." 414 So.2d at 212. Section 607.397 is for this very reason inapplicable to a promoter case; a person cannot "assume to act as a corporation" when both parties are fully aware that there is no corporation. See Sherwood & Roberts-Oregon, Inc. v. Alexander, 269 Or. 389, 525 P.2d 135, 138 (1974). If, in contrast, the person dealing with the promoter is unaware that there is no corporation, then Section 607.397 could apply; the promoter, knowing there is no corporation, can then be said to have "assume[d] to act as a corporation."[7]

IV.

Having concluded that the construction of Section 607.397 is a matter of first impression in this district, and being persuaded by the decision of our sister court in Mobil Oil that our Legislature did not intend to impose liability on persons who act as a corporation without knowing that no corporation exists, we affirm the judgment for Feinberg. Because, as the trial court found, this is not a case where the individual knew or should have known of the nonexistence of the corporation when he acted, Mobil Oil controls and Feinberg prevails.

Affirmed.

Comments and Questions

1. The decision in *Harry Rich Corp.* provides a nice contrast with that in *Timberline Equipment Company, Inc.*, read earlier in this chapter. In *Timberline Equipment Company, Inc.* the court goes to great pains, in construing the 1969 version of the Model Business Corporation Act, to declare that the common law doctrine of de facto corporation was dead in Oregon. Though the Oregon court declined to examine the continued vitality of the corporation by estoppel doctrine under the Model Business Corporation Act, other courts have concluded that corporation by estoppel is also foreclosed under the Model Business Corporation Act. *See Robertson v. Levy*, 197 A.2d 443 (D.C.Ct. of App. 1964) (discussed in both *Timberline Equipment Company, Inc.* and *Harry Rich Corp.*). On the other hand, in *Harry Rich Corp.*, the Florida court, construing substantially the same provisions, declined to consider whether the de facto corporation doctrine was dead in Florida, and concluded that the doctrine of corporation by estoppel survived the enactment of the Model Business Corporation Act approach. The

7. It is noteworthy that although Section 607.397, Florida Statutes, is without comment tacked onto two strings of cited promoter cases in Ratner, 414 So.2d at 212, neither Futch v. Southern Stores, Inc., Mobil Oil Corp. v. Thoss, nor any other case construing Section 607.397 is mentioned. This suggests to us that the Ratner court was deciding a promoter case and merely acknowledging the potential relationship of Section 607.397 to promoters who deal with people who are unaware that there is no corporation.

Florida court based its decision, in part, on the fact that the Florida legislature retained a statutory corporation by estoppel provision even as it enacted statutes based on the Model Business Corporation Act. In effect, a hybrid approach was created, retaining some of the common law notions of limitations of liability while adopting a different statutory basis for determining liability.

2. In footnote 6 of the court's opinion in *Harry Rich Corp.*, the court suggests that the hybrid approach required by Florida's statutory scheme is precisely the standard adopted by in the Revised Model Business Corporation Act in its 1984 amendment resulting in the creation of §2.04. "These amendments to the Act simply reflect the existing law in states, such as Florida, which recognize corporate liability by estoppel and thus the need to condition individual liability with the requirement of knowledge." *Harry Rich Corp.*, at note 6. Do you agree?

3. Subsequent to the decision in *Harry Rich Corp.*, Florida revised its corporate statutes and adopted the framework of the Revised Model Business Corporation Act, including §2.04. *See* Fla. Stat. Ann. §607.0204

C. Liability for Pre-Incorporation Transactions and Defective Incorporation in the European Union and Japan

1. *Liability for Pre-Incorporation Transactions in the EU*

Liability for pre-incorporation transactions in the European Union is subject to the national laws of the Member States. The law varies from state to state. In France, for example:

> The persons who carry out the steps necessary for the formation of a company are often, but not always, the future shareholders of the company. They must in any event take care not to carry out acts which might engage their future liability. Because the company is not yet formally in existence (which only occurs at the signature of the by-laws), its (future) officers cannot sign such agreements, which is therefore usually done by the incorporators.
>
> The 1966 Law [Law No. 66-537 of July 24, 1966] provides that all persons who acted in the name of a company in formation are jointly and severally liable for all such acts unless the company agrees to assume such obligations, in which case these agreements are retroactively deemed to have been entered into by the company itself. Once the company assumes the obligations of such agreements, these persons are freed from all obligations relating to those contracts. If the associates refuse to assume such agreements, the incorporators which signed them remain personally liable, unless they took the precaution of indicating that such obligations were entered into subject to the formation of the company.
>
> Prior to the signature of the by-laws, a list of agreements entered into (état des actes) and the consequences for the company is drawn up and presented to the associates. This list is then attached to the by-laws, and once the by-laws are

signed, the agreements contained in the list are automatically assumed by the company. Alternatively, the 1966 Law provides that these agreements can be ratified by the company once it has been registered on the Commercial Register. With respect to acts taken between the signature of the by-laws and registration on the Commercial Register, a power of attorney can be given by the commercial company which will signify the acceptance by the company of such acts taken during this period (once the company is registered on the Commercial Register). Otherwise, the persons having entered into them remain liable, as in the case of commitments taken prior to the signature of the bylaws, unless the company's associates explicitly agrees to assume such commitments after its registration on the Commercial Register.

Christopher Joseph Mesnooh, Law and Business in France: A Guide to French Commercial and Corporate Law 38–39 (1994).

The German approach is similar, although the extent of liability differs as between a public limited company (*Aktiengessellschaft*) and the private limited company (*Gesellschaft mit beschrankter Haftung*).

Nigel Foster, *German Legal System and Laws*

(2nd ed. 1996)

(excerpts from pages 334, 341; footnotes omitted)

[*Gesellschaft mit beschrankter Haftung*]

Prior to the notarisation of the articles, the members of the enterprise are treated in law as civil law partners with joint and several liability for pre-incorporation transactions, which is not disturbed by subsequent notarisation or registration.... If the shares have been subscribed to, the articles have been adopted and subjected to notarisation but the company has not been registered, the company is known as a pre-company (*Vorgesellschaft*). The provisions of the GmbHG apply where relevant. Paragraph 11 II renders any person, including members of the board of management, who make contracts on behalf of the *Vorgesellschaft* fully personally liable for those contracts. The management are also liable for all acts of misconduct. On registration, the company automatically assumes the liability for transactions entered into prior to incorporation and the liability of those who transacted prior to incorporation ceases.... This includes liability imposed by ¶ 11 II and personal liability.

Paragraph 13 provides that on registration the company acquires legal personality, limited liability of its members, and can sue and be sued in its own name.

* * *

[*Aktiengessellschaft*]

Pre-incorporation liability is determined by § 41 AktG. Incorporators are fully liable for transactions before the articles are notarised. Liability of individuals who have contracted on behalf of the *Vorgessellschaft* (pre-company) does not cease after registration, unlike the GmbH (§ 41 I 2). The extent of their liability differs according to opinion. Some argue there is full liability; other argue the incorporators are liable only to the extent of the subscribed capital, unless the company fails to come into existence in which case they will be fully liable. It is assumed that the distinction between the AG and the GmbH is the result of the concern for greater protection from liability for the shareholders of the AG. A clear ruling from the courts is, however, required to confirm this. Transactions prior to registration become the company's obligation only if accepted by the company (§41 II), which releases the incorporators' liability. Personal liability is likely to persist.

Whatever the details of the requirements of the national law of the Member States, such law must conform to the overall requirements of the First Company Law Directive. The Directive has imposed a uniform theory of liability for pre-incorporation transactions. Article Seven of the First Company Law Directive provides that:

> If, before a company being formed has acquired legal personality, action has been carried out in its name and the company does not assume the obligations arising from such action, the persons who acted shall, without limit, be jointly and severally liable therefor, unless otherwise agreed.

In examining the materials below, think about whether the standard for liability established through the First Directive is substantially the same as that generally recognized under U.S. common law. If there are differences, are they substantial?

Ubbink Isolatie BV v. Dak-en Wandtechniek BV

(Case 136/87)
Court of Justice of the European Communities (6th Chamber)
[1988] ECR 4665, [1990] 1 CMLR 262
20 September 1988

Sr. Jose Luis da Cruz Vilaca [the Advocate General]:

The Hoge Raad der Nederlanden (Supreme Court of the Netherlands) has submitted to the court of Justice for a preliminary ruling four questions concerning the rules governing the nullity of companies laid down in the First Council Directive (68/151) ([1968] OJ Spec Ed 41, [1978] 1 Commercial laws of Europe 325) on co-ordination of the safeguards required of companies by national law in order to protect the interests of members and others (which I shall refer to as the First Directive).

1. Summary of the facts leading to the request for a preliminary ruling

At the time of the facts which led to the proceedings before the national courts Ubbink Isolatie was registered in the commercial register of the Netherlands as a private limited liability company in the course of being formed, under the name 'Ubbink Isolatie BV, io.'

By contrast, there was no mention in the commercial register of a private limited liability company trading under the name of 'Ubbink Isolatie BV.' Ubbink failed to meet either of the two conditions laid down by Dutch law for the constitution of a private limited liability company: it had no authentic instrument of constitution and no ministerial authorisation. Nevertheless, it was able to operate lawfully as a partnership.

However, it was under the name of 'Ubbink Isolatie BV' (without the addition of 'io' meaning 'in formation') that Ubbink made an agreement with Dak-en Wandtechneik and it was thus under that name that an action was brought against it by the latter company before the Arrondissementsrechtbank (District Court) of Arnhem for termination of the agreement and for a determination of contractual liability thereunder. Ubbink Isolatie objected that the private limited liability company Ubbink Isolatie BV did not lawfully exist since it was neither constituted nor registered in the commercial register under that name; actions undertaken in that name had therefore been carried out unlawfully.

Before considering the substance of the case the national court decided that even if Ubbink Isolatie BV had never been constituted or if the instrument of constitution was defective, that did not mean that there was no private limited liability company of that name: it existed until such time as it was wound up in accordance with Dutch legislation (sections 181 and 182 of the Civil Code).

Ubbink Isolatie appealed against that decision first to the Gerechtshof (Regional Court of Appeal) Arnhem and then to the Hoge Raad. The latter considered that the interpretation of section 182 of the Civil Code depended on the scope of Section III of the First Directive, and therefore referred to this Court the four questions set out in the Report for the Hearing.

2. Examination of the questions referred by the Hoge Raad

The four questions referred by the Hoge Raad seek essentially to know whether and to what extent the rules contained in Section III of the First Directive apply to a company in formation which does not satisfy the requirements for valid constitution laid down by national law.

A

The first question referred by the national court is the most important one. It asks whether, when actions have been carried out in the name of a private limited liability company which has not been validly constituted, inasmuch as it does not satisfy either of the requirements for valid constitution laid down by national law, the rules laid down in Section III of the First Directive require that 'company' to be regarded as being in existence so long as its nullity has not been declared in proceedings initiated for that purpose.

Both the Commission and Ubbink suggest that the reply to that question should be in the negative.

The argument put forward by the Commission is particularly persuasive: it submits that, with the exception of some of its provisions, in particular Article 2(1) (a) and (d), Article 7 and Article 10, the First Directive applies solely to companies which exist and which have legal personality, and it may apply to those which have been entered in the commercial register as if they had legal personality.

One of the provisions of the directive applicable to such cases would be, precisely, Article 11, the purpose of which is, in order to protect the interests of third parties, to limit the cases in which the nullity of companies covered by the directive may be declared under the legislation of the various member-States.

The Commission submits that in principle Article 11 does not apply to a declaration of nullity in the case of an entity which has no legal personality.

Since the moment of acquisition of legal personality is a matter governed by national law, and the directive contains no provision in that respect, the first question put by the national court can only be answered in the negative.

That is also my view as regards the answer to be given to that question.

That is because, as the Commission rightly points out, the directive has nothing to say regarding the acquisition of legal personality or legal capacity for companies covered by its provisions: that is a matter which is left in principle to each national legal system to regulate as it will.

Thus whilst some legal systems—the majority—make the acquisition of legal personality subject to registration of the company in the commercial register, others do not.

Dutch legislation does not impose that condition, but requires private limited liability companies (of the type known in Portugal as 'sociedades por quotas') and public limited liability companies to satisfy two conditions in order to be validly constituted: an authentic instrument of constitution must have been executed and the company must have passed a prior administrative scrutiny, evidenced by a ministerial authorisation.

It may be said that a system of that type, in which the acquisition of legal personality for companies is not dependent on completing registration formalities, fits awkwardly into the scheme of the directive, which is conceived largely on the basis that the commercial register is an important means of safeguarding the interests of third parties and protecting business transactions, especially in international trade. It may be noted, for example, that the absence of such registration is not listed among the grounds of nullity in Article 11, a reflection of the fact that in most of the member-States there is legislation linking the acquisition of collective personality to registration on such a register.

However, that does not mean that the national legislation linking the acquisition of legal personality to events prior to registration is incompatible in any way with the directive.

On the other hand, the directive itself contains no provisions—whether procedural or substantive—concerning the conditions under which a company may be deemed to exist prior to the acquisition of legal personality.

Article 12 refers only to the effects of a declaration of nullity made in accordance with Article 11.

The latter does not require the national legislature—subject to the provision in Article 12—to choose between the various kinds of nullity which may attach to any of the defects listed in Article 11 (2) (nullity, declaration of nullity, non-existence). Similarly, as regards procedure, no preference is expressed in the directive for a system whereby such kinds of nullity may be pleaded by way of a preliminary objection or for a system whereby they may be declared only in the context of separate proceedings.

It is thus clear that the first question put by the national court cannot be answered in the affirmative: from the directive there is nothing to be inferred as to whether a company which does not fulfil the conditions for valid constitution laid down by national law may be regarded as a company in existence so long as it has not been the subject of a declaration of nullity and whether, in order to obtain such a declaration, separate proceedings must have been instituted for the purpose.

Such a matter must be governed by national legislation and the directive itself allows the member-States ample freedom in that respect.

That conclusion reduces the importance of the question—expressly dealt with by the Commission—whether the restrictions contained in the rules regarding nullity laid down in Article 11 apply only to companies having legal personality or whether they may be applied to companies which do not yet have legal personality but which exist, in so far as they have commenced business and acts have been done in their name.

In order to examine that question it is necessary to consider the question of nullity in the case of anomalous companies.

The general scheme of the directive and a number of its provisions indicate, in fact, that the Community legislature intended to define and co-ordinate national rules on nullity for companies having legal personality or entered on the commercial register as if they had it (since, as we have seen, national legislation most often makes the acquisition of legal personality subject to such registration). The wording of Article 11 itself, as we have seen, supports that interpretation; and Article 7, the only one which expressly envisages acts carried out in the name of a company before it has acquired legal personality, appears to confirm it.

However, I do not consider it necessary to resolve that question in these proceedings.

Not only did the national court not expressly refer the matter to this Court (that is, the question whether the grounds for nullity before the acquisition of legal personality are restricted to those set out in Article 11), but the question is not pertinent to the circumstances concerned in the main action.

In the first place, Ubbink was not entered on the commercial register as a private limited liability company, but only as a private limited company in formation, subject to the rules governing partnerships (the possibility that registration in that form might mislead third parties as to the true nature of the company falls outside the ambit of the questions referred by the national court); in the second place, the two acts necessary for the valid constitution of a company and which, it is agreed, were lacking—the authentic instrument of constitution and the certificate of approval—are expressly referred to in the grounds of nullity given in Article 11 (paragraph 2 (a)), and no other was mentioned in the course of the proceedings.

B

Do any of the circumstances referred to in the other three questions put by the national court affect the conclusion I have reached as to the first question?

It will be recalled that in those questions the Hoge Raad asked whether the reply to the first question would be otherwise if:

> there was no authentic instrument of constitution or the rules of preventive control were not complied with, or both;
>
> there was an organisation of persons and assets which had the outward appearance of a company, and in whose name legal actions had been carried out;
>
> activities had been carried on by an organisation having a legal form other than those referred to in the First Directive (for instance, a partnership) and registered in that legal form in the commercial register, but under a name which, save as regards the indication of the legal form, was identical to the name of the company covered by the directive but not yet properly constituted.

As regards the first question (Question (b) of the reference for a preliminary ruling), it has no influence on the reply to be given to Question (a) since both the requirements referred to therein must be satisfied, as appears to be the case in Dutch law, in order validly to constitute a company. It would only be otherwise if only one of those requirements sufficed for the valid constitution of a company under national law: the reply to Question (a) must therefore stand in any case as regards the consequences of failure to fulfil the requirements necessary for the valid constitution of a company.

As far as the other two questions are concerned, the national court was referring directly to the situation with which the main proceedings are concerned.

In the first place, legal actions were carried out in the name of a private limited liability company which had not yet been properly constituted since it failed to fulfil the two requirements for that purpose imposed by Dutch legislation.

Whether, and to what extent, it is particular important to recognize the outward appearance of a private limited liability company that might present, is a matter for national law, since the directive contains no information in that respect.

However, in the case of a company in formation which has not yet acquired legal personality, the directive requires national law to comply with Article 7 of the directive, which provides that 'if, before a company being formed has acquired legal personality, action has been carried out in its name and the company does not assume the obligations arising from such action, the persons who acted shall, without limit, be jointly and severally liable therefore, unless otherwise agreed.' That, and only that, is what the First Directive requires as far as safeguarding the interests of third parties in the case of companies still in formation is concerned.

In other words, it is for each member-State to determine by its legislation whether and to what extent, regardless of the fact that a company is 'in formation' and apart from the personal liability of those who have so acted (Article 7 of the directive), the fact that such actions have been carried out in the name of the company which has not been properly constituted constitutes in law sufficient legal grounds for a declaration of nullity in respect of the anomalous or de facto company and, in particular, whether for that purpose there must exist an organisation of persons or assets.

It appears from the documents on the file that Ubbink Isolatie was registered in the commercial register as a private limited liability company 'in formation' subject to the rules governing partnerships.

However, Article 11 of the directive makes no special provision for the case where a member-State's national legislation permits the registration of a company (whether public or private limited liability) yet to be constituted as a company 'in formation' regarding it as a partnership and having its own rules regarding the nullity of such an entity.

Moreover, the First Directive applies solely to the types of company referred to in Article 1, which do not include partnerships; consequently, the definition of the conditions to be satisfied for their constitution or their nullity falls, as a rule, outside the scope of the directive and is therefore a matter for national legislation to regulate.

I consider, however, contrary to the argument put forward by Ubbink, that when the existence of a partnership is equivalent, under an express disposition of national law or in accordance with the interpretation given of it by legal doctrine or the courts, to a company in formation, which is covered by the First Directive, Article 7 of the directive must apply. Were it otherwise, its aim of safeguarding the interests of third parties could be frustrated by the legal expedient of regarding such an organisation as a partnership. The national legislature is therefore not at liberty to organize at will the rules governing liability for such entities (for example, by making solely the management or the shareholders liable); it has already been stipulated, by Article 7, that the persons who acted in the name of the company must be made liable.

3. Conclusion

In the light of the foregoing I suggest that the replies to be given to the questions put by the Hoge Raad should be as follows:

1. Each member-State has power to lay down its own rules governing the nullity of companies in formation of the types listed in Article 1 of the first Council Directive of 9 March 1968 on co-ordination of safeguards, which, for the protection of the interests of members and others, are required by member-States of companies, provided that in so

doing they comply with Article 7 of the directive. Consequently, there is nothing in the provisions contained in Section III of the First Directive which makes it necessary to regard a private limited liability in formation which does not satisfy the conditions for valid constitution of such a company laid down by national law, but in whose name actions have been carried out, as a company which exists until a declaration of nullity has been made in proceedings instituted for that purpose.

2. That reply given above remains the same in all the circumstances referred to by the national court in the second, third and fourth questions.

DECISION [by the court]: By judgment of 24 April 1987, which was received at the Court on 30 April 1987, the Hoge Raad der Nederlanden referred to the Court for a preliminary ruling under Article 177 EEC four questions on the interpretation of the rules on nullity laid down in Section III of the First Council Directive (68/151) of 9 March 1968 on co-ordination of safeguards which, for the protection of the interests of members and others, are required of companies within the meaning of the second paragraph of Article 58 of the Treaty ([1968] OJ Spec Ed 41, [1978] 1 Commercial Laws of Europe 325) (hereinafter referred to as 'the First Directive').

Those questions arose in proceedings concerning the performance of a contract between Dak-en Wandtechniek BV and the company calling itself Ubbink Isolatie BV (hereinafter referred to as 'the appellant').

At the time of the contested contract, a partnership was registered in the Commercial Register under the name 'Ubbink Isolatie BV io' (Ubbink Isolatie, a private limited company in the course of formation), listing as partners Ubbink Nederland BV and Isetco BV, both private limited companies, and as general representative, with the title of director, a certain Mr. Juraske. However, there was no private limited company registered in the Commercial Register under the name 'Ubbink Isolatie BV'. The national court found that as there has been no notarial instrument establishing a private limited company under the name 'Ubbink Isolatie BV' the company had not been duly formed.

The appellant concluded the contested contract with Dak-en Wandtechniek under the name 'Ubbink Isolatie BV' without the addition of the expression 'in the course of formation' and proceedings were brought against it under that name by Dak-en Wandtechniek before the Arrondissementsrechtbank (District Court) Arnhem for the termination of that contract and to establish liability thereunder; the appellant also initially submitted its defence under that name.

During the proceedings before that court, the appellant contended that Dak-en Wandtechniek was wrong to bring its action against 'Ubbink Isolatie BV'. The summons issued upon the application of Dak-en Wandtechniek was void and the application could not be granted because 'Ubbink Isolatie BV' did not exist.

In an interlocutory judgment, the Arondissementsrechtbank Arnhem held that even if Ubbink Isolatie BV had not been formed at all or if the instrument intended to form it was defective, the private limited liability company could not be said not to exist merely on that ground. The company existed until such time as it was wound up or a declaration of nullity was made in accordance with the Dutch Civil Code. Section 182(1) of Book 2 of that Code provides that where business has been carried on in the name of a private limited liability company which has not been registered in the Commercial Register and before an instrument forming the company has been drawn up and certified by a notary or without a declaration that the Minister has no objection to the formation of the company, a declaration of nullity may be obtained on the application of any interested party or of the public prosecutor.

The appellant appealed against that judgment to the Gerechtshof (Court of Appeal) Arnhem, which confirmed the judgment at first instance. The appellant then appealed to the Hoge Raad, claiming to be 'the party to the proceedings which, at earlier instances, was named as defendant and appeared as Ubbink Isolatie BV, a private limited liability company'. According to the statement of the grounds of appeal, section 182 does not apply to a case such as this in which no private limited liability company has been constituted and where actions have been wrongfully carried out on behalf or in the name of a fictitious private limited liability company which does not have the structure which is essential for the existence of such a company and in regard to which no instrument constituting the company has been executed.

Since it considered that section 182 must be interpreted in the light of the provisions of Section III of the First Directive, in particular Articles 11 and 12 thereof, the Hoge Raad stayed the proceedings pending a preliminary ruling from the Court of Justice on the following questions:

1. Where business is carried on in the name of a company within the meaning of the First Directive which has not, however, been constituted under the applicable national law because no authentic instrument of constitution within the meaning of Article 11(2) (a) of the directive was executed or the rules of preventive control, also within the meaning of Article 11 (2)(a), were not complied with, do the rules laid down in Section III of the First Directive mean that in proceedings brought against it 'the company' must be treated as being in existence so long as its nullity has not been declared in separate proceedings for a declaration of nullity and for the winding up of 'the company'?

2. Does it make any difference to the answer to Question 1 whether (i) only the instrument of constitution was not executed or only the rules of preventive control were not complied with, or (ii) the instrument was not executed and the aforesaid rules were not complied with either?

3. Does it make any difference to the answer to Question 1 whether (i) business is carried on within the framework of an organisation of persons and assets which—apart from the fact that business is done in the name of a company—gives the outward appearance of a company or (ii) business is carried on where there is no question of the existence of such an organisation?

4. Is it relevant to the answer to Question 1 that business is carried on within the framework of an organisation which, according to the applicable national law, has a different legal form from that of a company within the meaning of the First Directive, for example the legal form of a "vennootschap onder firma' (partnership), and is registered as such in the Commercial Register under a name which, save as regards the indication of the legal form, is identical to the name of the unconstituted company under which business is carried on?

Reference is made to the Report for the Hearing for a fuller account of the facts of the case, the procedure and the observations submitted to the Court, which are mentioned or discussed hereinafter only in so far as is necessary for the reasoning of the Court.

The first two questions put by the national court, which should be considered together, seek essentially to ascertain whether the rules governing nullity laid down in the First Directive are applicable in a case in which acts have been carried out in the name of a limited liability company, a legal form covered by the First Directive, which has not been constituted in national law by reason of the feature to complete the formalities required by that law for the formation of a company. The third and fourth questions seek to determine whether the reply to the first two questions would be different where the outward appearance of a company within the meaning of the First Directive has been created by the existence of an organisation of persons or a company not covered by the First Directive.

It should be observed that the purpose of the First Directive is to co-ordinate the safeguards required by member-States of companies having a share capital and private limited liability companies in order to protect, in particular, the interests of third parties.

Section I of the First Directive provides for formalities in regard to disclosure intended to provide third parties with prior information on the essential features of companies within the meaning of the said directive. As is indicated in one of the recitals in the preamble to the directive, disclosure is intended to permit third parties to ascertain the contents of the basic documents of the company and other information concerning it, especially particulars of the persons who are authorized to bind the company.

Consequently, third parties may legitimately rely on the information concerning a company within the meaning of the First Directive when that information has been the subject of disclosure in accordance with the provisions of Section I of the First Directive. The purpose of the directive is not therefore to permit third parties to rely on appearances created by the company's organs or representatives if those appearances do not conform to the information contained in the public register.

Consequently, the rules concerning the nullity of companies laid down in Section III of the First Directive apply only where third parties have been led to believe by information published in accordance with Section I that a company within the meaning of the First Directive exists.

On the other hand, third parties are not in that position when no formal disclosure has been made concerning a company within the meaning of the First Directive, in particular when the formalities required by national law for incorporation—a certified instrument of constitution and a preventive administrative check—have not been completed and for that reason the company appears in the public register as a company in the course of formation.

The reply to the first two questions must therefore be that the rules on the nullity of companies contained in the First Directive do not apply where the acts involved were performed in the name of a private limited liability company whose existence is not confirmed by the public register because the formalities for incorporation required by national law have not been completed.

Since that reply permits the national court to resolve the question of Community law which has been raised, there is no need to consider the other circumstances set out in the questions.

However, it must be pointed out that in so far as acts performed in the name of a limited liability company not yet incorporated are regarded by the applicable national law as having been performed in the name of a company being formed within the meaning of Article 7 of the First Directive, it is for the national law in question to provide, in accordance, with that provision, that the persons who perform them are to be jointly and severally liable.

Costs

The costs incurred by the Kingdom of the Netherlands and the Commission of the European Communities, which have submitted observations to the Court, are not recoverable. Since these proceedings are, in so far as the parties to the main proceedings are concerned, in the nature of a step in the action pending before the national court, the decision on costs is a matter for that court.

On those grounds THE COURT (Sixth Chamber), in answer to the questions referred to it by the Hoge Raad der Nederlanden by judgment of 24 April 1987,

HEREBY RULES:

The rules on the nullity of companies contained in the First Council Directive of 9 March 1968 (68/151) do not apply where the acts in question were performed in the name of a private limited liability company whose existence is not confirmed by the public register because the formalities for incorporation required by national law have not been completed.

José Manuel Otero Lastres, *Company Law*

in SPANISH BUSINESS LAW 153 (Bernardo M. Cremades, Gen Ed. 1985)
(excerpts pages 157–158)

1.1.2.1. The Company Pending Incorporation

The fact that compliance with the above two requirements (public deed and its recording at the Mercantile Registry) is not simultaneous implies that, during a certain period of time, the company has already been defined in the incorporation agreement but lacks legal personality, since it has not yet been recorded. In this case, the company is described as 'pending creation' or 'in formation'. This is done when the founders agree to the creation of the company, in compliance with all regulations, as a prior step to starting up operations.

The major problem posed by a company 'pending creation' is regulating the contracts entered into by its promoters before the company has reached full legal personality upon recording. Article 7 of the Stock Company Law (Ley de Sociedades Anónimas, "LSA') and Article 6 of the Limited Liability Company Law (Ley de Sociedades de Responsabilidad Limitada, "LSRL') deal with this problem. The regulation of contracts entered into by companies 'pending incorporation' can be summarized in the following way:

Contracts which are not necessary for the creation of the company—those which are preparatory and facilitate the functioning of the future company—are transferred to the company once it obtains full legal personality, provided that two requirements are met: (a) the company is recorded; and (b) the company ratifies such contracts within three months of recording. If the company is not recorded or, once recorded, does not ratify the contracts, they will not be binding on the company. The promoters who entered into such contracts will be jointly and severally liable for them to the contracting parties.

On the other hand, the company will always be liable for acts and contracts necessary for creating the company—those which arise from the double requirement of a public deed and recording.

These rules are also applicable to general and limited partnerships, based on a joint interpretation of Articles 118–120 of the [*Codigo Comercial*], with the exception of the three-month term for ratifying non-necessary contracts entered into by the promoters. In general and limited partnerships, there is no fixed term for ratifying such contracts.

Nevertheless, such ratification or denial must take place within a reasonable period of time.

1.1.2.2. *De Facto* Companies

A *de facto* company exists when an incorporation agreement has been signed and an 'entity' distinct from its individual partners is operating, but this entity lacks legal personality due to non-fulfillment of one or both of the requirements set forth in Article 119 of the [*Codigo Comercial*] [preparation of a legally sufficient deed and recording of that deed in the appropriate Mercantile registry: Ed.]. These companies are not illegal, since the [*Codigo Comercial*] grants them a certain legal status. In order to study the legal status of *de facto* companies, a distinction must be made between whether they are stock companies, limited liability companies, or any other type of company.

As has been stated, in the case of stock companies and limited liability companies, the law provides for the constitutive nature of the double requirement of a public deed and its recording (Article 6 of the LSA and Article 5 of the LSRL). As a result, if both requirements are not met, the company does not exist. Thus, *de facto* stock companies or limited liability companies cannot exist. Third parties are protected by Article 120 of the [*Codigo Comercial*], which declares the promoters jointly and severally liable to third parties with whom they contracted, based on the appearance of legality.

In other types of companies, most treatise writers feel that *de facto* companies are full-fledged companies. A distinction must be made between internal and external effects, in order to determine the scope of the legal status of such companies.

For *internal* matters, the incorporation agreement remains valid despite the *de facto* nature of the company. The partners may mutually claim performance of the agreement, provided that it was executed in compliance with essential legal requirements (Article 117 [*Codigo Comercial*]).

Which legal provisions are applicable to the internal regulation of *de facto* companies is an issue which has not been settled in case law. On some occasions the courts have applied the provisions governing general partnerships, but many court opinions have applied the provisions of the [*Codigo Civil*] concerning community property (Articles 392 et seq. of the [*Codigo Civil*]).

For *external* matters relating to third parties, most treatise writers feel that *de facto* companies have three characteristics:

- Lack of legal personality, which implies the lack of company assets separate from the partners' assets.
- Nullity of contracts entered into by the company with third parties, since pursuant to Article 118 of the [*Codigo Comercial*], contracts are only enforceable when the requirements of Article 119 have been met (Public Deed and recording).
- Liability of the promoters to third parties with whom they have contracted in the name of the company (Article 120 of the [*Codigo Comercial*]).

Despite the above, the TS [*Tribunal Supremo*] has recognized in some of its opinions that a *de facto* company has 'personality to act in the business world,' and that '(it) cannot fail to recognize... (parties) who recognized it outside the lawsuit and contracted with it' (e.g., TS opinions of 8 February 1960, 6 April 1961 and 16 April 1980).

Phonogram Ltd. v. Lane

Court of Appeal, Civil Division
[1982] QB 938, [1981] 3 All ER 182, [1981] 3 WLR 736, [1982] 3 CMLR 615, (47 MLR 671)
9, 10 March 1981

Reread the case. It appears in Chapter 6 at page 628.

The imposition of the standard enunciated in the First Company Law Directive has garnered its share of critics, especially in Britain. Are the points made in the following excerpt valid?

Oshkosh B'Gosh, Inc. v. Dan Marbel, Inc. Limited

English High Court (Queen's Bench Division)
[1988] 3 CMLR 214
11 November 1987

Sir Neil Lawson:

This is an appeal by the second defendant, Mr. Edward Lewis Craze, against an order made by Master Grant on 9 June 1987, under Order XIV virtually, when he refused to set aside a judgment in default of some $192,000 plus interest which had been signed against the second defendant, Mr. Craze, on 29 December 1986. There is also an appeal by the same defendant against an order made by the Master on the same date whereby he gave leave to the plaintiffs, who are a company incorporated in the State of Wisconsin in the United States, Oshkosh B'Gosh Incorporated, leave to set aside a default judgment entered against the first defendant, a company of the name of Dan Marbel Incorporated Limited, also signed in default on 29 December 1986. There is also an application by the plaintiffs to be released from undertakings given to Master Grant on the same occasion whereby the plaintiffs undertook in fact to take the necessary steps to set aside the default judgment against the first defendant.

The action commenced by a specially endorsed writ issued on 12 September 1986 and it claimed the price of goods sold and delivered by the plaintiffs to the defendants during the period February 1984 to February 1985 in the total principal sum of $192,666.59. There is a schedule attached to the statement of claim endorsed on the writ which sets out in detail each of the orders, each of the invoices, the dates and the amounts involved in the total sum.

The writ was served on the defendants by their solicitors (the same soliciotrs at that stage acted for both defendants) on or about 30 September. So far as the first defendants are concerned, Dan Marbel Inc, Ltd., there was no acknowledge of service or notice of intention to defend but such an acknowledgement and notice was in fact filed in due time by the second defendant. The second defendant's defence became due, therefore, on 27 October 1986. He did not file any defence, and in default of defence judgment was signed against him on 29 December. It was also signed against the first defendants,

Dan Marbel Inc. Ltd., on the same day because there had been no acknowledgement of service or notice of intention to defend.

The first named defendant, Dan Marbel Inc. Ltd., is not involved or interested in the appeal.

The claim which the plaintiffs make in their specially endorsed writ against the second defendant is primarily under section 108 subsection (4) of the Companies Act 1948, which was the Act in force at the time of the relevant transactions, not then having been replaced by the Consolidation Act of 1985 or the Companies Act of 1985 which now replaces it in the same terms, or at least if there are differences they are of no importance.

A further claim is made not actually in the statement of claim specifically but I think it arises under the statement of claim, and it is a claim which is made against the second defendant under section 9 of the European Communities Act 1972, again which has now been replaced by section 36 subsection (4) of the Companies Act 1985. There is no material difference in the wording of these sections but, of course, it is the 1972 Act section which applies, since that was the Act in force at the time of the transactions in question. Involved in that claim, I think, also is a claim at common law which is expressed in a separate paragraph of the statement of claim really claiming against the second defendant for the price of the goods sold and delivered as if he were a principal to the contract.

....

Certain facts about the identity of the first defendants, Dan Marbel Inc. Ltd. There was a registered limited company named Egormite Ltd., which had been incorporated on 6 November 1979. By a special resolution Egormite resolved to change its name to Dan Marbel Incorporated Limited on 6 April 1980 when it is said, and it has not been disputed, that the company registrar was notified on the same date of the special resolution. But no certificate of incorporation of that company, that is Dan Marbel Inc. Ltd., was issued in accordance with section 18 subsection (3) of the 1948 Companies Act, which is a definite requirement for the incorporation of a company following a change of name, until 5 June 1985, that is to say, after these transactions the subject of the plaintiffs' claim had come to an end. That certificate bore the same number as the certificate of incorporation of Egormite. Again, this is in accordance with the usual practice. It is a company which has changed its name like some women change their name on marriage although they do not have to go through a special resolution notified to the Registrar of Companies.

Now, there is a case in the Court of Appeal Shakelford & Co v. Dangerfield ((1868) LR 3 CP 407), and this is the accepted authority that a change of name is not complete until a certificate of incorporation in the new name is issued, and therefore there was no company Dan Marbel Incorporated Limited in existence during the period February 1984 to February 1985 when the transactions the subject of this claim took place. Nevertheless, those who ran Egormite—and the second defendant, Mr. Craze, was quite clearly the main participant in the dealings with the plaintiff throughout the relevant period—used the new name and the old registration number printed on their business documents, and these documents bore no trace of the existence of Egormite Ltd. Included in the business documents were the order forms covering the goods the subject of the plaintiff's claim in this action, and these are an exhibit to an affidavit sworn in support of the plaintiff's claim and they speak for themselves. There is no mention or hint of the existence of Egormite, and there is no indication that Dan Marbel Inc. Ltd. is the name under which some other entity or individual is trading.

I must say, but of course I do not suggest this was done with any ulterior motive, that I cannot think of anything more likely to confuse a person with whom it was proposed to have dealings than to have the name of a non-existent company with the registration number of an existing company which had a name completely dissimilar to the name on the notepaper and did not indicate it was a 'trading as' position. It really is most misleading to a person with whom dealings are going to be proposed.

I now proceed on the basis that the second defendant, Mr. Craze, manifestly appears from the pages of exhibited documents as the person controlling the activities of Egormite in the relevant period.

Now, as to the grounds. First of all, section 108 subsection (4) of the Companies Act reads as follows, and I only read the relevant part: 'If an officer of a company or any person on its behalf'—(a) relates to the use of the seal which has not got the company's full and proper registered name on it, which includes the word 'Limited' or an abbreviation of 'Limited'—'(b) Issues or authorises the issue of any business letter of the company or any notice or other official publication of the company, or signs or authorises to be signed on behalf of the company any bill of exchange, promissory note, endorsement, cheque or order for money or goods wherein its name is not mentioned in manner aforesaid'—and then (c) is not here relevant—'he shall be liable to a fine not exceeding £50, and shall further be personally liable to the holder of the bill of exchange, promissory note, cheque or order for money or goods for the amount thereof unless it is duly paid by the company'.

The orders for goods sold and delivered in the present case which are exhibited to the plaintiffs' affidavits are, I think, business letters or company notices or official publications of a company, which did not exist, called Dan Marbel Incorporated Limited; but if they fall within (b) so that authorisation of their issue simpliciter is an offence this does not give rise to a civil liability. It is only the second limb of 4(b) which creates a civil liability. So the real question here is whether these orders for goods were signed, or authorized to be signed, by the second defendant, because lest this is shown there is no civil liability on him if, as was the case, the goods ordered were not paid for. I say 'if, as was the case, the goods ordered were not paid for,' because the subsection concludes by saying that there is personal liability on the person who signs or authorises signature unless it is duly paid by the company.

Now, on authority it is quite clear that the plaintiffs here are in the position of a holder of an order for goods, and therefore they come within the last part of subsection (4), that is to say, they are persons to whom there is personal liability because they are holders of an order for goods, and they are liable for the amount thereof unless it is duly paid and so forth.

Now, it seems that the relevant orders for goods bear the printed name of Dan Marbel Incorporated Limited, and not that of Egormite, in at least two places; but none of them appear to have any signature at all, as the word signature is commonly understood. Whilst I found it unnecessary to decide the point, I am of the opinion that the orders for goods exhibited do not fall within the wording of section 108(4)(b) because they do not bear any signature of any kind. The mere fact that the first defendants,' not Egormite's, name is printed on them does not constitute a signature, the point being that in my judgment not only is there a difficulty I think about printed signatures, especially when they are printed on a series of forms, as whether they are really an acknowledgement, but of course in this case for the reason that Dan Marbel Incorporated Limited is a non-existent person and it therefore could not sign.

Therefore, in my judgment this is not a case where section 108(4)(b) applies, and the second defendant is not liable on the basis that he signed, or authorized to be signed on behalf of the company, orders for goods. I think my reasoning about the necessity of a signature of some kind is really implicit in the reasoning of the Court of Appeal in the case of John Wilkes (Footwear) v. Lee International (a Court of Appeal case decided on 2 July 1985, of which I have a transcript).

I now turn to section 9 of the European Communities Act 1972. The relevant part of that is subsection (2) and, as I have said, this is reproduced in the corresponding section of the Companies Act 1985, but it is in the 1972 Act with which we are concerned. It reads:

> Where a contract purports to be made by a company or by a person as agent for a company at a time when the company has not been formed, then, subject to any agreement to the contrary, the contract shall have effect as a contract entered into by the person purporting to act for the company or as agent for it, and he shall be personally liable on the contract accordingly.

So the simple question (though perhaps the answer is not very simple) is whether the second defendant purported to act for an unformed company, a company not yet formed, when he purported to make the contracts by that company which are represented by the orders exhibited for the goods the purchase price of which is presently sued for. On the exhibited documents there can be no doubt at all that it was the second defendant in all cases who purported to act for the company in placing the orders, and that company was not existing. I say there is no doubt on the exhibited documents. I have not done the exercise in full, but in many, many cases it is possible to link up specific orders which are exhibited with specific letters or specific telexes which are signed by the second defendant in relation to that particular order. They specify the number of the order in many cases, they specify the goods and the subject of the order in many cases and therefore I have no doubt that it was the second defendant in all cases who was purporting to act, not as agent for the company, but purporting to act for the company, and the company was a company which was not formed. It was not formed until the new certificate with the incorporation of issue in 1985.

The plaintiffs' case in my judgment, therefore, exactly falls within section 9 subsection (2) of the 1972 Act. The fact that the plaintiffs never intended to contract with the second defendant personally, which would be fatal to a claim made at common law, is wholly irrelevant to situations to which section 9 subsection (2) applies. For that I rely on the decision of the Court of Appeal in Phonogram Ltd. v. Lane ([1982] 1 QB 928, [1982] 3 CMLR 615).

Therefore, in my judgment the learned Master was quite correct in refusing to set aside the default judgment against the second defendant on the ground that the second defendant could not raise any triable issue in answer to the claim that he was personally liable and in answer specifically to the claim that he was personally liable which is made in the statement of claim and which is supported by section 9 subsection (2) of the European Communities Act 1972.

As I say, I have not found it necessary to decide the point under section 108 subsection (4), but in my opinion the orders here do not fall within that because, as I said, they bear no signature and because, indeed, the person who purported to give the orders did not exist and could not sign anything. It therefore follows that the defendant's appeal is dismissed with costs.

Comments and Questions

1. As in the United States, the specifics of liability for pre-incorporation transactions varies among the Member States of the European Union. Some of the differences can be explained by differences in the incorporation process. German law makes a distinction between the liability of incorporators, whose exposure is usually limited to the time period before the new company's articles of incorporation are notarized, and all others who seek to contract on behalf of the company-to-be-formed. French law provides effectively for novation by action of the company-to-be-formed that has the effect of releasing the incorporators from all liability for the obligations assumed. The English approach is closer to that of the United States. Do the differences in the legal rules *de jure* result in significant differences in result?

2. The differences between the requirements for corporate formation in civil law countries, such as France and Germany, and the much simpler requirements for corporate formation in England and Ireland become important in the context of developing a harmonized law of pre-incorporation liability. One of the critical differences between the civil law incorporation process and that of the common law turns on the existence of a period of time in civil law incorporation when a corporation has been formed but is not yet fully recognized as an independent legal entity, that is, when a company is 'in formation.' The *Ubbink Isolatie* case provides an illustration of the importance of the 'in formation' concept for purposes of determining the application of the rules on pre-incorporation liability as well as the rules applicable to issues of corporate nullity. The Anglo-American system of incorporation recognizes no interim periods of corporate formation. A corporation does not exist until the time all documents are properly filed and accepted. But at the time such documents are properly filed and accepted, the corporation is fully formed and legally valid. Notions of special rules for pre-incorporation liability geared to interim periods of corporate formation make no sense in the Anglo-American incorporation process. The significance of the effect of these differences for purposes of harmonizing the law of pre-incorporation liability are described with respect to Spanish law in the excerpt by José Manuel Otero Lastres, above. But, even given these differences, would it still be possible to argue, on the basis of that excerpt and *Ubbink Isolatie*, that for all practical purposes, the law of pre-incorporation liability is converging in Europe?

3. Convergence, to the extent it is actually occurring, does not necessarily imply the sort of close harmonization that results in equivalent application of the legal principle across different legal systems. Thus, it is also possible to argue that the difference in the structure of the legal rules for incorporation suggests some of the limits of programs of legal harmonization. The materials you have read indicate that Member State courts have been able to bend harmonizing legislation to the needs of Member State law rather than interpret Member State law transposing a harmonization directive for consistency with the practice of other Member States. *Phonogram* provides a marvelous example of this tendency in the British courts. There, the court, per the late Lord Denning, refused to accord the text of the provision its contextual definition, and on that basis reduced the possibility of uniform application. Here is an instance where the peculiarities of transposition of directives had a substantive effect, reducing the likelihood of uniformity. The Company Law Directive, in its official French version (there was no official English version at the time) speaks of acts "accomplis au nom d'un société en formation," that is of acts realized in the name of a company in formation. But the term 'com-

pany in formation' makes no sense in English because the process of incorporation in England, as in the U.S., does not contemplate a period when the corporation has a semi-formal or contingent legal existence The English transposition of the Directive, therefore, speaks of contracts purporting to be made by a company "at a time when the company has not been formed." The result, as demonstrated in *Phonogram*, logically follows form this difference. A uniform standard of liability for pre-incorporation transactions is imposed with different effects in countries following the French model from the effect in countries following the English model. Lord Denning justifies this result, in part, by suggesting that, since a directive is meant to harmonize only with respect to the result to be achieved, variations in application should be expected.

4. If the purpose of harmonization, as was suggested in Chapter 6, was to provide a flexible system where the peculiarities of the laws of individual Member States were accommodated, but where such peculiarities would be subordinated to the overall goals of uniform application (and thus, harmonization), then perhaps the effort to harmonize the law of liability for pre-incorporation transactions can be judged a failure. Do you agree? Would Lord Denning agree?

5. Compare the analysis of the Supreme Court of Colorado in *Micciche*, above, with that of the English High Court (Queen's Bench) in *Oshkosh B'Gosh*. Would the Colorado Supreme Court have reached the same result as the English High Court had the facts of *Oshkosh B'Gosh* been before it? Would the English High Court have reached the same result as that of the Colorado Supreme Court had *Micciche* been decided under English law?

---

2. *Liability for Pre-Incorporation Transactions in Japan*

Liability for pre-incorporation transactions in Japan is both perhaps narrower in scope less forgiving than its American counterpart. Liability is concentrated on the promoter, who is responsible for her own transactions, but perhaps also for those which might otherwise adversely affect the to-be-formed entity. As you read the excerpt that follows, consider whether the Japanese approach is similar to the English approach, or provides a unique approach to the problem of assigning liability for pre-incorporation transactions.

Bruce W. MacLennan, *Establishing a Stock Corporation in Japan after the 1990 Revision of the Commercial Code*

1 Pac. Rim L. & Pol'y J. 127 (1992)
(excerpts pages 134–135)

Promoter Liability[44]

The 1990 Code revisions left intact provisions which require the promoters and directors of the new corporation to purchase any shares remaining unsubscribed when the cor-

---

44. Under U.S. law, incorporators do little more than sign the articles of incorporation and have no statutory liability. *See* 1 MBCA Ann 96. On the other hand, if the incorporator promotes the corporation, the incorporator may be liable for pre-incorporation contracts and secret profits. MBCA §2.04.

poration comes into existence,[45] and which make the promoters and directors liable for unreceived payments for shares.[46] The 1990 amendment added provisions making promoters and directors jointly and severally liable to the corporation for undelivered contributions in kind[47] and for any shortfall to the corporation in the event the value of any contributed property is lower than the value stipulated for it in the articles of incorporation.[48]

The 1990 revision did not change Code provisions governing promoter liability. Promoters are jointly and severally liable to the corporation for (1) damages accruing from their negligence in connection with the incorporation;[49] (2) their promotive acts[50] in the event the corporation does not come into existence;[51] and (3) damages accruing to third parties as a consequence of bad faith or gross negligence.[52] Promoters may also be held jointly and severally liable with directors and auditors as specified in other provisions of the Commercial Code.[53] Finally, any non-promoter who permits the use of his or her name on documents in connection with the incorporation[54] incurs the same liability as a promoter.[55]

Comments and Questions

1. The Japanese promoter, to a greater extent than in Western countries, assumes the role of guarantor of the proper completion of the incorporation process. To what extent does the imposition of this sort of specific liability help to ensure that companies are properly formed? Would your answer change if a promoter could insure against liability for faulty incorporation, or otherwise obtain indemnification against liability?

2. In what other respects does the Japanese system of promoter liability differ from that of the United States? Of the EU? Is the difference solely of form or does it have a substantial substantive component?

3. If there is substantial convergence of the nature of promoter or incorporator liability for pre-incorporation transactions between the United States, the Member States of the EU and Japan, does it follow that harmonization of the laws of these jurisdictions through an international treaty—creating obligations in the form of the EU directive—would be appropriate or desirable? What objections, if any, could be raised?

4. Think back to the discussion in Chapters 2 and three about the socio-economic context in which Japanese law, and particularly, Japanese corporate law, operates. This

45. Comm. Code Art. 192(1).
46. Comm. Code Art. 192(2).
47. *Id.*
48. Comm. Code Art. 192-2. The value of contributions in kind is determined at the time the corporation comes into existence. *Id.*
49. Comm. Code Art. 193(1).
50. Legal obligations under agreements executed in connection with the incorporation.
51. Comm. Code Art. 194(1).
52. Comm. Code Art. 193(2).
53. Comm. Code Art. 195.
54. Share application forms, advertisements soliciting share subscribers, a prospectus, etc.
55. Comm. Code Art. 198. Promoter liability extends to the attorney acting as a promoter for purposes of the incorporation as well, until the corporation comes into existence. The risk is minimal in most cases where no property is transferred to the new subsidiary. In the event of a property transfer, liability is customarily limited by a waiver of liability signed by an authorized official of the foreign parent corporation.

is a system in which the informal operates with a substantial amount of legitimacy. Does the approach taken by the Japanese fits naturally in this context? Does your answer affect, or is it affected by, your assumptions about the ease with which norms can be translated across cultures?

5. In a sense, the law of promoter liability can be understood as a peculiar subset of the law of contract involving agents and non-existent entities, or entities in the course of formation. It might be possible to argue, then, that the entire subject of promoter liability is unnecessary within corporate law and that states should shy away from specialized legislation with respect to promoter liability. Does the strength of this argument depend, in part, on the way in which one characterizes or understands the basic nature of corporations? In other words, would the approach to this question change depending on whether a fiction-concession or contract theory of the firm were adopted?

3. *The Effects of Defective Incorporation in the EU and Japan*

Frank Wooldridge, *Company Law in the United Kingdom and the European Community: Its Harmonization and Unification*

(1991)

(excerpts pages 23–24)

Nullity of the Company

The possibility that a company may be declared void as from its inception is a clear threat to its shareholders, creditors and employees. Although provisions of national law concerning the nullity of companies in existence before the First Directive came into effect did much to mitigate the possible effects of nullity, the possibility that discontented shareholders might bring an action for the nullity of the company based upon contractual grounds—as in France, where the theory that the company is a contract has persisted until recently, or on the basis for formal defects in the constitution, as in Germany and Italy—still remained. Articles 10–12 of the First Directive seek to co-ordinate national legal provisions concerning nullity, and to limit severely the grounds on which it can be declared. Article 10 of the Directive, which is intended to prevent the defective constitution of companies, represents a compromise between the legal provisions of the original Member States having this aim in view. Article 11 provides that the nullity of a company can be ordered only by a decision of a court on six carefully defined grounds. Article 121(1) provides that persons who contract with a company which has been annulled under the impression that it was validly incorporated receive the same protection in accordance with the provisions of Article 3 governing publicity as if the company has acted *ultra vires*. The nullity of a company entails its winding up, but does not affect the validity of any commitments entered into with it.

The view is generally taken that the question of the nullity of companies does not arise under British law. This is because § 13(3) and (4) of the Companies Act 1985 provide that a company comes into existence and becomes capable of exercising all the functions of an incorporated company as from the date of incorporation mentioned in the certificate of incorporation; furthermore, this certificate is stated by section 13(7)(a) to be conclusive evidence that the requirements of the Act in respect of registration and matters precedent and incidental thereto have been complied with, and that the association is a company authorized to be registered and is duly registered under the Act. It is thus in principle not possible to call in question matters which occurred prior to and contemporaneously with the registration, as is the case in many other Member States. It is therefore clear why the European Communities Act 1972 and the Companies Act 1985 contained no provisions implementing Articles 10–12.

Implementation in the Member States

As already pointed out, the First Directive was implemented in Great Britain by section 9 of the European Communities Act 1972. This section was repealed by Schedule 1 to the Companies Consolidation (Consequential Provisions) Act 1985. It was then replaced by sections 18, 35, 36(4), 42, 351, 711 of, and Schedule 12 to, the Companies Act 1985. The defects of implementation in Great Britain have been considered above. As already pointed out, section 35 has been replaced by sections 35–35B of the Companies Act 1988, which were incorporated therein by the Companies Act 1989. The latter Act, like its forerunners, applies to England and Wales and to Scotland but is in principle inapplicable in Northern Ireland. The Directive was implemented in France by Ordinnance no. 69-1176 of 20 December 1969, amending the law of 24 July 1966 concerning commercial companies, and also by Decree no. 69-1177 of 24 December 1969, amending Decree no. 66-236 of March 1967 on commercial registry. The implementing law was passed in the Netherlands on 29 April 1971. Implementation also occurred rather late in Belgium, by means of a law passed on 6 March 1973.

In the Republic of Ireland, pre-incorporation contracts and *ultra vires* transactions are governed respectively by section 37 and section 8(1) of the Companies Act 1963, which were enacted in anticipation of the First Directive. There are, not surprisingly, significant differences between important phrases in the Directive and those sections. It would thus seem desirable for account to be taken of the wording of the First Directive in interpreting these sections. However, Keane J. failed to adopt such an approach in the case of *Northern Bank Finance Corporation v. Quinn*. Further provisions of the First Directive were implemented in Ireland by the Statutory Instrument No. 163 of 1973 (the European Communities (Companies) Regulation 1973). The most important matters governed by this instrument would seem to be the publication of notices, and organs authorized to bind the company. In Italy, implementation took place by Presidential Decree no. 127 of 21 December 1969, which made a number of amendments to the Civil Code.

Germany was the only original Member to implement the Directive with the time limit provided for therein. This implementation took place by the so-called *Koordinierungsgesetz* of 15 August 1969. Implementation took place in Luxembourg by the law of 23 November 1972. In Denmark it took place first of all by Act no. 503 of 29 November 1972 and then by the Companies Acts nos 370 and 371 of 13 June 1973. Greece was slow to implement the First Directive, but two Presidential Decrees were enacted with this object in view on 28 November 1986 and 10 December 1986, respectively. The first of these Decrees amended the law of 1920 governing public limited companies whilst the second Decree amended the law of the same year governing private companies and partnerships limited by shares. The Directive was implemented in Portugal by means of Decree Law 282/86 of 2 September 1986 and Decree

Law 403/86 of 3 December 1986. It was implemented in Spain by Law 19/1989 of 25 July 1989.

Responsibility for Liabilities Incurred during the Period before Authorization

The above matter is dealt with in Article 4, which provides that responsibility for liabilities incurred by or on behalf of the company during the period before any authorization to commence business is granted must be specified by law, apart from liabilities incurred under contracts which are conditional on the commencement of business.

Comments and Questions

1. Compare the approaches of the European countries with that of Japan. Is it clear that there is much substantive difference in approach?

> The issue of the validity of promoters' contracts, in the American sense, is not a concern of Japanese corporation law. Only incorporators' contracts listed in a corporation's charter bind the corporation after it comes into existence. Otherwise, only promoters are bound in transactions intended for corporate formation. The promoter's liability is derived from the Civil Code[42] on obligations, not the corporate law.

Dan Fenno Henderson, *Security Markets in the United States and Japan: Distinctive Aspects Molded by Cultural, Social, Economic, and Political Differences*, 14 HASTINGS INT'L & COMP. L. REV. 263, 274 (1991).

2. Japan's approach effectively places liability on the promoter for all acts of a corporation that does not come into existence. Promoters are also liable to the corporation or to third parties for neglect of their duties in connection with the review of the incorporation procedures that must occur at the founding meeting which precedes the registration of incorporation.[1]

3. Do you think there is a strong link between liability for pre-incorporation transactions and the law of nullity (or defective incorporation)? For the suggestion of an answer in Europe, reread the *Ubbink Isolatie* case in the previous section. Can you explain the difference between a company 'in formation' and a company to which the law of nullity applies?

4. Does the concept of nullity arise under English law? American law? What are the consequences of defective incorporation under English law?

5. The People's Republic of China appears to take a very different approach to the issue of liability for pre-incorporation transactions and corporate nullity. Consider the Chinese approach in the excerpts that follows.

---

42. MINPO bk. III.

1. Bruce W. MacLennan, *Establishing a Stock Corporation in Japan after the 1990 Revision of the Commercial Code*, 1 PAC. RIM L. & POL'Y J. 127, 148–49 (1992).

D. Liability for Pre-Incorporation Transactions and Defective Incorporation in China

---

Howard Gensler, *Company Formation and Securities Listing in the People's Republic of China*

17 HOUS. J. INT'L L. 399 (1995)
(excerpts pages 401–427; some footnotes omitted)

Reread the excerpt which may be found in Chapter 3, above, at page 255.

Robert C. Art and Minkang Gu, *China Incorporated: The First Corporation Law of the People's Republic of China*

20 YALE J. INT'L L. 273 (1995)
(excerpts pages 288–291)

Reread the excerpt that may be found at Chapter 7.A.4, above.

Comments and Questions

1. To what extent are questions of pre-incorporation liability and nullity in China affected by concerns with the effectiveness of the Chinese legal system to enforce its statutory law? Would your answer depend on the relationship of the managers, promoters and incorporators with the Chinese Communist Party? "Although China has made valiant efforts to reform its legal system in the past decade and a half, courts continue to display slavish obedience to the Party's authority."[1]

2. As with enterprises in the West and Japan, the formation of a corporation requires incorporators, who Professor Gensler calls 'initiators.' To what extent would the creation of statutory liability for initiators be effective where a state owned enterprise is bring converted to a joint stock corporation? How would your answer change if the majority or controlling shareholder of the resulting enterprise continued to be the Chinese state itself?

3. Art and Gu suggest that the process of incorporation is still tightly controlled within China. The process of incorporation is involved and requires review of significant facets of corporate organization and capital structure. However, many of the state owned enterprises are 'owned' by provincial, local or municipal authorities, Donald C. Clarke, *What's Law Got to Do With It? Legal Institutions and Economic Reform in China*,

---

1. Michael Irl Nikkel, Note: *'Chinese Characteristics' in Corporate Clothing: Questions of Fiduciary Duty in China's Company Law*, 80 MINN. L. REV. 503, 514 (1995).

10 U.C.L.A. Pac. Basin L.J. 1, 5–6 (1991), or the People's Liberation Army, rather than the central government. To what extent can liability rules against state institutions be effective to protect non-state institutional investors or other (foreign) third parties? Would the possibility of punishing the managers of the state owned enterprises through intra-Party channels serve as an alternative deterrent to conduct resulting in liability?[2]

4. Recall the discussion of the position of 'legal representative' within Chinese corporate law in Kingley T.W. Ong and Colin R. Baxter, *A Comparative Study of the Fundamental Elements of Chinese and English Company Law*, 48 Int'l & Comp. L. Q. 88 (1999), excerpted in Chapter 3 above at page 433. The legal representative is personally subject to punishment for the misconduct of legal persons. Might the punishment of the legal representative serve as an adequate substitute or supplement to the law of pre-incorporation liability or nullity?

E. Ultra Vires Doctrines

1. *The Consequences of Ultra Vires Actions in the United States*

The concept of *ultra vires* is fairly simple to state: a corporation is incompetent to do any act which lies beyond the powers conferred upon it in the articles of incorporation. The classic formulation of the doctrine can be found in the English case, *Ashbury Railway Carriage & Iron Co. v. Riche*, 33 N.S. Law Times Rep. 450 (1875). The corporation, in that case, was authorized to engage in the business of (1) selling railway plant and (2) carrying on the business of mechanical engineers and general contractors. The corporation entered into a contract to purchase a concession to build a railway in Belgium under which it was to raise the capital for the construction of the railway to be constructed by one Riche. Prior to its completion, the corporation repudiated the contract. The House of Lords concluded that the corporation was not liable to Riche because owning and operating a railway was beyond the purposes of the corporation.

> * * * * I assume the contract in itself to be perfectly legal; to have nothing in it obnoxious to any of the powers involved in the expressions which I have used. The question is not the illegality of the contract, but the competency and power of the corporation to make the contract. I am of opinion that this contract was, as I have said, entirely beyond the objects of the memorandum of association. If so it was thereby placed beyond the powers of the company to make the contract. If so it is not a question whether the contract ever was ratified or not ratified. If it was a contract void at its beginning it was void for this reason—because the company could not make the contract. If every shareholder of the company had been in this room, and every shareholder of the company had said, "That is a contract which we desire to make, which we authorize the directors to make, to which we sanction the placing the seal of the company," the case would not have stood in any different

2. On the difficulty of third party recovery for loss, *see also id.*, at 515–516.

position to that in which it stands now. The company would thereby by unanimous assent have been attempting to do the very thing which by the Act they were prohibited from doing.

The notion that corporations might be able to avoid contractual obligations simply because they are legally incapable of performing acts beyond their powers (as set forth in their charters), has greatly disturbed modern American courts, legislatures and business. As a result, the greater part of the Twentieth century has seen the substantially complete erosion of the applicability of the doctrine of *ultra vires* in the United States, especially as might be applied to void contractual obligations with or to third parties. In addition, virtually all corporations have taken the invitation of modern corporate statutes by providing in their charters that the corporation shall have the authority to conduct "all lawful business." In considering the materials which follow, consider whether the language of the First Directive goes as far as American corporate law has gone to eliminate the threat of *ultra vires* in commercial settings.

Theodora Holding Corp., Plaintiff, v. Henderson, et al., Defendants

Court of Chancery of Delaware, New Castle
Sept. 18, 1969
257 A.2d 398

MARVEL, Vice Chancellor:

Plaintiff, which was formed in May of 1967 by the defendant Girard B. Henderson's former wife, Theodora G. Henderson, is the holder of record of 11,000 of the 40,500 issued and outstanding shares of common stock of the defendant Alexander Dawson, Inc. It sues derivatively as well as on its own behalf for an accounting by the individual defendants for the losses allegedly sustained by the corporate defendant and the concomitant improper gains allegedly received by the individual defendants as a result of certain transactions of which plaintiff complains. However, the basic relief sought by plaintiff after trial is the appointment of a liquidating receiver for the corporate defendant, such application being based on the alleged wrongs suffered by the corporate defendant at the hands of the individual defendants, which wrongs, according to plaintiff, if permitted to continue, threaten the very existence of such corporation.

As of September 30, 1968, Theodora G. Henderson, in addition to her interest in the plaintiff corporation, was the holder of the following shares of preferred stock of the corporate defendant, namely, 3,000 of first preferred, 12,000 of second preferred, and 22,000 of third preferred. She continues to receive dividends on such shares. Prior to plaintiff's formation in 1967 Mrs. Henderson had received dividends on both common and preferred shares of the corporate defendant until she transferred her 11,000 shares of the common stock of said company to plaintiff during the year 1967. Corporate dividends paid to Mrs. Henderson in recent years and now to plaintiff and Mrs. Henderson have increased substantially in recent years. As of December 3, 1968, dividends paid to plaintiff and Mrs. Henderson in that year totalled $385,240. In 1966, Mrs. Henderson had received dividends in the amount of $292,840, and in 1967, a year in which Alexander Dawson, Inc., made a controversial charitable contribution having a value of $528,000, the combined dividends of plaintiff and Mrs. Henderson totalled $286,240.

In January of 1955, the defendant Girard B. Henderson and his then wife, Theodora G. Henderson, had entered into a separation agreement looking towards a divorce, at which time Mrs. Henderson's dividends from the corporate defendant totalled approximately $50,000 per annum. Under the terms of such agreement Mrs. Henderson acknowledged that she had received from her then husband the shares of common stock of Alexander Dawson, Inc., here in issue as well as a number of shares of preferred stock of such corporation. Upon plaintiff's organization, it became the owner of Mrs. Henderson's 11,000 shares of common stock[1] on May 3, 1967. As of April 30, 1967, the shares of Alexander Dawson, Inc., to be turned over to the plaintiff corporation had a fair market value of $15,675,000 and an underlying net asset value of $28,996,000. Mrs. Henderson has since placed certain Dawson shares in trust for her own benefit and that of her two daughters and their issue.

The individual defendant Henderson by reason of the extent of his combined majority holdings of common and preferred stock of Alexander Dawson, Inc., each class of which has voting rights, exercises effective control over the affairs of such corporation, the net worth of the assets of which, at the time of the filing of this suit, was approximately $150,000,000.

It is claimed and the evidence supports such contention that on December 8, 1967, the defendant Girard B. Henderson, by virtue of his voting control over the affairs of Alexander Dawson, Inc., caused the board of directors of such corporation to be reduced in number from eight to three persons, namely himself, the defendant Bengt Ljunggren,[2] and employee of the corporate defendant, and Mr. Henderson's daughter, Theodora H. Ives. It is alleged that thereafter the defendant Girard B. Henderson (over the objection of the director, Mrs. Ives) caused the board and the majority of the voting stock of Alexander Dawson, Inc., improperly to contribute stock held by it in the approximate value of $550,000 to the Alexander Dawson Foundation, a charitable trust, the affairs of which were then controlled and continue to be controlled by Mr. Henderson. Another claim asserted by plaintiff is to the effect that in November or December of 1967, the defendant Henderson wrongfully transferred assets of Alexander Dawson, Inc., consisting of some $14,000,000 in cash, to accounts in Switzerland, where a portion of said moneys was converted or sought to be converted into silver bullion and Swiss francs at a cost to the corporate defendant of more than $2,500,000. It is also claimed that on November 10, 1958, the defendant improperly caused the board of the corporate defendant to acquire rights to a membership on the New York Stock Exchange for said Henderson's personal use, and that said membership having been thereafter sold on January 22, 1968, at a net profit of $330,000, such profit was thereupon appropriated by Mr. Henderson. Plaintiff argues that the transaction complained of oc-

---

1. Because it did not become a holder of Alexander Dawson, Inc., stock until May of 1967, the individual defendants contend that plaintiff cannot complain of corporate transactions which occurred prior to that date, Title 8 Del.C. § 327, and Rule 23.1, Del.C.Ann. This procedural rule, however, was designed to militate against the wrong of buying into a derivative law suit and should not be allowed to bar an action by a stockholder with a long standing equitable interest in a corporation, Rosenthal v. Burry Biscuit Co., 30 Del.Ch. 296, 60 A.2d 106, and Maclary v. Pleasant Hills, Inc., 35 Del.Ch. 39, 109 A.2d 830. Had the harsh rule of Myer v. Myer, 271 App.Div. 465, 66 N.Y.S.2d 83, been invoked, I would have entertained a motion for the joinder of Theodora G. Henderson as a party plaintiff in light of her continuing ownership of preferred stock of Alexander Dawson, Inc.

2. Mr. Ljunggren, whose forte appears to be that of public relations, joined Alexander Dawson, Inc., in 1966 at a salary of $12,000 per annum. He has since been rewarded with substantial raises and bonuses which have more than doubled his starting salary.

curred in 1968 when the Stock Exchange seat, allegedly the property of the corporation, was sold and the profit pocketed by Mr. Henderson. However, as noted earlier, I am of the opinion that a decision as to the precise time at which this transaction occurred is not required because Mrs. Henderson's direct interest in the defendant corporation as well as her indirect interest therein through the plaintiff corporation constitute compliance with the requirements of 8 Del.C. §327, and Rule 23.1. It is further claimed that in March 1968 the defendant Henderson caused some $1,400,000 of the corporate defendant's assets to be invested in an airplane servicing and mechanics training project known as Kensair Corporation and that said entire investment has been irretrievably lost. It is next alleged that in December, 1967, an additional sum of approximately $737,000.00 of corporate funds was lost by reason of Mr. Henderson's application of the corporate defendant's funds to a research project known as Credo, Inc. It is finally claimed that other sums in lesser amounts have been dissipated on other unprofitable projects; that Mr. Henderson has improperly paid to himself non-interest bearing corporate loans, and that on the basis of the many instances of gross mismanagement of Alexander Dawson, Inc. charged in the complaint that a liquidating receiver should be appointed. However, after trial, plaintiff now limits its application for relief to recovery of the profit gained by Mr. Henderson as a result of the sale of a New York Stock Exchange seat together with the commissions earned through the use of such seat, to an accounting for the alleged improper corporate gift of $528,000 to the Alexander Dawson Foundation in 1967, and finally to the appointment of a liquidating receiver on the ground of gross mismanagement and distortion of corporate purpose on the part of Mr. Henderson.

Alexander Dawson, Inc. has functioned as a personal holding company since 1935 when Mr. Henderson's mother exchanged a substantial number of shares held by her in a company which later became Avon Products, Inc., for all of the shares of her own company known as Alexander Dawson, Inc. Mr. Henderson and a brother later succeeded to their mother's interest in Alexander Dawson, Inc., the brother thereafter permitting his shares to be redeemed by the corporation. As noted earlier, Mr. Henderson, by reason of his combined holdings of common and preferred stock of the corporate defendant, is in clear control of the affairs of such corporation, which, for the most part, has been operated informally by Mr. Henderson with scant regard for the views of other board members. Some seventy-five percent of its assets consist of shares of Avon Products, Inc. stock, there having been some diversification, particularly in 1967, largely through the urging of officers of the United States Trust Company of New York who have served as advisors. Through exercise of such control, Mr. Henderson has, since 1957, caused the corporate defendant to donate varying amounts to a charitable trust organized in that year by Mr. Henderson, namely the Alexander Dawson Foundation, In 1957, $10,610 was donated to such trust. From 1960 to 1966 (except for the year 1965) gifts were in the range of approximately $63,000 to $70,000 or higher in each year other than 1963 when $27,923 was donated. In 1966, however, a gift in the form of a large tract of land in Colorado, having a value of some $467,750, was made.[3] All of these gifts through 1966 were unanimously approved by all of the stockholders of Alexander Dawson, Inc., including Mrs. Theodora G. Henderson. The gift now under attack, namely one of the shares of stock of the corporate defendant having a value of some $528,000, was made to the Alexander Dawson Foundation in December of 1967. Such gift was first proposed by Mr. Henderson in April 1967 before the board of the

3. Mr. Henderson also made a personal donation of $122,602 to the Foundation in 1966.

corporate defendant was reduced in number from eight to three. However, director reaction was thereafter confused, one of the directors, Mrs. Henderson's daughter, Theodora H. Ives, having expressed a desire that a corporate gift also be made to her own charitable corporation and that of her mother, Theodora G. Henderson. Accordingly, the matter was not pressed by Mr. Henderson until late December when the reduced board had taken over management of the corporate defendant. It is claimed and admitted that such gift had an effect on the equity and dividends of shareholders of the corporate defendant although the tax consequences of such gift clearly soften the apparent impact of such transaction. It is significant, however, as noted above, that the 1966 corporate gift, consisting of a ranch located in Colorado, had been approved by all of the directors and stockholders of the corporate defendant, and that the gift here under attack was apparently intended to be a step towards consummation of the purpose behind such grant of land, namely to provide a fund for the financing of a western camp for under privileged boys, particularly members of the George Junior Republic, a self-governing institution which has served the public interest for some seventy-five years at a school near Freeville, New York. Thus, in the summer of 1967, a small group of under privileged children had enjoyed the advantages of such camp in a test of the feasibility of such an institution. However, it is apparently Mr. Henderson's intention to continue and expand his interest in such camp where he maintains an underground home which he occupies at a $6,000 rental per annum, such house being occupied by him during some three months of the year. Plaintiff initially attacked such use. However, as in the case of charges made concerning the purchase of silver bullion and Swiss francs, as well as corporate investments in Credo, Inc., Kensair Corporation and other enterprises plaintiff seeks no accounting from the individual defendants concerned.

* * *

The next matter to be considered is the propriety of the December 1967 gift made by Alexander Dawson, Inc. to the Alexander Dawson Foundation of shares of stock of the corporate defendant having a value in excess of $525,000, an amount within the limits of the provisions of the federal tax law having to do with deductible corporate gifts, Internal Revenue Code of 1954 §§ 170(b)(2), 545(b)(2).

Title 8 Del.C. § 122 provides as follows: 'Every corporation created under this chapter shall have power to—(9) Make donations for the public welfare or for charitable, scientific or educational purposes, and in time of war or other national emergency in aid thereof.'

There is no doubt but that the Alexander Dawson Foundation is recognized as a legitimate charitable trust by the Department of Internal Revenue. It is also clear that it is authorized to operate exclusively in the fields of '* * * religious, charitable, scientific, literary, or educational purposes, or for the prevention of cruelty to children or animals * * *.' Furthermore, contemporary courts recognize that unless corporations carry an increasing share of the burden of supporting charitable and educational causes that the business advantages now reposed in corporations by law may well prove to be unacceptable to the representatives of an aroused public. The recognized obligation of corporations towards philanthropic, educational and artistic causes is reflected in the statutory law of all of the states, other than the states of Arizona and Idaho.

In A. P. Smith Mfg. Co. v. Barlow, 13 N.J. 145, 98 A.2d 681, 39 A.L.R.2d 1179, appeal dismissed, 346 U.S. 861, 74 S.Ct. 107, 98 L.Ed. 373, a case in which the corporate donor had been organized long before the adoption of a statute authorizing corporate gifts to charitable or educational institutions, the Supreme Court of New Jersey upheld a gift of $1500 by the plaintiff corporation to Princeton University, being of the opinion that the trend towards the transfer of wealth from private industrial entrepreneurs to corporate institutions, the increase of taxes on individual income, coupled with steadily increasing philanthropic needs, necessitate corporate giving for educational needs even were there no statute permitting such gifts, and this was held to be the case apart from the question of the reserved power of the state to amend corporate charters. The court also noted that the gift tended to bolster the free enterprise system and the general social climate in which plaintiff was nurtured. And while the court pointed out that there was no showing that the gift in question was made indiscriminately or to a pet charity in furtherance of personal rather than corporate ends, the actual holding of the opinion appears to be that a corporate charitable or educational gift to be valid must merely be within reasonable limits both as to amount and purpose. Compare Union Pacific R.R. v. Trustees, Inc., 8 Utah 2d 101, 329 P.2d 398.

The New Jersey statute in force and effect at the time of the Smith case gift provided that directors might cause their corporation to contribute for charitable and educational purposes and the like '* * * such reasonable sum or sums as they may determine * * *' provided, however, that such contributions might not be made in situations where the proposed donee owned more than 10% of the voting stock of the donor and provided further that such gifts be limited to 5% of capital and surplus unless '* * * authorized by the stockholders.'

Whether or not these statutory limitations on corporate giving were the source of the limiting language of the New Jersey Supreme Court is not clear, the point being that the Delaware statute contains no such limiting language and therefor must, in my opinion, be construed to authorize any reasonable corporate gift of a charitable or educational nature. Significantly, Alexander Dawson, Inc. was incorporated in Delaware in 1958 after 8 Del.C. § 122(9) was cast in its present form, therefor no constitutional problem arising out of the effect on a stockholder's property rights of the State's reserved power to amend corporate charters is presented.

I conclude that the test to be applied in passing on the validity of a gift such as the one here in issue is that of reasonableness, a test in which the provisions of the Internal Revenue Code pertaining to charitable gifts by corporations furnish a helpful guide. The gift here under attack was made from gross income and had a value as of the time of giving of $528,000 in a year in which Alexander Dawson, Inc.'s total income was $19,144,229.06, or well within the federal tax deduction limitation of 5% Of such income. The contribution under attack can be said to have 'cost' all of the stockholders of Alexander Dawson, Inc. including plaintiff, less than $80,000, or some fifteen cents per dollar of contribution, taking into consideration the federal tax provisions applicable to holding companies as well as the provisions for compulsory distribution of dividends received by such a corporation. In addition, the gift, by reducing Alexander Dawson, Inc.'s reserve for unrealized capital gains taxes by some $130,000, increased the balance sheet net worth of stockholders of the corporate defendant by such amount. It is accordingly obvious, in my opinion, that the relatively small loss of immediate income otherwise payable to plaintiff and the corporate defendant's other stockholders, had it not been for the gift in question, is far out-weighed by the overall benefits flowing from the placing of such gift in channels where it serves to benefit those in need of philanthropic or educational support, thus providing justification for large private holdings, thereby benefiting plaintiff in the long run. Finally, the fact that the interests of the Alexander Dawson Foundation appear to be increasingly directed towards the rehabilitation and education of deprived but deserving young people is peculiarly appropriate in an age when a large segment of youth is alienated even from parents who are not entirely satisfied with our present social and economic system.

* * *

On notice, an order in conformity with the holdings of this opinion may be presented.

A. Elihu Michelson v. Louis C. Duncan, et al.

Supreme Court of Delaware
Decided Oct. 2, 1979
407 A.2d 211

Horsey, Justice:

Plaintiff appeals the Court of Chancery's grant of summary judgment in a derivative shareholder's suit brought to set aside stock options granted by the defendants, officers and directors of Household Finance Corporation (hereafter, "HFC") to key employees, including themselves. The source of the controversy between the parties is action taken by the directors in 1971–1974 to modify the Company's 1966 stock option plan (sometimes hereafter, "the Plan") and their issuance of stock options under the Plan as modified. The principal issue on appeal is whether a 1977 non-unanimous shareholder ratification of the earlier modifications of the Plan and of the options granted under the modified Plan entitled defendants to a grant of summary judgment.

For the reasons hereafter stated, we affirm in part and reverse in part the holdings of the Vice Chancellor. More specifically, we hold (1) that the Complaint states a claim for gift or waste of corporate assets; (2) that such claim was not waived or conceded by plaintiff before the court below; (3) that ratification cured or overcame attack on the options granted under the Plan as modified on the ground of lack of director authority but does not dispose of the claim of gift or waste; and (4) as to the latter, trial is required as to the issue of existence and adequacy of consideration for the grant of the new or modified options, but shareholder ratification shifts the burden of proof of failure or inadequacy of consideration from defendants to plaintiff.

The relevant facts are lengthy but are set out in detail in the opinion below, Michelson v. Duncan, Del.Ch., 386 A.2d 1144 (1978) and need not be repeated here, except those that are pertinent to this decision.

In 1966, the Board of Directors of HFC authorized a stock option plan whereby certain key employees, including a number of the directors, were granted options to purchase stock in HFC following a two year waiting period after grant. Purchases under the non-tax qualified portion of the 1966 plan, with which we are concerned, were to be made at 90% Of the market price at the time of grant. A grant limit of 5,000 shares per year per optionee, later raised to 15,000 shares, was imposed. The options could be exercised at a rate of 10% a year after the second year with the final 30% exercisable following the ninth anniversary of the grant. The Plan was described in proxy materials, but not set out in toto, and was overwhelmingly approved by the shareholders at their 1966 annual meeting.

The transactions in question relate to conduct of the Board of Directors from 1971 to 1974. In 1971 and again in 1973 the Board, acting on the recommendation of the Compensation Committee,[1] amended the rate of exercise limit to increase that limit

1. The Compensation Committee was established under the 1966 Plan and was composed of non-employee directors. Under the terms of the Plan they were charged with selecting employees el-

from 10% Per year to 33⅓% Following each of the second, third and fourth anniversaries of a grant. The net effect of this modification was to reduce the minimum time necessary to exercise an entire option from nine years to four years.

In 1974, following a dramatic decline in the market price of HFC stock, the Board of Directors in order to restore incentive to exercise the options, developed and adopted a plan (sometimes hereafter referred to as "the Amended Plan") whereby the existing options would be cancelled and new options issued in their place at the current lower market price. The exercise price of the new options was some $7.00 to $18.00 below the price of the old options. At the same meeting of the directors, 304,900 old options were exchanged for new options and 25,000 new options were issued without exchange. During the next year an additional 71,800 options were granted without exchange.

The Complaint attacks the options granted after December 31, 1973, and specifically the exchange options granted in April, 1974 on essentially two grounds: (1) lack of authority of the Board of Directors to grant the options as modified without prior shareholder approval; and (2) the options issued were void for lack of consideration.

More specifically, plaintiff claims that the Board lacked authority: to grant options in excess of 15,000 shares per optionee per 12 month period; to reduce the option purchase price below that provided under the 1966 plan; to increase the yearly percentage limit of options exercisable; and to exceed the total number of shares available for option under the 1966 Plan. The Complaint seeks (a) cancellation of all the options issued to all optionees, including defendants; (b) an accounting by the individual defendants for all profits realized by them under any options received; and (c) recovery from the individual defendants of all losses and damages sustained by HFC.

Admitting generally the amendments to the 1966 Plan but claiming that they were not contrary to the Plan, defendants, shortly after answer and before any extensive discovery had been undertaken by plaintiff or defendants, moved for summary judgment. In their opening brief filed with their motion, defendants argued: (1) that the cancellation of existing stock options in exchange for the issuance of new stock options at reduced prices is permissible under Delaware law as stated in Dann v. Chrysler Corp., Del.Ch., 41 Del.Ch. 438, 198 A.2d 185 (1963); aff'd sub nom. Hoffman v. Dann, Del.Supr., 205 A.2d 343 (1964), cert. denied 380 U.S. 973, 85 S.Ct. 1332, 14 L.Ed.2d 269 (1965); (2) that there was consideration for the new grants in that the optionee-employees were induced to remain with the corporation for an additional two years; and (3) that the grant of the new options in exchange for the old was not in violation of the terms of the 1966 Plan.

Plaintiff countered with a cross-motion for summary judgment asserting a contrary position; but in his opening brief below, plaintiff did not argue lack of consideration for the options granted or that they represented gifts or waste of corporate assets. Instead, plaintiff limited his argument to alleged lack of director authority.

Defendants then proceeded to obtain from the shareholders of HFC at its up-coming 1977 annual meeting a ratification that was less than unanimous of the actions of the directors complained of in this lawsuit concerning the Amended Plan and stock op-

---

igible for the option plan, determining the number of shares to be granted and fixing the terms for exercising each option. Moreover, the Plan provided that the Compensation Committee could recommend to the Board to waive the exercise limitation for selected optionees.

tions issued thereunder by the directors over the period 1971–1974. More or less simultaneously with this shareholder action, defendants filed their reply brief in support of summary judgment, referred to the recently accomplished shareholder ratification and argued that such shareholder action constituted a complete defense to the instant action and in particular to plaintiff's claim of lack of shareholder authority for the Amended Plan and options issued thereunder. Defendants argued that the director action was, at most, voidable, rather than void, and as such, any alleged defect that was the subject of the Complaint was curable by shareholder ratification. Defendants added that plaintiff had, in his briefing of the cross summary judgment motions, abandoned any claim of gift or waste of corporate assets which might have constituted a non-ratifiable action.

Plaintiff responded by supplemental memorandum that the HFC shareholder ratification action had injected a new fact element into the litigation not present at time of filing of his answering brief; that he had not abandoned his claim that the new options were granted without consideration and constituted gifts or waste of corporate assets; and plaintiff proceeded to argue that non-unanimous shareholder ratification was not a legal defense to a claim of gift or waste of corporate assets, even if it were a defense to his claim of lack of shareholder authority.

The Vice-Chancellor, following oral argument, granted summary judgment on defendants' motion and denied summary judgment on plaintiff's cross-motion. The Vice-Chancellor stated that while he would have been required to deny defendants summary judgment had plaintiff alleged gift or waste of corporate assets and presented sufficient evidence in support of such claim, he concluded that plaintiff had failed to plead, or, if pleaded, had later abandoned any claim that the Amended Plan and options granted thereunder amounted to gift or waste of corporate assets. He then found the 1977 shareholder ratification of the directors' 1971–1974 actions to have been fair and complete and thus, the ratification to be "intrinsically valid." The Vice-Chancellor further found no evidence of breach of fiduciary duty by the directors in delegating authority to grant options to the compensation Committee of the Board; and the Vice-Chancellor concluded that the 1977 shareholder ratification cured all remaining challenges to the acts of the defendants-directors. It is that decision which is appealed by plaintiff, A. Elihu Michelson.

I

Michelson contends that the Court's initial error was its ruling that plaintiff had not alleged a claim of gift or waste of corporate assets. We agree. Paragraph 17 of the Complaint fairly clearly asserts two separate and distinct claims: First, that the Board's modifications of the option Plan were invalid because contrary to and not authorized under the terms of the 1966 Plan; and Second, that the "new" options granted in and subsequent to 1974 were without consideration.

* * *

...We conclude that plaintiff did assert a claim for gift or waste of corporate assets. See Gottlieb v. Heyden Chemical Corp., Del.Supr., 33 Del.Ch. 82, 90 A.2d 660 (1952), Rosenthal v. Burry Biscuit Corp., Del.Ch., 30 Del.Ch. 299, 60 A.2d 106 (1948). Since the Vice-Chancellor found to the contrary, his ruling must be reversed.

II

We next consider whether plaintiff, having pleaded a claim of gift or waste, waived, disavowed or abandoned such claim, as the Vice-Chancellor found he had....

...Based on the foregoing, we think it clear that plaintiff did not waive, abandon or concede his claim of gift or waste; and we hold that the Vice-Chancellor erred in his finding to the contrary.

III

We now consider the correctness of the Vice-Chancellor's ruling that the 1977 shareholder ratification was fairly accomplished and thus was sufficient to cure any invalidity of the Plan's amendments based on the contention that the 1971–1974 director action was contrary to the terms of the 1966 Plan.

In order to hold the 1977 ratification effective to cure otherwise wrongful acts of the defendant directors, the Vice-Chancellor found (1) that their 1971–1974 acts were merely voidable, not void; and (2) that the ratification was fairly accomplished. These are essential elements to an effective shareholder ratification.... We will separately consider these two elements of the decision below.

A.

The essential distinction between voidable and void acts is that the former are those which may be found to have been performed in the interest of the corporation but beyond the authority of management, as distinguished from acts which are ultra vires, fraudulent or gifts or waste of corporate assets. 19 Am.Jur.2d, Corporations, § 1247. The practical distinction, for our purposes, is that voidable acts are susceptible to cure by shareholder approval while void acts are not. See Kerbs, supra; Keenan v. Eshleman, Del.Supr., 23 Del.Ch. 234, 2 A.2d 904 (1938).

The parties disagree as to whether the Vice-Chancellor actually found the directors' action in amending the Plan and granting new options in exchange for outstanding, unexercised options to be contrary to the Plan's terms and therefore voidable. It would appear that he did,[3] but it would be sufficient that he made that assumption as a basis for determining the fairness of the ratification issue. Plaintiff also contends that even if the ratification were found to be fairly accomplished and to relate back to cure otherwise unauthorized director actions, actions for consequential damages against the directors survive.

It is the law of Delaware, and general corporate law, that a validly accomplished shareholder ratification relates back to cure otherwise unauthorized acts of officers and directors. Hannigan v. Italo Petroleum Corporation of America, supra; 19 Am.Jur.2d, Corporations, § 1241. As stated in 5 Fletcher, Cyclopedia of Corporations,

3. Vice-Chancellor Hartnett wrote: "It should be noted that Michelson's contention that the 1966 plan was violated in that there was no provision in it for cancellation and reissuance of options appears well-founded although of no legal importance in view of the stockholder ratification. Termination is provided for in Paragraph 10 of the tax qualified and non-tax qualified portions of the plan, but clearly, even by the most liberal definition of 'termination' there was no authority given to immediately reissue terminated options." 386 A.2d at 1152. He added later in his opinion by footnote: "As further evidence that the 'termination' provisions in the 1966 Plan did not authorize cancellation and reissuance of options, and perhaps did not envision such action, HFC's previous stock option plan of 1963 specifically provided for such a procedure. The proxy statement for the 1963 Plan provided: 'Although the Board of Directors has made no determination with respect to action to be taken in the event of market fluctuations, it is the duty of the Board to devise ways and means to provide adequate incentive to attract and retain the best management talent available. In this effort, the Board reserves the right, with optionee approval, to cancel and reissue options at a lower market price. The Board of Directors may terminate the Plan at any time by resolution which, however may not affect outstanding options.' " 386 A.2d at 1153, n.12.

§2139 (perm.ed.rev.1976): "Generally, any act of the board of directors or of any of the officers beyond the scope of their authority fixing or increasing compensation may be ratified by the stockholders when the stockholders have originally authorized such act, and this may be done even after suit is filed, provided the ratification is voted by bona fide stockholders.... (W)here a majority of the stockholders of the corporation at a special meeting ratify a stock option plan for key executives which was authorized by interested directors, such ratification cures any voidable defect in the action by the board of directors." It is only where a claim of gift or waste of assets, fraud or ultra vires is asserted that a less than unanimous shareholder ratification is not a full defense.

Plaintiff's argument and authority to the contrary are not persuasive. Plaintiff relies on Gottfried v. Gottfried Baking Co., N.Y.App.Div., 1 A.D.2d 994, 151 N.Y.S.2d 583 (1956); but that case is not contrary authority. Apart from the fact that New York, not Delaware, law was in issue, the Court recognized that the question of the effect of subsequent shareholder ratification upon an otherwise invalid act of directors was not before it. Furthermore, Michelson's argument that ratification may cure an invalid act of a director but leave open the question of his liability for consequent losses to the corporation must be rejected as inherently inconsistent. If shareholders have approved an otherwise voidable act, their approval extinguishes any claim for losses based on prior lack of authority of the directors to undertake such action.

We hold that the Vice-Chancellor properly found the directors' action to be voidable to the extent attack on the Plan was premised on lack of director authority and that after-the-fact shareholder ratification related back to cure such invalidity unless the ratification procedure proved to be lacking in fairness or procedurally defective.

B.

The second consideration in determining the effectiveness of the shareholder ratification is whether such ratification was fairly effected and intrinsically valid, as found by the Court below. Shareholder ratification is valid only where the stockholders so ratifying are adequately informed of the consequences of their acts and the reasons therefor. The settled rule in Delaware is that "where a majority of fully Informed stockholders ratify action of even interested directors, an attack on the ratified transaction normally must fail." (emphasis added). Gerlach v. Gillam, Del.Ch., 37 Del.Ch. 244, 139 A.2d 591 at 593 (1958).

Whether the shareholders were informed, and thus their ratification valid, turns on the fairness and completeness of the proxy materials submitted by the management to the HFC shareholders prior to the annual meeting in April, 1977. Plaintiff attacks the adequacy of that notice, which the Court below found to be complete and fair.

The notice of annual meeting stated that one of the purposes of the meeting was to seek ratification of corporate action relating to the 1966 Stock Option Plan; and a predominant portion of the proxy statement was devoted to this subject. The introductory explanation of the proposed resolution of the Board of Directors to be put to the stockholders provided, in part:

> "Household's Board of Directors proposes, and recommends that the stockholders vote for, the resolution (set forth in Appendix A hereto) authorizing, approving, ratifying and confirming the actions, described below, of the Board of Directors, its Compensation Committee and other Household officers and employees with respect to the cancellations and grant of new options on April 9, 1974 under

the 1966 Employee Stock Option Plan ("Plan") and the periodic waivers of share limitations and percentage limitations on exercise since inception of the Plan. Adoption of the resolution requires the affirmative vote of a majority of all shares represented at the meeting, a quorum being present. On April 9, 1974, the Corporation cancelled non-tax-qualified options to purchase 304,900 shares of the Corporation's common stock issued pursuant to the Plan then held by directors, officers and employees of the Corporation and its subsidiaries with the agreement of such optionees. Each individual whose non-tax-qualified options were cancelled was granted a new option for the same number of shares but with an exercise price equal to the fair market value of Household's common stock on April 9, 1974. The exercise price of the new options was substantially lower than the exercise prices of the cancelled options. The purpose of these actions was to restore the incentive value of the non-tax-qualified options, which value had been lost because the exercise prices of the options were considerably in excess of the then fair market value of Household's common stock. These actions were similar to actions taken by a number of other corporations and resulted in keeping Household's executive benefits comparable to those of other corporations. See 'Cancellations and Grant of Options' below. The Plan contemplates the waiver of certain limitations set forth in the Plan and, from time to time after November 1967, the Board of Directors and its Compensation Committee waived certain provisions of the Plan limiting the number of shares which can be subject to options granted to any one individual in any consecutive twelve month period and limiting the annual percentage rates at which the options may be exercised. See 'Waivers of Share Limitation and Exercise Rate Limitation' below. The April 9, 1974 cancellations and grant of new options increased the opportunity for directors, officers and other optionees to acquire shares of the Corporation's common stock and realize profits upon their subsequent resale, which profits may or may not exist or be substantial, depending upon prevailing market conditions after exercise of the options. The waivers of share limitations and percentage limitations on exercise may have further enhanced opportunities for such profits. See 'Stock Options of Directors and Officers' below. For additional information concerning directors' and officers' salaries and other employee benefits, see 'Remuneration of Officers and Directors' above."

The proxy statement then informed the stockholders of the Michelson suit, the acts of the directors complained of by Michelson and summarized the action of management for which ratification was sought. Particular focus was on the Board's action of April 9, 1974 as well as its related action of waiving share limitation and exercise rate limitations prior thereto. The resolution itself, a five page document, attached to the proxy statement, further detailed the past actions of the Board of Directors sought to be ratified. Of the 37,724,220 shares represented in person or by proxy at the 1977 meeting, 32,670,527 shares (about 87%) were voted in favor of the resolution, 2,444,172 shares (about 6%) were voted against, and the remaining 2,509,521 shares were not voted with respect to the resolution.

The Vice-Chancellor found that the proxy statement "described in detail the stock option plan, the present litigation, and the actions which led to this lawsuit. The proxy statement also contained the complete text of the Stock Option Plan and the Complaint in its appendix." 386 A.2d at 1150. He further found the proxy materials informed the shareholders that the exercise price of the new options was substantially lower than the exercise prices of the cancelled options; that the purpose of the April 9, 1974 action was to restore the incentive value of the options, (a value which had been lost because the exercise prices of the options were considerably in excess of the then fair market value of Household's common stock); that it was contended that the April 9, 1974 cancellations and grant of new options, as well as the periodic waivers of share limitations and percentage limitations on exercise by the Board of Directors and its Compensation Committee, violated the terms of the Plan; that the Board of Directors believed that both the cancellation and grant of new options and waivers were authorized by the Plan; and that the Complaint of Michelson alleged the action of management constituted a breach of the individual defendants' fiduciary duty, and the grant of the new options was without consideration.

In summary, the resolution sought ratification of all of the past action of management concerning the cancellation of existing options and the grant of new options and change in exercise limitations and waiver of grant limitations.

Plaintiff contended before the Court below, and before this Court similarly contends, that the proxy materials were defectively misleading in five principal respects so as to render the ratification ineffective: (1) it was misleading for management to state that they relied upon a provision in the 1966 Plan as to termination of options for the validity of their April 9, 1974 action without disclosing to the shareholders that the "termination" provision of the Plan had not been included in 1966 in the original proxy materials' description of the Plan; (2) management should have been required in the 1977 proxy materials to inform HFC shareholders that the 1966 Plan was not "intended" to permit the management to cancel options and reissue new options as done on April 9, 1974; (3) management should have informed the shareholders that management had "deliberately excluded" from the provisions of the 1966 Plan a provision that had been included in HFC's 1963 stock option plan permitting cancellation and reissuance of options at lower current market prices; (4) management should have informed shareholders that the Compensation Committee was both "interested" and "dominated" by management and that it had "abdicated" its duty in awarding options to determine a reasonable relationship between the value of the options granted and the particular optionee's future benefit to the Corporation; and (5) management had misled the shareholders to believe that the entire terms of the 1966 Plan had been submitted to them in 1966 when in fact substantial omissions were made in the 1966 proxy materials.

The Vice-Chancellor rejected each of plaintiff's contentions and found the proxy and accompanying resolution fully complied with the requirements set forth by this Court in Lynch v. Vickers Energy Corporation, Del.Supr., 383 A.2d 278 (1977) requiring not merely adequate but complete disclosure of all relevant matters. The Vice-Chancellor stated: "It is my opinion, however, that there was complete candor in the disclosure of the facts which a reasonable stockholder would consider important in making an informed decision to ratify the transactions at issue, and that defendants have met the burden of showing complete disclosure of all the germane facts.... I find that the stockholders were informed of the essential facts surrounding the instant suit. They were provided with the complete text of plaintiff's complaint, and, all alleged wrongs for which ratification was sought were enumerated in detail." 386 A.2d at 1154. We agree with the Vice-Chancellor that it was not error, as Michelson contends, for management to fail to inform the shareholders of the items enumerated by Michelson. We say so because it would have been wholly the unreasonable for management to be required to have made such declarations in 1977 proxy materials. Such statements (a) were not factual assertions; (b) in some respects were not factually correct; (c) were inconsistent with management's position; or (d) called for legal conclusions. Therefore, we affirm the Vice-Chancellor's holding that the ratification was effective and "intrinsically valid."

Having found (a) the 1971–1974 directors' actions to be voidable only to the extent such actions are claimed to have been contrary to the Plan's terms; and (b) the shareholder ratification thereof to have been intrinsically valid, we affirm the Vice-Chancellor's grant of summary judgment for defendants as to plaintiff's claim that the shareholder ratification was not adequate to rectify unauthorized director action. However, as previously stated, ratification does not dispose of plaintiff's claim that there was no consideration for the option grants and that they constituted gifts or waste of corporate assets.

IV

This brings us to the final question, namely, whether Michelson presented sufficient evidence as to gift or waste to preclude summary judgment in defendants' favor.

Defendants make essentially two arguments in support of their position that there is no triable issue as to gift or waste. First, they contend plaintiff has failed to establish any material issue of fact relating to the question of adequacy of consideration for the cancellation of the old options in exchange for grant of the new options. Second, defendants claim that there is sufficiency of consideration as a matter of law by application of the pertinent facts to Delaware statute law, 8 Del.C. § 157,[4] and decisional law under Hoffman v. Dann, supra. We will now take up each of these arguments.

A.

Defendants contend that... shareholder ratification shifted the burden of proof of lack of consideration to plaintiff. Since plaintiff has failed to offer any evidence thereof, defendants claim that summary judgment below should be affirmed.

Plaintiff does not agree that there is insufficient evidence in the record of gift or waste of assets to raise a triable issue of fact. Plaintiff states this evidence includes the following director action: across the board, indiscriminate modifications of the 1966 Plan; lowering the exercise prices; accelerating the exercise rates; and the granting of new options in 1974 with no parity of services rendered to value of options granted.

Delaware decisional law supports plaintiff's position. Claims of gift or waste of corporate assets are seldom subject to disposition by summary judgment; and when there are genuine issues of fact as to the existence of consideration, a full hearing is required regardless of shareholder ratification. See Kerbs v. California Eastern Airways, supra; Gottlieb v. Heyden Chemical Corp., supra. "The determination of whether or not there has been in any given situation a gift of corporate assets does not rest upon any hard and fast rule. It is largely a question of fact." Gottlieb v. McKee, Del.Ch., 34 Del.Ch. 537, 107 A.2d 240 at 243 (1954). In Saxe v. Brady, Del.Ch., 40 Del.Ch. 474, 184 A.2d 602 (1962), Chancellor Seitz stated, "Where waste of corporate assets is alleged, the court, notwith-

4. 8 Del.C. § 157 provides in pertinent part: "§ 157. Rights and options respecting stock. Subject to any provisions in the certificate of incorporation, every corporation may create and issue... rights or options entitling the holders thereof to purchase from the corporation any shares of its capital stock...." The terms upon which... such shares may be purchased from the corporation upon the exercise of any such right or option, shall be such as shall be stated in the certificate of incorporation, or in a resolution adopted by the board of directors.... In the absence of actual fraud in the transaction, the judgment of the directors as to the consideration for the issuance of such rights or options and the sufficiency thereof shall be conclusive."

standing independent stockholder ratification, must examine the facts of the situation." (184 A.2d at 610). In Heyden, this Court stated: "An important question, which is not yet answered, is whether these services and these options can sensibly be deemed to be the subject of a fair exchange. This is obviously not a mere question of law. An issue of fact is raised, as to which, as yet, no evidence has been taken." 33 Del.Ch. 177, 91 A.2d 57 at 59. Similarly, in Gottlieb v. McKee, supra, the Court of Chancery, finding affidavits insufficient and otherwise inadequate for determination of an issue of gift or waste of assets, denied summary judgment for defendants as to a corporate opportunity claim and held a full hearing was required, notwithstanding shareholder ratification. See also Gamble v. Penn Valley Crude Oil Corp., Del.Ch., 34 Del.Ch. 359, 104 A.2d 257 (1954), cross-motions for summary judgment as to right of plaintiff to exercise and receive stock options were denied on the state of the record, the Court stating, "Vital facts are either lacking or in conflict and it would therefore be inappropriate to attempt either to assume them or to evaluate them on cross-motions for summary judgment." 104 A.2d at 263.

While, of course, each case must be determined on its own facts, the above cases indicate a strong disfavor for summary judgment in stock option claims where waste of corporate assets is alleged. Here, Michelson has, by his Complaint and affidavit of his attorney, raised material issues of fact as to the existence of consideration for grant of options, thus making summary judgment inappropriate on the issue of waste of corporate assets.

B.

Defendants alternatively argue that 8 Del.C. § 157 rules out any fact issue by making any consideration sufficient as a matter of law, relying on the following language of that section: "In the absence of actual fraud in the transaction, the judgment of the directors as to the consideration for the issuance of such rights or options and the sufficiency thereof shall be conclusive." The meaning of the quoted sentence is clear. However, defendant goes too far in his reliance on this section. Implicit in that section is the existence of some consideration, and assuming that fact begs the question at issue in a challenge of wasting corporate assets. See Kerbs, supra; Frankel v. Donovan, Del.Ch., 35 Del.Ch. 433, 120 A.2d 311 (1956).

Section 157 was intended to protect directors' business judgment in consideration inuring to the corporation in exchange for creating and issuing stock options. However, to assert that there was no consideration for the cancellation of the existing options in exchange for new options as asserted here is far different from asserting that there was inadequate consideration for doing so. Whether or not § 157 disposes of an inadequacy of consideration claim is not the issue before us. Here, the contention is made that there was no consideration received by HFC from the grant of the new or exchange options in 1974. We do not read § 157 as intended to erect a legal barrier to any claim for relief as to an alleged gift or waste of corporate assets in the issuance of stock options where the claim asserted is one of absolute failure of consideration.

....

C.

We further hold, as the Vice-Chancellor ruled, that shareholder ratification shifted the burden of proof of want or inadequacy of consideration for the grant of the options from defendants to plaintiff. See Gottlieb v. Heyden Chemical Corporation, supra, and Kaufman v. Schoenberg, Supra. In Gottlieb, this Court stated that "...(T)he entire atmosphere is freshened and a new set of rules invoked where formal approval has been given by a majority of independent, fully informed stockholders. . . ." 91 A.2d at 59.

Similarly, in Kaufman, the Chancellor stated that in the absence of independent stockholder ratification, interested directors have the burden of showing that the consideration to be received for the grant of options represented a "fair exchange," but the burden shifts where there has been shareholder ratification: "Where there has been independent stockholder ratification of interested director action, the objecting stockholder has the burden of showing that no person of ordinary sound business judgment would say that the consideration received for the options was a fair exchange for the options granted." 91 A.2d 791. See also Fidanque v. American Maracaibo Co., Del.Ch., 33 Del.Ch. 262, 92 A.2d 311 (1952), stating: "Even in cases, such as a case involving interlocking directorates, where the burden is upon the directors to prove the validity of their action and their good faith, a stockholder ratification shifts the burden of proof to the objector. Gottlieb v. Heyden Chemical Co., supra." 92 A.2d at 321.

Affirmed in part and reversed in part.

Comments and Questions

1. Most corporate gift giving is now authorized by statutes similar to those considered in *Theodora Holding Corp.* But the authority of corporations to make gifts is not necessarily dependent on express statutory authorization. Cases such as *A.P. Smith Mfg. Co. v. Barlow*, 98 A.2d 681, discussed by Vice Chancellor Marvel in *Theodora Holding Corp.* suggested that charitable gifting would be within the powers of the corporation in the absence of express statutory authority. The courts, however, suggested that such gift giving has limitations. Gifts for purposes other than corporate purposes were beyond the powers of a corporation. The standard applied in *Theodora Holding Corp.* was one of reasonableness. What factors did the court use to determine reasonableness? Are there other factors, other than financial effect and duty of loyalty concerns that might or should be considered by a court?

2. *Theodora Holding Corp.* also suggested non-monetary, or duty of loyalty limitations on the general power of corporations to do certain acts. The most important of these was with respect to purpose. Gifts or other acts that did not benefit the corporation are beyond the powers of a corporation. But what constitutes benefit to the corporation? *A.P. Smith Mfg.* and *Theodora Holding Corp.* suggest a very tenuous relationship between purpose and the benefit which can be deemed minimally sufficient. Bolstering the free enterprise system and the general social climate of the nation appear to be accepted by courts as sufficient. Indeed, the *Theodora Holding Corp.* opinion suggested the peculiar appropriateness of programs of 'rehabilitation' and 'education' for segments of the population alienated from the 'present social and economic system.' Does this mean, though, that under this rule corporations are *not* permitted to make gifts or incur other expenditures for rehabilitation and education of the population if the purposes of those gifts and expenditures are to alienate people from the current social and economic system and indoctrinate them in the benefits of an alternative system of greater economic benefit to the corporation? Could it be forbidden under American law? Should it be forbidden?

3. But the 'reasonable corporate purpose' standard suggests an irony. If, indeed, corporations are authorized, perhaps even encouraged to devote resources to bolstering the present social and economic system, then in what way does the relationship of corpora-

tions to the state differ in the United States from that of the People's Republic of China? Recall that enterprises in the People's Republic of China are bound to act consistent with and for the purpose of fostering the current social and economic system of the state.

4. **Problem:** Inspired by the U.S. President's campaign to federally fund religious charitable organizations in their programs of aid to the poor, the Board of Directors of Conglomo Corp. authorizes a contribution of $1,000,000 to the Church of Satan for the purpose of expanding the Church of Satan's 'Soup Kitchen for the Needy' Program. Assume that Conglomo has a net worth of $100,000,000,000, and its annual profits for the last ten years averaged $100,000,000. Assume further that there are no personal connections between the Church of Satan and any officer, director or major shareholder of Conglomo. Lastly assume that three of the core religious beliefs of the Church of Satan are that (1) people owe a blind obedience to employers, (2) eternal union with Satan is possible only by spending all one's money in this life, (3) members of all other religious sects are evil and must be shunned to the extent possible. Can this gift be challenged successfully? Would your answer be different if any members of the Board of Directors were also members of the Church of Satan?

5. *Michelson* illustrates well the difficulties of applying the doctrine of ultra vires in the United States. It suggests that the doctrine of ultra vires amalgamates a number of different issues.

First, the court draws the generally accepted distinction between void and voidable acts. Acts which are beyond the authority of a corporation's managers, but would otherwise be deemed to further the interests of the corporation, are voidable. Why would an act be beyond the authority of corporate managers? Acts which are both beyond the authority of corporate managers and of no benefit to the corporation are void. As the *Michelson* court explains, only void acts are designated ultra vires. These include all acts which are deemed as a matter of law to constitute a waste of corporate assets. What standard is used to determine whether an act furthers the corporate interest? Would the standard of *Theodora Holding Corp.* be appropriately applied to determine this issue? Does this distinction suggest that it is more likely that an act will be determined to be voidable rather than void more often than not?

Second, the court explains the limitations of shareholder power to ratify void and voidable acts. Voidable acts can be ratified by shareholders. Ratification can be accomplished in the manner permitted under state statute and the corporation's articles and by-laws. Delaware's rules governing ratification illustrate the application of the rule followed in a great number of jurisdictions. Void acts generally cannot be ratified by shareholders in due course. However, in many jurisdictions, even ultra vires acts, acts that waste corporate assets can be ratified by unanimous shareholder consent. These rules suggest that, at least in theory, there are no limits to the power of a corporation to act, whether or not such acts are in the interests of the corporation. Does this mean that the notion of ultra vires is essentially dead in the United States? Whatever the fate of ultra vires as a matter of theory, the result of these rules suggests, at a minimum, the construction of a hierarchy of difficulty for approval with real practical effect. Acts which are in the corporate interest but merely beyond the capacity of the corporate managers to appropriately effectuate are relatively easy to ratify. Shareholder approval of all other acts are substantially more difficult, if not practically impossible in many cases, to obtain.

Lastly, the *Michelson* court explains the procedural effects of a claim of ultra vires. In many jurisdictions, claims of ultra vires—corporate waste—raise issues of fact, not issues of law. This characterization makes the granting of summary judgment difficult where an ultra vires claim has survived the pleading stages of a litigation. It is for this reason, perhaps, that plaintiffs' counsel might be attracted to claims of ultra vires. In addition, shareholder ratification itself has procedural consequences. Generally, the defendant corporate managers have the burden of proving corporate benefit where the defendant raises issues of corporate waste. Shareholder ratification shifts the burden to defendant to prove corporate waste, that is, the absence of corporate benefit in the transaction. This tends to be a very significant burden. Shifting it to defendants can effectively end the case for all practical purposes.

6. The materials that follow illustrate the way that issues of corporate waste, corporate capacity, and liability for acts of corporate waste and lack of capacity have developed in the EU, Japan and China. No single alternative approach has emerged. Even within the EU, and under the harmonizing requirements of the First Company Law Directive, some variation in the application of the rules continues to exist. The English, for example, continue to focus on issues of capacity. The Japanese, in contrast, focus more formally on ultra vires as a general concept. As you review the materials that follow consider whether the formal differences in focus and approach result in differences in application, or whether convergence is in fact proceeding despite formal differences in statutory approaches.

2. *The Consequences of Ultra Vires Actions in the EU*

The First Company Law Directive has substantially narrowed the power of a corporation to avoid liability for contracts entered into which might be *ultra vires.*

Frank Wooldridge, *Company Law in the United Kingdom and the European Community: Its Harmonization and Unification*

(1991)

(excerpts pages 19–22)

Validity of the Obligations Entered into by the Company

Pre-incorporation contracts

Article 7 of the First Directive provides that if, before a company being formed has acquired legal personality, action has been carried out in its name and the company does not assume the obligations arising from such action, the persons who acted shall without limit, be jointly and severally liable thereon, unless otherwise agreed. Article 7 would seem to have been inspired by German and Italian law. The meaning of the last three words thereof would seem to be far from clear. It is perhaps surprising that Article 7 does not deal with the questions of ratification of pre-incorporation contracts.

Contracts entered into by a company already in existence

Article 9(1) of the First Directive stipulates that acts done by the organs of the company shall be binding on it even if these acts are not within the objects of the company, unless such acts exceed the powers which the law confers, or allows to be conferred, on those organs. It continues by stating that Member States may provide that the company shall not be bound where such acts are outside the objects of the company, if it proves that the third party knew that the act was outside those objects or could not, in view of the circumstances, have been unaware of it; disclosure of the statutes shall not of itself be sufficient proof thereof. The provisions of Article 9(1) represent a compromise between the legal provisions which governed the present matter in the five original Member States which accepted the principle of *spécialité statutaire* (which is comparable with the British and Irish doctrine of *ultra vires*), according to which a company may not perform legal transactions outside the scope of its objects, and those which were operative in Germany, according to which limitations placed on these authority conferred by the statutes might be disregarded, provided that the organ which acts on behalf of the company has the necessary authority to bind it. According to German law, a legal person has an unlimited capacity to act through its organs. German law conceives that a company's will is formed through the acts of will of these organs. The other original Member States accepted the mandate theory deprived from Roman Law, and enshrined in the Napoleonic Codes, according to which the relationship between a company and the person or body which deals on its behalf with a third party was conceived as being in essence that between a principal and an agent. The traditional view is that, in such a relationship, the scope of the agent's authority to enter into binding contracts is determined by the mandate given to the principal. In recent times, French law has moved away from the mandate theory towards a more Germanic approach, according to which a specific statutory definition is provided of the powers of management and representation of the *conseil d'administration* and the *président* of a *société anonyme* where the traditional board structure is adopted, and also of those of the *directoire* and its chairman where a *société anonyme* adopts an optional two-tier structure.

The term organ has no precise meaning under United Kingdom law and, perhaps somewhat unfortunately, it has not been used in the Companies Act 1989. It seems that the term is used in the Directive to refer to the body which normally has the power to represent the company. In the United Kingdom and the Republic of Ireland, this is the board of directors: managing directors would not seem to be organs for the present purposes, but possibly to come with the provisions of Article 9(3), which is discussed below. It appears that Article 9(1) apply *inter alia* to the situation familiar to some small English companies, where the company has only one director, and to board meetings where one director constitutes a quorum under the company's Articles. The usual method of representation in German companies is by the board of directors [*Vorstand*] in accordance with Article 78(1) of the *Aktiengesetz* of 1965 but, if the Articles so provide, some companies may be represented by a single director, two or more directors acting together, or by a director acting together with a commercial agent called a *Prokurist*, who has extensive powers by virtue of Articles 49–53 of the Commercial Code. Private companies are also represented in similar ways. Thus German company law knows many kinds of representative organs, but not all of them appear to be treated as organs for the purposes of Article 9(1) which, as already indicated, appears to be referring to the organ which normally has the power to represent the company. This seems to follow from Article 9(3) which contains certain legal provisions governing the effect of norms of national law derogating from the legal rules generally operative concerning the authority to represent the company.

It appears that there are some defects in the wording of Article 9(1) of the First Directive, and it is well known that the implementing legislation in Great Britain has given rise to some problems. Thus it is not clear what was meant by good faith for the purposes of the old section 35 of the Companies Act 1985. Further difficulties also arose as to whether the old Section 35 applied only to persons dealing with the company for valuable consideration, and whether this section applied to transactions with single directors in all circumstances.

The law in Great Britain has recently been changed by the enactment of section 35-35B and 322A of the Companies Act 1985, which were incorporated therein by sections 108 and 109 of the Companies Act 1989. These new sections were influenced by the recommendations contained in the Prentice Report, which suggested the abolition of the *ultra vires* ruled as between the company and third parties. The new provisions are rather complex and still appear to have some unsatisfactory features. Section 35(1), which goes further than is required by Article 9(1) of the Directive, provides that the validity of an act done by a company shall not be called into question on the ground of lack of capacity or by reason of anything in the company's memorandum. The provisions of section 35(2) are so worded that it is likely that a shareholder will be able to sue personally to prevent an *ultra vires* transaction only in very limited circumstances. Section 35A(1), which corresponds to the old section 35 of the Companies Act 1985, still uses the phrase good faith and the presumptions regarding good faith may well be too favourable to the third party. It is clear from the wording of sections 35(1) and 35A(2) that these sections are applicable to acts done by a company, including transactions to which it is a party, and thus should be treated as applicable to persons who deal with the company otherwise than for valuable consideration.

The new section 35A, unlike paragraph 6(1) of the Irish European Communities (Companies) Regulations, fails to make use of the concept of organs. It allows for the board of directors to act along with anyone ostensibly, impliedly or expressly authorized by it. The wording of section 35(A)(1), which provides that in favour of a person dealing with a company in good faith, the power of the directors to bind the company shall be deemed to be free of any limitation under the company's constitution, may perhaps be unfortunate, as such a limitation is capable of being treated as referring *inter alia* to a provision in the Articles prescribing the size of the quorum.

The complex provisions of section 322A of the Companies Act 1985 stipulate that certain transactions involving directors are voidable at the instance of the company. Although this section has a wide ambit, it seems possible to reconcile it with Article 9 of the First Directive on the ground that in so far as it fails to confer the power on the corporate organ, the board of directors, of entering into binding transactions with directors and other stated persons, the imposition of such a legal limitation is compatible with the first sentence of Article 9(1). The alternative argument that, where the other party to a transaction with the company was a director of the company, or of its holding company, or was a person connected or associated with such a director in accordance with the terms of section 322A, he was not a third party in the sense of the Directive, may not, however, be sustainable.

According to Article 9(2) of the First Directive, the limits of the powers of the organs of a company arising from the statutes or from a decision of the competent organs, may never be relied on against third parties, even if they have been disclosed. The provision appears to have been influenced by the German theory concerning the power of representation of the company's organs. It was originally thought unnecessary to implement Article 9(2) in Great Britain, probably because the rule in *Royal British Bank v. Turquand* and the doctrine to bind the company in relation to persons dealing with it. However, sections 35A(3) of the Companies Act 1985 would appear to take account of Article 9(2). This provision stipulates that the references made to limitations under the company's constitution include limitations deriving from a resolution of the general meeting or any class meeting of the shareholders or from any agreement between the members of the company or any class shareholders.

Article 9(3), which represents a compromise, stipulates that if the national law provides that authority to represent a company may, in derogation from the legal rules governing the subject, be conferred by the statutes on a single person or on several persons acting jointly, that law may provide that such a provision in the statutes may be relied on against third parties, on condition that it applies to the general power of representation. This provision also states that the question whether it can be relied upon against third parties is governed by Article 3. Although Article 9(3) has been implemented, for example, in the Netherlands, it has not been implemented in Great Britain. However, although the new provisions described above have some unsatisfactory features, they would seem to comply with the requirements of the First Directive more faithfully than that of the old ones.

68/151/EEC: First Council Directive of 9 March 1968

On co-ordination of safeguards which, for the protection of the interests of members and others, are required by member states of companies within the meaning of the second paragraph of article 58 of the treaty, with a view to making such safeguards equivalent throughout the community.

* * *

Article 9

1. Acts done by the organs of the company shall be binding upon it even if those acts are not within the objects of the company, unless such acts exceed the powers that the law confers or allows to be conferred on those organs. However, member states may provide that the company shall not be bound where such acts are outside the objects of the company, if it proves that the third party knew that the act was outside those objects or could not in view of the circumstances have been unaware of it; disclosure of the statutes shall not of itself be sufficient proof thereof.

2. The limits on the powers of the organs of the company, arising under the statutes or from a decision of the competent organs, may never be relied on as against third parties, even if they have been disclosed.

3. If the national law provides that authority to represent a company may, in derogation from the legal rules governing the subject, be conferred by the statutes on a single person or on several persons acting jointly, that law may provide that such a provision in the statutes may be relied on as against third parties on condition that it relates to the general power of representation; the question whether such a provision in the statutes can be relied on as against third parties shall be governed by article 3.

Comments and Questions

1. How does the approach of the First Company Law Directive differ from that of American law as illustrated in cases like *Michelson*?

2. Prior to the enactment of the First Company Law Directive, German scholars suggested that German corporate law effectively rejected application of a doctrine of ultra

vires. Evidence of this rejection of the doctrine of ultra vires include German court cases in which the courts refused to set aside the purchase by an AG of a GmbH where the resulting combination was not permitted under the AGs objectives or purposes and the statutory law of the GmbH which, with respect to third parties, binds the GmbH by action, even action exceeding the authority, of its managers. Henry P. deVries and Friedrich K. Juenger, *Limited Liability Contract: The GmbH* 64 Colum. L. Rev. 866, 879 & n. 94 (1964) (citing Gesetz betreffend die Gesellschaften mit beschränkter Haftung (Statute Concerning the Limited Liability Companies) § 37(2), and Reichsgericht (II. Zivilsenat), Nov. 19, 1926, 115 R.G.Z. 246). Do the provisions of the First Company Law Directive effectively change that assessment?

TCB Ltd. v. VWA Gray

English High Court (Chancery Division)
[1986] 3 CMLR 439
21 November 1985

The Vice-Chancellor

In this action, the plaintiff company TCB Ltd. is suing the defendant Mr. Victor Gray on a guarantee dated 27 January 1982. Apart from two major issues of fact, the history of the matter is not seriously in dispute. I will start by setting out the main facts as I find them and then come back to the two major issues.

TCB is a secondary bank whose offices are in Brighton. The personnel of TCB involved in this case were two directors, Mr. Gordon and Mr. Burgess, and a solicitor, Mr. Horsepool, who had formerly been head of TCB's in-house legal department and at the material time was in private practice: he continued to act as a part time in-house lawyer to TCB.

Mr. Gray was a very successful businessman. Over the years, he had built up two prosperous private companies Graylaw Holdings Ltd. ('Graylaw') and Link Service Stations Ltd. ('Link'): Mr. Gray was the principal shareholder in both companies although there were minority shareholders in both. Mr. Gray also had business enterprises outside these two companies and was a wealthy man. The Finance Director of Graylaw was a Mr. Grafham to whom Mr. Gray habitually left the detail of his and his companies' financial dealings. The directors of Link were Mr. Gray and a Mr. Pond: Mr. Green was the secretary.

In January 1982 Mr. Gray wished to enter into a specific transaction through the medium of Graylaw and Link. For that purpose he needed to borrow £5 million. He instructed two loan brokers, a Mr. Nolborough and a Mr. Stark. In some way that was never clarified in evidence, they in turn contacted another loan broker, Mr. Gill.

The first TCB heard of the proposal was a telephone call from Mr. Gill followed by letter from him dated 18 January 1982. In that letter Mr. Gill asked TCB to give sympathetic consideration to a loan of £5 million on a two year basis, interest only. The letter contained the following passage:

It would be noted that Mr. Victor Gray is the principal shareholder and his guarantee would be available and I would like, if possible, for the other minority shareholders to be ignored. As additional security Mr. Gray has personally available the under noted share portfolio which currently values in total between £3,800,000 and £4m and would be offered to TCB Limited.

The letter then sets out particulars of certain shares belonging to Mr. Gray.

There was then a series of telephone calls between Mr. Gordon of TCB and Mr. Stark. Mr. Gordon made a file note on 20 January 1982 part of which reads as follows:

The security is undoubtedly bolstered by Mr. Gray's guarantee supported by a Charge over the shares listed in Mr. Gill's letter. These have a current market value of almost £4m and are totally unencumbered at the present time, although it has not yet been established what part of the equity in the various companies they represent, and hence their marketability must be in some doubt.

A meeting was arranged and took place at TCB's Brighton offices on Thursday, 21 January. There were present Mr. Burgess and Mr. Gordon (For TCB), Mr. Gray, Mr. Stark and (according to some accounts) Mr. Nolborough. The meeting lasted between 1 and 1 1/2 hours and the whole proposal was discussed. The first major issue of fact between the parties is what was said about TCB requiring a guarantee from Mr. Gray. Mr. Burgess and Mr. Gordon said that the matter was specifically raised and discussed in the body of the meeting, that Mr. Gray sought to persuade them not to insist on an unlimited guarantee but to accept a guarantee limited to the value of the shares to be deposited by him as collateral but that they insisted on a full guarantee. Mr. Gray, on the other hand, says that the question of the guarantee only came up in passing when the meeting was breaking up and that he was left with the impression that his guarantee was merely to be a device whereby his collateral security was to be charged. I will come back to this point. When the meeting ended, TCB had agreed in principle to make the loan and on the terms of the loan subject to TCB making further inquiries.

On the next day, Friday 22 January, Mr. Gordon made a note of the agreed proposal for consideration by the Board of TCB. I will quote two passages from that note: Mr. Gray has substantial assets outside Graylaw and is offering in support of his personal guarantee a charge over stock market shares having a current market value of about £4m...As it would not be practicable to take second charges over the two hundred or so properties in Graylaw, it has been agreed that we will simply lend to the company relying on its balance sheet's net worth, but at the same time Mr. Gray will further support his personal guarantee by charging the 85% shareholding which he owns in Graylaw. He will similarly charge his shareholding in Links Service Stations Limited.

The proposal was approved by the Board of TCB and on the same day, Friday 22 January, Mr. Gordon drafted and sent to Mr. Stark a letter confirming in principle that TCB were prepared to make an advance of £5m to Graylaw and Link jointly. The letter required payment of a commitment fee of £50,000 and continued:

On receipt of the commitment fee we would be prepared to issue a formal Letter of Offer and at such time instruct our Legal Department in view of the urgency which you have told us exists here. The general terms of the offer would incorporate the following:

1. The advance to be in favour of Graylaw Holdings Limited and Link Service Stations Limited jointly. A debenture to be granted by the latter company only.

2. Mr. Gray to charge his 8.4 million shares in Graylaw and his shares in Link Service Stations Limited.

3. Mr. Gray also to charge the following shares in support of his personal guarantee [there then follow particulars of four stock market shareholdings].

4. TCB to advance £5m on a 24 month period with interest being charged at 3% over three month capital LIBOR with appropriate rollsovers, such interest to be

> paid monthly in arrears. Repayment in part or full to be permitted without penalty at any time during the initial twelve month period, thereafter subject to 1/2% redemption fee.

Meanwhile, on the same day, Friday 22 January, Mr. Gray informed Mr. Grafham of his success in raising the loan and the terms of the loan. A meeting was arranged with Mr. Gray's solicitor, Mr. Rowan of Carter & Co, for that afternoon. At that meeting at Mr. Rowan's office, Mr. Gray explained to Mr. Grafham and Mr. Rowan what he had arranged with TCB. Mr. Grafham and Mr. Rowan found it difficult to operate without a formal offer document and put through a telephone call to Mr. Burgess of TCB. Over the telephone, Mr. Burgess read out the letter of 22 Janaury to Mr. Stark; all three present in Mr. Rowan's office (ie including Mr. Gray) heard the letter read out. Mr. Rowan made a note of what he heard. Mr. Rowan and Mr. Grafham both said in evidence (and I accept) that the question of Mr. Gray's guarantee was discussed at this meeting on Friday 22 January. Although it was clear that neither Mr. Gray nor Mr. Grafham liked the personal guarantee, both Mr. Grafham and Mr. Rowan understood Mr. Gray was to give his personal guarantee and thereafter proceeded on that basis.

Mr. Gray was insisting that the loan should go through with the greatest urgency. The commitment fee was paid on the afternoon of 22 January. Mr. Rowan agreed to prepare the necessary documents so as to enable completion to take place in the middle of the following week. Mr. Gray was planning to go to Switzerland during the following week and it was arranged that he should give a power of attorney to Mr. Rowan to enable Mr. Rowan to complete the matter. At the meeting at Mr. Rowan's office, his assistant, Mr. McGuiness, prepared a power of attorney which was signed by Mr. Gray. I will have to come back to the form of the power of attorney in detail; for present purposes it is sufficient to say that on its face there is no seal, wafer, locus sigilli or any other indication that a seal was affixed.

The preparation of the necessary documents in the limited time available was a major undertaking. In all some 100 documents had to be prepared and executed. In addition, it emerged that not all the securities which Mr. Gray had agreed to charge stood in his name: many were in the names of others. It was agreed between Mr. Rowan and TCB that this problem should be dealt with by each of the registered holders of the shares (whom I will call 'the third party mortgagees') entering into TCB's standard form of guarantee and depositing the securities registered in its name in support of its guarantee. Liability under the guarantees of each of the third party mortgagees was to be expressly limited to the value for the time being of the securities deposited by each of them. There is a telex from TCB to Mr. Rowan, paragraph 5 of which reads as follows:

> Form of guarantee from each third party mortgagee in the standard form subject to addition 'it is also expressly provided that the liability of the guarantor shall be limited to the value of any securities from time to time deposited by the guarantors with TCB'.

This paragraph is to be contrasted with the earlier part of the telex which reads as follows:

> My requirements are as follows
>
> 1. Guarantee in standard form executed by Mr. Rowan on behalf of Mr. Victor Gray as donee of general power of attorney.

TCB's standard form of guarantee is in unlimited form.

Monday, 25 January was a busy day. Mr. Rowan and Mr. McGuiness were preparing the necessary documentation, tracing the whereabouts of the securities to be deposited and in some cases arranging to clear off existing charges. At some stage during that day, one copy of TCB's standard form of guarantee was amended by typing at the end of it a clause 15 which reads as follows:

> 15. It is also expressly provided that the liability of the Guarantor shall be limited to the value of any securities from time to time deposited by the Guarantor with TCB.

The standard form of guarantee as so amended was then photostated. The transaction involved ten guarantees in all, one to be executed by Mr. Gray personally, the other nine to be executed by the third party mortgagees.

It was at this stage that the crucial mistake was made. Mr. Gray had not left for Switzerland by Monday night and various documents were sent to him for execution, including his guarantee. In error the form of guarantee sent for execution by Mr. Gray was one of the photostats containing the typed clause 15, which limited liability under the guarantee. Mr. Gray executed his guarantee in this form and the documents were returned to Mr. Rowan's office. Given the pressure of work, it is in no way surprising that this error was made. Moreover I have no doubt that, so far as Mr. Rowan was concerned, it was an error. At all times, rightly or wrongly, he intended Mr. Gray to sign the guarantee in unlimited form.

On the next day, Tuesday 26 January, the activity continued unabated in order to get the documents ready. Mr. Rowan and Mr. McGuiness started early. At some stage they were joined by Mr. Grafham. Later still (the time is of great importance) they were joined by Mr. Horsepool of TCB. Mr. Horsepool puts the time of his arrival at about 2 pm, with which Mr. Grafham agrees. Mr. Horsepool then sat down to check the documents on behalf of TCB. Very soon he came across Mr. Gray's personal guarantee and noticed the fact that an error had been made by including the limiting provisions of clause 15. He drew this error to Mr. Rowan's attention. Mr. Rowan at once agreed that there was an error. He thought he could correct it under the power of attorney he held but, as he said, to 'cover his back' he decided to ring Mr. Gray. There were present in the room at the time he made the telephone call the three solicitors (Mr. Rowan, Mr. McGuiness and Mr. Horsepool) and Mr. Grafham, Mr. Gray's own financial consultant. All are agreed that Mr. Rowan said he was going to ring up Mr. Gray, that he made a telephone call, ostensibly to Mr. Gray, that he explained the problem and appeared to get approval for deletion of clause 15. Mr. Rowan's evidence was that he did ring Mr. Gray at his flat in Regent's Park, spoke to Mr. Gray and got the necessary approval. Mr. Gray denies that any such telephone call took place and indeed says that it could not have done so as he was not in his flat at any time that day. That is the second major issue of fact to which I shall have to return. In the event, Mr. Rowan did delete clause 15 from the guarantee signed by Mr. Gray, initialling the deletion and adding the words 'deletion by Robert Rowan as attorney for Victor William Arthur Gray.'

By the later evening of Tuesday 26 January all the documents had been executed. The only other document that I need specifically mention is the debenture executed by Graylaw and Link and a deed supplemental thereto. Both documents purport to be executed by Link in the same way. The seal of Link is affixed and opposite it is signed as Director by Mr. Rowan as attorney for Mr. Gray and by Mr. Green as Secretary. Mr. Rowan was not a director of Link.

The full £5m was drawn down on the next day, Wednesday 27 January. A year later, following the collapse of the Isle of Man Bank, Savings and Investment Bank, Graylaw and Link collapsed and went into liquidation. The security proved inadequate to repay TCB in full. On 8 February 1983 payment was demanded on the guarantee, and when the demand was not met this action was begun. The amount claimed (but not yet proved or agreed) is approximately £1.8m.

At first sight this was a straightforward case. But Mr. Gray had put forward broadly two lines of defence. First, he says that the deletion by Mr. Rowan of clause 15 was not authorized by Mr. Gray either under the power of attorney or by the alleged telephone call on Tuesday 26 January. As a result, it is said, Mr. Gray's liability is limited as stated in clause 15 to the value of the securities deposited by him and he is under no further liability. The power of attorney is invalid since it was not sealed by Mr. Gray. The disputed telephone call on Tuesday 26 January never took place. The second line of defence was only put forward by amendment at the start of the trial and is more complicated. Mr. Gray personally only entered into the transaction on the basis that he was guaranteeing the liability of the principal debtors, Graylaw and Link, which liability was to be secured by a debenture granted by, inter alia, Link. Then, it is said, the debenture was not validly granted by Link since it was not validly executed by Link: Link's articles require the company seal to be signed by a director, and Mr. Gray as director could not delegate his duties and powers to Mr. Rowan. So, the argument runs, TCB having failed to acquire proper security from one of the principal debtors, Link, Mr. Gray either never came under any liability as guarantor or was discharged from such liability.

Before turning to these arguments in detail I must first make findings as to the two major issues of fact. First, what happened at the meeting in Brighton on Thursday 21 January? I have no doubt that the version given by Mr. Gordon and Mr. Burgess is correct. The letter from Mr. Gill of 18 January says in terms that Mr. Gray's guarantee 'would be available' without any reference to such guarantee being limited: on the contrary, the letter refers to Mr. Gray's own shares as being 'additional security'. Mr. Gray told me he knew nothing of Mr. Gill. I have considerable doubts whether this is true. But in any event Mr. Gill got his instructions from someone: if from Mr. Stark or Mr. Nolborough, their instructions must in turn have come from Mr. Gray. Not one of the three loan brokers was called by Mr. Gray to give evidence and the letter of 18 January was otherwise in accordance with his instructions. Therefore the proposition before the meeting of 18 January was for a full guarantee to be given by Mr. Gray.

It seems to me most likely that at a meeting lasting 1 to 1/2 hours the question of the guarantee was not discussed. I found both Mr. Gordon and Mr. Burgess convincing witnesses and I accept their evidence. They said that in a transaction involving private companies, it was the almost invariable practice of TCB to insist on an unlimited guarantee from the principal shareholder. In this case there was an additional reason to insist on this requirement since Mr. Gray declined to disclose the purpose for which he was going to use the money borrowed, beyond saying that it was to finance an acquisition. I accept that Mr. Gray tried to negotiate that the guarantee should be limited, but that it was made clear to him that a full guarantee was required. The evidence of Mr. Gordon and Mr. Burgess is borne out by the fact that both sides' lawyers and Mr. Grafham (Mr. Gray's own financial adviser) thereafter proceeded without any doubt that the guarantee was to be unlimited.

Against this weight of inherent probability and convincing evidence, there is only the evidence of Mr. Gray himself. I did not find him a very satisfactory witness, even after making due allowances for his illness, which obviously gave him considerable trouble while giving evidence. He is obviously a very shrewd man who could well appreciate the significance of the questions being put to him. The extent of his memory seemed to be directly proportional to the desirability of his having any recollection on the point. Although not demonstrated under cross-examination to have told any lies, I treat his evidence with very great reserve.

Therefore I find that on Thursday 21 January and at all times thereafter Mr. Gray well knew that he was being required to give an unlimited guarantee as a term of the loan and so instructed his advisers. I have found the second issue of fact much more difficult. It will be remembered that Mr. Rowan, Mr. McGuiness, Mr. Grafham and Mr. Horsepool all gave evidence as to a telephone call on the afternoon of Tuesday 26 January. According to Mr. Horsepool's recollection he did not arrive at the meeting in Mr. Rowan's office until 2 pm, and he put the time of the call between 2.30 and 3 pm. The others put the call a little earlier.

Mr. Gray says that on Tuesday 26 January he was on the British Airways flight from Heathrow to Zurich accompanied by a Mrs. Godfrey (travelling as Mrs. Gray), which flight departed at 3 pm. His evidence that he was on that flight was most strongly corroborated by a representative of the investigation branch of British Airways who produced photocopies of tickets in the name of Mr. and Mrs. Gray on the flight showing them with seat allocations on the plane, which allocations are made at the time of check-in. He also confirmed that the flight actually departed at 3 pm; the last time for check-in was half an hour before, ie 2.30 pm. I find this compelling evidence that Mr. Gray was on that flight. In those circumstances it was physically impossible for Mr. Gray to be at his flat in Regent's Park at 2.15 or 2.30 pm to receive a telephone call from Mr. Rowan and still be in time to check in at Heathrow before 2.30 pm.

Mr. Gray, supported, by Mrs. Godfrey, gave a detailed account of his journey to London Airport. They say that Mr. Gray picked up Mrs. Godfrey at her home in Loughton, Essex, which they left at around 9.30 am. They then drove in Mr. Gray's Rolls Royce to one of the airport hotels (The Sheraton, according to Mr. Gray) and arrived before the restaurant was open. When the restaurant opened, they had lunch, then drove to the terminal, parked the car and checked in. They then boarded the flight to Zurich. They never went anywhere near the Regent's Park flat. There was no opportunity for Mr. Gray to make or receive a telephone call.

Mr. Brodie (for Mr. Gray) submits that the only resolution of this conflict of evidence is that Mr. Rowan pretended to speak to Mr. Gray on the telephone but in fact did not do so. Mr. Brodie does not submit that Mr. McGuiness, Mr. Grafham and Mr. Horsepool were lying or mistaken in saying that Mr. Rowan made the call, but that Mr. Rowan deceived them as to who he spoke to, if anyone. I find this impossible to accept. So far as Mr. Rowan is concerned, when faced with the error which had been made by including clause 15, it was perfectly reasonable to 'cover his back' by seeking specific authority from Mr. Gray before altering a document which Mr. Gray himself had signed. But if he found Mr. Gray was not available when he rang, surely the others present in the room and listening would have heard something from Mr. Rowan's words on the telephone which would have alerted them to the fact that he had not got through to Mr. Gray. Why should Mr. Rowan go to the extraordinary lengths of a fictitious phone call, decided upon on the spur of the moment, when he held what he then thought was a valid power of attorney to put matters right?

I accept Mr. Rowan's evidence that he did in fact speak to Mr. Gray and get his approval to the deletion of clause 15. Mr. Brodie submitted that Mr. Rowan was an untruthful witness and relied heavily on the discrepancies between his evidence in the witness box and what he had earlier said in letters and an affidavit, viz that clause 15 was only typed on to the guarantee in error after Mr. Gray had signed it. But this seems to me a faulty recollection of detail which anyone could make. I have some reservation about Mr. Rowan's attendance notes of telephone calls between himself and Mr. Gray which took place in January 1983 after Mr. Rowan had received a letter from Mr. Gray's present solicitors alleging that the alteration was unauthorized: the attendance notes smack of self serving. But as to the events of Tuesday 26 January, I accept his evidence, consistent as it is with the evidence of the other witnesses.

I think the probable reconciliation of the conflicting evidence is that the account given by Mr. Gray and Mrs. Godfrey of their leisurely progress from Loughton to Heathrow is not true. Mr. Gray painted himself, I am sure correctly, as being a busy man. He was in the middle of setting up a loan for £5m and a bid of some sort for a company, now disclosed to have been St Pirran. It takes 45–60 minutes to get from Mrs. Godfrey's home to London, and at midday a similar time or less from central London to Heathrow. I find it improbable that a busy man would have allowed five hours to get to London Airport. I did not find the evidence of either Mr. Gray or Mrs. Godfrey convincing on this point. Their accounts of their movements on that morning were quite detailed, yet neither could give the name of the hotels they stayed in that night in Zurich. Their evidence seemed to me to be carefully collated and I do not accept it. I think the probability is that Mr. Gray did go to his flat and received the telephone call there just before he left. I think the call must have been made a little earlier than Mr. Horsepool and Mr. Grafham remember. I find therefore that Mr. Rowan was expressly authorized to delete clause 15 from the guarantee signed by Mr. Gray.

I turn to consider Mr. Gray's defenses in law. Mr. Brodie (for Mr. Gray) accepts that if, as I have found, Mr. Gray over the telephone expressly authorized the deletion by Mr. Rowan of clause 15 of the guarantee, then that deletion was validly made. Accordingly, it is not strictly necessary on this aspect of the case for me to consider the validity of the Power of Attorney. But since the Power of Attorney was also used in connection with the grant of the debenture by Link, I must decide the point.

The Power of Attorney

The Power of Attorney is described as being a general power of attorney made by Mr. Gray. It reads:

> I appoint Robert Rowan to be my attorney in accordance with section 10 of the Powers of Attorney Act 1971.
>
> IN WITNESS whereof I have here set my hand and seal the day and year first above written.

It is signed by Mr. Gray and opposite his signature there appear the words 'signed sealed and delivered by the said Victor William Arthur Gray in the presence of' and then Mr. McGuiness witnesses it.

Section 1(1) of the Powers of Attorney Act 1971 reads as follows:

> An instrument creating a power of attorney shall be signed and sealed by, or by direction and in the presence of, the donor of the power.

As I have said, there is no seal or other mark on the document to indicate that it has been sealed, nor is there any oral evidence to suggest that Mr. Gray did anything when executing it beyond signing it. On the contrary, Mr. McGuiness said that the lack of a seal or wafer on the document was an oversight on his behalf. Approaching this evidence on any normal basis I would be unable to find as a fact that anything constituting sealing took place. Indeed, on the ordinary test of balance of probabilities, I would hold that it did not.

I was pressed by Mr. Reid (for TCB) with a line of cases culminating in First National Securities Ltd. v. Jones ([1978] Ch 109) in which the Courts have adopted a benign approach in deciding that a document has been executed as a deed. The Courts have gone a long way towards holding that any document delivered as a deed (even though nothing is done to the document itself at the time of execution) is proved to have been executed under seal. Yet no case in the High Court has been cited to me in which the court has gone as far as it would be necessary to go in this case, there being nothing to indicate that something amounting to sealing took place beyond the fact that the words of the document refer to it having been sealed. If I were to hold that this document was in fact sealed, I would not only be flying in the face of what actually happened, but also disregarding the statutory requirement that the document should be sealed. I think it would be wrong to extend the legal fiction any further and I decline to do so. If it is open to Mr. Gray to raise the point, I would hold that the Power of Attorney had not in fact been sealed.

But is it open to Mr. Gray to raise the point? In my judgment the answer is 'No' since he is estopped from denying that the document was sealed. Mr. Gray has executed a document drafted as a deed and which says that he has thereunto set his hand and seal. The document states in terms that it was signed, sealed and delivered in the presence of Mr. McGuiness. There is therefore a representation of the fact that it was in fact sealed. Mr. Gray executed the document with the intention that it should be relied on as a Power of Attorney and knowing that ICB were going to rely on it as such. TCB in fact relied on it to their detriment, since they advanced money in reliance on documents executed under the power. The case therefore has all the necessary elements of a classic estoppel.

I am fortified in reaching this result by the alternative ground for decision given by Danckwerts J in Stromdale & Ball Ltd. v. Burden ([1952] Ch 223 at 230). In that case there was a wafer seal attached to the document and the first ground of decision was that the execution of a document with a wax or wafer or other indication of a seal is sufficient adoption or recognition of the seal to amount to execution as a deed. But at page 230 Danckwerts J treated the case as also raising 'the clearest case of estoppel possible.'

In First National Securities Ltd. v. Jones (At p 121C) Sir David Cairns said this:

> I am sure that many documents intended by all parties to be deeds are now executed without any further formality than the signature opposite the words 'signed, sealed and delivered' usually in the presence of a witness, and I think it would be lamentable if the validity of documents so executed could be successfully challenged.

I agree. But for myself I prefer to hold that in the ordinary case a person so executing a deed is subsequently estopped from denying that he has sealed it rather than to find as a fact that something has occurred which we all know has not occurred.

The debenture granted by Link

It will be recalled that Mr. Brodie's second line of defence was that the guarantee given by Mr. Gray was invalidated or discharged by the failure of TCB to obtain a valid debenture from one of the principal debtors, Link.

The articles of Link incorporate clause 113 of Table A, which provides:

> The Directors shall provide for the safe custody of the Seal which shall only be used by the authority of the Directors or a Committee of the Directors authorized by the Directors in that behalf, and every instrument to which the Seal shall be affixed shall be signed by a Director and shall be countersigned by the Secretary or by a second Director or by some other person appointed by the Directors for the purpose.

The debenture was not signed by any director of Link, but by an attorney for a director. There is no power in the articles of Link for a director to act by an attorney. Therefore, says Mr. Brodie, on the principle delegatus non potest delegare the seal was not affixed in accordance with the requirements of the articles: accordingly the debenture is not the act of Link.

Apart from section 9(1) of the European Communities Act 1982, there would be much force in these submissions. But in my judgment that section provides a complete answer. Under the old law, a person dealing with a corporation was required to look at the company's memorandum and articles to satisfy himself that the transaction was within the corporate capacity of the company and was to be carried through in accordance with the requirements of its articles. The rigour of those requirements was only tempered to the extent that the rule in Royal British Bank v. Turquand ((1856) 6 E & B 327) allowed third parties to assume that acts of internal management had been properly carried out.

It has been generally assumed that the old law has to a large extent been swept away by section 9(1) of the 1972 Act which provides as follows:

> In favour of a person dealing with a company in good faith, any transaction decided on by the directors shall be deemed to be one which it is within the capacity of the company to enter into, and the power of the directors to bind the company shall be deemed to be free of any limitation under the memorandum or articles of association; and a party to a transaction so decided on shall not be bound to enquire as to the capacity of the company to enter into it or as to any such limitation on the powers of the directors and shall be presumed to have acted in good faith unless the contrary is proved.

Section 9(1) was passed to bring the law of England into line with Article 9 of Council Directive 68/151 of the European Economic Community. Article 9 provides:

> 1. Acts done by the organs of the company shall be binding upon it even if those acts are not within the objects of the company, unless such acts exceed the powers that the law confers or allows to be conferred on those organs.
>
> However, Member-States may provide that the company shall not be bound where such acts are outside the objects of the company, if it proves that the third party knew that the act was outside those objects or could not in view of the circumstances have been unaware of it; disclosure of the statutes shall not of itself be sufficient proof thereof.
>
> 2. The limits on the powers of the organs of the company, arising under the statutes or from a decision of the competent organs, may never be relied on as against third parties, even if they have been disclosed.
>
> 3. If the national law provides that authority to represent a company may, in derogation from the legal rules governing the subject, be conferred by the statutes on a single person or on several persons acting jointly, that law may provide that such a provision in the statutes may be relied on as against third parties on condition that it relates to the general power of representation; the question whether such a provision in the statutes can be relied on as against third parties shall be governed by Article 3.) In approaching the construction of the section, it is in my judgment relevant to note that the manifest purpose of both the directive and the section is to enable people to deal with a company in good faith without being adversely affected by any limits on the company's capacity or its rules for internal management. Given good faith, a third party is able to deal

with a company through its 'organs' (as the directive describes them) or directors. Section 9(1) achieves this in two ways. First it 'deems' all transactions to be authorized. Second, it 'deems' that the directors can bind the company without limitations. The second part of the section reinforces this by expressly abolishing the old doctrine of constructive notice of the contents of a company's Memorandum and Articles. It being the obvious purpose of the section to obviate the commercial inconvenience and frequent injustice caused by the old law, I approach the construction of the section with a great reluctance to construe it in such a way as to reintroduce, through the back door, any requirement that a third party acting in good faith must still investigate the regulating documents of a company.

Mr. Brodie, whilst accepting that TCB had no actual or imputed knowledge of any irregularity in the execution of the debenture, at first submitted that TCB did not act 'in good faith' within the meaning of the section since TCB was put on inquiry by the unusual manner in which the debenture had been executed. He said that TCB should have looked at the articles and would then have discovered the irregularity. Accordingly, he submitted, they were not acting 'in good faith.' On further consideration Mr. Brodie abandoned this argument, to my mind rightly. The last words of the second part of the subsection expressly provide that good faith is to be presumed: the second part further provides that the person dealing with the company is not bound to inquire as to limitations on the powers of directors. In my judgment it is impossible to establish lack of 'good faith' within the meaning of the section solely by alleging that inquiries ought to have been made which the second part of the subsection says needs not be made.

Mr. Brodie's next submission was that, in order for the section to apply at all, the first requirement is that there must be a transaction by the company. Since Link never sealed the debenture in the only way authorized by the articles, there was here no transaction by Link at all: the debenture was not the act of Link. If this argument is right, it drives a coach and horses through the section: in every dealing with the company the third party would have to look at its articles to ensure that the company was binding itself in an authorized manner. In my judgment the section does not have that effect. The section is dealing with purported actions by a company which, having regard to its internal documents, may be a nullity eg acts outside its corporate capacity. In such a case under the old law the purported act of the company would not be the act of the company at all. Yet the first part of section 9(1) 'deems' it so to be. Similarly a document under seal by the company executed otherwise than in accordance with its articles was not, under the old law, the act of the company: but section 9(1) deems it so to be since the powers of the directors are deemed to be free from limitations, ie as to the manner of affixing the company's seal. In my judgment, section 9(1) applies to transactions which a company purports to enter into and deems them to be validly entered into.

Mr. Brodie also submitted that Article 113 (regulating the way in which Link can seal documents) is not a 'limitation' on the powers of directors to bind the company but a mandatory direction as to the only way in which the company can bind itself. I reject this submission also. Link has either actual or (under section 9(1)) deemed capacity to enter into the debenture. Being an artificial person, Link can only enter into debenture by its agents, the directors. Any provision in the articles as to the manner in which the directors can act as agents for the company is a limitation on their power to bind the company and as such falls within the first part of section 9(1). Finally, Mr. Brodie submitted that in order to rely on the section it has to be shown that the debenture was a transaction 'decided on by the Directors.' I agree. Then, says Mr. Brodie, the evidence shows that the directors of Link never did decide to enter into this debenture.

The facts as I find them are that on completion of the loan there was handed to TCB a Minute of a Board meeting of Link held on 25 January 1982. That Minute records that there were present Mr. Gray, Mr. Pond, Mr. Green and Mr. Rowan. Paragraph 2 of the Minute, after reciting the proposal to grant the debenture, continued:

It was therefore resolved that the facility be accepted and the Form of Debenture in favour of TCB be executed under the Common Seal of the Company in the presence of Messrs Rowan (as attorney for Mr. Gray) and Mr. Green.

Paragraph 5 of the Minute provided as follows:

> It was further resolved that Messrs Rowan and Green be authorized to deliver the said Debenture to TCB and that they may be also empowered to execute any other documents required by TCB to complete the security documentation.

The minutes are signed by Mr. Rowan 'as attorney for V Gray.' The evidence clearly established that no such meeting of the directors of Link ever took place. But in fact all the directors of Link individually had decided to grant the debenture, although not at a meeting at which they were all present.

It has to be borne in mind on this aspect of the case that I have to determine whether a valid debenture was granted by Link. In my judgment Link, having put forward the Minutes of the meeting of 25 January as one of the completion documents on the basis of which TCB made the loan, could not be heard to challenge the validity of that Minute by denying that such meeting ever took place. Therefore the Minute stands as irrefutable evidence against Link that the grant of the debenture was a 'transaction decided on by the Directors.' Accordingly the necessary basis for section 9(1) of the 1972 Act to apply as between Link and TCB exists. It follows that the debenture was valid, and Mr. Gray's second line of defence also fails.

A number of other alternative arguments were advanced on each side which it is unnecessary for me to deal with.

I accordingly hold that Mr. Gray is liable without limit on his personal guarantee. I will hear Counsel further as to the Order I should make to determine the quantum of his liability.

Comments and Questions

1. To what extent has European Union law effected the law of corporate capacity in England? Which approach makes more sense to you, that of England prior to the enactment of Section 9(1) of the European Communities Act of 1982, or the approach of Section 9(1)? The effect of the change is to benefit third parties in transactions with corporations. Does it make sense, as a matter of corporate policy, to shift the burden of capacity from third parties to the corporation?

2. Though EU harmonization efforts have regularized, to some extent, the consequences of acting outside the objects of the corporation, those harmonization efforts have left to state law the regulation of the objects and powers of corporations, and the manner in which such objects and powers are conferred. The result, in most of the EU

Member States is a legal regime in which careful drafting of the "objectives" and "powers" clauses of the corporate charter become important. The two English cases, excerpted below, provide an illustration of current practice and the problems that sometime arise.

3. As you read the materials that follow, consider whether there are ways in which a good lawyer can draft around the problems of "objects" and "powers" limitations. Do you think that the effort involved in dealing with this issue is worth the fuss? What value does this exercise serve? Does it protect shareholders? Third parties? The state? Does it serve as a substitute for some other limitation?

Rolled Steel, Ltd. v. British Steel Corp.

Court of Appeal (Civil Division)

[1986] 1 Ch 246, [1985] 3 All ER 52, [1985] 2 WLR 908, [1984] BCLC 466, [1983–85] BCC 99, 158, (48 MLR 109), (44 CLJ 39)

11 June 1984

SLADE LJ, (giving the first judgment at the invitation of Lawton LJ). This is an appeal by British Steel Corporation (BSC) and Mr. Vivian Rupert Vaughan Cooper, who were two of the defendants in two consolidated actions, from an order of Vinelott J made on 23 March 1983. There is also a cross-appeal from the order by Rolled Steel Products (Holdings) Ltd., which was the plaintiff in the action.

The appeal and cross-appeal raise important questions of principle concerning, inter alia, the capacity and powers of companies incorporated under the Companies Acts and the powers and authority of their directors. Section 9(1) of the European Communities Act 1972, which may be important when such questions nowadays fall to be considered as between a company and persons dealing with it in good faith, had not become law when the transactions in issue in the present case were effected. For the purposes of this present judgment this subsection therefore requires no further attention.

The trial of these consolidated actions lasted for about 19 days and ended on or about 7 April 1981. Judgment was given by Vinelott J on 2 December 1981. There then followed a number of disputes concerning the detailed terms required to give effect to this judgment. The matter having been brought back to the judge for the resolution of these disputes, he delivered a further judgment for this purpose on 23 March 1983, following which the order now under appeal was drawn up.

The judgment of 2 December 1981 (some parts of which are now reported: see [1982] 3 All ER 1057, [1982] Ch 478) occupies nearly 100 pages of transcript, and sets out very carefully and comprehensively the long and involved history of this case. Since various important findings of fact are challenged, I cannot avoid a similar, if briefer, recital of this history.

[omitted; for a brief recounting of the relevant facts see the opinion on Lawton LJ., below]

The course of the trial before Vinelott J [is omitted].

* * *

The issues on the appeal and the cross-appeal

* * *

Though a large number of subsidiary points have been raised and argued on both sides, I think that the principal issues that have fallen for decision on this appeal have resolved themselves to seven. (1) The shareholders' consent point. (2) The judge's finding that, of the directors of RSP, at least Mr. Shenkman had abused his powers in entering into the relevant transactions. (3) The judge's finding of knowledge of such abuse on the part of Colvilles, BSC and Mr. Cooper. (4) The no due authorisation and Turquand's case points. (5) The ultra vires point. (6) The constructive trust point. (7) The relief (if any) to be granted to the plaintiff. The first, second, third, fifth and sixth points are raised by the notice of appeal. The fourth is raised by the notice of cross-appeal. The last is raised by both notices.

(1) The shareholders' consent point

[omitted]

(5) The ultra vires point

For many years, the phrase 'ultra vires' has from time to time been used by company lawyers in two senses. Primarily it is used to describe acts which are beyond the capacity of a company. As is pointed out by the editors of Gore-Browne on Companies (43rd edn) para 3-1, the phrase is also sometimes used to describe acts which are not beyond the capacity of the company but simply beyond the authority of either the board of directors or a majority of the shareholders.

In many instances, the sense in which the phrase is being used is far from clear. However, I think it plain that paras 11 and 13 of the statement of claim in this case, in alleging that each of the guarantee and the debenture were 'ultra vires and void,' were intended to allege that their execution was beyond the corporate capacity of RSP, on the grounds that they were executed not for the purposes or benefit of RSP but for the purposes or benefit of Mr. Shenkman.

Subject to a point relating to the true construction of the words 'as may seem expedient' in cl 3(K) of the memorandum of association, there is no doubt that these two transactions fell within the letter of cl 3(K) and (L) of the memorandum. Accordingly, two important points of principle which arise in the present context may be expressed thus: Is a transaction which falls within the letter of the powers conferred on a company incorporated under the Companies Acts, but is effected for a purpose not authorised by its memorandum of association, properly to be regarded as being beyond the corporate capacity of the company? Apart from §9(1) of the European Communities Act 1972, is such a transaction capable of conferring rights on a third party dealing with the company and, if so, in what circumstances?

The legal personality of a company incorporated under the Companies Acts exists only for the purpose of its incorporation, as defined in the objects clause, which have to be set out in its memorandum of association in the manner required by §2(1)(c) of the Companies Act 1948. It does not, however, follow that any act is beyond its capacity unless expressly authorised by its objects clause. Any such company is treated as having implied powers to do any act which is reasonably incidental to the attainment or pursuit of any of its express objects, unless such act is expressly prohibited by the memorandum: see Re Horsley & Weight Ltd. [1982] Ch 442 at 448, [1982] 3 All ER 1045 at 1050 per Buckley LJ.Strictly, therefore, it is not essential for the memorandum to insert any reference at all to mere powers, as distinct from objects. Indeed, in Cotman v. Brougham [1918] AC 514 at 522–3, Lord Wrenbury deprecated the widespread practice of introducing what should properly be called mere powers in memoranda, as opposed to articles of association, though he confessed that, when a junior at the Bar, he himself had had to yield to it after 'a vain struggle'.

The statutory requirement that the objects of a company shall be specified in the memorandum marks one important difference between objects and powers. In my judgment, however, whether a particular transaction, carried out in purported exercise of an express or implied power contained in a company's memorandum of association, is within the capacity of the company must still depend on the true construction of that memorandum.

Correctly, therefore, in my opinion, counsel for the defendants' (Mr. Heyman QC) argument has focussed attention in the present context on the wording of the memorandum of RSP. His first submission has been that the guarantee was intra vires RSP as a matter of corporate capacity because the provisions of cl 3(K) of the memorandum of RSP, read together with the closing words of that clause, set out a separate independent object, which RSP was capable of carrying on as such, and that the execution of the guarantee fell within that provision.

If this submission as to the construction of cl 3(K) were well founded, I think the suggested conclusion would follow and that, while the relevant transactions might have involved breaches of duty on the part of the directors of RSP, there would be no possible question of their having been beyond its corporate capacity. For the recent decision of this court in Re Horsley & Weight Ltd. [1982] Ch 442, [1982] 3 All ER 1045 has made clear, if this was not clear before, that ([1982] Ch at 449, 454–5, [1982] 3 All ER at 1051, 1055–6)

> 'the doing of an act which is expressed (by the company's memorandum to be, and is capable of being, an independent object of the company cannot be ultra vires, for it is by definition something which the company is formed to do and so must be intra vires.'

Furthermore, I think this decision also shows that this same principle applies whether or not the transaction in question is of a gratuitous nature ([1982] Ch at 450, [1982] 3 All ER at 1052):

> 'The objects of a company do not need to be commercial; they can be charitable or philanthropic; indeed they can be whatever the original incorporators wish, provided that they are legal. Nor is there any reason why a company should not part with its fund gratuitously or for non-commercial reasons if to do so is within its declared objects.'

In the light of the observations of Buckley LJ in that case at [1982] Ch 452, [1982] 3 All ER 1053, of Pennycuick J in Charterbridge Corporation Ltd. v. Lloyds Bank Ltd. [1970] Ch at 69–71 [1969] 2 All ER at 1189–91, and of Oliver J in Re Halt Garage (1964) Ltd. [1982] 3 All ER at 1028–30, the three tests of ultra vires suggested by Eve J in an often-cited passage in his judgment in Re Lee, Behrens & Co Ltd. [1932] 2 Ch 46 at 51, should, in my opinion, now be recognised as being of no assistance, and indeed positively misleading, when the relevant question is whether a particular gratuitous transaction is within a company's corporate capacity. To this extent, the tests should, I think, be finally laid to rest, though they may well be helpful in considering whether or not in any given case directors have abused the powers vested in them by the company.

The question whether cl 3(K) of RSP's memorandum contains a separate independent object of the company is purely one of construction of that memorandum. The decision of the House of Lords in Cotman v. Brougham [1918] AC 514 requires that, in answering it, full force must be given, so far as possible, to the provision at the end of cl 3 of the memorandum, which directs that each sub-clause shall be construed independently of the other sub-clauses. I accept counsel for the defendants' (Mr. Heyman QC) submission that cl 3(K) must be treated as containing a substantive object unless either (i) the subject matter of this sub-paragraph is by its nature incapable of constituting a substantive object (as was the power to borrow in Re Introductions Ltd. [1970] Ch 199, [1969] 1 All ER 887), or (ii) the wording of the memorandum shows expressly or by implication that the sub-clause was intended merely to constitute an ancillary power only: (see for example the observations of Buckley J in the latter case, at first instance, [1968] 2 All ER 1221 at 1224).

Counsel for the defendants (Mr. Heyman QC) has submitted, and I agree, that there is no reason in principle why a company should not be formed for the specific purpose, inter alia, of giving guarantees, whether gratuitous or otherwise—rather unusual though such an object might be.

Attention, however, has to be directed to the particular wording of cl 3(K). The authority to give guarantees and become security conferred by the second limb of the sub-clause is not an unrestricted authority. It is merely an authority to give guarantees or become security for 'any such persons, firms or companies'. The six words just quoted echo the words of the first limb of the sub-clause, which authorise the company to

> 'lend and advance money or give credit to such persons, firms or companies and on such terms as may seem expedient, and in particular to customers of and others having dealings with the company.'

The phrase 'as may seem expedient' necessarily implies that there is some criterion by which expediency is to be tested. The only possible criterion, in my opinion, can only mean 'as may seem expedient for the furtherance of the objects of the company'. The references in cl 3(K) to the giving of credit and to customers of and persons having dealings with the company, make it additionally clear that the sub-clause in its context was intended to comprise merely a series of ancillary powers. It follows that, in my opinion, the power to give guarantees and become security, which are the relevant powers in the present case, are not to be construed as independent objects of RSP and the judge was right in so holding.Correspondingly, I think he was right to reject the defendants' argument that the relevant transactions were intra vires RSP, insofar as that argument was based on the hypothesis that the powers conferred by cl 3(K) were independent of RSP.

What, then, is the position if (as I have concluded) the power to give guarantees and to become security are to be regarded as mere powers ancillary to the objects of RSP? Even on this footing, RSP, in executing the guarantee and the debenture, was performing acts of a nature which, at least seemingly, it was expressly authorised by cll 3(K) and (L) of its memorandum to perform. The particular exercises of these powers were, on the face of them, well capable of falling within the objects of RSP.

The judge, as I have read his judgment, accepted that these transactions were capable of falling within the scope of the wording of the powers conferred on RSP by its memorandum. Nevertheless, he considered that there is a general principle of company law that a transaction, which ostensibly falls within the scope of the wording of a company's memorandum but is in fact entered into for some purpose not authorised by that memorandum, will be ultra vires the company in what he called the 'wider sense,' and will confer rights on another party only if he can show that he dealt with the company in good faith and did not have notice that the transaction was entered into for an unauthorised purpose. It was primarily on the basis of this principle that the judge ultimately held the defendants in the present case liable to restore the moneys which they had received.

As Lord Selborne said in Ashbury Railway Carriage and Iron Co v. Riche (1875) LR 7 HL 653 at 693:

> 'a statutory corporation created by Act of Parliament for a particular purpose is limited as to all its powers by the purpose of its incorporation as defined by that Act.'

Strict logic might therefore appear to require that any act purported to be done by a company in purported exercise of powers ancillary to its objects conferred on it by its memorandum of association, whether express or implied (eg a power to borrow) would necessarily, and in every case, be beyond its capacity and therefore wholly void if such act was in fact performed for purposes other than those of its incorporation. However, the practical difficulties resulting from such a conclusion for persons dealing with a company carrying on a business authorised by its memorandum, would be intolerable. As Buckley J put it, in regard to a power to borrow, Re David Payne & Co Ltd. [1904] 2 Ch 608 at 613:

> 'A corporation, every time it wants to borrow, cannot be called upon by the lender to expose all its affairs, so that the lender can say, "Before I lend you anything, I must investigate how you carry on your business, and I must know why you want the money, and how you apply it, and when you do have it I must see you apply it in the right way." It is perfectly impossible to work out such a principle.'

The David Payne decision, in my opinion, indicates the proper alternative approach. In that case, the company concerned had express power under its memorandum of association 'to borrow and raise money for the purposes of the company business'. It borrowed money and issued a debenture to secure the loan. Its liquidator claimed that the debenture was ultra vires and void because there was evidence that the borrowing had not in fact been made for the purposes of the company's business. Buckley J in his judgment considered the force of the phrase 'for the purposes of the company's business'. He asked the question ([1904] 2 Ch at 612):

> 'Is it a condition attached to the exercise of the power that the money should be borrowed for the purposes of the business or is that a matter to be determined as between the shareholders and the directors?'

In the course of answering this question he said:

> 'A corporation cannot do anything except for the purposes of its business, borrowing or anything else; everything else is beyond its power and is ultra vires. So that the words "for the purposes of the company's business" are a mere expression of that which would be involved if there were no such words.'

This passage has been frequently echoed in later cases and, perhaps not surprisingly, has on occasions been read as referring to the capacity of the company. However, I think that, in using the phrase 'ultra vires' in this particular context, Buckley J can only have meant 'ultra vires the directors'. This, in my opinion, is made clear by what followed. He accepted that, if the phrase 'for the purpose of the company's business' was a condition attached to the exercise of the power, a loan would be ultra vires and void if the condition had not been complied with. He did not, however, regard it as such a condition; in his view it did no more than state the obvious. In these circumstances, his conclusion was as follows ([1904] 2 Ch at 613):

> 'If this borrowing was made, as it appears to me at present it was made, for a purpose illegitimate so far as the borrowing company was concerned, that may very well be a matter on which rights may arise as between the shareholders and directors of that company. It may have been a wrongful act on the part of the directors. But I do not think that a person who lends to the company is by any words such as these required to investigate whether the money borrowed is borrowed for a proper purpose or an improper purpose. The borrowing being effected, and the money passing to the company, the subsequent application of the money is a matter in which the directors may have acted wrongly; but that does not affect the principal act, which is the borrowing of the money.'

In these circumstances, he held ([1904] 2 Ch at 614) that the defendants

> 'who have paid this money and taken this debenture without notice that the money was going to be applied as it was are not affected by anything arising in regard to that.'

The most relevant passages in the judgments of the Court of Appeal in the David Payne case are cited in Vinelott J's judgment and I will not repeat them. Vaughan Williams LJ and Cosens-Hardy LJ expressly approved the manner in which Buckley J had approached the problem. Vaughan Williams LJ expressly ([1904] 2 Ch at 615), and the other members of the court implicitly, rejected the borrower's first argument that, since the debenture was not issued to raise money for the purposes of the company, it was ultra vires altogether 'in the sense that nothing could make it right'. All three members of the court considered that the plaintiff company could succeed if, but only if, it showed that, at the time of the loan, the lending company knew that the money was going to be applied by the borrowers for an improper purpose and that this had not been proved.

The one crucially important point to which Buckley J and the Court of Appeal in David Payne did not expressly advert is the basis upon which the lenders would have lost their security if they had known of the improper purpose for which the moneys lent were going to be applied. The basis is, in my opinion, this. The directors of the borrowing company in fact had no authority from the company to take the loan and grant the debenture because these transactions were not effected for the purposes of the company. Nevertheless, as a general rule, a company incorporated under the Companies Acts holds out its directors as having ostensible authority to do on its behalf anything which its memorandum of association, expressly or by implication, gives the company the capacity to do. In David Payne the company's memorandum gave it the capacity to borrow. As a matter of construction of the company's memorandum, the court was not prepared to construe the words 'for the purposes of the company's business' as limiting its corporate capacity, but construed them simply as limiting the authority of the directors. In the absence of notice to the contrary, the lenders would thus have been entitled to assume, on the authority of the principle in Turquand's case, and on more general principles of the law of agency, that the directors of the borrowing company were acting properly and regularly in the internal management of its affairs and were borrowing for the purposes of the company's business: see for example Re Hampshire Lane Co (1896) 2 Ch 743, a decision of Vaughan Williams J which was cited in the David Payne case; see also Bowstead on Agency (14th edn), pp 241–2 and the cases there cited. However, a party dealing with a company cannot rely on the ostensible authority of its directors to enter into a particular transaction, if it knows they in fact have no such authority because it is being entered into for improper purposes. Neither the rule in Turquand's case nor more general principles of the law of agency will avail him in such circumstances (see Bowstead on Agency (14th edn), p 243). The various passages in the judgments in both courts in the David Payne case which refer to the extent of the lender's obligation (if any) to inquire as to the purposes for which the loan is to be used, in my opinion, are not directed at all to the corporate capacity of the borrowing company; they are directed to the right of the lender to rely on the ostensible authority of the borrower's directors.

In Re Introductions Ltd. [1970] Ch 199, [1969] 1 All ER 887, the Court of Appeal again had to consider the validity of debentures granted by a company as security for a loan. The company under cl(N) of its memorandum of association had a general ancillary power to borrow money and to issue debentures to secure its repayment. But this power was not an independent object of the company. As Harman LJ put it ([1970] Ch at 210, [1969] 1 All ER at 889): 'borrowing is not an end in itself and must be for some purpose of the company'. The power was not expressed in terms to be exercisable only 'for the purposes of the company' but, following the reasoning of Buckley J in Re David Payne Ltd. [1904] 2 Ch 612 the court held that the words necessarily had to be implied. The company had borrowed money from a bank and granted debentures to secure the loan. But the only business carried on by it was that of pig-breeding, which was a purpose not authorised by its memorandum of association. On the liquidation of the company, a question arose as to the validity of the debentures. Harman LJ, who gave the leading judgment, after deciding that the power to borrow conferred by the memorandum was a mere ancillary power not an independent object, proceeded to cite ([1970] Ch at 210, [1969] 1 All ER at 890) the following passage from the speech of Lord Parker of Waddington in Cotman v. Brougham [1918] AC at 521:

> 'A person who deals with a company is entitled to assume that a company can do everything which it is expressly authorised to do by its memorandum of association, and need not investigate the equities between the company and its shareholders.'

This passage, it will be seen, closely echoes some of the language used by Buckley J in his judgment in the David Payne case and is, I think, an expression of the rule in Turquand's case and the more general principles of agency to which I have already referred. Harman LJ went on to say this ([1970] Ch at 210, [1969] 1 All ER at 890):

> 'I would agree that, if the bank did not know what the purpose of the borrowing was, it need not inquire (the emphasis is mine) but it did know and I can find nothing in Cotman v. Brougham to protect it notwithstanding that knowledge.'

The words 'it need not inquire,' in my opinion, make it clear that Harman LJ did not regard the borrowing as having been beyond the capacity of the company. However, he then went on to point out that the David Payne decision shows that the protection afforded by the principle stated by Lord Parker affords no protection to a lender who knows that the money is intended to be misapplied. The absence of any express provision in the company's memorandum of association requiring the loan to be applied for the purposes of the company, in his judgment, did not improve the bank's position, since such a provision would fall to be implied anyway. He concluded ([1970] Ch at 211, [1969] 1 All ER at 890): 'This borrowing was not for a legitimate purpose of the company; the bank knew it and therefore (the emphasis is mine) cannot rely on its debentures.'

As I read his judgment, therefore, Harman LJ reached his decision that the bank could not rely on the debentures following the ratio of the David Payne decision, that is to say, not because they had been granted by the company in excess of its corporate capacity, but because the bank knew that the directors of the company, in purporting to grant them, had exceeded the authority conferred on them by the company by entering into the transaction for purposes other than the company's corporate purpose.

Russell LJ, in a very short judgment ([1970] Ch at 211, [1969] All ER at 890), reached the same conclusion but by rather a different route from that of Harman LJ. As I read his judgment, his view was that the borrowing and execution of the debentures were ultra vires the company as a matter of corporate capacity because it was an implicit condition attached to the power to borrow contained in the company's memorandum that moneys should not be borrowed for use in an undertaking ultra vires the company. Since the sole undertaking of that company was the pig-breeding business, which was beyond the company's corporate capacity, the loans taken for use in that business were likewise inevitably beyond its corporate capacity. I read Russell LJ's decision as being limited to the facts of that particular case and not in any way conflicting with my interpretation of the David Payne decision.

It follows that, in my opinion, the decisions of this court in Re David Payne Ltd. and Re Introductions Ltd., on their true analysis, lend no support to the plaintiff's submission that the relevant transactions in the present case were beyond the corporate capacity of RSP simply because they were effected for improper purposes not authorised by its memorandum of association. Nor does this argument derive any support from the powerful judgment of Pennycuik J in Charterbridge Corpn Ltd. v. Lloyds Bank Ltd. [1970] Ch 62 at 69, [1969] 2 All ER 1185 at 1189 where one finds the following statement of principle:

> 'Apart from authority, I should feel little doubt that where a company is carrying out the purposes expressed in its memorandum, and does an act within the scope of a power expressed in its memorandum, that act is an act within the powers of the company. The memorandum of a company sets out its objects and proclaims them to persons dealing with the company and it would be contrary to the whole function of a memorandum that objects unequivocally set out in it should be subject to some implied limitation by reference to the state of mind of the parties concerned.'

Where directors misapply the assets of their company, that may give rise to a claim based on breach of duty. Again, a claim may arise against the other party to the transaction, if he has notice that the transaction was effected in breach of duty. Further, in a proper case, the company concerned may be entitled to have the transaction set aside. But all that results from the ordinary law of agency and has not of itself anything to do with the corporate powers of the company.'

Pennycuik J, having subsequently proceeded to review the authorities cited to him, apparently saw no reason to qualify this statement of the law and neither do I. I respectfully agree with it in its entirety and would regard the principles stated in the David Payne case as giving effect to the 'ordinary law of agency'.

I also respectfully agree with the following observations made by Oliver J, after an extensive review of the authorities, in Re Halt Garage (1964) Ltd. [1982] 3 All ER 1016 at 1029–30:

> 'I cannot help thinking, if I may respectfully say so, that there has been a certain confusion between the requirements for a valid exercise of the fiduciary powers of directors (which have nothing to do with the capacity of the company but everything to do with the propriety of acts done within that capacity), the extent to which powers can be implied or limits be placed, as a matter of construction, on

express powers, and the matters which the court will take into consideration at the suit of a minority shareholder in determining the extent to which his interests can be overridden by a majority vote. These three matters, as it seems to me, raise questions which are logically quite distinct but which have sometimes been treated as if they demanded a single, universal answer leading to the conclusion that, because a power must not be abused, therefore, beyond the limit of propriety it does not exist.'

My conclusions from these authorities on these questions of principle may be summarised as follows:—

(1) The basic rule is that a company incorporated under the Companies Acts only has the capacity to do those acts which fall within its objects as set out in its memorandum of association or are reasonably incidental to the attainment or pursuit of those objects. Ultimately, therefore, the question whether a particular transaction is within or outside its capacity must depend on the true construction of the memorandum.

(2) Nevertheless, if a particular act (such as each of the transactions of 22 January 1969 in the present case) is of a category which, on the true construction of the company's memorandum, is capable of being performed as reasonably incidental to the attainment or pursuit of its objects, it will not be rendered ultra vires the company merely because in a particular instance its directors, in performing the act in its name, are in truth doing so for purposes other than those set out in its memorandum. Subject to any express restrictions on the relevant power which may be contained in the memorandum, the state of mind or knowledge of the persons managing the company's affairs or of the persons dealing with it is irrelevant in considering questions of corporate capacity.

(3) While due regard must be paid to any express conditions attached to or limitations on powers contained in a company's memorandum (eg a power to borrow only up to a specified amount), the court will not ordinarily construe a statement in a memorandum that a particular power is exercisable 'for the purposes of the company' as a condition limiting the company's corporate capacity to exercise the power; it will regard it as simply imposing a limit on the authority of the directors: see the David Payne case.

(4) At least in default of the unanimous consent of all the shareholders (as to which see below), the directors of a company will not have actual authority from the company to exercise any express or implied power other than for the purposes of the company as set out in its memorandum of association.

(5) A company holds out its directors as having ostensible authority to bind the company to any transaction which falls within the powers expressly or impliedly conferred on it by its memorandum of association. Unless he is put on notice to the contrary, a person dealing in good faith with a company which is carrying on an intra vires business in entitled to assume that its directors are properly exercising such powers for the purposes of the company as set out in its memorandum. Correspondingly, such a person in such circumstances can hold the company to any transaction of this nature.

(6) If, however, a person dealing with a company is on notice that the directors are exercising the relevant power for purposes other than the purposes of the company, he cannot rely on the ostensible authority of the directors and, on ordinary principles of agency, cannot hold the company to the transaction.

In the present case I construe the words 'as may seem expedient' in cl 3(K) of RSP's memorandum not as limiting the corporate capacity of RSP but as simply imposing a limit on the authority of its directors. To adapt the wording of Harman LJ in the Introductions case following the David Payne decision, the guarantee and pro tanto the debenture were not executed for a legitimate purpose of RSP; Colvilles and BSC knew it and, therefore, cannot rely on the guarantee and pro tanto the debenture. All this results from the ordinary law of agency, not from the corporate powers of RSP. The relevant transactions in the present case, in my opinion, were not beyond its corporate capacity.

The learned judge explained that the reason why he regarded a transaction which is within the powers, express or implied, of a company but which is entered into for a purpose which is not authorised by its memorandum of association as equated with one which is ultra vires in the narrow sense is that 'such a transaction like a transaction which is ultra vires in the narrow sense is incapable of being made binding on the company even by the assent of all the members'. We have had the benefit of extensive argument as to the extent (if any) to which the assent of all the members of a company is capable of binding it to a transaction of this nature. Since the shareholders' consent point is not open to BSC and Mr. Cooper on the facts of the present case, I wish to make only the following few (obiter) observations in the context of this argument. First, if an act is beyond the corporate capacity of a company, it is clear that it cannot be ratified. As against the company itself, 'an ultra vires agreement cannot become intra vires by means of estoppel, lapse of time, ratification and acquiescence or delay': York Corpn v. Henry Leetham & Sons Ltd. [1924] 1 Ch 557 at 583 per Russell J. However, the clear general principle is that any act that falls within the corporate capacity of a company will bind it if it is done with the unanimous consents of all the shareholders or is subsequently ratified by such consents: see for example Salomon v. A Salomon & Co Ltd. [1897] AC 22 at 57 per Lord Davey, Re Horsley & Weight Ltd. [1982] Ch 442 at 454, [1982] 3 All ER 1045 at 1055 per Buckley LJ, Multinational Gas and Petrochemical Co v. Multinational Gas & Petrochemical Services Ltd. [1983] Ch 258, [1983] BCLC 461. This last-mentioned principle certainly is not an unqualified one. In particular, it will not enable the shareholders of a company to bind the company itself to a transaction which constitutes a fraud on its creditors: (see, for example, Re Halt Garage (1964) Ltd. [1982] 3 All ER 1016 at 1037 per Oliver J). But none of the authorities which have been cited to us have convinced me that a transaction which (i) falls within the letter of the express or implied powers of a company conferred by its memorandum, and (ii) does not involve a fraud on its creditors, and (iii) is assented to by all the shareholders, will not bind a fully solvent company merely because the intention of the directors, or the shareholders, is to effect a purpose not authorised by the memorandum. The recent decision of this court in the Multinational case seems to me to point to a contrary conclusion: see also Attorney General's Reference (No 2 of 1982) [1984] 2 All ER 216 at 223, [1984] 2 WLR 447 at 461 per Kerr LJ [1984] BCLC 60 at 67–69). However, none of these matters relating to ratification, in my opinion, call for decision on this appeal. I have touched on them only because they weighed with the learned judge and have been covered fully in argument.

Whether or not in 1969 the consent or ratification of all the shareholders was incapable of rendering the transactions of 22 January 1969 binding on RSP, I myself think that the concept of ultra vires 'in the wider sense' embodied by the learned judge in his judgment carries with it some risk of confusion. If confusion is to be avoided, it seems to me highly desirable that, as a matter of terminology, the phrase 'ultra vires' in the context of company law should for the future be rigidly confined to describing acts which are beyond the corporate capacity of a company. Transactions entered into by a company, such as those considered in the David Payne case, and those under consideration in the present case, cannot, in my opinion, be properly regarded as beyond its corporate capacity (and, therefore, ex hypothesi wholly void) if they are capable of conferring rights on a third party—albeit only on a third party who dealt with the company in good faith and without notice that they were being entered into in furtherance of improper purposes.

To sum up, my conclusions on the ultra vires point are these: The relevant transactions of 22 January were not beyond the corporate capacity of RSP and thus were not ultra vires in the proper sense of that phrase. However, the entering into the guarantee and, to the extent of the sum guaranteed, the debenture was beyond the authority of the directors, because they were entered into in furtherance of purposes not authorised by RSP's memorandum. Despite this lack of authority, they might have been capable of conferring rights on Colvilles if Colvilles had not known of this lack of authority. Colvilles, however, did have such knowledge and so acquired no rights under these transactions. Even if the 'no due authorisation' point discussed earlier in this judgment were not open to the plaintiff, because Mr. Shenkman had duly declared his interest at the relevant board meeting, RSP could disclaim these transactions, which its directors had carried out on its behalf, as being unauthorised, inasmuch as they were carried out for improper purposes. The practical relevance of the 'no due authorisation' point discussed in an earlier section of this judgment is that it enables the plaintiff also to disclaim the borrowing of the £ 401,448 and the whole (as opposed to part only) of the security given by the debenture (as having been in each case entered into by the directors without its authority) and also to attack the validity of the receiver's appointment.

(6) The constructive trust point

[omitted]

(7) The relief to be granted

[omitted]

Subject to this,

(1) I would dismiss the appeal of BSC and the receiver;

(2) I would allow the cross-appeal of RSP;

(3) I would vary the judge's order so as to include

(a) a declaration that each of the agreement, the guarantee and the debenture of 22 January 1969 was not and is not the deed of RSP;

(b) a declaration that the purported appointment of Mr. Cooper as receiver was and is void and of no effect;

(c) an order for payment or repayment of

(i) the interest element received by BSC from the receiver in respect of the £401,448;

(ii) the £ 50,000 received by the receiver;

(iii) interest on these two last mentioned sums;

(d) a proviso of the nature which I have already indicated;

(4) I would in all other respects uphold the judge's order.

BROWNE-WILKINSON LJ. I have had the advantage of reading the judgment of Slade LJ, with which I agree. I add my own views only on the ultra vires and constructive trust points which, despite §9 of the European Communities Act 1972, are still of some general importance.

The judge drew a distinction between two meanings of ultra vires which he called the 'narrow sense' and the 'wider sense'. As I understand his judgment, he treated ultra vires in the narrow sense as covering any transaction outside the express or implied powers of a company stated in its memorandum of association and ultra vires in the wider sense as covering a transaction which, although within such powers, is entered into in furtherance of 'some purpose which is not an authorised purpose': [1982] 1 Ch at 497. Although it is not entirely clear, he appears to have treated transactions which are ultra vires in his narrow sense as being wholly void as opposed to those which are ultra vires in the wider sense, which are capable of conferring rights on third parties who have no notice of the invalidity: [1982] 1 Ch at 499. He then apparently held that the guarantee by RSP was ultra vires in the wider sense and, since BSC had notice of that fact, it was unenforceable by BSC.

In my judgment, much of the confusion that has crept into the law flows from the use of the phrase 'ultra vires' in different senses in different contexts. The reconciliation of the authorities can only be achieved if one first defines the sense in which one is using the words 'ultra vires.' Because the literal translation of the words is 'beyond the powers,' there are many cases in which the words have been applied to transactions which, although within the capacity of the company, are carried out otherwise than through the correct exercise of the powers of the company by its officers: indeed, that is the sense in which the learned judge seems to have used the words in this case. For reasons which will appear, in my judgment, the use of the phrase 'ultra vires' should be restricted to those cases where the transaction is beyond the capacity of the company and therefore wholly void.

A company, being an artificial person, has no capacity to do anything outside the objects specified in its memorandum of association. If the transaction is outside the objects, in law it is wholly void. But the objects of a company and the powers conferred on a company to carry out those objects are two different things: see Cotman v. Brougham [1918] AC 514 especially per Lord Parker at 520 and per Lord Wrenbury at 522. If the concept that a company cannot do anything which is not authorised by law had been pursued with ruthless logic, the result might have been reached that a company could not (ie had no capacity) to do anything otherwise than in due exercise of its powers. But such ruthless logic has not been pursued and it is clear that a transaction falling within the objects of the company is capable of conferring rights on third parties even though the transaction was an abuse of the powers of the company: see, for example Re David Payne & Co Ltd. [1904] 2 Ch 608. It is therefore established that a company has capacity to carry out a transaction which falls within its objectives even though carried out by the wrongful exercise of its powers.

In my judgment, for this purpose the position of a company is analogous to that of a human being who has fiduciary powers. If two trustees convey trust property in breach of trust, the conveyance is not void. As human beings they have the capacity to transfer the legal estate: their capacity to transfer flows from their status as human beings not from the powers conferred on them as trustees. Even if their powers under the trust instrument did not authorise the conveyance, the legal estate will vest in the transferee. Beneficiaries under the trust would be entitled, if they learnt in time, to restrain the execution of such conveyance in excess of the powers of the trustees. If the beneficiaries only discovered the position after the conveyance, the transferee, if he took with notice, would be personally liable as a constructive trustee and the property conveyed could be recovered: but the conveyance would not be a nullity. So in the case of a limited company, if a transaction falls within the objects of the company (and is therefore within its capacity) it is effective to vest rights in a third party even if the transaction was carried out in excess or abuse of the powers of the company. If the members of the company learn of what is proposed in time, they will be able to restrain such transaction: if they only discover the facts later, their remedy lies against those who have wrongly caused the company to act in excess or abuse of the company's powers. If a third party has received the company's property with notice of the excess or abuse of powers, such third party will be personally liable as a constructive trustee and the company will be able to recover the property: see Belmont Finance Corpn Ltd. v. Williams Furniture Ltd. (No 2) [1980] 1 All ER 393.

However, the analogy between companies and trustees is not complete. As an artificial person, a company can only act by duly authorised agents. Apart from questions of ostensible authority, directors like any other agents can only bind the company by acts done in accordance with the formal requirements of their agency, eg, by resolution of the board at a properly constituted meeting. Acts done otherwise than in accordance with these formal requirements will not be the acts of the company. However, the principles of ostensible authority apply to the acts of directors acting as agents of the company and the rule in Turquand's case established that a third party dealing in good faith with directors is entitled to assume that the internal steps requisite for the formal validity of the directors' acts have been duly carried through. If, however, the third party has actual or constructive notice that such steps had not been taken, he will not be able to rely on any ostensible authority of the directors and their acts, being in excess of their actual authority, will not be the acts of the company.

The critical distinction is, therefore, between acts done in excess of the capacity of the company on the one hand and acts done in excess or abuse of the powers of the company on the other. If the transaction is beyond the capacity of the company it is in any event a nullity and wholly void: Whether or not the third party had notice of the invalidity, property transferred or money paid under such a transaction (although in excess or abuse of powers) is within the capacity of the company, the position of the third party depends upon whether or not he had notice that the transaction was in excess or abuse of the powers of the company. As between the shareholders and the directors, for most purposes it makes no practical difference whether the transaction is beyond the capacity of the company or merely in excess or abuse of its power: in either event the shareholders will be able to restrain the carrying out of the transaction or hold liable those who have carried it out. Only if the question of ratification by all the shareholders arises will it be material to consider whether the transaction is beyond the capacity of the company since it is established that, although all the shareholders can ratify a transaction within the company's capacity, they cannot ratify a transaction falling outside its objects.

In this judgment I therefore use the words 'ultra vires' as covering only those transactions which the company has no capacity to carry out: ie those things the company cannot do at all as opposed to those things it cannot properly do.

The two badges of a transaction which is ultra vires in that sense are (1) that the transaction is wholly void and (consequentially) (2) that it is irrelevant whether or not the third party had notice. It is therefore in this sense that the transactions in Re David Payne & Co Ltd. [1904] 2 Ch 608 and Charterbridge Corpn Ltd. v. Lloyds Bank Ltd. [1970] 1 Ch 62, [1969] 2 All ER 1185 were held not to be ultra vires. The distinction between the capacity of the company and abuse of powers was also drawn by Oliver J in Re Halt Garages (1964) Ltd. [1982] 3 All ER 1016 at 1034. I consider the reasoning of the decision in Re Lee, Behrens & Co Ltd. [1932] 2 Ch 46 to be wrong for the reasons given by Pennycuik J in the Charterbridge case: the decision itself can only be justified (if at all) on the footing that the widow who was granted a pension had notice of the impropriety of the grant. The only other case which, at first sight, is difficult to reconcile with my views is Re Introductions Ltd. [1969] 1 All ER 887, [1970] Ch 199, which I will consider later.

For these reasons, in considering a claim based on ultra vires, the first step must be to determine what are the objects (as opposed to the powers) of a company. Not all activities mentioned in the objects clause are necessarily objects in the strict sense: some of them may only be capable of existing as, or on their true construction are, ancillary powers: Cotman v. Brougham [1918] AC 514 and Re Introductions Ltd. [1970] Ch 199, [1969] 1 All ER 887. And this may be the position even if the memorandum of association contains the usual 'separate objects' clause: such a clause is not capable of elevating into an object of the company that which is in essence a power: see Re Introductions.

If, on construction of the objects clause, the transactions fall within the objects (as opposed to the powers), it will not be ultra vires since the company has the capacity to enter into the transaction. If the objects clause contains provisions (whether objects or powers) which show that a transaction of the kind in question is within the capacity of the company, that transaction will not be ultra vires. Sometimes the drafting of the memorandum and articles may be such that they put third parties on notice of the fact that certain things can only properly be done subject to certain conditions being satisfied. If the third party is put on notice in this way, he will not be able to rely on any exercise of the power which he knew or ought to have discovered did not comply with such conditions. But a provision that a power can be exercised only 'for the purposes of the company's business' does not require a third party to satisfy himself that the power is in fact being exercised for that purpose.

In my judgment, the propositions in the last two paragraphs accord with the decisions in Re David Payne Ltd. and the Charterbridge cases. As Slade LJ has pointed out, in the David Payne case the objects clause of the company stated expressly that the power to borrow was 'for the purposes of the company's business': yet the borrowing (which was not in fact for the purpose of the company's business) was held not to be ultra vires. Buckley J ([1904] 2 Ch at 612) plainly treated the provision as a power not an object. Vaughan Williams LJ held ([1904] 2 Ch at 615) that the fact that the validity of the debenture depended on whether or not the lender had knowledge of the impropriety showed that the transaction was not ultra vires. Moreover, it was held that, knowledge being a necessary requirement to render the loan unenforceable, the lender was not put on inquiry whether the money was being borrowed for the purposes of the company's business, notwithstanding that the power to borrow was expressly limited to borrowing for those purposes. That case, therefore, is clear authority for two propositions: (1) that where there is a power to borrow for the purposes of the company's business (even if contained in the objects clause) and the borrowing is made otherwise than for those purposes, the borrowing is not void as being ultra vires; and (2) a third party is not put on notice by an express requirement that the power is only exercisable for the purposes of the company's business.

The main difficulty in reconciling the authorities is Re Introductions. In my judgment, however, the decision in that case accords with the views I have expressed. The bank seeking to enforce the debenture had actual knowledge that the company was going to use the borrowed moneys for a purpose (pig breeding) which was wholly outside its main objects. The provision relating to borrowing in the memorandum of association was construed as being an ancillary power to borrow for the purposes of the company's business. Accordingly, the lender had actual notice of all the facts necessary to appreciate that the borrowing was in excess of the powers, ie an abuse of powers. It is to be noted that in the Court of Appeal judgments the transaction is nowhere categorised as ultra vires and void. Indeed, as Slade LJ has pointed out, the Court of Appeal held that the liability of the bank depended on the fact that it had notice. Buckley J at first instance described the borrowing as being ultra vires: but, in my judgment, this was merely an unguarded use of language since he also regarded the bank's knowledge of the facts as being a crucial element rendering the debenture unenforceable: see [1968] 2 All ER at 1225. In my judgment, Re Introductions is not a decision relating to ultra vires in the strict sense: it is an example of a case in which a third party has entered into a transaction with a company with actual notice that the transaction was an abuse of power and accordingly could not enforce the transaction against the company.

I summarise my conclusions as follows:

(1) To be ultra vires, a transaction has to be outside the capacity of the company, not merely in excess or abuse of the powers of the company.

(2) The question whether a transaction is outside the capacity of the company depends solely upon whether, on the true construction of its memorandum of association, the transaction is capable of falling within the objects of the company as opposed to being a proper exercise of the powers of the company.

(3) Notwithstanding the fact that the provision authorising the company to enter into the particular transaction is found in the objects clause and there is a provision requiring each paragraph to be construed as a separate object, such provision may be merely a power (and not an object) if either it is incapable of existing as a separate object or it can only be construed as a power ancillary to the other objects in the strict sense.

(4) If a transaction falls within the objects (and therefore the capacity) of the company, it is not ultra vires the company and accordingly it is not absolutely void.

(5) If a company enters into a transaction which is intra vires (as being within its capacity) but in excess or abuse of its powers, such transaction will be set aside at the instance of the shareholders.

(6) A third party, who has notice (actual or constructive) that a transaction, although intra vires the company, was entered into in excess or abuse of the powers of the company, cannot enforce such transaction against the company and will be accountable as constructive trustee for any money or property of the company received by the third party.

(7) The fact that a power is expressly or impliedly limited so as to be exercisable only 'for the purposes of the company's business' (or other words to that effect), does not put a third party on inquiry as to whether the power is being so exercised, ie such provision does not give him constructive notice of excess or abuse of such power.

Applying those principles to the present case, in my judgment, no question of ultra vires arises. For the reasons given both by the learned judge and by Slade LJ the provisions of cl 3(K) of the memorandum of association of RSP do not constitute a separate object but can only be construed as a power. RSP had the capacity to enter into the transactions involving the giving of guarantees and could properly have done so if they had been expedient in the interests of RSP's business. If BSC had known no more than that RSP was purporting to give the guarantee as being expedient for RSP's business, the transaction would have been unimpeachable as against BSC.

But, as the learned judge and Slade LJ have demonstrated, BSC had actual knowledge of facts which showed that the giving of the guarantee and the debenture was an abuse of powers by the directors of RSP since the transaction was not even considered to be for the benefit of RSP. The borrowing by RSP from BSC of the £ 401,448 was formally invalid since such borrowing was not approved by a quorate board meeting of RSP and the defence based on the rule in Turquand's case was neither pleaded nor established. BSC had constructive knowledge of this formal invalidity. Accordingly, BSC and the receiver are accountable as constructive trustees for all the moneys of RSP received by them with such notice.

As to the relief to be granted, my views accord with those of Slade LJ. In particular, as at present advised, I agree with him that Reversion Fund and Insurance Co v. Maison Cosway Ltd. [1913] 1 KB 364 appears to establish that RSP is not entitled to recover the principle of £ 401,448 since the sum borrowed was used to discharge the indebtedness of RSP to SSS. However, the parties, if they wish, must have an opportunity to present further argument on the relief to be given.

Finally, I have not formed any view on the difficult problems which arise when shareholders consent to a transaction which (though intra vires) is an excess or abuse of the powers of the company. I therefore must not be taken to be either approving or disapproving the views on this point expressed by Slade LJ.

LAWTON LJ. Stripped of its legal complications, many of which were caused by the way the trial judge dealt with the defendants' applications to amend the pleadings, this case raises issues of fact. When the evidence is looked at in the round, there is revealed an unattractive story of a fairly common kind which shows how some business men manipulate limited liability companies to avoid their financial liabilities and what other business men are driven to do in order to get paid what they are entitled to receive.

In the 1960s Mr. Shenkman was an entrepreneur. He had ideas for selling steel on a large scale but no capital with which to set up a suitable selling organisation. He did what many entrepreneurs do: he used other people's money. Unlike some entrepreneurs, he used no deception to get it. He did not need to do so (and, on the judge's findings, he probably did not want to do so) because of the way Colvilles (then an independent steel company) went about their business of producing and selling steel. They seem to have been more interested in selling their steel than of being paid the price for it. The result was that, by the beginning of 1968, they had sold and delivered to Mr. Shenkman's order a vast quantity of steel and were owed just under £ 800,000 for it. When they began to press for the debt to be paid they became aware of the legal problems which faced them. Mr. Shenkman has operated behind a screen of small limited liability companies in which he and family interests controlled all the shares. The company which owed Colvilles this huge debt, SSS, had no assets. Mr. Shenkman himself had very few. What assets there were (and they were fairly substantial) were in another company, RSP, which had had no dealings with Colvilles but into which Mr. Shenkman has syphoned by way of a loan about £ 400,000 of SSS's money which that company should have paid to Colvilles in discharge of its debts. Mr. Shenkman owned 51% of RSP shares. The trustees of a settlement in favour of his children owned the remaining 49%.

When in 1968 the defendants, BSC, took over Colvilles under the nationalising legislation they were faced with a difficult debt collecting problem. By the late autumn of 1968 they had these options: they could make Mr. Shenkman bankrupt for defaulting on a personal guarantee which he had given in 2 May 1968 for SSS's debts. A bankruptcy order would have vested Mr. Shenkman's shares in RSP in his trustee but, on the most optimistic assessment, less than about half of SSS's debts would be recovered. The second option was to put SSS into liquidation and get the liquidator to press RSP to repay £ 400,000 which it had borrowed from SSS. Once again, the best which could have been attained was the repayment of this sum; and the chances of getting it were poor, as the only worthwhile asset RSP had was some land at Rainham which had been valued at about £ 800,000 if sold over a longish period but which would almost certainly bring in much less if there were a forced sale. Anyway, a sale of any kind was sure to generate a substantial liability on RSP for corporation tax arising from capital gains as the land had been bought for £ 8,000.

BSC had to solve this problem: how could they link Mr. Shenkman and SSS's liabilities to RSP's assets? Their own legal adviser, Mr. Edwards, considered the problem, as did their experienced solicitors and counsel instructed by them. All, of course, knew that in law RSP was a separate legal entity from Mr. Shenkman and SSS and that those who directed the affairs of RSP (and, as BSC knew, they were Mr. Shenkman and his father) had to do so in the interests of RSP and not of Mr. Shenkman himself or SSS. If they did not, any transactions carried out in breach of trust would be at least voidable, and might be void if, on the correct construction of RSP's memorandum of association, there were limitations on the powers of RSP to borrow money or give guarantees.

The scheme which was devised to attach Mr. Shenkman and SSS's liabilities to RSP's assets has been described in detail by Slade LJ in his judgment. This scheme was designed to enable BSC to strip RSP of nearly all its assets and what was left over was likely to be successfully claimed by the Inland Revenue for corporation tax. Such a scheme, approved by RSP's directors on 22 January 1969 could not possibly have been for the benefit of RSP, and BSC, through their advisers, knew that it was not. In my judgment, BSC regarded RSP as an alias for Mr. Shenkman. He owed them money under the guarantee he had given in May 1968. They felt justified in tearing away RSP's corporate veil which hid him from his creditors. I have much sympathy for BSC. They were being kept out of their money by the legal fiction that RSP was not Mr. Shenkman. Unfortunately for them it is a legal fiction which has been recognised by the law for over a hundred years. It is said to have helped the growth of innumerable new businesses. The fact that limited liability has all too often enabled many to enrich themselves at the expense of those who have given credit to the companies they control is the price the business world has to pay for the potentiality for growth and convenience which goes with limited liability. In my judgment, BSC will have to pay that price. What Mr. Shenkman and his father did on 22 January 1968 by giving the guarantee was a misfeasance and BSC knew it was. The legal consequences of what happened are set out in Slade LJ's judgment with which I agree.

I wish, however, to add a comment about the pleading points which have had to be considered in this appeal. From the way they were raised by counsel and dealt with by the trial judge I was left with the impression that neither the judge nor defending counsel appreciated as fully as they should have done the need for precision and expedition when dealing with pleading points. My recent experience in this court shows that some counsel and judges are not giving pleadings the attention which they should. Pleadings are not formal documents which have to be prepared at the beginning of litigation. They are essential for the fair trial of an action and the saving of time at trial. The saving of time keeps down the costs of litigation. A plaintiff is entitled to know what defences he has to meet and a defendant what claims are being made against him. If the parties do not know, unnecessary evidence may be got together and led or, even worse, necessary evidence may not be led. Pleadings regulate what questions may be asked of witnesses in cross-examination. When counsel raises an objection to a question or a line or questioning, as counsel for the plaintiff (Mr. Morritt QC) did on a number of occasions, the trial judge should rule on it at once. He should not regard the objection as a critical commentary on what the other side is doing. If the judge does not rule, counsel should ask him to do so. If a line of questioning is stopped because it does not relate to an issue on the pleadings, counsel should at once consider whether his pleadings should be amended. If he decides that they should, he should forthwith apply for an amendment and should specify precisely what he wants and the judge should at once give a ruling on the application. The principles upon which amendments should be allowed are well known and are set out in the current edition of the Annual Practice. Judicial insistence on precision in pleading should not take the courts back to the days when the successful taking of pleading points sometimes resulted in a denial of justice. The judge's powers of adjourning and ordering the payment of costs thrown away should stop this happening.

With regret, I feel it necessary to make one more comment about the way the judge conducted this case. At the outset of this appeal counsel for the defendants (Mr. Heyman QC) invited our attention to the fact that the submissions of counsel ended on 7 April 1982 but judgment was not delivered until 2 December 1982. He submitted that this long and, in my experience unprecedented, delay resulted in the judge making material findings which were not justified by the evidence. I am not satisfied that this was so. But the fact that responsible and experienced counsel, acting for a public corporation, felt it incumbent upon him to make this submission shows that long delays in delivering judgment can cause disquiet and suspicion amongst litigants who lose—and those who win may feel they have been deprived of justice far too long. Delays of this length should not occur unless there are compelling reasons why they should; and, if there are such reasons, it would be prudent of a judge to refer to them briefly.In this case, for all we know, there may have been such reasons. We have kept in mind that the parties had a most patient hearing and that the judge must have kept a very full note to deliver the judgment he did.

For these reasons and the reasons given in Slade LJ's judgment, I would dismiss this appeal, allow the cross-appeal and grant the relief suggested by Slade LJ.

Order accordingly.

Anglo-Overseas Agencies v. Green

Queen's Bench Div.

[1961] 1 QB 1, [1960] 3 All ER 244, [1960] 3 WLR 561, 176 EG 359

20 July 1960

SALMON, J., read the following judgment: The plaintiff company in this action claims damages for conspiracy and breach of contract against the defendants. It appears from the statement of claim that in the spring of 1959 the plaintiff company engaged the first defendant, who is an architect, and the second defendants, a firm of estate agents, to assist the plaintiff company on certain agreed terms to obtain from the Merton and Morden Urban District Council the building lease of a valuable site in a key position in the Morden Shopping Centre. The statement of claim alleges, in effect, that thereafter the defendants, with intent to defraud the plaintiff company, consipired together to assist a competitor of the plaintiff company to obtain the building lease to which I have referred. The plaintiff company alleges that, by reason of the defendants' conspiracy and breach of contract, the building lease went to a competitor of the plaintiff company and the plaintiff company lost the large profit which it would otherwise have made out of the development of the site in question. The defendants by their amended defence deny the alleged conspiracy and breach of contract, but also take the point that the acquisition of the building lease which I have mentioned would have been ultra vires the plaintiff company. It has been ordered that this point shall be tried as a preliminary issue, and it is this issue that I now have to decide.

The defendants rely on what is sometimes referred to as the "main objects" rule of construction, namely, that where a memoradum of association expresses the objects of the company in a series of paragraphs, and one paragraph, or the first two or three paragraphs, appear to embody the "main object" of the company, all the other paragraphs are treated as merely ancillary to this "main object," and as limited or controlled thereby. The principal purpose of this rule is for the protection of shareholders, so that they may know how the money that they invest is to be used. The defendants as champions of this rule have cast themselves in a novel and perhaps not overwhelemingly attractive role. They say, in effect—"Even if we have caused the plaintiff company, and accordingly their shareholders, serious damage by conspiracy to defraud them, yet we can escape all liability by reason of this very rule designed for the protection of the shareholders." Nevertheless, whatever the merits may be, if the "main objects" rule does in law apply in this case, then the piece of business in respect of which the plaintiff company purported to engage the defendants was ultra vires the plaintiff company, and the defendants would in law clearly be entitled to succeed in the action.

The objects for which the plaintiff company was established are to be found in cl. 3 of its memorandum of association. The following are the opening words of the clause, "The objects for which the company is established are:"—then are set out a number of paragraphs from (A) to (S). Paragraphs (A) and (B) of this clause[5] make it plain that the plaintiff company's main object was to act as exporters and importers of a wide variety of goods. It is plain that the business of property development per se cannot be regarded as ancillary to this "main object." Accordingly, the paragraphs of cl. 3 relied on by counsel for the plaintiff company to engage in the business of property development, cannot so empower the plaintiff company if the "main objects" rule is to be applied to them, that is to say, if these paragraphs are merely ancillary to, and limited by, paras. (A) and (B). Counsel for the plaintiff company, however, relies on the concluding words of cl. 3 as excluding the application of the "main objects" rule. I will read those words:

> "...the intention is that the objects specified in any paragraph of this clause shall, except where othewise expressed in such paragraph, be in no wise limited or restricted by reference to or inference from the terms of any other paragraph or the name of the company."

Counsel for the defendants, on the other hand, contends that in Stephens v. Mysore Reefs (Kangundy) Mining Co., Ltd,[6] Swinfen Eady, J, considered this very form of

5. (1) Paragraphs (A) and (B) provide as follows:—

"(A) To carry on business as importers, exporters, buyers and sellers of, and dealers in merchandise of all descriptions, including metals, machinery, plant, tools and metal goods generally, cotton, wool, worsted, silk, flax, hemp, jute, mesta, balata, fibrous material, rubber, sponges, cloth, clothes, leather and leather goods, furniture, electrical goods, ivory, jewellery, gold, silver, precious stones and gems, skins, fur, corn, hay, straw, hops, liquors, foods, provisions, wood and timber, coal, coke, patent fuel, olis, household goods and fittings, waste goods and offal, and generally any articles or goods of any kind, whether manufactured or not.

"(B) To carry on business as exporters and importers of, and dealers in, and agents for, home and foreign and colonial goods and produce of all descriptions, and particularly of and in goods and produce exported from or imported into the colonies."

6. [1902] 1 Ch. 745.

words, and held that it did not exclude the "main objects" rule. Counsel for the plaintiff company replies that Stephens v. Mysore Reefs (Kangundy) Mining Co., Ltd. must be regarded as overruled by the decision of the House of Lords in Cotman v. Brougham,[7] but that, even if he is wrong in this, Stephens v. Mysore Reefs (Kangundy) Mining Co., Ltd. ought not to be followed. If, as counsel for the plaintiff company suggests, Swinfen Eady, J, decided Stephens v. Mysore Reefs (Kangundy) Mining Co., Ltd. on the basis that no clause could effectively enact that each paragraph of the objects clause was to be read in isolation, then clearly Cotman v. Brougham n(3) overrules this decision. If, on the other hand, he was merely construing the words before him, Cotman v. Brougham n(3) leaves his decision standing.

The text-books support the argument that Stephens v. Mysore Reefs (Kangundy) Mining Co., Ltd. n(2) is no longer law; see, for example, PALMER'S COMPANY LAW (16th Edn.), p. 59; and 6 HALSBURY'S LAWS OF ENGLAND (3rd Edn.), p. 414. I must confess that I find it difficult to ascertain precisely the basis on which Swinfen Eady, J, did decide Stephens v. Mysore Reefs (Kangundy) Mining Co., Ltd. I incline to the view that he was merely deciding that the form of words before him (which is precisely the same as that before me) was not apt to exclude the "main objects" rule. I doubt whether he intended to convey that no form of words could exclude the rule. If this be so, Cotman v. Brougham leaves Swinfen Eady, J's decision untouched, since the House of Lords was considering a different form of words, which I will read. The words before the House of Lords read as follows:[8]

> " 'The objects set forth in any sub-clause of this clause shall not, except when the context expressly so requires, be in any wise limited or restricted by reference to or inference from the terms of any other sub-clause, or by the name of the company. None of such sub-clauses or the objects therein specified or the powers thereby conferred shall be deemed subsidiary or auxiliary merely to the objects mentioned in the first sub-clause of this clause, but the company shall have full power to exercise all or any of the powers conferred by any part of this clause in any part of the world, and notwithstanding that the business, undertaking, property or acts proposed to be transacted, acquired, dealt with or performed do not fall within the objects of the first sub-clause of this clause.' "

In that case the House of Lords held that those words were sufficient to exclude the "main objects" rule; whereas in Stephens v. Mysore Reefs (Kangundy) Mining Co., Ltd. Swinfen Eady, J, had held that the words before him were not sufficient to exclude the "main objects" rule. Had it been the intention of the House of Lords to overrule Stephens v. Mysore Reefs (Kangundy) Mining Co., Ltd., it is strange that it did not expressly do so. It appears to me that the House of Lords considered it unnecessary to express any opinion about the correctness of Swinfen Eady, J's decision, and accordingly it was not referred to in any of the speeches save that of Lord Parker of Waddington,[6] who expresses no concluded view on it.

If the words in this case, and in Stephens v. Mysore Reefs (Kangundy) Mining Co., Ltd. do not mean that each paragraph of the objects clause is to be read in isolation and is not to be limited or restricted by any other paragraph, I do not know what they do mean. Nor is any other meaning suggested by SWINFEN DADY, J. Any decision of this

7. [1918] A.C. at p. 514.
8. [1918] A.C. at p. 517.
6. [1918] A.C. at p. 520.

judge, of course, carries the greatest weight, and he speaks with especial authority on this branch of the law. Nevertheless, his decision in Stephens v. Mysore Reefs (Kangundy) Mining Co., Ltd. for the last forty-two years has been generally regarded as no longer law. Even if that case is not overruled by the House of Lords in Cotman v. Brougham I do not think that I should regard it as preventing me from giving effect to what, in my view, is the plain meaning of the words before me. In my view, the form of words used in Cotman v. Brougham was merely an amplification of the form of words used here and in Stephens v. Mysore Reefs (Kangundy) Mining Co., Ltd. I hold that these words do exclude the "main objects" rule.

The principal argument has centred round the points with which I have already dealt. Counsel for the defendants, has, however, also argued, with his usual skill, that, even if the "main objects" rule is excluded, yet no paragraph in cl. 3 is sufficiently wide to empower the plaintiff company to carry on the business of property development. Counsel for the plaintiff company relies principally on para. (E) of cl 3, the material words of which read as follows:

> "To...acquire any concessions, contracts, rights...and to perform and fulfil the terms and conditions thereof, and to carry the same into effect, operate thereunder, develop and turn to account, maintain and sell, dispose of and deal with the same."

In my judgment, these words are wide enough to cover the project on which the plaintiff company engaged the defendants.

I accordingly hold that this project was not ultra vires the plaintiff company, and I decide the issue before me against the defendants.

Order accordingly.

Comments and Questions

1. As in the US, the British have attempted to reduce the need for long statements of objects and purpose. But the effort has not been greatly successful. Professor Ferran's assessment of the recent effort in British was not hopeful of great change in prior practice:

> Companies are now permitted to state in their memorandum that their object is to 'carry on business as a general commercial company.' Where a memorandum contains this statement, by statute, the effect is that (a) the object of the company is to carry on any trade or business whatsoever and (b) the company has power to do all such things as are incidental or conducive to the carrying on of any trade or business by it. This model short form objects clause was introduced into the companies legislation in 1989 and it was commonly assumed that companies might adopt it instead of the traditional long objects. However, it is possible that a court could construe 'trade or business' in (a) restrictively.[45] Also, since limb (b) is worded in objective terms, it may be less flexible than the subjective incidental clause to which companies are accustomed. For these reasons, companies will hesitate to move to short form objects instead of the

---

45. For example, could a company which wished to dispose of its business safely rely on a clause which authorized it only to *carry on* a trade or business? Would such wording permit a company to make charitable donations?....

> traditional long form. Some companies have adopted a general commercial company object in addition to their existing long objects but this is an unfortunate response to a measure that was intended to reduce the length of corporate documentation....
>
> [T]he approach taken in the reforms introduced in 1989 was to leave the requirement for companies to state their objects largely unchanged save for two relatively minor points. The first change was the introduction of the general commercial company object, a development which has proved to have limited practical benefit. The second development related to the procedure for changing the objects. A company can now change its objects for any reason by passing a special resolution to that effect. A dissenting minority of shareholders comprising the holders of at least 15 per cent of its share capital (where the company is limited by shares) or 15 per cent of its members (where it is not) can apply to court to have the alteration cancelled. The court can confirm the alteration in whole or in part and can impose conditions. The considerations which the court may take into account in deciding whether to confirm an alteration are not specified.... The practice of drafting very long objects means that, in any event, most companies do not need to change their objects very often.... Thus the reform in this respect is limited in its real effect.

EILÍS FERRAN, COMPANY LAW AND CORPORATE FINANCE 88–90 (1999) (some footnotes omitted).

2. As you consider the excerpts below, think about whether the problem of ultra vires is universal, whether a "solution" can be devised, or whether the resistance to streamlining suggests a strong purpose to current practice.

---

3. *Ultra Vires in Japan*

The doctrine of ultra vires on Japan provides an interesting contrast to the doctrine in the United States. As you read the excerpt that follows, consider to what extent the doctrine has naturalized more completely in Japan than in the United States.

Akio Takeuchi, *How Should We Abolish the Ultra Vires Doctrine in Corporate Law?*

Dan Fenno Henderson (trans.)
2 LAW IN JAPAN 140 (1968)
Originally appearing as *Kaishahō ni okeru ultra vires no gensoku wa dono yō ni shite haiki subeki ka?* [1965] AMERIKA HŌ pp. 20–50
(excerpts pages 140–150; some footnotes omitted)

I. LOCATION OF THE PROBLEMS

The so-called doctrine of ultra vires, that the capacity of Juristic Persons (*hōjin*) is restricted by the purposes stated in their Charters (*teikan*), becomes a problem in the following cases: first with Juristic-Persons-for-Public-Interest (*kōeki hōjin*) under Civil

Code article 43; and second with general business corporations. Third, also some special problems arise in connection with corporations regulated by Enterprise Laws (*gyōhō*) such as corporations engaged in the banking, insurance, securities business, and the like. These special problems are: how do the statutory limits on charter purposes affect their interpretation and the effects of acts exceeding them. Fourth, since the law has provided the kinds of businesses that each of various types of Cooperatives (*kyōdō kimiai*) can undertake, it demands that associations specify their business in their charters; so it is necessary to consider separately the question whether the effect of transactions outside the scope of those charter purposes can be viewed in the same way as with general business corporations, and whether, as a matter of legislative policy, they should be given the same treatment.[4]

The meaning of this doctrine and the function which it might fulfill should naturally be considered to differ in nuance depending on the various kinds of juristic persons so that whether or how to abolish it is not a problem solvable in one stroke. Here, however, I wish to proceed with a consideration centered around general business corporations focusing on [proposed] legislative policy concerning how to abolish the doctrine. And though the conclusion reached concerning public interest juristic persons will depend principally on how we evaluate their public character, at least I think we must re-examine whether to retain the doctrine of ultra vires from the angle at which we will consider corporations below.

In its typical form this doctrine is questioned in court when a corporation is requested to perform a contract and the corporation defends alleging that the contract is void because it is outside the corporation's purpose. But at least for general corporations, it is hardly an exaggeration to say that, because the cases have interpreted purpose clauses quite loosely, defenses that contracts of any kind are outside the corporation's purpose are just no longer sustained.[5] In fact, if we look only at post-war cases, so far as I have seen there is not a single case where this defense has been recognized in favor of a corporation against transactional opponents in the broad sense.[6]

Also in scholarly theory, formulation of interpretive analyses do vary, but nearly all agree in supporting this trend in the cases.[7] In this sense, the differences in scholarly theory surrounding this problem do not go to the actual evaluation of the doctrine, but they originate in differences in thinking concerning limits of interpretive technique by which it can be expunged from the ambit of the law now in force; they seem to come from differences in thinking about the limits of techniques in interpretive theory. If this is so, viewed from this unified trend of the cases and scholarly theory (theoretical structure aside), it would seem that the principle of ultra vires has in the end been rejected by the case law and if so this problem has already been solved in this way.

4. Professor Katsuo Ueyanagi is against applying Civil Code Article 43 to business corporations in general as a matter of interpretive theory (Ueyanagi, *Kaisha no nōryoku* (Capacity of business corporations), 1 KABUSHIKI KAISHAHŌ KŌZA (Collected articles on stock corporation law) 85 (1960)....

5. For development of the cases, *see* K. Ōsumi, Kaisha no kenri nōyoku no han'i—toku ni mokuteki ni yoru seigen (Scope of the right-capacity of business corporations—in particular its restriction by the corporations' purposes), 2 Shoho (Commercial Law), SOGO HANREI KENKYŪ SOSHO (Synoptic case research series) (1957).

6. Here are twenty-seven cases finding the transactions concerned to be within the corporations' purposes....

7. The prevailing theory. But Sōzō Komachiya is against this sort of trend in the cases. S. KOMACHIYA, IGIRISU KAISHAHO GAISETSU (Outline of English Company Law) 77 (1962).

But the question whether corporations can refuse to perform contracts on grounds that they are outside the corporations' purposes is in fact disputed in court over and over again. This in itself shows better than any other evidence that it is still an actual problem today. Of course, this problem is not removed from the actual legal structure simply because scholars solve it in their interpretive theories. Since this is so, it is no credit to scholarly circles that, while they put this problem aside as a matter that can be disputed in court, they are fond of treating it as a handy topic for articles.

II. Peculiarities of Ultra Vires Problems in Japan

As is widely known, the doctrine of ultra vires first developed in the middle of the 19th century from the English cases concerning companies based on special statutes; then it moved to embrace general companies. And because it was introduced in to the U.S. and Japan, the important countries where this doctrine is now found are England, the U.S., and Japan.[8] The action and the reaction against it have shown these following striking differences between Japan on the one hand and the U.S. and England on the other. They seem to show the peculiarities of the legal process in our country.

1) *Legislative Process.* The Civil Code of 1896 as a whole was worked out on the model of the continental law of Germany and France; but for the capacity of juristic persons the English law principles were quite consciously brought in.[9] In this respect our attention is first drawn to one of the few provisions of this kind in our Civil Code. But what deserves our attention more is that in the drafting process this was handled as "decisively settled in law" and a naturally self-evident matter. Of course, the theoretical explanation was made from the standpoint of the Corporate Fiction Theory (*hōjin-gisei-setsu*) to the effect that:

> Juristic persons, as creations of the state, and the law, exist for certain purposes, and therefore their right capacity exists only within the provisions of laws and the scope of their purposes; they have no legal existence outside these bounds.[10]

The trend in the scholarly theory was indicated in the reasons given, as as:

> From time to time since the Middle Ages, the fiction of the juristic person has been improperly expanded and juristic persons have been regarded as having capacity equal to natural persons; but in the more recent era almost no one doubts that juristic persons have limited capacity and that their capacity is restrained by the purposes for their formation.[11]

And the actual need for such provisions was explained as follows:

> In both England and the U.S., actually many questions and suits have arisen; so we drafted it in this way.[12]

But we can find no clue that they had compared and examined other legal systems, especially those of Germany and France, which do not recognize this doctrine; and there

8. It appears that this doctrine has also been introduced in such countries of the Anglo-American system as Canada, India, New Zealand, the Republic of South Africa, and Palestine. *Cf.* Levy, Private Corporations and their Control 372 (1950).

9. T. Ishii, *Kaisha no kenri noryoku* (Right-capacity of business corporations), 76 Hogaku kyokai zasshi (No. 2) 171 (1959).

10. 4 Hōten Chōsakai Mimpō Shusakai Giji Sokkiroku (Code investigation committee—stenographic record of the proceedings of the committee in charge of the Civil Code) 127 (*shusa*).

11. *Id.*

12. 3 Hoten Chosakai Mimpo Sokai Giji Sokkiroku (Code investigation committee—stenographic record of the proceedings of the general assembly on the Civil Code) 92 (*sokai*).

seems to have been no weighing of the actual advantages. The provision is said to have been enacted because suits had arisen in England and the U.S., but the truth is more that because this doctrine was recognized, many suits later arose, as is well known. The decisive reason why this doctrine was introduced into Japan seems to have been the chance circumstance that the chapter of the Civil Code on juristic persons was drafted by Dr. Nobushige Hozumi, who had studied in England. Though the discussions in the drafting process inferable from the deliberative records were insufficient by present standards, they were doubtless unavoidable in our country then. However, this is a good example showing the special characteristics when Japan was adopting foreign laws.

Of course in England, the doctrine of ultra vires was not made by legislation. Since statutes recognized formation of corporations for purposes specified within the statutes themselves, the courts developed the doctrine of ultra vires, by way of interpretation of the legislators' intent to the effect that corporate funds must not be used for any other purposes other than the purposes specified in the statutes—contracts contrary to this are void. And it was pointed out early that this doctrine was for two purposes: to protect shareholders and to protect creditors;[13] but this is not to say the doctrine came into being after the interests of the investors and creditors were carefully compared and weighed against the interests of persons transacting with corporations. Also, Professor R.W. Jennings has suggested that behind the birth of this doctrine was hostility toward the stock corporation with its privilege of limited liability and a warning lest it oppress enterprises run by individuals and partnerships.[14] The courts from this sort of mentality seem to have tried to restrain, by using this doctrine, the activities of corporations formed under special statutes and later those of stock corporations in general. But, in any event, it should be noted that the English courts' interpretation of legislative purposes were introduced into our country and was adopted as an abstract principle, as though it stood universally for the nature of juristic persons without regard to the English history.

Because this doctrine was adopted in this way (i.e. considered to be in the general nature of juristic persons themselves), it came to be regarded as applicable to all juristic persons regardless of the nature of the particular Association (*shadan*). At least until quite recently, no one distinguished between Partnership Corporations (*gōmei-gaisha*) or Limited Partnership Corporations (*gōshi gaisha*) and Stock Corporations (*kabushiki kaisha*) or Limited Liability Corporations (*yugen-gaisha*) in applying this doctrine. But in a partnership the partners bear unlimited liability and can act as agents for each other, so that it is just several sole proprietorships operating under a single name. With partnerships there never was a demand for protecting investors and creditors or a risk of sole proprietorships being oppressed by corporations having the privilege of limited liability. Consequently, in both England and the U.S. the principle of ultra vires is never applied to partnerships. The question whether, in interpretive theory of existing law, Civil Code article 43 does not apply to partnership corporations and limited partnership corporations aside, we can say that the fact that the doctrine of ultra vires has so far been considered to apply even to personal corporations is an instance where a foreign law doctrine has been wrongly generalized because it was adopted without regard to its historical and social background.

---

13. According to Gower (Gower, Modern Company Law 79 (2d ed., 1957)), Lord Justice Cairns had already pointed this out in a famous case, Ashbury Carriage Co. v. Riche, L.R., 7 H.L. 653, 667–668 (1875).

14. This is a view shown by Professor Jennings in a staff seminar in comparative study of Japanese and American corporation law.

2) *Drafting.* The first peculiarity to be seen in the legal development after the enactment of the doctrine is the difference in the charter-drafting practice. In England, too, already by about 1880 purpose clauses stated in charters were interpreted loosely: a standard for interpretation had been established by the cases to the effect that anything that may be found to be incidental to the purposes stated in charters comes within their purposes.[17] In practice, however, drafters would not leave solution of this problem to court interpretation. They would state as many as twenty or thirty purposes,[18] and then add a general clause, "any and all other lawful transactions." If one could have no transaction except those stated in the charter, then the drafters would evade this restriction by stating anything and everything in the charter. In interpreting such general clauses, courts applied the "*ejusdem generis* rule." Even if drafters had used the all inclusive words "any and all other lawful transactions," courts took the attitude that it was limited to the matters similar to the enumerated items. So in response, the drafters then wrote into charters that in interpreting the charter such a standard for interpretation would not apply, aiming to enlarge the scope of the purposes in the charter.[20]

In the U.S., similarly the purpose clauses in charters (articles of incorporation) have become highly detailed and all inclusive; the purpose clause will usually take up half or two thirds of the total number of words in the charter. In paragraph (1) of article 3 of the charter of a broadcasting company shown on page 47 et seq. below as an example [omitted here],[21] items (a) through (e) lists acts involved in and related to broadcasting in detail, and item (g) provides that the corporaiton can engage in mercantile or manufacturing business of any kind or character whatsoever. Items (f) and (h) through (n) are related not to the business that is to be the corporation's purpose itself, but to the acts necessary for a corporation with any kind of business, such as to perform acts dealing with chattels and real property, to conclude contracts.... Paragraph (2) provides that the specified purposes and capacities in the foregoing items shall be independent of each other, that they are not to be limited or restricted by reference to, or inference from, other paragraphs; this clearly precludes the *ejusdem generis* rule referred to earlier.

In this way the U.S. and English drafting practice has created a custom of using so broad a purpose clause as makes limitation by purpose meaningless, so the possibility of this doctrine's actually functioning has shrunk to a minimum. With this background, it is said that in the present day, whatever the state-law provisions are, a charter that will allow a defense to be made out that a particular transaction is outside the corporation's purpose must have been either drafted by an utterly incapable lawyer or must never have been touched by a lawyer.

In our country, the purpose clauses in charters are in general quite simple and brief; article 2 of the charter of Yawata Seitsu K.K. [Yawata Steel], for example, simply states: "The purpose of this corporation is to engage in manufacture and sale of steel and other businesses incidental thereto."[23] On the one hand, such drafting has merit. In England purpose clauses are too detailed to disclose what the true purposes

17. Att.-Gen v. Great Eastern Ry., 5 App. Case 473 (1880)....
18. Gower, *supra* note 13, at 83.
20. In Coteman v. Brougham, [1918] A.C. 514 the court severely criticized inclusion of such a clause concerning standards of interpretation, but did sustain its validity.
21. Taken from Lattin & Jennings, Cases and Materials on Corporations 1402–05 (3rd ed. 1959).
23. Ishii (at page 189 in his article cited in note 9 supra) gives examples of purpose clauses used in our country for several kinds of businesses; they are concise, but not so much as this.

of a business are so that there is a question whether purpose clause should be made briefer from the viewpoint of investor protection.[24] In our country such problems do not arise. But on the other hand, once a dispute has arisen, the courts must resort to some far fetched arguments to go beyond the bounds of interpretative theory, depending on the case, in order to reach an equitable and just solution.[25] In the U.S. and England it seems universal to take an affirmative posture in practice to avoid the cause of these unreasonable disputes before they happen, but in our country this attitude has not developed. No matter how you take this, it is clear that the charter drafting practice of our country at best lacks the sophistication to try to overcome the unreasonable restriction imposed by the doctrine. "Aren't Japanese corporations trying to secure room to refuse to perform their contracts as much as they can, by making their purpose clauses short?"[26] Whether the answer is that the standard of charter drafting in our country is not even developed enough to be conscious of such problems, or the answer is that the drafters have left the expressions in the charter open to the courts' elastic interpretation, the state of drafting in our country on this problem is quite characteristic of Japanese drafting techniques in general; that is, underdeveloped.

3) *Development of cases.* The U.S. cases on this problem are said to have become so confused they cannot be grasped.[27] But even so, Professor Stevens said in 1927 that one can summarize the conclusion of detailed analysis of the cases as follows:[28] (a) The cases are almost all agreed that either party may assert its nullity if neither has performed that contract at all. (b) The cases are also almost all agreed that the contract is valid if both parties have completely performed it. (c) But the cases split over the remedy for the other party if one party has completely performed or if both parties have only partially performed. The federal courts and eight states including Illinois recognize the remedy of a quasi-contractual suit, or what would in Japan be called a suit demanding Restitution of Unjust Enrichment (*futō ritoku no henkan*); but the courts in the other states, including New York and California (they come to 80 percent) sustain claims based on the contract itself. In short, in cases coming under (c) the cases split over the extent of the remedy they recognize; in cases coming under (a) and (b) the rules have been settled.

24. Report of the Company Law Committee, Cmnd, 1749, paras. 43–54 (1962). Hereinafter this report is called the "*Jenkins Report*."

25. For example, in *Yamada Stocking K.K.* v. Kono Sangyo K.K., 6 Kakyū minshū 124 (Tokyo Dist. Ct., Jan. 28, 1955), a corporation with the purpose; "to engage in the warehouse business, leasing of buildings and facilities necessary for collection and storage of agricultural products, insurance agency business, sale and export of agricultural and marine products, transporting and forwarding business, and other business incidental to the businesses named above" tried to overcome troubles caused by a business slump by engaging in the broker business; the corporation bought 350 dozen pair of socks, but refused to pay when the price was demanded, on grounds that the deal was outside the corporation's purpose. The court found the corporation liable on the grounds that "Matters that do not prejudice the purposes stated... in the charter and that help the juristic person survive are all properly held to come within the scope of the corporation's purpose." This kind of theory formulation in any sense surely exceeds the framework for ultra vires doctrine. A. Takeuchi, *Note* [1955] SHŌJI HANREI KEMKYŪ (No. 28).

26. A question put by Professor Jennings to the participation in the seminar.

27. 'For example, S.D. Thompson, *The Doctrine of Ultra Vires in Relation to Private Corporations*, 28 AM. L. REV. 376 (1894), says: "...the law with reference to it is in a state of hopeless and inextricable confusion.."...

28. R.S. Stevens, *A Proposal as to the Codification and Restatement of the Ultra Vires Doctrine*, 36 YALE L.J. 297 (1927).

In our country by contrast, though the cases have something in common with the U.S. and English cases in that interpretation of purpose clauses has been relaxed, no attempt has been made to get highly sophisticated solutions by forming a ratification theory or using the estoppel doctrine, depending on how far the contract involved had been performed. A corporation's liability on a contract was always recognized by making it fit within the corporation's purpose; so far as substantive law is concerned, the logical conclusion is that if a corporation has continued certain transactions over and over again, the transactions always come within the corporation's purpose, and even suits by shareholders pursuing liability of the directors are judged to come within the corporation's purpose. It is doubtful whether this way of handling the problem to push back the ultra vires doctrine in all of its areas of operation was the most desirable case development; compared to the way the U.S. cases use several different means for solving questions depending on the peculiarities of the particular facts, the cases in our country lack flexibility, even though they produced one means of solution: elastic interpretation of purpose clauses.

4) *Legislation.* Finally, compared to the U.S. and England, what is most characteristic of the problems of our country is our late start in legislation. In the U.S. by 1915 the Vermont Corporation Law section 15 pioneered in limiting the doctrine of ultra vires; later other state laws sought to limit or abolish this doctrine in various forms. According to what I have found, only fourteen states have no special provisions to limit the doctrine; another thirty eight jurisdictions have limiting provisions in one form or another. In England the *Report of the Cohen Committee on Company Law Amendment* published in 1945 recommended abolition of this doctrine and contended that the purpose clauses should be operative merely to limit the powers of the directors.[31] This recommendation was not followed in the 1948 Companies Act amendments; they only relaxed the requisites for changing purpose clauses.[32] The *Jenkins Report* published in 1962 did not recommend complete abolition of the ultra vires doctrine, but it did claim that provisions should be enacted to save persons dealing with companies from suffering unfair consequences and submitted a detailed proposal....[33]

In the U.S., then, most states have already passed some legislation and the number of such states are increasing; and in England though legislation has not yet come, argument for this kind of amendment has been made in earnest for over twenty years. In our country, however, such an amendment has never been examined publicly; there seems to be no call for amendment either by the business world, which suffers injury to the security of transactions owing to this doctrine, or by the courts and lawyers, who are able to handle the disputes only by resorting to far-fetched theory. In fact, it seems that even the Ministry of Justice, a legislative bureau, which is supposed to have personal contact with the courts, has never asserted that amendments are needed. What is more, I think this phenomenon of delay in legislation is somehow connected with the state of scholarly theories in our country; the fine details of theory formulation and the way to achieve specific justice in results in this problem have been argued by several scholars, but the problems are always dealt with in such a way as to stay within the framework of Code interpretation; there has been no thorough-going solution suited to rid us of the problem completely. In the inclination toward the Juristic Person-Substance Theory [*hojin-honshitsu-ron*; cf. the Juristic

31. Report of the Committee on Company Law Amendment, Cmd. 6659, para. 2 (1945). Hereinafter this report is called the "*Cohen Report.*"

32. Companies Act, 1948, sec. 5.

33. *Jenkins Report*, para. 35–42.

Person-Fiction Theory], scholars tend to discuss this problem in the form of whether it is a juristic person's Right-Capacity (*kenri noryoku; Rechtsfähigkeit*) or Act-Capacity (*koi noryoku; Geschäftsfähikeit*) that is restricted by its purpose. This approach is not a proper one to meet the actual demands for removing the cause weakening the security of transactions. Nearly half a century has passed since Professor Seiji Tanaka argued that Civil Code Article 43 does not apply to business corporations;[34] but in that period of time whether the scholarly theory is viewed to have led the cases, or is viewed to have just followed the conclusion of the cases, I think that Japanese scholarly theory must bear some of the blame, together with drafting practices and legislative organizations, for not removing from the courts the burden of rendering decisions where the conclusions are already determined.

So considered, the state of things in our country where this doctrine is involved seems to be this: courts alone have been carrying the load of problems abandoned in corporate practices and legislative drafting agencies, silently handling them—silently to the point of being simpleminded. Thus concerning the problem of corporate law it must be admitted that there is some truth—of course with some reservations—in the ironic remark by Professor R. Braucher that in the field of commercial law the U.S. is now a statute-law country and Japan, like France, is a case-law country.[35]

Comments and Questions

1. We have grown used to the use of comparative materials by American scholars. The excerpt you just read presents an example of a Japanese scholar using the comparative method to explore the nature of an imported legal doctrine in Japanese corporate law. How does Professor Takeuchi approach the use of comparative material to understand his subject? Does the approach differ from that used by American authors in excerpts you have read in this casebook? Consider in particular the manner in which Professor Takeuchi approaches criticism of doctrine throughout the excerpted material.

2. Since the time of the writing of the excerpted article, the law in the United States has changed a bit with respect to purpose clauses. As Professor Takeuchi suggests, the problem of "ultra vires" has been solved by statute in the United States. The issue remains one of case law in Japan.

3. Professor Takeuchi suggests that "Japanese drafting techniques in general [are] underdeveloped." Can you suggest ways in which open questions left in formal writings are otherwise filled in? Is it possible that the elasticity of judicial interpretation of concise purpose clauses suggests that the courts are filling in the gaps in the writings by references to unwritten but well understood codes of conduct or communal understandings? Should it make a difference whether such codes and conduct norms appear in formal instruments of "official" law or remain uncodified though binding? Would your answer change if enterprise organization was open to people outside the Japanese community? Is there a generalizable theory one can draw from this problem?

---

34. Seiji Tanaka, *Note*, [1921] Hanrei Minjiho (No. 153), says just that he thought the theory that Civil Code article 43 does not apply to business corporations was correct; it was in his Kaishahō teiyō (Manual of corporate law) 79 (1927) that he went into detail....

35. Professor Baucher's views expressed at the staff seminar on U.S.-Japanese commercial transactions law held [in Tokyo] in 1959. See 1 Baucher & Michida, Amerika shotori-hikiho to nihon minshoho (U.S. commercial transactions law and the Japanese Civil and Commercial Code) 54 (1959).

4. *Ultra Vires in China*

Chinese corporate law appears to be silent with respect to ultra vires transactions and their effect on third parties. However, Chinese law, like that of Britain, appears to require attention to corporate objectives.

> Chinese legal and organizational culture is fixated on the precise limitations described in a given entity's "business scope," such that no enterprise is authorized to undertake an activity not specifically delineated and authorized in an approved scope. Thus, it is somewhat surprising that the Company Law does not provide any protection for third parties acting in good faith, where a company or its directors or officers are acting ultra vires or beyond their scope of authority.[78] Conversely, the Standard Opinion provided for liability for those parties responsible for companies acting outside of their registered scope of business or engaging in illegal business.[79]

Nicholas C. Howson, *China's Company Law: One Step Forward, Two Steps Back? A Modest Complaint*, 11 COLUM. J. ASIAN L. 127, 150 (1997).

However, China does appear to have attempted a formal elimination of the risk to third parties from the actions of company agents acting ultra vires. The reform has not come from the New Corporate law.

> The Uniform Contract Law provides another important provision. That provision stipulates that contracts entered into by legal representatives or responsible persons on behalf of legal persons or other organizations are valid despite the lack of authority of these people unless the other contractual party is significantly negligent.[106] On the surface, it seems that this provision also affirms the position of the Supreme People's Court on the abolition of the ultra vires rule in China.[107] While contracts exceeding the registered scope of business may not be void per se, they may be invalidated if they violate other laws or regulations that restrict certain business activities. However, further examination reveals that this provision incorporates the internal irregularity rule in the West.[108]

Zhong Jianhua and Yu Guanghua, *China's Uniform Contract Law: Progress and Problems*, 17 UCLA PAC. BASIN L.J. 1, 16 (1999).

---

78. The Company Law only contains the affirmative statement to the effect that a company's business scope must be specified in its articles of association, and that a company must conduct its activities in accordance with its registered scope of business. *See* [Company Law of the People's Republic of China (adopted by the 5th Session of the Standing Committee of the 8th National People's Congress on Dec. 29, 1993, and effective July 1, 1994)], Art. 11, para. 2.

79. *See* [Opinion Regarding Standards for Companies Limited by Shares promulgated on May 15, 1992], Art. 104(4).

106. [*See* PRC, Contract Law, CHINA LAW & PRACTICE, May 1999, at 19], Art. 50.

107. *See* Zui Gao Renmin Fayuan [Supreme People's Court], Quanguo Jingji Shenpan Gongzuo Tanhui Jiyao, in ZHONGHUA RENMIN GONGHEGUO FALU QUANSHU 137–43 (Wang Huai'an et al. eds., Jilin People's Press 1993).

108. Under the internal irregularity rule, a person who deals in good faith with a company in a manner consistent with the company's public documents is entitled to rely on a presumption that all matters of internal management will comply with said documents. *See* Royal British Bank v. Turquand, 6 E & B 327, 119 Eng.Rep.886 (1856).

The excerpt that follows suggests the approach to ultra vires, and its uses in other socialist economies within the Chinese orbit.

John Gillespie, *Private Commercial Rights in Vietnam: A Comparative Analysis*

30 STAN. J. INT'L L. 325 (1994)
(excerpt pages 360–361)

F. Indirect Control Through the Doctrine of Ultra Vires

Official ideology will be most influencial when the legal boundaries delineating acceptable commercial behavior are unclear. The uncertainties surrounding the "authorized" business of companies, private enterprises and registered sole traders illustrate this process. These licensed forms of commercial organization must strictly comply with the business objectives set out in their certificates of registration,[210] but a party dealing with one of these entities may not know the exact parameters of its business objectives. Questions such as whether a business permitted to operate a tourist hotel may also lease cars will arise. Experience in the West has shown that an objectives clause, no matter how carefully or broadly drafted, can never provide a comprehensive guide to all authorized business. In Vietnam, companies, private enterprises, and sole traders are usually only authorized to engage in one specified activity. Although all powers to carry out that object are granted on registration, these entities are not permitted to include a "shopping list" of associated objects in the business license.[211]

The penalty for exceeding authorized business objectives is an automatic invalidation of the contract(s).[212] Rescission of unauthorized contracts creates a powerful incentive to avoid activities that may exceed the registered description of a company: once stripped of the protection of the business license, the individual who entered into the contract on behalf of the commercial entity becomes personally liable.[213] For those unsure of their authorized business objectives, the freedom to "take initiatives in all registered business activities" set out in article 12(7) of the Law on Companies loses its effect.[214]

When an authorized business decides to expand its authorized range of activities, the company must notify an Economic Arbitrator and publish the changes. Practice suggests that this procedure is unlikely to succeed without the consent of the appropriate People's Committee, since Economic Arbitrators are a quasi-judicial arm of the local executive and do not act as independent organizations.[215] The supervising People's Com-

---

210. *See* Law on Companies, art. 13(1) (1990); Law on Private Enterprises, Art. 22(7) (1990).

211. [Interviews with Nguyen Lac, Deputy Director of Law Department, State Economic Arbitration, in Hanoi (Mar. 26 1992, Feb. 11 1993)].

212. Ordinance on Economic Contracts, Art. 8 (1989); Decree on Economic Contracts (1990).

213. In most Western jurisdictions, an authorized officer will not be personally liable, absent fraud or knowledge that the company is insolvent. Evidently, the strict doctrine of ultra vires applies to legal persons in China. *Cf.* Henry Zheng, *Business Organizations and Securities Laws of the People's Republic of China, in* LAW IN THE PEOFLE'S REPUBLIC OF CHINA 864–67 (R. Folsom ed., 1989).

214. [Interviews with Nguyen Lac, Deputy Director of Law Department, State Economic Arbitration, in Hanoi (Mar. 26 1992, Feb. 11 1993)].

215. For a discussion of the role of the Economic Arbitrator, see supra note 32 [Note 32 read as follows: "State Economic Arbitrators were formed on February 14, 1960. This is a three-tiered system (central, provincal and district levels) of dispute resolution established in the DRV in 1963 to oversee the management and performance of economic contracts between state enterprises. Since

mittee is empowered to withdraw or suspend business registration for recalcitrant offenders.[216]

The example of the tourist hotel demonstrates that a business license does not create immutable rights. The operators of the hotel may be regarded as obstructionist, trouble-makers or anti-social if they insist on leasing cars after the People's Committee has decided that this is an inappropriate activity. State policy is just as important as formal law; as soon as a right imbedded in a license or law conflicts with policy, it loses its validity and ceases to be a true right.

Comments and Questions

1. Issues of corporate waste in China are tied less to questions of capacity than to issues of legality. Acts of corporate waste would amount to the sort of illegal act that would subject the legal representative of the corporation to punishment. See, e.g., Kingley T.W. Ong and Colin R. Baxter, *A Comparative Study of the Fundamental Elements of Chinese and English Company Law*, 48 INT'L & COMP. L.Q. 88 (1999), excerpted in Chapter 3 above at page 433.

2. In the US, the EU and Japan, rules of ultra vires based on corporate capacity appear to be directed to give shareholders and third parties dealing with the corporation, a measure of control and protection. Shareholders have a means of monitoring corporate managers, and third parties have a set of rules for regularizing liability in transactions with corporations. In contrast, the rules of ultra vires in China and Vietnam appear to be used as a means of state control of corporations. Capacity, as a rule of corporate law, does not stand alone. Rather, it appears to be merely one aspect of a complicated system of governmental control of the activities of corporations. The nature of that control is nicely illustrated by John Gillespie, *Private Commercial Rights in Vietnam*, excerpted above. Have the US, the EU and Japan entirely abandoned the use of the law of corporate capacity for regulatory purposes? Can you think of examples of situations where corporate capacity is tied to issues of regulatory approval?

1989, with the introduction of the Ordinance on Economic Contracts, these forums have expanded their jurisdiction to adjudicate private economic disputes. Nguyen Lac, *supra* note [214]; John Gillespie, *Commercial Arbitration in Vietnam*, 8 J. INT'L ARBITRATION 3, 25, 55–57 (1991).″]

216. There are few reported cases where a People's Committee has revoked a license. This may, however, be due to the fact that most People's Committees lack the resources to adequately monitor the activities of private companies or private enterprise. Phan Huu Chi, *supra* note 41; Law on Companies, Art. 21 (1990); Law on Private Enterprise, Art. 15 (1990).

Chapter 8

On Capital Requirements

Chapter Eight introduces students to another area of difference in national systems of corporate law: corporate capital requirements. These requirements were developed as a means of mediating between the conflicting interests of shareholders and creditors. Shareholders are assumed to desire the distribution to themselves of the greatest amount of corporate capital that will not imperil the financial soundness of the company. The object of shareholders is thought to be to maintain the corporation with enough capital to maximize the income generated by their holdings—in effect, the corporation is treated somewhat like a large income generating machine. Such income maximization might also result in the maximization of the value of shareholder investment in the corporation, since the value of this investment is at least in part a function of its return. Creditors, on the other hands are assumed to desire only the payment of interest on their loan, and the return of their principal at the appropriate time. For creditors, income maximization for shareholders might reduce corporate wealth available for the payment of interest and principal. The more wealth a corporation retains, the greater the protection a creditor enjoys.

As you read this chapter, test the following hypothesis: Two fundamentally different approaches to the regulation of corporate capital are possible given the divergence in interests of shareholders and lenders. Where shareholders, as a group, are more powerfully involved in corporate capital raising, corporate law tends to favor rules giving preference to shareholder distributions. This is most likely to occur in places like the United States where capital markets are well developed. In contrast, where capital markets are less well developed, where lenders provide a more significant part of corporate capital, corporate law will tend to favor rules giving a greater preference to lenders' concerns.

In the United States two approaches are now common, both essentially favoring shareholders. The traditional approach, well illustrated by the corporate law of Delaware, is based on the retention by the corporation of a minimum capital account based on the 'par value,' that is the statutory minimum price, of each share sold by the corporation. The modern approach, represented by the Revised Model Business Corporation Act, is based on assessments of corporate solvency at the time of distributions to shareholders. Both of these approaches are modern in the sense that neither is based on the requirement that companies 'escrow' some minimum amount to guarantee their solvency. Capital requirements thus no longer form an important part of the economics of corporate organization in the United States. It has, instead, become a technical matter of significant concern only for the financially marginal corporation or the thinly capitalized venture.

In most other nations, however, an approach at least formally favoring lenders is the rule. Minimum capital requirements continue to play an important role in corporate formation. To varying degrees, most states mandate the retention by corporations, especially public limited corporations (SAs, AGs, KKs, and the like), of sometimes large amounts of capital for the benefit of third parties, including creditors and the state. Capital requirements continue to be imposed for reasons largely discredited or deemed irrelevant in the United States. But in these states, capital markets traditionally had been less well developed. While this is changing now with the phenomenal growth of interlinked global capital markets, these states continue to follow their traditional approach. Minimum capital rules function as a technical matter of concern to the marginal or insolvent corporation. More importantly, minimum capital rules have become an important means of distinguishing between 'private companies' whose minimum capital requirements are relatively small and whose access to the capital markets (principally lenders) are significantly restricted, and 'public companies' that enjoy full access to these capital markets.

This chapter first introduces the two significant American approaches to the regulation of legal capital and considers the policies each is meant to embody. The chapter then examines the European approach to capital requirements. This analysis is done in the context of the Second Company Law Directive, the EU's principle attempt to harmonize the rules of capital requirements within Europe. The understanding of the tensions inherent in, and the limitations of, the harmonization process studied in Chapter 6, should prove helpful in understanding the way in which the Second Company Law Directive has contributed to the convergence of European capital requirements regimes. The chapter ends with a look at the capital requirements regimes in Japan and China. Both jurisdictions have adopted the minimum capital requirements approach of Europe, but each with a twist. The Japanese system presents an interesting fusion of European minimum capital rules and the traditional American rule of 'par' value. The Chinese approach illustrates the tensions between the need to create independent economic enterprises with the superior public policy of maintaining a state controlled socialist economic system. To the extent that minimum capital requirements are 'window-dressing,' the Chinese version presents 'window-dressing' of a different kind.

A. Capital Requirements in the U.S.

American state corporate law has generally adopted one of two approaches to the regulation of corporate capital.[1] For purposes of this course of study the first is labeled the traditional approach and the second the modern approach. Each is considered in more detail in the sections that follow.

The traditional approach, well illustrated by the Delaware corporate law, is based on the idea that corporations ought to maintain some minimum amount, tied to share value, in their capital accounts. 'Par value' is the concept generally used to define the minimum price that must be paid for a share of stock, the aggregation of which provides the minimum capital which must be maintained by a corporation. Aggregate par value is used as a critical component of the determination of the authority of corporations to make distributions to its shareholders. In modern jurisdictions, par value, or minimum capital, is determined not by law, but by each corporation.

---

1. California's approach to the regulation of capital, which doesn't follow either the traditional approach or that of the Revised Model Business Corporation Act, can be treated as another significant technique of capital regulation.

The modern approach is exemplified by the Revised Model Business Corporation Act. This approach rejects the notion of 'par value' or minimum capital as the basis for the regulation of corporate assets preserved against distribution. It adopts a more flexible approach to the regulation of corporate capital retention based on notions of financial solvency.

Both approaches share a number of features. Neither approach specifies a certain minimum aggregate amount of capital to be contributed to the corporation as a general rule. Each corporation, even under the traditional approach, is free to determine its own minimum. Yet, all corporations are required to be adequately capitalized. The failure to adequately capitalize can have significant repercussions under corporate, tax and bankruptcy laws, but the determination of adequacy is made on a case by case basis. As we will study in Chapter 9, shareholders may face personal liability for corporate debts in certain cases, when a corporate is too thinly capitalized. The doctrine of equitable subordination in bankruptcy, also described in Chapter 9, can reduce the priority of shareholder rights to repayment from out of the bankruptcy estate. Tax authorities may recharacterize shareholder debt as equity under principles of federal tax law. However, under both approaches, the primary effect of the capitalization rules is to restrict the power of corporations to make distributions to shareholders or repurchase a corporation's own shares when such activity might imperil the solvency of the enterprise.

1. The Traditional Approach: Delaware

Delaware General Corporation Law (DGCL) sections 152, 154, 160, 170, 172–174, 242–244, set out the traditional approach to capital requirements and dividends. While the trend in many states is to abandon this approach in favor of the one set forth in the Revised Model Business Corporation Act, the Delaware approach remains highly significant. It is also the approach closest in spirit to that in Europe, Japan and China.

Folk on the Delaware General Corporation Law: A Commentary and Analysis

(Ernest L. Folk, III, et al., eds)
(3rd ed. 1992)
(excerpt Vol. I pages §154:2–§154:3)

Section 154, as revised in 1967, retains much of the language of its counterpart in the old statute. It has three basic provisions. First, the par value of the consideration received for the issuance of par stock constitutes capital, and the excess, if any, may be allocated to surplus. Second, the entire consideration received for the issuance of no par stock constitutes capital, unless the directors, at the time of issuing shares for cash or within 60 days after issuing shares for property other than cash, allocate a portion of the total consideration to capital. The 1973 amendment defined stated capital as the "amount of consideration determined by the board to be capital with respect to no par stock." The term "stated capital" had previously been used without definition in section 243 and is now used in revised section 244(a)(3). Third, the directors may transfer any part of surplus to capital, and can designate that part as capital in respect of any class of stock.

During the 1967 revision of the corporation statute, the draftsmen rejected a proposal based on the Model Act to adopt and define concepts of earned surplus, capital surplus, and variations of capital surplus. The legislature instead retained the vestigial noncomponent surplus approach—excess of net assets over capital—and codified the common definition of net assets. Net assets means "the amount by which total assets exceed total liabilities," which does not include capital and surplus.

However, the question of how to determine whether a surplus exists (or whether capital is impaired) is important for purposes of determining whether a corporation may repurchase its own shares under section 160 or pay dividends section 170. * * * *

Comments and Questions

1. Why do you think it is important to regulate the conduct of the board of directors with respect to the valuation of assets contributed to a corporation? Would it not be sufficient protection to allow ordinary rules of contract, in this case perhaps fraud, to apply in cases of contributions of overvalued assets?

2. Delaware, like most states, provides a system of rules for regulating non-cash contributions to a corporation. The regulations consist of two major parts: (1) description of the classes of property which may be lawfully contributed; and (2) the rules for assessing value of the non-cash or non-cash equivalent property contributed. Del.Corp.Code §152.[1] Delaware limits the classes of property that may lawfully be contributed to the following: cash, services rendered, personal property, real property, leases of real property or a combination thereof. Many jurisdictions differ on the characteristics of classes of property that may be lawfully contributed for shares. In jurisdictions adopting the Revised Model Business Corporation Act, for example, issuance of stock solely for future services would be valid consideration [Revised Model Business Corporation Act Section 6.21], though such consideration would be invalid under Delaware law.

3. Delaware also empowers the board of directors to determine, in the first instance, the value of property contributed. The determination by the Board, is conclusive, absent actual fraud. If both the contributor and the Board both know of the Board's false valuation of the property, the actual fraud requirement of Del.Corp.Code §152 will likely be met. Also, under Del.Corp.Code §162, the shares issued to a contributor of property would be invalidated where a deliberate inflation

---

1. Delaware § 152 provides that:

The consideration, as determined pursuant to subsections (a) and (b) of § 153 of this title, for subscriptions to, or the purchase of, the capital stock to be issued by a corporation shall be paid in such form and in such manner as the board of directors shall determine. In the absence of actual fraud in the transaction, the judgment of the directors as to the value of such consideration shall be conclusive. The capital stock so issued shall be deemed to be fully paid and nonassessable stock, if: (1) The entire amount of such consideration has been received by the corporation in the form of cash, services rendered, personal property, real property, leases of real property or a combination thereof; or (2) not less than the amount of the consideration determined to be capital pursuant to § 154 of this title has been received by the corporation in such form and the corporation has received a binding obligation of the subscriber or purchaser to pay the balance of the subscription or purchase price; provided, however, nothing contained herein shall prevent the board of directors from issuing partly paid shares under § 156 of this title.

of values could be proven. If the board knowingly overvalued an asset without the knowledge of the contributor, the board would be liable for fraud under Del.Corp.Code §152, but the contributor may not be liable for anything, since the actual fraud was not hers, though her shares would be invalidated, at least to the extent of the overstatement of value. If the Board mistakenly overvalued property at the time of contribution, it is unclear whether anyone would be liable under Del.Corp.Code §152, or whether the shares issued would be invalidated. A showing of the absence of actual fraud removes the case from consideration under Section 152, though an action may lie for breach of the board's fiduciary duty of care. This aspect is considered more closely in Chapter Ten.

---

a. *Valuing Assets*

Directors are given the power in Delaware to set the price of shares to be purchased, and to determine the value of non-cash consideration received for the stock issued. Such determinations are conclusive absent "actual fraud in the transaction." The purpose is the protection of shareholders and creditors by "preventing the issuance of stock without any consideration, or upon insufficient consideration, whereby the actual capital would be less than the amount represented by the shares issued and sold to by the corporation... [and to ensure that assets received are of] such character that they could not be readily subjected to the payment of corporate debts, but would also secure the rights of stockholders in such capital." *Sohland v. Baker*, 141 A. 277, 286 (Del. 1927).

The determination of the value of the assets of the corporation, for purposes of determining the capital of the corporation in connection with distributions, takes a different turn.

Morris v. Standard Gas & Electric Co.

31 Del.Ch. 20, 63 A.2d 577 (1949)

SEITZ, Vice-Chancellor.

Plaintiff seeks a preliminary injunction to prevent the defendant corporation from paying dividends declared on certain classes of its preferred stock on the ground that such action would violate the General Corporation Law of Delaware.

Section 34 of the General Corporation Law of Delaware sets forth the circumstances under which the directors of a Delaware corporation shall have the power to declare and pay dividends. Insofar as pertinent, Section 34 provides:

> 'The directors * * * shall have power to declare and pay dividends * * * either (a) out of its net assets in excess of its capital as computed in accordance with the provisions of Sections * * * or (b), in case there shall be no such excess, out of its net profits for the fiscal year then current and/or the preceding fiscal year; provided, however, that if the capital of the corporation computed as aforesaid shall have been diminished by depreciation in the value of its property, or by losses, or otherwise, to an amount less than the aggregate amount of the capital represented by the issued and outstanding stock of all classes having a preference upon the distribution of assets, the directors of such corporation shall not declare and pay out of such net profits any dividends upon any shares of any classes of its capital stock

until the deficiency in the amount of capital represented by the issued and outstanding stock of all classes having a preference upon the distribution of assets shall have been repaired.'

Under the power purportedly given by Section 34(b), the directors of the defendant corporation on December 20, 1948 declared a regular quarterly dividend on the $7 and the $6 prior preference cumulative stock to be paid on January 25, 1949. Shortly thereafter, plaintiff filed this action to enjoin the payment of the dividends on the ground that the requirements of Section 34(b) had not been met because the net value of the assets was less than the aggregate amount of the capital represented by the issued and outstanding stock of all classes having a preference upon the distribution of assets. This is the decision on the application for a preliminary injunction which was heard entirely on affidavits.

The defendant is a Delaware corporation and a public utility holding company. It has outstanding 368,348 shares of prior preference stock $7 cumulative, and 100,000 shares of prior preference stock $6 cumulative. Each of the series mentioned is entitled to cumulative dividends payable quarterly at the annual rate indicated before any dividend may be paid on any other class of stock. In the event of liquidation or dissolution, each share of both series is entitled to a $100 preference over the shares of any other class, plus all dividend arrearages. No dividends have been paid on either series since 1934 and as of September 30, 1948 the $7 series had a per share arrearage of $102.90, and the $6 series an arrearage of $88.20, or an aggregate arrearage on both series of $46,723,009.20.

Defendant also has outstanding 757,442 shares of $4 cumulative preferred stock. This stock has a yearly cumulative dividend preference of $4 per share over the common stock. Subject to the rights of the prior preference stock, this class is entitled to receive $50 per share, plus arrearages in the event of liquidation or dissolution before any distribution is made on the common stock. No dividends have been declared on this stock since 1933, and as of September 30, 1948, the arrearages on the class aggregated $47,213,884.67.

Defendant has outstanding 2,162,607 shares of common stock.

The defendant's board consists of 9 directors, 3 are elected by the holders of the $6 and $7 shares voting as a class, 2 by the $4 shareholders voting as a class, and 4 by the common stockholders voting as a class.

The facts surrounding the declaration of the dividend can best be presented in chronological order. The defendant by an agreement dated December 21, 1945, as amended, had borrowed $51,000,000 from a group of banks. Under this agreement the defendant was prohibited from paying any dividends so long as any of the notes issued under the agreement remained unpaid. In order to clear the way for the declaration of a dividend, the defendant negotiated a new bank loan agreement dated November 26, 1948, under which about $11,600,000 was secured to liquidate the balance of the 1945 obligation. The new agreement permitted the defendant to declare current quarterly dividends on its prior preference stock, provided the amount of the dividends so paid does not exceed the dividend income received by the defendant after September 30, 1948.

Once the defendant was assured that the new bank loan agreement would be signed, its directors met to consider the possibility of declaring the regular quarterly dividend on the $6 and $7 prior preference stock. At a directors' meeting held on November 17, 1948, the minutes recite that all the directors discussed at length various considerations arising in connection with the question of the declaration of current quarterly dividends on the company's prior preference stock. The directors were advised that the Rules of the S. E. C. prohibit a registered holding company from paying dividends out of unearned surplus or capital without the permission of the Commission. The minutes recite:

'* * * that the Company had on its balance sheet an item designated 'Earned Surplus since December 31, 1937,' the amount of which at October 31, 1948, was $25,602,663.61; and that in view of the qualification by the independent accountants of the Company to the effect that the investments of the Company are subject to such adjustment as may be required in the completion of the corporate simplification program under the Public Utility Holding Company Act of 1935 [15 U.S.C.A. § 79 et seq.], it appeared desirable that the Company obtain from the Securities and Exchange Commission, before the declaration by the Board of current quarterly dividends on the Prior Preference Stock, authority to declare and pay those dividends, which would be charged to that item.'

After a discussion by the directors, a resolution was passed authorizing the officers of the defendant to file with the Commission such papers as in their judgment would be necessary or advisable in respect to the proposed declaration of a dividend on the prior preference stock.

About November 24, 1948, the defendant filed an application with the Commission requesting authority to pay current quarterly dividends on its prior preference stock. The application made it clear that the defendant corporation did not concede that the payment would be out of capital.

On December 7, 1948, the directors met, and reference was made to the possibility mentioned at the November 17, 1948 meeting that a dividend might be declared on the prior preference stock. The meeting was advised that an application had been made to the Commission for authority to pay such dividend. The chairman advised the meeting that consideration had been given to the Delaware statute and that in order that the company might have evidence of its compliance with the Delaware statute, W. C. Gilman and Company, at his request, prepared an appraisal of the assets to determine whether in its judgment the assets less the liabilities exceeded $88,500,000—this figure is the approximate total of the aggregate capital represented by the $7, $6, and $4 preferred, plus the sum required to pay a quarterly dividend on the prior preference stock ($87,350,943.35 plus $794,609). It is not denied that W. C. Gilman and Company possesses expert competence in appraisal matters and is familiar with the defendant's assets by reason of having been engaged to study them for other purposes. The factual appraisal made by Gilman and Company and submitted to the meeting was necessarily somewhat general. This appraisal discussed the values of the various stocks owned by the defendant by reference to market value, past, present, and future earnings, percentage of stock owned and knowledge based on other studies and sources of information. The report concluded that the net assets of the defendant had a fair value substantially in excess of $88,500,000. The meeting also heard a report made by G. W. Knourek, Vice-President and Treasurer of the defendant corporation. Mr. Knourek was eminently qualified both in education and experience to make such a valuation. His complete familiarity with the defendant's assets is clearly demonstrated. This report dated December 6, 1948, also discussed the value of the stocks and concluded that the fair value of the defendant's net assets substantially exceeded $88,500,000. In this report Mr. Knourek stated that in appraising the assets he gave consideration to market prices, capitalization of current dividends, capitalization of average earnings for the two years nine months ending September 30, 1948, appraisals made in 1943 in connection with the defendant's recapitalization, and the recent orders of the S. E. C. with respect to Louisville Gas and Electric Co. (Del.) and a sale of Oklahoma Gas and Electric Co. stock. The chairman made a statement to the meeting that he had examined the Gilman and Company report and the statement by Mr. Knourek, and that in his opinion a fair value of the net assets was in excess of $88,500,000. He explained to the meeting the methods he used in his study and valuation.

The chairman also stated that since this was the first time this matter had come before the board in many years, he had obtained opinions from two Delaware attorneys and one Chicago attorney as to whether a dividend might legally be declared under the Delaware statute. The opinion, which was read to the meeting, stated that based on the assumptions contained therein the company might legally pay the dividend under the Delaware law.

The minutes recite that the board made numerous inquiries and discussed the asset value problem generally. A balance sheet of the company as of October 31, 1948, and a statement of its income for the twelve months ending that date were presented to the meeting. The chairman suggested an adjournment of the meeting with the hope that in the interim a Commission order would be entered permitting the proposed dividend declaration to become effective.

A public hearing was held by the Commission at which hearing the present plaintiff appeared and objected to the defendant's proposal. After considering the record, a memorandum by the present plaintiff opposed and a memorandum of the prior preference protective committee in support of the proposal, the Commission by order dated December 17, 1948, permitted the proposed dividend to become effective forthwith, but provided, inter alia, that the stockholders be advised 'that the Commission permitted the declaration to become effective without determining whether the payment is being made out of capital.'

The Commission's opinion contains the following language:

> '* * * David Morris & Co. has attacked the valuation and the witnesses who testified in support of it. Although we are not convinced that this issue raised by the objecting stockholder is relevant to these proceedings, nevertheless we have considered the record and are not persuaded that the objection is well founded in fact. However, it should be clearly understood that we are expressing no opinion as to whether this valuation should be accepted for any purpose other than that for which it was presented.'

In light of the Commission's conclusion that the dividend would be allowed without deciding whether the dividend payment would be out of capital, it is apparent that the quoted factual conclusion was in the nature of a 'factual dictum' by an administrative body. In view of my approach to the problem presented, it is unnecessary to consider what weight should be given to the Commission's remark.

The directors met on December 20, 1948, and having been advised of the Commission's approval of the proposed dividend, and after discussion, unanimously adopted a resolution providing for a dividend of $1.75 per share on the $7 and a dividend of $1.50 per share on the $6 cumulative preference stock to be paid January 25, 1949 out of the net profits of the defendant corporation accumulated since January 1, 1947, and to be charged to the earned surplus account.

On December 28, 1948, plaintiff filed this action seeking a temporary injunction against the payment of the dividend. As permanent relief, plaintiff requested that the defendant be enjoined from paying any dividend on its stock until the court determined that any such dividend would not constitute a payment out of capital or unearned surplus in violation of the Delaware law. Has plaintiff made out a case for interlocutory relief?

Plaintiff says that when the dividend was declared the capital of the defendant (its assets less its liabilities) was not equal to the aggregate amount of the capital represented by the issued and outstanding stock of all classes having a preference upon distribution. The defendants, of course, take a contrary view. I am not persuaded that the contention and the denial pose the precise issue this court must decide because it assumes that one objective value exists and is capable of being determined.

The defendant corporation concedes that the power to pay the proposed dividend must be found under Section 34(b) of the General Corporation Law of Delaware. It is clear that the net profits of the defendant corporation for the then current and/or the preceding fiscal year are more than sufficient to cover the proposed dividend, and it is clear that the proposed dividend will be charged to the earned surplus account. The sole question then is whether the conditions of the proviso contained in Section 34(b) have been met. Otherwise stated, at the time the board of directors declared the dividend in question were they entitled to conclude that the net assets of the defendant were at least equal to the aggregate amount of the capital represented by the issued and outstanding stock of all classes having a preference upon distribution? Stated with relation to the present facts, were the net assets worth at least $88,145,552.35—being the amount of capital represented by the outstanding stock having a preference on distribution, plus the proposed quarterly dividend.

The problem is one of valuation which is surpassed in difficulty only in the domestic relations law. The numerous and varied standards applied in the legal, accounting and business fields have mapped a wavering course for one required to resolve a substantial problem of valuation. Here the governing statute has declared that the capital must—roughly speaking—be valued at its dollar equivalent before a dividend can be declared out of net profits for a designated period. This duty falls to the directors. What legal standard will be applied in determining whether the directors have valued the corporate assets in a manner deemed sufficient to comply with the requirements of Section 34(b)?

The plaintiff's attorney stated at the oral argument that he did not charge that the directors were guilty of any fraud or bad faith in valuating the capital assets at a dollar value which would satisfy the provisions of Section 34(b). He appeared to take the position that based on the standards he would apply in evaluating the assets, they were not sufficient to comply with the requirements of the statute, and hence the action of the directors violated the statute. He also took the position that nothing short of an actual appraisal of the assets in the underlying companies whose stock was owned by the defendant would be sufficient. Let us consider the second problem first.

Initially, of course, reasonable men can differ as to what constitutes an appraisal. If by an appraisal plaintiff means that all the assets had to be viewed and evaluated separately by the directors or experts in a manner similar to a valuation for purposes of a reorganization of the type currently popular at least in the utility field, then I conclude that the statute imposes no such requirement on the directors as a prerequisite to the employment of the power granted in Section 34(b). In large companies, especially those such as the defendant, an appraisal of the type suggested by plaintiff would mean that as a practical matter the provisions of Section 34(b) would be unavailable. See generally II Bonbright, Valuation of Property, pp. 973–974. I prefer the view expressed in the following language of the New York Supreme Court in Randall v. Bailey, Sup., 23 N.Y.S.2d 173, 184, affirmed 288 N.Y. 280, 43 N.E.2d 43:

> 'I see no cause for alarm over the fact that this view [taking assets at actual value] requires directors to make a determination of the value of the assets at each dividend declaration. On the contrary, I think that is exactly what the law always has contemplated that directors should do. That does not mean that the books themselves necessarily must be altered by write-ups or write-downs at each dividend

period, or that formal appraisals must be obtained from professional appraisers or even made by the directors themselves. That is obviously impossible in the case of corporations of any considerable size.'

In concluding that a formal appraisal of the type mentioned is not required, I do not mean to imply that the directors are not under a duty to evaluate the assets on the basis of acceptable data and by standards which they are entitled to believe reasonably reflect present 'values.' It is not practical to attempt to lay down a rigid rule as to what constitutes prior evidence of value for the consideration of directors in declaring a dividend under Section 34(b). The factors considered and the emphasis given will depend upon the case presented. At the expense of brevity, let us consider what the directors of the defendant corporation actually did in connection with the declaration of the dividend under attack and then evaluate that action.

Since no dividend had been declared for a great many years, the directors proceeded with some caution. Having seen that the current net assets were more than sufficient to meet the dividend requirements of the $6 and $7 preferred stock, the directors considered the possibility of paying such dividends. The first obstacle to such payment was removed by negotiating a new bank loan. Plaintiff points out that defendant corporation was apparently required to pledge or restrict practically its entire portfolio for this loan of $11,600,000, callable on three days' notice for default. Plaintiff argues that the very fact that the banks required the defendant to pledge or restrict assets which the defendant values at over $100,000,000 to secure a loan of $11,600,000, is evidence that the assets were not worth anything near the value placed on them by the board of directors for dividend purposes. Nothing appears in the papers before me which would throw any light on the question as to why assets of the value alleged were pledged or restricted. Lacking particulars, I do not feel that I should give any particular weight to this argument advanced by the plaintiff. Moreover, plaintiff concedes that the assets are worth upwards of $50,000,000, yet there is no explanation as to why the banks would require a pledge or restriction on assets even at the value placed on them by plaintiff, which is many times the value of the loan.

The directors considered the value factor at three meetings and had available and personally studied the reports concerning the defendant's assets prepared by admitted experts in the field. They had the balance sheets and profit and loss statements. Moreover, evidence as to value became available through the hearing before the S.E.C. even though the issue there presented was not the one now before this court.

That then is what was done before directors representing all classes of stock unanimously declared the dividend now under attack. Let us examine the case presented by plaintiff.

Plaintiff relied on his sworn complaint and his two affidavits. Since October 27, 1947, plaintiff has been the holder of record of 100 shares of the defendant's $4 cumulative preferred stock. In his complaint the plaintiff sets forth his 'opinion' of the value of defendant's assets and arrives at a gross value of $82,109,858. After deducting liabilities of $11,242,729, the plaintiff determines the defendant's net worth to be $70,863,829. The complaint merely sets forth plaintiff's opinion of the value of each asset owned by the defendant, plus the following allegation:

'Complainant in arriving at the total of $82,109,858. used the figures shown on the left side of Exhibit 'B.' While recently 100 shares of Philadelphia Co. stock sold for $9.75 per share, he feels that a large block could not be sold at such price. Wisconsin Public Service stock pays 20 cents dividend, or 5% on a value of $1.00 [sic] Stocks just as sound, if not better, are yielding 7% and 8%. It has no market value. The stock showing 'no value' are considered valueless and have no market value. The other stocks are valued at market prices.'

Plaintiff's first affidavit recites once again his opinion of the value of the defendant's assets with one remarkable change. In his affidavit he states that 'Thru a clerical error, the value of Wisconsin Public Service was erroneously listed in Exhibit 'B' to the injunction bill at $1.00 per share, instead of $10.00 per share.' This error is the more remarkable because it amounted to an error of $12,375,000, and meant that in drawing his complaint plaintiff by his own statement under-estimated the value of the defendant's assets by that amount. Plaintiff in his first affidavit also revised his net asset value in several respects, but principally to correct the clerical error. After these revisions, plaintiff arrived at a figure of $81,728,640 which he designated as '(Net Assets (Appraised).' He then proceeded to deduct the sum of $25,244,457 from this figure and arrived at the sum of $56,484,183 which he describes as 'net assets with safety margin.' This item is explained by a note which says:

> 'Less for safety margin 33 1/3 % of $50,247,900 Phila stock and 20% of 42,475,785 other operating utility stock or total deduction of $25,244,457.'

The plaintiff's affidavit supplies plaintiff's explanation of the 'safety margin' deduction. It reads:

> 'At the moment we are, in my opinion, at a critical point in an inflated economy. Conditions are highly uncertain. Earnings are now high. If our economy contracts, stocks can go lower. I do not think that it would be prudent for a company like the respondent with relatively little cash, to pay a cash dividend at this time without allowing a margin of safety for its investments. I think that a fair margin for safety would be 33-1/3% for a utility holding company like the Philadelphia Company herein mentioned and 20% for the other operating utility companies such as Oklahoma Gas & Electric Co. and the others mentioned in Exhibit 'D.''

Plaintiff appraises the net assets at about $82,000,000 before his 'safety margin' deduction. There is no justification under Section 34(b) for requiring an arbitrary deduction from present value before ascertaining the value of the net assets. The safety factor mentioned by plaintiff actually is an element in present value, but there is no justification under the statute for determining present value, and then making an arbitrary deduction. This 'safety margin' deduction is actually an attack on the wisdom of the directors in declaring a dividend at the present time. Indeed, in attempting to justify his argument for a deduction plaintiff speaks of what is 'prudent.' Where, as here, the only question is one of compliance with the statute, and there is no suggestion that the directors have been guilty of fraud or bad faith in attempting to comply therewith, I do not believe this court can substitute its concept of wisdom for that of the directors.

Plaintiff's affidavit indicates that he arbitrarily applied a ten times earnings formula as a standard for valuing the principal assets of the defendant. Defendant's assets consist of the ownership of various stock interests in public utility companies providing gas, electricity, transportation and other services in at least seven states. Certainly this test may be one standard by which the value of such assets are weighed, but it is most assuredly not the only standard to be applied. Indeed, the assets sought to be valued may have such a factual background that the application of such a rule would be misleading and even fraudulent. Although a certain picked class of utility stocks may have an average value of ten times earnings, nevertheless, as counsel for the stockholders' committee pointed out, it is only an average. The values of the utilities chose to determine an average may vary widely. Consequently, plaintiff's assumption that this standard of valuing the assets is the only one to be applied is fallacious. The defendant corporation does not say that this arbitrary standard should not be considered. It merely says that it is only one criterion of value to be considered. I am in accord with the defendant's position. Compare generally In re General Realty & Utilities Corporation, Del.Ch., 52 A.2d 6.

We are left then with plaintiff's opinion that the net assets are worth about $82,000,000. This is about $6,500,000 less than the value admittedly necessary if a dividend is to be legally declared under Section 34(b). The plaintiff gives only his opinion of the value of the assets. As a basis for qualifying himself to give such opinion, plaintiff mentions his experiences in the investment field. His college education was in the business field, and for about 15 years he has operated an investment business in Wall Street, New York City. He holds official positions in the New York Security Dealers Association. He states that it is his business to know the value of securities, although he overlooked a 'clerical error' of $12,375,000, and confused a worthless stock in the defendant's portfolio with stock of another class having a value of about $600,000. Indeed, there is nothing in the plaintiff's papers to show any real familiarity with the corporations whose stocks are owned by the defendant. Plaintiff speaks of the stocks as though the defendant's business was trading in utility stocks. Such is not the case, and in consequence plaintiff loses sight of the value inherent in holding certain blocks of stock which give the defendant working control of such corporations.

Plaintiff also contends that the appraisals relied on by the defendant's directors erroneously took into consideration such factors as the future earnings and prospects of the stocks owned by the defendant. He urges that such elements may not be considered in determining present value under Section 34(b). I am unable to agree with plaintiff's contention. The factors mentioned certainly form elements to be considered in determining the present value of stock in a going concern. It is indeed common knowledge that future prospects often constitute a most important factor where present value is sought to be determined.

Plaintiff points out that the reputable accountants who prepared the defendant's balance sheet stated that the value of the defendant's assets was subject to such adjustment as might be required under a simplification program called for by the Public Utility Holding Company Act of 1935. From this and other statements plaintiff implies that the accountants were suggesting that the capital assets were overvalued. In my opinion, the statements made by the accountants merely constituted a caveat for their own protection and did not purport to go further. Nor in my opinion does the fact that the defendant applied to the S.E.C. for permission to declare the dividend constitute persuasive evidence that the directors felt that the value of the assets was such that the dividend would actually be paid out of capital.

Thus we have a situation where plaintiff seeks a preliminary injunction to prevent the directors from paying a dividend under Section 34(b) because he alone values the net assets at about $6,500,000 below the required value, while the defendant's directors have declared the dividend after having been presented with substantial data as to value compiled by admitted experts in the field. This data, along with the corporate records, indicate that the net assets are substantially in excess of the statutory requirement. I purposely refrain from placing too much reliance upon the more elaborate statements contained in defendant's affidavits showing the justification for the action of the directors because I prefer to evaluate the information presented to and the action taken by the directors prior to or at the time the dividend was declared. The information presented to and the action taken by the directors, when contrasted with plaintiff's case, permits of but one reasonable answer. The plaintiff has failed utterly to make out a showing which would entitle him to a preliminary injunction.

Plaintiff's case comes down to a disagreement with the directors as to value under circumstances where the directors took great care to obtain data on the point in issue, and exercised an informed judgment on the matter. In such a situation, I am persuaded that this court cannot substitute either plaintiff's or its own opinion of value for that reached by the directors where there is no charge of fraud or bad faith. As stated, the process of valuation called for by Section 34(b) of necessity permits of no one objective standard of value. Having in mind its function, the directors must be given reasonable latitude in ascertaining value. Such being the case, I conclude that the action of the directors in determining that the net assets were worth at least the aggregate amount of the capital represented by the issued and outstanding stock of all classes having preference upon the distribution of assets cannot be disturbed on the showing here made. Consequently, plaintiff is not entitled to a preliminary injunction restraining the payment of the dividend.

An order accordingly will be advised on notice.

Comments and Questions

1. The principles enunciated here have carried over to the successor provisions of Delaware corporate law. *See* Del. Gen. Corp. L. § 170. Why would a shareholder seek to prevent the payment of a dividend on the basis of the minimum capital rules of Delaware law?

2. In whose favor do the rules for asset valuation work under these principles of Delaware Law: shareholders; creditors; or the board of directors? Why should this favored group be protected by the courts?

3. How would you respond to the following argument: The rules with respect to capital requirements, and especially the asset valuation rules for purposes of limiting the power of a board of directors to declare and pay dividends to shareholders were meant to protect creditors. That being the case, creditors ought to have the power to approve the valuation of assets by a board of directors in all cases where creditors in good faith assert that the corporation may be insolvent.

4. If you think the argument made in Note 3 above has merit, how would you implement the rule? Would your reaction to the argument made in Note 3 above be different if the statute that permitted creditors the right to approve valuation also contained a provision permitting an action for triple damages in the event the shareholders could prove the bad faith of creditors? How would such a rule alter the relationships between shareholders, officers, directors and lenders?

b. Impairing Capital

The regulation of corporate capital under traditional systems is meant, in large part, to protect creditors. A large part of this protection comes from the 'par value' system for determining the amount of assets available for distribution. We will look more closely at this function in the next section. Equally important is the protection of creditors from the ability of corporate boards to get around capital account limitations by the use of other devices. Thus, a corporation otherwise unable to make a distribution to shareholders might effectively achieve the same result by repurchasing its shares from shareholders. If every shareholder held fifteen shares before the share repurchase, and if the corporation purchased five shares from each of the shareholders for $5.00 per share, then at the end of the transaction each shareholder will have received $25.00, and retain the same proportionate ownership of shares as immediately before the transaction. The corporation would have effectively distributed $25.00 to each shareholder without regard to the limitation of distribution rules of the corporate law. Such a transaction effects a fraud on the rights of the creditors,[1] even if undertaken in good faith. *Propp v. Sadacca*, 175 A.2d 33, 38 (Del.Ch. 1961) aff'd sub nom., *Bennett v. Propp*, 187 A.2d 405 (1962).

In order to regulate this practice and prevent the impairment of creditors' rights, Delaware statute prohibits the repurchase by a corporation of its own shares "when the capital of the corporation is impaired or when such [purchase] would cause any impairment of the capital of the corporation."[2] A determination of capital impairment is based on a finding of corporate insolvency. A company's capital is impaired if "the value of its assets is less than the aggregate amount of all the shares of its capital stock." *In re International Radiator Co.*, 92 A. 255, 256 (Del. Ch. 1914). Some Delaware courts[3] have more recently analogized the insolvency standard of § 160 to the principles of insolvency from the Uniform Fraudulent Conveyance Act:

> A person is insolvent when the present salable value of his assets is less than the amount that would be required to pay his probable liability on his existing debts as they become absolute and matured.[4]

The case that follows illustrates the problems posed by the impairment of capital doctrine as well as the relationship between the minimum capital rules and the rules limiting the impairment of capital.

Klang v. Smith's Food & Drug Centers, Inc.

702 A.2d 150 (Del. 1997)

Veasey, Chief Justice:

This appeal calls into question the actions of a corporate board in carrying out a merger and self-tender offer. Plaintiff in this purported class action alleges that a corporation's repurchase of shares violated the statutory prohibition against the impairment of capital. Plaintiff also claims that the directors violated their fiduciary duty of candor by failing to disclose material facts prior to seeking stockholder approval of the transactions in question.

No corporation may repurchase or redeem its own shares except out of "surplus," as statutorily defined, or except as expressly authorized by provisions of the statute not relevant here. Balance sheets are not, however, conclusive indicators of surplus or a lack thereof. Corporations may revalue assets to show surplus, but perfection in that process is not required. Directors have reasonable latitude to depart from the balance sheet to calculate surplus, so long as they evaluate assets and liabilities in good faith, on the basis of acceptable data, by methods that they reasonably believe reflect present values, and arrive at a determination of the surplus that is not so far off the mark as to constitute

---

1. Delaware courts have stated that corporations should not be able to manipulate the corporate law to perpetuate any fraud upon or unfairly impair the rights of creditors. *See, e.g.*, In re International Radiator Corp., 92 A. 255 (DelCh. 1914); Pasotti v. U.S. Guardian Corp., 156 A. 255 (Del.Ch. 1931); Hegarty v. American Commonwealth Powers Corp., 174 A. 273 (Del.Ch. 1934).

2. Del.Gen. Corp. L. § 160.

3. *See, e.g.*, Farland v. Wills, Del.Ch., 1 Del. J. Corp. L. 467, 475 (1975).

4. Del.Code tit. 6, § 1302(a).

actual or constructive fraud. We hold that, on this record, the Court of Chancery was correct in finding that there was no impairment of capital and there were no disclosure violations. Accordingly, we affirm.

Facts

Smith's Food & Drug Centers, Inc. ("SFD") is a Delaware corporation that owns and operates a chain of supermarkets in the Southwestern United States. Slightly more than three years ago, Jeffrey P. Smith, SFD's Chief Executive Officer, began to entertain suitors with an interest in acquiring SFD. At the time, and until the transactions at issue, Mr. Smith and his family held common and preferred stock constituting 62.1% voting control of SFD. Plaintiff and the class he purports to represent are holders of common stock in SFD. On January 29, 1996, SFD entered into an agreement with The Yucaipa Companies ("Yucaipa"), a California partnership also active in the supermarket industry. Under the agreement, the following would take place: (1) Smitty's Supermarkets, Inc. ("Smitty's"), a wholly-owned subsidiary of Yucaipa that operated a supermarket chain in Arizona, was to merge into Cactus Acquisition, Inc. ("Cactus"), a subsidiary of SFD, in exchange for which SFD would deliver to Yucaipa slightly over 3 million newly-issued shares of SFD common stock; (2) SFD was to undertake a recapitalization, in the course of which SFD would assume a sizable amount of new debt, retire old debt, and offer to repurchase up to fifty percent of its outstanding shares (other than those issued to Yucaipa) for $36 per share; and (3) SFD was to repurchase 3 million shares of preferred stock from Jeffrey Smith and his family. SFD hired the investment firm of Houlihan Lokey Howard & Zukin ("Houlihan") to examine the transactions and render a solvency opinion. Houlihan eventually issued a report to the SFD Board replete with assurances that the transactions would not endanger SFD's solvency, and would not impair SFD's capital in violation of 8 Del.C. § 160. On May 17, 1996, in reliance on the Houlihan opinion, SFD's Board determined that there existed sufficient surplus to consummate the transactions, and enacted a resolution proclaiming as much. On May 23, 1996, SFD's stockholders voted to approve the transactions, which closed on that day. The self-tender offer was over-subscribed, so SFD repurchased fully fifty percent of its shares at the offering price of $36 per share.

* * *

Plaintiff's Capital-Impairment Claim

A corporation may not repurchase its shares if, in so doing, it would cause an impairment of capital, unless expressly authorized by Section 160.[4] A repurchase impairs capital if the funds used in the repurchase exceed the amount of the corporation's "surplus," defined by 8 Del.C. § 154 to mean the excess of net assets over the par value of the corporation's issued stock.[5]

Plaintiff asked the Court of Chancery to rescind the transactions in question as violative of Section 160. As we understand it, plaintiff's position breaks down into two

4. The provisions of Section 160 permitting a corporation to purchase its shares out of capital under circumstances are not implicated in this case. See n.1 supra.

5. Section 154 provides, "Any corporation may, by resolution of its board of directors, determine that only a part of the consideration... received by the corporation for... its capital stock... shall be capital.... The excess... of the net assets of the corporation over the amount so determined to be capital shall be surplus. Net assets means the amount by which total assets exceed total liabilities. Capital and surplus are not liabilities for this purpose."

analytically distinct arguments. First, he contends that SFD's balance sheets constitute conclusive evidence of capital impairment. He argues that the negative net worth that appeared on SFD's books following the repurchase compels us to find a violation of Section 160. Second, he suggests that even allowing the Board to "go behind the balance sheet" to calculate surplus does not save the transactions from violating Section 160. In connection with this claim, he attacks the SFD Board's off-balance-sheet method of calculating surplus on the theory that it does not adequately take into account all of SFD's assets and liabilities. Moreover, he argues that the May 17, 1996 resolution of the SFD Board conclusively refutes the Board's claim that revaluing the corporation's assets gives rise to the required surplus. We hold that each of these claims is without merit.

SFD's balance sheets do not establish a violation of 8 Del.C. § 160

In an April 25, 1996 proxy statement, the SFD Board released a pro forma balance sheet showing that the merger and self-tender offer would result in a deficit to surplus on SFD's books of more than $100 million. A balance sheet the SFD Board issued shortly after the transactions confirmed this result. Plaintiff asks us to adopt an interpretation of 8 Del.C. § 160 whereby balance-sheet net worth is controlling for purposes of determining compliance with the statute.[6] Defendants do not dispute that SFD's books showed a negative net worth in the wake of its transactions with Yucaipa, but argue that corporations should have the presumptive right to revalue assets and liabilities to comply with Section 160.

Plaintiff advances an erroneous interpretation of Section 160. We understand that the books of a corporation do not necessarily reflect the current values of its assets and liabilities. Among other factors, unrealized appreciation or depreciation can render book numbers inaccurate. It is unrealistic to hold that a corporation is bound by its balance sheets for purposes of determining compliance with Section 160. Accordingly, we adhere to the principles of Morris v. Standard Gas & Electric Co.[7] allowing corporations to revalue properly its assets and liabilities to show a surplus and thus conform to the statute.

It is helpful to recall the purpose behind Section 160. The General Assembly enacted the statute to prevent boards from draining corporations of assets to the detriment of creditors and the long-term health of the corporation.[8] That a corporation has not yet realized or reflected on its balance sheet the appreciation of assets is irrelevant to this concern. Regardless of what a balance sheet that has not been updated may show, an actual, though unrealized, appreciation reflects real economic value that the corporation may borrow against or that creditors may claim or levy upon. Allowing corporations to revalue assets and liabilities to reflect current realities complies with the statute and serves well the policies behind this statute.

The SFD Board appropriately revalued corporate assets to comply with 8 Del.C. § 160.

Plaintiff contends that SFD's repurchase of shares violated Section 160 even without regard to the corporation's balance sheets. Plaintiff claims that the SFD Board was not

6. See, e.g., Wright v. Heizer Corp., N.D.Ill., 503 F.Supp. 802, 810 (1980); In re Kettle of Fried Chicken of America, Inc., 6th Cir., 513 F.2d 807, 811 (1975).

7. Morris v. Standard Gas & Electric Co., Del.Ch., 63 A.2d 577 (1949).

8. *See* Pasotti v. United States Guardian Corp., Del.Ch., 156 A. 255, at 257 (1931).

entitled to rely on the solvency opinion of Houlihan, which showed that the transactions would not impair SFD's capital given a revaluation of corporate assets. The argument is that the methods that underlay the solvency opinion were inappropriate as a matter of law because they failed to take into account all of SFD's assets and liabilities. In addition, plaintiff suggests that the SFD Board's resolution of May 17, 1996 itself shows that the transactions impaired SFD's capital, and that therefore we must find a violation of 8 Del.C. § 160.

We disagree, and hold that the SFD Board revalued the corporate assets under appropriate methods. Therefore the self-tender offer complied with Section 160, notwithstanding errors that took place in the drafting of the resolution. On May 17, 1996, Houlihan released its solvency opinion to the SFD Board, expressing its judgment that the merger and self-tender offer would not impair SFD's capital. Houlihan reached this conclusion by comparing SFD's "Total Invested Capital" of $1.8 billion—a figure Houlihan arrived at by valuing SFD's assets under the "market multiple" approach—with SFD's long-term debt of $1.46 billion. This comparison yielded an approximation of SFD's "concluded equity value" equal to $346 million, a figure clearly in excess of the outstanding par value of SFD's stock. Thus, Houlihan concluded, the transactions would not violate 8 Del.C. § 160.

Plaintiff contends that Houlihan's analysis relied on inappropriate methods to mask a violation of Section 160. Noting that 8 Del.C. § 154 defines "net assets" as "the amount by which total assets exceeds total liabilities," plaintiff argues that Houlihan's analysis is erroneous as a matter of law because of its failure to calculate "total assets" and "total liabilities" as separate variables. In a related argument, plaintiff claims that the analysis failed to take into account all of SFD's liabilities, i.e., that Houlihan neglected to consider current liabilities in its comparison of SFD's "Total Invested Capital" and long-term debt. Plaintiff contends that the SFD Board's resolution proves that adding current liabilities into the mix shows a violation of Section 160. The resolution declared the value of SFD's assets to be $1.8 billion, and stated that its "total liabilities" would not exceed $1.46 billion after the transactions with Yucaipa. As noted, the $1.46 billion figure described only the value of SFD's long-term debt. Adding in SFD's $372 million in current liabilities, plaintiff argues, shows that the transactions impaired SFD's capital .

We believe that plaintiff reads too much into Section 154. The statute simply defines "net assets" in the course of defining "surplus." It does not mandate a "facts and figures balancing of assets and liabilities" to determine by what amount, if any, total assets exceeds total liabilities.[9] The statute is merely definitional. It does not require any particular method of calculating surplus, but simply prescribes factors that any such calculation must include. Although courts may not determine compliance with Section 160 except by methods that fully take into account the assets and liabilities of the corporation, Houlihan's methods were not erroneous as a matter of law simply because they used Total Invested Capital and long-term debt as analytical categories rather than "total assets" and "total liabilities."

We are satisfied that the Houlihan opinion adequately took into account all of SFD's assets and liabilities. Plaintiff points out that the $1.46 billion figure that approximated SFD's long-term debt failed to include $372 million in current liabilities, and argues

9. *See* Farland v. Wills, Del.Ch., 1 Del.J.Corp.L. 467, 475 (1975).

that including the latter in the calculations dissipates the surplus. In fact, plaintiff has misunderstood Houlihan's methods. The record shows that Houlihan's calculation of SFD's Total Invested Capital is already net of current liabilities. Thus, subtracting long-term debt from Total Invested Capital does, in fact, yield an accurate measure of a corporation's net assets.

The record contains, in the form of the Houlihan opinion, substantial evidence that the transactions complied with Section 160. Plaintiff has provided no reason to distrust Houlihan's analysis. In cases alleging impairment of capital under Section 160, the trial court may defer to the board's measurement of surplus unless a plaintiff can show that the directors "failed to fulfill their duty to evaluate the assets on the basis of acceptable data and by standards which they are entitled to believe reasonably reflect present values."[10]

In the absence of bad faith or fraud on the part of the board, courts will not "substitute [our] concepts of wisdom for that of the directors."[11] Here, plaintiff does not argue that the SFD Board acted in bad faith. Nor has he met his burden of showing that the methods and data that underlay the board's analysis are unreliable or that its determination of surplus is so far off the mark as to constitute actual or constructive fraud.[12] Therefore, we defer to the board's determination of surplus, and hold that SFD's self-tender offer did not violate 8 Del.C. § 160.

On a final note, we hold that the SFD Board's resolution of May 17, 1996 has no bearing on whether the transactions conformed to Section 160. The record shows that the SFD Board committed a serious error in drafting the resolution: the resolution states that, following the transactions, SFD's "total liabilities" would be no more than $1.46 billion. In fact, that figure reflects only the value of SFD's long-term debt. Although the SFD Board was guilty of sloppy work, and did not follow good corporate practices, it does not follow that Section 160 was violated. The statute requires only that there exist a surplus after a repurchase, not that the board memorialize the surplus in a resolution. The statute carves out a class of transactions that directors have no authority to execute, but does not, in fact, require any affirmative act on the part of the board. The SFD repurchase would be valid in the absence of any board resolution. A mistake in documenting the surplus will not negate the substance of the action, which complies with the statutory scheme.

Plaintiff's Disclosure Claims

[Omitted]

Houlihan's equity valuations were not material

An "equity valuation" is an accounting, rather than a legal or economic, concept. Houlihan derived equity valuations of SFD in the course of rendering its solvency opin-

---

10. Morris, 63 A.2d at 582.

11. *Id.* at 583.

12. We interpret 8 Del.C. § 172 to entitle boards to rely on experts such as Houlihan to determine compliance with 8 Del.C. § 160. Plaintiff has not alleged that the SFD Board failed to exercise reasonable care in selecting Houlihan, nor that rendering a solvency opinion is outside Houlihan's realm of competence. Compare 8 Del.C. § 141(e) (providing that directors may rely in good faith on records, reports, experts, etc.).

ion. Plaintiff contends that the SFD Board should have disclosed the equity valuations prior to obtaining stockholder approval of the merger and self-tender offer. Plaintiff claims that Houlihan's equity valuations were material as indicators of SFD's "economic" or "intrinsic" value. At the same time, plaintiff acknowledges that Houlihan did not intend its equity valuations to serve as predictors of the market price of SFD shares, and that defendants neither accepted them as such, nor used the equity valuations to derive the price for the self-tender offer.

In Barkan[19] and again in Citron v. Fairchild Camera & Instrument,[20] we expressed our reluctance to force disclosure of data generated solely for accounting purposes. In Barkan, we held that an estimate of a corporation's "liquidation value" prepared as part of a capital-impairment test was not material.[21] Similarly, in Citron we held that valuation estimates "prepared primarily for accounting purposes rather than for establishing the fair market value of [the corporation's] share" were immaterial.[22] The holding in both cases was premised upon the sentiment that figures generated for purely accounting purposes are useless predictors of market value, and are at least as likely to mislead stockholders as to enlighten them. In light of Barkan and Citron, we defer to the finding of the Court of Chancery that Houlihan's equity valuations would not alter the "total mix" of information available to SFD's stockholders.[23]

The amount of pre- and post-transaction surplus was not material. For similar reasons, we hold that the SFD Board was not obliged to disclose the amount of pre- and post-transaction surplus. Surplus is a statutory construct that bears no necessary relation to the financial health of a corporation. And as in Barkan and Citron, we are skeptical that the exact amount of surplus would have been relevant to the average SFD stockholder in deciding how to vote on the merger and self-tender offer....

Accordingly, we hold that calculating surplus prior to executing a repurchase triggers no disclosure obligations on the part of the board.

The substitution of $75 million of debt for $75 million of preferred stock was not material

[Omitted]

The judgment of the Court of Chancery is affirmed.

Comments and Questions

1. How do the valuation rules for corporate repurchases of its own stock under Del. Gen. Corp. L. § 160 differ from the generally applicable rules for stock valuation by a board of directors? What is the relationship between the theory of corporate waste we studied in Chapter Seven, and the rules regulating impairment of capital under Del. Gen. Corp. L. § 160? Can you make an argument that the doctrine of corporate waste is as effective a means of protecting creditors as the corporate capital impairment rules we have been studying?

19. Barkan, 567 A.2d at 1289.
20. Del.Supr., 569 A.2d 53 (1989).
21. 567 A.2d at 1289.
22. 569 A.2d at 70.
23. Levitt, 287 A.2d at 673.

2. Most other systems of corporate governance, for example those of European civil law countries, prohibit corporate share repurchases. Do you think that a flat prohibition of repurchases, to protect lenders, is a more efficient alternative than the American approach? Does the American approach provide any benefit to the corporation? To lenders? Consider these questions in light of the material in Note 3, below.

3. In Kaplan v. Goldsamt, 380 A.2d 556 (Del. Ch. 1977), shareholders challenged a payment to repurchase the shares of a large dissident shareholder and director. The thrust of plaintiff's argument was that the price paid to Goldsamt, the dissident shareholder, was so high that it amounted to corporate waste. Plaintiff sought to recover from the board members individually the excess price paid to the dissident. In rendering judgment for the defendants, the Vice Chancellor explained that:

> In the area of valuation, wide discretion is allowed to directors, and as long as they appear to act in good faith, with honest motives, and for honest ends, the exercise of their discretion will not be interfered with by the courts. Muschel v. Western Union Corp., Del.Ch., 310 A.2d 904 (1973); Cole v. National Cash Credit Ass'n., 18 Del.Ch. 47, 156 A. 183 (1931). The presumption of sound business judgment reposed in a Board of Directors will not be disturbed if any rational business purpose can be attributed to its decision. Sinclair Oil Corporation v. Levien, Del.Supr., 280 A.2d 717 (1971); accord, Gimbel v. Signal Companies, Inc., Del.Ch., 316 A.2d 599, aff'd, Del.Supr., 316 A.2d 619 (1974).
>
> By statute a director is fully protected in relying in good faith on reports to the corporation made by an appraiser selected with reasonable care. 8 Del.C. § 141(e). While it was admittedly predisposed to do so, the Board here did not enter into the agreement with Goldsamt until it first obtained a comparison from Loeb, Rhoades as to the likely cost of a tender offer. Before it finally submitted the matter to the shareholders it obtained a similar opinion from Bache. Loeb, Rhoades had previously acted as the investment banking advisor for Medicorp, so it can hardly be assumed that it was selected as an advisor on this proposal in the absence of reasonable care. There is no challenge as to the qualifications of Bache. Plaintiff is primarily troubled by the lack of formality or detail with which these opinions were rendered. Yet the proxy statement was allowed to state that the $9.50 figure was an estimated tender offer price approved by each firm, a factor which would seem to indicate that each firm was content to stand behind its estimate regardless of how it was delivered. To the extent that the Board relied upon these reports in confirming its decision to go through with the Goldsamt transaction, I fail to see how the individual members can be held accountable for improper conduct.
>
> Furthermore, in making his arguments as to the waste of assets, plaintiff seems to take financial matters out of context and attempts to limit the issue to one of value alone. In so doing, he ignores the other considerations which motivated the Board as discussed previously herein. He ignores also the fact that the Board did not pay Goldsamt his precise asking price of $10.00 per share, but rather that it exacted from him an agreement not to compete with the corporation he founded and to be available for consultation purpose for a period of five years. The fact that the noncompetition and consultation agreement had a separate value to Medicorp is not seriously disputed and there is no proof that the total consideration of $275,000 attributed to it is unreasonable or excessive. Moreover, Goldsamt has since provided services to the corporation pursuant to this agreement which have been of financial benefit to its interest.

While plaintiff would have the cases distinguished for factual reasons, I am of the opinion that the decision here is controlled by the principle set forth in Cheff v. Mathes, Del.Supr., 41 Del.Ch. 494, 199 A.2d 548 (1964) and Kors v. Carey, 39 Del.Ch. 47, 158 A.2d 136 (1960). These cases stand for the proposition that the use of corporate funds to acquire the shares of a dissident stockholder faction is a proper exercise of business judgment where it is done to eliminate what appears to be a clear threat to the future business or the existing, successful business policy of a company and is not accomplished for the sole or primary purpose of perpetuating the control of management. In so doing, the fact that a price paid is in excess of market does not necessarily make the transaction improper. See also, Folk, the Delaware General Corporation law, § 160, at 156–157. As recognized in Cheff v. Mathes, supra, at 199 A.2d 555:

"...a substantial block of stock will normally sell at a higher price than that prevailing on the open market, the increment being attributable to a 'control premium.' Plaintiffs argue that it is inappropriate to require the defendant corporation to pay a control premium, since control is meaningless to an acquisition by a corporation of its own shares. However, it is elementary that a holder of a substantial number of shares would expect to receive the control premium as part of his selling price, and if the corporation desired to obtain the stock, it is unreasonable to expect that the corporation could avoid paying what any other purchaser would be required to pay for the stock."

In this case the price paid to Goldsamt is not even defended on the control premium theory. Rather it is based on the belief by both Goldsamt and the Board, supported by at least some evidence, that the stock was not overpriced at $9.50 per share despite existing market quotations. It was a determination made by a Board of Directors which felt that based on information then available it would have been of questionable propriety to make a tender for the same amount of shares at a price of $9.00 per share to Medicorp's public shareholders. The decision was made and consummated only after the Board investigated the possibility of legal obstacles and sought confirmation through comparative tender offer estimates. Although the Board deemed it unnecessary, it was persuaded by the New York Exchange (or compelled to do so as plaintiff would have it) to submit the matter to the vote of the stockholders. The result was stockholder approval. And finally, it was done for the announced purpose of removing Goldsamt as a threat to the future business of the corporation, a purpose for which there existed at least some factual basis.

In final analysis, I am satisfied that the defendant members of the Board of Directors acted in good faith and based upon reasonable investigation and advice under the circumstances. Viewed overall, I do not find that the price paid to Goldsamt for his 550,000 shares and the five-year noncompetition and consultation agreement to have been a waste of corporate assets.

Accordingly, for the reasons herein given, I conclude that the allegations of the amended complaint have not been established. Judgment will be entered in favor of the defendants. Order on notice.

c. *Distribution of Dividends, Calculations, Limitations, and Liability*

At the center of the traditional approach's system of protection for creditors is the regulation of dividend distributions by corporate boards of directors. The idea underlying this system is that while the board of directors ought to have discretion to determine whether to declare and pay dividends, and to determine the amount of such distributions, there ought to be a limit to this discretion. The need for the imposition of a statutory limit follows from the nature of the participation of shareholders, directors and lenders in the corporate enterprise. While shareholders and directors can assert a significant measure of control of corporate governance, lenders, as a general rule do not. Moreover, lenders may not constrain or otherwise limit the discretion of the board of directors to act for the benefit of the corporation and its shareholders. Because the interests of shareholders in maximizing distributions can be adverse to the interests of lenders in preserving corporate capital as security for their loans, and because shareholders, and not lenders, ultimately control the corporate machinery through the board of directors, most states have provided minimum statutory protections for lenders.

Delaware's approach to lender protection is based on regulation of a corporations legal capital—the conditions under which shares may be sold and on the restriction of the power of a corporation to make distributions to shareholders based on the nature of the consideration received for each share of stock. This per share restricted amount, share 'par value,' when multiplied by the par value of all shares issued, constitutes the minimum 'capital' of the corporation.[1] This capital constitutes the corpus of funds reserved for the benefit of corporate lenders and may not be invaded for the purposes of making distributions to shareholders. Should the corporation receive consideration for the sale of its shares in amounts greater than the par value of the shares, the board of directors may add this excess to the corporation's capital account. Alternatively, the corporation's board of directors may designate such amounts received for stock in excess of its par value as 'surplus.' Distributions to shareholders may be made out of income, or in the absence of income, out of surplus.[2]

The value of this reserve is possibly greater in theory than in fact. 'Par value' is set by the board of directors in its discretion. It is now common for par value to be set at a relatively low amount. As a result, most of the consideration for stock is usually available for the surplus account, and thus, potentially, for distribution back to shareholders. Lenders generally have no formal authority to compel the setting of a par value at any particular amount. Because corporate boards of directors owe a duty of loyalty to the corporation, and not to the corporation's lenders, even boards of directors inclined to favor a conservative policy of distributions must be wary of the allegation that such policies favor lenders at the expense of shareholders. The materials that follow provide a flavor of the issues involved in the regulation of legal capital under the Delaware approach.

---

1. Del. Gen. Corp. L. §§ 152–154.

2. For the rules regulating legal capital in Delaware, *see* Del. Gen. Corp. L. §§ 160, 170, 172–174, 242(a)(3), 244. For a classic account of this traditional system, see Bayless Manning and James J. Hanks, Legal Capital (3rd ed. 1990).

Folk on the Delaware General Corporation Law: A Commentary and Analysis

(Ernest L. Folk, III, et al., eds)
(3rd ed. 1992)
(Vol. I pp. §§178:2; :6; :9; footnotes omitted)

[Section 170] authorizes the directors to declare dividends from any legally available source, subject to any restrictions contained in the certificate of incorporation. The legally available sources for such dividends are the corporation's surplus, as defined in other sections of the statute, or, alternatively, the corporation's "net profits for the fiscal year in which the dividend is declared and/ or the preceding fiscal year." No dividends may be declared, however, if the capital of the corporation has been diminished to an amount less than the aggregate amount of capital represented by the issued and outstanding stock having a preference on distribution.

* * *

A cash dividend reduces the net assets of the corporation and transfers that amount of cash to its stockholders. Therefore, a cash dividend severs a portion of the corporation's profits from the corporation, and its stockholders receive a present return on their investment in the form of cash.

* * *

A fundamental rule of corporation law, codified by section 170 and its predecessors, is that, assuming a corporation is a going concern, the right to a dividend depends on the existence of a surplus or net profits. Generally accrued dividends may not be paid out of capital even on liquidation but only out of the normal dividend sources of surplus or net profits.

* * *

Penington v. Commonwealth Hotel; Coast. Corporation McTamney v. Broadway, Seventh Ave. & 56th Street Hotel Realty Corporation

17 Del.Ch. 394, 155 A. 514 (Del. 1931)

RODNEY, J. (delivering the opinion of the Court):

The consideration of the first two questions determined by the Chancellor and raised by this appeal will be consolidated. The consideration of these questions will not be drawn out at length. It is sufficient that the questions have been carefully considered by this Court and we are unanimously of the opinion that the Chancellor was correct in the determination of both questions. A more detailed reconsideration of the questions could add but little to the opinion of the Chancellor as reported in 151 A. 228.

We shall now address ourselves to the remaining and more important question presented by this appeal. This question is, in brief—Are the preferred stockholders entitled, in dissolution proceedings, to a preference in the payment of dividends in addition to the par value of the preferred stock where the assets of the company do not include profits from its management? If the answer to this question is in the affirmative, the further question then arises to what point of time are the unpaid dividends computed? The Chancellor determined that since no profits or surplus existed, no dividends on the preferred stock could have accrued and, therefore, no unpaid dividends could be given preference in the dissolution proceedings. The remaining question as to the computation of the time of preference of such unpaid dividends was, of course, not considered by him.

This Court does not agree with the conclusion reached by the Chancellor and in view of the importance of the question with relation to the corporate structures under the laws of this State, we have given the matter both serious and special consideration.

The matter has twice been ably argued in this Court, exhaustive briefs have been filed and the Court believes it is in possession of the references to all pertinent and material cases.

The consideration of the rights of holders of preferred stock of the corporation in question to dividends is largely covered by paragraphs A and E of the Article Fourth of the Certificate of Incorporation. These paragraphs cover fields entirely different. Paragraph A treats solely of the rights of preferred stockholders to dividends while the Company is a going concern. Of course, the right to dividends in such a case depends upon the existence of surplus or net profits. This requirement is not only expressly set out in paragraph A, but is also fundamental in the law of corporations.

Paragraph E, however, has no relation to the company as a going concern; it contemplates only the relation of stockholders inter sese after all creditors have been paid and the remaining assets of the corporation are distributable to the stockholders. There is no legal requirement, aside from contract or as set out in the certificate of incorporation, that in dissolution proceedings accumulated dividends could only be preferred from surplus or profits. In other words, it is universally conceded that the certificate of incorporation could provide that in dissolution proceedings the holders of preferred stock would be entitled to a preference of accumulated unpaid dividends before payments to common stockholders even though no surplus or profits existed or had existed. It is, therefore, true that the non-existence of profits creates no legal barrier to the preference of dividends in dissolution proceedings. The question is then one solely of contract between the stockholders. What did the stockholders mean when, in contemplating dissolution proceedings, after the payments of debts, they stipulated that the preferred stockholders should have a return of the par value of their stock together with 'unpaid dividends accrued thereon?'

Since, in this case no rights of creditors are involved, and the charter provision under discussion must, in the last analysis, be considered as a contract between the stockholders, let us briefly consider the theoretical position of the organizers of the company and the undertaking of the stockholders.

Shares of both common and preferred stock are created. Everyone understands that the risks assumed by the two classes of stock differ one from the other as do their prospects for profit. The annual income or return to be derived from the preferred stock is limited to seven per centum. Everyone knows that any great balance of profit, in the hope and prospect of which the company is formed, over and beyond this seven per cent., will be solely distributable among the common stockholders. Everyone knows too the cardinal principle that the capital of the company must not be reduced or impaired by the payment of any return or income to the stockholders on account of the money put into the company by them, but that such income or return can only legally be paid from current or accumulated profits.

This payment to the stockholders as a return upon their investment is, in general, termed a dividend. A dividend is a sum of money or portion of a divisible thing to be distributed according to some fixed scheme. So fundamental in the law of corporations is the thought that dividends can only legally be paid from profits or from net assets in excess of capital that the payment or division itself, i. e., the dividend, is sometimes treated as almost synonymous and often confused with the source from which the payment or division is legally made.

The stockholders, knowing the provisions of the law that the dividends on the preferred stock can only be paid from surplus or profits and having in mind the great disparity of prospective income, further agree that the preferred dividends shall be cumulative and that no payment of dividends shall be made on the common stock unless and until all arrearage or deficiency of the dividends on the preferred stock has been paid.

The decisional law of this State has considered the rights of a holder of cumulative preferred stock in a going concern. In Morris v. American Public Utilities Co., 14 Del. Ch. 136, 122 A. 696 at Page 703, the learned Chancellor says:

> '* * * That as soon as the agreed dividend which the preferred stockholder is to receive is matured by time, a right to its ultimate payment is against those who have agreed to its payment becomes a vested right. It is a present property interest.'

The Morris Case was not a case under dissolution proceedings like the present one and we mention it because of its excellent treatment of the rights of holders of cumulative preferred stock. In the cited case the right to cumulative preferred dividends was a right matured against common stockholders by the passage of time subject to the limitation that the dividend could only be paid when a legal fund existed for its payment. In the Morris Case, as a going concern, this fund could consist solely in the existence of surplus or net profits.

Turning again to the paragraph concerning dissolution proceedings, we find that the stockholders have agreed, after all creditors have been paid and other claims met, that the preferred stockholders shall receive the par value of their stock with 'all unpaid dividends accrued thereon.'

Applying then the law relative to cumulative preferred stock to the case at bar what is the situation at the arrival of the date fixed for the first payment of the preferred dividend? There is no legal fund (surplus or profits), in this going concern from which this preferred dividend can be paid. As against the common stockholders, however, the right to this dividend is fixed and vested but the payment must be postponed until there exists a fund from which payment can legally be made. Upon the arrival of the time fixed for the second and subsequent payments of cumulative preferred dividends the situation is identical. The dividend cannot be paid, but the claim exists and the dividend accrues and the amount accumulates awaiting the existence of a legal fund for its payment.

The Company now goes into the hands of the Receiver and turning again to the paragraph of the charter concerning liquidation proceedings, we find that the stockholders have agreed, after all creditors have been paid and other claims met, that the preferred stockholders shall receive the par value of their stock with 'all unpaid dividends accrued thereon.' At this point we must advert again to the basic principle heretofore mentioned, viz.: that in liquidation or dissolution proceedings there is no requirement that dividends be paid from profits and no inhibition against payment of dividends from any existing assets, including capital. All debts having been paid, all the assets are distributable in the manner agreed upon by the stockholders in paragraph E.

We, therefore, find the preferred stockholders, as against the common stockholders, with vested and fixed rights to certain dividends and there now exists a legal fund for their payment.

While it is tacitly conceded that paragraphs A and E relate to different situations, the one concerning the corporation as a going concern and the other relating to the corporation in dissolution or liquidation proceedings, yet it is assumed that the word 'dividend' appearing in both must be given the same construction in each. It is further argued that the word 'dividend' in paragraph A, relating to the corporation as a going concern, means a division of the profits of the company in excess of capital. Entirely disregarding for the moment the statutory and fundamental law that dividends can only legally be paid from some source other than capital, we see nothing in paragraph A making it obligatory to add to the definition of the word 'dividends' any suggestion of the source of the legal payment. The paragraph itself does that when it stipulates that the dividends shall only be paid 'from surplus or net profits.' That the word 'dividend' is often used with no reference to surplus or net profits or other source of funds from which payment is to be made is apparent from a consideration of cases where dividends were declared when no surplus or net profits existed. Cases abound where such dividends, although illegal, have been made. The Courts have uniformly applied the word 'dividend' to the illegal division to the stockholders....

It is suggested that the word 'dividends' in paragraph E must be construed in connection with the same word in paragraph F having to do with the redemption of capital stock. This merits some attention, for while paragraph E concerns solely liquidation or dissolution proceedings, it does contemplate a division of capital. The redemption of preferred stock provided for in paragraph F is expressly excepted from the operation of the provisions of paragraph E; yet because the redemption of preferred stock brings about a change in the capital structure, the sections E and F are possibly more analogous one to the other than are the other sections. Paragraph F, of course, refers to the redemption of the preferred stock while the Company is a going concern and it is certain that the dividends to be paid the owners of the stock redeemed must be dividends declared from profits or surplus and not from capital. Let us briefly consider the application of paragraph F when the preferred dividend is overdue and in arrears and no profits or surplus exist for their payment. Because there are no profits or surplus the dividend cannot be paid, but surely it cannot be argued that the stock can be redeemed unless or until the arrearage of preferred dividend is paid. Such a construction would defeat the benefit of all cumulative features or at least place it in the power of the Board of Directors to defeat these features. Kennedy v. Carolina Public Service Co. (D. C.) 262 F. 803; Sterling v. H. F. Watson Co., 241 Pa. 105, 88 A. 297. Assuming then that the preferred stock could not be redeemed until the dividends accrued thereon had been paid, we find this amount of preferred dividends accumulating and simply awaiting the existence of a legal fund for its payment. If it be true that these unpaid dividends accumulate under Paragraph F and redemption provision under that paragraph cannot be applied until these dividends are discharged, then it must be apparent that the dividends have accrued by the passage of time and are not dependent for their mere accrual upon the existence of surplus or profits for no surplus or profits have existed, but do depend upon the surplus or profits solely for payment.

It would be most anomalous to find that the Company as a going concern could not redeem its preferred stock under paragraph F because of an accumulation of preferred dividends in arrears and no profits or surplus for their payment but that by the simple expedient of liquidation proceedings and re-organization by the common stockholders under Paragraph E the entire arrearage of preferred dividends could be wiped out.

The learned Chancellor in his attempt to find the meaning of the word 'dividend' correctly seeks also to find the reason for the inclusion of the word 'accrued.' He correctly considers that 'accrued' must mean something beyond 'unpaid.' 'Accrued' is not synonymous with 'unpaid' and does not cover the same field for a dividend may have accrued and not be unpaid. The word 'accrued' itself is derived from the Latin—ad and cresco—to grow to—and in such a context as that under consideration and construed with the word 'thereon,' it means these claims for dividends that have grown to the par value of the stock and matured and become due by the passage of time by virtue of the provisions of the Certificate of Incorporation creating the cumulative and preferred rights.

Such is our conclusion of the case upon principle. While it is true that in cases such as this a correct determination depends upon the phraseology of the particular charter or written instrument, yet it is gratifying that in other jurisdictions in the consideration of analogous provisions we find an almost entire unanimity sustaining our views....

In the Dominion Tar and Chemical Co. Case, Eve., J., said:

> 'I think that the judgments of Neville, J., in the New Chinese Antimony Co., Ltd. (3), and of P. O. Lawrence, J., in Re Springbok Agricultural Estates, Ld. (1), indicate that in their opinion the real sum payable to the preference shareholders under clauses not distinguishable from the one which I have to construe was the full amount of the preferential dividend without any reference to the question whether the distributable fund represented any reserve of profits or surplus profits earned by the company. * * * In other words, it seems to me that the construction which they have put upon the words, 'all arrears of the said preferential dividend,' was not arrears of such sums as the preference shareholders would have received had the company been a going concern—had the company earned profits available for the preferential dividend and had they in fact declared their dividend—but all arrears of the interest payable to the preference shareholders at the rate fixed by the contract between them and the company, and that in truth and in substance the expression 'all arrears of the said preferential dividend' in a clause of this sort means a sum equal to the amount secured as preferential dividend to the shareholders by the contracts under which the preference shares were issued. In my opinion, an obligation, which the preference shareholders would be under in one set of circumstances, cannot be imposed on them by the Court in a different state of circumstances, and I think on these grounds, fortified by the decisions to which I have referred, the preference shareholders in this case are entitled to their full 7 per cent. dividend before the surplus assets are applied in making further payment to the ordinary shareholders.'

....

We are, therefore, of the opinion that in the present case the holders of the cumulative preferred stock are entitled in the liquidation proceedings to be paid in addition to the par value of their stock the unpaid dividends accrued thereon.

We have reached the foregoing conclusion after a due and careful consideration of the argument on the part of the common stockholders. Counsel for the common stockholders have ably emphasized the fact that at common law, and in the absence of any statute or agreement to the contrary, all stock enjoys equal rights and privileges, and that claims for special preferences must be clearly provided by the charter contract. Such was in effect the holding of Gaskill v. Gladys Belle Oil Co. (Del. Ch.) 146 A. 337.

Being of the opinion that the charter contract tract in the present case does clearly provide for the preferences claimed by the preferred stockholders, we are of the opinion that the requirement contended for is fully met.

The question then arises to what point are these dividends payable? Are they payable to the time of the appointment of the Receiver, or down to the time of the distribution by the Receiver?

Like the answer to the preceding question heretofore discussed, the answer to this last question lies in a large measure, in the agreement entered into by the stockholders through the medium of the Certificate of Incorporation.

It seems apparent that the real agreement of the stockholders provided (by paragraph A) that so long as the Company was a going concern the preferred stockholders would be entitled to a cumulative seven per cent. dividend; by paragraph E it was agreed that when the Company ceased to do business, or, in the words of the paragraph itself 'in the event of the liquidation, dissolution or winding up of the corporation, or upon any distribution of its capital * * *' the holders of the preferred stock were entitled to the par value of the stock 'and all unpaid dividends accrued thereon' before any amount should be paid or assets distributed to the common stockholders.

The dividends, we think, that were made payable under paragraph E were those dividends that had accrued under paragraph A and which were unpaid because of the lack of any legal fund for their payment. The dividends accrued before the appointment of the Receiver and while the Company was a going concern and would have been then paid had there then existed surplus or profits liable for their discharge and the liquidation proceedings merely furnished the fund legally available for their payment.

The agreement of the stockholders related to the Company as a going concern and simply provided (by paragraph E) for the distribution of assets after dissolution proceedings had been commenced. The agreement of the stockholders did not attempt to control the operation of the company during the liquidation proceedings, but in such proceedings merely regulated the distribution of assets. After the appointment of the Receiver the management of the Company was taken from the officers and stockholders and placed in 'custodia legis.' While the Company was in the hands of the Court, through the instrumentality of its Receiver, no dividend could be declared nor, do we think any could accrue as such terms were used in Paragraph E of the Charter.

While we have heretofore reached the conclusion that dividends on the preferred stock mentioned in the Charter under discussion could and did accrue periodically though no profits were made or surplus existed and that such accrued dividends could be paid on dissolution proceedings because, in our opinion, such was the agreement of the parties, yet we think the dividends so to be paid on the dissolution proceedings must, to be within the agreement of the parties, be those dividends which had accrued while the Company was a going concern and which would have been paid from surplus or profits had such funds existed.

We are not unmindful of the fact that a considerable period of time has elapsed since the appointment of the Receiver nor of the further fact that the appointment itself was that of a Receiver generally and that in the original order there was no specific authority to wind up the corporation. The Receiver, however, did not operate the company as a going concern and all his activities have been directed to collecting and conserving the assets for distribution.

We are of the opinion that the holders of the preferred stock are entitled to the par value of their stock together with all unpaid dividends accrued thereon up to the time of the appointment of the Receiver by the Delaware Court.

The authorities upon the latter point herein considered are quite limited in number. The conclusion reached by us finds support in Drewry-Hughes Co. v. Throckmorton, 120 Va. 859, 92 S. E. 818, and in the language of Lord Sterling in Re Chrichton's Oil Co., L. R. (1902), 2 Ch. 86.

Comments and Questions

1. *Penington* is noteworthy for the use of the comparative method by the Delaware court. For what purposes did the *Penington* court use the English cases it considered in its opinion? Does it strike you as odd that the Delaware Supreme Court should look to the English courts for guidance on a matter of Delaware corporate law?

2. The traditional approach is not purely mechanical. In addition to compliance with the formal requirements of Delaware statutes, a board of directors may be prevented from declaring and paying dividends where such an act otherwise violates the fiduciary duties of the board of directors. The case that follows, Sinclair Oil Corp. v. Levien, provides a clear statement of the rule in Delaware. In that case, a minority shareholder of a subsidiary brought an action against the parent company for damages sustained by subsidiary. He alleged that as result of dividends paid by the subsidiary, the parent company diminished the industrial development of the subsidiary.

Sinclair Oil Corp. v. Levien

280 A.2d 717 (Del. 1971)

* * * *

Since it is admitted that the dividends were paid in strict compliance with 8 Del.C. § 170, the alleged excessiveness of the payments alone would not state a cause of action. Nevertheless, compliance with the applicable statute may not, under all circumstances, justify all dividend payments. If a plaintiff can meet his burden of proving that a dividend cannot be grounded on any reasonable business objective, then the courts can and will interfere with the board's decision to pay the dividend.

Sinclair contends that it is improper to apply the intrinsic fairness standard to dividend payments even when the board which voted for the dividends is completely dominated. In support of this contention, Sinclair relies heavily on American District Telegraph Co. (ADT) v. Grinnell Corp., (N.Y.Sup.Ct. 1969) aff'd. 33 A.D.2d 769, 306 N.Y.S.2d 209 (1969). Plaintiffs were minority stockholders of ADT, a subsidiary of Grinnell. The plaintiffs alleged that Grinnell, realizing that it would soon have to sell its ADT stock because of a pending anti-trust action, caused ADT to pay excessive dividends. Because the dividend payments conformed with applicable statutory law, and the plaintiffs could not prove an abuse of discretion, the court ruled that the complaint did not state a cause of action. Other decisions seem to support Sinclair's contention. In Metropolitan Casualty Ins. Co. v. First State Bank of Temple, 54 S.W.2d 358 (Tex.Civ.App. 1932), rev'd. on other grounds, 79 S.W.2d 835 (Sup.Ct. 1935), the court held that a majority of interested directors does not void a declaration of dividends because all directors, by necessity, are interested in and benefited by a dividend declaration. See, also, Schwartz v. Kahn, 183 Misc. 252, 50 N.Y.S.2d 931 (1944); Weinberger v. Quinn, 264 A.D. 405, 35 N.Y.S.2d 567 (1942).

We do not accept the argument that the intrinsic fairness test can never be applied to a dividend declaration by a dominated board, although a dividend declaration by a dominated board will not inevitably demand the application of the intrinsic fairness standard. Moskowitz v. Bantrell, 41 Del.Ch. 177, 190 A.2d 749 (Del.Supr. 1963). If such a dividend is in essence self-dealing by the parent, then the intrinsic fairness standard is the proper standard. For example, suppose a parent dominates a subsidiary and its board of directors. The subsidiary has outstanding two classes of stock, X and Y. Class X is owned by the parent and Class Y is owned by minority stockholders of the subsidiary. If the subsidiary, at the direction of the parent, declares a dividend on its Class X stock only, this might well be self-dealing by the parent. It would be receiving something from the subsidiary to the exclusion of and detrimental to its minority stockholders. This self-dealing, coupled with the parent's fiduciary duty, would make intrinsic fairness the proper standard by which to evaluate the dividend payments.

Consequently it must be determined whether the dividend payments by Sinven were, in essence, self-dealing by Sinclair. The dividends resulted in great sums of money being transferred from Sinven to Sinclair. However, a proportionate share of this money was received by the minority shareholders of Sinven. Sinclair received nothing from Sinven to the exclusion of its minority stockholders. As such, these dividends were not self-dealing. We hold therefore that the Chancellor erred in applying the intrinsic fairness test as to these dividend payments. The business judgment standard should have been applied.

We conclude that the facts demonstrate that the dividend payments complied with the business judgment standard and with 8 Del.C. § 170. The motives for causing the declaration of dividends are immaterial unless the plaintiff can show that the dividend payments resulted from improper motives and amounted to waste. The plaintiff contends only that the dividend payments drained Sinven of cash to such an extent that it was prevented from expanding.

The plaintiff proved no business opportunities which came to Sinven independently and which Sinclair either took to itself or denied to Sinven. As a matter of fact, with two minor exceptions which resulted in losses, all of Sinven's operations have been conducted in Venezuela, and Sinclair had a policy of exploiting its oil properties located in different countries by subsidiaries located in the particular countries.

From 1960 to 1966 Sinclair purchased or developed oil fields in Alaska, Canada, Paraguay, and other places around the world. The plaintiff contends that these were all opportunities which could have been taken by Sinven. The Chancellor concluded that Sinclair had not proved that its denial of expansion opportunities to Sinven was intrinsically fair. He based this conclusion on the following findings of fact. Sinclair made no real effort to expand Sinven. The excessive dividends paid by Sinven resulted in so great a cash drain as to effectively deny to Sinven any ability to expand. During this same period Sinclair actively pursued a company-wide policy of developing through its subsidiaries new sources of revenue, but Sinven was not permitted to participate and was confined in its activities to Venezuela.

However, the plaintiff could point to no opportunities which came to Sinven. Therefore, Sinclair usurped no business opportunity belonging to Sinven. Since Sinclair received nothing from Sinven to the exclusion of and detriment to Sinven's minority stockholders, there was no self-dealing. Therefore, business judgment is the proper standard by which to evaluate Sinclair's expansion policies.

Comments and Questions

1. Does the result in *Sinclair Oil* favor shareholders or lenders? From a lender's perspective, might the opposite result have been better?

2. *Sinclair Oil* involved a dispute between shareholders. Is there ever a case in which a board of directors violates its fiduciary duties to lenders by declaring and paying dividends? Compare Francis v. United Jersey Bank, 87 N.J. 15, 432 A.2d 814 (1981) (fiduciary duty extends to third parties on whose behalf the corporation holds funds as well as to creditors when the corporation is insolvent). If the corporation's managers might have duties of care to lenders upon insolvency, might insolvency provide a better basis for the regulation of dividend distributions?

d. Nimble Dividends

Dividends payable out of current profits have been called "nimble dividends." Delaware, like other traditional jurisdictions provides its corporations with the power to, effectively, distribute dividends out of capital in years when the corporation is able to post a profit. Not all states permitting nimble dividends follow the same rules. For example, Nevada allows nimble dividends if the articles of incorporation specifically allow it. NEV. REV. STAT. § 78.288(3) (1999). Moreover, a corporation may restrict its power to authorize nimble dividends. This can some cause problems. Consider in that respect the materials that follow.

Weinberg v. Baltimore Brick Co.

114 A.2d 812 (1955)

SOUTHERLAND, Chief Justice.

The question in this case is whether the charter of the Baltimore Brick Company contains a restriction preventing the company from declaring preferred dividends out of current net earnings while there is a capital deficit in respect of the common stock. The company was incorporated in Delaware in September, 1902. It was organized to take over the assets and business of its predecessor, a New Jersey corporation of the same name. The company has outstanding 10,563 shares of first preferred stock and 8,344 shares of common stock. The rights of the first preferred stockholders under the Delaware charter are identical, we are advised, with their rights under the New Jersey charter. The dividend rights are as follows:

> 'Said First Preferred stock shall entitle the holder to receive each year, out of the net earnings of the company, a fixed yearly dividend of five per centum (5%) before any dividend shall be paid upon or set apart for the said Second Preferred or said common stock, and the dividends on the said First Preferred stock shall be cumulative, no dividend being paid upon the Second Preferred or Common stock until the arrears of the dividends due on the First Preferred stock shall first have been paid.'

The liquidation preference is as follows:

> 'The holders of the said First Preferred stock in case of liquidation or dissolution of the company, shall be entitled to be paid in full, before any amount shall be paid to the holders of the Second Preferred or Common Stock.'

The preferred shares have full voting rights. In addition, the preferred stockholders are entitled to elect six members of a board of nine directors. A considerable amount of first preferred stock had been issued by the New Jersey corporation in connection with a refinancing of its funded debt. In 1902 an arrangement was effected with the bondholders whereby the latter surrendered the six per cent bonds and received in lieu thereof a smaller principal amount of five per cent bonds and a large number of shares of first preferred stock. In 1902 all of the assets were transferred to the Delaware company.

The company has a large arrearage of accumulated and unpaid preferred dividends. In recent years, beginning in 1950, the company has declared several dividends on its preferred stock. On June 30, 1954, a further dividend of $2.50 a share was declared, payable August 2, 1954. This action was objected to by the directors elected by the common stockholders, including plaintiff, who is the owner of a majority of the outstanding common shares. Plaintiff thereafter brought suit in the court below to enjoin the payment of the dividend, alleging that the company had no 'net earnings,' that its common capital was impaired, and that the payment of the dividend would be in violation of law. The court declined to enjoin the payment of the dividend already declared, but temporarily restrained the declaration and payment of further dividends, and set the case down for hearing on a rule for preliminary injunction.

At the hearing the parties agreed that the company has net earnings for the current and preceding fiscal years available for the payment of dividends, and that the preferred capital is not impaired. They were and are in disagreement whether there is an impairment of the common capital. This latter issue the Vice Chancellor did not resolve, since he was of opinion that even if the common capital was impaired the dividend was nevertheless lawful, 108 A.2d 81. This holding plaintiff brings here for review.

The case turns upon the construction of the phrase 'net earnings' in the charter provisions relating to the preferred stock. At the time when the Brick Company was incorporated the Delaware statute regulating the payment of dividends was the General Corporation Law of 1901. 22 Del.L.Ch. 394. Section 34 of that act provided as follows:

> 'The Directors of every corporation created under this Act shall have power, after reserving over and above its capital stock paid in, such sum, if any, as shall have been fixed by the stockholders, to declare a dividend among its stockholders of the whole of its accumulated profits, in excess of the amount so reserved, and pay the same to such stockholders on demand; provided, that the corporation may, in its certificate of incorporation, or in its by-laws, give the Directors power to fix the amount to be reserved.'

Section 35 provided in part as follows:

> 'No corporation created under the provisions of this Act, nor the directors thereof, shall make dividends except from the surplus or net profits arising from its business. Dividends may be paid in cash or capital stock at par, but otherwise the corporation shall not divide, withdraw, or in any way pay to the stockholders, or any of them, any part of its capital stock, or reduce its capital stock, except according to this Act, * * *.'

In Wittenberg v. Federal Mining & Smelting Corporation, 1926, 15 Del.Ch. 147, 133 A. 48, 55, the Chancellor construed these statutes and held that in the light of the language of Section 34, the phrase 'net profits' in Section 35 meant 'such as appear from the entire business of the company from its inception.' Since the corporate capital was depleted, there were no net profits, and no dividends could be declared. The decision was affirmed by the Supreme Court.

Shortly thereafter these sections were amended by the act of 1927, 35 Del.L.Ch. 85, and again amended in 1929, 36 Del.L.Ch. 135. These amendments are now codified in 8 Del.C. § 170, which reads as follows:

> 'The directors of every corporation created under this chapter, subject to any restrictions contained in its certificate of incorporation, may declare and pay dividends upon the shares of its capital stock either (1) out of its net assets in excess of its capital as computed in accordance with the provisions of sections 154 and 242–244 of this title, or (2) in case there shall be no such excess, out of its net profits for the fiscal year then current and/or the preceding fiscal year.'

Then follows a provision that no dividends may be paid if preferred capital is impaired.

It is conceded that if the statute governs the matter, the dividend is legal, since clause (2) specifically removes the prior statutory requirement of the existence of a surplus for the payment of dividends from current profits.

All the provisions of the General Corporation Law are impliedly written into every corporate charter granted under it. Peters v. United States Mortgage Co., 13 Del.Ch. 11, 114 A. 598. But the expanded power over dividends contained in the 1927 and 1929 amendments is granted 'subject to any restrictions contained' in the charter. Hence the sole question presented is whether the language of paragraph Fourth of the Brick Company's charter relating to the First Preferred stock constitutes a 'restriction,' and if so, the nature and extent thereof. The language relied upon by plaintiff is—

> 'Said First Preferred stock shall entitle the holder to receive each year, out of the net earnings of the company, a fixed yearly dividend of five per centum' etc. ...

Plaintiff's argument that the quoted language embodies a restriction upon the payment of preferred dividends runs as follows:

The designation of 'net earnings' as the source from which the dividend may be paid necessarily means that such earnings constitute the exclusive source for payment. Moreover the phrase 'net earnings,' like 'net profits,' means earnings accumulated over the entire life of the corporation, i. e., earned surplus. This is so, because by judicial construction both the New Jersey and Delaware statutes, at the times when the charters were filed, forbade the payment of dividends if the corporate capital was impaired.

The provisions of Section 35 of the Delaware act of 1902 were copied from the comparable section of the New Jersey act of 1896 [N.J.S.A. 14:8–19], see Wittenberg v. Federal Mining & Smelting Co., supra, and the preferred stock provisions of the company's Delaware charter were copied from the New Jersey charter, and took with them the construction placed upon the phrase 'net earnings' by the New Jersey decisions.

Hence, plaintiff concludes, the language of the charter restricts the source of payment of preferred dividends to earned surplus. Plaintiff makes the subsidiary point that the word 'earnings' is narrower in scope than the word 'profits'; and its use impliedly forbids payment of the dividend not only from paid-in or capital surplus, but also from 'windfall profits.'

This argument requires anaylsis. What plaintiff is asserting is that the language of the charter—'out of the net earnings'—is doubly restrictive in meaning. His contention comes to this: that the phrase is expressly restrictive because it designates an exclusive source of the dividend—earnings as opposed to a balance sheet surplus; and impliedly restrictive because the phrase is used in the narrow sense of earned surplus.

Defendant replies that the phrase 'net earnings' is nothing more than a paraphrase of the statutory language and is not a 'restriction' within the meaning of Section 34; and that the use of the phrase in the charter was not intended as a restriction of any kind and should not be construed as such.

Let us consider first the question whether the phrase 'net earnings' restricts the source of payment, or whether the language is a mere paraphrase of the statute. The point is one of some importance in Delaware law, because of the 1927 amendment. It has been held by the District Court of Delaware, by way of dictum, in Barrett v. Denver Tramway Corporation, 53 F.Supp. 198, 200, that a mere incorporation in the charter of the statutory phrase—'surplus, or net profits'—is not a restriction within the meaning of § 170. We are in accord with Judge Leahy's views in that case. A mere incorporation of the statutory language is equivalent to a statement that dividends may be declared as provided by law. But there is difficulty in applying that holding to this case.

It is true that there has been much loose employment in American dividend law, both statutory and decisional, of the various phrases descriptive of the dividend fund—'net profits,' 'net earnings,' 'surplus profits,' 'surplus or net profits,' and the like. It has been said that in dividend statutes all these terms are usually construed as meaning the same thing—a balance sheet surplus. Ballantine, Corporations (Rev.Ed.), p. 574. In this view, there was but one source of dividends under the former Delaware and New Jersey statutes, and a designation of the dividend source by any of the usual terms might be said to be a mere reference to the controlling statutory provisions.

But other writers have pointed out the difference in the meaning and implications of these phrases, as bearing upon the different tests prescribed by the various dividend statutes. See Weiner, 'Theory of Anglo-American Dividend Law,' 29 Col.L.Rev. 461; Kehl, Corporate Dividends, Ch. 2. The latter writer is of opinion that a more likely construction attributes to 'net profits' some meaning dissociated from the corporation's original capital. P. 62. Certainly it requires some stretch of construction to say that 'net earnings,' as a dividend source, is the equivalent of capital surplus. And capital surplus, whether paid-in or reduction, may well have been a legal source for dividends under Section 35 of the former Delaware statute. The point was discussed by Chancellor Wolcott in the Wittenberg case, but was not decided. There is a very real difference, in business and accounting practice, between a dividend paid from current or accumulated earnings, and one paid from paid-in or reduction surplus. And the distinction has been held to be of legal importance in determining the dividend rights of non-cumulative preferred stock. See Dohme v. Pacific Coast Co., 5 N.J.Super. 477, 68 A.2d 490.

Moreover, plaintiff argues with much force: If the framers of the charter had intended to incorporate the statutory language, why did they not do so? Accordingly, defendant's contention that 'net earnings' is equivalent to the statutory phrase—'surplus or net profits' is open to doubt. In the view we take of this case, it is unnecessary to decide the question, and we do not decide it. We shall assume that the source of the preferred dividends of the defendant is restricted to 'net earnings,' and that this phrase was used advisedly.

The second restrictive meaning that plaintiff seeks to attach to the phrase 'net earnings' is that of accumulated earnings, i.e., earned surplus. This meaning, he says, necessarily excludes current earnings if there is no surplus. This interpretation is drawn, by equating net earnings to net profits, from the judicial construction of the former Delaware and New Jersey dividend statutes. The argument is, in effect, that when the New Jersey corporation was formed prior or contemporaneous judicial construction of the phrase 'net earnings' had attached to it the definite and restricted meaning of earned surplus and that its use in a corporate charter necessarily carried with it that restricted meaning.

This argument runs into difficulty at the start. The assertion that the phrase 'net earnings' has a fixed and settled meaning in dividend law is not correct. With respect to the words 'profits' and 'earnings' it has been remarked: 'There seems to be no settled usage regarding these terms in commerce, and the economists are at hopeless loggerheads.' 29 Col.L.Rev. 474. In statutes regulating the payment of dividends, the term has sometimes been held to be equivalent to surplus, and sometimes to current earnings, depending upon the background and context in which it is used. In Mangham v. State, 11 Ga.App. 440, 75 S.E. 508, 509, the statute forbade the declaration of dividends except from 'the actual legitimate net earnings of its investments.' Pen.Code Ga.1910, § 740. The term was held to be a synonym for surplus. In effect the court read into the statute the general rule that dividends cannot be paid unless a surplus exists. However, in United States v. Riely, 4 Cir., 169 F.2d 542, 543, involving the Virginia statute permitting dividends 'out of net earnings, or out of* * * assets in excess of* * * capital,' Code Va.1942, § 3840, net earnings was held to mean current earnings, and therefore current dividends could be paid notwithstanding capital impairment. To the same effect is Grand Traverse Hotel Co. v. United States, D.C.Mich., 79 F.Supp. 860, construing the Michigan statute.

These decisions illustrate the problem that has often arisen in the construction of dividend statutes—whether one or two funds are intended, and if two funds are intended, whether a surplus test is applicable to both. They support the statement above made, viz., that 'net earnings' standing alone, has no single or fixed meaning in dividend law. On this point, see also Kehl, Corporate Dividends, 26 and 26.1.

Unless there is some controlling authority to the contrary (a question reserved for later consideration), we are free to give to the term the meaning that appears most reasonably adapted to the context in which it is used.

Now, we are not confronted here with a question of statutory construction. The question concerns the meaning of the phrase 'net earnings' in the charter provisions creating the preferred stock. Is the phrase used in the restricted sense of earned surplus, so as to exclude current earnings if there is no surplus? Is it used in the restricted sense of current earnings only, so as to exclude accumulated earnings? Or is it unrestricted in meaning, so as to permit dividends to be declared from any earnings legally available?

Preliminarily it is to be noted that the word 'net' is, for our present purpose, of little significance. It signifies merely what is left after subtracting one sum from another. What sum is to be subtracted and from what it is to be subtracted depends upon the nature of the fund out of which a particular dividend is declared. The question here is whether any restriction is intended by the reference to earnings as the source of the dividend.

We are dealing with preferred dividends expressly made cumulative. As applied to such dividends the natural meaning of earnings includes both current and accumulated earnings. This is necessarily so, because of the very nature of cumulative preferred stock; the current earnings are first to be devoted to its payment, and, if they are insufficient or if the dividend is passed, all future earnings are also charged with the dividend, and must be used to pay before any dividend can be paid on the common stock.

This is the characteristic feature of cumulative preferred stock. In Garrett v. Edge Moor Iron Co., 22 Del.Ch. 142, 194 A. 15, 17, there was presented the question whether the preferred stock of the Iron Company was intended to be cumulative. Chancellor Wolcott said:

> 'Here the net earnings and surplus out of which the stipulated dividends were to be paid, were not the net earnings of each year to which each particular annual dividend was allocable. The dividends were chargeable against net earnings and surplus generally, which means for all time. Where such is the charter contract, the authorities are in unison in holding that the stipulated dividend is cumulative and is always payable ahead of dividends on subordinate stock, whenever a lawful fund is available for distribution to stockholders.' ...

The holding of the case is not in point here, but the last phrase of the quoted language suggests the underlying intent of the ordinary charter provision creating cumulative preferred stock. Certainly when the framers of this charter made the stock cumulative, they intended that the dividends should be currently paid if legally possible to do so. That the dividend statute then in force forbade the payment of any dividends while capital was impaired is in no way inconsistent with this general intention, nor did the statutory restriction affect the naturally broad meaning of the word 'earnings' as contemplating the use of current earnings for dividends to whatever extent legally available. In short the phrase 'net earnings' in this charter does not necessarily import a restriction.

And we perceive no reason here for adopting a restrictive construction. The charter contains no negative or restrictive language of any kind. It is permissive in form. Nor is there any specific language from which the restriction urged by plaintiff can be inferred. Dividend restrictions are frequently met with, but they are ordinarily carefully spelled out, e. g., a restriction that out of profits a reserve or sinking fund must be established; a restriction that dividends shall be withheld or limited in amount while funded debt is outstanding; and the like. See 19 Fletcher, Cyclopedia Corporations, § 9032. Such a restriction, we suppose, is the kind primarily contemplated by the language of § 170.

Of course, there is nothing to prevent the framers of a charter from expressly providing that no dividends on cumulative preferred stock shall be paid except out of a surplus of assets over capital, or except out of earned surplus. But a self-imposed restriction of that nature, that is, a restriction operative apart from the statute, ought not to rest in implication. In cases like the one at bar it tends to impose an unreasonable hardship on the preferred stockholders. This view is approved by Ballantine and Hills in a discussion of 'Corporate Capital and Restrictions Upon Dividends,' 23 Cal.L.Rev. 229, 247–248. The result would be in many cases to saddle the corporation with a steadily increasing burden of accrued and unpaid dividends despite the existence of current earnings from which dividends could be paid without further capital impairment. This result is manifestly undesirable. Why should such a restriction be read into the charter by implication?

This conclusion finds support, in this case, from the corporate history. In connection with a refinancing of funded debt the former bondholders of the New Jersey corporation accepted the original preferred stock in exchange for a large portion of their bonds, and agreed to a lower rate of return. They were also given control of the corporation. Assuming that they accepted a restriction excluding capital surplus as a source of dividends, we think it is unreasonable to conclude that a further restriction was intended. It is much more reasonable to say that they intended the meaning we have above attributed to net earnings—that the preferred dividends should be paid from any earnings legally available for the purpose.

We take up now the question noticed before and reserved for later discussion—whether there is any controlling authority against the conclusion already indicated.

Plaintiff insists that the New Jersey decisions foreclose the unrestricted interpretation of net earnings. The following cases are cited: Park v. Grant Locomotive Works, 1885, 40 N.J.Eq. 114, 3 A. 162; Colgate v. United States Leather Co., 1907, 73 N.J.Eq. 72, 67 A. 657; and National Newark and Essex Banking Co., etc., v. Durant Motor Co., etc., 1938, 124 N.J.Eq. 213, 1 A.2d 316. (Parenthetically, we observe that for the purpose of developing this argument plaintiff has largely ignored the distinction, elsewhere insisted upon, between profits and earnings, and equates the two terms—an inconsistency illustrating the lack of any fixed and settled usage.) The Park case [40N.J.Eq. 114, 3 A. 163] involved a reorganization agreement (not a charter provision) providing for the issuance of stock (evidently common stock) to creditors as security for their debts. The agreement further provided that "all the net profits of the company" after the payment of taxes, insurance and maintenance "shall be divided annually among the stockholders". The suit was one to compel the payment of a dividend, and the defense was that certain securities appearing on the balance sheet were of little value and that the book surplus might be non-existent. The court held in effect that 'net profits' was equivalent to surplus, and that the parties had intended to use the phrase in this sense, since it could not be supposed that gains that might never be realized were to be a source of profits.

The holding in this case falls far short of establishing, as settled law, the construction of 'net earnings' for which plaintiff contends. At the most it is a holding that ordinarily net profits means surplus. It does not govern the question before us, which concerns a corporate charter defining the attributes of cumulative Preferred Stock.

The Colgate case is cited as holding that net earnings are synonymous with accumulated earnings and that the use of the phrase in a charter is intended to 'regulate' the payment of dividends. We find no holding in the case to the effect that net earnings must necessarily mean accumulated earnings only. The case concerned the dissolution preferences of preferred stockholders upon consolidation or merger, and their right to require a distribution of earned surplus upon the consummation of the consolidation. It decides nothing to the point here.

The National Newark case, decided in 1938, presents no question of the interpretation of the term net earnings in a corporate charter apart from the statute. It merely construes the phrase 'net profits' in the New Jersey statute as meaning a balance of assets over liabilities, and holds that because of the statute a dividend cannot be earned if there is no surplus. These three decisions, which plaintiff cites as establishing a single fixed meaning for the term 'net earnings,' do not in our opinion bear out his contention. Certainly they do not establish the existence of any such settled rule prior to 1901, when the New Jersey charter of the Brick Company was amended.

The case of Goodnow v. American Writing Paper Co., 73 N.J.Eq. 692, 69 A. 1014, indicates the lack of certainty that characterizes the analogous phrase 'net profits.' And it is interesting to note that as late as 1925, Judge Learned Hand in Borg v. International Silver Co., 2 Cir., 11 F.2d 147, held that the New Jersey act of 1904, as construed in the Goodnow case, permitted payment of dividends from 'net profits,' i. e., current profits, despite an impairment of capital.

We are of opinion that there is no controlling authority inconsistent with the conclusion above set forth, i. e., that the term 'net earnings' in the Brick Company's charter is not restrictive of the use of current earnings for preferred dividends.

The use of current earnings is of course limited by any applicable statute. Formerly it was forbidden entirely if there was a capital deficit; now it is limited to earnings of the current and the preceding fiscal years. To the extent that the statutory prohibition is removed, the language of the charter may be given full effect. The Delaware statutory provision requiring a surplus having been withdrawn, there is no legal impediment to the payment of dividends from current earnings to the extent now permitted by the statute as amended.

We are aware that a different conclusion was reached in Seiberling Rubber Co. v. United States, D.C., 115 F.Supp. 798, affirmed 6 Cir., 207 F.2d 585. The District Court took the view that the accepted meaning of the phrase 'net earnings' was 'accumulated earnings,' and that the charter provision was a restriction. The Court of Appeals affirmed, apparently relying on Jones v. First National Building Corporation, 10 Cir., 155 F.2d 815, 816. The Jones case is distinguishable on its facts. It involved a Delaware corporation incorporated in 1930 under a charter providing that the preferred dividends were 'payable out of the surplus.' With the holding in the Seiberling case that net earnings necessarily means accumulated earnings we cannot agree, for the reasons above set forth. Before concluding this opinion we must notice some subsidiary arguments advanced by plaintiff.

It is said that if the charter phrase means current earnings, it would prevent the payment of any dividend out of earned surplus. Gallagher v. New York Dock Co., Sup., 19 N.Y.S.2d 789, is cited. That case concerned non-cumulative preferred stock, and is an example of the problems that often arise with respect to the liability of earned surplus for the payment of an annual dividend that has been earned but not declared. No such problem exists with respect to cumulative dividends. To reinforce this argument, plaintiff suggests that the Brick Company's charter does not provide that arrearages of dividends may be paid out of earnings of later years. If we understand this suggestion, it is an assertion that the stock is non-cumulative. On the contrary, the charter expressly provides that the stock shall be cumulative. As we have already said, this means that if a preferred dividend is passed it must be paid out of future earnings before any dividend can be paid on the common stock. This is elementary. Plaintiff suggests some hypothetical questions, e. g., for what period are current earnings available for dividends. This supposed difficulty appears again to stem from the assumption that the stock is non-cumulative and that accumulated earnings may not be used for dividends. This point we have already dealt with. In the absence of capital impairment any net earnings, current or accumulated, are available for the preferred dividend. If capital impairment exists, their use is limited by the present statute. Plaintiff seeks to build some arguments on language culled from the Delaware cases dealing with the liquidation rights of preferred stockholders under various charter provisions. In Gaskill v. Gladys Belle Oil Co., 16 Del.Ch. 289, 146 A. 337, the question was whether preferred stock was entitled to a preference on dissolution, no language to that effect appearing in the charter. Chancellor Wolcott held that they could not be paid from capital, the only source available, because the charter did not charge the dividends upon capital funds in the event of liquidation.

We are uncertain what use plaintiff seeks to make of this holding. Presumably he means that payment out of current earnings is a payment out of capital. But this is not so; the disbursement of current earnings for dividends leaves untouched the capital assets existing before payment. This is exactly what is contemplated by the present statute. A somewhat similar rule has long prevailed in England. See Ammonia Soda Co., Ltd. v. Chamberlain [1918] 1 Ch. 266, 281ff.

In Penington v. Commonwealth Hotel Construction Corp., 17 Del.Ch. 394, 155 A. 514, 516, 75 A.L.R. 1136, decided after the 1927 amendment to the dividend section, the question was whether on liquidation the unpaid and accrued dividends on the preferred stock could be paid out of capital, there being no accumulated earnings. Some point is attempted to be made of the use by the court of the words 'surplus or net profits,' appearing in the charter, as contemplating a restricted source of dividends while the corporation was a going concern. The court, in a later part of the opinion discussing the same subject, also used the phrase 'current or accumulated profits.' Obviously nothing of significance here can be drawn from the use of these different phrases.

Plaintiff quotes from the case of Garrett v. Edge Moor Iron Co., supra [22 Del.Ch. 142, 194 A. 17], substantially the same language we have quoted above. Presumably the point plaintiff makes is that the reference to a general charge against earnings and surplus 'for all time' is a holding that net earnings necessarily means earned surplus, and excludes current earnings. On the contrary, the Chancellor was merely saying that dividends were not limited to current earnings, and hence the stock was cumulative. What he also said was that arrears of cumulative preferred dividends may be paid 'whenever a lawful fund is available.' This is exactly what we have held that charter to mean, if we insert the words 'from earnings' after the word 'fund' in the quoted phrase.

Plaintiff asserts that the stockholders of the Brick Company have by practical construction adopted the restricted meaning for which he contends. This contention is based on an opinion of counsel, summarized in the company's annual statement, reading as follows:

> 'The Company has been furnished with an opinion of counsel to the effect that accumulated dividends are payable only to the extent of surplus or net earnings, even in the event of liquidation.'

This language does not purport to embody any specific construction of the phrase 'net earnings' in connection with the payment of dividends while the company is a going concern. The real point of the footnote appears to relate to the liquidation preferences of the preferred stock. Plaintiff asserts that the result of the Vice Chancellor's holding works unfairness to the common stockholders. This we cannot follow. On the contrary, as we have pointed out above, the withholding of current dividends from the preferred stockholders has an element of unfairness to them. And where is the unfairness to the common stockholders? Unless the dividends are paid they continue to accrue, and must be paid before any dividends are paid upon the common stock. So far as concerns the loss of common capital, why should it not fall upon the common stockholders?

The control of the corporation by the preferred stockholders is assailed as unusual and unfair. This is not correct, since a shift on control from common to preferred stockholders upon the existence of arrearages is one way of according special rights to preferred stock.... In the case at bar, in consideration of a permanent surrender of some creditors' rights, the preferred stockholders were given permanent control. This does not seem unduly oppressive; but in any event it was agreed to and must be adhered to. A question of constitutionality is discussed on the briefs. This question is raised by plaintiff upon the assumption that the Vice Chancellor's opinion held that the amendatory act of 1927 was an automatic amendment of defendant's charter. Since in our view the decision turns solely upon the meaning of the language of the charter, no question of constitutionality is presented.

We hold that the words 'net earnings' in defendant's charter do not restrict the source of the preferred dividends to earned surplus. Payment from current earnings is lawful.

The judgment of the Court of Chancery is affirmed.

e. Revaluing and Manipulating Surplus

Surplus is not a concept set in stone. Depending on the manner in which the capital account is created, it is possible for the board of directors to revalue the capital account. For instance, if the capital account includes amounts in excess of the aggregate par value of the outstanding shares, the capital account may be reduced, and surplus created, up to an amount equal to the aggregate par value of such outstanding shares. This can be done without modifying the par value of the corporation's shares. Under what circumstances would this be important? In what way does the ability to manipulate surplus affect planning for the capitalization of a corporation?

U.S. v. Archer-Daniels-Midland Company

United States Court of Appeals Eighth Circuit.
April 11, 1957.
243 F.2d 130

GARDNER, Chief Judge.

Taxpayer, a Delaware corporation, on June 20, 1949, pursuant to resolution of its board of directors transferred from its capital surplus account the amount of $1,269,706.49 and from its earned surplus account the amount of $21,688,254.55 to its capital stock account, which transfer resulted in making its capital stock account $32,694,960. It issued no additional stock or shares to its stockholders. Following this transaction and on or about the 29th day of August, 1951, the Commissioner of Internal Revenue purporting to act under authority conferred by Section 1802(a) of the Internal Revenue Code of 1939, 26 U.S.C.A. 1802(a) assessed a documentary stamp tax in the amount of $34,436.91 against taxpayer.

After due protest taxpayer paid the documentary stamp tax so assessed and duly filed a claim for refund which in due course was disallowed. Taxpayer then brought this action for a refund of taxes so paid by it. The basic facts were all stipulated and the court entered its findings based on the stipulated facts and concluded as a matter of law that the transfer of funds from taxpayer's capital surplus account and earned surplus account to its capital stock account was not a taxable transaction and accordingly entered judgment in favor of taxpayer for the recovery of said $34,436.91 so paid on account of said $34,436.91 so the Commissioner. The facts will be further developed in the course of this opinion.

The government seeks reversal on substantially the following ground: that taxpayer's dedication of amounts from its capital surplus and earned surplus accounts to its common stock account constituted an original issue of shares and/or of profits and/or of interest in property or accumulations taxable under Section 1802(a) of the Internal Revenue Code of 1939.

The taxpayer being a Delaware corporation, we must look to the statute of that state for the law controlling its internal government. The statute of Delaware providing for the transfer from surplus to capital reads as follows:

'The capital of the corporation may be increased from time to time by resolution of the Board of Directors directing that a portion of the net assets of the corporation in excess of the amount so determined to be capital be transferred to capital account.' Section 14, Chapter 65, Revised Code of Delaware of 1935, 8 Del.C. 154.

Manifestly, the transfer here was in strict compliance with the provision of the Delaware statute. In this connection it is to be noted that the directors of the taxpayer, with the approval of the stockholders, could restore the amount to surplus and again make it legally available for dividends, Section 28, Chapter 65, Revised Code of Delaware of 1935, 8 Del.C. 244, which, of course, could not be done had the company issued stock or shares to its stockholders upon the transfer to its capital stock account.

It is the contention of the government that the levy of the documentary stamp tax finds authority in Section 1802(a) of the Internal Revenue Code of 1939 which so far as here pertinent imposes a tax as follows: 'On each original issue, whether on organization or reorganization, of shares or certificates of stock, or of profits, or of interest in property or accumulations * * *.' In this connection we call attention to Treasury Regulations under this provision of the statute. Section 113.20 of the Regulations states that Section 1802(a) 'imposes a tax upon each original issue of certificates (or shares when issued without certificates).' Section 113.22 of the Regulations provides that 'Stock is deemed to be issued when it is subscribed for and the subscription is accepted.' Section 113.23 of the Regulations specifically requires that 'A separate computation of tax must be made with respect to each certificate regardless of the number of certificates which may be issued in a single transaction,' and provides that the subscription is the basis of the tax when shares are issued without certificates. Section 113.24 of the Regulations is entitled 'Issues subject to tax.' Section 113.25 is entitled, 'Issues not subject to tax.' Section 113.26 of the Regulations requires the stamps to be affixed to the stock book and 'not the certificates issued.' It should be noted that not only in the statute but in the Regulations the word 'issue' or 'issued' is consistently repeated. In the instant case we may well consider what the resolution of the directors with reference to the transfer of surplus funds to the capital stock account did not do. It did not increase the number of shares; it did not provide for the issuance of additional shares or certificates; it did not alter, change or affect the then outstanding certificates and it did not purport to create or grant to stockholders any new or additional rights. Not only did the resolution of the directors make no such provision but the transfer as provided created no new or additional shares or certificates of stock, nor did there result from such transfer any change or modification whatsoever in the number or form of certificates evidencing shares of taxpayer's common stock. This was a mere bookkeeping transaction and no one was enriched or impoverished by this transfer of funds. The situation in this regard is well reflected in the court's findings where among other things it is said:

'IV

'Archer-Daniels-Midland Company did not issue or create any additional shares of its capital stock by reason of said transfer of Capital Surplus and Earned Surplus to Capital Stock account.

'V

'Archer-Daniels-Midland Company has not at any time issued any shares or certificates of stock in respect to said transfer of Capital Surplus and Earned Surplus to its Capital Stock account.

'VI

'No change or modification whatsoever was made in the form of certificate evidencing shares of common stock of Archer-Daniels-Midland Company.

'VII

'Archer-Daniels-Midland Company had $1,634,748 shares of common stock outstanding immediately before said transfer of Capital Surplus and Earned Surplus to Capital Stock account and the same number immediately after such transaction took place.'

We are in accord with the decision of the trial court that these sections impose a tax upon the issuance of shares or certificates and not upon a transfer of surplus to capital and this view finds support in the following cases: American Steel Foundries v. Sauber, 7 Cir., 239 F.2d 300; United States v. National Sugar Refining Co., D.C.S.D.N.Y., 113 F.Supp. 157; F. & M. Schaefer Brewing Co. v. United States, D.C.E.D.N.Y., 130 F.Supp. 322; Empire Trust Co. v. Hoey, 2 Cir., 103 F.2d 430; United States Steel Corp. v. United States, Ct.Cl., 142 F.Supp. 948. In American Steel Foundries v. Sauber, supra, the facts so far as material to the issues here involved were identical with the facts in the instant case. The government there, as here, contended that a dedication of an amount from a corporation's surplus accounts to its capital stock account constitutes an issue of shares under Section 1802(a) of the Internal Revenue Code of 1939, regardless of whether such a dedication is accompanied by an increase in the number of shares outstanding or by a physical delivery to the stockholders of new or different certificates. In disposing of this contention of the government the court, inter alia, said:

'The basic question here presented is what constitutes an issuance of shares.

'Taxpayer points out that the word 'share' denotes a portion of something such as a corporation's assets and earnings. The statute speaks of an 'original issue * * * of shares.' After the transfer from the surplus account to the capital stock account the capital of the corporation was divided into the same number of shares as before, and each of such shares represented the same portion and interest in the corporation's assets and earnings as before.

'We think the transfer of surplus to capital in the present case did not result in the creation of any new or additional interest in the corporation. The number of plaintiff's outstanding shares and the percentage of its assets and earnings represented by each of said shares were not affected in any way by the transfer. The capital of the corporation was divided into the same number of shares after the increase in stated capital as before, and each of such shares represented the same portion and interest in the corporation's assets and earnings as before.

'We know of no authority and none has been cited to us sustaining the position of the government in this case. On the other hand, there are three District Court cases in addition to the decision in this case in the court below which sustain the position of the taxpayer.

'In United States v. National Sugar Refining Co., D.C.N.Y.1953, 113 F.Supp. 157, the taxpayer corporation had transferred nine million dollars from its surplus to its capital account without creating or delivering new certificates of stock or modifying the certificates then outstanding. The court granted the taxpayer's motion for summary judgment holding that a mere transfer of surplus to capital and an increase in the stated value of the outstanding no-par value shares of the taxpayer did not constitute an issuance of shares within the meaning of Section

1802(a) and that consequently no stamp tax was due. The court said, 113 F.Supp. at page 160: 'Section 1802(a) is a tax on an original issue of capital stock. It is not a tax on an addition to capital, made by a transfer from surplus to capital, where no new stock is issued. The cases show that the stamp tax is, as L. Hand, C.J., put it, 'an excise upon the act of issuance,' to be imposed only once when the original certificate is issued.'

'The National Sugar Refining Company case was approved and followed in F. & M. Schaefer Brewing Co. v. United States of America, D.C.N.Y.1955, 130 F.Supp. 322. In the Schaefer Company case as in the case at bar, the corporation had increased the state value of its no par value preferred stock by a transfer of surplus to capital without issuing new or additional certificates and without amending the certificates then outstanding. The Court held there was no liability under the documentary stamp tax.'

We are in entire accord with the decision of the Seventh Circuit in American Steel Foundries v. Sauber, supra, and the authorities therein cited. The judgment appealed from is therefore affirmed.

---

f. Protection for Creditors; Director Liability

Creditors generally have no right to make a determination with respect to the reasonableness of the par value of stock issued by Delaware Corporations, and therefore have no control of the size of the Capital and surplus accounts of the corporation. Creditors, however, have been given a means of policing the amounts distributed from out of the corporation. By common law, as codified in most traditional jurisdictions, such as Delaware, directors are made personally liable for distributions of dividends or repurchases of stock in violation of the limitations of the "impairment of capital" and "surplus" rules of Delaware law. On occasion, even shareholders may find themselves liable for the payments, especially where the interests of creditors and shareholders conflict.

In re Kettle Fried Chicken of America, Inc.

513 F.2d 807 (6th Cir. 1975)

ENGEL, Circuit Judge:

This is an appeal from a judgment of the district court requiring certain former shareholders of Kettle Fried Chicken of America, Inc. to refund to the trustee in bankruptcy payments they had received from the bankrupt corporation in repurchase of its capital stock at a time when its capital was found to be impaired. We affirm.

Kettle Fried Chicken of America, Inc., hereinafter Kettle, was incorporated under the laws of Delaware in March, 1968. After its initial incorporation, the authorized capital of Kettle was increased and several stock splits occurred. In October, 1968, the original investors sold approximately 50% of the equity of the corporation to a group of new investors known as the "Cincinnati group".

At a Board of Directors' meeting in February, 1969, it was decided that the corporation would attempt to buy back from some of the shareholders their common stock in

Kettle, the stock to be used as part of a plan to attract needed key personnel. This buy back program was initiated although the corporation then had in its treasury over 600,000 shares of its own stock. Between March 13 and March 19, 1969, 75,500 shares of stock were repurchased by Kettle from the five defendants here at ninety cents per share, for a total cash payment by Kettle of $67,950.

Of the 75,500 shares acquired by Kettle in March, 1969, from the defendants, 25,000 shares were resold and transferred to a Mr. Fishkin at $1.10 per share. Kettle apparently entered into contracts with two other persons for resale of the other purchased shares, but both deals ultimately fell through. Under the contracts of sale the purchasers had a right to cancel the agreement if Kettle failed to obtain approval of the Ohio Securities Commission for the stock sale within 45 days after the date of the agreement. It is clear that Mr. Flory canceled his contract to purchase 25,000 shares under this provision. Although there is some dispute as to whether Mr. Luby remains liable on his contract, he attempted to rescind by canceling payment on his check for the stock on March 31, 1969.

The corporation began to suffer more severe financial difficulties in 1969, caused at least in part by the depressed financial and economic conditions of the fast food industry. In October, 1969 several of Kettle's directors resigned and the Board discussed filing for the corporation a Chapter XI proceeding in bankruptcy. On March 5, 1970 Kettle made an assignment for the benefit of creditors under state law. On June 5, 1970 it was adjudged bankrupt.

The trustee in bankruptcy brought this action against the five shareholders who sold their stock back to the corporation in March, 1969. The action was brought under § 70(e) of the Bankruptcy Act, 11 U.S.C. § 110(e). That section provides in part:

"A transfer made or suffered or obligation incurred by a debtor adjudged a bankrupt under this title which, under any Federal or State law applicable thereto, is fraudulent as against or voidable for any other reason by any creditor of the debtor, having a claim provable under this title, shall be null and void as against the trustee of such debtor."

The trustee, in bringing his § 70(e) action, invoked Title 8, § 160, Delaware Statutes, which he claims allows a creditor to void the stock purchase which occurred here. At the times relevant to this litigation, § 160 provided:

> Every corporation may purchase, receive, take or otherwise acquire, own and hold, sell, lend, exchange, transfer or otherwise dispose of, pledge, use and otherwise deal in and with its own shares; but no corporation shall use its funds or property for the purchase of its own shares of capital stock when the capital of the corporation is impaired or when such use would cause any impairment of the capital of the corporation, except that it may purchase or redeem out of capital its own shares of preferred or special stock in accordance with section 243 of this title. Shares of its own capital stock belonging to the corporation or to another corporation, if a majority of the shares entitled to vote in the election of directors of such other corporation is held, directly or indirectly, by the corporation, shall neither be entitled to vote nor be counted for quorum purposes. Nothing in this section shall be construed as limiting the right of any corporation to vote stock, including but not limited to its own stock, held by it in a fiduciary capacity.[2]

---

2. Section 160 has since been amended by the Delaware legislature, 59 Del. Laws, c. 106, § 3.

The referee found as a matter of fact that the capital of the corporation was impaired at the time of the stock repurchase by Kettle. Damages of $45,450 were assessed pro rata against the five defendants.

Defendants raise four issues on this appeal. Their first contention is that the transactions involved here were not a "purchase" within the meaning of Section 160. Since Kettle had already lined up purchasers to buy the stock from the corporation at a higher price per share when it bought the stock from defendants, they contend that the transaction was a purchase not by the corporation, but rather by Messrs. Fishkin, Flory and Luby, the corporation merely acting as a conduit between the defendants and the subsequent purchasers.

We agree with the trustee that the term "purchase" as used in Section 160 must be given its normal meaning and that so construed, Kettle must be considered as the purchaser of the stock. It bought the stock directly from defendants. The sale was not conditioned upon Kettle's ability to resell the stock to any third party, although preliminary plans for the resale had been made. There was no contractual relationship, either written or verbal, between defendants and the three men who the corporation expected ultimately to acquire the stock.

In Alcott v. Hyman, 42 Del. Ch. 233, 208 A. 2d 501 (1965), the Delaware Supreme Court rejected a similar effort to place a strained interpretation on the use of the word "purchase" in Section 160. Plaintiffs argued there that the transaction in question did not constitute a "purchase" by the corporation of its own stock because the corporation had received cash and an assumption of liabilities as well as receiving its own stock. The Delaware Court held otherwise:

"They argue, however, that the transaction was not a 'purchase' because AAP received cash and an assumption of liabilities as well as its own stock. We find no merit in this contention." 208 A. 2d at 508.

Appellants' second contention is that the referee erred in finding that the capital of the corporation was impaired at the time the stock was repurchased by the corporation.

Appellants admit that if Kettle's assets are measured at book value as shown on the balance sheet of March 31, 1969, capital impairment is shown. However, they urge, if "fair market value of all assets as a package" is considered, then the evidence before the referee required him to hold that the capital was not impaired at the time of repurchase. Appellants rely especially upon the well-reasoned opinion of Judge Haynsworth in Mountain State Steel Foundries v. Commissioner of Internal Revenue, 284 F.2d 737 (4th Cir. 1960). There, construing a similar West Virginia statute, the court held:

> "At least until the highest court of West Virginia should otherwise decide, we think for our collateral purpose the statute should be construed as prohibiting the purchase of its own stock if the use of its funds for the purpose would deplete the realizable value of its assets to a point below the total of its liabilities and capital." 284 F.2d at 741 (emphasis added)
>
> However, Judge Haynsworth further commented:
>
> "If we are to look to actual values in applying the statute, the spirit of the statute requires that they be conservatively determined. Opinion evidence of appreciation should be received with skepticism if insolvency ensues..." 284 F.2d at 742

We are, of course, obliged to look to Delaware law. Capital impairment as such is not defined in the Delaware statutes. The Court of Chancery of Delaware has endeavored to define the term in In re International Radiator Company, 10 Del. Ch. 358, 92 A. 255 at 256 (1914):

In the statute the impairment of the "capital" of the company is mentioned. As here used, this means the reduction of the amount of the assets of the company below the amount represented by the aggregate outstanding shares of the capital stock of the company. In other words, a corporation may use only its surplus for the purchase of shares of its own capital stock. "Capital" does not in this connection mean the assets of the company, for, of course, the assets are reduced when any of it is used by a corporation to purchase shares of its own capital stock. It must have some other meaning then. The statute must mean, therefore, that the funds and property of the company shall not be used for the purchase of shares of its own capital stock when the value of its assets is less than the aggregate amount of all the shares of its capital stock. A use by a corporation of its assets to purchase shares of its own capital stock under such conditions impairs the capital of the company. 92 A. at 256.

The same construction of Delaware law has been recognized by this circuit in Ashman v. Miller, 101 F.2d 85 (6th Cir. 1939).

In re International Radiator Company, supra, did not present the precise issue of whether, if compelled to make a choice, the Delaware courts would use book or actual value in measuring assets for the purpose of determining whether the capital of the corporation was impaired, and we are unable to find any certain guidance either from the above quotation or from any other Delaware source. We conclude, however, as we believe the referee did, that the capital of Kettle was impaired under either test.

It is true that the referee relied primarily upon the March 31, 1969 balance sheet of Kettle as evidencing its capital impairment at the time of the purchases of stock earlier that same month. If a balance sheet test is employed, there was insufficient surplus in the usual sense to cover the purchase, and impairment resulted. The referee, however, did not stop there, nor did the proofs. He made pointed reference to the testimony of the company president, Paul T. Milliken, that the figures in the Price-Waterhouse report of March 31, 1969 fairly reflected the actual as well as the book value of the assets. Further, the referee expressly recognized appellants' argument. He cited Mountain State Steel Foundries, supra, with approval, and even paraphrased its language to observe that "The spirit of capital impairment statutes requires that actual values be conservatively determined." To all this, we can only observe additionally that the relatively brief span of time between the 1968 incorporation and the March, 1969 sale strengthens the likelihood that actual value would not have departed too drastically from book value in that period. What Judge Haynsworth was seeking was a "more objective standard than a computation which is the product of years of financial history of an enterprise." 284 F.2d at 741.

A further objection by appellants to use of the March, 1969 balance sheet as evidence of value was that it failed to include any "package" or "going concern" value of the corporation. While there is authority that in a proper case such values may be included among corporate assets when capital impairment is under consideration, Bishop v. Prosser-Grandview Broadcasters, Inc., 3 Wash. App. 43, 472 P. 2d 560 (Wash. 1970), we are satisfied that the referee did not err in rejecting it upon the evidence here. The record convincingly establishes that the enterprise never got off the ground and never produced anything but deficits. Under such circumstances to have attributed a solid cash value to the high hopes of speculators interested in investing in the enterprise is hardly consistent with the conservative determination of actual value which Mountain State Steel Foundries, supra, counsels.

Accordingly we conclude that the determination that Kettle's capital was impaired within the meaning of the Delaware statute was not clearly erroneous.

Appellants' third contention is that even if the purchase of stock was made at a time when the capital of the corporation was impaired, the repurchase did not cause any detriment to creditors of the corporation because, although the corporation paid appellants $67,950 for the stock, it had contracts with Mr. Fishkin, Mr. Luby and Mr. Flory to resell the stock for more than was paid for it.

Mr. Fishkin went through with his agreement to purchase 25,000 shares at $1.10 per share. Mr. Flory and Mr. Luby, however, refused to complete their contracts of purchase. Appellants contend that Mr. Luby remains liable on his contract to purchase the shares of stock in question and, therefore, since the corporation has a cause of action to collect this amount from him, it has suffered no detriment by its stock purchase from appellants. We cannot agree.

Since the trustee has filed no cross-appeal here, we do not reach the difficult legal question of whether the referee should have allowed any set-off. Cf. Lytle v. Andrews, 34 F.2d 252 (8th Cir. 1934), United Thacker Coal Co. v. Peytona Lumber Co., 15 F. Supp. 40 (D.C. W. Va., 1936). Here the referee reduced appellants' liability from $67,950 which they received to $45,450, thus crediting appellants with $22,500 of the money received when the 25,000 shares were resold to Mr. Fishkin.

Even if we assume that liability to return the moneys received here could in a proper case be the subject of setoff, the referee did not err in refusing to allow a setoff for the amount of stock purchased by Mr. Luby. Although Mr. Luby signed a contract to purchase the stock, he cancelled payment on the check for the stock and the stock was never issued to him. The corporation treated the stopping of payment on the check as a cancellation of the contract and never contemplated legal action to compel performance by Luby. We can think of no good reason for allowing credit for what was never received and have not been shown any authority for such a contention.

The referee found the corporation's "economic" damage to be $45,450 and judgment was entered in that amount against the defendants. Obviously in reaching this figure, the referee gave credit for the sale of the 25,000 shares to Mr. Fishkin. In doing so, however, he computed the credit on the basis of ninety cents per share, the price at which defendants sold the stock to Kettle, rather than $1.10, the price Kettle received from Fishkin. Defendants claim they were entitled to credit at $1.10 per share or $27,500 instead of at ninety cents, or $22,500. In their brief, they treat this difference as a mathematical error of the referee subject to mere technical correction on appeal. There was no error by the referee either in law or in computation. He simply refused to give them credit for the $5,000 profit on resale.

As mentioned earlier, there was no privity of contract between defendants and Fishkin. When we consider as well the objects of the statute and the interests of the creditors of the corporation, we find no good reason for giving the defendants the benefit of the additional $5,000 received by Kettle from Fishkin.

Finally, appellants contend that Section 160 should not be construed to permit a remedy for creditors against innocent shareholders who have sold stock to the corporation in good faith and without knowledge that the capital of the corporation was impaired at the time of the sale. We recognize that the referee made a specific finding that "defendants were not aware of the pall of illegality surrounding this transaction."[3]

Appellants rely particularly upon McDonald v. Williams, 174 U.S. 397, 43 L. Ed. 1022, 19 S. Ct. 743 (1899). In McDonald, the United States Supreme Court held that although the National Bank Act made it ultra vires for the directors of a national banking association to declare a dividend out of capital, innocent shareholders who received the dividend in good faith and believed it to come out of the surplus of the corporation would not be required to pay the amount of the dividend over to the receiver for the bankrupt corporation. Appellants also cite Bartlett v. Smith, 162 Md. 478, 160 A. 440 (Md. 1932); Bates v. Brooks, 222 Iowa 1128, 270 N.W. 867 (Ia. 1937), and Wood v. National City Bank, 24 F.2d 661 (2nd Cir. 1928). These cases, like McDonald, involve dividends rather than stock repurchases.

It may fairly be observed that these cases have but limited precedential value for, as noted by the trustee, "the purchase of its own stock by a corporation is not its usual or ordinary course of business and in no sense is comparable to the declaration of a corporate dividend." More to the point, we think, is Hamor v. Taylor-Rice Engineering Co., 84 F. 392 (Cir. Ct. Delaware, 1897). There a shareholder sold his stock back to the corporation at a time when the capital of the corporation was allegedly impaired and received the corporation's note. After the corporation became insolvent, the shareholder attempted to file a claim as a creditor of the corporation. The receivers objected, alleging that the stock purchase had occurred at a time when the capital of the corporation was impaired, though the corporation was not at that time insolvent. Construing the forerunner to Section 160 and the common law of Delaware, the court held:

> "But whether a corporation be solvent or insolvent, the fund represented by its capital stock must remain inviolate for the protection of its creditors. In the absence of statutory authority in that behalf a corporation has no legal power to reduce this fund by any formal or voluntary act or contract on its part, to the prejudice of its creditors either then or thereafter existing, whether by distributing any part of it by way of dividend, or by giving any part of it to one or more stockholders, or by disposing of it in any other manner, except by way of changing its form to meet the exigencies of the corporate business. Such an act or contract is ultra vires, not only of the directors or stockholders, but of the corporation itself."

84 F. at 397.

The court concluded that if the stock purchase had been made at a time when the capital of the corporation was impaired (which was not clear from the record), the transaction was void as against the trustee. Thus, the shareholder would have no right to assert his claim for the amount which the corporation owed him on the note. Cf. Gibbon v. Hill, 79 F.2d 288 (3rd Cir. 1935).[4]

---

3. Other than this, the referee made no finding relating to good faith and innocence of wrongdoing. All defendants except Lynch were original shareholders. Defendants Stanley and Scalf were vice-president and secretary-treasurer, respectively, of Kettle.

4. In Gibbon, a panel of the Third Circuit interpreting a similar New Jersey capital impairment statute, concluded that a shareholder who sold his stock to the corporation at a time when the capital of the corporation was impaired was liable to the creditors' representative in an action brought to recover those amounts. This conclusion was reached although, as here, the corporation was not rendered insolvent by the stock purchase.

While in Hamor, supra, the shareholder was filing a claim as a creditor, we think its logic is persuasive and is applicable here. Where the corporate act is illegal, the shareholder's lack of knowledge of the illegality cannot be controlling and the transaction is voidable by the trustee for the creditors.

Appellants contend that since the legislature has provided a specific remedy against the directors of the corporation under Section 174[5] and provided no express remedy against the shareholders under Section 160, we should not imply one.

An examination of the relevant case law indicates that appellants' contention on this point must also be rejected. In Powers v. Heggie, 268 Mass. 233, 167 N.E. 314 (Mass. 1929), and Bartlett v. Smith, 162 Md. 478, 160 A. 440 (Md. 1932), the Supreme Courts of Massachusetts and Maryland, interpreting the prior Delaware capital impairment statute, concluded that the legislature in providing a specific remedy against directors in no way intended to relieve shareholders of liability.

As did the courts in both Powers and Bartlett, supra, we find persuasive the following language from Williams v. Boice, 38 N.J. Eq. 364, 369:

> "The statute does not transfer the liability from the stockholders to the directors, but it creates a liability on the part of the latter in favor of the corporation or the creditors in certain events. * * * The stockholder who has received part of the capital by way of dividend, without legislative authority, has no right to it as against the creditors of the corporation, and no wrong is done him if he be compelled to repay it when it is required to pay the debts of the corporation. * * * But that provision does not, either in terms or by implication, exonerate the stockholders. * * * The remedy given by the statute is cumulative. The Legislature does not say that the stockholders shall be at liberty to keep the money, and that the creditors must have recourse to the directors alone."

Williams v. Boice, supra, as quoted in Powers v. Heggie, 167 N.E. at 318

To like effect under Illinois law, see Reilly v. Segert, 31 Ill. 2d 297, 201 N.E. 2d 444 (1964), in which the Supreme Court of Illinois held that "The existence of a statutory provision dealing with the liability of directors does not preclude a non-statutory liabil-

---

5. At the time relevant to the transactions involved here, § 174 provided:

"(a) In case of any willful or negligent violation of the provisions of sections 160 the directors under whose administration the same may happen shall be jointly and severally liable, at any time within six years after having such unlawful dividend or after unlawful stock purchase or redemption, to the corporation, and to its creditors in the event of its dissolution or insolvency, to the full amount of the dividend unlawfully paid, or to the full amount unlawfully paid for the purchase or redemption of the corporation's stock, with interest from the time such liability accrued. Any director who may have dissented from the act or resolution by which the same was done, may exonerate himself from such liability by causing his dissent to be entered on the books containing the minutes of the proceedings of the directors at the time the same was done, or immediately after he has notice of the same.

(b) Any directors against whom a claim is successfully asserted under this section shall be entitled to contribution from the other directors who voted for or concurred in the unlawful dividend, stock purchase or stock redemption.

(c) Any director against whom a claim is successfully asserted under this section shall be entitled, to the extent of the amount paid by him as a result of such claim, to be subrogated to the rights of the corporation against stockholders who received the dividend on, or assets for the sale or redemption of, their stock with knowledge of facts indicating that such dividend, stock purchase or redemption was unlawful under this chapter, in proportion to the amounts received by such stockholders respectively."

Section 174 has since been amended by the Delaware legislature, 59 Del. Laws, c. 106, § 6.

ity on the part of shareholders." Reilly v. Segert, supra, at 445. Thus, the court in Reilly held the shareholders could be held liable to the receiver for the creditors of the corporation.

The judgment of the district court is affirmed. Costs to appellees.

Ernest S. Johnston, et al. v. Emanuel L. Wolfe, et al.

487 A.2d 1132 (Del. 1985)

CHRISTIE, Justice:

This is an appeal from a decision of the Court of Chancery which granted summary judgment to the defendants-appellees. The complaint was brought as a class action under 8 Del.C. § 174.[1] The plaintiff class consists of those persons who claim to be either the creditors of Allied Artists Pictures Corporation (Allied or pre-merger Allied), a Delaware corporation which no longer exists, or of Allied's successor corporation of the same name (New Allied), also incorporated under the laws of this State. Named as defendants are Allied's former directors. Plaintiffs seek to collect money which they claim they are owed by one of the corporations from the directors of pre-merger Allied. It is alleged that the former directors are liable because they approved pre-merger Allied's redemption of all its outstanding preferred stock on January 19, 1976, as part of an overall plan of reorganization among Allied and certain affiliated corporations, whereby Allied ceased to exist and New Allied came into existence as a result of the merger.

(a) In case of any wilful or negligent violation of the provisions of § 160 or 173 of this title, the directors under whose administration the same may happen shall be jointly and severally liable, at any time within 6 years after paying such unlawful dividend or after such unlawful stock purchase or redemption, to the corporation, and to its creditors in the event of its dissolution or insolvency, to the full amount of the dividend unlawfully paid, or to the full amount unlawfully paid for the purchase or redemption of the corporation's stock, with interest from the time such liability accrued. Any director who may have been absent when the same was done, or who may have dissented from the act or resolution by which the same was done, may exonerate himself from such liability by causing his dissent to be entered on the books containing the minutes of the proceedings of the directors at the time the same was done, or immediately after he has notice of the same.

(b) Any director against whom a claim is successfully asserted under this section shall be entitled to contribution from the other directors who voted for or concurred in the unlawful dividend, stock purchase or stock redemption.

(c) Any director against whom a claim is successfully asserted under this section shall be entitled, to the extent of the amount paid by him as a result of such claim, to be subrogated to the rights of the corporation against stockholders who received the dividend on, or assets for the sale or redemption of, their stock with knowledge of facts indicating that such dividend, stock purchase or redemption was unlawful under this chapter, in proportion to the amounts received by such stockholders respectively.

---

1. 8 Del.C. § 174. Liability of directors for unlawful payment of dividend or unlawful stock purchase or redemption; exoneration from liability; contribution among directors; subrogation.

In mid-1975 Allied entered into a complex agreement and plan of reorganization which provided, among other things, that Allied was to be merged into a corporation known as Allied Artists of Delaware, Inc. This new corporation, in turn, changed its name after the merger to Allied Artists Pictures Corporation (New Allied).

As part of the reorganization plan, Allied redeemed all of its preferred stock prior to the merger which took place on January 19–20, 1976. Under the merger agreement, and also by operation of law, 8 Del.C. § 259(a), the creditors of pre-merger Allied became creditors of New Allied. New Allied continued business operations until April 4, 1979, when it filed a petition under Chapter XI of the Bankruptcy Act.

In their complaint, plaintiffs alleged that the redemption of preferred stock was accomplished in violation of 8 Del.C. § 160 which sets forth a corporation's rights and duties with respect to redemption of its own stock. Plaintiffs contend that this situation gives them the right, as corporate creditors, to look to the erring directors for payment of their claims under 8 Del.C. § 174. Appellants further claim that because New Allied is insolvent, they as creditors of New Allied (and on behalf of a class of such creditors) have the right to proceed under 8 Del.C. § 174 against the former directors of pre-merger Allied to recover the full amount of a deposit of corporate funds which was made in connection with the redemption of Allied's preferred stock prior to the merger.

The appellees moved to dismiss the complaint or in the alternative, for summary judgment. The grounds asserted in support of the motion were: (1) as creditors of New Allied (and not of pre-merger Allied), appellants lacked standing to maintain any action under 8 Del.C. § 174 against the directors of pre-merger Allied; and (2) the preferred stock redemption was, in any case, accomplished in accordance with the requirements of 8 Del.C. § 160 and other applicable sections of the Delaware General Corporate Law and so the former directors have no liability to anyone in connection therewith. There was no dispute as to the material facts pertinent to the issues on which the Court of Chancery based its decision.

The Court of Chancery granted summary judgment in favor of the appellees, holding that the provisions of 8 Del.C. § 174 may be invoked only by pre-merger creditors, and that post-merger creditors have no standing to invoke that statute. Since the Court of Chancery had entered summary judgment against appellants on the basis that plaintiffs had no standing to sue, it did not reach any of the other arguments presented.

Relying upon In Re International Radiator, Co., Del. Ch., 10 Del. Ch. 358, 92 A. 255 (1914), the Court of Chancery found that statutes (which correspond to current § 174) protecting the integrity of a corporation's stated capital aim at "... protecting those who have extended credit to a corporation ... [and] who have relied on stated capital ...'as a trust fund for the security of creditors....'" The court concluded:

The purpose of section 174, as this Court views the matter, is to provide a cause of action to creditors who have extended credit to a corporation based on that corporation's stated capital. And when the corporation impairs that capital by an illegal redemption of stock, it depletes the creditors' "trust fund" and seriously jeopardizes their means to recover their debts. * * * Under these circumstances, the Court concludes that the words "its creditors" in section 174 is meant to apply to creditors of pre-merger Allied; that is the corporation that allegedly illegally impaired its capital. Ernest S. Johnston, et al. v. Emanual L. Wolfe, et al., Del. Ch., Civ. No. 6682, Longobardi, V.C. (February 24, 1983). The court found that plaintiffs Johnston and Praught were creditors of post-merger New Allied only, and for that reason the court granted summary judgment to the defendants as to these two plaintiffs.

The entry of summary judgment against plaintiff Baron turned on the Chancery Court's conclusion that the prior judgment on which Baron relied was for attorney's fees and costs and such judgment ran in favor of Baron's lawyers and not Baron. See Baron v. Allied Artists Pictures Corp., Del. Ch., 395 A.2d 375 (1978), aff'd, Del. Supr., 413 A.2d 876 (1980). Baron attempted to reopen that prior litigation four years later by filing a motion asking the Court of Chancery to "clarify" its order so as to give Baron standing as a judgment creditor of pre-merger Allied (and, therefore, standing in this new action against the former directors), but no change in the prior order was made. Thus, as of the time this case was decided by Vice Chancellor Longobardi in the Court of Chancery on February 24, 1983, Baron had failed to establish that he had ever been a creditor of pre-merger Allied.

After Vice Chancellor Longobardi announced his decision against Baron in this case, Chancellor Brown again took up the matter of Baron's standing as a creditor of pre-merger Allied. He did this because Baron had again sought reargument in the prior litigation which Chancellor Brown had handled in 1976. By a letter order dated May 2, 1983 Chancellor Brown again refused to alter the judgment earlier entered. However, Baron filed additional evidence and by order dated October 6, 1983 Chancellor Brown:

(1) Indicated that he had considered a newly discovered affidavit which had been found in old files stored in the house of a now deceased attorney, and that the affidavit shed new light on the situation;

(2) Implied that if this evidence had been before him earlier, and he had been asked to enter judgment in favor of Baron instead of Baron's lawyers, he would have done so;

(3) Observed that there was no reason to enter such an order at this late date since it was unnecessary in the case before him, and such an order's significance would be confined to the case (this case) then pending in the Delaware Supreme Court;

(4) Observed that the facts of the matter are available to be argued in this Court;

(5) Declined to take any action based on the newly discovered evidence.

In view of this situation we have considered the facts of the matter as they are revealed in the court file of the prior case in the Court of Chancery. That case was a suit filed on February 20, 1974 by Baron against pre-merger Allied and its directors. The Court of Chancery rendered an opinion which included a judgment for fees and expenses in favor of Baron's lawyers on November 28, 1978. See Baron v. Allied Artists Pictures Corp., Del. Ch., 395 A.2d 375 (1978). It is that judgment upon which Chancellor Brown commented in his letter of October 6, 1983 referred to above, and it is on that judgment Baron now relies to establish that he was a creditor of pre-merger Allied.

Since the merger took place on February 19 and 20, 1976 and the judgment against pre-merger Allied was not rendered until November 28, 1978, those obtaining that judgment cannot be said to be creditors of pre-merger Allied at the time the merger, took place even though such judgment was later entered against pre-merger Allied (then out of existence for most purposes).

On appeal we find that the Court of Chancery correctly granted defendant's motion for summary judgment based on plaintiff's lack of standing and we affirm. However, our conclusion that Baron lacked standing is based on reasons different from those relied on by the trial court.

The statute here in question, 8 Del.C. § 174, provides in essence that directors who are guilty of "wilful or negligent violation" of the statutes governing the purchase or redemption by the corporation of its own stock or of the issuance of dividends on its own stock (8 Del.C. §§ 160, 173), "shall be jointly and severally liable at any time within 6 years after paying such unlawful dividend or after such unlawful stock purchase or redemption, to the corporation and to its creditors in the event of its dissolution or redemption..." (emphasis added).

The plaintiffs assert the claim that the directors of Allied wrongfully impaired the capital of that corporation When they made a deposit of pre-merger Allied's funds ($408,706) in trust, for the purchase of Allied's preferred stock held by a corporation which was about to merge with Allied to form New Allied. When the merger was completed the funds were returned to the treasury of New Allied since New Allied then included and controlled the assets of the merged corporation. The funds were in trust for about 12 hours and were never dissipated or improperly diverted in any way.

Since no plaintiff was a creditor of pre-merger Allied when the merger took place, no plaintiff extended any credit to pre-merger Allied on the basis of that corporation's stated capital. Plaintiffs Johnson and Praught are creditors of New Allied on account of certain trade indebtedness incurred in 1978 and 1979, after the reorganization. Neither of these plaintiffs even claims to have been a creditor of pre-merger Allied at any time. If they relied on the corporate structure of New Allied in extending credit to New Allied, such reliance had to have been based on the corporate structure of New Allied as it existed at the time the credit was extended.

Johnson and Praught, as creditors of New Allied, are deemed not to be "creditors" of pre-merger Allied within the meaning of 8 Del.C. § 174 because, in fact, they did not have a claim against pre-merger Allied when it went out of existence. When the statute seeks to protect "its creditors" such phrase refers to those creditors who were already creditors at the time of the action challenged under the statute; that is, in this case, to creditors of pre-merger Allied.

The Court of Chancery originally found that Baron's claim of standing which would entitle him to sue the directors of the former corporation was invalid because Baron was not a creditor of pre-merger Allied or of New Allied. We take notice of the fact that Baron was instrumental in obtaining a judgment against pre-merger Allied after the merger and that such judgment could have been obtained in Baron's own name (although it was not). We hold that Baron nevertheless lacks standing since the judgment on which he relies was not obtained until after the merger.

In view of the importance attached to the prior litigation, we here note some additional history of that litigation. Approximately one year after the mergers became effective, Baron's attorneys petitioned the Court of Chancery for fees and expenses which had been incurred in litigation conducted in 1976 against pre-merger Allied. The attorneys claimed that the litigation they conducted in 1976 had been the cause of Allied's merger. They filed affidavits in support of their petition setting forth the costs incurred and the hours spent in connection with that litigation. Included was a claim for expenses in the amount of $5,155.70 and a claim for attorneys' fees of $276,800. The Court of Chancery awarded the attorneys their expenses of $5,155.70 and attorneys' fees in the amount of $50,000. In connection with that award, the Vice Chancellor found that the merger had been prompted by the litigation and that the merger had accomplished Baron's goal of having all preferred stock dividend arrearages paid up and the stock redeemed. Baron v. Allied Artists Pictures Corp., Del. Ch., 395 A.2d at 378. It is this merger which Baron was found to have helped bring about for which his attorneys were granted expenses and fees. He now seeks to penalize the former directors for the way that merger was carried out.

In any event, the award of fees and costs was made by then Vice Chancellor Brown, directly to Baron's attorneys and not to Baron. The Court of Chancery then stated:

I note here without further comment that the petition for fees and expenses had not been filed on behalf of the plaintiff Baron. Rather his counsel have petitioned directly for such an award in their own right. Defendants have not challenged the propriety of this and consequently my decision herein should not be taken as passing upon it one way or the other, Baron v. Allied Artists Pictures Corp., Del. Ch., 395 A.2d at 383 n. 1. As indicated earlier, Baron's subsequent attempts to be recognized as the judgment creditor finally met with a measure of partial success on February 23, 1983, but this did not make him a pre-merger judgment creditor of Allied.

We are of the opinion that Baron had no standing to bring this action under 8 Del.C. § 174(a), but we base this decision on the fact that he was not a creditor of pre-merger Allied as of the date of the merger (even though at a later date after the merger he probably could have gotten a judgment against the corporation).

We hold that the Court of Chancery was correct when it determined that none of the plaintiffs are entitled to invoke the rights which the creditors of pre-merger Allied would have had under § 174, because none of the plaintiffs was a creditor of pre-merger Allied when the merger took place. Only the theory upon which Baron's disqualification is based differs from that announced by the Court of Chancery.

We do not reach other issues in the case.

* * *

AFFIRMED.

---

2. *The "Modern" Approaches*

The 1977 revisions to the California corporate law mark a substantial break with the traditional notions of capital requirements and the regulation of the payment of dividends. In the place of the regime of "stated capital" and "surplus" and "par value," California substituted a test to be applied on a case by case basis. The California Legislature adopted this new approach based on its belief that it better reflected the economic realities of corporate distributions and more soundly protected lender interests. Review California Corp. Code §§ 114, 166, 500–502, and 507, and RMBCA §§ 6.21, 6.22, and 6.40, and the materials that follow.

---

a. California

Cal Corp Code § 500 (2000)

§ 500. Distributions; Conditions; Exemptions

Neither a corporation nor any of its subsidiaries shall make any distribution to the corporation's shareholders (Section 166) except as follows:

(a) The distribution may be made if the amount of the retained earnings of the corporation immediately prior thereto equals or exceeds the amount of the proposed distribution.

(b) The distribution may be made if immediately after giving effect thereto:

(1) The sum of the assets of the corporation (exclusive of goodwill, capitalized research and development expenses and deferred charges) would be at least equal to 1 1/4 times its liabilities (not including deferred taxes, deferred income and other deferred credits); and

(2) Thse current assets of the corporation would be at least equal to its current liabilities or, if the average of the earnings of the corporation before taxes on income and before interest expense for the two preceding fiscal years was less than the average of the interest expense of the corporation for those fiscal years, at least equal to 1 1/4 times its current liabilities; provided, however, that in determining the amount of the assets of the corporation profits derived from an exchange of assets shall not be included unless the assets received are currently realizable in cash; and provided, further, that for the purpose of this subdivision "current assets" may include net amounts which the board has determined in good faith may reasonably be expected to be received from customers during the 12-month period used in calculating current liabilities pursuant to existing contractual relationships obligating those customers to make fixed or periodic payments during the term of the contract or, in the case of public utilities, pursuant to service connections with customers, after in each case giving effect to future costs not then included in current liabilities but reasonably expected to be incurred by the corporation in performing those contracts or providing service to utility customers. Paragraph (2) of subdivision (b) is not applicable to a corporation which does not classify its assets into current and fixed under generally accepted accounting principles.

(c) The amount of any distribution payable in property shall, for the purposes of this chapter, be determined on the basis of the value at which the property is carried on the corporation's financial statements in accordance with generally accepted accounting principles.

(d) For the purpose of applying this section to a distribution by a corporation of cash or property in payment by the corporation in connection with the purchase of its shares, there shall be added to retained earnings all amounts that had been previously deducted therefrom with respect to obligations incurred in connection with the corporation's repurchase of its shares and reflected on the corporation's balance sheet, but not in excess of the principal of the obligations that remain unpaid immediately prior to the distribution. In addition, there shall be deducted from liabilities all amounts that had been previously added thereto with respect to the obligations incurred in connection with the corporation's repurchase of its shares and reflected on the corporation's balance sheet, but not in excess of the principal of the obligations that will remain unpaid after the distribution, provided that no addition to retained earnings or deduction from liabilities under this subdivision shall occur on account of any obligation that is a distribution to the corporation's shareholders (Section 166) at the time the obligation is incurred.

(e) This section does not apply to a corporation licensed as a broker-dealer under Chapter 2 (commencing with Section 25210) of Part 3 of Division 1 of

Title 4, if immediately after giving effect to any distribution the corporation is in compliance with the net capital rules of the Commissioner of Corporations and the Securities and Exchange Commission.

Comments and Questions

1. The Legislative Committee comments suggest the ways in which this approach was to be implemented:

> Under prior law dividends may generally be declared only out of earned surplus. [Cal. § 1500.] There are several exceptions to this general rule. Dividends may be paid in some circumstances out of net profits for a six to twelve month period ("nimble" dividends), paid-in surplus or surplus resulting from the reduction of stated capital. [Cal. § 1500.] However, a dividend may not be declared in any event where the corporation would thereby be rendered insolvent. [Cal. § 1501.]
>
> As a practical matter, these general restrictions do not provide adequate protection to creditors, particularly trade creditors. This results from the fact that all but an insignificant amount of the money originally received from the shareholders can be designated as paid-in surplus rather than state capital.
>
> Similarly, the general rule under prior law is that a corporation may acquire shares issued by it only from earned surplus. [Cal. § 1707.] Exceptions to this rule permit purchases of such shares from reduction surplus, and redemption of shares subject to redemption from any surplus. [Cal. §§ 1706 and 1707.]
>
> This distinction between the sources from which shares may be purchased and those from which dividends may be paid is anomalous, as a purchase of shares on a pro rata basis has exactly the same effect as a dividend with regard to the protection of creditors and senior shareholders.
>
> For the purpose of establishing meaningful protection for creditors and shareholders and to rationalize restrictions upon the payment of dividends and repurchase of shares, this section provides restrictions upon a corporation in the making of any "distribution to its shareholders" based upon the current financial condition of the corporation. ["Distribution to its shareholder" is a defined term. See § 166.] This approach eliminates the concepts of "stated capital" and "surplus" in favor of balance sheet tests.
>
> The corporation may make a distribution to its shareholders if either of two tests is met. First, a corporation may make a distribution out of its retained earnings.
>
> Second, if there are not retained earnings, a corporation may make a distribution provided that after giving effect to the distribution the assets of the corporation (exclusive of certain intangibles) are at least equal to one and a quarter times its liabilities (excluding certain deferred items) and its current assets are at least equal to its current liabilities.
>
> With regard to the liquidity portion of this test, if the average of the earnings of the corporation before taxes on income and before interest expense for the two proceeding fiscal years is not at least equal to the average of the interest expense of the corporation for such years, the current assets must be at least one and quarter times the current liabilities. However, this liquidity test is inapplicable to any cor-

poration not classifying its assets into current and fixed under generally accepted accounting principles.

This section prohibits, in determining the amount of the assets of a corporation, the inclusion of any appreciation in value not yet realized (except with respect to readily marketable securities) and profits derived from exchange of assets unless the assets received are currently realizable in cash. Prior law provides a similar limitation with respect to the declaration of dividends. [Cal. § 1502] The amount of any distribution payable in property is the value at which such property is carried on the corporation's financial statements.[All references to financial statements, as well as other specified terms, mean consolidated financial statements or other items prepared or determined in accordance with generally accepted accounting principles then applicable. See § 114.]

In appropriate cases where income within a "current" period is definitely assured and determinable, such income although not yet received may be included in the calculation of current assets subject to certain adjustments.

Any distribution to the corporation's shareholders permitted by this section is subject to the solvency limitation of § 501.

Deering's California Codes Annotated, California General Corporation Law, § 500 (Official Comment; Legislative Committee Comment).

2. In reviewing the California approach, do you believe there is much practical difference between the results under Delaware law and under California law? Consider your answer in light of the reasoning of the case that follows. After you review the materials in subsection b, which follows, you will be asked to consider the problem of the leveraged buyout under the approach adopted in the Revised Model Business Corporation Act excerpted below.

Credit Managers Ass'n of Southern California v. Federal Co.

629 F.Supp. 175 (C.D.Cal., 1985)
Amended Memorandum Opinion

RAFEEDIE, District Judge:

....Plaintiff is a California citizen and defendant a citizen of Tennessee and Delaware. Diversity jurisdiction exists pursuant to 28 U.S.C. § 1332. Venue is proper in the Central District of California pursuant to 28 U.S.C. § 1391(a). The parties agree that California substantive law applies.

I. INTRODUCTION

Plaintiff Credit Managers Association of Southern California ("Credit Managers") is the assignee of an assignment for the benefit of creditors of Crescent Food Company ("Crescent"). Crescent sold and distributed gourmet foods, including imported cheeses, to delicatessens and supermarkets in California.

Prior to May 1982, defendant the Federal Company ("Federal") owned 100 percent of Crescent's stock. In May Federal sold the stock for $1,435,932 to Teeple-Reizer Acquisition Company ("TRAC"), an entity formed by the top management of Crescent for the purpose of acquiring Crescent. The sale of the stock by Federal to TRAC was what is commonly referred to as a leveraged buyout, the acquiring company (TRAC) financing the purchase of the stock by borrowing against the assets of the acquired company (Crescent).

On October 17, 1983, a year and five months after the buyout, Crescent was in financial difficulty and executed a general assignment for the benefit of creditors. Plaintiff Credit Managers is the assignee and brings this action seeking substantially to set aside the leveraged buyout and to bring back into Crescent certain assets transferred to Federal as payment for Crescent's stock. Plaintiff seeks to have these assets held in a constructive trust for the benefit of the unpaid claims of Crescent's creditors.

II. PLAINTIFF'S LEGAL THEORIES

In many ways, this is a case of first impression, there being no precedent directly on point.[3] While much has been written about fairness to shareholders when a public company "goes private" through a leveraged buyout,[4] little has been written about fairness to creditors.[5] Because a leveraged buyout by definition involves borrowing heavily against the assets of a company, the creditors of that company face a much more highly leveraged company after the buyout than before. If the company's cash flow cannot service this new debt—either because of the size of the debt service or a business downturn decreasing the company's income or a combination of the two—the company often must cease operations, leaving accounts payable unpaid. This, according to plaintiff, is what happened to Crescent. Plaintiff comes before this court seeking to undo the buyout proceeding under three legal theories: (1) the transfer of some of Crescent's assets to Federal as part of the purchase price for the Crescent stock was a fraudulent conveyance; (2) the transfer of some of these assets was an unlawful distribution to Crescent's shareholders; and (3) Federal's claims against Crescent should be equitably subordinated to the claims of Crescent's creditors. These theories will be examined infra. First the court will briefly review the details of the buyout and Crescent's subsequent financial difficulties.

III. FACTS

From November 1975 to May 1, 1982, Crescent was a wholly owned subsidiary of Federal. Crescent's major fixed asset was a warehouse in Vernon, California valued at approximately $2 million (hereinafter "the warehouse"). Crescent's major liability was approximately $7.25 million in debt owed to Federal. This intercompany loan was an unsecured demand loan bearing interest at a rate of ten percent per annum. In the early 1980's Federal decided to sell Crescent primarily because of Crescent's poor fi-

3. United States v. Gleneagles Inv. Co., Inc., 565 F.Supp. 556 (M.D.Penn.1983) (hereinafter "Gleneagles") also examines whether a leveraged buyout was a fraudulent conveyance. Gleneagles is different from the instant case because plaintiff there proved violations of Sections 6 and 7 of the Uniform Fraudulent Conveyance Act which require a showing of intentional fraud. Plaintiff Credit Managers alleges constructive fraud by defendant Federal, a violation of Section 5 of the Uniform Fraudulent Conveyance Act. Plaintiff does not allege intentional fraud.

4. *E.g.*, McCune and Van Kirk, "Leveraged Buyouts by Management," 16 Rev. of Securities Regulation, No. 22 at 769 (Dec. 22, 1983); Denham, "Going Private," Los Angeles Lawyer (June 1985).

5. *E.g.*, Baird & Jackson, "Fraudulent Conveyance Law and Its Proper Domain," 38 Vand.L.Rev., 829, 850–854 (1985); "Leveraged Buyout Alleged as Fraud in Bankruptcy Case," Legal Times of Washington at 1 (October 21, 1985). The latter article discusses the leveraged buyout of Table Talk, Inc., formerly the world's largest producer of pies, and its subsequent bankruptcy. Table Talk's trustee is attempting to set aside the leveraged buyout as a fraudulent conveyance. Cataldo v. Karol, No. 85-3618-Y, D.Mass. The trustee has sued both Squibb, the company that sold Table Talk, Inc., and Texas General Corp., the company that bought it. In the instant action plaintiff has sued only Federal, the company that sold Crescent, not TRAC, the company that bought it.

nancial performance and Federal's inability to do anything to improve that performance. While a number of companies expressed interest in Crescent, Federal ultimately decided to sell the company to its management in a leveraged buyout. To accomplish this, Crescent's management formed TRAC and capitalized it at $450,000. Teeple and Reizer, principals of TRAC and top management at Crescent, invested $85,000. Others invested the remaining $365,000. On May 1, 1982 Federal and TRAC entered into a stock purchase agreement for the sale of Crescent's stock to TRAC. The price for the shares was $1,435,932, the book value of Crescent. TRAC paid $235,932 in cash and executed a promissory note for $1.2 million in favor of Federal bearing interest at the rate of ten percent per annum for the balance. Both TRAC and Crescent executed the note.

On May 7, 1982, as security for the $1.2 million note, Crescent executed a First Trust Deed and Assignment of Rents ("Deed of Trust") in favor of Federal which placed a lien on the warehouse for the amount outstanding on the note.

Also as part of the TRAC-Federal transaction, Crescent paid off the $7.25 million intercompany debt owed to Federal. Crescent accomplished this by borrowing that amount from the General Electric Credit Corporation ("GECC"). The GECC loan was secured by all the assets of Crescent (e.g. accounts receivables, inventory, machinery, equipment and a second trust deed on all real property) and bore an interest rate generally ranging from 16 to 21 percent. The GECC line of credit to Crescent was for a maximum of $7.5 million. Exhibit 29. There were several other relatively insignificant cash adjustments between Federal and Crescent as part of the sale of Crescent's stock involving prepaid casualty insurance premiums and income tax refunds. See Plaintiff's Memorandum of Contentions of Fact and Law at 2 n. 3 (hereinafter "Plaintiff's Memorandum").

Shortly after the transaction, TRAC loaned $189,000, which was most of its remaining cash, to Crescent. Crescent's new management also changed the name of the company to Crescent Reese Foods ("Crescent Reese") and publicized the buyout to those it did business with.

It is obvious that Crescent was much more heavily leveraged after the stock sale than before. Crescent took on a $1.2 million lien against its warehouse and it refinanced a $7.25 million unsecured loan at 10 percent interest with a $7.25 million secured loan at 16 to 20 percent interest. It is not disputed that Crescent's debt service increased significantly because of the buyout.

In November of 1982, six months after the buyout, GECC extended Crescent an additional line of credit for $2.5 million bringing Crescent's total potential borrowing from GECC to $10.0 million.

After the May 1982 buyout, Crescent experienced four setbacks to its business: (1) Suppliers, concerned that Crescent was no longer part of Federal, a much larger company, extended less trade credit to Crescent, requiring earlier payment of bills; (2) Crescent's competitors started giving their customers a longer period in which to pay their bills, a practice that Crescent was forced to match; (3) Crescent workers went on strike which resulted in an interruption of the business for approximately two months and destruction of some Crescent property; and (4) Crescent lost business due to the shut down of some of its customers' stores. Defendant contends that these setbacks did Crescent in, not the leveraged buyout. Plaintiff contends that because Crescent had unreasonably small capital, it was unable to survive these four setbacks. Plaintiff further contends that even without these setbacks, the leveraged buyout and the concomitant increase in Crescent's debt service made Crescent's demise inevitable.

In October of 1983, with accounts payable at approximately $3.0 million and with insufficient cash to continue operations and no borrowing capacity, Crescent shut down, executing an assignment of its assets for the benefit of creditors, a statutory alternative to bankruptcy under California Code of Civil Procedure § 493.010. At the time of trial, plaintiff Credit Managers continued to operate Crescent's cheese importation and distribution business, deciding that continued operation was more beneficial to creditors than the other alternative, the bankruptcy of Crescent.

In reaching a decision in this case, the court was required to make a number of factual findings about how certain assets and liabilities should be valued and accounted for on Crescent's balance sheet. These findings are discussed again infra, but are stated below as specific findings of the court:

1. The present value (on May 7, 1982) of TRAC and Crescent's $1.2 million obligation to Federal, given the below market interest rate on the five-year loan, was $900,000;

2. The $189,000 "loan" from TRAC to Crescent was, in fact, a capital contribution to Crescent as TRAC never demanded repayment; and

3. The fair market value of Crescent's fixed assets on May 7, 1982 exceeded the $1,382,228 stated on Crescent's balance sheet in the fixed assets minus depreciation category.

IV. FRAUDULENT CONVEYANCE

A. Threshold Issues

In attempting to apply the law of fraudulent conveyances to a leveraged buyout, plaintiff seeks to apply a law with its origins in 16th century England[7] to a financial transaction which did not exist on a large scale until the 1980's. As a threshold matter, it is not at all clear that fraudulent conveyance law is broadly applicable to leveraged buyouts:

> The reach of fraudulent conveyance law has not been an issue for much of this century. The issue has become an important one in the 1980's however. Identifying the precise reach of fraudulent conveyance law is the crucial inquiry in several important legal disputes, such as whether... a leveraged buyout is a fraudulent conveyance.
>
> ....
>
> An important conceptual question is whether a leveraged buyout in fact presents fraudulent conveyance problems.... A firm that incurs obligations in the course of a buyout does not seem at all like the Elizabethan deadbeat who sells his sheep to his brother for a pittance.

Baird & Jackson, "Fraudulent Conveyance Law and Its Proper Domain," 38 Vand.L.Rev., 829, 832–33, 852 (hereinafter "Baird & Jackson"). As this "important conceptual question" was not briefed by the parties, and as there are other grounds for its decision, the court does not answer the question. It should be stated, however, that in analyzing plaintiff's claims, the court does not mean to suggest that it believes fraudulent conveyance law is generally and broadly applicable to leveraged buyouts. To the contrary, Baird & Jackson's article presents compelling arguments why it should not be.[8]

---

7. 13 Eliz., ch. 5. *See* In re Madrid, 725 F.2d 1197, 1199–200 (9th Cir.1984) (historical review of fraudulent conveyance law in the bankruptcy area).

8. Baird & Jackson's main point is that leveraged buyouts can be beneficial to creditors. A company can and often does do better under new management, especially when the new managers have personally invested in the enterprise. If creditors have the right to retroactively attack the buyout if

Assuming that fraudulent conveyance law is applicable to all leveraged buyouts, there is yet another threshold question—whether plaintiff represents creditors who have a right to complain about the conveyance that made TRAC's buyout of Crescent possible. Plaintiff proposes that the court make the following finding of fact: "As of May 7, 1982 and continuing thereafter through the present, there are one or more creditors of Crescent who hold matured claims against Crescent in excess of the total recovery sought herein and who are beneficiaries of the general assignment to Credit Managers for the benefit of creditors executed on October 17, 1983." Plaintiff's Proposed Finding of Fact 49. See also Plaintiff's Memorandum at 15–16 and n. 10. The implication of the proposed finding, if not its express wording, is that all creditors held substantial matured claims at the birth of Crescent Reese Foods (the date of the buyout) and at its death (the date of the assignment). There can be no quarrel that creditors held claims on the date of the assignment (October 17, 1983), but the evidence presented at trial did not show these creditors held substantial claims on the date of the buyout (May 7, 1982). In fact, most claims arose after the buyout.

Exhibit 143 is a balance sheet for Crescent and Crescent Reese prepared by an accounting firm retained by plaintiff. After adjustments it shows that Crescent owed about $2.5 million to trade creditors (accounts payable-trade) at the time of the buyout. An accountant retained by plaintiff, Kenneth Goldman, testified at trial that at the time of the assignment creditors' claims were approximately $3.0 million. This $500,000 increase shows that at least $500,000 of the unpaid accounts payable arose after the buyout. More importantly, plaintiff's accountant's testimony also shows that the creditors in 1983, for the most part, were not the same as those who were creditors in May of 1982 when the buyout occurred. Using Exhibit 151, plaintiff's accountant testified that there were three trade creditors who were owed money at the time of the buyout—Infofoods, Hertz, and Fromageries Bel. Exhibit 151 shows these three creditors were owed approximately $130,000. This evidence proves that much of the credit extended by existing creditors was extended after the buyout. Finally, plaintiff's accountant testified that the $130,000 in accounts payable that existed on May 7, 1982 was paid shortly after the buyout, proving that at that time the creditors plaintiff represents were owed no money at all and that their current claims arose exclusively from credit extended after the buyout.

The evidence shows that the creditors had knowledge of Crescent's new ownership and the change in the name of the company. Creditors had at least some knowledge of the financial impact the buyout had on the company because the creditors demanded quicker payment from the new Crescent (Crescent Reese) on accounts payable than they had from the old Crescent. These creditors made a post-buyout decision to extend credit on new terms to a new entity, an entity with a very different financial structure than its predecessor. As the creditors plaintiff represents did not have any substantial stake in Crescent at the time of the buyout, there does not appear to be a strong reason to give these creditors the right to attack the buyout as harmful to them. It would seem that if leveraged buyouts are to be susceptible to attack on fraudulent conveyance grounds, only those who were creditors at the time of the transaction should have a right to attack the transaction. The limited law and scholarship on the subject supports

---

the company fails, buyouts will be deterred even when they would be in the best interest of all involved. In fraudulent conveyance cases, courts only examine buyouts that fail. Rulings in such cases, however, affect all future leveraged buyouts by creating potential liability for stockholders of companies that go private.

this observation. In U.S. v. Gleneagles Investment Co., 565 F.Supp. 556 (M.D.Pa.1983), the earliest and apparently the only published case examining the leveraged buyout-fraudulent conveyance question, the court made specific findings that each creditor who sued to set aside the conveyance held a matured claim on the date of the conveyance. In separate findings of fact, the court stated the name of the creditor and the amount they were owed on November 23, 1973, the date of the alleged fraudulent conveyance in that case. Id. at 572, Findings of Fact 155–60. Plaintiff Credit Managers has not provided the court with evidence to make similar findings in this case (i.e. the names of each creditor and the amount owed on May 7, 1982, the date of the execution of the Deed of Trust). In fact, the evidence that was presented as analyzed above proves the October 1982 creditors were, for the most part, not creditors in May of 1983.

A similar conclusion that creditors must hold matured claims the day of the buyout is implied in Baird & Jackson's article. The transaction they examine involves general creditors who were owed $4 million at the time of the buyout and later sued to set aside the conveyance. Baird & Jackson, supra at 850.

It is unclear whether it is legally significant that plaintiff does not represent creditors who were creditors at the time of the buyout. Section 5 of The Uniform Fraudulent Conveyance Act under which plaintiff sues states:

> Every conveyance made without fair consideration when the person making it is engaged or is about to engage in a business or transaction for which the property remaining in his hands after the conveyance is an unreasonably small capital, is fraudulent as to creditors and as to other persons who become creditors during the continuation of such business or transaction without regard to his actual intent.

Cal.Civil Code § 3439.05 (emphasis added). The statute clearly covers future as well as existing creditors. However, when the California legislature passed this provision in 1939, it clearly did not intend to cover leveraged buyouts which are very public events. The legislature was addressing, instead transactions that have the earmarks of fraud. The conveyance in this case occurred in May of 1982. Despite the fact that creditors knew of the conveyance, creditors chose to wait two years, until May of 1984, to file this case challenging the buyout. This presents the question of whether defendant is entitled to raise a laches defense, an issue which both parties have discussed. If there is no limit on when a creditor can sue to set aside a transfer, fraudulent conveyance law becomes an insurance policy for creditors of companies that have gone private. Credit could liberally be extended to such companies regardless of their assets or cash flow with the knowledge that the buyout could always be attacked later if the company folded. A judicially created statute of limitations through the development of a laches defense might be appropriate to limit fraudulent conveyances actions so that they would not be brought each and every time a leveraged buyout failed. Bankruptcy law has such a limit under 11 U.S.C. § 548 allowing challenges only to conveyances made within one year of the filing of a bankruptcy petition. In the instant case, the date analogous to the filing of a bankruptcy petition would be the date of the assignment, October 17, 1983. The alleged fraudulent conveyance was more than one year before that date. There is no apparent reason why creditors of a company that has executed an assignment for benefit of creditors should have a longer period of time to set aside a conveyance than creditors of a company that has filed bankruptcy.

The two threshold issues discussed above are important conceptual and legal questions raised by this case. Because the parties did not brief the important questions of whether fraudulent conveyance law is generally and broadly applicable to leveraged buyouts and whether, if it is, creditors challenging the transaction must be creditors at the time of the transaction, the court does not rule on the fraudulent conveyance claim on these grounds.

B. Was There a Fraudulent Conveyance?

....

[Omitted.]

2. Unreasonably Small Capital

Whether Crescent was undercapitalized as a result of the buyout is "a question of fact that must be ascertained on a case by case basis." Wells Fargo Bank v. Desert View Building Supplies, Inc., 475 F.Supp. 693 (D.Nev.1978) aff'd 633 F.2d 225 (9th Cir.1980). Although the case law is not completely clear, the court assumes the burden of proof is on Federal to prove that Crescent was not left with unreasonably small capital because of the transfer. Neumeyer v. Crown Funding Corp., 56 Cal.App.3d 178, 188, 128 Cal.Rptr. 366, 372 (1976); Kirkland v. Risso, 98 Cal.App.3d 971, 978, 159 Cal.Rptr. 798, 801–02 (1979); Gleneagles, 565 F.Supp. at 577.

Federal relies primarily on GECC's analysis of Crescent's cash flow and the testimony of GECC officials to prove that Crescent was not undercapitalized at the time of the buyout when GECC studied the company and decided to lend it $7.5 million. Federal also relies on the testimony of Crescent's top management personnel who invested their own money in the Crescent and believed in May of 1982 that it was a viable entity with sufficient capital to generate income to cover the debt service and make a profit. Plaintiff counters this evidence with the opinion of an expert witness that, compared to others in the wholesale food business and under a variety of measures of financial health, Crescent was undercapitalized. Plaintiff does not dispute that the GECC cash flow analysis predicted that Crescent would have sufficient funds to carry on its operations but plaintiff contends that the underlying assumptions of the GECC analysis were wrong.

After considering the evidence, the court is persuaded by the GECC analysis and a review of Crescent's balance sheet that Crescent was not undercapitalized at the time of the buyout.

The testimony of GECC's manager for the Western Region, Stephen Read, is especially probative. Read testified that GECC only finances five percent of the leveraged buyouts it considers and that the projected cash flow of the company is among the most important factors they consider. Read further testified that although the assets of the borrower are an important consideration since the loan is secured, cash flow is more important, since without the cash flow to service the debt, the loan would not be made. Read testified that Crescent's assets (e.g. accounts receivable and real estate) were considered in the making of the Crescent loan, but it was the projected cash flow that was the determinative factor in deciding to make the loan. In sum, based on its analysis of Crescent as evidenced by its internal reports, the buyout "made sense" to GECC as they fully expected the cash flow to be sufficient to service the debt. GECC projected a positive monthly cash flow of $69,000 to $885,000 a month for the year following the buyout.

GECC examined Crescent's financial health again in July of 1982 and again determined that Crescent was adequately capitalized and had sufficient cash flow to service the debt though its projections on future cash flow were more pessimistic. Based on this second analysis, which took place after the buyout, GECC agreed in November to lend another $2.5 million to Crescent for a total secured line of credit of $10.0 million. The court finds, based on the testimony of the GECC employees and the reports done by GECC both before and after the buyout, that Crescent, though heavily in debt, was not undercapitalized and had sufficient expected cash flow to stay in business.

Plaintiff argues that the court should reduce the weight that is placed on the evidence presented by the GECC witnesses because of incorrect assumptions contained in the GECC reports. Plaintiff's expert witness, economics professor and consultant Michael Tennenbaum, challenges four projections made by GECC: (1) the sales forecast; (2) the gross profit margin; (3) inventory turnover; and (4) the average age of accounts receivable. While the court found Tennenbaum qualified as an expert witness on financial matters, the court notes for the record that Tennenbaum does not have any particular expertise in analyzing the wholesale food business.

a. Projected Sales

GECC forecast sales of $61 million for Crescent during the 12 months following the buyout. Tennenbaum testified that based on Crescent's historical sales experience he would have predicted total sales ranging from $55 to $57 million—$4 million less than GECC projected. Actual Crescent sales were $57 million. The question the court must decide is not whether GECC's projection was correct, for it clearly was not, but whether it was reasonable and prudent at the time it was made. The court finds that it was. The testimony of Crescent's president Stanley Teeple proved that the reason the projected sales figures were not met was because of two unforeseen events. Market Basket stores, a big customer of Crescent, shut down and Crescent was left with substantial excess inventory. Many of the products Crescent sold were perishable and had to be sold by a certain date and so Crescent had to sell the excess inventory at distress sale prices. Therefore, in addition to the ongoing loss of sales to a big customer, the closing of Market Basket stores created a surplus of product at Crescent which had a downward impact on prices generally for that period. The second event was the strike against Crescent in October through December of 1982. The Teamster's Union, which represented Crescent's drivers, struck and two other unions, representing Crescent warehousemen and administrative personnel, refused to cross the picket line. Teeple testified that the strike was "devastating" to Crescent. It occurred during Crescent's busy season. In addition to lost sales caused by the strike's disruptive effect on Crescent, Crescent's cost of operations went up due to the strike and a dozen Crescent trucks were either destroyed or damaged, apparently due to strike related violence.

Despite this testimony, plaintiff argued at trial that the strike had no impact on Crescent's sales. As proof plaintiff proved that during October through December 1981 Crescent had $15 million in sales while during the strike in October through December of 1982 plaintiff had $16.3 million in sales. These figures are accurate but they do not prove, as plaintiff contends, that the strike had no impact on sales. All these figures prove is that despite the strike Crescent was able to increase sales over the previous year. Teeple's testimony demonstrates that, but for the strike, Crescent's sales during that period would have been even higher than $16.3 million and the annual sales of Crescent would have been closer to the $61 million projected by GECC. Crescent's annual sales had been increasing prior to the buyout and it was prudent to project that those increases would continue.

Based on the evidence presented the court finds the forecast of $61 million in sales was not unreasonable. The strike, the loss of Market Basket stores as a customer, as well as the downturn in the economy in 1982–83 discussed by plaintiff's expert, caused sales to fall $4 million below projected figures. These were not predictable events when the buyout occurred.

Moreover, Tennenbaum testified that he did not recompute the cash flow analysis using the lower sales figure of $57 million so there is no basis for this court to reach the conclusion that the lower sales figure had any impact whatsoever on Crescent's cash flow, let alone a negative one. With $57 million in sales, Crescent was a smaller company than GECC predicted. Smaller companies need less capital to operate, so it is conceivable that lower sales, given that the amount of capital remained constant, made Crescent a healthier company rather than one that was less well capitalized.

b. Gross Profit Margins and Inventory Turnover

Plaintiff's expert testified that he disagreed with GECC's projections of Crescent's gross profit margin and inventory turnover. GECC forecast a gross profit margin of 17.8 percent and plaintiff's expert testified that that actual figure was between 17.5 and 18 percent. GECC forecast an inventory turnover of eight times a year and Crescent's actual inventory turnover was eight times a year. As the GECC projections were consistent with Crescent's actual operating results, there is no reason to reduce the weight the court places on the GECC analysis because of these projections.

c. Accounts Receivable Collection Period

Plaintiff's expert's most effective attack on the GECC analysis concerns GECC's initial assumption that Crescent's accounts receivable, on average, would be collected 26 days after being billed. In the year preceding the buyout, the collection period ranged from 26 days to 34 days. In the seven months following the buyout, the collection period ranged from 34 to 43 days, generally on the lower side. The industry average, according to Tennenbaum, was 7 to 34 days.

GECC's projection of a 26-day collection period was not unreasonable. Crescent had achieved that level before and it was well within the industry range. Crescent's main customers were the largest supermarket chains in Southern California and it was reasonable to predict a faster collection period after the buyout due to better management and more effective collection procedures. However, the court finds that it was not prudent to project an average 26-day collection period given Crescent's history and the fact that many Crescent customers were billed "net 30." The court agrees with plaintiff's expert that a 30-day accounts receivable collection period was consistent with Crescent's historical experience and a prudent projection. GECC came close to recognizing this itself after the buyout in July 1982 when it reviewed its cash flow projections and changed the projected average collection period from 26 days to 29 days. Crescent's actual average was slightly more than 30, due in part to delays caused by the strike affecting administrative staff in November and December of 1982. But for the strike, the accounts receivable collection period would have been shorter.

Tennenbaum recomputed the GECC cash flow analysis assuming a 30-day accounts receivable collection period. Exhibit 152, Schedule III. The recomputation demonstrates the dramatic impact a four-day increase in the collection period has on cash flows. A four day increase would mean that Crescent had to finance its $5 million in receivables for approximately a fifteen percent longer period of time. Unlike GECC's projected positive cash flow of $69,000 to $885,000 at the end of each month using a 26-day collection period, the Tennenbaum analysis of the same numbers with a 30-day collection period showed cash flows ranging from a negative $871,000 to a positive

$297,000 at the end of each month completing the year after the buyout with a projected $53,000 cash surplus in April 1983.

Despite the positive cash flow at the end of the year, and because of the projected one month deficit of $871,000, Tennenbaum concluded Crescent needed an additional $871,000 capital to operate assuming an average 30-day collection period. Tennenbaum also concluded that Crescent did not have "the reasonable prospect of being able to encumber sufficient assets to be able to borrow an additional $870,000 over and above what it had already borrowed from GECC and Federal." Exhibit 152 at 23. Therefore Tennenbaum concluded Crescent was undercapitalized.

Tennenbaum's opinion follows from his oft-stated belief that after the buyout, Crescent was fully encumbered and unable to borrow to cover short-term cash needs. Tennenbaum states that after the buyout it would be "difficult if not impossible [for Crescent] to arrange additional financing" and the "over-leveraged condition of Crescent precluded any reasonable probability of being able to borrow substantial amounts." Exhibit 152 at 12, 14. The court does not reach the same conclusion as Tennenbaum because after the buyout GECC agreed to increase its line of credit to Crescent by $2.5 million. The GECC decision was made after a study of Crescent's cash flow in July of 1982, which took into account projections of lower sales and a longer period of accounts receivable. Exhibit 50. GECC examined numbers similar to those produced by Tennenbaum and agreed to lend the funds. There could be no stronger evidence that Crescent had access to additional borrowing than GECC's decision to increase the line of credit. Consequently, Crescent did have the ability to borrow to cover a one month shortfall of $871,000. The $871,000 projected deficit would have been comprised largely of inventory and accounts receivable. Both were assets GECC was willing to loan funds against. Crescent's main cash flow problem, in Tennenbaum's analysis and in fact, was financing inventory and accounts receivable through the Thanksgiving-Christmas holiday season. After the holidays, Crescent would be back in the black. Tennenbaum's analysis showed Crescent with a $297,000 cash surplus in January when Crescent received payment for its holiday sales. In reviewing Tennenbaum's modifications of the GECC cash flow, it is clear that with the additional line of credit provided by GECC, Crescent had sufficient cash flow to pay its creditors and its debt service and keep operating. This was the conclusion of GECC in deciding to lend additional funds to Crescent and this is the conclusion of the court as well.

Plaintiff points to the fact that at the same time GECC extended the $2.5 million line of credit, GECC refused to extend a $350,000 term loan to Crescent. But GECC did extend a one month $100,000 loan to help finance inventory buildup for the peak season at Crescent. It was during that period, on October 13, 1985, that the strike disrupted Crescent's operations. Exhibit 56.

With 20-20 hindsight it is clear that Crescent's cash flows did not work out as projected by GECC. The strike in particular was a factor, hitting Crescent at the worst time of the year at a time when management clearly needed to be tending to arranging short-term financing, collecting accounts receivable and consolidating operations which was one of the efficiencies being implemented by the management. Instead, management was forced to worry about day-to-day operations, replacing striking workers, and maintaining the flow of business. The strike was a crippling blow from which Crescent never fully recovered according to the testimony received at trial.

As stated at the outset, the court's task in determining whether Crescent had sufficient capital as evidenced by cash flow projections is not to examine what happened to

Crescent, but whether the GECC projections, as modified, were prudent. The court finds that they were. GECC's analysis throughout, particularly the initial analysis of Crescent's business prospects in Exhibits 49A and 49C, convince the court that Crescent was not undercapitalized at the time of the buyout based on a review and an analysis of projected cash flows. Based on these projections, GECC was willing to lend substantial sums to Crescent both before and after the buyout. Plaintiff is correct (and it is obvious) that the projections were wrong and that Crescent had insufficient capital to withstand the strike and the other setbacks to Crescent's business. But the law does not require that companies be sufficiently well capitalized to withstand any and all setbacks to their business. The requirement is only that they not be left with "unreasonably small capital" at the time of the conveyance alleged as fraudulent. The cash flows prove that Crescent did have sufficient capital after the buyout to continue operating.

d. Crescent's Balance Sheet—Financial Ratios

Plaintiff's expert Tennenbaum examined a variety of financial ratios to show that Crescent was undercapitalized, though he concedes that because of increased reliance on leveraging, these traditional balance sheet ratios (e.g. debt/equity ratios) are less relevant today than they once were and that it is possible to overcome the negative conclusions of such ratios based on positive cash flow projections....

The court does not rely on these ratios in reaching its decision. First, plaintiff's own expert concedes that the negative implication of ratios can be overcome by a positive cash flow analysis. This view is consistent with the court's reliance on cash flow analysis above. Second, the evidence at trial casts serious doubt on the numbers plaintiff's expert used to produce the financial ratios. As the court has already stated, the $189,000 "loan" from TRAC to Crescent was in fact a contribution to capital. This adjustment in the balance sheet alone, deleting the loan as a liability because it did not have to be repaid, nearly doubles the capitalization of the company on the balance sheet. Additionally, the balance sheet understated the fair market value of Crescent's assets. There was repeated evidence presented that the value of the warehouse, carried on Crescent's books at $900,000, was worth about twice that amount. Plaintiff's own expert offered an opinion that the warehouse was worth $1.8 million. The book value of other assets was similarly below fair market value. Also, Crescent held a valuable asset in a cheese license from the United States Department of Agriculture which allowed Crescent to import cheese. Such licenses cannot be transferred and therefore have no market value in the traditional sense, but it is clear from the testimony that TRAC considered both the warehouse and the cheese licenses major assets of Crescent when TRAC agreed to purchase the company for over $1.4 million. Plaintiff Credit Managers too has recognized the value of the licenses, continuing to operate them for the benefit of creditors. The licenses, if they could be sold, according to defendant's expert, would have a value of $300,000. Other estimates were as high as $500,000. Despite the fact that they cannot be sold, they do generate a stream of income for plaintiff as they did for Crescent and have some value when analyzing Crescent's assets.

The upward adjustment in Crescent's assets, as compared to values reflected in the balance sheet and the downward adjustment in Crescent's liabilities due to the recharacterization of the TRAC loan, significantly effect most of the financial ratios computed by plaintiff's expert. For this reason, these computations are not relied on by the court in reaching its decision that Crescent was not undercapitalized after the May 7, 1982 leveraged buyout.

For all the above reasons, the court concludes that Crescent was not left undercapitalized after Crescent's stock was purchased by TRAC. This case presents the question of whether Crescent's former shareholder Federal was paid too much for Crescent's stock. Most of the case law examining leveraged buyouts examines the opposite question, whether shareholders, usually minority shareholders, were paid too little for their shares. E.g. Weinberger v. UOP, Inc., 457 A.2d 701 (Del.1983). Though these are different questions, they both require an examination of the value of a company to determine how much shareholders should get for their shares. A fraudulent conveyance case, of course, also involves an examination of the equity the new owners put into the company. Perhaps the ultimate test is whether the buyout gives shareholders a fair price for their shares—not too much creating fraudulent conveyance and other problems, and not too little leaving shareholders undercompensated. See McCune and Van Kirk, "Leveraged Buyouts by Management," 16 Rev. of Securities Regulation No. 22 at 769 (December 22, 1983). TRAC's principals testified at trial, as did GECC officials, that the buyout made sense and the prospects for Crescent at the time of the buyout were very good. TRAC purchased for book value an established company with assets carried on the books at below market value. There was no evidence at trial that the price paid for Crescent was out of line with what it was worth. There was substantial evidence that the transaction being attacked as fraudulent was, in fact, a fair transaction as a result of arms length negotiations between the seller Federal and the purchaser TRAC at a time when other potential purchasers were also interested in the company. The court concludes that the transaction should not be set aside.

V. UNLAWFUL DISTRIBUTION TO SHAREHOLDERS

Plaintiff's second claim is that the $10,904.41 monthly debt service payments to Federal pursuant to the Note and the Deed of Trust were unlawful distributions to shareholders in violation of California Corporations Code §§ 500 and 501. See Baird & Jackson, supra at 852 n. 51.

California Corporations Code § 506 states both who may bring an action under §§ 500 and 501 and against whom they may bring it. It provides that shareholders who knowingly received prohibited distributions are "liable to the corporation for the benefit of all the creditors." Cal.Corp.Code § 506(a). However, § 506(b) provides, "Suit may be brought in the name of the corporation to enforce the liability [of shareholders to creditors for violation of §§ 500 and 501] by any one or more creditors of the corporation whose debts or claims arose prior to the time of the distribution to shareholders." (emphasis added) Plaintiff Credit Managers is not a creditor of Crescent, it is an assignee for the benefit of creditors. Plaintiff argues that since creditors are the beneficiaries of the assignment to Credit Managers, Credit Managers may sue on their behalf. Plaintiff's Memorandum at 16, n. 10. Plaintiff's argument is not well taken. "In the absence of a statute conferring it, the assignee [Credit Managers] has no greater or better right of action than the assignor [Crescent] had or would have had if no assignment had been made." 6A C.J.S. Assign. Ben. Cred. § 106; Smith v. Kirkpatrick, 281 P. 616, 208 Cal. 417 (1929). Neither Crescent nor Credit Managers has a right of action under § 506. Only the creditors do.

By comparing the California fraudulent conveyance statute with the unlawful distribution to shareholders statute, it is clear that the legislature did not intend to give Credit Managers a right of action under § 506. The fraudulent conveyance statute begins by giving creditors a right of action. Cal.Civ.Code § 3439.09(a). It goes on to specifically provide a right of action for assignees of a general assignment for the benefit of creditors. Cal.Civ.Code § 3439.09(b). Corporations Code § 506 contains no similar provision authorizing suits by assignees.

Even if the court were to consider the unlawful distribution claim, it would fail for the reasons discussed below, and because of the value of Crescent's assets discussed supra.

VI. PAYMENTS ON THE NOTE

TRAC partially paid for Crescent's stock by executing a $1.2 million note in favor of Federal. Crescent signed the note and executed the Deed of Trust which placed a lien on the warehouse to secure the note. The court has concluded that the note and the lien were not fraudulent conveyances. Plaintiff also alleges that the monthly debt service payments on the note of $10,904.41 were fraudulent conveyances and, in addition, that these payments were unlawful distributions to shareholders. Plaintiff's arguments are not well taken. If the note and the lien are valid, so are the payments to reduce the amount of the note. The transfer to Federal can only be examined at the time Federal perfected its trust deed on the warehouse, May 7, 1982, not when the payments were made to reduce the note. In re Madrid, 725 F.2d 1197 (9th Cir.1984); Cf. In re Greenbrook Carpet, 722 F.2d 659 (11th Cir.1984). The fraudulent conveyance statute states that the creation of a lien is a "conveyance." Cal.Civ.Code § 3439.01. The payments on the note in this case merely reduce the amount of a valid lien. Finally, even if the court were to find the payments impermissible, the Deed of Trust would still be valid. Matter of National Tile and Terrazo Co., Inc., 537 F.2d 329 (9th Cir.1976). As Federal's $1.2 million note is secured by the warehouse, voiding the payments to Federal would simply increase the amount of the lien, leaving the parties in the same position in which they are currently. The court notes, in addition, that plaintiff did not present evidence at trial as to who was a creditor at the date of each payment to Federal as required by California Corporations Code § 506(b).

VII. EQUITABLE SUBORDINATION

Finally, plaintiff argues that the court should exercise its inherent equitable powers to subordinate Crescent's debt to Federal to Crescent's debts to its creditors. Consistent with the court's finding that the buyout was a valid and fair transaction and that Federal's Deed of Trust is valid, there is no equitable reason why Crescent's unsecured creditors should be favored over Federal, a secured creditor.

VIII. CONCLUSION

For all the reasons discussed above, the court finds and holds that TRAC's purchase of Crescent's stock from Federal by means of a leveraged buyout was neither a fraudulent conveyance nor an unlawful distribution to shareholders. Let judgment be entered accordingly.

Comments and Questions

1. The *Credit Managers* case has been rejected, or questioned, by some courts with respect to its views of the application of California's fraudulent Conveyance statute. *See* In re Morse Tool, Inc., 108 B.R. 389 (Bkrtcy.D.Mass.,1989). In In re Bay Plastics, Inc., 187 B.R. 315, 334 (Bankr.C.D.Cal. Sep 05, 1995) the court noted that: Most courts that have considered the issue have decided that fraudulent transfer law should apply to LBOs.... *See generally,* [4 James F. Queenan, Jr. et al., Chapter 11 Theory and Practice: A Guide to Reorganization ch. 27 (1994); 3 William L. Norton, Jr., Norton Bankruptcy Law and Practice ch. 58A (2d ed. 1994)]; In fact, despite the reservations expressed in... Credit Managers Ass'n of Southern California v. Federal Co., 629 F.Supp. 175 (C.D.Cal. 1985), there appears to be no published opinion to the contrary.

For a different view, see, Kaiser Steel Corp. v. Pearl Brewing Co. (In re Kaiser Steel Corp.), 952 F.2d 1230 (10th Cir.1991), cert. denied, 505 U.S. 1213, 112 S.Ct. 3015, 120 L.Ed.2d 887 (1992). In that case, the court held that the bankruptcy trustee could not recover from selling shareholders of a publicly traded corporation because the payments to the shareholders constituted non-avoidable "settlement payments" under Bankruptcy Code § 546(e), 11 U.S.C.A. § 546(e) (West 1993).

2. In Moody v. Security Pacific Business Credit, Inc., 971 F.2d 1056, 1072 (3rd Cir. 1992), the court interpreted *Credit Managers* to mean that the focus of the adequacy of capital inquiry in a leveraged buyout should be the reasonableness of the parties' cash flow projections, and the availability of credit to finance operations. The *Moody* court held that for purposes of applying the Uniform Fraudulent Conveyances Act, "the test for unreasonably small capital is reasonable foreseeability." As such, "The critical question is whether the parties' projections were reasonable." *Id.*, at 1073. The *Credit Managers* court suggested, 629 F.Supp. at 188–189, that its adequacy of capital analysis was essentially the same as the analysis required under California's approach to limiting unlawful distributions, § 500 et seq. Do you agree? Is the analysis compatible with the "impairment of capital" doctrine under Delaware law?

b. Revised Model Business Corporation Act

The California reforms proved to be quite influential. The Revised Business Corporation Act swept "away all the distinctions among the various types of surplus by retain[ed] restrictions on distributions built around both the traditional equity insolvency and balance sheet tests of earlier statutes."[1] As you review the Revised Model Business Corporation Act approach to the regulation of corporate capital, consider whether this approach is an improvement over the traditional approach of Delaware law or even the more 'modern' approach adopted by California.

Revised Model Business Corp. Act §6.21, 6.40 & Commentary

SUBCHAPTER B. ISSUANCE OF SHARES

§ 6.21 Issuance of Shares

(a) The powers granted in this section to the board of directors may be reserved to the shareholders by the articles of incorporation.

(b) The board of directors may authorize shares to be issued for consideration consisting of any tangible or intangible property or benefit to the corporation including cash, promissory notes, services performed, contracts for services to be performed, or other securities of the corporation.

(c) Before the corporation issues shares, the board of directors must determine that the consideration received or to be received for shares to be issued is adequate. That determination by the board of directors is conclusive insofar as the adequacy of consideration for the issuance of shares relates to whether the shares are validly issued, fully paid, and nonassessable.

1. Rev. Model Bus. Corp. Act § 6.40 (Official Comment).

(d) When the corporation receives the consideration for which the board of directors authorized the issuance of shares, the shares issued therefor are fully paid and nonassessable.

(e) The corporation may place in escrow shares issued for a contract for future services or benefits or a promissory note, or make other arrangements to restrict the transfer of the shares, and may credit distributions in respect of the shares against their purchase price, until the services are performed, the note is paid, or the benefits received. If the services are not performed, the note is not paid, or the benefits are not received, the shares escrowed or restricted and the distributions credited may be cancelled in whole or part.

OFFICIAL COMMENT

The financial provisions of the Model Act reflect a modernization of the concepts underlying the capital structure and limitations on distributions of corporations. This process of modernization began with amendments in 1980 to the 1969 Model Act that eliminated the concepts of "par value" and "stated capital," and further modernization occurred in connection with the development of the revised Act in 1984. Practitioners and legal scholars have long recognized that the statutory structure embodying "par value" and "legal capital" concepts is not only complex and confusing but also fails to serve the original purpose of protecting creditors and senior security holders from payments to junior security holders. Indeed, to the extent security holders are led to believe that it provides this protection, these provisions may be affirmatively misleading. The Model Act has therefore eliminated these concepts entirely and substituted a simpler and more flexible structure that provides more realistic protection to these interests. Major aspects of this new structure are:

(1) the provisions relating to the issuance of shares set forth in this and the following sections;

(2) the provisions limiting distributions by corporations set forth in section 6.40 and discussed in the Official Comment to that section; and

(3) the elimination of the concept of treasury shares described in the Official Comment to section 6.31.

Section 6.21 incorporates not only the elimination of the concepts of par value and stated capital from the Model Act in 1980 but also eliminates the earlier rule declaring certain kinds of property ineligible as consideration for shares. The caption of the section, "Issuance of Shares by the Board of Directors," reflects the change in emphasis from imposing restrictions on the issuance of shares to establishing general principles for their issuance. The section replaces two sections captioned, respectively, "Consideration for Shares" (section 18) and "Payment for Shares" (section 19) in the 1969 Model Act.

Since shares need not have a par value, under section 6.21 there is no minimum price at which specific shares must be issued and therefore there can be no "watered stock" liability for issuing shares below an arbitrarily fixed price. The price at which shares are issued is primarily a matter of concern to other shareholders whose interests may be diluted if shares are issued at unreasonably low prices or for overvalued property. This problem of equality of treatment essentially involves honest and fair judgments by directors and cannot be effectively addressed by an arbitrary doctrine establishing a minimum price for shares such as "par value" provided under older statutes.

Section 6.21(b) specifically validates contracts for future services (including promoters' services), promissory notes, or "any tangible or intangible property or benefit to the corporation," as consideration for the present issue of shares. The term "benefit" should be broadly construed to include, for example, a reduction of a liability, a release of a claim, or benefits obtained by a corporation by contribution of its shares to a charitable organization or as a prize in a promotion. In the realities of commercial life, there is sometimes a need for the issuance of shares for contract rights or such intangible property or benefits. And, as a matter of business economics, contracts for future services, promissory notes, and intangible property or benefits often have value that is as real as the value of tangible property or past services, the only types of property that many older statutes permit as consideration for shares. Thus, only business judgment should determine what kind of property should be obtained for shares, and a determination by the directors meeting the requirements of section 8.30 to accept a specific kind of valuable property for shares should be accepted and not circumscribed by artificial or arbitrary rules.

The issuance of some shares for cash and other shares for promissory notes, contracts for past or future services, or for tangible or intangible property or benefits, like the issuance of shares for an inadequate consideration, opens the possibility of dilution of the interests of other shareholders. For example, persons acquiring shares for cash may be unfairly treated if optimistic values are placed on past or future services or intangible benefits being provided by other persons. The problem is particularly acute if the persons providing services, promissory notes, or property or benefits of debatable value are themselves connected with the promoters of the corporation or with its directors. Protection of shareholders against abuse of the power granted to the board of directors to determine that shares should be issued for intangible property or benefits is provided in part by the requirement that the board must act in accordance with the requirements of section 8.30, and, if applicable, section 8.31, in determining that the consideration received for shares is adequate, and in part by the requirement of section 16.21 that the corporation must inform all shareholders annually of all shares issued during the previous year for promissory notes or promises of future services.

Accounting principles are not specified in the Model Act, and the board of directors is not required by the statute to determine the "value" of noncash consideration received by the corporation (as was the case in earlier versions of the Model Act). In many instances, property or benefit received by the corporation will be of uncertain value; if the board of directors determines that the issuance of shares for the property or benefit is an appropriate transaction that protects the shareholders from dilution, that is sufficient under section 6.21. The board of directors does not have to make an explicit "adequacy" determination by formal resolution; that determination may be inferred from a determination to authorize the issuance of shares for a specified consideration.

Section 6.21 also does not require that the board of directors determine the value of the consideration to be entered on the books of the corporation, though the board of directors may do so if it wishes. Of course, a specific value must be placed on the consideration received for the shares for bookkeeping purposes, but bookkeeping details are not the statutory responsibility of the board of directors. The statute also does not require the board of directors to determine the corresponding entry on the right-hand side of the balance sheet under owner's equity to be designated as "stated capital" or be allocated among "stated capital" and other surplus accounts. The corporation, however, may determine that the shareholders' equity accounts should be divided into these traditional categories if it wishes.

The second sentence of section 6.21(c) describes the effect of the determination by the board of directors that consideration is adequate for the issuance of shares. That determination, without more, is conclusive to the extent that adequacy is relevant to the question whether the shares are validly issued, fully paid, and nonassessable. Section 6.21(c) provides that shares are fully paid and nonassessable when the corporation receives the consideration for which the board of directors authorized their issuance. Whether shares are validly issued may depend on compliance with corporate procedural requirements, such as issuance within the amount authorized in the articles of incorporation or holding a directors' meeting upon proper notice and with a quorum present. The Model Act does not address the remedies that may be available for issuances that are subject to challenge. This somewhat more elaborate clause replaces the provision in earlier versions of the Model Act and many state statutes that the determination by the board of directors of consideration for the issuance of shares was "conclusive in the absence of fraud in the transaction."

Shares issued pursuant to preincorporation subscriptions are governed by section 6.20 and not this section.

The revised Model Act does not address the question whether validly issued shares may thereafter be cancelled on the grounds of fraud or bad faith if the shares are in the hands of the original shareholder or other persons who were aware of the circumstances under which they were issued when they acquired the shares. It also leaves to the Uniform Commercial Code other questions relating to the rights of persons other than the person acquiring the shares from the corporation. See the Official Comment to section 6.22.

Section 6.21(e) permits the board of directors to determine that shares issued for promissory notes or for contracts for future services or benefits be placed in escrow or their transfer otherwise restricted until the services are performed, the benefits received, or the notes are paid. The section also defines the rights of the corporation with respect to these shares. If the shares are issued without being restricted as provided in this subsection, they are validly issued insofar as the adequacy of consideration is concerned. See section 6.22 and its Official Comment.

Section 6.21(a) provides that the powers granted to the board of directors by this section may be reserved to the shareholders by the articles of incorporation. No negative inference should be drawn from section 6.21(a) with respect to the efficacy of similar Provisions under other sections of the Model Act.

SUBCHAPTER D. DISTRIBUTIONS

§6.40 Distributions to Shareholders

(a) A board of directors may authorize and the corporation may make distributions to its shareholders subject to restriction by the articles of incorporation and the limitation in subsection (c).

(b) If the board of directors does not fix the record date for determining shareholders entitled to a distribution (other than one involving a purchase, redemption, or other acquisition of the corporation's shares), it is the date the board of directors authorizes the distribution.

(c) No distribution may be made if, after giving it effect:

(1) the corporation would not be able to pay its debts as they become due in the usual course of business; or

(2) the corporation's total assets would be less than the sum of its total liabilities plus (unless the articles of incorporation permit otherwise) the amount that would be needed, if the corporation were to be dissolved at the time of the distribution, to satisfy the preferential rights upon dissolution of shareholders whose preferential rights are superior to those receiving the distribution.

(d) The board of directors may base a determination that a distribution is not prohibited under subsection (c) either on financial statements prepared on the basis of accounting practices and principles that are reasonable in the circumstances or on a fair valuation or other method that is reasonable in the circumstances.

(e) Except as provided in subsection (g), the effect of a distribution under subsection (c) is measured:

(l) in the case of distribution by purchase, redemption, or other acquisition of the corporation's shares, as of the earlier of (i) the date money or other property is transferred or debt incurred by the corporation or (ii) the date the shareholder ceases to be a shareholder with respect to the acquired shares;

(2) in the case of any other distribution of indebtedness, as of the date the indebtedness is distributed;

(3) in all other cases, as of (i) the date the distribution is authorized if the payment occurs within 120 days after the date of authorization or (ii) the date the payment is made if it occurs more than 120 days after the date of authorization.

(f) A corporation's indebtedness to a shareholder incurred by reason of a distribution made in accordance with this section is at parity with the corporation's indebtedness to its general, unsecured creditors except to the extent subordinated by agreement.

(g) Indebtedness of a corporation, including indebtedness issued as a distribution, is not considered a liability for purposes of determinations under subsection (c) if its terms provide that payment of principal and interest are made only if and to the extent that payment of a distribution to shareholders could then be made under this section. If the indebtedness is issued as a distribution, each payment of principal or interest is treated as a distribution, the effect of which is measured on the date the payment is actually made.

OFFICIAL COMMENT

The reformulation of the statutory standards governing distributions is another important change made by the 1980 revisions to the financial provisions of the Model Act. It has long been recognized that the traditional "par value" and "stated capital" statutes do not provide significant protection against distributions of capital to shareholders. While most of these statutes contained elaborate provisions establishing "stated capital," "capital surplus," and "earned surplus" (and often other types of surplus as well), the net effect of most statutes was to permit the distribution to shareholders of most or all of the corporation's net assets—its capital along with its earnings—if the shareholders wished this to be done. However, statutes also generally imposed an equity insolvency test on distributions that prohibited distributions of assets if the corporation was insolvent or if the distribution had the effect of making the corporation insolvent or unable to meet its obligations as they were projected to arise.

The financial provisions of the revised Model Act, which are based on the 1980 amendments, sweep away all the distinctions among the various types of surplus but retain restrictions on distributions built around both the traditional equity insolvency and balance sheet tests of earlier statutes.

1. The Scope of Section 6.40

Section 1.40 defines "distribution" to include virtually all transfers of money, indebtedness of the corporation or other property to a shareholder in respect of the corporation's shares. It thus includes cash or property dividends, payments by a corporation to purchase its own shares, distributions of promissory notes or indebtedness, and distributions in partial or complete liquidation or voluntary or involuntary dissolution. Section 1.40 excludes from the definition of "distribution" transactions by the corporation in which only its own shares are distributed to its shareholders. These transactions are called "share dividends" in the revised Model Business Corporation Act. See section 6.23.

Section 6.40 imposes a single, uniform test on all distributions. Many of the old "par value" and "stated capital" statute provided tests that varied with the type of distribution under consideration or did not cover certain types of distributions at all.

Equity Insolvency Test

As noted above, older statutes prohibited payment of dividends if the corporation was, or as a result of the payment would be, insolvent in the equity sense. This test is retained, appearing in section 6.40(c)(1).

In most cases involving a corporation operating as a going concern in the normal course, information generally available will make it quite apparent that no particular inquiry concerning the equity insolvency test is needed. While neither a balance sheet nor an income statement can be conclusive as to this test, the existence of significant shareholders' equity and normal operating conditions are of themselves a strong indication that no issue should arise under that test. Indeed, in the case of a corporation having regularly audited financial statements, the absence of any qualification in the most recent auditor's opinion as to the corporation's status as a "going concern," coupled with a lack of subsequent adverse events, would normally be decisive.

It is only when circumstances indicate that the corporation is encountering difficulties or is in an uncertain position concerning its liquidity and operations that the board of directors or, more commonly, the officers or others upon whom they may place reliance under section 8.30(b), may need to address the issue. Because of the overall judgment required in evaluating the equity insolvency test, no one or more "bright line" tests can be employed. However, in determining whether the equity insolvency test has been met, certain judgments or assumptions as to the future course of the corporation's business are customarily justified, absent clear evidence to the contrary. These include the likelihood that (a) based on existing and contemplated demand for the corporation's products or services, it will be able to generate funds over a period of time sufficient to satisfy its existing and reasonably anticipated obligations as they mature, and (b) indebtedness which matures in the near-term will be refinanced where, on the basis of the corporation's financial condition and future prospects and the general availability of credit to businesses similarly situated, it is reasonable to assume that such refinancing may be accomplished. To the extent that the corporation may be subject to asserted or unasserted contingent liabilities, reasonable judgments as to the likelihood, amount, and time of any recovery against the corporation, after giving consideration to the extent to which the corporation is insured or otherwise protected against loss, may be utilized. There may be occasions when it would be useful to consider a cash flow analysis. based on a business forecast and budget, covering a sufficient period of time to permit a conclusion that known obligations of the corporation can reasonably be expected to be satisfied over the period of time that they will mature.

In exercising their judgment, the directors are entitled to rely, under section 8.30(b) as noted above, on information, opinions, reports, and statements prepared by others. Ordinarily, they should not be expected to become involved in the details of the various analyses or market or economic projections that may be relevant. Judgments must of necessity be made on the basis of information in the hands of the directors when a distribution is authorized. They should not, of course, be held responsible as a matter of hindsight for unforeseen developments. This is particularly true with respect to assumptions as to the ability of the corporation's business to repay long-term obligations which do not mature for several years, since the primary focus of the directors' decision to make a distribution should normally be on the corporation's prospects and obligations in the shorter term, unless special factors concerning the corporation's prospects require the taking of a longer term perspective.

3. Relationship to the Federal Bankruptcy Act and Other Fraudulent Conveyance Statutes

The revised Model Business Corporation Act establishes the validity of distributions from the corporate law standpoint under section 6.40 and determines the potential liability of directors for improper distributions under sections 8.30 and 8.33. The federal Bankruptcy Act and state fraudulent conveyance statutes, on the other hand, are designed to enable the trustee or other representative to recapture for the benefit of creditors funds distributed to others in some circumstances. In light of these diverse purposes, it was not thought necessary to make the tests of section 6.40 identical with the tests for insolvency under these various statutes.

4. Balance Sheet Test

Section 6.40(c)(2) requires that, after giving effect to any distribution, the corporation's assets equal or exceed its liabilities plus (with some exceptions) the dissolution preferences of senior equity securities. Section 6.40(d) authorizes asset and liability determinations to be made for this purpose on the basis of either (l) financial statements prepared on the basis of accounting practices and principles that are reasonable in the circumstances or (2) a fair valuation or other method that is reasonable in the circumstances. The determination of a corporation's assets and liabilities and the choice of the permissible basis on which to do so are left to the judgment of its board of directors. In making a judgment under section 6.40(d), the board may rely under section 8.30 upon opinions, reports, or statements, including financial statements and other financial data prepared or presented by public accountants or others.

Section 6.40 does not utilize particular accounting terminology of a technical nature or specify particular accounting concepts. In making determinations under this section, the board of directors may make judgments about accounting matters, giving full effect to its right to rely upon professional or expert opinion.

In a corporation with subsidiaries, the board of directors may rely on unconsolidated statements prepared on the basis of the equity method of accounting (see American Institute of Certified Public Accountants. APB Opinion No. 18 (1971)) as to the corporation's investee corporations, including corporate joint ventures and subsidiaries, although other evidence would be relevant in the total determination.

a. Generally accepted accounting principles

The board of directors should in all circumstances be entitled to rely upon reasonably current financial statements prepared on the basis of generally accepted accounting principles in determining whether or not the balance sheet test of section 6.40(c)(2) has been met, unless the board is then aware that it would be unreasonable to rely on the financial statements because of newly discovered or subsequently arising facts or circumstances. But section 6.40 does not mandate the use of generally accepted accounting principles; it only requires the use of accounting practices and principles that are reasonable in the circumstances. While publicly-owned corporations subject to registration under the Securities Exchange Act of 1934 must, and many other corporations in fact do, utilize financial statements prepared on the basis of generally accepted accounting principles, a great number of smaller or closely-held corporations do not. Some of these corporations maintain records solely on a tax accounting basis and their financial statements are of necessity prepared on that basis. Others prepare financial statements that substantially reflect generally accepted accounting principles but may depart from them in some respects (e.g., footnote disclosure). These facts of corporate life indicate that a statutory standard of reasonableness, rather than stipulating generally accepted accounting principles as the normative standard, is appropriate in order to achieve a reasonable degree of flexibility and to accommodate the needs of the many different types of business corporations which might be subject to these provisions, including in particular closely-held corporations. Accordingly, the revised Model Business Corporation Act contemplates that generally acceptable accounting principles are always "reasonable in the circumstances" and that other accounting principles may be perfectly acceptable, under a general standard of reasonableness, even if they do not involve the "fair value" or "current value" concepts that are also contemplated by section 6.40(d).

b. Other principles

Section 6.40(d) specifically permits determinations to be made under section 6.40(c)(2) on the basis of a fair valuation or other method that is reasonable in the circumstances. Thus the statute authorizes departures from historical cost accounting and sanctions the use of appraisal and current value methods to determine the amount available for distributions. No particular method of valuation is prescribed in the statute, since different methods may have validity depending upon the circumstances, including the type of enterprise and the purpose for which the determination is made. For example, it is inappropriate to apply a "quick-sale liquidation" method to value an enterprise, particularly with respect to the payment of normal dividends. On the other hand, a "quicksale liquidation valuation" method might be appropriate in certain circumstances for an enterprise in the course of reducing its asset or business base by a material degree. In most cases, a fair valuation method or a going-concern basis would be appropriate if it is believed that the enterprise will continue as a going concern.

Ordinarily a corporation should not selectively revalue assets. It should consider the value of all of its material assets, whether or not reflected in the financial statements (e.g., a valuable executory contract). Likewise, all of a corporation's material obligations should be considered and revalued to the extent appropriate and possible. In any event, section 6.40(d) calls for the application under section 6.40(c)(2) of a method of determining the aggregate amount of assets and liabilities that is reasonable in the circumstances.

Section 6.40(d) also refers to some "other method that is reasonable in the circumstances." This phrase is intended to comprehend within section 6.40(c)(2) the wide variety of possibilities that might not be considered to fall under a "fair valuation" but might be reasonable in the circumstances of a particular case.

5. Preferential Dissolution Rights and the Balance Sheet Test

Section 6.40(c)(2) provides that a distribution may not be made unless the total assets of the corporation exceed its liabilities plus the amount that would be needed to satisfy any shareholders' superior preferential rights upon dissolution if the corporation were to be dissolved at the time of the distribution. This requirement in effect treats preferential dissolution rights of shares for distribution purposes as if they were liabilities for the sole purpose of determining the amount available for distributions, and carries forward analogous treatment of shares having preferential dissolution rights from earlier versions of the Model Act. In making the calculation of the amount that must be added to the liabilities of the corporation to reflect the preferential dissolution rights, the assumption should be made that the preferential dissolution rights are to be established pursuant to the articles of incorporation, as of the date of the distribution or proposed distribution. The amount so determined must include arrearages in preferential dividends if the articles of incorporation require that they be paid upon the dissolution of the corporation. In the case of shares having both a preferential right upon dissolution and other nonpreferential rights, only the preferential right should be taken into account. The treatment of preferential dissolution rights of classes of shares set forth in section 6.40(c)(2) is applicable only to the balance sheet test and is not applicable to the equity insolvency test of section 6.40(c)(2). The treatment of preferential rights mandated by this section may always be eliminated by an appropriate provision in the articles of incorporation.

6. Time of Measurement

Section 6.40(e)(3) provides that the time for measuring the effect of a distribution for compliance with the equity insolvency and balance sheet tests for all distributions not involving the reacquisition of shares or the distribution of indebtedness is the date of authorization, if the payment occurs within 120 days following the authorization; if the payment occurs more than 120 days after the authorization, however, the date of payment must be used. If the corporation elects to make a distribution in the form of its own indebtedness under section 6.40(e)(2), the validity of that distribution must be measured as of the time of distribution unless the indebtedness qualifies under section 6.40(g).

Section 6.40(e)(1) provides a different rule for the time of measurement when the distribution involves a reacquisition of shares. See below, Application to Reacquisition of Shares—Time of measurement.

7. Record Date

Section 6.40(b) fixes the record date (if the board of directors does not otherwise fix it) for distributions other than those involving a reacquisition of shares as the date the board of directors authorizes the distribution. No record date is necessary for a reacquisition of shares from one or more specific shareholders. The board of directors has discretion to set a record date for a reacquisition if it is to be pro rata and to be offered to all shareholders as of a specified date.

8. Application to Repurchases or Redemption of Shares

The application of the equity insolvency and balance sheet tests to distributions that involve the purchase, redemption, or other acquisition of shares creates unique problems; section 6.40 provides specific rules for the resolution of these problems as described below.

a. Time of measurement

Section 6.40(e)(1) provides that the time for measuring the effect of a distribution under section 6.40(c), if shares of the corporation are reacquired, is the earlier of (i) the payment date, or (ii) the date the shareholder ceased to be a shareholder with respect to the shares, except as provided in section 6.40(g).

b. When tests are applied to redemption-related debt

In an acquisition of its shares, a corporation may transfer property or incur debt to the former holder of the shares. The case law on the status of this debt is conflicting. However, share repurchase agreements involving payment for shares over a period of time are of special importance in closely held corporate enterprises. Section 6.40(e) provides a clear rule for this situation: the legality of the distribution must be measured at the time of the issuance or incurrence of the debt, not at a later date when the debt is actually paid. Of course, this does not preclude a later challenge of a payment on account of redemption related debt by a bankruptcy trustee on the ground that it constitutes a preferential payment to a creditor.

c. Priority of debt distributed directly or incurred in connection with a reacquisition of shares

Section 6.40(f) provides that indebtedness created to acquire the corporation's shares or issued as a distribution is on a parity with the indebtedness of the corporation to its general, unsecured creditors, except to the extent subordinated by agreement. General creditors are better off in these situations than they would have been if cash or other property had been paid out for the shares or distributed (which is proper under the statute), and no worse off than if cash had been paid or distributed and then lent back to the corporation, making the shareholders (or former shareholders) creditors. The parity created by section 6.40(f) is logically consistent with the rule established by section 6.40(e) that these transactions should be judged at the time of the issuance of the debt.

d. Treatment of certain indebtedness

Section 6.40(g) provides that indebtedness need not be taken into account as a liability in determining whether the tests of section 6.40(c) have been met if the terms of the indebtedness provide that payments of principal or interest can be made only if and to the extent that payment of a distribution could then be made under section 6.40. This has the effect of making the holder of the indebtedness junior to all other creditors but senior to the holders of all classes of shares, not only during the time the corporation is operating but also upon dissolution and liquidation. It should be noted that the creation of such indebtedness, and the related limitations on payments of principal and interest, may create tax problems or raise other legal questions.

Although section 6.40(g) is applicable to all indebtedness meeting its tests, regardless of the circumstances of its issuance, it is anticipated that it will be applicable most frequently to permit the reacquisition of shares of the corporation at a time when the deferred purchase price exceeds the net worth of the corporation. This type of reacquisition will often be necessary in the case of businesses in early stages of development or service businesses whose value derives principally from existing or prospective net income or cash flow rather than from net asset value. In such situations, it is anticipated that net worth will grow over time from operations so that when payments in respect of the indebtedness are to be made the two insolvency tests will be satisfied. In the meantime, the fact that the indebtedness is outstanding will not prevent distributions that could be made under subsection (c) if the indebtedness were not counted in making the determination.

Comments and Questions

1. The Revised Model Business Corporation Act approach is meant to sweep away the artifice of the traditional American approaches to the regulation of corporate capital and substitute a simple, efficient and equitable system in its place. But let us consider the extent to which the Revised Model Business Corporation Act approach actually succeeds. The balance sheet test provides a measure of certainty in the determination of capital available for distribution. Are there issues of precision with respect to the application of the balance sheet test? Can changing assumptions under GAAP affect the results under the balance sheet test?

2. The equity insolvency test may have its own problems of precision. How precisely or uniformly can the equity insolvency test be applied by a board of directors? How much guidance does a board of directors have with respect to the application of the equity insolvency test. Does the equity insolvency test require the board of directors effectively to guess in cases where a corporation is close to solvency? What exposure does a board of directors face if a court, after the fact, determines that the board of directors 'guessed wrong' with respect to the solvency of the corporation at the time the distribution was declared? Paid?

3. From the perspective of lenders, the imprecision and potential exposure of a board of directors to liability for careless or too aggressive an application of the balance sheet or equity insolvency tests, is a positive benefit of the Revised Model Business Corporation Act approach. Such imprecision may force a board of directors to act much more conservatively in its assumptions and calculations to avoid or minimize the risk of liability. This should be especially true in cases of marginally solvent corporations. The result should be a tendency to reduce distributions to shareholders in such cases. But, from the perspective of corporate actors, this result may be less satisfactory. The approach ultimately depends on courts to pass on the judgments of the board with respect to distributions. It is possible that courts would be willing in these circumstances to substitute their judgment for that of the board of directors. Will the effect of this approach produce the sort of interference in the internal affairs of corporations that American courts have sought to avoid? Will your answer depend on the applicability of the business judgment rule to distribution determinations using the balance sheet and equity insolvency tests of the Revised Model Business Corporation Act?

4. Even if the business judgment rule is not applicable, can the board of directors minimize their exposure to liability by effecting an addition to the articles of incorporation limiting their liability for breaches of the duty of care? See Rev. Model Bus. Corp. Act § 202(b)(4).[2] Would this protection in the articles of incorporation aid the director who is also a shareholder receiving a portion of the distribution?

---

2. The articles of incorporation may include "a provision eliminating or limiting the liability of a director to the corporation or its shareholders for money damages for any action taken, or any failure to take any action, as a director, except liability for (A) the amount of a financial benefit received by a director to which he is not entitled; (B) an intentional infliction of harm on the corporation or the shareholders; (C) a violation of section 8.33 [liability for unlawful distributions under section 6.40]; or (D) an intentional violation of criminal law...." Rev. Model Bus. Corp. Act § 2.02(b)(4).

Compare the Delaware exculpatory provision, Del. Gen. Corp. L. § 102(b)(7), which permits shareholders to adopt a provision in the articles of incorporation eliminating or limiting director liability for breaches of fiduciary duty other than for breaches of the duty of loyalty, for bad faith acts or intentional misconduct, for unlawful payments of dividends or stock repurchases under Del. Gen. Corp. L. § 174, or any transaction in which the director derived an improper personal benefit.

5. The Official Comment Section 8.33 states that in an action under § 8.33, a director should have "all defense which would ordinarily be available, including the common law business judgment rule." REV. MODEL BUS. CORP. ACT § 8.33 (Official Comment). How would this change your answer to the question in Note 4, above?

6. The case that follows, *C-T of Virginia, Inc.* picks up on an issue that had proven troublesome under the California approach in *Credit Managers of Southern California*—the applicability of the unlawful distribution rules in leveraged buy-outs. Leveraged buy-outs prove an excellent context for testing the utility of legal capital regimes in protecting creditors. As you read the *C-T of Virginia* case, consider the effectiveness the Revised Model Business Corporation Act approach in this context.

In re C-T of Virginia, Incorporated, formerly known as Craddock-Terry Shoe Corporation, Debtor

958 F.2d 606 (4th Cir. 1992)

WILKINSON, Circuit Judge:

This case presents the question of whether the leveraged acquisition of a corporation, structured in the form of a cash-out merger and consummated at arm's length, is subject to restrictions on distributions to shareholders under Virginia law. The case involves an action brought by an official committee of unsecured creditors of a corporation now in bankruptcy against the former directors of that corporation. The creditors, suing on behalf of the corporation, claimed that the leveraged acquisition created an illegal distribution to shareholders under the Virginia Stock Corporation Act, Va.Code Ann. § 13.1-601 *et seq.* (Michie 1989). We agree with the district court that the merger did not create a distribution under Virginia law and therefore affirm its judgment.

I.

The facts underlying this case are not in dispute. C-T of Virginia, Inc., formerly Craddock-Terry Shoe Corp., is a Virginia corporation engaged in the manufacture, wholesale, and mail-order sale of shoes. Prior to the purchase that is the subject of this action, C-T was a publicly owned corporation whose stock was traded on the over-the-counter market. In April 1985, C-T hired a financial adviser, Prudential-Bache Securities, Inc., to study the strategic alternatives available to the company. Prudential recommended that C-T's management pursue a leveraged buyout ("LBO") of the company. Prudential indicated that an LBO would both realize maximum value for C-T's shareholders and maintain the viability of the post-LBO enterprise.

On May 20, 1985, C-T's board of directors accepted Prudential's recommendation and authorized management to explore the possibility of a management-sponsored LBO at $15 per share. (C-T common stock was trading for $14.25 per share when this authorization was announced.) The board retained the right to consider other proposals made to the corporation. On June 12, 1985, Southwestern General Corp. made such an unsolicited offer, which proposed a merger at $17.50 per share. Southwestern withdrew this offer on August 26, 1985, however, after President Reagan refused to impose limitations on shoe imports.

C-T received a second unsolicited offer on November 11, 1985, from HH Holdings, Inc. Holdings is a Delaware holding company owned by Sidney Kimmel and Alan Salke. Neither Holdings, Kimmel, nor Salke had any prior relationship or contact with C-T or the members of its board of directors. Holdings proposed a cash merger in which C-T shareholders would receive $19 per share of common stock. After the directors announced this offer, several owners of substantial amounts of C-T common stock urged that the directors reject the offer and demand $20 per share instead. Holdings agreed to the merger at $20 per share, and an Agreement in Principle was signed on December 11, 1985.

The parties formalized the transaction in an Agreement and Plan of Merger executed on January 24, 1986. The merger agreement structured the purchase in the form of a reverse triangular merger. For purposes of the merger, Holdings formed HH Acquisition, Inc., a wholly owned subsidiary. The merger agreement provided that on April 30, 1986, Acquisition would merge into C-T, leaving C-T as the surviving corporation wholly owned by Holdings. The funds necessary to purchase all outstanding shares of C-T, about $30 million, would be deposited with the exchange agent, Sovran Bank, before or at the closing of the transaction. At the moment that the merger was effected, the outstanding shares of C-T common stock would be automatically canceled, and the former shareholders would receive the right to submit their canceled stock certificates to Sovran for payment of $20 per canceled share. Also at that time, the directors of C-T would resign and be replaced by Salke, John W. Baker, and Roland K. Peters.

The financing for the merger was arranged solely by Holdings. Holdings provided about $4 million of its own money. It obtained the balance, approximately $26 million, in the form of bank loans secured by C-T's assets. The pre-merger directors did not solicit proposed financing, negotiate the terms of the financing or of the security, or participate in or authorize the encumbering of C-T's assets. The merger agreement did obligate C-T to provide Holdings, Acquisition, and the financing banks access to C-T's properties, personnel, and books and records and to cooperate with Holdings' efforts to secure financing. Further, the pre-merger directors approved the repurchase of C-T's preferred stock, which was a prerequisite to effectuation of the merger.

C-T's board of directors approved the merger agreement and unanimously voted to recommend that the shareholders approve the merger, which they did on April 17, 1986. The transaction was consummated as planned on April 30. The surviving corporation struggled along for about eighteen months, and it filed for bankruptcy under Chapter 11 on October 21, 1987.

In October 1989, the Official Committee of Unsecured Creditors of C-T filed this action in federal court against the pre-merger directors and officers of the corporation. The complaint alleged that the directors and officers breached their fiduciary duties owed to the corporation and that the directors had approved a distribution in violation of Va.Code Ann. §§ 13.1-653 and 13.1-692 (Michie 1989). The district court granted the defendants' motion to dismiss the former claim. 124 B.R. 689, 692–93 (W.D.Va.1990). It denied the directors' motion to dismiss the unlawful distribution claim, however, finding that under some factual circumstances the merger might have been a distribution. Id. at 693–94.

Subsequently, the district court granted the directors' motion for summary judgment on the illegal distribution claim. 124 B.R. 694 (W.D.Va.1990). The court found application of the restriction on distributions "inconsistent with Virginia's statutory scheme," because the merger provisions of the Virginia Stock Corporation Act—unlike the sale of corporate assets provisions, *see* Va.Code Ann. § 13.1-724 (Michie 1989)—"make[ ] no mention of distributions." 124 B.R. at 696–97. The court also concluded that the transaction was not "a distribution clothed in the garb of a merger" to evade the distribution restrictions. Id. at 697. The court concluded, finally, that, even if the merger involved a distribution, the directors did not "vote[ ] for or assent[ ] to" it, a prerequisite to liability under Va.Code Ann. § 13.1-692(A) (Michie 1989). For the latter holding, the court relied on the fact that the directors did not authorize the encumbering of C-T's assets, which occurred after they had resigned their offices. 124 B.R. at 699.

C-T appeals the summary judgment against it on the distribution claim.

II.

Modern distribution statutes derive from eighteenth century restrictions on when a corporation could pay dividends to its shareholders. *See* Revised Model Business Corporation Act § 6.40 historical note 1 (1986) (hereinafter RMBCA). Restrictions on a corporation's purchase of its own shares, and on other forms of distributions, were enacted later. *See* J. Choper, J. Coffee, & C. Morris, *Cases and Materials on Corporations* 1007 (3d ed. 1989). All states now impose limitations on the power of a corporation to make various distributions to its shareholders, *see* RMBCA § 6.40 statutory comparison 1, and federal courts must, of course, pay strict attention to the language of the relevant state statute.

Virginia's corporate law statute, including the distribution provisions, was substantially revised in 1985. *See* 1985 Va. Acts 868 (codified at Va.Code Ann. §§ 13.1-601 to -800 (Michie 1989)). The Virginia statute defines "distribution" as follows:

> "*Distribution*" means a direct or indirect transfer of money or other property, except its own shares, or incurrence of indebtedness by a corporation to or for the benefit of its shareholders in respect of any of its shares. A distribution may be in the form of a declaration or payment of a dividend; a purchase, redemption, or other acquisition of shares; a distribution of indebtedness of the corporation; or otherwise.

Va.Code Ann. § 13.1-603 (Michie 1989). Not all distributions are unlawful. Rather, a distribution is prohibited only if, after it is made, the corporation fails either of two insolvency tests:

> No distribution may be made if, after giving it effect:
>
> 1. The corporation would not be able to pay its debts as they become due in the usual course of business; or
>
> 2. The corporation's total assets would be less than the sum of its total liabilities plus (unless the articles of incorporation permit otherwise) the amount that would be needed, if the corporation were to be dissolved at the time of the distribution, to satisfy the preferential rights upon dissolution of shareholders whose preferential rights are superior to those receiving the distribution.

Id. § 13.1-653(C).

Directors face potential personal liability when the corporation makes an unlawful distribution:

> Unless he complies with the applicable standards of conduct described in § 13.1-690,[3] a director who votes for or assents to a distribution made in violation of this

3. Section 13.1-690 establishes, *inter alia*, the following standard of conduct for directors: "A director shall discharge his duties as a director, including his duties as a member of a committee, in accordance with his good faith business judgment of the best interests of the corporation." Va.Code Ann. § 13.1-690(A) (Michie 1989). Because we hold that the merger in this case was not a distribution, we need not consider whether the actions of C-T's pre-merger directors satisfied § 13.1-690

chapter or the articles of incorporation is personally liable to the corporation and its creditors for the amount of the distribution that exceeds what could have been distributed without violating this chapter or the articles of incorporation.

Id. § 13.1-692(A). There is, however, no provision in the Virginia Stock Corporation Act by which creditors can recover a distribution from the shareholders directly. Rather, a creditor's only remedy is against the directors, who then may seek contribution from shareholders who received the distribution. *Id.* § 13.1-692(B)(2).

III.

We now address the central question in this case: whether the merger involved a distribution to shareholders within the meaning of § 13.1-603. For the reasons set forth below, we conclude that the transaction does not fall within the statutory definition of distribution and, therefore, that the directors cannot be subjected to potential liability under § 13.1-692.[4]

A.

Appellant argues that the plain meaning of the statute contradicts the district court's conclusion that the merger did not create a distribution under Virginia law. It claims that the purchase of the pre-merger shareholders' shares in C-T entailed a distribution because the payment of the purchase price of $20 per share was a "transfer of money... by a corporation to... its shareholders." Since this purchase was funded primarily through loans secured by the assets of C-T, the argument runs, the value of the corporation—and hence the financial position of its creditors—was diminished. According to appellant, it is irrelevant whether the funds that are transferred to shareholders derive from the corporation's capital surplus, retained earnings, or new loans secured by corporate assets, and it is likewise immaterial that the payment resulted from a cash-out merger; appellant claims that the legislature intended the statute to have "the broadest range of inclusion" and thereby "pick up all forms of transfer of the assets of a corporation to its shareholders."

We do not share appellant's view of the statute. The Virginia Stock Corporation Act provides a precise definition of the word "distribution": "[A] direct or indirect transfer of money or other property, except its own shares, or incurrence of indebtedness by a corporation to or for the benefit of its shareholders in respect of any of its shares." Va.Code Ann. § 13.1-603 (Michie 1989). Payment of the merger consideration to C-T's former shareholders simply does not fit within the plain language of this definition. The key language, for our purposes here, is the requirement that the transfer of money or property be "by a corporation to... its shareholders." When post-merger C-T transferred $20 per canceled share to C-T's pre-merger shareholders, they were no longer the corporation's—"its"—shareholders, for their ownership interest had been lawfully canceled as of the effective time of the merger.

Similarly, we must reject appellant's argument that the encumbering of C-T's assets to raise sufficient funds to pay for the merger was a distribution because it represented

4. Our resolution of this case makes it unnecessary to consider whether, if the merger did involve a distribution, the former directors of C-T "vote[d] for or assent[ed] to" it. Va.Code Ann. § 13.1-692(A) (Michie 1989).

In addition, appellant has not argued before this court, as it did before the district court, *see* 124 B.R. at 697, that the transaction was "a distribution clothed in the garb of a merger." *Id.* (citing Wieboldt Stores, Inc. v. Schottenstein, 94 B.R. 488 (N.D.Ill.1988)). Accordingly, we need not address whether §§ 13.1-653 and 13.1-692 apply when a transfer of money or property to shareholders is disguised as a merger in an attempt to avoid the statutory restrictions on distributions.

the "incurrence of indebtedness by a corporation... for the benefit of its shareholders." *Id.* The financing for the merger was negotiated not by C-T's pre-merger directors for the benefit of C-T's pre-merger shareholders, but by the new owners and directors of the corporation. Moreover, the financing closed simultaneously with the closing of the merger. Accordingly, at the time the encumbering was undertaken, the pre-merger shareholders' ownership interests were canceled and, therefore, C-T did not incur debt "for the benefit of its shareholders."

Appellant's attempt to shoehorn the payment of merger consideration into the statutory definition of distribution must thus prove unsuccessful, for its argument fails to appreciate the significance of the fact that the transaction at issue represented the arm's-length purchase of C-T by Holdings. The distribution statute is aimed by its terms at actions taken by a corporation to enrich unjustly its own shareholders at the expense of creditors and to the detriment of the continuing viability of the company. It does not cover third-party payments to acquire the stock of a corporation or the encumbering of assets after a change in corporate ownership, and it is not intended to obstruct an arm's-length acquisition of an enterprise by new owners who have their own plans for commercial success. The reason for this distinction is simple: A corporate acquisition, structured as a merger, is simply a different animal from a distribution. Distribution statutes, as noted above, derive from the regulation of corporate dividends and traditionally apply to situations in which shareholders, after receiving the transfer from the corporation, retain their status as owners of the corporation. Distribution statutes have not been applied to wholesale changes in corporate ownership, as is the case here, and C-T has presented no evidence that the Virginia legislature intended the statutory definition to expand the applicability of distribution restrictions beyond their traditional scope.

Appellant insists, however, that the text of the statute does not exclude from the definition of distribution transfers incident to changes in corporate control. Appellant relies on the fact that § 13.1-603 states that "[a] distribution may be in the form of... a purchase, redemption, or other acquisition of shares." This language, however, is not nearly as broad as C-T suggests. To begin with, it is subject to the general requirement that the corporation act for the benefit of its shareholders. Further, the language functions in this context to prevent a corporation from disguising a distribution in the form of a partial acquisition of shares—*e.g.*, by "purchasing" twenty-five percent of each shareholder's shares, which would have the effect of transferring corporate assets to the shareholders without the corporation receiving any consideration in exchange and without changing the ownership structure in the slightest. The inclusion of purchases, redemptions, and other acquisitions within the ambit of distributions, therefore, is not an indication that the statutory definition applies when all outstanding shares of the corporation are purchased at a market rate in the course of an arm's-length purchase of the corporation.

None of this discussion should suggest that the transaction in this case was not subject to extensive regulation. Article 12 of the Virginia Stock Corporation Act provides detailed procedures that govern mergers, *see* Va.Code Ann. §§ 13.1-716, -718 (Michie 1989), and mandates review of the articles of merger by the Virginia State Corporation Commission, *see id.* § 13.1-720(B). As the district court observed, Article 12 "makes no mention of distributions," and the Virginia legislature could easily have provided a cross-reference to the distribution statutes had it intended the latter to apply to mergers. 124 B.R. at 696–97. Further, Virginia law prohibits transfers of money or corporate shares that are made "with intent to delay, hinder or defraud creditors," Va.Code Ann. § 55–80 (Michie 1986), or that are "not upon consideration deemed valuable in law," *id.* §

55–81 (Michie Supp.1991). Finally, federal bankruptcy law provides that a trustee in bankruptcy may avoid any transfer made within one year before bankruptcy, if the debtor "received less than a reasonably equivalent value in exchange" and was insolvent at the time of, or became insolvent as a result of, the transfer. 11 U.S.C.A. § 548(a)(2)(A) and (B)(i) (West Supp.1991). The existence of other state and federal enactments that potentially address this kind of transaction suggests the inadvisability of importing the distribution statutes into a context that the legislature did not intend.

B.

Other reasons impel us to hold that the leveraged acquisition of C-T was not a distribution under Virginia law. In this case appellant asks a federal court to apply a state distribution statute in a wholly novel way. It has not directed our attention to any decision by any court, state or federal, that has applied distribution restrictions to an arm's-length merger. "Federal judges are disinclined to make bold departures in areas of law that we have no responsibility for developing." Afram Export Corp. v. Metallurgiki Halyps, S.A., 772 F.2d 1358, 1370 (7th Cir.1985). Moreover, the reach of the rule of law appellant seeks is extremely broad: appellant conceded to the district court that, under its interpretation of the statutory definition, *every* merger would henceforth be a distribution. *See* 124 B.R. at 696. Accepting appellant's argument, therefore, would expose the defendants and directors of other Virginia corporations to a wholly unanticipated form of personal liability and would place a cloud over all corporate acquisitions that have closed within the past two years, *see* Va.Code Ann. § 13.1-692(C) (Michie 1989) (two-year statute of limitations for actions alleging personal liability for illegal distributions).

More fundamentally, application of distribution restrictions in the context of changes in corporate control would place directors under conflicting legal duties. In this case, for example, the district court found that, after the announcement that the directors had authorized a management-sponsored LBO, the company was for sale. 124 B.R. at 692 (relying on In re Time, Inc., Shareholder Litig., 571 A.2d 1140 (Del.1989.)) Thus, under Revlon, Inc. v. MacAndrews & Forbes Holdings, Inc., 506 A.2d 173 (Del.1986), the fiduciary duties owed by the pre-merger directors to C-T's shareholders required that the directors "sell [the company] to the highest bidder," *id.* at 182, and seek the highest price possible from that bidder. By negotiating with Holdings and getting Holdings to increase its offer price from $19 to $20, C-T's pre-merger directors were simply fulfilling these well-recognized fiduciary duties. Indeed, had the directors refused to consummate the transaction because Holdings planned to acquire the bulk of the merger consideration by leveraging the company's assets, C-T's shareholders would likely have sued them for breach of fiduciary duty. If we accepted appellant's proffered interpretation of the definition of distribution, however, C-T's pre-merger directors would have been required not only to maximize the sale price, but also to ensure the solvency of the post-sale corporation. How directors could successfully navigate these narrow waters—subject to the possibility of massive personal liability should they falter on either side—is left unexplained.

Moreover, it is difficult for us to conceive how distribution restrictions would effectively function in the corporate acquisitions context. In determining whether a proposed distribution is legal, directors must apply two sophisticated insolvency tests. *See* Va.Code Ann. § 13.1-653(C) (Michie 1989). In applying these tests, directors must assess the future business prospects and decisions of the company. *See* RMBCA § 6.40 comment 2. When, after a distribution, directors continue to operate the company and set its business policy, such a task is manageable and within their competence. In cases involving corporate acquisitions, however, the pre-acquisition directors typically depart their positions in the corporation after the transaction. Not only do they therefore lack any control over the future course of the company's business, but they also may be fully unaware of new management's plans and strategies. Indeed, the primary rationale for a change in corporate ownership and control is the new owners' belief that, by altering the company's business strategy and structure, they can make the company more profitable than it was under old management. In this situation, it seems both unrealistic and perverse to charge the old directors under the distribution statute with knowledge and responsibility for the actions of the new owners. We cannot believe that the legislature intended such a result.

We also do not share appellant's view that non-application of the distribution statute would be unfair to creditors. In this case, it is possible that the leveraged acquisition of C-T hastened or caused the company's downfall. On the other hand, C-T's creditors may have actually benefitted from the acquisition. *See* Baird & Jackson, Fraudulent Conveyance Law and Its Proper Domain, 38 Vand.L.Rev. 829, 853 (1985). The infusion of $4 million in new capital and the presence of a more effective management team may have permitted C-T to survive longer than it otherwise would have and may also have increased the chances that the company would survive over the long-term. In other words, it is impossible to conclude *a priori* whether a leveraged transaction such as that here on balance benefits or harms creditors of the target corporation. It is possible to say, however, that a creditor cannot avoid bearing the risk that his debtor will make a bad business decision:

> A creditor who lends a debtor money is taking advantage of the debtor's comparative advantage in using that money productively. A creditor necessarily defers to the debtor's skills in converting the money into other assets. The risk that both the creditor and debtor take is that the use the debtor makes of the money will benefit both parties. The creditor provides the capital, the debtor provides the know-how. The creditor is relying on the debtor's skill and judgment when it makes the loan. Only by giving the debtor discretion can the creditor hope to profit. Giving a debtor discretion, however, necessarily gives him the ability not only to make good decisions, but bad ones as well.

Id. at 838. Finally, it is important to recognize that, since LBOs are a well-known element in contemporary business life, creditors are well-positioned to protect themselves. "[T]he debtor-creditor relationship is essentially contractual." *Id.* at 835. If a creditor fears the prospect of a future leveraged acquisition of its debtor, it can protect itself by bargaining for security interests or protective provisions in its loan agreements that restrict the ability of its debtor to subject itself to a leveraged acquisition without the creditor's approval. *See id.* at 834–36; *see also* Kummert, *State Statutory Restrictions on Financial Distributions by Corporations to Shareholders: Part I*, 55 Wash.L.Rev. 359, 374 n. 63, 395 (1980) (noting "the extensive use by large or long term creditors of contract provisions that supersede the statutory provisions with far more rigorous restrictions on financial distributions by the corporate debtor").

> In addition, we note that even if corporate acquisitions are not subject to state distribution restrictions, protection is accorded creditors by the law of creditors' rights, particularly fraudulent conveyance statutes. *See generally* Sherwin, Creditors' Rights Against Participants in a Leveraged Buyout, 72 Minn.L.Rev. 449, 464–505 (1988) (discussing the application of fraudulent conveyance law to leveraged buyouts); Note, Fraudulent Conveyance Law and Leveraged Buyouts, 87 Colum.L.Rev. 1491 (1987) (same). In contrast to state corporate law, the law of

creditors' rights is designed and better equipped to protect creditors in situations such as that presented here. For example, state fraudulent conveyance statutes, *see, e.g.*, Va.Code Ann. §§ 55–80, 55–81 (Michie 1986 & Supp.1991), and federal bankruptcy law, *see* 11 U.S.C.A. § 548(a) (West 1979 & Supp.1991), enable creditors to recapture transferred funds by attacking the transaction directly. In contrast, distribution restrictions merely impose personal liability on directors, without any provision for a direct recoupment of the distributed assets from the shareholders who received them. *See* Va.Code Ann. § 13.1-692(A) and (B) (Michie 1989).

In attacking the transaction here, appellant fails to acknowledge all the risks inherent in it. Holdings' acquisition of C-T was an uncertain financial proposition for C-T's shareholders as well as its creditors. Although the post-merger corporation failed in this case some eighteen months after the leveraged acquisition, it was anything but clear at the time of the transaction that the corporation would enter bankruptcy. Indeed, C-T's new owners were so confident of its future success that they invested $4 million of their own money in it. Thus, had the domestic shoe market rebounded after the acquisition, the market price of a share in C-T may have risen substantially above the $20 that the pre-merger shareholders received. In that situation, the shareholders—not C-T's creditors—would be complaining today. Both this corporate acquisition and the lending of money to pre-merger C-T involved risk—the same risk that inheres in all legitimate business activity. State distribution statutes simply do not authorize courts to rearrange the losses that inevitably result from risks taken in the hope of gains.

IV.

In sum, we conclude that Holdings' leveraged acquisition of C-T, accomplished in the form of an arm's-length merger between Holdings' subsidiary Acquisition and C-T, did not create a distribution under Virginia law. The judgment of the district court is therefore

AFFIRMED.

Comments and Questions

1. How do you think a court would rule on the issue of the applicability of the distribution rules to leveraged buy-outs under the traditional approach? *See* Munford v. Valuation Research Corp., 97 F.3d 456 (11th Cir. 1996). A panel of the Eleventh Circuit held that Georgia's stock distribution and repurchase statutes apply to leveraged buy-out merger transactions. At the time, Georgia statutes provided that the board of directors could make distributions to shareholders out of the capital surplus of the corporation, unless the corporation was insolvent at the time of the distribution, or unless such distribution would render the corporation insolvent. O.C.G.A. § 14-2-91 (1988). Georgia's stock repurchasing statute prohibited directors from repurchasing the corporation's shares when such purchase would render the corporation insolvent. In reaching this result the Eleventh Circuit rejected the reasoning of the Fourth Circuit in *C-T of Virgina.*

The bankruptcy court, in this case, rejected this line of reasoning, reasoning that the legislature enacted the distribution and share repurchase statutes of the Georgia Code to protect creditors "by prohibiting transfers at a time when a corporation is insolvent or would be rendered insolvent." Such intent, the bankruptcy

> court noted, "furthers the longstanding principle that creditors are to be paid before shareholders." We agree with the district court and the reasoning of the bankruptcy court and decline to join the Fourth Circuit in holding that "[a] corporate acquisition, structured as a merger, is simply a different animal from a distribution." *C-T of Virginia, Inc.*, 958 F.2d at 611.

97 F.3d at 460.

2. The court in *C-T of Virgina* give too little weight to the policy of the distribution statutes to provide creditors with protection against the overreaching of shareholders and managers when it suggests that "creditors are well-positioned to protect themselves." There may be something to the suggestion that it should not be for the corporate law to protect creditors. The corporate law is meant to regulate the relationship between managers, officers and shareholders. That relationship defines the heart of the internal affairs of the corporation. Creditors have little if any role in this matrix. Instead, it is understood that the law of the relationship between creditors and the corporation, including shareholders, managers and officers, falls outside of the purview of the 'corporate law.' If that is the case, that is, if a separate body of law dealing with the rights of creditors generally provides the bulk of the protection that the state is willing to accord creditors (outside of the rights granted to creditors within their agreements with their borrowers), then why regulate capital for the protection of creditors at all? Might your answer change if you believed that the regulation of capital protects shareholders as well as creditors?

B. Capital Requirements in Europe

Capital requirements in Europe present a very different ordering than in the United States. At the level of large well funded corporations, the differences are negligible. For small or start up corporations, or corporations thinly capitalized, the differences can be more significant. As you review the material that follows, consider whether the effort of the Europeans to construct these regimes is worth the effort.

1. National Law Rules

As we have seen in prior chapters, most Member States of the EU impose significant minimum capital requirements in connection with corporate formation. The most significant burden of capital requirements falls on public limited companies the shares of which are actually offered to the public (SAs, AGs, and the like). The least significant burden falls on private limited companies (SARLs, GmbHs and the like). Recall that one of the reasons for the formation of an English private limited company in *Centros* was to avoid the minimum capital requirements for private limited companies under Danish law. The materials that follow provide a taste of some of the issues that arise in connection with the capitalization of European companies, as well as a sense of some of the innovations being made, particularly in England and France, with respect to the regime of minimum capital, which has been the rule in Europe since the 19th century.

José Manuel Otero Lastres, Company Law

in SPANISH BUSINESS LAW 153 (Bernardo M. Cremades, gen. ed. 1985) (excerpts pages 179–180)

Contributions to stock companies may consist in either cash, or assets whose cash value is determinable. Cash contributions must be in pesetas. If foreign currency is contributed, its legally determined equivalent value in pesetas must be stated.

Non-monetary contributions raise two fundamental problems: regulation of their transfer to the stock company and their assessment.

Article 32 of the [Ley de Sociedades Anónimas (LSA)] lists three legal provisions applicable to the transfer of non-monetary assets:

- If the contribution is of personal property, real property or property rights, the contributor must deliver such property free from encumbrances as provided for in the [Codigo Civil] for sales contracts. Transfer of risk is governed by the provisions of the [Codigo Comercial] for sales contracts.
- If the contribution is of a credit right, the contributor must guarantee its legitimacy and the debtor's solvency.
- If the contribution is of a company or commercial or industrial establishment, the transfer is coverned by Article 1532 of the [Codigo Civil], by virtue of which the contributor is only liable in the case of eviction of all or most of the company or establishment.

The public deed[1] must contain the assignment of a value for non-monetary contributions. This initial value must be reviewed by the directors within four months of the founding of a stock company.

Within the following four months, any shareholder may request the appropriate judge of the first instance to appoint an expert to review the directors' assessment of the value of non-monetary contributions. If there is any discrepancy between the two assessments, the judge will decide which of the two is correct, and adjudicate costs.

If the review proves that the value of the assets is less than the originally assigned value, the contributor may choose one of three alternatives: (a) cancel the number of shares equivalent to the difference in value; (b) withdraw from the company; (c) pay the difference in cash.

In the first two cases, the company must reduce its capital in the corresponding amount if the shares are not subscribed in cash within one month.

Until the review has been complete or the term to request it has expired, contributing shareholders may not obtain their definitive shares.

---

1. [The public deed is a document, similar to the articles of incorporation in the United States, but with more extensive required disclosure, which must be recorded with the local Mercantile or Commercial registry as a prerequisite to the establishment of a corporation in many civil law countries. [Ed.]]

Comments and Questions: Valuing Assets

1. Spanish law provides that all *sociedades anónimas* ("SAs") will keep annual accounts consisting of the required financial statements and the annual report of management. These annual accounts form the basis on which management may determine whether, and to what extent, dividends may be declared and paid. Spanish limited liability companies, corresponding to the French SARL, are required to produce a much more abbreviated set of financial reports.[5] Dividend or other distributions proposed by management must be based on the financial statements, reviewed by statutory auditors and approved at the annual shareholder meeting. Dividends are generally payable out of profits, subject to a reduction of ten percent of earnings in every year in which the corporation's legal reserve account is less than twenty percent of the aggregate amount of the share capital account. Dividends may be paid out of revenues in excess of the legal reserve so long as the distribution does not reduce the net worth of the corporation below the amount of the aggregate share capital account (that is, the minimum capital that must be retained in the capital account). Reductions of capital are discouraged. Under many circumstances, most creditors whose claim would be admissible in a liquidation have the authority to object to reductions of corporate capital.

2. French law is similar to that of Spain. For minimum capital rules, reread the excerpt from CHRISTOPHER JOSEPH MESNOOH, LAW AND BUSINESS IN FRANCE: A GUIDE TO FRENCH COMMERCIAL AND CORPORATE LAW (1994) reproduced in Chapter 3.

3. Much of continental practice with respect to capital requirements is reflected in the Second Company Law Directive, discussed in the section that follows.

4. What are the differences between valuing assets under Delaware law and that under Spanish law? Do the differences suggest fundamentally different approaches or merely divergences in details? Can you think of cases where valuation would be different under Spanish and Delaware law?

5. From the perspective of lenders, does greater judicial involvement in the initial capitalization of the corporation provide a greater degree of protection?

Enno W. Ercklentz, Jr., 2 Modern German Corporate Law

(1979)
(excerpts pages 440–441; 443–450; 453–454; 457–461; 463–464; some footnotes omitted)

[Dividend Distributions in the AG]

Both the corporation laws in effect in the various jurisdictions within the United States and the German stock corporation law recognize as a matter of principle that the stockholder, as the beneficial owner of the enterprise, is entitled to the net earnings of the enterprise in proportion to his ownership interest. This conceptual agreement notwithstanding, however, substantial differences exist between the United States and the German practice with respect to the declaration of dividends. Thus, both the manner in which the amounts which are available for dividends are determined and the

5. CODIGO COMMERCIAL, Art. 103.

manner in which dividends are declared under the German statute differ significantly from the practice in the United States.

Under the Delaware law, for example, it is well settled that the stockholder has a right to a dividend only if one has been declared by the board of directors. By way of contrast, however, the stockholder of an AG may, under certain circumstances, act to enforce a claim for the payment of a dividend by legal action. Aside from this particular difference, a further difference will be found in the fact that, under the stock corporation law, it is the meeting of stockholders of the AG and not the management board of Board of Overseers which actually declares the dividend. While the stockholder in a Delaware corporation is thus entirely dependent on the discretion of the board of directors for the declaration of a dividend and cannot generally institute action to force the declaration and payment thereof, the stockholder of the AG not only has a hand in determining the payment of a dividend, but may in some cases even enforce the payment of one.

* * *

In general, the stock corporation law now proceeds from the premise that, subject to certain modifications, the management board should be entitled as a matter of business judgement to allocate up to 50% of the net earnings for a particular year to free reserves in connection with its adoption of the financial statements and that the meeting of stockholders should be entitled to dispose of the remaining 50%.[1] In applying such percentage to net earnings, the amount thereof is first adjusted by deducting therefrom the amount required to be allocated to the legal reserve, if any, the amount of any loss carry-over from the preceding year, and possibly one or more other deductions, if applicable.

In the more usual event of the adoption of the financial statements by action of the management board, such organ may thus allocate to free reserves up to 50% of the net earnings for the year, as adjusted, in its own discretion. For this purpose, no specific authority need be found in the Articles.[2] The Articles may, however, grant the management board specific authority to allocate a lager percentage of net earnings to free reserves up to a certain level.[3] Although some disagreement exists as to whether the contemplated larger percentage is subject to any limitation, the more prevalent view would permit the Articles to authorize an allocation of up to a full 100% of net earnings, as adjusted, to free reserves. However, allocations to free reserves by the management board on the basis of such a special provision in the Articles are permissible only to the extent the free resources so not exceed an amount equivalent to stated capital.[4] Once free reserves reach that amount, further allocations of free reserves would be limited to the 50% of net earnings otherwise permitted by the statute.

In the event, however, that the meeting of stockholders should adopt the financial statements, the right of that organ to allocate amounts to free reserves in connection with its adoption of the financial statements is conditioned upon the existence of specific authority therefor in the Articles, but the amounts allocable thereto would be limited to 50% of net earnings, as adjusted, in any event.[5] The remaining 50% of such net earnings, as adjusted, would then be subject to disposition by the meeting of stockholders in its annual resolution relating to the disposition of distributable net earnings.[6]

1. Section 58, AktG [Aktiengesetz].
2. Section 58(2), AktG.
3. Section 58(2), AktG.
4. Section 58(2), AktG.
5. Section 58(1), AktG.
6. Section 58(3), AktG.

In view of these changes, therefore, the meeting of stockholders can in most instances no longer be arbitrarily presented with financial statements showing no distributable net earnings.

(ii) Source of Dividends

The stock corporation law contains two separate provisions affecting the source out of which an AG may pay dividends. Not only does the statute contain a flat prohibition upon the distribution of any portion of capital to stockholders, but it also contains a provision to the effect that, prior to the liquidation of the AG, distributions to stockholders by way of dividends may be made only out of amounts arising out of net earnings.[7]

While on the surface this rule does not appear to differ too significantly from the rule prevailing in Delaware, an analysis of the provisions of both statutes will demonstrate that the sources out of which an AG may declare and pay dividends are in fact more limited than the sources out of which its Delaware counterpart may declare and pay dividends to stockholders. The principal reason for this difference will be found in the fact that dividends may be paid out of capital surplus in Delaware, while under the stock corporation law such amounts as would constitute capital surplus in Delaware are allocated to the legal reserve which may not be used for dividend purposes.[8]

Before turning to a discussion of the manner in which the amounts available for dividend purposes are determined under the stock corporation law, a brief comparison of the rules as to the possible sources of dividends under both the Delaware statute and the stock corporation law may be in order.

Under the Delaware corporation statute, the board of directors of a corporation may declare and pay dividends out of its net profits for the current and preceding fiscal year as well as out of its surplus [or retained earnings—ed.]. The concept of net profits is not defined in the law and the determination of the amount thereof is thus in effect left to the accounting profession. The concept of surplus, on the other hand, is viewed so broadly as to comprehend even capital surplus [i.e. amounts paid in for shares in excess of par value at the time of purchase from the company—ed.].

Surplus is defined in Delaware as being the excess of the net assets of the corporation over capital.[9] The capital of the corporation for this purpose amounts to the aggregate par value of the outstanding shares of its capital stock unless the board of directors has taken express action assigning additional sums to capital upon the issuance of such shares. Thus, for instance, in the absence of action by the board of directors, the capital attributable to 1,000 outstanding shares of capital stock of a par value of $1.00 each would amount to only $1,000 even though a total of $20,000 may have been paid in upon such shares [i.e., the issue price was $20 per share—ed.]. The difference between such capital and the amount paid in, i.e., $19,000, would then be regarded as capital surplus rather than capital.[10] Even though the corporation may not avail of either net profits for the year or an earned surplus, the Delaware statute would under such circumstances still permit the declaration of a dividend out of this capital surplus so long as the net assets of the corporation exceeded this nominal $1,000 capital by the amount of the dividend. The Delaware statute thus makes no distinction be-

7. Section 57 and 58(5), AktG.
8. Section 150, AktG.
9. Section 154, Delaware General Corporation Law.
10. Such would be the case for financial reporting purposes at least.

tween earned surplus and capital surplus or any other form of surplus for dividend purposes.[11]

Under the stock corporation law, on the other hand, dividends may in general be paid only out of current net earnings or free reserves. Since the latter can be created only out of actual earnings, such reserves may be regarded as being comparable to an earned surplus in a Delaware corporation. In this connection, it will be recalled that the stock corporation law specifically prescribes the format of both the profit and loss statement and the balance sheet for an AG and that the amount of net earnings available for distribution in any year is thus quite precisely defined by statutory means.[12]

According to the stock corporation law, therefore, the amount of net earnings available for the payment of dividends in any given year consists of the excess of income items over expense items during such year, with such modifications as the deduction therefrom of the amount, if any, required to be allocated to the legal reserve, the deduction therefrom of the amount of any carry over loss from the previous year and the deduction therefrom of any amounts which have been allocated to free reserves by action of either the management board or the meeting of stockholders in connection with the adoption of the financial statements.[13] The amount of such net earnings may also be modified by the addition thereto of any amounts theretofore carried as free reserves which were allocated to such reserves in previous years but not previously utilized to absorb losses and which are to be dissolved in any given year and carried over into earnings. It will thus be noted that, to the extent that a concept akin to surplus in Delaware can be identified under the stock corporation law, such surplus is strictly limited to earned surplus and clearly excludes what would amount to capital surplus in Delaware.

Although the premium, if any, paid to a corporation over the par value of its shares or convertible debentures upon their issuance would constitute capital surplus in Delaware, such amounts, when paid to an AG, are allocated to the legal reserve under the stock corporation law.[14] The legal reserve also represents the account to which 5% of the annual net earnings of the AG must be allocated until the amount of such legal reserve constitutes a sum equal to 10% of stated capital, or such greater percentage thereof as the Articles may provide.[15] Since the legal reserve may under no circumstances be utilized, either directly or indirectly, to facilitate the payment of dividends, the entire amount of this reserve is regarded as tantamount to capital for dividend purposes.[16]

The legal reserve may, in fact, be utilized only to absorb losses under specified circumstances. Where the legal reserve has not yet attained an amount equivalent to 10% of stated capital, or such greater percentage as the Articles may determine, it may be utilized to absorb losses only if all existing free reserves have previously been dissolved for the same purpose. On the other hand, should the amount of the legal reserve exceed such percentage of stated capital, the amount of the excess may be utilized to absorb losses even without the prior dissolution of all free reserves, but subject to the condition, however, that free reserves may not at the same time be dissolved in order to effect

11. Section 154, Delaware General Corporate Law.
12. Section 157, AktG.
13. Section 157, AktG.
14. Section 150(2), AktG.
15. Section 150(2), AktG.
16. Section 150, AktG.

a dividend distribution.[17] Next to the stated capital of the AG, the legal reserve is thus regarded as one of the last lines of financial defense available to the AG which may not be diminished by distributions to stockholders prior to its liquidation.

The actual determination of the availability of a specific amount for dividend purposes in a particular year commences with the proper adoption of the financial statements for such year. Once these statements have been so adopted, the amounts appearing for each item set forth on the prescribed format for profit and loss statements will be fixed and determined, including the amount of distributable net earnings over which the meeting of stockholders may dispose of in its discretion.

If the management board has adopted the financial statements in conjunction with the board of Overseers, the amount which may be disposed of in the discretion of the meeting of stockholders will consist of the net earnings for the year, as adjusted, less the amount which the management board has in its discretion already allocated to free reserves in connection with its adoption of such statements.[18]

Where the meeting of stockholders has adopted the financial statements, the amount over which it may dispose is arrived at in similar fashion, except that, before reaching its annual resolution relating to the disposition of distributable net earnings, it will be able to allocate amounts to free reserves as part of the adoption function only if the Articles so permit.[19]

It might be noted that, no matter by what organ the financial statements are ultimately adopted, the meeting of stockholders is not required by law to declare a dividend out of distributable net earnings remaining for disposition. In its annual resolution relating to the disposition of such distributable net earnings, it may thus choose instead to allocate additional sums to free reserves. However, where the reserves created thereby become excessive pursuant to a statutory standard and a sum equal to at least 4% of the par value of capital stock is not declared as a dividend, the right of certain stockholders... to challenge the resolution involved should not be overlooked.[20]

* * *

[I]n order to assure stockholders of at least some dividend should sufficient earnings exist, the stock corporation law provides for a means whereby the declaration and payment of a minimum dividend may be secured under certain circumstances. The method by which this is accomplished consists of the commencement of a legal action seeking determination that the resolution of the meeting of stockholders disposing of the net earnings of the AG without declaring a minimum distribution to the stockholders is void.[25]

Such an action, however, cannot be brought by any stockholder under all circumstances. In fact, this avenue of relief to the minority is quite narrowly circumscribed. An action of this kind can thus be brought only by a qualified stockholder minority and only under specified circumstances. For this purpose, the qualified minority consists of a stockholder or stockholders owning shares amounting to at least 5% of the outstanding shares of capital stock of the AG or having an aggregate par value of at least DM 1,000,000.[26] In this respect, the law proceeds from the premise that any stockholder

17. Section 150(3) and 150(4), AktG.
18. Sections 58 and 157, AktG.
19. Sections 58 and 157, AktG.
20. Section 254(1), AktG.
25. Sections 254 and 246, AktG.
26. Section 254(2), AktG.

challenging the allocation by majority stockholder action of distributable net earnings to free reserves rather than to dividends should have more than a nominal interest in the AG.

With respect to the conditions which give rise to this cause of action, two circumstances must coincide within the resolution of the meeting of stockholders before the action can be brought. Not only must the declaration have failed to declare a distribution equivalent to at least 4% of the par value of the shares of capital stock outstanding, but such resolution must simultaneously have allocated to free reserves, beyond the requirements of law or the Articles, an amount out of distributable net earnings which, in the judgement of an ordinarily prudent busienss man, is not required for the financial well being of the AG over the foreseeable future.[27] This test was devised in the belief that the meeting of stockholders should have some leeway in arriving at a business like determination, based on the financial needs of the AG, to allocate the required amounts to free reserves without becoming obligated to declare a dividend where the financial circumstances of the AG clearly called for further accumulation of reserves. At the same time, it was not felt desirable to permit the meeting of stockholders, which might possibly be dominated by a controlling person or group, arbitrarily and without economic justification to allocate all distributable net earnings to free reserves and thereby deprive the minority of a dividend.

* * *

[Dividend Distributions: GmbH]

In general, the approach of the GmbH law to the question of distributions by the GmbH to its members is based upon the same principles which underlie the comparable provisions of the stock corporation law. In other words, the maintenance of the stated capital of the GmbH as a minimum pool of assets available for the protection of creditors is the principle consideration. However, because of the nature of the GmbH, the provisions of the GmbH law relating to dividends and distributions are necessarily somewhat different from those of the stock corporation law.

The GmbH law thus prohibits any distributions to members of the GmbH which would have the effect of impairing the stated capital of the enterprise.[30] Accordingly, distributions to members are limited to amounts representing net earnings or the proceeds arising out of an ordinary reduction of stated capital.[31] However, since it is also possible to impose assessments upon the members of a GmbH if the Association Agreement so provides, the GmbH law contains a further provision, a counterpart of which does not exist in the stock corporation law, setting forth the circumstances under which the GmbH may effect a distribution to its members of the proceeds of the assessments which may no longer be required by the GmbH....[32]

Dividends

The GmbH law provides that, in principle, the members shall be entitled to the net earnings of the enterprise in proportion to their interests therein.[33] The Association Agreement may, however, provide otherwise, both as to the right to distributions per se and as to the proportion of any such distributions.[34]

---

27. Section 254(1), AktG.
30. Section 30, GmbHG [Gesetz betreffend die Gesellschaften mit beschraenkter Haftung].
31. [Baumbach-Hueck, "GmbH-Gesetz" (12th Ed., 1966)], Section 30, Comment 2, p. 114.
32. Section 30(2), GmbHG.
33. Section 29, GmbHG.
34. Section 29(2), GmbHG.

As in the case of the AG it is the ownership organ of the GmbH, i.e., the meeting of members, which actually declares dividends to its members. However, in contrast to the circumstances prevailing within the AG, the meeting of members of a GmbH is also the organ possessing the primary authority to adopt its financial statements.[35] This prerogative will be shifted away from the meeting of members to another corporate organ only if the Association Agreement specifically so provides. Although the meeting of members will thus generally have substantially more influence over the financial statements of the GmbH than does the meeting of stockholders within the AG, the minority rights within the GmbH are not as well developed. Consequently, no right to enforce the payment of a minimum dividend comparable to that exercisable by a qualified minority within the AG exists under the GmbH law....

The provisions of the GmbH law dealing with the source of dividends distributions to members are somewhat more limited than the provisions of the stock corporation law. Thus, the GmbH law simply prohibits the distribution to members of any amounts required to maintain the stated capital of the GmbH.[36] Since any sums in excess of those required to maintain stated capital, excluding amounts representing assessments, would in general be attributable to earnings, retained or current, the practical effect of this approach would seem to be the same.

Notwithstanding this fact, however, the determination of the amount, if any, which may be available for distribution to members of a GmbH at any given time differs quite substantially from the procedure to that effect within the AG. In the first place, the GmbH law does not prescribe any format for either the balance sheet or profit and loss statement for a GmbH as the stock corporation law does for the AG. As a result, the rules of the commercial Code applicable to any commercial enterprise, whether or not incorporated, will generally be applicable to the GmbH.[37] Furthermore, the GmbH law provides neither for the establishment and funding of a legal reserve nor for a prerogative on the part of management to establish free reserves up to a certain extent.

Accordingly, the amount out of which the meeting of members may declare dividends would consist of the net earnings for the particular year, as augmented or diminished by previous earnings or losses, but undiminished by adjustments attributable either to any required allocation to a legal reserve or to any discretionary allocation to free reserves. It should be borne in mind, however, that the Association Agreement may specifically authorize or even require any such allocation, in which case the provisions of the Association Agreement would control.[38]

The actual determination of the availability of a specific amount for dividend purposes commences, as in the case of the AG, with the adoption of the financial statements. While these statements are prepared by the managing director or directors, they will generally be adopted by action of the meeting of members.[39] According to applicable rules under the Commercial Code, in determining the amount available for distribution, the net earnings for the particular year are either increased or diminished by any

---

35. Section 46, GmbhG.
36. Section 30, GmbHG.
37. Section 142, GmbHG; Section 10 [Handelsgesetzbuch (Commercial Code)]; but note that, where Publicity Law applies, the format provided for by the stock corporation law becomes mandatory...
38. Sections 45 and 46, GmbHG.
39. Section 46, GmbHG.

carryover earnings or losses from previous periods. If, on the other hand, the particular year produced a loss, then a carryover profit or loss would, respectively, diminish or increase the loss for the year. Where, however, the meeting of members in a prior year allocated the undistributed portion, if any, of such prior year's earnings to reserves, no carryover profit to increase or diminish the net earnings or losses for the later year would exist from that year unless such action is reversed by dissolution of the reserve so created.[40] Any dissolution of reserves for this purpose would be effected within the framework of the adoption of the financial statements by the meeting of members. It should thus be borne in mind that the amount of distributable net earnings for any given year may amount to more or less than the actual net earnings for the year depending on whether or not carryover profits or losses exist which would increase or diminish such net earnings.

* * *

As indicated above, distributions by a GmbH to its members are limited to amounts representing earnings and, in the case of a reduction of capital, to the amount of the reduction thereof.

A GmbH may, however, effect a form of distribution to its members which is unknown under the stock corporation law. Such a distribution consists of the return to members of amounts previously paid in by them in response to assessments upon their capital participations.

The return of assessments to the members of a GmbH may be effected only under certain specified circumstances.[46] A prerequisite for any such return is that the entire amount of the stated capital of the GmbH has been paid in. In other words, where the members have not contributed the full amount of stated capital, assessments cannot be returned under any circumstances. Furthermore, assessments may be returned only if the amount thereof is not required to replenish an impaired stated capital. Assuming that these conditions are met, however, the meeting of members may adopt a resolution authorizing the return of assessments to the members. Actual distributions thereof, however, must await the passage of three months from the date upon which the resolution of the meeting of members authorizing the distribution was published in the official journals.[47]

As in the case of the AG, an unlawful distribution may sometimes be found in any distinguished payment to members in the form of such items as compensation or commissions if such payment is excessive in relation to the services rendered. However, where the GmbH receives full value from a member in return, no unlawful distribution would be involved even though stated capital may be impaired by the distribution involved.

Comments and Questions

1. It appears that German law, like the more traditional approaches in the United States, relies on capitalization rules as a touchstone for the determination of dividends. The basis of the policy underlying the traditional approach appears to be the need to

40. Baumbach-Hueck, Section 47, Comment 2(B), p. 202.
46. Section 30(2), GmbHG.
47. Section 30(2), GmbHG.

provide some assurance that, even after money is distributed to shareholders (the residuary corporate claimants) the enterprise retains at least some legally designated minimum amount of funds for its own use (and likely the use of creditors if all else fails). Because the minimum capital requirements are fixed and have no relation either to the size of corporate net worth, income or debt, the theory, while elegant, does not appear to provide much assurance in fact. Yet, this obvious fact has done little to reduce the appeal of this requirement. Can you think of reasons for the continued vitality of the minimum capital rules? Do the German requirements for additions to minimum capital through contributions of earnings and the like described in the excerpt above make a real difference in the utility of these amounts for the benefit of corporate participants other than shareholders (creditors, employees and the like)?

2. The German rules appear to give shareholders more control over dividend policy than do its American counterparts. Why are such rules necessary? If for the protection of shareholders, then is it not possible to argue that the managers fail in their fiduciary duty to the shareholders by denying them dividends? What is the usual counter to that argument in the United States? Do you think the control can be structured to be, in actuality, more theoretical than real?

3. Do you think the rules with respect to compulsory dividends in Germany provide an effective means of shareholder protection? Would such a provision violate the public policy underlying the dividend distribution rules in the Delaware corporate law? Would the same be true under the policy underlying the approach of the Revised Model Business Corporation Act?

4. Unlike the law in the United States, where accounting issues are still a matter of private regulation, German law prescribes the accounting conventions for the presentation of critical financial information, including the information on the basis of which amounts available for dividends are calculated. German law in this regard, then, is vulnerable to change with a change in the statutory conventions for accounting. As we will see in the next section, such accounting standards have been subject to harmonization by the EU. To the extent that accounting standards are now a matter of EU "federal" law, has Germany lost the power to control the calculation of dividends? Even if Germany must now conform its accounting standards to EU law, is there a way that Germany could preserve its system for determining amounts available for dividends as set forth in the old system without violating EU rules (assuming that the old conventions are no longer available under the EU standards)?

5. German law strictly controls the accounting (balance sheet and profit and loss statement) for the AG, but not for the GmbH. Can you justify the difference in treatment in this regard between the rules for the AG, prescribed by statute, and those for the GmbH, which are not prescribed?

6. While it appears that German shareholders have a significantly greater control of dividend policy than their counterparts in the United States, that control is not exercised with any degree of independence. Generally, shareholders determine dividend policy on the basis of recommendations submitted to them by the Management Board, which along with the report of the supervisory board and the financial statements are distributed to shareholders in advance of the meeting. Generally such recommendations are adopted. Even where dissident shareholders are present, the structure of shareholding in Germany ensures that the largest shareholders' views will be reflected in the recommendations of management before those are distributed to all shareholders. This also goes far to minimize deviation from the management board recommendations. In

this pattern of behavior, perhaps, German companies resemble their American counterparts, at least in which corporate managers control the proxy machinery with the result that shareholder independence is usually expressed as a function of the desires of the company's managers. Do you agree? Is this state of affairs a bad thing?

7. Is it possible for a German AG to pay dividends equal to the entire amount of the current year's earnings? How does the German rule compare to the rule in Delaware? California? Under the Revised Model Business Corporation Act? Which rule better protects lenders?

8. Were you to be advising an American company contemplating the establishment of a subsidiary in Germany that was interested in drawing out the maximun amounts of dividends possible for its worldwide operations, which form of German company organization do you think would be better suited? Would your answer change if the company you were advising contemplated owning less than 100% of the subsidiary's stock?

Bairstow and Others v. Queens Moat Houses plc

Court of Appeal (Civil Division)
[2001] EWCA Civ 712, [2001] 2 BCLC 531
17 May 2001

Robert Walker LJ.:

Introduction

[1] The background to this appeal is very clearly summarised in the judgment of Rix LJ given on 26 October 2000 when this court (Simon Brown and Rix LJJ) gave permission to appeal, on strictly limited grounds, against orders of Nelson J made on 23 September 1999. The appellants are three former directors of Queens Moat Houses plc ("Queens Moat"): Mr. John Bairstow (who was chairman and managing director), Mr. Martin Marcus (who was deputy chairman and joint managing director) and Mr. Alan Porter (who was assistant finance director). Mr. David Hersey, the former finance director, was a party to the first-instance litigation but is not a party to the appeals. The same is true of the trustees of Mr. Bairstow's occupational pension scheme.

[2] The brief summary that follows is based on the judgment of Rix LJ, to which reference may be made for further detail. In 1993 the four directors named above ("the former directors") were dismissed by Queens Moat and brought separate proceedings against Queens Moat for wrongful dismissal. This followed a major crisis in the financial affairs of Queens Moat and its group of companies, which had carried on a rapidly-expanding hotel business both in the United Kingdom and elsewhere.

[3] Queens Moat defended the proceedings brought by the former directors on the grounds that they had between 1991 and 1993 committed serious breaches of contractual, fiduciary and statutory duties as directors of Queens Moat. Queens Moat counterclaimed under various heads, the most important of which (and the only head directly relevant to this appeal) being a claim for payment to the company of preference and ordinary dividends paid out on the strength of the company's statutory accounts for 1990 and 1991 (Queens Moat's accounting date was at all material times 31 December).

[4] After a trial spread over about a year (during which the former directors appeared in person) Nelson J handed down a judgment in July 1999 ("the main judg-

ment") dismissing the claims for wrongful dismissal and making findings of fact relevant to the counterclaim. In September he heard three days of further argument at which Mr. Bairstow and Mr. Marcus were represented by leading counsel and in December 1999 Nelson J handed down two further judgments, one relating to the counterclaim for payment of dividends ("the dividends judgment") and the other relating to costs (the former directors other than Mr. Hersey were ordered to pay costs on the indemnity basis; Mr. Hersey was ordered to pay them on the standard basis).

[5] The effect of the order on the dividends counterclaim was that the former directors were jointly and severally liable to pay to Queens Moat, with interest, the sum of £26.728m being the aggregate of ordinary dividends paid out on 28 May 1992 (a final dividend of 1.54p per share for 1991 amounting to £13.834m) and on 23 October 1992 (an interim dividend of 1.395p per share for 1992 amounting to £12.894m). The judge declined to make an order for payment in respect of any ordinary dividends paid out during 1991 (the final dividend for 1990 of 1.40p per share, amounting £12.460m, paid on 29 May 1991 and the interim for 1991 of 1.342p per share, amounting to £12.048m, paid on 21 October 1991) or any preference dividends paid at any time. There are respondent's notices seeking to vary the judge's order in relation to (i) dividends received by the former directors personally between May 1991 and January 1993 and (ii) seven preference and ordinary dividends paid between October 1991 and January 1993.

[6] At 1 January 1990 Queens Moat had an allotted and fully-paid capital of approximately 727m ordinary shares of 5p each and 24m 7% convertible cumulative redeemable preference shares of £1 each. At 1 January 1991 the comparable figures were 890m and (as a result of the conversion of 7% preference shares) 20m. At 1 January 1992 the comparable figures were 898m and 19m. Moreover during 1991 Queens Moat made a rights issue of approximately 189m 7.5% convertible cumulative redeemable preference shares of £1 each, which first ranked for dividend on 21 October 1991.

[7] Although this appeal is directly concerned only with the dividends which Queens Moat claims were paid unlawfully, it will be necessary to make some reference to the judge's findings in his main judgment (running to nearly 500 pages) which he handed down in July 1999. Nelson J found that all four former directors had committed serious breaches of their contracts and had been guilty of gross misconduct and wilful neglect.

[8] In relation to the all-important statutory requirements that individual company accounts and consolidated group accounts shall give "a true and fair view" (see §§.226(3) and 227(3) of the Companies Act 1985 as amended—"the Act"—set out below) the judge found, in Rix LJ's summary, that the former directors:

> "...had each been responsible for the fact that the company's 1991 accounts did not present a true and fair view. Mr. Bairstow and Mr. Marcus had signed them, and Mr. Porter and Mr. Hersey had prepared them. Instead of published pre-tax profits of some £90 million for the year, a true and fair view ought to have limited profits to some £32 million only. He also found that in 1992 and the first three months of 1993 the claimants had dishonestly sought to foster false expectations of annual profits for 1992 of around £80/85 million, when in truth underlying profits were running at a very much lower level: so much so that, without exceptional or extraordinary profits, or artificial profits created by dubious or dishonest transactions, the company's profits would have turned out to be plus or minus zero. Ultimately, on 1 April 1993 the company had to ask for its shares to be suspended. The 1992 accounts were not completed until 1994, when the company had long been under new management."

[9] This court gave permission to appeal on the limited grounds mentioned in paras 51, 52 and 53 of the judgment of Rix LJ. Those grounds are, in brief summary, the contention that directors' liability to restore unlawfully-paid dividends arises only in the case of an insolvent company (since otherwise shareholders might get a windfall by receiving the same dividend twice); the significance of a sufficiency of distributable profits in the group (although not in Queens Moat, the holding company); and (following on from the last point) the judge's exercise of his discretion to grant relief under § 727 of the Act. This court specifically refused permission to appeal against the findings of breaches of duty and the former directors' responsibility for the deficiencies of the 1991 accounts.

[10] At the appeal hearing Mr. Bairstow was represented by Mr Charles Purle QC. Mr. Marcus and Mr. Porter appeared in person. Queens Moat was represented by Mr. David Richards QC and Mr. Paul Downes.

The Statutory Provisions

[11] In the course of the appeal hearing reference was made, naturally enough, to a large number of provisions of the Act. At this point it is convenient to set out or summarise the provisions which are of central importance to the appeal; some other provisions of less importance are referred to later. Part VII of the Act (§§ 221–262A) is concerned with accounts and audit. Part VIII (§§ 263–281) is concerned with distribution of profits and assets. The statutory safeguards in Pt VIII are closely linked to the statutory requirements in Pt VII.

[12] Section 226 (duty to prepare individual company accounts) provides as follows:

> "(1) The directors of every company shall prepare for each financial year of the company:
>
> (a) a balance sheet as at the last day of the year, and
>
> (b) a profit and loss account.
>
> Those accounts are referred to in this Part as the company's 'individual accounts.'
>
> (2) The balance sheet shall give a true and fair view of the state of affairs of the company as at the end of the financial year; and the profit and loss account shall give a true and fair view of the profit and loss of the company for the financial year.
>
> (3) A company's individual accounts shall comply with the provisions of Sch 4 as to the form and content of the balance sheet and profit and loss account and additional information to be provided by way of notes to the accounts."

Subsections (4) and (5) contain further provisions not directly relevant to these appeals. Section 227 (duty to prepare group accounts) provides as follows:

> "(1) If at the end of a financial year a company is a parent company the directors shall, as well as preparing individual accounts for the year, prepare group accounts.
>
> (2) Group accounts shall be consolidated accounts comprising:
>
> (a) a consolidated balance sheet dealing with the state of affairs of the parent company and its subsidiary undertakings, and
>
> (b) a consolidated profit and loss account dealing with the profit or loss of the parent company and its subsidiary undertakings.
>
> (3) The accounts shall give a true and fair view of the state of affairs as at the end of the financial year, and the profit or loss for the financial year, of the undertak-

ings included in the consolidation as a whole, so far as concerns members of the company.

(4) A company's group accounts shall comply with the provisions of Schedule 4A as to the form and content of the consolidated balance sheet and consolidated profit and loss account and additional information to be provided by way of notes to the accounts."

Again, subsections (5) and (6) are not directly relevant.

[13] Section 230 (treatment of individual profit and loss account where group accounts prepared) provides as follows:

"(1) The following provisions apply with respect to the individual profit and loss account of a parent company where—

(a) the company is required to prepare and does prepare group accounts in accordance with this Act, and

(b) the notes to the company's individual balance sheet show the company's profit and loss for the financial year determined in accordance with this Act.

(2) The profit and loss account need not contain the information specified in paragraphs 52 to 57 of Schedule 4 (information supplementing the profit and loss account).

(3) The profit and loss account must be approved in accordance with section 233(1) (approval by board of directors) but may be omitted from the company's annual accounts for the purposes of the other provisions below in this Chapter.

(4) The exemption conferred by this section is conditional upon its being disclosed in the company's annual accounts that the exemption applies."

This section explains why the published consolidated accounts of Queens Moat and its group did not contain an individual profit and loss account. (It was not demonstrated to the court that all the conditions for the exemption had been satisfied, but Mr. Richards did not make any positive case that those conditions had not been satisfied).

[14] By § 262(1) "annual accounts" are defined for the purposes of Pt VII and (see § 742(1)) Pt VIII as:

"(a) the individual accounts required by section 226, and

(b) any group accounts required by section 227.

(but see also section 230 (treatment of individual profit and loss account where group accounts prepared))."

Section 262(3) defines "realised profits" and "realised losses" for the purposes of Pt VII and (see § 742(2)) Pt VIII, in relation to a company's accounts, as:

"...such profits and losses of the company as fall to be treated as realised in accordance with principles generally accepted, at the time when the accounts are prepared, with respect to the determination for accounting purposes of realised profits or losses.

This is without prejudice to:

(a) the construction of any other expression (where appropriate) by reference to accepted accounting principles or practice, or

(b) any specific provision for the treatment of profits or losses of any description as realised."

[15] Section 263 (certain distributions prohibited) provides in subsection (1):

"A company shall not make a distribution except out of profits available for the purpose."

Subsection (2) contains an elaborate definition of "distribution"; for present purposes it is sufficient that it includes a dividend. Subsection (3) provides:

"For purposes of this Part, a company's profits available for distribution are its accumulated, realised profits, so far as not previously utilised by distribution or capitalisation, less its accumulated, realised losses, so far as not previously written off in a reduction or reorganisation of capital duly made."

Section 264 contains rather more far-reaching restrictions applicable to a public company (in that they impose requirements as to net assets also). These restrictions applied to Queens Moat but no reliance has been placed on them in these appeals. The assets of Queens Moat were drastically revalued downwards in the 1992 accounts (when eventually published in 1994) but that is not an issue in these appeals. §§ 265 and 266 contain special provisions applicable to investment companies.

[16] Section 270 (distribution to be justified by reference to company's accounts) is of central importance. It is the main link between the restrictive safeguards in Pt VIII and the mandatory requirements of Pt VII and Schs 4 and 4A. It provides as follows:

"(1) This section and sections 271 to 276 below are for determining the question whether a distribution may be made by a company without contravening sections 263, 264 or 265.

(2) The amount of a distribution which may be made is determined by reference to the following items as stated in the company's accounts:

(a) profits, losses, assets and liabilities,

(b) provisions of any of the kinds mentioned in paragraphs 88 and 89 of Schedule 4 (depreciation, diminution in value of assets, retentions to meet liabilities, etc) and

(c) share capital and reserves (including undistributable reserves).

(3) Except in a case falling within the next subsection, the company's accounts which are relevant for this purpose are its last annual accounts, that is to say those prepared under Part VII which were laid in respect of the last preceding accounting reference period in respect of which accounts so prepared were laid; and for this purpose accounts are laid if section 241(1) has been complied with in relation to them.

(4) In the following two cases:

(a) where the distribution would be found to contravene the relevant section if reference were made only to the company's last annual accounts, or

(b) where the distribution is proposed to be declared during the company's first accounting reference period, or before any accounts are laid in respect of that period, the accounts relevant under this section (called "interim accounts" in the first case, and 'initial accounts' in the second) are those necessary to enable a reasonable judgment to be made as to the amounts of the items mentioned in subsection (2) above.

(5) The relevant section is treated as contravened in the case of a distribution unless the statutory requirements about the relevant accounts (that is, the requirements of this and the following three sections, as and where applicable) are complied with in relation to that distribution."

(Section 241(1) requires the directors to lay the accounts, with directors' and auditors' reports, before the company in general meeting).

[17] Section 271 (requirements for last annual accounts) provides as follows:

"(1) If the company's last annual accounts constitute the only accounts relevant under section 270, the statutory requirements in respect of them are as follows.

(2) The accounts must have been properly prepared in accordance with this Act, or have been so prepared subject only to matters which are not material for determining, by reference to items mentioned in section 270(2), whether the distribution would contravene the relevant section; and, without prejudice to the foregoing:

(a) so much of the accounts as consists of a balance sheet must give a true and fair view of the state of the company's affairs as at the balance sheet date, and

(b) so much of the accounts as consists of a profit and loss account must give a true and fair view of the company's profit or loss for the period in respect of which the accounts were prepared."

Subsections (3), (4) and (5) contain requirements about auditors' reports which are not directly relevant to these appeals. Section 272 contains requirements about interim accounts prepared for a proposed distribution by a public company. No such accounts were prepared in this case (although the interim figures published by Queens Moat on 14 August 1991 have been relied on by Mr. Richards in some of his submissions).

[18] Section 277 (consequences of unlawful distribution) provides, so far as relevant, as follows:

"(1) Where a distribution, or part of one, made by a company to one of its members is made in contravention of this Part and, at the time of the distribution, he knows or has reasonable grounds for believing that it is so made, he is liable to repay it (or that part of it, as the case may be) to the company or (in the case of a distribution made otherwise than in cash) to pay the company a sum equal to the value of the distribution (or part) at that time.

(2) The above is without prejudice to any obligation imposed apart from this section on a member of a company to repay a distribution unlawfully made to him..."

[19] Finally § 727(1) (in Pt XXV, miscellaneous and supplementary provisions) provides as follows:

"(1) If in any proceedings for negligence, default, breach of duty or breach of trust against an officer of a company or a person employed by a company as auditor (whether he is or is not an officer of the company) it appears to the court hearing the case that that officer or person is or may be liable in respect of the negligence, default, breach of duty or breach of trust, but that he has acted honestly and reasonably, and that having regard to all the circumstances of the case (including those connected with his appointment) he ought fairly to be excused for the negligence, default, breach of duty or breach of trust, that court may relieve him, either wholly or partly, from his liability on such terms as it thinks fit."

Detailed Chronology of the Dividends

[20] During the hearing in this court a lot of time was taken up—more than should have been taken up at an appellate hearing—in establishing the basic facts as to what was shown by the published accounts of Queens Moat, on the basis of which the various disputed dividends were paid. One reason for this was the absence of Queens Moat's individual profit and loss accounts; apart from some limited information in notes they were excluded (under § 230 of the Act) from the published annual accounts, and apparently they were not put in evidence before the judge. Moreover the calculations at pp 19–20 of the dividends judgment are incorrect. It is therefore necessary to enlarge on the summary in para 5 above in what would otherwise be tedious detail.

[21] Until its affairs were finally engulfed in crisis at the end of March 1993, Queens Moat's financial affairs were conducted according to a very regular annual timetable. After the end of its accounting year on 31 December, it published its annual accounts at the end of April and held its annual general meeting at the end of May. Dividends on the 7% preference shares were paid half-yearly in January and July and dividends on the 7.5% preference shares (after their issue in mid-1991) were paid half-yearly in April and October. An interim ordinary dividend was paid in October (on account of profits for the then current accounting period, but on the basis of the accounts for the accounting period which had ended on the previous 31 December) The final ordinary dividend was (in 1991 and 1992) paid on the very same day as the AGM was held, so that the company's declaration of the final dividend must have been taken for granted, at any rate as regards the practicalities of preparing dividend warrants (this point emerged only on the second day of the hearing, and neither side sought to make anything of it).

[22] As from the beginning of 1991 and down to the crisis at the end of March 1993 the dividends paid by Queens Moat can be summarised as follows [omitted] ....

[23] The judge (having set out these figures in a slightly different format) stated that the 1990 accounts showed that Queens Moat had (individual company) distributable reserves of £11.9m but paid total dividends of £35.873m on the basis of those accounts, and on the 1991 accounts had distributable reserves of £11.5m but paid total dividends of £34.420m on the basis of those accounts. In my judgment that analysis is not correct, because it disregards provision for unpaid dividends proposed to be paid on the basis of the accounts in question. In the accounts for 1990 (notes 7 and 17) this provision appears as £13.164m, which can be recognised as providing (in full) for the proposed final dividend and (on an accruals basis) for the 7% preference dividend due on 7 January 1991. Similarly the accounts for 1991 (notes 7 and 15) provided for unpaid dividends of £18.0, which can be recognised as the proposed final dividend of £13.834m and about £4.2m for accruing preference dividends (on both 7% and 7.5% preference shares).

[24] The judge's presentation of the figures for dividends paid on the basis of the 1990 accounts must therefore be amended as in the following summary:.... [omitted]

[25] Similarly the summary for dividends paid on the basis of the 1991 accounts should be: [omitted]....

These figures may still not be wholly satisfactory if (as the court was told) the preference dividends were provided for on an accruals basis. But they give a much better general idea of the position. The total shortfall for the two years was a little under £16m rather than being in excess of £46m. The difference is significant, especially on the cross-appeal in relation to dividends paid on the basis of the 1990 accounts (see para 67 below).

[26] In the course of discussion of the accounts Mr Richards pointed out, correctly, that until a dividend has been formally declared by the company in general meeting, a shareholder does not actually become a creditor capable of suing for the dividend as a debt. But Sch 4, para 3(7) of the Act requires proposed dividends to be disclosed in the accounts (either in the profit and loss account or in a note) and it was not suggested that there was anything wrong in the treatment in Queens Moat's account of proposed dividends which were unpaid at the year-end accounting date.

[27] The figures mentioned above for distributable reserves are those of Queens Moat itself. The figures for distributable reserves in the group as a whole were £129.8m as at 31 December 1990 and £151.0m as at 31 December 1991, as appears from the consolidated balance sheets as at those respective dates. That has led Mr Purle to submit that any breaches of Pt VIII of the Act could be regarded as technical. He also submitted that even a technical breach might be avoided under the principle in Re Duomatic Ltd. [1969] 2 Ch 365, [1969] 1 All ER 161, on the basis that the action of Queens Moat in declaring dividends in excess of its own distributable reserves must be taken to have amounted to the informal declaration of dividends from its wholly-owned subsidiaries sufficient to cover Queens Moat's dividends.

[28] That is the first main issue in the appeals. The second main issue is whether the rule in Flitcroft's Case (see Re Exchange Banking Co, Flitcroft's Case (1882) 21 Ch D 519) applies to a company which is not in insolvent liquidation. The third main issue is whether the appellants' liability is limited (as a matter of principle rather than discretionary relief) to the difference between any unlawful dividends which they caused to be paid, and the dividends which could lawfully and would in fact have been made. The fourth main issue is relief under s.727 of the Act. There is some degree of overlap between these issues.

Unlawful Dividends

[29] It is important to note that although the judge found that unlawful dividends had been paid on the basis of both the 1990 accounts and the 1991 accounts, he reached these conclusions by significantly different routes. This difference was reflected in the pleadings (for example para 17C(3) of Queens Moat's re-re-amended defence and counterclaim in Mr. Bairstow's action). It was also reflected in the judge's decisions about relief under § 727. In relation to the first group of dividends (numbered 1, 2, 3 and 4 in the table at para 22 above) the judge held that they were unlawful because there was an insufficiency of distributable profits so that they infringed s.263 of the Act. He did not hold (indeed, it was not Queens Moat's case) that the 1990 accounts themselves failed to give a true and fair view so as to infringe § 227(3). But the judge did hold that the 1991 accounts infringed § 227(3), with the consequence that the dividends in the second group (numbered 5, 6, 7, 8 and 9) were unlawful not only because of § 263 but also because of § 270(5). Nevertheless he gave relief in respect of preference dividends (numbered 6, 7 and 9).

[30] In this court Mr. Richards has not sought to attack the 1990 accounts but he has mounted a strong attack on the former directors in respect of all dividends paid after the publication of the group's interim results (showing profits of £36.2m pre-tax, £30.8m after tax) for the first half of 1991. His contention is that those interim results are the real watershed since they depended on extraordinary and artificial transactions, not disclosed in the results, entered into for no purpose other than to inflate the group's apparent profits. It will be necessary to come back to that in connection with relief under § 727. At this stage it serves to explain why the battle lines have been drawn as they are.

[31] The provisions of § 270 of the Act are of central importance to this appeal. They ensure that a company's power to pay dividends (or make other distributions within § 263) is linked to and controlled by the very detailed codes for accounts laid down by ss.226 and 227 and Schs 4 and 4A These codes (originally enacted by the Companies Act 1980 and the Companies Act 1989 respectively) represent the implementation of the Fourth and Seventh Company Law Directives (78/660/EEC and 83/349/EEC).

[32] The purpose of those directives is (as appears from their recitals and also from Tomberger v. Gebruder von der Wettern GmbH [1996] All ER (EC) 805, [1996] 2 BCLC 457, 468 of the latter report (para 17) ECJ) to build on the basic need for "a true and fair view" by requiring a company's financial statements to conform to a uniform layout and terminology and to contain an irreducible minimum of information in the notes to the accounts. In the past it was often, as the Earl of Halsbury LC said in Dovey v. Cory [1901] AC 477, 486–7, difficult or even impossible to tell whether a distribution was being paid out of profit or out of capital. The stringent new accounting codes avoid that difficulty. As the judge said:

> "The statutory code is designed to avoid that difficulty by making it entirely clear on the face of the accounts whether or not a payment of a dividend is properly made. Furthermore the code is designed to be a major protection for creditors and members, as Dillon LJ stated in Precision Dippings."

In relation to the adjustments described in paras 23 to 25 above Mr. Richards argued, relying on the stringency of the new codes, that these adjustments would amount to an impermissible reconstruction which offended § 270(2). I cannot accept that submission since the unpaid dividends declared on the basis of the previous year's accounts were correctly shown as such (see Sch 4, para 3(7) referred to in para 26 above).

[33] The judge's reference was to Precision Dippings Ltd. v. Precision Dippings Marketing Ltd. [1986] 1 Ch 447, [1985] 3 WLR 812 in which Dillon LJ said of §§ 39 and 43 of the Companies Act 1980 (the predecessors of §§ 263 and 270 of the Act), at p 455 of the former report:

> "The term 'distribution' includes a dividend such as the dividend in the present case, and the effect of [§ 39(1)] is clearly, in my judgment, to make it ultra vires for a company to pay a dividend except out of profits available for the purpose, just as it has long been held to be ultra vires for a company to pay a dividend out of capital: see In re Exchange Banking Co (Flitcroft's Case) (1882) 21 Ch D 519."

[34] Dillon LJ then discussed §43 in its application to the facts of the case before him, and the argument that the absence of an auditors' statement (under what is now § 271(4) of the Act) was a mere irregularity. He continued at p 457:

> "I do not, however, regard compliance with section 43(3)(c) as a mere procedural matter which can be waived or dispensed with by the members entitled to vote. The group of sections beginning with section 39 and including section 43 is a major protection for creditors, and the requirement of paragraph (c) of an auditors' written statement, where the auditors' report in the relevant accounts has been qualified, is an important part of that protection."

[35] In the same way the requirement that any distribution should be made only in accordance with a company's financial statements, drawn up in the proper format and laid before the company in general meeting, cannot be regarded as merely a procedural technicality. Mr Purle made some submissions based on § 271(2), but that provision could assist only in relation to items which are not material to the process required by §

270(2). The items mentioned in § 270(2) are so comprehensive as to leave little room for immaterial items (particulars of staff numbers under Sch 4 para 56 is arguably an example of an item which would not be material). § 271(2) cannot assist the appellants in this case.

[36] The strict and mandatory character of § 270 must be fatal to Mr. Purle's argument based on Duomatic, not only in relation to the dividends based on the 1991 accounts but also in relation to those based on the 1990 accounts. The former directors could not go behind the figures for Queens Moat's distributable profits disclosed by the accounts which they had prepared (and in the case of Mr. Bairstow and Mr. Marcus, signed) and laid before the company in general meeting. Even if it could be shown that wholly-owned subsidiaries had distributable profits which could lawfully and prudently have been paid up by way of dividend to Queen's Moat, that would go to the issue of relief, not to that of liability.

The Principle in Flitcroft's Case

[37] This court has in Precision Dippings confirmed that directors are accountable to the company for unlawful dividends paid in contravention of the provisions of what is now Pt VIII of the Act, whether or not the dividends are demonstrably paid out of capital. But Mr. Purle (with support from Mr. Marcus and Mr. Porter, who concentrated their brief oral submissions on this point) has submitted that that principle, which is sometimes called the principle in Flitcroft's Case, applies only in the case of an insolvent company, where the payment of an unlawful dividend directly prejudices the interests of the company's creditors.

[38] Flitcroft's case (1882) 21 Ch D 519 was a case of an insolvent banking company. The liquidator issued a summons against five former directors who had between 1873 and 1878 been concerned, in varying degrees, in paying half-yearly dividends totalling £3,192 at a time when they knew that some items in the balance sheet were bad debts and irrecoverable, and that the company had no distributable profits. The company in general meeting declared the dividends, but on the basis of the misleading accounts presented by the directors. This court (affirming the order of Bacon V-C but with a variation as to the nature of the liability) held the directors jointly and severally liable for the amount of the dividends.

[39] Sir George Jessel MR expressed his conclusion as follows (at p 534):

> "It follows then that if directors who are quasi trustees for the company improperly pay away the assets to the shareholders, they are liable to replace them. It is no answer to say that the shareholders could not compel them to do so. I am of opinion that the company could in its corporate capacity compel them to do so, even if there were no winding-up. They are liable to pay, and none the less liable because the liquidator represents, not only shareholders, but creditors. The body of the shareholders no doubt voted for a declaration of dividend on the faith of the misrepresentation of the directors, so that there really was no ratification at all."

[40] Brett LJ agreed with that view. He said (at p 535):

> "In my opinion the corporation could at any time before the winding-up have compelled the directors to replace the moneys thus improperly expended, and the liquidator now can do so. Even if the shareholders had all sanctioned what was done, and had remained the same throughout, still the company could have sued the directors for a breach of trust. They are trustees for the company not for the individual shareholders."

[41] Cotton LJ expressed himself rather differently, and there has been some debate as to the real significance of what he said at p 536:

> "The argument that the money has in fact been received by the company, and that the company cannot get it back, is ingenious but unsound. The corporation is not a mere aggregate of shareholders. If the corporation were suing for the purpose of paying over again to the shareholders what the shareholders had already received the Court would not allow it. But that is not the case here, the company is insolvent, and there is no objection to allowing it to get back its funds for the purpose of paying debts. The case of the liquidator is stronger, for in some respects he, as a quasi trustee for creditors as well as shareholders, stands in a different position from the company. But I rely on this, that the money was not paid to the corporation, but was paid improperly to individuals, and the corporation can sue the directors to get it back that it may be applied in payment of the debts of the corporation. I do not see how to make any distinction between what the directors retained and what they paid to other shareholders."

[42] Mr. Richards suggested that Cotton LJ may have been directing his remarks to a particular situation, that is of a company which is in liquidation but which is expected to have surplus assets after paying all its creditors in full. In such a situation it might be either pointless or oppressive for a liquidator to cause the company to embark on a course of action which might in the end prove circuitous. If that was what Cotton LJ had in mind (Mr Richards submitted) then his remarks were correct. If not, his remarks were contrary to the views of the Master of the Rolls and Brett LJ, and this court should prefer the latter views.

[43] It is impossible to be confident whether that is what Cotton LJ had in mind. Neither he nor any other member of the court was proceeding on the basis that the delinquent directors could recover the unlawful dividends from other shareholders who had innocently received them. Cotton LJ, like the other members of the court, emphasised that the shareholders had been deceived. Yet he saw no difference between dividends paid to directors and dividends paid to other shareholders.

[44] In my judgment the point must be decided by reference to principle rather than authority. Queens Moat's case is founded on the fundamental proposition (which was affirmed by the House of Lords in Salomon v. Salomon [1897] AC 22 and which Cotton LJ had well in mind in Flitcroft's Case) that a corporation is a legal person separate from the persons who are from time to time its members (in the case of a company limited by shares, the shareholders). The basic rules about lawful and unlawful dividends, developed from the earliest days of company law and now elaborated in accordance with Community legislation, exist not only for the protection of creditors but also for the protection of shareholders. If directors cause a company to pay a dividend which is ultra vires and unlawful because it infringes these rules, the fact that the company is still solvent should not be a defence to a claim against the directors to make good the unlawful distribution. Against that both Mr. Purle and the litigants in person pressed the court with the prospect of shareholders receiving an unmerited windfall, if the amounts of unlawful dividends which they have received in the past were now restored to Queens Moat by the former directors and were again to be distributed (this time lawfully) by way of dividend.

[45] In considering this windfall objection it is no doubt right to ignore the fact that the appellants are in practice unlikely, in view of the very large sums involved and the costs orders already made against them, to be able to meet even a small part of any judgments

against them. It is not so easy to ignore the fact that the present shareholders in Queens Moat are probably a very different body of investors than those who received the unlawful dividends ten years ago. Some of those early investors may have cut their losses by selling their shares at the bottom of the market. Some of the present investors may have been astute enough or lucky enough to have bought their shares at the bottom of the market. Some may even have formed a view, in deciding to invest in Queens Moat, as to the prospects of a successful recovery on the counterclaim. These considerations put some flesh on the Salomon v. Salomon point. They are matters which the court cannot easily take into account, however strong its instinct to achieve a fair result and avoid anything which resembles double recovery. Nevertheless it may be assumed that some of the present shareholders did receive and benefit from unlawful dividends paid between 1991 and 1993.

[46] Even in relation to those long-term investors the objection taken by Mr. Purle and the litigants in person is in my judgment misconceived. If there is any unfairness in the situation it does not arise from the so-called windfall which (if and so far as it occurs) will be a distribution lawfully made on the basis of properly prepared accounts for 2001 or some later accounting period. It will be made out of distributable profits which are disclosed in those accounts. Any unfairness would, on the contrary, arise from long-term investors not being required to account for the unlawful dividends which they received in the past.

[47] The prospect of the former directors being able to claim contribution from innocent recipients of unlawful dividends was debated (somewhat inconclusively) in the course of the appeal hearing. The statutory remedy in § 277 of the Act is not in point (since it is available only to the company, and only against a shareholder with actual or constructive knowledge of the unlawfulness of this dividend). But it is stated to be without prejudice to any other obligation to repay an unlawful dividend. In Moxham v. Grant [1900] 1 QB 88 this court considered that the principle of equitable contribution as between delinquent trustees (Chillingworth v. Chambers [1896] 1 Ch 685) could apply as between company directors and shareholders who had received unlawful dividends with notice of the facts. Long-term investors in Queens Moat now know the facts as to the unlawful dividends, even though they did not at the time of their receipt. But they may long since have changed their positions.

[48] The debate was bound to be inconclusive since the possible liability of long-term investors was not an issue in the appeals. They were not parties to the appeals and the court heard no argument on their behalf. Conceivably the point may have to be considered, at some time in the future, in the context of the insolvency of one or more of the former directors. It is therefore better to say no more about it than that the possibility of such claims cannot be excluded. For all these reasons the windfall argument must in my judgment be rejected.

The Measure of Compensation

[49] Mr. Purle boldly attacked the proposition that delinquent company directors should be equated with trustees for the purposes of measuring their liability to make good losses caused by breaches of fiduciary duty. He submitted that all the earlier authorities on the topic must now be read in the light of the decision of the House of Lords in Target Holdings Ltd. v. Redferns (a firm) [1996] AC 421, [1995] 3 All ER 785. He also submitted that, if the court applies what is now seen to be the appropriate test, it is apparent that no actionable loss was occasioned by the unlawful dividends, since they could have been declared and paid in a lawful manner (that is, by first paying up distributable profits from subsidiaries).

[50] There is ample authority, spanning well over a century, establishing that although company directors are not strictly speaking trustees, they are in a closely analogous position because of the fiduciary duties which they owe to the company. Lord Porter put the matter succinctly in Regal (Hastings) Ltd. v. Gulliver [1967] 2 AC 134, [1942] 1 All ER 378, 159 of the former report:

> "Directors, no doubt, are not trustees, but they occupy a fiduciary position towards the company whose board they form."

[51] There is no need to multiply citations. One of the most recent reviews of the authorities is in the judgment of Nourse LJ in Re Duckwari plc [1998] 1 Ch 253, [1998] 2 WLR 913, 262 of the former report, citing Re Lands Allotment Co [1894] 1 Ch 616, 631, Belmont Finance Corporation v. Williams Furniture Ltd. (No 2) [1980] 1 All ER 393, 405 and (in relation to the measure of compensation appropriate to a delinquent trustee) Knott v. Cottee (1852) 16 Beav 77.

[52] The facts of Target Holdings are well known and it is not necessary to set them out in detail. The case concerned a claim against a firm of solicitors sued for its involvement in a mortgage fraud. Fraud as well as negligence was pleaded. On completion of the transaction the solicitors had (in breach of their instructions) parted with the mortgage advance before obtaining the security. Within a month, however, they did obtain the security. The claimant, as a possible short cut to having to prove fraud at trial, sought summary judgment on the basis of the unauthorised payment, despite the solicitors having obtained the security (which subsequently proved hopelessly inadequate). That is the explanation of the references in the speech of Lord Browne-Wilkinson (at pp 437 and 439) to "stopping the clock".

[53] The result reached by the House of Lords in Target Holdings has been generally welcomed but the route to that result has been much debated (see in particular Sir Peter Millett, Equity's Place in the Law of Commerce (1998) LQR 114 p 214–227; Professor C E F Rickett, Where are We Going with Equitable Compensation? in Trends in Contemporary Trust Law (1996) pp 183–9). In my view it is unnecessary to go far into that debate, since whereas the trust in Target Holdings was (as Professor Ricketts puts it) simply an aspect of a wider commercial transaction involving agency, the fiduciary obligations undertaken in this case by the former directors involved heavy and continuing responsibilities for the stewardship of the company's assets. They were not strictly speaking trustees, as title to the assets was not vested in them; but they had trustee-like responsibilities, because they had the power and the duty to manage the company's business in the interests of all its members. It may be that a more satisfactory dividing line is not that between the traditional trust and the commercial trust, but between a breach of fiduciary duty in the wrongful disbursement of funds of which the fiduciary has this sort of trustee-like stewardship and a breach of fiduciary duty of a different character (for instance a solicitor's failure to disclose a conflict of interest as in Canson Enterprises v. Boughton & Co (1991) 85 DLR (4th) 129, a decision of the Supreme Court of Canada discussed by Lord Browne-Wilkinson at pp 438–9).

[54] These points were not fully explored in the course of argument and it would not be right to express any definite view on points which are not necessary to the determination of this appeal. It is sufficient, in my view, to observe that this is a wholly different case from Target Holdings, in which (so far as concerned the application for summary judgment) the solicitors were shown to have done no more than to have acted imprudently in disbursing their client's funds before they obtained their client's security. In this case the former directors are liable for deliberately and (at least in relation to the 1991 ac-

counts) dishonestly paying unlawful dividends out of the company's funds which were in their stewardship. Those unlawful payments have never been reimbursed. Queens Moat's case does not depend on any artificial exercise in 'stopping the clock.' The judge (at p 42 of the dividends judgment) rejected the submission that there was no loss because lawful dividends could and would have been paid, had the 1991 accounts reflected the true position. But even in the absence of such a finding, the submission was in my view bound to fail.

[55] As a footnote to this part of the case I should mention a section of the judge's dividend judgment (at p 36) which is headed: "Breach of Contract (a) Fiduciary Duty". The judge found no breach of fiduciary duty in relation to "dividends paid under the 1990 accounts and the 1991 accounts when there were insufficient funds," but he did find a breach in relation to "dividends paid under the 1991 accounts when they did not give a true and fair view".

[56] The judge had a truly daunting task in preparing his three judgments in this case and I would be slow to criticise any presentational format which he adopted in order to ensure that he had covered all relevant issues. But I think that here and at some other points in his dividends judgment the multiplicity of sub-headings may not have assisted him. He had already considered "Breach of trust" under a separate heading (at p 29), similarly subdivided, and had concluded that the breach of trust in relation to dividends paid on the basis of the 1990 accounts (but not the 1991 accounts) could be termed a merely technical breach. Mr. Richards suggested, without dissent from Mr. Purle, that the heading "Breach of Contract (a) Fiduciary Duty" was addressed to the contractual duty of good faith or loyalty which every employee owes to an employer. These points are mainly relevant to the cross-appeal and the issue of relief, which are discussed next.

Relief under Section 727 of the Act

[57] As indicated in the summary at para 22 above, the judge found that nine dividends had been unlawfully paid, but he granted relief under § 727 of the Act in respect of seven of them: the interim ordinary dividend paid on 21 October 1991, and the six preference dividends (three in respect of the 7% and three in respect of the 7.5% preference shares) paid between 1 October 1991 and 7 January 1993.

[58] The judge's reasons appear at pp 43–9 of the dividends judgment. He began by directing himself, correctly, that the burden of proving honesty and reasonableness was on those who were asking for relief. He also directed himself that s.727 enabled the court "to consider the matter from an essentially subjective point of view". That cannot, with respect, be right as regards reasonableness. It is questionable whether it is right as regards honesty. As Lord Nicholls said in Royal Brunei Airlines v. Tan [1995] 2 AC 378, [1995] 3 All ER 97, 389 of the former report:

> "The standard of what constitutes honest conduct is not subjective. Honesty is not an optional scale, with higher or lower values according to the moral standards of each individual. If a person knowingly appropriates another's property, he will not escape a finding of dishonesty simply because he sees nothing wrong in such behaviour."

[59] The judge then considered the conduct of the former directors in relation to the various dividends which were challenged. Again he subdivided his consideration not only by reference to the two different years' accounts but also by reference to the type of dividend (preference or ordinary) and by reference to the reasons why the dividends

were unlawful. Again, I respectfully question whether this approach was not over-schematic and unhelpful.

[60] The judge decided in relation to the 1990 accounts and the insufficiency of reserves that the former directors had left that matter to Queens Moat's auditors, Bird Luckin, to deal with. He was prepared to accept that an honest and reasonable director might overlook his statutory obligations because he placed too much reliance on the auditors. He concluded, on the balance of probabilities, that the former directors:

> "...were neither dishonest nor unreasonable in being unaware that there were insufficient reserves available in the parent company to pay the dividends on the basis of the 1990 accounts, and that this rendered them unlawful under the Act."

Accordingly he gave relief in respect of the first four disputed dividends. This is challenged on the cross-appeal, especially by reference to the interim results for 1991 which had been published before any of these four dividends was paid.

[61] In relation to the dividends paid on the basis of the 1991 accounts the judge noted that they overstated the group's real profit very substantially (it was common ground that the true figure for the year's pre-tax profit should have been about £32.2m, against the published figure of £90.4m). He also held that none of the former directors had shown that he was acting honestly or in good faith; on the contrary, he was satisfied that their conduct had been dishonest. He refused relief in respect of the two ordinary dividends paid on the basis of the 1991 accounts. Nevertheless he granted relief in respect of the three preference dividends. He stated his reasons for this as follows:

> "In relation to preference dividends however it would have been possible, on the basis of Mr Spence's evidence, for an honest and reasonable director to have considered that the preference dividends should be paid, even on the basis of reduced profit, breach of the banking covenants and rising debt."

[62] Mr. Purle's appeal on the judge's refusal of relief for the last two ordinary dividends is in my view quite hopeless. The judge considered the 1991 final accounts in great detail (pp 57–170 of his main judgment). He reached clear conclusions which covered the personal involvement of each of the former directors. His conclusions were fully justified by the evidence (and there can be no appeal against them)....

[63] The judge made a specific finding that the former directors were dishonest in the preparation of the 1991 accounts, in order to deceive the market into the belief that the group was much more profitable than it actually was. Honesty and reasonableness are absolutely necessary preconditions for relief under § 727 (see, if authority is needed, National Trustees Co of Australia v. General Finance Co of Australia [1905] AC 373, 381, a case on the equivalent provision in the Trusts Act 1901 of Victoria). It was not open to the judge, having found that the former directors were guilty of dishonestly preparing false accounts for 1991, to find that they had acted honestly and reasonably in paying any dividends on the strength of those accounts. That disposes of the last point in the appeal, and it means that the Queens Moat must succeed on the cross-appeal in relation to the last three payments of preference dividends.

[64] Mr. Richards' case in relation to the other four dividends challenged on the cross-appeal is that although they were paid on the basis of the 1990 accounts, they were paid at a time when the former directors were well aware that the group's businesses (both in the United Kingdom and on the continent) were encountering very adverse trading conditions, and when they had already embarked on a large number of improper expedients in order to give a false picture of continuing profitability. Mr.

Richards pointed to the interim results for 1991 (published on 14 August 1991) as the watershed after which the appellants could not be said to have been acting either honestly or reasonably.

[65] The judge considered the 1991 interim accounts (as to their factual content) at pp 35–56 of his main judgment and (as to the former directors' responsibility for the accounts) later in that judgment. He held that the accounts were misleading in respects....

Some of the most blatantly improper transactions such as the Sloane Club episode (see pp 45–8 of the main judgment) had taken place during this half-year. The judge held that each of the appellants was personally responsible for the misleading accounts. Those findings of the judge are not open to appeal.

[66] How then did the judge conclude that he could and should grant relief in respect of any dividends paid after August 1991? I have already set out (in paras 60 and 61 above) the passage (at pp 44–6 of the dividends judgment) in which the judge set out his reasons. With great respect to the judge, who shouldered a huge burden in trying and deciding this difficult case, this part of his reasoning cannot stand. It involves the proposition that directors could act honestly and reasonably in paying one type of dividend, but not in paying another type of dividend, when all the dividends were paid either on the basis of annual accounts, or in informal reliance on interim accounts, which the directors had prepared in a way which was neither honest nor reasonable. That sort of schizophrenia is an impossible concept. The judge's reasoning also contains a false syllogism: the former directors paid preference dividends (based on false results); honest and reasonable directors might have paid preference dividends (based on true results); therefore the former directors were acting honestly and reasonably.

[67] So far as the appellants needed relief under § 727 I think the judge was wrong to grant it on any dividend paid after August 1991. But it is important to bear in mind that the judge did not find (and had not been asked to find) that the 1990 accounts failed to give a true and fair view; and that the judge substantially overestimated the shortfall in the distributable reserves because he overlooked the £13.164m provision for unpaid dividends as at 31 December 1990. The £11.9m of distributable reserves covered the preference dividends of £0.651m and £3.013m paid on 7 July and 1 October 1991. It also covered £8.236m (or thereabouts) of the interim dividend of £12.048m paid on 21 October 1991. Those distributions have not therefore been shown to be unlawful and it is not necessary for the appellants to make out a claim to relief in respect of them. I would allow the cross-appeal but only in relation to (i) the unfranked balance of the interim dividend, (ii) the two preference dividends paid in January and April 1992 and (iii) the three preference dividends paid in July and October 1992 and January 1993. It is not necessary to consider separately the claim (which is unanswerable) in respect of dividends received by the appellants themselves.

Conclusion

[68] For these reasons I would dismiss the appellants' appeal and allow Queens Moat's cross-appeal to the extent indicated above. Counsel should try to agree the figures to be inserted in the order on the cross-appeal.

SEDLEY LJ: I agree.

SIR ANDREW MORRITT V-C: I also agree.

Appeal dismissed.

Comments and Questions

1. U.K. law presents a system of national law in Europe closest in spirit to that of the United States. In what ways is the law in Britain different from that in the United States? On the liability of directors for unlawful distributions, Delaware provides by statute that directors are jointly and severally liable to the corporation generally, and its creditors in the event of the dissolution or insolvency of the corporation, for the payment of unlawful dividends or stock repurchases, at any time within six years of the payment or repurchase. DEL. GEN. CORP. L. § 174(a). Directors are entitled to seek contribution from other directors voting for or concurring in the action. *Id.*, §174(b). Directors found liable are subrogated to the extent of the amount paid by the director to the rights of the corporation against the stockholders who received the unlawful payment, dividend or distribution, but only to the extent that it can be shown that the stockholders had knowledge of facts which indicated that the dividend, distribution or repurchase was unlawful. *Id.*, at § 174(c). The Revised Model Corporation Act provision is similar. REV. MODEL BUS. CORP. ACT § 8.33. Under the Revised Model Business Corporation Act, however, actions against directors are barred unless commenced within two years of the unlawful distribution, and actions against shareholders for recoupment are barred unless commenced within one year of the final adjudication of the liability of the director. *Id.*, at §8.33(c).

2. Before the U.K.'s entry into the EU, the regulation of dividends was substantially a creature of common law. Membership in the EU has resulted in the recodification of much of British corporate law, currently subject to the Companies Act of 1985, and related acts.[1] U.K. corporations generally may not make a distribution except out of profits available for that purpose. Only realized profits are available for distribution; unrealized profit may not be used for purposes of calculating amounts available for distribution. *See* Companies Act of 1985, § 280. Available profits for distribution includes aggregate accumulated realized profits less aggregate accumulated realized losses. Companies Act of 1985, § 263.

Public companies are subject to further restrictions based on the transposition of the objectives of the Second Company Law Directive. Thus, distributions may not be made if giving effect to the distribution, the company's net worth is less than the minimum required to remain in the capital account and undistributable reserves. Companies Act of 1985, § 264(1). Undistributable reserves includes amounts in the capital surplus account,[2] a capital redemption reserve, and other accounts. The amount of the minimum capital account is based on art. 6 of the Second Company Law Directive, that harmonized the minimum capital rules for all public companies within the EU.[3] This minimum share capital, called the nominal capital of a company, is currently £50,000 for a public company.[4] Par value in the U.K., is equal to the aggregate shares of the company divided by the company's nominal capital. Thus, while

1. The Companies Act of 1985, like its 1980 predecessor was meant, in part, to transpose the requirement of the Second Company Law Directive, Second EC Directive of 13 December 1976, EC Council Directive 77/91, OJ L 26, 31.1.77, p. 1, as subsequently amended by EC Directive 92/101, OJ L 347, 28.11.92, p. 64.

2. This account includes funds received in consideration for shares in excess of the par value of the shares. Companies Act of 1985, § 130.

3. Originally the amount was 25,000 ecus (Second Company Law Directive, art. 6).

4. Companies Act of 1985, §118(1) (or such other sum as the Secretary of State may specify by order made by statutory instrument).

par value has lost much of its significance in the U.K., the concept of nominal capital has been strengthened as a result of the transposition of the Second Company Law Directive.

Share redemptions were originally prohibited in the U.K. but are now permitted under tightly regulated circumstances. First, the company's articles of incorporation must authorize repurchases.[5] Second the company must have authorized a certain number of non-redeemable shares.[6] For purchases of publicly traded shares, the terms of the repurchase must be approved by shareholders.[7] Repurchase by private companies and in off-market transactions require approval of the contract of purchase by the shareholders.[8] Such repurchases must be funded out of profits from which dividend payments could otherwise have been made or proceeds of an issue of shares sold for purposes of redemption.[9] In order to protect creditors from the possibility that the nominal capital will be affected by share repurchases, companies are required to establish a capital redemption reserve fund. An amount equal to the amount by which the company's share capital is diminished by the cancellation of the shares repurchased, if the repurchase was effected out of distributable profits, must be transferred to a capital redemption reserve. Only the difference between the aggregate price of shares sold to redeem other shares and the nominal value of shares repurchased need be included in the capital redemption reserve.[10] This reserve fund is then made unavailable for use in calculating the amounts otherwise available for dividend distributions.

Distributions from out of capital can be made under exceptional circumstances by a private company if authorized in its articles of incorporation, if all otherwise distributable profits are used first, and if the repurchase is authorized by shareholders.[11] Moreover creditors must be notified,[12] and given the right to object to a court for cancellation of the resolution authorizing repurchase out of capital.

Does the U.K. approach protect creditors better than its American counterparts? Are there other actors who the law is meant to protect?

3. How do the harmonization rules of the EU affect the nature of the British approach to director liability? It has been suggested that the Second Company Law Directive affected fundamental changes in British company law especially with respect to, among other things, "minimum subscribed capital, the distinction between private and public companies, distributions, considerations for shares generally and in particular the valuation of non-cash consideration." VANESSA EDWARDS, EC COMPANY LAW 52 (1999).

It is clear from the case that U.K. law regulating corporate capital in the context of shareholder distributions is now materially affected by not only the Second Company Law Directive, which is the subject of the section that follows, but also to a great extent by the EU's authority to harmonize accounting practices under the Fourth and Seventh Company Law Directives, which were introduced in Chapter 6, above. To this extent, at least, British law may begin to more markedly differ from the American.

5. Companies Act of 1985, §159(1) and 162(1).
6. *Id.*, at § 159(2).
7. *Id.*, at § 166.
8. *Id.*, at § 164.
9. *Id.*, at §§ 160, 162.
10. *Id.*, at § 170.
11. *Id.*, at § 171.
12. *Id.*, at § 175.

4. As you consider the materials in the section that follow, think about the ways in which EU harmonization efforts, especially with respect to the Second Company Law Directive, have played a part in shaping the U.K. approach to the protection of creditors and others through the regulation of corporate capital.

2. *Capital Requirements and EU Harmonization*

The capital requirements for the various forms of corporate entities permitted under national law is, in the first instance, strictly a matter of national law. We have seen how these rules form a core part of the regulation of companies throughout Europe, but especially in civil law countries.

The European Union's attempts to harmonize the various Member State rules relating to the capital requirements derive in large part from the Second Directive. The ECJ has, in a number of controversial decisions, directly and aggressively applied these provisions.

Second Council Directive 77/91/EEC of 13 December 1976

On coordination of safeguards which, for the protection of the interests of members and others, are required by Member States of companies within the meaning of the second paragraph of Article 58 of the Treaty, in respect of the formation of public limited liability companies and the maintenance and alteration of their capital, with a view to making such safeguards equivalent, as modified by Council Directive 92/101/EEC of 23 November 1992 amending Directive 77/91/EEC on the formation of public limited-liability companies and the maintenance and alteration of their capital.

(Selected portions; the full text of the Second Company Law Directive may be accessed from the official web site of the European Union: <http://www.europa.eu.int/eur-lex/en/lif/dat/1977/en_377L0091.html>).

Article 6

1. The laws of the member states shall require that, in order that a company may be incorporated or obtain authorization to commence business, a minimum capital shall be subscribed the amount of which shall be not less than 25,000 European units of account. The european unit of account shall be that defined by Commission Decision no 3289/75/ECSC (4). The equivalent in national currency shall be calculated initially at the rate applicable on the date of adoption of this directive.

2. If the equivalent of the european unit of account in national currency is altered so that the value of the minimum capital in national currency remains less than 22,500 European units of account for a period of one year, the Commission shall inform the member state concerned that it must amend its legislation to comply with paragraph 1 within 12 months following the expiry of that period. However, the member state

may provide that the amended legislation shall not apply to companies already in existence until 18 months after its entry into force.

3. Every five years the Council, acting on a proposal from the Commission, shall examine and, if need be, revise the amounts expressed in this article in european units of account in the light of economic and monetary trends in the community and of the tendency towards allowing only large and medium-sized undertakings to opt for the types of company listed in article 1 (4).

Article 7

The subscribed capital may be formed only of assets capable of economic assessment. However, an undertaking to perform work or supply services may not form part of these assets.

Article 8

1. Shares may not be issued at a price lower than their nominal value, or, where there is no nominal value, their accountable par.

2. However, member states may allow those who undertake to place shares in the exercise of their profession to pay less than the total price of the shares for which they subscribe in the course of this transaction.

Article 9

1. Shares issued for a consideration must be paid up at the time the company is incorporated or is authorized to commence business at not less than 25 % of their nominal value or, in the absence of a nominal value, their accountable par.

2. However, where shares are issued for a consideration other than in cash at the time the company is incorporated or is authorized to commence business, the consideration must be transferred in full within five years of that time.

Article 10

1. A report on any consideration other than in cash shall be drawn up before the company is incorporated or is authorized to commence business, by one or more independent experts appointed or approved by an administrative or judicial authority. Such experts may be natural persons as well as legal persons and companies or firms under the laws of each member state.

2. The experts' report shall contain at least a description of each of the assets comprising the consideration as well as of the methods of valuation used and shall state whether the values arrived at by the application of these methods correspond at least to the number and nominal value or, where there is no nominal value, to the accountable par and, where appropriate, to the premium on the shares to be issued for them.

3. The expert's report shall be published in the manner laid down by the laws of each member state, in accordance with article 3 of directive 68/151/EEC.

4. Member states may decide not to apply this article where 90 % of the nominal value, or where there is no nominal value, of the accountable par, of all the shares is issued to one or more companies for a consideration other than in cash, and where the following requirements are met : (a) with regard to the company in receipt of such consideration, the persons referred to in article 3 (i) have agreed to dispense with the expert's report; (b) such agreement has been published as provided for in paragraph 3;

(c) the companies furnishing such consideration have reserves which May not be distributed under the law or the statutes and which are at least equal to the nominal value or, where there is no nominal value, the accountable par of the shares issued for consideration other than in cash; (d) the companies furnishing such consideration guarantee, up to an amount equal to that indicated in paragraph (c), the debts of the recipient company arising between the time the shares are issued for a consideration other than in cash and one year after the publication of that company's annual accounts for the financial year during which such consideration was furnished. Any transfer of these shares is prohibited within this period; (e) the guarantee referred to in (d) has been published as provided for in paragraph 3; (f) the companies furnishing such consideration shall place a sum equal to that indicated in (c) into a reserve which may not be distributed until three years after publication of the annual accounts of the recipient company for the financial year during which such consideration was furnished or, if necessary, until such later date as all claims relating to the guarantee referred to in (d) which are submitted during this period have been settled.

Article 11

1. If, before the expiry of a time limit laid down by national law of at least two years from the time the company is incorporated or is authorized to commence business, the company acquires any asset belonging to a person or company or firm referred to in article 3 (i) for a consideration of not less than one-tenth of the subscribed capital, the acquisition shall be examined and details of it published in the manner provided for in article 10 and it shall be submitted for the approval of the general meeting. Member states may also require these provisions to be applied when the assets belong to a shareholder or to any other person.

2. Paragraph 1 shall not apply to acquisitions effected in the normal course of the company's business, to acquisitions effected at the instance or under the supervision of an administrative or judicial authority, or to stock exchange acquisitions.

Article 12

Subject to the provisions relating to the reduction of subscribed capital, the shareholders may not be released from the obligation to pay up their contributions.

Article 13

Pending coordination of national laws at a subsequent date, member states shall adopt the measures necessary to require provision of at least the same safeguards as are laid down in articles 2 to 12 in the event of the conversion of another type of company into a public limited liability company.

Article 14

Articles 2 to 13 shall not prejudice the provisions of member states on competence and procedure relating to the modification of the statutes or of the instrument of incorporation.

Article 15

1. (a) except for cases of reductions of subscribed capital, no distribution to shareholders may be made when on the closing date of the last financial year the net assets as set out in the company's annual accounts are, or following such a distribution

would become, lower than the amount of the subscribed capital plus those reserves which may not be distributed under the law or the statutes. (b) where the uncalled part of the subscribed capital is not included in the assets shown in the balance sheet, this amount shall be deducted from the amount of subscribed capital referred to in paragraph (a). (c) the amount of a distribution to shareholders May not exceed the amount of the profits at the end of the last financial year plus any profits brought forward and sums drawn from reserves available for this purpose, less any losses brought forward and sums placed to reserve in accordance with the law or the statutes. (d) the expression "distribution" used in subparagraphs (a) and (c) includes in particular the payment of dividends and of interest relating to shares.

2. When the laws of a member state allow the payment of interim dividends, the following conditions at least shall apply: (a) interim accounts shall be drawn up showing that the funds available for distribution are sufficient, (b) the amount to be distributed may not exceed the total profits made since the end of the last financial year for which the annual accounts have been drawn up, plus any profits brought forward and sums drawn from reserves available for this purpose, less losses brought forward and sums to be placed to reserve pursuant to the requirements of the law or the statutes.

3. Paragraphs 1 and 2 shall not affect the provisions of the member states as regards increases in subscribed capital by capitalization of reserves.

4. The laws of a member state may provide for derogations from paragraph 1 (a) in the case of investment companies with fixed capital. The expression "investment company with fixed capital," within the meaning of this paragraph means only those companies:—the exclusive object of which is to invest their funds in various stocks and shares, land or other assets with the sole aim of spreading investment risks and giving their shareholders the benefit of the results of the management of their assets, and—which offer their own shares for subscription by the public. In so far as the laws of member states make use of this option they shall (a) require such companies to include the expression "investment company" in all documents indicated in article 4 of directive 68/151/EEC; (b) not permit any such company whose net assets fall below the amount specified in paragraph 1 (a) to make a distribution to shareholders when on the closing date of the last financial year the company's total assets as set out in the annual accounts are, or following such distribution would become, less than one-and-a-half times the amount of the company's total liabilities to creditors as set out in the annual accounts; (c) require any such company which makes a distribution when its net assets fall below the amount specified in paragraph 1 (a) to include in its annual accounts a note to that effect.

Article 16

Any distribution made contrary to article 15 must be returned by shareholders who have received it if the company proves that these shareholders knew of the irregularity of the distributions made to them, or could not in view of the circumstances have been unaware of it.

Article 17

1. In the case of a serious loss of the subscribed capital, a general meeting of shareholders must be called within the period laid down by the laws of the member states, to consider whether the company should be wound up or any other measures taken.

2. The amount of a loss deemed to be serious within the meaning of paragraph 1 may not be set by the laws of member states at a figure higher than half the subscribed capital.

Article 18

1. The shares of a company may not be subscribed for by the company itself.

2. If the shares of a company have been subscribed for by a person acting in his own name, but on behalf of the company, the subscriber shall be deemed to have subscribed for them for his own account.

3. The persons or companies or firms referred to in article 3(i) or, in cases of an increase in subscribed capital, the members of the administrative or management body shall be liable to pay for shares subscribed in contravention of this article. However, the laws of a member state may provide that any such person may be released from his obligation if the proves that no fault is attributable to him personally.

* * *

Solred SA and Administración General del Estado

Case C-347/96
5 March 1998 (1)

Judgment:

1. By order of 3 July 1996, received at the Court on 21 October 1996, the Tribunal Superior de Justicia de Madrid (High Court of Justice, Madrid) referred to the Court for a preliminary ruling under Article 177 of the EC Treaty three questions on the interpretation of Articles 4(1)(a), 5(1)(a), 7 and 10(a) of Council Directive 69/335/EEC of 17 July 1969 concerning indirect taxes on the raising of capital (OJ, English Special Edition 1969 (II), p. 412), as amended by Council Directive 85/303/EEC of 10 June 1985 (OJ 1985 L 156, p. 23, 'the Directive').

2. Those questions were raised in proceedings between Solred SA and the Administración General del Estado ('the tax authorities') concerning payment of a charge on the notarial deed recording the subsequent contribution of part of the share capital, which had been fully subscribed when the company was formed.

3. The Directive is aimed in particular at achieving harmonisation of the factors involved in the fixing and levying of capital duty in the Community, by means of the elimination of tax obstacles which interfere with the free movement of capital.

4. Article 4(1)(a) of the Directive imposes capital duty on inter alia 'the formation of a capital company' and Article 4(1)(c) imposes it on 'an increase in the capital of a capital company by contribution of assets of any kind.'

5. In accordance with Article 5(1)(a) of the Directive, capital duty is charged, in the case of formation of a capital company or of an increase in its capital, on the actual value of assets of any kind contributed or to be contributed by the members, after the deduction of liabilities assumed and of expenses borne by the company as a result of each contribution. The provision states that Member States may postpone the charging of capital duty until the contributions have been effected.

6. Article 7(2) provides that Member States may either exempt from capital duty certain transactions referred to in the Directive or charge duty on them at a single rate not exceeding 1%.

7. The Directive also provides, in accordance with the final recital in its preamble, for the abolition of other indirect taxes with the same characteristics as capital duty or stamp duty on securities, the retention of which might frustrate the purpose of the measures provided for in the Directive. Those indirect taxes, collection of which is prohibited, are listed inter alia in Articles 10 and 11 of the Directive. Article 10 provides:

'Apart from capital duty, Member States shall not charge, with regard to companies, firms, associations or legal persons operating for profit, any taxes whatsoever:

(a)in respect of the transactions referred to in Article 4;

(b)in respect of contributions, loans or the provision of services, occurring as part of the transactions referred to in Article 4;

(c)in respect of registration or any other formality required before the commencement of business to which a company, firm, association or legal person operating for profit may be subject by reason of its legal form.'

8. The Spanish legislation applicable to the dispute in the main proceedings is contained in the consolidated version of the Ley del Impuesto sobre Transmisiones Patrimoniales y Actos Jurídicos Documentados (Law concerning duty on transfers of assets and documented legal transactions), approved by Royal Legislative Decree 3050/1980 of 30 December 1980, the amended version of which now in force was approved by Royal Legislative Decree 1/1993 of 24 September 1993 (Boletín Oficial del Estado, 20 October 1993) ('the Law').

9. Article 1 of the Law provides as follows:

'(1)Duty on transfers of assets and documented legal transactions is an indirect tax imposed, subject to the conditions set out in the provisions below, on:

1.transfers of assets for consideration;

2.company transactions;

3.documented legal transactions.

(2)In no circumstances may one and the same act be subject to duty on account of both transfers of assets for consideration and company transactions.'

10. Under the heading 'Rate of duty' and in the section relating to duty on 'documented legal transactions' in the paragraph 'Notarial deeds,' Article 31 of the Law provides:

'(...)

(2)Where original documents and notarial deeds have for their subject-matter a quantity or a thing of value, or contain acts or contracts required to be entered in the Commercial, Mercantile or Industrial Property Register and are not subject to inheritance tax or tax on gifts or the taxes referred to in Article 1(1) and (2) of this Law, they shall give rise in addition to the payment of duty of 0.5% for such acts or contracts. Copies of notices of protest shall be subject to the same duty at the same rate payable by means of stamped documents.'

11. Solred was formed by notarial deed of 21 November 1990, with share capital of PTA 300 000 000. On that date, the sum of PTA 180 000 000, that is to say 60% of the nominal value of the share capital, was contributed. On 28 November 1990 Solred paid the tax authorities the sum of PTA 3 000 000, equivalent to 1% of the nominal value of the share capital.

12. By notarial deed of 17 January 1991 the 40% of the capital not yet issued and paid up, that is to say PTA 120 000 000, was contributed to Solred. On 7 February 1991 Solred submitted to the tax authorities the assessment form for the tax payable for that second transaction, stating that it should not give rise to any duty, since 1% duty had already been paid on the whole of the share capital when the company was formed.

13. The tax authorities, however, calculated duty at the rate of 0.5% on the sum of PTA 120 000 000. They took the view that the duty on company transactions paid on the formation of the company did not mean that the document recording the paying-up of the part of the capital still to be contributed could not be liable to duty as being a 'documented legal transaction.'

14. Solred brought an action against that decision before the Tribunal Económico Administrativo Regional de Madrid (Madrid Regional Court for Economic Administrative Affairs) which was dismissed by decision of 13 December 1993. Solred appealed to the Tribunal Superior de Justicia de Madrid, which decided to stay proceedings and refer the three following questions to the Court of Justice for a preliminary ruling:

> '(1)Properly construed, does Council Directive 69/335/EEC of 17 July 1969 (as amended by Directives 73/79 and 73/80 of 9 April 1973, 74/553 of 7 November 1974 and 85/303 of 10 June 1985), in particular Articles 4(1)(a), 5(1)(a), 7 and 10(a), mean that, if the legislation of a Member State provides for a duty to be charged on the formation of a public limited liability company at the rate of 1%, calculable in all cases on the nominal value of the share capital, even where that capital has not been paid up in full, a duty of 0.5% may not then be levied on the contribution of the part of the capital not previously paid up?
>
> (2)Is the limitation in Article 10 of Directive 69/335 also applicable even though the second payment of duty does not specifically relate to a capital contribution but falls to be levied on the document recording that contribution, where the recording thereof is a mandatory requirement under domestic company law and the rate of 0.5% specifically relates to the amount of the contribution recorded in the document?
>
> (3)Does the aforesaid Directive 69/335 (as amended) have direct effect, and does it affect, and possibly prevail over, the provisions of national law in the event that those provisions cannot be interpreted in a manner compatible with the directive?'

The first two questions

15. By its first two questions, which it is appropriate to consider together, the national court is essentially asking whether the Directive precludes the charging of duty of 0.5% on the notarial deed recording the contribution of part of the share capital paid up after the formation of a capital company, where duty of 1% has already been charged on the whole of the nominal value of the share capital.

16. The Spanish Government observes first of all that the Law provides for an indirect tax imposed on transfers of assets for consideration and on company transactions and on documented legal transactions. Where a transaction formally recorded by notarial deed is subject to the duty under one of the first heads, the deed itself is exempt from the duty.

17. In this instance, the formation of the company, as being a company transaction, was subject to duty at the rate of 1% of the capital subscribed. Next, as a result of the decision to contribute the capital not paid up when the company was formed, which is a

subsequent and independent transaction, the notarial deed is subject to the duty on documented legal transactions because the transaction formally recorded therein is not liable to any other tax.

18. The Spanish Government makes it clear that the charge at issue in the main proceedings is levied on the notarial instrument and not the transaction itself, which is not liable to any taxation.

19. The Spanish Government goes on to state that neither the contribution of the capital not paid up at the time the company was formed nor its formal recording by notarial deed is a condition precedent for the company to commence business. The company is formed once the constituent document is registered in the Commercial Register and may then act freely.

20. Finally, the Spanish Government claims that this is not a formality to which companies are subject on account of their legal form, but a formality which is necessary where the share capital has not been paid up in full on the formation of the company. Whether or not there is a second payment depends solely on the wishes of the members.

21. Article 10 of the Directive, read in the light of the last recital in the preamble, prohibits in particular indirect taxes with the same characteristics as capital duty. It thus applies, inter alia, to taxes in any form which are payable in respect of the formation of a capital company or an increase in its capital (Article 10(a)), or in respect of registration or any other formality required before the commencement of business, to which a company may be subject by reason of its legal form (Article 10(c)). That latter prohibition is justified by the fact that, even though the taxes in question are not imposed on capital contributions as such, they are nevertheless imposed on account of formalities connected with the company's legal form, in other words on account of the instrument employed for raising capital, so that their continued existence would similarly risk frustrating the aims of the Directive (Case C-2/94 Denkavit Internationaal and Others v. Kamer van Koophandel en Fabrieken voor Midden-Gelderland and Others [1996] ECR I-2827, paragraph 23, and Case C-188/95 Fantask A/S and Others v. Industriministeriet (Erhvervsministeriet) [1997] ECR I-0000, paragraph 21).

22. Taxes paid on the registration of new public and private limited companies are directly referred to in the prohibition laid down by Article 10(c) of the Directive. A similar conclusion must also be reached where those charges are payable on the registration of increases in the capital of such companies, since they too are imposed on account of an essential formality connected with the legal form of the companies in question. While registration of an increase in capital does not formally amount to a procedure which is required before a capital company commences business, it is none the less necessary for the carrying on of that business (Fantask, cited above, paragraph 22).

23. Although the duty on documented legal transactions is a general indirect tax, it is none the less, in circumstances such as those of the dispute in the main proceedings, charged on the notarial deeds necessary for the registration of the payment of the part of the share capital yet to be contributed and, accordingly, for the paying up in full of the shares. It is therefore a tax imposed on account of an essential formality connected with a company's legal form.

24. Furthermore, even if neither the payment of the outstanding part of the share capital nor its recording by notarial deed constitutes a preliminary formality required before

a capital company can carry on business, the fact remains that in order for the company to carry on business it is necessary to register the contribution of previously unpaid share capital.

25. It follows that although the Member States may, in accordance with Article 5(1)(a) of the Directive, postpone the charging of capital duty until the contributions have been effected, they may not impose taxes on a document recording the subsequent contribution to a capital company of part of the share capital, which has already borne capital duty.

26. The answer to the first two questions must therefore be that, properly construed, Article 10 of the Directive precludes the levying of 0.5% duty on the notarial deed recording the contribution of part of the share capital paid up after the formation of a capital company, where duty of 1% has already been charged on the whole of the nominal value of the share capital.

The third question

27. By its third question, the national court asks whether the provisions of the Directive give rise to rights upon which individuals may rely before national courts and whether those courts are obliged to leave unapplied provisions of national law incompatible therewith.

28. It is settled case-law that where the provisions of a directive appear, as far as their subject-matter is concerned, to be unconditional and sufficiently precise, those provisions may be relied upon in national courts by individuals against the State where the State fails to implement the directive in national law by the end of the period prescribed or where it fails to implement the directive correctly (see, in particular, Fantask, cited above, paragraph 54).

29. In this case, it is sufficient to observe that the prohibition laid down in Article 10 of the Directive is expressed in sufficiently precise and unconditional terms to be invoked by individuals in their national courts in order to contest a provision of national law which infringes the Directive.

30. The Court has consistently held that every national court must, in a case within its jurisdiction, apply Community law in its entirety and protect rights which the latter confers on individuals and must accordingly set aside any provision of national law which may conflict with it, whether prior or subsequent to the Community rule (Case 106/77 Amministrazione delle Finanze dello Stato v. Simmenthal [1978] ECR 629, paragraph 21).

31. The answer to the third question must therefore be that Article 10 of the Directive gives rise to rights on which individuals may rely before national courts. Those courts are obliged to leave unapplied provisions of national law incompatible therewith.

Costs

32. The costs incurred by the Spanish Government and by the Commission of the European Communities, which have submitted observations to the Court, are not recoverable. Since these proceedings are, for the parties to the main proceedings, a step in the action pending before the national court, the decision on costs is a matter for that court.

On those grounds,

THE COURT (Sixth Chamber), in answer to the questions referred to it by the Tribunal Superior de Justicia de Madrid by order of 3 July 1996, hereby rules:

1. Properly construed, Article 10 of Council Directive 69/335/EEC of 17 July 1969 concerning indirect taxes on the raising of capital, as amended by Council Directive 85/303/EEC of 10 June 1985, precludes the levying of 0.5% duty on the notarial deed recording the contribution of part of the share capital paid up after the formation of a capital company, where duty of 1% has already been charged on the whole of the nominal value of the share capital.

2. Article 10 of Directive 69/335, as amended, gives rise to rights on which individuals may rely before national courts. Those courts are obliged to leave unapplied provisions of national law incompatible therewith.

Comments and Questions

1. The EU's harmonization legislation has had its most substantial effects on the direct legislation of company law capital requirements. It has influenced the indirect regulation of capital requirements as well. In this case, EU law reaches to affect the characterization, as a taxable event, of the act of notarial deed of share registration.

2. The Second Directive has had greater effect on the national legislation of the EU's Member States. This directive attempts to harmonize the capital requirements of companies within the European Union. As you read the excerpts and cases that follow, consider whether the sort of partial and focused harmonization efforts of the EU, reflected in the detail and narrowness of the Second Company Law Directive, provides a sound basis for supra-national intervention in national company law making. Do the materials that follow suggest that the EU ought to abandon the effort to harmonize company law and substitute for it a supra-national company law?

3. The Statute for a European Company, Council Regulation (EC) No 2157/2001 of 8 October 2001, which may be found at http://europa.eu.int/eur-lex/pri/en/oj/dat/2001/l_294/l_29420011110en00010021.pdf will enter into force on 8 October 2004. Under its provisions, a new form of corporate enterprise, not completely tied to the laws of any Member State, may be formed, the Societas Europaea (SE). The Statute provides with respect to capitalization that the capital of an SE shall be expressed in euros and that the subscribed capital shall not be less than EUR 120000. However, the Statute also provides that the laws of a Member State requiring a greater subscribed capital for companies carrying on certain types of activity shall apply to SEs with registered offices in that Member State. (Statute, Art. 4) Otherwise, the capital of an SE, its maintenance and changes thereto, together with its shares, bonds and other similar securities shall be governed by the provisions which would apply to a public limited-liability company with a registered office in the Member State in which the SE is registered. (Statute Art. 5) While this provision would appear to permit a wide variation in the treatment of capital depending on the Member State of residence of an SE, that may not be the case in fact. The Second Company Law Directive, discussed below, is intended to harmonize much of the law of capital regulation by the Member States.

Frank Wooldridge, Company Law in the United Kingdom and the European Community: Its Harmonization and Unification

(1991)
(excerpts pages 25–33; footnotes omitted)

THE SECOND DIRECTIVE

Enactment and Scope of the Second Directive

The Commission's proposal for a Second Directive was submitted to the Council on 9 March 1970. However, the Council failed to adopt it until 13 December 1976, and then only after amending it very radically. One interrelationship between the two Directives consists of the fact that the Second Directive contains certain provisions on disclosure in its introductory part which supplement those of the First Directive. Furthermore, as already pointed out, the full titles of both instruments are in similar terms. The Second Directive is principally concerned with the formation of public companies, and the maintenance and alteration of their capital. Member States may decide not to apply the Directive to investment companies with a variable capital and to co-operatives incorporated as public companies. In Great Britain, many of the provisions of the Second Directive have been made applicable to private companies. There is a fairly abundant literature on the Directive, which instrument unfortunately contains no subheadings.

Description of the Company

The enactment of the Directive makes it necessary for Member States to distinguish between public and private companies. Thus, in Great Britain a public company is one which satisfies certain rather complex requirements. Article I of the Second Directive requires that public companies be distinguished by name from private companies. This requirement is complied with in Great Britain by sections 25(1) and 27(4) of the Companies Act 1985, which require that the name of a public company shall end with the words 'public limited company,' which may, however, be abbreviated to p.l.c.

Disclosure Requirements

According to Article 2 of the Directive, the statutes or the instrument of incorporation must contain information concerning five matters. The name and type of the company must be disclosed, as also must the objects, the amount of the subscribed and if, applicable, authorized capital, and the duration of the company, if not indefinite. Article 2 also requires that the rules governing the number of and procedure for appointing members of the bodies responsible for representing the company with regard to third parties, administration, management, supervision or control of the company, and the allocation of powers among these bodies be disclosed, so long as they are not legally determined.

Article 3 requires the disclosure of eleven matters (some of which are irrelevant for British purposes), in the statutes, or in the instrument of incorporation, or in a separate document of which official notification in accordance with Article 3 of the First Directive, as well as registration are required. Disclosure is thus required of the nominal value of shares subscribed for, and at least once a year, the number thereof, for each class of shares. Furthermore, disclosure must be made of the amount of subscribed capital paid up at the time of incorporation or commencement of business; the total amount of all the costs of formation and preparation for the commencement of business; and any special advantages given to a promoter. Disclosure in respect of the last two items is required in Great Britain by section 117(3)(c) and (d) of the Companies Act 1985 (as amended).

Responsibility for Liabilities Incurred during the Period before Authorization

The above matter is dealt with in Article 4, which provides that responsibility for liabilities incurred by or on behalf of the company during the period before any authorization to commence business is granted must be specified by law, apart from liabilities incurred under contracts which are conditional on the commencement of business.

Dissolution of the Company

Article 5 is concerned with the winding up of the company if its membership falls below two. It provides that such an event does not lead to a dissolution ipso jure. Should a Member State's legislation provide for the dissolution of the company by order of the court under the latter circumstance, the company must be given time to regularize the situation. The Second Directive goes a considerable way towards recognizing one-man companies, which have long been permitted to exist in Germany and have also been introduced in Denmark, France, Belgium and the Netherlands in recent years.

Provisions Governing the Raising of Capital when the Company is Formed

Article 6 of the Directive provides that a public company may not be incorporated or be authorized to commence business, unless it has a minimum capital of at least 25,000 units of account. Shares may not be issued at a price lower than their nominal value, and the subscribed capital may consist only of assets capable of economic assessment.' An undertaking to perform work or supply services may not form part of these assets." Shares issued for a cash consideration must be paid up to the extent of 25 per cent of their nominal value at the time when the company is incorporated, or when it is authorized to do business. Shares issued for a non-cash consideration at either of these times must be fully paid up within five years of the relevant time. Articles 10(1) and (2) require detailed reports by experts on the nature and value of the non-cash consideration. Article 10(3) requires publicity to be given to the experts' report. A number of exemptions from the requirements of Articles 10(1)(3) are provided for by Article 10(4). The requirements of Article 19(1) and (2) have been implemented in Great Britain by sections 103 and 108 of the Companies Act 1985 (as amended), which may be criticized on the grounds of their undue complexity.

Article 11(1) is clearly influenced by the provisions of Article 52 of the Aktiengesetz concerning Nachgrundung, or secondary foundation. It provides that, should the company acquire any asset from any subscriber of its memorandum (or, at the option of each Member State, any shareholder or other person) within not less than two years of the incorporation for a consideration of 10 per cent or more of the subscribed capital, the issue must be examined published and approved by the general meeting. Article 11(2) contains certain exceptions to Article 11(1), one of which relates to acquisitions made in the ordinary course of business. Subject to the provisions relating to the reduction of subscribed capital, the shareholders may not be released from their obligation to pay up their contributions. The same safeguards as those which are provided for in Articles 2-12 must be operative in the event of the conversion of another type of company into a public company.

Increase of Capital

By Article 25(1), any increase of capital may be decided on by the general meeting. However, Article 25(2) provides that the statutes, the instrument of incorporation, or the general meeting may provide for increase up to an authorized amount, decided upon by the authorized body. This provision shows the influence of the German provisions concerning genehmigtes Kapital (approved capital) contained in Articles 202 et seq. of the German Aktiengesetz. As in the Federal Republic, the authorized body may be empowered to issue shares for a maximum period of five years; this authority may be renewed on one or more occasions by the general meeting. Article 25(3) requires meetings of every class of shareholders whose rights would be affected by the increase. The provisions already mentioned are said by Article 25(4) to apply to the issue of all securities which are convertible shares, or carry the right to subscribe for shares. Article 26 which, like Article 9, made certain changes in British law necessary—provides that shares assessed on an increase of subscribed capital must be paid up to the extent of 25 per cent of their nominal value, plus any premiums. The provisions of Article 27(1) and (2), which apply to contributions in kind made on an increase of capital, correspond with those of Articles 9(2) and 10(1)-(3), which are applicable to contributions in kind made at the time of the formation of the company. Member states are permitted to dispense with the valuation requirements contained in Article 27(2) in the event of a merger or public offer for the purchase or exchange of shares where the shareholders in the target company are paid with the shares issued.

Article 29(1) requires new issues of shares for cash to be offered to the existing shareholders on a pre-emptive basis. Such preemptive rights have existed in French, German and Italian public companies for a considerable period of time, 8% are common in American jurisdictions, and now exist in English public companies. Article 29(2) provides that pre-emptive rights need not be made applicable in the case of issues of preference shares and that, should there be different classes of shares, the right of preemption may initially be given to the members of the class issued. By Article 29(6), pre-emptive rights apply to convertible securities but not on their conversion. It is provided by Article 29(3) that the compulsory rights issue must be published in the national gazette, except when all a company's shares are registered (as is still frequently the case in the United Kingdom), in which case the shareholders must be informed in writing. The right of preemption must be exercised within at least fourteen days from the date of publication of the offer, or the date of posting of the letters to the shareholders.

Article 29(4) provides that the right of preemption may be excluded by the general meeting, on a written report of the administrative or management bodies. The general meeting must act by a majority of not less than two-thirds of the votes attached to the shares or to the subscribed capital represented, unless a simple majority would represent at least half the subscribed capital. Registration and official notification of such a decision are required. Furthermore, Article 29(5) provides that directors may be given the power to restrict or prevent a compulsory rights issue for up to five years, either in the company's statutes or instrument of incorporation, or by the general meeting acting at least by the majority indicated in Article 29(4). According to Article 29(7), underwriting commission in the form of shares is not to be taken as exclusion of the pre-emptive right.

Maintenance of Capital

The provisions governing the maintenance of capital cover a member of rather disparate topics. Article 15(1)(a) provides that no distribution may be made to shareholders if the net assets would then be lower than the subscribed capital and capital reserves. Uncalled capital is not normally to be included in subscribed capital. In addition, Article 15(1) provides that the amount of a distribution to shareholders may not exceed the amount of the profits at the end of the last financial year plus any profit brought forward and sums drawn from reserves available for this purpose, less any losses brought forward and sums placed to reserve in accordance with the law or the statutes. Member States may provide for certain derogations from the present rules for investment companies with a fixed capital complying with the requirements of Article 15(6). Article 15(2) contains special requirements governing the payment of interim dividends. By Article 16, any distribution in contravention of Article 15 must be returned by shareholders who have received it and know of the irregularity, or could not have been unaware of it. Furthermore by Article 17, a general meeting must be called to consider whether the company should be wound up or other measures taken when a serious loss of the subscribed capital, at most one-half, occurs. This provision would seem to be influenced by French and German law, and has not been very satisfactorily implemented in Great Britain by section 142 of the Companies Act 1985.

Article 18 provides that a company may not subscribe for its own shares. The acquisition by a company of its own shares by a Member State may be permitted subject to the stringent conditions mentioned in Article 19(1). Authorization must be given by the general meeting for a maximum period of eighteen months. The nominal value of all the shares acquired by the company must not amount to more than 10 per cent of the subscribed capital. The acquisitions must not have the effect of reducing the net assets below the amount of the subscribed capital and the distributable reserve. Only fully paid shares may be purchased by the company. Article 19(2) provides that the approval of the general meeting may be dispensed with when there is a need to prevent serious and imminent harm to the company. The phraseology used is reminiscent of Article 71(1) sentence 1 of the German Aktiengesetz. which permits a company to purchase its shares in order to prevent serious harm [schweren Schaden] to it.' In addition, Article 19(3) provides that the company may dispense with the approval of the general meeting where shares are purchased for distribution to its employees, or to the employee of an associated company, within one year of acquisition. The two permissive exceptions contained in Article 19 have not been adopted under British legislation.

Article 20 makes provision for further permissive exceptions to Article 19. These comprise the redemption of redeemable shares, the acquisition of shares on a reduction of capital; the acquisition of shares as a result of a universal transfer of assets; the issue of shares as underwriting commission; the purchase of shares as a result of a court order in order to protect minorities; the forfeiture of fully paid shares; the acquisition of shares to indemnify minority shareholders in associated companies; and other cases of less importance. Apart from redeemable shares or shares acquired on a reduction of capital, shares acquired in accordance with Article 20 must be disposed of within three years, in so far as they exceed 10 per cent of the subscribed capital. If they have not been disposed of, they must be cancelled. Shares acquired in contravention of Articles 19 and 20 must be disposed of within a year, or otherwise be cancelled.

The voting rights in respect of the shares acquired by a company in itself are suspended in accordance with Article 22, and so they cannot be used to increase the directors' control. If the shares are included among the assets shown in the balance sheet, a capital reserve of the same amount must be included among the liabilities. The company's annual report must give details of all such purchases. Subject to certain exceptions, a company may not advance funds, nor make loans nor provide security, with a view to the acquisition of its shares by a third party. The acceptance of the company's own shares as security is subject to similar conditions to the acquisition thereof. It is noteworthy that since the Second Directive is not concerned with groups of companies, it contains no general prohibition on a subsidiary purchasing shares in its holding company, which may be objectionable on similar grounds to the purchase by a company of its own shares. However, most Member States do in fact provide for such a prohibition and the omission, a necessary consequence of the 'salami' tactics of harmonization, is not an important one.

Reduction of Capital

By Article 30, a reduction in the subscribed capital must normally take place by a decision of a general meeting, taken at least by a majority of not less than two-thirds of the votes attaching to the securities and the subscribed capital represented. The notice convening the meeting must at least specify the purpose of the reduction, and the manner in which it is to be carried out. It follows from Articles 32 and 33 that the creditors have the right to protection if the reduction is due to over-capitalization, but not if it is to offset losses. This dichotomy is paralleled in the legal systems of Great Britain, France and Germany. It is provided by Article 31 that reductions of capital which affect a particular class of shareholders shall require a separate vote by that class."' Article 33 may be applied by those Member States, such as Germany, that wish to allow a reduction of capital in order to transfer the money into a statutory reserve, which may be used only to offset losses." Article 34 provides that the subscribed capital must not be reduced below the minimum permitted capital. The provisions of Article 35 would seem to relate to the parts de jouissance (reimbursed shares) known in France and Belgium. Those of Article 36 would seem to relate principally to the compulsory amortization [Einziehung] with a reduction of capital known to German law, according to which provision for such amortization may be made in the company's Articles. In the United Kingdom, the forfeiture of shares is permissible only in the event of the non-payment of calls." Articles 35 and 36 are both permissive provisions, and have not given rise to any changes in English law.

Final Provisions

Article 39 prescribes requirements for the redemption of redeemable shares; this provision is permissive in character, and seems to have been influenced by section 58 of the Companies Act 1948." Unlike the latter provision, however, it is not restricted to the redemption of redeemable preference shares. The rules contained in Article 39 are somewhat complex; this would seem to explain the complexity of the provisions of sections 159 and 160 of the Companies Act 1985 relating to the redemption of shares. As already indicated, Article 40 is concerned with the majorities required for certain decisions. Article 41 provides for exemptions from certain Articles in order to facilitate employee participation. Article 42 provides that for the purposes of the implementation of the Directive, the laws of the Member States shall ensure equal treatment to all shareholders who are in the same position. Recognition of this principle of non-discrimination occurs in British company law, and by the City Code on Take-Overs and Mergers. A corresponding principle known as Gleichsbehandlung is recognized under German company law."

Implementation

The Second Directive was implemented in Germany by a law passed on 13 December 1978." The next Member State to implement the Directive was the United Kingdom. Implementation occurred through the enactment of the Companies Act 1980. The Companies Act 1981 made 48 amendments to this Act, and repealed 24 of its provisions, one year later. The latter Act has now been replaced by the consolidating Act of 1985." Implementation took place in France by law no. 81-1162 of 30 December 1981." In Denmark, law no. 262, which amended the law governing public companies so as to give effect to the Second Directive, was passed on 9 June 1982. Implementation by a number of other Member States was also late. Thus in the Republic of Ireland it took place through the Companies (Amendment) Act 1983 of 5 June 1983. In Luxembourg, it occurred through the law of 24 April 1983, whilst in Belgium the implementing statute was passed on 5 December 1984. In Italy, implementation did not occur until the enactment of the Presidential Decree of 10 February 1986. In Greece, it occurred through the medium of the enactment of the Presidential Decree no. 409/86, whilst in Portugal it took place as the result of the passing of Decree Law no. 262/86 of 2 September 1986. Implementation in Spain took place as the result of the passing of Law 19/1989 of 25 July 1989 and Decree Law 1564/1989 of 22 December 1989, which have already been referred to in connection with the First Directive.

Comments and Questions

1. The Second Company Law Directive appears to have gone far to regularize the regulation of capital within the EU. To what extent do you think there is room for different forms of regulation of capital between the Member States?

2. The excerpt from Frank Woolridge, Company Law in the United Kingdom, above, suggests that the United Kingdom has had to do much to conform its statutes regulating corporate capital to conform to the basic requirements of the Second Company Law Directive. To what extent have these changes resulted in a system of capital regulation different from any of those in the United States?

3. While it has been a truism of sorts that the legal systems of the United States and the United Kingdom belonged to the same 'family'—the family of legal systems based on the English common law—the absorption of the United Kingdom into the EU has had a profound effect on lawmaking within the United Kingdom. It is possible to suggest now that British law is becoming more 'foreign' or different from that of the other members of the common law family. Membership in the EU has begun to reshape British law as it has had to absorb the continental—civil law—approaches to lawmaking, that strongly influence the EU. Do you agree with this characterization of the drift of British law? Can you make an argument that British law is really nothing more than a species of American law, having more in common with the law of Delaware than it has any independent features?

4. The institutions of the EU have sought to aggressively implement the Second Company Law Directive. The first case that follows, Commission v. Ireland, provides an example of that effort. The second case that follows, Karella and Karellas v. Organismos Anasygkrotiseos, illustrates the way that the European Court of Justice has made use of the direct effects doctrine to force implementation of the Second Company Law Directive, even when a Member State fails to act.

EC Commission v. Ireland

(Case 151/81)
European Court of Justice
[1982] ECR 3573
12 October 1982

* * *

Sir Gordon Slynn, the Advocate General, delivered his opinion at the sitting on 22 June 1982:

This is an application by the Commission, under Article 169 of the EEC Treaty, for a declaration that Ireland has failed to fulfil its obligations under the Treaty in that it has not brought into force the measures needed in order to comply with the Second Council Directive on Company Law Harmonization (No. 77/91 of December 13, 1976, O.J. 1977, L 26/1) within the period fixed for doing so by Article 43 of the latter. That period expired on 16 December 1978, two years after the date on which the Directive was notified to the Member States.

Ireland has not claimed, either in its written or in its oral submissions, that it has yet brought into force the measures required to comply with the Directive. It states that it has set in motion the drafting procedure necessary for that purpose. It draws the Court's attention to three difficulties to which it attributes the delay in implementing the Directive. The first is the complexity of the subject-matter, which entails substantial changes in Irish company law. The second is the time-limit prescribed by the Directive, which Ireland regards as excessively short, as is said to be demonstrated by the fact that other Member States have also failed to comply with it in time. The third is the Irish political situation, which has entailed the loss of a considerable amount of parliamentary time as a result of two general elections in seven months. In these circumstances, Ireland contends that the Court has jurisdiction to "give due weight to these realities," even though "they do not amount to a strictly legal justification." It stresses that it is Ireland's wish to implement the Directive as soon as possible and asks the Court to dismiss the application or to stay the proceedings pending the early enactment of the legislation.

In support of this argument, counsel for Ireland relied on a passage in the Opinion of Mr. Advocate General Gand in Case 31/69 Commission v. Italy (1970) ECR 25 at 42, where he concluded that the Court should not lightly censure the course of action of a Member State, when the latter has a "wide margin of error...in appraising a course of action." In that case, however, the Commission's complaint related to the delay occurring in practice in disbursing certain sums where it could be said that a margin of discretion existed. Here the obligation to implement the Directive is clear and not discretionary and the passage relied on does not assist in this case. Counsel for Ireland also relied on Case 91/79 Commission v. Italy (1980) ECR 1099 at 1104, where (according to counsel) the Court said that domestic circumstances peculiar to one Member State may be taken into account by the Commission, when the decision to commence or to continue the procedure laid down in Article 169 has to be taken. The passage relied on is, however, a summary of the Commission's argument and is not part of the Decision.

This Court has already stated, in Case 52/75 Commission v. Italy (1976) ECR 277 at 284, that any delays there may have been on the part of other Member States in performing obligations may not be invoked by a Member State in order to justify its own, even temporary, failure to perform its obligations. If the period allowed for the implementation of a directive proves to be too short, the appropriate means of action available to the Member State is to seek to obtain the necessary extension of the period by the competent Community institution. It has not been alleged that Ireland sought such an extension. Furthermore, it is well established by the cases decided by the Court that a Member State is not entitled to rely on circumstances or practices existing in its own internal system to justify failing to comply with obligations imposed on it by a directive.

Even if, as I said in Case 28/81 Commission v. Italy (not yet reported) the Court can of its own discretion delay the making of a declaration because of circumstances explained to the Court, it seems to me that the decision whether and when to refer a failure by a Member State to fulfil its obligations is eventually one for the Commission, and if the breach has been established in the ordinary way the Commission is entitled to its declaration, if it persists in the application.

The Court was informed at the hearing that Irish legislation to implement the Directive has now been drafted but was still awaiting parliamentary time.

By a telex message sent to the President of the Court dated 18 June 1982 the Chief State Solicitor has stated that a bill implementing the second company Directive was introduced in the Senate on 16 June 1982 and that it is confidently expected that the measure will have passed both houses towards the end of July 1982.

In the absence of an application by the Commission to discontinue the proceedings, it seems to me that, despite the steps which have been taken since the hearing, the Commission is entitled to the declaration sought and an order should be made in any event that Ireland should pay the costs. On the other hand, if an application were made by the Commission to discontinue the proceedings before the Court gave its judgment, that would be a matter for the Court to consider.

DECISION:

By application received at the Court Registry on 5 June 1981 the Commission brought an action under Article 169 of the EEC Treaty for a declaration that by not adopting within the prescribed period the national provisions needed to comply with Directive No. 77/91/EEC, the Second Council Directive of 13 December 1976 on co-ordination of safeguards which, for the protection of the interests of members and others, are required by Member States of companies within the meaning of the second paragraph of Article 58 of the Treaty, in respect of the formation of public limited liability companies and the maintenance and alteration of their capital, with a view to making such safeguards equivalent, (Official Journal, 1977, No. L 26, p. 1), Ireland had failed to fulfil one of its obligations under the EEC Treaty.

Pursuant to Article 43 of the directive, Member States were required to bring into force the laws, regulations and administrative provisions needed in order to comply with the directive within two years of its notification. It was notified to Ireland on 16 December 1976 and the above-mentioned period accordingly expired on 16 December 1978.

The Irish Government does not contest that it has not fulfilled that obligation. It emphasizes however that the delay in implementing the directive is due not to any lack of awareness on the part of Ireland or the competent Irish authorities of the need to implement the required legislation but rather to the complexity of the subject-matter, the directive, moreover, being only one of numerous complex measures adopted, at the

Community level, within the field of company law. The difficulties encountered in implementing the directive in Ireland and in several other Member States show that the period prescribed for implementation of the directive was insufficient.

Those circumstances cannot expunge the failure to fulfil one of its obligations with which Ireland is charged. According to well-established case-law of the Court, a Member State may not plead provisions, practices or circumstances existing in its internal legal system in order to justify a failure to comply with obligations and time-limits resulting from Community directives.

Attention should also be drawn to the fact that the governments of the Member States participate in the preparatory work for directives and must therefore be in a position to prepare within the period prescribed, the draft legislative provisions necessary for their implementation. It appears, however, from information produced in the course of the proceedings that no draft law had yet been placed before the Irish Parliament within the period prescribed for implementation of the directive or even when the Commission brought its action.

It must therefore be declared that by failing to adopt within the prescribed period the provisions needed in order to comply with Council Directive No. 77/91 of 13 December 1976, Ireland has failed to fulfil one of its obligations under the Treaty.

Costs

Under Article 69 (2) of the Rules of Procedure, the unsuccessful party is to be ordered to pay the costs. Since the defendant has failed in its submissions, it must be ordered to pay the costs.

On those grounds, THE COURT, hereby:

1. Declares that, by not adopting within the prescribed period the provisions needed in order to comply with Council Directive No. 77/91/EEC, the Second Council Directive of 13 December 1976 on co-ordination of safeguards which, for the protection of the interests of members and others, are required by Member States of companies within the meaning of the second paragraph of Article 58 of the Treaty, in respect of the formation of public limited liability companies and the maintenance and alteration of their capital, with a view to making such safeguards equivalent, Ireland has failed to fulfil one of its obligations under the EEC Treaty;

2. Orders Ireland to pay the costs.

Karella and Karellas v. Organismos Anasygkrotiseos Epicheiriseon AE

(Joined cases C19-20/90)
Court of Justice of the European Communities (6th Chamber)
[1993] 2 CMLR 865
30 MAY 1991

Sig Giuseppe Tesauro (Advocate General)

OPINION:

1. In this case, the Court is asked to interpret a number of provisions of the Second Council Directive 77/91 on co-ordination of safeguards which, for the protection of the

interests of members and others, are required by Member-States of companies within the meaning of Article 58(2) EEC, in respect of the formation of public limited liability companies and the maintenance and alteration of their capital, with a view to making such safeguards equivalent (hereinafter referred to as 'the Second Directive').

2. I shall briefly summarise the relevant national legislation and the background to the main proceedings.

Greek Act 1386/1983 of 5 August 1983 set up the Organismos Ikonomikis Anasygkrotiseos Epicheiriseon AE (Business Reconstruction Organisation, hereinafter referred to as 'the OAE'), a public limited liability company whose capital is entirely subscribed by the State and whose purpose is to contribute to the economic and social development of the country. To that end, the OAE may inter alia take over the administration and day-to-day operation of undertakings undergoing rejuvenation or nationalised undertakings. Section 8(8) of Act 1386/1983 provides that, during its provisional administration of the undertaking subject to the system established by the Act, the OAE may decide inter alia, by way of derogation from the provisions in force relating to public limited liability companies as regards the exclusive power of the general meeting, to increase the capital of the undertaking concerned. However, the original shareholders continue to have pre-emptive rights, which they must exercise within a certain period.

Act 1386/1983 was the subject of Commission Decision 86/167, which was adopted in the course of the procedure provided for in Article 93 EEC. In that decision, the Commission stated that it had no objections to the implementation of the Act, provided that, among other things, the Greek Government amended the provisions relating to capital increases in order to bring them into line with Articles 25, 26, 29 and 30 of the Second Directive. Subsequently, on 7 March 1989, the Commission initiated proceedings under Article 169 EEC on the ground that Greece had failed to fulfil its obligations under the Second Directive. Finally, on 10 March 1990, the Greek Parliament passed Act 1882/1990 amending the previous legislation as regards the point at issue in the way desired by the Commission.

3. The applicants in the main proceedings are shareholders in Klostiria Velka AE, a company subjected to the provisions of Act 1386/1983 by decision of 14 December 1983 of the State Secretary for Industry, Energy and Technology. On 28 May 1986 the OAE, which had taken over the administration of the company, decided to increase its capital of approximately 200 million dr by 400 million dr under Article 8(8) of the Act. The decision was ratified by the Greek authorities by Decree 162 of 6 June 1986.

The Council of State, to which the applicants applied for the annulment of the decree ratifying the increase in capital, which they claimed was unlawful on the ground that it infringed the Greek Constitution and the Second Directive, dismissed as unfounded their claims that the act was unconstitutional, but decided at the same time to stay the proceedings and submit three questions to the Court for a preliminary ruling on the interpretation of the relevant Community legislation.

4. In its first question, the national court refers impliedly to the Court's consistent case law on the direct effect of directives and asks whether Article 25 in conjunction with Article 41(1) and Article 42 of the Second Directive are free of conditions left to the discretion of the Member-States and are sufficiently precise for individuals to rely on them against the administration before the national courts, claiming that the rules set out in a legislative provision are incompatible with them.

For the moment, I shall not consider the question of the direct effect, if any, of Article 42, to which I reserve the right to return in the final part of my Opinion. In contrast, as far as Article 25 of the Second Directive is concerned, it must be observed that it lays down extremely clearly and precisely a general principle concerning capital increases of public limited liability companies in so far as the first paragraph states that 'any increases in capital must be decided upon by the general meeting.' This precept does not appear to be conditional on the provisions of the next paragraph, according to which the statutes, the instrument of incorporation or the general meeting may authorise an increase in the subscribed capital up to a maximum amount fixed by them with due regard for any maximum amount provided for by law. In fact, Article 25(2) provides for an individual, clearly defined derogation from the principle under which decisions to increase the company's capital are to be reserved for the general meeting, which itself precludes a national legislature from derogating from that principle above and beyond the cases for which express provision is made. Consequently, the derogation provided for in Article 25(2) is not such as to rule out the direct effect of Article 25(1).

5. The same applies to Article 41 of the Second Directive, under which the Member-States may derogate from Article 25 if such derogation is necessary for the adoption or application of provisions designed to encourage the participation of employees or other groups of persons defined by national law in the capital of undertakings. Whilst it is true that the provision does give the national authorities a discretion to derogate from the principle set out in Article 25, it is also true that such a possibility appears to be strictly limited to the case provided for, namely that of encouraging popular participation in companies' capital by facilitating share purchase on the part of a number of groups of people, in particular employees.

Apart from the express reference to employees, the aim pursued by the provision is also apparent from the fact that it also enables derogations to be made from Article 9(1) and Article 26, under which shares issued for a consideration must be paid up at not less than 25 per cent of their nominal value. This is intended in fact to facilitate share purchase by social groups which normally do not dispose of substantial sums.

Consequently, Article 41 does not enable Member-States to limit ad nutum the scope of the principle set forth in Article 25, but merely lays down a precise derogation with a view to the achievement of a specific social aim. The very reference to 'other groups of persons' must therefore be construed as referring to associations of employees or legal persons whose aim is in any event to foster popular shareholding and evidently not credit institutions or any entity governed by public or private law irrespective of the aims which they pursue. Consequently, the scope of Article 41 is not such as to preclude the direct effect of Article 25, apart from those cases for which express provision is made.

6. In its second question, the national court asks whether a legal provision comes within the scope of Article 25 of the Second Directive where it does not permanently govern matters relating to increases in the capital of a limited liability company but is intended to deal with the exceptional circumstances of over-indebted companies which are of particular economic and social importance for society as a whole and provides, in order to ensure the survival and continued operation of those companies, for the adoption by administrative act of a decision to increase the company capital, without prejudice, however, to the pre-emptive right of the existing shareholders when the new shares are distributed, and if so to what extent it is compatible with that provision in conjunction with Article 41(1) of the directive.

The first part of the question is concerned with the actual scope of Article 25 of the Second Directive. Indeed, as appears from the national court's order, the Greek Council of State is inclined to consider that Article 25 does not cover a national law which does not specifically govern increases in company capital but is intended to deal with exceptional situations in which some undertakings have found themselves on account of their over-indebtedness.

I shall say forthwith that I cannot agree with that view. The aim of the Second Directive consists in particular of ensuring minimum equivalence in terms of the protection afforded to shareholders. To concede that a Member-State was entitled, by means of special or exceptional legislation, to derogate from the provisions laid down at Community level to that end would considerably detract from the system of safeguards intended to be laid down by the directive and would therefore impair the uniformity of the minimum level of shareholder protection.

There is nothing in the wording or in logic to suggest that the Community legislature intended to restrict the scope of Article 25 to cases where undertakings are without difficulties, leaving the Member-States free to adopt special, exceptional provisions to cover crisis situations. On the contrary, the Second Directive expressly contemplates such situations but it does not mention any possible derogations from other provisions of the directive and merely provides that in the case of a serious loss of the subscribed capital a general meeting of shareholders must be called within the period laid down by national legislation to consider whether the company should be wound up or any other measures taken.

7. On the other hand, where the Treaty itself seeks to allow the Member-States to adopt particular measures in order to safeguard vital interests, it makes express provision for this and generally arranges for appropriate control mechanisms designed to obviate abuses.

It is in fact obvious that if every provision of Community law were to be regarded as being subject to a general reservation as regards exceptional events, this might impair the binding nature of Community law and its uniform application.

By way of confirmation of the legislative approach whereby any derogations are expressly set out, I would point to the Third Council Directive 78/855 concerning mergers of public limited liability companies, a special provision of which provides that Member-States need not apply the directive in cases where the company or companies which are being acquired or will cease to exist are the subject of bankruptcy, composition or other similar proceedings (Article 1(3)).

The absence of similar provisions in the Second Directive must lead one to the conclusion that the Community legislature intended to confer the greater scope on the provision which reserves to the general meeting decisions on increases in capital, precisely because of the major potential effects of such a change for the situation of the company.

8. As for the view that the national legislation at issue may fall within the derogations expressly provided for in Article 41 of the Second Directive, it must be observed that it emerges from an examination of the wording of Act 1386/1983 that transfers of shares, in particular to employees or their representative organisations, local authorities, other public-law entities, charitable institutions or social organisations or private individuals (Article 2(3)), constitutes just one of the possibilities and potential activities of the OAE and is not the principal purpose of its operations. Consequently, the provision is not such as to make the legislation at issue, taken as a whole, comply with the Second Directive.

The fact that the Greek Government amended the legislation at issue as regards the very point with which the Court is concerned is further confirmation, albeit not decisive in itself, of the observations which I have made in the foregoing.

9. The conclusions which I have reached regarding the interpretation of the provisions in question release me from having to consider the question on the direct effect of

Article 42 of the Second Directive as raised in the third question concerning the interpretation of that provision.

10. Before concluding, I shall briefly dwell on the Greek Government's request to the effect that the scope ratione temporis of the Court's judgment should possibly be limited.

In that connection, I would point out by way of preliminary that, according to the Court's case law, the interpretation which, in the exercise of the jurisdiction conferred upon it by Article 177 EEC, the Court of Justice gives to a rule of Community law clarifies and defines where necessary the meaning and scope of the rule in question as it must or ought to have been understood and applied from the time of its coming into force. It follows that the rule as thus interpreted may, and must, be applied by the courts even to legal relationships arising and established before the judgment ruling on the request for interpretation, provided that in other respects the conditions enabling an action relating to the application of that rule are to be brought before the courts having jurisdiction are satisfied.

It is only exceptionally that the Court may, in application of the general principle of legal certainty inherent in the Community legal order and in taking account of the serious effects which its judgment might have, as regards the past, on legal relationships established in good faith, be moved to restrict for any person concerned the opportunity of relying upon the provision as thus interpreted with view to calling into question those legal relationships.

The Court has made use of that possibility in very specific circumstances, that is to say a risk of serious economic repercussions due in particular to the large number of legal relationships established in good faith on the basis of the legislation deemed to be validly in force together with the consideration that individuals and the national authorities were moved to act inconsistently with the Community legislation in view of an objective, substantial uncertainty relating to the scope of the Community provisions, which uncertainty may possibly have contributed towards other Member-States or the Commission adopting that same conduct.

However, even in such circumstances, the Court has made an exception for the rights of persons who brought court proceedings or took equivalent action before the date of the judgment.

In this case, there is no element—in relation to either the interpretation of the provision at issue or the number of persons concerned—such as to justify derogating from principle of the retroactive nature of the interpretative rulings. I therefore propose that the Court should abide by the strict criteria which it has applied in its previous case law in this field and not limit the scope of its judgment ratione temporis.

In the light of the foregoing considerations, I propose that the questions referred by the Greek Council of State should be answered as follows:

1. Article 25 in conjunction with Article 41(1) of Council Directive 77/91 are unconditional and sufficiently precise, with the result that individuals may rely upon them before national courts as against the administration, claiming that rules set out in a legal provision are incompatible with them.

2. Article 25 in conjunction with Article 41(1) of Council Directive 77/91 must be interpreted as meaning that they preclude the application of national rules which, in order to regulate the administration of certain undertakings in crisis situations, provide for the adoption by administrative act, without a vote by the general meeting, of a decision to increase the company capital, without prejudice to the right of pre-emption of the original shareholders.

DECISION: By two judgments dated 25 May 1989 which were received at the Court on 22 January 1990, the Symvoulio Epikrateias (Council of State) referred to the Court pursuant to Article 177 EEC three questions for a preliminary ruling on the interpretation of Articles 25, 41 and 42 of the Second Council Directive 77/91 on co-ordination of safeguards which, for the protection of the interests of members and others, are required by Member-States of companies within the meaning of Article 58(2) EEC, in respect of the formation of public limited liability companies and the maintenance and alteration of their capital, with a view to making such safeguards equivalent (hereinafter referred to as 'the Second Directive').

Those questions were raised in two sets of proceedings between two shareholders in the company Klostiria Velka AE, on the one hand, and the Minister of Industry, Energy and Technology and Organismos Anasygkrotiseos Epicheiriseon AE (Business Reconstruction Organisation, hereinafter referred to as 'the OAE'), on the other. Those proceedings are concerned with an increase in that company's capital which was decided upon by the OAE and approved by the State Secretary for Industry, Energy and Technology.

The OAE is a public-sector body having the form of a public limited liability company which acts in the public interest under the control of the State. It was set up by Greek Act 1386/1983 of 5 August 1983. Under section 2(2) of that Act, the purpose of the OAE is to contribute to the economic and social development of the country through the financial rejuvenation of undertakings, the importation and application of foreign know-how and the development of Greek know-how and through the establishment and operation of nationalised or mixed economy undertakings.

Section 2(3) of Act 1386/1983 lists the powers conferred on the OAE in order to achieve those objects. It may take over the administration and day-to-day operation of undertakings undergoing rejuvenation or nationalised undertakings; participate in the capital of undertakings; grant loans and issue or agree certain loans; acquire bonds; and make over shares, in particular to employees or their representative bodies, local government bodies or other legal entities governed by public law, charitable institutions, social organisations or private individuals.

Under section 5(1) of Act 1386/1983, the Minister for the National Economy may make undertakings undergoing serious financial difficulties subject to the system established by the Act.

Under section 7 of Act 1386/1983, the competent minister may decide to transfer to the OAE the administration of the undertaking subject to the system established by the Act, deal with the undertaking's debts so as to secure its viability or wind it up.

Section 8 of Act 1386/1983 contains provisions on transferring the administration of the undertaking to the OAE. Section 8(1), as amended by Act 1472/1984 lays down the rules as to how the transfer is to be effected and governs relations between the persons appointed by the OAE to administer the undertaking and the undertaking's bodies. Accordingly, it provides that publication of the ministerial decision to subject the undertaking to the system established by the Act terminates the powers of the undertaking's administrative bodies and that the general meeting is to continue to exist but cannot terminate the appointment of the members of the administration appointed by the OAE.

Section 8(8) of Act 1386/1983 provides that, during its provisional administration of the company subject to the system established by the Act, the OAE may decide, by way of derogation from the provisions in force relating to public limited liability companies, to increase the capital of the company concerned. The increase, which has to be approved by the minister, may take the form of contributions in cash or in kind. The undertaking's capital may also be increased by set-off. However, the original shareholders retain their pre-emptive rights, which they may exercise within a time-limit laid down in the ministerial decision granting approval.

By decision of 14 December 1983 the State Secretary for the Economy subjected Klostiria Velka AE to the provisions of Act 1386/1983. The OAE took over the administration of that company in accordance with section 8 of the Act. During its provisional administration the OAE decided, under section 8(8) of Act 1386/1983, to increase the capital of the company subjected to the system established by the Act by 400 million dr. The State Secretary for Industry, Energy and Technology approved that decision. The decree provided that the original shareholders would have an unlimited pre-emptive right which they had to exercise within one month of the publication of the decision.

Marina Karella and Nikolaos Karellas, who are shareholders in Klostiria Velka AE, brought actions for the annulment of that decree in the Greek Council of State on the ground that it was contrary to the Greek constitution and the Second Directive.

In its judgments of 25 May 1989 the Council of State held that the applicants' pleas in law seeking the annulment of the decree on the ground of its unconstitutionality were unfounded. However, it decided that it should refer to the Court for a preliminary ruling the following questions—identically worded in the two cases—on the interpretation of the Second Directive:

(1) Are the provisions of Article 25 in conjunction with Article 41(1) and Article 42 of Council Directive 77/91 free of conditions which lie within the discretion of the Member-States and sufficiently precise that they can be relied upon against the State before a national court by an individual claiming that the provision of an Act is incompatible with those provisions of the directive?

(2) Does a legal provision come within the scope of Article 25 of Directive 77/91 where it does not permanently govern matters relating to increases in the capital of a limited liability company but is intended to deal with the exceptional circumstances of over-indebted companies which are of particular economic and social importance for society as a whole and provides, in order to ensure the survival and continued operation of those companies, for the adoption by administrative act of a decision to increase the company capital, without prejudice, however, to the pre-emptive right of the existing shareholders when the new shares are distributed, and if so to what extent is it compatible with that provision in conjunction with Article 41(1) of the directive?

(3) Is such a law compatible with the provisions of Article 42 of Directive 77/91 in view of the fact that it does not prescribe that the price of the shares is to be fixed by the State on the basis of the objectively established net worth of the undertaking and the resultant inherent value of the old shares but leaves it to the discretion of the administration to fix the price so as to make possible the necessary immediate inflow of capital into companies which, because of their difficulties, have had confidence in them shaken, although it does safeguard the pre-emptive right of existing shareholders when the new shares are distributed?

Reference is made to the Report for the Hearing for a fuller account of the facts in the main proceedings, the applicable legislation and the written observations submitted to the Court, which are mentioned or discussed hereinafter only in so far as is necessary for the reasoning of the Court.

The national court's questions essentially raise two issues. The first is concerned with Article 25(1) of the Second Directive. The national court wishes to establish whether, having regard to Article 41(1) of the Second Directive, Article 25(1) maybe relied upon against the administration by individuals in the national courts. It then asks whether Article 25(1), in conjunction with Article 41(1), is applicable with regard to public rules, such as those provided for in Act 1386/ 1983, which govern the completely exceptional cases of undertakings which are of particular economic and social importance for society and are undergoing serious financial difficulties.

The second issue is concerned with Article 42 of the Second Directive. The national court asks whether that provision may be relied upon by individuals and whether it has to be interpreted as precluding national rules of the type referred to above.

The Court will initially consider the first issue, since, in the cases at issue in the main proceedings, the lawfulness of the increase in capital predominates over the question of the value of the issue price.

The direct effect of Article 25(1) of the Second Directive

As the Court has consistently held, wherever the provisions of a directive appear, as far as their subject-matter is concerned, to be unconditional and sufficiently precise, individuals are entitled to invoke them against the State: see, in particular, Case 8/81, Becker v. Finanzamt Munster-Innenstadt.

Consequently, it should be examined whether Article 25(1) of the Second Directive, which provides that any increase in capital must be decided upon by the general meeting, satisfies those conditions.

It must be held in that connection that that provision is clearly and precisely worded and lays down, unconditionally, a rule enshrining the general principle that the general meeting has the power to decide upon increases in capital.

The unconditional nature of that provision is not affected by the derogation provided for in Article 25(2) of the Second Directive to the effect that the company's instrument of incorporation or the general meeting may authorise an increase in the subscribed capital up to a maximum amount which is to be fixed with due regard for any maximum amount provided for by law. That individual, clearly defined derogation does not leave Member-States any possibility of making the principle of the power of the general meeting subject to any exceptions other than that for which express provision is made. The same applies to Article 41(1) of the Second Directive, under which Member-States may derogate from Article 25(1) and Article 9(1) and the first sentence of Article 19(1)(a) and (b) to the extent that such derogations are necessary to encourage the participation of employees or other groups of persons defined by national law in the capital of undertakings. That derogation, too, is strictly confined to the case provided for.

Moreover, the fact that the Community legislature provided for precise, concrete derogations confirms the unconditional character of the principle set forth in Article 25(1) of the Second Directive.

It is appropriate therefore to answer the national court by stating that Article 25(1) of the Second Directive may be relied upon by individuals against the public authorities before national courts.

The scope of Article 25(1) of the Second Directive

As for the scope of Article 25(1) of the Second Directive with respect to an Act, such as Act 1386/1983, it should be examined in the first place whether such an Act falls within the field of application of the directive, since that legislation does not set out the basic rules on increases of capital and merely seeks to deal with exceptional situations. If that legislation falls within the field of application of the Second Directive, it should then be considered whether it can qualify for the benefit of the derogation provided for in Article 41(1) of that directive.

As far as the field of application of the Second Directive is concerned, it should be stated first of all that, in accordance with Article 54(3)(g) EEC, it seeks to co-ordinate the safeguards which, for the protection of the interests of members and others, are required by Member-States of companies and firms within the meaning of Article 58(2) EEC with a view to making such safeguards equivalent. Consequently, the aim of the Second Directive is to provide a minimum level of protection for shareholders in all the Member-States.

That objective would be seriously frustrated if the Member-States were entitled to derogate from the provisions of the directive by maintaining in force rules—even rules categorised as special or exceptional—under which it is possible to decide by administrative measure, outside any decision by the general meeting of shareholders, to effect an increase in the company's capital which would have the effect either of obliging the original shareholders to increase their contributions to the capital or of imposing on them the addition of new shareholders, thus reducing their involvement in the decision-taking power of the company.

However, that observation does not signify that Community law prevents Member-States from derogating from those provisions in any circumstances. The Community legislature has made specific provision for well-defined derogations and for procedures which may result in such derogations with the aim of safeguarding certain vital interests of the Member-States which are liable to be affected in exceptional situations. Instances of this are Articles 19(2) and (3), Article 40(2), Article 41(2) and Article 43(2) of the directive.

In this connection, it must be held that no derogating provision which would allow the Member-States to derogate from Article 25(1) of the directive in crisis situations is provided for either in the EEC Treaty or in the Second Directive itself. On the contrary, Article 17(1) of the directive provides expressly that, in the case of a serious loss of the subscribed capital, a general meeting of shareholders must be called within the period laid down by the laws of the Member-States to consider whether the company should be wound up or any other measures taken. Consequently, that provision confirms the principle laid down by Article 25(1) and applies even where the company concerned is undergoing serious financial difficulties.

The OAE further claimed at the hearing that the Second Directive could not apply to the special collective liquidation or rejuvenation procedures for companies incapable of meeting their commitments, since its field of application was confined to the normal operation of companies.

That objection cannot be accepted. The directive is intended to ensure that members' and third parties' rights are safeguarded, in particular in operations for setting up companies and increasing and reducing company capital. In order to be effective, that safeguard must be secured for members as long as the company continues to exist with its own structures. Whilst the directive does not preclude the taking of execution measures and, in particular, liquidation measures placing the company under compulsory administration in the interests of safeguarding creditors' rights, it nevertheless continues to apply as long as the company's shareholders and normal bodies have not been divested of their powers. Certainly, this is true where there is a straightforward rejuvenation measure involving public bodies or companies governed by private law where the members' right to the capital and to decision-making power in the company is in question.

It follows that, in the absence of a derogation provided for by Community law, Article 25(1) of the Second Directive must be interpreted as precluding the Member-States from maintaining in force rules incompatible with the principle set forth in that article, even if those rules cover only exceptional situations. To recognise the existence of a general reservation covering exceptional situations, outside the specific conditions laid down in the provisions of the Treaty and the Second Directive, would, moreover, be liable to impair the binding nature and uniform application of Community law: see, to this effect, Case 222/84, Johnston v. Chief Constable of the Royal Ulster Constabulary.

As for the idea that rules comparable to those set out in Act 1386/1983 might qualify under the derogation provided for in Article 41(1), it should be observed that that provision pursues a precise, well-defined social-policy aim, namely to encourage private individuals to hold shares. Like the exceptions provided for in Article 19(3) and Article 23(2) of the Second Directive, it is intended solely to encourage, in an objective and concrete manner, persons, such as employees, who generally do not have the means necessary to do so under the normal conditions of company law in the Member-States, to participate in the capital of undertakings.

Consequently, a national rule cannot take advantage of that derogation unless its practical application helps to achieve the objective of Article 41(1) of the Second Directive.

In that connection, it should be made clear that that condition is not fulfilled merely because rules, such as those contained in Act 1386/1983, provide for the possibility, as one of the available means of achieving their objective, of the public restructuring body's transferring shares to employees or to individuals. Such a possibility is merely hypothetical and ancillary.

It should further be made clear, as stated by the Advocate General in his Opinion, that the reference in Article 41(1) of the Second Directive to other groups of persons refers to shareholding by private individuals and is not concerned with the transfer of shares to credit institutions or to public-law bodies.

Consequently, the answer to the national court's second question must be that Article 25 in conjunction with Article 41(1) of the Second Directive must be interpreted as meaning that they preclude national rules which, in order to ensure the survival and continued operation of undertakings which are of particular economic and social importance for society as a whole and are in exceptional circumstances by reason of their excessive debt burden, provide for the adoption by administrative act of a decision to increase the company capital, without prejudice to the right of pre-emption of the original shareholders when the new shares are issued.

In view of the answers set out above there is no need to consider the national court's third question or the part of the first question which is concerned with the direct effect of Article 42 of the Second Directive.

Costs

The costs incurred by the Greek Government and the EC Commission, which have submitted observations to the Court, are not recoverable. As these proceedings are, in so far as the parties to the main proceedings are concerned, in the nature of a step in the proceedings pending before the national court, the decision on costs is a matter for that court.

On those grounds, THE COURT (Sixth Chamber), in answer to the questions referred to it by the Symvoulio Epikrateias by two judgments dated 25 May 1989,

HEREBY RULES:

1. Article 25 of the Second Council Directive 77/91 on Co-ordination of safeguards which, for the protection of the interests of members and others, are required by Member-States of companies within the meaning of Article 58(2) EEC, in respect of the formation of public limited liability companies and the maintenance and alteration of their capital, with a view to making such safeguards equivalent, may be relied upon by individuals against the public authorities before national courts.

2. Article 25 in conjunction with Article 41(1) of the Second Directive must be interpreted as meaning that they preclude national rules which, in order to ensure the survival and continued operation of undertakings which are of particular economic and social importance for society as a whole and are in exceptional circumstances by reason of their excessive debt burden, provide for the adoption by administrative act of a decision to increase the company capital, without prejudice to the right of pre-emption of the original shareholders when the new shares are issued.

Comments and Questions

1. What precisely did the European Court of Justice decide in this case?

2. The Karella case left some questions unanswered. Particularly important is the question of the power of Member States to order their national law in a way to minimize fraud within the context of their particular business culture. The case that follows required the European Court of Justice to consider that issue. In the process the European Court of Justice defined the powers of the Member States and their limits in the context of the capital requirements provisions of the Second Directive. Consider whether the explanation of the case that follows, clarifies the issues raised by the case.

Anastasia Samara-Krispis and Ernst Steindorff, Joined Cases C-19/90 and 20/90, M. Karella and N. Karellas v. Ypourgos viomichanias, energias kai technologias, Organismos Anasygkrotiseos Epicheiriseon AE, Preliminary ruling of 30 January 1991, requested by the Greek Council of State on the interpretation of Articles 25, 41 and 42 of the Second Directive on company law, not yet reported

1992 C.M.L. Rev. 615
(excerpt pages 619–24)

4. Karella and Karellas

The Karella case as reported above poses a similar problem and, thereby, leads to the conclusion that the handling of company law questions should be improved before the Community can continue to legislate in the field of company law. The Court, in Karella, is quite right if it holds that Article 25 of the Second Directive on company law,[48] according to its clear wording and its purpose, excludes national rules which provide for the adoption by administrative act of a decision to increase the company capital. Yet the clear words and even the purpose of an article may not suffice to solve a complicated company law question. Here again, a more subtle reasoning could have been envisaged. For this reason, we must focus our attention on Greek law, first.

(a) The rule of the Greek Law 1385/1983, the application of which is excluded by the Court's interpretation of the Second directive, is a part of a legal act, which aims at avoiding or overcoming particularly embarrassing insolvency cases.[49] It could be part of the legal infrastructure without which the functioning of enterprises and companies cannot be ensured. It has not been the subject of harmonization.

In its report of 7 June 1983 on the bill, which later became Law 1386/1983, the Greek government referred to large enterprises of "particular importance socially and economically" and which are deeply indebted. Importance depends on the product line of an enterprise and on the number of people employed. The report envisages "the uneconomical use of resources, the inefficient management, the unsound formation of capital, the combination of economic circumstances, the inefficient organization and the obsolete and uneconomical mechanical equipment" as causes of a crisis into which such enterprises have plunged. The enterprises, according to the report, should be subsidized for the purpose of reorganization, if considered "viable". Otherwise they should be dissolved.

In order to achieve this objective the Act established a special entity called "Organization for Economic Recovery of Business Enterprises" in the form of a company (société anonyme, capital amounting to two billion drachmae, payable by the Greek State), which has to operate in accordance with company law insofar as Law 1386/1983 does not provide otherwise. The legislator deemed it necessary to depart from the provisions of Commercial Law and Civil Procedure as well as from those of the specific law 3562/1956 "re: submission of companies under the management and administration of creditors and introducing a special liquidation," this latter being "inadequate" to achieve the objective referred to above. The Law transfers management to the Organization; it adopts a special credit policy, provides for a compulsory increase of share capital and/or liquidation for the reason of indebtedness.

The Law gives detailed regulations. Its Article 5 stipulates that an enterprise will be submitted to the application of the Law by decision of the Minister of National Economy. Thus far, 28 enterprises have submitted to that procedure pursuant to an application made by creditors. Seventeen enterprises have been sold out. At present 23 enterprises are considered to be non-viable within the meaning of the Law. It is within this context that the share capital of a company was increased in the Karella case, by administrative act, without approval of the shareholders. This obviously contradicts Article 25 of the Directive, according to which shareholders must decide.

(b) The Greek government has maintained, before the Court, that the Second Directive does not exclude such a special regime and that its Article 25 has no preeminence and does not exclude the administrative act according to which the share capital of the com-

48. O.J. 1976, L 226/1, latest amendment O.J. 1985, L 302/9.

49. For other legal possibilities cf. the contributions to Arbeiten zur Rechtsvergleichung, No. 129 Das Unternehmen in der Krise—Probleme der Insolvenzvermeidung aus rechtsvergleichender Sicht (1986).

pany was increased. One could have added that a special regime such as the one introduced by the Greek Law can be handled only under other provisions of Community law. Advocate General Tesauro and the Court have refused such arguments. The Court held, without further discussion, that the protection of shareholders, provided for by the Directive, must be guaranteed as long as a company exists with its proper structure.[50] We submit that this, again, is formalistic and that the Greek Government's countervailing argument merits further consideration. Here again, the legal debate should begin where the Court and the Advocate general have ended.

(c) Our argument is that directives harmonizing company law or other pieces of civil law should be interpreted as if these directives and other parts of national law are parts of one and the same body of law. Of course, directives may govern the interpretation of rules of national law. But if a directive should be in conflict with the policy of national rules, which have not been harmonized, the conflict cannot be solved by a recourse to the preeminence of Community law. A solution should be found rather by a reconciliation of directives and other pieces of national law, and this in the same way as it would be done by a national court where a rule of national company law is in conflict with special legislation applicable to specific cases of insolvency. Greek company law, even with provisions corresponding to the Directive, would not simply oust the Articles of Law 1386/1983. It would, according to the arguments of the Greek government, probably accept the rule that "lex specialix derogat legi generali." This rule should be appropriate for the interpretation of a directive also. The judgment seems to exclude the possibility that the Greek Court, the Symvoulio Epikrateias, in deciding the case applies such a rule.

The reason for our submission is that company law like the whole body of civil law and the law of procedure and bankruptcy law form part of the legal infrastructure, the functioning of which is a prerequisite for economic activity. This legal infrastructure did not begin to exist with the first measures of Community legislation. It functions in a complicated interaction following different rules of the whole body of law. Directives govern specific legislation as well as its interpretation. But hereby they also interfere with the interaction of rules of law. They may endanger the coherence of national law and, hereby, the legal infrastructure on which economic activity depends. In a recent case, though not in the context of harmonization of law, the Court has explicitly ruled that coherence must be safeguarded in the field of tax law.[51] The ratio decidendi applies for company law and its harmonization as well. This leads us to suggest that two conclusions must be drawn.

First, the interpretation of directives dealing with questions of private and of company law cannot be limited to what the clear words of a directive say or what can be deduced from the purpose of a directive. Where provisions of a directive collide with institutions of national law which have not been harmonized, interpretation should not be satisfied with the argument that Community law supersedes national law. It should rather aim at a reconciliation of the directive with national law in order to safeguard the coherence of legal institutions. This presupposes that the interpretation of directives must be handled with great care and on the basis of an exhaustive study of national company and civil law.

Second, with the interpretation incumbent on the Court, under Article 177 EEC, it may no longer be possible for the Court to exclude national law from its consideration. The preparation of the draft for a trademark regulation may be taken as evidence that

50. Para 30 of the judgment.
51. Case C-204/90, Bachmann v. Belgium, judgment of 28 Jan. 1992, para 23, not yet reported.

the Court will have to include national law in its considerations. If the interpretation of directives dealing with company law, as well as with other fields of private law, has to take into consideration the coherence of the whole body of law, then the Court must embrace that whole body of law in its reasoning, even if this body consists for a large or major part of national law rules. In the Bachmann case, the Court correctly discussed the law of Belgium. Advocate General Van Gerven has demonstrated, in the Marleasing case, how this task has to be approached.

We know that our submission calls into questions the system of Article 177 EEC, and that it would oblige the Court to tackle the more difficult problems of law, as embedded in civil and, specifically, in company law. But there are only three ways of solving the problems of Community legislation in the fields of private and company law. First the Court could restrict its own interpretation and leave it to the discretion of national courts under national law to see how to reconcile rules governed by a directive, and other parts of national law. This could make Community legislation ineffective. Second, if the Court wants to avoid ineffectiveness, it has to become a private and company law court, which avoids formalistic interpretation and itself develops these fields of law in their relations with national law. Hereby, the legal infrastructure, on which economy depends, will be preserved. We know that this would impose a burden on the Court exceeding the difficulties which the cases before the Court have caused thus far. The Court would even need judges who are experienced in private and company law. Third, the Court, confronted with such problems and, for this purpose, with national law and extricate itself from the difficulties by recourse to a more or less formalistic interpretation. Then it could be alleged that the judiciary of the Community cannot fulfill the tasks which the Community has taken on its shoulders be enacting directives in the fields of private as well as of company laws. Its reputation and its authority may be diminished. The least that would follow would be that national Courts, contrary to the cases dealt with here, in order to preserve coherence of legal rules, would be tempted to make use of the doctrine of "acte clair" and to resolve difficult, even important, questions within their own responsibility, without any reference to the Court.

We think that the progress of the Community will force the Court to shoulder the difficulties incumbent in harmonization of private and, specifically, company and law and, hereby, enable the Community to include private and, specifically, company law in its harmonization programme. Otherwise the Community should refrain from harmonizing private and, above all, company law until the judiciary can be adapted to the tasks which follow from such harmonization.

Dionisios Diamantis and Elliniko Dimosio (Greek State), Organismos Ikonomikis Anasinkrotisis Epikhiriseon AE (OAE)

Case C-373/97
23 March 2000 (1)

Judgment:

1. By order of 24 June 1997, received at the Court on 31 October 1997, the Polimeles Protodikio Athinon (Court of First Instance, Athens) referred to the Court for a preliminary ruling under Article 177 of the EC Treaty (now Article 234 EC) two questions on the interpretation of Articles 25 and 29 of the Second Council Directive 77/91/EEC of

13 December 1976 on coordination of safeguards which, for the protection of the interests of members and others, are required by Member States of companies within the meaning of the second paragraph of Article 58 of the Treaty, in respect of the formation of public limited liability companies and the maintenance and alteration of their capital, with a view to making such safeguards equivalent (OJ 1977 L 26, p. 1) and on the abuse of a right arising from those provisions.

2. Those questions were raised in proceedings between, on the one hand, Mr Diamantis and, on the other hand, the Greek State and Organismos Ikonomikos Anasinkrotisis Epikhiriseon AE (Organisation for the Restructuring of Undertakings, hereinafter 'the OAE).

Legal Background

Community law

3. Under Article 25(1) of the Second Directive:

> 'Any increase in capital must be decided upon by the general meeting. Both this decision and the increase in the subscribed capital shall be published in the manner laid down by the laws of each Member State, in accordance with Article 3 of Directive 68/151/EEC.'

4. Article 29(1) of the Second Directive provides that whenever the capital is increased by consideration in cash, the shares must be offered on a pre-emptive basis to shareholders in proportion to the capital represented by their shares.

5. It should be noted that the Second Directive does not provide for any penalty in the event of breach of any of its provisions. Furthermore, it does not require the Member States to introduce such penalties in the rules which they are to implement.

National law

6. Law No 1386/1983 of 5 August 1983 (FEK A' 107/8.8.1983, p. 14) applies to companies that are experiencing serious difficulties; it established the OAE, the object of which is to contribute to the financial and social development of the country (Article 2(2)). To that end, the OAE may, inter alia, take over the administration and day-to-day management of undertakings undergoing reorganisation or nationalised undertakings, take shares in the capital of undertakings, grant, issue or take out certain loans, acquire bonds and transfer shares, in particular to workers or to organisations representing them, to local authorities or to other legal persons constituted under public law, charitable institutions, social organisations or individuals (Article 2(3)).

7. Under Article 5(1) of Law No 1386/1983, the Minister for the National Economy may decide to place undertakings in serious financial difficulties under the scheme established by that Law.

8. Article 7 of Law No 1386/1983 provides that the competent Minister may decide to transfer to the OAE the administration of an undertaking subject to the scheme established by that Law, to reschedule its debts in such a way as to ensure its viability by way of a compulsory increase in its capital by way of subscriptions of capital or capitalisation of existing debts or by restructuring the debts, or to take steps to place the undertaking in liquidation in accordance with Article 9.

9. Under Article 8(8) of Law No 1386/1983, the OAE may decide, in the course of its provisional administration, to increase the capital of the company concerned by way of derogation from the legislation in force relating to public limited liability companies, which provides that the general meeting of shareholders is to have exclusive compe-

tence. The increase must be approved by the competent Minister. The former shareholders nevertheless retain their right of pre-emption and may exercise it within a period prescribed in the ministerial decision approving the increase.

10. On 7 March 1989, that is to say subsequent to the facts that gave rise to the main proceedings but prior to the order for reference, the Commission instituted proceedings for a declaration pursuant to Article 169 of the EC Treaty (now Article 226 EC) that the Hellenic Republic had failed to fulfil its obligations under the Second Directive. On 10 March 1990 the Greek Parliament adopted Law No 1882/1990 (FEK A' 43/23.3.1990). Since then, even during the provisional administration of a company pursuant to Law No 1386/1983, any alteration in its capital must be decided upon by the general meeting of shareholders.

11. Like the Second Directive itself, Law No 1882/1990 does not provide for any specific penalty for breach of any of its provisions, so that the normal penalties under private law could be applicable.

12. However, Law No 2685/1999 of 11 January 1999 (FEK A' 35/18.2.1999), which entered into force on the date of its publication, provides for a single remedy where an increase in capital has been decided upon in breach of the provisions of the Second Directive and, in particular, of Article 25(1), namely the right to full compensation for the damage suffered following such an increase. Under Article 28(2) of that Law, the action for compensation is directed exclusively against the Greek State rather than against the company concerned.

13. Lastly, mention must be made of Article 281 of the Greek Civil Code, according to which 'the exercise of a right is prohibited where it manifestly exceeds the bounds of good faith, morality or the social or economic purpose of that right.

Facts of the case and main proceedings

14. Mr. Diamantis was a shareholder in the public limited liability company Plastika Kavalas AE (hereinafter 'Plastika Kavalas), holding 1,000 shares with a nominal value of GRD 1,000 each, out of the initial capital of GRD 87,000,000, divided into 87,000 shares (or 1.15%).

15. At the beginning of the 1980s that company, which had been founded in 1973, was facing serious financial difficulties. In September 1982 its factory operations were suspended and in 1983, as a result of its over-indebtedness, it was close to bankruptcy. On 24 August 1983, 32 shareholders of Plastika Kavalas asked that it be placed under the scheme provided for by Law No 1386/1983. That request was repeated on 20 December 1983.

16. Following that request, the Advisory Committee provided for in Article 11 of Law No 1386/1983, having noted the extremely difficult situation in which Plastika Kavalas found itself, on 22 December 1983 issued an opinion recommending that the company be made subject to the special liquidation scheme provided for in Articles 7 and 9 of the Law.

17. The consequence of that scheme would have been the immediate liquidation of the assets of Plastika Kavalas and payment of its debts, which is what happened to a number of other over-indebted undertakings in difficulty.

18. Despite the opinion recommending and giving reasons for liquidation, by Decision No 212 of 3 February 1984 (FEK B' 60/8.2.1984) the Minister for the National Economy decided to place Plastika Kavalas under the scheme for provisional OAE administration provided for in Article 7 of Law No 1386/1983. That scheme was maintained until the beginning of January 1987.

19. On 28 May 1986, under that provisional administration, the OAE decided to increase the capital of Plastika Kavalas by GRD 177,000,000 by the issue of 1,770,000 new

shares with a nominal value of GRD 100 each. The capital of the company was thus increased to GRD 264,000,000. That decision was approved by the Minister for Industry by Decision No 155 of 6 June 1986 (FEK B' 414/11.6.1986).

20. Since the former shareholders did not exercise their right of pre-emption within the prescribed period of 45 days from publication of that ministerial decision, all the new shares were issued to the OAE, which accordingly held approximately 67% of the capital of Plastika Kavalas.

21. On 11 December 1986, by resolution of the general meeting of the shareholders, where the OAE held a majority of the votes, the capital of the company was reduced to GRD 5,000,000, the minimum allowed by law. That reduction was prompted by the negative nature of the net situation of Plastika Kavalas and was effected by the cancellation of all the former shares and the issue of 5,000 new shares with a nominal value of GRD 1 000 each, which were allocated between those who had held shares in the company until that date in proportion to their shareholding. That resolution of the general meeting was approved by the Prefect of Kavala by Decision No 882 of 4 March 1987 (FEK 262/19.3.1987).

22. By Decision No 14 of 9 January 1987, the Second Minister for Industry, Energy and Technology (FEK B' 25/16.1.1987) approved a further increase in the capital of the company. The increase amounted to GRD 1,262,200,000 and was the result of, first, the compulsory conversion into shares of debts amounting to GRD 972,000,000 and, secondly, a contribution of GRD 290,000,000 in cash from the OAE for the repayment of creditors.

23. Following those alterations, the capital of Plastika Kavalas amounted to GRD 1,267,200,000, divided into 1,267,200 shares. From that time Plastika Kavalas operated normally for more than four years. Pursuant to Ministerial Decision No 14, the provisions of Law No 1386/1983 ceased to apply. The administration and operation of Plastika Kavalas were governed from then on by the decisions of the general meeting of shareholders and its administrative board.

24. In 1991 the majority of shares in Plastika Kavalas were transferred to Plastika Makedonias AE at a price of GRD 860,000,000. Lastly, in February 1994, Plastika Kavalas was taken over by the Petzetakis Group.

25. On 22 February 1991 Mr Diamantis brought an action in the national court seeking a declaration that the alterations in the capital of the company (two increases and one reduction) were invalid, on the ground that they were contrary to Article 25 of the Second Directive. The Greek Government and the OAE pleaded abuse of rights by Mr Diamantis and asked that the action be dismissed.

26. In its order for reference the national court cited, first, the Court's previous case-law on the direct effect of Article 25 of the Second Directive (Joined Cases C-19/90 and C-20/90 Karella and Karellas v. Minister of Industry, Energy and Technology and Another [1991] ECR I-2691 and Case C-381/89 Sindesmos Melon tis Eleftheras Evangelikis Ekklisias and Others v. Greek State and Others [1992] ECR I-2111) and concluded that it was clear from that case-law that Articles 8 and 10 of Law No 1386/1983 were contrary to the provisions of the Second Directive.

27. The national court accordingly held that the action was well founded in law, but also considered that the plea of abuse of rights as provided for in Article 281 of the Civil Code was well founded in law and on the facts.

28. The facts on which that plea was based were as follows:

– Mr. Diamantis and 32 other shareholders asked for Plastika Kavalas to be made subject to the scheme under Law No 1386/1983,

– because of the difficult financial situation in which Plastika Kavalas found itself, Mr. Diamantis had not been in favour of increasing the capital of the company and therefore did not exercise the right of pre-emption granted to him at the time of the first increase,

– Plastika Kavalas was reorganised by means of capitalisation of its debts and the payment of its creditors, which had substantial and irreversible consequences as far as shareholdings in its capital were concerned, in view of the fact that periods of five years and four years elapsed after the above-mentioned increases and the intervening reduction.

29. The national court therefore accepted that Article 281 of the Civil Code could be applied to defeat rights arising under Community law when there was an abuse of rights within the meaning of that provision. However, in view of the attitude taken by the Court of Justice in Case C-441/93 Pafitis and Others v. TKE and Others [1996] ECR I-1347, paragraphs 68 to 70 in relation to the same plea raised pursuant to Article 281 of the Civil Code, the national court considered that it was faced with a problem of interpretation of Articles 25(1) and 29(1) of the Second Directive with regard to the plea of abuse of rights.

30. In the circumstances the Polimeles Protodikio Athinon decided to stay proceedings and refer the following questions to the Court of Justice for a preliminary ruling:

'1.In the specific factual circumstances set out in the grounds of this order, does a question arise as to the application, in law and in substance, of Article 281 of the Greek Civil Code concerning abuse of rights by a plaintiff in relation to Articles 25(1) and 29(1) of the Second Directive?,

2.Should the Court of Justice of the European Communities find the above plea well founded in law and in substance, how will that affect the validity of the ministerial decisions increasing and reducing the capital of the company in question, of which the plaintiff happens to be a shareholder, and, by extension, are Articles 8(8) and 10(1) of Law No 1386/1983 compatible with Community law, in view of the fact that, where Article 281 of the Civil Code does not come into play, it has been held in accordance with the above that those provisions are contrary to the Second Directive?

Question 1

31. By its first question the national court is asking, essentially, whether, in the light of the circumstances at issue in the main proceedings, a national provision which penalises abuse of rights may validly be relied on to defeat an action for a declaration that social measures are invalid brought by a shareholder on the basis of breach of a right conferred by Article 25 of the Second Directive.

32. The preliminary point must be made that, as the Court has already held in Case C-367/96 Kefalas and Others v. Greek State and Others [1998] ECR I-2843, paragraph 28, the objective of Article 25(1) of the Second Directive is to ensure, for the benefit of shareholders, that a decision increasing the capital of the company and, consequently, affecting the share of equity held by them, is not taken without their participation in the exercise of the decision-making powers of the company. According to the case-law, that objective would be seriously frustrated if the Member States were entitled to derogate from the provisions of the directive by maintaining in force rules—even rules

categorised as special or exceptional—under which it was possible to decide by administrative measure, outside any decision by the general meeting of shareholders, to effect an increase in the company's capital (Karella and Karellas, cited above, paragraph 26).

33. However, Community law cannot be relied on for abusive or fraudulent ends (see Kefalas and Others, cited above, paragraph 20, and the case-law cited there). That would be the case if a shareholder, in reliance on Article 25(1) of the Second Directive, brought an action for the purpose of deriving, to the detriment of the company, an improper advantage, manifestly contrary to the objective of that provision (Kefalas and Others, cited above, paragraph 28).

34. Although national courts may, therefore, take account—on the basis of objective evidence—of abuse on the part of the person concerned in order, where appropriate, to deny him the benefit of the provisions of Community law on which he seeks to rely, they must nevertheless assess such conduct in the light of the objectives pursued by those provisions (Case C-206/94 Paletta [1996] ECR I-2357, paragraph 25). The application of a national rule such as Article 281 of the Civil Code must not, therefore, detract from the full effect and uniform application of Community law in the Member States (Pafitis and Others, cited above, paragraph 68).

35. It is for the national court to determine whether, in the case before it, application of Article 281 of the Civil Code is compatible with that requirement. However, the Court has jurisdiction to provide the national court with guidance on interpretation to enable it to assess that issue of compatibility.

36. In that connection, it is clear from the above judgments in Pafitis and Others, Paragraph 70, and Kefalas and Others, paragraph 29, that a shareholder relying on Article 25(1) of the Second Directive cannot be deemed to be abusing his rights merely because he is a minority shareholder of a company subject to reorganisation measures, or has benefited from the reorganisation of the company, or has not exercised his right of preemption. Similarly, the fact that the plaintiff in the main proceedings asked that Plastika Kavalas be made subject to the scheme under Law No. 1386/1983 does not indicate an abuse of rights.

37. As the Advocate General observed in point 29 of his Opinion, once a company is placed under the scheme provided for under Law No 1386/1983, a wide range of solutions regarding the treatment to be applied to it is available, so that a request for that Law to be applied cannot be treated as agreement to the power to take decisions with regard to increases in capital being transferred to a body external to the general meeting. A shareholder relying on Article 25(1) of the Second Directive cannot, therefore, be said to be abusing his rights under that provision on the ground that he was one of the shareholders who asked that the company be placed under the scheme of Law No 1386/1983.

38. It must next be determined whether Community law precludes the national court from verifying whether, in choosing to bring an action for a declaration that the alterations in capital were invalid, after periods of five years and four years had elapsed, the plaintiff in the main proceedings was seeking to derive, to the detriment of Plastika Kavalas, an improper advantage manifestly contrary to the objective of Article 25(1) of the Second Directive, thus constituting an abuse of his rights under that provision.

39. On that point it must be observed that the fact of having instituted proceedings, even after a certain lapse of time, within the limitation period provided for under national law for such actions cannot, as such, be described as sufficient telling evidence of abuse of rights.

40. However, it appears from the order for reference that if the action brought by the plaintiff in the main proceedings for a declaration of invalidity in respect of the alterations in the capital of Plastika Kavalas when it was under provisional administration were upheld, several operations that took place during that period could be affected, in particular purchases, sales, enforcement measures, acquisitions of businesses and the merger of Plastika Kavalas with another company. Moreover, it is indisputable that the invalidity of those alterations would inevitably affect the rights of bona fide third parties.

41. In this connection it must be borne in mind that the Second Directive does not provide for any specific penalty for breach of any of its provisions, so that the normal penalties under private law could be applicable. When he instituted proceedings the plaintiff in the main proceedings was thus entitled to elect, as he did, from among the remedies in national law available for penalising a breach of Article 25 of the Second Directive, an action for a declaration that the alterations in the capital of the company that took place were invalid.

42. It must therefore be ascertained whether Community law precludes the national court from verifying whether, in view of all that has taken place, in law and in fact, since the alterations in the capital of the company, the type of reparation sought constitutes sufficient telling evidence, in the sense indicated above, of abuse of the shareholder's rights under Article 25(1) of the Second Directive.

43. In this case it would not appear that the uniform application and full effect of Community law would be compromised if it were to be held an abuse of rights for a shareholder to rely on Article 25(1) of the Second Directive on the ground that, of the remedies available for a situation that has arisen in breach of that provision, he has chosen a remedy that will cause such serious damage to the legitimate interests of others that it appears manifestly disproportionate. Such a determination would not alter the scope of that provision and would not compromise its objectives.

44. The reply to the first question must therefore be that Community law does not preclude national courts from applying a provision of national law which enables them to determine whether a right deriving from a Community law provision is being abused. However, in making that determination, it is not permissible to deem a shareholder relying on Article 25(1) of the Second Directive to be abusing his rights under that provision merely because he is a minority shareholder of a company subject to reorganisation measures, or has benefited from reorganisation of the company, or has not exercised his right of pre-emption, or was among the shareholders who asked for the company to be placed under the scheme applicable to companies in serious difficulties, or has allowed a certain period of time to elapse before bringing his action. In contrast, Community law does not preclude national courts from applying the provision of national law concerned if, of the remedies available for a situation that has arisen in breach of that provision, a shareholder has chosen a remedy that will cause such serious damage to the legitimate interests of others that it appears manifestly disproportionate.

Question 2

45. In view of the foregoing considerations there is no need to reply to the second question.

Costs

46. The costs incurred by the Greek Government and the Commission, which have submitted observations to the Court, are not recoverable. Since these proceedings are, for the parties to the main proceedings, a step in the action pending before the national court, the decision on costs is a matter for that court.

On those grounds,

THE COURT (Sixth Chamber),

in answer to the questions referred to it by the Polimeles Protodikio Athinon by order of 24 June 1997, hereby rules:

Community law does not preclude national courts from applying a provision of national law which enables them to determine whether a right deriving from a Community law provision is being abused. However, in making that determination, it is not permissible to deem a shareholder relying on Article 25(1) of the Second Directive 77/91/EEC of 13 December 1976 on coordination of safeguards which, for the protection of the interests of members and others, are required by Member States of companies within the meaning of the second paragraph of Article 58 of the Treaty, in respect of the formation of public limited liability companies and the maintenance and alteration of their capital, with a view to making such safeguards equivalent, to be abusing his rights under that provision merely because he is a minority shareholder of a company subject to reorganisation measures, or has benefited from reorganisation of the company, or has not exercised his right of pre-emption, or was among the shareholders who asked for the company to be placed under the scheme applicable to companies in serious difficulties, or has allowed a certain period of time to elapse before bringing his action. In contrast, Community law does not preclude national courts from applying the provision of national law concerned if, of the remedies available for a situation that has arisen in breach of that provision, a shareholder has chosen a remedy that will cause such serious damage to the legitimate interests of others that it appears manifestly disproportionate.

Comment and Questions

1. Do you think the approach of the European Court of Justice makes sense? How much guidance does the case provide to either corporations or governments with respect to the powers of Member States to control the activities of private companies in distress?

2. One possible justification of the result in the *Diamontis* case is that the European Court of Justice was seeking to confirm the power of state institutions to protect creditors and others from the overreaching of shareholders. *Diamontis* presented a case of a shareholder subverting the spirit of the law by precisely invoking the form of the law. Do you agree?

3. Not everyone has greeted warmly the ECJ's harmonization efforts, especially with respect to its enforcement of the capital rules of the Second Directive. Consider the arguments raised in the materials below in light of the purposes of the capital requirements. Do the capital requirements make sense from a business perspective? Who is supposed to be protected by the capital requirements? If, in fact, the requirements offer insubstantial protection, do they serve to create a false sense of security? Is the effectiveness of the approach any better than those of the United States?

4. The cases that follow illustrate some of the issues confronted by national courts as the Member States seek to adjust their legislation in response to EU the harmonization initiative under the 2nd Company Law Directive.

Re State Equity Holding: EC Commission v. Belgium

(Case 52/84)
Court of Justice of the European Communities
[1986] ECR 89, [1987] 1 CMLR 710
15 January 1986

Herr Carl Otto Lenz, Advocate General [delivered the following Opinion:]

The action on which I am giving my views today centres on the question whether the Kingdom of Belgium has failed to fulfil an obligation under the EEC Treaty by not complying with Commission Decision 83/130/EEC of 16 February 1983 on aid granted by the Belgian Government to a firm manufacturing ceramic sanitary ware ([1983] OJ L91/32).

1. Since 1979 a public regional holding company in Wallonia (Belgium) has been the main shareholder of Boch SA, a firm manufacturing ceramic sanitary ware. On 3 August 1981 the region decided to take a share amounting to 475 million Bfr in a new capital issue. This investment of capital by a public body in an undertaking which had been operating at a heavy loss over a number of years and which consequently found itself in serious financial difficulties was designed to assist it in reconstituting its capital and reserves and to enable it to continue operating until a reconstruction plan for the ceramics industry had been formulated.

The Commission of the European Communities (the applicant in these proceedings) learnt of the arrangement and, in April and June 1982, approached the Government of the Kingdom of Belgium (the defendant) in order to remind it that under Article 93(3) EEC it was required to give prior notice of aid measures. The applicant's telexes to that effect remained unanswered.

In September 1982 the applicant commenced the aid-review procedure under Article 93(2) of the Treaty. It found that the defendant had granted the aid without following the procedure under Article 93(3) (notification of the scheme to the applicant).

After completion of the aid-review procedure in accordance with Article 93(2), the applicant issued the aforesaid decision of 16 February 1983, the main terms of which are as follows:

> Article 1
>
> The aid granted by the Belgian Government to a firm manufacturing ceramic sanitary ware is incompatible with the Common Market within the meaning of Article 92 of the EEC Treaty, and must therefore be withdrawn.
>
> Article 2
>
> Belgium shall inform the Commission within three months of the date of notification of this decision of the measures it has taken to comply therewith.

In the preamble to the decision the applicant stated that the aid granted by the defendant was such as to affect trade between Member-States and to distort competition within the meaning of Article 92(1) EEC.

The applicant added that the prohibition on aid laid down in Article 92(1) applied to injections of capital both by the central government itself and by other public agencies under the central government's authority. In the circumstances of this case, a capital holding of 475 million Bfr in an undertaking whose capital and reserves amounted to 25.4 million Bfr constituted aid within the meaning of Article 92(1).

The purpose of the aid, according to the decision, was to permit the maintenance of production capacity, and this was likely to strike a particularly grave blow at conditions of competition, since free market conditions would normally require the closure of the firm in question so that, in a situation in which the industry was faced with over-capacity, more efficient competitors could expand.

The decision further set out the reasons why the aid could not be regarded as compatible with the Common Market by virtue of Article 92(3) of the Treaty. Lastly, the decision stated that developments in the ceramics industry showed that, particularly in view of the surplus capacity in the Community, to maintain production capacity through the grant of State aid would not be in the common interest.

The decision was not contested by the defendant within the two-month period laid down by Article 173(3). It therefore became unassailable.

After expiry of that period the defendant contacted the applicant by a letter of 3 June 1983, in which it attacked the decision, asserting inter alia that the arrangement did not constitute aid requiring notification under Article 93(3) of the Treaty. Moreover, the defendant claimed that the applicant had been wrong to conclude that the aid was not covered by the exemptions laid down in Article 92(3), according to which certain types of aid may be considered compatible with the Common Market. Furthermore, Belgian domestic law did not permit compliance with the decision because the reduction of capital which would be entailed by a refund of capital invested could not be allowed to impinge on the rights of third parties.

In conclusion the defendant called on the applicant to explain what it meant when it stated that the aid had to be withdrawn and what consequences that entailed.

In its reply of 22 July 1983 the applicant allowed the defendant a further period of 15 days in which to inform it of the measures adopted in order to comply with the decision. The letter did not contain the explanations requested by the defendant but merely stated that the first priority was to fulfil the Community obligations.

In a further letter to the applicant of 5 September 1983 the defendant maintained its earlier position and made no mention of measures—whether adopted or projected—for giving effect to the applicant's decision.

The applicant subsequently found that the defendant had not complied with the decision and had, without giving notice, granted the undertaking in question further aid to cover its losses. (One of those aids is the subject of Case 40/85, Belgium v. EC Commission, judgment delivered 10 July 1986: not yet reported.)

The applicant consequently brought the matter before the Court of Justice, pursuant to the second subparagraph of Article 93(2).

2. The applicant claims that the Court should:

Declare that, by not complying within the prescribed period with the Commission Decision of 16 February 1983 on aid granted by the Belgian Government to a firm manufacturing ceramic sanitary ware, the Kingdom of Belgium has failed to fulfil its obligations under the EEC Treaty;

Order the Kingdom of Belgium to pay the costs.

The defendant contends that the Court should:

Dismiss the application as unfounded;

Order the applicant to pay the costs.

3. (a) The applicant observes that, in the course of the procedure under Article 93(2) EEC, it established that the contested aid was incompatible with the Common Market within the meaning of Article 92. It was therefore obliged, in accordance with the first paragraph of Article 93(2), to require the Kingdom of Belgium to abolish or alter the aid within a period to be determined by the Commission.

The applicant adds that under Article 189 EEC a decision is binding in its entirety upon those to whom it is addressed. By the date on which the action was brought the defendant had still not complied with the decision communicated to it by letter of 24 February 1983, and at no time had it indicated the slightest intention of doing so. It had on the contrary granted the undertaking in question further aid in 1983 without notifying the applicant.

Furthermore, a Member-State to which the Commission has addressed a decision pursuant to Article 93(2) of the Treaty is precluded from challenging the validity of such a decision in legal proceedings instituted by the Commission under the second subparagraph of Article 93(2) of the Treaty if that State has allowed the period permitted under Article 173(3) to elapse without contesting the legality of the decision in the manner prescribed by that provision.

The applicant observes that the defendant may not plead provisions, practices or circumstances existing in its internal legal system in order to justify a failure to observe obligations arising from Community decisions.

According to the applicant, the content of the defendant's obligations is entirely clear, and the aid whose abolition is demanded by the Commission is readily identifiable since it involves a specific grant of 475 million Bfr in the form of the acquisition of a holding in the capital of the undertaking in question by a public body.

(b) The defendant reaffirms that it was not in breach of its obligations under Article 93(2) EEC by failing to give effect to Article 1 of the decision of 16 February 1983.

The reasons why it did not comply with the decision are the following:

The practice currently followed by the applicant as regards public participation makes it impossible, in the circumstances of this case, to give effect to the obligation imposed by Article 1 of the decision, namely to withdraw the alleged aid.

Despite repeated requests from the defendant, the applicant failed to supply the additional information needed to enable the defendant to establish what was meant by the obligation to withdraw the alleged aid.

The defendant points to the Second Report on Competition Policy, (ECSC, EEC & Euratom Commission: Second Report on Competition Policy (Annex to the 'Sixth General Report on the Activities of the European Communities') Brussels and Luxembourg, April 1973, paragraph 122 et seq.), in which for the first time the applicant stated its position on financial participation by public bodies. It is apparent from the report that Article 222 EEC does not in principle preclude State participation in undertakings. Admittedly, such participation may in certain cases constitute aid which is incompatible with the Common Market; that, however, does not mean that it may in itself be immediately and directly equated with aid. It is thus only in retrospect that the applicant can determine whether the participation had the same effect as aid. The Seventh Report on Competition Policy again refers to that stance on the part of the applicant. (Seventh Report on Competition, paragraph 232.)

According to the defendant, in so far as it cannot be determined—except in retrospect—whether such a holding is compatible with Article 92 of the Treaty, the imposition of an obligation to redeem the holding when the profits of the undertaking are insufficient to finance such a redemption seriously prejudices the rights of innocent third parties. The capital of a company is regarded in all Member-States as a security for creditors, and this means that any reduction of the capital necessarily requires the consent of the company's creditors and may only be effected from available profits. By compelling the defendant to withdraw from the company the applicant failed to take proper account of the special nature of the intervention of public bodies in cases in which that intervention takes the form of acquiring a capital holding in an undertaking.

According to the defendant, it is a fundamental principle of company law in all Member-States that the share capital constitutes a security for creditors which serves to offset the limits placed on shareholders' liability, and must remain intact. That principle is confirmed by the Second Council Directive of 13 December 1976 'on co-ordination of safeguards which, for the protection of the interests of members and others, are required by Member-States of companies within the meaning of the second paragraph of Article 58 of the Treaty, in respect of the formation of public limited liability companies and the maintenance and alteration of their capital, with a view to making such safeguards equivalent.' [1977] OJ L26/1, [1978] 1 Commercial Laws of Europe 83.)

It is not, according to the defendant, a valid answer to say that Article 92 of the Treaty must take priority over the interests of the undertakings' creditors. If that were so, innocent third parties would be affected whose good faith is unimpeachable in the absence of a criterion enabling the illegality of participation by a public body to be determined in advance.

The defendant further alleges that, despite its requests, the applicant supplied no further particulars as to the scope of the duty to withdraw the supposed aid. As the Court of Justice emphasized in its judgment of 12 July 1973 in Case 70/72 (Re Investment Grants for Mining: EC Commission v. Germany: [1973] ECR 813, [1973] CMLR 741), decisions taken under Article 93(2) of the Treaty can take full effect only on condition that the Commission indicates to the Member-State concerned in what respect it considers the aid incompatible with the Treaty and therefore in need of abolition or alteration.

Since the applicant failed to specify the scope of the obligation in question, the defendant cannot be criticised for not having fulfilled it.

In its rejoinder and in the oral procedure the defendant stated that it in no way questioned the legality of the decision of 16 February 1983. It claimed merely that, on account of the difficulties in giving effect to the contested decision, it was impossible to comply with it.

According to the defendant, the logic of the system of supervision created by Article 92 of the Treaty demands that Member-States shall know precisely, in advance, the circumstances in which plans to participate in companies must be notified in order that their compatibility with the Treaty may be assessed in good time. To date, however, the applicant has failed to lay down the criteria on the basis of which a Member-State may determine the cases in which participation on the part of a public body is subject to the duty of prior notification under Article 93(3) of the Treaty. As long as participation by public bodies continues to be reviewed for compatibility with Article 92 solely on the basis of an ex post facto assessment, the Commission cannot demand the subsequent withdrawal of a holding that is considered incompatible with Article 92 without interfering seriously with third-party rights, violating the principle of equality between shareholders, jeopardizing the interests of legal certainty and encountering insuperable difficulties in the implementation of the decision.

B

In setting out my views on this case I consider it appropriate to begin by clarifying the precise subject-matter of this dispute.

Since the defendant did not challenge the applicant's decision of 16 February 1983 within the period prescribed by Article 173(3) of the Treaty, the decision became unassailable. It is clear from the previous decisions of the Court... that the defendant may not thereafter challenge the legality of the applicant's decision. The defendant's submissions as to (a) whether the acquisition by a State of a holding in a company's capital constitutes aid, (b) whether the applicant should have been informed before the holding was acquired and (c) whether such aid could have been regarded as compatible with the Common Market under Article 92(3) of the Treaty, can no longer be considered in the present proceedings; the defendant's arguments on those points must therefore be disregarded.

All that remains to be considered is whether the applicant's decision was sufficiently specific to be complied with, and whether it was legally possible for the defendant to take the action required by the decision. [The Advocate General concluded that the decision was sufficiently specific to be compiled with].

* * *

2. Was it legally impossible to give effect to the decision of 26 February 1983?

The defendant has submitted that it would be legally impossible to withdraw the State's capital holding in the undertaking in question by securing repayment of the capital to its investor. That is—it argues—precluded by the provisions of both domestic (Belgian) and Community law. Under both systems, distributions to shareholders may be made only from an undertaking's profits, of which there are none in this case.

The first observation to be made on that argument is that the introduction of capital into the undertaking was not only a procedural infringement of Article 93(3) EEC but also a substantive infringement of Article 92.

Under Article 93(3) even the proposal to grant the aid should have been notified to the applicant, and the proposal should not have been put into effect before the applicant had issued a final decision. The defendant was in breach of both obligations, with the result that the capital was introduced illegally.

Moreover, the aid was illegal on substantive grounds, because it was not compatible with the Common Market within the meaning of Article 92 of the Treaty. As has been explained on several occasions, that point is established by the unassailable Commission decision of 16 February 1983.

As far as the recovery of the aid is concerned, the defendant invokes the Second Company Law Directive of 13 December 1976. (Second Council Directive no 77/91/EEC of 13 December 1976 on co-ordination of safeguards which, for the protection of the interests of members and others, are required by Member-States of companies within the meaning of the second paragraph of Article 58 of the Treaty, in respect of the formation of public limited liability companies and the maintenance and alteration of their capital, with a view to making such safeguards equivalent. [1977] OJ L26/1, [1978] 1 Commercial Laws of Europe 83.)

The defendant's line of argument does not carry conviction, however. It is true that the directive—particularly Articles 15 et seq and 32 et seq—contains provisions for the protection of creditors of public limited liability companies. Thus, Article 15 prohibits distributions to shareholders if net assets would thereby fall below the amount of the subscribed capital. Under Article 32, in the event of a reduction in capital, creditors must receive security for claims which have not fallen due, and no payment may be made to shareholders until the creditors have obtained satisfaction.

Those two provisions are undoubtedly based on the principle that the share capital of a public limited liability company has to serve as security for the creditors of the company, and therefore may not be reduced to their detriment. That rule does not, however, operate in the present case.

Article 15 governs distributions to shareholders, which may be paid only out of company profits. Since the undertaking concerned unquestionably has no profits at its disposal, there is no possibility of repaying the illegal capital holding by way of a distribution.

Article 32 cannot operate either, because the provisions on the reduction of capital can only refer to lawfully subscribed capital. However, since the present case concerns the recovery of capital unlawfully introduced, those provisions cannot operate in favour of the creditors of the company, because they are not entitled to demand the retention of unlawfully subscribed share capital as a security for their claims on the company.

The Second Council Directive admits of no other interpretation. A contrary interpretation would cast doubt on the validity of the directive, because it would then run counter to the provisions of Articles 92 and 93 of the EEC Treaty; Community institutions are prohibited from issuing rules of law which contradict the Treaty provisions or even impair their practical efficacy.

The defendant may not therefore plead the Second Council Directive of 13 December 1976 in order to evade the obligations incumbent upon it under Articles 92 and 93 of the Treaty.

The same is true of the submission that domestic law does not allow the aid to be recovered. In successive judgements the Court of Justice has held that a Member-State may not plead provisions, practices or circumstances existing in its internal legal system in order to justify a failure to comply with its obligations arising under Community law. (See for example Case 215/83: re Collective Redundancies: EC Commission v. Belgium: [1985] 3 CMLR 624.)

The general plea of protecting 'innocent third parties'—that is, the creditors of the undertaking—is equally unconvincing. The notion of protection may not be adduced in order to justify ex post facto an aid scheme adopted in breach of Community law. Should third parties have been harmed by the unlawful conduct of the Belgian authorities, they should be referred to the national courts and to the national provisions governing the liability of public bodies for unlawful acts.

C

I therefore propose that the Court should decide as follows:

1. By not complying with the Commission Decision 83/130/EEC of 16 February 1983 on aid granted by the Belgian Government to a firm manufacturing ceramic sanitary ware, the Kingdom of Belgium has failed to fulfil its obligations under the EEC Treaty.

2. The Kingdom of Belgium is ordered to pay the costs.

Decision: By an application lodged at the Court Registry on 28 February 1984, the Commission of the European Communities brought an action under the second subparagraph of Article 93(2) of the EEC Treaty seeking a declaration that, by not complying within the prescribed period with Commission Decision 83/130/EEC of 16 February 1983 on aid granted by the Belgian Government to a firm manufacturing ceramic sanitary ware ([1983] OJ L91/32), the Kingdom of Belgium had failed to fulfil its obligations under the EEC Treaty.

In the disputed decision the Commission found that the acquisition by a public regional holding company of a holding worth 475 million Bfr in the capital of an undertaking manufacturing ceramic ware at La Louviere constituted aid of a type which was incompatible with the Common Market within the meaning of Article 92 EEC and should therefore be withdrawn. The Commission further asked to be informed, within three months of the date on which the decision was notified to the applicant, of the measures which it had taken to comply therewith.

The preamble to the decision contains the following recital:

The purpose of the aid is to permit the maintenance of production capacity and this is likely to strike a particularly grave blow at conditions of competition since free market conditions would normally require the closure of the firm in question so that, in a situation in which the industry is faced with over-capacity, more efficient competitors could expand.

The decision was notified to the Kingdom of Belgium by letter of 24 February 1983. No action was brought before the Court to have the decision declared void.

By letter of 3 June 1983 addressed to the competent Member of the Commission, the Belgian Permanent Representative to the European Communities contested the accuracy of the statement of reasons given in the decision and stressed the serious social consequences of closing down the undertaking in question. He also observed that Belgian law did not allow share capital to be refunded except by way of withdrawal from company profits, which was precluded by the results reported by the undertaking. Lastly, the letter requested the Commission to explain to the Belgian authorities what it meant by 'withdrawal of the aid' and what consequences it thought its definition entailed.

By letter of 22 July 1983 the Member of the Commission replied, stating inter alia that the first priority was to fulfil the obligations arising under Community law. He went on to state that he would be grateful if the Permanent Representative would let him know within 15 days what measures the Belgian Government had adopted in order to comply with the Commission's decision.

By letter of 5 September 1983 the Belgian Permanent Representative once again criticised the reasoning given in the decision, and repeated his request for an explanation. The Commission took the view that its decision had not been put into effect and, alarmed at reports appearing in the Belgian press of further aid for the undertaking in question, it brought the present action without answering his letter.

In the proceedings before the Court the Commission stressed that, having found that the aid in question was incompatible with the Common Market, it was obliged under the first subparagraph of Article 93(2) EEC to require the Member-State concerned to abolish or alter the aid within a period determined by the Commission. The Commission asks whether the Belgian Government's submissions do not amount to challenging the validity of the decision, which according to the case law of the Court is no longer possible, since the decision was not contested within the period laid down by Article 173(3) of the Treaty.

In any event, the Commission maintains that the Belgian Government's submissions are unfounded. Unlike the decision in Case 70/72 (EC Commission v. Germany ([1973]

ECR 813, [1973] CMLR 741 (Re Investment Grants For Mining)), this decision clearly identified the aid to be abolished. It was thus sufficiently precise to be put into effect, and according to the case law of the Court the Belgian Government could not plead requirements of Belgian law in order to justify its failure to comply with the obligations arising from Community decision.

The Belgian Government contends that the Belgian authorities were not in breach of their obligations under Article 93(2) of the Treaty. In spite of their repeated requests the Commission, it claims, failed to supply the necessary particulars enabling them to establish what was entailed by the obligation to abolish the alleged aid. They could not therefore be criticised for not discharging that obligation.

The Belgian Government also refers to the Second and Seventh Reports on Competition Policy, in which the Commission defined its position as regards the acquisition of holdings by public bodies. In those reports the Commission stated that the conduct of bodies created and financed by the State for the purpose of acquiring holdings in the capital of certain undertakings can only be appraised ex post facto. By adopting that policy the Commission itself prevented the withdrawal of capital holdings, because to demand that the holdings should be redeemed would seriously harm the rights of innocent third parties whenever the profits of an undertaking were insufficient to permit such redemption.

In this particular case the undertakings did not, according to the Belgian Government, have the profits needed to cover the redemption, and it would therefore have been impossible to implement the decision to the letter without winding up the company. The decision, on the other hand, called for the withdrawal of the aid, not the winding up of the company. In any case, on 25 January 1985 a general meeting of shareholders passed a resolution winding up the company; the Belgian Government cannot understand what more the Commission expects.

The Court has consistently held, most recently in its judgment of 15 November 1983 (Case 52/83, EC Commission v. France ([1983] ECR 3707, [1985] 3 CMLR 278 (Re State Aids in The Clothing Industry)), that after the expiry of the period laid down in Article 173(3) EEC a Member-State which is the addressee of a decision adopted under the first subparagraph of Article 93(2) may not call in question the validity of that decision in the course of legal proceedings commenced pursuant to the second subparagraph of that Article. It must be concluded that such is indeed the situation in the present case.

In those circumstances the only defense left to the Belgian Government in opposing the Commission's application for a declaration that it failed to fulfil its Treaty obligations would be to plead that it was absolutely impossible for it to implement the decision properly. In this connection it should be noted that the decision demands the withdrawal from the undertaking of a capital holding of 475 million Bfr, the acquisition of which was decided upon by the regional authorities on 3 August 1981 and effected by a public regional holding company; that demand is sufficiently precise to be complied with. The fact that, on account of the undertaking's financial position, the Belgian authorities could not recover the sum paid does not constitute proof that implementation was impossible, because the Commission's objective was to abolish the aid and, as the Belgian Government itself admits, that objective could be attained by proceedings for winding up the company, which the Belgian authorities could institute in their capacity as shareholder or creditor.

As regards the Belgian Government's argument that the decision was in fact put into effect inasmuch as the company was wound up early in 1985, it should be noted that the application is concerned with the failure on the part of the Kingdom of Belgium to comply with the decision within the prescribed period and that the decision, which was notified by letter of 24 February 1983, enjoined the Belgian Government to inform the Commission, within three months of notification of the decision, of the measures which it had taken to comply therewith. It must therefore be held that, in any event, the decision was not put into effect within the prescribed period.

It should be added that the fact that the only defense which a Member-State to which a decision has been addressed can raise in legal proceedings such as these is that implementation of the decision is absolutely impossible does not prevent that State—if, in giving effect to the decision, it encounters unforeseen or unforeseeable difficulties or perceives consequences overlooked by the Commission—from submitting those problems for consideration by the Commission, together with proposals for suitable amendments. In such a case the Commission and the Member-State concerned must respect the principle underlying Article 5 of the Treaty, which imposes a duty of genuine co-operation on the Member-States and Community institutions; accordingly, they must work together in good faith to overcoming difficulties whilst fully observing the Treaty provisions, and in particular the provisions on aid. However, in the present instance, none of the difficulties referred to by the Belgian Government is of that nature, and that Government made no proposals whatever to the Commission for the adoption of other suitable measures; instead, acting through its Permanent Representative and after expiry of the period prescribed for compliance, it confined itself to contesting the accuracy of the reasons recited by the decision, to pleading that it was impossible to redeem the capital holding on account of Belgian legal provisions, and to requesting the Commission to clarify what it meant by 'withdrawal of the aid.' Such an attitude cannot be regarded as consistent with the duty of co-operation mentioned above.

It follows from the foregoing that the Court must hold, in the terms set out in the Commission's application, that the Kingdom of Belgium has failed to fulfil its Treaty obligations.

Costs: Under Article 69(2) of the Rules of Procedure the unsuccessful party is to be ordered to pay the costs. Since the defendant has failed in its submissions it must be ordered to pay the costs.

On those grounds THE COURT hereby:

1. Declares that, by not complying within the prescribed period with Commission Decision 83/130/EEC of 16 February 1983 on aid granted by the Belgian Government to a firm manufacturing ceramic sanitary ware, the Kingdom of Belgium has failed to fulfil its obligations under the Treaty.

2. Orders the Kingdom of Belgium to pay the costs.

Comments and Question

1. The immediately preceding case, *Re State Equity Holding*, provides an interesting example of unintended consequences of regulation where the regulatory state seeks multiple objectives in different fields of law.

2. On what basis do you think a court or legislature ought to decide which among competing objectives, ought to be given precedence, when application of the rules relating to each objective might lead to inconsistent results? Does the explanation of the advocate general effectively and fairly deal with the issue presented? Can you make a case

that corporate law ought to take precedence over the competition policy involved in the decision against the Belgian government in that case, that is, that Belgium did make a credible claim for impossibility?

3. The case that follows suggests another problem: harmonization does not necessarily displace national law. The result can be variance, and perhaps significant variance, between Member States in the implementation and administration of harmonizing goals.

In re Scandinavian Bank Group plc

Chancery Division
[1988] 1 Ch 87, [1987] 2 All ER 70, [1987] 2 WLR 752, [1987] BCLC 220, [1987] FTLR 224, [1987] BCC 93

15 December 1986

Harman J, read the following judgment.

I have before me a petition presented on 26 August 1986 by Scandinavian Bank Plc ("the company"). The company changed its name by special resolution as certified by a certificate of incorporation on change of name dated 24 October 1986 by adding the word "Group" after "Bank" and the company is now Scandinavian Bank Group plc. The company's petition was duly verified by an affidavit by Garrett Frank Bouton sworn on 26 August 1986; he is and has for several years been the managing director and chief executive of the company.

As set out in the petition, the company was incorporated in 1969 as Scandinavian Bank Ltd., but was re-registered as a public company on 28 July 1986. As appears from the evidence, the company is a recognised bank, that is the Bank of England has granted the company recognition under the Banking Act 1979. Exhibit "G" to Mr Bouton's affidavit was the published accounts of the company for the year to 31 December 1985. These show that the company's shares are held in varying amounts by five leading Nordic banks and that its total assets were then nearly £3.3 billion (I use the word "billion" in the sense of £1,000 million). Its growth has plainly been remarkable over its 16 year life. The petition sets out the company's authorised share capital starting at £3 million divided into 3 million shares of £1 each, increasing by seven successive steps to its present share capital of £75 million divided into 75 million shares of £1 each of which 64,370,000 shares have been issued and are fully paid-up.

On 26 August 1986 an extraordinary general meeting of the company was held on short notice. All the members of the company signed a consent to short notice and unanimously passed a special resolution that the capital of the company be reorganised so as to consist of shares denominated in different currencies. The means of the reorganisation was the reduction of the authorised capital from £75 million to £10,694,370. This reduction was achieved by the cancellation of similar proportions of the issued shares held by each of the five Nordic bank shareholders, leaving 64,370 issued shares of £1 each, making a total issued share capital of £64,370. The figure is of significance in relation to a public company such as the company, since by section 45(2)(a) of the Companies Act 1985 "the nominal value of the company's allotted share capital must be not less than the authorised minimum..." and by section 118(1) of the Act of 1985 "'the authorised' minimum means £50,000." Thus the company's allotted share capital after the cancellation of large parts of its issued share capital will remain above the "authorised minimum" for a public company.

The special resolution went on in part 2 to provide that contingently upon the above reduction of capital taking effect the 10,630,000 in issued shares be cancelled and that the 64,370 issued shares of £1 each be divided into 643,700 shares of 10p each by sub-dividing each of the £1 shares into 10 shares of 10p each. So far the proposals are entirely neutral transactions which would throw up large reserves on the left hand side of the company's next published balance sheet, but would alter its assets on the right hand side not at all. Each share would have become very much more valuable when considered as a fraction of the company's net assets, but the net asset value of each shareholder's holding would not have altered at all. As set out in paragraph 10 of the petition:

> "the proposed reduction of capital does not involve the return of any paid-up share capital, nor the diminution of liability in respect of unpaid capital."

The reduction does not affect creditors of the company at all.

It may be wondered why a petition for approval of a reduction of capital which, as so far set out, has no effect upon the world outside the company, is unanimously approved by the members of the company and involves merely a shifting of the position of figures on the left hand side of a balance sheet, without altering the totals at the foot thereof, should warrant an extended judgment. This court habitually considers petitions for the reduction of capital on Mondays in term time and, provided creditors are not affected and members do not object, such petitions are usually approved without any reasons being given by the judge. The machinery is familiar to company law practitioners and the specialist judges who have sat in this court.

This petition was presented by an extremely well known firm of City solicitors of the highest repute. It was called on before me in vacation, on special grounds, and argued by Miss Arden, who is as knowledgeable and skilled in this field as any judge could wish. However, Miss Arden's argument extended not only over the time available in vacation, but also on two further days at the start of the Michaelmas Sittings. The reason lay in paragraph 2(c) of the special resolution which provided that the capital of the company be increased to £30 million, US $30 million, Sw Fr 30 million, and Dm 30 million. Each of those four classes of shares, three of which are wholly new to the company, was divided into 300 million shares of respectively 10p each, US 10 cents each, 10 Swiss centimes each and 10 pfennigs each. The minute which the court was asked to approve set out this new share capital in multi-currency form.

If the petition had sought merely the court's sanction of the reduction and approval of a minute referring to the reduced issued capital of £64,370 divided into 643,700 shares of 10p each that would have sufficed so far as formal statutory requirements go. The court's approval of the increase of share capital, and more particularly of its division into four separate currencies with 300 million shares in each currency, is not necessitated by the Act of 1985. In that sense it could be said that the increase of share capital is not a matter with which the court need be concerned. Under section 121(2)(a) of the Act of 1985, "a company may increase its share capital by new shares of such amount as it thinks expedient." Once the reduction of share capital to £10,694,370 of which £64,370 had been issued was approved, the company could then proceed to increase its share capital under that section. However, the company is, as I have said, a recognised bank, and the Bank of England is greatly concerned with supervision of such entities. The question whether a company can lawfully have a multi-currency share capital is plainly of vital importance to the company for the purpose of satisfying the Bank of England, and given the responsible way in which the company has conducted itself, and its resultant standing, the lawfulness of its desired share capital is plainly a matter with which it is properly concerned.

As is usual on petitions to sanction reductions where all the members are in favour and no creditor is affected, the petition, although advertised and in a sense inter partes, came on before me with only the company represented. Miss Arden took me to all the points which might be relevant to the question and endeavoured to call my attention to any matters throwing doubt on the lawfulness of multi-currency share capital. However, the more I considered the admirable arguments advanced the more I felt that a point of considerable importance and public interest was involved. Since the company alone was represented it was obvious that if I was persuaded by the impressive argument advanced by Miss Arden, and approved the minute as asked, there was no prospect of any reconsideration of my decision by a higher court. It is also known among specialist company lawyers that eminent practitioners held opposing views and had advised clients to opposite effect as to the lawfulness of multi-currency share capital. All these considerations led me to follow the precedent set by Lord Brightman when sitting in the Companies Court as a judge of first instance (see Harris, In re Sheldon Group Ltd. [1971] 1 WLR 899, 900) and invite the assistance of an amicus curiae. The Attorney-General responded by nominating Mr. Weaver, who has argued the point for the assistance of the court.

The requirements for the memorandum of a company having a share capital are set out in section 2(5)(a) of the Act of 1985:

> "the memorandum must also... state the amount of the share capital... and the division of the share capital into shares of a fixed amount;..."

When the petition was restored for further argument, after the nomination of an amicus curiae, Mr. Potts appeared with Miss Arden, since she was unfortunately prevented from attending the resumed hearing. Mr. Potts submitted to me that the word "amount" must have the same meaning wherever it appeared in the paragraph of the subsection. He also submitted that "amount" must mean an amount expressed in money. The word could not apply to "amounts" or quantities in other sorts of measure, eg, the "amount" of the share capital could not be 100 troy ounces of gold, nor could it be one ton of potatoes, and the division into "shares of a fixed amount" would not be satisfied by providing that there should be 100 shares each of one troy ounce of gold, nor 160 shares each of one stone of potatoes. Mr. Weaver accepted and supported this argument. I am satisfied that it is correct and the subsection means that monetary amounts must be stated, both for the amount of the share capital and the fixed amount of each share.

The next question on the meaning of "a fixed amount" in section 2(5)(a) is whether the monetary amount has to be an amount in "lawful money," that is of an amount which can be paid in legal tender. Both counsel asserted that the requirement did not go so far. They cited the inconvenience and difficulty which would arise if all shares had to be expressed as a fixed amount of lawful money. Many companies had, in pre-decimilisation days, shares whose nominal amount was half-a-crown. That was simple to translate into shares of 12 1/2p each decimal currency, which was an amount capable of payment in legal tender at the time. However, the 1/2p has recently ceased to be legal tender. It would be extremely inconvenient if all companies with 12 1/2p shares had to alter the nominal amount fixed for their shares as a result of a change which had no bearing at all on the conduct of their business.

Further, some companies have shares with a nominal amount fixed at one 1/2p. In In re Rotaprint Plc (unreported), 21 July 1986, an order was made by Hoffmann J on a petition for the confirmation of a reduction of capital by Rotaprint Plc approving a minute showing the share capital divided into shares of 1/2p each. That order was made after the abolition of the 1/2p as legal tender. It would be strange if the order was wholly impossible to make and when made was of no effect because a company could not have the nominal amount of its shares expressed except in amounts capable of legal tender. Finally, at least one public limited company quoted on the Stock Exchange has its share capital divided into shares of a nominal amount of 0.1p each, an amount which has never been legal tender. The generality of practice, it was submitted, showed that although "amount" meant monetary amount, it did not mean an amount capable of payment in legal tender. Again, I accept counsel's joint persuasions.

The question then turns to two points: first, do the words "the amount," using the definite article, where they appear in the early part of section 2(5)(a) require a single total amount to be stated in the memorandum. As Mr. Potts expressed it "Do the words require an aggregate to be stated?"; as Miss Arden expressed it, does the Interpretation Act 1978 apply so that the singular includes the plural and "the amount" can be read as "the amount or amounts?" Secondly, do the words "the amount" and the phrase "of a fixed amount," both read as meaning "monetary amount," require a monetary amount in English currency, or can an amount expressed in any currency satisfy the meaning of the words in the statute?

On the first point I certainly, until the argument on this petition, have assumed that "the amount of the share capital" meant a single aggregate sum. It is clear, as Miss Arden submitted to me, that a company may have its share capital divided into several different classes of shares, each of a different nominal amount; for example a company could well have a share capital of £1,000 divided into 250 preference shares of £1 each, 1,000 ordinary shares of 50p each and 1,000 deferred shares of 25p each. Such a structure would be entirely conventional. But the question is whether the assumption that a total or aggregate of a company's share capital has to be stated is correct. Miss Arden submitted that section 6(c) of the Interpretation Act 1978 applies "unless the contrary intention appears"; in the Act of 1985 no contrary intention appeared and accordingly, although the assumption had commonly been that one expressed a company's share capital in one total, yet there was in law no requirement that that be so.

The question whether a "contrary intention" appears in an Act of Parliament so as to exclude the Interpretation Act 1978 was considered by the Privy Council in Blue Metal Industries Ltd. v. Dilley [1970] AC 827. The New South Wales Interpretation Act was in similar terms to the Act of 1978, and the Act under consideration was the New South Wales Companies Act 1961. The point arose under a section closely analogous to section 209 of the Companies Act 1948, that is the power of an acquiring company to compulsorily buy-in the shareholdings of a dissentient minority which held less than 10 per cent of the shares of the company acquired. The Privy Council delivered their advice to Her Majesty in a judgment of Lord Morris of Borth-y-Gest. The Board, upholding the decisions of both courts below, held that the references to "transferor company" in the section could only, in the light of the policy of the Act, refer to a single entity: see p 853C-D. The Board further stated the general point that the Interpretation Act is a drafting convenience and is not to be used to change the character of legislation: see p 848C-E. If there appeared a clear policy in the sections of the Act of 1985 concerning share capital I would be greatly assisted by the decision. Unhappily for me the statute does not, in my judgment, show any clear policy in this part of the field of company law.

* * *

I was taken by Miss Arden to the only observation directly upon the question of what currency can be utilised for expressing the capital of a company. In Adelaide Electric Supply Co Ltd. v. Prudential Assurance Co Ltd. [1934] AC 122 the House of Lords considered the liability of an English company whose articles of association provided that dividends should be paid in Australasia. The House held that payment in Adelaide in Australian currency was a good discharge of the English company's liability to its English shareholders because the contract constituted by the articles so provided. Lord Atkin considered the question of currency at pp 134–135. He observed, as it seems to me very accurately, that while both England and Australia were on the gold standard a pound in either country gave the same value and was the same pound. He also observed that he thought that at the time of the decision of the House the two "pounds" were no longer the same. However, he agreed with Lord Wright's observations with that reservation. Lord Warrington held that as a unit of account the pound was the same in both currencies and that the contract was discharged by payment in legal tender at the place where the payment was due, i.e., in Australia. He disregarded the fact, which he noted, that the rate of exchange between England and Australia was adverse to English shareholders, since the obligation was discharged in Australia. Lord Tomlin held, at pp 142–143, that at the date of the contract there was no distinction between the English and the Australian pound and that therefore the payment made in discharge of the contract was to be made in local currency which was legal tender where the payment was agreed to be made, notwithstanding later changes to the currencies. Lord Wright held, at p 155, that "the currencies of England and Australia are and were at all material times different currencies..." He thus differs in his reasoning, though not in the result, from the preceding speeches. However, there appears in Lord Wright's speech the following observations, at p 150:

"As the appellant company was registered in England, it is clear that its capital must be a fixed sum in British sterling... Similarly, all the returns and accounts required by the Companies Acts must have been rendered and kept according to the same currency."

Miss Arden, Mr. Potts and Mr. Weaver all submitted that this passage was an obiter dictum since the point did not arise for decision in the Adelaide Electric case. It is, however, an observation by a great lawyer and must be of great weight.

For myself I do not doubt that there was before and throughout the first half, of perhaps the first two-thirds, of the present century a usually unstated assumption that English companies must have their capital and draw their accounts in English currency. The pound had for so many years been properly called "a pound sterling"; that is a unit with a value in precious metal. Such a unit may fluctuate in internal purchasing power, but can be taken as having a stated value. But the United Kingdom went off the gold standard many years ago, and has ceased to have any fixed rate of exchange for the pound in any foreign currency since the collapse of the Bretton Woods Agreement in 1971. In these changed circumstances the law has had to adjust its perceptions so as not to cause injustice to individuals.

The House of Lords decided in Miliangos v. George Frank (Textiles) Ltd. [1976] AC 443 that the long established rule that an English court could only give judgment in what was called sterling, meaning pounds of Great Britain, should be altered. Judgment, it was held, could be given for a sum of money expressed in a foreign currency where the obligation under the contract sued upon was expressed in that foreign currency. The House recognised that the decision was a departure from a decision of the House itself, but that a new rule was needed to keep in step with commercial needs. Lord Wilberforce sets out, at pp 462H-467D, the reasons which led him to find a better rule. Lord Cross of Chelsea was of the same view (see pp 497E-498B, as were Lord Edmund-Davies and Lord Fraser of Tullybelton whose speeches follow his. The decision has had far-reaching effects and is applied very frequently nowadays.

That decision was followed and applied in Choice Investments Ltd. v. Jeromnimon [1981] QB 149 where it was held that a sum standing to the credit of a judgment debtor at an English bank in a foreign currency deposit account was a "debt" within the meaning of the Administration of Justice Act 1956 and the County Courts Act 1959. It is, in my judgment, clear that had the question arisen in the late 1950s or during the 1960s no court would have so construed the word "debt" in an English statute. But the Court of Appeal unanimously so held, basing themselves on the reasoning in the Miliangos v. George Frank (Textiles) Ltd. [1976] AC 443.

All this, submitted Miss Arden and Mr. Potts, pointed to the conclusion that Lord Wright's assertion in Adelaide Electric Supply Co Ltd. v. Prudential Assurance Co Ltd. [1934] AC 122 should no longer be accepted as correct. They submitted that the second point raised on the meaning of "amount" should be answered by saying that an amount in any currency was an amount within section 2(5)(a) of the Act of 1985. Mr. Potts went on to assert that the meaning of the word "amount" in section 121(2)(a) of the Act of 1985 was a fortiori not limited to an amount in English currency. And, he submitted, if it be possible to increase share capital by adding shares expressed in a nominal amount of foreign currency, why should it not be possible to have an original share capital expressed in a foreign currency. In Mr. Pott's submission the correct answer was that "amount" wherever it appeared in the statute could be read as meaning "any currency amount."

Mr. Weaver drew my attention in particular to section 117(3)(a) and section 118(1) of the Act of 1985 requiring a public limited company to have an authorised minimum issued capital of £50,000. He further drew my attention to article 6 of the second Council Directive (77/91/EEC), (Official Journal 1977 No L26, p 1). This Directive can be referred to as an aid to construction of the English statute, and to my mind does point to the conclusion that the requirement imposed by section 118(1) of the Act of 1985 can only be satisfied in pound terms. The references in the article to "national currency" seem to me to require member states to impose upon companies incorporated within them a minimum share capital in their own currency. I do not think, however, that this requirement prevents or militates against the possibility that a company can have its share capital expressed in more than one currency, so long, in the case of a public company, as at least £50,000 of its share capital is in sterling. However, the point does not directly arise on this petition since the company has and intends to have more than the required minimum of its share capital in pounds.

Mr. Weaver also called my attention to section 376(1)(b) of the Act of 1985 which specifies that requisitionists must be "not less than 100 members holding shares...on which there has been paid up an average sum, per member, of not less than £100." This, he suggested, was difficult to satisfy if the share capital held by some of the requisitionists was of nominal amount stated in a foreign currency. Miss Arden had anticipated this point and asserted that it was, first, mere machinery and the tail must not be allowed to wag the dog, and secondly that as in In re Simo Securities Trust Ltd. [1971] 1 WLR 1455 the court had had to find in the absence of any clear guidance in section 209 of the Act of 1985, the most practical date on which to measure a holding so the court would have, and be able, to work out a way of determining whether requisitionists were of adequate standing.

Mr. Weaver also referred me to Tables "B," "C" and "D" as prescribed by The Companies (Tables A to F) Regulations 1985 (SI 1985 No 805) and the references to pounds therein. However, he accepted that these were very slight pointers, although he submitted that they tended in the direction he was urging upon the court.

In my judgment, none of these pointers is a sufficient indication to determine that the law requires the capital of an English company to be in pounds. I should add that in In re Chase Manhattan Ltd. (unreported), 21 January 1986, where the company was a private company and so not within section 45(2)(a) of the Act of 1985, I myself sanctioned a reduction of capital in pounds to nothing and an increase in United States dollars. There was then cited to me Lord Wright's observations in Adelaide Electric Supply Co Ltd. v. Prudential Assurance Co Ltd. [1934] AC 122 and the decision in Miliangos v. George Frank (Textiles) Ltd. [1976] AC 443. Only one currency was proposed for the new share capital, and I then held that "amount" was adequately satisfied by a statement that the capital was so many thousand United States dollars, and that shares of US $1 each were shares of a fixed amount.

Mr. Weaver also referred me, as had more briefly Miss Arden, to Pattison v. Marine Midland Ltd., both in the Court of Appeal [1983] Ch 205 and in the House of Lords [1984] AC 362. The decision concerned the taxation of profits alleged by the Inland Revenue to have been earned by the respondent bank. The House of Lords dealt with the problem very shortly. Lord Templeman's speech was assented to by all the other members of the House who took part; he held that although the taxpayer bank in its accounts from year to year had translated both dollar assets and dollar liabilities into pounds, yet, since the bank had never actually converted its dollar assets into pounds, nor vice versa:

> "There never was any loss or profit from the lending and borrowing and there never was any exchange profit because the company did not make any relevant currency conversions:" see p 373

That decision is clear, easy to follow and has no effect on the point before me.

However, in the Court of Appeal Dillon LJ [1983] Ch 205, 212, who is more knowledgeable in the field of company law than most and a most accurate speaker, held first that "It seems to me, however, that there never has been any realisation [my emphasis] of any profit at all..." and therefore no taxable profit. This entirely accords with Lord Templeman's ruling. However, Dillon LJ added, at p 212:

> "It is a wholly unreal conception, in this day and age, that an English company can only carry on its business in sterling. Of course, an English company must convert into sterling the actual profits of its business activities carried on in other currencies..."

Those words indicate that an English company must keep its accounts in pounds. Griffiths LJ made no such comment. Sir John Donaldson MR however, said, at p 215:

> "...I know of no commercial reason why the company's own profit and loss account should be expressed solely in sterling. This is certainly customary and may

be a requirement of company legislation, although no one was able to refer us to any such provision."

That observation does not support Dillon LJ's words. In my judgment one must always recall, in considering any judgment, that it is based upon the facts of the particular case and addressed to the problems specifically raised. In Pattison v. Marine Midland Ltd. the accounts of the bank were in fact drawn in sterling and the question of what basis was proper for accounts was not in issue. Much as I respect Dillon LJ's opinion, I do not consider that his observation is very material to my decision in this case.

Mr. Weaver's main submission was not that an English company could not have a share capital measured by a foreign currency, and consequently shares fixed in amount by reference to a foreign currency, but that unless the currency in which the share capital was measured was only one currency and that the accounts of a company were drawn in the same currency as that in which its share capital was expressed, the amount of each share would not be fixed. As I see it, this argument depends upon the words "fixed amount" meaning "of a particular and unchanging value." Mr. Weaver observed to me, echoing Lord Halsbury LC in the Ooregum Gold Mines Co of India Ltd. v. Roper [1892] AC 125, that no creditor could look to the capital of a company with a multi-currency share capital and know what was his security. As he rightly said, it would be necessary to translate the balance sheet of any company into one currency at the balance sheet date in order to compare like with like and to obtain a true and fair view, as required of accounts, of the assets and liabilities of the company. As Mr. Weaver said, it is necessary to have a measuring rod in order to draw accounts, and one cannot have two measuring rods used in one comparable document.

True though that observation is, it does not seem to me to address the point here at issue. No one doubts that accounts must be drawn in one currency. It is probable that if a company has a multi-currency share capital the auditors will translate the left hand side of the balance sheet into the one currency used for the accounts at rates of exchange ruling at the balance sheet date. Such an observation is equally true of the right hand side of a balance sheet. If a company holds assets in Japan, in India, in France and in the United States, but draws its accounts in English pounds, all of those assets will have to be translated into English pounds at the relevant rate of exchange at the balance sheet date. If such a process is proper for the right hand side of a balance sheet, or for a statement of assets in a narrative form of accounts, I cannot see why it is inappropriate on the left hand side, or for debits in a narrative form of accounts.

As it seems to me, the amount of the share capital, and the fixed amount of each share, is not altered by the figures appearing in the successive annual accounts of a company. The figures in the accounts are a translation, no doubt at rates stated in the notes to the accounts of real assets and real liabilities. The translation is necessary for purposes of comparison, but it does not alter or affect the true nature or amount of the underlying asset or liability. A loan of US $1 million from a New York bank to an English company has to be repaid by payment of US $1 million, although in two successive balance sheets drawn in pounds at 31 December 1984 and 31 December 1985 it would have appeared as a liability of about £925,925 (assuming an exchange rate of US $1.05 to the £1 on 31 December 1984) and about £689,655 (assuming an exchange rate of US $1.45 to the £1 on 31 December 1985). Such translation differences do not, in my judgment, alter the true amount of a company's indebtedness, nor do they amount to a conversion of the US dollar liability into sterling. They are mere translation effects. If that company has always kept the $1 million which it borrowed in the United States and repays the $1 million out of those funds, it will not have made any profit or loss on its borrowings, notwithstanding the different figures in successive balance sheets.

I accept that although share capital appears on the left hand side of a balance sheet, yet it is not a true debit unlike borrowings by a company. A share represents a fraction of a company's net worth, as well as stating the nominal amount paid up on it, or for which the holder is liable to pay. But I reject the contention that a share has a value, in the sense of a monetary amount to which a shareholder is entitled, or upon which a creditor can truly look as a fixed sum in English pounds. There can be no doubt that the directors of a company can receive subscriptions for shares in a foreign currency—see section 738(4) of the Act of 1985 which provides that cash includes foreign currency and section 738(2) of the same Act which provides that receipt in good faith of a cheque is payment-up of the nominal amount (described as "nominal value") of any share. Those subscriptions in one foreign currency can at once be converted into another foreign currency, eg, a subscription in US dollars can be converted into a bank deposit in Swiss francs, by the directors of the company. Provided the objects of the company are appropriate, no creditor or shareholder could complain.

In my judgment, neither creditor nor shareholder is worse off if the payment-up of the share in US dollars is attributed to a share denominated in US dollars, rather than to a share in English pounds or a share in Swiss francs, and that notwithstanding that a company also receives subscriptions in those currencies for shares denominated in those currencies. In my judgment the words "the amount" in section 2(5)(a) of the Act of 1985 does not have to mean a single total amount where they are first used. I accept Mr. Potts' submission that the amount of the share capital is stated in the memorandum if on reading through the relevant clause (usually clause 5) one finds that the amount is £X million sterling, US $X million, and Sw Fr Y million. The memorandum does not have to state a single figure as a total of the share capital.

In my judgment, the amount of a share is a fixed amount if it is stated in the memorandum in monetary form. The fixed amount cannot be stated in two currencies, ie, a share of US $1 or £1—but it may be stated in different currencies for different shares. Each share is and remains of a "fixed amount," notwithstanding that the exchange rates vary. To hold otherwise is to confuse "value" with "amount," and to hold that restating, for purposes of comparison, amounts of share capital as different sums according to different rates of exchange at successive year ends, would make the amount of each share "unfixed," is to confuse the representation in the accounts with the actual nominal amount of a share for which a subscriber is liable. I do not accept that the reserve thrown up by alterations in accounts would be a reserve capable of application either before the Companies Act 1980 by way of dividend or now by capitalisation. To use the notional figure in that way would be to cause the accounts not to give a "true and fair view" of the company's affairs. The very well known firm of chartered accountants who are the auditors to the company are confident that they can assess the accounts with a multi-currency share capital on the true and fair view basis. I am satisfied that no such distortion as Mr. Weaver envisaged could be the result of a variation in rates of exchange applied to a multi-currency share capital.

The most helpful evidence produced by Mr. Weaver from the Registrar of Companies showed first that there are quite a large number, at least 125 companies, which already have foreign currency share capital, and probably two which have multi-currency share capital. The registrar's practice, based on advice, is that increases of capital under section 121 of the Act of 1985 will be accepted though in a different currency from that of the original share capital. The decision to which I have come supports the registrar's course of conduct. I was told that no public authority, notably the Bank of England and the Treasury, is concerned that a decision on the lawfulness of multi-currency capital such as I have reached will cause them problems, and the Official Receiver sees no difficulty in administering liquidations, although he expects, following In re Lines Bros Ltd. [1983] Ch 1, to draw the liquidation account of an insolvent company in sterling converted at the date of the winding up. As Brightman LJ put it, at p 15E: "The accounts of a liquidator can only be expressed in a single currency." But that very learned judge expressed it thereafter on the basis that he was "assuming...that sterling is the currency of the liquidation" (my emphasis). It follows that in my judgment a liquidation account does not have to be expressed in pounds, but it does have to be translated into one single currency. The Official Receiver's attitude is helpful in considering the exercise of my discretion to approve this petition.

In my judgment, Mr. Weaver was correct in saying that the point raised went to jurisdiction. I am satisfied for the reasons set out above that the court has jurisdiction to approve a minute referring to multi-currency share capital because such a form of share capital is lawful within the Act of 1985. As a matter of discretion, I am content to sanction the reduction, approve the minute as now proposed and direct advertisement as before in the same newspaper.

Order accordingly. No order as to costs.

C. Capital Requirements of Japanese Companies

The capital requirement rules of Japan are closer in spirit to those of Germany and France than they are to those of the United States. As in Continental European civil law states, scrupulous compliance with all legal formality is essential. Moreover, Japan, like its European counterparts, follows the regime of minimum capital. As you read the excerpts that follow, consider the ways in which the Japanese system is similar to and different from the other systems you have studied.

Dan Fenno Henderson, *Security Markets in the United States and Japan: Distinctive Aspects Molded by Cultural, Social, Economic, and Political Differences*

14 Hastings Int'l & Comp. L. Rev. 263 (1991)
(excerpts pages 266–273; some footnotes omitted)

II. Distinctive Sytemic Features in Corporate Law

A. Macro-Comparisons

Our study will begin with an overall comparison of the U.S. and Japanese corporate legal systems. This analysis, despite its intricacies, may be the easiest. Defining a security or an insider are technical problems of great specialized importance to securities regulations, whether national or international. But technical definitions do not travel well across national boundaries or across linguistic and cultural barriers, and are best dealt with by specialists. Here we will discuss four general differences in the corporate legal systems of the United States and Japan. The understanding of these differences is important to all efforts to standardize across national boundaries.

Turning first to the broadest contours of both nations' corporate laws, is the fact that Japan is a civil-law country with its own juristic method and structure of corporate law, typical of a code system, as opposed to American corporate law which is couched in a common-law context. Japanese corporate law is codified as Book II of a very systematic Commercial Code[8] with the usual general provisions (sosoku) and special divisions (hen: "books") integrated with special statutes (tokuho), in turn systematically interrelated to other codes in the civil-law system.[9] The Commercial Code was first enacted in 1898, mostly fashioned after German models. It was substantially amended before World War II in 1938 and again after World War II in 1951. The 1951 amendments strengthened the board of directors and also strengthened individual shareholder's rights. Under the auspices of the Allied Occupation, the 1951 amendments brought to the code a substantial overlay of American corporate law, drawn largely from Illinois state laws.[10] The amendment process has continued[11] right up to the present with amendments in 1990 which distinguish between the treatment of large and small corporations, and require higher minimal capital for stock corporations (kabushiki kaisha, KK), in an attempt to encourage small enterprises to use the Limited Liability Company (yugen-kaisha, YK). Despite the infusion of American law and the recent amendments, the corporate law, in concept and method, is essentially civil in nature.

American corporate law on the other hand, is a statutory overlay on the common-law system, consisting in part of state enabling statutes and of federal regulatory (public) law, and also of private law by way of private causes of action. The American corporate law is largely embodied in different state statutes with some diversity of language, rules, and case law interpretations, not to mention the federal overlay. Still further diversity may be expected by way of accruing and ongoing decisional law interpreting each state's statutes. Though Japan is developing significant case law, there remains a significant difference.

A second major systemic difference between American and Japanese corporate laws is that Japan's is a unitary system with one Commercial Code (including Book II on Corporations) for the entire country, whereas American enabling statutes are state laws. These vary from state to state, and there are thus fifty corporate statutes in the United States. So, except for the federal securities regulations enacted in the 1930s, it is not possible to speak of American corporate law as such when addressing a specific legal

---

8. Shoho (Commercial Code), Law No. 48 of 1899 [SHOHO] (Eibun-Horei-Sha trans. 1983). This is a convenient translation. However, as with any translation, it will prove inadequate when the operative Japanese is subjected to pressures in solving problems of interpretation and application.

9. As with all codes in the civil law system, the General Provisions may apply to all of the subdivisions of the code; in the case of juristic persons, the General Provisions of the whole Commercial Code apply, SHOHO Arts. 1-51; additionally, the General Provisions of corporate law will apply, SHOHO bk. II, and sometimes the General Provisions of the Civil Code must be applied, e.g., MINPO Arts. 33–84.

10. Blakemore & Yazawa, *Japanese Commercial Code Revision—Concerning Corporations*, 2 Am. J. Comp. L. 12 (1953).

11. *See* Zadankai, Kaisha-ho kaisei o megutte (Symposium: Concerning the Revision of the Corporate Law), Jurisuto, Sept. 15, 1990.

problem in one of the fifty states. Of course it is necessary to seek answers to these legal problems in the cases or provisions in the statutes of the specific state. For ultimate answers it is necessary to go to the supreme court of the specific state involved.

This said, two factors which have somewhat reduced the apparent diversity in American corporate law are worth emphasis. The first is the Revised Model Business Corporation Code (1984) sponsored by the American Bar Association (ABA). It has been followed to a great extent in the statutes of more than thirty-five states, and thus has had a unifying effect on states' corporate laws. Another unifying factor in American law can perhaps be identified in the work of the American Law Institute's project on Principles of Corporate Governance, which is important, ongoing, and too complex to measure in passing.

Two states especially influence American securities law. Delaware and California offer important variations in this area: California because it is such a large state with somewhat more concern in its law for shareholder protection, and Delaware because so many major listed corporations are established there to enjoy the flexibility which that state's law allows corporate management. Delaware has won the "race to laxity,"[14] though in the long competition, nearly all other states have gone the laxity route. New York also has many companies incorporated under its law.

Another unifying factor in American law is the Federal Securities Regulations, first enacted between 1933 and 1934. These regulations, after nearly sixty years of accruing administrative and judicial experience, have become the matrix for new private actions (unknown in Japan) which enable firms or individuals to sue for damages or enforce management liabilities for fraud or other corporate rights and obligations. This federalizing process has produced a body of national corporate law, eclipsing the diverse state law in several areas of interstate commerce.

The federal laws and regulations are administered initially by the Securities Exchange Commission (SEC), an independent federal regulatory agency, without parallel in Japan except possibly the unique Fair Trade Commission (Kosei Torihiki Iinkai) which is concerned with unfair trade practices and the antimonopoly law. Also accruing from the Federal Securities Regulations is an accumulation of case law refining these aspects of corporate law.

In a third area of comparison between Japanese and American corporations law, it is the Japanese law which is diverse and also more systematic. What its significance is, if any, to the securities trade, is difficult to assess in the abstract. But it is an important feature in the background.

Book II of the Japanese Commercial Code provides for three types of juristic persons (hojin): the partnership corporation (gomei-kaisha),[16] limited partnership corporation (goshi-kaisha),[17] and the stock corporation (kabushiki kaisha, KK).[18] In addition, the limited liability company (yugen-kaisha, YK)[19] was established by special statute in 1938. Only the KK is designed to be a publicly held entity with shares listed and sold on

14. This is Professor Conard's phrase, which he adopted from Justice Brandeis' dissent in Louis K. Liggett Co. v. Lee, 288 U.S. 517, 558–59 (1933) (Brandeis, J., dissenting). For certain, the laxity trend has produced the governance problem. *See* [Conard, *An Overview of the Laws of Corporations*, 71 Mich. L. Rev. 621, 624–31 (1973).], at 631–38....

16. SHOHO Arts. 62–145.

17. *Id.* Arts. 146–164.

18. *Id.* Arts. 165–456.

19. Yugen-kaisha-ho (Limited Liability Company Law), Law No. 74 of 1938.

the stock exchanges. The practice has departed from the design, however. Nearly a million tiny close corporations have been organized as KK, eschewing the legal entities provided for them in the law. Of course, none of them are listed.

In contrast, the corporate laws of the several American states have never envisaged but one corporate form, perhaps because, historically, partnerships were widely used and well-developed in practice and in the common law for small businesses and the professions. Practice soon necessitated special formulae for close corporations,[20] presumably as much for tax reasons as for limited liability. More than half of the state statutes contain special provisions or options for corporations with only a few shareholders, all or most of whom are to be active in the management of the corporate business. Nevertheless, the American law has not developed the dichotomy between public and private companies such as the German GmbH adopted by Japan.[21] Generally, American business corporate law envisages a single type of juristic person. But the general corporation must be tailored by contract and by provisions in the bylaws or articles (under special statutory rules in most states) for convenience in forming a close corporation, which until recently[22] was not a formal legal term in the statutes.

A new classification of KK was created in 1974 by amendment to the Commercial Code and by special statutes[23] enacted at the same time. Further amendments took place in 1981.[24] Under these changes all KKs are classified by size into three classes, each of which has different auditing regimes of increasing strictness by size:

1. 500 million yen or more in capital, or over twenty billion yen in borrowings;

2. 100 million yen to 500 million yen; and

---

20. Until the last 25 or 30 years, the close corporation has been a stepchild in American law. Close corporation has been but a term of convenience. Only recently has it begun to appear in statutes with new legal significance. *See* F. O'Neal & R. Thompson, O'Neal's Close Corporations (3d ed. 1987) (standard work). Del. Code Ann. tit. 8, §§ 341–356 (1974) was perhaps the first state statute to define and treat in detail close corporations as a separate legislative problem, though North Carolina and Florida pioneered in scattering helpful provisions in their general corporate laws. For a recent history of close corporations in the various American states, *see* Karjala, *An Analysis of Close Corporation Legislation in the United States*, 21 Ariz. St. L.J. 663 (1989). In Japan, the LLC is governed by a special statute, Yugen-kaisha-ho, supra note 19, but many entities are incorporated, instead, as stock corporations (kabushiki kaisha, KK). Many lucid comparative insights may be found in Shishido, *Problems of the Closely Held Corporation: A Comparative Study of the Japanese and American Legal Systems and a Critique of the Japanese Tentative Draft on Close Corporations*, 38 Am. J. Comp. L. 337 (1990); D. Henderson, Rethinking the Close Corporation in Japan (1990); Karjala, *The Closely Held Enterprise Under Japanese Law*, 7 B.U. Int'l L.J. 229 (1989).

21. The German Gesellschaft mit beschrankter Haftung (GmbH) is a juristic person specially designed for a limited number of shareholders and for situations similar to American close corporations. The GmbH was the model for the Japanese limited liability company (yugen-kaisha). In English, *see* Oliver, The Private Company in Germany: A Translation and Commentary (2d ed. 1986), for a description of the German GmbH.

22. Del. Code Ann. tit. 8, §§ 341–356 (1974). These 16 provisions are applicable to close corporations, as defined in the law, and comprise subchapter XIV of the Delaware Code. *See* Karjala, *An Analysis of Close Corporation Legislation in the United States*, *supra* note 20, at 670 (1989).

23. .... (Law to Amend a Part of the Commercial Code), Law No. 21 of 1974; .... (Law on Special Cases under the Commercial Code on the Audit of Stock Corporations), Law No. 22 of 1974; Shoho no ichibu o kaisei suru horitsu to no shiko ni tomonau kankei horitsu no seiri ni kansuru horitsu (Law Concerning Adjustments in Related Laws Accompanying the Enforcement of the Law to Amend a Part of the Commercial Code), Law No. 23 of 1974.

24. Law No. 74 of 1981. For a summary of the 1981 amendments to this law and other aspects of the Commercial Code and special laws, *see* Motoki, Kosugi, & Johnson, *Explanation of the Amended Stock Corporation Law*, 2 Japan Bus. L.J. 309 (1981).

3. under 100 million yen.

This reform in some ways resembles the additional auditing and accounting practices imposed on listed corporations by federal securities regulations in the United States, though the statutory methods and enforcement techniques are quite different.

The fourth systemic difference between the U.S. and Japanese corporate laws is the rigid mandatory nature of the Japanese code. This raises theoretical questions concerning the basis of a corporation and the role of contracts in its underpinning, an issue of great interest in both countries, particularly among academics, in recent years. In Japan, this rigidity of mandatory provisions is found primarily in the KK. Designed specifically to be a publicly held corporation, the KK is much more rigidly structured by mandatory rules and less subject to change by agreement than corporations set up under most American state statutes.

The following aspects of the KK are worth emphasizing: (1) the Japanese formation procedures are very formal as to initial organization, capital pay-in, and registration procedures for the charter;[25] (2) major changes such as amendments, mergers, and sale of assets require high fixed minimal votes and the like;[26] (3) accounting provisions in the Commercial Code are similarly formal and rigid compared to American statutes, though the SEC rules largely bridge this gap in the circumstances covered by federal law.

B. Micro-Comparisons

Switching now from macro-comparisons of the corporate law systems to micro-comparisons within the KK and the U.S. corporation, it is important to highlight a few salient differences of interest to those dealing with corporate law and securities. Of a multitude of such microdifferences in the rules and corporate institutions, the following features will at least indicate the importance of this aspect of harmonization. The features listed are only the more prominent humps and bumps, spots and stripes, which distinguish these two legal beasts. Taken together, they should be of interest to foreign investment counsel from both nations, though this listing is only indicative of many other corporate problems. Of course, a uniform corporate law such as that under consideration in the European Community[27] would be an ultimate solution for global trading, enabling the United States and Japan to trade shares with the same legal characteristics. The characteristics are as follows:

a. The legal conception of the KK, as noted, is a more mandatory structure, relatively less malleable by contract than the American corporation.

b. In the KK, formation is formal and rigid, with a number of specified prerequisites which must be satisfied punctiliously before the corporation can be registered, come into existence, and begin business.[29] Recent amendments to the Commercial Code, effective April 1, 1991, have relaxed some of these rigidities. Examples of these rigid formalities in corporate formation of the KK are:

25. *See* Henderson, *Threshold Advice to American Incorporation in Japan*, in CURRENT LEGAL ASPECTS OF DOING BUSINESS IN JAPAN AND EAST ASIA 76 (J. Haley ed. 1978).

26. D. HENDERSON, FOREIGN ENTERPRISE IN JAPAN: LAWS AND POLICIES ch. 13 (1985) [hereinafter D. HENDERSON, FOREIGN ENTERPRISE IN JAPAN].

27. Work on the European Corporation law is reviewed in Carreau & Lee, *Toward a European Company Law*, 9 NW. J. INT'L L. & BUS. 501 (1989).

29. *See* D. HENDERSON, FOREIGN ENTERPRISE IN JAPAN, *supra* note 26; SHOHO Art. 165.

1. At least seven incorporators[30] (hokkinin) must sign the charter (teikan), and there must be at least one subscriber[31] besides the seven incorporators (eight in all) in order to avoid the onerous court approvals required to assure compliance with formalities when only incorporators participate in formation.

2. The corporation's purpose clause must specifically describe the business in which the corporation will engage. The catchall enumeration or the broad generalizations of American state law may be unacceptable at the Japanese Registry.[32] This makes ultra vires more of a concern in Japan than in the United States, though in litigation ultra vires is seldom found against defendants.[33]

3. Certain items can only bind the corporation if they are inserted in the charter.[34] These include:

(i) contributions in kind;[35]

(ii) benefits to be received by incorporators;[36]

(iii) pre-incorporation arrangements by the corporation to take over property after it comes into existence; the property value and its transferor must be specified;[37] and

(iv) incorporation expenses to be borne by the new corporation.[38]

4. Before presentation to the Registry office, the charter must be notarized by a public notary (koshonin) and registered at the notary's office to assure compliance with all code requirements.[39]

5. One-fourth of a KK's authorized capital[40] must be paid into a designated bank account. The bank must certify its receipt before the Registry of the Ministry of Justice will formally register the company.

6. Court appointed inspectors must approve contributions in kind[41] and their values—a cumbersome, fixed procedure which takes time.

All of these and other rigidities of Japanese corporate formation law contrast sharply with the simple filing of a document of incorporation (often by a single incorporator)

---

30. The Japanese term "hokkinin" is translated "promoter" in EHS, but "incorporator" is preferable; hokkinin had quite different roles from our promoters. The standardized English equivalents, which I use for Japanese legal terms, may be found in D. Henderson, J. Haley & F. Rand, A Japanese-English Glossary (1985). Note that the recent amendments to the Commercial Code, effective April 1, 1991, have abolished the requirement seven incorporators; only one will be required.

31. SHOHO Art. 173.

32. For judicial discussion of ultra vires, *see* Arita v. Kojima, 24 Minshu 625 (June 24, 1970), aff'g 19 Kosai Minshu 7 (Jan. 31, 1966). English translations, T. Hattori & D. Henderson, Civil Procedure in Japan B-24 (1985).

33. Takeuchi, Kaishah ni okeru ultra vires no gensoku wa dono y ni shite haiki subeki ka?, 1965 Amerika Ho 20 (English translation by Henderson, *How Should We Abolish the Ultra Vires Doctrine in Corporation Law?*, 2 Law in Japan 140 (1968)).

34. SHOHO Art. 168.

35. *Id.* Art. 168(5).

36. *Id.* Art. 168(4).

37. *Id.* Art. 168(6).

38. *Id.* Art. 168(7).

39. *Id.* Art. 167. Note that the Japanese public notary (Koshonin) is a much more structured official of civilian origin than our notary public.

40. *Id.* Art. 166, ¶ 3.

41. *Id.* Arts. 173(1), 181(1). This requirement will be relaxed under the 1990 amendment, effective in 1991.

under American state statutes. Functional equivalents of these Japanese constraints on pay-in of capital are found in the United States, only in the federal securities law, if at all....

D. Capital Requirements of Chinese Companies

Chinese capital requirements to some extent mirror those of Europe. The complication in the Chinese system stems from the close relationship between the Chinese state and its corporations. In effect, the regulation of capital within China, like the regulation of other aspects of corporate law, can be reduced to the basic problem of socialist state regulation when the state regulates one of its organs. Corporations are those organs of the socialist state that can serve as the interface with the public and private economic institutions of capitalist states. Yet, it is not clear that this effort has been successful. As you read that material that follows, consider whether you think the Chinese State has successfully put a "global business practice" face on its business enterprises.

Nicholas C. Howson, *China's Company Law: One Step Forward, Two Steps Back? A Modest Complaint*

11 COLUM. J. ASIAN L. 127 (1997)
(excerpt pages 150; 163–167; 170–171; some footnotes omitted)

The Company Law requires, seemingly without exception, that a portion (five to ten percent) of a company's after-tax profits be first allocated to a "statutory common welfare fund."[76] The Standard Opinion merely provided for the establishment of such a fund, but required no minimum allocation to it.[77] While it is true that in the past the PRC Ministry of Finance had promulgated notices requiring such allocations for Chinese corporate entities, the Ministry was reportedly in the process of amending such regulations to do away with such requirements. However, with the promulgation of the Company Law, such allocations are locked into a statute of national application, binding on all companies in China.

***

vii. Formation of Companies Limited by Shares and Initial Public Offers. The Company Law provides for two methods of forming a company limited by shares: "offer" and "promotion."

Establishment by the "offer" method means "subscription by the promoters of part of the shares to be issued by a company (not less than 35%) and a public offer of the re-

76. *See* [Company Law of the People's Republic of China (adopted by the 5th Session of the Standing Committee of the 8th National People's Congress on Dec. 29, 1993, and effective July 1, 1994) [hereinafter Company Law]] Art. 177.

77. ["Opinion Regarding Standards for Companies Limited by Shares" promulgated May 15, 1992 [hereinafter the "standard Opinion"], Art. 74.

maining part of the shares" prior to formal establishment,"[137] i.e., the raising of funds from the public even before the company has been established.[138] (The provisions of the Standard Opinion resulted in the same anomaly.[139]) Few overseas jurisdictions allow the public offer of shares of a company that is not yet formed; it is highly unlikely that investors in China will, as the domestic capital market matures, engage in such risky purchases (even though the Company Law provides for a full refund of the public subscribers' payments—with bank interest—in the event a founding meeting is not held, the public shares have not been fully subscribed, or a resolution not to establish the company is adopted at the founding meeting).[140]

Establishment by the "promoter" method contemplates the subscription by the promoters of all initial shares issued by the company[141] (while subsequent issuances are restricted within any twelve-month period following).[142] Thus, an initial public offering using the first technique seems unpalatable, while the second seems impossible.

The Company Law further requires that companies limited by shares must have at least five promoters (more than half of which must be domiciled in China),[143] but that state-owned enterprises being re-organized into companies limited by shares may have fewer than five promoters, but only if they are established through the "offer" method.[144] Thus, the Company Law provision also represents a step back from the Standard Opinion, which allowed that "large scale" state enterprises being transformed into companies could, subject to approval, have only one promoter if the "offer" method was used.[145]

The combined implications of each of these provisions makes for very difficult promotion, establishment and initial public offering procedures. While the problem remains for wholly domestic companies, the CSRC provided a remedy in the Overseas Listing Rules. Pursuant to those Rules, a state-owned enterprise (i) may be converted

---

137. *See* Company Law, *supra* note [76], Art. 74. This provision represents a narrowing of options, as compared with the Standard Opinion, which described two kinds of "offers": (a) a public offer much like that described in Article 74 of the Company Law, and (b) a "directed share offer," allowing for subscription by the promoters, and non-public issuances to other legal persons and, subject to approval, employees (a kind of pre-establishment private placement). *See* Standard Opinion, *supra* note [77], Art. 7, para. 3.

138. *See* Company Law, *supra* note [76], Arts. 91–95 which mandate a founding meeting within 40 days of payment in full by the public subscribers, adoption of the issuer's articles of association at that meeting, submission of a company registration within 30 days of the founders' meeting, and a decision by the registration authority regarding formation of the company thirty days after that. *See also id.* Art. 136, which indicates that share certificates may not be issued prior to the registration and establishment of a company, and Art. 142, which requires that, in connection with an issuance of new shares, all money be paid in before shares are issued, and re-registration is effected.

139. *See* Standard Opinion, *supra* note [77], Arts. 19, 20, which contemplate a founding meeting forty days after payment for company shares is received in full, and formal registration and establishment of the company thirty days after that.

140. *See* Company Law, *supra* note [76], Arts. 91 (para. 2), 93.

141. *Id.*, at Arts. 74, 82.

142. As with the offer method of establishment, companies formed by promoters are established only after all promoters shares have been fully paid. Id. Art. 82, para. 2.

143. The Standard Opinion, *supra* note [77], required a minimum of three promoters.

144. *See* Company Law, *supra* note [76], Art. 75.

145. *See* Standard Opinion, *supra* note [77], Art. 9, para. 1. The [Addendum Regarding the Implementation of the Standard Opinion by Companies Listing in Hong Kong (May 24, 1993 by CRES) [hereinafter Addendum]] was even more favorable in such situations, allowing for one promoter, formal establishment and an immediate increase in capital followed by a public offer. See Addendum, . . . Art. 6.

into a company limited by shares by the promotion method with fewer than five promoters, and (ii) may issue new shares immediately after its formal establishment.[146] (The Standard Opinion,[147] the Issuance and Trading Regulations[148] and the Company Law all provide for certain restrictions on increases in capital and public flotations within a year of formation or any previous increase.[149]) The Overseas Listing Rules provide even greater flexibility for companies engaging in transformation and initial public offering by stating that "a company may increase its capital through an issuance of foreign-listed foreign-funded shares even when the issuance is within a period of less than twelve (12) months of a previous share issuance."[150] This offers the best of both worlds: formation by promoters and formal legal establishment of an issuer, followed by an increase in capital, and an initial public offering—i.e., the "offer" method, but with the legal establishment of the company sensibly coming after the promotion and before the offer.

viii. No Pricing Differential for Simultaneous Issuances. The Company Law states very clearly: "For share certificates...issued at the same time (tongci faxing de gupiao), each share shall have the same issue terms and price; the share price for each share purchased by any organization or individual must be the same."[151] This makes very difficult

146. *See* ["Special Regulations of the State Council on Foreign Offerings and Listings of Companies Limited by Shares," promulgated on Aug. 4, 1994 by the State Council of the PRC, but published only on August 19, 1994 in the People's Daily hereinafter "Overseas Listing Rules"],...Art. 6.

147. *See* Standard Opinion, *supra* note [77], Art. 62.

148. *See* CRES's letter to the Hong Kong Stock Exchange of June 10, 1993 (Tigaihansheng, No. 74, 1993) [hereinafter CRES Hong Kong Stock Exchange Letter]. In item 6 of the letter, CRES stated that: "the duty described in Article 62 of the Standard Opinion has the same meaning as the "Chengxin Zeren '[fiduciary duty]' of Hong Kong law." (Note the English words "fiduciary duty" are set out in the original Chinese form of the letter.) The equivalent concept exists in Taiwan's corporate law as "Shanliang Guanli."

149. The Company Law does stipulate that a company's articles of association are binding upon the company's shareholders, directors, members of the supervisory committee and senior managers (*See* Company Law, *supra* note [76], Arts. 11, 59). The Overseas Listing Rules, *supra* note 36, expanded the application of this concept to other senior officers, which includes the CFO, the secretary of the company and other officers specified in the articles of association. The Company Law does contain specific prohibitions against directors, supervisors and management personnel acting in an interest contrary to the company's: *See* Company Law, *supra* note [76], Arts. 59 (exploit position, accept bribes or take over company property), 60 (misappropriate company funds), 61 (enter into competition with, or sign contracts with, the company), 62 (disclose confidential company information), 118 (vote for resolutions which violate laws, the articles of association or result in serious losses), 128 (supervisors), 198 (members of the liquidation group) and 214 (misappropriations, etc.).

150. Company Law, *supra* note [76], Art. 59. Some analysts have understood this Article and all the other indications of responsibility in the Company Law as the concept of fiduciary duty. Even if this view is credible, it raises the question as to why the Overseas Listing Rules had to restate the Standard Opinion formulation (*See* Overseas Listing Rules, *supra* note [146], Art. 31) and why the former CRES-explicated language was dropped. In addition, there is continuing dispute among various analysts and regulators as to whom or what precisely such duty vided the amount of the dividends so paid does not exceed the dividend income received by the defendant after September 30, 1948.

151. *See* Overseas Listing Rules, *supra* note [146], Art. 23, para. 1. This provision refers to such persons' (including supervisory committee members') "fiduciary duty" and "duty of due care." There may be a problem of legislating logic in this case. The above-cited provision of the Overseas Listing Rules makes implicit reference to an interpretation of a statutory provision (*See* Standard Opinion, *supra* note [77], Art. 62) contained in a superseded law (the Standard Opinion) by a now seemingly dis-empowered authority (CRES—which is granted no power to explain the Company Law).

the previously accepted practice of simultaneous issuances of either (i) "A" and "H" (or "N"[152]) shares or (ii) "A" and "B" shares, at different issue prices, and explicitly overrules the very finely-drawn Article 27 (paragraph 3) of the Standard Opinion, which states only that: "the issue price of the same type of shares during the same issue by a company must be uniform (emphasis added)." This form of language allowed "A," "B" and "H" shares to be offered at different issue prices, based upon their characterization as different "types" of shares.

ix. Share Subscription Applications. The Company Law mandates that, in making a public offer of shares, promoters must publish a prospectus and prepare a share subscription application (rengushu), the latter of which must conform to detailed requirements.[153] However, this provision seemingly conflicts with accepted practice under the Standard Opinion, which required companies to issue "share subscription certificates" (gupiao rengouzheng). Apparently, these share subscription applications are not the same as share subscription certificates, as subscribers submitting the former are obligated to make payment for shares according to the number of shares they have subscribed for pursuant to the share subscription applications,[154] presumably eliminating any allocation among potential subscribers in the event of over-subscription.

* * *

xiv. Interim Dividends. Neither the Standard Opinion nor the Company Law provides an explicit legal basis for interim dividend distributions, or empowers the board of a company to declare such an interim dividend, absent the approval of the shareholders acting in general meeting.[166] The requirement that certain allocations be made annually to the statutory common reserve and welfare funds before the profits of the company may be distributed (and the "clawback" of dividends in the case of an under-allocation)[167] ensure that interim dividends will be difficult to effect, if they are not contrary to law. Thus, interim dividends, an important aspect of capital markets transactions in mature markets, and certain to become increasingly desirable to real PRC investors, are seemingly impossible or illegal to effect.

xv. Return of Mis-allocated Profits. The Company Law mandates that any company must, before distributing its annual after-tax profits, make allocations to the company's "statutory common reserve fund" (10% of after-tax profits) and "statutory common

152. Most Chinese legal theorists would think that, by default, it is the Standing Committee of the National People's Congress....

153. *See* the definitive work on this most important question, Donald C. Clarke, *Power and Politics in the Chinese Court System: The Enforcement of Civil Judgments*, 10 Colum. J. Asian L. 1 (1996).

154. *See* Company Law, *supra* note [76], Arts. 58 (with respect to the directors of limited liability companies), 123 (directors of companies limited by shares), 128, para. 2 (supervisors).

166. *See* Overseas Listing Rules, *supra* note [146], Art. 22. But note the curious formulation of this Article and the corresponding article of the Overseas Mandatory Articles (*supra* note 38, Art. 53), which asks for only 50% of the "shareholders who are planning to attend" (Nichuxi Huiyide Gudong) (which plans to attend must be confirmed in writing to the company at least twenty days before the meeting is convened per Article 20 of the Overseas Listing Rules). Thus, even if shareholders holding 90% of the stock of a company attend a meeting without having confirmed their desire to attend beforehand, while two of the remaining three shareholders holding in the aggregate 10% of the company stock and having confirmed their desire to attend, miss their bus, a quorum is not established.

167. *See* "Articles of Association for Overseas Listed Companies," promulgated by CRES and the State Council Securities Commission on Aug. 27, 1995 [hereinafter Overseas Mandatory Articles],... Arts. 49–55, 64, 70, 71, 78–85.

welfare fund" (5–10% of after-tax profits).[168] The provision is subject to a cap once the common reserve fund is funded to a certain level (50% of registered capital), and a carry-over funding obligation in the event of losses. However, the Company Law also contains the following extraordinary provision:

If a shareholders meeting or the board of directors violates the above provisions and profits are distributed to the shareholders before the company makes up losses or makes allocations to the statutory common reserve fund and the statutory common welfare fund, the profits distributed in violation of the provisions must be returned to the company.[169]

Not only is this "clawback" mechanism profoundly worrying to shareholders (as it raises the specter of having to disgorge already received and employed dividends), but it is almost impossible to implement in a true market context, where shareholders acquire and dispose of interests continuously. How likely is it that a company could reconstruct its year-end shareholders' list from several years previous, and then contact certain former shareholders (and recipients of wrongfully calculated dividend monies) to cause them to disgorge such monies to the company? The provision is plainly unworkable, and a holdover from a corporate regime that contemplates large, static shareholders: i.e., the state, or long-term foreign investors in joint ventures. It also represents a misconceived departure from the Standard Opinion, which required allocations to make up previous losses, and to the two statutory funds (with no minimum for the welfare fund),[170] before any dividend (or bonus) distributions—and in the event of a breach of such obligations by the company, then the conferring of a right on the company's creditors to request compensation (from the company, not the shareholders) for any losses incurred.

Comments and Questions

1. Consider the argument that China, by adopting the traditional Western European approach to capital requirements for corporations, has, in an ironic way, adopted the most class based approach to capitalization regulation. The capitalization requirements effectively make the corporate form unavailable to those without the money in China. In a sense, then, capitalization requirements provides a limitation to limited liability by denying the corporate form—with its limited liability—to all but those who can afford it. To the extent that such capitalization requirements prevent entrepreneurs from starting what would be successful, if risky, ventures, the system is ultimately inefficient. The United States has adopted the opposite approach—low or non-existent capitalization requirements makes the corporate form readily available. However, for unsuccessful ventures, veil piercing based on inadequate capitalization provides some protection. Veil piercing is discussed in more detail in Chapter 9, below. The excerpt below expands this argument. Do you agree?

In addition, the Company Law imposes relaxed capitalization requirements, ranging from 100,000 yuan to 500,000 yuan for limited liability companies and 10

---

168. *See* Company Law, *supra* note [76], Art. 177....

169. *See* Company Law, *supra* note [76], Art. 177, para. 3. *See* also Art. 216 which also commands that in such event the Company must make up (how and to whom?) "the exact amount which should have been allocated."

170. *See* Standard Opinion, *supra* note [77], Art. 73, para. 1.

million yuan for companies limited by shares.[47] Such a capitalization requirement has been commonplace since the beginning of China's open-door era economic legislation.[48] Though the minimum amount of registered capital varies with different laws, there seems to be a recognizable downward trend. The national level regulations on companies limited by shares promulgated by the PRC State Economic Commission required 10 million yuan for domestic incorporators and 30 million yuan for foreign-invested companies. In the same year, the Shanghai municipality issued provisional regulations that required at least 5 million yuan for limited liability companies and 30 million yuan for foreign-invested companies. So, the Company Law appears to have taken a considerable step forward in greatly reducing the capitalization requirement for limited liability companies and by disposing entirely of any such requirement for foreign-invested companies. Despite this, what remains is still a substantially higher standard than that under U.S. law. In the United States, virtually no capitalization is required for incorporation, [51] and the gap left by the absence of such requirement is arguably filled by the common-law doctrine of corporate-veil piercing. Empirically, inadequate capitalization may well be the most important substantive factor that U.S. courts rely on in finding personal liability of shareholders.[52] To the extent that post facto veil-piercing in the United States has enabled shareholders to enjoy the protection of limited liability until the corporate veil is pierced, the Chinese approach effectively precludes shareholders from availing themselves of the protection of limited liability if they cannot meet the capitalization requirement. The Company Law's capitalization requirement is also restrictive since it has essentially placed limited liability protection beyond the reach of a large portion of the population, considering the generally low level of income in China.

---

47. Company Law, Article 23 provides, in part:

> The registered capital of limited liability companies may not be less than the following minima:
>
> (1) for companies involved mainly in production and business operations, 500,000 yuan;
> (2) for companies involved mainly in wholesale of merchandise, 500,000 yuan;
> (3) for companies involved mainly in commercial retailing, 300,000 yuan;
> (4) for scientific and technological development, consultancy and service companies, 100,000 yuan.
>
> If the minima for registered capital of limited liability companies in special industries need to be higher than those set forth in the preceding paragraph, such higher minima shall be provided for separately in laws and administrative regulations.

[Zhonghua Renmin Gongheguo Gongsi Fa [Company Law of 1994], in FAGUI HUIBAN, translated in 2 CHINA L. & PRAC. 7 (1994) [hereinafter Company Law]], Art. 23.

Article 78 provides in part: "The minimum registered capital of a company limited by shares shall be 10 million yuan. If the minimum registered capital of a company limited by shares needs to be higher than the foregoing amount, such higher minimum shall be provided for separately in laws and administrative regulations." *Id.* Art. 78.

48. *See* James Fang & David Tang, *The Wholly Foreign-Owned Enterprise Law: Defining the Legislative History and Interpreting the Statute*, 2 J. CHINESE L. 153, 169, n.71 (1988); [Matthew Bersani, *Privatization and the Creation of Stock Companies in China*, 1993 COLUM. BUS. L. REV. 301 (1993)], at 314; Provisional Regulations of Shanghai Municipality on Limited Liability Companies (1992).

51. *See* [Matthew Bersani, *Privatization and the Creation of Stock Companies in China*, 1993 COLUM. BUS. L. REV. 301 (1993)], at 314. *See generally* N.Y. Bus. Corp. Law,...§402; Del. Code Ann.,...§§101–102.

52. *See* William Hackney & Tracey Benson, *Shareholder Liability for Inadequate Capital*, 43 U. PITT. L. REV. 837 (1982); CARY & EISENBERG, *supra* note 3, at200 (stating that "undercapitalization is actually one of the most significant factors in piercing").

Chuan Roger Peng, *Limited Liability in China: A Partial Reading of China's Company Law of 1994*, 10 COLUM. J. ASIAN L. 263, 272–273 (1996).

2. To what extent does the regulation of capital requirements in China reinforce state control over private economic activity, or rather, serve to strengthen state domination of all economic activity? It has recently been argued that:

> ...state-sector privatization in China is pursued only after a vibrant non-state sector has been established—not for the purpose of allowing private entities greater ownership and control over enterprises, but perversely and ironically the exact reverse—to allow the state to exercise greater ownership and control over a vast pool of privately-held capital hidden in the non-state sector. Secondly, state-sector privatization is limited and distorted, again by ideological constraints: (1) the number of state-owned enterprises that are privatized because of a quota system only recently abolished; (2) the type of enterprises that are allowed to be listed on the securities exchanges (state, not private, enterprises); and (3) the percentage (a strict minority) of shares in listed enterprises that can be privately owned and traded.

Lan Cao, *Chinese Privatization: Between Plan and Market*, 63 LAW & CONTEMP. PROBS. 13, 15–16 (2000). Can you suggest alternative arguments that support a contention that China is indeed building a strong non-state economic sector?

3. The Chinese Company Law describes the minimum capitalization requirements of corporations. Unlike the British and European civil law systems, in which minimum capital is based on the type of corporation created, the Chinese Company Law creates categories of legal capital based on the type of corporation created as well as on a classification system based on the industrial sector in which the corporation will operate. For limited companies manufacturing and wholesale industries require the highest minimum capital. The retail sector is required to maintain a smaller minimum capital and the smallest capital must be maintained by businesses in the technology, consultation and services sectors.[171] Limited stock companies, on the other hand, all must maintain a fairly high minimum capital.[172] The state reserves the right to raise the minimum capital requirements in "special cases."[173] Listed companies, those whose shares are traded on securities exchanges must maintain the highest minimum capital.[174] To what extent is this system more useful to state control of corporations than it is for the benefit of creditors or non-state shareholders?

---

171. *See* Howard Gensler, *Company Formation and Securities Listing in the People's Republic of China*, 17 HOUS. J. INT'L L. 399, 402 (1995) (ranging from a high of 500,000 yuan Renminbi to a low of 100,000 yuan Renminbi).

172. In the early 1990s that amount was set at 10,000,000 yuan Renminbi. See Howard Gensler, *Company Formation and Securities Listing in the People's Republic of China*, 17 HOUS. J. INT'L L. 399, 415 (1995).

173. *Id.*

174. *Id.*, at 426 (50,000,000 yuan Renminbi). In addition, under the rules, small listed companies must maintain a per share par value of 1,000 yuan Renminbi and one hundred shareholders, while large listed companies must have an aggregate minimum capital of 400,000,000 yuan Renminbi. *Id.*

Chapter 9

Limitations on Limited Liability

A general characteristic of corporate organization is that shareholders' liability for the obligations of the corporation are limited to the total amount contributed by each shareholder for the purchase of his shares. Creditors of the corporation cannot reach the personal wealth of shareholders to satisfy corporate debts. Every jurisdiction also permit creditors to each shareholder wealth, that is to pierce the corporate veil under certain circumstances. Though simple to state, the rule, and its exceptions, constitute a thorny problem in every jurisdiction. Moreover, the solutions created vary widely.

In this chapter we will explore the various approaches to the problems of limited liability and its exceptions that have been taken by the United States, the EU, Japan and China. In that connection we will continue to explore, now in a more particularized context, the ways in which different nations search for an acceptable balance between the interests of shareholders, on the one hand, and that of creditors (whether contract or tort creditors), on the other.

A. The American Approach

Just as the American federal system has left to the states the power to regulate its corporations, so has it left to the states, for the most part, the development of rules for determining under what circumstances the courts will disregard the separate personality of the corporations and reach to the shareholders for the payments of the obligations of the corporation. The notion of limiting the liability of shareholders of a corporation is neither ancient (in the United Kingdom it was established only in the second half of the 19th century, and only slightly earlier in the United States) nor universally lauded by academics (or litigants!). And yet, the notion, in one form or another, is firmly established in both the United States, the Member States of the EU, and Japan. It remains problematic in the People's Republic of China.

1. In General

John Laya and Thelma Laya, His Wife, v. Erin Homes, Inc., a Corporation, Michael Ferns, Individually, and Mike Ferns, dba Erin Homes, Inc.

Supreme Court of Appeals of West Virginia.
177 W.Va. 343, 352 S.E.2d 93 (1986)

McHUGH, Justice:

This action is before this Court upon appeal by the plaintiffs/appellants, John Laya and Thelma Laya, husband and wife, from a final order entered by the Circuit Court of Ohio County, West Virginia (the trial court), dismissing two of the named defendants, namely, Michael Ferns, individually, and Mike Ferns doing business as Erin Homes, Inc., leaving as a defendant only Erin Homes, Inc., a corporation. The appellants contend that the dismissal of these two defendants upon a motion for summary judgment was improper. We agree and reverse and remand.

I

Michael Ferns and Lawrence Finneran were the incorporators of Erin Homes, Inc. in May, 1978. Ferns was one of the initial directors of the corporation and initially was secretary-treasurer of the corporation. Finneran was one of the initial directors of the corporation and initially was president of the corporation. Finneran's wife was also one of the initial directors of the corporation. There is nothing in the record to indicate that any meetings of the directors or shareholders were held prior to January 2, 1980. On that date, at a special meeting of the shareholders, Finneran and his wife resigned as directors, Finneran resigned as president, and Ferns, his wife, and his then personal secretary, Rosemary Bodey (she is no longer an employee) were elected as the new directors. At that meeting Ferns became the president and his wife became the secretary-treasurer. There is no evidence that there have been any meetings of the directors or shareholders after January 2, 1980.

According to the stock records of the corporation, Ferns and Finneran on June 1, 1979 were each issued a stock certificate representing 100 shares of capital stock. The corporation was authorized to issue 500 shares of stock at a par value of $10.00. Finneran gave a promissory note for $1,000.00 to the corporation for his stock.[1] There is no evidence that the corporation ever received any cash payments from Finneran for his stock, and his promissory note was canceled upon his resignation as a director and president. Similarly, there is no evidence that Ferns ever paid any portion of the $1,000.00 for his 100 shares of $100.00 par stock.

According to undated "bills of sale," certain equipment (house-moving equipment, a highlift, a backhoe and miscellaneous equipment) was contributed to the corporation by Ferns shortly after incorporation. The house-moving equipment was purchased originally by Ferns for about $6,500–$6,700. The corporation according to the "bill of sale" assumed a debt of $5,220 on this equipment. Similarly, the corporation assumed

1. W.Va.Code, 31-1-82 [1974] provides, in relevant part: "Neither promissory notes nor future services shall constitute payment or part payment for the issuance of shares of a corporation."

liabilities of $5,995.94, $7,991.93 and $17,752.00, respectively, for the highlift, backhoe, and miscellaneous equipment. There is no record of any cash payments or issuance of shares of stock by the corporation for any of this equipment. The house-moving equipment was stored in Ferns' personal garage. The record is silent on where the other equipment was stored. The corporation purportedly paid $10,000.00 to an unrelated person for two parcels (five acres) of real estate, but there is no record of payment.

No corporate minutes were maintained after January 2, 1980. The corporate office was located in the same office as Ferns' other corporate business, Pike Homes, Inc., a dealer in mobile homes, formed in the year 1976. Ferns and Finneran are the only shareholders in Pike Homes, Inc. Erin Homes, Inc. was also a mobile home dealer until sometime in the year 1982, when the nature of the business was changed by Ferns to that of home remodeling.

The federal corporate income tax returns reflect "buildings and other assets." For example, at the beginning of the year 1980 such assets were listed at $61,455.00 and at the end of that year at $54,520.85. (The record does not indicate the amount of depreciation.) There is no evidence as to how these figures, or most of the other figures on the income tax returns for each year, were ascertained by the certified public accountant who prepared the tax returns. For example, there is no evidence of corporate records of any sales or other disposition of corporate assets. The 1980 federal corporate income tax return shows gross receipts of $463,987.65 from mobile home sales, and cost of goods sold in the amount of $374,256.62, for net sales proceeds of $89,731.03. The tax return shows $34,428.00 of interest incurred on loans to purchase the inventory of mobile homes. The record contains no information on these loans, such as the name of the lenders and whether there were any personal obligations for these loans imposed upon Ferns.

In his deposition testimony Ferns asserted that he never commingled his personal funds with the funds of Erin Homes, Inc. The corporation has always had its own checking account and all mobile home sales proceeds were deposited therein. The corporation leased in its own name from an unrelated person the real property upon which the mobile home sales business was located. Erin Homes, Inc. has filed federal income tax returns each year, using its own federal identification number. It has a West Virginia business registration certificate; it makes payments to the workers' compensation and unemployment compensation funds.

On October 1, 1980, John Laya and Thelma Laya, husband and wife, contracted with Erin Homes, Inc. to purchase from the latter a certain mobile home. Michael Ferns signed the contract as president of the corporation. The Layas "traded in" a certain pick-up truck and were given $5,000.00 credit toward the $17,500.00 purchase price of the mobile home; on October 31, 1980, the Layas also paid $12,500.00 in cash for the balance of the purchase price of the mobile home. The Layas shortly thereafter received the title to the mobile home.

The Layas allege that, contrary to the agreement, the mobile home was not subsequently delivered to them but was retained on the premises of Erin Homes, Inc. and was used by Erin Homes, Inc. as an unlocked exhibition model. The Layas allege that the trailer was allowed to fall into a state of disarray and disrepair, greatly impairing the value of the trailer.

In addition, the Layas incurred $8,500.00 in expenses for erection of a foundation for the trailer on their lot and for necessary excavation and earth moving to provide the proper ingress and egress to their lot for the equipment necessary to place the mobile home thereon.

The Layas also allege that the mobile home was moved by Erin Homes, Inc. at some time thereafter to another location, adjacent to a public highway, where it has been damaged by unknown persons (broken windows, stolen interior fixtures, etc.).

The Layas brought this action in August, 1981, against Erin Homes, Inc., a corporation, Michael Ferns, individually, and Mike Ferns, doing business as Erin Homes, Inc. For the alleged breach of contract by the defendants outlined above, the plaintiffs sought rescission of the contract and recovery of the $17,500.00 purchase price of the mobile home, together with the consequential damages of $8,500.00 for excavation and earth-moving.

The plaintiffs also sought $50,000.00 for pain, suffering and mental anguish caused by the defendants' conduct and $250,000.00 for punitive damages resulting from "the willful and deliberate misconduct of the defendants by refusing to perform the conditions of the contract and permitting the trailer to be wasted, for a total of $326,000.00 to be awarded unto the plaintiffs[.]"

The defendants' answers, each of which was prepared by the same attorney, denied the material allegations of the complaint with respect to the alleged breach of contract. The defendants later filed motions in limine, including a motion for summary judgment to prevent the plaintiffs from attempting to "pierce the corporate veil" of Erin Homes, Inc. to reach the personal assets of Michael Ferns.

The trial court granted the defendants' motion for summary judgment and dismissed Michael Ferns, individually, and Mike Ferns, doing business as Erin Homes, Inc., as defendants in this action. The trial court was of the opinion that the evidence relied upon by the plaintiffs (the deposition of Michael Ferns) was insufficient to justify Ferns' individual liability because there was no evidence of fraud and insufficient evidence to find that Michael Ferns had completely disregarded the corporate existence so that "piercing of the corporate veil" would be necessary to avoid an injustice to the plaintiffs.

The plaintiffs thereafter prosecuted this appeal. They claim that equity requires the corporate entity to be disregarded in this case to make the alleged real party in interest, the individual actor, liable.

II

W.Va.Code, 31-1-89 [1974] provides, in pertinent part: "A holder of or subscriber to shares of a corporation shall be under no obligation to the corporation or its creditors with respect to such shares other than the obligation to pay to the corporation the full consideration for which such shares were issued or to be issued." That is, a corporate shareholder's liability is usually limited to his or her capital investment in the corporation, and the shareholder is normally not liable individually to a creditor of the corporation. This limited liability is one of the legitimate advantages of doing business in the corporate form. "The organization of a corporation for the avowed purpose of avoiding personal responsibility does not of itself...justify disregard of the corporate entity." 1 W. Fletcher, Cyclopedia of the Law of Private Corporations §41.20 (rev.perm.ed. 1983). Professor David H. Barber, another leading authority in this area of the law, also recognizes this point: Given the purpose of promoting commerce by providing limited liability for shareholders in state corporation laws, courts have been reluctant to pierce the corporate veil, even when the express purpose of incorporation was to limit the liability of the incorporators. Indeed, courts of every jurisdiction have recognized the legitimacy of incorporating to avoid personal liability. Consequently, something more than the shareholders' desire to avoid personal liability must exist to justify piercing the corporate veil. Barber, Piercing the Corporate Veil, 17 Willamette L.Rev. 371, 373 (1981) (footnotes omitted). Accord, Note, Confronting Close Corporate Status in West Virginia: Alternative Theories to Prevent Abuse to the Detriment of Creditors, 86 W.Va.L.Rev. 139, 141 (1983). The concept of limited shareholder liability applies generally to a close corporation, as well as to a corporation whose shares are publicly traded. "Our state law [W.Va.Code, 31-1-26 [1974]] permits close corporations, with one shareholder, so we cannot [properly] disregard a corporation solely because it has one...shareholder[ ]." Southern Electrical Supply Co. v. Raleigh County National Bank,...320 S.E.2d 515, 524 (1984).

In addition to its recognition in the West Virginia Corporation Act, W.Va.Code, 31-1-1 to 31-1-158, as amended, the principle of limited shareholder liability is recognized in case law as a derivative of the principle that a corporation and its shareholder(s) are presumed to be separate legal entities. "The law presumes...that corporations are separate from their shareholders." Syl. pt. 3 (in part), Southern Electrical Supply Co. v. Raleigh County National Bank,...320 S.E.2d 515 (1984). "[T]he burden of proof is on a party soliciting a court to disregard a corporate structure." Id.,...320 S.E.2d at 522.

We use the term "close corporation" in this opinion to mean "a corporation whose shares are not generally traded in the securities markets. This definition seems to be most nearly in accord with the linguistic usages of the legal profession[.]" 1 F. O'Neal, Close Corporations § 1.02 (2d ed. 1971). Under exceptional circumstances, the corporate entity may be disregarded to remove the barrier to personal liability of the shareholder(s) actively participating in the operation of the business. "Justice may require that courts look beyond the bare legal relationship of the parties to prevent the corporate form from being used to perpetrate injustice, defeat public convenience or justify wrong. However, the corporate form will never be disregarded lightly." Southern States Cooperative, Inc. v. Dailey,...280 S.E.2d 821, 827 (1981). This Court expressed the principle of "piercing the corporate veil" in the following manner in syllabus point 10 of Sanders v. Roselawn Memorial Gardens, [Inc.,] 152 W.Va. 91, 159 S.E.2d 784 (1968): While, legally speaking, a corporation constitutes an entity separate and apart from the persons who own it, such is a fiction of the law introduced for purpose of convenience and to subserve the ends of justice; and it is now well settled, as a general principle, that the fiction should be disregarded when it is urged with an intent not within its reason and purpose, and in such a way that its retention would produce injustices or inequitable consequences. Accord, Southern Electrical Supply Co. v. Raleigh County National Bank,...320 S.E.2d 515, 521–22 (1984);...

"Piercing the corporate veil" is an equitable remedy, the propriety of which must be examined on an ad hoc basis. See 1 W. Fletcher, Cyclopedia of the Law of Private Corporations § 41.25 (rev.perm.ed. 1983). "[D]ecisions to look beyond, inside and through corporate facades must be made case-by-case, with particular attention to factual details." Southern Electrical Supply Co. v. Raleigh County National Bank,...320 S.E.2d 515, 523 (1984).

Some of the factors to be considered in deciding whether to pierce the corporate veil are:

(1) commingling of funds and other assets of the corporation with those of the individual shareholders;

(2) diversion of the corporation's funds or assets to noncorporate uses (to the personal uses of the corporation's shareholders);

(3) failure to maintain the corporate formalities necessary for the issuance of or subscription to the corporation's stock, such as formal approval of the stock issue by the board of directors;

(4) an individual shareholder representing to persons outside the corporation that he or she is personally liable for the debts or other obligations of the corporation;

(5) failure to maintain corporate minutes or adequate corporate records;

(6) identical equitable ownership in two entities;

(7) identity of the directors and officers of two entities who are responsible for supervision and management (a partnership or sole proprietorship and a corporation owned and managed by the same parties);

(8) failure to adequately capitalize a corporation for the reasonable risks of the corporate undertaking;

(9) absence of separately held corporate assets;

(10) use of a corporation as a mere shell or conduit to operate a single venture or some particular aspect of the business of an individual or another corporation;

(11) sole ownership of all the stock by one individual or members of a single family;

(12) use of the same office or business location by the corporation and its individual shareholder(s);

(13) employment of the same employees or attorney by the corporation and its shareholder(s);

(14) concealment or misrepresentation of the identity of the ownership, management or financial interests in the corporation, and concealment of personal business activities of the shareholders (sole shareholders do not reveal the association with a corporation, which makes loans to them without adequate security);

(15) disregard of legal formalities and failure to maintain proper arm's length relationships among related entities;

(16) use of a corporate entity as a conduit to procure labor, services or merchandise for another person or entity;

(17) diversion of corporate assets from the corporation by or to a stockholder or other person or entity to the detriment of creditors, or the manipulation of assets and liabilities between entities to concentrate the assets in one and the liabilities in another;

(18) contracting by the corporation with another person with the intent to avoid the risk of nonperformance by use of the corporate entity; or the use of a corporation as a subterfuge for illegal transactions;

(19) the formation and use of the corporation to assume the existing liabilities of another person or entity.[2]

Examination of the numerous relevant factors in a "totality of the circumstances" test provides a more enlightening analysis than merely applying metaphors, like "simu-

---

2. *See, e.g.*, Associated Vendors, Inc. v. Oakland Meat Co., 210 Cal.App.2d 825, 838–40, 26 Cal.Rptr. 806, 813–15 (1962) (collecting cases); Barber, *Piercing the Corporate Veil*, 17 WILLAMETTE L.REV. 371, 374–75 (1981). Associated Vendors is a forerunner of the modern cases analyzing the "totality of the circumstances" in order to pierce the corporate veil in a case involving an alleged breach of contract.

lacrum," "alter ego," "instrumentality," etc., to describe the unity of the shareholder(s) and the corporation justifying, where equitable, the piercing of the corporate veil in the case.[3] This totality of the circumstances approach also leads to a more informed balancing or weighing of the primary policy behind limited liability of the shareholder(s), specifically, a capital investment incentive, against the primary policy justifying piercing of the corporate veil, specifically, the avoidance of clearly inequitable consequences of not piercing. "This evidence must be analyzed in conjunction with evidence that a corporation attempted to use its corporate structure to perpetrate a fraud or do grave injustice on an innocent third party seeking to 'pierce the veil.' " Southern Electrical Supply Co. v. Raleigh County National Bank,... 320 S.E.2d 515, 523 (1984).

Thus, in a case involving an alleged breach of contract, to "pierce the corporate veil" in order to hold the shareholder(s) actively participating in the operation of the business personally liable for such breach to the party who entered into the contract with the corporation, there is normally a two-prong test: (1) there must be such unity of interest and ownership that the separate personalities of the corporation and of the individual shareholder(s) no longer exist (a disregard of formalities requirement) and (2) an inequitable result would occur if the acts are treated as those of the corporation alone (a fairness requirement). See, e.g., Automotriz Del Golfo De California v. Resnick, 47 Cal.2d 792, 796, 306 P.2d 1, 3 (1957) (en banc).[4] Most of the numerous factors listed previously are pertinent primarily to the disregard of formalities requirement, not because it is the more important requirement—it is not—but because it is easier to compile a list of typical corporate formalities than to anticipate and list types of inequitable and unfair consequences which could result from not piercing the corporate veil in a given case.[5]

---

3. In discussing the concept of piercing the corporate veil to hold the parent corporation liable for the debts of its subsidiary corporation, the renowned Benjamin N. Cardozo, then Chief Judge of the New York Court of Appeals, remarked that this concept "is still enveloped in the mists of metaphor. Metaphors in law are to be narrowly watched, for starting as devices to liberate thought, they end often by enslaving it." Berkey v. Third Avenue Ry., 244 N.Y. 84, 94, 155 N.E. 58, 61 (1926).

4. The cause of action in the case now before us sounds essentially in contract. Therefore, we do not address here the question of what is required to pierce the corporate veil in a tort case. In note 13 of Southern Electrical Supply Co. v. Raleigh County National Bank,... 320 S.E.2d 515 (1984), this Court recognized that "[s]ome courts will more readily disregard a corporate form in cases of tort liability than in contract cases because contracts are voluntarily entered into with the corporate structure."... n. 13, 320 S.E.2d at 522–23 n. 13.

5. Courts have discussed the significance of the disregard of formalities requirement. "The very nature of a closely held corporation militates against strict compliance with corporate formalities. However, the centralization of ownership is not a carte blanche to abrogate established procedure." In re County Green Limited Partnership, 438 F.Supp. 701, 707 (W.D.Va.1977), rev'd on other grounds, 604 F.2d 289 (4th Cir.1979). In the latter opinion it was "note[d] that a single factor will rarely, if ever, be sufficient to justify the drastic remedy of piercing the corporate veil. The trier of fact should look at all the circumstances in each case rather than relying on any single factor." Id., 604 F.2d at 292. In the context of a close corporation, the failure to follow corporate formalities is important because the trier of the facts may reasonably infer that such conduct springs not from merely innocent, overworked inattention to paperwork by the sole or controlling shareholder, but is indicative of the fact that such shareholder views the business as his or her own individual business so that there is no need to "go through the motions" of complying with formalities: Individuals who wish to enjoy limited personal liability for business activities under a corporate umbrella should be expected to adhere to the relatively simple formalities of creating and maintaining a corporate entity. In a sense, faithfulness to these formalities is the price paid for the corporate fiction, a relatively small price to pay for limited liability. Furthermore, the formalities are themselves an excellent litmus of the extent to which the individuals involved actually view the corporation as a separate

In a breach of contract case many of the commentators and a few of the cases suggest that there may also be a third prong to the test for piercing the corporate veil which must be hurdled by certain types, and only certain types, of contract creditors of the corporation, specifically, those capable of protecting themselves. When, under the circumstances, it would be reasonable for that particular type of a party entering into the contract with the corporation, for example, a bank or other lending institution, to conduct an investigation of the credit of the corporation prior to entering into the contract, such party will be charged with the knowledge that a reasonable credit investigation would disclose. If such an investigation would disclose that the corporation is grossly undercapitalized, based upon the nature and the magnitude of the corporate undertaking, such party will be deemed to have assumed the risk of the gross undercapitalization and will not be permitted to pierce the corporate veil. In such a case that type of a sophisticated party dealing with the corporation should, and ordinarily would, also, or in lieu thereof, enter into a contract with the shareholder(s). Cf. DeWitt Truck Brokers, Inc. v. W. Ray Flemming Fruit Co., 540 F.2d 681, 686 n. 13 (4th Cir.1976) (contract creditors impliedly assume the risk of gross undercapitalization); Hanson v. Bradley, 298 Mass. 371, 380–82, 10 N.E.2d 259, 264–65 (1937) (fair inference is that salaried employee of corporation knew worthlessness of corporation when he entered into contract for salary). On the other hand, "'the plaintiffs' lack of sophistication is equally tenable against the presumption [suggested by some commentators] that they [the plaintiffs as contract creditors] knowingly assumed the risk of the corporation's undercapitalization.'" Labadie Coal Co. v. Black, 672 F.2d 92, 100 (D.C.Cir.1982), quoting Barber, Piercing the Corporate Veil, 17 Willamette L.Rev. 371, 386 (1981).

Generally, the presumption is that the party dealing with the corporation did not assume the risk of grossly inadequate capitalization. "[I]n entering into such [contractual] relationships with corporate entities the parties are [generally] entitled to rely upon certain assumptions, one being that the corporation is more than a mere shell—that it has substance as well as form." Iron City Sand & Gravel Division of McDonough Co. v. West Fork Towing Corp., 298 F.Supp. 1091, 1099 (N.D.W.Va.1969), rev'd on other grounds, 440 F.2d 958 (4th Cir.1971). In other words, the incorporators who actively participate in the operation of the business are not entitled to personal immunity when they fail to provide the quid pro quo for such immunity, specifically, a reasonably adequate capital fund to which creditors may resort. See Hanson v. Bradley, 298 Mass. 371, 380, 10 N.E.2d 259, 264 (1937).

Close corporations are closely scrutinized to determine whether the corporate veil should be pierced. See Amfac Mechanical Supply Co. v. Federer, 645 P.2d 73, 81 (Wyo.1982). One of the principal reasons for this close scrutiny of close corporations is that grossly inadequate capitalization is more likely to occur in a close corporation than in a corporation whose shares are publicly traded, and grossly inadequate capitalization is a very important factor, as an element of the fairness prong, in determining whether to pierce the corporate veil. "One fact which all the authorities consider significant in the inquiry [of whether to pierce the corporate veil], and particularly so in the case of the one-man or closely-held corporation, is whether the corporation was grossly undercapitalized for the purposes of the corporate undertaking." DeWitt Truck Brokers, Inc.

---

being.... It is clearly not necessary that all of these factors be present in a given case to justify piercing the veil. Labadie Coal Co. v. Black, 672 F.2d 92, 96–97 (D.C.Cir.1982) (emphasis in original).

v. W. Ray Flemming Fruit Co., 540 F.2d 681, 685 (4th Cir.1976). An obvious inadequacy of capital, measured by the nature and magnitude of the corporate undertaking, has, according to Anderson v. Abbott, 321 U.S. 349, 362, 64 S.Ct. 531, 538, 88 L.Ed. 793, 803 (1944), frequently been an important factor in cases denying shareholders their defense of limited liability....[6]

The obligation to provide adequate capital begins with incorporation and is a continuing obligation thereafter during the corporation's operations. DeWitt Truck Brokers, Inc. v. W. Ray Flemming Fruit Co., 540 F.2d 681, 686 (4th Cir.1976). With respect to determining the adequacy of the corporation's capital, in light of the nature and magnitude of the corporate undertaking, there are several tests and factors which can be utilized to analyze the financial data of the corporation. For example, comparison with the capitalization of other corporations in the same or a similar line of business may be made. The capitalization of the corporation in question could be compared with the average industry-wide ratios (current ratio, acid-test ratio, debt/equity ratio, etc.) obtained from published sources (Dunn & Bradstreet, Moody's Manual of Investments, Standard and Poor's Corporation Records, etc.). These average ratios could be buttressed by expert testimony from certified public accountants, securities analysts, investment counselors or other qualified financial analysts. See Barber, Piercing the Corporate Veil, 17 Willamette L.Rev. 371, 392–94 (1981). "Grossly inadequate capitalization" for the purpose of piercing the corporate veil would generally be reflected by a substantial deficiency of capital compared with that level of capitalization deemed adequate in the case by the financial analyst experts.

It is clear that grossly inadequate capitalization combined with disregard of corporate formalities, causing basic unfairness, are sufficient to pierce the corporate veil in order to hold the shareholder(s) actively participating in the operation of the business personally liable for a breach of contract to the party who entered into the contract with the corporation. See, e.g., Labadie Coal Co. v. Black, 672 F.2d 92, 99–100 (D.C.Cir.1982); DeWitt Truck Brokers, Inc. v. W. Ray Flemming Fruit Co., 540 F.2d 681, 687 (4th Cir.1976); Automotriz Del Golfo De California v. Resnick, 47 Cal.2d 792, 796–98, 306 P.2d 1, 4 (1957) (en banc); Amfac Mechanical Supply Co. v. Federer, 645 P.2d 73, 79–82 (Wyo.1982). "The essence of the fairness test is simply that an individual businessman [or business

6. An often quoted statement of the vital importance of grossly inadequate capitalization as a factor in determining whether to pierce the corporate veil is set forth in 1 W. FLETCHER, CYCLOPEDIA OF THE LAW OF PRIVATE CORPORATIONS §44.1 (rev.perm.ed. 1983) (footnotes omitted): If a corporation is organized and carries on a business without substantial capital in such a way that the corporation is likely to have insufficient assets available to meet its debts, it is inequitable that the stockholders should set up such a flimsy organization to escape personal liability. The attempt to do corporate business without providing any sufficient basis of financial responsibilities to creditors is an abuse of the separate entity and will be ineffectual to exempt the stockholders from corporate debts. It is coming to be recognized as the policy of the law that stockholders should in good faith put at the risk of the business unencumbered capital reasonably adequate for its prospective liabilities. If the capital is illusory or trifling compared with the business to be done and the risks of loss, this is ground for denying the separate entity privilege. It has been stated that a corporation's capitalization is a major consideration of courts in deciding whether a legitimate separate corporate entity was maintained. Several of the commentators suggest that grossly inadequate capitalization per se should be sufficient to pierce the corporate veil, except when a contract creditor capable of protecting itself assumes the risk. *See, e.g.*, Gelb, *Piercing the Corporate Veil—The Undercapitalization Factor*, 59 CHI.KENT L.REV. 1 (1982); Note, *Disregarding the Corporate Fiction in Florida: The Need for Specifics*, 27 U.FLA.L.REV. 175 (1974).

woman] cannot [be allowed to] hide from the normal consequences of carefree entrepreneuring by doing so through a corporate shell." Labadie Coal Co. v. Black, 672 F.2d 92, 100 (D.C.Cir.1982) (emphasis in original).

It is also clear that the propriety of piercing the corporate veil should rarely be determined upon a motion for summary judgment. Instead, the propriety of piercing the corporate veil usually involves numerous questions of fact for the trier of the facts to determine upon all of the evidence. See Southern Electrical Supply Co. v. Raleigh County National Bank,... n. 5, 320 S.E.2d 515, 517 n. 5 (1984); Wheeling Kitchen Equipment Co. v. R & R Sewing Center, Inc., 154 W.Va. 715, 719–20, 179 S.E.2d 587, 589–90 (1971); Alorna Coat Corp. v. Behr, 408 So.2d 496, 498 (Ala.1981) (motion to dismiss); Curtis v. Vlotho, 313 N.W.2d 469, 472 (S.D.1981) (trial court in nonjury trial improperly considered only the evidence on lack of fraudulent representation, without analyzing other factors for piercing corporate veil); Amfac Mechanical Supply Co. v. Federer, 645 P.2d 73, 74–77, 82 (Wyo.1982) (motion to dismiss improperly granted in nonjury trial at close of plaintiff's evidence; trial court improperly relied exclusively on lack of fraud; prima facie case for piercing shown by evidence of grossly inadequate capitalization and disregard of corporate formalities).

* * *

Based upon all of the above, we reverse the order of the trial court granting the defendants' motion for summary judgment and remand this case for further proceedings consistent with the principles enunciated herein.

Reversed and remanded.

Sandra K. Miller, *Piercing the Corporate Veil among Affiliated Companies in the European Community and in the U.S.: A Comparative Analysis of U.S., German, and U.K. Veil Piercing Approaches*

36 Am. Bus. L.J. 73 (1998)
(excerpts pages 84–88; 91–95; some footnotes omitted)

Piercing the Corporate Veil of Affiliated Corporations under U.S. Law

The general rule that a corporation is a separate legal entity that limits the creditor's rights to the assets of the corporation lies at the core of corporate jurisprudence in the United States.[46] The limited liability of the shareholder for corporate debts was firmly

46. Interestingly, as of the beginning of the nineteenth century, it was common for shareholders to be directly liable for corporate debts. Spawned by the industrial revolution and the growing desire of the shareholders of manufacturing companies to obtain limited liability, limited liability became the rule by the 1850's. See Phillip I. Blumberg, *Limited Liability and Corporate Groups*, 11 J. Corp. L. 591, 591–95 (1986) (providing a detailed review of the emergence of limited liability in the United States). A minority of states retained unlimited liability. Rhode Island adopted limited liability as late as 1847 and California enacted limited liability in 1931. Personal liability of shareholders of banks remained until the Depression of 1929; Philip I. Blumberg, The Law of Corporate Groups § 2.01, at 30 (3d ed. 1997) (providing a historical overview of modern corporate law); Anderson v. Abbott, 321 U.S. 349 (1944) (imposing personal liability on shareholders of a bank holding company under the banking law in effect prior to the Depression); E. Merrick Dodd, Ameri-

established in the U.S. legal system by the mid-19th century.[47] At the time when the concept of limited liability became firmly entrenched in U.S. law, corporate groups were relatively uncommon.[48] Initially the corporate veil protected only the individual shareholder. By the late 19th century corporations became authorized to own stock in other corporations.[49] The rule of limited liability applicable to the individual shareholder was extended to the corporate shareholder, apparently with little controversy or analysis.[50]

Today, corporate conglomerates dominate the economy. The general rule is that business risk is limited on an entity-by-entity basis.[51] Yet, the veil-piercing doctrine remains one of the most litigated issues in corporate law.[52] In 1990, for example, a computerized survey found over 1600 cases that raised the doctrine of piercing the corporate veil.[53] More veil-piercing litigation can be expected with the growing use of limited liability companies, which combine the corporate shield of limited liability with the flow-through tax treatment traditionally associated with partnerships.

The case law emerging from the veil-piercing doctrine has long been criticized as being highly discretionary and unpredictable.[55] The prospect of parental liability for

---

CAN BUSINESS CORPORATIONS UNTIL 1860 (1954) (outlining the development of limited liability); Liggett v. Lee, 288 U.S. 517, 557–60 (1932) (tracing the evolution of the corporation dating from the early days when the corporation was a creature of state charter, in which Justice Brandeis explains that the public was slow to accept the corporate form, noting:

> Incorporation for business was commonly denied long after it had been freely granted for religious, educational and charitable purposes. It was denied because of fear. Fear of encroachment upon the liberties and opportunities of the individual. Fear of the subjection of labor to capital. Fear of monopoly. Fear that the absorption of capital by corporations, and their perpetual life, might bring evils similar to those which attended mortmain.

Id. at 548).

See also Michael J. Gaertner, *Reverse Piercing The Corporate Veil: Should Corporation Owners Have It Both Ways?*, 30 WM. & MARY L. REV. 667, 669–72 (indicating that in 1811 New York became the first state to enact a general incorporation law. General incorporation law became commonplace by about the middle of the nineteenth century).

47. BLUMBERG, LIMITED LIABILITY AND CORPORATE GROUPS, *supra* note 46, at 595 (1986) (indicating that there were isolated attempts to provide for unlimited shareholder liability but these came to an end by the 1850's).

48. [Adolf A. Berle, Jr., *The Theory of Enterprise Entity*, 47 COLUM. L. REV. 343 (1947)] at 344.

49. BLUMBERG, LIMITED LIABILITY AND CORPORATE GROUPS, *supra* note 46, at 605. Just as it has been said that the railways built the tort law, it may be said that the railways paved the way toward the emergence of corporate groups. Initially special charters for corporate ownership were obtained by the Baltimore & Ohio Railroad and the Pennsylvania Railroad. *Id.* at 595.

50. BLUMBERG, *supra* note 46, at 607....

51. ....*See* William O. Douglas & Carrol M. Shanks, *Insulation From Liability Through Subsidiary Corporations*, 39 YALE L.J. 193 (1929) (noting as early as 1929 that the affiliated business structure is used for a wide range of business reasons including: the avoidance of complications in the purchase of physical assets; the preservation of good will of an established business; the minimization of taxation; and the furtherance of management goals).

52. ....Veil-piercing litigation occurs in a wide variety of contexts in today's business environment. *See* Robert B. Thompson, *The Limits of Liability In The New Limited Liability Entities,* 32 WAKE FOREST L. REV. 1 (1997) (discussing veil-piercing in connection with limited liability companies and limited liability partnerships).

53. *See* [Robert B. Thompson, *Piercing The Corporate Veil: An Empirical Study*, 76 CORNELL L. REV. 1036 (1991)] (indicating that the initial pool of cases found in a Westlaw analysis revealed 2,000 cases involving veil-piercing terminology. The pool of veil-piercing cases which were eventually analyzed consisted of 1600 cases. In contrast, fewer than 300 cases were found on "corporate takeovers" or "hostile takeovers").

55. Justice Cardozo has been frequently quoted as criticizing the veil piercing doctrine. *See* Berkey v. Third Ave. Ry., 155 N.E. 58, 61 (N.Y. 1927)....

subsidiary obligations is troublesome to the U.S. parent company with either domestic or foreign subsidiaries. The litigation ranges in complexity from the mundane slip and fall case[56] to the highly complex environmental disaster.[57] In veil-piercing cases involving the piercing of a foreign subsidiary with a U.S. parent company, the litigation is frequently complicated by additional issues concerning jurisdiction, choice of law, and forum non conveniens.[58]....

Veil-Piercing Under U.S. Common Law: The Twin Elements of "Control" and "Improper Conduct"

* * *

Commentators and some judicial decisions have organized the prodigious case law into categories consisting of the "instrumentality" theory, the "alter ego" theory, and the "identity" theory.[71] However, such characterizations are not helpful in light of the

---

56. *See* Ioviero v. Ciga Hotels, 475 N.Y.S.2d 880 (N.Y. App. Div. 1984) (involving a plaintiff who fell at a hotel in Venice and attempted to use the veil-piercing doctrine to hold a related New York sales and promotional company liable).

57. The widespread use of subsidiaries which conduct business in diverse countries contributes significantly to the complexity of contemporary corporate veil-piercing litigation. *See* Giuseppinna Noto v. CIA Secula di Armanento, 310 F.Supp. 639 (S.D.N.Y. 1970) (involving a personal injury suit resulting from the explosion of an oil tanker. The oil tanker was owned by an Italian Corporation and was leased to a British subsidiary of British Petroleum Company Ltd. The oil terminal and loading facilities were under exclusive operation and control of a Dutch subsidiary of a British corporation whose shares were held directly and indirectly by many of the world's major oil companies which are members of the Iranian Oil Consortium of 1954. The plaintiffs sought to pierce the corporate veil of the Dutch subsidiary, and successive layers of subsidiary entities to ultimately reach the parent companies which were major oil corporations. The suit was instituted in New York because it was the place where the oil consortium agreement was executed. The twenty-three defendants included domestic U.S. companies, foreign corporations of Britain, the Netherlands, France, Italy, Iran, and the government of Iran); Fish & Neave v. Perovetz, L.P.I., No. 91 Civ 7047 (CSH), 1992 U.S.Dist. LEXIS 20228, at *1 (S.D.N.Y., Jan. 7, 1993) (involving a lawsuit initiated by a New York law firm seeking to pierce the corporate veil of a network of affiliated U.K., Netherlands Antilles, and Delaware companies arising out of legal services rendered in connection with patent matter); Japan Petroleum Co. (Nigeria Ltd.) v. Ashland Oil Inc., 465 F.Supp. 831 (D. Del. 1978) (involving a suit by a Nigerian corporation against a Kentucky parent company which owned two Nigerian subsidiaries. The subsidiaries lost an oil drilling rig in violation of a leasing agreement); O'Berry v. McDermott, Inc., 712 S.W.2d 206 (Tex. Ct. App. 1986) (involving the question of whether an employee who was injured on the job could sue the parent company in California even though he was employed by its subsidiary in Thailand where he was injured).

58. *See* In Re Union Carbide Corp. Gas Plant Disaster, 809 F.2d 195 (2d Cir.1987); Richard Schaffer et al., International Business Law and its Environment 26 (3d ed. 1996) (discussing the Bhopal industrial disaster which occurred in a plant owned by Union Carbide Corporation India Limited which was 51% owned by Union Carbide, a U.S. corporation. The 2d Circuit upheld the District Court's dismissal of the case on the basis of the doctrine of forum non conveniens. This doctrine states that where a case is properly heard in more than one court, it should be heard by the one that is most convenient. The case was eventually settled in India for $470 million. Interestingly, the plaintiff's argument was not premised on traditional concepts of respondeat superior. Instead, liability was premised on the single enterprise theory. The plaintiffs argued that Union Carbide is a multinational corporation with a global purpose, and as such, its parent and subsidiary companies should be treated as one unit);...; Daniel G. Brown, *Jurisdiction Over A Corporation On The Basis Of The Contracts Of An Affiliated Corporation: Do You Have To Pierce The Corporate Veil*, 61 U. Cin. L. Rev. 595 (1992) (providing an overview of jurisdictional questions concerning affiliated groups under U.S. law).

71. *See* Blumberg, The Law Of Corporate Groups, *supra* note 46, at § 2.02.

numerous descriptive phrases that are used, apparently interchangeably, by the courts.[72] Some courts have abandoned all efforts to articulate a theory and instead take a "laundry list" approach to the identification of factors[73] likely to justify veil-piercing, listing such factors as gross undercapitalization, nonobservance of corporate formalities, nonpayment of dividends, insolvency of the corporation, siphoning of corporation funds, non-functioning of corporate officers and directors, and the absence of corporate records.[74] Other courts emphasize the functional relationship between the parent and subsidiary, looking to a number of factors pointing to the proximity of the parent-subsidiary relationship ranging from parental voting control to shared use of common business departments.[75]

Evidence of inadequate capitalization or the depletion of corporate capital has led to veil-piercing in a variety of circumstances; however, veil-piercing has been successfully avoided where the subsidiary is well-capitalized and conducts its own daily operations.[76]

* * *

Some courts have stated that a showing of fraud is not required to trigger the piercing of the veil.[78] However, deception of some kind may be involved. For example, the

---

72. *See* R.W. Hamilton, Corporations Including Partnerships and Limited Partnerships 261(4th ed. 1990) (identifying twenty-five metaphors describing the prohibited manner in which the shareholder uses the corporation including as a "mere adjunct," "agent," "alter ego," "alter identity," "arm," "blind," "branch," "buffer," "cloak," "coat," "corporate double," "instrumentality," "mouthpiece," "name," "nominal identity," "phrase," "puppet," "screen," "sham," "simulacrum," "snare," "stooge," "subterfuge," or "tool").

73. Carte Blanche (Singapore) Pte. Ltd. v. Diners Club Int'l, 2 F.2d 24 (2d Cir.1993) (involving a dispute over the marketing and servicing of credit cards in which a number of veil-piercing factors were considered, including the absence of corporate formalities; inadequate capitalization; withdrawal of corporate funds for personal purposes; overlap of officers, personnel, office space, and addresses and telephones; exercise of discretion in business decision-making; occurrence of non-arms length transactions; payment or guarantee of debts by other corporations in the group; and whether the dominated corporation had property used by other corporations in the group).

74. Dewitt v. W. Ray Flemming Fruit Co., 540 F.2d 681 (4th Cir.1976).

75. United States v. Jon-T Chemicals, Inc., 768 F.2d 686, 691–692 (5th Cir.1985) (involving a civil action by the U.S. to recover damages from the erroneous payment of money pursuant to a federal agricultural subsidy program as the result of false information submitted by a corporate subsidiary of the defendant. The U.S. sought to hold the parent company liable. The court looked to whether the parent organized the subsidiary; the stock ownership of the parent; the use of common parent/subsidiary directors and officers; the use of common business departments; the preparation of joint financial statements and tax returns; the degree of parental financial assistance and the level of subsidiary capitalization; parental payment of subsidiary expenses; whether the subsidiary has business from sources other than from the parent; the observation of basic corporate formalities; and the degree to which the subsidiary conducts daily operations autonomously)....

76. *See* Amfac v. Int'l Systems & Controls Corp., 630 P.2d 868 (Ore. Ct. App. 1981) (involving a reversal by the Oregon Supreme Court in light of faulty instructions to the jury). Inadequate capital in relation to the magnitude of the enterprise has frequently been an important factor in the disregard of the corporate veil. *See* Anderson v. Abbott, 321 U.S. 349, 362 (1944) (expressing concern with capitalization); Francis O. Day Co. v. Shapiro, 267 F.2d 669, 672 (D.C. Cir.1959) (referring to inadequacy of capital as an issue of concern); Japan Petroleum Co. (Nigeria) v. Ashland Oil, 456 F.Supp. 831, 841 (D.Del..1978) (involving a suit by a Nigerian corporation against a Kentucky company and its two Nigerian subsidiaries arising out of the destruction of an offshore drilling unit. The court failed to pierce a well-capitalized subsidiary's corporate veil in spite of the existence of several common management and administrative functions).

78. *See* Nat'l Marine Serv. v. Thibodeaux & Co., 501 F.2d 940, 942 (5th Cir.1974) (involving a suit by a shipyard to recover compensation for repairs, indicating that fraud is a concern but not a

incorporation of an entity specifically to avoid paying a creditor has been grounds for piercing the corporate veil.[79]

Public representations of the corporation continue to be important in the consideration of whether to pierce the corporate veil. Business operations conducted among a large number of corporations whose identities and functions are easily confused are subject to particular scrutiny and skepticism.[80] The corporate veil has been pierced where the parent held out to the public that a subsidiary was a department of its own business.[81] It also has been pierced where an undercapitalized corporation made express representations that another individual or another corporation assumed responsibility for the contract at issue.[82] On the other hand, veil-piercing has been avoided upon a showing of public representations of the companies as separate entities.[83]

In light of the diversity of judicial approaches, the use of expansive rhetoric, and the sheer volume of legal opinions, veil-piercing jurisprudence in the U.S. lacks the degree of certainty and predictability that the modern business requires. The veil-piercing

---

prerequisite). It has been observed, however, that veil-piercing typically involves fraud, or something approaching fraud, such as commingling of assets, or dealings which otherwise mislead....

79. *See* Castleberry v. Byron, 721 S.W.2d 273 (Tex. 1986) (involving the creation of a new corporate entity to avoid paying the buy-out price to a minority shareholder. The business of the old corporation was essentially transferred to the new entity. The court observed that one common sham is for a closely-held corporation to avoid an obligation by siphoning off corporate revenues, selling off assets, and transferring the old business to a new start-up entity. The Texas statute was subsequently narrowed to make actual fraud a prerequisite to piercing. *See* Tex. Civ. Code Ann. Art. 2.21. (West 1997)).

80. *See* Francis O. Day Co. v. Shapiro, 267 F.2d 669, 672 (D.C. Cir.1959) (reversing the dismissal of a case where the functions of a real estate enterprise were divided among over five companies with similar names); Berger v. Columbia Broadcasting, 453 F.2d 991 (5th Cir.1972) (involving a suit against CBS for breach of a contract to air a fashion show executed by a subsidiary of CBS. When CBS, the parent company, executed a similar contract with another party, the court failed to pierce the corporate veil of the CBS subsidiary).

81. *See* Kissun v. Humana, Inc., 479 S.E.2d 751, 753 (Ga. 1997) (observing that even where parent and subsidiary have remained separate corporate entities both corporations may be liable where one corporation acts as the agent of another); Japan Petroleum Co. (Nigeria) v. Ashland Oil, 456 F.Supp. 831, 841(D.Del. 1978) involving contractual dispute in which the court emphasized that the fact that a parent holds out to the public that a subsidiary is a department of its own business increases the likelihood that the parent will be held liable for the subsidiary's acts).

82. *See* Weisser v. Mursam Shoe Corp., 127 F.2d 344, 348 (2d Cir.1942) (involving a representation that an individual and his brother stood behind a lease agreement, in which the court noted "the doctrine hardly seems challenged that a representation that the liability of the subsidiary is the same as that of its parent or affiliate will result in piercing of the corporate veil of a subsidiary which is in fact undercapitalized, dominated and used as an instrument of the parent"); Edwards Co. v. Monogram Indus., 730 F.2d 977, 984 (5th Cir.1984) (involving an unsuccessful attempt to pierce the corporate veil in a contract dispute wherein the court observed that the plaintiff had relied exclusively on the subsidiary's credit and there had been no assurance or representation that the parent would be responsible for the subsidiary's obligations).

83. *See* Ioviero v. Ciga Hotels, 475 N.Y.S.2d 880 (N.Y. Sup. Ct. 1984) (involving an infant who injured her hand when she slipped and fell while leaving the dining room at the Hotel Excelsior in Venice, Italy. The plaintiff sought to hold Ciga Hotels, a New York company, vicariously liable for the personal injuries sustained at the Venice hotel. The defendant successfully argued that Cigahotels, Inc. did not own, operate, manage or control the Venice hotel, but merely provided sales and promotional services to the hotel industry. The defendant emphasized that it had a contract which indicated that it was a separate company from Cigahotels, S.P.A., the Venice company. Although the defendant used the letterhead Cigahotels, S.P.A., as well as its trademark, the defendant's agency role was always disclosed at the bottom of each letter).

common law of torts and contracts remains highly discretionary and problematic for the business planner.

Limited liability is said to shift some of the costs of innovation, and its failure, to the customers (creditors) and employees of corporations. Without the protection afforded by concepts of limited liability, it is argued, people would be less eager to invest in large (and very risky) endeavors, and much human progress would be considerably slowed. Critics note, however, that the most efficient users of limited liability are the large corporations themselves. By permitting corporations to insulate lines of businesses by the creation of subsidiaries, the corporation can take advantage of employees, customers and creditors in a way not contemplated when the notion of limited liability gained acceptance. The modern multi-tiered corporation, then, is able to hide its assets from those who must look to it for satisfaction of all their claims. Is this fair? Does it make sense? Are there better, or more efficient alternatives?

The economic justification for the doctrine of limited liability rests on several factors. These are briefly described in the excerpt that follows.

Phillip I. Blumberg, *The Law of Corporate Groups: Tort, Contract, and Other Common Law Problems in the Substantive Law of Parent and Subsidiary Corporations*

(1987)

(excerpts pages 67–74; footnotes omitted or renumbered)

* * *

[Avoids exposure of risk of loss to absentee investors]. The widespread distribution of shares of the larger corporation makes the shareholder an investor without the opportunity (and presumably the interest) to participate in the management of the corporation. It leads to the separation of ownership and control; under such circumstances the imposition on absentee investors of liability for the debts of the corporation would expose such investors to business risks that originate out of a decisionmaking process from which they are far removed and for which they bear no realistic responsibility. This is not only hazardous for them, but is not compatible with generally accepted views of fairness.

* * *

[Facilitates investment in and therefor the existence of very large scale enterprises]. Limited liability in very large scale enterprises serves two distinct functions. First, as the scale of the enterprise increases, the significance of liability assumes even more dramatic dimensions. Large scale enterprise involves enormous risks dwarfing the financial resources of all but the wealthiest shareholder. Exposure to such level of risk would discourage investment. Second, the enormous amounts of capital required necessitates investment by thousands of investors. This further increases the widespread distribution of shares and the remoteness of the relationship of shareholders to managerial participation. Accordingly, it makes the absence of limited liability an even more significant deterrent to investment. [This argument is criticized as ignoring the very real increase in the proportion of corporate investment of financial institutions through debt as well as equity investment. With such wealth, the larger investing institutions may be able to diversify against risk. The problem remains joint and several liability—the risk decreases under a system of pro-rata liability.]

* * *

[Facilitates the diversification of portfolios]. Limited liability permits investors to invest with more assurance in enterprises in which they have no managerial participation. They can significantly increase the number of their investments and thereby achieve more extensive diversification of their portfolios, which is acknowledged to be a more efficient pattern for investment. It also facilitates optimal investment decisions because the availability of diversification will encourage economically useful risk-taking that would be discouraged under unlimited liability. [This argument has been criticized as having only limited applicability—to the small investor. The wealthy, including large financial institutions would be able to diversify irrespective of the availability of limited liability.]

* * *

[Avoids increased agency costs]. In the absence of limited liability, shareholders exposed to risk beyond their capital investment would reportedly be under great pressure to assert control; over the conduct of the business managers. Economists point out that even with limited liability, investors are under pressure to monitor the activities of the managers whose decisions will determine the profitability of the enterprise and the value of their investment. These economists assert that separation of ownership and control involves significant agency costs in the form of monitoring and bonding of managers and providing incentive compensation structures to assure a greater congruence between the objectives of shareholder-investors and managers. In the absence of limited liability, the situation would be even more serious. Management decisionmaking would not only determine the profitableness of shareholder investment but in addition would expose shareholders to the possibility of substantial liability above and beyond the loss of their investment. [The result according to economists is increased agency costs and inefficiency.].

* * *

[Minimizes impairment of capital markets]. It has been suggested that, in the absence if limited liability, an investment decision would involve a judgment on the financial condition of fellow shareholders as well as a judgment on the financial merits of the enterprise. Under this view, creditors would pursue wealthier shareholders first, and the relative conditions of shareholder wealth would influence the practical imposition of liability on particular shareholders.....Substantially increased information costs would arise from the cost of acquiring information about the wealth of fellow shareholders, in addition to the cost of acquiring information about the enterprise itself, when determining the selection of new investments and the retention of existing ones. Information costs for corporate creditors are less than for corporate investors. Capital raising would accordingly become less efficient, and the efficiency of the capital market would be impaired. Limited liability has, therefore, been termed indispensable for an organized securities market. [This notion is criticized as ignoring the history of the development of strong capital markets even during the period when limited liability was not available.

* * *

[Avoids increased collection costs for creditors]. Limited liability, it is claimed, avoids the need for corporate creditors to bring expensive and cumbersome individual collection suits against numerous scattered shareholders of corporations that have defaulted on their obligations. [This view is criticized for effectively ignoring the existence of the corporation and corporate wealth as the initial and primary source for meeting the corporations' obligations to third parties, and for ignoring advances in civil procedure which makes it relatively easy to consolidate proceedings against multiple parties].

* * *

[Avoids increased contracting costs by shareholders]. By including limited liability in the corporation law, the law in effect creates an efficient contract term applicable to all transactions. It eliminates the necessity for shareholders to incur the expense of contracting around the liability. [This position is criticized as lacking both theoretical and empirical justification.]

* * *

[Encourages risk taking].... [B]y accomplishing a risk-shifting that is not created in the marketplace, limited liability encourages business managers to venture into activities that they would not otherwise undertake. Although not all such ventures will be successful, investors can diversify against the risk and be reasonably sure of an overall positive outcome. Society as a whole then benefits from the increased production.... In this view, limited liability is a compensatory alteration to deal with the failure of the market to achieve adequate risk-shifting on its own. [Insurance might be a preferable alternative, but is not generally available].

The courts have tended to reach to the shareholders of a corporation when one or more of the following factors are deemed present: (i) fraud; (ii) failure to observe corporate formalities; (iii) undercapitalization; (iv) commingling of assets; (v) direct control. Usually the factors are mixed together, and courts have been quite "flexible" in discovering the existence of these factors. Consider whether or to what extent the presence of a single factor will be sufficient to "pierce the corporate veil."

2. *Contractual Actions Against the Corporation*

American courts are said to use a different set of criteria when determining whether to pierce the corporate veil in disputes of a contractual nature than when the underlying liability of the corporation is in tort. As you read the cases that follow, consider whether the courts are indeed applying a different standard.

Morris Gray v. Edgewater Landing, Inc.

Supreme Court of Mississippi
541 So. 2d 1044
April 5, 1989

ROBERTSON, J. The Court:

I.

This appeal arises from a breach of lease dispute between a landlord and his corporate restaurateur tenant. The landlord claims that the restaurateur's neglect resulted in severe damage to the leased premises. He seeks to hold the shareholders individually as well. After the Circuit Court had directed a verdict exonerating the shareholders, the jury found for the landlord and against his corporate ex-tenant. As it seems unlikely he will obtain any degree of satisfaction from the now-dormant corporation, the landlord appeals the discharge of the shareholders. We affirm.

II.

A.

Morris Gray lives in Rankin County, Mississippi, and owns a long-term leasehold interest in land bordering the Ross Barnett Reservoir. On March 8, 1977, Gray leased the premises and its improvements to Edgewater Landing, Inc. for five years, with an option to renew for a like term. Edgewater agreed to renovate the existing building at its expense, and to operate a restaurant therein. The lease contained a common clause that upon termination the lessee would return the premises in good condition, reasonable wear and tear excepted.

Edgewater successfully operated a restaurant and lounge on the premises for one and one-half years. At that point Billy Stegall, Edgewater's original shareholder, sold all of his shares in the corporation to Tom Bradley, who continued to run the restaurant. Sometime thereafter, Bradley transferred one-half of the stock to a third party. These shares eventually were acquired by Sandra Martin, Bradley's bookkeeper. Sandra Martin's husband, Randy, acted as the manager of the restaurant.

The corporate restaurateur exercised its option to continue occupancy for an additional five years, thus scheduling the leasehold to terminate on March 31, 1987. Prior to that time, however, on September 29, 1986, the restaurant's liquor license expired, and the corporation was unable to renew it. This contretemps triggered the termination of the lease.

Gray assumed control of the restaurant on September 30, 1986. He was unhappy with what he found. The roof leaked, causing tiles from the suspended ceiling to become water-soaked. The waterfront patio area was overgrown with weeds. Numerous floor tiles had peeled up. Much of the wooden trim on the outside of the building was rotted. Gray denied access to employees of Edgewater Landing, Inc. when they returned to clean the restaurant and to reclaim their personal effects and equipment.

B.

On October 6, 1986, Edgewater Landing, Inc. commenced this civil action by filing its complaint in the Circuit Court of Madison County, Mississippi, naming Morris Gray as defendant and asserting a claim for conversion. Gray filed a counterclaim charging breach of the lease agreement and joining individually as third party defendants on the lease breach claim Tom Bradley and Sandra L. Martin, shareholders of Edgewater Landing, Inc. Venue was changed to the Circuit Court of Rankin County, Mississippi.

Trial commenced on May 5, 1987, at the close of which the Circuit Court directed a verdict in favor of the individual third party defendants, holding Gray's evidence insufficient as a matter of law to "pierce the corporate veil." On Edgewater's conversion claim, the jury returned a verdict for Gray. On Gray's breach of lease counterclaim, the jury returned a verdict in his favor and against Edgewater and assessed damages in the amount of$ 102,342.00.

From the directed verdict for Bradley and Martin, Gray has perfected this appeal.

III.

Gray's four separate assignments may be reduced to a single complaint: that the Circuit Court erred when it refused to submit to the jury the matter of the personal liability vel non of the shareholders of Edgewater Landing, Inc., Sandra Martin and Tom Bradley....

Where, in the context of an action for breach of a lease or other similar consensual undertaking, a party seeks to pierce the veil of the corporation with whom he has contracted and to hold the shareholders personally liable, our focus is fixed upon the expectations of the parties in concluding the bargain. Since contract liability arises from an essentially consensual relationship, courts generally decline to disregard the corporate entity, choosing instead to enforce the contract as written. 1 Fletcher Cyc. Corp., §41.85 (perm. ed.1983).

As do most courts, this court has reserved piercing the corporate veil for factual circumstances which are clearly extraordinary—where to do otherwise would "subvert the ends of justice." Johnson & Higgins of Mississippi, Inc. v. Commissioner of Insurance, 321 So.2d 281, 284 (Miss.1975). Among this Court's reports may be found a long string of decisions reflecting our law's commitment to the legal integrity of the corporate entity—and the concomitant limited liability of shareholders....

Nothing in Thames & Co. v. Eicher, 373 So.2d 1033 (Miss.1979) is to the contrary. Moreover, this case is wholly distinguishable from Gibson v. Manuel, 534 So.2d 199 (Miss. 1988). In Gibson we held a corporate officer to a fiduciary obligation to the plaintiff who was pledgee of all corporate stock. Here we perceive no basis for charging Bradley and Martin with any fiduciary status vis-a-vis Gray.

A corollary point should be noted. The lease agreement sued upon was executed by the corporation only. Bradley and Martin, in addition to being shareholders, were agents of the corporation as well. Gray complains that Bradley and Martin were the individuals whose actions for the corporation offended the corporation's obligations under the lease agreement. As agents for a disclosed principal, however, they incur no individual liability, absent fraud or other equivalent conduct. Gardner v. Jones, 464 So.2d 1144, 1151 (Miss.1985); Thames & Co. v. Eicher, 373 So.2d 1033, 1035 (Miss.1979).

The prior holdings of this Court are consonant with the great weight of authority elsewhere to the effect that, in contract actions, the corporate fiction will not be disregarded in cases of simple negligence. See Kaites v. Dept. of Environmental Resources, 108 Pa. Commw. 267, 529 A.2d 1148, 1151 (Pa.Comwlth.1987) ("He may be held liable for misfeasance but not for simple nonfeasance." A corollary of this general statement is that the breach of a contract, without more (i.e., a showing of fraud) does not justify the disregard of the corporate entity. Grayson v. Nordic Construction Co., Inc., 22 Wash. App. 143, 589 P.2d 283, 286 (1978). As one authority has stated:

> The attempt to hold another party liable where the claim asserted is of contractual origin presents difficulties. The question which must be met and answered is why one who contracted with a selected party and received the promise he bargained for should be allowed to look to another merely because he is disappointed in the selected party's performance. The answer under contract law is that he may not hold the other liable without additional compelling facts. Fletcher Cyc. Corp., §41.85 (perm.ed.1983) (footnotes omitted); see also Condenser Service & Engineering Co. v. Brunswick Port Authority, 87 Ga.App. 469, 74 S.E.2d 398, 402 (1953) (finding no liability to a parent corporation for the negligent performance by its subsidiary under a leasing agreement).

Just as the corporation's negligent performance of contractual duties does not justify the disregard of the corporate entity, neither does the fact that the principal shareholder oversees the day-to-day operation. Because the cardinal rule of corporate law is that a corporation possesses a legal existence separate and apart from that of its officers and shareholders... the mere operation of corporate business does not render one personally liable for corporate acts.... Sole ownership of a corporation by one person or another corporation is not a factor, and neither is the fact that the sole owners uses and controls it to promote his ends. Amason v. Whitehead, 186 Ga.App. 320, 367 S.E.2d 107, 108 (1988) (citations omitted) (emphasis added).

To cause a court to disregard the corporate entity and justify shareholder liability, the complaining party must demonstrate: (a) some frustration of contractual expectations regarding the party to whom he looked for performance; (b) the flagrant disregard of corporate formalities by the defendant corporation and its principals; (c) a demonstration of fraud or other equivalent misfeasance on the part of the corporate shareholder. T.C.L., Inc. v. Lacoste, 431 So.2d 918, 922 (Miss.1983); Thames & Co. v. Eicher, 373 So.2d 1033, 1035 (Miss.1979). To present a jury issue on a demand that the corporate veil be pierced, a party must present some credible evidence on each of these points.

Applying these standards to today's case, we find that Gray has failed to offer proof sufficient to create a jury issue on any of these three requisites. First, Gray admits that, despite the change in ownership, he had no doubt that he was contracting with a corporate party, not Billy Stegall or Tom Bradley personally. As a businessman himself, Gray appreciated this distinction. Second, Gray offered no proof that corporate formalities were not followed by Edgewater Landing, Inc. Indeed, the evidence suggests the contrary, that formalities were at all times adhered to. Third, Gray has put forth no proof that the corporate agent/shareholders perpetrated upon him any fraud. To the contrary, the proof adduced at trial indicates that the lessee and its agents were guilty of no more than simple negligence in the maintenance of the leased premises.

Co-Ex Plastics, Inc. v. AlaPak, Inc. and Greg Gantt

Supreme Court of Alabama
536 So. 2d 37
September 23, 1988

ADAMS, J., for the Court:

Plaintiff, co-Ex Plastics, Inc. ("Co-Ex"), appeals from a judgment in favor of Greg Gantt in which the judge disallowed Co-Ex's request to pierce the corporate veil and allow recovery individually from Gantt. A judgment in favor of Co-Ex against defendant AlaPak, Inc. was granted. We affirm.

The facts of this case are largely undisputed and can be summarized as follows:

Gantt began a packaging and supply business in 1980, using the name Alabama Packaging and Supply, and he operated that business as a sole proprietorship until 1984, when he incorporated this business as AlaPak, Inc. Upon incorporation, Gantt transferred all assets and liabilities of "Alabama Packaging and Supply," sole proprietorship, to AlaPak, the corporation. As a result of this transfer, AlaPak assumed total assets of $591,894.55 and total liabilities of $580,054.48. The capital stock of the corporation was $1,000.00 and there existed $10,839.87 in paid-in capital. Soon after incorporation, Ala-

Pak entered a financing arrangement with national Acceptance Corporation ("NAC") and entered loan transactions with First Montgomery Bank.

AlaPak and Co-Ex, a Tennessee corporation, commenced a supplier-purchaser relationship (open account) in July 1985, which continued to January 1986, during which time Co-Ex sold over $127,000.00 worth of goods to AlaPak. By January 1986, the account was overdue by approximately $35,000.00.

Co-Ex sued AlaPak and Gantt to collect the $35,000.00 owed. After a non-jury trial, the court awarded Co-Ex $35,000.00 against AlaPak and entered judgment in favor of Gantt, refusing to pierce the corporate veil. Co-Ex filed a motion to alter, amend or vacate the judgment and for a new trial; the trial court amended its judgment to award Co-Ex a total of $41,825.00, which included interest, but again denied Co-Ex relief against Gantt.

Evidence was presented at trial indicating that Gantt, the sole stockholder and director and the principal officer of AlaPak:

1) could not produce a stock certificate;
2) had retained the "Alabama Packaging and Supply Company" bank account as AlaPak's bank account; and
3) had continued to use the "Alabama Packaging and Supply Company" checks because, he stated, he lost the AlaPak checks.

It was further shown that Gantt had not signed checks in a representative capacity and that Gantt also varied the manner in which he referred to the corporation, i.e., "AlaPak," "Alabama Packaging and Supply Co.," and "Alabama Packing and Supply, Inc."

AlaPak closed its doors in August 1986, after NAC withdrew its line of credit. A bankruptcy petition was prepared thereafter, but was not filed, which disclosed a total of $391,500.30 owed to unsecured creditors and $110,000.00 in accounts receivable subject to a security interest in favor of NAC and inventory of $72,000.00 existing.

Three issues are presented on appeal:

1) Did Gantt operate AlaPak in such a manner that the corporate veil should be pierced and he be held individually liable for the debts of the corporation?
2) Did the trial court erroneously apply the law, so that the ore tenus rule does not apply to this appeal?
3) Did the trial court err in allowing Gantt to prove AlaPak's corporate existence through use of parol evidence?

The concept that a corporation is a legal entity existing separate and apart from those who compose it is a well-settled rule in the State of Alabama. Cohen v. Williams, 294 Ala. 417, 420, 318 So. 2d 279, 280 (1975) (quoting 18 Am.Jur. 2d Corporations § 14 at 559 (1965)). It is also a well-settled rule in this State that the corporate form can be set aside, and the individual or individuals owning all of its stock and assets can be treated as the business entity, even in the absence of fraud, as a means of preventing injustice or inequitable consequences. Cohen, 299 Ala. at 421, 318 So. 2d at 281. This Court has also held:

A separate corporate existence will not be recognized when a corporation is so organized and controlled and its business so conducted as to make it a mere instrumentality of another or the alter ego of the person owning and controlling it. Woods v. Commercial Contractors, Inc., 384 So. 2d 1076, 1979 (Ala. 1980).

Co-Ex first contends that AlaPak was merely an instrumentality of Gantt, and that this was shown by Gantt's failure to follow corporate formalities in the course of its business, i.e., the failure of Gantt to produce a stock certificate; the retention of the Alabama Packaging and Supply Company bank account, and the continued use of the Alabama Packaging and Supply Company checks, which were never shown to have been signed in a representative capacity. Gantt, on the other hand, argues that Co-Ex knew or should have known that AlaPak was a corporation and acknowledged, AlaPak, as such, and therefore, that no fraud can be inferred from AlaPak's neglect of corporate formalities. We find AlaPak's argument persuasive on this issue. We have held that in the absence of fraud or inequity, the sole shareholder in a corporation will be protected from individual liability by the corporation entity, Washburn v. Rabun, 487 So. 2d 1361 (Ala. 1986). In this case, the mere fact that minor formalities, such as those cited by Co-Ex in the business operations of AlaPak, were not followed does not rise to such a level that the corporate veil should be pierced. There is no indication in the record that AlaPak attempted to fraudulently induce Co-Ex into any contractual arrangements, nor is there any indication that the ends of justice would be deserved if the corporate veil were not pierced.

Co-Ex also argues that AlaPak was under-capitalized and, therefore, that the corporate veil should be pierced. Co-Ex suggests that the $1,000.00 of capital stock and the $300,000.00 business credit line were inadequate to cover the potential debts of the corporation. Gantt counters by arguing that AlaPak conformed to the general operating standards of one-man corporations and argues that Co-Ex did not rely on any representation regarding AlaPak's financial condition when it contracted with it, and that Co-Ex initiated an inadequate inquiry into the financial status of AlaPak. Gantt further argues that at the time of incorporation, AlaPak's assets exceeded its liabilities. We find Gantt's argument persuasive. We recently held in East End Memorial Ass'n v. Egerman 514 So. 2d 38 (Ala. 1987), that "a party who has contracted with a financially weak corporation and is disappointed in obtaining satisfaction of his claim cannot look to the dominant stockholder or parent corporation in the absence of additional compelling facts." 514 So. 2d at 44, quoting Tigrett v. Pointer, 580 S.W.2d 375, 382 (Tex. Civ. App. 1978). No evidence was presented showing that Co-Ex inquired about the status of AlaPak, other than through a bank credit check, nor was there any evidence that Co-Ex requested a personal guarantee from Gantt.

Voluntary creditors of corporations are held to a higher standard because they "are generally able to inspect the financial structure of a corporation and discover potential risks of loss before any transaction takes place. Consequently, courts are less sympathetic with voluntary creditors who, having had the opportunity of inspection, nevertheless elected to transact with an undercapitalized corporation." Disregarding the Entities of Closely Held and Parent-Subsidiary Corporate Structures, 12 Cum.L.Rev. 155, 165 (1981). We, therefore, must affirm the trial court's refusal to pierce the corporate veil for the reasons advanced by Co-Ex.

The rule in Alabama as to ore tenus evidence, is, as stated in Barrett v. Odom, May & DeBuys, 453 So. 2d 729 (Ala. 1984), that "every presumption will be indulged in favor of the trial court, and its findings will not be disturbed on appeal unless palpably wrong or clearly erroneous." Co-Ex contends that the trial court erred in its reliance on Paddock, smith & Aydlotte v. WAAY Television, 410 So. 2d 106 (Ala. Civ. App. 1982), to decide the issues in this case because, it says, many evidentiary features distinguish the two cases. We must disagree. We find the following similarities in Paddock sufficient to uphold the trial court's reliance on that case:

1) Paddock, Smith & Aydlotte ("Paddock") was a duly formed corporation.

2) No evidence of Paddock's corporate status was intentionally concealed.

3) WAAY failed to make adequate inquiries into the financial status of Paddock.

Similar factors were present in the instant case. Therefore, we will not disturb the trial court's use of that precedent as a yardstick in evaluating the evidence in this case.

The final issue Co-Ex presents for our review is whether the trial court erred in allowing Gantt to present parol evidence to prove AlaPak's corporate existence.

[omitted]

For the foregoing reasons, the judgment of the trial court is affirmed.

3. *Tort Actions Against the Corporation*

A criticism of the doctrine of blanket limited liability involves the application of the doctrine against tort victims. While employees and creditors might be said to have accepted the risks inherent in limited liability, tort victims do not. One does not generally bargain to be the tort victim of the most solvent corporation. As such, is it fair for the shareholders of corporations that are tortfeasors to be permitted to shield their assets behind the doctrine of limited liability? Worse yet, should a corporation be able to shield its assets in this way by moving its assets as between any number of subsidiaries?

Given these criticisms, and the relative youth newness of the concept of limited liability, why ought it to remain a fixture of corporate law? The most lucid explanation of the economic purposes of the notion of corporate (shareholder) limited liability was expressed by Easterbrook and Fischel. How convincing is their explanation? Is the purpose of limited liability worth the cost? Can you justify your answer solely in economic terms? Alternatively, can you justify your answer in terms other than "pure" economics?

Courts in the United States have tended to take a more sympathetic view with respect to the imposition of liability on shareholders of corporations where the party seeking to impose the liability is a tort victim.

William Minton al., Plaintiffs and Respondents, v. Mauden N. Caveney, as Executrix, etc., Defendant and Appellant

Supreme Court of California
56 Cal. 2d 576; 364 P.2d 473; 15 Cal. Rptr. 641
September 5, 1961

Justice Traynor:

The Seminole Hot Springs Corporation, hereinafter referred to as Seminole, was duly incorporated in California on March 8, 1954. It conducted a public swimming pool that it leased from its owner. On June 24, 1954, plaintiffs' daughter drowned in the pool, and plaintiffs recovered a judgment for $10,000 against Seminole for her wrongful death. The judgment remains unsatisfied.

On January 30, 1957, plaintiffs brought the present action to hold defendant Cavaney personally liable for the judgment against Seminole. Cavaney died on May 28, 1958, and his widow, the executrix of his estate, was substituted as defendant. The trial court entered judgment for plaintiffs for $10,000. Defendant appeals.

Plaintiffs introduced evidence that Cavaney was a director and secretary and treasurer of Seminole and that on November 15, 1954, about five months after the drowning, Cavaney as secretary of Seminole and Edwin A. Kraft as president of Seminole applied for permission to issue three shares of Seminole stock, one share to be issued to Kraft, another to F. J. Wettrick and the third to Cavaney. The Commissioner of Corporations refused permission to issue these shares unless additional information was furnished. The application was then abandoned and no shares were ever issued. There was also evidence that for a time Seminole used Cavaney's office to keep records and to receive mail. Before his death Cavaney answered certain interrogatories. He was asked if Seminole "ever had any assets?" He stated that "insofar as my own personal knowledge and belief is concerned said corporation did not have any assets." Cavaney also stated in the return to an attempted execution that "[insofar] as I know, this corporation had no assets of any kind or character. The corporation was duly organized but never functioned as a corporation."

Defendant introduced evidence that Cavaney was an attorney at law, that he was approached by Kraft and Wettrick to form Seminole, and that he was the attorney for Seminole. Plaintiffs introduced Cavaney's answer to several interrogatories that he held the post of secretary and treasurer and director in a temporary capacity and as an accommodation to his client. Defendant contends that the evidence does not support the court's determination[1] that Cavaney is personally liable for Seminole's debts and that the "alter ego" doctrine is inapplicable because plaintiffs failed to show that there was "'(1)...such unity of interest and ownership that the separate personalities of the corporation and the individual no longer exist and (2) that, if the acts are treated as those of the corporation alone, an inequitable result will follow.'" (Riddle v. Leuschner, 51 Cal.2d 574, 580 [335 P.2d 107]; Automotriz etc. De California v. Resnick, 47 Cal.2d 792, 796 [306 P.2d 1, 63 A.L.R.2d 1042]; Minifie v. Rowley, 187 Cal. 481, 487 [202 P. 673].)

The figurative terminology "alter ego" and "disregard of the corporate entity" is generally used to refer to the various situations that are an abuse of the corporate privilege.... The equitable owners of a corporation, for example, are personally liable when they treat the assets of the corporation as their own and add or withdraw capital from the corporation at will...when they hold themselves out as being personally liable for the debts of the corporation...or when they provide inadequate capitalization and actively participate in the conduct of corporate affairs....

In the instant case the evidence is undisputed that there was no attempt to provide adequate capitalization. Seminole never had any substantial assets. It leased the pool that it operated, and the lease was forfeited for failure to pay the rent. Its capital was "'trifling compared with the business to be done and the risks of loss....'" (Automotriz etc. De California v. Resnick, supra, 47 Cal.2d 792, 797.) The evidence is also undisputed that Cavaney was not only the secretary and treasurer of the corporation but was also a director. The evidence that Cavaney was to receive one-third of the shares to be issued supports an inference that he was an equitable owner (see Riddle v. Leuschner, supra, 51 Cal.2d 574, 580), and the evidence that for a time the records of the corporation were kept in Cavaney's office supports an inference that he actively participated in the conduct of the business. The trial court was not required to believe his statement

1. Defendant did not request that the findings of the trial court be included in the record on appeal. It must be presumed therefore that the findings support the judgment. (*See* 3 Witkin, California Procedure, pp. 2238–2239.)

that he was only a "temporary" director and officer "for accommodation." In any event it merely raised a conflict in the evidence that was resolved adversely to defendant. Moreover, section 800 of the Corporations Code provides that "... the business and affairs of every corporation shall be controlled by, a board of not less than three directors." Defendant does not claim that Cavaney was a director with specialized duties (see 5 U.Chi.L.Rev. 668). It is immaterial whether or not he accepted the office of director as an "accommodation" with the understanding that he would not exercise any of the duties of a director. A person may not in this manner divorce the responsibilities of a director from the statutory duties and powers of that office.

There is no merit in defendant's contentions that the "alter ego" doctrine applies only to contractual debts and not to tort claims... that plaintiffs' cause of action abated when Cavaney died... or that the judgment in the action against the corporation bars plaintiffs from bringing the present action.... Defendant Cavaney waived the defense of the statute of limitations by failing to plead that defense in the answer to the complaint or by specifying the statute of limitations as a ground of its general demurrer....

In this action to hold defendant personally liable upon the judgment against Seminole plaintiffs did not allege or present any evidence on the issue of Seminole's negligence or on the amount of damages sustained by plaintiffs. They relied solely on the judgment against Seminole. Defendant correctly contends that Cavaney or his estate cannot be held liable for the debts of Seminole without an opportunity to relitigate these issues. (Motores De Mexicali v. Superior Court, 51 Cal.2d 172, 176 [331 P.2d 1]; see also Dillard v. McKnight, supra, 34 Cal.2d 209, 214.) Cavaney was not a party to the action against the corporation, and the judgment in that action is therefore not binding upon him unless he controlled the litigation leading to the judgment. (Motores De Mexicali v. Superior Court, supra, 51 Cal.2d 172, 175; Thomson v. L. C. Roney & Co., supra, 112 Cal.App.2d 420, 427; Mirabito v. San Francisco Dairy Co., 8 Cal.App.2d 54, 58–59 [47 P.2d 530]; see Rest., Judgments, § 84.) Although Cavaney filed an answer to the complaint against Seminole as its attorney, he withdrew before the trial and did not thereafter participate therein. The filing of an answer without any other participation is not sufficient to bind Cavaney. "In order that the rule stated in this section [that a person in control of the litigation is bound by the judgment] should apply it is necessary that the one in whose favor or against whom the rules of res judicata operate participate in the control of the action and if judgment is adverse, be able to determine whether or not an appeal should be taken. It is not sufficient that he supplies the funds for the prosecution or defense, that he appears as a witness or cooperates without having control." (Rest., Judgments, § 84, comment e; see Motores De Mexicali v. Superior Court, supra, 51 Cal.2d 172, 176.)

The judgment is reversed.

SCHAUER, J., Concurring and Dissenting.

[omitted]

Do you agree that public policy considerations favor the applications of principles of tort law in the construction of rules for the imposition of liability between related companies? The excerpt that follows suggests some of the policy concerns. Do these policy objectives suggest that a much more broad approach to the imposition of liability should be an affirmative goal of state policy?

Phillip I. Blumberg, *The Law of Corporate Groups: Tort, Contract, and Other Common Law Problems in the Substantive Law of Parent and Subsidiary Corporations*

(1987)

(excerpts pages 162–163; footnotes omitted or renumbered)

* * *

The problem of imposition of... tort liability can best be understood by recognizing that cases arise against a background of underlying conflict between principles tort law and traditional corporation law..... The issue transcends consideration of corporate law and requires courts to choose between tort law and traditional corporation law for a legal rule that will determine in many cases whether an injured plaintiff has an effective remedy.

Tort law principles that have become increasingly accepted strongly support the recognition of enterprise liability in place of traditional entity law. These principles rest not on one, but on several, major objectives:

(1) Tort law seeks to allocate to (that is impose on) the economic activity (that is, the enterprise) all the costs properly allowable to the product and to distribute all such costs to the consumers of the product.

(2) Tort law seeks to provide an effective remedy that will make whole the injured tort victim.

(3) Tort law seeks to allocate liability to a party involved in the economic process that has resources available ("the deep pocket") for satisfaction of such costs.

(4) Tort law recognizes that in "an increasingly complex system of manufacture and distribution, pinpointing fault has become increasingly difficult."[1] In the larger context, a plaintiff may not be able to identify the particular manufacturer responsible for the injury from a defective product, and liability accordingly may be imposed on all manufactures of the product. The same rationale in appropriate cases may point to the imposition of liability on the group, rather than resorting to elaborate discovery and litigation to fasten liability in a particular component.

(5) Tort law, fashioned as it is by the availability of insurance works toward the end of imposing liability where it can be absorbed by insurance and the ultimate costs borne by all insurance purchasers of the class involved.

But even sympathy for the victims of corporate torts have its limits in law, at least currently. Consider in this context the following cases:

---

1. *See* Subak, *Corporate Governance and Tort Law Reform—A Review of Two Contemporary Plays*, 40 Bus. L. xviii (1985).

Greer v. St. Joseph's Indian School

Supreme Court of South Dakota
438 N.W.2d 204
March 22, 1989

TIMM, Circuit Judge:

This is an action by the limited partners (Glanzers) against their general partner (Dehon) and the general partner's parent corporation (St. Joseph's[1]).

BACKGROUND AND PROCEDURAL HISTORY

On June 20, 1984, the Glanzers and Dehon formed a limited partnership, Glanzer Tackle Company, to manufacture and distribute fishing tackle and related products. In the four years preceding the partnership, the Glanzers operated a tackle-making business out of their home near Chamberlain. The assets of that business, including inventory, equipment, customer sales list, good will, and the Glanzer name, were contributed by the Glanzers to the partnership.

The partnership agreement required Dehon to contribute $30,000 in cash, provide accounting services for one year, provide space for one year, and pay utilities and property taxes for one year. Dehon also agreed to pay Glanzers $20,000 for contributing the assets of their tackle business to the partnership, $10,000 of which was due on or before July 1, 1984, and the remaining $10,000 was to be paid to the partnership and passed through to the Glanzers on or before April 1, 1985. Additionally, the partnership was to employ Alan Glanzer for three years with minimum compensation for each of the years being $20,000, $22,000 and $24,000.

The Glanzers did not receive the $10,000 due them on or before April 1, 1985. Three months later Alan Glanzer's employment was terminated by the partnership, and Glanzer Tackle Company sought bankruptcy protection.

On August 6, 1985, Glanzers commenced an action against Dehon and St. Joseph's alleging breach of the partnership agreement, negligent and intentional infliction of emotional distress, fraudulent and negligent misrepresentation, guarantee, and breach of fiduciary duty. St. Joseph's liability was predicated on theories of disregard of corporate entity and agency.

On August 25, 1985, St. Joseph's entered a special appearance and motion to dismiss. A hearing on the motion took place November 7, 1985. On January 6, 1986, the trial court dismissed the action against St. Joseph's. The action against Dehon was tried to a jury in December of 1987. The jury returned a verdict for Glanzers in the amount of $120,001.00. Both parties appeal. We affirm, in part, reverse, in part, and remand for a new trial.

ISSUE I: WHETHER THE TRIAL COURT ERRED IN GRANTING ST. JOSEPH'S MOTION FOR SUMMARY JUDGMENT.

---

1. St. Joseph's Indian School is the name under which the Congregation of the Priests of the Sacred Heart, Inc., a South Dakota corporation, is registered to do business in Brule County, the venue of this action. Dehon Industries, Inc., a South Dakota corporation, is a subsidiary of the Priests of the Sacred Heart, Inc.

The South Dakota Rules of Civil Procedure in circuit courts state that if, on a motion to dismiss for failure to state a claim upon which relief can be granted, matters outside the pleadings are presented to and not excluded by the trial court, the motion should be treated as one for summary judgment and disposed of as provided in SDCL 15-6-56.[2]

The record before us plainly indicates that matters outside the pleadings[3] were presented to the trial court. That they were considered is specifically mentioned in the trial court's order disposing of the motion. Accordingly, on review we treat St. Joseph's motion to dismiss as one for summary judgment and the disposition a grant of that motion.

* * *

Glanzers predicated St. Joseph's liability for the acts of Dehon upon the instrumentality exception to the rule of corporate separateness and agency. St. Joseph's bore the burden of showing there was no genuine issue of material fact under either theory. In determining whether that burden was met, we first examine those theories.

A parent corporation is liable for the acts of its subsidiary under the instrumentality exception when (1) the parent controls the subsidiary to such a degree as to render the latter the mere instrumentality of the former; and (2) adherence to the rule of corporate separateness would produce injustices and inequities. Larson v. Western Underwriters, 77 S.D. 157, 87 N.W.2d 883, 887, (1958); Mobridge Community Industries, Inc. v. Toure, Ltd., 273 N.W.2d 128, 132 (S.D. 1978). Similarly, a parent corporation is liable for the acts of its subsidiary when an agency relationship exists between them....

Under the first leg of the instrumentality exception, a number of factors have been identified which indicate the degree of control necessary to hold the parent liable:

(a) The parent corporation owns all or most of the capital stock of the subsidiary.

(b) The parent and subsidiary corporations have common directors or officers.

(c) The parent corporation finances the subsidiary.

(d) The parent corporation subscribes to all the capital stock of the subsidiary or otherwise causes its incorporation.

(e) The subsidiary has grossly inadequate capital.

(f) The parent corporation pays the salaries and other expenses or losses of the subsidiary.

(g) The subsidiary has substantially no business except with the parent corporation or no assets except those conveyed to it by the parent corporation.

(h) In the papers of the parent corporation or in the statements of its officers, the subsidiary is described as a department or division of the parent corporation, or its business or financial responsibility is referred to as the parent corporation's own.

(i) The parent corporation uses the property of the subsidiary as its own.

(j) The directors or executives of the subsidiary do not act independently in the interest of the subsidiary but take their orders from the parent corporation in the latter's interest.

---

2. SDCL 15-6-12(b).

3. The only pleading on file at the time of the trial court's disposition of St. Joseph's motion to dismiss was the complaint; neither Dehon nor St. Joseph's had filed an answer.

(k) The formal legal requirements of the subsidiary are not observed.

....

All of these factors need not be present for the trier of fact to conclude that the subsidiary is a mere instrumentality of its parent. Jackson, supra, at 1173. Nor is the list exhaustive. Duff, supra, at 763. Each case is sui generis and must be decided in accordance with its own underlying facts. Mobridge Community Industries, Inc., supra, at 132.

Upon finding instrumentality the trier of fact must then consider whether retention of corporate separateness would produce injustices and inequitable consequences. The second leg of the instrumentality exception is established where the wrong alleged is a result of fraudulent, unjust or illegal acts. Curtis v. Vlotho, 313 N.W.2d 469 (S.D. 1983); Curtis v. Feurhelm, 335 N.W.2d 575 (S.D. 1983); Farmers Feed & Seed, supra; Mobridge Community Industries, supra.

Liability on the agency theory is established if the following factual elements are present: (1) manifestation by the principal that the agent shall act for him; (2) the agent's acceptance of the undertaking; and (3) the understanding of the parties that the principal is to be in control of the undertaking. Southard v. Hansen, 376 N.W.2d 56, 58 (S.D. 1985); Kasselder v. Kapperman, 316 N.W.2d 628 (S.D. 1982); Watkins Company v. Dutt, 84 S.D. 453, 173 N.W.2d 41 (1969).

With these theories in mind, we turn to the facts presented by St. Joseph's to the trial court. At the hearing on the motion for summary judgment, St. Joseph's rested on the affidavit of Father Cassidy. The affidavit established that (1) St. Joseph's was operated by the Congregation of the Priests of the Sacred Heart, Inc.; (2) the Congregation of the Priests of the Sacred Heart, Inc., owned stock in Dehon; (3) Father Cassidy was superintendent of St. Joseph's, president of the board of directors of the Congregation of Priests of the Sacred Heart, Inc., and president of the board of directors of Dehon; (4) employees of St. Joseph's either had served or were currently serving as directors and officers of Dehon and the congregation of the Priests of the Sacred Heart, Inc. Additionally, the affiant drew the conclusion that St. Joseph's was not "a party to any agreement, contract or had any other relationship with the plaintiffs..." pertaining to the matters in issue in the lawsuit.

Although these meager facts coupled with a legal conclusion fall far short of the evidentiary mark established for a moving party by SDCL 15-6-56(e), the trial court refused to deny St. Joseph's motion and directed Glanzers to proceed with their resistance to the motion. Additional facts came to light: (1) Father Westhoven was the Director of Development of St. Joseph's and the Treasurer of the Board of Directors of Dehon; Cy Maus was the Senior Executive Officer for Development at St. Joseph's, the Executive Director of the St. Joseph's Lakota Development Council and the Secretary of the Board of Directors of Dehon; (2) the manager of Glanzer Tackle Company was an employee of St. Joseph's, receiving compensation solely from St. Joseph's; (3) Glanzer Tackle Company was located in the same building as the St. Joseph's Lakota Development Council; (4) St. Joseph's was a nonprofit corporation involved in helping Indian people and created the St. Joseph's Lakota Development Council to assist Indian business on the reservation; (5) Dehon was incorporated to develop Indian-oriented business ventures; (6) Cy Maus testified that the sole intent in creating Glanzer Tackle Company was to provide income, employment and business outlets for Indian people; (7) the Glanzers were insured through St. Joseph's medical insurer; (8) Alan Glanzer's W-2 for 1984 listed St. Joseph's as his employer; (9) Alan Glanzer was paid for work done for Glanzer Tackle

Company by checks drawn on St. Joseph's account; (10) Dehon paid St. Joseph's for some services provided Glanzer Tackle Company with stock or notes, while other services were provided in the form of "grants;" (11) St. Joseph's, in exchange for stock, capitalized Dehon; (12) Dehon used St. Joseph's stationery in transacting business; (13) the Lakota Development Council used Glanzer Tackle Company's secretary; (14) Alan Glanzer had been hired by the partnership with Dehon guaranteeing employment and salary for a minimum of three years; (15) Alan Glanzer's employment was terminated prior to the expiration of the term of employment; (16) Alan Glanzer did not receive $10,000 pursuant to the terms of the partnership agreement; (17) Dehon mismanaged Glanzer Tackle Company by (a) wasting partnership funds, (b) antagonizing partnership customers, (c) ignoring established markets, (d) improvidently discounting products, (e) failing to hire adequate sales personnel, (f) incurring excessive debt, and (g) failing to pay creditors; and (18) the partnership agreement provided that Dehon, St. Joseph's "or their subsidiaries or associated entities" would provide "space or equipment rental, accounting services, mailing services, computer time, and other... services" to Glanzer Tackle Company with approval of the partners at the lesser of market cost or the cost the provider charged others for the same service.[4]

Based on these facts there need not be a lengthy discussion of whether a question of material fact exists under the first leg of the instrumentality exception. The foregoing evidence addresses virtually every indicia of control previously listed.

Under the second leg of the instrumentality exception, questions of material fact are also revealed. While it is true that some courts are more hesitant to pierce the corporate veil in contract cases than tort cases, see e.g. Miller v. Dixon Industries Corp., 513 A.2d 597 (RI 1986), this case is not a mere contract action. Fraud, negligence and breach of fiduciary duty have also been pled. The evidence before the trial court on St. Joseph's control of Dehon, Dehon's mismanagement of Glanzer Tackle Company, failure to meet financial obligations to Glanzers, and self-dealing raises questions of injustice and inequity were St. Joseph's not held liable for the acts of Dehon. Accordingly, we find St. Joseph's reliance on Almac, Inc. v. JRH Development, Inc., 391 N.W.2d 919 (Minn.App. 1986) to be ineffectual. The fact that Glanzers chose to contract with Dehon rather than St. Joseph's is insufficient to support the court's award of summary judgment.

Glanzers' agency theory should also have survived the motion for summary judgment. Evidence of the formation of Dehon to accomplish St. Joseph's mission, Dehon's acceptance of that role and control of Dehon by St. Joseph's should have preserved this issue for jury resolution.

When measured against the previously defined theories of corporate liability, the evidence demonstrates issues of material fact as to Dehon's status as an instrumentality or agent of St. Joseph's. We are compelled to conclude that St. Joseph's failed to shoulder its burden of presenting a prima facie case for summary judgment. Thus, the trial court erred in granting the motion. Wm. Collins, Inc. v. S. D. State Bd. of Transp., 264 N.W.2d 491 (S.D. 1978). On remand, the question of St. Joseph's liability for the acts of Dehon must be placed before the jury.

* * *

---

4. The partnership agreement was not introduced into evidence at the motion hearing. However, the record indicates that the agreement was to be provided to the court subsequent to the hearing. The court's memorandum opinion alludes to the agreement and apparently was considered in granting the motion for summary judgment.

[The court then considered several issues relating to jury instructions, the isuues and the determination of damages]

We have reviewed the remaining issues and find that they are either addressed herein or are without merit.

Affirmed in part, reversed, in part and remanded for a new trial.

The courts do not always treat tort cases more sympathetically when a tort victim seeks to pierce the corporate veil than in a contract action in which a party seeks to pierce the corporate veil. Indeed, sometimes it is difficult to distinguish contract and tort actions at all. Is the case which follows distinguishable from those which preceded?

Jonas Jackson, Appellant, v. General Electric Company, Appellee

Supreme Court of Alaska
514 P.2d 1170
October 12, 1973

FITZGERALD, J.:

This appeal brings a single issue before us for determination. Under the facts here, is the parent corporation, General Electric Company,[1] to be held liable for the wrong of its wholly-owned subsidiary, General Electric Credit Corporation?[2] The essential facts giving rise to this case are not in dispute.

Appellant Jonas Jackson, a member of the armed forces, bought a General Electric appliance in 1962 from a retail store in Texas. The retailer made a credit arrangement with appellant to finance the purchase with appellant to finance the purchase through General Electric Credit Corporation. Two years after the sale of the appliance GECC sent a defamatory collection letter to appellant's military superiors. Although GECC made the defamation, appellant brought his action against the appellee GE. According to the record GE was licensed to do business in the State of Alaska when the action was filed but GECC did not obtain a license to do business in Alaska until after that date.[3] The appellant before the case came to trial moved to add GECC as a party defendant. This motion was successfully resisted by appellee.[4]

During trial, the judge held a hearing, out of the presence of the jury, on the question of appellee's responsibility for GECC's defamatory conduct. The judge reserved that issue to himself and submitted the case to the jury only on those issues relating to defamation and damages. A verdict of $5,000.00 in appellant's favor was returned by the jury. The judge then ruled on the reserved issue and dismissed appellant's claim against GE.

---

1. Hereinafter referred to as GE.
2. Hereinafter referred to as GECC.
3. It is possible that Jackson thought that the Alaska courts did not have jurisdiction over GECC since GECC was not then licensed by the State of Alaska to do business within the state.
4. Appellant did not petition for review under Rules 23 and 24 of the appellate rules from the ruling by the trial court which denied his application to make GECC a defendant nor has he made this ruling one of his specifications of error in this appeal.

The trial judge stated in a memorandum opinion the reasons for dismissal. The findings of the trial court are summarized as follows:[5]

GECC carries on two principal lines of business consisting of consumer financing and commercial and industrial financing. For the nine months ending September 26, 1970, 51% of GECC's receivables represented consumer financing (30% in home products of the character involved in the instant case).

GECC provides inventory financing for over 6,500 dealers of home products, most of whom sell a variety of home products purchased from various manufacturers. The great majority of such financing is for home products manufactured by GE.

In addition to its consumer credit involvement GECC maintains a very substantial operation in commercial and industrial financing, financing sales of heavy equipment, aircraft and other equipment, and leasing of aircraft and railroad rolling stock and industrial equipment. Receivables in this connection exceeded three-quarters of a million dollars on September 26, 1970. There is no evidence showing that any substantial amount of these receivables involve GE products.

As of September 26, 1970, approximately 7% of GECC's consumer time sales and other retail receivables outstanding were attributable to GE products and approximately 56% of its dealer inventory financing was related to GE products. In addition, management estimates that approximately 2% of its commercial and industrial receivables as of September 26, 1970 were attributable to the financing of GE equipment exclusive of GE components incorporated in equipment of other manufacturers.

There is recited [in the prospectus] an agreement, entered into in 1960 between GE and GECC concerning the repurchase of GE appliances and television sets repossessed by GECC from defaulting dealers, with $80,000,000 in receivables covered by the agreement, in addition to additional recourse rights against GE on certain other GE products of $23,000,000.

Consolidated income tax returns are filed by the two companies.

GE furnishes advisory services to GECC "including consulting services of specialists in treasury, accounting, tax, legal, marketing, employee and community relations, and auditing functions." GECC pays GE for these services, with slightly over $1,000,000 authorized in 1970. The directors and officers of GECC in 1970 were all officers or employees of GE except the president, Mr. Klock. Mr. Klock, however, is shown to have received incentive compensation of 474 shares of GE in addition to his salary. The prospectus reveals the option rights of key employees to purchase GE stock.

The earnings of the subsidiary are reflected in financial reports of the parent in determining the parent's income.[6]

GECC is not underfinanced, its creditors are not disadvantaged, and the corporation is unquestionably solvent.

On these findings the trial court concluded that GE should not be held responsible for GECC's defamatory letter.

---

5. Many of the findings of the trial court were derived from a GECC prospectus dated December 10, 1970, filed with the Securities Exchanges Commission. The prospectus which was offered by appellant was received into evidence as an exhibit. The trial court found the contents of the prospectus highly reliable.

6. Testimony of Mr. Richard Sassara, vice president and branch manager for Foster and Marshall Investment Bankers and Brokers.

There are a number of well-recognized exceptions to the rule that ordinarily the parent corporation will not be held liable for the wrongs of its wholly-owned subsidiary. For instance a parent corporation may be held liable for its subsidiary's conduct when the parent uses a separate corporate form to defeat public convenience, justify wrong, commit fraud, or defend crime.[7] The parent corporation may also be liable for the wrongful conduct of its subsidiary when the subsidiary is the mere instrumentality of the parent. Liability is imposed in such instances simply because the two corporations are so closely intertwined that they do not merit treatment as separate entities.[8]

Appellant did not attempt at trial to prove that the use of separate corporate forms by GE was to perpetrate fraud or inequities, although most of the authorities he cites to us in his brief involved such matters. Rather, he attempted to establish that the affairs of GE and its subsidiary, GECC, were so interdependent that the corporate status of GECC should be disregarded; to put it another way, that GECC was a mere instrumentality of GE when the defamatory letter was sent.

Professor Powell[9] has identified eleven factors which may be looked for in ascertaining whether a subsidiary is acting as the mere instrumentality of its parent:

(a) The parent corporation owns all or most of the capital stock of the subsidiary.

(b) The parent and subsidiary corporations have common directors or officers.

(c) The parent corporation finances the subsidiary.

(d) The parent corporation subscribes to all the capital stock of the subsidiary or otherwise causes its incorporation.

(e) The subsidiary has grossly inadequate capital.

(f) The parent corporation pays the salaries and other expenses or losses of the subsidiary.

(g) The subsidiary has substantially no business except with the parent corporation or no assets except those conveyed to it by the parent corporation.

(h) In the papers of the parent corporation or in the statements of its officers, the subsidiary is described as a department or division of the parent corporation, or its business or financial responsibility is referred to as the parent corporation's own.

(i) The parent corporation uses the property of the subsidiary as its own.

(j) The directors or executives of the subsidiary do not act independently in the interest of the subsidiary but take their orders from the parent corporation in the latter's interest.

(k) The formal legal requirements of the subsidiary are not observed.

It is not necessary, of course, that all eleven of these factors be found in order to conclude that the subsidiary is the mere instrumentality of its parent. A parent corporation

---

7. *See* Steven v. Roscoe Turner Aeronautical Corp., 324 F.2d 157, 160 (7th Cir. 1963).

8. To be distinguished from "mere instrumentality" situations are those cases where the subsidiary is an agent of the parent for some purposes. Such cases are not true "veil-piercing" cases at all; rather, recovery is had against the parent on traditional agency principles. *See e.g.*, Zaist v. Olson, 154 Conn. 563, 573–574, 227 A.2d 552, 557 (1967); Detroit Motor Appliance Co. v. General Motors Corp., 5 F. Supp. 27, 30–31 (E.D.Ill. 1933).

9. Powell, Parent and Subsidiary Corporations ¶¶ 5–6, at 9 (1931). This listing has been quoted approvingly by the courts. See Taylor v. Standard Gas & Electric Co., 96 F.2d 693, 704 (10th Cir. 1938); Steven v. Roscoe Turner Aeronautical Corp., 324 F.2d 157, 161 (7th Cir. 1963). *See also* Annotation, 7 A.L.R.3d 1343 (1966).

which does not permit its subsidiary to exercise an individual status may not expect that the subsidiary's independence will be recognized elsewhere.

It is true that the findings of the trial court disclose a good deal of interrelation in the financial affairs and management of GE with its subsidiary GECC. The principal business carried on by GECC is to provide financing. But a substantial amount of GECC consumer financing in 1970 involved home products of manufacturers other than GE. Most commercial and industrial financing done by GECC in the same year did not involve GE products.

It is significant that the 1960 agreements between GE and GECC for purchase of repossessed GE appliances and the agreement by which GECC obtains management consultant services from GE appear to establish rights and obligations as between separate corporate entities. Appellant offered no evidence to show that GECC was underfinanced, or that GE used the property of GECC as its own, or paid the salaries, losses or expenses of GECC.

Our responsibility is not to approve the result, and indeed in this case an opposite result could conceivably have been reached by us if we were serving as the trial court. We cannot say however that the findings of the trial judge were clearly erroneous.

We hold, therefore, that the trial court did not err in holding that appellant has failed to prove that GECC is the mere instrumentality of GE and hence responsible to appellant for the defamatory letter.

The judgment is affirmed.

---

4. *Liability for Obligations of Related Corporations*

The theory supporting notion of corporate limited liability might well be more attenuated when the issue revolves around the liability of a parent corporation for the obligations of its subsidiaries. In the materials that follow, consider whether, or to what extent, the fact that a corporation owns the shares of another ought to eliminate the protection of limited liability between the entities? Consider also whether the effect of enterprise liability is the functional elimination of legal personality of subsidiaries owned by corporations?

Sandra K. Miller, *Piercing the Corporate Veil among Affiliated Companies in the European Community and in the U.S.: A Comparative Analysis of U.S., German, and U.K. Veil Piercing Approaches*

36 AM. BUS. L.J. 73 (1998)
(excerpts page 95; some footnotes omitted)

The Erosion of The Single Entity Principle Under U.S. Statutory Law

....The emergence of "enterprise liability" has its roots in the Great Depression.[86] Beginning in the early Roosevelt administration from 1933 to 1935, several specific

86. [Phillip I. Blumberg, *The Increasing Recognition of Enterprise Principles Determining Parent and Subsidiary Corporation Liabilities*, 28 CONN. L. REV. 295 (1996) (providing an overview of fed-

statutes were passed dealing with the regulation of corporate groups involving securities, railways, and public utilities.[87] The statutory shift from entity to enterprise liability has been accomplished through the use of various statutory formulations of the definition of corporate "control."[88] Enterprise liability is applied in a wide variety of statutory contexts involving banking and loan institutions, insurance, securities and investment companies, employer-sponsored pension plans, federal taxation, state taxation, and environmental laws.

Phillip I. Blumberg, *The Law of Corporate Groups: Tort, Contract, and Other Common Law Problems in the Substantive Law of Parent and Subsidiary Corporations*

(1987)
(excerpt pages 94–97)

* * *

When we examine the advantages and disadvantages of limited liability in the special case where it is applied to protect the constituent corporations of a corporate group, the theoretical analysis largely becomes irrelevant by reason of a number of factors.

First, we are not concerned in any way with the imposition of liability on the ultimate investors of the enterprise. A rule imposing liability on the enterprise for the torts or other acts of its constituent corporations need involve no change in the rule of limited liability for ultimate investors.

Second, we are no longer faced with a universe of thousands of shareholders of varying degrees of wealth. Instead, the subsidiary in a corporate group typically has a single shareholder—its parent.

Third, we are no longer faced with public shareholders who are widely separated from participation in management or control. Within the group, the sole shareholder—the parent—in its role as manager of the group is almost invariably engaged in establishing policy, determining budget, providing administrative support, and participating extensively in the decisionmaking of the subsidiary corporation, with only the degree of intrusiveness varying in the individual case.

Fourth, the business of the parent will typically be integrated economically with the business of the subsidiary. Indeed, in many cases, the two affiliates will be conducting interrelated fragments of a single unitary business.

In view of these fundamental changes in the nature of the shareholder and of its relation to the subsidiary corporation, it should be immediately apparent that many of the presumed theoretical advantages of limited liability simply become irrelevant in the case of the corporate group.

In the following review, we will re-examine the theoretical discussion and seek to determine the extent to which the various advantages advanced in support of limited lia-

---

eral and state laws which expressly apply to corporate groups of affiliated business entities, and] tracing the development of federal and state laws which expressly apply to corporate groups of affiliated business entities).]

87. *Id.*[, at 304.]

88. *Id.*

bility in the simple model typically assumed by economists commentators continue to be relevant when limited liability is re-examined in the... structure of corporate groups.

Avoids Dangerous Exposure to Risk of Absentee Investors. Since the parent corporation is not an absentee owner, this consideration become irrelevant.

Permits Very Large Scale Enterprise. With the parent corporation as the sole shareholder, the concerns about encouraging widespread distribution of shares is also irrelevant.

Permits Diversification of Portfolios. The parent facing the risk of liability for the debts of its subsidiaries is in a position to diversify its portfolio and spread the risk. Economists recognize that a similar ability to diversify on the part of financial institutions that are ultimate investors would make the imposition of limited liability significantly less important than in the case of individual investors lacking the same ability to diversify. This factor would be as applicable to corporate groups as to financial institutions.

Avoids Increased Agency Costs. In the corporate group, the parent corporation is almost always engaged to some degree in the management of the subsidiary. The subsidiary is typically managed as part of the same enterprise with varying degrees of decentralization. Under such circumstances, the need to establish congruence of the interests of the manager and the owner-investor, with its attendant presumed agency and monitoring costs, simply does not arise. The agency costs of the senior management of the enterprise monitoring the acts of subordinate managers do not significantly change where part of the enterprise is operated as a subsidiary rather than as an unincorporated branch or division. Thus, this consideration too becomes largely irrelevant.

Avoids Increased Information Costs. Since as much information about the subsidiary's operations will be available as if this part of the enterprise were conducted as a branch or division, this concern is also irrelevant.

Avoids Impairment of the Efficiency of the Capital Market. In the case of the wholly owned subsidiary, which is the typical case, there is no market in the subsidiary's shares, and so this consideration is irrelevant as well. In the case of the partly owned subsidiary, however, there will frequently be a market in which the publicly held shares are traded. In that limited case, this advantage would still be relevant.

Avoids Enforcement Costs for Creditors. Creditors will be able to proceed directly against the parent, so the specter of litigation against innumerable shareholders to enforce their liability would not arise. This consideration is thus irrelevant as well.

Avoids Costs of Contracting Around Liability. Unlike so many other factors, this consideration would continue to be fully applicable.

Encourages Risk Taking. This factor is also relevant in the case of corporate groups. It is particularly important in the case of conglomerate enterprises considering investment in areas unrelated to the existing businesses of the group. In the integrated group where the additional investment represents a horizontal or vertical extension of activities already being undertaken, the factor is less significant. Professor Hadden points out that "it is arguable that [without limited liability] some worthwhile but risky ventures which might be undertaken by large groups would not be undertaken at all."[1] He reports that this factor has deterred legislators in Germany and in the European Economic Community from imposing absolute liability on holding companies for the debts

---

1. Hadden, *Inside Corporate Groups*, 12 Int'l J. Soc. L. 271, 281 (1984).

of their subsidiaries under existing German law and under the Proposed Ninth Directive of the European Economic Community.

* * *

Comments and Questions

1. Do you think Professor Blumberg's arguments can apply with equal force in the case of the closely held corporation? Apply the criteria listed by Professor Blumberg in his article. It is possible to argue that limited liability may be inappropriate or irrevelant in the case of closely held corporations. Yet, such arguments may hide a reality that in connection with closely held corporations, the size of the enterprise and the relationship between the amount of credit extended and the net worth of the enterprise may have a greater influence on the availability of limited liability than the statutory provision of limited liability. As such limited liability may be moot in a context in which shareholders of a closely held corporation may waive their limited liability as a condition to receiving credit from lenders.

2. Are there other arguments that you could make in support of limited liability for closely held corporations that would not apply in the context of corporate groups? In reviewing the materials which follow, ponder whether there is merit to the notion that limited liability ought to shield corporate parents from the liabilities of their subsidiaries, or vice versa.

Las Palmas Associates, et al., Appellants, v. Las Palmas Center Associates, et al., Respondents

Court of Appeal, Second District, Division 2
Nov. 5, 1991
1 Cal.Rptr.2d 301, 235 Cal.App.3d 1220

NOTT, Associate Justice:

This lengthy and acrimonious litigation involves the sale of the Rancho Las Palmas Shopping Center, a 165,472 square-foot commercial complex located in Rancho Mirage, California. Appellants Las Palmas Associates, et al., built and sold the property to respondents Las Palmas Center Associates, et al. When a dispute arose concerning their duty to guaranty the rents of two tenants, appellants commenced an action for declaratory relief. Respondents in turn filed a cross-complaint for, among other things, fraud and breach of contract. A jury rendered verdicts awarding respondents $232,393 for breach of contract, $1.27 million for fraud, and $10 million in punitive damages. In a separate trial, the court, sitting without a jury, denied appellants declaratory relief. The court then awarded respondents $352,918 in contractual attorney's fees and entered judgment in the sum of $11,622,918. Appellants now appeal.

Because the undisputed evidence establishes that respondents' fraud damages are identical to their losses under the breach of contract theory, we hold that the fraud award must be reduced to $232,393. Additionally, we find it necessary to lower the punitive damage award to $2 million. Lastly, inasmuch as respondents have elected to take under the tort claim, the award for contractual attorney's fees allocated to prosecute that action must be reversed. However, because respondents were the prevailing parties in appellants' declaratory relief lawsuit, which was an "action on the contract," respondents are entitled to recover their attorney's fees incurred in defense of that litigation.

CONTENTIONS

Appellants seek a reversal of the judgment on the basis that (1) the trial court erroneously denied their motion to bifurcate the punitive damage trial from respondents' underlying action for fraud, in violation of Civil Code section 3295, subdivision (d); (2) there are no grounds to hold respondent Hahn Devcorp as the alter ego of its sister corporation, respondent Ernest Hahn, Inc.; (3) the fraud verdict is unsupported by substantial evidence and is invalid as a matter of law; (4) respondents' trial counsel committed prejudicial misconduct; (5) the $1.27 million fraud award, among other things, improperly compensates buyers for a claim that they previously relinquished; and, (6) the punitive damage verdict is unsupported by the evidence, excessive, unconstitutional, and the product of the jury's passion and prejudice. Appellants do not, however, complain that the breach of contract award is defective.

INTRODUCTION

In 1978, Las Palmas Associates (Associates), a limited partnership, agreed to build and then sell the Rancho Las Palmas Shopping Center (shopping center) to Villa Pacific Building Company (Villa Pacific), a corporation. Villa Pacific's sole shareholder and board chairman was Ronald Waranch, a real estate developer. Under the terms of the purchase agreement, Villa Pacific acquired an 84 percent interest in the yet to be constructed shopping center. The remaining 16 percent share belonged to Stanley Gribble, president of Hahn Devcorp (Devcorp), a builder of community and neighborhood shopping centers. Gribble received his interest in the shopping center as part of his executive compensation package from Devcorp. Besides being Associates' general partner, Devcorp was also at the time a wholly owned corporate subsidiary of Ernest W. Hahn, Inc. (Hahn Inc.), a nationwide developer of regional shopping centers. Together, Gribble and Villa Pacific formed a general partnership known as Las Palmas Center Associates (Las Palmas), which would eventually hold title to the property.

For the sake of clarity, we will refer to Associates, Devcorp and Hahn Inc. collectively as "sellers." Similarly, we will identify Villa Pacific, Waranch, and Las Palmas jointly as "buyers."

FACTS

Viewing the evidence, as we must, in the light most favorable to the prevailing party (Mozzetti v. City of Brisbane (1977) 67 Cal.App.3d 565, 570, 136 Cal.Rptr. 751; Little v. Stuyvesant Life Ins. Co. (1977) 67 Cal.App.3d 451, 462, 136 Cal.Rptr. 653), the record reveals that the initial price for the shopping center was $10,727,499. That amount, though, was subject to being either increased or decreased, depending on the project's completion date and the rental income generated from the leases of commercial tenants. Buyers paid up-front $2 million in cash to sellers. To protect that investment, Hahn Inc. in 1978 issued two guaranties to assure buyers the cash payment would be refunded if the deal collapsed.

In conjunction with the sale, buyers leased back the property to sellers. The parties also entered into various other amended purchase agreements, the effect of which was to require sellers to secure construction and permanent financing, build the complex, and sublease the property to tenants meeting certain financial and operating specifications. As consideration for the lease, sellers promised to pay buyers a portion of the gross rentals beginning in March 1980. The parties, moreover, had title to the property placed into an escrow account scheduled to close upon the completion of the shopping center and the subleasing of the stores to tenants. At the end of escrow, the parties planned for buyers to assume the permanent financing and pay sellers another cash payment. They also agreed that after the transaction closed, sellers would manage the facility for a period of three years.

One component of the purchase price was the capitalization of the shopping center's rental income.

To establish the final purchase price, Waranch testified at trial that the parties selected a 7 percent capitalization rate. They then divided that percentage into the net operating income of the shopping center as of the date of closing. The parties defined net operating income as the actual rental income less operating expenses and debt service. The result of that operation was then multiplied by 84 percent, which represented buyers' interest in the property.

Capitalization is a method of establishing a present day price for an asset that produces future income, such as rental property. It has been defined as "The amount equal to the value of the sum of money that would earn a periodic interest return equal to the rent if invested at the current market rate of interest." (Dolan, Basic Economics (2d ed. 1980) ch. 32, Rent, Interest, and Profits, p. 554.)

In 1980, a dispute arose between the parties concerning the amount of rental income sellers had collected. Buyers contended they were entitled to approximately $1.6 million in rents. In contrast, sellers asserted there was no rental income because operating expenses exceeded rents by $400,000. As a compromise, buyers relinquished their claim for the rents in exchange for sellers taking $2,187,683 of the purchase price in the form of buyers' promissory note. The note had a rate of 7 percent interest and was secured by a deed of trust to the shopping center.

Sometime in either 1980 or 1981, Hahn, Inc. merged with Trizec Centers, Inc., a subsidiary of Trizec Corporation Ltd. At trial, the court admitted into evidence the proxy statement of that transaction. According to the document, Ernest Hahn, the board chairman and chief executive officer of Hahn, Inc., agreed to sell his 1.6 million shares of the company to Trizec Centers. The proxy statement further revealed that on May 19, 1980, Ernest Hahn executed an employment agreement to serve as chief executive officer for Hahn, Inc. and Trizec Centers. Under the employment agreement, the board of directors of Hahn, Inc. and Devcorp would consist of two persons appointed by Ernest Hahn and five directors named by Trizec Centers. It was also anticipated that Ernest Hahn would appoint himself and Robert W. Lees, the former president of Hahn, Inc., to both boards.

Furthermore, the proxy statement revealed that in 1980 Devcorp had 25 shopping centers either under development or in operation. The document stated Devcorp owed over $30 million in outstanding loans, had secured $43.2 million in loan commitments, and that Hahn, Inc. had fully guarantied the financing.

On March 20, 1981, Hahn, Inc. transferred all 10,000 of its shares of Devcorp to Trizec Centers. Three days later, Trizec Centers conveyed 659 shares of Devcorp to Goldlist Acquisition Corp. and the remaining 9,341 shares of Devcorp to Trizec Equities, Inc.

By early 1982, the shopping center had two problem tenants. Franchise Stores Realty Corp. (Franchise) held a ten-year lease that it assigned to one Robert Young. He, however, eventually abandoned the store, leaving the leasehold to revert back to Franchise with $6,000 owed in back rent. At the same time, Phanny's Phudge Pharlors (Phanny's Phudge), which had signed a 15-year lease, was out of business and attempting to sublet its store.

As the closing date approached, buyers objected to including Phanny's Phudge and Franchise into the capitalized purchase price. To persuade buyers to consummate the transaction, sellers had Devcorp guaranty the stores' two leases. Pursuant to the guaranties, Devcorp essentially pledged to pay all sums due under the leases until Phanny's Phudge and Franchise paid their rents for consecutive periods ranging from three to six months. The guaranties also obligated buyers not to unreasonably withhold their permission to assignments of the leases.[1]

With the rents capitalized, the total face value of the cash and financing paid by buyers was $15,046,800. Of that amount, $639,898 represented the capitalized rents from the Franchise and Phanny's Phudge leases.

Following the execution of the guaranties, Franchise sought to assign its lease to Riverco. Buyers rejected the assignment until sellers orally agreed that Riverco was covered by the Devcorp guaranty. After Riverco assumed the lease, it never once kept its rent payments current for the number of consecutive months required by the lease guaranty. Then, in December 1983, Riverco declared bankruptcy.

Meanwhile, Phanny's Phudge also had closed its doors and was attempting to locate a subtenant. In May 1982, buyers asked Devcorp to honor its commitment under the Phanny's Phudge guaranty. Devcorp refused the request, contending it had no obligation to pay the rent because buyers had unreasonably denied an assignment of the property to another tenant. Subsequently, in a July 1982 correspondence, Devcorp's corporate counsel, Vaughn Hapeman, disavowed the guaranty, claiming Phanny's Phudge had kept its rent current for the requisite three consecutive months ending that June. Buyers would later present evidence at trial that Hapeman made the assertion, despite the fact: (1) sellers' own management company served three-day notices to Phanny's Phudge demanding payment of the rents for May and June 1982; and, (2) that

1. Specifically, the lease guaranties provided: (1)—"Seller unconditionally guarant[ies] to Buyer the full and uninterrupted payment by Phanny's Phudge Pharlors ('Phanny's Phudge') of all amounts payable pursuant to its lease dated November 13, 1979, as amended July 1, 1981 (the 'Phanny's Phudge Lease'), of space within the Shopping Center (i) until such time as Phanny's Phudge shall not be delinquent in the payment of such amounts, or in the performance of their obligations under the Phanny's Phudge Lease to operate their business, for a period of any three (3) successive months from and after the date of this Sixth Amendment, or (ii) until the written approval by Buyer of any further assignment, subletting or termination of the Phanny's Phudge Lease, which approval shall not be unreasonably withheld, whichever first occurs, and Seller shall thereupon be automatically released from its obligations under this Paragraph 4." (2)—"Seller unconditionally guarant[ies] to Buyer the full and uninterrupted payment by Franchise Stores Realty Corp. ('Franchise Stores') of all amounts payable pursuant to its lease ('Franchise Stores Lease') of space in the Shopping Center (i) until Franchise Stores shall not be delinquent in the payment of such amounts for a period of any six (6) successive months from and after the date of this Sixth Amendment, or (ii) until Franchise Stores takes back possession and operates the premises covered by the Franchise Stores Lease for a period of any three (3) successive months, or (iii) until written approval by Buyer of any further assignment, subletting or termination of the Franchise Stores Lease, which approval shall not be unreasonably withheld, whichever first occurs, and Seller shall thereupon be automatically released from its obligations under this Paragraph 5."

Stanley Gribble, Devcorp's president, wrote margin notes to Hapeman on an internal copy of the letter stating he thought Phanny's Phudge rent was past due for the period in question.

By June 1983, Devcorp's board of directors was liquidating the company's assets and discharging its executives and employees. Eventually, Devcorp became a shell company with Hahn, Inc.'s staff transacting its remaining business.

Also that year, at the suggestion of Devcorp's attorney, buyers evicted Phanny's Phudge from the property and obtained a $34,814 unlawful detainer judgment. On November 8, 1983, buyers assigned the judgment to sellers because, as discussed in more detail below, buyers had been offsetting from their loan payments the rents left unpaid by Phanny's Phudge and Franchise.

In the summer of 1984, buyers notified sellers that they had located a tenant who desired to open a Greek restaurant in the Phanny's Phudge store. On July 23, 1984, Randy Brant, the director of leasing operations for Hahn, Inc., wrote to buyers' property manager, stating: "Please proceed to finalize the [deal for the Greek restaurant]. As the proposed rent will not reach our guarant[ied] rent until the third year Ernest W. Hahn, Inc. will agree to pick up the difference.... In addition Ernest W. Hahn, Inc. will agree to guarant[y] this lease and pay the commission amount of $7,235.00 to Weiman Property Management...." Relying on the offer, buyers entered into the lease with the new tenant.

On September 27, 1984, Jana Green, corporate counsel for Hahn, Inc., wrote buyers' management company using Devcorp's stationery. The letter rescinded the Hahn, Inc. guaranty and replaced it with one issued by Devcorp. The letter stated: "This letter supersedes that certain letter, dated July 24, 1984, from Mr. Randy Brant, Director of Leasing, rendering it void and of no force and effect. [¶] The purpose of this letter is to provide a new guarant[y] on the same terms and conditions of the 'Phanny['s] Phudge' lease guarant[y] which said terms and conditions are as set forth below...." Green signed the letter as corporate counsel for Devcorp.

A week later, Devcorp again changed its position and had Green write buyers that it was no longer responsible for any of the guaranties. First, she asserted buyers' eviction action had terminated the Phanny's Phudge guaranty. Her letter also announced that sellers were giving buyers a $34,814 credit against the promissory note, apparently in recognition of the tender of the unlawful detainer judgment. Secondly, the attorney insisted the lease assignments to Young, and then later to Riverco, had relieved sellers from their obligations under the Franchise guaranty.

As previously discussed, buyers were offsetting the uncollected rents from their loan payments. They started to take the deductions in August 1982 and continued the practice without objection from sellers until May 1984. At that time, sellers asked buyers to stop the deductions and instead bill them for the uncollected rents. Buyers complied with the request, but never received any remittances from sellers. Eventually, buyers reinstituted the offsets.

As events developed, it would not be until March 1986 before buyers located a tenant for the Franchise store who paid a sufficient number of consecutive rents to terminate that lease guaranty. Similarly, a tenant who paid the requisite number of consecutive rents for the Phanny's Phudge store was not found until October 1986.

Sellers commenced the present action in Riverside County. Their complaint sought a declaration that the lease guaranties had terminated and that buyers had defaulted on the promissory note by taking the offsets. After buyers succeeded in having venue for the lawsuit transferred to Los Angeles County, sellers initiated a nonjudicial foreclosure to collect the arrearages caused by the offsets. To cure the default, Buyers paid sellers $322,288, which included the offsets, plus interest. Buyers then filed a cross-complaint seeking, among other things, damages for breach of the lease guaranties. They also sought punitive damages for fraud, tortious breach of contract, and intentional infliction of emotional distress. In their fraud action, buyers alleged that sellers had misrepresented their intent to honor the guaranties in order to induce buyers into consummating the sale.

At the conclusion of extensive pre-trial proceedings, the court dismissed all the tort claims except for the fraud action. The court also decided to impanel a jury to hear both lawsuits and to return advisory verdicts on the equitable issues. The court further ruled on sellers' in limine motion to exclude buyers from introducing evidence on various matters. However, despite the fact that buyers were seeking punitive damages for fraud, sellers neglected to request a protective order to preclude buyers from introducing evidence of sellers' financial condition.

In opening statements to the jury, both sides announced that buyers were seeking punitive damages. In addition, buyers on two separate occasions during their opening statement informed the jury, without a challenge by sellers, that Hahn Inc. was a "billion-dollar company."

Sellers prosecuted their lawsuit first and called as a witness Vaughn Hapeman, general counsel for Devcorp. Under cross-examination by buyers, Hapeman acknowledged that Hahn, Inc. was a billion dollar company.[2]

To determine the shopping center's market value, sellers called as their expert witness Thomas Marshall, a member of the Appraisal Institute. He testified that in February 1982, he conducted an income, cost, and sales comparison analysis of the property. Having assumed a 6 percent vacancy rate, Marshall opined that under the income approach the shopping center's market value in 1982 was $16.4 million, or $13,776,000 for buyers' 84 percent interest. He further stated its present worth was $22.9 million.

On cross-examination, buyers questioned Marshall concerning his written appraisal report that claimed buyers actually had underpaid for the shopping center. Marshall arrived at that conclusion by reducing the face value of buyers' promissory note ($2,187,683) to $600,000. Because of favorable terms, Marshall opined that the note needed to be discounted by approximately $1.5 million to determine its present day value in 1982. Using the discounted value of the note, Marshall calculated that the consideration given by buyers was only $13,546,800. By subtracting that amount from the $13,776,000 appraised value of buyers' share of the shopping center, Marshall was able to demonstrate that buyers made an immediate $229,200 profit from the transaction. Marshall admitted, however, that in arriving at his opinion he did not include the fact that buyers had relinquished their claim for $1.6 million in back rents as consideration for the right to finance the final purchase price payment.

Sellers concluded their case on the sixth day of trial. The following morning, buyers brought a motion to have sellers make available their financial records. Buyers argued that

2. At oral argument before us, sellers' counsel represented that his clients had objected to the questions directed at their wealth. Actually, the record reflects that sellers objected to buyers' inquiry concerning the merger with Trizec Centers, Inc.

the motion should be granted because through cross-examination of sellers' witnesses they had presented a prima facie case for punitive damages. Buyers further informed the court that their first witness was Vernon Schwartz, the former senior vice-president and chief financial officer of Hahn Inc., who had traveled from San Francisco to be in court.

Sellers opposed the discovery motion, contending buyers had failed to meet their statutory burden to establish by clear and convincing evidence that sellers were guilty of acts justifying exemplary damages. During argument on this point, the trial court inquired: "I take it you did not ask for bifurcation [of the issue of the sellers' wealth under Civil Code section 3295, subdivision (d)]?"[3] Sellers answered in the negative because they believed there was insufficient evidence of fraud to warrant disclosure of their wealth.

The trial court ordered sellers to provide the financial records. Sellers then made an oral motion to exclude evidence of their finances from the jury under subdivision (d) of section 3295. The trial court denied the request.

Thereafter, during buyers' direct examination of Schwartz, the witness estimated that Hahn, Inc. owned more than 40 shopping centers and had assets in excess of a billion dollars.

The remainder of the trial lasted for nearly three weeks. During their case in chief, buyers attempted to prove the economic downturn of the early 1980's, along with unanticipated construction costs and higher interest rates, caused sellers to overestimate their profit margin. Under buyers' scenario, sellers needed the rents from Franchise and Phanny's Phudge to be capitalized into the final purchase price to keep the deal profitable. Buyers also sought to prove that after the issuance of the guaranties, sellers drained Devcorp of its assets and manpower for the purpose of leaving the company a mere shell corporation.

Before submitting the case to the jury, the parties stipulated the net value of Hahn Inc. was $497 million. They also agreed Devcorp had a total worth of $4.1 million.[4]

In closing summation to the jury, buyers argued that sellers owed them $232,292 for breach of the guaranty agreements. The amount represented uncollected rents, management fees, taxes, penalties, interest, and other miscellaneous costs due under the Franchise and Phanny's Phudge leases. Turning to the tort action, they asked the jury to find that sellers had fraudulently promised to guaranty the leases as an inducement for them to complete the deal. In addressing the issue of fraud damages, buyers' counsel first told the panel: "I could ask you for a million, two-seventy.... We're not going to do that because I think that is a—I think ridiculous, even though it works to our advantage at this point. I think it's a ridiculous theory. I don't think it's justified and I don't think it's right." He then urged the jury to find that the proper measure of the fraud damages was the capitalized cost of the two leases: $639,878 ($374,702 for Phanny's Phudge and $265,176 for Franchise).[6]

---

3. All further statutory references are to the Civil Code unless otherwise indicated. As explained later in our opinion, section 3295, subdivision (d) grants a defendant the option of requesting the trial court to exclude from the trier of fact evidence of the defendant's wealth until a verdict is rendered for plaintiff awarding actual damages and a finding has been made that defendant was guilty of malice, oppression, or fraud.

4. Apparently, half of Devcorp's net worth came from buyers' promissory note.

6. Buyers arrived at that figure by subtracting the appraised value of their share of the shopping center ($13,776,000) from the face value of the consideration they paid ($15,046,800).

On the other hand, sellers asserted in their closing argument that buyers had not suffered any fraud damages because the shopping center in 1982 was worth more than what buyers had paid. Then referring to the property's current value, sellers' attorney stated: "Of course, we also know that when we talk about market value, you heard the testimony of the appraiser, the market value conservatively appraised is $22.9 million. Far more than what [buyers] paid."

Seizing on sellers' closing argument, buyers' attorney on rebuttal told the jury: "I'm going to change my mind from yesterday. [Sellers' attorney] stands up here and he says that the real measure of damages on the shopping center is that [buyers get what they] paid for, and he says...today that the center was worth [$]22,900,000. You heard the appraiser. The appraiser said it was worth sixteen million four and 84 percent of it was that number. And that is what [buyers] paid, and that is what [they] overpaid. That theory is the dumbest theory in the world to base damages on. And the real theory, the second one that's easily had, and that is the one I told you about on the [$]639,000. You know, if he wants to be dumb enough to stand up and continue to argue that is the way to do it, then bury him with it, okay? On that verdict form when you put down how much is the guilt of fraud, don't put the [$]639,000, follow his instruction and put [$]1,270,000 down there. That is what he wants you to do."

After deliberating for only one day, the panel unanimously agreed sellers had breached the two guaranties. The jury set damages at $232,393. By a vote of 10 to 2, the jury also found (1) sellers had fraudulently misrepresented their intent to honor the guaranties, causing buyers to overpay $1.27 million for the shopping center; and (2) in making the guaranties, sellers acted with oppression, fraud, or malice. Voting 9 to 3, the panel assessed sellers $10 million in punitive damages. Finally, the jury also unanimously found that Devcorp was the alter ego of Hahn, Inc. and that Hahn, Inc. should be held liable for the obligations of Devcorp.

The court thereafter dismissed the jury and allowed the parties to address the merits of sellers' declaratory relief action. The parties also argued whether Hahn, Inc. should be held accountable for Devcorp's conduct. Following argument, the trial court determined that sellers had breached the guaranties. It further held there was a sufficient unity of interest and ownership between the two corporations to find Devcorp to be the alter ego of Hahn, Inc.

Sellers made various post-trial motions. In their request for a new trial, they contended, inter alia, that an award of $1.27 million in fraud damages was unsupported by the evidence and that the punitive damage verdict was excessive. The trial court took the motions under submission, remarking "...I have never seen a simple commercial real estate sale transaction screwed up so badly by so many members of the bar over a long period of time as I have in this situation. [¶] It is absolutely unbelievable what has happened to these parties over this period of time." Two days later, the trial court summarily denied the motions.

DISCUSSION

I. Whether The Fraud Verdict Should Be Affirmed

Sellers assert the evidence is insufficient to support a finding that at the time they initially entered into the lease guaranties they harbored an intent to defraud buyers. We conclude otherwise. [omitted]

* * *

II. Whether It Was Prejudicial Error to Allow the Jury Knowledge of Sellers' Wealth

Sellers argue the trial court committed prejudicial error when it failed to heed the mandatory language of section 3295 and grant them a protective order excluding evidence of their wealth from the jury until the panel found them liable for fraud. * * * *

* * *

* * * * Thus, we are convinced that the references to sellers' wealth in closing argument did not impermissibly sway the jury to render verdicts against the sellers.

III. Whether Buyers' Trial Counsel Committed Prejudicial Misconduct

Sellers complain they were denied a fair trial because in closing argument buyers' counsel committed purported acts of misconduct, to wit, he (1) suggested buyers sought a change of venue because sellers' attorneys used political contributions to exert influence over the judiciary in Riverside County; (2) intimated sellers paid their attorneys to lie for them in court and to conceal evidence; (3) misrepresented the amount of money buyers ultimately spent for the shopping center; (4) appealed to the jury to be sympathetic to Waranch; and, (5) implied that Waranch might donate an award of punitive damages to charity. Sellers also assert buyers' attorney poisoned the proceedings by abusing witnesses, making improper objections, and repeatedly propounding argumentative questions. We do not agree.

* * *

* * * * Here, there was substantial evidence of sellers' fraud. Thus, even if buyers' counsel was guilty of a pervasive pattern of misconduct, we think it had an innocuous effect on the jury's overall conclusion that sellers had committed a tortious act.

IV. Whether the Record Supports the Finding That
Devcorp Was the Alter Ego of Hahn, Inc.

Hahn, Inc. complains buyers cannot pierce its corporate veil because the undisputed evidence established that it had no interest in the corporation at the time the 1982 lease guaranties were created. We find the contention meritless.

"The law as to whether courts will pierce the corporate veil is easy to state but difficult to apply." (Talbot v. Fresno-Pacific Corp. (1960) 181 Cal.App.2d 425, 432, 5 Cal.Rptr. 361.) Because it is founded on equitable principles, application of the alter ego "is not made to depend upon prior decisions involving factual situations which appear to be similar.... 'It is the general rule that the conditions under which a corporate entity may be disregarded vary according to the circumstances of each case.'" McLoughlin v. L. Bloom Sons Co., Inc. (1962) 206 Cal.App.2d 848, 853, 24 Cal.Rptr. 311.... Whether the evidence has established that the corporate veil should be ignored is primarily a question of fact which should not be disturbed when supported by substantial evidence. (Jack Farenbaugh & Son v. Belmont Construction, Inc., supra, at p. 1032, 240 Cal.Rptr. 78.)

Hahn, Inc. relies on Riddle v. Leuschner (1959) 51 Cal.2d 574, 335 P.2d 107. There, the California Supreme Court reversed a judgment, based on an alter ego theory, against a manager of businesses owned by two corporations. The court stated: "It is undisputed that he held none of the stock, and there is no evidence that he had any interest as an owner in the business operated by either of the two corporations or that he had a right to share in any profits they might make. Instead, he received a monthly salary. Under all the circumstances, he is to be regarded as having been a managing employee of the two companies, and his control over their affairs must be treated as that which would be exercised by a managing agent rather than that of a shareholder or owner. It follows that there was not such unity of 'interest and ownership' between [the manager] and the corporations that the separate personalities of the corporations and the individual no longer existed, within the meaning of the rule...." (Id. at p. 580, 335 P.2d 107.)

Riddle stands for the proposition that it would be unfair to impose personal liability on an individual for corporate conduct unless he had an ownership interest in the company. At the same time, under the facts of this case, it would be as equally unfair to permit Hahn, Inc. to escape liability for the unperformed guaranties simply because it earlier had transferred ownership of Devcorp to, among others, a sister corporation within the Trizec family of companies.

"Usually, a disregard of the corporate entity is sought in order to fasten liability upon individual stockholders....'It has been stated that the two requirements for application of this doctrine are (1) that there be such unity of interest and ownership that the separate personalities of the corporation and the individual no longer exist and (2) that, if the acts are treated as those of the corporation alone, an inequitable result will follow.' [¶] However, only a difference in wording is used in stating the same concept where the entity sought to be held liable is another corporation instead of an individual. 'A very numerous and growing class of cases wherein the corporate entity is disregarded is that wherein it is so organized and controlled, and its affairs are so conducted, as to make it merely an instrumentality, agency, conduit, or adjunct of another corporation.' [Citations.]" (McLoughlin v. L. Bloom Sons Co., Inc., supra, 206 Cal.App.2d 848, 851–852, 24 Cal.Rptr. 311, emphasis added.)

Because society recognizes the benefits of allowing persons and organizations to limit their business risks through incorporation, sound public policy dictates that imposition of alter ego liability be approached with caution. (Cascade Energy and Metals Corp. v. Banks (1990) 896 F.2d 1557, 1576.) Nevertheless, it would be unjust to permit those who control companies to treat them as a single or unitary enterprise and then assert their corporate separateness in order to commit frauds and other misdeeds with impunity. Here, buyers essentially tried the case based on a single-enterprise theory of liability. In closing argument to the jury, buyers argued the evidence established that the line of command ran from Trizec at the top, with Hahn, Inc. in the middle, and Devcorp at the bottom.

Generally, alter ego liability is reserved for the parent-subsidiary relationship. However, under the single-enterprise rule, liability can be found between sister companies. The theory has been described as follows: " 'In effect what happens is that the court, for sufficient reason, has determined that though there are two or more personalities, there is but one enterprise; and that this enterprise has been so handled that it should respond, as a whole, for the debts of certain component elements of it. The court thus has constructed for purposes of imposing liability an entity unknown to any secretary of state comprising assets and liabilities of two or more legal personalities; endowed that entity with the assets of both, and charged it with the liabilities of one or both.' " (2 Marsh's Cal.Corp. Law (3d ed. 1990) § 16.23, p. 1416, quoting a law review article by Professor Berle found at 47 Colum.L.Rev. (1947) 343, 350.)

In Pan Pacific Sash & Door Co. v. Greendale Park, Inc. (1958) 166 Cal.App.2d 652, 333 P.2d 802, defendants formed Greendale Park, Inc. and the Ralmor Corporation to build homes on undeveloped lots. Defendants transferred the real property to Greendale Park and later had that corporation contract with Ralmor for the construction. Plaintiff sold sash doors, frames and jambs to Ralmor. When Ralmor did not pay for the goods, plaintiff sued each corporation asserting they were both one and the same. The trial court entered judgment against both corporations under the alter ego theory.

The Court of Appeal in Pan Pacific affirmed the judgment, stating: "Upon the basis of the... evidence the trial court was warranted in concluding, as it did, that each corporation was but an instrumentality or conduit of the other in the prosecution of a single venture namely, the construction and sale of houses upon the tract in question.... There was such unity of interest and ownership that the separateness of the two corporations had in effect ceased and an adherence to the fiction of a separate existence of the two corporations would, under the circumstances here present, promote injustice and make it inequitable for Greendale to escape liability for an obligation incurred as much for its benefit as for Ralmor." (Id. at pp. 658–659, 333 P.2d 802.)

We find there is substantial evidence to support the conclusion that Hahn, Inc. and Devcorp formed a single enterprise for the purpose of committing a continuing fraud against buyers. First, the evidence that Hahn, Inc. had guarantied $43.2 million in loans and loan commitments to Devcorp strongly suggests Devcorp was undercapitalized for a company in the business of developing shopping centers. Likewise, in 1978 Hahn, Inc. issued two guaranties to buyers to protect the $2 million cash downpayment they made to Devcorp. Moreover, besides the loan guaranties, Hahn, Inc. temporarily guarantied the Phanny's Phudge lease, despite the fact that Hahn, Inc. no longer had a stock ownership interest in Devcorp. These guaranties indicate that Devcorp's survivability as a developer was intertwined with its dependence on Hahn, Inc.

Furthermore, Ernest Hahn and Robert Lees sat as directors on the boards of Hahn, Inc. and Devcorp. When Devcorp's board of directors fired the corporation's executives and staff, Hahn, Inc. used its employees, including its corporate counsel, to continue to manage what remained of the business. In short, the trial court reasonably could have concluded that Hahn, Inc. and Devcorp were combined into a single enterprise to defraud buyers.

Sellers next assert that even assuming there was a unity of interest between Hahn, Inc. and Devcorp, the record lacks substantial evidence to support a finding that justice required the trial court to pierce the corporate veil. They premise their argument on the fact the parties stipulated at trial that Devcorp was worth $4.1 million, an amount sufficient to satisfy the $1.27 million award of compensatory damages and a suitable punitive damage award. They contend buyers dragged Hahn, Inc., with its sizeable assets, into the lawsuit only to increase the funds available for a punitive damage award. We are unpersuaded by the claim.

Sellers cite Walker v. Signal Companies, Inc. (1978) 84 Cal.App.3d 982, 149 Cal.Rptr. 119 in support of their argument. There, plaintiffs obtained a judgment awarding fraud and punitive damages against two affiliated corporations. The trial court, however, had entered a judgment of nonsuit in favor of the corporate parent. In affirming the judgment, the appellate court stated: "We conclude that more is required than solely a parent-subsidiary corporate relationship to create liability of a parent for the actions of its subsidiary. [¶]... The sole basis for holding [the parent] liable would be to enable the plaintiffs to obtain an increased award of punitive damages because of the substantial net worth of the parent. There is no factual justification to do so." (Id. at p. 1001, 149 Cal.Rptr. 119.) The present case is obviously distinguishable from Walker. Hahn, Inc. actively participated in the sale of the shopping center from the very beginning to the very end. Hence, there is a sufficient factual basis for allowing buyers to pierce the corporate veil of Devcorp.

Finally, as explained in the next section, we have reduced substantially the jury's award of compensatory and punitive damages. Still, we think it appropriate to maintain Hahn, Inc.'s liability for the judgment. Even though at trial the parties stipulated that Devcorp was worth $4.1 million, it is unclear from the record how much of that amount is composed of buyers' promissory note, which buyers presumably have been paying down throughout this litigation. Moreover, buyers suggest in their respondent's brief that by the time this appeal becomes final, sellers could totally deplete Devcorp of all its assets.

For all the above reasons, we will uphold the trial court's determination that Devcorp is the alter ego of Hahn, Inc.

V. Whether the $1.27 Million Fraud Award Is Excessive as a Matter of Law

We agree with sellers that the $1.27 million fraud award is excessive, but not on the grounds urged by them....

* * *

VI. Whether the Punitive Damage Award Must Also Be Reduced

Sellers insist the punitive damage award cannot be upheld because there is no reasonable relationship between the award's size and (1) the reprehensibility of their conduct; (2) the injuries suffered by buyers; and, (3) their net worth. (See Neal v. Farmers Ins. Exchange, supra, 21 Cal.3d 910, 928, 148 Cal.Rptr. 389, 582 P.2d 980.) In light of our holding that the jury's $1.27 million fraud award was not supported by substantial evidence, we agree that the $10 million award for punitive damage must be reduced.

* * *

VII. The Award of Contractual Attorney's Fee Must Be Reversed

A party is barred from collecting contractual attorney's fees in an action for fraud. (Schlocker v. Schlocker (1976) 62 Cal.App.3d 921, 133 Cal.Rptr. 485; see also Stout v. Turney, supra, 22 Cal.3d 718, 730, 150 Cal.Rptr. 637, 586 P.2d 1228.) In their respondent's brief, buyers in effect have stated they desire to take under their fraud action. The award of contractual attorney's fees allocated to prosecute that claim, therefore, must be reversed. However, sellers' declaratory relief lawsuit, which alleged that they had no liability to buyers due to the occurrence of certain events contemplated by the guaranties, clearly was "an action on the contract" within the meaning of subdivision (a) of section 1717. Hence, buyers as the prevailing party in that litigation are entitled to recover their reasonable attorney's fees incurred in the defense of that action.

* * *

VIII. Sellers' Other Contentions

Sellers have raised numerous other issues that we have reviewed and find unnecessary to discuss.

DISPOSITION

The judgment is modified to reflect our decision to reduce respondents' award of fraud damages to $232,393 and the award of punitive damages to $2 million. The matter is remanded to the trial court for its determination and award of attorney's fees incurred by respondents in defense of appellants' declaratory relief action. Each side is to bear their own costs of appeal.

GATES, Acting P.J., and FUKUTO, J., concur.

C.M. Corporation, Continental Manors, Inc. and Commercial Management, Inc. v. Oberer Dev. Co.

United States Court of Appeals, Seventh Circuit
631 F.2d 536
October 7, 1980

KILKENNY, J.:

STATEMENT OF THE CASE

This is an appeal in a diversity action from a judgment notwithstanding the verdict in favor of appellees and against appellants. Appellants, C M Corporation, Continental Manors, Inc. and Commercial Management, Inc., brought the action to recover damages for breach of contract and breach of warranty in the design and construction of three nursing homes. Named as defendants in the amended complaint were the appellees Gold Key Builders, Inc., Oberer Development Company, Creative Construction Company, and George R. Oberer. Creative Construction Company was dismissed from the case. Personal service was never obtained on George Oberer and he never formally appeared.

The issue presented at trial was whether the corporate veil between Gold Key Builders and Oberer Development Company should be pierced. Prior to trial, all the parties agreed that if the jury found it proper to pierce the corporate veil, the entire dispute between appellants and appellees would be referred to arbitration. Consequently, the jury was not presented with any issues on the substantive breach of contract claim or of damages.

At the close of all the evidence, appellees moved for a directed verdict, but the court reserved ruling on the motion. Following the instructions to the jury, the court submitted the issues to the jury on two special interrogatories; the first asking whether the corporate existence of Gold Key Builders was pierced during the relevant period, and the second asking whether Oberer Development Company was responsible for the obligations of Gold Key Builders and its predecessors. The jury answered each interrogatory in the affirmative.

Appellees forthwith moved for judgment notwithstanding the verdict. After extensive briefing the district court granted the appellees' motion and entered judgment accordingly. It is from this judgment that appellants appeal.

THE CORPORATIONS

Although raising one basic issue, this case is complicated by the number of corporations involved at one time or another. A brief description of the corporations and their relationships is required for an understanding of the issue.

Appellant C M Corporation (CM) owns the other appellants, Continental Manors, Inc. and Commercial Management, Inc. CM and its subsidiaries are in the business of offering expert advice to communities wishing to construct nursing homes. They also manage nursing homes for various clients.

CM is seeking damages from Gold Key Builders and Oberer Development Company in connection with the construction of three nursing homes; one in Piper City, Illinois, another in Newman, Illinois, and the third in West Liberty, Iowa. Because Gold Key Builders is insolvent, CM is attempting to pierce the corporate veil and hold Oberer Development liable for the obligations of its subsidiary, Gold Key Builders. It is important to note here that Gold Key Builders did not become a subsidiary of Oberer Development until after 1976, and after the projects were completed.

Gold Key Builders has not always been known by that name. In 1972, when the Piper City Project began, and in 1973, when the Newman Project started, Gold Key was known as Enco, Inc. By 1974, at the time the West Liberty Project was commenced, the name had been changed to Anco, Inc. Subsequently, Anco became Gold Key Builders. There is no question that Gold Key Builders is responsible for the obligations of Enco and Anco. The dispute is over whether Oberer Development Company can be held liable for the obligations of Gold Key Builders.

Enco and Anco contracted to build the three nursing home projects. Although not a party to this action, Creative Construction Company is in the picture because it contracted to design the Newman, Illinois Project. In 1976, Creative was merged into Oberer Development Company.

All these corporations have or have had certain features in common. All are or were among a group of ten to fifteen companies owned by George Oberer and members of his family. This group of companies was sometimes loosely referred to as "Oberer Enterprises." However, Oberer Enterprises was never a legal entity. Consequently, it could not be a party to this action. The corporations also shared some common directors, an occasional common officer, and a common Dayton, Ohio address.

ISSUE

Because the district court entered judgment notwithstanding the jury's verdict, the question before us is whether the evidence, together with all the inferences which may reasonably be drawn therefrom, when viewed in the light most favorable to appellants is insufficient to support the verdict piercing the corporate veil between Gold Key Builders and Oberer Development Company. Farmers State Bank of Valparaiso v. Dravo Corp., 321 F.2d 38 (CA7 1963); Sparrow v. Yellow Cab Co., 273 F.2d 1 (CA9 1959), rehearing denied (1960).

THE LAW

All parties contend, and we agree, that our analysis is controlled by the law announced in Steven v. Roscoe Turner Aeronautical Corp., 324 F.2d 157 (CA7 1963). In Turner, this court held that a parent corporation would be responsible for the obligations of its subsidiary when the subsidiary has become its mere instrumentality. In order to establish that a parent should be held liable for the obligations of its subsidiary, three elements must be proved: "control by the parent to such a degree that the subsidiary has become its mere instrumentality; fraud or wrong by the parent through its subsidiary, e.g., torts, violation of a statute or stripping the subsidiary of its assets; and unjust loss or injury to the claimant, such as insolvency of the subsidiary." Roscoe Turner, supra, at 160....

In determining whether the requisite degree of control has been maintained by the parent corporation, we have said that many factors are relevant, and that it is the presence of these factors in proper combination which would lead to a piercing of the corporate veil separating a corporation from its owner or owners. Among the factors considered controlling are:

"(a) The parent corporation owns all or most of the capital stock of the subsidiary.

"(b) The parent and subsidiary corporations have common directors or officers.

"(c) The parent corporation finances the subsidiary.

"(d) The parent corporation subscribes to all the capital stock of the subsidiary or otherwise causes its incorporation.

"(e) The subsidiary has grossly inadequate capital.

"(f) The parent corporation pays the salaries and other expenses or losses of the subsidiary.

"(g) The subsidiary has substantially no business except with the parent corporation or no assets except those conveyed to it by the parent corporation.

"(h) In the papers of the parent corporation or in the statements of its officers, the subsidiary is described as a department or division of the parent corporation, or its business or financial responsibility is referred to as the parent corporation's own.

"(i) The parent corporation uses the property of the subsidiary as its own.

"(j) The directors or executives of the subsidiary do not act independently in the interest of the subsidiary but take their orders from the parent corporation in the latter's interest.

"(k) The formal legal requirements of the subsidiary are not observed." Roscoe Turner, supra, at 161, quoting from Taylor v. Standard Gas & Electric Co., 96 F.2d 693 at 704–05 (CA10 1938), rev'd on other grounds, 306 U.S. 307, 59 S. Ct. 543, 83 L. Ed. 669 (1939) (quoting Powell, Parent and Subsidiary Corporations at 9 (1931)).

Stock control and common officers and directors are generally prerequisites to piercing the corporate veil. However, those factors are not sufficient by themselves to invoke the doctrine for "such factors are common business practice and exist in most parent and subsidiary relationships." Roscoe Turner, supra at 161.

We recognize that the equitable doctrine of piercing the corporate veil is not limited to the parent-subsidiary relationship. The separate identities of affiliated corporations owned by the same parent may be disregarded under proper circumstances. Matter of Bowen Transports, Inc., 551 F.2d 171, 179 (CA7 1977). In any event, it must be shown that another entity actually dominated a sham corporation. Bowen Transports, supra, at 179; Williams v. McAllister Bros., Inc., 534 F.2d 19 (CA2 1976).

ANALYSIS

When the law is applied to the facts of this case, viewed in the light most favorable to appellants, it is apparent that no reasonable jury, having been properly instructed in the law, could have rendered the verdict it did. An examination of the evidence introduced at trial reveals that there is no evidence that Gold Key Builders or its predecessors were shells or sham corporations during the period when appellants and their assignors were dealing with them. Nor is there any evidence of wrong suffered by appellants.

Therefore, at least two elements of appellants' case required by Roscoe Turner were not supplied. It must be conceded that appellants' argument is ingenious; but it is ingenious because it succeeded in confusing the issues and in exaggerating the importance of a few unconnected facts far beyond their real import.

The principal difficulty with appellants' case is the manner in which they seek to hold Oberer Development liable for the obligations of Gold Key Builders. They attempt to accomplish this by two avenues. First, they argue that there was substantial confusion of identity between Gold Key Builders' predecessors (Enco and Anco) and Creative Construction. Because Creative was merged into Oberer Development, they contend that Oberer Development can be held liable for the confusion. Second, they argue that there was a lack of separate identity between Gold Key's predecessors and Oberer Enterprises, and further confusion between Oberer Development. In short, appellants attempt to pierce through Gold Key and its predecessors to Oberer Development by way of Oberer Enterprises.

We deal first with the Creative approach. It is significant that all three of the construction projects were completed and total payment rendered prior to 1977. Although Creative was eventually merged into Oberer Development, until 1977 it was an independent and viable corporation. Oberer Development did not own stock in Creative and there is no evidence Oberer Development dominated Creative in any way. True enough, Creative and Oberer Development had common shareholders and directors, and were both in the business of general contracting and design. However, these facts alone are not sufficient to justify piercing the corporate veil.

Appellants vigorously contend that there was a complete lack of substantive corporate identity between Creative and Gold Key's predecessors. However, the undisputed evidence shows that Creative did remain separate from Gold Key's predecessors. Creative was given the design contract for one of the projects, and there is some evidence to show that it may have become tangentially involved in a consulting capacity with other projects, but absolutely no evidence was introduced to show that Creative was controlled in any way by Gold Key's predecessors. No evidence was introduced to show that Creative did not keep separate financial records, hold separate board and shareholder meetings, have business with corporations other than Gold Key's predecessors, maintain separate bank accounts, list separate phone numbers, or pay its own bills. There is some evidence that an officer of a Gold Key predecessor may have acted on one occasion for Creative during the transition period from his employment with Creative to his new position, but this cannot be considered sufficient to pierce a corporate veil. There is no evidence that either Creative or Gold Key's predecessors were grossly undercapitalized, nor was there any indication that during the period the projects were in progress Creative and Gold Key's predecessors tried to avoid their obligations by hiding behind each other's corporate structures.

There was an instance where Creative received a bill from another company with regard to an entirely different project; a bill which should have been directed to a Gold Key predecessor. However, the uncontradicted testimony revealed that this error by a third party was corrected. Creative did not pay the bill, Gold Key's predecessor paid. There were a couple of other instances of third parties' mistakes in sending documents to one corporation which should properly have been directed to another. Nevertheless, it is crystal clear that Creative maintained a separate corporate identity from Gold Key's predecessors.

We cannot help but note the abundant evidence in the record that CM's officers were experienced businessmen who fully understood the nature of related corporate structures. Time after time they demonstrated their understanding of the separate identities of Creative and Gold Key's predecessors by addressing separate correspondence to each. Moreover, it is not irrelevant that whatever minimal confusion existed between Creative and Gold Key's predecessors was created by the mistakes of third parties and related to entirely different projects. That CM understood the Oberer owned companies to be somewhat related, but was fully aware of their separate corporate identities, is obvious from the evidence.

A similar analysis applies to CM's attempts to reach Oberer Development through Oberer Enterprises, the large group of Oberer owned firms. Appellants failed to introduce any evidence that any of the Oberer group of firms owned the capital stock of each other. No evidence was introduced to show that any of the corporations financed each other or caused incorporation of other corporations. Absolutely no evidence was introduced to show that any of the Oberer Corporations were grossly undercapitalized. No showing was made that the directors or executives of the corporations did not act independently in the interest of each corporation. Finally, there was no evidence introduced to show that the formal legal requirements of the corporations were not observed or that Oberer Enterprises is an entity capable of being sued as a party.

Appellants rely heavily on a letter from George Oberer to a CM officer in which he said that a Gold Key predecessor was closely related to the other Oberer firms and that a problem with a Gold Key predecessor was considered an Oberer problem. This letter is insufficient to provide a basis for holding Oberer Development Company liable for the obligations of another corporation which was far from being a shell or sham corporation. Appellants introduced no evidence to show that Gold Key's predecessors were not observing corporate formalities, were grossly undercapitalized, did not pay their own expenses, did not act independently of the other Oberer firms, or were manipulated by other Oberer corporations.

Appellants also argue that a computer printout from an outside company shows payroll records of Oberer firms. They argue that because "Oberer Construction" was written across the top of the printout and because employees of several Oberer firms appear on the list, they have shown that there was intermingling of employees. However, an examination of the printout reveals that each Oberer firm was given a separate code number and that the employees were separated by the company codes.

We have noted that there was no evidence introduced to show that any of the Oberer firms were not viable corporations at the time the contracts on the nursing homes were signed and during the construction phases of the projects. We consider this lack of evidence important because it shows that appellants failed to meet their burden of showing that the predecessors of Gold Key Builders were shells or sham corporations. It is true that when this action was filed Gold Key Builders was insolvent. But no evidence was presented to show why Gold Key Builders became insolvent. If the assets of Gold Key were raided by Oberer Development, or if some fraud were perpetrated by an Oberer firm to make Gold Key insolvent, then an action to pierce Gold Key's veil might very well be justified. Without such evidence, there simply is no basis from which a jury could find that a wrong had been committed.

In sum, we recognize that one of the primary purposes of the corporate form of business is to insulate shareholders from unlimited liability, and that the power to pierce the corporate veil should be exercised reluctantly and cautiously. DeWitt Truck Brokers, Inc. v. W. Ray Flemming Fruit Co., 540 F.2d 681, 683 (CA4 1976).

CONCLUSION

Inasmuch as the record before us fails to contain substantial evidence of any one or more of the three requirements to pierce a corporate veil as outlined in Steven v. Roscoe Turner Aeronautical Corp., 324 F.2d 157 (CA7 1963), we agree with the district judge and hold that his judgment directing a verdict and giving judgment notwithstanding the verdict must be affirmed.

IT IS SO ORDERED.

SWYGERT, Circuit Judge, dissenting:

The evidence in this case demonstrates conclusively that the corporate veil should be pierced. All of the necessary indicia for such a result exists. Gold Key Builders is a mere instrumentality of the Oberer Development Company. The Oberer enterprises, comprising the parent company and all of the constituent companies (including Gold Key Builders), are owned and controlled by the Oberer family. Third parties dealing with the separate entities had every reason to believe that they were in reality dealing with George R. Oberer and members of his family through their corporate alter egos. Hypertechnical, legalistic distinctions, engaged in by the majority, ought not be used to immunize the Oberer Development Company from a liability it legally and morally owes.

I respectfully dissent.

B. The European Approach

The EC has not attempted to harmonize the law relating to the disregarding of the separate personality of a corporation. It continues to rely on the laws of the Member States for the determination of the circumstances under which the courts will impose liability for the obligations of the corporation. European notions of limiting the protections of limited liability share some commonalities with the American version; but the doctrines applied are not identical. In addition, the approach of the German and French systems are quite different. In considering the materials which follow, all of which concentrate on materials from the United Kingdom and Ireland, determine to what extent the differences in approaches might lead to different results under American and European approaches.

1. European Common Law Approaches

Company Law: Lifting the Veil

Estates Gazette
25 July 1992

Issue No 9229 p 115
SECTION: MAINLY FOR STUDENTS

In what circumstances may the directors of a company be sued rather than the company itself?

Inevitably in the course of professional life surveyors and other property specialists will deal with limited companies. If something goes wrong, who can be sued—the company or the directors?

In Salomon v. Salomon & Co [1897] AC 22, a landmark case, the matter was put beyond doubt. The company has a separate identity. The company is liable for company debts. Aron Salomon (and his boot-making business) achieved for company law what Mrs Carlill (and her smoke ball) achieved for contract law and what Mrs Donoghue (and her adulterated ginger beer) achieved for the law of torts. Salomon transferred his business to a private limited company, and he and six other members of his family subscribed to the company's memorandum; the purchase price was £38,782. Salomon took 20,001 shares and the six other family members took one share each. Debentures to the value of £10,000 were given (and cash was also paid) to Salomon as the balance of the purchase price. The business foundered and was wound up, with liabilities in excess of its assets by £7,733. The company's liquidator claimed the company's business was still Salomon's and that the company was merely a sham to limit Salomon's liability for debts incurred in carrying on the business. He argued that repayment of Salomon's debenture should be postponed until after the company's other creditors had been satisfied.

The House of Lords unanimously held that the company was a separate person in law. Thus was established one of the basic articles of faith of English company law, indeed of company law in all common law systems, that a company is a legal person, independent and distinct from its shareholders and its managers.

This principle of separate identity has been consistently applied. Thus, in the New Zealand case of Lee v. Lee's Air Farming [1961] AC 12 (which went to the Privy Council), Lee owned all the shares (but one) in the company which he founded; his wife held the other. Lee was governing director of the company (whose business was spraying crops from the air). When he was killed in a flying accident while on company business, his widow was held to be entitled to recover compensation from the company for his estate as the company was quite separate and distinct from her husband, its employee. However, like most legal principles, it is a rule that gives way to exceptions. Some of the exceptions have been found to be necessary to counteract specific dangers and abuses and are provided for in legislation. Others are provided for in judicial decisions.

Technical oversights

If a company carries on business without at lease two members, and does so for more than six months, any person who is a member of that company during any period thereafter and who knows that the company is carrying on business with one member, is liable (jointly and severally with the company itself) for any debts of the company contracted during that period: section 24 of the Companies Act 1985.

If a company's seal is used, or if a letter, notice, bill of exchange, order for goods, or money, etc. is issued on behalf of a company and it does not bear the correct company name, the officer or agent who took (or authorized) this action will be liable to the holder of the document bearing the incorrect name unless the company honours the obligation. He is also liable to a fine: section 349(4) of the Companies Act 1985.

Perhaps the most obvious instance of this would be where the word "limited" is omitted from the name of a limited company. Thus, in British Airways Board v. Parish [1979] 2 Lloyd's Rep 361, a director signed a company cheque and failed to put the word "limited" at the end of the company name. The cheque was dishonoured and the payee agreed with the company that it should pay the due amount by instalment. It was held that this did not absolve the director from his statutory liability.

Fraudulent trading

An important exception to the "Salomon" principle of separate identity is what is terms fraudulent trading. If the company's business has been carried on with intent to defraud creditors or for any other fraudulent purpose, the court, on the application of the liquidator, may declare that the persons who were knowingly parties to the fraud are liable to make such contributions (if any) to the company's assets as the court thinks proper: section 213 of the Insolvency Act 1986.

The concept of fraudulent trading was extended in 1985 to take into account wrongful trading. If the winding-up of an insolvent company a past or present director knew, or ought to have known before the commencement of the winding-up, that there was no reasonable prospect that the company could avoid the liquidation, but failed to take every reasonable step to minimise the potential loss to the company's creditors, then the court may declare (on the application of the liquidator) that that person is liable to make such contribution (if any) to the company's assets as the court thinks proper: section 214 of the Insolvency Act 1986.

Group enterprises

A very important exception to the principle of separate personality is provided by situations in which associated companies are treated as the same "group enterprise." Where a relationship of parent company and subsidiary exists (section 736 of the Companies Act 1985) then, in certain situations, the 1985 Act will specify that legal consequences are to follow, e.g. the obligation to prepare and present group accounts will apply to that group enterprise: sections 229 and 230 of the Companies Act 1985.

Some provisions of legislation on company law, particularly those providing remedies for shareholders, may require the courts to "lift the veil" to discover the relationship on which the company was founded. If the company was founded on the basis of participation in management by certain shareholders, this may persuade the court to grant a remedy to an excluded shareholder: see section 459 of the Companies Act 1985; section 122(1)(g) of the Insolvency Act 1986 and Re Westbourne Galleries [1970] 3 All ER 374.

There are other statutory examples of regulations requiring that the veil be lifted. One area where such rules abound is taxation. Legislation has sought to restrict the use of the corporate form to avoid taxation and in some situations a higher tax charge may result.

Apart from these statutory rules the courts have, in certain situations, treated a parent company and its subsidiaries as one entity if they carry on one business. There appears to be no consistent application of this principle, nor indeed any single device for achieving the identification of a "holding company" with a subsidiary. In Smith, Stone & Knight Ltd. v. Birmingham Corporation [1939] 4 All ER 116, the court treated a subsidiary company as the agent of its holding company (an approach which is at odds with the Salomon case). By contrast, in Harold Holdsworth & Co (Wakefield) Ltd. v. Caddies [1955] 1 WLR 352 and DHN Food Distributors Ltd. v. Tower Hamlets London Borough Council [1976] 3 All ER 462, a company was identified with its wholly-owned subsidiary on the basis of their being part of the same "group enterprise."

In the DHN case a company, DHN Food Products, was formed to carry on the business of importing and distributing groceries. The premises from which the company traded were, in fact, owned by Bronze, which became a wholly-owned subsidiary of DHN.' Bronze and DHN had the same directors. When the Tower Hamlets London

Borough Council acquired the property to build houses on the site, compensation was payable under the relevant legislation for loss of title and also for disturbance of the business. However, compensation for disturbance of the business was payable under the express wording of the legislation only if the business disturbed belonged to the titleholder, but in this case the operator of the business and the titleholder were different.

The Court of Appeal treated the companies as one entity. Lord Denning MR said at p 467:

> We all know that in many respects a group of companies are treated together for the purpose of general accounts, balance sheet, and profit-and-loss account. They are treated as one concern...This is especially the case when a parent company owns all the shares of the subsidiaries, so much so that it can control every movement of the subsidiaries.

However, the approach of the courts is not consistent. In Woolfson v. Strathclyde Regional Council (1978) 248 EG 777 the House of Lords refused to lift the veil in a situation that concerned a wholly-owned subsidiary and its holding company.

"Sham" companies

There is, therefore, no consistent thread running through the decided cases but the veil will be lifted to prevent fraud or sharp practice. Thus, in Jones v. Lipman [1962] 1 All ER 442, a vendor of land sought to evade specific performance of a contract for sale by conveying a piece of land to a company which he had specifically purchased for the purpose. The court held that the acquisition of the company and the conveyance of the land to it was a mere "cloak or sham" to evade the contract of sale.

Similarly, in Gilford Motor Co v. Horne [1933] Ch 935, an employee (who was subject to a restraint of trade clause) set up a company to circumvent its provisions. He claimed that the company could not be bound by the restraint clause because it was a separate legal person from himself and it was not a party to the contract between himself and his former employer. He then proceeded to operate from a garage in Highgate, through the company, in competition with his former employer. The company's shares were allotted to his wife and an employee of the company, who were appointed directors. The court held that, since the defendant controlled the company, its formation was a sham and an injunction was issued against him, restraining him from competing through the company.

A similar desire to prevent sharp practice motivated the decision in Re Bugle Press Ltd. [1960] 3 All ER 791. The issued capital of Bugle Press Ltd. was £10,000, of which the two directors (Jackson and Shaw) held £1,000. Jackson and Shaw formed another company, of which they were the only two members, and this company offered to acquire all the shares of Bugle Press Ltd. Jackson and Shaw accepted the offer in respect of their own shareholding and then the new company sought to acquire the applicant's 1,000 shares under the statutory procedure of sections 428 to 430F of the Companies Act 1985. These sections provide that, where a scheme or contract involving the transfer of shares in a company to another company has been approved by the holders of not less than nine-tenths of the shares, the other one-tenth can be compulsorily acquired. The court held that Treby was entitled to a declaration that Jackson and Shaw could not acquire shares because the offeror and the holders of 90% of the acquired company were in reality the same persons.

In housing law a landlord may be required to carry out expensive improvements to a property which is in need of repair. A landlord may be able to resist an order if he can show great hardship. When the landlord is a company with only a little capital the courts will look at the circumstances of those who control the company. As Lord Denning MR said in Hillbank Properties Ltd. v. Hackney London Borough Council (1978) 247 EG 807: He [the judge] should have set aside the corporate veil and have seen the strength of the resources at their [the controllers'] command.

Courts are willing to lift the veil under other circumstances too. Thus, for example, a decision of all the members of a company may be valid as a company decision. To determine whether the decision is one of all the members, the veil has to be lifted: see e.g. Re Express Engineering Works [1920] 1 Ch 466. The veil may also be lifted to determine a company's nationality by reference to the nationality of its members. This was the approach adopted in Re FG Films Ltd. [1953] 1 WLR 483, where the court held that the film Monsoon was not a British film; although the company producing it was incorporated in England, it was controlled by an American corporation. In Daimler Co Ltd. v. Continental Tyre & Rubber Co [Great Britain] Ltd. [1916] 2 AC 307, the House of Lords decided that the company, although incorporated in England, was an enemy alien as its shareholders were all German.

In the realm of criminal law and tort the veil may be lifted to determine whether an act by an individual is in fact the act of the directing mind and will of the company. The rules governing the lifting of the veil are, in general, random and haphazard although some underlying themes—to prevent fraud (and/or to help the Revenue!)—may be discerned. but it is not true to say that the corporate veil cannot be pierced. As Lord Denning said in Littlewoods Mail Order Store Ltd. v. McGregor [1969] 3 All ER 855:

The corporate veil has often been supposed to cast a veil over the personality of a limited company through which the courts cannot see. But this is not true. The courts can and often do draw aside the veil. They can and often do pull off the mask. They look to see what really lies behind.

Consider the differences between the American approaches to inter-corporate liability on a contract theory that we have been considering and those represented in the cases which follow:

Sidney Taylor, Plaintiff, v. Philip Smyth, Kape Investments Limited, Calla Associates Limited and Northern Bank Limited, Defendants

[1981 No. 4617P and S.C. Nos. 172/173/174 of 1989]
Supreme Court; [1991] IR 158
27 February 1990; 5 July 1990

PANEL: Finlay C.J., Hederman, McCarthy, JJ.

Finlay C.J. :

I agree with the judgment to be delivered by McCarthy J.

Hederman J.:

I agree.

McCarthy J.:

In his judgment in the High Court, Lardner J. detailed the somewhat complicated facts underlying these proceedings. Whilst the notices of appeal challenge in detail many of the inferences drawn from the facts as he found them, it is not suggested therein nor in the course of the hearing itself that any of the primary facts found by him are not open on the evidence. I therefore gratefully accept the summary of facts set out in his careful and comprehensive judgment delivered on the 20 December, 1988.

By agreement between the parties, the arguments on the hearing of this appeal were first presented on behalf of Kape. Mr. Brady S.C. submitted that Lardner J. was wrong in:-

(1) the finding of conspiracy;

(2) the finding of breach of contract;

(3) the assessment of damages;

(4) the order over for costs.

In supporting these submissions, in part, Mr. Callanan, counsel for Philip Smyth, stated that his client is sensitive to what is termed the opprobrium of being found party to a civil conspiracy. This, I think, springs from an understandable but mistaken belief that the word "conspiracy" in this context has overtones of the criminal law. This is not so. If a tort or a breach of contract be committed by two or more persons or bodies who agree to do the particular act or to do it in a particular way, who act, as it is said, in concert, then there is a conspiracy which may, in circumstances that I shall later outline, be an actionable wrong. If opprobrium there be, it derives more from the nature of the wrong agreed to be done rather than from the agreement to do it; this is all the more so where, as here, the conspiracy is alleged between Mr. Smyth as an individual and one or other or more of the companies which he controls, a question to which I now turn. It is argued that since, apart from the banks, the several companies involved in the transaction where wholly controlled by Mr. Smyth, he cannot, in law, so to speak, conspire with himself. He, it is said, is "the sole controlling agent and mind."

1. Conspiracy

(a) The legal fiction. The principle defined in Saloman v. Saloman & Co. [1897] A.C. 22, which was a case of a "one man" company, has been qualified on many occasions but, as I understand it, remains the law—that a company legally incorporated does not cease to be an independent legal entity, separate and distinct from the individual members of the company, simply because it is wholly controlled by one individual. But, it is said, Mr. Smyth cannot conspire with himself, which is the reality of the allegation insofar as it is said that he conspired with Kape, with Calla, or with Calder all of which companies he controls; reliance is placed upon a decision on trial made by Nield J. in Reg. v. McDonnell [1966] 1 Q.B. 233 where a criminal charge of conspiracy was brought against the defendant and it was contended that there could be no conspiracy because there were not two persons and two minds involved. Nield J. emphasized that it was not a company which was being proceeded against but an individual defendant and, of course, that it was a criminal trial. He concluded at p. 246 that, whilst an indictment for a common law conspiracy to defraud would lie against a limited company, "the true position is that a company and a director cannot be convicted of conspiracy when the only human being who is said to have broken the law or intended to do so is the one director, and that is the situation in the present case." No authority was cited in support of extending this proposition to an action for civil conspiracy. In principle, it would seem invidious, for example, that the assets of a limited company should not be liable to answer for conspiracy where its assets had been augmented as a result of the action alleged to constitute the conspiracy. Essentially, it would be permitting the company to lift its corporate veil as and when it suits. The matter is not devoid of authority. In Belmont Finance (No. 1) v. Williams Furniture [1979] Ch. 250, Williams Furniture owned City Industrial Finance which owned Belmont, whose majority directors were the seventh and eighth defendants. Four other defendants owned Maximum and wanted to purchase Belmont. They agreed to sell Maximum to Belmont for £500,000 and to purchase Belmont from City Industrial for £489,000. The Belmont directors resolved to implement this agreement and the transaction was completed. Belmont went into liquidation and its receiver sued alleging that the value of Maximum was only £60,000 but that the price of £500,000 for Maximum had been arrived at to enable those four defendants to purchase Belmont with money provided by Belmont, in contravention of the Companies Act. It was held that since Belmont was a victim of the alleged conspiracy and the essence of the agreement was to deprive it of a large part of its assets, the knowledge of its directors that the agreement was illegal was not to be imputed to Belmont merely because they were directors of Belmont. Therefore, Belmont was not a party to the conspiracy. The trial judge had held that the claim in conspiracy failed in limine on the ground that one party to a conspiracy to do an unlawful act cannot sue a co-conspirator in relation to that act. In the course of his judgment, Buckley L.J. said at p. 260:

> "I shall deal first with the conspiracy claim. The plaintiff company's argument is to the following effect: on the allegations in the statement of claim, the agreement was illegal, and they say that an agreement between two or more persons to effect any unlawful purpose, with knowledge of all the facts which are necessary ingredients of illegality, is a conspiracy; and we were referred to Crofter Hand Woven Harris Tweed Co. Ltd. v. Veitch [1942] A.C. 435 and Reg. v. Churchill (No. 2) [1967] 2 A.C. 224. The agreement was carried out, and damaged the plaintiff company.

In the course of the argument in this court counsel for the first and second defendants conceded that the plaintiff company is entitled in this appeal to succeed on the conspiracy point, unless it is debarred from doing so on the ground that it was a party to the conspiracy, which was the ground that was relied on by the judge.

The plaintiff company points out that the agreement was resolved on by a board of which the seventh and eighth defendants constituted the majority, and that they were the two directors who countersigned the plaintiff company's seal on the agreement, and that they are sued as two of the conspirators. It is conceded by Mr. Miller for the plaintiff company that a company may be held to be a participant in a criminal conspiracy, and that the illegality attending a conspiracy cannot relieve the company on the ground that such an agreement may be ultra vires; but he says that to establish a conspiracy to which the plaintiff was a party, having as its object the doing of an illegal act, it must be shown that the company must be treated as knowing all the facts relevant to the illegality; he relies on Reg. v. Churchill (No. 2) [1967] 2 A.C. 224.

The plaintiff in its reply denies being a party to the conspiracy and, says Mr. Miller, it would be for the defendants to allege the necessary knowledge on the part of the plaintiff company. But he further submits that even if the plaintiff company should be regarded as a party to the conspiracy, this would not debar it from relief; and he relies on Oram v. Hutt [1914] 1 Ch. 98."

The point now under consideration in this appeal did not expressly arise in Belmont Finance (No. 1) v. Williams Furniture [1979] Ch. 250, but it must underlie the entire of the argument and judgment in it. The basis of that case was that the separate legal entity of the company may, in law, conspire with those directors who, in effect, control it. In Lennard's Carrying Co. Ltd. v. Asiatic Petroleum Co. Ltd. [1915] A.C. 705 Viscount Haldane L.C. said at p. 713:-

> "...a corporation is an abstraction. It has no mind of its own any more than it has a body of its own; its active and directing will must consequently be sought in the person of somebody who for some purposes may be called an agent, but who is really the directing mind and will of the corporation, the very ego and centre of the personality of the corporation."

Judgment Accordingly.

In reading the case that follows, consider whether English courts make the distinction between contract and tort bases for piercing the corporate veil that American courts sometimes make.

Monarch Airlines Engineering Ltd. v. Intercon (Cattle-meats) Ltd.

Queen's Bench Division (Official Referees' Business)
(1986) 11 Con LR 58; 27 June 1985

His Honour Judge James Fox-Andrews QC

The plaintiff in this action, Monarch, applies for an Order under Order 15 that Herr Dieter Dobler, Herr Gunther Dobler, Friedrich Dobler, KG and Mr. Paedrig O'Toole, should be made parties to this action.

The provisions of Order 15 under which this application is made... provide:

> [4(2)] "Where the Plaintiff in any action claims any relief to which any other person is entitled jointly with him, all persons so entitled must, subject to the provisions of any Act and unless the Court gives leave to the contrary, be parties to the action and any of them who does not consent to be joined as a Plaintiff must, subject to any Order made by the Court on an application for leave under this paragraph, be made a Defendant.
>
> [6(2)] Subject to the provisions of this Rule, at any stage of the proceedings in any cause or matter the Court may on such terms as it thinks just and either of its own motion or on application:
>
> (b) Order any of the following persons to be added as a party, namely:
>
> (i) Any person who ought to have been joined as a party or whose presence before the Court is necessary to ensure that all matters in dispute in the cause of the matter may be effectually and completely determined and adjudicated upon, or
>
> (ii) Any person between whom and any party to the cause or matter there may exist a question or issue arising out of or relating to or connected with any relief or remedy claimed in the cause or matter which in the opinion of the Court it would be just and convenient to determine as between him and that party as well as between the parties to the cause or matter."

The object of making these persons additional parties is that in the event of Monarch succeeding on the defendant's counterclaim it may have other pockets out of which to obtain its costs than from the defendant, Intercon, which is insolvent.

The action arises out of an aircraft crash that occurred at Shannon on the 30 July 1977. The aircraft, a Britannia, was owned by Intercon. Monarch took proceedings against Intercon for monies allegedly due to it for maintenance and engineering services provided to Intercon. In those proceedings on 26 June 1978 by way of counterclaim Intercon sued Monarch for damages on the grounds that Monarch was responsible for the aircraft's loss.

In the event there was a split trial, the liability issue of which was determined by McCullogh J on 18 February 1982. He held in favour of Intercon.

An appeal to the Court of Appeal by Monarch against that decision failed. A petition to the House of Lords for leave to appeal was subsequently abandoned.

The result of McCullogh J's judgment was that Monarch paid Intercon approximately £297000. The effect of that judgment was that any cause of action Monarch had against Intercon merged in the judgment. The balance of Intercon's claim was transferred to an official referee. The quantum issue came before me on 20 May 1985.

I have already heard certain evidence in the course of this trial. What I say in the course of this judgment in no way constitutes findings of fact by me but merely provides the matrix in which I have considered this application. I have heard the evidence of Mr. O'Toole. He has had extensive experience in the cattle trade, both in the Republic of Ireland and elsewhere. He was the managing director of Intercon, which had been incorporated in 1973. This company, however, did not trade thereafter for some years. I have heard the evidence in chief of Herr Dieter Dobler and part of his cross-examination. Herr Dieter and his brother Gunther worked in a company called Friedrich Dobler KG, a company carrying on business in Bavaria, West Germany, and bearing their father's name.

Herr Dieter and Mr. O'Toole had a wide business relationship going back to 1971. The evidence I have heard so far indicates that Mr. O'Toole in his personal capacity probably acted as agent to Friedrich Dobler KG until the end of 1975 or early 1976.

It is unnecessary to describe fully this business relationship. It underwent change as the years went by.

As a result of discussions between the Doblers on the one hand and Mr. O'Toole on the other Intercon was activated in 1976 with finance provided from Herr Dieter and Herr Gunther from monies probably coming from Friedrich Dobler KG. With those moneys Intercon purchased an aircraft. That aircraft was to be used principally for the carriage of cattle for Friedrich Dobler KG for which services Intercon was to be paid.

The shareholding in Intercon is conveniently set out in paragraph 5 of the contributor's petition presented to the Irish High Court on 13 July 1979 by Herr Dieter and Herr Gunther Dobler. Suffice it is to say that the Dobler interest was 45 per cent of Intercon's issued share capital. The rest of the shares were held by Irish shareholders. It has not been suggested so far in this trial that Mr. O'Toole held his 22 per cent of these shares or any of the other Irish shareholders held their shares or any part of them in trust for the Dobler interest. Herr Dieter and Herr Gunther Dobler were directors of Intercon.

There is no evidence before me that Mr. O'Toole or Intercon were shareholders of Friedrich Dobler KG or any associated or subsidiary company of Dobler KG, nor is it suggested that Mr. O'Toole was a director in any of the Dobler Companies.

The audited accounts show that Intercon was indebted to Herr Dieter and Herr Gunther in very large sums of money. In comparison the company's indebtedness to Mr. O'Toole and other Irish directors was extremely modest.

This application is made under three heads: Order 15, r 4(2); Order 5, r 6(2)(b)(i) and r 6(2)(b)(ii).

Mr Sparrow in his application dealt with Order 15, r 6(2) first. Since it is convenient to do so I propose to follow that course.

Mr Sparrow contends that the objects of r 6(2)(b)(i) are to ensure both that the real parties are before the court and that there should be a final determination of all matters in dispute; r 6(2)(b)(ii) appears to me to be directed to achieving a similar result.

It is not contended that without the addition of some or all of these further persons Intercon's claim would be unenforceable. The duty of the court it appears to me is that, in the absence of special circumstances, the addition of parties, where they are necessary as set out in r 6(2)(b)(i) or between them and a party to the action there may exist a question or issue of the kind indicated in r 6(2)(b)(ii), should be allowed.

It is I think of some assistance to consider how Gower in his Principles of Modern Company Law, 4th edition at p 123 deals with the matter:

"UNDER CASE LAW

Efforts by the judges to lift the veil have, in general, been hamstrung by Salomon v. Salomon & Co Ltd. [1897] AC 22 which finally destroyed the possibility of regarding a 'one man company' as a mere alias of, or agent for, the principal shareholder...

Nevertheless, there have been exceptional cases in which the courts have felt willing or compelled to lift the veil and in recent years there have, perhaps, been signs of less reluctance to do.

AGENCY

In the first place, there is no reason why, in fact, a company should not act as an agent of its shareholders. Where there is an express agreement to this effect, no difficulty arises. This will be a rare occurrence. More often the courts will be asked to infer an agency relationship and Salomon shows how difficult it would be to persuade them to draw this inference. Nevertheless, they have always shown less reluctance to do so where the inference they are asked to draw is that a subsidiary company has acted as agent for its owning company. In this respect judicial action agitated the legislative intervention dealt with above. Examples are discussed below under the heading 'Associated Companies'.

When, however, they have been asked to treat the company as agent of its individual controlling shareholder and to make the shareholder liable on that basis then not being willing to do so except where that is necessary to frustrate some grave impropriety, and in such circumstances they have coupled the description of the company as an agent with more pejorative descriptions, such as 'share', 'cloak', 'device', 'stratagem', 'puppet', 'creature', etc. In truth they themselves seem to have been using a cloak, that of agency principles, to give respectability to the use of a sledge hammer. These examples are dealt with under the heading 'fraud' or 'improper conduct'.

This difference in practice between cases concerning controlling companies and those concerning controlling individuals is rarely made explicit in judgments but is clearly discernible and makes good sense. If a limited company is treated as an agent for whose acts its human corporators are liable as principals, the main object of incorporation is defeated: if, however, these corporators operate through a pyramid of limited companies, their objective is less likely to be defeated if the holding company is made responsible for the acts of its subsidiaries—it may indeed by promoted—and the corporators will not lose the advantage of limited liability."

The circumstances in which a corporate veil will be lifted can best be considered under a number of heads:

(1) Fraud or improper conduct

Monarch disclaimed that Intercon was a sham company or was an instrument of fraud. It is therefore unnecessary for me to consider the line of authorities on this aspect.

(2) Trust

As already indicated there has been no suggestion in this trial that Mr. O'Toole or any of the Irish directors held all or any of his or their shares in trust.

(3) Agents generally and associated companies in particular

Since it may be material on the question as to the time at which this application was made it is I think of assistance to indicate briefly the matters relied upon by Mr. Sparrow.

Reliance is placed first on certain statements made by Herr Dieter Dobler in the course of his evidence. The statements relied upon include:

"Our own transport system"; "buy our Airline"; "buy our own aeroplane"; "we were asked by the Authorities in Germany to show that we actually owned an aircraft and would do the work."

Second, reliance is placed on the fact that there had been a principal/agent relationship between Friedrich Dobler, KG and Mr. O'Toole prior to 1976 and that Herr Dieter Dobler in the course of his evidence had said that that relationship was still good today.

Third, reliance was placed upon a letter written by Friedrich Dobler KG to Jorg, a competitor, on 14 April 1977 where Friedrich Dobler KG used the expression "Our Irish airline Intercon."

Fourth, reliance is placed upon the audited accounts of Intercon which showed the Doblers to be creditors in the sum of £272 000 whereas the Irish directors were creditors only in very small amounts.

It was urged upon me by Monarch that I should look at the realities of the situation and although Mr. Sparrow was loath to use the expression "that I should pierce the corporate veil." In particular, he relied on a passage of Cotton LJ in Edison & Swan United Electric Light v. Holland [1889] 41 Ch 28.

The Court of Appeal was similarly and successfully urged in DHN Food Distributors Ltd. v. London Borough of Tower Hamlets [1976] 3 All ER 462. But the facts of that case and the present could hardly be more different.

I can find no common identity or community of interest between Intercon and the Dobler interests.

My attention has also been drawn to Salomon v. Salomon & Co Ltd. [1897] AC 22 at pp 30, 31 and 42. As Gower indicates Salomon has been distinguished in a number of respects. But it still remains fons et origo of the principle that in the absence of special circumstances the corporate entity of a limited company remains intact.

My attention was drawn to Smith Stone & Knight Ltd. v. Birmingham Corporation [1939] 3 All ER 116, at p 120. Reliance was also placed on the decision of the House of

Lords in Ebrahimi v. Westbourne Galleries [1973] AC 360 and, in particular, the speech of Lord Wilberforce.

In the ordinary way in the absence of express agreement in circumstances such as these agency is only likely to arise where the alleged principal holds a majority of the shares, that is to say has a controlling interest in the alleged agent. There may be circumstances where the absence of a controlling interest will not prevent the court from lifting the corporate veil. This may occur particularly where there is a dispute between shareholders such as was the case in Ebrahimi. However, it seems to me that in the absence of a controlling interest the circumstances where the veil would be lifted must be special and, indeed, rare. It is noteworthy in Stone & Knight Ltd. v. Birmingham Corporation that the parent company owned 497 of the 502 issued shares of the subsidiary.

I do not find that the presence before the court of these additional parties or any of them are or is necessary within Order 15, r 6(2)(b)(i) to ensure that all matters in dispute in the present case may be effectually and completely determined and adjudicated upon by the court. I am not satisfied there is any likelihood of further litigation if I refuse this application. There will be finality if the action proceeds as presently constituted.

I turn therefore to consider Order 15, r 6(2)(b)(ii). Although under r 6(2)(b)(i) the court should not go beyond enquiring whether there is a genuine issue to be tried—see Long v. Crossley [1879] 13 Ch D 388—it seems to me that different considerations arise where the application is under Order 15, r 6(2)(b)(ii) and, in particular, where the application is made in the course of a trial.

I do not find the matters relied upon by Mr. Sparrow raise a prima facie case of there being a principal/agent relationship from 1976 onwards. Deplorable though the lack of contemporaneous accounting documentation is, such documents as I have seen point strongly against any such relationship. The language used by Herr Dieter Dobler is just as consistent with an arm's-length business relationship as with one of principal/agent.

It is common for someone holding a substantial interest in a company to adopt a proprietorial attitude towards that company or its assets. I also have regard to the fact that all Herr Dieter's evidence has been given through an interpreter. The whole tenor of the evidence I have heard from Mr. O'Toole and Herr Dieter is strongly against the principal/agent relationship. The fact that it is sought to join so many additional parties is a significant factor indicating the uncertainty of the alleged relationships. A letter to Jorg and the audited accounts above referred to have been in the hands of Monarch for many months.

But for the decision I have reached, I would have adjourned the application so that it was supported by affidavit evidence as required by r 6(3).

The only cogent explanation as to why the application was not made until trial is that Herr Dieter Dobler made the statements above referred to together with others. But it is clear from much that was addressed to me by Mr. Sparrow that suspicions about the relationship between Dobler and Intercon had been harboured for a substantial period. The question or issue could and should have been raised a long time ago if it was to be raised at all.

The application was made on 4 June 1985. This was the fifth day of the trial which was adjourned on 23 May because of the Whitsun break. It is a trial which should have commenced many months ago.

The events giving rise to this quantum claim occurred some seven and three-quarter years ago. It is made three and a half years after the judgment on liability at a trial at which none of the proposed additional parties were represented. Monarch's cause of action against Intercon merged in the judgment of 18 February 1982. Such cause of action, if any, by Monarch against these additional parties based on a joint liability was also then extinguished. This application is really no more than an endeavour to obtain by one route what Monarch has already failed to obtain by another, namely, security for costs.

The delay that would result from acceding to this application must be considerable. A ten-day hearing estimate even without legal arguments was probably a substantial under-estimate. Obtaining a hearing date for a 15–20 day trial would be likely to result in a 1986 hearing. The time spent on the present trial with all its costs would be thrown away. Considerable costs in having further parties represented would be incurred. It may be that in any event these additional persons would have limitation defenses.

I do not consider it just or convenient to determine between these additional parties and existing parties the issue whether or not there was a principal/agent relationship at the material time. Indeed, I think it would be most unjust to do so and a grave embarrassment to Intercon.

I turn, therefore, finally to consider Order 15, r 4(2). It seems to me that this sub-rule is dealing with the position where either there is no dispute on joint entitlement or where, prima facie, two people are jointly entitled. I derive support for the latter from the third paragraph of note 15/4/9 on p 172 of the White Book.

Where there is no prima facie evidence of joint entitlement but its existence may be in issue then in an appropriate case an order may be made under Order 15, r 6(2)(b)(ii). But as I have already indicated I do not consider that this is an appropriate case for such an order.

On my interpretation of this sub-rule it has no application because there is no prima facie case that these parties or either of them are jointly entitled with Intercon.

But if I am wrong as to that, its apparent mandatory terms are qualified by the power given to the court to excuse the addition of a party. I exercise the discretion I have against Monarch for the reasons already indicated.

DISPOSITION:

In the ordinary way, in the absence of express agreement, a limited liability company will only be treated as agent of a shareholder where the alleged principal has a controlling interest in the alleged agent. In the absence of such a controlling interest the circumstances where the corporate veil will be lifted would be special and rare.

---

2. *Common Law Liability for Obligations of Related Corporations Outside the U.S.*

In the cases that follow, the courts considered the basis for liability between related entities. As you read the cases, think about whether the standard is the same in their context as applied when the ultimate liable party is a natural person.

The State [at the Prosecution of Thomas McInerney and Company Limited] v. The County Council of the County of Dublin

High Court
[1985] IR 1, [1985] ILRM 513
12 December, 1984

Carroll J.:

On the 26th January, 1982, Thomas McInerney and Company Limited [the prosecutor] entered into a contract to buy the lands comprised in Folio 1170 County Dublin comprising a property known as Cappagh House and approximately fifteen acres of land for £750,000.00. The prosecutor is a wholly owned subsidiary of McInerney Properties Limited [referred to as the parent company]. An application for planning permission was made on the 9th March, 1982. The sale of the property was completed on the 15th April, 1982, and the property was conveyed at the direction of the prosecutor to McInerney Construction Limited [referred to as the registered owner], which was another wholly owned subsidiary of the parent company. Planning permission was refused on the 4th June, 1982. An appeal against refusal to An Bord Pleanala [the Board] was refused on the 12th March, 1984.

A purchase notice dated the 4th April, 1984 was served by the prosecutor by registered post addressed to the County Manager at the principal office of the respondent [the County Council] in O'Connell Street, Dublin, and was delivered on the 5th April, 1984. It was received in the Planning Department of the County Council on the 9th April, 1984. The Planning Department, by letter dated the 10th April, acknowledged having received the notice on the 9th April. The County Council served notice on the 6th July, 1984, refusing to purchase the land.

The prosecutor's case is that the County Council had only three months from the service of the purchase notice to serve a notice refusing to purchase. Since it did not do so in time, it must now purchase the lands.

The prosecutor obtained a conditional order of mandamus on the 27th July, 1984. The County Council has shown cause by affidavit. A number of supporting affidavits were filed by both parties.

The relevant section is § 29 of the Local Government [Planning and Development] Act, 1963, as amended by § 14, subs. 5, of the Local Government [Planning and Development] Act, 1976, which transferred the functions of the Minister under § 29 to the Board....

The definition of owner in § 2 of the Local Government [Planning and Development] Act, 1963, is also relevant. In the Act "owner" , in relation to land, means a person, other than a mortgagee not in possession, who, whether in his own right or as trustee or agent for any other person, is entitled to receive the rackrent of the land or, where the land is not let at a rackrent, would be so entitled if it were so let.

There are four relevant points at issue between the parties.

[1] The County Council claims the notice was served by a person who is not the owner within the meaning of the section and the notice is therefore invalid. The prosecutor claims that because the prosecutor and the registered owner are subsidiaries of the

parent company, the corporate veil should be lifted and the prosecutor should be considered to be the "owner" within the meaning of section 29.

[2] The County Council claims that the purchase notice was not served until the 9th April, 1984, when it was received in the Planning Department. The prosecutor claims that service was effected when the letter was delivered at the principal office of the County Council on the 5th April.

[3] The County Council claims that the prosecutor has not exhausted all the remedies available and is therefore not entitled to the relief sought. The six month period from the refusal of the appeal by the Board had not elapsed and there was time to serve another purchase notice which would have been answered promptly. The prosecutor says that as the County Council failed to serve a notice refusing to buy within the statutory period there can be no valid hearing by the Board on the refusal to purchase. Therefore the statutory remedy provided by the Act cannot operate.

[4] The County Council claims there is no default procedure where the notice in reply to the purchase notice is not served within three months and that the prosecutor's remedy is for breach of statutory duty. The prosecutor claims that even though no default procedure is provided for on the failure of a planning authority to give notice, the logical consequence of failing to serve notice in time is that a valid notice refusing to purchase cannot be served out of time and therefore the County Council must purchase.

The first point concerns the identity of the "owner." One of the cases relied on by Mr. Blayney was Smith Stone and Knight Limited v. Birmingham Corporation [1939] 4 All E.R. 116. In a claim for compensation for disturbance on compulsory acquisition by a parent company in respect of land held by a subsidiary, it was held that possession by a separate legal entity was not conclusive on the question of a right to claim; and as the subsidiary company was not operating on its own behalf but on behalf of the parent company, the parent company was the party to claim compensation. Atkinson J. said that the subsidiary was the agent in all respects for the parent company and the parent company could at any time say they would carry on business in their own name.

I do not think this advances the prosecutor's claim. It merely establishes that if a subsidiary acts as agent, the principal/parent company is entitled to claim compensation. This would also be allowed under § 29 since the definition of "owner" allows the purchase notice to be served by the person who is or would be entitled to receipt of the rackrent whether as beneficiary, trustee or agent. In this case the prosecutor does not claim to be any of those.

Another case cited was D.H.N. Food Distributors Limited v. Tower Hamlets London Borough Council [1976] 1 W.L.R. 852. The passage relied on by Mr. Blayney is from the judgment of Lord Denning MR at p. 860:—

"Third, lifting the corporate veil. A further very interesting point was raised by Mr. Dobry on company law. We all know that in many respects a group of companies are treated together for the purpose of general accounts, balance sheet, and profit and loss account. They are treated as one concern. Professor Gower in Modern Company Law, third edition [1969], p. 216 says:—'There is evidence of a general tenancy to ignore the separate legal entities of various companies within a group, and to look instead at the economic entity of the whole group.'

This is especially the case when a parent company owns all the shares of the subsidiaries—so much so that it can control every movement of the subsidiaries. These subsidiaries are bound hand and foot to the parent company and must do just what the parent company says. A striking instance is the decision of the House of Lords in Harold Holdsworth and Co. [Wakefield] Ltd.v. Caddies [1955] 1 W.L.R. 352. So here. This group is virtually the same as a partnership in which all the three companies are partners. They should not be treated separately so as to be defeated on a technical point. They should not be deprived of the compensation which should justly be payable for disturbance. The three companies should, for present purposes, be treated as one, and the parent company D.H.N. should be treated as that one. So D.H.N. are entitled to claim compensation accordingly. It was not necessary for them to go through a conveyancing device to get it.

I realise that the President of the Lands Tribunal, in view of previous cases, felt it necessary to decide as he did. But now that the matter has been fully discussed in this court, we must decide differently from him. These companies as a group are entitled to compensation not only for the value of the land, but also compensation for disturbance. I would allow the appeal accordingly."

The facts in that case were that there were three companies—a parent company which ran the business, a subsidiary which owned the land, and another subsidiary which owned the vehicles. The lands were compulsorily acquired and as a result the business closed down and the three companies went into liquidation.

The considerations in this case are entirely different. In my opinion the corporate veil is not a device to be raised and lowered at the option of the parent company or group. The arm which lifts the corporate veil must always be that of justice. If justice requires [as it did in the D.H.N. Case] the courts will not be slow to treat a group of subsidiary companies and their parent company as one. But can it be said that justice requires it in this case?

We have here a parent company with thirty subsidiary companies forming the McInerney Group. According to Mr. Cody, the Finance Director of the parent company, it is group policy, depending on circumstances, to operate in the name of one of these companies on various sites throughout the country. He says that McInerney Construction Limited [the registered owner] has no resources other than those supplied by another subsidiary. The purchase moneys were provided by the prosecutor, "it being the intention that such moneys be repaid in due course out of the proceeds of realisation."

When those averments are considered, it appears to me that here there is a group of companies operated so as to maximise the benefits to be gained from the individual corporate identity of each subsidiary. If the purchase money was to be repaid out of the proceeds of realisation, it follows that the profits [or losses] remained with the registered owner. If the development was not profitable, the loss would be confined within the assets of that one company.

If the relationship of trustee and beneficiary exists between the registered owner and the prosecutor so as to entitle the prosecutor to receive the rents and profits as beneficial owner, that is not so stated. It appears that all the prosecutor is entitled to is to be reimbursed the purchase money out of the proceeds of realisation. If the prosecutor has lent the money to the registered owner secured by mortgage, then it is a mortgagee not in possession and is excluded from the definition of "owner." The affidavit of Mr. Cody is silent as to how the money is secured [if at all]. If the prosecutor has simply lent the money and it is not secured by mortgage, it has no right to receive the rents and profits. Nowhere is it averred that agency exists in relation to receipt of the rents and profits of these lands as between the prosecutor and the registered owner.

In my opinion this is not a case where justice demands that the corporate veil be lifted. The prosecutor, and through it the parent company and the McInerney Group, became aware in time to serve a purchase notice in the name of the "owner" as defined by the Act. But it refused to do so because the plum which it was believed had fallen into its corporate lap would be taken away and would not be permitted to fall again into the lap of the "owner." It is not for a corporate group to claim that the veil should be lifted to illuminate one aspect of its business while it should be left in situ to isolate the individual actions of its subsidiaries in other respects.

Therefore I am of opinion that the purchase notice to be served under §29 was not served by the "owner" as required by that section and the notice dated the 4th April, 1984, is therefore invalid.

* * *

Re A Company Ltd; SIB Ltd. v. Vwagh

Court of Appeal, (Civil Division)
[1985] BCLC 333, [1983–85] BCC 99, 421
3 April 1985

CUMMING-BRUCE LJ: On 22 October 1982 on the application of the plaintiffs, Sir Neil Lawson, sitting as a judge of the High Court, made a series of orders whereby he ordered discovery by interrogatories of an unusually extensive and detailed character, to be answered by the first defendant, and imposed injunctions against him restraining him from disposing of shares in foreign companies and of his rights, interests and benefits under the terms of trusts entitled to English assets or to shares in foreign or English companies entitled to any English assets, and from directing or procuring disposal or charge of English assets by any such company or trust. The terms of the orders are more far-reaching than is usual, as they extend to disclosure of information about the operation of foreign companies and trusts and restraints on the disposal by the first defendant of any of his shares of other interest in such foreign corporations or trusts.

The judge did not give any formal judgment when making an order in terms of the plaintiffs' amended summons. We have a note agreed by counsel for the plaintiffs and the first defendant. The note informs us that in the course of the argument and prior to making the order Sir Neil Lawson made the following observations: that on the evidence before the court with regards to trusts 1, 2, 3 and 4 it was perfectly plain that they were devices to conceal the assets of the first defendant and his relatives; that the activities of the first defendant had to be regarded with the greatest suspicion, and that he was satisfied that the plaintiffs were entitled to the relief sought in the amended summons, subject to a period of 42 days for the making and serving of the affidavit of the first defendant.

On the application of counsel for the first defendant for a stay pending appeal as to the order for discovery the judge made an observation that on the evidence before him he was quite satisfied that all the companies and bodies were vehicles for the defendant. By his order Sir Neil Lawson granted a stay on his orders for discovery.

The first defendant appeals. The grounds pleaded in the notice of appeal challenge the jurisdiction to make those orders, and plead that the orders are oppressive and unwarranted extension of the jurisdiction to make Mareva injunctions and of the power to order discovery in aid thereof. It is pleaded that the judge erred in treating the first defendant in effect as if he was a judgment debtor.

In order to appreciate and analyse the submissions made to us on the hearing of the appeal it was necessary first to consider the material before us in the pleadings in the action for deceit and/or compensation for breach of constructive trust and/or fiduciary duty, and the evidence filed in support of the applications before the judge. The evidence is somewhat massive and extremely detailed. It discloses an elaborate and most ingenious scheme brought into operation at the instance of the first defendant, whereby his personal assets were organised in such a way that they were held by foreign and English corporations and trusts in a manner that effectively conceals his true beneficial interest in English assets. At this stage the plaintiffs' case that the first defendant brought into existence an elaborate structure of corporations and trusts operated the same in order to make it impracticable for the liquidators of the plaintiff companies to reap the fruits of any legal proceedings they might take it necessarily founded on inference from such still incomplete material as the liquidators have been able to obtain. The affidavits of Mr. W, Mr. J and Mr. B with their exhibits afford strong primary evidence that at the date when the first defendant realised that the affairs of the plaintiff companies were insolvent the first defendant was procuring his agents and associates to ensure that all his interests in real property in England and other English assets were transferred out of his apparent legal and beneficial ownership. The network of interlocking companies and trusts had already been created; after the alleged fraud in the statement of claim the network appears to have been used as a device to prevent the plaintiffs from realising the fruits of the proceedings now brought, which proceedings were to be anticipated by the first defendant if and when the fraud instigated in December 1980 was discovered after the insolvency of the plaintiffs had led to the investigation by the liquidators of the affairs of those companies.

The evidence comprised in the plaintiffs' affidavits with their exhibits was for reasons of convenience illustrated by this court by three diagrams entitled figures 1, 2 and 3 appended to this judgment [see diagrams in original], which are designed to demonstrate the way in which the first defendant arranged his affairs so that his English assets should be put outside the reach of his creditors, including the plaintiffs as judgment debtors, in the contingency of judgment being given against him in proceedings instituted by the liquidators of the plaintiff companies. By the mechanism of shares held by nominees and of trusts in which the first defendant is nowhere named as beneficiary in trust deeds which give the trustees power to add to the beneficiaries an appearance is given of a legal and beneficial holding of the English assets which is independent of the first defendant. But the exhibits to the affidavits establish a strong prima facie case that the whole structure is but a facade behind which the first defendant was able to control and manipulate the operations of the company directors and trustees who purported to exercise independent powers. That was evidently the view of the judge is shown by his observation, in the course of argument before him and before making his order, to the effect that he was quite satisfied that on the evidence all the companies and bodies were vehicles for the first defendant, and that was perfectly plain that the trusts were devices to conceal the assets of the first defendant and his relatives.

There were inferences of fact which the judge was entitled to draw if the evidence of primary fact supported the inference. The order that he made, taken with his observations prior to making the order, shows that he drew these inferences. We have not found it easy to apprehend and analyse the evidence before the judge. The task of tracing the interest of the first defendant in English assets through the elaborate network used to conceal it involves some effort, due to the ingenuity of the legal and equitable construction. But the evidence is clear enough at this stage that the whole construction is but a facade used to place the English assets outside the reach of the first defendant's creditors, including the plaintiffs, if judgment is obtained by them as prayed in the statement of claim.

With these introductory observations we consider the submissions made on behalf of the first defendant.

Counsel for the first defendant (Mr Moss) founded his submission in relation to the limits of the judicial discretion conferred on the court by § 37 of the Supreme Court Act 1981 on propositions to be collected from the judgments and decision in four well-known cases: A v. C [1980] 2 All ER 347, [1981] 1 QB 956; Bekhor (AJ) & Co Ltd. v. Bilton [1981] 2 All ER 565, [1981] 1 QB 923; Z v. A-Z and AA-LL [1982] 1 All ER 556, [1982] QB 558 and Intraco v. Notis Shipping Corp of Liberia, The Bhoja Trader [1981] 2 Lloyd's Rep 256. He submitted that the principles to be collected from these authorities establish these propositions:

(a) Though as appears from the judgment in A v. C the court should exercise its powers to order discovery in order to ensure that the Mareva jurisdiction is properly exercised, the power should not be exercised to discover whether the defendant has assets within the jurisdiction. In order to establish a right of relief at all, the plaintiff has at least to give grounds for believing that the defendant has assets here.

(b) Shares held in a foreign corporation, themselves foreign assets, are to be distinguished from the corporation in which the shares are held. The evidence goes no further than showing that the first defendant holds shares registered in foreign corporations. Such shares confer on him no entitlement to the assets of the corporation concerned, whether held directly or indirectly through subsidiaries or by the medium of foreign trusts.

(c) There is a distinction between discovery, the object of which is to police a Mareva injunction which is not a proper exercise of the power to make an order ancillary to the injunction, and the power to order discovery in order to establish the nature and extent of the defendant's interest in assets within the jurisdiction which is a proper exercise of the power.

(d) The decisions have to be carefully examined to distinguish the powers of the court in tracing proceedings from simple Mareva situations.

Applying these propositions, counsel for the first defendant submitted that on the evidence the most that was established was that the English assets in question were vested in foreign corporations (or trusts in which the first defendant was not named beneficiary) and that the fact that he held shares in such corporations only showed entitlement to a foreign asset, namely the shares, without any sufficient proximity of interest in the assets to which the foreign corporation (or trusts) were directly or indirectly entitled. By way of illustration he gave as an example that on the orders made by the judge, a holding of a minority interest in a foreign corporation was sufficient to compel him to answer interrogatories directed to the entitlement of that corporation to English assets. In order to meet this objection, counsel for the plaintiffs (Miss Gloster) invited us to make orders more restrictive in their extent than the orders made by the judge. The significant amendment was to restrict the obligation to answer interrogatories to those English or foreign companies or trusts or other vehicles over which the first defendant has substantial or effective control which were entitled to English assets as at the date of the affidavit, whether directly or indirectly. She accepts and now seeks a similar restriction in relation to the orders made by the judge restraining the first defendant from disposing of shares in any foreign company or trust. So the orders now sought to be upheld are orders containing that important limitation.

The issue between the parties thus crystallised to a consideration of a distinction which was not, as far as we know, canvassed before the judge. The first defendant submitted that it was only if the evidence disclosed that the legal structure of the companies in which the first defendant had an interest (or the legal and equitable structure of trusts created at his instigation) was a complete sham that the court, exercising jurisdiction under § 37 of the Supreme Court Act 1981, would pierce the corporate veil and look beyond the legal entitlement to the English asset in question. Counsel for the plaintiffs contended that if, in the case of any corporation or trust, the court was satisfied that the legal structure has some reality but none the less was a vehicle over which the defendant exercised substantial or effective control, the Mareva injunction was appropriate in order to prevent disposal of English assets; and discovery by interrogatories was appropriate in order to ascertain the nature and extent of the first defendant's interest once it was demonstrated (as it was) that the vehicles were directly or indirectly entitled to English assets.

In our view the cases before and after Wallersteiner v. Moir [1974] All ER 217, [1974] 1 WLR 991 show that the court will use its powers to pierce the corporate veil if it is necessary to achieve justice irrespective of the legal efficacy of the corporate structure under consideration. As Lord Denning MR said ([1974] 3 All ER 217 at 238, [1974] 1 WLR 991 at 1013) the companies there identified were distinct legal entities and the principles of Salomon v. Salomon & Co Ltd. [1897] AC 22 prima facie applied. But only prima facie. On the facts of the Wallersteiner case, the companies danced to Dr Wallersteiner's bidding. Buckley LJ disagreed on the facts about the position of IFT, but Scarman LJ held that the evidence disclosed liability in Wallersteiner on the ground that he instigated the loan of £50,000.

We hold that the evidence sufficiently establishes that over a period of years the servants or agents of the first defendant have on the first defendant's instructions brought into existence the sophisticated and intricate network of interrelated English and foreign companies and foreign trusts as a mechanism through which the first defendant could at will dispose of his English assets. The evidence sufficiently establishes that when, after the fraud alleged in the statement of claim, the first defendant realised that insolvency of the plaintiffs was in sight, he either then arranged that his English assets should disappear into the network of interrelated English and foreign legal structures of such complexity that only he and/or his agents could disentangle his personal interest, of in the case of some English assets, he had already achieved this confusion against the contingency of a future judgment. In either case we hold that there is ample evidence to justify the orders now sought by the plaintiffs in their revised form.

We deal with three objections argued before us on behalf of the first defendant.

First, it is submitted that the order is premature. If the plaintiffs had sought for the voluntary co-operation of the first defendant after the orders made by Hirst J, they might have got all that they were entitled to by way of discovery. So the application for discovery and its attendant expense is quite unnecessary. The known facts tell a different story. Though the first defendant has filed an affidavit, he has never demonstrated any intention to disclose to the plaintiffs anything about the way he has organised his English assets. His defence to the statement of claim was and remains a masterpiece of the pleader's art of non-disclosure. He has instructed solicitors to represent him in these proceedings, but has discreetly established his residence in Spain.

Second, it has been submitted to us that on the information presently available to the plaintiffs and, through them, to the court, certain of the English assets alleged now to be under the first defendant's substantial or effective control are held directly or indirectly by companies in which at least one other has a substantial or equal shareholding. An example is a Panamanian corporate structure in which a third party N holds a 50% interest, that party apparently being the individual who procured the first defendant in the documentation described in his letter dated 3 December 1980 to S as the 'minimum two million valuation' used to engineer the deceit pleaded in the statement of claim. One KP also appears in the records held by the liquidators as having an interest in certain companies, as do the first defendant's wife and son. The answer is that these matters are no objection at this stage either to the order for interrogatories sought or for the injunctions sought or for the injunctions sought in the order now revised. If there are other genuine interests vested in third parties beneficially, the first defendant can state the facts in his answer to the interrogatories, and the notice of the injunctions can be served on the parties alleged to be beneficially interested, and their objection can be made to the court and its validity upheld. When there is such massive evidence of nominees, and puppet directors dancing to the first defendant's tune, it is for him to state on oath his belief, if he holds it, that one or more persons implicated in the silken skein of his spider's web has a genuine beneficial interest.

Third, it is objected that the interrogatories sought are on any view oppressive, in that they necessarily or probably compel the first defendant to undertake an enormous investigation involving also his various financial or legal advisers who have more detailed knowledge than the first defendant can be expected to have of the organisation of his financial affairs. And the investigation is likely to involve inquiry in territories all over the globe. The answer is that the complication of the answer to the interrogatories is no more than a reflection of the complexity of the structure which the first defendant has himself for his own purposes brought into existence.

Our conclusion is that the order should stand in the revised form now before us. It is in our view exceptional in its characteristics. It is exceptional because the facts are exceptional.

We move that, subject to the revisions appearing in the revised draft order before us, the appeal be dismissed.

DISPOSITION:

Appeal dismissed. 25 July. The Appeal Committee of the House of Lords (Lord Scarman, Lord Roskill and Lord Griffiths) dismissed a petition by the plaintiff for leave to appeal.

National Dock Labour Board v. Pinn & Wheeler Ltd. and Others

Queen's Bench Division
[1989] BCLC 647, [1989] BCC 75
10 November 1988

MACPHERSON J: The appellant, the National Dock Labour Board, seeks before me to overturn the decision of an industrial tribunal given in London on 9 December 1987.

The tribunal by a unanimous decision decided that 'the applicants are waterside manufacturers'.

This conclusion was reached in the joint application of three limited companies; Pinn & Wheeler Ltd. (Pinn); K & B Forest Products Ltd. (K & B) and the Sabah Timber Co Ltd. (Sabah). A second application launched by K & B alone was before the tribunal, but no decision was necessary in that application because of the tribunal's two conclusions. First that it was—

> 'wholly unrealistic to consider each applicant (in the first application) as a separate unrelated entity capable of carrying out its own operations without reference to the constraints imposed on the organisation by the Sabah Timber Co Ltd.'

And second that:

> 'We find that the three applicants qualify as waterside manufacturers because they do have a waterside facility, namely the Pinn & Wheeler Ltd's wharf, that cargoes belonging to the Sabah Timber Co are loaded and unloaded at this wharf. The cargo is then taken to the mill at K & B Forest Products Ltd. where it is processed and manufactured. For these reasons we find that the applicants listed in the first application are waterside manufacturers.'

I indicate at once that in my judgment that conclusion is flawed.

The applications came to the tribunal under the provisions of § 51(1) of the Docks and Harbours Act 1966 because there was a dispute between the National Dock Labour Board and the three companies 'about a question to which this section applies'.

The question stemmed from § 51(3) and was 'whether any work is dock work'. The relevant work was the unloading by Pinn's own employees, who were not registered dock workers, or a cargo of timber owned by Sabah on 27 July 1987. The timber was destined for K & B whose premises are about 500 yards away from the Pinn wharf, across a road, but no directly across, and without any actual waterside frontage of their own.

There was a threatened strike by dock workers which led to an injunction in the Court of Appeal to restrain the applicants from handling or loading cargo save by the use of registered dock labour. The cargo in question remained on the quay pending the determination of the case by the tribunal.

The specific question for determination by the tribunal was phrased more fully as follows:

> 'Whether the unloading and handling of cargoes of timber by the first applicant the majority of which is subject to a manufacturing process by the second applicant is dock work within the meaning of the Docks and Harbours Act 1966 section 58(1) and the Dock Workers Employment Scheme 1967 (SI 1967/1252). This scheme exempts waterside manufacturers from using registered dock transport workers except where such work is that of a Public Wharfinger and/or Master Lighterman and/or Master Stevedore.'

This is therefore a demarcation dispute and the National Dock Labour Board are fully entitled to put forward a case which, if correct, could further the cause of registered dock workers.

I was referred in argument to the relevant legislation and to its historical background and development. But I see no need to set that out in full, save to quote the definition of 'dock work' in § 58(1) of the 1966 Act which is as follows:

'"dock work" in relation to any port, means work which is treated for the purposes of any labour schemes as dock work at that port.'

The relevant scheme is the 1967 scheme (see Sch 2 to the Dock Workers (Regulation of Employment (Amendment) Order 1967, SI 1967/1252). And for the Port of London 'dock work' is equated with 'port transport work' which is accepted to mean:

'All work directly connected with the handling of cargo in or on ship, craft, quay or warehouse, and without prejudice to the generality of the above, includes in particular the unloading at a warehouse of cargo conveyed thereto by any means whatsoever and the loading of cargo for conveyance therefrom; and the expression "cargo" includes a part of any cargo.'

But the definition is subject to vital exceptions. The relevant one reads as follows:

'Port Transport shall not include work carried out by...(f) Waterside Manufacturers (except where such work is that of a Public Wharfinger, and/or Master Lighterman and/or Master Stevedore).'

Hence the question considered by the tribunal, and the focus is, as can be seen, on the work done and on who does it and where.

Under the Tribunals and Inquiries Act 1971, an application is available from the industrial tribunal only on a point of law. And of course this must always be remembered.

The position of the premises occupied by the two 'operating' companies is well illustrated in photographs which are before me. And the basic facts are set out by the tribunal. They do not require repetition by me.

It is of some significance that until May 1987 Pinn were public wharfingers, doing work for others. But the tribunal found, justifiably in my judgment, that by the relevant date the company had 'ceased to do work for others and they were using their waterside facility for the sole use of the second applicant'. It is true that the tribunal also concluded that a percentage of unprocessed material was sold on to another party. But in my judgment the finding of fact referred to above and the tribunal's conclusion namely that 'the presence of this additional material does not have the effect of removing the exemption' is fatal to the argument that Pinn remained a public wharfinger, and thus the National Dock Labour Board cannot in my judgment succeed in arguing that they are protected by what is in fact the exception to the exemption concerning such activity.

It seems to me next that logically the first question to consider is whether or not the tribunal were correct in law to consider the three companies as one. I have already indicated that the tribunal believed that it was 'unrealistic' to consider them as separate unrelated entities.

I take this point first since if the companies are regarded separately it seems to me impossible to argue that Pinn or K & B taken individually were waterside manufacturers. There is a finding of fact (para 16) that the premises of the second applicant are 'not on the waterside'. In para 21 the tribunal hold that:

'In order to satisfy the requirements of a waterside manufacturer, we find the premises must have a wharfing facility, that is they must abut the water's edge. They must also have a manufacturing process but that this, by its very nature, may well have to be some distance from the wharf.'

That finding, however, plainly lumps the two companies together. Looked at separately K & B did not work at premises on the waterside, and Pinn did not have a 'manufacturing process'. Pinn are in the phraseology of counsel for the board (Mr Beloff QC) geographically all right, but cannot satisfy the activity test since they have no factory or mill and do no manufacturing work. K & B are all right under the activity test, but are geographically excluded since (as expressly found by the tribunal) their premises and thus their work is 'not on the waterside'.

Was the tribunal therefore correct in law to consider the two 'operating' companies simply as divisions or subsidiaries of Sabah?

In my judgment that approach was incorrect.

It is only in special circumstances which indicate that there 'is a mere facade concealing the true facts' that it is appropriate to pierce the corporate veil. See per Lord Keith in Woolfson v. Strathclyde Regional Council (1978) 38 P & CR 521. It is true that the control of Sabah was analysed by the tribunal, and that the measure of control and ownership by that company of the other two was in analysis tighter than that apparent in the Woolfson case. But by the same token in my judgment the position did not approach that set out in DHN Food Distributors Ltd. v. Tower Hamlets London Borough [1976] 3 All ER 462, [1976] 1 WLR 852. And it must be noted that Lord Keith doubted the deciding force of that case, and readily distinguished it. For example also, Goff LJ himself had stressed in DHN [1976] 3 All ER 462 at 468, [1976] 1 WLR 852 at 861 that 'the two subsidiaries were both wholly owned...and had no separate business...whatsoever'. Shaw LJ referred to the matter thus ([1976] 3 All ER 462 at 473–474, [1976] 1 WLR 852 at 867–868):

> 'In this utter identity and community of interest between DHN and Bronze there was no flaw at all...It appears to me that it (the Lands tribunal) was too strict in its application to the facts of this case, which are, as I have said, of a very special character, for it ignored the realities of the respective roles which the companies filled.'

In Alec Lobb (Garages) Ltd. v. Total Oil GB [1985] 1 All ER 303 at 309, [1985] 1 WLR 173 at 178 Dillon LJ did refer to the proposition that: 'The court has ample power to pierce the corporate.' That is true; and in the context of that case he was referring to the unveiling of 'a palpable device in an endeavour to evade the doctrine of restraint of trade'. So that there was a facade concealing the true facts. Although it is to be noted that the case of Woolfson v. Strathclyde Regional Council was not cited to the Court of Appeal.

In my judgment there was (to quote Lord Keith's words) 'no basis consonant with principle' on which on the facts of this case 'the corporate veil can be pierced...' It does indeed seem to me perhaps to be unseemly that the three companies should be allowed to unveil themselves in order to try to avoid the effect of the Dock Labour Scheme. Sometimes, where an injustice may result as in DHN Food Distributors v. Tower Hamlets and where the factual circumstances as to control and so on are very strong, different considerations may of course arise.

But where the companies are kept alive as separate legal entities for good commercial or historical reasons in order to keep the company's name fully alive and in order to maintain the loyalty of employees for example, and also probably to avoid redundancy and other problems, I see no reason why the veil should be pierced. Certainly Lord Keith's words are strong and in my judgment support the argument of counsel for the board.

But even if the three companies are looked at as one I accept also counsel's argument that the tribunal's conclusion is logically and legally flawed.

He puts the matter very simply as follows: Aggregating the three companies does not of itself make Pinn's work 'dock work'. Even if by such a process K & B's manufacturing can be attributed to Pinn the manufacturing work or processes are not 'waterside'.

It is legitimate to find (see para 21) that 'there is a connection with the goods coming into the wharf and the manufacturing process being carried on, despite the distance between the wharf and the second applicant's mill'. But once it is accepted that 'In order to satisfy the requirements of a waterside manufacturer... premises must have a wharfing facility' it is illegitimate in my judgment to say that the work done is that of a waterside manufacturer if the 'manufacturing process... by its very nature, may well have to be some distance from the wharf'.

And the concluding paragraph of the decision is similarly flawed in my judgment. As soon as it is necessary to say that 'the cargo is then taken to the mill at K & B', and to accept (para 16) that the mill or manufacturing premises are 'not on the waterside', the flaw is apparent.

It is true that a manufacturing process or premises may extend a considerable distance inland from the water's edge. But where there is palpable and obvious division of the wharf and its attendant premises, and the manufacturing area is separated by 500 yards and a road, I cannot see how it can be said that the work done at Pinn's premises is that of a waterside manufacturer.

Assuming that Pinn and K & B had been separate entities I do not understand how, for example, the purchase of Pinn by K & B could suddenly make K & B 'waterside' if they were not 'waterside' before.

Counsel for the applicants strongly argues that the tribunal's conclusion was one of fact. Of course findings of fact were necessary to the conclusion. But the application of those facts to the plain statutory words is in my judgment a question of law, or mixed law and fact. And in any event in my judgment once the findings of fact are analysed their application by the tribunal to the words 'waterside manufacturer' giving those words their ordinary and natural meaning, was illogical and unreasonable to such an extent that it is attackable under the principles laid down in Edwards v. Birstow [1955] 3 All ER 48, [1956] AC 14 and Brutus v. Cozens [1972] 2 All ER 1297, [1973] AC 854. Taking the necessary and logical steps expounded to me by counsel for the board I believe that the decision was simply wrong and palpably so.

Whatever may be the view of those who disapprove of demarcation, Pinn's work done in June or July 1987 with the cargo of the Marie II was in my judgment dock work and should only have been done by registered dock labour.

In those circumstances in my judgment this appeal succeeds.

Appeal allowed.

Pinn and Wheeler & Others v. National Dock Labour Board

Court of Appeal (Civil Division)
(Transcript:Association)
15 March 1989

MAY LJ: In my earlier judgment in this appeal, I set out the corporate relationship between the four companies originally involved and the details of the substantial corporate re-organisation which took place at the end of 1988 and March 1989. I also recorded the approach adopted by the Industrial Tribunal on the hearing before them which was, as appears for instance from paragraph 10 of their decision: "We considered the relationship of the three applicant companies and the evidence was that the first and second applicants are wholly-owned subsidiaries of the third applicant along with the property holding company, William T Storer Ltd. For the purposes of reaching our decision we did not find it necessary to consider the position of the Sabah group within the Harrison and Crossfield company." Then in paragraph 14: "We find that in the circumstances of this case it would be wholly unrealistic to consider each applicant as a separate unrelated entity capable of carrying out its own operations without reference to the constraints imposed on the organisation by the Sabah Timber Co Ltd." Earlier the Industrial Tribunal had set out in even greater detail the close relationship between the limited companies concerned and the personalities of their directors.

On the substantive appeal from the Industrial Tribunal's decision to the Divisional Court, in addition to the point with which we have already dealt in the context of the corporate re-organisation, it was argued that the Industrial Tribunal had been wrong (as it was expressed) to pierce the corporate veil clothing all four limited companies. It was submitted to the learned judge that the Industrial Tribunal had had to deal with the companies as they were and in respect of one as a wharfinger and in respect of another as a manufacturer. Being different legal entities, it was wrong of the Industrial Tribunal to coalesce the two particularly relevant companies and conclude that together they constituted a waterside manufacturer and thus entitled to the exemption. With that submission the learned judge agreed. He expressed his decision in this way:

> "It is only in special circumstances which indicate that there 'is a mere facade concealing the true facts' that it is appropriate to pierce the corporate veil....
>
> In my judgement there was (to quote Lord Keith's words) 'no basis consonant with principle' upon which on the facts of this case 'the corporate veil can be pierced'. It does indeed seem to me perhaps to be unseemly that the three companies should be allowed to unveil themselves in order to try to avoid the effect of the Dock Labour Scheme."

It was argued in support of this particular aspect of the appeal to us from the decision of the Divisional Court that, contrary to the view taken by the learned judge below, the Industrial Tribunal were indeed justified in the circumstances of the instant case in not paying strict regard to the separate corporate identities of the respective companies and were correct in their common sense and, as it was suggested, realistic approach in looking at the commercial reality of the situation. There was, Mr. Field submitted, sufficient identity between at least the two material companies in a commercial sense, to entitle the Industrial Tribunal to consider the two together as constituting a waterside manufacturer. Indeed it was in the context of the whole scheme and the creation of this particular exemption that one should really look at the commercial reality of the situation and not allow oneself to be circumscribed by any strict adherence to the legal principle that the companies were each separate legal entities. Alternatively it was submitted that the Industrial Tribunal would have been correct to go behind the corporate veil and identify one particular company about which it could be said, construing the scheme realistically and from a commercial point of view, that it was the waterside manufacturer, and in the circumstances of this particular case it would have been the manufacturing company, K & B Forest Products Ltd.

In support of those submissions we were referred to two authorities. First, DHN Food Distributors Ltd. v. Tower Hamlets London Borough Council [1976] 1 WLR

852, 32 P & CR 240 and to various passages from the judgements of the court in that case. For present purposes I do not think it necessary to rehearse those passages in this judgment because we were also referred to a later decision in which that earlier decision was considered, namely Woolfson v. Strathclyde Regional Council 38 P & CR 521. It is unnecessary to go through the facts of that case, but in delivering the principal speech in the House of Lords, with which the remainder of their Lordships agreed, Lord Keith of Kinkel at 38 P & CR 521 page 525 referred to the DHN Food Distributors Ltd. and at page 526, in relation to the decision of the Court of Appeal in that case, said this:

> "I have some doubts whether in this respect the Court of Appeal properly applied the principle that it is appropriate to pierce the corporate veil only where special circumstances exist indicating that it is a mere facade concealing the true facts."

In my judgment, on this and other authorities to which I have taken the opportunity of looking, that is the basic principle by which one should be guided in deciding whether of not the corporate veil, enveloping separate corporate identities in law, should be pierced and that one should look at the realities of the situation, rather than the legal niceties. In the instant case there were no special circumstances which indicated that the separate companies were a mere facade concealing the true facts. There were originally, as I understand the situation, commercial and subsequently at least historical reasons why the four companies were retained in existence.

In those circumstances I respectfully agree with the learned judge that the Industrial Tribunal, although seeking very properly in other cases to look at the commercial reality of the situation, erred in law in this case in failing to recognise and separate the different legal corporate identities of the four companies concerned.

Accordingly, for those reasons I would dismiss the appeal against the learned judge on this particular point.

STOCKER LJ: I agree and there is nothing I wish to add.

TAYLOR LJ: I agree

Appeal dismissed. No order for costs. Application for leave to appeal to the House of Lords refused.

Professor Neil Hawke and John Marston, *Facades and Corporate Veils*

Law Society's Gazette, Vol. 86, No. 17, p. 32, 3 May 1989

The considerable uncertainty surrounding the court's willingness to pierce the corporate veil was again emphasized in the recent decision of the Queen's Bench Division in National Dock Labour Board v. Pinn and Wheeler Ltd. [1988] The Times, 17 November, denying the privilege of separate legal personality for the company.

The court was confronted by an appeal from the National Dock Labour Board in respect of a decision by an industrial tribunal on the status of a company and its wholly owned subsidiaries. The tribunal had held that the companies were within the term 'waterside manufacturer' so that their work was not 'dock work' for the purpose of §58(1) of the Docks and Harbours Act 1966 and the Dock Workers Employment Scheme 1967. Two of the companies, Pinn and K & B, were wholly owned subsidiaries of Sabah Timber Co Ltd. Cargoes owned by Sabah were loaded at a wharf in Pinn's ownership and taken to K & B's mill 500 yards away across a main road.

Abusive conduct

The decision of the court turns on the application of the House of Lords decision in Woolfson v. Strathclyde Regional Council (1978) 38 P & CR 521 to the effect that the veil should only be pierced where there are special circumstances amounting to a mere 'facade' disguising true facts. This principle might most easily be represented as depending on 'abusive' conduct. As a generalisation, any perceived abuse of separate legal personality may justify a lifting of the corporate veil by the court.

This approach has been applied only erratically by the court. They are often tempted, so it would seem, to reserve a wide discretion to permit the lifting of the veil in ignorance of the approach commended in Woolfson. Such a wide discretion has probably absolved the courts from undertaking necessary analysis of the policy justifications for the principle in Salomon v. Salomon and Co Ltd. [1897] AC 22 as well as the scope of statutory prescriptions for the removal of the veil.

It is the purpose of this article to review the law's uncertain view of the corporate veil, in order to emphasise the need for care in the design of corporate relationships if the uncertainties of the courts' approach are to be avoided.

Judicial confusion

It is not the intention of this article to attempt to reconcile the many different approaches to separate legal personality. Nevertheless one may be forgiven for thinking that the justification for a lifting of the veil in a particular case may depend simply on the court's view of the merits of the case. Indeed in DHN Food Distributors Ltd. v. Tower Hamlets London Borough Council [1976] 1 WLR 852 (CA), Goff LJ felt obliged to remark 'I wish to safeguard myself by saying...I am relying on the facts of this particular case'. If this is an accurate view then, again, it may be suggested that broader issues of policy already outlined may not have featured in the court's thinking. A cynical view of Pinn and Wheeler may be articulated on the basis of the court's opinion of the companies' attempts to avoid inclusion in the national dock labour scheme. In DHN the Court of Appeal concluded that a group company was not disabled from receiving disturbance compensation even though it had no interest in the subject land that had been compulsorily purchased from another (wholly owned) member of the group. The court rejected the lands tribunal's 'strict legalistic view' in favour of a conclusion that each of the companies should be seen as a group in order to allow DHN (the parent company) to receive the compensation. The court emphasized the need to avoid separate treatment so as to avoid defeat 'on a technical point'. Again, the court's departure from strict legal principles in Salomon was arguably influenced by the merits of DHN's claim. Unfortunately, such uncertainties of approach (as perceived by corporate strategists) do nothing to help either the development of a coherent policy attitude, through statute or otherwise, or the development of a consciousness of the need to make provision for difficulties that may arise from separate legal personality for the company.

Salomon upheld

The law reports contain a number of important decisions where the separate legal personality of the company has been upheld. Notable examples include Lonhro Ltd. v. Shell Petroleum Co Ltd. [1980] 1 WLR 627, affirming The decision of The Court of Appeal ([1980] QB 358) where the Court refused to order the discovery of certain documents held by subsidiaries. Interestingly, in the Court of Appeal, Shaw LJ (who was a member of the

Court in DHN) considered that there was no immediate or certain prospect of acquiring possession of The documents. Such a prospect, he said, might depend on an alteration of the articles of an unwilling or recalcitrant subsidiary followed by the removal of its then directors and their substitution by others more compliant. Again, in Multinational Gas and Petrochemical Co Ltd. v. Multinational Gas and Petrochemical Services Ltd. [1983] 2 All ER 563 (CA), it was held that the companies controlling the shareholdings in the subject company were not liable for negligent commercial transactions. This approach provides a firm foundation for the fundamental policy of the law, in favour of encouraging commercial risk under the protective privilege of separate legal personality for the company.

Agency and fraud

Agency and fraud represent the two possible bases on which to make inroads into the separation of the company from its owners. No doubt the wider company law definition of fraud was in mind when, in Woolfson, Lord Keith emphasized that '...it is appropriate to pierce the corporate veil only where special circumstances exist indicating...a mere facade concealing the true facts'. Accordingly, the veil should be lifted in the face of any evidence of an abusive exploitation of the corporate form.

There is, of course, a crucial distinction between abusive exploitation and the application of so-called 'agency' principles. Agency principles will, for example, fix the parent company with responsibility for a subsidiary's debts or distribute responsibility or entitlement. Such a process had depended on the Court's perception of control or the rather nebulous perception of group economic unity. In DHN the Court was arguably better able to justify its conclusion on the basis that The subsidiaries were all wholly owned. Indeed this was one of the factual grounds upon which Lord Keith distinguished DHN.

The distribution of liabilities or entitlements according to the agency principle is open to various criticism. The deployment of Lord Keith's principle in Woolfson also is subject to potential difficulty in so far as it is used in relation to facts which are not necessarily on all fours with an abusive use of the corporate form. In other words the Court may find 'special circumstances' justifying a lifting of the veil as a means of reorganizing group affairs where the parties, perhaps carelessly, fail to anticipate particular difficulties. The crucial difficulty therefore is in drawing a line between a situation where the veil is justifiably lifted because it is perceived that there has been some use of the corporate form for an improper (ie, fraudulent) purpose and a situation in which the Court perceives a necessity for a distribution of liabilities and entitlements.

This second situation requires, it is submitted, a strong policy stand against any such distribution. In other words, any certainty that the law may seek can only emerge from a clear confirmation of the Salomon principle. In Monarch Airlines Engineering Ltd. v. Intercon (Cattle-Meats) Ltd. (1986) 11 Con LR 58 it was held that in the absence of express agreement, agency will only arise where the alleged principal has a controlling interest will not prevent the Court from lifting the corporate veil, although those circumstances will be are. Such an approach emphasizes the following difficulties:

(a) there may be a temptation, from decisions like that in DHN to assume that the veil will be lifted if there is complete control;

(b) The Monarch decision, in its reference to mere control strengthens the DHN assumption just referred to but fails to address the often complex variables underlying the question of control, be it legal control or de facto control;

(c) it must be an untenable stance to suggest that, even exceptionally, lack of control may allow a lifting of the veil for agency purposes.

The decision in Monarch does recognise the possible significance of an express agreement, presumably a shareholders' agreement, often found in the private company sector. Clearly such an agreement may constructively anticipate problems and difficulties. Maintenance of a strong adherence to the Salomon principle should encourage those advising companies to crystallise relationships and liabilities in such agreements.

Effect of EC

It has been emphasized already that the 'agency' approach can facilitate a reorganisation or redistribution of corporate liabilities and entitlements at the instance of the Court. The advent of shareholders' agreements in the realm of private companies enables 'prepackaged' reorganisation and redistributions. Increasingly though, this process is seen to be generated by statute, sometimes in the wake of EC company law Directives. The government's new Companies Bill throws up a classic example based on the seventh Directive. The proposed legislation is generated by the perceived need to counter the practice of removing certain liabilities from a group's balance sheet while at The same time retaining profits from a subject transaction. The liabilities have been undertaken by companies created so that they are subsidiaries for tax purposes but not for Companies Act purposes. Retention of the grouped profits for tax purposes is particularly favourable because the tax regime applicable takes no account of the 'non-subsidiary subsidiary'. This practice will be dealt with through a redefinition of subsidiary companies as those companies which are controlled in fact through voting rights.

A second major development will be generated by the ninth EC company law Directive in the field of multi-national operations. The intention here is to remove the limit on a parent company's liability for a subsidiary. The limit (or even elimination) of the parent company's liability comes, of course, from the Salomon principle in English law. The intention is to enable the law to impose liability on the parent company in respect of redundancy compensation for workers dismissed by the subsidiary in a host country, for example. The law is walking a very sensitive policy tight-rope here, bearing in mind the need to encourage commercial and industrial risk-taking behind the twin privileges of separate legal personality and limited liability.

The issue probably becomes even more sensitive if potential liabilities are to be extended to include (for example) parent company liability for subsidiary company debts and protection of minority shareholders in a subsidiary. There are intriguing questions to be answered here. For example, if such redistributions of liability are to be anywhere near absolute should the subsidiary be wholly owned? If not, is it necessary to prescribe a scale of liability? If it is perceived to be necessary, how is that scale of liability defined in law?

Need for restraint

The law's uncertain view of the corporate veil emerges from the Court's failure to resist the temptation to interfere with the barrier between the company and its owners. While fraud may be a legitimate ground for interference by reference to the public policy justification for defending the statutory framework of incorporation, the same defence is not available in the so-called 'agency' cases. Here The Court is aiding the redistribution of corporate liabilities and entitlements. The courts have shown themselves to be unable to cope with the many variables involved such as the existence of wholly or partially owned subsidiary companies. In order to encourage a greater measure of self-regulation and self-reliance here the courts should refrain from veil lifting. Such restraint, it is suggested, may be doubly important in view of the growth of legislation governing corporate groups in particular. It is those who generate these statutory developments who are better able to evaluate and balance very sensitive issues of commercial policy.

---

3. European Civil Law Approaches

Not all of the Member States of the European Community have adopted the British approach to limited liability. In particular, both the French and German systems offer alternatives to the doctrine of "veil piercing." The first excerpt provides a description of the classical approach of civil law jurisdictions to the issue of piercing the corporate veil. There follows the emerging European continental approaches to extending liability to affiliated groups of corporations.

a. Veil Piercing

Continental jurisdictions have come to the concept of veil piercing with some reluctance. However, the continental systems have all come to recognize that there is nothing absolute about a corporate legal personality.

E. J. Cohn and C. Simitis, *"Lifting the Veil" in the Company Law of the European Continent*

12 INT'L & COMP. L. Q. 189 (1963)
(excerpts pages 190–198; 205–210; some footnotes omitted)

1. The problem of the "lifting of the veil" is known in Germany as that of the "breaching of the wall of the corporation." It is recognised that there are a number of cases when such a breach occurs. Many attempts have been made to find a principle behind the various lines of cases. So far none of them have been successful. We shall hereunder set out in the first instance the types fo cases in which the courts have lifted the veil of the corporation. This summary will be followed by a brief description of the search for a general formula.

2. It is now a recognised principle of German law that by way of exception from the rule which confines the liability of the shareholder for the debts of a company to the capital invested by him, there may be in certain cases a further liability. This exception is largely the work of the courts. It has found scant recognition by the legislature. A sole or controlling shareholder who has failed to distinguish between the assets and affairs of the corporation on the one hand and his own private assets and affairs on the other hand and who has derived advantage from doing so, may be personally liable for the debts of the corporation....

The principle however has its limits. It is said to be applicable only where the operations of the sole shareholder have resulted in rendering it impossible for the creditors to obtain satisfaction from the company's assets. The Federal Supreme Court has added that it applies only where the confusion of private assets and corporate assets was effected in intentional disregard of the interests fo the company's creditors. But this remark has been attacked by learned writers. Its validity is certainly not free from doubt.

Another field for the application of the principle that the sole controlling shareholder is responsible for the debts of the company ruled by him is in the sphere of undercapitalization. It is a well known habit of less scrupulous promoters to employ a company with small capital for the purpose of carrying on a large enterprise. Such capital as the company need is provided by loans from the sole or controlling shareholder. Thus A had formed the X company with the assistance of E and G, whose shared he purchases shortly after the formation of the company. The company's capital amounted to DM 20,000 only. It was utterly insufficient for the company's business, but A provided further capital by way of loans which he gave to the company. When things began to look bad, the company repaid the loans to A. As a result its other creditors were unable to obtain repayment of their debts. They asked the courts for an order that A should repay to the company the loans which he had given. They were successful. The loans, it was held, were to be treated as if they were the company's capital. The sole or controlling shareholder who had started the company in this manner had to be treated as if the loan capital was share-capital. He was under an obligaiton to repay the amount of the loans to the company. The situation, it seems, was in many ways similar to that in *Salomon v. Salomon.*[1] But the Federal Supreme Court, sitting in the twentieth century, was less impressed with the concept of corporate personality than had the House of Lords been in 1897.[5]

There is a statutory rule which establishes a liability of the shareholder for the debt of a company controlled by him. Article 101 of the *Statute on Joint Stock Corporations* provides that a person who, by exercising his influence on a company for that purpose, obtains for himself or a third party special advantages other than those which may naturally result from his participation in the company and thereby has caused damage to the company, is liable to compensate the company and is responsible for all the company's debts that remain unpaid in consequence of the damage and to the extent of it. This provision has remained a dead letter. It has been in force for fifteen years. There is no recorded decision in which it has been applied. It seems that the legislature has imposed too heavy a burden of proof on anyone wishing to rely on it.

3. The courts have naturally been far more reluctant to affirm the doctrine that a company may be liable for the debts of its sole or controlling shareholder. This doctrine, of course, pierces the veil of the corporation far more effectively than does the possibility that a shareholder may be liable for the company's debts. But there is a whole series of cases which have led to such drastic piercing. Admittedly the circumstances were unusual. However, we live in times when what once seemed unusual may in fact become recurrent. A number of companies were formed by the Germain Reich before or during the Second World War for the purpose of carrying out tasks connected with military operations. They were wound up after the end of the war. Their liquidators claimed payment of the debts owed to them. Many of the debtors, however, also owed debts to the German Reich. In other cases debtors of one company were creditors of other companies of the same type. They tried to set off these claims. This should in strictness not have been permitted because the claims may, of course, be set off only where the debtor and creditor on both sides are identical. The courts, however, permitted the set-off. The

1. [This case is discussed in *The Irish Permanent Building Society et al. v. Seamus Cauldwell* at Chapter 4. Ed.]
5. BGH, judgment of December 14, 1959 in (1960) *Neue Juristische Wochenschrift* 286; and also see the earlier judgment of the German Supreme Court (RG) of November 16, 1937 (1938) *Juristische Wochenschrift* 862 and of December 3, 1938, in (1939) *Juristische Wochenschrift* 355....

companies were not teated as independent legal entities but as mere departments of the State working with the full knowledge of the latter and—to a large extent—under its instructions.[6]

In a later decision, the Federal Supreme Court—somewhat surprisingly—declared the principle of these decisions to be inapplicable elsewhere.[7]...

4. There are a number of cases where the courts have disregarded the corporate entity in order to be able to grant a manner of protection to persons whose interests were to be secured by a statutory provision. Thus the statute protecting purchasers under a hire-purchase agreement was inapplicable to loans. It consequently failed to benefit a person who had acquired a motor-car from a corporation against cash, but who had obtained the cash on loan from another corporation, whose shares were owned by the same people who owned the selling corporation. The courts held that the two corporations were in reality one: the seller was in fact a party to the loan contract. This latter contract, too, was therefore subject to the provisions intended to protect the purchaser.[8] Today the lifting of the veil is no longer required to bring about this result. The courts have adopted a more extensive interpretation of the Act on Hire-Purchase Agreements, which renders it unnecessary top resort to it.[9]

In another case the defendant, who controlled as majority shareholder a number of companies, had appointed the plaintiff as his personal agent, promising him a share in the profits of his companies. The plaintiff asked to be entitled to inspect the books of these companies in order to ascertain the amount of the profits which had been earned. The defendant objected on the ground that the companies as separate legal entities could not be compelled to allow inspection. The exercise of the plaintiff's rights required a resolution of the boards of the companies. The former Supreme Court rejected this argument. In its view, "the realities of life and the power fo facts" had to be taken into account. The result was that the plaintiff was held liable to exercise his power of control over the companies in such a way as to compel them to allow inspection.[10]

The trend of decisions is, of course, counterbalanced by others in which the courts have insisted on the strict separation between the company and its controlling shareholder. Thus a sole shareholder cannot use the company's trademark. The forms required by company law must be observed.

5. There are, however, other cases[11] in which all formal requirements were dispensed with. *Fraus omnia corrumpit.* Among the concepts which fraud corrupts is, it seems, to some extent the corporate personality of a corporation. An agent under German law may not retain bribe money received by him. He must disclose and deliver it to the principal. In order to circumvent this liability, an agent arranged that bribe money should be paid to a company controlled by him and not to him personally. The former Supreme Court held that he was bound to pay over the money to his principal, although he personally had not received it.

Fraud, however, is a concept which must not be too strictly interpreted in this connection. At any event it is very nearly related to what is described as "abuse of the lib-

6. BGH, judgement of October 30, 1951, 3 *Entscheidungen in Zivilsachen* 316; judgment of July 3, 1953, 10 *Entscheidungen* 205; judgment of March 17, 1955, 17 *Entscheidungen* 19....

7. BGH, judgement of November 7, 1957, 26 *Entscheidungen in Zivilsachen* 31.

8. RG, judgement of January 30, 1931, 131 *Entscheidungen in Zivilsachen* 213, at 225....

9. RG judgement of May 26, 1922, (1922) *Juristiche Wochenschrift* 1520.

10. RG, judgment of July 9, 1926, 114 *Entscheidungen in Zivilsachen* 276....

11. RG, judgment of December 16, 1939 (1940) *Deutches Recht* 580.

erty to contract and to form corporations." This is shown by a case usually referred to as the *Toivoli Theatre* case [RG, judgment of May 5, 1932, (1933) *Höchstrichterliche Rechtsprechung* No. 299]. Here a company operated a theatre. The building had been lent to it by its sole shareholder who was also its managing director. When creditors obtained a judgment against the company and tried to enforce it, the shareholder terminated the contract with the company, took over the management of the theatre and thereby deprived the company of its chief asset. In these circumstances the court permitted the judgment to be enforced against the shareholder's personal property. He had, it was found, abused the forms of law in order to prevent creditors from obtaining satisfaction.

6. Bona fides is sometimes a requirement for the acquisition of rights. Thus A may be registered as owner of Blackacre in the register of immovable property while R is the real owner. B, who acquires Blackacre from A, acquires full ownership, if he relies in good faith upon the fact that A is registered in the register and in ignorance of R's title. The courts have restricted the applicability of this rule to cases where a sole shareholder acquires from his company or vice versa. His knowledge excludes good faith even though he may not be a director or member of the supervisory board of the company.[12] This doctrine, however, applies only where there is a complete identity between the natural person or persons on the one hand and the shareholder or shareholders of the corporation on the other hand. It was not applied in a case in which the sole shareholder of the transferor company owned only 75 per cent of the shares of the transferee company.[13]

The argument behind these cases is that there was economic identity between the interests of the shareholder and that of the corporation. This brings this line of cases into relationship with another line where legal identity was under discussion. Section 181 of the Civil Code provides that an agent cannot contract with himself on behalf of his principal. Does this mean that a company represented by its sole managing director and sole shareholder cannot a contract with him? Many writers of high authority had refused to go so far. Some had thought that this was permissible at least in those cases in which there was a resolution of the company in general meeting permitting the contract. The Federal Supreme Court disagreed with this view. Such contracting between the company and the shareholder was permissible only if the company was represented by another person as managing director or where it was permitted by the charter of the company.[14] In permitting the latter alternative the court relied on the publicity of the Commercial Registerwhere everyone may inspect the charter. This may, perhaps, not always be an effective way of stopping abuses.

If the sole shareholders are treated as being economically or even legally identical with the company, there is only a short step to treating them as if they were actually relatives of the company. This step has been taken by the legislature in section 108(2) of the Act of Settlement in cases of Insolvency. This Act says, in its section 4, that a debtor must disclose certain transactions with near relatives which were concluded during the two years preceding the proceedings. Section 108(2) prescribes that in some of these cases "shareholders are treated as if they were near relatives" and the same applies to near relatives of such shareholders. This rule has been extended to cases of bankruptcy and other cases where fraudulent preferences were given to sole or controlling shareholders.

12. RG, judgment of October 19, 1929, 126 *Entscheidungen* 46....
13. RG, judgment of November 26, 1927, 119 *Entscheidungen* 126 at 131.
14. BGH, judgement of October 6, 1960, (1960) *Neue Juristische Wochenschrift* 2285....

7. The rule of good faith applies to the interpretation of contracts. This rule may lead to a piercing of the veil. Where a contract in restraint of trade is permissible, its effect cannot be circumvented by the formation of a separate juridical entity. If A has promised not to compete with B, a company of which he is sole or controlling shareholder is bound by his promise.[16] The shareholders of a company which has concluded a non-competition agreement cannot escape the obligations that have been created by dissolving the company and forming a new company which competes with which the agreement was concluded.[17] Similarly, a liberal interpretation of legal provisions may result in the veil being lifted. Section 119 of the Civil Code enables a party to avoid an agreement which is affected by an error relating to "essential characteristics" of the other party. Where the "other party" is a company, the "essential characteristic," which results in the right to avoid, may be "essential characteristics" of the company's controlling shareholder. Thus X concluded an agreement with the B company whose controlling shareholder was Y. X had thought that Y was a man of excellent repute. In fact, he was a person well known to be entirely unreliable in all matters of business. X was held to be entitled to avoid the agreement with the company. The essential characteristics of the controlling shareholder had become essential characteristics of his company.[18]

8. The doctrine of "lifting of the veil" means ultimately a realistic treatment of the concept of the juristic personality. This realistic treatment may not only lead to an identification of the company with its controlling personalities. It may also result in a company being identified with the business which it conducts or with the property which it owns. The Civil Code provides certain statutory rights in favour of the purchaser to whom defective goods has been delivered or who receives possession of goods but a defective title. These rules might have been thought not to be applicable where a vendor sold the shares of a company which on its part owned a house affected by dry rot: strictly speaking the purchaser had been promised title to shares and he got what he had bargained for—at least in name. But the courts resisted the temptation to look at the shell instead of at its kernel and held that the sale of the shares was equal to the sale of the company's assets. Thus where a business was sold by way of the sale of shares in the company conducting it, the court could inquire whether the business was as good as had been promised.[19] This doctrine, according to the majority view remains, however, inapplicable where only part of the company's shares have been sold or where several transferees economically unconnected with each other were the purchasers.[20] But it is not certain whether this restriction will remain for long.[21] In fact, here, as elsewhere, the limits of the doctrine are ill-defined. If the company is identical with its assets the sale of all the shares in a company owning nothing but immovable assets should logi-

16. BGH, judgment of February 13, 1952, 5 *Entscheidungen* 68.

17. RG, judgment of June 10, 1926, 114 *Entscheidungen* 68.

18. RG, judgment of February 23, 1934, 143 *Entscheidungen* 429. The judgement, strangely enough, says very little as to the nature of the controlling shareholder's business unreliability, at least not in that part which alone has been published.

19. RG, judgment of March 9, 1928, 120 *Entscheidungen* 283, at 287; judgement of July 5, 1928, 122 *Entscheidungen*378, at p. 381.... In its judgement of March 16, 1928, in 98 *Entscheidungen* 289, at p. 292 the court used an entirely different argument to arrive at the same result: the function of the doctrine of the lifting of the veil can, it seems, be performed by many other doctrines of a similarly equitable character.

20. See, RG, judgment of January 3, 1944, (1944) *Deutches Recht* 485; judgment of December 5, 1928, 122 *Entscheidungen* 378, at 381.

21. See the article by Loos in 15 *Neue Juristiche Wochenschrift* 519.

cally be governed by the rules of the form applicable to the sale of immovables. The courts have not drawn this conclusion.[22] The sale of a business by a minor is subject to the permission of the guardianship court. This rule is extended to the sale of all shares in a company that runs a business.[23] To discover any difference between these two types of cases is hard. The decisions are difficult, if not impossible, to harmonize.

9. It is little to be wondered at that the courts have been unable to define in general terms with any claim of accuracy the nature and extent of the doctrine of the lifting of the veil. The Federal Supreme Court, following the precedent of the former German Supreme Court, has repeatedly used the following formula:

> The legal differentiation between a company and its sole participant cannot be taken into account without exceptions. The corporate entity and its sole participant must be treated as if they were one and the same entity, if the realities of life, the economic requirements and the power of facts render it imperative for the judge to disregard any differentiation between the personality and the assets of the corporation on the one hand and those of its sole shareholder on the other hand.[24]

The formula is obviously so wide and vague as to be practically meaningless. Professor Serick, who has written the leading monograph on the topic, has advocated a far narrower conception: in his view the doctrine is to be applied only where this was to be required in order to prevent intentional abuse of the concept of corporate personality. The Federal Supreme Court has, however, expressly rejected this view, notwithstanding the fact that it occasionally has based a decision on it, even after having rejected it.[25] At present it seems that the building up and defining of those various lines of cases in which the doctrine is applicable is the most hopeful approach to greater legal certainty which in this field is, no doubt, most desirable indeed....

* * *

Juan M. Dobson, *Lifting the Veil in Four Countries: The Law of Argentina, England, France and the United States*

35 INT'L & COMP. L.Q. 839 (1986)

(excerpts pages 839–846, 851–852, 853–854, 859–60; some footnotes omitted)

A variety of key expressions are associated with the problems caused by the abuse of corporate personality: "lifting the veil" in England, "disregard of the legal entity" in the U.S., "*abuso de la personalidad jurídica*" in Argentina, "*Durchgriff*" in Germany. These labels do not indicate an independent concept in law, but only a result which can be obtained through the medium of various other concepts....

Some typical factual situations illustrate the problems of "lifting the veil":

1. A company is formed or used to evade obligations owed to contracting or third parties.
2. The working capital of a company is brought in as a loan from the shareholders.

22. RG, judgment of January 30, 1925, (1925) *Juristiche Wochenschrift* 1109.
23. Kammergericht, judgments of October 7, 1926, (1927) *Juristiche Wochenschrift* 2578 and of October 15, 1925, (1926) *Juristiche Wochenschrift* 600.
24. BG, judgement of November 29, 1956, 22 *Entscheidungen* 226; the formula is no less than forty years old, see RG in 99 *Entscheidungen* 234....
25. E.g., BGH, judgement of March 12, 1959, 29 *Entscheidungen* 386, at 392.

3. The overwhelming majority of the capital of a company is in the hands of one person.

4. One company holds itself out as connected with another in an effort to convey to third parties that the latter has its economic support.

5. A company is dominated by the economic power of another company or by an individual.

6. A director or shadow director of a company uses the company's assets for his own benefit.

7. A director or shadow director continues to carry on a company knowing it to be insolvent.

8. The assets or management of a company are significantly co-mingled with those of another company or an individual.

These situations can be reduced to two broad headings: cases of abusive control of a company of a company, and cases of lack of separation of the assets that give rise to economic units.....

II. General Principles: Fraud and Agency

A. The Importance of Fraud

Fraud has relevance in all countries considered. Most of the decisions that will be examined make direct or indirect reference to fraud—the "disregard of legal entity" doctrinme of the US forms part of the law of fraud;[2] the notion of fraud is contained in most of the English decisions;[3] the Argentine Supreme Court has stated that fraud is a prerequisite of *abuso de la personalidad* remedies;[4] and, in France, the complementary doctrines of the *société fictive* and of *confusion des patrimoines* both involve the notion of fraud.[5]

This common tendency to use the concept of fraud has led to an unusual convergence of decisions handed down in countries with such dissimilar legal traditions as Argentina and the US and has assisted in the derivation of notions of considerable importance. However, solutions to the problems posed by abuse of corporate personality which might otherwise seem to arise from the remedies fo fraudulent acts prove on closer inspection to be inadequate.

1. Fraud Under French and Argentine Law.

Scholars in these jurisdictions have made some effort to set up a general theory of fraud in private law, comprehending all possible modes of fraud.[7] Such a theory would mark a reappearance of the general principle, *fraus omnia coorumpit*, and would empower judges to deny the normal consequences of the law even where a particular case

2. Most US courts will not disregard legal entity without evidence of fraud Berkowitz v. Allied Stores of Penn-Ohio, Inc., 541 F.Supp. 1209 (1982); Laborers' Local Union Nos. 472 and 172 v. Interstate Curb and Sidewalk, 488 A.2d 980 (1982)....

3. It is appropriate to lift the corporate veil only where special circumstances exist indicating that it is a mere facade concealing true facts: Woolfson v. Strathclyde Regional Council (1978) P. & C.R. 521 (HL); Wallersteiner v. Moir [1974] 1 W.L.R. 991 (CA); Smith, Stone and Knight Ltd. v. Lord Mayor etc. of the City of Birmingham [1939] 4 All E.R. 116; Jones and Another v. Lipman and another [1962] 1 W.L.R. 832; Ford Motor Co. v. Horne [1933] Ch. 935; Commissioner of Inland Revenue v. Sansom [1921] 2 K,B, 492.

4. CSJN, ED.69-427 (1976).

5. *Mary-Raynaud v. Maillard* (1908) D. 1910, 233, *note* Percerou: Aix-en-Provence (1981); *Banco Sudameris v. Vioncent es qual.* Cannes 16.10.81) D. 1982, I.R. 6....

7. Vidal, *Essai d'une théorie générale de la fraude en droit français* (1957); Ghestin, Goubeaux, *Traité de droit civil, introduction générale* (2nd ed., 1983), Vol. 1, pp. 663, 668.

would otherwise fall squarely within its scope. The general theory of "fraud on the law" has in this sense found its way into private international law, but the French and Argentinian courts do not seem to be using it in their internal law.

The distinction between simulation, *dolus* and *actio Pauliana* fraud is known in both countries and has substantially the same effects. The distinction concerns the available remedies.

(a) Simulation in sham or fictitious companies Problems relating to the control of companies have in the past been resolved in both Argentina and France under the rules on simulation.[8] A Company is deemed to be organised as a contract. Since plurality is considered to be an essential ingredient of the association (here, company) contract, lack of true membership in the form of at least two genuine members results in the company being treated as fictitious or *fictive*....

In Argentina, statute law does not allow a one-man company and there are few cases on the matter. In those that there are, one-man companies have beenfound to be fictitious.

France enacted a statute in 1985 allowing the one-man company—the *enterpriae unipersonnelle à responsibilité limité* (EURL).[10] Before then, a company was fictitious whenever the essential prerequisite of plurality was absent because there could be no *affectio scoietatis*. Indeed, the *Court de Cassation* stated that fictitious companies were a threat to the *ordre public* as they were expressions of fraud.[12] The courts adopted a very strict position on the one-man company—it was classed as "non-existent," a severe form of nullity. The new statute represents a change of attitude, though its scope is not yet entirely clear. The EURL was designed to allow individuals to limit their liability, but the wording gave rise to the opinion, even before enactment, that the one-man company could still be treated as fictitious.

The most striking cases to have come before the Argentinian courts on the issue of *abuso de la personalidad jurídica* have related to wholly owned subsidiaries where a company—often, but not always, a foreign multinational—owns 99.99% of the shares

8. Simulation is an operation through which an apparent legal situation, different from the real legal situation, is created. There is an uncharacteristic reluctance in Argentine authors to define simulation, given its multifarious expressions (see H., L., and J. Mazeaud, Chabas, *Leçons de droit civil* (7th ed., 1985), Tome II, Vol. 1, p. 907, n. 807; Borda, *Tratado de derecho civil, Parte General* (5th ed.), Vol. II, p. 335). The French Civil Code does not contain express provisions on simulation, but the rule of evidence indicated in art. 1321 has gioven rise to a whole doctrine accepted by the courts and legal writers (see Bredin, "Remarques sur la conception jurisprudentielle de l'acte simulé" [1956] Rev. trim. dr. civ. 261 et seq.). The Argentine Civil Code, following the Spanish tradition, describes different situaitons as "pretended trasnactions," stating that an act of the parties will be deemed to be simulated whenever its legal character is shown to have been disguised to look like another transaction, or whenever a deed contains false dates or provisions that are insincere, where a conveyance is made to someone who is a third party's stooge: Argentine Civil Code, art. 955. There has to be a contrast between the exterior facade put up by the parties and their real object. Ehenever the parties have used a contract to create an illusion, this is a *fictif* transaction, which is one of the varieties of simulation (Mazeaud, Chabas, supra). The purpose of an action on simulation is to render the hidden transaction visible: to "lift the veil" of the ostensible operation. Normally the fictitious transaction will be entered into to evade the normal consequences of the law applying to the real transaction. These will immediately become applicable (Civ. Ire., 22.10.75, Bull.Civ. I. 243....).

10. EURL loi no. 85-697, 11.7.85, O. 1985, 394.

12. Paris, 23.12.75, Gaz.Pal. 1976, I.361, note L.C.; Cass. 22.6.76, D.1977.619, note Diener; Gisserot, "La confusion des patrimoines est-elle une source autoinome d'extension de faillte?" [1972] Rev.trim.dr.comm. 56 n.17.

of the subsidiary. They involved making the parent company liable for the debts of its subsidiary or ignoring the legal boundaries between the two companies. However, the courts' decisions have been based on the rather ambiguous doctrine of "economic unity" . . . rather than on fictitiousness or simulation.

A possible reason for the courts to avoid the fictitiousness approach is that the consequences of a judicial declaration of nullity—even more so when the nullity is "non-existence"—are onerous. If the requisite of plurality in membership is not met and the company is declared null and void, the owner of the shares may incur unlimited liability for the fictitious company's debts.

The effects of finding fictitiousness or simulation are comparable to those of "lifting the veil." Its effects are extreme and do not take account of legitimate modern needs for limited liability. The tendency is towards recognition of the one man company, an example being the 1985 French statute, but legislative intervention is required to counteract the excesses of the traditional remedies for fraud.

Decisions of French courts in insolvency matters have made extensive use of the doctrine of simulation since at least the first decade of this century, adapting concepts that date from the last. As early as 1908, French judges were ready to admit that a director who has gone inot business personally under a company's cloak could be made personally bankrupt because he had identified himself with the company.[16] The decision drew upon the *fraus omnia corrumpit* rule and the *société fictive* principles, as did other decisions.

Both French and Argentine law recognises other kinds of fraud, however, which have no connection with fictitiousness or simulation.

(b) Dolus. This is perhaps the most usual meaning of the word "fraud." It refers to acts performed by a person actively appreciating the unlawful consequences of his actions, i.e. with intent, and is clearly part of French and Argentine law.[17] If a court finds that a contract has been concluded as a result of the intentional fraud of one of the parties, the innocent party may claim nullity of the contract and third parties may claim damages if they have been prejudiced.

In the company context, the concept of *dolus* can be used to solve problems arising from thge use of a company as a shelter to evade contractual obligations or to prejudice third parties, for instance by a person forming a company so that he can violate a contractual obligation restraining him from trading in a particular area. By claiming a traditional remedy, the result of an action for *dolus* would be to lift the veil of the company. For these cases, the remedy seems adequate.

---

16. *Mary-Reynaud v. Maillard*, 29.6.1908, D.1910, 233, note Percerou.

17. *Dolus* is an action on deceit, a variety of fraud where the relevant condition is a degree of consciousness on the part of the performer . . . that his action is against the law. . . . In the laws of France and Argentina, it must be shown that one of the parties to a contract has entered into it fundamentally as a result of the deliberate machinations and/or lies of the other. Where simple reticence may constitute *dolus*, see Mazeaud, Chabas, op. cit. supra n. 8, at p. 176, n. 193. Machinations and/or lies will be deemed to vitiate the consent of the other contracting party if they are grave and decisive. Whenever a party shows that he would not have entered the contract had it not been for the deceit (*dolus*), the principle of error and its resulting nullity will become applicable (arts. 931, 932, Argentine Civil Code; art. 1116, French Civil Code; Borda, *Tratado de derecho civil, Parte Gnereal* (5th ed.), Vol. II, at 311. . . . , The concept of *dolus* in the Argentine Civil Code has also been applied to control situations whereby one of the parties to a contract has performed operations with the specific intent of impeding the fulfillment of that contract (arts. 506, 507).

(c) Actio Pauliana. Both French and Argentine law embrace this special variation of fraud, adopting a traditional Roman law action recognised by most civil law systems.[18] In both systems, a declaration of fraud under the *actio Pauliana* results in property transfers amd the assumption of obligations being *inopposable* as against certain creditors (i.e. they are specifically invalid when set in opposition to creditors' claims). This is also called "revocation," since the validity of the act itself is not reviewed but its effects are curtailed. A typical case in which the *actio Pauliana* is available is where the debtor enters into a transaction with a third party who had knowledge of the debtor's insolvency at the time of the transaction. A creditor who is prejudiced by the transaction can get it set aside and exercise his rights of execution as if the debtor had not entered into the transaction; the transaction is *inopposable* as against the creditor.

The actio Pauliana provides useful legal protectionin cases where monies are put up by members of a company in financial difficulties and go into the company's funds, not as paid up capital, but as a loan. Here, if the company goes into liquidation, the lender can collect on distribution as a creditor. Were he to contribute paid-up capital, he would lose his standing as a creditor and would not be able to collect at all. This situa-

18. The *actio Pauliana* is designed to give relief to individual creditors against transactions made by the debtor which may prejudice their rights of execution. Insufficient assets in the hands of the debtor and prejudice to the creditor from the contested transaction must be proved....

(a) If the transaction is "onerous" (which roughly means "for valuable consdieration"), proof of "intentional conivance at the prejudice" between the debtor and the recipient is required. Thus, the constituent elements of the *actio Pauliana* are, in both Argentina and France: (1) prejudice to a creditor causing or aggravating insolvency (art. 962, Argentine Civil Code; Civ.Ire, 17.10.79, J.P.C. 1981.II. 19-267, *note* Ghestin); (2) the obligation to the creditor must pre-date the transaction (art. 962 Argentine Civil Code; Civ. Ire, 17.1.84, D. 1984, note Flash, n. 13); (3) fraudulent connivance of the debtor and the third party (art. 962, Argentine Civil Code; Civ. 7.7.1896, D.P. 96.1/519; 17.6.45, D. 1946, *Somm.* 2).

(b) In its remote origins, the *actio Pauliana* was designed as a penal remedy for fraudulent transactions, but, as early as the thirteenth century, its consequences were also used to remedy cases where fraud might well be absent, e.g. gifts made by an insolvent debtor. This implied a change in the conditions of the action as fraud in this context became irrelevant. Thus, the first variation that appeared was the case of gratuitous transactions (whereby the benefits of a conveyance were assured to a party without any reciprocal obligation). A daughter receiving a house from an insolvent father as a wedding gift might very well be ignorant of her parent's straits and would in no way be consenting to fraud. But in these cases, such as an absence of fraud is irrelevant to the availability to a creditor of the *actio Pauliana*: the transaction can nevertheless be set aside (art. 967, Argentine Civil Code; Civ. Ire, 23.4.81, D. 1981, 395).

(c) The *actio Pauliana*, for transactions for valuable consideration, proved to be too cumbersome for the practical Italian merchants of medieval times, as fraudulent connivance had to be proven in each case. This burden of proof was duly called the *diabolica probatio* owing to its intricacies: the necessity element of fraudulent intent was more often than not hidden under elaborate legal clothing. To circumvent this difficulty, a new legal instrument was drafted into the statutes on bankruptcy. These contained presumptions of fraud in bankruptcy, doing away entirely with the need for proof of fraud. Payments of debts before the maturing date, interests or charges (securities) given for the benefit of pre-existent non-secured debts, and payments in a mode other than that contracted for were all presumed to be fraudulent. There was also a presumption of fraud where the party to a transaction that was prejudicial to the creditors of the other party had entered it with knowledge of the insolvency of the latter.

(d) All these remedies are part of the law of both Argentina and France, and are of recurrent application (Ley 19.551, arts. 122, 123; Loi 85–98, arts. 107–108). The normal effect of *inopposabilité* was abandoned by the new French Insolvency Act of 1985 and nullity is now the penalty resulting from the presumptions of fraud in an insolvency context....Argentine law still maintains the traditional remedy.

tion—that of an *internal* creditor who is also a member fo the company—has particular significance in modern insolvency law.

The *actio Pauliana* has itself had its variants. One of them is found in French and Argentine insolvency law where the requirements for the action have been simplified to make it a more useful instrument to remedy fraud. Another variant contemplates transactions made with "fraudulent foresight": terms added to cover future contingencies may enabel creditors to have the transactions set aside. If granted, this remedy also results in a lifting of the veil *vis-a-vis* a loan made by a member to a company, so that it seems particularly apt for dealing with problems involving "internal" loans made by company members.

On the other hand, the remedy can prove excessive as a rigid application does not allow distinctions to be made between transactions made in good faith and those made in bad faith. A member ready to lend money to a company in difficulties might be discouraged from doing so by a wide interpretation of the rule and, since his very knowledge of the company's situation may lead to his future status as a creditor being challenged, a useful source of funds for rescuing enterprises in trouble may dry up. Distinctions, clearly defined by legislation, should be made so that the *actio Pauliana* does not have the exaggerated results.

These three variants of fraud each have a role to play in problems connected with lifting the veil. Each has different scope and consequences. Two need to be modified to be thoroughly useful. But the remedies available for fraud in any of these three variants are in marked contrast to the remedies provided for "fraud" in the laws of England and the US.

* * *

II. Company Control

In French and Argentine law, control by itself carries no connotation of, or even scope for, liability in agency for the undisclosed principal. This does not satisfy economic needs at a time when companies frequently have to conform to the wishes of another, often to the detriment of the company's creditors. Control by itself can be made to engender liability in agency for each undisclosed principal in English and US law. But even this does not adequately fulfil the needs of a society where limited liability has proved to be a most useful tool in the development fo the economy. A wall of insulation against liability provides too much protection, but an extension of liability results in an undermining of the legitimate protection offered by the use of the corporate form.

This unsatisfactory proposition, from a legal point of view, governs an area of utmost importance. A need for legal certainty is imperative in the face of increasing concentration of capital, with corporate mergers of spectacular dimensions happening with increasing frequency. Ownership of company shares is more and more in the hands of other companies in the West.

One of the questions this raises is whether the principle of limited liability should be forsaken in favour of a new, more appropriate standard. This might be: "Liability derives from control." This would mean that, whenever there was a finding of company control, liability for the debts of the controlled company would be placed upon the controller. This proposition has enjoyed the support of some legal writers, but until now the legal systems have been reluctant to adopt it. Perhaps the time has come for new modes of capital ownership to be developed. One of these could involve an adjustment of the traditional principles governing limited liability.

It is obvious that limited liability still has a major role to play in economic development—a purpose clearly of the utmost importance. These considerations notwithstanding, increasing abuse of the limited liability privilege presents legal scholars with a challenging need for checks and balances to safeguard the rights of creditors appropriately. It should be said that lifting the veil problems arise more often than not in the context of an abuse of limited liability.

* * *

B. Company Control Under French and Argentine Law

It should be noted that French and Argentine decisions have not used lifting of the veil solutions in the context of the "abuse of rights" theory, although some legal writers have suggested it.[43]

In its 1968 Civil Code Reform Act (Ley 17.711), Argentina introduced an express general provision that the law does not recognise the abusive exercise of rights. This would apply, for instance, when the purpose of the law granting the rights is contradicted, or when the limits imposed by good faith, morality or custom are exceeded.[44]

French statutes contain no express provision on the abuse of rights, but a strong and consistent line of cases has established the existence and application of the theory in French law.[45] It has become a versatile instrument in the hands of judges, who use it in all sorts of circumstances and without imposing rigid limits on it.

In Argentina, a finding of abuse of rights enables the judge to apply various remedies: (a) to make the person responsible liable in damages to the injured party; (b) to freeze any effects of the abusive act; and (c) to refuse to hear any legal action based on the abusive act. As a matter of law, a nullity will follow a finding of an abuse of rights because the relevant conduct is wrongful.

In both these legal systems, abuse of rights would seem to be the correct point from which to develop a doctrine of "abusive control."

* * *

IV. Economic Units

So far this article has examined, albeit briefly, the legal consequences of the relationship of control between a company and another person, whether individual or corporate. Separation has to be established—by definition, there has to be two persons. A different situation arises when such a separation is absent. Different remedies have to be used since unity has taken the place of separation. All four countries examined in this article have produced relevant case law.

A. French and Argentine Court Decisions on Unity

Since 1973 the Argentine courts have developed a doctrine under which insolvency proceedings may be extended from one company to another person (corporate or individual), where there has been *unidad jurídica* (legal unity) between them. It is not entirely clear what the prerequisites of this unity are, but the *Suprema Corte de Justicia de la Nación* has held that fraud must be shown for this remedy to become available. Another case referred

43. Serick, *Apariencia y realidad de las sociedades comerciales. El abuso del derecho por medio de la persona jurídica* (1958), p. 241.

44. Art. 1071, Argentine Civil Code: "*La ley no ampara el ejercicio abusive de los derechos. Se considerara tal al que contrarie los fines que aquélla tuvo en mira al reconocerlos o al que exceda los límites impuestos por la buena fe, la moral y las buenas costumbres*"; abuse of rights was made unconstitutional by express provision of the Argentine Constitution of 1949 (art. 35)....

45. Ghstin, Goubeaux, *Traité de driot civil, introduction générale* (2nd ed., 1983), p. 617, n. 697....

to the existence in fact of "only one enterprise."[66] It has also been decided that "independent policies" in the management of the companies making a group means that the concept of unity is inapplicable. In fact, there is great uncertainty in this area of the law.

A similar situation prevails in France, where court decisions have developed the doctrine of *confusion des patrimoines* (comingling of assets) to the same type of problem.[68] When this is applied, two or more companies can be made subject to common insolvency proceedings. There is no clear authority on the conditions under which this remedy becomes available. After initially adopting a broad approach, the courts have directed themselves towards a fraud approach, requiring "total confusion" of assets as the only cause for extending insolvency proceeding this way. The French courts seem to have reverted to a *société fictive* approach, which is itself an application of fraud principles. The present situation is uncertain, and French scholars say that the doctrine is in a state of flux.

Comments and Questions

1. To what extent, if any, are the continental approaches to "piercing the corporate veil" essentially a specialized species of fraud? How does fraud, simulation, and dolus differ in their application in continental law? If the corporation is merged with its shareholder for purposes of "piercing the veil" on grounds of fraud, ought a result of that merger be the nullity of the corporation in its entirety?

2. To what extent is the doctrine of "veil piercing" a means of regulating the use by sole shareholders, or by the limited participants of a closely held corporation of the corporate form? As you will see in the materials in the following section, the law with respect to the disregard of the corporate form in the context of multi-corporate enterprises may be different than that used in the case of shareholders who are natural persons.

3. What are the differences between the American, English, French and German approaches to the disregard of the corporate form? Are the differences merely of form or are there real substantive differences? How do you explain the different approaches? For a discussion of some of the issues, see Neil Hawke, Corporate Liability (London: Sweet & Maxwell 2000).

4. Messrs. Cohn and Simitis argue in the excerpt above that "the function of the doctrine of the lifting of the veil can, it seems, be performed by many other doctrines of a similarly equitable character." The same is true from the perspective of the American lawyer. For example, while German courts might apply the principles of disregarding the corporate form in connection with the sale of a controlling block of shares, an American lawyer would apply private law principles of contract as the basis on which to resolve disputes. In particular, the representations and warranties common to sale of stock agreements, rather than legal doctrine of "veil piercing" might form the heart of the American analysis. Looking at the other hypotheticals raised in that excerpt, can you suggest alternative's to the American doctrine of "veil piercing" that might have been applied.

5. Is there a parallel in U.S. law to the civil law concept of the *actio Pauliana*?

---

66. First instance, *Talleres Inglemere SA*, ED. 48-361.

68. Paris, 5.7.66 [1966] Rev.trim.dr.comm. 1006, obs. Houin; Cass. com. 15.3.82, D.1982, 404; idem, 11.4.82 [1983]. Rev.trim.dr.comm. 477.4; Paris, 12.7.76, D.1977, I.R. 42;....

In the United States, bankruptcy courts have subordinated the claims of shareholders to those of creditors where the courts conclude that shareholder equity investment in the bankrupt corporation was inadequate. This principle is known as the 'Deep Rock Doctrine' and originated in Taylor v. Standard Gas & Electric Company, 306 U.S. 307 (1939), in which the Supreme Court permitted courts to use their equity jurisdiction to subordinate shareholder debt claims against a bankrupt corporation to the claims of other creditors. The problem of adequacy of capitalization in a bankruptcy context continues to vex the courts. A number of approaches have been developed. Some courts have looked to the extent to which shareholders complied with corporate formalities when creating shareholder debt.[1] Others have looked to the capitalization of the corporation at the time the debt is incurred to apply a test based on the willingness of third party creditors to make a similar loan on equal terms at the times the shareholder debt is incurred.[2] Still other courts require, as a prerequisite to the assertion of a court';s equity power, proof of undercapitalization and a showing of some sort of suspicious, inequitable conduct.[3] Is subordination of shareholder debt an adequate alternative to piercing the corporate veil? Does your answer depend on the amount of corporate aseets available for distribution to creditors at the time of a bankruptcy?

b. Veil Piercing Among Related Companies

The problems of limited liability become especially acute when a corporation is owned by another. In this context the possibility for abuse becomes acute. It is possible, for example, for a corporation to limit its liability with respect to risky enterprises by placing those operations in a subsidiary. Should this subsidiary fail, its creditors would, absent guarantees or the like from the parent corporation, be able to look only to the resources of the subsidiary. The 20th century saw the beginning of a furious policy debate over the fairness of this possibility in enterprise organization. The excerpts below highlight the contours of that debate and the ways in which governments have responded. In reading the materials, think about which position you think is stronger, and what, if anything, should be the response of government? Consider also whether the potential abuses of the power to create groups of enterprises can be militated by private law means.

Jose Engracia Antunes, *The Liability of Polycorporate Enterprises*

13 CONN. J. INT'L L. 197 (1999)
(excerpts pages 203–215, 217–218, 221–223; some footnotes omitted)

C. The Polycorporate Enterprise

---

1. *See* In re Frett Roofing & Sheet Metal Co., Inc., 438 F.Supp. 726 (E.D. Va. 1977) aff'd 605 F.2d 1201 (4th Cir. 1979) (debt equity ratio of over 80 to 1 was alone not enough to undercapitalization, but when combined with a failure to observe corporate formalities in the creation of debt then evidence sufficient to subordinate the shareholders loans).
2. *See* In re Trimble Co., 479 F.2d 103 (3rd Cir. 1973).
3. *See* In re Branding Iron Steak House, 536 F.2d 299 (9th Cir. 1976).

1. The Rise of the Polycorporate Enterprise

This classical statutory model of enterprise, and its attached liability regime, has operated satisfactorily as long as the business enterprise has indeed been organized and conducted through a single independent corporation. However, if one looks to the modern world economy, one concludes that enterprises have increasingly chosen to organize and conduct their business operations in the form of a cluster of various separate corporations, rather than as a single corporate entity. Instead of the initial atomistic corporate world living under a perfect competition and free market model, the present century assisted the rise of an economic order largely dominated by multinational and multicorporate groups. Therefore, the major enterprise has typically evolved as a complex, large-scale business network, where the different parts of a unitary business are allocated to a group of affiliated corporations (subsidiary corporations), global co-ordination is obtained through the submission of such legally independent parts to a common economic strategy, and management of the whole is exercised by headquarters (parent corporation).

As a matter of fact, of the one hundred largest economic entities in the world, 50 are nations and 50 are multinational corporate groups. At the beginning of the 1970s, the total revenue of the eight largest multinational and multicorporate networks (Exxon, GM, Ford, General Electric, IBM, Chrysler, Texaco and Shell) was already some $118 billion, a monetary mass identical to the global budget expenses of six European member states together (Belgium, Germany, France, Italy, Luxembourg, Netherlands). Some of these networks are even stronger economically than individual nations. For instance, the annual revenue of General Motors is higher than the gross national product of Belgium, the annual revenue of Standard Oil corresponds to the one of a country such as Denmark, and the annual revenue of IBM to those of Portugal or Norway. No wonder "multinational corporate groups increasingly have become predominant in the world economy."[69]

The enterprise has thus entered a new evolutionary age of its structural organization: the earlier model of the individual singlecorporate enterprise has thus been simply superceded by the more complex model of the polycorporate enterprise, which represents what is, by and large, the dominant form of enterprise organization in the largest world-wide markets (the United States, EU, and Japan).[70]

2. The New Feature of Corporate Control

Surprisingly, this dramatic change of enterprise structures has been a result of the paradox rooted at the very core of modern Corporation Law. In fact, whereas the original regulatory framework of incorporated enterprises was firmly anchored on the dogmatic archetype of corporate autonomy (along with the fundamentals of legal personality and limited liability), legislators all over the world have tacitly begun to comply with some corporate practices and even to introduce new legal mechanisms which have brought about a new and emergent feature: corporate control.[71]

---

69. Phillip I. Blumberg, *The Increasing Recognition of Enterprise Principles in Determining Parent and Subsidiary Corporation Liabilities*, 28 Conn. L. Rev. 295, 297 (1996).

70. For a more extensive empirical analysis of the impact of the polycorporate enterprise in today's world economy, *see* Jose Engracia Antunes, *Liability of Corporate Groups*, *in* 10 Studies in Transnational Economic Law 37 (1994).

71. The term control is an elusive one, as elusive as the reality it describes. There is no satisfactory formula known to this author for defining the phenomenon of control as a power of dominance over the corporation, capable of embracing all its possible origins, mechanisms, forms, and effects. Although we can intuitively perceive it as a crucial phenomenon of the internal and external dynamics of modern corporations, control represents a manifold reality that is not susceptible to

Though not all appearing at the same time or having the same nature, nevertheless such mechanisms of control all had something in common. They opened up the possibility that corporations could be controlled by other corporations and governed according to alien business interests. These legal mechanisms of intercorporate control are now multiple, including those of a financial nature (namely intercorporate stock ownership, cross-shareholdings, concentration of voting rights),[72] a contractual nature (be that by the use of specific inter-enterprise contractual agreements[73] or of common commercial contracts[74]), a personal nature (interlocking directorships),[75] or an organizational nature (namely, those established through the corporate by-laws).[76]

---

being grasped by a bold theoretical definition. The works on this new feature of corporation law are rather fragmentary. *See* Claude Berr, *La Place de la Notion de Controle en Droit des Societes, in* MELANGES EN L'HONNEUR DE DANIEL BASTIAN 1 (1974) (Fr.); Michael Stork, *Definition Legale du Controle d'une Societe en Droit Francais*, 104 REVUE DES SOCIETES 385 (1986) (Fr.); Antonio Pavona La Rosa, *"Controllo" e "Gruppo" nella Fenomenologia dei Collegamenti Societari*, 1 DRITTO FALLIMENTARE 1 (1985) (Italy); Marchetti, *Note Sulla Nozione di Controllo nella Legislazione Speciale* 1 (Italy); Marco Lamandini, *Il "Controllo"—Nozioni e Tipo nella Legislazione Economica*, QUADERNI DI GIURISPRUDENZA COMMERCIALE (1995) (Italy); John H. Farrar, *Ownership and Control of Listed Public Companies: Revising or Rejecting the Concept of Control, in* COMPANY LAW IN CHANGE 39 (B.G. Pettet ed., 1987) (U.K.); Adolf Berle, *"Control" in Corporation Law*, 58 CORNELL L. REV. 1212 (1958) (U.S.); Daniel Fischel & Frank Easterbrook, *Corporate Control Transactions*, 91 YALE L.J. 698 (1982) (U.S.); Richard Jennings, *Trading in Corporate Control*, 44 CAL. L. REV. 1 (1956) (U.S.); EDWARD S. HERMAN, CORPORATE CONTROL, CORPORATE POWER (1981) (U.S.).

72. *See* Investment Trust Corp. v. Singapore Traction Co., 1 Ch. 615 (1935) (Eng.) (where only one share was capable of outvoting the remaining 399,999 shares; this still remains a paramount example of the revolutionary scope of this mechanism of intercorporate control in the realm of the classical model of the autonomous corporation).

73. Examples of such agreements are management control contracts, business transfer contracts, or profit pools. *See generally* PHILIPE ENGLISH, LES GROUPES D'ENTREPRISES A STRUCTURE CONTRACTUELLE (1980); BARTHELEMY MERCADAL & PHILIPPE JANIN, LES CONTRACTS DE COOPERATION INTERENTREPRISES (Juridiams Lefebure ed., 1974); Strobel, Unternehmensvertrag im deutschen und franzosichen Recht; G. VIRASSAMI, LES CONTRATS DE DEPENDANCE (1986); OTTO VON BREVERN, ALLGEMEINE GRUNDSATZE FUR UNTERNEHMENSVERTRAGE (1971).

74. Enterprises are increasingly cooperating through a variety of relationships organized by the use of common contractual forms, which are likely to alienate their power of economic self-determination. For instance, supply agreements (*"Lieferungsvertrage," "contrats de fourniture"*) may create a factual control between a corporation which is producing a very specialized product and its monopsonic buyer in the market. Loan contracts (*"Darlehensvertrage," "contrats de pret"*) may also create a factual control of the corporate lender over corporate borrower due to clauses eventually included in the contractual agreement attributing supervisory or monitoring rights to the former concerning the management of the latter's business (the German Cartel Commission disclosed that, in about 850 loan contracts, it has found the existence of clauses by which the corporation-borrower bound itself to supply 80% of its total production exclusively to the corporation-lender. See Bundeskartellamt, *"Tatigkeitbericht,"* 40. And the list goes on: technology transfer contracts (*"Lizenzvertrage," "accords de transfer de technologie"*), exclusivity contracts (*"Ausschließkeitsbindungen," contrat d'exclusivite d'achat ou vente"*), agency contracts (*"Besorgungsvertrage," "sous-traitance"*), franchising contracts, etc.....

75. Although positively rejected in earlier times, the possibility of the same physical persons integrating the organs of different corporations has led to the device of interlocking board directorates ("personelle Verflechtung," "unions personnelles") as a major institutional mechanism of intercorporate control. *See* JOHN ANDREWS, THE INTERLOCKING CORPORATE DIRECTOR (1982); Werner Ebke, *Interlocking Directorates*, 19 ZEITSCHRIFT FUR UNTERNEHMENS-UND GESELLSCHAFTSRECHT 50 (1990)....; FRANZ STOKMANN ET AL., NETWORKS OF CORPORATE POWER (1985).

76. Contrary to the original assumptions of the founding fathers of Corporation Law, the incorporated enterprise is not a democratic organization and the basic rule governing its functioning (the so-called majority principle) turns out to function essentially as a strategic mechanism for the appropriation of corporate control in the hands of a few wealthy investors. As Eisenberg put it, "what

With this growing statutory and jurisprudential acceptance of corporate control within the fold of classical Corporation Law, this branch lives under a truly schizophrenic paradox. The regulation of the incorporated enterprise is being achieved through a branch of law obeying opposite inspiring images of the corporation: the corporation as an autonomous and independent entity versus the corporation as an affiliated and controlled entity. This branch of law also promotes competing types of enterprise and economic organization: the single corporate enterprise versus the polycorporate enterprise.

3. The Liability of the Polycorporate Enterprise

Needless to say, with this deep mutation in the organization and structure of the modern enterprise, the original regulatory framework provided for by classical Corporation Law has thus become a matter of doubt. While the economic forms of enterprise organization have evolved in the direction of multicorporate structures, the legal forms of its organization have remained stuck to a statutory model designed and conceived exclusively for the case of single corporate enterprises. As a result of this decoupling between the legal and economic models of the enterprise, the polycorporate enterprise has thus become an "explosive shell of classical company law."

One of the areas where the challenge set by the polycorporate enterprise to Corporation Law is greater concerns the area of enterprise liability, that is, the treatment of liability issues of parent-subsidiary relationships. As it shall be shown further in detail, the crucial problem here obviously relates to the unsuitability of the classical liability standards of Corporation Law designed for the case of single corporate enterprises to the emergent phenomenon of the polycorporate enterprise. In reality, the automatic extension of these classical standards to the new reality of corporate groups leads inevitably to untenable distortions. The best proof of the inadequacy of such an extension lies in the incredible amount of cases dealing with liability issues in multicorporate networks, where the central question is invariably the plaintiff's complaint about the inequitable outcome of the formal liability insulation in the parent-subsidiary corporation relationship in spite of the existence of a real linkage of control between them.

III. The Polycorporate Enigma

The polycorporate enterprise is conventionally defined as a complex multinational and multi-unit business network, where the different parts of a unitary business are allocated to a group of affiliated corporations (subsidiary corporations), and where global co-ordination is obtained through the submission of such legally independent parts to a common economic strategy and management for the whole exercised by

---

counts is not shareholders, but shareholdings." MELVIN EISENBERG, THE STRUCTURE OF THE CORPORATION: A LEGAL ANALYSIS 44 (1976). Furthermore, the controlling and autarchic properties of the basic principle "one share-one vote" may even be strengthened by an appropriated design of the articles of association, which may ultimately enhance the control of one corporation over another, even in cases of minority stockholdings. Examples of this are, for instance, cumulative voting shares ("*Mehrstimmenrecht*," "*actions a vote plural*," "*azioni a voto plurimo*"), no voting shares ("*actions sans droit de vote*," "*azioni senza voto*"), "golden shares," the use of proxies, voting trusts, etc. A major example is given by the so-called "oligarchic clauses," well known in Dutch and German law, describing any kind of stipulation in the articles of association of a corporation conferring on the holder of a certain class of shares a casting vote regarding the nomination of the members of the board or special rights in the context of the general meeting. *See* Herman Biron, *Les Clauses Oligarchiques en Droit Neerlandais*, RPS 273 (1961); RENE RODIERE, LE DROIT DES SOCIETES DANS SES RAPPORTS AVEC LA CONCENTRATION 39 (1967).

headquarters (parent corporation). Thus, in its fundamentals, the polycorporate enterprise constitutes a new form of enterprise organization where a plurality of separate legal entities are submitted to a unitary economic direction.

A. Unity and Plurality of the Polycorporate Structure

Since it was discovered one century ago,[37] the problem of the polycorporate enterprise ("*groups of companies*," "*Konzern*," "*groupe de societes*," "*gruppi di societa*") has become one of the most controversial topics of modern private law.[38]

As a matter of fact, this controversy had a great deal to do with the distinctive and enigmatic feature of this phenomenon, the paradoxical tension or contradiction between plurality (multiplicity of legal entities) and unity (unity of economic entity) within the fold of the same enterprise. The problem, which attracted a whole generation of scholars, consists of the major challenge emerging from this contradiction: while traditional corporate laws were designed to regulate independent and individual incorporated enterprises, the polycorporate cluster represents a sort of "super-enterprise" without legal personality which exists and acts precisely through first-degree legally independent enterprises.

In a very famous expression coined by Ludwig Raiser more than twenty-five years ago, "the polarity between unity of the total and the multiplicity of the parts constitutes the central problem."[41]

B. Autonomy and Control of the Polycorporate Organization

The core of the problem is yet unresolved and the results achieved so far are rather unsatisfactory.[42] I submit that the enigmatic core of polycorporate enterprise, this polarity between "unity and diversity" (Einheit und Vielheit), is to be understood as being the ultimate result of the aforementioned paradoxical tension underlying modern Corporation Law, a branch between the two competing principles of corporate autonomy and of corporate control.

1. Legal Plurality and Corporate Autonomy

The typical legal plurality of multicorporate networks is nothing but the direct and necessary consequence of the existence of a principle of corporate autonomy.

Without the existence of this corporate autonomy, multicorporate groups as a particular form of enterprise organization would certainly be unthinkable. As a matter of

---

37. The concept of group has been employed for the first time in the legal doctrine by an Austrian lawyer. *See* Landesberger, *Welche Maßnahmen empfehlen sich fur die rechtliche Behandlung der industrielle Kartelle, in* GUTACHEN FUR DIE 26. DJT II 294, 301 (1902).

38. "The groups of companies," says Yves Guyon, "are at the very heart of all the problems of company law." Yves Guyon, *Examen Critique des Projects Europeens en Matiere de Groupes de Societes,* in GROUPS OF COMPANIES IN EUROPEAN LAW 155 (K. Hopt ed., 1982) (original in French). This is well illustrated by the more than one thousand articles that have been published on this subject in the last 35 years in Germany alone....

41. Ludwig Raiser, *Die Konzernbildung als Gegenstand rechts- und wirtschaftswissenschaftlicher Untersuchung, in* DAS VERHALTNIS VON WIRTSCHAFTSWISSENSCHAFT ZUR RECHTSWISSENSCHAFT 51, 54 (Raiser et al. eds., 1964).

42. *See* Wolfram Timm, *Minderheitenschutz und unternehmerische Entscheidungsfreiheit,* 153 ZEITSCHRIFT FUR DAS GESAMTE HANDELSRECHT 60 (1989) ("Despite numerous efforts during the last two decades on this topic, the basic problematic of group law has not yet been settled." (original in German)); Herbert Wiedemann, *Die Unternehmensgruppe* in PRIVATRECHT 5 (1988) ("In any case, for the time being, it seems not possible to present a "general theory' of group law, which would be valid for all the private law areas and in which could be founded the common root for the law of the affiliate enterprise." (original in German)).

fact, without corporate autonomy, corporations wishing to economically integrate their businesses or to submit them to a common business strategy could only resort to a merger. Accordingly, the historical evolution from the singlecorporate to the polycorporate enterprise that occurred throughout the present century would not have been possible. Enterprises undergoing a growing process would have had to choose between two rigid organizational options, either internal growth or fusion, and economic activity would then have been conducted by enterprises organized not as large multicorporate business networks, but instead as large monolithic single corporations.

2. Economic Unity and Corporate Control

The economic unity of multicorporate networks, crystallized in the existence of a unified management exercised as a rule by the parent corporation over its various subsidiaries, is also a result of the emergent feature of corporate control.

In fact, the exercise of this unified management by the group-headquarters presupposes that the parent corporation holds an ultimate power of domination over the business activities of the affiliated corporations. If this power does not exist, neither does unified management ("unified management is domination").[46] By expressly or tacitly recognizing a number of intercorporate control devices, namely intercorporate stockownerships, the law gave an institutional reality and a safe legal support to the organization of the parent-subsidiary links. Without such institutional devices of corporate control, the creation of stable polycorporate networks would have been completely unthinkable ("the vital link" would then be missing[48]) and corporations wishing to grow would be compelled either to choose the option of merger, where a safe legal basis for the concentration of both incorporated businesses is offered, or to embark in the pursuit of highly risky and unstable intercorporate relationships, since intercorporate ties would be lacking in any kind of formal-legal support. In other words, had the law not provided for the existence of judicially-based mechanisms of intercorporate control, it is most probable that the history of enterprise organization in the twentieth century would have been very different and that multicorporate and multinational business networks would have never succeeded to impose themselves as the major form of enterprise organization.[49]

C. Centralization and Decentralization in the Polycorporate Organization

Autonomy and control also represent the two basic operational patterns of decision-making power allocation within a polycorporate network. Actually, the polycorporate

---

46. Echard Rehbinder, Konzernrecht und allgemeines Privatrecht. Eine rechtsvergleichende Untersuchung nach deutschem und amerikanischem Recht 23 (1969).

48. *See* 2 Phillip I. Blumberg, The Law of Corporate Groups 14 (1982) (noting that this is the vital link: "[w]ithout the existence of control, the corporations do not constitute a corporate group.").

49. At best, one could imagine informal vehicles of intercorporate control being used to construct the ties of such networks and sustain their global coordination, as happened, for instance, with the old Japanese "zaibatsu," based as they are largely on a community of interest and a tradition of cooperation. *See* Jose Engracia Antunes, Structure and Organization of Japanese Multinational Enterprises: Some Features of Japanese Corporate Management (1988); Robert Tindall, Multinational Enterprises: Legal and Management Structures and Interrelationship with Ownership, Control, Antitrust, Labor, Taxation, and Disclosure 36 (1975). But in Western economies, these types of intercorporate control links would certainly have proved to offer a very unsafe and fragile basis for the coordination of group components and a rather unattractive basis for the creation and functioning of the polycorporate structure, as an alternative organizational form of enterprise activity.

enterprise is a new form of enterprise organization whose specificity consists of the conduct of a unitary business through extremely flexible governance structures where a constantly changing, ad-hoc, and opportunistic blend of the autonomy of parts and the control of the whole is being processed.

One should notice here that autonomy or control are all of one piece: full autonomy and full control represent just the polar situations of the broadest of spectrums for distribution of governance power in a parent-subsidiary relationship, as centralization and decentralization represent the outer limits of a scale of numerous alternative organizational structures for polycorporate enterprises. Reality is therefore always situated somewhere in between. What is more, the actual partition of decision-making power in complex business polycorporate networks (i.e. the concrete balance between autonomy-control found in parent-subsidiary relationships) or the concrete shape of its organizational structure (i.e. the degree of group centralization-decentralization) cannot be determined in general terms and in advance. This means that the organizational blend between autonomy/control and between decentralization/centralization varies from group to group: "there are no two identical groups." What is valid for one group may turn out to be invalid for another. Within the same group, what can be said about one subsidiary does not necessarily imply the same for other subsidiaries of the same group. Within the same subsidiary, what is true for one functional area or one decision-making area need not be for another.[56] Within a single decision-making area of a subsidiary, there can perfectly well coexist decisions made directly by group headquarters and others that are taken autonomously by the subsidiary management. Therefore, the inquiry into the concrete balance between autonomy-control and into the distinction between centralization-decentralization can only be objectively and meaningfully made regarding concrete acts or business decisions, and not in general for the all groups, for all parent-subsidiary relations, or even all functional areas of subsidiary management.

D. An Enigma Solved?

The polycorporate enterprise appears then as an enterprise form whose possibility and specificity results precisely from the creative and dialectical interplay of these two central and somewhat contradictory features of modern Corporation Law—corporate autonomy and corporate control. It can be considered neither as simply the result of the dogma of corporate autonomy nor as the product of the competing principle of corporate control, but instead precisely the outcome of the paradoxical combination between them. These principles thus constitute inseparable factors in the genesis of the group phenomenon and their simultaneous consideration is necessary for a full understanding of its nature.

From this perspective, it is also the traditional enigmatic core of the polycorporate problem which attracted an entire generation of scholars to the so-called dilemma between unity and diversity (Einheit und Vielheit) that looks rather plain. The paradoxical polarity between the juridical autonomy of the corporation's parts and the economic unity of the whole is nothing but the ultimate result of the paradoxical situation of a branch of law that at the same time promotes the autonomy of the corporation and permits the control of the same corporation, with the consequent virtual destruction of that autonomy.

---

56. For example, central control in one functional area of the subsidiary management, e.g., finance, marketing, personal, by no means implies the existence of a similar control in a different functional area of the same corporation.

IV. The Liability of the Polycorporate Enterprise: A Comparative Overview

This hybrid nature of polycorporate enterprises soon brought about the crucial problem of the unsuitability to polycorporate enterprises of the traditional liability standards, designed by classical corporation law for the case of singlecorporate enterprises.

In fact, by extending the traditional, highly formal concepts of legal personality and limited liability (fashioned to rule the relationships between independent corporations and its individual investors) uncritically to parent corporations, legal orders and courts have proceeded without any apparent recognition of the vitally different considerations involved in the regulation of the liabilities of sole independent corporations and of mere parts of a multi-corporate groups whose activity falls entirely under the control of the parent corporation. It soon became apparent that the automatic extension of these old archetypes to the new reality of corporate groups led inevitably to untenable distortions and could not be applied indiscriminately without leading to grossly unfair results.

The best proof of the inadequacy of such an extension lies in the incredible amount of cases dealing with intragroup liability issues, where the central question is invariably the plaintiff's complaint about the inequitable outcome of the formal liability insulation of the parent-subsidiary corporation relationship in spite of the existence of a real linkage of control. Far from being restricted to one single legal branch, such cases arise across the entire range of the law, covering areas as diverse as classical tort liability, contract liability, environmental liability, product liability, labor liability, tax liability, competition liability, penal liability, bankruptcy liability, and so on. Besides, the problem is likely to increase as it has been asserted by several studies that enterprises operating in many industrial sectors, such as the hazardous-waste, chemical, nuclear, aeronautical, biotechnology sectors, usually expand through insulating in subsidiaries their most risky ventures in order to avoid tort liability exposure. Catastrophes involving large multinational corporate groups, such as the "Bhopal" disaster in India, the "Amoco Cadiz" channel oil spill in France, or the chemical accidents involving "Sandoz" in Switzerland and "Hoffmann-La Roche" in Italy, constitute vivid and dramatic illustrations of that.

The central question which has been even considered as "one of the great unsolved problems of modern company law"[60] is: given a polycorporate enterprise, under what circumstances may the parent corporation be obliged to settle the liabilities and debts of its subsidiary corporations? Notwithstanding the different degree of legislative, judicial and doctrinal development among the various national legal orders, one may distinguish currently three major types of regulatory strategies in comparative law. These strategies are the traditional strategy of the "entity law approach," the revolutionary strategy of the "enterprise approach" and the mitigate strategy of the "dualistic approach."

A. The Entity Law Approach

The so-called entity law approach is the traditional and still-prevailing regulatory strategy concerning intragroup liability for the great majority of Common or Civil Law countries.

1. Entity Law and Piercing the Corporate Veil Jurisprudence

This approach consists of the position of those legal orders that decide intragroup liability questions on the basis of the fundamental principle according to which one mem-

60. Clive Schmitthoff, *Banco Ambrosiano and Modern Company Law*, J. Bus. L. 361, 363 (1982).

ber of a corporate group, namely the parent corporation, cannot be made liable for the debts or the acts of other group members for the reason that they are distinct legal entities.[61] Under this view, the imposition of liability on the parent corporation for debts of group affiliates is considered as a rule to be impossible. Only for the most extraordinary cases and in exceptional circumstances will this rule be set aside by disregarding the corporate entity of the corporations involved ("piercing the corporate veil" in the United States, "lifting the corporate veil" in the United Kingdom, "*superamento dello schermo della personalita giuridica*" in Italy, "*abuso de la personalidad juridica*" in Latin Countries).[62]

* * *

B. The Enterprise Approach

The so-called enterprise approach pleads for a new and revolutionary regulatory strategy on intragroup liability matters, and has found its most expressive recognition in several proposals initiated by EU law during the 1970s in the context of its attempts on the harmonization and co-ordination of company laws of European member states, namely, the proposals of a directive on groups of companies [69] and a regulation on the statutes of the European Company.[70]

1. The EU Legal System

This strategy pleads that intragroup liability problems should be decided according to the fundamental principle that the parent corporation shall be liable for all the unpaid debts and acts of its subsidiaries for the reason that the former controls the latter, forming thereby a unitary economic enterprise. While not yet having become positive law, this is an interesting approach since it symbolizes in a world-wide context the most far-reaching statutory undertaking against the prevailing traditional entity law approach.

By placing itself in the antipodes of the classical approach, this trend wants to decide intragroup liability cases on the basis of a rigid application of a rule of limited liability. This solution calls for an automatic application of the opposite rule—the unlimited liability of the parent corporation. It then became clear that, while the fundamental criteria underlying the classical entity law approach were given by the old dogma of corporate autonomy, this regulatory trend is now based on the emergent feature of corporate control. By conceiving the polycorporate group as a sort of vertically-controlled, unitary enterprise with a highly centralized governance structure whose organizational axle (parent corporation) exercises complete control over the various subunits (sub-

61. On this archetype of American law on corporations, see generally PHILLIP I. BLUMBERG, THE LAW OF CORPORATE GROUPS (1987); ALFRED F. CONARD, CORPORATIONS IN PERSPECTIVE 416 (1976); WILLIAM MEADE FLETCHER, CYCLOPEDIA OF THE LAW OF PRIVATE CORPORATIONS §25 (3d ed. 1981); HARRY G. HENN & JOHN R. ALEXANDER, LAWS OF CORPORATIONS AND OTHERS BUSINESS ENTERPRISES 15, 145, 344 (3rd ed. 1983); RICHARD W. JENNINGS & RICHARD M. BUXBAUM, CORPORATIONS: CASES AND MATERIALS (1979).

62. For curious legal-comparative undertakings on the topic, *see* Ulrich Drobnig, *The Disregard of Legal Entities in International Trade*, in THE LEGAL STRUCTURE OF THE ENTERPRISE (1985); E.J. Cohn & C. Simitis, *"Lifting the Veil" in the Company Laws of the European Continent*, 12 INT'L & COMP. L.Q. 189 (1963); Juan M. Dobson, *Lifting the Veil in Four Countries: The Law of Argentina, England, France and United States*, 35 INT'L & COMP. L.Q. 839 (1986).

69. *See* Proposal for a Ninth Directive Based on Article 54, 3(g) of the EEC Treaty on Links between Undertakings and, in particular, on Groups of Companies (EEC Doc. III-1639/84-E).

70. *See* Commission Proposal for a Council Regulation on the Statute for a European Company, O.J.E.C. 16/10/; 1989 O.J. (C 263) 41; 1991 O.J. (C 176).

sidiaries), this strategy imposes liability of the parent corporation as following automatically from the very existence of polycorporate group.

* * *

C. The Dualist Approach

Somewhere in between these two radical and opposite strategies, a third intermediate and differentiated regulatory strategy may be referred to: the so-called dualist approach. This approach can only be properly understood in the global context of a specific and comprehensive law on affiliated corporations. The landmark case is Germany (1965), followed closely by some other recent national legal orders recently, such as Brazil (1976)[81] and Portugal (1986).[82]

1. The German Legal System

The German law on affiliated companies and groups of companies ("Konzernrecht"), enacted with the Stock Corporation Law of 1965, develops essentially along a two-level structure, regulating group reality on the basis of a fundamental distinction between two types of groups. [83]

On the one hand, there are the so-called "contractual groups" ("*Vertragskonzerne*"), where parent's control has been embodied "de jure" in a special organizational contract, the contract of domination ("*Beherrschungsvertrag*"), following which the law has expressly recognized to parent corporations a broad legal power of control over its subsidiaries in open deviation from some of the classical canons of corporation law, and consequently imposed on the former a duty to cover all the annual losses or even a joint liability for the settlement of debts of the latter. On the other hand, there are the so-called "factual groups" ("*faktische Konzerne*"), where the parent's control is exercised as a mere "de facto" power, following which parent corporations found themselves bound basically to the traditional canons of corporation law, being permitted to use their controlling influence only in the best interests of the subsidiary, but being as well only obliged to a duty of compensation for single established detriments that have emerged from the use of such influence.[84]

Therefore, intragroup liability solutions will follow automatically from the accommodation of group reality within one of these two pre-established types of groups: either a system of global compensation in contractual groups (where the parent is bound

81. Cf. "Lei das Sociedades Anonimas," enacted by the Law n 6404, of 15.12.1976, Chapter XX-XXII, Arts. 243–270. On Brazilian law, see Fabio Konder Comparato, *Les Groupes de Societes dans la Nouvelle Loi Bresilienne des Societes par Actions*, 54 RS 845 (1978); Jose Imbid Irujo, *Los Grupos de Sociedades en la Nueva Ley Brasilena de Sociedades Anonimas, in* REVISTA DE DERECHO MERCANTIL 461 (1979); PIRAS, I GRUPPI DI SOCIETA NEL DIRITTO TEDESCO E BRASILIANO, 263.

82. Cf. "Codigo das Sociedades Comerciais," enacted by DL n 262/ 86, of 2.9.1986, Title VI, Arts. 481–508. On the Portuguese law, *see* Jose Engracia Antunes, *The Law of Affiliated Companies in Portugal*, in 1 GRUPPI DI SOCIETA 355 (1996)....

83. On the regulation of groups of companies provided for by the Stock Corporation Law of 6.9.1965 ("Aktiengesetz") for a general introduction, *see* ERNST GESSLER ET AL., KOMMENTAR ZUM AKTIENGESETZ Bd. 1, 178–291, Lief 6 (1973 and seq.) (with commentaries of Geßler and Kropff); KOLNER, KOMMENTAR ZUM AKTIENGESETZ BD. 1, 141–285, Bd. 6, 1–577 (Wolfgang Zollner ed., 1986–87) (with commentaries of H.J. Koppensteiner); MUNCHENER HANDBUCH DES GESELLSCHAFTSRECHT, Bd. 4- Aktiengesellschaft 705–898 (Michael Hoffman-Becking ed., 1988); VOLKER EMMERICH & JURGEN SONNENSCHEIN, KONZERNRECHT (1992)....

84. *See* §§291 ff. AktG (F.R.G.) (pertaining to "contractual groups"); §§311 ff. AktG (F.R.G.) (pertaining to "factual groups")....

to assume all the annual losses of its subsidiary), or a system of mere punctual compensation in factual groups (where the parent has only to compensate concretely established patrimonial prejudice caused to the subsidiary).[85]

Karl Hofstetter, *Parent Responsibility for Subsidiary Corporations: Evaluating European Trends*

39 Int'l & Comp. L. Q. 577 (1990)
(excerpt pages 579–586; footnotes renumbered or omitted)

* * *

[German Law]

In 1965 The German legislature enacted an amendment about corporate groups to its Stock Corporation Act. This statute is still unequalled by any other piece of legislation in the world.[1] The law applies only to the "*Aktiengesellschaft*," i.e. the (large) stock corporation. It's practical effect is said to have not been dramatic. Nonetheless it has been a milestone in European corporate group law. It has to be seen as the first... attempt to diminish greatly the role of traditional "piercing the corporate veil law" in the corporate group context....

To be sure, concern law ("*Konzernrecht*") has not pre-empted the whole field of parent liability law. Contract law, tort law, bankruptcy law (fraudulent conveyance and equitable subordination law) and even "piercing the corporate veil law"have continued to serve as functional equivalents to concern law....

The German Stock Corporation Act applies to all subsidiary companies in the form of the German stock corporation.[2] It divides corporate groups into three classes: integration concerns, contract concerns and *de facto* concerns. It imposes liability on parent corporations to their subsidiaries and subsidiary creditors as follows:

.... [Integration.] Where a parent holds between 95 and 100 per cent of the stock of the a subsidiary, the two companies can agree to integrate formally [this amounts to something approaching a classical Delaware merger]. Upon integration the parent acquires the basically unlimited power to direct its subsidiary.... the corollary of this authority is the joint and several co-liability of the parent company for all existing and future creditor claims against the subsidiary.

.....[Contract concerns.] The German legislature anticipated that corporate groups linked through "control agreements" would become the most popular form of corporate affiliation. This perception was based on two facts. First, control agreements can lead to preferential treatment under German tax laws. Second, except for integration,

---

85. While these rules represent the very core of the German intragroup liability system, one should be aware of the existence of other residual and functional equivalents, such as the jurisprudential "piercing the corporate veil."...

1. More recently Brazil and Portugal enacted corporate group laws but without the far reaching liability provisions....

2. Or in the form of the (less) important limited partnership corporation ("*Kommanditgesellschaft auf Aktien*"); except for some provisions, the legal form of the parent company is not the deciding factor in determining the application of the Act; where a subsidiary falls within its coverage, the Act also applies to corporate groups with foreign parent corporations....

control agreements are the only legal way for a parent to acquire broad managing power over its subsidiary corporations. In practice, control agreements have been rarely used. This is due to the fact that the provisions about the *de facto* concern...have turned out to be without "teeth."

A control agreement is concluded through shareholder resolutions in both the parent and subsidiary corporations....A parent's broad authority under a control agreement is balanced by its obligation to compensate the subsidiary for all (annual) deficits occurring during the contract period. Subsidiary creditors can enforce compensation claims against parents within the powers given to them by the bankruptcy law.....

[De facto concerns]. Most German parent and subsidiary companies are merely linked through stock ownership. Majority ownership triggers the presumption that subsidiaries are dependant on their parent....the law does not allow any disadvantageous interference with the subsidiary's business in a *de facto* concern, unless compensation is granted. At least in theory, a broad and systematic involvement by the parent in the subsidiary's affairs is prohibited. Where a parent fails to compensate the subsidiary for any inflicted disadvantages by the end of each business year, the subsidiary acquires a claim for consequential damages. Creditors can enforce this claim by way of derivative actions.

The provisions about the *de facto* concern in the German Stock Corporation Act have remained almost dead letter. Successful actions for damages under these provisions are apparently unknown. the reason lies in high enforcement costs and risks. Proof of detrimental interference on a transaction-by-transaction basis is very difficult to establish where the business of the parent and subsidiary corporations have been highly interconnected.....

The German Stock Corporation Act does not cover subsidiaries in the form of partnerships or close corporations ("GmbH"). The close corporation is, however, a particularly important vehicle for German business. The absence of codified concern law for corporate groups with close-corporation subsidiaries caused the courts to step in....

In the *ITT* decision the German Federal Court[3] held that a parent company with a controlling influence over a subsidiary has fiduciary duties to the subsidiary commensurate with its degree of involvement in the subsidiary's affairs. A violation of fiduciary duties can trigger damage claims for the subsidiary against the parent. Going one step further, the German Federal Court later enunciated its "qualified concern" doctrine. A qualified concern is a corporate group structure in which the parent, as a mere shareholder, exerts a longstanding and pervasive control pattern over the (daily) affairs of its subsidiary. After having paved the way in *Gervais*[4] the German Federal Court handed down its forceful *Autokran* decision.[5] It held that where a parent company was "permanently and extensively" involved in the management of a now bankrupt subsidiary, a rebuttable presumption exists that the parent did not show sufficient consideration for the subsidiary. Hence, unless the parent is able to defend itself successfully, it is directly liable to the subsidiary's creditors for the subsidiary's obligations. In this remarkable decision the German Federal Court designed a way around the notorious enforcement prob-

3. Bundesgerichtshof, 65 BGHZ 15.
4. BGH 1980, in Neue Juristiche Wochenschrift, NJW 231 (1979).....
5. 95 BGHZ 330 (1985).

lems in connection with parent liability provisions for highly integrated *de facto* concerns. It did this by resorting to two legal techniques: the shifting of the burden of proof top the parent company and the granting of a direct claim against the parent to subsidiary creditors. In its subsequent *Tiefbau* decision the Court confirmed its *Autokran* rationale.[6] At the same time it restricted the parents defense to situations in which the subsidiary's "losses were caused by circumstances outside the parent's managerial control." . . . .

[French Law]

French law has taken a restrained but conceptually interesting approach to parent company liability. It has not codified a comprehensive law for company groups but has made partial adjustments in its bankruptcy and labour laws. . . . .

. . . . Two basic categories of bankruptcy extension to the parent, i.e. substantive consolidation, have to be distinguished in French law: the commingling of assets cases and the statutory consolidation cases.

The commingling of assets cases under French law resemble their equivalents under the United States "piercing the corporate veil" doctrine. They provide for substantive consolidation where the assets and affairs of a parent and subsidiary corporation have been so closely intertwined that the latter is to be considered a mere instrumentality of the former.[7]

Statutory consolidation applies where a parent company has been acting as a director of a subsidiary. The subsidiary's bankruptcy extends to the parent company where the parent (as director):

(1) disposed of the assets of the subsidiary as if it were its own;

(2) used the subsidiary as a mask to achieve its own interests;

(3) used the assets and loans from the subsidiary in a way that impaired the latter's interests;

(4) exploited the subsidiary in a way that had to lead to bankruptcy;

(5) destroyed documents or failed to keep proper accountability of the subsidiary's affairs; or

(6) fraudulently depleted the subsidiary of its assets.[8]

A parent is considered a "director" where it administered the subsidiary's affairs like a director, notwithstanding its formal position. Thus a parent becomes a *de facto* director[9] if it involves itself in the subsidiary's day to day management without having been formally elected as a director.

The creative part of French substantive law lies in its recognition of the "*de facto* director" notion. Through its restriction of substantive consolidation to the described ex-

---

6. BGH ZIP 1989, 440z; NJW 1800 (1989).

7. Maurice Cozian and Alain Viandier, *Droit des societes* 440 (1987).

8. *Action en extension*, loi du 25 janvier 1985, Art. 182; [*see also* Maurice Cozian and Alain Viandier, Droit des Societes 441 (1987)].

9. *Dirigeant de fait.*

treme cases of parent misconduct it does, however, in effect not move significantly beyond, e.g., substantive consolidation law in the United States.

B. *Directors' Liability*

If a parent company acted as a formal or *de facto* director of a now bankrupt subsidiary, it can become liable under French law.[10] The establishment of parent liability requires that the parent violated its fiduciary duties as a director of the subsidiary.[11] Furthermore, proximate cause between the parent's action or inaction and the infliction of damage on the subsidiary must be proven. Subsidiary creditors do not have a direct claim against the parent; they can enforce parent liability only derivatively.....

In any case, parent directors' liability law has not been made use of frequently by French subsidiary creditors. The odds against bringing successful actions under this legal regime have proved to be overwhelming. Plaintiffs have the difficult task of establishing a parent's status as a director, its violation of fiduciary duties and proximate causation of damages to the subsidiary. Litigation risks are further amplified by the lack of direct claims of subsidiary creditors against the parent. In fact the enforcement problems which surround French parent directors' liability law mirror those for the *de facto* concern under the German Stock Corporation Act.

C. *Labour Law*

French Labour law has gone a significant step further than French Bankruptcy law in its provision for parent liability. It attaches parent liability whenever a parent has involved itself in the relationship between a subsidiary and its employees. If a parent has, e.g., directed its subsidiary in its hiring decisions or has directly addressed subsidiary employees by giving them work instructions, it automatically assumes joint and several liability to the subsidiary's employees.....

Sandra K. Miller, *Piercing the Corporate Veil among Affiliated Companies in the European Community and in the U.S.: A Comparative Analysis of U.S., German, and U.K. Veil Piercing Approaches*

36 Am. Bus. L.J. 73 (1998)
(excerpts pages 99–109, 111–114; some footnotes omitted)

PIERCING THE CORPORATE VEIL OF AFFILIATED CORPORATIONS UNDER GERMAN LAW

* * *

Limited Liability Under German Law

---

10. *Action en comblement du passif*, loi du 25 janvier 1985, Art. 180.....

11. *Faute de gestion.*

German corporate law provides for limited liability regarding the obligations of both the public AG and the private GmbH.[119] However, as in the U.S., there is a body of case law (referred to as "Durchgriffshaftung") which provides for piercing of the corporate veil in exceptional cases for serious reasons of equity and good faith.[120]

In addition to case law, Book III of the German Stock Corporation Law of 1965 provides a comprehensive set of rules governing controlling and controlled enterprises known as the "Konzern."[121] The "Konzernrecht," or law concerning controlling and controlled enterprises, is intended to protect shareholders and creditors of public companies largely by requiring the dominating company to compensate the dominated company for any annual net losses.[122]

---

119. *See* Gesetz betreffend die Gesellschaften mit beschränkter Haftung (Act on Limited Liability Companies) [hereinafter GmbH] v. 10.5 1994 (BGBI. I 2922), (F.R.G.), § 6 ¶ 1, translated in [1 Business Transactions in Germany (Matthew Bender) (Dennis Campbell et al. eds., 1994) at app. 6].... [The Aktiengesellschaft [hereinafter AG] is governed by the Stock Corporation Act or Aktiengesetz [hereinafter AktG],] *see* AktG § 1 ¶ 1, translated in 1 Business Transactions, *supra*, at app. 7; [Carston Alting, *Piercing The Corporate Veil in American and German Law-Liability of Individuals and Entities: A Comparative View*, 2 Tulsa J. Comp. & Int'l L. 187, 190 (1984)] (providing an overview of the German and U.S. laws regarding entity recognition and the disregard of the corporate entity in the case of the individual and corporate shareholder).

120. *See* Alting, *supra* note [119], at 190 (describing the veil-piercing jurisprudence in Germany).

121. *See* AktG § 15–19, 290–338, translated in 1 Business Transactions, *supra* note [119], at app. 7 (describing four different parent-subsidiary relationships which require one AktG to be dominated by another business enterprise). *See also* 2 Business Transactions, *supra* note [119], § 24.05 at 24–148 (Apr. 1994) (indicating that Section 15 Stock Corporation Act 1937 provided:

> If legally independent enterprises are combined under a centralized management for economic purposes, they form a Konzern; the individual enterprises are Konzern companies. If a legally independent enterprise is controlled by another enterprise because of participations or otherwise, the controlling and the controlled enterprise together are deemed to form a Konzern and to be individually Konzern companies).

See Alting, *supra* note [119], at 233 (indicating that the term "Konzern" usually refers to the affiliated group of companies and the law is known as the "Konzernrecht"). *See also* 2 Business Transactions, *supra* note [119], § 24.05 at 24–148 (Apr. 1994) (discussing the history of the Konzern and indicating that originally the Konzern received preferential tax treatment under the Corporation Tax Act of 1920. The 1920 tax code exempted from corporate taxable income dividend income received from companies in which a 25% interest or more was held. The tax rules were changed in 1977 and the corporate level tax on income which is distributed to shareholders has been completely eliminated).

122. *See* AktG § 302, translated in 1 Business Transactions, *supra* note 42, at app. 7 providing:
Assumption of Losses

> (1) In the case of a control agreement or profit transfer agreement, the other contracting party shall compensate any annual net loss occurring during the term of the agreement to the extent that such loss is not compensated by withdrawing amounts from the profit reserves which were transferred to such reserves during the term of the agreement.
> (2) If a controlled company has leased or otherwise surrendered the operation of its business to its controlling enterprise, such controlling enterprise shall compensate any annual net loss occurring during the term of the agreement to the extent that the consideration agreed upon for such lease or surrender does not constitute adequate compensation.
> (3) The company may only waive or compromise any claim for compensation after the expiration of three years from the date on which the registration of the cancellation or termination of the agreement in the commercial register shall be deemed to have been announced pursuant to § 10 of the Commercial Code. The foregoing shall not apply if the party obligated to compensate is insolvent and enters into composition with his creditors

The Konzernrecht provides a broad array of rules governing the affiliated group's structure, governance, auditing, information reporting, and liability to creditors. The statute applies only to the public stock company or partnership limited by shares. However, case law has developed similar rules by analogy in the case of the controlled privately-owned GmbH.[123] As the world's only codification systematically governing the parent-subsidiary relationship, the German Konzernrecht has served as a model for several European proposals concerning the affiliated group of companies.[124]

A Konzern is created if a controlling enterprise and one or more controlled enterprises are combined under the centralized management of the controlling enterprise.[125] The controlled company must be a publicly-owned corporation or AG, although the controlling enterprise may take any form and need not necessarily be a corporation.[126] A rebuttable presumption of control exists in the case of majority ownership.[127] In the absence of majority ownership, control exists if the minority has direct influence, through a contractual relationship or because of strong representation on the Supervisory Board.[128]

The German statute provides two methods of regulating controlling and controlled enterprises. In the case of the contractual Konzern, the controlling and controlled companies enter into an express contract or enterprise agreement. In the absence of an express contract, a de facto Konzern is created and the statute imposes a variety of rules designed to protect both the shareholder and creditor.

The Contractual Konzern

If a contractual Konzern is created, the terms of the enterprise agreement are of public record.[129] The most common types of agreements are the domination agreement[130]

> to avoid or terminate bankruptcy proceedings. Such waiver or composition shall only become effective if the outside shareholders consent thereto by separate resolution and no minority whose holding in aggregate equals or exceeds one-tenth of the share capital represented at the passing of the resolution has recorded an objection.

123. *See* Alting, *supra* note [119], at 234 (noting that the concept of a qualified de facto domination has no statutory basis but has been developed in case law by the Bundesgerichtshof in the context of a dominated GmbH).

124. *See* [Hiroshi Motomura, *Protecting Outside Shareholders In A Corporate Subsidiary: a Comparative Look At The Private and Judicial Roles In The United States and Germany*, 61 Wis.L.Rev. 61 (1980)] (exploring the German and U.S. approach to minority shareholders).

125. *See* AktG § 290, translated in 1 Business Transactions, *supra* note [119], at app. 7 providing in part:

> (1) An agreement in which a stock corporation or partnership limited by shares submits the direction of the company to another enterprise ("control agreement") or undertakes to transfer its entire profits to another enterprise ("profit transfer agreements") shall constitute enterprise agreements.

126. Motomura, *supra* note [124], at 66 n.20 (citing H. Wurdinter, Aktien- Und Konzernrechtt 283 (3rd ed. 1973)).

127. AktG § 17(2), translated in 1 Business Transactions, *supra* note [119], at app. 7.

128. 2 Business Transactions, *supra* note [119], at § 24.05 at 24–152 (Apr. 1994) (indicating that in determining whether a loan of a stockholder can be regarded as a contribution to capital, the Federal Court of Justice (Bundesgerichtshof) has ruled that influence can only be presumed if the enterprise holds at least 25 percent of the stock of a corporation, citing BGH WM 1984, 625).

129. AktG § 294 ¶ 2, translated in 1 Business Transactions, *supra* note [119], at app. 7 (providing that the agreement only becomes effective upon its registration in the commercial register of the company's domicile).

130. The domination agreement or domination contract is referred to as the Beherrschungsvertrag. *See* Motomura, *supra* note [124], at 68.

and the profit transfer agreement.[131] The domination agreement gives the controlling enterprise the right to give instructions to management of the controlled company.[132] The profit transfer agreement requires one enterprise to transfer its entire profits to the other.[133] The two agreements are not mutually exclusive. In the case of a profit transfer agreement, reasonable amounts must be provided by periodic payments to shareholders based on the par value of shares.[134] If a domination agreement or profit transfer agreement has been executed, the dominating company is required to compensate the dominated company for the annual net loss occurring during the term of the agreement.[135] Thus, the annual balance sheet of the controlled company will show no losses.[136] The dominating company also must establish a legal reserve for the amounts which are payable.[137]

The contractual Konzern protects creditors in a number of important ways. The dominating company must create a legal reserve for amounts payable to the controlled company to compensate for its losses. The executed enterprise contract must be pub-

---

131. *Id.* The profit transfer agreement is known as the Gewinnabfuehrungsvertrag. *See* AktG §291, translated in 1 BUSINESS TRANSACTIONS, supra note [119], at app. 7.

132. *See* AktG §308, translated in 1 BUSINESS TRANSACTIONS, *supra* note [119], at app. 7 providing in part:

Power To Direct

> (1) In the case of a control agreement, the controlling enterprise shall be entitled to issue instructions to the management of the controlled company with respect to management of the controlled company. Unless otherwise provided in such agreement, instructions may be issued which are disadvantaged to the interest of the controlling enterprises or of affiliated enterprise and such controlled company.
>
> (2) The management board of the controlled company shall be obligated to comply with the instructions of the controlling enterprise. The management board may not refuse compliance with an instruction on the grounds that such instruction does not in its opinion serve the interests of the controlling enterprise or of affiliated enterprises which are members of the same group as such controlling enterprises and such controlled company unless such instructions manifestly do not serve such interests.

133. AktG. §291, translated in 1 BUSINESS TRANSACTIONS, *supra* note [119], at app. 7, provides:

Control Agreement; Profit Transfer Agreement

> (1) An agreement in which a stock corporation or partnership limited by shares submits the direction of the company to another enterprise ("control agreement") or undertakes to transfer its entire profits to another enterprise ("profit transfer agreements") shall constitute enterprise agreements. An agreement in which a stock corporation or partnership limited by shares agrees to conduct its business on behalf of another enterprise shall also constitute a profit transfer agreement.

Several other types of enterprise agreements are provided for in AktG §292 entitled "Other Enterprise Agreements." These other agreements include various types of profit sharing agreements including a pooling of profits into a profit pool; a profit arrangement involving a sharing of profits of a segment of the business; the leasing of one business to another; profit agreements which share profits with members of the management or supervisory board, or with individual employees; and certain business lease arrangements. *See* AktG §292, translated in 1 BUSINESS TRANSACTIONS, *supra* note [119], at app. 7.

134. *See* AktG §304, translated in 1 BUSINESS TRANSACTIONS, *supra* note [119], at app. 134 (providing for adequate compensation to be paid to outside shareholders in the case of a profit transfer agreement or control or domination agreement).

135. *See* AktG §302, translated in 1 BUSINESS TRANSACTIONS, *supra* note [119], at app. 134.

136. From an accounting standpoint, any deficits are effectively eliminated through the creation of an amount receivable from the controlling company. *See* 2 BUSINESS TRANSACTIONS, *supra* note [119], at §24.05[4] at 24–162 (Apr. 1994).

137. *See* AktG §300, translated in 1 BUSINESS TRANSACTIONS, *supra* note [119], at app. 7 (providing for the creation of legal reserves).

lished in the commercial register to give creditors information about the existence and form of the enterprise agreement.[138] The creditor also is protected if an enterprise agreement is terminated. Termination is made public through publication in the commercial register.[139] In the event of termination, the dominating company must provide security to the creditors whose claims arose prior to the date on which the cancellation was published in the commercial register.[140] In lieu of providing security, the dominating party may provide a guarantee to the creditors.[141]

Both shareholders and creditors are protected by standards of conduct applicable to management. Members of the management board and the supervisory board are jointly and severally liable if they have not employed the care of the diligent and conscientious manager.[142] The supervisory board, which oversees the conduct of management, is designed to provide increased accountability for corporate decisions.[143] Moreover, the legal representatives of a controlling enterprise must exercise the care of the diligent and conscientious manager in issuing instructions to the controlled company.[144]

The De Facto Konzern

If one enterprise controls the other and an enterprise agreement is not executed, the German statute creates a De Facto Konzern and requires the controlling enterprise to compensate the controlled enterprise for any disadvantageous transaction.[145] In addition, in the absence of a control agreement, the management board of the controlled company must provide an annual report on the company's relations with affiliated enterprises.[146]

---

138. 1 Business Transactions, *supra* note [119] at § 294.

139. 1 Business Transactions, *supra* note [119] at § 298 (requiring termination to be promptly reported in the commercial register).

140. 1 Business Transactions, *supra* note [119] at § 303(1).

141. 1 Business Transactions, *supra* note [119] at § 303(3).

142. 1 Business Transactions, *supra* note [119] at § 310 providing in part:

> (1) The members of the management board and supervisory board of the company shall, in addition to any person liable pursuant to § 309, be jointly and severally liable if they have acted in violation of their duties. In the event of a dispute as to whether they have employed the care of diligent and conscientious manager, they shall bear the burden of proof.
>
> (2) The consent of the supervisory board to such act shall not preclude liability for damages....

143. The existence of the Supervisory Board, which is a separate board that oversees the direction of the company, is attractive in Germany apparently because many German banks hold equity interests and seek additional protection for their investments. *See* [Vassil Breskovski, *Directors' Duty of Care in Eastern Europe*, 29 Int'l Law. 77, 91 (1995)], at 85 (indicating that a number of Eastern European countries have followed the German legal system which provides for both a Supervisory Board and a Board of Directors, offering a system which provides additional supervision desired by German banks).

144. *See* AktG. § 309, translated in 1 Business Transactions, *supra* note [119], at app. 7 (providing that the legal representatives of the controlled enterprise have the burden of proving that they acted with the care of a diligent and conscientious manager).

145. *See* AktG. § 311, translated in 1 Business Transactions, *supra* note [119], at app. 7 (requiring that if compensation is not made during the fiscal year in which the controlled company has incurred the disadvantage, the time and means of the compensation shall be determined no later than by the end of the fiscal year).

146. *See* AktG. § 312, translated in 1Business Transactions, *supra* note [119] (providing detailed rules governing the report on relations with affiliated enterprises). *See* 2 Business Transactions, *supra* note [119], at § 24.05[6] at 24, 170–171(Apr. 1994) (discussing the reporting and auditing requirements of the De Facto Konzern). *See* Alting, *supra* note [119], at 238 (indicating that because of the difficulty of stating a cause of action and proving specific damages, commentators

In the annual report on relations with affiliated enterprises, all transactions entered into with the controlling enterprise must be addressed and analyzed to determine whether a disadvantage was incurred.[147] The report must comply with the principles of conscientious and accurate accounting.[148] If the controlled enterprise is required to have audited financial statements, the report on transactions with affiliates must be submitted to the auditors together with the annual financial statements.[149] The supervisory board of the controlled corporation also must review the report on relations with affiliated enterprises.[150]

The shareholders may request that the court conduct a special audit if the external auditor has restricted the wording of, or has refused to confirm, the report on relations with affiliated enterprises.[151] A special audit also may be commissioned if the supervisory board has objected to the management's comments or if the management board states that a disadvantage has been incurred without compensation.[152]

In contrast to the contractual Konzern, the rights and responsibilities of members of a De Facto Konzern are not clearly identified.[153] In the absence of an enterprise agreement, the controlled entity must prove that the controlling enterprise caused it to be put at a disadvantage in a specific transaction. Damages must be proved. Under the German legal system this burden of proof may be difficult to sustain, particularly in light of the lack of pretrial discovery allowable and the absence of corporate rules permitting the shareholders to obtain comprehensive information.[154]

The Qualified De Facto Konzern

Although the contractual Konzern and the De Facto Konzern apply by operation of statute to controlled corporations that are public corporations, the qualified De Facto Konzern arises by judicial construction typically in the context of the private limited liability company or GmbH.[155] If a controlling enterprise permanently interferes with the conduct of business by a controlled GmbH, a qualified DeFacto Konzern may be created and the controlling enterprise may be liable to the controlled GmbH's creditors. A Qualified De Facto Konzern also may be created in certain cases where an individual exercises control over a GmbH.

Unlike the De Facto Konzern created by statute, the judicially-created qualified De Facto Konzern does not require proof of a specific detrimental transaction.[156] Rather, the focus is on whether an individual or a company has exerted a material influence

---

have criticized the de facto Konzern as being ineffective. In addition, the controlling company is not directly liable to creditors of the controlled company).

147. *See* AktG § 312 at ¶ 1, translated in 1 BUSINESS TRANSACTIONS, *supra* note [119], at app. 7.

148. *See* AktG. § 312 at ¶ 2, translated in 1 BUSINESS TRANSACTIONS, *supra* note 42, at app. 7.

149. *See* AktG § 313, translated in 1 BUSINESS TRANSACTIONS, *supra* note [119], at app. 7 (referring to Audit By External Auditors).

150. *See* AktG § 314, translated in 1 BUSINESS TRANSACTIONS, *supra* note [119], at app. 7 (referring to Examination By Supervisory Board).

151. *See* AktG § 315, translated in 1 BUSINESS TRANSCTIONS, *supra* note [119], at app. 7 (referring to Special Audit).

152. *See* AktG § 315, translated in 1 BUSINESS TRANSACTIONS, *supra* note [119], at ¶ 1–3.

153. *See* AktG § 311, translated in 1 BUSINESS TRANSACTIONS, *supra* note [119].

154. *See* Alting, *supra* note [119], at 240 (indicating that there are no German rules comparable to the broad discovery rulesapplicable under Fed. R. Civ. P. 26–37 and that AktG §§ 313–15 gives the shareholder rights to information at the shareholders meeting but that unlike accountants, who are entitled to comprehensive information, shareholders' rights to information are restricted except for the ability to demand the court appointment of accountants for special purposes under AktG § 315).

155. *See* Alting, *supra* note [119], at 241.

156. *See* Alting, *supra* note [119], at 242–43.

upon the dominated entity.[157] The extensive control creates the presumption that its exercise has been detrimental and specific damages need not be proved.[158]

In Autokran,[159] the seminal case involving the creation of a qualified De Facto Konzern, the Bundesgerichtshof (Federal Supreme Court) held that a controlling enterprise was liable to the dominated companies' lessor for lease amounts payable. The plaintiff was a lessor of cranes which it leased to seven GmbHs. The seven GmbHs were required to make lease payments for the use of the cranes. Upon default by the GmbHs the plaintiff obtained judgments for lease payments totaling 700,000 DM but was able to collect only 44,000 DM. The plaintiff was successful in recovering the balance owed from the defendant company which controlled the delinquent GmbHs.[160]

The court held that the defendant exercised such tight control over the GmbHs that a qualified De Facto relationship was created. The controlling defendant company had entered into a contract with all of the GmbHs under which it received the right to amounts receivable from the customers of the GmbHs. It also received the right to profits. In return, the controlling defendant company was obligated to assume all debts of the GmbHs including wages owed. Under these circumstances the court applied the statutory provisions pertaining to a contractual Konzern by analogy and held the controlling company liable for the obligations of the controlled GmbHs.[161]

In light of the contractual agreement between the controlling enterprise and the GmbHs in the Autokran case, the analogy to a contractual Konzern is readily apparent. However, the judiciary has stretched the analogy to the contractual Konzern even in the absence of formal contracts between the dominant and subservient companies.

In Tiefbau[162] the Bundesgerichtshof held a bank that was one of several owners of a GmbH liable to the liquidator of a GmbH because the bank controlled all of the financial affairs of the GmbH. The court applied AktG, § 302 by analogy and held that the bank was liable for losses incurred by the dominated GmbH.[163]

The court also has stated that a dominating corporation which exercised abusive control could be liable for the losses of its subsidiary. In TBB,[164] the parent and its subsidiary or "daughter" company were engaged in the construction business. A creditor

---

157. *See* Alting, *supra* note [119], at 242–43.

158. *See* Alting, *supra* note [119], at 242–43.

159. BGHZ 95, 330, 1986 NJW 188.

160. *See* Alting, *supra* note [119], at 244 (discussing Autokran case). *See also* [Dr. Thomas Stohlmeier, *German Limited Liability Company—Unlimited Liability of Parent Company?*, 21 Int'l Bus. Law. 135 (1993)] at 135 (providing an overview of German corporate law and the potential liability of a parent company under both statute and case law).

161. *See* AktG § 303, translated in 1 Business Transactions, *supra* note [119], at app. 7 (providing in part, that upon termination or cancellation of a control agreement or a profit transfer agreement, the controlling enterprise must provide security for the debts owed to creditors as of the time of the cancellation of the agreement. In lieu of security, the controlling enterprise may guarantee the debts).

162. BGHZ 107, 7, 1989 NJW 1800; Alting, *supra* note [119], at 245 (discussing the court's analogy of the facts to AktG 302). *See also* Stohlmeier, *supra* note [160] at 135 (discussing the case and its business implications).

163. AktG. § 302, translated in 1 Business Transactions, *supra* note 42, at app. 7 (providing that in the case of a control agreement or a profit transfer agreement the dominating enterprise must compensate the dominated company for annual net losses). *See* Alting, *supra* note 28, at 245 (discussing the control agreements).

164. T-Baubetreuungsgesellschaft mit schrankter Haftung (TBB), BGHZ, 1993 NJW 1200. This is a decision of the Bundesgerichtshof.

sued the parent company for the liability owed by the subsidiary. The court stated that the dominating company would be liable if control over the GmbH was abusive. The court noted, "The dominating company of a GmbH is liable if it exercises management in a way without regard to the interest of the dependent companies and without compensation of their inflictions."[165] The court also emphasized the importance of keeping separate and accurate books for the GmbH, noting, "The correct bookkeeping of the individual companies should be secured so that each company can only be charged with a part of the entire obligation so that assets of the dependent companies cannot be touched."[166] Ultimately, the defendant prevailed because the plaintiffs failed to prove that there was any wrong-doing or incorrect bookkeeping.[167]

In a more recent 1994 decision, the court re-stated its position that an individual could be personally liable if he exercised "abusive" control over a company. In a case commentary, the defendant was an individual who was part owner of a holding company that owned two GmbHs, referred to as HGmbH and B GmbH.[168] The companies were in the construction business. The defendant transferred 10 million DM from HGmbH to BGmbH, presumably to enable BGmbH to pay salary expenses. However, the defendant needlessly drained the capital of H GmbH because BGmbH only owed 200,000 DM in salary. Eventually, HGmbH went bankrupt, and its employees sued it as well as the defendant in his individual capacity for back wages and severance pay. The court held the individual defendant personally liable because his control was abusive. The court indicated that the defendant failed to give "appropriate respect to the interests of the HGmbH during exercising his position as manager."[169]

Unfortunately, as in prior decisions, the court fails to provide guidance on the nature of the control that justifies the creation of a qualified De Facto Konzern and the imposition of liability upon the dominating business entity or dominating individual. The earlier cases such as Autokran and Tiefbau suggest a liberal application of the piercing concept which does not require a particular showing of abusive parental control. The more recent decisions of TBB and Case Commentary 1994 NJW 2980 suggest that parental liability will be imposed upon the controlling shareholder of a GmbH only when the control is exercised in a manner which is not in the interests of the GmbH and which may be described as abusive.

4. *Application of Member State Limited Liability Rules to EU Matters*

The European Community has yet to harmonize the law relating to the limitation of liability of companies. The closest the Community has come has been in the proposals for the creation of a European Company Statute and in the proposal for a new Ninth

165. *Id.*

166. *Id.* at 1203.

167. *Id.*

168. *See* Case Commentary, 1994 NJW 2980. This is a decision of the Rechtsprechung der Oberlandesgrerichte in Zinilsachen (OLGZ), a trial court in Munich. *See* Alting, *supra* note 28, at 246 (indicating that the case affirmed TBB, 1993 NJW 1200, which required "abusive control" to justify the creation of a Qualified De Facto Konzern).

169. *See* Case Commentary, 1994 NJW 2980, 3246.

Directive on groups of companies. The Company Statute remains in draft form and revolves around the creation of a Societas Europa. The Ninth Directive has met substantial opposition since its re-introduction in 1985, especially from Common Law Member States who see in the Ninth Directive an attempt to force the Member States to adopt a hybrid of (the as yet not particularly effective) French and German law with respect to the liability of parent companies for the obligation of their subsidiaries.

Draft Proposal for a Ninth Directive Pursuant to Article 54(3)(G) of the EEC Treaty Relating to Links Between Undertakings and in Particular to Groups

Business Guide to EC Initiatives
1991 Spring

SECTION: I. COMPANY LAW; 2. Relationships Between Parent Companies and Their Subsidiaries ("Ninth"); Pg. 3

PUBLISHED: No official publication has been released

STATUS: Awaiting Commission approval for submission to The Council.

CONTENTS: The objective of the Ninth Directive on company law, which would apply to public limited companies, would be to define the legal relationship between parent companies and their subsidiaries in both formal and informal entities. In the first case, the formal control contract establishing the grouping would grant the parent company the right to exert influence on the running of the subsidiary, where the interests of the group as a whole took precedence over the interests of the individual subsidiary. However, the contract would also award the minority shareholders and creditors of the subsidiary an extensive range of closely defined legal rights with respect to the parent company. In the case of informally established groups of companies, where no formal control contract exists, the proposed Directive aims at greater transparency of the relationship between the companies, with the subsidiary company obliged to make available to the general public, an annual dependency report on the relationship between itself and its parent.

PROSPECTS: The future of the proposal is largely dependent upon the outcome of the consultations with Member States initiated by Commissioner Narjes in December 1984. The only governments to have voiced their opinions so far have been the UK and the Netherlands. The UK Government issued a hostile response to the draft proposal, based upon the views put forth by British employers and trade union groups. A consultative document was distributed by the UK Department of Trade and Industry (DTI) in early 1985, precisely for the purpose of eliciting these views. The UK position continues to stress the need for legislation in this area but argues that it should not be coordinated at Community level. The 1985 White Paper on Completing the Internal Market envisaged the submission of a formal proposal on the relationship of undertakings in a group by 1988. However, this deadline was not met. The Commission projected, in its fourth annual progress report concerning the implementation of the White Paper that the proposal would be put forward in 1990. Although discussion papers are in circulation, the draft proposal has still not acquired formal status. It is hoped that some change will occur by the end of 1990.

BUSINESS PERSPECTIVE: One of the major concerns of the business community would be the administrative, auditing and legal costs associated with implementation of this draft proposal which would apply to more than 500,000 companies throughout the Community. More fundamentally, the draft proposal threatens to undermine the concept of limited liability—the very basis of company law. UNICE considers that the introduction of the draft Ninth Directive is unnecessary, and will damage the competitiveness of groups operating in the EC. It suggests that the requirement of a special report on relations between the parent and subsidiary in non-formalized company groupings be dropped. The Confederation of British Industry (CBI) also objects to the use of a system of law familiar to only one of the Member States as a basis for harmonization.

Brian Harris, *"Social Charter": The Legal Basis*

New Law Journal, Vol. 139
Vol. 139, No. 6410, p. 764
2 June 1989
SECTION: EEC NEWS

TEXT: On May 17, 1989, the Commission of the European Communities put forward a "Community Charter of Fundamental Social Rights": more concisely, its proposal for a Social Charter. This has been greeted by a range of criticisms from the political suggestion that this is "socialism by the backdoor" to the legal suggestion that the Commission is extending its activities beyond the powers conferred by the Treaties. It is not the primary purpose of this article to comment on the political aspects of the argument, but rather to look at the legal basis for the various components of the Community's social policy.

* * *

Proposals

The Commission proposed a Ninth Company Law Directive in 1975, part of which has been brought into effect by Directive 88/62 and the Companies Acts 1985 and 1989 concerning the disclosure of interests in shares to the company which issued the shares. The remaining parts of the proposed Ninth Directive concern the relationship between parent companies and their subsidiaries, but remain proposals, because they reflect the existing national legislation of only one state—Germany—and are not backed by other member states. In fact, the proposals would not have much practical effect in the UK.

The forgoing materials suggest the reasons the EU failed to harmonize the law of limited liability. Despite this failure, the concepts of limited liability have crept into Community decisionmaking, and the decision making of the courts of the member states, as the following materials highlight:

Rolls Royce plc v. Mrs. D. Doughty
Employment Appeal Tribunal

[1988] 1 CMLR 569
28 July 1987

GARLAND J: This is an appeal from the Industrial Tribunal at Birmingham whose decision was sent to the parties on 16 October 1986. The issue before the Tribunal is summarised in paras 1 and 2 of the Reasons as follows:

1. Mrs Doughty was born on 7 February 1926. She worked for Rolls Royce plc and its predecessor, in such circumstances that her employment is continuous employment, from 14 November 1977 until 28 February 1986. She had a contract of employment with Rolls Royce as a Grade 6 clerk. The provisions of the company's Staff Handbook were incorporated into her contract of employment. In relation to Termination of Employment, the Staff Handbook contained a provision that:

> 'Employment ceases at normal retirement date, which is 65 for men and 60 for women'.

On the evidence, that policy is rigidly enforced. On 2 September 1985 Mrs Doughty received a note from the personnel officer which (inter alia) said:

> 'I understand our records show that you are approaching your 60th birthday and I wish to advise you that arrangements are being made for you to retire from Rolls Royce on 28 February 1986'.

That was a dismissal, the only reason for which was that Mrs Doughty was a woman who had passed the retiring age applicable to women. Rolls Royce would not have dismissed her when it did had she been a man. At the date of dismissal Mrs Doughty was able and willing to continue in her employment and would, if she had been allowed to do so, have so continued until she had reached the age of 65. As a consequence, Mrs Doughty has suffered financial loss, being the difference between what she would have earned in employment with Rolls Royce and her pension.

2. Mrs Doughty complains to the Tribunal, in her amended originating application, that she was first, unfairly dismissed under the provisions of § 54 et seq of the Employment protection (Consolidation) Act 1978; secondly, that she has been discriminated against contrary to the provisions of § 6(2)(b) of the Sex Discrimination Act 1975; and thirdly that in the circumstances of her case she is entitled to ask the Tribunal to give effect to the provisions of Article 5(1) of Council Directive 76/297 of 9 February 1976 being part of European Community Law.

The evidence on which the Tribunal finally reached the conclusion that Rolls Royce plc was 'an emanation of the State' so that the applicant was entitled to rely on Council Directive 76/207 is set out in paras 4, 5, 6 and 7 of the Reasons. Since we are asked to reconsider the legal inferences and conclusions which the Tribunal drew from that evidence, we recite it below:

4. Rolls Royce's principal business is the design, development, manufacture and sale of gas turbine engines and ancillary equipment for aircraft and for industrial and marine applications. Rolls Royce was formed in 1971 as a consequence of the insolvency of the former Rolls Royce Limited. On 4 February 1971 the former Rolls Royce Limited went into receivership. The business of that company consisted of the gas turbine business already described and the manufacture of motor cars and diesel engines. The motor car and diesel engine business was transferred by the receiver to a newly formed

company named Rolls Royce Motors Limited. By the Rolls Royce (Purchase) Act 1971 the Government was authorized to acquire for the benefit of the Crown any part of the undertaking and assets of Rolls Royce Limited. Under this authority the Government caused the formation of Rolls Royce (then named Rolls Royce (1971) Limited) as a private limited company in which all the shares were held by nominees on behalf of the Crown. The company then purchased from the receiver the undertaking and assets of Rolls Royce Limited relative to the turbine business. The transfer of the gas turbine business to the company became effective on 23 May 1971. On that day all employees of Rolls Royce Limited in Receivership became employees of Rolls Royce on the same terms and conditions as applied to their previous employment and with continuity of service. Rolls Royce's shares have at all times been held on behalf of the Crown. From 1 April 1976 until 2 August 1980 all the shares were held by the national Enterprise Board under the provisions of the Industry Act 1975. On 21 March 1977 Rolls Royce changed its name from Rolls Royce (1971) Limited to Rolls Royce Limited and on 1 May 1986 re-registered as Rolls Royce plc. None of these changes of name or the changes in the manner in which the shares have been held have changed the status of the terms and conditions of employees of the company. Rolls Royce has continued to recognise and negotiate with the trade unions previously recognised by its predecessor the former Rolls Royce Limited. For works employees the principal trade union is the AEU although a number of other trade unions are represented. As far as staff employees are concerned the principal recognised trade unions are the ASTMS, TASS and APEX. The company has at all times remained in membership of the Engineering Employers Federation and has adhered to agreements negotiated by the EEF on behalf of its member companies. No civil service trade unions have ever been recognised by Rolls Royce, and civil service terms and conditions have never been applied to its employees. Rolls Royce has at all times been registered as a limited company and has complied with the requirements of the Companies Acts. In the last three years the company has reduced staff substantially by voluntary severance. All employees released have received statutory redundancy payments and the company has claimed and received the appropriate rebates from the Department of Employment. Rolls Royce has at all times traded as a commercial company competing for business worldwide and a substantial proportion of its business consists of the production and support of engines for civil aircraft. In particular, the company trades with the State under terms and conditions negotiated at arms length in the same way as other private sector companies, and does not enjoy the benefit of any special exclusion of liability which are not available to other private sector companies in the aerospace industry. When required the company tenders for State business on a competitive basis. There is no duty placed on the State to manufacture gas turbine engines, consequently, the company does not discharge any duty laid upon government. We discuss the question of a duty imposed on the State later in this decision. We do not regard it as significant that the shares were at one time held by the National Enterprise Board or that Civil Service Trade Unions do not operate at Rolls Royce, or that Civil Service terms and conditions do not apply to employees.

5. The Memorandum and Articles of Association of Rolls Royce are in a form which could be applicable to many companies and contains no unusual provisions in relation to shareholders. Unfortunately, the Articles of Association produced at the hearing were those adopted on 22 April 1986 and we have had to proceed on the basis that the former Articles of Association did not contain any provision which might affect our decision or, in particular, limit the rights and powers of the shareholders. The respondents accept that in law the ultimate power in relation to the company and its business rests

with the shareholders by virtue of their ability to pass resolutions in General Meeting, which they can compel Rolls Royce to comply with Article 74 of the Articles of Association of Rolls Royce specifically provides for directions to be given to the directors by special resolution of the shareholders.

6. In December 1980, a 'Memorandum of Understanding with Rolls Royce—Relationship with Government' was promulgated. That provided:

> 'In its relations with the company, the Government has three separate roles—that of 100 per cent shareholder, that of principal customer for the development and production of military engines and that of its overall sponsorship of the aerospace industry. A sole shareholder, the Government expects the Board of the Company to operate as far as possible as if it were the Board of a privately owned company established under the Companies Act; it is not the intention of the Government to concern itself with the day to day management of the Company, or to diminish in any way the responsibility of the Board for the conduct of the Company's affairs. The Government requires the Company to act commercially, and to seek a commercial return, to be defined from time to time, on the capital employed in its operations.

As regards the military role, whilst the ratio of military to civil business may alter with changing circumstances, the Board should assume that orders placed by the Ministry of Defence and overseas military sales will continue to be an important part of the future activities of Rolls Royce. In the light of the importance of the defence interests served by the Company, the Board should ensure that appropriate attention is given to this side of the business. It should discuss with the Government any proposals for reorganisation or for changes in commercial strategy of the Company or any of its subsidiary or associated companies which could impinge substantially on the defence interests.

The Government expects the Company to consult with it about future plans and the way in which it proposes that they should be financed. Such consultations will be primarily based on the provision each year of a medium/long term corporation plan dealing with the strategic options available to the Company and a short term operating plan and annual budget. Once agreement has been reached, the Board will be responsible for reporting progress promptly in its quarterly accounts and will inform the Government of any significant changes in relation to the agreed plans and of any decisions which could have major economic or political implications.

The Government expects the Board to seek its approval before extending the Company's activities into new areas of business, or disposing of significant existing interests and before launching any new engine projects or major developments of existing projects, or making any major capital investments, and will expect satisfactory rates of return over the life of such projects.

The Secretary of State for Industry would appoint directors to the Board on the basis of recommendations from the Chairman, and the Board will consult the Secretary of State before appointing a chairman, deputy chairman, managing director, chief executive or finance director and before fixing directors' remuneration.

The Chairman will have access to the Minister responsible to discuss any matters he or the Board wish to raise with the Government'.

We find that the provisions of that memorandum might well be such as might be found between a company and a 100 per cent shareholder, whoever that shareholder might be. They indicate an interest in the company and the expectation of influencing the affairs of that company beyond those which would normally apply to a small investor.

7. We also had produced to us Minutes of Evidence taken before the Trade and Industry Committee on 11 June 1986 when the Chairman of Rolls Royce, Sir Francis Tombs, gave evidence, in which he indicated the effects of what was then called Government ownership upon the Company. We conclude from that evidence that the character status and power exercised by Rolls Royce's sole shareholder in practice significantly influence the policies of the Board of Directors and the business carried on by Rolls Royce.

Council Directive 76/207 of 9 February 1976 provides as follows:

Article 2

1. For the purposes of the following provisions, the principle of equal treatment shall mean that there shall be no discrimination whatsoever on grounds of sex either directly or indirectly by reference in particular to marital or family status.

Article 5

1. Application of the principle of equal treatment with regard to working conditions, including the conditions governing dismissal, means that men and women shall be guaranteed the same conditions without discrimination on grounds of sex.

2. To this end, member-States shall take the measures necessary to ensure that

(a) any laws, regulations and administrative provisions contrary to the principle of equal treatment shall be abolished.

It is now established law that where a member-State has been placed under a duty by a Council directive to adopt a certain course of action but has failed to do so, a private individual may rely on the directive as against the defaulting State: See Becker v. Finanzamt Munster-innenstadt ([1982] ECR 53 [1982] 1 CMLR 499) where the Court said

Thus, wherever the provisions of a directive appear, as far as their subject matter is concerned, to be unconditional and sufficiently precise, those provisions may, in the absence of implementing measures adopted within the prescribed period, be relied on as against any national provision which is incompatible with the directive or in so far as the provisions define rights which individuals are able to assert against the State.

The question posed is, what is the State if one is not dealing with it directly? In Auer v. Ministere Public ([1983] ECR 2727, [1985] 1 CMLR 123.) the examining committee of the Ordre national des Veterinaires de France were regarded as 'exercising public powers conferred on them by national laws which govern the recognition of diplomas' and although not an 'organ of the State in the true sense of the term, in one way or another implementing the policy of the State'. In Broekmeulen v. Huisarts Registratie Commissie ([1981] ECR 2311, [1982] 1 CMLR 91.) the respondents were the Dutch General Practitioners Registration Committee. An appeal lay to the Appeals Committee for General Medicine. Both were set up under the internal rules of the Royal Netherlands Society for the Promotion of Medicine. The Court in fact treated them as part of the State legal system saying they 'must be considered as a Court or tribunal of a member-State within the meaning of Article 177'.

Against this European background we come to Marshall v. Southampton and SW Hampshire Area Health Authority ([1986] ICR 335, [1986] 1 CMLR 688.) where the same issue concerning discrimination in the retiring age arose on a reference by the Court of Appeal. It was conceded that the Area Health authority was 'the State' following Wood v. Leeds Area Health Authority ([1974] ICR 535.) where a Health authority employee was held to be a Crown servant because the Authority was acting on behalf of a Minister of the Crown. The issues in *Marshall* were whether the *Becker* principle was available where the retiring age was a matter of national law and whether a distinction would be drawn between the State as an employer and the State as a public authority. The European Court decided both issues in favour of the applicant. Since it was conceded that the health authority was the State, the case affords little guidance on the issue in the present appeal as to what is and what is not the State.

The Tribunal found that Rolls Royce was 'an emanation of the State' after appearing to place considerable emphasis on their view of the State's power as sole shareholder to, if we may so put it, direct the directors. In paragraph 8 they said,

The State as the sole shareholder of Rolls Royce had the power, lawfully exercisable under the provisions of the Companies Acts and the Articles of Association of Rolls Royce to require the Directors to make provision in its contracts of employment with employees so as to comply with Article 5(1) of Council Directive 76/207.

In paragraph 12 they refer to Lonrho Ltd. v. Shell Petroleum Co Ltd. ([1980] QB 358.) (which deals with whether documents of a wholly owned subsidiary are in 'the possession custody or power' of the parent company for the purposes of order 24 Rule 2(1) of the RSC) and conclude 'we find that the power exercisable by Rolls Royce's shareholder was a presently enforceable and immediately indefeasible legal right'. This appears to be a reference to the judgment of Shaw LJ at page 375.

We pause at this stage to comment that Rolls Royce has now of course been privatised and the default of the State in failing to implement the directive has been remedied by the 1986 Act which comes into force in November of this year. However, this appeal is of importance to the applicant and others and we have to consider whether the Tribunal was correct in law in reaching the conclusion that it did.

The phrase 'emanation of the State' was derived from Gilbert v. Corporation of Trinity House ([1886] 17 QBD 795.) where Trinity House was referred to as an 'amanation of the Crown'. The phrase was severely criticised as 'inappopriate and undefined' in International Railway Company v. Niagara Parks Commission ([1941] AC 328.) where it was said that 'servant or agent' was more accurate. In BBC v. Johns ([1965] Ch 32.) 'emanation of the Crown' was roundly dismissed as of no assistance in deciding the question before the Court (which was whether or not the BBC enjoyed Crown immunity), Diplock LJ saying, 'I hope that no one will ever again in a Court of law use so imprecise a metaphor as 'emanation of the Crown'. The test adopted by the Court of Appeal was whether the BBC's activities were 'within the province of or a function of government'. It could not be said to be acting as an agent for the government. The same approach has been adopted by Denning LJ in Tamlin v. Hannaford ([1950] 1 KB 18.) (the issue being whether the British Transport Commission was entitled to Crown immunity); he said that the proper question was whether the BTC was a servant or agent of the Crown.

...It was submitted on behalf of Rolls Royce that the correct test is to ask whether the body concerned is an organ or agent of the State carrying out a State function. Rolls Royce was a commercial company in which the State was interested and which it was capable of influencing, but the company is distinct from its members and is not the agent of its members: Salomon v. Salomon & Co Ltd. ([1897] AC 22). Even a 100 per cent shareholding does not create agency: Ebbw Vale Udc v. South Wales Traffic Area Licensing Authority. ([1931] 2 KB 366). In addition, Counsel pointed to the period between 1 April 1976 and 2 August 1980 when the shares were held by the National Enterprise Board which was expressly declared not to be a servant or agent of the Crown nor to enjoy any status immunity or privilege of the Crown. Was the status of Rolls Royce different before and after those dates? So far as the Tribunal thought that Rolls Royce had 'the power lawfully exercisable' (Reasons, paragraph 8) or a presently enforceable and indefeasible legal right (Reasons, paragraph 12) to control the directors, they were plainly wrong in law and had misread the decision in Lonrho v. Shell. The relevant passages are in the judgment of Lord Denning at page 374 and Shaw LJ at pages 375 and 376. At page 374, Lord Denning said:

> 'The directors, under their articles, are the managers of the companies. Shell and BP are only shareholders. Unless and until those directors are removed, they must do their duty by their companies. How then can it be said that Shell and BP, as mere shareholders, have power over these documents when the managing director and the other directors have refused point blank to produce them—and for good reason?

Then it said, 'It is all very well, but Shell and BP have good resources at their command. Looking at the articles, if they take proper steps, they can remove those directors and replace them with others who would do their will'. Is that likely? It has to be remembered that, if new directors are appointed, they will owe a duty to their companies—either the Rhodesian or South African companies.

They are not to be dictated to by Shell or BP if it is not in the interests of those companies.

We considered the position of directors of companies in Scottish Co-operative Wholsesale Society Ltd. v. Meyer [1959] AC 324. We went into it closely at pp 366 and 367. It is quite plain to me that if any new directors are put into these Rhodesian and South African companies, it would be their first duty to consider the interests of those companies: and to consider the legislation of Rhodesia and South Africa. If they, in good faith, said, 'we are not going to produce them or let you have them', their decision cannot be overruled by the shareholders.

Then it said, 'Shell and BP could change the articles. The articles already give power over some books. The articles could be changed to give the shareholders the right to inspect these documents. If the articles were altered accordingly, that would give them this power'.

It seems to me that there is a complete answer to all these suggestions: namely, that the only documents which Shell and BP have to disclose are those which are in their immediate power. If they have to take further and other steps to get them, then they are not in their immediate power, and are not to be disclosed.

At page 375 Shaw LJ said:

> I have come to the view that a document can be said to be in the power of a party for the purpose of disclosure only if, at the time and in the situation which obtains at the date of discovery, that party is, on the factual realities of the case virtually in possession (as with a one-man company in relation to documents of the company) or otherwise has a present indefeasible legal right to demand possession from the person in whose possession or control it is at that time.

In the present case no such sure or direct route to acquiring possession existed or exists. The relationship between Shell and BP, on the one hand, and, on the other hand, the various subsidiaries, including those which are wholly owned by the two parent companies, may afford an ultimate but not an immediate or certain prospect of acquiring possession of documents which belong to and are in the possession and control for the time being of a subsidiary. The realisation of that prospect might involve the alteration of the articles of an unwilling or recalcitrant subsidiary followed by the removal of its then directors and their substitution by others more compliant. This would involve a radical transformation of the local scene within the subsidiary company. It would involve not merely raising the corporate veil, but committing an affront on the persona of the company itself. Even then, the directors who are substituted for the recalcitrant ones may find that there exists a conflict of duty so that they have no right to comply with the requirement. It would follow that the outcome of such a procedure would be at the best dubious.

He added:

> There are no doubt situations, such as existed in B v. B (MATRIMONIAL PROCEEDINGS: DISCOVERY) [1978] Fam 181, where on the established facts a company is so utterly subservient or subordinated to the will and the wishes of some other person (whether an individual or a parent company) that compliance with that other person's demands can be regarded as assured. Each case must depend upon its own facts and also upon the nature, degree and context of the control it is sought to exercise.

The Applicant's Case. This was most helpfully summarised in writing and amplified in argument:

> Has the State, and 'State' must be viewed broadly, power to require the body to carry out its will so it can be said that its failure to exercise that power is causal of the applicant's inability to exercise her rights under the directive? The question is whether the State has the power to amend the contract of employment.

The power must be a lawful power to instruct, exercisable directly by or on behalf of the appropriate State authority to the body, and enforceable directly in the case of refusal to carry out the instruction by direct mechanisms of authority (rather than by indirect pressure or punishment by refusing further contracts, withdrawing grants etc).

The instruction must be within the lawful capacity of the body to carry out (ie within the legal constraints on the body imposed or recognised by the State).

In the present case the State plainly has the power to instruct the body how to conduct its business generally; in particular it has the power to instruct the body to vary the contract of employment (in accordance with Mrs Doughty's wishes) so as to comply with the directive.

'Power to instruct' means using powers as 100 per cent shareholder under the Companies Act. The 'servant or agent' test is far too narrow—a broad brush European approach is required when the substance of the matter is that the State is seeking to take advantage of its own default.

We were referred to a number of other authorities and had the advantage of reading in draft the decision of this Tribunal in Foster v. British Gas ([1987] ICR 904.) and the authorities referred to in it. We were also shown the decision of the London (Central) Industrial Tribunal in Reith & Others v. British Airways Plc. We do not propose to comment in detail on all the cases cited by Counsel or referred to in those authorities. However, some should be mentioned. In Johnston v. Chief Constable Ruc ([1987] ICR 831, [1986] 3 CMLR 240.) the European Court of Justice said of the RUC: 'Whatever its relations may be with other organs of the State, such a public authority, charged by the State with the maintenance of public order and safety does not act as a private individual'. It was said that this decision was not easily reconciled with R v. Commissioner of Police of the Metropolis ex Parte Blackburn. ([1968] 2 QB 118). We do not think so. That case was concerned with the degree of discretion enjoyed by the Commissioner in the maintenance of public order and safety. In Tunstall v. Steigmann ([1962] 2 QB 593.) the Court of Appeal had to consider whether, for the purposes of section 30(1)(g) of the Landlord & Tenant Act 1954, a landlord who proposed to carry on business in the holding by a company in which she owned 98 shares, the other 2 being owned by nominees, 'intended to occupy the holding for the purposes of a business to be carried on by her'. The Court held that the landlord and her company were quite separate legal entities and that the principle in Salomon v. Salomon & Co Ltd. would only be departed from where the company was 'a mere facade'. This is not, of course, the same point that we have to decide, but the passage from the judgment of Shaw LJ in *Lonrho* at page 376 points the way, particularly the phrase: 'compliance with that other person's demands can be regarded as assured'. We take the view that there is a substantial difference between the mere exercise of influence over a separate and independent legal persona, and assured control of a servant or agent. In addition, it is necessary to consider whether what is being done is, in the broad sense, a function of the State.

We have come to the conclusion that the arguments advanced on behalf of Rolls Royce are correct and that the Tribunal misdirected itself in law both when considering the position of Rolls Royce vis-a-vis its sole shareholder under the Companies Act and the effect of the decision in *Lonrho*. The use of the phrase 'emanation of the State' was regrettable, but we note that unfortunately it has been used by the European Court in *Johnston*. We take the view that the correct approach is to ask whether the body concerned can be said to be an organ or agent of the State carrying out a State function. In answering that question when the body is a commercial trading company, the passage in Shaw LJ's judgment in *Lonrho* can provide a useful test. Rolls Royce was not an organ or agent of The State, nor was it carrying out a State function. The appeal is allowed.

Appeal allowed.

Istituto Chemioterapico Italiano SpA and Commercial Solvents Corporation v. EC Commission

(Joined Cases 6 and 7/73)
European Court of Justice
[1974] ECR 223, [1974] 1 CMLR 309
6 March 1974

J. P. Warner (Advocate General)

The Advocate-General delivered his opinion at the hearing on 22 January 1974.

In these actions, which are brought under Article 173 of the EEC Treaty, the Applicants challenge a Decision of the Commission dated 14 December 1972 which was addressed to them. That Decision was based, or purportedly based, on Article 86 of the Treaty and on Regulation No 17 of the Council, of 6 February 1962.

The facts as found by the Commission may be summarized as follows.

A group of companies headed by the Applicant in Case 7/73, that is Commercial Solvents Corporation, of New York, which I shall refer to as CSC, at present has a world monopoly in the production on an industrial scale of products derived from the nitration of paraffin. These products include 1-nitropropane which is the raw material for the production on an industrial scale of aminobutanol. Aminobutanol, apart from having limited uses as an emulsifier, is in its turn the raw material for the industrial production of ethambutol, a compound used in the treatment of pulmonary tuberculosis.

Although the master patents relating to the method of production of 1-nitropropane have expired, the CSC group is able to maintain its monopoly by virtue of its know-how and because a newcomer in this industry would be faced with obstacles such as the high cost and complexity of the necessary equipment and the difficulty of finding outlets for the products other than 1-nitropropane that are derived from the nitration of paraffin, namely 2-nitropropane, nitromethane and nitroethane.

Up to the beginning of 1970 the CSC group supplied aminobutanol to customers in the EEC through subsidiaries and through independent distributors. In particular it supplied the Italian market through the Applicant in Case 6/73, Istituto Chemioterapico Italiano, of Milan, which I shall, like the Commission, refer to as 'ICI', without, I hope, thereby causing it to be confused with a more famous chemical company. ICI is an Italian company limited by shares, 51% of which are owned by CSC. This gives CSC, among other powers, that of appointing the directors of ICI and of determining its policy. ICI has a board of ten directors, five of whom are executives of CSC. The chairman of the board is the president of CSC. Although this is not mentioned in the Decision, it is admitted on the pleadings that, as chairman, he has a casting vote. The executive committee of ICI consists of six members, three of whom are representatives of C.C. In its report for 1972 CSC referred to ICI as its subsidiary. In a previous report it had stated that ICI's laboratories were the base for CC's research in Europe.

Supplies of ethambutol in the EEC come from three main producers. These producers use part of their production for the manufacture of their own pharmaceutical 'specialties' and sell the rest. They are:

1. The CSC group, through ICI;

2. Cyanamid Italia, of Catania, which is a subsidiary of the American Cyanamid Company, of New Jersey; and

3. Another Italian company, Laboratorio Chimico Farmaceutico Giorgio Zoja SpA, which I shall call 'Zoja'. It was this company that triggered off the present proceedings, by making an application to the Commission against CSC and ICI under Article 3 (2) of Regulation No 17.

Zoja has been since 1966 the main customer of ICI for aminobutanol. During 1968 and 1969 there were abortive negotiations for a merger between ICI and Zoja.

In May 1969 ICI informed Zoja that CSC had decided to increase its price for aminobutanol. Zoja accepted this increase although its current contract with ICI made no provision for it. In November 1969, however, Zoja discovered that it could obtain aminobutanol more cheaply from other sources and it availed itself of these sources until the middle of 1970, cancelling, with the assent of ICI, a substantial part of its contract with that company.

In the second half of 1970 supplies of aminobutanol and of 1-nitropropane suddenly began to dry up on the market and, in a short time, they disappeared altogether. Zoja sought supplies from numerous sources, both within and outside the EEC, without success. Some of the firms to which it applied said that they had none because CSC had stopped delivery, others that they were forbidden to sell the products in question for pharmaceutical use.

In July and October 1970 ICI bought from a small producer of ethambutol, bulciago, of Como, some 35 000 kg of 1-nitropropane which it re-sold as an emulsifier to various small manufacturers of paint, exacting from them an undertaking not to re-sell it for pharmaceutical use.

(My Lords, I would interpose here that this finding is said by ICI to be based on a misunderstanding by the Commission of something that was stated on behalf of ICI during the proceedings before the Commission. According to ICI the Undertaking exacted was that the 1-nitropropane in question should not be exported outside the EEC. As Your Lordships will see, I do not think that, at the end of the day, anything turns on this issue.)

In November 1970 Zoja asked ICI for a supply of 120 000 kg of aminobutanol for 1971. ICI said that it would have to refer the request to CSC. In January 1971 ICI informed Zoja that it had been told by CSC that CSC no longer had aminobutanol available for sale.

Subsequent attempts by Zoja during 1971 to obtain aminobutanol from sources in the EEC and elsewhere ended with the same negative result. Enquiries made from traders and through Italian embassies and through the Istituto per il commercio estero in every case led back to a single source of supply, CSC.

On 8 April 1971 Zoja lodged its application under Article 3 of Regulation No 17 with the Commission. In October 1971 it made a last request to ICI for a supply of aminobutanol or of 1-nitropropane. To this ICI replied that for some time it had been informed by its supplier, CSC, that CSC no longer had these products available for ICI.

The position at the time of the Commission's decision was that Zoja had up to then been able to continue production of ethambutol at a reduced rate but that it would have to cease production when its reserves of raw materials were exhausted unless it could in the meantime obtain a regular supply.

The Commission held:

A) That CSC was able to exercise and did exercise such a degree of control over ICI that the two companies should be treated as forming, in their relations with Zoja and for the purposes of Article 86, a single undertaking;

(B) That this single undertaking, referred to by the Commission as the CSC-ICI group, held a dominant position, namely a world monopoly of the supply of 1-nitropropane and aminobutanol, which were the essential raw materials for the manufacture of ethambutol on an industrial scale;

(C) That the CSC-ICI group had abused its dominant position in ceasing to supply raw materials to one of the principal producers of ethambutol in the EEC, conduct which must lead to the elimination of that producer and so to a reduction in competition;

(D) That such abuse affected trade in Ethambutol between Member States, in particular since Zoja exported it to France and to Germany.

In Its Decision The Commission:

(By Article 1)

—declared that the cessation from November 1970 of the supply to Zoja of raw material for the production of ethambutol constituted an infringement by CSC and ICI of Article 86;

(By Article 2)

—required CSC and ICI to bring such infringement to an end and in particular:

(a) to supply at once to Zoja 60 000 kg of 1-nitropropane or 30 000 kg of aminobutanol at a price no higher than the maximum price that they charged for those products; and

(b) to submit within two months for the approval of the Commission proposals for the subsequent supply of Zoja;

(By Article 3)

—imposed on CSC and ICI jointly and severally a fine of 200 000 u.a. payable within three months; and

(By Article 4)

—imposed on them jointly and severally penalties of 1 000 u.a. per {261} day of delay in complying with either of the requirements as to the supply of Zoja.

Soon after the issue of the Commission's Decision CSC complied, albeit under protest, with the requirement as to the immediate supply to Zoja of 60 000 kg of 1-nitropropane or 30 000 kg of aminobutanol.

The applications originating these actions were lodged at the Registry on 17 February 1973 and were accompanied by Applications for a stay of execution of the Decision of the Commission pending the proceedings before the Court in so far as that Decision required the submission of proposals for the further supply of Zoja and the payment of the fine.

Soon after proceedings were begun Zoja applied to intervene in them and that application was granted. I need not take up your Lordships' time with a detailed recital of the subsequent course of the proceedings, but I should mention that one result of them was the signature at Milan on 10 April 1973 of a contract for the supply of aminobutanol by CSC to Zoja. This contract is for a term of two years beginning 1 January 1973 and is to continue in force from year to year thereafter until cancelled by either party. Zoja is satisfied with its provisions as to quantities, price and so forth; and it has been approved by the Commission as meeting the requirements of its Decision. Following its signature Zoja applied for leave to discontinue its intervention. This, in the absence of any opposition, was granted.

My Lords, the Decision of the commission is attacked by CSC and by ICI on many grounds and it is, I conceive, my duty to consider these grounds one by one.

Competence of the Commission

1. Are CSC and ICI a single 'undertaking'?

CSC contends that the Commission had no competence in the matter, so far as CSC is concerned, because CSC is a company established under the law of Maryland and having its principal office in New York. CSC's only relevant connexion with the EEC, it says, is that it once sold nitropropane and aminobutanol into the EEC fob United States ports and later made the policy decision to discontinue such sales. It denies ever having had that measure of control over ICI that would enable it and ICI to be treated for the purposes of Article 86 as a single undertaking. It cites in that connexion the decisions of this Court in Case 22/71 Beguelin Import Co. v. S.A.G.L. Import Export (Rec. 1971, p. 949), in the 'dyestuffs cases'—Case 48/69 Imperial Chemical Industries Ltd. v. Commission (Rec. 1972, p. 619), Case 52/69 J. R. Geigy AG v. Commission (ibid. p. 787) and Case 53/69 Sandoz AG v. Commission (ibid. p. 845)—and in Case 6/72 Europemballage Corporation and Continental Can Company Inc. v. Commission [1973] E.C.R. 215.

What those authorities show to my mind is that the mere fact that a parent company and its subsidiary are separate legal persons does not mean that they are separate 'undertakings' for the purposes of Articles 85 and 86. Thus an agreement between them is not in general within the prohibition contained in Article 85 (that was the decision in the Beguelin case). Conversely the parent cannot shelter from the prohibitions contained in Articles 85 and 86 by saying that the only acts done within the Community were those of the subsidiary. There are indications in the judgments in those cases that the position may be different where the subsidiary is allowed to manage its business autonomously, and it is upon those indications that the argument of CSC rests. That argument is that, in order for parent and subsidiary to be treated as a single undertaking, 'there must be (a) power of direction of the parent company over the subsidiary and also (b) the actual exercise of the parent's control to such an extent that the subsidiary does not determine its behaviour on the market in an autonomous manner, but essentially carries out the instructions given to it by the parent company. 'The yardstick', it is said, 'is the complete absence in a subsidiary of the power to determine its own market behaviour. The possibility of control by the parent is not sufficient; what is needed is the actual exercise of such control to the extent that the subsidiary loses its market autonomy'. And, so the argument runs, it is for the Commission to show that those conditions exist. I can see, my Lords, that the judgments in the cases referred to could be open to that interpretation. But in my opinion such an interpretation of them would be erroneous.

One starts to my mind from this, that neither Article 85 nor Article 86 anywhere refers to 'persons'. In both Articles the relevant prohibitions are directed to 'undertakings', a much wider and looser concept. This indeed is what one would expect, because it would be inappropriate to apply rigidly in the sphere of competition law the doctrine referred to by English lawyers as that of Salomon v. Salomon & Co. Ltd. [1897] A.C. 22—i.e. the doctrine that every company is a separate legal person that cannot be identified with its members. Basically that doctrine exists in order to preserve the principle of limited liability. It is concerned with the rights of creditors in the context of company law. It has been applied, with more or less happy results, in other spheres, such as those of conveyancing, of contracts and of liability for tort. But to export it blindly into branches of the law where it has little relevance, could, in my opinion, serve only to divorce the law from reality.

Suppose, my Lords, that CSC had traded in Italy through a branch office. There could have been no doubt then that it was amenable to the jurisdiction of the Commission and of this Court. Could it have made any difference if CSC has chosen to trade in Italy through a wholly-owned subsidiary? The difference would have been one only of legal form, not of reality. Why then should it make any difference that it chose to trade in Italy through a subsidiary that it controlled by a 51% majority rather than by a 100% majority? What matters in this field, in my view, is control, not extent of beneficial ownership.

My Lords, I would respectfully adopt the words of Lord Denning M.R. when he said in Littlewoods Mail Order Stores v. C.I.R. [1969] 1 W.L.R. at p. 1254:

> 'The doctrine laid down in Salomon v. Salomon & Co. [1897] A.C. 22, has to be watched very carefully. It has often been supposed to cast a veil over the personality of a limited company through which the courts cannot see. But that is not true. The courts can and often do draw aside the veil. They can, and often do, pull off the mask. They look to see what really lies behind. The legislature has shown the way with group accounts and the rest. And the courts follow suit.'

In his references to 'group accounts and the rest' Lord Denning was of course, in characteristic manner, compendiously describing a whole mass of 20th century legislative reaction against the consequences of an unbridled and unthinking extension of the doctrine of Salomon v. Salomon & Co. into fields where it should be applied, if at all, only with caution. In this respect, the field of fiscal law is a notorious example. So is that of competition law. Thus for instance the very recent Fair Trading Act 1973 of the United Kingdom contains passim provisions for the treatment as 'one person' of the 'members of one and the same group of interconnected bodies corporate'. The drafting technique of that Act is very different from that of the EEC Treaty, but the underlying sentiment is manifestly the same.

My Lords, the law, if it is to retain respect, must accord with common sense and with reality. It should not, in my opinion, allow its own principles to be misapplied to the point where they provide opportunities for the adoption of devices designed to defeat its own ends.

It is, my Lords, with these considerations in mind that I approach the argument of CSC in the present case. In my opinion those considerations import at least:

1. that there is a presumption that a subsidiary will act in accordance with the wishes of its parent because according to common experience subsidiaries generally do so act;

2. that, unless that presumption is rebutted, it is proper for the parent and the subsidiary to be treated as a single undertaking for the purposes of Articles 85 and 86 of the EEC Treaty; and

3. that the presumption can only be rebutted if it is shown affirmatively, by those concerned to rebut it, that the subsidiary in fact conducted its business autonomously. I confess that to my mind this must be a very difficult ones to discharge. I can conceive of its being discharged in such a case as that of (say) an insurance company, or of a company which is a trustee of a pension fund, acquiring by way of investment a controlling interest in a trading company, or in a case where what is at first sight the subsidiary of one company is shown to be in reality a joint venture between that and another company in unequal shares. But I would think it almost impossible to discharge in the ordinary case of a parent and subsidiary carrying on related businesses.

The arguments of CSC and of ICI as contained in their pleadings, consist in the main of mere assertion, unsupported by evidence, that CSC did not control ICI's 'behaviour on the market'. A number of pages in CSC's Reply are also taken up by an attempt to show that, in the law of none of the Member States, including Italy, does the control of a majority of the votes attached to shares in a company carry control of that company. This is plainly wrong. CSC does point out, and it produces a certificate of Arthur Young & Company to substantiate the fact, that over 75% of ICI's turnover is derived from the sale of products neither produced by CSC nor based on raw materials produced by CSC. This seems to me, with respect, inconclusive. Even less persuasive is the fact, relied upon by CSC, that the managing directors of ICI have remained unchanged since before 1962 when CSC acquired its 51% interest in ICI. Lacking throughout is the slightest evidence that ICI was ever able or willing to negotiate at arm's length with CSC, in the way that an autonomous trader would. Indeed there is in the summary of the facts contained in CSC'S application (at p. 4) a passage which seems to me significant in this connexion, albeit unintentionally so. It reads: 'Early in 1970 CSC decided, for commercial and technical policy reasons, that in principle it would no longer supply nitropropane and aminobutanol to the EEC, but would instead supply dextro-aminobutanol, an upgraded intermediate product which [ICI] would convert to bulk Ethambutol for sale in the EEC and elsewhere, and for the production of its own specialties.'

At the hearing Counsel for ICI started, no doubt on instructions, that at the time of the purchase by CSC of its 51% interest in ICI an agreement was entered into of which the purpose was to ensure that ICI 'would not lose its economic independence.' Your lordships will find the terms of that alleged agreement at page 5 of the transcript of the hearing. I do not think that it would be right for me to take up time by reading them. There is no mention of this agreement in the pleadings, nor was any evidence adduced about it. We do not even know whether it is alleged to have been oral or in writing, let alone what was supposed to be its duration. Nor of course has the Commission had the opportunity of affording us its considered comments on its significance. In my opinion, my Lords, this Court ought not in a case such as this, to be asked to found its decision on assertions made by Counsel, unpleaded and unsupported by any evidence.

In the result I am of opinion that CSC's challenge to the competence of the Commission and to the jurisdiction of this Court should be held to fail.

* * *

DECISION:

* * *

(e) CSC and Istituto as an economic unit

36. The applicants refer to the case law of the Court and in particular to Judgments 48/69, 52/69 and 53/69 of 14 July 1972 (Rec. 1972, p. 619, 787 and 845), and dispute whether CSC effectively exercises a power of control over Istituto and whether these constitute an economic unit. The two companies have always acted independently, so that CSC cannot be deemed responsible for the acts of Istituto nor Istituto for those of CSC. Therefore even if CSC holds a dominant position within the world market in raw materials for the manufacture of ethambutol, it has not acted within the Community, and therefore the author of the conduct complained of can only be Istituto which however does not have a dominant position within the market in question.

37. In the disputed, Decision in Section II-A CSC's holding of share capital and involvement in the administration of Istituto are set out. It is pointed out in that section that the annual reports of CSC show Istituto as one of its subsidiaries. It is inferred from the prohibition issued in 1970 by CSC to its distributors on reselling nitropropane and aminobutanol for the manufacture of ethambutol that CSC was not abstaining from exercising its power of control over Istituto. It takes note of an attempt on the part of Istituto to take over Zoja by means of a merger in which it is unlikely that CSC played no {253} part. The conclusion is reached that 'CSC holds the power of control of Istituto and exercises its control in fact at least with respect to Istituto's relations with Zoja's and it is therefore proper 'to treat the companies of CSC and Istituto as constituting in their relations with Zoja and for the purposes of the application of Article 86 a single undertaking or economic unit'.

38. It follows from the passages quoted that there is no foundation in the complaint, which must therefore be rejected, that the Commission altered its position during the course of the present proceedings in that after having agreed in its Decision that the two companies constituted an economic unit in every respect, it restricted its position to the argument that in any case they acted as such a unit in their relations with Zoja.

39. As to the substance of the submission, besides the particulars given in Section II-A, the disputed Decision contains other particulars which are capable of showing that the argument that, in their conduct vis a vis Zoja, CSC and Istituto act as one economic unit, is well-founded. In this respect the coincidence pointed out in Section

II-A of the periods when CSC decided to prolong its production to a stage beyond finishing and Istituto, a former distributor of nitropropane aminobutanol, began its activities as a producer of ethambutol is highly significant. It is difficult not to associate the decision by CSC no longer to sell nitropropane and aminobutanol with the fact it made an exception in favour of Istituto, which was supplied with dextroaminobutanol for the purposes of its own production of ethambutol and specialities based on this product.

40. The fact, pointed out in Section III-A of the Decision, that Istituto bought quantities of nitropropane which was still available on the market for resale to paint manufacturers who were forbidden to resell for pharmaceutical purposes outside the Common Market is likewise significant.

41. As regards the market in nitropropane and its derivatives the conduct of CSC and Istituto has thus characterized by an obviously united action, which, taking account of the power of control of CSC over Istituto, confirms the conclusions in the Decision that as regards their relations with Zoja the two companies must be deemed an economic unit and that they are jointly and severally responsible for the conduct complained of. In these circumstances the argument of CSC that it did not do business within the Community and that therefore the Commission lacked competence to apply Regulation No 17/63 to it must likewise be rejected.

C. Japan and Limited Liability

The American occupation of Japan produced many changes in Japanese Company Law. Among them was the introduction of the American concept of veil piercing. As a result, the issue of the extent to which shareholders can insulate their personal property from corporate creditors is highly fact specific. Although a number of factors tend to be considered important in the determination, the bad motives of the shareholder seems to play a critical role in the determination by Japanese courts to pierce the corporate veil.

As you read the materials that follow, consider whether the Japanese application of this doctrine parallels that of the United States. Are the same facts that have become critical in United States courts to a determination that a shareholder ought to be held liable for the debts of the corporation also critical in the determination to pierce the corporate veil in Japan? How important are equitable considerations to the determination to pierce the corporate veil, that is, are the bad motives of the shareholders as in American law as they appear to be in Japanese law?

J. Mark Ramseyer and Minoru Nakazato, Japanese Law: An Economic Approach

(1999)

(excerpts pages 117–119; some footnotes omitted)

1. Piercing the Corporate Veil

"When a corporation is a complete shell or is abused to evade the law," wrote the Supreme Court in 1969, "a court must disregard its corporate form. To recognize it would violate the very purpose behind the institutional distinctions."[36] The firm in question had run an electrical appliance store, and the owner (one man) had organized it as a corporation to evade taxes. Apparently because of his tax fraud, the court pierced the corporate veil. Although piercing the corporate veil is always an exceptional remedy, courts have pierced corporate veils where firms confused the roles of their officers, skipped required meetings, or co-mingled funds. As in the United States, they pierce the veil in both tort and (more dubiously) contract cases and use a heavily fact specific inquiry.[37]

Take the 111 employees discharged when their corporate employer dissolved. Because the firm had been a wholly owned subsidiary of another, they tried to pierce the corporate veil and collect their back pay from the parent. The court let them proceed: the subsidiary's officers had been seconded from the parent, the business of the two firms had often been intermingled and the parent firm had made all significant (and even many minor) business and personnel decisions for the subsidiary.[38]

Or take the suit by Sayoko Goto, a former member of the Takarazuka Revue. The all-woman troop specializes in cross-dressed actresses doing plays ranging from *West Side Story* to the *Tale of Genji* to *mon Paris*. According to one anthropologist, the "oppositional construction of gender was refracted through the Takarasiennes who embodied the eroticized tension between sexual and gender transgression and repression."[39] Maybe so. In any case, Goto had retired and wanted to open a 'café.' Quite what she planned to offer in her new establishment the court did not say. But to run it the way she wanted, she needed an adult entertainment license from the local policed station.

For this 'café' Goto planned to lease space from a lawyer named Yoshikiyo Tsuchida. Tsuchida claimed to own the entire building. He used the third and fourth floors for his law office and offered Goto the ground floor. Goto liked it. Tsuchida explained that title was in a travel agency he owned, so she signed a lease with the agency and remodeled the premises.

When Goto went to the police station for her licence, however, she found that she needed elaborate documentation from her landlord. Tsuchida promised the documents, but never delivered. Apparently his travel agency had never obtained the obligatory construction inspections on the building. In fact, it had not even paid the contractor. Within a few months, the contractor claimed to succeed to title and evicted her.

Unable to run her 'café,' Goto sued both Tsuchida's travel agency and (that firm being broke) Tsuchida himself. The court found the company liable and let Goto pierce its corporate veil. Tsuchida had run several firms but had made little effort to keep them distinct: he had ignored corporate formalities, his law office staff had paid corporate bills, his corporate directors had been directors in name only, and his travel agency had had no assets and had defaulted on its taxes.[40]

Although Japanese courts may pierce the corporate veil to hold shareholders liable, they also disregard the corporate form for other quite sensible reasons. Lone shark Taro

36. K.K. Yamayoshi shokai v. Kishi, 551 Hanrei jiho 80, 81 (Sup. Ct. Feb. 27, 1969).

37. E.g. Shigatame, K.K. v. Marusho sangyo, K.K., 663 Hanrei jiho 88 (Sup. Ct., March 9, 1972) (shareholder and director meetings missed).

38. [No name given] v. Kawagishi kogyo, K.K., 558 Hanrei jiho 38 (Sendai D. Ct. March 26, 1970).

39. Jennifer Robertson, *mon Japan: The Revue Theater as a Technologyof Japanese Imperialism*, 22 AM. ETHNOLOGIST 970, 972 (1995).

40. Goto v. Tsuchida, 598 Hanrei jiho 77 (Osaka D. Ct. May 14, 1969).

Kono had long patronized Hanako Otsuyama at her geisha house. Business was apparently business, even if Otsuyama was very much married to Jiro Heikawa. Heikawa himself ran a tropical fish store but ran it unsuccessfully. He was heavily in debt, and Otsuyama and her father were guaranteeing his loans. To her, Kono now made a proposition: Divorce Heikawa and live with me, and I will repay his debts. She agreed, and they lived together at her geisha house for three years.

Kono did not repay Heikawa's debts directly. Instead, he used his "financial services" firm. After he and Otsuyama had cut their ties, he used that firm to sue her and her father for indemnity. Their agreement with Kono himself was irrelevant, this "firm" argued, because the firm was legally distinct from Kono. It had paid their debt, and it had not agreed to forgive that debt; hence it could now sue for indemnity. Not so fast held the court. One suspects it could have found more than one way to throw out Kono's claim, but it chose to pierce the corporate veil: the firm was a one man operation, Kono effectively owned all the stock, he was the sole director, he was the sole employee, and he held no shareholder meetings. Any promise he made on his own behalf bound the firm. As he had agreed to pay the debt and she had kept her half of the bargain, he could not now manipulate his shell company to escape his half.[41]

D. China and the Porous Company

China has proven to be the limiting case for the convergence of company law. Or has it? Issues relating to the ownership of enterprises has proven, in the context of liability for corporate obligations, to be a thorny issue, conceptually and practically, within the People's Republic of China. Because the state remains the ultimate owner of property, and thus stands in the shoes of the shareholders, piercing the corporate veil in the Western sense is impossible. The State, as the embodiment of the vanguard of workers and peasants, whose genius is exercised through the organs of the Chinese State and Communist Party, is hardly to be liable to itself for the bad acts of its servants. Another path has to be taken. In the People's Republic of China, that path leads to liability of managers and foreigners when the "fiction" of the corporate form needs to be abandoned. The readings that follow attempt to flesh out this approach. As you read what follows, consider whether you agree with this characterization of reaching through the corporate form to find liability for corporate acts with one or another of the corporate actors in China.

Tingmei Fu, *Legal Person in China*

41 Am. J. Comp. L. 261 (1993)

(excerpts pages 289–295; some footnotes omitted)

The GPCL [General Principles of Civil Law] employs the notion of "independent liability" to describe the liability feature of all Chinese legal persons. However, within Chi-

41. [Name deleted] shoji Y.G. v. Otsuyama, 694 Hanrei jiho 109 (Omura Summary Ct. September 25, 1972).

nese legal circles, considerable confusion exists as to the exact meaning of this term. In particular, this term has been misunderstood by some as being equivalent to "limited liability."[144] In fact, "independent liability" and "limited liability" differ in their meaning and substance.[145] Fundamentally, "independent liability" is reserved for legal persons, whereas "limited liability" is meant for shareholders of companies. For example, an unlimited company as legal person is able to bear "independent liability," but its shareholders may nevertheless be obliged to bar unlimited liability. Moreover, to hold that a comoany (legal person) bears limited liability is not only against the law,[146] but also detrimental to the interests of the shareholders.[147]

In an attempt to clarify the meaning of "independent liability," the GPCL defines the scope of civil liability for several types of enterprise legal persons.[148] Therefore, collective enterprises and foreign investment enterprises, if qualified as legal persons, shall be responsible with all the property which they own. But in the case of state enterprises, the extent of their civil liability is the property which the state has authorized them to manage and administer. As such, despite the fact that the state is the sole owner of state enterprises, it is no longer responsible for the debts of the latter. Such limitation of the state's liability contrasts greatly with the situation before the economic reform, when the state actually bore unlimited liability for state enterprises.

The concept of independent liability is also significant in that organizations which do not have legal personality are not able to bear independent liability. For example, as indicated earlier, not all cooperative joint ventures may qualify as Chinese legal persons. For those that are not legal persons, the liability has to be determined in accordance with relevant contracts or general law governing partnerships.[149]

The notion of independent liability has paved the way for the development of enterprise bankruptcy in Chinese law. For many years following the foundation of the PRC, the concept of bankruptcy was not applicable in China. But in just a few months after the adoption of the GPCL, the Enterprise Bankruptcy Law was promulgated.[150] Due to the enormous controversies involved, this law was meant for trial implementation and only

---

144. An example can be found in the Regulations Concerning Foreign-Related Companies in the Special Economic Zones of the Guangdong Province (adopted on September 28, 1986, effective from Jan. 1, 1987). While Art. 3, para. 2 of the Regulations assumes that "all foreign-related companies in the Special Economic Zone are limited liability companies," Art. 149 seems to impose unlimited liability on partners of cooperative joint ventures. For a brief discussion, see Edward J. Epstein, "China and Hong Kong: Law, Ideology and the Future Interaction of the Legal Systems," in Raymons Wacks (ed.), *The Future of the Law in Hong Kong*, 37–75, at 73: "Here, if Art. 2 had been expressed as "all foreign-related companies...are companies assuming *independent* liability," then there would not have been such conceptual confusion.

145. *See Farrar's Company Law*, at 67–8 (1988).

146. *See* Art. 48, GPCL. *See also* Art. 106 of the Implementing Regulations of the Law on Equity Joint Ventures, which states that an equity joint venture shall be liable with "all its assets."

147. *See Boyle and Bird's Company law*, at 49 (1987) ("It is wrong to insert, as has been done, "The Liability of the Company is Limited." Such a variation, if passed by the Registrar, might produce results disastrous to the members."). Compare with the misleading expression that "a legal person has limited liability," in [Henry Zheng, *China's Civil and Commercial Law*, (1988)] at 310.

148. *See* Art. 48, GPCL.

149. The GPCL only makes stipulations concerning partnership between natural persons (*see* Arts. 30–35). Therefore a partnership between enterprises may have to be decided by reference to the rules concerning "economic associations" (*see* Arts. 53-3, GPCL).

150. Adopted on December 2, 1986, effective from Nov. 1, 1988. For an introduction to this Law, *see* Henry Zheng, "Bankruptcy Law in the People's Republic of China—Principles, Procedure and Practice," 19 *Vand. J. Trans. L.* 683 (1986).

applicable to state enterprises.[151] Nevertheless, the newly adopted Civil Procedure Law contains a chapter "Chapter Nineteen" regarding the "Procedures for the Repayment of Debts Owed by Bankrupt Enterprise Legal Persons." This chapter consists of eight articles containing provisions similar to those stipulated by the enterprise Bankruptcy Law,[153] and is applicable to all enterprises possessing legal personality other than state enterprises, which are still under the exclusive jurisdiction of the Enterprise Bankruptcy Law. [154]

2. Piercing the Corporate Veil

In the West, in the early days after the recognition of corporate personality, it was taken for granted that the legal personality of corporations should be preserved in determining their civil liability. Shareholders should not be made accountable, in excess to their promised contribution, for the debt liability of corporation which possessed legal personality. From the early Twentieth century, however, courts in many jurisdictions have followed the American experiences in lifting corporate veil which has been abused. "Piercing the veil" is both possible and desirable when, for example, corporate personality is used for the purpose of fraud or as a means to avoiding legal obligations, or when the legal person is controlled by another legal person in the same group, with the latter being potentially made liable for the former's debt.[155] For some observers, "piercing the veil jurisprudence" has initiated a new enterprise theory concerning corporate personality.[156]

In China, piercing the veil jurisprudence is still largely unknown. In fact, both the Enterprise Bankruptcy Law and the State Enterprise Law[157] have in principle denied any civil liability owed by the state (or government) to a state enterprise or its creditors in case the former's actionable interference lead to the latter's bankruptcy. In theory, there-

151. For a detailed review of the drafting process of the Chinese Enterprise Bankruptcy Law, *see* Ta-Kuang Chang, "The Making of the Chinese Bankruptcy Law: A Study of the Chinese Legislative Process," 28 *Harv. Int'l L.J.* 333–72 (1987).

Many restrictions have been imposed on by this bankruptcy law. For example, state enterprises as debtors have to get the approval from relevant government departments in charge before they are able to file for bankruptcy (*see* Art. 8). In addition, government departments are also entitled to play an important role in the process of reorganization and liquidation. In addition, due to the grave concern over various issues such as unemployment and social instability, the Enterprise Bankruptcy Law remains far from effectively enforced in China. According to the information provided by the Economic Chamber of the Supreme People's Court, by the end of 1991, the number of bankruptcy cases accepted by courts at local levels was just 252. In 1991, the courts declared bankruptcy on 57 enterprises. For the source of this information, see *Baokan Wenzhai* (Digest of Newspapers and Periodicals), Mar. 24, 1992 at 1. (The report did not indicate whether all these cases were concerned with state enterprises. It is possible that other types of enterprises may have also been involved).

153. For example, apart from the absence of the requirement "due to poor management," the test for enterprise bankruptcy as adopted in the Civil Procedure Law (Art. 199) is similar to that provided in the Enterprise Bankruptcy Law (Art. 3). In addition, the order for the repayment of debts as provided in the Civil Procedure Law (Art. 204) is the same as that provided in the Enterprise Bankruptcy Law (Art. 37).

154. *See* Art. 206, Civil procedure Law (1991)....

155. For a summary of European Continental law on this issue, *see* E.J. Cohn & C. Simitis, "Lifting the Veil" in the Company Laws of the European Continent," 12 *Int'l & Comp. L. Q.* 189–225 (1963). For an account of English law, see *Farrar's Company Law, supra* n. 145 at 73–81.

156. [Philip I. Blumberg, "The Corporate Personality in American Law: A Summary Review," 38 *Am. J. Comp. L.* 49–69 (Supplement 1990)].

157. Adopted on Apr. 13, 1988 and effective as of Aug. 1, 1988. For an English translation, *see* *China L. & Prac.* 35–50 (No. 5, 1988).

fore, enterprise legal persons should only be responsible for their debts to the extent of all the property which they own or "manage."

In practice, however, corporate personality has been lifted at least once. In August 1987, the Supreme People's Court issued an "Opinion" (*pifu*) on the debt liability of enterprises and companies promoted by administrative organs or enterprises.[158] According to this Opinion, while the debts of "enterprises" or "companies" established by administrative units should be the first paid out of the property of the enterprises or companies, the part they could not afford to pay had to be made up for by those administrative units that approved and established the enterprises or companies, or that reported the establishment of the enterprises or companies. On the other ad, when a "branch enterprise" (*fenzhi qiye*) was established by an enterprise, if the branch enterprise was actually qualified as a legal person, its debt should be paid with its own independent assets; if the "branch enterprise" was not qualified as a legal person, the enterprise which established the branch enterprise should have joint and several liability with the branch. But if the branch was a "company" (*gongsi*), "*regardless of its being qualified as a legal person or not,*" the enterprise that promulgated the branch company had to be responsible for making up the debts which the branch company could not afford to pay in full.[159] As such, the Opinion of the Supreme People's Court actually lifted corporate personality by asking certain connected entities (including administrative units and "enterprises") that established the bankrupt enterprises and companies in question to be responsible for their debts.

The move towards lifting the corporate veil immediately caused great concern and shock among Chinese lawyers.[160] They argued strongly that as legal persons should bear "independent liability," their corporate veil should not be lifted. As such, they resorted to the notion of independent liability to defend the corporate veil of legal persons.

In fact, one has to look at the general background underlying the move towards lifting the corporate veil. At the time when the Supreme People's Court issued its Opinion, China had just begun to "consolidate" (*zhengdun*) enterprises, especially "companies" formed by administrative organs. This consolidation was a mass movement launched under the guidance of the Party and state policies. Indeed, the Supreme People's Court, in its Opinion, directly cited and referred to thos epolicy documents jointly issued byu the State Council and the Central Committee of the Chinese Communist Party. Accordingly, these policy documents to a great extent formed the very basis of the Opinion issued by the Supreme People's Court. The Opinion also expressed the intentional differentiated treatment between ordinary "enterprises" (*qiye*) and "companies" (*gongsi*)[162] in

---

158. *See Zhonghua Renmin Gongheguo Zuigao Renmin Fayuan Gongbao* (Bulletin of the Supreme People's Court of the PRC), at 21 (No. 4, 1987).

159. *Id.*

160. *See, e.g.*, Lin Yi, "Guanu Qiye Kaiban De Gongsi Daobi Hou Zhaiwu Qingchang Wenti de Jidian Sikao (Some thought about the Payment of Debts Sustained by Bankrupt Companies Promoted by Enterprises)," in *Faxue Pibglun*, at 84–88 & 69 (no. 1, 1991).

162. The relationship between "enterprise" and "company" is very controversial in the Chinese context. Generally speaking, except for some "administrative companies" which have both business and administrative functions, "enterprises" are usually understood to include "companies." However, for certain purposes such as registration, "companies" may be put under different legal regime from that governing ordinary "enterprises." In fact, the controversial relationship between "enterprise" and "company" has been one of the major obstacles frustrating the promulgation of company law in China. For the purpose of "consolidating companies," "companies" referred to enterprises whose titles included the term "company" (*gongsi*), though in fact those companies might belong to neither limited liability companies nor companies limited by shares as prevailing in the West.

the case of enterprises that functioned as their "promoters and sponsors" (*kaiban ren*). The fact that "enterprises" were discriminately held liable to pay up the debts of the "companies" which the enterprises had promoted, regardless of the companies being legal persons or not, can only be explained as a kind of penalty imposed on those enterprises which were keen to establish "companies" in order to make profits.

It is therefore clear that the decision to lift the corporate veil as instructed by the Opinion was taken less on the basis of logical and legal reasoning than under the guidance of the particular state policy. As a result, the challenge made by Chinese lawyers against this move sounds understandable.

Indeed, as a response to the concerns expressed over the lifting of the corporate veil, on December 21, 1990, the State Council issued a Circular concerning the settlement of debts of abolished or merged companies in the campaign to consolidate companies.[163] This Circular to a considerable extent modified the position set by the Opinion of the Supreme People's Court. It required that companies which met the requirements of a legal person as provided by the GPCL, and "which had dissociated themselves from the Party or government organisations as their promoters or sponsors," should as a rule pay their debts with the property they were authorised by the state to manage or which they owned.[164] As such, the shock caused by the Supreme Court's Opinion was partially redressed. Although it seems that the Circular to lift the veil of companies that failed to disconnect themselves from government or Party authorities, it is clear that many other companies whose veil would have been lifted in accordance with the Opinion were eventually relieved by the new state policy as recognised in this Circular.

The campaign to consolidate companies was officially ended in late 1991. But the experience during this campaign clearly demonstrates that corporate personality in China is not so absolute as to be preserved in all circumstances. The corporate veil can be lifted as a result of special state policy. Furthermore, it has also been suggested by some Chinese lawyers that the idea of holding both natural and legal persons behind the veil liable for the debts of subordinate legal may be relevant both in domestic civil law[165] and even in foreign investment enterprise law.[166] However, the opposition to the practice of lifting the corporate veil canjnot be underestimated. This is not only because some factors such as conceptual confusion are present, but because some factors such as conceptual confusion are present, but because many Chinese lawyers still tend to overemphasize the function of legal personality in separating enterprises and their investors (shareholders or owners).[167] Consequently, it remains to be seen whether piercing the

---

163. For the text, *see* [Circular Concerning Several Issues Regarding Approving Business Capacity (see the text in Chinese, in *Zhonghua Renmin Gongheguo Gongsi Fagui Huibian* (Collection of PRC Company Laws and Regulations (1991)] at 316.

164. *Id.*

165. It may be necessary to ask holding companies to be responsible for the debts of their subsidiaries. For a discussion, *see* Wang Baoshu, "Woguo Qiye Lianhe Zhong de Kangcaien Jiqi Falü Duice (On Newly Emerged Concern and Legal Disposition in China)," in *Faxue Yanjiu*, 47 (No. 6, 1990).

166. The corporate veil may be lifted as a matter of reference to "international practice." Consequently, foreign investors may be held liable for the debts of foreign investment enterprises established in China. For a brief mention, *see* Yao Meizhen (ed.), *Waishang Touzi Qiyefa Jiaocheng* (Textbook on Foreign Investment Enterprise Law), at 67 (1990).

167. One Chinese Scholar has this comment on the Western concept of piercing the corporate veil "considering the (low) standard of our legal system and the (inadequate) professional knowledge of judges, the adoption of this theory or practice (i.e. piercing the corporate veil) is likely to produce considerable discretion and to reduce the positive function of the legal person system." *See*

corporate veil jurisprudence will be introduced in Chinese law on legal grounds similar to those already widely accepted in the West.

Robert C. Art and Minkang Gu, *China Incorporated: The First Corporation Law of the People's Republic of China*

20 YALE J. INT'L L. 273 (1995)
(excerpts pages 293–294; some footnotes omitted)

C. Liability for Corporate Obligations: Shareholders and "Legal Representatives"

One particularly important element of the 1993 Corporation Law is its adoption of the principle of limited liability for shareholders—a concept fundamental to Western corporate law, but relatively new to China. The Corporation Law does not adopt limited liability wholesale, however. Instead, the law provides for the distinctively Chinese concept of a human "legal representative" who is subject to sanction for improper corporate activities.

The idea that those operating a business should be entitled to enjoy the profits if it succeeds, but be insulated from liability for losses if it fails, is neither intuitively appealing nor obvious. The concept inevitably denies recovery not only to contract claimants, but also to personal injury tort victims when the corporation is bankrupt. Western capitalist countries decided long ago that the benefits to society of encouraging commerce in this manner outweighed the detriment to such claimants. Only the long history of that policy decision in capitalist countries makes the principle appear basic or commonplace. In China, which lacks a comparable history of orientation toward private enterprise, acceptance of the limited liability principle could not be assumed. Earlier versions of company regulations provided for limited liability in only some forms of company organization.[126]

It is therefore significant that the Corporation Law adopted principles of liability for corporate obligations parallel to Western—in particular American—practice in key respects. For instance, the Corporation Law adopts the familiar principle that a corporation is a "legal person," an entity that enjoys civil rights and owes civil responsibilities to the full extent of its assets.[127] In addition, the law explicitly protects shareholders from liability beyond their capital contributions,[128] and does not mention "piercing the corporate veil" or any other limitation on shareholder immunity.

Shi Jichun, "Woguo Jiben Jiti Jingji Lifa Chuyi (My Humble Opinion on Basic Legislation Concerning Collective Economy in China)," *Zhongguo Faxue*, 33–41, at 39 (No. 2, 1992).

126. The 1951 regulation, for example, provided for some companies with limited liability, others with unlimited liability, and others with a combination of the two. *See supra* note 41. [The 1951 rules provided for five business forms: a limited liability company, an unlimited liability company, a company established by both a limited and an unlimited liability company, a company with limited liability and ownership by shares, and a company established by both unlimited and limited liability shareholders. The regulations were Siying Qiye Zanxing Tiaoli [The Provisional Regulation on Private Enterprises] (promulgated Dec. 30, 1950) Siying Qiye Zhanxing Tiaoli Shixing Banfa [The Implementing Measures for the Provisional Regulations on Private Enterprises] (promulgated Mar. 3, 1953), cited in [Alison W. Conner, To Get Rich is Precarious: Regulation of Private Enterprise in the People's Republic of China, 5 J. Chinese L. 1 (1991)] at 4 n.9.]

127. Corporation Law, Arts. 3 and 4....

128. Article 3 provides that shareholders in an LLC assume liability limited to "the amount of capital that they invested," and that shareholders in a Joint Stock Company "assume... liability equal to the amount of shares purchased." The difference in phrasing might suggest that capital can be

Nevertheless, the Corporation Law integrates the distinctively Chinese concept of the *fading daibiaoren*, or "legal representative," as an encroachment on limited liability. A legal representative is the natural person authorized to act on behalf of and to bind the company[130] in a manner similar to the "agent" in American corporate law. The Chinese legal representative, however, serves an expanded role bearing greater risks than an agent under American law. The legal representative of a corporation is the chairman of the board of directors or president,[131] or, in a small LLC that chooses not to have a board, the executive director.[132] He or she must perform such functions as applying for a certificate for a branch company.[133]

Most importantly, the Civil Code subjects a legal representative to sanctions for the legal person's misconduct.[134] For example, the legal representative is personally at risk if the corporation engages in business beyond its authorized scope, conceals facts from registration and tax authorities, or hides property to evade repayment of debts.[135] While the legal representative is not personally liable for corporate debts, the extent of responsibility is nevertheless serious. He or she may be fined or subjected to administrative sanctions, including warnings, reprimands, probation, and dismissal from office,[136] with attendant loss of prestige, status, and face. Moreover, if the offense constitutes a crime, the legal representative may be prosecuted.

Chuan Roger Peng, *Limited Liability in China: A Partial Reading of China's Company Law of 1994*

10 COLUM. J. ASIAN L. 263 (1996)
(excerpts pages 267–274; some footnotes omitted)

III. THE COMPANY LAW OF 1994

A. Embracing Limited Liability

Probably the most important feature of the Company Law's concept of limited liability is that it expressly stipulates that entities formed under the Company Law "shall be enterprise legal persons." Shareholders of a limited liability company or of a company limited by shares shall be "liable toward the company" to the extent of their "capital

---

contributed to an LLC in a form other than share purchases, but the Law does not reflect that concept elsewhere.

130. The "legal representative" concept has a long history in Chinese law. For the current general statement of the rule, see The General Principles of Civil Law of the People's Republic of China, art. 43, Apr. 12, 1986, available in Lexis, Chinalaw library, File No. 346 [hereinafter Civil Law].

131. Corporation Law, arts. 45 (applicable to most LLC's), 68 (applicable to LLC's wholly owned by the state), 113 (applicable to joint stock companies).

132. *Id.* Art. 51.

133. *Id.* Art. 96.

134. *Id.* Art. 49.

135. *Id.*

136. *Id.* (stating that legal representative is subject to administrative sanctions). The term "administrative sanctions" is defined in, for example, Zhonghua Renmin Gongheguo Xingzheng Jiancha Tiaoli (The Provisions of Administrative Supervision of PRC), passed on November 23, 1990 by the State Council and issued on December 9, 1990 by the 69th decree of the State Council of PRC. Sanctions include warning, minor and severe reprimands, probation, demotion, dismissal, and discharge.

contributions" or "shareholdings," respectively.[24] This represents a significant alignment of Chinese corporate law with the prevalent American corporate law in terms of shareholder limited liability.[25] Given the failure to address such a concept in the historic development of enterprise law in China, this step indicates China's recognition that, in balancing the benefits of encouraging commerce and entrepreneurship with the evils of the society bearing the costs of externalities created by individuals, the former outweighs the latter. This recognition is also reflected in the law's conferring "legal person" status on all entities formed under it, thus making the enterprise an entity with "full rights" in its property and all civil rights and liabilities "according to law," as distinct from those rights and liabilities of the individual shareholders.[27]] Compared with historic practice before the Company Law, the inclusiveness of the law in conferring "legal person" status and limited liability protection has a twofold effect in the standardization of treatment of enterprises.

The first equalizing effect is that the Company Law does not distinguish between purely domestic enterprises and those receiving foreign investment (hereinafter "foreign-invested companies"). Previously, foreign investors generally had the advantage of electing to be a limited liability company. This difference seems motivated by the government's desire to attract foreign investment and at the same time to keep tight control over domestic enterprises. While the protection of limited liability is available to foreign investors, the specific entity form of "foreign enterprise" offers an extra layer of protection if investors are uncomfortable with the uncertainty in the interpretation of Chinese foreign investment laws. A "foreign enterprise" may elect to incorporate under a foreign jurisdiction (e.g. Delaware, Hong Kong, or the Cayman Islands) and be controlled by the laws of the foreign jurisdiction instead of by Chinese law. However, although the Company Law does not make a distinction between foreign and domestic enterprises, the actual effectiveness

24. [Zhonghua Renmin Gongheguo Gongsi Fa [Company Law of 1994], in FAGUI HUIBIAN, translated in 2 CHINA L. & PRAC. 7 (1994) [hereinafter Company Law]], Art. 3:

> Limited liability companies and companies limited by shares shall be enterprise legal persons.
>
> In the case of a limited liability company, shareholders shall be liable toward the company to the extent of their respective capital contributions, and the company shall be liable for its debts to the extent of all its assets.
>
> In the case of a company limited by shares, all of the company's capital shall be divided into equal shares, shareholders shall be liable toward the company to the extent of their respective shareholdings, and the company shall be liable for its debts to the extent of all its assets.

The distinction between a "limited liability company" and a "company limited by shares" is similar to that between a close corporation and a corporation in U.S. terms. The Chinese term of "limited liability company" should be distinguished from the same term used in American law, which describes unincorporated entities with specific governance structures.

25. [Robert Art & Minkang Gu, *China Incorporated: The First Corporation Law of the People's Republic of China*, 20 YALE J. INT'L L. 273 (1995).] at 293–294. Although limited liability has arguably been available to certain purely private enterprises since 1951, its impact on the economic system was negligible. Under the new Company Law, all eligible entities, including private enterprises, are afforded limited liability protection, but various requirements, such as capitalization, tend to exclude most private enterprises.

27. Company Law, Article 4, states in part: "...Companies shall possess full rights in the legal person property formed by the investments of their shareholders, and shall possess civil rights and bear civil liability according to law." Company Law, *supra* note 2, Art. 4. *See also* Art & Gu, *supra* note 5, at 293; DONG, *supra* note [24], at 34 (citing from the General Principles of Chinese Civil Law, Arts. 22–34, the definition of "legal person," which includes the quality of being "able to assume civil obligations independently").

of such equal treatment remains to be seen. The Chinese government generally takes a permissive view of existing laws, in the sense that existing laws are controlling if not overruled expressly by new laws. Therefore, in the areas not covered expressly in the Company Law, unequal treatment of domestic and foreign enterprises may still prevail.

The second equalizing effect of the Company Law is that among domestic enterprises, no distinction is drawn among enterprises of different ownership structures, i.e. state-owned, collectively-owned, and private or individual enterprises. The significance of this effect is not so much the equality between private and public enterprises (state-owned and collectively-owned) but rather the equality among private enterprises themselves. Because the issue of limited liability appears moot in public enterprises, it is difficult to evaluate the implications of limited liability between public and private enterprises. However, it is clear that before the Company Law, only a portion of China's private enterprises enjoyed the status of a "legal person" and the protection of limited liability. The effort not to distinguish between the different types of domestic enterprises in the Company Law essentially means that the protection of limited liability is now available to all domestic enterprises, including all domestic private enterprises.

B. Limitations on Limited Liability

Notwithstanding the broad recognition of limited liability in the Company Law, the law imposes a number of limitations on the limited liability doctrine. These limitations substantially offset the protection offered by limited liability to companies, shareholders, and officers, thereby effectively reducing the step toward virtual alignment with Western and U.S. corporate law to a half-step. One significant limitation is the consistent application of the concept of "legal representative" throughout the Company Law.[34] Although the enterprise is a distinctive "legal person" with independent rights and liabilities in all corporate affairs and transactions, under the Company Law, as well as traditional practice in China, at least some essential aspects of the legal person are condensed and attached to a "legal representative," who is a natural person representing and acting on behalf of the enterprise. No comparable concept exists in American corporate law; the closest similarity is found in the concept of "agency." Under U.S. law, the agent of a corporation is generally an officer of the corporation, authorized to represent the corporation in transactions and affairs, and afforded greater protection under agency principles than that afforded to a director of the corporation. The "legal representative" in a Chinese enterprise is usually the chairperson of the board. The scope of duty and liabilities of the legal representative are not delineated in the Company Law, but are found in the Civil Law of the PRC. This law provides that a legal representative is subject to various types of administrative sanctions, including "warning, minor and severe reprimands, probation, demotion, dismissal, and discharge." Although the law excludes personal liability for enterprise debt, the enumerated liabilities of the legal representative are generally severe and disproportionate to her/his shareholdings in the en-

---

34. *See* [Robert Art & Minkang Gu, *China Incorporated: The First Corporation Law of the People's Republic of China*, 20 Yale J. Int'l L. 273 (1995)], at 293–294; Company Law, *supra* note [24], Art. 45 (chairperson of the board shall be the legal representative of a limited liability company); *id.* Art. 51 ("If a limited liability company does not have a board of directors, the executive director shall be the legal representative of the company"); *id.* Art. 68 (chairperson of the board shall be the legal representative of a wholly state-owned limited liability company); *id.* Art. 94 (application for registration of establishment shall include "the name and domicile of the legal representative"); *id.* Art. 96 (the legal representative has the duty to apply for registration for a branch of a company limited by shares); *id.* Art. 113 (chairperson of the board shall be the legal representative of a company limited by shares).

terprise. Although sanctions are administrative in nature, the whole concept of a "legal representative" singularly bearing the consequences of enterprise conduct is not only a serious limitation to the limited liability doctrine, but a virtual disregard of the "legal person" delineation under the Company Law.

Apart from the sharp restrictions on the limited liability doctrine caused by the concept of the legal representative, the Liability section of the Company Law also imposes stringent personal liability imposed on officers and directors of the enterprise.[40] While U.S. corporate law generally describes duties of corporate directors and officers broadly as the "duty of care" and allows substantial discretion under the rubric of the "business judgment rule," the Company Law takes a different approach. In the Liability section, the law specifically lists various types of prohibited conduct and the available sanctions attached to each. There are four types of sanctions: fines levied on the enterprise, fines levied on individuals, administrative sanctions and criminal liability. While fines are levied mostly when finances are involved and administrative sanctions are only imposed on state employees, criminal sanctions are attached to almost every article in this section as the most severe alternative to imposing liability on enterprise personnel. Two aspects of such liability provisions appear to be overly harsh and with no comparable counterparts in American corporate law. One is the imposition of additional sanctions outside of the governance structure of the enterprise, which usually happens to state personnel in a company partially or wholly-owned by the state. Aside from internal actions of the company, the state is free to apply additional sanctions. In such situations, the individuals involved completely lose the protection of limited liability. The other aspect is that sanctions are imposed on relatively medium or low-level personnel. Considering the basic lack of discretion and the follow-the-instructions nature of medium and low-level positions in the enterprise, such sanctions represent a severe infringement on the protection of limited liability through the agency theory. In the United States, due to the predominantly private nature of corporations, administrative sanctions are uncommon. Also, corporate personnel not authorized for high-level decision-making are protected from liability except for criminal conduct.[46]

* * *

A final, and perhaps more fundamental, limitation on the availability of limited liability is not expressly associated with such concepts as personal liability or capitalization, but is embedded in the spirit of the entire statute. This is the great power of state control over incorporation.[54] This essentially deems incorporation, and the rights and

---

40. Company Law, *supra* note [24], Arts. 206–228 (each article typically includes: "...administrative sanctions shall be imposed according to law on the personnel in charge that are directly responsible and on other directly responsible personnel. If a criminal offence is constituted, criminal liability shall be pursued according to law.").

46. *See* SEC v. Texas Gulf Sulphur Co., 401 F.2d 833 (1968) (en banc) (Friendly, J., concurring); cert. denied, 394 U.S. 976 (1969).

54. According to the Company Law, the state retains control over various corporate issues, including registration, amendment to the certificate of incorporation, public stock offering, etc. *See* Art & Gu, *supra* note [34], at 288 (stating that the Company Law "tightly regulates incorporation, maintaining state control over this form and its attendant privilege of limited liability...The process of incorporation, operation, and capitalization of a business are thus plainly matters of government control and permission, not of right"); Company Law, *supra* note 2, Art. 8 (registration is subject to examination and approval under prior laws or administrative regulations); *id.* Art. 11 (amendment of the company registry to change the scope of business requires approval by both the approval and registration authority); *id.* Art. 27 (requiring capital contribution to be verified by a statutory investment verification organization and approved by the registration authority and relevant authorities via examination and approval if provided by other laws and regulations); *id.* Art. 77 (establish-

benefits thereof, privileges subject to state approval. The broad language of Article 8 of the Company Law makes an individual's right to incorporate contingent upon the amorphous content and interpretation of existing laws and regulations.[55] According to the Company Law, while the power to "examine and approve" the establishment of limited liability companies is entrusted to "relevant authorities," that concerning the establishment of companies limited by shares can be ultimately traced to the PRC State Council or the "People's Government at the provincial level."[56] What is not detailed in the Company Law, but in the Administrative Regulations of PRC Concerning the Registration of Corporations, is a list of the more specific and demanding requirements necessary to obtain such approval.[57] Prevalent U.S. law, on the other hand, makes incorporation a right rather than a privilege,[58] and grants the protection of limited liability and other incidental benefits of incorporation upon completion of minimal formalities. Hence, the limited availability of limited liability to individuals in China is just another indication of a centralized government experimenting with a uniquely Chinese model of a market economy without relinquishing control from the top.

Comments and Questions

1. In the People's Republic of China, it could be argued that the state is the ultimate and true owner of property, state enterprises are owned directly ad indirectly by the state and its organs. Moreover, the state reserves the right, through its organs directly, and through the disciplinary functions of the Communist Party and its functionaries indirectly, to exercise authority over enterprises as and when required by state or Party policy. Do you think the People's Republic of China will be able to reconcile the idea of legal personality separate from the state, limited liability and the disregard of limited liability for shareholders under certain circumstances? If the state is insulated from liability with respect to its "investment" can individual investors who are not acting as State or Party functionaries also limit their exposure to liability when acting in a similar capacity? Does this mean that while the state can intervene, only non-state actors can be reached if the veil is pierced?

2. Consider the following critique of the rules of "veil piercing" in China:

---

ment of company limited by shares msut be approved by the State Council or a provincial government).

55. *See* Company Law, *supra* note [24], Art. 8; *supra* note 54.

56. Company Law, *supra* note [24], Arts. 27, 77.

57. Articles 19 and 73 of the Company Law provide general requirements for establishing a limited liability company and a company limited by shares, respectively. The Administrative Regulations of the PRC Governing the Registration of Legal Corporations (promulgated by the State Council, 1988) and the Administrative Regulations of the PRC Concerning the Registration of Corporations (promulgated by the State Council, 1994) provide a more detailed list of requirements: (1) Own name, organizational structure, and articles of association; (2) fixed place of business and physical facilities; (3) funds and personnel conforming with state regulations and proportionate with the scale of production and services; (4) ability to bear civil liability independently; and (5) scope of business conforming with state laws, statutory regulations, and policies. *See* Art & Gu, *supra* note [34], at 96.

58. The Delaware General Corporations Law § 101 provides: "Any person, partnership, association or corporation, singly or jointly with others... may incorporate or organize a corporation under this chapter by filing with the Secretary of State a certificate of incorporation which shall be executed, acknowledged, filed and recorded in accordance with section 103 of this title." § 103 merely provides certain requirements clerical or formal in nature. DEL. CODE ANN.,... §§101,103

> B. Piercing the Corporate Veil "With Chinese Characteristics": The State Reaches Through to "its" Assets. No doubt to provide comfort to conservative figures who did not welcome the lessening of state control and the advent of corporations in China, the Company Law states: "the state-owned assets of a company belong to the state."[46] This stipulation is nonsense, as a corporation's assets should belong to the corporation, which corporation in turn belongs to all of the shareholders, it being impossible to identify a portion of the company's assets that belong exclusively to certain shareholders participating in the corporation. There was no similar concept in the Standard Opinion. Thus, pursuant to the terms of the Company Law, if a company limited by shares is owned 60% by a state entity or state proxy, yet all of the factory, capital equipment and fixed assets of the company were contributed to the corporation by such state entity or proxy (the other shareholders contributing cash), conceivably the 60% shareholder would own 100% of the assets of the corporation, or the corporation would not be able to dispose of such assets without the approval of the state-owned assets bureau.

Nicholas C. Howson, *China's Company Law: One Step Forward, Two Steps Back? A Modest Complaint,* 11 COLUM. J. ASIAN L. 127, 142 (1997).

3. Theories of legal personality are intimately tied to the issues of piercing the corporate veil. This connection is exposed in Chinese theory of liability for corporate liability. The use of the "legal representative" in Chinese corporate law suggests a hierarchy of personality which suggests that "legal persons" mat be accorded little effect in law. Do you agree? Can you explain the theory and use of the "legal representative" in Chinese corporate law theory? Can the concept of the "legal representative," as the physical representation of the legal personality on the body of a natural person be explained by reference to the theories of legal personality we have studied?

46. *See* [Company Law of the People's Republic of China (adopted by the 5th Session of the Standing Committee of the 8th National People's Congress on Dec. 29, 1993, and effective July 1, 1994)], Art. 4, para. 3.

Chapter 10

Regulating the Conduct of Managers

One of the fundamental objects of internal corporate governance concerns the duties of corporate managers. This chapter considers the different ways in which states define and regulate the fundamental obligations of managers to the corporation. We will first consider the regulatory pattern applicable generally. We will then study the differences in duty, if any, where an enterprise comprises one part of a multi-corporate enterprise.

A. Approaches to the Regulation of the Conduct of Managers

The materials which follow provide an overview of the different approaches to the regulation of the behavior of managers. Three primary approaches are considered: common law, civil law and socialist law approaches. As you read through the materials consider whether, or to what extent, the differences between the approaches of the common law and civil law countries are converging. Consider also whether there is substantial difference in the approaches of capitalist and socialist systems with respect to the disciplining of managers, even managers with substantial economic power.

1. *The Common Law Approach*

The common law approach to the regulation of the conduct of managers is distinctive among systems of corporate governance. This approach is shared by common-law countries, including the United States, Great Britain, Ireland, Australia, New Zealand, and many of the former British colonies in Asia and Africa. The approach is based on the imposition of "fiduciary" duties on managers, principally the directors of a corporation derived from and similar (but not identical) to the duties imposed on trustees generally under the common law. In addition, in the common law systems of federal states, provision has to be made for the determination of the level of government at which such duties will be governed. In the United States, the states have primary responsibility for the regulation of the conduct of managers as part of the internal affairs of a corporation. However, the federal government may impose such additional duties as it likes in connection with its regulation of corporations, principally through the federal securities laws.

a. The United States

Restatement (Second) Conflict of Laws

§ 309 & comment

> The local law of the state of incorporation will be applied to determine the existence and extent of a director's or officer's liability to the corporation, its creditors and shareholders, except where, with respect to the particular issue, some other state has a more significant relationship under the principles stated in §6 to the parties and the transaction, in which event the local law of the other state will be applied.

Comment:

a. Scope of section....

Liability will typically be imposed upon directors under the rule of this Section for such matters as the fraudulent or negligent mismanagement of the corporation's affairs, the unlawful declaration of dividends, the making of false returns, the unlawful acquisition of treasury stock and unlawfully profiting at the corporation's expense.

Melvin A. Eisenberg, *Corporate Law and Social Norms*

99 Colum. L. Rev. 1253 (1999)
(excerpts 1265–1278)

A. Fiduciary Duties

The major fiduciary duties of corporate actors are the duty of care and the duty of loyalty. The duty of care concerns the standards that apply to the conduct of corporate actors who are free of self-interest. My theses concerning the duty of care are as follows: The level of directorial care is largely driven by social norms, rather than by the threat of liability or the prospect of gain. Within the last ten years, an inefficient nonobligational norm that licensed and insulated a low level of directorial care has been replaced by a more efficient obligational norm that requires a higher level of care. This norm-shift was in significant part the result of a change in belief-systems. The change in belief-systems, in turn, was partly induced by the expressive effect of legal authorities, which clarified and added moral force to the social norm of care.

The duty of loyalty concerns the standards that apply to the conduct of corporate actors who are not free of self-interest. My theses concerning the duty of loyalty are as follows: Adherence to the duty of loyalty is driven by both the threat of liability and social norms. The legal rules in this area serve both regulatory and norm-supporting and norm-defining functions. Although the regulatory function of these legal rules is important, the social norm of loyalty that the legal rules support and define is critical to the efficient operation of the duty of loyalty.

Standards of care and loyalty potentially apply to all major types of corporate actors, although often in somewhat different ways to different actors. I will focus on the application of the duty of care to directors and the application of the duty of loyalty to directors and officers.

1. The Duty of Care.—The common experience of informed observers is that the level of directorial care has risen significantly in the last ten years or so; that directors today are more attentive to their responsibilities, more ready to displace inefficient CEOs, more concerned about corporate structure, more active in setting agendas and determining corporate strategy, and so forth.[30]

What has caused this shift to a greater level of care? Pretty clearly, not an increased threat of liability. It is true that during this period the meaning of the duty of care was greatly clarified and elaborated: Smith v. Van Gorkom made clear that reasonable inquiry by a director was a condition to the invocation of the business judgment rule.[31] The ALI's Principles of Corporate Governance formulated the first clear statement of the business judgment rule as a special standard of review—that is, a rationality rather than a reasonability standard—and the conditions that had to be satisfied to qualify for application of the special standard of review.[32] Cede & Co. v. Technicolor, Inc. made clear that if the conditions to invoking the business judgment standard of review are not satisfied, the standard of review is reasonableness or some equivalent.[33] The monitoring duty of the board was made explicit and strongly supported, first in Francis v. United Jersey Bank[34] and later and more comprehensively in the Caremark case.[35]

From a liability perspective, however, the developments during this period were overshadowed, if not overwhelmed, by the adoption of director-shield statutes that permit a corporation's certificate of incorporation to eliminate the liability of directors for violation of the duty of care. Delaware Section 102(b)(7) is typical. This section provides that the certificate of incorporation may include:

> A provision eliminating or limiting the personal liability of a director to the corporation or its stockholders for monetary damages for breach of fiduciary duty as a director, provided that such provision shall not eliminate or limit the liability of a director: (i) For any breach of the director's duty of loyalty to the corporation or its stockholders; (ii) for acts or omissions not in good faith or which involve intentional misconduct or a knowing violation of law; (iii) [for improper distributions]; or (iv) for any transaction from which the director derived an improper personal benefit.[36]

The shield statutes have important exceptions. For example, the statutes typically do not apply to an officer acting in her capacity as an officer. This exception, however, does not affect directors acting in their directorial capacities. In addition, the statutes generally concern only liability, not the validity of directorial action, so that although the directors are protected against liability for an action, the action itself may be deemed invalid. There are many important contexts in which the standard of care may affect validity; among the most important are decisions by disinterested directors to approve

30. See, e.g., Ira M. Millstein & Paul W. MacAvoy, The Active Board of Directors and Performance of the Publicly Traded Corporation, 98 Colum. L. Rev. 1283, 1283–86 (1998). My claim here is not that directors are now performing just as they should. See, e.g., Charles Gaparino and Pui Wing Tam, Mutual-Fund Boards: No Comfort?, Wall St. J., Feb. 5, 1999, at C1. Rather, my claim is that directorial performance has significantly improved.

31. 488 A.2d 858, 872–73 (Del. 1985).

32. ALI, Principles of Corporate Governance, supra note 26, § 4.01.

33. 634 A.2d 345, 360–61, 371–73 (Del. 1994).

34. 432 A.2d 814, 822–23 (N.J. 1981).

35. In re Caremark Int'l, Inc. Derivative Litig., 698 A.2d 959, 968–70 (Del. Ch. 1996).

36. Del. Code Ann. tit. 8, § 102(b)(7) (1991).

interested-director transactions or to take defensive actions against a takeover bid. The validity exception, however, does not reduce the statutes' protection against liability.

The statutes also typically have exceptions, like those in Delaware Section 102(b)(7), for acts or omissions not "in good faith," or which involve "intentional misconduct," or the like. The meaning of these terms in this context will have to be developed by judicial interpretation, but a lot can be packed into the concept of good faith. In In re RJR Nabisco, Chancellor Allen stated that an action by a director is not in good faith if it is based on "any human emotion [that] may cause a director to place his own interests, preferences or appetites before the welfare of the corporation" including "hatred, lust, envy, revenge, ... shame or pride."[38] In Gagliardi v. Trifoods International, Inc., Chancellor Allen stated: "I include within the category of improper motivation those cases in which particularized claims of director entrenchment are made... [o]r in which, relatedly, transfers of corporate control by the board... are involved."[39] In Caremark, Chancellor Allen stated that "a sustained or systematic failure of the board to exercise oversight—such as an utter failure to attempt to assure a reasonable information and reporting system exists—will establish the lack of good faith."[40] The meaning of "intentional misconduct" is also unclear. For example, a complete failure to act might be construed as intentional misconduct within the meaning of the statutes. The not-in-good-faith and intentional-misconduct exceptions therefore somewhat diminish the protection the shield statutes afford against directorial liability for breach of the duty of care. Even when these exceptions are taken into account, however, the result of the shield statutes is to drastically reduce the threat of such liability. Accordingly, if directorial care was based solely on the threat of liability we would expect the level of care to have gone drastically down in the last ten or so years, rather than significantly up.

A possible incentive for care even when there is no significant threat of liability is the prospect of individual gain. This factor, however, is insufficient to account for the increase in directorial care over the last ten or so years. To begin with, a director's compensation is normally unrelated to his performance. Such compensation is almost invariably uniform for all directors on a given board (subject perhaps to extra compensation for committee service). Extra care by a particular director is therefore unlikely to lead to increased compensation. A director might have an incentive to exercise care so that he will be reappointed or will be more attractive as a directorial candidate for other corporations, but few directors fail to be reappointed for lack of care and there is little or no evidence that there is a market in careful directors. Under very recent practice, directors may receive part of their compensation in the form of stock or stock options. Some believe that this practice will increase directorial care. That may or may not be true, but the practice is too new and too limited to account for the general increase in the level of directorial care over the last ten or so years.

Since the increased level of directorial care over the last ten or so years cannot be accounted for either by an increase in the threat of liability or by the prospect of gain, and since, indeed, the threat of liability has been substantially reduced if not virtually eliminated, it is difficult to avoid the conclusion that the level of directorial care is determined in significant part not by the threat of liability or the prospect of gain, but by so-

38. In re RJR Nabisco, Inc. Shareholders Litig., 14 Del. J. Corp. Law 1132, 1159 (Del. Ch. 1989).
39. Gagliardi v. Trifoods Int'l, Inc., 683 A.2d 1049, 1051 n.4 (Del. Ch. 1996).
40. Caremark, 698 A.2d at 971.

cial norms concerning the directorial role, and that the increased level of care is due to a shift in these social norms.

What has led to this shift? One factor may be the role of the media. The business press, like the general press, has become increasingly willing, and indeed eager, to report on the shortcomings of directors and officers. A juicy story about feckless directors on page one of the Wall Street Journal is the equivalent of a picture of Brad Pitt on the cover of Vanity Fair. The increased likelihood of such stories, with their consequence of shaming and the loss of esteem, may have been one factor in making directors more attentive. Another factor is that directorial performance has come under closer scrutiny from institutional investors, who may either put direct pressure on directors or present another possible source of bad publicity.

But something more significant seems to be operating; that is, a shift in the social norm governing directorial duties, from a nonobligational practice norm that insulated inactive directors from criticism and self-criticism, to an obligational norm that requires a higher level of care. This shift in norms, in turn, largely resulted from a change in the belief-system of the business community concerning the nature of the obligations associated with the directorial role. The issue then is what elements led to this change in the belief-system. One possible element was new information. Some of this information was provided by the rise of the takeover-bid institution. The enormous discrepancy between takeover-bid prices and market prices conveyed the information that there was a lot of managerial inefficiency, and that something in addition to takeover bids needed to be done about it. The relative decline of such corporate giants as General Motors and Sears conveyed the same information.

The law may also have contributed to the change in directors' belief-systems. Recall that at the same time the shield statutes virtually eliminated liability for the director's breach of the duty of care, the courts were greatly clarifying the meaning of that duty. To understand the impact of this clarification, a distinction must be drawn between standards of conduct and standards of review. A standard of conduct states how an actor should conduct a given activity or play a given role. A standard of review is the test a court applies when it reviews an actor's conduct to determine whether to impose liability or grant injunctive relief.

Typically, the elements of a standard of conduct and a correlative standard of review are the same. For example, the standard of conduct for an actor in driving a car is to drive carefully, and the correlative standard of review to determine whether liability should be imposed is whether the actor drove carefully. In corporation law, however, the standards of conduct and review pervasively diverge. For example, in the area of duty of care the standard of conduct is "act reasonably," but the standard of review is often the much looser business judgment standard of rationality. Similarly, the elimination of liability under the shield statutes did not affect the director's standard of conduct, but only the liability for failure to adhere to that standard.

Although legal standards of conduct are characteristically accompanied by liability rules or other enforcement regimes, even a legal standard of conduct that is unaccompanied by such a regime may be effective because of its impact on social norms. While social norms differ from legal rules, there is often a symbiotic relationship between legal rules and social norms. On the one hand, legal rules are often based on social norms. On the other hand, many legal rules have an expressive effect—that is, in addition to their regulatory effects, legal rules send messages of various kinds. Adoption of a legal rule that is based on a social norm sends a message that the community regards the norm as especially important. This message increases both the likelihood that the norm will be internalized and the reputational penalties for violating the norm. Furthermore, legal rules add, to the force of a specific obligational norm, the force of the general norm of obedience to law, which is one of the most powerful norms of our society.

Legal rules may also serve to clarify social norms by providing focal points for their meaning. The clarifying function of legal rules has obvious relevance to the duty of care, because one function of the cases that clarify the meaning of that duty, especially in a directorial context, is to tell directors how to play their directorial role. Thus one way of looking at the change in the social norm concerning directorial care is that directors who once believed, as a result of an earlier prevailing practice, that they could properly satisfy the demands of the directorial role with minimal attention, have been instructed by the courts—or perhaps more accurately, by their lawyers—that this view is wrong. Having been so instructed, directors who wanted to perform their role properly made appropriate adjustments in their conduct—not necessarily to avoid liability, but just because they wanted to play their roles properly. Ed Rock, in a notable article, shows how much of the Delaware case law on takeovers, and by extension the duty of care generally, can be understood as directed in significant part toward instructing directors on how to play their role in that context and publicly admonishing those directors who failed to properly play that role.[45]

Legal rules may also be effective, even without an enforcement strategy, because they facilitate the effectiveness of informal sanctions by norm-compliers against norm-violators. For example, Cooter points out that if smoking in public places like airports violates a social norm but not a legal norm, some norm-compliers will attempt to enforce the norm by sanctioning smokers with words or looks, but others will not. If a legal rule is adopted to ban smoking in such places, many of the norm-compliers who previously had kept silent will now speak out. This effect may be especially important where a relatively small number of additional informal norm-enforcers may tip the balance in a way that makes norm violations too uncomfortable to be worth the trouble. Correspondingly, the adoption of a legal rule, even without formal enforcement, can cause actors to correctly believe that there will be more social enforcement of the norm. This aspect of the effect of legal rules on social norms is particularly salient to the duty of care, because the development of the meaning of that duty in the case law gave institutional investors, the media, and, for that matter fellow directors, a better purchase for criticism of laggard directors.

The history of the norms concerning the duty of care illustrates that nonobligational practice norms can have significant consequences. The prior social norm concerning the director's role was the nonobligational practice norm that directors do not do much. Although this norm was not obligational it had a significant effect on conduct, because it permitted a low level of directorial care by insulating directors who did not do much from both external criticism and self-criticism.

This history also illustrates that social norms may be inefficient. There is sometimes a tendency to view social norms as good, efficient, or both; in particular, to view social norms as a form of private action that does a better job of regulating conduct, just because it is private action, than governmental action. But social norms are not necessarily either good or efficient. They may be morally bad, or at least insulate morally bad

45. See Edward B. Rock, *Saints and Sinners: How Does Delaware Corporate Law Work?*, 44 UCLA L. Rev. 1009 (1997).

conduct from criticism, as in the Jim Crow South. They may promote inefficient behavior, or at least insulate inefficient behavior from criticism, as did the prior social norm concerning the director's role.

Bad or inefficient social norms may result from a variety of causes, including self-interest, inertia, and bad or inefficient belief-systems. Bad or inefficient belief-systems, in turn, may result from bad information or from persuasion that is founded on false premises or developed by fallacious or incomplete reasoning. Whatever the origin, it is important that social norms not be treated as intrinsically more desirable than legal regulation in governing conduct. Rather, the issues raised by social norms, for those concerned about the law, are how social norms operate in a field that is within the scope of law; whether, in any given area, social norms potentially have advantages over legal rules in governing conduct; and whether the social norms that prevail in an area are good or bad, efficient or inefficient.

2. The Duty of Loyalty.

a. Authentic Loyalty and Instrumental Loyalty.—The duty of loyalty is a shorthand expression for the duty of fair dealing by, and the trustworthiness of, directors, officers, and controlling shareholders when they are financially interested in a matter affecting the corporation. A useful entry point into the relationship between law and social norms in this area is provided by an important article by Jonathan Macey and Geoffrey Miller.[48] This article was triggered by the Supreme Court's decision in Basic, Inc. v. Levinson,[49] which held that a corporation that denies that it is in merger negotiations violates Rule 10b-5 if the denial is false and the information is material.[50] Macey and Miller criticize this result. They begin by arguing, as others have, that from an economic perspective, fiduciary principles are essentially contractual devices:

> This economic perspective is important because it generates a mechanism by which courts can decide cases. In particular, when scrutinizing managerial behavior, courts should treat an allegation of a breach of fiduciary duty as they would treat any alleged breach of contract. This analytic method often is described as the "hypothetical bargain" approach. Under this approach to fiduciary duty, courts would evaluate whether the managers' actions were consistent with the terms of a hypothetical fully specified, contingent contract that informed, value-maximizing investors would have agreed to ex ante.[51]

Based on this perspective, Macey and Miller argue that lies by corporate officials should be exempt from liability if they are made with the good faith intention of furthering the shareholders' interests, and do not create negative externalities and thereby reduce allocative efficiency. Accordingly, Macey and Miller conclude, the issue that arose in Basic should have been resolved by asking whether a rational shareholder group would endorse a corporation's strategy of publicly and falsely denying that it was involved in merger negotiations. Based on this standard, Macey and Miller conclude that a corporation should be able to falsely deny that it is in merger negotiations, because nondisclosure facilitates merger negotiations, merger negotiations facilitate mergers, and mergers increase shareholder wealth.

---

48. Jonathan R. Macey & Geoffrey P. Miller, *Good Finance, Bad Economics: An Analysis of the Fraud-on-the-Market Theory*, 42 STAN. L. REV. 1059 (1990).

49. 485 U.S. 224 (1988).

50. The Court added that materiality in a merger context depends on the probability that the merger will be consummated and its significance to the corporation if it is consummated. See id. at 238–39.

51. Macey & Miller, supra note 48, at 1068–69 (citations omitted).

There are important problems with the Macey and Miller analysis even when the analysis is taken on its own terms. One of these problems is that if the Macey and Miller rule prevailed, then whenever a corporation made a statement, investors could not know whether the statement was true or was the kind of lie that would be permissible under the Macey and Miller rule. Since the Macey and Miller rule is not limited to statements concerning merger negotiations, investors would have to discount all corporate statements because they might be permissible lies. Discounting all corporate statements, however, would make the market significantly less efficient, if not positively inefficient, which would be bad for shareholders as a class.[54] Moreover, unless a corporation can commit itself to honesty, under the Macey and Miller rule the corporation could not convincingly make a truthful statement that it was not engaged in merger negotiations—or for that matter, in any other rumored-but-untrue value-enhancing transaction.

The most fundamental problem with the Macey and Miller analysis, however, is that it ignores the expressive function of law. If the Macey and Miller rule was adopted, the message that the law would send is that there is nothing wrong with lying—that truth-telling is valued not for its own sake, but only instrumentally. Such a message would significantly diminish the force of the social norm of truth-telling. Just as the law can add to the force of an obligational norm by throwing its support to the norm, so it can reduce the force of an obligational norm by withdrawing support. Even if the result of sanctioning lies was good for shareholders in their shareholder role, it still would be bad for shareholders in their larger role as members of society.

There is also a strictly economic reason why the law should not send such a message. The corporate system operates most efficiently where corporate actors act loyally—that is, deal fairly and in a trustworthy manner—and are perceived to do so. One way to achieve loyalty is by legal sanctions. Taken alone, this way is very expensive and probably has limited effectiveness, because of the difficulty of detecting breaches of the duty of loyalty and the cost of legal enforcement. A second way to achieve loyalty is to install intracorporate monitoring and bonding systems. This way is somewhat more effective than a legal regime alone, but it is also very expensive—and the more effective it is to be, the more expensive it must be.

In contrast, the operation of the social norm of loyalty is very inexpensive. Of course, if the loyalty norm is adhered to only because the actor fears reputational sanctions, the problem of detection remains significant. Drawing on terminology used by Bruce Chapman, I will refer to loyalty that is based on an internalized norm—particularly a norm that shapes character—as authentic, and to loyalty that is based on reputational concerns as instrumental.[56] Instrumental loyalty is good, but authentic loyalty is better. Instrumental loyalty will be forthcoming only when disloyalty is easy to observe. Authentic loyalty will be forthcoming even when disloyalty is difficult to observe.

---

54. Another, related point is made by Ian Ayres. Assuming that a rule that permitted a corporation to lie would be a default rule, then a corporation could vary the rule by committing itself to honesty. If a corporation did not commit to honesty, the market would simply assume that any statements the corporation made were dishonest. This assumption, in turn, would induce a majority of corporations to commit to honesty, which would more or less bring us back to where we are now. See Ian Ayres, *Back to Basics: Regulating How Corporations Speak to the Market*, 77 VA. L. REV. 945, 947–59 (1991).

56. See Bruce Chapman, *Trust, Economic Rationality, and the Corporate Fiduciary Obligation*, 43 U. TORONTO L.J. 547, 580 (1993).

To put the extreme case, if all corporate actors fully internalized the social norm of loyalty and gave full effect to that norm, the costs of both legal sanctions and monitoring and bonding systems would be unnecessary, and the levels of loyalty would be much higher than those sanctions and systems can achieve. Accordingly, whatever the law does do to increase the force of the social norm of loyalty, and further its internalization, will lead to greater efficiency and will therefore benefit shareholders as a class. Whatever the law does to diminish the force of the social norm of loyalty, and lessen its internalization, will have the opposite effect. Therefore, even taking the interests of shareholders as a class apart from their interests as members of society, a legal regime that promoted the view that the social norm of loyalty is only instrumental, and which thereby diminished both the force of the norm and its internalization, would reduce the efficiency of the corporate system.

What is true of the corporate system in particular is also true of the economic system in general. As stated by Casson:

> Overall economic performance depends on transaction costs, and these mainly reflect the level of trust in the economy. The level of trust depends in turn on culture. An effective culture has a strong moral content. Morality can overcome problems that formal procedures—based on monitoring compliance with contracts—cannot. A strong culture therefore reduces transaction costs and enhances performance—the success of an economy depends on the quality of its culture.[57]

An analogous objection applies to the conception, adduced by Macey and Miller in support of their argument that the duty of loyalty is essentially contractual. The duty of loyalty is seldom, if ever, imposed by a real contract. Directors and officers do not agree that they will be bound by a duty of loyalty. Instead, the duty is imposed by law. As the Delaware Supreme Court said in Guth v. Loft, "[a] public policy, existing through the years, and derived from a profound knowledge of human characteristics and motives, has established a rule that demands of a corporate officer or director, peremptorily and inexorably, the most scrupulous observance of his duty...."[58]

It is true that the duty of loyalty, and the corresponding rights it creates, may be limited in certain respects by agreement. However, that a right or a duty may be limited by agreement does not make the right or duty contractual. For example, the general duty to exercise reasonable care can be contracted around, within certain limits, but that does not make the law of negligence contractual. Similarly, the right to a jury trial can be waived, but that does not make the Sixth Amendment contractual. Nor is a right or a duty contractual because it is imposed on the basis of what courts or legislators believe the parties would want to do if they had addressed the issue. Since it is impossible to determine what terms actors with unknown preferences and potentially different bargaining power would actually agree upon, rules that purport to be based on hypothetical bargains are actually based on collective action. Furthermore, if the duty of loyalty was contractual, it would follow that the duty could be not only limited but completely waived by agreement. Generally speaking, however, it cannot be.

A more fundamental problem with the contractual conception of the duty of loyalty is that the critical role of trust in the success of the corporate system would be signifi-

57. Mark Casson, The Economics of Business Culture: Game Theory, Transaction Costs, and Economic Performance 3 (1991).

58. 5 A.2d 503, 510 (Del. 1939) (emphasis added).

cantly undermined if the law sent a message that the duty of loyalty was essentially a contractual duty, not a duty imposed by law. As Bruce Chapman has stated:

> [C]ompetitive corporate contracting cannot achieve all that this [contractual] view promises unless it is aided by the very value that a contractual understanding of the fiduciary obligation denies, namely, the duty of loyalty and trust. Trust plays an essential role in all modern economies, and without it, or without the coordination that is provided by institutional loyalty, even efficient wealth-maximizing corporate contracting can make us all worse off.... Nor can the concept of trust be very easily accommodated into the contractual model of the corporation. Properly interpreted, the concepts of trust and loyalty present a deep challenge not only to that contractual model, but also to the very conventions of instrumental rationality upon which the model is based.[61]

In short, the duty of loyalty is almost never the result of a real contract, and the adoption by the legal system of the contractual conception of the duty of loyalty, like the adoption of an instrumental conception of truth-telling, would disserve efficiency interests.

b. Sanctions.—Another role of the social norm of loyalty is to up the ante for violating the duty of loyalty for those corporate actors who have not internalized the duty. Generally speaking, the legal sanctions for violating the duty of loyalty are inefficiently low. The primary legal sanctions are rescission and restitution. Normally, however, these sanctions merely put the fiduciary back to where he would have been if he had not violated his duty. Because not all violations will be detected, a fiduciary whose only objective was to maximize his wealth, and who only feared legal sanctions for violating the duty of loyalty, would have an incentive to violate the duty—for example, by taking a corporate opportunity, or dealing unfairly with the corporation in a self-interested transaction. If the violation is undetected, the fiduciary comes out ahead. If it is detected, the fiduciary is normally no worse off under the legal sanctions than he would have been if he had not violated his duty. Although additional legal sanctions are sometimes imposed—for example, loss of salary or punitive damages—these sanctions are atypical and it is therefore doubtful that the prospect of such sanctions, discounted by the likelihood that they will be imposed, change the picture that much.

Therefore, if the only reason for not violating the duty of loyalty was the prospect of a legal sanction, fiduciaries would regularly violate that duty. The social norm of loyalty, however, adds the sanction of loss of reputation to the legal sanctions. Because the legal sanctions are set at an inefficiently low level, the increase in sanctions provided by the social norm is necessary if the total sanctions for breach of the duty of loyalty are to approximate an efficient level. To put this differently, in the absence of the social norm of loyalty, the costs of enforcing the duty of loyalty would be prohibitively high. Either corporate law would need to systematically impose huge punitive damages in loyalty cases to effectively deter breach, or corporations would be required to incur huge monitoring costs, or both.

c. Concretization.—In the case of the duty of care, the present posture of the law is essentially to support the social norm of care with a legal standard of conduct that is unaccompanied by an enforcement strategy. In the case of the duty of loyalty, the legal rules are accompanied by an enforcement strategy. Thus, the legal rules in this area achieve their ends partly by regulation and partly by the support they give to social norms. The latter, expressive function of the legal rules in the loyalty area is analogous

61. Chapman, supra note 56, at 549....

to the expressive function provided by many other legal rules. However, the expressive function of the legal rules of loyalty has a special cast, because those rules not only support the norm but make it operational and meaningful through concretization.

In this connection, McAdams draws a useful distinction between general norms, like "friends should be loyal," and concrete norms, like the obligations "to listen attentively to a friend's troubles, to water her plants when she is away, to drive her home when she is intoxicated," and so on.[62] "Narrow, concrete norms," he points out, "often define the meaning of a specific behavior by defining that behavior as complying with or violating an internalized abstract norm. Thus, an antilittering norm may work because a consensus arises that littering violates the internalized norm to be a 'good neighbor.'"[63]

Similarly, a general duty of loyalty is one thing; a web of specific duties that particularize the general duty is another. Few if any philosophers specialize in delineating the meaning of loyalty in the corporate context. Rather, it is the courts that have made the general principle of loyalty fully meaningful by spinning out the principle into specific rules governing such matters as the fairness of self-interested transactions, disclosure, corporate opportunities, the use of corporate assets, and so forth. Once these rules have been developed, they serve to support the social norm of loyalty in a variety of ways—for example, by giving clarity to the norm and by providing a focal point around which overlapping instantiations of the norm can cohere. These messages, in turn, are amplified by corporate codes of conduct and by stories in the business media that discuss particular transgressions. Thus, in the loyalty area the specific rules developed by courts simultaneously regulate the conduct of corporate actors, and are transmuted into social norms concerning the conduct of corporate actors.

The role of the law in developing specific social norms in the loyalty area is important in itself. It also bears on the evaluation of shareholder suits. For at least fifty years, shareholder suits have come under criticism based on cost-benefit analyses that purport to show that on average the financial benefits of such suits are less than their costs. There are a number of problems with these studies, but the most basic flaw is that in calculating benefits, these studies count only immediate financial benefits. This approach ignores two of the most important benefits of shareholder suits to shareholders as a class. The first and most obvious of these benefits is the deterrent effect of shareholder suits. The second and even more important benefit is that it is through shareholder suits that the specific legal rules of the duty of loyalty have been shaped. Those legal rules, in turn, have given specific meaning not only to the legal duty of loyalty, but to the social norm of loyalty. The social norm, in turn, provides an extremely effective and low-cost way to achieve loyalty. Thus shareholder suits, whatever their short-term purpose and result, have the long-term result of creating an extremely valuable public good. The desirability of such suits cannot be measured without counting the value of that good.

Comments and Problem

1. Professor Eisenberg suggests that social norms and legal norms work together to account for the particular state of corporate governance, and in the excerpt provided

---

62. [Richard H. McAdams, *The Origin, Development, and Regulation of Norms*, 96 Mich. L. Rev. 338, 341 (1997)] at 382.
63. Id. at 383.

above, of fiduciary duty. The Restatement Second Conflict of Laws, reminds us that corporate law is essentially local. Yet, the legal norms Professor Eisenberg highlights appear to be national in scope. Does this suggest that state law making in the area of corporate law is more fictive than substantive, that is, that state law in this field has necessarily converged because of the normative harmonization of enterprise practice in the United States? Conversely, does Professor Eisenberg's hypothesis suggest that supra-national harmonization will follow from the harmonization of enterprise behavior across national boundaries?

2. **Problem:** You are the chief of staff to the newly elected governor of Wyoming. The Governor was elected, in part, on her promise to revamp the corporate laws of fiduciary duty. She has argued, during the campaign, that the corporate laws of Wyoming, based on the Revised Model Business Corporation Act, have become captive to nationalizing law making which is repugnant to the free citizens of Wyoming. The norms expressed in this law, like the norms of the Delaware law copied by many other jurisdictions, do not express the deeply held beliefs of the people of Wyoming. She has proposed the elimination of all laws of fiduciary obligation in Wyoming. Instead, any obligation of the board to shareholders, employees and others, will be limited to that expressly provided in the articles of incorporation. Voters in Wyoming have been ecstatic about this proposal. The business community has been less enthusiastic. Should the Governor introduce legislation to adopt her plan? Be prepared to discuss the arguments for and against the proposal.

---

b. Other Common Law Approaches

The fiduciary duties of directors and officers in other common law countries is based on a similar grounding as that on which American corporate fiduciary principles arise. However, other common law countries have tended to resist either an expansion of the behavior norms inherent in fiduciary duties in the enterprise context, or the temptation to codify the obligation. The materials set forth below provide a taste of the common law approach to fiduciary duty outside the United States.

Bristol and West Building Society v. Mothew (t/a Stapley & Co)

Court of Appeal, (Civil Division)
[1998] Ch 1, [1996] 4 All ER 698, [1997] 2 WLR 436, 75 P & CR 241
24 July 1996

Millett, LJ, (giving the first judgment at the invitation of Staughton LJ).

* * *

[For a description of the facts and disposition of this case, deferred for consideration in connection with our study of the Duty of Loyalty, see section C.1.b]

Breach of fiduciary duty

Despite the warning given by Fletcher Moulton LJ in Re Coomber, Coomber v. Coomber [1911] 1 Ch 723 at 728 this branch of the law has been bedevilled by unthinking resort to verbal formulae. It is therefore necessary to begin by defining one's terms.

The expression 'fiduciary duty' is properly confined to those duties which are peculiar to fiduciaries and the breach of which attracts legal consequences differing from those consequent upon the breach of other duties. Unless the expression is so limited it is lacking in practical utility. In this sense it is obvious that not every breach of duty by a fiduciary is a breach of fiduciary duty. I would indorse the observations of Southin J in Girardet v. Crease & Co (1987) 11 BCLR (2d) 361 where she said:

> 'The word "fiduciary" is flung around now as if it applied to all breaches of duty by solicitors, directors of companies and so forth... That a lawyer can commit a breach of the special duty [of a fiduciary]... by entering into a contract with the client without full disclosure... and so forth is clear. But to say that simple carelessness in giving advice is such a breach is a perversion of words.'

These remarks were approved by La Forest J in Lac Minerals Ltd. v. International Corona Ltd. (1989) 61 DLR (4th) 14 at 28, where he said:

> '... not every legal claim arising out of a relationship with fiduciary incidents will give rise to a claim for a breach of fiduciary duty.'

It is similarly inappropriate to apply the expression to the obligation of a trustee or other fiduciary to use proper skill and care in the discharge of his duties. If it is confined to cases where the fiduciary nature of the duty has special legal consequences, then the fact that the source of the duty is to be found in equity rather than the common law does not make it a fiduciary duty. The common law and equity each developed the duty of care, but they did so independently of each other and the standard of care required is not always the same. But they influenced each other, and today the substance of the resulting obligations is more significant than their particular historic origin. In Henderson v. Merrett Syndicates Ltd., Hallam-Eames v Merrett Syndicates Ltd., Hughes v. Merrett Syndicates Ltd., Arbuthnott v. Feltrim Underwriting Agencies Ltd., Deeny v. Gooda Walker Ltd. (in liq) [1994] 3 All ER 506 at 543, [1995] 2 AC 145 at 205 Lord Browne-Wilkinson said:

> 'The liability of a fiduciary for the negligent transaction of his duties is not a separate head of liability but the paradigm of the general duty to act with care imposed by law on those who take it upon themselves to act or advise others. Although the historical development of the rules of law and equity have, in the past, caused different labels to be stuck on different manifestations of the duty, in truth the duty of care on bailees carriers, trustees, directors, agents and others is the same duty: it arises from the circumstances in which the defendants were acting, not from their status or description. It is the fact that they have all assumed responsibility for the property or affairs of others which renders them liable for the careless performance of what they have undertaken to do, not the description of the trade or position which they hold.'

I respectfully agree, and indorse the comment of Ipp J in Permanent Building Society (in liq) v. Wheeler (1994) 14 ACSR 109 at 157 where he said:

> 'It is essential to bear in mind that the existence of a fiduciary relationship does not mean that every duty owed by a fiduciary to the beneficiary is a fiduciary duty. In particular, a trustee's duty to exercise reasonable care, though equitable, is not specifically a fiduciary duty...'

Ipp J explained this (at 158):

> 'The director's duty to exercise care and skill has nothing to do with any position of disadvantage or vulnerability on the part of the company. It is not a duty that stems from the requirements of trust and confidence imposed on a

> fiduciary. In my opinion, that duty is not a fiduciary duty, although it is a duty actionable in the equitable jurisdiction of this court...I consider that Hamilton owed PBS a duty, both in law and in equity, to exercise reasonable care and skill, and PBS was able to mount a claim against him for breach of the legal duty, and, in the alternative, breach of the equitable duty. For the reasons I have expressed, in my view the equitable duty is not to be equated with or termed a "fiduciary" duty.'

I agree. Historical support for this analysis may be found in the passage in Viscount Haldane LC's speech in Nocton v. Lord Ashburton [1914] AC 932 at 956, [1914–15] All ER Rep 45 at 54. Discussing the old bill in Chancery for equitable compensation for breach of fiduciary duty, he said that he thought it probable that a demurrer for want of equity would always have lain to a bill which did no more than seek to enforce a claim for damages for negligence against a solicitor.

In my judgment this is not just a question of semantics. It goes to the very heart of the concept of breach of fiduciary duty and the availability of equitable remedies.

Although the remedy which equity makes available for breach of the equitable duty of skill and care is equitable compensation rather than damages, this is merely the product of history and in this context is in my opinion a distinction without a difference. Equitable compensation for breach of the duty of skill and care resembles common law damages in that it is awarded by way of compensation to the plaintiff for his loss. There is no reason in principle why the common law rules of causation, remoteness of damage and measure of damages should not be applied by analogy in such a case. It should not be confused with equitable compensation for breach of fiduciary duty, which may be awarded in lieu of rescission or specific restitution.

This leaves those duties which are special to fiduciaries and which attract those remedies which are peculiar to the equitable jurisdiction and are primarily restitutionary or restorative rather than compensatory. A fiduciary is someone who has undertaken to act for or on behalf of another in a particular matter in circumstances which give rise to a relationship of trust and confidence. The distinguishing obligation of a fiduciary is the obligation of loyalty. The principal is entitled to the single-minded loyalty of his fiduciary. This core liability has several facets. A fiduciary must act in good faith; he must not make a profit out of his trust; he must not place himself in a position where his duty and his interest may conflict; he may not act for his own benefit or the benefit of a third person without the informed consent of his principal. This is not intended to be an exhaustive list, but it is sufficient to indicate the nature of fiduciary obligations. They are the defining characteristics of the fiduciary. As Dr Finn pointed out in his classic work Fiduciary Obligations (1977) p 2, he is not subject to fiduciary obligations because he is a fiduciary; it is because he is subject to them that he is a fiduciary.

(In this survey I have left out of account the situation where the fiduciary deals with his principal. In such a case he must prove affirmatively that the transaction is fair and that in the course of the negotiations he made full disclosure of all facts material to the transaction. Even inadvertent failure to disclose will entitle the principal to rescind the transaction. The rule is the same whether the fiduciary is acting on his own behalf or on behalf of another. The principle need not be further considered because it does arise in the present case. The mortgage advance was negotiated directly between the society and the purchasers. The defendant had nothing to do with the negotiations. He was instructed by the society to carry out on its behalf a transaction which had already been agreed.)

The nature of the obligation determines the nature of the breach. The various obligations of a fiduciary merely reflect different aspects of his core duties of loyalty and fidelity. Breach of fiduciary obligation, therefore, connotes disloyalty or infidelity. Mere incompetence is not enough. A servant who loyally does his incompetent best for his master is not unfaithful and is not guilty of a breach of fiduciary duty.

[The rest of the discussion, dealing with the duty of loyalty, is continued below at Section C.1.b of this Chapter]

Comments and Questions

1. In what ways does the approach of the English courts differ from that of their American counterparts? Which standard is better suited to fair enforcement?

2. Applying Professor Eisenberg's thesis with respect to fiduciary duty principles, do the differences between English and American approaches suggest social rather than political or "legal" differences? If so, would harmonization be harder to achieve? Should harmonization be an objective in any case?

---

2. The Civil Law Approach

a. France and Germany

The civil law tradition of continental Europe has evolved an approach to the duties of directors that are different in form to those of common law countries like the United States and England. As you read the materials that follow, consider whether the differences are merely skin deep, that is, whether directors in civil law systems are required to adhere to conduct norms substantially the same as in common law regimes. The first excerpt, by David Berger considers director duties in French system countries by looking at the directors' duties in the context of tender offers. The second excerpt, from a much longer work by Thomas Andre, considers the problems of translating common law approaches to director duties into German corporate law. Specifically, he argues that efforts of California Public Employees' Retirement System (CalPERS) to impose U.S. governance standards on foreign companies are likely to fail because such efforts do not take sufficient account of cultural differences between German and American corporate governance regimes.

David J. Berger, *Exporting the Twin Towers: The Development of a Transnational Business Judgment Rule*

9 St. Louis U. Pub. L. Rev. 169 (1990)
(excerpts pages 175–177; some footnotes omitted)

B. France

While there presently is no separate legal category for securities law in France, the Commission des Operations de Bourse (COB) is charged with policing securities transactions.[26] The COB ensures compliance with the provisions of the various company by-laws relating to securities and must approve any prospectus issued during a takeover by both the offeror and by the target company. There is no specific parliamentary law or government decree which regulates takeovers in France. The concept of fiduciary duty does not exist as a general rule in French law; rather, minority shareholders' rights are protected through general principles of law.[28] Stockholders may bring a direct action against directors for losses suffered as a result of poor management.[29] Article 244 of the 1966 Act makes directors and managers of a company jointly or severally liable to the company or creditors for all losses due to (1) a violation of the statutory or regulatory provision of laws or decrees relating to stock companies, or (2) a violation of the company's charter and by-laws, or (3) any negligence in management.[30] No defense is available, and article 244 is broadly interpreted by French courts. The most typical defensive provisions adopted by directors are amendments to a company's articles of association prior to a takeover offer. These amendments may limit the number of voting shares per stockholder regardless of the amount of stock held, or authorize the issuance of shares with double voting rights. Companies may adopt amendments which specifically limit takeover attempts by non-EEC investors, while a number of government regulations also make the acquisition of companies significantly more difficult for non-EEC nationals.

Once a hostile tender offer has been launched, the board's ability to take defensive action is severely constrained. The COB has held that once a tender offer has commenced, the interests of shareholders must remain the dominant concern, and the target must exercise prudence in redeploying assets or taking other extraordinary corporate actions. These rules act as a significant deterrent to a board considering the adoption of some of the defensive measures available in the United States after a hostile offer is made public.

---

26. The COB was created in 1967 and began operations on January 1, 1968. See Ordinance 67-833 of September 28, 1967, art. 2 [hereinafter 1967 Ordinance]. Other regulatory agencies include the Conseil des Bourses de Valeurs (Stock Exchange Council) a professional agency consisting of 12 members (10 of whom are appointed by the Stock Exchange), which is responsible for the analysis and approval of the price of a cash offer and the terms and conditions of a share exchange offer. The contents of the information statement to be submitted, as well as guidelines for its drafting, are described in an Instruction issued by the COB in 1973. See COB, Instruction Relative Aux Notes D' Information (1973). The 1973 Instruction was updated in 1980 to increase the amount and type of information required, making it roughly comparable to the Williams Act disclosure requirements in the United States.

28. For example, Act 66-537 of July 24, 1966 (1966 Act) and Decree 67-236 of March 23, 1967 (Decree 67-236), as amended, allow shareholders holding 10 percent or more of a company's capital to call a general meeting, see 1966 Act at art. 158; Decree 67-236 at art. 122. Shareholders may also ask a commercial court to appoint an expert to report any alleged mismanagement or the poor business judgment of a particular decision, see 1966 Act at art. 222; Decree 67-236 at art. 195. In the event of a merger, both target and offeror must appoint special auditors to report to a special meeting of stockholders, 1966 Act at arts. 376–77; Decree 67-236 act arts. 255–60. See generally E. Stein, Harmonization of European Community Laws (1971).

29. The 1966 Act forbids a company from preventing such suits against directors in its by-laws or amendments, see supra 1966 Act, note 28, at art. 245; see generally Miller, France, in International Capital Markets and Securities Regulation, §§7.01–.26 (H. Bloomenthal ed. 1988).

30. Article 244 relates to the traditional form of stock companies in France (e.g., single-tier administrative council run by a president-general manager). Each member of the council may be held liable. Articles 249 and 250 of the 1966 Act extend article 244 to the newer form of stock companies, which typically consist of an executive board (directoire) and a supervisory council (counseil de surveillance). While executive board members are liable on the same basis as directors under article 244, members of the supervisory council are only liable for negligent actions. See 1966 Act, supra note 28, at art 244–50; see generally Miller, *supra* note 29, at §§7.07–.15.

C. Belgium

Until recently, takeover activity in Belgium was rare and occurred almost entirely on a friendly basis. Although the recent hostile bid for Societe General de Belgique may mark the beginning of a new era, takeover regulations remain virtually nonexistent. Currently there is no detailed takeover law or disclosure regulation in Belgium, and one leading commentator has bluntly stated that "there is no law in Belgium governing takeovers."[38]....

Takeover bids in Belgium are under the general jurisdiction of the Commission Bancaire (Commission), which is given broad responsibility for supervising securities issues. In theory the Commission has limited powers. For example, it cannot carry out independent investigations into the circumstances of an offer: it has no executive powers, and its rules have no formal legal force. At least prior to de Benedetti's bid for Societe General de Belgique, the Commission's decisions are usually followed. Consistent with the informal regulatory procedure governing takeovers, there are no specific restrictions on defensive tactics which directors may employ. In addition, there are no expressed private remedies provided to stockholders under the Belgium securities laws, and little case law to support the position that directors are liable for their negligence.[42] A similar freedom of action exists for an offeror since there are no limitations on the offeror's acquisition of shares in the target and no requirement to disclose holdings or the acquisition of shares in listed companies prior to the offer being made.

Thomas J. Andre, Jr., *Cultural Hegemony: the Exportation of Anglo-Saxon Corporate Governance Ideologies to Germany*

73 Tul. L. Rev. 69 (1998)

(excerpts pages 151–156; some footnotes omitted)

B. The Independence of Directors

A basic plank in any modern governance platform in the United States is, of course, that a majority of the board should be "independent."[409] To CalPERS "independence" generally means "the absence of any monetary, financial or commercial relationship with the company that might impair the duty of loyalty to shareholders."[410]

---

38. There are general principles which bidders are required to follow in a takeover including treating all shareholders equally, offering a price "which reflects the value of each share so far as practicable," and, in the case of a counter-offer, exceeding the prior offer by at least five percent (while further increases must be by at least 2.5 percent). See generally Wtterwulghe [*Takeover Bids in Belgium*, 5 J. Comp. Bus. & Cap. Mrkt. L. 41 (1983)], at 47–52. However, these are not legal obligations but merely rules of conduct and are difficult to enforce.

42. Wymeesch, *Belgium*, *in* International Capital Markets and Securities Regulation, §§ 8A.09–12. (H. Bloomenthal ed. 1988).

409. See Alexander Hageluken, *Das Thema Des Tages: Bankenmacht*, Suddeutsche Zeitung, Nov. 7, 1997, available in LEXIS, World Library, Allwld File (recognizing that the most important governance concern of American pension funds is the independence of directors).

410. See California Pub. Employees' Retirement Sys., Why Corporate Governance Today? A Policy Statement 9 (1995). For a more complete version of CalPERS' definition of "independence," see Archer Daniels Midland, SEC No-Action Letter, July 29, 1996, available in LEXIS, Fedsec Library, Noact File.

In Germany, any question of independence must focus on the supervisory board rather than on the Vorstand, which by definition consists of the most senior corporate employees. In considering supervisory board independence, as a matter of German law, one starts with the proposition that as many as one-half of the board consists of labor representatives. While it is true that not all of these representatives are employees of the company, one could not reasonably stretch the definition of "independence" to encompass even the non-employee directors. Short of legislation changing the co-determination laws,[411] which seems very unlikely even in the long run, in most of CalPERS' portfolio companies one half of the board will not be independent. Second, as a strictly legal matter, Vorstand members may not simultaneously sit on both the Vorstand and the supervisory board.[413] Indeed, German company law contains a number of provisions that emphasize the strict separation of the functions of the management and supervisory boards.[414] In familiar terms, German supervisory boards are not, therefore, dominated by inside directors, and are at least formally independent of the management boards they are supposed to supervise and monitor. Moreover, German law also prohibits certain board relationships that would tend to undermine the independence of a given supervisory board member.[415]

Of course, the fact that supervisory board members are by law outside directors does not make such directors "independent" as CalPERS and other institutions would define the term. Indeed, consistent with the prevailing view of the larger societal role of the company, it is fair to suggest that at least some supervisory board members are chosen for the very reason that they are not independent; that is, because they or the particular constituency they represent has an existing financial or similar relationship to the company.[416] Bank representatives are of course the principal examples. There can be little question that individual bank Vorstand members who sit on the supervisory board of

---

411. It has been reported that CalPERS eschews legislation as a method of changing the boardroom, preferring instead peer group pressure. See Lisa Buckingham, Labour Reforms of Boardrooms Opposed in U.S., Guardian (London), Oct. 12, 1995, at 21, available in LEXIS, World Library, Allwld File. Obviously peer group pressure will not change the reality of labor representation on German supervisory boards. However, it seems more probable that CalPERS or other institutional investors would in fact support legislation that furthered their governance goals. See German Governance Principles, supra note 54 ("CalPERS... encourages the use of legislation, if necessary" to improve governance).

413. There is a minor exception for short-term situations where a management board member is absent or incapacitated. See AktG §105, P2.

414. See, e.g., id. §111 ("Management responsibilities may not be conferred on the supervisory board.").

415. See id. §100. CalPERS has stated that German Vorstand members "have often served on the supervisory boards of the very companies whose representatives sit on their own supervisory board, creating a system of interlocking directorships accompanied with special relationships." German Governance Principles, supra note 54. Section 100 of the Aktiengesetz would appear to prohibit the relationship CalPERS describes. That section would prohibit, for example, the appointment of a member of the Siemens Vorstand to the supervisory board of Deutsche Bank, if a member of the Vorstand of Deutsche Bank already sits on the Siemens supervisory board. See AktG §100. Thus, German law parallels a portion of the definition of "independence" that CalPERS has recommended: an individual is not independent if he is "employed by a public company at which an executive officer of the Company serves as a director." California Pub. Employees' Retirement Sys., Corporate Governance Core Principles & Guidelines app. B-1 (1998); see also Archer Daniels Midland, Proxy Statement (1996), available in LEXIS, Fedsec Library, Proxy File (disclosing that CalPERS utilizes a similar standard in shareholder proposal under Rule 14a-8).

416. See Carl Kester, Governance, Contracting and Investment Horizons: A Look at Japan and Germany, in Studies in International Corporate Finance and Governance Systems 227, 237 (Donald H. Chew ed., 1997) (suggesting that supervisory board members "typically are not strictly disinter-

companies that have banking relationships with the company would not be considered "independent" under any but the narrowest definition of the term. Of course, because the principal German banks are universal banks, it is not merely the credit relationships with their corporate clients that undermine their independence. For example, the independence of bank Vorstand members may also be compromised because German banks provide investment banking and brokerage services on behalf of their industrial clients on whose boards they are represented. But while there has been some apparent recognition of the possible benefits of independence, and while there have been some calls for more independent directors,[418] particularly in light of some of the recent financial "scandals," it remains the case that most German companies are still a long way from achieving the kind of independent boards that some institutional investors like CalPERS seek. Moreover, problems of board independence are more intractable in Germany than in the United States. For example, a supervisory board member may be an executive of another company that has a commercial relationship to the company and for that reason would not be "independent." It may also be the case, however, that the individual's own company has an equity interest in the company on whose board that individual sits. This is most obviously the case with some banks and their industrial clients, but it is also true to a more limited extent outside the banking area. Thus, a member of the Vorstand of industrial company A may sit on the supervisory board of industrial company B, not only because of some existing commercial relationship, but also because Company A owns an equity stake in company B. Such relationships do not appear to be particularly common, at least among the major German public industrial companies, but such dual equity and commercial relationships among companies are simply one of the complicating factors that international institutional investors will have to account for in assessing the independence of board members.

Barring legislation that would reduce the size of supervisory boards, most of the AGs in which CalPERS and other institutional investors are likely to invest will have at least six and more likely either eight or ten equity representatives on the supervisory board. These boards cannot be expanded to add more independent directors. It has been suggested elsewhere that some contemporary German supervisory boards may in fact already be too small to accommodate all of the interests that a given company might like to accommodate. If this is correct, and if a greater percentage of independent board members is nevertheless to be achieved, German supervisory boards will have difficult choices to make in nominating new board members. Almost inevitably some traditional relationships will have to be reconfigured if greater independence is to be achieved. But even if it is too much to expect that all supervisory board members be independent, at most companies there should be a sufficient number of positions to accommodate truly independent directors (including representatives of large stockholders who have no other relationship to the company) as well as those who have commercial or similar ties to the company.

Of course, institutional investors rarely if ever demand that an entire board consist of independent directors. One question that institutional investors may want to address, therefore, is whether they wish to target directors representing specific constituencies. For example, given the obvious lack of independence of bank Vorstand members in most cases, should an effort be directed at reducing the numbers of such representa-

---

ested experts in some field appointed to give their presumably objective points of view," but rather "tend to mirror the company's most important investor and business relationships").

418. See, e.g., Geoffrey Owen, No Solution Perfect, Fin. Times, June 29, 1994, at XI.

tives? That question in turn would raise other issues. Given the history of bank supervisory board representation, what steps are realistically available to public stockholders who would seek to reduce bank board representation, and would shareholder initiatives have a reasonable likelihood of reducing the number of bank Vorstand members on the boards of industrial companies? A related question that institutional investors will inevitably have to consider is how much it ultimately matters if bank Vorstand members are not weaned from the boards of industrial companies? Finally, given that the absolute number of bank representatives is not that significant, is it ultimately worth potentially antagonizing much of the German corporate establishment by insisting on a reduction in number of bank representatives, when in fact there may be easier targets?

Aside from representatives of banks, as in the United States, there are a few obvious areas where changes could be made to achieve more independent boards. First, the standard practice whereby retiring senior Vorstand members, and in particular the Chairman of the Vorstand, are elected to the supervisory board[423] could be eliminated.[424] Second, any positions reserved for representatives of customers or suppliers, for example, at least when they are not also shareholders, could also be allocated to more independent individuals. Third, individuals who serve as lawyers,[425] investment bankers or other professionals for the company might be gradually purged to make room for independent directors. Finally, while it would be more politically sensitive, and perhaps more difficult to achieve, companies might be persuaded to reduce the number of representatives of political entities who serve on the boards of a number of prominent companies, and who may tend to favor the economic interests of the particular constituents whom they represent.[426]

Ultimately, however, the major problem with German supervisory boards may not prove to be the explicit, formal relationships that exist among companies and their board members or between their board members and other entities that do business with the company. Quite aside from the number of supervisory board positions that can be attributed to the equity positions of the banks and the larger insurance companies, it is apparent that a surprisingly small number of individuals comprise a significant percentage of the available supervisory board positions that can be filled by share-

---

423. See, e.g., Andrew Fisher, A Reluctant Departure: With So Many Changes Still to Come, the Chairman of Deutsche Bank Regrets That It Is Time to Step Down, Fin. Times, May 13, 1997, at 21 (describing a retiring chief executive moving to chairmanship of supervisory board); Linde Chairman to Move to Supervisory Board, Handelsblatt, Mar. 21, 1997, available in LEXIS, World Library, Allwld File; MAN's Goette Elected as Head of Supervisory Board, AFX News, Dec. 10. 1996, available in LEXIS, World Library, Allwld File.

424. See Deutsche Bank to Expand AGM Agenda, Handelsblatt, Apr. 24, 1997, available in LEXIS, World Library, Allwld File (reporting on shareholder organization, which proposed that no supervisory board member could have served on Vorstand within the last five years).

425. According to the Association of German Banks, supra note 351, nearly 10% of the positions on the supervisory boards of the 100 largest companies are filled by lawyer-notaries. Whether most of these individuals represent the company in some way is not clear, but it does not seem unreasonable to surmise that many do. The survey can be found at <http://www.bankenverband.de/daten/zahlen/bankenim.htm>.

426. The classic case is that of Volkswagen AG. See, e.g., John Templeman, Commentary: It's Time for German States to Go Out of Business, Bus. Wk. Int'l, July 8, 1996, at 17 (describing supervisory board influence of representatives of state of Lower Saxony, which controls 20% of Volkswagen shares); David Woodruff, Commentary: Stop Using VW as a State Job Mill, Bus. Wk. Int'l, Aug. 3, 1998, at 25 (same); cf. Graham Bowley, German State Beats Rival to Preussag, Fin. Times, Feb. 6, 1998, at 27 (describing role of prominent state prime minister and powerful state-controlled bank in arranging sale of company assets to protect jobs and avoid foreign control).

holder representatives at major German companies. While undoubtedly a number of individuals who do serve are selected because they are in fact both appropriately credentialed and superbly qualified, surely the pool of qualified individuals must be larger. One can only conjecture as to the possible reasons why so few individuals control so many board positions. One can speculate that, as in the United States, some individuals will be selected to serve because they are considered "trophy" directors as a result of the prominence of their existing connections.[428] Moreover, considering that new supervisory board members must at least in a general way be satisfactory to the labor representatives on the board, some individuals with a proven track record at other companies may be appointed because they are deemed "safer" than those without a similar history. Some existing board members may view a board membership as a kind of public service and seek to reward those who have paid their dues as part of the system, while others may view it as a kind of sinecure for their friends or colleagues. But whether in fact directors are chosen on the basis of these or similar considerations, one certainly does get the impression from looking at German supervisory boards that there is a potentially unhealthy concentration of a relatively few individuals selected for board membership because they are already part of an elite fraternity. As Professor Brudney observed a number of years ago, "[n]o definition of independence yet offered precludes an independent director from being a social friend of, or a member of the same clubs, associations, or charitable efforts as, the persons whose [performance]...he is asked to assess."[429]

Comments and Questions

1. An argument can be made for the proposition that independent directors on a board minimize problems of duty of loyalty in corporations. Do you agree?

2. Are the problems of translation of director norms described in the excerpts above explainable by the theory of 'path dependance' which you first encountered in Chapter 1 of these materials? Are there better explanations for resistence to convergence of the norms of director duties? Consider the following argument in that connection: "A nation's culture can be perceived as the mother of all path dependencies. Figuratively, it means that a nation's culture might be more persistent than other factors believed to induce path dependence. Substantively, a nation's unique set of cultural values might indeed affect—in a chain of causality—the development of that nation's laws in general and its corporate governance system in particular." Amir N. Licht, *The Mother of All Path Dependencies Toward a Cross-cultural Theory of Corporate Governance Systems*, 26 Del. J. Corp. L. 147, 149–150 (2001).

3. The excerpt from the work of Thomas Andre suggests, like many of the excerpts you have already read, that convergence appears to be weighted in favor of the American model of corporate governance. A factor favoring this form of convergence may be

---

428. See Judith H. Dobrzynski, When Directors Play Musical Chairs; Seats on Too Many Boards Spell Problems for Investors, N.Y. Times, Nov. 11, 1996, §3, at 1 (describing "trophy" directors as those "who sit on many boards and can navigate corporate America's wood-paneled board rooms as easily as their own homes").

429. See Victor Brudney, *The Independent Director—Heavenly City or Potemkin Village?*, 95 Harv. L. Rev. 597, 613 (1982).

the move in many countries toward more developed capital markets. As countries adopt an approach to share liquidity similar to that in the United States, that adoption may create strong incentives to mimic the form of corporate governance in effect in the national system with 'model form' of capital markets. Are there other bases for explaining this pattern? In that connection reconsider the excerpt from Colin J. Bennett, *Regulating Privacy: Data Protection and Public Policy in Europe and the United States*, excerpted in Chapter 1.

---

b. Japan

Like the Civil Code systems of Continental Europe, the Japanese system creates a statutorily based system of duties and responsibilities of members fo the board of directors. Like the systems in France and Germany, those duties are not comprehensive in the manner of the American and English systems of fiduciary duty. Yet, Japan has also adopted a form of the system of fiduciary governance received from the United States during the Allied Occupation. The readings that follow provide a basic description of the model used in Japan.

Thomas J. Blackmore and Makoto Yazawa, *Japanese Commercial Code Revisions Concerning Corporations*

2 Am. J. Comp. L. 12 (1953)
(excerpts from pages 20–21; 23–24; some footnotes omitted).

[A portion of this article was reproduced at Chapter 2, supra, with respect to the reception of American corporate law in Japan during the Allied Occupation of Japan after the end of the Second World War.]

A shareholder was given certain direct controls over management in cases of illegality or unfairness. In this connection, the thorniest issue was that of the right to inspect the files and books of a corporation. Under [previous law], shareholders had no right of access to corporate records beyond the opportunity to approve the annual financial statement at a shareholders meeting. Under the amendment of 1950, shareholders having more than one tenth of all outstanding shares of a corporation are given a right to examine the corporate books of account and records and make extracts therefrom. The one tenth requirement is an amendment inserted by the Legislative Counsel which refused to accept the original draft giving such right without limitation to every individual shareholder.... Fiduciary responsibilities of directors to their corporations have been established, and the liabilities of directors for improper acts have been increased. Also, director liabilities cannot be released or satisfied except by unanimous consent of all shareholders.[53]

53. Arts. 254-2, 266.

Liabilities of directors may be enforced by shareholders' representative suits, injunctions, or actions instituted by minority shareholders to force resignation.[54] Any shareholder who has been a shareholder for six months may institute an action against a director on behalf of the corporation, either within thirty days of the after the date on which he had demanded such action of the director in the case of emergency.... Now when a director makes an ultra vires act or any illegal act and thereby gives rise to a reasonable fear that irreparable damage will be done to the corporation, any shareholder having the same six months qualification may demand on behalf of the corporation that the director refrain from such acts and, if necessary, take such a demand to a court....

* * *

Almost equally and uniformly, Japanese have opposed the new remedies of shareholders which are patterned on the classical remedies of the United States. The requirements for the amendment of corporate articles to provide for pre-emptive rights, and the need to exclude or limit cumulative voting and to provide for the quorum of shareholders, have necessitated the revision of the articles of incorporation of every corporation in Japan, which has caused great inconvenience to registry offices and expense to corporations which have been forced to hold special meetings for this purpose. To practicing attorneys, of course, these requirements have constituted a windfall.

The remedies of shareholders which are the cause of such criticism are accepted and acknowledged to be sound in theory, and if properly interpreted and applied by courts trained to act and having practical knowledge of corporate management, they might eventually be generally accepted. Unfortunately, in Japan the present judiciary finds such cases strange, and there is no supporting body of tradition or flexible case law comparable to that of England and the United States.

Another unfortunate result of the strengthening of individual shareholder's rights has been an increase in the use of blackmailing tactics on the part of professional agitators and, at times, an improper exertion of pressure by labor representatives. Quite frequently, it seems, managers of Japanese corporations have, with tacit consent of their boards of directors, used their authority in ways which might be questioned or might appear to afford them personal advantage. The new and powerful remedies of stockholders afford to the individual, with inside information and the desire, an opportunity to force concessions from corporate management. The view that blackmail is best cured by the elimination of sin is, of course, a sound one, but it does not provide much comfort o corporations whose managers are pressed for hush money or for concessions beyond what would result from direct bargaining.

Actually, the need for a strengthening of the individual shareholder's position, which SCAP asserted, does not now exist in Japan. Blue Sky laws such as the Security and Exchange Act of 1948,[66] the Investment Trust Act of 1951,[67] and the Corporate Reorganization Act of 1952,[68] afford effective protection against abuses far beyond the shareholder

54. Art. 257. An action to enforce a resignation may be instituted only when a majority of the shareholders have rejected the removal of a director, notwithstanding dishonest or illegal conduct of such director.

66. Law No. 25 of 1948.

67. Law No. 198 of 1951.

68. Law No. 172 of 1952.

remedies for self-defense of the revised Commercial Code through measures based on the principle of full disclosure to a regulatory body.

Comment and Question

1. As it turns out, the predictions made in 1951 about the use of shareholder remedies for unscrupulous ends turned out to be correct, and the Japanese government spent decades attempting to curtail the practices which sprang up around the threat of use of shareholder remedies against managers, and the control by managers of legitimate shareholder dissent.

> Another major reason for the lack of shareholder participation has been the presence at meetings of "professional shareholders" known as "*sokai-ya*." The *sokai-ya* are hired by management to attend meetings to ensure that no debate takes place, that no embarrassing questions are asked, and that the meeting runs smoothly and ends quickly. These men each own a few shares to gain entrance to the meeting, and are paid handsomely from corporate funds funneled through some nondescript account. They have been described as "gangster-type groups... who are hired by the company to 'preserve order' at these meetings."[236] *Sokai-ya* also make money by posing as a threat to management. They are "large men in flashy clothes who are professional blackmailers. They make a living out of extortion; managements pay for their silence on such matters as pollution, etc."[237]

Christopher Lee Heftel, Survey, *Corporate Governance in Japan: The Position of Shareholders in Publicly Held Corporations*, 5 U. Haw. L. Rev. 135, 170 (1983).

Hiroshi Oda, Japanese Law (2nd ed. 1999)

(excerpt page 251)

In addition to the liability of directors to the company, directors are also liable to third parties in certain cases. Generally, when a director causes loss to a third party, the company and not the director is liable to the third party (article 261, para. 3, art. 78). However, where a director acted in bad faith, or was seriously at fault in exercising his power, he is personally liable to a third party (art. 266-3, para. 1). Moreover, if a director makes a false entry on significant matters in an application for shares or bonds, a certificate for pre-emptive rights, a prospectus, etc., he is liable to a third party unless he proves that he was not at fault (art. 266-3, para. 2).

In most cases, the third party will be either a creditor or a shareholder. In one case, A, a representative director of a company purchased steel on behalf of the company. A used the seal of another representative director and president B, and issued a promissory note to the seller. B had been asked to become a managing director by A to give credibility to the company. B left the management of the company to A and authorized him to issue promissory. The seller failed to cash the promissory note and therefore

236. [Browne, *The Capital Structures of Japanese Corporations*, Asian Finance, Aug. 15, 1980, at 32].

237. [H. Stokes, The Japanese Competitor (1976)] at 11.

sued B. The Supreme Court acknowledged the liability of B on the ground of article 266-3.[44]

Sometimes, those who have agreed to have their names registered as directors, but are only nominal directors, are held liable under this provision. There was a case where a person who was appointed external director failed to oversee the managing of the company by the representative director, did not ask for board meetings to be convened and left the company to the arbitrary management of this representative director. In the meantime, the representative director purchased goods which the company could not afford and the company collapsed. The seller sued this external director. The Supreme Court found him liable to the seller for his failure to oversee the management.[45]

One of the aims of imposing liability on directors to third parties s to protect creditors of small and medium sized companies. The majority of Japanese companies are small or medium sized and are run by a small number of individuals, often a family. Assets of these companies can be very small, and without a provision enabling creditors to claim against directors, it is difficult for them to recover their money from the company itself. The Supreme Court ruled that the loss does not have to be directly caused by the director to the third party. Even where the director caused a loss to the company by neglect of duty, as a result of which the third party suffered a loss, this person is entitled to claim against the director.[46]

Comments and Questions

1. In Japan, to whom are a corporate manager's duty owed—the shareholders, the corporation itself, the creditors, the employees, the business community of which it is a part, the general community, or the nation? If the duty runs to more than one of these groups, what mechanisms can be used to mediate disputes between the groups to ensure that managerial decisions do not breach a duty to any of the communities?

2. How do you think the nature of the duties owed are framed? In the United States, such duties are framed in the context of hierarchical relationships between independent parties, bound only by the nature of the relationship between them—master and servant, principle and agent, trustor and trustee, bailor and bailee. Regulation has as one of its objects, the description of the nature of the hierarchy between these bi-polar relationships, usually translated as the duties of each. Do these relationships translate in a similar manner in Japan? Consider your answer in light of the following statement:

> As in America, the board of directors in Japan is responsible for management of the corporation,[47] though the Japanese board is normally made up of insiders who are corporate managers as well. Strictly speaking, Japanese directors do not have fiduciary duties. The duties of American directors are derived from trust principles, in turn derived from the historical Anglo-American division of law and equity. Equity of this sort is, of course, unknown to the civil

44. Judgment of the Supreme Court, November 26, 1969 (Minshu 23-11-2150).
45. Judgment of the Supreme Court, March 18, 1980 (Hanji 971–101).
46. Judgment of the Supreme Court, November 26, 1969 (Minshu 23-11-2150).
47. SHOHO art. 260.

law tradition.[49] Instead, the Japanese director's duties to the corporation are defined in terms of the law of mandates[50] from the Civil Code, and special provisions in the corporate law define other duties.[51] Whether the differences in abstract verbal formulae make for any distinctions between U.S. and Japanese practice is questionable, given massive U.S. legal dilution in the name of the business judgment rule.

Dan Fenno Henderson, *Security Markets in the United States and Japan: Distinctive Aspects Molded by Cultural, Social, Economic, and Political Differences*, 14 HASTINGS INT'L & COMP. L. REV. 263, 276 (1991)

3. *Socialist Approaches*

The question of managerial duty plays a special role in Marxist/Socialist systems such as those of the People's Republic of China. The basic reason springs from the theoretical basis of social organization of such systems, so fundamentally different from those of Europe and most Western Hemisphere political communities.

Kingsley T.W. Ong and Colin R. Baxter, *A Comparative Study of the Fundamental Elements of Chinese and English Company Law*,

48 INTERNATIONAL & COMPARATIVE LAW QUARTERLY 88 (1999)
(excerpts from pages 121–122 some footnotes omitted)

C. *Punishment for Misconduct*

The punishments imposed by the Chinese system on misbehaving company officers are severe by English standards. China's socialist ideologies emphasise utilitarian collectivism.[230] This justifies heavy punishments for offenders who harm society as a whole. On the other hand, England's strong democratic principles emphasise individualism. This difference in emphasis between collectivism and individualism has resulted in different conceptions of human rights and consequently different standards of punishment.

China's enforcement scheme is based on progressive discipline. As a first step, those making false reports relating to matters like registration and capital, accounting, etc.

49. Kondo, *The Management Liability of Directors*, 20 LAW IN JAPAN 150 (1987). The dilution of the fiduciary duties of the American boards of large American corporations is still a problem, crying for solution. See generally Takeuchi, *Should There be a General Provision on the Social Responsibility of Enterprises in the Commercial Code*, 11 LAW IN JAPAN 37 (1978) (general aspects of the Japanese debate); C. Heftel, *Corporate Governance in Japan: The Position of Shareholders in Publicly Held Corporations*, 5 U. HAW. L. REV. 135 (1983).

50. MINPO arts. 643–56.

51. SHOHO arts. 254-3, 264, 265, 266(1), 293-5(5). *See* Kondo, *supra* note 49.

230. For a further discussion of the Marxist approach to punishment, see J.G. Murphy, "Marxism and Retribution," in A. Duff and D. Garland (Eds.), A Reader on Punishment (1994).

will be ordered to correct their mistakes.[231] Fines are imposed where cheating creditors, investors or society in general is involved.[232] Fine levels are defined by the CL—between RMB 10,000 and RMB 100,000,[233] or between 1 and 5 percent of illegally raised capital,[234] or between 5 and 10 percent of illegally withdrawn subscription money.[235]

Directors, supervisors and managers are also subject to "administrative sanctions." These include penalties like probation, demerits, demotion, and dismissal.[236] These actions threaten the individual's position and career, which is severe given the great emphasis placed on respect and "face-saving" in the Chinese culture. Improper gains are also subject to forfeiture.[238]

Criminal liability results from almost all violations of the CL.[239] Punishment for white collar crimes can be severe, including the death penalty. For example, the Xinhua News Agency reported that the president of a Chinese company who embezzled about £250,000 was executed in April 1994. A deputy-minister was sentenced to twenty years in prison in the same case. In another case, Shen Taifu, former president of the Beijing Great Wall Machinery & Electronics Group, was convicted of embezzling about £154,000 and a 10 percent patent commission on all company transactions. He also devised a national pyramid scheme, selling bonds by promising interest rates of 43 per cent and defrauding approximately 100,000 investors of more than £76 million. Shen was executed and all his personal property was confiscated. His wife, a vice-president of the company, was convicted of converting about £77,000 of company money. She was sentenced to 15 years in jail and deprived of political rights for three years. In a more recent case, a businesswoman found guilty of defrauding investors of £28 million was executed.

These severe punishments, if applied in the United Kingdom, would almost certainly result in public outcry. While the UK Companies Act 1985 sets out over 200 kinds of offense with which a director can be charged, none has been enforced as vigorously, or results in sanctions as severe as the Chinese CL. The human rights situation in China has already created much tension between China and developed nations. On human rights, China and the United Kingdom have different national requirements and policies. There are still 70 million Chinese living in poverty. Eradicating poverty is thus the biggest "human rights aim" of China. China adopts a socialist utilitarian collectivist approach and views the human rights of millions of poor Chinese as outweighing the human rights of a few offenders. Owing to its different ideologies and economic position, English society can afford to focus on individualism.

It is clear that the Chinese system incorporates greater safeguards against malfeasance than the English system. Traditional Marxism is primarily against the company concept. Therefore, it does not comment much on the internal governance of the company. In incorporating the concept of the legal person, the Chinese have chosen a pref-

---

231. CL, Arts. 206, 209, 211.

232. CL, Arts. 206–212.

233. CL, Art. 206. This is about £ 750 to £ 7,500.

234. CL, Art. 210.

235. CL, Art. 209.

236. The term "administrative sanctions" is defined in *Zhonghua Renmin Gongheguo Xingzheng Jiancha Tiaoli* (The Provisions of Administrative Supervision of PRC), passed on 23 Nov. 1990 by the State Council.

238. CL, Arts. 214, 215.

239. At least 15 arts. state that, in addition to other more specific sanctions, criminal liability (not defined in CL) applies in accordance with the law: CL, Arts. 206–214, 217–224.

erence that would ensure greatest directors' accountability—the managerial approach, under which shareholders receive primacy.

Comments and Questions

1. To whom are fiduciary duties owed when the nation-state is the majority shareholder of an enterprise—the corporation as an independent organ, the shareholders, or the state? Would your answer make a difference in terms of the way directors would have to approach corporate decision-making?

2. Consider again the Constitution of the People's Republic of China, excerpted in Chapter 2 of these materials. Ong and Baxter suggest that Chinese socialist utilitarian collectivism is the basis of a system of duty very different from that which has developed in the West and accepted, to some extent, in Japan. The Chinese system is based on a concept of fiduciary duty running from every natural and legal person to the state. The nature of that duty is defined not by the courts or statutes, but by the Chinese Communist Party. In such a system, characterized by a paramount legal duty to the state, the primary duty of business enterprises organized as corporations must also be to the state. Corporate managers, as fiduciaries of investors and shareholders thus owe, in addition to their personal duty, a collective duty to manage the corporation primarily for the benefit of the state. Maximization of shareholder value in the enterprise, then, can be measured in the way in which the corporation maximizes its contribution to the state consistent with its secondary obligation to those particular individuals that have invested in the corporation. Indeed, operating a corporation primarily for the purpose of maximizing shareholder value, if such operation contributes no value to the state or threatens the Communist Party, would not maximize the economic utility of the corporate enterprise as an autonomous unit of the state economic apparatus. As such, conduct of that sort would constitute action in breach of the managers' duty to the state and the Communist Party as well as a breach of the corporation's duty to the state as a dependent legal personality. Here, then, is a method of conceptualizing managerial duty in which Western forms of capital organization and capitalist theory have been adapted to a socialist state whose normative foundations are irreconcilable with that of the West. By adopting Western forms, the subversion of Western substance can be obscured. Do you think borrowing on this basis furthers convergence? Is the alternative illustrated by the People's Republic of China an example of the way in which globalization can be turned against itself?

B. Duty of Care

1. The Common Law Approach

a. The United States

What is the duty of care? It is a conduct norm applicable to corporate directors, and sometimes officers, which essentially requires a director to exercise reasonable care when carrying out his duties. The failure to carry out those duties with the requisite amount of care will lead to personal liability for the director to the extent of the losses to the corporation flowing from or arising from the decisions made in breach of this duty. If he does so, and if he has a reasonable basis for his decisions, a doctrine called the Business Judgment Rule will protect him from personal liability for financial loss arising from those decisions. From this little kernel springs the greater body of the law governing the conduct of officers, directors and shareholders outside of the closely held corporation environment—all of which is applicable to all corporations.

Alden Smith and John W. Gosselin, Plaintiffs Below, Appellants v. Jerome W. Van Gorkom, et al., Defendants Below, Appellees

Supreme Court of Delaware.
488 A.2d 858 (1985)
(some footnotes omitted)

HORSEY, Justice (for the majority):

This appeal from the Court of Chancery involves a class action brought by shareholders of the defendant Trans Union Corporation ("Trans Union" or "the Company"), originally seeking rescission of a cash-out merger of Trans Union into the defendant New T Company ("New T"), a wholly-owned subsidiary of the defendant, Marmon Group, Inc. ("Marmon"). Alternate relief in the form of damages is sought against the defendant members of the Board of Directors of Trans Union, New T, and Jay A. Pritzker and Robert A. Pritzker, owners of Marmon.[1]

Following trial, the former Chancellor granted judgment for the defendant directors by unreported letter opinion dated July 6, 1982.[2] Judgment was based on two findings: (1) that the Board of Directors had acted in an informed manner so as to be entitled to protection of the business judgment rule in approving the cash-out merger; and (2) that the shareholder vote approving the merger should not be set aside because the stockholders had been "fairly informed" by the Board of Directors before voting thereon. The plaintiffs appeal.

Speaking for the majority of the Court, we conclude that both rulings of the Court of Chancery are clearly erroneous. Therefore, we reverse and direct that judgment be entered in favor of the plaintiffs and against the defendant directors for the fair value of the plaintiffs' stockholdings in Trans Union, in accordance with Weinberger v. UOP, Inc., Del.Supr., 457 A.2d 701 (1983).

---

1. The plaintiff, Alden Smith, originally sought to enjoin the merger; but, following extensive discovery, the Trial Court denied the plaintiff's motion for preliminary injunction by unreported letter opinion dated February 3, 1981. On February 10, 1981, the proposed merger was approved by Trans Union's stockholders at a special meeting and the merger became effective on that date. Thereafter, John W. Gosselin was permitted to intervene as an additional plaintiff; and Smith and Gosselin were certified as representing a class consisting of all persons, other than defendants, who held shares of Trans Union common stock on all relevant dates. At the time of the merger, Smith owned 54,000 shares of Trans Union stock, Gosselin owned 23,600 shares, and members of Gosselin's family owned 20,000 shares.

2. Following trial, and before decision by the Trial Court, the parties stipulated to the dismissal, with prejudice, of the Messrs. Pritzker as parties defendant. However, all references to defendants hereinafter are to the defendant directors of Trans Union, unless otherwise noted.

We hold: (1) that the Board's decision, reached September 20, 1980, to approve the proposed cash-out merger was not the product of an informed business judgment; (2) that the Board's subsequent efforts to amend the Merger Agreement and take other curative action were ineffectual, both legally and factually; and (3) that the Board did not deal with complete candor with the stockholders by failing to disclose all material facts, which they knew or should have known, before securing the stockholders' approval of the merger.

I.

The nature of this case requires a detailed factual statement. The following facts are essentially uncontradicted:

-A-

Trans Union was a publicly-traded, diversified holding company, the principal earnings of which were generated by its railcar leasing business. During the period here involved, the Company had a cash flow of hundreds of millions of dollars annually. However, the Company had difficulty in generating sufficient taxable income to offset increasingly large investment tax credits (ITCs). Accelerated depreciation deductions had decreased available taxable income against which to offset accumulating ITCs. The Company took these deductions, despite their effect on usable ITCs, because the rental price in the railcar leasing market had already impounded the purported tax savings.

In the late 1970's, together with other capital-intensive firms, Trans Union lobbied in Congress to have ITCs refundable in cash to firms which could not fully utilize the credit. During the summer of 1980, defendant Jerome W. Van Gorkom, Trans Union's Chairman and Chief Executive Officer, testified and lobbied in Congress for refundability of ITCs and against further accelerated depreciation. By the end of August, Van Gorkom was convinced that Congress would neither accept the refundability concept nor curtail further accelerated depreciation.

Beginning in the late 1960's, and continuing through the 1970's, Trans Union pursued a program of acquiring small companies in order to increase available taxable income. In July 1980, Trans Union Management prepared the annual revision of the Company's Five Year Forecast. This report was presented to the Board of Directors at its July, 1980 meeting. The report projected an annual income growth of about 20%. The report also concluded that Trans Union would have about $195 million in spare cash between 1980 and 1985, "with the surplus growing rapidly from 1982 onward." The report referred to the ITC situation as a "nagging problem" and, given that problem, the leasing company "would still appear to be constrained to a tax breakeven." The report then listed four alternative uses of the projected 1982–1985 equity surplus: (1) stock repurchase; (2) dividend increases; (3) a major acquisition program; and (4) combinations of the above. The sale of Trans Union was not among the alternatives. The report emphasized that, despite the overall surplus, the operation of the Company would consume all available equity for the next several years, and concluded: "As a result, we have sufficient time to fully develop our course of action."

-B-

On August 27, 1980, Van Gorkom met with Senior Management of Trans Union. Van Gorkom reported on his lobbying efforts in Washington and his desire to find a solution to the tax credit problem more permanent than a continued program of acquisitions. Various alternatives were suggested and discussed preliminarily, including the sale of Trans Union to a company with a large amount of taxable income.

Donald Romans, Chief Financial Officer of Trans Union, stated that his department had done a "very brief bit of work on the possibility of a leveraged buy-out." This work had been prompted by a media article which Romans had seen regarding a leveraged buy-out by management. The work consisted of a "preliminary study" of the cash which could be generated by the Company if it participated in a leveraged buy-out. As Romans stated, this analysis "was a very first and rough cut at seeing whether a cash flow would support what might be considered a high price for this type of transaction."

On September 5, at another Senior Management meeting which Van Gorkom attended, Romans again brought up the idea of a leveraged buy-out as a "possible strategic alternative" to the Company's acquisition program. Romans and Bruce S. Chelberg, President and Chief Operating Officer of Trans Union, had been working on the matter in preparation for the meeting. According to Romans: They did not "come up" with a price for the Company. They merely "ran the numbers" at $50 a share and at $60 a share with the "rough form" of their cash figures at the time. Their "figures indicated that $50 would be very easy to do but $60 would be very difficult to do under those figures." This work did not purport to establish a fair price for either the Company or 100% of the stock. It was intended to determine the cash flow needed to service the debt that would "probably" be incurred in a leveraged buy-out, based on "rough calculations" without "any benefit of experts to identify what the limits were to that, and so forth." These computations were not considered extensive and no conclusion was reached.

At this meeting, Van Gorkom stated that he would be willing to take $55 per share for his own 75,000 shares. He vetoed the suggestion of a leveraged buy-out by Management, however, as involving a potential conflict of interest for Management. Van Gorkom, a certified public accountant and lawyer, had been an officer of Trans Union for 24 years, its Chief Executive Officer for more than 17 years, and Chairman of its Board for 2 years. It is noteworthy in this connection that he was then approaching 65 years of age and mandatory retirement.

For several days following the September 5 meeting, Van Gorkom pondered the idea of a sale. He had participated in many acquisitions as a manager and director of Trans Union and as a director of other companies. He was familiar with acquisition procedures, valuation methods, and negotiations; and he privately considered the pros and cons of whether Trans Union should seek a privately or publicly-held purchaser.

Van Gorkom decided to meet with Jay A. Pritzker, a well-known corporate takeover specialist and a social acquaintance. However, rather than approaching Pritzker simply to determine his interest in acquiring Trans Union, Van Gorkom assembled a proposed per share price for sale of the Company and a financing structure by which to accomplish the sale. Van Gorkom did so without consulting either his Board or any members of Senior Management except one: Carl Peterson, Trans Union's Controller. Telling Peterson that he wanted no other person on his staff to know what he was doing, but without telling him why, Van Gorkom directed Peterson to calculate the feasibility of a leveraged buy-out at an assumed price per share of $55. Apart from the Company's historic stock market price,[5] and Van Gorkom's long association with Trans Union, the

5. The common stock of Trans Union was traded on the New York Stock Exchange. Over the five year period from 1975 through 1979, Trans Union's stock had traded within a range of a high of $39 1/2 and a low of $24 1/4 . Its high and low range for 1980 through September 19 (the last trading day before announcement of the merger) was $38 1/4–$29 1/2 .

record is devoid of any competent evidence that $55 represented the per share intrinsic value of the Company.

Having thus chosen the $55 figure, based solely on the availability of a leveraged buy-out, Van Gorkom multiplied the price per share by the number of shares outstanding to reach a total value of the Company of $690 million. Van Gorkom told Peterson to use this $690 million figure and to assume a $200 million equity contribution by the buyer. Based on these assumptions, Van Gorkom directed Peterson to determine whether the debt portion of the purchase price could be paid off in five years or less if financed by Trans Union's cash flow as projected in the Five Year Forecast, and by the sale of certain weaker divisions identified in a study done for Trans Union by the Boston Consulting Group ("BCG study"). Peterson reported that, of the purchase price, approximately $50–80 million would remain outstanding after five years. Van Gorkom was disappointed, but decided to meet with Pritzker nevertheless.

Van Gorkom arranged a meeting with Pritzker at the latter's home on Saturday, September 13, 1980. Van Gorkom prefaced his presentation by stating to Pritzker: "Now as far as you are concerned, I can, I think, show how you can pay a substantial premium over the present stock price and pay off most of the loan in the first five years. * * * If you could pay $55 for this Company, here is a way in which I think it can be financed."

Van Gorkom then reviewed with Pritzker his calculations based upon his proposed price of $55 per share. Although Pritzker mentioned $50 as a more attractive figure, no other price was mentioned. However, Van Gorkom stated that to be sure that $55 was the best price obtainable, Trans Union should be free to accept any better offer. Pritzker demurred, stating that his organization would serve as a "stalking horse" for an "auction contest" only if Trans Union would permit Pritzker to buy 1,750,000 shares of Trans Union stock at market price which Pritzker could then sell to any higher bidder. After further discussion on this point, Pritzker told Van Gorkom that he would give him a more definite reaction soon.

On Monday, September 15, Pritzker advised Van Gorkom that he was interested in the $55 cash-out merger proposal and requested more information on Trans Union. Van Gorkom agreed to meet privately with Pritzker, accompanied by Peterson, Chelberg, and Michael Carpenter, Trans Union's consultant from the Boston Consulting Group. The meetings took place on September 16 and 17. Van Gorkom was "astounded that events were moving with such amazing rapidity."

On Thursday, September 18, Van Gorkom met again with Pritzker. At that time, Van Gorkom knew that Pritzker intended to make a cash-out merger offer at Van Gorkom's proposed $55 per share. Pritzker instructed his attorney, a merger and acquisition specialist, to begin drafting merger documents. There was no further discussion of the $55 price. However, the number of shares of Trans Union's treasury stock to be offered to Pritzker was negotiated down to one million shares; the price was set at $38—75 cents above the per share price at the close of the market on September 19. At this point, Pritzker insisted that the Trans Union Board act on his merger proposal within the next three days, stating to Van Gorkom: "We have to have a decision by no later than Sunday [evening, September 21] before the opening of the English stock exchange on Monday morning." Pritzker's lawyer was then instructed to draft the merger documents, to be reviewed by Van Gorkom's lawyer, "sometimes with discussion and sometimes not, in the haste to get it finished."

On Friday, September 19, Van Gorkom, Chelberg, and Pritzker consulted with Trans Union's lead bank regarding the financing of Pritzker's purchase of Trans Union. The bank indicated that it could form a syndicate of banks that would finance the transaction. On the same day, Van Gorkom retained James Brennan, Esquire, to advise Trans Union on the legal aspects of the merger. Van Gorkom did not consult with William Browder, a Vice-President and director of Trans Union and former head of its legal department, or with William Moore, then the head of Trans Union's legal staff.

On Friday, September 19, Van Gorkom called a special meeting of the Trans Union Board for noon the following day. He also called a meeting of the Company's Senior Management to convene at 11:00 a.m., prior to the meeting of the Board. No one, except Chelberg and Peterson, was told the purpose of the meetings. Van Gorkom did not invite Trans Union's investment banker, Salomon Brothers or its Chicago-based partner, to attend.

Of those present at the Senior Management meeting on September 20, only Chelberg and Peterson had prior knowledge of Pritzker's offer. Van Gorkom disclosed the offer and described its terms, but he furnished no copies of the proposed Merger Agreement. Romans announced that his department had done a second study which showed that, for a leveraged buy-out, the price range for Trans Union stock was between $55 and $65 per share. Van Gorkom neither saw the study nor asked Romans to make it available for the Board meeting.

Senior Management's reaction to the Pritzker proposal was completely negative. No member of Management, except Chelberg and Peterson, supported the proposal. Romans objected to the price as being too low;[6] he was critical of the timing and suggested that consideration should be given to the adverse tax consequences of an all-cash deal for low-basis shareholders; and he took the position that the agreement to sell Pritzker one million newly-issued shares at market price would inhibit other offers, as would the prohibitions against soliciting bids and furnishing inside information to other bidders. Romans argued that the Pritzker proposal was a "lock up" and amounted to "an agreed merger as opposed to an offer." Nevertheless, Van Gorkom proceeded to the Board meeting as scheduled without further delay.

Ten directors served on the Trans Union Board, five inside (defendants Bonser, O'Boyle, Browder, Chelberg, and Van Gorkom) and five outside (defendants Wallis, Johnson, Lanterman, Morgan and Reneker). All directors were present at the meeting, except O'Boyle who was ill. Of the outside directors, four were corporate chief executive officers and one was the former Dean of the University of Chicago Business School. None was an investment banker or trained financial analyst. All members of the Board were well informed about the Company and its operations as a going concern. They were familiar with the current financial condition of the Company, as well as operating and earnings projections reported in the recent Five Year Forecast. The Board generally received regular and detailed reports and was kept abreast of the accumulated investment tax credit and accelerated depreciation problem.

Van Gorkom began the Special Meeting of the Board with a twenty-minute oral presentation. Copies of the proposed Merger Agreement were delivered too late for study before or during the meeting.[7] He reviewed the Company's ITC and depreciation prob-

6. Van Gorkom asked Romans to express his opinion as to the $55 price. Romans stated that he "thought the price was too low in relation to what he could derive for the company in a cash sale, particularly one which enabled us to realize the values of certain subsidiaries and independent entities."

7. The record is not clear as to the terms of the Merger Agreement. The Agreement, as originally presented to the Board on September 20, was never produced by defendants despite demands by the plaintiffs. Nor is it clear that the directors were given an opportunity to study the Merger Agreement

lems and the efforts theretofore made to solve them. He discussed his initial meeting with Pritzker and his motivation in arranging that meeting. Van Gorkom did not disclose to the Board, however, the methodology by which he alone had arrived at the $55 figure, or the fact that he first proposed the $55 price in his negotiations with Pritzker.

Van Gorkom outlined the terms of the Pritzker offer as follows: Pritzker would pay $55 in cash for all outstanding shares of Trans Union stock upon completion of which Trans Union would be merged into New T Company, a subsidiary wholly-owned by Pritzker and formed to implement the merger; for a period of 90 days, Trans Union could receive, but could not actively solicit, competing offers; the offer had to be acted on by the next evening, Sunday, September 21; Trans Union could only furnish to competing bidders published information, and not proprietary information; the offer was subject to Pritzker obtaining the necessary financing by October 10, 1980; if the financing contingency were met or waived by Pritzker, Trans Union was required to sell to Pritzker one million newly-issued shares of Trans Union at $38 per share.

Van Gorkom took the position that putting Trans Union "up for auction" through a 90-day market test would validate a decision by the Board that $55 was a fair price. He told the Board that the "free market will have an opportunity to judge whether $55 is a fair price." Van Gorkom framed the decision before the Board not as whether $55 per share was the highest price that could be obtained, but as whether the $55 price was a fair price that the stockholders should be given the opportunity to accept or reject.[8] Attorney Brennan advised the members of the Board that they might be sued if they failed to accept the offer and that a fairness opinion was not required as a matter of law.

Romans attended the meeting as chief financial officer of the Company. He told the Board that he had not been involved in the negotiations with Pritzker and knew nothing about the merger proposal until the morning of the meeting; that his studies did not indicate either a fair price for the stock or a valuation of the Company; that he did not see his role as directly addressing the fairness issue; and that he and his people "were trying to search for ways to justify a price in connection with such a [leveraged buy-out] transaction, rather than to say what the shares are worth." Romans testified:

> I told the Board that the study ran the numbers at 50 and 60, and then the subsequent study at 55 and 65, and that was not the same thing as saying that I have a valuation of the company at X dollars. But it was a way—a first step towards reaching that conclusion.

Romans told the Board that, in his opinion, $55 was "in the range of a fair price," but "at the beginning of the range."

Chelberg, Trans Union's President, supported Van Gorkom's presentation and representations. He testified that he "participated to make sure that the Board members collectively were clear on the details of the agreement or offer from Pritzker;" that he "participated in the discussion with Mr. Brennan, inquiring of him about the necessity for valuation opinions in spite of the way in which this particular offer was couched;" and that he was otherwise actively involved in supporting the positions being taken by Van Gorkom before the Board about "the necessity to act immediately

---

before voting on it. All that can be said is that Brennan had the Agreement before him during the meeting.

8. In Van Gorkom's words: The "real decision" is whether to "let the stockholders decide it" which is "all you are being asked to decide today."

on this offer," and about "the adequacy of the $55 and the question of how that would be tested."

The Board meeting of September 20 lasted about two hours. Based solely upon Van Gorkom's oral presentation, Chelberg's supporting representations, Romans' oral statement, Brennan's legal advice, and their knowledge of the market history of the Company's stock,[9] the directors approved the proposed Merger Agreement. However, the Board later claimed to have attached two conditions to its acceptance: (1) that Trans Union reserved the right to accept any better offer that was made during the market test period; and (2) that Trans Union could share its proprietary information with any other potential bidders. While the Board now claims to have reserved the right to accept any better offer received after the announcement of the Pritzker agreement (even though the minutes of the meeting do not reflect this), it is undisputed that the Board did not reserve the right to actively solicit alternate offers.

The Merger Agreement was executed by Van Gorkom during the evening of September 20 at a formal social event that he hosted for the opening of the Chicago Lyric Opera. Neither he nor any other director read the agreement prior to its signing and delivery to Pritzker.

* * *

On Monday, September 22, the Company issued a press release announcing that Trans Union had entered into a "definitive" Merger Agreement with an affiliate of the Marmon Group, Inc., a Pritzker holding company. Within 10 days of the public announcement, dissent among Senior Management over the merger had become widespread. Faced with threatened resignations of key officers, Van Gorkom met with Pritzker who agreed to several modifications of the Agreement. Pritzker was willing to do so provided that Van Gorkom could persuade the dissidents to remain on the Company payroll for at least six months after consummation of the merger.

Van Gorkom reconvened the Board on October 8 and secured the directors' approval of the proposed amendments—sight unseen. The Board also authorized the employment of Salomon Brothers, its investment banker, to solicit other offers for Trans Union during the proposed "market test" period.

The next day, October 9, Trans Union issued a press release announcing: (1) that Pritzker had obtained "the financing commitments necessary to consummate" the merger with Trans Union; (2) that Pritzker had acquired one million shares of Trans Union common stock at $38 per share; (3) that Trans Union was now permitted to actively seek other offers and had retained Salomon Brothers for that purpose; and (4) that if a more favorable offer were not received before February 1, 1981, Trans Union's shareholders would thereafter meet to vote on the Pritzker proposal.

It was not until the following day, October 10, that the actual amendments to the Merger Agreement were prepared by Pritzker and delivered to Van Gorkom for execution. As will be seen, the amendments were considerably at variance with Van Gorkom's representations of the amendments to the Board on October 8; and the amendments

9. The Trial Court stated the premium relationship of the $55 price to the market history of the Company's stock as follows:

* * * the merger price offered to the stockholders of Trans Union represented a premium of 62% over the average of the high and low prices at which Trans Union stock had traded in 1980, a premium of 48% over the last closing price, and a premium of 39% over the highest price at which the stock of Trans Union had traded any time during the prior six years.

placed serious constraints on Trans Union's ability to negotiate a better deal and withdraw from the Pritzker agreement. Nevertheless, Van Gorkom proceeded to execute what became the October 10 amendments to the Merger Agreement without conferring further with the Board members and apparently without comprehending the actual implications of the amendments.

* * *

Salomon Brothers' efforts over a three-month period from October 21 to January 21 produced only one serious suitor for Trans Union—General Electric Credit Corporation ("GE Credit"), a subsidiary of the General Electric Company. However, GE Credit was unwilling to make an offer for Trans Union unless Trans Union first rescinded its Merger Agreement with Pritzker. When Pritzker refused, GE Credit terminated further discussions with Trans Union in early January.

In the meantime, in early December, the investment firm of Kohlberg, Kravis, Roberts & Co. ("KKR"), the only other concern to make a firm offer for Trans Union, withdrew its offer under circumstances hereinafter detailed.

On December 19, this litigation was commenced and, within four weeks, the plaintiffs had deposed eight of the ten directors of Trans Union, including Van Gorkom, Chelberg and Romans, its Chief Financial Officer. On January 21, Management's Proxy Statement for the February 10 shareholder meeting was mailed to Trans Union's stockholders. On January 26, Trans Union's Board met and, after a lengthy meeting, voted to proceed with the Pritzker merger. The Board also approved for mailing, "on or about January 27," a Supplement to its Proxy Statement. The Supplement purportedly set forth all information relevant to the Pritzker Merger Agreement, which had not been divulged in the first Proxy Statement.

* * *

On February 10, the stockholders of Trans Union approved the Pritzker merger proposal. Of the outstanding shares, 69.9% were voted in favor of the merger; 7.25% were voted against the merger; and 22.85% were not voted.

II.

We turn to the issue of the application of the business judgment rule to the September 20 meeting of the Board.

The Court of Chancery concluded from the evidence that the Board of Directors' approval of the Pritzker merger proposal fell within the protection of the business judgment rule. The Court found that the Board had given sufficient time and attention to the transaction, since the directors had considered the Pritzker proposal on three different occasions, on September 20, and on October 8, 1980 and finally on January 26, 1981. On that basis, the Court reasoned that the Board had acquired, over the four-month period, sufficient information to reach an informed business judgment on the cash-out merger proposal. The Court ruled:

> ...that given the market value of Trans Union's stock, the business acumen of the members of the board of Trans Union, the substantial premium over market offered by the Pritzkers and the ultimate effect on the merger price provided by the prospect of other bids for the stock in question, that the board of directors of Trans Union did not act recklessly or improvidently in determining on a course of action which they believed to be in the best interest of the stockholders of Trans Union.

The Court of Chancery made but one finding; i.e., that the Board's conduct over the entire period from September 20 through January 26, 1981 was not reckless or improvident, but informed. This ultimate conclusion was premised upon three subordinate findings, one explicit and two implied. The Court's explicit finding was that Trans Union's Board was "free to turn down the Pritzker proposal" not only on September 20 but also on October 8, 1980 and on January 26, 1981. The Court's implied, subordinate findings were: (1) that no legally binding agreement was reached by the parties until January 26; and (2) that if a higher offer were to be forthcoming, the market test would have produced it, and Trans Union would have been contractually free to accept such higher offer. However, the Court offered no factual basis or legal support for any of these findings; and the record compels contrary conclusions.

* * *

The plaintiffs contend that the Court of Chancery erred as a matter of law by exonerating the defendant directors under the business judgment rule without first determining whether the rule's threshold condition of "due care and prudence" was satisfied. The plaintiffs assert that the Trial Court found the defendant directors to have reached an informed business judgment on the basis of "extraneous considerations and events that occurred after September 20, 1980." The defendants deny that the Trial Court committed legal error in relying upon post-September 20, 1980 events and the directors' later acquired knowledge. The defendants further submit that their decision to accept $55 per share was informed because: (1) they were "highly qualified;" (2) they were "well-informed;" and (3) they deliberated over the "proposal" not once but three times. On essentially this evidence and under our standard of review, the defendants assert that affirmance is required. We must disagree.

Under Delaware law, the business judgment rule is the offspring of the fundamental principle, codified in 8 Del.C. § 141(a), that the business and affairs of a Delaware corporation are managed by or under its board of directors.[11] Pogostin v. Rice, Del.Supr., 480 A.2d 619, 624 (1984); Aronson v. Lewis, Del.Supr., 473 A.2d 805, 811 (1984); Zapata Corp. v. Maldonado, Del.Supr., 430 A.2d 779, 782 (1981). In carrying out their managerial roles, directors are charged with an unyielding fiduciary duty to the corporation and its shareholders. Loft, Inc. v. Guth, Del.Ch., 2 A.2d 225 (1938), aff'd, Del.Supr., 5 A.2d 503 (1939). The business judgment rule exists to protect and promote the full and free exercise of the managerial power granted to Delaware directors. Zapata Corp. v. Maldonado, supra at 782. The rule itself "is a presumption that in making a business decision, the directors of a corporation acted on an informed basis, in good faith and in the honest belief that the action taken was in the best interests of the company." Aronson, supra at 812. Thus, the party attacking a board decision as uninformed must rebut the presumption that its business judgment was an informed one. Id.

The determination of whether a business judgment is an informed one turns on whether the directors have informed themselves "prior to making a business decision, of all material information reasonably available to them." Id.

---

11. 8 Del.C. § 141 provides, in pertinent part:

(a) The business and affairs of every corporation organized under this chapter shall be managed by or under the direction of a board of directors, except as may be otherwise provided in this chapter or in its certificate of incorporation. If any such provision is made in the certificate of incorporation, the powers and duties conferred or imposed upon the board of directors by this chapter shall be exercised or performed to such extent and by such person or persons as shall be provided in the certificate of incorporation.

Under the business judgment rule there is no protection for directors who have made "an unintelligent or unadvised judgment." Mitchell v. Highland-Western Glass, Del.Ch., 167 A. 831, 833 (1933). A director's duty to inform himself in preparation for a decision derives from the fiduciary capacity in which he serves the corporation and its stockholders. Lutz v. Boas, Del.Ch., 171 A.2d 381 (1961). See Weinberger v. UOP, Inc., supra; Guth v. Loft, supra. Since a director is vested with the responsibility for the management of the affairs of the corporation, he must execute that duty with the recognition that he acts on behalf of others. Such obligation does not tolerate faithlessness or self-dealing. But fulfillment of the fiduciary function requires more than the mere absence of bad faith or fraud. Representation of the financial interests of others imposes on a director an affirmative duty to protect those interests and to proceed with a critical eye in assessing information of the type and under the circumstances present here....

Thus, a director's duty to exercise an informed business judgment is in the nature of a duty of care, as distinguished from a duty of loyalty. Here, there were no allegations of fraud, bad faith, or self-dealing, or proof thereof. Hence, it is presumed that the directors reached their business judgment in good faith, Allaun v. Consolidated Oil Co., Del.Ch., 147 A. 257 (1929), and considerations of motive are irrelevant to the issue before us.

The standard of care applicable to a director's duty of care has also been recently restated by this Court. In Aronson, supra, we stated:

> While the Delaware cases use a variety of terms to describe the applicable standard of care, our analysis satisfies us that under the business judgment rule director liability is predicated upon concepts of gross negligence. (footnote omitted)

473 A.2d at 812.

We again confirm that view. We think the concept of gross negligence is also the proper standard for determining whether a business judgment reached by a board of directors was an informed one.

In the specific context of a proposed merger of domestic corporations, a director has a duty under 8 Del.C. §251(b), along with his fellow directors, to act in an informed and deliberate manner in determining whether to approve an agreement of merger before submitting the proposal to the stockholders. Certainly in the merger context, a director may not abdicate that duty by leaving to the shareholders alone the decision to approve or disapprove the agreement. See Beard v. Elster, Del.Supr., 160 A.2d 731, 737 (1960). Only an agreement of merger satisfying the requirements of 8 Del.C. §251(b) may be submitted to the shareholders under §251(c). See generally Aronson v. Lewis, supra at 811–13; see also Pogostin v. Rice, supra.

It is against those standards that the conduct of the directors of Trans Union must be tested, as a matter of law and as a matter of fact, regarding their exercise of an informed business judgment in voting to approve the Pritzker merger proposal.

III.

The defendants argue that the determination of whether their decision to accept $55 per share for Trans Union represented an informed business judgment requires consideration, not only of that which they knew and learned on September 20, but also of that which they subsequently learned and did over the following four-month period before the shareholders met to vote on the proposal in February, 1981. The defendants thereby seek to reduce the significance of their action on September 20 and to widen the time frame for determining whether their decision to accept the Pritzker proposal was an informed one. Thus, the defendants contend that what the directors did and learned subsequent to September 20 and through January 26, 1981, was properly taken into account by the Trial Court in determining whether the Board's judgment was an informed one. We disagree with this post hoc approach.

The issue of whether the directors reached an informed decision to "sell" the Company on September 20, 1980 must be determined only upon the basis of the information then reasonably available to the directors and relevant to their decision to accept the Pritzker merger proposal. This is not to say that the directors were precluded from altering their original plan of action, had they done so in an informed manner. What we do say is that the question of whether the directors reached an informed business judgment in agreeing to sell the Company, pursuant to the terms of the September 20 Agreement presents, in reality, two questions: (A) whether the directors reached an informed business judgment on September 20, 1980; and (B) if they did not, whether the directors' actions taken subsequent to September 20 were adequate to cure any infirmity in their action taken on September 20. We first consider the directors' September 20 action in terms of their reaching an informed business judgment.

-A-

On the record before us, we must conclude that the Board of Directors did not reach an informed business judgment on September 20, 1980 in voting to "sell" the Company for $55 per share pursuant to the Pritzker cash-out merger proposal. Our reasons, in summary, are as follows:

The directors (1) did not adequately inform themselves as to Van Gorkom's role in forcing the "sale" of the Company and in establishing the per share purchase price; (2) were uninformed as to the intrinsic value of the Company; and (3) given these circumstances, at a minimum, were grossly negligent in approving the "sale" of the Company upon two hours' consideration, without prior notice, and without the exigency of a crisis or emergency.

As has been noted, the Board based its September 20 decision to approve the cash-out merger primarily on Van Gorkom's representations. None of the directors, other than Van Gorkom and Chelberg, had any prior knowledge that the purpose of the meeting was to propose a cash-out merger of Trans Union. No members of Senior Management were present, other than Chelberg, Romans and Peterson; and the latter two had only learned of the proposed sale an hour earlier. Both general counsel Moore and former general counsel Browder attended the meeting, but were equally uninformed as to the purpose of the meeting and the documents to be acted upon.

Without any documents before them concerning the proposed transaction, the members of the Board were required to rely entirely upon Van Gorkom's 20-minute oral presentation of the proposal. No written summary of the terms of the merger was presented; the directors were given no documentation to support the adequacy of $55 price per share for sale of the Company; and the Board had before it nothing more than Van Gorkom's statement of his understanding of the substance of an agreement which he admittedly had never read, nor which any member of the Board had ever seen.

Under 8 Del.C. § 141(e),[15] "directors are fully protected in relying in good faith on reports made by officers." .... The term "report" has been liberally construed to in-

15. Section 141(e) provides in pertinent part:
A member of the board of directors...shall, in the performance of his duties, be fully protected

clude reports of informal personal investigations by corporate officers, Cheff v. Mathes, Del.Supr., 199 A.2d 548, 556 (1964). However, there is no evidence that any "report," as defined under § 141(e), concerning the Pritzker proposal, was presented to the Board on September 20.[16] Van Gorkom's oral presentation of his understanding of the terms of the proposed Merger Agreement, which he had not seen, and Romans' brief oral statement of his preliminary study regarding the feasibility of a leveraged buy-out of Trans Union do not qualify as § 141(e) "reports" for these reasons: The former lacked substance because Van Gorkom was basically uninformed as to the essential provisions of the very document about which he was talking. Romans' statement was irrelevant to the issues before the Board since it did not purport to be a valuation study. At a minimum for a report to enjoy the status conferred by § 141(e), it must be pertinent to the subject matter upon which a board is called to act, and otherwise be entitled to good faith, not blind, reliance. Considering all of the surrounding circumstances—hastily calling the meeting without prior notice of its subject matter, the proposed sale of the Company without any prior consideration of the issue or necessity therefor, the urgent time constraints imposed by Pritzker, and the total absence of any documentation whatsoever—the directors were duty bound to make reasonable inquiry of Van Gorkom and Romans, and if they had done so, the inadequacy of that upon which they now claim to have relied would have been apparent.

The defendants rely on the following factors to sustain the Trial Court's finding that the Board's decision was an informed one: (1) the magnitude of the premium or spread between the $55 Pritzker offering price and Trans Union's current market price of $38 per share; (2) the amendment of the Agreement as submitted on September 20 to permit the Board to accept any better offer during the "market test" period; (3) the collective experience and expertise of the Board's "inside" and "outside" directors; and (4) their reliance on Brennan's legal advice that the directors might be sued if they rejected the Pritzker proposal. We discuss each of these grounds seriatim:

(1)

A substantial premium may provide one reason to recommend a merger, but in the absence of other sound valuation information, the fact of a premium alone does not provide an adequate basis upon which to assess the fairness of an offering price. Here, the judgment reached as to the adequacy of the premium was based on a comparison between the historically depressed Trans Union market price and the amount of the Pritzker offer. Using market price as a basis for concluding that the premium adequately reflected the true value of the Company was a clearly faulty, indeed fallacious, premise, as the defendants' own evidence demonstrates.

---

in relying in good faith upon the books of accounts or reports made to the corporation by any of its officers, or by an independent certified public accountant, or by an appraiser selected with reasonable care by the board of directors..., or in relying in good faith upon other records of the corporation.

16. In support of the defendants' argument that their judgment as to the adequacy of $55 per share was an informed one, the directors rely on the BCG study and the Five Year Forecast. However, no one even referred to either of these studies at the September 20 meeting; and it is conceded that these materials do not represent valuation studies. Hence, these documents do not constitute evidence as to whether the directors reached an informed judgment on September 20 that $55 per share was a fair value for sale of the Company.

The record is clear that before September 20, Van Gorkom and other members of Trans Union's Board knew that the market had consistently undervalued the worth of Trans Union's stock, despite steady increases in the Company's operating income in the seven years preceding the merger. The Board related this occurrence in large part to Trans Union's inability to use its ITCs as previously noted. Van Gorkom testified that he did not believe the market price accurately reflected Trans Union's true worth; and several of the directors testified that, as a general rule, most chief executives think that the market undervalues their companies' stock. Yet, on September 20, Trans Union's Board apparently believed that the market stock price accurately reflected the value of the Company for the purpose of determining the adequacy of the premium for its sale.

In the Proxy Statement, however, the directors reversed their position. There, they stated that, although the earnings prospects for Trans Union were "excellent," they found no basis for believing that this would be reflected in future stock prices. With regard to past trading, the Board stated that the prices at which the Company's common stock had traded in recent years did not reflect the "inherent" value of the Company. But having referred to the "inherent" value of Trans Union, the directors ascribed no number to it. Moreover, nowhere did they disclose that they had no basis on which to fix "inherent" worth beyond an impressionistic reaction to the premium over market and an unsubstantiated belief that the value of the assets was "significantly greater" than book value. By their own admission they could not rely on the stock price as an accurate measure of value. Yet, also by their own admission, the Board members assumed that Trans Union's market price was adequate to serve as a basis upon which to assess the adequacy of the premium for purposes of the September 20 meeting.

The parties do not dispute that a publicly-traded stock price is solely a measure of the value of a minority position and, thus, market price represents only the value of a single share. Nevertheless, on September 20, the Board assessed the adequacy of the premium over market, offered by Pritzker, solely by comparing it with Trans Union's current and historical stock price. (See supra note 5 at 866.)

Indeed, as of September 20, the Board had no other information on which to base a determination of the intrinsic value of Trans Union as a going concern. As of September 20, the Board had made no evaluation of the Company designed to value the entire enterprise, nor had the Board ever previously considered selling the Company or consenting to a buy-out merger. Thus, the adequacy of a premium is indeterminate unless it is assessed in terms of other competent and sound valuation information that reflects the value of the particular business.

Despite the foregoing facts and circumstances, there was no call by the Board, either on September 20 or thereafter, for any valuation study or documentation of the $55 price per share as a measure of the fair value of the Company in a cash-out context. It is undisputed that the major asset of Trans Union was its cash flow. Yet, at no time did the Board call for a valuation study taking into account that highly significant element of the Company's assets.

We do not imply that an outside valuation study is essential to support an informed business judgment; nor do we state that fairness opinions by independent investment bankers are required as a matter of law. Often insiders familiar with the business of a going concern are in a better position than are outsiders to gather relevant information; and under appropriate circumstances, such directors may be fully protected in relying in good faith upon the valuation reports of their management. See 8 Del.C. § 141(e). See also Cheff v. Mathes, supra.

Here, the record establishes that the Board did not request its Chief Financial Officer, Romans, to make any valuation study or review of the proposal to determine the adequacy of $55 per share for sale of the Company. On the record before us: The Board rested on Romans' elicited response that the $55 figure was within a "fair price range" within the context of a leveraged buy-out. No director sought any further information from Romans. No director asked him why he put $55 at the bottom of his range. No director asked Romans for any details as to his study, the reason why it had been undertaken or its depth. No director asked to see the study; and no director asked Romans whether Trans Union's finance department could do a fairness study within the remaining 36-hour[18] period available under the Pritzker offer.

Had the Board, or any member, made an inquiry of Romans, he presumably would have responded as he testified: that his calculations were rough and preliminary; and, that the study was not designed to determine the fair value of the Company, but rather to assess the feasibility of a leveraged buy-out financed by the Company's projected cash flow, making certain assumptions as to the purchaser's borrowing needs. Romans would have presumably also informed the Board of his view, and the widespread view of Senior Management, that the timing of the offer was wrong and the offer inadequate.

The record also establishes that the Board accepted without scrutiny Van Gorkom's representation as to the fairness of the $55 price per share for sale of the Company—a subject that the Board had never previously considered. The Board thereby failed to discover that Van Gorkom had suggested the $55 price to Pritzker and, most crucially, that Van Gorkom had arrived at the $55 figure based on calculations designed solely to determine the feasibility of a leveraged buy-out.[19] No questions were raised either as to the tax implications of a cash-out merger or how the price for the one million share option granted Pritzker was calculated.

We do not say that the Board of Directors was not entitled to give some credence to Van Gorkom's representation that $55 was an adequate or fair price. Under § 141(e), the directors were entitled to rely upon their chairman's opinion of value and adequacy, provided that such opinion was reached on a sound basis. Here, the issue is whether the directors informed themselves as to all information that was reasonably available to them. Had they done so, they would have learned of the source and derivation of the $55 price and could not reasonably have relied thereupon in good faith.

None of the directors, Management or outside, were investment bankers or financial analysts. Yet the Board did not consider recessing the meeting until a later hour that day (or requesting an extension of Pritzker's Sunday evening deadline) to give it time to

---

18. Romans' department study was not made available to the Board until circulation of Trans Union's Supplementary Proxy Statement and the Board's meeting of January 26, 1981, on the eve of the shareholder meeting; and, as has been noted, the study has never been produced for inclusion in the record in this case.

19. As of September 20 the directors did not know: that Van Gorkom had arrived at the $55 figure alone, and subjectively, as the figure to be used by Controller Peterson in creating a feasible structure for a leveraged buy-out by a prospective purchaser; that Van Gorkom had not sought advice, information or assistance from either inside or outside Trans Union directors as to the value of the Company as an entity or the fair price per share for 100% of its stock; that Van Gorkom had not consulted with the Company's investment bankers or other financial analysts; that Van Gorkom had not consulted with or confided in any officer or director of the Company except Chelberg; and that Van Gorkom had deliberately chosen to ignore the advice and opinion of the members of his Senior Management group regarding the adequacy of the $55 price.

elicit more information as to the sufficiency of the offer, either from inside Management (in particular Romans) or from Trans Union's own investment banker, Salomon Brothers, whose Chicago specialist in merger and acquisitions was known to the Board and familiar with Trans Union's affairs.

Thus, the record compels the conclusion that on September 20 the Board lacked valuation information adequate to reach an informed business judgment as to the fairness of $55 per share for sale of the Company.

(2)

This brings us to the post-September 20 "market test" upon which the defendants ultimately rely to confirm the reasonableness of their September 20 decision to accept the Pritzker proposal. In this connection, the directors present a two-part argument: (a) that by making a "market test" of Pritzker's $55 per share offer a condition of their September 20 decision to accept his offer, they cannot be found to have acted impulsively or in an uninformed manner on September 20; and (b) that the adequacy of the $17 premium for sale of the Company was conclusively established over the following 90 to 120 days by the most reliable evidence available—the marketplace. Thus, the defendants impliedly contend that the "market test" eliminated the need for the Board to perform any other form of fairness test either on September 20, or thereafter.

Again, the facts of record do not support the defendants' argument. There is no evidence: (a) that the Merger Agreement was effectively amended to give the Board freedom to put Trans Union up for auction sale to the highest bidder; or (b) that a public auction was in fact permitted to occur. The minutes of the Board meeting make no reference to any of this. Indeed, the record compels the conclusion that the directors had no rational basis for expecting that a market test was attainable, given the terms of the Agreement as executed during the evening of September 20. We rely upon the following facts which are essentially uncontradicted:

The Merger Agreement, specifically identified as that originally presented to the Board on September 20, has never been produced by the defendants, notwithstanding the plaintiffs' several demands for production before as well as during trial. No acceptable explanation of this failure to produce documents has been given to either the Trial Court or this Court. Significantly, neither the defendants nor their counsel have made the affirmative representation that this critical document has been produced. Thus, the Court is deprived of the best evidence on which to judge the merits of the defendants' position as to the care and attention which they gave to the terms of the Agreement on September 20.

Van Gorkom states that the Agreement as submitted incorporated the ingredients for a market test by authorizing Trans Union to receive competing offers over the next 90-day period. However, he concedes that the Agreement barred Trans Union from actively soliciting such offers and from furnishing to interested parties any information about the Company other than that already in the public domain. Whether the original Agreement of September 20 went so far as to authorize Trans Union to receive competitive proposals is arguable. The defendants' unexplained failure to produce and identify the original Merger Agreement permits the logical inference that the instrument would not support their assertions in this regard. Wilmington Trust Co. v. General Motors Corp., Del.Supr., 51 A.2d 584, 593 (1947); II Wigmore on Evidence § 291 (3d ed. 1940). It is a well established principle that the production of weak evidence when strong is, or should have been, available can lead only to the conclusion that the strong would have been adverse. Interstate Circuit v. United States, 306 U.S. 208, 226, 59 S.Ct. 467, 474, 83 L.Ed. 610 (1939); Deberry v. State, Del.Supr., 457 A.2d 744, 754 (1983). Van Gorkom, conceding that he never read the Agreement, stated that he was relying upon his understanding that, under corporate law, directors always have an inherent right, as well as a fiduciary duty, to accept a better offer notwithstanding an existing contractual commitment by the Board. (See the discussion infra, part III B(3) at p. 55.)

The defendant directors assert that they "insisted" upon including two amendments to the Agreement, thereby permitting a market test: (1) to give Trans Union the right to accept a better offer; and (2) to reserve to Trans Union the right to distribute proprietary information on the Company to alternative bidders. Yet, the defendants concede that they did not seek to amend the Agreement to permit Trans Union to solicit competing offers.

Several of Trans Union's outside directors resolutely maintained that the Agreement as submitted was approved on the understanding that, "if we got a better deal, we had a right to take it." Director Johnson so testified; but he then added, "And if they didn't put that in the agreement, then the management did not carry out the conclusion of the Board. And I just don't know whether they did or not." The only clause in the Agreement as finally executed to which the defendants can point as "keeping the door open" is the following underlined statement found in subparagraph (a) of section 2.03 of the Merger Agreement as executed:

> The Board of Directors shall recommend to the stockholders of Trans Union that they approve and adopt the Merger Agreement ('the stockholders' approval') and to use its best efforts to obtain the requisite votes therefor. GL acknowledges that Trans Union directors may have a competing fiduciary obligation to the shareholders under certain circumstances.

Clearly, this language on its face cannot be construed as incorporating either of the two "conditions" described above: either the right to accept a better offer or the right to distribute proprietary information to third parties. The logical witness for the defendants to call to confirm their construction of this clause of the Agreement would have been Trans Union's outside attorney, James Brennan. The defendants' failure, without explanation, to call this witness again permits the logical inference that his testimony would not have been helpful to them. The further fact that the directors adjourned, rather than recessed, the meeting without incorporating in the Agreement these important "conditions" further weakens the defendants' position. As has been noted, nothing in the Board's Minutes supports these claims. No reference to either of the so-called "conditions" or of Trans Union's reserved right to test the market appears in any notes of the Board meeting or in the Board Resolution accepting the Pritzker offer or in the Minutes of the meeting itself. That evening, in the midst of a formal party which he hosted for the opening of the Chicago Lyric Opera, Van Gorkom executed the Merger Agreement without he or any other member of the Board having read the instruments.

The defendants attempt to downplay the significance of the prohibition against Trans Union's actively soliciting competing offers by arguing that the directors "understood that the entire financial community would know that Trans Union was for sale upon the announcement of the Pritzker offer, and anyone desiring to make a better offer was free to do so." Yet, the press release issued on September 22, with the authorization of the Board, stated that Trans Union had entered into "definitive agreements" with the Pritzkers; and the press release did not even disclose Trans Union's limited right to receive and accept higher offers. Accompanying this press release was a further public announcement that Pritzker had been granted an option to purchase at any time one million shares of Trans Union's capital stock at 75 cents above the then-current price per share.

Thus, notwithstanding what several of the outside directors later claimed to have "thought" occurred at the meeting, the record compels the conclusion that Trans Union's Board had no rational basis to conclude on September 20 or in the days immediately following, that the Board's acceptance of Pritzker's offer was conditioned on (1) a "market test" of the offer; and (2) the Board's right to withdraw from the Pritzker Agreement and accept any higher offer received before the shareholder meeting.

(3)

The directors' unfounded reliance on both the premium and the market test as the basis for accepting the Pritzker proposal undermines the defendants' remaining contention that the Board's collective experience and sophistication was a sufficient basis for finding that it reached its September 20 decision with informed, reasonable deliberation.[21] Compare Gimbel v. Signal Companies, Inc., Del. Ch., 316 A.2d 599 (1974), aff'd per curiam, Del.Supr., 316 A.2d 619 (1974). There, the Court of Chancery preliminary enjoined a board's sale of stock of its wholly-owned subsidiary for an alleged grossly inadequate price. It did so based on a finding that the business judgment rule had been pierced for failure of management to give its board "the opportunity to make a reasonable and reasoned decision." 316 A.2d at 615. The Court there reached this result notwithstanding the board's sophistication and experience; the company's need of immediate cash; and the board's need to act promptly due to the impact of an energy crisis on the value of the underlying assets being sold—all of its subsidiary's oil and gas interests. The Court found those factors denoting competence to be outweighed by evidence of gross negligence; that management in effect sprang the deal on the board by negotiating the asset sale without informing the board; that the buyer intended to "force a quick decision" by the board; that the board meeting was called on only one-and-a-half days' notice; that its outside directors were not notified of the meeting's purpose; that during a meeting spanning "a couple of hours" a sale of assets worth $480 million was approved; and that the Board failed to obtain a current appraisal of its oil and gas interests. The analogy of Signal to the case at bar is significant.

(4)

Part of the defense is based on a claim that the directors relied on legal advice rendered at the September 20 meeting by James Brennan, Esquire, who was present at Van Gorkom's request. Unfortunately, Brennan did not appear and testify at trial even though his firm participated in the defense of this action. There is no contemporaneous evidence of the advice given by Brennan on September 20, only the later deposition and

21. Trans Union's five "inside" directors had backgrounds in law and accounting, 116 years of collective employment by the Company and 68 years of combined experience on its Board. Trans Union's five "outside" directors included four chief executives of major corporations and an economist who was a former dean of a major school of business and chancellor of a university. The "outside" directors had 78 years of combined experience as chief executive officers of major corporations and 50 years of cumulative experience as directors of Trans Union. Thus, defendants argue that the Board was eminently qualified to reach an informed judgment on the proposed "sale" of Trans Union notwithstanding their lack of any advance notice of the proposal, the shortness of their deliberation, and their determination not to consult with their investment banker or to obtain a fairness opinion.

trial testimony of certain directors as to their recollections or understanding of what was said at the meeting. Since counsel did not testify, and the advice attributed to Brennan is hearsay received by the Trial Court over the plaintiffs' objections, we consider it only in the context of the directors' present claims. In fairness to counsel, we make no findings that the advice attributed to him was in fact given. We focus solely on the efficacy of the defendants' claims, made months and years later, in an effort to extricate themselves from liability.

Several defendants testified that Brennan advised them that Delaware law did not require a fairness opinion or an outside valuation of the Company before the Board could act on the Pritzker proposal. If given, the advice was correct. However, that did not end the matter. Unless the directors had before them adequate information regarding the intrinsic value of the Company, upon which a proper exercise of business judgment could be made, mere advice of this type is meaningless; and, given this record of the defendants' failures, it constitutes no defense here.[22]

* * *

We conclude that Trans Union's Board was grossly negligent in that it failed to act with informed reasonable deliberation in agreeing to the Pritzker merger proposal on September 20; and we further conclude that the Trial Court erred as a matter of law in failing to address that question before determining whether the directors' later conduct was sufficient to cure its initial error.

A second claim is that counsel advised the Board it would be subject to lawsuits if it rejected the $55 per share offer. It is, of course, a fact of corporate life that today when faced with difficult or sensitive issues, directors often are subject to suit, irrespective of the decisions they make. However, counsel's mere acknowledgement of this circumstance cannot be rationally translated into a justification for a board permitting itself to be stampeded into a patently unadvised act. While suit might result from the rejection of a merger or tender offer, Delaware law makes clear that a board acting within the ambit of the business judgment rule faces no ultimate liability. Pogostin v. Rice, supra. Thus, we cannot conclude that the mere threat of litigation, acknowledged by counsel, constitutes either legal advice or any valid basis upon which to pursue an uninformed course.

Since we conclude that Brennan's purported advice is of no consequence to the defense of this case, it is unnecessary for us to invoke the adverse inferences which may be attributable to one failing to appear at trial and testify.

-B-

We now examine the Board's post-September 20 conduct for the purpose of determining first, whether it was informed and not grossly negligent; and second, if informed, whether it was sufficient to legally rectify and cure the Board's derelictions of September 20.

(1)

First, as to the Board meeting of October 8: Its purpose arose in the aftermath of the September 20 meeting: (1) the September 22 press release announcing that Trans Union

---

22. Nonetheless, we are satisfied that in an appropriate factual context a proper exercise of business judgment may include, as one of its aspects, reasonable reliance upon the advice of counsel. This is wholly outside the statutory protections of 8 Del.C. § 141(e) involving reliance upon reports of officers, certain experts and books and records of the company.

"had entered into definitive agreements to merge with an affiliate of Marmon Group, Inc.;" and (2) Senior Management's ensuing revolt.

* * *

The press release made no reference to provisions allegedly reserving to the Board the rights to perform a "market test" and to withdraw from the Pritzker Agreement if Trans Union received a better offer before the shareholder meeting. The defendants also concede that Trans Union never made a subsequent public announcement stating that it had in fact reserved the right to accept alternate offers, the Agreement notwithstanding.

The public announcement of the Pritzker merger resulted in an "en masse" revolt of Trans Union's Senior Management. The head of Trans Union's tank car operations (its most profitable division) informed Van Gorkom that unless the merger were called off, fifteen key personnel would resign.

Instead of reconvening the Board, Van Gorkom again privately met with Pritzker, informed him of the developments, and sought his advice. Pritzker then made the following suggestions for overcoming Management's dissatisfaction: (1) that the Agreement be amended to permit Trans Union to solicit, as well as receive, higher offers; and (2) that the shareholder meeting be postponed from early January to February 10, 1981. In return, Pritzker asked Van Gorkom to obtain a commitment from Senior Management to remain at Trans Union for at least six months after the merger was consummated.

Van Gorkom then advised Senior Management that the Agreement would be amended to give Trans Union the right to solicit competing offers through January, 1981, if they would agree to remain with Trans Union. Senior Management was temporarily mollified; and Van Gorkom then called a special meeting of Trans Union's Board for October 8.

Thus, the primary purpose of the October 8 Board meeting was to amend the Merger Agreement, in a manner agreeable to Pritzker, to permit Trans Union to conduct a "market test." Van Gorkom understood that the proposed amendments were intended to give the Company an unfettered "right to openly solicit offers down through January 31." Van Gorkom presumably so represented the amendments to Trans Union's Board members on October 8. In a brief session, the directors approved Van Gorkom's oral presentation of the substance of the proposed amendments, the terms of which were not reduced to writing until October 10. But rather than waiting to review the amendments, the Board again approved them sight unseen and adjourned, giving Van Gorkom authority to execute the papers when he received them.[25]

Thus, the Court of Chancery's finding that the October 8 Board meeting was convened to reconsider the Pritzker "proposal" is clearly erroneous. Further, the consequence of the Board's faulty conduct on October 8, in approving amendments to the Agreement which had not even been drafted, will become apparent when the actual amendments to the Agreement are hereafter examined.

---

25. We do not suggest that a board must read in haec verba every contract or legal document which it approves, but if it is to successfully absolve itself from charges of the type made here, there must be some credible contemporary evidence demonstrating that the directors knew what they were doing, and ensured that their purported action was given effect. That is the consistent failure which cast this Board upon its unredeemable course.

The next day, October 9, and before the Agreement was amended, Pritzker moved swiftly to off-set the proposed market test amendment. First, Pritzker informed Trans Union that he had completed arrangements for financing its acquisition and that the parties were thereby mutually bound to a firm purchase and sale arrangement. Second, Pritzker announced the exercise of his option to purchase one million shares of Trans Union's treasury stock at $38 per share—75 cents above the current market price. Trans Union's Management responded the same day by issuing a press release announcing: (1) that all financing arrangements for Pritzker's acquisition of Trans Union had been completed; and (2) Pritzker's purchase of one million shares of Trans Union's treasury stock at $38 per share.

The next day, October 10, Pritzker delivered to Trans Union the proposed amendments to the September 20 Merger Agreement. Van Gorkom promptly proceeded to countersign all the instruments on behalf of Trans Union without reviewing the instruments to determine if they were consistent with the authority previously granted him by the Board. The amending documents were apparently not approved by Trans Union's Board until a much later date, December 2. The record does not affirmatively establish that Trans Union's directors ever read the October 10 amendments.

The October 10 amendments to the Merger Agreement did authorize Trans Union to solicit competing offers, but the amendments had more far-reaching effects. The most significant change was in the definition of the third-party "offer" available to Trans Union as a possible basis for withdrawal from its Merger Agreement with Pritzker. Under the October 10 amendments, a better offer was no longer sufficient to permit Trans Union's withdrawal. Trans Union was now permitted to terminate the Pritzker Agreement and abandon the merger only if, prior to February 10, 1981, Trans Union had either consummated a merger (or sale of assets) with a third party or had entered into a "definitive" merger agreement more favorable than Pritzker's and for a greater consideration—subject only to stockholder approval. Further, the "extension" of the market test period to February 10, 1981 was circumscribed by other amendments which required Trans Union to file its preliminary proxy statement on the Pritzker merger proposal by December 5, 1980 and use its best efforts to mail the statement to its shareholders by January 5, 1981. Thus, the market test period was effectively reduced, not extended. (See infra note 29 at 886.)

In our view, the record compels the conclusion that the directors' conduct on October exhibited the same deficiencies as did their conduct on September 20....

We conclude that the Board acted in a grossly negligent manner on October 8; and that Van Gorkom's representations on which the Board based its actions do not constitute "reports" under § 141(e) on which the directors could reasonably have relied. Further, the amended Merger Agreement imposed on Trans Union's acceptance of a third party offer conditions more onerous than those imposed on Trans Union's acceptance of Pritzker's offer on September 20. After October 10, Trans Union could accept from a third party a better offer only if it were incorporated in a definitive agreement between the parties, and not conditioned on financing or on any other contingency.

The October 9 press release, coupled with the October 10 amendments, had the clear effect of locking Trans Union's Board into the Pritzker Agreement. Pritzker had thereby foreclosed Trans Union's Board from negotiating any better "definitive" agreement over the remaining eight weeks before Trans Union was required to clear the Proxy Statement submitting the Pritzker proposal to its shareholders.

(2)

Next, as to the "curative" effects of the Board's post-September 20 conduct, we review in more detail the reaction of Van Gorkom to the KKR proposal and the results of the Board-sponsored "market test."

The KKR proposal was the first and only offer received subsequent to the Pritzker Merger Agreement. The offer resulted primarily from the efforts of Romans and other senior officers to propose an alternative to Pritzker's acquisition of Trans Union. In late September, Romans' group contacted KKR about the possibility of a leveraged buy-out by all members of Management, except Van Gorkom. By early October, Henry R. Kravis of KKR gave Romans written notice of KKR's "interest in making an offer to purchase 100%" of Trans Union's common stock.

Thereafter, and until early December, Romans' group worked with KKR to develop a proposal. It did so with Van Gorkom's knowledge and apparently grudging consent. On December 2, Kravis and Romans hand-delivered to Van Gorkom a formal letter-offer to purchase all of Trans Union's assets and to assume all of its liabilities for an aggregate cash consideration equivalent to $60 per share. The offer was contingent upon completing equity and bank financing of $650 million, which Kravis represented as 80% complete. The KKR letter made reference to discussions with major banks regarding the loan portion of the buy-out cost and stated that KKR was "confident that commitments for the bank financing * * * can be obtained within two or three weeks." The purchasing group was to include certain named key members of Trans Union's Senior Management, excluding Van Gorkom, and a major Canadian company. Kravis stated that they were willing to enter into a "definitive agreement" under terms and conditions "substantially the same" as those contained in Trans Union's agreement with Pritzker. The offer was addressed to Trans Union's Board of Directors and a meeting with the Board, scheduled for that afternoon, was requested.

Van Gorkom's reaction to the KKR proposal was completely negative; he did not view the offer as being firm because of its financing condition. It was pointed out, to no avail, that Pritzker's offer had not only been similarly conditioned, but accepted on an expedited basis. Van Gorkom refused Kravis' request that Trans Union issue a press release announcing KKR's offer, on the ground that it might "chill" any other offer. Romans and Kravis left with the understanding that their proposal would be presented to Trans Union's Board that afternoon.

Within a matter of hours and shortly before the scheduled Board meeting, Kravis withdrew his letter-offer. He gave as his reason a sudden decision by the Chief Officer of Trans Union's rail car leasing operation to withdraw from the KKR purchasing group. Van Gorkom had spoken to that officer about his participation in the KKR proposal immediately after his meeting with Romans and Kravis. However, Van Gorkom denied any responsibility for the officer's change of mind.

At the Board meeting later that afternoon, Van Gorkom did not inform the directors of the KKR proposal because he considered it "dead." Van Gorkom did not contact KKR again until January 20, when faced with the realities of this lawsuit, he then attempted to reopen negotiations. KKR declined due to the imminence of the February 10 stockholder meeting.

GE Credit Corporation's interest in Trans Union did not develop until November; and it made no written proposal until mid-January. Even then, its proposal was not in the form of an offer. Had there been time to do so, GE Credit was prepared to offer between $2 and $5 per share above the $55 per share price which Pritzker offered. But GE

Credit needed an additional 60 to 90 days; and it was unwilling to make a formal offer without a concession from Pritzker extending the February 10 "deadline" for Trans Union's stockholder meeting. As previously stated, Pritzker refused to grant such extension; and on January 21, GE Credit terminated further negotiations with Trans Union. Its stated reasons, among others, were its "unwillingness to become involved in a bidding contest with Pritzker in the absence of the willingness of [the Pritzker interests] to terminate the proposed $55 cash merger."

* * *

In the absence of any explicit finding by the Trial Court as to the reasonableness of Trans Union's directors' reliance on a market test and its feasibility, we may make our own findings based on the record. Our review of the record compels a finding that confirmation of the appropriateness of the Pritzker offer by an unfettered or free market test was virtually meaningless in the face of the terms and time limitations of Trans Union's Merger Agreement with Pritzker as amended October 10, 1980.

(3)

Finally, we turn to the Board's meeting of January 26, 1981. The defendant directors rely upon the action there taken to refute the contention that they did not reach an informed business judgment in approving the Pritzker merger. The defendants contend that the Trial Court correctly concluded that Trans Union's directors were, in effect, as "free to turn down the Pritzker proposal" on January 26, as they were on September 20.

Applying the appropriate standard of review set forth in Levitt v. Bouvier, supra, we conclude that the Trial Court's finding in this regard is neither supported by the record nor the product of an orderly and logical deductive process. Without disagreeing with the principle that a business decision by an originally uninformed board of directors may, under appropriate circumstances, be timely cured so as to become informed and deliberate, Muschel v. Western Union Corporation, Del. Ch., 310 A.2d 904 (1973), we find that the record does not permit the defendants to invoke that principle in this case.

The Board's January 26 meeting was the first meeting following the filing of the plaintiffs' suit in mid-December and the last meeting before the previously-noticed shareholder meeting of February 10. All ten members of the Board and three outside attorneys attended the meeting. At that meeting the following facts, among other aspects of the Merger Agreement, were discussed:

(a) The fact that prior to September 20, 1980, no Board member or member of Senior Management, except Chelberg and Peterson, knew that Van Gorkom had discussed a possible merger with Pritzker;

(b) The fact that the price of $55 per share had been suggested initially to Pritzker by Van Gorkom;

(c) The fact that the Board had not sought an independent fairness opinion;

(d) The fact that, at the September 20 Senior Management meeting, Romans and several members of Senior Management indicated both concern that the $55 per share price was inadequate and a belief that a higher price should and could be obtained;

(e) The fact that Romans had advised the Board at its meeting on September 20, that he and his department had prepared a study which indicated that the Company had a value in the range of $55 to $65 per share, and that he could not advise the Board that the $55 per share offer made by Pritzker was unfair.

* * *

We must conclude from the foregoing that the Board was mistaken as a matter of law regarding its available courses of action on January 26, 1981. Options (2) and (3) were not viable or legally available to the Board under 8 Del.C. §251(b). The Board could not remain committed to the Pritzker merger and yet recommend that its stockholders vote it down; nor could it take a neutral position and delegate to the stockholders the unadvised decision as to whether to accept or reject the merger. Under §251(b), the Board had but two options: (1) to proceed with the merger and the stockholder meeting, with the Board's recommendation of approval; or (2) to rescind its agreement with Pritzker, withdraw its approval of the merger, and notify its stockholders that the proposed shareholder meeting was cancelled. There is no evidence that the Board gave any consideration to these, its only legally viable alternative courses of action.

But the second course of action would have clearly involved a substantial risk—that the Board would be faced with suit by Pritzker for breach of contract based on its September 20 agreement as amended October 10. As previously noted, under the terms of the October 10 amendment, the Board's only ground for release from its agreement with Pritzker was its entry into a more favorable definitive agreement to sell the Company to a third party. Thus, in reality, the Board was not "free to turn down the Pritzker proposal" as the Trial Court found. Indeed, short of negotiating a better agreement with a third party, the Board's only basis for release from the Pritzker Agreement without liability would have been to establish fundamental wrongdoing by Pritzker. Clearly, the Board was not "free" to withdraw from its agreement with Pritzker on January 26 by simply relying on its self-induced failure to have reached an informed business judgment at the time of its original agreement. See Wilmington Trust Company v. Coulter, Del.Supr., 200 A.2d 441, 453 (1964), aff'g Pennsylvania Company v. Wilmington Trust Company, Del.Ch., 186 A.2d 751 (1962).

Therefore, the Trial Court's conclusion that the Board reached an informed business judgment on January 26 in determining whether to turn down the Pritzker "proposal" on that day cannot be sustained. The Court's conclusion is not supported by the record; it is contrary to the provisions of §251(b) and basic principles of contract law; and it is not the product of a logical and deductive reasoning process.

* * *

Upon the basis of the foregoing, we hold that the defendants' post-September conduct did not cure the deficiencies of their September 20 conduct; and that, accordingly, the Trial Court erred in according to the defendants the benefits of the business judgment rule.

IV.

Whether the directors of Trans Union should be treated as one or individually in terms of invoking the protection of the business judgment rule and the applicability of 8 Del.C. §141(c) are questions which were not originally addressed by the parties in their briefing of this case. This resulted in a supplemental briefing and a second rehearing en banc on two basic questions: (a) whether one or more of the directors were deprived of the protection of the business judgment rule by evidence of an absence of good faith; and (b) whether one or more of the outside directors were entitled to invoke the protection of 8 Del.C. §141(e) by evidence of a reasonable, good faith reliance on "reports," including legal advice, rendered the Board by certain inside directors and the Board's special counsel, Brennan.

The parties' response, including reargument, has led the majority of the Court to conclude: (1) that since all of the defendant directors, outside as well as inside, take a unified position, we are required to treat all of the directors as one as to whether they are entitled to the protection of the business judgment rule; and (2) that considerations of good faith, including the presumption that the directors acted in good faith, are irrelevant in determining the threshold issue of whether the directors as a Board exercised an informed business judgment. For the same reason, we must reject defense counsel's ad hominem argument for affirmance: that reversal may result in a multi-million dollar class award against the defendants for having made an allegedly uninformed business judgment in a transaction not involving any personal gain, self-dealing or claim of bad faith.

In their brief, the defendants similarly mistake the business judgment rule's application to this case by erroneously invoking presumptions of good faith and "wide discretion":

> This is a case in which plaintiff challenged the exercise of business judgment by an independent Board of Directors. There were no allegations and no proof of fraud, bad faith, or self-dealing by the directors....

The business judgment rule, which was properly applied by the Chancellor, allows directors wide discretion in the matter of valuation and affords room for honest differences of opinion. In order to prevail, plaintiffs had the heavy burden of proving that the merger price was so grossly inadequate as to display itself as a badge of fraud. That is a burden which plaintiffs have not met.

However, plaintiffs have not claimed, nor did the Trial Court decide, that $55 was a grossly inadequate price per share for sale of the Company. That being so, the presumption that a board's judgment as to adequacy of price represents an honest exercise of business judgment (absent proof that the sale price was grossly inadequate) is irrelevant to the threshold question of whether an informed judgment was reached....

V.

The defendants ultimately rely on the stockholder vote of February 10 for exoneration. The defendants contend that the stockholders' "overwhelming" vote approving the Pritzker Merger Agreement had the legal effect of curing any failure of the Board to reach an informed business judgment in its approval of the merger.

The parties tacitly agree that a discovered failure of the Board to reach an informed business judgment in approving the merger constitutes a voidable, rather than a void, act. Hence, the merger can be sustained, notwithstanding the infirmity of the Board's action, if its approval by majority vote of the shareholders is found to have been based on an informed electorate. Cf. Michelson v. Duncan, Del.Supr., 407 A.2d 211 (1979), aff'g in part and rev'g in part, Del. Ch., 386 A.2d 1144 (1978). The disagreement between the parties arises over: (1) the Board's burden of disclosing to the shareholders all relevant and material information; and (2) the sufficiency of the evidence as to whether the Board satisfied that burden.

* * *

The settled rule in Delaware is that "where a majority of fully informed stockholders ratify action of even interested directors, an attack on the ratified transaction normally must fail." Gerlach v. Gillam, Del.Ch., 139 A.2d 591, 593 (1958). The question of whether shareholders have been fully informed such that their vote can be said to ratify director action, "turns on the fairness and completeness of the proxy materials submitted by the management to the... shareholders." Michelson v. Duncan, supra at 220. As this Court stated in Gottlieb v. Heyden Chemical Corp., Del.Supr., 91 A.2d 57, 59 (1952):

> [T]he entire atmosphere is freshened and a new set of rules invoked where a formal approval has been given by a majority of independent, fully informed stockholders....

In Lynch v. Vickers Energy Corp., supra, this Court held that corporate directors owe to their stockholders a fiduciary duty to disclose all facts germane to the transaction at issue in an atmosphere of complete candor. We defined "germane" in the tender offer context as all "information such as a reasonable stockholder would consider important in deciding whether to sell or retain stock." Id. at 281. Accord Weinberger v. UOP, Inc., supra; Michelson v. Duncan, supra; Schreiber v. Pennzoil Corp., Del.Ch., 419 A.2d 952 (1980). In reality, "germane" means material facts.

Applying this standard to the record before us, we find that Trans Union's stockholders were not fully informed of all facts material to their vote on the Pritzker Merger and that the Trial Court's ruling to the contrary is clearly erroneous.

* * *

The burden must fall on defendants who claim ratification based on shareholder vote to establish that the shareholder approval resulted from a fully informed electorate. On the record before us, it is clear that the Board failed to meet that burden. Weinberger v. UOP, Inc., supra at 703; Michelson v. Duncan, supra.

* * *

For the foregoing reasons, we conclude that the director defendants breached their fiduciary duty of candor by their failure to make true and correct disclosures of all information they had, or should have had, material to the transaction submitted for stockholder approval.

VI.

To summarize: we hold that the directors of Trans Union breached their fiduciary duty to their stockholders (1) by their failure to inform themselves of all information reasonably available to them and relevant to their decision to recommend the Pritzker merger; and (2) by their failure to disclose all material information such as a reasonable stockholder would consider important in deciding whether to approve the Pritzker offer.

We hold, therefore, that the Trial Court committed reversible error in applying the business judgment rule in favor of the director defendants in this case.

On remand, the Court of Chancery shall conduct an evidentiary hearing to determine the fair value of the shares represented by the plaintiffs' class, based on the intrinsic value of Trans Union on September 20, 1980. Such valuation shall be made in accordance with Weinberger v. UOP, Inc., supra at 712–715. Thereafter, an award of damages may be entered to the extent that the fair value of Trans Union exceeds $55 per share.

* * *

REVERSED and REMANDED for proceedings consistent herewith.

McNEILLY, Justice, dissenting:

The majority opinion reads like an advocate's closing address to a hostile jury. And I say that not lightly. Throughout the opinion great emphasis is directed only to the negative, with nothing more than lip service granted the positive aspects of this case. In my opinion Chancellor Marvel (retired) should have been affirmed. The Chancellor's opinion was the product of well reasoned conclusions, based upon a sound deductive process, clearly supported by the evidence and entitled to deference in this appeal. Because of my diametrical opposition to all evidentiary conclusions of the majority, I respectfully dissent.

It would serve no useful purpose, particularly at this late date, for me to dissent at great length. I restrain myself from doing so, but feel compelled to at least point out what I consider to be the most glaring deficiencies in the majority opinion. The majority has spoken and has effectively said that Trans Union's Directors have been the victims of a "fast shuffle" by Van Gorkom and Pritzker. That is the beginning of the majority's comedy of errors. The first and most important error made is the majority's assessment of the directors' knowledge of the affairs of Trans Union and their combined ability to act in this situation under the protection of the business judgment rule.

Trans Union's Board of Directors consisted of ten men, five of whom were "inside" directors and five of whom were "outside" directors. The "inside" directors were Van Gorkom, Chelberg, Bonser, William B. Browder, Senior Vice-President-Law, and Thomas P. O'Boyle, Senior Vice-President-Administration. At the time the merger was proposed the inside five directors had collectively been employed by the Company for 116 years and had 68 years of combined experience as directors. The "outside" directors were A.W. Wallis, William B. Johnson, Joseph B. Lanterman, Graham J. Morgan and Robert W. Reneker. With the exception of Wallis, these were all chief executive officers of Chicago based corporations that were at least as large as Trans Union. The five "outside" directors had 78 years of combined experience as chief executive officers, and 53 years cumulative service as Trans Union directors.

The inside directors wear their badge of expertise in the corporate affairs of Trans Union on their sleeves. But what about the outsiders? Dr. Wallis is or was an economist and math statistician, a professor of economics at Yale University, dean of the graduate school of business at the University of Chicago, and Chancellor of the University of Rochester. Dr. Wallis had been on the Board of Trans Union since 1962. He also was on the Board of Bausch & Lomb, Kodak, Metropolitan Life Insurance Company, Standard Oil and others.

William B. Johnson is a University of Pennsylvania law graduate, President of Railway Express until 1966, Chairman and Chief Executive of I.C. Industries Holding Company, and member of Trans Union's Board since 1968.

Joseph Lanterman, a Certified Public Accountant, is or was President and Chief Executive of American Steel, on the Board of International Harvester, Peoples Energy, Illinois Bell Telephone, Harris Bank and Trust Company, Kemper Insurance Company and a director of Trans Union for four years.

Graham Morgan is a chemist, was Chairman and Chief Executive Officer of U.S. Gypsum, and in the 17 and 18 years prior to the Trans Union transaction had been involved in 31 or 32 corporate takeovers.

Robert Reneker attended University of Chicago and Harvard Business Schools. He was President and Chief Executive of Swift and Company, director of Trans Union since 1971, and member of the Boards of seven other corporations including U.S. Gypsum and the Chicago Tribune.

Directors of this caliber are not ordinarily taken in by a "fast shuffle." I submit they were not taken into this multi-million dollar corporate transaction without being fully informed and aware of the state of the art as it pertained to the entire corporate panorama of Trans Union. True, even directors such as these, with their business acumen, interest and expertise, can go astray. I do not believe that to be the case here. These men knew Trans Union like the back of their hands and were more than well qualified to make on the spot informed business judgments concerning the affairs of Trans Union including a 100% sale of the corporation. Lest we forget, the corporate world of then and now operates on what is so aptly referred to as "the fast track." These men were at the time an integral part of that world, all professional business men, not intellectual figureheads.

The majority of this Court holds that the Board's decision, reached on September 20, 1980, to approve the merger was not the product of an informed business judgment, that the Board's subsequent efforts to amend the Merger Agreement and take other curative action were legally and factually ineffectual, and that the Board did not deal with complete candor with the stockholders by failing to disclose all material facts, which they knew or should have known, before securing the stockholders' approval of the merger. I disagree.

* * *

[The dissent of Justice Christie is omitted]

b. The Business Judgement Rule in the United States

If the breach of the duty of care is the sword available to the shareholders for ensuring that directors act always in the best interests of the corporation at a certain level of competence, the business judgment rule is the shield afforded to directors by the corporate law to prevent directors from facing liability for bad or unprofitable business decisions made in good faith and on the basis of the information reasonably available to them. What is the business judgment rule? It is sometimes thought of as a presumption that the business decision made by the directors was reasonable, and not a basis for liability, where the plaintiff is unable to show that, in making the business decision complained of, the directors failed to act on an informed basis (that is they arrived at their decision in a deliberate manner and considering all reasonable facts reasonably available to them at the time of the decision), in good faith and in the honest belief that the action taken was in the best interests of the company. To claim the presumption, the director must be (i) disinterested, (ii) independent, and (iii) informed. What happens when the presumption is removed? The court must then inquire into the fairness of the director's decision.

Gregory V. Varallo and Daniel A. Dreisbach, Fundamentals of Corporate Governance: A Guide for Directors and Corporate Counsel

(1996) (excerpts from pages 55–61; some footnotes omitted)

Much has been written about the so-called "business judgement rule." There is at least one entire treatise devoted to the subject,[90] and the articles in print on the topic

90. DENNIS J. BLOCK, ET AL., THE BUSINESS JUDGMENT RULE (3rd ed. 1989) [hereafter THE BUSINESS JUDGMENT RULE at ___"]; and see E. Norman Veasey, in 1 R. FRANKLIN BALOTTI & JESSE

run into the hundreds, if not thousands. Here, we address the topic in only brief form, trusting that the interested reader will pursue the subject at greater length in the wealth of available resources.

The Nature of the Rule

At its simplest, the business judgment rule is a series of presumptions relating to decisions made by directors. It should be noted that the presumptions constituting the rule attach only to a director's *judgment*, although a conscious decision not to act is entitled to exactly the same treatment as a decision to take action.[91] To be entitled to rely on the protections of the rule, however, a director must have made a decision.[92]

A board's decision will be protected unless it is shown that a majority of the directors on the board were not disinterested with respect to that decision; the decision was made without prior consideration of all reasonably available material information; or a majority of the board is shown to have failed to act in the honest belief that the decision was in the best interests of the corporation. In a leading case, the Delaware Chancellor has described the rule from the perspective of a reviewing court:

> The business judgment form of judicial review encompasses three elements: a threshold review of the objective financial interests of the board whose decision is under attack (i.e. independence), a review of the board's subjective motivation (i.e., good faith), and an objective review of the process by which it reached the decision under review (i.e., due care).[93]

The rule, when invoked to shield a decision made outside the control context provides a powerful presumption that, in making a decision, the directors acted "on an informed basis, in good faith, and in the honest belief that the action taken was in the best interests of the company."[94] If a plaintiff is unable to rebut the presumption inherent in the rule at trial (and it is plaintiff's burden to do so), the directors are protected from liability arising out of that decision, even if it later proves to be unwise.[95]

The rationale that supports such a sweeping limitation on judicial review of directors' decisions often is stated in different ways. First, the rule is said to encourage competent individuals to serve as directors by limiting liability and recognizing "human fallibility." Second, the rule recognizes that business decisions involve a certain degree of risk and that a system of law that subjects the risk takers to constant second-guessing by courts and shareholders alike would be highly inefficient. Third, the rule reflects the in-

---

A. Finkelstein, The Delaware Law of Corporations and Business Organizations (2d ed. Supp. 1995) at chapter] 4.

91. Aronson v. Lewis, 473 A.2d 805, 813 (Del. 1984) (the rule "operates only in the context of director action...It has no role where directors have either abdicated their functions, or absent a conscious decision, failed to act") (footnote omitted); Rabkin v. Philip A. Hunt Chem. Corp., 547 A.2d 963, 972 (Del.Ch. 1986) (the rule "may apply to a deliberate decision not to act, but it has no bearing on a claim that directors' inaction was the result of ignorance").

92. Balotti & Finkelstein, *supra* note [90], at 4–41; The Business Judgment Rule at 12.

93. *In re* RJR Nabisco, Inc. Shareholders Litig., C.A. No. 10389, slip op. At 34–35 (Del. Ch. Jan. 31, 1989), *appeal denied*, 556 A.2d 1070 (Del. 1989).

94. *Aronson*, 473 A.2d at 812; and see Smith v. Van Gorkum, 488 A.2d 858, 872 (Del. 1985). The authors of *The Business Judgment Rule, supra* note 90, note that courts in at least sixteen states other than Delaware have described the rule in terms of these presumptions. *Id.*, at 8–9.

95. *See* Growbow v. Perot, 526 A.2d 914, 928 (Del. Ch. 1987) Rule protects decision "however controversial, unpopular, or even wrong such a decision might turn out to be...."), *aff'd* 539 A.2d 180 (Del. 1988).

stitutional shortcomings of the courts, which are not well suited to review often complex and technical business decisions.[96]

The Prerequisites for Invoking the Rule

When and under what circumstances may this powerful series of presumptions be invoked to shield a board's decision? In the ordinary course of business, the presumptions of the rule protect director decision making provided the four elements of the rule are present. In each case, the reviewing court will seek to determine whether the board made a decision to act or refrain from acting; whether a majority of the board was disinterested with respect to the decision in the sense that it had no financial interest in the outcome; whether the board carefully considered the issue and all reasonably available material information before acting; and whether the decision was taken in the good-faith belief that it was appropriate and in the best interests of the corporation. Here we examine briefly each of these elements in light of the relevant law.

Did the board make a decision?

The law does not protect directors' inaction. The law does, however, distinguish between inaction and a conscious decision to refrain from acting. As noted previously, the latter decision is entitled to the presumptions of the rule, just as any other business decision of the board.

Was a majority of the board financially interested in the decision?

The decision of a director who has a financial interest in the underlying transaction is not entitled to the benefit of the business judgment rule. The rule proceeds from the commonsense observation that an "interested" director is likely to be affected by that personal interest. The courts also have held that the presence of fewer than a majority of "interested" directors will not strip the board's decision of the protection of the business judgment rule, without special circumstances.[97] The special circumstances under which the interest of less than a majority of the board could deprive the board's decision of the protection of the business judgment rule were described in *Cinerama, Inc. v. Technicolor, Inc.* In that case, the court concluded that the financial interest of one or more (but less than a majority of) directors stripped board action of the presumptions of the business judgment rule where the interested director "*controls* or *dominates* the board as a whole "or where the interested director fails to disclose his or her interest to the board and a reasonable director would have regarded the existence of the interest "as a significant fact in the evaluation of the proposed transaction."[98] Under either circumstance, the burden then shifts to the full board to show that the transaction is entirely fair to the corporation. This is so even where a single director fails to disclose his or ger interest to the board. In such a situation, the good faith or "innocence" of the other board mem-

96. *See* The Business Judgment Rule, *supra* note 90, at 6; *In re J.P. Stevens & Co., Inc. Shareholders Litig.*, 542 A.2d 770, 780 (Del. Ch.), *appeal denied* 540 A,2d 1088 (Del. 1988); Solash v. Telex Corp., C.A. Nos. 9518, 9525, 9528, slip op. At 19 (Del. Ch. Jan. 19, 1988) ("Because businessmen and women are correctly perceived as possessing skills, information and judgment not possessed by reviewing courts and because there is great social utility in encouraging the allocation of assets and the evaluation and assumption of economic risk by those with such skill and information, courts have long been reluctant to seocnd guess such decisions when they appear to have been made in good faith.").

97. Aronson v. Lewis, 437 A.2d 805, 812 (Del. 1984); Cinerama, Inc. v. Technicolor, Inc., C.A. No. 8358 (Del.Ch. Oct. 6, 1994), *aff'd* 663 A.2d 1156 (Del. 1995).

98. *Cinerama, Inc.*, slip op. At 51.

bers, while relevant in the court's creation of a remedy, does not impact the necessity of showing the entire fairness or inherent fairness of the transaction.[99]

What constitutes "interest"? Directors are ordinarily thought to be "interested" in a decision if they have a direct financial interest in the outcome or stand on both sides of the transaction.[100] Put differently, a director is "independent" when "he or she is in a position to base his or her decision on the merits of the issue rather than being governed by extraneous considerations or influences."[101] The mere receipt of customary fees for services as a director does not render a director "interested."[102] Nonetheless, the payment of elaborate perquisites to board members may call into question their "interestedness," at least in the context of a suit challenging the award of such perquisites.[103] Moreover, to deprive the director or the board of the presumptions of the business judgment rule, the interest must be "material."[104]

Several corporations have attempted to define independent or disinterested directors in their bylaws. Section 2.12 of the GM bylaws requires that a majority of the board be made up of independent directors, which it defines as directors who have not been employed by the corporation within five years, are not "significant" advisors or consultants, are not affiliated with significant customers or suppliers, do not have significant personal services contracts with the company, are not affiliated with a tax-exempt entity that receives significant contributions from the company, and are not closely related to insiders at the company....

More difficult issues arise in connection with what could fairly be termed directors' "indirect" interest in particular decisions. For example, in the *Revlon* case, the Delaware Supreme Court suggested that the board might not be entitled to the presumptions of the business judgment rule because several of the directors "were associated at some point with entities that had various business relationships with Revlon."[105] In a different case, the independence of a board composed of various professionals who rendered accounting, legal, and consulting services to the corporation or its dominant director was called into question where the case challenged the issuance of supervoting stock designed to assure the success of the incumbent board in a proxy fight.[106]

Before leaving the subject of director interest, however, it should be noted that the special scrutiny afforded to cases arising against the backdrop of a proxy or written consent

---

99. *Cinerama, Inc.*, slip op. At 52.

100. Note that in this regard, Delaware, as most states, has statutorily mandated that the interest of some members of the board in a particular decision is not necessarily fatal to the decision. Where the interested directors disclose their interest to their fellow board members and the board acts by an independent majority, or by an independent committee of the board, or the director's interest is disclosed and the shareholders vote to approve the transaction, or the transaction itself is objectively fair to the corporation, it is not "void or voidable" solely because of the participation of "interested" directors. 8 Del. Code Ann. § 144.

101. Kaplan v. Wyatt, 499 A.2d 1184, 1189 (Del. 1985).

102. Growbow v. Perot, 539 A.2d 180, 188 (Del. 1988).

103. Heineman v. Datapoint Corp., C.A. No. 7956 (Del.Ch. Oct. 9, 1990) (finding that pleading that recited receipt of annuities by all directors and severance contracts by two members of the board created a reasonable doubt regarding the director's disinterest); *and see* Tate & Lyle PLC v. Staley Continental, Inc., C.A. No. 9813 (Del. Ch. May 9, 1988) (enjoining funding of $65 million irrevocable "rabbi trust" designed to preserve director benefits adopted in the face of a hostile takeover proposal).

104. Cede & Co. v. Technicolor, Inc., 634 A.2d 345, 363 (Del. 1993).

105. Revlon, Inc. v. MacAndrews & Forbes Holdings, Inc., 506 A.2d 173, 176 note 3 (Del. 1986).

106. Packer v. Yampol, C.A. No. 8432 (Del. Ch. Apr. 18, 1986).

fight and alleging manipulation of the election by the incumbent board also may be reflected in findings regarding the "interestedness" of directors who act to frustrate a proxy or consent fight. In one "franchise" case, for example, the court concluded that all directors were "interested" in the decision to postpone an annual meeting where the decision was made after the company's proxy solicitor informed the board that it would be likely to lose a proxy fight for control of the company if the scheduled meeting went forward.[107]

Did the board act with due care?

Directors owe a duty to consider all reasonably available material information on a topic prior to making a decision,. At least under Delaware law, without a provision in the certificate of incorporation of the company exculpating directors from monetary liability for breach fo the duty of care, a director may be held to respond in damages for a breach of his or her duty of care. Moreover, a decision taken in the absence of due care is not one to which the business judgment rule will attach.

Nonetheless, the courts have recognized that assembling information has certain costs and, in some circumstances, risks as well.[108] Take, for example, the case where a bidder offers to buy the company for a substantial premium to market at what appears to be a very attractive price but makes clear that if the offer is not accepted unconditionally in some short period of time (for example, forty-eight hours) it will expire, not to be renewed. The board faced with such an offer is put to a difficult choice. While it appears relatively clear that a decision to reject such an offer on the grounds that the board has insufficient time in which to become fully informed would not be a basis for director liability,[109] a good faith decision that the company should be sold at the price offered could be subject to judicial second-guessing on the grounds that the board could not have had sufficient time to become fully informed prior to making a decision about such a critically important matter. In fact, this "hypothetical" tracks closely the facts of the *Van Gorkom* case, in which the directors were ultimately found personally liable for accepting an offer made at a not insubstantial premium to market by an acquirer who insisted on a response in a short period of time.

More recent decisions appear to provide some further elucidation. In *RJR Nabisco Shareholders Litigation*, for example, the Delaware court stated that "where an arm's-length negotiating adversary imposes time limits a board is forced to contend with that circumstance. If it exercises informed judgment in the circumstances, considers the risks posed by the deadline imposed, and concludes that it is prudent to act and acts with care, it has satisfied its duty."[110]

---

107. Aprahamian v. HBO & Co., 531 A.2d 1204 (Del. Ch. 1987); and cf. Packer v. Yampol. In a similar case, Good v. Texaco, C.A. No. 7501 (Del. Ch. May 14, 1984), the court concluded preliminarily that the allegations of a complaint sufficiently plead director "interest" where the board, in connection with corporate repurchase of approximately 5 percent of Texaco's common stock would be voted as the board directed for some period f time. The court's preliminary findings as to the interest of the board in this setting was buttressed by the fact that the company's stock was widely held and the 5 percent voting block dramatically exceeded the small individual stockholdings of the directors, thus greatly magnifying their ability to cause their own reelection, entirely at corporate expense. *See also* Abajian v. Kennedy, C.A. No. 11425 (Del. Ch. Jan. 17, 1992).

108. *See In re* RJR Nabisco Shareholders Litig., C.A. No. 10389 (Del. Ch. Jan. 31, 1989), *appeal denied* 556 A.2d 1070 (Del. 1989).

109. *See* Lewis v. Honeywell, C.A. N0. 8651 (Del. Ch. July 28, 1987).

110. RJR Nabisco Shareholders Litg., C.A. No. 10289, slip op. At 52 (Del. Ch. Jan. 31, 1989), *appealed denied* 556 A.2d 1070 (Del. 1989). In Citron v. Fairchild Camera & Instrument Corp., 569 A.2d 53 (Del. 1989), the Delaware Supreme Court revisited the case where a board was forced with a tight deadline to accept or reject a premium offer for the company. Although it cautioned that in

Did the board act in the honest belief that its decision would benefit the corporation?

The requirement of "good faith" has been expressed in various ways. Put most simple, directors must act "in the honest belief that their actions are in the corporation's best interests" and not for any personal gain.[111] Also subsumed within the notion of "good faith" is that the action taken has a "rational business purpose." Where the court concludes that a board's decision is not rational, it likewise may conclude that the decision was [not] in good faith.[112]

The Delaware Modification of the Rule and Other Approaches to Business Judgment in the Takeover Context

As we noted previously, directors confronted with a takeover proposal must show that before acting they reasonably perceived a "danger to corporate policy and effectiveness" and that the action was "reasonable in relation to the threat posed."[113] If a majority of the board is able to make these showings, the board will be entitled to the presumptions of the business judgment rule, provided that all of the prerequisites for invocation of the rule are present. The imposition of the threshold requirements in the takeover area is a judicially crafted attempt to acknowledge the "omnipresent specter" of self-interest implicated whenever a board is required to make decisions that directly implicate its own tenure.

Not all jurisdictions track the Delaware approach to judicial review of director decision making in the takeover context. Indiana has enacted legislation rejecting the Delaware approach.[114] Pennsylvania also appears to have rejected the *Unocal* approach by statute.[115] New York, California and New Jersey all appear to approach the subject somewhat differently from the Delaware model. While less than clear, it appears that neither New York nor California law places any *Unocal*-type threshold burden on directors, regardless of whether the directors act in the face of a takeover threat or not. Under this approach, however, once a plaintiff is able to make a prima facie showing that the board used its corporate powers to retain control, the burden falls on the directors to prove the intrinsic fairness of the transaction.[116] Courts interpreting New Jersey law have been less clear, one applying the Delaware approach, one following more closely the New York approach.[117]

The American Bar Association (ABA) Committee on Corporate Laws, which is the drafter of the Model Business Corporation Act, set out to codify the business judgment rule in connection with its overhaul of the Model Act during the 1980s. The project eventually was abandoned, apparently in light of concerns that no codification of the

---

the past, boards who allowed themselves to be rushed in decision making were more likely to be subject to criticism for failing to exercise due care, the court nonetheless affirmed the lower court's decision, finding that in the circumstances the board could have concluded that it had sufficient information to sell the company, notwithstanding the very short time frame involved.

111. *See* Aronson v. Lewis, 473 A.2d at 812.

112. *See* Sutton Holding Corp. v. DeSoto Inc., C.A. No. 11221, slip op. At 20 (Del. Ch. Feb. 5, 1990). *See also In re* RJR Nabisco Shareholders Litig., slip op. At 36–37 note 13 (noting that the court, in the appropriate circumstance, could infer bad faith from "an 'egregious' or 'irrational' decision.").

113. *See* Unocal Corp. v. Mesa Petroleum Co., 1493 A.2d 946, 955 (Del. 1985).

114. 35 Ind. Code Ann. § 23-1-35-1(f) (Burns 1988).

115. 15 Pa. Stat. Ann. § 1715(d) (Purdon's 1988).

116. *See* Hanson Trust PLC v. ML SCM Acquisition, Inc., 781 F.2d 264, 273 (2d Cir. 1986) (New York); cf. Klaus v. Hi-Shear Corp., 528 F.2d 225 (9th Cir. 1975) (California law); E. Norman Veasey, in Baloti & Finkelstein, Ch. 4, *supra* note [90], at 4-54, 4-55.

117. *Compare* Asarco Inc. v. M.R.H. Holmes A Court, 611 F. Supp. 468 (D.N.J. 1985); Minstar Acquiring Corp. v. AMF Inc., 621 F. Supp. 1252 (D. N.J. 1985).

rule can accommodate all of the circumstances that a board might possibly address.[118] The American Law Institute (ALI) was not similarly dissuaded from its attempts to codify the rule, however. Section 4.01(c) of the *Principles of Corporate Governance: Analysis and Recommendations*, approved by the members fo the ALI in May, 1985, provides:

> A director or officer who makes a business judgment in good faith fulfills his duty [of care] if:
>
> (1) he is not interested [a defined term] in the subject of his business judgment;
>
> (2) he is informed with respect to the subject of his business judgement to the extent he reasonably believes to be appropriate under all the circumstances; and
>
> (3) he rationally believes that his business judgment is in the best interests of the corporation.[119]

This formulation has been the subject of extensive critique and debate.[120]

---

c. *Critiques of the Duty of Care and the Business Judgment Rule in the United States*

The Business judgment rule and the duty of care as currently constituted in the United States has been subject to some criticism. Some of the criticism is systemic—the argument is made that if the separation between ownership and control decreased, the need for the duty of care would decrease as well. Others are based on broader policy concerns—the need, for example, to consider the rule in the context of a general approach to tort liability in enterprise law. As you read the excerpts of the articles that follow, consider whether or not you agree with their premises and conclusions.

R. Franklin Balotti, Charles M. Elson, J. Travis Laster, *Equity Ownership and the Duty of Care: Convergence, Revolution, or Evolution?*

55 Bus. Law. 661 (2000)
(661–662; 680–691; some footnotes omitted)

The fiduciary duty of care is one of the pillars of Delaware corporate law. In conjunction with the duty of loyalty, the duty of care ensures that directors serve the interests of the corporation and its stockholders by making informed decisions on the corporation's

118. *See* E. Norman Veasey & Julie M.S. Sietz, *The Business Judgment Rule in the Revised Model Act, The Trans Union Case, and the ALI Project—A Strange Porridge*, 63 Tex. L. Rev. 1483, 1496 (1985); and see The Business Judgment Rule, *supra* note 90, at 24–25.

119. *Principles of Corporate Governance: Analysis and Recommendations* §4.01(c) (Tentative Draft No. 4 Apr. 12, 1985); and see The Business Judgement Rule, *supra* note 90, at 25–26.

120. *See, e.g.*, Michael P. Dooley & E. Norman Veasey, *The Role of the Board in Derivative Litigation: Delaware Law and the Current ALI Proposals Compared*, 44 Bus. Law. 503 (Feb. 1989); Roswell B. Perkins, *The ALI Corporate Governance Project in Midstream*, 41 Bus. Law. 1195 (Aug. 1986); E. Norman Veasey & Julie M.S. Sietz, *The Business Judgment Rule in the Revised Model Act, The Trans Union Case, and the ALI Project—A Strange Porridge*, [63 Tex. L. Rev. 1483 (1985)].

and stockholders' behalf. If directors fail to fulfill this duty, then an action or transaction may potentially be enjoined, or the directors themselves subject to financial liability.[1] Under the traditional corporate law model, courts police the duty of care by examining the information the directors had available and the process they followed in rendering a decision. The procedural model has numerous and substantial weaknesses, including the ease with which an adequate record may be constructed and the lack of any necessary connection between procedural rituals and optimal decision making. A viable and compelling alternative to the traditional process-oriented model would be for a court examining a challenged corporate decision first to consider whether the directors making the decision also were substantial stockholders. If so, then the directors' enlightened self-interest should have operated to ensure that the decision reached was the best option available and in the company's best interest, thereby resolving the challenge. Courts, therefore, could adopt a rebuttable presumption that directors acted with due care where the directors also are substantial stockholders, potentially rendering process-oriented review initially unnecessary.

This proposed approach is not as radical as it might seem. Three lines of authority are converging in support of an equity-based presumption of care. First, a commission established by the National Association of Corporate Directors (NACD)[2] has suggested that such an approach is worthy of "close examination and consideration."[3] Second, Delaware courts have recognized the important incentives that equity ownership creates. Finally, current empirical and sociological research indicates that ownership of a substantial equity stake materially enhances director decision making. These authorities provide strong support for an equity-based presumption of care that would dispense with the traditional process-oriented approach, unless the plaintiff successfully rebutted the presumption. Rather than a revolutionary change, the proposed presumption represents an evolutionary development in the analysis of directors' fiduciary duties.

* * *

The Operation of a Potential Equity-based Presumption of Care

The operation of a potential equity-based presumption of care hinges on the role of the duty of care and its relationship to the business judgment rule.

---

1. See Smith v. Van Gorkom, 488 A.2d 858, 893 (Del. 1985) (imposing potential liability for breach of the duty of care; remanding case for determination of damages). Under Delaware law, a corporation may enact a charter provision "eliminating or limiting the personal liability of a director to the corporation or its stockholders for monetary damages for breach of fiduciary duty as a director, provided that such provision shall not eliminate or limit the liability of a director" for breaches of the duty of loyalty and in other identified scenarios. Del. Code Ann. tit. 8, § 102(b)(7) (1974). "Personal monetary exposure for directors for due care violations may thus be eliminated by a provision in a certificate of incorporation. Section 102(b)(7) does not, however, eliminate the requirement that directors act with due care." R. Franklin Balotti & Jesse A. Finkelstein, The Delaware Law of Corporations and Business Organizations § 4.34, at 4–215 (3d ed. Supp. 1999).

2. Founded in 1977, the NACD is a not-for-profit organization focused on meeting the needs of individuals serving on and working with corporate boards. The NACD's membership includes over 2000 chairmen, chief executive officers, presidents, vice-presidents, chief financial officers, and others who serve on, or deal with, corporate boards of directors. The NACD Best Practices Council (NACD Council) was established in 1997 to provide guidance and counsel to fast-growing, entrepreneurial companies. See Report of the NACD Best Practices Council: Coping with Fraud and Other Illegal Activity (1998) [hereinafter NACD REPORT]. Two of this Article's authors, Mr. Balotti and Professor Elson, served on the NACD Council.

3. Id. at 16.

> The business judgment rule is an acknowledgment of the managerial prerogatives of... directors.... It is a presumption that in making a business decision the directors of a corporation acted on an informed basis, in good faith and, in the honest belief that the action taken was in the best interests of the company. Absent an abuse of discretion, that judgment will be respected by the courts. The burden is on the party challenging the decision to establish facts rebutting the presumption.[98]

Proof of gross negligence sufficient to establish a breach of the duty of care is one way of rebutting the presumption.[99]

Delaware law distinguishes between the application of the business judgment rule in "transactional justification" cases and personal liability cases.[100] In transactional justification cases, the business judgment rule operates potentially to protect a board's decision from challenge, such as when a plaintiff seeks a preliminary injunction to prevent a transaction from closing that allegedly was approved by the board without exercising due care.[101] In personal liability cases, the rule potentially "shields directors from personal liability" as long as their decisions "can be attributed to any rational business purpose," such as when a derivative or class action plaintiff seeks to recover money damages from directors for allegedly taking action or allowing a harm to befall the corporation because of a failure to exercise due care.[102] Although generally the same standards and criteria are applied in both the transactional justification and personal liability contexts,[103] courts have recognized that both the business judgment rule and the duty of care may operate differently based on the factual, legal, and procedural circum-

98. Aronson v. Lewis, 473 A.2d 805, 812 (Del. 1984) (citations omitted).

99. See, e.g., Stepak v. Ross, Civ. A. No. 7047, slip op. at 14 (Del. Ch. Sept. 5, 1985) (observing in evaluating the strength of claims for purposes of approving a settlement that "to rebut the defense that the individual defendants are protected by the business judgment rule... plaintiffs would have to show that the individual defendants acted with gross negligence"). See also Rabkin v. Philip A. Hunt Chem. Corp., 547 A.2d 963, 970 (Del. Ch. 1986) ("Gross negligence is the standard to be applied in deciding first, whether the directors' decisions were informed, and, if so, whether the directors may be held liable for reaching the wrong decision." (citation omitted)).

100. See Unitrin, Inc. v. American Gen. Corp., 651 A.2d 1361, 1374 (Del. 1995).

101. Transactional justification cases most commonly have involved corporate takeovers or other change of control situations in which enhanced scrutiny under Unocal Corp. v. Mesa Petroleum Co., 493 A.2d 946 (Del. 1985), or Revlon, Inc. v. MacAndrews & Forbes Holdings, Inc., 506 A.2d 173 (Del. 1986), and their progeny has been applied as a precursor to business judgment review. Not all transactional challenges take place in a takeover environment, and enhanced scrutiny is not a prerequisite for a transactional justification case. See, e.g., Gimbel v. Signal Cos., 316 A.2d 599, 609 (Del. Ch.) (examining sale of assets under business judgment rule in transactional justification context; enjoining transaction pending development of record on valuation), aff'd, 316 A.2d 619 (Del. 1974).

102. Unitrin, 651 A.2d at 1374; see also Joseph Hinsey IV, Business Judgment and the American Law Institute's Corporate Governance Project: The Rule, the Doctrine, and the Reality, 52 GEO. WASH. L. REV. 609, 611–12 (1984); Thomas S. Leo, Potential Remedies in Acquisition Transactions, in ACQUISITIONS AND MERGERS IN A CHANGING ENVIRONMENT, at 609, 645–46 (PLI Corp. Law & Practice Course Handbook Series No. 700, 1990) (distinguishing between the business judgment rule, which "[shields] individual directors against liability for damages," and the business judgment doctrine, which "protects the decision itself"). The business judgment rule also functions in a third role as "the scope of review applied by the courts in cases involving the termination of derivative actions upon the motion of a special litigation committee." E. Norman Veasey et al., Counseling Directors on the Business Judgment Rule and the Duty of Loyalty, in CONTESTS FOR CORPORATE CONTROL 1991, at 475, 503 (PLI Corp. Law & Practice Course Handbook Series No. 731, 1991).

103. See Veasey et al., supra note 102, at 503 ("[C]ourts usually analyze transactional justification cases by applying the criteria traditionally employed under the business judgment rule.").

stance of a given case.[104] Section 102(b)(7) of the Delaware General Corporation Law confirms this distinction by allowing a Delaware corporation to include a provision in its certificate of incorporation to shield directors from personal liability for breaches of the duty of care. Section 102(b)(7) does not eliminate the obligation to act with due care and thus is inapplicable in transactional justification settings.[106]

In the transactional justification context, where a majority of the directors on a board each individually owns stock in the corporation representing a material amount of his or her personal wealth, the directors could be entitled to a presumption that they acted with due care for purposes of the business judgment rule. The proposed requirement that a majority of directors hold material amounts of stock before the equity-based presumption will apply in a transactional justification context draws on existing principles of Delaware law and provides a practical and administrable standard. Several alternative positions are available, including requiring all directors to be substantial stockholders or granting the presumption where only one director is a substantial stockholder. At the one extreme, it can be argued that Delaware law requires informed action by the board of directors as a whole, not merely a portion of the directors, and therefore the presumption only should apply if the entire board can invoke it.[107] At the other extreme, it can be argued that a director who is a substantial stockholder will not approve a transaction that results in self injury, and thus if even one director who is a substantial stockholder goes along with a decision, that is sufficient evidence that the directors as a whole acted with due care. Although each position has some logical force, a middle position requiring a majority of the board appears more prudent. Assuming a majority of votes are needed for the board to act, then the majority requirement for directors who are substantial stockholders parallels the voting requirement and ensures that the transaction could have been approved by the vote of the substantial stockholding directors. The majority standard also is analogous to the standard for analyzing director disinterestedness and independence under the business judgment rule, where Delaware law has settled on a majority requirement.[108] The majority standard also avoids the extremes of having the potential presumption of care cut too narrowly (for a unanimous board rule) or extend too broadly (for a solitary director standard).

---

104. See Hanson Trust PLC v. ML SCM Acquisition, Inc., 781 F.2d 264, 275 (2d Cir. 1986) (enjoining challenged lock-up transaction because of a breach of the duty of care, but finding that the breach did "not rise to that level of gross negligence found in Smith v. Van Gorkom"); Moran v. Household Int'l Corp., 490 A.2d 1059, 1076 (Del. Ch.) ("The strength of the [business judgment rule's] presumption may vary according to the procedural context in which it is raised as a defense."), aff'd, 500 A.2d 1346 (Del. 1985).

106. See Michael P. Dooley & E. Norman Veasey, The Role of the Board in Derivative Litigation: Delaware Law and the Current ALI Proposals Compared, 44 BUS. LAW. 503, 510 n.31 (1989) (explaining that § 102(b)(7) "permits a corporation to protect its directors from personal liability for (among other things) gross negligence in the decisionmaking process.... But this statute does not apply to protect the decision in an injunction proceeding.").

107. See Kumar v. Racing Corp. of Am., Civ. A. No. 12,039, slip op. at 12 (Del. Ch. Apr. 26, 1991) ("Defendants seem to be suggesting that, since the Veale family directors had discussed this matter and given it some thought prior to the board meeting, it does not matter that Kumar was left out of these 'deliberations.' I think that it does. The board of directors, as a whole, must be informed.").

108. See, e.g., Cinerama, Inc. v. Technicolor, Inc., 663 A.2d 1156, 1170 (Del. 1995) (recognizing that "as to the duty of loyalty, approval of a transaction by a board of which a majority of directors is disinterested and independent" is sufficient to trigger the protections of the business judgment rule).

Existing Delaware precedent suggests a different approach in personal liability settings. Delaware law appears to contemplate the possibility of analyzing each director's conduct individually when determining whether to impose personal liability for a breach of the duty of care. In Smith v. Van Gorkom,[109] the Delaware Supreme Court considered "[w]hether the directors of Trans Union should be treated as one or individually in terms of invoking the protection of the business judgment rule."[110] The court concluded that "since all of the defendant directors, outside as well as inside, take a unified position, we are required to treat all of the directors as one as to whether they are entitled to the protection of the business judgment rule."[111] On motion for reargument, one of the defendant directors argued that "his undisputed absence due to illness from [both of] the... meetings of the directors of Trans Union [where the challenged merger was considered] entitles him to be relieved from personal liability for the failure of the other directors to exercise due care at those meetings."[112] The court did not reject or criticize this argument as a legal matter, but rather found that the argument had been waived because it had not been raised earlier and because counsel for the individual defendants had represented to the court that there were no relevant distinctions among the directors.[113] The Delaware Supreme Court took a similar approach in Cheff v. Mathes.[114] In Cheff, the Delaware Court of Chancery had found liable certain directors who were aware of an alternative transaction structure, but exonerated other directors who were unaware of the alternative. The Delaware Supreme Court did not criticize the concept of differential treatment but rather found that knowledge of the alternative transaction structure was irrelevant to the core legal issue presented by the case.[115] In Propp v. Sadacca,[116] the Delaware Court of Chancery in fact declined to hold one director liable for a challenged transaction where the director "abstained from voting in good faith because he honestly believed" he had a conflict of interest.[117] The court found "[o]n the basis of all relevant facts of record" that the director was "not legally responsible for the transaction under attack."[118]

In addition to implying that some directors may be subject to liability for duty of care violations while others may not, Delaware law also recognizes that different standards may be applied to different directors in determining liability for breaches of the duty of care based on the directors' role in a challenged transaction. In Cheff, the Delaware Supreme Court observed that all of the directors had a degree of self-interest in protecting their positions by repurchasing company stock using corporate funds in response to a hostile takeover attempt. In articulating the burden of proof to be placed on the target company's directors, the court distinguished among: (i) the company's chief executive officer, (ii) a director who also was the company's regular outside counsel, and (iii) the remaining outside directors.[119] The court then held that although the outside directors would be "called upon to justify their actions," they would not be

---

109. 488 A.2d 858 (Del. 1985).
110. Id. at 888.
111. Id. at 889.
112. Id. at 898.
113. See id. at 898–99.
114. 199 A.2d 548 (Del. 1964).
115. See id. at 556
116. 175 A.2d 33 (Del. Ch. 1961), aff'd in part, rev'd in part sub nom. Bennett v. Propp, 187 A.2d 405 (Del. 1962).
117. Id. at 39.
118. Id.
119. See id. at 554–55

"held to the same standard of proof required of those directors having personal and pecuniary interest in the transaction."[120] One treatise has stated this rule generally: "The degree of care for directors... has been said to accommodate the various levels of director involvement in management...."[121]

These authorities indicate that in a personal liability setting, the proposed equity-based presumption of care should be applied on an individual basis to each defendant director to determine whether that director should be insulated from personal liability.[122] If a director possesses a material amount of stock, then that director could be presumed to have exercised a level of due care sufficient to avoid the imposition of personal liability, even if the board as a whole was found to have failed to exercise due care in approving the challenged transaction. This aspect of the proposed presumption admittedly creates potentially counter-intuitive results. It envisions, for example, that directors with substantial equity holdings who attended the same meetings, received the same materials, and participated in the same discussions as other directors could be insulated from liability, while directors without substantial equity holdings could be held liable. It also envisions that in rare situations, the directors most capable of satisfying a judgment may be insulated from recovery. On balance, however, the empirical benefits of improved director monitoring and oversight should outweigh the additional protection from liability that the presumption confers.[124] The material stock ownership requirement also should operate most often to insulate directors with moderate personal

---

120. Id. Although the Delaware Supreme Court did not explore the concept further, the three levels of involvement in the challenged transaction by the directors in Cheff suggest that a different standard would apply for analyzing the duty of care not only between insiders and outsiders, but also among insiders, outsiders, and quasi-insiders like the company's outside counsel. See, e.g., Sanjai Bhagat and Bernard Black, *The Uncertain Relationship Between Board Composition and Firm Performance*, 54 Bus. Law. 921, 923 (1999). Professors Bhagat and Black note the

> common practice of dividing directors into inside directors (persons who are currently officers of the company), affiliated outside directors, (former company officers, relatives of company officers, and persons who [have or] are likely to have business relationships with the company, including commercial bankers, investment bankers and lawyers) (sometimes called grey directors), and independent directors (outside directors without such affiliations).

Id.

121. 18B Am. Jur. 2d Corporations § 1710 (1985).

122. A competing view is possible. Under § 144 of the Delaware General Corporation Law, the fully informed vote of a majority of disinterested directors, even though less than a quorum, is sufficient to bring a self-dealing transaction between a corporation and one or more of its officers and directors within the scope of the business judgment rule. See Del. Code Ann. tit. 8, § 144(a) (1974 & Supp. 1998); Oberly v. Kirby, 592 A.2d 445, 466 (Del. 1991) (noting that compliance with the procedures of § 144 is sufficient to "bring [an interested transaction] within the scope of the business judgment rule"). By analogy, the approval of a transaction by a majority of directors with substantial equity holdings could be deemed sufficient to protect all directors from liability, including directors without substantial equity holdings. The rule in the personal liability context thus would resemble the rule in the transactional justification context. This approach cuts against authority recognizing the difference between the transactional justification and personal liability contexts and against precedent that supports treating directors individually for purposes of assessing personal liability. In addition, the language of § 144, which speaks of whether a transaction "shall be void or voidable," seems primarily focused on transactional justification, rather than personal liability issues. An all-or-nothing liability rule also imposes greater restrictions on the ability of plaintiffs to obtain redress for their injuries. For these reasons, an individualized approach seems preferable.

124. To the extent that fear of liability currently spurs directors to comply with the duty of care, the incentives it creates are minimal. A combination of § 102(b)(7) provisions, indemnification rights, and directors and officers liability insurance largely eliminates the threat of liability as a practical matter. From a liability perspective, therefore, the cost of moving to an equity-based system seems marginal at best.

wealth who have accumulated equity through customary and reasonable director compensation plans in amounts that are nonetheless material because of the director's personal financial situation. Further empirical study of these issues would be beneficial.

In light of the potential effects of the proposed equity-based presumption of care, the level of financial interest that is necessary for directors to invoke the presumption becomes crucial. The empirical studies of director decision making indicate that on average, a financial stake of $100,000 or more has a material effect on director action. This general finding does not necessarily show, however, that a $100,000 stake always has a beneficial effect. For directors with substantial wealth, a $100,000 stake in a specific company may have minimal importance.

Existing Delaware Court of Chancery precedent suggests that each director's equity position should be evaluated as a portion of that director's wealth to determine whether the stake will have a material effect on the director's decision making. In In re General Motors Class H Shareholders Litigation,[125] a class of holders of a tracking stock designed to derive its value from the performance of Hughes Electronic Corporation (Hughes), a wholly-owned subsidiary of General Motors Corporation, alleged that the GM board of directors was self-interested in the sale of Hughes because all of the directors owned substantially more GM $1 2/3 shares than Hughes tracking stock shares. The Delaware Court of Chancery held that

> [t]o show that a GM director's independence was compromised by her ownership of greater amounts of GM $1 2/3 stock, the plaintiffs must plead that the amount of such holdings and the predominance of such holdings over [Hughes] holdings was of a sufficiently material importance, in the context of the director's economic circumstances, as to have made it improbable that the director could perform her fiduciary duties to the [Hughes] shareholders without being influenced by her overriding personal interest in the performance of the GM $1 2/3 shares.[126]

The court reached the same conclusion in Solomon v. Armstrong,[127] in which holders of a different series of GM tracking stock argued that the GM board of directors was self-interested in a split-off transaction because "the outside directors held a disproportionate number of shares of GM 1 2/3 common stock." The Delaware Court of Chancery held that "when a party challenges a director's action based on a claim of the director's debilitating pecuniary self-interest, that party must allege that the director's interest is material to that director."[128] The court dismissed the claims because the plaintiffs had failed to make the necessary allegation of material self-interest. These cases suggest that if a director wishes to show that his or her substantial stock ownership is sufficient to eliminate an otherwise "debilitating... self-interest," then the director must show that the value of his or her equity position is "material to that director" when judged "in the context of the director's economic circumstances."[131]

---

125. Civ. A. No. 15,517 (Del. Ch. Mar. 22, 1999).
126. Id., slip op. at 14.
127. Consol. Civ. A. No. 13,515 (Del. Ch. Mar. 25, 1999).
128. Id., slip op. at 30.
131. See generally Cinerama, Inc. v. Technicolor, Inc., 663 A.2d 1156, 1167 (Del. 1995) (adopting "actual person" standard for determining materiality of director self-interest); Cede & Co. v. Technicolor, Inc., 634 A.2d 345, 364 (Del. 1993) (adopting requirement that director self-interest be material and rejecting use of a "reasonable person standard" in making the materiality determination), modified, 636 A.2d 956 (Del. 1994). See also HMG/Courtland Properties, Inc. v. Gray, Civ. A. No. 15,789, slip op. at 46–47, 65 (Del. Ch. July 12, 1999) (finding that an "affluent" director who had invested "$355,000 of his [own] and his sister's money" in certain challenged transactions had a

Under this standard, a director who wishes to invoke the substantial equity ownership presumption should have the burden to prove that he or she holds equity having a value that is material "in the context of the director's economic circumstances." This will require some level of disclosure of each director's personal finances and a concomitant opportunity for discovery by plaintiff's counsel. This in turn creates the danger of fishing expeditions into the personal lives of board members as well as the risk that courts will be dragged into valuation disputes over individual assets or the aggregate value of a director's wealth. Directors who do not wish to divulge the necessary information about their personal assets could choose to forgo the defense and rely on the traditional business judgment rule. Courts also may need to develop procedures to limit the extent of litigation over valuation issues. At some level of financial involvement, courts could presume that a director's equity interest in the corporation is material. Thus in Unitrin, neither the Delaware Supreme Court nor the Delaware Court of Chancery analyzed whether the stockholder directors' investment in Unitrin was a material portion of their personal wealth. One director held 400,000 shares, representing a $20.1 million investment at the American General offer price; another held 1,062,335 shares, representing a $53.5 million investment at the offer price, and a third director held 7,242,260 shares, representing a $365 million investment at the American General offer price. The Delaware Supreme Court understandably accepted these amounts as constituting substantial investments sufficient to align the directors' interests with those of the stockholders generally. Courts also could rely on the empirical studies of the effect of equity ownership on director decision making to consider recognizing a presumption that equity holdings worth $100,000 or more in value are material.

Finally, as suggested by the NACD Council, a party seeking to overcome the equity-based presumption of care in either the transactional justification or personal liability setting may rebut the presumption by alleging and proving either: (i) that "the directors intentionally acted contrary to their own economic interests," or (ii) that "damages resulted from a sustained and systematic failure of the directors to exercise oversight."[132] The second test adopts the standard established in In re Caremark International, Inc. Derivative Litigation[133] for establishing a breach of fiduciary duty based on a board's uninformed failure to act. Where this standard is met, a board necessarily lacks the information needed to meet its duty of care, and the equity-based presumption is irrelevant.

The first test, by contrast, represents a new standard based on the possibility that even equity-owning directors might conceivably act contrary to their own economic interests. Importantly, however, the types of evidence that a plaintiff may use to establish this presumption should be narrowly curtailed. Two methods in particular are contrary to the spirit of the business judgment rule and the nature of the equity-based presumption of care. First, a plaintiff should not be able to investigate the information that an equity-holding board had available to argue that the directors rejected an option that

---

material personal interest in the transactions that created a disabling conflict); In re Dairy Mart Convenience Stores, C.A. No. 14,713, slip op. at 53 n.57 (Del. Ch. May 24, 1999) (rejecting claim that directors had disqualifying self-interest in transaction that involved granting stock options to directors where plaintiffs "failed to plead the materiality of that potential self-interest"); Cinerama, Inc. v. Technicolor, Inc., Civ. A. No. 8358, slip op. at 35 (Del. Ch. June 24, 1991) ("Plainly, a $150,000 cash payment contingent upon the closing of the deal is a circumstance that has a substantial probability of affecting the independence of Mr. Sullivan's judgment to the detriment of the company's shareholders, given all of the circumstances (i.e., his very modest stock holding in the company)."), aff'd in part, rev'd in part sub nom. Cede & Co, 634 A.2d at 345.

132. NACD Report, supra note 2, at 16.

133. 698 A.2d 959, 967–68 (Del. Ch. 1996)....

would better serve their economic interests. This method simply would reintroduce the current procedural approach under a new guise, in which rather than attempting to determine whether directors were informed, a court would attempt to determine whether the directors were informed of a superior alternative. To evaluate such a claim, the court would conduct the same type of procedural exegesis that it currently uses to analyze the duty of care, including examining the materials presented at meetings, the length of discussions on various subjects, and the advice received from investment bankers and other experts. The purpose of the equity-based presumption is to avoid precisely this type of ritualistic inquiry unless the presumption is rebutted. Second, a plaintiff should not be able to argue that an alternative course rejected by an equity-holding board was substantively superior to the option the board in fact selected. This would require the court to substitute its own business judgment for that of the directors without any preliminary indication or finding that the board had breached its fiduciary duties, an approach which is squarely contrary to the business judgment rule. Although future cases necessarily will flesh out the standard, the types of situations in which a plaintiff can show that equity-holding directors acted "contrary to their own economic interests" likely only will be cases in which a court can infer from the objective facts surrounding a transaction that an otherwise disinterested board nevertheless acted with an improper motive. Cases of this nature should be comparably rare. In any event, plaintiffs should have the burden of proving the exception and should not be permitted to conduct discovery into a director's purportedly contrarian motivations unless they have pled specific facts which, if true, would establish that the director acted contrary to his or her economic interests. As with the business judgment rule generally, absent specific allegations to the contrary, directors should be presumed to have acted "on an informed basis, in good faith and in the honest belief that the action taken was in the best interests of the company."[137]

The proposed equity-based presumption of care has potentially dramatic consequences for fiduciary duty litigation. In transactional settings, once a majority of the board has made the necessary showing, the effects of the presumption should significantly limit the scope of permissible discovery and the range of issues that a court needs to consider. Issues such as the number and length of meetings held, the types of materials received, the advice given by investment bankers or other experts, the questions asked by the board, and the length of time for deliberations all will be irrelevant to the court's analysis. Even serious allegations of egregious conduct that under current procedural standards would almost certainly result in a finding that the duty of care was breached should not be entertained if the requirements for the presumption have been met. Absent such a rule, the courts quickly will find themselves recreating the current procedural approach to due care issues under the guise of determining whether a particular action or specific information was so significant that the presumption should not apply. The only hallmarks a court would have to make such a determination are the same procedural rituals that have given rise to the current due care system. To protect the viability of the equity-based rule, the presumption should cut off all inquiry into the procedural steps actually taken by the board, unless the presumption is rebutted. This will have the concomitant benefit of enabling courts to dispose of cases through motions for summary judgment, judgment on the pleadings, or through limited evidentiary hearings.

The Potential Equity-based Presumption Should Not Extend to the Duty of Disclosure or the Duty of Loyalty

137. Aronson, 473 A.2d at 812.

Importantly, the proposed equity-based presumption only should apply to the duty of care. Substantial equity ownership should have no bearing on the duty of disclosure. Substantial equity ownership also should not give rise to any presumption for the duty of loyalty, and plaintiffs still may attempt to rebut the protections of the business judgment rule by showing director disloyalty or self-interest.

The inapplicability of a presumption based on substantial equity ownership to the duty of disclosure follows naturally from the established legal principle that, as a general matter, the business judgment rule does not apply to disclosure issues.[138] Although it could be argued that directors who will benefit substantially from a transaction have an interest in ensuring that the transaction is accomplished and therefore will make sure that all material facts are disclosed to avoid any potential challenge on duty of disclosure grounds, the indirect incentives for fulfilling the duty of disclosure seem less compelling than the direct incentives for fulfilling the duty of care. Moreover, courts can evaluate disclosure issues efficiently by examining proxy statements and other disclosures issued in connection with a transaction. Disclosure cases have not devolved into the checklist of procedural rituals that currently marks the analysis of the duty of care. As a result, there does not appear to be a compelling reason to depart from the existing rule of law that makes the duty of care and other business judgment principles generally inapplicable in disclosure cases.

The application of the potential equity-based exception to the duty of loyalty presents a more difficult issue. The Delaware cases that recognize the incentives created by substantial equity ownership could be read as supporting an exception to the duty of loyalty where the enlightened self-interest of the directors aligns with the interests of the stockholders. Some Delaware decisions even suggest that the incentives created by substantial equity ownership will be sufficient to overcome and sterilize competing influences that could create self-interested behavior. In Unitrin, Inc. v. American General Corp.,[139] the Delaware Supreme Court held that directors who were also substantial stockholders would not be influenced by the "[p]restige and [p]erquisites" of board membership in deciding how to vote in a proxy contest, but rather would vote "in their own best economic interests."[140] In Giammargo v. Snapple Beverage Corp.,[141] the Delaware Court of Chancery found that the directors' 68% stock ownership rendered "very strained" the claim that side-payments had influenced the directors to favor an otherwise inadequate transaction.

Unfortunately, this view of director incentives may well be incorrect. Even directors who are substantial stockholders potentially have an incentive to divert transaction proceeds to themselves through consulting agreements, accelerated vesting of options, or other side arrangements. Insider directors have even greater opportunities to obtain special consideration in the form of employment contracts, severance agreements,

---

138. See Bear, Stearns & Co. v. Anderson, Clayton & Co. (In re Anderson, Clayton Shareholders' Litig.), 519 A.2d 669, 675 (Del. Ch. 1986) ("[T]he question [of] whether shareholders have, under the circumstances, been provided with appropriate information upon which an informed choice on a matter of fundamental corporate importance may be made, is not a decision...of the kind the business judgment rule is intended to protect...."); see also Stroud v. Grace, 606 A.2d 75, 89 (Del. 1992) (holding that business judgment rule would apply to a decision not to disclose confidential information only where information was shown to be material, had been requested by the stockholder plaintiff, and the stockholder plaintiff had refused to sign a reasonable confidentiality agreement).

139. 651 A.2d 1361 (Del. 1995).

140. Id. at 1380.

141. Civ. A. No. 13,845 (Del. Ch. Nov. 15, 1994).

covenants not to compete, and other mechanisms. Even with an ownership stake as great as in Giammargo, directors potentially have an incentive to divert transaction proceeds. Under Giammargo's facts, the directors' 68% stock ownership meant that every dollar increase in merger consideration would give the directors only 68 cents in value, versus the possibility of a full dollar through a side agreement. While it is possible that the Giammargo directors owned so many shares that they could obtain a larger aggregate amount through an increase in the merger consideration rather than a direct side payment, the validity of that proposition would depend on the dynamics of the negotiation and encompass a variety of factual issues.

More importantly, as the Delaware courts have recognized, the incentives created by substantial equity ownership may themselves cause duty of loyalty problems. Substantial stockholdings may create a conflict of interest that requires disclosure or which results in the application of the entire fairness standard.[143] The unique circumstances of a substantial stockholder also may cause a director's interests to depart from those of the stockholders as a whole. For example, a director who is a substantial stockholder may prefer for personal reasons a non-taxable transaction or a pricing structure that would offer a lower gross pre-tax value to all stockholders but a higher net after-tax value to that director. Duty of loyalty questions thus encompass a variety of factual issues that undercut the efficacy of an equity-based presumption.

Because of these concerns, an equity-based presumption should apply only to the duty of care. The connection between equity ownership and the duty of disclosure is too tenuous and the connection between equity ownership and the duty of loyalty too problematic to merit a potential presumption at this time.

Franklin A. Gevurtz, *The Business Judgment Rule: Meaningless Verbiage or Misguided Notion?*

67 S. Cal. L. Rev. 287 (1994)
(excerpts 321–327; some footnotes omitted)

B. Testing the Justifications in Specific Situations

Perhaps the ultimate test of these various justifications for a special liability standard for directors is to examine whether they would be persuasive in distinguishing between directors and other defendants in specific contexts. Consider first the situation in Smith v. Van Gorkom.[163] One aspect of the case relevant here is the guidance the directors of Trans Union received from an outside counsel brought in to advise them on the proposed sale of the company. The attorney evidently did not warn the directors they were about to breach their duty of care by acting on the limited information before them. On the contrary, the attorney purportedly advised the board members that they did not

143. See Oberly v. Kirby, 592 A.2d 445, 468 (Del. 1991) (applying entire fairness standard where equity holdings of directors created incentives that "could have induced them to advance Allegheny's interests at the expense of the Foundation and its beneficiaries"); Eisenberg v. Chicago Milwaukee Corp., 537 A.2d 1051, 1061 (Del. Ch. 1987) (finding that directors' substantial equity holdings raised a potential conflict of interest that should have been disclosed in connection with a self-tender offer for the defendant company's preferred stock).

163. 488 A.2d 858 (Del. 1985).

need an investment banker's fairness opinion regarding the proposed sale and, what is more, he stated they might be sued if they voted not to sell.[164]

These facts lead one to wonder what would have happened had either the directors or the shareholders sued this attorney for malpractice. The standard against which the court would have measured the attorney's advice presumably would be the familiar skill and care ordinarily possessed and exercised by attorneys in the locality.[166] No court has ever suggested the business judgment rule would provide a defense for a corporation's outside counsel.[167] In contrast, the Delaware Supreme Court held that under the business judgment rule the directors of Trans Union could not be liable unless they were grossly negligent. Why the difference? Can any of the previously discussed justifications explain such a result?[169]

To begin with, would after-the-fact judicial review of the attorney's advice pose any lesser problem here than did review of the directors' decision? The decision of what and how much legal advice to give is a question of judgment. In Van Gorkom, the attorney had to weigh the risk (ultimately realized) that he would fail to warn the directors of an action which would lead to their liability versus the risk that if he urged too much caution upon the directors they could lose the opportunity for a highly desirable sale. This substantially parallels the judgment the directors of Trans Union had to make. Indeed, it is difficult to see—especially given the narrow margin by which the directors lost this case, as well as the general uncertainty in this whole area of law—how the attorney's decision was much less intuitive and judgmental than the directors'.[174] Litigation over whether the

---

164. Id. at 881. The court characterized the attorney's purported advice as literally true. This was being too kind. Whether or not the advice was literally true, the failure to warn the directors that they were about to breach their duty by acting on inadequate information clearly raises the issue of malpractice. See, e.g., Bukoskey v. Walter W. Shuham CPA, P.C., 666 F.Supp. 181 (D. Alaska 1987).

166. See, e.g., McClain v. Faraone, 369 A.2d 1090 (Del. 1977); Mallen & Smith, supra note 95, at 856–57. While some archaic legal-malpractice cases refer to a standard of gross negligence, this usage has disappeared. Id. at 884–87.

167. Cf. Holland v. Stenhouse, 1991 WL 30138 (N.D.Ill. 1991). In this case, the trustee for a bankrupt insurance company sued both the former directors for breach of their duty of care and the company's attorney for legal malpractice for, among other things, failing to advise the directors of their duty. The directors moved to dismiss based upon Delaware's business judgment rule. There is no indication any party considered the business judgment rule at all relevant to the claim against the attorney.

169. [The previously discussed justifications were: (1) difficulties with after-the-fact review of business decisions; (2) nature of the damages and its impact on the willingness of qualified directors to serve; (3) the plaintiffs are generally not sympathetic and their motives for suing suspect; and (4) the compensation and deterrence value of the duty of care: Editor]. One might be more sympathetic to the directors than the attorney because they were operating based upon his poor advice. This, however, goes to the question of whether there was reasonable reliance upon advice so as to preclude a finding of negligence. E.g., Cal. Corp. Code § 309(b) (West 1992). It does not justify applying a standard for liability other than ordinary negligence. See, e.g., Frances T. v. Village Green Owners Ass'n, 723 P.2d 573, 584 (Cal. 1986) (holding that directors' reasonable reliance on expert advice should be taken into account under an ordinary negligence standard).

174. Admittedly, one might distinguish the attorney, who was only advising, from the directors, who were deciding whether to delay and seek more information. It is unrealistic, however, to argue the corporation's attorney does not need to exercise judgment in giving advice because the ultimate decision rests with the board. For one thing, it is questionable whether the Trans Union board would have had the nerve to go ahead with immediate approval when confronted with an attorney's opinion that it faced liability. Cf. SEC v. National Student Marketing Corp., 457 F.Supp. 682, 713 (D.D.C. 1978) (speculating that board might not have violated securities law if attorney had objected). Moreover, an attorney who avoids exercising judgment by attempting to warn clients about every contingency risks finding those warnings ignored when the client should heed them.

attorney negligently advised the Trans Union board would risk the fact finder confusing bad results (the board was held liable) with negligence and would be expensive even if the attorney won. This prospect, in turn, creates an incentive for attorneys to avoid the risk of liability for themselves by always warning the client of any potential hazard. The result of such a practice, however, is to undermine the utility of the attorney's advice to the client, who is left to figure out what warnings to take seriously. About the only thing one could say is that judges (at least in Delaware) have some expertise in providing legal advice to corporate boards. Yet, expertise cannot explain a different standard here. Consider the fact that had the board received poor advice from a professional other than an attorney—such as an opinion on valuation from an investment banker—the standard in a malpractice suit presumably still would not have the business judgment rule.

If problems of after-the-fact judicial review would not have justified different treatment of the lawyer in Van Gorkom, neither would the nature of the damages or the plaintiff. The damages faced by the attorney presumably would have been the same as faced by the directors he advised. Similarly, if the shareholders of Trans Union sued the attorney, there would be no difference in the plaintiff to explain the different standard applied.

Is there any difference in terms of the economic utility of compensation or deterrence? In a suit against either the directors or the attorney, compensation would come largely from insurance. While the attorney's policy would not have been purchased directly by the corporation, as were the directors', the corporation (along with the law firm's other clients) paid for the attorney's policy through the fees the attorney charged. In either event, liability for negligence is an expensive way to achieve loss spreading.[178] As far as deterrence is concerned, the attorney, like the directors, faces market incentives. After all, the mergers and acquisitions field is one in which a reputation for good results can dictate economic success for a lawyer. Conversely, one might suspect boards would be leery of hiring an attorney who previously led his clients into a well publicized fiasco.

As a second test of these justifications, consider the following hypothetical, somewhat inspired by recent events. Suppose a corporation operates oil tankers. Due to a decision by one of the company's captains as to speed, course, or whatever, a company ship runs aground, resulting in an oil spill. If coastal-property owners damaged by the spill sue the corporation, the issue will be whether the captain's decision was negligent. The corporation would hardly get anywhere by arguing for a "nautical judgment rule" under which it could avoid liability unless the captain acted in bad faith, or with gross rather than ordinary negligence, or which confined the fact finder to focusing exclusively or primarily upon the methodology by which the captain reached the decision rather than upon the

178. Some writers have argued that directors are poorer "loss avoiders" than outside attorneys or accountants because directors do not spread the loss over a large base of clients. E.g., Coffee, supra note 140, at 802. Why this makes any difference is obscure. Cf. Robinson, supra note 112, at 180–82 (challenging the notion that doctors are cheaper loss-avoiders because of their ability to spread costs among their patients). Either director—and officer—or legal-malpractice insurance spreads the loss—albeit in either case through an administratively expensive system. In either case, there is some "social accounting." The consumers, here the corporations, will pay for the injuries which may occur to themselves by virtue of the legal or managerial services they are buying—either through higher fees to cover the legal-malpractice insurance or by directly paying for the directors' liability policy. Hence, in both cases liability serves the same possible function of avoiding overconsumption of services which do not reflect their full cost. Moreover, even if there is some utility to imposing the cost of injuries on enterprises able to disperse those costs in the price of goods or services charged to a wide customer base, liability for negligence has never been so limited. E.g., Brown v. Kendall, 60 Mass. (6 Cush). 292 (1850).

decision itself. Moreover, since the corporation's liability is vicarious, the captain could be personally liable to the damaged coastal property owners for negligence. The captain, too, would not get far arguing for a different threshold for liability.

Now suppose the corporation sued its captain to indemnify it for the judgment it paid the property owners or even for loss of the ship and cargo. Again, the standard upon which the captain's liability will hinge is simple negligence. There appears to be little or no authority for applying the business judgment rule to accidents caused by corporate employees below top management.

To introduce the business judgment rule, let us change the facts of the hypothetical. To keep things simple, assume the grounding was the result of a storm or, in any event, not the result of any person's negligence. Assume also, however, that had the tanker possessed a double hull, it would have survived the grounding without a spill. Further, let us suppose the corporation's board of directors made the decision to purchase single—rather than double-hulled oil tankers. This was a business decision in which the board had to balance the protective advantages of double hulled tankers against their added costs and lower cargo-carrying capabilities. What would the result be if the damaged-coastal-property owners sued the corporation? Again, the standard for liability would be simple negligence, not the business judgment rule.[185] The same would be true if the damaged property owners sued the directors personally: Courts do not apply the business judgment rule to suits by third parties against directors whose decisions have caused injury.[186]

Now, however, consider what would happen if the corporation sued the directors, either to indemnify if for any payment to the injured property owners or for loss of the ship and cargo. This would seem to call for application of the business judgment rule. The incongruities are striking. The same board decision about double hulls which a court would have no trouble scrutinizing under an ordinary negligence standard in a suit brought by third parties—either against the corporation or against the directors person-

---

185. This is the sort of corporate-safety-versus-cost decision toward which Judge Hand directed his formula in United States v. Carroll Towing Co., 159 F.2d 169 (2d Cir.1947).

186. E.g., Frances T. v. Village Green Owners Ass'n, 723 P.2d 573, 582–83 (Cal. 1986) (stating that the court was unaware of any case from any jurisdiction in which the business judgment rule governed a director's liability in tort to third persons); Bowes v. Cincinnati Riverfront Coliseum, Inc., 465 N.E.2d 904 (Ohio Ct.App. 1983).

A potential source of confusion when discussing third-party claims against corporate directors comes from the rule that directors generally are not liable to third parties for breaching the duty of care owed to the corporation. E.g., Newman v. Forward Lands, 418 F.Supp. 134, 137 (E.D.Pa. 1976). This is simply part of the rule of agency law that the mere failure to perform an agent's duty to his or her principal does not, except in certain cases, render the agent liable to a third party injured by the neglect. E.g., Restatement (Second) of Agency §352 (1984). On the other hand, neither directors nor other agents can escape liability for conduct which would otherwise constitute a tort toward a third party just because the director or agent was acting on behalf of the corporation. E.g., Frances T., 723 P.2d at 582–83; Restatement (Second) of Agency §§343, 350. Difficulties in reconciling these two propositions occur primarily when the claim involves inaction by the director or agent and economic loss rather than physical injury. See, e.g., Newman, 418 F.Supp. at 136–37; Restatement (Second) of Agency §§354, 357. However, the hypothetical in the text involves a decision to purchase single-hulled tankers rather than inaction, which results in physical injury to coastal property rather than merely economic loss. More fundamentally, this whole issue goes to whether there is any duty to the third party at all; it does not act, as does the business judgment rule, to alter the standard of fault required.

ally—would suddenly demand the lesser scrutiny of the business judgment rule when the corporation brought the suit. Moreover, any qualms about the corporation suing those acting on its behalf would fade immediately if the suit was against the captain rather than the directors.[188]

Can any of the proffered justifications possibly explain the distinctions here? Would after-the-fact judicial review of the directors' decision regarding double hulls present that much greater probability of error or of deterring worthwhile risk taking than would review of the ship captain's judgment? Even if so, the difficulties of after-the-fact review cannot explain the different standards applied to the double-hull decision depending upon whether the suit is by the injured property owners or by (or on behalf of) the corporation. Clearly, the nature of the damages cannot explain the results: The damages are substantially the same throughout.

The difference in the nature of the plaintiff might account for the different standards applied to the directors' decision; but then what about the corporation's action against the ship captain? Perhaps one might argue that the business judgment rule should insulate all corporate employees from liability for ordinary negligence. Suppose, in that event, the grounding resulted from the decision of a harbor pilot who was working for the company as an independent contractor? Alternately, suppose a partnership or sole proprietorship operated the tanker: Should employees have a different standard of liability depending upon whether they work for a corporation or an unincorporated employer? In short, once one starts suggesting corporations should be unable to sue some of their employees for ordinary negligence, it is difficult to know where to stop.

Finally, what about compensation or deterrence? Putting aside the questions of whether the injured coastal property owners might just as well have purchased insurance for themselves, or whether their need for compensation exists even if the spill was not the result of negligence, it is clear that the corporation's need for compensation cannot explain the difference in the standard between the corporation's suit of the ship captain and of the directors. As for deterrence goals, how this distinguishes the appropriate standard for the captain versus the directors is a mystery.

The bottom line is that utilizing the business judgment rule to insulate directors from liability for ordinary negligence creates differences in treatment between individuals which cannot be explained by any policy justifications. That alone should be enough to condemn this approach.

---

188. The situation facing the Massachusetts Supreme Court in Uccello v. Gold'N Foods, Inc., 90 N.E.2d 530 (Mass. 1950), came tantalizingly close to creating such a paradox. Uccello, a minority shareholder in Gold'N Foods, sued the directors for mismanagement. Gold'N Foods manufactured salad dressing. Due to use of poor ingredients, Gold'N Foods suffered numerous complaints and returns of spoiled dressing, and ultimately went out of business. The directors knew of the problem but continued manufacturing without solving it. The court applied a gross negligence standard under its interpretation of the business judgment rule and exonerated the directors. Fortunately, the spoilage did not create a health hazard. Had the spoilage done so, then the Massachusetts court would have confronted the situation in which the same board decision would face review under a gross or under an ordinary negligence standard—this case having arisen before strict products liability—depending upon who brought the action. Moreover, had an ordinary employee's negligence caused the spoilage, the business judgment rule presumably would not apply even to an action by the company against the employee.

Comments and Questions

1. Do you agree with the criticisms of the business judgment rule articulated in the excerpts? Are there strong public policy arguments in favor of insulating directors from liability in duty of care cases by limiting liability to those cases where the gross negligence of the directors can be demonstrated or by creating a presumption of care in cases of directors with economic interests in the enterprise?

2. If directors' substantial interests in the corporation can act as a shield against liability under the duty of care, can the same rationale be used to shield the directors from breaches of other duties, perhaps even the duty of loyalty? Would by the creation of a shield against liability based on ownership create a need for the state to regulate the duties of shareholders with managerial authority? Should that affect the scope of the business judgment rule or its "reform".

---

d. American Statutory Exculpation Provisions

Since the decision in *Smith v. Van Gorkom*, many state legislatures enacted provisions which ameliorated the effect of the decision, or otherwise limited the extent of liability of directors to shareholders and the corporation for breaches of the duty of care. The Delaware provision, excerpted below, is fairly typical.

Delaware Code Annotated

TITLE 8. CORPORATIONS
CHAPTER 1. GENERAL CORPORATION LAW
SUBCHAPTER I. FORMATION

§ 102 Contents of certificate of incorporation.

* * *

(b) In addition to the matters required to be set forth in the certificate of incorporation by subsection (a) of this section, the certificate of incorporation may also contain any or all of the following matters:

* * *

(7) A provision eliminating or limiting the personal liability of a director to the corporation or its stockholders for monetary damages for breach of fiduciary duty as a director, provided that such provision shall not eliminate or limit the liability of a director: (i) For any breach of the director's duty of loyalty to the corporation or its stockholders; (ii) for acts or omissions not in good faith or which involve intentional misconduct or a knowing violation of law; (iii) under § 174 of this title; or (iv) for any transaction from which the director derived an improper personal benefit. No such provision shall eliminate or limit the liability of a director for any act or omission occurring prior to the date when such provision becomes effective. All references in this paragraph to a director shall also be deemed to refer (x) to a member of the governing body of a corporation which is not authorized to issue capital stock, and (y) to such other person or persons, if any, who, pursuant to a provision of the certificate of incorporation in ac-

cordance with s 141(a) of this title, exercise or perform any of the powers or duties otherwise conferred or imposed upon the board of directors by this title.

Michael Bradley and Cindy A. Schipani, *The Relevance of the Duty of Care Standard in Corporate Governance*

75 Iowa L. Rev. 1 (1989)

(excerpts pages 3–9; 70–72; some footnotes omitted)

Casual empiricism suggests that contrary to the predictions of its skeptics, the large-scale public corporation has thrived. In 1988 corporate activity in the United States accounted for more than 60 percent of total Gross Domestic Product.[10] Furthermore, there is no evidence to suggest that the corporate form is losing its prominence as the most important mechanism for the organization of production.

Thus, the interesting question is not whether the corporation will survive; rather, the question is how does it survive? What legal, institutional, and economic factors account for the continued existence of this organizational form? And what factors constrain the agency costs of the large-scale public corporation, so that it has become the most important organizational form for the provision of goods and services?

There has always been a certain tension among students of the modern corporation as to whether legal rules or economic forces are more responsible for the corporation's continued existence. There are those like the drafters of the American Law Institute Project on Corporate Governance who argue that the agency costs of the large-scale corporation are solved largely through the constraints imposed by liability rules and judicial review.[11] Citing the traditional arguments for the inefficiencies arising from absentee stockholders and unbridled corporate managers, they propose, inter alia, to strengthen the role of legal rules in constraining corporate managerial behavior.[12] Those who hold this view and stress administrative solutions might be referred to as "institutionalists."

There is an alternative explanation for the survival of the large-scale corporation. This argument, often referred to as the "contractarian" view, recognizes that market forces act to discipline corporate managers and cause the managers to align their inter-

---

10. 68 Survey of Current Business 4, 5 (Feb. 1989).

11. The American Law Institute (ALI) was founded in 1923 for the purpose of remedying the "increasing uncertainty and complexity" of American law through the establishment of a "Restatement of the Law." The ALI has produced numerous restatements of the common law and has joined the Commissioners on Uniform State Laws in drafting the Uniform Commercial Code. See generally American Law Institute, The American Law Institute 50th Anniversary (1973). Their proposals consist of seven tentative drafts and one discussion draft....

12. See Staff of Securities and Exchange Commission, Senate Comm. on Banking, Housing & Urban Affairs, 96th Cong., 2d Sess., Report on Corporate Accountability (Comm. Print 1980); Blumberg, *A Need for Supplementary National Legislation, in* Commentaries on Corporate Structure and Governance: The ALI-ABA Symposiums 1977–1978, at 343 (D. Schwartz ed. 1979); Brudney, *Corporate Governance, Agency Costs, and the Rhetoric of Contract*, 85 Colum. L. Rev. 1403, 1434–43 (1985); Buxbaum, *Corporate Legitimacy, Economic Theory, and Legal Doctrine*, 45 Ohio St. L.J. 515, 542–43 (1984); Cary, *Federalism and Corporate Law: Reflections Upon Delaware*, 83 Yale L.J. 663, 700–03 (1974); Ratner, *Regulating Management Through Corporate Law, in* Commentaries on Corporate Structure and Governance: The ALI-ABA Symposiums 1977–1978, at 138, 139–41 (D. Schwartz ed. 1979); Comment, *Law for Sale: A Study of the Delaware Corporate Law of 1967*, 117 U. Pa. L. Rev. 861, 897–98 (1969).

ests with those of the firm's security holders. These forces stem from competition in the capital, labor, and product markets, as well as competition in the market for corporate control. This view of the large-scale corporation follows from the works of Coase,[13] Manne,[14] Alchian and Demsetz,[15] Jensen and Meckling,[16] Fama,[17] and Fama and Jensen.[18]

The distinction between these two views is the mechanism believed to be primarily responsible for the continued existence of the public corporation. Institutionalists exalt the importance of legal rules and judicial review; contractarians focus on voluntary contracting and the market forces that work to constrain the behavior of corporate managers. The two theories generate drastically different implications for public policy.

According to the legal constraint theory, judicial and legislative intervention is needed to protect the interests of absentee owners. According to this view, corporate managers are accountable to neither their stockholders nor to society in general. Their behavior, therefore, must be held in check by legal rules and judicial review. In contrast, the market constraint theory states that public policy should facilitate contracting among self-interested individuals. Judicial or legislative constraints imposed on this contracting process disadvantage all corporate stakeholders.

The objective of this Article is to gain insight into the relative importance of legal rules on the one hand, and economic forces on the other, in explaining the continued prosperity of the public corporation. While the two schools of thought generate distinctly different predictions for public policy, subjecting these hypotheses to empirical tests is very difficult. It is undoubtedly the case that both liability rules and market forces are important in constraining the behavior of corporate officials. The contractarian and institutionalist views are abstract, polar extremes.

Reality lies somewhere in between. Nevertheless, it is important to examine the relevance of each at the margin. Given a change in environment, which of the two is a better predictor of subsequent events and effects? The effects of a series of events between January 1985 and July 1986 afford a rare opportunity to examine one aspect of this debate.

On January 29, 1985, the Delaware Supreme Court in Smith v. Van Gorkom (the Trans Union Case)[23] reversed a lower court decision and ruled that the directors of Trans Union Corporation had violated their fiduciary duty by accepting a merger proposal after only two hours of deliberation and without review of the relevant documentation. It was irrelevant to the court that the offer was at a substantial premium over market. The court's analysis focused on the board's decisionmaking process as opposed to the outcome. The court found that by making an important decision in such an impulsive fashion, and without ascertaining the intrinsic value of the corporation, the directors violated the duty of care owed the firm's security holders. Eventually, the case was settled out of court for a reported $23,500,000.

---

13. Coase, *The Nature of the Firm*, 4 ECONOMICA 386 (1937).
14. Manne, *Mergers and the Market for Corporate Control*, 73 J. POL. ECON. 110 (1965).
15. Alchian & Demsetz, *Production, Information Costs and Economic Organization*, 62 AM. ECON. REV. 777 (1972).
16. [Jensen & Meckling, *Theory of the Firm: Managerial Behavior, Agency Costs and Ownership Structure*, 3 J. FIN. ECON. 305 (1976)].
17. Fama, *Agency Problems and the Theory of the Firm*, 88 J. POL. ECON. 228 (1980).
18. Fama & Jensen, *Separation of Ownership and Control*, 26 J.L. & ECON. 301 (1983).
23. 488 A.2d 858 (Del. 1985).

Trans Union came as a complete shock to the corporate community. There was widespread concern that the decision had undermined the business judgment rule and had exposed corporate managers to intolerable levels of liability. Many predicted that the decision adversely would affect the ability of corporations to attract qualified individuals to serve on their boards of directors.

In direct response to these concerns, the Delaware Legislature enacted section 102(b)(7), effective July 1, 1986, which allowed firms to "opt" out of the strengthened duty of care standard established by the Trans Union court. In fact the legislation went further. The statute allows Delaware firms to amend their articles of incorporation to eliminate monetary liability of directors to the corporation and its shareholders for breach of the duty of due care. In other words, the statute allows each firm to adopt its own (explicit) business judgment rule.

The two theories outlined above generate contrasting predictions regarding the economic effects of this chain of events. According to the contractarians, the corporation is nothing more than a nexus of contracts made between and among self-interested individuals. The agency costs of the corporate form are held in check through the workings of competitive markets. Within this context, the liberties afforded corporate managers by the business judgment rule represent a mutually advantageous relationship between stockholders and managers. Consequently, Trans Union should have had a detrimental effect on the wealth of all corporate stakeholders, including equity holders. To the extent that the decision constrained the ability of corporate stockholders to contract freely, the agency costs of the corporate form would increase and the value of equity claims would decrease.

Because the Trans Union decision pertains exclusively to firms incorporated in Delaware, the market constraint theory predicts that the decision would reduce the equity values of Delaware corporations relative to firms incorporated elsewhere. This effect, however, may be dampened by the tendency of courts in other jurisdictions to consider Delaware case law in interpreting their own corporate laws. The market may expect that other state courts will follow the Trans Union interpretation of the duty of care standard and the business judgment rule. Thus, Trans Union may not significantly affect the stock prices of Delaware corporations vis-a-vis other corporations. Yet, because of the controversy surrounding the decision, it is also plausible that some jurisdictions would take a wait-and-see attitude before adopting the Trans Union rule. Under this scenario, we expect to see a difference in the returns to Delaware firms relative to firms incorporated elsewhere.

In a similar vein, the market constraint theory predicts that this wealth loss would have been reversed with the passage of section 102(b)(7). To the extent that the law unexpectedly negated the stricter and inefficient fiduciary standard articulated by the Trans Union court, the value of the equity of Delaware firms should have increased in the wake of the legislation.

In contrast, the legal constraint theory predicts just the opposite pattern in the relative value of Delaware firms. The theory holds that stronger liability rules favor (absentee) stockholders. Thus, the Trans Union decision should increase the relative value of Delaware firms and the subsequent legislation should have the opposite effect.

* * *

Our empirical analysis of the market reaction to Delaware's enactment of section 102(b)(7) leads us to conclude that liability rules are important for efficient corporate governance. The significant decrease in the relative value of Delaware firms after enactment of section 102(b)(7), together with the negative market reaction to the announcement that a Delaware firm decided to adopt the provisions of the Delaware statute, support the conclusion that relaxed liability exposure for duty of care violations is detrimental to shareholder wealth. Section 102(b)(7) apparently increased the agency costs of the corporate form by increasing managerial discretion which in turn has led to a decrease in the value of the equity of these firms.

The negative market response to the enactment of section 102(b)(7) is a curious result, because in order to take advantage of the provisions of the statute, shareholders must approve an enabling charter amendment. Of course, this is not the first study to document a negative stock market reaction to the adoption of a charter amendment. Gregg Jarrell and Annette Poulsen find a negative market response to the adoption of certain antitakeover amendments, which they more generally refer to as "shark repellents."[366]

There are (at least) two "explanations" for this apparent failure of the corporate proxy machinery. One could argue either that the observed decrease in market value would have been even greater if the firm's stockholders had not adopted the given charter amendment, or that the decrease in the value of the stock is less than the costs investors would have had to incur to prevent it. On balance, we favor the latter explanation.

It has long been recognized that information is an economic good and as such, individuals will "produce" information up to the point where marginal costs equal marginal (expected) benefits.[367] Under reasonable assumptions, individuals will "produce" a finite amount of information, which is to say they will decide to remain rationally ignorant about some things. If voting with management increases shareholder wealth, "on average," then investors will find it uneconomical to investigate and weigh the merits of each proxy proposal. They will simply follow management's recommendation.

Moreover, modern portfolio theory prescribes that investors hold well-diversified portfolios. As a result, stockholders care little about the fortunes of any one firm. The external monitoring of managerial behavior is left to institutions and individuals with significant holdings of the firm's stock.[369] John Pound argues and presents consistent evidence that institutions and large shareholders may support management-sponsored proxy issues even when they fully recognize that the result will be a decrease in the market price of the firm's stock.[370] Thus, while it seems paradoxical that stockholders would vote for charter amendments that decrease their wealth, with diffuse stockholders, the costs of waging a campaign to defeat a management sponsored proxy is far greater than the slight decrease in market value that we document in this Article.

That managers can use the proxy machinery to extract wealth from their stockholders creates a demand for a regulatory environment that will facilitate such activity. As a result, there will be an incentive for states to satisfy this demand by enacting "promanagement" legislation. The debate concerning the social welfare of competition among states for corporate charters has a long history in corporate law. The arguments on both sides of the so-called "race to the bottom versus race to the top" debate are well documented and well known. The negative economic effects incurred in the wake of Delaware's enactment of section 102(b)(7) are more consistent with William Cary's thesis that competi-

366. [Jarrell & Poulsen, Shark Repellents and Stock Prices: The Effects of Antitakeover Amendments Since 1980, 19 J. Fin. Econ. 127 (1987)] at 127–28.

367. Stigler, *The Economics of Information*, 69 J. Pol. Econ. 213, 216 (1961).

369. See Shleifer & Vishny, *Large Shareholders and Corporate Control*, 94 J. Pol. Econ. 461, 461–63 (1986).

370. Pound, *Takeover Defeats Hurt Stockholders: A Reply to the Kidder Peabody Study*, Midland Corp. Fin. J., Summer 1986, at 33.

tion among states can be characterized as a race to the bottom. We end by noting that since July 1, 1986, the effective date of the Delaware statute, 37 states have enacted similar legislation.

Comments and Questions

1. Michael Bradley and Cindy Schipani suggest that the Delaware legislature's reaction to the decision in Van Gorkom served to increase the value to managers of serving on corporate boards while reducing the value of Delaware corporations to shareholders. One can argue thst provisions such as Del. Code tit. 8, section 102(b)(7) represent a transfer of wealth from shareholders to managers. They suggest that managers will exercise their power to extract wealth from shareholders to press for a regulatory environment that facilitates this extraction of wealth. Do managers pay a price for this power to enlist the state in their extraction of shareholder wealth? Consider in this connection whether the relaxation of liability for breaches of the duty of care has come at a time when the breadth of the duty of loyalty has been broadened, especially in the context of sales of control. Perhaps states have discounted the practical effect of traditional monitoring by shareholders. Can you make an argument that in lieu of traditional monitoring by shareholders, states have moved to monitoring by competitor managers? In thinking about your answer, think about the extent to which manager on manager monitoring is encouraged through contests for control, especially tender offers, in which incumbent managers are limited by their duty of loyalty to the corporation to act solely in the best interests of the corporation. Shareholders participate passively in this form of monitoring. Shareholders are limited to the exercise of their right to 'exit' the corporation—sell their shares. This accords with the current American ideal of shareholder participation in an era of open and active markets for shares (see Justice Scalia's opinion in *Austin*, excerpted in Chapter 4 of these materials).

2. The wave of statutory reform following the *Van Gorkom* opinion has generated additional criticism on other grounds. Consider the following argument:

> Provisions in the certificate of incorporation limiting director liability for negligence present the same fundamental issue as contractual waivers of negligence liability in other contexts.[231] That issue is the need to reconcile the goal of allowing individuals to adjust their relationships to suit themselves by contract with the concern that individuals not lose protection against negligent injury as a result of economic coercion or the failure to fully appreciate the impact of what they are doing.[232] While the basic issue is the same when dealing with different groups of prospective defendants, the resolution need not be. On the contrary, the prospect for waiver by coercion or confusion may depend upon the specific context.[233] When dealing with director liability, this calls for evalua-

---

231. E.g., Fidelity Storage Co. v. Kingsbury, 79 F.2d 705 (D.C.Cir.1935) (bailment); Tunkl v. Regents of the Univ. of California, 383 P.2d 441 (Cal. 1963) (medical care); Wagenblast v. Odessa School Dist., 758 P.2d 968 (Wash. 1988) (participation in interscholastic sports).

232. E.g., Tunkl, 393 P.2d at 445–46 (outlining six factors largely going to the bargaining power of the parties for determining if an exculpatory contract violates public policy); Allright, Inc. v. Schroeder, 551 S.W.2d 745 (Tex.Civ.App. 1977) (not enforcing an exculpatory clause written in fine print on a claim ticket).

233. In fact, courts have traditionally enforced exculpatory clauses for some categories of defendants but not for other categories. E.g., Keeton et al., supra note 57, at 482–83; see also N.Y.

> tion of the processes of shareholder voting and purchasing decisions—a subject about which much has been written.[234] Whatever the appropriate balance here, there is no logical reason it need be the same as when dealing with, say, waivers by those seeking emergency medical care (when the prospects for coercion are of a different order of magnitude). Accordingly, if a legislature decides to allow liability waivers in articles of incorporation, this is not necessarily creating an unjustified differentiation in the treatment of corporate directors. Indeed, to the extent courts generally uphold liability waivers in employment contracts,[235] such legislation actually serves to correlate the treatment of directors with that of other agents.
>
> Unfortunately, similar kind remarks cannot be made about those statutory provisions which automatically limit director liability for all corporations in a jurisdiction. Such provisions are symptomatic of the ad hoc approach to tort law reform under which various groups of prospective defendants—doctors, directors or whoever—lobby the legislature for special treatment. If, as suggested above, the possible problems created by director liability for ordinary negligence parallel the problems of negligence liability for many other groups, any legislative action should deal with the issues across the board.

Franklin A. Gevurtz, *The Business Judgment Rule: Meaningless Verbiage or Misguided Notion?*, 67 S. Cal. L. Rev. 287, 335–336 (1994). Do you agree with Professor Gevurtz's argument? Are issues relating to the relations between the primary corporate actors—directors, shareholders and officers—unique and worthy of ad hoc regulation?

3. Can you think of reasons that share values would have dropped on the adoption of director exculpatory amendments to a corporation's articles of incorporation other than disapproval of such amendments? Does your answer depend on the composition of the shareholder population: for example, would disapproval reflected in lower stock prices be more likely in corporations where ownership is largely dispersed or where there are one or more shareholders, whether natural persons or institutional investors with large blocks of stocks?

4. Delaware courts have developed a number of rules relating to the pleading and proof of applicability of the protection of exculpation provisions. These rules were nicely summarized in O'Reilly v. Transworld Healthcare, Inc., 745 A 2d 902 (Del. Ch. 1999):

> B. The Exculpation Clause in HMI's Certificate of Incorporation Tracking 8 Del.C. Section 102(b)(7)
>
> The HMI directors argue that the claims against them must be dismissed because they are immunized from personal liability by HMI's Certificate of Incorporation, which tracks the provisions of 8 *Del.C.* § 102(b)(7). Article XI of HMI's Certificate of Incorporation, as amended on March 27, 1992, provides:
>
>> A director of the Corporation shall not be personally liable to the Corporation or its stockholders for monetary damages for breach of fiduciary duty as a directors [sic], except for liability (i) for any breach of

---

Gen.Oblig. Law §§ 5-321 to 5-326 (McKinney 1992) (listing activities in which exculpatory clauses are contrary to public policy).

234. For a sampling of this literature see Symposium, *Contractual Freedom in Corporate Law*, 89 Colum.L.Rev. 1395 (1989).

235. E.g., Griffiths v. Henry Broderick, Inc., 182 P.2d 18 (Wash. 1947); Restatement (Second) of Agency § 379 cmts. a–d (1984).

> the director's duty of loyalty to the Corporation or its stockholders, (ii) for acts or omissions not in good faith or which involve intentional misconduct or a knowing violation of law, (iii) under Section 174 of the Delaware Corporation Law, as the same exists or hereafter may be amended, or (iv) for any transaction from which the directors derived an improper personal benefit.

(the "Exculpation Provision").

It is settled that 8 *Del.C.* § 102(b)(7) ("Section 102(b)(7)") and provisions tracking its language exculpate directors from liability where the factual basis for a claim for breach of fiduciary duty against the directors solely implicates a violation of the duty of care made in good faith.[8] Most recently in *Emerald Partners v. Berlin,* the Supreme Court said,

> the shield from liability provided by a certificate of incorporation provision adopted pursuant to 8 *Del.C.* § 102(b)(7) is in the nature of an affirmative defense. Defendants seeking exculpation under such a provision will normally bear the burden of establishing each of its elements. Here, the Court of Chancery incorrectly ruled that [plaintiff] was required to establish at *trial* that the individual defendants acted in bad faith or in breach of their duty of loyalty. To the contrary, the burden of demonstrating good faith, however slight it might be in given circumstances, is upon the party seeking the protection of the statute. Nonetheless, where the factual basis for a claim *solely* implicates a violation of the duty of care, this Court has indicated that the protections of such a charter provision may properly be invoked and applied.[9]

With the benefit of the Supreme Court's guidance, I now conclude that claims against directors can be dismissed pursuant to certificate of incorporation provisions tracking Section 102(b)(7) only where the complaint fails to plead sufficiently that the directors' conduct falls into at least one of the exceptions under which the directors are not afforded the provisions' protection.[10] Both Counts I and II of O'Reilly's Complaint meet this standard.

O'Reilly's Complaint sufficiently pleads that the directors' alleged disclosure violations were a violation of the duty of loyalty. While the HMI directors seem to contend that all disclosure claims involve only breaches of the fiduciary duty of care, that contention is wrong. Directors' disclosure obligations arise out of both the fiduciary duty of care and loyalty."[11] A claim for breach of the fiduciary duty of disclosure implicates only the duty of care when the factual basis for the al-

---

8. *See* Emerald Partners v. Berlin, Del. Supr., *726 A.2d 1215, 1224 (1999); See also* Frank v. Arnelle, *1998 Del. Ch. LEXIS 176,* *37–39, Del. Ch., C.A. No. 15642, Chandler, C. (Sept. 16, 1998).

9. *Emerald Partners, 726 A.2d at 1223–24* (citations omitted).

10. I note that this pleading standard comports with the Supreme Court's statement in Arnold v. Society for Savings Bancorp., Del. Supr., *650 A.2d 1270, 1287 (1994),* that "claims alleging disclosure violations that do not otherwise fall within any exception [of Section 102(b)(7)] are protected by Section 102(b)(7) and any certificate of incorporation provision ... adopted pursuant thereto."

11. *See* Malone v. Brincat, *Del. Supr., 722 A.2d 5, 11 (1998)* ("The duty of directors to observe proper disclosure requirements derives from the combination of the fiduciary duties of care, loyalty and good faith.") (citations omitted); *See also Cinerama Inc. v. Technicolor, Inc., Del. Supr., 663 A.2d 1156, 1163 (1995)* ("A combination of the fiduciary duties of care and loyalty gives rise to the requirement that 'a director disclose to shareholders all material facts bearing upon a merger vote....'").

leged violation suggests that the violation was made as a result of a good faith, but nevertheless, erroneous judgment about the proper scope or content of the required disclosure.[12] However, where a complaint alleges or pleads facts sufficient to support the inference that the disclosure violation was made in bad faith, knowingly or intentionally, the alleged violation implicates the duty of loyalty.[13]

The Complaint in this instance alleges that the HMI directors "breached their fiduciary duty of disclosure to plaintiffs in a knowing, intentional and bad faith manner...." While the HMI directors argue that O'Reilly's allegation of their bad faith, knowledge and intent is a conclusory allegation on which I should not rely in determining whether O'Reilly's disclosure claims against the HMI directors should be dismissed pursuant to the Exculpation Provision, I disagree with their characterization of the allegations. Given the allegations in the Complaint of self-interest among two of HMI's four board members and the reasonable inference that the pleaded disclosure allegations were part of a plan to deceive HMI's stockholders in order to consummate the Merger and fulfill the two HMI directors' and Transworld's self-interests, I cannot conclude at this stage of the proceedings that O'Reilly's allegations of bad faith, knowledge and intent are merely conclusory. O'Reilly, therefore, has sufficiently pleaded that the HMI directors' alleged disclosure violations implicated the duty of loyalty. The Exculpation Provision, now known to be an affirmative defense, does not act as a bar as a matter of law.

As already discussed in the preceding paragraph, the Complaint sufficiently pleads that the HMI directors knowingly, intentionally and in bad faith failed to meet their disclosure obligations. Aside from supporting the conclusion that O'Reilly's disclosure claim implicates the duty of loyalty, this pleading also calls into play the Exculpation Provision's second exception for "acts or omissions not in good faith or which involve intentional misconduct or a knowing violation of law." Furthermore, O'Reilly's allegations of self-interest among two of HMI's directors further implicates the Exculpation Provision's fourth exception. Count I of O'Reilly's Complaint, therefore, meets the pleading requirements to survive a motion to dismiss the disclosure claims against the HMI directors despite the looming spectre of the Exculpation Provision.

Count II of the Complaint sets forth an entire fairness claim. As explained later in this opinion,[14] O'Reilly has sufficiently pleaded that two of HMI's four board members were self-interested, and that the Merger was the result of an unfair process and unfair price. This claim against HMI's directors, therefore, impli-

---

12. *See* Zirn v. VLI Corp., Del. Supr., *681 A.2d 1050, 1061–62 (1996)* ("We agree with the Defendants and hold that the VLI directors are shielded from liability by 8 *Del.C.* § 102(b)(7) and the amendment to VLI's Certificate of Incorporation giving effect to that statutory provision. The record reveals that any misstatements or omissions that occurred were made in good faith. The VLI directors lacked any pecuniary motive to mislead the VLI stockholders intentionally and no other plausible motive for deceiving the stockholders has been advanced. A good faith erroneous judgement as to the proper scope or content of required disclosure implicates the duty of care rather than the duty of loyalty. Arnold I, *650 A.2d at 1287–1288 & n.36*. Thus, the disclosure violations at issue here fall within the ambit of the protection of section 102(b)(7).")

13. *See id.*

14. *See* 1999 Del. Ch. LEXIS *185*, *72.

> cates the duty of loyalty, and the Exculpation Provision cannot act as a bar as a matter of law. Although not raised by the Defendants, within O'Reilly's allegation that the Merger price resulted from an unfair process is an allegation that the HMI directors breached their duty of care when approving the Merger price. Unlike the disclosure claims, this allegation is not accompanied by an express allegation that the breach was made in bad faith, knowingly or intentionally. Again, however, it is reasonable to infer from the two HMI directors' self-interest and Transworld's self-interest and alleged threats, that these alleged violations of the duty of care were made to consummate the Merger and to fulfill their respective self-interests. As a result, these allegations of the directors' breach of their duty of care fall within the Exculpation Provision's second and fourth exceptions, and therefore, the Exculpation Provision cannot at this stage in the proceedings be a basis for dismissing that claim against the HMI directors.

O'Reilly V. Transworld Healthcare, Inc., 745 A.2d 902, 914–916 (Del. Ch. 1999) [Ed: other portions of this case are reproduced below in Part D—Duty of Disclosure]. Do you think that the effect of these rules is to narrow or broaden the scope of the protection sought to be afforded under the Delaware exculpatory provision? Do the rules create traps for the unwary drafter of exculpatory language for insertion in the articles of incorporation?

---

e. Other Common Law Approaches

In re Equitable Fire Insurance Co., Ltd.

[1925] Ch. 407
(Chancery Division)
(excerpt pages 424–430; footnotes omitted)

May 22. Romer, J. On June 27, 1916, Gerrard Lee Bevan became a director of the City Equitable Fire Insurance Company, Ltd. The company at that time was carrying on successfully the business of reinsurance of fire and marine risks, and was in a sound financial condition. On February 14, 1922 an order was made for the winding up of the company by the Court. A searching investigation of the affairs of the company was then made, and this investigation disclosed a shortage in the funds of which the company should have been possessed of over 1,200,000*l.* This deplorable state of affairs was in no way due to the company's trading operations as a reinsurance company. From the year 1916 onwards to February 28, 1921, which is the date of the copany's last published balance sheet, there was a steady and most remarkable increase in the premium income of the company, due principally to the fact that it had been able to secure a large part of the business of the Munich Reinsurance Company, who, before of the outbreak of the war, had done most of the reinsurance business in this country. For the year ending February, 1916, the company's premium income from all classes of insurance was 363,000*l.* For the year ending February, 1919, the premium income on fire and general account was 613,483*l.*, and on marine account was 1,351,000*l.* For the year ending February, 1920, the corresponding figures were 1,189,759*l.* and 1,422,471*l.*, and for the year ending February, 1921, they were 2,071,515*l.*, and 1,469,197*l.* In each of the years 1919, 1920 and 1921 there was a large and progressive trading profit. The collapse of the company was not, therefore, due to its reinsurance business. It was entirely due to the following causes. Various industrial investments of the company, of which the net cost to the company had been 701,739*l.*, have realized or are estimated to realize 202,373*l.*, representing a loss of close upon 500,000*l.* Over 445,000*l.* of the company's funds had been applied in acquiring an interest in certain lands in Brazil, and this interest is estimated at the present time to be worth about 100,000*l.* only. No less a sum than 110,000*l.* had found its way into the hands of the company's manager in circumstances to be detailed hereafter, and none of that money is recoverable. A sum of 385,000*l.* odd was due from Ellis & Co., the company's brokers of which firm Bevan was the senior partner. And against this indebtedness the company held collateral security that has realized under 31,000*l.* In respect of the balance, it is estimated that only about 14,000*l.* will ultimately be received as dividend in the bankruptcy of that firm. Beavan himself had misappropriated other moneys of the company amounting to nearly 7,000*l.*, and some 9,000*l.* had been lent by Bevan or Ellis & Co. to a company known as Saskatoon Grain Co. without any authority whatever. Little, if anything, will ever be recovered in respect of these two sums. Nearly the whole of these enormous losses were brought about through Bevan's instrumentality, and a large part of them by his deliberate fraud. For that fraud he had been tried, and convicted, and is now suffering the just penalty. But the question not unnaturally arises as to whether, during the period covered by Bevan's nefarious activities, the other directors and the auditors of the company were properly discharging the duties they owed to the company's shareholders. The Official Receiver, as the liquidator of the company, alleges that they were not. He has accordingly included them, or such of them as are still living, as respondents to the summons which he issued against Bevan under s. 215 of the Company's Act; and whilst admitting, and rightly admitting, that they have acted honestly throughout, he claims that they have been guilty of such negligence as to render themselves liable to the company in damages. Whether they are, or are not so liable, is the question that I have to determine. It will be convenient to consider the case of the directors and the case of the auditors separately, and I propose to begin with the directors. But before investigating the facts it will be convenient to consider the law applicable to the case.

It has sometimes been said that directors are trustees. If this means no more than that directors in the performance of their duties stand in a fiduciary relationship to the company the statement is true enough. But if the statement is meant to be an indication by way of analogy of what those duties are, it appears to me to be wholly misleading. I can see but little resemblance between the duties of a director and the duties of a trustee of a will or of a marriage settlement. It is indeed impossible to describe the duty of directors in general terms, whether by way of analogy or otherwise. The position of a director of a company carrying on a small retail business is very different from that of a director of a railway company. The duties of a bank director may differ widely from those of an insurance director, and the duties of a director of one insurance company may differ from those of a director of another. In one company, for instance, matters may normally be attended to by the manager or other members of the staff that in another company are attended to by the directors themselves. The larger the business carried on by the company the more numerous, and the more important, the matters that must of necessity be left to the managers, the accountants and the rest of the staff. The manner in which the work of the company is to be distributed between the board of directors and the staff is in truth a business matter to be decided on business lines. To use the words of Lord Macnaghten in Dovey v. Cory: "I do not think it desirable for any tribunal to do that which Parliament has abstained from doing—that is, to formulate precise rules for the guidance or embarrassment of businessmen in the conduct of business affairs. There never has been, and I think there never will be, much difficulty in dealing with any particular case on its own facts and circumstances; and, speaking for myself, I rather doubt the wisdom of attempting to do more ."

In order, therefore, to ascertain the duties that a person appointed to the board of an established company undertakes to perform, it is necessary to consider not only the nature of the company's business, but also the manner in which the work of the company is in fact distributed between the directors and the other officials of the company, provided always that this distribution is a reasonable one in the circumstances, and is not inconsistent with any express provisions of the articles of association. In discharging the duties of his position thus ascertained a director must, of course, act honestly; but he must also exercise some degree of both skill and diligence. To the question of what is the particular degree of skill and diligence required of him, the authorities do not, I think, give any very clear answer. It has been laid down that so long as a director acts honestly he cannot be made responsible in damages unless guilty of gross or culpable negligence in a business sense. But as pointed out by Neville J. in In re Brazilian Rubber Plantations and Estates, Ld., one cannot say whether a man has been guilty of negligence, gross or otherwise, unless one can determine what is the extent of the duty which he is alleged to have neglected. For myself, I confess to feeling some difficulty in understanding the difference between negligence and gross negligence except insofar as the expressions are used for the purpose of drawing a distinction between the duty that is owed in one case and the duty that is owed in another. If two men owe the same duty to a third person, and neglect to perform that duty, they are both guilty of negligence, and it is not altogether easy to understand how one can be guilty of gross negligence and the other of negligence only. But if it be said of two men one is only liable to a third person for gross negligence, and the other is liable for mere negligence, this, I think, means no more than that the duties of the two men are different. The one owes a duty to take a greater degree of care than does the other.... If, therefore, a director is only liable for gross or culpable negligence, this means that he does not owe a duty to his company, to take all possible care. It is some degree of care less than that. The care that he is bound to take has been described by Neville J. in the case referred to above as "reasonable care" to be measured by the care an ordinary man might be expected to take in the circumstances on his own behalf. In saying this Neville J. was only following what was laid down in Overend Gurney Co. v. Gibb as being the proper test to apply, namely: whether or not the directors exceeded the powers entrusted to them, or whether if they did not so exceed their powers they were cognizant of circumstances of such a character, so plain, so manifest, and so simple of appreciation, that no men with any ordinary degree of prudence, acting on their own behalf, would have entered into such a transaction as they entered into?"

There are, in addition, one or two other general propositions that seem to be warranted by the reported cases: (1) A director need not exhibit in the performance of his duties a greater degree of skill than may reasonably be expected from a person of his knowledge and experience. A director of a life insurance company, for instance, does not guarantee that he has the skill of an actuary or of a physician. In the words of Lindley M.R.: "If directors act within their powers, if they act with such care as is reasonably to be expected from them, having regard to their knowledge and experience, and if they act honestly for the benefit of the company they represent, they discharge both their equitable as well as their legal duty to the company.".... It is perhaps only another way of stating the same proposition to say that directors are not liable for mere errors of judgment. A director is not bound to give continuous attention to the affairs of his company. His duties are of an intermittent nature to be performed at periodical board meetings, and at meetings of any committee of the board upon which he happens tobe placed. He is not, however, bound to attend all such meetings though he ought to attend whenever, in the circumstances, he is reasonably able to do so. In respect of all duties that, having regard to the exigencies of business, and the articles of association, may properly be left to some other official, a director is, in the absence of grounds for suspicion, justified in trusting that official to perform such duties honestly. In the judgment of the Court of Appeal in In re National Bank of Wales, Ld..., the following passage occurs in relation to a director who had been deceived by the manager, and managing director, as to matters within their own particular sphere of activities: "Was it his duty to test the accuracy or completeness of what hewas told by the general manager and the managing director? This is a question on which opinions may differ, but we are not prepared to say that he failed in his legal duty. Business cannot be carried on upon principles of distrust. Men is responsible positions must be trusted by those above them, as well as by those below them, until there is reason to distrust them. We agree that care and prudence do not involve distrust; but for a director acting honestly himself to be held legally liable for negligence, in trusting the officers under him not to conceal from him what they ought to report to him, appears to us to be laying too heavy a burden on honest businessmen." That case went to the House of Lords... Lord Davey, in the course of his speech to the House, made the following observations: "I think the respondent was bound to give his attention to and exercise his judgment as a man of business on the matters which were bound to be brought before the board at the meetings which he attended, and it is not proved that he did not do so. But I think he was entitled to rely upon the judgment, information and advice, of the chairman and general manager, as to whose integrity, skill and competence he had no reason for suspicion. I agree with what was said by Sir George Jessel in Hallmark's Case...and by Chitty J. in In re Denham & Co...., that directors are not bound to examine entries in the company's books. It was the duty of the general manager and (possibly) of the chairman to go carefully through the returns from the branches, and to bring before the board any matter requiring their consideration; but the respondent was not, in my opinion, guilty of negligence in not examining them for himself, notwithstanding that they were laid on the table of the board for reference."

These are the general principles that I shall endeavor to apply in considering the question whether the directors of this company ave been guilty of negligence.

Comments and Question

1. The English standard imposes a subjective standard for breaches of a duty of care. To what extent are the standards applicable to an inside director different from that imposed on an outside director? Consider the following explanation of an Australian court:

> The standard of reasonableness to be applied is that of a director of reasonable competence, exercising the care and diligence that a reasonable person might be expected to take in the same circumstances, acting on his or her own behalf.... The director is not expected to have any particular expertise or qualifications;.....But the director is expected to be capable of understanding the company's affairs, to the extent of reaching a reasonably informed opinion of its financial capacity.... So in this case, the level of competence and care of a director to be assumed for the purposes of this provision is that appropriate to the complexity of [the company's] affairs, and having regard to the constitution and organisation of that company....

> The degree of involvement assumed is that of a non-executive director.....I accept that the standard must be applied with due regard to the exigencies of business, although it should not be assumed that the reasonable director has other commitments which prevent due attention being given to the affairs of the company in question. I accept also that undue effect should not be to the wisdom of hindsight.

Standard Chartered Bank of Australia Ltd. v. Antico and Others, 131 A.L.R. 1 (!995) (Supreme Court of New South Wales).

3. Convergence, and the utility of the comparative method with respect to the duty of care are nicely illustrated in Daniels v. Anderson (1995) 13 ACLC 614, 16 ACSR 607 (Supreme Court New South Wales), in which the court, after a long discussion of the nature and scope of the duty of care citing English and American cases, derived a standard for the duty of care. The *Daniels* court determined that:

> A person who accepts the office of director of a particular company undertakes the responsibility of ensuring that he or she understands the nature of the duty a director is called upon to perform. That duty will vary according to the size and business of the particular company and the experience or skills that the director held himself or herself out to have in support of appointment to the office. None of this is novel. It turns upon the natural expectations and reliance placed by shareholders on the experience and skill of a particular director. The duty is a common law duty to take reasonable care owed severally by persons who are fiduciary agents bound not to exercise the powers conferred upon them for private purpose or for any purpose foreign to the power and placed... at the apex of the structure of direction and management. The duty includes that of acting collectively to manage the company. Breach of the duty will found an action for negligence at the suit of the company.

Id., 13 ACLC at 667–68.

2. Breaches of the duty of care are classified as a wrong done to the company. As a result, only the company generally has the sole right to seek recovery against directors for any loss it may have suffered. "[W]here the alleged wrong is a transaction which might be made binding on the company or association and on all its members by a simple majority of the members, no individual member of the company is allowed to maintain an action in respect of that matter for the simple reason that, if a mere majority of the members of the company or association is in favour of what has been done, then *cadit quaestio*." Edwards v. Halliwell [1950] 2 All ER 1064, 1066 (per Jenkins, LJ).

3. A derivative action, however, may be asserted by shareholders under very limited circumstances. Generally shareholders may bring actions in the name of the company only with respect to actions that cannot be ratified by the company or its shareholders. Generally, such acts, commonly known in England as 'frauds on the minority,' include conduct generally understood to constitute breaches of the duty of loyalty in the United States. "Apart from the benefit to themselves at the company's expense, the essence of the matter seems to be an abuse or misuse of power. 'Fraud' in the phrase 'fraud on a minority' seems to be being used as comprising not only fraud at common law but also fraud in the wider equitable sense of that term, as in the equitable concept of a fraud on a power." Estmanco (Kilner House) Ltd. v. Greater London Council [1982] All ER 437, 445 (per Sir R. Megarry) (abuse or misuse of power). Thus, mere negligence is generally held to be an insufficient ground for bringing an action within

the 'fraud on the minority' exception. Pavlides v. Jenson [1956] 2 All ER 518 (sale of property for less than market value can be ratified). However, where the negligence results in profit to one or mor of the corporate managers, directors, or shareholders, then even negligence may be sufficient to assert a derivative action on grounds of 'fraud on the minority.' Daniels v. Daniels [1978] 2 All ER 89 (sale of property to a director for substantially less than market value). How would Van Gorkom have been decided under principles of English law?

4. Section 459 of the Companies Act of 1985 may provide an additional avenue for shareholder action. Section 459 provides, in subpart (1), that a member of a company may petition a court for an order "on the ground that the company's affairs are being or have been conducted in a manner which is unfairly prejudicial to the interests of its members generally or some part of its members (including at least himself) or that any actual or proposed act or omission of the company (including an act or omission on its behalf) is or would be prejudicial." Where negligence is substantial enough, a court may entertain a petition based on unfairly prejudicial conduct. This statutory provision has proven to be useful in the context of small private companies and will be treated in more detail in Chapter 11.

2. Civil Law Approaches

a. The Approach in Germany

The European approaches can be divided into three broad categories. The first is that of Common Law countries, discussed above. The second is that of the civil law countries, principally France and Germany. The last are those of the former Socialist countries of Eastern Europe.

Enno W. Ercklentz, Jr., 1 Modern German Corporate Law

(1979)
(excerpts pages 161–164; 172–173; 180–182; 189; 209–212, 222–224; some footnotes omitted)

Liability of Members of Board of Overseers [AG]

[S]ervice on the Board of Overseers of an AG is not without potential liability. Members of this body who fail to discharge their duties with the requisite standard of care will be liable to the AG for any loss or damage suffered by the AG arising out of such failure.

The standard of care which a member of the Board of Overseers is expected to exercise is generally the same as the standard of care required of a member of the management board, except that the different functions of each body is taken into account in applying this standard.[40] Thus, while a member of the management board must exercise the care of a normally conscientious manager, the member of the Board of Overseers is bound to exercise the care of a normally conscientious Overseer. This represents an ob-

40. Sections 116 and 93, AktG.

vious distinction, since the duties of a member of the management board quite clearly differ from those of a member of the Board of Overseers.

While loss or damage may be incurred by an AG as a result of the failure of members of the Board of Overseers to properly discharge their obligations in a wide range of circumstances, the law specifically enumerates a number of actions which will result in liability on the part of members of this body if a proper discharge of their duties would have been able to prevent the action form taking place.[41] All of the actions enumerated in this manner are such as would tend to impair the stated capital or the credit of the AG and include, for instance, the unlawful payment of interest or dividends, the unlawful reimbursement of capital contributions of shareholders, the unlawful distribution of assets of the AG, the unlawful grant of credit, as well as the unlawful payment of compensation to members of the Board of Overseers.

The standard of care expected of members of the Board of Overseers, in addition to contemplating close attention to the operations of the AG, also requires affirmative action on their part to prevent possible loss or damage to the AG under the circumstances. Should a member of the Board of Overseers obtain information to the effect that action of the kind enumerated in the law may be taken, it would be the duty of the member to take all reasonable steps to cause the full Board of Overseers to take appropriate preventive steps. Such steps might consist of the removal of the management board from office and may even extend to such measures as the obtaining of an injunction or other form of legal redress. If, after obtaining such information, the member of the Board of Overseers takes all steps reasonably within his power in an attempt to avert the illegal action, such member will be regarded as having discharged his obligation and would be absolved from any liability even if the Board of Overseers subsequently fails to act and loss is actually incurred by the AG.

Members of the Board of Overseers will also be absolved of liability, at least toward the AG, if the loss ro damage in question arises out of an action which is based upon a lawful resolution of the meeting of stockholders.[42] Thus, a resolution of the meeting of stockholders authorizing, for example, a dividend or payment contrary to law will not shield members of the Board of Overseers against possible liability. In such an instance, the members of the Board of Overseers would be required to take whatever steps are in their power to prevent effectuation of the prohibited act.

In general, any liability of members of the Board of Overseers can be asserted only by the AG and cannot be asserted either by stockholders or by third parties. However, such liability may also be asserted by creditors of the AG under some circumstances if the AG is unable to satisfy the claims of creditors.[43] The right of creditors to assert a possible liability of members of the Board of Overseers is thus only a conditional right. Given the existence of such condition, creditors will be able, in the case of loss or damage arising out of the aforementioned actions enumerated in the statute, to assert claims against members of the Board of Overseers where merely ordinary neglect of duty is involved. In all other cases, however, assertion of liability against members of the Board of Overseers by creditors is limited to circumstances involving gross neglect of duty.

In an action against members of the Board of Overseers seeking to impose liability for loss or damage arising out of their alleged failure to meet the required standard of

41. Section 93(3), AktG.
42. Section 93(4), AktG.
43. Section 93(5), AktG.

care in the discharge of their duties, whether such action is brought by the AG or by its creditors, the burden of proof is reversed.[44] Both the AG and the creditors need merely show that the AG has suffered loss or damage by reason of action or inaction on the part of the members of the Board of Overseers, whereupon the burden of affirmatively demonstrating that the required standard of care has been satisfied shifts to the members of the board of Overseers. Accordingly, depending on the circumstances and the nature of the plaintiff, the defendant members of the Board of Overseers will have to demonstrate that they did not either ordinarily or grossly neglect their duties to the AG. Thus, they will be absolved of liability toward creditors, for instance, where they could show that they were not culpable or ordinary neglect of their duties, in the case of loss arising out of the actions enumerated in the statute, or where they could show that they did not grossly neglect their duties in the case of loss arising out of other circumstances.

Claims against members of the Board of Overseers based on these provisions are subject to a statute of limitations of five years.[45] On the other hand, the right to contribution existing among jointly and severally liable members of the Board of Overseers is subject to a statute of limitations of thirty years.[46]

* * *

Liability of Members of Board of Overseers [Voluntary Board; GmbH]

Although the extent of potential liability of members of a Board fo Overseers is not as great in the case of the GmbH as it is in the case of the AG, service on a voluntary Board of Overseers of a GmbH also entails the risk of some possible liability. However, the member of a voluntary board of Overseers will not be subject to any liability to the creditors of the GmbH as in the case of the members of the Board of Overseers of an AG.

Members of a voluntary Board of Overseers of a GmbH who fail to discharge their duties with the requisite standard of care will be liable to the GmbH for loss or damage suffered by ut arising out of such failure.[63] As in the case of an AG, however, a distinction is drawn between the function of the member of the Board of Overseers and the function of the managing director or directors. While the member of the Board of Overseers is bound to exercise the care of a normally conscientious Overseer, he is not expected to observe the care required of a managing director since the functions of a managing director and an Overseers are of a different nature.

Liability toward the GmbH for loss or damage arising out of certain corporate actions which tend to impair its stated capital rests primarily upon the managing director or directors.[64] Even though not specifically made liable therefor by the statute as in the case of the AG, members of a voluntary Board of Overseers may nevertheless become liable for any such loss toward the GmbH if they could have prevented the action giving rise to the loss. As indicated above, however, they will not become liable toward creditors of the GmbH.

Notwithstanding this more limited liability of the member of a voluntary Board of Overseers, the normal burden of proof remains reversed wherever liability is

44. Section 93(2), AktG.
45. Section 93(6), AktG.
46. [von Godin & Wilhelmi, "Kommentar zum Aktiengesetz vom 6. September 1965" (4th ed., 1971)]Section 93, Comment 31, p. 507/8; RG 159, 86.
63. Section 52, GmbHG; Sections 116 and 93, AktG.
64. Section 31(6) GmbHG.

sought to be imposed upon a member for loss or damage arising out of an allegesd failure to meet the requisite standard of care.[65] Accordingly, were a claim for such liability is made, it is up to the member of the Board of Overseers to affirmatively demonstrate that he has satisfied the standard of care required under the circumstances.

Claims against members of the Board of Overseers based on these provisions are subject to a statute of limitations of five years.[66]

* * *

Liability of Members of Board of Overseers [Mandatory Board; GmbH]

The potential liability of a member of a Board of Overseers constituted under the 1952 Codetermination Law is almost coextensive with that of a member of the Board of Overseers of an AG, because the 1952 Codetermination Law has imposed upon the Board of Overseers of a GmbH the standards of liability of the stock corporation law.[80]

Accordingly, members of such a Board of Overseers who fail to discharge their duties with the requisite standard of care will be liable to the GmbH and, under some circumstances, to the creditors of the GmbH as well, for any loss or damage suffered by the GmbH arising out of such failure. The standard of care to be exercised by a member of this body is the care of a normally conscientious Overseer.

Although that provision of the stock corporation law imposing liability in the case of certain specifically enumerated actions which would tend to impair the stated capital or the credit of the corporate entity applied to a Board of Overseers created under the 1952 Codetermination Law, the actions covered by such provision cannot directly be applied to the GmbH, since the measures involved constitute violations of the stock corporation law rather than of the GmbH law. However, similar provisions of the GmbH law would be read into this provision by analogy ion order to satisfy the intent of the law.

The right of creditors of a GmbH to assert liability against members of the Board of Overseers based on loss or damage to the GmbH arising out of the failure of the members to properly discharge their obligations is, as in the case of the AG, only a conditional right, since it is conditioned on the inability of the GmbH to satisfy the claims fo creditors directly.[81] Moreover, except in the case of violations of the GmbH law similar to those enumerated in the stock corporation law, creditors would also be unable to assert any liability against members of the Board of Overseers unless a gross violation of duties were involved. A simple violation of the duties of a member would thus support liability toward creditors only where the violation involved an unlawful impairment of the stated capital of the GmbH.

As in the case of the AG, the normal burden of proof is reversed where liability is sought to be imposed upon members of a Board of Overseers of a GmbH established under the 1952 Codetermination Law.[82] The GmbH or its creditors need merely establish that the GmbH has suffered loss or damage by reason of an alleged action or inaction on the part of the members of the Board of Overseers. The latter would then be required to affirmatively demonstrate that they had met the required standard of care under the circumstances.

---

65. Section 52, GmbHG; Section 93(2), AktG.
66. Section 31(5), GmbHG.
80. Section 77(1), 1952 Codetermination Law; Section 116 AktG.
81. Section 77(1), 1952 Codetermination Law; Sections 116 and 93(5), AktG.
82. Section 77(1), 1952 Codetermination Law; Section 116 and 93(2), AktG.

Claims against members of the Board of Overseers based on these provisions are subject to a statute of limitations of five years.[83]

* * *

As in the case of the Board of Overseers formed under the 1951 Codetermination Law and Supplementary Codetermination Law, the potential liability of members of a Board of Overseers of GmbH under the 1976 Codetermination Law is coextensive with the liability of members of the Board of Overseers of an AG.[98]

* * *

Liability of Members of Management Board [AG]

In view of the wide range of authority and discretion exercised by the management board, the law imposes a fairly strict standard of liability upon members of this organ. In principle, the members of the management board are liable to the AG, and in some cases to the creditors of the AG, for any loss or damage arising out of a breach of their duty toward the AG.[29] For this purpose, the duty of members of the management board is to manage the AG with the care of an ordinary and conscientious manager.

In any action against members of the management board seeking the imposition of liability upon a member, the normal burden of proof is reversed. Accordingly, where the AG establishes that a loss has been sustained because of action or inaction on the part of the management board, the members of the management board must then affirmatively show that they have met the necessary standard of care in connection with the transaction at issue.[30]

The members of the management board are not, of course, insurers of the financial success of the AG and liability will attach to them only where a loss has been sustained by the AG either as a result of deliberate injury to the AG or by negligence on the part of members of the management board. In this respect, the statute enumerates various actions which may result in liability on the part of the management board.[31] Such actions are of a kind tending to impair the stated capital of the AG and include such actions as the unlawful repayment of subscriptions to stockholders, the unlawful payment of dividends, the unlawful acquisition by the AG of its own capital stock, the unlawful distribution of corporate assets, the unlawful issuance of shares before the par value thereof has been paid in, as well as some other actions of similar nature.

As has been indicated above, the liability of members of the management board is toward the AG in most cases. In some cases, nevertheless, creditors of the AG may also directly assert liability against the members of the management board.[32] The assertion of any such claim by creditors, however, is subject to two conditions. The primary condition to such assertion is that the creditors are unable to obtain satisfaction of their claims from the AG itself. Thus, where the AG is able to meet its obligations toward creditors, the latter would have no right to assert any claims against the management board. A second condition to the liability of the management board toward creditors arises out of one or more of

83. Section 77(1), 1952 Codetermination Law; Sections 116 and 93(6), AktG.
98. Section 116 and 93, AktG.
29. Section 93, AktG ["Aktiengesetz"].
30. Section 93(2), AktG.
31. Section 93(3), AktG.
32. Section 93(5), AktG.

the aforementioned actions specifically enumerated in the statute, the management board must have been guilty of a gross breach of duty toward the AG. Therefore, unless one of these specifically enumerated actions is involved, the management board will not be liable to creditors, even under the circumstances in which the AG is unable to satisfy their claims, if no more than a simple breach of its duties toward the AG was involved.

Where actions giving rise to a claim of liability against members of the management board was effected on the basis of lawful action by the meeting of stockholders, the members of the management board will be relieved of liability toward the AG.[33] Such action by the meeting of stockholders does not, however, relieve the members of the management board from potential liability towards creditors. In view of the fact that the meeting of stockholders cannot exercise management prerogatives, this insulation of the management board from liability toward the AG by reason of action by the meeting of the stockholders occurs only where the management board has exercised its right to request action on the part of the meeting of stockholders with respect to a particular transaction. It is, of course, obvious that, in order to enjoy relief from liability on the basis of action of the meeting of stockholders, the management board must effect the particular transaction within the framework of the resolution adopted by the stockholders. By way of contrast, it might be noted that approval of a transaction by the Board of Overseers, which approval may be required pursuant to the Articles or pursuant to action taken by the Board of Overseers, will not relieve the management board from potential liability toward the AG. This state of affairs serves to underscore the fact that it is the management board which bears the primary responsibility for the management of the affairs fo the AG and that approval of a particular transaction by the Board of Overseers has no effect on the liability of the management board.

Claims against the management board based on these provisions are subject to a five year statute of limitations.[34]

* * *

Liability of Managing Directors [GmbH]

The liability of which the GmbH law imposes upon the managing director or directors of the GmbH is similar to the liability of the members of the management board of an AG. Thus, the GmbH law requires the managing director or directors to manage the affairs of the GmbH with the care of an ordinary business man and subjects the managing director or directors to liability for loss sustained by the GmbH as a result of a failure to observe the standard.[47] Unlike the case of the AG, however, the GmbH law does not provide for any direct liability on the part of the managing director or directors toward creditors. Accordingly, any claims for damages sustained as a result of a violation of any duty by the managing directors can only be asserted by the GmbH.

The managing director or directors are relieved of liability toward the GmbH where the action complained of was taken pursuant to direction of another corporate organ binding upon the executive organ by law or provision of the Association Agreement. The only exception to this rule exists where the direction involved is a prima facie violation of law or of the Association Agreement. In such a case, it would be the duty of the managing director or directors to decline to carry out the direction.

33. Section 93(4), AktG.
34. Section 93(6), AktG.
47. Section 43, GmbhG.

The GmbH law enumerates some specific acts which would be a basis for liability on the part of the managing director or directors. These acts are similar in nature to those enumerated in the stock corporation law for the same purpose but are not as extensive. Thus, the acts referred to in the statute consist of the effectuation of any payments tending to impair the stated capital of the GmbH in violation of the applicable principles of law.[48] It should be noted that, in these particular situations, the managing director or directors will be relieved of liability toward the GmbH on the grounds that the action was taken on the basis of direction by the meeting of members or Board of Overseers if the GmbH must assert the liability to satisfy the claims of creditors.[49]

As in the case of the AG, where the GmbH alleges that it has sustained a loss as a result of negligent action or inaction by the executive organ, the burden of proof is reversed. The mere showing of such a loss is thus sufficient and the managing director or directors will then be required to affirmatively demonstrate that they have satisfied the applicable standard of care.[50]

Where there is more than one managing director, all managing directors will in principle be jointly and severally liable to the GmbH. Where, however, the management of the GmbH has been divided among a number of managing directors, the individual managing director will be directly liable only for his own violation of duties and will be liable for the violation of duty by another managing director only to the extent that he failed to properly inform himself as to the management activities of such other managing directors.[51]

Claims against the managing director or directors expire five years from the date on which the claims may be deemed to have arisen.[52]

Comments and Questions

1. What is the difference in the way that German and American law approach the burden of proof in cases where a plaintiff seeks to impose liability on a director for breach of the duty of care? How does the rule of shareholder ratification in Germany differ from that in the United States?

2. Is the duty of care in Germany analogous to that in the United States? Is the duty of care the same for AGs and GmbHs? Can you explain the basis for the difference in treatment?

---

b. The European Union

Overlaying the approaches of the French, English and German approaches is the potential for harmonization at the "federal" level through the proposed Fifth Company Law directive of the European Union.

---

48. Sections 30, 31, and 43, GmbH.
49. Section 43(3), GmbH.
50. Section 43, GmbH....
51. Section 43, GmbH....
52. Section 43(4), GmbH.

As you read the materials that follow, consider how the English approach differs from that of the proposed Fifth Company Law Directive, how the German and French approaches contribute to the Fifth Directive, and how the Eastern European approaches borrow from the civil law and European approaches.

Vassil Breskovski, *Directors' Duty of Care in Eastern Europe*

29 Int'l Law. 77 (1995)
(excerpts from pages 91–92; some footnotes omitted)

E. THE DRAFT FIFTH DIRECTIVE AND THE EUROPEAN COMPANY STATUTE

The Draft Fifth Directive and the European Statute do not articulate a standard of care and skill for board members.[105] Nevertheless, both regulations provide for civil liability of members of management and supervisory boards for "breaches of... [duty] in carrying out their [[functions]."[106] It may be inferred that provisions scattered throughout the Draft Directive bear upon the so-mentioned duties and functions. As far as the one-tiered board is concerned, all management members have the same basic duty. According to article 21q(2) they shall "carry out their functions in the interest of the company having regard [in particular] to the interest of the shareholders and the employees." We may conclude that by this wording article 21q(2) includes the use of due care in making business decisions.[107]

Liability is joint and several without limit, but individual directors can escape liability if they prove that no fault is personally attributable to them. "Fault" seems to be equivalent to the meaning and use of "negligence" in the U.K. and U.S. law. This minimum liability presumably covers any damages sustained by the company as a result of a breach of duty by members of the governing organs in performing their functions.[108]

The authorization of a transaction by the supervisory organ (or presumably by the nonmanagement members of the administrative organ) shall not of itself exempt the management directors from liability.[109] Similarly, under article 14(5) of the Draft Directive the authorization by the general meeting of the shareholders of a transaction that causes damages to the company does not itself exempt any members of the board or boards of directors from liability.[110] Article 18(1) implies that the general meeting of shareholders can renounce the right to bring proceedings on behalf of the company to enforce the joint and several liability without limit. Nevertheless, such a refusal is ineffective against any shareholder entitled to maintain a suit to enforce article 14 liability,

---

105. [Jane Welch, *The Fifth Draft Directive—A False Dawn?*, 8 EUR. L. REV. 83 (1983)] at 91.
106. [Amended Proposal for a Fifth Directive Founded on Article 54(3)(g) of the EEC Treaty Concerning the Structure of Public Limited Companies and the Powers and Obligations of Their Organs, 1983 O.J. (C 240)] at art. 14.
107. *Id.* art. 21q(2).
108. See, e.g., [2 GORE-BROWNE ON COMPANIES 38-001 (A. J. Boyle & Richard Sykes eds., 44th ed. 1986)] at 39–007,—024; M. Raaijmakers, *European Harmonization: Quo Vadis?*, *in* HARMONIZATION OF COMPANY AND SECURITIES LAW 64, 85 (1989).
109. 1983 O.J. (C 240), supra note [106], art. 14(4).
110. Id. art. 14(1), (5).

that is, a shareholder who holds shares of 10 percent or more of subscribed capital.[111] Finally, advance renunciation is prohibited, since article 18(2) provides that damage to the company must have occurred in order for the renunciation to be effective.[112]

The provisions of the Draft Directive and the European Statute clearly impose a much more severe standard than the existing U.K. and U.S. law and one similar to German and French statutory law. Nevertheless, the provisions in the Draft Directive and the European Company Statute are problematic.[113]

One difficulty is the absence of a definition of the duty of care as well as what constitutes a breach of that duty. Therefore, it is certainly necessary to extend harmonization in respect to directors' duty of diligence.[114]

Second, several provisions relating to the directors' duties are ambiguous. For example, article 21q(1) provides that all "members of the administrative organ shall have the same rights and duties, without prejudice to" delegation of the conduct of management of the company or to allocation of functions among the members of that organ.[115] This nebulous provision might be interpreted to the effect that no difference exists between the rights and duties of management and nonmanagement directors other than those arising from the delegation of management functions.

Comments and Questions

1. The draft Fifth Company Law Directive would modify the company laws of the Member States closer to the German model of corporate governance. As the materials suggest, this movement would significantly change the English approach. Can you articulate some of the ways English law would have to change under the Fifth Company Law Directive?

2. The draft Fifth Company Law Directive was fiercely opposed by Britain. After several largely unsuccessful attempts to modify the draft to meet the objections of Britain, efforts to enact this draft directive appear to have stalled. However, the EU Commission appears to continue to work on harmonizing rules relating to director conduct. For a brief commentary, see VANESSSA EDWARDS, EC COMPANY LAW 387–390 (1999).

c. A Note on Eastern European Systems

The harmonization attempts of the European Union have had an influence well beyond the borders of the European Union. In particular, many of the states of the formerly socialist Eastern Europe have begun to modify their corporate law in significant respect. In some respects, this influence has a practical political dimension: many of the Eastern European states hope to become members of the EU. Membership will require conformity to EU law. It may also require the conformity of basic norms of corporate governance that those generally prevailing among the EU Mem-

111. Id. art. 16(1), (2).

112. Id. art. 18(1), (2).

113. 2 GORE-BROWNE ON COMPANIES, supra note [108], at 39–026.

114. [EUROPEAN BUSINESS LAW, LEGAL AND ECONOMIC ANALYSES ON INTEGRATION AND HARMONIZATION 199–226 (Richard Buxbaum et al. eds., 1991)] at 212.

115. 1883 O.J. (C 240), supra note [106], art. 21q(1).

ber States, even if such conformity is not legally required. To that end, these states have been receptive to corporate law developments in Germany and the European Union. Consider the extent of the influence of Western European norms and governance ideals within Eastern Europe in the excerpt below.

Vassil Breskovski, *Directors' Duty of Care in Eastern Europe*

29 Int'l Law. 77 (1995)

(excerpts from pages 92–94; some footnotes omitted)

1. Bulgaria

The Bulgarian Law on Commerce, which follows closely the Draft Directive, does not contain any distinct provisions that elaborate the standard of care to be followed by the directors and management of the public limited company. Nevertheless, under article 240(2), members of the management board and the supervisory board are jointly liable for any damages caused by their fault.[116] A member of the board will not be held liable if the court finds that the board member has no fault connected to the damage.[117] Interestingly enough, the board members have to deposit security for their potential liability in an amount specified by the general meeting but not less than their remuneration for a three-month period. This indemnity may be in stocks or in bonds.[118]

2. The Czech Republic and the Republic of Slovakia

As already mentioned, under the law of the Czech Republic and the Republic of Slovakia the administration of public limited companies (joint stock companies) is based on a two-tiered system. Members of the board of directors and the supervisory board are obliged to fulfill their duties with due care and to maintain confidentiality of information and facts, the disclosure of which to third parties could cause the corporation to suffer damage.[119] As far as liability is concerned, section 66 of the Commercial Code states that the relations between the corporation and the members of its corporate bodies are primarily ruled by provisions on mandated contracts.

3. Hungary

According to Hungarian law, a member of the board of directors or the supervisory board, or an auditor, "shall be obliged to act with the care generally expected from persons in such positions."[120] If such persons breach their duties, they will be held liable for damages under the general provisions of the civil law. A contract with

---

116. [Turgovski Zakon [Law on Commerce], Durzhaven Vestnik No. 48 (1991), translated in 1 Central and Eastern European Legal Materials (Vratislav Pechota ed., 1993) [hereinafter Bulgarian Law on Commerce].].

117. Article 240(3), sent. 1 of the Law on Commerce, supra note [116].

118. Article 240(3), sent. 2 of the Law on Commerce, supra note [116].

119. [Obchodni Zakonik [Czechoslovak Commercial Code of 1991)] [hereinafter Czechoslovak Commercial Code], translated in 2 David E. Birenbaum, Business Ventures in Eastern Europe and Russia (2d ed. 1992) [hereinafter Business Ventures in Eastern Europe and Russia]. The Commercial Code continues to be effective in the territories of the Czech Republic and the Republic of Slovakia as long as it is not repealed by the National Councils] at § 194(5).

120. [Torveny a Gazdasagi Tarsasagokrol [Act VI of 1988 on Business Organizations], translated in 3 Hungarian Rules of Law in Force No. 3–4 (Feb. 1–15, 1992), reprinted in Business Ventures in Eastern Europe and Russia, supra [hereinafter Hungarian Company Act]] at art. 32(1).

the company cannot waive liability. The liability of the senior officers is joint and several.[121] However, a director who objects to a decision and reports the objection either to the supervisory board or to the general meeting of shareholders will not be held liable.[122]

4. Poland

Polish law requires that directors carry out their duties with the "diligence of a conscientious merchant," but does not precisely define the meaning of the quoted phrase. It is not clear whether this test is objective. If it is, this test implies that directors will be held to no higher standard than an average businessman and are not required to have specific expertise.[123] The liability of the directors is joint and several.

---

d. Japan

Japan's approach to the issue of director duty is a blend of continental and American notions, modified to suit the social tastes of the Japanese. The blending, however, has not been easy, and the process is not complete.

Mitsuo Kondō, *The Management Liability of Directors*

(Torishimariyaku no keiel sekinin)
Donald C. Clarke, trans.
20 Law in Japan 150 (1987)[*]
(excerpts pages 150–158; 170–172; some footnotes omitted)

The Duty of Care[a] and the Duty of Loyalty

The Commercial Code provides that the rules of mandate in the Civil Code [articles 643–656] shall apply to the legal relationship between the company and the director (Commercial Code, article 24[3]). As a result, directors perform their functions subject to the duty of care (Civil Code, article 644). The commercial Code stipulates separately, however, that directors have a duty to perform their functions loyally for the sake fo the company (Commercial Code, article 254-3). Commonly called the director's duty of loyalty, this duty has been the subject of a lively theoretical debate over whether it is distinct and different from the duty of care.

Among scholars and courts the majority view (the "theory of similarity") has been that the rule of article 254-3 of the Commercial Code amplifies the duty of care, serving

---

121. [Gyula Gayer, *Changes in Hungarian Corporate Law*, De Droit Des Affaires Internationales 526 (No. 4/5, 1990)] at 523.

122. Hungarian Company Act, supra note [120], art. 32(3).

123. See, e.g.,[William Sievers & Andre Spark, *Directors' Duties in Selected Markets: Poland*, 8 Int'l Company & Com. L. Rev. 311 (Aug. 1993)].

*. From 3 Gendai Kōgyō hō kōza (Lectures on Contemporary Busienss Enterprises) 293 (Takeuchi & Tatsuda eds. 1985).

a. *Zenkan gimu* and *zenkan chūi gimu* have been uniformly translated in thuis article as "duty of care." Both are abbreviations of *zenryō naru kanrisha no chūi gimu (the "duty of care of a virtuous manager"), an expression appearing in article 644 of the Civil Code.*

only to clarify it further, and that it cannot be interpreted to provide for a duty that is separate from and higher than the normal duty of care in a mandatory relationship.[1] Opposed to this view is a widely held theory (the ":theory of difference") that the duty of loyalty is distinct from the duty of care: the duty of care does nothing more than prescribe the degree of care that should be used by directors in performing their functions, while the duty of loyalty obligates directors not to use their position to advance their personal interests at the expense of the company's interests. This theory views the two duties as different in kind and as functioning in different situations. Under the continental law of mandate, there might be a moral requirement that the mandatory not sacrifice the interests of the mandator, but this has not been elevated into a legal duty. The duty of loyalty is considered separate from the mandate relationship and as stemming from the trust relationship in Anglo-American law.[2]

In recent years, the theory of difference has gained steadily in strength. However, generally accepted doctrine has never denied that the director has a duty not to seek to advance his own interests at the expense of the interests of the company. For this reason, the issue of whether the duty of loyalty is subsumed under the duty of care has recently come to be an issue of whether this is not simply a semantic problem. Is there any real difference between the theory of difference and the theory of similarity? In concrete terms, is there any difference in result?[3] In response to these doubts, the majority view first denies the difference [between the two duties] set forth above. Article 644 of the Civil Code, it is argued, provides for the degree of care to be exercised by mandatories so that generally in carrying out the purpose of the mandate they may fulfill their task in the most rational way; thus the duty of directors to perform their functions faithfully for the benefit of the company where there is a conflict between their interests and those of the company can be understood as included in the duty set out in article 644 of the Civil Code.[4] Under the majority view no duties arise from the duty of loyalty additional to those arising from each of the concrete rules, including the rules relating to man-

1. Among cases holding to this effect are Artita v. Kojima, 24 Minshū (No. 6) 625 (Sup. Ct., June 24, 1960) and Nakamoto v. Koizumi Seima K.K., 27 Kakyū minshū (Nos. 5–8) 387 (Kōbe Dist. Ct., June 18, 1975). As for theories, see inter alia, K. Ōsumi, SHIMPAN KAISHAHŌ GAIRON (Outine of company law, new edition) 119 (1967); 1 T. Ishii, KAISHAHŌ (company law) 311 (1967); T. Suzuki, SHIMPAN KAISHAHŌ (Company Law, new edition) 183 (revised 2nd ed. 1982); Morimoto, TORISHIMARIYAKU NO ZENKAN CHŪI GAMU TO CHŪJITSU GIMU (The director's duty of care and duty of loyalty), 81 Min Shō (No. 4) 29 (1980).

2. For theories taking this type of stand, see, intr alia, Ōsakadani, *Torishimariyaku no sekinin* (The director's responsibility), in 3 KABUSHIKI KAISHAHŌ (Lectures on the law of stock corporations) 117 (1956); AKABORI (Shibuya), *Torishimariyaku no chūjitsu gimu* (The director's duty o loyalty), 85 HŌGAKU KYŌKAI ZASSHI (No. 4) 72–73 (1968); C. HOSHIKAWA, TORISHIMARIYAKU CHŪJITSU GIMU RON (On the director's duty of loyalty) (1972); 2 Y. KANZAKI, SHIMPAN SHŌHŌ (KAISHAHŌ) Commercial law (new edition)) 372 (1982); 1 S. TANAKA, SAI ZENTAI KAISHAHŌ SHŌRON (Revised treatise on company law) 593 (1982). In the last book, the following reasons for taking this stand are adduced: first, the Commercial Code sets up article 254-3 separately from article 254(3). Second, the principles of interpretation of received law [support sucha stand]. Third, in the 1950 revision of the Commercial Code, which put in article 254-3, the duties and liabilities of directors were toughened. Fourth, it is necessary to prevent directors from seeking to advance their private interests, and in particular to curb the abuse of expense accounts. And fifth, it makes clear the director's duty outside cases provided for in the written law.

3. *See* Morimoto, *supra* note 1, at 4. In addition, according to Shibuya, whether or not the duty of loyalty is included within the duty of care should be viewed as a terminological question; the more important question concerns the extent to which the content of the duty of loyalty in Anglo-American law can be adopted in Japanese law. *See* Shibuya, *supra* note 2, at 45–46.

4. *See* Morimoto, *supra* note 1, at 19.

date.[5] Thus, in this view, even the director's duty to refrain from competing is taken to be a particular form of the duty of care.[6]

In opposition to this is the position that the duty of loyalty is different in kind: while the duty of care is concerned with the degree of care and skill used by directors in the course of performing their functions for the company, the duty of loyalty is not concerned with the acts *per se* undertaken by directors in their capacity as organs of the company. This theory maintains that there is a great difference between the two.[7] It sees the need for distinguishing between the two duties in the following three points. First, negligence is an issue with respect to the duty of care, but not with respect to the duty of loyalty. If directors, through conduct opposed to the interests of the company, inflict a loss on the company, then as a matter of course they become liable for compensation.[8] Second, the scope of a director's liability for violation of the duty of loyalty is not limited to compensation for the amount of the loss suffered by the company; it extends to repayment to the company of all gains acquired by the director.[9] Third, unlike in cases where a violation of the duty of care is alleged, courts have no difficulty in finding violations of the duty of loyalty.[10] Moreover, the theory holds that the very existence of article 254-3 serves to highlight the problem of the conflict of interests between the director and the company outside of situations where the Commercial Code establishes concrete duties by express rules.[11]

Certainly, to label as "the duty of loyalty" the duty of directors not to take action to advance their own interests in situations where their interests and the interests of the company conflict and to distinguish it from the duty of care may be useful as a heuristic device, and it is easy to extract a duty apart from those severally stipulated in the Commercial Code. It is not impossible, however, to understand the above duty as one form of the duty of care. The duty of care in the broad sense should be understood to comprise both the duty of care in the narrow sense and the duty of loyalty. Furthermore, it is untrue that only the duty of care, and not the duty of loyalty, is at issue with respect to the acts *per se* undertaken by directors in their capacity as an organ of the company.[12] A clear line cannot be drawn between cases where the duty of care is at issue

---

5. *See* KAWAMOTO, GENDAI KAISHAHŌ (Modern compoany law) 371 (newly revised 2d ed. 1982).

6. See Morimoto, supra note 1, at 19. Against this, Professor Kanzaki holds that because there is no overlap between acts belonging in the category of business that the director, in violation of the duty of care, fails to undertake for the company, and acts belonging in the category of business of the company that the director, in violation of the duty of loyalty, undertakes for the benefit of himself or a third party, the duty to refrain from competing cannot be understood as one particular form of the duty of care. *See* Y. Kanzaki, *Torishimariyaku no chūjitsu gimu—sono gutaiteki hatsugen* (The director's duty of loyalty—its concrete manifestation), in YOSHIDA EISUKE SENSEI KOKI KINEN RONBUN RHŪ (Essay in honor of the 70th birthday of Professor Eisuke Yoshida), SHINTEN SURU KIGYŌHŌ, KEIZAIHŌ (Enterprise law and economic law on the advance) 101 (1982).

7. See C. HOSHIKAWA, *supra*, note 2, at 131; Y Kanzaki, *supra* note 6, at 87–88.

8. Hoshikawa holds that if one takes the position that negligence is required, then the reasons for the existence fo the duty of loyalty are manifestly weakened. See C, Hoshikawa, *supra*, note 2, at 27.

9. *See* M. KITAZAWA, *supra* note 2, at 372.

10. See Y. Kanzaki, *supra* note 6, at 88; M. KITAZAWA, *supra* note 2 at 372. The reasons for this is said to be that the court need not worry that its judgment as to whether the acts of the director were or were not undertaken as part of the proper performance of his duties will unduly restrict the director's business activities.

11. See Shibuya, *supra* note 2, 85 HŌGAKU KYŌKAI ZASSHI (No. 1) 3; S. TANAKA, supra, note 2 at 596. The taking of corporate opportunities, the prohibition of profiting from secrets, and the transfer and control over the company are given as examples of thin kind of problem.

12. For example, in what are called indirect transactions under article 265(1), where it is not the director with the conflict of interest but another director who undertakes transactions with third

and cases where the duty of loyalty is at issue. Moreover, to lay down a rule that there should always be strict liability for violation of the duty of loyalty could lead in some cases to harsh results for directors. In addition, as will be discussed in detail in the following section, I find unconvincing that position that the courts' readiness to find violations of the duty of loyalty is nothing more than the flip side of their excessive deference to the director's business judgment with respect to the alleged violations of the duty of care.[13] When the matter is considered in this way, the theory of the distinct nature of the duty of loyalty appears unsuited to thinking about the liability of directors in Japan.

The Scope of the Director's Liability

When a director violates the duty of care or the duty of loyally, he is liable not only to the company but also to third parties (Commercial Code articles 266, 266-2). Cases where a director is liable can be broadly divided into those where liability stems from an affirmative act and those where it stems from a failure to act.

In the latter case, liability is sought largely in terms of the the director's duty to supervise: Directors have been sued not only for actions undertaken directly by them, but also on the grounds that they failed to stop unlawful acts (*ihō kōi*) committed by other directors. This is precisely because a duty is imposed on directors to supervise other directors in the exercise of their functions (*shokumu shikkō*), Commercial Code , article 260(1)). As it is difficult however, to define the scope of liability for violation of the duty to supervise,[14] attention must be paid to the danger of an inappropriate expansion of such liability. This is because where this type of liability is concerned, it is difficult as a practical matter (*jijitsu jō*) to establish strictly the cause- and-effect relationship between the director's violation of duty and the harm to the company or the third party, and liability can be found solely on the basis of the director's being employed as such or being listed as a director in the Company Register.

The Supreme Court has construed the director's duty to supervise as not limited to matters brought before the board of directors, but extending generally to the exercise of functions (*sokumu shikkō*) by representative directors and others.[15] In lower court decisions as well, the director's duty to supervise has, based on the above position, been strictly construed, and the director has in most cases been found liable. In particular, this kind of liability has come to be frequently attached to the dummy directors of close corporations who actually have almost nothing to do with the management of the company. Directors of this kind, because they have absolutely no intention of paying attention to the exercise of functions by other directors, can therefore be said to be potentially liable to suit for violation of the duty to supervise any time between the time they

---

parties as a representative fo the company, then with respect to the acts he undertakes as an organ of the company, it is possible to say that the duty of loyalty is at issue.

13. According to Morimoto, the emphasis on the fact that article 254-3 of the Commercial Code imported the Anglo-American duty of loyalty opens the way to an undue expansion of the theory of relaxation of the director's duty of care, with the danger that the legal treatment of transactions affecting the interests of directors will be unduly severe. *See* Morimoto, *supra* note 1, at 29.

14. If it were seriously required that a causal relationship be shown between the violation of the duty to supervise and harm suffered, there is the problem of the unreasonable result that the more a director habitually paid attention to the exercise of functions by other directors, because that would mean that the probability of his being able to stop improper actions by other directors was large, the more easily he could be found liable for overlooking such actions. See 1 A. Takeuchi, Hanrei Shoho (Commercial Code cases) 310 (1976).

15. See Hasimoto v. Kobayashi, 27 Minshū (No. 5) 655 (Sup. Ct., May 22, 1973).

take up their post and the time they leave it. Rigorously imposing liability on directors of this kind can be supported as giving a warning to those who lightly lend their names out as directors.

Nevertheless, several recent cases, while affirming as a general matter the director's duty to supervise, have at the same time seemed in specific situations to countenance a director's failure to carry out the duty to supervise. It would appear that special consideration was made for the fact that the director in question perhaps served without compensation, lived far away from the company, or had little influence over the company.[16] Obviously, if one takes into account the individual circumstances of this kind of director to end up denying the director's liability, the director's duty to supervise is emasculated and the whole point of the law becomes lost.[17] In this sense, the holdings of these of these cases can be questioned. However, it is also possible to consider the decisions as correct if one thinks of the courts as being worried about the liability of directors becoming too severe. It is difficult to see where liability grounded on a violation of the duty to supervise might end; in an extreme case, it would be easy to find liability merely when another director violated the duty.

In contradistinction to this liability stemming from a failure to act, liability in the former case stemming from an affirmative act turns on (*mondai ni suru*) a violation of duty by the director in the concrete performance of his functions. A director becomes liable when in the course of performing his functions he causes harm to the company through negligence, to say nothing of when he deliberately engages in actions that bring harm to the company. This type of liability, like liability for violation of the duty to supervise, is frequently, is frequently pursued under article 266-3 by creditors of the company. In particular, when the director has made out a check that was unlikely to be paid and ultimately was not paid or when the company has fallen into bankruptcy through the careless management of the director, the courts have imposed a heavy liability on the director.

Even in these cases, however, where the director, moved solely by concern for the god of the company, makes out a check, it is often possible to say that he is managing the company. In other words, there will be cases where despite the fact that the director exercises his business judgment with the interests of the company at heart, through misfortune he ends up only bringing harm to it. In such a case, to impose liability on the director to compensate for the above harms would seem, depending on the circumstances, an extremely harsh result from the standpoint of the director. Moreover, judges, who do not necessarily possess specialized management knowledge, in many cases probably experience difficulty in passing on the correctness of the judgments made by directors, who are management specialists, using their specialist knowledge.

16. See, for example, the following cases all denying liability grounded on the duty to supervise: Tokyo Toyota Karōra K.K. v. Tokyo Auto K.K., KIN SHO HAN (No. 561) 38 (Tokyo Dist. Ct., March 16, 1978) (nominal director living at a great distance away from the company); Koshi v. Kōgu K.K., HANREI JIHO (No. 931) 119 (Osaka High Ct., March 23, 1979) (director virtually in name only neither was an investor nor received compensation and who had no specialized knowledge of the company's business); Yamashita v. Segawa, HANREI JIHŪ (No. 963) 96 (Osaka Dist. Ct., March 28, 1980) (nominal directors who received no compensation and did not participate in planning unless they had invested).

17. *See* Shimura, *Torishimariyaku no kanshi oimu no han'i* (The scope of the director's duty to supervise), Shōji hōmu (No. 843) 24 (1979); Y. KANZAKI, TORISHIMARIYAKU SEIDO RON (Treatise on the director system) 76 (1981).

This kind of concern is developed in the United States into the business judgment rule. According to this rule, when the director, within the scope of the company's and his own authority, makes certain management decisions, if those decisions have a rational basis and he makes those decisions as a result of his own judgment and discretion, uninfluenced by concerns other than those he honestly believes to be in the best interests of the company, the courts will not interfere in internal management affairs and the judgment of the judge will not be substituted for the judgment of the director.[18] Even in Japan, there have for some time been theories calling for the introduction of this rule and the adoption of its thinking.[19] In addition, there are several Japanese court decisions where this rule appears to have been used.[20]

However, scholarly theories differ not only over whether the rule may be applied, but also over the proper way to understand it and the scope of its application. In particular, there is disagreement—linked with the opposition of theories regarding the duty of loyalty described above—over whether the business judgment rule should be applied when a violation of the duty of loyalty is alleged. In American law, as noted above, for this rule to apply, the director must have considered only the best interests of the company and not have made an insincere judgment under the influence of any other factors. Thus, where a business judgment is made, this rule is not applied if the interests of the director and those of the company conflict. There is, however, some disagreement on this point. In recent American cases, it has become an issue whether or not the business judgment rule may be applied to the judgment of directors as to whether the company should terminate derivative suits pursuing the liability of directors or whether the company should adopt countermeasures in the face of a tender offer (*kokai kaitsuke*). In these situations, there is a danger that the director's both in avoiding pursuit of the liability of other directors which might give rise to his own liability and maintaining his control over the company might lead to a conflict with the best interests of the company. But the courts, even in these kinds of circumstances, have affirmed the applicability of the business judgment rule.[23] Moreover, even when the director is in a position

18. See W. KNEPPER, LIABILITY OF CORPORATE OFFICERS ANDDIRECTORS 20 (3rd ed. 1978); H. HENN & J. ALEXANDER, THE LAW OF CORPORATIONS AND OTHER BUSINESS ENTERPRISES 661 (3d ed. 1983).

19. See Yoshinaga, *Torihimariyaku no ippanteki gimu* (The general duties of directors), 29 HITOTSUBASHI RONSHŪ (no. 4) 300-01 (1953); Ōsakandi, *Torihimariyaku no sekinin* (The liability of director), in 3 KAUSHIKI KAISHAHŌ KŌZA (Lectures on the law of stock corporations) 1124, 1127 (1956); Namiki, Amerik*a ni okeru keiei jō no handan no gensoku no hattan* (The development of the business judgment rule in America), in KEIŌ GIJUKU DAIGAKUIN HŌGAKU KENKYUKA RONBUNSHU, SHOWA 53 NENDO (Collected essays from the legal research department of the graduate school of Keiō University, 1978) 69 (1978); Y. Kanzaki, *Beikoku ni okeru keiei handan no gensoku no tenkai* (The evolution of the business judgment rule in America), in 2 GENDAI SHIHO SHIHOGAKU NO KADAI TO TENBŌ (Issues and prospects in modern private law) 255 (1982); Y. Kanzai, supra note 17, at 83; Namiki, *Amerika no keiei jō no handan no gensoku* (The American business judgment rule), HAN HŌ (No. 126) 1 (1983); Kondo, *Torihimariyaku no sekinin to sono kyūsai* (The liability of directors and relief therefrom), 99 HŌGAKU KYŌKAI ZASSHI (No. 7) 122 (1982).

20. See, e.g., Tokōzai K.K. v. Eda, HANREI JIHŌ (No. 771) 77 (Tokyo High Ct., January 29, 1975); Daiwa Kōgyō K.K. v. Tezuka, HANREI JIHŌ (No. 1005) 161 (Tokyo Dist. Ct., September 30, 1980); Kitahara v. Ohashi, HANREI JIHŌ (No. 909) 95 (Tokyo Dist. Ct., March 2, 1978); Nara Shinrin Kainatsu K.K. v. Matsumoto, HANREI TAIMUZU (No. 437) 159 (Osaka Dist Ct., November 18, 1980).

23. For examples of derivative suits, see Gall v. Exxon Corp., 418 F.Supp. 508 (S.D.N.Y.) 1976); Maldonado v. Flynn, 485 F.Supp. 274 (S.D.N.Y. 1980). Regarding control of the company, see Johnson v. Trueblood, 629 F.2d 287 (3rd Cir. 1980), cert. denied , 450 U.S. 999 (1981); Panter v. Mar-

where his interests are opposed to those of the company, the courts have not uniformly denied the applicability of the business judgment rule, but have instead made a judgment as to whether the [director's] interest is of such a nature and degree as to preclude application of the business judgment rule.[24]

Most theories advocating application of the business judgment rule in Japanese law, particularly those advocating the different nature of the duty of loyalty, accept the way of thinking of American law and hold that this rule should not be applied where liability is grounded in the director's duty of loyalty. With respect to this problem, their understanding is as follows.

As company management has become more complex and a matter for specialists, it has become more difficult for courts to pass judgement after the fact on the appropriateness of business judgments made by directors. Moreover, because an element of risk unavoidably accompanies the activities of an enterprise, it is not always appropriate to criticize a director's judgment after the fact, and violations [of the duty of care] are rarely pursued. It is in this sense that there is a trend toward the relaxation of the director's duty of care.[25] On the other hand, because it is necessary to protect the company from a director's malfeasance (*fusei na kōi*), the doctrine of the director's duty of loyalty has developed in order to prevent his judgment from being warped when his activities on behalf of the company are influenced by his own personal interests or those of a third party. Under the duty of care, business judgments are to be respected to the extent that they constitute the performance of functions pursuant to laws and the company charter, and to that extent the duty of care is relaxed. In contrast, the demands of the duty of loyalty should be strict in order to secure the director's impartial performance of his functions, and the applicability of the business judgment rule should be denied.[26]

Moreover, in cases where the duty of loyalty is at issue, the courts ave no special difficulty in finding a violation of that duty, because the director has used his position to advance the interests of a third party at the expense of the company. That is to say, because there is no need for concern that the judgment of the courts as to whether the acts of the director were undertaken in the proper performance of his functions might excessively (*futō ni*) restrict his managerial activities,[27] it is thought that the rule should not be applied in determining liability predicated on a violation of the duty of loyalty. In other words, the rationales advanced by the position denying the applicability of the business judgment rule in cases where the duty of loyalty is at issue are mainly (1) that it is technically an easy matter for a court to determine whether there has been a violations of the duty of loyalty and (2) that it is necessary to regulate conflicts of interest strictly.

Against this, the position of the theory of similarity is that the concept of transaction affecting a director's interests is a relative one; except in paradigm cases, it is impossible to distinguish strictly between cases where the duty of care is at issue and cases where the duty of loyalty is at issue. This school argues that it is rarely true that violations of

---

shall Field & Co., 646 F.2d 271 (7th Cir. 1981), cert. denied, 454 U.S. 1092 (1981). Conflicting views are set forth in the latter two opinions: They hold that in circumstances creating this kind of conflict of interest, the applicability of the business judgment rule should not be denied. For further detail, see Kondō, *Amerika ni okeru keiei handan no hōsoku no tekiyō genkai* (The limits of the applicability of the business judgemnt rule in America), 32 Kōbe Hōgaku (No. 4) 767 (1983).

24. See T. Namiki, Amerika ni okeru torishimayaku no keiei sekinin no hōri (The jurisprudence of the business liability of directors in America) 141 (1983).

25. See M. Kitazawa, supra note 2, at 372.

26. See Shibuya, supra note 2, at 46.

27. See Y. Kanzai, supra note 6, at 101–102.

the duty loyalty, unlike violations of the duty of care, can be found by courts with no special difficulty.[28] The theory of difference is also criticized for opening the door to an unduly (*futō na*) expansion of the doctrine of the relaxation of the duty of care, with the danger that the legal treatment of transactions affecting a director's interests would become unduly strict.[29]

The two rationales advanced by the position holding that the business judgment rule should not be applied in cases involving the duty of loyalty seem not to be decisive. That is, against the claim that the inquiry of the court as to whether there has been a violation of the duty of loyalty is easy, the theory of similarity claims that except in paradigmatic cases, it will not always be possible to distinguish clearly between cases involving the duty of care and cases involving the duty of loyalty. For example, in the indirect transactions of article 265 the Commercial Code, when a director other than the director with a conflict of interest represents the company and must decide whether or not to undertake the transaction, does his potential liability arise solely out of the duty of care? Moreover, it cannot be said that when a director in the performance of his functions encounters a conflict of his interests with those of the company, he will always sacrifice the best interests of the company and put his own interests first.

Even if we sum up the situation as "conflict of interest," there is still a question as to whether it reaches a level where the impartial judgement of the director is warped. It would clearly be overprotective of the directors if in cases of [alleged] violation of the duty of care, the courts, provided certain procedural conditions had been satisfied, thoroughly respected the business judgment of the director and made absolutely no inquiry into the substance of that judgment. If the business judgment rule is to be understood in the above manner, not only should it not be applied to [alleged] violations of the duty of loyalty, but it should also not be applied to [alleged] violations of the duty of care. But if this rule is understood as an effort, through according a certain level of respect to the director's business judgment, to prevent reliability of the director from being too severe when the determination of that liability comes to be made, then it covers not only cases where the duty of care is at issue but also, allowing for differences of degree, cases where the duty of loyalty is at issue.

If the business judgment rule understood in this way is adopted in Japan, I believe it should be applied to alleged violations of the duty of loyalty. Even if understood in this way, it will not be an obstacle to the strict regulation of the duty of loyalty. The position denying the applicability fo the business judgment rule to the duty of loyalty merely underscores the act that the duty of care is overly protective of directors. The thinking behind the business judgment rule is such that in cases involving the duty of loyalty as well, the necessity of a according a certain level of respect to the judgment of the director cannot be denied.

* * *

Appendix

Statutes referred to in this article are supplied below. The translations are from the *Eibun Hōrei Sha* series, with minor alterations to correct the occasional infelicity and to conform statutory references to *Law in Japan's* usage.

28. See Morimoto, supra note 1, at 26.
29. See *id.*, at 29.

CIVIL CODE (*mimpō*, in 2 EHS No. 2100–2101 (1981))

Art. 644 A mandatory is bound to manage the affairs entrusted to him with the care of a good manager in accordance with the tenor of the mandate.

COMMERCIAL CODE (*Shoho*, in 2 EHS No. 2200 (1982))

Art. 254(3). The relations between the company and the directors shall be governed by the provisions relating to mandates Art. 254-3. The directors shall be obliged to obey any law or ordinance and the articles of incorporation as well as resolutions adopted at a general meeting and to perform their duties faithfully on behalf of a company. Art. 260(91). The board of directors shall decide the administration of affairs of the company, and supervise the directors' execution of their duties. (2) . The board fo directors may not have a director decide the following matters or other important aspects of administration of affairs:

(i) Disposition and taking over of important property;

(ii) Loan of large amount;

(iii) Appointment and dismissal of an important employee such as a manager;

(iv) Establishment, change, and discontinuance of an important organ such as a branch.

Art. 264(1). A director who intends to effect on his behalf or on behalf of a third person a transaction that comes under a class of business carried on by the company shall disclose all material facts relating to said transaction at a meeting of the board of directors and obtain its approval.

(2). The director having effected the transaction in the preceding paragraph shall report important matters as to the transaction to the board of directors without delay.

(3). If a director has, in contravention of the provisions of paragraph 1, effected a transaction on his own behalf, the board of directors may treat such transactions as effected on behalf of the company.

(4) The right mentioned in the preceding paragraph shall lapse where one year has elapsed from the time fo the transaction.

Art. 265(1). When a director intends to acquire the company's products or other properties by transfer or to transfer his own products or other properties to the company or to receive loans from the company or to affect any transaction with the company on his own behalf or on that of a third person, he shall obtain the approval of the board of directors. The same shall apply in the case where the company guarantees liability of the director or otherwise affects with a person other then the director a transaction in which interests are contrary between the company and the director.

(2) In the case where there has been approval under the first sentence of the preceding paragraph, the provision of article 108 of the Civil Code shall not apply.

(3) The provision of paragraph 2 of the preceding article shall apply *mutatis mutandis* to the director having effected the transaction of paragraph 1.

Art. 266(1). In the following cases, directors who have done any one of the acts mentioned there shall be jointly and severally liable in effecting performance or in damages to the company, in the case of item (i) for the amount which has been distributed or divided illegally, in the case (ii) for the amount of the interests offered, in the case of item (iii) for the amount of loans yet not repaid, or in the case of item (iv) and item (v) for the amount of any damage caused the company:

(i) where they have submitted to a general meeting the proposal for the distribution of profits in contravention of the provision of article 290(1), or they have distributed money in contravention of the provision of article 293-5(3);

(ii) where they have offered the interest on property in violation of the provision of article 294-2(1);

(iii) where they have loaned money to another director;

(iv) where they have effected any transaction mentioned in paragraph of the preceding article;

(v) where they have done any act which violates any law or ordinance or the articles of incorporation.

(2) In cases where any acts mentioned in the preceding paragraph has been done in accordance with the resolution of the board of directors, the directors who have assented to such resolution shall be deemed to have done such act.

(3) The directors who have participated in the resolution mentioned in the preceding paragraph and who have not expressed their dissent in the minutes shall be presumed to have assented to such resolution.

(4) If the director has effected a transaction in violation of the provision of article 264(1), the amount of the profit acquired due to the transaction by the director or the third party shall be presumed to be the amount of damage imposed to the company in paragraph 1. Provided that, this shall not apply if the right prescribed in paragraph 3 of said article has been exercised.

(5) The liability of directors mentioned in paragraph 1 cannot be released (*menjo*) except by the unanimous consent of all the shareholders.

(6) The liability of directors in respect to the transaction mentioned in item (iv) of paragraph 1 may be released by a majority of two-thirds or more of the votes of the total number of the issued shares, notwithstanding the provisions of the preceding paragraph. In this case, the directors shall disclose all material facts as to such transaction at a general meeting of shareholders.

Art. 266-3(1). If directors have been guilty of wrongful intent or of gross negligence in respect to the assumption of their duties, they shall be jointly and severally liable in damages to third persons also.

(2). It shall be the same as the preceding paragraph where the director has made a false entry as to the important matters to be stated in the application for shares, certificate for preemptive right, application for debentures, or the prospectus or in the documents of article 281(1), or made a false registration or public notice. Provided that, this shall not apply in the case where the director proves that he was not negligent of care in making the entry, registration, or public notice.

(3). The provisions of article 266(2) & (3) shall apply *mutatis mutandi* to the cases mentioned in the preceding two paragraph [sic].

Comments, Questions, and Problem

1. Is there a practical difference between the "theory of similarity" (that the duty of loyalty is merely an amplification of the duty of care) and the "theory of difference" (that the duty of care and of loyalty describe two distinct bases for regulating director

conduct)? Can you think of situations where the application of the different theories would lead to different results? Professor Kondo discounts the occurrence of these differences in Japan. Yet in the United States, it is undisputed that the duty of loyalty is not a subset fo the conduct subsumed under the duty of care.

2. Compare Civil Code articles 644–656 and Commercial Code article 254[3] to the Revised Model Business Corporation Act Articles and Subchapter (F). Do they provide an equivalent regulatory basis for director conduct? Do the statutory approaches suggest different theories of the regulation of director conduct underlying each act? IS it possible to harmonize the approaches of both statutes?

3. The theory of difference is based on the supposition that the Japanese law of managerial regulation is based on a conglomeration of continental theories of mandate and Anglo-American theories of trust. How successfully have those theories been blended into a law of managerial regulation in Japan? In that light consider the earlier readings on managerial culture in Japan. Do the earlier readings suggest that if the formal rules of managerial conduct are unsuccessfully developed they might be treated as irrelevant, or communally "reinterpreted" in a more felicitous manner by both managers and courts?

4. Professor Kondo tells us that a "duty is imposed on directors to supervise other directors in the exercise of their functions" under Japanese law. Is there a similar duty imposed on a director under U.S. law? If so, what are a director's obligations where the directors believes that other directors are breaching their obligations to the corporation? Are they obligations the same as those imposed on a Japanese director under the same circumstances?

5. Students of comparative law are usually concerned about their ability to correctly understand the laws of foreign jurisdictions. It is interesting, at the same time, to consider whether foreign comparativists understand principles of American law as American's understand them. With this in mind, consider whether Professor Kondo correctly restates the law of the "business judgment rule" in the excerpted materials above.

6. **Problem:** A newly elected governor of the State of Delaware proposes to seek amendment of the Delaware corporations code by imposing a new exclusive basis of director liability as follows: "A director becomes liable when in the course of performing his functions he causes harm to the company through negligence, or when he deliberately engages in actions that bring harm to the company." You are counsel to the trade association representing many of the larger national corporations incorporated in Delaware. Prepare an analysis of this change in law for your clients concentrating on the way in which the law might change the results under current law.

---

3. *Socialist Approaches*

Review the materials on Socialist approaches to monitoring managers, Chapter 10, Section A.3.

Comments and Questions

1. To whom would a Communist party member who is appointed to a management position of a company owe her duty in the management of that company? What would

be the nature of that duty? Would your answer to these questions depend on the extent to which the state holds an ownership interest in the company?

2. Consider the nature of conflicts of interest for managers in the People's Republic of China. If a company manager's primary duty is to maximize collective shareholder wealth, the duty to manage with due care extends to the shareholders. Yet if the state is a large shareholder of a number of companies that compete against each other, a conflict of duty, even of the duty of care, may arise as the manager attempts to maximize the wealth of the company she directs. Where the company competes against other companies whose primary shareholder is also the state, it may be possible to characterize actions which optimize one particular company's wealth at the expense of that of another company, especially where the collective wealth of both companies decreases as the one company prospers against the other, as adversely affecting the collective investment of the state in its companies. If the manager owes a duty to the state at least equal to that she owes to the company, then it may constitute a breach of the duty of care to engage in such actions without first determining the collective effect on the state. Do you agree? If this is the case, then to what extent can one actually consider the imposition of a duty of care on managers as window dressing?

C. Duty of Loyalty in General

Corporate directors do not exist in a vacuum. Successful people engaged in business usually have interests which may be substantially broader than their relationship to the corporation on whose boards of directors they may serve. The problem of defining, and enforcing the bona fides of the relation between director and company in this context has been among the most difficult tasks of corporate law. In the United States it has given rise to a highly complex and nuanced law of the fiduciary duty of loyalty. In Civil Law countries, a less comprehensive statutory based approach has been attempted. Neither system has proven to be perfect. Socialist countries like China face additional problems because managers may have conflicting official duties as well as conflicts between these duties and their personal interests.

1. Common Law Approaches

a. The American Approach

The duty of loyalty is at the center of a director's duty to the corporation. The duty of loyalty has proven to be an elastic concept in the United States. It has been formulated in ways which permit its use from simple transactions in which a director stands on both sides of a simple transaction, to the most sophisticated forms of corporate reorganization. The complexity of the situations in which it may be applicable has, in turn, created a doctrine which is itself complex.

Guth et al. v. Loft, Inc.

Supreme Court of Delaware
23 Del.Ch. 255, 5 A.2d 503
April 11, 1939.

LAYTON, Chief Justice, delivering the opinion of the Court:

In the Court below the appellants took the position that, on the facts, the complainant was entitled to no equitable relief whatever. In this Court, they seek only a modification of the Chancellor's decree, not a reversal of it. They now contend that the question is one of equitable adjustment based upon the extent and value of the respective contributions of the appellants and the appellee. This change of position is brought about, as it is said, because of certain basic fact findings of the Chancellor which are admittedly unassailable in this Court. The appellants accept the findings of fact; but they contend that the Chancellor's inferences from them were unwarrantable in material instances, and far more favorable to the complainant than they would have been had not he felt justified in penalizing Guth for what seemed to him serious departures from a strict standard of official conduct. They say that this attitude of mind of the Chancellor was brought about by attacking Guth's official conduct in such manner as to create an impression of ruthlessness, thereby causing the Chancellor to be less critical of equitable theory, and more inclined to do what amounted to an infliction of a penalty.

As stated by the appellants, there were certain questions before the Chancellor for determination: (1) was Guth at the time the Pepsi-Cola opportunity came to him obligated, in view of his official connection with Loft, to take the opportunity for Loft rather than for himself? On this point the appellants contend no finding was made.

(2) Was Guth, nevertheless, estopped from denying that the opportunity belonged to Loft; and was he rightfully penalized to the extent of his whole interest therein, merely because resources borrowed from Loft had contributed in some measure to its development; and did Loft's contributions create the whole value behind the interests of Guth and Grace in Pepsi, thereby constituting Loft the equitable owner of those interests? These questions were answered in the affirmative; and because of the answers, the Chancellor, it is said, did not answer the last question before him, that is, upon what theory and to what extent should Loft share in the proceeds of the Pepsi-Cola enterprise?

The appellants contend, at length and earnestly, that the Chancellor made no finding of fact with respect to corporate opportunity. They admit that if the Chancellor had found, or if this Court should find, that the Pepsi-Cola opportunity was one which Guth, as president and dominant director of Loft, was bound to embrace for it, such finding would create, as it is said, an obstacle to the appellants' right to a reappraisement of the Loft contributions to the Pepsi-Cola enterprise; and as the oral argument is remembered, it was stated in more direct and explicit terms, that if the Chancellor had so found, or if this Court should find, in favor of Loft upon the issue, the case would be at an end.

The appellants offer a comparison of the preliminary draft of a decree, submitted by the complainant as Finding A, with the final draft of that finding. Briefly, the substantial difference is, that in the preliminary draft it was stated that the opportunity to acquire the formula, goodwill and business incident to the manufacture and sale of Pepsi-Cola, belonged to the complainant; whereas, in the decree as signed, it was stated that Guth was estopped to deny that he had received the opportunity on behalf of the complainant. The appellants say that strenuous objection was made to the draft submitted by the appellee on the ground that nowhere in the Chancellor's opinion did it appear that he had found, as a fact, that the opportunity belonged to Loft, and after full consideration, the Chancellor acquiesced, and the modification was made. The appellee contends that the chancellor did find that the Pepsi-Cola opportunity belonged to it, and that the modification was made for other reasons.

In these circumstances of contention, certain questions suggest themselves for consideration, and some of them for answer: Did the Chancellor make an explicit finding that the Pepsi-Cola opportunity belonged in equity to Loft, and if so, was such finding justifiable in fact and in law? If the Chancellor made no such explicit finding, should he have done so, or should this Court make such finding? Assuming that the Chancellor made no explicit finding and that this Court should not feel justified in making such finding, was, and is, the doctrine of estoppel properly invocable in favor of the complainant?

The complainant is not, of course, precluded from making the argument that, upon the law and the facts, the Pepsi-Cola opportunity belonged to it; nor is this Court prohibited from so finding.

It is necessary briefly to notice what the Chancellor said with respect to the question of corporate opportunity. As a preliminary to the discussion of the question, the Chancellor stated generally the principles governing officers and directors of a corporation with respect to their fiduciary relation to the corporation and its stockholders, and their liability to account to the corporation for profits and advantages resulting from unlawful acts and breaches of trust done and committed in the promotion of their own interests. He then proceeded to say that Guth, being not only a director of Loft but its president as well, and dominant in the management of its affairs, the principles and rules governing trustees in their relations with their correlates applied to him with peculiar and exceptional force. He particularly noticed a proposition of law stated by the defendants, that when a business opportunity comes to an officer or director in his individual capacity rather than in his official capacity, and is one which, because of its nature, is not essential to the corporation, and is one in which it has no interest or expectancy, the officer or director is entitled to treat the opportunity as his own. As stated, he found the proposition acceptable in the main; but he observed that the cases cited by the defendant recognized as true also the converse of the proposition, and that in all of them the fundamental fact of good faith was found in favor of the officer or director charged with the dereliction. He then proceeded to say [2 A.2d 240]:

> 'Now the evidence in the case subjudice does not warrant the view that any one of these features may be affirmed as existing here. The brief review of some of its salient features which I have hereinbefore made, shows the opposite of every one of them to have been the fact. That Loft had the means to finance and establish the business is clearly demonstrated. In every aspect of essential fact it did so. That Guth did not use his own funds and risk his own resources in acquiring and developing the Pepsi business is equally demonstrated. He was in fact unable to do so. I dismiss from consideration his claim of a parol contract of guaranty with Loft by which he engaged to save it harmless from any loss it might suffer from its advances. I conclude that no such guaranty was given. Even if it was, it was worthless. That the business of producing Pepsi-Cola syrup was in the line of Loft's business and of practical and not theoretical interest to it, is shown by the fact that Loft was engaged in manufacturing fountain syrups of numerous kinds to supply its own extensive needs. Indeed the outstanding justi-

> fication which Guth offers for his utilization of Loft's resources on the scale he did, was Loft's need for a constant and reliable supply of Pepsi-Cola syrup. The former directors now allied with Guth, a minority of the former board, offer a like justification for their alleged approval of Guth's acts in plunging Loft deep into the Pepsi venture. It does not become either Guth or the minority group of directors now associated with him to claim that Pepsi was an enterprise which was foreign to Loft's purposes and alien to its business interests. The very claim, if accepted, denounces as a shocking breach of their duty as directors their act of agreeing, as they now say they did, to Guth's free use of Loft's resources of all kinds to an unlimited extent to promote and develop the enterprise.'
>
> 'I am of the opinion that under such circumstances as are disclosed in this case, Guth is estopped by what he subsequently caused Loft to do, to deny that when he embraced the Megargel offer he did so in behalf of Loft. The offer cannot be viewed in any light other than an expectancy that was Loft's. Guth is estopped to contend to the contrary. The case of Bailey v. Jacobs, 325 Pa. 187, 189 A. 320, cited at an earlier point in this opinion, is a pertinent and persuasive authority in support of that view.'

Manifestly, the Chancellor found to exist facts and circumstances from which the conclusion could be reached that the Pepsi-Cola opportunity belonged in equity to Loft.

Corporate officers and directors are not permitted to use their position of trust and confidence to further their private interests. While technically not trustees, they stand in a fiduciary relation to the corporation and its stockholders. A public policy, existing through the years, and derived from a profound knowledge of human characteristics and motives, has established a rule that demands of a corporate officer or director, peremptorily and inexorably, the most scrupulous observance of his duty, not only affirmatively to protect the interests of the corporation committed to his charge, but also to refrain from doing anything that would work injury to the corporation, or to deprive it of profit or advantage which his skill and ability might properly bring to it, or to enable it to make in the reasonable and lawful exercise of its powers. The rule that requires an undivided and unselfish loyalty to the corporation demands that there shall be no conflict between duty and self-interest. The occasions for the determination of honesty, good faith and loyal conduct are many and varied, and no hard and fast rule can be formulated. The standard of loyalty is measured by no fixed scale.

If an officer or director of a corporation, in violation of his duty as such, acquires gain or advantage for himself, the law charges the interest so acquired with a trust for the benefit of the corporation, at its election, while it denies to the betrayer all benefit and profit. The rule, inveterate and uncompromising in its rigidity, does not rest upon the narrow ground of injury or damage to the corporation resulting from a betrayal of confidence, but upon a broader foundation of a wise public policy that, for the purpose of removing all temptation, extinguishes all possibility of profit flowing from a breach of the confidence imposed by the fiduciary relation. Given the relation between the parties, a certain result follows; and a constructive trust is the remedial device through which precedence of self is compelled to give way to the stern demands of loyalty....

The rule, referred to briefly as the rule of corporate opportunity, is merely one of the manifestations of the general rule that demands of an officer or director the utmost good faith in his relation to the corporation which he represents.

It is true that when a business opportunity comes to a corporate officer or director in his individual capacity rather than in his official capacity, and the opportunity is one which, because of the nature of the enterprise, is not essential to his corporation, and is one in which it has no interest or expectancy, the officer or director is entitled to treat the opportunity as his own, and the corporation has no interest in it, if, of course, the officer or director has not wrongfully embarked the corporation's resources therein.... But, in all of these cases, except, perhaps, in one, there was no infidelity on the part of the corporate officer sought to be charged. In the first case, it was found that the corporation had no practical use for the property acquired by Harris. In the Pioneer Oil & Gas Co. case, Anderson used no funds or assets of the corporation, did not know that the corporation was negotiating for the oil lands and, further, the corporation could not, in any event have acquired them, because their proprietors objected to the corporation's having an interest in them, and because the corporation was in no financial position to pay for them. In the Stubbs case, the railroad company, desiring to purchase from Porter such part of his land as was necessary for its right of way, station, water-tank, and woodshed, declined to accede to his price. Stubbs, a director, made every effort to buy the necessary land for the company and failed. He then bought the entire tract, and offered to sell to the company what it needed. The company repudiated expressly all participation in the purchase. Later the company located its tracks and buildings on a part of the land, but could not agree with Stubbs as to damages or terms of the conveyance. Three and one-half years thereafter, Stubbs was informed for the first time that the company claimed that he held the land in trust for it. In the Lancaster Loose Leaf Tobacco Co. case, the company had never engaged in the particular line of business, and its established policy had been not to engage in it. The only interest which the company had in the burley tobacco bought by Robinson was its commissions in selling it on its floors, and these commissions it received. In the Lagarde case, it was said that the proprietorship of the property acquired by the Legardes may have been important to the corporation, but was not shown to have been necessary to the continuance of its business, or that its purchase by the Legardes had in any way impaired the value of the corporation's property. This decision is, perhaps, the strongest cited on behalf of the appellants. With deference to the Court that rendered it, a different view of the correctness of the conclusion reached may be entertained.

On the other hand, it is equally true that, if there is presented to a corporate officer or director a business opportunity which the corporation is financially able to undertake, is, from its nature, in the line of the corporation's business and is of practical advantage to it, is one in which the corporation has an interest or a reasonable expectancy, and, by embracing the opportunity, the self-interest of the officer or director will be brought into conflict with that of his corporation, the law will not permit him to seize the opportunity for himself. And, if, in such circumstances, the interests of the corporation are betrayed, the corporation may elect to claim all of the benefits of the transaction for itself, and the law will impress a trust in favor of the corporation upon the property, interests and profits so acquired....

But, there is little profit in a discussion of the particular cases cited. In none of them are the facts and circumstances comparable to those of the case under consideration. The question is not one to be decided on narrow or technical grounds, but upon broad considerations of corporate duty and loyalty.

As stated in 3 Fletcher Cyclopedia, Corporations, § 862, an authority seemingly relied on by the appellants, 'There is a vast field for individual activity outside the duty of a director, yet well within the general scope of the corporation's business. The test seems to be whether there was a specific duty, on the part of the officer sought to be held liable, to act or contract in regard to the particular matter as the representative of the corporation—all of which is largely a question of fact'.

Duty and loyalty are inseparably connected. Duty is that which is required by one's station or occupation; is that which one is bound by legal or moral obligation to do or refrain from doing; and it is with this conception of duty as the underlying basis of the principle applicable to the situation disclosed, that the conduct and acts of Guth with respect to his acquisition of the Pepsi-Cola enterprise will be scrutinized. Guth was not merely a director and the president of Loft. He was its master. It is admitted that Guth manifested some of the qualities of a dictator. The directors were selected by him. Some of them held salaried positions in the company. All of them held their positions at his favor. Whether they were supine merely, or for sufficient reasons entirely subservient to Guth, it is not profitable to inquire. It is sufficient to say that they either wilfully or negligently allowed Guth absolute freedom of action in the management of Loft's activities, and theirs is an unenviable position whether testifying for or against the appellants.

Prior to May, 1931, Guth became convinced that Loft was being unfairly discriminated against by the Coca-Cola Company of whose syrup it was a large purchaser, in that Loft had been refused a jobber's discount on the syrup, although others, whose purchases were of far less importance, had been given such discount. He determined to replace Coca-Cola as a beverage at the Loft stores with some other cola drink, if that could be accomplished. So, on May 19, 1931, he suggested an inquiry with respect to desirability of discontinuing the use of Coca-Cola, and replacing it with Pepsi-Cola at a greatly reduced price. Pepsi-Cola was the syrup produced by National Pepsi-Cola Company. As a beverage it had been on the market for over twenty-five years, and while it was not known to consumers in the area of the Loft stores, its formula and trademark were well established. Guth's purpose was to deliver Loft from the thraldom of the Coca-Cola Company, which practically dominated the field of cola beverages, and, at the same time, to gain for Loft a greater margin of profit on its sales of cola beverages. Certainly, the choice of an acceptable substitute for Coca-Cola was not a wide one, and, doubtless, his experience in the field of bottled beverages convinced him that it was necessary for him to obtain a cola syrup whose formula and trademark were secure against attack. Although the difficulties and dangers were great, he concluded to make the change. Almost simultaneously, National Pepsi-Cola Company, in which Megargel was predominant and whom Guth knew, went into bankruptcy; and Guth was informed that the long established Pepsi-Cola formula and trademark could be had at a small price. Guth, of course, was Loft; and Loft's determination to replace Coca-Cola with some other cola beverage in its many stores was practically co-incidental with the opportunity to acquire the Pepsi-Cola formula and trademark. This was the condition of affairs when Megargel approached Guth. Guth contended that his negotiation with Megargel in 1931 was but a continuation of a negotiation begun in 1928, when he had no connection with Loft; but the Chancellor found to the contrary, and his finding is accepted.

It is urged by the appellants that Megargel offered the Pepsi-Cola opportunity to Guth personally, and not to him as president of Loft. The Chancellor said that there was no way of knowing the fact, as Megargel was dead, and the benefit of his testimony could not be had; but that it was not important, for the matter of consequence was how Guth received the proposition.

It was incumbent upon Guth to show that his every act in dealing with the opportunity presented was in the exercise of the utmost good faith to Loft; and the burden was cast upon him satisfactorily to prove that the offer was made to him individually. Reasonable inferences, drawn from acknowledged facts and circumstances, are powerful factors in arriving at the truth of a disputed matter, and such inferences are not to be ignored in considering the acts and conduct of Megargel. He had been for years engaged in the manufacture and sale of a cola syrup in competition with Coca-Cola. He knew of the difficulties of competition with such a powerful opponent in general, and in particular in the securing of a necessary foothold in a new territory where Coca-Cola was supreme. He could not hope to establish the popularity and use of his syrup in a strange field, and in competition with the assured position of Coca-Cola, by the usual advertising means, for he, himself, had no money or resources, and it is entirely unbelievable that he expected Guth to have command of the vast amount of money necessary to popularize Pepsi-Cola by the ordinary methods. He knew of the difficulty, not to say impossibility, of inducing proprietors of soft drink establishments to use a cola drink utterly unknown to their patrons. It would seem clear, from any reasonable point of view, that Megargel sought to interest someone who controlled an existing opportunity to popularize his product by an actual presentation of it to the consuming public. Such person was Guth, the president of Loft. It is entirely reasonable to infer that Megargel approached Guth as president of Loft, operating, as it did, many soft drink fountains in a most necessary and desirable territory where Pepsi-Cola was little known, he well knowing that if the drink could be established in New York and circumjacent territory, its success would be assured. Every reasonable inference points to this conclusion. What was finally agreed upon between Megargel and Guth, and what outward appearance their agreement assumed, is of small importance. It was a matter of indifference to Megargel whether his co-adventurer was Guth personally, or Loft, so long as his terms were met and his object attained.

Leaving aside the manner of the offer of the opportunity, certain other matters are to be considered in determining whether the opportunity, in the circumstances, belonged to Loft; and in this we agree that Guth's right to appropriate the Pepsi-Cola opportunity to himself depends upon the circumstances existing at the time it presented itself to him without regard to subsequent events, and that due weight should be given to character of the opportunity which Megargel envisioned and brought to Guth's door.

The real issue is whether the opportunity to secure a very substantial stock interest in a corporation to be formed for the purpose of exploiting a cola beverage on a wholesale scale was so closely associated with the existing business activities of Loft, and so essential thereto, as to bring the transaction within that class of cases where the acquisition of the property would throw the corporate officer purchasing it into competition with his company. This is a factual question to be decided by reasonable inferences from objective facts.

It is asserted that, no matter how diversified the scope of Loft's activities, its primary business was the manufacturing and selling of candy in its own chain of retail stores, and that it never had the idea of turning a subsidiary product into a highly advertised, nation-wide specialty. Therefore, it had never initiated any investigation into the possibility of acquiring a stock interest in a corporation to be formed to exploit Pepsi-Cola on the scale envisioned by Megargel, necessitating sales of at least 1,000,000 gallons a year. It is said that the most effective argument against the proposition that Guth was obligated to take the opportunity for Loft is to be found in the complainant's own assertion that Guth was guilty of an improper exercise of business judgment when he replaced Coca-Cola with Pepsi-Cola at the Loft Stores. Assuming that the complainant's argument in this respect is incompatible with its contention that the Pepsi-Cola opportunity belonged to Loft, it is no more inconsistent than is the position of the appellants on the question. In the Court below, the defendants strove strenuously to show, and to have it believed, that the Pepsi-Cola opportunity was presented to Loft by Guth, with a full disclosure by him that if the company did not embrace it, he would. This, manifestly, was a recognition of the necessity for his showing complete good faith on his part as a corporate officer of Loft. In this Court, the Chancellor having found as a fact that Guth did not offer the opportunity to his corporation, it is asserted that no question of good faith is involved for the reason that the opportunity was of such character that Guth, although Loft's president, was entirely free to embrace it for himself. The issue is not to be enmeshed in the cobwebs of sophistry. It rises far above inconsistencies in argument.

The appellants suggest a doubt whether Loft would have been able to finance the project along the lines contemplated by Megargel, viewing the situation as of 1931. The answer to this suggestion is two-fold. The Chancellor found that Loft's net asset position at that time was amply sufficient to finance the enterprise, and that its plant, equipment, executives, personnel and facilities, supplemented by such expansion for the necessary development of the business as it was well able to provide, were in all respects adequate. The second answer is that Loft's resources were found to be sufficient, for Guth made use of no other to any important extent.

Next it is contended that the Pepsi-Cola opportunity was not in the line of Loft's activities which essentially were of a retail nature. It is pointed out that, in 1931, the retail stores operated by Loft were largely located in the congested areas along the Middle Atlantic Seaboard, that its manufacturing operations were centered in its New York factory, and that it was a definitely localized business, and not operated on a national scale; whereas, the Megargel proposition envisaged annual sales of syrup at least a million gallons, which could be accomplished only by a wholesale distribution. Loft, however, had many wholesale activities. Its wholesale business in 1931 amounted to over $800,000. It was a large company by any standard. It had an enormous plant. It paid enormous rentals. Guth, himself, said that Loft's success depended upon the fullest utilization of its large plant facilities. Moreover, it was a manufacturer of syrups and, with the exception of cola syrup, it supplied its own extensive needs. The appellants admit that wholsesale distribution of bottled beverages can best be accomplished by license agreements with bottlers. Guth, president of Loft, was an able and experienced man in that field. Loft, then, through its own personnel, possessed the technical knowledge, the practical business experience, and the resources necessary for the development of the Pepsi-Cola enterprise.

But, the appellants say that the expression, 'in the line' of a business, is a phrase so elastic as to furnish no basis for a useful inference. The phrase is not within the field of precise definition, nor is it one that can be bounded by a set formula. It has a flexible meaning, which is to be applied reasonably and sensibly to the facts and circumstances of the particular case. Where a corporation is engaged in a certain business, and an opportunity is presented to it embracing an activity as to which it has fundamental knowledge, practical experience and ability to pursue, which, logically and naturally, is adaptable to its business having regard for its financial position, and is one that is consonant with its reasonable needs and aspirations for expansion, it may be properly said that the opportunity is in the line of the corporation's business.

The manufacture of syrup was the core of the Pepsi-Cola opportunity. The manufacture of syrups was one of Loft's not unimportant activities. It had the necessary resources, facilities, equipment, technical and practical knowledge and experience. The tie was close between the business of Loft and the Pepsi-Cola enterprise. Beatty v. Guggenheim Exploration Co., 225 N.Y. 380, 122 N.E. 378; Transvaal Cold Storage Co., Ltd., v. Palmer, [1904] T. S. Transvaal L. R. 4. Conceding that the essential of an opportunity is reasonably within the scope of a corporation's activities, latitude should be allowed for development and expansion. To deny this would be to deny the history of industrial development.

It is urged that Loft had no interest or expectancy in the Pepsi-Cola opportunity. That it had no existing property right therein is manifest; but we cannot agree that it had no concern or expectancy in the opportunity within the protection of remedial equity. Loft had a practical and essential concern with respect to some cola syrup with an established formula and trademark. A cola beverage has come to be a business necessity for soft drink establishments; and it was essential to the success of Loft to serve at its soda fountains an acceptible five cent cola drink in order to attract into its stores the great multitude of people who have formed the habit of drinking cola beverages. When Guth determined to discontinue the sale of Coca-Cola in the Loft stores, it became, by his own act, a matter of urgent necessity for Loft to acquire a constant supply of some satisfactory cola syrup, secure against probable attack, as a replacement; and when the Pepsi-Cola opportunity presented itself, Guth having already considered the availability of the syrup, it became impressed with a Loft interest and expectancy arising out of the circumstances and the urgent and practical need created by him as the directing head of Loft.

As a general proposition it may be said that a corporate officer or director is entirely free to engage in an independent, competitive business, so long as he violates no legal or moral duty with respect to the fiduciary relation that exists between the corporation and himself. The appellants contend that no conflict of interest between Guth and Loft resulted from his acquirement and exploitation of the Pepsi-Cola opportunity. They maintain that the acquisition did not place Guth in competition with Loft any more than a manufacturer can be said to compete with a retail merchant whom the manufacturer supplies with goods to be sold. However true the statement, applied generally, may be, we emphatically dissent from the application of the analogy to the situation of the parties here. There is no unity between the ordinary manufacturer and the retailer of his goods. Generally, the retailer, if he becomes dissatisfied with one supplier of merchandise, can turn to another. He is under no compulsion and no restraint. In the instant case Guth was Loft, and Guth was Pepsi. He absolutely controlled Loft. His authority over Pepsi was supreme. As Pepsi, he created and controlled the supply of Pepsi-Cola syrup, and he determined the price and the terms. What he offered, as Pepsi, he had the power, as Loft, to accept. Upon any consideration of human characteristics and motives, he created a conflict between self-interest and duty. He made himself the judge in his own cause. This was the inevitable result of the dual personality which Guth assumed, and his position was one which, upon the least austere view of corporate duty, he had no right to assume. Moreover, a reasonable probability of injury to Loft resulted from the situation forced upon it. Guth was in the same position to impose his terms upon Loft as had been the Coca-Cola Company. If Loft had been in servitude to that company with respect to its need for a cola syrup, its condition did not change when its supply came to depend upon Pepsi, for, it was found by the Chancellor, against Guth's contention, that he had not given Loft the protection of a contract which secured to it a constant supply of Pepsi-Cola syrup at any definite price or for any definite time.

It is useless to pursue the argument. The facts and circumstances demonstrate that Guth's appropriation of the Pepsi-Cola opportunity to himself placed him in a competitive position with Loft with respect to a commodity essential to it, thereby rendering his personal interests incompatible with the superior interests of his corporation; and this situation was accomplished, not openly and with his own resources, but secretly and with the money and facilities of the corporation which was committed to his protection.

Although the facts and circumstances disclosed by the voluminous record clearly show gross violations of legal and moral duties by Guth in his dealings with Loft, the appellants make bold to say that no duty was cast upon Guth, hence he was guilty of no disloyalty. The fiduciary relation demands something more than the morals of the market place. Meinhard v. Salmon, supra. Guth's abstractions of Loft's money and materials are complacently referred to as borrowings. Whether his acts are to be deemed properly cognizable in a civil court at all, we need not inquire, but certain it is that borrowing is not descriptive of them. A borrower presumes a lender acting freely. Guth took without limit or stint from a helpless corporation, in violation of a statute enacted for the protection of corporations against such abuses, and without the knowledge or authority of the corporation's Board of Directors. Cunning and craft supplanted sincerity. Frankness gave way to concealment. He did not offer the Pepsi-Cola opportunity to Loft, but captured it for himself. He invested little or no money of his own in the venture, but commandeered for his own benefit and advantage the money, resources and facilities of his corporation and the services of its officials. He thrust upon Loft the hazard, while he reaped the benefit. His time was paid for by Loft. The use of the Grace plant was not essential to the enterprise. In such manner he acquired for himself and Grace ninety one percent of the capital stock of Pepsi, now worth many millions. A genius in his line he may be, but the law makes no distinction between the wrong doing genius and the one less endowed.

Upon a consideration of all the facts and circumstances as disclosed we are convinced that the opportunity to acquire the Pepsi-Cola trademark and formula, goodwill and business belonged to the complainant, and that Guth, as its President, had no right to appropriate the opportunity to himself.

The Chancellor's opinion may be said to leave in some doubt whether he found as a fact that the Pepsi-Cola opportunity belonged to Loft. Certain it is that he found all of the elements of a business opportunity to exist. Whether he made use of the word 'estopped' as meaning that he found in the facts and circumstances all of the elements of an equitable estoppel, or whether the word was used loosely in the sense that the facts and circumstances were so overwhelming as to render it impossible for Guth to rebut the conclusion that the opportunity belonged to Loft, it is needless to argue. It may be said, however, that we are not at all convinced that the elements of an equitable estoppel may not be found having regard for the dual personality which Guth assumed.

The decree of the Chancellor is sustained.

Allen Nixon, et al., Defendants Below, Appellants, v. Guy C. Blackwell, et al., Plaintiffs Below, Appellees.

Supreme Court of Delaware
626 A.2d 1366
June 22, 1993, Decided

VEASEY, Chief Justice:

In this action we review a decision of the Court of Chancery holding that the defendant directors of a closely-held corporation breached their fiduciary duties to the plaintiffs by maintaining a discriminatory policy that unfairly favors employee stockholders over plaintiffs. The Vice Chancellor found that the directors treated the plaintiffs unfairly by establishing an employee stock ownership plan ("ESOP") and by purchasing key man life insurance policies to provide liquidity for defendants and other corporate employees to enable them to sell their stock while providing no comparable liquidity for minority stockholders. We conclude that the Court of Chancery applied erroneous legal standards and made findings of fact which were not the product of an orderly and logical deductive reasoning process. Accordingly, we REVERSE and REMAND to the Court of Chancery for proceedings not inconsistent with this opinion.

I. FACTS

This case involved a five-day trial before the Vice Chancellor. The record is detailed, but only a brief discussion of the salient facts is necessary to an understanding of the issues before us.

A. The Parties

Plaintiffs are 14 minority stockholders of Class B, non-voting, stock of E. C. Barton & Co. (the "Corporation"). The individual defendants are the members of the board of directors (the "Board" or the "directors"). The Corporation is also a defendant. Plaintiffs collectively own only Class B stock, and own no Class A stock. Their total holdings comprise approximately 25 percent of all the common stock outstanding as of the end of fiscal year 1989.

At all relevant times, the Board consisted of ten individuals who either are currently employed, or were once employed, by the Corporation. At the time this suit was filed, these directors collectively owned approximately 47.5 percent of all the outstanding Class A shares. The remaining Class A shares were held by certain other present and former employees of the Corporation.

B. Mr. Barton's Testamentary Plan

The Corporation is a non-public, closely-held Delaware corporation headquartered in Arkansas. It is engaged in the business of selling wholesale and retail lumber in the Mississippi Delta. The Corporation was formed in 1928 by E. C. Barton ("Mr. Barton") and has two classes of common stock: Class A voting stock and Class B non-voting stock. Substantially all of the Corporation's stock was held by Mr. Barton at the time of his death in 1967. Mr. Barton was survived by his second wife, Martha K. Barton ("Mrs. Barton") who died in 1985, and by Dorothy B. Rebsamen and Mary Lee Marcom, his daughter and granddaughter, respectively, from his first marriage. Pursuant to Mr. Barton's testamentary plan, 49 percent of the Class A voting stock was bequeathed outright to eight of his loyal employees. The remaining 51 percent, along with 14 percent of the Class B non-voting stock, was placed into an independently managed 15-year trust for the same eight people. Sixty-one percent of the Class B non-voting stock was bequeathed outright to Mrs. Barton. Mr. Barton's daughter and granddaughter received 21 percent of the Class B stock in trust. The non-voting Class B shares Mr. Barton bequeathed to his family represented 75 percent of the Corporation's total equity.

Ownership interests in the Corporation began to change in the early 1970s following the distribution of Mr. Barton's estate. Mrs. Barton gave certain shares of Class B non-voting stock to her three children, Guy C. Blackwell, Owen G. Blackwell and Martha G. Hestand (the "children"). In 1973 the Corporation purchased all of the Class B stock held in trust for Mr. Barton's daughter and granddaughter at a price of $ 45 per share.[2] Mrs. Barton sold the remainder of her Class B shares to the Corporation in January 1975 at a price of $ 45 per share. These transactions left Mrs. Barton's three children collectively with 30 percent of the outstanding Class B non-voting stock. The children

2. The Internal Revenue Service valued the stock at $ 45 per share at the time of Mr. Barton's death.

have no voting rights despite their substantial equity interest in the Corporation. The children are also the only non-employee Class B stockholders.

There is no public market for, or trading in, either class of the Corporation's stock. This creates problems for stockholders, particularly the Class B minority stockholders, who wish to sell or otherwise realize the value of their shares. The corporation purported to address this problem in several ways over the years.

C. The Self-Tenders

The Corporation occasionally offered to purchase the Class B stock of the non-employee stockholders through a series of self-tender offers. During the late 1970s the Corporation attempted to purchase the outstanding Class B shares held by Guy C. Blackwell, Owen G. Blackwell and Martha G. Hestand, the Corporation's only non-employee stockholders. The Corporation first offered to repurchase the children's stock at $ 45 per share shortly after they acquired it from Mrs. Barton. The children rejected the offer and the stock subsequently split 25-for-1 in 1976. A second unsuccessful repurchase offer was made in 1977. At that time, the Corporation offered the children $ 8.22 per share. In light of the stock split, this price appears to be approximately four times the amount the Corporation paid for Mrs. Barton's Class B shares three years earlier. In 1979 the Corporation again approached the children and offered to repurchase their stock at a price of $ 15 per share. Martha Hestand accepted the offer and tendered her shares to the Corporation. Guy and Owen Blackwell, however, refused to sell their shares at that price. The Corporation made no further repurchase offers until May 1985, when the ESOP undertook a tender offer to repurchase 48,000 shares of Class B stock, concurrently with a tender offer by the Corporation for 39,000 Class A and 100,000 Class B shares at a price of $ 25 per share. The book value of the Class A stock and the Class B stock at that time was $ 38.39 and $ 26.35, respectively. The remaining children and the other plaintiffs in the present action refused to sell.

D. The Employee Stock Ownership Plan ("ESOP")

In November 1975 the Corporation established an ESOP designed to hold Class B non-voting stock for the benefit of eligible employees of the Corporation. The ESOP is a tax-qualified profit-sharing plan whereby employees of the Corporation are allocated a share of the assets held by the plan in proportion to their annual compensation, subject to certain vesting requirements. The ESOP is funded by annual cash contributions from the Corporation. Under the plan, terminating and retiring employees are entitled to receive their interest in the ESOP by taking Class B stock or cash in lieu of stock. It appears from the record that most terminating employees and retirees elect to receive cash in lieu of stock. The Corporation commissions an annual appraisal of the Corporation to determine the value of its stock for ESOP purposes. Thus, the ESOP provides employee Class B stockholders with a substantial measure of liquidity not available to non-employee stockholders. The Corporation had the option of repurchasing Class A stock from the employees upon their retirement or death. The estates of the employee stockholders did not have a corresponding right to put the stock to the Corporation.

E. The Key Man Insurance Policies

The Corporation also purchased certain key man life insurance policies with death benefits payable to the Corporation. Several early policies insuring the lives of key executives and directors were purchased during Mr. Barton's lifetime with death benefits payable to the Corporation. In 1982 the Corporation purchased additional key man policies in connection with agreements entered into between the Corporation and nine key officers and directors. Each executive executed an agreement giving the Corporation a call option to substitute Class B non-voting stock for their Class A voting stock upon the occurrence of certain events, including death and termination of employment, so that the voting shares could be reissued to new key personnel. In return, the Board adopted a resolution creating a non-binding recommendation that a portion of the key man life insurance proceeds be used to repurchase the exchanged Class B stock from the executives' estates at a price at least equal to 80 percent of their ESOP value. The minutes of a special meeting of the Board on June 26, 1982, provide:

> BE IT RESOLVED that the Board of Directors of E C. Barton & Company recommends and strongly urges the E. C. Barton & Company Employee Stock Ownership Plan Committee and the Trustees of the E. C. Barton & Company Employee Stock Ownership Trust, upon receipt of life insurance funds, resulting from the death of any one of the said nine controlling Class "A" stockholders, that said life insurance funds be used as next set out: 40% for the purchase of shares of E. C. Barton & Company stock from the estate of the deceased stockholder; 35% for the purchase of shares of E. C. Barton & Company stock from the remaining controlling Class "A" stockholders on a pro rata basis; 25% retained by the Employee Stock Ownership Trust for liquidity....

Despite the strong recommendation, the ultimate decision on the use of insurance proceeds for this purpose was left to the discretion of the Corporation's management or the Board.

In 1985 the Corporation purchased eight $ 300,000 keyman life insurance policies and adopted a plan in connection with its June self-tender. The Corporation's tender offer was for both Class A and Class B stock. The intended use for the proceeds of the keyman life insurance policies was to fund the retirement of any unpaid principal and interest on promissory notes issued in payment for Class A stock acquired in one of the self-tenders. A resolution of the Board facilitating this end was unanimously adopted at the December 17, 1985 meeting. The minutes of that meeting provide:

> IT IS THEREFORE RESOLVED that the death benefits inuring to the Company from the proceeds of the [eight keyman] insurance policies shall first be applied to the unpaid balance of principal and interest of the Promissory Note issued in June of 1985 to the deceased, and the balance of said proceeds prorated and applied to the unpaid principal and/or interest of such Promissory Notes held by the survivors of the aforementioned insured key men.

In the five-year period, 1985 to 1989, the Corporation paid approximately $ 450,000 in net key man premiums. The premiums exceeded the Corporation's declared dividends in 1986 and 1989, even after the earnings on the policies were deducted (1986—premiums, $ 146,614, dividends, $ 93,133; 1989—premiums, $ 144,704, dividends, $ 143,374). The reasonableness and significance of these facts is not clear in the record or the findings of the trial court.

The record and the findings of the trial court are not precisely clear on the issue of corporate benefit compared with individual benefit to the defendants with respect to the proceeds of the key man insurance policies. The death benefits of such policies, as here, are normally payable to the Corporation and are designed to benefit the Corporation by providing some measure of compensation for the loss of productive corporate executives. Here the two resolutions recited above show a desire to earmark the proceeds. On the death of each individual, the 1985 resolution would apply the proceeds to liquidation of at least part of the corporate debt (i.e., the corporate promissory note issued to the deceased in connection with that employee's previous tender of stock). Certainly that would provide "liquidity" to the employee's estate by paying off a corporate debt, but presumably that obligation was owing in any event and was a liability on the corporate balance sheet. Liquidation of it would improve the corporate balance sheet and would also put cash in the hands of the employee's estate.

The analysis of this issue would seem to call for a disciplined balancing test by a court reviewing the mailer for entire fairness. As we note hereafter, we find such an analysis to be lacking in the trial court's opinion.

F. Dividend Policy and Compensation

The Board from time to time paid modest dividends. Because the earnings were solid in many years and dividends relatively low, the retained earnings of the Corporation continued to increase at a relatively high level. Plaintiffs challenged these corporate decisions as unfair to the minority. There was also a challenge at trial by plaintiffs to the compensation level of the defendants. In view of the ruling of the Vice Chancellor in defendants' favor on the dividend policy and against the plaintiffs on the claim of excessive compensation, from which rulings no appeal was taken by plaintiffs, there is no need to detail the facts relating to those issues, except to the extent, hereinafter discussed, that the trial court referred to the dividend policy in connection with other issues or fairness generally.

II. PROCEEDINGS IN THE COURT OF CHANCERY

[The Court described the proceedings in the trial court in some detail]

III. RATIONALE OF THE VICE CHANCELLOR'S DECISION

[omitted]

IV. SCOPE AND STANDARD OF REVIEW

The threshold question is the applicable standard by which the defendants' conduct is to be judged. This is a legal question and therefore is subject to de novo review by this Court. Fiduciary Trust Co. v. Fiduciary Trust Co., Del. Supr., 445 A.2d 927, 930 (1982). The ultimate determination of the trial court involved mixed questions of fact and law. The trial court made findings of fact upon which its conclusion that defendants had violated their fiduciary duties was predicated. This Court reviews the entire record and the sufficiency of evidence to test the propriety of those findings, and will review the factual findings of the trial court to determine if they are sufficiently supported by the record and are the product of an orderly and logical deductive process. *Levitt v. Bouvier, Del. Supr., 287 A.2d 671, 673 (1972); Smith v. Van Gorkom, Del. Supr., 488 A.2d 858, 871 (1985).*

V. APPLICABLE PRINCIPLES OF SUBSTANTIVE LAW

Defendants contend that the trial court erred in not applying the business judgment rule. Since the defendants benefitted from the ESOP and could have benefitted from the key man life insurance beyond that which benefitted other stockholders generally, the defendants are on both sides of the transaction. For that reason, we agree with the trial court that the entire fairness test applies to this aspect of the case. Accordingly, defendants have the burden of showing the entire fairness of those transactions. Sinclair Oil Corp. v. Levien, Del. Supr., 280 A.2d 717 (1971) ("Levien"); Weinberger v. UOP, Inc., Del. Supr., 457 A.2d 701 (1983) ("Weinberger").

> When directors of a Delaware corporation are on both sides of a transaction, they are required to demonstrate their utmost good faith and the most scrupulous inherent fairness of the bargain... The requirement of fairness is unflinching in its demand that where one stands on both sides of a transaction,

> he has the burden of establishing its entire fairness, sufficient to pass the test of careful scrutiny by the courts.

Weinberger, 457 A.2d at 710.

Weinberger explains further the two aspects of entire fairness, fair price and fair dealing:

> The concept of fairness has two basic aspects: fair dealing and fair price. The former embraces questions of when the transaction was timed, how it was initiated, structured, negotiated, disclosed to the directors, and how the approvals of the directors and the stockholders were obtained. The latter aspect of fairness relates to the economic and financial considerations of the proposed merger, including all relevant factors: assets, market value, earnings, future prospects, and any other elements that affect the intrinsic or inherent value of a company's stock.... All aspects of the issue must be examined as a whole since the question is one of entire fairness.

Id. at 711. The case before us involves only the issue of fair dealing.

It is often of critical importance whether a particular decision is one to which the business judgment rule applies or the entire fairness rule applies. It is sometimes thought that the decision whether to apply the business judgment rule or the entire fairness test can be outcome-determinative.

Because the effect of the proper invocation of the business judgment rule is so powerful and the standard of entire fairness so exacting, the determination of the appropriate standard of judicial review frequently is determinative of the outcome of derivative litigation. Mills Acquisition Co. v. MacMillan, Inc., Del. Supr., 559 A.2d 1261, 1279 (1988) ("MacMillan") (quoting AC Acquisitions v. Anderson, Clayton & Co., Del. Ch., 519 A.2d 103, 111 (1986) ("Anderson Clayton")). Application of the entire fairness rule does not, however, always implicate liability of the conflicted corporate decisionmaker, nor does it necessarily render the decision void.[6]

The entire fairness analysis essentially requires "judicial scrutiny." Weinberger, 457 A.2d at 710. In business judgment rule cases, an essential element is the fact that there has been a business decision made by a disinterested and independent corporate decisionmaker. Aronson v. Lewis, Del. Supr., 473 A.2d 805, 812 (1984); Smith v. Van Gorkom, Del. Supr., 488 A.2d 858, 872–73 (1985). When there is no independent corporate decisionmaker,[7] the court may become the objective arbiter. Marciano, 535 A.2d at 404.

The trial court in this case, however, appears to have adopted the novel legal principle that Class B stockholders had a right to "liquidity" equal to that which the court found to be available to the defendants. It is well established in our jurisprudence that stockholders need not always be treated equally for all purposes. See Unocal Corp. v. Mesa Petroleum Co., Del. Supr., 493 A.2d 946, 957 (1985) ("Unocal") (discriminatory

6. See 8 Del. C. § 144; Marciano v. Nakash, Del. Supr., 535 A.2d 400, 403–05 (1987) ("Marciano") (loans made to a corporation by its half owners with the bona fide intention of assisting the corporation are valid and enforceable debts notwithstanding their origin in self-dealing); Rosenblatt v. Getty Oil Co., Del. Supr., 493 A.2d 929 (1985) (arm's length bargaining is considered to be strong evidence of the fairness of a merger ratio). But see, Rabkin v. Philip A. Hunt Chemical Corp., Del. Supr., 498 A.2d 1099 (1985) (a corporation that manipulated the timing of a proposed merger to avoid certain commitments rendered the transaction unfair).

7. This could be a disinterested and independent majority of the board of directors or the stockholders. See Fliegler v. Lawrence, Del. Supr., 361 A.2d 218 (1976).

exchange offer held valid); and Cheff v. Mathes, 41 Del. Ch. 494, 199 A.2d 548, 554–56 (1964) (selective stock repurchase held valid). To hold that fairness necessarily requires precise equality is to beg the question:

> Many scholars, though few courts, conclude that one aspect of fiduciary duty is the equal treatment of investors. Their argument takes the following form: fiduciary principles require fair conduct; equal treatment is fair conduct; hence, fiduciary principles require equal treatment. The conclusion does not follow. The argument depends on an equivalence between equal and fair treatment. To say that fiduciary principles require equal treatment is to beg the question whether investors would contract for equal or even equivalent treatment.

Frank H. Easterbrook and Daniel R. Fischel, The Economic Structure of Corporate Law 110 (1991) (emphasis in original). This holding of the trial court overlooks the significant facts that the minority stockholders were not: (a) employees of the Corporation; (b) entitled to share in an ESOP; (c) qualified for key man insurance; or (d) protected by specific provisions in the certificate of incorporation, by-laws, or a stockholders' agreement.

There is support in this record for the fact that the ESOP is a corporate benefit and was established, at least in part, to benefit the Corporation. Generally speaking, the creation of ESOPs is a normal corporate practice and is generally thought to benefit the corporation.[9] The same is true generally with respect to key man insurance programs. If such corporate practices were necessarily to require equal treatment for non-employee stockholders, that would be a matter for legislative determination in Delaware. There is no such legislation to that effect. If we were to adopt such a rule, our decision would border on judicial legislation. See Providence & Worcester Co. v. Baker, Del. Supr., 378 A.2d 121, 124 (1977).

Accordingly, we hold that the Vice Chancellor erred as a matter of law in concluding that the liquidity afforded to the employee stockholders by the ESOP and the key man insurance required substantially equal treatment for the non-employee stockholders. Moreover, the Vice Chancellor failed to evaluate and articulate, for example, whether or not and to what extent (a) corporate benefits flowed from the ESOP and the key man insurance; (b) the ESOP and key man insurance plans are novel, extraordinary, or relatively routine business practices; (c) the dividend policy was even relevant; (d) Mr. Barton's plan for employee management and benefits should be honored; and (e) the self-tenders showed defendants' willingness to provide an exit opportunity for the plaintiffs.

In a case where the court is scrutinizing the fairness of a self-interested corporate transaction the court should articulate the standards which it is applying in its scrutiny of the transactions. These standards are not carved in stone for all cases because a court of equity must necessarily have the flexibility to deal with varying circumstances and issues. Yet, the standards must be reasonable, articulable, and articulated. While the court is not expected to substitute its business judgment for that of the directors in areas where particular business expertise is an ingredient of the decision,[14] the reasonableness of the business judgment of the conflicted directors' decision must be examined searchingly through a principled and disciplined analysis. The decision of the trial court did not plainly delineate and articulate findings of fact and conclusions of law so

---

9. See Shamrock Holdings, Inc. v. Polaroid Corp., Del. Ch., 559 A.2d 257, 271–76 (1989) (properly adopted ESOP can be fair even if it has anti-takeover consequences). See also Henry C. Blackiston III, Linda E. Rappaport, and Lawrence A. Pasini, ESOPs: What They Are and How They Work, *45 Bus. Law. 85 (1989).*

14. See Auerbach v. Bennett, 47 N.Y.2d 619, 419 N.Y.S.2d 920, 393 N.E.2d 994, 1000-002 (1979) (courts are "ill-equipped" to make business decisions).

that this Court, as the reviewing court, could fathom without undue difficulty the bases for the trial court's decision.[15] The court's decision should not be the product solely of subjective, reflexive impressions based primarily on suspicion[16] or what has sometimes been called the "smell test."[17]

We hold on this record that defendants have met their burden of establishing the entire fairness of their dealings with the non-employee Class B stockholders, and are entitled to judgment. The record is sufficient to conclude that plaintiffs' claim that the defendant directors have maintained a discriminatory policy of favoring Class A employee stockholders over Class B non-employee stockholders is without merit. The directors have followed a consistent policy originally established by Mr. Barton, the founder of the Corporation, whose intent from the formation of the Corporation was to use the Class A stock as the vehicle for the Corporation's continuity through employee management and ownership.

Mr. Barton established the Corporation in 1928 by creating two classes of stock, not one, and by holding 100 percent of the Class A stock and 82 percent of the Class B stock. Mr. Barton himself established the practice of purchasing key man life insurance with funds of the Corporation to retain in the employ of the Corporation valuable employees by assuring them that, following their retirement or death, the Corporation will have liquid assets which could be used to repurchase the shares acquired by the employee, which shares may otherwise constitute an illiquid and unsalable asset of his or her estate. Another rational purpose is to prevent the stock from passing out of the control of the employees of the Corporation into the hands of family or descendants of the employee.

---

15. To be sure, the trial court undertook to explain its rulings in a written opinion, so that our criticism of the court's ruling is not that there was no written basis for the decision. See Redden v. McGill, Del. Supr., 549 A.2d 695 (1988). Our concern is that the written decision is imprecise, and the same principles of appellate review apply:

> In order for this Court to discharge its appellate responsibilities it must be supplied with the bases for the decision of the trial court. A decision without reasons borders on the arbitrary and is not subject to meaningful review. This Court has repeatedly cautioned trial courts on the need to supply reasons for their rulings.

Id. at 698.

16. We note that the Vice Chancellor, as the trier of fact, expressed what can best be described as "suspicions" about the motivation for the key man insurance. Slip op. at 12, quoted supra, 626 A.2d at 1375. This Court respects and gives deference to findings of fact by trial courts when supported by the record, and when they are the product of an orderly and logical deductive reasoning process, especially when those findings are based in part on testimony of live witnesses whose demeanor and credibility the trial judge has had the opportunity to evaluate. Footnote 3 at page 12 of the Vice Chancellor's opinion is a demonstration of credibility issues properly left to the trial court, but otherwise the crucial findings in the Vice Chancellor's opinion are somewhat vague and the opinion does not crisply and clearly set forth findings of fact in a form which we believe is entitled to such deference. See pages 26–27, supra. Thus, we hold that these findings are not the product of an orderly and logical deductive reasoning process.

17. We are mindful of the elasticity inherent in equity jurisprudence and the traditional desirability in certain equity cases of measuring conduct by the "conscience of the court" and disapproving conduct which offends or shocks that conscience. Yet one must be wary of equity jurisprudence which takes on a random or ad hoc quality.

> Equity is a rougish [sic] thing. For law we have to measure, know what to trust to; Equity is according to the conscience of him that is Chancellor, and as that is larger or narrower, so it Equity. 'Tis all one as if they should make the standard for the measure we call a "foot" a Chancellor's foot; what an uncertain measure would this be. One Chancellor has a long foot, another a short foot, a third an indifferent foot. 'Tis the same thing in the Chancellor's conscience.

John Selden, 1584–1654 "Equity," Table-Talk, 1689 The Quotable Lawyer 97 (David S. Shrager and Elizabeth Frost eds., 1986).

The directors' actions following Mr. Barton's death are consistent with Mr. Barton's plan. An ESOP, for example, is normally established for employees. Accordingly, there is no inequity in limiting ESOP benefits to the employee stockholders. Indeed, it makes no sense to include non-employees in ESOP benefits. The fact that the Class B stock represented 75 percent of the Corporation's total equity is irrelevant to the issue of fair dealing. The Class B stock was given no voting rights because those stockholders were not intended to have a direct voice in the management and operation of the Corporation. They were simply passive investors—entitled to be treated fairly but not necessarily to be treated equally. The fortunes of the Corporation rested with the Class A employee stockholders and the Class B stockholders benefitted from the multiple increases in value of their Class B stock. Moreover, the Board made continuing efforts to buy back the Class B stock.

We hold that paragraphs 4 and 5 of the March 10, 1992 order of the trial court and the order of May 20, 1992, awarding fees and costs to plaintiffs, are reversed and remanded with instructions to conform the judgment to the findings and conclusions in this opinion.

VI. NO SPECIAL RULES FOR A "CLOSELY-HELD CORPORATION" NOT QUALIFIED AS A "CLOSE CORPORATION" UNDER SUBCHAPTER XIV OF THE DELAWARE GENERAL CORPORATION LAW.

[omitted here; reproduced and discussed in Chapter 11, which follows]

VII. CONCLUSION

We hold that the Court of Chancery correctly determined that the entire fairness test is applicable in reviewing the actions of the defendants in establishing and implementing the ESOP and the key man life insurance program. The Vice Chancellor erred, however, as a matter of law in concluding on this record that the defendants had not carried their burden of showing entire fairness. The trial court erroneously undertook to create a novel theory of corporation law and erroneously failed to set forth and apply articulable standards for determining fairness. Moreover, certain findings of fact by the trial court were not the product of an orderly and deductive reasoning process.

In a case such as this where the business judgment rule is not applicable and the entire fairness test is applicable, the imposition of the latter test is not, alone, outcome-determinative. The doctrine of entire fairness does not lend itself to bright line precision or rigid doctrine. Yet it does not necessarily require equality, it cannot be a matter of total subjectivity on the part of the trial court, and it cannot result in a random pattern of ad hoc determinations which could do violence to the stability of our corporation law.

Accordingly, we REVERSE the judgment of the Court of Chancery and REMAND the matter for proceedings not inconsistent with this opinion.

---

b. Other Common Law Approaches

The English approach to the duty of loyalty is at once similar to but not identical with the American approach. After reading the materials which follow, can you articulate the differences in approaches? Are the differences fundamental or merely ones of application?

Bristol and West Building Society v. Mothew (t/a Stapley & Co)

Court of Appeal, (Civil Division)
[1998] Ch 1, [1996] 4 All ER 698, [1997] 2 WLR 436, 75 P & CR 241
24 July 1996

Millett, LJ, (giving the first judgment at the invitation of Staughton LJ).

This is an appeal brought by the defendant with the leave of the single Lord Justice from an order for summary judgment given initially by the district judge and affirmed (for different reasons) by Chadwick J. It raises important questions of principle in relation to a claim by a mortgagee to recover from the solicitor who was acting for both mortgagor and mortgagee the loss arising from the mortgagor's subsequent default.

The collapse in the property market which accompanied the recession at the beginning of the present decade caused mortgage lenders to suffer serious losses. Unable to recover their advances from the borrowers or by the enforcement of their security they have sought to recover them from the valuers or solicitors on whose valuations or advice they have relied. In some cases they have been the victims of a fraud to which the valuers and solicitors have been parties. In other cases, such as the present, they have been unable to accuse their solicitor of anything more serious than negligence. Believing that the common law rules of causation and remoteness of damage might not enable them to recover the whole amount of their loss they have turned to equity and alleged breach of trust or fiduciary duty. We have thus been concerned to decide just what is involved in these concepts.

THE FACTS

The facts are not in dispute. The defendant is a solicitor. In August 1988 he acted for a Mr. and Mrs. Towers in the purchase of 17 Thameshill Avenue, Romford (the property) for £ 73,000. In accordance with the usual practice he also acted for the Bristol and West Building Society (the Society) to which the purchasers had applied for an advance of £ 59,000 in order to finance the purchase. (This was the Cheshunt Building Society, but its rights have since vested in the society.) In their application form the purchasers had stated that the balance of the purchase price of £ 14,000 was being provided by them personally and that they were not applying elsewhere for financial assistance towards the purchase price.

The Society offered to advance to the purchasers £ 59,000 on the security of a first mortgage of the property on the express condition that unless otherwise agreed in writing the balance of the purchase price was to be provided by the purchasers personally without resort to further borrowing and that no second mortgage or other loan was being arranged or contemplated in connection with the purchase. The defendant was provided with the offer of advance (but not with the purchasers' application).

The Society's standing instructions to solicitors acting for the Society required them to report to the society prior to completion (inter alia):

> '(viii) Any proposal that the applicant may create a second mortgage or enter into a promissory note or otherwise borrow in order to finance part of the purchase price. (ix) Any incorrect information given in the solicitor's instructions. (x) Any other matters which ought to be brought to the notice of the Society as prospective mortgagee.'

The solicitor was required to submit a report on title and request for advance cheque to the Society at least five clear working days before the cheque was required. This was done on a form by which the solicitor was asked to confirm (inter alia) that the title was good and marketable and might safely be accepted by the society; that to the best of his knowledge and belief the balance of the purchase money was being provided by the applicant personally without resort to further borrowing; and that the special conditions attached to the offer of advance had been, or would be, complied with.

Mr. and Mrs. Towers intended to provide the balance of the purchase price from the net proceeds of sale of their existing property after discharging a subsisting mortgage. As it happens, they owed money to Barclays Bank which was secured by a second charge on that property. They arranged with the bank to allow a small part of the debt (£ 3,350) to remain outstanding after the sale of the existing property and to be secured by a second charge on the new property. The defendant was informed of these arrangements and gave an undertaking to the bank to hold the title deeds to its order pending registration. Unfortunately, he either failed to appreciate that, although they related to old borrowing, these arrangements were a matter which he was required to report to the Society, or he had forgotten or overlooked them when he made his report.

By his report dated 2 August 1988 the defendant confirmed that to the best of his knowledge and belief the balance of the purchase money was being provided by the applicants personally without resort to further borrowing and that the special conditions attached to the offer of advance had been or would be complied with. He failed to disclose the fact that Mr. and Mrs. Towers were making arrangements for a second mortgage in connection with the purchase.

It is conceded by the defendant that his statements were untrue and that his failure to report the purchasers' arrangements for a second mortgage was a breach of his instructions. The Society alleges that the defendant acted negligently and in breach of contract, and this is admitted. There is no allegation of dishonesty or bad faith, and if any such allegation were made it would be strongly resisted. The Society does not allege that the defendant made the statements in question knowing them to be untrue. It alleges only that he 'knew or ought to have known' that they were untrue, and this is consistent with oversight.

Following the receipt of the report the Society forwarded a cheque for the amount of the advance to the defendant in readiness for completion on 30 August. Completion took place on that date when the mortgage advance was released to the vendor's solicitors as part of the purchase price for the property. Mr. and Mrs. Towers executed a first charge in favour of the Society and a second charge in favour of the bank. On 25 November the defendant applied to the Society for its consent to the registration of the second charge in favour of the bank. The Society granted its consent on 10 March 1989. It does not appear that the Society was aware of the date of the bank's charge (and so was aware that it constituted a breach of the conditions of the advance) when it gave its consent, but it is alleged that the Society must have learned of it shortly afterwards and nevertheless took no action.

The purchasers defaulted after making only small repayments and the Society enforced its security. The property was sold on 6 February 1991 and realised net proceeds of a little under £ 53,000. The Society claimed to recover the whole of its net loss on the transaction from the defendant, alleging breach of contract, negligence and breach of trust. As I have already indicated, breach of contract and negligence are admitted; breach of trust is denied.

It has always been the defendant's case that the Society would not have been concerned by the purchasers' proposal to grant a second charge to the bank if this had been disclosed to it in August 1988; that it would still have proceeded with the transaction; and that it would have suffered precisely the same loss in that event. It is alleged that, in the heady days of 1988, when the property market was at its height and mortgage lenders were falling over themselves to advance money to house purchasers, the Society would not have been concerned by a proposal to grant a second charge to secure a relatively trivial indebtedness which did not even represent fresh borrowing; and it is contended that this is demonstrated by the lack of concern shown by the Society when it was asked to give its consent to the registration of a second charge in March 1989. Despite the submissions of the Society to the contrary, I am satisfied that, if legally relevant, these allegations raise a triable issue.

The course of the proceedings below

It was common ground below that no damages would be recoverable at common law for breach of contract or tort unless the Society could show that it would not have proceeded with the transaction if it had been informed of the facts. The Society, however, submitted that the position was different in equity. It alleged that the defendant had committed a breach of trust or fiduciary duty, and submitted that common law principles of causation and remoteness of damage have no application in such a case so that it was not necessary for the Society to show that it would not have proceeded with the transaction if it had been informed of the facts.

The district judge accepted these arguments. In respect of the common law claims for breach of contract and negligence she gave summary judgment for damages to be assessed. This was apparently on the basis that the judgment would leave it open to the defendant to contend that no loss was caused by the breach.

The district judge also gave summary judgment for the Society for breach of trust for the sum of £ 59,000 less the sums received by the Society on the sale of the property, and this was affirmed by the judge, who was satisfied that there was no question or issue to be tried in the action and dismissed the appeal.

The course of the appeal

In the course of the appeal the defendant submitted that, by consenting to the registration of the second charge, the Society waived the breaches of which complaint is made; and that this raises a triable issue on liability which entitles him to unconditional leave to defend in relation to all the pleaded causes of action. In the absence of any evidence or reason to suppose that the Society was aware of the date of the second charge when it gave its consent to its registration, I am not persuaded that there is a triable issue on waiver, and I would not disturb the order below on this ground.

When the appeal was first argued before us it was still conceded by the Society that it could not recover damages at common law for breach of contract or negligence unless it could show that it would not have proceeded with the mortgage advance if it had been informed of the facts. The Society, however, maintained that it could escape this principle because the defendant was also guilty of a breach of trust and that common law rules of causation and remoteness of damage have no application in such a case. The critical questions, therefore, appeared to be whether the defendant was guilty of a breach of trust or fiduciary duty and, if so, whether the Society needed to prove that it would not still have proceeded with the transaction if it had been told of the facts.

After we had reserved judgment on the appeal, however, the Society informed us that it wished to resile from its concession. Relying on the recent decision of this court in Downs v Chappell [1996] 3 All ER 344, delivered on 3 April 1996, the Society submitted that it was entitled to recover the whole of its net loss on the transaction by way of damages for negligence at common law without having to establish that it would not have proceeded with the transaction if it had been informed of the facts. If correct, it submitted, this would be determinative of the case, and it would not be necessary for the Society to rely on any breach of trust or fiduciary duty. Before the defendant's advisors could respond to this, speeches were delivered in the House of Lords in South Australia Asset Management Corp v. York Montague Ltd., United Bank of Kuwait plc v Prudential Property Services Ltd., Nykredit Mortgage Bank plc v Edward Erdman Group Ltd. [1996] 3 All ER 365, [1996] 3 WLR 87. These were relevant to the common law position. For the reasons given by Staughton LJ, however, we decided that it was not necessary to restore the appeal for further argument. This was because the assessment of damages at common law is still pending. They will have to be assessed in conformity with the decision of the House of Lords in the South Australia case and not with any gloss which, in the absence of argument, we may inadvertently have put upon that decision.

THE CLAIMS AT COMMON LAW

The Society has served a respondent's notice, in which it contends that it is entitled to judgment for the sum claimed, and not merely for damages to be assessed, in respect of its common law claims. If this is correct, then the Society does not need to establish that the defendant was guilty of a breach of trust or fiduciary duty.

* * *

The Society has proved the causal link between the defendant's negligence and the making of the mortgage advance but it has not yet established the amount of its loss (if any) which is properly attributable to the defendant's negligence. Damages remain to be assessed. We are bound by the decision of this court in Downs v. Chappell to hold that the Society will not have to prove that it would not have made the mortgage advance if it had known the true facts; but it will be required to establish what it has lost as a result of the existence of the second charge and the purchasers' indebtedness to the bank. It can maintain the money judgment which it has obtained below only if it can invoke equitable principles.

THE CLAIMS IN EQUITY

The judge's reasoning

The judge found that, in the events which happened, the defendant committed a breach of trust by applying the mortgage advance in the purchase of the property; that he was accordingly liable to restore the trust property, viz the £ 59,000 with interest less receipts; that no question of damages at common law or of compensation for loss arose; and that it was irrelevant whether, had it been told of the position, the Society might still have chosen to make the advance notwithstanding the arrangements which had been made with the bank. Accordingly, the judge concluded that there was no question or issue to be tried in the action and gave summary judgment for the whole of the Society's claim.

The judge's conclusion that the defendant had committed a breach of trust in applying the mortgage advance in the purchase of the property was based on the fact that he had obtained payment of the mortgage advance by misrepresentation....

* * *

Breach of fiduciary duty

[For the judge's general discussion of fiduciary duty, see section A.1.b, above]

* * *

Before us the defendant submits that, while he was guilty of negligence and breach of contract, he was not guilty of a breach of trust or fiduciary duty. It is convenient to take first the question of fiduciary duty, and then to consider the question of breach of trust.

In the present case it is clear that, if the defendant had been acting for the Society alone, his admitted negligence would not have exposed him to a charge of breach of fiduciary duty. Before us counsel for the Society accepted as much, but insisted that the fact that he also acted for the purchasers made all the difference. So it is necessary to ask: why did the fact that the defendant was acting for the purchasers as well as for the Society convert the defendant's admitted breach of his duty of skill and care into a breach of fiduciary duty? To answer this question it is necessary to identify the fiduciary obligation of which he is alleged to have been in breach.

It is at this point, in my judgment, that the Society's argument runs into difficulty. A fiduciary who acts for two principals with potentially conflicting interests without the informed consent of both is in breach of the obligation of undivided loyalty; he puts himself in a position where his duty to one principal may conflict with his duty to the other: see Clark Boyce v. Mouat [1993] 4 All ER 268, [1994] 1 AC 428 and the cases there cited. This is sometimes described as 'the double employment rule'. Breach of the rule automatically constitutes a breach of fiduciary duty. But this is not something of which the Society can complain. It knew that the defendant was acting for the purchasers when it instructed him. Indeed, that was the very reason why it chose the defendant to act for it. The potential conflict was of the society's own making (see Finn p 254 and Kelly v. Cooper [1993] AC 205, [1993] 3 LRC 476).

It was submitted on behalf of the Society that this is irrelevant because the defendant misled the Society. It did not know of the arrangements which the purchasers had made with their bank, and so could not be said to be 'fully informed' for the purpose of absolving the defendant from the operation of the double employment rule. The submission is misconceived. The Society knew all the facts relevant to its choice of solicitor. Its decision to forward the cheque for the mortgage advance to the defendant and to instruct him to proceed was based on false information, but its earlier decision to employ the defendant despite the potentially conflicting interest of his other clients was a fully informed decision.

That, of course, is not the end of the matter. Even if a fiduciary is properly acting for two principals with potentially conflicting interests he must act in good faith in the interests of each and must not act with the intention of furthering the interests of one principal to the prejudice of those of the other (see Finn p 48). I shall call this 'the duty of good faith'. But it goes further than this. He must not allow the performance of his obligations to one principal to be influenced by his relationship with the other. He must serve each as faithfully and loyally as if he were his only principal. Conduct which is in breach of this duty need not be dishonest but it must be intentional. An unconscious omission which happens to benefit one principal at the expense of the other does not constitute a breach of fiduciary duty, though it may constitute a breach of the duty of skill and care. This is because the principle which is in play is that the fiduciary must not be inhibited by the existence of his other employment from serving the interests of his principal as faithfully and effectively as if he were the only employer. I shall call this 'the no inhibition principle'. Unless the fiduciary is inhibited or believes (whether rightly or wrongly) that he is inhibited in the performance of his duties to one principal by reason of his employment by the other, his failure to act is not attributable to the double employment.

Finally, the fiduciary must take care not to find himself in a position where there is an actual conflict of duty so that he cannot fulfil his obligations to one principal without failing in his obligations to the other: see Moody v. Cox [1917] 2 Ch 71, [1916–17] All ER Rep 548 and Commonwealth Bank of Australia v. Smith (1991) 102 ALR 453. If he does, he may have no alternative but to cease to act for at least one and preferably both. The fact that he cannot fulfil his obligations to one principal without being in breach of his obligations to the other will not absolve him from liability. I shall call this 'the actual conflict rule'.

In the present case the judge evidently thought that the defendant was in breach of both the duty of good faith and the actual conflict rule. In Bristol and West Building Society v. May May & Merrimans (a firm) [1996] 2 All ER 801 at 817–818 he said:

> '...there can be no doubt that the requirement of unconscionable conduct is present where a solicitor who is acting for both borrower and lender misrepresents to the lender some fact which he knows, or must be taken to know, will or may affect the lender's decision to proceed with the loan. In those circumstances the solicitor is abusing his fiduciary relationship with one client, the lender, to obtain an advantage for his other client, the borrower. It is as much "against the dictates of conscience" for a solicitor knowingly to prefer the interests of one client over those of another client as it is for him to prefer his own interests over those of his client.' (My emphasis.)
>
> I respectfully agree; but no such allegation is made in the present case.
>
> As to the actual conflict rule, the judge said (at 832):
>
> 'First, in Mothew, the "agent" was a fiduciary who had put himself in a position in which his duty to the lender was in conflict with the interests of his other client, the borrower.' (My emphasis.)

I do not accept this. By instructing him to act for them, the purchasers must be taken to have authorised the defendant to complete the report without which the mortgage advance would not have been forthcoming; and to complete it truthfully. The defendant was required by the society to report on the purchasers' title as well as to confirm the absence of any further borrowing. The two stood in exactly the same case. The defendant would not have been in breach of his duty to the purchasers if he had disclosed the facts to the society any more than if he had reported a defect in their title.

This proposition can be tested by considering what the defendant's position would have been if he had acted for the purchasers and another solicitor had been instructed to act for the Society. He would have been required to deduce the purchasers' title to the satisfaction of the Society's solicitor, and to confirm to him that no further borrowing or second charge was in contemplation. His duty to the purchasers would have required him to ascertain the facts from them and to report them to the Society. Unless they told him the facts and instructed him to lie to the Society, instructions which he would be bound to refuse, his duty to the purchasers would not inhibit him in providing full and truthful information to the solicitor acting for the Society.

In my judgment, the defendant was never in breach of the actual conflict rule. It is not alleged that he acted in bad faith or that he deliberately withheld information because he wrongly believed that his duty to the purchasers required him to do so. He was not guilty of a breach of fiduciary duty.

The judge relied on Nocton v. Lord Ashburton [1914] AC 932, [1914–15] All ER Rep 45 and Commonwealth Bank of Australia v. Smith (1991) 102 ALR 453 to hold that a party who pays money to his solicitor in reliance on a representation known by the solicitor to be false has a remedy in breach of fiduciary duty. Neither case is authority for the proposition (though its correctness is not in issue); certainly neither is authority for the proposition that a party who pays money to a solicitor in reliance on a representation which the solicitor ought to have known to be false has such a remedy.

In Nocton v. Lord Ashburton a solicitor had an undisclosed personal interest in a transaction on which he gave his client advice which was to his own advantage and the disadvantage of his client. The plaintiff pleaded breach of the duty of good faith. In fact this was unnecessary; the existence of the defendant's undisclosed interest was enough: see Lewis v. Hillman (1852) 3 HL Cas 607, 10 ER 239. The plaintiff was entitled to receive, and thought that he was receiving, the disinterested advice of a solicitor with no other interest in the transaction. Commonwealth Bank of Australia v. Smith involved a breach of the actual conflict rule. The defendant, who was acting for both parties to a proposed transaction, placed himself in an impossible position by undertaking to advise one of them on the merits of the transaction.

In Moody v. Cox [1917] 2 Ch 71, [1916–17] All ER Rep 548 a solicitor, who was acting for both vendor and purchaser, was in possession of valuations which showed that the property was not worth the price which the purchaser had agreed to pay. He did not disclose them to the purchaser, and claimed that his duty to the vendor precluded him from doing so. The purchaser was allowed to rescind. The case bears a superficial resemblance to the present but there are two crucial differences: (i) the vendor was under no obligation to disclose the valuations to the purchaser and did not wish his solicitor do so; and (ii) the vendor and the solicitor tacitly agreed to conceal the valuations from the purchaser. The solicitor was in breach of both the duty of good faith and the actual conflict rule; his defence fell foul of the no inhibition principle.

That was a case of deliberate concealment. Non-disclosure and concealment are two very different things. This has been a truism of the law from the time of Cicero, citing Diogenes of Babylon (see De Officiis, lib 3, c 12, 13). It is even enshrined, like other such truisms, in a Latin tag: aliud est celare, aliud tacere.

The Society placed much reliance on a dictum by Lord Jauncey in Clarke Boyce v. Mouat [1993] 4 All ER 268 at 275, [1994] 1 AC 428 at 437, where he said:

> 'Another case of breach [of fiduciary duty] is where a solicitor acts for both parties without disclosing this to one of them or where having disclosed it he fails, unbeknown to one party, to disclose to that party material facts relative to the other party of which he is aware.' (My emphasis.)

But I do not think that Lord Jauncey meant to include an inadvertent failure which owes nothing to the double employment. Where such failure is to the advantage of the other party, the court will jealously scrutinise the facts to ensure that there has been nothing more than inadvertence, but there can be no justification for treating an unconscious failure as demonstrating a want of fidelity.

In my judgment the distinction drawn by Ipp J in Permanent Building Society (in liq) v. Wheeler (1994) 14 ACSR 109 is sound in principle and is decisive of the present case. On the Society's pleaded case the fact that the defendant was acting for the purchasers played no part in his failure to report the true state of affairs to the Society. It did not inhibit him from fulfilling his obligations to the Society. It is consistent with its pleaded case that the defendant would have done so but for a negligent oversight. It would have been exactly the same if he had failed to notice and report the existence of a defect in the purchasers' title. To characterise either such failure as a breach of fiduciary duty because he was acting for both parties in a situation where that fact did not contribute to his failure is, in my opinion, to substitute a verbal formula for principle.

In my judgment the judge's conclusion that the defendant was in breach of fiduciary duty cannot be supported. It follows that it cannot be sustained as a ground for holding the defendant to be in breach of a constructive trust of the mortgage money.

Breach of trust

[The discussion on beach of trust is omitted]

Conclusion

In my judgment the defendant was not guilty of breach of trust or fiduciary duty. This makes it unnecessary to consider what the consequences of such a breach would have been. I would allow the appeal and set aside the money judgment. I would leave undisturbed the judgments for damages to be assessed for breach of contract and negligence, but make it clear that it does not follow that the society will establish any recoverable loss.

OTTON LJ. I have read with advantage the judgments of Millett and Staughton LJJ. I agree with the analysis and reasoning regarding breach of trust and of fiduciary duty. I wish only to add a few words on the extant common law claims.

[The discussion is omitted].

STAUGHTON LJ. Mr. Mothew made his report to the Chestnut Building Society on 2 August 1988. In it he answered one of the questions asked as follows:

'[Q.] Please confirm that (to the best of your knowledge and belief) the balance of the purchase money is being provided by the applicant(s) personally without resort to further borrowing. If not please give details. [A.] Confirmed.'

That was untrue. There were other aspects of the same error, but I need not go into them in detail. Although Mr. Mothew had the means of knowledge in his possession, which could have brought the error to his attention, it is not said that he acted fraudulently or in bad faith.

The ordinary remedy of a client who has received wrong information or advice from his solicitor is to claim damages for negligence, whether as a breach of contract or as a tort. For such a claim to give rise to substantial damages the building society would have to show that the breach of contract or negligence caused them loss. By their respondent's notice they seek to say that, if they had known the true facts, they would not have lent any money to Mr. and Mrs. Towers.

The judge regarded that point as immaterial, since the building society succeeded on other grounds. If it is material, in my opinion it raises a triable issue. According to Samantha Bennett of the Society's advances department, the offer of advance would have immediately been withdrawn if the Society had known that even £ 3,350 was being borrowed elsewhere. In the nature of things Mr. Mothew is unlikely to have evidence which directly controverts that statement. But there are grounds for supposing that it may be open to question. I would not give judgment under RSC Ord 14 on the basis that it is true. If it is critical, the case must go to trial, perhaps with the aid of interrogatories and discovery of documents.

However, in this particular case the building society were not the sole clients of Mr. Mothew; he was also the solicitor acting for Mr. and Mrs. Towers. That is said to make all the difference, because Mr. Mothew then became under a fiduciary duty to the building society. And the argument is that for breach of fiduciary duty the remedy does not depend on causation or remoteness; all that is necessary is that the loss would not have occurred but for the breach of duty.

It seems to me wrong that a breach of contract or tort should become a breach of fiduciary duty in that way. I am glad to find that the authorities relied on by Millett LJ show that it is wrong. In my judgment Mr. Mothew was in breach of a duty of care and nothing more. True he was in a situation where he owed duties to two clients, and those duties might conflict with each other. But he did not prefer the interest of one client to that of another; at most he was guilty of negligence which had that unintended effect.

Alternatively it is said that Mr. Mothew was in breach of trust because he paid away the trust fund contrary to his instructions. He did indeed hold the £ 59,000 in trust; it was not his own money. There was in my opinion an express or implied trust, and not (as the judge held) a constructive trust. But he did not pay it away contrary to the society's instructions. The cheque reached Mr. Mothew with a letter dated 23 August 1988, which in effect instructed him to use it for completion of the proposed purchase. That was what he did.

There being in my opinion no breach of fiduciary duty or breach of trust, it is unnecessary to consider what remedy such a breach might have afforded.

Thus far the appeal succeeds, but there remains judgment on the cause of action at common law for damages to be assessed.

[This section of the opinion is omitted].

I would allow the appeal and remit the assessment of damages, either to Chadwick J or to another judge of the Chancery Division as the exigencies of business may require. The cross-appeal should be dismissed.

DISPOSITION:

Appeal allowed. Cross-appeal dismissed.

---

2. *Civil Law Approaches*

The civil law countries have not developed a focused and comprehensive law for the regulation of the conduct of managers equivalent to the common law's duty of loyalty. The materials excerpted below provide a view of the more focused, and some would argue, more limited approach to the problem of "managerial loyalty" in civil law countries.

Juan M. Dobson, *Lifting the Veil in Four Countries: The Law of Argentina, England, France and the United States*

35 INT'L & COMP. L.Q. 839 (1986)
(excerpts pages 856–857; some footnotes omitted)

2. Control In French and Argentine insolvency laws.

Both French and Argentine insolvency legislation contains provisions referring to abusive control. In France, the *extension de la faillite au maitre de l'affaire* (extension of insolvency proceedings to the controller) doctrine is based on a statutory definition of control. The present Act on the Salvage and Liquidation of Enterprises (loi 85–98 of 25 Jan. 1985, *relative au redressement at a la liquidation judiciaire des enterpirses*) preserves the doctrine first introduced in 1935 as a reform of article 437 of the *Code de commerce.* The 1985 Act extends *redressement* (restitution) proceedings to any director or shadow director who has

(1) disposed of the company's assets as if they were his own;

(2) used the cloak of the company to perform commercial acts in his own interests;

(3) used the credit or assets of the company in his own interest, or to advance interests in conflicts with those of the company, or to benefit another company in which he is directly or indirectly interested; or

(4) pursued an unprofitable operation abusively and in his own interest that could have led to the company's insolvency.

The Act refers expressly to the interests of the *company* as opposed to the interests of the controller (*maitre de l'affaire*).

The Argentine Insolvency Act 1972 introduced a similar extension of proceedings in solvency (later modified by the Insolvency Reform Act 1983, Ley 22.917). Among the situations expressly provided for the legislation makes bankrupt those who, under the cloak of a company, have acted in their own personal interest and have dealt with the company's assets as if they were their own. It also extends insolvency process to a company controller who has imposed unity of direction on a company in the interest of the controller who has imposed unity of direction on a company in the interest of the controller or the group to which it belongs, improperly and against the interests of the company (1983 Act, art. 165).[54]

Both the French and the Argentine statutes embody broad notions of control, as well as the concept of abusive control. "Control" covers internal and external control, and both are precisely defined. A person who can "dispose of the company's assets as if they were his own", or who can "use the company's name to carry to carry out his own commercial acts" has to be in full control of the company. Likewise, to be able to use the company's credit for personal purposes necessarily entails having control. That control is described in the French Act as *dirigeant de droit ou de fait* ("director or shadow director" under ss. 741 and 7472 of the English Companies Act of 1985), and is equivalent to the terms "internal or external control"....

3. *Duty of Loyalty in Japan and China*

The notion of fiduciary duty as a normative basis for managerial control, as Americans understand it, is essentially foreign to Japanese and Chinese. Yet these notions have been incorporated, in naturalized form, in both countries to a certain extent. The naturalization of fiduciary notions of loyalty as a regulatory mechanism has been easier in Japan than in the People's republic of China.

---

54. "*La quiebra se extiende: (1) A toda personal que, bajo la apariencia de la actuación de la fallada, ha efectuado los actos en su interes personal y dispuesto de los bienes como si fueron propios, en fraude de sus acreedores; (2) A toda persona controlante de la sociedad fallida, cuando ha desviado indebidamente el interes social de la controlada, sometiendola a una dirección unificada en interés de la controlante o del grup económico del que forma parte.*"

a. Japan

Japan provides an excellent example of the ability of a complex and sophisticated society to import and harmonize legal norms. As you read the materials that follow, think about why the Japanese chose harmonization, and naturalization of foreign norms, rather than resistance. Consider also whether the price for joining the global trading community is assimilation of the basic norms of that community. To what extent is assimilation, chronicled below, a product of this price paying? To what extent is assimilation merely a reordering of traditional patterns to fit the vocabulary of the international enterprise community?

Mark D. West, *The Pricing of Shareholder Derivative Actions in Japan and the United States*

88 Nw. U.L. Rev. 1436 (1994)
(excerpt pages 1478–1484; some footnotes omitted)

The Japanese expression of directors' duties in the derivative action context is much more complicated and much less definitive than the American delineation.[199] Part of the problem lies in poor drafting, as is expressed by Takeo Suzuki, one of the drafters of the 1950 Code revisions:

> Shareholder derivative actions are designed to enforce the responsibility of directors, but what sort of responsibility does that provision have in mind? If a director borrows money from a company and doesn't return it, wouldn't it be strange if you couldn't sue him derivatively? This sort of problem was never even a real issue when we were drafting the legislation. When we discovered that problems such as this could arise, we were really surprised. [200]

Thus, lack of legislative foresight has led to a piecemeal, common-law-like approach to directorial duties[201] in the derivative action context as lawyers and judges try to figure out exactly what the drafters could have meant. Through this interpretative process, two separate lines of reasoning have emerged. Some scholars argue that the appropriate lens is the general principles of the Commercial Code governing the conduct of directors. The first such principle is in Article 254(3), which establishes that directors are governed by the provisions relating to mandates. This is a roundabout way of imposing on directors the Civil Code standard of care for mandates[202] as opposed to the lower Civil Code standard of care one would use in one's own affairs. The effect is to make directors subject to the "duty of care of a good manager" (*zenkan gimu*) under Article 644 of the Civil Code.[203] The second principle is found in Commercial Code Article 254-3, which

---

199. American duties of care and loyalty are likewise rather vague, but case law seems to provide more definitive "signposts" of liability than exist in the Japanese system.

200. [Takeo Suzuki, *Shoho to Tomo ni Ayumu* Walking with Commercial Law 146-96 (as told to Akio Takeuchi, 1977)] at 184.

201. Directors in Japan are not subject to fiduciary duties, but to civil law trust principles. See Dan F. Henderson, *Security Markets in the United States and Japan: Distinctive Aspects Molded by Cultural, Social, Economic, and Political Differences*, 14 Hastings Int'l & Comp. L. Rev. 263, 276 (1991).

202. Minpo Civil Code arts. 643–656.

203. Id. at art. 644. This principle is derived from the Roman law maxim "diligentia boni patris familias."

Some Japanese commentators have called for the introduction of the business judgment rule in requires directors to "perform their duties faithfully on behalf of the company," thus subjecting directors to a sort of duty of loyalty (*chujitsu gimu*).[204] This delineation of directorial duties is not as clear-cut as it seems. In the general context, courts and commentators have had a difficult time determining the coterminous scope of the two duties. The majority view is that the duty of loyalty imposed by Article 254-3 merely amplifies the duty of care of a good manager; [205] however, a sizeable minority asserts that the two duties are distinct.[206]

Other scholars argue that the appropriate lens is not the broad-based duty principles, but the provisions of the Commercial Code that apply specifically to derivative actions. Article 267 says that derivative actions may be brought to "enforce the liability of directors" (*torishimariyaku no sekinin wo tsuikyu suru*).[207] The provision immediately preceding this one makes clear to what actions the term "liability" refers; Article 266 specifies that "liability to the company" includes situations in which directors, inter alia, violate the sokaiya provisions, loan money to other directors, engage in self-interested transactions as specified in Article 265(1),[208] or violate any law, ordinance, or the articles of incorporation.[209]

Japanese courts have been unclear regarding the scope of actionable duties and have mixed and matched the director's broad duties (care of a good manager and loyalty) with the derivative action or specific liability provisions of Article 266, as well as adding a few extra bases of liability. Some courts and commentators take a narrow approach, arguing that the only bases for liability are the provisions of Article 266 and Article 280(13) liability to secure subscription of unsubscribed shares.[210] This approach can

---

Japan, and several court decisions appear to have incorporated the rule. See, e.g., Judgment of Jan. 29, 1975 (Tokozai K.K. v. Eda), Tokyo Kosai Tokyo High Court, 771 Hanji 77; Judgment of Sept. 30, 1980 (Daiwa Kogyo K.K. v. Tezuka), Tokyo Chisai Tokyo District Court, 1005 Hanji 161; Kazushi Yoshihara, *Torishimariyaku no Chui Gimu to Keiei Handan Kisoku* Directors' Duty of Care and the Business Judgment Rule, 116 Bessatsu Jurisuto 118 (Tsuneo Otori et al. eds., 1992) (discussing Judgment of Oct. 8, 1980, Fukuoka Chisai Fukuoka District Court, 1012 Hanji 117). However, the rule has not gained widespread acceptance in Japan and has not even a hint of the impact that it has in American jurisprudence. See Mitsuo Kondo, *Torishimariyaku no Keiei Sekinin Managerial Liability of Directors, in* 3 Gendai Kigyoho Koza 293, 301 (Misao Tatsuta et al. eds., 1985).

204. Shoho Commercial Code art. 254-3. *See* Hiroyuki Kansaku, *Torishimariyaku no Chujitsu Gimu* The Duty of Loyalty of Directors, 116 Bessatsu Jurisuto 120 (Tsuneo tori et al. eds., 1992); Mitsuko Akabori Shibuya, *Torishimariyaku no Chujitsu Gimu* The Duty of Loyalty of Directors, 32 Shiho 153 (1970).

205. See, e.g., Judgment of Apr. 5, 1963 (Arita v. Kojima, or the Yawata Steel Case), Tokyo Chisai Tokyo District Court, 14 Kaminshu 657, rev'd, Judgment of Jan. 31, 1966, Tokyo Kosai Tokyo High Court, 19 Kominshu 7, aff'd, Judgment of June 24, 1970, Saikosai Supreme Court, 24 Minshu 625.

206. See Kondo, supra note 203, at 293–94.

207. Shoho Commercial Code art. 267(1).

208. Directors can be released from this liability by a two-thirds vote of holders of the outstanding stock. Id. at art. 266(6). All other forms of liability in this article can be released only by a unanimous vote. Shoho Commercial Code art. 266(5).

209. Id. at art. 266(1). When such acts are done in accordance with a resolution of the board of directors, the directors who assent are deemed to have done the act. Id. at art. 266(2). Those who do not dissent are presumed to have assented. Id. at art. 266(3). Article 266-3 sets out liabilities to third parties. Because the derivative action is brought on behalf of the company, it cannot be used to enforce Article 266-3 liability.

210. See [Masahiro Kitazawa, *Kabunushi no Daihyo Sosho Shareholder Derivative Actions, in* 6 Shinpan Chushaku Kaishaho Company Law Commentary, New Edition 354, 355 (Akio Takeuchi et al. eds., 1987)], at 362. On the debate in general, see Kondo, supra note 11, at 70–71; Naohide Saeki, *Daihyo Sosho ni Yotte Tsuikyu Shiuru Torishimariyaku no Sekinin no Han'i Pursuing* the Boundaries of Director Liability with Derivative Actions, in Jurisuto Zokan: Shoho no Soten

lead to awkward results, as in Huang v. Li.[211] In Huang, the director-defendant had purchased a building on the account of the corporation and registered it in his own name. Shareholders brought suit, asking the court to compel the director to transfer title to the corporation. Because nothing in Articles 266 or 280(13) specifically prohibits a director from holding on to the property, the court refused to compel such action.[212] Other courts have held that such an approach is too limited; the derivative action should be enforceable over a broader range of directorial misdeeds.[213] Still another judicial approach is to avoid the derivative-action-specific liability provisions altogether and follow the general-principle-based approach to "mandatory" duties.[214] At least one case lies somewhere in the middle. The court in Fujita v. Shiokawa [215] adopted a narrow statutory base, holding that derivative actions are limited to Articles 266 and 280(13) actions, yet, interpreting that narrow range broadly, found that the duty of a director to transfer title to corporate property is included in those duties.[216]

Gauging the effect of the directorial duty issue is a bit like debating over the chicken and the egg. On the one hand, the lack of a cohesive directorial duty doctrine may deter shareholder derivative actions. Certainly, for the individual shareholder contemplating litigation today, the lack of a cohesive doctrine effectively raises the price of a derivative action. Because the rule is so uncertain, derivative actions are a crap shoot for most shareholders.[217] If the privilege of rolling were free or at least cheap, many shareholders

---

JURISUTO SPECIAL EDITION: POINTS OF DISPUTE IN COMMERCIAL LAW 118 (Masahiro Kitazawa ed., 1978).

211. Judgment of Oct. 19, 1956 (Huang v. Li), Tokyo Chisai Tokyo District Court, 7 Kaminshu 2934.

212. See id. This is probably the problem to which Suzuki was referring in his comment on the lack of foresight in drafting the provisions. *See supra* note 200 and accompanying text.

213. See Judgment of Oct. 30, 1979 (Kinoshita v. Katayama), Osaka Kosai Osaka High Court, 954 Hanji 89 (enforcing director's duty to restore property deed); [TAKEO SUZUKI & TERUHISA ISHII, KABUSHIKI KAISHAHO KAISETSU COMMENTARY ON COMPANY LAW 180 (1950)], at 180; KEN'ICHIRO OSUMI & HIROSHI IMAI, KAISHAHO RON COMPANY LAW COMMENTARY 272 (3d ed. 1992); [SEIJI TANAKA ET AL., CONMENTAARU KAISHAHO COMPANY LAW COMMENTARY 868 (4th ed. 1984)], at 862. Regarding the Kinoshita Case, see Masao Kishida, *Daihyo Sosho to Torishimariyaku no Han'i* Derivative Actions and the Limits of Director Liability, in KAISHA HANREI HYAKUSEN, BESSATSU JURISUTO, supra note 203, at 122.

214. See supra TAN. See also, e.g., Judgment of Apr. 5, 1963 (Arita v. Kojima, or the Yawata Steel Case), Tokyo Chisai Tokyo District Court, 14 Kaminshu 657, rev'd, Judgment of Jan. 31, 1966, Tokyo Kosai Tokyo High Court, 19 Kominshu 7, aff'd, Judgment of June 24, 1970, Saikosai Supreme Court, 24 Minshu 625 (holding that political contribution out of corporate funds does not violate director's duty of loyalty if amount is reasonable).

215. Judgment of Aug. 10, 1963 (Fujita v. Shiokawa), Osaka Chisai Osaka District Court, 14 Kaminshu 1585.

216. Id. See also Eiji Hattori, Shoji Hanrei Kenkyu Commercial Law Case Research, 344 Jurisuto 130, 132 (explaining why both camps dislike the decision).

217. Some scholars have argued that "whether wealth-maximizing disputants sue or settle depends as much on their ability to agree on the likely litigated outcome as on the costs and pay-offs from litigation." [J. Mark Ramseyer, *Reluctant Litigant Revisited: Rationality and Disputes in Japan*, 4 J. JAPAN. STUD. 111 (1978)], at 114. See also George Priest and Benjamin Klein, *The Selection of Disputes for Litigation*, *13* J. LEGAL STUD. 1 (1984). By this theory, the lack of a well-defined directorial duty doctrine should lead to more, not less, derivative litigation. Parties will be unable to agree on the likely litigated outcome and thus will ex ante perceive litigating more profitable than settling. However, the nature of the derivative action differs from other forms of litigation to such an extent that a divergent outcome is not surprising. Unlike plaintiffs in, say, automobile accident litigation, derivative action plaintiffs are less likely to be sure of their injuries; they might not even know that they have a redressable injury at all. The lack of concrete directorial duty rules thus means that shareholder-plaintiffs may not even be aware that a dispute has arisen.

might take their chances. But institutional barriers make derivative suits expensive. Moreover, the price is raised still higher by limited awareness of directorial duties among the public, and even among many Japanese attorneys.[219]

On the other hand, if the problem is viewed through a historical lens, the lack of derivative litigation may in fact be not a result but a cause of the vague status of directorial duties. Derivative actions serve an "educational and socializing" function, since such suits help make more concrete the duties of directors.[220] Fewer derivative suits means fewer concrete rules, because courts have fewer chances to define the scope of the applicable law. In other words, it may be precisely because Japanese shareholders do not sue that Japan, even after fifty years of experience with derivative suits, has no explicit statement of directorial duties.

Regardless of the rules' effect on shareholders, directors may also be affected by the rules. Director behavior may be affected ex ante, as the director weighs the implicit price of infringing upon shareholder entitlements.[221] As regards the duty of care, it is unlikely that directors consciously decide to be negligent; however, the lack of a precise rule certainly does nothing to discourage sloth. As for the duty of loyalty, the director is in some ways in the same position as the shareholder, in that committing a misdeed is like rolling the dice. If the roll is a good one, the director may profit handsomely; if not, he could lose even more.

Legal provisions aside, directors are also subject to a variety of extralegal constraints that often fall under the rubric of "culture." First, public apology and resignation play an important role in the Japanese management monitoring process. [222] More so than in the United States, directors of large Japanese corporations often assume personal responsibility (usually in the moral rather than the legal sense) for the actions of their companies and for their own actions by issuing public apologies and resigning from their positions. Thus, some would argue, derivative litigation in Japan is supplanted by a cultural remedy.[223]

Also of importance is the relationship of the parties in the derivative litigation context. Shareholders and directors, though perhaps strangers on a personal level, are in an ongoing relationship. Unlike two disputing strangers, it may be more profitable for shareholders and directors to maintain their relationship by utilizing other mechanisms, such as settlement, or in the shareholder's case, exit. Moreover, the director-shareholder relationship is one of informational asymmetry; shareholders often do not have access to the information necessary to pursue a derivative action. Thus, the appropriate query in the derivative action context is not "How are disputes selected for litigation?" but rather "How is ordinary human behavior selected for disputes?" When the rule is as unclear as the one described above, very few directorial actions will result in shareholder-director disputes, which in turn will lead to lower litigation rates.

219. See, e.g., [Makoto Yazawa, *The Legal Structure for Corporate Enterprise: Shareholder-Management Relations Under Japanese Law, in* Law in Japan 547 (Arthur T. von Mehren ed., 1963)], at 559–62.

220. [American Law Institute, Principles of Corporate Governance: Analysis and Recommendations 601 (Proposed Final Draft 1992)], Introductory Note, at 597.

221. Shareholders, too, are affected ex ante; they receive a premium in the form of a reduced stock price for accepting the systemic risk caused by the lack of a comprehensive legal rule.

222. See John O. Haley, *Sheathing the Sword of Japanese Justice in Japan: An Essay on Law Without Sanctions*, 8 J. Japan. Stud. 265, 275–76 (1982). A recent example is the resignation and public apology of Setsuya "Big" Tabuchi on July 22, 1991, to atone for the loss compensation scandal. See *infra* TAN; see also Hisanobu Ohse, *Record Number of Japanese Company Chiefs Resign*, Reuters Asia-Pacific Business Report, June 3, 1993, available in LEXIS, ASIAPC Library, APBRPT File.

223. See Robert A.G. Monks & Nell Minow, Power and Accountability 167 (1991); Yo Makino, *Antei Kabunushi ni "Anju"* A Safe Abode for Safe Shareholders, Nihon Keizai Shinbun, June 24, 1992, at 1 (Part 2 of Haiiro no "Keiei Sekinin" The Grey Areas of Managerial Liability).

A more complete analysis of director apology requires an examination of the underlying financial incentives of such a policy. Recognizing the cost of bringing derivative actions, Japanese shareholders are quite satisfied when a director apologizes and resigns to atone for misconduct, because this removes the need for any sort of costly action on their part to "throw the bums out." In other words, ex post, "buying" an apology is cheap compared to buying a high-priced judicial remedy.[224] From the corporation's standpoint, director apology and resignation is also preferred for economic reasons. As in the shareholder case, managers prefer apology and resignation because it deters other forms of shareholder remedies that might be more costly to the corporation. In addition, it lets management control the form of the information that is to be distributed, thus reducing the chances of repercussions from negative publicity. [225] From the director's point of view, apology and resignation often result merely in a transfer to a subsidiary's board, while more severe consequences can result if one has to be forced out. Although culture may play some part in the calculus, it is clear that both sides also have economic incentives to favor the apology system.

A second factor, also often labeled as "cultural," is the concept of director loyalty to the corporation. Employee loyalty, from the lowest ranked workers to senior management, has long been cited as both a cause of Japanese success and a prominent feature of Japanese society.[226] Although early accounts focused on cultural explanations for the phenomenon,[227] recent scholarship has argued that loyalty is the product of economic incentives created by bonus payments and firm-specific human capital investments incident to lifetime employment guarantees.[228] Other studies have noted that the lifetime employment system is not steeped in cultural tradition, but rather is a postwar development that was apparently designed to combat capital shortages, not to satisfy cultural mores. Directors are loyal because it is more profitable to be loyal than not.

Could it be that lifetime employment-based loyalty means that, ex ante, Japanese directors are less likely to decide to commit transgressions against the corporation than are their counterparts in the United States?[229] On the one hand, directors may avoid

224. This theory also explains why American directors rarely get off the hook with an apology and resignation. The costs of other judicial forms of relief are much lower in the United States....

225. Some argue that directors in Japan feel more of a sense of guilt than directors in the United States, and thus Japanese directors apologize and resign in instances in which the American directors might not take such drastic action. See TAKEO DOI, AMAE NO KOZO The Structure of Amae 199 (1971) (directors resign out of strong sense of guilt); see also Toni M. Massaro, *Shame, Culture, and American Criminal Law*, 89 MICH. L. REV. 1880, 1906–10 (1991) (presenting Japan as having a shame culture). Though shame and guilt may play some role in the resignation decision, it should be noted that Japanese directors usually apologize and resign only as the result of major incidents that have consequences resting on legal rules or the lack thereof.

226. See, e.g., EZRA F. VOGEL, JAPAN AS NUMBER ONE: LESSONS FOR AMERICA 146–50 (5th ed. 1980).

227. See, e.g., CHIE NAKANE, JAPANESE SOCIETY 3–4, 70–74 (1970).

228. See Masahiro Okuno, *Corporate Loyalty and Bonus Payments: An Analysis of Work Incentives in Japan*, in THE ECONOMIC ANALYSIS OF THE JAPANESE FIRM 387 (Masahiko Aoki ed., 1984).

229. See [AMERIKA TO NIHON NO KAISHAHO Corporation Law in the United States and Japan 303–21 (Richard W. Jennings & Masahiro Kitazawa eds., 1965)], at 354 (statement of Richard W. Jennings, querying the same). Or as one popular novelist put it, "the executives feel they are part of a family. And they'd never betray their own family." MICHAEL CRICHTON, RISING SUN 103 (1993).

Advocates of the cultural theory of Japanese management might argue that fewer duty violations occur in Japan because of the diffused decision-making process employed in Japanese firms. See RONALD DORE, TAKING JAPAN SERIOUSLY: A CONFUCIAN PERSPECTIVE ON LEADING ECONOMIC ISSUES 54, 142 (1987). In such a structure, the argument goes, fraud is much more difficult because so many participants are required. But even in this scheme duty violations can occur easily. Individual misdeeds because they know that if they are found out, they will lose the center of their lives, their jobs, and finding future employment will be extremely difficult. On the other hand, if corporations do not take such transgressions seriously, directors may have incentives to take all they can. Although no empirical studies have been conducted,[230] anecdotal evidence[231] and scholarly opinion[232] suggest that the latter is more plausible, or at least that these two forces mitigate each other to produce an intermediate level of enforcement that is roughly comparable to that of the United States.[233]

S. Todd Huckaby, *Note: Defensive Action to Hostile Takeover Efforts in Japan: The Shuwa Decisions*

29 COLUM. J. TRANSNAT'L L. 439 (1991)
(excerpts pages 443–461; some footnotes omitted)

I. SHUWA AND THE LEGALITY OF DEFENSIVE ACTION TO HOSTILE TAKEOVERS IN JAPAN

In Japan, defensive actions to repel hostile takeovers[29] traditionally have been accepted by the courts due to the customary judicial and cultural aversion to hostile cor-

---

directors can still breach their duties without ever reaching the point of a board-wide fraud conspiracy, and entire boards can violate duties by simple mismanagement.

230. The data on this point are almost impossible to collect. Three research methods seem plausible, though each is flawed. First, an examination of white collar crime figures would be of little use because those figures may reflect decisions of resource allocation as much as actual incidence of crime and fiduciary duties may be violated without crimes being committed. Second, an examination of the frequency of lawsuits against directors would be imperfect, since issues of price make systematic comparisons impossible. Finally, polling directors as to their misdeeds would be unlikely to achieve accurate results.

231. In the normal case, internal corporate discipline amounts only to pay cuts or withholding of bonuses. On at least one occasion, a director has resigned only to resurface on the board of a subsidiary. See Makino, *supra* note 223.

232. See [Yasuhei Taniguchi, *Kabunushi no Daihyo Sosho* Shareholder Derivative Actions, in 5 JITSUMU MINJI SOSHO KOZA Lectures on the Practice of Civil Procedure 95 (Chuichi Suzuki & Akira Mikazuki eds., 1969)], at 99.

233. American managerial practices are no more virtuous; Japanese commentators have noted that golden parachutes may have the same effect in the United States. See AKIO MORITA & SHINTARO ISHIHARA, "NO" TO IERU NIHON The Japan That Can Say No 93 (1989) (Japanese version only; Morita's comments not translated in English version).

29. Defensive tactics may include the use of dormant charter and by-law provisions, "white knights," "poison pills," "greenmail," and restructuring strategies.

First, corporations may include provisions to provide for (1) supermajority requirements for approval of mergers; (2) "fair price" amendments waiving the supermajority requirement if a "fair price" is offered to the shareholders; and (3) staggered board provisions making a complete takeover of the board more difficult. J. CHOPER, J. COFFEE & R. MORRIS, CASES AND MATERIALS ON CORPORATIONS 1125 (3d ed. 1989) [hereinafter CORPORATIONS].

"White knight" is the name given a friendly corporation to which a substantial block of shares is issued or an option to purchase shares is granted with the intent of diluting the corporate raider's holdings and placing greater control of the target company in friendly hands. Id.

"Poison pills" are convertible securities or warrants used to deter the hostile acquisition and force the buyer to negotiate with the management. They usually have provisions activating a right to purchase stock at an advantageous price. Id.

Corporate "greenmail" refers to the "selective repurchase by the target corporation of a potential bidder's stock, usually at a premium over the market." Id. at 1132. See generally Note, *Greenmail:*

porate action. These defenses are available in the United States and are currently being considered by corporations in Japan.[30]

Provided that repelling the takeover is not the primary purpose of the issuance, defensive action to takeover attempts through the issuance of new shares is not illegal under Japanese[31] or American law.[32] In both countries, the legitimacy of the defensive tactic depends on the business purpose stated to justify such action.[33] A fiduciary duty is imposed on those deciding to issue the shares to act in the interest of the company and the shareholders instead of acting to entrench themselves in control of the corporation.[34] However, in Japan, this duty has not been strictly enforced historically. Although the basic rules protecting shareholders from such defensive tactics existed,[35] until the

---

Targeted Stock Repurchases and the Management Entrenchment Hypothesis, 98 HARV.L.REV. 1045 (1985).

Restructuring defenses usually consist of the implementation of some of the acquiror's proposals before the merger. The most common technique is a leveraged-buyout (LBO), whereby management of the target corporation creates a new corporation which competes with the raider. However, this defensive tactic recently has become less useful because junk bonds, high-risk bonds earning a high rate of return and the usual financing tool in LBOs, are currently disfavored by investors due to their riskiness. CORPORATIONS, at 1132.

30. In Japan, defensive actions are currently being studied by the corporate community to determine whether they are legally feasible or useful. Takahashi, *Japan Not Immune from Mergermania*, NIHON KEIZAI SHIMBUN (Japan Econ.J.), Aug. 12, 1989, at 1. Nevertheless, even if they would be legal, most have never been used.... These types of defensive tactics were not considered before because of the absence of hostile takeover activity in Japan....

Japanese corporations receive an additional layer of protection from foreign hostile takeovers through the Foreign Exchange and Commerce Law (FECL) which requires notification to the MOF once a non-Japanese corporation holds more than 10% of a Japanese company. *Gaikoku Kawase oyobi Gaiboku Boeki Kanri ho* (Foreign Exchange and Foreign Trade Control Law), art. 26, § 3, Law No. 228 of 1949, as amended [hereinafter FECL], translated in 5 EHS L.BULL. SERIES (AA); Tatsuta, Proxy Regulation, Tender Offers, and Insider Trading, in JAPANESE SECURITIES REGULATION 159, 175–76 (L. Loss, M. Yazawa & B. Banoff eds. 1983) [hereinafter JAPANESE REGULATION]. The foreign investor may not proceed with the transaction until 30 days after such notification is filed, unless authorized to do so. Note, *Prying Open the Japanese Market: Tender Offers and the Legal System in Japan*, 11 LOY.L.A.INT'L & COMP.L.J. 579, 585 (1989) (citing Legal Division, International Finance Bureau, Ministry of Finance, Commentary on the Amendment of the Foreign Exchange and Foreign Trade Control Law 1, 34 (1980)). In addition, the MOF may "deem it necessary to make an inquiry." The MOF may take up to five months to issue a response to suggest changes in the transaction. FECL art. 27, para. 2–3; Note, *Prying Open the Japanese Market*, at 586.

31. Article 280-2 outlines the procedure for such transactions. SHOHO art. 280-2.

32. Unocal Corp. v. Mesa Petroleum Co., 493 A.2d 946, 955 (Del.1985). U.S. corporate law depends on state law. In many ways, the reasoning of the Shuwa decision is similar to the court's reasoning in Unocal. In Unocal, the court decided that defensive actions to hostile takeovers must be reasonable in light of the threat presented to the corporation to be consistent with the business judgment rule. Under the business judgment rule, a board of director's actions are justified if it acts in what it reasonably believes to be the corporation's and the shareholder's best interests. Unocal, 493 A.2d at 955. See Moran v. Household Int'l, Inc., 500 A.2d 1346 (DelSup.1985)....

33. ....Under Japanese law, management is required to have a valid business purpose to issue shares at a "specially advantageous price." SHOH art. 280-10. Business judgment in Japan is proscribed by the duty of good faith imposed on the directors of a corporation. Id. art. 254-3 (interpreting MINPO (Civil Code) art. 644). The duty is phrased as a duty to be a "good manager." MINPO art. 644.

34. Unocal, 493 A.2d at 955; Chujitsuya-Inageya Shinkabu Hakko Sashitome Karishobun Jiken (Preliminary Injunction Judgment Against Chujitsuya and Inageya's Issuance of New Shares), 1317 HANREI JIHO [HANJI] 28 (Aug. 21, 1989) [hereinafter Sashitome Karishobun], at 35.

35. SHOH art. 280-2, para. 2 & art. 280-10

Shuwa Decisions, the Japanese courts had been reluctant to enforce the fiduciary duty in cases where stock dilution mechanisms were used to repel unsolicited takeovers.

A. The Facts of Shuwa

The Shuwa Decisions were decided by the 8th Civil Section of the Tokyo District Court[37] on July 25, 1989. Presiding Judge Kazuo Yamaguchi granted a preliminary injunction to Shuwa denying the right of the two target companies, Inageya and Chujitsuya, to issue new stock to each other in an attempt to dilute Shuwa's takeover attempt.[38]

Shuwa, a closely held real estate development corporation, began the takeover attempt[39] by buying shares of Inageya in January of 1988 and of Chujitsuya from June 1987 to February 1988. Shuwa remained anonymous during the acquisition period by purposely failing to change the registry of the stock. In all, Shuwa purchased 33.4% of Chujitsuya's shares and 21.4% of Inageya's shares, which made Shuwa a major shareholder in both corporations.

The first major problem for Shuwa in its takeover attempt arose in early July 1989 when it changed the registry of the stock to its own name in order to influence the policies of Chujitsuya and Inageya. Immediately thereafter, the boards of directors of both Inageya and Chujitsuya met to discuss a capital lock-up intended to repel Shuwa's takeover attempts. As a result of this meeting, Chujitsuya's and Inageya's boards agreed to exchange stock at a reduced price. Specifically, Chujitsuya offered its shares at $11,120 per share and Inageya exchanged its shares at $11,580 per share when the market prices for these shares were $15,050 and $14,150 per share, respectively.

This transaction was designed to grant each company a 19.5% stake in the other's stock, considerably diluting Shuwa's holdings. The defensive action against Shuwa's acquisition attempt was to be completed through the payment of the $15 billion difference in the price between Chujitsuya and Inageya stock exchanged. However, after close ex-

37. Japan's legal structure is characteristic of civil law countries. The Japanese legal system combines its Germanic origins with a common law statutory system similar to that in the United States. These legal structures were assimilated and applied in Japan in accordance with the unique Japanese cultural and social traditions. Happe, *Inside the Japanese Stock Market: An Assessment*, 5 Am. U. J. Int'l L. & Pol'y 87, 99 (1987).

In Japan, previous case decisions do not have precedential value. The Supreme Court (Saiko Saibansho), High Courts (Koto Saibansho), District Courts (Chiho Saibansho), Family Courts (Katei Saibansho) and Summary Courts (Kan'i Saibansho) form the judiciary structure of Japan. Saibansho Ho (Courts Act), art. 26, §2, Law No. 59 of 1947. Japanese District Courts have either one or three judges depending on the importance and nature of the case. Id. Thus, the Shuwa court had three judges. For a discussion of the Japanese judicial structure, see Organization of Courts, in The Japanese Legal System: Introductory Cases and Materials 48, 48–53 (H. Tanaka & M. Smith eds. 1976) [hereinafter Japanese System].

38. Sashitome Karishobun, supra note [34], at 30.

39. According to allegations in the press, Shuwa's purchase of shares was linked to its president's close friendship with Nobotsugu Shimizu, the chairman of Life Stores. In 1988, business difficulties led Shimizu to search for business partners in an effort to invigorate the operations of Life Stores. Shuwa's president acquired the shares through Shimizu and furthered Shimizu's purposes after the transaction. Kobayashi met with Yoshimoto Takagi, Chujitsuya's president, as early as October 1988 to discuss the possibility of a merger, but Takagi rejected the proposal. Shuwa Mo Kime Te Kaku (Shuwa Does Not Have Reason For Its Decision Either), Nihon Keizai Shimbun, July 26, 1989, at 1 [hereinafter Kime Te Kaku]. This factual background was considered by the court in determining the business purpose of the Shuwa takeover attempt.

amination of the transaction, the Ministry of Finance (MOF) warned the issuer in the transaction, Nomura Securities, against issuing the shares at such an unreasonably low price that it would threaten the existing shareholders' interests. To ensure that the shares of Chujitsuya and Inageya's shareholders would not be deprived of their value, it was imperative that the court grant the injunction before the exchange of shares took place.

B. The Legal Framework

In Japan, mergers and acquisitions exclusively between Japanese parties[51] are regulated by the Commercial Code,[52] the Antimonopoly Law[53] and the Securities and Exchange Law.[54] In the Shuwa Decisions, the plaintiff requested the enforcement of shareholder rights provided for in the Commercial Code.[55]

1. The Japanese Commercial Code

The Commercial Code regulates capitalization, shareholder rights, restructuring and dissolution of Japanese companies. However, the vagueness of the Commercial Code requires judicial interpretation of its provisions. For instance, the Code terms "specially favorable issue price" in Article 280-2, paragraph 2 and "grossly unfair manner" in Article 280-10 are not defined in the Code. In addition, the Code is subject to administra-

51. In Shuwa, the parties to the transaction were all Japanese. If there had been a foreign party involved, the FECL would apply. The FECL covers areas such as capital transactions and investments in Japan involving foreign nationals. FECL, supra note 30, arts. 20–46.

52. The Commercial Code says that if the shareholder holds the stock for over six months he, or she, may: (a) make proposals to the agenda for shareholder meetings and inspect the register with 1% ownership or three hundred shares (SHOHO art. 232-2); (b) convene a meeting of shareholders with 3% ownership (id. art. 237); (c) inspect and make copies of accounting and other company records with 10% ownership (id. art. 293-6); (d) veto two-thirds majority decisions such as the issuance of stock at a "specially favorable issue price" with 33.4% ownership (id. art. 280-2, para. 2 & art. 343); (e) appoint directors with 50% ownership (id. art. 256-3); and (f) remove directors (id. art. 257), change the articles of incorporation (id. art. 343), and approve mergers and the transfer of substantial assets (id. art. 245) with 66.7% ownership. [JAPAN ECONOMIC INSTITUTE, PATTERNS AND IMPLICATIONS OF JAPANESE STOCKHOLDING 6 (Japan Economic Institute Report No. 3A, 1991) [hereinafter JEI 1991 REPORT]], at 8.

53. Shiteki Dokusen no Kinshi oyobi Kosei Torihiki no Kakuho ni Kansuru Horitsu (Law Concerning Prohibition of Private Monopoly and Maintenance of Fair Trade), Law No. 54 of 1947, as amended, translated in H. IYORI & A. UESUGI, THE ANTIMONOPOLY LAWS OF JAPAN 213 (1983), and in ANTIMONOPOLY LEGISLATION OF JAPAN (M. Nakagawa ed. 1984). The Antimonopoly Law is patterned after the U.S. antitrust laws and regulates unfair business concentrations and restraints on competition....

54. Shoken Torihikiho (Securities and Exchange Law), Law No. 25 of 1948, as amended [hereinafter JSEL], translated in JAPANESE SECURITIES REGULATION appendix A (L. Loss, M. Yazawa & B. Banoff eds. 1983)....In the Shuwa transactions, Chujitsuya and Inageya were not required to register with the MOF because the issue qualified as a private offering. Under the JSEL, a private offering is an issuance to less than "an unspecified large number of persons." JSEL, arts. 2, 3. This statutory provision is generally interpreted by the MOF to mean fewer than "around 50 persons." KANZAKI, SHOKEN TORIHIKI HO (Stock Exchange Law) 249 (1st ed. 1987) (citing Ministry of Finance, Securities Division, Tsutatsu (Administrative Guidance Directive) No. 2272 (Sept. 6, 1971)).

U.S. securities laws were used as the pattern for the development of the JSEL. Shimada, *A Comparison of Securities Regulation in Japan and the United States*, 29 COLUM. J. TRANS-NAT'L L. 319 (1991). However, the JSEL has been drafted and interpreted differently because of: (1) the Japanese unitary system of government; (2) the drafters' awareness of the unique corporate structure of Japan (discussed infra note 83); and (3) the lack of litigation concerning the interpretation of the JSEL and a judicial preference for administrative resolution of such conflicts resulting from the absence of the level of precedent found in the United States. Happe, *supra* note 37, at 124.

55. SHOHO arts. 280-2, 280-10.

tive guidance[58] in its interpretation.[59] Therefore, the ultimate enforcement of the statutory language of the Code remains uncertain in many instances.

Article 280 of the Commercial Code regulates the issuance of new shares by corporations.[60] Under Article 280, the board of directors of a corporation can issue new stock to any party and determine the price,[61] payment day, and quantity issued of that stock, so long as the stock is already authorized and unissued,[62] and its preemptory rights [63] are not granted to the current shareholders through the articles of incorporation.[64] Despite these broad powers granted to the board of directors, the shareholders are entitled to notification from the board in the event of such an issuance.[65] These offerings are usually made within the keiretsu (industrial family) corporate structure,[66] a structure of companies affiliated through an extensive network of cross-shareholding.

---

58. ....There are three principal types of guidance depending on the purpose of the government officials: (1) advisory, (2) regulatory and (3) reconciliatory. Yeomans, *Administrative Guidance: A Peregrine View*, 19 LAW IN JAPAN 125, 135–36 (1986). Compliance with administrative guidance is "purely voluntary" only in the sense that there is no statutory penalty for non-compliance. However, failure to comply will result in embarrassment to the government agency and in the subsequent denial of future services to the non-complying party. Luney, Book Review, 10 N.C.J. INT'L & COM.REG. 297, 298 (1983) (L. Loss, M. Yazawa & B. Banoff eds. 1983) (reviewing JAPANESE SECURITIES REGULATION).

Administrative guidance derives its authority from broad legislative mandates establishing the agency. Happe, *supra* note 37, at 117....

59. The warnings given to Chujitsuya and Inageya by the Ministry were administrative guidance in the interpretation of the Commercial Code.

60. SHOHO art. 280. Article 280 of the Commercial Code is not the only section of the Code that affected the transaction at issue in Shuwa. Articles 343, 347 and 348 are also relevant to this discussion. First, Article 348 requires a 50% vote of a quorum of two-thirds of the corporation's shareholders when making changes to the articles of incorporation. Id. art. 343. Second, Article 347 provides that the number of shares authorized to be issued cannot be increased to exceed four times the total amount of shares already issued. Id. art. 347. Finally, Article 348 requires a 50% vote of a quorum of two-thirds of the corporation's shareholders for the passage of a resolution to alter the articles of incorporation to require the approval of the board of directors for transferring the shares, notwithstanding the requirements of Article 343. Id. art. 348.

61. The Code requires that the price be set at "fair value." Id. art. 280-2, para. 2.

62. Articles 166 and 347 of the Code allow corporations to authorize capital up to four times their paid-in capital. Id. arts. 166 & 347.

63. Id. art. 280-2, para. 1. Preemptory rights are the rights given to shareholders to purchase an amount of the new shares to be issued commensurate to the shareholder's holdings ratio before the new issuance. J. DOWNES & J. GOODMAN, DICTIONARY OF FINANCE AND INVESTMENT TERMS 299 (2d ed. 1987). Preemptory rights are not established as a shareholder right in the Commercial Code.

64. SHOHO art. 280-3-3.

65. Id. arts. 232, 280-3-2.

66. The keiretsu corporate structure, a network of interrelated companies which assist each other as clients, suppliers, purchasers, distributors and banks, operates so that the members of the "group" hold a large portion of each other's stock. There are three major types of keiretsu: financial, industrial and subsidiary. The financial keiretsu is organized around a large bank with financial links to a wide variety of companies. The traditional pre-World War II zaibatsu (holding companies) have survived in modern Japan as financial keiretsu (e.g., Mitsui, Sumitomo, Mitsubishi) despite the legal prohibition against holding companies in the Antimonopoly Law. JAPAN ECONOMIC INSTITUTE, KEIRETSU AND OTHER LARGE CORPORATE GROUPS IN JAPAN (Japan Economic Institute Report No. 2A, 1990) [hereinafter JEI 1990 REPORT]. The industrial keiretsu is organized around a large manufacturer or independent firm (e.g., Sony, Daie, Hitachi, Tokyu) that has a greater percentage of control of its related companies than the financial keiretsu leader since no legal limits on ownership exist. Id. The subsidiary keiretsu are organized around a manufacturer using the services of many, different subcontractors (e.g., Toyota). Id. at 4.

In Shuwa, the new issuance was offered at a "specially favorable issue price" which, under Article 280-2, paragraph 2 of the Code, requires a vote of approval of over fifty percent of a quorum of at least two-thirds of the corporation's shareholders. Despite this Code requirement, however, the Inageya and Chujitsuya transfers were never submitted for shareholder approval.

Besides outlining the procedures required for shareholder approval of the corporation's stock transactions, the Commercial Code also provides for an injunction against stock transactions if the price is determined to be unfair to the shareholders.[69] The shareholders are allowed to apply to the courts for an injunction any time before the issuance and may petition the court to declare the transaction invalid any time within six months of the transaction.[70] Thus, in Shuwa, the court enforced these Code sections protecting shareholders against unfair issuances and granted the preliminary injunction sought by the main shareholder, Shuwa.

2. Prior Cases

Prior to Shuwa, several decisions by Japanese courts had allowed the issuance of new stock at a discounted rate when the purpose of that issuance was explicitly approved by the court. In these earlier cases, the courts determined that the Commercial Code's prohibition of issuances in an "unfair manner" was the equivalent of a requirement that a proper business purpose be shown. The following cases reflect the legal atmosphere in which the Shuwa transaction took place.

The 1987 Takuma v. Cosmopolitan[72] case involved an exchange of stock at an undervalued price similar to the Chujitsuya-Inageya exchange. In Takuma, the court decided that the transaction was valid.[73] The key distinction between Takuma and Shuwa is that management of the Takuma Corporation (Takuma) issued stock to a related bank in response to a greenmail attempt by known figures of the Yakuza (the Japanese mafia). The court accepted Takuma's stated business purpose for the issuance; namely, that the issuance was necessary to raise additional financial resources for capital investments.[75] The court in Takuma was very sympathetic to the stated business purpose of the target corporation because of its inherent bias against the Yakuza and the notion of an investor greenmailing a company.

In Nakajima v. Sony,[77] the court allowed the undervalued issuance of shares to a third party where the discount was roughly half the market price but the purpose of the transaction was to permit Sony to save Aiwa from certain bankruptcy. The Nakajima court allowed the issuance because it was for the benefit of the shareholders. As in the previous Takuma case, the court looked behind the transaction to determine its purpose.

Finally, in an important pre-Shuwa decision, the Minebea case,[81] the medium-sized Minebea Corporation (Minebea), a world leader in the production of precision ball-

---

69. SHOHO art. 280-10.

70. Id. art. 280-15.

72. Shinkabu Hakko Sashitome Karishobun Shinse Kyakka Kettei (New Issuance of Stock Provisional Injunction Decision), 47 SHOJI HOMU 34 (1988) [hereinafter Shinkabu Hakko].

73. Id. at 39.

75. Shinkabu Hakko, supra note 72, at 39.

77. Shoji (Business), 679 HANJI 70 (1972). Mr. Nakajima represented the shareholders of Aiwa Corporation. Id.

81. Tokyo Gets Its First Taste of Greenmail, BUS. WEEK, Sept. 23, 1985, at 56. For a discussion of the Minebea case, see Abell & Kitaarai, *Japanese M & A: The Barriers to Hostile Takeovers*, 8 INT'L FIN. L. REV. 11, 13 (Feb. 1989).

bearings and a takeover target of Trafalgar Holdings, Ltd. (Trafalgar), an American corporation, and Glen International (Glen), a British corporation,[82] issued shares to its stable shareholders[83] and proposed a merger with Kanemori Company, Ltd., in an effort to dilute the two foreign companies' existing interests. This defensive action by Minebea to Trafalgar and Glen's hostile takeover attempt was very similar to the plan adopted by Chujitsuya and Inageya in response to Shuwa's hostile takeover attempt. However, contrary to the result in the later Shuwa Decisions, the court in Minebea approved the transaction and recognized the merger as legitimate under the business purpose rule. The Minebea court explicitly supported Minebea's efforts to retain control of the strategic ball bearings industry, especially since two percent of its business was with the Japanese military. Thus, the courts in Takuma, Nakajima and Minebea viewed the managements' motivations for the issuance of shares as the crucial factor in determining "fairness" in the transactions.

C. The Shuwa Decisions

In the Shuwa Decisions, the court did not interpret the Commercial Code to permit a Minebea type of defensive action to hostile takeovers. The rationale for applying the law differently in Minebea and Shuwa suggests that the courts are interpreting the Com-

---

82. Trafalgar Holdings, Ltd. ("Trafalgar") and Glen International ("Glen") held 23% of the outstanding shares of the Minebea Corporation ("Minebea") in the form of warrants and convertible bonds. Glen owned an additional ten million shares outright. These holdings jointly made Trafalgar and Glen the largest shareholders of Minebea. Crabb, supra note 67, at 123. The situation was even more interesting since Minebea itself had attempted a hostile takeover of Sankyo Seiki Manufacturing Company five years before. Hostile Takeovers Shaking Traditional Ties, Nihon Keizai Shimbun (Japan Econ.J.), Mar. 17, 1990, at 19 [hereinafter Shaking Traditional Ties].

83. In general, Japanese companies are owned by a network of "stable shareholders." In other words, the largest shareholders in a particular company are likely to be associated with that company through pre-existing business relationships. Nearly 65% of shares of the Japanese companies listed on the Japanese stock exchanges are owned by other companies and organizations with close relationships (31% by financial institutions and 26% by corporations). Abell & Kitaarai, supra note 81, at 11. The remaining 27% is held by individual investors. Id. The holdings of related companies are not traded and constitute a stable controlling interest which prevents any individual shareholder from acting as a real hostile takeover threat. Id. at 12. Most stable shareholders view their role as "subordinate to another non-shareholding relationship," such as the keiretsu (industrial family) relationship, the bank-client relationship and the supplier-purchaser relationship. Nishimura, Corporate Acquisitions in Japan: Impediments and Opportunities 2 (Mar. 8, 1989) (unpublished paper presented at Business Week Symposium on U.S.-Japan Relations in New York City; on file at the Columbia Journal of Transnational Law). In fact, most large Japanese companies sell controlling blocs of their stock to their clients, suppliers and banks to protect themselves from takeovers. Lehner, Japan's Bias Against Domestic Takeovers May Become a Trade Issue, Wall St. J., Dec. 1, 1988, at A18. Only one restriction on the creation of a stable shareholder network exists: banks and insurance companies are limited in their holdings of shares of any one company to 5% and 10%, respectively. JEI 1990 REPORT, supra note 66, at 3.

Stable shareholders usually give blank proxies to management in exchange for the same type of treatment in their own corporations. Failure to follow this practice is considered an insult and jeopardizes the relationship. Heftel, *Corporate Governance in Japan: The Position of Shareholders in Publicly Held Corporations*, 5 U. Haw. L. Rev. 135, 165 (1983). Stable shareholding groups usually conduct joint meetings, form interlocking directorates and engage in joint internal and external business dealings. See Note, *Mergers and Acquisitions in Japan: New Options for Foreign Companies?*, 26 Colum. J. Transnat'l L. 575, 587 (1988). Stable shareholders have also provided the management of target corporations, such as Chujitsuya and Inageya, with a guarantee against takeovers since these shareholders generally do not trade their shares with a potential corporate raider. For instance, even though Shuwa is currently the largest shareholder in the Nagasakiya Company (Nagasakiya) with over 15% ownership, it has been unable to force a merger because 75% of the shares are held by stable institutional shareholders who will always support Nagasakiya's management....

mercial Code more favorably to the hostile raider when the takeover has a constructive economic effect.[86] The Shuwa Decisions also signal a new judicial concern for, and willingness to expand, shareholder rights in Japan.

As previously discussed, Shuwa's petition for relief requested the court to declare that Article 280-2, paragraph 2 of the Commercial Code prohibited the reciprocal stock issue at such a "specially favorable" issue price. Shuwa further requested a temporary injunction stating that the transaction was grossly unfair because it was intended as a defensive action to retain corporate control and, therefore, was not made for a valid business purpose. In its decision, the Shuwa court explicitly considered each element of the complaint: (1) how the valuation of the shares was reached, (2) the stated business purposes of the transaction for all the parties involved and (3) the ultimate effect of the transaction on the shareholders of Chujitsuya and Inageya.

1. Valuation of Shares

First, the Shuwa court had to determine the value of the shares exchanged to decide whether the issue price was "specially favorable" in violation of Article 280-2 of the Code. In making its determination, the court compared the stock issue prices of 1,120 yens and 1,580 yens with the market prices of 5,050 yens and 4,150 yens on the Tokyo Stock Exchange on the day that Chujitsuya and Inageya decided to issue the stock to each other. The 4:1 and 3:1 reduction ratios were declared "specially favorable"[88] issue prices as defined in Article 280-2 of the Code. This finding by the court triggered the Commercial Code's requirement that the companies' managements obtain shareholder approval before executing the transaction.[89] Since both companies failed to submit the proposal to their shareholders for approval, the court declared the transaction illegal and issued the injunction.[90]

The main point of dispute in the valuation of the shares was whether market prices should be considered in determining the actual value of the stock. The defendants requested the court to adopt a valuation figure determined by the market price of the companies' shares prior to the stock purchases by Shuwa. Alternatively, they suggested the application of an objective value price—the price of the shares if the companies were not listed on the Tokyo Stock Exchange. The defendants emphasized to the court that valuation issues for this type of stock "sale" had been viewed with leniency in the past. In addition, counsel for Chujitsuya and Inageya presented stock performance charts for the entire Japanese supermarket industry to argue that the recent rise in the price of the stock was not consistent with the overall supermarket industry performance. These arguments were not accepted by the court.

The Shuwa court ruled that the current market value at the time the board of directors set the issuing price was the best indicator of actual value even though takeover speculation may have previously inflated the market price.[94] The court ruled that both

86. This rationale can be inferred by the allowance of similar dilution tactics in Takuma, where greenmail was at issue, and the denial of such defensive action in Shuwa, where the raider was attempting to help restructure the supermarket industry.

88. SHOHO art. 280-2, para. 2.

89. Sashitome Karishobun, supra note [34], at 30.

90. Id. However, the finding that the issue prices were "specially favorable" was not dispositive under Japanese law at the time since previous courts had determined that a legitimate business purpose for the transaction was sufficient to justify the issuance despite a "specially favorable" price. See supra Section I(B)(2).

94. This determination was in accordance with the pre-Shuwa understanding of the law. Judgment of July 27, 1973, Koto Saibansho (High Court), Tokyo, 715 HANJI 100. However, the Shuwa court, contrary to these earlier decisions, disregarded the inflationary effect on the stock price

the market value of the shares prior to the purchases by Shuwa and the objective market value based on overall performance of the supermarket industry would be very difficult to determine effectively because of price fluctuations and the lack of objectivity by the parties in pricing the stock. Instead, the court determined that the market value should be the stocks' prices on July 10, 1989, the date of the target companies' decision to issue the stock to each other.[95]

The court's decision to adopt the most recent market price as its valuation standard was influenced by the continuity of the higher price—the stock performance for both companies had remained stable at this higher level for over a year and five months for Chujitsuya and over ten months for Inageya.[96] The most recent market price was seen by the court as the best indicator of future performance and the only truly objective indicator available for companies listed on the Tokyo Stock Exchange.[97]

2. Business Purpose

In addition to the stock valuation issue, the court examined the business purposes of Shuwa, Chujitsuya and Inageya for participating in the various transactions leading up to the litigation. Shuwa's purpose for the purchases of the shares was not mentioned in the final decision. However, it was reviewed by the court in the earlier stages of the litigation. On the other hand, the business purposes of Chujitsuya and Inageya were scrutinized closely by the court and were ultimately rejected as insufficient to justify their attempt to dilute Shuwa's control.

a. Shuwa's Purpose

Shuwa defended its acquisition of shares of Chujitsuya and Inageya on the grounds that a restructuring of the medium size supermarket retail industry was necessary to increase competition and to improve the inefficient distribution system. Shuwa's president Shigeru Kobayashi expressed an intent to create a company with annual sales of over 1 trillion yens by integrating Chujitsuya, Inageya, Nagasakiya and Life Stores. Shuwa argued that, in the end, this restructuring would "increase consumer purchasing power and resolve trade friction."

b. Chujitsuya and Inegeya's Purpose

Chujitsuya and Inageya claimed very similar reasons for their attempted lock-up of each other. However, the court scrutinized the purposes of these two parties more closely and required that they demonstrate a proper business purpose for their lock-up, which would justify the manner of the issuance. The court concluded that the defendants failed to do so.

In framing their arguments, the target companies claimed to have formed the lock-up to restructure themselves and to increase competition in the supermarket industry,

---

caused by the suspicion of a hostile takeover and did not allow any modification of the market price as a result. Sashitome Karishobun, supra note [34], at 30.

95. Sashitome Karishobun, supra note [34], at 28.

96. Id. at 32, 35.

97. The court would have undermined the reliability of the Japanese stock exchanges in allowing this defensive dilution of Shuwa's holdings. In fact, the court in its decision stated that "there [was] a high probability" that the Tokyo Stock Exchange's value of Shuwa's stock would decrease if the proposed stock swap was allowed. Id. at 31.

In addition, if the stock market price is ignored, the stock exchanges cease to be reliable pricing mechanisms and investors will seek alternatives to obtain a better price. Investors in the stock market will not buy stock at the exchange prices if they cannot rely on the accuracy of the stock exchange itself to determine the fair market price. In Shuwa, the court noted that, if the company's shares were not listed on the Tokyo Stock Exchange, the valuation would have been based on the objective value of the target company. Id. at 31.

placing their emphasis on the joint transfer of business know-how. They claimed to have formed a joint project team in December 1988, to exchange knowledge and to establish a closer business relationship. However, the court found as a factual matter that the lock-up had been established with the only intention of retaining corporate control when faced with the realization that Shuwa was gaining control of their shares. The court granted the injunction to Shuwa after it determined that the sole business purpose of retaining corporate control was an improper one.

3. Effect on Shareholders: The Enforcement of Art. 280-10

The court's analysis of stock valuation and business purpose was closely linked to its analysis of the lock-up's effect on the rights of Chujitsuya and Inageya shareholders. The court concluded that minority shareholders in these companies were being directly harmed by the stock issuance and held that any valuation of new offerings had to be done in a manner impartial to both old and new shareholders in the interest of fairness to all. Thus, the undervalued price at issue was declared unfair to the existing shareholders who had paid full market price because its direct effect was to cause the market price of both stocks to fall.

In addition, the Shuwa court found that another effect of the lock-up was the dilution of the relative holdings ratios of all the shareholders. Because the transaction involved the transfer of little cash, the court noted that the issuance would dilute all the existing shareholders' stock without contributing any real value to either Chujitsuya or Inageya.[105]

In the past, Japanese courts had allowed the issuance of shares as a defensive action to hostile takeovers despite the provisions of the Commercial Code regarding shareholder rights. However, the Shuwa Decisions effected a marked change in the law. Shuwa imposed a greater fiduciary duty on Japanese management and demonstrated the court's willingness to favorably interpret the legal norms protecting shareholders, even in the event of a hostile takeover defense. As a result of the Shuwa Decisions, Japanese management can no longer issue stock as a defensive action without shareholder participation if such an issuance would be extremely unfair to those shareholders.

D. The Shuwa Test and Its Application: Miyari Valve

1. The Shuwa Test

The Shuwa Decisions set forth a two-part test[108] applicable to all transactions involving a new issuance of shares to third parties in the context of a defensive action by companies listed on the First Section of the Tokyo Stock Exchange. To be allowed, the issuance must be necessary for business. The stock may not be issued at a specially advantageous price without prior shareholder approval. This general rule reflects a new judicial commitment to interpret the Commercial Code more favorably for shareholder rights, even if it benefits a corporate raider.

2. The Miyairi Valve Case

In Miyairi Valve Mfg. Co. v. Takahashi Sangyo Co.,[112] the Tokyo District Court had the first opportunity to apply the Shuwa test shortly after its formulation. Miyairi Valve Manufacturing Co. (Miyairi) was the target of a hostile takeover attempt by Takahashi Sangyo Co. (Takahashi), which held forty-seven percent of Miyairi's outstanding shares at the time of the new stock's issuance. The new offering by Miyairi increased its capital

105. Sashitome Karishobun, supra note [34], at 35.
108. Sashitome Karishobun, supra note [34], at 29.
112. Hanrei Tokuho (Special Report of Decisions), 1323 HANJI 48 (1989) [hereinafter Tokuho].

by eighteen percent. The stock was allegedly issued to third parties to raise funds for the purchase of the Hsinglung Company (Hsinglung), a Taiwanese valve maker. As a result of the new issuance, Takahashi's holdings were reduced from a forty-seven percent ownership interest to a forty percent interest.] Despite this dilution of Takahashi's interest, its petition for an injunction against Miyairi's issuance of the stock was denied by the court in August 1989.

The Miyairi Valve court applied the second prong of the Shuwa test first by determining that the issuance was not at a "specially advantageous" price since it was within the allowable discount margin set by the Japanese Securities Dealer's Association (JSDA).[117] The central controversy in the case related to the first prong of the Shuwa test, the requirement that the issuance be necessary for business. The court accepted Miyairi's argument that it was issuing the new stock to raise funds for the purchase of Hsinglung and, thus, was unwilling to protect Takahashi from a dilution of its holdings because Miyairi had an adequate rationale for raising its capital levels. The purpose for the issuance was found to be fair to all of Miyairi's shareholders and allowable even under the stricter test formulated in the Shuwa Decisions. Thus, the Miyairi Valve case applied the Shuwa test to allow third party stock issues where it was not altogether clear that the issuance was, in effect, a defensive action to a hostile takeover.[119]

Because the Shuwa Decisions are distinguishable from Miyairi Valve, the Shuwa test itself remains the judicial standard for the scrutiny of new issuances to third parties. In other words, if the shareholders will not gain anything from the issuance, as in the Shuwa Decisions, the courts will not allow the dilution of their stock.

Comments and Questions

1. Recall the excerpt from John Owen Haley, Authority Without Power: Law and the Japanese Paradox, which you studied in Chapter 2 of these materials. To what extent does Japanese cultural norms affect the way in which what appear to be Western style rules are applied by Japanese courts? Is this effect better demonstrated by the reluctance of parties to bring cations in court or by the way in which Japanese courts apply the law to cases brought before them? Consider in this regard the effect of director apology and resignation as an alternative to suit, as described in the excerpt by Mark West.

2. Mark West explains the two schools of scholarly thought regarding the extent of director duties in the context of derivative suits. Which of the two schools of thought more closely resembles the American approach? Does the narrower approach, that is that the scope of director duties is limited to those actions with respect to which directors are made liable to the company by statute, provide significantly less protection to shareholders?

3. What are the differences between permissible defensive tactics in the United States and Japan? Do the similarities suggest convergence as an achievable goal in this regard?

117. An allowable discount, as stated in a directive of the Japan Securities Dealer's Association, is up to ten percent of the market price during the previous six months. Japan Acts to Make Takeovers Easier..., Asian Wall St. J., Aug. 7, 1989, at 1 [hereinafter Japan Acts]....

119. In Miyairi Valve, the same district court denied the request for an injunction in circumstances similar to Shuwa. Id. at 48. Yet, the cases are distinguishable by the facts mentioned above.

b. China

China presents a system of regulation at once similar to but very different from that in other systems of enterprise governance. As you read through the materials that follow, consider whether the regulation of managers in the Chinese system is not more closely linked to Western notions of the regulation of government functionaries than of the regulation of business managers.

Robert C. Art and Minkang Gu, *China Incorporated: The First Corporation Law of the People's Republic of China*

20 YALE J. INT'L L. 273 (1995)
(excerpts pages 299–300; some footnotes omitted)

D. Safeguards Against Malfeasance

The Corporation Law specifies in detail the penalties for violating its various rules, duties, and requirements. Enforcement of these specific provisions is based on administrative and criminal processes rather than on derivative civil liability actions brought by shareholders. The Law does not even mention derivative actions, and such actions, if allowed, would in all likelihood be unsuccessful. Under current conditions, few if any Chinese corporate officers or directors would be financially able to pay a substantial civil judgment for breach of a fiduciary duty and thus could provide little relief to aggrieved shareholders suing derivatively.

The enforcement scheme of the Law relies on progressive discipline. As a first step, those who make false reports or statements relating to such matters as registration capital and accounting shall be, in the statute's terms, "ordered to correct their mistakes."[176] When the offense involves cheating creditors, investors, or society, fines are imposed.[177] The Law defines the range of fines by amount (typically between 10,000 and 100,000 yuan[178]) or percentage (such as between 1% and 5% of illegally raised capital,[179] or between 5% and 10% of illegally withdrawn subscription amounts[180]).

Directors, supervisors, and managers are subject to "administrative sanctions," which pose a serious threat to the individual's position and career. Other laws lend meaning to this term, specifying as included in "administrative sanctions" such penalties as probation, demerits, demotion, and dismissal.[181] In addition, any improper gains, i.e., those

---

176. Corporation Law, arts. 206, 209, 211.

177. See, e.g., id. arts. 206–12

178. Fines between 10,000 and 100,000 yuan may be imposed for submitting false documents relating to registration, id. art. 206, keeping a false set of accounting records, id. art. 211, and providing false reports of financial affairs, id. art. 212.

179. Id. art. 210.

180. Id. art. 209.

181. For a definition of "administrative sanctions" see supra note 136 [The term "administrative sanctions" is defined in, for example, Zhonghua Renmin Gongheguo Xingzheng Jiancha Tiaoli (The Provisions of Administrative Supervision of PRC), passed on November 23, 1990 by the State

derived from accepting bribes, appropriating corporate capital or lending it to others,[182] or operating a business in competition with the corporation,[183] are subject to forfeiture.

Criminal liability potentially attaches to all violations of the Corporation Law.[184] The punishment for white-collar crimes can be severe, including the death penalty.[185] For example, a corporate president convicted of embezzlement, bribery, and selling bonds through a pyramid scheme was executed in 1994.[186]

Short of these extreme sanctions, the Law imposes procedures and requirements in an effort to minimize the opportunities for abuse. Such safeguards are deemed necessary to prevent fraud and misappropriation in the creation and operation of corporations. The danger of such abuses is apparent, particularly because potential investors are not yet sophisticated and because control by private parties of the state's property invites misappropriation.

To safeguard against these abuses, the Law precludes individuals from holding office as a director or manager if they have committed any crime involving corruption, embezzlement, or offenses against the social economic order, or if they have held office in a company whose operating license was revoked for illegal acts. [187] State officials are also disqualified,[188] presumably to reduce the risk of improper influence. Corruption of government officials, in forms including insider trading of securities,[189] has been a serious problem.[190]

Council and issued on December 9, 1990 by the 69th decree of the State Council of PRC. Sanctions include warning, minor and severe reprimands, probation, demotion, dismissal, and discharge].

182. Corporation Law, art. 214.

183. Id. art. 215.

184. At least 15 separate articles state that in addition to the other more specific sanctions, criminal liability (which is not defined in the Corporation Law) applies "in accordance with the law." Id. arts. 206-14, 217-24.

185. Robert Steiner, *Big Chinese Bank, Citing Fraud, Won't Honor Letter of Credit*, ASIAN WALL ST. J. , June 23, 1993, at 3. For instance, the Xinhua News Agency reported that the president of a Chinese company who embezzled about $375,000 was executed in April 1994; that a vice-minister was sentenced to 20 years in prison in the same case; and that a company president was executed for embezzlement and bribery totaling $373,500. *Chinese Executive Convicted of Embezzlement Executed*, OREGONIAN , Apr. 12, 1994, at A4.

186. Shen Taifu, former president of the Beijing Changcheng [Great Wall] Machinery and Electronics Group, was convicted of embezzling two million yuan and taking a ten percent patent commission on all company transactions. He also devised a national pyramid scheme, selling bonds by promising interest rates of 43% and defrauding approximately 100,000 investors of more than one billion yuan. Finally, he paid bribes for favors. Shen was executed, and all of his personal property was confiscated. His wife, Sun Jihong, a vice president of the company, was convicted of converting one million yuan of company money, sentenced to fifteen years in jail, and deprived of political rights for three years. Jiang Jiang, *Finally, Alarm Bells Sound*, BEIJING REV. , May 2–8, 1994, at 13.

187. Corporation Law, art. 57.

188. Id. art. 58.

189. Investors in A-share stock markets, which are open only to Chinese citizens, frequently complain of rampant insider trading by government officials and private citizens such as business leaders and stockbrokers who have undisclosed information about regulatory policies and corporate developments. One brokerage firm has been found guilty of trading on advance knowledge of a corporate takeover, forced to disgorge its profits, fined, and shut down for two months. Joseph Kahn, *China Fines Broker in First Crackdown on Insider Trading*, WALL ST. J. , Feb. 7, 1994, at A11. In 1993, the Communist Party's top disciplinary committee formally banned party officials from playing the stock market. [Marcus W. Brauchli, *Chaotic Change: Beijing's Grip Weakens as Free Enterprise Turns into Free-for-All*, WALL ST. J. , Aug. 26, 1993], at A1.

190. President Jiang Zemin has warned that corruption has grown so common that it threatens to ruin the Communist Party. Party and army officials have stolen billions of yuan, engaged in mas-

Besides requiring corporate officers to have clean records and imposing general principles of fiduciary duty, the statute specifically prohibits misappropriation of company funds, deposit of company funds in personal bank accounts, and use of company assets as surety for a director's personal debts.[191] Directors may not conduct business with the company except as provided in the bylaws or in resolutions promulgated by the shareholders.[192]

Nicholas C. Howson, *China's Company Law: One Step Forward, Two Steps Back? A Modest Complaint*

11 Colum. J. Asian L. 127 (1997)

(excerpt pages 142–146; footnotes omitted)

C. Fiduciary Duty. Before the earliest "H" share offerings, the Hong Kong securities authorities demanded that PRC directors and officers of Chinese companies be subject to some strong and credible notion of fiduciary duty. So it was that the Standard Opinion,[47] in conjunction with an explanation rendered to the Hong Kong Securities and Exchange Commission by CRES on the meaning of Article 62 thereof, established the notion of "fiduciary duty" (chengxin zeren) for directors and senior managers in Chinese law for the first time.[48] Sadly, the Company Law eliminated this key concept (and phraseology), and thus any commonly accepted notion of how, or in whose interest, such key personnel should act.[49] (Instead, directors, supervisors and managers are to

---

sive smuggling and other rackets, and sought bribes and payoffs. [Nicholas Kristof, *China Sees 'Market-Leninism' as Way to Future*, N.Y. Times, Sept. 6, 1993], at 5.

191. Corporation Law, art. 60.

192. Id. art. 61.

47. See ["Opinion Regarding Standards for Companies Limited by Shares," promulgated on May 15, 1992 [hereinafter Standard Opinion]. A separate opinion on standards applicable to "limited liability companies" was also promulgated on the same day [hereinafter Limited Liability Company Standard Opinion]], art. 62. [Editor's note: The author explains that the Standard Opinion was issued to provide national standards for corporations wishing to have their shares traded on exchanges outside of the People's Republic of China and that "issuers which listed almost simultaneously on the Shanghai and Hong Kong exchanges ("A" and "H" share issuers), and the first direct issuer on the New York Stock Exchange (an "N" share issuer, with no underlying tranche inside the PRC or in Hong Kong), were established pursuant to the Standard Opinion." *Id.*, at 137–138 The Standard Opinion served and the precursor to the national Company Law of China. See supra at 137–139].

48. See CRES's letter to the Hong Kong Stock Exchange of June 10, 1993 (Tigaihansheng, No. 74, 1993) [hereinafter CRES Hong Kong Stock Exchange Letter]. In item 6 of the letter, CRES stated that: "the duty...described in Article 62 of the Standard Opinion has the same meaning as the" Chengxin Zeren [fiduciary duty]' of Hong Kong law." (Note the English words "fiduciary duty" are set out in the original Chinese form of the letter.) The equivalent concept exists in Taiwan's corporate law as "Shanliang Guanli."

49. The Company Law does stipulate that a company's articles of association are binding upon the company's shareholders, directors, members of the supervisory committee and senior managers (See Company Law, supra note 2, arts. 11, 59). The Overseas Listing Rules ["Special Regulations of the State Council on Foreign Offerings and Listings of Companies Limited by Shares" promulgated on Aug. 4, 1994 by the State Council of the PRC, but published only on August 19, 1994 in the People's Daily [hereinafter Overseas Listing Rules], supra note 36, expanded the application of this concept to other senior officers, which includes the CFO, the secretary of the company and other officers specified in the articles of association. The Company Law does contain specific prohibitions against directors, supervisors and management personnel acting in an interest contrary to the company's: See Company Law, supra note 2, arts. 59 (exploit position, accept bribes or take over com-

"protect the company's interests.")[50] The exact concept (and phraseology) was recovered, and only with respect to companies issuing stock overseas, in the Overseas Listing Rules of August 1994.[51] The damage in this regard is significant. First, it may have retarded the wide and undisputed application of a key concept of corporate responsibility which ensures that the board and management of a corporate entity will act in the interests of the entity, not the particular shareholder who has appointed such director or executive (or the state). Second, the omission leaves a mystery as to the exact standard which directors and senior executives of PRC companies must measure up to. Contrary to the U.S. and English systems, there is no common law system in China which will in time produce jurisprudence explaining and amplifying such a key concept; like the continental system, an authoritative explanation will have to be rendered—difficult, even if the substantive omission is remedied, because the Company Law designates no authoritative interpreter of the Law.[52] Of course, even if an authoritative body was anointed to explain the Law, and develop a coherent jurisprudence, there would remain the nettlesome problem of how, and who would enforce the duty so identified.[53]

D. State Officials. As China makes the transition from a Party-led, state-mandated economy to a "socialist market economy," various state officials have been placed in positions of "leadership" (i.e., managerial control) of newly transformed enterprises. In many cases, such newly-minted managers are simply the senior cadres of the enterprise's previous "leading department." As the underlying assets have become corporatized, so the leading department's relationship with the assets has changed from one of administrative control to share ownership. Thus, the laudable prohibition in the Company Law against "state officials" (guojia gongwuyuan) acting as directors, supervisors or managers of Chinese companies seems strange and certain to be widely dishon-

---

pany property), 60 (misappropriate company funds), 61 (enter into competition with, or sign contracts with, the company), 62 (disclose confidential company information), 118 (vote for resolutions which violate laws, the articles of association or result in serious losses), 128 (supervisors), 198 (members of liquidation group) and 214 (misappropriation, etc.)

50. [Company Law of the People's Republic of China (adopted by the 5th Session of the Standing Committee of the 8th National People's Congress on Dec. 29, 1993, and effective July 1, 1994) [hereinafter Company Law]], art. 59. Some analysts have understood this Article and all the other indications of responsibility in the Company Law as the concept of fiduciary duty. Even if this view is credible, it raises the question as to why the Overseas Listing Rules had to restate the Standard Opinion formulation (See Overseas Listing Rules, supra note 36, art. 31) and why the former CRES-explicated language was dropped. In addition, there is continuing dispute among various analysts and regulators as to whom or what precisely such duty is owed: the company, the shareholders or—in the most conservative view—the state.

51. See "Special Regulations of the State Council on Foreign Offerings and Listings of Companies Limited by Shares" promulgated on Aug. 4, 1994 by the State Council of the PRC, but published only on August 19, 1994 in the People's Daily [hereinafter Overseas Listing Rules], art. 23, para. 1. This provision refers to such persons' (including supervisory committee members') "fiduciary duty" and "duty of due care." There may be a problem of legislating logic in this case. The above-cited provision of the Overseas Listing Rules makes implicit reference to an interpretation of a statutory provision (See Standard Opinion, supra note 30, art. 62) contained in a superseded law (the Standard Opinion) by a now seemingly dis-empowered authority (CRES—which is granted no power to explain the Company Law).

52. Most Chinese legal theorists would think that, by default, it is the Standing Committee of the National People's Congress....

53. See the definitive work on this most important question, Donald C. Clarke, *Power and Politics in the Chinese Court System: The Enforcement of Civil Judgments*, 10 COLUM. J. ASIAN L. 1 (1996).

ored,[54] and contributes to the sense that the Company Law is not to be understood as a statute that has close connection with "actual circumstances" in China. (The Standard Opinion had no such provision.)[55] Unfortunately, the term "state officials" remains undefined, and worse, the underlying concept is presently honored mostly in the breach, where all of the directors, supervisors and managers of countless companies in the PRC also serve in government positions, or as the local or enterprise Communist party officials.[56]

Comments and Questions

1. Nicholas Howson suggests that Chinese systems of managerial control suffer deficits both under a "rule of law" yardstick, as well as in the way the rules, such as they are, have been implemented. Do you think that special problems of fiduciary duty exist where the national government is the principal shareholder of a corporation, and that its officials will be designated to serve as managers of the company? Would it make a difference if those government officials serving as managers also retained regulatory authority over some aspect of the activity of the corporation? Can you offer justifications based on the political system in place in China? Would your answer change if the basis of your defense were principles of Western corporate governance?

2. How does the regime of administrative sanction differ from the systems of liability under Western fiduciary duty principles?

3. Both Chinese and Japanese systems of fiduciary duty are based on adopting approaches received from the West. The Chinese adopted a company law and omitted statutory treatment of the duty of managers to the company. Japanese company law has incorporated the concept of managerial duty. To what extent are the approaches adopted in each transplants? To what extent have the two nations taken 'foreign' ideas and reconstituted them to make them compatible with the cultural and political norms of each of these states?

4. Nicholas Howson notes that the Company Law of the People's Republic leaves unclear to whom any managerial duty is owed—the company, the shareholders or the state. What difference does this make in terms of the nature of conduct expected of managers? Would your answer change if the state was a significant shareholder of a company? Many companies? If the primary obligation of managers is to the state, what is the position of individuals who are minority shareholders in corporations in which the state is a shareholder?

---

54. See Company Law, supra note [50], arts. 58 (with respect to the directors of limited liability companies), 123 (directors of companies limited by shares), 128, para. 2 (supervisors).

55. See Standard Opinion, supra note [47], art. 61, which restricts certain individuals—incompetents, bankrupts, criminals, etc.—from serving as directors. The Company Law retains this concept, both with respect to limited liability companies (See Company Law, supra note 2, art. 57) and companies limited by shares (id. art. 123).

56. Of course, an argument can be made that "party" officials are not "state" officials, in a society and political system that confers separate status on party and state. The easy rejoinder to this argument is that China is a one-party state, where the party acts as a kind of executive, which ensures that its policies are implemented by the state.

D. Duty of Disclosure

The duty of disclosure can be understood as a more precisely focused subset of the duties of care and loyalty. Among American jurisdictions, Delaware courts have identified and refined this obligation to a greater degree than any other. The duty is a conditional duty—it applies only in the context of decision-making, either at the level of the managers or shareholders, and relates directly to that decision-making. The materials in this section describe the duty of disclosure as articulated by the Delaware courts and then suggests some analogies to this duty outside the United States.

1. The American Articulation of the Duty of Disclosure

Much like other fiduciary duty in general in traditional jurisdictions like Delaware, the duty of disclosure is substantially a creature of the courts. The legislature has intervened only marginally in the construction and regulation of this doctrine in the courts. It is a doctrine perfectly suited to the habits and predilections of American enterprise regulation—constructed as it is with strong resonances to the policy of disclosure underlying the federal regulation of securities.

O'Reilly v. Transworld Healthcare, Inc.

Court of Chancery of Delaware, New Castle
745 A.2d 902
August 20, 1999, Decided
(some footnotes omitted)

STEELE, V.C.

Defendants Transworld Healthcare, Inc. ("Transworld") and the former directors of Health Management Inc. ("HMI") move to dismiss pursuant to Court of Chancery Rule 12(b)(6) this individual and stockholder class action against them, which challenges the fairness of HMI's merger with a subsidiary of Transworld. HMI's directors approved a merger between HMI and Transworld's wholly-owned subsidiary at $ 2 per share, but agreed to reduce the merger consideration to $ 1.00 per share, and then to $ .30 per share after two revelations of accounting errors in HMI's financial statements. During HMI and Transworld's negotiations, a second bidder, Counsel Corp., opened up acquisition talks with HMI. HMI did not pursue merger negotiations with Counsel Corp. After HMI's stockholders approved the merger with Transworld's subsidiary, but before the merger was consummated, Transworld agreed to sell HMI's assets to Counsel Corp. Following the merger, Transworld sold HMI's assets to Counsel Corp. at a profit.

Plaintiff O'Reilly alleges that Transworld leveraged its 49% ownership of HMI's outstanding voting stock, its option to purchase 2% of HMI's stock, and its $ 49 million in

HMI debt holdings at the time of the renegotiations to squeeze unfair concessions from a financially ailing HMI and to prevent HMI from negotiating with Counsel Corp. so that Transworld could resell HMI's assets to Counsel Corp. at a higher price. She alleges that the Defendants breached their duty of disclosure in a Proxy Statement issued in connection with the merger and that the merger process and price were unfair.

Because O'Reilly asserts well-pleaded allegations that: (i) Transworld was an HMI controlling stockholder with concomitant fiduciary status; (ii) the HMI directors' conduct falls within the exceptions of HMI's certificate of incorporation's exculpation provision tracking the language of 8 Del.C. § 102(b)(7); (iii) the merger's Proxy Statement contained false statements regarding Transworld's purpose for engaging in the merger and the "arms-length" nature of the merger negotiations; and (iv) the merger process and price were unfair, I deny in part Defendants' motion to dismiss.

Because O'Reilly fails to set forth well pleaded allegations in support of certain other claims against Defendants for breach of the fiduciary duty of disclosure, I grant in part Defendants' motion.

I. Background[1]

A. The Parties

Defendant HMI, a Delaware corporation, provided pharmaceutical management to patients with long-term medical conditions and similar health-related services. Defendants Nicol, Dimitriadis, Triche, and Weinberg were HMI's four directors. On October 1, 1997, HMI merged with a wholly owned subsidiary of Defendant Transworld (the "Merger"). Transworld is a New York corporation that is a regional provider of a broad range of healthcare services and products. Plaintiff O'Reilly owned 2,600 shares of HMI stock at the time of the Merger.

B. The Events Leading up to Merger Negotiations

In the Spring of 1996, HMI's board of directors learned that HMI's financial statements going back to 1994 were inaccurate. HMI restated its financials, which revealed significant deterioration in HMI's financial condition. To account for the restated finances, HMI recorded special charges in 1995 and 1996 including reductions in working capital, retained earnings and stockholders' equity. For 1996, HMI reported a net operating loss of over $ 8 million, reflecting, among other things, a $ 2.8 million write off for medical device inventory, a $ 3.6 million charge for reorganizational costs, and an $ 8.4 million reserve to allow for an increase in doubtful accounts. As a result, HMI defaulted on its loan agreements. The board responded to this crisis by hiring National Westminster Bank Plc ("NatWest") to assist HMI in evaluating a number of strategic and financial options. After rejecting the possibility of a private security placement, HMI's board began looking for someone willing to acquire the ailing company.

C. HMI's Negotiations And Agreements with Transworld

In October 1996, HMI met with Transworld. On November 13, 1996, HMI and Transworld entered into a stock purchase agreement (the "Stock Purchase Agreement")

1. The facts recited are as alleged in the Complaint and the Proxy Statement. It is appropriate for me to consider the Proxy Statement in this instance because it is integral to Plaintiff's claim and is incorporated into the Complaint. See Vanderbilt Income and Growth Assoc., L.L.C. v. Arvida/JMB Managers, Inc., Del. Supr., 691 A.2d 609, 613 (1996) (citing In re Santa Fe Pac. Corp. Shareholder Litig., Del. Supr., 669 A.2d 59, 70 (1995). O'Reilly in her Complaint relies on the Proxy Statement to set forth the facts surrounding the merger. The alleged misdisclosures underlying O'Reilly's claim for breach of the fiduciary duty of disclosure, furthermore, were made in the Proxy Statement.

and a merger agreement (the "Merger Agreement"). Pursuant to the Stock Purchase Agreement, Transworld agreed to acquire 49% of HMI's outstanding voting stock and Transworld acquired an option to purchase an additional 2% of HMI's outstanding voting stock. Transworld paid the following consideration for the HMI stock under the Stock Purchase Agreement: (i) $ 1 per share; (ii) Transworld's agreement to execute the Merger Agreement; (iii) Transworld's purchase of the rights of HMI's senior lenders under HMI's credit agreements; (iv) Transworld's extension of the expiration of a forbearance agreement which HMI had entered into with its senior lenders; (v) Transworld's agreement to lend additional amounts under HMI's revolving credit facility, subject to certain conditions; and (vi) Transworld's cancellation of warrants held by the lenders that Transworld was effectively replacing. Pursuant to the Merger Agreement, Transworld agreed to acquire HMI's publicly-traded stock for $ 2.00 per share. HMI's board obtained an opinion from NatWest which stated that from a financial perspective the $ 2.00 per share Merger price was fair to HMI's stockholders other than Transworld.

As contemplated by the Stock Purchase Agreement, Transworld: (i) acquired HMI's bank debt; (ii) extended the termination date of the pre-existing forbearance agreement HMI had entered with its senior lenders, which was to terminate on November 15, 1996, to December 12, 1996; and (iii) promised to lend up to an additional $ 3 million to HMI under HMI's revolving line of credit. In November and December 1996, Transworld's principal stockholder, Hyperion Partners II L.P., acquired approximately $ 18 million in additional debt which HMI owed to various entities. As a result, Transworld and one of its affiliates owned virtually all of HMI's debt.

In January of 1997, Transworld informed HMI that because of HMI's "adverse business results," Transworld would exercise its right to decline to consummate its agreement to purchase 49% of HMI's stock and the Merger Agreement, unless the Merger price were renegotiated to $ 1.50 per share. The HMI board unanimously agreed, and on January 13, 1997, Transworld and HMI signed an amended merger agreement reflecting, among other things, the reduced Merger price. The HMI board received another "fairness opinion" from NatWest declaring the $ 1.50 per share Merger price to be fair. Also on January 13, 1997, Transworld consummated the purchase of 49% of HMI's outstanding voting stock that the Stock Purchase Agreement contemplated.

After reviewing Transworld's due diligence findings, on January 14, 1997, HMI hired BDO Seidman, LLP ("BDO Seidman") to review HMI's accounts receivable. BDO Seidman discovered that HMI's financial statements for the first three-quarters of fiscal 1997 were inaccurate. Written analyses of BDO Seidman's findings were distributed to the HMI board and Transworld. After reviewing the analyses, Transworld concluded that HMI's equity had no value. Transworld informed HMI that, if Transworld had not already had a substantial equity investment in HMI, it would not wish to pursue the Merger.

According to the Proxy Statement, on March 13, 1997, Transworld demanded that HMI drop the Merger price for the public shares to $ .05 per share or it would not consummate the Merger. HMI responded with a counteroffer of $ 1 per share. Transworld refused, making a "last and final offer" of $ .30 per share. HMI's board accepted. On March 26, 1997, a second amendment to the Merger Agreement was executed, reflecting the reduction in the Merger price from $ 1.50 per share to $ .30 per share. HMI did not obtain a fairness opinion with respect to the reduced $ .30 per share Merger price.

D. Counsel Corp. Expresses Interest in HMI

On March 26, 1997, one of HMI's competitors, Counsel Corp., sent HMI a letter expressing an interest in discussing the acquisition of a primary line of HMI's business. Initially HMI's board did not respond to the letter. On May 8, 1997, a representative of Counsel Corp. contacted HMI's lawyers to express again Counsel Corp.'s interest in acquiring a primary line of HMI's business. Counsel Corp.'s representative indicated that Counsel Corp. could make a cash offer, but that Counsel Corp. would have to conduct a due diligence investigation before it could make any type of proposal. On May 10 and May 19, 1997, the HMI board met and decided not to pursue further discussions with Counsel Corp. At these board meetings, the HMI board considered the fact that the Merger Agreement contained provisions expressly limiting any discussions with potential acquirers and that Transworld had indicated that at that late date the disclosure of confidential information to, and HMI's continuing discussions with, Counsel Corp. would jeopardize the Merger. According to the Proxy Statement, the HMI board also considered the following: (i) Counsel Corp. had extensive discussions with HMI in July and November of 1996, and in each case indicated that any transaction with Counsel Corp. would yield no value to HMI's stockholders; (ii) HMI's financial condition actually was less favorable than that presented in July and November of 1996, as indicated in part by the restatements of the first and second quarter 1997 financial statements; and (iii) Counsel Corp.'s expression of interest was for only a portion, but not all, of HMI. The Proxy Statement also stated that the HMI board concluded that the potential damage of providing additional confidential information to Counsel Corp., a competitor, and of jeopardizing the Merger was greater than the possibility that a transaction with the competitor would actually occur and would actually result in additional value to HMI's stockholders and creditors.

E. The Proxy Statement & HMI Directors' Conflicts of Interest

On June 16, 1997, HMI mailed its stockholders the Proxy Statement for the Merger in which the HMI board recommended that the HMI stockholders vote in favor of the Merger. The Proxy Statement noted that two of HMI's four directors had possible conflicts of interest in approving the Merger. Defendant Nicol, HMI's CEO, President and board member, agreed to continue in his officer positions until HMI filed a certificate of merger with the Delaware Secretary of State and he stood eligible to receive cash payments contingent upon consummation of the Merger. Nicol had also been advised that the value of his employment contract in a bankruptcy scenario, the likely alternative to the Merger, was dubious. Defendant Dimitriadis, HMI's Chairman, was a defendant in a derivative lawsuit. HIM management believed that the plaintiffs in that action might lose their standing if the Merger were consummated. Furthermore, Dimitriadis would be at a substantial risk of losing an advance toward legal fees and indemnification if HMI were to file for bankruptcy. Thus, the Proxy Statement revealed that Dimitriadis stood in a much better position to receive advanced fees and/or indemnification if HMI merged with Transworld's subsidiary.

F. HMI Stockholders Approve the Merger & Transworld Agrees to Sell Assets to Counsel Corp.

On July 11, 1997, HMI had a special stockholders meeting at which the HMI stockholders approved the Merger. On August 1, 1997, however, Transworld announced that its bank disapproved financing for the Merger. HMI announced that if the Merger fell through and Transworld enforced its creditor rights, HMI might be required to file for bankruptcy. Two weeks later, Transworld entered into an agreement with Counsel Corp. pursuant to which Counsel Corp. agreed to purchase HMI's assets, either from Transworld or directly from HMI, for $ 40 million. On October 1, 1997, Transworld consummated the Merger and on October 10, 1997, Transworld sold HMI's assets to Counsel Corp.

G. HMI Stockholders Exercise Appraisal Rights & O'Reilly Files this Action

Certain HMI stockholders dissented from the Merger and sought appraisal. That action, filed February 3, 1998, currently lacks a plaintiff. O'Reilly, meanwhile, filed this action. She challenges the Merger on two grounds: (1) that HMI's directors and Transworld, its alleged controlling stockholder, breached their duty of disclosure by failing to disclose accurately material aspects of the Merger and (2) that the negotiation process and Merger price were unfair. Defendants believe Plaintiff inadequately pleaded both claims, that they, therefore, fail to state claims upon which relief may be granted and that the Complaint should be dismissed.

II. LEGAL STANDARD

In evaluating Defendants' motion to dismiss, I assume the truthfulness of all well-pleaded, nonconclusory allegations found in the Complaint, and I extend the benefit of all reasonable inferences that can be drawn from the pleadings to the non-movant, O'Reilly....

III. PARTIES' CONTENTIONS & RULINGS OF LAW

* * *

C. O'Reilly's Disclosure Claims

O'Reilly claims that the Defendants breached the fiduciary duty of disclosure, a subset of the duty of loyalty arising when stockholder action is sought or required.[15] Corporate fiduciaries, including corporate directors, majority stockholders, and presumably minority controlling stockholders, have a duty to disclose all material facts when seeking stockholder action.[16] Material facts are those facts for which "there is a substantial likelihood that a reasonable shareholder would consider [them] important in deciding how to vote."[17] Corporate fiduciaries can breach their duty of disclosure under Delaware law in a number ways—by making a materially false statement, by omitting a material fact, or by making a partial disclosure that is materially misleading.[18] O'Reilly alleges that Defendants breached their fiduciary duty of disclosure in all three ways.

One should note that trial judges approaching issues similar to the appropriate analysis of directors' disclosure obligations in the context of a motion to dismiss a pleading feel much like field mechanics attempting triage on a disabled vehicle. The trial judge under enormous pressures of time and conflicting advice on how to diagnose and then make the repairs, has only experience and a sketchy field manual from the factory with which to work. Certain knowledge that the owners will immediately take the vehicle back to the factory for repair and that there are three or more mechanics, who prepared the field manual, who will then assess the nature and quality of the field repairs, make changes to them and/or send the vehicle back with instructions for additional work (often accompanied by a previously unknown, newly published supplement to the existing manual in the field) makes the task even more daunting. Nonetheless, the work must be done and I do so with an introductory attempt to outline principles that I think I have correctly discerned from the current version of the field manual.

These are:

15. Malone, 722 A.2d at 10; Jackson National Life Insurance Co. v. Kennedy, et al., 741 A.2d 377, 1999 Del. Ch. LEXIS 154, *32, Del. Ch., C.A. No. 16472, Steele, V.C. (July 15, 1999).

16. See Malone, 722 A.2d at 11 & n. 21.

17. Rosenblatt v. Getty Oil Co., Del. Supr., 493 A.2d 929, 944 (1985) (citations omitted).

18. In re the Walt Disney Co. Derivative Litig., Del. Ch., 731 A.2d 342, 376 (1998).

1. The duty of disclosure is a subset of the more general duties of loyalty, "good faith," and care and is implicated only when stockholder action is contemplated, i.e. requested or required. Disclosure violations arising out of communications not contemplating stockholder action implicate the broader fiduciary duties of loyalty, "good faith" and care.

2. Breaches of the duty of disclosure always impinge upon the stockholder franchise and stockholders' right to make an informed decision on corporate affairs. A plaintiff, therefore, is entitled to *per se* nominal damages for a breach of the duty of disclosure. So long as the plaintiff pleads sufficiently the other specific elements of a breach of the fiduciary duty of disclosure arising from a false statement, omission or partial disclosure, a plaintiff may request nominal damages, without pleading causation or actual quantifiable damages.

3. A plaintiff who seeks more than nominal damages for breach of the duty of disclosure, however, must set forth in a well-pleaded complaint allegations sufficient to support the remedy sought. As a result, when a plaintiff requests more than nominal damages, a plaintiff also will have to plead causation and identify actual quantifiable damages in order to survive a motion to dismiss. Furthermore, in the event that the claim for breach of the fiduciary duty of disclosure arises from the misdisclosure of wrongdoing that underlies an accompanying claim challenging the fairness of the same transaction, the plaintiff will have to plead that the breach of the duty of disclosure created a cognizable harm discrete from the harm that the underlying wrongdoing caused, as well as the requisite causation and damages to support its request for more than nominal damages.

4. A well-pleaded disclosure claim arising out of a communication that does not contemplate stockholder action and which implicates the broader duties of loyalty, "good faith" and care, as opposed to the more narrow duty of disclosure, must identify a disclosure violation through which corporate fiduciaries misinformed stockholders and set forth allegations that support the remedy sought. A plaintiff then will have to plead causation and identify actual quantifiable damages in order to plead sufficiently this category of disclosure violation.

I reach the above conclusions from what now appears to be a distinction between "the fiduciary duty of disclosure" and disclosure violations that implicate fiduciary duties in the broad sense but do not involve communications that contemplate stockholder action.

In the Supreme Court's most recent opinion discussing the fiduciary duty of disclosure, the Court stated, "an action for a breach of fiduciary duty arising out of disclosure violations in connection with a request for stockholder action does not include the elements of reliance, causation and actual quantifiable monetary damages."[19] In support of this statement, the Supreme Court cited the portions of Cinerama Inc. v. Technicolor, Inc.[20] and In re Tri-Star Pictures, Inc. Litig.[21] which stand for the proposition that under Delaware law there is a rule of *per se* damages for breach of the fiduciary duty of disclosure.[22] The Supreme Court also cited the portion of Loudon v. Archer-Daniels-Midland

19. *Malone, 722 A.2d at 12* (citations omitted).
20. *Del. Supr., 663 A.2d at 1163.*
21. *Del. Supr., 634 A.2d 319, 333 (1993).*
22. *Malone, 722 A.2d at 12 n. 27.*

Co.[23] in which the Supreme Court limited Tri-Star's *per se* rule of damages to the narrow proposition that, "where directors have breached their disclosure duties in a corporate transaction that has in turn caused impairment to the economic or voting rights of stockholders, there must be at least be an award of nominal damages...." I note that this express limitation of *Tri-Star's per se* rule of damages arose from the Loudon Court's desire to limit *Tri-Star* to the facts of *Tri-Star,* which the *Loudon* Court summarized as a, "case involving stockholder approval of an improperly manipulated transaction implicating cash values and voting rights."[24] Malone does not cite the portion of the *Loudon* opinion in which the Supreme Court addressed the pleading requirements for damages in the category of disclosure claims to which the limited *per se* rule of damages did not apply under its ruling (i.e. claims not involving stockholder approval of an improperly manipulated transaction through disclosure violations). In that portion of Loudon, the Supreme Court stated that damages would be awarded in those disclosure claims only if the disclosure violation impaired stockholder voting rights or deprived stockholders of their economic interests, and the complaint contained well-pleaded allegations sufficient to warrant the remedy sought.[25] Through its limitation of Tri-Star's *per se* rule of damages, the Loudon Court distinguished between disclosure violations associated with stockholder action and those that are not, strongly suggesting that both types of disclosure violations implicate the fiduciary duty of disclosure. Unlike *Malone,* to follow, Loudon did not narrowly limit the duty of disclosure to stockholder action scenarios.

Malone's statement that causation and actual quantifiable damages are not elements of a claim for breach of the fiduciary duty of disclosure, and, more significantly, its citations in support of that statement, constitute a retreat to Tri-Star's *per se* rule of damages for *all* violations of the fiduciary duty of disclosure. While this statement appears to be inconsistent with *Loudon's* limitation of the *per se* rule of damages and Loudon's heightened pleading standard for claims of breach of the fiduciary duty of disclosure not covered by the limited *per se* rule of damages, any such inconsistency becomes transparent when one considers Malone's contemporaneous limitation on the circumstances in which the duty of disclosure applies. Under Malone, the "duty of disclosure" is implicated only in communications that request stockholder action.[26] If a corporate fiduciary violates the duty of disclosure, as Malone now narrowly defines that duty, it is axiomatic that stockholders' voting rights are impaired. Even under Loudon, the stockholder would be entitled to nominal damages. In essence, Malone's explicit limitation of the duty of disclosure to those instances in which stockholder action is requested dispels the apparent dichotomy that the Supreme Court created in Loudon for the treatment of disclosure violations arising out of communications requesting stockholder action and disclosure violations arising out of communications that do not request stockholder action. This *per se* rule of damages for violations of the duty of disclosure makes sense so long as Delaware law continues to attach value to a stockholder's right to make an informed decision on corporate

23. *Del. Supr., 700 A.2d 135, 142 (1997).*

24. Id.

25. *Id. at 147.* It appears that under *Loudon's* pleading standards even a claim for nominal damages would need to be accompanied by an allegation that the disclosure violation impaired stockholder voting rights or impaired stockholders of their economic interests. This view, however, is inconsistent with *Malone's* pronouncement that causation is not an element of a claim for breach of the fiduciary duty of disclosure.

26. *See infra n.* 15.

affairs and continues to protect stockholders from the impairment of their voting rights, even in the absence of quantifiable economic harm to the stockholders.[27]

As has always been the case, since Tri-Star's pronouncement of the *per se* rule of damages for violations of the duty of disclosure, the *per se* rule of damages in this context encompasses only nominal damages.[28] In *Tri-Star* the Court suggested that a request for anything more than nominal damages (i.e. compensatory damages) would require substantive proof of those damages, most likely through an expert opinion.[29] The *Loudon* Court seemed to affirm this portion of Tri-Star when it said, "in *every* case, a plaintiff stating a claim against directors for violation of the duty of disclosure must set forth in a well-pleaded complaint allegations sufficient to warrant the remedy sought."[30] Presumably, a claim for breach of the fiduciary duty of disclosure that sufficiently pleads the other specific elements of the breach arising from a false statement, omission, or partial disclosure will support a request for nominal damages, without the need to plead causation or actual quantifiable damages. Since Malone did not overrule Loudon, however, a plaintiff may want to allege impairment of stockholder voting rights or deprivation of stockholder economic interests in order to assure survival of even a claim limited to a request for nominal damages.[31] Under Tri-Star, a request for compensatory damages will have to be supported by allegations in the complaint sufficient to warrant the damages sought. Again, since Malone did not overrule Loudon, in order for a request for *compensatory damages* arising from a violation of the duty of disclosure to survive, a plaintiff will have to set-forth in a well-pleaded complaint allegations to support those damages.[32] As a result, causation and actual quantifiable damages are elements of the *compensatory damages portion* of a claim for breach of the fiduciary duty of disclosure. Following this Court's recent holding in Brown v. Perrette, et al., furthermore, a well-pleaded request for more than nominal damages for breach of the duty of disclosure arising from the misdisclosure of wrongdoing that underlies an accompanying claim challenging the entire fairness of the same transaction will require a plaintiff to plead that the disclosure violation created a cognizable harm discrete from the harm caused by the underlying wrongdoing in the entire fairness claim, in order for the disclosure claim to survive a motion to dismiss.[33]

---

27. See e.g., Malone, 722 A.2d at 12; Loudon, 700 A.2d at 142 ("Where directors have breached their disclosure duties in a corporate transaction that has in turn caused impairment to the *economic or voting* rights of stockholders, there must at least be an award of nominal damages.) (emphasis added); *Tri-Star, 634 A.2d at 334* ("In all of these cases, the courts recognized some value associated with a stockholder's right to make an informed decision on corporate affairs. That issue is squarely raised here.")

28. See Loudon, 700 A.2d at 142 ("The Tri-Star Court held that, under the circumstances of that case involving stockholder approval of an improperly manipulated transaction implicating cash values and voting rights, there should be some damage award. The [Tri-Star] Court cautioned, however, that if plaintiff sought more than nominal damages, proof (including expert testimony) would have to replace "hypothetical estimates.") (citations omitted); See also Tri-Star, 634 A.2d at 333–334 & n. 18.

29. Id. As a result, I think the rule is more appropriately termed "the *per se* rule of nominal damages."

30. Loudon, 700 A.2d at 147 (emphasis added).

31. See id; See also infra n. 25.

32. I note that under Tri-Star it did not appear that at the pleading stage a request for compensatory damages needed to be supported by allegations sufficient to warrant those damages. See Tri-Star, 634 A.2d at 333–334 & n. 18.

33. 1999 Del. Ch. LEXIS 92, *19, Del. Ch., C.A. No. 13531, Chandler, C. (May 14, 1999). I conclude that in order for *Brown* to be consistent with *Malone's* retreat to *per se* damages for breach of

The *per se* rule of damages does not apply to disclosure violations that arise out of communications that do not contemplate stockholder action and that, therefore, implicate only the broader fiduciary duties of loyalty, "good faith" and care and not the narrower fiduciary duty of disclosure. Disclosure claims based upon violations that do not implicate stockholder action are among the category of claims discussed in Loudon. Loudon, a case decided before Malone limited the duty of disclosure to communications contemplating stockholder action, concluded that the *per se* rule of damages did not apply to disclosure claims arising out of communications that did not contemplate stockholder action. Malone's more narrow characterization of the "duty of disclosure" should have no impact on Loudon's treatment of these claims. Therefore, disclosure claims arising out of communications that do not contemplate stockholder action and which implicate only the broader fiduciary duties of loyalty, "good faith" and care, as opposed to the fiduciary duty of disclosure, must be supported, under Loudon, by a well-pleaded complaint with allegations sufficient to warrant the remedy sought, regardless of whether the requested remedies are for nominal damages, compensatory damages or some other type of relief. This rule makes sense because unlike a disclosure violation arising out of a communication contemplating stockholder action, which automatically impairs stockholder voting rights, a disclosure violation arising out of a communication that does not contemplate stockholder action neither automatically impairs stockholder voting rights nor automatically deprives stockholders of their economic interests. The only salient distinction, then, between Loudon and Malone is Malone couching the duty of disclosure in terms of contemplated stockholder action and Loudon using a broader rubric encompassing all disclosure violations as violations of the "duty of disclosure" whether stockholder action is contemplated or not.

With that exhausting, if not exhaustive, discussion in mind, I will turn to the sufficiency of O'Reilly's specific claims of breach of the fiduciary duty of disclosure.

1. O'Reilly's Claims of False Statements or Representations

To state a claim for breach of the fiduciary duty of disclosure on the basis of a false statement or representation, a plaintiff must identify (1) a material statement or representation in a communication contemplating stockholder action (2) that is false.[34] If the plaintiff requests more than nominal damages, the complaint must allege facts sufficient to support the damages requested.[35] O'Reilly alleges that the Defendants made several false statements in the Proxy Statement.

(a) Transworld's Purpose for Engaging in the Merger

---

the now more narrow fiduciary duty of disclosure, *Brown's* holding on damages can only apply to compensatory damages—not both nominal *and* compensatory damages.

34. Some cases imply in dicta that knowledge is an element of the breach of the fiduciary duty of disclosure through false or misleading statements. *See, e.g.*, Havens v. Attar, 1997 Del. Ch. LEXIS 12, *24, Del. Ch., C.A. No. 15134, Chandler, V.C. (Jan. 30, 1997); Marhart, Inc. v. Calmat Co., 1992 Del. Ch. LEXIS 85, *10, Del. Ch., C.A. No. 11820, Berger, V.C. (Apr. 22, 1992). I conclude that after *Malone* knowledge is no longer an element. The duty of disclosure itself requires directors, and presumably other corporate fiduciaries, "to provide shareholders with all information that is material to the action being requested and to provide a balanced, *truthful* account of all matters disclosed in the communications with shareholders." Malone, 722 A.2d at *12* (emphasis added). According to this statement, corporate fiduciaries have an obligation to confirm that statements in communications contemplating stockholder action are true before disseminating the communications to the stockholders. I note, however, that "knowledge" that the statement is false or misleading would be relevant to a claim to exempt directors from liability for the breach of the duty of disclosure pursuant to exculpatory charter provisions authorized by 8 Del.C. § 102(b)(7).

35. See 1999 Del. Ch. LEXIS 185, *61.

O'Reilly alleges that the disclosure of Transworld's purpose for the Merger was materially false and misleading. The Proxy Statement described Transworld's intention to integrate HMI's business lines into Transworld's operations. O'Reilly asserts that this purpose was false, claiming that Transworld intended to sell, not synergize, HMI's assets. This disclosure claim is pleaded in three sequential versions:

(a) *Fraudulent intent at the* time—Transworld intended to sell HMI's assets to Counsel Corp. at the time it issued the Proxy Statement, but falsely reported otherwise.

(b) *Failure to update before vote on Merger*—The Proxy Statement was accurate at the time issued, but Transworld's plans changed materially when it learned of Counsel Corp.'s interest. Transworld failed to update its disclosure and inform HMI's stockholders of this material change in its purpose for engaging in the Merger before the stockholders voted on the Merger.

(c) *Failure to hold second vote on Merger*—O'Reilly alleges that if Transworld did not change its purpose for the Merger until after the HMI stockholders approved the Merger, that change of direction was such a fundamental event that not only should Transworld have disclosed the sale of assets to Counsel Corp., but the new plan triggered a duty to allow HMI's stockholders to vote on what had become a substantially different business plan underlying the Merger.

Defendants attack the first two versions of the disclosure claims for failure to allege that any agreement between Transworld and Counsel Corp. had been reached—or had even been discussed or contemplated—before the Proxy Statement was issued on June 16, 1997 or before the stockholders' meeting took place on July 11, 1997. Defendants argue that without this allegation, the Complaint fails to allege any facts to show that the Proxy Statement was false at the time it was issued or at the time of the July 11 stockholders' meeting. Contrary to Defendants' contention, however, O'Reilly does not need to allege the existence of a pre-July 11 agreement or discussions between Transworld and Counsel Corp. in order to maintain that the Proxy Statement's representations regarding Transworld's purpose for engaging in the Merger were false at the relevant times. Rather, O'Reilly must allege that Transworld's purpose on June 16 or July 11 for engaging in the Merger was to turn around and sell HMI's assets to Counsel Corp. at a profit following the Merger, or plead facts that can be construed reasonably to support that inference. While allegations that an agreement between Transworld and Counsel Corp. existed or allegations that discussions between Transworld and Counsel Corp. took place before July 11 would bolster O'Reilly's pleadings, those allegations are not necessary for this portion of O'Reilly's disclosure claim to survive this motion to dismiss. It certainly is possible that before July 11 Transworld intended to sell HMI's assets, but had refrained from contacting Counsel Corp. until the HMI stockholders approved the Merger under the alleged guise that Transworld intended to integrate HMI into its operations. Under this scenario, the Proxy Statement's representations would be false, despite the fact that Transworld had not yet had any contact with Counsel Corp.

The Complaint pleads facts that support the inference that at the relevant times Transworld intended to sell HMI's assets following the Merger as opposed to integrating them into Transworld's operations. The Complaint alleges that: (i) between January 13, 1997 and March 13, 1997, Transworld informed HMI that it believed that the equity of HMI had no value, and that if Transworld did not already have a significant equity investment in HMI, it would no longer wish to pursue the Merger; (ii) on March 26, 1997, HMI and Transworld amended the Merger Agreement to reduce the Merger price from $ 1.50 to $ 0.30 in response to Transworld's March 13, 1997 "threat" that it would not pursue the Merger otherwise; (iii) on March 26, 1997, Counsel Corp. contacted HMI and expressed an interest in discussing the acquisition of a primary line of HMI's business; (iv) before issuing the Proxy Statement and despite Transworld's representation that it would prefer not to proceed with the Merger, Transworld represented to HMI that discussions between HMI and Counsel Corp. would place the Merger at risk; (v) the Proxy Statement was issued on June 16, 1997; (vi) the HMI stockholders approved the Merger on July 11, 1997; (vii) on August 1, 1997, Transworld issued a press release stating that it had been unable to obtain the bank consent necessary to complete the Merger; and (viii) on August 14, 1997, Transworld announced that it had entered an agreement with Counsel Corp. relating to the sale of all of HMI's businesses and operations. A reasonable inference to draw from these allegations is that when Transworld learned, in March of 1997, of Counsel Corp.'s interest in acquiring a primary line of HMI's business, Transworld immediately began to plan the eventual sale of HMI's assets to Counsel Corp. Specifically, this inference is supported by the allegations that: (i) Transworld expressed disinterest in the Merger, (ii) Transworld then discouraged HMI from negotiating with Counsel Corp. upon Counsel Corp.'s expression of its interest in acquiring a primary line of HMI's business (an acquisition that could have released Transworld from the need to consummate the Merger); and, (iii) six weeks after the HMI stockholders approved the Merger, Transworld entered into an agreement with Counsel Corp. to sell HMI's assets to Counsel Corp. Again, while one could draw an inference from these allegations that is less favorable to O'Reilly, at this stage of the proceeding I am to draw all reasonable inferences from well-pleaded facts in the light most favorable to O'Reilly. I conclude, therefore, that O'Reilly has pleaded sufficiently that the Proxy Statement's representations regarding Transworld's purpose for engaging in the Merger were false at the relevant times.

I also conclude that this alleged false statement is material. If in fact Transworld's purpose for engaging in the Merger was to sell HMI's assets to Counsel Corp., that is a fact that a reasonable stockholder would consider important in deciding how to vote. Since O'Reilly sufficiently pleads these two elements of this disclosure claim based on materially false statements, the Complaint sufficiently supports, under Malone, a request for at least nominal damages. In any event, O'Reilly pleads that the false statement, along with the other violations of the duty of disclosure, deprived HMI stockholders of their right to cast an informed vote and their right to make an informed investment decision in connection with the Merger.

O'Reilly also pleads that this false statement, along with the other disclosure violations, caused a quantifiable economic loss to her and requests more than nominal damages. O'Reilly alleges that but for all of the disclosure violations, it is reasonably likely that Transworld would have ultimately been forced to pay $ 1.50 per share, as opposed to $ .30 per share, to acquire HMI's publicly-held common stock. O'Reilly also alleges that the HMI stockholders suffered pecuniary economic damages equal to at least the difference between the value of the Merger consideration and HMI's fair value. Finally, O'Reilly alleges that Transworld and at least two of HMI's four directors obtained profits and benefits as a result of the Merger which constitute unjust enrichment and which they are required to disgorge separate and apart from any transactional or pecuniary damages suffered by the HMI stockholders. These requests for additional damages, however, fall short of Brown's pleading requirement.[36] Count II of the Complaint chal-

36. See 1999 Del. Ch. LEXIS 185, *36.

lenges the fairness of the Merger and includes claims against Transworld for unfair dealing and usurpation of corporate opportunity. These claims encompass Defendants' alleged concealment from the HMI stockholders of Transworld's true purpose for engaging in the Merger, which, in turn, is the topic of the alleged false statement in this portion of O'Reilly's claim for breach of the fiduciary duty of disclosure. The alleged harm that resulted from the Defendants' violations of the duty of disclosure, however, is essentially the same as the alleged harm that was caused by the Defendants' wrongdoing underlying Count II's unfairness claim: an unfair price and a diversion to the Defendants of monies that belong to HMI. O'Reilly, therefore, fails to plead that the Defendants' misdisclosure of Transworld's purpose created a cognizable harm discrete from the alleged usurpation of corporate opportunity and unfair dealing that proper disclosure would have revealed. The compensatory damages that the HMI stockholders could be awarded if they succeed on their claims regarding the unfairness of the Merger would compensate the HMI stockholders for the harm alleged in this portion of the Complaint. As a result, I grant Defendants' motion with regard to O'Reilly's request for compensatory damages arising out of this portion of O'Reilly's disclosure claim, but I deny Defendants' motion to dismiss the remainder of the first two versions of this portion of O'Reilly's disclosure claim.

Before leaving this portion of O'Reilly's disclosure claim, I note that O'Reilly's third variation on the same theme falls short of the mark. [Omitted]. Thus, I conclude that this version of O'Reilly's first portion of her claim for breach of the fiduciary duty of disclosure fails to state a valid legal cause of action, and, therefore, I dismiss it.

(b) Threats of Bankruptcy

[Omitted]

(c) Contradictory Statements About HMI's Liquidation Value

[Omitted]

(d) Arm's Length Negotiations

O'Reilly alleges the Proxy Statement's representation that Transworld and HMI's negotiations were "conducted on an arms length basis" was false. In the Complaint, she cites Webster's Ninth New Collegiate Dictionary: "The generally accepted definition of 'arms length' is 'the condition or fact that the parties to a transaction are independent and on an equal footing.'"

Defendants argue that this claim should be dismissed because all the facts upon which O'Reilly relies in claiming that the negotiations in fact were not "arm's length" are in the Proxy Statement. Defendants would like me to conclude, therefore, that despite the fact that the representation in the Proxy Statement that the negotiations were "conducted on an arm's length basis" may have been false, the Defendants have fulfilled their fiduciary duty of disclosure because the Proxy Statement provided sufficient information for the stockholders to conclude that the statement was false. This proposition is completely inconsistent with Delaware's fiduciary duty of disclosure which requires corporate fiduciaries to "provide a balanced, truthful account of all matters disclosed in the communications with shareholders,"[41] when requesting stockholder action. Stockholders should be entitled to rely on the truthfulness of statements in communications from corporate fiduciaries without having to question each representation

41. Malone, 722 A.2d at 12.

against potentially conflicting statements or facts that would lead to conflicting conclusions.

Defendants' citation to Wilen v. Pollution Control Indus.[42] does not support their argument. Wilen involved an allegation that a proxy statement omitted disclosure that one of a corporation's directors was "subservient" to the corporation's acquirer.[43] This Court confirmed that the omission was not material because it was a legal conclusion and all of the underlying facts establishing the claim of subservience had been disclosed.[44] In this case, however, O'Reilly does not allege an omission of a legal conclusion. Rather, she alleges an affirmative misrepresentation of facts—the existence of "arm's length" negotiations—which cannot be cured by reference to underlying facts. Once the corporate fiduciaries in this case decided to take the next step and communicate whether or not the negotiations were "arm's length" (the omission of which *may* not have been material if the disclosure on Transworld's status and influence and the conflicts of two of HMI's four directors were an adequate basis for HMI's stockholders to conclude that the negotiations were not "arm's length"), they had a duty to do so truthfully. The fact that the Proxy Materials contained adequate information for stockholders to conclude that this representation was false or questionable does not diminish the materiality of the false statement. Despite the presence of other contradictory information, there is a substantial likelihood that a reasonable investor relied on the "arm's length" statement in deciding to approve the Merger.

Defendants go on to challenge O'Reilly's definition of the term "arm's length" and argue that this claim is merely a disagreement over the definition of the term "arm's length," which, they claim is insufficient to support a disclosure claim. Regardless of the parties' preferred definition of the term "arm's length," O'Reilly's allegations, if true, would support a finding that in fact the negotiations were not "arm's length" and that the Proxy Statement's representation on this issue was false.

Again, because O'Reilly pleads that this statement was false, and material, she has a well pleaded claim for nominal damages arising from the alleged breach of the fiduciary duty of disclosure. For the same reasons set forth earlier in this opinion,[45] O'Reilly has failed to plead sufficiently her request for additional damages. One of the essential allegations underlying O'Reilly's claim in Count II that the Merger was unfair is that the Merger negotiations were not "arm's length," and resulted in unfair dealing and a usurpation of corporate opportunity by Transworld. O'Reilly's Complaint fails to plead *prima facie* facts that this false statement created a cognizable harm discrete from the harm caused by the alleged unfair negotiations that honest disclosure would have revealed and which also underlies O'Reilly's entire fairness claim. I, therefore, dismiss under *Brown* O'Reilly's request for compensatory damages arising out of this false statement, but I deny the Defendants' motion to dismiss the remainder of this portion of O'Reilly's disclosure claim.

(e) Funding source .

Although Defendants' brief does not address this claim, I raise this portion of O'Reilly's disclosure claim *sua sponte.* She alleges the statement, "Transworld will use

42. 1984 Del. Ch. LEXIS 550, *12, Del. Ch., C.A. No. 7254, Hartnett, V.C. (Oct. 15, 1984).
43. Id.
44. 1984 Del. Ch. LEXIS 550, *12–13.
45. See 1999 Del. Ch. LEXIS 185, *47–48.

available working capital to fund the Merger Consideration of approximately $ 2.8 million in the aggregate and expenses of approximately $ 1.7 million relating to the merger," was false because Transworld intended to either borrow the funds or raise it by selling HMI's assets. I dismiss this claim because so long as Transworld raised the cash it needed to buy HMI, the source was immaterial to the stockholders' vote. To the extent that this claim could be linked to an effort to conceal Transworld's purpose for engaging in the Merger, any concerns arising from that link will be addressed sufficiently by the disclosure claim that the statements regarding Transworld's purpose were false.

2. O'Reilly's Claim of Omission

[omitted]

D. O'Reilly's Entire Fairness Claim

[omitted]

III. CONCLUSION

For the reasons stated above, I grant in part and deny in part Defendants' motion to dismiss Count I of the Complaint, and I deny Defendants' motion to dismiss Count II of the Complaint.

IT IS SO ORDERED.

---

2. *Other Approaches to Disclosure*

Outside of the United States, actions based on a duty of disclosure are rare. An alternative set of remedies have arisen around the obligations of statutory auditors and their mandatory report to the shareholders on the state of the company. As you read the materials that follow, consider whether the statutory procedures described, especially those based on mandatory audits and auditor reports, resemble, in some way, the duty of disclosure constructed by the Delaware courts.

Dan Fenno Henderson, *Security Markets in the United States and Japan: Distinctive Aspects Molded by Cultural, Social, Economic, and Political Differences*

14 HASTINGS INT'L & COMP. L. REV. 263 (1991)
(excerpts pages 277–279; some footnotes omitted)

There are some major differences between the Japanese and U.S. legal systems for large public corporations. The formal differences, not discussed in this Article, include substantive variations, as well as differing means and, indeed, differing degrees of legal enforcement.[56] The Japanese Commercial Code provides for a corporate ac-

---

56. See Baum, *Japanese Capital Markets: New Legislation*, 22 LAW IN JAPAN (1989) (assessment in English of Japan's recent rules for insiders); Note, *Regulation of Inside Trading in Japan*, 89 COLUM. L. REV. 1296 (1989) (authored by Tomoko A. Kashi); K. OKAMURA & C. TAKESKITA, LAWS AND REGULATION RELATING TO INSIDER TRADING IN JAPAN (Tokyo 1989) (part I includes English translations of the new ministerial ordinances; part II is a synopsis of the changes; and part III has the laws in the official Japanese language). For pre-amendment law, see Ishizumi, *Insider Trading*

counting officer known as an auditor (*kansayaku*),[57] and for special accountant auditors (*kaikei kansanin*) for larger corporations,[58] all of whom are perceived as representing the shareholders' interests inside the corporate law, and not in the regulatory law as American certified public accountants (CPAs) are. The Commercial Code also requires reports (balance sheets, profit and loss statements, proposals for distribution of surplus profits, and operating reports) to issue from the board to the auditor (and accounting auditor), and then to the shareholders for approval.[59] These reports must be approved by the board and the auditors (and accountant auditors) before they are presented to the general shareholders' annual (in practice often semiannual) meeting.

These provisions for accounting and operational supervision by auditors within the KKs become more stringent for KKs of larger capitalizations (or borrowings). The law requires that CPAs staff the accountant auditor's positions.[60] Powers of examination and supervision of directors' operations are also included in the laws.

Without elaborating here on the considerable complexity of these accounting mechanisms within the Commercial Code and subsidiary statutes, it is sufficient to state that accountability is built into the Commercial Code and special statutes for corporations, rather than imposed largely from the outside by regulatory law as in the American federal rubric.[61] Japanese law does, however, impose further regulation of accounts, and mandates disclosure for listed corporations, by way of the securities regulations,[62] which are patterned after the American practice. Prior to various amendments in 1974 and 1981, the CPA's audit, under the Japanese securities regulations, occurred after the shareholders had approved the board's accounts as reported to them by the board and examined by the auditor, making it difficult to rectify errors at that late date.

Comments and Questions

1. The Japanese system provides an important role for independent auditors to provide for corporate accounting for the benefit of shareholders. Do these systems of independent auditor reports provide a substitute for a duty of disclosure? In one sense the

Regulation: An Examination of Section 16(b) and a Proposal for Japan, 47 FORDHAM L. REV. 449 (1979).

57. SHOHO arts. 273....

58. Large corporations are those with 500 million yen equity capital, or borrowings of twenty billion yen. Smith, The 1974 Revision of the Commercial Code and Related Legislation, 7 LAW IN JAPAN 113, 120 (1974); see also Kabushiki keisha no kansa to ni kansuru shoho no tokurei ni kansuru horitsu (Law for Special Exceptions to the Commercial Code Concerning Audits of Stock Corporations), Law No. 22 of 1974, art. 2 [hereinafter Law No. 22 of 1974].

59. SHOHO art. 281.

60. Law No. 22 of 1974, arts. 2, 4.

61. See L. LOSS & J. SELIGMAN, supra note 15, at 687–743 (1989). Note however, that the ABA recommendations for an audit committee within the board of directors, comprised of outside directors, are a similar attempt to avoid management's (inside directors') self-serving control of audits. *Corporate Director's Guidebook*, 32 BUS. LAW. 5, 36 (1976).

62. Shoken torihiki-ho (Securities Exchange Law), Law No. 25 of 1950, art. 193-2(1). See M. TATSUTA, SECURITIES REGULATION IN JAPAN 57 (1970). For an authoritative commentary, see W. HORIGUCHI, KOMMENTARU SHOKEN TORIHIKI-HO (rev. ed. 1985). See Also JAPANESE SECURITIES LAW (L. Loss, M. Yazawa, & B. Banoff eds. 1983) (the material in this book is largely from the 1970s and not up to date, but it contains much valuable information in English.).

shareholder auditor function serves a significant disclosure function—at least with respect to the financial performance of the company. But in another sense it provides little in the way of the sort of disclosure at the heart of the Delaware disclosure duty—that is full disclosure to shareholders in connection with actions requiring shareholder approval.

2. In the United States, at least with respect to companies subject to the registration and reporting requirements of federal securities laws, shareholders must also receive detailed financial information prepared in accordance with complex rules (based in part on Generally Accepted Accounting Principles). But in the United States, the auditors represent management's interests, rather than those of the shareholders. Shareholders can discipline auditors through legal actions for fraud in connection with the preparation of the financial statements.

3. In Britain, the courts have long imposed a requirement that directors give shareholders enough information to understand the implications of any proposed transaction. Peel v. London and North Wester Rly Co., [1907] 1 Ch 5 (Court of Appeals). As long as the directors comply with this common law requirement, they are free to use company funds to press their position on the matter coming before the shareholders for their approval. Shareholders opposing the board's position have a limited statutory right to have a brief statement of their views circulated.

4. The EU has also imposed disclosure obligations running parallel to that of Japan in the Fourth, Seventh and Eighth Company Law Directives. The Fourth Directive harmonized the preparation of financial reports by limited liability companies, as well as the preparation of an annual report containing "a fair review of the development of the company's business and of its position."[1] These financial statements and the annual report must be made a matter of public record after approval by shareholders at a duly convened meeting. The Seventh Company Law Directive extends the Fourth Company Law Directive's reporting requirements, particularly with respect to consolidated accounts. The Eighth Company Law Directive imposes a harmonized standard fr auditor qualifications. The mandatory disclosures required by these directives, and the manner in which disclosure is to take place is governed to a large extent by the First Company Law Directive. In addition, of course, the share exchanges in the various Member States have imposed their own disclosure requirements. These are similar in scope to those of the national American exchanges. These provisions, like those in Japan, may provide a substitute for a duty to disclose with respect to actions requiring shareholder approval, but are not as broadly applicable as Delaware's duty to disclose. In particular, disclosure obligations contained in the EU Directives are generally not applicable to private companies, and many jurisdictions have not extended these obligations to private companies on a permissive basis. Can you think of other provisions that might cover this duty? The duty of loyalty? Any duty running to the corporation?

---

1. Fourth Company Law Directive, Art. 46(1). For the English implementation, see Companies Act of 1985, section 234.

Chapter 11

Fiduciary Duties of Shareholders

Notions of fiduciary duty, or of categories of duties owed to the corporation by various participants in the corporate enterprise, are not limited to directors and officers. Over the course of the last century, different systems of corporate governance have begun to develop a legal basis for regulating the conduct of majority or controlling shareholders in the corporation. The problems of regulating the conduct of controlling shareholders arise in two distinct forms. The first, and simplest, involves the regulation of non-governmental parties who are shareholders. More difficult problems arise in connection with the regulation of controlling shareholders who are also governmental units. This problem is particularly acute in Socialist states, such as the People's Republic of China, or in state with transitional economies, like Russia. This chapter introduces you to the major comparative trends in the area of shareholder regulation.

A. The American Common Law Models

There is no single approach to the understanding, definition, or regulation of shareholder obligations to the corporation, or to other shareholders in American law. The materials that follow explore the problems attendant on the regulation of shareholder conduct to the corporation and her fellow shareholders in two contexts. First, it highlights the different approaches courts have taken to the construction of a fiduciary duty of shareholders. At one end of the spectrum stands states, led by Massachusetts, that have imposed strong fiduciary duties on controlling, or at least majority, shareholders of corporations the shares of which are not publicly traded. The other end of the spectrum is represented by the courts of Delaware, that have rejected the Massachusetts style construction of general fiduciary duties of controlling shareholders, but nonetheless have extended at least some of the fiduciary duties of directors to controlling shareholders . Second, the materials suggest the different analysis that some courts have followed when confronted with issues of fiduciary duty in the face of one or more agreements between the shareholders who are parties to the dispute.

1. A Generally Applicable Shareholder Duty?

American courts and legislatures have struggled with the problem of the control of shareholder activity for the greater part of the last century. As the materials that follow demonstrate, American courts and legislatures are far from reaching any consensus on the problem or its solution.

Stanley J. Wilkes v. Springside Nursing Home, Inc. & Others[1]

Supreme Judicial Court of Massachusetts
370 Mass. 842; 353 N.E.2d 657
August 20, 1976, Decided

HENNESSEY, J.:

On August 5, 1971, the plaintiff (Wilkes) filed a bill in equity for declaratory judgment in the Probate Court for Berkshire County,[2] naming as defendants T. Edward Quinn (Quinn),[3] Leon L. Riche (Riche), the First Agricultural National Bank of Berkshire County and Frank Sutherland MacShane as executors under the will of Lawrence R. Connor (Connor), and the Springside Nursing Home, Inc. (Springside or the corporation). Wilkes alleged that he, Quinn, Riche and Dr. Hubert A. Pipkin (Pipkin)[4] entered into a partnership agreement in 1951, prior to the incorporation of Springside, which agreement was breached in 1967 when Wilkes's salary was terminated and he was voted out as an officer and director of the corporation. Wilkes sought, among other forms of relief, damages in the amount of the salary he would have received had he continued as a director and officer of Springside subsequent to March, 1967.

A judge of the Probate Court referred the suit to a master, who, after a lengthy hearing, issued his final report in late 1973. Wilkes's objections to the master's report were overruled after a hearing, and the master's report was confirmed in late 1974. A judgment was entered dismissing Wilkes's action on the merits. We granted direct appellate review. Mass. R. A. P. 11, 365 Mass. 854 (1974). On appeal, Wilkes argued in the alternative that (1) he should recover damages for breach of the alleged partnership agreement; and (2) he should recover damages because the defendants, as majority stockholders in Springside, breached their fiduciary duty to him as a minority stockholder by their action in February and March, 1967.

---

1. Barbara Quinn (executrix under the will of T. Edward Quinn), Leon L. Riche, and the First Agricultural National Bank of Berkshire County and Frank Sutherland MacShane (executors under the will of Lawrence R. Connor).

2. Wilkes urged the court, inter alia, to declare the rights of the parties under (1) an alleged partnership agreement entered into in 1951 between himself, T. Edward Quinn (see note 3 *infra*), Leon L. Riche and Dr. Hubert A. Pipkin (see note 4 *infra*); and (2) certain portions of a stock transfer restriction agreement executed by the four original stockholders in the Springside Nursing Home, Inc., in 1956.

3. T. Edward Quinn died while this action was sub judice. The executrix of his estate has been substituted as a party-defendant. See note 1 *supra*.

4. Dr. Pipkin transferred his interest in Springside to Connor in 1959 and is not a defendant in this action.

We conclude that the master's findings were warranted by the evidence and that his report was properly confirmed. However, we reverse so much of the judgment as dismisses Wilkes's complaint and order the entry of a judgment substantially granting the relief sought by Wilkes under the second alternative set forth above.

A summary of the pertinent facts as found by the master is set out in the following pages. It will be seen that, although the issue whether there was a breach of the fiduciary duty owed to Wilkes by the majority stockholders in Springside was not considered by the master, the master's report and the designated portions of the transcript of the evidence before him supply us with a sufficient basis for our conclusion.

In 1951 Wilkes acquired an option to purchase a building and lot located on the corner of Springside Avenue and North Street in Pittsfield, Massachusetts, the building having previously housed the Hillcrest Hospital. Though Wilkes was principally engaged in the roofing and siding business, he had gained a reputation locally for profitable dealings in real estate. Riche, an acquaintance of Wilkes, learned of the option, and interested Quinn (who was known to Wilkes through membership on the draft board in Pittsfield) and Pipkin (an acquaintance of both Wilkes and Riche) in joining Wilkes in his investment. The four men met and decided to participate jointly in the purchase of the building and lot as a real estate investment which, they believed, had good profit potential on resale or rental.

The parties later determined that the property would have its greatest potential for profit if it were operated by them as a nursing home. Wilkes consulted his attorney, who advised him that if the four men were to operate the contemplated nursing home as planned, they would be partners and would be liable for any debts incurred by the partnership and by each other. On the attorney's suggestion, and after consultation among themselves, ownership of the property was vested in Springside, a corporation organized under Massachusetts law.

Each of the four men invested $ 1,000 and subscribed to ten shares of $ 100 par value stock in Springside.[6] At the time of incorporation it was understood by all of the parties that each would be a director of Springside and each would participate actively in the management and decision making involved in operating the corporation.[7] It was, further, the understanding and intention of all the parties that, corporate resources permitting, each would receive money from the corporation in equal amounts as long as each assumed an active and ongoing responsibility for carrying a portion of the burdens necessary to operate the business.

The work involved in establishing and operating a nursing home was roughly apportioned, and each of the four men undertook his respective tasks.[8] Initially, Riche was elected president of Springside, Wilkes was elected treasurer, and Quinn was

6. On May 2, 1955, and again on December 23, 1958, each of the four original investors paid for and was issued additional shares of $ 100 par value stock, eventually bringing the total number of shares owned by each to 115.

7. Wilkes testified before the master that, when the corporate officers were elected, all four men "were... guaranteed directorships." Riche's understanding of the parties' intentions was that they all wanted to play a part in the management of the corporation and wanted to have some "say" in the risks involved; that, to this end, they all would be directors; and that "unless you [were] a director and officer you could not participate in the decisions of [the] enterprise."

8. Wilkes took charge of the repair, upkeep and maintenance of the physical plant and grounds; Riche assumed supervision over the kitchen facilities and dietary and food aspects of the home; Pipkin was to make himself available if and when medical problems arose; and Quinn dealt with the personnel and administrative aspects of the nursing home, serving informally as a managing director. Quinn further coordinated the activities of the other parties and served as a communication

elected clerk.[9] Each of the four was listed in the articles of organization as a director of the corporation.

At some time in 1952, it became apparent that the operational income and cash flow from the business were sufficient to permit the four stockholders to draw money from the corporation on a regular basis. Each of the four original parties initially received $ 35 a week from the corporation. As time went on the weekly return to each was increased until, in 1955, it totaled $ 100.

In 1959, after a long illness, Pipkin sold his shares in the corporation to Connor, who was known to Wilkes, Riche and Quinn through past transactions with Springside in his capacity as president of the First Agricultural National Bank of Berkshire County. Connor received a weekly stipend from the corporation equal to that received by Wilkes, Riche and Quinn. He was elected a director of the corporation but never held any other office. He was assigned no specific area of responsibility in the operation of the nursing home but did participate in business discussions and decisions as a director and served additionally as financial adviser to the corporation.

In 1965 the stockholders decided to sell a portion of the corporate property to Quinn who, in addition to being a stockholder in Springside, possessed an interest in another corporation which desired to operate a rest home on the property. Wilkes was successful in prevailing on the other stockholders of Springside to procure a higher sale price for the property than Quinn apparently anticipated paying or desired to pay. After the sale was consummated, the relationship between Quinn and Wilkes began to deteriorate.

The bad blood between Quinn and Wilkes affected the attitudes of both Riche and Connor. As a consequence of the strained relations among the parties, Wilkes, in January of 1967, gave notice of his intention to sell his shares for an amount based on an appraisal of their value. In February of 1967 a directors' meeting was held and the board exercised its right to establish the salaries of its officers and employees.[10] A schedule of payments was established whereby Quinn was to receive a substantial weekly increase and Riche and Connor were to continue receiving $ 100 a week. Wilkes, however, was left off the list of those to whom a salary was to be paid. The directors also set the annual meeting of the stockholders for March, 1967.

At the annual meeting in March, Wilkes was not reelected as a director, nor was he reelected as an officer of the corporation. He was further informed that neither his services nor his presence at the nursing home was wanted by his associates.

The meetings of the directors and stockholders in early 1967, the master found, were used as a vehicle to force Wilkes out of active participation in the management and operation of the corporation and to cut off all corporate payments to him. Though the board of directors had the power to dismiss any officers or employees for misconduct or neglect of duties, there was no indication in the minutes of the board of directors' meeting of February, 1967, that the failure to establish a salary for Wilkes was based on

---

link among them when matters had to be discussed and decisions had to be made without a formal meeting.

9. Riche held the office of president from 1951 to 1963; Quinn served as president from 1963 on, as clerk from 1951 to 1967, and as treasurer from 1967 on; Wilkes was treasurer from 1951 to 1967.

10. The by-laws of the corporation provided that the directors, subject to the approval of the stockholders, had the power to fix the salaries of all officers and employees. This power, however, up until February, 1967, had not been exercised formally; all payments made to the four participants in the venture had resulted from the informal but unanimous approval of all the parties concerned.

either ground. The severance of Wilkes from the payroll resulted not from misconduct or neglect of duties, but because of the personal desire of Quinn, Riche and Connor to prevent him from continuing to receive money from the corporation.

Despite a continuing deterioration in his personal relationship with his associates, Wilkes had consistently endeavored to carry on his responsibilities to the corporation in the same satisfactory manner and with the same degree of competence he had previously shown. Wilkes was at all times willing to carry on his responsibilities and participation if permitted so to do and provided that he receive his weekly stipend.

1. We turn to Wilkes's claim for damages based on a breach of fiduciary duty owed to him by the other participants in this venture. In light of the theory underlying this claim, we do not consider it vital to our approach to this case whether the claim is governed by partnership law or the law applicable to business corporations. This is so because, as all the parties agree, Springside was at all times relevant to this action, a close corporation as we have recently defined such an entity in Donahue v. Rodd Electrotype of New England, Inc., 367 Mass. 578, 585–586 (1975).

In Donahue,[12] we held that "stockholders in the close corporation owe one another substantially the same fiduciary duty in the operation of the enterprise that partners owe to one another." Id. at 593 (footnotes omitted). As determined in previous decisions of this court, the standard of duty owed by partners to one another is one of "utmost good faith and loyalty." Cardullo v. Landau, 329 Mass. 5, 8 (1952), and cases cited. DeCotis v. D'Antona, 350 Mass. 165, 168 (1966), quoting from Mendelsohn v. Leather Mfg. Corp., 326 Mass. 226, 233 (1950). Thus, we concluded in Donahue, with regard to "their actions relative to the operations of the enterprise and the effects of that operation on the rights and investments of other stockholders," "[s]tockholders in close corporations must discharge their management and stockholder responsibilities in conformity with this strict good faith standard. They may not act out of avarice, expediency or self-interest in derogation of their duty of loyalty to the other stockholders and to the corporation." 367 Mass. at 593 n.18.

In the Donahue case we recognized that one peculiar aspect of close corporations was the opportunity afforded to majority stockholders to oppress, disadvantage or "freeze out" minority stockholders. In Donahue itself, for example, the majority refused the minority an equal opportunity to sell a ratable number of shares to the corporation at the same price available to the majority. The net result of this refusal, we said, was that the minority could be forced to "sell out at less than fair value," 367 Mass. at 592, since there is by definition no ready market for minority stock in a close corporation.

"Freeze outs," however, may be accomplished by the use of other devices. One such device which has proved to be particularly effective in accomplishing the purpose of the majority is to deprive minority stockholders of corporate offices and of employment with the corporation. F.H. O'Neal, "Squeeze-Outs" of Minority Shareholders 59, 78–79 (1975). See 367 Mass. at 587, 589. This "freeze-out" technique has been successful because courts fairly consistently have been disinclined to interfere in those facets of internal corporate operations, such as the selection and retention or dismissal of officers, directors and employees, which essentially involve management decisions subject to the principle of majority control. See Note, 35 N.C. L. Rev. 271, 277 (1957). As one authori-

12. For legal commentary relating to the *Donahue* case, see 89 Harv. L. Rev. 423 (1975); 60 Mass. L. Q. 318 (1975); 21 Vill. L. Rev. 307 (1976).

tative source has said, "[M]any courts apparently feel that there is a legitimate sphere in which the controlling [directors or] shareholders can act in their own interest even if the minority suffers." F.H. O'Neal, *supra* at 59 (footnote omitted). Comment, 1959 Duke L.J. 436, 437.

The denial of employment to the minority at the hands of the majority is especially pernicious in some instances. A guaranty of employment with the corporation may have been one of the "basic reason[s] why a minority owner has invested capital in the firm." Symposium—The Close Corporation, 52 Nw. U.L. Rev. 345, 392 (1957). See F.H. O'Neal, supra at 78–79; Hancock, Minority Interests in Small Business Entities, 17 Clev.-Mar. L. Rev. 130, 132–133 (1968); 89 Harv. L. Rev. 423, 427 (1975). The minority stockholder typically depends on his salary as the principal return on his investment, since the "earnings of a close corporation... are distributed in major part in salaries, bonuses and retirement benefits." 1 F.H. O'Neal, Close Corporations § 1.07 (1971).[13] Other noneconomic interests of the minority stockholder are likewise injuriously affected by barring him from corporate office. See F.H. O'Neal, "Squeeze-Outs" of Minority Shareholders 79 (1975). Such action severely restricts his participation in the management of the enterprise, and he is relegated to enjoying those benefits incident to his status as a stockholder. See Symposium—The Close Corporation, 52 Nw. U.L. Rev. 345, 386 (1957). In sum, by terminating a minority stockholder's employment or by severing him from a position as an officer or director, the majority effectively frustrate the minority stockholder's purposes in entering on the corporate venture and also deny him an equal return on his investment.

The Donahue decision acknowledged, as a "natural outgrowth" of the case law of this Commonwealth, a strict obligation on the part of majority stockholders in a close corporation to deal with the minority with the utmost good faith and loyalty. On its face, this strict standard is applicable in the instant case. The distinction between the majority action in Donahue and the majority action in this case is more one of form than of substance. Nevertheless, we are concerned that untempered application of the strict good faith standard enunciated in Donahue to cases such as the one before us will result in the imposition of limitations on legitimate action by the controlling group in a close corporation which will unduly hamper its effectiveness in managing the corporation in the best interests of all concerned. The majority, concededly, have certain rights to what has been termed "selfish ownership" in the corporation which should be balanced against the concept of their fiduciary obligation to the minority. See Hill, The Sale of Controlling Shares, 70 Harv. L. Rev. 986, 1013–1015 (1957); Note, 44 Iowa L. Rev. 734, 740–741 (1959); Symposium—The Close Corporation, 52 Nw. U.L. Rev. 345, 395–396 (1957).

Therefore, when minority stockholders in a close corporation bring suit against the majority alleging a breach of the strict good faith duty owed to them by the majority, we must carefully analyze the action taken by the controlling stockholders in the individual case. It must be asked whether the controlling group can demonstrate a legitimate business purpose for its action.... In asking this question, we acknowledge the fact that the controlling group in a close corporation must have some room to maneuver in

13. We note here that the master found that Springside never declared or paid a dividend to its stockholders.

establishing the business policy of the corporation. It must have a large measure of discretion, for example, in declaring or withholding dividends, deciding whether to merge or consolidate, establishing the salaries of corporate officers, dismissing directors with or without cause, and hiring and firing corporate employees.

When an asserted business purpose for their action is advanced by the majority, however, we think it is open to minority stockholders to demonstrate that the same legitimate objective could have been achieved through an alternative course of action less harmful to the minority's interest.... If called on to settle a dispute, our courts must weigh the legitimate business purpose, if any, against the practicability of a less harmful alternative.

Applying this approach to the instant case it is apparent that the majority stockholders in Springside have not shown a legitimate business purpose for severing Wilkes from the payroll of the corporation or for refusing to reelect him as a salaried officer and director. The master's subsidiary findings relating to the purpose of the meetings of the directors and stockholders in February and March, 1967, are supported by the evidence. There was no showing of misconduct on Wilkes's part as a director, officer or employee of the corporation which would lead us to approve the majority action as a legitimate response to the disruptive nature of an undesirable individual bent on injuring or destroying the corporation. On the contrary, it appears that Wilkes had always accomplished his assigned share of the duties competently, and that he had never indicated an unwillingness to continue to do so.

It is an inescapable conclusion from all the evidence that the action of the majority stockholders here was a designed "freeze out" for which no legitimate business purpose has been suggested. Furthermore, we may infer that a design to pressure Wilkes into selling his shares to the corporation at a price below their value well may have been at the heart of the majority's plan.[14]

In the context of this case, several factors bear directly on the duty owed to Wilkes by his associates. At a minimum, the duty of utmost good faith and loyalty would demand that the majority consider that their action was in disregard of a long-standing policy of the stockholders that each would be a director of the corporation and that employment with the corporation would go hand in hand with stock ownership; that Wilkes was one of the four originators of the nursing home venture; and that Wilkes, like the others, had invested his capital and time for more than fifteen years with the expectation that he would continue to participate in corporate decisions. Most important is the plain fact that the cutting off of Wilkes's salary, together with the fact that the corporation never declared a dividend (see note 13 *supra*), assured that Wilkes would receive no return at all from the corporation.

2. The question of Wilkes's damages at the hands of the majority has not been thoroughly explored on the record before us. Wilkes, in his original complaint, sought damages in the amount of the $ 100 a week he believed he was entitled to from the time his salary was terminated up until the time this action was commenced. However, the record shows that, after Wilkes was severed from the corporate payroll, the schedule of salaries and payments made to the other stockholders varied from time to time. In addi-

14. This inference arises from the fact that Connor, acting on behalf of the three controlling stockholders, offered to purchase Wilkes's shares for a price Connor admittedly would not have accepted for his own shares.

tion, the duties assumed by the other stockholders after Wilkes was deprived of his share of the corporate earnings appear to have changed in significant respects.[15] Any resolution of this question must take into account whether the corporation was dissolved during the pendency of this litigation.

Therefore our order is as follows: So much of the judgment as dismisses Wilkes's complaint and awards costs to the defendants is reversed. The case is remanded to the Probate Court for Berkshire County for further proceedings concerning the issue of damages. Thereafter a judgment shall be entered declaring that Quinn, Riche and Connor breached their fiduciary duty to Wilkes as a minority stockholder in Springside, and awarding money damages therefor. Wilkes shall be allowed to recover from Riche, the estate of T. Edward Quinn and the estate of Lawrence R. Connor, ratably, according to the inequitable enrichment of each, the salary he would have received had he remained an officer and director of Springside. In considering the issue of damages the judge on remand shall take into account the extent to which any remaining corporate funds of Springside may be diverted to satisfy Wilkes's claim.

So ordered.

Comments and Questions

1. A few states have adopted the Massachusetts position. Some of them rely on the finding of equivalence between the duty imposed by law between partners and that which ought to be imposed between shareholders of a closely held corporation. For an example see Daniels v. Thomas, Dean & Hoskins, Inc., a corporation et al., 246 Mont. 125; 804 P.2d 359 (1990).

2. Other states, led by Delaware, have rejected the approach of the Massachusetts courts. The case that follows sets forth the basic rationale of the Delaware courts in this regard. These states resist imposing any sort of heightened duty on majority shareholders to other shareholders in a closely held corporation. In considering the Delaware response to the protections which should be made available to Delaware shareholders of closely held corporations ask yourself the following questions:

A. Is the reasoning of the Delaware court more convincing than that of the Massachusetts court?

B. Is it possible, under the Delaware standard, to contractually adopt, as between the shareholders of a closely held corporation, the Massachusetts standard of fiduciary duty *inter se?* Would it make a difference if the shareholders adopted an amendment to the articles of incorporation to that effect? Would it make a difference if the corporation elected close corporation status under the Delaware statute?

15. In fairness to Wilkes, who, as the master found, was at all times ready and willing to work for the corporation, it should be noted that neither the other stockholders nor their representatives may be heard to say that Wilkes's duties were performed by them and that Wilkes's damages should, for that reason, be diminished.

Allen Nixon, et al., Defendants Below, Appellants, v. Guy C. Blackwell, et al., Plaintiffs Below, Appellees.

Supreme Court of Delaware
626 A.2d 1366
June 22, 1993, Decided

VEASEY, Chief Justice:

[The facts of the case are set for in the excerpt in chapter 10 above.].

VI. NO SPECIAL RULES FOR A "CLOSELY-HELD CORPORATION" NOT QUALIFIED AS A "CLOSE CORPORATION" UNDER SUBCHAPTER XIV OF THE DELAWARE GENERAL CORPORATION LAW.

We wish to address one further matter which was raised at oral argument before this Court: Whether there should be any special, judicially-created rules to "protect" minority stockholders of closely-held Delaware corporations.[18]

The case at bar points up the basic dilemma of minority stockholders in receiving fair value for their stock as to which there is no market and no market valuation. It is not difficult to be sympathetic, in the abstract, to a stockholder who finds himself or herself in that position. A stockholder who bargains for stock in a closely-held corporation and who pays for those shares (unlike the plaintiffs in this case who acquired their stock through gift) can make a business judgment whether to buy into such a minority position, and if so on what terms. One could bargain for definitive provisions of self-ordering permitted to a Delaware corporation through the certificate of incorporation or by-laws by reason of the provisions in 8 Del. C. §§ 102, 109, and 141(a). Moreover, in addition to such mechanisms, a stockholder intending to buy into a minority position in a Delaware corporation may enter into definitive stockholder agreements, and such agreements may provide for elaborate earnings tests, buy-out provisions, voting trusts, or other voting agreements. See. e.g., 8 Del. C. § 218; Sonitrol Holding Co. v. Marceau Investissements, Del. Supr., 607 A.2d 1177 (1992).

The tools of good corporate practice are designed to give a purchasing minority stockholder the opportunity to bargain for protection before parting with consideration. It would do violence to normal corporate practice and our corporation law to fashion an ad hoc ruling which would result in a court-imposed stockholder buy-out for which the parties had not contracted.

In 1967, when the Delaware General Corporation Law was significantly revised, a new Subchapter XIV entitled "Close Corporations; Special Provisions," became a part of that law for the first time. While these provisions were patterned in theory after close

---

18. Compare Robert B. Thompson, The Shareholder's Cause of Action for Oppression, 48 Bus. Law. 699 (1993) and F. Hodge O'Neal and Robert B. Thompson, O'Neal's Close Corporations: Law and Practice, §§ 8.07–8.09 (3d ed. 1987) (favoring court formulation of a special rule protecting the minority from oppression) with Frank H. Easterbrook and Daniel R. Fischel, The Economic Structure of Corporate Law 228–52 (1991) (noting that "courts have found the equal opportunity rule... impossible to administer," id. at 247).

corporation statutes in Florida and Maryland, "the Delaware provisions were unique and influenced the development of similar legislation in a number of other states...." See Ernest L. Folk, III, Rodman Ward, Jr., and Edward P. Welch, 2 Folk on the Delaware General Corporation Law 404 (1988). Subchapter XIV is a narrowly constructed statute which applies only to a corporation which is designated as a "close corporation" in its certificate of incorporation, and which fulfills other requirements, including a limitation to 30 on the number of stockholders, that all classes of stock have to have at least one restriction on transfer, and that there be no "public offering." 8 Del. C. § 342. Accordingly, subchapter XIV applies only to "close corporations," as defined in section 342. "Unless a corporation elects to become a close corporation under this subchapter in the manner prescribed in this subchapter, it shall be subject in all respects to this chapter, except this subchapter." 8 Del. C. § 341. The corporation before the Court in this matter, is not a "close corporation." Therefore it is not governed by the provisions of Subchapter XIV.[19]

One cannot read into the situation presented in the case at bar any special relief for the minority stockholders in this closely-held, but not statutory "close corporation" because the provisions of Subchapter XIV relating to close corporations and other statutory schemes[20] preempt the field in their respective areas. It would run counter to the spirit of the doctrine of independent legal significance,[21] and would be inappropriate judicial legislation[22] for this Court to fashion a special judicially-created rule for minority investors when the entity does not fall within those statutes, or when there are no negotiated special provisions in the certificate of incorporation, by-laws, or stockholder agreements. The entire fairness test, correctly applied and articulated, is the proper judicial approach.

---

19. We do not intend to up imply that, if the Corporation had been a close corporation under Subchapter XIV, the result in this case would have been different.

> Statutory close corporations have not found particular favor with practitioners. Practitioners have for the most part viewed the complex statutory provisions underlying the purportedly simplified operational procedures for close corporations as legal quicksand of uncertain depth and have adopted the view that the objectives sought by the subchapter are achievable for their clients with considerably less uncertainty by cloaking a conventionally created corporation with the panoply of charter provisions, transfer restrictions, by-laws, stockholders' agreements, buy-sell arrangements, irrevocable proxies, voting trusts or other contractual mechanisms which were and remain the traditional method for accomplishing the goals sought by the close corporation provisions.

David A. Drexler, Lewis S. Black, Jr., and A. Gilchrist Sparks, III, Delaware Corporation Law and Practice § 43.01 (1993).

20. It is to be noted that Delaware statutory law provides for many forms of business enterprise: partnerships pursuant to 6 Del. C. §§ 1501–43; limited partnerships pursuant to 6 Del. C. § 17-101–1109; limited liability companies pursuant to 6 Del. C. §§ 18-101–1106; business trusts pursuant to Title 12, §§ 3801–20. Compare the Close Corporation Supplement to the Model Business Corporation Act, especially Section 20 relating to "Shareholder Agreements."

21. See Rothschild Intern. Corp. v. Liggett Group, Inc., Del. Supr., 474 A.2d 133, 136 (1984); Orzeck v. Englehart, 41 Del. Ch. 361, 195 A.2d 375, 378 (1963); Hariton v. Arco Electronics, Inc., 41 Del. Ch. 74, 188 A.2d 123 (1963); Federal United Corp. v. Havender, 24 Del. Ch. 318, 11 A.2d 331 (1940). See David A. Drexler, Lewis S. Black, Jr., and A. Gilchrist Sparks, III, Delaware Corporation Law and Practice § 4.02 (1993).

An important tool to practitioners in the use of the General Corporation Law is the principle of "independent legal significance." The principle holds that the validity of a transaction accomplished pursuant to a specified section or sections of the statute will be tested by the standards applicable to those sections and not by those of other provisions, even though the ultimate economic results could have been achieved through use of procedures authorized by such other provisions and even though use of such other procedures might have created different rights among those affected by the transaction.

22. Providence & Worcester Co. v. Baker, 378 A.2d at 124.

Shell Petroleum, Inc. v. Raymond A. Smith

Supreme Court of Delaware
606 A.2d 112
April 23, 1992, Decided

MOORE, Justice.

Shell Petroleum, Inc., the successor to SPNV Holdings, Inc. ("Holdings"), appeals a decision of the Court of Chancery awarding the class plaintiffs, all former minority shareholders of Shell Oil Company ("Shell"), damages for material misstatements made to the latter in connection with a short form "freeze-out" merger initiated by Holdings. We agree that the misstatements were material and that Holdings must bear responsibility for them. Accordingly, we affirm.

I.

In early 1984, Royal Dutch Petroleum Company ("Royal Dutch"), through various subsidiaries, controlled approximately 70% of the outstanding common shares of Shell. On January 24, 1984, Royal Dutch announced its intention to merge Shell into Holdings (now Shell Petroleum, Inc.)[1] by offering the minority $ 55 per share. However, Shell's board of directors rejected the offer as inadequate.

Royal Dutch then withdrew the merger proposal and initiated a tender offer at $ 58 per share.[2] As a result of the tender offer, Holdings' ownership interest increased to 94.6% of Shell's outstanding stock. Holdings then initiated a short-form merger pursuant to 8 Del. C. § 253.

Under the terms of the short-form merger, Shell's minority stockholders were to receive $ 58 per share. However, if a shareholder waived his right to seek an appraisal before July 1, 1985, he would receive an extra $ 2 per share. In conjunction with the short-form merger, Holdings distributed several documents to the minority, including a document entitled "Certain Information About Shell" ("CIAS").

The CIAS included a table of discounted future net cash flows ("DCF") for Shell's oil and gas reserves. However, due to a computer programming error, the DCF failed to account for the cash flows from approximately 295 million barrel equivalents of U.S. proved oil and gas reserves. Shell's failure to include the reserves in its calculations resulted in an understatement of its discounted future net cash flows of approximately $ 993 million to $ 1.1 billion or $ 3.00 to $ 3.45 per share. Moreover, as a result of the error, Shell stated in the CIAS that there had been a slight decline in the value of its oil and gas reserves from 1984 to 1985. When properly calculated, the value of the reserves had actually increased over that time period.

---

1. Holdings was formed for the purpose of obtaining the Shell stock owned by minority shareholders. Shell Petroleum, Inc. and Holdings will be referred to simply as Holdings.

2. The tender offer generated a significant amount of litigation regarding the fairness of the offer price and the adequacy of the disclosure materials. See Joseph v. Shell Oil Company, Del. Ch., 482 A.2d 335 (1984). The litigation was settled in early 1985. The settlement provided for cash payments to class members of approximately $ 190 million or $ 2 per share.

Shell's minority shareholders sued in the Court of Chancery asserting that the error in the DCF along with other alleged disclosure violations constituted a breach of Holdings' fiduciary "duty of candor"[3] After trial, the Court of Chancery held that the error in the DCF was both material and misleading. Moreover, the trial court concluded that Holdings, by virtue of its substantial role in preparing and distributing the disclosure materials, was liable to the minority shareholders for the error. The court then awarded the shareholder class $ 2 per share.

II.

We first consider Holdings' argument that the billion dollar understatement of Shell's oil and gas reserves was not material, and therefore, the Court of Chancery erred in finding a breach of fiduciary duty.

A.

The question whether the disclosures to Shell's minority shareholders were adequate is a mixed one of law and fact, requiring an assessment of the inferences a reasonable shareholder would draw and the significance of those inferences to the individual shareholder. Rosenblatt v. Getty Oil Co., Del. Supr., 493 A.2d 929, 944–45 (1985); see also Kahn v. Household Acquisition Corp., Del. Supr., 591 A.2d 166, 171 (1991) (quoting TSC Industries, Inc. v. Northway, Inc., 426 U.S. 438, 450, 48 L. Ed. 2d 757, 96 S. Ct. 2126 (1976)). Therefore, "this Court has the authority to review the entire record and to make its own findings of fact in a proper case." *Levitt v. Bouvier, Del. Supr., 287 A.2d 671, 673 (1972).* However, if the findings of the trial judge "are sufficiently supported by the record and are the product of an orderly and logical deductive process,... we accept them, even though independently we might have reached opposite conclusions." Id.

B.

Holdings' duty with respect to disclosure is clear. As the majority shareholder, Holdings bears the burden of showing complete disclosure of all material facts relevant to a minority shareholders' decision whether to accept the short-form merger consideration or seek an appraisal. Bershad v. Curtiss-Wright Corp., Del. Supr., 535 A.2d 840, 846 (1987) (citing Weinberger v. UOP, Inc., Del. Supr., 457 A.2d 701, 703 (1983)). Thus, the question is one of materiality. Id. (citing Smith v. Van Gorkom, Del. Supr., 488 A.2d 858, 890 (1985)). A fact is considered material if there is a "substantial likelihood that the disclosure of the omitted fact would have been viewed by the reasonable investor as having significantly altered the 'total mix' of information made available." Id. (quoting Rosenblatt, 493 A.2d at 944); see also TSC Industries, 426 U.S. at 449. "While it need not be shown that an omission or distortion would have made an investor change his overall view of a proposed transaction, it must be shown that the fact in question would have been relevant to him." Barkan v. Amsted Industries, Inc., Del. Supr., 567 A.2d 1279, 1289 (1989).

---

3. Recently, we noted that the term "duty of candor" does not import a unique or special rule of disclosure. "It represents nothing more than the well-recognized proposition that directors of Delaware corporations are under a fiduciary duty to disclose fully and fairly all material information within the board's control when it seeks shareholder action." Stroud v. Grace, Del. Supr., 606 A.2d 75, 84, Moore, J. (1992). Thus, we considered the term "duty of candor" to be both "confusing and imprecise given the well-established principles and duties of disclosure that otherwise exist." Id. Accordingly, we stated that it is more appropriate to speak of a duty of disclosure based on a materiality standard rather than unhelpful terminology having no well accepted meaning in the disclosure context. Id. We do so here.

C.

The Court of Chancery concluded that "the understatement of Shell's oil and gas reserves by 294.6 million barrel equivalents, with a value of approximately $ 1 billion ($ 3.00–$ 3.45 per share)... would have been viewed by a reasonable investor as significantly altering the 'total mix' of information available." Smith v. Shell Petroleum, Inc., Del. Ch., C.A. No. 8395, 1990 Del. Ch. LEXIS 82, Hartnett, V.C. (June 19, 1990) ("Smith") (citing Rosenblatt, 493 A.2d at 944). It is clear from the Vice Chancellor's decision that he applied the proper legal standards and carefully considered the evidence presented. However, Holdings argues that the court's decision was incorrect because: 1) the error was insignificant when viewed in context; 2) the error was not significant enough to affect a shareholder's decision whether to seek an appraisal; and 3) the error was not material because the DCF was only an estimate.

Holdings contends that the billion dollar error was insignificant because it resulted in only a 5.5% understatement in the total discounted cash flows reported. However, the significance of the error is clearly demonstrated by the fact that a Shell executive vice president stated in the Wall Street Journal that a 220 million barrel discovery in the Gulf of Mexico was considered a major find. Thus, it is difficult to accept Holdings' argument that the failure to report cash flows from 295 million barrels was insignificant, when the discovery of 220 million barrels was considered important enough to merit coverage on the first page of the Wall Street Journal.[4]

Holdings also argues that a $ 3 per share error was not significant enough to make a reasonable stockholder change his decision and seek an appraisal. However, the question is not whether the information would have changed the stockholder's decision to accept the merger consideration, but whether "the fact in question would have been relevant to him." Barkan, 567 A.2d at 1289. "The real worth of an oil company is centered in its reserves." Rosenblatt, 493 A.2d at 941. We cannot agree that a billion dollar understatement of the value of Shell's reserves would have been anything but highly relevant and material to a reasonable stockholder.

Finally, Holdings contends that the DCF is only an estimate of future cash flows and, therefore, it would be unreasonable for a shareholder to conclude that Shell's oil and gas reserves were worth the amount presented in the DCF. In fact, according to Holdings, a reasonable shareholder should anticipate a certain margin of error simply due to the uncertainties inherent in the estimate process.

Although the DCF presents an estimate of future cash flows, a shareholder could reasonably conclude that the DCF was accurately prepared based on all available information. Moreover, a reasonable shareholder could conclude that the 1985 DCF was prepared in a manner consistent with the 1984 DCF. Thus, a comparison of the 1984 and 1985 DCFs should present an accurate indication of whether the value of Shell's reserves was increasing or decreasing. Such was not the case. A comparison of the 1984 and 1985 DCFs inevitably leads to the erroneous conclusion, as stated in the CIAS, that the value of Shell's reserves had declined. Most importantly, the misleading statement that the value of the reserves had declined was not based upon the inherent

---

4. Holdings attempts to diminish the importance of the story in the Wall Street Journal by noting that the discovery involved actual barrels of oil, whereas the DCF only presented estimated cash flows from oil reserves. This argument is unpersuasive. The inherent value of any oil discovery is not the oil itself, but rather, the cash and profits expected to be generated by the oil. Thus, the estimated cash flows from oil and gas reserves are important to a reasonable investor, and a billion dollar understatement of those cash flows would be significant.

inaccuracies of the estimate process, but upon an error made by Shell. The fact that the error was included in a schedule which contained estimates does not diminish its materiality.

In the final analysis, the question is not whether this Court agrees or disagrees with the trial court's decision. Rather, the question is whether the Vice Chancellor's findings are "supported by the record and are the product of an orderly and logical deductive process." Levitt, 287 A.2d at 673. After reviewing the record, we conclude that the Vice Chancellor's decision was both supported by the record and well-reasoned.

III.

Holdings also argues that the Court of Chancery erred in finding it liable for the understatement contained in Shell's disclosure materials. Essentially, Holdings contends that it should not be held liable for an error made by Shell. Holdings argues that the trial court's decision makes it the insurer of the accuracy of the information provided by its subsidiary. This argument is unpersuasive and suggests a misunderstanding of the trial court's decision.

It is undisputed that Holdings, as Shell's majority shareholder, owed a duty to Shell's minority shareholders to disclose information, within its knowledge, which might assist the minority shareholders in responding to the proposed merger. Kahn, 591 A.2d at 171. However, Holdings contends that it neither knew nor should have known of the error and, therefore, was under no duty to disclose it. See Van Gorkom, 488 A.2d at 864. In response to Holdings' claim that it had no reason to know of the error in the DCF, the trial court noted that "Holdings had control over [the DCF's] preparation and sent it to the stockholders." Smith, slip op. at 43. Thus, Holdings should have known about the error. Accordingly, Holdings' liability was not premised solely upon its fiduciary duty as a majority shareholder, rather Holdings' liability was based on the substantial role it played in the preparation and distribution of the disclosure materials.

In support of its conclusion that Holdings had control over the preparation and distribution of the disclosure materials, the trial court referred to the deposition testimony of Holdings' lawyer, Steward R. Bross, Jr. ("Bross"), in which he stated that the CIAS was prepared by Shell at Holdings' request. In addition, with Royal Dutch's Chairman L.C. van Wachen presiding as chairman, Shell's board of directors gave Holdings a virtual "blank check" to do whatever Holdings felt necessary in directing Shell's preparation of the disclosure materials.[6] Finally, Holdings organized a series of timetables to coordinate all work related to the disclosure materials. Thus, the record fully supports the trial court's conclusion that Holdings had control over the preparation of the CIAS.

It is only logical that a majority shareholder who directs a subsidiary to prepare certain disclosure materials and then distributes those materials to minority shareholders should be held accountable for any errors contained therein. Based upon the significant role played by Holdings in the preparation and distribution of the disclosure materials,

6. The following resolution was unanimously adopted by Shell's Board of Directors:
RESOLVED, That the proper officers of the Company be, and each of them hereby is, authorized and empowered, if SPNV Holdings, Inc. effects a merger of the Company under Section 253 of the Delaware Corporation Law, i) to take any and all action with respect to persons who were shareholders immediately before the merger, including furnishing notice of the merger, rights of appraisal, the procedures concerning payment for shares, and certain other information and ii) to permit SPNV Holdings, Inc. to perform any part of such action, in the name and on behalf of the Company, as is deemed or considered necessary, appropriate, advisable or prudent....

we find the decision of the Court of Chancery finding Holdings liable for the error in the DCF to be manifestly correct.

IV.

In addition to the billion dollar understatement of Shell's oil and gas reserves, the trial court found two other minor disclosure violations in the 1985 disclosure documents which were "indicative of a conscious decision of [Holdings] to be less than candid." Smith, slip op. at 49. The minor disclosure violations included: 1) the failure to update Shell's 1984 asset evaluations; and 2) the failure to disclose that Morgan Stanley's valuation assumptions differed from Shell's assumptions. Although not the basis for the trial court's decision that Holdings breached its fiduciary duty of disclosure, it appears that the two minor violations were considered when determining damages.

Holdings argues that the Court of Chancery erred in concluding that the failure to update the 1984 asset evaluations or disclose Morgan Stanley's valuation assumptions constituted separate disclosure violations. However, because the trial court's determination that Holdings breached its duty of disclosure is adequately supported by the billion dollar understatement of Shell's oil and gas reserves, we find it is unnecessary to consider Holdings' arguments regarding the minor disclosure violations.

Finally, the finding of the two minor disclosure violations did not alter the trial court's decision that Holdings breached its duty of disclosure. At most, the other disclosure violations were considered by the trial court when ascertaining damages. In determining the appropriate remedy for a disclosure violation, the Court of Chancery has broad discretion. Weinberger, 457 A.2d at 714. We conclude that the trial court's consideration of Holdings' less than candid approach to disclosure was not an abuse of that discretion.

V.

Holdings contends that the Court of Chancery's decision to award interest from the date of the filing of the amended complaint was an abuse of discretion. We disagree.

[The discussion of the court is omitted]

Accordingly, the judgment of the Court of Chancery is AFFIRMED.

Comments, Questions and Problem

1. Are you more convinced by the arguments of the Delaware or the Massachusetts courts?

2. Can you harmonize the Delaware court's decisions in *Nixon* and *Shell Petroleum* excerpted above? Does the difference depend on the public policy constructed by Delaware courts with respect to the importance of disclosure in the regulation of the "shareholder democracy" model of corporate law?

3. In Sinclair Oil Corp. v. Levien, 280 A.2d 717 (Del. 1971), Sinclair Oil Corp. owned about 97% of the stock of Sinclair Venezuelan Oil Company (Sinven). Sinclair Oil nominated all of Sinven's directors and generally dominated the subsidiary. The minority shareholders alleged that the parent caused Sinven to pay out excessive dividends, effectively preventing the development of Sinven. The Delaware Court agreed that the parent corporation owed the subsidiary a fiduciary duty.

> The Chancellor hled that because of Sinclair's fiduciary duty and its control opver Sinven, its relationship with Sinven must meet the test of intrinsic fairness. The standard of intrinsic fairness involves both a high degree of fairness and a shift in the burden of proof. Under this standard the burden is on Sinclair to prove, subject to careful judicial scrutiny, that its transactions with Sinven were objectively fair.
>
> * * *
>
> When the situation involves a parent and a subsidiary, with the parent controlling the transaction and fixing the terms, the test of intrinsic fairness, with its resulting shifting of the burden of proof, is applied.... The basic situation for the application of the rule is the one in which the parent has received a benefit to the exclusion and at the expense of the subsidiary.
>
> * * *
>
> This standard will be applied only when the fiduciary dutyt is accompanied by self-dealing—the situation when a parent is on both sides of a transaction with its subsidiary. Self-dealing occurs when the parent, by virtue of the domination of the subsidiary, causes the subsidiary to act in such a way that the parent receives something from the subsidiary to the exclusion of, and detriment to, the minority stockholders of the subsidiary.
>
> * * *
>
> [Because] Sinclair received nothing from Sinven to the exclusion of its minority shareholders... these dividends were not self-dealing. We hold therefore that the Chancellor erred in applying the intrinsic fairness test as to these dividend payments. The business judgement standard should have been applied.

In Weinberger v. UOP, Inc., 457 A.2d 701 (Del. 1983), the Delaware Court applied a similar standard to a cash out merger of the minority shareholders of a subsidiary. "Given the absence of any attempt to structure this transaction on an arm's length basis, Signal [the parent company] cannot escape the effects of the conflicts it faced, particularly when its designees on UOP's board did not totally abstain from participation in the matter." In a self-dealing situation, such as that in UOP, the court required the parent company to proof the entire fairness of the transaction.

> "The concept of fairness has two basic aspects: fair dealing and fair price. The former embraces questions of when the transaction was timed, how it was initiated, structured, negotiated, disclosed to the directors, and how the approvals of the directors and the stockholders were obtained. The latter aspect of fairness relates to the economic and financial considerations of the proposed merger, including all relevant factors: assets, market value, earnings, future prospects, and any other elements that affect the intrinsic or inherent value of a company's stock.... All aspects of the issue must be examined as a whole since the question is one of entire fairness. However, in a non-fraudulent transaction we recognize that price may be the preponderant consideration....

Although compensation is usually the remedy accorded to minority shareholders, the Delaware courts have on occasion enjoined a transaction. *See* Sealy Mattress Company of New Jersey v. Sealy, Inc., 532 A.2d 1324 (Del.Ch. 1987) (extreme set of circumstances including no informed board decision and no disclosure of material facts to the minority shareholders).

4. **Problem:** You are the lawyer for a person who contemplating investing a sizeable portion of her wealth in a closely held Delaware corporation—Kimba Corp. She understands the limitations of the *Nixon* case. She has been convinced by you that private law, that is an agreement between all shareholders, can be used to essentially import the fiduciary duty rules of Massachusetts into Kimba Corp. She asks that you draft provisions to accomplish this purpose. She also wants you to be prepared to explain to her where such provisions are best placed—shareholder agreement, bylaws or articles of incorporation.

---

2. *Shareholder Duty and Contractual Bargaining*

What happens when the parties contract for certain events? May shareholders be protected against the aggressive use of contractual provisions to avoid the consequences of their contracts? What if these contracts include provisions of shareholder agreements? Or the bylaws? New York courts have dealt with this question. In reading the case that follows, consider whether you agree more with the dissent or the majority opinion.

Phillip B. Ingle, Appellant, v. Glamore Motor Sales, Inc., et al., Respondents. (Action No. 1.); Phillip B. Ingle, Appellant, v. James H. Glamore et al., Respondents. (Action No. 2.)

Court of Appeals of New York
73 N.Y.2d 183; 535 N.E.2d 1311
February 21, 1989

BELLACOSA, J.:

Without a contract for a definite period of employment or some other legally recognized limitation on an employer's unqualified right to discharge an at-will employee who also happens to be a minority shareholder in a close corporation, there is no insulation under the contractual and employment relationships alleged in this case from being fired or from having invoked a stock-repurchase option.

In 1964, plaintiff-appellant Ingle sought to purchase an equity interest in respondent Glamore Motor Sales, Inc. from its then sole shareholder, respondent James Glamore. Ingle was not sold an interest in the corporation initially, but he was hired as sales manager. There was no express agreement between the parties establishing either the duration or conditions of employment.

In 1966, Glamore and Ingle entered into a written shareholders' agreement which provided that Ingle would purchase 22 of Glamore's 100 shares in the corporation, that Ingle would have a five-year option to purchase an additional 18 shares, and that Glamore would nominate and vote Ingle as a director and secretary of the corporation. The agreement also gave Glamore the right to repurchase all of Ingle's stock if "Ingle shall cease to be an employee of the Corporation for *any reason*" (emphasis added). Ingle later purchased the 18 additional shares and the parties executed a new shareholders' agreement, which updated some facets and eliminated outdated ones. The repurchase provision of the 1973 agreement tracked identically the 1966 version.

On January 1, 1982, the corporation issued 60 additional shares of stock. Glamore purchased 22 shares of the new issue and his two sons (respondents William and Robert Glamore) each purchased 19 shares. The three Glamores and Ingle, the only four shareholders, entered into a third agreement reflecting the corporate relationship. The repurchase provision pertinent to this litigation is: "(b) *Termination of employment.* In the event that any Stockholder shall *cease to be an employee of the Corporation for any reason*, Glamore shall have the option, for a period of 30 days after such termination of employment, to purchase all of the shares of stock then owned by such Stockholder" (emphasis supplied).

At a special meeting of the board of directors held on May 9, 1983, Ingle was voted out of his corporate posts and fired from his employment as operating manager of the business. The termination was effective May 31, 1983. On June 1, Glamore notified Ingle that he was exercising the repurchase-upon-termination-of-employment option and in due course paid Ingle $ 96,000 for his 40 shares in the corporation.

Plaintiff argues that as a minority shareholder of a closely held corporation, employed without the benefit of a contract containing a durational employment protection and without any limitation on the employer's right to discharge, he is nevertheless entitled by reason of his minority shareholder status to a fiduciary-rooted protection against being fired. His theory is that his employment status should not be governed by the employment at-will doctrine but, rather, that as a minority shareholder in a close corporation he should be treated as a co-owner, equivalent to a partner, whose employment rights flow from a special duty of loyalty and good faith. He next urges that an implicit covenant of good faith and fair dealing under the shareholders' agreement precluded his termination without cause, despite the express language and nature of the agreement in that regard. He concludes that even if he is an at-will employee, an action properly lies for the respondents' breach of fiduciary duties and for wrongful interference with his employment. Ingle started two separate actions seeking damages via seven causes of action alleging breach of fiduciary duty and of contract. Eventually all causes of action were dismissed—we believe correctly.

A minority shareholder in a close corporation, by that status alone, who contractually agrees to the repurchase of his shares upon termination of his employment for any reason, acquires no right from the corporation or majority shareholders against at-will discharge. There is nothing in law, in the agreement, or in the relationship of the parties to warrant such a contradictory and judicial alteration of the employment relationship or the express agreement. It is necessary in this case to appreciate and keep distinct the duty a corporation owes to a minority shareholder *as a shareholder* from any duty it might owe him as an employee.

Both lower courts agree, as do we, that Ingle did not sufficiently present facts raising a triable issue regarding the existence of either an oral or written employment contract fixing employment of a definite duration.... Under the established common-law rule—and without any reference to the shareholders' agreement—the corporation had the right to discharge plaintiff at will....

The twist in this fact pattern is an asserted liability based on allegations that the corporate officers breached fiduciary duties of good faith and fair dealing arising from the shareholders' agreement and on tortious interference with Ingle's employment. The twist does not support a deviation from the governing principle in this case.

In Murphy v American Home Prods. Corp. (58 NY2d 293, supra), we concluded that there is no implied obligation of good faith and fair dealing in an employment at will, as that would be incongruous to the legally recognized jural relationship in that kind of employment relationship (id., at 304–305; see, Sabetay v Sterling Drug, 69 NY2d 329, 335–336, supra). In holding that there is no cause of action in tort for abusive or wrongful discharge of an at-will employee, we declined to allow the use of substitute nomenclature or causes, such as a prima facie tort or intentional infliction of emotional distress, to bootstrap the threshold deficiency in a wrongful discharge claim (Murphy v American Home Prods. Corp., supra, at 303–304; see, James v Board of Educ., 37 NY2d 891, 892). Similarly, the plaintiff here cannot be allowed to evade the employment at-will rule and relationship by recasting his cause of action in the garb of a tortious interference with his employment *(see, Inselman* & Co. v FNB Fin. Co., 41 NY2d 1078, 1080).

Plaintiff confuses and tries to avoid the sequential relationship of his employment status to his shareholders' agreement by extracting an obligation from the agreement to manufacture a legally unrecognized employment security. Divestiture of his status as a shareholder, by operation of the repurchase provision, is a contractually agreed to consequence flowing directly from the firing, not vice versa. The dissent similarly confuses and inverts the Appellate Division's and our holding (dissenting opn, at 195).

As noted, Ingle argued that the corporation discharged him because James Glamore would then have a right to repurchase his shares under the terms of the shareholders' agreement. Notably, however, Ingle never asserted that the $ 2,400 per share paid to him upon termination was not fairly representative of his equity interest in the corporation. He does not contend that the corporation undervalued his shares, and he accepted payment from Glamore without reservation. Indeed, that, too, was fixed by the parties' buy-out agreement. We have no occasion to address issues involved in cases where the minority shareholders may be discharged solely to avoid assertion of the legal rights afforded to them under Business Corporation Law §§ 1104-a and 1118 and our decision in Matter of Pace Photographers (Rosen) (71 NY2d 737), because no such matter has been pleaded and that is not this case.

Ingle's and the dissent's reliance on *Fender v Prescott* (101 AD2d 418, 422, expressly affirmed on grounds other than the corporate relationship discussion 64 NY2d 1077, 1078–1079) for an exception based on the close corporate form in which this employer and employee find themselves is unavailing. No duty of loyalty and good faith akin to that between partners, precluding termination except for cause, arises among those operating a business in the corporate form who "have only the rights, duties and obligations of stockholders" and not those of partners *(see, Weisman v Awnair Corp., 3 NY2d 444, 449–450).*

Finally, the dissent essentially invokes an equity appeal. While we have no quarrel whatsoever with that magnificent juridical jewel applied in its proper setting, this lawsuit does not qualify. Here, fair principles of well-settled law, affecting employment and contractual relationships between private parties, govern and are entitled to respect and efficacy from this court. We cannot merely substitute our preferred notions for those of the parties themselves in such matters.

The pleading here does not support the conclusion that respondents breached a fiduciary duty as corporate officers by dismissing an at-will employee and exercising an agreed-upon repurchase-upon-termination clause (see, Bevilacque v Ford Motor Co., 125 AD2d 516, 519–520). "[There] is no reason why an appeal to general fiduciary law should be used *** as a pretext for evading *** contractual obligations" (*see*, Coleman v Taub, 638 F2d 628, 636; Jenkins v Haworth, Inc., 572 F Supp 591, 601).

If there was no protection against discharge of an at-will employee in *Murphy (supra)* and *Sabetay (supra)*, where there was no contractual arrangement at all, there surely can be none here where the related contract expressly confirms the unavailability of that protection. Moreover, to hold otherwise on the facts and pleadings of this case would confuse our recent holdings in an area of the law where certainty, predictability and reliability are highly prized common-law goals.

We have carefully and thoroughly considered all of appellant's arguments and additionally conclude that his remaining arguments are also unavailing.

Accordingly, the order of the Appellate Division should be affirmed, with costs.

DISSENT:

Hancock, Jr., J. (dissenting). This appeal presents a clear-cut legal question: whether plaintiff's status as an officer, director, substantial part owner and active participant in the affairs and management of Glamore Motor Sales, a close corporation, gives him equitable rights and remedies which are not subject to the ordinary legal rules of master and servant? The majority answers "no" and writes off the case as a routine application of New York's employment at-will rule. Because this produces a result which is egregiously unfair and one which, I am convinced, is not warranted under existing case law, I respectfully dissent.

By treating the essence of plaintiff's complaints as a claimed breach of a hiring contract by the employer rather than an unfair squeeze-out of a minority shareholder in a close corporation by the majority, the court simply concludes that plaintiff has no rights at all. It does so by applying the rule of Martin v New York Life Ins. Co. (148 NY 117), "that where an employment is for an indefinite term it is presumed to be a hiring at will which may be freely terminated by either party at any time for any reason *or even for no reason* [emphasis added]" (Murphy v American Home Prods. Corp., 58 NY2d 293, 300; see, Sabetay v Sterling Drug, 69 NY2d 329, 333; Weiner v McGraw-Hill, Inc., 57 NY2d 458). These cases, in my view, are totally inapposite. But in reliance on Martin, Weiner, Murphy and Sabetay, plaintiff's complaints are dismissed in their entirety, without a trial, on motions for summary judgment and dismissal (CPLR 3212, 3211 [a] [7]).

* * *

II

New York, like many other States, unquestionably recognizes that the status of a minority shareholder in a close corporation requires special protection from the courts. Indeed, in Matter of Kemp & Beatley (Gardstein) (64 NY2d 63, 71), Chief Judge Cooke, speaking for a unanimous court stated: "'Unlike the typical shareholder in a publicly held corporation, who may be simply an investor or a speculator and cares nothing for the responsibilities of management, the shareholder in a close corporation is a co-owner of the business and wants the privileges and powers that go with ownership. His participation in that particular corporation is often his principal or sole source of income. As a matter of fact, providing employment for himself may have been the principal reason why he participated in organizing the corporation. He may or may not anticipate an ultimate profit from the sale of his interest, but he normally draws very little from the corporation as dividends. In his capacity as an officer or employee of the corporation, he looks to his salary for the principal return on his capital investment, because earnings of a close corporation, as is well known, are distributed in major part in salaries, bonuses and retirement benefits' (O'Neal, Close Corporations [2d ed], § 1.07)"....

Thus, for purposes of asserting rights as a minority shareholder under Business Corporation Law § 1104-a, we have held that a shareholder "who reasonably expected that ownership in the corporation would entitle him or her to a job, a share of corporate earnings, a place in corporate management, or some other form of security, would be oppressed in a very real sense when others in the corporation seek to defeat those expectations and there exists no effective means of salvaging the investment" (Matter of Kemp & Beatley [Gardstein], supra, at 72–73).

The singular vulnerability of the minority in a close corporation has prompted courts of equity to impose fiduciary obligations on the majority shareholders in their dealings with the minority and to require "a high degree of fidelity and good faith" *(Fender v Prescott, supra, at 422)*. This same need for protection from the majority is reflected in the "solicitude toward the rights of minority shareholders" *(Matter of Kemp & Beatley [Gardstein], supra, at 70)* shown by our Legislature in enacting Business Corporation Law §§ 1104-a, 1118 *(see, Matter of Pace Photographers [Rosen], 71 NY2d 737, 744–745, supra)* and by Legislatures in other jurisdictions in enacting similar statutes.... The need for special protection of a minority shareholder could not be better illustrated than in the case at bar.

A person who, like plaintiff, buys a minority interest in a close corporation does so not only in the hope of enjoying an increase in value of his stake in the business but for the assurance of employment in the business in a managerial position. In addition to the security of long-term employment and the prospect of financial return in the form of salary, his expectancy includes a voice in the management and operation of the business and in the formulation of its plans for future development and growth *(see, e.g.,* Matter of Kemp & Beatley [Gardstein], supra, at 71–72). The anticipated rewards for his efforts differ markedly from those of the typical salaried corporate employee in a large company...and encompass much more than the promised salary or other immediate remuneration: e.g., the prospect of participating in the growth and the increased value of the business, and the challenge, the independence, the prestige, the feeling of achievement, and the other intangible benefits of being part of the management of a successfully run small company....

Not surprisingly, the losses which a minority shareholder in a close corporation may suffer in a squeeze-out by the majority have been characterized as "catastrophic" (1 O'Neal & Thompson, Oppression of Minority Shareholders § 1:03). It is because of the difficulty in valuing these expectancies and the inadequacy of an action at law for damages as a remedy for their loss and the fact that the majority may inflict such losses on a minority shareholder through the sheer exercise of voting power, that resort to equitable remedies is necessary.... Thus, the relationship of a minority shareholder to a close corporation, if fairly viewed, cannot possibly be equated with an ordinary hiring and, in the absence of a contract, regarded as nothing more than an employment at will. But this is exactly how the majority of the court has treated plaintiff's association with Glamore Motor Sales. And it has done so by not addressing the multiple relationships and the expectancies and vulnerabilities peculiar to the status of a minority shareholder in plaintiff's position—those very considerations which call for the relief that only a court of equity can give. By simply considering the case as one at law for breach of contract, the majority makes defendants impervious to suit by placing them under the protective mantel of the Sabetay, Murphy, Weiner and Martin rule. This result, I submit, is not only unfair but amounts to an extension of the employment at-will doctrine over a situation which, I believe, it was never intended to cover.

III

Assuming for the moment that the case could properly be viewed merely as one at law for breach of a hiring contract, the application of the employment at-will rule in this context would still be particularly inappropriate and unfair. Nor is such application supported by our precedents.

There can be little question that the basis for the traditional employment at-will rule is in the contractual principle of mutuality of obligation, "that if the employee can quit his job at will, then so, too, must the employer have the right to terminate the relationship for any reason or no reason" (Blades, Employment At Will vs. Individual Freedom on Limiting the Abusive Exercise of Employer Power, 67 Colum L Rev 1404, 1419; Minda, The Common Law of Employment At-Will in New York: The Paralysis of Nineteenth Century Doctrine, 36 Syracuse L Rev 939, 975–978). Indeed, the Supreme Court, in Adair v United States (208 U.S. 161), stated the general rule thus: "the right of the employee to quit the service of the employer, for whatever reason, is the same as the right of the employer, for whatever reason, to dispense with the services of such employee" (208 U.S., *supra*, at 174–175).[4]

To be sure, this court in recent years has shied away from the "mutuality" doctrine in favor of the doctrine of contractual consideration as the basis (*see,* Weiner v McGraw-Hill, Inc., supra, at 463–464) for its "sharply scrutinized" employment at-will rule (*see,* Sabetay v Sterling Drug, 69 NY2d 329, 333, supra; Murphy v American Home Prods. Corp., supra, at 308–309, and n 4 [Meyer, J., dissenting in part]). Nevertheless, in adhering to the principle that "the law accords the employer an unfettered right to terminate the employment at any time" (*see,* Murphy v American Home Prods. Corp., supra, at 304), rejecting the tort of abusive discharge (id., at 300–301), and declining to read into an indefinite employment contract an implied obligation of fair dealing (id., at 304, 305), the decisions have done so in recognition of the continued vitality of "the freedom of contract underpinnings of the [employment at-will] rule" (id., at 301). And it has been observed that any modification of the rule should be left to the Legislature, because "stability and predictability in contractual affairs is a highly desirable jurisprudential value" (Sabetay v Sterling Drug, supra, at 336). Thus—despite recent pronouncements *(see, e.g.,* Weiner v McGraw-Hill, Inc., supra, at 463)—there clearly remains at the core of the employment at-will rule at least a hard residue of the mutuality notion—the idea, simply, that if the employee can quit at any time for any reason he can be discharged at any time for any reason.

But whether it be lack of mutuality or lack of consideration, the rationale for the employment at-will rule does not fit the situation of the typical minority shareholder-participant in a close corporation. For such participant is *not truly free* to quit at any time; and *there is consideration* which would support an implied understanding that, at least,

4. In Adair v United States (208 U.S. 161), a Lochner-era decision (see, Lochner v New York, 198 U.S. 45), the Supreme Court struck down a statute making it a Federal offense to fire a worker because of his union membership upon the ground that the statute interfered with the employer's constitutional substantive due process and contractual rights to discharge an at-will employee at any time for any reason. Professor Blades cites *Adair,* the first case in which the Supreme Court addressed the employment at-will rule, as illustrative of the traditional basis for the rule in the common law of contracts *(see,* Blades, Employment At Will vs. Individual Freedom on Limiting the Abusive Exercise of Employer Power, 67 Colum L Rev 1404, 1416–1417, 1419–1421). Commenting on the freedom of contract underpinnings of the employment at-will rule, Justice Holmes, in dissent, stated: "I confess that I think that the right to make contracts at will that has been derived from the word liberty in the amendments has been stretched to its extreme by the decisions; but they agree that sometimes the right may be restrained" (208 U.S., at 191).

the majority owner will not discharge him arbitrarily or in bad faith and without some legitimate business reason. Unlike the employee of a large corporation, the minority shareholder in a close corporation has typically invested a large percentage of his financial wherewithal in the business. He has been willing to do so because of what he expects will be his long-term association with the business and his ability to protect his investment and, he hopes, to make it grow. The same features of the minority owner-participant's status which make him particularly vulnerable to action by the majority obviously work to compel him to stay on the job. He needs to do so to protect his investment and to share in any increase in its value.

In short, there are strong financial and other pressures operating to prevent a minority shareholder from deciding to leave voluntarily. To treat plaintiff's position in Glamore Motor Sales as though it entailed the same freedom to leave as that of the large company mid-level employees in Murphy, Weiner and Sabetay is to ignore the substantially different factors in plaintiff's situation which curtailed his freedom to leave and which, as a practical matter, bound him to the job. Thus, application of the employment at-will rule in this case would, I submit, be clearly inconsistent with its "freedom of contract underpinnings" (Murphy v American Home Prods. Corp., supra, at 301), whether those "underpinnings" are lack of mutual promises or want of consideration.

IV

In concluding that plaintiff has no basis for a claim against the individual defendants for interference with plaintiff's employment by unlawfully inducing the corporation to discharge him, the majority reasons that to allow him to recast his claim "in the garb of a tortious interference" would permit him to "evade the employment at-will rule and relationship" (majority opn, at 189). This court has long held, however, that a cause of action for tortious interference with contract may exist even where the underlying contract is terminable at will (*see,* Guard-Life Corp. v Parker Hardware Mfg. Corp., 50 NY2d 183, supra; A. S. Rampell, Inc. v Hyster Co., 3 NY2d 369, supra). Although interference with a terminable at-will contract, like interference with a prospective contract, requires proof that wrongful means were used (*see,* Guard-Life Corp. v Parker Hardware Mfg. Corp., supra, at 190–191), such wrongful means include "violation of a duty of fidelity owed to the plaintiff by the defendant" (*id.*, at *194,* citing A. S. Rampell, Inc. v Hyster Co., supra; and Duane Jones Co. v Burke, 306 NY 172. . . .). Here it is alleged that the individual defendants, as majority shareholders, acted in violation of their fiduciary duty to plaintiff as a minority shareholder. Thus, even if it is assumed that plaintiff's relationship with Glamore Motor Sales amounted to no more than a legal hiring at will, his causes of action against the individual defendants for inducing his discharge willfully and in bad faith for the purpose of triggering the buy-back provision should not have been dismissed.

In sum, I believe that plaintiff has valid claims arising out of his discharge in bad faith by the controlling shareholders in violation of their fiduciary duty owed to him as a minority shareholder in a close corporation. Also, plaintiff has valid claims against the individual defendants for wrongfully inducing the corporation to terminate his employment. The record demonstrates clearly that there are factual issues requiring that plaintiff be given the opportunity to prove these claims at trial. The order should, therefore, be reversed, the motions denied, and plaintiff's complaints reinstated.

B. Statutory Approaches in the United States

Many states have adopted statutes to regulate the relations between shareholders of closely held corporations. The effect of those statutes is to create a statutory fiduciary obligation among shareholders of closely held corporations to each other. The statutes, of course, while settling the significant question of whether such obligations exist between shareholders leave unanswered a host of questions pertaining to the contours and limits of the obligations created by statute. The case which follows, Exadaktilos v. Cinnaminson Realty Co. 400 A.2d 554, 561–62 (N.J. Super. 1979), aff'd, 414 A.2d 994 (N.J. 1980), provides an example of the problems and possibilities offered by these statutes. As you read the case, consider form of standard created by the court with respect to a plaintiff's reasonable expectations.

Leonidas Exadaktilos, Plaintiff, v. Cinnaminson Realty Co., Inc. A/K/A Hathaway's Lodge, Inc., A New Jersey Corporation, and Others

Superior Court of New Jersey, Law Division, Burlington County
167 N.J. Super. 141; 400 A.2d 554
March 2, 1979, Decided

Haines, J.:

The "oppressed shareholder" is a litigant newly created by Legislative amendment to the New Jersey Corporation Act. See N.J.S.A. 14A:12-7. Plaintiff Leonidas Exadaktolis, claims to be one. He alleges that he purchased a 20% interest in defendant corporation, which owns and operates a restaurant. The corporation has three other stockholders, the respective owners of 20%, 20% and 40% of its stock. George Skordas holds the 40% interest. That a stock certificate representing 20% of the corporation's outstanding shares was issued to plaintiff at a cost of $ 20,000 is undisputed, but defendants allege that the stock was actually paid for by defendant Skordas, plaintiff's father-in-law. As a consequence, it is said that the stock is subject to a resulting trust. Since plaintiff seeks to qualify for the relief afforded "oppressed" shareholders, resolution of the dispute concerning ownership necessarily precedes an evaluation of the merits of this claim.

Plaintiff traced the money he used to purchase the stock to several sources. Five thousand dollars, saved from wages earned by working on ships, accompanied plaintiff when he entered this country. Upon marrying Skordas' daughter in 1969, cash wedding gifts in the amount of $ 3,800 were received and set aside. During that same year he saved $ 100 a week from his wages, a total of $ 5,200. In 1970 his income increased and he was able to save $ 7,800 from his wages. In 1969 and 1970 he sold a truck for $ 1,200, saving all the proceeds as well as $ 1,800 awarded to his wife because of her involvement in an accident. Plaintiff testified that after 1970 he was unable to save money because his wife had a child and stopped working. All of these monies reportedly were kept in a box in plaintiff's closet because he did not trust banks. His savings totalled $ 24,000, more than enough to enable him to advance the $ 20,000 necessary to purchase the stock.

On cross-examination plaintiff's income tax returns were introduced into evidence. The 1969 return reflected an income for both him and his wife of $ 8,695, with $ 5,620.90 representing his wife's earnings. A saving of $ 5,200 in that year would have left only $ 3,495.10 available for living expenses. The only wages listed for plaintiff was the year's total of $ 286 paid by a painter for whom plaintiff had worked. This return contradicted plaintiff's testimony that he had earned $ 120 to $ 135 a week as a painter, plus $ 45 to $ 60 a week by working in a diner during that year. The 1970 return showed total earnings of $ 8,619.31 of which his wife accounted for $ 6,210.47. Had plaintiff saved $ 7,800 that year, the family would have had $ 819.31 left for living expenses. Plaintiff said that he made over $ 180 a week as a partner with his brother in a painting business during that year. The partnership information return showed only $ 1,480 paid to him. Plaintiff did not produce any records to support his claim of receiving over $ 180 a week. Nor did his brother, who testified as to other matters, verify this statement. Finally, no income tax return disclosed the sale of a truck for $ 1,200. Plaintiff explained these discrepancies by claiming that the tax returns were "wrong," that he depended on his wife to prepare them or have them prepared, and that he was not aware that he had to report all of his income for federal tax purposes.

Plaintiff admitted he had not declared his possession of $ 5,000 when he entered this country. The $ 1,800 saved from his wife's accident was reflected in a check to her actually totalling $ 1,942.47. The check was dated March 16, 1973. The $ 20,000 in cash advanced for the stock was paid prior to December 1972; the accident monies could not have been available to plaintiff at that time.

Plaintiff justified the risky arrangement of keeping money in a closet on the ground that he did not trust banks. It developed, however, that he had several bank accounts. Although he claimed that the accounts were used merely to establish credit, they also were used to accumulate savings.

On cross-examination plaintiff said the monies saved in the closet amounted to exactly $ 20,000. On redirect he amended this testimony and said the amount may have varied either way by about $ 200. Each of these statements stand in contradiction to his testimony on direct examination.

Skordas, on the other hand, had substantial monies and was plaintiff's father-in-law at the time of the stock transaction. No testimony indicated any rift between them at the time the stock was purchased. The opportunity to make an investment in the restaurant was provided to plaintiff by Skordas. He defended his son-in-law from criticism by other principals of the corporation. After the restaurant had been purchased, improvements were made, the cost being borne in part by the corporation's principals and in part with borrowed money. Skordas loaned his son-in-law $ 20,000 to cover his share of the improvements, taking an unsecured promissory note as payment for the loan. These facts demonstrate that Skordas was interested in plaintiff's welfare and generous in making money available on an informal basis.

The only person present at the time plaintiff supposedly gave the $ 20,000 in cash to his father-in-law, according to plaintiff's testimony, was his wife. She was not produced as a witness to this transaction or to any other relevant fact, although she was available since she was, in fact, in the courtroom during most of the trial. Apparently, she was not deposed. These circumstances may be explained by the fact that plaintiff and his wife were then involved in divorce proceedings so that she may have been a hostile witness, but this was not shown. It was revealed in the course of the trial that she had certain relevant records, not subpoenaed by plaintiff, which may not have been privileged. See *Evid. R.* 28. These matters damage plaintiff's credibility. Skordas' credibility is also tarnished; he, too, failed to produce his daughter as a witness.

Plaintiff's testimony is so riddled with contradictions and qualifications as to lead to the conclusions that he is not a credible witness, that he did not have $ 20,000, and that he did not pay for the stock. Consequently, it must be Skordas alone who advanced money from his adequate funds to purchase the stock. These findings, however, do not carry the day for defendants. Legal title to the stock resides in plaintiff and his claim of "oppression" must be considered unless the stock is subject to a resulting trust that vests beneficial ownership thereof in Skordas.

It is a general rule that "a resulting trust will be declared in favor of the one paying the purchase price of property transferred to another unless it is shown that the one paying the price manifested an intention that no resulting trust should arise." *Weisberg v. Koprowski, 17 N.J. 362, 371 (1955).* This rule raises only a rebuttable presumption, however, designed to provide guidance to the court in determining true intent. Fowler v. Scott, 8 N.J. Super. 490 (Ch. Div. 1950); Turro v. Turro, 38 N.J. Super. 535 (App. Div. 1956). A contrary presumption, namely, that a gift or advancement was intended and not a resulting trust, arises when certain relationships, such as blood or marriage, exist between the payor and the transferee. [T]he application of the rule inferring a gift to a transferee related to the payor is not to be determined on considerations of the closeness of the relationship or the extent of natural affection, nor by reason of any legal obligation to furnish support *** [it is] the preference of modern decisions for a determination based upon whether the grantee is a natural object of bounty of the payor, that is, *** whether he stands in such a relationship "that it is probable that the payor intends to make a gift to the transferee" * * *. [Weisberg v. Koprowski, supra at 372–373]

See Turro v. Turro and Fowler v. Scott, supra. The presumption of a gift, when such a relationship is present, supersedes the presumption of a resulting trust and casts the burden of proof upon the party attempting to establish the trust. Turro v. Turro, supra. Plaintiff was married to Skordas' daughter and had fathered his grandchild at the time the monies were advanced. This relationship made plaintiff the natural object of Skordas' bounty, raising a presumption that the monies used to purchase the stock were given or advanced to plaintiff. See Restatement, Trusts 2d, Comment to §442. The burden of overcoming this presumption was upon Skordas. *Id.*, §443.

Skordas' testimony was not helpful to his cause. At best, it provided limited support for a claim, not made by Skordas in this suit and later rejected in this opinion, that he loaned the money to plaintiff. He testified that he agreed to "put up" the money to enable plaintiff to go into the restaurant business with him when plaintiff said he had no funds. On cross-examination, he said that he had told plaintiff the $ 20,000 could be paid back later, but denied any discussion concerning the ownership of the stock. This testimony is contrary to his deposition in which he said the stock was to be turned over to plaintiff only if he learned the business and paid his father-in-law back the monies advanced. A revealing parallel circumstance involves a loan by Skordas to Peter Marlas, another principal in the corporation, not related to Skordas. When Skordas was deposed, he testified that the loan to Marlas was made upon the understanding that the latter's shares belonged to Skordas until the loan was repaid. At trial, however, he said that Marlas' shares were not subject to any reservation of title. This evidence not only affects Skordas' credibility, but also makes it seem unlikely that he would have intended to hold title to his son-in-law's stock when he did not do so with someone who was not related to him. William Malanos, another principal of the corporation, testified that he did not know of any arrangement under which Skordas was to have the beneficial interest in the shares issued to plaintiff, although Skordas had told him about a "loan" to Exadaktolis.

After the stock certificate was delivered to plaintiff, he became comaker of a corporate note given to a bank to secure a loan of $ 220,000, as to which he also signed a personal guarantee. The assumption of that liability by one who had no interest in the corporation is most unlikely. There is a similar inconsistency in Skordas' loan of $ 20,000 to plaintiff for his contribution to corporate improvements and the assertion by Skordas that he did not intend plaintiff to obtain a beneficial interest in the stock. No evidence indicates any action or statement by Skordas evincing any interest in the stock until this suit was commenced. It is an inescapable conclusion that no resulting trust arose with respect to plaintiff's stock. In fact,. Skordas' own testimony denies any intention on his part to have his son-in-law hold the stock in his name for Skordas' benefit.

Nor does Skordas' testimony, or any other evidence, provide adequate proof that the $ 20,000 was loaned to his son-in-law. When he advanced these monies he took no note or other evidence of indebtedness from plaintiff and required no security; he has never received any interest on the money and has made no claim for repayment in his pleadings or otherwise. The only testimony concerning a possible loan is Skordas' statement on cross-examination that he told plaintiff the money could be paid back later. He said nothing about this in his direct testimony. Although Malanos said he had been told by Skordas that the money was loaned, that testimony is admissible as a declaration against interest regarding Skordas' trust claim but is inadmissible hearsay on the loan question. I conclude that the evidence was entirely inadequate to support the claim that the $ 20,000 was loaned to plaintiff. The presumption of gift has not been overcome.[1]

It follows from this analysis that plaintiff must be treated as the owner of a 20% interest in defendant corporation. Consequently, the merits of his oppression claim require consideration. N.J.S.A. 14A:12-7(1)(c) provides as follows:

> 1. The Superior Court, in an action brought under this section, may appoint a custodian, appoint a provisional director, order a sale of the corporation's stock as provided below, or enter a judgment dissolving the corporation, upon proof that
>
> * * * (c) In the case of a corporation having 25 or less shareholders, the directors or those in control have acted fraudulently or illegally, mismanaged the corporation, or abused their authority as officers or directors or have acted oppressively or unfairly toward one or more minority shareholders in their capacities as shareholders, directors, officers, or employees.

No New Jersey decision has interpreted this statutory provision. Many other jurisdictions have enacted provisions similar to that which took effect in New Jersey in 1974. See Note, "Oppression of Minority Shareholders: A Proposed Model and Suggested Remedies," 44 Miss. L.J. 476, n. 1 (1976). Nonetheless, relatively few cases have discussed the concept of "oppression."

---

1. This conclusion may well be immaterial. Any future suit brought to collect the $ 20,000 probably would be barred by the single controversy doctrine. *The Malaker Corporation v. First Jersey Nat'l Bk., 163 N.J. Super. 463, 496 (App. Div. 1978).*

In Illinois, the first American jurisdiction to adopt this type of provision, *id. at 476*, the courts have proceeded more by saying what oppression is not than what it is: We have held that the word "oppressive" as used in this statute, does not carry an essential inference of imminent disaster; it can contemplate a continuing course of conduct. The word does not necessarily savor of fraud, and the absence of "mismanagement, or misapplication of assets," does not prevent a finding that the conduct of the dominant directors or officers has been oppressive. It is not synonymous with "illegal" and "fraudulent." [Gidwitz v. Lanzit Corrugated Box Co., 20 Ill. 2d 208, 170 N.E. 2d 131, 135 (Sup. Ct. 1960)] See Central Standard Life Insurance Company v. Davis, 10 Ill. 2d 566, 141 N.E. 2d 45, 50 (Sup. Ct. 1957). The Illinois courts have also expressed a concern that corporate formalities be obeyed, see Gidwitz v. Lanzit Corrugated Box Co., supra, and an Illinois appellate court has held that corporate decisions within the "business judgment rule" cannot be made the basis of an oppression claim, see Polikoff v. Dole & Clark Building Corp., 37 Ill. App. 2d 29, 184 N.E. 2d 792, 795–96 (App. Ct. 1962). The business judgment rule instructs that a decision made by a board of directors pertaining to the manner in which corporate affairs are to be conducted should not be tampered with by the judiciary so long as the decision is one within the power delegated to the directors and there is no showing of bad faith. See Sarner v. Sarner, 62 N.J. Super. 41, 60 (App. Div. 1960), rev'd and rem. on other grounds, 38 N.J. 463 (1962); Edison v. Edison United Phonograph Co., 52 N.J. Eq. 620, 626–27 (Ch. 1894). The possibility raised in Gray v. Hall, 10 Ill. App. 3d 1030, 295 N.E. 2d 506, 509 (App. Ct. 1973), however, that corporate salary and dividend policy might constitute oppressive behavior under certain circumstances, casts considerable doubt on the continued validity of this business judgment exclusion in Illinois.

The Supreme Court of Virginia has adopted the Illinois reasoning and in addition has quoted with approval language from English cases interpreting the term "oppression" in a similar enactment. In this context it has been held that oppressive means "*** a visible departure from the standards of fair dealing, and a violation of fair play on which every shareholder who entrusts his money to a company is entitled to rely." Elder v. Elder & Watson, Ltd. (1952) Sess. Cas. 49, 55. It has also been held to mean "*** a lack of probity and fair dealing in the affairs of a company to the prejudice of some of its members." Scottish Co-op. Wholesale Society, Ltd. v. Meyer (1958), 3 All. E.R. 66, 86 (H.L.). [White v. Perkins, 213 Va. 129, 189 S.E. 2d 315, 319–320 (Sup. Ct. 1972)]

The Supreme Court of Oregon also turned to the English cases for guidance in Baker v. Commercial Body Builders, Inc., 264 Or. 614, 507 P. 2d 387, 393 (Sup. Ct. 1973). While the terminology employed by both the statute and case law certainly provides the court with the latitude necessary to deal with all the circumstances peculiar to any case brought to its attention, it fails to suggest any perspective from which to judge what is oppressive or unfair. Such perspective can be attained through a reading of the statute as a whole and of comments pertaining to it and similar enactments.

The oppression remedy is available only to individuals participating in corporations with less than 25 shareholders. The Commissioners' Comment appended to *N.J.S.A. 14A:12-7* indicates that this limitation was imposed to preclude strike suits against large corporations. Additionally, in most instances the market place provides a remedy for those shareholders who feel that they are being oppressed by a large corporation, *i.e.*, they can sell their stock. That remedy is not readily available to minority shareholders in close corporations. The statute was designed therefore to solve a problem peculiar to them.

That problem arises in "shareholder 'freeze out' situations", see Final Report of the Corporate Law Revision Commission 12, *N.J.S.A.* 14A (cum. supp. 1978), defined by one commentator as meaning *** a manipulative use of corporate control or inside information to eliminate minority shareholders from the enterprise, or to reduce to relative insignificance their voting power or claims on corporate earnings and assets or otherwise to deprive them of corporate income or advantages to which they are entitled. [2 O'Neal, Close Corporations (2d ed. 1971), § 8.07 at 43]

A host of techniques can be employed to freeze out minority shareholders. See O'Neal, Oppression of Minority Shareholders, cc. 2–6 (1975). The Commissioners' Comment to this section points to removal of minority shareholders from corporate offices and substantial diminution of their power or compensation as examples of freeze-out techniques. In determining whether oppression is present, the statute expressly authorizes an examination of corporate conduct toward a minority shareholder in the role of shareholder, director, officer or employee. In this regard New Jersey is almost unique because most oppression provisions limit the examination to the effect of corporate conduct on a minority shareholder in his guise of shareholder and no more. See *Id.* at 484 and n. 42.

The focus and scope of this inquiry recognizes that the different circumstances impelling the formation of large as opposed to close corporations lead their shareholders to harbor different expectations. Large corporations are usually formed as a means of attracting capital through the sale of stock to investors, with no expectation of participation in corporate management or employment. Profit is expected through the payment of dividends or sale of stock at an appreciated value. See Tinney, "Oppressive Conduct by Majority Shareholders, Directors, or Those in Control of Corporation," 5 Proof of Fact, 2d 645, 652 (1975). Close corporations, in contrast, are frequently formed by individuals most aptly described as partners. See Note, "Relief to Oppressed Minorities in Close Corporations: Partnership Precepts and Related Considerations," *1974 Ariz. St. L.J. 409, 411–413.* These persons desire the tax benefits, the insulation from personal liability and the perpetual life that flows from the corporate form. See Cary, Corporations, 20–21, 362–63 (1969). The amassing of capital through the sale of stock to investors is at best of secondary importance. The personal relationship between shareholders which is more or less peculiar to and usually antedates the formation of close corporations, see O'Neal & Magill, "California's New Close Corporation Legislation," 23 U.C.L.A. L. Rev. 1155, 1166–1169 (1976), makes it impossible to hypothesize a set of expectations that will be held in common by all minority shareholders in these corporations. Unlike their counterparts in large corporations, they may expect to participate in management or to influence operations, directly or indirectly, formally or informally. See Tinney, "Oppressive Conduct by Majority Shareholders, Directors, or Those in Control of Corporation," *supra*. Furthermore, there generally is an expectation on the part of some participants that their interest is to be recognized in the form of a salary derived from employment with the corporation. See Note, "Relief to Oppressed Minorities in Close Corporations: Partnership Precepts and Related Considerations," *supra* at 412.

Thus, the statutory language embodies a legislative determination that freeze-out maneuvers in close corporations constitute an abuse of corporate power. Traditional principles of corporate law, such as the business judgment rule, have failed to curb this abuse. Consequently, actions of close corporations that conform with these principles cannot be immune from scrutiny. To implement the intent of the Legislature, a method must be developed whereby it can be decided when a particular course of corporate conduct has resulted in the oppression of a minority shareholder.

The special circumstances, arrangements and personal relationships that frequently underly the formation of close corporations generate certain expectations among the shareholders concerning their respective roles in corporate affairs, including management and earnings. These expectations preclude the drawing of any conclusions about the impact of a particular course of corporate conduct on a shareholder without taking into consideration the role that he is expected to play. Accordingly, a court must determine initially the understanding of the parties in this regard. Armed with this information, the court can then decide whether the controlling shareholders have acted in a fashion that is contrary to this understanding or in the language of the statute, "have acted oppressively *** toward one or more minority shareholders."

The expectations of the parties in the instant suit with regard to their participation in corporate affairs are not established by any agreement; they must be gleaned from the evidence presented. Here the corporation is close and small and operates a single restaurant. Three of its shareholders had lengthy experience in the restaurant business prior to the corporation's formation. Although the corporation operates, technically, with one director who is not the largest stockholder, its business decisions actually have been made informally by these three shareholders. Except for its organizational meeting, no director or shareholder meetings have been held since the corporation's inception in 1972. Plaintiff, the fourth shareholder, had no restaurant experience at the time he received his stock as a gift from his father-in-law. By giving him the stock, Skordas sought to provide him with an opportunity to learn the restaurant business and eventually take part in its management.

There is some indication that plaintiff's opportunity was extended over the objections of the other two shareholders and it is clear that they never welcomed him as a fellow participant in the enterprise. The evidence shows that plaintiff failed to get along with employees, causing the loss of key personnel, that he quit on more than one occasion, without reason or notice, and that he was not compatible with the other principals. Plaintiff's discharge from employment with the corporation, therefore, was because of his unsatisfactory performance. The circumstances under which the parties' expectations in these areas were disappointed do not establish oppressive action toward plaintiff by the controlling shareholders. The promise of employment was honored, the opportunity being lost to plaintiff through no fault of defendants. The parties' expectation that plaintiff would at some time participate in management was likewise thwarted by plaintiff's failure to satisfy the condition precedent to participation, *i.e.*, that he learn the business.

Although it would seem too early in the life of this corporation to expect dividends, the facts on that issue are not in. Claims of plaintiff regarding irresponsible fiscal policies and management improprieties were deferred until the decisions contained in this opinion were made. The proof to be offered in these areas may establish a case of corporate mismanagement or of oppression, entitling plaintiff to relief.[2]

---

2. One point in that connection should be mentioned: plaintiff and the other 20% shareholders, when compared with Skordas, a 40% shareholder, contributed a disproportionate amount of money to the corporation for improvements. If there is no explanation for that circumstance in the testimony to be presented, some adjustment may be necessary.

Comments and Questions

1. The New Jersey court's interpretation of the statutory imposition of a duty of those in control of closely held corporations to minority shareholders provides an excellent example of the use of the comparative method in interpreting statutes that we first encountered in Chapter 1. To what courts did the New Jersey court turn in order to interpret its statute? Why did the New Jersey court look to the English cases?

2. To what extent is the statutory provision similar to the judicially constructed rules of majority shareholder duty to minority shareholders described by the Massachusetts Supreme Judicial Court in *Wilkes*?

3. The fiduciary duty created by cases like *Wilkes* or the statute discussed in *Exadaktilos* are limited to closely held corporations. Is there a reason for this limitation? Shareholders in corporations with many shareholders are usually able to sell their shares more easily than shareholders of closely held corporations. To that extent, at least, shareholders of corporations whose shares are widely held have a protection against the bad acts of directors that shareholders of closely held corporations do not have. In effect, protection for shareholders of publicly held corporations is essentially limited to exit. There is little in the corporate statutes or case law that provides greater protection for shareholder voice within the corporate context, and little to foster shareholder loyalty. The protection that courts or legislatures are willing to provide shareholders of closely held corporations appears to be similar to that available to shareholders of corporations whose shares are widely held: the sale of stock or liquidation of the corporation. Should exit or dissolution be the preferred remedy in cases of majority shareholder overreaching or oppression? Can you think of an alternative approach that values voice and shareholder loyalty over exit rights?

C. Other Common Law Approaches

As the New Jersey court noted in *Exadaktilos*, England has rejected both that approach of Massachusetts—creating a judicial doctrine of protection for minority shareholders—as well as the approach adopted in Delaware—no 'special' statutory or judicial protection of minority shareholders in closely held corporations. Instead, the English have modified their company law to create a protection similar to the statutory approaches of New Jersey, Illinois, Virginia and other states. Subsection (1) of section 459 of the Companies Act of 1985 provides:

> A member of a company may apply to the court by petition for an order... on the ground that the company's affairs are being or have been conducted in a manner which is unfairly prejudicial to the interests of its members generally or of some part of its members (including at least himself) or that any actual or proposed act or omission of the company (including an act or omission on its behalf) is or would be so prejudicial.

As you read the materials that follow, consider relationship between the similarity of legal systems and the ease of translation of legal doctrine. Is the English approach easier toi adopt in the United States because both legal systems are similar? Would a transposition of standards from Germany to the United States have been more difficult? Is the issue one of similarity of systems of law or similarities of language? In other words, if English were the national language of Germany, would American courts find it easier to consider arguments and examples from the German system in interpreting their own?

Re Saul D. Harrison & Sons plc [1995] 1 BCLC 14 (C.A.)

NEILL, HOFFMANN, WAITE LJJ HOFFMANN LJ HOFFMANN LJ, (Giving the first judgment at the invitation of Neill LJ): This is an appeal from an order of Vinelott J striking out as an abuse of process a contributory's petition for an order under §459 of the Companies Act 1985 and to wind up on the just and equitable ground.

1. THE COMPANY

The company was formed in 1947 to take over the business founded by the petitioner's great-grandfather in 1891 and subsequently carried on by four of his sons. Its original and until recently main business was the manufacture and sale of industrial cleaning and wiping cloths made from waste textiles. But it also sells Johnson & Johnson J-Cloths and wiping products made from paper and it sorts and sells second-hand clothing (mainly for export to Africa).

For many years the company owned a factory called the Stronghold Works in West Ham. In December 1989 London Regional Transport promoted a bill in Parliament for the extension of the Jubilee Line which included a power compulsorily to purchase the Stronghold Works. The company negotiated with London Regional Transport in advance of the passage of the bill, and in October 1990 it entered into an agreement to sell the Stronghold Works for £2,750,000 and at the same time bought new premises in Hackney for the same price. The move to Hackney was completed in October 1991.

In 1960 the company's shares were reorganised into three classes. There are 30 A shares, 174,300 B shares and 815,670 C shares. The A shares carry votes but no right to dividend. The B and C shares carry no votes but are entitled to a dividend, with the B shareholders entitled to 10% before payment to the C shareholders. For the purpose of avoiding estate duty, most of the C shares were allotted to or in trust for the grandchildren of Saul Harrison's sons including the petitioner. But the A shares were allotted to the three surviving sons of the founder, including the petitioner's grandfather Alfred. They have since devolved upon the petitioner's aunt Marion and her second cousin Alan. The petitioner's 87,563 C shares represent 8.76% of the issued share capital of the company, all of which is still held by or on trust for members of the family. At the time of the hearing before Vinelott J the directors were Alan, his son Stephen and the petitioner's first cousin David.

1. THE ALLEGATIONS

The essence of the petitioner's complaint is that although the company has substantial net assets, the prospects for its business have for some years been so poor that by the time the petition was presented any reasonable board would have closed it down and distributed the assets to the shareholders. Instead, the directors have allowed the assets to be dissipated in losses in order to preserve their own inflated salaries and perquisites. The petitioner relies in particular upon the purchase of new premises in 1990. She says that any reasonable board would have regarded the proposed compulsory purchase by London Regional Transport as a golden opportunity to realise the company's principal asset and cease trading. The decision to buy new premises to continue a loss-making trade could not have been bona fide.

In addition to these central allegations the petition also complains that the directors have caused the company to pay substantial salaries and benefits to their wives for little or no consideration. The accounts are said to be deficient; first, because the Stronghold Works were shown until sale at historic cost (£456,000) when they were plainly worth a great deal more, and secondly, because proper particulars of the directors' remuneration were not given. Finally, it is said that the accounts for periods up to 31 March 1989 were qualified because the directors did not keep proper accounting records.

On these grounds the petitioner says that the affairs of the company have been conducted in a manner unfairly prejudicial to the C shareholders, including herself, within the meaning of § 459 of the Companies Act 1985 and that it is just and equitable that the company should be wound up.

3. 'UNFAIRLY PREJUDICIAL' AND 'JUST AND EQUITABLE'

What must a petitioner show in order to justify an order under § 459 or an order to wind up? The grounds for winding up are that it is 'just and equitable' to do so. The grounds for an order under § 459 are that

> 'the company's affairs are being or have been conducted in a manner which is unfairly prejudicial to the interests of its members generally or of some part of its members (including at least [the petitioner])'.

If these grounds are made out, the court has a discretion to make such order as it thinks fit for giving relief in respect of the matters complained of, including in particular the relief sought in this case, which is an order that other members or the company itself buy the petitioner's shares: see § 461(2)(d).

'Unfairly prejudicial' is deliberately imprecise language which was chosen by Parliament because its earlier attempt in § 210 of the Companies Act 1948 to provide a similar remedy had been too restrictively construed. The earlier section had used the word 'oppressive', which the House of Lords in Scottish Co-op Wholesale Society Ltd. v Meyer [1958] 3 All ER 66, [1959] AC 324, [1958] 3 WLR 404 said meant 'burdensome, harsh and wrongful'. This gave rise to some uncertainty as to whether 'wrongful' required actual illegality or invasion of legal rights. The Jenkins Committee on Company Law, which reported in 1962, thought that it should not. To make this clear, it recommended the use of the term 'unfairly prejudicial', which Parliament somewhat tardily adopted in § 75 of the Companies Act 1980. This section is reproduced (with minor amendment) in the present § 459 of the Companies Act 1985.

Mr Purle, who appeared for the petitioner, said that the only test of unfairness was whether a reasonable bystander would think that the conduct in question was unfair. This is correct, so far as it goes, and has some support in the cases. Its merit is to emphasise that the court is applying an objective standard of fairness. But I do not think that it is the most illuminating way of putting the matter. For one thing, the standard of fairness must necessarily be laid down by the court. In explaining how the court sets about deciding what is fair in the context of company management, I do not think that it helps a great deal to add the reasonable company watcher to the already substantial cast of imaginary characters which the law uses to personify its standards of justice in different situations. An appeal to the views of an imaginary third party makes the concept seem more vague than it really is. It is more useful to examine the factors which the law actually takes into account in setting the standard.

In deciding what is fair or unfair for the purposes of §459, it is important to have in mind that fairness is being used in the context of a commercial relationship. The articles of association are just what their name implies: the contractual terms which govern the relationships of the shareholders with the company and each other. They determine the powers of the board and the company in general meeting and everyone who becomes a member of a company is taken to have agreed to them. Since keeping promises and honouring agreements is probably the most important element of commercial fairness, the starting point in any case under §459 will be to ask whether the conduct of which the shareholder complains was in accordance with the articles of association.

The answer to this question often turns on the fact that the powers which the shareholders have entrusted to the board are fiduciary powers, which must be exercised for the benefit of the company as a whole. If the board act for some ulterior purpose, they step outside the terms of the bargain between the shareholders and the company. As a matter of ordinary company law, this may or may not entitle the individual shareholder to a remedy. It depends upon whether he can bring himself within one of the exceptions to the rule in Foss v Harbottle (1843) 2 Hare 461. But the fact that the board are protected by the principle of majority rule does not necessarily prevent their conduct from being unfair within the meaning of §459. Enabling the court in an appropriate case to outflank the rule in Foss v Harbottle was one of the purposes of the section. So in Re a Company (No 00370 of 1987), ex p Glossop [1988] BCLC 570, [1988] 1 WLR 1068, where the complaint was of a consistent refusal by the board to recommend payment of a dividend, Harman J said that such conduct could make it just and equitable to wind up the company. He did so by reference to the seminal judgment of Lord Wilberforce in Howard Smith Ltd. v Ampol Petroleum Ltd. [1974] 1 All ER 1126, [1974] AC 821 on the principles by which the court decides whether the board has acted within its fiduciary powers and said that on the facts alleged it was arguable that the board had exceeded them. This seems to me in principle the correct point at which to start the inquiry into both whether the conduct in question could justify a just and equitable winding up and also whether it is unfair for the purposes of §459. It seems clear that but for a technical objection which was removed when the section was amended in 1989, Harman J would have allowed the petition to proceed on both grounds, as Peter Gibson J did before the amendment in Re Sam Weller & Sons Ltd. [1990] BCLC 80, [1990] Ch 682. I should however add that while I respectfully think that Harman J was right in asking himself whether the board had abused its fiduciary powers, I would not necessarily subscribe to the theory of corporate hubris on which he decided that it arguably had.

Although one begins with the articles and the powers of the board, a finding that conduct was not in accordance with the articles does not necessarily mean that it was unfair, still less that the court will exercise its discretion to grant relief. There is often sound sense in the rule in Foss v Harbottle (1843) 2 Hare 461. In choosing the term 'unfairly prejudicial', the Jenkins Committee (para 204) equated it with Lord Cooper's understanding of 'oppression' in Elder v Elder and Watson 1952 SC 49:

> 'a visible departure from the standards of fair dealing and a violation of the conditions of fair play on which every shareholder who entrusts his money to a company is entitled to rely'.

So trivial or technical infringements of the articles were not intended to give rise to petitions under §459.

Not only may conduct be technically unlawful without being unfair: it can also be unfair without being unlawful. In a commercial context, this may at first seem surprising. How can it be unfair to act in accordance with what the parties have agreed? As a general rule, it is not. But there are cases in which the letter of the articles does not fully reflect the understandings upon which the shareholders are associated. Lord Wilberforce drew attention to such cases in a celebrated passage of his judgment in Ebrahimi v Westbourne Galleries Ltd. [1972] 2 All ER 492 at 500, [1973] AC 360 at 379, which discusses what seems to me the identical concept of injustice or unfairness which can form the basis of a just and equitable winding up:

> 'The words [just and equitable] are a recognition of the fact that a limited company is more than a mere judicial entity, with a personality in law of its own: that there is room in company law for recognition of the fact that behind it, or amongst it, there are individuals, with rights, expectations and obligations inter se which are not necessarily submerged in the company structure. That structure is defined by the Companies Act 1948 and by the articles of association by which the shareholders agree to be bound. In most companies and in most contexts, this definition is sufficient and exhaustive, equally so whether the company is large or small. The "just and equitable" provision does not, as the respondents suggest, entitle one party to disregard the obligation he assumes by entering a company, nor the court to dispense him from it. It does, as equity always does, enable the court to subject the exercise of legal rights to equitable considerations; considerations, that is, of a personal character arising between one individual and another, which may make it unjust, or inequitable, to insist on legal rights or to exercise them in a particular way.'

Thus the personal relationship between a shareholder and those who control the company may entitle him to say that it would in certain circumstances be unfair for them to exercise a power conferred by the articles upon the board or the company in general meeting. I have in the past ventured to borrow from public law the term 'legitimate expectation' to describe the correlative 'right' in the shareholder to which such a relationship may give rise. It often arises out of a fundamental understanding between the shareholders which formed the basis of their association but was not put into contractual form, such as an assumption that each of the parties who has ventured his capital will also participate in the management of the company and receive the return on his investment in the form of salary rather than dividend. These relationships need not always take the form of implied agreements with the shareholder concerned; they could enure for the benefit of a third party such as a joint venturer's widow. But in Ebrahimi v Westbourne Galleries Ltd. ([1972] 2 All ER 492 at 500) Lord Wilberforce went on to say:

> 'It would be impossible, and wholly undesirable, to define the circumstances in which these considerations may arise. Certainly the fact that the company is a small one, or a private company, is not enough. There are very many of these where the association is a purely commercial one, of which it can safely be said that the basis of association is adequately and exhaustively laid down in the articles. The superimposition of equitable considerations requires something more. . . .'

Thus in the absence of 'something more', there is no basis for a legitimate expectation that the board and the company in general meeting will not exercise whatever powers they are given by the articles of association.

In this case, as the judge emphasised, there is nothing more. The petitioner was given her shares in 1960 pursuant to a reorganisation of the share capital which vested the entire control of the company in the A shareholders and the board whom they appointed. This scheme is binding upon her and there are no special circumstances to modify its effects. Although the petition speaks of the petitioner having various 'legitimate expectations', no grounds are alleged for saying that her rights are not 'adequately and exhaustively' laid down by the articles. And in substance the alleged 'legitimate expectations' amount to no more than an expectation that the board would manage the company in accordance with their fiduciary obligations and the terms of the articles and the Companies Act.

Thus it seems to me that in this case one can be a good deal more precise than to ask in general terms, as Mr Purle suggested, whether a bystander would think that the board had been unfair. As there are no grounds for saying that it would be unfair for the board to act in accordance with the bargain between the petitioner and the company, the very minimum required to make out a case of unfairness is that the powers of management have been used for an unlawful purpose or the articles otherwise infringed. Hence the allegation in the petition that the board acted in bad faith, carrying on the business in order to provide themselves with salaries rather than because they genuinely thought that it was in the interests of the shareholders as a whole.

Mr Purle said that it was not necessary for this purpose that the petitioner should have to show that the board was motivated by self-interest. It would be sufficient that the decision to continue the business was irrational: one which no reasonable board of rational businessmen could have thought was in the interests of the company. There may be cases in which this distinction makes some sense but in this one it does not. If no rational board could honestly have thought that carrying on the business was in the interests of the company, the conclusion must inevitably follow that the board acted from some improper motive of their own. The petition recognises this and squarely alleges bad faith. In my judgment the claims for relief under § 459 and winding up stand or fall by whether this allegation can be made out.

[The rest of the opinion is omitted]

Comments and Questions

1. As the case relates it, under earlier English law, minority shareholders had been protected against oppression. That term was interpreted by the House of Lords to include acts which were wrongful. The statute was thereafter amended to substitute 'unfair prejudice' for 'oppression' for the purpose of broadening the reach of the provision. Which English provision is closer to the American concepts of oppression of minority shareholders—the older provision limited to 'oppression' or the new standard of 'unfair prejudice'?

2. Is there a reason the concepts of unfair prejudice or oppression ought not to be applied with equal force to corporations whose shares are widely held and actively traded on an established securities market?

3. Notions of legal personality affected the determination of the English court in interpreting the statutory provision providing protection for minority shareholders. Where corporations are considered little more than a collective form of individual endeavor, it is possible for courts to more readily intervene in contests for advantage between groups of shareholders. The language of American and English cases treating minority shareholders' rights is full of these notions. It finds expression in the American cases in the way courts attempt to draw analogies between closely held corporations and partnerships. How does it find expression in the English case you have just read?

4. It is possible to argue that the nature of corporate personality is dependent on the nature of the investment in the corporation—that publicly traded corporations are more likely to approach the 'independent entity' ideal, while closely held corporations more closely approach the 'partnership in corporate clothing' ideal. Does acceptance of these fundamental differences of corporate personality justify greater legislative intrusion into the relationship between shareholders of closely held corporations, and a hands off treatment for publicly traded corporations?

D. The Civil Law Countries and Shareholder Duty

1. *Europe*

European approaches to the protection of minority shareholders in closely held corporations are very different than those being developed in the United States. The German approach, in particular, as well as that of the United States, has become influential in the reception of Western forms of enterprise organization of those countries formerly operating under a Soviet-Socialist style of political and economic organization. Neither approach is without its problems. As you consider the materials that follow, think about the points of convergence and divergence of problems facing lawyers in similar situations in different countries. For example, does the American lawyer representing interests in a closely held corporation face the same sorts of choices, legal and practical solutions, as the German lawyer drafting a charter for a GmbH?

Henry P. deVries and Friedrich K. Juenger, *Limited Liability Contract: The GmbH*

64 Colum. L. Rev. 866 (1964)
(Excerpts 881–885; some footnotes omitted)

The statute provides that normally "the appointment of a manager may be revoked at any time."[107] However, the charter may limit dismissal to cases in which "important reasons require it."[108] The term "important reasons" encompasses a great variety of grounds not subject to more precise definition.[109] Dismissal for an important reason

107. GmbH Statute § 38, para. 1.

108. GmbH Statute § 38, para. 2. The German term "*wichtige Gründe*" has been translated as "cogent grounds." *See* Falkenhausen and Steefel, *Shareholders' Rights in German Corporations (AG and GmbH)*, 10 Am. J. Comp. L. 407 (1961)... We prefer the literal translation since outside the German legal context this term is meaningless in any event....

109. The statute mentions as examples of "important reasons" the gross violation of duties and the lack of capacity to manage the company properly. Other reasons would be the acceptance of bribes, continued sickness, juggling of the company's books, use of the company's funds for improper purposes, lack of necessary expertise and indebtedness. The standards to be applied vary with the size and type of business....

does not require beach or fault on the part of the manager, nor is it necessary that the reason even relate to him.

The right to terminate for "important reasons" is considered a rule of public policy, and cannot be waived in advance. Thus, a charter provision purporting to guarantee a quota holder the right to be a manager for a period of time or for life or which requires unanimity, cannot effectively bar his dismissal for "important reasons."

* * *

H. Dissolution and Expulsion of Quota Holders

The statutory reasons for the dissolution of a GmbH are expiration of the duration specified in the charter,[115] resolution of a majority of three fourths of the votes cast in a meeting called to decide on such resolution,[116] petition in bankruptcy,[117] and a judgement in a case of impossibility of achieving the corporate objectives or a judicial finding of "important reasons" for dissolution.[118]

This last provision, which has already been mentioned as one of the statutory minority rights, was thought a sufficient safety valve to the enforced intimacy of a closed corporation. Examples of the meaning of impossibility include nullity of a patent for the exploitation of which the GmbH was organized or a legal prohibition. However, a temporary impossibility to continue production because of wartime regulations does not suffice. "Important reasons" include complete lack of profitability for the foreseeable future, total obsolescence of the facilities or know how, loss of customers, and personal disputes between the quota holders leading to corporate deadlock.

The remedy of dissolution upon a finding of "important reasons" is subject to certain restrictions. It is not available to a plaintiff who is solely or primarily responsible for such reasons. Furthermore, since the statute refers to "important reasons relating to the condition *of the company*," the personal condition of plaintiff does not justify the finding of an important ground.

The German courts felt that dissolution of the GmbH was not a desirable method of solving internal conflicts in view of the possible destruction fo the enterprise. On the other hand, they were reluctant to force the members of a close company to remain partners when their relationship had deteriorated. The reach of statutory provisions permitting the expulsion of a quota holder or the cancellation of his quota was too limited to solve this problem. The former German Supreme Court found a solution by fashioning a new rule out of whole cloth. According to this rule, a GmbH can expel an individual quota holder for an "important reason" and "important reason" was said to exist if the other quota holders cannot reasonably be required to continue their association with him because of his conduct or personality and if, therefore, the continued existence of the GmbH could be endangered. The present German Supreme Court accepted and institutionalized this novel remedy by filling in the details the *Reichsgericht* had left open. Drawing an analogy to the case of expulsion of members of a commercial partnership, the *Bundesgerichtshof* has held that the ousting of a quota holder requires that the company bring an action and that the decree expelling the quota holder be conditioned on compensation within a specified period of time. The German commenta-

115. GmbH Statute § 60....
116. GmbH Statute § 60....
117. GmbH Statute § 60....
118. See GmbH Statute § 60, para. 1, No. 3, and § 61, para. 1.

tors accept this rule. A number of problems remain, however, particularly regarding the two man company.

As a counterpart to the rule, disgruntled quota holders would apparently have a right to resign from the GmbH whenever they cannot reasonably expect to remain members.

The very ingenuity with which the German courts have attempted to solve the problem of incompatible quota holders suggests the need for careful drafting and adequate provisions in joint venture agreements. As a practical matter, charter clauses permitting a minority to quit and a majority to oust dissenter and to break a deadlock by a put or take provision, recourse to arbitration, vote of a third party, or even flipping a coin, may offer a more acceptable solution to typical close corporation problems than a court order.

Sandra K. Miller, *Minority Shareholder Oppression in the Private Company in the European Community: A Comparative Analysis of the German, United Kingdom, and French "Close Corporation Problem"*

30 Cornell Int'l L.J. 381 (1997)
(excerpts from pages 393, 396–399,401,
403–406, 408–409; some footnotes omitted)

II. The Corporate Structure and the Close Corporation Problem: A Comparative Analysis of German, UK, and French Law

A close look at the corporate structures under German, French, and UK law reveals significant differences in corporate organization. Germany and France tend to have the most formalistic corporate structures while the UK has the least restrictive organizational form. In all countries considered, the public corporation is subject to considerable formalities. The private limited liability companies enjoy a considerable degree of informality in the way in which business may be conducted.

With regard to standards of conduct for shareholders, German law is the most exacting of all three countries. All three countries have developed equitable remedies to resolve shareholder disputes (i.e., shareholder buy-outs, corporate dissolutions). Under German law, a shareholder may withdraw himself, or may seek an expulsion of a fellow shareholder upon a showing of "substantial causes." The substantial causes pertain largely to the personal characteristics of the shareholder and focus on the personal relationship between the parties. In contrast, equitable remedies under UK law do not focus on the personal characteristics of the shareholder, but rather on the conduct of the shareholder in the course of managing the business. UK law broadly provides for equitable remedies where the shareholder's conduct of the company's affairs has been "unfairly prejudicial" to the other members. France has also enacted remedies for the shareholder of the private company. French law provides for anticipatory dissolution of a company for "valid reasons" including nonperformance of one's obligations or discord among members.

* * *

C. The German Close Corporation Problem

German law provides highly discretionary judicial remedies when the shareholder has a dispute with other GmbH shareholders. To some extent the judicial remedies function as a source of additional regulation of shareholder conduct. Section 61 of the GmbH law provides that: (1) The company may be dissolved by a court decision in which case it becomes impossible to accomplish the purpose of the company or when there are substantial causes (*wichtige Grund*) for the dissolution resulting from the conditions of the company.[78]

Because the dissolution remedy is so severe, the German courts have developed two additional remedies, the withdrawal (*Austritt*) and the expulsion (*AusschlieBung*).[79] Under the withdrawal concept, the aggrieved shareholder seeks to withdraw from the company and is entitled to obtain the fair market value of his or her interest in the company. In an expulsion, the aggrieved shareholder seeks to expel the other shareholder or shareholders. The right to obtain either a withdrawal or an expulsion is premised on a showing that there is a "substantial basis" or "*wichtige Grund*" for the remedy.[80]

There are three possible grounds for establishing a "substantial basis" for a withdrawal: 1) objectionable personal characteristics of the shareholder; 2) the arbitrary exercise of management by the shareholder; and 3) the existence of special factors unique to the facts and circumstances. Personal circumstances of the withdrawing shareholder which may serve as a substantial basis include extreme financial need, a lengthy and expensive illness, relocation abroad, or the inability to perform the requisite duties. An analysis of the shareholder's misconduct is made if it is alleged that the shareholder exercises majority power in an arbitrary fashion.[81] Special factors can operate as a substantial basis where the shareholder's financial return is undesirable, or where the company's purposes change and pose additional risks to the shareholder. The articles of incorporation may not restrict or eliminate the right to withdraw.

If an expulsion is sought, the party seeking to expel another shareholder may do so based on personal factors relating to the shareholder or based on the shareholder's conduct. Advanced age, extended illness, or mental derangement may be cited as personal factors which justify an expulsion. A variety of shareholder conduct can also justify an expulsion. The aggrieved party may argue that the shareholder has disorganized financial circumstances, lacks trustworthiness or creditworthiness, or has lost personal qualifications required by the articles. An expulsion can be sought if the shareholder has been derelict in his duties, breaches trust, causes incurable dissension, or makes improper sexual advances. The mechanism for expulsion is through a court order.

---

78. See Gesetz betreffend die Gesellschaften mit beschrankter Haftung (Act on Limited Liability Companies) §61(1), v.10.5.1995 (BGBI. I 2911), translated in[1 Business Transactions in Germany App. 6 (Dennis Campbell et al., 1994)].

79. It has been observed that the leading post-war German decision on the dissolution remedy emphasizes that dissolution leads to a loss of business and a loss of jobs. Hence, over a seventy year period Courts have developed the withdrawal and expulsion remedies as an alternative to the action for dissolution. See Scogin, supra note 5, at 132–33, 152 n.101 citing BGHZ 9, 157. For an excellent explanation of the withdrawal and exclusion, see 1 Business Transactions in Germany §§ 23.09(1), 23.09(3) n.7 (pointing out that the leading cases on these remedies are Supreme Court of the German Reich, decision of August 13, 1942, RGZ 169, 330; Federal Court of Justice, decisions of April 1, 1953, BGHZ 9, 157; February 5, 1955, BGHZ 16, 317; and February 23, 1981, NJW 1981, 2302 (F.R.G.).

80. [Hugh T. Scogin, *Withdrawal and Expulsion in Germany: A Comparative Perspective on the "Close Corporation Problem,"* 15 Mich. J. Int'l L. 127 (1993)] at 154–60 [the next two paragraphs of text are based on this work].

81. *Id.*

The remedies of withdrawal and expulsion illustrate the importance of case law in Germany. It is frequently said that common law systems rely on case law precedents and civil law systems do not. Yet, the German close corporation remedies are based on case law rather than statute.[88]

The broad scope of the definition of a "substantial basis" justifying a withdrawal or expulsion gives rise to considerable uncertainty in shareholder relations and operates as an added dimension of the regulation of shareholder conduct. The GmbH shareholder must not only monitor his or her conduct, but must also make sure that personal circumstances do not develop which arguably could be regarded as grounds for withdrawal or expulsion. The GmbH shareholder who also functions as a member of the Board of Directors bears an even greater burden because the Director must comply with a separate set of stringent standards of conduct applicable to Board Members.[89]

The character of the shareholder, his or her personal circumstances and personal relationships are scrutinized by a court which is entertaining a petition for an expulsion or withdrawal. The inquiry is not confined to the shareholder's conduct in managing the business. For example, in a 1953 German GmbH decision involving a dispute between two owners of a cabaret-dance bar, the defendant's extramarital affairs were relevant to a determination of whether he should be expelled from the corporation.[90] The plaintiff sought to expel the defendant because the defendant failed to credit the company with certain funds, and purchased a car without consulting the plaintiff. In addition, the defendant had been found guilty of adultery. In determining whether the remedy should be given, the court evaluated the character of both parties and the defendant's adultery became relevant to the evaluation of his character. The defendant argued that he should be permitted to continue in the business. He maintained that his own behavior was neutralized by the behavior of the plaintiff, because the plaintiff had also committed adultery. The court ultimately concluded that the plaintiff was entitled to an expulsion.

The sweeping scope of judicial discretion, and its potential for bending to serve political and/or governmental policies is illustrated by the application of the withdrawal and expulsion remedies during the reign of the Third Reich. During this period, Jewishness constituted a "substantial basis" for expulsion. The leading case was decided in 1942.[92] In 1937, the Jewish plaintiff was expelled by the defendants and sued to obtain a

---

88. *Scogin, supra* note [80], at 133–34.

89. The standards of conduct of the Directors of the GmbH are quite strict and are virtually identical to those applicable to the AG. The managing directors of the GmbH must employ the diligence of an orderly business man in the matters of the company. See Gesetz betreffend die Gesellschaften mit beschrankter Haftung (Act on Limited Liability Companies) §43(1), v.10.5.1994 (BGBI. I 2911), translated in Business Transactions in Germany, supra note 19. The German Stock Corporation Act (Aktiengesetz or AktG) requires managers and directors to apply the care of the orderly and prudent business manager. If a Supervisory Board is used in the GmbH, the standards of care applicable to Supervisory Board members of the AG apply to the GmbH's Supervisory Board members. See also id. §51(1). A business judgment rule may not be invoked to shield directors from liability for their business decisions. As one commentator noted:

> The burden of proof is on the directors and managers, that is, they have to show that they have adhered to the duty of due care. The due care requirement is absolute and any negligence, however slight, can give rise to damages. Thus, the burden imposed on the directors is reduced by the fact that while they have certain discretion in the exercise of their judgment, the scope of their discretion is probably narrower than under the business judgment rule in the United States.

See Vassil Breskovski, *Directors' Duty of Care in Eastern Europe*, 29 INT'L LAW. 77, 89 (1995).

90. Federal Court of Justice, decision of April 1, 1953, BGHZ 9, 157 (F.R.G.).

92. Judgment of Aug. 13, 1942, RGZ 169, 334 (F.R.G.).

determination that his expulsion was null and void. The defendants had taken the position that the plaintiff's Jewishness was an economic disadvantage and was grounds for expulsion. Although the plaintiff won in the trial court, upon appeal the expulsion of the plaintiff was upheld. The court reasoned that the GmbH must have the opportunity to eliminate a partner if the character of the partner becomes intolerable. The court of appeal concluded that the plaintiff's affiliation with the Jewish race was intolerable.

After World War II when the political climate changed, the decision holding Jewishness as a "substantial basis" was condemned and the expulsion remedy became controversial. However, in 1953 the Court upheld the expulsion remedy.[95] Although Jewishness is no longer grounds for expulsion, the courts continue to award expulsions based on the rationale that a shareholder should not be trapped in an unbearable commercial relationship.

The close corporation remedies under German law are clearly broader than those found in most states in the United States. In contrast to the German remedies of withdrawal and expulsion, equitable remedies under U.S. law are typically, although not exclusively geared to alleviating the problems of the minority shareholder. U.S. remedies focus rather narrowly on the shareholder's conduct in the business, rather than on the shareholder's overall character. Finally, while U.S. partnership law provides a mechanism for the expulsion of a partner, shareholder expulsion has not been adopted as a remedy in the U.S. corporate context.

* * *

E. The UK Close Corporation Problem

Because the shareholder of a private UK company may not freely transfer his or her corporate interest, the shareholder of a private company is vulnerable in the event of a dispute with other shareholders. The minority shareholder is particularly at risk where there is misconduct by the majority owner. Disagreements among shareholders can bring corporate operations to a grinding halt.

* * *

A new provision was inserted into the 1980 Companies Act to provide assistance to the minority shareholder. The new formulation, now found in Section 459 of the Companies Act 1985 provides:

> A member of a company may apply to the court by petition for an order under this Part on the ground that the company's affairs are being or have been conducted in a manner which is unfairly prejudicial to the interests of some part of the members (including at least himself) or that any actual or proposed act or omission of the company (including an act or omission on its behalf) is or would be so prejudicial.[121]

Section 461(1) provides the court with wide discretion to award a remedy.[122] If the court is satisfied that a petition is justified the court may fashion a remedy in any number of ways including, but not limited to: 1) issuing an order regulating the conduct of the company's affairs in the future; 2) requiring the company to refrain from certain conduct; 3) ordering civil proceedings; and 4) ordering one or more members to purchase the shares of other members.[123]

---

95. See Judgment of Apr. 1, 1953, BGHZ 9, 157 (F.R.G.).
121. See Companies Act 1985, pt. XVII, § 459(1).
122. Id. § 461(1).
123. Id. § 461(2).

The intent of the change was to provide a more comprehensive remedy to minority shareholders and to broaden the circumstances under which relief would be granted.[124] The revised provisions have now opened up a floodgate of litigation and the new rules have been widely criticized for producing lengthy and costly litigation.

Unfairly prejudicial conduct has been asserted in a wide variety of circumstances. Unfairly prejudicial conduct has been alleged where: 1) one member prevents another from participating in the management of the company;[125] 2) one member has seriously mismanaged a business;[126] 3) a member improperly uses corporate assets;[127] 4) one member misappropriates sums of the company's money;[128] and 5) a member diverts substantial profits from the company to himself.[129]

The judicial construction of the definition of unfairly prejudicial conduct has been purposely vague. As noted in Burr v. Harrison:[130]

> 'Unfairly prejudicial' is deliberately imprecise language which was chosen by Parliament because its earlier attempt in § 210 of the Companies Act 1948 to provide a similar remedy had been too restrictively construed... [i]n deciding what is fair or unfair for the purposes of § 459, it is important to have in mind that fairness is being used in the context of a commercial relationship.[131]

Recently in the UK, as in the United States, the British courts have looked to the legitimate expectations of the shareholder to define unfairly prejudicial conduct.[132]

---

124. [*Minority Shareholders: What Protection, If Any, Does English Law Give to Minority Shareholders?*, ESTATES GAZETTE, July 27, 1991, at 154].

125. Re Haden Bill Electrical Ltd. [1995] 2 BCLC 280 (Ch. Eng.) (holding that a plaintiff who was removed as chairman and as director of a private company had a legitimate expectation that he would continue to participate in the management of the company); Re Bird Precision Bellows, Ltd. [1985] 3 All E.R. 523 (C.A.) (holding that unfair prejudice existed where the petitioners were minority shareholders and the majority removed them from the board of directors).

126. Re Macro (Ipswich) Ltd. [1994] 2 BCLC 354 (Ch. Eng.) (substantial mismanagement of the real estate business occurred where the defendant failed to get competitive bids on construction work, failed to refurbish properties, failed to properly supervise repair work, obtained poor terms for leases, mismanaged litigation, and overpaid insurance).

127. See Re Elgindata Ltd. [1993] 1 All E.R. 232 (C.A.) (holding that serious mismanagement occurred where majority shareholders bought an expensive car, had company pay for construction costs of a home, and used corporate assets for personal purposes). See also In re Sam Weller & Sons Ltd. [1990] Ch. 682, [1989] 3 W.L.R. 923 [1990] B.C.L.C. 80 (Eng.) (involving a director who had the company purchase a holiday home for his sons, and refused to pay dividends).

128. Adam Wilson Young and Others v. Falkirk Football and Athletic Club Ltd. Outer House Cases (involving allegations of improper personal expenditures, incompetent management causing loss of goodwill, and misappropriation of funds).

129. Lowe v. Fahey and others [1996] 1 BCLC 262 ((Ch. Eng.) (alleging that substantial profits from two development projects were diverted from the company). See also In Re London School of Electronics Ltd. [1986] 1 Ch 211, [1985] 3 WLR 474, [1985] BCLC 273, [1983–85] BCC, 394 (Ch. Eng.) (involving a diversion of the company's students from the company's program to a different program).

130. Re Saul D. Harrison & Sons [1995] 1 BCLC 14, 17 (C.A. Eng.).

131. *Id.*

132. Re Postgate & Derby (Agencies) Ltd. [1987] BCLC 8, [1986] BCC 99, 353 (Ch. Eng.) in which the court reviewed a management buy-out which was in which the directors had an interest. In articulating the legal standard required under Section 459 of the Companies Act 1985 the court explained: "The concept of unfair prejudice which forms the basis of the jurisdiction under § 459 enables the court to take into account not only the rights of members under the company's constitution, but also their legitimate expectations arising from the agreements or understandings of the members inter se." Id.

Under the legitimate expectations analysis, the court may look beyond the intentions of the parties as reflected in the articles of incorporation. The court will attempt to discern the fundamental understanding of the parties as to the nature of their relationship and the conduct of the business. Thus, the court may conclude that part of the unwritten, but fundamental understanding between the parties is that they will both participate in management, receive dividends, or conduct business in a certain manner. Violations of this fundamental understanding may be regarded as unfairly prejudicial conduct.

While the law was revised with the best of intentions to provide aggrieved shareholders with fair access to a remedy, the new provision has lead to an overwhelming amount of lengthy and costly litigation. The definition of "unfairly prejudicial" must be decided on a case by case basis and has created a considerable degree of uncertainty involving the resolution of shareholder disputes.[135] The UK Law Commission is currently studying the provision and is expected to develop recommendations for improvement in the law.

* * *

G. The French Close Corporation Problem

The owners of a SARL face the same potential problems faced by investors who own shares in an illiquid private corporation. If the owners have a dispute, the company may be deadlocked, or one or more members may be squeezed out of the business enterprise. Dissolution is a remedy available to shareholders of the SARL who have irreconcilable grievances with one another. The company law provides for anticipatory dissolution of the company by tribunal upon demand of one of the members, where there are: "valid reasons, especially in the event of nonperformance of obligations by one of the members, or of discord among the members paralyzing the operation of the company."[148]

Unfortunately, the statute provides no guidance as to the definition of "valid reasons" and there is virtually no case law to elaborate on the concept. Further, the remedy provided under French law is more severe than that provided under German or UK law. The French remedy is dissolution—a dramatic measure that extinguishes the corporation. In contrast, the German remedies of expulsion or withdrawal change the composition of shareholders, but leave the business entity intact. Similarly, the UK remedies for unfairly prejudicial conduct may include but are not limited to dissolution of the

---

135. See J.C. Bruno, "Reasonable Expectations"—A Primer on an Oppressive Standard, 71 Mich B.J. 434 (1992) (Part 1); 71 Mich B.J. 566 (1992) (Part 2) (discussing the uncertainty in the law created by the use of the reasonable expectation standard).

148. See Law No. 78-9 of January 4, 1978, art. 1844-7, providing:

The company terminates:

1. Upon expiration of the time for which it was established, except where it has been extended in accordance with article 1844-6;

2. Upon accomplishment or extinguishment of its object;

3. Upon annulment of the company contract;

4. Upon anticipatory dissolution (dissolution anticipate) agreed to by the members;

5. Upon anticipatory dissolution pronounced by the tribunal upon demand of one of the members for valid reasons (justes motifs), especially in the event of nonperformance of his obligations by one of the members, or of discord among the members paralyzing the operation of the company;

6. Upon anticipatory dissolution pronounced by the tribunal in the case specified in article 1844-5;

7. (Law No. 88-15 of Jan. 5, 1988.) By the effect of a judgment ordering the judicial liquidation or the complete transfer of the assets of the company;

8. For any other cause specified in the statutes. It should be noted that these provisions apply to the SA and the SARL.

corporation. Under UK law, equitable solutions far short of dissolution may be fashioned, such as shareholder buy-outs.

The only other remedy available under French law short of anticipatory dissolution, is an order for the majority to prepare reports on specific matters of concern to the minority shareholders. The French law provides that ten percent of the shareholders may obtain an order from the Commercial Court to appoint an expert to prepare a report on one or more issues which concern the corporation.[149] Upon completion of the report it must be sent to the petitioning shareholder, the corporation's statutory auditor, and if appropriate, the public prosecutor. The report must be published along with the annual report or notice to shareholders of the next annual meeting.[150]

Juan M. Dobson, *Lifting the Veil in Four Countries: The Law of Argentina, England, France and the United States*

35 Int'l & Comp. L.Q. 839 (1986)
(excerpts pages 854–856; some footnotes omitted)

1. Abuse of rights and the "interests of the company"

Analyses based on abuse of rights have been used to solve problems arising from abuses of the controlling majority vis-a-vis minority shareholders in both French and Argentine company law. The same approach can be used to solve problems arising from abuses committed by the controller of a company vis-a-vis third parties, e.g. creditors.

The abuse of rights approach may be combined with another well-established concept—the "interests of the company".[48] This concept allows a company's activities and assets to be protected by the law as a matter separate and distinct from the protection of the activities and rights of the members of the company, even if forming a majority.

French law contains no statutory definition of the phrase. During the Senate reading of the Companies Act 1967, it was suggested that the "interests of the company" are either (a) the interests of the shareholder, or (b) the interests of the company as such, separate and in possible conflict with those of the shareholders.[49] The courts have not established a clear-cut definition. The Paris *Cour d'appel* has stated that the interests of the company are the interests of the "enterprise,"[50] while the *Cour de Cassation* has adopted a more restricted view, confining it to the interests of the shareholders.[51] A similar concept in insolvency law.

149. [See 1 Simeon & Assoc. et al., Doing Business in France § 5.01 (1996)] at 5–50.

150. Law No. 66-537 of July 24, 1966, art. 226. See David J. Berger, Guidelines For Mergers and Acquisitions in France, 11 Nw. J. Int'l L. & Bus. 484, 493 (1991) (discussing the major provisions of the SA).

48. The *Cour de Cassation* has held that an abuse of rights occurs when a resolution is taken contrary to the "general interests" of the company: Cass.Com. 18.4.61 [1961] Rev. trim.dr.comm. 634, obs. Houin; Cass.com. 22.4.76, D.1977.4, note Bousquet.

49. Hemard, Terré, Mabiltat, *Sociétés commerciales* (1972), Vol. I, p. 803, n. 940.

50. *Société Fruehauf Corp. v. Massardy et autres*, Paris, 22.5.68, D.1969, 147, *note* Contin.

51. Contin, *loc. cit. supra* n.50…

Argentine law provides that a shareholder placed in a position which conflicts with the interests of the company must abstain from participating in any decisions relating to that position (*Ley de sociedades*19.550/1972, art. 248). The courts have not yet reacted a consensus but scholarly opinion that the view that the "interests of the company" cover all matters leading to, and concerned within, the fulfillment of the purposes of the company: conflicting interests may appear not only when the company makes a loss but also when its ability to make a profit has been impaired.[52]

As a basic minimum, the interests of the company must refer to the inherent purposes and aspirations of every possible member of a company, and signify the duty of management and others in control of the company's operations to make a profit from carrying out the company's objects.[53] For a satisfactory definition, those purposes and aspirations have to be balanced against the needs of the company to survive as a going concern. The short-term interests of the member are balanced against the long-term interests in the operation of the company.

The theory of abuse of rights is based on the notion that the rights have to be exercised according to the purposes for which they were conferred by law. When this approach has been applied to the rights of a dominant majority over a dissenting majority in a company, it has enabled an oppressive resolution adopted by general meeting to be annulled.

The two concepts (abuse of rights and the interests of the company) can provide a sound basis for a theory of abusive control of companies. While internal control—that exercise through voting power at company meetings—may or may not be abusive, a member can also use the rights conferred on him by the law either way. If he uses his power in the company's interests it is not abusive, but, if he uses it inconsistently with the company's interests (e.g. by using the company's assets as his own), it becomes abusive.

External control, on the other hand, is always abusive. Where control is exercised as a result of economic dominance, it involves an abuse of contractual rights and is therefore clearly an abuse of rights generally.

Comments and Problem

1. One of the purposes of examining shareholder protection in the context of closely held corporations is to determine whether other related systems of corporate regulation have attempted solutions to problems which might be worth transplanting, in one way or another. Another reason is, perhaps, the converse of the first, to determine whether transplanting corporate regulatory schemes make sense. The Europeans have been active in the comparative study of regimes of corporate regulation. The countries of Eastern Europe have been especially sensitive to the possibilities offered by other systems as these nations attempt to significantly modify their regulatory regimes to accord to the great changes in their political and economic systems after 1989.

---

52. Halperin, *Curso de derecho comercial*, Vol. II, pp. 225, 227; Zaldivar, Manovil, Ragazzi, Rovira, *Cuadernos de derecho societario*, Vol. III, IV, p. 33; Roimisier, *El interés social en la sociedad anónima* (1979), pp 52, 60.

53. Dobson, *El abuso de la personalidad jurídica* (1985), p. 407.

2. Another reason for transplanting systems is the need to harmonize systems of governance. Harmonization, as we have seen, can be important to facilitate trade. Harmonization can also have significant political impetus. We have already seen how military occupation and the need to rebuild the society of the occupied nation, as in Japan, can result in significant harmonization of laws. We have also now seen how political revolution, as in China, can create within the victorious faction, a need to modify law to conform to the new economic and political bases of institutional ordering. The excerpt that follows shows the way in which nations may choose to harmonize their systems of enterprise regulation in anticipation of joining supra-national organizations. In this case, the Czechs, anticipating admittance into the European Union have had to conform their laws with that in mind.

3. Do you think that the notions of minimum protections for shareholders of closely held corporations can be universalized?

4. **Problem:** You are the assistant to the new President of the Republic of Turkmenistan, a predominantly Muslim country of ethnic Turks, only recently separated from the Soviet Union. At the suggestion of the American Ambassador to Turkmenistan, the President has received a delegation of American law professors eager to reform the corporate law of this country. You know that the President receives a significant amount of support for loan requests at the World Bank from the Americans. The American professors, full of a belief in the genius of the American system of protection for shareholders of closely held corporations, have submitted a plan to rewrite the company law of Turkmenistan. They argue that the current system is horribly unfair to shareholders and must be changed. Under current Turkmenistan law, shareholders of companies whose shares are not publicly held have an unlimited right to require the company to repurchase their shares by application to a court. If the company is unable to purchase the shares, the government is permitted to loan funds to the company in an amount sufficient to effect the purchase. Shareholders have no other rights. You know that American investment in Turkmenistan is currently quite low and may not increase for a number of years. The largest trading partners of the country are Iran, China and Turkey. Turkish investment, however, is primarily from subsidiaries of European Companies based in the European Union. That investment will grow substantially as these nations have admitted as refugees a large number of former citizens of Turkmenistan. Traditionally, before the Russian occupation of Turkmenistan in 1770, the great legal influence in Turkmenistan was that of the Ottoman Turks. The President has asked that you be prepared to defend this system. Prepare a memorandum of points in support of the current law.

Carol L. Kline, *Protecting Minority Shareholders in Close Corporations: Modeling Czech Investor Protections on German and United States Law*

23 B.C. Int'l & Comp. L. Rev. 229 (2000)
(excerpts from pages 236–238; 255–261; some footnotes omitted)

3. Structure of Legal Business Entities

The four legal business entities established by the Commercial Code are the limited liability company (*spolecnost s rucenim omezenym*), joint stock company (*akciova spolecnost*), general partnership (*verejna obchodni spolecnost*), and limited partnership (*ko-*

manditni spolecnost an akcie).[65] The limited liability company and the joint stock company are the two most common business entities.[66]

In a limited liability company, a shareholder is only liable for any unpaid capital.[67] Each shareholder must invest at least 20,000 Czech crowns (Kc),[68] and the number of shareholders is limited to fifty.[69] The minimum capitalization requirement for a limited liability company is 100,000 Kc.[70] A shareholder in a limited liability company may not withdraw from the company, but the shareholder may be expelled by the other shareholders.[71] Limited liability companies have a flexible management structure—management may be effectuated however the shareholders determine.[72]

For a joint stock company, the major requirement is a net capitalization of one million Kc.[73] A shareholder is not personally liable for any of the company's obligations.[74] Joint stock companies must have a supervisory board.[75] Shareholders may pass resolutions with a simple majority vote if a quorum of 30% of the shareholders are present.[76]

4. Minority Shareholder Protections

In 1996, the Czech government introduced amendments to the Commercial Code that were designed to provide minority shareholder protections.[77] These amendments were also intended to afford protections similar to other European countries.[78] Effective

---

65. [Sergio Salani & Jerry Sloan, *An Overview of Legal and Financing Aspects for Doing Business in Hungary, Poland, and the Czech Republic*, 9 Temp. Int'l & Comp. L.J. 27 (1995)] at 45.

66. [Karel Fiala & Filip Hruska, *Current Financial and Investment Environment in the Czech Republic*, 49 Consumer Fin. L.Q. REP. 296 (1995)] at 297.

67. [Richard Pivnicka & Mark Kreist, *Czech Republic: Investment in Freedom and the Future*, 1 Int'l Dimensions 6 (1997)] at 6; Salani & Sloan, supra, note [65] at 45.

68. As of Thursday, April 1, 1999, one United States dollar would purchase 35.788 Czech crowns (Koruna). See Currency Trading—Exchange Rates, WALL ST. J., Apr. 1, 1999, at C11.

69. Fiala & Hruska, supra, note [66] at 297.

70. See *id.*

71. [Sarah Andrus, *The Czech Republic and Slovakia: Foreign Participation in Changing Economies*, 17 Hastings Int'l & Comp. L. Rev. 611 (1994)] at 623 & n. 100.

72. See Salani & Sloan, supra note [65], at 45.

73. See Fiala & Hruska, supra note [66], at 297; Pivnicka & Kreisl, supra note [67], at 7.

74. See Pivnicka & Kreisl, supra note [67], at 7.

75. See Salani & Sloan, supra note [65], at 45.

76. See Andrus, supra note [71], at 625.

77. See Act No. 142/1996 *Sbirka zakon* (Collection of Laws) Amending the Commercial Code and the Civil Code, cited in [John Regis Coogan et al., *International Legal Developments in Review: 1996—Central European Law*, 31 Int'l Law. 495, 495 (1997)] at 499; *Legislative Changes Will Bring Greater Transparency and Shareholder Protection to Czech Capital Market*, E./w. Executive Guide, July 1, 1996 [hereinafter Legislative Changes]. Foreign investors are equally protected by the amendment because the Commercial Code provides that all foreign investors may conduct business under the same conditions as Czech investors. See Fiala & Hruska, supra note [66], at 297.

78. ....These amendments were modeled on both European Union guidelines and German law. See Susan Tietjen, *Recent Amendments to the Czech Commercial Code and Securities Act*, Cent. Eur. L. Committee News I. (Am. Bar Ass'n Section of Int'l Law and Practice, Washington, D.C.), Summer 1996, at 2. It is important that the Czech Republic model its protections on those of other European states because it currently seeks admission into the European Union. Significantly, the European Union has proposed the adoption of stronger minority shareholder protections as a short-term objective for accession. See Accession Partnership-Czech Republic-October 1999-Draft (visited Dec. 8, 1999) <http://europa.eu.int/comm/enlargement/docs/index.htm> [hereinafter Accession Partnership]. For more specific examples of these similarities, compare infra notes 79-86 and accompanying text with Miller, supra note 13, at 393, 396, 403 (discussing buyout remedies in Germany and the United Kingdom).

July 1, 1996, these amendments introduced strict buyout rules in takeovers.[79] At any time a takeover occurs, the person effectuating the takeover must offer to purchase the shares of the remaining shareholders for the average market price of those shares.[80] This buyout remedy now affords minority shareholders an opportunity to exit the corporation. Furthermore, the amendments create limitations on minority shareholder squeeze-outs.[82] Prior to the amendments, minority shareholders were subject to squeeze-outs when corporations canceled the ability to publicly trade shares or imposed restrictions on the transfer of shares. Due to this imposed lack of liquidity, minority shareholders were pressured to sell their shares on majority shareholders' terms. The amendments now require shareholder votes to either cancel the public tradeability of shares or to impose limitations on the transferability of shares.[85] If the corporation obtains shareholder approval for either of these changes, it must offer to purchase the shares of all shareholders who did not vote for the change.[86]

* * *

III. COMPARATIVE ANALYSIS OF MINORITY SHAREHOLDER PROTECTIONS IN THE CZECH REPUBLIC, GERMANY, AND THE UNITED STATES

A. Remedies Available

In the Czech Republic, minority shareholders are protected through the recent amendments to the Commercial Code and the expulsion rights of a limited liability company.[265] The amendments to the Commercial Code permit shareholders to obtain fair market value for their shares in the event of a takeover of the business entity. The amendments also provide for shareholder votes whenever a corporation wishes to cancel the public tradeability of shares or limit the transferability of shares. If the corporation receives the requisite vote, it must then offer to purchase the shares of those who did not vote for the change. In addition, shareholders in a limited liability company may be expelled from the company. These remedies permit the business entity to continue, but do not permit the aggrieved minority shareholder to continue in the business. Although these remedies guarantee that the minority shareholder receives fair market value, problems of valuation and the loss of future earnings and good will place the departing minority shareholder in a disadvantageous position.

---

79. See Coogan et al., supra note [77], at 499; Legislative Changes, supra note 77. Any acquisition by a person of more than one-half, two-thirds, or three-fourths of the aggregate nominal value of a company's voting shares constitutes a takeover....

80. See Legislative Changes, supra note 77. The average market price for the purpose of the shareholder buyout is calculated according to the price of the stock over the previous six months. See id. Furthermore, in order to prevent circumvention of the strict buyout requirement, the amendment considers a "shareholder" to include any group acting in accord. See id.

82. See Coogan et al., supra note [77], at 499;....

85. [Tietjen, supra note 78, at 4.] A majority vote of the shareholders (where each shareholder has one vote regardless of how many shares he or she holds) and a three-fourths vote of those shareholders who will be affected by the change are required in order to cancel the public tradeability of shares. See id. To limit the transferability of shares, a corporation must obtain a two-thirds vote of the shareholders and a three-fourths vote of those shareholders who will be affected by the change. See id.

86. See Tietjen, supra note 78, at 5.

265. See supra notes 71, 77–86 and accompanying text.

German minority shareholders in a GmbH are granted several remedies: dissolution, withdrawal, and expulsion. The dissolution remedy prevents the majority shareholder from continuing the business, so the minority shareholder faces a proportional loss. Minority shareholders may even be able to continue in the business without the complications of dealing with the majority shareholder if an expulsion remedy is granted.

In the United States, minority shareholders have been able to obtain dissolution and buyout remedies, but the basis for granting such remedies is narrower than the German *wichtige Grund.* This is because U.S. courts, unlike the German courts, refrain from looking at the personal characteristics of shareholders when determining whether remedies should be granted. In addition to these remedies, some courts in the United States have recognized fiduciary duties owed to minority shareholders. Fiduciary duties, stemming from duties owed to partners in partnerships, are unique as compared to the Czech Republic, but they may be analogous to the German concept of *wichtige Grund.*[278] On the other hand, fiduciary duties contrast with German remedies because while fiduciary duties may be contractually waived by the shareholders, the rights to withdrawal or expulsion on the basis of *wichtige Grund* may not be contractually waived.

B. Enforcement of Remedies

As compared to Germany and the United States, the Czech Republic has the weakest enforcement of minority shareholder protections. The Czech Republic was still developing its Securities and Exchange Commission by mid-1997, and the introduction of statutory minority shareholder protections did not occur until 1996. The relative novelty of the Czech Republic's system for enforcing minority shareholder protections results in an undeveloped and untested set of protections.

Germany has a well-established system for granting minority shareholder remedies. The courts have been extremely active in this area, but the treatment of Jews during the Third Reich remains a shadow on the judicial enforcement of minority shareholder protections. The breadth of *wichtige Grund* has contributed to uncertainty in the law. Although judicial discretion and the broad reach of *wichtige Grund* permit a more flexible analysis of shareholder relationships, the uncertainty of the legal doctrine may adversely affect these relationships.

The United States does not have a uniform system for enforcing minority shareholder protections because each state within the United States enacts its own legislation. Some jurisdictions within the United States, however, have developed broad bases for granting minority shareholder remedies. In Illinois, oppressive conduct (a basis for granting dissolution) only requires a finding of heavy-handed or arbitrary conduct. New York's reasonable expectations standard (a basis for granting a buyout) allows a court to consider the bargain of the parties. Finally, Massachusetts fiduciary duties allow a court to probe into the good faith and loyalty of the shareholders. Both the number of remedies that may be available, and the broad scrutiny used to determine whether remedies should be granted, provide U.S. courts with similar enforcement power and discretion as German courts.

---

278. ....Some breaches of fiduciary duties in the United States may be similar to what would constitute wichtige Grund for withdrawal or expulsion in Germany....

C. Adequacy of Remedies

The Czech Republic's remedies do not appear to adequately protect minority shareholders. Although shareholders in a limited liability company may be expelled, and shareholders may seek fair market value in the event of a takeover, shareholders have no other option but to take the money and leave the company. Furthermore, buyout remedies are only triggered upon takeovers, cancellation of the public tradeability of shares, or limitation of share transferability. As the Czech Republic is trying to attract investors, particularly foreign investors, allowing only the option of expulsion or buyout removes the incentive to make the effort to invest in the first place. This is most contrary to one of the goals of the Commercial Code: fostering public confidence in capitalism and private business ownership. Czech citizens have only recently been introduced to the investment arena. If their first glimpses of shareholding are dominant investment funds capable of controlling business decisions and illiquid shares, they may be unwilling to enter the investment arena again. Foreign investors, with their numerous opportunities for investment in other countries, will seek more protective states.

German minority shareholders appear to be adequately protected—they are afforded several remedies and a broad means through which to obtain them. The problem, however, is that the remedies available to minority shareholders may also be used against them. As *wichtige Grund* may be established based on personal characteristics of a shareholder, majority shareholders might try to expel a minority shareholder for one of these characteristics—being uncooperative, for example.

The adequacy of remedies in the United States varies depending on the state in which the business entity is formed. In general, the major failure of remedies in the United States is that courts have been unwilling to expel a heavy-handed majority shareholder. From a minority shareholder's point of view, either the minority shareholder can seek dissolution or a buyout (thereby losing all hopes of future profits and participation), or the minority shareholder can remain with the corporation with the majority shareholder (possibly seeking damages based on violations of fiduciary duties). In neither of these scenarios may a minority shareholder continue in the business without the heavy-handed majority shareholder.

IV. SUGGESTIONS FOR IMPROVING MINORITY SHAREHOLDER PROTECTIONS IN THE CZECH REPUBLIC

In order to alleviate some of the deficiencies of minority shareholder protections and attract foreign investors, the Czech Republic should adopt several aspects of minority shareholder protections already established by Germany and the United States. If German and U.S. investors look to the Czech Republic and find similar protections to those in their home states, they may feel more comfortable making an investment there. Increasing minority shareholder protections, therefore, may attract foreign investors and enable the Czech Republic to compete with Poland and Hungary.

A. The Relationship Between the Czech Republic, Germany, and the United States

Several factors point to Germany and the United States as candidates for emulation by the Czech Republic. First, Germany and the United States rank first and second respectively in foreign investment in the Czech Republic. German investment accounts for 30% of the total foreign investment, and the United States accounts for 14%. Germany has already been moving capital and technology into the Czech Republic because of the low wages there.

Next, the Czech Republic has already looked to Germany and the United States as models for change. The Czech Republic's corporation laws closely model U.S. and German corporation laws.[318] The Czech Republic planned to create its Securities and Exchange Commission partly based on the U.S. Securities and Exchange Commission. Furthermore, as a condition for providing much needed capital, U.S. institutions have demanded that host countries assimilate to their styles of doing business. According to Mr. Richard Salzman, head of the Prague Stock Exchange, "[Czechs] speak English, we take advice from Americans, but look at the map. We are going towards the German system."

Finally, as Germany is a dominant member of the European Union, and the Czech Republic is currently seeking admission into the European Union, emulating German standards may make transition into the European Union easier. Already, the Czech Republic has signed an association agreement with the European Union.[323] During the term of this agreement, the Czech Republic has begun to bring its laws into compliance with European Union guidelines.

B. Improving Shareholder Protections in the Czech Republic— Providing Broader Bases for Buyout Remedies

In order to improve shareholder protections, the Czech Republic may wish to broaden the availability of buyouts. Currently, buyouts are only available in the context of takeovers or corporate actions to cancel the public tradeability of shares or limit the transferability of shares. In both Germany and the United States, buyouts are available when conduct of a majority shareholder becomes intolerable.

Broadening the availability of buyouts and imposing fiduciary duties on shareholders, however, implicates a need to develop judicial standards for those concepts. Furthermore, the Czech Republic will have to establish a procedure for review. Within the past five years, both the Ministry of Finance and the Securities and Exchange Commission have played a role in overseeing the trading of shares. In addition to granting oversight powers to the Ministry of Finance or the Securities and Exchange Commission, the Czech judiciary could be granted a role in review.

Although dissolution may be considered as an alternative remedy, the Czech Republic's need to support competitive enterprises, thereby enhancing its market economy and inspiring investor confidence, may preclude this remedy. Upon dissolution, the corporate entity ceases to exist. Even with expulsion, if the minority shareholder does not have sufficient capital to compensate the expelled majority shareholder, the corporation will be dissolved. As the Czech Republic wants to encourage business, it may not want to introduce remedies that destroy business.

Perhaps the most effective way to institute change will be to adopt an amendment to the Commercial Code. This is the means by which the Czech Republic adopted its most recent minority shareholder protections. As the Commercial Code governs business activities, passing an amendment to the Commercial Code to provide broader bases for

---

318. See Vassil Breskovski, *Directors' Duty of Care in Eastern Europe*, 29 INT'L LAW. 77, 78 (1995). The recent amendments to the Commercial Code are based on European Union guidelines and German law, See Tietjen, supra note 78, at 2.

323. See generally, Europe Agreement establishing an association between the European Communities and their Member States, of the one part, and the Czech Republic, of the other part, 1994 O.J. (L 360/2), as amended by 1996 O.J. (L 343/1) and explained in 1997 O.J. (C 141/5), *available in* ENCYCLOPEDIA OF EUROPEAN UNION LAW, vol. 3, § 43.2660, et seq.

buyouts is an adequate means to both protect minority shareholders and inspire investor confidence.

---

2. *Japan*

Protection of shareholders, especially of minority shareholders, is becoming a more dynamic area of concern in Japan. Its boundaries are intimately tied to notions of director duty. If directors owe a greater duty to constituencies other than shareholders, it may well be that majority shareholders owe greater duty to the minority shareholders. Indeed, majority shareholders may owe a greater duty to employees and creditors than to the desires of the minority. The readings that follow suggest an answer, or at least an approach, to an understanding of these issues.

Dan Fenno Henderson, *Security Markets in the United States and Japan: Distinctive Aspects Molded by Cultural, Social, Economic, and Political Differences*

14 Hastings Int'l & Comp. L. Rev. 263 (1991)
(excerpts pages 274–276; some footnotes omitted)

d. It is probably fair to say that the implementation of corporate democracy by the shareholders' meetings of large corporations is the major unsolved problem in both the U.S. and Japanese corporate law systems, and resides at the core of the ongoing discussion of corporate governance. In both nations, shareholders must and do rely on representation by management. Issues genuinely contested by shareholder votes are exceptional, and center around rare intraboard rivalries expressed by a proxy contest. Recent American institutional investors' use of the proxy system[43] has not been emulated in Japan.

Otherwise, shareholders concerned about mismanagement simply vote by selling on the stock exchange. Even the rash of leveraged buy outs, takeovers, and tender offers in America in the 1980s is but another manifestation of voting by selling as the only meaningful expression of shareholder concern. The fact that control is in essence, a stake, raises a host of other unrelated issues related to minority protection.

Equity (and therefore the shareholder) is not nearly as important in Japan as it is in the United States; rather, debt is predominant. This lends to another difference: Japanese management manages shareholders differently, not in law, but in practice. One management technique is the "stable shareholder," explained more fully below, which is implemented by cross-shareholdings within the establishment. Another technique is more directly concerned with the managing of shareholder meetings, and centers around a professional shareholder. These sokai-ya, or shareholder meeting operators, extort favors from management in exchange for not causing trouble at shareholder meetings, or for facilitating, by a sort of guerrilla tactic, smooth and short shareholder meetings. By 1981 sokai-ya practices had become truly institutionalized in many corpo-

---

43. See Institutions Expected to Pursue Shareholder Proposals Agressively, 21 Sec. Reg. & L. Rep. (BNA) No. 21, at 202 (Feb. 3, 1989).

rations. The purpose of sokai-ya is to enable management to avoid criticism and to get through meetings quickly, generally under thirty minutes.[44]

> In 1981 attempts were made, by amendment to the Commercial Code, to thwart the illegal activities of sokai-ya and managers alike. The changes have apparently been successful to curtail, if not completely eradicate, the sokai-ya.[45]

In the American practice there has been no exact equivalent to sokai-ya working with management to manage the shareholders. But in the 1980s plenty of management and financial practices were costly to the public shareholders, not to mention the taxpayer. There are ample ill-defined conflicts of interests and malpractices of management which the law has yet to fully sort out and rectify. In the areas of leveraged buy outs, two-tiered tender offers, poison pills, green mail, and golden parachutes, as well as programmed trading, insider trading, and savings and loan fiascos accompanied by junk bond speculations, a host of legal problems have been raised in the courts, running about a decade behind the fast deals. Thus, American individual shareholders have their problems too, despite the absence of the sokai-ya, and the general shareholder meeting certainly holds little promise of becoming useful to the ordinary shareholder any time soon. There is, however, an enormous difference in the use of equity finance in Japan and the United States, and therefore in the role of the shareholder. The difference inheres in the sociology of the corporate world and the mechanisms of finance within the politicobusiness establishment.

S. Todd Huckaby, Note: *Defensive Action to Hostile Takeover Efforts in Japan: the Shuwa Decisions*

29 Colum. J. Transnat'l L. 439 (1991)
(excerpts pages 443–461; some footnotes omitted)

Reread the excerpts reproduced in Chapter 10, with a focus on the construction and interpretation of majority shareholder duty.

E. Socialist Approaches

The problem posed by the theory of the "state" is fundamental to the difficulties of creating a legal basis for organizing enterprises on a Western model. The deficiencies of the company law adopted by the People's Republic of China is illustrative. Where the "state" constitutes the majority or controlling shareholder of a going concern organized as a corporation, the foundational bases upon which Western corporate governance operates is lost. Moreover, if the state is based on the notion that individuals and legal per-

44. A good summary of the sokai-ya institution before the 1981 amendments is found in Japan v. Yasumo, 23 Keishu 1359 (Oct. 16, 1969), a criminal case wherein SHOHO arts. 494(1)(1) and (2) were applied to convict a corporate officer who dealt with sokai-ya.

45. SHOHO arts. 294-2, 237-4(3), 497. See Takeuchi, Shareholders Meetings Under the Revised Commercial Code, 20 Law in Japan 173 (1987).

sons owe the highest fiduciary duty to the state, the basis on which monitoring of corporate managers is grounded becomes irrelevant. On the other hand it may be possible to argue that China has begun to travel down a path at the end of which will be a revolutionary new way of conceiving the enterprise organized as a corporation by operation of law, in which the state serves both as regulator of the legal context in which the corporation operates and controller of the operations of each enterprise which it has permitted to exist. The state is its own regulator; truly a self-referential system operating on multiple levels of the sort that perhaps lies at the limit of enterprise theory such as that we considered in Chapter 4.[1]

The reading that follows highlights what may well be the Achilles heel of Chinese corporate governance. The failure to create effective regulation, governed under the rule of law, of the relationships between the state as majority shareholder, and the directors and minority shareholders of Chinese corporations, will create the danger that such corporations will ultimately be deemed a sham.

The result—China may well be the first state in which the concepts of multi-tiered conglomerate and political unit merge.

> The Party Committee Secretary, Chairman and General Manager of the Shenyang Materials Development Corporation wrote that in joint-stock companies "party organizations [must] play their role as the political nucleus; and for the party organizations to play this role they must, based on the characteristics of a joint-stock enterprise, carry out and implement the party's line, principles, and policies in the enterprise."[2]

A brave new world indeed.

Michael Irl Nikkel, Note: *"Chinese Characteristics" in Corporate Clothing: Questions of Fiduciary Duty in China's Company Law*

80 Minn. L. Rev. 503 (1995)

(excerpts pages 522–528; 530–539; some footnotes omitted)

II. ENTER THE NEW COMPANY LAW

A. The Company Law's Underpinnings

The Company Law is another sign of China's shift away from the command economy advanced under Mao toward one driven by market-oriented forces.[96] The Company Law

---

1. *See* Gunther Teubner, *Enterprise Corporatism: New Industrial Policy and the "Essence" of the Legal Person*, 36 Am. J. Corp. L. 130 (1988).

2. [Wang Linhua, Characteristics of and General Plan for Party Committee's Leadership of Joint-Stock Enterprises, Lingdao Kexue [Leadership Sci.], Jan. 11, 1995, at 36, 36–37, translated in and microformed on F.B.I.S.-CHI 95-067, Article on Party Role in Joint-Stock Enterprises, Apr. 7, 1995, at 33], at 34, *quoted in* Michael Irl Nikkel, Note: *"Chinese Characteristics" in Corporate Clothing: Questions of Fiduciary Duty in China's Company Law*, 80 Minn. L. Rev. 503 & n. 179 (1995).

96. ....Through March 1994, there were more than 7 million registered enterprises in China and, according to official Chinese statistics, 1.44 million of those were "corporate companies with State, collective, Sino-foreign or private investment." Ma Zhiping, *State Eases Restrictions on Forming Companies*, China Daily, July 1, 1994, available in WESTLAW, INT-NEWS Database. By July 31, 1994, an estimated 54,500 of these 1.44 million enterprises were operational shareholding com-

provides a legal framework for the protection of individual and institutional investors, whether they are foreign or domestic. Additionally, the Company Law establishes a mechanism for a shareholding system to transform state-owned enterprises into market-oriented companies.[98]

The heart of the Law's progressivity is Article 102. It provides that shareholders, rather than the state, "shall be the organ of authority of the company."[99] Article 14 of the Law,[100] however, retains the spirit of the original model of Communism in China that commentators refer to as the "Chinese characteristics" of reform. The provision states that the new "companies must... strengthen the establishment of a socialist spiritual civilization, and accept the supervision of the government and the public."[102] Although the statement is probably closer to Maoist hyperbole than to enforceable law, it continues a Party-centered dynamic under which China's court system and administrative agencies will likely operate—and a risk of which investors should be aware.

---

panies. Figures Show Shareholding Enterprises Prospering, Xinhua, Nov. 3, 1994, translated in and microformed on F.B.I.S.-CHI 94-213, Nov. 3, 1994, at 46. In a study by the China Enterprise Evaluation Center, Chinese enterprises recorded greater economic efficiency after they adopted the shareholding system. Id.

There is significant confusion inside and outside of China as to what makes a company. An example of the mayhem created by the misconceptions is that many of the farm collectives in rural China are converting themselves into "companies" where the shareholders are the local villagers and the farmers. Interview with Tahirih V. Lee, Associate Professor of Law, University of Minnesota Law School, in Minneapolis, Minn. (Apr. 27, 1995). That these "companies" have shareholders might lead a visitor to believe that they are in fact true companies. This is not necessarily the case, however, because a company is merely an entity created by the state—a fiction for the carrying on of business. If an entity fails to comply with regulations designed to provide for that fiction (the structural faculties and registration procedures laid out in the law) then the "company" is not a company at all, but merely an amalgamation of individuals who are doing business together. A problem develops when another entity or individual attempts to bring a suit against the "company" for breach of contract, or other reason, and finds to its embarrassment that the "shareholders" of that "company" are not registered in compliance with any regulation. The individual or entity is thereafter forced into multiple suits against the "shareholders" of the "company." Visitors would do well, therefore, to seek actual registration documentation from the "company," and go one step further by investigating at the local registry whether the document given them is legitimate.

98. [China's Company Law: The New Legislation 7 (Guiguo Wang trans., 1994) [hereinafter Company Law]], art. 81. Such a mechanism provides ample justification for the Company Law's formation. See supra text accompanying notes 78–85 (discussing the status of state-owned enterprises).

On July 20, 1994, China's State Council released company registration procedures for the Company Law. Regulations of the People's Republic of China for Administering Company Registration, Xinhua News Agency, translated and available in, LEXIS, WORLD Library, BBCSWB File [hereinafter Registration Regulations]. The Registration Regulations establish that China's State Administration for Industry and Commerce is in charge of company registration work around the country. Id. art. 5. Items needed for a company to register include name, address, statutory representative, registered capital (at least 100,000 RMB), enterprise category, scope of operation, period of business operation and names of stockholders or the name of the promoter of the company. Id. art. 9. Under article 3 of the Regulations, a company only receives its coveted "enterprise legal-person business license" once it registers "in accordance with the law." Id. art. 3.

99. Company Law, supra note [98], art. 102.

100. Id. art. 14.

102. Company Law, supra note [98], art. 14. Some commentators consider this provision closer to canonical law than corporate law because it seems almost ecclesiastical with its spiritual language. Rowan Callick, China: Credibility of Chinese Laws Under Scrutiny, Australian Fin. Rev., Dec. 9, 1994, at 23. They explain that the provision serves to raise questions about the status of companies in China and the law's legitimacy. Id.

B. Company Structure Under the New Law

The Company Law creates two classes of companies: limited liability companies[103] and companies limited by shares.[104] Companies limited by shares are commonly referred to as joint-stock companies. This Note focuses on the Company Law's treatment of these joint-stock companies because of their wide investment potential.[106]

The Company Law guarantees a joint-stock company limited liability and provides for the division of its registered capital into shares.[107] Like American corporations, shareholders exercise control over their contributions and receive a share of profits from the enterprise[108] in proportion to the number of shares they own.[109] Under the Company Law, shareholders elect directors in accordance with the number of voting shares owned by each shareholder.[110]

---

103. Limited liability companies are sometimes seen as something akin to closely held corporations in the United States. See Vivienne Bath, *Introducing the "Limited Company,"* CHINA BUS. REV., Jan.–Feb. 1993, at 50, 52–53 (comparing new Chinese security regulations to existing regulations in the United States). "The terminology used in this area can be confusing.... The term "limited liability company,' used in Hong Kong and certain states in the United States, also refers to a form of corporate organization that is treated as a partnership for tax purposes." [Matthew D. Bersani, *Privatization and the Creation of Stock Companies in China*, 1993 COLUM. BUS. L. REV. 301], at 308 n.16. For an illuminating side-by-side comparison of the two classes of new companies see Preston M. Torbert, *Broadening the Scope of Investment*, CHINA BUS. REV., May–June 1994, at 48, 49.

104. Company Law, supra note [98], art. 2.

106. Limited liability companies must have more than two, but less than fifty shareholders. Company Law, supra note 12, art. 20. Only joint-stock company promoters can make public offerings for sale of a company's stock. Id. art. 74. Shareholders in both forms of companies are liable to the company to the extent of their capital contribution. Id. art. 3. In cases where an SOE is reorganized to become a wholly state-owned, limited liability company that produces products determined by the State Council to be of national importance, or is involved in a similarly special industry, the new company is not obligated to establish a shareholder's general meeting. Id. arts. 64, 66. These wholly state-owned limited liability companies must have boards of directors, not simply executive directors. Id. art. 68.

107. Id. arts. 19–36....

108. Id. art. 103. Shareholders can then assign these shares, subject to certain restrictions, and the company, can repurchase the shares in some situation. Id. arts. 143–147, 149. Importantly, an SOE or an entity formed under the Company Law can invest up to 50% of its net assets in another company. Id. art. 12. In this way, an SOE actually can have the controlling share in a new enterprise formed under the Company Law. Id. Because this 50% figure does not include the profit from asset investment the company returns into the new enterprise to provide additional capital for it to operate, i.e., profit capitalization, an investing company's share of the new enterprise could grow over time. Id.

109. Shareholders enjoy rights and assume obligations based on the number of shares owned. Id. art. 106. They exert a degree of control over the operations of the company through their ability to attend and vote at shareholders' meetings. Id. art. 103. Like shareholders of U.S. companies, shareholders in the new Chinese companies have the right to attend meetings in person or by proxy, inspect corporate records, receive dividends, and receive the residual value of the company's assets in the event of liquidation. Id. arts. 108, 110, 177, 195. The shareholders may approve matters involving the company's finances and profit distribution plans, including amendment of the company's articles of association and approval of mergers and liquidations. Id. art. 103. More than two-thirds of those shareholders in attendance at the general meetings must adopt amendments to the articles. Id. art. 107. If subscribers representing more than half of the total number of outstanding shares are present, the shareholders can meet for the first time. Id. art. 92. By a simple majority vote of those in attendance, the shareholders at this inaugural meeting can approve the articles and elect board and supervisory board members. Id. art. 92(2)–(4). Shareholders owning 10% or more of the company's equity also have the right to convene an extraordinary shareholders' meeting to discuss important issues. Id. art. 104(3).

110. Id. art. 103(2).

The board of directors[111] in the newly formed company has the responsibility of appointing and removing management at its highest level.[112] Similar to the bylaws of most United States corporations, the company's articles of association set forth management's rules for operation.[114] Shareholders elect directors, but cannot remove them except for cause.

Directors and managers ultimately must answer to shareholders under the Company Law. Accordingly, the members of management are supposed to make decisions based on the best interests of shareholders, instead of the members' or third parties' personal concerns. Article 123 of the Company Law states that "the directors and the manager shall... faithfully perform their duties and protect the interests of the company." [117] Yet, by simultaneously maintaining the company's duty to the "socialist spiritual civilization,"[118] the Company Law provides the Party with a justification for upholding a director or manager's decision that the Party deems to be in the best interests of the country, but not necessarily of the company.

The Company Law sets out several provisions, however, that could ultimately work to protect the fiduciary relations inherent in a corporate setting. The Company Law requires directors to execute their official duties and to protect the company's interests without exploiting their position and power in the company.[119] Similarly, the law contains duty of loyalty provisions like those found in U.S. corporate law.[120] Commentators practicing under the common law system see these new provisions as "a step further towards the concept of "fiduciary duties' under common law."

Other provisions in the Company Law also work specifically to protect investors from possible breaches of fiduciary duty. The Company Law sets forth a series of prohibitions that, among other things, disqualify government officials from serving concurrently as directors or general managers,[122] prohibit directors and managers from taking

---

111. Id. art. 112(8)–(10). Unlike the U.S. model, a supervisory board, of which the shareholders and the company's workers elect constituent parts, can oversee the board of directors. Id. arts. 124, 126....

112. Company Law, supra note 12, art. 112(9). The management office, under the direction of the board of directors, runs these companies. Id. art. 119. The manager attends the directors' meetings as a nonvoting attendee. Id. art. 119. Depending on the company's articles, the board or manager can appoint deputy managers. Id. art. 119(6). The promoters, through the company's articles, can vest in the manager hiring and firing authority. Id. art. 119(8). The manager can in this way have broader powers than his or her SOE counterparts.

114. Company Law, supra note [98], art. 79.

117. Company Law, supra note [98], art. 123. In the United States, a fiduciary obligation exists when someone has a duty to subordinate his or her own personal interests in favor of another's benefit. Black's Law Dictionary 625 (6th ed. 1990). This "is the highest standard of duty implied by law." Id.

118. Company Law, supra note [98], art. 14.

119. Id. arts. 214–215.

120. Under the Company Law, directors or managers may not engage in the same type of business as the company for which they work. Id. arts. 61, 123. For similar U.S. provisions, see Corporate Director's Guidebook, 33 Bus. Law. 1591, 1599 (1978) [hereinafter Guidebook] ("When the corporate director has a material personal interest in a contract or transaction to which the corporation is to be a party,... the director should disclose the existence of such an interest.").

122. Company Law, supra note 12, arts. 58, 123. In addition, directors cannot lend or misappropriate company funds, open their own accounts for deposit of company funds, or use company equity as security for debts of shareholders or other persons. Id. arts. 60, 123. The Company Law also prevents directors from disclosing company secrets unless allowed to do so by law or according to the shareholders' wishes. Id. arts. 62, 123.

bribes or accepting illegal income,[123] and preclude directors and managers from entering contracts with the company except in limited circumstances.[124] For example, a director may not contract with the company to supply equipment directly to the company from the director's own business without the authorization of the company's articles or its shareholders. The Company Law also holds directors, supervisors, and general managers liable for violations of the Company Law's duty of care and loyalty provisions.[126]

Finally, the Company Law requires a Chinese joint-stock company to maintain a supervisory board.[127] Shareholders and the company's staff and workers elect constituent parts of this board.[128] The board's functions are to supervise staff and ensure that the actions of the directors and management are in compliance with other PRC laws and the company's articles.[129] The supervisory board has the authority to require a director or manager to "correct" an illegal act or one that violates the joint-stock company's articles.[130] Overall, the Company Law represents a good foundation for the beginnings of corporate activity in China despite provisions favoring the central government.[131]

* * *

III. Fiduciary Duty in the Ownership and Control of China's Companies

Still unclear under China's system of corporate governance is whether the steps taken by the new Company Law will provide sufficient protection to investors, especially minority shareholders in majority state-held joint-stock companies. The Company Law must protect the "lawful rights and interests of companies, shareholders and creditors" if China hopes to use effectively the fiduciary relationship that exists in company settings.[141] The Company Law must ensure that minority shareholders in majority state-held companies have a right of recourse to directors or managers who breach their fiduciary duty to the company.

A. An Example Amplifying the Shareholder Protection Enigma in China

Recall the inconsistency of Articles 14 and 102. While the Company Law provides that shareholders "shall be the organ of authority of the company,"[142] the Law also man-

---

123. Id. arts. 59, 123.

124. Id. arts. 61, 123.

126. Company Law, supra note [98], art. 63. Under the current state of the court system in China, it is hard to determine the exact loss to the company. . . .

127. Company Law, supra note [98], art. 124.

128. Id. Although the promoters set out the general composition of the supervisory board in the company's articles of association, the Company Law requires that the staff and workers elect an "appropriate proportion" of the members of the board. Id. In addition, the supervisory board must have at least three members, who serve three years with the possibility of reelection. Id. art. 125.

129. Id. art. 126(2).

130. Id. art. 126(3). In doing so, the supervisory board has the right to examine the company's books and propose interim shareholders' meetings. Id. art. 126(1), (4). Like a company manager, supervisory board members must attend meetings of the board of directors as nonvoting attendees. Id. art. 126. What effect the supervisory board will have on the amelioration of a breach of fiduciary responsibility in a new company is uncertain. . . .

131. Although joint-stock companies have been operating in China for some time now, the government has only recently promulgated measures regulating their establishment and operation. Vivienne Bath, *Introducing the "Limited Company"*, China Bus. Rev., Jan.–Feb. 1993, at 50, 50–51; see also supra text accompanying notes 69–71 (discussing the limited privatization of domestically traded companies).

141. Company Law, supra note [98], art. 1 ("This Law is formulated in accordance with the Constitution in order to suit the requirements of establishing a modern enterprise system.").

142. Id. art. 102.

dates that new companies should build the "socialist spiritual civilization, and accept the supervision of the government and the public."[143] The following scenario illustrates the contradiction this creates.

In August 1995, Ford Motor Company announced plans to purchase a twenty percent equity stake in the Chinese company Jiangling Motors Corporation to produce minivans for the Chinese market.[144] Jiangling is a light-truck manufacturer located in Nanchang, the capital of Jiangxi province in southern China. Ford paid $ 40 million for a twenty percent stake in Jiangling when Jiangling issued new shares on Shenzhen's B-share market—the only shares that foreigners may purchase.[145] The Jiangling Motors Corporation Group (JMCG) retains a fifty-one percent controlling interest in the corporation with another seventeen percent owned by local investors through Shenzhen's A-share market—shares that only Chinese may purchase.[146] The agreement to purchase the equity stake entitles Ford to three directors on Jiangling's nine-member board and five senior management positions. A Ford spokesperson said that the company could have purchased a greater stake in Jiangling, "but we saw no real advantage in that. We can't get a controlling interest in any case." That interest, of course, stays with JMCG, a state-controlled entity. Jiangling remains a majority state-owned joint-stock company publicly listed on the Shenzhen stock exchange.[149]

Assume that all goes well for Ford in its new venture and that the new minivans become quite popular for domestic Chinese consumers.[150] Jiangling begins to make a profit. In fact, it is so profitable that by the end of the partnership's first year of business, Jiangling has money to spare. Assume that at that point, local Jiangxi officials ask Jiangling's board to make a loan to one of Jiangxi's failing SOEs. In keeping with China's tight money policy of the past few years, the SOE has been unable to secure enough credit through its usual channel, the central government. The local officials sell the loan as a way to "strengthen the establishment of a socialist spiritual civilization" and diversify Jiangling's investments.[152] In addition, the officials promise the JMCG majority directors that the SOE will make every effort to pay back the credit. The Jiangxi officials convince the JMCG directors that an operating loan to the SOE, full of would-be unemployeds, is the "right" thing to do. Jiangling's board, including the three Ford directors, performs the usual due diligence as to the SOE's credit-worthiness and determines that a loan to the SOE is not in Jiangling's best interests. But because of the symbiotic relationship that exists between the Jiangxi officials and the JMCG directors—and much to the chagrin of the Ford directors—the JMCG directors approve the loan.

---

143. Id. art. 14.

144. Angelo B. Henderson & Craig S. Smith, Ford to Purchase 20% Equity Stake in Jiangling Motors, Wall St. J., Aug. 23, 1995, at A5.

145. Id.

146. Tony Walker, Ford Skates Around Chinese Freeze—Share-buying Avoids the Joint Ventures Ban, Fin. Times, Sept. 7, 1995, at 34, available in LEXIS, WORLD Library, ALLWLD File.

149. Christine Chan, Ford Stake Puts Brakes on Jiangling, S. China Morning Post, Aug. 24, 1995, at 4, available in LEXIS, WORLD Library, ALLWLD File.

150. Apparently, at the time of the Ford announcement, Jiangling was not the healthiest of companies. The company had debts of over 2.5 billion yuan, including a 1.9 billion yuan foreign currency loan. Renee Lai, Jiangling B Shares Raise $ 352m, S. China Morning Post, Sept. 15, 1995, at 3, available in LEXIS, WORLD Library, ALLWLD File. In addition, its operating profit was down from a year before and the Shenzhen exchange rules did not require the company to make a profit forecast for the subsequent year. Id.

152. See Company Law, supra note [98], art. 14.

As expected, the SOE defaults on the loan and Jiangling is out the money it could have used for development purposes. The Ford directors strenuously objected to the loan, but, in an effort not to waste the good guanxi[153] they have built with local Jiangxi officials, they decide against bringing an action for breach of duty. They realize that "it's going to take time and money [because] "the transition is still occurring from a socialist economy to a socialist market economy, and that has its difficulties."[154]

Assume further that Jiangling, in spite of the bad loan, continues to be profitable. [155] Other local SOE managers notice, and soon the JMCG directors have approved three more similar loans that are all outstanding and in various stages of default. Tired of what they see as an abuse of discretion by the JMCG directors,[156] and clearly wanting to return to the business of manufacturing minivans, the Ford directors decide to test the Company Law's fiduciary duty provisions in court. They bring a case for breach of Article 123's duty to "protect the interests of the company."[157]

This sets up the dilemma for the Company Law. The JMCG directors must decide whether to work toward the company's profitability or answer the requests of the Jiangxi officials. A joint-stock company's business decisions do not "reflect fully those of a shareholding company in the developed countries"[158] because of the Chinese government's presence in the management of Jiangling, and, arguably, in all aspects of the economy.[159]

B. The Ill-effects of Limited Privatization on China's Corporate Sector

The long-term viability and legitimacy of companies in China depends on the ability of shareholders to make the new companies respond to market forces. Unfortunately, the Chinese government, whether on the local or national level, has an overriding influence in economic decisions made by majority state-owned companies.[160] The influence

153. "In short, Ford is entering traditional joint ventures with key Chinese companies—thereby pleasing a demanding Chinese government and building guanxi, or connections—while working hard to modernize and expand those companies." Keith Naughton et al., *Ford Opens the Throttle: It's Challenging Toyota's Dominance in the Far East*, Bus. Wk., Sept. 18, 1995, at 66, 68.

154. Keith Naughton et al., *Ford Opens the Throttle*, Bus. Wk. (Int'l ed.), Sept. 18, 1995, at 24, available in LEXIS, WORLD Library, ALLWLD File.

155. "Amazingly, no listed company has admitted that their [sic] decline in profits could be the result of... misguided operating decisions." Shuang Mu, *Seven Listed Companies Report Losses in First Half*, Bus. Wk. (China Daily Supp.), Sept. 10, 1995, available in LEXIS, WORLD Library, ALLWLD File.

156. A similar occurrence is quite likely to happen in more and more situations as Chinese "companies [use] their funds in high-risk stock and futures trading." Id.

157. See Company Law, supra note [98], art. 123.

158. [Andrew Xuefeng Qian, *Riding Two Horses: Corporatizing Enterprises and the Emerging Securities Regulatory Regime in China*, 12 UCLA Pac. Basin L.J. 62 (1993)], at 92.

159. Mr. Jiang Zemin, Communist Party chief, president, military leader, and heir-apparent to senior leader Deng Xiaoping, continues to take a conservative approach to governing China. His speeches have focused on the theme of protecting state enterprise's role as the core to the Chinese economy and building discipline in the Communist Party. Kathy Chen & Joseph Kahn, Mr. Weather Vane: A Pliant Technocrat is in Line to Become Next Leader of China, Wall St. J., Feb. 3, 1995, at A1, A8.

160. According to an interview with Hong Hu, China's Vice Minister of the State Commission for Restructuring the Economy, China is now concentrating on improving the state-owned sector to insure that the "public sector—including the State-owned sector and collectively-owned sector—holds a dominant position in China's economy." Privatization Not "Orientation' for Restructuring—Xinhua, June 20, 1995, translated in and microformed on F.B.I.S.-CHI 95-118, June 20, 1995, at 31 [hereinafter Hong Hu]. Consequently, the state-owned sector plays a leading role in China's economic growth. Id....

emanates from "Chinese characteristics" of reform and the conception of management and control of joint-stock companies that pervades business in China.

Management accountability is viewed in a different light than in fully market-based economies, and management in majority state-owned companies sometimes overlooks the interests of minority shareholders they are supposed to protect. Concepts such as public disclosure of financial records,[164] accountability to shareholders, and equal shares/equal votes are alien in China. Former SOE managers-turned-joint-stock company directors in companies where the state has a controlling interest too often continue to answer the requests of the state or the Party.

China's continuing state control ideology pervades decisions made by the courts and government in China. Government officials within China believe the "joint-stock system is just a property organization form and does not mean private ownership."[169] A possible effect of the relationship between state control and actual private ownership is that the profits in state controlled joint-stock companies have begun to falter, while joint ventures and privately owned companies in China are prospering. A far more deleterious effect, however, is that the state's overwhelming presence as a company shareholder might render the new Company Law's fiduciary provisions meaningless.

1. Protection of Fiduciary Interests Through Shareholder Meetings?

The Company Law provides a good basis on which to build China's corporate structure.[171] When events similar to those in the Jiangling example occur, however, protection for investors is inadequate. Under the Company Law, as in the United States, the shareholders' first line of control and financial protection emerges from their right to vote at company shareholder meetings. Unfortunately, in those companies where a majority of the shares are controlled by a government entity, the meetings are often a rubber stamp for previously decided state actions.[173]

The Company Law, like Western corporate law, effectively excludes minority shareholders from determining the business policies and plans of the company.[174] Although minority shareholders have a right under the Company Law to call an extraordinary board meeting to consider an issue,[175] the shareholders cannot change the course of business de-

---

164. One commentator has stated:

> Although Chinese stocks that are listed abroad have to meet local standards on releasing information, "the level of disclosure is still very poor.... There are still massive problems in understanding what is going on with these companies.... Domestic accounting varies from the international accounting systems, so most companies have two sets of books. Once a year, in theory, you should get accounts that have been audited by international auditors, but there are gaps in those accounts, and it is still a struggle."

Harvey D. Shapiro, *The Tao of Investing*, HEMISPHERES, Jan. 1995, at 50.

169. Hong Hu, *supra* note 160, at 31.

171. See [David Ho, China's Company Law: Something Concrete to Go By, E. Asian Executive Rep., Feb. 15, 1994, available in LEXIS, NEXIS Library, EASIAN File.], at 9 (noting that the Company Law gives foreign investors "something more concrete to go by than mere opinions and unpublished rules vaguely quoted by state officials").

173. "Theoretically investors are supposed to be able to select top officers and managers in a company, influence the annual report, discuss future investment, and so forth.... Yet a Huadong University Professor of Politics and Law, described a shareholders' meeting he had attended as a 'joke,' followed by a banquet." [Solomon M. Karmel, Note, *Emerging Securities Markets in China: Capitalism with Chinese Characteristics*, 140 CHINA Q. 1105, 1105 (1994)], at 1113 n.35.

174. Directors are elected by the shareholders; thus, the same situation occurs when minority shareholders attempt to replace certain directors. Company Law, supra note [98], art. 103(2).

175. See id. art. 104(3) (requiring an extraordinary shareholders' meeting if requested by shareholders owning 10% or more of the company's shares).

cisions made by the board or dismiss a director without cause.[176] Thus, the shareholder's minority status, like that of the Ford directors in the hypothetical, eliminates an important means of recourse against the management of the company through the shareholding system itself.

2. Protection of Fiduciary Interests Through Supervisory Boards?

A second possible avenue for minority shareholders might come through notifying the company's supervisory board about the situation so that the supervisory board can "correct" the decision.[177]

Unfortunately, under the Law a "proportion"[178] of the supervisory board are also shareholders, and most likely majority shareholders. If, as in the Jiangling example, the majority is representative of a state entity that controls the board of directors, the supervisory board's own willingness to remedy a minority shareholder's complaint proves problematic. This is especially true where the head of the supervisory board is a Party member.[179] It is unlikely that the supervisory board will provide recourse for a minority stock owner because the supervisory board in a majority state-controlled company almost always will be made up of Party members.

3. Other Avenues of Possible Fiduciary Protection

Likewise, unless the directors simultaneously serve as government officials or in some other way violate the Company Law's explicit prohibitions, those stipulations do not provide any recourse either. Minority shareholders inevitably have little or no recourse to the management of a majority state-owned company through the channels explicitly provided in the Law.

The "limited privatization" of companies saps the vitality of a market that could protect minority rights. If a large number of share subscriptions existed such that a majority of the shareholders in the Jiangling example were private individuals or non-state-controlled institutions, the situation could change because private shareholders would theoretically demand profitability in cases where the state would balk.[183] Because the Party is still prone to serve its own interests when the situation demands, rather than the interests of profitability, minority shareholders in a majority state-owned joint-stock company must turn to China's judicial system or guanxi to resolve business disputes.

---

176. See id. art. 39 (requiring that resolutions be adopted by two-thirds or more of voting shareholders).

177. Id. art. 126(3). If some minority shareholders are employees of the company, they can be elected by their coworkers to serve on the supervisory board and thereby take up the issue. Id. art. 124.

178. Id.

179. The Party Committee Secretary, Chairman and General Manager of the Shenyang Materials Development Corporation wrote that in joint-stock companies "party organizations [must] play their role as the political nucleus; and for the party organizations to play this role they must, based on the characteristics of a joint-stock enterprise, carry out and implement the party's line, principles, and policies in the enterprise." [Wang Linhua, Characteristics of and General Plan for Party Committee's Leadership of Joint-Stock Enterprises, Lingdao Kexue [Leadership Sci.], Jan. 11, 1995, at 36, 36–37, translated in and microformed on F.B.I.S.-CHI 95-067, Article on Party Role in Joint-Stock Enterprises, Apr. 7, 1995, at 33], at 34.

183. For a different view, see Lincoln Y. Rathnam & Viswanath Khaitan, Privatization: An Investor's Perspective, Pub. Util. Fort., Jan. 1, 1994, at 17 (outlining the benefits of state, as opposed to private ownership). "Investors are generally better off with offerings where 1) the government continues to own a majority of the shares... [and] 2) new management runs the business as a business." Id.

C. Justice Through the Chinese Judiciary?

Although the decision in the Jiangling example may remain standard in China, it would not be considered "business as usual" in developed countries. Assume that the loan to the fictional Jiangxi SOE would be considered a gross abuse of discretion by U.S. courts. Under the "legal person" status provided for in the Company Law, and guaranteed under China's Civil Law,[188] Ford's minority directors should be able to bring a derivative suit as agents on the company's behalf against the JMCG directors.[189] While it appears Ford may have a valid claim against the JMCG directors, that may not be the case in China.

The conflicting language of the Company Law and the subordinate position of the judiciary in China's governmental hierarchy hampers a shareholder's legal recourse. Article 123 of the Company Law requires directors and managers to protect the company's interests. This requirement is offset by Article 14's duty to "strengthen the establishment of a socialist spiritual civilization, and accept the supervision of the government and the public." Due to the difference between the Chinese concept of fiduciary responsibility and that of their Western counterparts, it is doubtful that a Chinese People's Court would find a loan to a failing SOE sufficient to penalize the directors. Moreover, the conflicting language of the Law adds to the difficulty by allowing directors a great deal of flexibility when making business decisions. Chinese courts, especially local ones,[196] likely would uphold the decision of the directors based on the directors' responsibility to the state.[197]

---

188. Included in the Civil Law is a description of the rights and obligations of an agent to their principal, the enterprise legal person. Civil Law, supra note 32, ch. IV, II. Unlike agency principles in the United States, see, e.g., Restatement (Second) of Agency 160–161, 194 (1958), the Chinese principal has the power to repudiate the agent's acts committed outside the scope of the agency relationship:

> With respect to acts committed without the power of agency, beyond the power of agency or after the termination of the power of agency, the principal shall bear civil liability therefor only after such acts have been ratified by the principal. The actor shall bear civil liability for any act that has not been ratified. Any principal who is aware that another person is implementing civil acts in the name of the principal and does not make a declaration of repudiation shall be deemed to have consented thereto.
>
> Any agent who fails to perform his duties causing losses to the principal as a result thereof should bear civil liabilities.

Civil Law, supra note 31, ch. VI, II, art. 66. "An agent's acts that are ultra vires are, seemingly, not binding on the principal unless the principal ratified or acquiesced to the agent's acts." Gary J. Dernelle, Direct Foreign Investment and Contractual Relations in the People's Republic of China, 6 Depaul Bus. L.J. 331, 344–45 (1994). If such an act occurs, the Civil Law provides that the agent assumes civil liabilities. Civil Law, supra note 31, ch. VI, I, art. 106. These civil liabilities can take several forms and can include compensation for losses. Id. ch. VI, IV, art. 134.

189. Although the Company Law does not set out an explicit provision guaranteeing the right to bring a suit derivatively by a shareholder, especially a foreign minority shareholder, Article 111 of the Law appears to grant that right. Article 111 provides that "where a resolution of the... board of directors... infringes the lawful rights and interests of the shareholders, the shareholders concerned shall be entitled to apply for an injunction in a People's court to terminate the violation or infringement." Company Law, supra note [98], art. 111. When read together with the Civil Law and the Company Law's mandate on directors to "faithfully perform their duties and protect the interests of the company" under Article 123, it appears that minority shareholders can at least bring an injunction against the board for a breach of fiduciary duty and then seek damages on behalf of the company for that infringement.

196. For example, local exchange officials in Shanghai were able to protect "big local traders during a bond-futures scandal last February that nearly toppled the city's leading broker." Bruce Einhorn & Dexter Roberts, China's Other Exchange Reaches for the Spotlight, Bus. Wk., Sept. 25, 1995, at 106.

197. See Company Law, supra note [98], art. 14 (explaining the responsibilities companies have to the state).

Alternatively, in the event that a judge decides to interpret the Company Law to actually create director liability to shareholders for a board of directors' poor business judgment, local Party officials could step in and override the ruling. The Party has ultimate control over court decisions because the Party remains at the top of the Chinese hierarchy. Using the Ford fiction, if the Party believes that the JMCG directors' decision to loan money to the failing SOE was good for the Jiangxi community, Ford is probably not assured of adequate recourse through the Chinese court system. Thus, China's laws "do not adequately protect shareholders, especially the minority shareholders."[199]

A Note on Post-socialist Transitional Economies, the Case of Russia

While China remains committed to its Marxist/Socialist structure, most other once Marxist/Socialist states have begun the process of transforming their political and economic systems to ones based on the principles of democracy and free enterprise. The problems encountered by these economies in transition has been great, no more so than in the area of the control of managers and shareholders. The reading that follows suggests some of the difficulties in the greatest post Marxist/Socialist state—Russia.

Andrei A. Baev, *The Transformation of the Role of the State in Monitoring Large Firms in Russia: From the State's Supervision to the State's Fiduciary Duties*

8 Transnat'l Law. 247 (1995)
(excerpts pages 278–93; some footnotes omitted

A. Sovereign Immunity, Reasonable Politics and the Fiduciary Duties of the State

The doctrine of "sovereign immunity," based on the postulate that "the King can do no wrong," formed part of the English common law heritage. Thus, under common law, the state has been held to be immune from tort liability. In Kawananakoa v. Polyblank,[124] Justice Holmes articulated the underlying basis for such immunity: "A sovereign is exempt from suit, not because of any formal conception or obsolete theory, but on the logical and practical ground that there can be no legal right as against the authority that makes the law on which the right depends." The immunity of the state is also recognized in the U.S. Constitution. The Eleventh Amendment proscribes suits by citizens in federal courts against their own state unless the affected state consents. Although many U.S. state courts have abolished the blanket tort immunity of the states, this doctrine is still present in U.S. law in a reduced form.

In contrast, the institutionalization of state fiduciary duties would not contradict the civil law system, which traditionally recognizes the state as an immediate subject of civil

---

199. [Andrew Xuefeng Qian, *Riding Two Horses: Corporatizing Enterprises and the Emerging Securities Regulatory Regime in China*, 12 UCLA Pac. Basin L.J. 62, 65 (1993)], at 92.
124. 205 U.S. 349 (1907).

law in the non-public relations of the state with its citizens and juridical entities.[128] As an independent, non-sovereign participant in occasional business transactions with private entities, the state has certain rights and incurs specific obligations.[129] Moreover, in Russia, the state's liability might also emerge from instances of malicious prosecution, political repression or other state actions. The state's obligations might arise from torts caused by the state or the state's agents during the scope of their employment. Furthermore, according to Russian law, the state may be liable for damages that have not been caused by the state or its agents. For instance, the new Russian Law On Ownership in the RSFSR [hereinafter The Law] imposes civil liability on the state for general damages caused to individuals by crimes. The Law expressly proclaims that "damage caused to an owner by a crime shall be compensated by the state by decision of a court. The expenditures incurred by the state in this connection shall be recovered from the guilty person in a judicial proceeding in accordance with RSFSR legislation."[131] Thus, imposition of fiduciary duties upon the state should not create many special problems for civil law countries, since general liability of the sovereign is traditionally recognized in these countries.

However, application of the theory of fiduciary duties to the state as a shareholder might be problematic from the point of view of supervision, particularly in former socialist countries with the civil law tradition of "conceptual jurisprudence." Intuition and common sense, despite their powerful influence on everyday human affairs, are excluded from the legal thinking. Thus, due to the vague, open-ended concept of loyalty, the idea of fiduciary duties, as well as trust, were absent from civil and Russian law. Moreover, the problems of conceptualizing a doctrine of fiduciary duty and trust become even more serious in former socialist countries, which, because of their ideological commitment, have adhered more strictly to the civil law tradition. The socialist countries were also culturally adherent to the principles of social consciousness, mutual aid, community interaction, socialist trustworthiness, and other ethical norms that were not formulated in law. As a result, there are certain technical problems with respect to the definition of fiduciary duties and their judicial enforcement in the former socialist countries that may not be apparent to common law lawyers.[133]

---

128. See, e.g., MICHAEL BRAGINSKY, THE SOVIET STATE AS A SUBJECT OF CIVIL LAW 14–34 (Progress ed., 1988); R. KHALFINA, STATE PROPERTY IN THE USSR 48–59 (Progress ed., 1980).

129. It is fair to note that distinctions between "governmental" and "proprietary" functions have also been recognized in American common law. See, e.g., Edgar Fuller & A. James Casner, *Municipal Tort Liability in Operation*, 54 HARV. L. REV. 437 (1941). "Proprietary" functions have been construed as "those functions that a city performs, but which could as well be provided by a private corporation." MARC A. FRANKLIN & ROBERT L. RABIN, TORTS 187 (1993).

131. [LAW ON ENTERPRISE IN THE USSR, adopted by the USSR Supreme Soviet, June 4, 1990, Vedomosti SND SSSR, No. 25, Item 460, translated in W.E. BUTLER, BASIC LEGAL DOCUMENTS OF THE RUSSIAN FEDERATION 301–19 (W.E. Butler trans. and ed., Oceana Publications Inc., 1992)] at art. 30, para. 3

133. For example, a problem may arise with construing the terms "special advantage" and "self-interest," which are ambiguous as applied to the state as sovereign. This is particularly so when the state is considered, constitutionally, the state of the whole people. What is the "self-interest" and the "self-dealing" of the whole people's state? Do shareholders receive some advantages from the reasonable politics of the government? What is the "public interest," and when should the pursuit of profit maximization by particular enterprises (which until privatization had been enterprises of the entire populace) be sacrificed for the public interest? May evil be committed against a public entity for the sake of the universal good? What, ultimately, is the state? Should we construe "the state" broadly as a nation, or narrowly as a political unit comprising a federation, or even more narrowly as a particular government ministry in charge of monitoring the mixed joint-stock enterprises with partial government participation in the equity? Are liability rules and legal remedies any different if a "spe-

* * *

Arguably, the democratic state has a duty to all its citizens, including shareholders, who are fortunate enough to share equity in an enterprise with their state. However, democratic participation is defined in terms of the process, rather than in terms of the outcome of the process. Accordingly, democracy does not necessarily safeguard the interest of everyone in society. It inevitably presumes that the decision-making process will lead to outcomes not desired by some citizens who happen to be part of a minority. In a sense, democracy might well turn into an autocracy of the majority or of well-organized groups, either of which is equally deleterious. While the autocracy of the majority leads to the neglect or abuse of minorities, the influence of interest-groups contributes to the corruption and degradation of the notion of democracy. If the latter is true, as some public choice literature suggests, we might conclude that legislatures and politicians speak only for well-organized groups rather than for the general public. In order to prevent the influence of groups organized against corporations, there should be certain limitations on the range of governmental appropriation of corporate resources when government acts as an ordinary shareholder.

On the other hand, the government should not be allowed to exercise protectionism toward a corporation in which the state holds an equity stake. The legislation of many countries expressly prohibits the state from acting in a protectionist fashion towards particular companies. In the United States, for instance, the Constitution of New Jersey provides that "no donation of land or appropriation of money shall be made by the State or any county or municipal corporation to or for the use of any society, association or corporation whatever."[139] Although the Russian Constitution does not contain a similar postulate, Russian civil law provides companies with the right to be treated equally by the state, without regard to the basis of their ownership. The Law of the Russian Federation, "On Ownership in the RSFSR" (adopted on December 24, 1990), proclaims that "the establishment by the State in any form whatever of limitations or privileges with respect to the right of ownership dependent upon whatever property is in private, State, or municipal ownership or the ownership of social associations (or organizations) shall not be permitted."[140] The preamble of another Act of the Russian Federation, "On Enterprises and Entrepreneurial Activity," the major Russian corporate and business law act, also declares that the same law should apply "to all subjects of entrepreneurial activity and enterprises, irrespective of the form of ownership and sphere of activity, including juridical persons and citizens of other Union Republics and foreign States...."[141] The law guarantees "equal rights of access of all subjects of entrepreneurial activity to material, financial, labour, informational, and natural resources, and equal conditions of activity of enterprises irrespective of their type of ownership and organizational-legal forms thereof."[142] Thus, in Russia, it is well recognized that the state cannot grant special privileges to any specific enterprise or organization.

---

cial advantage" was pursued by democratically elected politicians rather than by the government's agents? What difference does it make, if any, if "advantages" were sought through a democratic procedure, such as referendum or initiative, rather than by political leaders? What are the criteria for imposing fiduciary duties on the state for self-dealing by government employees? Who is empowered to express an official state resolution? Is the government's action "advantageous" to the state if it promotes unpopular political or economic measures? Should "advantages" be construed only as pecuniary benefits? Indeed, there are plenty of unanswered questions and a great deal of confusion

139. N.J. Const., art. VIII, §III, para.3.

140. The Law on Ownership in Rsfsr, supra note [131], art. 2, para. 3, at 13–14,

141. The Law on Ownership in Rsfsr, supra note [131].

142. The Law on Ownership in Rsfsr, supra note [131], art. 20, para. 1.

However, the analysis becomes more complicated if we assume that not every governmental action is self-dealing per se. The government should not be punished as a shareholder of a public corporation simply because it pursues some public interest which might be collaterally beneficial to the government and detrimental to the shareholders. Equally important, the government should not be precluded from participating in the equity of a particular enterprise simply because it carries specific sovereign functions. For example, government should not be automatically accused of self-dealing if it decreases federal interest rates, unintentionally affecting the value of its stock in mixed-ownership enterprises. But, of course, the government should not intentionally change interest rates in order, for example, to maximize its benefits during the conversion of its golden shares into ordinary shares when the time for such conversion has arrived.

The most difficult problem is distinguishing whether the government functions at a particular moment as the sovereign or whether it acts in a private capacity. Since it is nearly impossible to separate the capacity of the government as sovereign from the government's capacity as shareholder, it is inefficient to impose a burden of proof on the government to justify legitimate government regulation.... If we consider every government action that is detrimental to the shareholders of a corporation in which the government has a controlling interest as a violation of its fiduciary duties, the government would hardly be able to impose taxes, modify liability rules or issue regulations; that is, to act in its capacity as sovereign.... According to this view, the corporation is not strictly private but is "tinged with a public purpose" and "thus, corporate purpose can be seen as including the advancement of the general welfare" as well as bearing certain "moral obligations" towards society.[146]....

To eliminate problems of determining whether government acts of monitoring a corporation are in "good faith and inherent fairness" to the minority shareholders, we might as well adopt the common law reasoning for fairness articulated in cases of government taking of private property. As was expressed by the U.S. Supreme Court, the constitutional guarantee against government taking of private property "was designed to bar Government from forcing some people alone to bear public burdens which, in all fairness and justice, should be borne by the public as a whole."[148] Thus, applying this test to corporate action, one should conclude that when acting in its shareholder's capacity, the government must not force the minority shareholders to bear public burdens which should be borne by the public as a whole.

Accordingly, government pressure on a public corporation (in which the government has a controlling interest) to enter into a contract with a government entity that is wholly owed by the government is not a violation of the fiduciary duty owed to the minority shareholders as long as the terms of the contract are not so unfair as to make the minority shareholders alone bear the public burden of subsidizing the government entity, which should be borne by society as a whole.

* * *

Nonetheless, due to the current socio-political atmosphere in Russia and other former socialist countries, the rule-bound system might currently be more appropriate than the general casuistic system. Aside from the civil law tradition, there are several reasons for this conclusion.

---

146. William T. Allen, *Our Schizophrenic Conception of the Business Corporation*, 14 CARDOZO L. REV. 261, 264–76 (1992).

148. Armstrong v. United States, 364 U.S. 40, 49 (1960) (emphasis added)

First, fiduciary duties, like duties of agents, are normally designed as "catchall" rules intended to fill the gaps in a contract between parties. Theoretically, if there is a complete contract and there are no regulatory gaps, fiduciary duties are not needed. This notion, however, is based on the assumption that fully informed, competent parties voluntarily enter into contractual relations with each other, and are professionally advised regarding the legal consequences of such relations. When there are doubts about the fair and independent bargaining between the parties, mandatory rules are preferable. In Russia, the state along with the managers and employees of privatized enterprises are in better bargaining positions than outside shareholders. Yet bargaining games, in which the parties possess asymmetric information, are bound to fail. Due to the absence of adequate legal requirements for disclosure, unregulated advertisement procedures and undeveloped capital markets, Russian managers are in exclusive possession of the information regarding the performance, finances and management of the enterprise.

Second, democracy requires predictability. Rules of law, as opposed to precedents, might better serve to achieve "procedural justice" under conditions of political instability, social and political uncertainty, and an undeveloped judicial system with corruptible judges. Rules of law, as complete specification of the content of law, provide constituents with the right to know in advance about their rights and obligations.

Third, Russian judges, educated in a traditional civil law manner, are not ready to exercise broad judicial discretion in construing issues of ethics and public policy. Moreover, as elsewhere, there is no consensus in Russian society regarding public morals. There are no jury trials in civil cases, as there is no independent judicial system. Disputes regarding corporate matters are still decided by state arbitration, rather than by the people's courts, which are relatively independent and separated from the government.

In this author's view, the judicial and legal systems in Russia are not yet ready to adopt the casuistical system of judicial discretion, which might be, in the end, an optimal system for the enforcement of various types of fiduciary duties. The rule bound system is preferable for Russia in its current social and political situation. However, to preserve the general principles of democracy, including the freedom of contract, it may be advisable to introduce the mandatory "menu" system, which, besides establishing "fiduciary" patterns for articles of incorporation, would open some space for private negotiations.

The issue of fiduciary duties with regard to the state as a shareholder may arise in the following situations: (1) when the state acts entirely in the capacity of an ordinary shareholder (controlling or minority); (2) when the state acts only as a "special shareholder" without possessing any equity interest in the corporation; and (3) when the state acts in its double capacity as both an ordinary shareholder and a special shareholder. The determination of the state's fiduciary duties in these situations also depends on whether we are dealing with a public corporation or a close corporation. Therefore, it makes sense to analyze the question of the state's fiduciary duties along these lines.

B. Fiduciary Duties of the State as an Ordinary Shareholder

1. In Public Corporations

a. Government as a Controlling Shareholder

Generally, the concept of open-ended fiduciary duties, generated within the common law system of trust, is not known in civil law. Even though rapid changes in the legislation of many civil law countries are under way, the development of a theory of fiduciary duties in these countries is far from its logical completion.[150] Although a new Russian law has reproduced the traditional U.S. (common law) variant of the duty of loyalty, it has been applied exclusively to the directors of corporations. [151] Russian civil law does not yet recognize the fiduciary duties of controlling shareholders in public corporations; neither does it acknowledge the existence of shareholders' fiduciary duties in close corporations. Therefore, normative perspectives for developing the legislative base make it is necessary to analyze the concept of the fiduciary duties of the state from the point of view of U.S. corporate law.

Under common law, the concept of fiduciary duties applies to shareholders to the extent that a shareholder holds the power to control a corporation or has some other practical ability, as in a close corporation, to substantially affect or block the decision-making process. As a general rule, controlling shareholders in conventional U.S. corporations must refrain from using their control to obtain special advantages for themselves at the expense of minority shareholders. This fiduciary obligation is frequently construed by the courts as an obligation to act in "good faith and inherent fairness" toward the minority in the course of transactions where control of the corporation is material, i.e., when the controlling shareholder enters into business dealings with the corporation or when the controlling shareholder causes the corporation to make fundamental changes, such as mergers or amendments of the articles of corporation, that may promote the controlling shareholder's own self-interest at the expense of the minority.

It is unclear why this standard cannot be applied to the state when it acts as an ordinary controlling shareholder without a golden share. Yet, the government is more predisposed to relinquishing the pursuit of earnings optimization than are private shareholders. Government has objectives that may not coincide with the profitable operation of corporations. Government is inevitably concerned with combating inflation, unemployment, balancing the budget, defense spending, social services, regional development and obtaining the maximum number of votes during elections.

The state should not be allowed to accomplish its pecuniary or non-pecuniary public policy goals at the expense of the other shareholders. In other words, the state should be precluded from abusing its position as the dominant shareholder in a mixed-ownership corporation. Otherwise, privatization and transformation of SOEs into publicly-held corporations would not be a significant improvement over the formerly state-centralized enterprises.

For example, if a contract is unfair—as when the state, by utilizing its controlling power, compels a corporation to enter into a contract with another SOE or government entity for the purchase of obsolete and unmarketable equipment or of useless services

150. For instance, Japanese corporate law still does not recognize the distinction between the duty of care and the duty of loyalty (emphasis added). See SHOHO (Commercial Code), art. 254-3. Japanese corporate law also does not recognize the fiduciary duties of shareholders. See Kondo, Torishimariyaku *No Keiei Sekinin [Directors' Duties]*, 3 GENDAI KIGYO HO KOZA [LECTURES IN CONTEMP. BUS. ENTERPRISE] 293, 295–299 (A. Takeuchi & M. Tatsuta eds., Tokyo University Press, 1985). On the distinction between the fiduciary duty of loyalty and the duty of care in U.S. corporate law, see Kenneth E. Scott, The Role of Preconceptions in Policy Analysis in Law: A Response to Fischel and Bradley, 71 CORNELL L. REV. 299 (1986).

151. See, e.g., MODEL STATUTE OF PUBLICLY-HELD JOINT-STOCK COMPANY, art. 7, Supplement to the RF President's Edict On Organizational Measures for Transforming State Enterprises and Voluntary Associations of State Enterprises into Joint-Stock Companies, No. 721, July 1, 1992, in ROSSIJSKAJA GAZETA, July 6, 1992, available in LEXIS, World Library, Allwld File.

for a price that is well above that which would be set in an arm's-length bargain—the state has breached its fiduciary duty to the minority shareholders. In this situation, the government's objective in entering into this kind of transaction is irrelevant, as long as the government cannot offer a satisfactory business justification for the particular deal.

Furthermore, government does not participate directly in the decision-making process of corporations in which it holds a controlling interest, but acts through its authorized agents, who often have distinctive interests clashing with the profitmaximizing goals of the corporation. If a fiduciary duty is not imposed on these decision makers, they might be tempted to maximize their own benefit at the cost of the corporation. Even if the state or the corporation provides these agents with some equity interest, the problem is not eliminated entirely, since managers personally will bear only a fraction of the costs of the pecuniary or non-pecuniary benefits they take out of the corporation in maximizing their own utility.

Therefore, the authorized representatives of the government who sit on a corporation's board of directors should first represent the interests of the corporation and of its shareholders....

Thus, in order to preclude the influence that political parties may have on corporate directors, it would be feasible to create some legal mechanisms that would give directors independence from local and central governments. For instance, relations between directors and the government may be specified in a contract, which would be subject to mandatory legislative requirements due to the unequal bargaining position of the parties.

b. Government as a Non-Controlling Shareholder

Generally, non-controlling shareholders in a public corporation do not owe a fiduciary duty to majority shareholders. This is logical, since fiduciary duties are a judicial creation, constructed in order to preclude possible abuses of representatives by their agents. Since minority shareholders do not have enough voting power to represent those who have a majority equity stake, they cannot possibly abuse their power. Thus, it is not possible to misuse something that you do not have.

Nonetheless, the state in its position as a non-controlling shareholder, even without a golden share, enjoys a unique bargaining situation and ability to influence the decision-making process. The government inevitably possesses more material information than any single shareholder or entity. Moreover, the government has the power of legislative initiative; it determines financial policy; it controls judicial and law enforcement agencies; it establishes tariffs, quotas and taxes; it regulates labor relations; and it imposes zoning regulations. For example, in Russia the government is empowered to issue binding law-implementing resolutions and directives aimed at particular enterprises or organizations.[160] The President of Russia has the power to issue decrees and directives binding throughout the Russian Federation, so long as they are not "at variance with the Constitution of the Russian Federation or federal laws."[161] In other words, the Russian government and President possess an enormous capacity to influence the board of directors of almost any national corporation by issuing an individual decree pertaining to the specific business matters of the particular company.

In such circumstances, the law should expressly provide for legal remedies that would preclude the state from exercising undue influence over the shareholders and of-

160. See Konst. RSFSR, art. 115

161. Id. art. 90, para. 2–3.

ficers of corporations. Thus, the state as a non-controlling shareholder should still have the fiduciary duties of "business judgment" and "entire fairness" toward the other shareholders and the company.

2. In Close Corporations

It is well recognized in U.S. corporate law that shareholders of a close corporation owe each other a fiduciary duty of "utmost good faith and loyalty."[162] This duty is imposed on all shareholders of a close corporation, majority or minority. As one court held, shareholders in a close corporation "may not act out of avarice, expediency or self-interest in derogation of their duty of loyalty to the other shareholders and to the corporation."[163] The rationale of this holding is obvious: there is no practical market for the stock of a close corporation and the abused shareholders cannot easily extricate themselves from the corporate venture.[164] One solution to this problem is a buy-out agreement. Another solution is to establish fiduciary duties.

By analogy, the state as an ordinary shareholder in a close corporation should not be allowed to act out of expediency or self-interest in derogation of its duties of good faith and loyalty to the other shareholders and to the company. For instance, the state, as a minority shareholder, should not exercise its veto power unreasonably. An example of an unreasonable veto in the Russian context is when the state as a shareholder refuses to change an existing unprofitable line of production, or blocks a decision made for business reasons, in order to switch the national flag of the carriers of a shipping corporation, which the government believes harms the national interest. Although the state may legally block these decisions when it possesses the golden share, the government should not be allowed to employ the same technique when it acts in its exclusive capacity as an ordinary shareholder if the veto is unduly prejudicial to the rest of the shareholders. After all, in the case where the state holds the golden share, prospective shareholders will realize that the government as a special shareholder can exercise its veto power with respect to certain matters, and, hence, the price which they will pay for the shares will reflect the effect of the divergence between the state's interest and theirs. In contrast, when the government participates in a joint-stock company as an ordinary shareholder, the other shareholders should be entitled to expect that the general rules of fiduciary duties apply to all shareholders and directors, including the government and its agents.

C. Fiduciary Duties of the State as a Special Shareholder

The concept of special shareholder, or golden shareholder, originated during the British privatization of the 1980s, when the then-state-held firms, such as Britoil and Jaguar, were sold off by Prime Minister Margaret Thatcher's Conservative government. The British Government retained so-called golden shares in both these enterprises, allowing the government to outvote all shareholders regardless of the number of shares held by the government. This technique has been employed during privatization by the governments of many countries. In Russia alone, by the beginning of 1994, golden shares had been issued to the government by 125 joint-stock companies.

In short, the provisions regarding the golden share enable the government to exercise a certain control over a privatized enterprise after the state has become a mi-

162. Donahue v. Rodd Electrotype Co. of New England, 367 Mass. 578, 593 (1975), 328 N.E.2d 505 (Mass. 1975).

163. Id. at 593.

164. See, e.g., Sugarman v. Sugarman, 797 F.2d 3 (1st Cir. 1986) (discussing the freeze-out of minority shareholders).

nority shareholder or even after total privatization. Thus, a golden share empowers the state with a control disproportionate to the state's equity in an enterprise. This "authority-giving" quality of the share makes it "golden" in the eyes of ordinary shareholders.

Because of its special extraordinary powers and the goal it tends to achieve, the golden share can only be held by the government. This requirement restricts the transferability of the golden share, which is not tradable on secondary markets and not consignable to non-government entities.

With respect to the fiduciary duties of the state, it is one thing when the state acts entirely in its traditional shareholder capacity, and another when the state acts as a special (golden) shareholder. Presumably, when the state has a conventional equity interest in a corporation (no golden share), it should owe the usual duty of fairness to the other shareholders. But when the state exercises its right of veto in its capacity as a special shareholder, it cannot be forced to act fairly towards other shareholders if the vetoed action would have been contrary to the national interest or to some other purposes for which the golden share was established. Otherwise, the purpose of the golden share in preserving strategic national or public policy interests would be undermined, since practically all government vetoes might be construed as inherently unfair to the minority shareholders, while beneficial to the state. For example, suppose that in the case of the company Zim, in which the Israeli government retains a golden share in order to require the company's ships to remain under Israel's flag, the government exercises its right to veto a proposal to change the flag. The shareholders might argue that such a veto is detrimental to them because the corporation incurs continuous losses due to burdensome national labor laws, strong trade unions and high taxation and tariffs. Nonetheless, the requirement for Zim to preserve the national flag was the purpose of retaining the golden share by the Israeli government. By requiring its carriers to remain under Israel's national flag, the government secures its ability to call them into requisition in case of a national emergency. The shareholders were aware of such requirement and the price they paid for their shares of stock certainly reflected the inability of the company to change the flag under which its carriers sailed.[170]

Of course, the provisions of the golden share must necessarily be disclosed in a company's prospectus. Since the provisions for a golden share are pronounced in legislative acts and corporate documents, the shareholders by buying stocks in such a company are deemed to have consented to such provisions. Therefore, the shareholders are not actually damaged by the government's veto, unless the government's action is completely unreasonable, arbitrary or unrelated to the purpose of the golden share.

The "reasonableness" test should remain as a means of evaluating governmental actions as a special shareholder. The test might include the requirements that a legitimate governmental objective be demonstrated for a particular veto and that a rational rela-

170. However, the government should also be precluded from granting to the company any cargo preferences, direct shipping subsidies, tax benefits or other economic benefits. Arguably, in advancing the company's competitiveness, the government pursues its own pecuniary interest, since the government has an equity interest in the company. However, in what other manner can the government provide for the profitable operation of the shipping company which loses money by remaining under the national flag? This question goes to the problem of distinguishing the government's role as sovereign from its capacity as a shareholder, which should be resolved on a case-by-case basis.

tions hip exist between the means (veto) and the state's objective. In other words, a veto should be upheld if it is rationally related to the legitimate governmental purpose of retaining the golden share preliminarily specified in the prospectus. Of course, the reasonableness of governmental actions should be challengeable before independent judicial organs.

D. Fiduciary Duties of the State When It Acts in a Double Capacity as a Special and Ordinary Shareholder

In certain situations, the government wants not only to retain veto power over specific strategic decisions made by management but also to retain the right to participate in the profit of a privatized enterprise (as when a government holds an equity stake in an enterprise and receives dividends). To accomplish its goals, the government may use the golden share technique together with an equity share in the corporation.

For instance, during the privatization of the steel company Siderurgia Nacional, the Portuguese government retained a twenty-five percent golden share in the company, but decided to hold only a ten percent golden share in Petrogal and the gas supply consortium. The Hungarian government retains twenty-five percent and a golden share in its non-nuclear state electricity companies, but considers the retention of only one golden share in the gas distribution companies sufficient to exercise control over certain strategic decisions. In Russia, during privatization of the national gold industry, the government retained thirty-eight to fifty-one percent of the equity stock in twenty-five companies, while retaining only a single golden share in seventeen other companies. Indeed, as a general rule, holding the golden share alone provides the government with substantial powers to veto management decisions regardless of the percentage of the equity the government possesses in the enterprise. However, if the government wants to participate in a company's profit, a single golden share will not be sufficient.

Thus, when the government holds equity stock in an enterprise plus a golden share, the fiduciary duties of government towards shareholders should be the same as in the case when government retains only the golden share. Additional duties and liabilities should not be imposed upon the government simply because it decides to preserve some equity in an enterprise. As long as the decision to retain a golden share is publicly disclosed, shareholders should not have undue expectations about the future development of an enterprise, and this would be reflected in the price they are willing to pay for the shares. Since the main purpose of a golden share is to preserve the status quo of the present industrial activity of an enterprise, the future profitability of the company is not obscure. As a rule, the golden share is preserved by the government for a short period of time and for strictly specified purposes. Investors who do not want to participate together with the government in such a venture may choose other alternatives for investments. Moreover, the government itself will be interested in exercising its veto right in the most prudent manner, because a government veto that prevents more profitable activity will also harm the state, which would have an equity interest in the enterprise.

Comments and Questions

1. Michael Irl Nikkel argues that the tension between the Chinese Company Law's premise that the shareholders are the organ of corporate authority and that the Chinese government and public have the authority to supervise corporations has created a pos-

sibility that non-state shareholders may have little protection for their interests under Chinese Company Law, even as the form of the Chinese Company Law appears to mimic that of the West. But, if the largest shareholder of a Chinese corporation is an organ of the state, can you argue that there is no tension between the provisions? Does your answer depend on how strongly you believe in the principle of majority rule?

2. If corporations owe the greatest duty to the state, is there a reason that minority shareholders need protection for corporate action that may hurt them but increase the value of the state? It is possible to conceive of a regime in which the interests of shareholders must be the same as the interests of the state. When the state is satisfied, then it may be possible to believe that shareholders have no reason to complain, whatever the effect of the state's satisfaction on the value of the holdings of non-state shareholders. In effect, the state is the ultimate residuary under Chinese corporate law, rather than the shareholder as under Western theories of the corporation. On the other hand, is the prior explanation only viable if one accepts the paramount place of the state in the relationship between shareholders, and managers? But if the viability of the Chinese approach is based on acceptance of the position of the state, then is there any reason that placing shareholders in the paramount place within corporations as is done in the West any more compelling?

3. What are the differences in the approaches taken by post-Socialist Russia described in the excerpt of Andrei Baev and the modern People's Republic of China? Can the differences be explained on a cultural basis? Does the Russian approach suggest a different way of conceiving of the role fo the state as shareholder?

4. Do you think that any of the solutions proposed for the emerging Russian economy might have application for the economic reforms of the People's Republic of China?

Index